The Handbook of Physical Education

The Handbook of Physical Education

Edited by
David Kirk, Doune Macdonald and
Mary O'Sullivan

Los Angeles | London | New Delhi
Singapore | Washington DC

THE HENLEY COLLEGE LIBRARY

SAGE Publications Ltd
1 Oliver's Yard
55 City Road
London EC1Y 1SP

SAGE Publications Inc.
2455 Teller Road
Thousand Oaks, California 91320

SAGE Publications India Pvt Ltd
B 1/I 1 Mohan Cooperative Industrial Area
Mathura Road
New Delhi 110 044

SAGE Publications Asia-Pacific Pte Ltd
3 Church Street
#10-04 Samsung Hub
Singapore 049483

British Library Cataloguing in Publication data

A catalogue record for this book is available from
the British Library

ISBN 978-0-7619-4412-6
ISBN 978-1-4462-7050-9 (pbk)

Library of Congress Control Number: 2006920927

Typeset by C&M Digitals (P) Ltd., Chennai, India
Printed by MPG Printgroup, UK
Printed on paper from sustainable resources

MIX
Paper from
responsible sources
FSC® C018575
www.fsc.org

Contents

Introduction

DAVID KIRK, DOUNE MACDONALD AND MARY O'SULLIVAN

The curriculum historian Ivor Goodson (1988) has argued that school subjects and university disciplines are social constructs rather than naturally occurring phenomena. What he means by this is that fields of study would not exist but for contestation and struggle among and between vying groups and individuals over resources of various kinds, including material resources, rewards and status. As fields gain a foothold in universities, groups and individuals may struggle, not merely to thrive, but also to survive. A whole literature on the rise and fall of particular school subjects and university fields of study now exists to provide a strong empirical base to Goodson's claim (e.g. see the *Falmer Studies in Curriculum History* series). What is clear from this literature is that while there are broad trends and patterns to the rise and fall of particular fields of study, each has its own individual trajectory. Sometimes a field bursts on to the scene to become immediately popular (e.g. sport and exercise sciences may be a case in point), some seem to be firmly entrenched but are suddenly under threat (witness the case of physics and chemistry in UK universities), and some may now only be able to reflect on former glories (e.g. Latin and Greek, once the centrepiece of university education).

The study of educational issues in physical education and sport is an interesting case when set beside Goodson's theory. In Australia, New Zealand and the UK, for instance, the educational mission of physical education was the key rationale for the field in higher education institutions up until the early 1970s. There was up to this time little research conducted around this educational mission, and when research did begin in earnest from the 1950s in the UK and the 1960s in the USA it was in the fields of exercise physiology, biomechanics, history and philosophy (Henry, 1978). While these subdisciplines of the sport and exercise sciences have thrived in universities around the world, the educational mission of university departments has been displaced from its central role to become one of several aspects of the work of these departments. In some places, the educational aspects of sport and exercise has been marginalized, and is viewed as of lesser academic worth than some of the other subdisciplines. Part of the rationale for such a view was that education workers in the sport and exercise field did not do research.

Since the 1970s, this situation has changed dramatically. In order to retain their place in university departments, and to gain access to the same rewards as fellow academics, such as promotion, staff development opportunities, support to attend conferences, and so on, education workers began to carry out research. The production of this handbook is a measure of the progress that has been made in terms of the development of the field. Moreover, evidence of the emergence of a critical mass of researchers can be found in the strong and continuing presence of special interest groups within the major educational research associations in the USA (American Educational Research Association, AERA) and Australia (Australian Association for Research in Education, AARE) and the recent establishment of a similar group in the UK within British Educational Research Association (BERA). There are also parallel research groups in the professional associations in each of these countries. Countries such as France also have parallel specialist educational research associations such as Association pour la Recherche sur l'Intervention en Sport (ARIS), while international bodies such as the Association Internationale pour les Ecoles Superieur d'Education Physique (AIESEP) holds regular conferences with an educational research focus around the world. As language barriers are overcome, many Asian countries are attracting multinational participants to their conferences and increasingly joining international forums. There are established chairs held by educational researchers in many of the leading university departments in Australia, Ireland, France, the USA, and the UK, and there has been an increasing flow of completed doctoral theses in these countries since the late 1980s.

There is also a buoyant book market for research-based material on physical education, with Human Kinetics and Routledge/Falmer currently possessing the strongest lists. In addition, the field is served by several English-language specialist scholarly journals. The *Journal of Teaching in Physical Education* was originally established in 1981 to provide a forum for the publication of pedagogical research mainly in North America, and now serves an international audience. Another North American journal, the *Research Quarterly for Exercise and Sport*, has a well-supported pedagogy section, while the long-established journal *Quest* provides a medium for conceptual and theoretical essays in physical education. Other English language outlets for educational research include the *European Physical Education Review*. The publication of two new specialist scholarly journals, *Sport, Education and Society* in 1996 and *Physical Education and Sport Pedagogy* more recently in 2004, provides an illustration of the continuing consolidation and expansion of the field. Review articles published periodically since the 1970s, including Locke (1977), Placek and Locke (1986), Hellison (1989), O'Sullivan et al. (1992), Rovegno and Kirk (1995), Kirk (1997), and Macdonald et al. (2002), provide a clear illustration of the ongoing maturation of the field, some of the major points of debate, and some of the key issues and challenges for future development.

Reflecting Goodson's thesis, these review articles show that these 30 or so years of progress have not been smooth and linear. Educational researchers have had to fight for their place in the academy, and colleagues in other subdisciplines have not readily been willing to give up resources. This struggle continues in university departments around the world. One of the most significant areas of contestation has been focused around the name of the field of study and proper topics and methods of study that are the primary responsibility of educational researchers. For some time, educational researchers persisted with the term "physical education" to identify the boundaries of their expertise and field of interest. However, it eventually became clear that the older connotations of this terms as synonymous with the fledgling field of sport and exercise sciences made the continuing use of this term difficult to sustain in a university environment. Too many others could claim to own this term, so it lacked the exclusivity that is essential for the survival of fields of study in universities (see e.g. Bernstein, 1971). Alternatively, the term was viewed as out of date and old fashioned, concerned only with mere physical activity and so academically disreputable. We have continued to use the term physical education in this handbook as a means of identifying a key process of being educated in, about and through movement as a medium. The term physical education is also commonplace in school systems around the world, and much of the research reported here has been concerned with the practices that constitute and construct this school subject.

While we have retained the use of the term physical education to denote this specific process, in the face of the challenges just outlined, increasingly educational researchers in English-speaking countries began to use the term "pedagogy" to describe their work and to locate themselves as a subdiscipline of the sport and exercise sciences. Consistent with this development, we have located the term pedagogy at the centre of this handbook, as a means of providing an organizing principle for the text. The notion of pedagogy we are working with here can be defined by its three key elements of learning, teaching and curriculum. We understand these three elements to be interdependent, though not all pedagogy research has necessarily been carried out with an understanding of the nature of this interdependence. Sections 3, 4 and 5 of this handbook deal in turn with each of these key elements. We have grouped chapters thematically around these key elements in order to make the authors' task manageable and the readers' task sensible. At the same time, many of the authors have succeeded in keeping each of the elements of pedagogy in view while they explore some dimensions of one element in detail.

Section 2 provides evidence of Goodson's thesis that scholars with particular perspectives have had interests in educational work within physical education, though in the case of the chapters included here we can see that these perspectives and interests need not be negative. Indeed, as the chapters show, philosophers, sociologists, psychologists, historians and public health researchers have done much to enrich our understanding of pedagogy in school and other sites.

An important element of marking a field of study's identity is its subject matter, which as we have already claimed is pedagogy. A further element is the theoretical perspectives researchers employ to study this topic. Section 1 includes chapters that provide us with insights into the breadth of perspectives pedagogy researchers have used to study their subject. What we learn from reading these chapters is that, perhaps more so than other sub-disciplines in sport and exercise sciences, pedagogy research has used a wide range of theoretical perspectives. There are risks and benefits attached to the existence of this range. A key benefit is that researchers are able to draw on a pool of epistemologies, methodologies and methods to design studies that can cope with the complexity of learning, teaching, and curriculum and their interdependence. A risk to a field that is still in the process of establishing itself in the academy is that it is seen to lack a distinctive approach to research. The chapters in this section provide a rich source of arguments for and against such a position.

Section 6 offers insights into areas of research that we believe are breaking new ground in our field of study. Interestingly, although some of the chapter topics have been of long-term interest to educational researchers, they nevertheless continue to prompt the development and application of new theoretical and methodological perspectives. These chapters also provide important insights into the interdependence of the key elements of pedagogy as they are instantiated in terms of sexuality, girls, boys, disability and race.

This handbook is an expression, however limited, of a view of knowledge about physical education pedagogy as we begin this new century. Choices of topics, authors, chapter foci, are meant to be inclusive and international in scope though we readily admit not everything is included. These are the authors and the knowledge we have available but they are not the only or final answers on the many educational issues in physical education. As co-editors, we have attempted to represent the different research traditions and emerging areas on interest across the global scholarly community.

References

Berstein, B. (1971). On the classification and framing of educational knowledge, In M.F.D. Young (Ed.), *Knowledge and control: New directions in the sociology of education*. London: Collier-Macmillan.

Goodson, I.F. (1988). *The making of curriculum*. Lewes: Falmer.

Hellison, D. (1989). Our constructed reality: some contributions to an alternative perspective to physical education pedagogy. *Quest, 40*, 84–90.

Henry, F.M. (1978). The academic discipline of physical education. *Quest, 29*, 13–29. (first published 1968)

Kirk, D. (1997). Sociology of physical and health education. In L. Saha, (Ed.), *International encyclopaedia of the sociology of education* (pp. 193–201). London: Elsevier.

Locke, L.F. (1977). Research on teaching physical education: New hope for a dismal science. *Quest, 28*, 2–16.

Macdonald, D., Kirk, D., Metzler, M.W., Nilges, L.M., Schempp, P. and Wright, J. (2002). 'It's all very well in theory': A review of theoretical perspectives and their applications in contemporary pedagogical research. *Quest, 54*(2), 133–156.

O'Sullivan, M., Siedentop, D. and Locke, L. (1992). Towards collegiality: Competing viewpoints among teacher educators. *Quest, 44*, 266–280.

Placek, J.H. and Locke, L.F. (1986). Research on teaching physical education: New knowledge and cautios optimism. *Journal of Teacher Education, 37*(4), 24–28.

Rovegno, I. and Kirk, D. (1995). Articulations and silences in socially critical work on physical education: toward a broader agenda. *Quest, 47*(4), 447–474.

Contributors

Chantal Amade-Escot is Professor of Education and Co-Director of the Laboratoire d'Etudes des Méthodes Moderne d'Education (LEMME), a multidisciplinary research center on sciences education, mathematics education, and sport education at Paul Sabatier University, Toulouse, France. Her research focuses primarily on "didactics" as a paradigm to study the situated process of teaching and learning. She co-chairs the French association for comparative research in "didactics" (ARCD) which members are from different school disciplines. Her academic background is in Sport Pedagogy. She has authored over 50 refereed papers on didactics, physical education, sport pedagogy, and teachers education. She is associate editor of the French multidisciplinary journal "Science et Motricité", and member of the advisory board of "Physical Education and Sport Pedagogy".

Kathleen Armour is Reader in the School of Sport and Exercise Sciences at Loughborough University.

Daniel Behets teaches in the Faculty of Kinesiology and Rehabilitation Sciences at the Katholieke Universiteit Leuven.

Don Belcher is Assistant Professor in the Department of Kinesiology at the University of Alabama.

Mike Brown teaches in the Faculty of Education at Monash University.

Ralph Buck is head of the Department of Dance Studies at the University of Auckland.

Mark Byra is Professor and Director of the Division of Kinesiology and Health, University of Wyoming. His research interests include models of teaching, specifically those teaching styles associated with the Spectrum, and how teacher knowledge is development over time in preservice teachers as reflected in their thoughts and behaviours.

Ching Wei Chang graduated from the doctoral Sport Pedagogy Programme of National Taiwan Normal University. He is also a doctoral student at University of Franche-Comté (France). His research interest focuses on children's tactical game play learning using a constructivist approach (tactical and decision) and on its associated PE Teacher Education Programme.

Gill Clarke teaches in the Research and Graduate School of Education at the University of Southampton.

Connie Collier is an Associate Professor in the School of Exercise, Leisure, and Sport at Kent State University. Connie's scholarship focus is the preparation and professional development of physical education teachers, with an emphasis on the development of pedagogical practices and curricula that are sensitive and responsive to issues of social justice. She develops and studies pedagogical methods in teacher education, including the use of the case method approach and integration of technology. She was the 2003–4, Chair of AAH-PERD Curriculum and Instruction Academy and currently serves on the editorial board of *The Journal of Teaching in Physical Education.*

Brian Davies is Professor of Education in the School of Social Sciences, Cardiff University, Wales. Since his *Social Control and Education* he has taught and written widely on social theory and research, educational policy and pedagogic practice. His special interest in the work of Basil Bernstein is reflected in many publications including, Muller, J., Davies., B., and Morias, A., *Reading Bernstein, Researching Bernstein* (London: Routledge, 2004) and Fitz., J., Davies., B and Evans, J., *Educational Policy and Social Reproduction. Class Inscription and Symbolic Control* (London: Routledge, 2006).

Kristine De Martelaer finished her studies in Physical Education (Master) in Gent in 1989 together with her Teacher Diploma (Aggregate). She started working at the Vrije Universiteit Brussel (VUB) as an assistant specializing in swimming for students PE and physiotherapy and as swimming coach for athletes. In 1991 she achieved her Master in Leisure Agogics at the VUB. During 12 years she focused on the didactics and coaching aspects of swimming while she was Technical Director for the trainer courses in Flanders. This fieldwork was combined with (interuniversity) research projects in the domain of youth sport policy and youth sport leadership. In these years her special interest went to the rights of children in sport and a youth-centred approach in organized sport. With this topic she achieved her PhD in Physical Education in 1996 (VUB). From 1997 until 2000 she was also a part time assistant at the University of Gent, responsible for the co-ordination of the option "Training & Coaching" and the use of a quality instrument for sport clubs (IKSport) in an interuniversity research project. Since December 2001 she is professor at the department of Movement education and sports training (VUB). She currently teaches sport history, didactics, curriculum development and first aid, together with the co-ordination of the courses on dance. She is participating in a central VUB project on portfolio and the use of ICT during the Teacher Education Training. Her actual academic interest is situated within pedagogy: experiences and expectations of children and teachers/coaches with PE and sport, competences and job profile of teachers PE and youth coaches, physical education teacher education, motor development of young children in relation with the movement culture, and education through dance. The output of research is about 37 articles (national and international), 28 contributions in proceedings, 19 chapters in books, five books as (co)-author and many congress presentations. As president of the committee of education at the faculty of Physical Education and Physiotherapy she is co-ordinating the transition between the actual education system (licentiate) and the future Bachelor-Master.

José Devís Devís is Director of the "Theory and Pedagogy of PE and Sport Research Unit" at the Facultat de Ciències de l'Activitat Física i l'Esport Universitat de València (Spains), and member of the Editorial Board/Refereering of *Sport, Education and Society* and *Physical Education and Sport Pedagogy'* journals. His main academic interests are teaching and teacher education in PE, themes he has published papers in Spanish and English. He has also edited several books in Spanish as 'Nuevas perspectivas curriculares en educación física', 'Actividad física, deporte y salud's and 'La educación física, el deporte y la salud en el siglo XXI', as well as authored the text, 'Educación física, deporte y currículum. Investigación y desarrollo curricular'.

Patt Dodds, Ph.D., is a Professor Emerita at the University of Massachusetts – Amherst. Her research interests include socialization of physical education teachers and teacher educators, the lives and career pathways of teacher educators, and women in the professoriate. She has served as editor or co-editor of several physical education pedagogy journals and is a recipient of the AAHPERD Curriculum & Instructiona Academy Honor Award as well as current Past President of AAHPERD's Research Consortium.

Jim Dollman is currently a lecturer in exercise physiology and anthropometry at the School of Health Sciences, University of South Australia. In the past decade he has conducted extensive research into trends and patterns of distribution of children's physical activity and health-related fitness, with a particular emphasis on the impact of socioeconomic status. As a member of the Australian Child and Adolescent Obesity Research Network (ACAORN) he has worked with other paediatric physical activity researchers towards standardizing self-report instruments for physical activity.

John Dolly is Professor in the Department of Educational Studies in Psychology, Research Methodology and Counseling at the University of Alabama.

Ben Dyson teaches in the Dept of Human Movement Sciences at the University of Memphis.

Joey C. Eisenmann is Assistant Professor of Health and Human Performance at Iowa State University.

John Evans is Professor of Sociology of Education and Physical Education at Loughborough University, England. He teaches and writes on issues of equity, education policy, identity and processes of schooling. He has authored and edited a number of papers and books in the Sociology of Education and Physical Education and co authored with Dawn Penney, *Politics, Policy and Practice in Physical Education* (E & FN Spon, 1999) and with John Fitz and Brian Davies, *Educational Policy and Social Reproduction. Class Inscription and Symbolic Control* (Routledge, 2006)

Hayley Fitzgerald teaches in the Carnegie Faculty of Sport and Education at Leeds Metropolitan University.

Anne Flintoff is currently Reader in Physical Education in the Carnegie Faculty of Sport and Education, Leeds Metropolitan University, England. She has been involved in school PE – as a teacher, teacher trainer, and researcher for over 20 years. Her higher education teaching, research and consultancy has centred on issues of equity and social inclusion, and she publishes regularly in the both academic and professionaljournals in the area of PE and sport. She is a member of the Advisory Board of the *PE and Sport Pedagogy* journal. Recent publications include Scraton and Flintoff (eds) 2002, *Gender and Sport: A Reader*, Routledge; Flintoff, A. and Scraton, S. (2005) *Gender and PE* in Green, K. and Hardman (eds) (2005) *Physical Education: Essential Issues*, Sage, Flintoff, A.Hylton, K. and Long, J (eds) (2005)*Young people and active leisure: participation, policy and evaluation*, Leisure Studies Association, Brighton.

Michael Gard is a senior lecturer in dance, physical and health education at Charles Sturt University's Bathurst campus. He teaches and writes about the human body, gender and sexuality, the shortcoming's of biological determinism in all its forms, and the use and misuse of dance within physical education. He is the author of two books: *The Obesity Epidemic: Science, Morality and Ideology* (with Jan Wright) and *Men Who Dance: Aesthetics, Athletics and the Art of Masculinity.*

Wade Gilbert is an Associate Professor in the Department of Kinesiology at California State University, Fresno. He directs the Sport & Exercise Psychology Lab and is the project coordinator for SHAPE (School-based Healthy Activities Program for Exercise). Dr. Gilbert is the editor of a special issue of *The Sport Psychologist* on Coach Education. His work has been published in a wide array of scientific outlets including *Research Quarterly for Exercise and Sport, The Sport Psychologist, and the Journal of Teaching Physical Education.*

Louis Harrison teaches in the Department of Kinesiology at Louisiana State University.

Peter Hastie teaches in Department of Health and Human Performance at Auburn University.

Peter Hay is Associate Lecturer in Pedagogy at the University of Queensland.

Gary Hellison is a Professor in the Jane Addams College of Social Work at the University of Illinois at Chicago.

lisahunter researches in the areas of middle schooling, young peoples' subjectivity and engagement with society, transition and extreme lifestyle sports. She is playing with research as activism for and by students and preservice teachers, lecturing in teacher education, middle schooling, and health and physical education.

Gary D. Kinchin is Deputy Head of School within the School of Education at the University of Southampton. He received an MA and PhD from The Ohio State University and has held academic positions at Illinois State University and De Montfort University. Gary's research interest is in sport education with over 40 journal articles, chapters and conference papers related to this topic. He is a co-editor of the text *Sport Education in Physical Education: Research Based Practice* and a member of the BERA Special Interest Group in Physical Education and Sport Pedagogy. Gary also serves on the Editorial Board of the *Physical Education and Sport Pedagogy* journal.

Bomna Ko is a graduate teaching associate in the College of Education at Ohio State University.

Cathy Lirgg is Associate Professor in the Department of Health Science at the University of Arkansas.

Tom Martinek is a Professor in the Department of Exercise and Sport Science. During his 30-year tenure at UNCG, Tom has focused his research efforts on the social and psychological dynamics of teaching and coaching. Dr. Martinek's work has been published in journals such as *Research Quarterly for Exercise and Sport, Journal of Teaching in Physical Education, Journal of Exercise and Sport Psychology, Quest, Urban Review, Physical Education and Sport Pedagogy, International Journal of Sport Science,* and *Community Youth Development Journal.* He has also authored or co-authored four books. He has spent the past 12 years directing and teaching in youth development programs which have served over 300 underserved youth. He also provides pre-service and in-service staff development programs for practitioners who work with at-risk, underserved children and youth. The basis of his work with children evolves from his past sequential research on teacher expectancy effects, learned helplessness, and resiliency of children and youth.

Steve Mitchell is a Professor of Sport Pedagogy in the School of Exercise, Leisure and Sport. He is in his fourteenth year at Kent State, having previously completed Doctoral work at Syracuse University, and Masters and Bachelors degrees at Loughborough University, England. With colleagues Judy Oslin and Linda Griffin, Steve has authored numerous articles and book chapters related to tactical games teaching. The trio has also co-authored three textbooks related to game teaching within public school physical education, including one that is now into its second edition.

William Mosrgan is a Professor in the School of Educational Policy and Leadership at the Ohio State University.

Lynda Nilges is a Professor in the Department of Physical Education at the University of South Carolina.

Judy Oslin is a Professor in the School of Exercise, Leisure, and Sport at Kent State University. Her scholarship is in student-centred curricular approaches, specifically the tactical approach to games education, with a secondary line of research in the role of assessment in student learning. Judy is an active member in the Ohio Association of Health, Physical Education, Recreation and Dance, American Alliance of Health, Physical Education, Recreation, and Dance, National Association of Kinesiology and Physical Education in Higher Education, and American Education Association. Judy also served as a member of the Editorial Board for *The Journal of Teaching in Physical Education* from 2000–2004. She continues to serve as a Guest Reviewer for *The Journal of Teaching in Physical Education as well as Physical Education and Sport Pedagogy.*

Dawn Penney is a Senior Lecturer at the School of Education, Edith Cowan University, Australia. Dawn has been a key figure in research on policy and curriculum development in physical education and junior sport since gaining her doctorate from Southampton in 1994. Dawn has subsequently held positions at the University of Queensland, De Montfort University and Loughborough University and is a fellow of the Physical Education Association of the United Kingdom. Dawn has published extensively in physical education and mainstream education journals, is co-author of *Politics, Policy and Practice in Physical Education* (E&FN Spon, London, 1999), editor of *Gender and Physical Education: Contemporary Issues and Future Directions* (Routledge, London, 2002); co-editor of *Sport Education in Physical Education: Research based practice* (Routledge, London, 2005) and a co-author of senior physical education texts designed to support studies in Queensland and the UK.

Murray Philips teaches in the School of Human Movement Studies at The University of Queensland.

Clive Pope completed his PhD at the Ohio State University, USA. He is currently a Senior Lecturer at the University of Waikato and teaches about sport for children and youth at undergraduate and graduate level. His main research interests are the development of sport academies in schools, sideline behaviour at children's sport, sport ethnography, the affective domain in physical education and sport, coach effectiveness and the changing nature of youth sport. He has presented and published in England, North America, Europe, Australia and New Zealand.

Emma Rich is a lecturer in physical education, Gender, Identity and Health in the School of Sport and Exercise Sciences at Loughborough University. Her research interests are oriented towards issues of equity, education policy, identity and processes of schooling, with a specific focus on gender issues, and health and identity. She has published in refereed journals and books in sociology, physical education, health and feminist studies. She is the founder of the Gender Sport and Society Forum (GSSF).

Alexander Paul Roper is a Doctoral Research student at the University of Queensland, where he also lectures in the business of sport. His research interests are his area, but his PhD examines sports political utilization in Malaysia. His research interests include the socio-cultural/historical role of sport in SE Asia.

Inez Rovegno is Professor of Teacher Education at the University of Alabama.

Rachel Sandford is a Research Associate in the School of Sport and Exercise Sciences at Lough borough University. Her doctoral research was concerned with issues relating to young people, embodied identity and physical culture, and she has also been involved with research projects focusing on the relationship between formal education and disordered eating. Her current research interests are built around an evaluation of physical activity programmes designed to re-engage disaffected youth, and include a focus on the processes of informal education and mentoring. She has published in refereed journals and books in the areas of sociology, physical education and health.

Sheila Scraton is a Professor in the Carnegie Faculty of Sport and Education at Leeds Metropolitan University.

Daryl Siedentop is a Professor at The Ohio State University.

Melinda Solmon teaches in the Department of Kinesiology at Louisiana State University.

Sandra Stroot teaches in the College of Education at the Ohio State University.

Marc Theeboom is Assistant Professor at the Faculty of Physical Education and Physiotherapy at the Vrije Universiteit Brussel, Belgium (Free University of Brussels). He obtained a PhD in physical education and a master's degree in leisure agogics. His research primarily focuses on pedagogical and policy related aspects of youth sport in general and underprivileged youth, martial arts, physical education and school sport in particular.

Richard Tinning is a Professor in the School of Human Movement Studies at The University of Queensland.

Stewart Trost is an Associate Professor at Kansas State University with dual appointments with the Department of Kinesiology and K-State Community Health Institute. A native of Brisbane, Australia, Trost completed his BS in Health Education and Promotion and MS in Exercise Physiology at Oregon State University and received his PhD in Exercise Physiology from the School of Public Health at the University of South Carolina. His research interests include (a) assessment of physical activity in children and adolescents; (b) the prevention and treatment of childhood obesity and its associated metabolic disorders; (c) the psychosocial and environmental determinants of physical activity behavior; (d) community- and school-based promotion of physical activity; and (e) the relationship between physical activity and other health behaviors.

Pierre Trudel is a Professor at the School of Human Kinetics, University of Ottawa, Canada. In the last 15 years his research group has been funded by the Social Sciences and Humanities Research Council of Canada to conduct research on coaching and coach education. He has published 60 articles in a variety of journals and books. Dr. Trudel, has been a consultant for many sport organizations, developing programs and supervising coaches.

Niki Tsangaridou is an Assistant Professor in the Department of Education at the University of Cyprus. She has a BSc in Physical Education from the Department of Physical Education and Sport Science of the National and Kapodistrian University of Athens, MSc from the Department of Curriculum and Teaching Human Movement of Boston University, and PhD in Physical Education Teacher Education from The Ohio State University. Her research interests revolve around instructional and curriculum analysis, teachers' thinking and reflection, teachers' beliefs, teacher effectiveness, and learning to teach. She is a recipient of the "Young Researcher Award" from the International Association for Physical Education in Higher Education (AIESEP) in 2001 and the "Metzler-Freedman Exemplary Paper Award" from the *Journal of Teaching in Physical Education* in 2004. She is editorial board member of the *Journal of Teaching in Physical Education* and guest reviewer for other research journals. Dr. Tsangaridou has published extensively on teaching and teacher education in physical education and made numerous presentations on teacher education topics at international conferences and professional workshops.

Hans van der Mars received his PhD from The Ohio State University (1984). At Oregon State University he teaches in the physical education teacher education program, advises a small cadre of doctoral students and serves as Graduate Program Coordinator. Previously he taught at Arizona State University and the University of Maine-Orono. He has been an active researcher in sport pedagogy/physical education teacher education having (co-)authored and published over 60 research and professional papers, a textbook and several book chapters. He has published in the *Journal of Teaching in Physical Education (JTPE), Adapted Physical Activity (APAQ), Pediatric Exercise Science (PES), Physical Educator, Strategies, Palaestra, Journal of Sport Pedagogy, and Research Quarterly for Exercise & Sport (RQES)*. Recently, he co-authored the *Complete Guide to Sport Education* and served as Co-Editor of the Journal of Teaching in Physical Education (JTPE). A frequent presenter at international, national regional and state level conferences, Dr van der Mars also delivers workshops for K-12 physical educators. He enjoys spending time with his family, playing golf, jogging, listen to music, keeping up with world affairs and urging on his beloved New York Mets.

Lieven Vergauwen is Professor of Sports Pedagogy in the Faculty of Kinesiology and Rehabilitation Sciences at the Katholieke Universiteit Leuven (Belgium). He is also Lecturer and Sport Pedagogy researcher in the Department of Teacher Education at the Karel de Grote-college. His research areas include Sports Pedagogy, Teacher Education, PE didactics, Cooperative learning and Tennis.

Natalie Wallian is Associate Professor at the University of Franche Comte (France) and has been successively elementary teacher, PE teacher at the International College of Strasbourg, and finally in charge of PE Teacher Education at the Department of Physical Education.

After a thesis about a historical approach on the game place at school, she now teaches educational sciences, swimming and research methodology in PE. She is also in charge of the Masters Degree of PE named "Sports, Language and Intervention". Her research interest is now on language interactions within the teaching/learning system, where she develops a semioconstructivist and student-centered approach of teaching.

Phillip Ward is an Associate Professor of Sport and Exercise Education at The Ohio State University. Phillip teaches and studies curriculum, instruction and professional development in physical education settings. He is the author of *Teaching Tumbling* and co-author of *Physical Education in the 21st Century*. He has published more than 50 papers in the field of sport pedagogy and is a member of the editorial review boards of several journals. He is a Fellow of AAHPERD's Research Consortium. With his wife Marie, and sons Robert and Trevor, Phillip likes to play tennis, to kayak and to travel.

Gregory J. Welk is Assistant Professor with the Department of Health and Human Performance at Iowa State University.

Jan Wright is Professor and Associate Dean Research in the Faculty of Education, the University of Wollongong. Her research draws on feminist and poststructuralist theory to critically engage issues associated with the body, health and physical activity. Her most recent work investigates the place and meaning of physical activity and health in the lives of young people from different social, cultural and geographical locations as they move through and beyond school.

SECTION I

Theoretical Perspectives in Physical Education Research

This opening section of the handbook is perhaps the most contentious and complex. What questions researchers have asked, how they have addressed these questions, what sense they have made of their investigations and to what end, reflect particular positions, priorities, and traditions in seek a "truth". However, the language and frameworks available to us to talk about the research process are very slippery. Should we talk in terms of paradigms, perspectives, and theories, or more specifically about ontologies, epistemologies, methodologies, and methods? As with Macdonald et al. (2002), this handbook uses the term "theoretical perspectives" to frame this section given that these words connote a view of the human world that broadly informs the research process and provides an orientation for systematic explanation. "Theoretical perspectives" contrasts the more general term "paradigm", which, while also suggesting a particular world view that permeates the inquiry process, can signify a strong, often dualistic, research affiliation (e.g. quantitative – qualitative; objectivist – subjectivist; hierarchical – collegial) that is not always helpful (Husen, 1997).

Some chapters within this section refer to paradigms and, on occasions, allude to a brief time in the early 1990s when physical education research experienced a microcosm of what has been called in the broader education literature, the paradigm wars (see Walker and Evers, 1997, or in physical education, the paradigm debate, Sparkes, 1992). For some researchers, paradigmatic allegiances or resistance to them self-consciously directs their research while for others, their assumptions and actions are unconscious. It is a goal of this section to illuminate five theoretical perspectives that are currently shaping physical education research and, in doing so, bring to the fore the richness of the assumptions and approaches underpinning research in the field.

The five theoretical perspectives around which this section is organized are: behavioural, interpretative,

critical, "post", and feminist. These are by no means the only perspectives to inform physical education research and, as will become clear, they do not sit in isolation from each other. The sequence of chapters should not be read as a chronology from the established to the new, or from quantitative to qualitative methods, though there is some basis for seeing such continua. Each chapter introduces the key concepts of the perspective and highlights international research that represents the perspective, some of which is reintroduced in subsequent sections that look at the substantive issues being researched.

Ward outlines the behavioural theoretical perspective as the philosophy, science and application of behavioural analysis. This dimension of the positivist paradigm has a strong tradition in physical education, reflecting what Good, in 1929, celebrated as education having reached a stage in its development when it may be considered a science given that it possessed both a systematic and orderly arrangement of knowledge and a scientific method (Good, 1929). Pope's chapter on the interpretative perspective shifts us away from objectivist epistemologies, experimental design, and measurement to a subjectivist epistemology that values people's meaning making by employing generally, though not exclusively, qualitative methods.

The next three perspectives that follow are "newer kids on the block" in physical education research yet each has rapidly accumulated a body of knowledge. Devis explains how the critical perspective in physical education research is concerned with more equitable physical education outcomes, particularly for those who occupy less powerful positions such as women, ethnic minorities, or those with disabilities. The feminist perspective (Nilges) takes the focus more closely to power relationships surrounding gender that work in ways to oppress women. Finally, readers looking for insight into the complex "post" perspectives of postmodernism, poststructuralism, and postcolonialism will find it in Wright's chapter. Together these perspectives provide new ways of considering power relationships, and the subjectivities and embodiment of teachers, teacher educators, and students of physical education. The critical, "post" and feminist chapters lay a strong foundation for Section 6 that looks at difference and diversity in physical education.

The inter-relationship of these theoretical perspectives is a recurrent theme of the chapters in this section. While the authors recognize the importance of researchers being cognizant and reflective of the theoretical perspectives upon which they draw, they are also mindful that the field should not stagnate. The field needs new ways of working across the perspectives, with new alliances in the research process and mixed methods of research (Johnson and Onwuegbuzie, 2004). That said, the authors also reinforce the "need to ask good questions, seek well-considered ways of coming to know, and communicate in ways that are inclusive if the field is to progress as strong and cohesive" (Macdonald et al., 151).

References

Good, C. (1929). *How to do research in education*. Baltimore, MD: Warwick and York.

Husen, T. (1997). Research paradigms in education. In J. Keeves (Ed.), *Educational research, methodology, and measurement: An international handbook* (pp. 16–21). Oxford: Elsevier.

Johnson, R. and Onwuegbuzie, A. (2004). Mixed methods research: A research paradigm whose time has come. *Educational Researcher, 33*, 14–26.

Macdonald, D., Kirk, D., Metzler, M.W., Nilges, L.M., Schempp, P. and Wright, J. (2002). 'It's all very well in theory': A review of theoretical perspectives and their applications in contemporary pedagogical research. *Quest, 54*, 133–156.

Sparkes, A. (1992). *Research in physical education and sport: Exploring alternative visions*. London: Falmer Press.

Walker, J. and Evers, C. (1997). Research in education: Epistemological issues. In J. Keeves (Ed.), *Educational research, methodology, and measurement: An international handbook* (pp. 22–30). Oxford: Elsevier.

1.1 The philosophy, science and application of behavior analysis in physical education

PHILLIP WARD

The sentiments of Pasteur highlight two key values of behavior analysis: valuing the individual and recognizing the enormous potential in humankind. These roles manifest themselves in an applied science that is both pragmatic and empowering. Findings from the science of behavior analysis have successfully made the transfer from research to practice and into everyday usage by the public. This homogenization[1] of behavior analysis can be seen everywhere. For parents, behavior analysis has developed proactive and positive child rearing strategies (Azrin, 1981; Becker, 1972; Latham, 1993; Maag, 1996). For teachers, behavior analysis has both created procedures and refined guidelines for what have become essential instructional elements such as feedback, prompts, and cues (Cooper et al., 1987) as well as developing highly generalizable instructional strategies (Becker and Carnine, 1981; Greenwood et al., 1991; Keller and Sherman, 1982; Lindsley, 1990). It also has contributed significantly to a vision of an inclusive society with the development of technologies to enable individuals with disabilities to maximize the quality of their lives (Heward, 2003).

Behind these practices is a rigorous science. Ward and Barrett (2002: 244–245) described three independent assessments of the contributions of behavior analysis in the field of education.[2]

First, Walberg (1984) analyzed 3000 studies on the effects of teacher and instructional methods factors on student achievement of K-12 students. The effects of behavioral strategies such as cues, corrective feedback, and reinforcement were large with a mean effect of one standard deviation (ranging from +.88 to +1.17). In practical terms this means that in a normal distribution students at the 50th percentile would have their score raised to the 84th percentile ...

Second, Direct Instruction (Becker and Carnine, 1981) an elementary school curriculum in language, reading and math has produced effect sizes that are two to four times greater than other curriculums (ABT associates, 1977). In their national evaluation of Project Follow Through[3] the independent evaluation agency ABT Associates concluded: "Critics of the model have predicted that the emphasis on tightly controlled instruction might discourage children from freely expressing themselves, and thus inhibiting the development of self-esteem and other affective skills. In fact, this is not the case" (ABT Associates, 1977: 73). Not only did students in the direct instruction model perform well on cognitive as well as affective tests, subsequent evaluation of these students indicated that they continued to perform well in middle and high school maintaining their academic performance over their peers. Direct Instruction Follow-Through students also had higher college acceptance rates than their peers (Kinder and Carnine, 1991).

Finally, Forness et al. (1997) in their review of 18 meta-analyses of interventions of over 1000 studies in special education reported that behavioral interventions had a mean effect size of +.93. What is impressive is not merely the size of this statistic, but rather that the next most effective treatments in special education settings were drugs with an effect size of +.58. Providing teachers with effective pedagogical practices represents a significant social contribution by behavior analysis toward the empowerment of students with special needs.

Despite both the strength of findings and the widespread homogenization of behavior analysis it is still widely misunderstood and thus misrepresented (Todd and Morris, 1992). The major purposes of this chapter are to share with the reader the epistemological foundations of behavior analysis, its empirical contributions, and its current and potential contributions to the field of physical education.

A brief historical and epistemological perspective

Different sciences often hold different assumptions about the nature of knowledge and the criteria used for scientific explanation. Making the distinction between epistemologies and methodologies is important, because while many of the behavioral sciences share some epistemological assumptions they also hold other very divergent assumptions. Thus their methodologies vary accordingly. From an epistemological perspective O'Donohue and Kitchener (1998) identify 14 versions of Behaviorism. Two of the most common include the "Methodological Behaviorism" of John Watson (1913)[4] and the "Radical Behaviorism" of B.F. Skinner[5] (1974).

Methodological behaviorism represents a line of inquiry that in its initial iteration in the early 20th century emphasized observable behaviors and eschewed all non-observable behavior. It relies on truth by agreement[6] as its criteria for empiricism. However, as Moore (2000) observed, as methodological behaviorism moved into the mid and late 20th century its scientists, mostly psychologists, have also pursued a strategy of including in their theories unobservable constructs that have been operationally defined. The inclusion of hypothetical constructs has made methodological behaviorism a root theory for many modern psychological practices.

In stark contrast to methodological behaviorism, is Skinner's radical behaviorism (1974). Many writers, both scientific and lay, confuse radical behaviorism with the early practices of methodological behaviorism suggesting, for example, that radical behaviorism eschews non-observable behavior such as feelings and thinking which it does not. Both in practice and from an ontological perspective, however, the two behaviorisms share little in common. Skinner called his philosophy of the science of behavior, radical behaviorism in the sense that the term "radical" meant a comprehensive explanation of behavior (Skinner, 1974). Comprehensive in that Skinner's radical behaviorism:

> does not insist on truth by agreement and can therefore consider events taking place within the private world within the skin. It does not call these events unobservable, and it does not dismiss them as subjective. It simply questions the nature of the objects observed and the reliability of the observations. The position can be stated as follows: what is felt or introspectively observed is not some non-physical world of consciousness, mind, or mental life but the observer's own body. (Skinner, 1974: 18–19)

Thus rather than acting as a causal agent of behavior a private event is:

> At best no more than a link in the causal chain, and it is usually not even that. We may think before we act in the sense that we may behave covertly before we behave overtly, but our action is not an 'expression' of the covert response or the consequence of it. The two are simply attributable to the same variables. (Skinner, 1953: 279)

As an example of Skinner's point consider a teacher observing a student's interaction with the task. She may think about an appropriate strategy to use to help the student, and then act accordingly, but the thinking and the acting were occasioned by the observation of the student's interaction. Skinner's second point is that in many cases thinking is a behavior that occurs at the same time as a teacher's behavior. Both are occasioned by the observation, but thinking may not be part of the causal sequence for the resultant teacher behavior. For Skinner the skin is not a barrier in the examination of behavior. He called behavior that occurred outside of the skin "overt" and behavior inside of the skin "covert" (Skinner, 1974). His point was that regardless of where the behavior occurred it was subject to the same principles. Skinner was most interested in an explanation of the behavior. Thus relative to a covert behavior such as thinking, the question is not "Does thinking occur?" but rather "Why does it occur?" and "What are its distinguishing characteristics" (Skinner, 1974).

Radical behaviorism differs from many views of contemporary psychology on this point. By eschewing a non-physical world within the skin, it stands apart from the Cartesian dualism of a mind as a separate and distinct substance from a physical world, a mind not subject to causal laws. Moreover, the epistemological roots of radical behaviorism are not to be found in logical positivism as is sometimes asserted (Moore, 2000). For many authors behavior analysis and logical positivism are synonymous. At a superficial level it is possible to see why. Both positions share assumptions about determinism, empiricism, and experimentation. Certainly, several behaviorisms have been front and center of the logical positivist position such as methodological behaviorism and neo-behaviorism. However, radical behaviorism holds very different assumptions than logical positivism and ought not to be described as a logical positivist position (Moore, 2000; O'Donohue and Ferguson, 2001; Skinner, 1974; Smith, 1986). In addition to the rejecting the truth by agreement criterion of the logical positivists, radical behaviorism views verbal behavior as learned behavior, a consequence of genetic predispositions and the influence of a social environment. As such verbal behavior is not regarded as providing evidence of underlying mental processes or mental phenomena; it is instead analyzed as a behavior in terms of the events that caused its occurrence (Moore, 2000).

The epistemology of radical behaviorism has been influenced by the works of the English philosopher Francis Bacon, by the Austrian physicist Ernst Mach and it is grounded in the natural sciences. Bacon's insistence on the inductive method as a strategy for science influenced Skinner to discard theories that were not inductively derived and to emphasize observation as a central strategy in data collection for the science of behavior analysis (Skinner, 1950).

Mach's influences on Skinner were not as much ontological as methodological (Chiesa, 1992). Causality as a mechanistic push–pull, cause and effect, was replaced by Mach's notion of functional relations. Chiesea (1992: 1290) notes: "In the Skinnerian system, a cause is replaced with a 'change in the independent variable' and an effect is replaced with a 'change in the dependent variable,' transforming the cause-effect into a 'functional relation'." This emphasis on relational characteristics of events is also underscored in the assumption that like a snowflake, no two humans are the same. It is possible that a current set of circumstances is common to many people (such as everyone who reads these words) but the histories of each reader are unique. Thus the unit of analysis in behavior analysis is the unique behavior of the individual which is a function of the intersection in time of the current context, the history of the individual and their genetic predispositions (such as intelligence). This recognition of the uniqueness of individuals led to the use of single subject methodology as the strategy for both measuring individual behavior and demonstrating functional relations.

In books (Skinner, 1953, 1974) and papers (Skinner, 1966, 1981) Skinner outlined his rationale situating behavior analysis as a selectionist science akin to biology as the parent science for evolutionary change. He drew upon evolutionary theory in describing selection occurring at the biological level where some species characteristics and not others are selected over the course of multiple generations (Glenn, 1988). Skinner (1974) proposed that at the behavioral level, selection operated in an analogous manner where some behaviors are selected by the environment and others are not as a result of individual adaptation within the course of a lifetime. He also proposed that the analogy extended to the cultural level referring to cultural practices that occur in different societies, some of which are selected because of their consequences and some of which are not (Skinner, 1974).

Regardless of the level of analysis (evolutionary, behavioral or cultural) the basic processes are variation and selection. In each case, selection must wait for variation to occur. At the evolutionary level the evolutionary history of a species or phylogeny is a product of the selection of genotypes by the environment. Such selection is contingent upon the variability in the species. At the behavioral or ontogenic level some behaviors are more likely to survive than others as a result of their consequences. For example, the chain of behaviors and consequences that leads you to travel to your school or office one way rather than another. Unlike evolutionary changes that occur over generations, individuals can adapt quickly to changes such as when road repairs or the influence of traffic at a particular time of day creates potential consequences that from experience you might wish to avoid. Similar outcomes can occur from advice-giving leading to the following of rules; such as listening to the traffic report and adjusting the route you travel accordingly. New behaviors are emitted by individuals all the time, but only some are selected (such as when an infant is learning to walk or when a student in physical education is learning to evade a defender in tag rugby for the first few times). We typically call this trial and error, and the outcome is that successful actions tend to be repeated.

Cultural selection occurs when some cultural practices are selected over others within particular cultures. As ontogenic (operant) selection is explainable in the context of phylogenic (natural) selection, cultural selection is explainable in terms of ontogenic selection. A culture consists of the learned behavior and the products of that behavior (Glenn, 2003). Glenn (1988: 167) defined a cultural practice as a "set of interlocking contingencies of reinforcement in which the behavior and the behavioral products of each participant function as environmental events with which the behavior of other individuals interacts". For example, the cultural practice of education in a university is arranged in such a way as to offer a variety of educational choices. Though the content of these choices varies greatly (for example majors in biology, education, anthropology), the choices have much in common. Many students take introductory classes in these various content areas. Thus, faculty in different departments all contribute to the undergraduate experience of a student. Faculty may be unaware of the contributions of others such as an instructor teaching introduction to exercise physiology may be unaware of what was taught in introduction to anthropology. Yet the combined coursework that a student completes produces a cultural outcome called a "university education". An individual's courses are interconnected in multiple ways most commonly seen in the curriculum and in the rules that define the progress through the curriculum. The organization of the components and the rules of the curriculum may be considered a meta-contingency.

A meta-contingency then, describes the relations between the interlocking behavioral contingencies in the curriculum such as rules and courses. Meta-contingencies exist in many institutionalized forms in societies and they not only explain cultural practices of individuals who collaborate and contribute to cultural outcomes, such as education, but also the maintenance of cultural practices such as sexual, gender, and racial discrimination, as well as practices such as tolerance, equity, and equality (Harris, 1989). In a number of areas such as participation in sport, access to health care, and equitable opportunities for education, the meta-contingencies are arranged in such a way as to favor some groups over others such as boys over girls, the wealthy over the poor, the able-bodied over the disabled, or one ethnicity over another. Meta-contingencies can also explain cultural practices that attempt to overcome these practices, such as legislation, or non-legislative policies in workplaces, schools and also the collective acts of small groups.

Essential concepts of behavior analysis[7]

Behavior analysis is both a basic and an applied science. Basic laboratory research is known as the experimental analysis of behavior. Applied research is known as applied behavior analysis (ABA). The subject matter of this science is behavior. Behavior can be simply defined as everything that a person does. This includes, as discussed earlier, covert behavior such as thinking and feeling that a person can self-observe as well as overt behavior such as writing, speaking and moving that can be observed by others. The purpose of behavior analysis is to seek explanation and description to enable the prediction and control of behavior.

Prediction allows us to have advance knowledge of what will happen in certain situations (O'Donohue and Ferguson, 2001). Teachers often behave on the basis of their past experiences with similar situations. For example, a teacher who has had experience teaching the overhand pass in volleyball will also have had experience with which cues and prompts work in teaching the skill (this is the pedagogical content knowledge that the teacher "knows"). When teaching the overhand pass in the present the teacher is likely to use such cues again. Reflecting on the pedagogical content knowledge that might best suit a student is an example of everyday prediction. That is on the basis of experience with past students we predict that the circumstances are similar and that this cue we are about to give the student will likely work. The cue may not work because the situation may have changed, or the student's difficulty with the skill may not be at all similar to what the teacher has encountered in the past with other students. With increasingly complex behavior prediction becomes less predictable, but not less determined (Chisea, 2003).

The use of the term "control" indicates that the controlling variables for a particular situation are understood and such knowledge allows one to change the controlling variables to improve a situation. For many individuals hearing the term "control" suggests to them some nefarious purpose and raises questions about the purposes of control. Often these positions are phrased in terms of political and social issues and correctly so! What is often

not recognized is that knowing the controlling variables empowers individuals to pursue their change of the conditions in their own lives. For example, we often rely on the prediction of weather reports to control our dress for the next day; and we rely on our experiences in dealing with children or colleagues to allow us to control our actions as parents or peers. If one assumes orderly rather than capricious relations among phenomena, then one cannot step outside of the causal stream. As Skinner (1974: 209) explains "We cannot choose a way of life in which there is no control. We can only change the controlling conditions". Thus a person can in this sense control the world around them by controlling the variables that are responsible for the behaviors. Setting a schedule for oneself places priority on some events and less on others. A lesson plan operates in the same manner allowing teachers to manage how and where they spend their time. Teachers often rely on their experiences in dealing with children to inform them of how they might behave when a similar situation occurs again.

Two classes of behavior

Basic and applied researchers in behavior analysis study two general classes of behavior called respondent and operant behavior. The controlling mechanisms for each of these behaviors are fundamentally different.

Respondent behavior

Behavior that is under the control of the autonomic nervous system, commonly called reflexes, is a class of behavior called respondent behavior. Reflexes are elicited by a stimulus. Some reflexes are unlearned such as blinking when you see a bright light in a dark room or an infant's startle reflex. These reflexes are congenital and are shared by most members of a species. Respondent behaviors comprise only a small portion of the human behavioral repertoire. The forms (topography) of respondent behavior, once they are developmentally capable of being elicited, are stable/do not increase across the life span (i.e., new respondent behaviors are not developed). What changes is the spread of stimuli that will elicit the respondent behavior. We do not learn new physiological and emotional responses, rather new stimuli become conditioned to elicit those responses. Over the course of a person's life some physiological and emotional responses become conditioned respondent behavior.

Martin (2003) explains:

> Consider a plausible example of reflexive learning in sport. Let's suppose that a beginning gymnast experiences several bad falls while practicing a back

flip on the balance beam, each fall causing both feelings of fear and considerable pain. The principal of Pavlovian learning states that if a neutral stimulus (practicing a back flip on the balance beam) is closely followed by an unconditioned response (feelings of fear). Then the previously neutral stimulus (practicing a back flip on the balance beam) will also tend to elicit that response (feelings of fear). Now when the young gymnast is about to practice the back flip on the balance beam, she is likely to become fearful and tense. (Martin, 2003: 11).

In order to reduce the pain and fear the gymnast is displaying, coaches often pad the balance beam to make it softer when struck and they also physically support the gymnast as she performs the skill. In so doing, coaches "end" the relationship between performing the back flip and the pain and fear. Technically this would be called respondent extinction (for more detailed discussion of respondent principles see Martin, 2003). Respondent processes can provide an explanation for situations such as: "Why do so many individuals" get nervous before speaking in public?" and "Why do some athletes tense up before performance?" In many cases the explanation lies in the relationships established between stimuli and behavior that over time become conditioned respondent behavior.

Operant behavior

In contrast to respondent behaviors, "operants" are a class of behaviors whose occurrence is not elicited by stimuli (that is stimulus–response), but are controlled by the consequences of the behavior (that is response–consequence). Many behaviors are emitted for the first time as a result of following instructions, or as variations of previous behaviors as one experiments in a trial and error fashion, or perhaps as an accident where a person was trying to perform one action, but performed another because their timing may have been off. In each of these cases the behavior comes under the control of its consequences. In some cases the behavior will not be repeated, or repeated very infrequently and in others it will be repeated frequently. One way to think of operants is as a genetic susceptibility of a voluntary behavior to be affected by its consequences. Thus any behavior that varies as a function of its consequences may be said to be an operant. This is called the "law of effect" (Thorndike, 1932) and is a primary assumption of the determinism of radical behavior analysis.

A principle of behavior is a description of nature expressed as a basic functional relation between a behavior and its controlling variables. Principles of operant behavior (such as reinforcement, punishment, extinction) are functionally defined by behavior environment interactions; specifically, the occurrence of a behavior and a consequence that immediately follows that behavior. The behavior–environment interaction produced reinforcement when because of the consequence, the person emits that behavior more frequently in the future when experiencing a similar environmental context. Behavior–environment interactions can be broadly described as increasing the occurrence of the behavior, decreasing the occurrence of a behavior and maintaining a behavior. When a behavior increases in its occurrence it is said to be reinforced. This is seen often when a student performs a technique repeatedly because it is successful. When a behavior decreases its occurrence it may have occurred because a new environmental event occurred in which case this process is called punishment. This often occurs in trial and error learning where a student tries different ways to perform a skill and stops using some in favor of others. Sometimes a behavior decreases because a reinforcer previously present is no longer provided. When this happens the process is described as extinction.

A good example of extinction occurs when a teacher who has in the past reinforced with her attention a student who repeatedly interrupts during demonstrations, decides to ignore future interruptions. In such a case, the teacher might look for conversation with the student at another time in the lesson. There are a number of research-based behavior change procedures that derive from these principles such as shaping, backward chaining, differential reinforcement, generalization and discrimination (see Cooper et al. (1987), for more details on principles and behavior change procedures).

While a behavior can be explained by its consequences, behavior most often occurs in a context. Commonly called antecedents, this context occasions the behavior. Antecedents do not function as a stimulus to elicit behavior as is the case with respondent behavior, but it does make the behavior more probable. The antecedent has been present in the past when the behavior was reinforced (Cooper et al., 1987). Thus when a student enters a gymnasium it is more likely that physical activity is going to occur than a math class. The student is able to discriminate between contexts because of the antecedent. A physical education teacher who has taught her students to enter the gymnasium and to move to one of the existing stations to begin warm-up and to do so as long as the music is playing has established a set of antecedents that students can discriminate, each with a behavior and an associated consequence.

Antecedents can also include motivating variables called "motivating operations" (Laraway et al., 2003). A motivating operation produces two behavioral effects. First, it momentarily alters the reinforcing effectiveness of consequent events. Second, it momentarily alters (increases or decreases) the frequency of responses that have been reinforced by those consequent events. An example of a motivating operation might occur when during a basketball practice a coach puts three minutes on the shot clock for the two teams to score as many points as is possible in that available time. This has the effect of momentarily increasing the frequency of shots on goals during the three minutes available.

Major findings in physical education and sport pedagogy

The history of ABA in phsysical education owes much to Daryl Siedentop. An early book *The Development and Control of Behavior in Sport and Physical Education* co-authored with Brent Rushall (1972) introduced behavior analysis to coaches and physical educators. Siedentop's (1976) first and subsequent editions of *Developing Teaching Skills in Physical Education* provided practical guidelines incorporating the research on effective teaching and the application of behavior analysis in physical education contexts. In a series of papers Siedentop (1981, 1982, 1983, 1984) described a research agenda that both conceptually and methodologically influenced and supported the work of at least three decades of graduate students at The Ohio State University (OSU), as well as faculty and students elsewhere in the USA and overseas.

While Siedentop was a professor at OSU a number of individuals were concurrently contributing to behavior analysis in physical education, adapted physical education and in coaching. Eitan Eldar in Israel at the Zinman College of Physical Education developed an applied behavior analysis program which has simultaneously served as a teacher training program as well as an outreach and engagement program. The program uses movement and sport taught by preservice and inservice teachers as a context for behavior change for children and youths with particular attention to those at risk of school failure and those who have special needs. Along with a number of publications, Eldar has authored two books in Hebrew *Effective Teaching in Physical Education* (Eldar, 1997) and more recently, *Applied Behavior Analysis* (Eldar, 2002).

Ron French at Texas Women's University and Barry Lavay at California State University Long Beach have been writing and teaching behavior analysis for students with disabilities in the USA for nearly two decades. In 1990 French and Lavay edited *A Manual of Behavior Management Techniques for Physical Educators and Recreators* and later that decade Lavay, French and Henderson (1997) wrote a physical education specific behavior management text for teachers. Brent Rushall, an Australian, now at San Diego State University has been writing,

teaching, and conducting workshops in behavioral sports psychology around the world since the late 1960s. The focus of much of Rushall's 74 books and manuals, and his more than 300 articles has been on coaches and athletes (http://www-rohan.sdsu.edu/dept/coachsci/rushall/about.htm). Garry Martin, a Canadian, at the University of Manitoba has used behavior analysis in two fields: developmental disabilities and sport psychology. He has authored the popular book for teachers, *Behavior Modification: What it is and How to do it?* (Martin and Pear, 2003), and several books specific for coaching settings (Martin and Hrycaiko, 1983; Martin and Lumsden, 1987) including his most recent *Sport Psychology: Practical Guidelines from Behavior Analysis* (Martin, 2003). Together with Dennis Hrycaiko, Martin has published widely in the field of sports psychology.

Since 1980, there have been several major reviews of the behavioral literature of physical education (Ward and Barrett 2002), of sport and physical education (Donahue, et al., 1980; Martin, 1992), of behavioral coaching interventions (Lee, 1993; Martin and Tkachuk 2000; Tkachuk et al., 2003) of behavioral interventions in youth sport (Smith et al., 1996) and of behavioral procedures used to teach motor skills to individuals with severe disabilities (Demchack, 1993). This section begins with a survey of studies using applied behavior analysis techniques and using single subject designs to determine their effectiveness. Intervention studies in both physical education and sport are reported because increasingly, studies in these areas are being cross-cited, and techniques developed in one area such as coaching are being more frequently used in physical education.

Research in physical education settings

There is a strong literature base in K-12 physical education. Ward and Barrett (2002) reported on 34 intervention studies conducted from 1976–2000, and since then there have been a further five studies that have been published.[8] Demchack (1993) reviewed 34 intervention studies focusing on behavioral procedures to teach motor skills to individuals with severe disabilities not included in Ward's and Barrett's analysis.

One focus of behavioral researchers has been directed toward improving teaching behavior of preservice and inservice teachers. A number of behavioral strategies have been used to improve teaching behaviors using variations of systematic feedback such as verbal and graphic feedback (Darst, 1976; Darst and Steeves, 1980; Dunbar and O'Sullivan, 1986; Grant et al., 1990; Lounsbery and Sharpe, 1999; Pease, 1984; Sharpe et al., 1997,

2002); audiocueing (e.g., van der Mars, 1987, 1988; Kahan, 2002); use of videotape (Sharpe et al., 1996) and self-monitoring (Eldar, 1990).

Feedback of teaching performance has also been studied using principals as change agents (Ratliffe, 1986); and in a procedure called directed rehearsal, which is a positive practice procedure to develop competency of basic teaching skills (Ward et al., 1998, 1997); and feedback and modeling of teaching behaviors (Sharpe et al., 1989). Systematic models of behavioral supervision have also been developed and assessed (Ocansey, 1988). In addition, a training program to help preservice teachers improve their qualitative analysis of motor skills has been validated (Wilkinson, 1991).

A second focus of researchers has been class management. Here the goal has been to reduce off-task behavior and increase on-task behavior. Researchers have assessed the effects of independent variables such as group contingencies (Jeltma and Vogler, 1985; Pease, 1982; Patrick et al., 1998; Ward and Dunaway, 1995), individual contingencies (Vogler and French, 1983; White and Bailey, 1990), cross-group feedback (Ryan and Yerg, 2001), a public address system (Ryan et al., 2002), and teacher proximity (Sariscsany et al., 1995; Schuldheisz and van der Mars, 2001). In this line of inquiry researchers have also focused on teaching proactive social skills to students using a sportsmanship curriculum (Sharpe et al., 1995), and social skills training (Giebink and McKenzie, 1985).

A number of studies have validated the effectiveness of using peers in physical education using various arrangements such as: classwide peer tutoring (Johnson and Ward, 2002); peer-mediated accountability (Crouch et al., 1997; Ward et al., 1997, 1998); and the use of typical functioning peers as tutors for students with disabilities (Houston-Wilson et al., 1997; Lieberman et al., 2000; Webster, 1987).

Studies using behavioral interventions in both integrated and segregated physical education settings have examined instructions that promote inclusion. There have been studies on the effects of teaching students with disabilities how to self-pace their aerobic exercise (Ellis et al., 1993); on the efficacy of a four-step instructional strategy on the motor performance of students with mild–moderate disabilities (Yang and Poretta, 1999); and an assessment of an integrated versus a segregated setting on preschool students' motor performance (Zittel and McCubbin, 1996).

In her review of behavioral procedures to teach motor skills to individuals with severe disabilities, Demchak (1993) described antecedent and consequent conditions that have been demonstrated to improve the acquisition of basic yet critical motor skills. Antecedents typically included systems of prompts including verbal instructions, gestures, modeling, and physical guidance. Consequences such as social reinforcers and corrective feedback were commonly used. Instructional strategies included "shaping" a procedure in which successive approximations of the behavior are reinforced. The instructors in these studies were typically not physical educators, but physical therapists. The results were very positive. Many of the participants in these studies required considerable ongoing support to function in society. Teaching them motor skills such as walking, stationary bike riding, and running provides these individuals with some control over their environments. Demchak (1993) argued that individuals with severe disabilities are often able to be taught motor skills when other approaches such as neuromotor programming, sensory integration, and naturalistic programming have been unsuccessful.

Research in sport settings

The earliest behavioral study in sports was conducted by Rushall and Pettinger (1969). They investigated the effects of various reinforcers on the performance of swimmers. Since then, there has been a decade by decade increase in the number of behavioral studies published with a wide variety of foci. Many studies have been completed using systematic observation techniques derived from behavior analysis such as the Smith and Smoll series of studies using the Coaching Behavior Assessment System (Smith et al., 1977) focusing on behavioral interventions in youth sport (see Smith et al., 1996 for a review). Martin and Tkachuk (2000) categorized intervention studies using applied behavior analysis techniques as those that focused on (a) behavioral coaching versus standard coaching, (b) self-management interventions to improve performance, (c) interventions designed to improve competitive performance, and (d) changing the behavior of coaches.

In behavioral coaching studies interventions often consisting of differential and contingent reinforcement are compared to standard coaching using athlete behaviors as a dependent variable. Examples of these variables include performance of offense skills in a youth football team (Komaki and Barnett, 1977); swimming stroke performance by youth swimmers (Fitterling and Ayllon, 1983; Koop and Martin, 1983); correct relay tag technique by competitive inline-roller speed skaters (Anderson and Kirkpatrick, 2002); foul shooting performance of a women's collegiate basketball team (Kladopoulos and McComas, 2001); swimming practice and social behaviors by members of a youth swim team (Vogler and Mood, 1986); and the technique of youth tennis players (Buzas and Ayllon, 1981).

One promising pedagogical strategy used by coaches that is also being used by teachers in physical education is the "freeze technique". In this strategy the coach calls a freeze to the play in a scrimmage or drill and players are questioned about their current physical placements relative to the play. This is followed by modeling and then a replay of the events. The freeze technique has been used successfully to improve performance of technical skills and the use of tactics in gymnastics, tennis, and football (Allison and Allyon, 1980); and with youth soccer players (Rush and Ayllon, 1984); and youth track athletes (Shapiro and Shapiro, 1985).

An increasingly studied area of feedback has been publicly posting information about athlete performance. The effects of public posting have been assessed on the practice of set plays in scrimmages with measures of generalization to game performances in collegiate football (Brobst and Ward, 2002, Ward and Carnes, 2002, Ward et al., 1997); on reducing un-sportsperson-like conduct in tennis (Galvin and Ward, 1998); and on body checks during collegiate hockey games (Anderson et al., 1988).

Another form of feedback has been the use of self-management interventions using goal setting and self monitoring to increase the frequency of previously learned skills with youth swimmers (Critchfield and Vargas, 1991; McKenzie and Rushall, 1974); youth figure skaters, (Hume et al., 1985); and with female youth gymnasts (Wolko et al., 1993). Goal setting has also been used as a standalone intervention in collegiate basketball (Swain and Jones, 1995). There are also some unique feedback studies including assessments of the use of videotaping feedback on performance of youth swimmers (Hazen et al., 1990); a shaping procedure with a photoelectric beam to improve the technical skill and performance of a pole vaulter (Scott et al., 1997), musical reinforcement to improve swimming behaviors (Hume and Crossman, 1992), and stimulus cueing and discrimination training to improve the performance of tennis players (Ziegler, 1987) and soccer players (Ziegler, 1994).

There have been a number of package interventions using various combinations of goal setting, relaxation, imagery, self monitoring, and self talk that have been assessed with track and field athletes in Special Olympics (Gregg et al., 2004; Wanlin et al., 1997); adult tri-athletes and runners (Patrick and Hrycaiko, 1998; Thelwell and Greenlees, 2003); youth figure skaters (Ming and Martin, 1996); youth hockey goaltenders (Rogerson and Hrycaiko, 2002); and with collegiate basketball players (Hamilton and Fremouw, 1985; Kendall et al., 1990).

Summary

There are at least five conclusions that can be derived from this survey of applied behavior analytic research in physical education and sport. First, applied behavior analytic studies have made major contributions to the field of physical education by establishing an empirical base for many teacher education, teaching, and coaching practices. The independent variables in these studies (such as differential reinforcement) demonstrate utility in both teaching and coaching settings. In particular, coaching studies have shown that interventions using behavioral principles have effectively improved the performances of youth and college athletes, in both individual and team sports, focusing on both the techniques of skill performance and the tactics of game play. In addition, researchers investigating teaching strategies in coaching settings have validated those interventions by assessing the extent to which the performances occur during games (for example, Ward and Carnes, 2002). Such studies have strong application to physical education settings. For example, one behavioral strategy the "freeze technique" (Allison and Allyon, 1980; Rush and Ayllon, 1984; Shapiro and Shapiro, 1985) has recently been used by Lee (2004) to assess the use of supporting behavior of middle school students learning to play rugby. Lee's data show that performances from teaching scrimmages where teachers used the freeze technique to stop the play and replay player movements generalized to games where students demonstrated supporting tactical play more appropriately than when the focus was on only technical performance.

Second, the research questions that have been asked in these studies have focused on pragmatic challenges in teaching and coaching. Changes in the dependent variables as a result of the independent variables have demonstrated meaningful change in the participants' behavior. There is evidence in various forms including follow-up data, and social validity questionnaires, that these procedures are used by teachers teaching in K-12 physical education settings and by coaches in recreation through collegiate levels of competition. The research questions posed in these physical education and coaching studies emphasize the tradition of induction and have been open-ended, asking: "What are the effects of an independent variable on a dependent variable?" While, the data in these studies demonstrate the efficacy of the pedagogical strategies, it is only recently that measures of maintenance and generalization have occurred with any consistency (Lee, 1993; Ward and Barrett, 2002). Research questions are now moving beyond simply "Can this performance be improved?" to including "What evidence is there that behavior has been maintained over time or used in another setting?" Importantly, the questions and the studies used to answer them show a programmatic theme that includes the systematic replication of findings with different participants, settings, and behaviors.

Third, compared to earlier decades, researchers in the past decade have used designs with increasing levels of sophistication including the use of reversals of interventions (where treatments are withdrawn or the contingencies reversed), the counterbalancing of interventions, and the combination of two or more design types such as using a reversal or multi-treatment design within a multiple baseline design. While it is true that the studies by and large show substantive effects from baseline conditions to intervention, the rigor of these studies varies. Single subject designs by their very nature, emphasize internal validity. If one applies the design rules (Cooper et al., 1987) to some of these studies, limitations appear. Most problematic for physical education researchers has been the answer to the question "When to intervene?" There are several threats to internal validity associated with this question. One of these threats is intervening before a stable baseline has been achieved and similarly introducing a second intervention before the previous intervention has demonstrated stability. One requirement for single-subject designs is the establishment of stability of data during various conditions. This stability allows for the underlying inductive rationale for the experimental designs to be made (Cooper et al., 1987). In some instances interventions occurred when there was quite large variability in the baseline data. Typically, the variability reduced following intervention and the interpretation between levels of performance in each condition was more easily determined. While this is acceptable in some instances, not all studies were able to demonstrate such strong effects of an intervention. In such cases waiting longer for the data to become stable would have been a better design option.

The most serious threat to internal validity has been the commonplace decision to intervene on all of the participants in a class at the same time. A typical study selects a purposive sample per class of usually two to four students. These students along with the rest of the class receive an intervention such as feedback at the same time. Since each student is unique, their behaviors in baseline often vary. If treated individually, the decision to intervene on each student might not occur on the same day. Logistically however, teachers cannot implement the interventions to some students and not to others. Thus, researchers have in the name of efficiency frequently made the decision to intervene on all students at the same time. It is often unclear in some studies, on what criteria the decision to intervene has been made.

Both of the problems described here are often a consequence of the researcher's struggle with creating a good design relative to the number of lessons in a unit of instruction. Most studies are less than 20 days in length because most units of instruction are less than 20 days. In the interest of ecological validity researchers have "crammed" studies into the available time. What this limitation of time has meant is that introductions of interventions and baselines have occurred before the previous condition's data were fully stable. These are common challenges in many research designs. But because of the emphasis in single-subject designs on stable data

these common problems become threats to internal validity.

Fourth, the dependent variables that have been used over the last few decades have improved in their descriptions and measurement. There has been a trend away from interval recording toward event recording of behaviors. A common strategy is to choose high- and low-skilled, male and female students in a study in order to show the differential effects of the intervention on ability and gender. Also occurring in the design of studies has been the inclusion of measures of social validity. To assess social validity an investigator invites participants and experts to examine the goals, procedures, and outcomes of the study. In their review of physical education literature from 1979–2000, Ward and Barrett (2002) reported that only 17% of studies used measures of social validity, but that more recent studies were likely to have included these measures than older studies. Several coaching studies (for example, Kendall et al., 1990; Patrick and Hrycaiko, 1998; Thelwell and Greenlees, 2003) have demonstrated the use of independent variables not commonly associated with behavior analysis. Relaxation training, self-talk, and goal setting are all effective strategies that have been used as independent variables to improve performance.

Fifth, there is surprisingly little analysis of the functional aspects of interventions in these studies beyond a description of their effects. One explanation may lie in the fact that many are "packaged" interventions involving several components. For example, in providing feedback to students several researchers in physical education used verbal and graphic feedback. Determining the individual effects of the intervention components is not possible in such studies. It is however, necessary to begin to conduct such analysis if the functional relationships among variables and behavior are to be well elucidated. Related to this last point, is an absence of explanation of behavioral principles underlying these studies. It is unclear beyond some gross indicators what behavioral principles are operating in some of these studies. Researchers would do well to explain the rationales for their independent variables not just in terms of their use in other studies, but also in terms that describe the behavioral principles.

What is not apparent from this review is the effect to which behavioral strategies and procedures have become embedded into everyday practice and into the research of non-behavioral researchers. As one example of the contributions and embedded nature of behavior analysis consider the following abridged history of supervision in physical education. In 1980, one of the most influential milestones in supervision research was the creation of an observation instrument that used interval recording to record student and teacher behaviors. Academic Learning Time in Physical Education or ALT-PE

(Siedentop et al., 1982) used a set of variables that has served to focus the profession's attention on the effects of teacher behavior on student behavior and visa versa. Soon after that, training procedures for this instrument were standardized. The manual was created as public domain so that it could be distributed widely. Today many systematic observation instruments used to assess student teaching are based on the ALT-PE instrument.

In 1981 Siedentop published a paper titled *The Ohio State University supervision research program* describing dissertation research that had been conducted in the area of student teacher supervision. Drawing the growth in systematic observation instruments, a collection of systematic observation instruments using event, duration and interval recording procedures was published in 1983 by Darst et al. An updated version appeared again in 1989 by Darst et al. These books helped define the dependent variables of interest in the area of supervision research, and this in turn had the effect of further focusing attention on what teachers and students do, rather than making reference to psychometric measures as other professions have used.

In 1988, Ocansay described a systematic process for using data obtained by systematic observation which served to show teacher educators how data from ALT-PE and other instruments could be incorporated into a systematic supervision plan. Also in 1988, Taggart described a set of sequential field experiences designed to systematically generalize teaching skills across teaching settings. The first book on supervision was published by Metzler (1990), followed by similar texts by Randall (1992), Boyce (2003), and Senne (2004). The references and practices in these books have drawn heavily on procedures developed from the work of the previous decades of behavioral researchers. In short, much of the supervision literature in physical education is derived in part or whole from behavioral research in physical education.

Applications of behavior analysis in physical education

In this section of the paper, drawing upon behavior analysis theory and recent directions in research I illustrate three applications of behavior analysis: (a) the teaching of tactics, (b) peer-assisted learning, and (c) social skills training.

The teaching of tactics

Historically, the teaching of games in physical education has proceeded from motor skill training to game play with little emphasis given to the tactical components of a game. This has produced critiques of this process that make the case students lack

knowledge of what to do when confronted with tactical situations within the game (Holt et al., 2002). From a behavioral perspective an execution of tactical performance reflects the accumulation of a person's history of discrimination and generalization responses in similar conditions. Such discrimination and generalization are predicated on contextual stimuli. For example, the position of members of the offense during corner kick in a game of soccer are stimuli for a defender's positioning. In addition, when the ball is kicked, the speed, direction and trajectory function as typographic stimuli for all of the players' resultant movements. Movements by players can also be affected by the rules they are following such as person to person or zone defense, or the instructions that if a particular situation occurs then do this. Such rules can be provided by teammates or by the coach, or they might be formed from past experiences. The degree to which these rules are followed depends to the extent that the rules have consequences. Consequences in this instance might include the ability of the defenders to steal the ball, whether possession is kept following the corner kick and whether a kick on goal occurred. A teacher may also provide feedback or prompts during a corner kick for players to get into position if they are not in the correct position.

The task for successful players can be described in terms of both stimulus and response generalization. Stimulus generalization occurs when a behavior that has been reinforced only in the presence of a given antecedent condition occurs with an increased frequency in the presence of different, but similar stimuli (Cooper et al., 1987). This occurs when a player who practices a drill in a 2-on-3 situation moves to a 3-on-3 or applies a tactic previously practiced only during a scrimmage for the first time during a game. Response generalization occurs when in a given antecedent condition a player's repertoire of available behaviors to pass, to maintain possession of the ball, or to take a kick on goal, evokes similar, but different responses (Cooper et al., 1987).

The behavioral view emphasizes the use of specific skills to specific situations that have been previously explicitly taught and where students are following rules such as "If this … do this or this …". Emphasis is also placed on the generalization of existing skills to new scenarios. As Siedentop (1983: 14) noted:

> "Clearly, not all situations can be identified and taught as rule governed sport behavior. But the fact that not all situations can be anticipated does not mean that frequently occurring and occasionally occurring important situations should not be identified and courses of action prescribed".

It is also very important to respond to novel conditions that students have not encountered before.

Siedentop (1983) suggested that the best way to prepare for novel situations was to build a repertoire of discriminated behavior in which the player is able to respond appropriately to unencountered complex situations. An example of this process is well reflected in Launder's (2001) Play Practice instructional model which uses rules of play that emphasize scenario tactics consistent with the overall character of the game (for example, rugby is a running game while basketball is a passing game). In play practice tactics are applied to increasingly more complex game-like scenarios.

Peer-assisted learning

A major problem that teacher's encounter is finding adequate time to monitor and to provide feedback and reinforcement for students in their classes. Peer-Assisted Learning (PAL) strategies are very effective ways to allow students to receive instruction, feedback and reinforcement from group members much more frequently than a teacher could provide. Peer-Assisted Learning occurs in small groups and in dyads. It is most commonly seen in forms such as tutoring and cooperative learning, but it is also a component of instructional models such as Teaching Games for Understanding (Bunker and Thorpe, 1982), Sport Education (Siedentop, 1994), and Social and Personal Responsibility (Hellison, 2003). Activities such as tutoring and cooperative learning also involve discrimination and generalization by students. Examples of discrimination include when a tutor observing two students playing tennis praises one student's technique, but corrects the other's technique; and when a student passes the ball in basketball to a player in the open, but not to another who is being covered by an opponent. Examples of generalization occur when a tutor who has been praising a friend during a game in physical education who then praises that friend during a recess game.

Tutors are taught to behave one way such as to praise or to otherwise identify the performance as correct when a certain performance occurs, and to behave differently when that performance does not occur. This differential behavior of the tutor functions as one consequence of the tutee's behavior. Other consequences present in the environment might include positive outcomes such as successfully shooting a basket or acing a serve in tennis or punitive outcomes such as missing the block in volleyball or missing the basket in a shot in basketball.

The contingencies in PAL are often arranged in the form of group contingencies (Cooper et al., 1987). In a group contingency, students work toward common goals such as taking on roles as members of a sport education team. In these roles opportunities are provided to develop co-operation, accountability, and responsibility. There are three types of group contingencies: independent, dependent, and interdependent. In an independent group contingency, the same behavior, criteria, and reinforcer apply to each student. Access to the reinforcer is based on each student's own performance. Holding students accountable for the completion of a task card is an example of independent group contingencies. In a dependent group contingency an individual member of the group must meet the criterion for all members to receive the reinforcement. A student may be randomly selected by the teacher as the "focus student" for the group. If the student completes the task for the day or demonstrates the behaviors stated by the teacher then the group receives the reinforcer. Since no team member knows the identity of the focus student, they all work toward accomplishing the task. In an interdependent group contingency, group members both individually and as a group must accomplish the task. A good example of an interdependent group contingency is the jigsaw cooperative learning strategy where each student is reliant in part on their own contributions and the contributions of everyone else to complete the task.

Social skills

Establishing and maintaining meaningful relationships with peers is a critical social skill for students. Such relations are often necessary for children and youths to accept others, demonstrate interpersonal sensitivity, perspective taking, and shared values (Sheridan, 1995). Successful peer relations are also positively correlated with children's academic achievement, as well as their adjustment in childhood and into adulthood (Walker and Holmes, 1987). Socially competent children and youths use a variety of strategies to initiate interactions, maintain social interactions, deal with disagreements, and manage conflict (Sheridan, 1995). In contrast, socially incompetent children engage in behaviors that can lead them to become increasingly withdrawn and in some instances aggressive. Research has shown that social skills are situation-specific and that they can be taught to students (Walker and Holmes, 1987).

From a behavioral perspective, social skills are very much like motor skills. Few people believe that one is born with the ability to correctly perform a motor skill such as a jump shot. Such learning at the very least requires practice opportunities and feedback. Moreover when a student performs the jump shot in class, most teachers assume that any errors made were not made on purpose. Teachers most often assume that the errors were the product of a particular learning history that has not taught the student the correct technique. In contrast, social skills are often assumed by teachers to have been learned elsewhere, that the learning history was appropriate, and that students are purposely misbehaving. Thus social skills are often treated differently than motor skills. Misbehavior is often punished with no opportunity provided for feedback and practice. Moreover, social skills are seldom explicitly taught.

To develop and maintain friends and to cooperate in class, students must learn to behave in ways appropriate for the context of a situation. The phrase "learn to behave in ways appropriate for the context of a situation" is another way of saying that individuals must discriminate and generalize from one social situation to another. For example, we often behave differently in the company of close friends than in the company of colleagues; and differently on vacation with our family, than when instructing in a class. For some individuals, social skills are modeled by others and they are in turn imitated. For others, instruction and feedback are needed to assist with the acquisition of social skills or to assist those who have the skills in their repertoire, but use them inappropriately.

In physical education, studies show that students are not very supportive of their classmates during lessons and that negative comments by students such as sarcasm and criticism often occur at a higher frequency than positive comments (Giebink and McKenzie, 1985; Patrick et al., 1997). The most relevant social behaviors in physical education are fair play behaviors such as showing respect to opposing teams, officials, accepting losses without complaint, or victory without gloating. These fair play behaviors are important social skills for students to acquire in physical education and they are important skills for students to learn to use in sport-related activities outside of the school. In behavioral studies to date these social skills are used as dependent variables and various forms of group contingencies have been used as independent variables. Future studies are likely to explore the arrangement of contingencies that operate within existing curricula frameworks as sport education and cooperative learning.

Current trends and future directions for behavior analysis in physical education

The past three decades have established applied behavior analysis as an applied science in the study of physical education and physical education teacher education. This section of the chapter is devoted to forecasting the direction future inquiry may take. This is a bit like guessing where the golf ball is going to lie after you hit it. Your history provides some indication, but until the ball touches down it is wishful thinking. This forecast can be

organized into four categories focusing on (a) the development and/or refinement of behavioral strategies in the general area of physical education and physical education teacher education, (b) the transfer of pedagogies used in coaching settings to physical education and visa versa, (c) the study of meta-contingencies in physical education, and (d) investigation of rule-governed behavior. As is the character of applied behavior analysis, these forecasts are driven by instructional, motivational, and managerial challenges facing practitioners.

First, researchers are likely to continue to assess and refine instructional strategies such as peer-assisted learning, group contingencies, skill analysis, inclusion practices, as well as improving teacher education strategies such as supervisory practices. As this chapter shows, an extensive research program has been developed grounded in experimental research and behavioral principles. Despite this success, there is clearly a need for evidence of generalization across participants and settings, as well as studies which show the maintenance of these strategies by teachers.

Two emerging areas of inquiry are social skills training and the teaching of tactics in games. Research in these two areas will extend the scope of behavior analysis because they use dependent measures such as social conduct and decision making often considered not to be in the purview of behavior analysis. Thus in addition to contributing to and extending the literature in physical education such studies will broaden the scope of behavior analysis in physical education.

Second, a major influence area of physical education research in the next decade is likely to come from the migration of effective practices from coaching settings to teaching. The freeze technique has been described previously, but another useful strategy that has been used in coaching is teaching players to self-manage their emotional, social, and psychomotor behavior. Self-management strategies enable individuals to monitor and take control of their behaviors. These strategies generally include such techniques as self-monitoring and self-evaluation. This in turn leads to individuals arranging their environments to occasion and reinforce the behaviors being monitored, such as eating choices, exercise, social behaviors, and reflection. There are two good examples of self-management applications in physical education. Eldar's (1990) study of the effects of self-management of teacher behaviors demonstrated that preservice teachers can self-manage their instructional and managerial behaviors to in turn create changes in student behavior. Another good example of self-management is the student self-management program of the Sports, Play, and Recreation for Kids (SPARK) curriculum (McKenzie and Rosengard, 2000). This is a system of self-management that has been carefully developed using behavioral principles and represents a significant step forward in helping students to take personal responsibility for their out-of-school physical activity behaviors.

Third, within the behavioral community there is a growing interest in examining the role of meta-contingencies in the cultural selection of behavior. A number of researchers are turning their attention to sociocultural contingencies. Biglan (1995) describes research strategies designed to address pressing social problems including childrearing practices, sexist practices, and environmentally harmful practices. In an edited text by Mattaini and Theyer (1996) authors discuss meta-contingencies relative to issues such as sexism, racism, youth violence, teenage sexuality, and loneliness. In physical education one prominent leader of the field, Thom McKenzie, has argued for some time now that meta-contingencies ought to be the focus of change efforts for systemic health-related change in society (McKenzie, 2001). Included in his suggestions is the reallocating of resources at local, state, and federal levels to create "invitational environments" to promote engagement in physical activity, the linking of schools with communities to better integrate in- and out-of-school physical activity, and the teaching of self-management skills to our children and youths to provide them with some control over their choices.

Finally, rules, instructions, and advice are verbal stimuli that describe environmental contingencies (Skinner, 1957). When a teacher provides instructions to her class such as "fix the defender by moving toward him" she is describing the behavior to be performed and a consequence of the behavior. The student could learn how to do this from experience, in which case he would be shaped by the consequences of this behavior over time. In the case of students learning this for the first time, rules and instructions help accelerate learning. Thus rule-governed behavior is shaped in cultural contexts. Individuals follow rules and also generate rules. The consequence of this is that individuals are able to examine the contingencies associated with behaviors without having to experience the actual contingencies themselves (Skinner, 1957). For example, most of us do not have direct experience with the effects of electricity contacting our bodies, yet we follow rules that ensure that we avoid such contact. Young children are given rules such as "do not place anything in the outlet socket" or "do not use a knife to lift the bread out of the toaster".

Rule-governed behavior offers a number of advantages: it allows behavior to be acquired more quickly than behavior shaped by contingencies and it also allows us to avoid aversive contingencies and come into contact with positive contingencies much more efficiently than by trial and error (Plaud and Plaud, 1998). In many studies in physical education,

rules are given to the participants but they are usually part of the independent variable. Important questions here include "Why does rule-governed behavior occur?", "What are the controlling variables?", and "What are the distinguishing characteristics of rule-governed behavior?" Rules are particularly useful and are likely to play a critical component to social skills training and in the teaching of tactics.

Concluding comments

Many individuals lack familiarity with behavior analysis. Sometimes this is because they have not studied the science, but also because many accept as true, folklore that misrepresents the science's assumptions, findings, and goals, such as confusing radical behaviorism with methodological behaviorism or incorrectly associating it with logical positivism. This chapter shows how behavior analysis has developed and accumulated a highly generalizable body of knowledge that is relevant to physical educators and to teacher educators. This knowledge has been based on a foundation of basic and applied research, situated within a comprehensive philosophy called radical behaviorism. What behavior analysis offers to physical education and to society at large are principles that can be used to assess the issues that confront us. "The important thing is not so much to know how to solve a problem, as to know how to look for a solution" (Skinner, 1971: 161).

Notes

1 Daryl Siedentop first brought this concept to my attention using the old bumper sticker expression "Have you hugged your child today?" as an example of how homogenization occurs.

2 Ward and Barrett (2002: 244) also note that the "majority of the studies in these reviews were not conducted by behavior analysts, but rather by investigators who were assessing behavioral procedures (e.g., principles, interventions and curriculums) or by investigators who had used these procedures as components of their studies. Such studies have typically employed group designs and have often been part of large-scale research projects."

3 Project Follow Through was a large-scale, national, longitudinal evaluation study conducted in the 1970s of over 20 different approaches to teaching economically disadvantaged children K-3. The Direct Instruction model referred to here is a behavioral curriculum and should not be confused with the direct instruction pedagogical strategies derived from process-product research.

4 Watson was a strict environmentalist and firmly believed that experience only and not heredity influenced learning.

5 Skinner's impact in science includes 30 honorary degrees around the world, 18 books, approximately 200 articles. His citation count is among the highest in psychology. See O'Donohue and Ferguson (2001) for more details.

6 Truth by agreement refers to the practice of determining the truth of an event by reaching some form of consensus. Skinner rejected this process of determining truth arguing that what matters is whether a scientist can successfully influence the variables being studied.

7 Given the limitations of space in this chapter it is not possible to provide detailed descriptions of behavioral processes therefore I refer the reader to the references that provide more detail.

8 By using single subject designs as one of the criteria for the selection of studies the number of behavioral interventions reported in the literature has been narrowed significantly. Many group designs and descriptive studies use dependent measures, measurement strategies, and independent variables that are behavioral in nature.

Acknowledgments

I am grateful for the comments of Tim Barrett, John O. Cooper and Daryl Siedentop on earlier drafts of the manuscript.

References

ABT Associates (1977). *Education as experimentation: A planned variation model* (Vol. 4). Cambridge, MA: Authors.

Allison, M.G. and Ayllon, T. (1980). Behavioral coaching in the development of skills in football, gymnastics, and tennis. *Journal of Applied Behavior Analysis, 13,* 297–314.

Anderson, C.D., Crowell, C.R., Doman, M. and Howard, G.S. (1988). Performance posting, goal setting, and activity-contingent praise as applied to a university hockey team. *Journal of Applied Psychology, 73,* 87–95.

Anderson, G. and Kirkpatrick, M.A. (2002). Variable effects of a behavioral treatment package on the performance of inline roller speed skaters. *Journal of Applied Behavior Analysis, 35,* 195–198.

Azrin, N. (1981). *Toilet training in less than a day.* New York: Pocket Books.

Becker, W.C. (1972). *Parents are teachers.* Champaign, IL: Research Press.

Becker, W.C. and Carnine, D. (1981). Direct instruction: A behavior theory model for comprehensive educational intervention with the disadvantaged. In S.W. Bijou and R. Ruiz (Eds.), *Behavior Modification: Contributions to Education* (pp. 145–210). Hillsdale, NJ: Erlbaum.

Biglan, A. (1995). *Changing cultural practices: a Contextualist framework for intervention research.* Reno, NV: Context Press.

Boyce, B.A. (2003). *Improving your teaching skills: a guide for student teachers and practitioners.* Boston, MA: McGraw-Hill.

Brobst, B. and Ward, P. (2002). Effects of public posting, goal setting, and oral feedback on the skills of female soccer players. *Journal of Applied Behavior Analysis, 35* (3), 247–257.

Bunker, D.J. and Thorpe, R.D. (1982). A model for teaching of games in secondary schools. *Bulletin of Physical Education, 18,* 5–8.

Buzas, H.P. and Allyon, T. (1981). Differential reinforcement in coaching tennis skills. *Behavior Modification, 5,* 372–385.

Chiesa, M. (1992). Radical behaviorism and scientific frameworks: From mechanistic to relational accounts. *American Psychologist, 47,* 1287–1299.

Chiesa, M. (2003). Implications of determinism: Personal responsibility and the value of science. In K.A. Lattal and P.C. Chase (Eds.), *Behavior theory and philosophy* (pp. 243–258). New York: Kluwer/Plenum.

Cooper, J.O., Heron, T.E. and Heward, W.L. (1987). *Applied behavior analysis.* Columbus, OH: Merrill.

Critchfield, T.S. and Vargas, E.A. (1991). Self-recording, instructions, and public self-graphing: Effects on swimming in the absence of coach verbal interaction. *Behavior Modification, 15,* 95–112.

Crouch, D.W., Ward, P. and Patrick, C.A. (1997). The effects of peer-mediated accountability on task accomplishment during volleyball drills in elementary physical education. *Journal of Teaching in Physical Education, 17,* 26–39.

Darst, P.W. (1976). Effects of competency-based intervention on student-teacher and pupil behavior. *Research Quarterly for Exercise and Sport, 47,* 336–345.

Darst, P.W., and Steeves, D. (1980). A competency-based approach to secondary student teaching in physical education. *Research Quarterly for Exercise and Sport, 51,* 274–285.

Darst, P.W. Mancini, V.H. and Zakrajsek, D.B. (Eds.) (1983). *Systematic observation: Instrumentation for physical education.* West Point, NY: Leisure Press.

Darst, P.W., Zakrajsek, D.B., and Mancini, V.H. (Eds.), (1989) *Analyzing physical education and sport instruction.* Champaign, Ill.: Human Kinetics Publishers.

Demchak, M.A. (1993). A review of procedures to teach motor skills to individuals with severe disabilities. *Journal of Behavioral Education, 3,* 339–361.

Donahue, J., Gillis, J. and King, K. (1980). Behavior modification in sport and physical education: A review. *Journal of Sport Psychology, 2,* 311–328.

Dunbar, R.R. and O'Sullivan, M.M. (1986). Effects of intervention on differential treatment of boys and girls in elementary physical education lessons. *Journal of Teaching in Physical Education, 5,* 166–175.

Eldar, E. (1990). Effect of self-management on preservice teachers performance during a field experience in physical education. *Journal of Teaching in Physical Education, 9,* 307–323.

Eldar, E. (1997 – Hebrew). *Effective teaching in physical education.* Netanya, Israel: Tamuz.

Eldar, E. (2002 – Hebrew). *Applied behavior analysis – principles and procedures.* Beerotaim, Israel: Behavior Analysis.

Ellis, D.N., Cress, P.J. and Spellman, C.R. (1993). Training students with mental retardation to self pace while exercising. *Adapted Physical Education Quarterly, 10,* 104–124.

Fitterling, J.M. and Ayllon, T. (1983). Behavioral coaching in classical ballet: Enhancing skill development. *Behavior Modification, 7,* 345–368.

Forness, S.R., Kavale, K.A., Blum, I., and Lloyd, J.W. (1997). What works in special education and related services: Using meta-analysis to guide practice. *Teaching Exceptional Children, 29* (6), 4–9.

French, R. and Lavay, B. (1990). *A manual of behavior management techniques for physical educators and recreators.* Kearney, NE: Educational Systems Associates.

Galvan, Z.J., and Ward, P. (1998). Effects of public posting on inappropriate on-court behaviors by collegiate tennis players. *The Sport Psychologist, 12,* 419–426.

Giebink, M.P. and McKenzie, T.L. (1985). Teaching sportsmanship in physical education and recreation: An analysis of interventions and generalization effects. *Journal of Teaching in Physical Education, 4,* 167–177.

Glenn, S.S. (1988). Contingencies and metacontingencies: Toward a synthesis of behavior analysis and cultural materialism. *The Behavior Analyst, 11,* 161–179.

Glenn, S.S. (2003). Operant contingencies and the origin of cultures. In K.A. Lattal and P.C. Chase (Eds.), *Behavior theory and philosophy* (pp. 223–242). New York: Kluwer/Plenum.

Grant, B.C., Ballard, K.D. and Glynn, T.L. (1990). Teacher feedback intervention, motor-on-task behavior, and successful task performance. *Journal of Teaching in Physical Education, 9,* 123–139.

Gregg, M.J., Hrycaiko, D., Dennis, W., Mactavish, J.B. and Martin, G.L. (2004). A mental skills package for Special Olympics athletes: a preliminary study. *Adapted Physical Activity Quarterly, 21,* 4–18.

Greenwood, C.R., Maheady, L. and Carta, J.J. (1991). Peer tutoring programs in the regular education classroom. In G. Stoner, M.R. Shinn, and H.M. Walker (Eds.), *Interventions for achievement and behavior problems* (pp. 179–200). Washington, DC: National Association for Psychologists.

Hazen, A., Johnstone, C., Martin, G.L. and Srikameswaran, S. (1990). A videotaping feedback package for improving skills of youth competitive swimmers. *The Sport Psychologist, 4,* 213–227.

Hamilton, S.A. and Fernouw, W.J. (1985). Cogntive behavioral training for college basketball free throw performance. *Cognitive Therapy and Research, 9,* 479–483.

Harris, M. (1989). *Our Kind.* New York: Harper Perennial.

Hellison, D. (2003). *Teaching responsibility through physical activity.* Champaign, IL: Human Kinetics.

Heward, W.L. (2003). *Exceptional children: An introduction to special education edition*: 7th edn. Upper Saddle River, NJ: Prentice Hall.

Holt, N.L., Strean, W.B. and Bengoechea, E.G. (2002). Expanding the teaching of games for understanding model: New avenues for future research and practice. *Journal of Teaching in Physical Education, 21,* 162–176.

Houston-Wilson, C., Dunn, J.M., van der Mars, H. and McCubbin, J. (1997). The effect of peer tutors on motor performance in integrated physical education classes. *Adapted Physical Education Quarterly, 14,* 298–313.

Hume, K.M. and Crossman, J. (1992). Musical reinforcement of practice behaviors among competitive swimmers. *Journal of Applied Behavior Analysis, 25,* 665–670.

Hume, K.M., Martin, G.L., Gonzalez, P., Cracklen, C. and Genthon, S. (1985). A self-monitoring feedback package for improving freestyle figure skating practice. *Journal of Sport Psychology, 7,* 333–345.

Jeltma, K. and Vogler, E.W. (1985). Effects of an individual contingency on behaviorally disordered students in physical education. *Adapted Physical Education Quarterly, 2,* 127–135.

Johnson, M. and Ward, P. (2002). Effects of classwide peer tutoring on correct performance of striking skills in third grade physical education. *Journal of Teaching in Physical Education, 20,* 247–263.

Kahan, D. (2002). The effects of a bug-in the ear device on intralesson communication between a student teacher and a cooperating teacher. *Journal of Teaching in Physical Education, 22,* 86–104.

Keller, F.S. and Sherman, J.G. (1982). *The PSI handbook: Essays on personalized instruction.* Lawrence, Kansas: TRI Publications.

Kendall, G., Hrycaiko, D., Martin, G.L. and Kendall, T. (1990). The effects of an imagery rehearsal, relaxation, and self-talk package on basketball game performance. *Journal of Sport & Exercise Psychology, 12,* 157–166.

Kinder, D. and Carnine, D.W. (1991). Direct instruction: What it is and what it is becoming. *Journal of Behavioral Education, 1,* 193–214.

Kladopoulos, C.N. and McComas, J.J. (2001). The effects of form training on foul-shooting performance in members of a women's college basketball team. *Journal of Applied Behavior Analysis, 34,* 329–332.

Komaki, J. and Barnett, F.T. (1977). A behavioral approach to coaching football: Improving the play execution of the offensive backfield on a youth football team. *Journal of Applied Behavior Analysis, 7,* 199–206.

Koop, S. and Martin, G.L. (1983). A coaching strategy to reduce swimming stroke errors with beginning age-group swimmers. *Journal of Applied Behavior Analysis, 16,* 447–460.

Laraway, S., Snycerski, S., Michael, J. and Poling, A. (2003). Motivating operations and terms to describe them: Some further refinements. *Journal Of Applied Behavior Analysis, 36,* 401–410.

Latham, G.I. (1993). *The Power of Positive Parenting.* Logan, UT: P and T.

Launder, A.G. (2001). *Play practice: The games approach to teaching and coaching sports.* Champaign, IL: Human Kinetics.

Lavay, B.W., French, R. and Henderson, H.L. (1997). *Positive behavior management strategies for physical education.* Champaign, IL: Human Kinetics.

Lee, C. (1993). Operant strategies in sport and exercise: Possibilities for theoretical development. *International Journal of Sports Psychology, 24,* 306–325.

Lee, M-A. (2004). *Generalization of supporting movement in tag rugby from practice to games in 7th and 8th grade physical education.* Unpublished Doctoral Dissertation. The Ohio State University.

Lieberman, L.L., Dunn, J.M., van der Mars, H. and McCubbin, J. (2000). Peer tutors effects on activity levels of deaf students in inclusive elementary physical education. *Adapted Physical Education Quarterly, 17,* 20–39.

Lindslay, O.R. (1990). Precision teaching: By teachers for children. *Teaching Exceptional Children, 22,* 10–15.

Lounsbery, M. and Sharpe, T. (1999). Effects of sequential feedback on preservice teacher instructional interactions and students' skill practice. *Journal of Teaching in Physical Education, 19,* 56–78.

Maag, J. (1996). *Parenting without punishment: Making problem behavior work for you.* Philadelphia, PA: The Charles Press.

Martin, G.L. (1992). Applied behavior analysis in sport and physical education: Past, present, and future. In R.P. West and L.A. Hamerlynk (Eds.), *Designs for excellence in education: The legacy of B.F. Skinner* (pp. 223–260). Longmont, CO: Sopris West.

Martin, G.L. (2003). *Sport psychology: Practical guidelines from Behavior Analysis.* Winnipeg, Canada: Sport Science Press.

Martin, G.L. and Hrycaiko, D. (1983). *Behavior modification and coaching: Principles, procedures, and research.* Springfield, IL. : Charles Thomas.

Martin, G.L. and Lumsden, J.A. (1987). *Coaching an effective behavioral approach.* St. Louis, MO: Mosby.

Martin, G.L. and Tkachuk, G.A. (2000). Behavioral sport pyschology. In J. Austin and J.E. Carr (Eds.), *Handbook of applied behavior analysis* (pp. 399–422). Reno, NV: Context Press.

Martin, G.L. and Pear, J.J. (2003). *Behavior modification: What it is and how to do it.* Upper Saddle River, NJ: Prentice Hall.

Mattini, M.A. and Thyer, B.A. (1996). *Finding solutions to social problems: Behavioral strategies for change.* Washington, DC: American Psychological Association.

McKenzie, T. and Rosengard, P. (2000). *SPARK physical education program Grades 3–6.* San Diego, CA: San Diego State University Foundation.

McKenzie, T.L. (2001). Back to the future: health-related physical education. In P. Ward and P. Doutis (Eds), Physical Education in the 21st Century (pp. 113–131). Lincoln, NE: Univeristy of Nebraska.

McKenzie, T.L. and Rushall, B.S. (1974). Effects of self-recording on attendance and performance in a competitive swimming training environment. *Journal of Applied Behavior Analysis, 7,* 199–206.

Metzler, M. (1990). *Instructional supervision for physical education.* Champaign, IL: Human Kinetics.

Ming, S. and Martin, G.L. (1996). Single-subject evaluation of a self-talk package for improving figure skating performance. *The Sport Psychologist, 10,* 227–238.

Moore, J. (2000). Thinking about thinking and feeling about feeling. *The Behavior Analyst, 23,* 45–56.

Ocansey, R.T. (1988). The effects of a behavioral model of supervision on the supervisory behaviors of cooperating teachers. *Journal of Teaching in Physical Education, 8,* 46–63.

O'Donohue, W. and Ferguson, K.E. (2001). *The psychology of B.F. Skinner.* Thousand Oaks, CA: Sage.

O'Donohue, W. and Kitchener, R. (Eds.) (1998). *Handbook of behaviorism.* San Diego: Academic Press.

Paese, P. (1982). Effects of interdependent group contingencies in a secondary physical education setting. *Journal of Teaching in Physical Education, 2,* 29–37.

Paese, P. (1984). The effects of cooperating teacher intervention and a self-assessment technique on the verbal interactions of elementary student teachers. *Journal of Teaching in Physical Education, 3,* 51–59.

Patrick, T. and Hrycaiko, D. (1998). Effect of a mental training package on an endurance performance. *Sports Psychologist, 12,* 283–299.

Patrick, C.A., Ward, P. and Crouch, D.W. (1998). Effects of holding students accountable for social behaviors during volleyball games in elementary physical education. *Journal of Teaching in Physical Education, 17,* 143–156.

Plaud, J.J. and Plaud, D.M. (1998). Clinical behavior therapy and the experimental analysis of behavior. *Journal of Clinical Psychology, 54,* 905–921.

Todd, J.T. and Morris, E.K. (1992). Case histories in the great power of steady misrepresentation. *American Psychologist, 47,* 1441–1253.

Randall, L.E. (1992). *Systematic supervision for physical education.* Champaign, IL: Human Kinetics.

Ratliffe, T. (1986). The influence of school principals on management time, and student activity time for two elementary physical education teachers. *Journal of Teaching in Physical Education, 5,* 117–125.

Rogerson, L.J. and Hrycaiko, D.W. (2002). Enhancing competitve performance of ice hockey goaltenders using centering and self-talk. *Journal of Applied Sport Psychology, 14,* 14–26.

Rush, D.B. and Allyon, T. (1984). Peer behavioral coaching: Soccer. *Journal of Sport Psychology, 6,* 325–334.

Rushall, B.S. and Pettinger, J. (1969). An evaluation of the effect of various reinforcers used as motivators in swimming. *Research Quarterly, 40,* 540–545.

Rushall, B.S. and Siedentop, D. (1972). *The Development and control of behavior in sport and physical education.* Philadelphia, PA: Lea and Febiger.

Ryan, S. and Yerg, B. (2001). The effects of crossgroup feedback on off-task behavior in a physical education setting. *Journal of Teaching in Physical Education, 20,* 172–187.

Ryan, S., Ormond, T., Imwold, C. and Rotunda, R.J. (2002). The effects of a public address system on the off-task behavior of elementary physical education. Students. *Journal of Applied Behavior Analysis, 35,* 305–308.

Sariscsany, M.J., Darst, P.W. and van der Mars, H. (1995). The effects of three teacher supervision patterns on student on-task and skill performance in secondary physical education. *Journal of Teaching in Physical Education, 14,* 179–197.

Schuldheisz, J.M. and van der Mars, H. (2001). Active supervision and students' physical activity in middle school physical education. *Journal of Teaching in Physical Education, 21,* 75–90.

Scott, D., Scott, L.M. and Goldwater, B. (1997). A performance improvement program for an international-level track and field athlete. *Journal of Applied Behavior Analysis, 30,* 573–575.

Senne, T. (2004). *On you mark, get set, go: A guide for beginning physical education teachers.* Reston, VA: American Alliance for Health Physical Education Recreation and Dance.

Siedentop, D. (1976). *Developing teaching skills in physical education.* Boston: Houghton-Mifflin.

Siedentop, D. (1981). The Ohio State University supervision research program summary report. *Journal of Teaching in Physical Education, 1,* 30–38.

Siedentop, D. (1982). Teaching research: The interventionist view. *Journal of Teaching in Physical Education, 1,* 46–50.

Siedentop, D. (1983). Research on teaching in physical education. In T. Templin and J. Olson (Eds.), *Teaching in Physical Education* (pp. 3–15). Champaign, IL: Human Kinetics.

Siedentop, D. (1984). The modification of teacher behavior. In M. Pieron and G. Graham (Eds.), *Sport Pedagogy* (pp. 3–18). Champaign, IL: Human Kinetics.

Siedentop, D., Tousignant, M. and Parker, M. (1982). *Academic learning time-physical education coding manual* (Rev. ed.). Columbus, OH: The Ohio State University, School of Health, Physical Education, and Recreation.

Shapiro, E.S. and Shapiro, S. (1985). Behavioral coaching and the development of skills in track. *Behavior Modification, 9,* 211–224.

Sharpe, T.L., Hawkins, A. and Wiegand, R. (1989). Model/practice versus verbal/rehearsal introductions of systems skills within an individually prescribed instructional system. *Journal of Teaching in Physical Education, 9,* 25–38.

Sharpe, T., Brown, M. and Crider, K. (1995). The effects of a sportsmanship curriculum intervention on generalized positive social behavior of urban elementary school students. *Journal of Applied Behavior Analysis, 28,* 401–416.

Sharpe, T., Spies, R., Newman, D. and Spickelmier-Vallin, D. (1996). Assessing and improving the accuracy of inservice teachers' perceptions of daily practice. *Journal of Teaching in Physical Education, 15,* 297–318.

Sharpe, T., Lounsbery, M. and Bahls, V. (1997). Description and effects of sequential behavior practice in teacher education. *Research Quarterly for Exercise and Sport, 68,* 222–232.

Sharpe, T., So, H., Mavi, H. and Brown, S. (2002). Comparative effects of sequential behavior feedback and goal-setting across peer-teaching and field based practice teaching. *Journal of Teaching in Physical Education, 15,* 297–318.

Sheridan, S. (1995). Building social skills in the classroom. In S. Goldstein (Ed.), *Understanding and managing children's classroom behavior* (pp. 375–396). New York: John Wiley.

Skinner, B.F. (1950). Are theories of learning really necessary? *Psychological Review, 57,* 193–216.

Skinner, B.F. (1953). *Science and human behavior.* New York: Appleton-century-Crofts.

Skinner, B.F. (1957). *Verbal behavior.* Englewood Cliffs, NJ: Prentice Hall.

Skinner, B.F. (1966). The phylogeny and ontogency of behavior. *Science, 153,* 1205–1213.

Skinner, B.F. (1974). *About behaviorism.* London: Jonathan Cape.

Skinner, B.F. (1971). *Beyond freedom and dignity.* London: Jonathan Cape.

Skinner, B.F. (1981). Selection by consequences. *Science, 213,* 501–504.

Smith, L.D. (1986). *Behaviorism and logical positivism.* Stanford, California: Stanford University Press.

Smith, R.E., Smoll, F.L. and Hunt, E. (1977). A system of behavioral assessment of athletic coaches. *Research Quarterly for Exercise and Sport, 48,* 401–407.

Smith, R.E., Smoll, F.L. and Christensen, D.S. (1996). Behavioral assessments and interventions in youth sports. *Behavior Modification, 20,* 3–44.

Swain, A. and Jones, G. (1995). Effects of goal-setting interventions on selected basketball skills: a single-subject design. *Research Quarterly for Exercise and Sport, 66,* 51–63.

Taggart, A. (1989). The systematic development of teaching skills: A sequence of planned pedagogical experiences. *Journal of Teaching in Physical Education, 8,* 73–86.

Thelwell, R.C. and Greenlees, I.A. (2003). Developing competitive endurance performance using mental skills training. *Sport Psychologist 17,* 318–337.

Thorndike, E.L. (1932). *The fundamentals of learning.* New York: Columbia University.

Tkachuk, G., Leslie-Toogood, A. and Martin, G.L. (2003). Behavioral assessment in sport psychology. *Sport Psychologist 17,* 104–117.

Todd, J.T. and Morris, E.K. (1992). Case histories of the steady power of misrepresentations. *American Psychologist, 47,* 1441–1453.

van der Mars, H. (1987). Effects of audio-cueing on teacher verbal praise of student managerial and transitional task performance. *Journal of Teaching in Physical Education, 6,* 157–165.

van der Mars, H. (1988). The effects of audio-cueing on selected teaching behaviors of an experienced elementary physical education specialist *Journal of Teaching in Physical Education, 8,* 64–72.

Vogler, E.W. and French, R.W. (1983). The effects of a group contingency strategy on behaviorally disordered students in physical education. *Research Quarterly for Exercise and Sport, 54,* 273–277.

Vogler, W.E. and Mood, D.P. (1986). Management of practice behavior in competitive age group swimming. *Journal of Sport Behavior, 9,* 160–172.

Walberg, H.J. (1984). Improving the productivity of America's schools. *Educational Leadership, 41,* 19–27.

Walker, H.M. and Holmes, D. (1987). *The access program: Adolescent curriculum for communication and effective social skills.* Austin, TX: PROED.

Wanlin, C., Hrycaiko, D., Martin, G.M. and Mahon, M. (1997). The effects of a goal setting package on the performance of young speed skaters. *Journal of Applied Sports Psychology, 9,* 212–228.

Ward, P. (2002). A case for cultural interdependence: Behavior analysis and the zeitgeist. Paper presented at *The Ohio State University 3rd Focus on Behavior Analysis in Education Conference.* Columbus, OH.

Ward, P. and Barrett, T. (2002). A review of behavior analysis research in physical education. *Journal of Teaching in Physical Education, 21,* 242–266.

Ward, P. and Carnes, M. (2002). Effects of posting self-set goals on collegiate football players' skill execution during practice and games. *Journal of Applied Behavior Analysis, 35,* 1–12.

Ward, P. and Dunaway, S. (1995). The effects of contingent music on laps run in a high school physical education class. *The Physical Educator, 52,* 2–7.

Ward, P., Johnson, L.A., Ward, M.C. and Jones, D.L. (1997a). Comparison of the effects of formal and informal accountability on the task accomplishment of a lifeguard rescue. *Journal of Behavioral Education, 7,* 359–371.

Ward, P., Smith, S. and Sharpe, T. (1997). The effects of accountability on task accomplishment in collegiate football. *Journal of Teaching in Physical Education. 17,* 40–51.

Ward, P., Smith, S. and Makasci, K. (1997b). Teacher training: Effects of directed rehearsal on the teaching skills of physical education majors. *Journal of Behavioral Education, 7,* 505–517.

Ward, P., Johnson, M. and Konukman, F. (1998a). Directed rehearsal and preservice teachers' performance of instructional behaviors. *Journal of Behavioral Education, 8,* 369–380.

Ward, P., Smith, S.L., Makasci, K. and Crouch, D.W. (1998b). Differential effects of peer-mediated accountability on task accomplishment in elementary physical education. *Journal of Teaching in Physical Education, 17,* 442–452.

Watson, J.B. (1913). Psychology as the behaviorist views it. *Psychological Review, 20,* 158–177.

Webster, G.E. (1987). Influence of peer tutors upon academic learning time-physical education of mentally handicapped students. *Journal of Teaching in Physical Education, 6,* 393–403.

White, A.G. and Bailey, J.S. (1990). Reducing disruptive behaviors of elementary physical education students with sit and watch. *Journal of Applied Behavior Analysis, 23,* 353–359.

Wilkinson, S. (1991). A training program for improving undergraduates' analytic skill in volleyball. *Journal of Teaching in Physical Education, 11,* 177–194.

Wilkinson, S. (1996). Visual analysis of the overarm throw and related sport skills: training and transfer effects. *Journal of Teaching in Physical Education, 16,* 66–78.

Wolko, K.L., Hrycaiko, D.W. and Martin, G.L. (1993). A comparison of two self-management packages to standard coaching for improving practice performance of gymnasts. *Behavior Modification, 17,* 209–223.

Yang, J-J. and Porretta, D.L. (1999). Sport/Leisure skill learning by adolescents with mild mental retardation: A four step strategy. *Adapted Physical Education Quarterly, 16,* 300–315.

Ziegler, S.G. (1987). Effects of stimulus cueing on the acquisition of ground strokes by beginning tennis players. *Journal of Applied Behavior Analysis, 20,* 405–411.

Ziegler, S.G. (1994). The effects of attentional shift training on the execution of soccer skills: A preliminary investigation. *Journal of Applied Behavior Analysis, 27,* 545–552.

Zittel, L. and McCubbin, J.A. (1996). Effect of an integrated physical education setting on motor performance of preschool children with developmental delays. *Adapted Physical Education Quarterly, 13,* 316–333.

1.2 Interpretive perspectives in physical education research

CLIVE POPE

We can, and I think must, look upon human life as chiefly a vast interpretive process in which people, singly and collectively, guide themselves by defining the objects, events, and situations which they encounter … Any scheme designed to analyze human group life in its general character has to fit this process of interpretation (Blumer, 1956: 686).

Introduction

The emergence of interpretive research methods has expanded significantly over the last 30 years. That expansion has been accompanied by an increasing acceptance of and interest in qualitative research forms by educational researchers, including those who work in the wider areas of physical education and sport pedagogy. Through exploration within the interpretive paradigm our field has been able to ask new and different questions and adopt newer and perhaps more sophisticated tools to answer those questions. Looking at the world through different paradigmatic lenses has shed new light on what we have come to know about physical education. However, before embarking on this paradigmatic journey, I would like to address three pertinent issues. The first concerns an issue raised by Eliot Eisner (1990) who cautioned of the need to separate so one may analyze. Therefore, any perspective or paradigmatic approach to research in physical education does not fall into neatly demarcated discrete cells but rather targets a common and wide-ranging attempt to individualize one research approach that falls under the guise of "interpretive". The boundaries between interpretivism and positivism on the one side and interpretivism and subjectivism on the other are not water-tight, rather they are permeable and lithe.

The second issue relates to the ambiguity of the terms interpretive and qualitative. Neither "qualitative research" nor "interpretivism" are precise ors agreed expressions and are often used interchangeably.

However, the term "qualitative" should not be adopted as a synonym for "interpretive". A qualitative research study may be interpretive, positivist, or critical, dependent largely on the philosophical disposition of the researcher. Qualitative is an adjective often adopted as a blanket descriptor for anything that is non-numeric data (Schwandt, 1997). However elusive a definition may be, I have attempted to characterize the term qualitative in relation to how it is germane to this chapter. In general, qualitative research can be portrayed as a process to obtain an in-depth understanding of the meanings and descriptions of situations presented by people. Primacy is allocated to the subjective interpretations of the participant(s) rather than theoretical knowledge of the researcher or previously held "truths" about a selected phenomenon. Alternatively:

Qualitative research is a situated activity that locates the observer in the world. It consists of a set of interpretive, material practices that make the world visible … qualitative researchers study things in their natural settings, attempting to make sense of, or to interpret, phenomena in terms of the meanings people bring to them (Denzin and Lincoln, 2000: 3).

The third issue also relates to terminology. The terms selected align with those used by Crotty (1998), Sparkes (1992), and Erickson (1986). Interpretivism is addressed as a theoretical perspective having three major constituents: symbolic interactionism, hermeneutics, and phenomenology. While critical inquiry, feminism, and postmodernism align with this perspective, each will be addressed in subsequent chapters.

Exploring interpretivism and interpretivists

At a simplistic level the difference between positivist and interpretive research goals often address the distinction between aiming for explanation compared to aiming for understanding; and the distinction between the personal and impersonal role of the researcher. Interpretive researchers are excavators: they adopt methods to get inside the way others see the world or construct meanings of their worlds. The goal of interpretive researchers is to explore what actions mean to people who partake in them. They seek to know why things are happening in a particular society. The subjective process promotes communication with the cultural conditions of a society and an understanding of why things operate. They would argue that humans act in accordance with their subjective understanding of the world and its associated phenomena (Blaikie, 1993). Furthermore, they would argue that if we want to understand people's actions we have first to understand those actions in the way that the participants do.

Interpretivism does not concern itself with the pursuit of universally applicable laws and rules, but rather seeks to construct descriptive analyses that emphasize deep, interpretive understandings of social phenomena. Interpretivists consider any analysis of human action, to use Geetz's words "interpretive science in search of meaning, not an experimental science in search of laws" (Geertz, 1973: 5). The interpretive philosophy is founded on the belief that science is subjective and therefore permits alternative models of reality. It gives emphasis to the creative aspects of science, and could be the polar opposite of the positivist philosophy. The interpretive orientation conceives multiple realities, each of which is relative to a particular context or frame of reference.

Interpretive researchers embrace the maxim that all knowledge is essentially subjective and support the idea that the conduct of research is also subjective and interactive (Markula et al., 2001). The interpretivist paradigm thus generally leads to the adoption of qualitative research methods that allow the researcher to gain a descriptive understanding of the values, meanings and actions of the subjects under study. It is important to explore and focus on how knowledge is constructed (epistemology) rather than methods associated with research approaches (Erickson, 1986). The epistemology of qualitative researchers can be described as existential (non-determinant) and constructivist. A constructivist epistemology means knowledge is viewed as something that is actively constructed, historically and culturally grounded and loaded with moral and political values (Howe, 2001). As Schwandt (1994) asserts, an interpretivist (or constructivist) believes that understanding of the world is achieved through interpretation. These two views are associated with an expectation that phenomena are intricately related to many coincidental actions and that understanding them requires thorough attention to contexts: temporal and spatial, economic, social, cultural, historical, political, and personal.

The epistemology that underpins interpretivism also recognizes that knowledge is derived from the day-to-day concepts and meanings. The interpretivist paradigm thus generally leads to the adoption of qualitative research methods that allow the researcher to gain a descriptive understanding of the values, meanings, and actions of the subjects under study. Personal experience will therefore often act as a starting point because:

> Experience addresses the ongoingness of life as it is registered through the filter of culture – that is, through acts we have already learned to interpret as experiences or, in the case of shock, surprise, embarrassment, or trauma, through acts we reprocess as experiences after the fact, by talking about them and thus making them seem less personal, more typical (Abrahams, 1986: 55).

The important distinction here is between an event and an experience. The act of teaching is an event, it is something that happens and we know a significant amount about the act of teaching. This is something that could for instance, be explored in the positivist paradigm. By contrast, an experience is teaching as an act we are involved in, it happens to us or others and we therefore see it as meaningful. The task of the interpretive researcher is to excavate how the meaning of teaching is created within a natural setting. The process of meaning making (how does the teacher establish meaning about teaching) becomes the focus of investigation.

Interpretivism therefore calls for a different notion of "scientific inquiry" when the study of human lived experience is conducted. It contends that traditional scientific methods are not pertinent to the investigation of human social behaviour. They reject the notion that humans can be studied using the same philosophical base as is used in studying physical objects. Moreover, interpretivists accept that there can be multiple interpretations of reality but argue that such interpretations are in and of themselves a part of the knowledge they are pursuing. They believe that knowledge and meaning are acts of interpretation and therefore there is no objective knowledge that is independent of thinking, reasoning individuals.

Interpretivism involves an *ontology* whereby social reality is seen as the product of processes through which participants collectively negotiate and produce socially constructed meanings for actions and situations. "Interpretive practice engages both the *hows* and the *whats* of social reality; it is centered both in how people methodically construct their experiences and their worlds and in the configurations of meaning and institutional life that inform and shape their reality-constituting activity" (Gubrium and Holstein, 2000: 488). Such a process encourages communication with the cultural conditions of a society and a subsequent understanding of how things operate. Crotty (1998) explicates the interpretivist approach "*looks for culturally derived and historically situated interpretations of the social life-world* [italics original]" (p. 67).

An interpretive approach to research employs a practical orientation. It will often involve "getting out there" and investigating everyday life. Social scientists, including educationists, don't just want descriptions they want reasons; they endeavour to gain access to the "meaning" behind peoples actions. Interpretation is the attempt to extract meaning and to do so requires an empathy with who and where they research. It is concerned with the specifics of meaning and action in social life that takes place in concrete scenes of face-to-face interaction, and that takes place in the wider society surrounding the scene of action (Erickson, 1986). This often requires talking with and/or observing individuals or groups to learn about their worlds, the issues they confront, the perspectives they hold, or the experiences they endure. Such insights can shed light on how people generate and make sense of forms of social action. The study of phenomena in their natural settings is vital to the interpretivist philosophy. Given the strong interaction between the researcher and actors in the field and elsewhere, along with an agreed constructivist orientation to knowledge, given the attention to actor intentionality and a sense of self, the researcher ultimately comes to share a personal view. Traditionally, this is done either linguistically or through observation.

A brief historical perspective

The historical roots of interpretivism can be traced back to the nineteenth century and link to sociology, anthropology, and linguistics. It is argued "interpretivism was conceived in reaction to the effort to develop a natural science of the social. Its foil was largely logical empiricist methodology and the bid to apply that framework to human inquiry" (Schwandt, 1994: 125). A distinction thus was advocated between the natural sciences, *Naturwissenschaften,* and the human sciences, *Geisteswissenschaften. Geist* refers to the mind, our thoughts, feelings, emotions, values, and consciousness. By contrast natural science focuses on the nature of objects, things themselves and the manner in which things behave. While nature can be explained, human life must be understood. This perspective was expounded by Dilthey and taken up by Weber and Schultz. Much of the interpretivist perspective is tied to *Verstehen* a German term

to mean "understanding" advocated by German philosopher and historian William Dilthey (1833–1911). Dilthey advocated for the need to understand meaning from the perspective of the individual as the basis of the human sciences. This he contrasted with the natural sciences that developed causal explanations through the adoption of universal laws. In essence, the social world of the actors is interpreted before the researcher arrives:

> The difference between the social and the natural world is that the latter does not constitute itself as 'meaningful': the meanings it has produced by men [sic] in the course of their practical life, and as a consequence of their endeavours to understand or explain it for themselves. Social life – of which these endeavours are a part – on the other hand, is *produced* by its component actors precisely in terms of their active constitution and reconstitution of frames of meaning whereby they organise their experiences (Giddens, 1974: 79).

As Schwandt (2000) proposes, interpretivism normally embraces two dimensions of *Verstehen* as expounded by Schutz (1962). First, *Verstehen* is that process whereby people derive meanings of their own everyday actions as well as those of others with whom they interrelate. But *Verstehen* can also mean "a method peculiar to the social sciences" (Schutz, 1962: 57) that involves the researcher coming to know the first dimension. *Verstehen* has figured significantly in the works of Dilthey, Schutz and Heidegger.

The two principal traditions associated with interpretivism are hermeneutics and phenomenology which (together with symbolic interactionism) will be examined later in this chapter. The principal distinction between phenomenology and hermeneutics is "phenomenology describes how one orients to lived experience, hermeneutics describes how one interprets the 'texts' of life" (van Manen, 1997: 4). Both traditions have their intellectual roots in German and British philosophy. Proponents of the interpretive movement attempted to establish an objective way of understanding the subjective nature of social reality. The British influence was mostly attributed to the work of Winch (1958) who argued social science should not be based on natural science. Rather he argued that human behaviour is best understood as rule-following that is learned and not behaviour that is established by cause (Blaikie, 1993).

More recent historical concepts

Prior to the 1980s, the positivist approach to research into teaching and learning physical education and sport had influenced the questions being asked by researchers and how their findings were represented and reported. There was a tendency for research to focus on measuring things, account for how things happened and to predict and/or control things. The psychometric model had dominated the social and behavioural sciences including education. During the 1970s and 1980s important concerns were raised about the restrictive nature of quantitative data and methods that were often connected with positivism, the prevailing paradigm at that time. The principal argument was that positivistic methods ignored the crucial meaning of contexts in favour of accumulating quantified measures of phenomena (Guba and Lincoln, 1994).

It was during this period that physical education began to embrace interpretive research as an alternative process. The adoption of observation at research sites yielded insights into the nature of teaching and learning of physical education. Evidence of this trend was marked in Templin and Olson's text *Teaching in Physical Education* (Templin and Olson, 1983). This publication included Griffin's work on student interaction patterns. This qualitative study adopted observation protocols likened to those of ethnography and included daily field notes that were analysed inductively to establish participation patterns amongst a middle school physical education class. Her observations were augmented by teacher interview data. Griffin revealed that student opportunities to learn were hobbled by gender-based stereotyped perceptions of what tasks were considered to be relevant or appropriate by boys and girls (Griffin, 1983). Several similar issues were presented in subsequent publications each revealing pertinent and quite disquieting aspects to the physical education ecology (Griffin, 1984, 1985a, 1985b).

Templin and Olson's text also revealed Kollen's study of student experiences of physical education. Through interviews conducted with 20 high school students, Kollen was able to reveal that for many students, physical education was characterized by embarrassment and/or humiliation (Kollen, 1983). The above results were published using detailed description, a characteristic of interpretive studies. The nature and presentation were quite different to that of quantitative works.

The emergence of qualitative research as an alternative process received attention in special sections within *The Journal of Teaching in Physical Education* (Earls, 1986) and *Research Quarterly for Exercise and Sport* (see Locke, 1989). Moreover, Locke, Griffin and Templin edited a section on "Profiles of Struggle" in *The Journal of Physical Education, Recreation and Dance* (see Locke and Griffin, 1986). This monograph presented seven examples of realistic human encounters with teaching physical education experienced by selected teachers and their everyday battles with policy, compromise, priority, and change. These portraits highlight the resilience teachers must often construct to endure the harsh realities of real world teaching. Perhaps the strength of these portraits are the actual words and actions of the profiled teachers, something an interpretive approach can reveal.

More recently interpretive studies have addressed issues like marginality. Sparkes et al. (1990) described how teachers of varying degrees of experience coped with their concerns about teaching a subject perceived as marginal. This study called for a re-look at how teacher education programmes are structured and the need to address the micro-political forces that operate within educational systems.

In the research community, like other aspects of life, times have changed and as a result we have seen more and more researchers inhabit the interpretive nest. So why is this? Eisner (2001) offers five possible reasons. First, the chance to get up close and personal to the research process as it occurs in classrooms (among other settings) has become appealing. Such an attraction is fortified by a realization that a "one-shot commando raid as a way to get the data and get out no longer seems attractive" (p. 137). A second proposed reason for change is a growing enthusiasm by researchers to accept and embrace pluralism as part of social life. Such a perspective has been assisted by the multiple ways of knowing advocated by movements such as feminism (see Chapter 5). Third, previous forms of research have not been completely successful which has prompted the search for alternative models of inquiry, including qualitative and interpretive options. Fourth, the dynamic nature of education means conditions cannot be held constantly so problems may be found and solutions created. Rather, there is a need for research to deal with situations that may help us "develop some insights we can work with" (p. 138). The fifth reason is attributed to form. Eisner reminds us that form and content hold a symbiotic relationship and different forms can communicate different meanings. It was "the gloves are off" call that celebrated the questioning of traditional research conventions and a call for "anything goes" coupled with the chaotic inference of what would count as research.

Denzin and Lincoln (2000) define seven moments of inquiry, all of which operate in the present. These moments have acted as a heuristic for the evolution of research that addresses the human sciences. They illustrate the diversity and development of theoretical and philosophic shifts that have occurred during the last century.

The traditional (1900–1950). During this period, qualitative researchers sought to produce objective accounts of naturalistic reports fashioned by the dominant scientist paradigm: "They were concerned with offering valid, reliable, and objective interpretations of their writings. The 'other' who was studied was alien, foreign, and strange" (Denzin and Lincoln, 2000: 12).

The modernist (1950–1970). This phase was marked by a formalization of qualitative method, building on the traditional moment. The most notable work of this period is perhaps *Boys in White* (Becker et al., 1961) an indicative example of the drive by qualitative researchers to emulate the rigor of quantitative work. Denzin and Lincoln argue: "This did work in the modernist period clothe itself in the language and rhetoric of positivist and post-positivist discourse" (p. 14).

Blurred genres (1970–1986) This period derived from the seminal work of Clifford Geertz who called for the need to elicit "thick descriptions" of specific events, rituals, and customs. Geertz argued that traditional, functional, behavioural, and authoritarian approaches toward human science were yielding to a sizeable number of alternative approaches. This period marked the ascendency of the postpositivistic, constructivist, and naturalistic paradigms and a legacy of competing perspectives including phenomenology, symbolic interactionism, ethnomethodology, structuralism, poststructuralism, constructionism, deconstructionism, semiotics, neopostivism, and neo-Marxism to name a few. This period gave researchers wide-ranging choices between paradigms, arenas, strategies, and methods. Moreover, a softening of the boundaries between disciplines, in particular the social sciences and humanities was in evidence. It was a period of blurring of boundaries, leading to what Larry Locke described as "a field marked by zesty disarray" (Locke, 1989: 2). The appearance of several qualitative journals also marked this period. As Denzin and Lincoln (2000) exclaim: "The golden age of the social sciences was over, and a new age of blurred, interpretive genres was upon us" (p. 15).

The crisis of representation (1986–1990) was marked by a series of texts that addressed the consequences of Geetz's blurred genres (Clifford, 1988; Clifford and Marcus, 1986; Marcus and Fisher, 1986; Turner and Bruner, 1986). These works focused on issues of reflexivity, race, gender, power, and privilege. As Sparkes (2002) declares: "The crisis of representation remains with us today in the form of a continued questioning of the assumption that qualitative researchers can directly capture lived experience" (p. 5).

In addition to the crisis of representation, Denzin and Lincoln offer two supplementary crises. The crisis of legitimation invites a reappraisal of terms like *validity, generalizability,* and *reliability,* artifacts of earlier moments. If such terms are deemed irrelevant, what should take their place? Hence this crisis asks what criteria should determine how qualitative studies are evaluated? These two crises align

with the third: the crisis of praxis. This crisis poses the question, "Is it possible to effect change in the world if society is only and always a text?" (p. 17). To summarize, Denzin and Lincoln (1994) describe this period as "[a] messy moment, multiple voices, experimental texts, breaks, ruptures, crises of legitimation and representation, self-critique, new moral discourses, and technologies" (p. 581).

Postmodern or experimental (1990–1995). This period heralded the appearance of experimental writing styles (see Richardson, 1994, 1996) as a response to concerns over representation of the other: "We care less about our 'objectivity' as scientists than we do about providing our readers with some powerful propositional, tacit, intuitive, emotional, historical, poetic, and emphatic experience of the Other via the texts we write" (Lincoln and Denzin, 1994: 582).

Postexperimental (1995–2000). Denzin (1997) described this moment of inquiry as a period marked by intense reflection, "messy texts" (Marcus, 1994) and experimentation in writing styles. He clarifies this statement by adding: "messy texts are many sited, open ended, they refuse theoretical closure, and they do not indulge in abstract, analytic theorizing" (p. xvii). In essence, writers are encouraged to write well and move away from writing styles that have been described as atrociously dull (Atkinson, 1990). Denison and Markula support the idea of learning from other writing genres and argue "there is much to learn from fiction and non-fiction writers about how to write more emotionally sensitive, dynamic, sociologically imaginative, visceral texts, particularly from a craft, style, and technical standpoint" (Denison and Markula, 2003: 18). The many styles and techniques associated with writing and representation have been explored cogently by Sparkes (2002) who offers guidelines for researchers wishing to attempt new writing styles.

The future (2000–?) This is understandably an undefined period. In terms of direction however, Norman Denzin argues that: "this is an ethnography that refuses abstractions and high theory. It is a way of being in the world that avoids jargon and huge chunks of data. Viewing culture as a complex process of improvisation, it seeks to understand how people enact and construct meaning in their daily lives" (Denzin, 1999: 510). Moreover, the seventh moment is seen as "sites for critical conversations about democracy, race, gender, class, nation, freedom, and community" (Lincoln and Denzin, 2000: 1048). There is little doubt that the interpretive paradigm will see numerous methods and styles being adopted by researchers to produce robust, vital, and profound contributions to our collective understanding of human meaning and practice.

Finally, as we enter a new era, it is suggested that there is a need to reflect on the issues we should bring forward into the twenty-first century (Lincoln and Denzin, 2003). Consideration must be assigned to the changing nature of research and the extent to which such change can expand and deepen our understanding of social life. Clearly how we perceive research will continue to change, a time for experimentation, but interesting times all the same. The interpretive paradigm has seen the emergence of narrative, the telling of stories and sharing of experiences. As a representational tool narrative holds great potential because "when well crafted, is a spur to imagination, and through our imaginative participation in the worlds that we create we have a platform for seeing what might be called our 'actual worlds' more clearly" (Eisner, 1997: 264).

Before closure of the historical progression of interpretivism, it is pertinent to visit and acknowledge what many educators believe to be a vital contribution to the nature of contemporary educational research. One of the crucial beacons for interpretive research in education was the seminal work of Frederick Erickson (1986) who argued that interpretation was central to qualitative research. He proposed that the intense interaction that often marks this form of research marked by a constructivist orientation to knowledge and strong attention to the participant's sense of self, the researcher ultimately arrives at a shared personal view. His argument drew on the tenets of ethnography that acknowledged the emic or behaviours or language of those being studied as opposed to the etic or only the researcher's interpretation of the same customs, beliefs, or actions. In other words it is acceptance of the insider's versus the outsider's perspective (Geertz, 1973). Erickson also highlighted the need for "thick description", the expectation of multiple realities and alternative interpretations in keeping with traditional ethnographic accents. Erickson argued the case for a new approach to research based on the natural settings of classrooms and the interactions between students and teachers, what those interactions meant and, on a macro level, how such interpretations related to social action and structure. It was a call for the need to examine the culture of classrooms and especially the meanings shared between researcher and researched. Since the publication of that chapter, educational research is replete with examples based on interpretive perspective and ethnographic methods.

Core concepts to interpretivism

Interpretive research generally follows an inductive process. Schwandt (1997) warns that inductive analysis is however not unique to qualitative forms of research. Indeed he suggests "Qualitative analysis often (but not

always) seeks to construct hypotheses by mucking around for ideas and hunches in the data rather than deriving those hypotheses in the first instance from established theory" (p. 70). At the heart of this form of research is the rejection of causal and theoretical laws to explain human science but rather human action can only be understood by exploring intersubjective meanings derived from lived experience.

Principal components

Possible constituents of the interpretive paradigm are ethnography, hermeneutics, naturalism, phenomenology, symbolic interactionism, constructivism, ethnomethodology, case study and qualitative research. However, Crotty would argue that ethnography is a methodology while case study is a method utilised in interpretive research. As signalled in the introduction to this chapter I have aligned my approach to that of Crotty (1998) and addressed three theoretical perspectives of interpretivism: hermeneutics, phenomenology and symbolic interactionism.

Hermeneutics

Interpretive research is associated with *hermeneutics*, a premise that evolved from the nineteenth century. The term draws from the Greek god Hermes, who was charged with the task of communicating the wishes of the gods to mortals. In essence, it refers to seeking clarity from the obscure. At the heart of hermeneutics is the notion of language. Understanding is often associated with linguistics for it helps people to understand themselves and the world around them. But we should not confuse the relationship between the two. Hermeneutics is not linguistics rather it is concerned with the interpretation of meaning through text and/or conversation. "Thus, hermeneutic science involves the art of reading a text so that the intention and meaning behind appearances are fully understood" (Moustakas, 1994: 9).

Hermeneutics is a term used to refer to the many faces of interpretation. This includes the philosophy, theory, and application of interpretation that can be manifested through speech, text, or action (Schwandt, 1997). Exact definition is problematic as the term is used in many forms by many commentators. We can however extract a working conception of hermeneutics from the complex history and widespread definitional vagueness. Friedrich Schleiermacher (1768–1834) is generally acknowledged as the architect of hermeneutic theory. He defined hermeneutics as an art or practice of understanding, often associated with biblical, classical, or legal texts. William Dilthey later extended

Schleiermacher's perspective to a methodology of the human sciences that could improve the art of understanding. Since its early beginnings, hermeneutics has evolved into a variety of theories, principles, and methods. While the term dates back to the seventeenth century, it was Dilthey who in 1900 composed an essay that changed the meaning of *Hermeneutics*, expanding the original meaning as applied to law and religion to understanding human expression in general. Dilthey drew on the work of Kant and Hume to argue that understanding contributes to knowing social action.

Gallagher (1992) offers an example of the evolution of hermeneutics marked by four distinguishing approaches. The traditional approach based on the work of Schleiermacher and Dilthey is termed *conservative hermeneutics*. Using this approach the interpreter would follow correct procedure and be able to move away from their personal historical status and "understand the author or as the author intended" and "reproduce the meaning or intention of the author" (p. 9) to establish a universal or even an objective truth.

Moderate hermeneutics marked by the work of Hans-Georg Gadamer and Paul Ricoeur who contend that no process can guarantee a complete objective interpretation of a specific author because of the influence of our historical circumstances which can reveal prejudices. A moderate perspective would argue that the reader adopts a somewhat creative approach to the text thereby making an objective interpretation untenable.

Radical hermeneutics endeavours to deconstruct the meaning of the text through the adoption of a less formalized and more playful interpretation of the words instead of seeking truth from the text. This approach is informed by the work of Nietzsche and Heidegger. The aim of this approach is "deconstructing the meaning of a text, not in order to analyze it or to reconstruct a different meaning" (Gallagher, 1992: 10).

The final approach is *critical hermeneutics* that has evolved through the work of Habermas and Apel. Hermeneutics is adopted as a means of addressing issues of power, exploitation, and injustice by examining individual belief systems. Moreover, the argument aligned with this approach focused on how beliefs and ideas reflect the holder's social class interests. Any interpretation is therefore constrained and biased by social, political, and economic forces.

The purpose of hermeneutics is to enhance our understanding of other individuals, groups or cultures. Hermeneutic understanding is characterized by a "hermeneutic circle" or spiral where pre-understanding is influenced by understanding which is in turn interpreted to create a new understanding. This process is indicative of everyday life

that all human beings experience meaning we are all 'interpretive' beings (Schwandt, 1997). Moreover hermeneutics "regards understanding and interpretation as endemic to and a definitive mark of human existence and social life" (Odman and Kerdeman, 1997: 185).

Hermeneutics can help us to deepen our understanding of physical education. For example, a hermeneutically oriented physical educator would endeavour to interpret the meaning that physical educational practices and principles hold for those who experience and participate in them. Hermeneutics can also act as a valuable tool for sport and physical education research by explicating the meanings attached by students and staff toward specific educational policy and practice. For example, MacPhail et al. (2003b) adopted a Nominal Group Technique of interviewing to ascertain how young people believed participation in sport could be enhanced. The findings gleaned from this study draw attention to what is considered to be relevant by young people. This in turn could influence the future content and delivery of physical education policy and programmes. Laker et al. (2003) discovered that while their physical education teacher education programme promoted gender equity, student teacher interviews revealed the powerful socializing influences of school culture. Their research revealed that in schools where student teachers were placed, content of programmes and staff status were influenced by significant gender issues, namely a strong male orientation.

Relevant questions with a hermeneutic flavour might include: How has the new curriculum influenced the way teachers teach? What kinds of messages do the topic selections made by teachers portray to students? What might be the reasons that students avoid participation in some physical education activities? How do students account for their excitement in class? Such questions seek meaning from those affected or require the researcher to account for what they have reported.

Phenomenology

Phenomenology has almost adopted a chameleon status as it is often labelled a philosophy, a methodology, a paradigm and even a qualitative method. So many allocations by authors have contributed to a rather confused status. Its standing is further perplexed by the internal derivatives outlined below. The term however literally means the study of phenomena, arguably an important perspective because "phenomena are the building blocks of human science and the basis of all knowledge" (Moustakas, 1994: 26).

Phenomenology seeks to describe the important, invariant qualities of everyday phenomenon, without attempting to explain how or why an experience occurs. The aim of phenomenology "is to construct an animating evocative description (text) of human actions, behaviours, intentions, and experiences as we meet them in the lifeworld" (van Manen, 1997: 19). Phenomenological descriptions have the potential to offer us sensitive portrayals and interpretations of likely life experiences. Put simply and directly, phenomenological inquiry focuses on the question: "What is the structure and essence of experience of this phenomenon for these people?" The phenomenon being experienced may be an emotion – loneliness, jealousy, anger. The phenomenon may be a relationship, a marriage, or a job. The phenomenon may be a program, an organisation, or a culture (Patton, 1990, p. 69).

van Manen (1997) argues that phenomenology holds an unusual status as a methodology because it provides only description of how people experience the world in a manner that is raw. Such descriptions are not subjected to taxonomies, classifications, or abstractions, rather, they are explications of phenomena themselves, the exalted states of consciousness while running, playing, or dancing, the altered perceptions of surroundings, the almost spiritual sporting moments, to appreciate and reflect on the almost mystical moments that can occur, to discover such experiences and perhaps most importantly to understand them, that is the promise of phenomenology. This status is in keeping with Husserl's call of *Zu den Sachen* or getting "back to the things themselves". Things may include experiences, situations, concepts, emotions or events.

Phenomenology is the first method of knowledge because it begins with "things themselves"; it is also the final court of appeal. Phenomenology, step by step, attempts to eliminate everything that represents a prejudgment, setting aside presuppositions, and reaching a transcendental state of freshness and openness, a readiness to see in an unfettered way, not threatened by customs, beliefs, and prejudices of normal science, by the habits of the natural world or by knowledge based on unreflected everyday experience (Moustakas, 1994: 41).

Phenomenological data are drawn from language and discourse thereby giving it a qualitative status (Polkinghorne, 1989). Language is utilized to create a description of a selected phenomenon. The focus is on what individuals experience, not why or how, presented in a textual manner which might include "thoughts, feelings, examples, ideas, [and] situations that portray what comprises an experience" (Moustakas, 1994: 47). And as van Manen (1997) highlights, "the meaning of the lived experience is usually hidden or veiled" (p. 27).

Merleau-Ponty (1962) proposed four related themes that are common to the adoption and practice of phenomenology. The object of phenomenology is the *description* of phenomena as opposed to explanation. Any description is based on the notion of personal experience that becomes the nucleus of the phenomenon. A second theme is the notion of *reduction* that requires the known or given assumptions and presuppositions of a certain phenomenon to be excluded or "bracketed". In so doing, any theoretical bias that could contaminate description is ensured. Merleau-Ponty (1962) argues that phenomenology is the study of *essence*. By essence he refers to the derivative of the Greek term *ousia*, which is concerned with the inner nature of a thing. It is something that makes a thing what it is, something that is described as it is experienced. The crucial imperative lies in the need to focus not on the things themselves but to their meaning based on ingredients like feelings, perceptions, decisions and memories. To understand the meaning of a phenomenon, you must pursue the essential structure or *essence*. Finally, *intentionality* acknowledges Husserl's argument that individuals are always conscious of something. What Husserl discovered when he considered the content of his mind were such acts as remembering, desiring, and perceiving and the abstract content of these acts, which Husserl called meanings. These meanings, he claimed, enabled an act to be directed toward an object under a certain aspect; and such directedness, termed intentionality, he held to be the quintessence of consciousness. Husserl (cited in Moustakas, 1994: 29) developed the concepts of *noema* and *noesis* to present meaning to acts of consciousness. These terms distinguish between the initial meanings that surface intuitively when something is perceived, and the components of understanding that evolve in our consciousness through reflection on the phenomena:

> The noesis refers to the acts of perceiving, feeling, thinking, remembering, or judging – all of which are embedded with the meanings that are concealed and hidden from consciousness. The meanings must be recognized and drawn out.
>
> The other central concept of intentionality is that of noema. The noema corresponds at all points to the noesis. Wherever a noesis exists it is always directly related to a noema. The noema, in perception, is its perceptual meaning … (Moustakas, 1994: 69).

The noema conveys *what* is being experienced or the object of the experience, whereas the noesis is *how* it is being experienced or the subjective experiencing of the phenomena.

The future impact of phenomenology will depend on its resonance with the needs, wants, and aspirations of physical education and sport pedagogy researchers. Perhaps one of the most promising options is that proposed by Kretchmar (2000) who advocates the need for teachers to develop a better understanding of how to cultivate meaning for our students. The internal values of many activities offered to young people are not necessarily acknowledged because they have failed to be engaged with them at a reflexive level. Movement experiences are personal and "from a phenomenological view it becomes the purpose of the physical educator to develop, encourage, and nurture this awareness of and openness to self–this understanding of self" (Kleinman, 1979: 179). Moreover, the potential of phenomenology to elevate our understanding of movement experiences is indeed significant. But to address any potential our field must pay credence to how such experiences are shared. This would require moving beyond mediocrity and focusing on the unique qualities of movement that can be shared and explored by many for no other reason than "we are obliged to adopt an animating, narratively rich, description of experience as the method of studying the life-world of physical education" (Smith, 1992: 87).

One of the few authentic studies to have employed a phenomenological perspective is Wessinger's (1994) study of scoring in physical education games. The goal of this study was to explore the experience of scoring as it was seen as a manifestation of "doing it well". The author presents a practical explanation of the procedural steps taken to derive meaning from the children in her study. Wessinger offers some salient questions based on the use of games in physical education. She invites teachers to introspectively question their reasons for the inclusion of games based on a personal philosophy and perhaps more importantly, what alignment exists between how games are presented to children and what they attach credence to. While this study is an exemplar of a phenomenological project marked by rich description, it also illustrates how such a study can enhance the practice of teaching physical education.

More recently, Nilges (2004) adopted transcendental phenomenology to examine the meanings of movement for a fifth grade class who completed a contemporary dance unit. Through the use of videotape, student journaling and semi-structured interviews Nilges was able to reveal the complexity of student interpretations of their dance experiences and the importance of exploring and understanding student consciousness at an individual level.

However, while this form of interpretive inquiry seldom appears as journal manuscripts, Kerry and Armour (2000) warn that many examples of projects that have adopted an explicit phenomenological perspective are unpublished or stored on microfiche. They lament the dearth of research studies that have by-passed the potential of phenomenology and its vital connection to meaning and movement.

Symbolic Interactionism

Because there are many varieties to this research approach, any brief summary is often problematic. Nevertheless, this popular approach to interpretive research was championed by sociologists as a derivative of the Chicago School characterized initially by the work of G. H. Mead (1934) and more recently by Blumer (1969). The symbols that formed the basis of study included signs, gestures, language and anything that may convey meaning to the interpreter who in turn adjusts their actions in accordance with newly interpreted structures and meanings. This evolving process of adjustment and interaction in turn promotes the development of cultures or their constitutive parts. For the Chicago School, studying this process required venturing out into the city that became the venue (a social laboratory) for their research. The Chicago School provided the platform for a series of studies by British interactionists who shifted the laboratory to the school. These studies focused on how action was constructed within classrooms and were accompanied by publications on methodological issues (Burgess, 1985, 1984a, 1984b; Hammersley and Atkinson, 1983; Hammersley and Woods, 1984; Woods, 1983).

Denzin (1992) argues that interactionists have a reluctance for theories that disregard personal biographies and lived experiences or any attempt to quantify such experiences. How can you measure the mind? Symbolic interactionism favours asking "how" questions rather than "why". According to Blumer (1969) symbolic interactionism sees human beings confront the world they have to interpret so they can act as opposed to the need to respond to environmental stimuli.

> Symbolic interaction rests in the last analysis on three simple premises. The first premise is that human beings act toward things on the basis of meanings they have for them ... The second premise is that the meaning of such things is derived from, or arises out of, the social interaction that one has with one's fellows. The third premise is that these meanings are handled in, and modified through, an interpretative process used by the person in dealing with the things he [sic] encounters (Blumer, 1969, quoted in Prus, 1997: 5).

Any social situation is marked by interpretations, a teacher must interpret the behaviour of the student, students interpret the actions of fellow students, students responding to teacher action, all interpretations and actions are constantly changing and interacting. Such interpretations and interactions contribute to a constructive process. Different interactions can result in different constructions be they objects or situations (a pair of sport shoes may be a status symbol, an allegiance to one brand or just a pair of shoes). Any or all such interpretations help shed light on what actually occurs in physical education and sport settings, how teaching and learning is perceived or experienced, how curriculum is interpreted and implemented, how policy is enacted, how settings are organized, how subcultures are created or cultivated. For example, Pope and O'Sullivan (2003) observed "Free Gym" (that consisted entirely of pick-up basketball) in an urban American high school over a period of five months. The observation gradually revealed a student imposed hierarchy based on gender, age, skill, and clothing accompanied by a code of rules that determined each student's position on the hierarchy and how movement within such a structure required a required level of "street literacy" or social learning among students. While this gym time was free of teacher influence, the self-imposed code of conduct ensured time and space only for the strongest and fittest, exhibiting a Darwinian-based environment.

Major findings

Interpretive researchers who have chosen to represent the experiences and interpretations of individuals have found themselves stuck between a rock and a paradigmatic hard place. This relatively recent development has occurred because:

> "Researchers attempting to study life-worlds of others are apt to find themselves having to fend off the critiques of positivist social scientists and [more recently] deal with the confusions generated by the postmodernists, as well as the efforts any variety of moralists or control agents who may attempt to tell researchers how they should proceed and what questions they should be asking of the other" (Prus, 1997: 21).

Irrespective of this, perceived dialectic utilization of interpretive frameworks has aided researchers to gain a deeper understanding of life in sport and physical education settings. Interpretive research derivatives have been employed to analyze the ecologies of sport and physical education settings (Carlson and Hastie, 1997; Griffin, 1984, 1985a, 1985b; Hastie, 1995, 2000; James, 1999; Pope and O'Sullivan, 2003; Tousignant, 1982), to acknowledge the voices of students (Bramham, 2003; Carlson, 1995a, 1995b; Dyson, 1995; Flintoff and Scratton, 2001; Gard and Meyenn, 2000; Graham, 1995a, 1995b; Hastie, 1998; Kinchin and O'Sullivan, 2003; Kristen et al., 2002; Langley, 1995, 1996; Macphail et al., 2003a; Nugent and Faucette, 1997; Pope and Grant, 1996; Portman, 1995; Sanders and Graham, 1995; Suomi et al., 2003;

Williams and Woodhouse, 1996), student physical activity choices (Wright et al., 2003), student learning strategies, (Azzarito and Ennis, 2003) and student thinking (Ennis, 1991; Hare and Graber, 2000; Lake, 2001; Macphail et al., 2003).

There are probably two significant areas where interpretive research can promote our understanding. The first is student experiences. Students are an integral part of the learning environment. They have been described as "active receivers and mediators of classroom events" (Mitman and Lash, 1988: 55). Any educator can test students to ascertain exactly what they have gained from work that has been completed as part of their learning. However, at the conclusion of any learning episode measures of student learning cannot reveal the variety and quality of experiences that students may have had during their learning. However, interpretive practices hold considerable potential to assist educators to learn more about the experiences of their students. Perhaps alternative approaches are required to gain a better understanding of the impact of curricular on recipients. Weinstein (1983) called for an integration of student, teacher and observer perspectives of classroom (or gymnasium) phenomena. Although classrooms are described as busy places hosting considerable interaction (Jackson, 1968), little is known about the activity or the reasons for its existence.

The enigmatic nature of student experience of the curriculum appears to represent an educational black hole inviting exploration. The temptation to explore has been largely stonewalled by educationists (Graham, 1995a, 1995b). Although curriculum study should have an illuminating effect on the black hole that characterizes research on student experiences, insufficient attention has been accorded to those who eventually receive, interpret, and define curricula. Despite their dynamic role as part of the learning process, students have traditionally been treated as passive recipients of curriculum and instruction. Although there has been considerable research into the thought processes of students (Wittrock, 1986), the same can not be said for the experiential aspect of learning. There is evidence to reveal that not all physical education experiences are positive. In physical education students may often experience lessons that are different to what a teacher has intended (Graber, 1988; Wang, 1977). Moreover, for some students experiences of physical education have been quite negative. Kollen's (1983) investigation involved interviewing 20 high school students about their responses to physical education. Her work revealed that participants found the programme to be "characterized by embarrassing situations, public humiliation, not being believed, unrealistic expectations" (p. 87). The dominance of masculine, competitive and athletic norms proved to be an alienating experience for many students. Kollen (1983) suggests that movement activities need to be of an integrated nature rather than fragmented, which was the perception of the participants of her study.

There is still little known about how the experiences of students are interpreted other than through an acknowledged dialogue such as interviewing. To fully ascertain the type of subjective experiences students receive in physical education researchers must pursue appropriate forms of inquiry. Smith (1991) purports that by applying appropriate research tools it is possible to make a connection between school physical education curricula and "the concrete experiences through which children first come to appreciate physical activity" (p. 46). In order to understand more about student experiences there is a need to pursue this essential aspect of curriculum further (for further discussion on this topic see Chapter 3.8).

Interpretive work has also shed light on the varied nature of physical education teachers' worlds. For example, Sparkes (1994) explored the teaching life of a lesbian physical educator and the associated strategies she employed to retain a position of safety. Pissanos and Allison (1993) examined influences on the continued professional development of an experienced elementary physical education specialist using life history interviewing. Specifically, researchers have employed interpretive tenets to investigate teacher reflection (Tsangaridou and O'Sullivan, 1997), teacher action (Tsangaridou and O'Sullivan, 2003), management issues (Stort and Sanders, 2002), teacher knowledge (McCaughtry, 2004; Rovegno, 1986; Rovegno, Chen, and Todorovich, 2003), equity issues (Laker, Laker, and Lea, 2003), teacher socialization (Naess, 2001) teacher change (Bechtel, 2002; Flintoff, 2003; Kirk and Macdonald, 2001; Laws, 1998; Pope and O'Sullivan, 1998) and teachers' lives (Armour and Jones, 1998; O'Sullivan, 1994; Sparkes, 1994; Templin, Sparkes, Grant, and Schempp, 1994; Williamson, 1988).

Recently Byra and Goc Karp (2000) have summarized data collection techniques in physical education teacher education research as presented in two refereed journals. Their findings indicate a vibrant and varied representation of qualitative studies many of which employ an interpretive perspective. Their findings are indicative of how our field can gain from a divergence of paradigmatic and methodological approaches.

Major trends and future directions

Interpretive forms of inquiry proffer no panaceas for issues and problems that mark the world of physical education and sport. Researchers working within the interpretive paradigm are often faced with demanding and excessive time commitments, their work is still regarded by some as "unscientific", but there is an ever-increasing acceptance of the work they do. Interpretivists are today confronted with opportunities to pursue their interests, develop their strengths, expand their understanding, take risks and experience the promise and perils of conducting research. The versatility of this approach is still being realized. The arrival of *Telling Tales in Sport and Physical Activity* (Sparkes, 2002) has shed light on how research findings can be represented. Andrew Sparkes invites researchers to explore the many options now available to researchers. He proclaims: "My hope is that in the coming years a variety of representational forms will come to be valued in their own right for the powerful ways in which they can enhance and extend our understanding of sport and physical activity" (Sparkes, 2002: 234).

The optimism that currently abounds contrasts with earlier vacillation. Larry Locke once warned:

"Qualitative research has a future in sport and physical education; it is the kind of future which remains in doubt. If procedural and theoretical problems are not resolved by adherents, trained and productive young scholars are not attracted, and broad acceptance as a legitimate form of research is not won, qualitative research may end as a small footnote to our professional history" (Locke, 1989: 13).

Over the course of the last 20 years interpretive approaches to research have rapidly established legitimacy as a means to understanding teaching and learning in physical education and sport. The real life descriptions, personal stories, shared meanings, and shifting worlds that have become the hallmarks of interpretive research ring true for many teachers, teacher educators, and researchers and as a consequence, is seen by many as an essential *way of knowing*. Interpretive accounts have helped us to realize that reality is not something to be taken for granted, rather, we must accord attention to multiple realities and socially constructed meanings that mark the many and varied social contexts associated with physical education.

The interpretive paradigm has allowed us to gain a greater and more powerful understanding of what sport and physical education means to participants. By championing the interpretive paradigm researchers have been able to gain a more enriched sense of what physical education and sport means to individuals and how those meanings can be adopted to enhance future curriculum and policy initiatives.

Eisner (2001) describes qualitative (read interpretive) research as "a domain that is vibrant and growing" (p. 142) evidenced by the plethora of books, journals, conference presentations, and articles that address this area of research. It is perhaps timely to note that in the third *Handbook of Research on Teaching*, published in 1986, two chapters addressed interpretive research and its associated methods. Fifteen years later the fourth edition of the *Handbook* is marked by a proliferation of paradigmatic and methodological chapters, particularly those concerned with the interpretive paradigm. As a result, "today we can scarcely imagine research on teaching without the interpretive perspective or ethnographic procedures of data collection and analysis" (Eisenhart, 2001: 209). The shifting landscape has led to the realization that "it is clear that Geertz's (1988, 1993) prophecy about the 'blurring of genres' is rapidly being fulfilled. Inquiry methodology can no longer be treated as a set of universally applicable rules and abstractions" (Lincoln and Guba, 2000: 164). The caution however must be that a paradigmatic equilibrium is maintained.

Linda Bain (1995) has argued for a balance of scientific and subjective knowledge. Each theoretical perspective discussed in this volume provides a different set of lenses, while some take on the characteristics of a telescope others resemble a microscope but perhaps more importantly, all lenses help us to see the world more completely. Multiple lenses help to create that balance. And while some would argue there is still a paradigmatic imbalance to research in sport and physical education, it is important to acknowledge the significant and salubrious shifts that the interpretive perspective has achieved. But before repudiating the methodological singularism of positivism and advocating the use of multiple interpretive methodologies, researchers would do well to avoid blindly adopting an interpretive philosophy without due consideration to the limitations, assumptions, and relevance of their decision.

Talk of paradigm shifts is convenient and often savvy. However, the caveat we must attach to such maxims is that paradigms may shift, but any movement occurs at a pedestrian rate. Movement ascribed to epistemologies requires change and acceptance by the relevant players who must base such shifts on well-informed decisions because "… one's method must be congruent with both one's world-view and the subject to be studied. When a research topic and method are in accord with one's intrinsic interests there is a personal investment in the ideas to be investigated" (Dudley, 1992: 328). Perhaps most crucial is not so much what position to take but why. Who we are and what we want to know should drive the approach we should take. Perhaps the most important advice we can embrace is that offered by Daryl Siedentop who, in his reflective professional account of "lessons learned", exclaims that the most important lesson to learn about how the world can be explained according to a chosen perspective is to "Have one!". Siedentop (2002) cautions that to move beyond your own paradigmatic space is good but do not forget where you come from.

The interpretive paradigm and its associated derivatives have irrevocably changed our understanding of physical education contexts, the people within those contexts and the relationship of such contexts with society. There is much to celebrate but we can do better. The challenge for interpretivists will be to accrue a greater understanding of and sensitivity towards the needs of teachers and learners within educational settings. While interpretivism has often been presented as a challenge to the canonical authority of positivism a more sanguine perspective might address the potential such a standpoint has in helping us come to know about the richness of teaching and physical education.

References

Abrahams, R.D. (1986). Ordinary and extraordinary experience. In V.W. Turner and E.M. Bruner (Eds.), *The anthropology of experience* (pp. 45–72). Urbana, IL: University of Illinois Press.

Armour, K.R. and Jones, R.L. (1998). *Physical education teachers' lives and careers*. London: Macmillan.

Atkinson, P. (1990). *The ethnographic imagination*. London: Routledge.

Azzarito, L. and Ennis, C.D. (2003). A sense of connection: Toward social constructivist physical education. *Sport, Education and Society, 8* (2), 179–198.

Bain, L. (1995). Mindfulness and subjective knowledge. *Quest, 47,* 238–253.

Bechtel, P. (2002). Understanding the teacher change process for urban secondary physical education teachers. *Microform Publications Bulletin: Health, Physical Education, Recreation, Exercise and Sport Sciences., 15*(1), 1.

Becker, H.S., Greer, B., Hughes, E.C. Strauss, A.L. (1961). *Boys in white: Student culture in medical school.* Chicago: University of Chicago Press.

Blaikie, N. (1993). *Approaches to social enquiry.* Cambridge: Polity Press.

Blumer, H. (1956). Sociological analysis and the variable. *American Sociological Review, 21,* 683–690.

Blumer, H. (1969). *Symbolic interactionism.* Englewood Cliffs, NJ: Prentice-Hall.

Bramham, P. (2003). Boys, masculinities and PE. *Sport, Education and Society, 8* (1), 57–71.

Burgess, R. (1985). Issues and problems in educational research: An introduction. In R. Burgess (Ed.), *Issues in educational research: Qualitative methods* (pp. 1–17). London: Falmer Press.

Burgess, R. (Ed.). (1984a). *In the field: An introduction to the field research.* London: George Allen & Unwin.

Burgess, R. (Ed.). (1984b). *The research process in educational settings: Ten case studies.* Lewes: The Falmer Press.

Byra, M. and Goc Karp, G. (2000). Data collection techniques employed in qualittaive research in physical education teacher education. *Journal of Teaching in Physical Education, 19,* 246–266.

Carlson, T. (1995a). "Now I think I can." The reaction of eight low skilled students to sport education. *The ACH-PER Healthy Lifestyles Journal, 42* (4), 6–9.

Carlson, T. (1995b). We hate gym : student alienation from Physical Education. *Journal of Teaching in Physical Education, 14,* 467–477.

Carlson, T.B. and Hastie, P.A. (1997). The student social system within sport education. *Journal of Teaching in Physical Education, 16,* 176–195.

Clifford, J. (1988). *The predicament of culture.* Cambridge, MA.: Harvard University Press.

Clifford, J. and Marcus, G.E. (Eds.). (1986). *Writing culture.* Berkeley, CA: University of California Press.

Crotty, M. (1998). *The foundations of social research: Meaning and perspectives in the research process.* Crows Nest, NSW: Allen & Unwin.

Denison, J.D. and Markula, P. (2003). Introduction. In J.D. Denison and P. Markula (Eds.), *Moving writing: Crafting movement in sport research* (pp. 1–24). New York: Peter Lang Publishing.

Denzin, N. (1997). *Interpretive ethnography – Ethnographic practices for the 21st century.* Thousand Oaks, CA: Sage.

Denzin, N.K. (1992). *Symbolic interactionism and cultural studies.* Oxford: Blackwell Publishing.

Denzin, N.K. (1999). Interpretive ethnography for the next century. *Journal of Contemporary Ethnography, 28* (5), 510–519.

Denzin, N.K. and Lincoln, Y.S. (2000). Introduction: The discipline and practice of qualitative research. In N. Denzin and Y. Lincoln (Eds.), *Handbook of qualitative research* (2nd. ed., pp. 1–28). Thousand Oaks, CA: Sage.

Dudley, N.Q. (1992). Participatory principles in human inquiry: Ethics and methods of a study of the paradigm shift experience. *Qualitative Studies in Education, 5* (4), 325–344.

Dyson, B.P. (1995). Students' voices in two alternative elementary physical education programs. *Journal of Teaching in Physical Education, 14,* 394–407.

Earls, N. (1986). Naturalistic inquiry: Interactive research and the insider-outsider perspective [Special monograph]. *Journal of Teaching in Physical Education, 6,* 1.

Eisenhart, M. (2001). Changing conceptions of culture and ethnographic methodology: Recent thematic shifts and their implications for research on teaching. In V. Richardson (Ed.), *Handbook of research on teaching* (4th ed., pp. 209–225). Washington, D.C.: American Educational Research Association.

Eisner, E.W. (1990). The meaning of alternative paradigms for practice. In E. Guba (Ed.), *The paradigm dialogue* (pp. 88–102). London: Sage.

Eisner, E.W. (1997). The new frontier in qualitative research methodology. *Qualitative Inquiry, 3* (3), 259–273.

Eisner, E.W. (2001). Concerns and aspirations for qualitative research in the new millennium. *Qualitative Research, 1* (2), 135–145.

Ennis, C. (1991). Discrete thinking skills in two teachers' Physical Education classes. *The Elementary School Journal, 91* (5), 473–487.

Erickson, F. (1986). Qualitative methods in research on teaching. In M. Wittrock (Ed.), *Handbook of Research on Teaching* (pp. 465–485). New York: Macmillan.

Flintoff, A. (2003). The school sport co-ordinator programme: Changing the role of the physical education teacher? *Sport, Education and Society, 8* (2), 231–250.

Flintoff, A. and Scratton, S. (2001). Stepping into active leisure? Young women's perceptions of active lifestyles and their experiences of school physical education. *Sport, Education and Society, 6* (1), 5–21.

Gallagher, S. (1992). *Hermeneutics and education.* Albany, NY: State University of New York Press.

Gard, M. and Meyenn, R. (2000). Boys, bodies, pleasures and pain: Interogating contact sports in schools. *Sport, Education and Society, 5* (1), 19–34.

Geertz, C. (Ed.). (1973). *The intepretation of cultures: selected essays.* New York: Basic Books.

Geertz, C. (1988). *Works and Lives: The Anthropologist as Author.* Cambridge: Polity Press.

Geertz, C. (1993). *Local knowledge: Further essays in interpretive anthropology.* London: Fontana.

Giddens, A. (1974). *Positivism and sociology.* London: Heinemann.

Graber, K. (1988). *Making the grade: A qualitative study of teacher preparation.* Paper presented at the American Educational Research Association, New Orleans.

Graham, G. (1995a). Physical education through students eyes and in students voices: Implications for teachers and researchers. *Journal of Teaching in Physical Education, 14,* 478–482.

Graham, G. (1995b). Physical Education through Students' eyes and in students voices: introduction. *Journal of Teaching in Physical Education, 14,* 364–371.

Griffin, P.S. (1983). "Gymnastics is a girls thing": Student participation and interaction patterns in a middle school gymnastics unit. In T. Templin and J. Olson (Eds.), *Teaching in Physical education.* Champaign, IL: Human Kinetics.

Griffin, P.S. (1984). Girls' participation patterns in a middle school team sports unit. *Journal of Teaching Physical Education, 4,* 30–38.

Griffin, P.S. (1985a). Boys' participation patterns in a middle school team sports unit. *Journal of Teaching Physical Education, 4,* 100–110.

Griffin, P.S. (1985b). Teachers' perceptions of and responses to sex equity problems in a middle school physical education program. *Research Quarterly for Exercise and Sport, 56,* 103–110.

Guba, E.G. and Lincoln, Y.S. (1994). Competing paradigms in qualitative research. In N.K. Denzin and Y.S. Lincoln (Eds.), *Handbook of qualitative research* (pp. 105–117). Thousand Oaks, CA: Sage.

Gubrium, J.F. and Holstein, J.A. (2000). Analyzing interpretive practice. In N.K. Denzin and Y.S. Lincoln (Eds.), *Handbook of qualitative research (second edition)* (pp. 487–508). Thousand Oakes, CA: Sage Publications.

Hammersley, M. and Atkinson, P. (Eds.). (1983). *Ethnography: Principles in practice.* London: Tavistock.

Hammersley, M. and Woods, P. (Eds.). (1984). *Life in school : The sociology of pupil culture.* Milton Keynes, UK: Open University Press.

Hare, M.K. and Graber, K.C. (2000). Student misconceptions during two invasion game units in physical education: A qualitative investigation of student thought processing. *Journal of Teaching in Physical Education, 20,* 55–77.

Hastie, P. (1995). An ecology of a secondary school outdoor adventure camp. *Journal of Teaching in Physical Education, 15,* 79–97.

Hastie, P. (1998). *Skill & tractical development during a sport education frisbee season.* Paper presented at the A.E.R.A., San Diego, CA.

Hastie, P.A. (2000). An ecological analysis of a sport education season. *Journal of Teaching in Physical Education, 19,* 355–373.

Howe, K.R. (2001). Qualitative educational research: The philosophical issues. In V. Richardson (Ed.), *Handbook of research on teaching* (4th ed., pp. 201–208). Washington, DC.: American Educational Research Association.

Jackson, P.W. (1968). *Life in classrooms.* New York: Holt, Rinehart and Winston.

James, K. (1999). "I feel really embarrassed in front of the guys!" Adolescent girls and informal school basketball. *The ACHPER Healthy Lifestyles Journal, 46* (4), 11–16.

Kerry, D.S. and Armour, K.M. (2000). Sport sciences and the promise of phenomenology: Philosophy, method, and insight. *Quest, 52,* 1–17.

Kinchin, G.D. and O'Sullivan, M. (2003). Incidences of student support for and resistance to a curricular innovation in high school physical education. *Journal of Teaching in Physical Education, 22,* 245–264.

Kirk, D. and Macdonald, D. (2001). Teacher voice and ownership of curriculum change. *Journal of Curriculum Studies, 8* (2), 271–298.

Kleinman, S. (1979). The significance of human movement: A phenomenological approach. In E.W. Gerber and W.J. Harper (Eds.), *Sport and the body.* (pp. 177–180). Philadelphia, PA.: Lea & Febiger.

Kollen, P. (1983). Fragmentation and integration in movement. In T.J. Templin and J.K. Olsen (Eds.), *Teaching physical education* (pp. 86–93). Champaign, IL: Human Kinetics.

Kretchmar, R.S. (2000). Movement subcultures: Sites of meaning. *Journal of Physical Education, Recreation, and Dance, 71* (5), 19–25.

Kristen, L., Patriksson, G. and Fridlund, B. (2002). Conceptions of children and adolescents with physical disabilities about their participation in a sports programme. *European Physical Education Review, 8* (2), 139–156.

Lake, J. (2001). Young people's conceptions of sport, physical education and exercise: implications for physical education and the promotion of health-related exercise. *European Physical Education Review, 7* (1), 80–91.

Laker, A., Laker, J.C. and Lea, S. (2003). School experience and the issue of gender. *Sport, Education and Society, 8* (1), 73–89.

Langley, D. and Knight, S.M. (1996). Exploring practical knowledge: a case study of an experienced senior tennis performer. *Research Quarterly for Exercise and Sport, 67* (4), 433–448.

Langley, D.J. (1995). Examining the personal experience of student skill learning: A narrative perspective. *Research Quarterly for Exercise and Sport, 66,* 116–128.

Laws, C. (1998). Physical education, curriculum change and individualism. *European Journal of Physical Education, 3* (1), 114.

Lincoln, Y.S. and Denzin, N.K. (1994). The Fifth Moment. In N. Denzin and Y. Lincoln (Eds.), *Handbook of qualitative research* (pp. 575–585). Thousand Oaks, CA: Sage Publications.

Lincoln, Y.S. and Denzin, N.K. (2000). The seventh moment: Out of the past. In N.K. Denzin and Y.S. Lincoln (Eds.), *Handbook of qualitative research* (2nd. ed., pp. 1047–1065). Thousand Oaks, CA: Sage.

Lincoln, Y.S. and Denzin, N.K. (Eds.). (2003). *Turning points in qualitative research: Tying knots in a handerchief.* Walnut Creek, CA: Altira Mira Press.

Lincoln, Y.S. and Guba, E.G. (2000). Paradigmatic controversies, contradictions, and emerging confluences. In N. Denzin and Y. Lincoln (Eds.), *Handbook of qualitative research* (2nd ed., pp. 163–188). Thousand Oaks, CA: Sage.

Locke, L.F. (1989). Qualitative research as a form of scientific inquiry in sport and physical education. *Research Quarterly For Exercise and Sport, 60,* 1–20.

Locke, L. and Griffin, P. (1986). Profiles of struggle: Introduction. *Journal of Physical Education, Recreation, and Dance, 57* (4), 32–33.

MacPhail, A., Kinchin, G.D. and Kirk, D. (2003a). Students' conceptions of sport and sport education. *European Physical Education Review, 9* (3), 285–299.

MacPhail, A., Kirk, D. and Eley, D. (2003b). Listening to young people's voices: youth sports leaders' advice on facilitating particpation in sport. *European Physical Education Review, 9* (1), 57–73.

Marcus, G. (1994). What comes (just) after "post"? The case of ethnography. In Y. Lincoln and N. Denzin (Eds.), *Handbook of Qualitative Research* (pp. 563–574). Thousand Oaks, CA: Sage.

Marcus, G. and Fisher, M. (1986). *Anthropology as cultural critique.* Chicago, IL: Chicago University Press.

Markula, P., Grant, B.C. and Denison, J.D. (2001). Qualitative research and aging and physical activity: Multiple ways of knowing. *Journal of Aging and Physical Activity, 9,* 245–264.

McCaughtry, N. (2004). The emotional dimensions of a teacher's pedagogical content knowledge: Influences on content, curriculum, and pedagogy. *Journal of Teaching in Physical Education, 23,* 30–47.

Mead, G.H. (1934). *Mind, self and identity.* Chicago, IL: University Press.

Merleau-Ponty, M. (1962). *The phenomenology of perception.* New York: Humanities Press.

Mitman, A.L. and Lash, A.A. (1988). Students' perceptions of their academic standing and classroom behavior. *The Elementary School Journal, 89* (1), 55–68.

Moustakas, C. (1994). *Phenomenological research methods.* Thousand Oaks, CA: Sage Publications.

Naess, F.D. (2001). Narratives about young men and masculinities in organized sport in Norway. *Sport, Education and Society, 6* (2), 125–142.

Nilges, L.M. (2004). Ice Can Look Like Glass: A Phenomenological Investigation of Movement Meaning. *Research Quarterly for Exercise and Sport, 75* (3), 298–314.

Nugent, P. and Faucette, N. (1997). *Preadolscent females' voices: Preferred curricula, class organizational strategies, and teaching behaviors during elementary physical education.* Paper presented at the A.E.R.A., Chicago, Illinois.

Odman, P.-J. and Kerdeman, D. (1997). Hermeneutics. In J.P. Keeves (Ed.), *Educational research, methodology, and measurement: An international handbook.* (pp. 185–192). New York: Pergamon Press.

O'Sullivan, M. (1994). High school physical education teachers: Their world of work. *Journal of Teaching in Physical Education, 13* (4), 323–441.

Patton, M.Q. (1990). *Qualitative evaluation and research methods* (2nd ed.). Newberry Park: Sage.

Pissanos, B.W. and Allison, P.C. (1993). Student constructs of elementary school physical education. *Research Quarterly for Exercise and Sport, 64* (4), 425–435.

Polkinghorne, D. (1989). Phenomenological research methods. In R. Vale and S. Halling (Eds.), *Existential-Phenomenological perspectives in psychology exploring the breadth of human experience* (pp. 41–60). New York, Plenum Press.

Pope, C.C. and Grant, B.C. (1996). Student experiences in sport education. *Waikato Journal of Education, 2,* 103–118.

Pope, C. and O'Sullivan, M. (1998). Culture, pedagogy and teacher change in an urban high school: How do you want your eggs done? *Sport Education and Society, 3* (2), 210–226.

Pope, C.C. and O'Sullivan, M. (2003). Darwinism in the gym. *Journal of Teaching in Physical Education, 22,* 311–327.

Portman, P. (1995). Who is having fun in physical education classes? Experiences of six grade students in elementary and middle schools. *Journal of Teaching in Physical Education, 15,* 445–453.

Prus, R. (1997). *Subcultural mosaics and intersubjective realities.* New York: State University of New York Press.

Richardson, L. (1994). Writing: A method of inquiry. In N. Denzin and Y. Lincoln (Eds.), *Handbook of qualitative research* (pp. 516–529). Thousand Oaks, CA: Sage.

Richardson, L. (Ed.). (1996). *Fields of play constructing an academic life.* New Brunswick, NJ: Rutgers University Press.

Rovegno, I. (1986). *Preservice physical education teachers' knowledge, attitudes, and actions during their elementary physical education methods course and embedded field experiences.* Unpublished Dissertation Proposal PhD, University of North Carolina, Greensboro.

Rovegno, I., Chen, W. and Todorovich, J. (2003). Accomplished teachers' pedagogical content knowledge of teaching dribbling to third grade children. *Journal of Teaching in Physical Education, 22,* 426–449.

Sanders, S. and Graham, G. (1995). Kindergarten children's initial experiences in physical education: The relentless persistence for play clashes with the zone of acceptable responses. *Journal of Teaching Physical Education, 14,* 372–383.

Schutz, A. (1962). *Collected papers* (Vol 1; M. Natanson, Ed.). The Hague: Martinus Nijhoff.

Schwandt, T. (2000). Three epistemological stances for qualitative inquiry: Interpretivism, hermeneutics, and social constructionism. In N. Denzin and Y. Lincoln (Eds.), *Handbook of qualitative research* (2nd Ed., pp. 189–213). Newberry Park: Sage.

Schwandt, T.A. (1994). Constructivist, interpretivist approaches to human inquiry. In N.K. Denzin and Y.S. Lincoln (Eds.), *Handbook of qualitative research* (pp. 118–137). Thousand Oakes, CA: Sage.

Schwandt, T.A. (1997). *Qualitative inquiry: A dictionary of terms.* Thousand Oaks, CA: Sage.

Siedentop, D. (2002). Lessons learned. *Journal of Teaching in Physical Education, 21,* 454–464.

Smith, S.J. (1991). Where is the child in physical education. *Quest, 43,* 37–54.

Smith, S.J. (1992). Studying the lifeworld of physical education: A phenomenological orientation. In A. C. Sparkes (Ed.), *Research in physical education and sport* (pp. 61–89). London: The Falmer Press.

Sparkes, A. (1994). Self, silence and invisibility as a beginning teacher: A life history of a lesbian experience. *British Journal of Sociology of Education, 16,* 93–118.

Sparkes, A.C. (2002). *Telling tales in sport and physical activity.* Champaign, IL: Human Kinetics.

Sparkes, A.C. (Ed.). (1992). *Research in Physical Education and Sport: Exploring alternative visions.* London: The Falmer Press.

Sparkes, A., Templin, T.J. and Schempp, P.G. (1990). The problematic nature of a career in a marginal subject: Some implications for teacher education programmes. *Journal of Education for Teaching, 16* (1), 3–28.

Stort, S. and Sanders, S.W. (2002). Why can't students just do as they're told?! An exploration of incorrect repsonses. *Journal of Teaching in Physical Education, 21,* 208–228.

Suomi, J., Collier, D. and Brown, L. (2003). Factors affecting the social experiences of students in elementary physical education classes. *Journal of Teaching in Physical Education, 22,* 186–202.

Templin, T.J. and Olson, J.K. (Eds.). (1983). *Teaching in physical education.* Champaign, IL: Human Kinetics.

Templin, T., Sparkes, A., Grant, B. and Schempp, P. (1994). Matching the self : the paradoxical case and life history of a late career teacher/coach. *Journal of Teaching in Physical Education, 13,* 274–294.

Tousignant, M.G. (1982). *Analysis of the task structures in secondary school physical education.* University Microfilms Int No 82–22–191. Ann Arbor, Michigan.

Tsangaridou, N. and O'Sullivan, M. (1997). The role of reflection in shaping physical education teachers' educational values and practices. *Journal of Teaching in Physical Education, 17,* 2–25.

Tsangaridou, N. and O'Sullivan, M. (2003). Physical education teachers' theories of action and theories-in-use. *Journal of Teaching in Physical Education, 22,* 132–152.

Turner, V. and Bruner, E. (Eds.). (1986). *The anthropology of experience.* Urbana, IL: University of Illinois Press.

van Manen, M. (1997). *Researching lived experience: Human science for an action sensitive pedagogy.* London, Ontario: The Althouse Press.

Wang, B. (1977). *An ethnography of a physical education class: An experiment in integrated living.* Unpublished Ed. Dissertation: University Microfilms International, The University of North Carolina at Greensboro.

Weinstein, R.S. (1983). Student Perceptions of Schooling. *The Elementary School Journal, 83* (4), 287–312.

Wessinger, N.P. (1994). "I hit a home-run!" the lived meaning of scoring in games in Physical Education. *Quest, 46,* 425–439.

Williams, A. and Woodhouse, J. (1996). Delivering the discourse – Urban adolescents' perceptions of physical education. *Sport, Education and Society, 1* (2), 201–213.

Williamson, K.M. (1988). *A phenomenological description of the professional lives and experiences of physical education teacher educators.* Unpublished Ed. University of Massachusetts.

Winch, P. (1958). *The idea of social science and its relation to philosophy.* London: Routledge & Kegan Paul.

Wittrock, M.C. (1986). Student thought processes. In M.C. Wittrock (Ed.), *Handbook of research on teaching (3rd Ed.)* (pp. 297–314). New York: Macmillan.

Woods, P. (1983). *Sociology and the school.* London: Routledge & Kegan Paul.

Wright, J., Macdonald, D. and Groom, L. (2003). Physical activity and young people: Beyond participation. *Sport, Education and Society, 8* (1), 17–33.

1.3 Socially critical research perspectives in physical education

JOSÉ DEVÍS-DEVÍS

Introduction

The last 25 years have witnessed the emergence of socially critical research as an important perspective within the domain of qualitative research and across a range of disciplines including education and physical education (Kirk, 1997a; Sparkes, 1992). Interest in this perspective has been stimulated, within the field of physical education and sport, by a concern to acknowledge and address the inequalities and injustices inherent in the practices, pedagogies, and policies of this field with a view to developing an emancipatory agenda. This said, it was not until the end of the 1980s that the first review paper to focus specifically on critical research was published by Bain (1989) in which she identified the main characteristics of this perspective and outlined its current use within physical education. In a handbook chapter of research on physical education teacher education (PETE), Bain (1990a) also introduced critical social research in her analysis. However, in general reviews of teaching and curriculum studies in the early 1990s, the socially critical perspective was still signalled as deserving attention in the future (Silverman, 1991; Steinhardt, 1992).

Against this backdrop, it is necessary to begin this chapter by focusing on the purposes of socially critical research. This is not an easy task because there is no single, unique form of this kind of research that is characterized by a plurality of concerns revolving around issues of social justice, equality, and emancipation (Guba, 1990; Sparkes, 1992). Thus, the socially critical perspective is best understood as a dynamic activity that constantly redefines and transforms itself in response to emergent (and often opposing) theoretical movements, responses to critics, and societal changes in advanced capitalist societies (Kincheloe and McLaren, 2000; Morrow, 1991). This dynamic aspect makes it difficult to offer singular and all-encompassing definitions of just what socially critical research is. This is particularly so given its ongoing and emerging relationships with other dynamic fields such as interpretive inquiry, feminist, poststructuralist, and postcolonial research. For example, a particular study may adopt an ethnographic approach and draw upon neo-Marxist concepts to analyze and interpret the data, or poststructuralist textual theory may be applied to real and problematic contexts with a view to generating politically transformative action.

Socially critical research is also difficult to define, not just for methodological reasons, but also because of the outcomes required. Thus, this kind of research should result in the emancipation of those involved and should lead to radical challenges in their conclusions and practices (Macdonald, 1997). With this in mind, my tactic in this chapter is to present its main features and offer a panoramic view of different trends and investigations in order to give a flavour of this approach. However, in some cases, it is difficult to define boundaries from other perspectives mentioned in this handbook because the ideas and theories that inform sociocritical pedagogic inquires are likewise closely interconnected. Here, the work of theorists, practitioners, and researchers also interact to shape a multiple and complex universe of discourses and cultural productions of sociocritical activities. Therefore, although the focus in this chapter is on critical theory and socially critical research in physical education and PETE, rather than critical pedagogy, it is inevitable that the latter be touched upon.

Brief historical overview

It was at the beginning of the 1980s when some physical education academics, the majority of them from English-speaking countries, directed their research towards equality, social justice, and emancipation objectives. This emergence was preceded by important critiques around traditional ways of understanding physical education and PETE teaching and research, as well as by their correspondent alternative proposals in these domains.

Early critiques on the teaching domain addressed the technical approach to physical education curriculum planning and effective PETE. These critiques also reclaimed greater teachers' sensitivity to social and cultural problems, such as inequalities and discrimination in physical education and sport, along with a more decisive role to act as problem-setters and not only problem-solvers in relation to their professional practices (Fitzclarence, 1987; Harris, 1987; Kirk and Smith, 1986; Lawson, 1984; Tinning, 1985). These critiques and demands were followed by alternative proposals of pedagogy in order to overcome previous limitations, achieve greater personal and social responsibility values among students, and help teachers to become agents of social change (Hellison, 1978, 1985; Kirk, 1986, 1988; Tinning, 1987a; Tinning et al., 1993).

In the research domain, some critical voices on dominant inquiry emerged from different places, emphasizing limitations of positivist research in understanding and improving physical education and PETE (Beamish, 1982; Crum, 1986; Kirk, 1989; Lawson, 1990b). Some authors assumed the challenge to find new research paradigms for teachers and teaching in physical education in order to reflect the new professional demands and theoretical contributions (Lawson, 1983a, 1983b, 1984, 1985) and others initiated open discussion with advocates of a positivist mode of research (Schempp, 1987, 1988; Siedentop, 1987). It was part of an increasing debate within social sciences, about the epistemological unity or diversity of educational research. In the meantime, a plethora of reasons and counter-reasons among advocates of different research paradigms (mainly positivist, interpretative, and critical) appeared, becoming what has been called "the paradigm wars" (Gage, 1989). In the physical education and sport field the acknowledgement and celebration of the diversity approach was proposed because it offered different visions of the field and allowed a greater understanding and theory development (Sparkes, 1991, 1992). Paradigmatic debate contributed, at least, to understanding the interests, assumptions and purposes of each other and clarifying some confusion among them. It also helped to improve the field's research situation and prepare its "transition from adolescence to adulthood" (Lawson, 1990a: 6).

From my point of view, both critiques about the professional and research domains and their alternatives were of great relevance to the creation of an environment on behalf of constructivist social positions. New inquiry methods and perspectives were also used to address professional reclaims arisen. The emergence of the first group of socially critical studies not only established links between what happened in physical education or PETE classrooms and wider social problems, but also encouraged social action for professional improvement and emancipation.

The collection of studies edited by Evans (1986, 1988) gathered a substantial number of critical studies on curriculum innovation, ideology, gender, and coeducation, written by different European authors, emphasized issues of power and control. Furthermore, Tinning's (1987b, 1988) work on emancipatory action research represented initial attempts to use research in order to change the understanding and teaching practices of student teachers from Deakin University (Australia), an international focus of development and diffusion of this kind of research in education and physical education. The early critical qualitative research, conducted by Griffin (1983, 1984, 1985a, 1985b) in the USA, emphasized equity, gender, and ability, as well as the power of contextual factors in the physical education classes (Griffin, 1985c). Dewar's (1985, 1987) studies on curriculum materials and social construction of gender in North America showed an initial influence of critical sociology and neo-Marxist theories that later evolved, like Griffin's work, towards a feminist position. Another edited book by Kirk and Tinning (1990) included different critical contributions written by an international group of authors from English-speaking countries. Contributors tried to submit for critical examination the new ideas that appeared during the years before, such as hidden curriculum, health, gender, pedagogy, teaching, and innovation. As the editors suggested, it meant to look into the substantive issues of physical education and PETE and, at the same time, to look out to connect these issues with contemporary social and cultural movements.

The 1990s and the early 2000s are characterized by an expansion and development of socially critical research perspectives in physical education and PETE. For instance, over this period there has been an increasing presence of sociocritical studies in consolidated international journals of the field (*Quest, Journal of Teaching in Physical Education, Research Quarterly for Exercise and Sport* or *European Physical Education Review*) and new ones especially sensitive to sociocultural issues as *Sport, Education and Society*. Other international edited books have included new critical research chapters on gender, curriculum, and life history, and action research themes (Sparkes, 1992), different equality issues in teaching and teacher education (Evans, 1993), and new sociocritical perspectives under the influence of postmodernism (Fernández-Balboa, 1997a). During these years, a new generation of authors have addressed their research toward critical purposes, some from the very beginning of their academic careers and others reorienting their previous positivist socialization toward alternative paradigms more committed to social issues. Sociocritical research perspectives also initiated an internationalization process beyond the English-speaking countries, mainly due to a literature diffusion and the translation of books and papers, as well as direct contacts with authors from the first or second generation of critical research.[1] From revisiting papers of previous critical pedagogy work and attempts for broadening its agenda (Fernández-Balboa, 1993a; Kirk, 2001; Rovegno and Kirk, 1995), new sociocritical research avenues have emerged around caring, student learning, physical culture and responsibility teaching models, as well as ecological issues. This broader conception has been an object of recent internal contestation because it potentially confuses the early political agenda or emancipatory politics that characterize the discourse and practice of critical pedagogy and research (Tinning, 2002). Nevertheless, stronger contestation has been generated by the critiques from different theoretical positions such as empiricism, feminism, and post-structuralism. These critiques have informed and provoked new challenges on the recent and future development of sociocritical research.

Core concepts and characteristics

Socially critical research, as any other kind of inquiry, is carried out and based on a series of shared assumptions regarding ontology, epistemology, theory, purposes, and methodology. These suppositions shape a paradigm or a disciplinary matrix of assumptions (Kuhn, 1975), a world view (Patton, 1978), a basic belief system (Guba and Lincoln, 1989), or a particular set of lenses to see and understand the world (Sparkes, 1992). The ways in which these assumptions operate together in a complex manner shape the research questions asked and the approaches chosen to answer them. As such, each paradigm or tradition operates as a coherent whole.

Ontology, epistemology, and social theory

Ontology refers to the study of being and nature, that is, to questions about what it means to be a human being and what is the nature of reality or the very nature of the research subject matter. It is also concerned about the relationships between our ways of making sense of the world and its material reality. Ontology falls on a realist-relativist dimension that assumes the world has a true nature, which is knowable and real, or that we can never know the true nature of the world because all we have are accounts of what it is. In this sense, the main ontological issue about how we understand reality moves between an external and previously determined position, and an internal and individual consciously derived one.

In contrast, epistemology refers to the nature of knowledge, its production and communication. In other words, it is about what is known and who can

know, what kinds of knowledge are possible and accepted, how we go about obtaining and transmitting that knowledge. The main epistemological question about the nature of knowledge moves between positions considering it as something objective, tangible, and attainable, and another one that regards it as something subjective, transcendental, and personally experienced (Smith, 1989; 1993; Sparkes, 1992). Within the critical research paradigm, social reality is much more than behaviour patterns, and concepts and ideas created by symbolic interactions. This reality is also conceived as a product of social, material and historical conditions based on a holistic idea of social phenomena.

Knowledge, on the other hand, is considered as socially constructed and value-based, not discovered and value-free as the positivist research paradigm or created and value-laden as the interpretive one. From critical research paradigm, there is a rejection of the innocence and neutrality of knowledge and it is taken to be inevitably political since it represents the interests of certain groups, usually powerful ones (Carr and Kemmis, 1988; Popkewitz, 1988). Nevertheless, a deeper understanding of these assumptions requires looking towards two primary forms of ontological and epistemological issues. This first is a radical structuralist strand that "adopts an external-realist ontology, an objectivist epistemology, and holds a somewhat deterministic view of people that leads them to concentrate upon structural relationships within a realist social world via the analysis of deep-seated internal contradictions and the analysis of power relationships". The second is a radical humanism strand "which has much in common with the interpretive paradigm in that it adopts an internal-idealist ontology, a subjectivist epistemology, and a more voluntaristic view of people" (Sparkes, 1992: 38).

As it can be observed, these two onto-epistemological strands are connected with certain theories or philosophical stances, ways of viewing the world and understanding social life that inform sociocritical inquiry. Social theories or groups of social theories that are connected with these strands are: Marxism, neo-Marxism, feminism, and the new sociology of education (NSE).[2] These links appear because main liberatory research perspectives are debtors of many of their concepts. In this sense, Marxism, instigated by Karl Marx and his followers, is related to radical structuralist positions that see social issues as being shaped by underlying structures (social class, economical level, ideological identification, or sex), in ways that explain the social organization. For example, schooling has been considered an ideological state apparatus that contributes to maintain the capitalist system, and a correspondence has been established between social relationships in schools and relationships in the productive labour system (in Kemmis and Fitzclarence, 1988).

Neo-Marxism was understood as a cluster of theoretical contributions from the Frankfurt School until Giddens' structuration theory emerged. This theory has had a substantial impact on educational and physical education researchers. Related to the radical humanism strand of onto-epistemological character, neo-Marxism criticizes positivism and Marxist structuralism, for being mechanistic, determinist, and pessimistic. It considers social order to be created by persons in constant interaction within historical and social conditions they have to live with. In this sense, individual agency is always subscribed within larger structures and, therefore, it cannot be known completely nor can its consequences. Of great importance has been, for example, the Freirian empowering concepts of *oppression, conscientization and dialogue* that allow knowing the world and acting in it (Freire, 1973, 1974). Other relevant concepts are *hegemony*, that facilitates power analysis and group confrontation in the study of society and curriculum (Apple, 1986), as well as *resistance* against domination, *voice* to participate in the social sphere, and the notion of *teachers as intellectuals* that implies a commitment with emancipation (Giroux, 1983, 1990).

As a body of thought to explain woman's oppression and eliminate it, feminism is shaped by different theoretical perspectives (e.g. liberal, radical, Marxist). Although feminism is developed in Chapter 5, I would emphasize here that, from an onto-epistemological point of view, those perspectives connected to structuralism see education as a key institution in the maintenance of social and sexual divisions in the labour market. Those ones related to humanism see schools as important places in the construction of male supremacy over female (Scraton, 1990).

Another group of NSE contributions, structuralist and non-structuralist, has also been decisive in the theoretical development of education and physical education critical research perspectives. Among the main concepts, the *social construction* notion appears applied to knowledge and curriculum, as well as its relationships with social and economic structures (Young, 1972). *Habitus* is another important concept referring to social and cultural structures internalized by people (Bourdieu, 1972, 1988). *Code* is also a relevant notion used to refer to the implicit and differentially acquired grammar by different social classes (Bernstein, 1989a, 1989b).

Finally, I would highlight that these theoretical and onto-epistemological issues become a driving force in guiding and clustering different aspects of the inquiry process, such as purposes, method, data collection techniques, ways of analyzing and interpreting data, and even the written presentation form, within a coherent particular sociocritical research.

Purposes

Research that aspires to be critical seeks to confront injustices in society, that is to say, it aims to analyse how present unjust conditions are produced and maintained in order to understand, criticize, and change them. It should be stressed that understanding is only a first step towards addressing such injustices since critical research has a political and transformative outcome, compared with interpretative research that is more concerned with description and understanding of subjective meanings of action (Carr and Kemmis, 1988; Popkewitz, 1988). Therefore, the ultimate goal that underpins and guides socially critical research perspectives is *emancipation*, connected with a commitment to social justice, equity and social change (Carr and Kemmis, 1988; Kincheloe and McLaren, 2000; Macdonald et al., 2002). In its broadest sense, human emancipation is a personal and social process of liberation, from sources of domination, which affects social action. According to Habermas' theory of knowledge-constitutive interests (1982), adaptation to new social circumstances and challenges, and an ability to change, are vital necessities in contemporary life. In this sense, adaptation and change become daily concerns of those who participate in physical education and sport domains.

Socially critical researchers that seek an emancipatory purpose are deeply concerned about issues of ideology and power. As a system of ideas, beliefs, values, commitments, and patterns of thought and social practices, ideology operates dialectically between individuals and structures to reproduce and maintain social characteristics. Therefore, it is a mediator through which personal consciousness and social practices and relationships are created (Kemmis and Fitzclarence, 1988; Kincheloe and McLaren, 2000). It is then not a separate system of ideas, beliefs, and commitments that could be contrasted with another system as, for example, science, but "an aspect of every system of signs and symbols in so far as they are implicated in an asymmetrical distribution of power and resources" (McLellan, 1986: 83). In this sense, ideology is twofold since it functions as a necessary shared system of symbols and social practices that would make many social situations incomprehensible without it, and as a system embedded in power relationships and sedimented forms of thought of everyday life that can distort communication and understanding. This second function is of primary interest and concern to socially critical researchers because it reduces emancipatory possibilities and desires.

Nevertheless, emancipatory purposes and issues of ideology and power are addressed differently by different socially critical research perspectives. For some neo-Marxists, the main critical research purpose consists of a social and cultural critique of ideologies and power relationships. The point is not simply to expose ideologies and power relationships, but to embed this knowledge in the consciousness of the unprivileged and provoke social action that assists in their self-emancipation (Carr and Kemmis, 1988). Therefore, critique not only will allow to understand beyond the surface of the physical education and sport's world but to act positively for a better possible future.

In contrast, other neo-Marxists are more concerned with the empowerment potential of critical research in order to increase the capacity of participants, individuals, or groups, to take greater control of their decisions so they might challenge relationships and structures of power. They blur the separation between research and action by combining education, socio-political action, and inquiry (Fals-Borda, 1992). Due to a wide usage of the term empowerment, it should be emphasized that empowerment can take many forms and it does not only occur at the level of individual consciousness but also at institutional and social structural levels. Recently, in the physical education field, Kirk (2001) has stated that self-consciousness is a necessary aspect of empowerment though not sufficient in itself since it needs social change. Moreover, empowerment is not something transmitted from one person to another but a shared experience where power is redistributed among participants and enhanced to take greater control of their life. As a process, empowerment in critical research implies listening and understanding social conditions, dialogue to identify inquiry problems, and social action to change those problems (Freire, 1973, 1987).

Feminist researchers' general goal seeks "to correct both the invisibility and distortion of female experience in ways relevant to ending women's unequal social position" (Lather, 1991: 71). However, as neo-Marxist critical researchers, they have purposes of socio-cultural critique and empowerment though focused upon gender as a fundamental category to understand the social order. In this sense, contemporary feminist research in physical education and sport is focused on women's empowerment, as practitioners and as research participants, with an overt political commitment to ensuring their voices within the making of knowledge, and contributing to take greater control of their lives (see, for example, Clarke and Humberstone, 1997; Scraton and Flintoff, 1992).

Finally, critical researchers' purposes from the perspective of the NSE, including later works of Bernstein (1989a, 1989b, 1993) and Bourdieu (1988), address the role schooling and education play in the transmission and reproduction of dominant culture. In the field of physical education, some research contributions have used Bernstein's concept of pedagogical discourse to study how knowledge production of different curriculum innovations and reforms is created outside educational places (Evans and Clarke, 1988; Penney and Evans, 1999). In a similar vein, recent studies use Bourdieu's contributions for providing explanations of the social construction of the body and gender and, in doing so, assist in finding ways to interrupt the habitus for facilitating students' physical empowerment (e.g. Gorely et al., 2003).

Methodological issues

According to the onto-epistemological questions and purposes of socially critical research mentioned in the previous sections, and derived from their assumptions, a number of methodological issues that affect the research process emerge. One issue is related to the researcher–researched relationship. Emancipatory purpose and issues of power in this kind of inquiry not only address social reality but also are central to the research process itself. Critical researchers need to adapt and develop methodological ways to overcome the marginalization of those persons that are objects of study. Therefore, persons or social actors need to participate in the inquiry process to become partners in the knowledge production and utilization in order to eliminate imbalances in the research power relationships. *Collaborative*, *dialogic* and *participatory* have been terms used to characterize a more democratic way of having relationships that break asymmetries in the research process and introduce participants from disempowered groups (Fals-Borda, 1992; McLaren, 1995). *Reciprocity* is another term used here to refer to a mutual negotiation of meaning and power during the research process. It avoids imposition from the part of the researcher and provides participants with insights for action and social change (Lather, 1991). On the contrary, traditional relationships are conceived as an act of colonization (Stavenhagen, 1992) or vampirism of social knowledge (McLaren, 1995), due to the pursuit of objectivity in positivist research and of neutrality in much of the interpretative research that in the end justifies and supports the *status quo* (Zamosc, 1992). Therefore, socially critical inquiry perspectives that foster emancipation are using a range of generally qualitative methods that emphasize a more egalitarian researcher–researched relationship.

Within education, critical ethnography, curriculum history, life history, collaborative research, action research and case studies informed by different critical concepts are used as the main methodological strategies. Examples of methodological strategies are also provided within the field of physical education and sport (e.g. Curtner-Smith, 2002; Evans, 1988; Kirk and Tinning, 1990; Sparkes,

1992). They offer a varied degree of collaboration, participation or reciprocity within a continuum of possibilities according to different distributions of power relationships between researchers and participants. At the traditional pole, those methodologies with a researcher's controlled investigation processes would be located and, at the experiential pole, those with a community controlled investigation processes (Heron, 1981). Neil Pateman (1989), after a comparison of three different collaborative projects with teachers, suggests that varied forms of collaborative research depend on the following dimensions: (a) the extent of participation of people involved during different stages of the collaborative project; (b) the degree of autonomy achieved by participant teachers in the project; (c) the extent that participants take researched problems as their own; and (d) the symmetry in researcher–teacher relationships during different phases of collaborative project development. If these dimensions are not identified by researchers, the use of the terms "collaborative research" and "action research" become misleading. This is why Tinning (1992) suggests that epistemological assumptions of particular physical education collaborative projects or action researches should be specified. Then it would be possible to know whether onto-epistemological issues and purposes according to a critical social science guide a particular research.

Another important methodological issue of critical inquiry perspectives is related to the analytical process with the collected data. For some authors, this issue is a distinctive feature of this research approach compared with other forms of qualitative research (Caspecken and Apple, 1992). *Ideological critique* (Carr and Kemmis, 1988), *relational analysis* (Apple, 1986; Kirk, 1999) and *intertextual* and *intercontextual* modes of analysis (Goodson, 1995) are various strategies used within critical perspectives. All of them try to situate educational phenomena within a wider social context to present a holistic view more sensitive to complex relationships between social structure and human agency. They interact, during the data-gathering process, with critical concepts that guide the whole inquiry. These strategies provide sophisticated understandings of physical education and sport practices that inform innovations for social and professional transformation.

An issue of truth or validity is another key methodological aspect that requires reconceptualization within socially critical research. Some critical researchers use the term "validity" but others prefer the word "trustworthiness" as a more appropriate term since the former one maintains its connection to positivist definitions of internal and external validity. Nevertheless, the basic question remains the same, "What criteria can critical researchers use to assess trustworthiness of data and to guard against personal biases in this form of inquiry?"

Patti Lather (1991) has offered four criteria that may be employed to address validity in emancipatory or praxis-oriented research: (a) triangulation that allows to contemplate reality from different sources, methods, and theoretical frames; (b) construct validity or systematized reflexivity that gives some indication of how an a priori theory has been changed by the logic of the data; (c) face validity or member checks during the process of data analysis; and (d) catalytic validity that refers to the degree research process reorients, focuses, and energizes participants to alter their consciousness toward knowing reality and better transform it.

The three first notions offered are similar to the ones used within the interpretive paradigm, but the catalytic validity is specific to sociocritical research. This notion is similar to criteria developed by participatory action research authors when they refer to efficacy of inquiry in changing social practices (McTaggart, 1997; Zamosc, 1992). In this sense, efficacy should occur at the ideological representations level and the political level, as Zamosc (1992) suggests in the context of a participatory action research with fique peasants in Colombia. At the former level, efficacy occurs when actors perceive and understand factors operating in their own reality in such a way that new attitudes or values emerge. At the second level, efficacy is expected to produce changes in actors' real situation for reaching their collective goals. Nevertheless, Zamosc later says that difficulties arise in knowing to what degree ideological and political changes are due to the research or to other influencing factors. As technical control is not possible in the naturalistic contexts of participatory action research, he considers validity will ultimately depend upon trust in the researchers' integrity and their self-critique and reflexivity.

Research trends in socially critical physical education

My intention in this section is to trace the main research trends and developments during the last two decades. While Kirk's (1997a) work has served as an important guide in this section, modifications and additions have been collated in the following themes: (a) social construction of physical education and PETE; (b) teacher's socialization; and (c) policy and practice in physical education.

Social construction of physical education and PETE

Physical education and PETE are historical products that are shaped by ever-changing social, political, economical, and cultural, as well as educational, forces. At any point in time they are the legacy of struggles and contestation among rival groups. As far as socially critical inquiry is concerned, its researchers have paid special attention to meanings, values, beliefs, interactions, and practices, because of their potential to reproduce or challenge existing power relationships in the profession. Therefore, socio-historical analyses and ideologies and social relations arise as important areas of study.

Socio-historical analyses

Studies within this sociocritical research trend emphasize a social history of the school subject in different countries. This kind of research locates physical education practices and language within a sociocultural net of relationships that is likely to connect different levels of the profession (schools, PETE, community, and outdoor activities) with social categories such as the body and gender.

Several historical works, developed in France, have addressed the relationships between physical education and social conceptions of work, as well as, regimes of truth and the language structure of physical education classes. It has also delineated the discourses on the body in physical education through the analysis of different written texts, from mid-nineteenth to mid-twentieth century, with the steam engine emerging as the main scientific metaphor for the human body (Gleyse et al., 2002).

One of the few Spanish socio-historical works analyses how the medical knowledge, dominant in physical education nowadays, developed a powerful socio-moral discourse in the nineteenth century to regulate the bodies and control society (Barbero, 1993). Not only does it suggest issues of power relationships among different kinds of physical education disciplinary knowledge, but also professional dependence on medicine. In a similar vein, feminist historical research shows how the male medical discourse of this century has affected Anglo-American middle class women's body and exercise prescription and, in doing so, this discourse has worked as an instrument of social control (Vertinsky, 1990). Male medical discourse has been a result of the interaction among scientific knowledge, medical practices and social perception, in such a way that reflects the "popular beliefs about the nature of women, their biological purpose and their social role" (p. 1). Despite some women's struggles to enter the medical profession and their fighting against the orthodoxy, medical definitions of women's health and exercise regulation operate as a form of consciousness to protect the female reproductive systems. Its influence has contemporary echoes when the risk of reproductive impairment appears, very often, among the health hazards of high-performance women, but never among the hazards for men. As Vertinsky suggests, medical protection of women

can perpetuate old prejudices denying them control over their own bodies and lives.

Jennifer Hargreaves (1994) also provides a social history of female sport and physical education development in the United Kingdom from the late 1800s to the Second World War. She illustrates how the improvements in sport and physical education for women, embedded in the contested atmosphere of social conservatives and medical authorities, were reflected in two different kinds of physical education curriculum for girls: (a) the gymnastics and dance-centred curricula of the elite day schools; and (b) the games-centred one of the public boarding schools. Nevertheless, by the time the physical education profession seemed to be established, Hargreaves shows how Swedish gymnastics were the dominant activities provided for the girls with a science-for-health professional legitimacy. As the author points out, women had to struggle against popular, middle-class definitions of their biologies in order to participate in physical activities and sports.

In Australia, Wright's (1996) investigation shows how, between the 1880s and 1980s, the dominant masculine tradition developed around sport and movement sciences, marginalized other forms of physical activity associated with women such as gymnastics and dance. She contends that this situation forced girls to share the resources and opportunities available to the boys "without questioning the assumptions on which the practices of this tradition are based; or questioning the contribution these practices themselves make to girls' disaffection with physical education" (p. 347).

The work developed by Kirk (1990, 1992b) on physical education curriculum history in post-war Britain exposes the processes of selecting, organizing, and distributing knowledge and how these processes are part of and, at the same time, contribute to the power production in the profession and society. He highlights the ways in which physical education definitions were contested by different gendered gymnastic traditions, the male games and sport ethic, and the scientific functionalism linked to the health and fitness movement. In a later study, more centred in Australia, Kirk (1998a) considers physical education as a field of corporeal knowledge manifested through physical training, medical inspection and sport discourses. He also suggests that the changes towards looser forms of corporeal power and the increasing relevance of popular physical culture demand a reforming agenda for physical education in postmodern times (Kirk, 1997b). This research is especially important because Kirk uses the historical material to interrogate contemporary curriculum problems, and shows an explicit political endeavour because it has the potential to generate critical and reflective awareness among physical educators.

Ideologies and social relations

Gathering and naming contemporary large-scale social systems of beliefs, structures, and practices in physical education and PETE is the aim of this subsection. Ideologies exert a systematized influence in the social construction of physical education and PETE, and their analyses represent a first step for challenging these systematized influences and for proposing counter-hegemonic pedagogies.

Early Marxist analyses from the 1970s and 1980s consider sport and physical education as state ideological apparatuses, pervaded by the bourgeois values and the technocentric consciousness which reflect and maintain the unequal distribution of power and economic resources of capitalist societies (Brohm, 1984; Brohm et al., 1978; Charles, 1979; Hargreaves, 1977). These mechanistic analyses gave way to a neo-Marxist perspective, adopting a more complex view of the relationships between physical education and the capitalist mode of production. One of the early analysis, developed by Kirk et al. (1986) in Australia, shows how play-like activities have been trivialized and marginalized in favour of work-like activities, and how this situation reproduces the hegemonic social order. Another Australian analysis, this time on PETE, contends that the hegemonic technocracy "closes off rather than opens the mind, depoliticises rather than politicises, and disempowers rather than empowers learners" (McKay, et al., 1990: 57).

In the qualitative study developed by George and Kirk (1988), three main in-subject ideologies, named healthism (the belief that health is an unquestionable self-evident good), individualism (related to the self-effort and discipline of everyday life), and recreationalism (the enjoyment and trivialization of physical activities), appear as substantial barriers to the development of a critical pedagogy in Australian schools. Linda Bain (1990b), in a critical review of the hidden curriculum in physical education, conducts a meta-analysis of the US observational research on physical education and sport, and identifies three main ideological themes namely, meritocracy, technocentric ideology, and the construction of social relations. Meritocracy refers to the unchallenged emphasis on motorelitism. Technocentric ideology relates to the taken-for-granted goals of an education that is judged by its efficiency and effectiveness in producing measurable outcomes. Social relations refer to the patterns of interaction that reproduce or challenge existing power relations. In doing so, she has connected classroom interactions with wider social issues in order to contribute to the transformation of teaching and achieve a more just and equal physical education and society (also see Fernández-Balboa, 1993b; Kirk, 1992a).

Some qualitative studies have addressed the influence gender exerts on students' interactions and subsequent opportunities to learn. US research shows how interactions among girls are cooperative, verbal, and private, while boys' interactions tend to be physical and combative. In this cluster of studies, hardly ever do girls begin interactions with boys, whose actions are especially aggressive, although there are some cases of highly skilled girls' resistance to the pattern of male domination (Griffin, 1983, 1984, 1985a, 1985b). Similar conclusions were obtained a decade later where students who resist the dominant gender patterns exert oppositional behaviours such as objections to teachers' team selections and objections to inequitable game play (Chepyator-Thomson and Ennis, 1997). Other qualitative studies, developed in British and Australian school playgrounds, show that boys monopolize the space to play football and exclude those girls who desire to participate (Renold, 1997; Williams, 1989) and how this activity works to reinforce hegemonic masculinity (Branham, 2003; Burguess et al., 2003; Skelton, 2000).

Other studies concentrate on the role health and the body play as social and cultural mediators in the enactment of ideologies in physical education. For instance, Colquhoun's (1990) qualitative research illustrates how biophysical knowledge has become the basis for an Australian health-based physical education programme. He also shows how self-control and release are present in this curricular initiative via an imagery that supports healthism (body as machine metaphor, adherence to healthy habits, discipline, well-being, fun, and contentment). Following Bernstein's ideas, the instructional discourse of this initiative is embedded in the regulative discourse of healthism through a corporeal and individualistic conception of health in which body shape and fatness play a central role (Kirk and Colquhoun, 1989). Results from a Spanish interview study about social representation of body and health in 11 physical education undergraduates show a negative attitude toward fat persons, a positive or less negative one toward slender people, and a better attitude toward athletic bodies. The authors contend that the ideology of shapism is manifested through a naturalization process of body normality, which is equated to health and is represented by a mesomorphic body in men and by a more slender body in women (Devís-Devís et al., 1994).

Beyond the ideologies mentioned in this section, recent studies are still identifying new ideologies that, especially surrounding gender, sexuality and ethnicity interactions, contribute to foreground patterns of inequality and structural influences within physical education and sport field (see Chapter 5).

Teacher socialization

The lifelong, subjective, and dialectical process of teacher socialization is, from a sociocritical perspective, historically produced and culturally constructed in such a way that dominant meanings and values of the physical education profession are negotiated and contested. Sociocritical research contributions are mainly centred on initial teacher education, entrance to teaching and teacher's work, lives, and careers.

Initial teacher education

PETE programmes looking at the evolution of pre-service teachers' beliefs and values report that initial beliefs held by the students remain largely unchanged throughout the programme (Doolittle et al., 1993). This is supported by the critical case study, developed by Fernández-Balboa (2000) on Australian prospective teachers, which emphasizes the lack of micropolitical consciousness of teaching work among student teachers, facilitating the perpetuation of traditional values and practices. These results are similar to those from a critical ethnography that considers an Australian PETE programme as utilitarian, sexist, scientistic, technocratic, and absent of a socially critical endeavour (Macdonald and Tinning, 1995). In this study, the authors also contend that the isolated and personal incidents of resistance have little impact on social practices, in particular, the positioning of women, both faculty and students. They finally suggest that the professional disempowerment observed could be interrupted through a structural redefinition of the nature of PETE and an alternative critical pedagogy throughout the programme.

Tinning's (1987b) action research project in the early 1980s initiated several Australian critical pedagogy research-based experiences in PETE. They are evaluative, qualitative and action research oriented studies, committed to the improvement of a critical agenda. For instance, the qualitative case study developed by Macdonald and Brooker (1995) identifies tensions and barriers from students and university practices when adopting critical approaches. For some students this pedagogy is perceived as peripheral to their major interests probably because it is an isolated experience within the university programme. Class size in introductory and intermediate levels, large facilities for teaching and learning, lack of collaborative academic work, and the requirement to grade student learning according to relatively traditional statistical distributions make the introduction of alternative teaching and learning procedures difficult. However, the main barriers to critical pedagogies revolve around both the structures of university life, "which reflect rationalist discourses", and the intensification of academic work due to the "specialization and fragmentation of knowledge as it is packaged in the modern university" (Macdonald and Brooker, 1995: 107). The authors suggest that a critical orientation requires

much unlearning to occur among students and academics, as well as political work beyond the pedagogical procedures within the classroom.

In a later action research study, conducted by the same authors in developing socially responsible professionals, they comment upon their disappointment with "the extent that technical knowledge dominated the subject matter" of their student teachers. For them, student resistance in this study raises issues about curriculum negotiation, which is related to the decisions made in wider contexts such as state education and professional organizations. Nevertheless, they also conclude that "For those students who could make sense of the critical subject matter, the outcomes seemed to be worthwhile in that they had grasped fresh perspectives on taken-for-granted practices" (Macdonald and Brooker, 1999: 57).

More recently, Hickey (2001) presents, in a qualitative case study on two student teachers during a year-long physical education unit, a tempered optimism about the potential of critical perspectives within PETE. Among the limitations to the uptake of critical perspectives are the students' instrumental demands, and their feelings of frustration and lack of support when attempting to engage in critical praxis. Hickey also refers to uncertain and non-rational dimensions of the human enterprise such as traditional views of good practices and embodied forms of knowledge that come from students' physical activity backgrounds.

The early case study, conducted by Gore (1990) to evaluate her reflective teaching as a form of critical pedagogy, reveals how student teachers elaborate multiple readings of a programme based on their different subjectivities. She identifies three groups of students labelled as "recalcitrant", "acquiescent", and "committed" who differ according to "*how* they reflect and *on what* they reflected" (p. 119). While the three groups reflected on technical skills of teaching, the recalcitrant group was not beyond it, the acquiescent group was also "concerned about *what* and *how* kids were learning" (p. 123), and the committed "tended to be more concerned about their role as teachers in the broader context of society" (p. 124). She also uses the notion of pedagogy as text to enable a more complex understanding of the research process and the promotion of reflexivity.

In an evaluative case study of a Spanish PETE programme on reflective teaching influenced strongly by Gore's work, Pascual (1993) finds that this programme is not long enough to stimulate critical reflection among her student teachers, and they are not prepared to play a critical friend role within the student teacher-as-researcher context. With these problems in mind, she considers that more reflexivity is required among researchers and suggests the necessity of teacher educators' self-questioning when working with critical programmes. More recently, in an interview study with 17 Spanish PETEs who claim to practice critical pedagogy, Muros and Fernández-Balboa (2005: 257) indicate that many of them "seemed to be guided more by good intentions than by real knowledge of this type of pedagogy", particularly its principles, purposes and methods. Authors finally recommend caution and reflection when engaging in critical pedagogy, and provide some implications for PETE.

The practice of critical pedagogy in a USA PETE course was examined in an action research project by Fernández-Balboa (1998). This author outlines the difficulties of facilitating critical dialogue in classrooms due to several incidents that emerged during teachers' and students' interactions. This evidences problematic issues surrounding questions of authority, language, and voice. Another study developed by Curtner-Smith and Sofo (2004) about the impact of a critically oriented method course on 20 preservice teachers, highlights content, context and duration of the course, teachers' conservative socialization, and marginal status of critical concepts, as crucial issues to explain the influence of the technical focus of the course compared to the virtually null impact of the critical focus.

Teacher's induction, work conditions, and careers

As part of the socially critical agenda, teachers' research focuses especially on different structural constraints, and considers the dialectics between the individual's agency and structural influences. In other words, sociocritical researchers try to relate physical education teachers' identities with the contexts in which these identities are constructed and situated. In doing so, more possibilities emerge to help teachers become agents of social change.

Some studies address beginning teachers' lives and workplace conditions. For instance, in a life history research, Schempp et al. (1993) illustrate the micropolitics of induction process of three English teachers. Data analysis reveals how biographies and previous teaching experiences in school and university are important influences on beginners' thoughts and actions. The occupational demands teachers face are assessed in relation to classroom management and committee assignments. Data also indicate that joining committees and remaining silent are beginners' main strategies to gain power and be accepted in schools. Teachers' willingness and lack of initiative during their induction process manifest difficulties to challenge the *status quo* in schools. An Australian study shows that beginning teachers abandon the profession as a consequence of the disempowering proletarianization process experienced. It is characterized by the following: (a) lack of status; (b) routine and fragmented nature of teachers' work; (c) limited authority and autonomy; (d) personal and professional surveillance; and

(e) unprofessional staffroom culture (Macdonald, 1995). A subsequent study, developed by the same author and carried out with six teachers from the 22 participants of the previous one, reveals that beginners receive a variety of pressures regarding their isolation, professional status, and lifestyle choices. In this study, physical appearances emerge as "key sites of struggle and negotiation of their self and social identities" (Macdonald and Kirk, 1996: 73). Further, surveillance and control are experienced by young female teachers due to the existence of patriarchal values in the community and the workplace.

The marginalization of physical education has attracted the attention of some researchers since it affects the teachers' socialization process. Evans and Williams (1989) developed a questionnaire-based research project with British physical education teachers from 72 comprehensive schools. It reports the problems and difficulties physical educators face from teaching a low-status subject. Female teachers in particular have been victimized in their careers while working within a meritocratic and patriarchal school system. Other studies, developed by Sparkes and colleagues and drawing on life history interview data, contend that the dynamics of the socialization process become increasingly complex when a combination of marginalizing factors appear (Sparkes and Templin, 1992; Sparkes et al., 1990, 1993). Particularly, they refer to the powerful pressures exerted upon those physical educators as the intersection of a number of marginalities: a low-status subject, being a female teacher, and being a lesbian within a patriarchal and heterosexist system. These and other studies centred on the experiences of lesbian and gay students and teachers (see Chapter 5), have important political consequences since they can contribute not only to breaking silences and empowering these people, but also to fostering alternative and anti-oppressive physical education programmes and practices.

Another group of sociocritical investigations has focused on experienced physical educators who have power, as full members of the school culture, to reproduce or transform physical education in schools. In an early biographical interview-based study, complemented with a questionnaire, Sikes (1988) observes a decline in teaching commitment among middle-age British men teachers in favour of more administrative tasks, and a women's subordinate professional role to men in their entire careers. On the contrary, Macdonald's (1999) qualitative interview-based study on Australian experienced teachers reveals great commitment and satisfaction with their job. She reports, as main reasons for satisfaction, teachers' gratification of gaining important support from schools and the autonomy they have to control programme content, teaching tasks, time management and the like, albeit under prescribed centralized policies, programme outcomes, and school routines. Differences in the outcomes of both studies can be understood by taking into account different historical and sociocultural contexts. However, in other occasions these differences can be a question of perspective depending upon which theoretical concept their respective inquiries are based. This issue is emphasized in the case of Dowling's (2002) study on a Norwegian female teacher who tells of a perfect teaching career, a fulfilling vocation with a strong commitment to help young people. However, as the researcher suggests, she is ignoring structural constraints as if the teacher was living in a silky cocoon. As Dowling indicates, it is necessary to attend to the dialectics among teachers' selves and their social structures.

There are also two case studies in which a life history approach is used with two male physical educators close to retirement (Templin et al., 1991, 1994). The first one, situated in Great Britain, refers to a teacher that was impressed upon the importance his students gave to fitness and discipline. He had experienced powerful negative constraints and influences within the workplace and felt victimized by many curricular and school changes during his career. In contrast, the second case study, located in the USA, shows a physical educator with a strong sense of self who enjoyed his career and combined multiple roles. He had no conflictual experiences between teacher/coach roles after accepting a high school physical education teacher position that involved a strong commitment to coaching. These studies highlight teachers' experiences and the interpretation of their voices, a political statement in itself as teachers have been historically silenced. The studies are also especially relevant because teachers' accumulated knowledge can be instructive for improving teachers' working conditions and physical education programmes.

Policy and practice in physical education

Educational policies are general guides or proposals to order educational matters, while educational practices are actual developments that depend on the complex and uncontrollable joint of relationships that are produced inside and outside of an educational system. In between, and embedded within social, economic, and political contexts, conflicts and contradictions emerge to give insight on important aspects of a sociocritical agenda such as power, control, and ideology. I have divided this research trend into two groups of studies, many of them based on ideology critique and relational analysis. The first one is addressed to school reforms and innovations, and another one especially focused on critical pedagogy developments in schools.

School reforms and innovations analyses

Reforms or innovations are, from a sociocritical perspective, strategic arenas open to the interests and struggles of different social groups and institutions. In this sense, Evans and Penney's (1995, 1998) and Penney and Evans' (1999) investigation into the policy making and implementation of the National Curriculum Physical Education for England and Wales, focuses on the struggles to define physical education curriculum and how certain discourses have been privileged and others marginalized in the official documents. The shaping and re-shaping process has resulted in a document that determines which knowledge is worthwhile to be taught in physical education (competitive games, sex and ability differentiation, and Victorian ideals) and its pedagogy and assessment.

Drawing on data from documents and other empirical research sources, Devís-Devís (1997) and Molina and Devís-Devís (2001) have developed a critical analysis of physical education within the 1990s Spanish education reform. Conflicts and tensions among different groups interested in education are driven by a perceived need to achieve a strong competitive position in the international market, and thereby gain a better place in the new European Union. Contradictions and gaps in the official documents ensue and a traditional view of sport together with a functionalist health-related-fitness view become prevalent.

Lisette Burrows and Jan Wright (2001) have critically examined the developmental discourses of the 1987 New Zealand health and physical education syllabus for junior and secondary school years through the lens of poststructuralism and critical psychology. They conclude the document reflected a hierarchy of narrow developmentally defined norms, heavily relying on age and motor performance, that classified and marginalized some groups of children whose developmental patterns fell outside the norms. The authors consider that new curriculum documents offer better alternatives to developmentalism by providing a rationale that facilitates the use of different pedagogies in classroom.

A group of critical analyses on contemporary innovations has been developed on a variety of issues and in different places. For example, the widespread health-based physical education innovations that emerged from the 1980s new health consciousness in Western societies, have been critically studied because of their narrow fitness focus (Colquhoun, 1990; Penney, 1998). In a similar vein, analyses of co-education initiatives show that mixed-sex groupings do not necessarily equate with co-education since equal access rhetoric means, very often, equal access to male versions of physical education, reproducing gender ideologies and conflicts (Evans et al., 1987; Nilges, 1998; Scraton, 1993; Wright and King, 1991). Other pedagogical innovations such as Teaching Games for Understanding (TGfU) and sport education have also been criticized. TGfU is said to fail to challenge the profound structure of classroom communication and the oppression generated by sport

(Evans and Clarke, 1988; Kirk, 1988). Sport education can, from a critical perspective, represent an ideological apparatus for the reproduction of competitive capitalism in the playground (Shehu, 1998).

Other studies have focused on the innovation process itself instead of a particular content or issue. This is the case of the large qualitative research, developed by Sparkes (1988a, 1988b, 1989b, 1990), to understand a teacher-initiated innovation in a British comprehensive school from different theoretical approaches. One of the approaches is centred on a social and micropolitical understanding of change, and the uneven distribution of power between participants. Another is focused on the different subjective meanings participants give to the innovation, depending on the role they play in the innovation context and the costs and rewards it represents to them. The last approach used highlights the process of change, in this case centred on the superficial rhetoric employed to conceal that there is innovation without change.

Critical pedagogy developments in school physical education

Since sociocritical research is committed to emancipatory change, some studies have investigated critical pedagogy initiatives. These evaluative studies have focused on the strengths and weaknesses of these initiatives in order to enhance the educational potentials of physical education. They have also centred on curricular developments which, on a collaborative partnership base, have aimed to students' and teachers' empowerment. For instance, the introduction of critical consciousness within a health-based physical education programme in a Spanish secondary school is examined in a collaborative case study by two teachers and a university lecturer (Peiró-Velert and Devís-Devís, 1993). Since critical consciousness was not an issue to be developed as an official teaching content, some problematic aspects arose during its implementation in the classroom. These included: (a) teacher found a lack of edited critical readings for secondary students, difficulties to elaborate new ones and he considered a dilemma the sequence of their presentation; (b) students' opinions about their group discussion experiences were not registered, when they can be a crucial source of information; (c) difficulties in developing critical issues within a physical activity-based examinable subject; and (d) criticial issues were selected by the teacher, although he found students' social beliefs could be used as more close issues to them to be discussed in the group debates.

Qualitative research developed by Oliver (2001) in the USA on the usage of teenage magazines to engage adolescent girls in critical inquiry/reflection about their bodies, shows possibilities and problems in this type of curriculum work. She considers that this initiative provides spaces for these girls to connect critical issues with their body experiences, though among the problems, are some dominant body narratives from popular culture and some feelings of frustration girls can experience with this type of critique.

Another research example is based on an innovative sport-curriculum, named *Sport for Peace*, developed by Ennis (1999) to enhance the participation levels of adolescents in urban secondary schools of the USA. This initiative enrolls different joint agencies from schools, community, and university groups for curriculum development, resulting in a better sport environment for girls, enjoyment and perceptions of success in girls, cooperation for boys and girls, and boys' positive attitudes towards girls' ability. Inez Rovegno and Dianna Bandhauer's (1998) collaborative study between a teacher and a researcher in the USA examines the effect of a long collaboration on the professional-academic development of both participants. The authors contend how both share privilege since researcher gains time for inquiry and learning from literature and theory exemplification while teacher gains time and freedom to explore in her teaching and a positive administrative school context. They also share empowerment since both transform their respective practices by critiquing and exploring ideas about curriculum and instruction, as well as communicating their story to a wider audience by writing for journal publications.

On the contrary, action research projects, developed by Tinning et al. (1996) for implementing a new national curriculum in Australia, are less promising than their initial critical purposes. Although the projects had positive professional development outcomes for participant teachers, authentic engagement in emancipatory action research was problematic for them. Intensification of teachers' work, professional stress, a lack of outside assistance and action research extra demands on teachers' time were the main barriers identified by the authors. As they contend, "some of the project team actually considered the emancipatory claim for action research to be flawed and certainly not relevant to the concerns of many teachers" (p. 393). In a similar vein, recent research has also submitted under scrutiny the partnership notion and reveals the emergence of problems related to power relationships among participants, teacher ownership, project structure and other institutional influences (Kirk and Macdonald, 2001).

Critiques, challenges and future developments

Different authors, mainly from empiricist, feminist, and poststructuralist or postmodernist[3] theoretical positions, have roundly criticized socially critical research and pedagogy. Empiricists criticize it for being too unfounded, provocative, sweeping, and even offensive. For instance, O'Sullivan et al. (1992) considered that there was no available empirical evidence to support many of the sociocritical advocates' claims, at least at that particular moment. These scholars also suggested that some radical authors use polemical presentation and vitriolic language in the pursuit of their purposes reflecting their perceived high moral ground. As the authors of the critique contend, "some of their assertions about the new discourse have at times made us frustrated, uncomfortable, and even angry" (pp. 267–8).

Feminist and postmodernist critiques focus on theoretical abstraction and onto-epistemological issues on the basis that sociocritical research does not connect with daily practices nor sufficiently consider multiplicity, difference, and particularity. For example, Ellsworth (1989: 297) claims that critical pedagogy (and research) has taken a "highly abstract and utopian line which does not necessarily sustain the daily workings of the education its supporters advocate". She also asks why it does not feel empowering and "which do they [critical advocates] silence and marginalize, and what interests do they appear to serve?" (p. 298). Further critique alleges that socially critical research is gender and race blind, and omits the existence of possible conflicting oppressed groups. That is to say, it is necessary to consider that an individual can experience oppression in one sphere while being oppressive in another depending on the social category considered, such as class, gender, race, age, or place (Weiler, 1995). Jennifer Gore (1992), an early advocate of sociocritical research and pedagogy, claims from a Foucaultian perspective that critical work also functions as a regime of truth or system of power that operates producing and maintaining certain truths. In other words, a researcher that is sharing power to contribute to participants' empowerment is inevitably implicated in power, so his/her efforts to liberate them can, on the contrary, facilitate relations of dominance. Gore and other poststructuralist authors also criticize sociocritical advocates who fail to locate themselves reflexively within their research analyses (Gore, 1996; Lather, 1991).

Socially critical theorists and researchers, such as Kincheloe and McLaren (2000: 294), consider these critiques, especially postmodernist ones, as "a site of both hope and fear". Fear of the limited interest postmodernism manifests in social affairs, and the reduced view of history as a play of language and textuality. This is mainly due to a shortened relationship postmodernism establishes with wider dominating structures of oppression. Conversely, hope is manifested by the possibility of synergism between critical theory and poststructuralism, only if the latter serves as a transformative critique and a stimulus for political action. When this occurs, a postmodernization of the socially critical paradigm

and perspective is being produced in such ways that affect its main assumptions and represent important challenges for the future. In this sense, many concepts are introduced to attend increasing social complexity, such as difference, particularity, language, subjectivity, and power, together with social categories as class, gender, race, age, or place (see Freire, 1990; Quantz, 1992). Even traditional critical concepts are affected. For example, ideology not only refers to social practices but also language and discourses in the construction of collective symbolisms as some authors have advanced in physical education and PETE (e.g. Kirk, 1992a; Tinning, 1991; Whitson and Mcintosh, 1990).

For the challenges mentioned above to be afforded, research humility and reflexivity are demanded. Research humility, suggested by Kincheloe and McLaren (2000), refers to the modesty the sociocritical researchers should display during the whole inquiry process, from its epistemological foundations to its final product. It means, for instance, to accept that emancipation is a never-ending process, that socially critical research has its own fallibility, and it is historically and locally developed since what is emancipatory in one situation can be oppressive in another. It also affects the way critical researchers analyze and interpret empirical data, since they should recognize their dependence on the theoretical frames chosen and their individual ideological assumptions and biographies. Finally, it also means to assume that there is not a dominant explanatory system but a range of socially critical perspectives and social interpretations of sociocultural phenomena such as physical education and sport.

Reflexivity, the second notion, is understood as a strategy that entails an awareness of researchers as knowledge producers. Smyth and Shacklock (1998) see it as a disclosure of the researcher's beliefs, values, and interests, and a self-questioning strategy or a deliberate process to look for the tensions and contradictions in the research practice, as well as to be aware of the researchers' own complicity in what they critique.

Along this section I have intended to present the external critiques socially critical research has received, as well as the challenges to be faced in the future. Before this scenario and taking into account several internal attempts to broaden socially critical research agenda (e.g. Fernández-Balboa, 1993a; Kirk, 2001; Rovegno and Kirk, 1995), I have identified the following new topics to extend the current main research trends:

1. *Students' voices and identities.* Though there is some physical education research on students' voices from a liberal perspective, this area still remains underdeveloped within socially critical research. The few existing contributions are dispersed among

several research trends reviewed in this chapter (see also Brooker and Macdonald, 1999). More studies are necessary to know how students contribute to the social construction of physical education and PETE, and their role in the reproduction and transformation of critical forms of pedagogy. Taking their lead from feminist and poststructuralist theory, critical researchers should acknowledge the role subjectivities play in these processes. They also should be aware that students' voices are largely based on the researcher's agenda and new methodological strategies are necessary to provide authenticity and validity of those voices.

2. *Students' learning.* This research area is even more neglected than the previous one. The critical agenda needs a coherent theory of learning in physical education and PETE since the ability to think and act critically requires the development of a theory of learning applicable to both the learning of student teachers and school students (Kirk, 2001). Literature suggests that situated cognition and situated learning may provide theoretical advances for sociocritical empirical research to foster pedagogies that facilitate creative thinking (Kirk and Macdonald, 1998; Rovegno, 1995; Rovegno and Kirk, 1995). From these theoretical positions, learning is assumed to be multidimensional and that students are active learners who learn different things at the same time. Recent studies are using these approaches in school physical education, more specifically in the context of TGfU and sport education units (e.g. Kirk and MacPhail, 2002; Brunton, 2003).

3. *Identity interfaces.* Most of the literature dealing with the social construction of physical education is centred in one socially mediated category of analysis, such as class, gender, or race. There is consequently a necessity to acknowledge and investigate the social complexity associated with the interface that race, culture, social class, location, gender, age, religion, ability, and sexuality have in students' and teachers' subjectivities and the oppression and inequities which are concealed in-between such dynamic interactions. This is the case of current sociocritical research that, for instance, studies physical education's intergenerational links in the reproduction of masculinity and femininity (Brown and Evans, 2004) or the impact that location, gender, and culture play in the students' access to and engagement opportunities in physical activity (Wright et al., 2003).

4. *Social construction of the bodies.* As a part of human selves, the body is everywhere, in-between any social interaction and identity. There is probably no better place to illustrate the self than in body changes. Nevertheless, social scientists in general and physical education and sport researchers in particular have neglected it. Until recently, sociocritical researchers have not paid attention to the role school sport and physical education play in the process of socially constructing and constituting the body, embodied identities and their relationships with health, since it can either enable or constrain bodies. The book *Body Knowledge and Control*, edited by Evans et al. (2004), is an example of this new research interest, influenced by different neo-Marxist, NSE, feminist, and poststructuralist theoretical approaches.

5. *Social setting interfaces.* Knowledge in the physical education and sport field is constructed in many different sites like schools, playgrounds, universities, media, and so on, and socially critical studies are mainly located in one or another of these places. Therefore, to understand how physical education and sport discourses are constructed, transmitted, and transformed within the complex and related settings mentioned before, inquiries need to be addressed towards the interfaces among these settings. Of special interest are the dialectic relationships and mutual influences between universities and physical education, exercise and sport professions to attend community needs, especially those people underserved by these professions traditionally focused on the talented, skilled, fit, and able-bodied persons (Lawson, 2005). An example of this new trend explores the school–university interface using, in a complementary fashion, the theoretical frameworks of socialization into an occupation, enculturation into communities of practice, and Bernstein's theory on pedagogic discourse (Macdonald et al., 1999).

6. *Popular culture and physical education.* Another special social interface of recent interest is the school physical education–popular culture relationship because cultural materials that make sense of physical education (sport, exercise, play) are located outside the school. To avoid school programme's isolation from the society in which they are embedded it is necessary to understand the effects and influences of popular culture on school students and their views of physical education (Fernández-Balboa, 1997b). Therefore, dialectic communication between school physical education and physical culture is needed to reach social legitimacy and strengthen ways of social transformation beyond the school walls (Kirk, 1998b; Macdonald, 2003). Some advanced research stresses these relationships. For instance, Kunz's (1991) case study analysed tensions, complementarities, and functions between students' physical education practices and their movement culture in two Brazilian schools, and proposed a curriculum from this empirical data. Another research project, developed by Tinning and Fitzclarence (1992) in Australia, studied the relationships between physical education, the media, and the lives of Victorian students to engage them as critical consumers of physical activity outside the school system. Current research is based on the communities of practice framework and the connective specialism concept to understand and develop social strategies and

programmes to encourage physical education–popular culture connections (Kirk and Macdonald, 1998; Penney et al., 2002).

7. *Ethic of care and responsibility.* New areas of research, focused on emotion and caring of humans and environment, have been open to scrutiny because an ethic of care and responsibility has been proposed as the moral basis for sociocritical work, in addition to the traditional ethic of justice and emancipation. A recent qualitative research project has studied the role emotional understanding plays in teaching physical education and its influence on content, pedagogy and curriculum (McCaughtry, 2004). An emotional dimension also arises in a Spanish biographical study as a consequence of a student's identity crisis that emerged within PETE critical pedagogy practices (Devís-Devís and Sparkes, 1999). Caring has additionally been the central concept of certain physical educators and researchers in their work with disengaged adolescent girls to challenge the *status quo* and build social change and empowerment (e.g. Ennis, 1999; Ennis et al., 1997). This work is related to Hellison's social responsibility model (see Chapter 34), developed for working with at-risk youngsters, whose effectiveness has been empirically supported in the USA and elsewhere in different areas to promote personal and social values (DeBusk and Hellison, 1989; Escartí et al., 2005; Hellison and Walsh, 2002; Wright et al., 2004). Some critical research on pedagogies of responsibility has recently been explored about the impact human actions (i.e. sport, exercise, recreation activities) produce on the environment (Lake et al., 2001). Others have used narrative strategies to challenge hegemonic masculinity and heterosexism in physical education and PETE, and create links between graduate students' sport experiences and critical theoretical positions from the course readings (Hickey and Fitzclarence, 1999; Liberti et al., 2004; Sparkes, 1997, 2002).

These seven interrelated topics form, in my view, the new signposts for future socially critical research developments that I envision can contribute to a more just, democratic, equitable, safe, and responsible society. In a globalized world with its cultural, economic, and ecological problems, sociocritical research and its political action are not only intellectually exciting and challenging, but necessary. I hope this chapter stimulates readers to become active participants in order to reach the very potentialities these research perspectives anticipate.

Notes

1 I am aware of the limitations of this chapter in representing literature from a wide range of languages. Although it mainly draws upon work in the English language, I have observed an increasing number of sociocritical publications from non-English speaking countries since the 1990s. During the elaboration of this chapter, I have also had the opportunity to access some sociocritical inquiry from Romance languages. For instance, I have consulted some Brazilian contributions, such as a comparative case study on physical education and community physical culture (Kunz, 1991), a critical ethnography that reconstructs the professional culture of the physical education teachers in a city (Molina-Neto, 1996), and an action research for the professional development of an in-service teachers' group (Bracht et al., 2002). Among other Spanish works, beyond the few examples reviewed in this chapter, there is: early action research (Fraile, 1990) and collaborative research on teacher development (Devís-Devís, 1996); a focus group investigation on student teachers' beliefs (Martínez, 1994); a case study on reflective teaching in PETE (Pascual, 1996); a physical education reform analysis (Hernández, 1996); and a hidden physical education curriculum analysis (Barbero, 1996). These contributions have created a milieu for future sociocritical research developments in these countries.

2 I cannot do justice here to the diversity of conceptual contributions the different social theories have made to the study of education and physical education. I only mention some basic concepts of the main socially critical theories that I consider necessary to better understand the physical education literature.

3 Postmodernism is the name used by authors working in North America and poststructuralism by those working in Europe. Although some people present differences between them, I will use both terms interchangeably as some others have previously done in education and physical education (Lather, 1991; Macdonald et al., 2002).

Acknowledgements

I would like to thank Carmen Peiró-Velert and Andrew Sparkes for early suggestions and the English translation of several parts of this chapter, as well as to Vicente Molina-Neto for his assistance and accessibility to the Brazilian literature. I would also like to thank the editors for giving me the opportunity to participate in the project of this handbook and for their helpful comments on an earlier draft of this chapter.

References

Apple, M.W. (1986). *Ideología y currículo.* Tr. R. Lassaletta. Madrid: Akal.

Bain, L.L. (1989). 'Interpretive and critical research in sport and physical education', *Research Quarterly for Exercise and Sport,* **60**, 21–24.

Bain, L.L. (1990a). Physical education teacher education. In W.R. Houston (Ed.), *Handbook of research on teacher education* (pp. 758–781) New York: Macmillan.

Bain, L.L. (1990b). A critical analysis of the hidden curriculum in physical education. In D. Kirk and R. Tinning (Eds.), *Physical education, curriculum and culture: critical issues in the contemporary crisis* (pp. 23–42). London: The Falmer Press.

Barbero, J.I. (1993). Las redes de la cultura física. Aproximación genealógica al saber médico en educación física. In J.I. Barbero (Ed.), *Investigación alternativa en educación física* (II Encuentro Unisport sobre sociología deportiva) (pp. 7–30). Málaga Spain: Unisport.

Barbero, J.I. (1996). Cultura profesional y curriculum (oculto) en educación física. Reflexiones sobre las (im)posibilidades de cambio. *Revista de Educación*, 311, 13–45.

Beamish, R. (1982). 'A critical examination of the epistemological limitations of the positivist approach to comparative sport studies'. In J.C. Pooley and C.A. Pooley (Eds.), *Proceedings of the second international seminar on comparative physical education and sport* (pp. 131–162). Halifax UK: Dalhousie University Printing Center.

Bernstein, B. (1989a). *Clases, códigos y control I. Estudios teóricos para una sociología del lenguaje*. Tr. R. Feito. Madrid: Akal.

Bernstein, B. (1989b). *Clases, códigos y control II. Hacia una teoría de las transmisiones educativas*. Tr. R. Feito. Madrid: Akal.

Bernstein, B. (1993). *La estructura del discurso pedagógico. Clases, códigos y control IV*. Tr. P. Manzano. Madrid: Morata.

Bourdieu, P. (1972). Systems of education and systems of thought. In M.F.D. Young (Ed.), *Knowledge and control: New directions in the sociology of education*. (2nd edn. pp. 189–207). London: Collier-Macmillan.

Bourdieu, P. (1988). *La distinción: criterio y bases sociales del gusto*. Tr. Mª del Carmen Ruiz. Madrid: Taurus.

Bracht, V., Pires, R., García, S.P. and Sofiste, A.F.S. (2002). A prática pedagógica em educação física: a mudança a partir da pesquisa-ação. *Revista Brasileira de Ciências do Esporte*, 23(2), 9–29.

Branham, P. (2003). Boys, masculinities and PE. *Sport, Education and Society*, 8(1), 57–71.

Brohm, J.-M. (1984). *Sociología política del deporte*. Tr. D. Álvarez and R. Palacios. México: Fondo de Cultura Económica.

Brohm, J.-M., Laguillaumie, P., Gantheret, F. and Berthaud, G. (1978). *Deporte, cultura y represión*. Tr. A. Szpunberg. Barcelona, Spain: Gustavo Gili.

Brooker, R. and Macdonald, D. (1999). Did *we* hear *you*?: issues of student voice in a curriculum innovation. *Journal of Curriculum Studies*, 31(1), 83–97.

Brown, D. and Evans, J. (2004). Reproducing gender? Intergenerational links and the male PE teacher as a cultural conduit in teaching physical education. *Journal of Teaching in Physical Education*, 23, 48–70.

Brunton, J.A. (2003). Changing hierarchies of power in physical education using sport education. *European Physical Education Review*, 9(3): 267–284.

Burguess, I., Edwards, A. and Skinner, J. (2003). Football culture in an Australian school setting: the construction of masculine identity. *Sport, Education and Society*, 8(2), 199–212.

Burrows, L. and Wright, J.E. (2001). Developing children in New Zealand school physical education. *Sport, Education and Society*, 6(2), 165–182.

Carr, W. and Kemmis, S. (1988). *Teoría crítica de la enseñanza. La investigación-acción en la formación del profesorado*. Tr. J.A. Bravo. Barcelona, Spain: Martínez Roca.

Carspecken, P.F. and Apple, M. (1992). Critical qualitative research: theory, methodology, and practice. In M. D. LeCompte, W. L. Millroy and J. Preissle (Eds.), *The Handbook of qualitative research in education* (pp. 507–553). San Diego, CA: Academic Press.

Charles, J.M. (1979). Technocentric ideology in physical education. *Quest*, 31(2): 277–284.

Chepyator-Thomson, J.R. and Ennis, C.D. (1997). Reproduction and resistance to the culture of femininity and masculinity in secondary school physical education. *Research Quarterly for Exercise and Sport*, 68(1), 89–99.

Clarke, G. and Humberstone, B. (1997) (Eds.), *Researching women and sport*. London: Macmillan.

Colquhoun, D. (1990). Images of healthism in health-based physical education. In D. Kirk and R. Tinning (Eds.), *Physical education, curriculum and culture* (pp. 225–251). London: The Falmer Press.

Crum, B. (1986). Concerning the quality of the development of knowledge in Sport Pedagogy. *Journal of Teaching in Physical Education*, 5, 211–220.

Curtner-Smith, M. (2002). Methodological issues in research. In A. Laker (Ed.), *The sociology of sport and physical education. An introductory reader* (pp. 36–57). London: Routledge/Falmer.

Curtner-Smith, M. and Sofo, S. (2004). Influence of a critically oriented methods course and early field experiences on preservice teachers' conceptions of teaching. *Sport, Education and Society*, 9(1): 115–142.

DeBusk, M. and Hellison, D. (1989). Implementing a physical education self-responsibility model for delinquency-prone youth. *Journal of Teaching in Physical Education*, 8, 104–112.

Devís-Devís, J. (1996). *Educación física, deporte y currículum*. Madrid: Visor.

Devís-Devís, J. (1997). Policy, practice, and reconversion in Spanish educational reform: teaching and teacher education in physical education. *The Curriculum Journal*, 8(2), 213–230.

Devís-Devís, J. and Sparkes, A.C. (1999). Burning the book: a biographical study of a pedagogically inspired identity crisis in physical education. *European Physical Education Review*, 5, 135–152.

Devís-Devís, J., Perdiguero, E., Silvestre, A. and Peiró-Velert, C. (1994). La representación social del cuerpo en un grupo de estudiantes de educación física. In A. Clemente, G. Musitu and M. Gutiérrez (Eds.), *Intervención educativa y desarrollo humano* (pp. 147–155). Valencia: Set i Set ediciones.

Dewar, A.M. (1985). Curriculum development and teachers' work: The case of the Basic Stuff Series in physical education. In M.M. Carnes (Ed.), *Proceedings of the fourth conference on curriculum theory in physical education* (pp. 158–167). Athens: University of Georgia.

Dewar, A.M. (1987). The social construction of gender in physical education. *Women's Studies International Forum*, **10**, 453–465.

Doolittle, S.A., Dodds, P. and Placek, J.H. (1993). Persistence of beliefs about teaching during formal training of preservice teachers. *Journal of Teaching in Physical Eduation*, **12**(4), 355–365.

Dowling, F. (2002). Sharing stories about the dialectics of self and structure in teacher socialization: revisiting a Norwegian physical educator's life. *European Physical Education Review*, **7**(1), 44–60.

Ellsworth, E. (1989). Why doesn't this feel empowering? Working through the repressive myths of critical pedagogy. *Harvard Educational Review*, **59**(3), 297–324.

Ennis, C.D. (1999). Creating a culturally relevant curriculum for disengaged girls. *Sport, Education and Society*, **4**(1), 31–50.

Ennis, C.D., Cothran, D.J., Davidson, K.S., Loftus, S.J., Owens, L., Swanson, L. and Hopsicker, P. (1997). Implementing curriculum within a context of fear and disengagement. *Journal of Teaching in Physical Education*, **17**, 52–71.

Escartí, A., Pascual, C. and Gutiérrez, M. (2005). *Responsabilidad personal y social a través de la educación física y el deporte*. Barcelona: Graó.

Evans, J. (1986) (Ed.), *Physical education, sport and schooling. Studies in the sociology of physical education*. London: The Falmer Press.

Evans, J. (1988) (Ed.), *Teachers, teaching and control in physical education*. London: The Falmer Press.

Evans, J. (1993) (Ed.), *Equality, education and physical education*. London: The Falmer Press.

Evans, J. and Clarke, G. (1988). Changing the face of physical education. In J. Evans (Ed.), *Teachers, teaching and control in physical education* (pp. 125–143). London: The Falmer Press.

Evans, J. and Penney, D. (1995). The politics of pedagogy: making a National Curriculum Physical Education. *Journal of Education Policy*, **10**(1), 27–44.

Evans, J. and Penney, D. (1998). Policy, process and power. In K. Green and K. Hardman (Eds.), *Physical education. A Reader* (PP. 71–83). Oxford: Meyer and Meyer Sport.

Evans, J. and Williams, T. (1989). Moving up and getting out: the classed and gendered career oportunities in physical education. In T. J. Templin and P. G. Schempp (Eds.), *Socialization into physical education. learning to teach* (pp. 235–250). Indianápolis IN: Benchmark Press.

Evans, J., Lopez, S., Duncan, M. and Evans, M. (1987). Some thoughts on the political and pedagogical implications of mixed sex grouping in physical education. *British Educational Research Journal*, **13**(1), 59–71.

Evans, J., Davies, B. and Wright, J. (2004) (Eds.) *Body control and knowledge. Studies in the sociology of physical education and health*. London: Routledge.

Fals-Borda, O. (1992). La ciencia y el pueblo: nuevas reflexiones. In M. C. Salazar (Ed.), *La investigación acción participativa. Inicios y desarrollos* (pp. 65–84). Madrid: Popular-OEI-Quinto Centenario.

Fernández-Balboa, J.M. (1993a). Aspecto crítico y cívico del rol de los/las profesionales de la educación física y el deporte: conexiones con la política, la economía y el medio ambiente. *Apunts. Educació Física*, **34**, 74–82.

Fernández-Balboa, J-M. (1993b). Sociocultural characteristics of the hidden curriculum in physical education. *Quest*, **45**, 230–254.

Fernández-Balboa, J-M. (1997a) (Ed.), *Critical postmodernism in human movement, physical education and sport*. Albany, NY: SUNY.

Fernández-Balboa, J-M. (1997b). Physical education teacher preparation in the postmodern era: toward a critical pedagogy. In J-M. Fernández-Balboa, (Ed.), *Critical postmodernism in human movement, physical education and sport* (pp. 121–138). Albany: SUNY.

Fernández-Balboa, J-M. (1998). The practice of critical pedagogy: critical self-reflection as praxis. *Teaching Education*, **9**(2), 47–53.

Fernández-Balboa, J-M. (2000). Prospective physical educators' perspectives on school micropolitics. *Journal of Sport Pedagogy*, **6**(2), 1–33.

Fitzclarence, L. (1987). The physical education curriculum: A cultural perspective. In R. Tinning (Ed.), *Teaching physical education reader* (pp. 66–73). Deakin, Australia: Deakin University Press.

Fraile, A. (1990). La investigación-acción en la educación corporal. In M.G. Pérez (Ed.), *Investigación-acción. Aplicaciones al campo social y educativo* (pp. 259–277). Madrid: Dykinson.

Freire, P. (1973). *Pedagogía del oprimido*. 8th edition. Tr.J. Mellado. México: Siglo XXI.

Freire, P. (1974). *Concientización*. 3rd edn. Tr.M. Agudelo. Bogotá: Asociación de Publicaciones Educativas.

Freire, P. (1987). *L'educació com a pràctica de la llibertat*. Tr.A. Roca. Vic: Eumo-Diputació de Barcelona.

Freire, P. (1990). *La naturaleza política de la educación: cultura, poder y liberación*. Tr.S. Horvath. Barcelona: Paidós.

Gage, N. (1989). The paradigm wars and their aftermath. A 'historical' sketch of research on teaching since 1989. *Educational Researcher*, **18**(7), 4–10.

George, L. and Kirk, D. (1988). Limits of change in physical education: ideologies, teachers and the experience of physical activity. In J. Evans (Ed.), *Teachers, teaching and control in physical education* (pp. 145–155). London: The Falmer Press.

Giroux, H.A. (1983). *Theory and resistance in education: A pedagogy for the opposition*. London: Heinemann.

Giroux, H.A. (1990). *Los profesores como intelectuales. Hacia una pedagogía crítica del aprendizaje*. Tr.I. Arias. Barcelona: Paidós-MEC.

Gleyse, J., Pigeassou, C., Marcellini, A., De Léséleuc, E. and Bui-Xuân, G. (2002). Physical education as a subject in France (school curriculum, policies and discourse): the body and the metaphors of the engine- Elements used in the analysis of a power and control system during the

Second Industrial Revolution. *Sport, Education and Society,* 7(1), 5–23.

Goodson, I. (1995). 'The story so far': personal knowledge and the political. In T. Tiller, A. Sparkes, S. Karhus and F. Dowling-Naes (Eds.), *The Qualitative challenge. Reflections on educational research* (pp. 61–79). Landås: Caspar Forlag.

Gore, J. (1990). Pedagogy as text in physical education teacher education: beyond the preferred reading. In D.Kirk and R. Tinning (Eds.), *Physical education, curriculum and culture* (pp. 101–138). London: The Falmer Press.

Gore, J. (1992). What can we do for you! What can "we" do for "you"? Struggling over empowerment in critical and feminist pedagogy. In C. Luke and J. Gore (Eds.), *Feminisms and critical pedagogy* (pp. 54–73). London: Routledge.

Gore, J. (1996). *Controversias entre las pedagogías.* Tr.P. Manzano. Madrid: Morata.

Gorely, T., Holroyd, R. and Kirk, D. (2003). Muscularity, the habitus and the social construction of gender: towards a gender-relevant physical education. *British Journal of Sociology of Education,* 24(4), 429–448.

Griffin, P. S. (1983). Gymnastics is a girl's thing': Student participation and interaction patterns in a middle school gymnastics unit. In T.J. Templin and J.K.Olson (Eds.) *Teaching in physical education* (pp. 71–75). Champaign, IL: Human Kinetics.

Griffin, P.S. (1984). Girls' participation patterns in a middle school team sports unit. *Journal of Teaching in Physical Education,* 4, 30–38.

Griffin, P.S. (1985a). Boys' participation styles in a middle school physical education team sports unit. *Journal of Teaching in Physical Education,* 4, 100–110.

Griffin, P.S. (1985b). Teachers' perceptions of and responses to sex equity problems in a middle school physical education program. *Research Quarterly for Exercise and Sport,* 56, 103–110.

Griffin, P. S. (1985c). Teaching in an urban, multiracial physical education program: the power of context. *Quest,* 37, 154–165.

Guba, E.G. (1990). *The Paradigm Dialog.* London: Sage.

Guba, E.G. and Lincoln, Y. (1989). *Fourth generation evaluation.* London: Sage.

Habermas, J. (1982). *Conocimiento e interés.* Tr. M. Jiménez, J.F. Ivars and L. Martín. Madrid: Taurus.

Hargreaves, J. (1977). Sport and physical education: autonomy or domination. *Bulletin of Physical Education,* 13(1), 19–28.

Hargreaves, J. (1994). *Sporting females. critical issues in the history and sociology of women's sports.* London: Routledge.

Harris, J.C. (1987). Social contexts, scholarly inquiry, and physical education. *Quest,* 39, 282–294.

Hellison, D.R. (1978) *Beyond balls and bats: Alienated (and other) youth in the gym.* Washington, DC: AAHPER.

Hellison, D.R. (1985). *Goals and strategies for teaching physical education.* Champaign, IL: Human Kinetics.

Hellison, D. and Walsh, D. (2002). Responsibility-based youth programs evaluation: investigating the investigations. *Quest,* 54, 292–307.

Hernández, J. (1996). La construcción histórica y social de la educación física: el currículo de la LOGSE, una nueva definición de la educación física escolar. *Revista de Educación,* 311, 51–76.

Heron, J. (1981). Philosophical basis for a new paradigm. In P. Reason and J. Rowan (Eds.), *Human inquiry. A sourcebook of new paradigm research* (pp. 19–35). Bath: Pitman Press.

Hickey, C. (2001). 'I feel enlightened now, but … ' The limits to the pedagogic translation of critical social discourses in physical education. *Journal of Teaching in Physical Education,* 20, 227–246.

Hickey, C. and Fitzclarence, L. (1999). Educating boys in sport and physical education: using narrative methods to develop pedagogies of responsibility. *Sport, Education and Society,* 4, 51–62.

Kemmis, S. and Fitzclarence, L. (1988). *El currículum: más allá de la teoría de la reproducción.* Tr. P. Mazano. Madrid: Morata.

Kincheloe, J.L. and McLaren, P.L. (2000). Rethinking critical theory and qualitative research. In N. Denzin and Y. Lincoln (Eds.), *Handbook of qualitative research.* (2nd edn. pp. 279–313). Beverly Hills, CA: Sage.

Kirk, D. (1986). A critical pedagogy for teacher education: toward an inquiry-oriented approach. *Journal of Teaching in Physical Education,* 5, 230–246.

Kirk, D. (1988). *Physical education and curriculum study. A critical introduction.* London: Croom Helm.

Kirk, D. (1989). The orthodoxy in RT-PE and the research/practice gap: a critique and alternative view. *Journal of Teaching in Physical Education,* 8, 123–130.

Kirk, D. (1990). Defining the subject: gymnastics and gender in British physical education. In D. Kirk and R. Tinning (Eds.), *Physical education, curriculum and culture* (pp. 43–66). London: The Falmer Press.

Kirk, D. (1992a). Physical education, discourse, and ideology: bringing the hidden curriculum into view. *Quest,* 44, 35–56.

Kirk, D. (1992b). *Defining physical education. The social construction of a school subject in postwar britain.* London: The Falmer Press.

Kirk, D. (1997a). Sociocultural research in physical and health education: recent trends and future developments. In J. Wright (Ed.), *Researching in physical and health education* (pp. 5–21). Wollongong: University of Wollongong.

Kirk, D. (1997b). Schooling bodies in new times: the reform of school physical education in high modernity. In J-M. Fernández-Balboa (Ed.), *Critical postmodernism in human movement, physical education and sport* (pp. 39–63). Albany, NY: SUNY.

Kirk, D. (1998a). *Schooling bodies. School practice and public discourse, 1880–1950.* London: Leicester University Press.

Kirk, D. (1998b). Educational reform, physical culture and the crisis of legitimation in physical education. *Discourse: Studies in the Cultural Politics of Education,* 19(1): 101–12.

Kirk, D. (1999). Physical culture, physical education and relational analysis. *Sport, Education and Society,* 4(1): 63–74.

Kirk, D. (2001). Fundamentos para una pedagogía crítica en la formación del profesorado de educación física. In J. Devís-Devís (Ed.), *La educación física, el deporte y la salud en el siglo XXI* (pp. 101–209). Alcoi: Marfil.

Kirk, D. (2002). The social construction of the body in physical education and sport. In A. Laker (Ed.), *The sociology of sport and physical education. An introductory reader* (pp. 79–91). London: Routledge Falmer.

Kirk, D. (2003) (Ed.). Special issue: situated learning in physical education: explorations of the sport education model. *European Physical Education Review, 9*(3).

Kirk, D. and Colquhoun, D. (1989). Healthism and physical education. *British Journal of Sociology of Education, 10*(4): 417–434.

Kirk, D. and Macdonald, D. (1998). Situated learning in physical education. *Journal of Teaching in Physical Education, 17*: 376–387.

Kirk, D. and Macdonald, D. (2001). Teacher voice and ownership of curriculum change. *Journal of Curriculum Studies, 33*(5): 551–567.

Kirk, D. and MacPhail, A. (2002). Teaching games for understanding and situated learning: rethinking the Bunker-Thorpe model. *Journal of Teaching in Physical Education, 21*(2): 177–192.

Kirk, D., McKay, J. and George, L.F. (1986). 'All work and no play? Hegemony in the P.E. curriculum. In *Trends and developments in P.E.: Proceedings of the VIII Commonwealth and International Conference on Sport, P.E., Dance, Recreation and Health* (pp.170–177). London: E. and F.N. Spon.

Kirk, D. and Smith, S. (1986). How objective are ROSBA objectives? A critique of objectivism in curriculum design. Curriculum Perspectives, 6(2): 32–36.

Kirk, D. and Tinning, R. (1990) (Ed.), Physical education, curriculum and culture: Critical issues in the contemporary crisis. London: The Falmer Press.

Kuhn, T.S. (1975). *La estructura de las revoluciones científicas.* Tr. A. Contin. Madrid: Fondo de Cultura Económica.

Kunz, E. (1991). *Educaçao física: ensino e mudanças.* Ijuí: Unijuí.

Lake, J.R., Stratton, G., Martin, D. and Money, M. (2001). Physical education and sustainable development: an untrodden path, *Quest, 53*: 471–482.

Lather, P.A. (1991). *Getting smart. Feminist research and pedagogy with/in the postmodern.* New York: Routledge.

Lawson, H.A. (1983a). New directions for research on teacher education and school practice in physical education. *International Journal of Physical Education, 3–4*: 10–15 and 8–14.

Lawson, H.A. (1983b). Paradigms for research on teaching and teachers. In T.J. Templin and J.K. Olson (Eds.), *Teaching in physical education* (pp. 339–358). Champaign, IL: Human Kinetics.

Lawson, H.A. (1984). Problem-setting for physical education and sport. *Quest, 36*: 46–60.

Lawson, H.A. (1985). Knowledge for work in the physical education profession. *Sociology of Sport Journal, 2*: 9–24.

Lawson, H.A. (1990a). Sport Pedagogy research: from information-gathering to useful knowledge. *Journal of Teaching in Physical Education, 10*: 1–20.

Lawson, H.A. (1990b). Beyond positivism: research, practice, and undergraduate professional education. *Quest, 42*: 161–183.

Lawson, H.A. (2005). Empowering people, facilitating community development, and contributing to sustainable development: the social work of sport, exercise, and physical education programs. *Sport, Education and Society, 10*(1): 135–160.

Liberti, R.M., Kunz, M., Swantek, D. and Sullivan, S. (2004). 'Forbidden Narratives': Exploring the use of student narratives of self in a graduate sport sociology course. *Quest, 56*: 190–207.

Macdonald, D. (1995). The role of proletarianization in physical education teacher attrition. *Research Quarterly for Exercise and Sport, 66*(2): 129–141.

Macdonald, D. (1997). 'Researching PETE: an account of explicit representations and covert knowledges. In J. Wright (Ed.), *Researching in physical and health education* (pp. 23–37). Wollongong: University of Wollongong.

Macdonald, D. (1999). The "professional" work of experienced physical education teachers. *Research Quarterly for Exercise and Sport, 70*(1): 41–54.

Macdonald, D. (2003). Curriculum change and the post-modern world: is the school curriculum-reform movement and anachronism? *Journal of Curriculum Studies, 35*(2), 139–149.

Macdonald, D. and Brooker, R. (1995). Professional education: tensions in subject design and implementation. *Education Research and Perspectives, 22*(2): 99–109.

Macdonald, D. and Brooker, R. (1999). Articulating a critical pedagogy in physical education teacher education. *Journal of Sport Pedagogy, 5*(1): 51–64.

Macdonald, D. and Kirk, D. (1996). Private lives, public lives: surveillance, identity and self in the work of beginning physical education teachers. *Sport, Education and Society, 1*(1): 59–75.

Macdonald, D. and Tinning, R. (1995). Physical education teacher education and the trend to proletarianization: a case study. *Journal of Teaching in Physical Education, 15*: 98–118.

Macdonald, D., Kirk, D. and Braiuka, S. (1999). The social construction of the physical activity field at the school/university interface. *European Physical Education Review, 5*(1): 31–51.

Macdonald, D., Kirk, D., Metzler, M., Nilges, L.M., Schempp, P. and Wright, J. (2002). It's all very well, in theory: theoretical perspectives and their applications in contemporary pedagogical research. *Quest, 54*: 133–156.

Martínez, L. (1994). Influencia de las creencias implícitas en la formación inicial de los especialistas en educación física. In S. Romero (coord.) *Didáctica de la educación física: diseños curriculares en primaria* (pp. 225–232). Sevilla, Spain: Wanceulen.

McCaughtry, N. (2004). The emotional dimensions of a teacher's pedagogical content knowledge: influences of content, curriculum, and pedagogy. *Journal of Teaching in Physical Education, 23*: 30–47.

McKay, J., Gore, J. and Kirk, D. (1990). Beyond the limits of technocratic physical education. *Quest, 42*: 52–75.

McLaren, P.L. (1995). Collision with otherness: 'traveling' theory, postcolonial criticism, and the politics of ethnographic practice: The mission of the wounded ethnographer., In P.L. McLaren and J.M. Giarelli (Eds.), *Critical theory and educational research* (pp. 271–300). Albany, NY: SUNY Press.

McLellan, D. (1986). *Ideology*. Milton Keynes: Open University Press.

McTaggart, R. (1997). Reading the collection. In R. McTaggart (Ed.), *Participatory action research* (pp. 1–24). Albany: SUNY.

Molina, J.P. and Devís-Devís, J. (2001). La educación física en la reforma educativa actual: análisis crítico. In B. Vázquez (Ed.), *Bases educativas de la actividad física y el deporte* (pp. 301–331). Madrid: Síntesis.

Molina-Neto, V. (1996). La cultura docente del profesorado de educación física de las escuelas públicas de Porto Alegre. Tesis doctoral inédita (PhD), Universitat de Barcelona, Barcelona.

Morrow, R.A. (1991). Critical theory, Gramsci and cultural studies: from structuralism to poststructuralism. In P. Wexler (Ed.), *Critical theory now* (pp. 27–69). London: The Falmer Press.

Muros, B. and Fernández-Balboa, J-M. (2005). Physical education teacher educator's personal perspectives regarding their practice of critical pedagogy. *Journal of Teaching in Physical Education*, 24(3): 243–264.

Nilges, L.M. (1998). I thought only fairy tales had supernatural power: a radical feminist analysis of Title IX in physical education. *Journal of Teaching in Physical Education*, 17: 172–194.

Oliver, K.L. (2001) Images of the body from popular culture: engaging adolescent girls in critical inquiry. *Sport, Education and Society*. 6(2): 143–164.

O'Sullivan, M., Siedentop, D. and Locke, L. (1992). 'Toward collegiallity: competing viewpoints among teacher educators. *Quest*, 44: 266–280.

Pascual, C. (1993). La evaluación de un programa de educación física para la formación inicial del profesorado: algunos problemas, dilemas y/o contradicciones. In J.I. Barbero (Ed.), *Investigación alternativa en educación física* (pp. 183–202). (II Encuentro Unisport de Sociología del Deporte). Málaga: Unisport.

Pascual, C. (1996). Reflecting on teaching a course in physical education teacher education. Paper presented at the AIESEP International Conference, Lisbon, Portugal.

Pateman, N.A. (1989). On collaboration with teachers. In J. Allen and J. Preissle (Eds.), *Qualitative research in education Teaching and learning qualitative traditions*. Athens: (pp. 127–145). The University of Georgia.

Patton, M.Q. (1978). *Qualitative evaluation methods*. Beverly Hills, CA: Sage.

Peiró-Velert, C. and Devís-Devís, J. (1993). Innovación en educación física y salud: el estudio de un caso en investigación colaborativa. In J.I. Barbero (Ed.), *Investigación alternativa en educación física* (II Encuentro Unisport de Sociología del Deporte). (pp. 249–270). Málaga, spain Unisport.

Penney, D. (1998). Positioning and defining physical education, sport and health in the curriculum. *European Physical Education Review*, 4(2): 117–126.

Penney, D. and Evans, J. (1999). *Politics, policy and practice in phycial education*. London: E & FN Spon.

Penney, D., Clarke, G. and Kinchin, G. (2002). Developing physical education as a 'connective specialism': is sport education the answer?. *Sport, Education and Society*, 7(1): 55–64.

Popkewitz, T.S. (1988). *Paradigma e ideología en investigación educativa*. Tr. A. Ballesteros. Madrid: Mondadori.

Quantz, R.A. (1992). On critical ethnography with some postmodern considerations. In M.D. LeCompte, W.L. Millroy and J. Preissle (Eds.), *The Handbook of qualitative research in education* (pp. 447–505). San Diego, CA: Academic Press.

Renold, E. (1997). 'All they've got on their brains is football'. Sport, masculinity and the gendered practice of the playground relations. *Sport, Education and Society*, 2(1): 5–23.

Rovegno, I. (1995). Theoretical perspectives on knowledge and learning and a student teacher's pedagogical content knowledge of dividing and sequencing subject matter. *Journal of Teaching in Physical Education*, 14, 284–304.

Rovegno, I. and Bandhauer, D. (1998). A study of the collaborative research process: shared privilege and shared empowerment. *Journal of Teaching in Physical Education*, 17: 357–375.

Rovegno, I. and Kirk, D. (1995). 'Articulations and silences in socially critical work on physical education: toward a broader agenda. *Quest*, 47: 447–474.

Schempp, P.G. (1987). 'Research on teaching physical education': Beyond the limits of natural science. *Journal of Teaching in Physical Education*, 6: 111–121.

Schempp, P.G. (1988). Exorcist II: a reply to Siedentop. *Journal of Teaching in Physical Education*, 7: 79–81.

Schempp, P.G., Sparkes, A.C. and Templin, T. (1993). The micropolitics of teacher induction. *American Educational Research Journal*, 30(3): 447–472.

Scraton, S. (1990). *Gender and physical education*. Deakin University, Australia: Geelong.

Scraton, S. (1993). Equality, coeducation and physical education in secondary schooling. In J. Evans (Ed.), *Equality, education and physical education* (pp. 139–153). London: The Falmer Press.

Scraton, S. and Flintoff, A. (1992). Feminist research and physical education. In A. Sparkes (Ed.), *Research in physical education and sport. Exploring alternative visions* (pp. 167–187). London: The Falmer Press.

Shehu, J. (1998). Sport Education: ideology, evidence and implications for physical education in Africa. *Sport, Education and Society*, 3(2): 227–235.

Siedentop, D. (1987). Dialogue or exorcism? A rejoinder to Schempp. *Journal of Teaching in Physical Education*, 6, 373–376.

Sikes, P.J. (1988). Growing old gracefully? Age, identity and physical education. In J. Evans (Ed.), *Teachers, teaching and control in physical education* (pp. 21–40). London: The Falmer Press.

Silverman, S. (1991). Research on teaching in physical education. *Research Quarterly for Exercise and Sport*, 62(4): 352–364.

Skelton, C. (2000). 'A passion for football': dominant masculinities and primary schooling. *Sport, Education and Society, 5*(1): 5–18.

Smith, J.K. (1989). *The Nature of Social and Educational Inquiry*. Norwood, NJ: Ablex.

Smith, J.K. (1993). *After the Demise of Empirism*. Norwood, NJ: Ablex.

Smyth, J. and Shacklock, G. (1998). Behind the 'Cleansing' of socially critical research accounts. In G. Shacklock and J. Smyth (Eds.), *Being reflexive in critical educational and social research* (pp. 1–12). London: The Falmer Press.

Sparkes, A.C. (1988a). The micropolitics of innovation in the physical education curriculum. In J. Evans (Ed.), *Teachers, teaching and control in physical education*. (pp. 157–177). London: The Falmer Press.

Sparkes, A.C. (1988b). Strands of commitment within the process of teacher initiated innovation. *Educational Review, 40*(3): 301–317.

Sparkes, A.C. (1989a). Paradigmatic confusions and the evasion of critical issues in naturalistic research. *Journal of Teaching in Physical Education. 8*(2): 131–151.

Sparkes, A.C. (1989b). Towards an understanding of the personal costs and rewards involved in teacher initiated innovations. *Educational Management and Administration, 17*: 100–208.

Sparkes, A.C. (1990). Power, domination and resistance in the process of teacher-initiated innovation. *Research Papers in Education, 5*(2): 153–178.

Sparkes, A.C. (1991). Toward understanding, dialogue, and polyvocality in the research comunity: extending the boundaries of the paradigms debate. *Journal of Teaching in Physical Education, 10*: 103–133.

Sparkes, A.C. (1992). The paradigms debate: an extended review and a celebration of difference. In A. Sparkes (Ed.), *Research in physical education and sport. exploring alternative visions* (pp. 9–60). London: The Falmer Press.

Sparkes, A.C. (1997). Ethnographic fiction and representing the absent other. *Sport, Education and Society, 2*(1): 25–40.

Sparkes, A.C. (2002). *Telling tales in sport and physical activity*. Champaign, IL: Human Kinetics.

Sparkes, A.C. and Templin, T.J. (1992). Life histories and physical education teachers: exploring the meanings of marginality. In A.C. Sparkes (Ed.), *Research in physical education and sport. Exploring alternative visions* (pp. 118–145). London: The Falmer Press.

Sparkes, A., Templin, T. and Schempp, P. (1990). The problematic nature of a career in a marginal subject: some implications for teacher education programmes. *Journal of Education for Teaching, 16*(1): 3–27.

Sparkes, A., Templin, T. and Schempp, P. (1993). Exploring dimensions of marginality: reflecting on the life histories of physical education teachers. *Journal of Teaching in Physical Education, 12*(4): 386–398.

Stavenhagen, R. (1992). Cómo descolonizar las ciencias sociales. In M.C. Salazar (Ed.), *La investigación acción participativa. Inicios y desarrollos* (pp. 37–64). Madrid: Popular-OEI-Quinto Centenario.

Steinhardt, M.A. (1992). Physical education. In P.W. Jackson (Ed.), *Handbook of research on curriculum*. (pp. 964–1001). New York: Macmillan.

Templin, T., Sparkes, A.C. and Schempp, P. (1991). The professional life cycle of a retired physical education teacher: a tale of a bitter disengagement. *Physical Education Review, 14*(2): 143–156.

Templin, T., Sparkes, A.C., Grant, B. and Schempp, P. (1994). Matching the self and aging gracefully: a life history of a late career teacher/coach. *Journal of Teaching in Physical Education, 13*(3): 274–294.

Tinning, R. (1985). Physical education and the cult of slenderness. A critique. *The ACHPERD National Journal, 107*: 10–13.

Tinning, R. (1987a). *Improving teaching in physical education*. Deakin, Australia: Deakin University Press.

Tinning, R. (1987b). Beyond the development of a utilitarian teaching perspective: an Australian case study of action research in teacher preparation. In G.T. Barrette, R.S. Feingold, C.R. Rees and M. Piéron (Eds.), *Myths, models and methods in sport pedagogy*. (pp. 113–122). Champaign, IL: Human Kinetics.

Tinning, R. (1988). Student teaching and the pedagogy of necessity. *Journal of Teaching in Physical Education, 7*(2): 82–89.

Tinning, R. (1991). Teacher education pedagogy: dominant discourses and the process of problem solving. *Journal of Teaching in Physical Education, 11*(1): 1–20.

Tinning, R. (1992). Action research as epistemology and practice: towards transformative educational practice in physical education. In A. Sparkes (Ed.), *Research in physical education and sport* Exploring Alternative visions. (pp. 188–209). London: The Falmer Press.

Tinning, R. (2002). Toward a "Modest pedagogy": reflections on the problematics of critical pedagogy. *Quest, 54*: 224–240.

Tinning, R. and Fitzclarence, L. (1992). Postmodern youth culture and the crisis in Australian secondary school physical education. *Quest, 44*: 287–303.

Tinning, R., Kirk, D. and Evans, J. (1993). *Learning to teach physical education*. Sydney: Prentice Hall.

Tinning, R., Macdonald, D., Tregenza, K. and Boustead, J. (1996). Action research and the professional development of teachers in the health and physical education field: the Australian NPDP experience. *Journal of Educational Action Research, 4*(3): 389–405.

Vertinsky, P. (1990). *The eternally wounded woman. Women, doctors and exercise in the late Nineteenth Century*. Manchester: Manchester University Press.

Weiler, K. (1995). Freire and a feminist pedagogy of difference. In J. Holland and M.Blair with S. Sheldon (Eds.), *Debates and Issues in Feminist Research and Pedagogy* (pp. 23–44). Clevedon: Multilingual Matters and The Open University.

Whitson, D.J. and Mcintosh, D. (1990). The scientization of physical education: discourses of performance. *Quest, 42*: 40–51.

Williams, A. (1989). Girls and boys come out to play (but mainly boys) – Gender and physical education. In

A. Williams (Ed.), *Issues in physical education for the primary years* (pp. 145–159). London: The Falmer Press.

Wright, J.E. (1996). Mapping the discourses in physical education: articulating a female tradition. *Journal of Curriculum Studies, 28*: 331–351.

Wright, J.E. and King, R.C. (1991). 'I say what I mean,' said Alice: an analysis of gendered discourse in physical education. *Journal of Teaching in Physical Education, 10*: 210–225.

Wright, J.E., Macdonald, D. and Groom, L. (2003). Physical activity and young people: beyond participation. *Sport, Education and Society, 8*(1): 17–33.

Wright, P.M., White, K. and Gaebler-Spira, D. (2004). Exploring the relevance of the personal and social responsibility model in adapted physical activity: a collective case study. *Journal of Teaching in Physical Education, 23*: 71–87.

Young, M.F.D. (1972) (Ed.). *Knowledge and control: New directions in the sociology of education.* 2nd edn. London: Collier-Macmillan.

Zamosc, L. (1992). Campesinos y sociólogos: reflexiones sobre dos experiencias de investigación activa. In M.C. Salazar (Ed.), *La investigación acción participativa. Inicios y desarrollos* (pp. 85–134). Madrid: Popular-OEI-Quinto Centenario.

1.4 Physical education research from postmodern, poststructural and postcolonial perspectives

JAN WRIGHT

Introduction

Physical education research drawing on poststructuralist and postmodernist approaches is relatively new. At this point in time there seems to be a notable absence of research in physical education drawing on postcolonial theory and agendas, although the relevance of such an approach to research in the field is one that will be argued in this chapter. Whether researchers describe their work as postmodern or poststructural tends to be determined by whether they are researching in a North American context or UK, European, Australian and New Zealand context. In many cases, there is no explicit indication as to whether researchers identify their work as drawing on either of these perspectives. And so the decision to include research in this chapter has been based on the theorists researchers draw on, the technical language that they use, and on my judgements as to whether their approach is consistent with the ontological and epistemological parameters of a postmodernist/poststructuralist perspective. In addition, it is likely that there will be considerable overlap in this chapter with research reported in other chapters on "approaches" and disciplinary contributions. Poststructuralist and postmodernist perspectives also inform other types of emancipatory research including feminist research (Macdonald, 1993; Oliver and Lalik, 2004), research from a critical theory perspective and sociological research (Evans et al., 2002, 2003; Gilroy and Clarke, 1997; Penney and Evans, 1999; Penney and Glover, 1998). In addition, very few qualitative methodologies have been untouched by shifts towards an understanding of the constructed and unstable nature of "truth" and subjectivity; an understanding which has usually been drawn from poststructuralist or postmodernist theorists (Denzin, 2000). As Sparkes (1992) argues "the post-structuralist turn has the potential to provide us with insights into our own engagement in the research process because it brings to the fore the relationships between language, meaning and power as they act to influence the interpretation of any text" (p. 274). This makes it difficult at times to draw the line on what to include and what not. However, that being said, research which draws on a poststructuralist and postmodernist framework will have characteristics that are recognizable and one of the main purposes of this chapter is to demonstrate what these are.

Core concepts

The term "post" suggests a temporal relationship with an "other" that came before. However, this fails to capture the complexity of the "post" relationship with those theories and forms of practice that have this prefix. While the "post" form has only been able to come into existence because of a preceding perspective or theory, it has not come to replace that perspective; instead it stands in a critical relation to it. "Post" in this way signifies a disjunction, a disruption, a critical engagement with an existing "set of ideas" or, with postcolonialism, a set of circumstances which have produced a particular set of ideas and social relationships (colonialism). Indeed one of the important tenets of a "post" perspective is the fluidity of boundaries; as Usher and Edwards (1994) suggest, postmodernism "is complex and multiform, resisting reductive and simplistic explanation" (p. 7). The terms postmodernism, poststructuralism, and postcolonialism are thus hard to pin down. As constructs they are used differently by authors and researchers, and this use changes over time as ideas evolve, and are reinterpreted. In addition, the terms postmodernism and poststructuralism are often used interchangeably. According to Scheurich (1997), North American educational and social science researchers have little familiarity with the term poststructuralism, although many draw on what, in the European tradition, are known as "key poststructuralist texts", in particular, the work of

Michel Foucault. The term poststructuralism is more widely used in educational research in the UK, Europe, Australia and New Zealand to describe work which draws on Foucault, Derrida and Lacan, and that takes a particular interest in how "texts" "in both the narrow sense of written, electronic, spoken texts, and in the broader sense, of discourses, practices, institutions, produce particular subjects, subjectivities and social relations". In this sense poststructuralism comes closer to providing a specific methodology, "a way of analysing and asking questions by anyone in *any* field" (Marshall, 1992, cited in Usher and Edwards 1994: 18). However, the same "deconstructive" approach in North American contexts might be described as postmodernist (e.g. Nilges, 2000; Rail, 1998). What seems to be particularly foregrounded in self-described postmodernist research is the explicit challenge to "received" knowledge, and the desire to "transgress boundaries" in the ways of *doing* research, "including the ways in which researchers write reality and people's understanding of it" (Rail, 1998: xii). But then again many poststructuralist researchers in Europe, UK, Australia and New Zealand would describe themselves as taking up the same challenge.

Despite these difficulties in pinning down definitions, there are some understandings about knowledge and the self that characterize all of the "post" perspectives and which provide guidance to the choice of research to be included in the chapter. For example, one would expect such work to critique essentialist notions of identity/self, to be working from a premise that reality is not fixed, and to be based on an assumption that it is important to understand how relations of power work in determining what meanings have precedence in particular contexts. In education and physical education research, postmodernist and poststructuralist research seems generally to have an emancipatory purpose; that is, to make visible the ways in which power and knowledge operate to privilege certain practices and forms of subjectivity and to examine their effects on the lives of individuals and groups. Such a process also has a purpose of opening spaces for alternative ways of "knowing" and "being" that provide new possibilities for practice in physical education and related fields.

Scheurich (1997) suggests that "postmodernism is Western civilization's best attempt to date to critique its own most fundamental assumptions, particularly those assumptions that constitute reality, subjectivity, research, and knowledge" (p. 2). Critiquing well-established practices and theories is not always an easy or popular task. However, a reflexive approach to the assumptions which underpin physical education practice and research seems important if we are to avoid a position which continues to endorse, unquestioningly, deep-seated biases based on the centrality of certain kinds of thinking – for instance, Eurocentric, scientific,

patriarchal views of the world. As Foucault (1997) points out:

> If one is to challenge the domination of particular truths/a particular truth regime then they must do so by playing a certain game of truth, by showing its consequences, by pointing out that there are other reasonable options, by teaching people what they don't know about their own situation, their working conditions and their exploitation. (pp. 295–6)

What poststructuralism, postmodernism, and postcolonialism share is the notion that "truth" is a fiction, that it is complex and constructed in relation to context, and that certain "truths" have more power to affect practice and self-constitution than others. The process of identifying poststructuralist, postmodernist, and postcolonial work is further complicated, however, by the ways in which researchers draw on concepts, technical terms and so on without explicitly situating themselves in relation to these perspectives. In reviewing research which draws on postmodern or poststructural theory and approaches, I will use these terms as the researchers themselves use them or if this is not made explicit, as the research exemplifies specific poststructuralist or postmodernist tasks and/or methodologies. The distinctions between the terms, as they are used by physical education researchers, will not always be pursued. What is important here is the work these perspectives do in assisting researchers to set problems, design and conduct research, and interpret their findings in the context of physical education research. In physical education poststructuralist/postmodernist research, it is the work of Michel Foucault or the work from key researchers in physical education who have drawn directly on Foucault (e.g. Kirk, 1998; Wright, 1995), or indirectly (Tinning, 1990) on some of the key ideas from Foucault which have been most influential. In addition, it is possible to characterize some of the sociological research using Bernstein's more recent conceptualizations of discourse (e.g. Evans and Penney, 1995; Kirk et al., 1997; Penney and Evans, 1999; Penney and Glover, 1998) as poststructuralist research.

By way of clarifying the differences in the research covered in this chapter the main ideas associated with each perspective will be briefly described before turning to examples of research in physical education. A discussion of postcolonialism as a perspective will begin this section, more to point to its potential for research in physical education than as an introduction to existing work.

A postcolonial perspective

Postcolonialism as research perspective has been included in this chapter, not because it is widely used by physical education researchers, indeed a fairly comprehensive search suggests its absence (with the one exception, Hastie et al., (in press), but because of its potential as an important perspective for interrogating discourses and practices where issues of race and ethnicity/cultural diversity/minorities arise. This applies in relation to groups within countries such as the USA, Canada, the UK, Australia and New Zealand, and to those countries which are traditionally recognized as struggling with the effects of colonization. Postcolonial theory, and related areas of research, such as subaltern studies, provide a way of examining the influence of globalization and colonization on what counts in relation to physical education curriculum and pedagogies.

Postcolonialism as a perspective is derived from the influential work in the 1970s of Edward Said. Since the publication of his book *Orientalism* in 1978, which critiqued the Western construction of the Orient, there has been widespread use of the term postcolonialism in the academy. Again, "the 'post' in postcolonial is not to be understood as a temporal register but as a sign and cultural marker of a spatial challenge and contestation with the occupying powers of the West in the ethical, political, and aesthetic forms of marginalisation" (McCarthy et al., 2003: 459). Although postcolonialism began as a study of interactions between European nations and the societies they colonized in the modern period, it has been expanded to encompass dominant and subordinate relations produced through the effects of globalization and the dominance of particular cultures in and between nations. This position is exemplified in the following quote from McCarthy and his colleagues (McCarthy et al., 2003) in their "Afterword" to a collection of papers on postcolonialism and education in the *Harvard Education Review*:

> By postcolonial theory we are referring to the practice(s) of systematic reflection on dominate/subordinate relations produced in colonial and neo-colonial relations and encounters between metropolitan industrial and industrialized countries. These relations are properly but not exhaustively understood as center-periphery because they continue to be asymmetrical in their organization and their character. (p. 459)

Postcolonial studies therefore challenge notions of singular identity and ancestry and essentialist notions of identity and confront discrimination on the basis of race/ethnicity. In relation to education, postcolonial writers and researchers challenge monologic interpretations of culture and the dominant Eurocentric curriculum. In relation to physical education, postcolonial theory can help to take up the same work and to challenge the dominance of practices based on Eurocentric meanings about health and physical activity, and what, arguably, is

"an unremitting whiteness" (Olesen, 2000: 220) in physical education research.

Poststructuralism as methodology: discourse and discourse analysis

While both postmodernist and poststructuralist researchers are concerned with meanings as produced in "text", it does seem that poststructuralism is able to provide more specific analytical tools to interrogate texts, in the form of "discourse analysis" (Wetherell et al., 2001). "Discourse analysis" is a term used to describe the process of identifying regularities of meaning (patterns in language use) as these are "constitutive of discourses and to show how discourses in turn constitute aspects of society and the people within it" (Taylor, 2001: 9). The term "discourse(s)", here, captures the relationship between meaning and power; it is used to refer to systems of beliefs and values which produce particular social practices and social relations. According to Stephen Ball (1990), "(d)iscourses are about what can be said and thought, but also who can speak, when and with what authority" (p. 2). Foucault (1972) describes discourse as "practices that systematically form the objects of which they speak ... Discourses are not about objects; they constitute them and in the practice of doing so conceal their own intervention" (p. 49). It is through discourse that meanings, subjects, and subjectivities are formed. Although in this sense discourse is not equivalent to language, choices in language – for instance, choosing to define health in terms of fitness – point to those discourses being drawn upon by writers and speakers, and to the ways in which they position themselves and others.

Discourse analysis, then, is a process designed to capture regularities of meaning (generally patterns of language use). What a discourse analysis takes as its unit of analysis depends on what forms of meaning making are being explored. In most cases researchers draw on the tools of linguistics (Wright, 1993, 1997, 2000) or critical discourse analysis (Clarke, 1992; Lupton, 1992, 1999), however, Nilges (2001) in a particularly innovative analysis of meaning, has used bodily movements as recorded by Laban notation. Key to most forms of poststructuralist analysis, then, is the notion that all forms of meaning production, including "lived experience", can be treated as texts. Thus, ethnographies, interviews, journals, narratives, even physical movements as they are documented by video or in the form of field notes can be systematically analysed as texts (written, spoken, or visual), as they are constituted in and by specific social and cultural contexts.

Within physical education the term "discourse" has a history which begins with the work of John Evans in the UK in the 1980s. For Evans and those who have followed his lead in interrogating policy and practices in physical education, Bernstein's notion of pedagogic discourse has been the key conceptual tool in this process. "Discourse" as used by Bernstein, incorporates notions of meaning and power in ways similar to the use of discourse by Foucault. However, for those working with Bernstein's notion of "pedagogic discourse" and related concepts such as instructional and regulatory discourse, these are highly theorized and modelled concepts relating specifically to education (increasingly in the broadest possible sense). Increasingly those drawing on Bernstein are using his later work to ask questions about the "body", that is "how *'knowledge of the body'* is produced, transmitted and 'received' and embodied through PEH and sport in schools" (Evans and Davies, 2004b: 4, italics in the original). The kinds of projects such theoretical resources make possible have much in common with research that I would characterize as falling within a poststructuralist approach: they seek to interrogate the ways the social practices associated with schooling shape "consciousness and social relations". What seems to be different about those working within a Bernsteinian framework is that there is a search for specific regularities, an interest in defining codes and in mapping relationships that have some stability. Evans and Davies (2004a) for example ask "how are particular forms of knowledge and discourse encoded and translated into pedagogical practices and with what consequences for identity and consciousness?" (p. 207). They criticize Foucault for failing to address these issues and argue that he does not provide the theoretical resources to do so:

> We share Bernstein's view that Foucault's analysis of power, knowledge and discourse is a mighty attempt to show the new forms of the discursive positioning of subjects. Yet there is no substantive analysis of the complex of agencies, agents, social relations through which power, knowledge and discourse are brought into play as regulatory devices; nor any discussion of modalities of control. It is a discourse without social relations. Furthermore Foucault ignores almost completely any systematic analysis of the common denominator of all discourses, education and the modalities of its transmission. (Bernstein, 1996) (Evans and Davies, 2004b: 207)

Most researchers working with Foucault would argue that such a criticism is missing the point. Foucault provides a more fluid and flexible way of working with the notion of "power", one which is concerned with the exercise of power in all of its guises, through language, action, and events. This is not to say that "power" cannot be exercised by institutional structures and practices (material and discursive), nor does it ignore the effects of power in creating relations of subordination. For Foucault:

> Power is an effect of the operation of social relationships, between groups and between individuals. It is not unitary it has no essence. There are as many forms of power as there are types of relationship. Every group exercises power and is subjected to it. (Sheridan, 1980: 218)

'Post' research in physical education

An historical perspective: "posts" in physical education

Prior to 1990, one would have been hard pressed to find a reference to postmodernism, poststructuralism, or postcolonialism in the English language physical education research literature. A comprehensive search suggests that postcolonial and related perspectives such as subaltern studies are still notable by their absence. This is not all that surprising given the late entry of these perspectives into educational research, despite their having a considerable impact in social sciences and humanities research.

Poststructuralist and postmodernist perspectives are still relatively marginal in mainstream physical education research in the USA, although they have a stronger following in the UK, Canada, Australia and New Zealand. Their marginality is not simply to do with their relative newness in the field but also because like "critical theory" these perspectives, by their very nature, trouble taken-for-granted ways of thinking about and doing physical education, and traditional approaches to research in physical education. They challenge the implicit positivism that has underpinned physical education research reported in the major journals such as the *Journal of Teaching in Physical Education.* Despite a major shift in this journal to a welcoming of qualitative research in the late 1980s, the strong and important relationship in the journal between research and classroom practice appears to allow little room for theories which raise fundamental questions about the relationship between physical education as a social practice and the formation of the self and culture/society.

Before discussing the empirical research in physical education which has been influenced by a poststructuralist/postmodernist perspective, some mention needs to be made of another body of work in physical education which refers in one way or another to postmodernism or poststructuralism but do not report on empirical research. The books and papers which fall into this category are usually informed by a critical pedagogy perspective. Some like the edited collection by Juan-Miguel Fernandez-Balboa (1997) raise questions about the nature of physical education in post- or high modernity. Others question the relevance of traditional forms of physical education for young people whose lives, expectations, and interests are shaped by postmodern times and the influences of globalization (e.g. Tinning and Fitzclarence, 1992), provide commentary on curriculum and curriculum change processes in a postmodern context (e.g. Macdonald, 2003a, 2003b), or critically examine pedagogical practices using poststructuralist concepts of governmentality and performativity (e.g. Kelly, Hickey, and Tinning, 2000; Macdonald and Tinning, 2003).

The first two *research* papers which, arguably, draw explicitly on a poststructuralist or postmodernist methodological perspective are found in two edited collections: the first, *Teachers, Teaching and Control* (Evans, 1988) edited by John Evans from the UK; and the second, *Physical Education, Curriculum and Culture* (Kirk and Tinning, 1990), by David Kirk and Richard Tinning, both in Australia at the time. Evans' book collects together papers that have been written primarily from a sociological perspective about teachers' work and careers in physical education. There is one chapter, however, by Evans and Gill Clarke (1988) which reports on the results of research interrogating physical education as a social practice. This chapter examines how the "new privileging texts" of health-related fitness (HRF) and teaching games for understanding (TGFU) are taken up in classrooms at a case study school. Using Bernstein's understanding of pedagogic discourse the authors examine "not only how children are differently positioned in '*relation to*' the privileging text by virtue of their cultural habitus but also the '*relations within*' the text" (p. 127). They describe through extracts of teacher talk the ways in which teachers control classroom discourses; that is, how "the discourse routinely demonstrates the teacher's authority, knowledge and power" (p. 136). Their conclusion from this analysis is that "substantial curricular and organisational change has left largely unchanged relations between teacher and taught and pupils and knowledge" (p. 137).

The collection of papers in *Physical Education, Curriculum and Culture* is framed by the authors as "critical studies of curriculum" with all of the papers taking up the task of examining how the knowledge in physical education is "selected, organized, appropriated, legitimated and evaluated" (Kirk and Tinning, 1990: 3). In the introduction to their collection, Kirk and Tinning explicitly make reference to Foucault's work as a way of analysing the relationship between the body, movement, and culture. However, it is only Jennifer Gore's chapter (1990), "Pedagogy as text in physical education teacher education", that explicitly draws on Foucault to interrogate her practice as a physical educator and researcher. In this chapter she analyses a scenario drawn from her work as a physical education teacher educator as a "pedagogical text" using theories of "reading" from cultural studies and Foucault's notion of relations of power. The purpose of her analysis is to go beyond the preferred or dominant reading to a reading from a "critical perspective". A critical perspective in this case is one which focuses on "issues of knowledge and issue of power relations" (p. 111). The poststructuralist (Gore describes her position as one aligned with cultural studies) aspects of the paper are recognizable in her secondary analysis of her initial interpretations of the research she conducted on her pedagogical practice. In her research on the lesson, Gore uses methods which both answer questions about the effectiveness of the lesson and the ways in which the students engaged with the lesson. She used interviews with students, students' written work completed for the subject (journal entries, lesson critiques, and photograph comments), and questionnaires to collect demographic data and evaluate the course. From these data she categorized the responses of the students to her pedagogical approach (which emphasized reflective practice and student-centred learning) into three types: recalcitrant, aquiescent, and committed. Reflecting on her processes of categorization and indeed on her own expectations of her practice as an academic as "transformative", she concludes that research approaches to pedagogy which draw only on technical or even transformative perspectives, close down multiple readings, multiple ways of understanding students' responses, and ways of recognizing changing and partial subjectivities. She argues that researching "pedagogy as text" points to "overlooked or marginalized readings" which in turn can point to "inequities and injustices, the acknowledgement and correction of which depend on the audience, on its moral and political commitments" (p. 134). Although not elaborated in this chapter (see Gore, 1998), Gore signals the importance of Foucault's notion of "regimes of truth" to an understanding of the relationship between power knowledge and social practice.

The more detailed work of elaborating this relationship and the ways in which physical education has been shaped by particular social, economic, and political circumstances has been a major part of the influential work of David Kirk. His first book on the social construction of the British curriculum, *Defining Physical Education* (Kirk, 1992), introduced a genealogical approach to the study of physical education which has proved to be the model for those interpreting physical education curriculum from both a historical and contemporary perspective. His second book, *Schooling Bodies* (Kirk, 1998), which provided an analysis of school practice and public discourse in physical education and related fields, extended this analysis to the Australian context (Kirk, 2003, 2004).

Although the research reported thus far challenged the nature of "truth" and interrogated the production of truth in the context of relations of power, no research in physical education to this point explicitly identified itself as drawing on a poststructural or postmodern approach. The first paper to do so was one published by Wright and King in *Journal of Teaching in Physical Education* in 1991, which reported on research analysing teachers' talk for the ways it contributed to the construction of gendered subjectivities. This paper was followed by another by Wright in 1995 which laid out a framework for a poststructuralist approach to research in physical education. This paper reported on the methodology employed in a study which investigated the (re)production of femininity and masculinity in three secondary schools through an analysis of teacher–student interactions in coeducational and single-sex physical education lessons. Using Foucauldian notions of subjectivity and discourse and the analytic tools of systemic functional linguistics, the study involved the analysis of physical education lessons as specific genres or texts jointly constructed by teachers and students. The power of the texts to position students in relation to particular forms of masculinity and femininity was interpreted through an investigation of the likely institutional and cultural discursive resources available to students to take up or challenge such positionings. These resources were identified through an analysis of media sporting texts and interviews with teachers and students.

There have been a few papers since in the *Journal of Teaching in Physical Education*. In 1996, the British-based journal, *Sport Education and Society*, was established to provide a context for the reporting of research which dealt with sport and physical education and "a wide range of associated social, cultural, political and ethical issues in physical activity, sport and health" (*Sport Education and Society* inside cover). This journal has provided a forum for socially informed research and since its establishment the number of research articles in the physical education domain, drawing on poststructuralist and postmodernist perspectives has grown.

A survey of recent research suggests that certain "technical" terms, such as "discourse" derived from postmodernist and poststructuralist theories have come into common usage in research papers that do not explicitly locate themselves as drawing on these perspectives. These have come into use through the influence of writers, such as David Kirk (corporeal discourse), John Evans and Dawn Penney (official and unofficial discourses of physical education) and Richard Tinning (performance and participation discourses). They have also come into use through slippages from earlier work using the term "ideology" (1990) to later work where discourse is now used in a very similar context (Tinning et al., 2001),

and/or from feminist theory where terms such as gender discourses, or (hegemonic) discourses of femininity and masculinity have become common currency. Williams and Woodhouse (1996), for example, report on their investigation of the match between students "feelings" about physical education, as determined by their responses to a survey, and the "official" (and contradictory) discourses of physical education. While "discourse" is used here in the poststructuralist (Foucauldian/Bernstein) sense of meanings constructed in relations of power there is no other indication that the research has been conducted within the parameters of a "post" perspective.

This slippage in the use of what have been "post" technical terms has made choosing what should and should not be included in the survey of physical education literature drawing on "post" perspectives a challenge. In addition, as a perspective that critiques the taken-for-granted and thereby prompt changes in social practice, there is a considerable overlap between physical education research which draws on, or names itself feminist, critical, and/or emancipatory research. Further, there is no research design/paradigm that is particularly unique to "post" work. In general, it is likely to be qualitative, although not always (see, for example, Nilges, 2000), and to be interested in text(s). It is likely to take account of relations of power between participants and the researcher, it often explores different ways of representing information, drawing on narrative inquiry and life history research (which have in turn been informed by postmodernism), and at its best it should be reflexive (Gore, 1998; Scheurich, 1997).

In surveying the work in physical education research which has drawn on a poststructuralist, postmodernist, I will for the most part only refer to that work which explicitly frames the project of the research in poststucturalist terms, that is, is specifically concerned with investigating the nature of knowledge as discursively constructed, the relationship between knowledge/discourse and the constitution of selves and social relations. What this means is that I will primarily (but not only) be reporting on work from researchers located in the UK, Australia and New Zealand, which generally identifies itself as poststructuralist, and draws on the work of Foucault and/or Bernstein.

There are now also a number of papers which describe the process of doing poststructuralist work in physical education research: using a genealogical discourse analysis to interrogate curriculum texts (Burrows, 1997), using a close interrogation of interview texts to investigate the process of subjectification (Wright, 2004); designing a poststructuralist analysis of classroom talk (Wright, 1995) and a comparative analysis of classroom talk (Wright, 2000a,b); and the use of observation and notation to demonstrate how quantitative data can be used to investigate the construction of gendered identities (Nilges, 2000).

Mapping the discourses of physical education: genealogies of physical education

In his early work, Foucault (1979) was interested in mapping or constructing a genealogy of the emergence of particular "technologies of power" in institutional contexts, specifically in relation to the science, medicine and, particularly in *The Birth of the Clinic*, psychiatry. For Foucault (1997), "technologies of power are, 'those technologies which determine the conduct of individuals and submit them to certain ends or domination, an objectivising of the subject'" (p. 225). In undertaking a genealogy, Foucault sought to show the "specificity and materiality" of the interconnections between power and knowledge (Dreyfus and Rabinow, 1986: 203). Power in this sense is understood as not primarily located in structures or in all-powerful state apparatuses, but rather institutions act as specific sites where particular techniques of power are channelled and brought to bear on individuals in systematic ways. In this way a school, through its architecture, its organization, its curriculum and daily practices, becomes a disciplinary site that draws on particular regimes of truth (discourses) to legitimate its existence and to define what it does. Thus, for example, particular pedagogical practices in physical education, such as those associated with assessment, the organization of classes based on ability and the measuring of bodies for weight and fitness work to produce particular kinds of bodies as normal and thereby construct for individuals, particular opportunities for forming an understanding of themselves in relation to others (particular forms of subjectivities) (Burns, 1993).

Foucault uses the term "genealogy" to differentiate between the more traditional "narrative" histories and investigations of historically situated social practices in specific political, social, and economic contexts. Genealogies interrogate operation of power in constructing knowledge; as a form of research a genealogical approach provides "an incisive strategy for getting at and disturbing the seemingly unalterable form of truth" (Harwood and Rasmussen, 2003: 1). Most of the genealogical work in physical education is interested in physical education as a curriculum text and a social practice. Indeed, most of the contemporary critical policy and curriculum analysis in physical education is interested in the conjunction of power, the production of particular "truths" in relation to physical education and the practices they effect. This research examines the ways physical education discourses and practices have come to be as they are,

why and how some forms have come to prominence (in what social, political, and cultural contexts) and others not, and with what consequences for individuals and social groups. In addition, it is interested in interrogating physical education curriculum and policy texts to identify the work of discourses in constituting particular "subjects".

The two major areas of research in this area are those which look historically at physical education (e.g. Burrows, 2000; Burrows and Wright, 2001; Kirk, 1998, 2003, 2004; Kirk and Twigg, 1994; Wright, 1996) and those which examine contemporary shifts in policy and curriculum construction and the consequences of these for physical education practice (Gilroy and Clarke, 1997; Glover, 2001; Lupton, 1999; Macdonald and Kirk, 1998; Penney and Evans, 1999; Penney and Glover, 1998; Penney and Harris, 2004; Thorpe, 2003). The first tends to draw primarily on Foucault and the second, primarily on Bernstein's later work (with some exceptions) where it moves away from a more structuralist approach with its focus on language and social class to "his later poststructuralist attention (to) text, voice and discourse [which] could, in fact, be termed "postmodern" (Tyler, 2004, p. 16). In Australia, research on the ways in which particular discourses (e.g. those associated with "health") have influenced the curriculum have often combined the two (e.g. Evans et al., 2002; Tinning and Glasby, 2002).

The two most influential researchers in this area have been David Kirk and John Evans. Kirk has used Foucault's work on "disciplining the body" and his notion of "biopower" to examine how school-based physical education has been implicated in regulating and normalizing the bodies of students (e.g. Kirk, 1998, 2003, 2004). In *Schooling Bodies*, Kirk draws together a number of papers published in various chapters and articles, to provide a genealogy of physical education in Australia from 1880–1950. Although his method of collecting data is that of historical research, he is more interested in physical education as "a field of corporeal knowledge that provides valuable insights into the social construction of bodies" (p. 2). He collects archival materials, like school magazines, education department memoranda and policy documents, and reports from school inspectors, which are then examined to identify the impact of public discourses, such as those associated with nationalism and eugenics, on how physical education, physical activity, and bodies were understood. He uses his analysis of historical documents to demonstrate the shift in the schooling of bodies, from "the meticulous, detailed and precise" forms of regulation associated with the militarized physical training and school medical inspections of the nineteenth and early twentieth century to one which was "increasingly individualized, internalised and diffused" (p. 3). He argues that the move from drill and exercise to a greater emphasis on games signalled a shift from predominantly external forms of regulation to self-regulation. In his later work (2003, 2004) he explores this shift as signalling, a wider social shift in the ways power operates in society in relation to the body. Drawing on Foucault's concept of "biopower", that is the integration of two forms of power – one that operates at the level of the material body and the other of the social body – he demonstrates how shifts in "biopower" from the "heavy ponderous and meticulous" to "a looser form of power over the body" can be identified in the shifts in physical education from an emphasis on drill and exercise to games (Kirk, 2003, 2004). His main point however in this later work is that a "looser" form of power does not necessarily mean that bodies are free from the exercise of power (nor should they be). Instead games, particularly as practiced in the formal environment of physical education and school sport have their own embedded techniques of power – the regulation of time and space, the objectives of the game and the requisite training of bodies to achieve mastery. He suggests that while they may seem to have offered a liberating and more individualized, experience, there are forms of regulation and "hazards" associated with games as they are currently taught (and coached) that are rarely acknowledged. Kirk (2004) concludes that:

> a necessary component of the process of schooling bodies is both their empowerment and their regulation; empowerment in the sense that practices such as physical education provide opportunities for young people to develop and realise particular movement capacities of their bodies; regulation in the sense that the development of some forms of movement expertise inevitably delimits other movement capacities young people might develop. (p. 131)

Wright's (1996) paper, "Mapping the discourses", builds on Kirk's earlier genealogical work on British and Australian physical education to examine the social construction of the New South Wales (Aust) physical education curriculum from a feminist poststructuralist perspective. Archival material and interviews with those who took part or were subjected to physical education as a social practice prior to the 1980s were collected and analysed to identify how particular cultural and institutional discourses operated to marginalize female physical educators and students and to the forms of practice historically associated with women. In a similar vein, Burrows (2000; Burrows and Wright, 2001) draws on the poststructuralist analyses of development psychology to inform her interrogation of the ways in which developmental discourses and discourses of childhood shaped the New Zealand curriculum and create particular notions of "normality".

In one of the rare reports in English from European researchers in physical education drawing on a poststructuralist perspective, Gleyse and colleagues (Gleyse et al., 2002), analyse the influential texts which have contributed to "the development of physical education in France from the mid nineteenth century to the 1960s" to show the shifts from the conceptualization of the body as "a steam engine and then as a machine" to more generalized notions of "humanized productivity" and how these "were to express and often to influence the reality of the practice put into effect and sometimes even the programs and policies themselves" (pp. 6–7).

Whereas the research doing genealogical work thus far reported has been historical, there is also research which takes a similar approach – that is, interrogates institutionally produced texts but which is primarily concerned with contemporary curriculum and policy. This research examines how particular conjunctions of meaning and power come together to constitute physical education in the context of policy, syllabus and in one case popular media texts, and with what likely effects for practice. Much of this work is influenced by Basil Bernstein's concept of "pedagogic discourse", as well as, or instead of, Foucault's theorizing of the relationship between knowledge and power.

One of the recent focuses of work on the physical education curriculum has been to investigate the influence of health discourse particularly as health becomes incorporated into or joined with contemporary physical education syllabuses as physical education and health education (e.g. Penney and Glover, 1998; Penney and Harris, 2004; Tinning and Glasby, 2002). Drawing on both the work of Bernstein and Stuart Hall, Penney and Harris (2004), for example, examine the representations of the body and health in texts derived from recent physical education policy documents produced by the government in England. They use physical education policy documents from New Zealand to highlight the cultural specificity of each and to demonstrate which discourses are "variously included, privileged and marginalised or excluded" (p. 98). From their analysis of the official curriculum texts they argue that the NCPE uncritically promotes particularly narrow gendered conceptualizations of health, physical activity, and the body. Their analysis of support materials and inspectors' reports suggests that these conceptualizations of physical education are unlikely to be challenged and indeed may be further restricted and constrained by influences on teachers, such as the privileging of sport in the UK, as these texts are "recontextualized" into classroom practice.

Using the theoretical resources from Foucault ("governmentality"), Beck (1992) and Giddens (1991) ("risk society") and the "new public health"

(Lupton, 1995; Petersen and Bunton, 1997; Petersen and Waddell, 1998), Tinning and Glasby (2002) analyse the Queensland Health and Physical Education (HPE) curriculum for the ways in which it constructs particular notions of the body and the healthy person. Their purpose is to "understand why HPE continues to be implicated in the reproduction of values associated with the cult of the body" (p. 109). They demonstrate how, through the privileging of "expert" knowledge about food, exercise and the body, particular forms of pedagogical work are performed by the Qld HPE syllabus and the teachers who organize learning experiences from its expected outcomes. This pedagogical work serves to regulate and govern body practices in ways which continue to reinforce the "cult of the body" and which silence alternative ways of thinking about health and the body.

One of the recurrent themes in physical education commentary is that the profession and/or the subject is in crisis (Glover, 1993; Kirk, 1996; Kirk and Tinning, 1990; Tinning and Fitzclarence, 1992). In a paper entitled 'Crisis discourse in physical education and the laugh of Foucault', Stephen Thorpe (Thorpe, 2003) examines a particular instance of the "crisis discourse" for its "effects" (p. 131). Using as his text the Four Corners Program, "Fools Gold", a 1992 ABC documentary which tapped "into national sentiments surrounding the then approaching Olympic games in Barcelona" (p. 134), he demonstrates how particular "truths" about physical education are mobilized through the articulation of "exercise, fitness, public health and national success in elite sport" with the "four key interrelated discourses of nationalism, militarism, eugenics and capitalism (Kirk, 1998b)" (p. 134). He demonstrates how this articulation allows ways of understanding children's participation in physical activity and their health as being in decline, with school physical education being held largely responsible. This analysis is juxtaposed with an analysis of the crisis discourse as it was manifested in the report of the 1992 Commonwealth Senate Inquiry into sport and physical education and the parliamentary commentary which followed. Thorpe identifies similar "truths" about physical education as being mobilized in these texts. On the basis of his analysis, Thorpe concludes that those within physical education who are concerned to bring about change should be more concerned with "problematizing" (Foucault, 1985) the crisis discourse; that is, asking "*why the word crisis is used*" and "*the consequences of its use*", than investigating "*the nature of the crisis*" (p. 147). He argues that there is no end to the "crisis" and that the role for "critical intellectuals" is one of ongoing critique, "an incessant activism" which is alert to self-evident and commonplace knowledge.

Governmentality: how discourses and subjectivities are called into practice

The work described above has helped to begin the process of mapping the discourses that have shaped and continue to shape physical education and to explain the *potential* of these discourses for constructing particular kinds of subjects. Another body of work has explored how these and other cultural and institutional discourses are implicated in constituting particular subjectivities in and through physical education as a social practice in schools. This research falls under two main categories: that which is interested in how discourses taken up by teachers and students as they talk about physical education and related topics – for example, health, fitness, the body; and that which is interested in how particular subjectivities and social relations are constructed in the context of physical education classes. The first category of research tends to use interviews as a way of identifying what institutional and cultural discourses teachers and/or students draw on to make sense of physical education (e.g. Lupton, 1999; Macdonald and Kirk, 1996, 1999; Olafson, 2002; Wright, 1996); the second usually involves an analysis of texts derived from teacher–pupil interactions in physical education lessons (e.g. Davies, 2001; Delamont, 1998; Gore, 1990; Prain and Hickey, 1995; Ronholt, 2002; Wright, 1997, 2000). In both cases from a poststructuralist perspective the interest lies in how particular "subjectivities" are formed in relation to competing discourses and how power relations and particular discourses are enacted to constitute physical education lessons.

Teachers' and students' subjectivities

Any interrogation of the ways in which teachers take up particular notions of physical education generally requires some discussion of the discursive resources available for making meaning. In some cases, this is limited to material published in other papers. In other cases, the specific nature of the context requires a brief genealogy of the syllabus or related documents to provide context and a comparison between the possible readings of the institutional texts and their interpretations by teachers. This latter project is exemplified by Lupton's (1999) investigation of the ways teachers negotiated the discourses embedded in the Victoria health and physical education curriculum, as instantiated in the Victorian Board of Studies Curriculum and Standards Framework (CSF) published in 1995. She describes her method as follows:

> These texts were analysed for the appearance of key words, phrases and ideas, and the formation of such words, phrases and ideas into larger

discourses. In the context of the present discussion, the texts were read with the following questions in mind: How do the texts represent the objectives and concerns of the health and physical education curriculum? What dominant principles do they espouse? How do they represent students and teachers? What notion of health is privileged in the texts? What are the broader discourses (those 'outside' the texts) evident that are structuring these representations? (p. 290)

Using this approach Lupton demonstrates how the neo-liberal tenets of "the new public health", which inform the CSF, can be identified in the teachers' talk as they described their idea of the "good student". These tenets are particularly exemplified in both sites by "notions of ethical self-management and citizenship" (p. 290). She argues from her analysis that "while the curriculum document represents such objectives as unproblematic and taken for granted", there are tensions between these "ideals" and the practices of teachers; tensions which are related to the everyday contexts of teachers' lives and work. This was particularly evident in the teachers' struggle to reconcile what they perceived health education sets out to achieve ("the development of the social, emotional and communicative capacities of students") and a traditional emphasis in physical education on "demonstrating superiority over others" (p. 298–299). She concludes that the teachers' responses demonstrate the extent to which "disciplinary strategies", such as those embedded in curriculum documents, meet with resistance and fail at the site of the school and warns against any assumption that curriculum imperatives in any way point to practice.

In a rather different example, Macdonald and Kirk (1996) investigated how the nature of physical education teachers work and the expectations of how physical education teachers should be, as these are shaped by the institutional and corporeal discourses associated with sport and physical education, effect teachers' identity and their relation to the profession, to their work environments and so on. In the context of teacher socialization, they use Foucauldian notions of discourse and identity, to explain how particular forms of embodiment are enforced through the social practices of those around them. For example, in the context of a larger study on physical education teacher attrition, they use Foucault's notions of regulation and surveillance to explore the pressures to conform on beginning physical education teachers in remote and isolated schools in Queensland. They describe the consequences of these pressures for the ways the beginning teachers were able to construct their professional and personal identities. Data were collected through semistructured interviews, conversations, and notes taken on field visits. The main

theme that emerged was that the teachers regarded themselves as being under constant surveillance with their private and public lives monitored by students and teachers. They were expected to embody the community's ideas of the sporting healthy body, and to conform to local conservative expectations in terms of expressions of sexuality, lifestyle, dress, and grooming. As a consequence several of the beginning teachers chose to leave physical education teaching "due, in part, to the negative effects of the surveillance". (p. 74)

School physical education as social practice

For the researchers investigating school physical education as social practice, the texts of interest are those derived from the interactions between teachers and students in lessons. In many cases the focus has been on the construction of gender, that is, how particular notions of masculinity and femininity have been constituted in and through the social practices (the language and non-verbal behaviours) enacted in lessons. In some cases, the focus has been on how bodies and/or specific forms of movement practice are constituted in the classroom language and the bodily movements of students. Most of those involved in conducting this form of analytic work are not so much concerned with providing definitive and generalizable information about gender differences, or about the ways in which the body is used in physical education, but want to provide a way of recognizing how language and other social practices work to position "subjects" in relation to specific discourses. The papers from these studies often conclude with a comment that the insights provided into localized practices can provide a basis for reflection whereby teachers may develop a better understanding of their own practice.

The analytic tools to conduct this research have been drawn variously from linguistics, semiotics, discourse analysis, Laban notation, and phenomenology. The use of Laban notation and phenomenology point to ways of being able to document systematically the "language" choices in movement. In all cases there is a detailed analysis of text, ranging from a close analysis of the section of one lesson to particular linguistic or non-verbal phenomena across a number of lessons.

Jan Wright's series of papers (Wright, 1993, 1997, 2000; Wright and King, 1991) on the language of physical education lessons exemplifies the use of linguistics to demonstrate how teachers' choices of language contribute to the construction of gendered subjectivities and social relations. The teachers in her study agreed to wear tape recorders with lapel mikes (with current technology, less intrusive forms of recording are available). The tapes were then transcribed and analysed systematically for language choices in terms of grammatical (such as, speech functions and modality) and lexical (vocabulary) patterns. The lessons were video-recorded for context and to assist in interpretation of the transcripts derived from the tapes. The video recordings also provided possibilities for the analysis of non-linguistic aspects of lessons such as the students' use of space, choices of activities, and so on. Wright used this analysis to demonstrate how female and male teachers constructed very different language environments for female and male students, that is, how the language that they used with female students as compared with male students anticipated a different subject – one who was less capable, less skilled, less interested in physical activity and who needed cajoling into action. The following quote sums up the main conclusions of this work:

> A detailed analysis of lessons reveals complexities and contradictions – on the one hand the female teachers provide more explicit instruction, more praise and encouragement and attempt to create more personalised relationships with their female students. On the other hand, their use of language also attempts to more closely control students' behaviour through regulatory statements about appropriate attitudes to physical education and the proper comportment of their bodies.
> The boys appear to be allowed more freedom. On the other hand their compliance with the discourses and practices of physical education is assumed (except in dance where they are expected to be resistant). For a boy to be non-compliant is not so much to identify himself as a poor or problem student but to bring into question his masculinity, his very identity as male. For girls, resistance to the discourses of physical education brings no similar risk, rather resistance can ironically confirm their positioning as feminine in a patriarchal gendered discourse. (Wright, 1997: 69)

An examination of the ways in which gendered subjectivities are constituted is also the focus of Ronholt's (2002) "critical classroom study" of teaching and learning. In this paper, the emphasis is on the association between discourses of physical education and gender, how this association is constructed through the structures of the physical education lesson and how it influences children's learning. Ronholt uses a phenomenological and "critical discourse analysis" of a video recording of a primary/elementary school lesson (Grade 2) taught by a female teacher to identify how physical education and gendered discourses are embedded in children's and teachers' discursive practices. She points to the importance of language, in this case a sequence of exchanges about who in the class can and can't take breaks during an extended run. The comment by one of the boys in the class that "It's

only the sissies ... [who cannot run without breaks]", encapsulates the nature of the group and then determines who will opt for which group: the boys all run without breaks (despite an early indication that some may have opted otherwise), and all except one girl join the group who takes breaks. Ronholt uses the concept of "situated learning" to link her analysis of the classroom practices to the children's learning about what matters in physical education and in the wider society as they participate in their social world in the case of a physical education lesson. Like most poststructuralist researchers one of the purposes of her analysis is to make "visible what is usually hidden" so that in through their awareness of how discourses work teachers can "critically reflect and react pedagogically in an educational situation" (Ronholt, 2002: 34).

While the focus of Wright and Ronholt's work is physical activity-based lessons, Deana Leahy and Lyn Harrison (Leahy and Harrison, 2004) use Foucault's (Foucault, 1988, 1991) notions of "governmentality" and "technologies of the self", together with contemporary social analyses of "risk" (Beck, 1992) to investigate the ways in which risk discourses (re)constituted in HPE lessons work "to shape and produce particular kinds of people" (p. 130). They analyse texts derived from teacher and key informant interviews, classroom observations, and curriculum documents to demonstrate how the "expert knowledge" deployed in the physical education classroom constitutes the "at risk" student, that is, ensures that students understand themselves as being "at risk" or in danger of being at risk (p. 133). This is accomplished by drawing on "hybrid risk knowledges", where melodramatic and often mythical risk narratives (supported by popular cultural images) are mixed with scientific information to persuade young people of the risks that face them.

Whereas there have been analytical tools readily available to do the work of analysing language from a poststructuralist perspective, the analysis of physical education as an embodied practice has required other ways of working. In an innovative study of students' use of their bodies in educational gymnastics tasks, Nilges draws on the work of Kirk, Fernandez Balboa, and Hall to construe "movement as a nonverbal discourse that is capable of (a) enfleshing bodies with gender knowledge and (b) serving as a cultural medium through which the inequities of traditional gender knowledge are displayed or actively resisted". She uses these constructs to understand "the moving body" as "situated as a discursive arena for studying gender where bodies are socially constructed and take an active role in constituting and shaping the social systems in which they exist". (p. 288). What is particularly innovative about Nilges' work is her use of Laban notation as the basis of an interpretive framework for systematically analysing the ways in which male and female undergraduate students use their bodies to construct movement sequences. The interpretive framework involved the identification of parameters for coding and recording the data in ways that could be analysed quantitatively. The dimensions of "effort analysis" were used to provide:

> ... a link between theorizing the embodiment of gender and studying the embodiment of gender. Effort analysis allowed the body's ever-changing use of weight (strong/light), time (sudden/sustained), space (direct/indirect), and flow (bound/free) to be abstracted from movement. A coding system for quantifying and interpreting the embodiment of gender in student sequence work was constructed by overlaying the effort aspect with a gender reference imparted by historical images of masculinity and femininity. (p. 296)

The data collected through the coding of students movements were analysed using

> a three-stage, chi-square analysis to determine whether males as a group were significantly more likely to use strong, sudden, direct and bound movements actions in their sequences than females ... and whether females as a group were significantly more likely to use light, sustained, indirect, and free actions in their sequences than males. (p. 299)

Her hypothesis was confirmed.

Like much of the research in this area which wants to compare female and male behaviour (language included), this research has to argue that its purpose is not to contribute to an essentialized notion of female and male behaviour. Rather it is about demonstrating how particular practices in physical education continue to reproduce narrow and limiting notions of what it means to be and move as a woman or a man. In this case Nilges argues that her research provides:

> a postmodern framework for the studying the embodiment of gender ... to establish a lens for examining ways in which traditional images of masculinity and femininity are nonverbally constructed and communicated through the discourse of bodily movement in the educational gymnastics setting. (pp. 303–4)

While Nilges' work is the only example of postmodernist research which specifically uses bodily movement as the unit of analysis, the body is certainly not absent from other poststructuralist work. Indeed the notion of "embodied subjectivity", the body as the object of/subjected to power (biopower) and the body as constructed in and by particular

social and cultural contexts is an integral part of much of the poststructuralist analysis in physical education (and related fields such as sociology of sport and health). For example, Wright (2000a, b) uses Jennifer Gore's (1995) categories derived from Foucault's "techniques of power" to analyse the ways the social practices (in this case specifically language) work to constitute particular embodied subjectivities and social relations in a physical education lesson. This work is extended in Wright (2000a) where the meanings about bodies in a physical education lesson are compared to those in a Feldenkrais lesson. These analyses led Wright to suggest that physical educators should pay close attention to the forms of embodiment that are produced by the kinds of interactions and language use which are generic in physical education lessons and be alert to the possibilities of alternative forms of movement practices. Hunter (2005) draws on the work of Bourdieu to explore how "discourses associated with the body, both within the classroom context and the *field* of physical education, create discursive spaces for constituting the *embodied subjectivities* of those within the social space" (p. 183). She interviewed students during their last year of primary school and first year of high school and their teachers, conducted field observations and collected journals, photographs and video footage. The data derived from these procedures were analysed by a variety of methods including critical discourse analysis and drawing on the theoretical perspectives of critical pedagogy, poststructural feminism, cultural studies, and youth studies. Her analysis demonstrates what has also been discussed in relation to other studies above, that physical education through its association with sport and other discourses which constitute a particular kind of "ideal body", marginalizes "many young people from physical education, physical activity, health and their bodies, and reduce(s) positive spaces for different subjectivities to exist" (p. 24). She suggests that by "redefining what a good student in PE could *be* like or *look* like, within and outside sport discourses, there may be spaces for more students to successfully position themselves (and be positioned by others)" (p. 25) as worthy and as able to participate "successfully" in physical education and physical activity.

In a last example which does not fall neatly into either the category of classroom research or subjectivities as they are constituted in and through discourses associated with physical education and/or health is a very evocative paper by Halas and Hanson titled "Pathologising Billy", who uses autoethnography and Foucault's concept of governmentality to examine how the pathologizing of a young native American student, diagnosed with attention deficit disorder, living in foster care, shapes what it is possible for him to be and do. Halas describes how she uses shooting hoops in her efforts to connect with Billy. Over a long and difficult period Billy manages to stay in school and make it to the end of the year through the care of the teacher and the opportunity to shoot hoops and attend extra PE. In the following year Billy discovers volleyball and in an unprecedented (for Billy) opportunity is permitted to play volleyball in an interschool game. The team wins and Billy is "a winner in every sense of the word" (p. 121). Within a week he is expelled from school. Halas and Hanson conclude Billy's story as follows:

> Forced to attend a treatment centre and living in foster care, the institutional parameters of Billy's day-to-day reality attempt to mold him into a body which complies to society's norms. Athletic, young and slight he is marked by not only the physical forces his body has been subjected to but also the effects of power, that is the knowledge relations which turn him into an object of focus for the justice and educational systems and services ... Eventually ... the young man who wasn't allowed in a regular physical education class has progressed to becoming a participant in an interschools competition. All the while he never transcends the subjectivity of a special student, the pathologized behavior problem, the Young Offender soon to have a record. ... he cannot escape larger discursive conditions that find expression in the material realities of his existence. (p. 122)

This paper points to the possibilities of a post-structuralist approach to help understand the multifaceted relationships between teachers and their pupils and to examine these in the complex context of students' and teachers' subjectivities and the cultural and institutional discourses and material circumstances which shape both.

Postcolonial research in physical education

At the time of writing this chapter, it was possible to identify only one published research paper in physical education which drew on postcolonial theory. The paper, by Hastie, Martin and Buchanan (Hastie et al., 2006), describes how two Anglo teachers came to understand "their *praxis* as they attempted to present a culturally relevant physical education program to a class of African-American sixth-grade students" (295). The program, a unit on "stepping" (a form of African-American vernacular dance), was designed to challenge physical education as a practice that reflects "a Euro-American hegemony that proscribes certain cultures ... as backward and marginal". The paper draws on the reflections of the teachers (two of the authors) as they interrogate the legitimacy of white teachers teaching "stepping" to

African-American children in a rural elementary school, and on the ethnographic data collected by the third author as observer. The authors describe how by adopting a postcolonial frame of reference they were able to develop a deeper consciousness of the implications of their innovation. They argue on the basis of their experience and reflections that if teachers are to implement (and they argue that they should) culturally relevant curriculum where there are questions about their legitimacy to do so they must be:

> At least, ... a willing participant in the act of praxis, not only engaging in the cycle of looking, thinking, acting, reflecting (Stringer, 2004), but also extending the process to consider the political and social aspects that impact curriculum and pedagogy, and indeed, the students we teach. (p. 21)

Directions for the future

Researchers in physical education have barely tapped the potential of a post approach, although it is clear that poststructural, postmodern, and postcolonial perspectives provide powerful theoretical and empirical frameworks for addressing important questions associated with the production of knowledge, the formation of subjectivities and an understanding of embodiment. These are all fundamental to understanding the ways in which policy, curriculum, and pedagogy are shaped in specific social and cultural contexts and with what effect for all of those involved in any way in the field of physical education. Although "post" perspectives eschew grand narratives and totalizing explanations of any phenomenon, as is obvious from the work described above, in making visible the ways in which power and knowledge are joined to construct particular social practices, subjectivities, and social relations, research informed by "post" perspectives clearly has an emancipatory purpose. The work of identifying the operation of discourses as they impact on all levels of practice is important ongoing work. In the immediate future the impact of health discourses on physical education is an area of obvious need. This challenge has been taken up by some of the authors discussed earlier in this chapter (e.g. Leahy and Harrison, 2004; Penney and Harris, 2004), however, the increasing salience of health discourses associated with the "obesity epidemic" with young people and "risk" in the context of physical education, requires further empirical work. An Australian longitudinal qualitative study of the place and meaning of physical activity, physical culture, and health in young peoples' lives has begun this task. This study has interviewed young people from a range of geographical, social, and cultural locations to understand how young peoples' identities and practices are shaped by their experiences of schooling, by their families and by the social and cultural contexts in which they live. From a different perspective a postcolonial perspective is being employed by researchers at The University of Queensland to better understand the relationships between Aboriginal and Torres Strait Islander's subjectivities, ethnicity, and physical activity.

It is also worth pointing at this stage to some of the work of doctoral students that is beginning to address this need. Louise McCuaig's study, for example, analyses the Queensland Health and Physical Education curriculum as it is explicitly engaged in deploying biopower technologies to construct healthy citizens of the future. Gabrielle O'Flynn uses Foucault's concept of the "technologies of the self" to explore how health and physical activity discourses operate in different school and community settings to construct different kinds of selves and different relations to the body and Seth Brown (2002) draws on "technologies of power" to understand the patterns of privilege and marginalization of young men in a vocationally oriented physical education curriculum. Further, Kelly Hunt is using Foucauldian theory alongside postcolonial perspectives in her work with young Muslim women's subjectivities in relation to physical activity, physical education, and health. From a different perspective, in addressing a young indigenous Australian's growing problem with early-onset diabetes, postcolonial theory is being employed by researchers at The University of Queensland to better understand the relationships between Aboriginal and Torres Strait Islander's subjectivities, ethnicity, and physical activity.

What is obviously missing from this review of physical education research informed by post perspectives is work informed by a postcolonial perspective. Whereas poststructuralist and postmodernist theory has been coupled with feminist theory to make visible the means by which gender is constructed in and through physical education, with the one exception cited above, this has not been the case with race and ethnicity. There is obviously considerable potential for deconstructing the way in which curriculum has been constructed and physical education has been taught in ways which privilege Eurocentric notions of the self, of physical activity, and learning; and which interrogate the "effects" of globalization and European and American hegemony on physical education and physical activity participation internationally. Physical education researchers might well look to research in the sociology of sport (e.g. Bale and Cronin, 2002) and in education (e.g. McCarthy et al., 2003; *Journal of Postcolonial Education*) to assist in the raising of problems and the setting of research agendas.

Finally, "post" researchers in physical education should be beware of falling into the complacency of the same patterns of research. Theorizing in the areas of postmodernity, poststructuralism, and postcolonialism continue apace. A key to "post" work is the need to keep "troubling" the taken-for-granted and the familiar, to engage what Foucault describes as "an ethic of discomfort", that is, "to never consent to being completely comfortable with your own certainties" (Foucault, 1997, quoted in Harwood and Rasmussen, 2004, p. 305). This includes the research methods that are employed as well as the questions that are asked.

References

Bale, J. and Cronin, M. (Eds.). (2002). *Sport and postcolonialism.* Oxford: Berg.

Ball, S.J. (Ed.). (1990). *Foucault and education: Disciplines and knowledge.* London: Routledge.

Beck, U. (1992). *Risk society.* London: Sage.

Bernstein, B. (1996). Pedagogy, symbolic control and identity: Theory, research and critique. London: Taylor & Francis.

Brown, S. (2002). *Governing the recreational self.* Paper presented at the Australian Association for Research in Education Annual Conference, December, Brisbane, QLD, Australia.

Burns, R. (1993). Health fitness and female subjectivity: what is happening to school health and physical education. In L. Yates (Ed.), *Feminism and education.* Melbourne: La Trobe University Press.

Burrows, L. (1997). Analysing developmental discourses in physical education. In J. Wright (Ed.), *Proceedings of the researching in physical and health education conference,* Wollongong, Australia: Faculty of Education.

Burrows, L. (2000). Fictions, factions and frictions: Constructing the 'child' in school physical education. *Journal of Physical Education New Zealand, 33* (2), 22–36.

Burrows, L. and Wright, J. (2001). Developing children in New Zealand school physical education. *Sport Education and Society, 6* (2), 165–182.

Clarke, G. (1992). Learning the language: discourse analysis in physical education. In A.C. Sparkes (Ed.), *Research in physical education and sport: Exploring alternative visions.* London: Falmer Press.

Davies, B. (2001). Literacy and literate subjects in a health and physical education class: A poststructuralist analysis. *Linguistics and Education, 11* (4), 333–352.

Delamont, S. (1998). 'You need the leotard'. Revisiting the first PE lesson. *Sport, Education and Society, 3* (1), 5–17.

Denzin, N.K. (2000). The practices and politics of interpretation. In N.K. Denzin and Y.S. Lincoln (Eds.), *Handbook of qualitative research* (2nd Ed., pp. 897–922). Thousand Oaks, CA: Sage.

Dreyfus, H.L. and Rabinow, P. (1986). *Michel foucault: Beyond structuralism and hermeneutics.* Brighton, UK: The Harvester Press.

Evans, J. (Ed.). (1988). *Teachers, teaching and control in physical education.* London: Falmer Press.

Evans, J. and Clarke, G. (1988). Changing the face of physical education. In J. Evans (Ed.), *Teachers, teaching and control in physical education* (pp. 125–143). London: Falmer Press.

Evans, J. and Davies, B. (2004a). Endnote: the embodiment of consciousness: Bernstein, health and schooling. In J. Evans, B. Davies and J. Wright (Eds.), *Body, knowledge and control: Studies in the sociology of physical education and health.* London: Routledge.

Evans, J. and Davies, B. (2004b). Pedagogy, symbolic control, identity and health. In J. Evans, B. Davies and J. Wright (Eds.), *Body, knowledge and control: Studies in the sociology of physical education and health.* London: Routledge.

Evans, J. and Penney, D. (1995). Physical education, restoration and the politics of sport. *Curriculum Studies, 3* (2), 183–196.

Evans, J., Evans, B. and Rich, E. (2002). Eating disorders and comprehensive ideals. *Forum for promoting 3–19 comprehensive education, 44* (2), 59–65.

Evans, J., Evans, B. and Rich, E. (2003). Let them eat chips. *Pedagogy, Culture and Society, 12* (2), 215–240.

Fernandez-Balboa, J.-M. (Ed.). (1997). *Critical postmodernism in human movement, physical education and sport.* Albany, NY: SUNY Press.

Foucault, M. (1972). *The archaeology of knowledge.* New York: Pantheon.

Foucault, M. (1979). *Discipline and punish: The birth of the prison.* Hammondsworth, UK: Penguin.

Foucault, M. (1985). The use of pleasure: The history of sexuality, Vol. 3, R. Hurley (Trans.). London: Penguin.

Foucault, M. (1988). Technologies of the self. In L.H. Martin, H. Gutman and P. Hutton (Eds.), *Technologies of the self: A seminar with Michel Foucault.* London: Tavistock Publications.

Foucault, M. (1991). Governmentality. In G. Burchell, C. Gordon and P. Muller (Eds.), *The Foucault effect* (pp. 87–194). Brighton, UK: Harvester Wheatsheaf.

Foucault, M. (1997). *Ethics: subjectivity and truth* (R. Hurley and others, Trans.). New York: The New Press.

Giddens, A. (1991). *Modernity and self-identity: Self and society in the late modern age.* Cambridge, UK: Polity Press.

Gilroy, S. and Clarke, G. (1997). 'Raising the game': Deconstructing the sporting text – from Major to Blair. *Pedagogy in Practice, 3* (2), 19–37.

Gleyse, J., Pigeassou, A., Marcellini, A., De Lesleleuc, E. and Bui-Xuan, G. (2002). Physical education as subject in France (school curriculum, policies and discourse: The body and the metaphors of the engine – elements used in the analysis of power and control during the second industrial revolution. *Sport Education and Society, 7* (1), 5–23.

Glover, S. (1993). National curriculum comment: Creating opportunity or crisis for physical education and physical educators. *The ACHPER National Journal, 40* (2), 19–21.

Glover, S. (2001). *Social construction of pedagogic discourse in health and physical education: A study of the writing the National Statement and Profile 1992–1994.* Unpublished PhD, University of Queensland, Brisbane.

Gore, J. (1990). Pedagogy as text in physical education teacher education: beyond the preferred reading. In D. Kirk and R. Tinning (Eds.), *Physical education, curriculum and culture.* Basingstoke, Hampshire, UK: Falmer Press.

Gore, J. (1998). Disciplining bodies: On the continuity of power relations in pedagogy. In T.S. Popkewitz and M. Brennan (Eds.), *Foucault's challenge: Discourse, knowledge and power in education* (pp. 231–251). New York and London: Teachers College Press.

Halas, J. and Hanson, L. (2001). Pathologising Billy: Enabling and constraining the body of the condemned. *Sociology of Sport Journal, 18* (1), 115–126.

Harwood, V. and Rasmussen, M.L. (2003). *Applying Foucaultian angles of scrutiny to qualitative data analysis.* A paper presented at the Annual Meeting of the American Educational Research Association, April, New Orleans.

Harwood, V. and Rasmussen, M.L. (2004). Studying schools with an 'ethics of discomfort'. In B. Baker and K. Heyning (Eds.), *Dangerous coagulations? The uses of Foucault in the study of education* (pp. 305–321). New York: Peter Lang.

Hastie, P.A., Martin, E. and Buchanan, A.M. (2006). Stepping out of the norm: An examination of praxis for a culturally relevant pedagogy for African-American children. *Journal of Curriculum Studies, 38* (3), 293–306.

Hunter, L. (2005). Who gets to play? Kids, bodies and schooled subjectivities. In J. Vadeboncoeur and L. Patel Stevens (Eds.), *Re/Constructing 'the adolescent: Sign, symbol and the body* (pp. 181–210). New York: Peter Lang.

Kelly, P., Hickey, C. and Tinning, R. (2000). Producing knowledge about physical education pedagogy: Problematizing the activities of expertise. *Quest, 52,* 284–296.

Kirk, D. (1992). *Defining physical education: The social construction of a subject in postwar Britain.* Basingstoke, UK: Falmer Press.

Kirk, D. (1996). The crisis in school physical education: An argument against the tide. *ACHPER Healthy Lifestyles Journal, 43* (4), 25–27.

Kirk, D. (1998). *Schooling bodies: School practice and public discourse, 1880–1950.* London, UK: Leicester University Press.

Kirk, D. (2003). Beyond the academic curriculum: the production and operation of biopower in the less studied sites of schooling. In B. Baker and K. Heyning (Eds.), *Dangerous coagulations? The uses of Foucault in the study of education* (pp. 117–134). New York: Peter Lang.

Kirk, D. (2004). Towards a critical history of the body, identity and health: corporeal power and school practice. In J. Evans, B. Davies and J. Wright (Eds.), *Body knowledge and control: Studies in the sociology of physical education and health.* London: Routledge.

Kirk, D. and Tinning, R. (Eds.). (1990). *Physical education, curriculum and culture: Critical issues in contemporary crisis.* London: Falmer Press.

Kirk, D. and Twigg, K. (1994). Regulating the Australian body: eugenics, anthropometrics and school medical inspection in Victoria, 1990–1945. *History of Education Review, 23*, 19–37.

Kirk, D., Macdonald, D. and Tinning, R. (1997). The social construction of pedagogic discourse in physical education teacher education. *The Curriculum Journal, 8* (2), 271–298.

Leahy, D. and Harrison, L. (2004). Health and physical education and the production of the 'at risk self'. In J. Evans, B. Davies and J. Wright (Eds.), *Body, knowledge and control: Studies in the sociology of physical education and health* (pp. 130–139). London and New York: Routledge.

Lupton, D. (1992). Discourse analysis: a new methodology for understanding the ideologies of health and illness. *Australian Journal of Public Health, 16* (2), 145–150.

Lupton, D. (1995). *The Imperative of health: Public health and the regulated body.* London: Sage.

Lupton, D. (1999). Developing the "whole me": citizenship, neo-liberalism and the contemporary health and physical education curriculum. *Critical Public Health, 9* (4), 287–300.

Macdonald, D. (1993). Knowledge, gender and power in physical education teacher education. *Australian Journal of Education, 37* (3), 259–278.

Macdonald, D. (2003a). Curriculum change and the post-modern world: is the school curriculum-reform movement an anachronism? *Journal of Curriculum Studies, 35* (2), 139–149.

Macdonald, D. (2003b). Rich task implementation: modernism meets postmodernism. *Discourse, 24* (2), 248–262.

Macdonald, D. and Kirk, D. (1996). Private lives, public lives: surveillance, identity and self in the work of beginning physical education teachers. *Sport, Education and Society, 1* (1), 59–75.

Macdonald, D. and Kirk, D. (1998). *Complementary and contested discourses: Australian PETE programs and their relationship to school health and physical education.* Paper presented at the AIESEP International Conference, July, New York.

Macdonald, D. and Kirk, D. (1999). Pedagogy, the body and Christian identity. *Sport Education and Society, 4* (2), 131–142.

Macdonald, D. and Tinning, R. (2003). Reflective practice goes public: Reflection, governmentality and post-modernity. In A. Laker (Ed.), *The Future of physical education: Building a new pedagogy* (pp. 82–101). London: Routledge.

McCarthy, C., Giardina, M.D., Harewood, S.J. and Park, J.-K. (2003). Contesting culture: Identity and curriculum dilemmas in the age of globalization, postcolonialism, multiplicity. *Harvard Educational Review, 73* (3), 449–465.

Nilges, L. (2000). A nonverbal discourse analysis of gender in undergraduate educational gymnastic sequences using Laban Effort Analysis. *Journal of Teaching in Physical Education, 19* (3), 287–310.

Olafson, L. (2002). 'I hate phys. ed.': Adolescent girls talk about physical education. *Physical Educator, 59* (2), 67–74.

Olesen, V.L. (2000). Feminisms and qualitative research at and into the millennium. In N.K. Denzin and Y.S. Lincoln (Eds.), *Handbook of Qualitative Research* (pp. 215–255). Thousand Oaks, CA: Sage.

Oliver, K.L. and Lalik, R. (2004). Critical inquiry on the body in girls' physical education classes: A critical post-structuralist perspective. *Journal of Teaching in Physical Education, 23* (2), 162–195.

Penney, D. and Evans, J. (1999). Naming the game. Discourse and domination in physical education and sport in England and Wales. *European Physical Education Review, 3* (1), 21–32.

Penney, D. and Glover, S. (1998). Contested identities: A comparative analysis of the position and definitions of physical education in National Curriculum developments in England and Wales and Australia. *European Journal of Physical Education, 3*, 5–21.

Penney, D. and Harris, J. (2004). The body and heath in policy: Representations and recontextualisation. In J. Evans, B. Davies and J. Wright (Eds.), *Body, knowledge and control: Studies in the sociology of physical education and health* (pp. 96–111). London and New York: Routledge.

Petersen, A. and Bunton, R. (Eds.). (1997). *Foucault, health and medicine.* London and New York: Routledge.

Petersen, A. and Waddell, C. (1998). *Health matters: A sociology of illness, prevention and care.* Sydney: Allen and Unwin.

Prain, V. and Hickey, C. (1995). Using discourse analysis to change physical education. *Quest, 47* (1), 76–90.

Rail, G. (1998). Introduction. In G. Rail (Ed.), *Sport and postmodern times* (pp. ix–xxi). Albany, NY: SUNY Press.

Ronholt, H. (2002). 'It's only the sissies …': Analysis of teaching and learning processes in physical education: a contribution to the hidden curriculum. *Sport Education and Society, 7* (1), 25–39.

Scheurich, J.J. (1997). *Research method in the postmodern.* London: Falmer Press.

Sheridan, A. (1980). *Michel Foucault: The will to truth.* London and New York: Routledge.

Sparkes, A.C. (1992). Writing and the textual construction of realities: Some challenges for alternative paradigms research in physical education. In A.C. Sparkes (Ed.), *Research in physical education and sport: Exploring alternative visions* (pp. 271–297). London: Falmer Press.

Stringer, E.T. (2004) Action research in education. Upper Saddle River, NJ: Pearson Merrill Prentice Hall.

Taylor, S. (2001). Locating and conducting discourse analytic research. In M. Wetherell, S. Taylor and S. Yates (Eds.), *Discourse as data: A guide for analysis.* London: Sage.

Thorpe, S. (2003). Crisis discourse in physical education and the laugh of Michel Foucault. *Sport Education and Society, 8* (2), 131–151.

Tinning, R. (1990). *Ideology and physical education.* Geelong, Vic.: Deakin University Press.

Tinning, R. and Fitzclarence, L. (1992). Postmodern youth culture and the crisis in Australian secondary school physical education. *Quest, 44* (3), 287–304.

Tinning, R. and Glasby, T. (2002). Pedagogical work and the 'cult of the body': considering the role of HPE in the context of the new 'public health'. *Sport Education and Society,* 7 (2), 109–119.

Tinning, R., Macdonald, D., Wright, J. and Hickey, C. (2001). *Becoming a physical education teacher.* Sydney: Prentice-Hall.

Tyler, W. (2004). Silent, invisible, total: Pedagogic discourse and the age of information. In J. Muller, B. Davies and A. Morais (Eds.), *Reading Bernstein, researching Bernstein.* London: Routledge/Falmer.

Usher, R. and Edwards, R. (1994). *Postmodernism and education.* London and New York: Routledge.

Wetherell, M., Taylor, S. and Yates, S. (Eds.). (2001). *Discourse as data: A guide for analysis.* London: Sage.

Williams, A. and Woodhouse, J. (1996). Delivering the discourse – urban adolescents' perceptions of physical education. *Sport, Education and Society,* 1 (2), 210–213.

Wright, J. (1993). Regulation and resistance: the physical education lesson as speech genre. *Social Semiotics,* 3 (1), 23–56.

Wright, J. (1995). A feminist post-structuralist methodology for the study of gender construction in physical education: description of a case study. *Journal of Teaching in Physical Education,* 15 (1), 1–24.

Wright, J. (1996). Mapping the discourses in physical education. *Journal of Curriculum Studies,* 28 (3), 331–351.

Wright, J. (1996). The construction of complementarity in physical education. *Gender and Education,* 8 (1), 61–79.

Wright, J. (1997). The construction of gendered contexts in single sex and coeducational physical education lessons. *Sport, Education and Society,* 2 (1), 55–72.

Wright, J. (1997). The construction of gendered contexts in single sex and coeducational physical education lessons. *Sport, Education and Society,* 2 (1), 55–72.

Wright, J. (2000a). Bodies, meanings and movement: A movement comparison of the language of a physical education lesson and a Feldenkrais movement class. *Sport Education and Society,* 5 (1), 35–49.

Wright, J. (2000b). Disciplining the body: power, knowledge and subjectivity in a physical education lesson. In A. Lee and C. Poynton (Eds.), *Culture and Text.* Sydney: Allen and Unwin.

Wright, J. (2004). Post-structural methodologies: the body schooling and health. In J. Evans and B. Davies (Eds.), *Body, knowledge and control: Studies in the sociology of physical education and health* (pp. 19–31). London and New York: Routledge.

Wright, J. and King, R.C. (1991). "I say what I mean," said Alice: an analysis of gendered discourse in physical education. *Journal of Teaching in Physical Education,* 10 (2), 210–225.

1.5 Feminist strands, perspectives, and methodology for research in physical education

LYNDA M. NILGES

Introduction

Feminists contend that no single word, such as feminism, can be used to name a broad heterogeneous social movement aimed at the betterment of women's lives (DeVault, 1996; Howard and Allen, 2000). Feminism itself is not a monolithic ideology and all feminists do not think alike. It's impossible, therefore, to speak of a single feminist perspective. Over the past 40 years a range of perspectives have surfaced within feminist theory in an attempt to more fully explain women's oppression and offer solutions for its elimination (Tong, 1998; Weedon, 1999; Whelehan, 1995). Broadly speaking these perspectives have increasingly differentiated women's lives and their subjectivities as opposed to viewing "women" as a universal and homogeneous category. Relative to the range of perspectives that are discernable in feminist research, Olesen and Clarke suggest:

> It is important to recognize that knowledge is continually dynamic – new frames open which give way to others, which in turn open again and again …. What is important for concerned feminists is that new topics, issues of concern and matter for feminist inquiry are continually produced and given attention to yield more nuanced understandings of actions on critical issues. (1999: 356)

Although the term feminism needs more careful consideration now than it did when second wave feminism emerged in Western societies during the 1960s, feminist researchers (1) share a commitment to centering and making problematic the experiences of girls and women and/or the institutions and discourses that frame those experiences and (2) use research to set the stage for "praxis," defined here as other research or action that helps transcend and transform gender through institutional and/or personal change (Olesen, 2000). By nature, feminist research is political in that it seeks to promote awareness and change relative to women's lives as well as gender relations between males and females. Applied to physical education, feminist praxis means unity rather than disjuncture should exist between research and practice (Hall, 1996; Macdonald, 2002). Feminist research should contribute to an informed knowledge and understanding about gender and/or gender difference that will help shape and/or alter schooling practices and policies in ways that promote equity and justice (Scraton and Flintoff, 1992).

Feminist research gives voice to women in a school subject and a profession that historically developed in explicitly gendered ways. In the UK for example, Kirk (2002) discusses how gender shaped the development of physical education in the early to mid 20th century. He outlines how women such as Marjorie Randall had an early voice in the direction of physical education through the development of educational gymnastics. As the focus of physical education in the UK shifted from gymnastics systems to sports and games this voice was eventually lost to "masculine" curricula that focused heavily on specific skill development and competition. Educational gymnastics as a child-centered, process-oriented approach to gymnastics instruction had little or no competition and emphasized movement exploration and body awareness. This approach was congruent with cultural views of femininity at the time that situated vigorous and competitive physical activity for girls and women as likely to produce manliness and dangerous to reproductive health. The prevailing historical sentiment was "if one believed that sport built men then one probably believed that women should have nothing to do with it" (Mechikoff and Estes, 2002: 260).

Like women in the UK, women in the United States in the early to mid 20th century also worked within the constraints imposed by cultural beliefs about femininity to shape the profession. As gymnastics systems were replaced by sports and dance, pioneers such as Isadora Duncan and Delphine Hanna were instrumental in giving voice and direction to women's physical education. Isadora Duncan established dance as an integral part of women's physical education and Delphine Hanna promoted a system of "appropriate" activity for females that included anthropometric measurements and corrective exercises. Efforts to establish athletics for women in the United States were conceived more slowly. In the 1930s, for example, the "Play Day" model for school athletics endorsed by Helen Smith focused on social mingling among schools rather than strategy and precision play (Park and Hult, 1993). Gender differences were clearly recognized and maintained by early physical educators in both the US and the UK, yet by the 1960s women's voice in the direction of physical education had been largely subdued by the masculinized, sport-specific version of physical education that had achieved dominance. As Kirk (2002: 35) suggests, physical education had developed in such a way that, "in order to be successful in the subject girls and women needed to perform in a masculinized way, and furthermore, a particular masculinized way".

With a history that cast women as separate and unequal, physical education has become a rich context for scholarship from different feminist perspectives. For example, recent research in physical education has used various feminist perspectives and concepts to place gender at the center of analysis in studying student constructions of masculinity and femininity (e.g., Brown, 1999; Chepyator-Thompson, Jepkorir and Ennis, 1997; Nilges, 1998; Paechter, 2003), teacher's sexuality (e.g. Clarke, 1998; Lenskyj, 1997; Sykes, 1998, 2001), gender differences in children's attitudes toward physical activity (e.g. Luke and Sinclair, 1991) and gendered subjectivity as constituted through the body (e.g. Gard, 2003; Oliver and Lalik, 2001; Nilges, 2000; Wright, 1996). While feminist research itself will be dealt with in greater detail in other areas of this book, this chapter provides an overview of the various feminist perspectives and presents key issues and debates that currently surround the design and conduct of feminist research in physical education. First, I present three broad strands (liberal, structural, and deconstructive) to outline the scope and types of feminist research indicating how these strands emerged over time and in response to the limitations of the feminist thinking that preceded it. These strands represent the major frameworks under which most feminist research that has been conducted in physical education can be located. Each of these strands, in turn, encompasses certain feminist perspectives that contain theoretical commitments and ways of thinking about gender and

oppression that have led to the production of particular types of feminist research in physical education. Second, I discuss feminist methodology focusing on feminist epistemology and methodological issues researchers often confront. I conclude with some speculation about the status and future of feminist research in physical education.

The diversity of feminist thinking: strands and perspectives

Most feminist scholars consider the growing range of feminist perspectives to be a healthy sign (Evans, 1997; Tong, 1998). Feminist theory is now old enough to have a history and dynamic enough to have sustained its innovativeness in offering a variety of perspectives for investigating relationships between gender and the social world. To discuss the feminist perspectives it's important to consider why theory is needed anyway. While some contend that categorizing thinking as "x" or "y" can be problematic in that such categorization may artificially limit inquiry, Guba and Lincoln (1994: 105) speak favorably of theory as a "basic belief system or world view that guides the investigator not only in choices of method but in ontologically and epistemologically fundamental ways." Theory, therefore, is beneficial in that it provides a unified and systematic explanation of phenomena that can be used to inform questions, aid in prediction, and offer a lens for interpretation. Assuming that "good" theory has strong explanatory and interpretive power, Hall (1996) suggests the value of feminist theory in physical education and sport is that it offers a variety of perspectives designed to enhance our understanding of our gendered human movement culture, pick apart how it works, and unravel the various interconnections that keep it together.

The feminist perspectives can be organized by three broad strands; the liberal strand, the structural strand, and the deconstructive strand. While these strands represent the broad frameworks under which most feminist research in physical education can be located, each strand also encompasses various perspectives that further define and delimit the strand (see Table 1.5.1). I chose this method of organization because it is clear there has been both "tight" and "loose" applications of feminist theory in physical education. Some researchers have very specifically identified and theorized from the feminist perspectives (e.g. Nilges, 1998; Sykes, 2001; Wright, 1995) while others have more broadly located their scholarship within the general ideas and concepts associated with particular strands. For example, what I term here as a "loose" application of feminist theory in

Table 1.5.1   General Overview of the Feminist Strands and Perspectives

Definitional Component	Liberal Strand	Structural Strand	Deconstructive Strand
Source of oppression	Oppression located in the lack of opportunity and access on the basis of biological sex and/or patterns of socialization that promote biological determinism as status quo	Oppression located in social and economic structures which construct the sex/gender system in ways that support the inequitable distribution of power	Oppression is situational, provisional and located in shifting language systems and discourses that control power and constitute gender in highly variable ways
Strategy to eliminate oppression	Removal of outdated discriminatory practices and assimilation	Structural analysis and critique of power relations leading to consciousness raising and change	Interruption leading to the undercutting and deconstruction of received categories
Criticisms/ limitations	• Does not view gender as a constructed category • Situates categories of "women" and "men" as universal	• Situates categories of "women" and "men" as universal • Focuses on gender oppression in terms of "sameness" rather than difference • System constructs the person rather than the person constructing the system; removes human agency	• Because gender oppression is situational and provisional, no definite program for change can be offered • Originates in the academy; language is so specific that it becomes irrelevant to everyday individuals.
Associated perspective(s)	• Liberal Feminist Perspective	• Radical Feminist Perspective • Marxist Feminist Perspective • Socialist Feminist Perspective	• Male Feminist Perspective • Lesbian Feminist Perspective • Poststructural Feminist Perspective
Sample physical education research within the strand	ILEA, 1984 Luke & Sinclair, 1992 Macdonald, 1990 Smeal & Carpenter, 1993	Chepyator-Thompson & Ennis, 1997 Hargreaves, 1986, 2002 Nilges, 1998, 2001 Santina et al., 1998 Scraton, 1986, 1987, 1989 Flintoff & Scraton, 2001	Clarke, 1998 Gard, 2003 Bramham, 2003 Oliver & Lalik, 2001 Nilges, 2000 Olafson, 2002 Parker, 1996 Sykes, 1998, 2001 Wright, 1996

physical education might include addressing a broad concept from the liberal strand such as gender difference (e.g. Shuiteman and Knoppers, 1987) or the structural strand such as patriarchy (e.g. Chepyator-Thompson et al., 1997) without necessarily defining the work as feminist. Like Olesen (2000), I adopted the perspective in preparing this chapter that feminist

research has many variants and a feminist study is one that develops the insights of feminism. Under this premise some researchers in physical education have utilized feminist theory in their work more "tightly" and explicitly than others.

While the strands and perspectives share a similar ontological position that gender reality is constructed in ways that oppress women, women's experiences of oppression are viewed differently and believed to extend from different circumstances depending on the strand and/or feminist perspective taken (Tong, 1998; Whelehan, 1995). The differences within the strands and perspectives will be discussed next relative to (1) how oppression is defined, (2) where the source of oppression is located, and (3) the strategies that are recommended to eliminate oppression. As Whelehan (1995) suggests, "when it comes to isolating causes and posing solutions to oppression there seems to be little or no agreement within feminist thinking" (p. 26). Similar to the concern expressed by Scraton and Flintoff (2002), I recognize that the strands and perspectives identified here do not do justice to the overlap and complexity within and across variations of feminist thinking. After nearly 40 years of scholarship, feminism is extremely sophisticated, complex, and varied. My goal is to provide a starting point for understanding how and why different feminist perspectives arose and came to give primacy to different factors that surround questions of gender and oppression.

Strand 1: Liberal

How is oppression defined?

As the one of the earliest organizing strands of feminist scholarship the liberal strand is informed by the political ideology of liberalism that places individual freedom and flourishing at the heart of a just social order (Thompson, 2003; Tong, 1998). Liberalism places a high priority on rationality (i.e., the ability to reason) as the capacity that distinguishes human beings from animals. Significant to the liberal ideology is the concept of metaphysical dualism. Metaphysical dualism supports a biologically determined distinction between male and female "nature" where the capacity for reason is believed to rest "naturally" in men as opposed to women. As a result, universal principles of the social order have historically granted men access to the public sphere where rationality is awarded with social power and advancement while simultaneously restricting women to the private sphere (i.e., encompassing home and family responsibilities) where the irrational side of human nature (e.g., nurturance and emotion) prevails. In this way the liberal concept of female "nature" is largely biologically endowed and assumes women's innate irrationality. Oppression, therefore, is a result of women being excluded from the societal rights and privileges men are granted "naturally" including education and workplace rights (Whelehan, 1995) and of interest here, physical education and sporting rights and access.

Where is the source of oppression located?

Unlike the two other strands discussed in this chapter, liberal feminism is the only feminist perspective that falls under the liberal strand. Liberal feminists contend the "oppressor" relative to women in sport and physical education is the lack of opportunity on the basis of biological sex. For liberal feminists, therefore, oppression is located in the lack of opportunity and access that results from biological determinism and the patterns of socialization that perpetuate biological determinism as status quo. By locating oppression in this manner, liberal feminists believe that women's oppression, in physical education and sport or otherwise, is a product of intentional actions in a society that values equality in terms of sameness. In other words, oppression will be alleviated when women and men are given access to the same goods, services, rights, and physical opportunities.

Liberal feminist research in physical education has been referred to as "distributive" in that it attempts to empirically demonstrate gender difference in terms of biological sex (Hall, 1996). For instance, researchers in physical education and sport have empirically documented gender differences in children's attitudes toward physical activity (Luke and Sinclair, 1991), activity selection, and socialization (ILEA, 1984), the scholarly productivity of university professors in health, physical education, recreation and dance (Shuiteman and Knoppers, 1987), teacher attention to boys and girls in physical education (Macdonald, 1990), and the preferred teaching strategies of physical educators (Vertinsky, 1984). In addition, Smeal and Carpenter (1993) considered how gender stereotypes perpetuate liberal notions of equality while Nilges (1998) exposed the limitations of Title IX as a purportedly liberal emancipatory policy in the United States. In these studies gender role differentiation and/or patterns of socialization on the basis of biological sex are a key focus.

Strategies to eliminate oppression

Whelehan (1995) identifies the language of liberty, rights, and legal equality as the currency of liberal feminism. The strategy to eliminate oppression within a liberal feminist perspective assumes that the social order within democratic societies is fundamentally sound but certain adjustments need to be made to remove outdated discriminatory practices (Scraton and Flintoff, 1992). Liberal feminists, therefore, work within the system to bring about change. Strategies to eliminate oppression frequently result in quantitative change and include increasing women's access to the rights, privileges, and social spaces that have historically been held by men.

In the arena of physical education and sport, liberal interventions include political activity to increase women's access to the activities, facilities, and/or funding that if left unsecured create barriers to developing physical competence. Liberal interventions of this nature can be thought of as "assimilationist" in that they seek to achieve numerical equality and representation between men and women in the realm of sport and physical education without viewing gender itself as a problematic and/or constructed identity category. For example, equal opportunity initiatives for women's participation in sport and physical activity were widely legislated in the 1970s and 1980s, including Title IX in the United States, anti-discrimination Acts in the United Kingdom and Australia, and the Canadian Charter of Rights and Freedoms.

Limitations of liberal feminist research

Liberal feminist research provides a useful starting point for exposing androcentric (i.e., male) bias in physical education and sport resources and opportunities for the purpose of initiating changes to legislation, policies and practices. Feminists in the late 1960s and early 1970s, however, recognized two primary shortcomings to liberal feminist thinking. First, giving women access and opportunity to a "man's world" (sometimes referred to as the mix and stir approach) does nothing to alter prevailing power relations between men and women. In physical education, for example, the door can be opened for females to participate in a range of activities but it has to be questioned whether simply opening the door will lead to (1) the increased physical confidence and competence of girls and (2) their acceptance as "equals" by their male peers relative to their sporting efforts. Second, liberal feminism is largely based on the assumption that women's experiences with oppression are the same regardless of race, class, ethnicity, and/or sexuality. Thus, the tendency of liberal feminism to situate women as a universal and homogeneous category is a frequently cited limitation (e.g. Evans 1997; Tong, 1998; Thompson, 2003; Whelehan, 1995). The structural strand of feminist thinking evolved after the liberal strand and largely in response to these limitations.

Strand 2: Structural

How is oppression defined?

Structural feminists fault liberal feminist thinking for failing to capture gender as a socially constructed, human practice with a historical and cultural dimension. For structural feminists, inclusion and opportunity within the liberal framework is merely "token" in that it may give the illusion that the system is open but does nothing to change the system itself (Thompson, 2003). Structural feminists, therefore, differ from liberal feminists in that they focus on how the political, social, and economic structures in which women live construct the sex/gender system in ways that support the inequitable distribution of power. Power can be defined as "something one group exercises over another; a kind of property legitimized by laws, standards, hegemonic practices and institutional relations" (Thompson, 2003: 17). Oppression within the structural strand, therefore, is not biologically defined but constructed by various structural systems of society (e.g., patriarchy, capitalism, and class). These systems transform biological sex into a product of structural activity with "haves" and "have nots" relative to power. In this way the more or less stable structures of society construct gender reality by regulating and controlling the distribution of power and privilege (Pinar et al., 1996). For structural feminists, social structures constitute reality and in doing so replace human agency in the construction of gender meaning.

Where is the source of oppression located?

Three feminist perspectives can be delineated under the broad goals of the structural strand including (1) the radical feminist perspective, (2) the Marxist feminist perspective, and (3) the Socialist feminist perspective. Each of these perspectives differs based on the perception of the universal social structure or structures that contribute to the oppressive distribution of power between men and women.

Radical feminist perspective

Radical feminists locate oppression within patriarchal gender relations that use certain facts about male and female sexuality to construct masculine and feminine identity in ways that empower men and disempower women. Patriarchal gender relations are constructed around ideologies that associate masculinity with characteristics such as power, strength, aggression, and autonomy and femininity with characteristics such as subordination, appearance, frailty, and emotionality (Tong, 1998). Masculinity and femininity under patriarchy become relationally defined hegemonic constructions that result in the structuring of personal and social relationships that empower men as a group and justify the subordination of women as a group (Macdonald et al., 2002). Significant to radical feminist analysis in physical education, patriarchal gender relations historically constructed masculinity to encompass physicality in ways that excluded women from participation in sport and physical activity by virtue of the structure of the sex/gender system. The historical disassociation of femininity and physicality within patriarchal gender relations is evident in the following early excerpt from the *American Physical Education Review*:

> While the boy may indulge in vigorous effort to the limit of his strength, the girl must husband her resources. Woman represents the conservative tendency, man the progressive. Grace, poise and good form are important in the training of the female. The man must learn to achieve, accomplish and conquer. For the female, games should be played with caution … [Because] of the inability to stand prolonged physical strain, frequent intervals of rest should be given. (Orr, 1907: 56)

Orr's statement is relevant to understanding modern day radical feminist thinking in that it demonstrates how patriarchal ideologies when taken as "real" can create and recreate cultural practices that maintain gender oppression as status quo. Contemporary radical feminist research in physical education shows continuing evidence of patriarchal gender differentiation in physical education. For example, Nilges (1998, 2001) identified gender discrimination as a radical issue of power distribution rather than a liberal issue of opportunity by exposing a largely unchallenged "we–they" dichotomy in a physical education class (4th grade) in the United States.

This "we–they" dichotomy not only situated boys and girls as separate and different along patriarchal lines but also as largely unequal with physical power and space being surrendered to boys. Chepyator-Thompson et al. (1997) studied how patriarchal differentiation influenced secondary school students' constructions of gender. It was concluded that the majority of students selected activities and participated in physical education in ways that reflect the broadly accepted gender patterns of patriarchy in the larger society. Likewise, Santina et al. (1998) used patriarchal consciousness as a frame to study patterns of gender inequity in four middle schools in the United States. Findings indicated that the denial of girls' access to selected curriculum offerings, voluntary gender segregation by students during instruction, and perceptions of male superiority and female inferiority by students and teachers, led to alienation of girls and the perpetuation of patriarchy in physical education. While the last two studies (i.e., Chepyator-Thompson et al., 1997; Satina et al., 1998) do not specifically claim radical feminism as a frame, they clearly extend our knowledge of patriarchy as a potentially oppressive structure in physical education. These studies are examples of what I termed earlier to be "loose" applications of feminist theory.

Marxist feminist perspective

Marxist feminists locate oppression within the sexual division of labor that structures capitalist class relations (Whelehan, 1995). The economic structure of capitalist societies becomes central to investigating the source of women's oppression:

> The sexual division of labor is fundamental to this [Marxist] approach and focuses on how capital benefits from women's unpaid domestic labor and their maintenance of the future labor force (children) and the day to day care of male laborers. (Scraton and Flintoff, 2002: 36)

In this way, Marxist feminists see capitalist divisions in the labor force as the primary cause of oppression because such divisions exploit women by removing them from, or limiting their participation in, the "productive" workforce.

Historical analysis is fundamental to the Marxist feminist perspective. Hargreaves (1986, 2002) has contributed the most detailed application of Marxist feminism in sport and physical education to date. Working from a historical perspective, Hargreaves suggests the way capitalist economic structures historically promoted the "Victorian ideal" where women's dependent role as wife and mother left men free to accumulate capital, influenced the early direction of girls' physical education. Because a woman's work role was always secondary to her role in the family within the Victorian ideal, early physical education came to be designed to ensure girls the physical health necessary to produce strong and able workers. For example, exercise itself was believed to help a woman organize the perfect home while gymnastics was considered to be an ideal form of training for duties related to child bearing and motherhood.

Empirically the Marxist feminist perspective has not been well developed in physical education. It's interesting to note however that recent data from the United States Department of Health and Human Services (1996) not only outlines the health benefits of regular participation in physical activity for American citizens but also clearly indicates that engagement in physical activity is not equally distributed across gender and/or socioeconomic groups. At a historical point in time where obesity in the United Stated has reached epidemic proportions, this situation would appear to open itself nicely to Marxist feminist analysis.

Socialist feminist perspective

Socialist feminists contend Marxist feminists have said too little about women's oppression by men and therefore locate oppression in the intersection of both capitalism and patriarchy (Tong, 1998). Relative to physical education and sport, Bray (1988) suggests capitalism creates the structures within which physical education and sport must operate but patriarchy prepares and selects people for those structures. The example that follows demonstrates the intersection of capitalism and patriarchy within the dual systems theory of oppression endorsed by socialist feminists:

> The patriarchal imperative (articulated by a leadership that is primarily male) demand that men engage in physically aggressive, non-nurturing activities – such as sport – which do not prepare them for reproductive labor. Conversely, patriarchal leadership controls a society in which women learn nurturing behaviors, rather than aggressive behaviors, so they will continue to perform devalued labor [such as reproductive labor]. … Because boys and men are not expected to take on a major role in reproductive labor in capitalist patriarchy, there is no need to foster nurturing behaviors and nonviolent behavior in young boys. Indeed, preparation for the productive job market entails an emphasis on aggressiveness and independence. Such behaviors are thought to be fostered through sport participation and boys are often encouraged to participate in sports to prepare for their role as productive laborers. (Bray, 1988: 51)

Although socialist feminists use a dual systems approach in their theorizing, it has been argued that the socialist feminist perspective continues to give primacy to capitalism while underplaying patriarchy. As Scraton and Flintoff (2002: 36) indicate, "A major problem with socialist feminism is how the relationship between class and gender can be theorized without giving primacy to one or the other."

Scraton (1986, 1992) has contributed substantial socialist feminist research to physical education. This research centers on how girls' experiences in physical education and leisure are related to patriarchal images of masculinity and femininity as well as class location. Scraton emphasizes the relationship between physicality, sexuality, and motherhood in her analyses. More recently, Flintoff and Scraton (2001) used a structural analysis of economic and gender relations to understand how girls negotiated and managed their decisions to be physically active. Findings indicate that adolescent girls (15 years) from four case study schools in the UK, often cited structural constraints such as cost and transportation to and from a sporting venue to be deterrent from engaging in an active lifestyle outside of school physical education. Overall, the results were encouraging, however, in that many girls made positive choices about physical activity involvement both inside and outside of physical education regardless of the structural and social constraints identified.

Strategies to eliminate oppression

Because structural oppression builds exclusion into the legitimate knowledge structures of gender, class and/or capitalism it masquerades as status quo and can be difficult to recognize. Structural feminists use explicit structural analysis to document oppression and how, in everyday sites such as physical education, oppression has served the interests of those in power. Structural feminists endorse critique and consciousness-raising as a strategy to eliminate oppression. In doing so, they hope to give women the ideological tools needed to question gender, class and economic structures and patterns in light of the interests they serve. For structural feminists, therefore, oppression will be eliminated as women are helped to form a representation of reality that is not distorted in ways that empower men over women. As Whelehan (1995: 71) states, "Consciousness-raising was conceived as the most effective means of encouraging all women to acknowledge their entrenched secondary status." It is possible that broad efforts at consciousness-raising have begun to alter patriarchal gender ideologies. For example, at least some schoolage girls in the US (e.g. Chepyator-Thompson et al., 1997; Nilges) and the UK (e.g., Cockburn and Clarke, 2003) are actively resisting patriarchal notions of femininity by associating strength, sport participation, and physicality with femininity. In addition, more girls than ever in the UK are participating in physical activity outside of school, as well as, participating in a wider variety of activities (Flintoff and Scraton, 2001).

Limitations of the structural feminist perspectives

A primary limitation of the structural feminist perspective is that individual differences are obscured within structurally driven theories of oppression that situate "woman" and "man" as universal and homogeneous categories. Because gender reality within the structural feminist strand is determined by societal structures it tends to be ahistorical, deterministic, and leaves little room for taking into account the sociopolitical construction of the structural systems themselves (Pinar et al., 1996; Tong, 1998; Whelehan, 1995). As feminist theory continued to evolve from the early 1980s to the present time this was viewed as problematic to understanding gender oppression in terms of difference rather than sameness. Said another way, if underlying structures are believed to constitute gender reality, then the languages and discourses that circulate within and around a given structure and how they come to influence people in different ways remain concealed. Thus, deconstructive feminists began to define perspectives that challenged this limitation.

Strand 3: Deconstructive

How is oppression defined?

To understand how oppression is defined in the deconstructive strand, the shift that occurred in the theoretical understanding of the world in the late 20th century requires consideration. Two major changes occurred including globalization and the shift from moderninity to post-modernity (Evans, 1997). Globalization in the late 20th century prompted a feminist reconceptualization of the concept of identity. As global markets and economies united countries and cultures more closely it became evident that differences between women and men within and across multiple identity categories (e.g. race, class, sexual orientation) were great. As a result feminists began to view the concept of identity as shifting and negotiable thus problematizing early feminist notions of "woman" and "man" as universal categories.

Also supporting the notion of shifting identities was the onslaught of postmodern thinking and living in much of the Western world. This shift, although far too complex to capture here, carried important features within which deconstructive feminists came to define their perspectives including the endorsement of "truth" as local and subjective (therefore capable of shifting within time and place) and a decentralized view of power (as opposed to centrally located power on the basis of biology or the overarching structures of society). The postmodern era came to mark a new point in social history where "being, thinking and speaking allowed for openness, plurality, diversity and difference" (Tong, 1998: 195). It is within the social climate of postmodernism that deconstructive feminist thought emerged in ways that challenged the universal and essentialist treatment of gender in the liberal and structural strands.

Deconstructive feminists and structural feminists both understand power in relational terms but their analysis of power differs significantly. Thompson explains:

> Whereas for structural theorists the operations of power can be understood as conforming to fairly regular patterns that maintain a particular balance (or rather, imbalance) between dominant and subordinate groups, for deconstructive theorists the permutations of oppressive power relations are endlessly variable, and therefore more difficult to challenge or change. (2003: 34)

Deconstructive feminists, therefore, believe it is no longer relevant or possible to seek a single "truth" or explanation of a particular issue such as gender or oppression. They locate gender meaning within language systems and discourses where meaning can never be fully present but only understood in relation to an infinite network of other words in a language and discourses that shift over time and place. Discourses form the subjects and objects of which they speak in that words, written or spoken, which group themselves according to certain rules established within the discourse, make their existence possible (Pinar et al., 1996). Discourses, revealed in and through language, are taken by deconstructive feminists to constitute gender in highly variable ways.

Deconstructive feminists argue strongly against dualistic constructions such as masculinity–femininity, where *this* construction of femininity can only be produced through reference to *that* masculinity. Derrida (1981) refers to such dualistic constructions as logocentric in that they presuppose truth. As presupposed truths, dualistic notions of gender, according to deconstructive feminists, universally entrap men and women in largely white, heterosexual, and Western (structural) recreations of the self. Since gender knowledge from a deconstructive standpoint is discursively mediated and located, women's experiences with oppression are likely to vary substantially over time and place.

Three feminist perspectives can be delineated under the broad tenets of the deconstructive strand, (1) the male feminist perspective, (2) the lesbian feminist perspective, and (3) the poststructural feminist perspective. It is evident within these perspectives that feminists began to focus on identity politics and conceive the potential for studying gender outside the boundaries of the political orientations that characterized earlier strands (Olesen, 2000; Whelehan, 1995). Broadly speaking these perspectives have increasingly differentiated the lives and subjectivities of women and men through discourse and language analysis. While it is not possible to pinpoint an exact definition and location of oppression within these perspectives due to the underlying tenets of the strand, each perspective does work from a particular starting point that distinguishes it from other deconstructive perspectives.

Male feminist perspective

The male feminist perspective centers on masculinity discourses and their impact on boys and physical activity. Male feminists explore how various discourses shape the lives of boys and how hegemonic masculinity, in particular, can act in both stifling and empowering ways (Whelehan, 1995). While there has been substantial debate over whether feminists should welcome the entrance of men into feminism or treat it with caution (e.g. Ramazanoglu, 2002; Robinson, 2003), male masculinity theorists have become increasing visible in feminism over the past two decades. Feminist theory was initially a space for women to theorize about and for women. Feminists are divided as to whether men and masculinity studies should be part of the feminist agenda. Some feminists contend that such inclusion diverts interest from women and does little more than re-establish women as the patriarchal "other" (e.g. Robinson, 2003). Other feminists are more positive and suggest that a clearer picture of gender relations can only be gained by considering femininity and masculinity relationally. For example, it has been suggested that the infiltration of men's feminism into gender research in physical education has added to the increasing complexity of gender as a discursive construct. As Scraton and Flintoff (2002: 37) offer, "the research and writing of profeminist men have contributed to our [physical education] knowledge of men's power and how men have to change if gender relations are to be equalized". Not only is it important for women to be conscious of the part played by men and masculinity in the production and reproduction of gender inequalities but it is also important that men begin to accept the challenge of working toward social change. Hall (1987, 2002) reinforces this notion indicating that slowly but surely feminist study in physical education and sport is moving away from an exclusive and restrictive focus on women and femininity to the relational nature of the gendered social behavior of both sexes.

Recent studies in physical education have focused on the impact of masculinity discourses on boys and their participation in physical activity. This work demonstrates how schooling practices and/or athletics teach boys manhood and the enactment of masculinity in multiple and shifting ways (e.g., Bramham, 2003; Gard, 2003; Parker, 1996). For example, Bramham (2003) used a profeminist perspective to deconstruct the concept of dominant hegemonic masculinity with boys (15-year-olds) in four inner city schools uncovering the ways in which physical activity is shaped by masculine identities and mediated through discursive processes that include staff, student friendship networks, class membership, and ethnic identity. Bramham concluded, "Individuals are not universally or inextricably determined by class and race identities, as boys negotiate individual ways through the demands of masculinity, with the help of friends, families and teachers" (p. 70). Connell endorses this type of non-universalizing view of masculinity:

> It is clear from the new social research as a whole that there is not one pattern of masculinity that is found everywhere. We need to speak of 'masculinities', not masculinity. Different cultures and different periods of history construct gender differently. (2000, 2002: 263)

In a case study of a multi-ethnic, inner city secondary school, Parker (1996) studied how popular sporting forms determine the masculine identities of adolescent males. Although masculinities were not found to differ among students of varying ethnic origin they were defined differentially across three groups on the basis of athletic ability (1) the hard boys, (2) the conformists, and (3) the victims. Reinforcing dominant images of masculinity and sport, the hard boys were the most athletic students. The hard boys were also the most likely to display aggressive and violent behavior in physical education and equate a lack of sporting ability with homosexuality. Although students displayed differing masculinities, the findings of this study support that the "hard boys" (or athletes) perpetuated dominant forms of masculinity to a greater extent than did their less physically competent peers.

Lesbian feminist perspective

The lesbian feminist perspective criticizes early liberal and structural feminist work for being far too heterogeneous. Like male feminists, lesbian feminists challenge the macro analyses of structural approaches to gender oppression. Lesbian feminists seek to disrupt the largely unconditional endorsement of heterosexuality (often described as "heteroreality") that exists elsewhere in feminism by discursively critiquing its part in women's oppression:

> [Lesbian feminists] recognize that lesbian sexual orientation affects all aspects of one's life, because people commonly perceive homosexuality as a sickness which incapacitates' people in all other areas of their lives – their eligibility for jobs, their fitness for parenthoods, and so forth. Therefore, these perceptions and the ideology of a heteroreality must be the focus for lesbian feminist politics. (Whelehan, 1995: 90)

Research in physical education from a lesbian feminist perspective has focused primarily on the lives of physical education teachers. For example, Clarke (1998) illustrated the complexities of the teaching and sporting lives of secondary physical education teachers in England emphasizing how multiple identities are constructed and managed in the workplace. Likewise, Sykes (2001) used deconstruction to investigate the homophobic silences of both lesbian and heterosexual physical education teachers in Canada focusing on the role of institutional discourses such as "women's team sports", "adolescent dating", and "whiteness". Sparkes (1994) also investigated the discursive construction of the life of a lesbian physical educator in the UK focusing on how what is said and not said relative to sexuality influences identity management.

Sykes (1998, 2001) reinforces the deconstructive positioning of lesbian feminist research suggesting it is always unfinished and partial in that language, speech, and discourses do not mirror lesbian experience but rather create it. The challenge for lesbian feminist researchers becomes providing insight into lesbian experiences in ways that help eliminate sexism, heterosexism, and homophobia in physical education and sport while resisting essentialist notions of lesbian identity that reinforce dualistic thinking about sexuality (Griffin, 1992, 2002; Veri, 1999).

Poststructural feminist perspective

The poststructural feminist perspective situates oppression in the discourses and languages through which certain identities, situations, and relationships come to be accepted as natural or normal. Poststructural feminists frequently draw from Michel Foucault's (1980, 1984) theorizing about power. Foucault argues against a view of power that is top down and centralized in favor of a decentralized view of power that circulates and shifts in ways that place subjects in the simultaneous position of undergoing and exercising power. Therefore, poststructural understandings of oppression must be considered on an individual basis and require analyzing the discourses through which subjects and their worlds are empowered, disempowered or come to actively resist the effects of power. For poststructural feminists research becomes an avenue for investigating how:

> … selves and social relations are constituted in particular relations of power-knowledge. Rather than being fixed or constituted in specific emobodied individuals, selves are taken to be constructs. The terms 'subject' and 'subjectivity(ies)' are used to denote ways in which selves are formed in and through language and other systems of meaning. (Macdonald et al., 2002: 142–143)

Feminist poststructural research has made a considerable contribution to our understanding of how social practices and discourses affect gender relations in physical activity settings (Wright, 1995). It is often entwined with other perspectives in situating feminist research. For example, Sykes (2001) used both poststructural and lesbian feminist perspectives in researching lesbian and heterosexual physical education teachers. Because power and the effects of power on the body are central to Foucault's thinking and physical education focuses directly on the body (Paechter, 2003), a good deal of poststructural research in physical education has taken an interest in how physical education and

sport discourses contribute to embodied meaning. For example, Oliver and Lalik's (2001) ongoing work with developing a critical "body" curriculum for adolescent girls in physical education demonstrates how and where girls learn to experience their bodies and come to adopt and/or resist forms of oppressive body enculturation. Likewise Wright (1996) studied how student talk and talk between teachers and students construct male and female bodies. Wright emphasized how the language students use to construct male and female bodies as largely opposite discursively maintains gender relations as complementary (i.e., where girls are situated as weaker and less skilled than boys and boys are situated as stronger and more highly skilled than girls). Also interested in embodiment, Nilges (2000) examined how gender is constructed within undergraduate students' educational gymnastics work through the non-verbal discourse of the moving body while Olafson (2002) investigated how adolescent girls' bodies are schooled into resistance in physical education through interactions with various social and cultural discourses (e.g., peers, the formal curriculum and instructional methods, and cultural messages about femininity).

Feminist theorizing about the body has also been used to study female athletes. For example, Rail (1990, 1992) studied how women basketball players embody and use physicality in the game, the emotions that surround it and the ways in which it helps them learn about and question their subjectivities and identities. Theberge (1997) studied how female ice hockey players in Canada embody gender and physicality. The results of this study deconstruct hegemonic views of femininity in that the athletes expressed empowerment and enjoyment in using their body assertively and aggressively at times in sport. Krane et al. (2004), investigated how female athletes ($n = 21$) negotiate and reconcile social expectations surrounding femininity and athleticism. They found that female athletes' perceptions of their bodies and their subjectivity in sport and society were not passive representations of hegemonic femininity. The athletes studied negotiated their femininity. They chose multiple definitions of femininity and actively shifted between these definitions. Thus, the sportswomen in this study, in different ways across different sports, developed and performed two identities – athlete and woman. This finding supports deconstructive feminist thought in that femininity and the body are defined in multiple, contextually specific, and shifting ways.

Strategies to eliminate oppression

Deconstructive feminists support deconstructionism as a strategy to eliminate oppression with the caveat that any effort to eliminate oppression can be only addressed locally and within the present historical moment because oppression itself is a situational and shifting discursive construction. Deconstructionism involves undercutting the "giveness" of received categories such as "masculinity– femininity", "heterosexuality–homosexuality", or "the body" with a focus on interrupting rather than critiquing power relations. As Thompson (2003: 20) explains, "Since our habits and expectations organize what and how we see, interruptions create a momentary, admittedly fragile, space for the development of new possibilities and ideas". Rather than accepting meaning as ready-made, deconstruction leads to provisional, situated, and multiple meanings that generate new perceptions of gender and/or the discourses around which it is constructed. Through alternative texts and explanations, deconstructive feminists attempt to empower women and men by redefining universal and logocentric presuppositions of truth in ways that do not reinvoke dominant discourses.

Deconstructionism as a change strategy is evident in Oliver and Lalik's (2001) study of the implementation of a critical body curriculum for girls in physical education and Gard's (2003) work with use of dance as a movement form to problematize the taken-for-grantedness of male embodiment. In Oliver and Lalik's (2001) study, the body is situated as a discursive site through which culture potentially perpetuates the oppression of women. The authors assist adolescent girls in critically deconstructing their concerns with their body through a planned curriculum where students critically interpret body texts, relate body texts to personal experiences, and discuss various ideas with their classmates about their body experiences. A primary goal of the curriculum is to help girls "disrupt" how they experience their bodies in dominant culture through a largely deconstructive process. Likewise Gard (2003) discusses the use of dance in anti-oppressive teaching, as opposed to more familiar movement forms, to help boys deconstruct the "giveness" of heterosexual male embodiment. According to Gard (2003: 220), "Dance movement is likely to be (at least initially) an uncomfortable experience for some students and that, whether we acknowledge it or not, much of the discomfort will be related to the gendered identities of these students". Because many boys continue to associate dance movement with femininity and homosexuality, dance itself presents an opportunity for deconstructing identity and "allowing students the pleasure (and pain) of being someone else" (Gard, 2003: 220). In each of these examples, deconstruction is used as a pedagogical tool for effecting change in local educational sites.

Limitations of the deconstructive feminist perspectives

While the perspectives of the deconstructive strand avoid the biological determinism of liberal feminism

and resist situating "man" and "woman" as universal categories, several criticisms often surface relative to this strand. First, because oppression within the deconstructive strand is situational and provisional, deconstructive feminists cannot offer a definite program for change (Thompson, 2003). If change can only occur within the here and now, there is reason to argue that the deconstructive perspectives overemphasize identity politics to the extent that any sense of the collectivity and common purpose in the feminist community is largely lost. The danger of situating difference as a primary concern becomes that concrete rallying points for justice are lost in a loosely defined feminism shaped only by fleeting moments of power, identity, and oppression. Ramazanoglu and Holland (2002) indicate that women can only constitute the subject of feminism if they share at least some degree of gendered social position.

In an effort to disrupt and deconstruct the "giveness" of many of the core tenets of earlier feminist strands, Whelehan argues that deconstructive feminist thought has also produced a "garden of intellectual delights" (1995: 207) with language being used in such a specific way that it becomes increasingly irrelevant to everyday individuals. Much deconstructive feminist thinking, therefore, is accused of originating in the academy and being too academic in content to be practical to, or practicably applied by, most women and men (Tong, 1998).

Feminist strands: concluding comments

Prior to turning to methodological issues in feminist research a few closing comments relative to the strands are needed. Flintoff and Scraton (2001) indicate that feminist theorizing in physical education and sport has been substantial over the last 30 years. They credit the increasing volume and sophistication of feminist work in physical education to key theoretical developments in feminism at large. Therefore, understanding key differences between the strands and perspectives is valuable for feminist scholars in physical education who are attempting to locate their work. The strands were reviewed here in the order in which they broadly appeared in feminist thought. Each strand increased in theoretical complexity and emerged in response to particular issues identified in feminist thinking and writing at large. This is not to suggest, however, that one replaced the other. All strands and perspectives continue to inform feminist research. Recognizing the strengths, limitations and key tenets of each is important to making informed choices about the design and conduct of feminist research not only now but in the future as feminism continues to evolve.

Doing feminist research: epistemology and methodology

Feminist methodology is concerned with epistemological questions relative to how we come to know and the procedures and processes that are used to make knowledge valid and authoritative (Campbell and Wasco, 2000; Naples, 2003; Ramazanoglu and Holland, 2002). The production of feminist knowledge has contributed to a shift in research practices in many disciplines, including physical education. Largely challenging traditional notions of scientific method, feminist scholars have developed alternative epistemologies to guide research and have articulated new visions for the process of doing research. Ramazanoglu and Holland state:

> The academic area of feminist methodology was initiated primarily as a way of characterizing existing methods of producing knowledge as masculine and of challenging existing gendered understandings of social life. In general feminists were critical of ways of producing supposedly scientific knowledge of social life that claimed to be politically neutral, or gender neutral, while in practice promoting, reproducing or ignoring men's appropriation of science and reason. (2002: 15)

Well-designed feminist research is more than simply adopting a feminist perspective; it requires explicit consideration of how knowledge is produced and how inquiry is conducted. Epistemological and methodological issues related to feminist research are outlined next.

What is feminist epistemology?

The epistemological question in social research centers on the nature of knowledge and how knowledge is constituted in the research process (Campbell and Wasco, 2000; DeVault, 1996). There are three epistemological positions that can be used to situate the nature of knowledge within feminist work, *feminist empiricism, feminist standpoint,* and *feminist postmodernism.* Each epistemological position generally (but not exclusively) aligns with a particular feminist strand and is concerned with the link between knowledge and experience and what will be the basis for legitimate authority in feminist research.

Feminist empiricism

Feminist empiricism is the least radical of the epistemological positions in terms of its disruption of traditional notions of science. Feminist empiricism does not call for structural changes to science itself.

This epistemological stance is typically taken in liberal feminist research where (1) an objective gender reality is assumed to exist, the (2) research design tends to be more traditional, and (3) the researcher retains a detached subject–object relationship. Because feminist empiricism assumes that a real, objective world does exist, it is the researchers' responsibility to capture that world in a way that doesn't reflect gender bias. As part of the inquiry process, a researcher grounded in an epistemology of feminist empiricism might explicitly examine research questions to ensure they don't reflect gender stereotypes, ensure gender fair sampling, and neither ignore nor overemphasize gender difference in analyses. In this way feminist empiricism promotes authority in feminist knowledge by ensuring it was generated through a "gender-fair" research process.

Feminist standpoint

Structural feminists who view gender as unjustly constructed by the political, social, and/or economic structures in which women live often work from an epistemology grounded in feminist standpoint. Feminist standpoint signals two critical epistemological assumptions about the nature and production of feminist knowledge.

First, valid feminist knowledge is subjectively determined and must start with the experiences of women and how their experiences extend from and/or are related to their particular gendered, raced, or classed position (or standpoint). This assumes that valid feminist knowledge is (1) grounded in the actual voices of women and their experiences and (2) that a direct connection exists between experience and knowledge (Harding, 1987; Stanley and Wise, 1993). Researchers, therefore, situate women themselves as knowing subjects and by getting inside their lives attempt to understand the structural workings of power and its influence on gender construction. DeVault (1996) suggests standpoint provides an appropriate site for viewing social organization because it locates the researcher and the researched in the material places in which they live as opposed to a contrived or distanced research setting.

Second, standpoint epistemology positions the researcher as an active, rather than detached, participant in the construction of feminist knowledge. Knowledge produced from an epistemology of feminist standpoint necessitates that the researcher reflect on how her/his own social positioning potentially influences their interpretations. Because the feminist researcher can "know" only from a specific and partial social location, making the "self" visible in the research process is critical to valid knowledge claims. From an epistemological perspective, feminist standpoint attempts to produce a less distorted view of scientific knowledge by situating "science itself as a social product, that scientists are socially constructed human beings with a partial vision and that no scientific method ensures access to some incontrovertible truth" (Ramazanoglu and Holland, 2002: 44). For example, as feminist researchers in physical education, Scraton and Flintoff (2002) discuss how their work is necessarily grounded in their lives as white, middle class, heterosexual women and the particular location and realities of the women with whom they conduct research. It follows that there are multiple feminist standpoints, each necessarily dependent on specific situations and researchers.

Feminist postmodernism

Feminists working within the deconstructive strand believe it is neither relevant nor possible to seek a single "truth" or explanation of a particular issue such as gender or oppression. As an epistemological position, feminist postmodernism aligns with the deconstructive strand of feminism. Feminist postmodernism challenges the authority of feminist knowledge undercutting the notion that valid feminist knowledge is grounded in the experiences of women. It not only rejects the fundamental assumptions and values of science but also questions whether a distinct feminist science is even possible.

Feminist postmodernism situates valid feminist knowledge as grounded in the world and endless stories, or texts, that are capable of being told based on our interaction with various discourses. In this way, authoritative knowledge from an epistemological position of feminist postmodernism is inherently subjective and bound by the limitations of language. This means a direct connection between experience and knowledge does not exist (it is mediated through language) and knowledge claims must always (1) be taken as partial and incomplete and (2) be represented in ways that resist finality and are open to multiple readings (in physical education see Sykes, 2001). Knowledge claims of this sort that place authority in partiality and a lack of finishness sharply contrast the direct connection between knowledge and truth that characterizes traditional science. Ramazanoglu and Holland state:

> Once any direct connection between truths produced by scientific methods and some true, external reality are denied, feminist knowledge, like other claims to knowledge of social life, are just political fictions that cannot have a testable relationship with an external, real world. (2002: 86–87)

In this sense, any suggestion of "truth" in feminist research becomes what Olesen (2000) calls a destructive illusion because feminists can never produce more than a partial story of women's lives. *Why think epistemologically?* For researchers

unfamiliar with epistemological debates in social science, the notion of feminist epistemology might appear removed from the practical demands of designing and conducting research. Different epistemological positions have different implications for explicating the kind of relationships that exist between knowledge and power. Situating a research question in relation to epistemology means deciding what constitutes authoritative knowledge of gender and/or oppression and under what conditions it can be judged as believable or valid (Naples, 2003; Ramazanoglu and Holland, 2002). Since different feminist epistemologies establish different "rules" for what counts as "good" knowledge, epistemological positions serve to authorize feminist knowledge. Feminist research that is conducted using a clear perspective and epistemological position is less likely to have its authority and believability challenged or discredited as mere opinion.

What is feminist methodology?

Olesen (2000) indicates that variations in feminist thinking have "opened and upended" taken-for-granted conceptualizations of doing research. To create feminist approaches to research, feminist scholars have not only redefined the nature of knowledge (epistemology) but articulated new and/or reworked methodological processes for conducting research (Campbell and Wasco, 2000). These processes are considered next including locating the researcher, voice and representation, emotionality, and praxis.

Locating the researcher

Research from a feminist perspective resists situating the researcher as an all-knowing and distanced seeker of objective knowledge. Because gendered lives are difficult to access directly, much feminist research is done in a face-to-face context. Like all social researchers feminist researchers must carefully establish trust and rapport with participants particularly when techniques are used that involve direct personal contact. Ramazanoglu and Holland indicate traditional hierarchies between the researcher and the research do little to encourage trust and rapport:

> In social research, the researcher and the researched always stand in some social relationship to each other but these relationships are rarely balanced, or ones with fully shared meanings. Feminist research relationships need critical examination rather than any prior assumption of shared identity. (2002: 106)

Since researchers have a history and a gender that enter into any research interaction, feminists often foreground their own subjectivity within their work to establish rapport with participants. This strategy is believed to help level hierarchy and control in research relationships. Oleson (2000), however, notes that this development did not go unmarked by more traditional social scientists that tend to link subjective measures of establishing rapport with in inherent bias. To combat the "how close is too close" argument in feminist research, Harding (1993) argues for the use of "strong objectivity" in feminist research where the relationship between the researcher and participants is investigated and acknowledged from a situated perspective rather than denied any existence at all. To balance power in research relationships it is recommended that feminist researchers locate themselves decisively "inside" the research account rather than on the "outside looking in". In physical education, the accounts of Sykes (1998, 2001) and Oliver and Lalik (2001) clearly position the researchers inside the research agenda, thus a sense of how the knowledge was produced and how research interactions took place is continually evident.

Voice and representation

The politics of representation in feminist research involve how and where researchers potentially exercise power in turning peoples lives into authoritative texts. Since a primary goal of feminist research is to give voice to women, decisions relative to how participant voices are heard, with what authority, and in what form are critical elements of the feminist research process. Sykes (2001: 16) contemplated the dilemma of voice when researching life histories of heterosexual and lesbian physical education teachers indicating she was "painfully aware that not foregrounding the women's stories 'as they were told' risked subjecting the women to textual erasure and silencing". Feminist researchers need to be sensitive to the ongoing tensions between making voices heard in research accounts and the potential that exists for exploiting or misrepresenting voices particularly when differences (e.g., gender, race, class, sexuality) exist between the researcher and those that are researched. Fine (1992) identifies worrisome issues of voice for feminist researchers including the use of pieces of narratives out of context, taking individual voices to reflect the ideas of groups (overgeneralizing), and assuming that voices are free of power relations. To acknowledge and manage the exercise of power in knowledge production, Fine (1992) encourages feminist researchers to indicate as part of their methodology how and within what limits voices are framed and used in a particular research account.

Related to voice are issues of representation in feminist research. A substantial body of experimental writing in feminist research and the social

sciences at large has recently emerged (Richardson, 2000). Experimental writing alters the distant and omniscient writing style and textual form of traditional research using poetry, fiction, narrative, and/or performance texts to represent knowledge. While experimental forms of representation are becoming an increasingly visible methodological strategy in feminist research at large (see Richardson, 2000 for a review) and physical education and sport research at large (see Sparkes, 2002 for a review), they are just beginning to emerge in feminist research in physical education. An example here includes Nilges' (2001) use of an experimental writing format referred to as an impressionist tale to textualize a study of patriarchal gender construction in physical education. This account demonstrates how opening qualitative feminist research to a wider variety of rhetorical devices can change what is "known" about gender construction in elementary school physical education. Nilges' (2001) impressionist tale contrasts more traditional styles of writing research using metaphor and the temporal sequencing of fact and fiction to provide an imaginative rendering of fieldwork that allows readers to directly see, hear, and feel what occurred in the physical education class that was studied. Sparkes alludes to the powerful decisions related to voice and representation that confront feminist researchers in physical education:

> No textual staging can ever be innocent. Whose voices are included in the text, how they are given weight and interpreted, along with questions of priority and juxtaposition, are not just textual strategies but are political concerns that have moral consequences. (1999: 159)

Emotionality

The dismissal of emotions from the research process is typically connected to the pursuit of academic objectivity. However, feminist research assumes researcher subjectivity thus freeing up emotions to become a crucial part of the research process (Campbell and Wasco, 2000). Reger (2001) identifies emotions as physical and mental responses that are grounded in social contexts and interactions. Researchers often find feminist research to be an emotional experience with some sense of attachment felt toward the topic or the participants. Acknowledging a space for emotions in the production of feminist knowledge can make using an objective voice in accounts not only difficult for researchers but incongruent with feminism's attempt to establish a relationship between the researcher and the researched:

> Difficult for many feminist researchers is adopting an objective academic voice, devoid of emotion, while addressing the feminist research imperative

of attending to the relationship between the researcher and the researched. (Reger, 2001: 606)

From a methodological standpoint the question becomes (1) what to do with the emotions that arise from the research process and (2) how the process of feminist research can be used to link emotions and knowledge (Campbell and Wasco, 2000). By situating emotions as data and exploring their affective roots, new types of subjective knowledge can be authorized. Rather than viewing emotions as a violation of objectivity, Ramazanoglu and Holland (2002) suggest that emotions provide valuable spaces to think differently and make new connections about a topic of study and the emotional intensity of a researcher being in meaning laden spaces. Although the role of the emotional dimension in the conduct of feminist research has surfaced in a good deal of writing about feminist methodology, emotional analysis has yet to surface in a feminist research project in physical education. Reger's (2001) investigation of the emotions that were experienced (i.e., fear, guilt, and anger) during a study of a local women's bookstore provides an excellent example of emotional analysis and offers additional references.

Praxis

A key methodological feature of feminist research is that it should promote praxis defined here as other research or action that helps transcend and transform gender through institutional and/or personal change. According to Hall:

> Praxis acknowledges that what goes on in academe, at least as far as feminism is concerned, should be directed at producing the kind of useful knowledge wanted and needed by those outside academe who are working for social change. The [methodological] issue then is how to connect theory and research to the real world. (1996: 78)

By implication there are many kinds of change that could result from feminist research in physical education including bringing new topics to the discipline, initiating consciousness-raising on the basis of research findings, and/or influencing policy decisions as a result of research.

There is no shortage of feminist research in physical education that concludes with a call for political and social action (see for example, Cockburn and Clarke, 2003) and/or modifications in curricular content and/or teaching strategies (see, for example, Chepyator-Thompson et al., 1997; Flintoff and Scraton, 2001; Gard, 2003; Nilges, 1998; Wright, 1995). However, Devault (1996) suggests change should not merely be a slogan in feminist methodology making the larger issue related to praxis whether or not feminist research in physical education does in fact influence actual change. For example, Chepyator-Thompson et al. (1997) conclude their study of reproduction and resistance to cultures of masculinity and femininity in secondary school physical education with suggestions for reforming practices in teacher education and school physical education. It's difficult to know, however, if the results of the research and the suggestions for change that are offered did initiate any changes in the teacher education practices of the researchers or the day-to-day practices of the secondary teachers involved in the study. In this regard, Macdonald (2002) raises speculation as to whether gender research in physical education has effectively changed what goes on in schools and suggests that many schools continue to look for strategies and practices that promote equity and justice despite the research that has been produced. From a methodological perspective, feminist research should not lose sight of its indebtedness to change and researchers must work toward accountability and change if the principle of feminist praxis is to be upheld to the fullest extent.

There are notable examples of praxis in feminist research in physical education. Scraton and Flintoff (1992) discuss a study in which they investigated how images of femininity and the social construction of gender-appropriate behavior are reinforced or challenged by the structure, content and teaching of girl's physical education in secondary schools. Reflections by one of the researchers on this project demonstrate a commitment to using research to influence change:

> ... although I felt unable to intervene during the research process, I thought it important to not only 'take' from the research situation. Thus having made contacts throughout the schools, I tried to 'pay back' by becoming involved in various anti-sexist/equal opportunity initiatives that began in the years to follow. (Scraton and Flintoff, 1992: 183)

Wright's (1999) work also demonstrates how research can be used to change gendered practices in physical education. As part of a funded research development grant by the Department of Education and Training (DET) in Australia, teachers ($n = 120$) underwent a workshop designed to help increase their awareness of gender issues and the construction of gender in physical education. Survey follow-up to the workshop showed at least some teachers were positively influenced by the workshop and had either begun to implement some changes or indicated they were making plans to introduce gender reform strategies in their classes. Thus, in its initial stage, Wright's (1999) project appeared "praxis-oriented" in that it led to actual changes in teachers' instructional practices.

Feminist epistemology and methodology: concluding comments

Taken together feminist epistemology and feminist methodology provide an alternative to the often dispassionate, distanced and objective positioning and procedures of traditional science. DeVault (1996: 45) reminds us "theory does not translate unproblematically to questions of empirical investigation". Feminist scholars in physical education should carefully consider not only the feminist strands and perspectives in designing and conducting inquiry but epistemological and methodological issues as well. Like the feminist strands and perspectives the epistemological and methodological issues surrounding feminist research have diversified. As the nature of science continues to shift in the social context of the 21st century, researchers need to be increasingly more skilful at speaking to the validity and authority of feminist knowledge and the ways in which feminist knowledge claims are methodologically generated.

Problems, possibilities and feminist research in physical education

The volume of writing on feminist theory and methodology has increased dramatically in recent years. It would be misleading to suggest that the information presented here is all encompassing. This chapter is necessarily short and therefore relatively selective. For any feminist strand, perspective or epistemological, or methodological issue that was presented there have been volumes written. In addition, there are many overlapping features within the strands and perspectives that are lost by separating out and labeling the different feminisms for discussion purposes. Readers are encouraged to use the information here not as an ending point but as a starting point for more fully investigating feminism as a complex, diverse, and evolving research perspective. In this regard I agree with Tong (1998: 9) who states, "My overriding hope is that this [chapter] will prompt its readers to think themselves into the fullness of being feminism intends". With that said three concluding thoughts, however, seem appropriate.

First, although feminist research itself was not the objective of this chapter, it will be further dealt with in other areas of this book including the chapters on post-structuralism, sexuality, masculinities, and physical activity for girls and women. In detailing the strands, perspectives and methodological issues related to feminist research, however, it is evident that much feminist research in physical education is what I termed earlier as "loosely" defined. I found myself continually referring to the well-developed feminist work of Flintoff and Scraton (2001), Wright (1995), Oliver and Lalik (2001) and Sykes (1998, 2001) when exemplifying various aspects of the feminist research process. I hope this chapter reminds feminist scholars that well-designed feminist research is a process rather than merely a perspective. Well-articulated (or tight) feminist research requires solid theoretical, epistemological, and methodological positioning as the strands and/or perspectives in and of themselves do not translate easily to questions of empirical investigation. Researchers, consumers of research, and reviewers should be cautious of any study that claims to sit in a broad feminist frame as the implications of such broadness render any knowledge claim nearly meaningless.

Second, Kirk (2002) in reference to physical education in Great Britain and O'Sullivan, Ghering and Bush (2002) in reference to physical education in the United States, provide compelling evidence that although progress has been made toward more inclusive schooling, many students leave schools with traditional conceptions of masculinity and femininity relative to sport and physical activity unchallenged. Therefore, the ongoing need for feminist research to make a commitment to influencing actual change (praxis) is critical to helping students of the future transcend and transform such conceptions. There should not be a gap between feminist theory and feminist practice in physical education although such a disjunction has been argued to exist (Hall, 1996; Macdonald, 2002). Feminist researchers need to continue to expand inquiry beyond students in schools to include teachers and teachers' lives, as well as the factors and/or discourses that influence student and teacher identities relative to gender and physical activity outside of schools. Only then might feminism help physical educators develop a more complete understanding of the contexts and processes through which social change may be promoted. At the same time teacher educators need to understand the ways schools operate to reconstitute gender inequality in order to intervene at the level of teacher preparation (Mahony, 2000). This type of understanding could also be implicated through feminist research designed with praxis in mind. As Tinning (2002: 24) argues, "issues related to gender equity, equality, quality of opportunity, catering to diversity and challenging unjust practices should be an integral part of physical education". Macdonald (2002), however, issues caution suggesting that the increasing complexity of feminist research in terms of the questions being asked and the perspectives being used might do little to influence meaningful change as many schools remain conservative in their orientation, while Dewar (1991) acknowledges that encouraging students to critically examine and reflect on their own oppressive beliefs related to sexism, classism, and/or heterosexism can be challenging. Change itself has proven difficult in physical education particularly when set by the parameters of feminist thinking and unfortunately, as Hall (1996) indicates, many sport and physical educators continue to view feminism as a dirty word.

Finally, it is important that scholars do not lose sight of how feminist theory has evolved over the last 40 years particularly in relation to its move from focusing on all men and all women as universal to increasingly differentiating the subjectivities of both women and men. Understanding the history of feminism and what research has been done in physical education in the name of feminism is critical to moving into the future without undue repetition, as new feminisms will undoubtedly continue to emerge from existing theoretical positions.

Acknowledgment

I would like to thank Dr. Susan K. Lynn for providing me with access to The Florida State University library system while gathering literature for this chapter.

Please send correspondence regarding this chapter to Lynda M. Nilges, University of South Carolina, Department of Physical Education, Columbia, SC, USA 29208, lnilges@gwm.sc.edu.

References

Bramham, P. (2003). Boys, masculinities and PE. *Sport, Education and Society*. *8*(1), 57–71.

Bray, C. (1988). Sport and social change: Socialist feminist theory. *Journal of Physical Education, Recreation and Dance*, *59* (1), 50–53.

Brown, D. (1999). Complicity and reproduction in teaching physical education. *Sport, Education and Society*, *4* (2), 143–159.

Campbell, R. and Wasco, S. (2000). Feminist approaches to social science: Epistemological and methodological tenets. *American Journal of Community Psychology*, *28* (6), 773–791.

Chepyator-Thompson, P., Jepkorir, R. and Ennis, C. (1997). Reproduction and resistance to the culture of masculinity and femininity in secondary school physical education. *Research Quarterly for Exercise and Sport*, *68* (1), 88–99.

Clarke, G. (1998). Queering the pitch and coming out to play: Lesbians in physical education and sport. *Sport, Education and Society*, *3* (2), 145–160.

Cockburn, C. and Clarke, G. (2002). Everybody's looking at you!: Girls negotiating the "femininity deficit" they incur in physical education. *Women's Studies International Forum*, *25* (6), 651–665.

Connell, R.W. (2002). Debates about men, new research on masculinities. In S. Scraton and A. Flintoff (Eds.), *Gender and sport: A reader* (pp. 161–168) New York: Routelege. (Reprinted from *Men and the boys*, 2000, 3–5, 10–14 and 29–32).

DeVault, M. (1996). Talking back to sociology: Distinctive contributions of feminist methodology. *Annual Review of Sociology*, *22*, 29–50.

Derrida, J. (1981). *Dissemination*. (B. Johnson, Trans.). London: Athlone.

Dewar, A. (1991). Feminist pedagogy in physical education: Promises, possibilities and pitfalls. *Journal of Physical Education, Recreation and Dance*, *62* (1), 68–77.

Evans, M. (1997). *Introducing contemporary feminist thought*. Cambridge, UK: Polity Press.

Fine, M. (1992). Passions, politics and power: Feminist research possibilities. In M. Fine (Ed.), *Disruptive voices: The possibilities of feminist research* (pp. 205–232). Ann Arbor, MI: University of Michigan Press.

Flintoff, A. and Scraton, S. (2001). Stepping into active leisure: Young women's perceptions of active lifestyles and their experiences of school physical education. *Sport, Education and Society*, *6* (1), 5–21.

Foucault, M. (1980). *Power/knowledge: Selected interviews and other writings 1972–1977* In C. Gordon (Ed.), (C. Gordon, L. Marshall, J. Mepham and K. Soper, Trans.). New York: Pantheon Books. (Original works published 1972, 1975, 1976, 1977).

Foucault, M. (1984). In P. Rainbow (Ed.), *The Foucault Reader*. New York: Routelege.

Gard, M. (2001). Dancing around the "problem" of boys and dance. *Discourse*, *22* (2), 213–225.

Gard, M. (2003). Being someone else: Using dance in anti-oppressive teaching. *Educational Review*, *55* (2), 211–223.

Griffin, P. (2002). Changing the game: Homophobia, sexism and lesbians in sport. In S. Scraton and A. Flintoff (Eds.), *Gender and sport: A reader* (pp. 193–208). New York: Routelege. (Reprinted from *Quest*, 1992, *44* (2), 251–265).

Guba, E. and Lincoln, Y. (1994). Competing paradigms in qualitative research. In N. Denzin and Y. Lincoln (Eds.), *Handbook of Qualitative Research* (pp. 105–117). Thousand Oaks, CA: Sage.

Hall, M.A. (1996). *Feminisms and sporting bodies: Essays on theory and practice*. Champaign, IL: Human Kinetics.

Hall, M.A. (2002). The discourse of gender and sport: From femininity to feminism. In S. Scraton and A. Flintoff (Eds.), *Gender and sport: A reader*, (pp. 6–17). New York: Routelege. (Reprinted from *Sociology of Sport Journal*, 1988, 5: 330–340).

Harding, S. (1987). *Feminism and methodology*. Bloomington, IN: Indiana University Press.

Harding, S. (1993). Rethinking standpoint epistemologies: What is strong objectivity?. In L. Alcoff and E. Potter (Eds.), *Feminist epistemologies*. London: Routeledge.

Hargreaves, J. (1986). *Sport, power and culture*. Cambridge: Polity Press.

Hargreaves, J. (2002). The Victorian cult of the family in the early years of female sport. In S. Scraton and A. Flintoff (Eds.), *Gender and sport: A reader* (pp. 53–65). New York: Routelege. (Reprinted from *The Sports Process* by E. Dunning, Ed., 1993, Champaign, IL: Human Kinetics).

Howard, J. and Allen, C. (2000). Introduction: Feminisms at the millenium. In J. Howard and C. Allen (Eds.), *Feminisms at the millennium* (pp. 5–18). Chicago, IL: University of Chicago Press.

ILEA (1984). *Providing equal opportunities for boys and girls in physical education.* London: ILEA.

Krane, V., Choi, Y.L., Baird, S., Aimar, C. and Kauer, K. (2004). Living the paradox: Female athletes negotiate femininity and muscularity. *Sex Roles, 50* (5–6), 315–329.

Kirk, D. (2002). Physical education: A gendered history. In D. Penny (Ed.), *Gender and physical education: Contemporary issues and future directions* (pp. 24–37). New York: Routledge.

Lenskyj, H. (1997). No fear? Lesbians in sport and physical education. *Women in Sport and Physical Activity Journal, 6* (2), 7.

Luke, M. and Sinclair, C. (1991). Gender differences in adolescents' attitudes toward school physical education. *Journal of Teaching in Physical Education, 11*: 31–46.

Markula, P. (2003). The technologies of self: Sport, feminism and Foucault. *Sociology of Sport Journal, 20* (2): 87–107.

Macdonald, D. (1990). The relationship between sex composition of physical education and teacher/pupil verbal interaction. *Journal of Teaching in Physical Education, 9* (2), 152–63.

Macdonald, D. (2002). Extending agendas: Physical culture research in the 21st century. In D. Penny (Ed.), *Gender and physical education: Contemporary issues and future directions.* (pp. 208–222). New York: Routledge.

Macdonald, D., Kirk, D., Metzler, M., Nilges, L., Schempp, P. and Wright, J. (2002). It's all very well in theory: Theoretical perspectives and their applications in contemporary pedagogical research. *Quest, 54* (2), 133–156.

Mahony, P. (2000). Teacher education and feminism. *Women's Studies International Forum, 23* (6), 767–775.

Mechikoff, R. and Estes, S. (2002). *A history and philosophy of sport and physical education: From ancient civilization to the modern world* (3rd Ed.). New York: McGraw-Hill.

Naples, N. (2003). *Feminism and method.* New York: Routledge.

Nilges, L. (1998). I thought only fairy tales had supernatural power: A radical feminist analysis of Title IX in physical education. *Journal of Teaching in Physical Education, 1* (2), 172–194.

Nilges, L. (2000). A nonverbal discourse analysis of gender in undergraduate educational gymnastics sequences using Laban effort analysis. *Journal of Teaching in Physical Education, 19* (3), 287–310.

Nilges, L. (2001). The twice told tale of Alice's physical life in Wonderland: Writing qualitative research in the 21st century. *Quest, 53,* 231–259.

Nilges, L. (in press) Ice can look like glass: A phenomenological investigation of movement meaning in one fifth-grade class during a creative dance unit. *Research Quarterly for Exercise and Sport.*

O'Sullivan, M., Bush, K. and Gehering, M. (2002). Gender equity and physical education: A USA perspective. In D. Penny (Ed.), *Gender and physical education: Contemporary issues and future directions* (pp. 163–189). New York: Routledge.

Olafson, L. (2002). I hate phys. ed.: Adolescent girls talk about physical education. *The Physical Educator, 59* (2), 67–74.

Olesen, V. (2000). Feminism and qualitative research at and into the millennium. In N. Denzin and Y. Lincoln (Eds.), *Handbook of qualitative research* (2nd Ed.) (pp. 215–255). Thousand Oaks, CA: Sage.

Olesen, V. and Clarke, A. (1999). Resisting closure, embracing uncertainties, creating agendas. In A.E. Clarke and V.L. Olesen (Eds.), *Revisioning women, health and healing: Feminist, cultural and technoscience perspectives,* (pp. 355–357). New York: Routledge.

Oliver, K.L. and Lalik, R. (2001). The body as curriculum: Learning with adolescent girls. *Journal of Curriculum Studies, 33* (3), 303–333.

Orr, W. (1907). The place for athletics in the curriculum of secondary schools for girls and boys. *American Physical Education Review, 12* (1), 49–59.

Paechter, C. (2003). Power, bodies and identity: How different forms of physical education construct varying degrees of masculinity and femininity in secondary schools. *Sex Education, 3* (1), 47–59.

Park, R. and Hult, J. (1993). Women as leaders in physical education and school-based sports, 1985 to the 1930s. *Journal of Physical Education, Recreation and Dance, 64* (3), 35–40.

Parker, A. (1996). The construction of masculinity within boys physical education. *Gender and Education, 8* (2), 141–157.

Pinar, W., Reynolds, W., Slattery, P. and Taubman, P. (1996). *Understanding curriculum.* New York: Peter Lang.

Ramazanoglu, C. (2002). What can you do with a man: Feminism and the critical appraisal of masculinity. *Women's Studies International Forum, 15* (3), 339–350.

Ramazanoglu, C. and Holland, J. (2002). *Feminist methodology: Challenges and choices.* Thousand Oaks, CA: Sage.

Rail, G. (1990). Physical contact in women's basketball: A first interpretation. *International Review for the Sociology of Sport, 25,* 269–285.

Rail, G. (1992). Physical contact in women's basketball: A phenomenological construction and contextualization. *International Review for the Sociology of Sport, 27,* 1–27.

Reger, J. (2001). Emotions, objectivity and voice: An analysis of a "failed" participant observation. *Women's Studies International Forum, 24* (5), 605–615.

Richardson, L. (2000). Writing: A method of inquiry. In N. Denzin and Y. Lincolon (Eds.), *Handbook of qualitative research* (2nd Ed. pp. 923–948). Thousand Oaks, CA: Sage.

Robinson, V. (2003). Radical revisionings?: The theorizing of masculinity and (radical) feminist theory. *Women's Studies International Forum, 26* (2), 129–137.

Santina, B., Solmon, M., Cothran, D., Loftus, S. and Stockin-Davidson, K. (1998). Patriarchal consciousness: Middle school students' and teachers' perspectives of motivational practices. *Sport, Education and Society, 3* (2), 181–200.

Schacht, S. (1997). Feminist fieldwork in the misogynist setting of the rugby pitch: Temporarily becoming a sylph to survive and personally grow. *Journal of Contemporary Ethnography, 26*, 338–363.

Scraton, S. (1986). Images of femininity and the teaching of girls physical education. In J. Evans (Ed.), *Physical education, sport and schooling: Studies in the sociology of physical education* (pp. 71–94). Lewes: Falmer Press.

Scraton, S. (1992). *Shaping up to womanhood: Girls and physical education.* Milton Keynes: Open University Press.

Scraton, S. and Flintoff, A. (1992). Feminist research and physical education. In A. Sparkes (Ed.), *Research in physical education and sport: Exploring alternative visions* (pp.167–187). London: Falmer Press.

Scraton, S. and Flintoff, A. (2002). Sport feminism: The contribution of feminist thought to our gender understanding of sport. In S. Scraton and A. Flintoff (Eds.), *Gender and sport: A reader* (pp. 30–46). New York: Routledge.

Shuiteman, J. and Knoppers, A. (1987). An examination of gender differences in scholarly productivity among physical educators. *Research Quarterly for Exercise and Sport, 60*, 159–165.

Smeal, G. and Carpenter, B. (1993). Feminism, physical education and the realities of the classroom. *Feminist Teacher, 7* (3), 33–41.

Sparkes, A. (1994). Self, silence and invisibility as a beginning teacher: A life history of lesbian experience. *British Journal of Sociology of Education, 15* (1), 93–118.

Sparkes, A. (1995). Writing people: Reflections on the dual crisis of representation and legitimation in qualitative inquiry. *Quest, 47* (2), 158–195.

Sparkes, A. (2002). *Telling tales in sport and physical activity: A Qualitative journey.* Champaign, IL: Human Kinetics.

Stanley, L. and Wise, S. (1993). *Breaking out again: Feminist ontology and epistemology.* London: Routledge.

Sykes, H. (1996). Constr(i)(u)cting lesbian identities in physical education: Feminist and poststructural approaches to researching sexuality. *Quest, 48* (4), 459–469.

Sykes, H. (1998). Turning closets inside/out: Towards a queer-feminist theory in women's physical education. *Sociology of Sport Journal, 15* (2), 154–173.

Sykes, H. (2001). Understanding and overstating: Feminist-poststructural life histories of physical education teachers. *Journal of Qualitative Studies in Education, 14* (1), 13–31.

Theberge, N. (1997). It's part of the game: Physicality and the production of gender in women's hockey. *Gender and Society, 11*: 69–87.

Thompson, A. (2003). Caring in context: Four feminist theories on gender and education. *Curriculum Inquiry, 33* (1), 9–65.

Tinning, R. (2002). Toward a "modest pedagogy": Reflections on the problematics of critical pedagogy. *Quest, 54* (3), 224–240.

Tong, R. (1998). *Feminist thought: A more comprehensive introduction* (2nd ed.). Boulder, CO: Westview Press.

United States Department of Health and Human Services. (1996). *Physical activity and health: A report of the surgeon general.* Washington, DC: US Government Printing Office.

Veri, M.J. (1999). Homophobic discourse surrounding the female athlete. *Quest, 51*, 355–368.

Vertinsky, P. (1984). In search of a gender dimension: An empirical investigation of teacher preferences for teaching strategies in physical education. *Journal of Curriculum Studies, 16* (4), 425–430.

Weedon, C. (1999). *Feminism, theory and the politics of difference.* Malden, MA: Blackwell Publishers.

Whelehan, I. (1995). *Modern feminist thought: From the second wave to post-feminism.* Washington Square, New York: New York University Press.

Wright, J. (1995). A feminist poststructuralist methodology for the study of gender construction in physical education: Description of a study. *Journal of Teaching in Physical Education, 15* (1), 1–24.

Wright, J. (1996). The construction of complementarity in physical education. *Gender and Education, 8* (1), 61–79.

Wright, J. (1999). Changing gendered practices in physical education: Working with teachers. *European Physical Education Review, 5* (3), 181–197.

SECTION II

Cross-Disciplinary Contributions to Research on Physical Education

In 1969, American curriculum theorist Joseph Schwab pronounced the curriculum field to be "moribund". The cause of its untimely demise, according to Schwab, was the invasion and colonization by a range of disciplines such as psychology, sociology and history. Schwab claimed that this discipline-based research fragmented the curriculum field, proposed competing and contradictory explanations for curricula phenomena, and was too theoretical to inform practitioners' deliberations on curriculum practice.

More than 35 years later, we can say with some confidence that Schwab's pronouncement was perhaps premature. Both curriculum and education more broadly have survived what appeared at the time to be a colonization and have thrived as fields of study with their own particular theories, issues, problems, and methods (e.g. Kirk, 1994). Moreover, the resurgence of curriculum and education as fields of study has not been at the expense of discipline-based study, as Schwab's analysis might have led us to expect. As we can see in this section, the application of theories, issues, problems, and methods from a range of disciplines has the potential to enrich our understanding of physical education as an educational phenomenon.

Philosophy, history and psychology can probably lay claim to the longest running lines of research in physical education, with sociology emerging to significance in the 1980s, and with public health the relative newcomer. Perhaps in some respects consistent with Schwab's critique, both Morgan's and Phillips and Roper's chapters reveal a diminution in the amount of attention given to physical education by philosophers and historians respectively as sport has grown in importance within their research agendas. At the same time, both Morgan and Phillips and Roper argue for the continuing relevance of philosophical and historical studies of physical education and suggest that ongoing developments in their fields can provide new insights into physical education. In a somewhat contrasting situation, and in many respects matching the dominance of psychology in educational research more generally, the

continuing proliferation of psychological studies in physical education settings leads Lirgg to focus on just one prominent line of inquiry centred around the concept of motivation. Again qualifying Schwab's analysis, Lirgg shows that social psychologists have often sought to provide advice to physical education practitioners on how studies of concepts such as motivation can inform their deliberations on practice. Evans and Davies' chapter provides an overview of sociological contributions to physical education, and like Lirgg's account of social psychology, their chapter reveals burgeoning sociological interest in physical education, particularly since the body and concepts such as embodiment became central to contemporary mainstream sociological inquiry. Finally, Trost's contribution reveals that physical education is of key and growing interest to researchers in the field of public health, in so far as physical education is viewed as both a source of the problem and as a possible solution to alleged increases in childhood obesity and sedentariness.

Each of these authors shows that, far from providing contradictory findings for physical education, their disciplines provide particular perspectives that enrich our understanding. They also provide repositories of theories and methods that pedagogy researchers can plunder and apply to specific problems in their fields of interest within physical education. And the histories of each discipline remind us that we must study physical education in the round, from as many salient perspectives as possible, and that we should not base policy and practice on whichever perspective happens to be fashionable at any given time.

References

Kirk, D. (1994). A journal and its field: The impact of the *Journal of Curriculum Studies*. *Journal of Curriculum Studies, 26*(5), 535–547.

Schwab, J. (1969). The practical: A language for curriculum. *School Review, 78*, 1–24.

2.1 Philosophy and physical education

WILLIAM J. MORGAN

Brief historical perspective

Strictly speaking, the philosophy of physical education is a sub-discipline of the philosophy of education, which, in turn, is a division of philosophy proper. So conceived, the philosophical issues pursued in the philosophy of physical education take their point of departure from the main issues that enliven the philosophy of education. And it was precisely this pedagogical perspective that informed most philosophical considerations of games, sports, exercise, dance, and other related physical fare on both sides of the Atlantic (mainly, the US and Great Britain) up to the late 1960s or so.

But beginning in the late 1960s (in the US) and the 1970s (in Britain), however, the field of the philosophy of physical education gradually gave way to a new, upstart area called the philosophy of sport. This change was by no means merely a linguistic or semantic one, but a thorough-going theoretical and practical one that reflected, no doubt, the growing prominence of sport as a social practice in the Anglo-American world, to say nothing of Europe and the rest of the world. In any event, it signaled the break of philosophic considerations of games and sports, and to a lesser extent exercise and dance, from the philosophy of education. This meant that the philosophical examination of human movement phenomena was no longer considered beholden to the philosophy of education, and thus no longer considered its sub-discipline but a bonafide philosophical subject in its own right. This put it on a par not only with the philosophy of education but as well with the philosophy of art, science, and religion. More particularly, it also meant that analyses of human movement phenomena came to have less and less to do with issues like knowledge (what counts as knowledge?, by what mechanisms do we obtain knowledge of such phenomena?, and what constitutes the logical organization of such knowledge?) and more and more to do with issues of value, especially ethical value (for a large part of the increased philosophical attention sports attracted in the last few decades of the past century had to do with their hard-to-miss moral debauchery).

In locating this break in the disciplinary identity and focus of philosophic examinations of human movement in the 1960s and 1970s, of course, I do not mean to imply that all philosophical work in physical education ceased at that point, and that everyone from that point on trained their philosophical sights on sports. Drawing boundaries that are too neat and tidy, of course, is the danger of any effort to periodize an academic enterprise or any other reasonably complex enterprise for that matter. So philosophical work dealing with physical education proper has persisted up to the present, but it has been clearly dwarfed by the work devoted to sports, and by the concern with ethical inquiries that defined and continues to define much of that work.

In order to appreciate the full significance of this break, however, it would be wise to briefly characterize the focus and content of philosophical inquiry in physical activity and sports prior to the 1960s and to do the same for the immediately following period which saw the birth and eventual hegemony of the philosophy of sport.

To begin at the beginning then, the philosophy of physical education in the pre-1960s looked rather different depending on whether one's frame of reference was the American or the English scene. With regard to the American scene, the body of literature reveals an eclectic mix of philosophical studies of physical education, and one which favored the use of so-called philosophic schools of thought. By schools of philosophic thought I mean things like pragmatism, naturalism, realism, idealism, and existentialism, which consist of a collection of concepts that examine phenomena like physical education from one or more of these standpoints. So, for instance, an existentialist analysis of physical education would take as its point of departure the unique being of the individual (what Heidegger called "Dasein", which literally translated means "being there," and by which Heidegger tried to convey the idea that what distinguishes the particular being of humans is the care they take regarding their own existence, not only its mere sustenance but its perfection), and judge the relative worth of physical education by how, and in what way, it hooks up with this existential project. The point of analyses like these was no mere scholastic one, however, but an effort to construct a coherent philosophy to live one's life by. The work of Davis, Miller, and Zeigler formed the nucleus of this early work; and more contemporary examples of it can be found in Charles's and Kretchmar's recent books.

On the other side of the Atlantic, however, the early work in the philosophy of physical education was a far less eclectic mix owing to the dominance of analytic philosophy. From the outset, this body of work reflected an unmistakable analytic bent, one that favored conceptual analyses of key terms associated with education, and one that was directly carried over into the philosophy of physical education. This explains why the latter was largely given over to considerations as to what extent physical education could itself legitimately be called an educational subject, a question prompted by the work of classical analytical philosophers of education like Peters who claimed that anything worthy of the name education must possessive both a cognitive orientation and content. For Peters that meant that education was a matter of inducting the uninitiated into intrinsically valuable forms of knowledge that together go to make up the rational mind (MacNamee, 1998). This suggests that because physical education is preeminently a practical rather than a theoretical endeavor, meaning that while it is not averse to theoretical treatment (whether it be biological, chemical, biomechanical, historical, sociological, or philosophical in character) such treatment is not central to what it is or what it does, it lacks the cognitive orientation and propositional content befitting education. Unsurprisingly, this grand dismissal of physical education prompted a basic rethinking of what constitutes education proper by philosophers of physical education. It was with this aim in mind that Arnold, Aspin, Best, and Reid, and more recently McNamee and Parry, turned out their own expanded conceptions of education, conceptions that left room according to Reid, for pleasurable human activities; according to Aspin and Best, for esthetic endeavors; according to Arnold, for moral practices; and according to Parry and McNamee, for activities that involve practical, tacit knowledge. They thus argued that if the mark of an educated person could not be reduced to the capacity to wield propositional knowledge, but included as well the ability to suffuse one's intentions and actions with esthetic, moral, and practical know-how, and to provide pleasurable experiences that people regard as intrinsically worthwhile, then physical education should most definitely not be denied entrance into the pantheon of education.

While these philosophers critically, and I think successfully, challenged Peters' sweeping and uncompromising rejection of the educational pedigree of physical education as an academic and,

therefore, appropriate school subject, the same cannot be said for their response to Peters heavy reliance on language analysis in his treatment of education, which for the most part they aped (Kirk, 2001). This led to a certain scholastic preoccupation with definitional issues, whose practical import was not always easy to fathom. However, taking its cue from its intellectual cousin the sociology of education, whose respective theorists heretofore largely ignored one another, physical educationists began to take up in the mid-1980s critical questions concerning the social construction and production of knowledge. Rather than focusing on a conceptual analysis of key notions of education, these thinkers turned their attention, among other things, to the ideological and political uses of education, and in physical education circles to the social "normalization" and regulation of "schooling bodies" (Evans and Davies, 1986; Kirk, 2001).

In the late and post-1960s, as previously noted, the philosophy of sport gradually eclipsed the philosophy of physical education in both the US and Britain as well as larger Europe. It should also be said, however, that American-educated theorists embraced this new philosophical emphasis on sport more quickly and enthusiastically than their British counterparts. This might explain why the impetus for this break originated in the US with the publication of Slusher's *Man, Sport, and Existence* (1967) and Metheny's *Movement and Meaning* (1968). These two books helped put the philosophical examination of human movement and mostly sport on the intellectual map, and signaled the beginning of the end of the reign of the philosophy of education and of its preoccupation with issues of knowledge.

But it was Paul Weiss's important book *Sport: A Philosophical Inquiry*, published in the following year of 1969, that gave the philosophy of sport the philosophical cachet it needed to prosper. This had as much or perhaps more to do with Weiss's stature in the philosophical community, where he was widely regarded as one of America's premier philosophers and the co-founder of one of its most prestigious journals, the *Review of Metaphysics*, as it did with the philosophic brilliance of his book. In any event, the publication of his book on sport finally brought attention to this seemingly trivial slice of human life to the attention of philosophers themselves, who had long steered clear of anything having to do with popular culture, let alone vulgar matters of the body. It was his example that further inspired philosophically inclined and sometimes philosophically trained theorists in physical education departments (where Slusher and Metheny, for instance, were housed), who also in the 1960s were likewise trying to break away from what they regarded to be the staid pedagogical tradition of physical education, to take up the serious philosophic study of sport. And in the important year of 1972, these two groups (philosophers and former physical educationists), led by Weiss himself, banded together to form the Philosophic Society for the Study of Sport (the name has recently been changed to the International Association of the Philosophy of Sport). Weiss was installed as its first president in 1974, and in that same year the society began publishing the *Journal of the Philosophy of Sport*, which to this day remains the most important journal in the field.

Core concepts

While attempts to define philosophy, and so the philosophy of physical education or the philosophy of anything else, are notoriously difficult, and usually fail, owing, among other things, to its great complexity and diversity, efforts to encapsulate its central questions, concerns, issues, and concepts are, fortunately, not as ominous. In fact, the core questions and concepts of the philosophy of physical education center on three key themes. But before we try to explicate them and stake out the intellectual territory they demarcate, it is first important to distinguish the character of philosophical questions themselves that distinguish them from other types of inquiry.

Generally speaking, and somewhat crudely put, there are three kinds of questions one can ask when inquiring into some matter. The first kind of question is an objective one in which both what is being asked and what counts as a good answer to it is clear and agreed upon by just about all. More importantly, answers to objective questions admit of, and converge to one right answer from which, therefore, wrong answers can be unambiguously distinguished. And, finally, and relatedly, answers to objective questions brook no dissent, or at least no plausible dissent. So if I want to know what the atomic weight of hydrogen is, or what the chemical composition of water is, or how many feet there are in a yard, I can count on the fact that there is an objectively right answer to each of my questions. All that is required is to look it up, or to carry out some more or less complex empirical procedure or mathematical computation. And if I claim, despite evidence to the contrary, that the chemical makeup of water is not two parts hydrogen and one part oxygen, then everyone is justified in thinking me wrong, or, if I carry my contrarism too far, off my rocker.

The second kind of question is a subjective one and asks after people's personal tastes and preferences. Here there is not one objectively correct answer for every question asked, and indeed the answer given in each case is highly likely to be different. Since the point here is to find out someone's opinion, belief, or desire, no justification of one's answer is expected or warranted. So if I ask people what their favorite movie is, or their favorite ice cream, I will in most cases get different answers to my queries and yet be entirely satisfied with their veracity because my aim was simply to determine people's subjective views about some matter.

The third kind of question is a normative one in which we are intent on probing people's reasons for the actions they undertake. Here while there is no objectively right answer to the questions asked, there are better and worse answers to them, in which what counts as a better or worse reason is its persuasive power. By persuasive power here is meant their argumentative force to effect some intersubjective consensus among those one is trying to persuade to act in one way or another. In this case, justification, the ability to back up what one is claiming with convincing arguments is everything, since this is the only way, short of physical force or terror, we have available to us to figure out what we should do and how we should act. In fact, most of life's most vexing and messiest questions fall into this category. So if I am trying to decide whether to go to graduate school, or to get married, or to embark on a different career, justifying my decisions to the argumentative satisfaction of myself and my peers is paramount. More dauntingly, if I am trying to resolve whether to follow through on my terminally ill father's request to terminate his life because he can no longer bear his suffering, I face a decision that requires me to think carefully about what I will do and what reasons I might have for acting one way or another. Cavalier, ill-considered actions in the face of serious and perplexing questions like these will simply not pass muster.

In the case of philosophy generally and the philosophy of physical education/sport particularly, the questions asked are all of this latter third kind. That means that the issues taken up in philosophy, no matter the type, call for careful reasoning and the marshalling of the best arguments available to persuade others of the validity and soundness of one's views. And it is in this sense that Socrates's well-known maxim that an unexamined life is not worth living is to be taken. To which we can add, in a more contemporary vein, that an unexamined life is, in addition, not a free one, since if one simply acts on whatever beliefs and values cross one's mind one can hardly call oneself the author of the actions they give rise to.

However, knowing that philosophical inquiry is committed to normative kinds of questions does not yet tell us just what those questions are, that is, just what sorts of issues philosophers deal with and consider their bailiwick. Fortunately, we can speak with some precision here because there are three themes central to philosophical inquiry. The first has to do with questions of reality, or of what is technically known as metaphysics. This question, in turn, can be asked in three yet more specific ways depending on what is regarded as the referent of reality in each instance. If by reality one means what are the basic constituents or building blocks of nature, then we are dealing with the sub-field of cosmology; if by reality one means the non-human constitution of the world, then we have entered the province of theology; and finally, if by reality one means the being of human beings, the essential features that mark us off from other creatures, then we have encroached into the study of what is called ontology. Since in modern times the study of cosmology has been for the most part ceded to physics, and since the study of the non-human constitution of the world has been delegated to theology and distinguished from philosophy proper, the study of metaphysics today is largely limited to ontological inquiry.

The second major theme of philosophy is the study of knowledge, which goes by the formal name of epistemology. Here the concern is not with the psychological organization of knowledge, but its logical organization and the sorting out of different claims to knowledge, for instance, knowledge bequeathed to us by sense perception, intuition, abstract conception, scientific conjecture, and revealed truth.

The third and final major theme of philosophy is the study of value, which is formally called axiology. The study of value falls into two sub-categories. The first is the study of value in the sense of what is right or wrong, good or bad, noble or ignoble. This is known as ethics, and is mainly concerned with, among other things, just what it is we morally owe to one another. The second sub-area of value considers value from the standpoint of what is beautiful or not. This is called esthetics and it is primarily interested in what marks off esthetic practices from other kinds of practices, and what makes something esthetically pleasing or valuable.

Major research areas and applications

In light of our above discussion of core concepts in philosophy, we can better see and appreciate the intellectual shift philosophy of physical education underwent when it morphed into the philosophy of sport. In the pre-1960s heyday of philosophy of physical education, the central theme that drove philosophic inquiry was epistemology. As such, philosophers of this era took seriously the epistemological challenges posed by a practical, evidently atheoretical, subject like physical education. Most of their effort, therefore, as previously noted, was geared toward justifying physical education as an intellectually reputable enterprise, one in which the study of physical education rivaled in importance the study of any other academic subject. And most of this research was applied, in the sense that even at its most abstract it kept a close eye on the practice of physical activity in school settings. So it was precisely this practical focus that anchored its theoretical efforts to portray physical education as an integral part of the educational landscape.

By contrast, the burgeoning of the philosophy of sport not only resulted in its cutting ties with the philosophy of education, but as well with physical activity and sports conducted primarily in educational settings. Instead, it directed most of its attention to elite sports, which even in their collegiate settings in the US have at best a tenuous relation to educational institutions and their main educational missions. And much of its philosophical interest in elite sports was fueled by its diffusion across the world and by the great attention lavished on it worldwide. Since the growing social and cultural significance of these sports occurred at a time when they were going through one moral travail after another, it was hardly surprising that interest in the ethical study of sports grew by leaps and bounds while interest in epistemological issues waned appreciably. It also explains why much of this philosophic research was far less applied than its physical education predecessor, though, as I shall argue below, the practical potential of this rapidly growing body of research is great, and, if tapped, offers an important corrective to the earlier philosophy of physical education's neglect of ethical issues in school-based physical activity and sports.

But I am already getting ahead of myself in laying out the major research agenda of this new philosophy of sport, which as I have been arguing all along is the only philosophical game, as it were, left in town at the moment.

So let me start again, this time at the beginning. For the turn away from epistemological issues in this second wave of the philosophy of sport not only inaugurated ethics as an important field of research, but also ontological investigations. These took the form of conceptual investigations that tried both to demarcate the differences as well as establish the relationships between human movement phenomena like play, game, and sport, and occasionally exercise and dance, and to explicate the particular forms of life, of being, represented by each.

To begin with play, the preponderance of the literature suggests that play is best characterized as a quality of action as opposed to a full-blown action itself, and one which captures a certain way of engaging in human movement phenomena like sport. That mode of engagement has to do with a certain motivational state one brings to games and sports, and a certain way of intrinsically valuing them. To play sports with a capital P then (to distinguish it from play with a small p, in which it merely serves as a synonym for the common verb perform or operate, as in the phrase to play a musical instrument), is to value them as ends in themselves as opposed to means that can be used to secure ends that are, strictly speaking, external to sports (many of the very things earlier physical educationists stressed could be had by engaging in physical activity, such as health, skill and character development, social learning skills, as well as some things these very same physical educationists denounced, such as winning at all costs, and the pursuit of the almighty dollar). Some theorists, like Suits for example, further claim that intrinsically valuing something picks out only one feature of play, and that the other equally important feature that must also be accounted for is that the resources deployed in play (time, space, equipment, etc.) must be reallocated from their primary use in everyday life to intrinsically valued activities. That means, for instance, that since eating mashed potatoes honors their primary instrumental purpose, which is to furnish us the nutrition we need to live and function adequately, it is not play. But that also means that when we reshape these same mashed potatoes into hills and valleys in order to engage in a pleasurable activity we find intrinsically rewarding, it is play.

By contrast, games and sports are treated in the literature as complex social practices. The most distinctive feature of these practices, which like most other activities are governed by certain goals and certain characteristic means of achieving these goals, is their defining rules, what Searle and others call constitutive rules. For these rules could not be more different than their everyday counterparts, since the role they perform in games is the very opposite of the role rules they perform in everyday life. Whereas in everyday life the rules we follow are designed to allow us to realize our ends as efficiently and as smoothly as possible (if I need to drive a nail in a piece of wood I use a hammer to do so), in games they are designed to make it as difficult as possible to realize their goals (to put the ball in the hole in golf I must stand some considerable distance from it and limit myself to using hard to manage clubs). So the fastest, easiest, most efficient means available to us in seeking to achieve game goals are always ruled out in favor of some less easy and less efficient way of doing so. And the point of these rules, as strange as they might at first seem, is readily and perfectly intelligible; for were it not for these means-limiting rules the goals we face in games would hardly hold our interest because we would hardly find them challenging (imagine a game of golf where hand-carrying the ball to the hole and stuffing it in were allowed, and so, were its main point. True, this would considerably lower every golfer's score, but it would also considerably lower, if not extinguish, every golfer's interest in playing golf).

If sports differ from games at all, the literature further suggests, they differ only in the skills that are central to them. This means that all sports are games, but not all games are sports. And what marks sporting games off from other sorts of games is that they are games of skill as opposed to chance (which distinguishes dice games from sporting ones), and further, that those skills are of a decidedly physical character (which distinguishes games of skill like bridge from sporting games like basketball).

So the current philosophical research suggests that play, game, and sport, though in many respects closely related, are each different animals. For each demarcates a different way of being-in-the-world, of living one's life. At the same time, the close relations between them are undeniable, and serve, interestingly enough, to separate them all off from the routine instrumental activities we take up in our daily lives. This suggests, from an ontological standpoint, that there is something quite unique about play, game, and sport, about the ways of being that they provide us, and that this uniqueness is apparently what accounts both for their great allure and charm and for their vulnerability to exploitation and corruption.

But does it offer anything of practical import? For though it might be conceded that while some of this philosophic research appears quite sophisticated and even perhaps interesting, for example, in its explanation of what it is that makes these phenomena so different from the rest of our lives, it seems, nonetheless, an awfully slim reed to hang anything of truly educational significance on. It might even be objected further that most of this literature lacks substance, that it comes off as so much aimless intellectualizing, so much conceptual tomfoolery. I think, however, that both of these charges are unfounded, and that if this literature is guilty of anything it is not lack of practical substance but of understating or simply ignoring its educational utility. Let me explain.

It is commonplace in physical education, and in academic areas in general, that when asked to justify its inclusion in the curriculum, in other words its educational value, its proponents immediately and instinctively reach for an instrumental answer. So it is that physical education is touted for its contribution to health and fitness, motor learning, social cooperation, intellectual revitalization, ad infinitum, and some would even say, ad nauseam. These ends are, no doubt, serious and important ones, and what makes them so is their contribution to our ordinary lives. For in order to live well and productively, it is important, among other things, to be physically fit and to know how to interact with our peers so that we can get things done collectively that we could not achieve on our own. This means that physical education is a serious and important matter, but, and here is the rub, only in a secondhand, marginal way. For the things that are most serious and important in our lives are the things we do to secure our survival and well-being, which is why in contemporary capitalist societies like ours that tie personal fortune and welfare to work it is practices like these that assume such a commanding and prominent place in our lives. Physical education in this scheme can be regarded as serious but only in a derivative way, that is, only if it furthers our work-lives and the other instrumental pursuits that dominate our everyday life. Hence, when push comes to shove, what is most serious always takes precedence over what is serious only in a derivative way, which is why an instrumental justification of physical education always comes up on the short end of the stick. No matter how hard and how ingeniously we pitch such justificatory efforts, then, play, game, and sport remain second-class, second-rate endeavors, endeavors about which it can be said that there are always other things that outrank them in importance and value.

If the previously discussed ontological investigations of these human movement phenomena are right, however, such efforts to show the educational utility of these phenomena are misguided because they get it exactly backwards. That is to say, those things which we take seriously in our daily work lives are important only insofar as they make it possible to engage in things like play, games, and sports. To put the same point otherwise, the purpose of life is to accomplish those things that we *have* to do in order to be able to do those things we *want* to do. So the point of working is to get to the point that we do not have to work any longer so that we can devote ourselves to those things that we find intrinsically rewarding. The same goes, for instance, for the deadly serious business of political diplomacy, whose important task of securing the peace is important precisely because it makes it possible for us to engage our attention and devote our energy to those select human activities that give our life meaning. After all, what would be the point of work or of political brinkmanship or, for that matter, of life, if there were no pursuits we humans find intrinsically satisfying that make life worth living in the first place, that is, worth all the struggle and hardship that are an inescapable part of life. And since play, game, and sport are best conceived, as the philosophical literature suggests, as just such intrinsically good things, they are among the most important and serious of human activities, and they are the very activities which things like work derive whatever seriousness they possess. All of which suggests, that when physical educationists endeavor to secure the academic legitimacy of their subject in the instrumental ways described above they are barking up the wrong tree.

They are also, as it turns out, skating on very thin ice. For instrumental justifications of physical education programs not only relegate them to second-class status and importance but also open them to the objection that there might well be better ways to accomplish the ends they supposedly help to realize. For example, if physical education programs are justified because they are conducive to intellectual revitalization, it might easily and persuasively be countered that word games that break the tedium of classroom instruction or meditation exercises that relieve intellectual stress are far more effective ways to accomplish this outcome. So attempts that purport to demonstrate the educational utility of physical education can easily backfire with disastrous results.

If I am right about the superiority of intrinsic over instrumental defenses of physical education, then even seemingly abstruse because abstract ontological inquiries into the place of play, game, and sport in our lives bear practical fruit. That said, however, it must at once also be said that most of the real action in the philosophy of sport lies in the ethics of sports. And here it will be much more transparent, I trust, that ethical research of this kind has all sorts of practical implications for physical activity and sports conducted in school settings despite its preoccupation with elite sports. However, because much of the practical relevance of this ethical research, like its ontological counterpart, remains understated or unstated, it will still be necessary to flesh it out.

The kind of ethical inquiry relevant here focuses on how participants should treat one another in sport settings, and more particularly, on what kinds of conduct and assists to performance are morally permissible in seeking bodily excellence. The first question raises a host of questions regarding matters like sportspersonship, fair play, athletic success, cheating, the moral standing of competition, and gender issues of sexual identity and equity; and the second raises a narrower range of issues that have to do with the present epidemic of doping in sports and the moral problems it poses.

Some of the most interesting ethical research in sports grows out of the first question noted above, and suggests that notions like sportspersonship, fair play, athletic success, and cheating are intimately bound up with one another. That is because sportspersonship is often defined in terms of fair play, and cheating is commonly thought to involve a violation of both. Much of this literature tries to spell out just what virtues and moral qualities are central to conceptions of sportspersonship and fair play. Some argue that fair play is a virtue that must be acquired in learning sports, and in trying to meet the standards of excellence they put in place. Others claim that fair play has to do with general notions like moral respect, and, therefore, includes a bundle of moral qualities like benevolence, generosity, and equanimity. Still others regard fair play as a contractual notion, as an agreement we tacitly enter into when we agree to play a game and try to realize its goals.

In this connection, I would be remiss if I did not say something about the remarkable impact Alasdair MacIntyre's important book, *After Virtue*, has had in philosophy of sport circles. MacIntyre's treatise on moral virtues, published in 1981, singled out the importance of what he calls social practices, which include things like architecture, music, painting, science, and most importantly for our purposes games and sports. According to MacIntyre, social practices are defined by three main features: the standards of excellence they seek, the goods that are internal to their pursuit, and the virtues that are necessary to achieve these internal goods. The standards of excellence tell us both what kinds of activities fall under certain social practices, and how those practices are to be judged especially in moral terms. The internal goods of a practice are those goods that can only be attained by participation in a practice. So in the case of sports, they would include such things as the intrinsic pleasure of performing a sport's skill well, the meshing of the intentions and actions of an entire team as if they were one person, the self-awareness and self-knowledge gained by pushing one's body to the limit. Moreover, in trying to realize the standards of excellence of a social practice and the goods internal to them, one must be willing to take whatever risks they require, be willing to give "what is due to whom," and be able to listen to and constructively respond to criticisms of one's shortcomings. In other words, one must be prepared to exercise virtues like courage, justice, and honesty.

MacIntyre's linkage of moral virtues to social practices like sports immediately caught the eye of philosophers of sport because it helped to explain both the present moral malaise of sports and how they might once again, if practiced, structured, and organized in the right way, become vehicles of moral expression. Siedentop explored these issues in youth and junior sports, and Morgan in elite sports themselves. In the former case, Siedentop put MacIntyre's ideas to effective use in touting the educative potential of youth sports to inculcate virtues like self-discipline, humility, and sensitivity to the needs and values of others. The rub, he noted, is that in order to turn youth sports in this ethical direction they would have to change, and in some cases completely transform, the way they are practiced in elite circles, which are noted not only for their moral slackness but their downright indifference to moral concerns. In the latter case, Morgan explored, with MacIntyre as his guide, the way in which the goods internal to elite sports are compromised by external goods like money that are offered as rewards for successful athletic achievement. By promoting the latter at the expense of the former, social institutions such as, for instance, the International Olympic Committee, which like other such institutions oversee and regulate social practices, are often themselves responsible for the moral decline of the very sports they were designed and entrusted to safeguard.

It is also evident from the literature that getting clear as to just what moral features fair play, and notions like it, entail, goes a long way as well in explaining athletic success. For it has been frequently and forcefully argued that athletic success cannot be simply equated with winning or failure with losing. That is because there are a number of respects in which athletic contests can fail, that is, fall short of the excellence they are designed to showcase. Such failures might be owed to refereeing errors, cheating, the use of tactics like taunting, or just plain bad luck, in which the winner of the contest does not deserve this acclaim because s/he was not the most excellent. The upshot of such arguments is that athletic success is not simply a technical matter, but a moral one. For unless one shows moral respect for one's opponent, which precludes treating one's opponents as mere obstacles to be overcome, and moral respect for the game itself, which precludes separating winning from the play of the game, one cannot succeed in sport.

Another issue of concern in this regard is the moral status of competition itself. Many have claimed that any form of competition is morally problematic because of its egoistic bent, because the point of competition is the self-interested one of demonstrating one's athletic superiority over others, and of achieving a goal, winning, that once achieved is the exclusive possession of the person or team who has achieved it. If this account of competition is right, then sports can not be regarded as moral ventures because they leave no room for the moral consideration of others.

The literature suggests, however, that instead of a knockdown argument against the moral credentials of competitive sports what we actually have here is an impoverished conception of competition itself, one that fails to see that competitive sports at their best involve what Simon and others call a mutual quest for excellence. The mutuality in question occurs at two levels. On the first level, any competition rightly understood cannot be properly construed as a war of all against all because competitors must cooperate with one another if there is to be a contest at all. That is, they must agree to abide by the rules and the standards of excellence that define the contest. Further, and more importantly, it is my competitors that supply me with the challenge against which I prove my athletic mettle, and it is only by striving together with them to realize that excellence that I can gauge how well I measure up athletically speaking, and they are able to do the same. In this sense, then, competition involves not only pitting myself against others but competing with them, and it is in this reciprocal give and take with these others that I am pressed and obligated to give them their moral due.

Cheating looms large in all of these analyses if for no other reason than, as already noted, it is commonly held to be a violation of the moral debt we owe to others in sports. But what, exactly, is cheating, and what sort of moral offense does it represent. To the first question, the literature gives a fairly definitive response, even though it concedes there are border situations in which it is difficult to say with any reasonable degree of certainty whether cheating has occurred. The most effective argumentative strategy in this regard equates cheating with lying. Just as telling something to someone that is untrue does not in itself count as lying, similarly simply breaking a rule in sport does not in itself count as cheating. What is missing in both cases is any mention of intention, and of an intention of a certain sort. So what turns telling something to someone that is untrue into a bald-faced lie as opposed to a simple mistake or misconception, is that one does so deliberately and deceitfully. In other words, I know what I am conveying to others is untrue and I purposefully do so in order to mislead them. The same applies to cheating, which is distinguished from mere rule breaking because I both intended to break the rule and to get away with it. So understood, it becomes fairly easy to see what sort of moral offense cheating constitutes. It violates a moral trust I enter into with others as a condition of playing the game in the first place by seeking to gain an unfair advantage over them by hook and crook, by disguising what my true intentions are. Such deceitful acts, then, fail in two important moral senses: first, they fail to show moral respect for my competitors as persons in their own right, and second, they fail to show moral respect for the perfectionist demands of the game itself.

A related and especially important moral concern in this regard is the complex issue of sexual identity and equity in sport. With regard to the first point, it is clear that in spite of the impressive inroads women have recently made in sports, these physical practices have not been especially kind to them. By that I mean specifically that when women engage in sports, this is perhaps most true at the elite level, they can expect either to have their own sexual identity questioned (the same occurs, for example, to gender-bending male athletes who play what are traditionally and rather pejoratively referred to as "feminine" sports) or that of the athletic stature of the sports they participate in (the claim, for instance, that synchronized swimming and their ilk are not real sports).

That women in sport continue to be subject to such hurtful stereotypes complicates the second issue in question here, the matter of sexual equity. For if sports are themselves morally problematic practices, beset as they seem to be by things like homophobia, then the question arises of why women and other vulnerable groups should seek access to them at all. It may well be better, or so this

line of argument intimates, for them to pursue less morally compromised endeavors. There is the additional complication, which may well in part explain the high incidence of sexual animus in practices like these, that since most sports were created by men for men they naturally enough privilege the male body (emphasizing as they do qualities like strength, power, and speed). That means that even if women were granted equal opportunity to participate in sports, invidious comparisons between their athletic accomplishments and those of their male peers would be inevitable – making an already inhospitable environment even more so.

The literature reveals three possible responses to these knotty problems. The first concedes the criticism that sports are morally challenged practices, but argues against the inference that, therefore, women should steer clear of them. So Francis, for instance, powerfully argues that while such unpleasant facts about sports weakens the case for sexual equality it does not eliminate it. Rather, we still have good reason to seek equity for women in sports as long as men are allowed to participate in these morally unwholesome practices. The idea seems to be the simple one that even in the moral realm what is good for the gander is good for the goose.

The second response challenges the claim that sports fall short of the mark morally and argues that they provide important benefits for their participants that it would be wrong to bar women from acquiring. Those benefits include what philosophers like Jane English call basic benefits (things like health, skill, self-respect, fun) and scarce benefits (things like fame and wealth). The moral case varies depending on what set of benefits one has in mind. So in the case of basic benefits, English argues that everyone is morally entitled to achieve these benefits and, therefore, that it would be wrong to deny them to women on the basis of their lesser skill (obviously, she has in mind here programs like intramural sports whose purpose is to offer participants, regardless of their race, ethnicity, sexual identity, or level of skill a chance to garner these benefits). In the case of scarce benefits, claims English, since skill is relevant here in a way it is not in the former instance, not everyone is entitled to obtain these benefits. But the relevance of skill can not, she argues further, be used to deprive women of equal opportunity to achieve these benefits. Rather, it suggests that there ought to be segregated and protected sports for able, elite women athletes that elite male athletes are barred from participating in. And the reason why elite male athletes should be prevented from seeking access to these women's sports is itself for English a decidedly moral one: namely, that the self-respect of all women would suffer if there were no women role models in high-performance sports.

The third response also finds moral fault with contemporary women's sports but is mostly agnostic on the question of whether women should or should not seek access to them because it regards the entire matter of access as morally beside the point. Instead, it goes in a different and in many ways more obvious even if more radical direction. For since, it argues, there is a built-in moral bias in the present batch of women sports it is necessary to invent a new batch that privileges women's bodies. So understood, the proper moral antidote to the masculinist bias of actually existing sports lies in fashioning new ones that accent things like grace and dexterity rather than power and speed. The added moral advantage of this strategy is that it confronts headlong the idea that women's sports are a poor imitation of men's sports, which will go a long way, or at least English claims, in stemming the invidious comparison of women's to men's sports.

This takes us to the second major area of ethical inquiry in sports that considers what aids to performance in this realm are morally permissible. The main target here is, unsurprisingly, the use of performance-enhancing drugs in sports, although the even thornier and scarier issue of genetic interventions to boost performance is beginning to attract some attention in the literature – however, because gene technology is still in its infancy many of these issues are not yet clearly understood. The argument over drug use pits libertarians, defenders of individual freedom, against paternalists, defenders of regulating individuals' lives to protect their and our welfare. In the particular case of sports, the issue boils down to how much risk athletes should be allowed to take in their efforts to improve their performance. Unfortunately, the literature reveals no clear consensus here. On the one hand, defenders of individual liberty argue that as long as one is a competent moral agent and knows the risks involved, it should be left to the individual to decide whether they wish to chemically augment their performance. That means doping should be legalized so that athletes can exercise their individual discretion whether to take them or not. Paternalistic critics of doping, however, argue that athletes should not be allowed to play, so to speak, Russian Roulette with their sporting lives. They worry especially about the coercive environment of sports where athletes are pressured to do whatever it takes to come out on top, which makes it exceedingly difficult to say no to things like drugs, and about the fairness of doping, which is alleged to give drug-takers an unfair advantage over their non-drug taking peers. These are vexing issues, and there are good arguments on each side that have led to the present stalemate.

As I have already argued, the relevance of both of these areas of ethical inquiry to educational practice seems obvious on its face, especially when compared to its ontological counterpart. And its preoccupation with elite sports in this regard need not be as problematic as it might at first appear. Let me explain.

For starters, if an important part of the educational significance of practices like sports is to convey moral lessons, that is, to teach moral virtues like honesty, fairness, and a sense of justice, a reasonable position I believe, then the ethics in sport literature seems just what the doctor ordered. This is so in at least two senses. First, in its no-holds barred critical depiction of elite sports, warts and all, it sketches a vivid picture of how not to morally do sports. That is, it shows in stark detail how sports go morally bad when, for instance, winning is granted too much importance and when external rewards like money command too much attention from the participants. There are important moral lessons, then, to be learned from this sort of moral debauchery that physical education can afford to ignore only at its own peril. Second, in subjecting elite sports to withering moral criticism, as the literature does, it also provides important lessons about how to redesign sports to avoid these sorts of undesirable moral consequences. So, for example, in showing why the dominant view of athletic success, which as we have seen simply reduces it to winning, can not hold a moral candle to conceptions of athletic success that emphasize the importance of worthy opponents who morally respect both their opponents and the game itself, this literature more than meets halfway practitioners keen on using sports to good moral effect.

It should also be said in this same vein that the ethical literature in sports provides valuable insights as to how sports might be morally restructured without denuding sports of the very qualities that attract us so to them. I am thinking here of the literature's defense of the morality of competition, which suggests that as we ponder how to redesign sports to good moral effect we do not give short shrift to the idea that there are morally valuable lessons to be learned by exposing people to the heat of competition. This suggests that there is indeed something to be said, after all, for the old adage that if you want to see what someone is really like engage them in a competitive game, and that that something has a moral dimension to it if properly handled. For learning to deal with one's own frailties, and so with disappointment and defeat, which are a constant in competitive sports, and learning to do so in ways that give both oneself and others their proper moral due, is a moral lesson whose importance would be hard to exaggerate. The moral of this moral, then, is that there is no need to turn sports into half-hearted, feckless affairs, in order to make them morally relevant to our lives.

The ethical sports literature also has an important role to play in dispelling certain morally repugnant stereotypes of vulnerable groups. Here again the focus of this literature on elite sports does not detract from its practical utility, since the parading of such stereotypes in the very public setting of top-level sports is used to tar all the members of these targeted groups not just their athletic representatives. I have in mind in this regard the stereotyping of elite women's sports as athletically inferior versions of elite men's sports, which, in turn, as just noted, is used to put all women down with its not so subtle intimation that what goes for women in sports goes for women in all walks of life. The idea is as simple as it is pernicious, namely, that women lack the manly virtues required not just to succeed in sports but in life itself. This is why many critics have accused sports of being the last male bastion, the one place left men to lord their dominance over the opposite sex.

As the literature so deftly shows, however, nothing could be further from the truth. For this claim of male superiority rests on a bad inference, one that falsely claims that the present male advantage in sports is itself evidence that women are naturally inferior to men in the athletic realm. When, in fact, all that can be legitimately inferred from men's present dominance over women in these sports is the much more modest and homely point that, surprise, surprise, men are more adept at sports that were conceived with them in mind. In other words, because we live in patriarchal societies, and because in such societies men have the greater say in how social practices and institutions get put together, it is no coincidence that we ended up with sports that stress qualities like power and speed which suit men well and women ill. So there is a simple explanation for the present dominance of men in sports and it has nothing to do with biology and everything to do with social dominance. It thus stands to reason that if matriarchal societies were the rule rather than the rare exception, our major sports would not look anything like American football, basketball, soccer, or rugby, but exactly like the sports of synchronized swimming and the balance beam in gymnastics. In other words, if the athletic shoe were on the other foot, then the stereotype of athletic inferiority would be as well – in which case we would have to disabuse men of the specious claim that they are naturally inferior to women in sports.

Finally, the literature's fixation on the moral dilemmas of elite sport does not short-circuit its practical utility for physical education because the problems of the former are not as far removed from those of the latter as is commonly thought. That is because like it or not high-performance sports sets the tone, both morally and non-morally, for the rest of the sports world, to include the world of physical education. How else to explain the recent estimate that as many as a quarter of million kids in the US under the age of 16 use aids like anabolic steroids either to bolster their athletic performance or to improve their physical appearance. Performance-enhancing drugs are, of course, but one example of the hold elite sports have on young people. They are,

however, one of the more worrisome of such examples. And despite the previously discussed lack of consensus regarding the moral permissibility of doping for adult sports in the literature, there is a clear consensus in that same literature that doping has no legitimate moral place in youth sports. The reason why is because young people are not adjudged, either by defenders of freedom or their paternalistic opposite numbers, to be competent moral agents owing largely to their immaturity and ignorance, to the fact that they seldom consider the long-term effects of their actions. On this, and many other moral issues like it, then, the sport ethics literature has much to offer the physical education practitioner.

Major trends and future directions

In one respect, I have already tipped my hand regarding major trends and future directions in the philosophy of physical education. For it is clear from my above remarks that the research that feeds the philosophy of physical education will come largely from the philosophy of sport rather than the philosophy of education literature. It is also clear that much of this research will be centered on ethical inquiry in sports, as opposed to the older epistemological research paradigm favored in philosophy of education circles. So there is good reason to think this emphasis on ethics and de-emphasis on theory of knowledge will continue into the foreseeable future.

But there has also been a recent shift in the parent discipline of philosophy itself (at present more evident in the US and Europe than Great Britain) that is already shaping philosophic inquiry in sports and will likely set much of its research agenda in the coming years. I am referring to the upsurge of pragmatism in philosophy, a movement that challenges headlong what many see as the sterile scholasticism of analytic philosophy, of its preoccupation with technical and rather arcane conceptual issues (for example, the controversy over whether the "truths" of mathematics are explicative or ampliative, that is, whether they merely make explicit what we already know implicity or whether they extend our present stock of knowledge).

What is noteworthy about this recent pragmatic turn is its reconception of philosophy itself, of what its main tasks are. For on a pragmatic reading of philosophy of the sort one finds in the classical pragmatist John Dewey, the central aim of philosophy is to apply critical intelligence to the resolution of social problems. That means, as Richard Rorty, a contemporary philosopher whose widely read books and essays have helped rekindle interest in pragmatism, once put it, "philosophy is always parasitic on, always a reaction to, developments elsewhere in culture and society." So understood, philosophy is best conceived not as a technical discipline that possesses its own special concepts and issues, but as a critical response to problems that arise from the social and historical circumstances in which we live. In other words, philosophy can only do its work profitably on this view if it eschews the intellectual comforts and consolations of disciplinary insularity and goes social and historical, that is, if it makes every effort to get a critical handle on the forms of life in which these problems come wrapped. This is what Wittgenstein famously meant when he said that "understanding a language-game is sharing a form of life," and that concepts are "patterns which recur, with different variations, in the weave of our life."

It is precisely this pragmatic spirit that informs much of the current philosophy of sport literature, and much of the recent work in sports ethics. Further, it is this same spirit, I conjecture, that will guide its future work. And this is as good a point as any to end my chapter on, if for no other reason than this refocusing of philosophy on the social and historical lives we actually live bodes well for the future fruitful collaboration between philosophy of sport theorists and physical education practitioners.

Acknowledgments

I want to thank David Kirk for his many insightful comments on an earlier draft of this manuscript and Lana Mink for her assistance in compiling the accompanying bibliography.

References

Arnold, P. (1983). The approaches toward an understanding of sportsmanship. *Journal of the Philosophy of Sport*, X, 61–70.

Aspin, D. (1976). 'Knowing How' and 'Knowing That' and Physical Education.' *Journal of the Philosophy of Sport*, 3, 97–117.

Belliotti, R. (1979). Women, sex, and sports. *Journal of the Philosophy of Sport*, VI, 67–72.

Best, D. (1978). *Philosophy and human movement*. London: Allen & Unwin.

Brown, M. (1984). Paternalism, drugs, and the nature of sports. *Journal of the Philosophy of Sport*, XI, 14–22.

Carlisle, R. (1969). The concept of physical education. *Proceedings of the Philosophy of Education Society of Great Britain*, 3, 1–11.

D'Agostino, F. (1981). The ethos of games. *Journal of the Philosophy of Sport*, VIII, 7–18.

Delattre, E. (1975). Some reflections on success and failure in competitive athletics. *Journal of the Philosophy of Sport*, II, 133–139.

Dixon, N. (1992). On sportsmanship and "running up the score". *Journal of the Philosophy of Sport*, XIX, 1–13.

Duncan, M. (1994). The politics of women's body images and practices: Foucault, the Panopticon, and *Shape* magazine. *Journal of Sports and Social Issues*, 18, 48–65.

English, J. (1978). Sex equality in sports. *Philosophy and Public Affairs*, 7, 269–277.

Evans, J. and Davies, B. (1986). Sociology, schooling and physical education. In J. Evans (Ed.), *Physical education, sport and schooling: Studies in the sociology of physical Education*, (pp. 11–37) London: Falmer.

Feezell, R. (1986). Sportsmanship. *Journal of the Philosophy of Sport*, VIII, 1–13.

Fraleigh, W. (1982). Why the good foul is not good. *Journal of physical education, recreation, and dance*, 53, 41–42.

Francis, L. (1993–4). Title IX: Equality for Women's Sports?. *Journal of the Philosophy of Sport*, XX–XXI, 32–47.

Gardner, R. (1989). On performance-enhancing substances and the unfair advantage argument. *Journal of the Philosophy of Sport*, XVI, 59–73.

Gorn, E. and Oriard, M. (1995). Taking sports seriously (Point of View). *Chronicle of Higher Education*, 52a.

Gruneau, R. (1983). *Class, sports, and social development*. Amherst, MA: University of Massachusetts Press.

Hoberman, J. (1995). Sport and the technological image of man. In W.J. Morgan and K.V. Meier (Eds), *Philosophical inquiry in sport* (pp. 202–208). Champaign, IL: Human Kinetics.

Hyland, D. (1984). Opponents, contestants, and competitors: the dialectic of sport. *Journal of the Philosophy of Sport*, XI, 63–70.

Hyland, D. (1990). *Philosophy of Sport*. New York: Paragon House.

Keating, J. (1964). Sportsmanship as a moral category. *Ethics*, LXXV, 25–35.

King, R. (1991). Environmental ethics and the case against hunting. *Environmental Ethics*, 13, 59–85.

Kirk, D. (2001). Schooling bodies through physical education: Insights from social epistemology and curriculum history. *Studies in the Philosophy of Education*, 20(6), 475–487.

Kirk, D. (2002). Junior sport as a moral practice. *Journal of Teaching in Physical Education*, 21(4), 402–408.

Kretchmar, S. (1982). Distancing: an essay on abstract thinking in sport performances. *Journal of the Philosophy of Sport*, IX, 6–18.

Kretchmar, S. (1989). On beautiful games. *Journal of the Philosophy of Sport*, XVI, 34–43.

Kretchmar, S. (1994). *Practical philosophy of sport*. Champagne, IL: Human Kinetics.

Lavin, M. (1987). Sports and drugs: are the current bans justified? *Journal of the Philosophy of Sport*, XIV, 34–43.

Leaman, O. (1981). Cheating and fair play in sport. In W.J. Morgan (Ed.), *Sport and the humanities: A collection of original essays* (pp. 25–30). Knoxville, TN: Bureau of Educational Research and Service, University of Tennessee.

Lehman, C. (1981). Can cheaters play the game?. *Journal of the Philosophy of Sport*, VIII, 41–46.

Lurie, Y. (2002). The ontology of sports injuries: Professional ethics of sports medicine, *International Journal of Applied Philosophy, 16*, 265–276.

McNamee, M. (1998). Education, philosophy, and physical education: analysis, epistemology and axiology. *European Physical Education Review, 4*(1), 75–91.

Messner, M. (1988). Sports and male domination: the female athlete as contested ideological terrain. *Sociology of Sport Journal, 5*, 197–211.

Metheny, E. (1968). *Movement and meaning.* New York: McGraw-Hill.

Morgan, W. (1994). *Leftist theories of sport: A critique and reconstruction.* Urbana and Chicago: University of Illinois Press.

Morgan, W. and Meier, K.V. (1995). *Philosophic inquiry in sport.* Champaign, IL: Human Kinetics.

Morgan, W., Meier, K., Schneider, A. (2001). *Ethics in sport.* Champaign, IL: Human Kinetics.

Osterhoudt, R. (1991). *The philosophy of sport: an overview.* Champaign, IL: Stipes.

Pearson, K. (1973). Deception, sportsmanship, and ethics. *Quest, XIX*, 115–118.

Perry, C. (1983). Blood doping and athletic competition. *The International Journal of Applied Philosophy, 1*, 39–45.

Regan, T. (1983). Why hunting and trapping are wrong. In T. Regan (Ed.), *The Case for Animal Rights.* Berkeley, CA: University of California Press.

Rorty, R. (1982). *Consequences of pragmatism.* Minneapolis, MN: University of Minnesota Press.

Rorty, R. (1995). Philosophy and the future. In H.J. Saatkamp (Ed.). *Rorty and pragmatism: The philosopher responds to his critics* (pp. 197–205). Nashville, TN: Vanderbilt University Press.

Scherer, D. (1991). Existence, breeding, and the rights: the use of animals in sports. *Between the species,* Summer: 132–137.

Sheridan, H. (2003). Fair play: A review of the literature. *European Physical Education Review, 9*(2), 163–184.

Siedentop, D. (2002). Junior sport and the evolution of sport cultures. *Journal of Teaching in Physical Education, 21*(4), 392–401.

Simon, R. (1984). Good competition and drug-enhanced performance. *Journal of the Philosophy of Sport, XI*, 6–13.

Simon, R. (1993–4). Gender equity and inequity in athletics. *Journal of the Philosophy of Sport, XX–XXI*, 6–22.

Singer, P. (1973). Animal liberation. *The New York Review of Books,* 5 April.

Slusher, H. (1967). *Man, sport, and existence: A critical analysis.* Philadelphia PA: Lea & Febiger.

Stornes, T. (2001). Sportspersonship in elite sports: on the effects of personal and environmental factors on the display of sportspersonship among elite male handball players. *European Physical Education Review, 7*(3), 283–304.

Suits, B. (1973). The elements of sport. In R. Osterhoudt (Ed.), *The philosophy of sport: A collection of original essays* (pp. 48–64). Springfield, IL: Charles C. Thomas.

Suits, B. (1988). Tricky triad: games, play, and sport. *Journal of the Philosophy of Sport, XV*, 1–9.

Theodoulides, A. and Armour, K.M. (2001). Personal, social and moral development through team games: some critical questions. *European Physical Education Review, 7*(1), 5–23.

Thompson, P. (1982). Privacy and the urinalysis testing of athletes. *Journal of the Philosophy of Sport, IX*, 60–65.

Weiss, P. (1969). *Sport: A philosophic inquiry.* Carbondale, IL: Southern Illinois Press.

Wittgenstein, L. (1953). *Philosophical investigations.* Oxford: Basil Blackwell.

Young, I. (1979). The exclusion of women from sport: conceptual and existential dimensions. *Philosophy in Context, 9*, 44–53.

2.2 The sociology of physical education

JOHN EVANS AND BRIAN DAVIES

A brief history: sociology and the sociology of physical education

It is now over 20 years since the publication of Physical Education, Sport and Schooling. Studies in the Sociology of Physical Education and Sport (Evans, 1986), our modest contribution toward the development of a sociology of physical education in the UK and elsewhere. There we lamented the near absence in mainstream sociology, its sub-discipline the sociology of education and in educational research of any significant interest in how physical education (PE) was implicated in processes of socio-cultural reproduction or, in current speak, how "the body is schooled" (Evans, 1988; Evans et al., 2004; Hargreaves, 1982; Jenkins, 1982; Kirk, 1993; Laker, 2002; Shilling, 1993). As professionals interested in what schools do to pupils we felt limited in our capacity to understand the nature of teaching, learning and educational innovation and their relation to social and cultural progress and change. We pointed to obvious reasons for this lacuna. Rarely had physical education enjoyed high status either within political discourse or formal education in Europe or elsewhere. This was reflected in the perspectives of educational and social researchers and funding agencies. It was of low priority, unfashionable and inconsequential to display interests in a low-status subject area and none were lower than PE. These subject hierarchies in school reached out to wider status hierarchies in society that privileged intellectual over physical/manual labour and to a dominant tradition of Western philosophy and thought which persistently "marginalized and separated body from mind matters on the assumption that it is the mind that makes us distinctively human" (Shilling, 2004: xvi) and celebrated its cultivation as the primary educational aim. Body/physical/practical matters were sidelined, positioned on the subject margins, a domain

unworthy of educational activity, scholarship and research. All too few scholars were inclined to lay bare the fallacy of mind/body, intellectual/physical dualisms or expose their attendant elitism. As Shilling has pointed out, there was little justification for this dichotomous way of thinking as, "all education involves a physical education of the body" (Shilling, 2004: xv) and its neglect had very serious implications for our understandings of how teachers teach and pupils learn.

Without taking into account the corporeal preconditions and characteristics of social action, and the ways in which structures of power and control impacted on the bodies of those subject to them, its [the Sociology of Education's] multiplying perspectives were fated to construct partial explanations which misrepresented the mechanisms associated with the organisation, delivery and reception of education. In these cases it was never properly clear how educational outcomes actually occurred because it was never properly clear how the *physical* habits, senses and dispositions of embodied students responded to and were shaped by the organisation and transmission of knowledge within schools. (2004: xv)

If we did not understand "embodiment" we could not claim to understand the nature of "knowing", or the requirements of learning and teaching at all. However, during the 1980s and 1990s the study of "the body" became fashionable, a respectable element of scholarship and a plethora of writing and research on the way in which it was configured in society through the practices of formal education began to emerge.

The sociological reasons for the emergence of "the body" both as a major issue in contemporary society and an important research area need not be detailed here (see Evans and Davies, 2004: Hunter, 2004; Kirk, 1993; Shilling, 1993). It reflected fast-changing social, cultural and political circumstances globally, a political culture of individualism that centred attention on the individual rather than government or "the State" as the main locus of responsibility when dealing with "health" and other "risks" of modern society and burgeoning commercial and political interests in exploiting the investment possibilities in any number of "body matters" and concerns across westernized worlds. Together, these factors ensured that, by the mid 1980s, there had emerged not just widespread public interest in all matters physical (sex, diets, fitness, exercise regimes, body modification techniques) but an intellectual "community" of researchers in sociology and what we might loosely call "the sociology of PE", applying various forms of social theory and the methodologies of the social sciences to the study of the body in contemporary society. How "body knowledge" is produced, transmitted and received in and through the practices of education, physical education and health (PEH) and sport in and outside schools became a fashionable research concern.

Not everyone belonging to this intellectual "community" using social science tools to study education and PE would call themselves a "sociologist". Indeed to refer to them as "a community" as if they had distinct boundaries of interest, meeting points and social relations is somewhat problematic (see Bain, 1997). The sociology of physical education was fashioned in the 1970s and has fragmented, re-branded and internally differentiated ever since. It is much more appropriate to refer to "sociologies of physical education" than "a sociology of physical education", given that the discipline, reflecting mainstream sociology and the sociology of education more generally, is both more extensive than ever in terms of its subject matter and research and complex in the range of theoretical approaches it brings to bear upon its interests (see Ball, 2004; Reid, 1982). Indeed we would echo Ball's (2004) comments on the sociology of education generally, in saying that any attempt to encompass or sum up the sociology of physical education "within a single framework is fraught with difficulties" (Ball, 2004: 1). "What actually counts as the sociology of education is a construction" (Apple, 1996), made up of "shifting amalgamations of subgroups and traditions" (Godson, 1983: 3; quoted in Ball, 2004: 1). These are dynamic, shifting identities and research positions. Researchers may operate more or less comfortably (at various times and locations) under the mantles of critical curriculum historian (see Kirk, 1992, 1997a/b, 2004), curriculum theorist (Bain, 1990, 1997; Ennis, 1999; Kirk and Tinning 1990), feminist scholar/educator (Dodds, 1993; Clarke and Humberstone 1997; Humberstone and Pederson, 2001; Scraton, 1992) or define their identity with reference to one of the variants of social theory (see, Evans and Davies, 2004; Hunter, 2004) that characterize sociology, e.g., poststructuralist

(Wright, 2004), critical theorist (Fernandez Balbao, 1997), race or gender theorist (Harrison et al., 2002; Hickey and Fitzclarence 1999; Oliver and Lalik 2004) or figurational sociologist (Green, 2000, 2002). Others may locate their work within thematic strands, for example, the sociology of knowledge (Glyse et al., 2002), teacher education (Cassidy and Tinning, 2004 Curtner-Smith, 2001; Macdonald, 2003), professional and career development in PE (Armour and Jones, 1998), or health and physical education (see Becket, 2004). Or they may eschew labels altogether preferring, instead, to work pragmatically across social theories, in the interests of problem solving in education and PE (for example, Hellison, 1997; Hellison and Templin, 1991; Laker, 2003; Locke et al., 1998; O'Sullivan et al., 1992). What they all have in common is their use of concepts and methodologies of the social sciences to do either one or two things, sometimes simultaneously: contribute to our professional understandings of the embodied nature of educational phenomena and add to the body of knowledge called sociology.

Some writers and researchers may seem primarily concerned to shed light on, for example, the nature of teaching (Capel, 2004; Hardy and Mawer, 1990), "situated learning" (see Kirk and Macdonald, 1998), innovative pedagogy (Laker, 2003), curriculum or policy development in educational settings (Curtner-Smith, 1999; Ennis, 1999; Penney and Evans, 1999; Wright et al., 2004), deploying and refining sociological concepts and ideas toward this end. Others seem more concerned to interrogate how the variants of physical education found in schools and other institutions are implicated in processes of social and cultural reproduction; in the nature of class, gender, race, ability, amongst other social relations (see Azzarito and Solomon, 2005; Hayes and Stidder, 2003, Hunter, 2004); in social change, order and continuity; how power, authority and control are expressed in society and schools; and how all these complex processes, when expressed in physical education, help define how consciousness and desire are given specific forms, evaluated, distributed, challenged and changed (Evans et al., 2004; Wright et al., 2004). In order to do so, they are inevitably concerned with what and how teachers and pupils learn.

A distinction is sometimes invoked in overview discussions of this kind between "the sociology of education" and "educational sociology". The latter has a distinctive North American flavour, originating as it did in the USA as a marriage of educationalists and sociologists (see Reid, 1982) long before the emergence of the sociology of education within the then embryonic but thriving institutions of teacher education in the UK, Australia and elsewhere in the 1960s and 1970. While educational sociology tried to "solve educational problems in a practical way using sociology", as Reid (1982: 17) pointed out, sociologists of education endeavoured to go beyond this to offer theoretical explanations not simply with reference to an event's own characteristics but to factors, forces and influences that lay outside of and beyond them. These involved empirical investigations seeking to verify explanation through data gathering increasingly aware of its "relative objectivity", recognizing the effects of researchers' attitudes and values on what is observed and the importance of others' culturally determined attitudes and viewpoints. Theorizing, empirical investigation and relative "objectivity" constituted the claims of sociology of education to be "scientific" and distinct from educational sociology. However, this simple division is somewhat misleading. People and problems do not fall into neat categories of either "the sociology of education" or "educational sociology". Those interested in social theory for example, in explaining the nature of power, order and control in society and schools, are not just engaged in a sociological challenge but a set of moral, educational, professional and practical problems.

Any worthwhile sociology of physical education is grounded both in educational agendas, whether defined by teachers, pupils, parents, politicians, or sociologists and a sociological imagination that seeks "to grasp history and biography and the relation between the two within society" (Mills, 1959: 6). This means tracing connections between the personal issues or problems of pupils, teachers, teacher educators and others as they relate, for example, to success, failure, achievement, health/ill health and events, forces, policies and processes in the wider public domain (locally, nationally and internationally). It means making "visible what is rendered invisible through the society's institutional procedures, and through the daily practices of its members" (Bernstein, 1977: 157), including those found in school physical education and teacher education. This is a moral as well as an educational enterprise. There is no such thing as a value disinterested sociology of physical education or one divorced from the interests of teachers, children, parents, business, governments and others involved in its production, transmission and evaluation. Its research agendas and choices of research focus and subjects invariably generate descriptions of the social world that will not only define what knowledge, or the individual, or society, "is", but uncover and illuminate what it is held that they "ought to" be.

Core concepts: the "sociologies of physical education" – theory first?

It is not then, our intention here to overview the variety of sociological perspectives or social theories that have been brought to bear on the study of physical education during the last 20 or so years. That has been very ably accomplished elsewhere, for example, by Macdonald et al. (2002) who categorized the variety of theoretical perspectives that have informed physical education research in recent years as positivist, interpretive, socially critical, poststructuralist and feminist and pointed to the attendant shortcomings of blind allegiance to any one of these perspectives. Instead, they argue for the kind of "polyvocality" in social science research favoured by Sparkes (1992, 2002). Alternatively, we could eschew labels altogether and attempt to range across the fields of social theory and research pragmatically in the study of PE. It is perhaps worth noting that many of the most recent thinkers in the social sciences – Said, Sontag, Raymond Williams, Habermas, Foucault, Bourdieu, Bernstein – resisted any conventional label. For more explicit post-modern doubters, theory became "just a provisional name for the space you were left with when classical academic categories began to crumble. In this respect, the more traditional title for the theorist was the intellectual" (Eagleton, 2003: 22).

In our view, theory has an integral part to play not only in our understanding of education and physical education but also in its development and enhancement. In Australia, Luke (1999) has vividly illustrated how the detailed and conceptually dense theoretical sociological work of the British sociologist Basil Bernstein can both enhance understanding of social and cultural production and contribute substantially to policy initiatives and practices inside schools. Others have drawn on the work of the French social theorists Pierre Bourdieu (for example, see Brown 2005; Hunter, 2004) and Michel Foucault to understand and inform policy and practice in Physical Education, as it occurs in and outside schools (Wright, 2004; Wright et al., 2004). We should also remind ourselves that 'doing theory' is itself a form of labour involving investments of time, emotional energy and social relations and that it is not simply the preserve of academics in universities. What Terry Eagleton (2003) calls "lower case theory" goes on all the time. When viewing and interpreting the "abilities" or "health" of children, or explaining ill discipline, or reading the timetable, we are making basic assumptions about these everyday things, perhaps attempting to explain them and even predict what might happen next. All forms of practice are theory laden; rarely, if ever, is our thinking "theory free". Indeed, one of the key interests of a reflexive sociology of physical education is to document the nature of "lower case" theory, or what we would prefer to call "first-order theory" that professionals and others draw on in schools and elsewhere to make sense of their social worlds and explore its relationship with the "second-order" theories that sociology and others disciplines provide. Why do some achieve status and recognition, others not?

In fairness, the sociology of physical education is a relatively new subject area, its fields of research embryonic and much remains to be achieved. There is too little evidence of a cumulating body of knowledge in the sociology of physical education though on "situated learning", gender relations, policy development, curriculum innovation and the nature of power and control, there is shape to be discerned. There are attendant dangers, then, in providing overviews of the kind that simply catalogue changing theoretical perspectives. Inevitably they create the impression that a field is characterized either by rational, chronological development in which new and better theories replace old redundant ones, or that its scholars and researchers are merely followers of fad or fashion, their research product ever interesting but inconsequential, destined to offer hubris, news or poetry rather than enduring and cumulative knowledge to the field. Both have an element of truth that falls more readily into place when we consider more deeply the nature of knowledge in the social sciences. If there is lack of accumulated wisdom in the sociology of physical education the fault may not lie entirely with researchers in the field. In mainstream sociology, the turning away from classical figures in sociology and the crucial categories of the grand narratives of class, race, gender and ability in recent years may have been at the expense of important insights on issues, such as equity and justice in education, morality, poverty, that should touch the interests of all in education and PE (Eagleton, 2003; Shilling, 2004). As Eagleton (2003: 22) pointed out, many in academic work believed that "over the 1980s and 1990s theory had ceased to act as a critique and had become a branch of commodity production". History had ended, truth and totality were out, pleasure and pluralism were in, and "grand narratives were for the sad types with leather patches on their jacket elbows and Biros in their top pockets. Suddenly everyone was working on vampires and sadomasochism". Less histrionically, sociologists in PE have largely avoided such trends, remaining grounded in the interests and agendas of education and its practitioners in schools and elsewhere. Though invigorated and deriving insights from "new" social theory, theirs has been an enduring commitment to issues of prejudice, class, sexism, racism and elitism, always with an eye on their educational implications, on teaching and how children learn, succeed or fail.

It is also worth noting that the emergence of "new theory" and "new allegiances" in the sociology of physical education, as in sociology generally, may as Bernstein (2000) pointed out, have much to do with the nature of knowledge in the social sciences. Sociology is characterized by what Bernstein (2000: 163) referred to as "horizontal knowledge structures" featuring horizontal discourse and weak grammar.

The segmental organization of the knowledge/s of horizontal discourse leads to "segmentally structured acquisition" (p. 159). Students of sociology and the sociology of physical education are required to learn to speak particular social theoretical languages, for example, of Marxism, or post-structuralism, or figurational, interpretive, or critical social theory and tend to become socialized deeply into the underlying codes and modes of their (or more particularly, their teachers') perspectives.[1] Intellectual capital (that is to say, value, status and reward) is bound up with the language and, therefore, with its defence of the challenge to other languages (Bernstein, 2000: 162). Bernstein pointed out that one of the problems of acquiring a horizontal knowledge structure is the range of languages which has to be managed, each having its own procedures for doing theory and research (p. 163). Segmental competencies/literacies are culturally localized, "evoked by *contexts whose reading is unproblematic*" (p. 159). Furthermore, the more members that are isolated or excluded from each other, the weaker will be the social base for the development of either repertoires or reservoirs of knowledge with which to interrogate and understand the social world. One learns a particular gaze, "how to recognise, regard, realise and evaluate legitimately the phenomenon of concern" (p. 171). Theorizing is weak, even regarded with suspicion.

"Developments" in the sociology of physical education, as in sociology generally, sometimes are often no more than the introduction of new language/s offering the *potential* of a fresh perspective "rather than the development of theory which is more general, more integrating than previous theory" (Bernstein, 2000: 162). Some evidence of this in the sociology of physical education is to be found, for example, in its embracing of the theories of post structuralism (see Fernandez Balboa, 1997; Wright, 2004) and "situated learning" (Kirk, 2003; Kirk and Macdonald, 1998) in recent years, which have provided valuable new insight and knowledge on gender, "ability", health and teaching and learning in physical education in schools. But these features of horizontal knowledge/s and the social relations which support them also have the potential "to shatter any underlying sense of unity" among researchers in a way which may inhibit progress. The social worlds of PE are always "imaged by the complex, projections arising out of the relationships between individuals and groups in research communities" (ibid: 171). As Bernstein pointed out "imaging" "shows the potential of the social in its different modes of realisation and above all else it is a reminder that all knowledge is social in its production and realisation" (ibid: 171). This is true of sociology and all the other disciplines, for example, of psychology, physiology, etc., that inform the practices of PE. Reviewing any body of knowledge produced by sociology or psychology or another discipline must, then, be accompanied by an awareness of its social bases and the basic theoretical stance or perspective from which research is produced.

On such a view, while segmentation may be a feature of doing social *theory*, doing *research* in sociology and the sociology of physical education, if it is to be most productive, requires a shift from commitment to a language to "dedication to a problem and its vicissitudes":

> Latour makes a distinction between the science and research. Science refers to established canons, research refers to a dynamic interactional process. In the case of sociology and many of its 'ofs' the specialised languages are the equivalent of science. What is being advocated here is linguistic challenge by the dynamic interactional process of research; not a displacement but a repositioning of the role of specialised languages. (Bernstein, 2000: 171)

The challenge then, is "to combat fundamentalism" in research and theory with something "less brittle than post-modern relativism and scepticism". As Eagleton (2003: 22) argued, it is a "question of being deep without being dogmatic" and that we must "strike out from well trodden paths of class, race, gender, and look again at questions that have been shelved". Bernstein insisted that we must be concerned not only with "analysis of the 'message' of pedagogy (class, gender, race, region, nation, religion)" but its

> 'voice' that is never heard, only its realisations; that is, its messages. The 'voice' is constituted by the pedagogic device … a grammar for producing specialised messages, realisations … which regulates what it processes … orders and positions and yet contains the potential of its own transformation … the fundamental theoretical object of the discipline. (1990: 190)

The pedagogic device is shaped and contested as both official (central and local state) and pedagogic (higher education, specialized media producers and others exerting influence upon education) recontextualizing agencies rework newly produced discourse in forms fit for transmission by teachers, the reproducers of the system.

Very little of the detailed work required to fulfil Bernstein's project of analysis of "relations within" education has been undertaken, as yet, in physical education. As theoretical fashions have changed in mainstream sociology and have been productively reflected in the sociology of physical education, they have hardly diverted study from its "relations to", core socio-educational problems of class inequality, prejudice, gender and other stereotyping and

poverty that stubbornly fail to go away. We have hardly begun to elucidate the grammar of the device that generates them.

Major interests and agendas of the sociology of physical education

Who or what defines the interests and agendas of the sociology of physical education? At one level the answer is to be found in the discipline of sociology itself whose core interest lies with understanding the nature of social and cultural production and reproduction and the part played by schools and other fields of education in such processes. In contexts of formal education this is to focus on what Bernstein (1977: 85) refers to as the three message systems of education – *the curriculum* which defines what counts as valid knowledge, *pedagogy* which defines what counts as valid transmission of knowledge, and *evaluation* which defines what counts as a realization of this knowledge on the part of the taught. All are contexts of communication through which social reproduction and production occur and they together are major regulators of the structure of experience. The forms of instructional discourse that we operate always presuppose or can be regarded as being embedded in regulative ones. Understanding them requires that we focus on the forms of organization, administration, governance and government that influence these message systems, features of education that are all too rarely addressed in research in the sociology of physical education.[2]

Within the broad frame of sociological research outlined above, what we choose to focus on is as likely to be guided by altruism, financial and p/Political expediency, as any theoretical or substantive interest, or pressing educational concern. Even the enduring themes of sociology are fashioned and shaped by prevailing social and political educational agendas, along with current vogue methodologies and theories. For example, in the 1970 s the agendas of the sociology of physical education, reflecting those of the sociology of education and educationalists at the time, centred largely on what went on inside schools and classrooms, on pupil–teacher interaction, curriculum innovation and development, ability grouping policies and on issues relating to class and gender. Race, sexuality and education policy rarely entered the frame as serious research concerns until the 1980s. Interpretive sociologies and methodologies (for example, ethnography, ethnomethodology, phenomenology) often flavoured with variants of Marxism were, for many, the theoretical order of the day. By the mid-1980s, however, the focus then shifted away from classroom processes toward the study of policy, as the educational terrain became saturated with government policy and with issues of "difference", identity and "the body", as new forms of theory, such as that encapsulated in the writing of the French social theorist Michel Foucault and variously defined as post structuralism or postmodernism, became fashionable.

At another level, however, what we chose to focus upon in research in physical education will reflect, at least in part, our definition of and involvement with what education and physical education are and where we think it occurs. As with other school subjects, physical education is a social and affective process. It is as much concerned with the transmission of technical skills, competences and knowledge as it is with rules of behaviour and values. It socializes as its skills, helps lay down the rules of belonging to culture and class. It is also a process that is productive of culture, having the capacity, albeit limited, to alter and change how individuals think and act. But how and where does this occur? And what are its relative impacts on different social fields? If we see physical education as occurring only in the "communities of practice" of schools, clubs or universities, that is where research will be located. If, in contrast, we see physical education as occurring wherever there is enacted an intention on the part of one person to bring about change, amelioration and enhancement in the way in which another thinks about, uses and understands their body in relation to physical culture in all its prevailing forms we will also look beyond those formal institutions of education to embrace, for example, the formal and informal cultures of families, young people, clubs and associations, representations in the media and, perhaps, more importantly to the relationships between these diverse fields. We believe that this is prerequisite to appreciating the complexity of physical education and the ways in which individuals experience its message systems, within and across different fields. For example, in recent years "the media" (our TV screens, websites, newspapers, magazines, advertising outlets) have been filled with advice on how to get and stay healthy, eat "properly", exercise and get thin and how to avoid the purported "risks" of (post) modern society (see Gard, 2004). In doing so they are involved substantially in "physical education", both informally (in a routine, unorganized, casual fashion) through their impact on the thinking/mind sets of individuals and more formally where it is further mediated through Government policies on health and education and translated into a curriculum in schools. Indeed the fabrication and genesis – globally, locally, institutionally – of "risk" and its impact on the curriculum and pedagogies of teachers, parents and pupils in and outside schools, has become an important element of the interests of many in the sociology of PE in recent years (see Evans et al., 2004; Gard and Wright, 2001, 2005; Leahy and Harrison, 2004;

Tinning and Fitzclarence, 1992). Indeed, Tyler has suggested that if the boundaries of educational institutions are continually eroded through the applications of technology-driven and neo-liberal reform, the foundational claims of the socially productive functions of schooling, on which the sociology of education have been hitherto based, become increasingly destabilized and problematic.

> If pedagogic principles are so ubiquitous and pervasive in contemporary culture, then what are conventionally accepted as to be the social and communicative relations between school and society are inverted. No longer do educational processes merely reproduce society but, in some sense, they constitute and legitimate that society. (2004: 15–16)

Sociology is, by definition, "relational", its theoretical concerns displaying or focussing upon relationships between structure and agency and between micro, meso and macro fields of practice. Recent research in physical education, for example, by Holroyd (2003), some of it drawing on the theoretical work of Elias, Bourdieu and Foucault, has highlighted how important relationality is to sociological and educational understandings of how and what children learn in physical education and sport in schools and other social contexts. Others have attempted, empirically and conceptually, to trace the relationships between curriculum developments in schools and leisure, sport and health cultures outside them (Kirk, 2003), and between systems of governance and government policy and what goes on in PE (Leahy and Harrison, 2004). But effective empirical investigation of such relationality, of how practices and processes in one context, for example, in the family (see Kay, 2003), amongst peers, intersect with those in another, is rarely achieved. For example, how parents invest in the physical education of their children may have a powerful bearing on how their offspring are perceived in schools, how included they may feel, how they may succeed or fail. We have all too few empirical studies in physical education that offer such scope or perspective that not only enables us to make connections between levels of analysis (e.g., micro, meso and macro) but also traces actions and interactions across diverse fields (see Ball et al., 2000; Hunt, 2003; Macdonald, 2003; Wright, 2003).

The form and content of physical education has changed historically and varies across cultures so that in some contexts and periods, sport rather than health education, gymnastics rather than sport may feature more prominently than other physical activities. Indeed, one of the aspirations of the sociology of physical education is the investigation of the changing forms and definitions of physical education, of what is to count as valid physical education and why, at any given time. History is not a foreign place in the sociology of physical education,

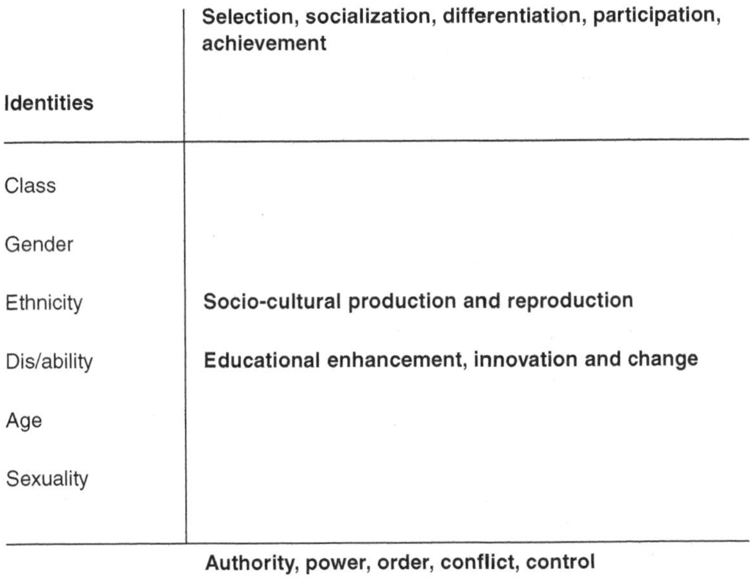

Identities | Selection, socialization, differentiation, participation, achievement

Class

Gender

Ethnicity   Socio-cultural production and reproduction

Dis/ability   Educational enhancement, innovation and change

Age

Sexuality

Authority, power, order, conflict, control

Figure 2.2.1   The sociology of physical education – conceptualizing social and cultural production and reproduction and educational change

any more than what goes on in other cultures, in the home, among families, in clubs and playgrounds. All are fundamental to our understanding of how the pedagogies, curriculum and assessment policies of the present day are shaped and shape the teachers and pupils who are subjected to them. And, as we have contended, schools and institutions of teacher education are not the only places where physical education occurs. In the sociology of physical education we should extend our perspectives to include all its forms, however configured and wherever they occur. Indeed, this is even more important in the world that Tyler (2004: 1) conjectures. "We" (in westernised societies) live in societies that are becoming "totally pedagogised" (see Bernstein, 2001). Pedagogised activity occurs across a variety of sites and is a lifetime process. We share Tyler's Bernsteinian view that we therefore need a firm understanding of the articulation of "the relations within" pedagogic processes and their "relations to" (i.e. of education to other relationships based on gender, class, race, and ethnicity) as they are articulated in and outside schools and how these together constitute the embodied self (see Evans and Davies, 2004; Hunter, 2004).

Trends and directions: socialization, identity, power and control

The sociology of physical education has, then, at its core, interests in how formal and informal forms of

physical education are implicated in social and cultural production and reproduction and how these processes of forming knowledge and identity contribute towards educational enhancement, progress, stability, innovation and change. To this end, we suggest that its research agenda should focus on the five interrelated processes of selection, socialization, differentiation, participation and achievement. This would involve investigating the ways in which these express, produce and reproduce relations of authority, power, conflict, order and control and would contribute in the social construction and production of embodied identity. None are separate or distinct social processes either conceptually or empirically. We might represent the complexity of their relationships as in Figure 2.2.1.

A research interest in, for example, any one of the five processes identified across the upper horizontal axis inescapably touches others along it. For example, it would be difficult to say anything about how teachers identify and select pupils in physical education without offering comment on socialization and differentiation. Equally, although each of these processes can be studied in its own right, we are unlikely to gain purchase on their complexity unless we also consider how each, alone or together, reflects and is the "effect of" relations of authority, power, order and control in society and schools and how these dynamic processes help construct or are constructed by the relations of class, gender, ethnicity, "ability"/disability, sexuality and age, with which they intersect. No process along the upper horizontal axis occurs outside or independently of relations of authority, power, order, conflict and control, represented along the bottom axis; or without either framing or being framed by the multiple characteristics of identity, represented along the vertical axis. That axis is not intended to represent a hierarchy of identity or influence, though we claim elsewhere in this book that in the "last instance" social class is the most powerful influence on individuals' life chances (for example, in education, employment and health) both in and outside schools.

As sociologists of physical education we may, for example, have as our prime concern issues of gender and physical education. Their investigation would be incomplete unless it also considered how processes of gender construction were mediated by class, ethnicity and other dimensions of identity and implicated in relations of power, order and control. As yet, few investigations in physical education have achieved such a complex relational perspective.

But what of the five core social processes?

Socialization

Socialization refers to the processes by which we learn to become members of the social groups, communities, societies to which we belong. It does not only occur in schools but in all social spheres of life and it is in the relationships between fields of socialization that new insights are to be found (Humberstone and Pedersen, 2001). Nor does it involve only imposition of values, as it is a productive process in which cultures may be consolidated, changed, refined or re-defined. It is also a process in which there is likely to be conflict and tension as cultures are resisted, adapted, fought over and challenged; a "sociology of transgression and deviancy" must feature routinely in the sociology of physical education. We might consider schools as "social worlds or social systems" comprising social interactions which shape and are shaped by prevailing (and emerging) mores, values and norms. We can approach this via studies of the cultures of schools, their departments, subject communities, teachers, pupils, peers, other educational workers, all the while bearing in mind that education occurs in "learning communities" that extend beyond schools (Lave and Wenger, 1991) and that there are formal as well as informal aspects of socialization; for example, what pupils learn "formally" in the classroom may be more or less important in terms of its impact on their embodied consciousness, as what they learn "informally" behind the bicycle shed or from the influences of TV. Research in the sociology of physical education has revealed that historically physical education has not only reflected but also privileged certain values and interests that might fairly be described as those of

middle class, able-bodied, heterosexual, mesomorphic, males and rejected others. We have a number of studies of how middle class or hegemonic masculine values are reproduced and embodied through the formal and informal apparatus of schools (e.g., Hickey et al., 1998; Kirk, 1993). We also know much about sport as a socialization agency (Rees, 1995; Stroot, 2002). But we have yet to explore how the variety of sub-cultural identities that defines contemporary societies intersect and are reflected and represented in physical education in and outside schools. And we have barely begun to capture the dynamic between the informal and formal cultures of parents, pupils, peers, and teachers (see MacDonald, 2003; Wright, 2003; Light, 2006). Yet as Luke (1999: 20) has pointed out, we ought not to begin to decide what to do educationally or plan where to put resources and programmes unless we know something about the students we are teaching and the communities we work in, though many politicians and teachers continue to do so. He is also right to suggest that terms like middle class, masculinity, femininity, can get in the way of achieving this, unless our descriptions begin to uncover their nuance and variety. Given the vibrancy of the sociology of physical education, we perhaps now have a remarkable opportunity to study changes in pedagogic discourse and processes as they are occurring in and outside schools and which control the body as message systems. In schools, amongst other things, this will mean tracing the significance over the past decades of the transformation of physical training into physical education (see Kirk, 1992) and back again, in the UK, in the reclassification of teacher education as teacher training. It will mean tracing the transformation in some contexts of physical education to "sport education", in others, the infusion of health education into its curriculum. What shifts in regulative and instructional principles are involved in these changes? What body pedagogies (and their derivative, body pedagogics) do they generate? A shift from the body abstracted from pupils' experience (as something to be trained) to the body as a critical realization of pupils' experience (as something to be constantly worked on and improved) (Beckett, 2004; Bernstein, 1990; Evans et al., 2004) involves a shift from one dominant discourse to another, emerging from conflict and competition between official and pedagogic agents and implying changes in relations of power and control, practices and values. Identities do not shift with the wind. We need to turn to study of the three message systems of education, curriculum, pedagogy and evaluation, the internal grammar of their hierarchical distributive, recontextualizing and evaluative rules and their organizational and administrative forms and governance (in and outside schools) if we are to provide more complete and complex understanding of how they are experienced, resisted, received and shape subjectivity and identity.

Differentiation

How are children categorized in and through the formal and informal practices and processes of physical education by teachers, coaches, pupils, peers, parents, others; and what principles underpin and regulate such processes. How do these processes relate to differentiation in the social structures of schools and society? What are the reference points in the differentiation process – social class, "ability", gender, ethnicity, age, sexuality, body appearance, personality? What are the social cues, bodily demeanours, predispositions, that teachers, pupils, others, use to categorize themselves and others? What social and emotional as well as technical attributes lead teachers to identify themselves or their peers and their pupils as successes or failures in physical education? How is "ability" configured and identified in relation to the message systems of schooling? How are teachers and others expected to differentiate their charges for policy makers, parents and others with vested interests in education, in and outside school? Although researchers in physical education have gone some way toward documenting how children and young people are categorised and differentiated by gender in physical education (for example, see Clarke and Humberstone, 1997; Flintoff and Scraton, 2001; Penney, 2002) we have few studies of class, ethnicity (for example, Benn, 1996; Zaman, 1997), sexuality (Clarke, 2004) and disability (DePauw, 2000; Smith, 2004; Sparkes, 2004) or of how teachers are socialized in schools and institutions of teacher education (Brown and Evans, 2004; Rich, 2001). And it is quite extraordinary that we have had so few studies since the 1970s of how in physical education, teachers and pupils are categorized by "ability" (see Bailey and Morley, 2003; Brittain, 2004; Sparkes, 2004; Penney and Hunter, 2006), especially as "tracking" and other forms of grouping for teaching in other subject areas have been a considerable research concern (see Hallam, 2002; Kulik and Kulik, 1982). Consequently we know very little of what, and how, organisational practices in schools and teacher education reflect and endorse particular conceptions of "ability", or how tracking, streaming, mixed ability, or banding, bear on how pupils think about their own and others' bodies in relation to learning, achievement and participation in physical activity. Teachers are also differentiated and regulated within school and teacher education subcultures by conceptions of "ability" through processes that reflect and recreate relations of power, order and control.

Selection

It is now over 70 years since Willard Waller wrote his seminal exposition on the sociology of teaching, in which he argued that in the US:

the amount of schooling which children undergo foreshadows, and some would say determines, their future earning capacity and the level of society on which they will find their life. A crude selection, then, goes on in schools, a social selection of those destined to fulfil certain predetermined social functions. Partly it is schools themselves that select. The native intelligence of children sets certain absolute limits to their achievements. No amount of schooling can make the moron perform satisfactorily above his fated level – the school must sort all the human material that comes to them.

The children of the rich are carried by express elevators of prep schools that do not stop below the college levels. The most stupid, indeed, sometimes fall off the elevator, but even these may ultimately ascend to the higher floors by dint of much tutoring and the offices of friends. But the children of the poor tend to drop out early, and very frequently for reasons quite other incapacity to learn; they drop out because their labour is needed at home, because they are ashamed to attend school in shabby clothes, because there is no tradition in their group of going beyond the literacy stage in education. (1932: 20)

After 70 years of "progressive" educational change little in the way of relative poverty and achievement in formal education has changed. It is still the case that we are more likely to enjoy better health, live longer, take part in more sport and organized leisure and enjoy a higher income, the more years of formal education we have experienced. Want health and longevity? Forget health education, fitness regimes and expensive diets; just avoid being working class. But what is the nature of selection in physical education in and outside school? What principles underscore and regulate selection procedures amongst teachers, pupils, peers, others, and what organizational (grouping policies), curriculum, pedagogical and assessment practices do they reflect and endorse? In the UK for example, policies have emerged that ask teachers to identify the 'gifted and talented', while simultaneously embracing "inclusion" as an educational ideal. How, in the increasingly competitive environments of schools, are equality and equity to be achieved (see Penney, 2003)? How are the gifted and talented identified and categorized? Who are the "new professionals" the Sports Development Officers, the "link teachers"who are to perform these deeds? How are they selected and with what consequence for whom? (see Penney and Houlihan, 2003). Are particular forms of body perfection (slender ideals) providing criteria for selection in PE and health settings inside schools? (Rich et al., 2004).

Achievement

Given the emphasis on "performance" in sport and other physical activities and the place and position it has enjoyed in physical education in recent years, it is not surprising that "achievement" has been defined in terms of "ability" to perform or that it plays such a large part in categorization. But how are "ability" and achievement configured through the message systems of physical education and by the policies, forms of government and administration that help shape them? How is achievement defined within the cultures and sub-cultures of schools, in the home, amongst peers, in formal and informal cultures? Why is achievement defined in terms of "ability" rather than, say "desire", or aptitude, or empathy? How have definitions of achievement changed over time and across cultures, and what are the social, emotional, personal, embodied reference points for its recognition? What is the nature of skill, knowledge and competence; what and whose corporeal dispositions (i.e. skills, body shapes or sizes) are recognized as being of value and are nurtured and how does this relate to processes occurring outside schools amongst peers, in family life? Does physical education inside schools interrupt or support processes of "achievement" occurring elsewhere? How are "abilities", desires and "pleasures" configured in relation to economic, social, and political interests and who, socially, politically and educationally, is to decide? (see Pronger, 2002). Again, we cannot begin to understand these processes unless we see them relationally, with reference to multiple identities and relations of power, authority, order, conflict and control.

Participation

This is not just a matter of documenting who does what in terms of involvement in physical activity in, outside or after school; it is also to interrogate the trajectories of people's lives, their interruptions, conflicts, tensions, transgressions and obstructions. How, for example, do pupils progress through school systems, from primary to secondary, on to university or college, through the physical education curriculum, pedagogies and evaluation schemes, into the parallel worlds of leisure in clubs or the home, then into physical activity after school and into later life? What are the critical incidents or critical phases in their careers in physical education and sport and other leisure forms? Beyond knowing who does what in terms of class and gender, race and participation, we know next to nothing of the reasons why, or how individuals make decisions in and out of school (or of the pleasures and pains that may accompany such decisions). Again, we need to ask how these processes are cross-cut by relations of authority, power, order, conflict and control, and how they construct and are constructed by particular forms of consciousness, subjectivity and identity.

We can not study any of these processes independently of an analysis of the curriculum, pedagogies and assessments that pupils experience in schools, or of the policy contexts, government and administrative processes that define and help shape each of these aspects of education. All are communicative contexts and forms of action regulated by principles in which meanings are attributed to actions and ultimately embodied. As such we need constantly remind ourselves (*pace Bernstein*), of the sociological questions that must lie at the heart of any project calling itself a sociology of physical education:

> First, how does a dominating distribution of power and principles of control generate, distribute, reproduce and legitimate dominating and dominated principles of communication? Second, how does such a distribution of principles of communication regulate relations within and between social groups? Third, how do these principles of communication produce a distribution of forms of pedagogic consciousness? (2000: 4)

In summary, how does power and control translate into principles of communication, and how do these principles of communication differentially regulate forms of embodied consciousness with respect to their reproduction and the possibility of change? How do these processes enhance social and educational progress, innovation and change in society and schools? Whether our theoretical interest is positivist, poststructuralist, interpretative, functionalist, figurational or Marxist, each in its own way is interested in issues such as these, in how formal and informal processes of education impact the subjectivities and embodied identities of teacher and pupils in and outside schools.

Conclusion

The sociology of physical education was a practice born of the modernist project (see Evans and Davies, 1993; Fernandez-Balbao, 1997; Laker, 2002), its endeavour to help make things "better" for more pupils in schools and PE. Its agendas are not exhausted or redundant despite the advent of what some call "new times" (Kirk, 1997a). Equity and social justice are still prime educational issues and motivating forces for those embarking on research in PE (Hayes and Stidder, 2003; Laker, 2002; Penney, 2002; Wright et al., 2004). As Luke (1999: 2) reminded us, "it is imperative that we understand exactly who is being left out and left behind, educationally, economically and socially". In some respects, in some cultural contexts, we do live in "new times" and it is, therefore, important that we provide close and detailed analysis of how new community and cultural configurations bear on these matters. But we also need "finer grained analysis of how social class, location, gender and poverty and culture blend and mix – and how particular blends of these actually are at the basis of the failure and alienation that many people still experience" (Luke, 1999: 3).

Of course the sociology of physical education is limited in its capacity to achieve this. It stands as only one among many influences and social practices acting upon the lives of teachers, pupils and others in and outside schools. But schools, and physical education within them, are key institutions in processes of social and cultural reproduction and the sociology of physical education has a part to play in our understanding of how these processes occur and what potentially they mean and can achieve in educational terms. In short, its concepts and methods can inform the nature of pedagogy (see Wright et al., 2004). Indeed, we share Luke's view, that change for the better will only occur if there are particular alignments of elements of regulative and instructional practices within the three message systems curriculum, pedagogy and evaluation and some understanding of how these are configured in schools and wider social systems, constrained or framed by the play of power, authority and control.

> We can't begin to change outcomes, and we can't begin 'making a difference' with the most at risk kids and generating different patterns of results within individual classrooms and across systems unless we get the three message systems working in a coordinated, principled and educationally constructive way. (Luke, 1999: 5)

Morais and her colleagues would agree.[3] In the future, the use value of sociology of physical education may be defined in terms of how well it can contribute to the achievement of this worthy ideal.

Notes

1 Larry Locke provides an interesting, constructively critical illustration of this phenomenon with reference to the journal, Sport, Education and Society (see http://www.unlockresearch.com/content/articl/3/26/).

2 These are beginning to be addressed quite systematically in some others, such as science education, through the work of researchers like Morais, Neves and their associates in Portugal. Their work can be most readily accessed in Morais and Neves (2001); Morais et al. (2004); Neves and Morais (2001); and Neves et al. (2004).

3 Morais and her co-workers would claim that their studies have shown that a mixed pedagogic practice with quite specific features, such as open teacher–child and child–child communicative relations, explicit evaluation criteria, weak pacing of learning, strong intradisciplinary relations and high level of conceptual demand and investigative proficiency can promote high levels of scientific development in primary school children that can overcome a disadvantaged student background even with respect of complex cognitive competences.

References

Apple, M. (1996). Power, meaning and identity: Critical sociology of education in the United States. *British Journal of Sociology of Education, 17* (2), 125–144.

Armour, K.A. and Jones, R.J. (1998). *Physical education and teacher's lives and careers.* London: The Falmer Press.

Azzavito, L. and Solomon, M.A. (2005). A reconceptualization of physical education: The intersection of gender/race/social class. *Sport, Education and society special issue, 10* (1), 25-49.

Bain, L. (1997). Transformation in the postmodern era: A new game plan. In J.M. Fernandez-Balboa (Ed.), *Critical postmodernism in human movement, physical education and sport.* Albany: State University of New York Press, pp. 183–197.

Bain, L. (1998). A critical analysis of the hidden curriculum in physical education, in D. Kirk and R. Tinning (Eds.), *Physical education, curriculum and culture.* London: The Falmer Press, pp. 23–43.

Bailey, R. and Morley, D. (2003). Towards a model of talent development in physical education. Paper presented as the annual conference of the British Educational Research Association, Edinburgh.

Ball, S. (2003). *The more things change. Educational research, social class and 'interlocking' inequalities.* Stevenage: Pear Tree Press.

Ball, S. (2004). The sociology of education. A disputational account. In S. Ball (Ed.), *The Routledge/Falmer reader in sociology of education.* London: Routledge/Falmer.

Ball, S., Maguire, M. and Macrae, S. (2000). *Choice, pathways and transitions post 16.* London: Routledge/Falmer.

Becket, L. (2004) (Ed.). Health, the body and identity work in health and physical education. *Sport, Education and Society,* Special Edition, *9* (2), 171–175.

Benn, T. (1996). Muslim women and physical education in initial teacher training. *Sport, Education and Society, 1* (1), 5–23.

Bernstein, B (1977). *Class, codes and control. towards a theory of educational transmission. Volume III Class, codes and control.* London: Routledge & Kegan Paul.

Bernstein, B. (1990). *The structuring of pedagogic discourse. Volume IV Class, codes and control,* (2nd ed.). London, Routledge.

Bernstein, B. (2000). *Pedagogy, symbolic control and identity.* New York, Oxford: Rowman and Littlefield Publishers Inc.

Bernstein, B. (2001). From pedagogies to knowledge. In A. Morais, I. Neves, B. Davies and H. Daniels (Eds.), *Towards a sociology of pedagogy: The contribution of Basil Bernstein to research.* New York: Peter Lang.

Brittain, I. (2004). The role of schools in constructing self-perceptions of sport and physical education in relation to pupils with disabilities. *Sport, Education and Society, 9,* 1, 75–95.

Brown, D. (2005). An economy of gendered practices? Learning to teach physical education from the perspective of Pierre Bourdieu's embodied sociology. *Sport, Education and society, 10* (1), 3–25.

Brown, D. and Evans, J. (2004). Reproducing gender? Intergenerational links and the male PE teacher as a cultural conduit in teaching physical education. *Journal of Teaching Physical Education, 23* (1), 48–71.

Capel, S. (2004). Teachers, teaching and pedagogy in physical education. In K. Green and K. Hardman (Eds), *Physical Education. Special Issues.* London: Sage.

Cassidy, T. and Tinning, R. (2004). Slippage is not a dirty word: Considering the usefulness of Giddens' notion of knowledgeability in understanding the possibility for teacher education. *Teaching Education, 15* (2), 175–188.

Clarke, G. (2004). Threatening space. (Physical) education and homophobic body work. In J. Evans, B. Davies and J. Wright (Eds.) (2004) *Body Knowledge and control. Studies in the sociology of physical education and health,* pp. 191–205. London: Routledge.

Clarke, G. and Humberstone, B. (1997). *Researching women and sport.* London: Macmillan.

Curtner-Smith, M. (1999). The more things change the more they stay the same: factors influencing teachers' interpretation and delivery of national curriculum physical education. *Sport, Education and Society, 4* (1), 63–75

Curtner-Smith, M. (2001). The occupational socialisation of a first year physical education teacher with a teaching orientation. *Sport Education and Society, 6* (1): 81–101.

DePauw, K.P. (2000). Social-cultural context of disability: Implications for scientific inquiry and professional preparation. *Quest, 52* (4): 358–368.

Dodds, P. (1993). Removing the ugly isms from your gym, in J. Evans, (Ed.) *Equality, education and physical education,* (pp. 28–43). London: The Falmer Press.

Eagleton, T. (2003). Bin Laden sure didn't read any beer mats. *The Times Higher Educational Supplement,* October 3, p. 22.

Ennis, C. D. (1999). Creating a culturally relevant curriculum for disengaged girls. *Sport, Education and Society, 4,* 1, 31–51.

Evans. J. (1988). Body matters: towards a socialist physical education. In H. Lauder and P. Brown. (Eds.), *Education in search of a future* (pp. 174–192). London: The Falmer Press.

Evans, J. (1986). *Physical education, sport and schooling. studies in the sociology of physical education.* London: The Falmer Press.

Evans, J. and Davies, B. (1993). Physical education post ERA., in a postmodern society. In J. Evans (Ed.) (1993) *Equality, Education and Physical Education,* pp. 233–238. London: The Falmer Press.

Evans, J. and Davies, B. (2004). Pedagogy, symbolic control, identity and health. In J. Evans, B. Davies and J. Wright (Eds.) (2004) *Body Knowledge and control. Studies in the sociology of physical education and health.* London: Routledge.

Evans, J. and Davies, B. (2004). The embodiment of consciousness. *Bernstein, health and schooling.* In J. Evans, B. Davies and J. Wright (Eds.) (2004) *Body Knowledge and control. Studies in the sociology of physical education and health,* pp. 207–218. London: Routledge.

Evans, J., Davies, B. and Wright, J. (Eds.) (2004). *Body knowledge and control. Studies in the sociology of physical education and health.* London: Routledge.

Ennis, C.D. (1999). Creating a culturally relevant curriculum for disadvantaged girls, *sport education and society, 4* (1): 31–51

Fernandez-Balbao, J.M. (1997). *Critical Postmodernism in Human Movement, Physical Education and Sport.* Albany: State University of New York Press.

Flintoff, A. and Scraton, S. (2001). Stepping into active leisure? Young women's perceptions of active lifestyles and their experiences of school physical education. *Sport, Education and society, 6* (1), 5-21.

Gard, M and Wright, J. (2001). 'Managing uncertainty: Obesity discourses and physical education in a risk society', *Studies in the Philosophy of Education,* 20: 535–549.

Gard, M. and Wright, J. (2005). *The obesity epidemic. Science, morality and ideology.* London: Routledge.

Goodson, I. (1983). *School subjects and curriculum change.* Beckenham: Croom Helm.

Green, K. (2000). Exploring the everyday philosophies of physical education teachers from a sociological perspective. *Sport, Education and Society, 5* (2): 109–131.

Green, K. (2002). Physical education teachers in their figurations. A sociological analysis of everyday Philosophies. *Sport, Education and Society, 7* (2), 65–85.

Glyse, J., Pigeassou, C., Marcellini, E., De Leseleuc and Bui-Xuan, G. (2002). Physical education as a subject in France (school curriculum, policies and discourse): The body and the metaphors of the engine – elements used in the analysis of a power and control system during the second industrial revolution. *Sport, Education and Society, 7* (1), 5–25.

Hallam, S. (2002). *Ability grouping in schools.* London: Institute of Education, University of London.

Hardy, C.A. and Mawer, M. (Eds) (1999). *Learning and teaching in physical education.* London: The Falmer Press.

Harrison, L., Harrison, C.K. and Moore, L. (2002). African American racial identity and sport. *Sport, Education and Society, 7* (2), 121–135.

Hargreaves, J. (1982). *Sport, culture and ideology.* London: Routledge and Kegan Paul.

Hayes, S. and Stidder, G. (2003). *Equity and inclusion in physical education.* London: Routledge/Falmer.

Hellison, D. (1997). A practical inquiry into the critical-postmodernist perspective in physical education. In J.M. Fernandez-Balbao (Ed.) (1997). *Critical Postmodernism in Human Movement, Physical Education and Sport,* pp. 197–207. Albany: State University of New York Press.

Hellison, D. and Templin, T. (1991). *A reflective approach to physical education,* Leeds, UK: Human Kinetics.

Hickey, C., Fitzclarence, L. and Mathews, R. (1998). *Where the boys are: Masculinity, sport and education.* Deakin: Deakin Centre for Education and Change.

Hickey, C., and Fitzclarence, L. (1999). Educating boys in sports and physical education. *Sport, Education and Society, 4* (1), 51–63.

Holroyd, RA. (2003). Fields of experience: Young people's construction of embodied identities. Unpublished thesis, Loughborough: Loughborough University,

Hunt, K. (2003). Young muslim women, physical activity and physical culture: dispelling myths, or reinforcing stereotypes, paper presented at the NZARE/AARE conference. *Educational research risks and dilemmas.* Auckland.

Hunter, L. (2004). Bourdieu and the social space of the PE class: Reproduction of Doxa through practice. *Sport, Education and Society, 9* (2), 175–192.

Humberstone, B. and Pedersen, K. (2001). Gender, class and outdoor traditions. *Sport, Education and Society, 6* (1), 23–35.

Jenkins, C. (1982). Sociology and physical education, In A. Hartnett, (Ed.), *The social sciences in educational studies: A selective guide to the literature* (pp. 275–283) London, Heineman.

Kay, T. (2003). The family factor in sport. A review of family factors affecting sports participation. Institute of sport and leisure policy. Loughborough: Loughborough University.

Kelly, P. (2000). The dangerousness of youth-at-risk: the possibilities of surveillance and intervention in uncertain times. *Journal of Adolescence 23,* 463–476.

Kirk, D. (1992). Defining physical education. *The social construction of a subject in post war Britain.* London: Falmer Press.

Kirk, D. (1993). *The body schooling and culture.* Geelong, Victoria: Deakin University Press.

Kirk, D. (1997a). Schooling bodies in New times: The reform of physical education in high modernity. In J.M. Fernandez-Balbao (Ed.) (1997). *Critical Postmodernism in Human Movement, Physical Education and Sport,* pp. 39-65. Albany: State University of New York Press.

Kirk, D. (1997b). Socio-cultural research in physical education and health education: recent trends future developments. In J. Wright (Ed.), *Researching in physical and health education* pp. 5–23. Woollangong: University of Wollongong.

Kirk, D. (2003). The social construction of physical education. Legitimation crises and strategic intervention in education reform. In K. Hardman (Ed.), *Sport science studies. Physical education: Deconstruction and reconstruction – issues and directions, 12,* ICSSPE. pp. 153–171.

Kirk, D. (2004). Toward a critical history of the body, identity and health: corporeal power and school practice. In J. Evans, B. Davies and J. Wright (Eds.) (2004) *Body Knowledge and control. Studies in the sociology of physical education and health,* pp. 52–68. London: Routledge.

Kirk, D. and Macdonald, D. (1998). Situated learning in physical education. *Journal of Teaching in Physical Education, 17* (3), 376–387.

Kirk, D. and Tinning, R. (1990). *Physical education, curriculum and culture.* London: The Falmer Press.

Kulik, C-L.C. and Kulik, J.A. (1982). Effects of ability grouping on secondary school students. A meta analysis of evaluation findings. *American Educational Research Journal, 19,* 415–428.

Laker, A. (2002). The sociology of physical education. *An introductory reader,* London: Routledge/Falmer.

Laker, A. (2003). *The future of physical education.* London: Routledge.

Lave, J. and Wenger, E. (1991). *Situated learning: legitimate peripheral participation.* New York: Cambridge University press.

Leahy, D and Harrison, L. (2004). Health and physical education and the production of the 'at risk self'. In J. Evans, B. Davies and J. Wright (Eds.) (2004) *Body Knowledge and control. Studies in the sociology of physical education and health,* pp. 130–140. London: Routledge.

Light, R. (2006). Situated learning in an Australian surf club. *Sport, Education and society, 11* (2), 155–173.

Luke, A. (1999). Education 2010 and new times: Why equity and social justice still matter, but differently, paper prepared for the Education Queensland online conference, 20/10/99.

Locke, L.F., Siverman, S.J. and Spirduso, W.W. (1998). *Reading and understanding research.* Thousand Oaks, CA: Sage Publications

Locke, L. (2003). Research journal of the month, November 2003, '*Sport, Education and Society*', http://www.unlockresearch.com/content/article/3/26.

MacDonald, D. (2003). Families and physical activity: fortification, facilitation and a 'forbidden thing', paper presented at the NZARE/AARE conference Educational Research Risks and Dilemmas, Auckland, November, 2003.

MacDonald, D., Kirk, D., Metzler, M., Nilges, L.M., Schempp, P. and Wright, J. (2002). It's all very well in theory. Theoretical perspectives and their application in contemporary pedagogic research, *Quest, 54* (2), 133–157.

Marshall, G. (1998). *Oxford dictionary of sociology.* Oxford: Oxford University Press.

Mills, C.W. (1959). *The sociological imagination.* Harmondsworth: Penguin.

Morais, A. and Neves, I. (2001). Pedagogic social contexts: Studies for a sociology of learning. In A. Morais, I. Neves, B. Davies and H. Daniels (Eds.) *Towards a sociology of pedagogy: The contribution of Basil Bernstein to research.* New York: Peter Lang.

Morais, A., Neves, I., Davies, B. and Daniels, H. (Eds.) (2001). *Towards a sociology of pedagogy. The contribution of Basil Bernstein to research.* New York: Peter Lang.

Morais, A., Neves, I. and Pires, D. (2004). The *what* and the *how* of teaching and learning: Going deeper into sociological analysis and intervention. In J. Muller, B. Davies and A. Morais (Eds.) (2004). *Reading Bernstein, Researching Bernstein,* pp. 75–91. London: Routledge/Falmer.

Neves, I. and Morais, A. (2001). Texts and contexts in educational systems: Studies in recontextualising spaces. In A. Morais, I. Neves, B. Davies and H. Daniels (Eds.) *Towards a sociology of pedagogy: The contribution of Basil Bernstein to research,* pp. 185-221. New York: Peter Lang.

Neves, I. Morais, A. and Alfonso, M. (2004). Teacher training contexts: Study of specific sociological characteristics. In J. Muller, B. Davies and A. Morais (Eds.) (2004). *Reading Bernstein, Researching Bernstein,* pp. 168–189. London: Routledge/Falmer.

Oliver, K. and Lalik, R. (2004). The beauty walk. Interrogating whiteness as the norm for beauty within one school's hidden curriculum. In J. Evans, B. Davies and J. Wright (Eds.) (2004) *Body Knowledge and control.*

Studies in the sociology of physical education and health, pp. 157–173. London: Routledge.

O'Sullivan, M., Siedentop, D. and Locke, L.F. (1992). Toward collegiality. Competing viewpoints among teacher educators. *Quest*, 44 (2), 266–280.

Penney, D. (2002). *Gender and physical education. Contemporary issues and future directions.* London: Routledge.

Penney, D. (2003). Can we promote collaboration amidst a culture of performativity? Paper presented at the NZARE/AARE conference, Educational Research Risks and Dilemmas, Auckland, November 2003.

Penney, D. and Evans, J. (1999). *Politics, policy and practice in physical education.* London: E&FN Spon.

Penney, D. and Houlihan, B. (2003). Specialist colleges national monitoring and evaluation research report: First National Survey report. Loughborough. Institute of Youth Sport.

Penney, D. and Hunter, L. (2006). Ability, curriculum and pedagogy. *Sport, Education and society special issue, 11* (3).

Pronger, B. (2002). *Body fascism.* London: University of Toronto Press.

Rees, R. (1995). What price victory? Myths, rituals, athletics and the dilemmas of schooling. In A. Sadonovik (Ed.), *Knowledge and pedagogy.* Norwood, NJ: Ablex Publishing Corporation.

Reid, I. (1982). *Sociological perspectives on school and education.* Somerset, UK: Open Books.

Rich, E. (2001). Gender positioning in teacher education. *International Studies in Sociology of Education, 11* (2), 131–157.

Rich, E., Holroyd, R. and Evans, J. (2004). Hungry to be noticed: Young women, anorexia and schooling. In J. Evans, B. Davies and J. Wright (Eds.) (2004) *Body Knowledge and control. Studies in the sociology of physical education and health,* pp. 173-191. London: Routledge.

Smith, A. (2004). The inclusion of pupils with special educational needs in secondary school physical education, *Physical Education. and Sport Pedagogy, 9* (1), 37–55.

Sparkes, A. (1992). The paradigms debate. In A. Sparkes (Ed.), *Research in physical education and sport* (pp. 9–60). London: The Falmer Press.

Sparkes, A. (2002). *Telling tales in sport and physical activity, a qualitative journey.* Leeds, UK: Human Kinetics.

Sparkes, A. (2004). From performance to impairment. A patchwork of embodied memories. In J. Evans, B. Davies and J. Wright (Eds.) (2004) *Body Knowledge and control. Studies in the sociology of physical education and health,* pp. 115–130. London: Routledge.

Scraton, S. (1992). Shaping up to womanhood. Buckingham, UK: Open University Press.

Shilling, C. (1993). *The body and social theory.* London: Sage.

Shilling, C. (2004). Educating bodies: schooling and the constitution of society. In J. Evans, B. Davies and J. Wright (Eds.) (2004) *Body Knowledge and control. Studies in the sociology of physical education and health,* pp. xv–xxii. London: Routledge.

Stroot, S.A. (2002). Sport as a socialising agency. In A. Laker, (Ed.), *The sociology of sport and physical education* (pp. 129–148). London: The Falmer Press.

Tinning, R. and Fitzclarence, L. (1992). Postmodern youth culture and the crisis in Australian secondary school physical education. *Quest, 44*: 287–304.

Tyler, W. (2004). Silent, invisible, total: Pedagogic discourse and the age of information. In J. Muller, B. Davies and A. Morais (Eds.) (2004). *Reading Bernstein, Researching Bernstein,* pp. 15–30. London: Routledge/Falmer.

Waller, W. (1932). *The sociology of teaching.* London: John Wiley and Sons.

Wright, J. (2003). Becoming somebody. Changing priorities and physical activity, paper presented at the NZARE/AARE conference Educational Research Risks and Dilemmas, Auckland, November, 2003.

Wright. J. (2004). Post-structural methodologies: the body, schooling and health. In J. Evan B. Davies and J. Wright (Eds.), *Body knowledge and control. Studies in the sociology of physical education and health* (pp. 19–33). London: Routledge.

Wright, J., Macdonald, D. and Burrows, L. (2004). *Critical enquiry and problem solving in physical education.* London: Routledge.

Zaman, H. (1997). Islam, well being and physical activity: Perceptions of muslim women, In Clarke, G. and B. Humberstone (Eds.) (pp. 50–68). *Researching women and sport.* London: MacMillan Press.

2.3 History of physical education

MURRAY G. PHILLIPS AND ALEXANDER PAUL ROPER

Brief historical perspective

There is a long history of material, starting in the last couple of decades of the 19th century, which has examined the history of physical education (Ainsworth, 1930; Hartwell, 1886, 1905; Leonard, 1905, 1915, 1923; Rice, 1926, Schwendener, 1942). Nancy Struna has argued that the growth in the research on the history of physical education reflected an increased interest in physical education both publicly and institutionally at schools, colleges and universities. She also notes that the writers of these early history treatises had little or no formal training in history; they were not trained historians, but physical educators with an interest and a desire to record history. These writers worked without support from their own departments, probably little or no collaboration or advice from historians working in other areas, and did not have access to formal associations for like minded physical educators to discuss their interests. As Struna (1997: 151) summarizes, these physical educators worked in an academic vacuum, and perhaps it is not surprising that: "The books on history from this period were descriptive chronicles" in which "events unfolded; connections and explanations were left untold".

The history of physical education became an increasingly popular topic from the late 1950s through to the 1980s. The field was marked by the emergence of the first major histories of physical education. Pioneering amongst these world histories of physical education were Van Dalen et al. (1953) *A World History of Physical Education: Cultural, Philosophical, Comparative* and Dixon et al. (1957) *Landmarks in the History of Physical Education*. These were the most comprehensive surveys of physical education from the ancient societies through the Middle Ages, to modern Europe, the United States and a host of other contemporary nations. What these sources had in common were their attempts to survey the international developments of physical education with a heavy focus on

linking physical activities in ancient, pre-modern and modern societies. Not surprisingly, given their pioneering status and their internationalist approaches, both of these sources went through numerous reprints and editions.

Another important aspect of the history of physical education, typified by Peter McIntosh's (1952; 1962; 1963; 1971, 1981) and Earl Zeigler's (1973; 1975; 1979; 1988) work, was its diversification to include the emerging topic of the history of sport. In fact, some of the physical educationalists have been acknowledged as the founders of the modern discipline of the history of sport (Huggins, 2001). There was a greater appreciation of sport as a related but separate academic pursuit to physical education. As the preface to Zeigler's (1979: vii) *History of Physical Education and Sport* argues: "the term 'sport' is gaining broad recognition and use as an area of intensified study, research, and practice" to the point where "some authorities now conceive of the term 'sport' as being separate, or different, from the term 'physical education'". Whereas the history of physical education was originally a diverse field which focused on physical education but also encompassed historical aspects of sport, sport was now seen as having an independence deserving of separate academic status. Zeigler was forecasting the emergence of the history of sport, which as we shall see, eventually outstripped and consumed the history of physical education.

While Dixon, McIntosh, Van Dalen and Zeigler were writing the early editions of their histories of physical education, there were no formal associations specifically representing their interests. North Americans, for instance, presented their work at the College of Physical Education Association, but institutional development lacked until 1960. Seward Stanley, an early advocate of the history of physical education, along with his former doctoral student, Marvin Eyler and Zeigler initiated the History of Sport section at the College of Physical Education Association. Similar processes were occurring in other countries with the formation of the International Committee for the History of Physical Education and Sport in 1967 and the International Association for the History of Physical Education and Sport in 1973. Eventually a range of physical education conferences/associations created sections or chapters dedicated to the pursuit of the history of physical education and sport (Struna, 1997).

In many countries in the 1970s and 1980s, the history of sport sections broke away from their physical education associations and established sport history societies such as the North American Society for Sport History (NASSH) in 1972 and the Australian Society for Sport History (ASSH) in 1983. These societies initiated journals including the *Journal of Sport History* (1974) and *Sporting Traditions* (1984) respectively that exclusively focused on the new subdiscipline. These societies and associations, which also developed in Britain, Europe and Asia, attracted a broader clientele than those involved in physical education departments including historians working in other related fields. In Australia, for example, historians of physical education formed a special interest group within the Australian Council for Physical Education, Dance and Recreation devoted to the history of physical education and they merged with interested social, economic and Australian historians, who had conducted small conferences and produced two edited collections from the late 1970s, to form the Australian Society for Sport History. The implication of societies like NASSH and ASSH, as well as similar organizations in Asia, Britain and Europe and their associated journals were very important: they resulted in a burgeoning sport history discipline and a decline in the development of the history of physical education. Struna (1997: 158) summarized the long term effect: "the history of physical education was subsumed within the broader history of sport". Interest in history of sport boomed; history of physical education slumped.

While Roland Naul (1990) has argued that there has been a renaissance in the history of physical education in Germany, other countries do not confirm this trend (Kirk, 1998a). Whereas the 1970s and 1980s was a period that not only produced many manuscripts, but also a considerable body of theses from institutions like the University of Manchester which produced at least seven PhD and masters thesis (see Crunden C (1972); Deasey E (1972); Moore JD (1968); Wilson M (1974); Woodward AC (1964, 1968); Wright EP (1969)), there has been diminishing postgraduate work and few published manuscripts in the history of physical education from the 1990s. For instance it is difficult to find books beyond Bailey and Vamplew's (1999) *100 Years of Physical Education*, Kirk's (1998b) *Schooling Bodies: School Practice and Public Discourse, 1880–1950* and Kruger and Trangbaek's (1999) *The History of Physical Education & Sport from European Perspectives*. These three sources, as worthy as they are in their own right, pale into insignificance in terms of the sheer bulk of work produced in previous decades.

The dramatic decline in the volume of historiography of physical education was most likely related to two issues. Firstly, there were structural, educational and ideological changes occurring in the discipline of physical education. What has been termed the "scientization of physical education" (Whitson and Macintosh, 1990) witnessed the emergence of specialist subdisciplines in biomechanics, exercise physiology, sport psychology and motor learning, accompanied by niche academic journals, which epitomized a growing emphasis on sporting performance and a marginalization of the social dimensions of physical education (Kirk et al., 1997). Accompanying these changes was the renaming of former schools and departments of Physical Education to Schools of Exercise Science, Human Movement Studies, Kinesiology, and Sport Studies (Kirk, 2000b; Tinning, 1993). This transition is described in the Australian context: "In keeping with trends worldwide, the emergence of the discipline of human movement studies in Australia came many years after, and derived its roots from, the physical education profession" (Abernathy, 1996: 24). The history of physical education became unfashionable as it was subordinated by the new disciplines that appeared under a range of guises mentioned previously (McKay et al., 1990).

Secondly, and working at precisely the same time, the field of sport history continued to grow and many of the practitioners in the schools of physical education broadened their interests to the history of sport rather than exclusively focusing on physical education. As Kirk (1998a: 52) summarizes: "historians and sociologists have abandoned school sport and physical education for the apparently more appealing topics of community based sport and exercise". Consequently advertised positions in the newly renamed schools were in the broader field of sport history rather then the history of physical education. At this point physical educationalists had lost the battle over defining the focus of historical pursuits (Huggins, 2001). These sport historians, with their sport history societies and specialist national and international journals, were interested in a wide range of topics, reflecting many of the concerns of social history, of which physical education only represented the periphery (Parratt, 1998; Phillips, 2001; Struna 2000). In summary, changes in the academic discipline of physical education and the emergence and growth in the history of sport resulted in diminished interest in the history of physical education. That interest has not been reinvigorated in the new millennium.

Core concepts

There are many important concepts in the history of physical education including social class, gender, the body, athleticism, muscular Christianity, social Darwinism, eugenics amongst others; however, the focus in this section is on what we consider the single most crucial core term. That core concept is actually the term "physical education". How you define physical education constructs the parameters of the historical field. Does physical education encompass virtually every activity that is an acquired physical skill such as running, riding and sporting participation? Or should the emphasis be on physical activity in education settings? Should that educational setting be informal such as social situations or formal as occurs in schools, universities and other institutions?

Most historians defined physical education in a way that included virtually any physical activity. Recorded in historical writings are experiences of primitive man, the Egyptians, Greeks, and Romans, peoples of the Middle Ages, Renaissance, and Industrial Revolution. There seems little doubt in the works of historians that physical education, like all human endeavours, was (and is) unequivocally a part of man's cultural development. It is an activity that Siedentop (1972: 10) believes "Man [sic] as a species has always been engaged in" and which Van Dalen and Bennett (1971) contend is so inextricably interwoven with the progress of civilization that it can be assumed that one never existed without the other. As Siedentop (1972: 10) contended: "It is highly probable that endeavours which might legitimately be called physical education were the first systematic attempt at instruction in the history of man". Duncan and Watson (1960: 3) certainly seem to agree with this argument:

> physical education has a cultural heritage and background that began at the dawn of civilisation. Broadly interpreted it is one of the most ancient phases of man's [sic] education. Primitive man [sic] had to be very active physically to survive. Simple, natural, and necessary physical activity was a continuous part of his experience, and through it he [sic] gained many of the same values that are claimed for the physical education programs of today.

When used in this sense, the concept of physical education embraces all the numerous and diverse names, titles and viewpoints under its own banner. Assertions such as these do little other than testify to the ambivalence of the term physical education when used in its historical context. Amongst a plethora of historians it would seem that collaboration between brain and brawn serves as the only rationale for defining physical education. Since these early definitions, however sport historians and sociologists have contested the views that promote sport and physical education as a timeless and cultural universal (Guttman, 1978; McKay, 1991).

Osterhoudt (1991) is one of the few academics who has attempted to be more specific about defining physical education from a historical perspective. He ascertains the term "physical education" is derived from the Greek word *physika*, meaning "material" and the Latin, *educare*, again, effectively meaning "to rear", the most literal interpretation of physical education sees it as attempting *to rear in the form of our material element.* (Osterhoudt, 1991: 402). Specifically he defined the global historical development of physical education as taking three main forms. It has been characterized in turn as *physical training* in which it is thought of as an agent (a means to) bio-psychological health and fitness; as *physical culture,* in which it is thought of as an acculturative agent (a means to social ends); and as *physical education* in itself, in which it is thought of as the composite of sporting activities and dance (Osterhoudt, 1991: 346). With the development of both physical training and physical culture to physical education, there is certainly evidence that the basic motif underlying the predominance of exercise and games were raised to a higher level. Osterhoudt argues that physical education itself completes the development toward which both physical training and physical culture were predisposed by making fully human their strictly biological and strictly social orientations.

These prevalent definitions of physical education are incredibly important because they have shaped the historical field. By providing very few limits to what can be classified as physical education, the historical field is all encompassing including physical activities from primitive societies – walking, running, riding, hunting, dancing, fishing as well as games, athletic events and sporting activities – to a range of activities in modern societies, most notably physical education at schools and sport in all its varieties: male, female, amateur, professional, community, school, college, junior and mature aged. It is not surprising that the following section, which summarizes the history of physical education, reads like a history of virtually every physical activity throughout time.

Major findings

While the accepted definitions have been all encompassing, it can not be assumed that all historians have applied the nebulous concept of physical education equally, consistently or uniformly. In fact, the historiography of physical education has several defining and differentiating features. The first feature is the scope of the historiography. Many histories of physical education start somewhere with one of the ancient societies ranging from the Egyptians to the Greeks and finish with contemporary times featuring the history of physical education in a specific nation or a group of nations. It is usually in the period of the 19th century that historians mark as the emergence of physical education in the modern world. From this vantage, sources focus on national or multi-national histories on physical education in Australia (Crawford, 1981; Kirk, 1998b), England (Bailey and Vamplew, 1999; Fletcher 1984a,b; McIntosh, 1952; Smith, 1974), Europe (Kruger and Trangbaek, 1999) and North America (Ainsworth, 1930; Leonard, 1915, 1923; Lockhart and Spears, 1972; Rice, 1926; Schwendener, 1942; Zeigler, 1975). The second feature of the historiography of physical education is that its temporal origins vary between historians. Van Dalen and Bennett's (1971) *A World's History of Physical Education* begins with the exploits of "primitive" societies, Zeigler's (1979) *History of Physical Education and Sport* starts his edited volume with the ancient Sumerians, while McIntosh et al. (1981) *Landmarks in the History of Physical Education* situates the earliest physical education with the ancient Greeks. In essence, the historiography of physical education displays multiple births.

The third feature is the degrees of intensity accorded to historical periods. Not all historical periods are treated equally by historians. Consider, for example, the third edition of Mechikoff and Estes' (2002) *A History and Philosophy of Sport and Physical Education*. In this popular source, the physical activities of the Egyptians, Sumerians, Babylonians, Hittites, Assyrians, Persians, Hebrews, Mycenaeans and Minoans stretching over 3000 years is given 13 pages, the 1000-year Greek civilization is discussed over 27 pages, the 1000-year reign of the Romans is accorded 19 pages, the Dark Ages that existed for 400 years is not covered at all, and the 600 years of the Middle Ages takes up 16 pages. Some historical periods are remembered more intensely than others, while some are not remembered at all. Their perceived value or lack of value to historians determines the intensity of their coverage.

The fourth feature is the trajectories of the histories of historical accounts. Trajectories of historical narratives can take a number of shapes including progression toward an ultimate goal, decline into an abyss, or zig-zag narratives where progress and decline are alternated. The historical narratives of physical educational represent a zig-zag narrative in which physical education is perceived to rise, fall and then be rejuvenated again. As Mechikoff and Estes' history highlights, physical education rises during the early civilizations of the Tigris, Euphrates and Nile rivers, reaches a pinnacle during the Greek civilization, gradually slides downwards with the Romans and hits a nadir during the Dark Ages, only to be revived and continued to rise from the Middle Ages.

These four features of the historiography of physical education reinforce the central message of *Time Maps* in which Eviatar Zerubavel argues that memory "is patterned in a highly structured manner that both shapes and distorts what we actually come to mentally retain from the past" (Zerubavel, 2003: 11). Given these defining features of the historiography of physical education, the findings of historians will be summarized accordingly to the accepted periodization that has understood physical education in the context of:

- Ancient societies
- Middle Ages to Reformation
- Modern physical education.

Ancient societies

As indicated in Mechikoff and Estes' (2002) *A History and Philosophy of Sport and Physical Education* the intensity of research and writing on the early river civilizations of the Tigris, Euphrates and Nile is far less than that of other historical periods, specifically the work carried out on the ancient Greek civilization. For this reason, any discussion of the Egyptians, Sumerians, Babylonians, Hittites, Assyrians, Hebrews and Persians civilizations, stretching over 3000 years, can only be cursory. People of these civilizations participated in a range of physical activities that were mediated by social, cultural, economical, gender and political factors. Physical activities in these early civilizations were closely tied to survival (boating, fishing, fowling, hunting and swimming), recreation and entertainment (acrobatics, board games, chance games, guessing games, bull games and toreador sports), and military training (archery, boxing, chariot racing, gladiatorial events, jumping contests, running, horse events and wrestling). Access to these activities were determined by citizenship, social status and wealth, rights of manhood (not of womanhood), and in many cases these events were linked to religious rights, rituals and celebrations (Van Dalen and Bennett, 1971; Howell and Howell, 1988; Mechikoff and Estes, 2002; Zeigler, 1973).

Some of these civilizations, particularly the Assyrians, Egyptians, Hebrews and Persians, coexisted and influenced Greek civilization. The physical activities of the Greeks has attracted so much attention, or as Zerubavel contends a great deal of intensity, because aspects of their sport appealed to 19th and 20th century sport and physical education advocates and historians. There is little doubt that physical education constituted a central component of life in ancient Greece. Athletic activities of the early Homeric Age are traced from the *Iliad* and the

Odyssey. In these literary masterpieces, the heroes Achilles and Odysseus represented "the man of action" and "the man of wisdom", and participated in chariot races, boxing, dancing, discuss, javelin, leaping, running and wrestling. Physical education was designed to develop "the man of action" as every male in Homeric Greece was destined at some point in their life to be a warrior required to fight in the intermittent warfare that characterized the era (Van Dalen and Bennett, 1971). As Greece moved from pastoral, agricultural communities to an alliance of city states, physical education emerged as a central cultural component of the rival and contrasting political entities of Sparta and Athens.

Sparta was an autocratic, state-supervised and warrior-orientated city state. Spartan society, consisting of a ruling class, intermediate class and slaves, educated its male citizens to be "obedient soldiers, capable commanders and conscientious citizens" (Van Dalen and Bennett, 1971: 39). State-regulated, age-determined education in Sparta focused on respect for authority, physical fitness and military skill with little emphasis placed on the arts, sciences, philosophy and literature. Physical activities such as gymnastics, running, jumping, boxing, wrestling and pankration (a brutal combination of boxing and wrestling) were geared toward producing warriors. What is unique about Spartan education is that young male and females shared similar educational experiences. While girls did not live in public military barracks like the boys, they participated in discus, gymnastics, horse riding, javelin, swimming, running and wrestling at separate training grounds. The objective for women's physical education was to enable them to produce healthy, strong and virile potential warriors (Willets, 1981).

In contrast to Sparta, Athens was a more liberal, progressive and democratic society, a society noted for its art, literature and philosophy as well as its political system. Citizens, foreign settlers and slaves constituted Athenian society, yet only citizens were provided with educational opportunities. Education was very different in Athens when compared to Sparta. Athenian women had virtually no physical education and, while the objective of preparing male warriors was similar to Sparta, Athenian education was a balance between music (including poetry) and gymnastics which encompassed a range of physical activities. Less regulated than in Sparta, physical education provided students with a range of graded activities at the palestra and gymnasium which included boxing, discus, javelin, pankration, pentathlon, running and wrestling with the ultimate goals of developing the virtues of citizenship, loyalty and courage (Willets, 1981). Many of these athletic events were part of the four great sport and religious festivals which comprised the Olympic, Isthmian, Pythian and Nemean Games. These games began as simple athletic contests dedicated to Greek gods, but over 1000 years the Olympic Games, in particular, became increasingly complex, encompassing events for boys and men in running over different distances, pentathlon, wrestling, races in armour, chariot races with horses and mules, and pankration (Howell and Howell, 1988).

The explicit objectives of physical education in Athens, as of education more broadly, was to educate the mind and the body, to unite "the man of action" with "the man of wisdom", to produce a well-integrated person. In the late Athenian period, these ideals were distorted as the role of the palestra and gymnasium changed, as professional athletes, valued and rewarded for winning, replaced the objective of all-round physical excellence. Van Dalen and Bennett (1971: 47) summarized the relevance of early Athenian sporting cultures to Western sport:

> They gave to all future civilizations important aesthetic ideals: the ideals of harmonized balance of mind and body, of body symmetry, and of bodily beauty in repose and in action. To these contributions may be added educational gymnastics, the competitive sports of track and field, the classic dance, and the Olympic Games.

The reverence held for the athletic ideals of the Greeks helps explain the intensity of writing by historians on their physical activities.

The Roman civilization, as vast as it was stretching from Scotland to Turkey to North Africa over almost a thousand years, and as difficult as it is to generalize about such a complex civilization that incorporated many other cultures, was noticeably different to the Greeks. Unlike the Greeks who were interested in the abstract and the aesthetic, as well as scientific and philosophic thought, the Romans were ordered, practical and pragmatic, less recognized for their philosophical or scientific contributions. Utilitarian achievements were their forte. While the Greeks are remembered for their intellectual contributions to later civilizations, the Romans are remembered more for their engineering, architectural and administrative feats.

With such differing perceptions of life, it is not surprising that physical education and physical activities for the Romans took on different forms than the Greeks. During the early years of the Republic (509–27 BC), Van Dalen and Bennett (1971: 70) argue the purpose of physical education was "to develop strength of body, courage in battle, agility in arms and obedience to commands". At the Campus Martius, a large open area on the banks of the Tiber River, under guidance from fathers, and at the military camps, young male Romans were taught archery, ball games, fencing, javelin, horse riding, jumping and running. While the Greeks valued participation for all-round development of the individual, the Romans were far more utilitarian with the specific objective of physical training to make strong, adept and ready soldiers (Van Dalen and Bennett, 1971).

During the later Republic and Empire (27 BC–476 AD), physical education continued to remain important for military men and the growing band of professional athletes, but for most Romans physical activities consisted of exercises at modest (*balneae*) and often lavish (*thermae*) public and private baths. In 33 BC there were 170 baths in Rome, 300 years later the city could boast 856 such institutions. These baths were more like recreational centres comprising different forms of indoor and outdoor baths, rooms of varying temperature, areas for ball playing and even shops, lounges, libraries, art galleries and dining venues. It was here that Romans took their physical education in the form of exercises with weights, jumping, running, wrestling and a number of ball games. Participants followed their exercise with a bath and massage. Mild exercise was preferred to the competitive version of sport championed by the Greeks. This reflected, in part, the ideas of philosopher and physician Claudius Galen who recognized the health giving qualities of physical exercise. The baths were the venues that made the lives bearable for male and female Romans who lived in an extremely crowded city, over one million people in an area less than 12 miles square, under very uncomfortable conditions (McIntosh, 1981).

Another dimension of the sporting lives of the Romans was their penchant for spectator orientated activities that were epitomized in chariot racing at the circuses and gladiatorial battles at the amphitheatres. Probably reflecting the influence of the Etruscans who loved chariot racing and participated in armed combat between warriors, Romans took these activities to a new level (Howell and Howell, 1988). Chariot racing and gladiator battles were popular all over the Roman Empire but it was Rome that housed the greatest of these facilities with the Circus Maximus and the Colosseum (Flavian Amphitheatre). At the Circus Maximus, as many as 250 000 spectators on permanent, three tiered grandstands could watch chariot races, horse events and boxing contests, while at the Colosseum 50 000 spectators witnessed animal fights, naval battles and gladiatorial contests. Chariot racing was serviced by specialized personnel including trainers, veterinarians, jockeys, grooms and stable police, while gladiators were trained to master a range of weapons at gladiator schools. Events at the various amphitheatres were particularly gruesome affairs, costing both animal and human lives, watched by spectators seated according to wealth, gender and citizenship. These spectacles at both the circuses and the amphitheatres, sponsored by politicians, were the "bread and circuses" that fulfilled the utilitarian service of ridding society of unwanted slaves and prisoners at the same time as pacifying and entertaining an idle Roman public during their ever-growing number of holidays. Chariot racing and the gladiatorial battles typified the dominant characteristics of Roman physical activities, as Mechikoff and Estes (2002: 75–6) argue: "Aside from the warriors, the Romans grew into a nation of spectators, not participants, who enjoyed watching slaves and professional athletes perform as competitors while the less fortunate Christians, criminals and political prisoners were unwilling participants".

Middle Ages to Reformation

Following the collapse of Rome in AD 476, many institutions including the unique form of popular spectator sports ceased. One institution that survived was the Church (incorporating both the Papacy and Holy Roman Empire) which reached its height in Europe in this period. Here, "the influence of the Catholic Church on European culture … cannot be overestimated. It permeated every aspect of culture – scholarship, politics, economics, and even one's private life" (Mechikoff and Estes, 2002: 104). The prominence of the Church is vitally important when discussing the role of physical education in this period, especially so, given the prominence of the Catholic Church to medieval philosophy and whereby the philosophical position of the body reflected theological beliefs. What is interesting here is the obvious fact that there was a paucity of literature on which early medieval philosophies had access to. Christian theologians did, however, both recognize and incorporate the works of Aristotle and Plato and as such, as Copleston (1961) ascertains, were compelled to embrace specific attitudes about the philosophy of the ancient Greeks to reconcile Greek philosophy with Christian theology. Similarly to Socrates' concerns in the *Phaedo* the early Christians saw the achievement of physical perfection and moreover the practice of worshipping (pagan gods), which pre-occupied the Greeks, as focusing too much on secular concerns whilst neglecting spiritual concerns. Simply, "The majority of Christians believed that to participate in athletics or engage in physical training to glorify the body would contaminate the body, which 'housed' the soul, and would make the soul impure. The negative attitude that Medieval Christians had toward the body was in no small part the result of a reaction to paganism" (Mechikoff and Estes, 2002: 87).

Most early Christians held the body in contempt. Whilst it is certainly true that some Orthodox Christians consistently rejected this belief, it remains equally true that they were also in the minority. Despite the writings of Saints Thomas Aquinas and Bonaventure, as well as the noted Jewish philosopher and physician, Moses Maimondes, the most commonly held view during this period – and certainly one espoused by Frank Bottomley (1979) – saw the human body as vile, corrupt and beyond redemption – a view only enhanced by the spread of the bubonic plague across Europe during the 14th century. The body became an "instrument of sin" (Van Dalen and Bennett, 1971: 90). Perhaps, it is not too surprising to note then that the consensus among some medieval historians is that, with the exception of ritual dancing and manual labour, Christians were encouraged to avoid the pleasures of the flesh (Ballou, 1968; Bottomley, 1979; Carter, 1980, 1981, 1984; Cripps-Day, 1980; Henderson, 1947; Hoskins, 1958; Pole, 1958; Strutt, 1876). As Van Dalen and Bennett (1971: 90) state, in such an environment "even the most worthy ideals of physical education could not exist". This is not to say that physical education and sporting activities (not including military activities) were entirely absent from the Middle Ages, but it should certainly be noted that they were tolerated (grudgingly) more than condoned.

This negative attitude towards sport did, however, as John Marshall Carter (1981) highlights, change in the 11th and 12th centuries. During this period, primarily because of the manner in which property was inherited, many nobles elected to become monks. Mechikoff and Estes (2002: 93) illustrate how:

Secular habits such as hunting, falconry, and perhaps, even the combat sports used to train knights, remained popular. Young nobles who became priests introduced these activities into the ecclesiastical community, [which] with the passage of time were slowly accepted by the church.

In addition to these sports – and with the permission of the local church authority – ball games were also popular during the Middle Ages. Indeed, as Mechikoff and Estes (2002: 95) continue:

The apparent universality of ball games, their popularity with the peasant serfs, the interest of the tradesmen and upper classes, their association with Christian holidays, and the long tradition of quiet acceptance of such games by church authority made it extremely difficult for the church to end its association with these games.

It did intervene, however, with the deterioration of the games into violent, drunken, lewd affairs with a swift reminder of appropriate conduct and some fairly vehement chastisement. Likewise, the more aristocratic sports which centred round the medieval tournaments also faced the Church's wrath due to the inherent carnage and brutality that were often present. Although it should be noted that during the Crusades such condemnations were largely absent.

It was roughly a decade or so after the ending of the Crusades (1096–1291) that one can identify the beginnings of the Renaissance (circa 1300–1550). Caused in part by the reintroduction in intellectual circles of both Greek and Roman thought, the Church had to now compete with the literature, philosophies and paganism of these two great ancient cultures. Here, new rationalizations for considering the body were developed which subsequently set down the foundations for the development and evolution of a new attitude towards both physical education and sport. Indeed, it can certainly be argued that Renaissance philosophy led to the justification in Western civilization of both physical education and sport (Bronowski and Mazlish, 1960; Durant, 1957; Calhoun, 1981; Hackensmith, 1966; Rice et al., 1969; Woodward, 1921). Perhaps the most fundamental change here was an increase in the importance attached and placed on the body – Mechikoff and Estes (2002: 119) certainly seem to think so:

With the reading of the classic Greek and Roman philosophers, scholars began to re-examine all aspects of their lives in classical perspective … Like Plato and Aristotle, the intellectuals of the Renaissance placed an emphasis on living in this world as opposed to living in the next world, or heaven. This philosophy, known as humanism, emphasised our "humanness" rather than our spiritual selves. As a direct consequence of this type of thinking, affairs of the human body were considered much more acceptable. Sport and physical education were direct beneficiaries of this type of thought.[1]

Vittorino da Feltre was one of the first educators during the Renaissance to introduce physical education as an important part of an educational programme – which would subsequently become the model upon which physical education curricula were based. For two or more hours each day da Feltre's students would engage in such physical activities as ball games, fencing, leaping, riding and running under the watchful gaze of teachers skilled in such manners. Da Feltre effectively brought together the humanist ideals of body, mind, and spirit for the first time in an attempt to develop the ideal citizen. With Sparta as his model (and heavily influenced by Plato), Petrus Paulus Vergerius, one of the first of the great Italian humanists, provides another example of a leading educator of this period introducing physical education into their educational curriculum. Although very similar to educators of the Middle Ages (in that he saw the principal function of physical education as helping to prepare one for the military), the fact that he incorporated physical education into the education of the total individual also helped mark a new chapter in physical education.

In a world where trade and commerce were becoming integral parts of everyday life, education (whose benefits were evident among the upper classes and aristocracy) came to be seen as a necessity. With its incorporation and utilization in the educational curriculum, physical education obviously became more common in the curriculum of both the Renaissance and Reformation than it had been in the Middle Ages. It should, however, be stated quite clearly here, that this incorporation equated to only a small part of the overall educational programme and "where it did exist it was usually associated with the education of the wealthy" (Mechikoff and Estes, 2002: 112). Sport was not a part of college life in the new modern universities such as Oxford and Cambridge – simply, the mind and its education was still the fundamental undertaking of educators. Additionally, the influence of the Church (and more specifically its admonishment that the body was not to be used for pleasure) was still strong enough to restrict sporting activities. With the Reformation and the identification of hard work and industriousness with good work and prayers – religion as a tool to gauge conduct – play and games were sinful. Although the theology of the Reformation and that of the early Christian monks were very different in their view of the value of the body, both theologies worked against play, sport, and physical education (Calhoun, 1981; Gerber, 1971; Hackensmith, 1966; Rice et al., 1969; Mechikoff and Estes 2002; Schmidt, 1960; Van Dalen et al., 1953; Woodward, 1921).

Indeed, despite the different propositions and philosophies that subsequently occurred during both the Age of Science and the Enlightenment – and the evolution of the notion that humans were able to both comprehend and influence their environment – it was only really with Johann Friedrich GutsMuths that physical education was actually professionalized. At the Schnepfenthal Educational Institute, Germany, GutsMuths continued and developed the programme that Christian Andre (Schnepfenthal's original physical education teacher) had founded. In time, these programmes, alongside his teaching techniques and writings became the benchmark by which ensuing physical educators were judged.

GutsMuths used a number of ideas to develop his syllabus. He was acutely aware that the majority of educational institutions did not value (or were even aware) of the benefits of physical education and believed that the best way to develop health was through his gymnastics programme. At around this same time, the Universal German Institute was established by Friedrich Wilhelm August Froebel, meanwhile Johann Heinrich Pestalozzi in French-annexed-Switzerland oversaw the establishment of a physical education programme at Yverdon, and in Denmark, Franz Nachtegall established and operated "the first institution for physical training to be opened in modern times" (Gerber, 1971: 178). Here in northern Europe, and primarily in Germany, Sweden and Denmark, physical education, and perhaps as importantly its justification and development, benefited greatly from the philosophy of idealism (Butler, 1957; Hoernle, 1927; Kleinman,

1986). As Froebel highlighted, "without such cultivation of the body, education can never attain its object, which is perfect human culture" (Froebel, 1887: 250).

In Germany, Sweden and Denmark the promotion of physical education (confirming previous era's beliefs in its primary purpose) was not so much for its educational and health value, but rather for its military purposes. Gymnastics under Friedrich Ludwig Jahn exemplifies this dimension of physical education. Following on from GutsMuths teachings (which Jahn applied to his own works), physical education was used to pursue German national unity and freedom from French control. To Jahn, there was a direct correlation between the cultural influences of the French occupation and a loss of German national pride. As a result he saw the need for a nationwide programme of physical education – supported in Prussia by Wilhelm Schroder, who (as school inspector) publicly called for schools to accept gymnastics as part of their curricula – and the birth of the German turnverein movement in the spring of 1811. Due to its overtly political nature and in no small way to its nationalistic stance, by 1820 a Prussian royal decree had been issued banning all gymnastics and closing over 100 gymnastic fields. Jahn himself was imprisoned. What this movement had achieved is noteworthy. Between 1811 and 1819 it not only served as a catalyst for social change in the German states, but also for the call for a unified democracy of these same states. Buoyed by the ideals of independence and freedom from French rule, the Turners practiced their gymnastics in order to be both mentally and physically prepared to liberate their nation. Notwithstanding these achievements, the Turners by exporting their gymnastic methods to the United States, as will be shown in more detail shortly, catalysed the emergence of physical education in other nations.

The promotion of the health dimensions of physical education was central in the career of Per Ling who established in Sweden the medical and scientific benefits of exercise (Thulin, 1931). Indeed, what is interesting is how much alike the physical education curricula were to contemporary physical education (Kindervater, 1926; Schwendener, 1942). Essential to the newly introduced bachelor's degree in physical education (to which the Turners had so greatly contributed) were such subjects as anatomy, educational psychology, first aid, health, history and philosophy, physiology, and sports skills. Such fundamental changes in the scope of physical education can be seen to have first been discussed in a conference organized by William G. Anderson, MD. Here on November 27, 1885, a group of 49 people (mostly physicians) made the first real attempt to develop, as a legitimate profession, physical education (Harris, 1890; Park, 1985). This trend in expertise and specialization reflected the general trends in society at that time. From a view in which the nature of health was deemed by those in the medical profession as, "manifest in a balanced constitution (the body) and temperament (the mind and spirit)" there arose a situation whereby science "focussed on the organic development of the individual, which provided a great deal of impetus in defining the role and scope of physical education." Simply, prevention was better than cure and in the doctors who attended Anderson's conference we are able to see "a beginning point for the body of knowledge in physical education based on health and the prevention of disease" (Mechikoff and Estes, 2002: 192). Physical education and educators were now fundamentally concerned with (this changing concept of) health, whereby moral indiscretions could no longer be blamed for an individual's physical shortcomings. Science, it had been proven with its capacity to control, cure and restore health had not only earned society's confidence but became the dominant force in research into physical education.

Modern physical education

In the remaining section of this synopsis of physical education, we will limit our discussion to the history of physical education in America, Australia and Great Britain until the Second World War. The reasons for this selection are purely practical and functional: there is considerable material available on these nations and this material is readily accessible in English. In essence, we are simply following the pattern established by previous historians who have examined some eras and specific nations rather than others. We will leave it to other historians to break this trend by adding to the intensity of research of those eras and nations that have not been examined in great detail.

When considering the development of physical education in America, Australia and Britain, there are obvious similarities. The similarities primarily resided in the popular, available and accessible systems of physical education. All three nations at various times adopted forms of gymnastic exercises originating from Germany, Sweden and Denmark, as well as supporting hybrid and unique systems of gymnastics developed by individuals including, amongst others, Dio Lewis and Dudley Sargent in America, Gustav Techow in Australia, and Archibald Maclaren in England. The importance of games as part of school life which had its origins in England also found resonance in America and Australia. Beyond these similarities, however, physical education in these countries was individually shaped by debates about the body, eugenics, health concerns, nationalism and militarism, and interwoven in unique ways with class, gender and race. While it is possible to identify similarities in systems of physical education, each country developed specific forms that were moulded by distinct social, economical and political environments.

The European influence on physical education in America, Australia and Great Britain was unmistakable. National forms of gymnastics in Germany, Sweden and Denmark, in particular, under the initiatives of Gutsmuths, Jahn, Franz Nachtegall, Ling and Adolf Spiess were catalysts to physical education in other countries. In America, the form of gymnastics, based on apparatus, that gained official support and a large degree of acceptance in the education system was the German mode advocated by Gutsmuths, Jahn and their disciples. Gymnastics was introduced at the Round Hill School in 1825 and in the following year at Harvard by political exiles and former Turner members from Germany (Gerber, 1971). Two decades later, as a consequence of a wave of German immigrants, the first Turnverein was formed in 1848 and, within 2 years, an association of Turnverein was established which eventually evolved into the American Gymnastic Union in 1919 (Munrow, 1981).

The Turner movement provided gymnastic teacher training before any other organization, offered public schools the expertise of its instructors, and schools from Milwaukee, Chicago, Davenport, Cleveland, St Louis, Denver, Columbus, Dayton, Buffalo to Indianapolis employed teachers in German gymnastics. While American physical education was largely influenced by German gymnastics, acceptance of Swedish gymnastics, a rigid programme of routine callisthenics with little apparatus, was more limited with less official support. Swedish immigrants were fewer in number than the Germans, they came later to America, and their influence was minimal. Americans, rather than immigrant Swedes, proselytized Swedish gymnastics through private sponsorship and the provision of teacher education. Swedish gymnastics was practiced in eastern cities of America, such as Boston, and were popularized by female physical education students rather than their male colleagues. Geographically more isolated and practiced more by women than men, Swedish gymnastics never gained the acceptance of the German system in America (Munrow, 1981; Van Dalen and Bennett, 1971).

The British like many others employed specific European systems as well as creating amalgamations of their own (Smith, 1974). Initially military drill was promoted by authorities, and then German gymnastics gained favour up until Swedish gymnastics was officially sanctioned in the schools, and eventually hybrid forms of "British" regimes of physical exercises were created (McIntosh, 1963, 1968, 1971, 1987). In contrast to America, German gymnastics was quickly usurped by the Swedish system which became physical education for the majority of students in government-funded schools (Smith, 1974). The Public Schools, catering for wealthier sections of society as will be shortly discussed, endorsed the games ethic exemplifying the class-based nature of physical education in Britain.

Swedish gymnastics gained a fillip by the appointment of Swedes as the Lady Superintendents of Physical Exercises starting with Concordia Lofving and then the famous Martina Bergman (later Madame Bergman Osterberg). These individuals were crucial in shifting the regime of physical education to the Swedish system and were indicative of a strong tradition of training women in physical education in Britain as was the case in the USA (Kirk, 2000b). Their appointments signalled the dominant role of female physical educators as individuals, as instructors in training colleges, as administrators in professional organizations, as publishers of professional journals, and as agitators to educational authorities and Members of Parliament advocating Swedish gymnastics (Bailey and Vamplew, 1999). Swedish gymnastics was primarily an activity for students at elementary and secondary schools with mostly female instructors as very few males were provided with opportunities to develop the necessary expertise. The female-dominated aspect of physical education did not significantly change until after the Second World War when Swedish gymnastics lost favour as other forms of physical education and games gained ascendancy in the curricula (McIntosh, 1981).

Not surprisingly given the British colonial legacy in Australia, physical education in the Antipodes was heavily influenced by the British model. Australians followed with interest the various reports, Acts and Royal Commissions in Britain, and implemented the recommendations from manuals, syllabi and books on physical training. Like the British, Australians preferred the Swedish system, rather than the German model of gymnastics adopted by the Americans. It was not until the publication of the "Grey" Book in 1946 that educational authorities in Australia consciously moved away from British syllabi and developed a system of physical education distinctly different to the British model (Kirk, 1998b).

The contours of physical education in Australia, nevertheless, displayed different dimensions than the British system because physical education was heavily influenced by localized social, cultural and political issues. For example, unlike Britain, Australia did not develop a tradition of training female physical educators (Kirk, 2000a) and the shortage of women teachers "had important implications for the gender appropriateness of physical education offered to girls" (Kirk, 2000b: 21). Another issue of difference centred on the relationship between education and militarism. Militarism was incredibly important in both Britain and Australia, resulting in physical education being closely aligned and, in some cases, virtually indistinguishable from physical training. Militarist physical training in Britain indelibly shaped physical education either side of the 20th century, but one thing the militarist lobby never achieved was compulsory military training

in the schools. In Australia, the militarist lobby directly influenced physical education for two decades beyond the British experience and pressured government and educational authorities to create various forms of military training for schoolage children. Colonial authorities – concerned about the removal of British forces from 1870, the imperialistic tendencies of Asian countries and Russia, and with no standing army for defence – perceived schools as an appropriate institution to train citizen armies. The most significant of these schemes was the compulsory junior cadet training introduced across the country in 1911. Under this scheme, boys between the ages of 12 and 14 were provided with a mixture of marching, squad drill and rifle shooting. The total physical experiences accompanying this military training included gymnastics of the Ling system as well as some swimming, running and organized games (Kirk, 1998b). As this example illustrates, while Australia took the lead from Britain until the Second World War, the forms of physical education popular in Australia displayed unique features that differentiated it from the British model.

Likewise the games ethic that originated in the United Kingdom took different forms in America and Australia. In Britain many modern sports underwent codification and it was in English Public Schools that the games ethic germinated, developed and disseminated. The games ethic referred to the preference for team games, in particular, and the perceived ability of these activities not only to develop the physical dimensions of the participants, but to foster desirable character traits that encompassed obedience, leadership, courage, morality and perseverance. All of these were developed within dominant notions of heterosexual masculinity (Mangan 1981, 2000). Many of these schoolboys educated in the character-building and masculine qualities of games became the merchants, missionaries and administrators who advocated the games ethic as they travelled to all parts of the British Empire and the Americas (Mangan 1988, 1992, 1998).

The games cult, however, was not established with any sort of homogeneity in the school systems of the Empire and the Americas. It was initially considered almost exclusively a middle-class phenomenon in Britain until the Second World War as the working-class education system, without the material resources in playing fields and teaching expertise in games, did not have the opportunity or desire to expose children to the perceived benefits of games playing. More recent research, nevertheless, points to the existence of games in elementary schools either side of the 20th century (Mangan and Hickey, 2000). Similarly the games cult in Britain was gendered. For young private-school boys, games developed many of the characteristics described above; for women the experience was different. Public boarding schools for girls mimicked their male equivalents in their commitment to games playing in a series of inter-form, inter-house and inter-school competitions rewarding their athletes with colours, cups and uniforms (McCrone 1987, 1998). Yet, "loyalty, co-operation, smartness, cleanliness, fairness, exemplary manners and a strict inner discipline of moderation, self-control and respect for authority were celebrated in sport as female virtues" (Hargreaves, 1994: 111). The games cult conformed to and contributed to stereotypical dimensions of gendered identity.

The character-developing dimensions of the games ethic were equally important in the USA. As Dudley Sargent, a pioneer physical educator, declared: "The grand aim of all muscular activity from an educational point of view is to improve conduct and develop character" (cited in Van Dalen, 1971: 398). One of the manifestations of this sporting ideology in the American context was the development of competitive sports at schools and universities. Interscholastic and intercollegiate sport developed during the second half of the 19th century as exclusively male activities and grew into massive industries that raised large amounts of revenue for their institutions from paying spectators, radio coverage, and television coverage as well as associated marketing and merchandising. Like the games ethic in Britain, the industry of interscholastic and intercollegiate sport was heavily gendered. Intramural sport was encouraged for women, under the mantra "a sport for every girl and every girl in a sport" (Mechikoff and Estes, 2002: 261–2), but competitive interscholastic and intercollegiate sport was opposed for many years.

Opposition to women's competitive sport, emanating from both male administrators and female physical educationalists, was framed around idealized, perceived stereotypical notions of femininity that would be allegedly destroyed by the elitist, masculine, and commodified nature of interscholastic and intercollegiate sport. Challenges to these gendered beliefs were mounted in the political struggles between those attempting to control women's sport during the 20th century. More opportunities were gradually made available for school and college female athletes. Title IX of the Educational Amendments Act of 1972 provided the antidiscrimination legislation that has encouraged a wider range of competitive sports for women, albeit with all the inherent problems of male sports in schools and colleges (Mechikoff and Estes, 2002).

The games ethic in Australia exhibited different manifestations. University (college) sport never developed along the commodified lines of the USA model, nor did interschool sport, particularly at the government-funded schools, follow the highly competitive, hierarchical American model. Influenced by the British educational system and the associated value system surrounding participation in games, Australians etched a version of the games ethic that

was grafted onto traits of the emerging nation. Teamwork, leadership, courage and comradeship remained from the British games ethic, but added to these traits were self-reliance and a form of rugged, frontier manliness as well as a passion for success in sporting contests (Crawford cited in Kirk, 1998b: 137). This tailored games ethic was also gendered. For boys at middle-class private schools, team games "were from the beginning gendered practices, explicitly designed to promote physical strength, aggression, competitiveness, courage and loyalty as defining characteristics of masculinity" (Kirk, 2000a: 60). For girls at equivalent schools, games helped challenge stereotypical versions of femininity that "positioned women and girls as fragile, co-operative, loyal and dexterous" (Kirk, 2000a: 60).

Equally importantly, as Kirk's (1998b) analysis of school sport in Australia illustrates, the benefits attributed to games were never stagnant and altered continually according to prevailing social and cultural forces. For working class boys, and to a lesser extent girls, of the government schools, the justifications for advocating games did not centre on preparing leaders for government, the professions or the armed forces as it was for the middle class children of the fee paying private schools. During the first World War, the emphasis for working class boys was on physical development through games, and in the next decade participation centred on social and moral factors: countering unwanted behaviour such as cheating in games. In the 1930s and 1940s games were advocated for both boys and girls to develop self-confidence, foster enjoyment and promote play. The games ethic, gendered and class specific, shifted over time to accommodate larger social trends and was specifically interpreted against the canvas of national identity.

Obviously this synopsis of physical education in America, Australia and Great Britain up until the Second World War is not representative of physical education throughout the world, nor is it meant to be, but the theme that runs through this section could easily be applied in other historical contexts of physical education. As has been shown from the ancient civilizations to the modern era, physical education has never been stagnant, varying between segments of societies and between civilizations themselves, always a contest between competing versions of physical education, and has represented a struggle between those who have wanted to define, control and implement physical education. America, Australia and Great Britain provide examples of the struggles over physical education, examples which exemplify similar power struggles in Europe, Africa and Asia.

Major trends

While the findings of a range of historians of physical education have been summarized, the following section will critically analyse the underlying assumptions that have guided some of these histories. The approach to this section is stimulated by the debate over the last decade centring on the processes of the production of history. Out of this debate, several key questions have been posed: Is history a separate empiricist discipline? Or is history another form of the constructionist social sciences? Or, alternatively, is history a form of literature? Finally, and crucially, does history have its own, unique epistemology? In attempting to answer these questions, Alun Munslow has identified three dominant approaches to historical knowledge which he categorizes as reconstructionism, constructionism and deconstructionism. Reconstructionist historians rely on empiricism which assumes that historians interrogate the evidence by comparison, verification and contextualization and explain the past by assuming a disinterested, rational and non-judgmental position. In this way, the objective historian can directly infer meaning from voices of the past and the interpretation inherent in the sources (Munslow, 2000). Constructionist historians attempt to understand historical events by placing them in pre-existing frameworks, which involves a range of theories, ideologies and social categories, in a way that still allows for human agency, intentionality and choice. Constructionist histories have often been ideologically self-conscious advocating the political agendas of marginalized groups from women to blacks to immigrants to colonized peoples to the working classes (Munslow, 2000). The final category, deconstructionist historians, rely far less on traditional empiricism and explicit social theories emphasizing, instead, the form of history – the centrality of language, representation and narrative – over reconstructionist and contructionist fascination with content.

Reconstructionist histories of physical education

A great deal of the histories of physical education from the earliest sources in the late 19th century through to the new millennium have been written within a reconstructionist framework. These histories range in their commitment to reconstructionist ideals, but there are at least three features that are epitomized in specific histories. These features are a commitment to the sanctity of "primary sources" and the methodological principles that follow from this priority, an aversion to discussing the philosophy of history that underpins their work and, finally, a distrust of any attempt to apply social theory to their historical endeavours.

Lockhart's and Spears' (1972) *Chronicle of American Physical Education 1855–1930* epitomizes the importance placed on primary sources by reconstructionist historians. While recognizing the impositionalist role of historians in relation to

evidence, Lockhart and Spears (1972: xv) prioritize primary sources as privileged forms of evidence for historians in the justification for their book by providing: "The unique purpose of the opportunity for students to begin the exciting exploration of the development of physical education in the United States through *primary sources*". The *Chronicle of American Physical Education* provides a collection of primary sources including eyewitness accounts, diaries, memories and the writings of men and women chronologically arranged in three separate time frames from 1855–1930. The editors specifically point out that they did not alter these sources, retaining the original language, author identification and reprinting them in full. Contributions from early influential identities, EM Hartwell, Fred Eugene Leonard and G Stanley Hall, are interspersed with original documents about amateurism, anthropometry, athletics, basketball, college sport, competition, gymnastics, physical training, play, research methodologies, rowing, swimming, volleyball and women's sport. As Lockhart and Spears (1972: xi) summarize: the "*Chronicle of American Physical Education* provides a selection of primary sources so that the reader may examine directly the writer's approach to his subject and the development of his ideas".

The approach in *Chronicle of American Physical Education* exemplifies the reconstructionist belief in the "correspondence theory of empiricism" which stresses that "truthful meaning can be directly inferred from the primary sources" (Munslow, 1997: 20). Inferences gained from the evidence can be attained by evaluating the intentions of the author and by placing the primary sources in context by putting other pieces of the jigsaw together. By critically and forensically evaluating the evidence, through the craft-like skills of historical analysis, historians get nearer to the truth, closer to fulfilling Ranke's maxim of knowing history "as it actually happened" (Munslow, 1997). Lockhart and Spears promote primary sources, as unique and singular relics of the past, which are used by reconstructionist historians to justify the rejection of theoretical paradigms as violating the sanctity and independence of the past. Critics of reconstructionist history question the ability to understand the intentionality of the author of the sources and the historian's ability to provide explanation by contextualization (Munslow, 1997).

Another feature of the majority of the histories written during the field's boom period from the 1950s to the 1980s, with the exception of McIntosh's and Zeigler's histories, is the absence of discussions about their own production of history. In most sources, there is no mention of methodology, epistemology or ontology. To be fair, this silence about the processes of historical production in the early editions of these books preceded the prominent Carr–Elton debate, but later editions of original volumes and most history of physical education books were written following this seminal debate and the "cultural turn" initiated by Hayden White, Clifford Geertz and others from the 1970s (Bonnell and Hunt, 1999). One reading of this situation, and the one we side with, is that physical education historians assumed, like many other historians in other fields, that there was a single, dominant and appropriate way of historical research. This approach was based on empiricism and assumed that historians interrogate the evidence by comparison, verification and contextualization and explain the past by assuming a disinterested, rational and non-judgmental position. In this way, the objective historian directly inferred meaning from voices of the past and the interpretation inherent in the sources (Munslow, 2000).

Rather than tackling issues centred on the production of history, the emphasis was placed on justifying the value of history to physical education studies. As Zeigler (1973: vii) argued: "The profession and (perhaps) discipline of physical education and sport most assuredly needs to know 'where it has been, and how it got there.' By continuous, careful assessment of 'where and what we are at present,' the guideposts for the future should be somewhat more readily apparent ... A careful study of history is a first prerequisite along the way to full understanding". This rationale was most likely associated with establishing the worth of history in the emerging field of physical education, trying in essence to stake out some "turf" in the curriculum politics of the period. Even though hard-lined reconstructionist historians would disagree, history is always written from a particular standpoint, for a particular reason, and for a particular group in mind (Jenkins, 1997). All history is political (Southgate, 2001).

The remaining feature of the reconstructionist histories of physical education is the lack of theoretical approaches. Most sources are totally devoid of Marxist, feminist, cultural, figurationalist and other theoretical approaches that characterized other fields within sport studies, such as sociology and pedagogy, at the same time. While the likes of Gerber and Van Dalen did not justify this approach, there were other prominent historians who did. As GR Elton propounded, preconceived theories of explanation were to be avidly avoided because they threatened both the inferential qualities of the empirical method and the independence of the evidence, as well as the objectivity of the historian, and combined to produce a degraded form of history from one particular perspective. This typifies the approach of many early physical education historians. Some were atheoretical, while others were openly and trenchantly anti-theoretical. Both atheoretical and anti-theoretical positions have attracted the ire of sport sociologists who have described history without theory as an anodyne version of the heritage industry (Horne et al., 1999).

An example of the history of physical education that eschewed social theory, but at the same time proffered a philosophy of history, illustrating different positions within the reconstructionist paradigm, is Gerber's (1971) *Innovators and Institutions in Physical Education*. Gerber (1971: vi), for example, prefaces her book, by citing English historian, Thomas Carlyle: "The history of the world is but the biography of great men". Carlyle's "great men" theory of history postulated that "Universal History, the history of what man has accomplished in this world is at bottom the History of the Great Men who have worked here" (Carlyle cited in Fulbrook, 2002: 122). Gerber (1971: vii) subsequently challenges the gendered essence of Carlyle's theory and contextualizes his theory in the history of physical education: "The events and ideas which constitute the history of physical education can be traced back to the individual men and women who helped to formulate them. Insights into the patterns of physical education in the Western World can be gained therefore from a study of the people who were primarily responsible for proffering its ideas. The book contains biographical information about the innovators and presents their most important and relevant theories ... ". *Innovators and Institutions in Physical Education* is a gender-sensitive version of Carlylian history.

Gerber (1971) provides biographical material on over 50 individuals considered influential either in a positive or negative light in terms of the historical development of physical education. The individuals include the early Greek authors, Homer and Plato, concerned physicians, Claudius Galen and Hieronymous Mercurialis, influential churchmen, Aeneas Piccolomini, Martin Luther, John Calvin, Ignatius de Loyola, and educational protagonists from Vittorino da Feltre to Jean Jacques Rousseau to John Dewey. Emphasis then shifts to European physical educators which included the Germans Guts Muths and Jahn, the Swedes including Ling and his son Hjalmar, the Dane Nachtegall as well as other individuals from Switzerland, France, England and Austria. Reflecting the intended readership for the book, a great deal of attention is given to individuals from America. The only other moderating dimension to Carlyle's approach to history is that Gerber provides analysis of pivotal institutions in the development of physical education such as the Philanthropinum (1774), the Schnepfenthal Educational Institute (1784) and Royal Central Gymnastic Institute (1851) in Germany, the Royal Gymnastic Institute (1814) in Sweden, the Bergman-Osterberg Physical Training College (1885) in England, the Round Hill School (1823) and the Harvard Summer School of Physical Education (1887) amongst others in America.

This approach is very informative because she overtly states her philosophy of history as well as detailing the commitment of these individuals, their personalities and beliefs, their access to power, and the impact of their decisions. Her work is in fact a harbinger for contemporary academics who value biography and life-histories of sports people from reflective and critical positions (Bale et al., 2004). The limitations of the "Great Men" theory are as equally obvious as its assets. By placing so much emphasis on agency, structural issues are minimized. Emphasis on the individual devalues the world historical situation of their existence. The impact, importance and success of individuals depend on a variety of specific historical circumstances that not only produce these individuals but also provide them with the power to act. What is often minimized in a series of biographical accounts, as Gerber has produced, are collective beliefs and mentalities, social, cultural and economic conditions as well as political institutions and developments. Mary Fulbrook (2002: 134) summarizes the limitations of the "Great Men" theory of history: "There is, in short, a lot more to historical explanation than the motives and actions of individuals, however important these may sometimes be in affecting the course of historical development".

Constructionist histories of physical education

The reconstructionist approach to history represents a large bulk of the early sources and their subsequent newer editions. Some historians, however, have challenged this approach to historical production, particularly the rejection of any form of preconceived theories of explanation or any overt philosophy of history by reconstructionist historians. Zeigler was one prominent historian who was willing to clearly articulate his philosophy of history. Zeigler, who wrote both historical and philosophical treatises, argued that historical production had several defending features. He recognized that history is written in the present with little chance of avoiding the mood of the times or the predispositions of the historian. In his philosophy of history, objectivity was illusory: "thus we might agree that complete objectivity of history is an impossibility" (Zeigler, 1988: 249). Emphasis in the research process was on primary sources with Zeigler (1988: 248), arguing "that historical writers need to uncover as many primary sources as possible to write the best history", yet he did not eschew social theory and looked to anthropology, sociology, psychology as well as philosophy to provide theoretical concepts. Dogmatic or rigid theories were to be avoided while pragmatic, pluralistic and flexible theories were recommended as long as they helped understand and explain historical phenomena. Theoretical and philosophical positions were perceived as moving historical investigation toward a scientific base, a worthwhile objective in his view.

Zeigler's philosophical approach as applied to the history of physical education was eclectic, drawing mostly on sociology and philosophy. Specifically he combined Talcot Parsons' theory of action with a particular focus on values and norms, and a series of recurring issues or problems in physical education. His approach critically analysed material from primary and secondary sources and organized these material data around what Zeigler considered to be major social forces such as values, politics, nationalism, economics, religion and ecology, and a series of perennial problems/issues specific to physical education including curriculum, instruction, preparation, the body, dance, leisure, amateurism and professionalism, management and the concept of progress. He summarized: "this technique of 'doing' history may be called 'vertical' as opposed to a 'horizontal' traditional approach – a 'longitudinal' treatment of history in contradistinction to a strictly chronological one … a conscious effort is made to keep the reader from thinking that history is of antiquarian interest only" (Zeigler, 1988: 257).

Different to Zeigler, because he does not overtly articulate his philosophical approach to history in similar detail, is Tony Mangan's acclaimed expose of athleticism in the English Public School system. Mangan's path-breaking work on athleticism was published in 1981 (and republished in 2000) and is still hailed as an exemplary example of sport history. As an early reviewer stated: "I do not think I can overrate the value of Mangan's contribution to sport studies" (Freeman, 1983: 72). Following from the early work of PC McIntosh and others, Mangan examined the dominant educational philosophy of the English Public School system: athleticism. Athleticism was interpreted as a complex ideology which had several characteristics: "Physical exercise was taken, considerably and compulsorily, in the sincere belief of many, however romantic, misplaced or myopic, that it was a highly effective means of inculcating valuable instrumental and impressive educational goals: physical and moral courage, loyalty and co-operation, the capacity to act fairly and take defeat well, the ability to both command and obey" (Mangan, 2000: 9). Athleticism, as embodied by the headmasters, masters and boys, and expressed in speeches, poems and other literature, was examined through a comparative analysis of six schools from different forms of public schools. This methodological approach enabled Mangan to tease out variations in the motivations of boys, masters and schools, differences in the timing of adoption of athleticism as well as assessing the degrees of resistance to the dominant educational philosophy. Part of this comparative analysis details the contributions of the relative headmasters including the famous Thomas Arnold of Rugby School. Mangan debunked the myth that Arnold was the pivotal figure of athleticism in the public schools. As Feeman commented Mangan showed us that

"Arnold is to public school athleticism as Abner Doubleday is American baseball: a popular myth" (Freeman, 1983: 71).

From a methodological and epistemological perspective, Mangan's work is heavily grounded in empiricism epitomized by an extensive and exhaustive evaluation of primary source material which included magazines, registers, manuscripts, official documents as well as journals and newspapers. Where Mangan's work differs from many reconstructionist historians and shifts his book into the category of constructionist history is that the research material is filtered through a number of conceptual tools. Mangan's approach to history has been depicted as one "which constructs histories through an interpretive process and not simply recording 'facts'" (Girginov, 2003: 98). The central and defining conceptual tool is ideology which in its various guises helps make sense of athleticism as the dominant educational philosophy in the public schools. Complementing ideology is the concept of power which describes the structural relations of the educational system though the processes of enculturation and acculturation (Griginov, 2003). Other conceptual tools employed to analyse athleticism are symbol, ritual, muscular Christianity, manliness, social Darwinism and social class. What appeals to many reviewers is Mangan's application of rhetoric, discourse and semiotics "so often conducted in a wash of unfathomable jargon, is here performed with skilful clarity, and is cleverly and smoothly woven into an analysis of the practices that both flowed from and underlay the language of athleticism" (Crotty, 2001: 86).

The final example of a constructionist approach to history is David Kirk's (1998b) *Schooling Bodies: School Practice and Public Discourse, 1880–1950*. Like Mangan, Kirk's approach is empirical in the sense that he infers his findings from primary and secondary sources, but where his work contrasts from Mangan as well as Zeigler is that he openly places himself into the history, he writes in the first person and thereby declares himself to be part of the process of historical production. Equally obvious, Kirk utilizes theory as a central epistemological instrument rather than a series of conceptual tools as Mangan has: "I will try to convince the reader that the emergence and consolidation of militarized physical training and school medical inspection by the end of the first decade of this century represented both the ultimate achievement and the beginning of the decline of a phase of modernity Foucault describes as disciplinary society" (Kirk, 1998b: 3). Within a Foucauldian framework, three prominent schooling practices in the history of physical education in Australia – physical training, medical inspections and school sport and games – were analysed in relation to the theoretical knowledge centring on the social construction of the body, biopower and disciplinary technology, and discourse. The chapter headings are indicative of both the content material and the importance of the body to the historical approach: "Schooling Bodies", "Drilling Bodies", "Examining Bodies", "Resisting Bodies", "Civilising Bodies" and "Liberating Bodies". Kirk articulates physical education as a field of corporeal knowledge which contributes to the understanding of the social construction of the body. The degree to which Kirk's history is wedded to the Foucauldian framework unsettles reconstructionist historians aversion to social theory, an issue which underpins a review of *Schooling Bodies*: "Although it is always likely to be difficult to read an historical text through what, I would argue, becomes a very restrictive framework at times, it is also the case that Kirk has been completely open in his presentation of that framework" (Armour, 1999: 207).

Deconstructionist histories of physical education

Deconstructionist histories are distinct from reconstructionist and constructionist histories on at least two issues. Firstly, the emphasis on the divinity of the sources in reconstructionist and constructionist history is undermined because deconstructionists understand sources as "texts" that potentially provide a range of realities and possible alternatives. Secondly, deconstructionists argue that historians don't automatically discover a narrative story in the past, rather they have no choice but to impose a narrative on event that is intended to resemble the past. Textuality of the sources and the unavoidable, impositionalist role of the historian create a relativism of meaning and elevates the importance of form, a neglected issue in both reconstructionist and constructionist history, over content.

The interesting feature of deconstructionist history is that examples are very hard to find in the history of physical education. Those examples that do exist have been created by academics working more broadly in pedagogy who have adopted antifoundationalist positions – poststructuralist, postmodern, and postfeminist – in their work. In the Australian context, Kirk (1992; 2001), Kay Whitehead and Stephen Thorpe (2004) and Janice Wright (1996) have brought anti-foundationalist positions to the history of physical education. Kirk, for example, applies some of the principles of curriculum history to the understanding of physical education from past eras. He understands that any history is the history of the "here and now" as much as it is about the past, he recognizes the importance of historians' biographies and their rationales for research, he eschews making any claims to political neutrality, and he argues that there is no objective primacy of facts, as facts only makes sense within individual and collective frames of reference. Kirk (1992: 215) summarizes:

This is not to say that scholarship or respect for the compelling weight of evidence are any less important in curriculum history than traditional history. But it is to say that notions like 'scholarship' and 'the compelling weight of evidence', and what actually counts as evidence, only make sense within a person's biographically produced frame of reference, and the matrices of cultural norms, beliefs and values in which such frames of reference are embedded.

These principles have much in common with Munslow's typology of deconstructionist history.

These relatively few examples highlight that the history of physical education displays features very similar to the field of the history of sport more broadly which until very recently has been reluctant to embrace what has been termed the literary, cultural and rhetoric turns (Phillips, 2001). The future directions of the history of physical education will hopefully witness some more examples that engage with the anti-foundationalist positions which have been argued are reflective of life in contemporary times (Poster, 1997).

Note

1 For a more detailed account of humanist thought the following Renaissance authors are recommended. Baldassare Castiglione's, The Courtier; Aenas Silvio Piccolomini's, De Liberorum Educatione; Pietro Pomponazzi's, De immortalitate animae; Petrus Paulus Vergerius, De Ingenius Moribus.

References

Abernathy, B., Kippers, V., Mackinnon, L.T., Neal, R.J. and Hanrahan S.J. (1996). *The biophysical foundations of human movement.* South Melbourne: Macmillan.

Ainsworth, D. (1930). *A history of physical education in colleges for women.* San Diego: Barnes.

Armour, K. (1999). Schooling bodies. School practice and public discourse 1880–1950. (Book Review). *Sport, Education and Society,* 4(2), 204–207.

Bailey, S. and Vamplew, W. (1999). *100 years of physical education.* Reading, UK: Physical Education Association.

Bale, J., Christensen, M.K and Pfister, G. (Eds). (2004). *Writing lives in sports: Biographies, life-histories, and methods.* Aarhus, Denmark: Aarhus University Press.

Ballou, R. (1968). *Early Christian society and its relationship to sport.* National College Physical Education Association for Men 71st Proceedings.

Bonnell, V.E. and Hunt, L. (Eds). (1999). *Beyond the cultural turn: New directions in the study of society and culture.* Berkeley, CA: University of California Press.

Bottomley, F. (1979). *Attitudes to the body in western Christendom.* London: Lepus Books.

Bronowski, J. and Mazlish, B. (1960). *The Western intellectual tradition: From Leonardo to Hegel.* New York: Harper & Brothers.

Butler, D.J. (1957). *Four philosophies and their practice in education and religion.* New York: Harper & Row.

Calhoun, D.W. (1981). *Sports, culture and personality.* West Point; New York: Leisure Press.

Carter, J.M. (1980). Sport in the Bayeux Tapestry. *Canadian Journal of History of Sport and Physical Education, XI* (1), May, 36–60.

Carter, J.M. (1981). *Ludi Medi Aevi: Studies in the history of medieval sport.* Kansas: Kansas University Press.

Carter, J. M. (1984). *Sports and pastimes of the middle ages.* Columbus, Georgia: Brentwood University.

Castiglione, B. (1974). *The book of the courtier.* London: Dent.

Copleston, F.C. (1961). *Medieval philosophy.* New York: Harper.

Crawford, R. (1981). *A history of physical education in Victoria and New South Wales 1872–1939:* with particular reference to the English precedent, La Trobe University.

Cripps-Day, F.H. (1980). *The history of the tournament in England and France.* London: Bernard Quartich.

Crotty, M. (2001). J.A. Mangan. Athleticism in the Victorian and Edwardian public school: the emergence and consolidation of an educational ideology. (Book Review). *Sporting Traditions,* 17(2), 85–87.

Crunden, C. (1972). The effect of formal and informal influences upon physical education in england between 1870 and 1920. Manchester, UK: University of Manchester.

Deasey, E. (1972). The contribution of the organisers to the development of physical education in England and Wales, 1870–1939. Manchetser, UK: University of Manchester.

Dixon, J.G., McIntosh, P.C., Munrow, A.D. and Willetts, R.F. (1957). *Landmarks in the history of physical education.* London: Routledge & K Paul.

Duncan, R.O. and Watson, H.B. (1960). *Introduction to physical education.* New York: Ronald Press.

Durant, W. (1957). *The Reformation.* New York: Simon and Schuster.

Fletcher, S. (1984a). *The making and breaking of a female tradition: women's physical education in England, 1880–1980.* Women, sport and history. Proceedings of the Second Annual Conference of the British Society of Sports History, Chester, UK

Fletcher, S. (1984b). *Women first: The female tradition in physical education 1880–1980.* London: Athlone Press.

Freeman, W.H. (1983). Mangan, J.A. Athleticism in the Victorian and Edwardian public school. (book review). *Journal of Sport History,* 10 (2), 70–72.

Froebel, F. (1887). *The education of man.* New York: D. Appleton.

Fulbrook, M. (2002). *Historical theory.* London: Routledge.

Gerber, E.W. (1971). *Innovators and institutions in physical education.* Philadelphia, PA: Lea & Febiger.

Girginov, V. (2003). Sport, society and militarism. In Pursuit of the democratic soldier: J.A. Mangan's exploration of militarism. *The International Journal of the History of Sport,* 20(4), 90–117.

Guttman, A. (1978). *From ritual to record: The nature of modern sports.* New York: Columbia University Press.

Hackensmith, C.W. (1966). *History of physical education.* New York: Harper & Row.

Hargreaves, J. (1994). *Sporting females: Critical issues in the history and sociology of women's sports.* London: Routledge.

Harris, W.T. (1890). Physical training. *Physical training: A full report of the papers and discussions of the conference held in Boston in November, 1889.* Boston: Press of George H. Ellis.

Hartwell, E.M. (1886). *Physical training in American Colleges and Universities.* Washington DC.: U.S. Government Printing Office.

Hartwell, E.M. (1905). On physical training (pp. 721–757). Washington, DC.: Government Printing Office

Henderson, R.W. (1947). *Bat and Bishop: The origin of ball games.* New York: Rockport.

Horne, J., Tomlinson, A. and Whannel, G. (1999). *Understanding sport : An introduction to the sociological and cultural analysis of sport.* London: Spon Press.

Hoernle, R.F.A. (1927). *Idealism as philosophy.* New York: Doubleday.

Hoskins, C.H. (1958). *The Latin literature of sport: Studies in medieval culture.* New York: Roderick Ungar.

Howell, M.L. and Howell, R. (1988). Physical activities and sport in early societies. In E.F. Zeigler (Ed), *History of physical education and sport.* Champaign, IL: Stipes Publishing Company.

Huggins, M. (2001). Walking in the footsteps of a pioneer: Peter McIntosh – Trailblazer in the history of sport. *The International Journal of Sport History 18*(2), 136–147.

Huggins, M. (2003). Direct and indirect influence: J.A. Mangan and the Victorian middle classes. *The International Journal of the History of Sport, 20*(4), 26–45.

Jenkins, K. (Ed.) (1997). *The postmodern history reader.* London: Routledge.

Kindervater, A.G. (1926). Early history of physical education in the public schools of America. *Mind and Body, 33,* 97–103.

Kirk, D. (1992). Curriculum history in physical education: A source of struggle and a force for change. In A.C. Sparkes (Ed.), *Research in physical education and sport: Exploring alternate visions.* London: Falmer Press.

Kirk, D. (1998a). School sport and physical education in history. *International Journal of Physical Education, XXXV* (2), 44–56.

Kirk, D. (1998b). *Schooling bodies: School practice and public discourse, 1880–1950.* London: Leicester University Press.

Kirk, D. (2000a). Gender associations: Sport, state schools and Australian culture. *The International Journal of Sport History, 17*(2/3), 49–64.

Kirk, D. (2000b). The reconfiguration of the physical activity field in Australian higher education, 1970–1986. *Sporting Traditions, 16* (2), 17–38.

Kirk, D. (2001). Schooling bodies through physical education: Insights from social epistemology and curriculum history. *Studies in Philosophy and Education, 20,* 475–487.

Kirk, D., Macdonald, D. and Tinning, R. (1997). The social construction of a pedagogic discourse in physical education teacher education in Australia. *The Curriculum Journal, 8* (2), 269–296.

Kleinman, S. (Ed.). (1986). *Mind and body: East meets West.* Champaign, IL: Human Kinetics Publishers.

Kruger, A. and Trangbaek, E. (Eds). (1999). *The history of physical education & sport from European perspectives.* Copenhagen: European Committee for the History of Sport in Europe.

Leonard, F.E. (1905). The first introduction of the Jahn gymnastics into America. *Mind and Body. 12,* 193–98, 217–223, 249–254, 281–287, 313–319, 345–351.

Leonard, F.E. (1915). *Pioneers of modern physical training.* New York: Association Press.

Leonard, F.E. (1923). *A guide to the history of physical education.* Philadelphia PA: Lea & Febiger.

Lockhart, A.S. and Spears, B. (1972). *Chronicle of American physical education: Selected readings, 1855–1930.* Dubuque, Iowa: W.C. Brown Company.

Mangan, J.A. (1981). *Athleticism in the Victorian and Edwardian public school.* Cambridge, UK: Cambridge University Press.

Mangan, J.A. (Ed.) (1988). *Pleasure, profit, proselytism: British culture and sport at home and abroad, 1700–1914.* London: Frank Cass.

Mangan, J.A. (Ed.) (1992). *The cultural bond: Sport, empire, society.* London: Frank Cass.

Mangan, J.A. (1998). *The games ethic and imperialism: Aspects of the diffusion of an ideal.* London: Frank Cass.

Mangan, J.A. (2000). *Athleticism in the Victorian and Edwardian public school : The emergence and consolidation of an educational ideology.* Cambridge, UK: Cambridge University Press.

Mangan, J.A. and Hickey, C. (2000). Athleticism in the service of the proletariat: preparation for the elementary school and the extension of middle-class manliness. *The European Sports History Review, 2,* 112–139.

McCrone, K.E. (1987). Play up, play up and play the game': Sport at the late Victorian Girls' Public School. in J.A. Mangan and R.J. Park (Eds), *From "Fair Sex" to feminism: Sport and the socialization of women in the industrial and post-industrial eras.* London: Frank Cass.

McCrone, K.E. (1988). *Sport and the physical emancipation of English women, 1870–1914.* London: Routledge.

McIntosh, P.C. (1952). *Physical education in England since 1800.* London: Bell.

McIntosh, P.C. (1962). *Games and sports.* London: Educational Supply Association Ltd.

McIntosh, P.C. (1963). *Sport in society.* London: C.A. Watts & Co. Ltd.

McIntosh, P.C. (1971). *Sport in society.* London: C. A. Watts & Co. Ltd.

McIntosh, P.C. (1981). Games and gymnastics for two Nations in one. In P.C. McIntosh, J.G. Dixon, A.D. Munrow and R.F. Willetts, *Landmarks in the history of physical education.* London: Routledge & Kegan Paul.

McIntosh, P.C. Dixon, J.D., Munrow A.D. and Willetts, R.F. (1981). *Landmarks in the history of physical education.* London: Routledge & Kegan Paul.

McKay, J. (1991). *No pain, no gain? : Sport and Australian culture.* London: Prentice Hall.

McKay, J., Gore, J. and Kirk, D. (1990). Beyond the limits of technocratic physical education. *Quest, 42*(1), 52–75.

Mechikoff, R.A. and Estes, S.G. (Eds) (2002). *A History and philosophy of sport and physical education. From ancient civilizations to the modern world.* Boston: McGraw Hill.

Moore, J.D. (1968). *Social objectives in english physical education since 1870.* Manchester, UK: University of Manchester.

Munrow, A.D. (1981). Physical education in the USA. In P.C. McIntosh, J.G. Dixon, A.D. Munrow and R.F. Willetts, *Landmarks in the history of physical education* (pp. 156–164). London: Routledge & Kegan Paul.

Munslow, A. (1997). *Deconstructing history.* London: Routledge.

Munslow, A. (2000). *The Routledge companion to historical studies.* London: Routledge.

Naul, R. (1990). The renaissance of the history of school sports: Back to the future? *Journal of Sport History, (2),* 199–213.

Osterhoudt, R.G. (1991). *The philosophy of sport: An overview.* Champaign, IL: Stipes.

Park, R.J. (1985). Science, service, and the professionalization of physical education: 1885–1905. Research Quarterly for Exercise and Sport Centennial Issue, 1985: 13.

Parratt, C.M. (1998). About turns: Reflecting on sport history in the 1990s. *Sport History Review, 29* (1), 4–17.

Phillips, M.G. (2001). Deconstructing sport history: The postmodern challenge. *The Journal of Sport History, 28* (3), 327–345.

Pole, A.L. (1958). The renaissance. In A.L. Pole, *Medieval England* (p. 1). Oxford: Clarendon Press.

Poster, M. (1997). *Cultural history and postmodernity: Disciplinary readings and challenges.* New York: Columbia University Press.

Rice, E.A. (1926). *A brief history of physical education.* New York: A.S Barnes and Company.

Rice, E.A., Hutchinson, J.L. and Lee, M. (1969). *A brief history of physical education.* New York: John Wiley & Sons.

Schmidt, A.M. (1960). *John Calvin and the Calvanist tradition.* New York: Harper & Brothers.

Schwedener, N. (1942). *A history of physical education in New York.* New York: Barnes.

Siedentop, D. (1972). *Physical education: Introductory analysis.* The big ten symposium on the history of physical education and sport, Ohio State University, Columbus, Ohio: William C. Brown Co. Publishers.

Smith, W.D. (1974). *Stretching their bodies: The history of physical education.* London: David & Charles.

Southgate, B. (2001). *History: what & why? Ancient, Modern, and postmodern perspectives.* London: Routledge.

Struna, N.L. (1997). Sport history. In J.D. Massengale and R.A. Swanson (Eds), *The history of exercise and sport science.* Champaign, IL: Human Kinetics.

Struna, N.L. (2000). Social history and sport. In J.J. Coakley and E. Dunning (Eds), *Handbook of sports studies.* London: Sage.

Strutt, J. (1876). *The sports and pastimes of the people of England.* London: Chatto and Windus.

Thulin, J.G. (1931). The application of P. H. Ling's system to modern Swedish Ling gymnastics. *Mind and Body, 38,* 625–631.

Tinning, R. (1993). Physical education and the sciences of physical activity and sport: Symbiotic or adversarial knowledge fields, Paper presented at the Congreso Mundial de Ciencias de la Actividad Fisica y el Desporte, Grandala, Espana.

Van Dalen, D.B. and Bennett, B.L. (1971). *A world history of physical education: Cultural, philosophical, comparative.* Englewood Cliffs, NJ: Prentice Hall.

Van Dalen, D.B., Mitchell, E.D. and Bennett, B.L. (1953). *A world history of physical education: Cultural, philosophical, comparative.* Englewood Cliffs, NJ: Prentice Hall.

Whitehead, K. and Thorpe, S. (2004). The problematic place of a woman physical instructor: An historical case study. *Gender and Education, 16* (1), 77–95.

Whitson, D. and MacIntosh, D. (1990). The Scientization of physical education: discourses of performance. *Quest, 42*(1), 40–51.

Willetts, R.F. (1981). Social aspects of Greek physical education. In P.C. McIntosh, J.G. Dixon, A.D. Munrow and R.F. Willetts Eds, *Landmarks in the history of physical education.* London: Routledge & Kegan Paul.

Wilson, M. (1974). The provision of in-service training courses for teachers of physical education before 1925. Manchester, UK: University of Manchester.

Woodward, A.C. (1897). *Vittorino da Feltre and other humanist educators: Essays and versions : An introduction to the history of classical education.* Cambridge: University Press.

Woodward, A.C. (1964). The development of physical education in England as shown in the parliamentary debates and the National Press during the period 1870–1918. Manchester, UK: University of Manchester.

Woodward, A.C. (1968). The development of physical education in England in schools in England and Wales. Manchester, UK: University of Manchester.

Woodward, W.H. (1921). *Vittorino da Feltre and humanist educators.* Cambridge: The University Press.

Wright, E.P. (1969). The organisers of physical education – Their origins, developments and possible role in the future. Manchester, UK: University of Manchester.

Wright, J. (1996). Mapping the discourses of physical education: Articulating a female tradition. *Journal of Curriculum Studies, 28* (3), 331–352.

Zeigler, E.F. (Ed.). (1973). *A history of sport and physical education to 1900 (selected topics).* Champaign, IL: Stipes Publishing Company.

Zeigler, E.F. (Ed.). (1975). *A history of physical education & sport in the United States and Canada.* Champaign, IL: Stipes Publishing Company.

Zeigler, E.F. (Ed.). (1979). *History of physical education and sport.* Englewood Cliffs, NJ: Prentice Hall.

Zeigler, E.F. (Ed.). (1988). *History of physical education and sport.* Champaign, IL: Stipes Publishing Company.

Zerubavel, E. (2003). *Time maps: Collective memory and the social shape of the past.* Chicago: University of Chicago Press.

2.4 Social psychology and physical education

CATHY LIRGG

Introduction

Social psychology is basically concerned with how individuals think about, influence, and relate to one another (Myers, 1987). Specifically, emphasis is placed on trying to understand the underlying processes associated with the impact that the social situation has upon individual behavior. While sociologists study the structure of groups, social psychologists study not only how the individual can be influenced by another individual or by the group, but also how the individual can influence the group as well. The key difference between social psychology and sociology is that a social psychologist places the emphasis on the individual. Obviously, social psychology is a very broad field. Social psychology research agendas range from attitudes, to group dynamics, to moral behavior with a multitude of topics in between. Some issues within the physical education arena with a social psychological bent would be social situations within a classroom such as leadership issues of the teacher, teacher efficacy, reinforcement issues, teacher–student and student–student interactions, and teacher expectancies. Other major areas of recent concern are aggression/morality themes such as moral and character development and how they can be addressed within the physical education classroom (see Auweele et al., 1999 for a discussion of many of these issues). A common thread running through the research, though, is the attempt to discern why people act; that is, what impacts people's decisions to act. In essence, what outside influences motivate people and through what processes does that happen?

Whole books have been written about the impact of social psychological research in physical education in many and varied areas of the field. This chapter does not pretend to capture all of the research or even all of the issues. Given the broad nature of social psychology, this chapter will narrow its focus as to research on how certain motivated behaviors have been studied within the physical education classroom. Also included will be a discussion of research examining the ways in which the social setting can affect motivation.

Brief historical perspective

Why should physical educators be concerned with research on motivation? Certainly motivation is a complex phenomenon, although one which has been studied in a wide variety of situations. Unfortunately, it is also one which is still poorly understood by the people who need it most: those responsible for helping others achieve (Roberts, 1992). What physical educator would not want a class full of highly motivated students who work hard to better themselves physically? If we can understand the factors influencing an individual's motivation in a specific situation, we should be able to increase that motivation. It is important to understand that we are not necessarily increasing achievement. Roberts suggests that achievement is individually subjective and too often research has used performance as an exclusive measurement variable. However, an understanding of motivation can certainly help physical educators improve the quality of their instruction as well as design programs that work (Fox, 1988). If we can increase students' motivation, we have given the students a wider range of choices that they can make. It is then up to the student to decide in what venue to strive, with confidence, to achieve.

Cognitive theory has been the dominant perspective in the study of motivated behavior from a social psychological perspective in recent years (Roberts, 1992). From Weiner's (1972) theory of attributions that marked the beginning of recognizing the role of cognitions in behavior, to Bandura's (1986) social cognitive theory that says that a person's behavior, cognitions and other personal factors, and the environment are inextricably interrelated, social psychologists have moved away from personality theories (e.g. Eysenck and Eysenck, 1968) or hypotheses that the environment alone acts upon the individual (e.g. Skinner, 1969). Social psychology research has, therefore, become more complex. A host of mediating factors must be taken into account and a myriad of motivation theories have been proposed to attempt to make sense of an individual's behavior. Although we can study complex situations in laboratories, they eventually must all play out in social settings.

There is no doubt the physical education class is a social setting. Therefore, the importance of social psychology research in physical education is obvious. What we have learned about human nature and what drives us has been studied in everyday relationships, in the workplace, in the classroom, and on the athletic field. What we have learned can be transferred to other achievement settings such as the physical education classroom. Indeed, the physical education classroom has been the site of various research studies examining specific social psychological topics.

Because the underlying theme throughout this chapter will be motivation, the next section will briefly review theories pertaining to motivation that have impacted social psychological research in physical education. It is not the aim of this chapter to judge the merits, strengths, or weaknesses of any of these theories. Refer to the bibliography for more detailed presentations of each theory.

Core concepts

In this section, several theories of motivation will be briefly outlined. Each theory has implications for physical education and will set the stage for a discussion of important social psychological issues in the field. While less-recent theories may seem to be too simplistic and lack the ability to explain behavior fully, they are important for early insight into motivation, parts of which have been incorporated into many of the more recent theories of today (Roberts, 1992).

Need achievement theory

One of the earliest theories of motivation that considered both personal and environmental factors was need achievement theory (Atkinson, 1957; McClelland, 1961). Basically, the theory states that people are motivated by one of two achievement motives (personal factors): motive to achieve success or motive to avoid failure. The probability of success and the incentive value of success (situational factors) are then taken into consideration by the person. The result is to either approach success or avoid failure. Finally, the theory hypothesizes that certain emotions (pride or shame) will arise from

that choice. High achievers will focus on pride while low achievers will focus on shame. Therefore, high achievers will seek out achievement challenges and intermediate risks and will enhance their performance under evaluation. Low achievers will tend to avoid challenging tasks, avoid risks, and perform poorly when evaluated. Need achievement theory has served as a valuable framework for many of the theories that have come after it, the most important of its contributions being task preference and performance predictions (Weinberg and Gould, 2003).

Attribution theory

The earliest theory of attribution was conceived by Heider (1958). Heider believed that to understand behavior, one must first understand how the environment is perceived. He assumed that individuals seek stable environments, attempt to control their environments, and anticipate others' behaviors. He further felt that to understand behavior, knowing the dispositional qualities of an individual was important. Although Heider is seen as the founding father of attribution theory, the most significant work concerning attribution theory, formulated originally to explain academic success and failure in the classroom, is generally credited to Bernard Weiner (Weiner, 1979; Weiner et al., 1972). Weiner and colleagues (1972) originally identified four basic attributions (a person's schema as to the cause or explanation of an outcome): ability, effort, task difficulty, and luck. They categorized these attributions into two dimensions: locus of control (internal versus external) and stability (stable versus unstable). Internal attributions were those that were attributed to ability or effort. Task difficulty and luck were deemed to be external attributions. Stable attributions were ability and task difficulty, while unstable ones were effort and luck. In 1979, Weiner added the dimension of controllability, whether the factor was perceived to be under one's control or not. He also renamed the "locus of control" dimension as "locus of causality" to differentiate it from "controllability".

An important part of this theory is its attribution–emotion relationship (Weiner and Handel, 1985; Weiner et al., 1972). A person who succeeds and attributes that success to internal factors should feel pride, whereas one who attributes failure to internal factors should experience shame. Conversely, if one succeeds but attributes that success to external factors, pride should be reduced. If one fails but blames it on external factors, shame should be reduced. Attributing success or failure to controllable factors should increase motivation, while attributing success or failure to uncontrollable factors should decrease motivation. Lastly, attributing success (or failure) on stable factors will increase the expectancy of future success (or failure). Likewise, expectancies of success or failure should be reduced if the attribution made was one of unstable factors. Research has found that emotions are likely to be generated when the outcomes are unexpected, negative, or important (Biddle et al., 2001).

Social learning theory/social cognitive theory

Social leaning theory as formulated by Bandura (1977a) and its redefinition, social cognitive theory (Bandura, 1986) will be discussed together. The difference between social learning theory and social cognitive theory is essentially semantic, with the title "social learning theory" simply putting an emphasis on learning. Classic social learning theory was concerned with expectancies (Rotter, 1954), reinforcement (Patterson, 1982) and observational learning or modeling (Bandura, 1973; Bandura et al., 1966). Bandura (1986) believed that the scope of his social learning theory went farther than a conditioning model of response acquisition. The title "social cognitive theory'" denotes knowledge acquisition through cognitive processing. Although these pathways have always been a part of Bandura's social learning theory, social cognitive theory suggests a wider scope than learning, encompassing motivation and self-regulatory mechanisms. Although Bandura (1986) claims that the relabeling of social learning theory "carries no claim of theoretical parentage" (p. xii), these two theories will, in most cases throughout this chapter, be treated as one and referred to as social cognitive theory.

Social cognitive theory is a broad theory that supports the notion of an interrelationship between behavior, cognitions and other personal factors, and environmental events. According to the theory, people are motivated not simply by their cognitions, as attribution theory suggests, or by external forces such as expectancy of reinforcement (Crandall, 1963; Skinner, 1971, 1974) would suggest. Instead, there is a complex triadic reciprocity among internal and external forces and the behavior that that relationship produces. Therefore, behavior is not an outcome in itself but an interacting determinant along with the person and the situation.

Social cognitive theory makes the following important assumptions. First, individuals are able to symbolize, which gives them the ability to internalize experiences, plan new courses of action, and predict outcomes. Secondly, individuals can analyze their own feelings which is important for controlling thoughts and behaviors. Next, individuals are capable of self-regulation by which they can control their own actions, change their environments, set their own standards and evaluate themselves on the basis of those standards, and create personal incentives to motivate and guide their actions. Finally, social cognitive theory posits that people learn by observing others' behaviors.

Self-efficacy theory

Self-efficacy, as conceptualized by Bandura (1977b), refers to people's judgments of their capabilities to organize and execute courses of action to attain specific performances. It is not a perception of personal skills as much as it is a judgment of one's ability to use the skills one possesses. Bandura's theory posits that efficacy is affected by several diverse antecendents or sources. The most powerful source is past performance. If one has done well in a similar situation in the past, one is likely to be higher in efficacy than if one has previously failed. However, the influence of past performance may depend on the effort expended, perceived task difficulty, guidance received, temporal patterns of success and failure (Bandura, 1997), and the individual's conception of ability, that is, whether one views ability as inherent or acquired (Lirgg et al., 1996).

A second powerful source is observing the performance of others. Although vicarious sources are weaker than past performances, they can be strengthened by providing models similar to the observer (George et al., 1992; McCullaugh, 1986, 1987; Weiss et al., 1998). Self-modeling, watching oneself perform correctly, has also shown promise as being more powerful than simply watching another person (Starek and McCulllagh, 1999). Maddux (1995) also suggests that imaginal experiences, i.e., imaging success or failure, can be an additional source of efficacy.

Other sources of efficacy include verbal persuasion, and acknowledgment of one's physiological and emotional states. The effectiveness of verbal persuasion may depend on the prestige, credibility, expertise, and trustworthiness of the persuader (Bandura, 1997). In terms of physiological states, one's level of fitness or fatigue may impact efficacy beliefs as well as positive or negative affective states like happiness, depression, or anxiety (Maddux and Meier, 1995; Schunk, 1985).

According to the theory, high or low efficacy will in turn affect levels of motivation through behavior and thought patterns. High or low efficacy should influence the tasks one chooses (or if one indeed chooses a certain task at all), and the effort and persistence put forth in that task when chosen. In addition, one's efficacy in a situation will influence one's goals involving that task, the worry one has concerning that task, and the attributions one makes about the outcome. Bandura (1986, 1997) cautions that efficacy beliefs will be a major determinant of behavior only to the extent that a person has sufficient incentives to perform a task and that no physical or social constraints are put upon the performance. Also, the person must have some information on which to base efficacy judgments. Thus, when tasks are ambiguous or when first learning a task, there will be a discrepancy between efficacy judgments and performance.

Competence motivation theory

Competence motivation theory (Harter, 1978) arose as an outgrowth of White's (1959) model of effectance motivation which describes a person's desire to deal effectively with his or her environment and gain pleasure from it. Harter's competence motivation theory is of value in physical education because it seeks to explain mastery strivings of children across three domains: social, cognitive, and physical. Like need achievement theories, this theory is based on the idea that individuals inherently want to experience feelings of competence and will experience positive affect (e.g. pride) when mastery attempts are successful. If the mastery attempt is successful, perceived competence and intrinsic pleasure should increase, thus increasing competence motivation. High competence motivation will enable the child to try old or new tasks. However, if the mastery attempt is a failure, the child will perceive his or her ability as low, with a resultant increase in anxiety and decrease in competence motivation. The child then may not attempt new challenges. However, a unique aspect of the theory is the role that parents and significant others play. After initial mastery attempts by the child, positive encouragement and support from important others will increase a child's intrinsic motivation toward competence and lead the child to perceive his or her ability as competent, irrespective of the outcome of the attempt. Conversely, if negative influences are shown after mastery attempts, the child will have less intrinsic motivation, or develop an extrinsic motivational orientation, as well as perceive his or her ability as low. According to Harter, parents can nudge the child toward higher competence motivation even if the outcome of the mastery attempt is failure by giving positive feedback. Competence motivation theory has been widely tested in classroom achievement situations and has been the basis for much of the developmental research in children's sport.

Expectancy-value theory

Another theory that incorporates parental influence is Eccles' expectancy-value theory (Eccles and Harold, 1991; Eccles-Parsons et al., 1983). It has been primarily used to explain children's gender differences of success expectancies, perceptions of value, motivation, and activity choices. The theory posits that parents' beliefs about the child's attitudes, temperament, and abilities impact their support and encouragement as well as the opportunities they provide to the child. Parents also help the child interpret his or her own perceptions of competence, expectations for future success, and attributions for performance. Additionally, children will be influenced by and will eventually internalize parent's beliefs and values as to the worthiness of a pursuit. Investigations on gender stereotypes in all types of achievement settings have relied heavily upon expectancy-value theory to guide the research (Brustad, 1993; Eccles, 1987; Eccles-Parsons et al., 1982; Kimiecik and Horn, 1998).

Achievement goal theory

Achievement goal theory, as conceptualized by Nichols (1984), identifies two achievement goals that individuals may adopt depending on how they view competence. Task involvement goals (also called mastery or learning goals) are ones in which the individual seeks to improve performance and master the task. Ego involvement goals (also called performance, outcome, competitive, or ability goals) focus on demonstrating competence and avoiding negative judgments of ability. Individuals will vary in their task and ego orientation and it is thought that these variations are a result of childhood socialization (Nichols, 1989).

According to the theory, an individual's goal orientation will affect effort expended on a task, perceptions of competence, and attributions for success or failure. These influences will in turn affect performance, task choice, persistence, and achievement-related affect (Duda, 1992). Task-oriented individuals of all levels of competence, then, will choose moderately challenging tasks or opponents, maintain intrinsic interest, and be less likely to drop out because their focus is on effort instead of outcome. The same pattern should be found with an ego orientation, but only for those with high perceived competence. Low-competence ego-oriented individuals will choose tasks that are too easy or too hard, display a lack of persistence especially following failure, and make attributions concerning ability. While task and ego orientations have been found to be independent constructs, it has also been found that individuals can possess high or low amounts of both orientations or neither (Fox et al., 1994).

In addition, the motivational climate of a situation can be considered task- or ego-oriented. Situations where the value is placed on competition with others constitutes an ego focus. Situations where learning is the focus or where the competition is within the individual are considered to be task-oriented. Not only can the overall motivational climate affect individuals in the same manner as an individual's orientations can (Ntoumanis and Biddle, 1997), but also the motivational climate can influence the type of achievement goals that an individual adopts (Duda and Hall, 2001).

Cognitive evaluation theory (self-determination theory)

Cognitive evaluation theory suggests that an important determinant of an individual's intrinsic motivation is his or her perception of autonomy (Deci and Ryan, 1985). Individuals have a basic need to feel competent, self-determined, and connected to others. There are three states of self-determination. Amotivation is when there is no reason for doing the activity or doing the activity is outside the individual's control. The other two states are extrinsic motivation (motivated by external factors) and intrinsic motivation (motivated by factors within the individual). External motivation can occur for the achievement of external rewards, when external pressures are internalized, or when participation is voluntary but not chosen for enjoyment. Intrinsic motivation is also multifaceted. One can participate for learning or understanding, to accomplish things, or to experience stimulation.

Major findings

This section will be systematically divided into topics from two areas of social psychological research of interest to physical educators: the broad category of motivation and the impact of the social context. As discussed earlier in the chapter, both of these areas and the individual topics included under them in some way have been influenced by one or a combination of motivational theories. The majority of the research reviewed here will be research from within physical education classes.

Motivation

There is little debate that motivation is essential in any achievement area. There is also little debate that motivation of schoolchildren in physical education is a concern (e.g. Carlson, 1995). The topics that follow will discuss motivation on an individual level. These topics will include research in physical education or other education settings involving attributions, goal orientations, and perceived competence.

Attribution research

Original research in attribution theory took place in classroom settings. In the classroom, attribution research has found that as children come to believe that increasing their effort will produce success, children increase their persistence on a task (e.g. Weiner, 1979). In the physical activity realm, most of the research has been conducted in terms of sport. While this research will not be presented here, Biddle et al. (2001) have summarized some of the findings. While more diverse attributional responses seem to be made in sport as compared to classroom research, those perceiving success make attributions more to internal controllable factors than do those perceiving failure. Attributions are more likely to be made with unexpected outcomes or unreached goals. Although attributions are associated with emotional responses, perceived performance is a better predictor of emotion. Finally, research into attribution retraining in sport is promising. Biddle et al. also feel that using attribution research as a foundation for investigating teacher–pupil relationships has merit.

However, to date, little research has been conducted with children in a physical education setting. To study the relationship between attributions and emotion, Vlachopoulos et al. (1997) had British 11–14-year-olds participate in either a 400m run or an endurance shuttle run as part of their normal physical education lesson. They found that positive affect was best predicted by perceptions of success and high task involvement, with internal attributions contributing to a small amount of the variance. Because negative affect was not predicted by attributions, the authors concluded that attributions play a secondary role in the emotional experience of physical activity of children. However, Vlachopoulos and Biddle (1997) asked over a thousand 11–16-year-old students who had been attending physical education classes for the past 2 years to state the reasons for their success or failure in those classes. They found that personally controllable attributions augmented positive emotion and minimized negative affect.

A third study within the physical education arena sought to examine the causal attributions and levels of persistence of learned helpless and mastery-oriented students (Martinek and Griffith, 1994). Learned helplessness is created when failure is attributed to lack of ability and increased effort is not seen as helpful. Martinek and Griffith identified 14 elementary and 13 middle schools students as either learned helpless or mastery-oriented. The students then took part in six lessons of volleyball and six lessons of gymnastics. All lessons were videotaped and edited for each student to view personal segments of success or failure. Each student was interviewed and asked three questions during the viewing. They were first asked to describe what they were doing in the scene. Next, they were asked how they thought they did on the task. Finally, they were asked why they thought they succeeded or failed on the task. Results showed that elementary learned helpless and mastery-oriented students did not differ in their attributions for success or failure. The same result was found for middle school students in their attributions for success. However, there was a significant relationship between the older student groups and failure attributions. Learned helpless students attributed failure mostly to lack of ability (64%) and effort and task difficulty least (9% each). Mastery-oriented students attributed failure to lack of effort 54% of the time, while attributing it to ability only 9% of the time. The authors suggest two reasons for the age differences. First, younger children (younger than age 12) have difficulty differentiating between effort and ability (Nichols and Miller, 1983, 1984). In their eyes, people who try harder have more ability. Secondly, older students have had more time to experience success and rewards (mastery-oriented students) or failure (learned helpless students) than younger students.

According to attribution theory, effort is an attribution that is important when failure is the outcome. In an interesting twist in attribution research, Biddle and Goudas (1997) asked elementary student teachers, part of whom were physical education specialists, and secondary certified physical education teachers to rate the degree to which they would rather work with five hypothetical students who varied in effort (high/low), ability (high/low), and success (success/failure). The results showed that effort was clearly valued over the other variables, probably because it is controllable.

Robinson (1990) has called for increased attention to student attributions in physical education as a way to stem student demoralization. He felt that attribution retraining could play a very important part in helping to motivate all students, not just the ones who excel. Attribution retraining has been studied with various groups: poor readers (Cavanaugh, 1991), college students (Perry et al., 1993; Perry and Penner, 1993), learning disabled (Okolo, 1992) and the learned helpless (Fowler and Peterson, 1991). Classroom attribution retraining specifically with children has shown that getting children to attribute their failures to effort increases persistence (Andrews and Debus, 1978; Craske, 1985; Dweck, 1975; Medway and Venino, 1982; Schunk and Cox, 1980). However, Curtis (1992) cautions against solely attributing failure to lack of effort, especially if it is apparent to the performer that maximal effort is being given. She suggests, instead, that attributing failure to poor strategy is more appropriate.

Unfortunately, little research has been conducted specifically in physical education classes to examine attribution retraining programs. In one of those studies, college recreational basketball players were assigned to either a controllable and unstable attributional orientation, an uncontrollable and stable orientation, or a non-attributional orientation (Orbach et al., 1997). They then completed a basketball dribbling task, after which they were given negative feedback that was about 25% higher than a stated goal. After failing (and perceiving their performance as a failure), they were queried as to their attributions for the failure. They then participated in the appropriate intervention program based on their random group assignment and allowed to complete the task a few more times. Results showed that those in the controllable, unstable condition made more controllable unstable attributions and also performed the task better than the other two groups. In a similar study with beginning

tennis players, Orbach et al. (1999) found similar attributional results. They also found that the controllable, stable attribution group had more positive affect than either of the other two groups.

Two attribution retraining studies have been done with participants younger than college age. Miserandino (1998) gave high school basketball players feedback that contained effort encouragement or technique feedback. After a 4-week training session during their regular practice, the effort feedback group improved their performance and had a stronger mastery orientation than the technique feedback group. Similarly, Sinnott and Biddle (1998) retrained six 11–12-year-olds who had maladaptive attributions after performing a dribbling task. After the retraining, these children showed obvious changes in attribution and increased their perception of success.

Perceptions of ability

Self-confidence has been the subject of much research in recent years in social psychology research in sport and physical education. The perception of one's own abilities has been frequently cited as both a mediating construct in achievement strivings and as a psychological factor affecting athletic performance. However, confidence has been operationalized in numerous ways. For example, the constructs of self-efficacy (Bandura, 1977b), perceived competence (Harter, 1982; Nichols, 1984), sport confidence (Fox and Corbin, 1989; Vealey, 1986), expectancies (Rotter, 1954), and movement confidence (Griffin and Keough, 1984) have all been proposed as measuring an individual's perception of his or her abilities. Regardless of the theoretical orientation by which it is measured, self-confidence has been shown to be an important variable. However, the most useful theoretical veins have tended to come from an achievement goal perspective, competence motivation theory, self-efficacy theory, and self-determination theory.

Nicholls' (1989) research has clearly shown that young children are not able to distinguish effort from ability. When asked to choose the most skilled between two people who complete a task equally well, children will choose the individual who shows the most effort, in spite of the fact that the other person is seen doing the same task without difficulty. It is not until late elementary age that children are able to distinguish between effort and ability. For this reason, many studies have found that young children are task-oriented; basically, in their eyes, it is the effort that counts.

Also, because young children do not have a differentiated concept of ability, they often overestimate their own abilities (Lee et al., 1983; 1988; Phillips, 1984). Therefore, as children grow older and they are able to understand ability better, their perceptions of their abilities tend to fall more in line with their actual abilities (Horn and Weiss, 1991). McKiddie and Maynard (1997) surveyed 160 British children in Year 7 (age 11–12) and Year 10 (ages 14–15). Ratings were obtained from each student as to their perceived physical competence as measured by Harter's (1982) Perceived Competence Scale. Teacher ratings were used to assess actual competence of each student. Low Pearson correlations for Year 7 students (r_{males} = 0.25 and $r_{females}$ = 0.15) showed that there was little relationship between actual and perceived measure of ability. However, Year 10 students produced quite high correlations for both boys and girls, with coefficients of 0.96 and 0.84 respectively. They also found that although there were no gender differences in accuracy at Year 7, by Year 10 boys were significantly more accurate than females. In addition, children who were more accurate in their assessment of their own abilities indicated that they relied more heavily upon peer comparison while inaccurate children relied more often on adult feedback.

In comparison, a qualitative study of American children in 4th, 8th, and 11th grades found that children at all grade levels tended to rate their abilities based on social comparison (Xiang, Lee et al., 2001). Rudisill et al. (1993) found that 9–11-year-olds did not differ by gender in the amount of over- or under-estimating of their competence. McKiddie and Maynard (1997) suggest that as children get older, gender differences will appear. Their study provides some support for this idea in that they found gender differences in accuracy of assessment with 14–15-year-olds but not with 11–12-year-olds.

Gender differences in perceptions of ability have been shown to be related not only to age, but to stereotypic beliefs. In a 1991 meta-analysis across a wide range of ages, Lirgg found support for the lower confidence beliefs of females when tasks are stereotypically male. More recently, Solmon et al. (2003) found that males were more confident than females in learning an ice hockey skill, but females who viewed ice hockey as gender neutral were more confident than those who viewed ice hockey as a male activity. Stereotyping activities starts at a young age. Lee et al. (1999) found that 5th graders held stereotypic views of basketball and dance. They concluded that a sense of gender-appropriateness drives competence beliefs as well as other motivational beliefs of students with well-established sex-role ideas. This is unfortunate because if girls believe that physical education is more for boys, as Solmon (1997) has found, the motivation of girls toward participating in physical education classes may be compromised.

Xiang et al. (2003) found support for achievement goal theory and the expectancy-value model in their study with third and fourth graders and their parents. The children in their study were involved in a year-long running program at their elementary school that was also familiar to their parents. Xiang et al. questioned parents concerning their beliefs about their children's goal orientations and competence, and also about their own gender-stereotypic beliefs about running and the importance and usefulness of the running program. Correlational analyses found that all of these beliefs were important sources of parental influences on children's motivation and behavior. However, regression analyses showed that only parents' competence beliefs predicted persistence, effort, and performance in the mile run. Interestingly, parent's gender-stereotypic views were related to their own achievement goals for their children. Parents who considered running to be appropriate for both sexes also held task-oriented achievement goals for their children, while those who thought of running as being more appropriate for boys held ego-oriented goals.

Some studies have examined the impact of beliefs about the origin of ability on self-efficacy (Journden et al., 1991; Lirgg et al., 1996). Findings from these studies have shown that efficacy is positively affected in individuals who believe that ability can be acquired as opposed to being innate. After viewing ten skills from a masculine task (kung fu) and ten skills from a feminine task (baton twirling), Lirgg and colleagues had students rate their efficacy to perform those skills if they were given lessons and a chance to practice. Analyses indicated that females were less efficacious only when they were contemplating a masculine task and believed that ability was innate. Self-efficacy of males was not affected by either conception of ability or sex-type of task.

From a self-determination perspective, the importance of perceived competence in physical activity cannot be underestimated. Goudas and Biddle (1994) found that 68% of the variance in intrinsic motivation was explained by perceived competence. In Ntoumanis' (2001) model of motivational processes in physical education using British teenagers, competence was also a strong positive predictor of intrinsic motivation, as well as identified regulation (indicating self-regulatory behavior), and, in a negative manner, amotivation.

Goal orientation

One of the most researched areas in achievement motivation in recent years has been goal orientations. Research in academic classrooms has overwhelmingly shown that a task orientation will increase children's involvement in learning and the quality of that involvement (Ames, 1992). This research has also spawned an enormous body of literature from the world of sport and physical activity. We know that having a task orientation is linked to enjoyment, satisfaction, and interest in an activity (Boyd and Callahan, 1994; Duda et al., 1995; Newton and Duda, 1999) as well as intrinsic motivation (Doubrant and Biddle, 1997; Duda et al., 1995; Kavussanu and Roberts, 1996; Seifriz et al., 1992). Many studies have supported the relationship between task orientation and the belief that to be successful in sport, one must work hard and work with others (e.g. Biddle et al., 1996; Duda et.al., 1992; VanYperen and Duda, 1999). Task orientation has also been related to giving more effort (Duda et al., 1989) while ego orientation has shown positive relationships to a lack of persistence such as dropping out of sport (Duda, 1989, Ewing, 1981; Whitehead, 1989). Goal orientations have also been shown to affect performance. Taking a social cognitive perspective, Hall (1990) showed the impact of the interaction between perceived ability and goal orientation. Low ability participants who were in an experimentally induced ego orientation condition performed worse than their counterparts in the assigned task orientation condition. Hall speculated that this low performance could be a result of an increase in anxiety (Duda et al., 1990; Hall and Kerr, 1997).

Physical education research has generally supported the findings from academics and sport. Walling and Duda (1995) extended research on the purpose of sport to the physical education classroom. They found students' views of the purposes of physical education to be more diverse than from results of similar studies from the sport domain. However, in accordance with previous sport research, task orientation was found to be correlated with trying hard and collaborating with others. Ego orientation was related to the view that physical education should be an easy class whose purpose is to make students more competitive. It was also negatively related to enjoyment and the teaching of rules and strategies. Predictably, high ego-oriented students believed that high ability leads to success more so than did students with a low ego orientation.

Goudas et al. (1994a) examined the motives of 85 12–14-year-old English schoolchildren participating in football, netball, and gymnastics during their physical education classes. They found that the higher the level of task orientation reported, the higher the levels of intrinsic interest. In addition, the effects of ego orientation were mediated by perceived competence. They also found differences in motivational orientations toward the different activities, suggesting that motivation in physical education may not be a global concept.

Vlachopoulos et al. (1996) examined children's affect following physical exercise (800m run) in a physical education class. They found that positive engagement, tranquility, and revitalization were predicted by task orientation. Similar to the previous study's findings, an ego orientation combined with high perceptions of competence was also

related to those variables. However, task orientation but not ego orientation negatively predicted physical exhaustion.

The impact of goal orientation on effort was examined by Goudas et al. (1994b). They found that children who had high task orientation and low ego orientation also displayed more effort during fitness testing and reported greater enjoyment than those children who held high-ego and low task orientations. Interestingly, these findings were true regardless of their perceptions of success. Similarly, Papaioannou (1995) found that, regardless of level of perceived ability, task orientation was a strong predictor of intrinsic motivation, interest in the lesson, and intentions for high effort and participation in physical education class.

Cury and Sarrazin (1998) examined goal orientations of French children in relation to feedback, strategy, and task choice. In a series of three studies, 13–15-year-old males participated in climbing or basketball activities. They found that boys who were high ego involved with low perceptions of ability chose extremely hard or extremely easy tasks (as opposed to moderately difficult ones), spent less time in training, and rejected information that would have helped them progress compared to high ego/high perceived ability boys or task oriented boys of both high and low perceived ability.

In the Vlachopoulos and Biddle (1997) British study of physical education classes referred to earlier, task but not ego orientation was positively related to success perception. In addition, for the low perceived ability group, ego orientations were related to personally uncontrollable attributions while the opposite was true for high perceived ability group. They argue that the goal structure created in physical education be examined specifically to understand emotion in the physical education context.

While many studies on goal orientation have come from an achievement goal perspective, some recent studies have followed a self-determination theoretical perspective (Deci and Ryan, 1985). One such study was conducted by Standage and Treasure (2002). Surveying 318 youths from two American middle schools, they found that task orientation was positively related to more self-determined types of motivation such as intrinsic motivation and negatively related to external regulation and amotivation, while an ego orientation was weakly related to less self-determined motivation. They also found that a high task orientation, or one that is combined with an ego orientation will promote self-determination behaviors in a physical education context.

Prusak et al. (2004) also conducted a study within the framework of self-determination theory to investigate the effect of choice on the motivations of adolescent girls in physical education. Participants in this study were 1110 girls in all-girl junior high physical education classes. The girls participated in a walking unit within either a choice or a no-choice condition. The choice condition was offered a variety of choices throughout their unit such as with whom they would be participating. The no-choice group was given numerous cues that conveyed the message that they had no choice about the activities. Results showed that girls in the choice condition were more intrinsically motivated, experienced less external control, and were less amotivated than those in the no-choice group.

Although an individual will possess an affinity for being either task or ego involved, the classroom structure can certainly focus on one motivational goal or the other. Much has been written about the "motivational climate" of the physical education classroom, that is, whether its goals are task or ego oriented. For example, Cury and Biddle (1996) found that situational class climate influenced student interest in physical education more than did individual goals. Motivational climate will be discussed in the next section concerning the social setting.

Social setting

Much research in physical education has examined the gymnasium as a classroom and its effects on individual achievement. The topics in this area will include motivational climate, cooperative learning, and coeducation.

Motivational climate

The research on goal orientations shows clearly that a task orientation is conducive to increased motivational states. However, the situation itself can be considered to be competitive (ego orientation climate) or a learning environment (task orientation climate). Predictably, research from the sport environment has shown that an ego-involving climate is maladaptive. Andree and Whitehead (1996) found that British teenagers who dropped out of their sport considered themselves to be low ability and the environment to be ego-involving. In another study involving British athletes, Ntoumanis and Biddle (1998) found that there was no direct relationship between motivational climate and anxiety. However, they did find that the impact of ego orientation on anxiety was mediated by perceptions of ability, suggesting that motivational climate may have an indirect effect on affective responses through individual goal orientations. Attributions can also be affected by the motivational climate. Papaioannou (1995) found that students attributed success to effort when the climate was perceived to be task-oriented.

In a study of 600 French female handball players, those perceiving a task climate on their team perceived greater progress, while those who perceived

an ego climate perceived themselves as having lower autonomy (Guiller and Sarrazin, 1999). Lower autonomy was related to less self-determination which in turn was related to higher intentions to drop out of the sport. A US study of elite youth soccer players found that a high perceived task climate and a low perceived ego climate were related to high intrinsic motivation (Treasure et al., 1999). However, Chaumeton and Duda (1988), not surprisingly, found that as children move up through the ranks of organized sport from elementary to high school in the US the motivational climate becomes more ego-involved. In a study of junior swimmers that examined achievement goal theory from a cognitive evaluation perspective, Petherick and Weigand (2002) found that a task-oriented climate was a predictor of internally regulated motivation, while an ego-oriented climate predicted externally regulated behaviors.

Although, intuitively, physical education classes do not have the competitive bent that sport teams have, the teacher is important in influencing the motivational climate as either competitive or task-oriented (Walling and Duda, 1995). Several studies have examined motivational climate in physical education classes and how teachers can affect this climate by such things as their choice of activities. Papaioannou and Kouli (1999) involved 239 junior high students from Greece in several ego- and task-oriented drills during volleyball instruction in their physical education classes. The students responded to questionnaires after experiencing each type of task. After the task-oriented activities, students had higher self-confidence, lower somatic anxiety, and perceived a higher task-oriented environment than after the ego-involved activities. Task orientation and task-oriented climate were predictors of concentration and loss of self-consciousness. Boys perceived both lessons to be more ego-involved than did girls.

Also, in terms of gender, girls may actually benefit more by a task-oriented climate than boys. In a 2002 British study of 818 middle school students, researchers clustered students into high, moderate, or low motivation for physical activity (Wang et al., 2002). Not surprisingly, they found that a task orientation was related to self-determined motivation and a belief that learning can change ability. However, they also found that boys were disproportionately represented in the highly motivated group. The authors agree with Ames (1992) that to specifically motivate girls in physical activity, the classroom structure might need to be changed to support an increase in an autonomy-supporting environment.

Teaching style may also impact the motivational climate and, eventually, the motivation of the individual students. In a British study (Goudas et al., 1995), track and field was taught to teenagers using either a direct style of teaching or an inclusion style (Mosston and Ashworth, 1986). Results showed that the inclusion style was related to higher levels of intrinsic motivation and task orientation and lower levels of work avoidance.

Motivational climate may also affect students' perceptions about their teachers. Papaioannou (1998) found that 10–15-year-old students who perceived the class climate to be ego-oriented also perceived teaching strategies to be promoting an external locus of causality; that is, the teacher was seen as imposing rules to counter misbehavior and seemed to make students feel ashamed when they misbehaved. Students who perceived a task-oriented climate were more self-determined; they wanted to behave and cooperate with others.

A task-oriented physical education environment has also been shown to be related to less boredom (Carpenter and Morgan, 1999; Treasure, 1997), greater enjoyment in the activity (Goudas and Biddle, 1994; Kavussanu and Roberts, 1996; Pappaioannou, 1994), greater intrinsic interest (Cury and Biddle, 1996; Cury et al., 1996), greater effort ((Pappaioannou et al., 2004), less tension and anxiety (Goudas and Biddle, 1994; Kavussanu and Roberts, 1996; Pappaioannou, 1994, 1995); and a more orderly classroom (Pappaioannou, 1998) than an ego-oriented climate. In additon, Pappaioannou's (1995) study of Greek schoolchildren found that perceiving the physical education class climate as ego-oriented was related to the perception that the teacher was favoring high-over low-ability students.

In a recent study, Pappaioannou et al. (2004) examined whether students with a task orientation would be disadvantaged by being in an ego-oriented climate and visa versa. Data were gathered from almost 3000 students as to, among other things, their individual goal orientations and their perceptions of the motivational climates of their classes. The study found no support for the matching hypothesis that said that students would be advantaged if their goal orientation matched the classroom climate. However, they did find some support for a negative incompatibility. They also found that dual high task- and ego-oriented climates positively affected both task orientation and enjoyment.

Cooperation versus competition

In a topic similar to motivational climate, much has been written about the virtues of (or debilitating effects of) competition in life in general (e.g. Kohn, 1986). In education, cooperative learning (Johnson and Johnson, 1975) has been studied extensively from four perspectives: motivational, social cohesion, cognitive, and developmental (Slavin, 1996). Cooperative learning places the student at the center of learning, where all students contribute to the group and students rely on one another to complete tasks (Dyson et al., 2004). Cooperative learning seems to have its greatest effects on student learning when groups are rewarded based on individual learning within the group (Slavin, 1996). While most educational cooperative learning studies have found benefits for all achievement groups, some studies have found that high achievers benefit most (Terwel et al., 2001; Webb, 1992). In general, heterogeneous groups in terms of skill level are desirable. Also in the classroom setting, pairs seem to perform better than groups of four and all-boy or all-girl groups perform better than heterogenous gender groups (Moody and Gifford, 1990).

The classic example of competition versus cooperation occurred in a social psychology experiment that was conducted at a summer camp (Sherif, 1978). Boys were divided into two groups and were involved daily in sport competitions between the groups. Before long, hostility was noticed not only within the competition arena, but in other areas of camp life. Only when the groups were forced to work together to repair the camp's water and food transportation system did they work out their differences.

In social psychology research in sport, most of the emphasis has been placed on the good and the bad of competition within the youth sport setting (Brown and Branta, 1988; Martens, 1978; Roberts, 1980). By the very nature of sport, cooperation has not been much of a topic in the sport world. However, not surprisingly, educational research concerning cooperative learning has been extended to the physical education classroom setting. However, this research is sparse.

While many textbooks in physical education discuss cooperative learning (e.g. Harrison et al., 1996; Rink, 1998; Siedentop and Tannehill, 2000), little actual research has been conducted on cooperative learning in the physical education classroom. Ben Dyson (2001, 2002) studied the effects of cooperative learning programs in several elementary school physical education classes (third through fifth grades). Using qualitative methods, Dyson found in both studies that teachers and students held similar perceptions about the program. He also found that implementation for such programs may take time. One teacher was initially frustrated with the amount of time it took to organize her students in a 30-minute class, decreasing practice time. However, this frustration lessened as time went on and students became familiar with organization features and their own roles. Overall, elementary students and teachers using cooperative learning strategies emphasized improving motor skills, developing social skills, working together as a team, helping others improve, and taking responsibility for one's own learning. The teacher in Dyson and Strachan's (2000) study at the high school level similarly reported that cooperative learning helped her to help students develop motor skills, develop game strategies, actively participate, and improve communication skills.

In a 2000 dissertation, Barrett utilized two cooperative learning strategies (PACER and Jigsaw II-PE) to study the effects of cooperative learning in sixth graders. Both strategies resulted in increased correct trials and total trials. These results were also found for low skilled boys and girls. Cooperative learning has also been found to enhance social interactions and physical fitness of elementary students and preschoolers (Grinski, 1989) and social reasoning skills, interactions, and social participation of 5th graders (Smith et al., 1997).

Marsh and Peart (1988) found differences in self-concept of ability between cooperative and competitive classes. Participants in their study were 8th grade Australian girls who were either in a 6-week, cooperative aerobics fitness program, a similar but competitive fitness program, or a control group. While both fitness groups improved fitness scores from pretest to post-test more so than the control group, the cooperative group also improved in physical ability self-concept and physical appearance self-concept. The competitive group actually decreased in both of those scales.

Certainly the sport education model (Siedentop, 1994) lends itself to the use of cooperation in a competitive environment. Individual teams must work as a group to increase skill and to be successful within a sport season. The entire class must also work together to make the sport season successful. However, research concerning the sport education model will not be discussed here, as it will be covered in more detail in another section of this book.

A final type of cooperation found in physical education that will be mentioned here is peer teaching. A component of Mosston and Ashton's (1994) teaching styles, originally labeled reciprocal teaching, peer teaching could properly be assumed to be a teaching model as opposed to a learning style. However, because it involves cooperation on the part of the students, it will be briefly reviewed here. Little empirical evidence for the efficacy of peer teaching in physical education has been reported due to the dearth of research in this area. Most peer teaching studies have paired students with disabilities with non-disabled students (Halle et al., 1989; Houston-Wilson et al., 1997; Webster, 1987). Generally, these studies have found peer tutoring to be successful in these situations, although results are mixed as to whether trained tutors improve performance more than untrained tutors (DePaepe, 1985; Webster, 1987).

Two studies have used multiple baseline designs to test the efficiency of peer tutoring. In a master's thesis, Konukman (1998) assessed the effects of peer tutoring with 6th grade girls during a team handball unit. He showed that ALT-PE and total and correct trials were all improved from baseline. In a more recent study, during a 20-lesson striking unit Johnson and Ward (2001) found that during the intervention phase, 3rd grade girls had fewer total trials, more correct trials, and a higher percentage of correct trials than during baseline. They also found that peer tutoring similarly affected high- and low-skilled girls. Also, students were able to accurately determine each other's performance over 90% of the time, supporting past research (Crouch et al., 1997; Konukman, 1998).

Coeducation versus same-sex classes

The make-up of any class certainly influences the individuals within the class. Nowhere can this be seen more prominently than in physical education classes. Prior to 1972, most physical education classes in the United States were same sex. However, Title IX of the Education Amendments of 1972 sought to eliminate sex discrimination among students and had important implications for physical education. It stated:

> No person in the United States shall, on the basis of sex, be excluded from participation in, or be denied the benefits of, or be subjected to discrimination under any educational program or activity receiving federal financial assistance.

Although the most familiar stipulations of Title IX concerned athletic teams, under the provisions of Title IX, physical education classes were to be available to all students, allowing both boys and girls the opportunity to participate in all physical education activities. Some contact sports (boxing, wrestling, ice hockey, football, basketball, and rugby) could be segregated for class competition, but were to be integrated for instruction. Either male or female teachers could teach the classes, provided some provision was made regarding supervision of the locker rooms. Locker rooms and facilities were to be similar for both boys and girls. Title IX also stipulated that standards of individual performance (i.e. grading policies) should be developed and applied without regard to sex.

The stipulations of this act, however, have not proceeded smoothly. The Office of Civil Rights (OCR) reports that among the most common complaints against Title IX infractions are those that arise from same-sex physical education classes (US General Accounting Office [GAO], 1996). According to the OCR, many of the schools involved in these complaints do not even realize that they are in non-compliance with Title IX.

The question of which class environment is better is difficult to answer. The dependent variables in research studies have included such things as performance, social psychological variables such as confidence and attitudes, teacher support, and interactions with students. Although research studies have looked at mixed sex groupings in athletics and college physical education classes, the studies examined in this chapter will reflect those from only K-12 physical education and only social psychological variables will be reported.

At a very basic level, some researchers have simply asked students about their instructional preferences. A survey in one high school showed that 76% of the girls and 52% of the boys supported coeducational physical education classes (Mikkelson, 1979). However, those girls who perceived themselves as not being good in sports favored same-sex instruction. A study of 602 urban and rural high school students found that 77% liked their physical education classes because they were coeducational (Rice, 1988). A study of over 300 10th and 11th grade students also found that 69% liked physical education because it was coeducational (Tannehill et al., 1994). While these figures seem to overwhelmingly support coeducation, it should be noted that all of these studies were at the senior high level. In contrast, Lirgg (1993) found that although high school students in her study similarly preferred coeducational classes, middle school students preferred same-sex ones. In support of this, Treanor et al. (1998) found that middle school students who attended a half year of coeducational classes and a half year of same-sex classes showed a preference for same-sex classes but, unlike previous research (Griffin, 1984, 1985a), this preference was not correlated to ability.

Just as in the United States, coeducational physical education has not been embraced by all. Teachers in Germany are also somewhat skeptical about teaching coeducational physical education. Schmidt (1985) interviewed 456 physical education teachers and asked them in which classes would they like to teach physical education to mixed groups. While 87% of the teachers stated they would prefer to teach coeducational groups in the 5th and 6th grades, only 34% indicated they preferred to teach boys and girls together in the 7th to 10th grades. Reservations by the teachers had much to do with their feeling of a lack of sufficient training to teach in coeducational settings. In addition, German researcher Gertrude Pfister (1983) noted that girls who were anxious and less skilled in sport tended to reject coeducation for fear of failure to meet high standards and fear of being laughed at.

Drawing from self-efficacy and expectancy-value theory, Lirgg (1993) examined both the self-perceptions of students in same-sex and coeducational physical education at the middle and high school levels during a 10–week unit of basketball. Boys in coed classes reported being more confident in their abilities to learn basketball skills than did those in same-sex classes. While girls in same-sex classes showed a trend to being more confident than their coeducational counterparts, this difference was not quite significant. Between boys and girls in coeducational classes confidence differences appeared. Boys in these classes were much more confident than were the girls, which could result in a situation where the boys may dominate the activities in class. The confidence differences between students in coed and same-sex classes, while noteworthy, does not create a problem in a particular class because the students in these classes are actually in different classes.

Girls in the Treanor et al. (1998) study believed that they performed skills better, thought that they received more practice opportunities, and were less afraid of injury in same-sex classes than in coeducational ones. However, they thought that they competed harder in coeducational classes, a finding that might represent the possibility of a competitive (e.g., ego-oriented) environment aided by the presence of boys. Hastie (1998) found that middle school girls who participated in a sport education unit of floor hockey generally enjoyed playing on coeducational teams. Even so, boys tended to dominate decisions and took over the roles of captain and referee.

Other studies have looked beyond preferences to the quality of students' interactions and class environment as measures of the successfulness of coeducational physical education. In a playground setting, Lever (1976) noted that boys controlled ten times as much space as girls and invaded girls' games and scenes of play more often than girls invaded those of the boys. However, Sarkin et al. (1997) found that while 5th grade boys were more active than girls during recess, boys and girls did not differ in activity level during physical education class.

Although the studies are somewhat dated, three researchers have provided extensive information about the efficacy of coeducational classes in physical education. Griffin (1983) investigated participation patterns in a coeducational gymnastics unit and found that boys and girls participated seriously in gymnastics only in events that they perceived as gender-appropriate. She also noted that while boys limited opportunities of girls to learn by hassling them, girls did not limit the boys' opportunities. Griffin (1985b) found through interviews that gender-role stereotypes of teachers appeared, even when they were sincerely trying to be fair. Pfister (1983, 1985a,b), whose research has taken place in Germany, has noted similar findings. Boys are noticed, attended to, rewarded, and punished more than girls in coeducational physical instruction. In part to keep boys from becoming troublemakers, teachers tend to accommodate their interests more so than girls.

Solomons (1980) conducted an extensive study that examined both high- and low-ability boys and girls in an elementary physical education unit, as well as the interaction between ability, gender, and teacher feedback. In a catching and throwing game, she found that, in general, girls had no contact with the ball other than to serve; therefore, they had relatively few decisions on whether to pass or try to score. Overall, the girls received only about one-third as many passes as the boys. Even girls who were successful in their tries to score did not continue to receive passes, while boys who failed in their attempts were still supplied with opportunities to pass and score. Both the girls and the boys perceived the boys as more highly skilled, even when actual performance did not support this assumption.

She also found that boys of high ability were more active in class and received more passes than girls of high ability, while girls with high ability gave away twice as many passes rather than try to score than did boys of high ability. Boys of high ability encouraged and helped low-ability boys but girls of either ability level did not receive this encouragement. However, very low-ability boys were the most viciously attacked verbally, especially by the girls.

In regard to teacher feedback, Solomons also noticed gender differences. Teachers would provide extra practice for low-ability boys but not for low-ability girls. Girls were congratulated for doing something not nearly as well as boys were expected to do. Moreover, when a girl performed poorly, it was ignored or patronized (e.g. "nice try"); boys who were performing poorly were criticized and corrected. Overall, Solomons concluded that those who were already skilled seemed to benefit more from coeducational classes.

Lirgg (1994) also found that same-sex and coeducational physical education classes revealed quite different climates, although boys and girls in the same coeducational classes generally viewed their environments similarly. Teacher gender was not a factor in the coeducational classes; that is, students in coeducational classes taught by either male or female teachers generally perceived the environment similarly. Overall, girls' same-sex classes were perceived most favorably, while boys' same-sex classes were perceived least favorably. For example, girls in same-sex classes believed that students in their classes displayed more helping behaviors than did girls in coeducational classes or boys in either class type. Also, girls felt that they received more teacher support than did boys, especially girls in same-sex classes. Finally, both boys and girls felt that students in same-sex classes were more involved in the class than did those in coeducational ones.

A study that found teacher gender differences was conducted in Australia by Macdonald (1990). Students in both same-sex and coeducational classes were taught 18 lessons on hockey by both male and female teachers. Macdonald found that in the coeducational and all-girl classes, female teachers gave more skill-based interactions. Boys had more verbal and more positive interactions with the teacher in coeducational classes than did girls. Also, while most girls did not perceive favoritism given to boys, about half the teachers expected boys to perform the skills better than girls.

An abundance of research on coeducational physical education has been conducted in Germany. Pfister (1983) suggested that around 20 large size experiments have been conducted in schools. Contrary to many of the findings in the United States, these projects have produced consistently positive results, including changes in students' attitudes. However, according to Pfister, much of the credit for the success of these experimental programs belongs to the teachers and leaders in charge and their positive stance towards coeducational physical education. Most importantly, the needs and wishes of the students were taken into consideration before introducing coeducational physical education lessons. Pfister, as well as others such as Griffin, have consistently emphasized that if a positive attitude among the teachers is lacking, then coeducational physical education is a liability for both sexes, especially for girls.

Clearly, social psychology research on motivation has impacted research in physical education. In the next section, ideas for practitioners based on this research will be proposed.

Application to practice

From the preceding summary of relevant research, it is clear that social psychology has left its thumbprint on physical education research. At first glance, practitioners might be overwhelmed by the volume of information specifically concerning motivation that has been gathered within the last 30 years. However, as many theories have been proposed, this section of the chapter will attempt to integrate knowledge to make it useful for teachers so that the gymnasium can be a better place to be for students.

What have we learned from studies from each of these theories? Research from need achievement and achievement goal theory make it clear that having a task orientation, that is, putting the emphasis on mastering a task instead of comparing skill to another, is by far the best way of thinking. We know that most young children have a task orientation and work hard to show effort. Somewhere along the path to growing up, coupled with the cognitive understanding that ability and effort are not the same thing, many children develop an ego orientation. It is quite likely that the nature of organized sport that so many children enjoy today values competition against another person and that value has socialized children to develop an ego orientation.

Even youth sport leagues that have "fun" as the primary goal also keep league standings for children as young as five. No one, not even achievement goal researchers, would argue that competition should be banned. Competition is a part of sport. However, the physical education arena is somewhat different. The key is where to place the competition emphasis. Teachers can help their students by valuing improvement over outcome, by focusing on teaching skills instead of just playing games, and by emphasizing the cooperation needed instead of the competition expected.

Children are not born with an ego orientation. According to social cognitive theory, they develop their ideas about the world from the world itself and process those through their own cognitions. It would be wise for physical educators to acknowledge that how students view physical education and their own abilities can be shaped by the physical education environment. The seemingly innocuous use of relay races during the learning of a new skill will seem out of place when teachers realize that they are promoting not the learning of the skill but valuing the competition that will inevitably be won by the more experienced group. A better idea might be to form similar groups, have students time their group, give their group ample individual practice time to help make their individual group better (cooperative learning), and then retime to see how well they improved. There is still competition, but the competition is within the individual, or in this case, the individual groups.

The sport education model, reviewed elsewhere in this handbook, is an example of how competition can be valued but the focus is on the process. Siedentop (1994) developed the model from observing that many children enjoyed sport competition but not physical education. His model encourages a variety of fair competitions, but a big part of the working model is the emphasis on having students create the situation and make it work for all. Students referee games, keep statistics, coach, and run practices. Students can get caught up and excited about so much more than the competition, and the competitions can then be viewed as a team effort, a feeling often lacking in a physical education class.

It is often said that it is not competition itself that is bad, but the social milieu in which it is found. This idea is especially salient for physical education. Given that so many good outcomes can be achieved with a task orientation, physical educators need to try their best to reexamine their own philosophies and then structure their classrooms to match those philosophies. Whether it is the type of activities offered, the words that the teacher uses, the skills and activities planned, or the way assessments are done, teachers need to think about what message they are sending to their students. Everything they do, at every grade level, will help shape how students feel about physical education and their own abilities.

In many of the theories (self-efficacy theory, competence motivation theory, achievement goal theory), self-confidence, in one of its many theoretical forms, is a key construct. Self-efficacy theory posits that an individual's confidence will affect his or her persistence, effort, task choice, attributions, and emotions. Goal orientation theory shows how low confident ego-oriented individuals are severely affected in terms of those same variables. And perception of ability is at the core of competence motivation theory. While goal orientation research especially makes it clear that low confidence is detrimental to an individual's motivation, self-efficacy theory and competence motivation theory outline the paths as to how confidence is developed. Both theories show how important past success is for increasing confidence or competence. Harter's (1982) model of competence motivation, and to some extent Bandura's theory of self-efficacy, clearly shows that positive social influences from others can increase competence.

Ideally, physical education teachers can create situations where all students can be successful. This may mean breaking down skills into more manageable parts for students, moving more slowly with one group than another, using multiple teaching styles to reach all students, or redefining the meaning of success. As research has shown, this is vitally important to increase student motivation. However, what if a student does fail? The teacher has a few options other than the ones mentioned previously. First, the student can be encouraged to try harder (attribution theory). If the student thinks that his or her failure is due to lack of ability, the game is over. But if the student can attribute failure to lack of effort, the game is still on. At this point, the teacher had better have an alternate strategy because if the student is then giving maximum effort and still failing, it's game over again. Borrowing from achievement goal theory, you emphasize competition within–getting better than you were before. This chapter did not cover goal setting which is a useful tool to get athletes off plateaus and increase confidence. The reader is referred to the bibliography for information about goal-setting programs. Goal-setting works because it creates many successively harder steps in order to get to the final goal. Accomplishing each step allows for mini-successes, thus increasing confidence. And once a success is noted, the teacher should help the student attribute that success to internal attributes such as ability or effort.

Competence motivation theory says that after mastery attempts are made, one route that can lead to increased motivation is positive social influences from others. Praise for the effort, good feedback, spending time with the student going over errors, telling students that you know they can do it, all fall under the category of positive influences that are well within the realm of a physical education teacher. Harter's model makes it clear that this influence can increase feelings of competence, even without a successful mastery attempt. Self-efficacy theory, while acknowledging that past success is the strongest influence on increasing confidence, also says that confidence can be increased by verbal persuasion from a significant other (e.g. a teacher) or by vicarious success, that is, watching a similar other succeed (for more information on modeling, see the bibliography). If motivation keeps one trying, and if a student can be motivated to keep trying, eventually success will come. It would be wrong for the teacher to expect all students to be successful all the time. Harter's model especially gives hope that students who don't quite get it can feel good enough about themselves to be motivated to keep trying until they do.

Major trends and future directions

Physical education researchers are steadily incorporating social psychological research into their knowledge base. Physical education research is not uncommon in predominantly psychological research journals such as the *British Journal of Educational Psychology* and *Journal of Sport and Exercise Psychology* and, in turn, physical education journals like *Journal of Teaching in Physical Education* have opened their doors to psychology researchers. The marriage appears to be very compatible. Both fields need to continue to cooperate and share ideas so that researchers can both test theory and also apply it to the classroom. But there is still much work to be done.

The biggest challenge to physical educators is not so much what to do, but how to do it. If we concede that task-oriented climates offer students a better chance of enjoying physical education and being successful, we need to define positive classroom climates in behavioral terms so that teachers can recognize specific aspects of the environment to reproduce in their own gymnasiums. How can we teach youngsters to collaborate, cooperate, and compare themselves to their own previous skills at all age levels? On one level, this seems to be a curricular problem, but on an individual level, teachers need effective strategies that they can actually use, not just great philosophies. Teacher education programs should consciously incorporate discussions about positive class environments into all of their preservice teaching classes and then give their students the skills to be able to create those environments.

Teachers need to pay more attention to the psychological well-being of all their students. Not long ago, athletics trainers were concerned only with getting athletes back in the action by accelerating their physical healing. Now, they are trained to deal with the psychological issues that have always been there but were largely ignored until it was realized that the body might heal but the mind certainly has a part in the healing. Teaching in physical education is no different. We teach our teachers to be good clinicians by being able to plan an active class, teach skills correctly, and give adaptive feedback. All are important in teaching. However, many teachers fall short of reaching as many students as they could by failing to understand that motivation is as much their jobs as it is the students' responsibility. Teachers need to create environments that foster motivation. At the very least, every teacher should be able to describe several strategies for such things as: (a) creating a task-oriented environment, (b) teaching using cooperative instead of competitive procedures, (c) retraining students to use attributions effectively, and (d) creating successful situations during units for all individuals regardless of level of skill.

Researchers may need to evaluate the types of programs offered at different age levels. Children have specific psychological needs at all age levels and teachers need to be aware of those. The one-size-fits-all curriculum, even at the elementary level, is not appropriate. A task-oriented environment for 1st graders, while similar, will look different than one for 5th graders. Preservice teachers need to be able to try out new ideas, such as cooperative games and sport education units, during their learning years so that their first few years of teaching are not met with frustration.

One concern that still needs researched is the arguments for and against coeducation. If physical education classes are traditionally taught, coeducation, at least at some age levels, appears doomed. However, if the classroom climate is changed to reflect a more motivationally enriched situation, coeducation can be a great experience. The two seem inextricably linked. Before throwing out the baby with the bath water, so to speak, physical education classes must be safe for all students, and teachers must have a working understanding of how to create situations in their classes that will benefit and motivate all. This statement may seem like a broken record, but the fact is that far too few teachers know much about social psychology. Therefore, teachers teach in their multi-activity units where a few drills are performed and games are played, and then complain about having to teach students with diverse skill levels in a coeducational setting. Anecdotal evidence suggests that teachers are running successful programs (e.g. McDonald, 1997), but the word is not getting out to the vast majority. Teacher education programs need to be very sure that they construct their curricula in such a way that future teachers know that enhancing motivation is as important as teaching a proper tennis serve.

The study of motivation in physical education classes is unique when compared to both athletic teams and academic classrooms. Much can be learned from social psychology research in those other areas but care must be taken so that the findings are not automatically extrapolated to the gymnasium. As sport psychologists were warned to create their own theories and test them relative to sport instead of relying on psychology research (Landers, 1982), social psychology researchers should engage in creating theories specific to the social milieu within the physical education classroom. Pedagogists have typically been the primary researchers in the social psychology area within the physical education classroom. However, more and more researchers in the area of sport and exercise psychology are conducting research that was previously within the pedagogy domain (e.g. the work in teacher efficacy by Martin and Kulinna (2003) and Chase et al., 2003). While some might view this as a turf war, the significance of this overlap between disciplines is significant. The physical education classroom is a very multidisciplinary place and examining factors taking place in the classroom, especially within social psychological parameters, should be viewed from multiple perspectives. This multisided viewing, so to speak, can only be good for the field. We should expect to see more importance being afforded pedagogy research from within the ranks of social psychology researchers in physical activity in future research.

In short, the "future direction" that needs to be taken is primarily to educate teachers thoroughly on what the research so clearly suggests. Pedagogists and master practitioners in physical education should make available examples of programs that create positive motivational climates for students. Researchers in physical education pedagogy as well as those in allied areas should continue to help us all understand the dynamics of the physical education arena and how we can put that research into practice. But the bottom line is that physical education teachers must first be aware of how their philosophies, their class contents, and their class environments can significantly impact their students' motivations and learning. And then they must act on those realizations.

References

Ames, C. (1992). Achievement goals, motivational climate, and motivational processes. In G.C. Roberts (Ed.), *Motivation in sport and exercise* (pp. 161–176), Champaign, IL: Human Kinetics.

Andree, C. and Whitehead, J. (1996). The interactive effect of perceived ability and dispositional or situational achievement goals on persistence in young athletes. Paper presented at the annual meeting of the North American Society for the Psychology of Sport and Physical Activity, Asilomar, CA.

Andrews, S.R. and Debus, R.L. (1978). Persistence and the causal perception of failure: Modifying cognitive attributions. *Journal of Educational Psychology, 70,* 154–166.

Atkinson, J.W. (1957). Motivational determinants of risk-taking behavior. *Psychological Review, 64,* 359–372.

Atkinson, J.W. (Ed.) (1958). *Motives in fantasy action and society.* Princeton, NJ: Van Nostrand.

Auweele, Y.V., Bakker, F., Biddle, S., Durand, M. and Seiler, R. (Eds.), (1999). *Psychology for physical educators.* Champaign, IL: Human Kinetics.

Bandura, A. (1973). *Aggression: A social learning analysis.* Englewood Cliffs, NJ: Prentice-Hall.

Bandura, A. (1977a). *Social learning theory.* Englewood Cliffs, NJ: Prentice-Hall.

Bandura, A. (1977b). Self-efficacy: Toward a unifying theory of behavioral change. *Psychological Review, 84,* 191–215.

Bandura, A. (1986). *Social foundations of thought and action: A social cognitive theory.* Englewood Cliffs, NJ: Prentice-Hall, Inc.

Bandura, A. (1997). *Self-efficacy: The exercise of control.* New York: W. H. Freeman and Co.

Bandura, A., Grusec, J.E. and Menlove, F.L. (1966). Observational learning as a function of symbolization and incentive set. *Child Development, 37,* 499–506.

Barrett, T. (2000). *Effects of two cooperative learning strategies on academic learning time, student performance, and social behavior of sixth grade physical education students.* Unpublished doctoral dissertation, University of Nebraska, Lincoln.

Biddle, S.J.H., Akande, A., Vlachopoulos, S. and Fox, K.R. (1996). Toward an understanding of children's motivations for physical activity: Achievement goal orientations, beliefs about the causes of success, and sport emotion in Zimbawean children. *Psychology and Health, 12,* 49–55.

Biddle, S. and Goudas, M. (1997). Effort is virtuous: teacher preferences of pupil effort, ability, and grading in physical education. *Educational Research, 39,* 350–355.

Biddle, S.J.H., Hanrahan, S. J. and Sellars, C. N. (2001). Attributions: Past, present, and future. In R. Singer, H. Hausenblas and C. Janelle (Eds.), *Handbook of sport psychology* (2nd ed., pp. 444–471). New York: Wiley.

Boyd, M. and Callaghan, J. (1994). Task and ego goal perspectives in organized youth sport. *International Journal of Sport Psychology, 22,* 411–424.

Brown, E.W. and Branta, C.F. (Eds.). (1988). Competitive sports for children and youth: An overview of research and issues. Champaign, IL: Human Kinetics.

Brustad, R.J. (1993). Who will go out and play? Parental and psychological influences on children's attraction to physical activity. *Pediatric Exercise Science, 5,* 210–223.

Burton, D., Naylor, S. and Holliday, B. (2001). Goal setting in sport: Investigating the goal effectiveness paradox. In R.Singer, H. Hausenblas and C. Janelle (Eds.), *Handbook of sport psychology* (2nd Ed., pp. 497–528). New York: Wiley.

Carlson, T.B. (1995). We hate gym: Student alienation from physical education. *Journal of Teaching in Physical Education, 14*, 467–477.

Carpenter, P.J. and Morgan, K. (1999). Motivational climate, personal goal perspectives, and cognitive and affective responses in physical education classes. *European Journal of Physical Education, 4*, 31–44.

Cavanaugh, D.P. (1991). The effects of strategy changing and attributional retraining on poor readers. *Dissertation Abstracts International, 51* (7), 2328–A.

Chase, M.A, Lirgg, C. D. and Sakelos, T.J. (2003). Teacher efficacy and effective teaching behaviors in physical education. Paper presented at AAHPERD meeting, Philadelphia, PA.

Chaumeton, N. and Duda, J.L. (1988). Is it how you play the game or whether you win or lose? The effect of competitive level and situation on coaching behaviors. *Journal of Sport Behavior, 11*, 157–175.

Crandall, V.C. (1963). Reinforcement effects of adult reactions and nonreactions on children's achievement expectations. *Child Development, 34*, 335–354.

Craske, M.L. (1985). Improving persistence through observational learning and attribution retraining. *British Journal of Educational Psychology, 55*, 138–147.

Crouch, D.W., Ward, P. and Patrick, C.A. (1997). The effects of peer-mediated accountability on task accomplishment during volleyball drills in elementary physical education. *Journal of Teaching in Physical Education, 17*, 26–39.

Curtis, K.A. (1992). Altering beliefs about the importance of strategy: An attributional intervention. *Journal of Applied Social Psychology, 22*, 953–972.

Cury, F. and Biddle, S. (1996). Personal and situational factors influencing intrinsic interest of adolescent girls in school physical education: A structural equation modelling analysis. *Educational Psychology, 16*, 305–315.

Cury, F., Biddle, S., Famose, J.P., Goudas, M., Sarrazin, P. and Durand, M. (1996). Personal and situational factors influencing intrinsic interest of adolescent girls in school physical education: A structural equation modeling analysis. *Educational Psychology, 16*, 305–315.

Cury, F. and Sarrazin, P. (1998). Achievement motivation and learning behaviors in sport tasks. *Journal of Sport and Exercise Psychology, 20*, S11.

Deci, E.L. and Ryan, R.M. (1985). *Intrinsic motivation and self-determination in human behavior*. New York: Plenum Press.

Deci, E.L. and Ryan, R.M. (1992). The initiation and regulation of intrinsically motivated learning and achievement. In A.K. Boggiano and T.S. Pittman (Eds.), *Achievement and motivation: A social-developmental perspective* (pp. 9–36). Cambridge, MA: Cambridge University Press.

DePaepe, J.L. (1985). The influence of three least restrictive environments on the content motor-ALT and performance of moderately mentally retarded students. *Journal of Teaching in Physical Education, 5*, 34–41.

Dobrantu, M. and Biddle, S.J.H. (1997). The influence of situational and individual goals on intrinsic motivation of Romanian adolescents towards physical education. *European Yearbook of Sport Psychology, 1*, 148–165.

Duda, J.L. (1989). Goal perspectives, participation and persistence in sport. *International Journal of Sport Psychology, 20*, 42–56.

Duda, J.L. (1992). Motivation in sport settings: A goal perspective approach. In G.C. Roberts (Ed.), *Motivation in sport and exercise* (pp. 57–91), Champaign, IL: Human Kinetics.

Duda, J.L. (1992). Maximizing motivation in sport and physical education among children and adolescents: The case for greater task involvement. *Quest, 48*, 290–302.

Duda, J.L., Chi, L., Newton, M.L., Walling, M.D. and Catley, D. (1995). Task and ego orientation and intrinsic motivation in sport. *International Journal of Sport Psychology, 26*, 40–63.

Duda, J.L., Fox, K.R., Biddle, S.J.H. and Armstrong, N. (1992). Children's achievement goals and beliefs about success in sport. *British Journal of Educational Psychology, 62*, 313–323.

Duda, J.L. and Hall, H. (2001). Achievement goal theory in sport: Recent extensions and future directions. In R. Singer, H. Hausenblas and C. Janelle (Eds.), *Handbook of sport psychology* (2nd ed., pp. 417–443). New York: Wiley.

Duda, J.L., Newton, M. and Chi, L. (1990). *The relationship of task and ego orientation and expectations to multidimentional state anxiety*. Paper presented at the annual meeting of the North American Society for the Psychology of Sport and Physical Activity, Houston, TX.

Duda, J.L. and Nichols, J.G. (1992). Dimensions of achievement motivation in schoolwork and sport. *Journal of Educational Psychology, 84*, 1–10.

Duda, J.L., Smart, A. and Tappe, M. (1989). Personal investment in the rehabilitation of athletic injuries. *Journal of Sport and Exercise Psychology, 11*, 367–381.

Dweck, C.S. (1975). The role of expectations and attributions in the alleviation of learned helplessness. *Journal of Personality and Social Psychology, 31*, 674–685.

Dyson, B. (2001). Cooperative learning in an elementary physical education program. *Journal of Teaching in Physical Education, 20*, 264–281.

Dyson, B. (2002). The implementation of cooperative learning in an elementary physical education program. *Journal of Teaching in Physical Education, 22*, 69–85.

Dyson, B., Griffin, L. L. and Hastie, P. (2004). Sport education, tactical games, and cooperative learning: Theoretical and pedagogical considerations. *Quest, 56*, 226–240.

Dyson, B. and Strachan, K. (2000). Cooperative learning in a high school physical education program. *Waikato Journal of Education, 6*, 19–37.

Eccles, J. (1987). Gender roles and women's achievement-related decisions. *Psychology of Women Quarterly, 11*, 135–172.

Eccles, J. and Harold, R.D. (1991). Gender differences in sport involvement: Applying the Eccles' expectancy-value model. *Journal of Applied Sport Psychology, 3*, 7–35.

Eccles-Parson, J., Adler, T.F., Futterman, R., Goff, S.B., Kaczala, C.M., Meece, J.L. and Midgley, C. (1983). Expectancies, values, and academic behaviors. In J. Spence and R. Helmreich (Eds.), *Achievement and achievement motives: Psychological and sociological approaches* (pp. 75–146). San Francisco, CA: Freeman.

Eccles-Parson, J., Adler, T.F. and Kaczala, C.M. (1982). Socialization of achievement attitudes and beliefs: Parental influences. *Child Development, 53*, 310–321.

Ewing, M.E. (1981). *Achievement motivation and sport behavior of males and females*. Unpublished doctoral dissertation, University of Illinois-Champaign.

Eysenck, H.J. and Eysenck, S.B,G. (1968). *Eysenck personality inventory manual.* London: University of London Press.

Fowler, J.W. and Peterson, P.L. (1981). Increasing reading persistence and altering attributional style of learned helpless children. *Journal of Educational Psychology, 73*, 251–260.

Fox, K.R. (1988). The child's perspective in physical education: I. The psychological dimension in physical education. *British Journal of Physical Education, 19* (1), 34–38.

Fox, K.R. and Corbin, C.B. (1989). The physical self-perception profile: Development and preliminary validation. *Journal of Sport Psychology, 11*, 408–430.

Fox, K.R., Goudas, M., Biddle, S.J,H., Duda, J.L. and Armstrong, N. (1994). Children's task and ego goal profiles in sport. *British Journal of Educational Psychology, 64*, 253–261.

George, T.R., Feltz, D.L. and Chase, M.A. (1992). Effects of model similarity on self-efficacy and muscular endurance: A second look. *Journal of Sport and Exercise Psychology, 14*, 237–247.

Goudas, M. and Biddle, S. (1994). Perceived motivational climate and intrinsic motivation in school physical education classes. *European Journal of Psychology of Education, 9*, 241–250.

Goudas, M., Biddle, S. and Fox, K. (1994a). Perceived locus of causality, goal orientations, and perceived competence in school physical education classes. *British Journal of Educational Psychology, 64*, 453–463.

Goudas, M., Biddle, S. and Fox, K. (1994b). Achievement goal orientations and intrinsic motivation in physical fitness testing with children. *Pediatric Exercise Science, 6*, 159–167.

Goudas, M., Biddle, S., Fox, K. and Underwood, M. (1995). It ain't what you do, it's the way that you do it! Teaching style affects children's motivation in track and field lessons. *The Sport Psychologist, 9*, 254–264.

Griffin, N.S. and Keough, J.F. (1984). A model for movement confidence. In J. A.S. Kelso and J. Clark (Eds.), *The development of movement control and coordination* (pp. 213–236). New York: Wiley.

Griffin, P.S. (1983). "Gymnastics is a girl's thing": Student participation and interaction patterns in a middle school gymnastics unit. In T.S. Templin and J. Olson (Eds.), *Teaching physical education* (pp. 71–85). Champaign, IL: Human Kinetics Publishers.

Griffin, P.S. (1984). Girls' participation patterns in a middle school team sport unit. *Journal of Teaching in Physical Education, 4*, 30–38.

Griffin, P.S. (1985a). Boys' participation styles in a middle school physical education team sports unit. *Journal of Teaching in Physical Education, 4*, 100–110.

Griffin, P.S. (1985b). Teachers' perceptions of and responses to sex equity problems in a middle school physical education program. *Research Quarterly for Exercise and Science, 56*, 103–110.

Grinski, S. (1989). Children, games and prosocial behavior: Insights and connections. *Journal of Physical Education, Recreation, and Dance, 60* (8), 20–25.

Guillet, E. and Sarrazin, P. (1999). *L'influence du climate de l'extraineur sur le processus motivatioannel de l'abandon: Un test du modele hiearchique deVallerand (1997)*. In the Proceedings of the 8th International Congress of the Association for Research on Physical Activity and Sport (pp. 110–112). Macolin, Switzerland: Universities of Generva and Lausanne.

Hall, H. (1990). *A social-cognitive approach to goal setting: The mediating effects of achievement goals and perceived ability*, Unpublished doctoral dissertation, University of Illinois-Champaign.

Halle, J.W., Gabler-Halle, D. and Bembren, D.A. (1989). Effect of a peer-mediated aerobic conditioning program on fitness measures with children who have moderate and severe disabilities. *The Journal of the Association for Persons with Severe Handicaps, 14*, 33–47.

Hall, H.K. and Kerr, A.W. (1997). Motivational antecedents of precompetitive anxiety in youth sport. *The Sport Psychologist, 11*, 24–42.

Harrison, J.M., Blakemore, C.L., Buck, M.M. and Pellett, T.L. (1996). *Instructional strategies for secondary school physical education*. Madison, WI: Brown and Benchmark.

Harter, S. (1978). Effectance motivation: Toward a developmental model. *Human Development, 21*, 34–64.

Harter, S. (1982). The perceived competence scale for children. *Child Development, 53*, 87–97.

Hastie, P.A. (1998). The participation and perceptions of girls within a unit of sport education. *Journal of Teaching in Physical Education, 17*, 157–171.

Heider, F. (1958). *The psychology of interpersonal relations.* New York: Wiley.

Horn, T.S. and Weiss, M.R. (1991). A developmental analysis of children's self-ability judgements in the physical domain. *Pediatric Exercise Science, 3*, 310–326.

Houston-Wilson, C., Dunn, J., van der Mars, H. and McCubbin, J. (1997). The effect of peer tutors on motor performance in integrated physical education classes. *Adapted Physical Education Quarterly, 14*, 298–313.

Johnson, D.W. and Johnson, R.T. (1975). *Learning together and alone*. Englewood Cliffs, NJ: Prentice-Hall.

Johnson, M. and Ward, P. (2001). Effects of classwide peer teaching on correct performance of striking skills in 3rd grade physical education. *Journal of Teaching in Physical Education, 20*, 247–263.

Jourden, F.J., Bandura, A. and Banfield, J.T. (1991). The impact of conception of ability on self-regulatory factors and motor skill acquisition. *Journal of Sport and Exercise Psychology, 13*, 213–226.

Kavussanu, M. and Roberts, G.C. (1996). Motivation in physical activity contexts: The relationship of perceived motivational climate to intrinsic motivation and self-efficacy. *Journal of Sport and Exercise Psychology, 18*, 254–280.

Kimiecik, J. C. and Horn, T. S. (1998). Parental beliefs and children's moderate-to-vigorous physical activity. *Research Quarterly for Exercise and Sport, 69*, 163–175.

Kohn, A. (1986). *No contest: The case against competition.* Boston, MA: Houghton Mifflin.

Konukman, F. (1998). *The effects of classwide peer tutoring on team handball skills in sixth grade physical education classes.* Unpublished master's thesis, University of Nebraska, Lincoln.

Landers, D.L. (1982). Whatever happened to theory testing in sport psychology? In L. M. Wankel and R. B. Wilberg (Eds.), *Psychology of sport and motor behavior: Research and practice* (pp. 88–104). Edmonton, Canada: University of Alberta.

Lee, A.M., Fredenburg, K., Blecher, D. and Cleveland, N. (1999). Gender differences in children's conceptions of competence and motivation in physical education. *Sport, Education, and Society, 4*, 161–174.

Lee, A.M., Hall, E. G. and Carter, J.A. (1983). Age and sex differences in expectancy for success among American children. *The Journal of Psychology, 113*, 35–39.

Lee, A.M., Nelson, K. and Nelson, J.K. (1988). Success estimates and performance in children as influenced by age, gender, and task. *Sex Roles, 7*, 719–726.

Lever, J. (1976). Sex differences in the games children play. *Social Problems, 23*, 479–488.

Lirgg, C.D. (1991). Gender differences in self-confidence in physical activity: A meta-analysis. *Journal of Sport and Exercise Psychology, 13*, 294–310.

Lirgg, C.D. (1993). Effects of same-sex versus coeducational physical education on the self-perceptions of middle and high school students. *Research Quarterly for Exercise and Science, 64*, 324–334.

Lirgg, C.D. (1994). Environmental perceptions of students in same-sex and coeducational physical education classes. *Journal of Educational Psychology, 86*, 183–192.

Lirgg, C.D., George, T.R., Chase, M.A. and Ferguson, R.H. (1996). Impact of conception of ability and sex-type of task on male and female self-efficacy. *Journal of Sport and Exercise Psychology, 18*, 426–434.

Macdonald, D. (1990). The relationship between the sex composition of physical education classes and teacher/pupil verbal interaction. *Journal of Teaching in Physical Education, 9*, 152–163.

Maddox, J.E. (1995). Self-efficacy theory: An introduction. In J.E. Maddox (Ed.), *Self-efficacy, adaptation, and adjustment: Theory, research, and application* (pp. 3–33). New York: Plenum Press.

Maddox, J.E. and Meier, L.J. (1995). Self-efficacy and depression. In J.E. Maddox (Ed.), *Self-efficacy, adaptation, and adjustment: Theory, research, and application* (pp. 143–172). New York: Plenum Press.

Marsh, H.W. and Peart, N.D. (1988). Competitive and cooperative physical fitness training programs for girls: Effects on physical fitness and multidimentional self-concepts. *Journal of Sport and Exercise Psychology, 10*, 390–407.

Martens, R. (Ed.), *Joy and sadness in children's sport.* Champaign, IL: Human Kinetics.

Martin, J.J. and Kulinna, P.H. (2003). The development of a physical education teachers' self-efficacy instrument. *Journal of Teaching in Physical Education, 122*, 219–232.

Martinek, T.J. (1991). Psycho-social dynamics of teaching physical education. Dubuque, IA: Brown and Benchmark.

Martinek, T.J. and Griffith, J.B. (1994). Learned helplessness in physical education: A developmental study of causal attributions and task persistence. *Journal of Teaching in Physical Education, 13*, 108–122.

McClelland, D.C. (1961). *The achieving society.* New York: Free Press.

McCullagh, P. (1986). Model status as a determinant of attention in observational learning and performance. *Journal of Sport Psychology, 8*, 319–331.

McCullagh, P. (1987). Model similarity effects on motor performance. *Journal of Sport Psychology, 9*, 249–260.

McCullagh, P. and Weiss, M.R. (2001). Modeling: Considerations for motor skill performance and psychological responses. In R. Singer, H. Hausenblas and C. Janelle (Eds.), *Handbook of sport psychology* (2nd Ed., pp. 205–238). New York: Wiley.

McDonald, S. (1997). *New model P.E. class promotes participation.* [on-line]. Available: http://www.nando.net/newsroom/sports/pressbox.html

McKiddie, B. and Maynard, I. W. (1997). Perceived competence in schoolchildren in physical education. *Journal of Teaching in Physical Education, 16*, 324–339.

Medway, F.J. and Venino, G.R. (1982). The effects of effort feedback and performance patterns on children's attributions and task persistence. *Contemporary Educational Psychology, 7*, 26–34.

Mikkelson, M.D. (1979). Coed gym – It's a whole new ballgame. *Journal of Physical Education, Recreation, and Dance, 50* (8), 63–64.

Miserandina, M. (1998). Attributional retraining as a method of improving athletic performance. *Journal of Sport Behavior, 21*, 286–297.

Moody, J.D. and Gifford, V.D. (1990). *The effect of grouping by formal reasoning ability levels, group size, and gender on achievement in laboratory chemistry.* Paper presented at the annual meeting of the Mid-South educational Research Association, New Orleans.

Mosston, M. and Ashton, S. (1986). *Teaching physical education.* Columbus, OH: Merrill.

Myers, D.G. (1987). *Social psychology.* New York: McGraw-Hill.

Newton, M.L. and Duda, J.L. (1999). The interaction of motivational climate, dispositional goal orientation and perceived ability in predicting indices of motivation. *International Journal of Sport Psychology, 30*, 63–82.

Nichols, J.G. (1984). Achievement motivation: Conceptions of ability, subjective experience, task choice, and performance. *Psychological Review, 91*, 328–346.

Nichols, J.G. (1984). Conceptions of ability and achievement motivation. In R. Ames and C. Ames (Eds.), Research on motivation in education: Vol. 1 (pp. 39–73), *Student motivation*. New York: Academic Press.

Nichols, J.G. (1989). *The competitive ethos and democratic education*. Cambridge, MA: Harvard University Press.

Nichols, J.G. and Miller, A. T. (1983). The differentiation of the concepts of difficulty and ability. *Child Development, 54*, 951–959.

Nichols, J.G. and Miller, A.T. (1984). Reasoning about ability of self and others: A developmental study. *Child Development, 55*, 1990–1999.

Ntoumanis, N. (2001). A self-determination approach to the understanding of motivation in physical education. *British Journal of Educational Psychology, 71*, 225–242.

Ntoumanis, N. and Biddle, S.J.H. (1997). A review of psychological climate in physical activity settings with specific reference to motivation. *Journal of Sport Sciences, 17*, 643–665.

Ntoumanis, N. and Biddle, S.J.H. (1998). The relationship between competitive anxiety, achievement goals, and motivational climates. *Research Quarterly for Exercise and Sport, 69*, 176–187.

Okolo, C.M. (1992). The effects of computer-based attribution retraining on the attributions, persistence, and mathematics computation of students with learning disabilities. *Journal of Learning Disabilities, 25*, 327–334.

Orbach, I., Singer, R.N. and Murphey, M. (1997). An attribution retraining program and achievement in sport. *The Sport Psychologist, 11*, 294–304.

Orbach, I., Singer, R.N. and Price, S. (1999). An attribution retraining program and achievement in sport. *The Sport Psychologist, 13*, 69–82.

Papaioannou, A. (1994). The development of a questionnaire to measure achievement orientations in physical education. *Research Quarterly for Exercise and Sport, 65*, 11–20.

Papaioannou, A. (1995). Differential perceptual and motivational patterns when different goals are adopted. *Journal of Sport and Exercise Psychology, 17*, 18–34.

Papaioannou, A. (1998). Goal perspectives, reasons for being disciplined, and self-reported discipline in physical education lessons. *Journal of Teaching in Physical Education, 17*, 421–441.

Papaioannou, A. and Kouli, O. (1999). The effect of task structure, perceived motivational climate, and goal orientations on students' task involvement and anxiety. *Journal of Applied Sport Psychology, 11*, 51–71.

Papaioannou, A. and Theodorakis, Y. (1996). A test of three models for the prediction of intention for participation in physical education lessons. *International Journal of Sport Psychology, 27*, 383–399.

Papaioannou, A., Marsh, H.W. and Theodorakis, Y. (2004). A multilevel approach to motivational climate in physical education and sport settings: An individual or a group level construct? *Journal of Sport and Exercise Psychology, 26*, 90–118.

Patterson, G.R. (1982). *A social learning approach* (Vol. 3). *Coercive family process*. Eugene, O: Castalia.

Perry, R.P., Hechter, F.J., Menec, V.H. and Weinberg, L.E. (1989). Enhancing achievement motivation and performance in college students: An attributional retraining perspective. *Research in High Education, 34*, 687–723.

Perry, R.P. and Penner, K.S. (1990). Enhancing academic achievement in college students through attributional retraining and instruction, *Journal of Educational Psychology, 82*, 262–271.

Petherick, C.M. and Weigand, D.A. (2002). Goals, motivational climates and motivation. *International Journal of Sport Psychology, 33*, 218–237.

Pfister, G. (1983). *Geschlechtsspezifische Sozialisation und Koedukation im Sport*. Berlin: Bartels and Wernitz.

Pfister, G. (1985a). Zur Ausgrenzung von Weiblichkeit. Entwicklungen und Verhinderungen des Koedukativen Unterrichts. In, S. Kröner. and G. Pfister (Eds.), *Nachdenken über Koedukation im Sport* (pp. 11–37). Ahrensburg: Czwalina.

Pfister, G. (1985b). Als mädchen darf mann kein fußball spielen – Über das Eiüben der Geschlechterrollen im Sportunterricht. In R. Valtin and U. Warm (Eds.), *Fauen machen Schule* (pp. 42–52). Frankfort: Bartels and Wernitz.

Phillips, D. (1984). The illusion of competence among academically competent children. *Child Development, 55*, 2000–2016.

Prusak, K. A., Treasure, D.C., Darst, P.W. and Pangrazi, R.P. (2004). The effects of choice on the motivation of adolescent girls in physical education. *Journal of Teaching in Physical Education, 23*, 19–29.

Rice. P.L. (1988). Attitudes of high school student toward physical education, education activities, teachers, and personal health. *The Physical Educator*, 94–99.

Rink, J.E. (1998). *Teaching physical education for learning*. Boston: WCB, McGraw-Hill.

Roberts, G.C. (1980). Children in competition: A theoretical perspective and recommendations for practice. *Motor Sksills: Theory into Practice, 4*, 37–50.

Roberts, G.C. (1992). Motivatin in sport and exercise: Conceptual constraints and convergence. In G. C. Roberts (Ed.), *Motivation in sport and exercise* (pp. 3–29). Champaign, IL: Human Kinetics.

Roberts, G.C. (Ed.), *Motivation in sport and exercise*. Champaign, IL: Human Kinetics.

Robinson, D.W. (1990). An attributional analysis of student demoralization in physical education settings. *Quest, 42*, 27–39.

Rotter, J.B. (1954). *Social learning and clinical psychology*. Englewood Cliffs, NJ: Prentice-Hall.

Rotter, J.B. (1966). Generalized expectancies for internal and external control of reinforcement. *Psychological Monographs, 80*(1, Whole No. 609).

Rudisill, M.E., Mahar, M.T. and Meaney, K.S. (1993). The relationship between children's perceived and actual motor competence. *Perceptual and Motor Skills, 76*, 895–906.

Schmidt. W. (1985). Die Einstellung von Lehrpersonen zur Koedukation im Schulsport. In S. Kröner and G. Pfister (Eds.), *Nachdenken über Koedukation im Sport* (pp. 122–137). Ahrensburg: Czwalina..

Sarkin, J.A., Mckenzie, T.L. and Sallis, J.F. (1997). Gender differences in physical activity during fifth-grade physical education and recess periods. *Journal of Teaching in Physical Education, 17*, 99–106.

Schunk, D.H. (1985). Self-efficacy and classroom learning. *Psychology in the Schools, 22*, 208–223.

Schunk, D.H. and Cox, P.D. (1980). Strategy training and attributional feedback with learning disabled students. *Journal of Educational Psychology, 78*, 201–209.

Seifritz, J., Duda, J.l. and Chi, L. (1992). The relationship of perceived motivational climate to intrinsic motivation and beliefs about success in basketball. *Journal of Sport and Exercise Psychology, 14*, 375–391.

Sherif, C. (1978). The social context of competition. In R. Martens (Ed.), *Joy and sadness in children's sport* (pp. 81–97). Champaign, IL: Human Kinetics.

Shulman, L. (Ed.) (1977). Review of research in education (Vol. 4). Ithaca, IL: Peacock.

Siedentop, D. (1994). *Sport education.* Champaign, IL: Human Kinetics.

Siedentop, D. and Tannehill, D. (2000). *Developing teaching skills in physical education.* Mountain View, CA: Mayfield.

Sinnot, K. and Biddle, S. (1998). Changes in attributions, perceptions of success and intrinsic motivaation after attribution retraining in children's sport. *International Journal of Adolescence and Youth, 7*, 137–144.

Skinner, B.F. (1969). *Contingencies of reinforcement: A theoretical analysis.* New York: Appleton-Cenury-Crofts.

Skinner, B.F. (1971). *Beyond freedom and dignity.* New York: Knopf.

Skinner, B.F. (1974). *About behaviorism.* New York: Knopf.

Slavin, R.E. (1996). Research on cooperative learning and achievement: What we know, what we need to know. *Contemporary Educational Psychology, 21*, 43–69.

Smith, B., Markley, R. and GocKarp, G. (1997). The effect of a cooperative learning intervention on the social skill enhancement of a third grade physical education class. *Research Quarterly for Exercise and Sport, 68* (Suppl.), A-68.

Solmon, M.A. (1997). *Students' goals in physical education classes.* Paper presented at the annual meeting of the American Educational Research Association, Chicago.

Solmon, M.A., Lee, A.M., Belcher, D., Harrison, L. and Wells, L (2003). Beliefs about gender appropriateness, ability, and competence in physical activity. *Journal of Teaching in Physical Education, 22*, 261–279.

Solomons, H.H. (1980). Sex role mediation of achievement behaviors and interpersonal interactions in sex-integrated team games. In E. A. Pepitone (Ed.), *Children in cooperation and competition: Toward a developmental social psychology* (pp. 321–364). Lexington, MA: Lexington Books.

Standage, M. and Treasure, D.C. (2002). Relationships among achievement goal orientations and multidimensional situational motivation in physical education. *British Journal of Educational Psychology, 72*, 87–103.

Starak, J. and McCullagh, P. (1999). The effect of self-modeling on the performance of beginning swimming. *The Sport Psychologist, 13*, 269–287.

Tannehill, D., Romar, J. and O'Sullivan, M. (1994). Attitudes toward physical education: Their impact on how physical education teachers make sense of their work. *Journal of Teaching in Physical Education, 13*, 406–420.

Terwel, J., Gillies, R.M., van den Eeden, P. and Hoek, D. (2001). Cooperative learning processes of students: A longitudinal multilevel perspective. *British Journal of Educational Psychology, 71*, 619–645.

Treanor, L., Graber, K., Housner, L. and Wiegand, R. (1998). Middle school students' perceptions of coeducational and same-sex physical education classes. *Journal of Teaching in Physical Education, 18*, 43–56.

Treasure, D.,C. (1997). Perceptions of the motivational climate and elementary school children's cognitive and affective response. *Journal of Sport and Exercise Psychology, 19*, 278–290.

Treasure, D.C., Standage, M. and Lochbaum, M. (1999). *Perceptions of the motivational climate and situational motivation in elite youth sport.* Paper presented at the annual meeting of the Association for the Advancement of Applied Sport Psychology, Banff, Canada.

US General Accounting Office. (1996). *Public education: Issues involving single-gender schools and programs.* (Report Number: GAO/HEHS-96–122).

Van Yperen, N.W. and Duda, J.L. (1999). Goal orientations, beliefs about success, and performance among young elite Dutch soccer players. *Scandanavian Journal of Medicine and Science in Sport, 9*, 358–364.

Vlachopoulos, S. and Biddle, S.J.H. (1997). Modeling the relation of goal orientations to achievement-related affect in physical education: Does perceived ability matter? *Journal of Sport and Exercise Psychology, 19*, 169–187.

Vlachopoulos, S., Biddle, S.J.H. and Fox, K. (1996). A social-cognitive investigation into the mechanisms of affect generation in children's physical activity. *Journal of Sport and Exercise Psychology, 18*, 174–193.

Vlachopoulos, S., Biddle, S.J.H. and Fox, K. (1997). Determinants of emotion in childrens physical activity. *Pediatric Exercise Science, 9*, 65–79.

Vealey, R.S. (1986). Conceptualization of sport-confidence and competitive orientation: Preliminary investigation and instrument development. *Journal of Sport Psychology, 8*, 221–246.

Walling, M.D. and Duda, J. L. (1995). Goals and their associations with beliefs about success in and perceptions of the purposes of physical education. *Journal of Teaching in Physical Education, 14*, 140–156.

Wang, C.K.J., Chatzisarantis, N.L.D., Spray, C.M. and Biddle, S.J.H. (2002). Achievement goal profiles in school physicl education: Differences in self-determination, sport ability beliefs, and physical activity. *British Journal of Educational Psychology, 72*, 433–445.

Webb, N.M. (1992). Testing a theoretical model of student interaction and learning in small groups. In R. Hertz-Lazarowitz and N. Miller (Eds.), *Interaction in cooperative groups: The theoretical anatomy of group learning* (pp. 102–119). New York: Cambridge University Press.

Webster, G.E. (1987). Influence of peer tutors upon academic learning time-physical education of mentally handicapped students. *Journal of Teaching in Physical Education*, 7, 393–403.

Weinberg, R. (1992). Goal-setting and motor performance: A review and critique. In G.C. Roberts (Ed.), *Motivation in sport and exercise* (pp. 177–198), Champaign, IL: Human Kinetics.

Weinberg, R.S. and Gould, D. (2003). *Foundations of sport and exercise psychology*. Champaign, IL: Human Kinetics.

Weiner, B. (1986). An attributional theory of motivation and emotion. New York: Springer-Verlag.

Weiner, B. (1972). *Theories of motivation: From mechanics to cognition*. Chicago: Markham.

Weiner, B. (1979). A theory of motivation for some classroom experiences. *Journal of Educational Psychology*, 71, 3–25.

Weiner, B. (1985). An attributional theory of achievement motivation and emotion. *Psychological Review*, 92, 548–573.

Weiner, B. (1995). Human motivation. Newbury Park, CA: Sage.

Weiner, B., Frieze, I.H., Kukla, A., Reed, L., Rest, S. and Rosenbaum, R.M. (1972). In E.E. Jones, D.E. Kanouse, H.H. Kelley, R.E. Nisbett, S. Valins and B. Weiner (Eds.), *Attributions: Perceiving the causes of behavior* (pp. 95–120). Morristown, NJ: General Learning Press.

Weiner, B., Graham, S. and Chandler, C. (1982). Pity, anger, and guilt: An attributional analysis. *Personality and Social Psychology Bulletin*, 8, 226–232.

Weiner, B. and Handel, S. (1985). A cognition-emotion-action sequence: Anticipated emaotional consequences of causal attributions and reported communication strategy. *Developmental Psychology*, 21, 102–107.

Weiss, M.R., McCullagh, P., Smith, A.L. and Berlant, A.R. (1998). Observational learning and the fearful child: Influence of peer models on swimming skill performance and psychological responses. *Research Quarterly for Exercise and Sport*, 69, 380–394.

White, R.W. (1959). Motivation reconsidered: The concept of competence. *Psychological Review*, 66, 297–333.

Whitehead, J. (1989). *Achievement motivation and persistence in adolescent sport*. Paper presented at the symposium on Motivation in Sport and Exercise, University of Illinois, Urbana.

Xiang, P., McBride, R. and Bruene, A. (2003). Relations of parents' beliefs to children's motivation in an elementary physical education program. *Journal of Teaching in Physical Education*, 22, 410–425.

Xiang, P., Lee, A. and Williamson, L. (2001). Conceptions of ability in physical educatioin: Children and adolescents. *Journal of Teaching in Physical Education*, 20, 282–294.

2.5 Public health and physical education

STEWART G. TROST

Introduction

School physical education programs have long been concerned with the health and well-being of young people. The link between school physical education and public health can be traced back to as early as 1850, when Lemuel Shattuck recommended that schools provide physical training as a means of promoting personal and public health in the state of Massachusetts (Shattuck, 1850). The German and Swedish gymnastics systems, which dominated school physical education programs during the latter half of the 19th century, were based on the premise that personal health and well-being were achieved through rigorous exercise (Welch, 1996). The development of the AAHPER Youth Fitness Test and the introduction of mass fitness testing into the physical education curriculum during the 1950s were fueled by concerns that the health of American children was inferior to that of European children (Welch, 1996).

Brief historical perspective

In the United States, recognition of the contribution of school physical education programs to public health is evidenced by the existence of national public health objectives related to school physical education programs (USDHHS, 2000). Moreover, the landmark US Surgeon General's report on physical activity and health specifically identified school physical education as one of the most important vehicles for promoting health-enhancing physical activity in young people.

> With evidence that success in this arena is possible, every effort should be made to encourage schools to require daily physical education in each grade and to promote physical activities that can be enjoyed throughout life. (USDHHS, 1996, p. 6)

While acceptance of physical education's notional public health role is almost universal, commentators from a diverse range of academic disciplines have been quick to criticize physical education's contribution to public health (Corbin, 2002; Pate et al., 1995; Sallis and McKenzie, 1991; Simons-Morton, 1994). In their critique of school physical education as a legitimate public health entity, these commentators have drawn attention to the historically low rates of enrollment, lackluster levels of physical activity during class time, and chronic failure to teach the behavioral skills associated with lifetime participation in sport and physical activity. With widespread childhood obesity looming on the horizon, these concerns prompted public health authorities to call for and support school-based intervention trials testing the effects of modified physical education curricula, changes in teacher behavior, and/or changes to the school environment, on physical activity behavior in and outside of school physical education.

Core concepts

This chapter reviews the research on physical activity and health in young people and discusses the contribution of school physical education programs to public health. The chapter comprises four major subtopics. First, it summarizes the evidence linking youth physical activity to short- and long-term health outcomes. Second, it reviews current public health guidelines related to young people's participation in physical activity and examines the proportion of children and adolescents meeting them. Third, it summarizes the research literature pertaining to school-based physical activity interventions. And fourth, it scrutinizes the public health impact of school physical education through an application of a recognized public health evaluation framework.

The review of evidence will demonstrate that regular physical activity is associated with significant short-term health benefits during childhood and adolescence, but the evidence is weak and mostly cross-sectional in nature. While there remain compelling reasons to promote physical activity in young people, there is currently little evidence to suggest that childhood physical activity has a significant influence on health outcomes during adulthood. Research findings from a collection of descriptive epidemiological studies indicate that sizeable percentages of children and adolescents fail to meet contemporary guidelines for participation in moderate-to-vigorous physical activity. There is consistent evidence that boys are more active than girls and that the age-related decline in physical activity evident in both genders is more marked in girls than in boys. Findings from school-based intervention studies show that behaviorally oriented physical education curricula can be successfully implemented and that teacher behavior in physical education can be modified so as to increase student physical activity during physical education classes. However, the long term effects of these interventions and their impact on physical activity behavior outside of school are not clear. Lastly, the results of population-level surveys conducted over the last three decades would suggest that school physical education has failed to meet public health goals related to enrollment in school physical education, the proportion of children and adolescents exposed to daily physical education, and the amount of physical activity provided by an average physical education lesson. Application of a recognized public health evaluation framework to high school physical education in the United States suggests that, in its current state, a minuscule percentage of young people in grades nine through twelve derive health benefits from school physical education.

Definition of terms

Physical activity has been defined as any bodily movement produced by skeletal muscle action that results in energy expenditure above resting (USDHHS, 1996). As a result, the term physical activity includes virtually all forms of human movement, including occupational activities (e.g., lifting, digging, sweeping), household tasks (e.g., sweeping, mowing), transportation (e.g., walking to school or work), and leisure pursuits (e.g. recreational walking, basketball, and soccer). Exercise is a specific type of physical activity that has been defined as planned, structured, and repetitive bodily movement done to improve or maintain one or more components of physical fitness (USDHHS, 1996). The distinction is an important one, as only a small percentage of young people participate in physical activity for the sole purpose of improving fitness. It is also important to distinguish "physical activity" from "physical fitness". Physical fitness is defined as a set of attributes that persons have or achieve that relates to their ability to perform physical activity (USDHHS, 1996). Health-related components of

fitness include body composition, cardiorespiratory endurance, flexibility and muscular strength and endurance (USDHHS, 1996). Among children and adolescents, physical fitness is only weakly associated with physical activity, accounting for less than 5% of the variance in physical activity behavior (Morrow and Freedson, 1994; Trost, 1998). Hence, the frequent practice of using the terms physical activity and physical fitness interchangeably should be avoided. When quantifying physical activity behavior in young people, a variety of measurement units are used. These include energy expenditure per unit of time (kcal/h or kcal/kg/min); metabolic equivalents (METs), minutes or time blocks spent in moderate, hard, very hard, or total activity; frequency of continuous bouts of activity; and ordinal activity classifications or ratings such as low, moderate, and highly active. A MET approximates the energy expenditure associated with quiet sitting and is used as an index of physical activity intensity. By convention, moderate-intensity physical activities are those that require approximately 3 to 6 times as much energy as rest (3–6 METs), while vigorous physical activities are those that require greater than six times as much energy as rest (USDHHS, 1996).

Physical activity and health

Adults

Among adults, regular participation in physical activity has been shown to provide an array of important health benefits. These include reduced risk of coronary heart disease, hypertension, Type II diabetes mellitus, obesity, certain cancers, and some mental health problems (National Institutes of Health, 1996; USDHHS, 1996). Long-term prospective studies have consistently demonstrated that the risk of all-cause mortality is significantly lower in physically active and/or fit adults relative to their sedentary counterparts (Blair et al., 1989; Paffenbarger et al., 1986) and that mid-life increases in physical activity or fitness are associated with significant reductions in risk for all-cause mortality (Blair et al., 1995, Paffenbarger et al., 1994). This scientific evidence has prompted several medical and public health organizations to issue position statements and official recommendations endorsing promotion of physical activity for enhancement of public health (NIH, 1996; Pate et al., 1995; USDHHS, 1996).

Children and adolescents

Among children and adolescents, the relationship between physical activity and health is less well understood. Blair et al. (1989b) proposed a conceptual model illustrating the relationship between childhood physical activity and health status. According to the model, childhood physical activity

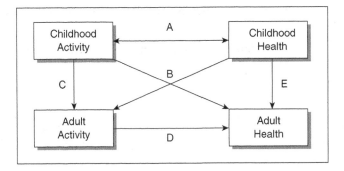

Figure 2.5.1   Conceptual model illustrating the relationship between childhood physical activity and health status (Blair et al., 1989)

may influence adult health status either directly (Path B) or indirectly through its beneficial effects on childhood health outcomes (Paths A and E). Alternatively, childhood activity may indirectly influence adult health status through its positive effects on physical activity levels during adulthood (Path C). This association is commonly referred to as the tracking of physical activity from childhood to adulthood (Figure. 2.5.1).

With respect to Path B, there is little evidence to suggest that childhood physical activity is directly associated with adult health status. The Harvard Alumni Study found sports participation early in life to be unassociated with morbidity and mortality from cardiovascular disease later in life (Paffenbarger et al., 1994). In addition, prospective epidemiological data from the Coopers Institute for Aerobic Research show sports participation during youth to be unrelated to coronary risk factor status during middle age (Brill et al., 1989).

With respect to the indirect effects of childhood physical activity on adult health status (Paths A and E), there is a growing body of evidence linking childhood physical activity with a number of important childhood health outcomes, which in turn, are known to influence health status during adulthood. To date, the most frequently studied childhood health outcomes include blood pressure, blood lipid and lipoprotein levels, adiposity, skeletal health, and psychological health. The evidence linking physical activity to these outcomes during childhood and adolescence is summarized in Table 2.5.1.

There is consistent evidence that physical activity has beneficial effects on adiposity, skeletal health, and psychological health in young people. Evidence related to physical activity and blood lipids and lipoproteins is mixed, with physical activity having a modest beneficial effect on blood triglyceride and HDL cholesterol levels, but little consistent effect on total, LDL, and VLDL cholesterol levels. Among healthy children, physical activity does not appear to

be related to resting blood pressure (Boreham and Riddoch, 2001; Trost, 2004).

Although promising, the data presented in Table 2.5.1 prompts the question: Why is the evidence so weak? Perhaps the first reason is that most children and adolescents are inherently healthy and that biological risk factors for chronic disease are generally observed to be at favorable levels in young people. Hence, the weak associations may be, in part, attributable to lack of variation with respect to physical activity and the health endpoint under examination. A second important reason is that the endpoints examined are influenced not only by physical activity, but also growth and maturation. Thus, without appropriate study designs, it is difficult to know if changes in biological risk factors are related to physical activity participation or are the result of normal growth and maturation. A third reason is that physical activity in children and adolescents is difficult to measure. Because all measures, to varying degrees, contain random measurement error, any association between physical activity and health will be biased towards the null. Hence, the associations summarized in Table 2.5.1 are likely to be an underestimation of its true relationship with physical activity.

Given the relatively weak evidence linking childhood physical activity with long-term health outcomes, on what scientific basis should we recommend that children and adolescents be physically active on a regular basis? First and foremost, it is intuitively sensible and biologically plausible that preventive health measures such as fostering a physically active lifestyle should begin early rather than later in life. It should never be forgotten that atherosclerosis is a process that begins early in life (Stary, 1989). Secondly, it is clear that participation in physical activity *is* associated with some important health benefits in young people. There is currently sufficient evidence to conclude that physical activity is positively associated with bone mass and inversely associated with adiposity and overweight/obesity. Notably, both of these health outcomes track rather

Table 2.5.1 Summary of the associations between physical activity and health outcomes in children and youth

Outcome	Strength of association	Dose of physical activity required
Blood pressure	↔/–	No indication
Blood lipids	+/–	No indication
Adiposity	– –	Long duration, moderate intensity
Skeletal health	++	Weight bearing exercise important
Psychological health	+	No indication
Cardiorespiratory fitness	+	Vigorous sustained activity

(– –) repeatedly documented inverse association; (–) weak or mixed evidence of an inverse association; (↔) evidence of no association; (+) wesak or mixed evidence of a positive association; (++) repeatedly documented evidence of a positive association

strongly from childhood into adulthood. Considering the dramatic rise in the prevalence of overweight and obesity in children and adolescents worldwide (Ebbeling et al., 2002), one could easily argue that the promotion of regular physical activity in young people has never been more important.

Tracking of physical activity

Path C of Blair's conceptual framework addresses the concept of tracking. Tracking, or stability of a characteristic, refers to the maintenance of relative rank or position within a group over time. From a public health perspective, the concept of tracking is of considerable utility as it implies that health behaviors established early in life are carried through into adulthood. The notion that physical activity behavior tracks from childhood into adolescence provides a strong rationale for school-based physical education programs and the promotion of physical activity in children and adolescents. To date, a relatively small number of studies have examined the tracking of physical activity. Most studies have examined the tracking of physical activity *during* childhood and adolescence, and information about the tracking of physical activity from childhood into adulthood is lacking.

As part of the Cardiovascular Risk in Young Finns Study, Raitakari et al. (1994) examined the long-term tracking of physical activity behavior in Finnish youth. Leisure-time physical activity was assessed via self-report questionnaire in randomly selected population-representative samples of youth aged 3 to 19 years. Baseline assessments were performed in 1980, with follow-up assessments performed in 3-year intervals in 1983 and 1986. Rank order correlations between physical activity at baseline and 3-years follow-up were statistically significant and ranged from 0.33 to 0.54. Rank order correlations between physical activity at baseline and 6-years follow-up, while statistically significant, were smaller in magnitude, ranging from 0.17 to 0.43. Tracking coefficients were

generally stronger among males and older age groups. To examine the stability of active and sedentary behavior, participants were classified as active or sedentary. Forty-one percent of males and 29% of females classified as active at age 12 remained active at age 18. Conversely, 56% of males and 63% of females classified as sedentary at age 12 remained inactive at age 18.

In a follow-up study of the Young Finns cohort, Telama and colleagues (1997) assessed the stability of physical activity behavior after 9 and 12 years of follow-up. This is an important study because it provides an assessment of the tracking of physical activity from childhood into adulthood. Rank order correlations for baseline physical activity (1980) and physical activity assessed 9 and 12 years later ranged from 0.18 to 0.47 and 0.00 to 0.27, respectively, indicating a low to moderate degree of tracking.

Another study that provides information about the long-term tracking of physical activity from childhood and adolescence into early adulthood is the Amsterdam Growth Study (van Mechelen and Kemper, 1995). The study examined both the short- and long-term tracking of total weekly energy expenditure and energy expenditure in organized sports. For time periods of approximately 5 years, there was suggestive evidence of tracking for total energy expenditure in both males ($r = 0.32$–0.44) and females ($r = 0.25$–0.58). For weekly energy expenditure in organized sports, short-term interperiod correlations (~ 5 years) were higher at 0.53 and 0.59 for males and females, respectively. For longer periods of follow-up (10–15 years), there was little evidence of tracking for any of the physical activity variables ($r < 0.20$). The investigators also examined the stability of membership in the highest and lowest quintile for total weekly energy expenditure. Among males, nine out of the 21 participants (42.8%) in the highest quintile for weekly energy expenditure at baseline (age 13) remained in the highest quintile at 4-years follow-up (age 16). Similarly, 12 of the 21 males (57.1%) in the lowest quintile for weekly energy expenditure at baseline remained in the lowest quintile at 4-years follow-up. Among females, seven out of the 24 participants (29.2%) in the highest quintile for weekly energy expenditure at baseline (age 13) remained in the highest quintile at 4-years follow-up (age 16). Seven of the 24 females (29.2%) in the lowest quintile for weekly energy expenditure at baseline remained in the lowest quintile at 4-years follow-up.

Saris et al. (1980) examined the stability of physical activity behavior in a cohort of 217 boys and 189 girls. Data were collected every 2 years beginning at age 6 and ending at age 12. Total energy expenditure and energy expenditure in activities above 50% of aerobic capacity were estimated from 24-hour heart rate monitoring using the individual regression equation between heart rate and oxygen consumption. Tracking coefficients for total energy expenditure ranged from 0.30 to 0.42. Tracking coefficients for energy expenditure in activities above 50% of aerobic capacity were less than 0.20, indicating a low degree of tracking.

Pate et al. (1996) investigated the tracking of physical activity in 47 3- to 4-year-old children over a 3-year period. Physical activity was assessed via continuous heart rate monitoring on at least 2 and up to 4 days per year. Participation in physical activity was quantified as the percentage of observed minutes between 3:00 p.m. and 6:00 p.m. during which heart rate was 50% or more above individual resting level (PAHR-50 Index). The spearman rank order correlation between the PAHR-50 index in year one and year three was 0.57 (P < .0001). In an additional tracking study involving middle-school aged children, Pate et al. (1999) examined the tracking characteristics of physical activity across the 5th, 6th and 7th grades in a cohort of rural, predominantly African-American children. Tracking coefficients for vigorous physical activity, moderate to vigorous physical activity, and after school energy expenditure ranged from 0.63 to 0.78, indicating a moderate to strong degree of tracking over the 3-year study period.

Sallis et al. (1995) examined the tracking of physical activity at home and recess in 351 Mexican-American and Anglo-American children (mean age 4.4 years). Physical activity was directly observed over a 2-year period. Measurement waves occurred every 6 months, with each wave consisting of 2 days of observation within 1 week. Children were observed for up to 60 minutes at home on a weekday evening and up to 30 minutes during recess at preschool or school. Tracking coefficients (Pearson r's) for physical activity performed at home were 0.16 (based on 1 day of observation) and 0.27 (mean of 2 days observation). Tracking coefficients for activity at recess were 0.04 (1 day of observation) and 0.12 (mean of 2 days observation), indicating a low degree of tracking.

Kelder et al. (1994) studied the tracking of physical activity in adolescents residing in two communities participating in the Minnesota Heart Health Program study. Physical activity was assessed via self-report questionnaire on an annual basis, beginning in 7th grade and ending in 12th grade. Tracking was analyzed by (a) dividing baseline physical activity values into quintiles; (b) computing the mean in each quintile; and (c) ascertaining whether the mean for each activity quintile maintained its relative position over time. Tracking was most apparent in the extremes of the physical activity distribution – those with the highest (> 6 h) and the lowest (< 1 h) weekly exercise time.

Janz et al. (2000) assessed the tracking of physical activity and sedentary behavior from childhood to adolescence in a cohort of 53 boys (mean age at baseline = 10.8 years) and 57 girls (mean age at baseline = 10.3 years). Vigorous physical activity, television watching and video game playing were assessed via self-report every 3 months over a 5-year follow-up period. Among boys, tracking coefficients (Spearman rho's) for vigorous physical activity ranged from 0.32 (Yr 1–Yr 5) to 0.52 (Yr 3–Yr 5 and Yr 4–Yr 5). Among girls, tracking coefficients for vigorous physical activity ranged from 0.43 (Yr 1–Yr 5) to 0.65 (Yr 4–Yr 5). Tracking coefficients for television watching and video game playing among boys ranged from 0.40 (Yr 2–Yr 5) to 0.65 (Yr 3–Yr 5). Among girls, tracking coefficients for television watching and video game playing ranged from 0.16 (Yr 1–Yr 5 and Yr 3–Yr 5) to 0.59 (Yr 4–Yr 5). Forty-seven percent of boys and 38% of girls in the lowest tertile for vigorous physical activity baseline remained in the lowest tertile at 5-years follow-up, while 36% of boys and 42% of girls in the highest tertile for vigorous physical activity remained in the highest activity tertile at 5-years follow-up. Forty-one percent of boys and 44% of girls in the lowest tertile for television watching and video game playing at baseline remained in the lowest tertile at 5-years follow-up, while 73% of boys and 21% of girls in the highest tertile for television watching and video game playing remained in the highest activity tertile at 5-years follow-up.

Although studies vary considerably with respect to length, age group studied, measurement of physical activity, and method used to assess tracking, there is consistent evidence that, over short time periods (3–5 years), physical activity behavior tracks well. However, over longer periods of follow-up (6–12 years) there is little evidence that physical activity behavior tracks during childhood and adolescence. Presently, there is no strong evidence to support the notion that physical activity tracks from childhood to adulthood. However, future longitudinal studies using more sophisticated measures of physical activity may provide a more definitive answer to this important question.

PA guidelines and recommendations for young people

While direct evidence linking childhood physical activity behavior to health outcomes during adulthood is currently lacking, numerous scientific and professional organizations have issued recommendations and/or guidelines regarding the amount of physical activity needed for good health in children and adolescents.

The 1994 International Consensus Conference on Physical Activity Guidelines for Adolescents (Sallis and Patrick, 1994) represents one of the most extensive efforts to develop guidelines on the types and amounts of physical activity needed by young people. Based on an extensive review of the pertinent scientific literature, a panel of leading scientists, healthcare providers, and public health officials issued the following recommendations for physical activity participation during adolescence.

- All adolescents should be physically active daily, or nearly every day, as part of play games, sports, work, transportation, recreation, physical education, or planned exercise, in the context of family, school, and community activities.
- Adolescents should engage in three or more sessions per week of activities that last 20 minutes or more at a time and that require moderate to vigorous levels of exertion.

Healthy People 2010 (USDHHS, 2000) which outlines the health promotion and disease prevention goals for United States of America in the year 2010, includes a number of physical activity objectives pertinent to young people. Of the five objectives related to physical activity and young people, objectives 22-6 and 22-7 serve as "guidelines" as to the amount and type of physical activity in which young people should participate. Notably, they differ little from adult physical activity guidelines.

22–6   Increase to at least 30% the proportion of adolescents who engage in moderate physical activity for at least 30 minutes on 5 or more of the previous 7 days.

22–7   Increase to at least 85% the proportion of adolescents who engage in vigorous physical activity that promotes cardiorespiratory fitness 3 or more days per week for 20 or more minutes per occasion.

Another approach to forming quantitative physical activity guidelines for young people has been to examine the type and amount of physical activity recommended for the adult population and extrapolate this amount back to children and adolescents, taking into account the decline in physical activity that occurs from childhood to adulthood.

Blair and coworkers (1989b), working from the epidemiological literature linking physical activity to health benefits in adults, estimated that a daily energy expenditure in physical activity of 12.6 kilojoules per kilogram of body weight (3 kcal/kg/day) was an appropriate target. This level of activity, when extrapolated to children, corresponds to 20–30 minutes of moderate to vigorous physical activity per day. To account for the hypothesized decline in physical activity between childhood and adulthood, the authors suggested applying a 33% adjustment, yielding an activity recommendation of 16.8 kilojoules per kilogram of body weight (4 kcal/kg/day) (approximately 30–40 minutes of moderate-to-vigorous physical activity per day).

In similar fashion, Corbin et al. (1994), proposed a "lifetime physical activity" guideline based on daily energy expenditure. It recommended that, at a minimum, children and adolescents accumulate 30 minutes of moderate physical activity daily (3–4 kcal/kg/day). For optimal benefit, however, the authors recommended an accumulation of 60 minutes of moderate to vigorous physical activity daily (6–8 kcal/kg/day). The emphasis on the accumulation of moderate to vigorous physical activity throughout the day differed from traditional prescription-based activity guidelines which stressed the importance of sustained bouts of physical activity.

In 1997, the Health Education Authority (HEA) in England initiated a process of expert consultation and review of evidence surrounding the promotion of health-enhancing physical activity for young people (Cavill et al., 2001). A primary objective of the project was to establish expert consensus on the recommended level and type of physical activity for young people. After taking into consideration the current physical activity patterns of young people and the scientific evidence linking physical activity to health outcomes in young people, the following recommendations were made:

- All young people should participate in physical activity of at least moderate intensity *for 1 hour per day.*
- Young people who currently do little activity should participate in physical activity of at least moderate intensity for *at least half an hour a day.*
- *At least twice a week,* some of these activities should help enhance and maintain muscular strength and flexibility, and bone health.

The National Association for Sport and Physical Education (NASPE) in the United States has issued two sets of physical activity guidelines for young people: one for children birth to 5-years of age and another for elementary school children aged 5–12 years (1998, 2002). The following recommendations were made for children aged 5–12 years.

- Elementary school aged children should be active at least 30 to 60 minutes on all, or most days of the week.
- An accumulation of more than 60 minutes, and up to several hours per day is encouraged.
- Some of the child's activity each day should be in periods lasting 10 to 15 minutes or more and include moderate to vigorous physical activity.
- Extended periods of inactivity are inappropriate for children.
- A variety of physical activities selected from the Physical Activity Pyramid is recommended for elementary school children.

In 2002 NASPE released *Active Start: A Statement of Physical Activity Guidelines for Children Birth to Five Years* (NASPE, 2002) recommends that all children birth to age 5 should engage in daily physical activity that promotes health-related fitness and movement skills. Guidelines are issue for infants, toddlers, and preschoolers, respectively. For preschoolers, NASPE recommended the following:

1. Preschoolers should accumulate at least 60 minutes daily of structured physical activity.
2. Preschoolers should engage in at least 60 minutes and up to several hours of daily, unstructured physical activity and should not be sedentary for more than 60 minutes at a time except when sleeping.
3. Preschoolers should develop competence in movement skills that are building blocks for more complex movement tasks.
4. Preschoolers should have indoor and outdoor areas that meet or exceed recommended safety standards for performing large muscle activities.
5. Individuals responsible for the well-being of preschoolers should be aware of the importance of physical activity and facilitate the child's movement skills.

Canada's Physical Activity for Children (2002) represents one of the most recent, and perhaps the most innovative approach to providing guidelines for children's participation in physical activity. Accompanied by a state-of-the-art social marketing campaign, the guidelines take an "individualized" approach to recommending a dose of physical activity for children and youth. It states that children should *increase* time currently spent on physical activity, starting with 30 minutes *more* per day (20 minutes of moderate activity and 10 minutes of vigorous activity). Consistent with the behavioral attributes of children's physical activity, the guide recommends building up physical activity throughout the day in periods of at least 5–10 minutes. In addition, the guide calls for children to reduce "non-active" time spent on TV, video, computer games, and surfing the internet, starting with 30 minutes

less per day. Importantly, the guide provides a progressive stepwise 5-month program to increase daily physical activity and decrease "non-active" pursuits. At the end of the 5 months, it is recommended that children accumulate at least 60 minutes of moderate physical activity daily (e.g. brisk walking, skating, bike riding, swimming, playing outdoors), 30 minutes of vigorous activity (e.g. running, soccer), and reduce "non-active" time by 90 minutes.

Descriptive epidemiology of physical activity in young people

Information regarding the percentage of children and adolescents meeting the above recommendations for participation in physical activity is available from two major sources: population-based surveys utilizing self-report measures of physical activity and small group studies employing more burdensome measures of physical activity such as direct observation, accelerometers, and heart rate monitors. The following section summarizes the major findings from population-based studies conducted over the last two decades as well as the growing number of studies using objective measures to investigate the physical activity behavior of children and adolescents.

Population surveys

The National Children and Youth Fitness Study

The National Children and Youth Fitness Study (NCYFS), assessed physical activity in a national probability sample of youths aged 10 to 18 (Ross and Gilbert, 1985). Students provided detailed information about the types, frequency, and duration of physical activity engaged in during the previous 12–month period. On average, students reported being engaged in sports, active games, and exercise for 760 minutes per week (approximately 1.8 hours/day), with boys reporting approximately 10% greater participation in physical activity than girls. Defining appropriate physical activity as exercise involving large muscle groups in dynamic movements for 20 minutes or longer, three or more times weekly, at intensity requiring 60% of maximal aerobic capacity, NCYFS estimated that approximately half of boys and girls in grades 5 through 12 were achieving at least the minimum weekly requirement.

In a secondary analysis of NCYFS-I data, Pate et al. (1994) combined estimated physical activity during physical education with physical activity performed outside the school. Using a conservative estimate of one-third of class time engaged in physical activity, it was estimated that youngsters spent an average of 1.8 hours per day engaged in physical activity. It was noted, however, that the standard deviation was considerable (50–60% of the mean), indicating that there was considerable variability in the physical activity habits of US adolescents.

Phase II of the NCYFS examined the physical activity habits and physical fitness of a representative sample of US children aged 6 to 9. In contrast to NCYFS-I, which utilized self-report data from students, physical activity information for NCYFS II was provided by parents and teachers. Items pertinent to children's participation in physical activity included: (a) the parent's and teacher's rating of the child's physical activity level relative to same-sex peers; (b) involvement in community organizations through which the child engaged in physical activity at least three times a week in the past year; (c) the child's five most frequent physical activities in these community organizations; and (d) the number of days per week that each parent exercised with the child for 20 minutes or more. Unfortunately these items did not allow the investigators to estimate time spent in moderate to vigorous physical activity (Ross and Pate, 1987).

Relative to their same sex peers, parents and guardians rated males above average in physical activity level and females as average. Teachers rated boys as much more active than girls. Among all children aged 6 through 9 years of age, nearly all (84.3%) reported participation in at least one community organization in the previous year. These organizations included public parks and recreation programs (65.3%), community-based sports programs (31.9%), churches and other places or worship (24.2%), private health clubs and spas (18.9%), and scouting groups (14.6%). Activities that were most frequently performed in these community organizations were swimming, running/sprinting, baseball/softball, bicycling and soccer. On average, parents and guardians reported exercising with their children less than 1 day per week (Ross et al., 1987).

Child and Adolescent Trial for Cardiovascular Health (CATCH)

Simons-Morton et al. (1997) performed structured physical activity interviews in 2410 3rd grade students from 96 schools in four distinct regions in the United States. On average, students reported 89.9 minutes of moderate to vigorous physical activity daily and 34.7 minutes of vigorous physical activity daily. Approximately 37% of 3rd graders reported less than 60 minutes of moderate to vigorous physical activity, with 12.8% reporting less than 30 minutes. Boys reported significantly greater participation in physical activity than girls and White children reported more physical activity than African-American or Hispanic children. The prevalence of moderate to vigorous physical activity was highest in California and lowest in Louisiana. The results indicated that, as early as the 3rd grade, many children are low active and in need of intervention programs to increase physical activity.

The Health Survey for England

The Health Survey for England (1999) comprises a series of annual surveys measuring a range of health outcomes in a population-representative sample of children and adults in England. The 1997 Health Survey collected information about the activity of children aged 2–15 in four main categories: walking, sports and exercise activities, housework and gardening, and active play. The reference period was taken as the 7 days before the interview. On average, 78% of boys and 70% of girls participated in some physical activity on 5 or more days in the last week. The most common type of activity was active play (53% of boys, 41% of girls) followed by walking (29% of boys and girls). Boys reported a mean of 10.4 hours per week doing any kind of physical activities. The mean time spent by girls was significantly lower at 7.69 hours. Around three-quarters of boys and girls had spent at least 60 minutes "sitting" on 5 days or more in the last week. This proportion increased steadily with age. Only 55% of boys and 39% of girls met the guideline of 60 minutes or more of at least moderate intensity activity on most days of the week.

Youth Risk Behavior Surveillance System (YRBSS)

In 1990, the US Centers for Disease Control and Prevention (CDC) initiated the Youth Risk Behavior Surveillance System (YRBSS). The goal of the YRBSS is to monitor the health risk behaviors that contribute to the leading causes of mortality and morbidity among youth and adults: tobacco use, alcohol and other drug use, sexual behaviors that contribute to unintentional pregnancy and sexually transmitted diseases including HIV infection, behaviors that contribute to unintentional and intentional injuries, unhealthy dietary behaviors, and physical inactivity. The YRBSS has three complementary components: national school-based surveys, state and local school-based surveys, and a national household-based survey. Each of these components is hypothesized to provide unique information about different populations of adolescent youth in the United States (Kolbe et al., 1993).

The national school-based survey includes several items to measure physical activity behaviors relevant to national health objectives. These include: participation in structured vigorous physical activity, participation in light to moderate physical activity, participation in physical activity to promote strength and flexibility, participation in school and community-based sports teams, and participation in school physical education. Data from the most recent school-based survey conducted in 2001 will be discussed in this section.

In the 2001 school-based survey (Grunbaum et al., 2000), nearly two-thirds (64.6%) of students in grades 9 through 12 reported participation in vigorous physical activity for at least 20 minutes on three or more of the 7 days preceding the survey. Across all racial/ethnic and grade level groups, male students (72.6%) were significantly more likely than female students (57.0%) to report sustained participation in vigorous physical activity. Among female students, participation in vigorous physical activity was significantly more likely among White students (59.8%) than African-American (47.8%) and Hispanic (52.4%) students, and more likely among 9th grade students (67.3%) than 12th grade students (45.4%). Approximately one-quarter (25.5%) of students in grades 9 through 12 reported participation in moderate physical activity on 5 of the 7 days preceding the survey. Overall, 55.2% of students reported playing on at least one sports team during the 12 months preceding the survey. The percentage of students reporting sports participation declined with grade level and was higher among White students than African-American and Hispanic students. Across all racial/ethnic and grade level groups, male students (60.9%) were significantly more likely than female students (49.9%) to report participation in organized sport.

WHO Health Behavior in School-aged Children Survey

The World Health Organization's cross-national survey on health and health behaviors assessed youth physical activity behavior in 26 nations from Europe and North America (World Health Organization, 2000). Students were asked how often and how many hours a week they participated in vigorous physical activity outside of school hours. Vigorous physical activity was defined as equivalent to slow jogging which might be expected to leave students feeling out of breath and sweaty. Across all nations and age groups, boys were more likely than girls to report exercising vigorously two or more times a week and vigorously exercising for 2 or more hours per week. Based on the weekly duration of vigorous physical activity, the most physically active countries were Austria, Germany, Norway, Denmark, and Switzerland. In these countries, the prevalence of vigorously exercising 2 or more hours

per week ranged from 60% to 80%. Latvia, Portugal, Russia, and Israel exhibited the lowest participation in vigorous physical activity, with prevalence estimates well under 40%.

Studies employing objective measures of physical activity

Given the limitations associated with self-reported measures of physical activity in children and adolescents (Trost, 2001), a preferable approach is to assess physical activity using objective monitoring techniques. Direct observation techniques or monitoring devices such as heart rate monitors and accelerometers can be used, with minimal subject reactivity, to quantify accumulated participation in physical activity at selected intensity levels. A general limitation of these studies is that they involve relatively small, non-representative samples of youth. Yet, despite this limitation, they provide a valuable opportunity for researchers to assess, in an indirect manner, the validity of self-report data obtained in population surveys. Moreover, they provide valuable physical activity data in populations of youth for whom self-report methods are not feasible, i.e., young children.

Trost and Pate (1999) reviewed the results of ten objective monitoring studies. Estimates of daily participation in moderate to vigorous physical activity ranged from 8 to 122 minutes, with an average approximating 40 minutes per day. In contrast to the findings of population-based surveys, objective monitoring studies consistently reported that only a small percentage (< 20%) of children and adolescents engaged in sustained 20-minute bouts of moderate to vigorous physical activity. However, there was consistent evidence that relatively large percentages of children and adolescents engaged in moderate to vigorous physical activity for 5- and 10-minute periods.

Two recently conducted objective monitoring studies have demonstrated that accelerometer-based assessments of physical activity are feasible alternatives to self-report methods in small- to medium-sized population-based samples of children and adolescents. Trost et al. (2002) evaluated age and gender differences in objectively measured physical activity in a population-based sample of public school students in grades 1 through 12. Daily participation in MVPA exhibited a significant inverse relationship with grade level, declining from just under 200 minutes per day in grades 1–3 to approximately 50 minutes daily in grades 10–12. On average, boys and girls from all grade levels exhibited few vigorous 20-minute bouts of physical activity over the 7-day monitoring period. In contrast, boys and girls exhibited frequent 5- and 10-minute bouts of MVPA.

Riddoch et al. (2004) objectively assessed physical activity in 2185 children aged 9 and 15 years from Denmark, Portugal, Estonia, and Norway. Among 9-year-olds, the average daily participation in MVPA for boys and girls was 192 and 160 minutes, respectively. Among 15-year-olds, the average daily participation in MVPA for boys and girls was 99 and 73 minutes, respectively. Nearly all (97.4–97.6%) of 9-year-olds met the United Kingdom Expert Consensus Group (HEA) guideline of 60 minutes of at least moderate physical activity per day. The percentage of male and female 15-year-olds meeting the guideline was significantly lower at 81.9% and 62.0%, respectively. The authors did not examine sustained bouts of MVPA. Although statistically significant differences were detected between countries, the level of physical activity across the four countries was considered similiar.

Physical activity levels during physical education class

Studies examining the amount of physical activity performed during physical education class have consistently shown that students spend a limited amount of time engaged in moderate to vigorous physical activity (MVPA) (Lee et al., 1987). Simons-Morton et al. (1993) systematically observed physical activity levels during 5th grade physical education in 20 elementary schools. On average, the students spent 8.5% of class time in MVPA, 23.3% in minimal activity, and 68.1% in sedentary activity. This proportion of class time amounted to just 10.4 minutes of MVPA per week. McKenzie et al. (1995) systematically observed student's physical activity during 293 3rd-grade physical education lessons from 95 geographically dispersed elementary schools in the United States. Across all schools, the average physical education lesson provided just 10.6 minutes of MVPA. The proportion of class time devoted to MVPA was, on average, 36.2%, a figure well-short of the recommended 50% of class time. In a similar study, McKenzie et al. (2000) directly observed student physical activity levels in 430 middle school physical education lessons conducted in 25 different schools. On average, daily physical education contributed 25 minutes of vigorous physical activity and 83 minutes of MVPA weekly – much less than the recommended 150 and 50 minutes of vigorous physical activity and MVPA, respectively. More recently, Scruggs and colleagues (2003) observed MVPA levels during 1st and 2nd grade physical education classes. On average, students were engaged in MVPA for 35% of lesson time. Based on a reported mean lesson duration of 29.5 minutes, this translated to just over 10 minutes of MVPA per lesson.

Summary of the descriptive epidemiology of physical activity in youth

Evidence from large population-based surveys using self-report methods and smaller group studies using objective measures of physical activity suggests that a large percentage of children and adolescents meet accepted guidelines for daily participation in moderate intensity physical activity. However, the sizeable standard deviations reported for daily physical activity suggests that a substantial number of children and adolescents are low active. There is also consistent evidence that boys are more active than girls and that participation in physical activity declines with age, more so in girls than boys. However, there is considerable disagreement between study types regarding the percentage of youth meeting guidelines for moderate to vigorous physical activity. Results from population-based studies conducted in the United States indicate that approximately two-thirds of adolescent youth engage in three or more 20-minute sessions of vigorous physical activity per week. In contrast, evidence from studies using objective measures of physical activity suggests that a small percentage of children and adolescents (< 20%) engage in sustained 20-minute bouts of moderate to vigorous physical activity. This suggests that the self-report methods employed in population-based surveillance studies may be providing overestimates of the percentage of youth meeting guidelines for moderate to vigorous physical activity. Observational studies on the amount of physical activity performed in an average school physical education lesson have consistently shown that students receive little health-enhancing physical activity in this setting.

Physical education and public health

Over the years the public health role of school physical education has been scrutinized by numerous authors and scientific/professional organizations (American Academy of Pediatrics Committees on Sports Medicine and School Health, 1987; American College of Sports Medicine, 1988; Centers for Disease Control and Prevention, 1997; Pate and Hohn, 1994; Sallis and McKenzie, 1991; Shilton and Naughton, 2001; Simons-Morton et al., 1987). In general, these reports come to the same conclusion – that school physical education program can best contribute to public health by: (1) providing frequent exposure to enjoyable and developmentally appropriate physical activity; and (2) preparing students for a lifetime of regular physical activity.

In the United States, the importance of school physical education in promoting lifelong physical activity in young people is underscored by the existence of national public health objectives related to the quality and quantity of physical activity during physical education (USDHHS, 2000).

22–8.   Increase the proportion of the nation's public and private school that require daily physical education for all students.

22–9.   Increase to at least 50% the proportion of adolescents who participate in daily school physical education.

22–10. Increase to at least 50% the proportion of adolescents who spend 50% of school physical education class time being physically active.

The CDC's *Guidelines for School and Community Programs to Promote Lifelong Physical Activity among Young People* (1997) lists ten recommendations for school and community programs to promote physical activity. Summarized in Table 2.5.2, the recommendations address policy, environment, school physical education, health education curricula, extracurricular activities, parental involvement, and community programs. Recommendations directly related to school physical education programs include:

• Require comprehensive, daily physical education for students in kindergarten through grade 12.
• Require the hiring of physical education specialists to teach physical education in kindergarten through grade 12.
• Require that physical activity instruction and programs meet the needs and interests of all students.
• Provide planned and sequential physical education curricula from kindergarten through grade 12 that promote enjoyable, lifelong physical activity.
• Use physical education curricula consistent with the national standards for physical education.
• Use active learning strategies and emphasize enjoyable participation in physical education class.
• Develop students' mastery of and confidence in motor and behavioral skills for participating in physical activity.
• Provide a substantial percentage of each student's recommended weekly amount of physical activity in physical education classes.
• Promote participation in enjoyable physical activity in the school, community, and home.

While the promotion of physical activity through school physical education programs has been widely endorsed, the quality of existing programs continues to be questioned by many organizations and individual experts. Organizations such as the American Academy of Pediatrics (1987) and the American College of Sports Medicine (1988) have called for substantial modifications of school physical education programs. In addition, over the past decade, many experts have recommended that physical education de-emphasize exposure of youngsters to competitive team sports and place much greater emphasis on promotion of life-long physical activity (Corbin, 2002; Sallis and McKenzie, 1991; Simons-Morton, 1994). While these recommendations seemingly have been well accepted within the public health and medical communities, they have not yet been widely implemented in the schools (Pate et al., 1995).

School-based physical activity interventions

School-based intervention studies have demonstrated that behaviorally oriented health and physical education curricula can be successfully implemented and that teacher behavior in physical education can be modified so as to increase student physical activity during physical education classes. A description of these studies is provided in Table 2.5.3.

Stone, et al. (1998) reviewed the results of 22 physical activity intervention studies conducted in school and/or community settings. Intervention studies targeting upper elementary schoolchildren were generally successful in increasing the amount of physical activity performed during physical education; however, very few studies reported positive changes in out-of-school physical activity. The majority of studies were successful in increasing knowledge and positive attitudes towards physical activity. The most effective studies employed randomized study designs, valid and reliable measures of physical activity, and more extensive interventions.

The US Task Force on Community Preventive Services (Kahn et al., 2002) conducted a systematic review of 14 published studies evaluating the effectiveness of strategies to increase the amount of class time engaged in MVPA. In the five studies measuring physical activity during physical education, all reported increases in the number of minutes spent in MVPA, the percent of class time spent in MVPA, and the intensity level of physical activity during class. All 14 studies reported an increase in physical fitness. Across all studies, the median increase in physical fitness was 8%. Based on strong evidence of effectiveness, the Task Force issued a recommendation to implement programs that increase the length of, or activity levels in, school-based physical education classes.

Table 2.5.2   CDC Guidelines for School and Community Programs to Promote Lifelong Physical Activity among Young People

---

Recommendation 1. Policy: Establish policies that promote enjoyable, lifelong physical activity among young people.

- Require comprehensive, daily physical education for students in kindergarten through grade 12.
- Require comprehensive health education for students in kindergarten through grade 12.
- Require that adequate resources, including budget and facilities, be committed for physical activity instruction and programs.
- Require the hiring of physical education specialists to teach physical education in kindergarten through grade 12, elementary school teachers trained to teach health education, health education specialists to teach health education in middle and senior high schools, and qualified people to direct school and community physical activity programs and to coach young people in sports and recreation programs.
- Require that physical activity instruction and programs meet the needs and interests of all students.

Recommendation 2. Environment: Provide physical and social environments that encourage and enable safe and enjoyable physical activity.

- Provide access to safe spaces and facilities for physical activity in the school and community.
- Establish and enforce measures to prevent physical activity-related injuries.
- Provide time within the school day for unstructured physical activity.
- Discourage the use or withholding of physical activity as punishment.
- Provide health promotion programs for school faculty and staff.

Recommendation 3. Physical education: Implement physical education curricula and instruction that emphasize enjoyable participation in physical activity and that help students develop the knowledge, attitudes, motor skills, behavioral skills, and confidence needed to adopt and maintain physically activity lifestyles.

- Provide planned and sequential physical education curricula from kindergarten through grade 12 that promote enjoyable, lifelong physical activity.
- Use physical education curricula consistent with the national standards for physical education.
- Use active learning strategies and emphasize enjoyable participation in physical education class.
- Develop students' mastery of and confidence in motor and behavioral skills for participating in physical activity.
- Provide a substantial percentage of each student's recommended weekly amount of physical activity in physical education classes.
- Promote participation in enjoyable physical activity in the school, community, and home.

Recommendation 4. Health Education: Implement health education curricula and instruction that help students develop the knowledge, attitudes, behavioral skills, and confidence needed to adopt and maintain physically active lifestyles.

- Provide planned and sequential health education curricula from kindergarten through grade 12 that promote lifelong participation in physical activity.
- Use health education curricula consistent with the national standards for health education.
- Promote collaboration among physical education, health education, and classroom teachers as well as teachers in related disciplines who plan and implement physical activity instruction.
- Use active learning strategies to emphasize enjoyable participation in physical activity in the school, community and home.
- Develop students' knowledge of and positive attitudes towards healthy behaviors, particularly physical activity.
- Develop students' mastery of and confidence in the behavioral skills needed to adopt and maintain a healthy lifestyle that includes regular physical activity.

Recommendation 5. Extracurricular activities: Provide extracurricular physical activity programs that meet the needs and interests of all students.

- Provide a diversity of developmentally appropriate competitive and noncompetitive physical activity programs for all students.
- Link students to community physical activity programs, and use community resources to support extracurricular physical activity programs.

Table 2.5.2 (Continued)

Recommendation 6. Parental involvement: Include parents and guardians in physical activity instruction and in extracurricular and community physical activity programs, and encourage them to support their children's participation in enjoyable physical activities.

- Encourage parents to advocate for quality physical activity instruction and programs for their children.
- Encourage parents to support their children's participation in appropriate, enjoyable physical activities.
- Encourage parents to be physically active role models and to plan and participate in family activities that include physical activity.

Recommendation 7. Personal training: Provide training for education, coaching, recreation, health care and other school and community personnel that imparts knowledge and skills needed to effectively promote enjoyable, lifelong physical activity among young people

- Train teachers to deliver physical education that provides a substantial percentage of each student's recommended weekly amount of physical activity.
- Train school and community personnel how to create psychosocial environments that enable young people to enjoy physical activity instruction and programs.
- Train school and community personnel how to involve parents and the community in physical activity instruction and programs.
- Train volunteers who coach sports and recreation programs for young people.

Recommendation 8. Health Services: Assess physical activity patterns among young people, reinforce physical activity among young people, counsel inactive young people about physical activity, and refer young people to appropriate physical activity programs.

- Regularly assess the physical activity patterns of young people, reinforce physical activity among active young people, counsel inactive young people about physical activity, and refer young people to appropriate physical activity programs.
- Advocate for school and community physical activity instruction and programs that meet the needs of young people.

Recommendation 9. Community programs: Provide a range of developmentally appropriate community sports and recreation programs that are attractive to all young people.

- Provide a diversity of developmentally appropriate community sports and recreation programs for all young people.
- Provide access to community sports and recreation programs for young people.

Recommendation 10. Evaluation: Regularly evaluate school and community physical activity instruction, programs and facilities.

- Evaluate the implementation and quality of physical activity policies curricula, instruction, programs, and personnel training.
- Measure students' attainment of physical activity knowledge, achievement of motor skills and behavioral skills, and adoption of healthy behaviors.

Ringuet and Trost (2003) reviewed the peer-reviewed literature pertinent to school-based physical activity interventions for children and adolescents. In order to provide a quantitative conclusion regarding the effectiveness of these interventions, a meta-analytic approach was utilized in which effect sizes from each study were pooled to provide a global estimate of effectiveness. Studies were included if: (1) the target population was children or adolescents; (2) physical activity was the primary outcome variable; and (3) an experimental or quasi-experimental study design was used. The authors did not include studies that used a single group, pre–post study design. In addition, studies examining changes in cardiovascular risk factors or changes in cardiorespiratory fitness in the absence of an appropriate physical activity outcome measure were not included. The efficacy of each intervention or magnitude of the intervention effect was expressed as a standardized effect size. Across all studies, the mean effect size was 0.47 (95% C.I. 0.28–0.66), indicating that school-based interventions have produced statistically significant but moderate changes in physical activity (Table 10.4). Consistent with the conclusions of previous reviews, the pooled effect size for interventions

Table 2.5.3 Description of school- and community-based physical activity intervention studies

Authors	Purpose	Results
Donnelly et al. (1996)	A nutrition and physical activity program was designed to attenuate obesity and improve physical and metabolic fitness in elementary schoolchildren	The intervention group showed a small but significantly greater 2-year average in physical activity in physical education class. However, this was offset by lower levels of physical activity outside of the classroom
Sallis et al. (1997) McKenzie et al. (1993)	This study evaluated a physical education program designed to increase physical activity during physical education classes and out of school. Health related physical education was taught by physical education specialists or trained teachers, and students in these classes were compared with those in control schools	Students in the specialist-led and teacher trained classes spent more time (40 minutes and 33 minutes per week respectively) being physically active than students in control groups. There was also a significant difference in both the frequency and mean length of the specialist-led, teacher trained, and control classes (PES 26.7 min; TT 23.4 min, CO 18.9 min)
Kelder et al. (1993)	This study was designed to test the efficacy of a school-based health promotion program embedded in a whole community program to reduce cardiovascular disease. Self-reported physical activity data were collected, including hours of exercise engaged in per week and duration and intensity of regular physical activity	Physical activity levels were significantly higher in the intervention group for females in grades 8 to 11. Male's average values were higher in the intervention group but not statistically significant. A downward trend in exercise outside of class (hours of exercise per week) was evident for both males and females in 7th grade, accelerating through the high school years
Simons-Morton et al. (1991)	This study tested the effects of a school-based program to improve elementary schoolchildren's diet and physical activity behavior. The intervention included classroom health education, vigorous health education, and lower-fat, lower-sodium school lunches	The percent of time children engaged in moderate to vigorous physical activity (MVPA) during physical education increased from less than 10% of classtime at post-test, and were higher in intervention schools than control schools. At baseline, mean MVPA was less than 3-minutes at each school and at post-test it increased in school 3 to 11.7 (3rd grade) and 15.0 (4th grade) minutes, and in school 4 to 16.2 (3rd grade) and 16.1 (4th grade) minutes per class.
Luepker et al. (1996)	This study was designed to assess the outcomes of health behavior interventions for the primary prevention of cardiovascular disease (CATCH). The intervention focused on the elementary schoolenvironment, and included school food service modifications, enhanced physical education, and classroom health curricula, plus family education	The intensity of physical activity in physical education classes increased significantly in the intervention schools compared with the control schools (P < 0.02). A significant increase in daily vigorous activity was reported by the intervention students compared with students in the control schools (58.6 minutes versus 46.5 minutes, P < 0.003)
Manios et al. (1999)	The school-based health education intervention program was primarily aimed at improving children's diet, fitness, and physical activity	Intervention group students showed a significantly greater increase in time spent in MVPA over the 3-year period, compared to control group (adjusted increases of 2.0 versus 0.4 hours/week, P < 0.0005).

Table 2.5.3 (Continued)

Authors	Purpose	Results
Killen et al. (1988)	This cardiovascular disease risk-reduction trial was designed to assess the effectiveness of a special 20-session risk reduction trial on health behaviors	A higher proportion of subjects in the treatment group who were not exercising regularly at baseline reported regular exercise at follow-up compared with controls (treatment group 30.2%; control group 20%, $P < 0.0003$)
Baranowski et al. (1990)	A center-based program was designed and implemented to promote aerobic physical activity among families with children. The program included one education and two fitness sessions per week for 14 weeks.	The experimental group showed a decrease in activity levels compared with the control group. The control children increased calorie expenditure more than the experimental children. However, the frequency of aerobic activity post-assessment was highest ($P < 0.05$) among children in the experimental group.
Nader et al. (1999)	This study was designed to assess the maintenance of intervention effects targeting diet and physical activity behaviors (CATCH)	Intervention students maintained significantly higher self-reported daily vigorous activity than control students ($P = 0.001$), although the difference declined from 13.6 minutes in grade 5 to 11.2, 10.8, and 8.8 minutes in grade 6, 7, and 8 respectively
Harell et al. (1996)	Examined the effects of an 8-week intervention delivered to all children and selected high-risk children. Twelve elementary schools from three regions in North Carolina. American Heart Association classroom curriculum was taught two times/week with a focus on nutrition, physical activity and smoking. Aerobically oriented PE classes taught by PE specialist three times per week	Children in the intervention group had significantly greater exercise knowledge and self-reported physical activity than children in the control group. Intervention group exhibited a 22.7% increase in physical activity compared to a 15.1% change in controls
Gortmaker et al. (1999a)	Evaluated the impact of a school-based health behavior intervention known as Planet Health on obesity among boys and girls in grades 6 to 8. Intervention was implemented as part of normal school curriculum including school physical education. PE sessions focused on decreasing sedentary behavior and increasing vigorous physical activity	Prevalence of obesity among girls in the intervention schools was reduced compared to controls. The intervention reduced television hours among boys and girls and increased fruit and vegetable consumption. The intervention did not have significant positive effects on daily participation in moderate and vigorous physical activity
Gortmaker et al. (1999b)	Evaluated the impact of a school-based interdisciplinary health behavior intervention on diet and physical activity among children in grades 4 and 5. A portion of the intervention was delivered during physical education and focused on nutrition issues and increasing physical activity through safe and enjoyable movement experiences	The intervention had a significant impact on total energy intake from fat, energy intake from saturated fat, and fruit and vegetable intake. No significant differences were observed with respect to participation in vigorous physical activity. The intervention resulted in reductions in television watching, but the difference was of marginal statistical significance

Table 2.5.4 Summary statistics for effect sizes from school-based physical activity intervention studies, PE only interventions, and interventions targeting overall physical activity (Ringuet and Trost, 2001)

Summary statistics	All studies	PE only	Overall activity
Maximum	2.5	2.5	1.6
Quartile 3 (Q3)	0.83	0.77	0.83
Median (Q2)	0.41	0.58	0.24
Quartile 1 (Q1)	0.07	0.37	0.05
Minimum	−0.61	0.05	−0.61
Q3–Q1	0.76	0.40	0.78
% positive	86.7	100	86.1
Mean	0.47	0.85	0.39
SD	0.62	0.80	0.53
N	44	9	36

targeting activity during physical education class (0.85 ± 0.8) was significantly greater than the effect size observed for interventions targeting overall physical activity 0.39 ± 0.5 (t43 = 2.12, P = .04).

The public health impact of physical education – a case study

Most researchers and practitioners from public health would agree that school-based physical education programs have enormous capacity to promote physical activity and prepare students for a lifetime of regular physical activity. Nevertheless, it could be argued that school physical education programs have not "delivered the goods" when it comes to promoting lifelong physical activity. This contention is based on: (1) physical education's consistent failure to meet public health objectives related to the quality and quantity of physical activity during physical education; and (2) physical education's enduring emphasis on competitive team sports rather than true lifetime activities.

Figure 2.5.2 depicts enrollment rates for high school physical education in the United States between 1991 and 2001. The data clearly show that enrollment in physical education has changed very little since 1991, averaging just over 50%. Taking the "half empty" view, one could conclude that school physical education has consistently failed to reach nearly half of all students attending public and private high schools in the United States. The situation becomes even bleaker when enrollment rates are examined by grade level. Examining grade level data from the school-based surveys conducted between 1993 and 2001, it is clear that enrollment in school physical education drops precipitously between grades 9 and 12 (Figure 2.5.3). Across all sex and racial/ethnic groups, the average grade-related decline in physical education enrollment was, in absolute terms, 39.6% ± 4.0%. This translates to an average relative decrease of approximately 54%. More importantly, within each survey year, the bulk of the decline occurs during grades 9 and 10, accounting for approximately 90% of the total decline in enrollment between grades 9 and 12. Of concern, since 1993, approximately two-thirds of high school seniors in the United States are not involved in school physical education of any kind (Kann et al., 1995, 1996, 1998, 2000; Grunbaum et al., 2000).

While rates of enrollment speak to the important issue of reach, the national health objectives specifically address young people's exposure to daily physical education and the amount of physical activity delivered during a typical physical education lesson. Figure 2.5.4 shows 10-year trend data for participation in daily school physical education among high school students in the United States. Between 1991 and 1995, the percentage of students participating in daily physical education declined from 41.6% to 25.4%. Since 1997, participation in daily physical education has increased modestly from 27.4% to 32.2% (Kann et al., 1995, 1996, 1998, 2000; Grunbaum et al., 2000). Consequently, national surveillance data collected over the decade indicate that a relatively small percentage of students attending public and private high schools in the United States are exposed to physical education on a daily basis. Importantly, the prevalence of daily physical education falls well short of the 50% level identified in *Healthy People 2010* Objective 22–9.

Figure 2.5.5 depicts grade level trend data for participation in daily physical education. Just as enrollment in physical education declines with increasing grade level, so too does the percentage of high school students exposed to daily physical education. Notably, only 9th grade students participating in the

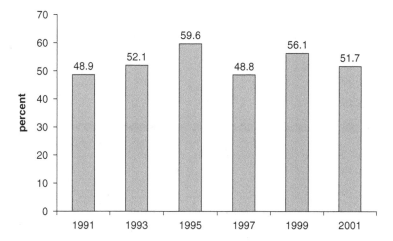

Figure 2.5.2 Percentage of high school students enrolled in physical education

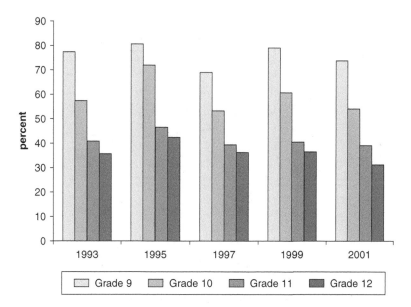

Figure 2.5.3 Percentage of high school students enrolled in physical education by grade level

1993 school-based survey exceeded the national health objective related to daily physical education. Considering that most students elect to fulfill their physical education requirement in the 9th grade, it is of great concern that less than half of these students received physical education on a daily basis. The percentage of students in grades 11 and 12

reporting participation in daily physical education has consistently remained around 20% or less (Kann et al., 1995, 1996, 1998, 2000; Grunbaum et al., 2000).

Healthy People 2010 objective 22–10 pertains to the amount of physical education class time engaged in physical activity. Figure 2.5.6 shows trend data for the percentage of high school students reporting

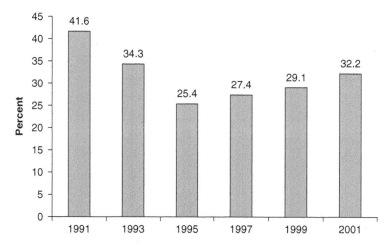

Figure 2.5.4   Percentage of high school students attending physical education class daily

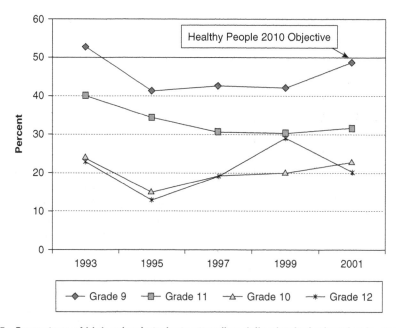

Figure 2.5.5   Percentage of high school students attending daily physical education by grade level

greater than 20 minutes of physical activity during an average physical education lesson. Between 1995 and 2001, the percentage of students meeting the criterion of 20 minutes or greater of physical activity during an average physical education lesson has steadily risen from 69.7% to 83.4% (Kann et al., 1995, 1996, 1998, 2000; Grunbaum et al., 2000). While the trend data suggest that students enrolled in school physical education are receiving substantial amounts of physical activity, it is important to

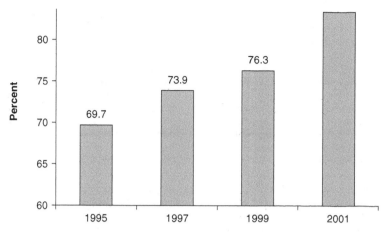

Figure 2.5.6   Percentage of high school students >20 min of physical activity during an average PE class

note that only half of the national student body is actually enrolled in physical education and that even fewer students attend physical education on a daily basis. For example, in the 1995 school-based survey, 69.7% of high school students enrolled in physical education reported being physically active for 20 minutes or longer (about half of a typical class period). Taking into account the relatively small proportion of students enrolled in and exposed to daily physical education, it was estimated that only 18.6% of all high school students were sufficiently active on a daily basis as part of school physical education (USDHHS, 1996).

The School Health Policies and Programs Study (SHPPS) is a national survey conducted by the CDC to assess school health policies and programs at the state, district, school, and classroom levels (Smith et al., 2001). In addition to evaluating other components of the comprehensive school health program (health education, health services, food service, and policies prohibiting tobacco use, alcohol and other drug use, and violence), SHPPS provides comprehensive multilevel information regarding policies and practices in school physical education. SHPPS data are a particularly useful tool for evaluating progress towards *Healthy People 2010* Objective 22–8 which calls for an increase in the proportion of public and private schools requiring daily physical education for all students.

According to SHPPS 2000, virtually all states and school districts in the United States require some form of physical education from kindergarten through grade 12. However, consistent with the grade-level trends observed in the YRBS and NCYFS, the percentage of schools that require physical education declines dramatically with grade level, from just over 50% in grades 1 through 5 to less than 10% in grades 10 through 12. With respect to exposure to daily physical education, SHHPS 2000 indicated that only 8.0% of elementary schools, 6.4% of middle/junior high schools, and 5.8% of senior high schools provide daily physical education or its equivalent for the entire school year for students in all grades in the school (Burgeson et al., 2001).

A second major factor that has limited physical education's contribution to public health is the profession's enduring preoccupation with competitive team sports. Many physical educators would surely disagree with this statement and point to the numerous policy documents and most recent national physical education standards calling for teachers to emphasize lifetime activities over competitive team sports (NAPSE, 1995). However, survey data collected over the last three decades would suggest that the physical education curriculum has primarily consisted of competitive team sports such as basketball, football, and volleyball. As a result, physical education programs have primarily served the needs and interests of athletically gifted children at the expense of less athletic children whose need for regular physical activity and positive movement experiences is much greater.

Ross (1994) analyzed data from the two National Children and Youth Fitness Studies to determine the most prominent activities performed in school physical education during the 1980s. Among students in grades 5 through 12, the largest portion of class time in school physical education was spent in basketball, calisthenics/exercises, volleyball, baseball/softball, and jogging. Among students in grades 1 through 4, the five most prominent activities were movement experiences, soccer, jumping/skipping rope, gymnastics and basketball. It was noted that as early as the 3rd and 4th grades, the focus of school physical education had shifted dramatically from movement education and fitness to competitive team sports such as soccer and basketball.

Pate and colleagues analyzed data from the physical education component of the 1994 CDC SHPPS to determine which activities were most frequently taught in school physical education (Pate et al., 1985). The top five activities performed by middle and high school students were basketball, volleyball, baseball/softball, football, and soccer. The percentage of all physical education courses devoting more than one class period to these activities ranged from 65.2% for soccer to 86.8% for basketball. In contrast, the percentage of courses devoting more than one class to activities such as aerobic dance, walking, swimming, handball, racquetball, hiking, and cycling ranged from 1.3% (cycling) to 29.6% (aerobic dance).

In a secondary analysis of the 1994 SHPPS data, Simons-Morton et al. (1999) classified basketball, baseball/softball, soccer, and volleyball as lifetime activities and concluded that such activities were being taught in more than 80% of middle and senior high schools across the nation. However, it is important to note that, according to the most recent physical activity surveillance data in the United States, less than 6% of the adult population participates in such activities (basketball (5.9%), baseball/softball (2.9%), volleyball (1.7%), football (1.5%) and soccer (1.4%) (USDHHS, 2000)). Moreover, of the six most prevalent physical activities reported by US adults (walking, gardening/yard work, stretching, weightlifting, cycling, jogging/running), only jogging/running made the list of the top 15 activities taught in school physical education (Simons-Morton et al., 1999; USDHHS, 2000). This discrepancy clearly demonstrates that physical educators and public health authorities operationalize the term "lifetime activity" very differently. Physical educators tend to view individual and team sports such as badminton, basketball, and volleyball as lifetime activities, despite the fact that very few adults do such activities. In contrast, the CDC guidelines for promoting lifelong physical activity in young people identifies activities such as dance, strength training, jogging, swimming, cycling, cross-country skiing, walking, and hiking as lifetime activities (Centers for Disease Control and Prevention, 1997). Notably, these activities figure prominently among the top ten leisure time physical activities performed by adults (USDHHS, 2000).

Does the emphasis on competitive sport in school physical education exist in the new millennium? Data from the most recent SHPPS 2000 would suggest that competitive team sports such as baseball/ softball, basketball, volleyball, and soccer continue to dominate the school physical education curriculum. However, on the positive side, nearly all physical education teachers participating in the 2000 SHPPS reported a significant allocation of instructional time to individual or paired activities such as walking/running and jumping rope (Burgeson et al., 2001).

RE-AIM evaluation of school physical education

The results of population-level surveys conducted over the last three decades would suggest that school physical education has failed to meet public health goals related to enrollment in school physical education, the proportion of children and adolescents exposed to daily physical education, and the amount of physical activity provided by an average physical education lesson. In addition, the available evidence indicates that school physical education programs have historically offered students a steady diet of competitive team sports (basketball, baseball/softball, volleyball, and soccer) instead of true lifetime physical activities (e.g. dance, strength training, jogging swimming, cycling, and walking). A tradition that, despite policy changes at the national, state, and school district levels, continues to this day.

From a public health perspective, the implications of these shortcomings can most effectively be illustrated through the application of a true public health evaluation framework. The RE-AIM framework was developed by Glasgow to determine the impact of health promotion programs and policies in real-world settings (Glasgow et al., 1999). The framework utilizes five distinct elements to evaluate public health impact: (1) *Reach*, the proportion of the target population (students) that participated in the intervention; (2) *Efficacy*, the success in promoting behavior change (physical activity) or the percentage of the target population meeting guidelines after completing the intervention; (3) *Adoption*, the proportion of settings (schools) that use the intervention; (4) *Implementation*, practitioners ("teachers") fidelity to the interventions protocol; and (5) *Maintenance*, the extent to which the intervention is sustained over time (grade levels).

An application of the RE-AIM framework in relation to school physical education's impact on physical activity among young people is illustrated Figure 2.5.7. The analysis is modeled after the hypothetical evaluation described by Dzewaltowski

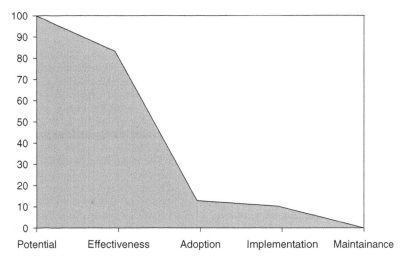

Figure 2.5.7   Public health impact of high schoool physical education

et al. (2004). Because the indicators needed to address all five elements of the RE-AIM framework were available for high school physical education programs, the illustration is delimited to students from this population. However, the framework could readily be applied to physical education policies and practices at the elementary and middle school levels.

The evaluation begins with the assumption that school physical education has the potential to reach the entire student population in grades 9 through 12 (100%). This assumption may seem somewhat unrealistic taking into account current enrollment levels and resources available for school physical education. However, for the purpose of determining potential public health impact, it is a reasonable assumption because nearly all children and adolescents are required to attend public or private school. If we adhere to the national public health objectives and equate efficacy with the proportion of high school students engaged in physical activity for 20 minutes or longer during a typical physical education lesson (~50% of lesson time), we can optimistically estimate (from the most recent YRBS data) that physical education has an 83% rate of effectiveness. Therefore, if all public and private schools offered physical education on a daily basis to all students in all grades, approximately 83% of students would be sufficiently active. Equating adoption with the most recent SHPPS data regarding the percentage of high schools requiring students to take a single course in physical education (16.4%), the percentage of the target population impacted by the intervention drops dramatically to

13%. Implementation addresses the issue of fidelity to the intervention protocol. If we generously assume that 75% of physical educators are providing sufficient physical activity time and teaching true lifetime activities instead of competitive team sports, the percentage of the target population impacted falls to 10%. Finally, equating maintenance with the percentage of senior high schools providing daily physical education or its equivalent for the entire school year in all grade levels (5.8%), the percentage of the target population impacted is 0.6%. Thus, taking into account the five elements of the RE-AIM framework, it is estimated that less than 1% of the target population will benefit from school physical education.

Recommendations and future directions

School physical education programs are uniquely situated to address the epidemic of obesity and sedentary behavior plaguing our youth worldwide. However, it is apparent that only a small percentage of school-aged young people are exposed to physical education programs for prolonged periods of time. Moreover, despite reform at the policy level, the physical activity experiences provided to young people as part of school physical education are, in many cases, not optimal and not consistent with the goal of promoting lifelong physical activity. Consequently, policies and practices related to school physical education need to be carefully scrutinized and modified so that a greater proportion of the student population are exposed to quality daily physical education.

To help facilitate this process, teacher education programs in physical education need to bring a legitimate public health perspective to their students. Prospective physical education teachers need to become "tuned in" to the global epidemic of physical inactivity and the biological, psychosocial, and environmental factors contributing to this epidemic. Physical education teachers need to become more familiar with the population-level monitoring and surveillance data related to children's exposure to daily physical education and the amount of physical activity provided by the average physical education lesson. They also need to become critical consumers of scientific information pertaining to youth physical activity and public health. They need to know the short- and long-term consequences of participation in regular physical activity, the influence of growth and maturation on health endpoints, and what is "best practice" regarding promoting physical activity in and outside of physical education. Most of all, there is an urgent need for physical educators to know and understand health behavioral change theory (e.g. social cognitive theory) and how to plan, implement and evaluate theory-based strategies to promote physical activity behavior in school physical education.

Finally, given that there is ample evidence that physical education programs can be modified so as to increase student physical activity in and outside of school physical education; studies are needed to determine the optimal way to disseminate new approaches to schools and teachers. Priority should be given to identifying communication channels and systems that optimize awareness and adoption of innovative physical education policies and programs.

References

American Academy of Pediatrics Committees on Sports Medicine and School Health. (1987). Physical fitness and the schools. *Pediatrics, 80,* 449–450.

American College of Sports Medicine. (1998). Physical fitness in children and youth. *Medicine and Science in Sports and Exercise, 20,* 422–423.

Baranowski, T., Simons-Morton, B., Hooks, P. et al. (1990). A center-based program for exercise change among Black-American families. *Health Education Quarterly, 17,* 179–196.

Biddle, S., Cavill, N. and Sallis, J.F. (1997). Policy framework for young people and health-enhancing physical activity. In S. Biddle, J.F., Callis, N. Cavill, N. (Eds.), *Young and Active.* London: Health Education Authority.

Blair, S.N., Kohl, H.W., Barlow, C.E., et al. (1995). Changes in physical fitness and all-cause mortality. *Journal of American Medical Association, 273,* 1093–1098.

Blair, S.N., Kohl, H.W., Paffenbarger, R.S. et al. (1989a). Physical fitness and all-cause mortality. *Journal of American Medical Association, 262,* 2395–2401.

Blair, S.N., Clark, D.G., Cureton, K.J. and Powell, K.E. (1989b). Exercise and fitness in childhood: Implications for a lifetime of health. C.V. Gisolfi D.R Lamb, (Eds), Indianapolis In *Perspectives in Exercise Science and Sports Medicine.* Indianapolis Benchmark Press,

Boreham, C. and Riddoch C. (2001). The physical activity, fitness and health of children. *Journal of Sports Sciences, 19,* 915–929.

Brill, P.A., Burkhalter, H.E., Kohl, H.W., Goodyear, N.N. and Blair, S.N. (1989). The impact of previous athleticism on exercise habits, physical fitness, and coronary heart disease risk factors in middle-aged men. *Research Quarterly for Exercise and Sport, 60,* 209–215.

Burgeson, C.R., Wechsler, H., Brener, N.D., Young, J.C. and Spain C.G. (2001). Physical education and activity: results from the school health policies and programs study 2000. *Journal of School Health, 71,* 279–293.

Canada's Physical Activity Guide to Healthy Active Living. (2002). *Canada's Physical Activity Guide for Children.*

Cavill, N., Biddle, S. and Sallis, J.F. (2001). Health enhancing physical activity for young people: Statement of the United Kingdom expert consensus conference. *Pediatric Exercise Science, 13,* 12–25.

Centers for Disease Control and Prevention. (1997). Guidelines for school and community programs to promote lifelong physical activity among young people. *Morbidity and Mortality Weekly Report, 46*(No. RR–3), 1–36.

Corbin, C.B., Pargrazi, R.P. and Welk, G.J. (1994). Toward an understanding of appropriate physical activity levels for youth. *Physical Activity and Fitness Research Digest, 1*(8), 1–8

Corbin, C.B. (2002). Physical education as an agent of change. *Quest, 54,* 182–195.

Donnelly, J.E., Jacobsen, D.J., Whatley, J.E. et al. (1996). Nutrition and physical activity program to attenuate obesity and promote physical and metabolic fitness in elementary school children. *Obesity Research, 4,* 229–243.

Dzewaltowski, D.A., Estrabrooks, P.A. and Glasgow R.E. (2004). The future of physical activity behavior change research: What is needed to improve translation of research into health promotion practice? *Exercise and Sports Sciences Reviews, 32,* 57–63.

Ebbeling, C.B., Pawlak, D.B. and Ludwig, D.S. (2002). Childhood obesity: public-health crisis, common sense cure. *Lancet, 360* (9331) 473–482.

Glasgow, R.E., Vogt, T.M. and Boles, S.M. (1999). Evaluating the public health impact of health promotion interventions: The RE-AIM framework. *American Journal of Public Health, 89,* 1322–1327.

Gortmaker, S.L., Cheung, L.W., Peterson, K.E. et al. (1999a). Impact of a school-based interdisciplinary intervention on diet and physical activity among urban primary school children: eat well and keep moving. *Archives of Pediatric and Adolescent Medicine 153,* 975–983.

Gortmaker, S.L., Peterson, K., Wiecha, J. et al. (1999b). Reducing obesity via a school-based interdisciplinary intervention among youth: Planet Health. *Archives of Pediatric and Adolescent Medicine, 153*, 409–418.

Grunbaum, J.A., Kann, L., Kinchen, S. et al. (2002). Youth Risk Behavior Surveillance – United States, 2001. *Morbidity and Mortality Weekly Report, 51* (SS–4), 1–64.

Harrell, J.S., McMurray, R.G., Bangdiwala, S.I. et al. (1996). Effects of a school-based intervention to reduce cardiovascular disease risk factors in elementary-school children: the Cardiovascular Health in Children (CHIC) study. *Journal of Pediatrics, 128*, 797–805.

Janz, K.F., Dawson, J.D. and Mahoney, L.T. (2000). Tracking physical fitness and physical activity from childhood to adolescence: the muscatine study. *Medicine and Science in Sports and Exercise, 32*, 1250–1257.

Kann, L., Warren, C.W., Harris, W.A. et al. (1995). Youth Risk Behavior Surveillance – United States, 1993. *Morbidity and Mortality Weekly Report, 44* (SS–1), 1–56.

Kann, L., Warren, C.W., Harris, W.A. et al. (1996). Youth Risk Behavior Surveillance – United States, 1995. *Morbidity and Mortality Weekly Report, 45* (SS–4), 1–86.

Kann, L., Kinchen, S.A., Williams, B.I. et al. (1998). Youth Risk Behavior Surveillance – United States, 1997. *Morbidity and Mortality Weekly Report, 47* (SS–3), 1–92.

Kann, L., Kinchen, S.A., Williams, B.I. et al. (2000). Youth Risk Behavior Surveillance – United States, 1999. *Morbidity and Mortality Weekly Report, 49* (SS–5), 1–96.

Kelder, S.H., Perry, C.L. and Klepp, K. (1993). Community-wide youth exercise promotion: Long-term outcomes of the Minnesota Heart Health Program and the Class of 1989 Study. *Journal of School Health, 63*, 218–223.

Kelder, S.H., Perry, C.L, Klepp, K-I. and Lytle, L.L. (1994). Longitudinal tracking of adolescent smoking, physical activity and food choice behaviors. *American Journal of Public Health*, 1121–1126.

Killen, J.D., Telch, M.J., Robinson, T.N. et al. (1988). Cardiovascular disease risk reduction for tenth graders: A multiple-factor school based approach. *Journal of the American Medical Association, 260*, 1728–1733.

Kolbe, L.J., Kann, L. and Collins J.L. (1993). Overview of the Youth Risk Behavior Surveillance System. *Public Health Reports, 108* (suppl), 2–10.

Lee, A.M., Carter, J.A. and Greenockle, K.M. (1987). Children and fitness: A pedagogical perspective. *Research Quarterly for Exercise and Sport, 58*, 321–325.

Luepker, R.V., Perry, C.L., McKinlay, S.M. et al. (1996). Outcomes of a field trial to improve children's dietary patterns and physical activity: The Child and Adolescent Trial for Cardiovascular Health (CATCH). *Journal of the American Medical Association, 275*, 768–776.

Manios, Y., Moschandreas, J., Hatzis, C. and Kafatos, A. (1999). Evaluation of a health and nutrition education program in primary school children of Crete over a three-year program. *Preventive Medicine, 28*, 149–159.

McKenzie, T.L., Sallis, J., Faucette, N., Roby, J.J. and Kolody, B. (1993). Effects of a curriculum and inservice program on the quantity and quality of elementary physical education classes. *Research Quarterly for Exercise and Sport, 64*, 178–187.

McKenzie, T.L., Feldman, H., Woods, S.E. et al. (1995). Children's activity levels and lesson context during third-grade physical education. *Research Quarterly for Exercise and Sport, 66*, 184–193.

McKenzie, T.L., Marshall, S.J., Sallis, J.F. and Conway, T.L. (2000). Student activity levels, lesson context, and teacher behavior during middle school physical education. *Research Quarterly for Exercise and Sport, 71*, 249–259.

Morrow, J.R. and Freedson, P.S. (1994). Relationship between habitual physical activity and aerobic fitness in adolescents. *Pediatric Exercise Science, 6*, 315–329.

Nader, P.R., Stone, E.J., Lytle, L.A. et al. (1999). Three-year maintenance of improved diet and physical activity: The CATCH cohort. *Archives of Pediatric and Adolescent Medicine, 153*, 695–704.

National Association for Sport and Physical Education. (1995). *Moving into the future: national standards for physical education.* National Association for Sport and Physical Education Reston: VA,

National Association for Sport and Physical Education. (1998). *Physical activity for children: A statement of guidelines.* NASPE Publications. Reston, VA

National Association for Sport and Physical Education. (2002). *Active Start: A statement of physical activity guidelines for children birth to five years.* NASPE Publications Reston, VA

NIH Consensus Development Panel on Physical Activity and Cardiovascular Health. (1996). Physical activity and cardiovascular health. *Journal of the American Medical Association, 276*, 241–246.

Paffenbarger, R.S., Hyde, R.T., Wing, A.L. et al. (1986). Physical activity, all-cause mortality and longevity of college alumni. *New England Journal of Medicine, 314*, 605–613.

Paffenbarger, R.S., Kampert, J.B., Lee, I-M. et al. (1994). Changes in physical activity and other lifeway patterns influencing longevity. *Medicine and Science in Sports Exercise, 26*, 857–865.

Pate, R.R., Baranowski, T., Dowda, M. and Trost, S.G. (1996). Tracking of physical activity in young children. *Medicine and Science in Sports and Exercise, 28*, 92–96.

Pate, R.R., Long, B.J. and Heath G.W. (1994). Descriptive epidemiology of physical activity in adolescents. *Pediatric Exercise Science, 6*, 434–447.

Pate, R. R., Pratt, M., Blair, S. N. et al. (1995). Physical activity and public health. A joint recommendation from the Centers for Disease Control and Prevention and the American College of Sports Medicine. *Journal of the American Medical Association, 273*, 402–407.

Pate, R.R., Trost, S.G., Dowda, M. et al. (1999). Tracking of physical activity, inactivity, and physical fitness in rural youth. *Pediatric Exercise Science, 11*, 364–376.

Pate, R.R. and Hohn, R.C (1994). A contemporary mission for physical education. In R.R. Pate and R.C. Hohn (Eds.), *Health and fitness through physical education.* (pp. 1–8) Human Kinetics. Champaign.

Pate, R.R., Small, M.L., Ross, J.G. et al. (1995). School physical education. *Journal of School Health, 65,* 312–318.

Raitakari, O.T., Porkka, K.V.K., Taimela, S. et al. (1994). Effects of persistent physical activity and inactivity on coronary risk factors in children and young adults: The Cardiovascular Risk in Young Finns Study. *American Journal of Epidemiology, 140,* 195–205.

Riddoch, C.J. Andersen L.B., Wedderkopp, N., et al. (2004). Physical activity levels and patterns of 9- and 15-yr-old European children. *Medicine and Science in Sports and Exercise, 36,* 86–92

Ross, J.G. and Gilbert G.G. (1985). The national children and youth fitness study: A summary of findings. *Journal of Physical Education Recreation and Dance, 56,* 45–50.

Ross, J.G., Pate, R.R., Caspersen, C.J., Damberg, C.L. and Svilar, M. The national children and youth fitness study II: home and community in children's exercise habits. *Journal of Physical Education Recreation and Dance, 58,* 85–92.

Ross, J.G. and Pate R.R. (1987). The national children and youth fitness study II: A summary of findings. *Journal of Physical Education Recreation and Dance, 58,* 51–56.

Ross, J.G. (1994). The status of fitness programming in our nation's schools. In R.R. Pate and R.C. Hohn (Eds.), *Health and fitness through physical education.* (pp. 21–30). Human Kinetics, Champaign.

Ross, J.G., Dotson, C.O., Gilbert, G.G. and Katz, S.J. (1985). What are kids doing in school physical education? *Journal of Physical Education Recreation and Dance, 56,* 73–76.

Ross, J.G., Pate, R.R., Corbin, C.B., Delpy, L. A. and Gold R.S. (1987). What is going on in the elementary physical education program? *Journal of Physical Education Recreation and Dance, 58,* 78–84.

Sallis, J.F. and McKenzie T.L. (1991). Physical education's role in public health. *Research Quarterly for Exercise and Sport, 62,* 124–137.

Sallis, J.F. and Patrick, K. (1994). Physical activity guidelines for adolescents: Consensus Statement. *Pediatric Exercise Science, 6,* 302–314.

Sallis, J.F., Berry, C.C., Broyles, S.L. et al. (1995). Variability and tracking of physical activity over 2 yr in young children. *Medicine and Science in Sports and Exercise,* 1042–1049.

Sallis, J.F., McKenzie, T.L., Alcaraz, J.E. et al.(1997). The effects of a 2–year physical education program (SPARK) on physical activity and fitness in elementary school students. *American Journal of Public Health, 87,* 1328–1334.

Saris, W.H.M., Elvers, J.W.H., van't Hof, M.A. and Binkhorst R. A. (1980). Changes in physical activity of children aged 6 to 12 years. In F. Rutenfranz, R. Mocellin, F. Klimmt (Eds). *Children and Exercise XII.* Human Kinetics, Champaign, IL.

Scruggs, P. W., Beveridge, S. K., Eisenman, P. A. et al. (2003). Quantifying physical activity via pedometry in elementary physical education. *Medicine and Science in Sports and Exercise, 35,* 1065–1071.

Shattuck, L. (1850). *Report of a general plan for the promotion of public and personal health, devised, prepared, and recommended by the commissioners appointed under a resolve of the legislature of the State Boston.* Dutton and Wentworth, Boston.

Shilton, T. and Naughton, G. (2001). *Physical activity and children: A statement of importance and call to action from the heart foundation.* Heart Foundation of Australia.

Simons-Morton, B.G., Taylor, W.C., Snider, S.A. and Huang, I.W. (1987). The physical activity of fifth-grade students during physical education classes. *American Journal of Public Health, 83,* 262–264.

Simons-Morton, B.G., McKenzie, T.J, Stone, E. et al. (1997). Physical activity in a multiethnic population of third graders in four states. *Amercian Journal of Public Health, 87,* 45–50.

Simons-Morton, B.G., Parcel, G.S., Baranowski, T., Forthofer, R. and O'Hara, N.M. (1991). Promoting physical activity and a healthful diet among children: Results of a school-based intervention study. *American Journal of Public Health, 81,* 986–991.

Simons-Morton, B. (1994). Implementing health-related physical education. In R.R. Pate and R.C. Hohn (Eds.), *Health and fitness through physical education* (pp. 137–145). Human Kinetics, Champaign, IL.

Simons-Morton, B., Eitel, P. and Small, M.L. (1999). School physical education: Secondary analyses of the School Health Policies and Programs Study. *Journal of Health Education, 30,* S21–S27.

Simons-Morton, B., O'Hara, N. M., Simons-Morton, D. and Parcel, G.S. (1987). Children and fitness: A public health perspective. *Research Quarterly for Exercise and Sport, 58,* 295–302.

Smith, T.K., Brener, N.D., Kann, L. et al. (2001). Methodology for the School Health Policies and Programs Study 2000. *Journal of School Health, 71,* 261–265.

Stary, H.C. (1989). Evolution and progression of atherosclerotic lesions in coronary arteries of children and young adults. *Arteriosclerosis, 9* (suppl 1), 19–32.

Stone, E.J., McKenzie, T.L., Welk, G.J. and Booth, M.L. (1998). Effects of physical activity interventions in youth: review and synthesis. *American Journal of Preventive Medicine, 15,* 298–315.

Telama, R., Yang, X., Laakso, L. and Viikari J. (1997). Physical activity in childhood and adolescence as predictor of physical activity in young adulthood. *American Journal of Preventive Medicine, 13,* 317–323.

The Department of Health. (1999). Health Survey for England: The health of young people '95–97. The Stationery Office, London: UK.

Trost, S.G. (1998). *The association between physical activity and cardiorespiratory fitness in children and adolescents: A meta-analytic review.* Report prepared for the University Of South Carolina School Of Public Health. Columbia, SC.

Trost S.G. (2001). Objective measurement of physical activity in youth: Current issues, future directions. *Exercise Sports Sciences Reviews, 29,* 32–36.

Trost, S.G. (2004). Discussion paper for the development of recommendations for children's and youths' participation in health promoting physical activity. Report for Commonwealth Department of Health Ageing, Canberra, Australia.

Trost, S.G. and Pate, R.R. (1999). Physical activity in children and youth. In J.M. Rippe (Ed). *Lifestyle Medicine* (pp. 663–673). Blackwell Science, Malden: MA.

Trost, S.G., Pate, R.R., Sallis, J.F. et al. (2002). Age and gender differences in objectively measured physical activity in youth. *Medicine and Science in Sports and Exercise*, *34*, 350–355.

U.S. Department of Health and Human Services. (1996). *Physical activity and health: A report of the Surgeon General*. Atlanta, U.S. Department of Health and Human Services, Centers for Disease Control and Prevention, National Center for Chronic Disease Prevention and Health Promotion.

U.S. Department of Health and Human Services. (2000). Healthy people 2010: *Understanding and improving health*. 2nd edition. *With understanding and improving health* and *objectives for improving health*, 2 vols. Government Printing Office. Washington, DC: US.

Van Mechelen, W. and Kemper, H.C.G. (1995). Habitual physical activity in longitudinal perspective. In: Kemper H.C.G (Ed). *The Amsterdam Growth Study. A longitudinal analysis of health, fitness, and lifestyle* (pp. 135–158). Human Kinetics, Champaign, IL.

Welch, P.D. (1996). *History of American Physical Education and Sport* (2nd ed). Charles Thomas Publishers. Springfield, IL.

World Health Organization (2000). Health and Health Behavior among Young People. Health Policy for Children and Adolescents Series No 1. World Health Organization.

SECTION III
Learners and Learning in Physical Education

According to Rink (1999), few theories of teaching have been informed, explicitly at least, by theories of how individuals learn. This is an insightful observation and, in some respects, a surprising one. Given the long history of research on teaching in physical education and in other subject areas, it might be reasonable to expect a theory of teaching to contain a concept of learning since progress in learning appears to be the obvious, even if often unstated, objective of teaching. While Rink does not attempt to prescribe which theory or theories of learning should inform teaching, she does make a strong case that in any theory of teaching there should be an explicit and coherent concept of learning.

The conceptualization of learning in physical education has been adversely affected by the complex and enduring problem of mind-body dualism. Even though philosophers have debated this issue in relation to physical education for many years, and some believe they have resolved it, at least to their own satisfaction (e.g. Carr, 1981), there has nevertheless been little gain in terms of the practice of physical education in schools. The rhetoric of educating the whole child, attractive though it seems, has not assisted physical educators to think clearly about how we should shape educational experiences to achieve this goal. Nor has a mere listing of the various dimensions of human life, the physical, social, moral, emotional, and so on, been of much practical help. This is not to say that these claims have not been valid. Rather, it is to assert that they have not been useful in clarifying how we might think about learning and the practical consequences of our understanding of learning for designing learning experiences for young people.

As the chapters in this section show, we have now reached a situation in physical education where lack of research and a surfeit of sophisticated ideas can no longer be blamed for slow progress in addressing problems of mind-body dualism or improving practice in physical education classes. Van der Mars' overview of time-based research shows that from the late 1970s this early research on learning in physical education was dominated by the process-product paradigm. This research focused on the relationships between teacher behaviour (process variables) and student achievement (product variables). While time-based research produced valuable descriptive information on how teachers and students spend their time in the gym, it was gradually supplanted by research within the classroom ecology (Hastie and Siedentop) and mediating process paradigms (Solmon), each of which revealed and explored complex process variables that influence student learning, such as the structure of learning tasks, the student social system, and the role of cognition in learning and its relationships to motivation and a range of other student characteristics.

By seeking to explain learning as a complex social phenomenon, the studies overviewed in the chapters by Hastie and Siedentop and Solmon opened the way for more radical criticisms of mind-body dualism than had been possible with the mainly behaviourist orientation of time-based studies. They also encouraged a proliferation of theoretical perspectives that researchers in physical education have taken up with enthusiasm. Situated and constructivist theories, as the chapters by Rovegno reveal, have had a considerable impact on recent studies in physical education. These theories have impacted widely in physical education. As the chapter by Wallian and Chang shows, there are important synergies between traditional concerns for motor learning in physical education and new concepts that feature in situated and constructivist approaches. Further synergies are evident from Sandford and Rich's chapter on learners and popular physical culture. In each of these chapters, we can see a movement away from the learner as the isolated, sovereign individual to a concept of the learner engaged with and embedded in profoundly social and collective activity.

The chapters by Hay and Dyson explore topics that have been relatively neglected by physical education researchers. Hay's focus on assessment for learning shows that explicit discussion of the nature of learning has rarely featured until recently in literature on assessment. On the face of it, this is an even more astonishing oversight than the omission of learning from theories of teaching. Dyson points out in similar fashion that it is only relatively recently that researchers have sought out the views and perspectives of young people as a means of better understanding the learning process in physical education classes.

Finally, Amade-Escot provides new insights into the didactique tradition of research, much of it conducted in the Francophone world. Since this work has mostly been reported in French, Amade-Escot does English-speaking researchers a huge service in opening up this body of research on learning and physical education. The studies she overviews assist us to understand the strong emphasis in this research tradition on the interdependent relationships between learning, subject matter knowledge, and instruction.

Taken together, the chapters in this section present a thriving, diverse and sophisticated field of research in physical education that is rapidly gaining momentum and maturity as researchers increasingly recognize that a focus on learning brings into view the bigger picture of physical education and the relationships between its various component parts.

References

Carr, D. (1981) On mastering a skill. *Journal of Philosophy of Eduction, 15* (1): 87–96.

Rink, J.E. (1999). Instruction from a learning perspective, pp. 149–168. In C.A. Hardy and M. Mawer (Eds.) *Learning and teaching in physical education.* London: Falmer.

3.1 Time and learning in physical education

HANS VAN DER MARS

Introduction

The study of time-based variables in Sport Pedagogy has a much-celebrated history as part of a developing understanding of daily life for teachers and students in physical education. Initial studies on time made it abundantly clear that time is a precious resource for teachers. As in classroom research, time-based research provided one of the most widely recognized variables relative to teacher effectiveness in physical education: Academic Learning Time-Physical Education (ALT-PE). A derivative of the classroom-based Academic Learning Time (ALT) variable, ALT-PE is defined as the time students spend appropriately/successfully engaged in a subject matter-related task (Siedentop et al., 1982). This temporal dimension of appropriate motor engagement is considered a key indicator of teacher effectiveness, because of its relationship with student achievement. It is now accepted as a process indicator of student learning

This chapter will include a general introduction to the variable of time at the class level in physical education, and how decisions (i.e. public policy/mandates) at one level affect time resources at levels below; a brief historical overview of time-based variables; a review of the theoretical frameworks that have formed the basis for much of the time-based research; review some of the core concepts; the measurement tactics relative to time-based research in physical education; major findings relative to time-based variables and their relationship to student learning; and finally suggested directions for future research.

The reader should note that this chapter will include not only research with time-based measures of learning, but also gives attention to research that measured frequency-based measures. Hence, throughout there will be reference made to the construct of "opportunity to learn." Furthermore, the chapter's focus is limited in two ways. First, the reviewed research will only include studies that linked time-/opportunity-to-learn variables with outcomes measures in the skill learning domain. The emergence of a public health orientation in

physical education over the past two decades has also produced a sizable empirical base relative to students' time spent in moderate to vigorous physical activity both during class and beyond. This important area of research is discussed elsewhere in this handbook. Second, there is mounting evidence demonstrating the influence of school-, school district-, state- and government-level policy decisions directly influence students' actual opportunity to learn. However, space limitations prevent its review in this chapter.

Class level influences on instructional time

In sport pedagogy, time variables have been studied mostly at the class level and have demonstrated how teachers' use of time directly influences how students spend their time, and consequently their opportunity to learn. Berliner (1979) went so far as to argue that at this level, teachers can more directly influence students' achievement, by arranging their instruction in ways that maximize the time that students spend in direct and successful contact with learning tasks. Metzler's (1979) clever metaphor, called the "Funnel effect" demonstrated the role of time usage relative to students having direct and successful contact with the subject matter during class. As shown in the lower half of Figure 3.1.1 (Program/Class level), of a finite amount of available class time, some is taken up by managerial and organizational teacher directions and related activities. The remaining time is then divided between teachers' instructions about the subject matter and various forms of activity time. This would be considered "allocated" time. Time spent on instruction would include explanations (and demonstrations) of techniques, tactics, rules, scorekeeping, officiating, etc.

Activity time would be that part of class time where students actually are offered the chance to practice skills; engage in game play or scrimmage, practice their dance steps, complete fitness task and so on. It is not unusual to hear physical education teachers verbalize the importance of providing their

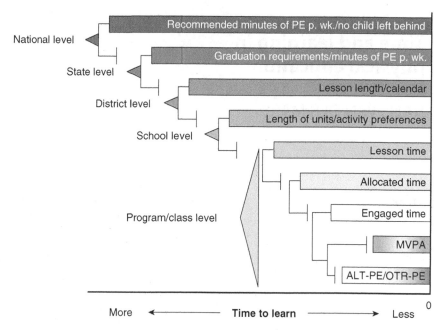

Figure 3.1.1 **Multi-level influences on student time/opportunity to learn**

class "with lots of activity time", which implies that they may view this as a primary criterion of a lesson's quality (Metzler, 1989). However, for individual students, merely having a high amount of activity time says nothing about the next two layers in the funnel. First, the amount of activity time says nothing about an individual student's actual task engagement. Even if the class group has the opportunity to be engaged, individual students either cannot or choose not to actively engage in assigned learning tasks. And second, even when actively engaged it is not necessarily the kind that would indicate learning is taking place. That is, the task may be either too easy or too difficult.

As shown in Figure 3.1.1, the upper limit of time within each layer of class time logically is always less than the layer above. Teachers who employ effective class management strategies through the development of routines will be able to maximize the available class time for content instruction and activity. The degree to which individual students are actively engaged in learning task and the appropriateness of that engagement is more dependent on the actual arrangement, the design of the learning tasks, and student interest in the task

Poor management (either because of lack of skill or by choice) increases the slippage between available class time and content-related instruction and activity time, thereby reducing students' opportunity to be in direct contact with the subject matter. The slippage between activity time and engaged time, as well as between engaged time and ALT-PE

will be greater if teachers' instructional design skills are not well developed (Siedentop and Tannehill, 2000). As will be noted later, students also influence how they spend their time based on their teacher's task directions and accountability practices.

Brief historical background on time and learning research in physical education

Sport pedagogy's efforts to study time were indeed revolutionary. Until the late 1970s, time-related variables had never been the focus of any systematic research in physical education. The Teachers College Data Bank project, headed by William Anderson at Columbia University (Anderson and Barrette, 1978) produced the first descriptive time data. The primary emphasis was on how teachers spent their time. The evidence showed that teachers were busy performing multiple pedagogical functions simultaneously, but that much of this was not necessarily "instructional" in nature. Much of the time teachers were occupied with organizing equipment and students, silently watching students, and/or managing students' general class behavior.

At about the same time, research projects were started at Ohio State University that borrowed heavily from the work done in the Beginning Teacher Evaluation Study (BTES) which produced initial evidence on the role and influence of time-based

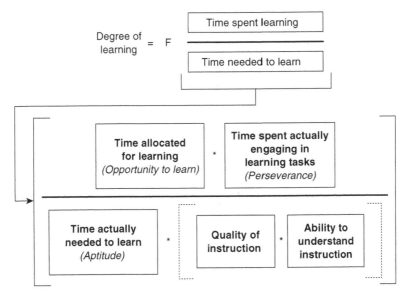

Adapted from Carroll (1963)

Figure 3.1.2   Carroll's model for school learning

variables and their relationship with student achievement in classroom subjects (Berliner, 1979; 1990; Fisher et al., 1980). The emphasis on time-based dimensions of students' engagement was a logical start. But two factors contributed to also studying opportunity to learn from a frequency perspective. First, the Juniper Gardens research project at the University of Kansas had developed the Opportunity-to-Respond (OTR) variable which measured student engagement from the perspective of how many words were read/spelled correctly and its link with academic achievement (Greenwood et al., 1984). Second, physical education content was mostly taught from a technique perspective, where students would practice individual skills (i.e. throw, catch, pass serve, etc.) that were short in duration and discrete. Thus, the frequency of the engagement for most skills was considered a more accurate measure. This gave rise to a series of studies that still focused on students' (appropriate) engagement, but used frequency instead of time as a measure of opportunity to learn.

Time and learning: Its theoretical bases

The time–learning relationship is rooted in the theoretical bases of the Model of School Learning (Carroll, 1963), Mastery Learning (Bloom, 1968), and Harnischfeger and Wiley's (1985) efforts related

to "Quantity of Schooling." Their common thread lies in seeking to understand schooling, and, thus, learning from the student's perspective, while also recognizing the variance in the rate at which people master a particular area of content. By taking this perspective, Berliner (1990) pointed out that the key to explaining student achievement (i.e. an albeit narrow indicator of learning) lies in determining the amount and quality of active involvement in their learning. More recently (though not in the context of school learning), time spent is a key dimension of the "deliberate practice" variable made prominent in the research on the development of expertise (i.e. elite level of performance) (Eriscsson et al., 1993).

Model of school learning

Carroll (1963) and Bloom (1968) recognized that students require different amounts of time to learn. Both models explain differences in learning between individuals using five central variables. These variables are: Aptitude, Perseverance, Opportunity to Learn, Quality of Instruction, and the Ability to Understand Instruction. The first three can all be expressed in unit of time measures. The latter two are not explained in terms of time, but strongly influence the time needed to learn/master content. The full Carroll model is presented in Figure 3.1.2, where learning is explained as an equation that incorporates these five variables.

The "Time Spent Learning" metric (the numerator) is determined by the students' opportunity to learn and their willingness to actually engage in the learning activity, where the former is influenced by the school's and teachers' decisions to allocate certain amounts of time to specific content. Because schools are expected to cover varied content areas, school days generally are divided into dedicated blocks of time devoted to math, science, physical education and so forth. Students' willingness to spend time actually engaged in a learning task is the metric used to reflect "perseverance."

The "Time Needed to Learn" metric (the denominator) is based on students' aptitude for learning the content, their ability to understand instruction and the quality of that instruction. Students requiring less time to learn/master content are said to have a higher aptitude. This is, of course, influenced by such factors as previous experiences with the content, the level of abstractness and/or complexity of the content. An example in physical education would be task of learning to guard/mark space or an opponent. Students who have demonstrated they know how and when to defend space versus an opponent in soccer may require less time to reach the same level of mastery when learning to play another invasion game such as basketball.

If the "quality of instruction" is high, the time needed to learn also would be less. That is, a 9-year-old student learning to shoot in basketball can master the appropriate technique at a faster rate if the learning conditions have been matched with his/her developmental characteristics by way of lower baskets, smaller/lighter balls and/or smaller teams.

The ability to understand instruction also influences the time required to learn. If students have difficulty understanding directions, they will require more time. This becomes especially pertinent in situations where tasks might be less explicit (i.e. that is where students are left more on their own to determine the important concept or ideas).

Active learning time

Harnischfeger and Wiley (1985) borrowed from the Mastery Learning model and coined the concept of "Active Learning Time", by placing its variables in the broader context of school learning. Their work is important, because it demonstrated how time spent by students actively engaged in learning in class is influenced by policy decisions, mandates and political pressures made at multiple levels, as depicted in Figure 3.1.1. That is, at the class level, time allocated for learning and the actual engagement by students is dependent on how teachers organize their content, time and students, and the extent to which they closely supervise their students' work. But the sheer volume of allocated time for learning at the school and district level (typically expressed in "number of minutes per week" or "needed credits for graduation") is dependent on policy decisions made at state and national levels. An excellent example is the No Child Left Behind (NCLB) act (US Department of Education, 2002) aimed at (a) improving academic achievement in "core" subjects (e.g. science, reading, and mathematics), and (b) closing the achievement gap between students of differing racial, ethnic, and economic background. Without manipulating either the length of the school year and/or school day, such federal mandates by definition necessitate the squeezing of available teaching positions and learning time and opportunity for students in physical education.

The work by Carroll (1963), Bloom (1968), Harnischfeger and Wiley (1985) formed the basis for the research conducted by Fisher et al. (1980) in the Beginning Teacher Evaluation Study (BTES). This project produced important markers relative to the relationship between various time variables and students' academic achievement. The work in the BTES Project constituted a departure from the "process – product" research paradigm (see Figure 3.1.3) that dominated the teacher effectiveness literature in the 1960s and early 1970s.

BTES researchers recognized the mediating role of students' behavior within the classroom and thus allowed for the study of relationships between teachers' instructional behavior (and the environment they arranged!) and students' behavior, as well as students' classroom behavior and their academic performance.

Findings were such that in classes where teachers actively monitor students and have high rates of content-relevant interactions with students, the students exhibit higher levels of active learning task engagement. Furthermore, the teachers' ability to both diagnose the students' skill level and, on this basis, assign more appropriate learning tasks, was strongly associated with higher student success rates (Fisher et al., 1980). Specifically, each of the following time-based variables were positively associated with student achievement: (a) classroom time allocated to content instruction; (b) class time during which students were actually engaged in content-related tasks, and (c) the class time during which the engagement in content produced high success.

Thus, looking through Mastery Learning's lenses one starts to appreciate the complex tasks that physical education teachers face in guiding students to acceptable levels of initial competency/proficiency in the psychomotor learning domain, all in the context of often increasingly limited resources, not the least of which is time. Interestingly enough, research on the development of expertise constitutes a logical extension of research on teaching–learning processes in classrooms. While classroom research has targeted mostly the development of basic

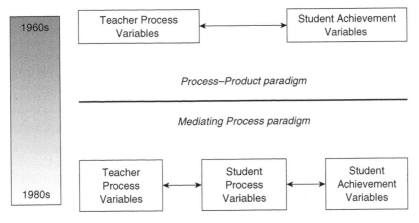

Figure 3.1.3   Main paradigms for research on teaching (1960–1980s)

academic skills, research on expertise in domains such as music, medicine and sport targets the few persons who reach unparalleled levels of performance (e.g. Ericsson, 1996). Time spent in "deliberate practice" is the centerpiece variable in this emerging line of inquiry.

Data collection tactics used in time-/opportunity-based research

Most all Sport Pedagogy research on time/opportunity to learn has relied on direct systematic observation (e.g. Darst et al., 1989). This research was focused largely on the learning of sport-related psychomotor skills. Borrowing extensively from colleagues involved in classroom teaching research and Applied Behavior Analysis, research programs at Boston University, Teachers College-Columbia University, University of Massachusetts and Ohio State University effectively promoted the use of direct observation tactics. These tactics included Event Recording, Duration Recording, Interval Recording, and Momentary Time Sampling (e.g. Siedentop and Tannehill, 2000; van der Mars, 1989a). Direct observation tactics are used to measure/estimate the frequency and/or duration of teacher and student behavior. Early studies on time-based variables employed duration recording (e.g. Anderson and Barrette, 1978).

Subsequent research depended more heavily on Interval Recording. When using Interval Recording, observers record the (non-)occurrence of predefined behavior based on the passage of intervals of time. As such, both the frequency and duration of behavior are estimated. Since the actual recording of the event(s) is dependent on the passage of time,

there is a built-in susceptibility to either over- or underestimation of the occurrence.

Despite these limitations, interval recording became a widely used tactic, because it allowed for a greater number of behaviors to be observed simultaneously and offered more rigorous measures of observer reliability/consistency (van der Mars, 1989b). Generally, time intervals range in length from 3 to 10 seconds.

The Academic Learning Time-Physical Education (ALT-PE) observation system

Researchers at Ohio State University developed the Academic Learning Time-Physical Education (ALT-PE) observation instrument (Siedentop et al., 1982). Key BTES variables were adapted for use in physical education contexts. It employs an alternating 6 seconds "observe"/6 seconds "record" interval, and enables an analysis of both contextual and learner involvement variables.

At the contextual level, observers select from the following groups of categories: (a) General Content variables (i.e. events unrelated to student learning of content); (b) Subject Matter Knowledge variables (i.e. time spent by a teacher explaining and/or demonstrating subject matter content, and (c) Subject Matter Motor variables (i.e. measures of available time for students to be in contact with motor tasks).

Learner involvement level categories capture the nature of individual students' task engagement. Not-Motor-Engaged categories include "waiting", "on-task", "off-task", "cognitive" and "interim" (i.e. preparatory tasks). Motor-Engaged categories include three types of active engagement in physical activities, including "motor appropriate", "motor inappropriate", and "supporting". The "motor appropriate" category represents the type of engagement that reflects learning, and thus constitutes ALT-PE. For ALT-PE to be coded the student has to be actively engaged in a motor task; the task needs to be aligned with the intended outcomes and the engagement needs to be appropriate/successful. It is the latter criterion that becomes the critical judgment for the coder.

The appropriateness of a student's motor engagement can be based on the technical execution (i.e. "form") of the task, the outcome of the task (or product), or a combination of the two. When first designed, the coding rule relative to the quality or appropriateness of a student's motor engagement was that the task needed to be sufficiently "easy" so the student could be successful approximately 80% of the time. Rink (2003) has argued that this criterion, while perhaps appropriate for math content, would be unreasonable in the psychomotor domain especially if one were to use an outcome-based criterion for judging success. That is, expert performers in sport (i.e. collegiate, professional and elite athletes) generally do not meet the 80% success level.

Consequently, the dominant criterion for judging the appropriateness of students' motor engagement has been the technical execution of the task. This requires observers to have clearly defined descriptors of the critical elements of the possible skills exhibited. The breadth of physical education content therefore requires an equally broad array of content specific definitions of what constitutes "appropriate" engagement by students.

In initial research with the ALT-PE instrument, ALT-PE encompassed both "motor" and "cognitive" engagement in relevant content. But since cognitive engagement was always recorded at an "easy" level of difficulty (required criterion for it to be considered ALT-PE), it tended to spuriously increase the total amount of ALT-PE. As noted by Metzler (1983), it was quickly decided that only "Motor-ALT-PE" would be used as it would be more congruent with and reflective of students' opportunity to learn motor skills, and is reflected in the revised ALT-PE system (Siedentop et al., 1982).

The validity of the interval recording-based ALT-PE instrument was established (Silverman et al., 1991) lending confidence that well-trained observers could capture a key process indicator of student learning. However, later work by Silverman and Zotos (1987) also demonstrated the limitations of using the 6 seconds, "observe"/6 seconds "record" recording format across a variety of learning tasks. Physical education learning tasks differ widely in terms of their natural frequency and duration. For tasks such as striking, passing, kicking, shooting and rebounding, frequency is the most representative dimension. Tasks such as dribbling a ball, jogging, swimming, juggling and rope-jumping are continuous in nature and thus their duration best represents their occurrence. Given the wide variety of tasks seen in typical physical education classes, interval recording was the logical observation tactic of choice.

Although the revised ALT-PE instrument manual offered event recording as an alternative observation tactic, the interval recording version was the observation tactic of choice. As early as 1983, several researchers urged that the "standard" ALT-PE observation instrument be adapted and customized for different learning content and contexts (e.g. Parker and O'Sullivan, 1983; Siedentop, 1983). These recommendations contributed to the rise of the frequency-based "Opportunity to Respond-Physical Education" (OTR-PE). Event recording still analyzes students' opportunity to learn and is a more sensitive metric if learning tasks are discrete (i.e. short duration) in nature.

Measurement of student learning in physical education

A key feature of teacher effectiveness research has been the definition of student learning. Teacher effectiveness research in the early 1970s depended on standardized achievement tests as the primary measure of learning; a narrow definition of learning especially by today's standards of authentic assessment.

Given the absence of such tests in physical education, Sport Pedagogy researchers often relied on compact research designs called Experimental Teaching Units (ETUs). ETUs provide teachers with a specific learning objective and a set of contextual parameters (e.g. availability of time per lesson, number of lessons and equipment). Teachers are then given the freedom to plan their series of lessons. At the end of the lesson series, learning is assessed through the use of a formal psychomotor skill achievement test (e.g. AAHPER, 1965) or an achievement test around a "novel skill".

In the 1960s, the American Alliance for Health, Physical Education and Recreation (AAHPER) developed performance tests for individual techniques in a variety of sports (e.g. volleyball set and forearm pass). The assistance of measurement experts in developing the test protocols enabled users to claim test reliability. For example, the serve test component of the AAHPER Volleyball Skills test (AAHPER, 1965) was used in the work by Silverman and colleagues as the indicator of student learning (e.g. Silverman, 1985a, 1990; Silverman et al., 1988, 1992).

Prior learning by students poses a problem in teacher effectiveness research, making it more difficult to attribute learning to the instructional efforts. To address this problem, pretests were employed to determine students' incoming levels of performance. Incoming ability was then "controlled" statistically to manage its confounding influence on learning. The use of "novel" skills tests such as the soccer tip-up accuracy test used by Ashy et al. (1988) or a hockey accuracy test (Metzler, 1983) offered an alternative approach to measuring student learning. Novel skills test were employed to ensure that learners participating in the study could be considered true novices thus negating the need for pretest, and minimize any additional practice opportunity prior to instruction.

As discussed in a later section on "Work yet to be done," the use of formal skill tests on technique performance in largely de-contextualized conditions really only capture only a small portion of the broad repertoire of performance indicators within game play. Consequently, it likely suppressed the strength of the relationship between appropriate motor engagement and student achievement measures. That is, the achievement measures used to indicate learning focused solely on "on-the-ball" techniques, leaving students' learning of "off-the-ball" moves completely out of the equation.

Time and learning in physical education: major findings

Correlational and experimental work has shown that (a) physical education teachers' actions do influence how students spend their time, and (b) what students do in class affects their achievement. As this research line developed the role and importance of student characteristics variables (e.g. gender, skill level, and special needs status) became a key feature of this research as well.

The review of findings is organized as follows: (a) Research linking time- and frequency-related variables with student skill learning indicators, (b) findings on the mediating influence of select contextual and student characteristics variables on the time–learning relationship, (c) experimental research findings around efforts to increase students' in-class task engagement, and (d) findings relative to the association between time spent in physical education and cognitive functioning/academic achievement.

Time/opportunity and learning in physical education

There are over 15 studies in physical education that support the association between how students spend their time and their performance on a skill achievement test. Methodologically, these studies differ in several ways. Some employed microteaching with pre-service teachers, while others took place with intact classes. Many projects used the ETU design (Graham, 1983) protocols, while others used longer units of time and licensed specialists. In other studies, post-test results were used to group more and less effective teachers, and determine differences in instructional processes retrospectively. Learners ranged in age from elementary to University levels. Despite these variations, the results generally support the link between time and learning in physical activity contexts.

In one of the first ever studies of its kind in physical education, Yerg (1981) used an Experimental Teaching Unit (ETU) to study differences in teaching process behaviors between more and less effective teachers. Using a pretest–post-test design, 40 pre-service teachers taught the cartwheel in a 20 minute lesson. Each teacher instructed three students (between grades 3 and 6). When separated into two groups, based on the actual number of skill attempts by students during the 20 minutes, several differences were found. In lessons with greater opportunity to practice, students performed better on both the pretest and post-test. Teachers in that same group spent less time on task presentations. Using residual gain scores from a regression analysis on the students' performance, the ten most and ten least effective teachers were selected from the total sample. No statistically significant differences were found between these two groups, and the analysis showed that students with higher incoming skill levels (based on the pretest) had more skill attempts and higher post-test score points to the powerful role of incoming ability.

In a physical education teacher education (PETE) program, ten male student teachers taught two lessons of 9 minutes on the handstand rollout to three male peers (Pieron, 1982a). Students in the more effective classes had significant gains from pretest to post-test, while those in the less effective classes did not. Residual gain scores were used to split more and less effective classes. Although there were no significant differences in instruction time, time allocated for skill practice, and actual engaged time, students in the more effective classes spent less time waiting and had higher rates of criterion skill practice trials.

In another study of low- and high-achieving students (based on observed skill level differences as determined by teachers) Pieron (1982b) studied performances of 224 high school-aged male and female students in both gymnastics and volleyball lessons. Significant differences occurred in the percent of on-task time and success rate in both volleyball and gymnastics favoring the higher-achieving students. Furthermore, these same students spent less time waiting.

Young and Metzler (1982) employed a novel skill (an accuracy task combining a hockey and golf skill) in an ETU context with a pretest and post-test to study the association between ALT-PE and achievement. Four teachers taught one lesson on the target skill to 90 elementary-aged students. Teachers were allowed to design and organize the lesson however they wished, but the lesson had to focus on teaching content related to the target skill. While the relationship between achievement scores and ALT-PE was not strong, it was statistically significant and in the desired direction.

Metzler (1983) re-analyzed data from another study using a similar hockey/golf skill in which two graduate students taught 77 elementary-level students. In addition, the students were divided into two groups, with one receiving instruction using the "reverse chaining" instructional strategy and the other group being exposed to a lecture/demonstration instructional strategy. This was done to create a greater variance in accumulated ALT-PE in the whole student group. The ETU format was used again with time lengths of 20, 30 and 40 minutes, respectively. An extra group of students was allowed to only take the pretest and post-test. Students who accumulated lower levels of ALT-PE performed poorer in terms of gain scores compared to those with higher ALT-PE levels. However, the results also hinted at a possible point of diminished benefits. That is, when students were separated in low, medium and high ALT-PE groups, the gain scores in the latter group were actually lower than the medium ALT-PE group.

Wurzer (1983) conducted a study in the context of the Red Cross' teaching of cardiopulmonary resuscitation (CPR). Twelve Red Cross CPR instructors and 36 students were observed during a standard course format over three 3-hour sessions, following a pretest. The correlation between ALT-PE and ability to perform one-rescuer CPR (based on gain score) was .75.

Graham et al. (1983) were the first to demonstrate the use of an ETU in the context of regular physical education classes at the elementary school level. Following a pretest on a similar task as the one employed by Metzler (1983), 11 teachers taught one lesson on the hockey/golf skill task. Class sizes ranged from 14 to 30 4th and 5th grade students. Using residual gain scores, teachers were grouped as more ($n = 4$) and less ($n = 4$) effective teachers. The three middle teachers were left out of the analysis. The difference in post-test scores between the two groups was significant. However, although students in classes of more effective teachers spent more time engaged in activity, less time in instruction and waiting, none of these differences reached statistical significance.

Phillips and Carlisle (1983) employed a pretest–post-test design with 18 teachers (across elementary, junior high and middle school levels) who taught ten lessons of volleyball. Other than being directed on which volleyball skills to teach, teachers were free in terms of planning and implementing the lessons. Achievement was assessed using gain scores from five skills tests that had been reported as being valid. A cluster analysis of skill achievement scores determined the five most and 13 least effective teachers. Students' performance on the achievement tests prior to the ten lessons was similar across the five skills. Following the ten lessons the two groups differed significantly in their achievement scores, favoring the more effective teachers group. Along with significant differences between the two groups on select teacher process variables (e.g. positive performance feedback), students in the most effective teacher group spent a significantly higher amount of time in engaged skill learning time, and were also more successful.

DePaepe (1985) completed the first study where students with disabilities served as participants. Using static and dynamic balance as achievement measures, DePaepe studied the effects of varying degrees of least restrictive environments on students' ALT-PE. Students (ages 5–12) were separated in three instructional format groups: peer-tutoring, self-contained, and mainstreamed. ALT-PE levels favored the peer tutored students. The mainstreamed students accumulated the lowest levels. A moderate positive correlation was found between ALT-PE and static balance. DePaepe emphasized the strength of peer tutoring in this context. Later research by Ward and his colleagues (e.g. Ward et al., 1998) built on this early effort.

Using a more general time variable than ALT-PE, DeKnop (1986) studied eight teachers of novice university-aged students over a series of five 3-hour tennis lessons. Teachers were grouped into more and less effective teacher groups according to the differences on the post-tests on three tennis skills. The more effective teachers were better able to transform the total available class time into "useful time" and "information time."

Moving from time to frequency

According to Silverman (1985a), physical education's efforts in demonstrating the link between student engagement in learning tasks and achievement were not as conclusive as those reported in classroom studies. Following these initial studies on the association of time and learning in physical education settings, a series of studies were completed where researchers chose criterion skill trials as the process variable measure.

Dugas (1983) used criterion trials (as opposed to pure time) as the measure of appropriate motor engagement in a high school-level study on archery. Significant relationship between criterion skill trials and performance on an archery achievement test, were found both when using the student and the class as the unit of analysis.

Silverman (1985a) used both duration recording (engaged time) and event recording (appropriate and inappropriate practice trials) in a pretest–post-test university level swimming context. Students were instructed over two sessions (15 minutes each) on the survival float. Based on their pretest performance, students were grouped as low, medium, and high skilled. Using a multiple regression analysis, engaged time did not predict post-test performance, but appropriate skill trials did, while the rate of inappropriate skill trials predicted lower performance.

Ashy et al's. (1988) study with 4th-grade students produced similar findings using a soccer skill. Preservice teachers taught the kick-up skill over two lessons (20 minutes each), and skill trials were judged on appropriateness in terms of the technical execution. A post-test only design was employed as the study focused on a novel skill. Regardless of the unit of analysis used (class versus student), appropriate trials correlated strongly with achievement, while total trials correlated negatively (but nonsignificantly) with achievement.

Silverman (1988) studied the relationship of several time and context variables with learning in the volleyball context at the middle school level. Using serving and forearm passing as the target skills, students were instructed over seven regular physical education classes. Although in earlier studies time spent on instruction/demonstration did not correlate with student achievement (e.g., Pieron, 1982a,b), in this study, at least for passing, instruction time rated as adequate or good did correlate with residual learning gain scores. Some of the main practice time variables correlating with achievement included: (a) higher amounts of total time spent in passing and serving practice (with teacher feedback), (b) time spent practicing the pass and serve individually (with teacher feedback); (c) higher amounts of time spent in reciprocal teaching practice of the serve, and (d) time spent in scrimmage (a negative correlation).

Finally, in their 4-day study of 6th-grade students on the volleyball forearm pass, Solmon and Lee (1996) investigated the relationship of students' cognitive mediation and in-class task engagement variables to residual achievement. They found that engaged time during practice, total trials and correct trials all correlated significantly (and more strongly than perceived competence) with achievement.

Is more better?

Sport Pedagogy researchers were quick to warn that this small but important database should not be interpreted as meaning that the relationship between appropriate motor engagement and achievement is linear in nature. Similar to Metzler's (1983) study, Silverman's (1990) work showed how there is a point of diminishing returns. Using the same videotapes of the aforementioned middle school volleyball study, he demonstrated positive curvilinear relationships between residual achievement scores and appropriate still attempts for the forearm pass and serve. The general pattern that emerged suggests that increased appropriate practice levels will first produce higher performance scores, but this is followed by a leveling off and then even a decrease in achievement. For both serving and forearm passing, similar patterns were found when calculating a ratio of appropriate to inappropriate skill attempts.

When considering total skill attempts (appropriate and inappropriate skill attempts combined), Silverman (1990) found a negative curvilinear relationship for the serve, but not for the forearm pass; indicating an initial decrease in performance was followed by a gradual upturn in the performance. Inappropriate practice (i.e. poor technical execution) showed a negative curvilinear relationship with residual achievement for the serve, but not the forearm pass.

The role of student characteristics and contextual variables

Numerous studies have incorporated contextual and student characteristic variables as mediators of the relationship between student opportunities to learn and achievement. This section will include a review of findings on the following mediating variables: student skill level, sex, disability, lesson content, instructional formats employed by teachers, and the accountability mechanisms in effect.

Student skill level

Most studies that included students' skill level as a variable were completed at a the elementary school level, where ALT-PE levels are generally higher than in secondary school classes. Generally, researchers left the decision of determining students' skill levels up to teachers. Most studies reported both the total engaged time and ALT-PE. While data are not consistent across all studies, the following general patterns emerge for students of varying skill levels:

1. With some exceptions (e.g. Shute et al., 1982; Silverman, 1993; Silverman et al., 1984), lower-skilled students generally have fewer opportunities to practice (regardless of the unit of measure used) than their higher-skilled counterparts. From a time perspective, such differences can vary from 2 to 10% (e.g. Graham, 1987; Grant et al., 1989; Shute et al., 1982; Silverman, 1985b; Telama et al., 1987).
2. Regardless of the school level studied, these differences remain quite consistent. Lower-skilled students accumulate lower levels of ALT-PE

(and OTR-PE) across K-12 grade levels and even in college-level activity classes (e.g. Buck et al., 1991).

3. Especially for lower-skilled students it is critical for the practice engagement to be appropriate (Silverman, 1993), as they tend to derive more benefit from appropriate practice.

The importance of these findings lies in cumulative deficit that emerges over the course of the students' entire K-12 physical education experience. Lesser-skilled students fall further behind their higher-skilled classmates as they move through grade levels, thus, perpetuating the "rich get richer and poor get poorer" phenomenon (Corbin, 2002).

Student sex

Depending on the school level, differences in time/opportunity to learn do appear when comparing male and female students. While ALT-PE levels at the elementary school level generally are similar (e.g. Shute et al., 1982; Silverman et al., 1984), as students move into secondary school, gender becomes an influential mediating variable. Using his original middle school volleyball data set, Silverman (1993) found that females had significantly more inappropriate skill trials and low-skilled males had higher rates of appropriate skill trials and the strongest correlation with achievement.

Student disability

Several scholars in both Sport Pedagogy and Adapted Physical Education have studied the teaching and learning processes in classes that include students with disabilities, including a focus on time-related variables. With few exceptions (e.g. Aufderheide et al., 1982), students with disabilities accrue less ALT-PE compared to their typically developing peers (Aufderheide, 1983; Gagnon et al., 1989; Shute et al., 1982; Silverman et al., 1984; Temple and Walkley, 1999; Vogler et al., 1990, 1992, 1998). Aufderheide et al. (1982) demonstrated that in elementary classes ALT-PE levels for mainstreamed students was similar to those of their typically developing peers, and that individualized instruction aided both groups. School level appears to influence mainstreamed students' ALT-PE levels as well. ALT-PE levels of mainstreamed students at elementary levels generally are higher than at the junior high school level (e.g. Aufderheide, 1983; Vogler et al., 1990, 1998).

Using both years of teaching experience and Berliner's (1994) classification of levels of expertise, Vogler et al. (1992) compared ALT-PE levels of mainstreamed ambulatory students and their typically developing peers. Differences in ALT-PE favoring the typically developing peers were not affected by either teachers' experience or level of expertise.

Lesson content

The varied content taught in physical education in part creates built-in variability in the opportunity that students have to accumulate ALT-PE. Some activities by their nature offer more engaged time/opportunity than others. For example, fitness (i.e. aerobics) and rhythm activities generally provide higher levels, followed by individual sports. Team sports and gymnastics produce the lowest levels of ALT-PE. However, one should remember that the data of sport-related lessons reflect a time where especially in secondary classes the typical focus was on more technique-based instruction. That is, the sequence of learning tasks in a unit of volleyball likely included the practice of isolated techniques (i.e. set, forearm pass, serve) followed by instruction on the rules of the (parent) game and then full-sided game play. In recent years, alternative curriculum models and instructional formats have emerged that potentially allow for increased and continuous opportunities for students to actively engage in learning activities. The Sport Education model (Siedentop et al., 2004) reflects many of the features of cooperative learning and small group instruction formats (i.e. teams competing in modified game structures). Likewise, the tactical games format of instruction (e.g. Griffin et al., 1997) employs a more games-based approach to foster students' understanding and use of more tactical features of game play. This has implications for coding protocols when measuring students' appropriate involvement within game play. What remains largely unanswered at this time is whether such approaches also translate to higher levels of ALT-PE and OTR-PE and student achievement measures.

Teachers' organization and management skills

Teachers' ability to effectively organize students and equipment plays a crucial role in creating time for students to learn. The professional literature used in the preparation of today's physical education offers numerous effective strategies that will help minimize the unproductive time during class (e.g. Graham et al., 2004; Rink, 2002; Siedentop and Tannehill, 2000; Siedentop et al., 2004). Managerial routines for student grouping, equipment dispersal and return, and gaining students' attention are vitally important in creating more time and opportunity for actual engagement by students. However, effective organization and management of students, equipment and time is merely a prerequisite for creating the time and opportunity. And, although there is support for maximizing practice time at the class level (e.g. Silverman, 1985b; Silverman et al., 1988), as noted previously, not all students benefit equally.

Research on increasing students' appropriate task engagement

The early descriptive evidence of low ALT-PE levels quickly prompted studies designed to demonstrate the efficacy of interventions aimed at increasing those levels. There is now a considerable body of evidence across studies using varied methodologies indicating that such increases are well within reach. The types of strategies used to demonstrate such improvements have included changes in select teaching behaviors, instructional formats, modified games conditions (e.g. use of modified equipment, rules and team size), strengthened accountability mechanisms, and changes in the overall curricular focus.

Changing teaching behavior

A substantial amount of research has been conducted in which changes in teaching behaviors (e.g. management strategies, feedback, and enthusiasm) were manipulated or where different task progressions of teachers were modified to determine their relationship with students' opportunity to practice and their achievement. The behavior analysis research program at Ohio State University included several studies aimed at increasing students' ALT-PE by way of changes in selected teacher behaviors (Siedentop and Tannehill, 2000) with each reporting varying levels of success. While Whaley (1980) saw no increases in ALT-PE when teachers received feedback on their students' ALT-PE levels, Birdwell (1980) produced increases in students' ALT-PE by changing teacher behaviors that helped reduce management time and increased their verbal feedback to students. Beamer's (1982) in-service education had mixed results when applied at two middle schools.

Mancini et al. (1984) provide systematic feedback (based on interaction analysis data) to teachers exhibiting signs of burnout. Increases in students' ALT-PE levels were attributed to the intervention which resulted in teachers changing their interaction patterns with their students by using more praise, questions and being more accepting of students' ideas. Similarly, Randall and Imwold (1989) employed a systematic feedback intervention along with goal setting with student teachers. The intervention produced significant differences (13%) in ALT-PE levels favoring the student teachers who received the intervention.

Opportunities for appropriate practice are enhanced as well through the use of appropriate task progressions. For example, employing refinement tasks in developing (game) skills has been shown to be essential (e.g. Rink et al., 1992; Pellett and Harrison, 1995a). French et al. (1991) studied the role of task progressions in volleyball and determined that while good use of task progressions is important, a critical criterion is that the task difficulty is matched to the learners' incoming capabilities.

Teacher feedback and its relationship to student achievement in physical education has been studied extensively. Lee et al. (1993) noted that although teachers' use of instructional feedback is generally accepted as an essential teaching function, its real contribution may not be as prominent as once believed. However, there is evidence that successful/appropriate skill trials are more likely to occur if teachers' feedback immediately prior to them was specific and congruent (e.g. Pellett and Harrison, 1995b).

Instructional formats

Over the years, physical educators have been introduced to numerous instructional formats, ranging from more teacher-directed ones to more student-directed arrangements (Metzler, 2000). Well-known formats include (Class-Wide) Peer Tutoring (also referred to as reciprocal teaching), Cooperative Learning, Mastery Learning/Personalized System for Instruction (PSI), Tactical Games Model, and Programmed Instruction. Most formats have their roots in classroom instruction, but have been adapted for use in physical education settings. Experts generally recognize: (a) the value of the various formats, (b) that one format is not inherently better than the other, and (c) that decisions on which format to employ should be in large part dependent on the overall goals and objectives of the chosen content (Metzler, 2000). Along with their promotion in professional publications, there is also a growing database for them from the 'time/opportunity and learning' perspective.

Findings from classroom-based research on *peer tutoring* indicate strong support relative to student achievement (e.g. Delquadri et al., 1986; Greenwood et al., 1984, 1991). Improvements in achievement are generally attributed to increased use of individualized instruction and higher levels of opportunity to respond (as well as the provision of quality teacher feedback).

In physical education, variations of peer tutoring have produced increases in ALT-PE, OTR-PE, including Peer Tutoring (e.g. DePaepe, 1985; Fernandez-Vivo, 2002; Houston-Wilson et al., 1997; Lieberman et al., 2000; Webster, 1987); Classwide Peer-Tutoring (CWPT) (e.g. Johnson and Ward, 2001); and a derivative version of CWPT, called Peer-Mediated Accountability (PMA) (e.g. Crouch et al., 1997; Ward et al., 1998).

In peer tutoring, one student is paired with another student, where one serves as a surrogate teacher for the other. In cases where these roles are reversed it has become known as reciprocal teaching (e.g. Ernst and Byra, 1998). In CWPT, the entire class serves in the role of either tutor and/or tutee. PMA is an instructional format where teachers present students with specific performance targets, peers chart each other's progress, results get posted publicly, and performance is recognized. Johnson and Ward (2001) recommended CWPT for use when students are being introduced to skills they have not yet learned, while PMA would be appropriate for situations where students have reached a basic level of mastery, but where teachers might wish to focus on repetition or further refine of the performance of students.

There is good evidence to show that the various versions of peer-tutoring strategies influence students' appropriate task engagement favorably across settings and types of students. Many of the studies on (CW)PT have been conducted in settings where students with disabilities were paired with typically developing peers. The five studies listed above that employed a peer tutoring intervention each demonstrated increased levels of appropriate task engagement. In an elementary level study on striking skills where CWPT was employed, Johnson and Ward (2001) showed that while the time spent on subject matter-related task did not change, and the total number of skill trials actually decreased during the tutoring condition, the percent of appropriate trials increased compared to the baseline condition. Furthermore, the tutoring benefited both lower- and higher-skilled girls.

The efficacy of the PMA format was demonstrated in two studies relative to total skill trials and correct (or appropriate) skill trials in elementary-level classes with volleyball skills as the target skills. Crouch et al. (1997) demonstrated dramatic increases in both total trials and correct trials when employing 1-minute timed practice tasks. A second study at the same school level focused on students of varying skill levels with the basketball lay-up as the target skill (Ward et al., 1998). During PMA conditions, total trials for average- and low-skilled students increased, but the percent of correct trials did not change, supporting the notion that PMA would not be appropriate in cases where students are learning new skills.

Harrison et al. (1999) compared *command style* (akin to direct instruction) and *mastery learning* formats in beginning college-level volleyball classes. Players in both formats had similar averages for number of total trials, similar rates of improvement on the pass, serve and spike skills tests and their percentage of correct passes, sets, or serves in game play, suggesting that both formats allowed for improvement in game play.

Metzler (1986) compared a combination of the Mastery Learning and *PSI* format with traditional teacher-directed skill drill practice-oriented format in tennis. Over 9 days of data collection, average ALT-PE levels in the Mastery Learning/PSI format course were almost 15% higher than in the other course. The former group performed significantly better on isolated skills than did the non-mastery and control groups. However, there was no significant difference between groups in the performance of skills in a competitive game situation.

The principles and philosophy behind *games-based instructional formats* are rooted in the work of Thorpe, Bunker and Almond (1986) in Great Britain. In North America it has emerged as the Teaching Games for Understanding (TGfU) model (e.g. Griffin et al., 1997; Mitchell et al., 2003). Similarly, Launder (2001) proposed the Play Practice approach to teaching sport where a central goal is the development of "Game Sense". "Game Sense" reflects the players' ability to orchestrate their use of techniques, tactics and their understanding of game rules, so they can make better decisions in game play.

These approaches to teaching sports/games, by definition, expand not only the content taught, they also change the measurement of students' opportunity to learn. Beyond students' technique execution (i.e. how they pass, catch, set, volley etc.), measurements now also need to be made of their ability to mark/guard opponents, cover and support teammates, and their decision-making. Although the volume of professional literature continues to outweigh the research base, the latter is getting increased attention. Rink (1996) and her colleagues compared students' achievement and game play over the course of 3-week and 6-week badminton units taught using either a tactical or technique approach, and a combination of the two. They suggested that, if instructed well, both technical and tactical approaches (and a combination thereof) can produce improvement in achievement scores. They reported that the high amounts of motor engaged time and opportunity for appropriate practice were likely explanations for improvements in achievement scores. Furthermore, both lower- and higher-skilled students demonstrated improvements in achievement, but the former group still lagged behind the latter.

Research by McKenzie and his colleagues (McKenzie, 1983) at the university level demonstrated the efficacy of various forms of *programmed instruction* formats. The use of program boards in swimming produced higher levels of performance (defined as laps completed and practice tasks completed) (McKenzie and Rushall, 1974). In fencing, machine-based verbal cues on pre-recorded audio-cassettes were used during drill practice and (a) freed the instructor from having to verbally cue the entire class, (b) provided greater opportunity for the instructor to move about provide better-quality feedback to individual students, (c) allowed students to work at their own individual pace, and (d) produced higher levels of ALT-PE than during teacher-paced sessions (McKenzie et al., 1984).

Modified game conditions

Early research in this area indicated that during regulation-type games most students get exceedingly few opportunities to respond (e.g. Brown, 1986; Buck et al., 1991; Parker, 1984). This prompted a series of studies that focused on the influence of modifying different aspects of the game play context. Research on the effects of reducing team sizes has shown that at the 5th and 6th grade level regardless of skill level or gender, it improved both ALT-PE and OTR-PE for volleyball but not soccer and softball (Brown, 1986; Davis, 1991; Parker, 1984). When specific sequenced modified games in volleyball were employed, students also reached higher rates of OTR-PE compared to the regulation game (Davis, 1991).

In 6th grade volleyball, modified rules (e.g. allowing one bounce; requiring two touches per side) did not change OTR-PE levels, but changes in the type of equipment in volleyball did (Lawless, 1984). Pellett and Lox (1998) showed that the use of racquets with larger head-size produced higher rates of appropriate trials (even though the total rate of trials was not different) and better end-of-course achievement scores than regular-sized racquets. Changing racquet length did help players perform better on a forehand achievement test in tennis (favoring the shorter racquet length), but during game play, total trials and successful trials were similar regardless of racquet length (Pellett and Lox, 1997). Pellett et al. (1994) also found that differently weighted balls in middle-school volleyball influenced the success rate of sets and underhand serves, with higher success coming in games with lighter balls, supporting the notion that "slowing the game down" in the early stages of learning may help students.

Accountability mechanisms

The ecological task system framework, first proposed by Doyle (1979) and adapted for physical education (Tousignant and Siedentop, 1983), formed the basis for a series of research studies that demonstrated the reciprocal nature of influence among teachers' and students' actions and pointed to the central role of teachers' active supervision function as an informal accountability mechanism. The level of explicitness, clarity and risk that teachers convey when assigning learning tasks influences the students' initial attempts at the task. However, it is the teachers' level of active supervision (coupled with more formal accountability mechanisms) that will determine the degree to which students will modify the assigned task to make it either easier or more challenging (e.g. Graham, 1987; Hastie and Saunders, 1990, 1991; Jones, 1992; Lund, 1990; Marks, 1988; Schuldheisz and van der Mars, 2001; Sariscsany et al., 1995; Silverman et al., 1995, 1998; van der Mars et al., 1994, 1998). Related to this, the importance of clear and explicit communication with students through the use of effective learning cues and demonstrations is well documented (Rink, 2003).

The aforementioned work by Ward and his colleagues in which Peer Mediated Accountability (PMA) formats were employed aligns very well with this research. The strength of these findings lies in the fact that this relationship between accountability and opportunity to respond holds across content, students of different skill levels and grade levels.

In summary, Sport Pedagogy research on time/opportunity to learn has amassed a sizable empirical base. It verifies that teachers' curricular and instructional decisions directly influence students' learning opportunities in class, and performance on learning outcome measures.

Physical education and academic achievement

Currently, the public health agenda is the dominant basis for defending physical education's presence in schools. As noted earlier, NCLB has increased pressures on schools to improve academic performance for all students (US Department of Education, 2002). Consequently, school districts have reconsidered how the available resources (including school time) can be best utilized, and allocated physical education time (in addition to other subject matters such as art, music, and foreign languages) are obvious targets for reduction. This has renewed the interest in studying the link between physical activity and cognitive functioning, as well as between time in physical education and academic achievement.

Historically, both physical education teachers and professional organizations have argued that quality daily physical education is vital to students' academic performance in the classroom. That is, the time spent in physical education contributes to students' cognitive functioning which will help improve performance on academic achievement tests. A distinction is made here between the variables "cognitive functioning" and "academic achievement", because of the way in which studies have been designed methodologically. For example, in the research linking physical activity and cognitive functioning, cognitive functioning often is measured in ways other than the typical standardized academic achievement tests. In that same line of research, physical activity is often operationalized in ways other than "time allocated to physical education per week", and some studies have actually been conducted in more laboratory-based settings.

Physical activity and cognitive functioning

Arguments for the link between physical activity and cognitive functioning use two distinct lines of reasoning. The first notes how physical exertion produces changes in selected physiological mechanisms, including increased blood flow to the brain, changes in brain neurotransmitters, and arousal levels. Students' cognitive function is purportedly improved as a consequence of these physiological changes. The second explanation is based more on learning and developmental mechanisms, where it is argued that movement stimulates cognitive development (e.g. Pica, 1997).

Two meta-analyses have been completed that focused specifically on studies linking physical activity (either acute or long-term) with cognitive functioning measures. Etnier et al. (1997) reviewed 135 studies that when taken together provided mixed results. Given the reported overall effect size (0.25), the authors concluded that exercise has a small but positive influence on cognition, with the caveat that many studies (especially those with larger effect sizes) lacked experimental rigor.

More recently, Sibley and Etnier (2003) completed a meta-analysis with more rigorous study inclusion criteria. The studies included ($n = 44$) had a range of physical activity protocols ranging from 10 minutes of circuit training, 6 weeks of strength training, 9 months of daily physical education classes to 6 years of daily physical education classes. Cognitive functioning measures ranged from intelligence quotient measurement, memory tests, math tests, verbal tests, creativity tests, concentration tests to perceptual skills tests. The overall effect size was 0.32, again pointing to a small but positive association with cognitive functioning. Furthermore, the association was stronger for middle and elementary school students than for high school students. The type of physical activity (aerobic- versus strength-related) did not change the relationship and the relationship holds true for student with physical and mental disabilities, and the strongest associations occurred when using academic achievement and IQ as indicators of cognitive functioning. However, the authors also warned that these results are by no means an indication that physical activity *causes* improved cognitive functioning (Sibley and Etnier, 2003).

Time in physical education and academic achievement

A small number of large school-based research projects have been conducted over the last three decades in France, Canada, Australia, and the United States linking time in physical education and academic achievement. In France, students who received 8 hours of physical education per week were compared to students in a 1 hour per week physical education program on achievement. Although questioned in terms of scientific rigor (Shephard, 1997), the former group performed better in academic subjects, as well as on indicators of physical and psychological health).

The Trois-Rivières project (Shephard et al., 1994, 1984) in Canada in the 1970s showed that students (Grades 1–6) who had received increased time in physical education and decreased time in classroom subjects performed better both on physical fitness and motor skills indicators, had increased levels of physical activity outside of school (especially on weekends) and higher achievement scores in math compared to students receiving less time in physical education. At the same time, the almost 14% drop in time allocated for academic classroom subjects in the experimental group produced no reduction in academic achievement for other subject areas.

Although more viewed from a health perspective, recent follow-up studies of the participants showed that: (a) females were more active, (b) men and women perceived themselves as more healthy, (c) females reported fewer lower back problems, (d) fewer men smoked cigarettes, (e) men and women reported greater dependence on exercise, and (f) had a higher proportion of participants who viewed the elementary school physical education experience as "very satisfying" (Shephard and Trudeau, 2000; Trudeau et al., 1998, 1999). While it would be difficult to argue that even the strongest of elementary physical education programs could exert such long-term influence, these studies at the very least demonstrate that strong physical education programs can/may serve as a foundation for developing the needed physical activity habits that reap health benefits later on in life.

In South Australia, an experimental study at the elementary school level students by Dwyer et al. (1983) compared classes of students with increased time allocated to physical education to those with increased time for academic subjects. Improvements in performance on physiological and physical fitness indicators favored those students who received more time in Physical Education. As was the case in the Trois-Rivières project, no differences were found between the two student groups on academic grades. However, Maynard et al. (1987) conducted a follow-up study showing that students in the experimental group (more physical education) received higher grades in mathematics and reading and were rated higher by their teachers on overall classroom conduct.

In the United States, Sallis et al. (1999) demonstrated that elementary school students who were exposed to the SPARK curriculum taught by licensed physical education specialists over a 2-year period (which doubled the amount of physical education class time per week) performed better on reading tests. Furthermore, the increased time in physical education did not correlate with poorer achievement in other academic subjects. The authors suggested that increased time in health-related physical education may have positive effects on students' academic achievement.

Finally, Wilkins et al. (2003) conducted a state-wide project in the state of Virginia to study: (a) the effects of the implementation of "high-stakes" testing in academic subjects on class time allocated to art, music and physical education (taught by specialists only), and (b) whether any decreases in time allocated to these three subjects were accompanied by better student performance on the state-wide core subject tests. Results showed that in schools where the time for art, music and physical education was either reduced or eliminated in favor of more time for academic subjects, students did not perform any better on the statewide tests.

Thus, given the "best available knowledge" to date, it appears that (a) increased time in physical education does not impede students' performance in classroom academic performance, (b) increased time in physical education may make small positive contributions to academic performance, and (c) decreased time allotments for physical education in favor of academic subject does not necessarily translate into improved academic performance.

The link between time in physical education (or time in physical activity) and academic achievement is clearly not linear, and presenting it as such may do more harm than good. If it were a linear relationship, most high schools in the United States should be overrun with athletic geniuses, based on the time spent by high school athletes in daily practices …

Research on time and learning: its critics

Classroom research scholars have voiced doubt about the value and importance of the research on instructional time and learning and the resulting knowledge base. Critics have used words such as "truisms", "trivial" and "commonsensical" to describe the overall findings (e.g. Jackson, 1985; Philips, 1985). Jackson lamented the fact that the interest in research on time represented a questionable return to an efficiency-driven perspective of schooling, and doubted that continued efforts in this line of research would further a genuine understanding and insight into the teaching–learning process.

Karweit (1984) noted the difficulties involved in translating seemingly practical research findings on instructional time into practice for the purpose of improving schooling. Borrowing from the emerging ecological perspective of classroom dynamics (Doyle, 1979) she pointed out that in the BTES research program the relationship between teacher and student activities was viewed from a one-directional perspective (i.e. the teacher governs the students' actions).

One of the key concerns voiced about research on student engagement in learning tasks variables is related to its measurement. For example, Karweit (1985) has argued that when students are observed, using a definition of attention-to-task behavior that includes eye movement and/or eye contact with the teacher, the possibility that a student might be thinking about something entirely unrelated to the topic at hand in the lesson is ignored. That is, attention to the task can at best only be inferred.

Shulman (1986) noted that despite the effort to move beyond the process–product research paradigm, the ALT research efforts continued to focus on individual students, rather than the classroom as the unit of analysis and viewed the learning process rather passively, as opposed to one of active cognitive processing; a view rooted in cognitive psychology.

Though not always pointing specifically to the line of research on time and learning, Sport Pedagogy scholars have also offered criticisms and critiques of this type of research, given its underlying deterministic and technocratic orientation (e.g. Kirk, 1989; Schempp, 1987; Tinning, 1987). However, Sparkes (1991) recognized the strength, limits and contributions of multiple research traditions, and sought balance in this discourse by arguing for the need for poly-vocality among the varying perspectives.

Why the time/opportunity to learn findings are important

With the emergence of new research paradigms in the 1980s, interest in studying time-based variables waned. And while the research on variables that influence students' OTR-PE continues, numerous other lines of inquiry have blossomed. As the Sport Pedagogy research community matures beyond the point where theoretical perspectives are viewed hierarchically (i.e. "Mine is better than yours"), the call for the development and maintenance of "collective memory" is essential (Macdonald et al., 2002). Thus, it is appropriate to emphasize the reasons why research findings of time-based dimensions are still important today.

First, the strength of the relationships between classroom processes and students' achievement were by all standards very strong, especially given the complex and dynamic nature of classroom life. Especially in the case of lower-ability students in reading and math, instructional time variables explained as much as 36% of the variance in achievement measures. Previously, no other group of variables (and few since!) has managed to demonstrate such predictive power. While in physical education contexts the variance explained by ALT-PE and/or OTR-PE never reached the same levels, it is likely that this is partly the result of both how appropriate student engagement and achievement were conceptualized and measured. This will be addressed further in a later section.

Second, the research findings on time/opportunity and learning demonstrated that there are tangible and observable process indicators of student learning. As such, appropriate/successful task engagement (expressed in either time or frequency) is now widely accepted as a "proxy" indicator for learning (Siedentop, 2002a). It has been argued that ALT-PE and OTR-PE are perhaps better indicators of learning than students' performance on achievement test, especially in the case where the match between the content covered in the classroom and that on the achievement test is low (Berliner, 1990). From a practical perspective, where formal achievement tests generally occur toward the end of a grading period or school year, data on students' appropriate/successful task engagement offers teachers an on-going indicator of student learning.

Third, it offers a strong evidence base for current professional textbooks used in physical education teacher education courses provide extensive information on this important dimension of the teaching– learning process (e.g. Darst and Pangrazi, 2002; Graham, 2001; Rink, 2002; Siedentop and Tannehill, 2000; Siedentop et al., 2004). They include extensive information on developing management and organizational routines, and how these can be taught to students.

Fourth, the research on time-/opportunity-based variables and student learning in classrooms demonstrates conclusively that the quality of instruction does make a significant difference. The manner in which teachers plan and design their instruction, deliver content, monitor their students' classroom work, provide feedback to their students and so on directly influences both the quantity and quality of the engagement. This is especially important for physical education programs. In the current political and economic climate for education, where improvement in academic achievement and increased accountability for teacher performance reigns, increases in the frequency or duration of physical education lesson are highly unlikely. And, thus, it is essential that programs offer students the maximum opportunity that is realistically possible.

Fifth, from a measurement perspective it would appear that sport pedagogy researchers have at least one advantage over those conducting teaching research in classrooms. As noted earlier, when collecting data in classrooms observers have to infer that a student is "attending to" or engaged by looking at a book or worksheet. In physical education, learning tasks in the psychomotor domain are movement-based, and, thus, directly observable.

Time and learning in physical education: work yet to be done

In his pessimistic (by his own admission) closing comments of a review of research on time in Sport Pedagogy, Metzler (1989) noted that Sport Pedagogy researchers often focus on a particular line of research for a short while, only to move on to study, other perhaps more sexy, variables. Although research on time-based variables has waned, efforts using the frequency-based OTR-PE measure have continued steadily.

What follows is not a long laundry list of specific research questions, but rather suggestions for general directions that take into consideration where the field is now, compared to the earliest days of research on time and learning.

As noted earlier, early research on time and learning in physical education was focused entirely on skill learning outcomes. Our historic allegiance to teaching sport content, and the manner in which it is typically taught is reflected in both the focus and design of the research. Sport has been taught by way of technique-oriented approaches. This approach has directly influenced how studies on time/opportunity and learning were designed.

Two interrelated developments in our field should help jumpstart the time/opportunity and learning line of research. They include the recent proliferation of games-based instruction by way of the Teaching Games for Understanding (TGfU) model and Play Practice (e.g., Griffin et al., 1997; Kirk and McPhail, 2002, Launder, 2001; Mitchell et al., 2003) and the emergence of authentic assessment practices.

In games-based teaching of sports much greater emphasis is placed on developing students' understanding of and performance in the many tactical aspects of game play. Tactical tasks of creating space, supporting and covering teammates, playing/returning to base position, decision-making are as fundamental to game play as is learning to effectively trap, catch, pass, field and so on. A typical lesson has students play in modified games where specific tactical features are accentuated. This is followed by a brief period of teacher questioning/discussion with students to contextualize the subsequent skill practice, and a return to additional game play where it is presumed that students, now with better understanding, will improve their game play. Over time, teachers raise the tactical complexity of modified games.

Future teacher effectiveness research would need to solve two problems. The first is the development and use of developmentally appropriate assessment tasks, in which students can demonstrate their learning as players. And second, effective assessment tools need to be developed that teachers and researchers can employ to provide credible evidence of learning. Historically, measurement experts involved in developing such tools have concentrated largely on problems of instrument validity and reliability. Given the predominant emphasis on learning mostly isolated techniques, it is not surprising that the skills assessment tasks that dominated the landscape also tested exactly that: the ability to perform the technique (e.g. volleyball forearm pass). Fundamentally, this enabled measurement experts to claim skill test validity. The emergence of Teaching Games for Understanding and Play Practice approaches to instruction (along with the authentic assessment movement) has prompted an interest in developing more ecologically valid assessment tools.

Relative to developing appropriate assessment tasks, Kirk (2005) points to promising efforts in England. Assessment tasks have been developed as a result of implementation of a National Curriculum for Physical Education (England and Wales). The assessment tasks (in the form of modified games) become increasingly complex as students progress through the physical education program.

With regard to the development of assessment templates, games-based instruction proponents have developed various assessment protocols. For example, the Games Performance Assessment Instrument (GPAI) (Oslin et al., 1998) offers quantitative information about learners' game involvement and game performance on both technical and tactical components of game play. Formative assessment tools with similar performance indices have been developed in Canada and France (Gréhaigne and Godbout 1998; Richard et al., 1999). These research tools would provide the type of authentic achievement indicators that have been missing from previous teacher effectiveness studies in physical education. Other, more teacher-friendly tools might include rating scale-based assessment templates (Siedentop et al., 2004). Such ratings templates would include key descriptors for each rating level that provide observable indicators of student learning. Such are sorely needed if we expect teachers to actually incorporate assessment of student learning in their programs.

Rink (1996) and her colleagues conducted a series of studies comparing technical and tactical approaches to teaching sports and games to determine differential learning experiences of students. Their choice of data collection instruments, inclusion of gender and skill level as mediating variables and length of the units of instruction are three important features that can serve as a guide for future teacher effectiveness research within games-based instruction.

As research surrounding games-based teaching develops further at a more fine-grained level, the measurement tools need to be equally sensitive. The research by Rink and her colleagues is a good example of connecting established variables of student learning opportunities (i.e. engaged time, OTR-PE) with newer variables (e.g. Game decisions, execution) (Rink, 1996).

Choosing observation tactics

A related measurement question that deserves to be revisited is the question about choosing the more appropriate observation tactic. The GPAI (and others like it) is an event recording tool, where marking/guarding of opponents, covering and supporting teammates, and decision-making are measured as if they are discrete occurrences. However, in the case of invasion games such as soccer, netball, rugby, basketball, and ultimate Frisbee, play tends to be more continuous; it has flow. During that time, even in a modified 4 versus 4 game, players will spend the majority of their time not in possession of the ball. Based on the lenses of tactical awareness, they actively engage in positioning, guarding, supporting and so on. In the ALT-PE and OTR-PE observation instruments these tactical components were never explicitly mentioned or included in any of the definitions of "appropriate task engagement". Thus, a student observed in a soccer or softball game who was not actually passing, striking, controlling, fielding or shooting a ball likely was not coded as accruing ALT-PE. It may prove fruitful, to resurrect time-based measurements of these same aspects of game play. An example of this already exists for a study on net games (i.e. badminton) (Graham et al., 1996).

Analysis of gender and skill level

That same study also offers a reminder that future research within games-based instruction must include student gender and skill level as mediating variables. Graham et al. (1996) reported positive results on students' affective components for both gender and skill level.

Length of units

One of the recognized limitations of Sport Pedagogy teacher effectiveness has been the short duration of the instruction during which learning was to occur. Many studies producing non-significant differences likely have ended up in file drawers as a consequence of units being too short. Considering the "time needed to learn" component of Carroll's (1963) Mastery Learning model, the comment made by Rink et al. (1996b) relative to the 6-week unit of badminton is most poignant: "The students in this study needed 6-weeks of good instruction to get out of the cooperative stage of development and into the competitive play". (p. 502). Taking this a step further, the development of 'Game Sense' (Launder, 2001) likely requires multiple years of good instruction.

This last point is, of course, closely related to program/school level time allocation for physical education. Physical education teachers have to work within the confines of a set number of minutes per week. How they build the curriculum within those available minutes will influence if/how many students will experience the early onset of game sense. More extensive research on the effective implementation of curriculum models such as Sport Education (Siedentop et al., 2004) can offer insight into what is reasonable to expect from teachers' efforts.

Conclusion

This chapter provided an overview of research in physical education on the link between time (and opportunity) and student learning from a skill outcomes perspective. Of the many lines of inquiry in Sport Pedagogy, this one has had an enormous impact on how we converse about teaching and how we prepare teachers. While time and opportunity are certainly not the sole variables of importance, they do tell an important story:

1. Over the last two decades much has been learned about time and opportunity for learning at the individual and class level, what variables will influence both, as well as effective strategies to increase students' learning opportunities.
2. There is a descriptive database on time variables in physical education at state/national levels.
3. Physical education programs are viewed as key points of impact in national efforts to reverse trends of obesity and physical activity.
4. Decisions made at each level (i.e. state, district, school, class) impact students' learning time and opportunity at the next level below.
5. Sport Pedagogy research in this line of inquiry should expand its focus to the following areas: effectiveness of strategies aimed at increasing physical activity beyond class periods (most notably at the high school level); impact of strategies aimed at changing public policy relative to learning time and opportunity in school physical education.

Time is a precious resource for student learning in physical education. Over the past decades physical education has lost significant ground in allocated curriculum time during the school week. It is imperative that further loss is eliminated, and that the time we can give to students is used wisely.

References

AAHPER (1965). *Volleyball skills test manual.* Reston, VA.

Anderson, W.G. and Barrette, G.T. (Eds.), (1978). *What's going on in gym: Descriptive studies of physical education classes.* Newton, CT: Motor Skills-Theory into Practice.

Aufderheide, S. (1983). ALT-PE in mainstreamed physical education classes. *Journal of Teaching in Physical Education,* 1(Summer Monograph): 22–26.

Aufderheide, S., McKenzie, T.L. and Knowles, C. (1982). Effects of individualized instruction on handicapped and nonhandicapped students in elementary physical education. *Journal of Teaching in Physical Education,* 1(3): 22–26.

Ashy, M.H., Lee, A.M. and Landin, D.K. (1988). Relationship of practice using correct technique to achievement in a motor skill. *Journal of Teaching in Physical Education,* 7: 115–120.

Beamer, D.W. (1982). The effects of an inservice education program on the academic learning time of selected students in physical education. *Dissertation Abstracts International,* 43: 08A. (UMI No. 8300208).

Berliner, D.C. (1979). Tempus educare. In P.L. Peterson and H.J. Walberg (Eds), *Research on teaching: Concepts, findings, and implications* (pp. 120–135). Berkeley, CA: McCutchan.

Berliner, D.C. (1990). What's all the fuss about instructional time? In M. Ben-Peretz and R. Bromme (Eds.), *The nature of time in schools: Theoretical concepts, practitioner perceptions* (pp. 3–35). New York: Teachers College Press.

Berliner, D.C. (1994). Expertise: The wonder of exemplary performance. In J.N. Mangieri and C. Collins-Block (Eds.), *Creating powerful thinking in teachers and students* (pp. 161–186). Fort Worth, TX. Holt, Rinehart & Winston.

Birdwell, D. (1980). The effects of modification of teacher behavior on the academic learning time of selected students in physical education. *Dissertation Abstracts International,* 41: 1472A. (UMI No. 8022239).

Bloom, B.S. (1968). Learning for mastery. *Evaluation comment,* 1(2), University of California at Los Angeles, Center for the Study of Evaluation. Reprinted in the C.W. Fisher and D.C. Berliner (Eds.), (1985), *Perspectives on instructional time* (pp. 73–93). New York: Longman.

Brown, W.E. (1986). The effects of volleyball and soccer game modifications on student opportunity to participate in fifth grade physical education classes (time-on-task). *Dissertation Abstracts International, 42,* 08A. (UMI No.8625185).

Buck, M.M., Harrison, J.M. and Bryce, G.R. (1991). An analysis of learning trials and their relationship to achievement in volleyball. *Journal of Teaching Physical Education,* 10: 134–152.

Carroll, J.B. (1963). A model of school learning. *Teachers College Record,* 64: 723–733.

Corbin, C.B. (2002). Physical activity for everyone: What every physical educator should know about promoting lifelong physical activity. *Journal of Teaching in Physical Education,* 21: 128–144.

Crouch, D.W., Ward, P. and Patrick, C.A. (1997). The effects of peer-mediated accountability on task accomplishment. *Journal of Teaching in Physical Education,* 17: 26–39.

Darst, P.W. and Pangrazi, R.P. (2002). Dynamic physical education for secondary school students. 4th ed. Needham Heights, MA: Allyn & Bacon.

Darst, P.W., Zakrajsek, D. and Mancini, V.H. (Eds.) (1989). *Analyzing physical education and sport instruction* 2nd edn. Champaign, IL: Human Kinetics.

Davis, C.I. (1991). The effects of game modifications on opportunities to respond in elementary volleyball classes. *Dissertation Abstracts International, 52:* 02A. (UMI No.9120650).

DeKnop, P. (1986). Relationship of specified teacher behaviors to student gain on tennis. *Journal of Teaching in Physical Education,* 5: 71–78.

Delquadri, J., Greenwood, C., Whorton, D., Carta, J. and Hall, R. (1986). Class-wide peer tutoring. *Exceptional Children, 52*: 535–542.

DePeape, J. (1985). The influence of three least restrictive environments on the content motor-ALT and performance of moderately mentally retarded students. *Journal of Teaching in Physical Education, 5*: 34–41.

Doyle, W. (1979). Classroom tasks and students' abilities. In P.L. Peterson and H.J. Walberg (Eds.), *Research on teaching: Concepts, findings, and implications* (pp. 183–209). Berkeley, CA: McCutchan.

Dugas, D. (1983). Relationships among process and product variables in an experimental teaching unit. *Dissertation Abstract International, 44*: 2709A. (UMI No. 8400193).

Dwyer, T., Coonan, W.E., Leitch, D.R., Hetzel, B.S. and Baghurst, P.A. (1983). An investigation of the effects of daily physical activity on the health of primary school students in South Australia, *International Journal of Epidemiology, 12*: 308–312.

Ericsson, K.A. (Ed.) (1996). *The road to excellence: The acquisition of expert performance in the arts and sciences, sports and games.* Mahwah, NJ: Lawrence Erlbaum.

Ericsson, K.A., Krampe, R.T. and Tesch-Römer, C. (1993). The role of deliberate practice in the acquisition of expert performance. *Psychological Review, 100*: 363–406.

Ernst, M. and Byra, M. (1998). Pairing learners in the reciprocal style of teaching: Influence on student skill, knowledge, and socialization. *Physical Educator, 55*: 24–37.

Etnier, J.L., Salazar, W., Landers, D.M., Petruzello, S.J., Han, M. and Nowell, P. (1997). The influence of physical fitness and exercise upon cognitive functioning: a meta-analysis. *Journal of Sport & Exercise Psychology, 19*: 249–277.

Fernandez-Vivo, M. (2002). The effects of peer tutoring on the academic learning time in physical education (ALT-PE) of elementary school students with visual impairments in inclusive physical education classes. *Dissertation Abstracts International, 63*: 09A. (UMI No. 13065487).

Fisher, C.W., Berliner, D.C., Filby, N.N., Marliave, R., Cahen, L.S. and Dishaw, M.M. (1980). *Teaching behavior, academic learning time, and student achievement: An overview.* Washington, DC: National Institute of Education.

French, K.E., Rink, J.E., Rikard, L., Mays, A., Lynn, S. and Werner, P. (1991). The effects of practice progressions on learning two volleyball skills. *Journal of Teaching in Physical Education, 10*: 261–274.

Gagnon, J., Tousignant, M. and Martel, D. (1989). Academic learning time in physical education classes for mentally handicapped students. *Adapted Physical Activity Quarterly, 6*: 280–289.

Graham, G. (1983). Review and implications of physical education experimental teaching unit research. In T. Templin and J. Olson (Eds.). *Teaching in physical education* (pp. 244–253). Champaign, IL: Human Kinetics.

Graham, G. (2001). *Teaching physical education: Becoming a master teacher* (2nd ed.). Champaign, IL: Human Kinetics.

Graham, G., Soares, P. and Harrington, W. (1983). Experienced physical education teachers' effectiveness with intact classes of fourth and/or fifth grade students: An ETU study. *Journal of Teaching in Physical Education, 2(2)*: 3–14.

Graham, G., Holt-Hale, S.A. and Parker, M. (2004). *Children moving: A reflective approach to teaching physical education.* 6th ed. Boston, MA: McGraw Hill.

Graham, K.C. (1987). A description of academic work and student performance during a middle school volleyball unit. *Journal of Teaching in Physical Education, 7*: 22–37.

Graham, K.C., Ellis, S.D., Williams, C.D., Kwak, E.C. and Werner, P.H. (1996). High- and low-skilled target students' academic achievement and instructional performance in a 6–week badminton unit. *Journal of Teaching in Physical Education, 15*: 477–489.

Grant, B., Ballard, K. and Glynn, T (1989). Student behavior in physical education lessons: A comparison among student achievement groups. *Journal of Educational Research, 82*: 216–226.

Greenwood, C.R., Delquardi, J.C. and Hall, R.V. (1984). Opportunity to respond and student academic performance. In W.L. Heward, T.E. Heron, D.S. Hill and J. Trap-Porter (Eds.), *Focus on behavior analysis in education* (pp. 58–88). Columbus, OH: Merrill.

Greenwood, C.R., Maheady, L. and Carta, J.J. (1991). Peer tutoring programs in the regular education classroom. In G. Stoner, M. Shinn and H. Walker (Eds), *Intervention for achievement and behavior problems* (pp. 179–200). Washington, DC: National Association for Psychologists.

Grehaigne, J.-F. and Godbout, P. (1998). Formative assessments in team sports in a tactical approach context. *Journal of Physical Education, Recreation, and Dance, 69(1)*: 46–51.

Griffin, L.L., Mitchell, S.A. and Oslin, J.L. (1997). *Teaching sports concepts and skills: A tactical games approach.* Champaign, IL: Human Kinetics.

Harnischfeger, A. and Wiley, D.E. (1985). Origins of active learning time. In C.W. Fisher and D.C. Berliner (Eds.), *Perspectives on instructional time* (pp. 133–156). New York: Longman.

Harrison, J.M., Preece, L.A., Blakemore, C.L., Richards, R.P., Wilkinson, C. and Fellingham, G.W. (1999). Effects of two instructional models–skill teaching and mastery learning–on skill development, knowledge, self-efficacy, and game play in volleyball. *Journal of Teaching in Physical Education, 19*: 34–57.

Hastie, P.A. and Saunders, J.E. (1990). A study of monitoring in secondary school physical education. *Journal of Classroom Interaction, 25*: 47–54.

Hastie, P.A. and Saunders, J.E. (1991). Accountability in secondary school physical education. *Teaching and Teacher Education, 7*: 373–382.

Houston-Wilson, C., Dunn, J., van der Mars, H. and McCubbin, J. (1997). The effect of peer tutoring on motor performance in integrated physical education classes. *Adapted Physical Activity Quarterly, 14*: 298–313.

Jackson, P. W. (1985). Time off-task at a time-on-task conference. In C.W. Fisher and D.C. Berliner (Eds.)

(1985). *Perspectives on instructional time* (pp. 301–307). New York: Longman.

Johnson, M. and Ward, P. (2001). Effects of classwide peer tutoring on correct performance of striking skills in 3rd grade physical education. *Journal of Teaching in Physical Education, 20*: 247–263.

Jones, D.L. (1992). Analysis of task systems in elementary physical education classes. *Journal of Teaching in Physical Education, 11*: 411–425.

Karweit, N. (1984). *Time-on-task: A research review.* Research Report No. 332. Baltimore, MD: The Johns Hopkins University, Center for Social Organization of Schools.

Karweit, N. (1985). Timescales, learning events, and productive instruction. In C.W. Fisher and D.C. Berliner (Eds.) (1985). *Perspectives on instructional time* (pp. 169–185). New York: Longman.

Kirk, D. (1989). The orthodoxy in RT-PE and the research/practice gap: A critique and an alternative view. *Journal of Teaching in Physical Education, 8*: 123–130.

Kirk, D. (2005). Model-based teaching and assessment in physical education: The Tactical Games model. In K. Green and K. Hardman (Eds.), *Physical education: Essential issues* (pp. 128–142). London: Sage.

Kirk, D. and MacPhail, A. (2002). Teaching games for understanding and situated learning: Rethinking the Bunker-Thorpe model. *Journal of Teaching in Physical Education, 21*: 177–192.

Launder, A.G. (2001). *Play practice: The games approach to teaching and coaching sports.* Champaign, IL: Human Kinetics.

Lawless, S.J. (1984). The effects of volleyball game modifications on children's opportunity to respond and academic learning time (behavior analysis, elementary). *Dissertation Abstracts International, 45*: 08A. (UMI No. 8426431).

Lee, A.M., Keh, N.C. and McGill, R.A. (1993). Instructional effects of teacher feedback in physical education. *Journal of Teaching in Physical Education, 12*: 228–243.

Lieberman, L., Dunn, J.M., van der Mars, H. and McCubbin, J. (2000). The effect of trained hearing peer tutors on the physical activity levels of deaf students in inclusive elementary school physical education classes. *Adapted Physical Activity Quarterly, 17*: 20–39.

Luke, M. (1989). Research on class management and organization: Review with implications for current practice. *Quest, 41*: 55–67.

Lund, J. (1990). Student performance and accountability conditions in physical education. *Dissertation Abstracts International. 51*: 3358A. (UMI No. 9105161).

Macdonald, D., Kirk, D., Metzler, M., Nilges, L.M., Schempp, P. and Wright, J. (2002). It's all very well, in theory: Theoretical perspectives and their applications in contemporary pedagogical research. *Quest, 54*: 133–156.

Mancini, V.H., Wuest, D., Vantine, K. and Clark, E. (1984). The use of instruction and supervision in interaction analysis on burned-out teachers: Its effects on teaching behaviors, level of burnout, and academic learning time. *Journal of Teaching in Physical Education, 3(2)*: 29–46.

Marks, M. (1988). Development of a system for the observation of task structures in physical education. *Dissertation Abstracts International, 49*: 09a. (UMI No. 8824565).

Maynard, E., Coonan, W., Worsley, A., Dwyer, T. and Baghurst, P. (1987). The development of the lifestyle education program in Australia. In B.S. Hetzel and G.S. Berenson (eds.), *Cardiovascular risk factors in children: Epidemiology and prevention* (pp. 123–149). Amsterdam: Elsevier.

McKenzie, T.L. (1983). Machine-paced instruction: Innovations for improving teaching in physical education. In T. Templin and J. Olson (Eds.), *Teaching in physical education* (pp. 224–231). Champaign, IL: Human Kinetics.

McKenzie, T.L. and Rushall, B. (1974). Effects of self-recording on attendance and performance in a competitive swimming training environment. *Journal of Applied Behavior Analysis, 7*: 199–206.

McKenzie, T.L., Clark, E.K. and McKenzie, R. (1984). Instructional strategies: Influence on teacher and student behavior. *Journal of Teaching in Physical Education, 3(2)*: 20–28.

Metzler, M.W. (1979). *The measurement of academic learning time in physical education.* Unpublished doctoral dissertation, The Ohio State University, Columbus.

Metzler, M.W. (1983). Using academic learning time in process-product studies with experimental teaching units. In T. Templin and J. Olson (Eds.), *Teaching in physical education* (pp. 185–196). Champaign, IL: Human Kinetics.

Metzler, M.W. (1986). Analysis of a Mastery Learning/Personalized System of Instruction for teaching tennis. In M. Pieron and G. Graham (Eds.), *The 1984 Olympic scientific congress proceedings, volume 6: Sport Pedagogy* (pp. 63–70). Champaign. IL: Human Kinetics.

Metzler, M.W. (1989). A review of research on time in sport pedagogy. *Journal of Teaching in Physical Education, 8*: 87–103.

Metzler, M.W. (2000). *Instructional models for physical education.* Boston MA: Allyn and Bacon.

Mitchell, S.A., Oslin, J.L. and Griffin, L.L. (2003). *Sport foundations for elementary physical education.* Champaign, IL: Human Kinetics.

Oslin, J.L., Mitchell, S.A. and Griffin, L.L. (1998). The Game Performance Assessment Instrument (GPAI): Development and preliminary validation. *Journal of Teaching Physical Education, 17*: 231–243.

Parker, M. (1984). The effects of game modifications on the nature and extent of the skill involvement of students in volleyball and softball (opportunity, respond, academic learning time)'. *Dissertation Abstracts International, 46*: 01A. (UMI No. 8504064).

Parker, M. and O'Sullivan, M. (1983). Modifying ALT-PE for game play contexts and other considerations. In P. Dodds and F. Rife (Eds.), Time to learn in physical education: History, completed research, and potential future for academic learning time in physical education. *Journal of Teaching in Physical Education,* 3(Monograph 1): 8–10.

Pellett, T.L. and Harrison, J.M. (1995a). The influence of refinement on female junior high school students' volleyball practice success and achievement. *Journal of Teaching in Physical Education, 15:* 41–52.

Pellett, T.L. and Harrison, J.M. (1995b). The influence of a teacher's specific, congruent, and corrective feedback on female junior high school students' immediate volleyball practice success. *Journal of Teaching in Physical Education, 15:* 53–63.

Pellett, T.L. and Lox, C.L. (1997). Tennis racket length comparisons and their effect on beginning college players' playing success and achievement. *Journal of Teaching in Physical Education, 16:* 490–499.

Pellett, T.L. and Lox, C.L. (1998). Tennis racket head-size comparisons and their effect on beginning college players' achievement and self-efficacy. *Journal of Teaching in Physical Education, 17:* 453–467.

Pellett, T.L., Henschel-Pellett, H.A. and Harrison, J.M. (1994). Influence of ball weight on junior high school girls' volleyball performance. *Perceptual and Motor Skills, 78:* 1379–1384.

Phillips, D.A. and Carlisle, C. (1983). A comparison of physical education teachers categorized as most and least effective. *Journal of Teaching Physical Education, 2(3):* 55–67.

Phillips. D.C. (1985). The uses and abuse of truisms. In C.W. Fisher and D.C. Berliner (Eds.), *Perspectives on instructional time* (pp. 309–316). New York: Longman.

Pica, R. (1997). Beyond physical development: Why young children need to move. *Young Children, 52(4):* 4–11.

Pieron, M. (1982a). Effectiveness of teaching a psychomotor task: Study in a micro-teaching setting. In M. Pieron and J.T.F. Cheffers (Eds.), *Studying the teaching in physical education* (pp. 79–89). Liege, Belgium: Association Internationale des Escoles Superieures d'Education Physique.

Pieron, M. (1982b). Behaviors of low and high achievers in physical education. In M. Pieron and J.T.F. Cheffers (Eds.), *Studying the teaching in physical education* (pp. 53–60). Liege, Belgium: Association Internationale des Escoles Superieures d'Education Physique.

Randall, L.E. and Imwold, C.H. (1989). The effect of an intervention on academic learning time provided by preservice physical education teachers. *Journal of Teaching in Physical Education, 8:* 271–279.

Richard, J., Godbout, P., Tousignant, M. and Gréhaigne, J.-F. (1999). The try-out of a team sport performance assessment procedure in elementary and junior high school physical education classes. *Journal of Teaching in Physical Education, 18:* 336–356.

Rink, J. (Ed.), (1996). Tactical and skill approaches to teaching sport and games – Monograph. *Journal of Teaching in Physical Education, 15:* 397–516.

Rink, J. (2002). *Teaching physical education for learning* 4th ed. Boston, MA: McGraw Hill.

Rink, J. (2003). Effective instruction in physical education, In S.J. Silverman and C.D. Ennis (Eds.), *Effective instruction in physical education* (pp. 165–186). 2nd ed. Champaign, IL: Human Kinetics.

Rink, J., French, K.E. and Tjeerdsma, B.L. (1996a). Foundations for the learning and instruction of sports and games. *Journal of Teaching in Physical Education, 15:* 399–417.

Rink, J.E., French, K.E. and Graham, K.C. (1996b). Implications for practice and research. *Journal of Teaching in Physical Education, 15:* 490–502.

Rink, J.E., French, K.E., Werner, P.H., Lynn, S. and Mays, A. (1992). The influence of content development on the effectiveness of instruction. *Journal of Teaching in Physical Education, 11:* 139–149.

Sallis, J.F., McKenzie, T.L., Kolody, B., Lewis, M., Marshall, S. and Rosengard, P. (1999). Effects of health-related physical education on academic achievement: Project SPARK. *Research Quarterly for Exercise and Sport, 70:* 127–134.

Salter, W.B. and Graham, G. (1985). The effects of three disparate instructional approaches on skill attempts and student learning in an experimental teaching unit. *Journal of Teaching in Physical Education, 4:* 212–218.

Sariscsany, M.J., Darst, P.W. and van der Mars, H. (1995). The effects of three teacher supervision patterns on student on-task and skill performance in secondary physical education. *Journal of Teaching in Physical Education, 14:* 179–197.

Schempp, P.G. (1987). Research on teaching in physical education: Beyond the limits of natural science. *Journal of Teaching in Physical Education, 6:* 111–121.

Schuldheisz, J. and van der Mars, H. (2001). Managing students' physical activity levels through active supervision in middle school physical education. *Journal of Teaching in Physical Education, 21:* 75–90.

Shephard, R. (1997). Curricular physical activity and academic performance. *Pediatric Exercise Science, 9:* 113–126.

Shephard, R. and Trudeau, F. (2000). The legacy of physical education: Influences on adult lifestyle. *Pediatric Exercise Science, 12:* 34–50.

Shephard, R., Volle, M., LaVallee, H., LaBarre, R. JeQuier, J. and Rajic, M. (1984). Required physical activity and academic grades: A controlled study In J. Ilmarinen and I. Valimaki (Eds.), *Children and sport.* (pp. 58–63). Berlin: Springer Verlag.

Shephard, R., LaVallee, H., Volle, M., LaBarre, R. and Beaucage, C. (1994). Academic skills and required physical education: The Trois-Rivières experience. *CAPHER Research Supplement, 1(1):* 1–12.

Shulman, L.S. (1986). Paradigms and research programs in the study of teaching: A contemporary perspective. In M.C. Wittrock (Ed.), *Handbook of research on teaching* (pp. 3–36). 3rd ed. New York: MacMillan.

Shute, S., Dodds. P., Placek., Rife, F. and Silverman, S. (1982). Academic learning time in elementary school movement education: A descriptive analytic study. *Journal of Teaching in Physical Education, 1(2):* 3–14.

Sibley, B.E. and Etnier, J.L. (2003). The relation between physical activity and cognition in children: A meta-analysis. *Pediatric Exercise Science, 15*: 243–256.

Siedentop, D. (1983). Academic learning time: Reflections and prospects. In P. Dodds and F. Rife (Eds.), 'Time to learn in physical education: History, completed research, and potential future for academic learning time in physical education, *Journal of Teaching in Physical Education, 3*(Monograph 1): 3–7.

Siedentop, D. (2002a). Ecological perspectives in teaching research. *Journal of Teaching in Physical Education, 21*: 427–440.

Siedentop, D. (2002b). Content knowledge for physical education. *Journal of Teaching in Physical Education, 21*: 368–377.

Siedentop, D. and Tannehill, D. (2000). *Developing teaching skills in physical education*. 4th ed. Mountain View, CA: Mayfield.

Siedentop, D., Tousignant, M. and Parker, M. (1982). *Academic learning time-physical education coding manual: 1982 Revision*. Unpublished manual, School of Health, Physical Education & Recreation. Columbus, OH: The Ohio State University.

Siedentop, D., Hastie, P. and van der Mars, H. (2004). *Complete guide to sport education*. Champaign, IL: Human Kinetics.

Silverman, S.J. (1985a). Relationships of engagement and practice trials to student achievement. *Journal of Teaching in Physical Education, 5*: 13–21.

Silverman, S.J. (1985b). Student characteristics mediating engagement-outcome relationships in physical education. *Research Quarterly for Exercise and Sport, 56*: 66–72.

Silverman, S.J. (1988). Relationships of presage and context variables to achievement. *Research Quarterly for Exercise and Sport, 59*, 35–41.

Silverman, S.J. (1990). Linear and curvilinear relationships between student practice and achievement in physical education. *Teaching and Teacher Education, 6*: 305–314.

Silverman, S.J. (1993). Student characteristics, practice, and achievement in physical education. *Journal of Educational Research, 87*: 54–61.

Silverman, S.J. and Zotos, C. (1987). Validity of interval and time sampling methods for measuring student engaged time in physical education. *Educational and Psychological Measurement, 47*: 1005–1012.

Silverman, S., Dodds, P., Placek, J., Shute, S. and Rife, F. (1984). Academic learning time in elementary school physical education (ALT-PE) for student subgroups and instructional activity units. *Research Quarterly for Exercise & Sport, 55*: 365–370.

Silverman, S.J., Tyson, L. and Marrs-Morford, L.M. (1988). Relationships of organization, time, and student achievement in physical education. *Teaching and Teacher Education, 4*: 247–257.

Silverman, S.J., Devillier, R. and Ramirez, T. (1991). The validity of academic learning time-physical education (ALT-PE) as a process measure of student achievement. *Research Quarterly for Exercise and Sport, 62*: 319–325.

Silverman, S.J., Tyson, L. and Krampitz, J. (1992). Teacher feedback and achievement: Interaction with student practice. *Teaching and Teacher Education, 8*: 333–344.

Silverman, S.J., Kulinna, P.H. and Crull, G. (1995). Skill-related task structures, explicitness, and accountability: Relationships with student achievement. *Research Quarterly for Exercise and Sport, 66*: 32–40.

Silverman, S.J., Subramaniam, P.R. and Woods, A.M. (1998). Task structures, student practice, and skill in physical education. *Journal of Educational Research, 91*: 298–306.

Solmon, M. and Lee, A.M. (1996). Entry characteristics, practice variables, and cognition: student mediation of instruction. *Journal of Teaching in Physical Education, 15*: 136–150.

Sparkes, A.C. (1991). Toward understanding, dialogue, and polyvocality in the research community: Extending the boundaries of the paradigms debate. *Journal of Teaching in Physical Education, 10*: 103–133.

Telama, R., Varstala, V., Heikinaro-Johansson, P. and Utriainen, J. (1987). Learning behavior in PE lessons and physical and psychological response to PE in high-skill and low-skill pupils. In G. Barrette, R. Feingold, C. Rees and M. Pieron (Eds.), *Myths, models and methods in sport pedagogy* (pp. 239–248). Champaign, IL: Human Kinetics.

Temple, V.A. and Walkley, J.W. (1999). Academic learning time-physical education (ALT-PE) of students with mild intellectual disabilities in regular Victorian schools. *Adapted Physical Activity Quarterly, 16*: 64–74.

Tinning, R.I. (1987). Beyond the development of a utilitarian teaching perspective: An Australian case study of action research in teacher preparation. In G.T. Barrette, R.S. Feingold, C.R. Rees and M. Pieron (Eds.), *Myth, models, & methods in sport pedagogy* (pp. 113–122). Champaign, IL: Human Kinetics.

Thorpe, R., Bunker, D. and Almond, L. (1986). *Rethinking games teaching*. Loughborough: UK Loughborough University.

Tousignant, M. and Siedentop, D. (1983). A qualitative analysis of task structures in required secondary physical education classes. *Journal of Teaching in Physical Education, 3*: 47–57.

Trudeau, F., Laurencelle, L., Tremblay, J., Rajic, M. and Shephard, R. (1998). A long-term follow-up of participants in the Trois-Rivières semi-longitudinal study of growth and development. *Pediatric Exercise Science, 10*: 366–377.

Trudeau, F., Laurencelle, L., Tremblay, J., Rajic, M. and Shephard, R. (1999). Daily primary school physical education: Effects on physical activity during adult life. *Medicine and Science in Sports & Exercise, 31*: 111–117.

U.S. Department of Education. (2002). *Public law 107–110, the No Child Left Behind Act of 2001*. Retrieved January 12, 2004 from http://www.ed.gov/policy/elsec/leg/esea02/index.html

van der Mars, H. (1989a) Basic recording tactics. In P.W. Darst, D. Zakrajsek and V.H. Mancini (Eds.), *Analyzing physical education and sport instruction* (pp. 19–53). 2nd ed. Champaign, IL: Human Kinetics.

van der Mars, H. (1989b). Observer reliability: Issues and procedures. In P.W. Darst, D. Zakrajsek and V.H. Mancini (Eds.), *Analyzing physical education and sport instruction* (pp. 54–80). 2nd ed. Champaign, IL: Human Kinetics.

van der Mars, H., Darst, P.W., Vogler, E.W. and Cusimano, B.E. (1994). Active supervision patterns of physical education teachers and their relationship with student behaviors. *Journal of Teaching in Physical Education, 14*: 99–112.

van der Mars, H., Vogler, E.W., Cusimano, B.E. and Darst, P.W. (1998). Teachers' active supervision patterns and students' activity levels during fitness activities. *Journal of Teaching in Physical Education, 18*: 57–75.

Vogler, E.W., van der Mars, H., Darst, P.W. and Cusimano, B.E. (1990). Relationship of presage, context, and process variables to ALT-PE of elementary level mainstreamed students. *Adapted Physical Activity Quarterly, 7*: 298–313.

Vogler, E.W., van der Mars, H., Cusimano, B.E. and Darst, P.W. (1998). Analysis of student/teacher behaviours in junior high physical education classes including children with mild disability. *Journal of Sport Pedagogy, 4*: 43–57.

Ward, P., Smith, S.L., Makasci, K. and Crouch, D.W. (1998). Differential effects of peer-mediated accountability on task accomplishment in elementary physical education. *Journal of Teaching in Physical Education, 17*: 442–452.

Webster, G. (1987). Influence of peer tutors upon academic learning time-physical education of mentally handicapped students. *Journal of Teaching in Physical Education, 7*: 393–403.

Whaley, G.M. (1980). The effect of daily monitoring and feedback to teachers and students on academic learning time – physical education. *Dissertation Abstracts International, 41*: 04A. (UMI No. 8022365).

Wilkins, J.B., Graham, G., Parker, S., Westfall, S., Fraser, R. and Tembo, M. (2003). Time in the arts and physical education and school achievement. *Journal of Curriculum Studies, 35*: 721–734.

Wurzer, D.J. (1983). Correlations between academic learning time-physical education and student achievement in cardiopulmonary resuscitation. In R. Telama, V. Varstala, J. Tiainen, L. Laakso and T, Haajanen (Eds.), Research in school physical education; (pp. 197–202). Proceedings of the International Symposium on Research in School Physical Education. Jyvaskyla, Finland: AIESEP.

Yerg, B.J. (1981). The impact of selected presage and process behaviors on the refinement of a motor skill. *Journal of Teaching in Physical Education, 1(1)*: 38–46.

Young, J. and Metzler, M.W. (1982). Correlation between academic learning time and achievement in a novel skill experimental teaching unit. *Abstracts: Research Papers 1982 AAHPERD Convention* (p. 105). Reston, VA: AAHPERD.

3.2 The classroom ecology paradigm

PETER A. HASTIE AND DARYL SIEDENTOP

Introduction

Initial research in physical education was handicapped by lack of a theoretical base, and the lack of a research tradition for investigators to follow (Locke, 1977). Limitations included the absence of replicative studies, and no collections of studies from which to derive future topics for research. In fact, Locke (1977) claims that prior to 1970, only 10% of all physical education research (of which no more than 5% was published) could be defined as fitting the model developed by Dunkin and Biddle (1974) to conceptualize the study of teaching in classrooms, and could therefore qualify as research on *teaching*. Indeed, it was not until 1986 that Placek and Locke (1986: 27) were confident enough to announce that "physical education has been the beneficiary of the same dramatic advances in research on teaching that have revolutionized our understanding of instruction in the classroom".

In subsequent reviews of research on teaching physical education. Silverman (1991) commented that still to that point, research had been mostly descriptive. Nonetheless, Silverman did identify a number of research streams that were beginning to take hold in the field, one of which was the classroom ecology stream. One of the research streams cited by Silverman (1991) was the classroom ecology model. Griffey (1991), in his reaction to the Silverman review, claimed had the potential for understanding the complex dynamics of instructional physical education. Griffey noted, however, that there was a paucity of research on this topic. While that may have been the case prior to 1990, in the decade since then there has been an abundance of research in physical education using the classroom ecology model, and a substantive database has been developed upon which to base this review. For the purposes of this chapter, this review will explain the fundamental concepts of the classroom ecology model, describe and account for the studies in physical education that have used

the model as their theoretical base, and, following the guidelines for reviews proposed by Cooper (1989), will examine topics that have not yet been explored. Papers for this reviews were selected through an examination of four sources; the *Dissertations Abstracts* database, the journals of *Research Quarterly for Exercise and Sport* and the *Journal of Teaching in Physical Education*, and through an ERIC search using the terms tasks, accountability, ecology and physical education as the main identifiers.

Brief historical perspective

The "classroom ecology paradigm" (Doyle, 1977: 183) was developed from a concern with the process–product paradigm, a paradigm that attempts to link teacher classroom behaviors directly with student learning or growth. The first of these concerns was the lack of explanation of *how* teaching behaviors are or might be linked to students' learning. In other words, most of the studies reported correlational data without explaining why the variables discovered should be related to achievement. As Doyle (1977: 167) commented, "in the absence of formal explanatory propositions, it is difficult to interpret contradictory findings or select potentially fruitful avenues for investigation".

Doyle's second concern was with an almost exclusive focus on the *teacher* in classrooms. This was manifest in two important ways. The first of these was in the neglect of pupil classroom processes. In this form of research, student data had been compiled mostly from classroom tests or other such product variables. Students' classroom behaviors (or process variables) had been neglected or at least de-emphasized. The second was in the assumption that the teacher is directly causing student outcomes. As Doyle reported, several studies have demonstrated the reverse, that is, that teacher behavior is often the result of (or coerced by) student classroom behaviors.

As an alternative to the process–product paradigm, Doyle (1977) proposed two other strategies for investigating effectiveness. These were the mediating process paradigm and the classroom ecology paradigm. Mediating process research is defined as the study of "the implicit human processes that mediate instructional stimuli and learning outcomes" (Levie and Dickie, 1973: 877), while the classroom ecology paradigm focuses on "the repetitive demands work makes on people and the ways in which they come to adjust, in myriad ways, to those demands" (Lortie, 1973: 485).

Doyle focused on the classroom environment as an active force in affecting behavior. He stated that classrooms have characteristics of multidimensionality, simultaneity, and unpredictability. Being multidimensional means that the classroom serves a variety of purposes, and contains a variety of events and processes that are not all related. The fact that many of these events occur at the same time leads to simultaneity and results in unpredictability in the sequence of events. Doyle (1979: 183) concludes that the "environmental demands which accompany teaching in classrooms interact with performance both to shape observed behavior and to establish limits on the range of response options".

Studies utilizing the classroom ecology paradigm focus upon the tasks that operate in classrooms and the environmental demands that are in place and act to restrict teacher and student actions. Research in this paradigm uses a combination of quantitative and qualitative techniques in order to make interpretative findings about the richness and complexity of learning environments.

Core concepts

The classroom ecology model portrays the behavioral dynamics of classrooms in a way that helps teachers interpret, predict and respond to those dynamics (Siedentop, 1988). The model focuses on teachers and students as they interact, rather than distal outcomes such as achievement or learning. The model then, is a study of classroom life as it naturally unfolds, and in that sense, represents an anthropological view which can only be accomplished through regular and long-term observation of that life.

The model represents class life as a set of three interrelated systems, managerial, instructional, and student social, in which changes in one system are likely to influence changes in another. Clearly, order and academic work are the two key issues in the ecological model, and the two are intimately linked (Doyle, 1986). For example, changes in student behavior (either positively or negatively) have clear implications for the amount of academic work that can be achieved. If students begin to misbehave, it is more likely that the teacher will act to restore order, thereby temporarily suspending the instructional focus of that lesson. Likewise, if teachers maintain rigorous standards for performance in the managerial system, opportunities for student socializing may be diminished. Indeed, findings from the earliest studies in physical education using this model confirmed that the compelling agenda for physical education teachers is the establishment and maintenance of order through a managerial system that typically focuses on cooperation rather than compliance (see Tousignant and Siedentop, 1983). However, it has also been noted that many teachers gain and maintain such cooperation in the managerial system by reducing the demands in the instructional system.

For the purposes of describing the completed work in this paradigm, the concept of the program of action (Doyle, 1986) needs to be foregrounded. The term "program of action" is used to identify that place where the notions of subject matter content and management come together in ways that are not easily separated. It could be postulated that it is within these notions that the quality of instruction and the attractiveness of the content can be linked to issues of class management. The program of action, then, encompasses the positioning and sequencing of content and management within lessons. Having a specific direction, momentum and energy, the program of action determines appropriate behaviors for students during different instructional contexts.

Merritt (1982) suggests that classroom activities contain vectors that, once entered into, pull events and participants along their course. The term vector is used purposefully, suggesting that the program of action draws events and participants along its course. Primary vectors are manifested in those agendas that the teacher has for the lesson, and define both action and the order necessary for the action to move forward smoothly. Secondary vectors are typically student initiated, and serve to test the robustness of the primary vector with its teacher-controlled or content-embedded accountability. Students initiate secondary vectors for a variety of purposes: to reduce the demands of a task, to lessen the chances of being held accountable, to seek a more interesting task, to engage socially with peers, or even out of boredom. Teachers often react to these secondary vectors, and how and when they do will "define the boundaries and strength of the primary direction vector and shape its direction" (Doyle, 1986: 420).

The program of action is presented through a series of tasks which focus attention on three aspects of student's work: (1) the products students are to formulate, (2) the operations used to generate these products, and (3) the resources available for these products. Whatever the task, there will be some response by the students, ranging from full engagement to passive or active non-engagement, and this will be followed by some teacher response. Thus, the program of action is not a fixed commodity set in place and left undisturbed, but rather a dynamic vector, the direction and momentum of which is determined by how some teachers monitor and respond to the potential or presence of student-initiated secondary vectors. It should be noted that secondary vectors initiated by students might have the potential to improve or strengthen the program of action, although most research reveals that the more frequent effort is to weaken the primary vector.

This understanding of how students attempt to influence the subject-matter demands of the class is seen clearly in Alexander's (1983) initial evidence of a contingency-developed tasks system. The extent to which a task initially explained by a teacher becomes the "actual" task practiced by students and accepted by the teacher depends upon the teacher's supervision and accountability practices. A program of action that has a strong work orientation, especially when students work toward some authentic curricular goal, typically results in high congruence between tasks as stated and those practiced by students. Without the content-embedded accountability, however, a strong work orientation typically requires active supervision and strong teacher imposed accountability.

Negotiation is also less likely to take place where the stated task involves little risk. Where the teacher has not specified the condition or criteria for successful completion, then almost any answer becomes acceptable, and hence students do not need to reduce the task demand. That is what Doyle (1986) meant when he said that without accountability the instructional task system is suspended. A teacher's skill and will to anticipate and then deal with negotiations typically reveals the likelihood of a strong or weak program of action.

Trading-off is that situation where teachers negotiate with students to produce the necessary cooperation in the managerial system by reducing the demands of the instructional system. Teachers also might allow for certain kinds of student social interaction to gain the necessary cooperation (as found by Jones, 1992, in the elementary setting, and Hastie and Pickwell, 1996, in the secondary school setting). At times, teachers might even suspend the instructional task system and allow students to engage in non-disruptive socializing tasks, provided they complete the managerial tasks as was found to be the case with one teacher in the study of Hastie and Saunders (1991).

The degree to which teachers trade-off depends upon the difficulty of the context in which the teaching is taking place, as well as the intention and expectations of the teacher for learning and achievement. Sanders and Graham (1995) found that teachers have a "zone of acceptable responses" for the tasks they present to children. In their study, on some occasions, teachers allowed significant adaptation when children made attempts to change a particular task, but then allowed no freedom for other tasks.

A further factor affecting teacher negotiation is the degree to which the teacher possesses effective teaching skills. Doyle (1986) notes that effective teachers in difficult situations tend to push students through the curriculum as a way of achieving and sustaining order. This notion of teaching skills was wholly supported in the study of effective elementary physical education specialists (O'Sullivan et al., 1989). For these teachers, one could contend that the overall program of action had the capacity to engage students and keep them engaged enthusiastically. However, where teachers encounter difficulty in gaining the cooperation of students in the intended tasks, they often retreat to a "curricular zone of safety" (Rovegno, 1994). Here teachers often restrict their content to application tasks (nearly always game play) and reduce the level of accountability to simply one of compliance in the managerial system.

Doyle (1980, 1983) has made a number of important statements relating to accountability. First, accountability drives a task system, be it managerial or instructional. Without accountability there is no task, and students will only do as much as they are motivated to by their own interests. In addition, the student response a teacher accepts and rewards defines the real tasks in classes, and the strictness of the criteria a teacher uses to judge the acceptability of these responses has consequences for task accomplishment. Thus it is only the tasks for which students are held accountable that they tend to treat seriously: "If no answers are required or any answer is accepted, then few students will actually attend to the content" (Doyle, 1983: 186).

The level of accountability will determine the difference between the "stated task" (that is, the instructions given to the student by the teacher) and the "real task" (that is, what the students are allowed to produce and what is accepted by the teacher). Teacher consequences determine the nature of tasks more than teacher instruction, and students often learn more about the tasks required from a teacher's reactions to performance than they did from the teacher's original instructions. Alexander (1983) refers to this as a contingency-developed instructional task system.

To understand a program of action, however, it is critical to note that class ecology is a dynamic, interdependent process. It should not be construed as being unidirectional. Indeed, Doyle was particularly concerned with research that focused only on teacher variables. He argued that an assumption of unidirectionality, that the teachers were directly causing student outcomes, was an oversimplification of how work gets produced in classrooms. According to Doyle (1977), several studies demonstrated the reverse, that is, that teacher behavior is often influenced by student behavior.

Task and task presentation

Fundamental to the study of a classroom ecology is the notion of tasks and task systems. Doyle (1980) was the first to produce an examination of classroom tasks. With reference to instruction, Doyle (1983) invoked a concept of "academic work", and stated that the curriculum can be seen as a collection of "academic tasks" or subject-matter tasks. The task designates the situational structure that organizes and directs student thought and action (Doyle and Carter, 1984).

Tousignant and Siedentop (1983) first identified three dimensions that define task systems in physical education: managerial, transitional, and instructional. Managerial tasks are those which relate to attendance, behavior, and in some subject areas, appropriate dress. Transitional tasks are defined as "the operation that the students were expected to do to accomplish the instructional tasks" (Tousignant, 1982: 99). Instructional tasks are those related to the achievement of subject-matter goals. Within the physical education context, there are several options for categorizing these tasks. One way is to focus on whether the task represents practice, scrimmage or game situations. Rink (1993) has proposed that instructional tasks can be categorized by the instructional purpose related to skill development: informing tasks, those which provide information to students about the upcoming task, particularly an explanation of task requirements, refining tasks, those concerned with improving the quality of the performances by the students, applying tasks, those which provide students with opportunities to apply their skills in game or scrimmage situations, and extending tasks, which are progressions of previous tasks which challenge students to perform in more difficult situations.

Following the category development of Tousignant and Siedentop (1983), Graham (1987) provided the first account within physical education of how the nature of the tasks influences the pattern of motor skill responses for students. Graham (1987) expressed concern with research in physical education that had examined end-of-instruction performance scores, claiming a need to focus on the subject-matter work of students in physical education. Using Rink's categories of instructional tasks, and examining student engagement and success rates during instruction, Graham demonstrated that teachers frequently differentiated movement tasks for high- and low-skilled students to allow for similar response rates. Jones (1992) followed

Graham's study on teacher and student performance through the analysis of the task systems operating in elementary physical education. Jones showed that students produced minimal task modification in the managerial task system, and produced high levels of compliance in instructional tasks. However, while students were consistently on task, they were successful only between 18 and 35% of the time. Several studies have shown that the most typical task development pattern is informing, followed by applying tasks, with less attention paid to extending tasks and very little to refining tasks, which, arguably, are the building blocks of successful skill development. Hastie and Vlaisavljevic (1999) showed a relationship between subject-matter expertise and the conduct of a teacher's instructional task system. Nine teachers were studied when teaching activities with which they self-reported as having higher or lower levels of subject matter expertise. Hastie and Vlaisavljevic's findings suggest that higher levels of expertise by teachers in certain areas result in two specific changes in the academic work of physical education. The first is a provision of more tasks, and particularly more extending tasks, while the second is an accountability focus centred more so on the quality of the performance than a level of participation or effort.

Descriptions of academic tasks have also been presented in a number of settings outside the physical education class. For example, Tinning and Siedentop (1985) examined the characteristics of the task systems that operate in student teaching. In this study, it was shown that the student teacher must balance the demands of those task systems that have consequence for pupils, but also those task relevant to the cooperating teacher and the university supervisor. In other words, the student teacher is both master and servant, putting in place tasks for pupils and responding to their outcomes, while at the same time attempting to fulfill tasks set by the higher authority. The work of Tinning and Siedentop (1985) has been adapted for use in training cooperating teachers and university supervisors by Ocansey (1989).

Hastie and Saunders (1992) and Griffin et al. (1998) have examined the task systems operating in sports teams. Similarities between teaching and coaching were identified in that managerial, transitional and instructional task systems were operational in both settings. However, in Hastie and Saunders' (1992) study, an additional task system emerged in the coaching setting, the "match play task system". A subset of instructional tasks, "role specific instructional tasks", was also identified. These role-specific tasks were tasks designed for certain players, and were not practiced by all team members. Examples include being the specialist setter on a volleyball team or the quarterback on an American football team.

The Griffin et al. (1998) study described the instructional ecology of a high school sport setting involving four players from a ten-player team and their coach. Systematic observation strategies were used to detail 44 practices. Post-season focus group interviews were conducted with the team and, individually, with the coach. The managerial, instructional, and student social systems in this volleyball setting interacted intimately. The quiet practice expectations, the posting of fast-paced practice tasks, and the coach clearly "in charge" all speak to orderly management. This system supports the explicitness and specificity of tasks and the clear, differentiated expectations of players by role and responsibility within the instructional task system. Both systems were interwoven and operated jointly to increased player cooperation and practice involvement. Nonetheless, Hastie (1993) found that athletes in these sport settings seemed more task oriented than reliant on external sanctions.

In a recent study adopting an ecological perspective, done in a non-physical education setting, Pope and O'Sullivan (2003) describe the ecology of "free gym" as it occurred in both school lunch-hour and after-school community settings. A period of sustained observation revealed a student-imposed hierarchy that was dominated by skilled male African-American basketball players. Status was gained through what occurred within the free-gym ecology. Students often had to learn the system by "serving time" before they could join a desired level of the hierarchy. While a few students thrived in this environment, most merely survived or were marginalized.

The social nature of physical education

The ecological paradigm provides an analysis of collective life in classes, both in its academic and social dimensions, and how those dimensions interact. Life in classes across time with children and adolescents is highly social. Allen (1986) first foregrounded the importance of a student social system by suggesting that students had two major goals, those of socializing and of passing the course. Siedentop (1988) argued that the student social agenda could be interpreted a task system, one that has strong potential to interact with the managerial and instructional task systems in ways that influence the ecology of class life.

The student social system in physical education has received considerably less attention than the managerial and instructional task systems. While some research has mentioned the influence of student's social agenda in affecting classroom processes (e.g. Jones, 1992; Son, 1989), only the studies of Hastie and Pickwell (1996) and Carlson

and Hastie (1997) have focused on this system. Nevertheless, this research on the student social system shows it to be a no less critical component in determining the nature and extent of subject-matter work within physical education.

In a systematic study of a dance unit within an 11th-grade physical education class, Hastie and Pickwell (1996) identified a number of strategies that the boys used to get out of instructional tasks they deemed uninviting or unimportant. These strategies allowed them to attend to their social agenda. Indeed, inventing and testing strategies to reduce their involvement in dance tasks actually became part of this social agenda. Furthermore, since the number of boys exceeded the number of girls in this class the teacher informally accepted much of this behavior provided it did not interrupt the smooth running of the lesson. As Hastie and Pickwell (1996:183) comment with reference to Placek's (1983) "busy, happy, good" findings; by being busy, happy, and good, the students can give the teacher what he or she wants, that is, the absence of critical events that lead to misdemeanors and deviant student behavior. The student social system, then, was confirmed as a strong influence in the ecology of this class.

The study of Supaporn et al. (2003) in a middle school setting indicated that their teacher's weak managerial task system, coupled with vague and incomplete instructional tasks, interacted with a student social system grounded in various forms of talk as social tasks to support a social program of action. Both teacher and student actions jointly created a primary social vector characterizing the overall program of action.

The student social system has been determined as a powerful driving force in other activity-based settings. In particular, the student social system has been seen as a key impulse in the accomplishment of managerial and instructional tasks during units of sport education (Carlson and Hastie, 1997), and off-campus in adventure education settings (Hastie, 1995). In both these studies, the social nature of the settings tended to promote students' involvement in the instructional and managerial tasks. In both sport and adventure education, working with one's friends to achieve instructional objectives was an attractive part of the setting. Students enjoyed the significant peer interaction that was available either at the climbing wall or ropes course in the adventure setting, or in developing team strategies and skill during peer coach-led practices in sport education. Further studies in sport education (e.g. Hastie, 1996, 1998a) have confirmed the key role that student leadership and responsibility plays in maintaining, and even strengthening, the primary vector for subject-matter work.

From these findings, it is reasonable to suggest that some curriculum models may have features embedded within them that produce a program of action that has considerable strength; for example, sport education (Siedentop, 1994) or adventure education. These models seem to have explicit goals that students see as authentic, and reasonably clear paths to attaining these goals, which no doubt helps sustain the primary vector of the program of action. Hastie's (2000) study of the ecology of sport education revealed that the high level of enthusiastic student engagement was due to the presence of three vectors, all of which make positive contributions to sustaining the program of action. These vectors include the teacher's managerial task system, the student social system, and the content-embedded accountability inherent in the curriculum model. Content-embedded accountability can be described as accountability intrinsic to the manner in which the activities develop and the goals are to be achieved. The models of sport and adventure education also tend not only to accommodate, but also indeed to explicitly depend upon, the student social system as a positive attribute of the learning ecology. They help define the social system in ways that contribute to rather than detract from the work agenda. Both provide a multidimensional program of action, in contrast to more traditional physical education settings, where teachers either push students through the curriculum with strong external accountability as a way of achieving and sustaining order, or retreat to a curricular zone of safety and negotiate minimum student work for cooperation in the managerial system.

Students' responses to tasks

Irrespective of the type of task system, tasks vary with the amount of information that they detail. This in turn sets the boundaries within which students can provide acceptable responses. Instructional tasks, and the subsequent student work related to them, depend mostly on the program of action. If that program of action is strong and there is strong accountability (either intrinsic to the curriculum or extrinsically developed by the teacher), then students will tend to demand that tasks be explicit. Explicit tasks are those where operational and outcome criteria are clear to the students.

A further component of a task, which affects potential student involvement, is the ambiguity and risk associated with that task. Ambiguity refers to the extent to which a precise answer can be defined in advance or a precise formula for generating an answer is available. Risk refers to the stringency of the evaluative criteria a teacher uses and the likelihood that these criteria can be met on a give occasion (Doyle, 1983).

Other tasks may be implicit or general. Implicit tasks are those students have previously practiced and in which they know how to play the role of a participant. Some researchers have labeled these as routine tasks. When tasks are presented so that the skill, tactic, or knowledge to be acquired is described in general, researchers typically categorize them as general rather than specific. These tasks are often high in ambiguity, but just as often low in risk, and students can be free to modify them without risking corrective reactions from the teacher. Instructional tasks are frequently less explicit than managerial tasks, and often carry less risk for accountability. This is particularly true for those managerial tasks that are introduced early in the term and counted on to become routine (Fink and Siedentop, 1989).

Despite the explicitness of a task, students can choose between a number of behavioral responses, and Marks (1998) has outlined a list of possible responses. In deriving the first instrument for the systematic observation of classes using the ecological model, Marks (1988) developed categories, which included off-task (including deviant or nonparticipant), task modification (where a student alters the stated task to make it either more difficult or easy) and on-task.

Son (1989) introduced the concept of "task congruence" in order to determine the extent to which the initial response of students corresponded to teachers' stated tasks. Son's analysis was made on two levels: responses to antecedent task statements, and subsequent consequences. The results of this investigation demonstrated that congruent student responses to stated tasks were more likely to be influenced by informal contingencies and/or other important variables, such as the nature of sport activities or student interest, than by antecedent task statements such as a task specification or the formal accountability system. Son (1989) showed that in the Korean context, one of the most important of those informal contingencies was aversive control, where teachers would threaten and physically punish inappropriate behavior.

Doyle (1986) notes that order can often exist in a class without full and continuous engagement by all students. He adds that "passive nonengagement is not necessarily problematic in establishing and sustaining order even though it may be unsatisfactory for learning" (Doyle, 1986: 396). In physical education, there is also the possibility of "fake engagement". Tousignant and Siedentop (1983) have described the "competent by-stander"; those students who are extraordinarily skilled at staying well within the boundaries of the managerial system but cleverly avoid participation in the instructional system. Son (1989) also showed how some skilled students participate in a practice task appropriately and successfully for a few repetitions, then reduce the task demands subtly and continue participation but also engage in social conversation with their partner(s). When such activities persist or become too widespread, and become noticed by the teacher, the managerial cohesion of the class becomes threatened, even though there is not overt misbehavior, often influencing the teacher to reduce the instructional demands or change the task.

Doyle (1986) notes that students' responses to work create pressures on the management system of a class. Where these threats are problematic, teachers often simplify task demands and lower the risk for mistakes. Where tasks are relatively simple and routine, classes tend to proceed smoothly with little hesitation or resistance.

In the development of tasks, then, a considerable degree of negotiation can occur. First identified by Woods (1978), negotiation is defined as any attempt by students to change the performance standards task completion is judged by. Students negotiate in various ways. While in classrooms negotiations are typically verbal interchanges, in physical education they are more often accomplished through student modification of learning tasks. Students modify tasks to make them more or less challenging, to increase their chances of success, or to hide their social interactions. Students may also try to avoid participating in tasks and try to hide their non-participation from the teacher.

If there is accountability for task performance, students will typically seek to increase the explicitness of the task demands (e.g. reduce ambiguity) and will also seek to reduce demands, typically by seeking to perform an easier version of the tasks. Students learn about tasks in various ways other than listening to teacher explanations. They can ask peers about tasks during transitions from explanations to participation, or they "hang back" and watch the eager performers make their first practice trials.

Research on ambiguity, risk, negotiation and trading-off within physical education is scarce. This is perhaps because, particularly within the secondary school setting, tasks usually appear to contain little risk. In US high schools, this teaching/learning environment has been described as "no sweat" (Siedentop et al., 1994), by which these authors referred to classes characterized by modest task demands, little student disruption, and a strong social orientation. In a French setting, Amade-Escot (2000) investigated how and why students modified instructional tasks, explaining modifications using the concept of the didactic contract. The didactic paradigm examines relationships among teachers, students, and the content embedded in tasks during academic work. Amade-Escot noted that continual, inevitable changes in the content taught were observed when it was brought into play in the instructional system. She further remarks that students stretched the didactic contract to test their capabilities in successfully completing the task. This caused a breach in the didactic contract, and such breaches were due to the teaching–learning process

itself rather than poor accountability. Where more rigorous expectations for learning are in place, such as in the UK and Australia, different levels of negotiation and trading-off may exist. Currently, however, we have no data on those settings.

The intervention study of Hastie (1997) outlines the key factors involved in the process of moving students from this position of no sweat to a level of quality performance. Through an action research methodology, Hastie (1997) identified three factors that seemed crucial for such a change. These included recognizing how students see that particular subject in the perspective of schooling, the provision of instructional tasks, which contain variety, uncertainty and challenge, and creating a class climate in which students want to be engaged.

Teacher response and accountability

When students are (or are not) performing classroom tasks, the teacher makes a number of decisions about their performance. Should the students' responses to the task be satisfactory, the decision most likely is to continue with the task. At the other extreme, where students are not responding to a satisfactory degree, the teacher may stop the task and present a new task. A less drastic measure would be to modify the task without abandoning it altogether. Doyle (1986) comments that when order becomes unstable, a more sensible option is this one of repair, since he claims that even in the best circumstances, transitions to new work are difficult to manage.

Nevertheless, regardless of the nature of the original task, and how explicit the original task might be, it is the subsequent supervision and accountability that determines the work students accomplish. Teachers communicate evaluations to students during practice periods by commenting on the appropriateness of behavior, effort, or performance, and by offering general or specific information relative to those. Doyle (1983) states that this evaluative climate connects tasks to a reward structure, which defines the accountability system operating in the class. Becker et al. (1968) originally referred to student accountability in this context as existing where there was an exchange of rewards or grades for performance. It is important to note, however, that grades are not solely the marks on a report card. It is more relevant to think of grades as one form of reward structure. This reward structure may be formal, where the performance counts towards a final grade, such as an examination, a skills test, or a squash tournament. More common in physical education, however, is informal accountability, where the performance does not directly contribute towards a grade. Indeed, in Jones's (1992) study of elementary school classes, no instances of formal accountability were identified. Examples of informal accountability in physical education include a practice exam, active monitoring and commentary, sitting out, public recognition, and teacher feedback (Lund, 1991).

When teachers in physical education hold students accountable only for managerial tasks (i.e. dressing and attendance), the instructional tasks system is suspended. Students then are able to do only as much of the instructional task as they wish, a situation Lund (1992: 353) defines as "pseudoaccountability". Siedentop (1988) has commented that it would appear that good teachers have a knack of stating tasks in ways that allow for minimal modification to match abilities and interests, but move quickly to redirect modifications that wander too far from the stated task. This reinforces the critical link between curriculum and ecology. Where a program of action is weak (from a motivational perspective), supervision and accountability become paramount, since when students do modify tasks they tend to do this rather quickly, adjusting for a variety of reasons, many of which promote secondary vectors which diminish the momentum of the primary vector. Teachers who do not supervise carefully inevitably suspend the informal accountability system, with the result that boundaries for acceptable responses become distanced from the stated task (Hastie, 1994a; Lund, 1992).

On the other hand, where the program of action is based on a strong, authentic curricular model, much of the accountability is embedded in tasks leading to the unit goals, requiring less teacher supervision. Indeed, sport education and adventure education programs typically use peer accountability mechanisms to motivate student work toward unit goals. Interestingly, both of these curricular models also shape the student social system so that it strongly supports the program of action, rather than being a potential distraction to it.

Research on accountability within physical education was initially descriptive. For example, Tousignant (1982) outlined a continuum of accountability within the instructional task system of physical education. She stated that students might be held accountable at four levels. At the lowest level, students can be held accountable for "minimal participation", no matter how good or average the performance. In this case, the students are expected to present themselves at class ready to participate. At the next level, students are held accountable for their "effort", so that the student is at least engaged in the task. At the next stage on the continuum, some "performance" level is expected. At this level, the teacher is likely to either chastise students for sloppy work, or alternately praise students for a "great move" or "good extension". "Evaluation" of how the performance was achieved is the fourth

stage of the accountability continuum described by Tousignant.

In accountability research dealing with the managerial task system, Fink and Siedentop (1989) found that good class managers had clear, consistent, and fairly rigid boundaries for managerial tasks and gave students sufficient practice and support that the tasks became routinized. A positive effect of formalizing teacher expectations for the performance has also been demonstrated (Hastie, 1994a). In this study, the teacher who achieved the highest degree of task compliance and student involvement was that teacher who most often stopped the class to reinforce his behavioral and performance standards.

Studies on accountability have also examined the links between teacher and student behaviors. These studies have focused more on the accountability systems that were teacher-focused rather than content-embedded. In these cases, Lund (1992) found that monitoring is the precursor of accountability and, as the instructional task system becomes more demanding, the complexity of this monitoring increases. The act of supervising student work was also found to be a strong factor in the accountability system operating in the classes investigated by Hastie and Saunders (1990). However, an intricate interrelationship between supervision, student involvement, and the opportunity to respond was identified. In terms of accountability, students were least likely to be off-task when the teacher was working directly with the students, and most likely to be off-task when the teacher could not see the student. Non-supervised students tended to avoid involvement where the opportunity to respond was low (such as when required to wait for a turn to participate).

Van der Mars and his colleagues (1994, 1998) examined the monitoring and supervision patterns of physical educators in relation to the work involvement patterns of students in their classes. Three key variables seemed to provide positive outcomes, (1) teacher location, (2) rate of movement, and (3) the provision of verbal feedback. When the teachers spent more time along the periphery and the sides of the activity area, actively moved from place to place, and were enthusiastic in providing verbal feedback, their students were more engaged in activity and were more on-task.

While monitoring has been shown to be the basis of most accountability, higher response rates and greater percentages of correctness and success have been achieved with accountability systems that had more than just this (Lund, 1992). In studies of secondary physical education (Hastie, 1994a, 1998a,b; Hastie and Saunders, 1991), active supervision was demonstrated to be a powerful determinant of students' task involvement. Active supervision, then, has become a key factor in the development of teaching effectiveness. While passive supervision is characterized by low rates of teacher interaction, active supervision consists of teaching patterns that include higher rates of interaction with students (such as prompting, encouragement, feedback), as well as greater movement about the work area. In active supervision contexts, teachers constantly and verbally reinforce task demands and the desired standards of performance, behaviors which have been determined as a common component of more effective teachers.

In one study of five high-school teachers in volleyball units (Lund, 1991), the most effective teacher had the *lowest* amount of practice time, but within that time student responses occurred at a higher rate, and a higher proportion of those responses were appropriate and successful, for more- and for less-skilled students. This was accomplished through a pedagogical strategy where each instructional task had an individual or group challenge as part of the task demands, and the teacher took time after each short practice bout to assess performance through public reporting and recognition.

Studies focusing on accountability have also been conducted that examine dependent variables other than student engagement in instructional tasks. For example, Patrick et al. (1998) examined the effects of a semiformal accountability intervention (a modified version of the good behavior game) on the occurrence of appropriate and inappropriate social behaviors, and appropriate skill attempts during a 20-lesson volleyball unit. These authors found that the intervention was effective in reducing inappropriate social behaviors and increasing appropriate social behaviors, but did not affect the number of correct volleyball skills performed.

The essential message from all the studies that focus on accountability seem to be that the work that eventually gets done in classes depends upon the strength of the program of action. That is, where the primary vector contains sufficient strength (one which contains achievable yet challenging tasks) and durability (in which there is some authentic outcome which can accommodate students' social agendas), it is capable of pulling events and participants along a course toward quality performance.

While active teaching behaviors have been associated with higher levels of student intensity in physical education, the effect of lesson context does, however, seem to mediate student responses and subsequent teacher accountability. In a study examining student and teacher behaviors during task contexts including skill practices, small-sided games and full games, Hastie (1998b) found that students provide more task-congruent responses in game play conditions than they do in skill practice settings, and that accountability strategies used by teachers are more influential in promoting task congruence in skill practice. Nevertheless, those teachers who employed more consistent and demanding accountability systems promoted greater student involvement and task congruence across all task conditions.

Doyle (1986) suggests a delicate balance exists between attending to the primary vector and attention to inappropriate behavior. To date, little or no research exists within physical education as to how teachers achieve this balance. While it is known that many classes lack intensity, and require little effort from students, research is warranted into those settings characterized by strong programs of action. The idea here seems to be that technically sound teaching is not sufficient, in and of itself, to sustain a program of action, especially in situations where an ordinary multiactivity curricular format is in place. Teachers certainly can create strong accountability systems that keep a less-than-exciting instructional program going forward (Siedentop, 1988), verification of which was presented in Hastie's (1997) study, but the question is whether it can be sustained over long periods of time and at what cost to the teacher, and also to student learning.

Applications to practice/policy

The main benefit of research using the ecological model is that it presents a realistic description of "life in the gym". It highlights that considerable negotiation takes place within many classes, where teachers trade-off a reduction in the demands of the instructional system and any rigorous accountability for cooperation in the management system. The student social system is generally allowed to flourish, as teachers are more concerned with creating and maintaining a classroom environment where they and their students can live peacefully throughout the year. As noted, many teachers gain and maintain student cooperation in the managerial system by reducing demands in the instructional system, with these trade-offs or treaties (Tomlinson, 1992) more evident in middle and secondary physical education than in elementary physical education.

A second key benefit of the applying research using this paradigm is that it forces us to examine not only teacher's actions, but also those of students through the analysis of tasks. One particularly rich example of this comes from Romar's (1995) study of middle school teachers. In this work, one teacher described her purpose of a basketball unit as helping children to play a well-played game, a most praiseworthy goal. Nevertheless, in an analysis of the instructional tasks of this teacher, it was revealed that there were no student learning tasks that had a tactical focus, and even the skill tasks were not game contextualized. As a result, the games played toward the end of the unit saw poor levels of play, and the teacher was disappointed. Notably, the teacher, like all the teachers in Romar's study saw herself as a good teacher because she performed many of what we know are appropriate teaching skills. All Romar's teachers had good demonstrations, clear explanations and they gave quality feedback. These self-perceptions were, for the most part, accurate. Many teachers do use skills appropriately and their students do typically enjoy classes. The point here is that these self-evaluations are based on perceptions of their own teaching behavior rather than estimates of student performance gains. However, there was little concern with the tasks the students were being asked to perform. This focus on tasks has shown that teachers in physical education generally do not ask students to complete difficult work. Accountability is primarily to keep students within the managerial boundaries of lessions, rather than to drive any significant production of motor skill performance. This underscores one of the most important lessons we have learned; to whit, if you want to understand the effectiveness of a teacher, don't watch the teacher, watch the students.

Major trends and future directions: what's missing within research on physical education?

Doyle has written in considerable depth about the importance of establishing and maintaining order in classes. Studies in physical education have shown consistently that the instructional task system is frequently low risk. There is some evidence that this can be partially attributed to the marginalization of the subject within schools (O'Sullivan et al., 1994). We have little evidence about how some teachers manage to break out of his marginalization and build and sustain strong programs of action, although our speculation at present is that the nature of the curriculum model may be a promising answer. Curricula that present authentic activities with real outcomes tend to motivate students and sustain them in participation without high levels of teacher supervision. Certainly, in the sport education literature there is evidence that teachers shifted their roles from traffic directors and policing to being content and strategy resource persons (Grant, 1992). Further, these teachers felt tested in this new role because of the demands students placed on them for content-related information and support, which leads us to believe that in such situations students have taken over the sustaining of the momentum of the primary vector.

As described, much of the research on teaching in physical education has been descriptive, with little taking an interventionist approach. Furthermore, much of the research has been completed on cohorts of teachers best described as solid or mainstream. Where studies have used the best-available teachers, these teachers have been chosen based upon teaching skills rather than the nature of their program. More attention needs to be given to those teachers who produce high levels of student work, not just high levels of behavioral cooperation. Of particular interest would be to examine how these good teachers develop and sustain a primary vector devoted to learning and skill performance. Valuable questions include; what is the nature of the curricular model?, how do teachers sell it to students?, how do teachers establish and maintain cooperation towards the models goals?, and how do students become important factors in sustaining the momentum of the program of action related to the model?

The essential goal of the classroom ecology paradigm is to investigate how teachers and students operate together to get work done. To understand life in physical education classes, one has to observe and analyze the ecology over extended periods of time. Teachers and their students live together for long periods of time and that collective life has to be reasonably peaceful. Peace is achieved through orderliness, predictability and a balance of subject-matter demands that is negotiated between students and teacher.

Those studies that have examined either teacher behaviors or student performance without examining the classroom behaviors of the other face the risk of making claims that are trivial, or altogether misleading. Moreover, of critical consequence is the examination of the tasks being set for students. Since performance in the subject matter is the salient criterion for judging teaching effectiveness, to neglect this aspect of the program of action, and failure to use response-based protocols to examine student work, is both unfair and conceptually counterproductive.

To understand teaching, one has to understand it as work. While there are clear performance aspects to teaching, and there are skills to be learned and perfected, it is a mistake to view teaching primarily from a performance aspect, as for example, one might judge a musical recital. It is rather the class-to-class, day-to-day, week-to-week work of teachers that needs to be foregrounded, and it is their perseverance in that context that needs to be analyzed.

References

Alexander, K. (1983). Behavior analysis of tasks and accountability in physical education. Doctoral dissertation, The Ohio State University, 1982, *Dissertations Abstracts International, 43*: 3257A.

Allen, J.D. (1986). 'Classroom management: Students' perspective, goals, and strategies'. *American Education Research Journal, 23*: 437–459.

Amade-Escot, C. (2000). *How students manage the didactic contract? Contribution of the didactic perspective to research in physical education classroom*. Paper presented at the Annual Meeting of the American Educational Research Association (New Orleans, LA, April 24–28, 2000).

Becker, H.S., Geer, B. and Hughes, E. (1968). *Making the grade: The academic side of college life*. New York: Wiley.

Carlson, T.B. and Hastie, P.A. (1997). The student-social system within sport education. *Journal of Teaching in Physical Education, 16*: 176–195.

Cooper, H.M. (1989). *Integrating research: A guide for literature reviews*. Newbury Park, CA: Sage Publications.

Doyle, W. (1977). Paradigms for research on teacher effectiveness. In L.S. Shulman (Ed.), *Review of research in education*, (pp. 163–198). Itasca, IL: F.E. Peacock.

Doyle, W. (1979). Classroom tasks and students' abilities. In P.L. Peterson and H.J. Walberg (Eds.), *Research on teaching: Concepts, findings and implications*. Berkeley, CA: McCutchan.

Doyle, W. (1980). *Student mediating responses in teacher effectiveness: Final report*, unpublished paper, North Texas State University. (ERIC Document Reproduction Service No. ED 187 698).

Doyle, W. (1983). Academic work. *Review of Educational Research, 53*: 159–199.

Doyle, W. (1986). Classroom organization and management. In M.C. Wittrock (Ed.), *Handbook of Research on Teaching*, 3rd ed., (pp. 392–431). New York: Macmillan.

Doyle, W. and Carter, K. (1984). Academic tasks in classrooms. *Curriculum Inquiry, 14*: 129–149.

Dunkin, M.J. and Biddle, B.J. (1974). *The study of teaching*. New York: Holt, Rinehart and Winston, Inc.

Fink, J. and Siedentop, D. (1989). The development of routines, rules, and expectations at the start of the school year. *Journal of Teaching in Physical Education, 8*: 198–212.

Graham, K.C. (1987). A description of academic work and student performance during a middle school volleyball unit. *Journal of Teaching in Physical Education, 7*: 22–37.

Grant, B.C. (1992). Integrating sport into the physical education curriculum in New Zealand secondary schools. *Quest, 44*: 304–316.

Griffey, D. (1991). The value and future agenda of research on teaching physical education. *Research Quarterly for Exercise and Sport, 62*: 380–383.

Griffin, L.L., Siedentop, D. and Tannehill, D. (1998). Instructional ecology of a high school volleyball team. *Journal of Teaching in Physical Education, 17*: 404–420.

Hastie, P.A. (1993). Players' perceptions of accountability in school sports settings. *Research Quarterly for Exercise and Sport, 64*: 158–166.

Hastie, P.A. (1994a). Selected teacher behaviors and student ALT-PE in secondary school physical education classes. *Journal of Teaching in Physical Education, 13*: 42–59.

Hastie, P.A. (1994b). Improving monitoring skills in physical education: A case study in student teaching. *Journal of Classroom Interaction, 13*(2): 11–20.

Hastie, P.A. (1995). An ecology of a secondary school outdoor adventure camp. *Journal of Teaching in Physical Education, 15*: 79–97.

Hastie, P.A. (1996). Student role involvement during a unit of sport education. *Journal of Teaching in Physical Education, 16*: 88–103.

Hastie, PA. (1997). Factors affecting the creation of a new ecology in a boys-only physical education class at a military school. *Research Quarterly for Exercise and Sport, 68*: 62–73.

Hastie, P.A. (1998a). The participation and perceptions of girls during a unit of sport education. *Journal of Teaching in Physical Education, 18*: 157–171.

Hastie, P.A. (1998b). Effect of instructional context on teacher and student behaviors in physical education. *Journal of Classroom Interaction, 33*: 24–31.

Hastie, P.A. (2000). An ecological analysis of a sport education season. *Journal of Teaching in Physical Education. 19*(3): 355–373.

Hastie, P.A. and Pickwell, A. (1996). A description of a student social system in a secondary school dance class. *Journal of Teaching in Physical Education, 15*: 171–187.

Hastie, P.A. and Saunders, J.E. (1989). Coaching behaviours and training involvement in elite junior rugby teams. *Journal of Physical Education and Sports Science, 1*(1): 21–32.

Hastie, P.A. and Saunders, J.E. (1990). A study of monitoring in secondary school physical education. *Journal of Classroom Interaction, 25*(1–2): 47–54.

Hastie, P.A. and Saunders, J.E. (1991). Accountability in secondary school physical education. *Teaching and Teacher Education, 7*: 373–382.

Hastie, P.A. and Saunders, J.E. (1992). A study of tasks and accountability in elite junior sports settings. *Journal of Teaching in Physical Education, 11*: 376–388.

Hastie, P.A. and Vlaisavljevic, N. (1999). The relationship between subject-matter expertise and accountability in instructional task. *Journal of Teaching in Physical Education, 19*: 22–33.

Jones, D.L. (1992). Analysis of task systems in elementary physical education classes. *Journal of Teaching in Physical Education, 11*: 411–425.

Levie, W.H. and Dickie, R.G. (1973). The analysis and application of media. In: R.M.W. Travers (Ed.), *Second handbook of research on teaching*. Chicago, IL: Rand McNally.

Locke, L.F. (1977). Research on teaching physical education: New hope for a dismal science. *Quest, 28*: 2–16.

Lortie, D.C. (1973). Observations on teaching as work. In: R.M.W. Travers (Ed.), *Second handbook of research on teaching*. Chicago, IL: Rand McNally.

Lund, J. (1992). Assessment and accountability in secondary physical education. *Quest, 44*: 352–360.

Lund, J.L. (1991). Student performance and accountability conditions in physical education. Doctoral dissertation, The Ohio State University, 1990, *Dissertations Abstracts International, 51*: 3358A.

Marks, M.C. (1988). Development of a system for the observation of task structures in Physical Education.

Doctoral dissertation, The Ohio State University, 1990, *Dissertations Abstracts International*, 51: 3358A.

Merritt, M. (1982) Distributing and directing attention in primary classrooms. In: L.C. Wilkinson (Ed.), *Communicating in the classroom*, (pp. 223–244). New York: Academic Press.

Ocansey, R. (1989). A systematic approach to organizing data generated during monitoring sessions in student teaching. *Journal of Teaching in Physical Education*, 8: 312–317.

O'Sullivan, M., Siedentop, D. and Tannehill, D. (1994). Breaking out: Codependency of high school physical education. *Journal of Teaching in Physical Education*, 13: 421–428.

O'Sullivan, M., Stroot, S.A. and Tannehill, D. (1989). Elementary physical education specialists: A commitment to student learning. *Journal of Teaching in Physical Education*, 8: 261–265.

Patrick, C.A., Ward, P. and Crouch, D.W. (1998). Effects of holding students accountable for social behaviors during volleyball games in elementary physical education. *Journal of Teaching in Physical Education*, 17: 143–156.

Placek, J. (1983). Conceptions of success in teaching: Busy, happy and good?' In T. Templin and J. Olson (Eds.), *Teaching in physical education*, (pp. 46–56). Champaign, IL: Human Kinetics.

Placek, J. and Locke, L.F. (1986). Research on teaching physical education: New knowledge and cautious optimism. *Journal of Teacher Education*, 37(4): 24–28.

Pope, C.C. and O'Sullivan, M. (2003). Darwinism in the gym. *Journal of Teaching in Physical Education*, 22: 311–327.

Rink, J. (1993). *Teaching physical education for learning*. St Louis MO: Mosby.

Romar, J.-E. (1995). *Case studies of Finnish physical education teachers: Espoused and enacted theories of action*. Abo, Finland: Aba Akademi University Press.

Rovegno, I. (1994). Teaching within a curricular zone of safety: School culture and the situated nature of student teachers' pedagogical content knowledge. *Research Quarterly for Exercise and Sport*, 65: 269–280.

Sanders, S. and Graham, G. (1995). Kindergarten children's initial experiences in physical education: The relentless persistence for play clashes with the zone of acceptable responses. *Journal of Teaching in Physical Education*, 14: 372–383.

Sariscsany, M.J., Darst, P.W. and van der Mars, H. (1995). The effects of three teacher supervision patterns on student on-task and skill performance in secondary physical education. *Journal of Teaching in Physical Education*, 14: 179–197.

Schuldheisz, J.M. and van der Mars, H. (2001). Active supervision and students' physical activity in middle school physical education. *Journal of Teaching in Physical Education*, 21: 75–90.

Siedentop, D. (1988). An ecological model for understanding teaching/learning in physical education. In *New Horizons of Human Movements: Proceedings of the 1988 Seoul Olympic Scientific Congress*. (Seoul: SOSCOC).

Siedentop, D. (1994). *Sport education: Quality PE through positive sport experiences*. Champaign, IL: Human Kinetics.

Siedentop, D. (1998). *In search of effective teaching: What we have learned from teachers and students*. Paper presented at the National Convention of the American Alliance for Health, Physical Education, Recreation and Dance, Reno, NV, 5–9 April.

Siedentop, D., Doutis, P., Tsangaridou, N., Ward, P. and Rauschenbach, J. (1994). 'Don't sweat gym: An analysis of curriculum and instruction. *Journal of Teaching in Physical Education*, 13: 375–394.

Silverman, S. (1991). Research on teaching in physical education. *Research Quarterly for Exercise and Sport*, 62: 352–364.

Son, C.T. (1989). Descriptive analysis of task congruence in Korean middle school physical education classes. Doctoral dissertation, Ohio State University, completed 1988, *Dissertations Abstracts International*, 50: 23 79A.

Supaporn, S., Dodds, P. and Griffin, L. (2003). An ecological analysis of middle school misbehavior through student and teacher perspectives. *Journal of Teaching in Physical Education*, 22: 328–349.

Tinning, R.I. and Siedentop, D. (1985). The characteristics of tasks and accountability in student teaching. *Journal of Teaching in Physical Education*, 4: 286–299.

Tomlinson, T.M. (1992). *Hard work and high expectations: Motivating students to learn*. Washington, DC: US Dept. of Education.

Tousignant, M. (1982). Analysis of the task structures in secondary physical education classes. Doctoral dissertation, Ohio State University, *Dissertations Abstracts International*, 43: 1470A.

Tousignant, M. and Siedentop, D. (1983). A qualitative analysis of tasks structures in required secondary physical education classes. *Journal of Teaching in Physical Education*, 3: 47–57.

van der Mars, H., Darst, P., Vogler, B. and Cusimano, B. (1994). Active supervision patterns of physical education teachers and their relationship with student behaviors. *Journal of Teaching in Physical Education*, 14: 99–112.

van der Mars, H., Vogler, B., Darst, P. and Cusimano, B. (1998). Students' physical activity levels and teachers' active supervision during fitness instruction. *Journal of Teaching in Physical Education*, 18: 57–75.

Woods, P. (1978). Negotiating the demands of school work. *Journal of Curriculum Studies* 10: 309–327.

3.3 Learner cognition

MELINDA A. SOLMON

Introduction

Cognition is defined by Gage and Berliner (1992) as "all the ways in which people think". As can be inferred from this definition, that terminology encompasses a broad range of constructs that affect student learning. The cognitive strategies and processes that are used to facilitate learning are critical components in the study of learner cognition (Pintrich and Garcia, 1991). In educational research literature, the term cognition is generally used interchangeably with thought processes (Peterson, 1988; Wittrock, 1986b). A wide range of thought processes and cognitive strategies have been studied in an effort to better understand how teachers and other practitioners can best structure the learning environment to facilitate student engagement in the content that will foster learning. Individuals engage in a wide array of cognitive processes during teaching and learning, including perceiving the environment, attending to and concentrating on instructional cues, and making decisions about their interactions during class that have a direct impact on what they learn. For example, they decide whether to exert effort, whether to seek help and employ strategies when they encounter difficulty, and whether or not to persist on a task.

Frameworks that incorporate a cognitive approach are based on the assumption that action is governed by thought (Roberts, 1992). It has to be acknowledged, however, that we may not always be thinking, and that sometimes our actions may be reactions that occur with little or no awareness of our thoughts (Schutz, 1992). When we do think, we make decisions about our actions, but sometimes we may act without really thinking. The rationale for using a cognitive approach in educational research is the supposition that a better understanding of how cognitive processes affect learning will enable researchers and practitioners to incorporate the findings into their daily practice in ways that will

optimize student cognition and ultimately facilitate learning. By learning more about how cognition affects learning, we hope to figure out how to first get students to think about what they are doing in achievement contexts, and then how to help them to think in ways that will facilitate their learning.

Over the past two decades, social cognitive theories have played an increasingly important role in educational research as investigators have recognized the value of studying the thoughts of learners and the social factors that affect cognitive processes as individuals acquire new information and skills. In their discussion of cognitive and situative perspectives on learning, thinking, and activity, Anderson et al. (2000) conclude that the study of individual and social perspectives should be vigorously pursued, as they are both of fundamental importance in educational processes that enlighten different aspects. The social and situated factors that are so important in cognition are addressed in many other chapters in this handbook, and although important findings relative to social factors and learner cognition will be examined, the focus here will be on individual cognition. It is crucial to point out, however, that both individual and social factors impinge on cognition and it is not possible to isolate those influences. The purpose of this chapter is to review and synthesize research literature that is related to learner cognition in physical education. I begin with a brief historical overview in order to provide a context for this body of work, with the intention of situating the findings within the existing literature. Next, theoretical bases that serve as a framework for this line of investigation are presented and the assumptions that underlie the study of learners' self-regulation of their cognitions are clarified. The major findings of the research in physical education settings are summarized, and then implications for practice that are supported by the research are examined. I conclude by pointing out directions for future research and identifying important questions that need to be investigated.

Brief historical perspective

The role of cognition in research on teaching physical education has its earliest roots in the motor learning literature. The initial phase of learning a motor skill is dominated by cognitive concerns (Magill, 2001). Models of skill acquisition describing the stages of learning characterize the first stage in cognitive terms (Fitts and Posner, 1967; Gentile, 1972) and those models recognize that considerable cognitive activity is required during initial phases while the learner's primary concern is understanding the elements of the task and what is required. As learners progress, motor performance becomes more automated, and cognition is refined so that the learner's attention can be directed toward finer points of technique or strategies. According to Nixon and Locke (1973), much of the early research on teaching in physical education focused on the acquisition of motor skills. They cautioned, however, that simply knowing how individuals acquire skill is not equivalent to knowing how to help them learn skills. They urged researchers to move beyond the methodological difficulties evident in this line of research to ask substantive questions about how teachers can best help students learn in physical education classes.

The role of cognition in skill acquisition has been recognized as an important component that must be investigated. In research on teaching physical education, however, as well as in classroom-based research, it became evident that learner cognitions in educational settings were far more complex than simply understanding the cognitive aspects of skill acquisition. The need to incorporate cognitive approaches in educational research paradigms evolved in large part from dissatisfaction with earlier approaches that failed to take into account students' thoughts in the teaching–learning process (Shulman, 1986). Early educational research efforts focused on differentiating more effective teachers from less effective ones. The process–product paradigm was adopted in the early 1970s as a reaction to criticism of existing research that did not examine teaching and learning in authentic field-based settings (Putnam et al., 1990). The goal of process–product studies was to identify relationships between teacher behaviors as instructional processes and student achievement as product variables. This paradigm dominated educational research during this period, and reviews (Rosenshine, 1976; Rosenshine and Furst, 1973) synthesizing this body of work categorized process variables based on their perceived potential to predict product outcomes.

Although this line of research made a contribution to the knowledge base about teaching, as it evolved there were many criticisms, most notably inconsistent findings that were often of little practical significance. The basic assumptions inherent in the process–product paradigm were called into serious question, and its lack of a theoretical basis is viewed as a major deficiency. The shortcomings of this paradigm are documented in several reviews (e.g. Doyle, 1977; Lee and Solmon, 1992; Shulman, 1986; Wittrock, 1986b) and will not be reiterated in detail here. Marx and Winne (1987) in summarizing the critiques conclude the process–product approach represents a simplistic view of teaching and learning that lacks the complexity to explain what makes teaching effective. Shulman (1986), while acknowledging the process–product paradigm has provided a solid foundation for further study, argues that its reliance on overt, observable behaviors fails to examine how students actually learn from teaching and disregards the cognitive activities of both students and teachers. Floden (2001) asserts that focusing on the effects of teaching on student achievement, when conducted using sound methodologies and linked to theory, continues to be a viable line of inquiry, especially in the current political climate and its focus on accountability and standardized tests. It is widely acknowledged, however, that a clear understanding of how students learn from teaching must include the investigation of learner cognition.

The move to incorporate the study of cognition into investigations of the teaching and learning process closely parallels what MacKeachie (2000) refers to as the cognitive revolution in psychology, or the paradigm shift from behaviorism in the 1950s and 1960s to a greater emphasis on human cognition and the acceptance of field-based research. As Peterson (1988) observed, a review of the chapter titles in the first three editions of the *Handbook of Research on Teaching* (Gage, 1963; Travers, 1973; Wittrock, 1986a) reveals that the first two editions were dominated by a focus on teachers and teaching with virtually no mention of students or learning. In the third edition, however, an emphasis on cognition student issues was evident, as Wittrock (1986b) provides a review of the research on students' thought processes and several other chapters address issues related to student learning and cognition. The most recent edition of that handbook (Richardson, 2001) continues to reflect an emphasis on learners and how their cognitions affect their learning.

There has been a preponderance of research in various academic disciplines related to cognition, instruction, and learning during the last two decades (Greeno et al., 1996; Wittrock, 1986b). The research on learner cognition specific to physical education has lagged behind that in other academic content areas such as science and mathematics. Luke and Hardy (1999) describe the interest in students' thought processes in physical education as "limited". There have been several scholars, however, who have conducted studies on learner cognition in physical education classes and that work has made a contribution to what we know about effective teaching (Lee, 1997).

Examining the progress in research on learner cognition thus far provides a basis for understanding the direction that current research is taking. Brown et al. (1983) in their chapter on learning, remembering, and understanding, described academic cognition as effortful, isolated and cold. They discounted the effect of emotions and motivation, and identified the knowledge and strategies necessary for efficient cognition as the principal concern in this line of inquiry. Based on the evidence that has been produced 20 years later, Pintrich (2003) concluded that Brown et al. (1983) were correct in characterizing cognition as effortful and complex, but he indicated they had been somewhat off the mark with regard to its being cold and isolated.

Rather than being cold, cognition is hot in the context of motivational and emotional factors, and rather than being isolated, it is clear that cognition is socially mediated (Pintrich, 2003). As research on learner cognition has evolved, those two threads have emerged as focal points in the research, and at present are influential avenues in this broader line of inquiry. The first thread centers on the relationship between cognition and motivation. In the general education literature, much research on motivation from a cognitive perspective has been conducted and motivation is recognized as a cognitive process (Roberts, 1992). The relationship between motivation and cognition, and the manner in which they are intertwined, has emerged as an important area of inquiry in learner cognitions as this research continues. In physical education research, as in research conducted in classrooms, investigations of motivation have flourished, but the relationship between motivation and other cognitive processes is not well understood. The second thread is the need to investigate cognition within frameworks that allow for consideration of multiple variables rather than studying aspects of cognition in isolation. Increasingly metacognition and self-regulation have been examined as a means of providing a framework to integrate cognitive, motivational, social and behavioral threads (MacKeachie, 2000). The strength of this trend is evident in the *Handbook of Self-Regulation* (Boekaerts et al., 2000). Luke and Hardy (1999) criticized the existing research in physical education for a tendency to "reduce the complexity of learning to a number of isolated variables, such as motivation, that remain adrift from any wider conceptual framework" (p. 175). They advocate for the use of a metacognitive ability

conceptual framework as a means to understand students' thought processes in physical education. Although researchers in physical education have not vigorously pursued approaches that investigate metacognition and self-regulation, there are a few scholars who are beginning to do so.

Core concepts

Three broad categories of theories have been used to frame the study of cognition: cognitive mediation, constructivism, and critical theories such as post-structuralism. Though these are distinctly different approaches to the study of the teaching and learning process, they share parallel views of the learner as an active and controlling agent in the learning process. The focus of this chapter is research that investigates learner cognition from a mediational perspective, as constructivist and post-structuralist views are presented in other chapters in this volume. It is important, however, to briefly relate cognitive mediation to constructivism and critical theories. From a cognitive constructivist viewpoint, learners adapt and refine knowledge through active restructuring of existing knowledge in highly individual ways (Windschitl, 2002). Meaningful learning is grounded in personal experience, and understanding of formal instruction is mediated by myriad influences, consistent with the cognitive mediational perspective. Feminist post-structuralism presents learners not as passive participants in institutionalized processes, but as active subjects who make choices and participate in structuring their identities (Weedon, 1997). These theoretical views are other ways of examining cognition that provide complementary perspectives to the cognitive mediational framework, and all recognize that learning requires active, effortful involvement on the part of the learner.

Cognitive mediation

The evolution of the mediating processes paradigm is described by Doyle (1977). He explains that this three-factor model represents a fundamentally different approach to the study of how teacher effects occur as compared to the two-factor process–product paradigm. Research from this perspective is grounded in the belief that learning does not automatically occur from teaching. The link between teacher behavior and student learning is not viewed as direct, but rather mediating factors intervene in that relationship. From this perspective, teacher behaviors can affect student learning only to the degree to which they activate information processing responses. Then learning occurs based on how the student actively engages those process.

Doyle (1977) was critical of the early work using the mediating processes paradigm for its limited conceptualization of student mediating responses, which at that time had consisted of overt, observable variables such as time utilization, estimates of attention, and task completion rates. He advocated the use of methodologies that would support the investigation of cognitive processes. The cognitive mediational model extends a performance-based model of teaching effectiveness by adding two important components: (a) the cognitive element, recognizing that students can have different cognitive responses to teacher behaviors and other events that occur in classes, and (b) the mediational element, recognizing that students' interpretations of instructional behaviors and environments serve as a filter for information and mediate their responses (Marx and Winne, 1987). The students' active and controlling role in mediating the effects of teaching is a critical link between teacher behavior and their learning. From this perspective, the role of the teacher is redefined. Rather than causing learning directly, the teacher's goal is to create an environment that encourages and enables students to think and act in ways that enable them to learn (Schuell, 1986).

Lee and Solmon (1992) presented cognitive mediation as a framework for the study of students' thought processes in physical education. They provide evidence supporting the notion that students play an active role in their learning in physical education through their cognitive processes and advocate for the investigation of cognitive conceptions as a means of gaining a clearer understanding of how students learn from teaching. Though they recognize that Lee and Solmon's cognitive mediational model addresses the complexities and interconnections among components of cognition such as attention, perception, affect and motivation, Dodds et al. (2001) point out that little attention has been given to the exploration of the content of learners' domain specific knowledge. They argue there is a need to pursue a research agenda on the development of student knowledge to complement the work that has been done using the cognitive mediational framework, which they describe as an instruction oriented (as opposed to a learner oriented) perspective. This contention is similar to Shulman's (1986) criticism that process–product research failed to consider the subject matter being taught, and their concern is valid. It is difficult to fully understand learner cognition without considering the development of student knowledge. Dodds et al. (2001) suggest that incorporating information-processing theories from cognitive psychology and alternative conceptions research from science education has the potential to make a significant contribution in the effort to fully understand learner cognition.

Underlying assumptions

Pintrich (2003) provided a general framework for self-regulated learning that, given the evolution of this line of research, has particular relevance to the study of learner cognition. He identifies four basic assumptions about learning and regulation that underlie models of self-regulation. Those assumptions are important core concepts within cognitive mediational paradigms that frame the study of learner cognition and characterize ways that cognitive processes function. The first assumption is that learners are viewed as active participants who construct individual meanings, goals, and strategies. This active construction of knowledge is based on information from both the external environment, as well as information from the individual's mind, which Pintrich refers to as the internal environment. Learners are characterized as active agents who make or construct meanings as they learn, rather than as passive recipients of information.

The second assumption builds on the first one by asserting that the potential for control over cognitive processes exists (Pintrich, 2003). This is not to say that individuals exert control over their cognition, motivation, and/or behavior at all times, or even that they are always able to do so if they chose to. Rather, this assertion recognizes only that some monitoring, control, and regulation is possible, while acknowledging that individual differences and contextual constraints can impede or facilitate regulation of cognitive processes.

All models of self-regulation also assume that there is some goal, or reference point that exists which serves as a comparison standard (Pintrich, 2003). Based on the goal that has been identified, progress is assessed and decisions are made concerning whether or not to continue or to change the course of action. Individuals set goals or identify standards they wish to achieve, begin to work toward those goals, and monitor their progress. Cognition, motivation, and behavior can be adapted or regulated so that individuals can reach their goals.

The fourth assumption underlying these models is that self-regulatory processes serve as mediators between individual characteristics and performance. Consistent with a cognitive mediational paradigm, models of self-regulation acknowledge that the relationships between the person, the context, and what is achieved in a learning context are mediated by individuals' self regulation of their cognition, motivation, and behavior.

In addition to the assumptions underlying self-regulation that Pintrich (2003) outlined, two other assertions are important in framing the study of learner cognition. First, as Rink (2001) points out, instructional approaches or methodologies are rooted in learning theories, and all teaching approaches and learning theories recognize the need for high levels of learner involvement with the content. She concludes, however, there is not a clear consensus on the level of cognitive processing that is requisite for learning, and argues that teachers and researchers cannot assume a particular teaching method or approach will elicit a particular learning process. She asserts that research studies that investigate teaching must also investigate learning and the processes that are associated with eliciting thought processes. Second, researchers who have studied motivational climates in physical education classes have concluded that a task-oriented climate focusing on individual improvement and mastery of a task will facilitate learning for a broad range of learners (Biddle, 2001). A task-involved goal orientation is associated with an adaptive pattern of behaviors that leads to achievement, including a willingness to exert effort, to work at a challenging level, to persist in the face of difficulty, and a belief in the efficacy of effort. There is clear evidence that this pattern of behaviors will lead to achievement. What is important in this chapter is to examine the literature on learner cognition with the goal of learning how to create an environment that will elicit student thoughts that will result in an adaptive motivational pattern.

Measurement issues and concerns

Investigation of learner cognition must rely in large measure on the analysis of self-report data, and the problems associated with accepting self-reports as evidence are well documented (see Lee and Solmon, 1992 for a discussion). Though Doyle (1977) criticized the initial work using the mediating processes paradigm as being limited to conceptualizing mediators as overt, observable variables, one explanation for using those variables may be found in the difficulty of establishing valid and reliable measures of cognition. Identifying those measures, however, is the cornerstone of conducting quality research. Several methodologies have been successfully employed to investigate learner cognitions including open-ended questionnaires (Rukavina et al., 2001), surveys (Solmon and Lee, 1997), stimulated recall interviews (Lee et al., 1992), interviews and narrative perspectives (Langley, 1995a), thought sampling techniques (Locke and Jensen, 1974), and think-aloud procedures (Langley, 1995b). The criticisms that have been leveled at self-report measures revolve around the issue of whether or not individuals accurately report their thoughts, or whether they are producing what they believe to be socially desirable responses. Another issue is whether these methods of data collection assess what individuals are actually thinking, or if by the very act of inquiring about thoughts, we introduce a form of metacognition and encourage people to evaluate or assess the situation in ways that might not occur if data were not being collected. Despite these criticisms, there is general agreement among scholars that, when collected with care, self-report can be used to collect valid and reliable data.

Major findings

Analyzing learner cognitions is a very complex process, which is not surprising given the complexity of the learning environment and the countless factors that influence how and what students learn. In the following section, the findings from the existing studies in the physical education literature are synthesized by examining various facets of cognition. Key findings from classroom literature are included when appropriate, but the studies cited are by no means exhaustive, given the volume of literature that exists. It is important to note that learner cognition is a multifaceted process that does not occur in a linear fashion. Perceptions, attention and concentration, interactive decisions, conceptions of the content, motivation, and self-regulation do not occur in isolation. Learner cognition is multiplicitous, and these factors interact with and affect one another in very complex ways.

Learner perceptions

Students enter instructional settings with entry characteristics, prior knowledge and experiences that serve as a lens or filter through which they view events that occur in the classroom or gymnasium. Studies using a cognitive mediational paradigm provide evidence that the same stimulus can lead to very different perceptions by individual learners (Luyten et al., 2001). There is a well-developed body of literature relevant to students' perceptions that is the focus of Dyson's chapter in this volume, so a relatively brief account of that topic is included here. It is important, however, to provide a brief summary because of the powerful influence that student perceptions have on their thought processes. What students bring with them to the learning environment, sometimes referred to as "baggage", provides the basis for their cognitions, and it is critical for teachers and researchers to consider their perspectives and viewpoints if we are to learn more about designing optimal learning environments. In this limited discussion of student perceptions, I address how perceptions of competence and initial skill level affect cognition during learning, and ways that prior knowledge and experience affect students' interpretations of instructional behaviors to demonstrate how critical student perceptions are in learner cognition.

Perceptions of competence

Perceptions of competence are core components in a variety of conceptual frameworks and several different terms are used to describe beliefs about one's level of ability. Although there are subtle differences between these terms, such as self-efficacy (Bandura, 1986) and competence as defined in Harter's (1985) competence motivation theory, there is strong agreement that self-confidence in one's ability is a very influential factor in cognition. When individuals enter classroom settings with the expectation of success, they try harder, persist longer, and perform better (Pintrich and Schunk, 2002). Lee and her colleagues (Lee 1997; Lee et al., 1999) have examined the effects of self-confidence on children's experiences in physical education, and there is clear evidence that students who believe they have the ability to be successful are more successful than those who do not.

Solmon and Lee (1997) developed and validated a questionnaire to assess students' cognitive processes in physical education classes. Confidence-efficacy was one of five factors that emerged as important components of cognition. Higher levels of confidence and efficacy were positively related to attention-concentration, willingness to engage, use of strategies, self-regulation, a mastery orientation, and attributing success to effort. The effect of students' ability perceptions on cognition during skill learning was demonstrated in a study by Lee et al. (1992). Using stimulated recall interviews, they investigated student thoughts during tennis instruction with a group of fourth grade students. When students' thoughts focused on negative self-evaluation, reflecting a lack of confidence and worry that they would be unable to perform the task, they were less successful during practice. Solmon and Lee (1996) report similar results with older children learning a volleyball skill. Low-ability students were unlikely to report high levels of motivational thoughts, were unable to identify and correct the errors that they made, and were unsuccessful in practice. Conversely, high ability students were able to detect and correct their errors and reported high levels of motivation and engagement.

Hebert et al. (2000) provide further evidence that it is important to consider perceptions of ability and initial skill level in their study with college students. They also demonstrate how instruction can be designed to facilitate positive cognitions based on entry characteristics. Participants in their study practiced the tennis serve under one of three conditions: the criterion skill (from the baseline), a part–whole progression, and a simplification condition, where students started serving closer to the net and moved back toward the baseline as they mastered the skill. Student thoughts varied as a function of entry skill level, with low-skill students reporting lower levels of

efficacy. It is important to note, though, in this study that the task progression mediated this effect. Low-skill students who practiced under the progressive conditions had higher levels of self-efficacy than those who practiced the criterion task. This study demonstrates how considering student entry characteristics and designing instruction so that students can experience success during practice can foster a positive pattern of cognitions.

Perceptions of instruction

Students enter instructional settings not only with beliefs about their ability to be successful, but also a powerful set of beliefs about schooling and the nature of the content to be learned based on their prior experiences and existing knowledge. Even very young children come to school with strongly held conceptions about physical education and physical activity that must be considered in attempts to facilitate learner cognitions that will enable students to learn (Solmon and Carter, 1995). As children progress through school and are exposed to a wide array of instructional practices and experiences in physical education classes, their prior knowledge and the conceptions that they hold about physical education continue to be a strong influence on how they perceive instruction. There is evidence that individuals in the same classes do not perceive the same instruction in the same ways, and also that they often do not perceive the teachers' behaviors and actions in the manner in which the teacher intends (Wittrock, 1986b). That is to say, individuals, based on their existing knowledge and beliefs, filter instructional information and interpret it in unique ways. From a cognitive mediational perspective, students mediate incoming information and construct individual meanings, and these meanings and interpretations may be quite different from what the teacher meant.

Gender, ethnicity, educational background, socioeconomic status, and a multitude of other variables can affect how students perceive instructional behaviors. Several examples can be found in the literature that demonstrate this phenomenon. Martinek (1988) identified high- and low-expectation students based on the teacher's ratings and investigated their perceptions of teacher feedback. He coded teacher feedback statements and compared the objective measure to student perceptions of feedback. High-expectation students actually received more corrective feedback than praise, but these students indicated they thought they were praised more than corrected. They seemed to be able to dismiss or ignore corrective behavior feedback by attributing it to teacher characteristics, suggesting the teacher had been in a bad mood. Low-expectation students' perceptions of feedback more closely corresponded to the coded observations, in that they received more praise than corrective behavior feedback. The low-expectation students tended to take the corrective feedback more personally. Using stimulated recall interviews to directly compare teacher and student perspectives of task-related events in physical education classes, Tjeerdsma (1997) concluded that in many ways students and teachers experience different realities in physical education classes. Perceptions of task difficulty, performance and effort, and teacher feedback were described as incongruent.

Students do not always accurately understand instructional information, even when the instruction is scripted and seemingly very clear. In the Lee et al. (1992) study, when asked if they understood what the teacher told them, students indicated they had. Follow-up questions, however, revealed their comprehension varied in terms of completeness and accuracy, and that none of the children in their study could recall a complete explanation. As mentioned earlier, student perceptions and the factors that influence them are explored in far greater detail in Dyson's chapter. Although there is much more research that is relevant to student perceptions, the important point here is that these perceptions are of considerable importance in understanding how students' cognitions mediate instruction and translate to learning.

Attention and concentration

Consideration of students' perceptions of their competence and how they perceive instructional stimuli is closely related to another aspect of cognition, what they attend to and whether or not they concentrate. Attentional demands during the acquisition of motor skills have been studied extensively. Attention is characterized by Magill (2001) as a limited capacity resource. Motor skill acquisition is facilitated by the ability to select and attend to meaningful information. As learners advance through the stages of learning motor skills, their performance becomes more automated, and because the basic elements of the skill demand less cognitive involvement, more attention can be directed to other aspects of the task, such as finer points of techniques or strategies. Another analogy can be drawn based on prior experience or existing knowledge. When individuals are exposed to information with which they are totally unfamiliar, they are likely to remember only isolated bits and pieces, because of the overload on their attentional demands created by the volume of new material. In contrast, an individual who has some prior knowledge may be able to attend to, and process, much more of the information because of the different demands on their attention.

In order to profit from instruction, students must have the opportunity to actively engage in learning activities. Allocated time for learning emerged from the process–product studies as a variable showing a promising relationship with student achievement (Rosenshine and Furst, 1973), and in the initial applications of the mediating processes paradigm, time on task was consistently identified as a mediating variable (Doyle, 1977). It is very logical that observed time on task predicts student achievement, but a rationale for studying student reports of their thoughts and cognitions as opposed to observer estimates of attention is found in the work of Peterson and her colleagues (Peterson and Swing, 1982; Peterson et al., 1984). In their studies, students' reports of the attention during stimulated recall interviews were more accurate predictors of student achievement than overt observers' estimates of time on task.

Consistent with the classroom studies, several studies in physical education settings have demonstrated that students are aware of their attentional levels and are able to report them with sufficient accuracy to provide valuable information about learning. Locke and Jensen (1974), in an early study of college students' thoughts in physical activity settings, used a thought sampling technique to investigate student attention. They categorized thoughts according to the level of attention directed toward the task. Median levels of attention varied according to the class and the nature of instruction. Higher levels of attention were reported during active practice than instructor talk, and there was evidence that the structure of the class and instructor variables affected level of attention.

Attention-concentration was one of the factors that emerged in the Solmon and Lee (1997) study as an important component of student cognition. Higher levels of attention were positively associated with other cognitive processes as well as a mastery orientation. In the Lee et al. (1992) study, the primary focus of thoughts reported in the stimulated recall interviews was skill-related thoughts focused on outcome or technique. Students who reported task-related thoughts were more successful during practice. Langley (1995b) used questionnaires, interviews, and think-aloud techniques in his study of student cognition during bowling instruction. He classified student thoughts in that skill setting as task-focused and reported a fundamental concern about errors.

There is clear evidence that attention to the elements of the task will facilitate appropriate cognitive involvement and skill acquisition. In some ways, then, the question becomes how to direct students' attention to the critical elements of the instructional environment. The study by Solmon and Lee (1996) provides an interesting perspective on student attention as an aspect of cognition. Students who had low perceived competence and initial skill levels were attentive during instruction, both by their own self-reports and according to observer estimates of attention, while those with higher perceived competence and initial skill level tended to be less attentive during the teacher's demonstration, again both by their own reports and according to observer estimates. During practice, however, high-ability students were on task and able to direct their attention to detecting and correcting errors. The high-ability students seemingly were able to discern salient information about the task quickly from the teacher's demonstration, and were soon bored with the explanation. Conversely, low-ability students expected to experience difficulty, focused intently on the instructor's demonstration and explanation, but were frustrated during practice when they encountered difficulty.

Interactive decisions and engagement

Research confirms the intuition that appropriate attention and concentration during instruction and practice facilitates learning. From a cognitive mediational perspective, it becomes important to understand how to structure the learning environment in a way that encourages students to make decisions during class to concentrate, direct their attention to the appropriate cues in the learning environment, and engage in tasks with sufficient levels of effort and persistence to learn. Students' perceptions of the task are related to decisions they make about their learning activities (Luyten et al., 2001). Students make choices concerning how they interact in class. For example, it is clear that there is tremendous variability in the numbers and quality of practice trials that students execute in physical education settings (Solmon and Lee, 1996). In physical education class settings, students can choose to actively engage in the content, or if they want to avoid participating, they are often able to do so by acting as competent bystanders (Tousignant and Siedentop, 1983). Byra and Jenkins (1998) investigated students' thoughts and behaviors during a short instructional unit using the inclusion style of teaching. When given the opportunity, learners in their study selected differing levels of task difficulty during practice. Students made their decisions based on their perceptions of success and challenge.

It is clear that students who engage in successful practice are those who learn, so the important issue with regard to cognition and engagement is to create an environment that fosters cognition that will lead to active, effortful engagement. The link between learner cognition and active engagement in classes has been demonstrated in several studies. Students who enter an instructional setting with higher levels of perceived competence and initial skill report higher levels of effort, are able to detect

and correct their errors during practice, and are more persistent and successful during skill practice (Solmon and Lee, 1996). Students who indicate they are cognitively engaged at a high level are more likely to work at a challenging level (Solmon and Boone 1993). When individuals experience some level of success during practice, they report that they are more willing to exert effort during practice (Hebert et al., 2000). Taken together, the results of these studies suggest that when the learning environment is structured to provide students with opportunities to be successful, and the opportunity to vary task difficulty is available, they are more likely to engage at appropriate levels of practice, and to be willing to exert effort and seek out challenge.

Conceptions and meanings

Individuals' ideas and beliefs about the nature of a content area are formulated based on a wide variety of information sources and prior experiences. They enter instructional settings with characteristics and prior experiences that affect how they perceive class events and the meanings they construct relevant to the content, and consequently how they interact and what they learn. Understanding how conceptions develop and how they affect the ways learners interact with the content is an important aspect of cognition that has, until recently, been understudied in physical education (Hare and Graber, 2000; Dodds et al., 2001). Langley (1995a) used a narrative perspective to investigate the meanings students constructed as they learned to bowl. This approach provided insight into the distinct individual experiences in the social context related to how they constructed realities in the learning environment. A complete understanding of learning cognition cannot be developed without considering students' conceptions that are relevant to physical education and how their domain specific knowledge develops.

Conceptions of ability

One area of learner conceptions that has received considerable attention in the classroom literature is conceptions of ability. The influence of beliefs about whether ability is a stable factor that cannot be changed, or a malleable factor that can be improved with effort, has been studied extensively. Dweck (2000) and Nicholls (1984) present frameworks for the study of conceptions of ability. Although they employ different terminology, their views are parallel. Nicholls (1984) presents a developmental approach and characterizes conceptions of ability as undifferentiated (ability cannot be differentiated from effort, so ability can be improved with effort) and differentiated (ability is stable and distinct from effort). He asserts that children begin with undifferentiated conceptions, and as they mature and are able to socially compare, they are able to differentiate effort from ability. Dweck (2000) labels the belief that ability cannot be changed as an entity belief, and the belief that ability can be improved through effort as an incremental conception. Regardless of the terminology used, a belief in the efficacy of effort to improve ability or performance is associated with a more adaptive pattern of cognitions.

Conceptions of ability have been studied by several researchers in physical education settings, and their findings are largely consistent with those from the classroom literature. Older children are better able to differentiate effort from ability, but they can maintain their belief in the efficacy of effort to improve their performance (Lee et al., 1995; Xiang and Lee, 1998; Xiang et al., 2001). Factors such as the nature of the activity, race, gender, and prior experience affect individuals' conceptions of ability in physical activities (Li et al., 2004, 2006). Nurturing a belief that ability can be improved with effort, or that individuals can be successful at an activity if they are willing to exert effort and persist, has the potential to foster a positive pattern of cognition and motivation (Li et al., 2005; Wang and Biddle, 2001).

Knowledge-related conceptions

The importance of understanding how students' knowledge-related conceptions develop has been demonstrated in content areas such as science and mathematics (Perkins and Simmons, 1988). If teachers are to construct learning environments that will enable students to engage in cognitions that will foster knowledge development, they must understand how conceptions and misconceptions about the content evolve. To correct mistakes and clarify misconceptions, it is essential to understand how conceptions of knowledge develop, so that activities can be designed to facilitate the construction of knowledge. The literature related to the cognitive aspects of knowledge construction is reviewed in the chapter on constructivist and situated approaches, so only a short overview is presented here.

Although research in this area was notably lacking in the earlier studies of learner cognition, several scholars have recently begun to pursue this line of inquiry (Griffin and Placek, 2001). Their work, even in its initial stages, demonstrates the importance of investigating this aspect of learner cognition and provides a sound basis for further inquiry. Collectively, this research illustrates that if teachers are to clearly and effectively communicate content and help students develop their knowledge, they must understand students' beliefs and conceptions. Hare and Graber (2000) investigated student misconceptions during invasion game units and

concluded that the level of instruction directly influenced the development or clarification of students' understandings. Misconceptions were more likely to emerge and remain unclarified during instruction from a student teacher, while students tended to exhibit fewer misconceptions about lesson content when they were taught by an experienced teacher.

The understanding and development of learners' domain-specific knowledge was the subject of a monograph edited by Griffin and Placek (2001). Investigation of students' conceptions of soccer demonstrated that students held alternative conceptions about the content, defined as ideas that are reasonably different than those presented in formal instruction, and that those alternative conceptions were related to difficulties observed in being able to move without the ball and the overall use of space (Griffin et al., 2001). The importance of studying the content of prior knowledge and giving students the opportunity to share that knowledge and relate it to new information was evident. Another series of studies in the monograph used situated and constraints theoretical perspectives to study how children learned tactics and skills in invasion games during a 12-lesson unit of instruction (Nevett et al., 2001a,b; Rovegno et al., 2001). Taken together, these studies suggested that students had difficulties in solving tactical games problems, and that a better understanding of their conceptions is an essential element in designing effective instruction.

Conceptions and development of knowledge have also been investigated in the content area of fitness. Although middle school students indicated an awareness that exercise is good for everyone, their knowledge and understanding related to fitness was described as lacking and/or incomplete (Placek et al., 2001). In their study with high school students, Stewart and Mitchell (2003) characterized conceptions of fitness concepts as narrow, vague, and often incorrect. This series of studies demonstrates the need for further investigation of the cognitive processes that affect the development of students' content knowledge. A better understanding of how students' misconceptions and conceptions evolve is an essential component in learning how to design instruction that can clarify misconceptions and facilitate students' active construction of knowledge.

Motivation

Motivation is defined by Roberts (2001) as the "dispositions, social variables, and/or cognitions that come into play when a person undertakes a task at which he or she is evaluated, or enters into competition with others, or attempts to attain some standard of excellence" (p. 6). He asserts that a comprehensive view of motivation includes three elements: the energization, direction, and regulation of behavior. Motivation is clearly an influential factor, characterized by Solmon (2003) as a construct that underlies more global cognitive processes. There is a large volume of research that addresses many facets of motivation in physical education and physical activity, and it is not possible to even begin to include a summary of that work. I will focus only on studies that have included motivation as it relates to other cognitive processes, but refer the reader to the following authors for comprehensive theoretical perspectives that are based on learner cognitions related to motivation.

Within the motivational frameworks, perhaps the most prolific line of research has been related to achievement goal theory. Biddle (2001) provides a careful analysis of the work that has been done using this theoretical perspective in physical education settings. He concludes that using teaching strategies that promote a mastery climate and a task orientation will increase children's motivation. Subramaniam and Silverman (Silverman and Subramaniam, 1999; Subramaniam and Silverman, 2000, 2002) have investigated the role of student attitude in physical education, and positive attitudes are associated with increased motivation and engagement. Both program and student characteristics are important influences on student attitude, and there is evidence that attitudes are malleable. Further investigation of student attitudes could inform teachers and researchers as they strive to design learning environments that will foster positive attitudes, which could provide a basis for positive learner cognitions. Chen (2001) has investigated the role of interest in motivation. He concludes activities that are novel, cognitively challenging, and generate instant enjoyment are likely to foster student engagement and advocates linking motivation to the learning setting, the curriculum, and the cultural environment through interest. Xiang and her colleagues (Xiang et al., 2003, 2004) have used the expectancy-value framework to investigate motivation in physical education classes. Consistent with research conducted in classrooms, expectancies for success and task values predicted intention to engage in physical activity.

There is evidence from these lines of investigation that achievement goals, attitudes, interest, value, and expectations for success are all important influences on the cognitions related to motivation. Specific studies in physical education settings support the notion that individuals' reports of their motivation can provide valuable insight into why some individuals are motivated to learn while others are not. Willingness to engage was one of five factors on the cognitive processes questionnaire developed by Solmon and Lee (1997). This factor was positively associated with higher levels of confidence, attention, self-regulation, a task orientation, and a belief that success is attributable to effort. Self-reported levels of motivation were positively associated with higher levels of perceived competence, initial skill level, and engagement during instruction and practice in the study by Solmon and Lee (1996). Individuals who practiced the criterion task, which was more difficult, reported lower levels of motivation than those who practiced in conditions that incorporated task progressions, which translated to more success during practice (Hebert et al., 2000).

Although the important role that motivational factors play in cognitive processes is recognized, the links between motivation and other cognitive processes such as attention, reasoning, and use of strategies has not been investigated in great detail (Pintrich, 2003). Pintrich indicates that the interaction between motivation and the activation and acquisition of knowledge is not really clear, and suggests that examining the relationship between other cognitive processes and motivation is an important area for further study.

Learning strategies

Learning strategies are defined by Weinstein and Mayer (1986) as learners' actions and thoughts that influence the acquisition, retention, and transfer of information or skills. Rehearsal, elaboration, imagery, help-seeking, and relating new information to prior knowledge are examples of strategies that can be used to facilitate learning. The use of specific cognitive strategies has been related to achievement in the classroom (Peterson and Swing, 1982; Peterson et al., 1984), and there is evidence that teaching learning strategies to students can facilitate attention, motivation, learning, memory, and comprehension (Weinstein and Mayer, 1986; Wittrock, 1986b). The use of learning strategies emerged in the Solmon and Lee (1997) study as an influential factor in students' cognition in physical education that was positively related to higher levels of attention and concentration and a task orientation. Several studies have investigated the role of learning strategies in skill acquisition using surveys and open-ended questionnaires to elicit self-reports of strategy use. Learners' reports of the strategies they use have provided valuable insight into how instructional strategies can be used in physical education classes to elicit various types of learning strategies. To date, however, the effectiveness of teaching learning strategies in physical education settings has not been fully investigated.

In the early stages of the acquisition of a new skill, more successful students are able to articulate specific strategies they use to learn the skill (Lee et al., 1992). Solmon and Lee (1996) provide insight into strategy use and skill level, and demonstrate how individual learner characteristics influence the ways students mediate instruction. Students with higher initial skill and perceptions of competence were successful during practice and did not report using strategies. Students with lower initial skill levels and perceptions of competence experienced difficulty during practice and reported attempts to use strategies during practice. Examining the use of learning strategies at a class level, without consideration for individual characteristics that affect learning, might suggest that the use of learning strategies was negatively related to achievement. By examining individual learner characteristics in relation to cognition, it becomes apparent that learning strategies are only effective when they are needed. Higher skilled students were able to successfully perform the task without using strategies because the task was easy for them. In contrast, students with lower initial skill levels encountered difficulties and evoked strategies in their attempts to learn the skill.

In a series of studies, Rukavina and his colleagues (Rukavina, 2003; Rukavina et al., 2001, 2004) investigated how task communication strategies affect the kinds of learning strategies students employ during the acquisition, retention, and transfer of a novel motor skill. Both open-ended questionnaires about strategy use, as well as surveys with likert-like response scales, clearly demonstrate that students' strategies vary based on the manner in which the task was communicated to the learner. In the initial study, students who viewed a correct model or a learning model receiving feedback statements focused on the technical elements of the task. Students who viewed a learning model without the benefit of hearing the feedback statements identified comparatively fewer strategies and focused less on technique (Rukavina et al., 2001). When direct and indirect task communication strategies were compared, similar results were evident (Rukavina et al., 2004). Students in the discovery condition reported using the learning strategy of relating the skill to prior knowledge more than those in conditions where the parameters of the task were made explicit through direct communication strategies. Learners who had access to visual models and verbal information about the task tended to mimic the model rather than explore and solve problems related to the movement task using trial and error strategies.

In an extension of this line of investigation, Rukavina (2003) incorporated scaffolding movement challenges into a guided discovery condition, and compared that to both a discovery condition and a direct instruction model. Learners in the scaffolding condition reported more frequent use of strategies related to the movement challenges they were asked to solve as compared to a direct instruction condition, even though participants in the direct instruction condition had access to the information included in the scaffolding condition. The use of learning strategies is an important aspect of learning a skill or improving one's performance, especially in a difficult task, and it is clear that instructional conditions can facilitate the use of certain kinds of strategies during skill learning. Although the research that has been conducted in physical education settings regarding learning strategies has shown promise, further investigation is needed to clarify how teachers can structure the learning environment to facilitate students' effective use of learning strategies.

Metacognition and self-regulation

Investigation into learner cognition is grounded in the assumption that learners can exert some control over their cognitions. Metacognition is defined by Wittrock (1986b) as the learner's knowledge about and control over their cognitive processes. Self-regulation of cognitive processes involves planning, monitoring, control, and reaction and reflection (Pintrich, 2000). There is a large and diverse body of research on self-regulatory processes and metacognition in the educational psychology literature (Boekaerts et al., 2000), and much of the recent research on learner cognition in classrooms has been folded into a self-regulation framework (Pintrich, 2003). Relatively little research in physical education settings, however, has addressed issues of metacognition and self-regulation. Luke and Hardy (1999) present a metacognitive ability conceptual framework incorporating metacognitive knowledge, strategies and experiences. They argue that the concept of metacognitive ability is important in understanding the complexity of learning in physical education and encourage researchers to use this framework to study learner cognition.

Luke and Hardy (1999) point out that there has been limited investigation of metacognitive processes in physical education, but several researchers have begun to address this. In an early study, Bouffard and Dunn (1993) investigated children's self-regulated learning of movement sequences. Older children demonstrated superior recall as compared to younger children, as they employed a greater variety of strategies and were able to use them more effectively. Self-regulation emerged as an influential factor in students' cognitive processes in the study by Solmon and Lee (1997). Students who reported being engaging in self-regulatory processes such as monitoring effort, seeking help, and problem solving had higher levels of confidence and attention, were willing to exert more effort, and use strategies. College students who had higher scores on a cognitive processes questionnaire, indicating an awareness of and willingness to engage in a positive pattern of cognitions, demonstrated higher levels of achievement (Solmon and

Boone, 1993). Rukavina (2003) investigated how college students' cognitions differed as a function of skill level under different teaching approaches. In the discovery and direct instruction conditions, participants with higher skill levels reported they engaged at a higher level of critical thinking. When a scaffolding approach was used to communicate task information in a guided discovery condition, however, the cognitive involvement in critical thinking did not differ as a function of skill level. Low-skill learners were able to engage in higher levels of cognition when the learning environment was structured to facilitate cognitive engagement.

Investigations specifically designed to investigate metacognition and self-regulation in physical education classes are just beginning. Luke's study (as cited in Luke and Hardy, 1999) is perhaps the first to examine students' metacognitive abilities in this setting. He concluded that students demonstrated poor metacognitive knowledge and inefficient metacognitive strategies. They seemed to be unaware that poor cognition hindered their performance, failed to regulate their cognitive activities, and believed they understood lesson content when assessments indicated they did not. Ommundsen (2003) recently investigated the relationship between implicit theories of ability and self-regulation strategies in physical education classes. Findings indicated that when students expressed the belief that ability can be improved with effort they were more likely to use metacognitive strategies, to better regulate their effort, and to seek help from classmates and teachers when needed. These initial studies demonstrate the utility of this line of investigation, and provide a basis for further inquiry into self-regulation and metacognition in physical education classes.

Implications for practice

Although much remains to be learned about learner cognition in physical education, the existing body of research provides a sound basis for several implications for teaching practice. It is apparent that learning requires cognitive effort and involvement, so the problem posed to the researchers and practitioners is how to structure the learning environment in ways that will foster high levels of cognitive engagement that will lead to achievement. Pintrich (2003) points out that there are multiple pathways for the energization and direction of behavior. General principles are supported by research using various theoretical frameworks, but the manner in which these principles applies to specific contexts may vary.

One key factor that has emerged is the need to consider previous experience, entry characteristics, and prior knowledge of the learner in the design of instruction. Students who enter achievement settings with high levels of confidence, who believe they have some level of control over the situation, and who value the task are more likely to be cognitively engaged in ways that translate to learning (Pintrich, 2003). By considering what students already know, and do not know, as well as how their prior experiences affect their perceptions of instruction and their expectations for success, practitioners can design learning activities that build on existing knowledge structures, enable students to have successful experiences, and foster their confidence. Fostering a belief in the efficacy of effort is an important component in this process. In addition to insuring that students feel they can be successful, it is also important to address the value component in the learning environment. Cognitive engagement is enhanced when individuals find some form of value in the task, whether it is intrinsic interest or enjoyment, or finding the activity useful in achieving a goal. Students are more likely to be cognitively engaged when they are motivated, and they are more likely to be motivated in activities when they find some value in the activity and they believe that they can be successful.

The research on learner cognition demonstrates the importance of directing the learner's attention to appropriate elements of the task. In order to accomplish that, it is important to develop an understanding of the learner's knowledge-related conceptions and misconceptions of the content. An understanding of how students' construct their knowledge is an essential element in designing an effective learning environment. Helping students link new information to prior knowledge, chunking information, and relating it to prior experience can help make knowledge more meaningful to students. It is also important not to overload students with so much information that they cannot process it. Asking questions to check for understanding is an effective instructional tool. It has the potential not only to provide information to the teacher about the learners' understanding, but also to help students clarify their knowledge and understanding in their own minds.

There is clear evidence that teaching approaches affect students' cognitions and the learning strategies that they use. Incorporating strategies and approaches that foster self-regulation and metacognition have the potential to enhance learner cognition which will ultimately affect student learning. According to Luke and Hardy (1999), one of the most challenging issues we face in this regard is to get students to start "thinking about thinking" in physical education classes. Approaches that involve guided discovery and problem solving, and those that require students to set goals, and monitor and evaluate their progress have the potential to accomplish that.

Future directions

Current research provides a sound basis for future study, but many questions about learner cognition remain. Several issues emerged in the review of this body of work. In much of the general education literature, as well as much of the research conducted in physical activity settings, the participants are college students. This work has made a valuable contribution to our understanding of learner cognition, but it does not automatically transfer to K-12 practice. There are studies that have been conducted with schoolchildren, but if we are going to make application of this work to school settings, it is important to generate a larger database of studies involving schoolchildren.

Another issue is the duration of the studies, and the settings in which they are conducted. Many studies are correlational studies relying solely on self-report measures collected in a single session. Others involve short instructional sessions with novel activities using researchers as teachers. Clearly these studies have made a valuable contribution to the knowledge base, but if we are to further our understanding of learner cognition it is imperative that we conduct studies in schools that extend over a period of time and involve schoolchildren and their teachers. The reward system in higher education does not necessarily foster a disposition to conduct that kind of research, as it is expedient and convenient to use college students as participants and to conduct studies of a short duration, and I readily acknowledge that much of my work falls into this category. If we are to move forward in this research agenda, however, it is important to conduct long-term studies in field-based contexts. A related issue mentioned earlier but reiterated here is the need to investigate the cognitive aspects of domain- specific knowledge. The studies published in the Griffin and Placek (2001) monograph demonstrate the contribution that line of inquiry can make, and more investigation of how domain-specific knowledge develops is warranted.

Researchers in physical education have begun to investigate self-regulation and metacognition, and that line of research also shows much promise. We need studies concerning the feasibility of teaching learning strategies to students in physical activity settings and how that will affect achievement, especially for individuals who begin with low levels of initial skill and perceived competence. It is also important to pursue a research agenda that explores the relationship between cognition and motivation, and how those complex processes interrelate.

Acknowledgment

I gratefully acknowledge the thoughtful and insightful comments of Amelia Lee and Charity Bryan on an earlier draft of this manuscript.

References

Anderson, J.R., Greeno, J.G., Reder, L. M. and Simon, H. A. (2000). Perspectives on learning, thinking, and activity. *Educational Researcher, 29(4)*: 11–13.

Bandura, A. (1986). *Social foundations of thought and action: A social cognitive theory.* Englewood Cliffs, NJ: Prentice Hall.

Biddle, S.J.H. (2001). Enhancing motivation in physical education. In G.C. Roberts (Ed.), *Advances in motivation in sport and exercise*, (pp. 101–127). Champaign, IL: Human Kinetics.

Boekaerts, M., Pintrich, P.R. and Zeidner, M. (Eds.). (2000). *Handbook of self-regulation.* San Diego, CA Acadmic Press.

Bouffard, M., and Dunn, J.G.H. (1993). Children's self-regulated learning of movement sequences. *Research Quarterly for Exercise and Sport, 64*: 393–403.

Brown, A.L., Bransford, J.D., Ferrara, R.A. and Campione, J.C. (1983). Learning, remembering, and understanding. In J.H. Flavell and E.M. Markman (Eds.), *Handbook of child psycholOlgy: Cognitive development* (Vol. 3, pp. 77–166). New York: Wiley.

Byra, M. and Jenkins, J. (1998). The thoughts and behaviors of learners in the inclusion style of teaching. *Journal of Teaching in Physical Education, 18*: 260–42.

Chen, A. (2001). A theoretical conceptualization for motivation research in physical education: An integrated perspective. *Quest, 53*: 59–76.

Dodds, P., Griffin, L.L. and Placek, J.H. (2001). A selected review of literature on the development of learners' domain-specific knowledge. *Journal of Teaching in Physical Education, 20*: 301–313.

Doyle, W. (1977). Paradigms of research for teacher effectiveness. *Review of Research in Education, 5*: 163–198.

Dweck, C.S. (2000). Self-theories: *Their role in motivation, personality, and development.* Philadelphia PA. Taylor and Francis.

Fitts, P.M. and Posner, M.I. (1967). *Human performance.* Belmont, CA: Brooks/Cole.

Floden, R.E. (2001) Research on effects of teaching: A continuing model for research on teaching. In V. Richardson (Ed.), *Handbook of research on teaching* (4th ed., pp. 3–16). Washington, DC.: American Educational Research Association.

Gage, N.L. (Ed.) (1963). *Handbook of research on teaching.* Chicago, IL: Rand McNally.

Gage, N.L. and Berliner, D.C. (1992). *Educational psychology.* Fifth edition. Boston, MA: Houghton Mifflin.

Gentile, A.M. (1972). A working model of skill acquisition with application to teaching. *Quest*, Monograph, *17*: 3–23.

Greeno, J.G., Collins, A.M. and Resnick, L.B. (1996). Cognition and learning. In D.C. Berliner, and R.C. Calfee, (Eds.), *Handbook of educational psychology* (pp. 15–46). New York: Simon and Schuster Macmillan.

Griffin, L.L. and Placek, J.H. (Eds.). (2001). The understanding and development of learners' domain-specific knowledge [Monograph]. *Journal of Teaching in Physical Education, 20*: 299–406.

Griffin, L.L., Dodds, P., Placek, J.H. and Tremino, F. (2001). Middle school students' conceptions of soccer: Their solutions to tactical problems, *Journal of Teaching in Physical Education, 20*: 324–340.

Hare, M.K. and Graber, K.C. (2000). Student misconceptions during two invasion game units in physical education: A qualitative investigation of student though processing. *Journal of Teaching in Physical Education, 20*: 55–77.

Harter, S. (1985). Competence as a dimension of self-evaluation: Toward a comprehensive model of self-worth. In R. Leahy (Ed.), *The Development of the self* (pp. 55–121). New York: Academic Press.

Hebert, E., Landin, D. and Solmon, M.A. (2000). The impact of task progressions on students' practice quality and thought process. *Journal of Teaching in Physical Education, 19*: 338–354.

Langley, D.J. (1995a). Examining the personal experience of student skill learning: A narrative perspective. *Research Quarterly for Exercise and Sport, 66*: 116–128.

Langley, D.J. (1995b). Student cognition in the instructional setting. *Journal of Teaching in Physical Education, 15*: 25–40.

Lee, A.M. (1997). Contributions of research on student thinking in physical education. *Journal of Teaching in Physical Education, 16*: 262–277.

Lee, A.M. and Solmon, M.A. (1992). Cognitive conceptions of teaching and learning motor skills. *Quest, 44*: 57–71.

Lee, A.M., Landin, D.K. and Carter, J.A. (1992). Student thoughts during tennis instruction. *Journal of Teaching in Physical Education, 11*: 256–267.

Lee, A.M., Carter, J.A. and Xiang, P. (1995). Children's conceptions of ability in physical education. *Journal of Teaching in Physical Education, 14*: 384–393.

Lee, A., Fredenburg, K., Belcher, D. and Cleveland, N. (1999). Gender differences in children's conceptions of competence and motivation in physical education. *Sport, Education and Society, 4*: 161–174.

Li, W., Lee, A.M. and Solmon, M. A. (2006). Gender differences in beliefs about the influence of ability and effort on performance in sport and physical activity. *Sex Roles, 54*: 147–156.

Li, W., Lee, A. M. and Solmon, M.A. (2005). Examining the relationships between dispositional ability conceptions, intrinsic motivation, perceived competence, experience and performance. *Journal of Teaching in Physical Education, 24*: 51–65.

Li, W., Lee, A.M. and Solmon, M.A. (2004). *Examining the relationships between dispositional ability conceptions, intrinsic motivation, perceived competence, experience, and performance.* Paper presented at the annual meeting of the American Educational Research Association, San Diego, CA.

Locke, L.F. and Jensen, M.K. (1974). Thought sampling: A study of student attention through self-report. *Research Quarterly, 45*: 263–275.

Luke, I.& Hardy, C. (1999). Appreciating the complexity of learning in physical education: The utilization of a metacognitive ability conceptual framework. *Sport, Education and Society, 4*: 175–191.

Luyten, L., Lowyck, J. and Tuerlinckx, F. (2001). Task perception as a mediating variable: A contribution to the validation of instructional knowledge. *British Journal of Educational Psychology, 71*: 203–223.

MacKeachie, W.J. (2000). Foreword. In M. Boekaerts, P.R. Pintrich, and M. Zeidner, (Eds.), *Handbook of self-regulation* (pp. xxi–xxiii). New York: Academic Press.

Magill, R.A. (2001). *Motor learning: Concepts and applications* (6th Ed). Bostonm MA: McGraw Hill.

Martinek, T.J. (1988). Confirmation of a teacher expectancy model: Student perceptions and casual attributions of teaching behaviors. *Research Quarterly for Exercise and Sport, 59*: 118–126.

Marx, R.W. and Winne P. H. (1987). The best tool teachers have–their students' thinking. In D. C. Berliner, and B.V. Rosenshine (Eds.), *Talks to teachers* (pp. 267–304). New York: Random House.

Nevett, M., Rovegno, I. and Babiarz, M. (2001a). Fourth-grade children's knowledge of cutting, passing and tactics in invasion games after a 12-lesson unit of instruction. *Journal of Teaching in Physical Education, 20*: 389–401.

Nevett, M., Rovegno, I., Babiarz, M. and McCaughtry, N. (2001b). Changes in basic tactics and motor skills in an invasion-type game after a 12-lesson unit of instruction. *Journal of Teaching in Physical Education, 20*: 352–369.

Nicholls, J.G. (1984). Conceptions of ability and achievement motivation. In R. Ames and C. Ames (Eds.), *Research on motivation in education*: Vol 1. *Student Motivation* (pp. 39–68). New York: Academic Press.

Nixon, J.E. and Locke. L. (1973). Research in teaching in physical education. In R.M.W. Travers (Ed.), *Second handbook of research on teaching* (pp. 1210–1242). Chicago, IL: Rand McNally.

Ommundsen, Y. (2003). Implicit theories of ability and self-regulation strategies in physical education classes. *Educational Psychology, 23*: 141–157.

Perkins, D. N. and Simmons, R. (1988). Patterns of misunderstanding: An integrative model for science, math, and programming. *Review of Educational Research, 58*, 303–326.

Peterson, P.L. (1988). Teachers' and students' cognitional knowledge for classroom teaching and learning. *Educational Researcher, 17*(5): 5–14.

Peterson, P.L.and Swing, S.R. (1982). Beyond time on task: Student's reports of their thought processes during classroom instruction. In W. Doyle and T.L. Good (Eds.), *Focus on teaching: Readings from the elementary School Journal* (pp. 228–238). Chicago, IL: The University of Chicago Press.

Peterson, P.L., Swing, S.R., Stark, K.D. and Waas, G.A. (1984). Students' cognition and time on task during mathematics instruction. *American Educational Research Journal, 21*: 497–515.

Pintrich, P.R. (2000). The role of goal orientation in self-regulated learning. In M. Boekaerts, P.R. Pintrich and M. Zeidner (Eds.), *Handbook of self-regulation* (pp. 451–502). New York: Academic Press.

Pintrich, P.R. (2003). A motivational science perspective on the role of student motivation in learning and teaching contexts. *Journal of Educational Psychology,* *95*: 667–686.

Pintrich, P.R. and Garcia, T. (1991). Student goal orientation and self-regulation in the college classroom. In M. Maehr and P.R. Pintrich (Eds.), *Advances in motivation and achievement, Vol. 7: Goals and self-regulatory processes* (pp. 371–402). Greenwich, CT: JAI.

Pintrich, P.R. and Schunk, D.J. (2002). *Motivation in education: Theory, research, and applications* (2nd Ed.), Upper Saddle River, NJ: Prentice Hall.

Placek, J.H., Griffin, L.L., Dodds, P., Raymond, C., Tremino, F. and James, A. (2001). Middle school students' conceptions of fitness: The long road to a healthy life style. *Journal of Teaching in Physical Education, 20*: 314–323.

Putnam, R.T., Lampert, M. and Peterson, P.L. (1990). Alternative perspectives on knowing mathematics in elementary schools. *Review of Research in Education, 16*: 57–150.

Richardson, V. (Ed.) (2001). Handbook of research on teaching (4th Ed.), Washington, DC.: *American Educational Research Association.*

Rink, J.E. (2001). Investigating the assumptions of pedagogy. *Journal of Teaching in Physical Education, 20*: 112–128.

Roberts, G.C. (1992). Motivation in sport and exercise: Conceptual constraints and convergence. In G.C. Roberts, (Ed.), *Motivation in sport and exercise* (pp.3–29), Champaign, IL: Human Kinetics.

Roberts, G.C. (2001). Understanding the dynamics of motivation in physical activity: The influence of achievement goals on motivational processes. In G.C. Roberts (Ed.), *Advances in motivation in sport and exercise* (pp. 1–50). Champaign, IL: Human Kinetics.

Rosenshine, B. (1976). Classroom instruction. In N.L. Gage (Ed.), *The psychology of teaching methods.* 75th Yearbook of the National Society for the Study of Education, Pt. 1. Chicago, IL: University of Chicago Press.

Rosenshine, B. and Furst, N. (1973). The use of direct observation to study teaching. In R.M.W. Travers (Ed.), *Second handbook of research on teaching* (pp. 122–183). Chicago,IL: Rand McNally.

Rovegno, I., Nevett, M., Brock, S. and Babiarz, M. (2001). Teaching and learning basic invasion-game tactics in 4th grade: A descriptive study from situated and constraints theoretical perspectives. *Journal of Teaching in Physical Education, 20*: 370–388.

Rukavina, P.B. (2003). *The effect of scaffolding movement challenges on students' task-related thoughts and performance.* Unpublished doctoral dissertation, Louisiana State University, Baton Rouge.

Rukavina, P.B., Lee, A.M. and Solmon, M.A. (2001). Maximizing student learning: A comparison of task communication strategies. *Journal of Sport Pedagogy, 7*: 61–75.

Rukavina, P., Lee, A.M. and Solmon, M.A. (2004). *Cognitive processes in direct and indirect task communication strategies.* Manuscript submitted for publication.

Schuell, T.J. (1986). Cognitive conceptions of learning. *Review of Educational Research, 56*: 411–436.

Schutz, P.A. (1992). Goals as the transactive point between motivation and cognition. In P.R. Pintrich, D.R. Brown and C.E. Weinstein (Eds.), *Student motivation, cognition, and learning: Essays in honor of Wilbert J. McKeachie* (pp. 135–156). Hillsdale, NJ: Lawrence Erlbaum.

Shulman, L.S. (1986). Paradigms and research programs in the study of teaching: A contemporary perspective. In M.C. Wittrock (Ed.), *Handbook of research on teaching* (3rd ed. pp. 3–36). New York: MacMillan.

Silverman, S. and Subramaniam, P.R. (1999). Student attitude toward physical education and physical activity: A review of measurement issues and outcomes. *Journal of Teaching in Physical Education, 19*: 97–125.

Solmon, M. (2003). Student issues in physical education classes: Attitude, cognition, and motivation. In S.J. Silverman and C.D. Ennis (Eds.), *Student learning in physical education: Applying research to enhance instruction* (2nd ed., pp. 147–163). Champaign, IL: Human Kinetics.

Solmon, M.A. and Boone, J. (1993). The impact of student goal orientation in physical education classes. *Research Quarterly for Exercise and Sport, 64*: 418–424.

Solmon, M.A. and Carter, J.A. (1995). Kindergarten and first-grade students' perceptions of physical education in one teacher's classes. *Elementary School Journal, 95*: 355–365.

Solmon, M.A. and Lee, A.M. (1996). Entry characteristics, practice variables, and cognition: Student mediation of instruction. *Journal of Teaching in Physical Education, 15*: 136–150.

Solmon, M.A. and Lee, A.M. (1997). Development of an instrument to assess cognitive processes in physical education classes. *Research Quarterly for Exercise and Sport, 68*: 152–160.

Stewart, S. and Mitchell, M. (2003). Instructional variables and student knowledge and conceptions of fitness. *Journal of Teaching in Physical Education, 22*: 533–551.

Subramaniam, P.R. and Silverman, S. (2000). Validation of scores from an instrument assessing student attitude toward physical education. *Measurement in Physical Education and Exercise Science, 4*: 29–43.

Subramaniam, P.R. and Silverman, S. (2002). Using complementary data: An investigation of student attitude in physical education. *Journal of Sport Pedagogy, 8*: 74–91.

Tjeerdsma, B.L. (1997). A comparison of teacher and student perspectives of tasks and feedback. *Journal of Teaching in Physical Education, 16*: 388–400.

Tousignant, M. and Siedentop, D. (1983). A qualitative analysis of task structures in required secondary physical education classes. *Journal of Teaching in Physical Education, 3*: 47–57.

Travers, R.M.W. (Ed.) (1973). *Second handbook of research on teaching.* Chicago, IL: Rand McNally.

Wang, J.C.K. and Biddle, S.J.H. (2001). Young people's motivational profiles in physical activity: A cluster analysis. *Journal of Sport & Exercise Psychology, 23*: 1–22.

Weedon, C. (1997). *Feminist practice and poststructuralist theory.* Malden, MA: Blackwell Publishers Inc.

Weinstein, C.E. and Mayer, R.E. (1986) The teaching of learning strategies. In M.C. Wittrock (Ed.), *Handbook of research on teaching* (3rd ed. pp. 315–327). New York: MacMillan.

Windschitl, M. (2002). Framing constructivism practice as the negotiation of dilemmas: An analysis of the conceptual, pedagogical, cultural, and political challenges facing teachers. *Review of Educational Research, 72*: 131–175.

Wittrock, M.C. (Ed.), (1986a) *Handbook of research on teaching* (3rd ed.). New York: MacMillan.

Wittrock, M.C. (1986b). Students' thought processes. In M.C. Wittrock (Ed.), *Handbook of research on teaching* (3rd ed. pp. 297–314). New York: MacMillan.

Xiang, P. and Lee, A. (1998). The development of self-perceptions of ability and achievement goals and their relations in physical education. *Research Quarterly for Exercise and Sport, 69*: 231–241.

Xiang, P., Lee, A. and Williamson, L. (2001). Conceptions of ability in physical education: Children and adolescents. *Journal of Teaching in Physical Education, 20*: 282–294.

Xiang, P., McBride, R., Guan, J. and Solmon, M. (2003). Children's motivation in elementary physical education: An expectancy-value model of achievement choice. *Research Quarterly for Exercise and Sport, 74*: 25–35.

Xiang, P., McBride, R., Guan, J. (2004). Children's motivation in elementary physical education: A longitudinal study. *Research Quarterly for Exercise and Sport, 75*: 71–80.

3.4 Constructivist perspectives on learning

INEZ ROVEGNO AND JOHN P. DOLLY

Introduction

This chapter reviews research in physical education conducted from constructivist perspectives. Although much if not most research on teaching, learning, and curriculum in physical education owes an allegiance to some theoretical orientation, this review is limited to those studies that explicitly used a constructivist perspective to guide the design of the study or interpret the findings. This limitation resulted in an incomplete portrayal of what research has reported about particular topics because many topics studied from a constructivist perspective have been studied from other perspectives. Because physical education researchers are interested in studying learning by both students in physical education settings and by pre-service and in-service teachers in teacher education settings, this review includes studies of physical education and teacher education.

A constructivist perspective offers a theoretical perspective on learning; it does not provide a theory of curriculum or instruction. As Rink (2001) suggests, however, all instructional approaches are based either implicitly or explicitly on some learning theory. There is a long history of curriculum work in physical education that has linked teaching and curriculum to a theoretical perspective on learning. Thus it is not surprising that many of the papers reviewed in this chapter directly examined a combination of learning, teaching, and curriculum.

This chapter focuses on theory most of which has been developed in the field of psychology. Many of the principles discussed are derived from research conducted on cognition and in classrooms. This work is relevant to physical education for several reasons. Cognitive knowledge of movement and fitness concepts and cognitive and social processes (e.g. analysis, decision making, social responsibility, effective group interactions, etc.) are critically important in physical education and are explicitly part of the national curriculum standards or curriculum guidelines in Scotland, England, Australia, and the USA. In addition, theories of learning developed within the motor domain have long been either directly based on theories developed in general psychology or strongly resemble such theories. For example, information processing and schema theories in the motor domain are both based on the same theories in cognitive science.

We believe it is counterproductive to claim that if we do not have substantial testing of a learning theory across physical activities, that we should not apply that theory without proof of its general effectiveness across all situations. There is little proof in physical education that any learning theory is most effective. The general principles of constructivism that learning is an active process, learners construct knowledge in relation to their prior knowledge, and knowledge is socially constructed have substantially more support in psychology research than the equally accurate and well-accepted principle that practice is essential in order to learn motor skills. The principles of constructivism have been generalized from a large body of research conducted in laboratories, everyday settings and school classrooms across subject domains. It seems unproductive to ignore this body of work. What we need to consider, however, is how, when, and to what extent these principles apply to particular physical education content and in which settings. For example, constructivist principles may very well play an insignificant role in explaining the development of walking, but they are likely to be very relevant and helpful in understanding the learning of complex motor activities in the social and cultural environments of schools. The tradition in physical education to apply research on classroom learning (e.g. academic learning time) has been and we believe will continue to be beneficial.

Multiple theories called constructivism

A number of different theories of knowledge and learning are termed constructivist (Phillips, 1995). Cognitive constructivism, focusing on psychological perspectives, can be organized under three general categories: (a) modern information processing theory, (b) radical constructivism, and (c) cognitive schema theory (Derry, 1996). Derry explained, "Cognitive constructivism is not a unique theoretical framework, pedagogical approach, or epistemology, but a general, metaphorical assumption about the nature of cognition that virtually all cognitive educational researchers accept. Despite this unifying assumption, there are many different cognitive constructivist research programs and theories within the community at large" (p. 163). Constructivism, however, is also a label for perspectives that focus on (a) "the construction of human knowledge in general" (Phillips, 1995, 7) such as scholars who focus on the social and cultural construction of knowledge, for example, feminist epistemologies, (b) social interactions as a primary mechanism for learning, (c) the way knowledge is represented culturally, and (d) the ways individuals are acculturated into cultural practices (Cobb, 1994a; Phillips, 1995). Phillips (1995) also notes the current use and impact of constructivist epistemologies of Immanuel Kant, Thomas Kuhn, John Dewey, and William James.

The arguments about the meaning of constructivism to different theorists often is based on their view of knowledge, for example, is knowledge socially constructed or situated or is it an individual process? (Derry, 1996). Cobb (1994b) addressed this distinction and advocated a viewpoint that combines social, sociocultural, and cognitive perspectives, a viewpoint we find reasonable. Nevertheless, other scholars disagree. According to Marshall (1996) "Using the term constructivism to refer to different approaches masks important differences, not just in meaning and assumptions, but also in how these various approaches are implemented in classrooms and their consequences for learners" (p. 238).

Constructivism: a theory of learning, not a prescription for teaching

In this section we focus on constructivist principles derived from research on learning mainly from psychology and social psychology. The situated perspectives, sometimes described as constructivist (Kirk and MacDonald, 1998) are discussed in a separate chapter. We begin by describing the contributions of Piaget and Vygotsky as these theorists are widely cited as the original source of many constructivist ideas.

Before doing so, we want to emphasize that constructivism is a theory of learning and is not a prescriptive set of instructional strategies. Cobb (1994a) explained his stance.

> The various versions of constructivism discussed in this issue do not constitute axiomatic foundations from which to deduce pedagogical principles. They can instead be thought of as general orienting frameworks within which to address pedagogical issues and develop instructional approaches. (p. 4)

Similarly, Driver et al. (1994) pointed out that constructivism is a theoretical perspective and any relationship between views of learning and pedagogy is problematic. As a theory of learning, constructivism provides no simple rules for pedagogical practice. Finally, the National Research Council (1999) stated, "Theoretical physics does not prescribe the design of a bridge, but surely it constrains the design of successful ones. Similarly, learning theory provides no simple recipe for designing effective learning environments, but it constrains the design of effective ones" (p. xvi).

Early constructivist theorists

Piaget and Vygotsky are the two leading theorists who most visibly represent the constructivist perspective as it has been applied in education. Jean Piaget created a theory around children's stages of development (Piaget and Inhelder, 1969). Of particular importance are his conclusions that children learn best when they are active and seek their own solutions to problems. He emphasized an active learner who makes discoveries, reflects on them and discusses them with others. He was concerned with developmentally appropriate activities taking into account the students' current readiness for learning and thinking. He believed for students truly to learn, they need to be personally engaged in the learning activity. Observing someone else doing a task has little meaning until the student demonstrates the ability to perform the task (Piaget, 1973).

In general, there is research supporting Piaget's conceptualization of how abilities emerge (Flavell, 1996; Schneider and Lockl, 2002; Seigler and Richards, 1982). Although researchers have challenged the more rigid stage process of development since his original work, Piaget created a theoretical perspective that has generated much research across education and psychology. In summarizing his comments about Piaget, Flavell (1996) indicates that Piaget is the most important person the field of cognitive development has known.

I think we are in more danger of underappreciating Piaget than overappreciating him, for much the same reason that fish are said to underappreciate the virtues of water. That is, many of Piaget's contributions have become so much a part of the way we view cognitive development nowadays that they are virtually invisible. (p. 202)

Piaget (1971) was one of the earliest theorists to describe how children perceive their environment and represent it cognitively. He describes a process of continual accommodation to and assimilation of information as a means of knowledge acquisition. He emphasized the learner as active in the learning process. "In short, elementary knowledge is never the result of a mere impression made by the object or the sensoral organs, but it is always due to an active assimilation of the subject who incorporates the objects to his sensorimotor schemes" (pp. 107–108).

In 1973, Piaget emphasized the close relationship between thought and language and their impact on the construction of knowledge. According to Youniss and Damon (1992), Piaget's theory remains important and valuable for those interested in the construction of knowledge. "With the single exception of Vygotskian theory, it stands alone among developmental approaches in its capacity to explain how the quality of particular social experiences influences the nature of ideas and values that arise from that experience" (p. 284). Piaget not only influenced the entire field of cognitive development, he also influenced some of the thinking of the other great theorist L. S. Vygotsky who often refers to Piaget's earlier work in his writing (1986, 1987).

Vygotsky (1986) was the other strong influence on constructivist theory. Like Piaget, Vygotsky (1987, 1997a) believed that children construct their own knowledge (Minick, 1987). Although Vygotsky emphasized language development, he also emphasized that cognitive skills are mediated by discourse and further they have their origins in social relations and a sociocultural backdrop. Vygotsky saw the child's development as inseparable from social and cultural activities.

Only when we learn to see the unity of generalization and social interaction do we begin to understand the actual connection that exists between the child's cognitive and social development. Our research is concerned with resolving both these fundamental problems, the problem of the relationship of thought to word and the problem of the relationship of generalization to social interaction. (Vygotsky, 1987: 49)

Vygotsky's theory, sometimes referred to as a social constructivist theory, suggests that knowledge and understanding can be best advanced through interactions with others in cooperative activities (Miller, 2003). These experiences in social contexts provide opportunities for students to develop their own views and construct their own knowledge.

Vygotsky's theoretical framework, which has been widely applied in education, had as a central component the analysis of transformations in children's personalities caused by the relationship between individual and social forces. Vygotsky provides a solid foundation for building teaching–learning classrooms that honor cultural and linguistic diversity and strive to educate and assess the whole child. (Mahn, 2003: 135–136)

Vygotsky's (1986) theory of cognitive development emphasizes the social origins of cognition. Vygotsky believed that children master activities and refine their thinking as a result of joint activities with more competent members of society. Vygotsky (1998, 1999) also placed a great deal of emphasis on action in the developmental process. In talking about words and actions, he pointed out that actions occur before speech. According to Jacobs and Eccles (2000), two of the critical features of his theory are intersubjectivity and scaffolding. "Intersubjectivity refers to the process of two people who begin a task with different conceptualizations coming to a shared understanding of the task as each person adjusts to the perspective of the other. … The concept of scaffolding refers to the social support provided by adults in any learning situation" (p. 424). According to Vygotsky (1997b), "For us to call a process 'external' means to call it 'social.' Every higher mental function was external because it was social before it became an internal, strictly mental function; it was formerly a social relation of two people" (p. 105).

In the application of both Piaget's and Vygotsky's theoretical models, the teacher is viewed as a facilitator who helps students learn new knowledge by creating positive learning environments that take into account the child's prior knowledge, experience, developmental level, and culture. The learner needs to have the opportunity to ask questions, generate hypotheses, and test their own ideas (Fosnot, 1996).

Core ideas of constructivism

Since the cognitive revolution beginning in the late 1950s a considerable amount of research has supported a set of core constructivist ideas. These ideas have been applied in research and also in a wide range of practitioner books and articles aimed at synthesizing and simplifying the research for teachers to a small set of recommendations (Fosnot, 1996; Grennon-Brooks and Brooks, 1993). We discuss the core ideas below.

Deep understanding and multiple connections support transfer to other contexts

Developed from studies of expertise across domains, research shows that successful learning results in: (a) a deep understanding of a body of knowledge, (b) chunks of information that are well-connected and organized around broad, meaningful, and important concepts and principles within the domain, and (c) knowledge that can be flexibly and accurately applied and transferred to other contexts (Chi et al., 1981, 1982; deGroot, 1965; Glaser, 1984, 1987). The idea of helping learners develop a deep, holistic, meaningful, well-connected understanding of school content has been a consistent suggestion by scholars attempting to provide teachers with guidance on using constructivist principles in their classrooms (Grennon-Brooks and Brooks, 1993; Fosnot, 1996; Prawat, 1992). The National Research Council (1999) recommends carefully planning instruction to insure that students develop more than a surface-level understanding. The goal is for students to develop a deep, meaningful grasp of concepts and be able to generalize concepts and knowledge to new settings and situations. Scholars have similarly advocated for Jerome Bruner's (1960) related ideas about the structure of the disciplines each having overarching structures that organize the knowledge of a domain. He proposed that teaching learners about the structures of the discipline at developmentally appropriate levels would help learners understand the meaning of concepts they were learning.

Research has shown that for learning to be applicable and generalizable it must be guided by general principles (National Research Council, 1999). When the learner understands underlying principles, transfer to new problems and new situations is more likely to occur; rote memory, as a form of knowledge, rarely transfers (National Research Council, 1999). Moreover, knowledge transfer in complex content domains requires cognitive flexibility, that is, the ability to create new representations by reorganizing, reordering, and flexibly applying pre-existing knowledge (Spiro, et al., 1987). In their summary of the research on transfer, the National Research Council (1999) suggests that transfer is facilitated by the degree to which people master and understand the original subject, apply the subject in multiple contexts, understand the abstract and underlying principles, and understand the conditions under which a concept or principle can be applied appropriately.

Prior knowledge and experiences

[Humans] come to formal education with a range of prior knowledge, skills, beliefs, and concepts that significantly influence what they notice about the environment and how they organize and interpret it. This, in turn, affects their abilities to remember, reason, solve problems, and acquire new knowledge. (National Research Council, 1999: 10)

Pre-existing knowledge changes through the processes of accretion, tuning, and restructuring (Rumelhart and Norman, 1978). These processes are an extension of Piaget's notions of assimilation and accommodation (Piaget and Inhelder, 1969). Based on their experiences, learners' initial conceptions can be inaccurate, naive, or incomplete and these initial conceptions can seem reasonable and be useful for interpreting experience or understanding a concept (Shuell, 1986).

We can see evidence for this even in the early work of Piaget who spent much time assessing these misconceptions trying to align them with a child's cognitive development (Piaget and Inhelder, 1969). Misconceptions can be difficult to change and have a negative impact on learning (Confrey, 1990).

There is a good deal of evidence that learning is enhanced when teachers pay attention to the knowledge and beliefs that learners bring to a learning task, use this knowledge as a starting point for new instruction, and monitor students' changing conceptions as instruction proceeds. (National Research Council, 1999: 11)

Moreover, a considerable amount of research indicates that students' prior knowledge is culturally based and acquired in the social practices within families, social communities, and ethnic and religious communities where race, gender, class, and sexuality are relevant (National Research Council, 1999). Thus, cultural practices and beliefs combined with prior academic knowledge are critical pieces of information to enable a teacher to develop instruction that is relevant, appropriate and challenging for the learner. Culture plays a major role in how we approach, present, and interpret new knowledge. Both teacher and student bring their own cultural beliefs and expectations to the classroom, both impact children's success.

Constructivism is often used to support the idea that teaching should be child-centered or learner-centered. This does not mean children determine the content and whatever they discover through hands–on activities is acceptable–a misconception about constructivism. What this means is that teachers focus on what students know, believe, can do, and bring to the classroom and then on how children are understanding, interpreting, thinking and feeling about the content being taught. Being learner-centered means asking, how does this student understand the content at this moment? What is this child's level of development and how will that impact her or his response to this task? How is the current classroom environment supporting or not supporting student learning? What content or instructional strategy will best help this child learn?

Learning is an active process of constructing knowledge

The hallmark of constructivist perspectives from the beginning is that learning is an active process of constructing knowledge. "The educational philosophy of John Dewey and the developmental psychologists Lev Vygotsky, Jean Piaget, and Jerome Bruner, among others, propose that children actively construct knowledge, and that this knowledge is constructed in a social context" (Zuckerman, 2003: 177).

> Broadly speaking, cognitive science confirms Piaget's claim that people must *construct* their understanding; they do not simply register what the world shows or tells them, as a camera or a tape recorder does. To "know" something, indeed, even simply to memorize effectively, people build a mental representation that imposes order and coherence on experience and information. (Resnick and Williams-Hall, 1998: 100)

Constructivist perspectives on learning emphasize the importance of students actively engaged in constructing knowledge and understanding. This places the teacher in a new role where he or she is seen as encouraging students to explore their world, discover knowledge, set and solve problems, and then to reflect and think critically (Grennon-Brooks and Brooks, 1993). Central to the idea of learning as an active process are both the self-regulatory cognitive processes (such as metacognition) and the knowledge that is the focus of instruction. Knowledge and cognitive processing are intertwined (Resnick and Williams-Hall, 1998). Resnick and Williams-Hall (1998) summarized the research and proposed that effective learning relies on learners actively engaging various cognitive processes to understand, reason about, reflect on, evaluate, and analyze information that is critical to learn. Moreover, effectiveness relies on learners self-monitoring and self-regulating what they are learning and the cognitive strategies, orientations, and dispositions they are employing during the learning process and evaluating if these strategies are effective (e.g. if they are confused or not, making connections or not, comprehending or not). There is considerable research supporting a range of teaching practices that include explicitly teaching cognitive processes along with self-regulation strategies as effective across subject matter domains (National Research Council, 1999; Perkins and Salomon, 1989).

The social and cultural construction of knowledge

Social interactions as a setting for learning

Social constructivist perspectives focus on learning in social settings. In discussing the collected works of Vygotsky, et al. (1993) summarized his central idea, "The source of development in mental processes is always social. Only later do these processes acquire individual psychological characteristics" (p. 306). The work of Vygotsky (1986) and Rogoff (1990) provide theoretical principles for how learning occurs through social interactions. The effectiveness of learning in groups has been well established across subject fields (National Research Council, 1999; Slavin, 1996). Through dialog, synthesizing and summarizing ideas to peers, explaining and justifying beliefs, making their thoughts and ideas explicit, negotiating conflicts, and resolving differing viewpoints students effectively learn through social interactions.

Knowledge is socially constructed

The value of having students construct knowledge through social interactions is further justified as this form of knowledge construction reflects the way knowledge is constructed within the disciplines. In making this argument for teaching science, Driver et al. (1994) describe how scientists initially constructed and socially negotiated scientific facts and principles. Teaching students science, they claim, should also include teaching students the processes that are used within the discipline to construct scientific knowledge – from hypotheses, to experiments, to the social construction, negotiation, and refinement of scientific knowledge. Similar arguments have been made for history and mathematics (Ball, 1993; Leinhardt and Greeno, 1991, 1994).

Cultural representations

Knowledge is not only socially constructed but arises within particular cultures and reflects the shared understandings of that culture. Social norms, ethnic values, religious values, media representations, and popular culture are among the culturally and publicly shared conceptions that can impact what and how students learn. These cultural constructions are particularly important in physical education with the pervasive interest in and powerful influence of professional and collegiate sport in societies and media representations of the body (Kirk, 1994, 1999).

The remainder of this chapter reviews the work in physical education based on constructivist perspectives. It is organized in the following sections: (a) curriculum theorizing based on a constructivist perspective, (b) curriculum theorizing of content, (c) descriptions of teaching based on constructivist principles of learning, (d) analyzing teaching using constructivist principles, (e) research on naive conceptions and misconceptions, (f) constructivist research on students' perspectives, (g) research on teacher learning, (h) social interactions as a setting for learning, and (i) studying programmatic components in undergraduate physical education teacher education.

Research in physical education

Curriculum theorizing based on a constructivist perspective

There is a problem in reviewing curriculum theorizing based on constructivist perspectives for this Handbook, which is limited to research. In the past 50 years our ideas about what constitutes research have changed and broadened considerably. We now view a range of conceptual, theoretical, and philosophical analyses as research and these analyses are regularly published in our research journals. Moreover, the field of curriculum has developed modes of inquiry for curriculum theorizing along with a host of journals publishing this work. When curriculum scholars first used constructivism as a theoretical perspective to guide their work there were no research journals in physical education devoted to curriculum scholarship nor was there a tradition of curriculum theorizing as a form of inquiry for publication. The outcomes of early curriculum scholarship and theorizing were applied and then disseminated in textbooks designed for teachers and undergraduates.

In these avenues of dissemination, the use of a constructivist perspective in curriculum scholarship has a long history in physical education especially at the elementary level and in curriculum designed in women's physical education college programs. For over 50 years curriculum writers have based their work on constructivist principles beginning with principles derived from the work of Piaget. For example, Mauldon and Redfern's text *Games Teaching* (1969) cites Piaget's work extensively in their framework of four stages of game development – which is a description of children's development related to games and the implications for the kinds of game experiences appropriate for teachers to provide at each stage. Similarly, Piaget's emphasis on children as active learners, explorers and discovers is evident in modern educational dance and modern educational gymnastics developed in England in the 1950s and 1960s (Morison, 1960). A similar

link between the then-emerging consensus about students as active, thinking, exploring learners and the use of teaching styles that would support these conceptions was discussed explicitly by Bilborough and Jones (1963) in England and Mosston (1966) in the US. This tradition continues today, especially with movement approaches at the elementary level, which are all heavily based on principles applied from constructivist theory (Allison and Barrett, 2000; Graham et al., 2004).

Teaching Games for Understanding (TGfU)

Several authors have noted that TGfU is consistent with constructivist principles. Kirk and MacPhail (2002) described how the methods of TGfU require the learner to be actively engaged in understanding the subject matter through the social interactions within group discussions. They note that TGfU proposes that first, teachers consider the learners' prior knowledge, experience, and developmental level and then modify the game form to match learners' levels of development. Finally, they discuss how teachers design tasks or game forms to focus learners' attention and guide their explorations and understanding of the tactical content that is the objective of the lesson.

Light and Fawns (2003) conducted the most thorough theorizing of TGfU to date. They drew on philosophical, psychological, and sociocultural research to describe the potential of TGfU as a curricular model for facilitating a deep, holistic understanding of games that also can contribute to students' skillfulness in games, higher-order thinking skills, social interactions, and positive affective experiences. They describe how structural aspects of TGfU facilitate students' active and social construction of knowledge. In terms of the social construction of knowledge, these include: (a) learners interacting within groups to solve problems; (b) an action–discussion cycle (game play followed by student group analysis of the game); (c) the use of cognitive processes during group discussions such as analysis, reflection, and critical thinking; and (d) a focus on the meaning of skills in the context of use. In terms of the active construction of knowledge, structural aspects of TGfU include: (a) teachers attending to students' prior knowledge and experiences as critical starting points for instruction; (b) the teacher as a facilitator of student learning by the use of open-ended questions; (c) the teacher setting tasks to focus students' attention and exploration of critical tactical concepts in game environments, and (d) the use of multiple instructional strategies based on the ways students are understanding the content being taught. Finally, TGfU facilitates the construction of holistic, connected knowledge through the simultaneous teaching of skills and tactics as they are applied in games.

Sport for Peace and Sport Education

Sport for Peace (Ennis, 1999) and Sport Education (Siedentop, 1994) are also secondary curriculum models with structures designed to support students' knowledge construction. Many of these structures require students to interact in groups and socially construct knowledge (such as generating the strategies and tactics they plan to employ in their games). These curriculum models also require individual students to be self-directed in constructing learning opportunities (e.g. when the captain or coach designs the content and tasks for practice sessions).

Ennis (1999) expanded on these underpinnings of constructivism in her description of Sport for Peace. It includes a focus on conflict negotiation, caring for other students, and social responsibility that is taught explicitly to students. Students are responsible for constructing a social environment that is safe, caring, and cooperative with opportunities for all team members to contribute and succeed. As Ennis indicates, sport environments are often inequitable environments that are not only dominated by males but reinforce alienation and marginalization of girls and the privileging of boys. Sport for Peace was designed to resist and contradict this social construction of the sport environment. The social construction of knowledge in Sport for Peace focuses on community, caring, enhancing the skill and game play ability of all teammates, and cooperative interdependence. Nevertheless, Ennis acknowledges that sport itself is a masculinist domain and Sport for Peace does not overcome these gender inequities. "Although Sport for Peace enhances girls experiences in sport, like other coeducational sport models, it fails to overcome repressive social constraints on girls' construction of their subjective identity as an active, engaged mover" (Ennis, 1999: 46). Other authors discuss these models in detail in other chapters of this handbook and we will not review them further here. The point here is that similar to TGfU, Sport for Peace and Sport Education are constructivist in their orientation through structures that require students to construct knowledge through social interactions.

Movement approaches

Chen et al. (2002) applied a biofunctional, "whole theme" constructivist approach (Iran-Nejad, 1994) to the movement approach for elementary physical education. The biofunctional, whole theme approach emphasizes learners' propensity to create themes, which are broad organizations of the learners'

intuitive knowledge base (Iran-Nejad, 1989). The whole theme approach views learning as multi-sourced (from both external and internal sources) and involves the learner's self-regulation, active attention to external sources, and active re-organization of their pre-existing knowledge (Iran-Nejad, et al., 1990). The implications are for teachers to elicit learners' knowledge (which is often tacit or held intuitively) and help learners connect their lived experiences with content being taught. The focus is on creating a thematic body of knowledge and helping learners understand the concepts of a domain within authentic contexts and broader themes. As opposed to a piecemeal approach (i.e. presenting concepts in a decontextualized way), a whole theme approach is based on simplification by integration (Iran-Nejad et al., 1990). Connecting the movement approach to biofunctional, whole theme constructivism, Chen et al. described the thematic organization of movement concepts based on Laban's framework for identifying content in movement approaches. Some movement approaches further organize concepts into smaller themes that can be the bases for lessons and units, while other movement approaches develop themes that integrate movement, social, and thinking processes (Logsdon et al., 1984; Hoffman et al., 1981). Chen et al. then analyzed a dance lesson and explained how the content and instructional techniques in the lesson were connected to whole theme constructivism.

Curriculum theorizing of content

A second way scholars have applied constructivist principles in curriculum work is in the analysis of subject matter for teaching. One purpose for this work is to give teachers and scholars a deeper understanding of the possibilities for learning within that content or approach and to provide content guidelines for teachers (Amade-Escot, 2000). An excellent example of such research was the analysis of tactical knowledge in team sports by Grehaigne and Godbount (1995). They first analyzed strategic and tactical (invasion) game play as a complex system where the actions of players were contingent upon and adaptive to other players. During matches, players must be able to react to unexpected situations, which they cannot precisely predict and practice during training. Through their research working with coaches and teachers and by observing game play, they identified a set of action rules or principles of action that outline the tactical content appropriate for teaching in team games. Based on these descriptions of the content of tactical game play, they propose that constructivist principles of learning are relevant to tactical knowledge. Due to the perceptual and decision-making components of tactics, learning involves "an adaptation to an environment perceived as a system of constraints and resources"

(p. 501) and learners must self-regulate (rather than simply reproduce what the teacher said) within game environments. Critical to their analysis was their claim that learning tactics is a constructive process that is more than the prescription of acquired knowledge but "constructed knowledge resulting from repeated hypothesis–verification cycles during practice" (p. 502).

Grehaigne and Godbount's (1995) analysis is an example of research from the Didactics Program (Amade-Escot, 2000). Amade-Escot (2000) explains how didactics research focuses on three levels of analysis. The macro level examines how disciplinary knowledge is constructed as social practices or by scholars within a discipline as it is transformed into knowledge taught in schools. The meso level examines how knowledge is adapted to learners and the micro level examines knowledge as it is negotiated and situated in physical education lessons. Both situated and constructivist principles are evident in this work. Fortunately, for those of us who cannot read French, another chapter reviews this body of research.

Descriptions of teaching based on constructivist principles of learning

In addition to describing curriculum, several studies have been conducted that describe teaching based on constructivist principles. What is significant about these studies is that they were conducted in the naturalistic setting and provide detailed accounts of how teachers can enact teaching methods, set an instructional environment, and select content that reflects constructivist views of learning. Most researchers have sought out accomplished or expert teachers for their studies.

Ennis (1991) conducted one of the first such studies on two expert teachers using a movement approach integrating thinking skills and content. The teachers used instructional techniques to facilitate children's use of thinking skills such as metacognition and focusing their attention on their movements while moving. They also attempted to help children use self-regulatory processes to monitor, assess, and adjust their work; explore and draw conclusions about movement responses; and think about and analyze movement to solve problems and acquire a deeper understanding.

In a series of studies, Weiyun Chen described critical aspects of constructivist-oriented teaching. The first study compared novice student teachers and expert teachers of constructivist-oriented movement approaches (Chen and Rovegno, 2000). Expert novice comparisons allow researchers to document, in a broad way, the beginning and end points of how teachers' knowledge can be expected to develop over time. Using a coding instrument, three experts and three novices were compared on three principles applied from constructivism (a) "engaging students in active and self-regulated construction of knowledge", (b) "activating students' prior knowledge and emerging relevance", and (c) "facilitating students' social interactions among groups and joint problem solving-settings" (p. 362). Although the novices used exploration tasks and asked children questions to engage their thinking about these activities, the expert teachers more extensively facilitated children's self-regulation and critical thinking and had a far more in-depth understanding. The experts knew that simply providing activities that had the possibility of facilitating the active construction of knowledge was not enough to insure that these learning processes occurred. The novices held what Prawat (1992) termed "naive" constructivist views. Similarly, the experts had far more differentiated and extensive ways to both activate children's prior knowledge and help them understand connections to their lives outside of school, while the novices focused primarily on activating prior knowledge. In addition, the experts used more group work and more extensively facilitated children's social interactions than the novices.

In the second study, Chen (2001) described the practices of an expert teacher of children's dance. The teacher (a) focused on connecting the content of dance to children's lives, (b) linked dance movement and shape to children's interpretations of picture books helping children elaborate and embody their interpretations of the story, (c) helped children generate ideas and then intentionally incorporated their ideas into the lesson and (d) encouraged children to respond to each others' ideas. Across lessons, the teacher facilitated the development of children's creative processes. These included (a) generating many varied responses, (b) expressing their interpretation of the dance material or the content of a poem or story, (c) elaborating, transforming, and organizing movements in their dance sequences, and (d) responding to the compositions of other children. She also worked explicitly on helping children self-regulate their practice and self-assess their dances.

In a third study, Chen and Cone (2003) studied the relationship between the expert teachers' instructional strategies and two kinds of knowledge construction by children: (a) the generation of divergent/original movements and (b) the refinement of dance quality. First, when the teacher used a scaffold to teach the exploration process and broke the content down into a sequence of tasks (for example, exploring a movement with one body part, then a second, then another and finally the whole body) and then asked children to generate their own divergent and original movements, the children succeeded in doing so. Similarly, when the teacher gave open-ended tasks along with demonstrating (or having children demonstrate), giving verbal cues, and asking questions, the children responded with divergent and original movements. In contrast, when the teacher presented either open-ended tasks without scaffolding the exploration process or tasks constrained to limited movements without relevant verbal cues, the children responded with a limited range of movements. The study also reported that the teacher used verbal cues and images to help the children refine the quality of their movements to become more expressive. In other words, teaching creative dance was not simply asking children to explore and design their own dances (constructive processes), but to help children refine and clarify their knowledge constructions.

These are important findings as they clarify that instructional techniques associated with constructivism when presented in limited or constrained ways will not automatically elicit the desired knowledge construction in children (in this case dance movement variety). To elicit knowledge construction in children requires the teacher go beyond simply presenting an activity. Further, the findings show that constructivist-oriented teaching includes instructional techniques such as demonstrating, verbal cues, refining cues, and breaking down content to scaffold cognitive processes–techniques that are sometimes misunderstood as not part of constructivist teaching.

Dyson (2002) described a teacher's implementation of cooperative learning and her students' responses to the lessons in terms of constructivist ideas about active, social learning. The teacher believed in a holistic approach that included motor, cognitive and affective goals, a belief recognized and verified by the students in her classes. In implementing her goals she used cooperative learning techniques in which students worked in pairs or small groups using task sheets to assess each other and help in developing skills. Thus, students engaged in active thinking about and critically analyzing performance and constructing knowledge through social interactions. Similar to the teacher described by Chen and Cone (2003) above, the teacher in Dyson's study learned that simply providing cooperative learning structures did not mean these structures would automatically work to insure learning. Socially constructing knowledge relied on students' communication skills and communication did not always go smoothly. Over time, the teacher modified her instruction, provided more guidance during group work, taught students explicitly how to perform their roles within group work, and taught students how to communicate better.

Azzarito and Ennis (2003) studied how two teachers used strategies associated with social constructivism in middle school physical education and their students' responses to these strategies. Major strategies were peer teaching and group tasks with assigned leadership roles so that students shared knowledge, collaborated on a common goal to understand tactics in a game, supported classmates' learning, and were responsible for attending to the needs of their classmates in equitable ways. Both teachers and students valued these experiences as it helped students feel a sense of community and connection. Reflecting the emphasis in social constructivism on social communities, the teachers focused on helping students connect what they were doing in physical education with their lives outside of school. For example, one teacher helped students develop individual fitness plans, emphasized life skills, and stressed the importance of how physical education related to their lives now and in the future. The other taught a self-defense unit so students could feel safer in their community. During the unit they discussed the meaning of self-defense in their lives, community, and broader culture. One teacher also designed community service projects and organized events in the community for students and their families.

The final constructivist study described how four accomplished teachers taught dribbling to third-grade children (Rovegno et al., 2003). Three themes, all linked to constructivism, emerged. First, the teachers analyzed and taught dribbling content as a web of connected concepts–connecting movement technique, tactics, movement concepts, children's participation in basketball when they were older, and their lives outside of school. Second, the teachers began their unit by eliciting students' prior knowledge, planning tasks that were based on what students already knew and could do, and by using metaphors, images, and stories that helped children learn, value, and find meaning in the content. Third, the teachers integrated dribbling movement and cognitive processes. A major focus of their teaching approach was to teach explicitly: (a) self-regulation and metacognition, (b) analysis of and critical thinking about movement and tactical situations, (c) decision making as an individual and in groups, and (d) a learning orientation focused on helping children be independent learners oriented toward self-referenced improvement, persistence and effort-based learning.

In summary the accomplished teachers used social and cognitive constructivist approaches. They did not simply use structures such as group work and activities such as exploration, problem solving, and discovery tasks. As Resnick and William-Hall (1998) suggest and in keeping with well-researched approaches in other subject areas (Beck et al., 1996; Cobb et al., 1991; Fennema et al., 1996; Palinscar and Brown, 1984) the accomplished teachers taught cognitive and social interaction processes explicitly and in an integrated way while retaining a focus on acquiring subject matter knowledge.

strength. They had no knowledge about intensity and proposed a wide range of recommendations for time (5–60 minutes per session and 1 month to 1 year to develop fitness).

Griffin (2001) examined middle-school students' knowledge of soccer using interviews to assess students' knowledge. The researchers categorized the sophistication of students' knowledge at four levels. The majority were at levels 2 and 3. The percentages of girls at levels 1 and 2 were higher than boys and the percentage of boys at levels 3 and 4 were higher than girls. Students provided a wide variety of solutions to tactical problems. Their solutions to offensive scenarios were sounder and less convoluted than their solutions to defensive scenarios. They scored higher on offensive tactics related to scoring goals then midfield offensive play. Students' knowledge at level 1 was primarily isolated information about rules, positions, skills, and how to score. Students' knowledge at the higher levels was more connected to the game and more conditional, that is, they knew how to apply knowledge appropriately in different conditions.

The researchers reported four conceptions that were not well understood: (a) off the ball movements (cutting into open spaces, defensive marking), (b) appropriate passing during midfield play, (c) knowledge of opponents' options, and (d) effective use of the width and depth of the field. The study, however, did not examine if or how students could apply their knowledge in actual games or if cognitive knowledge correlated with the use of tactics in game play.

Hare and Graber (2000) studied the responses of 29 5th grade students with four students studied in depth. The researchers focused on student misconceptions while learning two invasion games units taught by a cooperating teacher and student teacher. Misconceptions appeared throughout the study but were highly idiosyncratic. They point out that this is consistent with constructivist theory attributing these differences to knowledge as individually constructed. They classified the misconceptions into four categories, misunderstandings about (a) motor skill execution, (b) terminology, (c) tactics, and (d) instructional tasks. Many of the misunderstandings or misinterpretations they uncovered were directly linked to the teachers' lack of clarity in task presentations and lack of explicitness in feedback. For example, one finding was the students' misunderstanding of terminology. This was linked, in one instance, to the teacher using two different terms that meant the same thing. When the teacher and students both understood the terms being used, the chances for misconceptions were reduced. The student teacher perceived the misunderstandings to be behavioral problems not problems of poor instruction. The cooperating teacher was better able to communicate to students how to respond appropriately. Further, the student teacher and cooperating teacher made no attempts to determine if students were correctly learning the intended content thus allowing misconceptions to go uncorrected.

In a study with similar findings, Stork and Sanders (2002) found that 2nd- and 4th-grade children were not "blank slates" and interpreted instructions in ways different from each other and from the ways the teacher intended. Children responded at their developmental level of understanding and ability to perform the task. Students could not remember sequences of instruction and needed constant reminders. Although students were easily distracted, they were aware of the teacher's behavioral expectations and knew these better than the teacher's expectations for skill performance. It appears from the study that the teacher did not share her expectations for skill development, but did make classroom management goals explicit. Because there was no attempt to provide developmentally appropriate expectations, it was not surprising when students ignored the teacher's directions.

Thus, it appears that in some cases poor instruction causes inaccurate understandings (Hare and Graber, 2000; Stork and Sanders, 2002). This included teachers failing to present tasks and expectations explicitly and clearly, teachers failing to assess students' prior and current knowledge and developmental readiness to learn a skill, teachers failing to make the goals of instruction clear enough for students to understand what was expected, and failure to provide consistent use of terminology and monitor if students understood the concepts taught.

Other studies, however, documented inaccurate conceptions that arose that were not linked to poor instruction. As the knowledge on misconceptions across subject fields indicates, many misconceptions arise from individual experiences in the physical world and are reported consistently across cultures. For example, young children believe the earth is flat despite accurate instruction (Vosniadou and Brewer, 1992). When presented with information that the earth is round, they conceive of the earth as a flat, circular plate. When shown a clay sphere representing the earth, they take a two-earth view with one earth being a sphere and the other earth being the flat one on which they were standing. Other lines of research on misconceptions that arise during medical school education despite accurate instruction, analyzed how knowledge acquisition mechanisms that learners use to understand complex information can lead to misconceptions (Spiro et al., 1987, 1988).

Based on the medical education research, Rovegno (1992a, 1993b) documented how the same or similar knowledge acquisition mechanisms contributed to partial and inaccurate understandings of a movement approach. In the first study, Rovegno

(1992a) documented how undergraduates initially conceived of movement variety and movement quality as mutually exclusive and gave no feedback on movement quality during movement variety tasks. This was an example of rigid compartmentalization of knowledge components, one of the mechanisms described by Spiro et al. (1987, 1988). The second knowledge acquisition mechanism, over reliance on a single basis for representation, was evident when undergraduates focused solely on movement variety tasks in planning lessons. Third, the undergraduates generalized ideas in the movement approach like asking questions, problem solving, and exploration tasks to mean, "don't tell children what to do". Using a process similar to medical students (Spiro et al., 1987, 1988), they initially overgeneralized this idea inappropriately to a range of teaching situations the movement approach recommends the reverse (such as giving specific feedback to improve skill performance and presenting clear instructional cues). In a second study focused on the pre-service teachers' knowledge of tactics and game play, students relied on a rigid compartmentalization of the movement and traditional approaches and because they knew tactics and game play were part of traditional approaches, they initially assumed these were not included in the movement approach (despite faculty and cooperating teachers demonstrating and discussing game play and tactics) (Rovegno, 1993a). The beginning teachers' knowledge was not differentiated (i.e. detailed nor in depth), thus they initially rejected content, such as game strategy and teaching the role of captains, as appropriate for the movement approach because they associated words such as "strategy" and "captain" with elite sport models. Finally, they overrelied on bottom–up thinking in planning units, that is, building a unit beginning with the content they needed to teach about the motor skills and did not reflect on the content they needed to teach about the game they planned for the end of the unit, thus they left tactics out of their plans.

Over time the undergraduates developed their partial and inaccurate conceptions to be accurate, more complex understandings of the movement approach. Development resulted from faculty and cooperating teachers facilitating more robust understanding during later coursework and experiences teaching during student teaching and in their first year as teachers. It is important to note that the claims in these studies that the students developed inaccurate and partial understandings despite accurate instruction were based on data and claims made by the undergraduates themselves (Rovegno, 1992a, 1993b). In fact, most of the identification of inaccurate conceptions came directly from the undergraduates after their conceptions changed and they looked back and said "I used to think this way, but that was inaccurate, now I have a better understanding and I remember faculty or cooperating teachers accurately teaching or demonstrating this information". This is critical because unlike the misconceptions identified by Placek et al. (2001), there are no universally accepted facts that describe a movement approach. The standards for determining accurate knowledge in Placek et al. (2001) and Griffin et al. (2001) were based on well-accepted and sometimes scientifically based information about fitness and soccer tactics.

Thus, misconceptions can be accounted for by superficial or poor teaching (Hare and Graber, 2000; Stork and Sanders, 2002), knowledge acquisition mechanisms learners use to make initial sense of complex information (Rovegno, 1992a, 1993b), and through their experiences in the world. For example, it is easy to speculate that the students' misconceptions about fitness documented in Placek et al. (2001) arose in part from the ways fitness is presented in the media and popular culture. This suggests it is critical for teachers to recognize the role of prior knowledge and experiences in generating misconceptions, monitor how students are making sense of information during the learning process, and understand that acquiring in-depth, accurate knowledge within a complex domain takes considerable time and instruction.

Constructivist research on students' perspectives

Another way researchers have applied constructivism to research on students, is to examine students' perspectives as individual constructions of what they experienced. These descriptive studies offer information on how a group of students experienced the same situation or viewed the same topic in similar ways.

Pissanos and Allison (1993) conducted a follow-up study of ten students who all had the same elementary physical education teacher 6 years earlier. The goal was to see how these students constructed for themselves the meaning of their elementary school physical education experiences. The results indicated the students were able to relate how their teacher had clear expectations for their performance and was seen as supportive and enthusiastic. Females better identified the different sports in which they engaged and described them in richer detail. The authors speculated that the males might have viewed participation in sport lessons taught by a female teacher as perfunctory. Believing they already knew how to play the sports, males may not have thought the teacher had anything new or meaningful for them.

Turner et al. (2001) examined how students constructed a concept of skillfulness in invasion games. They found that students defined successful performance based on game play performance, not the learning and development of specific skills.

Constructivist theory grounded a study by Solmon and Carter (1995). They explored 104 first-grade students' perspectives of physical education and suggested that if we want to understand how students learn from teaching we need to first determine how they assign meaning to events. Students defined physical education as following rules and waiting in line but this was not seen as negative. Children perceived physical education as fun and "something that made them feel good and special" (Solmon and Carter, 1995: 363). Even though the teacher focused on equity, she still made the experience different for girls and boys in terms of her expectations and what she reinforced. Sixteen female but no male students said following directions were what they were supposed to learn. Researchers noted that the teacher was always positive, but reinforced girls for good behavior and was more likely to give positive feedback to boys for skill performance.

Coelho (2000) used a constructivist framework to study the perceptions of 236 students at the United States Military Academy toward physical education. Students who had a supportive physical education instructor who was encouraging but had high expectations saw the experience as positive. Students also reacted positively to teachers who provided extra help when the students had difficulty with a task and rated positively instructors who actively demonstrated the skills being taught. Negative responses focused on unfair grading, public embarrassment, and belittling by the teacher. Students who had instructors they perceived as adversarial also rated the experience as negative. Whether students found activities relevant, depended on a student's personal view based on individual experience. Social interactions were important especially when given positive support by upper-class students. The author concluded that there is a potential benefit in incorporating an emphasis on cooperative and social responsibility in the curriculum.

Research on teacher learning using constructivist perspectives

The lead author of this chapter recently reviewed the research on teachers' knowledge construction including studies from all theoretical perspectives and many of the findings reported here we based on that review (Rovegno, 2003). As mentioned earlier, this chapter is constrained to constructivist work although the findings from socialization and critical perspectives substantiate the work from constructivist perspectives.

Deep understanding and connection

One core concept of constructivism, discussed above, is that successful learning leads to deep, well-connected knowledge organized by broad concepts and principles and can be applied flexibly. Constructivist-based research in physical education reports that salient learning for teachers is when they learn that disconnected concepts were not only connected but were organized under broader, overarching themes (Ennis et al., 1991; Rovegno, 1992a, 1993a, 1998; Sebran, 1995; Woods et al., 2000). Specific content included how movement concepts are connected within the Laban framework, how skills connect to movement concepts, how movement concepts connect to sport, and how lessons can connect to broader educational goals such as social responsibility and thinking skill development. Experience in school settings facilitated making connections and understanding content, learners, and teaching in relation to broader educational goals. Learning occurred through accretion, tuning, or restructuring processes identified by Rumelhart and Norman (1978) (Ennis et al., 1991; Rovegno, 1991).

Prior knowledge and learning as an active process of constructing knowedge

One of the most robust findings of research on teacher education across theoretical perspectives is that pre-service and in-service teachers' prior knowledge and experiences impact their learning–sometimes in positive ways and sometimes in negative ways. Due to teacher educators' interest to change the viewpoints of prospective teachers from an elite-sport orientation to a professional, educational orientation, to teach them effective teaching practices that they will continue to utilize after graduation, and to teach new curricular approaches that undergraduates did not experience as K-12 pupils, what has been examined most often is the constraining impact of prior knowledge.

Constructivist research examining the impact of prior knowledge has sought to identify instances of both successful and unsuccessful learning during methods courses, pre-service teaching in field experiences, in-service teaching, and professional development settings. These studies are significant in that they identify pre-existing conceptions that are difficult to change, new concepts that are difficult to learn and the role of pre-existing knowledge in the learning process, knowledge that is constructed at different stages in teachers' careers, and the factors that facilitate or constrain learning. We organize the findings in four major topics.

First, several studies have reported changes in pre-service teachers' conceptions of pupils as a result of student research projects, teacher educators' interventions, and teaching in school settings (McCaughtry and Rovegno, 2003; Rovegno, 1991; Woods et al., 2000). Pre-service teachers acquired a more realistic understanding of students and a better understanding of how teaching, learning, content, and pupils interacted (Woods et al., 2000). They changed their interpretations from blaming the students for problems and thinking students were misbehaving, not trying or not listening, to recognizing students' responses were due to their content or instructional approach or were simply immature movement patterns that are part and parcel of the learning process (McCaughtry and Rovegno, 2003; Rovegno, 1991).

A second topic was progression or sequencing of content. While beginning teachers, especially during early field experiences, reported they initially had problems developing content progressions, they learned to organize content into smaller-stepped progression, build these progressions based on long-term objectives, and analyze the culminating activities of the unit and then find an effective way to identify and sequence the critical content that would enable children's successful learning (Pissanos and Allison, 1996; Rovegno, 1992a, 1992b, 1993a, 1993b, 1998; Sebran, 1995). Dividing and sequencing content, were salient concepts teachers learned in university settings, but they came to understand those concepts well and meaningfully through experience teaching in field settings. In other words, understanding did not come from simply analyzing content and then writing lesson and unit plans in university contexts. Understanding developed when what they knew about dividing and sequencing content was actually applied in schools and they contextualized their knowledge in terms of how the children responded to their tasks and either learned well or poorly. Light (2002) examined the prior knowledge and dispositions that primary-level classroom teachers, who would be responsible for teaching physical education to children, brought to a TGfU unit that shifts to a more holistic, contextualized way of dividing and sequencing content. Most had positive dispositions with some being ambivalent saying they would probably not teach games, and a few being very negative toward sports and physical education. With the exception of those entering with very negative attitudes, by the end of the unit the other student teachers reported positive feelings about TGfU and a favorable disposition to teach using this approach. Some reported the connection they saw between TGfU as a constructivist approach and the constructivist approaches they were being taught in other subject areas.

A third topic was the role of broader value orientations and cultural representations. Ennis et al. (1990) reported how in-service teachers' value orientation toward a disciplinary mastery approach constrained what they learned about and their acceptance of an innovative teaching approach. Rovegno (1993a) described cultural templates that undergraduates held when they entered a teacher education program. Foremost among these templates were elitist sport practices associated with professional and collegiate sport, negative stereotypes associated with physical educators, and the marginal status of the field. The pre-service teachers constructed a new understanding of what physical education could be as a result of faculty confronting their conceptions, persisting in advocating for and teaching an alternative view, and setting up field experiences that helped the undergraduates to elaborate their knowledge through learning by doing.

The fourth topic was teachers' responses and changes in teachers' pre-existing knowledge as they learned or adopted constructivist-oriented approaches. In a series of studies, Rovegno (1992a, b, c, 1998) described how pre-service and in-service teachers changed from focusing on presenting lesson activities to focusing on what children were actually learning during those activities and the detailed content children needed to learn that was part of the activity. A second change was a shift from thinking that constructivist-oriented teaching meant simply asking questions and presenting problems to solve or concepts to explore. Teachers learned that constructivist-oriented teaching includes giving children information when it is needed, explicitly teaching cognitive processes embedded in the activity, and monitoring and guiding student learning to insure a deep understanding of content. These changes are significant as they represent overcoming common misinterpretations of constructivism across subject areas (National Research Council, 1999).

Research on adopting teaching practices associated with constructivist approaches has consistently reported that changing their teaching is a difficult long-term process for teachers that requires persistence, a willingness to self-critique, and years of trial and error, adapting their approach, experimenting again and again without giving up on the new teaching approach until they held a deep, contextual understanding of how the new approach worked in practice (Barrett and Turner, 2000; Pissanos and Allison, 1996; Rovegno, 1998; Rovegno and Bandhauer, 1994, 1997a, b). Supportive colleagues and administrators, school norms that supported teacher development, university teacher educators, and professional reading supported the teachers' knowledge construction. For example, Dyson's (2002) 2-year study of how a teacher learned to implement cooperative learning reported that the teacher initially had problems reconciling the time it takes to teach social skills with the time needed for practicing motor skills. She learned she needed to teach interpersonal skills explicitly and that these take time to develop with students. She learned the importance of assigning and teaching different roles within group work and figured out ways to hold students accountable for learning.

One study looked at both teachers' adoption of a national curriculum including constructivist-oriented practices and also the impact on students' achievement on national exams. Thorburn and Collins (2003) studied the ways teachers from ten schools in Scotland implemented a national, year-long secondary curriculum that integrated and assessed both students' competence in performing physical activities and also their conceptual knowledge and ability to analyze physical activity in writing. The national policy "advises that indirect constructivist teaching approaches are the most effective teaching and learning environment, with teachers shaping the nature of each learner's activity, through, for example, adopting practical workshops with a problem-solving focus" (p. 188). The researchers reported that teachers found it difficult to develop students' critical thinking and analytical abilities. Factors contributing to this difficulty were time constraints, workload, timetable scheduling, lack of structures for holding students accountable for homework and learning, the need to cover course content, students' writing abilities, and students' abilities to understand essay test questions. When faced with problems some teachers used an approach that was completely teacher directed with teachers in two schools resorting to rote learning to the extent of preparing essay answers in advance and helping students rehearse these answers. Teachers in four schools viewed the curriculum and instructional methods favorably, but due to factors discussed above did not achieve a satisfactory level of success. Teachers in two schools, however, were successful in implementing the curriculum with positive achievement outcomes for students including outperforming students in schools with higher socioeconomic status.

Social interactions as a setting for learning

Another core concept of constructivism is that learners acquire knowledge through social interactions. In a study based on a social constructivist perspective, Tjeerdsma (1998) described the impact of student teachers on seven cooperating teachers' beliefs and perceptions. At the end of the student teachers' practicum, four said they had increased their reflections on their own teaching, five described feeling revitalized, and six said they did not change their teaching when they worked with a student teacher. A negative theme discussed by six was their concern about giving up their classes to student teachers because this meant giving up control of management and discipline; while two were concerned that the quality of pupil learning would decrease. Tjeerdsma suggested that in terms of a social constructivist perspective, individuals' experiences vary due to differences in the context and the social interactions within these contexts.

Studying programmatic components in undergraduate physical education teacher education

This final section describes a set of studies by teacher educators on their own students. Many researchers in physical education are also teacher educators with the same need to understand the learning processes of their students as K-12 teachers. We believe this kind of research offers a promising avenue for teacher educators to both understand more about the effectiveness of program components and to understand the conceptual frameworks from which students interpret their teacher education experiences. Other excellent studies of this sort have also been conducted from Critical perspectives (e.g. Brown, 1999; Hickey, 2001) and thus are not included in this chapter.

Allison, et al. (2000) examined beginning pre-service teachers' knowledge and beliefs about skillfulness and compare these to the goals of their program and the theoretical base that supports these goals. They found that their pre-service teachers (a) thought that above average ability was "*enough*" (p. 149) to characterize someone as skillful, (b) connected skillfulness with effort, commitment, and persistence in a physical activity, and (c) discussed skillfulness as a natural, inborn talent and a static trait ("either *you have it or you don't*") (p. 151). They also found that their students were most knowledgeable about games and least knowledgeable about gymnastics with dance in the middle. Although their analysis is far more detailed than can be summarized here, they concluded that the knowledge and beliefs their students brought to their program did not match with their program's emphasis on "the art and science of human movement" (p. 158) and an equal emphasis on games, dance, and gymnastics. Their students did, however, connect skillfulness to teaching, which is in keeping with program objectives, but viewed skillfulness as a static trait implying that the teacher education program needs to help undergraduates perceive that teachers can help all children develop skill in a variety of content areas.

In an enlightening study, Woods et al. (2000) examined how a teacher research project on high school pupils impacted what their pre-service teachers learned in an early field experience. The researchers/teacher educators designed the assignment to be in keeping with constructivist principles (Fosnot, 1996) that learners need to ask questions; test their own hypotheses; recognize, explore and confront possible misconceptions they might hold; reflect on experience and generalize principles and make connections; and engage in social interactions to construct, evaluate, and communicate ideas among peers. The research project required the undergraduates to first identify their prior knowledge and experiences with secondary pupils, generate questions about pupils, and through group discussion generate a research question. Then, in field experiences, they used multiple methods to refine their questions, design data collection methods, collect data, and prepare written and oral reports of findings. This was all supplemented with class discussions. Although the research project was difficult for the pre-service teachers, it facilitated their development in critical ways. Not only did they learn more about high-school students, but what they learned challenged their prior beliefs and helped them understand high-school pupils in a deeper more connected way.

Bolt (1998) studied the impact of case discussions on pre-service teachers' cognitive growth and found case-based learning facilitated an increase in their ability to identify problems, solutions, and concepts. The use of case-based learning has been promoted as a tool for helping people apply knowledge in complex, real-world settings and is a hallmark of education in law and business. Cases present concepts and actions within a context, thus reflecting the constructivist emphasis on deep, well-connected knowledge that learners can flexibly apply.

Summary and conclusions

Constructivist perspectives focus on learning in relation to the social environment. They portray the learner as actively engaged in the environment constructing knowledge. Constructivist work primarily focuses on knowledge and how knowledge is constructed and changes over time. It also incorporates the cognitive and social processes that regulate learning.

As noted in this chapter, constructivist perspectives have in the past and continue today to be a basis for research in physical education that address the curriculum, student learning and knowledge, teacher learning and knowledge as well as content. The early emphasis among constructivist theories to study learning and the acquisition of knowledge in naturalistic settings has been of major importance to researchers and teachers in physical education where our learning and teaching activities occur in complex learning environments often involving large numbers of students learning and developing skills in a complex system of interpersonal and contextual interactions.

What we have learned from constructivist theory over the years is the importance of students actively constructing knowledge and getting students actively engaged in learning. The research has also shown us the difficulty of overcoming misinformation from the media and naive conceptions or misconceptions held by students that need to be addressed by teachers to facilitate learning. The research that shows how more effective experienced teachers can be when compared to novices or student teachers is critical in helping us understand that good pedagogy develops over time and requires that teachers are willing to commit the time, effort and perseverance necessary to become successful and effective teachers.

Acknowledgment

We thank Margaret Stran, Department of Kinesiology, The University of Alabama for her assistance with this chapter.

References

Allison, P.C. and Barrett, K.R. (2000). *Constructing children's physical education experiences: Understanding the content for teaching.* Boston, MA: Allyn and Bacon.

Allison, P.C., Pissanos, B.W., Turner, A.P. and Law, D. R. (2000). Preservice physical educators' epistemologies of skillfulness. *Journal of Teaching in Physical Education, 19*: 141–161.

Amade-Escot, C. (2000). The contribution of two research programs on teaching content: 'Pedagogical content knowledge' and 'didactics of physical education.' *Journal of Teaching in Physical Education, 20*: 78–101.

Azzarito, L. and Ennis, C.D. (2003). A sense of connection: Toward social constructivist physical education. *Sport, Education and Society, 8*: 179–198.

Ball, D.L. (1993). With an eye on the mathematical horizon: Dilemmas of teaching elementary school mathematics. *The Elementary School Journal, 93*: 373–397.

Barrett, K.R. and Turner, A.P. (2000). Sandy's challenge: New game, new paradigm <a correspondence>. *Journal of Teaching in Physical Education, 19*: 162–181.

Beck, I.L., McKeown, M.G., Sandora, C., Kucan, L. and Worthy, J. (1996). Questioning the author: A yearlong classroom implementation to engage students with text. *The Elementary School Journal, 96*: 385–414.

Bein, E.S., Vlasova, T.A., Levina, R.E., Morozova, N.G. and Shif, Zh. I. (1993). Afterword. In R.W. Rieber and A.S. Carton (Eds.), (J.E. Knox and C.B. Stevens, Trans.), *The collected works of L.S. Vygotsky: The fundamentals of defectology* (abnormal psychology and learning disabilities) (Vol. 2, pp. 302–314). New York: Plenum.

Bertone, S., Meard, J., Euzet, J.P., Ria, L. and Durand, M. (2003). Intrapsychic conflict experienced by a preservice teacher during classroom interactions: A case study in physical education. *Teaching and Teacher Education, 19*: 113–125.

Bilborough, A. and Jones, P. (1963). *Physical education in the primary school.* London: University of London Press.

Bolt, B. (1998). Encouraging cognitive growth through case discussions. *Journal of Teaching in Physical Education, 18*: 90–102.

Brown, S. (1999). Complicity and reproduction in teaching physical education. *Sport, Education and Society, 4*: 143–159.

Bruner, J. (1960). *The process of education.* New York: Vantage.

Chen, W. (2001). Description of an expert teacher's constructivist-oriented teaching: Engaging students' critical thinking in learning creative dance. *Research Quarterly for Exercise and Sport, 72*: 366–375.

Chen, W. and Cone, T. (2003). Links between children's use of critical thinking and an expert teacher's teaching in creative dance. *Journal of Teaching in Physical Education, 22*: 169–185.

Chen, W. and Rovegno, I. (2000). Examination of expert and novice teachers' constructivist-oriented teaching practices using a movement approach to elementary physical education. *Research Quarterly for Exercise and Sport, 71*: 357–372.

Chen, W., Rovegno, I. and Iran-Nejad, A. (2002). Application of a wholetheme perspective to the movement approach for teaching physical education in elementary schools. *Education, 123*: 401–415.

Chi, M., Feltovich, P. and Glaser, R. (1981). Categorization and representation of physical problems by experts and novices. *Cognitive Science, 5*: 121–152.

Chi, M., Glaser, R. and Rees, E. (1982). Expertise in problem solving. In R. Sternberg (Ed.), *Advances in the psychology of human intelligence* (pp. 7–76). Hillsdale, NJ: Erlbaum.

Cobb, P. (1994a). Constructivism in mathematics and science education. *Educational Researcher, 23* (7): 4.

Cobb, P. (1994b). Where is the mind? Constructivist and socioculutural perspectives on mathematical development. *Educational Researcher, 23*(7): 13–20.

Cobb, P., Wood, T., Yackel, E. et al. (1991). Assessment of a problem-centered second-grade mathematics project. *Journal for Research in Mathematics Education, 22*: 3–29.

Coelho, J.D. (2000). Student perceptions of physical education in a mandatory college program. *Journal of Teaching in Physical Education, 19*: 222–245.

Confrey, J. (1990). A review of the research on student conceptions in mathematics, science, and programming. In C.B. Cazden (Ed.), *Review of research in education 16* (pp. 3–56). Washington, DC: F.E. Peacock.

d'Arripe-Longueville, F., Gernigon, C., Huet, M.L., Cadopi, M. and Winnykamen, F. (2002). Peer tutoring in a physical education setting: Influence of tutor skill level on novice learner's motivation and performance. *Journal of Teaching in Physical Education, 22*: 105–123.

Davydov, V.V. (1995). The influence of L.S. Vygotsky on education theory, research, and practice. *Educational Researcher, 24* (3): 12–21.

deGroot, A.D. (1965). *Thought and choice in chess.* The Hague, The Netherlands: Mouton.

Derry, S.J. (1996). Cognitive schema theory in the constructivist debate. *Educational Psychologist, 31*: 163–174.

Driver, R., Asoko, H., Leach, J., Mortimer, E. and Scott, P. (1994). Constructing scientific knowledge in the classroom. Educational Researcher, 23 (7): 5–12.

Dyson, B. (2002). The implementation of cooperative learning in an elementary physical education program. *Journal of Teaching in Physical Education, 22*: 69–85.

Ennis, C.D. (1991). Discrete thinking skills in two teachers' physical education classes. *The Elementary School Journal, 91*: 473–487.

Ennis, C.D. (1999). Creating a culturally relevant curriculum for disengaged girls. *Sport, Education and Society, 4*: 31–49.

Ennis, C.D., Mueller, L.K. and Hooper, L.M. (1990). The influence of teacher value orientations on curriculum planning within the parameters of a theoretical framework. *Research Quarterly for Exercise and Sport, 61*, 360–368.

Ennis, C.D., Mueller, L.K. and Zhu, W. (1991). Description of knowledge structures within a concept-based curriculum framework. *Research Quarterly for Exercise and Sport, 62*: 309–318.

Fennema, E., Carpenter, T., Franke, M., Levi, L., Jacobs, V. and Empson, S. (1996). A longitudinal study of learning to use children's thinking in mathematics instruction. *Journal for Research in Mathematics Education, 27*: 403–434.

Flavell, J.H. (1996). Piaget's legacy. *Psychological Science, 7*: 200–203.

Fosnot, C.T. (1996). Constructivism: A psychological theory of learning. In C.T. Fosnot (Ed.), *Constructivism: Theory, perspectives, and practice* (pp. 8–33). New York: Teachers College Press.

Glaser, R. (1984). Educational thinking: The role of knowledge. *American Psychologist, 39*: 93–104.

Glaser, R. (1987). Thoughts on expertise. In C. Schooler and W. Schaie (Eds.), *Cognitive functioning and social structure over the life course* (pp. 81–94). Norwood, NJ: Ablex.

Graham, G., Holt-Hale, S.A. and Parker, M. (2004). *Children moving: A reflective approach to teaching physical education* (6th ed.). Boston: McGraw Hill.

Grehaigne, J.-F. and Godbount, P. (1995). Tactical knowledge in team sports from a constructivist and cognitivist perspective. *Quest, 47*: 490–505.

Grennon-Brooks, J. and Brooks, M.G. (1993). *In search of understanding: The case for constructivist classrooms.* Alexandria, VA: Association for Supervision and Curriculum Development.

Griffin, L.L, Dodds, P., Placek, J.H. and Tremino, F. (2001). Middle school students' conceptions of soccer: Their solutions to tactical problems. *Journal of Teaching in Physical Education* [Monograph], *20*: 324–341.

Hare, M. and Graber, K. (2000). Student misconceptions during two invasion game units in physical education: A qualitative investigation of student thought processing. *Journal of Teaching in Physical Education, 20*: 55–77.

Hickey, C. (2001). 'I feel enlightened now, but…': The limits to the pedagogic translation of critical social discourses in physical education. *Journal of Teaching in Physical Education, 20*: 227–246.

Hoffman, H.A., Young, J. and Klesius, S.E. (1981). *Meaningful movement for children: A developmental theme approach to physical education.* Boston: Allyn and Bacon.

Iran-Nejad, A. (1989). A nonassociative schema theory of cognitive incompatibility. *Bulletin of the Psychonomic Society, 27:* 429–432.

Iran-Nejad, A. (1994). The global coherence context in educational practice: A comparison of piecemeal and whole-theme approaches to learning and teaching. *Research in the Schools, 1:* 63–76.

Iran-Nejad, A., McKeachie, W.J. and Berliner, D. C. (1990). The multisource nature of learning: An introduction. *Review of Educational Review, 60:* 509–515.

Jacobs, J.E. and Eccles, J.S. (2000). Parents, task values, and real-life achievement-related choices. In C. Sansone and J.M. Harackiewicz (Eds.), *Intrinsic and extrinsic motivation* (pp. 405–439). San Diego, CA: Academic Press.

Kirk, D. (1994). Making the present strange: Sources of the current crisis in school physical education. *Discourse, 15:* 46–63.

Kirk, D. (1999). Physical culture, physical education and relational analysis. *Sport, Education and Society, 4:* 63–73.

Kirk, D. and Macdonald, D. (1998). Situated learning in physical education. *Journal of Teaching in Physical Education, 17:* 376–387.

Kirk, D. and MacPhail, A. (2002). Teaching games for understanding and situated learning: Rethinking the Bunker-Thorpe model. *Journal of Teaching in Physical Education, 21:* 177–192.

Leinhardt, G. and Greeno, J.G. (1991). The cognitive skill in teaching. In P. Goodyear (Ed.), *Teaching knowledge and intelligent tutoring* (pp. 233–268). Norwood, NJ: Ablex.

Leinhardt, G. and Greeno, J.G. (1994). History: A time to be mindful. In G. Leinhardt, I.L. Beck, and C. Stainton (Eds.), *Teaching and learning in history* (pp. 209–225). Hillsdale, NJ: Erlbaum.

Light, R. (2002). The social nature of games: Australian pre-service teachers' first experiences of Teaching Games for Understanding. *European Physical Education Review, 8:* 286–304.

Light, R. and Fawns, R. (2003). Knowing the game: Integrating speech and action in games teaching through TGfU. *Quest, 55:* 161–176.

Logsdon, B.J., Barrett, K.R., Ammons, M. et al. (1984). *Physical education for children: A focus on the teaching process* (2nd Ed.). Philadelphia, PA: Lea & Febiger.

Mahn, H. (2003). Periods in child development: Vygotsky's perspective. In A. Zoulin, B. Gindis, V.S. Ageyev and S.M. Miller (Eds.), *Vygotsky's educational theory in cultural context* (pp. 119–137). Cambridge, UK: Cambridge University Press.

Marshall, H.H. (1996). Clarifying and implementing contemporary psychological perspectives. *Educational Psychologist, 31:* 29–34.

Mauldon, E. and Redfern, H.B. (1969). *Games teaching: A new approach for the primary school.* London: Macdonald & Evans.

McCaughtry, N. and Rovegno, I. (2003). Development of pedagogical content knowledge: Moving from blaming

students to predicting skillfulness, recognizing motor development, and understanding emotion. *Journal of Teaching in Physical Education, 22:* 355–368.

Miller, S.M. (2003). How literature discussion shapes thinking: ZPDs for teaching/learning habits of the heart and mind. In A. Zoulin, B. Gindis, V.S. Ageyev and S.M. Miller (Eds.), *Vygotsky's educational theory in cultural context* (pp. 289–316). Cambridge, UK: Cambridge University Press.

Minick, N. (1987). The development of Vygotsky's thought: An introduction. In R.W. Rieber and A.S. Carton (Eds.), *The collected works of L.S. Vygotsky: Problems of general psychology, including the volume 'Thinking and speech'* (Vol. 1, pp. 17–38). New York: Plenum.

Morison, R. (1960). *Educational gymnastics* (7th impression). London: Ling Book Shop.

Mosston, M. (1966). *Teaching physical education: From command to discovery.* Columbus, OH: Merrill.

National Research Council. (1999). *How people learn: Brain, mind, experience, and school.* Washington, DC.: National Academy Press.

Palinscar, A.S. and Brown, A.L. (1984). Reciprocal teaching of comprehension-fostering and monitoring activities. *Cognition and Instruction, 1:* 117–175.

Perkins, D.N. and Salomon, G. (1989). Are cognitive skills context-bound? *Educational Researcher, 18* (1): 16–25.

Phillips, D.C. (1995). The good, the bad, and the ugly: The many faces of constructivism. *Educational Researcher, 24* (7): 5–12.

Piaget, J. (1971). *Psychology and epistemology* (A. Rosin, Trans.). New York: Grossman.

Piaget, J. (1973). *The child and reality* (A. Rosin, Trans.). New York: Grossman.

Piaget, J. and Inhelder, B. (1969). *The psychology of the child* (H. Weaver, Trans.). New York: Basic Books.

Pissanos, B.W. and Allison, P.C. (1993). Students' constructs of elementary school physical education. *Research Quarterly for Exercise and Sport, 64:* 425–435.

Pissanos, B.W. and Allison, P.C. (1996). Continued professional learning: A topical life history. *Journal of Teaching in Physical Education, 16:* 2–19.

Placek, J.H., Griffin, L.L., Dodds, P., Raymond, C., Tremino, F. and James, A. (2001). Middle school students' conceptions of fitness: The long road to a healthy lifestyle. *Journal of Teaching in Physical Education [Monograph], 20:* 314–323.

Prawat, R.S. (1992). Teachers' beliefs about teaching and learning: A constructivist perspective. *American Journal of Education, 100:* 354–495.

Resnick, L.B. and Williams-Hall, M. (1998). Learning organizations for sustainable education reform. *Daedalus 127* (4): 89–118.

Rink, J.E. (2001). Investigating the assumptions of pedagogy. *Journal of Teaching in Physical Education, 20:* 112–128.

Rogoff, B. (1990). *Apprenticeship in thinking: Cognitive development in social context.* New York: Oxford University Press.

Rovegno, I. (1991). A participant-observation study of knowledge restructuring in a field-based elementary physical education methods course. *Research Quarterly for Exercise and Sport, 62*: 205–212.

Rovegno, I. (1992a). Learning a new curricular approach: Mechanisms of knowledge acquisition in preservice teachers. *Teaching and Teacher Education, 8*: 253–264.

Rovegno, I.C. (1992b). Learning to teach in a field-based methods course: The development of pedagogical content knowledge. *Teaching and Teacher Education, 8*: 69–82.

Rovegno, I. (1992c). Learning to reflect on teaching: A case study of one preservice physical education teacher. *The Elementary School Journal, 92*: 491–510.

Rovegno, I. (1993a). Content knowledge acquisition during undergraduate teacher education: Overcoming cultural templates and learning through practice. *American Educational Research Journal, 30*: 611–642.

Rovegno, I. (1993b). The development of curricular knowledge: A case study of problematic pedagogical content knowledge during advanced knowledge acquisition. *Research Quarterly for Exercise and Sport, 64*: 56–68.

Rovegno, I. (1998). The development of in-service teachers' knowledge of a constructivist approach to physical education: Teaching beyond activities. *Research Quarterly for Exercise and Sport, 69*: 147–162.

Rovegno, I. (2003). Teachers' knowledge construction. In S.J. Silverman and C.D. Ennis (Eds.), *Student learning in physical education: Applying research to enhance instruction* (2nd ed., pp. 295–310). Champaign, IL: Human Kinetics.

Rovegno, I. and Bandhauer, D. (1994). Child-designed games—Experience changes teachers' conceptions. *Journal of Physical Education, Recreation and Dance, 65*: 60–63.

Rovegno, I. and Bandhauer, D. (1997a). Norms of the school culture that facilitated teacher adoption and learning of a constructivist approach to physical education. *Journal of Teaching in Physical Education, 16*: 401–425.

Rovegno, I. and Bandhauer, D. (1997b). Psychological dispositions that facilitated and sustained the development of knowledge of a constructivist approach to physical education. *Journal of Teaching in Physical Education, 16*: 136–154.

Rovegno, I., Chen, W. and Todorovich, J. (2003). Accomplished teachers' pedagogical content knowledge of teaching dribbling to third grade. *Journal of Teaching in Physical Education, 22*: 426–449.

Rumelhart, D.E. and Norman, D.A. (1978). Accretion, tuning, and restructuring: Three modes of learning. In J.W. Cotton and R.L. Klatzky (Eds.), *Semantic factors in cognition* (pp. 37–53). Hillsdale, NJ: Erlbaum.

Schneider, W. and Lockl, K. (2002). The development of metacognitive knowledge in children and adolescents. In T.J. Perfect and B.L. Schwartz (Eds.), *Applied metacognition* (pp. 224–257). Cambridge, UK: Cambridge University Press.

Shuell, T. (1986). Cognitive conceptions of learning. *Review of Educational Research, 56*: 411–436.

Sebren, A. (1995). Preservice teachers' reflections and knowledge development in a field-based elementary physical education methods course. *Journal of Teaching in Physical Education, 14*: 262–283.

Siedentop, D. (1994). *Sport Education: Quality PE through positive sport experiences.* Champaign, IL: Human Kinetics.

Siegler, R. S. and Richards, D.D. (1982). The development of intelligence. In R.J. Sternberg (Ed.), *Handbook of human intelligence* (pp. 897–960). Cambridge, UK: Cambridge University Press.

Slavin, R.E. (1996). Research on cooperative learning and achievement: What we know, what we need to know. *Contemporary Educational Psychology, 21*: 43–69.

Solmon, M.A. and Carter, J.A. (1995). Kindergarten and first-grade students' perceptions of physical education in one teacher's classes. *The Elementary School Journal, 95*: 354–365.

Spiro, R.J., Coulson, R.L., Feltovich, P.J. and Anderson, D.K. (1988). Cognitive flexibility theory: Advanced knowledge acquisition in ill-structured domains. In *Tenth annual conference of the Cognitive Science Society* (pp. 375–383). Hillsdale, NJ: Erlbaum.

Spiro, R.J., Vispoel, W.P., Schmitz, J.G., Samarapungavan, A. and Boerger, A.E. (1987). Knowledge acquisition for application: Cognitive flexibility and transfer in complex content domains. In B.C. Britton (Ed.), *Executive control processes* (pp. 177–199). Hillsdale, NJ: Erlbaum.

Stork, S. and Sanders, S.W. (2002). Why can't students just do as they're told?! An exploration on incorrect responses. *Journal of Teaching in Physical Education, 21*: 208–228.

Thorburn, M. and Collins, D. (2003). Integrated curriculum models and their effects on teachers' pedagogy practices. *European Physical Education Review, 9*: 185–209.

Tjeersdsma, B.L. (1998). Cooperating teacher perceptions of and experiences in the student teaching practicum. *Journal of Teaching in Physical Education, 17*: 214–230.

Turner, A.P., Allison, P.C. and Pissanos, B.W. (2001). Constructing a concept of skillfulness in invasion games within a games for understanding context. *European Journal of Physical Education, 6*: 38–54.

Vosniadou, S. and Brewer, W.F. (1992). Mental models of the earth: A study of conceptual change in childhood. *Cognitive Psychology, 24*: 535–585.

Vygotsky, L. (1986). *Thought and language* (Revised and edited by A. Kozulin). Cambridge, MA: MIT Press. (Original work published in 1962)

Vygotsky, L.S. (1987). The problem and method of investigation. In R.W. Rieber and A.S. Carton (Eds.), (N. Minick, Trans.), *The collected works of L. S. Vygotsky: Problems of general psychology, including the volume 'Thinking and speech'* (Vol. 1, pp. 43–51). New York: Plenum.

Vygotsky, L.S. (1997a). The historical meaning of the crisis in psychology: A methodological investigation. In R.W. Rieber and J. Wollock (Eds.), (R. Van Der Veer, Trans.), *The collected works of L.S. Vygotsky: Problems of the theory and history of psychology, including the chapter on the crisis in psychology* (Vol. 3, pp. 233–344). New York: Plenum.

Vygotsky, L.S. (1997b). Genesis of higher mental function. In R.W. Rieber (Ed.), (M.J. Hall, Trans.), The collected works of L.S. Vygotsky: *The history of the development of higher mental functions* (Vol. 4, pp. 97–120). New York: Plenum.

Vygotsky, L.S. (1998). Development of higher mental functions during the transitional age. In R.W. Rieber (Ed.), (M.J. Hall, Trans.), *The collected works of L.S. Vygotsky: Child psychology* (Vol. 5, pp. 83–149). New York: Plenum.

Vygotsky, L. (1999). The problem of practical intellect in the psychology of animals and the psychology of the child. In R.W. Rieber (Ed.), (M.J. Hall, Trans.), *The collected works of L. S. Vygotsky: Scientific legacy* (Vol. 6, pp. 3–26). New York: Plenum Press.

Woods, M., Goc Karp, G. and Escamilla, E. (2000). Preservice teachers learning about students and the teaching-learning process. *Journal of Teaching in Physical Education, 20*: 15–39.

Youniss, J. and Damon, W. (1992). Social construction in Piaget's theory. In H. Beilin and P. Pufall (Eds.), *Piaget's theory prospects and possibilities* (pp. 267–286). Hillside, NJ: Lawrence Erlbaum.

Zuckerman, G. (2003). The learning activity in the first years of schooling: The developmental path toward reflection. In A. Zoulin, B. Gindis, V.S. Ageyev and S.M. Miller (Eds.), *Vygotsky's educational theory in cultural context* (pp. 177–199). Cambridge, UK: Cambridge University Press.

3.5 Situated perspectives on learning

INEZ ROVEGNO

Historical overview

Situated perspectives are relative newcomers to theoretical perspectives used explicitly as a basis for research in physical education. New perspectives on learning develop as researchers uncover the limits of current theories and seek to address questions they cannot address adequately with current theory. The need to understand learning in different ways or in different circumstances also arises as national priorities, political agendas, and goals for education broaden or change and demand new curricular and instructional approaches. "A fundamental tenet of modern learning theory is that different kinds of learning goals require different approaches to instruction; new goals for education require changes in opportunities to learn" (National Research Council, 1999: xvi).

There are many different situated perspectives from a range of fields including education, psychology, anthropology, and artificial intelligence (Clancey, 1997; Greeno, 1997; Rovegno et al., 2001). The roots of situated cognition lie in the work of activity theorists such as Vygotsky and ideas proposed by Dewey, Piaget, and Gibson (Brown et al., 1989; Clancey, 1997; Greeno, 1997). Much of the recent interest in situated views, however, began with the work of Jean Lave, Barbara Rogoff, and the debate in *Educational Researcher* initiated by Brown et al. (1989).

Many of the core theoretical concepts of situated perspectives are similar to or the same as core concepts of ecological psychology based on the pioneering work of J. J. Gibson (1979/86) and E. J. Gibson (1969) and the dynamical systems approach in the motor control domain with its roots in Bernstein (Kugler et al., 1980, 1982; Newell, 1986, 1996). Motor control is discussed elsewhere in this handbook; however, several core concepts from this work have been used in research and theorizing about physical education teaching and curriculum. The relevant core concepts from both the cognitive and motor domains will be discussed next.

The unit of analysis

In describing her theory of situated cognition, Lave (1988) proposed a unit of analysis in which the individual, activity in which he or she is engaged, and the sociocultural environment are inseparable. The unit of analysis has been a contentious issue among psychology researchers since the time of nonsense syllables and the black box of behaviorism because if you get the wrong unit of analysis your findings maybe useless by failing to take into account the culture, context, and interactions with others that all impinge on what is labeled cognition. Lave's proposal was based on a series of her own and other researchers' studies comparing adults' knowledge of mathematics as demonstrated on school arithmetic tests and their use of mathematical concepts and processes in everyday activities such as shopping in the supermarket, dieting, cooking, family money management, and loading dairy cartons. She reported that people could consistently arrive at accurate mathematical solutions in practice while at the same time producing inaccurate solutions on school tests of the same problems. She further described how people solved calculation problems in their everyday lives using processes far different from simply applying the relevant algorithm. Rather, people created units for calculation that were structured by the tasks in which they were engaged and they offloaded calculations on tools and the environment. Lave also studied how conflicting social norms and personal goals impacted the ways individuals characterized and solved calculation problems.

Her conclusion and the core concept underlying her arguments, which have sparked considerable interest in educational research, is that:

There is reason to suspect that what we call cognition is in fact a complex social phenomenon. The point is not so much that arrangements of knowledge in the head correspond in a complicated way to the social world outside the head, but that they are socially organized in such a fashion as to be indivisible. "Cognition" observed in everyday practice is distributed – stretched over, not divided among – mind, body, activity and culturally organized settings (which include other actors). (Lave, 1988: 1)

Thus, Lave (1988) proposes a unit of analysis as a person acting in a context or setting and the activity in which they are engaged. She argues against cognitive theory that analyzes cognition apart from the cultural context and the activity. She also argues against socialization (the transmission and then internalization of cultural norms) as a primary mechanism for describing the interaction between an individual and the cultural context as this too implies a separation of the individual, activity, and environment. Finally, she critiques cultural theorizing from the same stance.

The culture and cognition paradigm assumes that its polar concepts define the limits of analysis beyond which no other theoretical terms and relations are required. But no matter how comprehensive the theory, "culture" by itself cannot provide the underpinnings for a social analysis of people acting and their activity. (p. 177)

Lave focuses instead "on relations between sociocultural structure and social practice" (p. 177) and the indivisibility of body, cognition, feeling, activity, and the sociocultural world.

This focus on the inseparability of the individual, activity, and environment is also a hallmark of Rogoff's (1990) work on children's cognitive development as an apprenticeship.

The individual and the social are not analytically separate influences in the course of development. Neither is the relation an interaction, because that still implies separability of individuals and the social context. Instead, I view the individual child, social partners, and the cultural milieu as inseparable contributors to the ongoing activities in which child development takes place. (p. 18)

Within the motor control community, Newell (1986) also proposed the individual, task, and environment as the critical unit of analysis. He claimed that individual constraints (such as height, strength, and neural development), task constraints (such as the goal of the activity), and environmental constraints (including gravity, surface, and light) determined the movement patterns that would emerge in a given situation.

A relational perspective and the mutuality of individual and environment

As Rogoff (1990) suggests, a critical aspect of the indivisibility of individual, activity, and environment is the idea that development and learning emerge from the relations among rather than interactions between individual, activity, and environmental factors. Similarly, Newell (1986) suggests that the motor skill responses that an observer sees emerge from the relations among individual, task, and environment. This relational perspective is a core concept of situated perspectives. Gibson (1979/86), whose work has influenced many situated cognition scholars, describes the mutuality of the individual and environment in terms of affordances. An affordance is the possible use, meaning, or function of something in the environment in relation to the individual's capabilities, goals, and intentions. For Gibson, the environment is defined in terms of what it functionally affords for an individual engaged in a particular activity. Thus, individual action and the environment are not defined without the other; rather, Gibson defines the environment and individual in terms of their mutuality. Clancy (1997), and Pea (1993) explicitly acknowledge their debt to Gibson's ideas in developing their work on situated cognition.

Focus on the activity within a relational perspective

Reflecting the unit of analysis, what distinguishes situated perspectives is their focus on individuals participating in activities and events that are culturally situated practices (Cobb and Bowers, 1999; Pea, 1993). This is a shift in emphasis from more cognitive, constructivist perspectives that focus on individuals' cognitive representations or cultural representations of those social practices (Clancey, 1997). This is also a shift from understanding an action as a knowledge-based prescription for action to understanding actions as emerging from the relations among individual, task, and environmental constraints (Newell, 1986). The activity (or task) is essential as it sets or constrains the goals of the individual (Newell, 1986; Rogoff, 1990). Individuals attend to the environment in relation to their goals, intentions, and capabilities for engaging in the task at hand (E.J. Gibson, 1969; J.J. Gibson, 1979/86). Theoretical analyses of what happens in an event cannot be described independently of an individual's goals for the activity and the activity's constraints (Newell, 1986, Rogoff, 1990).

Distributed cognition

Another core concept of situated perspectives is the idea of distributed cognition. As discussed above, Lave (1988) claims that cognition is distributed across the individual, activity, and environment and that knowledge does not reside only in the brain nor does cognition occur simply in the heads of individuals, rather, individuals off-load cognitive work on the environment. Cognition can be distributed across the physical, symbolic, and social environment.

> Knowledge is commonly socially constructed, through collaborative efforts toward shared objectives or by dialogues and challenges brought about by differences in persons' perspectives. Intelligence may also be distributed for use in designed artifacts as diverse as physical tools, representations such as diagrams, and computer–user interfaces to complex tasks. In these cases, intelligence is often distributed by off-loading what could be elaborate and error-prone mental reasoning processes as action constraints on either the physical or symbolic environments. (Pea, 1993: 48)

Authenticity

The role and importance of authentic activities also appears across the work of situated scholars. The most prominent spokespersons were Brown et al. (1989) in *Educational Researcher*. Building on the work of Lave and other situated researchers, Brown et al. critiqued educational practices that teach content in decontextualized ways and claimed that "by ignoring the situated nature of cognition, education defeats its own goal of providing useable, robust knowledge" (p. 32). They proposed that educators view knowledge as a tool not simply to be acquired, but to be used and the understanding of it developed through use. Knowledge, being socially constructed, reflects the culture and its value as a tool for the learner depends on the learner's understanding of the concept in relation to its use in an activity within a cultural setting. Thus, they argue that school-based learning of subject matter needs to reflect, in substantive ways, how the subject matter is used outside of school and in broader communities of practice. The basis for their claims is the critical issue of facilitating transfer, claims that were debated in later issues of *Educational Researcher* (Anderson et al., 1996).

Communities of practice and legitimate peripheral participation

The final two concepts of situated perspectives that physical education researchers have applied are legitimate peripheral participation and communities of

practice. Lave and Wenger (1991) propose legitimate peripheral participation as an "analytical viewpoint on learning" (p. 40). The unit of analysis shifts from the individual learner to describing how newcomers move from peripheral positions through meaningful, authentic participation to become full participants in communities of practice. Like other situated concepts, legitimate peripheral participation shifts from focusing on individual learning of in-the-head knowledge and cognition, to learning as increased participation in a social practice. Lave and Wenger foreground the meanings an individual make of the social structures of social practices. They also focus on describing the social structures of communities of practice and how these structures function sometimes to deny access to newcomers and sometimes to facilitate it.

The review of the work in physical education based on situated perspectives is divided into four sections. These are (a) research on curriculum, (b) research on student learning and knowledge, (c) research on teaching and teachers' knowledge, and (d) research on teacher learning.

Research in physical education

Research on curriculum based on situated perspective

Teaching and curriculum are implicitly or explicitly based on a theory of learning (Kirk and Macdonald, 1998; Rink, 2001). One major task of curriculum theorists is to design and analyze curriculum and instruction in terms of the underlying theoretical basis and to apply the most current research and theory on learning to curriculum models. Theories provide images, guidelines, concepts, metaphors, and frameworks for how teachers might think about content, teaching, and learning. This section summarizes those papers that explicitly used situated perspectives to theorize about or describe curriculum and educational processes.

One of the earliest curriculum theory papers based on a situated perspective was Ennis's (1992) discussion of dynamical systems theory as a heuristic for understanding educational processes. She focused on attractors and constraints and their impact on stability and change. Some attractors are deep, stable, and resistant to change, while small changes in other attractors or constraints can lead to instability and change. Ennis describes how teachers' value orientations can serve as powerful attractors that can result in stability and contribute to teachers using consistent instructional approaches while resisting change to novel approaches. She suggests that dynamical systems theory not only offers a way to understand highly complex systems, but also suggests that researchers focus on critical junctures when apparently stable attractors become unstable and lead to change.

In another early paper, Rovegno and Kirk (1995) promoted an ecological perspective on learning for guiding curriculum and instruction. They suggest that prescriptive motor learning theories, which focus on feedback and error correction (Newell, 1986), imply that feedback and error correction are central to teaching. An ecological perspective focuses on learners' active explorations and search strategies and hence characterizes the learner as active and tasks as central to teaching. Like Ennis (1992), Rovegno and Kirk suggest the images of learning portrayed by dynamical systems and ecological psychology can be powerful because these images portray the learner as an active part of a holistic, dynamical system reflective of the complexity of the physical, social, and cultural school environment.

More recently, curriculum scholars have discussed curricular models in terms of situated theory. The first include Sport Education developed by Siedentop (1994) and Sport for Peace (Ennis, 2000), which incorporates many Sport Education structures. The second is Teaching Games for Understanding developed by Bunker and Thorpe (1983). These models are described in other chapters and will not be reviewed here. The focus in this chapter is on the analysis of these models in terms of situated theory.

Sport education and sport for peace

Ennis (2000) developed Sport for Peace in accord with the benefits situated and social constructivist perspectives have shown for learners to participate in a community of learners, to engage in authentic, legitimate activities within that community, and to interact within a cooperative, caring, interdependent, social group. Kirk and Macdonald (1998) explored several major concepts from a situated perspective using Sport Education as an example of how these concepts might be applied. They introduce Lave and Wenger's (1991) ideas of "legitimate peripheral participation and communities of practice" as potentially powerful notions for physical education. Kirk and Macdonald propose that sport, exercise and physical recreation are communities of practice with relevance to physical education although (citing Brooker and Macdonald, 1995; Kirk, 1994) commercial exercise and recreation facilities and outdoor adventure activities (such as whitewater rafting) are well beyond the resources of school-based physical education. However, physical education can reproduce some aspects of these communities of practice and provide authentic experiences that enable learners to acquire knowledge and skills for meaningful participation. Kirk

and Macdonald then make a case for Sport Education as a viable curricular model that provides legitimate peripheral participation in a school-based community of practice. The Sport Education model reproduces many of the positive, beneficial aspects of the community of practice of community sport while eliminating negative aspects. They claim part of the success of Sport Education is this very authenticity. Alexander and Luckman (2001) support this claim based on their survey study of 377 teachers who agreed that Sport Education provides opportunities for, in Lave and Wenger's terms, legitimate peripheral participation.

Responding to Kirk and Macdonald (1998), Penny et al. (2002) question the extent to which Sport Education provides legitimate peripheral participation in a community of practice. While they applaud the ways Sport Education stands in opposition to the institutionalized, elite sport culture based on exclusion, they note that this opposition means Sport Education is very disconnected from the culture of sport. They argue for Sport Education to become more connected to sport communities of practice not to reproduce these communities, but to transform them to be more equitable.

Taking a different tack, Kirk and Kinchin (2003), cite MacIntyre's analysis that separates the extrinsic rewards (e.g. prestige) accruing from excellence in a community of practice from the more central and critical internal goods of that practice. Kirk and Kinchin argue that Sport Education focuses on the internal goods of the community of sport such as the benefits of performance excellence, knowledge of the sport, affiliation, and health-related physical activity. They analyze how these internal goods have the potential for transfer beyond school settings.

Debate and further research on the relation between the community of sport and school-based sport and physical education is critical in that students always have some form of prior personal and cultural knowledge of sport that will impact how they experience school-based physical education (Rovegno, 1999). It is likely that students' prior knowledge is influenced heavily by media sport (Kirk, 1999). One benefit of using the idea of communities of practice as a conceptual tool for curriculum work is that it focuses our attention on the multiple communities of practice, such as youth and collegiate sport, community sport, physical recreation, exercise, media sport, and elite sport that are related to the subject matter we teach and that form the cultures students bring to our programs—not only the communities we are preparing young people to enter but also those that impact their lives before entering our classes (Kirk, 1999; Kirk and Macdonald, 1998; Kirk and MacPheil, 2002). As Lave and Wenger (1991) point out, everyone is a member of multiple communities of practice and Kirk (1999) suggests it is essential we "identify as precisely as possible the *relationships* between curriculum and learning in school physical education, allied practices in other sites and their cultural significance" (p. 70).

Teaching Games for Understanding (TGfU)

TGfU (Bunker and Thorpe, 1983) is a second curriculum model that has been analyzed in terms of situated learning theory. Kirk and MacPhail (2002) describe how TGfU provides authentic learning experiences; focuses on learning as active, rather than passive; and attends to the physical, sociocultural, and institutional environments in which learners' experiences are situated. The hallmark of TGfU is that lessons begin with authentic game experiences and tactics and skills are then taught in relation to that game environment. In other words, from the start skills and tactics are situated. Teachers modify games so that the game form itself structures learners' experiences in such a way as to focus their attention, perception, and thinking on some aspect of tactical content and related skills that the teacher aims to teach. Kirk and MacPhail explain that rather than teaching skills in isolation disconnected from learners' understanding of games and sports, the aim is to situate knowledge and experiences in an authentic context meaningful for the learner.

Light and Fawns (2003) also argue that a situated perspective can be a basis for TGfU. (Their discussion of how TGfU is constructivist is summarized elsewhere in this handbook.) They focus on the inseparability of body and mind, individual and environment and describe how TGfU is situated in that it focuses on the learner's perceptions and skills as actions situated within game environments. For the learner, the approach is holistic in that movement, higher-order thinking skills, perception, and affect are all developed through social interactions and facilitate the development of more holistic knowledge.

Research on student learning and knowledge based on situated perspectives

Few studies have examined student learning from a situated perspective. Those studies that have used the core concepts of affordances; the unit of analysis as the individual, activity, and environment; and distributed cognition to interpret the data. In a series of studies, David Langley and his colleagues used a situated perspective to account for what and how individuals learned and functioned in sport settings. In one study, Langley (1995) described students' thoughts about the learning process during a bowling course. The most important and frequently

discussed theme was errors in performance. Students discussed the causes of errors, the conditions that had an impact on errors, and their strategies for reducing errors. Langley showed how students' thoughts were constituted in part by the nature of the activity and sociocultural environment, that is, cognition was situated. Specifically, students' thoughts about the theme of errors were embedded in the nature of the activity of bowling (i.e. the way the game is played and scored with its emphasis on strikes and perfect scores), the sociocultural atmosphere of bowling alleys (with individual performance clearly visible and center stage), and the instructional process (e.g. the teacher's emphasis on correcting errors). Langley (2001) also used a situated perspective to describe how the learning of a golf swing by a senior adult beginning golfer was bounded by three categories of interacting constraints (Newell, 1986). These included a variety of physical ailments and injuries (physical constraints), his limited selection of clubs (task constraints), and his selection of only short golf courses (environmental constraints).

In another study Langley and Knight (1996) examined a successful, senior competitive tennis player's practical knowledge and used the idea of affordances to describe his knowledge. The individual's success was due to his keen knowledge of his capabilities to perform different shots in relation to both the game situation and his perceptions of his opponent's strengths and weaknesses. In theoretical terms, he perceived the affordances of the environment (Gibson, 1979/86). He quickly and accurately perceived the tactical possibilities in relation to his own and his opponents' capabilities. While his weaknesses constrained these possibilities, his strong self-knowledge and ability to quickly perceive his opponents' weaknesses allowed him to exploit their weaknesses using his strengths. Langley and Knight suggest that his success was due to his ability to perceive the environmental affordances at a highly differentiated level. Their descriptions of the tennis player's tactical knowledge and game play well illustrate how a situated perspective is suited for describing and theorizing about performance and tactics within game play.

A conceptual framework for categorizing dimensions of situated learning

Other researchers have found a situated perspective to be useful for interpreting student learning of skills and tactics in school settings. Kirk et al. (2000) used a situated perspective to gain insight into how Junior High students learned during a TGfU unit on basketball. They proposed a powerful framework for categorizing dimensions of situated learning (a) perceptual-physical, (b) social-interactive, and

(c) institutional-cultural. Each of these dimensions impacted students' responses and learning. In terms of the perceptual-physical dimensions, they described how students accurately remembered game tactics related to faking, sending lead passes, and defending a fake, but students could not perform these tactics in game situations. Kirk et al. suggested the problem was players' inability to perceive information in the environment that indicated when and where to pass. In other words, students understood the tactic before they could reliably perform this in game situations – a finding also reported in other studies on student learning of game tactics (Rovegno et al., 2001).

Second, in terms of the social-interactive dimension, students had problems passing due to the interactions among players and the distance between passer and receiver in relation to the passer's ability to throw an accurate pass at the appropriate moment. This finding was also reported in Rovegno et al. (2001) and reflects the relational aspects of game play. Tactical game play requires students to perceive and understand the relations among teammates and opponents within the game environment.

The third dimension, institution-cultural, was evident in that students participated in drills, but did not understand how these drills connected to basketball. Kirk et al. (2000) interpreted this finding as students solely conceptualizing the drill as school work and doing what the teacher told them to do, that is, working within the institutional community of practice of schools that was disconnected to basketball.

Kirk et al. (2000) suggest these three dimensions offer a valuable conceptual framework for further research on students' learning. For example, one possible explanation for students' resistance to drills and their desire to play the real game of basketball might reside in cultural-institution dimensions and be due to the way television portrays the game. Television shows basketball as an exciting game devoid of drills and repetitious practice (Brooker et al., 2000). A three-dimensional framework can help researchers identify multiple factors that impact learning.

Focusing on the institutional-cultural dimensions, Ronholt (2002) conducted a discourse analysis on a community of practice (Lave and Wenger, 1991) in a 2nd-grade physical education lesson. She showed how groups of children positioned themselves more or less peripherally in relation to the community of practice and the extent to which they could or did resist cultural discourses on gender. In brief, the children were given the option to run for two kilometers through a forest either without stopping or with breaks. The boys (with the exception of two) and one girl chose to run without breaks and were given status and rewarded by being allowed to play soccer when they were done. Two boys commented that "It's only the sissies" that take breaks

while "only the good ones" run without stopping making explicit to their peers the traditional masculine discourse associated with high status. The last four girls chose to walk, talk, laugh and were excited that they caught a frog. Ronholt discussed how their actions successfully challenged the dominant discourse. Using Wenger's (1998) notion that identity is developed through experiences participating in communities of practice, Ronholt discussed the implications for the different groups of children, in terms of dominant gendered patterns. She analyzed the teacher's discourse of health-related exercise, the boys' competitive perspective, the hidden curriculum, the ways the teacher negotiated differently with boys and girls, and the unequal opportunities for boys and girls to challenge the dominant discourse. She thus provided a theoretical explanation at the institutional-cultural level for what happened in the physical education lesson.

A final study on students was conducted by Pope and O'Sullivan (2003). They described the ecology of "free gym" basketball during lunch hour and after school in community settings. Although Lave and Wenger's (1991) work was not the theoretical framework for their study, they claimed that the ecology they described was akin to an apprenticeship and that individuals who wanted to participate in the basketball games engaged in what they labeled a "limited" form of legitimate peripheral participation although these opportunities were not available for most students.

Studies describing the link between teaching and students' movement responses

Situated perspectives have also been helpful for understanding how the tasks and the learning environment teachers design impact the movement responses of the children. Barrett and Collie (1996) described the connections between children's movement patterns of the lacrosse cradle and teachers' actions using Halverson's (1966) idea of eliciting tasks, that is, tasks designed to elicit particular movement patterns within a skill and Newell's (1986) constraints theory in which the task, individual, and environmental constraints influence the movement patterns that emerge. This study showed how, for example, organizational patterns that provided adequate space (environmental constraints) affected the speed of the run. A faster run elicited a full cradle and opposition of the legs and cradle (more mature patterns). Having the children put their hands close together on the stick and run easily holding the stick vertical (task constraints) elicited a more mature oppositional pattern. In contrast, having the children keep their hands apart (the mature pattern) had negative effects on three other components of cradling; (a) arms and hands moving in concert, (b) opposition of the cradle and legs, and (c) the size of the cradle. When a teacher described the mature pattern to swing the arms and turn the shoulders (a task constraint) this also elicited less mature patterns in the children – a finding also reported by Wulf and Weigelt (1997) who studied a simulated skiing task in the laboratory and Roberton et al. (1997) who studied kindergarteners hopping.

Barrett and Collie's (1996) study showed how changing environmental and task constraints changed the developmental level of different components of the children's cradle and facilitated better practice conditions. Because this study took place in the naturalistic setting, it offers powerful information about teaching lacrosse and adapting individual, task, and environmental constraints to elicit the movement patterns the teacher wants to develop. Moreover, Barrett and Collie propose the study implies a powerful principle to guide teaching, that is, teachers need to understand that the movement pattern the child exhibits results from the relationships among the child, task, and environment – not simply the child's ability level. "It is the teachers' responsibility to observe these relationships or interactions, recognize the effect they have on the children's movement pattern(s), and then, if necessary, change the task and/or environment to optimize developmental progress" (pp. 306–7). This situated conception of teaching goes well beyond a conception that teachers look for and then correct errors through feedback.

Similar to Barrett and Collie (1996), Chen et al. (2003), described children's dribbling and how dribbling responses varied with changes in task constraints. When teachers presented more difficult tasks such as dribbling at a fast speed, on angular pathways, with a crossover dribble, under and between the legs, at very low levels, following a leader, and while performing a second task (such as tossing and catching with the non-dribbling hand), there were more instances when children slapped with their palm rather than pushing the ball with their finger pads and the children had more problems maintaining contact with the ball on consecutive bounces (both less mature movement patterns). In contrast, more difficult tasks also elicited more instances of looking up (a more mature pattern) for low, typical, and high-skilled children. Low-skilled children rarely looked up unless the task required them to do so. Although some motor development research has shown task constraints had little or no impact on different components of striking or throwing (Langendorfer, 1987; Roberton, 1987), other studies found task constraints had a differential impact on components of throwing, dribbling, and catching (Burton and Welch, 1990; Burton et al., 1992; Langendorfer, 1990; Strohmeyer et al.,

1991). Chen et al., 2003 suggest that teachers need to consider different tasks for developing different components of dribbling.

A final project examining the relation between teaching and children's responses described how the researchers and on-site teachers team taught a unit on basic invasion-game tactics to fourth-grade children and what and how children learned (Nevett et al., 2001a,b; Rovegno et al., 2001). Using an approach similar to TGfU but for elementary school children, the unit focused on teaching passing and cutting to receive a pass in game-like situations and on the meaning of these tactical movements but not on throwing and catching techniques. The unit also emphasized children's decision making in groups about the rules, boundaries, and structures of the modified games and used a play–discuss–play cycle for children to analyze their game structures and tactical play. Finally, the teachers based content and teaching on children's emerging understanding of the social, thinking, and tactical movement skills embedded in the game-like tasks.

In terms of children's learning, pre- and post-test data showed significant improvement in lead passes, appropriate use of a back pass, appropriate scoring attempts, and appropriately holding the ball when no teammate was free (Nevett et al., 2001b). In addition, children sent more catchable passes and fewer passes that were too long, forceful, short, or behind the receiver. Good cutting decisions and successfully catching passes also showed significant increases. Nevertheless, there were variations within each child's response – sometimes he or she made good passing and cutting decisions and sometimes not. Thus the study suggests learning of cutting and passing requires extensive practice before these responses develop to the level of consistency and automaticity. The quantitative data also suggest an interaction between cutting, passing, and catching. The authors suggested that children's decisions in games cannot be assessed outside of the relations among players in the game. Children also scored significantly higher at the end of the unit on a multiple-choice knowledge test and on the quantity and quality of their descriptions of tactical actions and concepts in interviews (Nevett et al., 2001b).

Rovegno et al. (2001) derived three principles of curriculum and instruction based on situated perspectives and the findings of the study. First, passing and cutting were learned by the children, and taught and viewed by the teachers as situated, relational content. For example, at the start of the study, the children passed behind the receiver and with too much force and blamed receivers for not catching the ball. They did not understand that passing and cutting were relational and situated, that is, a good pass is defined in relation to the receiver's ability to catch the ball and the game environment. Based on the children's responses, the teachers responded by approaching passing explicitly as a relational skill by teaching that a good pass was a "catchable" pass in terms of the receiver's ability to catch the ball (e.g. not too forceful, high, etc.) and in terms of whether the receiver was free from defenders. Children's cutting and passing developed across the unit and the changes in the immature components of cutting and passing were described in relation to the content and tasks designed by the teachers. Development was not described as an individual process, rather, the researchers proposed development was in the relation between passer, receiver, and the immediate game environment – a conception of development in keeping with Rogoff (1990).

A second principle of instruction was to offload children's cognition on task constraints and the environment thus leading to economy of teaching (i.e. presenting tasks that elicited appropriate practice with few or no explanations from the teacher). It also led to constraining children's actions freeing cognitive resources to enable children to attend to the most relevant aspects of the game-like environment and also to enable children to understand the meaning of tactics because the environment made the meaning self-evident. This principle is based on the situated stance that cognition is distributed and thus can be offloaded onto tools, task constraints, and the environment (Lave, 1988; Pea, 1993).

A third principle of teaching was to pay careful attention to relationships among task and environmental constraints and children's capabilities in tactics and skills and to set and modify tasks and the environment to afford children's learning most productively. Modifications included the size of the boundaries, the number of goals, rules about whether play stopped or not after interceptions, whether to allow dropped balls to be free balls or turnovers, and the extent to which the intensity of the defense should be constrained. Data indicated it was difficult to get good games working as productive learning environments for all nine groups of children (each group consisting of six children). Different combinations of modifications were needed for different groups of children, for different children within each group, and at different times in the unit. Teaching tactical game play was complex in that it required the teachers to maintain a delicate balance among children's capabilities and task and environmental constraints.

As Kirk et al. (2000) indicate, cognitive and behavioral theories provide explanations for aspects of learning in physical education, Nevertheless, these accounts of learning when applied to game play are incomplete. The use of situated perspectives to examine the learning of tactical game play is helpful because tactics are the actions of individuals in relation to other individuals within a particular game situation and thus are relational and situated. Situated perspectives offer a broader, more comprehensive framework for understanding the learning of complex tactical physical activities.

Studies on teaching and teacher's knowledge

Researchers have also used situated perspectives as a basis for analyzing teaching and teachers' knowledge. Flavier et al. (2002) focused on teachers' actions during disruptive conflicts with students. They cited Theureau's "course of action" as their theoretical framework explaining that this framework was derived from the situated stance that the minimum unit of analysis must be individuals acting within a particular context. They found that disruptive conflicts were rare (only nine occurred across 138 lessons) and the archetype course of action included three phases. In the first phase teachers monitored students trying to maintain an environment focused on learning, recognized a disruptive event, and interrupted the event. In phase 2, teachers focused on getting the disruptive student to accept punishment. In phase 3, teachers exploited what they perceived as a teachable moment by reviewing class rules with the remainder of the students and warning them of the consequences.

In a study of pedagogical content knowledge, Rovegno (1995) described a student teacher's conceptions of learning and his resultant teaching decisions. The student teacher held a decontextualized, error-oriented view of skills in which all movements, other than the most efficient form, were considered errors. He also assumed skills would transfer to games without attention to the perceptual aspects of skills and the situated use of skills in games. The study showed how a teacher's view of learning impacted content, task design, and instruction. Rovegno analyzed and critiqued his progressions and discussed the theoretical bases for different ways to break down and sequence content and the possible implications of using a situated perspective. A situated perspective calls into question the assumption that teachers should control the complexity of content by primarily controlling the complexity of the environment and perceptional aspects of motor skills. It also questions an error perspective that focuses on providing prescriptive information about the most efficient form of performing a skill without recognizing that the movement that emerges results from the individual, task and environmental constraints. Ecological and dynamical systems perspectives describe learning as individuals actively exploring the environment in a more holistic way and using search strategies in relation to the task, environment, and learners' goals, capabilities, and intentions.

Research on teacher learning using situated perspectives

Researchers studying teacher learning using situated perspectives have used the following concepts for interpreting their data: (a) communities of practice, (b) the individual engaged in a meaningful activity within a social context as the unit for analysis, (c) the situated nature of knowledge, and (d) attractors and constraints within complex environments. They have studied what teachers learn more generally and also teachers' responses to situated curricular approaches.

Ennis et al. (1992) studied the role of teachers' value orientations on their expectations and goals for student learning and students' perceptions of their teachers' goals. Teachers with a Disciplinary Mastery/Learning Process (DM/LP) orientation taught in ways consistent with their value orientation and students' reports of their teaching were also consistent. Ennis et al. characterized DM/LP as a strong attractor that consistently affected many of the teachers' decisions and thus was recognized by students. Teachers with an Ecological Integration/Social Reconstruction (EI/SR) value orientation, however, reported that they were constrained in teaching in ways consistent with their philosophy and students' perceptions of their teachers were inconsistent with the teachers' goals. Ennis et al. suggested that the EI/SR value orientation was a weak attractor for those particular teachers who may not have the knowledge or instructional techniques necessary to put their goals into practice or articulate their goals to students.

Macdonald et al. (1999) used the situated concept of communities of practice and discussed the discontinuities and continuities between the communities of practice college students experienced in high school and their first year of college. The major discontinuity was the lack of practical experiences in sport and physical activities in their first year as Human Movement Studies majors in college, activities that were substantial aspects of physical education and sport in high school. A major continuity between high school and college was the emphasis on biophysical aspects and the marginalization of socio-cultural concepts of physical education. Students did not perceive general science coursework (such as chemistry, physics, and plant biology) to be relevant to their future careers, to other and future course work in Human Movement Studies, or to their high school physical education community of practice. Their frame of reference was whether information was useful in relation to future jobs. While there were some continuities between the high school and college communities of practice, undergraduates did not easily see the connections and experienced disconnected, contradictory messages. These findings are similar to those of Dewer (1987) who described undergraduates'

perceptions of what they were learning and reported students considered biophysical concepts directly related to the body and sport to be useful and beneficial to their future careers, while socio-cultural concepts were marginalized or disconnected.

Rovegno (1994) used the unit of analysis and a situated, relational view to explain and account for her findings on student teachers' pedagogical content knowledge. The unit of analysis was defined as student teachers, engaged in the activity of teaching, within the sociocultural communities of practice in their school settings. In one study, the most salient aspect of the student teachers' pedagogical content knowledge was a "curricular zone of safety". The curricular zone of safety was defined as a social affordance (Gibson, 1979/86; Valenti and Good, 1991), that is, what the student teachers perceived the social environment of the school afforded in relation to their capabilities and status as student teachers. The social environment included administrators who did not support physical education, cooperating teachers who joked about student teachers using the latest research and allowed a recreational rather than learning orientation in lessons, and a pupil subculture focused on recreation. Constrained by their weak and underdeveloped pedagogical content knowledge and their novice teaching capabilities, the student teachers taught content and used instructional techniques within a curricular zone of safety that little resembled the units they wanted to teach and believed reflected good teaching. Pedagogical content knowledge was thus constituted by the cultural aspects of the setting in relation to the student teachers' capabilities and knowledge and thus was defined as a situated (rather than in-the-head) form of knowledge.

In a second study using the same unit of analysis, Rovegno (1992) showed how pre-service teachers' pedagogical content knowledge developed as they perceived in a more detailed, differentiated way the relations among content, teaching, and children's learning. For example, the pre-service teachers all discussed how their teaching improved because they learned more about how the children learned the specific content they were teaching and how this was affected by the extent to which they broke content down in relation to the children's ability levels. They also recognized they were constrained by what they were capable of doing on-their-feet as beginning teachers and learned to improve their lessons and children's learning in relation to their individual teaching capabilities.

Reporting similar findings, Rolfe (2001) identified the factors that influence classroom teachers' confidence to teach dance. She interpreted her findings based on Brown et al.'s (1989) work on cognitive apprenticeship and the importance of authentic experiences. Both the quality of cognitive apprenticeship in terms of the cooperating teachers' demonstrating and assisting with ways of teaching dance and the quality and amount of authentic dance teaching experiences were positively linked to student teachers' confidence to teach dance.

Finally, in one study Rovegno (1993) described how distributed cognition enabled a student teacher to better understand how teachers could teach for multiple goals. The student teacher used her cooperating teacher's lesson objective format, which clearly listed on a clipboard the skill development content, movement concept, broad social responsibility goal, behaviors to be taught related to the social goal, cognitive content, and affective content that were embedded in lesson tasks. The student teacher did not have to figure out how to integrate multiple goals in her head; rather she offloaded cognitive work onto the clipboard. Her understanding and teaching of multiple, integrated goals was distributed across a tool and her thinking.

The use of situated perspectives in physical education teacher education offers scholars a different way to think about prospective teachers' knowledge and learning. Much of the teacher education curriculum in higher education rests on the supposition that knowledge, once acquired, will be transformed and then used by undergraduates in other courses or in their jobs after graduation. General science courses, foundational courses, methods courses, curriculum courses, and disciplinary-based courses are all taught in one community of practice, that is, the university. We assume that what undergraduates learn will be used later in the community of practice in schools. This assumption presumes knowledge is easily decontextualized from one setting and contextualized in another. The evidence from situated studies and a host of constructivist and socialization studies suggest the reverse. What situated studies offer is a different theoretical perspective for explaining both successful and unsuccessful learning in teacher education. These studies highlight the critical importance of communities of practice in structuring knowledge and learning.

Summary and conclusions

Situated perspectives focus on individuals acting in sociocultural settings and the impact of the activity (or task) and the physical, social, and cultural environment on individuals' meanings, actions, development, and learning. It offers a perspective on learning that is well supported by research and has been successfully applied across subject-matter domains in education. In concert with constructivist perspectives, the situated perspectives consider it critically important for researchers and teachers to understand how children learn in school settings. It suggests that researchers and teachers need to understand learners' pre-existing knowledge and how this facilitates and impedes learning. In particular, situated perspectives have illustrated the need to understand the multiple cultures of the learner, teacher, school, and society; how these impact learners; and how to plan curriculum and instruction that leads to robust, meaningful knowledge useful in multiple contexts.

What is significant for our field is that studies using a situated perspective signal an increased interest in studying learning, learning connected to teaching and programmatic elements, and learning connected to content and curriculum. Equally important is the emphasis on the learner interacting with multiple cultures in the environment not just the skills to be learned or the impact of teaching techniques.

Although any chapter organized around a theoretical perspective is bound to review an eclectic set of studies, the themes that cross these studies suggest researchers are interested in examining the learning process in detail and depth to better inform curriculum and instruction in school and teacher education settings. They are also interested in studying the multiple factors that impact learning not only, as has been in the past, to show what teaching techniques are effective, but to explore what learning experiences mean to learners. Many of the studies examined a combination of learning, teaching, content and/or context simultaneously and within naturalistic settings where teaching is neither contrived nor tightly controlled. This reflects the trend in educational psychology to study learning in naturalistic settings. Most were small-scale studies conducted by individuals or small teams of researchers without funding. This status is similar to much of the research on teacher education and teacher learning in other subject domains. Where we differ from our classroom colleagues is in the quantity of school-based research examining learning. This is both due to national funding priorities and to the shear number of researchers in those fields. In science, mathematics, history, geography, and all areas of literacy there are literally thousands of studies of small-scale teaching and curricular approaches aimed at examining the teaching and learning of a particular topic, set of skills, or cognitive processes and can serve as models for similar work in physical education (cf. Beck et al., 1996; Cobb et al., 1991; Fennema et al., 1996; Palinscar and Brown, 1984).

To close, I share the optimism of the National Research Council (1999) and Resnick and Williams-Hall (1998) that the substantial body of research on learning developed within the past 30 years offers critical information that can guide the design of curriculum and instructional approaches. The task of designing, evaluating, and disseminating these approaches is, of course, formidable as are the far

Analyzing teaching using constructivist principles

Using an approach that offers an alternative to simply connecting constructivist principles to teaching, Bertone et al. (2003) presented an analysis of the "intrapsychic conflicts" experienced by a student teacher during a badminton lesson. Such studies are significant in that they identify aspects of instruction and the possible role of teacher education in guiding pre-service teachers in their acquisition. The researchers based their analysis on Vygotskian conceptions of the relation between actions taken and the possible actions considered. They explain how a Vygotskian approach in teacher education would include helping novice teachers understand (i.e. internalize) the information experienced teachers seek in assessing what is happening in a lesson, what factors influence the teachers' choice of actions, and the possible actions a teacher can take to resolve problems and further lesson objectives. They explain that this is difficult because of the complexity of teaching and because pre-service teachers may not internalize possible actions they do not understand or perceive to be useful. Teaching is complex and different teaching actions can be associated with conflicting goals. Teachers may decide on one course of action within a lesson that is in conflict with other actions the teacher could take. They may or may not be aware of these inconsistencies but the intrapsychic conflict in assessing competing actions is considered "the foundation of teaching activity and not as a contradiction to be avoided" (p. 114).

In their study, the student teacher experienced intrapsychic conflicts among three actions (Bertone et al., 2003). First, she wanted students to find their own solutions to the tactical problem in badminton to force the opponent to move about the court as much as possible. However, in her critical feedback to students it was apparent that the one solution she wanted them to discover and use was to move their opponent on the diagonals (front side to back side on the diagonal). Finally, she wanted to maintain discipline and control and her actions to do so were sometimes in conflict with her other intentions.

The conflicts the student teacher experienced suggested to the researchers that she needed to understand a greater range of options for resolving conflicts and to learn to resolve these conflicts on-her-feet while teaching. Bertone et al. (2003) suggest that experience is crucial for developing the ability to make decisions about which course of action to use during teaching, but they do not claim that all experience is beneficial. In keeping with Vygotsky's theory that individuals internalize knowledge due to the scaffolding provided by more experienced individuals through social interactions (Davydov, 1995), the researchers suggest cooperating teachers scaffold their decision making-process through modeling, concrete analyses of classroom episodes, discussing problems, and helping pre-service teachers evoke a range of possible actions during teaching.

In another study based on Vygotsky's theory and his idea of a zone of proximal development, d'Arripe-Longueville et al. (2002), studied the impact of peer tutors on novice swimmers' performances. As the authors predicted, peer tutors who were intermediate and high-skilled performers of the swimming task had a greater impact on girls than tutors who were also novice swimmers. Tutors who were high-skilled swimmers also led to better performances in novice boys than the tutors who were also novices.

Research on naive conceptions and misconceptions

Based on the robust body of literature that pre-existing knowledge can constrain learning new information and the research identifying misconceptions that arise during learning or as a result of experience in the world, researchers have begun to identify misconceptions and the pre-existing knowledge of learners in physical education. These studies have been significant across subject domains and have generated curricular and instructional approaches (e.g. conceptual change approaches in science) that have successfully improved student learning. These studies also identify for teachers specific topics and concepts they can anticipate will be problematic for students.

Placek et al. (2001) identified several misconceptions about fitness held by middle school students. The 6th graders equated fitness to physical appearance. Most students believed that if you are thin you are fit. A major theme of fitness was weight loss and weight control. Students also equated strength with looking good not fitness. Other misconceptions included spot reduction (i.e. that exercising a particular muscle group such as the abdominal muscles, would reduce fat at that site) and sweating burns off fat. Students were confused about terminology with many not understanding terms such as cardiovascular endurance. Although the students had a reasonably accurate conception that exercise is beneficial, they were vague about the link between exercise and health. They had little knowledge of the aspects of fitness (cardiovascular endurance, muscular strength, muscular endurance, and flexibility) and were confused about which exercises would be beneficial for each aspect often providing incorrect answers. In general, the sixth graders knew that exercise was good but had an incomplete understanding of what constituted an appropriate exercise program. They were reasonably accurate in prescribing the frequency of aerobic activities but not more monumental challenges of teacher education and changing the culture of schools so that curriculum and instructional approaches based on current learning perspectives can be implemented in schools.

Acknowledgment

I thank Margaret Stran, Department of Kinesiology, The University of Alabama for her assistance with this chapter.

References

Alexander, K. and Luckman, J. (2001). Australian teachers' perceptions and uses of the sport education curriculum model. *European Physical Education Review, 7:* 243–267.

Anderson, J.R., Reder, L.M. and Simon, H.A. (1996). Situated learning and education. *Educational Researcher, 25*(4): 5–11.

Barrett, K.R. and Collie, S. (1996). Children learning lacrosse from teachers learning to teach it: The discovery of pedagogical content knowledge by observing children's movement. *Research Quarterly for Exercise and Sport, 67:* 297–309.

Beck, I.L., McKeown, M.G., Sandora, C., Kucan, L. and Worthy, J. (1996). Questioning the author: A yearlong classroom implementation to engage students with text. *The Elementary School Journal, 96:* 385–414.

Brooker, R., Kirk, D., Braiuka, S. and Bransgrove, A. (2000). Implementing a game sense approach to teaching junior high school basketball in a naturalistic setting. *European Physical Education Review, 6:* 7–26.

Brooker, R. and Macdonald, D. (1995). Mapping physical education in the reform agenda for Australian education: Tensions and contradictions. *European Physical Education Review, 1:* 101–110.

Brown, J. S., Collins, A. and Duguid, P. (1989). Situated cognition and the culture of Learning. *Educational Researcher, 18*(1): 32–42.

Bunker, D. and Thorpe, R. (1983). A model for the teaching of games in secondary schools. *Bulletin of Physical Education, 19:* 5–8.

Burton, A.W., Greer, N.L. and Wiese, D.M. (1992). Changes in overhand throwing patterns as a function of ball size. *Pediatric Exercise Science, 4:* 50–67.

Burton, A.W. and Welch, B.A. (1990). Dribbling performance in first-grade children: Effect of ball and hand size and ball-size preferences (Revision). *Physical Educator, 47:* 48–51.

Chen, W., Rovegno, I., Todorovich, J. and Babiarz, M. (2003). Third grade children's movement responses to dribbling tasks presented by accomplished teachers. *Journal of Teaching in Physical Education, 22:* 450–466.

Clancy, W.J. (1997). *Situated cognition: On human knowledge and computer representations.* Cambridge, UK: Cambridge University Press.

Cobb, P. and Bowers, J. (1999). Cognitive and situated learning perspectives in theory and practice. *Educational Researcher, 28*(2): 4–15.

Cobb, P., Wood, T., Yackel, E. et al., (1991). Assessment of a problem-centered second-grade mathematics project. *Journal for Research in Mathematics Education, 22:* 3–29.

Dewar, A. (1987). The social construction of gender in physical education. *Women's Studies International Forum, 10:* 453–465.

Ennis, C.D. (1992). Reconceptualizing learning as a dynamical system. *Journal of Curriculum and Supervision, 7:* 115–130.

Ennis, C.D. (2000). Canaries in the coal mine: Responding to disengaged students using theme-based curricula. *Quest, 52:* 119–130.

Ennis, C.D., Ross, J. and Chen, A. (1992). The role of value orientations in curricular decision making: A rationale for teachers' goals and expectations. *Research Quarterly for Exercise and Sport, 63:* 38–47.

Fennema, E., Carpenter, T., Franke, M., Levi, L., Jacobs, V. and Empson, S. (1996). A longitudinal study of learning to use children's thinking in mathematics instruction. *Journal for Research in Mathematics Education, 27:* 403–434.

Flavier, E., Bertone, S., Hauw, D. and Durand, M. (2002). The meaning and organization of physical education teachers' actions during conflict with students. *Journal of Teaching in Physical Education, 22:* 20–38.

Gibson, E.J. (1969). *Principles of perceptual learning and development.* Englewood Cliffs, NJ: Prentice-Hall.

Gibson, J.J. (1979/86). *The ecological approach to visual perception.* Boston, MA: Houghton Mifflin.

Greeno, J.G. (1997). On claims that answer the wrong questions. *Educational Researcher, 26*(1): 5–17.

Halverson, L.E. (1966). Development of motor patterns in young children. *Quest, (VI, Spring):* 44–53.

Kirk, D. (1994). Making the present strange: Sources of the current crisis in school physical education. *Discourse, 15:* 46–63.

Kirk, D. (1999). Physical culture, physical education and relational analysis. *Sport, Education and Society, 4:* 63–73.

Kirk, D. and Kinchin, G. (2003). Situated learning as a theoretical framework for sport education. *European Physical Education Review, 9:* 221–235.

Kirk, D. and Macdonald, D. (1998). Situated learning in physical education. *Journal of Teaching in Physical Education, 17:* 376–387.

Kirk, D. and MacPhail, A. (2002). Teaching games for understanding and situated learning: Rethinking the Bunker-Thorpe model. *Journal of Teaching in Physical Education, 21:* 177–192.

Kirk, D., Brooker, R. and Braiuka, S. (April, 2000). *Teaching games for understanding: A situated perspective on student learning.* Paper presented at the Annual Meeting of the American Educational Research Association, New Orleans, LA. (ERIC Document Reproduction Service No. ED442761).

Kugler, P.N., Kelso, J.A.S. and Turvey, M.T. (1980). On the concept of coordinative structures as dissipative structures: I. Theoretical lines. In G.E. Stelmach and J. Requin (Eds.), *Tutorials in motor behavior* (pp. 3–37). Amsterdam: North-Holland.

Kugler, P.N., Kelso, J.A.S. and Turvey, M.T. (1982). On the control and coordination of naturally developing systems. In J.A.S. Kelso and J.E. Clark (Eds.), *The development of movement control and co-ordination* (pp. 5–78). New York: Wiley.

Langendorfer, S. (1987). Prelongitudinal screening of over-arm striking development performed under two environmental conditions. In J.E. Clark and J.H. Humphrey (Eds.), *Advances in motor development research* (Vol. 1, pp. 17–47). New York: AMS Press.

Langendorfer, S. (1990). Motor-task goal as a constraint on developmental status. In J.E. Clark and J.H. Humphrey (Eds.), *Advances in motor development research* (Vol. 3, pp. 16–28). New York: AMS Press.

Langley, D.J. (1995). Student cognition in the instructional setting. *Journal of Teaching in Physical Education, 15*: 25–40.

Langley, D.J. (2001). The influence of functional constraints on sport-skill learning in a senior adult. *Journal of Aging and Physical Activity, 9*: 269–284.

Langley, D.J. and Knight, S.M. (1996). Exploring practical knowledge: A case study of an experienced senior tennis performer. *Research Quarterly for Exercise and Sport, 67*: 433–447.

Lave, J. (1988). *Cognition in practice: Mind, mathematics and culture in everyday life.* Cambridge, UK: Cambridge University Press.

Lave, J. and Wenger, E. (1991). *Situated learning: Legitimate peripheral participation.* Cambridge, UK: Cambridge University Press.

Light, R. and Fawns, R. (2003). Knowing the game: Integrating speech and action in games teaching through TGfU. *Quest, 55*: 161–176.

Macdonald, D., Kirk, D. and Braiuka, S. (1999). The social construction of the physical activity field at the school/university interface. *European Physical Education Review, 5*: 31–51.

National Research Council. (1999). *How people learn: Brain, mind, experience, and school.* Washington, DC.: National Academy Press.

Nevett, M., Rovegno, I. and Babiarz, M. (2001a). Fourth-grade children's knowledge of cutting, passing and tactics in invasion games after a 12-lesson unit of instruction. *Journal of Teaching in Physical Education* [Monograph], *20*: 389–401.

Nevett, M., Rovegno, I., Babiarz, M. and McCaughtry, N. (2001b). Changes in basic tactics and motor skills in an invasion-type game after a 12-lesson unit of instruction. *Journal of Teaching in Physical Education* [Monograph], *20*: 352–369.

Newell, K.M. (1986). Constraints on the development of coordination. In M.G. Wade and H.T.A. Whiting (Eds.), *Motor development in children: Aspects of coordination and control.* Amsterdam: Martinus Nijhoff.

Newell, K.M. (1996). Change in movement and skill: Learning, retention, and transfer. In M.L. Latash (Trans.) and M.T. Turvey (Eds.), *Dexterity and its development.* Mahwah, NJ: Lawrence Erlbaum.

Palinscar, A.S. and Brown, A.L. (1984). Reciprocal teaching of comprehension-fostering and monitoring activities. *Cognition and Instruction, 1*: 117–175.

Pea, R.D. (1993). Practices of distributed intelligence and designs for education. In G. Salomon (Ed.), *Distributed cognitions: Psychological and educational considerations* (pp. 47–87). Cambridge, UK: Cambridge University Press.

Penney, D., Clarke, G. and Kinchin, G. (2002). Developing physical education as a 'connective specialism': Is Sport Education the answer? *Sport, Education and Society 7*: 55–64.

Pope, C.C. and O'Sullivan, M. (2003). Darwinism in the gym. *Journal of Teaching in Physical Education, 23*: 311–327.

Resnick, L.B. and Williams-Hall, M. (1998). Learning organizations for sustainable education reform. *Daedalus 127*(4): 89–118.

Rink, J.E. (2001). Investigating the assumptions of pedagogy. *Journal of Teaching in Physical Education, 20*: 112–128.

Roberton, M.A. (1987). Developmental level as a function of the immediate environment. In J. E. Clark and J.H. Humphrey, (Eds.), *Advances in motor development research* (Vol. 1: pp. 1–15). New York: AMS Press.

Roberton, M.A., Halverson, L.E. and Harper, C.J. (1997). Visual/verbal modeling as a function of children's developmental levels in hopping. In J.E. Clark and J.H. Humphrey, (Eds.), *Motor development research and reviews* (Vol. 1, pp. 122–147). Reston, VA: National Association for Sport and Physical Education.

Rogoff, B. (1990). *Apprenticeship in thinking: Cognitive development in social context.* New York: Oxford University Press.

Rolfe, L. (2001). The factors which influence primary student teachers' confidence to teach dance. *European Physical Education Review, 7*: 157–175.

Ronholt, H. (2002). 'It's only the sissies…': Analysis of teaching and learning processes in physical education: A contribution to the hidden curriculum. *Sport, Education and Society 7*: 25–36.

Rovegno, I.C. (1992). Learning to teach in a field-based methods course: The development of pedagogical content knowledge. *Teaching and Teacher Education, 8*: 69–82.

Rovegno, I. (1993). Content knowledge acquisition during undergraduate teacher education: Overcoming cultural templates and learning through practice. *American Educational Research Journal, 30*: 611–642.

Rovegno, I. (1994). Teaching within a curricular zone of safety: School culture and the situated nature of student teachers' pedagogical content knowledge. *Research Quarterly for Exercise and Sport, 65*: 269–279.

Rovegno, I. (1995). Theoretical perspective on knowledge and learning and a student teacher's pedagogical content knowledge of dividing and sequencing subject matter. *Journal of Teaching in Physical Education, 14*: 284–304.

Rovegno, I. (1999). What is taught and learned in physical activity programs: The role of content. In J. -F. Grehaigne, N. Mahut, and D. Marchall, (Eds.), *Qu'apprennnent les eleves en faisant des activities physiques et sportives?* Besancon, France: L'Institut Universitaire de Formation des Maitres de Franche-Comte.

Rovegno, I. and Kirk, D. (1995). Articulations and silences in socially critical work on physical education: Toward a broader agenda. *Quest, 47*: 1–28.

Rovegno, I., Nevett, M. and Babiarz, M. (2001). Learning and teaching invasion-game tactics in 4th grade: Introduction and theoretical perspective. *Journal of Teaching in Physical Education* [Monograph], *20*: 341–352.

Rovegno, I., Nevett, M., Brock, S. and Babiarz, M. (2001). Teaching and learning basic invasion-game tactics in 4th grade: A descriptive study from situated and constraints theoretical perspectives. *Journal of Teaching in Physical Education* [Monograph], *20*: 370–388.

Siedentop, D. (1994). *Sport Education: Quality PE through positive sport experiences.* Champaign, IL: Human Kinetics.

Strohmeyer, H.S., Williams, K. and Schaub-George, D. (1991). Developmental sequences for catching a small ball: A prelongitudinal screening. *Research Quarterly for Exercise and Sport, 62*: 257–266.

Valenti, S.S. and Good, J.M.M. (1991). Social affordances and interaction: Introduction. *Ecological Psychology, 3*: 77–98.

Wenger, E. (1998). *Community of practice: Learning, meaning, and identity.* Cambridge, UK: Cambridge University Press.

Wulf, G. and Weigelt, C. (1997). Instructions about physical principles in learning a complex motor skill: To tell or not to tell. *Research Quarterly for Exercise and Sport, 68*: 362–367.

3.6 Learners and popular culture

RACHEL SANDFORD AND EMMA RICH

Introduction

Recent times have seen something of an explosion of interest in relation to the study of young people's social practice, and the impact of these experiences on their understandings of self and identity. In particular, concerns over young people's involvement in "unhealthy" or "antisocial" behaviours, as well as their perceived lack of participation in physical activities, has caused much attention to be directed specifically at youth leisure and lifestyle practices (e.g. Macdonald, 2002; Wright et al., 2003). At the same time, however, there have been significant changes within the nature of contemporary society that have included, in part, a growth in the accessibility and availability of social and cultural discourses, and these are seen to represent significant resources by which individuals, young people in particular, make sense of the social world following the perceived demise of previously solid institutions such as the family, religion, and local community networks (e.g. Brettschneider and Heim, 1997; Giddens, 1991; Kellner, 1992). In today's consumer culture, these discourses of popular culture are perceived as significant in terms of transmitting, representing, and reproducing dominant beliefs, values, and ideologies, particularly in relation to individuals' constructions of embodied identities. As such, it could be argued, they represent an important avenue of learning.

Within this chapter, the aim is to explore how young people in contemporary society learn in, about, and through their engagements with popular physical culture, and the bearing that these learning experiences have upon their relationships with physical education (PE). Throughout the discussion, learning is taken to be an implicit, situated and contextual process that takes place in both formal and informal settings. The centrality of the body to this process necessitates that learning is understood as an inherently embodied practice, one that is written into the body through the inculcation of values regarding appropriate behaviour, comportment, and action.

To summarize then, within this chapter we are concerned with defining, examining, and expanding upon the embodied learning that young people experience in contemporary culture. In order to do this we will highlight some of the key issues involved in the debate, define core concepts central to the discussions, and identify some of the past, recent and ongoing research undertaken and presented in this area. The issues raised will then be considered in light of their implications for and applications to practice and policy, before the discussion moves on to identify major trends within the field and potential future directions for subsequent research and theory development. The discussion will begin, however, with a brief historical overview of how embodied learning has been conceptualized with the concept of embodied learning.

Brief historical overview

The developing body of research exploring embodied learning within physical education and physical culture, which has emerged over the last two decades, has tended to draw upon a range of fields including sociology, education, gender and youth studies. Much of this has been aided (and indeed prompted) by recent developments in methodology within the field of physical education, which have seen much greater legitimacy given to qualitative research methods and have provided opportunities to examine young people's understandings, meanings and experiences of physical cultures. This paradigmatic shift within the field, towards social theories that embrace epistemologies and ontologies of a more "interpretive" nature, has led researchers to draw upon the tools of a range of social theories, including constructivism, postmodernism and poststructuralism, in order to provide a more complex insight into the relationships that young people have with PE. The changing perspective inherent within this evolution has facilitated developments within physical education research, which in turn have allowed researchers to explore and address some of the problematic issues that led, during the last decade, to intense discussion concerning a perceived "crisis" within the field (Kirk, 1994; Kirk and Tinning, 1990; Tinning and Fitzclarance, 1992; Thorpe, 2000).

Towards the end of the 1990s, researchers such as Penney and Evans (1999) and Brustad (1997) noted that despite significant social and cultural changes over the previous decades the structure of PE within schools had altered little, and that until recently much of the research conducted within the field of physical education had been somewhat decontextualized. They were not alone in this opinion, and such views were reinforced by calls for more detailed examinations of the context of physical education, which would involve, among other things, a shift away from the mediating paradigm to a conception of learning as socially constructed, situated, reflexive and embodied (Kirk and Macdonald, 1998). Research drawing on the post-structuralist concept of "discourse" has led to a growing recognition of the potential impact of implicit meanings transmitted through the PE context, and the implications of this process for young people's identities, the reinforcement of corporeal control, and the reproduction of inequalities. Through this work, meaning has come to be understood not as fixed, but as historically and culturally specific. Research within the fields of sociology, education, gender and youth cultural studies, drawing more or less on the work of Foucault's concept of discourse, has also made more complex our understanding of identity and the body, its social construction, and how this might relate to young people's engagement with physical cultures.

For example, the salience that particular discourses have for young people has been a useful way of exploring how and why young people disengage with PE and engage with other physical cultures. As Burrows (2004) reminds us, understanding cultures as relational and imbued with a variety of discourses invites us to interrogate the plurality of meaning that physical education and health practices have in relation to the various cultural resources that are brought to PE from other physical cultures.

An exploration of "embodiment" and "embodied learning" has also been central to the field of physical education. The social construction of bodies has emerged as a topic of significance within social research over the last few decades, thanks to authors such as Giddens (1991), Shilling (1993) and Turner (1996). Collectively, their work has helped to articulate and expand upon earlier philosophical and sociological theories of individuals such as Goffman (1959), Foucault (1977), and Bourdieu (1977). As such, it is now increasingly recognized that it is through the body that individuals experience, act, and actively construct understandings of both self and others, and that, given the complex nature of

social life in contemporary society, these processes contribute to an individual's development of multidimensional embodied identities (Holroyd, 2003; Hunter, 2004). The recognition that the body can be simultaneously present in both nature and culture, is perhaps another reason for why researchers are now beginning to stress the value of a constructivist approach for understanding the learning process within PE (e.g. Kirk and Macdonald, 1998). A social constructivist approach is perceived to be valuable because it recognizes that learning takes place within an environment that is saturated with social and cultural meaning, and in which societal discourses can help to promote and give value to particular body types over others. In this sense, it is taken that biology does not determine social behaviour in an absolute sense. As Shilling (1993) suggests, whilst we are born with physical differences, the construction of our bodies doesn't finish there. In much of the literature relating to the sociology of the body, the body itself is explored as a product of discourse and as an object of practice and of power (e.g. Frank, 1990; Shilling, 1993), and these notions are now being drawn upon within the field of physical education to make sense of young people's experience of implicit corporeal regulation, their management of the self, and their construction of embodied identities (Armour, 1999; Evans, 1986; Hunter, 2004; Kirk, 1998; Penney, 2002; Tinning, 1985).

In many respects, the physical education research can be seen to reflect and relate to some of the core themes being raised by researchers within the fields of social studies, youth studies, and media studies, particularly regarding the changing face of youth leisure/physical activity participation (e.g. Hendry et al., 1993), the centrality of the body in popular cultural discourses (e.g. Featherstone, 1982; Kellner, 1992), consumerism as a significant element of youth physical culture (e.g. Miles, 1998; Miles et al., 1998), and the recognition of young people's multidimensional social lives (e.g. Brettschneider, 1992). Several authors, for example, have drawn attention to the centrality of the body in popular physical culture, and the role of young people's engagement with various social sites such as the media, family, peers, and school in shaping their activity choices and participation (Holroyd, 2003; Kirk, 1993; Macdonald, 2002). In addition, a number of studies have looked at the influences of media discourses upon young people's identities and, in particular, the reproduction of dominant cultural norms through the promotion and veneration of specific bodily forms (Flintoff and Scraton, 2001; Kirk and Colquhoun, 1989; Oliver and Lalik, 2000; Tait, 2000; Tinning and Fitzclarence, 1992; Vertinsky, 1992). Research has suggested that physical activity as a marketable commodity is a central feature of media representations (Kirk, 1993; Tinning and Fitzclarence, 1992) and that "popular physical culture saturates young people's lives and provides both structure and substance to their attempts to make sense of themselves and others around them" (Kirk and Tinning, 1994, p. 620). Furthermore, it has been recognized that the increased spending power of young people within contemporary society has positioned them as a valuable market for the "commercialized and commodified offshoots of physical culture" (Kirk, 1999c, p. 71).

However, whereas there is a growing body of research that recognizes the multidimensional nature of young people's social lives and their engagement with physical culture in a number of social sites, it should be noted that there remains, perhaps understandably, a strong focus on the influence of the school within the physical education and pedagogy literature. Moreover, despite this wealth of research relating to the construction of the body and embodied experiences, it is still argued that the body as a domain of social practice, particularly in relation to (physical) educational practice, remains an area of comparative neglect by theorists (e.g. Kirk, 2004; Symes and Meadmore, 1999). Nonetheless, as the recent methodological and theoretical progressions outlined above indicate, physical education theorists are now beginning to make more connections between the body, education, and physical culture. As such, these areas of "neglect" can be seen to represent core areas for both current and future research within PE.

Core concepts

The information outlined above indicates that there is a wealth of research that focuses on the areas of young people, popular physical culture and embodied learning, and that it is a vast, diverse and complex field. Nonetheless, there are common elements within this body of research, and a number of identifiable factors that underpin much of the focus of academic interest in this area. In this next section of the chapter, we move on to a presentation and explanation of six of these core concepts, examining why they are so central to the discussion concerning young people, popular culture and embodied learning.

Habitus and physical capital

Within the literature on the sociology of the body and the construction of embodied identities within PE, one concept that has gained much currency in recent times is that of *"habitus"*. Drawn primarily from the work of French sociologist Pierre Bourdieu, this term helps to define the process by which the social is written into the corporeal and embodied identities are established (Bourdieu, 1990). Habitus is a central concept in Bourdieu's attempt to overcome the problematic binary between structure and agency, and to demonstrate

the "ontological complicity" that defines the relationship between agents and their social worlds (Bourdieu and Wacquant, 2002). A product of an individual's entire social experiences, habitus can perhaps be thought of as embodied sensibility (Calhoun, 1998), a result of them 'culturally learning, refining, recognising, recalling and evoking dispositions to act' (Jarvie and Maguire, 1994, p. 186). It is not overtly observable but is instead manifested through the development of "tastes", defined by Laberge (1995) as "dispositions and schemes of perception and appreciation" (p. 136), which help structure, as well as reflect, individuals' choices and lifestyles. Moreover, the habitus can also be seen to influence the body more directly through the influence on an individual's behaviour, deportment, and attitudes. In this way, it is possible to understand Bourdieu's (1990) comment that "habitus is not something that one has, like knowledge that can be brandished, but something that one is" (p. 73).

Within Bourdieu's theoretical approach, a concept that is closely aligned with that of habitus is what he referred to as "physical capital" (Bourdieu, 1986). A concern with the development of thebodies through social experiences led Bourdieu to examine the way in which the body could be seen to possess power and status, and through the embodiment of distinctive symbolic forms could contribute to the accumulation of various resources for the individual. However, as Shilling (1991) has noted, the opportunities to accumulate and exchange physical capital are unequal, as they are dependent to some extent upon an individual's particular social characteristics (e.g. class, gender). Physical capital, then, can be understood as comprising those physical attributes and abilities such as strength and skill that are embodied through engagement with particular sporting and social practices, and that can be readily converted into other forms of capital, i.e. economic (e.g. money), social (e.g. status) or cultural (e.g. qualifications) (Light, 2001). Moreover, it is evident that for young people clothing, body image, and sporting accessories are also imbued with cultural meaning (implying status, value or particular lifestyle choices) and provide a means by which an individual can acquire (or indeed lose) capital within the peer group. As such, it is argued that these elements of physical culture can also function as a form of physical capital for young people (e.g. Holroyd, 2003).

The inherent value of these concepts for understanding an individual's experiences of physical culture was highlighted by Bourdieu himself, when he sought to understand differences in sport participation on the basis of embodied class-based values (Bourdieu, 1978). However, these elements of Bourdieu's theory have been taken on and developed further by researchers within the field of physical education (e.g. Shilling, 1993) particularly, more recently, through the medium of doctoral theses (Brown, 2001; Holroyd, 2003; Hunter, 2002; Light, 1999).

Hidden curriculum

Coined by Philip Jackson in his (1968) study of classroom life, the term "hidden curriculum" has attained considerable currency within educational discourse over the past three decades, and is now firmly established within the jargon of researchers, policymakers and practitioners alike. The term itself entered the physical activity and pedagogy literature via a social psychology route, principally through the work of Linda Bains who attempted to outline an understanding of the term in relation to PE (Bain, 1975, 1985, 1990). However, despite this early work Kirk (1992) noted that there had been some confusion and ambiguity over its usage and perceived meaning within the physical education field. As such, he argued that there was a need to reassess understanding of the term, and to identify the hidden curriculum by focusing on communication and meaning-making through the discourses and ideologies of PE teaching and learning. Other researchers have picked up on this usage of the concept, and have sought to understand more of the attitudes, norms, and beliefs that are communicated unconsciously, unintentionally and unavoidably through both the formal and informal curriculum within schools (e.g. Chen, 1999; Rønholt, 2002). In particular, recent studies have looked at the significance of the hidden curriculum in relation to the transmission of knowledge and learning (e.g. Brustad, 1997), the reproduction and reinforcement of inequalities (e.g. Fernández-Balboa, 1997; Oliver and Lalik, 2004), and the implications for PE teacher education programmes (e.g. Schwager, 1997).

Corporeal regulation

As has been outlined above, the hidden curriculum is understood as distinguished from, but complementary to, the explicitly stated aims of the educational institutions, and is viewed as an effective means by which young people can assimilate the cultural norms, beliefs and values of the institution. The hidden curriculum is perhaps so "pedagogically influential" (Oliver and Lalik, 2004: 115) because there are significant implications for students' acquisition of knowledge and construction of embodied understandings of self. It is argued, for example, that the implicit and unspoken values of the school system, regarding issues such as appropriate behaviour, dress, and interactions with staff, etc., become ingrained through years of required conformity, so that young people, to an extent, embody the hidden curriculum at a deep level. Moreover, it is suggested that this process of

implicitly "schooling" the body via the hidden curriculum involves an element of corporeal regulation, and as such the embodiment of structure and regulations by young people can be seen as a way of constructing bodies that are productive yet controlled (Evans, 1988a,b; Hopkins, 1999; Kirk, 1993, 1998, 1999a; Tait, 2000; Thorpe, 2000). As with much of the recent literature relating to the sociology of the body, in which the body itself is explored as a product of discourse and as an object of practice and of power (e.g. Frank, 1990; Shilling, 1993), the understanding of bodily regulation within the physical education literature draws heavily upon the work of Foucault (1980, 1991). Foucault's contention that a shift in the locus of control in contemporary society, from external to internal, has meant that the body can now be perceived as the ultimate site for discipline, regulation and control, is seen to represent a valuable way in which the implicit processes of the hidden curriculum can be identified, examined, and understood.

Popular culture and physical culture

A number of authors within the fields of youth studies, sociology of education, and physical education and pedagogy have highlighted the significance of popular physical culture for young people. Given that, broadly speaking, the term culture denotes the knowledge, technologies, values, beliefs and customs that are common to a set of people, it follows that popular culture can be understood as the elements of the above that are widespread across societies and that are accessible to large numbers of people. The principal role of popular culture is entertainment, channelled primarily through the various forms of the mass media, and for young people in contemporary Western society the main elements are perceived to be popular music, television, films, fashion, and sport (e.g. McRobbie, 1994; Ralph et al., 1999). Many of the earlier studies in this area, undertaken primarily by sociologists working within the fields of youth studies, were influenced by the subcultural theories of the Centre for Contemporary Cultural Studies (CCCS), although some authors are now highlighting the limitations of this approach and are looking for alternative theoretical understandings of young people's affiliations and engagement with popular culture (e.g. Hodkinson, 2001; Tait, 2000). In addition, theorists within the field of physical education and pedagogy have also begun to consider the influence of popular culture on young people's construction of embodied identities, and to develop a more specific notion of physical culture.

Kirk (1999c) has defined physical culture as being "a range of practices concerned with the maintenance, representation and regulation of the body centred on three highly codified, institutionalized forms of physical activity – sport, physical recreation and exercise" (pp. 65–66), and the concept has been identified by many as representing a primary site for the construction of embodied identities (e.g. Kivel, 1998; Light, 2001; Oliver and Lalik, 2000). Building upon this definition of the term, and a broader recognition that young people are clearly influenced by the discourses of physical activity, health and fitness, an increasing number of researchers are taking the concept of physical culture into account when attempting to make sense of young people's leisure and lifestyles (e.g. Flintoff and Scraton, 2001; Wright et al., 2005). This can also be seen to reflect a growing recognition that it is impractical for physical activity contexts to be considered as removed from the influences of wider socio-cultural factors (e.g. Azzarito and Ennis, 2003; Roberts, 1996), and, more specifically, that previous participation research has generally not taken account of the cultural contexts in which young people engage with physical activity.

This notion of physical culture is significant here, in that it can be seen to link with the issues of the hidden curriculum and corporeal regulation. The discourses that shape young people's experiences of sport, physical recreation and exercise are concerned in part with the production of particular bodies, and are thus understood as significant influences that are imbued with meaning. In contemporary culture, for example, the archetypal masculine body is seen as being strong and muscular, and the feminine body slender and submissive (Bordo, 1993; Connell, 1995; Tinning, 1985). Moreover, popular culture has also been utilised as a medium through which to construct and (re)produce health messages associated with these "body ideals" (Evans et al., 2004; Kirk, 1999b; Kirk and Colquhoun, 1989).

Identity and subjectivities

Recent years have seen a discursive explosion regarding the notion of identity (Hall et al., 1999), and social theorists such as Jenkins (1996) have argued that the concept can now be regarded as a "touchstone of the times" (p. 8). Identity in pre-modern societies was perceived to be largely unproblematic, a fixed, enduring, and pre-given entity not open to the revision and reflection espoused in the later sociological theories of individuals such as Goffman (1959), Giddens (1991), and Beck (1992). Moreover, contemporary understandings of identity have viewed it as a more fluid, reflexive and ephemeral concept, inherently embodied, multidimensional by nature, and determined in part by situation and context (see also Foucault, 1991; Shilling, 1993). The subjective, transient and constructed nature of identity is highlighted within much of the literature regarding young people and

popular physical culture, and is significant here in that there are implications for the influence of young people's diverse experiences on their embodied constructions of self.

The notion of identity is of particular relevance when considering young people and popular physical culture, as the period of youth, more specifically adolescence, is widely considered a vital time in the identity formation process as well as a peak time for leisure needs (Bromnick and Swallow, 1999; Hendry et al., 1993). A period of intense transition, this stage in a young person's life sees them surrounded by a number of often competing and conflicting influences, i.e. in relation to interactions with family, school, peers, media and popular/physical culture. Indeed, in order to understand fully the lifestyle experiences of young people, it is now deemed essential to take account of the various social spaces that constitute their day-to-day lives (e.g. Brettschneider, 1992; Hendry et al., 1998; Wright et al., 2005). This is particularly significant in relation to the notion of embodied identity, when it is considered that the particular environments that comprise an individual's social experience can be seen to influence the body, and induce certain dispositions or habits (Laberge, 1995).

Situated learning and communities of practice

Recent years have seen changes within the theories of learning in physical education, with researchers moving away from the traditional mediating paradigm to embrace and develop a more constructivist approach to learning. In these approaches, learning focuses on the interaction of the individual with their environment, and involves a personal construction of meaning i.e. it is active, multidimensional, developmental and situated. A number of researchers have contributed to this area (e.g. Azzarito and Ennis, 2003; Brustad, 1997; Langley, 1997; Rovegno and Kirk, 1995), with many drawing on and developing the concept of situated learning as a tool for understanding the relational experience of the learning process (Kirk and Macdonald, 1998; Kirk and MacPhail, 2002; Penney, 2002; Rønholt, 2002) Developed in relation to the educational context of apprenticeships, Lave and Wenger's (1991) concept of situated learning outlines a situation in which the learner is seen to play an active rather than a passive role in the learning process. Adopting a relational view in which agent, activity and world are interrelated, learning is viewed as an inherently social experience, i.e. it is situated, and the learner is thus perceived as a practitioner in a particular "community of practice". Although learning is at first legitimately peripheral, through their ongoing membership individuals are able to acquire knowledge concerning the skills, discourses and techniques central to the practices of the community, and hence establish an identity within the broader setting of that social context. The concept of situated learning is useful in relation to PE, as it is perceived to facilitate an understanding about issues such as the hidden curriculum (Rønholt, 2002) and physical activity programmes that utilize the principle of community learning such as Sport Education (Kirk and Macdonald, 1998; Penney, 2002) and Teaching Games for Understanding (Kirk and MacPhail, 2002). Many of these more recent theories of learning potentially pave the way for students own cultural heritages, social backgrounds and preferences in health and PE to be valued and included in the PE curriculum and learning practices (Burrows, 2004: 105).

Major themes and links with practice

Two key issues that emerge from an examination of the notions of learners and popular culture are: the need to establish clear and systematic links between research, practice and policy; and the need to better understand young people's engagement with a range of physical cultures. The necessity for action here is clear, for there are many who highlight an evident divide between these facets of the physical educational field, and who explicitly articulate the need for closer collaboration between policymakers and practitioners (e.g. Evans and Penney, 2002; Macdonald, 2002). Moreover, there are numerous examples of researchers pointing out the similarities between their own analyses and the data from previous research endeavours, providing a striking illustration that the findings from research are simply not impacting on practice – the consistent identification of a PE uniform as a problematic issue for girls is perhaps a fitting example here (e.g. Flintoff and Scraton, 2001). Taking note of these key issues, in the following section we attempt to adopt a holistic approach to the themes under discussion in two ways: firstly, by teasing out potential implications for policy and practice; and secondly, by outlining the importance of collaborations between key organisations within future research agendas.

Young people, learning and physical activity

Broadly speaking, traditional models of PE have retained an activity-based curriculum, comprising long-established areas of activity and privileging games, with a view primarily on performance in sport. While there have been some initiatives to shift curricula to more socially critical outcomes (e.g. Wright, 1997) many still position sporting performance as central. Moreover, PE programmes

comprising sports and fitness related activities still take a central position in the curriculum in many schools in the UK, Australia and USA, despite evidence to suggest that young people are demonstrating a preference towards alternative individual recreational activities and physical cultures (Burrows, 2004; Tinning and Fitzclarence, 1992; Penney, 2002). Many of these practices are substantiated by claims relating to health benefits that are portrayed as "scientific fact", despite recent evidence suggesting there are contestable and contradictory findings around health and physical activity (Gard and Wright, 2001, 2005).

Within the sociology of physical education literature there have been increasing calls for PE (both in terms of curriculum and ITT) to draw from a wider spectrum of activities and physical cultures already represented in society (Kirk, 1999c; Wright et al., 2005) and, as Penney and Chandler (2000) note, to call into question the activity-based framework which currently dominates. In relation to popular culture and learners, this raises two key points. Firstly, in the development of this curriculum pupils have been largely absent from debates about its focus and form. As such, many of the physical cultures which young people are engaging with outside of PE are not represented within the curriculum. Secondly, and inter-related, such narrow offerings of physical activity within schools have had a bearing on how those within the PE context have come to understand young people's involvement in physical activity. To some extent, this situation has resulted in inaccurate and overly pessimistic views concerning young people's declining engagement with physical activity, physical education and school sport (Armstrong and McManus, 1994; DoH, 2002; Jowell, 2004). These claims have, for example, impacted upon the way in which girls' disengagement in Physical Education has been understood. Over the past decade, a number of studies have revealed the ways in which girls continue to be positioned as a "problem" within physical education (Flintoff & Scraton, 2001; Rich, 2003, 2004), suggesting that they are turned off physical activity and need to be motivated into participating. However, by examining girls' participation in a wider range of activities, a very different picture emerges, which suggests that young women are not simply disinterested in physical activity per se, but rather are disengaged from the current structure and format of Physical Education. Indeed, evidence indicates that more young people than ever before, both boys and girls, are taking part in a wide range of physical activities (e.g. Green, 2004; Roberts, 1996). Researchers have suggested that a key issue in relation to this debate is the fact that activities out of school would appear to have a far greater appeal than those within the curriculum (Flintoff & Scraton, 2001; Wright et al., 2005). Findings such as these would appear to reinforce the need, highlighted earlier, for physical education to draw from a wider range of activities and physical cultures in the construction of more contemporary, engaging and inclusive curricula.

School as a site of embodied learning and regulation

The above discussion has highlighted some of the factors that have contributed to an understanding of young people, learning and popular physical culture within the discipline of PE. As has been seen, knowledge has been influenced by somewhat restrictive discourse, and this has resulted in a relatively narrow, prescriptive curriculum in which the body is closely regulated. Before going on to discuss this in more detail, it is worth first outlining the role of the school more broadly as a site for embodied learning.

It is evident from the vast body of relevant literature in this area that the school is an important and influential social site for young people (Adler and Adler, 1998; Kirk, 1998). As a context in which it is obligatory for them to spend much of their time during what are perhaps the most developmental years of their lives, it is perhaps unsurprising that the school plays such a formative role in the lives of young people (Wren, 1999; Wyness, 1999). Moreover, the interactions that take place within the school environment ensure that for young people it is both an explicit and implicit learning experience. As Frost (2001) has noted:

> The institution (school) in which young people of both sexes spend a highly significant part of their lives plays an important part in the circulation of meanings and messages about what a young person can and should be, as well as serving to generate and reinforce elements of this identity. Relations of power, control and resistance are highly visible in these hierarchical settings, and the policing of behaviour and attitudes undertaken formally by staff and informally within group and pupil inter-relations is evident. (p. 111)

Research has suggested that a defining feature in the structuring of the school experience, and the regulation of those individuals located within it, is the precise management and organization of space and time (Jackson, 1968; Kirk, 1999a, 1999b; Marsland, 1993). Moreover, the arrangement of young people's bodies via temporal and spatial regulation within the school allows for those with power (i.e. staff, other adults) to maintain a degree of order and control (Foucault, 1991; Kirk, 1999b; Tait, 2000). Although not an explicit element of the educational curriculum, practices such as the use of timetables, implementation of school rules, and the hierarchical structure of social positions (all identified as common features of schools) also represent elements of the hidden curriculum. Through acceptance of and conformity to these practices, and, perhaps more importantly, an embodiment of the implicit values that they promote, recent studies show that young people develop an appropriate habitus which allows them to function effectively (and appropriately) within the field of school (Holroyd, 2003).

In addition to the embodiment of appropriate behaviours and dispositions, research suggests that another significant element to this acquisition of bodily knowledge within the school context relates to the regulations on clothing. The practice of wearing school uniforms originated initially in the public schools of the UK, although it is now widespread within most modern educational systems. The benefits of having a school uniform are often cited as including creating a sense of collective identity, encouraging a sense of school pride, and even contributing to a more constructive learning environment and enhancing student achievement. However, researchers exploring issues of the body within education contend that the school uniform is also seen to represent a tool for regulating and managing behaviour (e.g. Dussel, 2004; Symes and Meadmore, 1996) a reason that can perhaps be seen to underpin recent moves within the US to introduce more formal uniform policies. It is argued that a uniform can be seen to reflect the values, norms, and ideals of a school and can represent the literal embodiment of corporeal control. There are echoes of Foucault's (1991) notion of "surveillance" here, as through the regulation of the body the controlling authority of the school can transcend the physical boundaries of the institution and influence individuals' perceptions of appropriate behaviour (Holroyd, 2002). This implicit regulation of the body is discussed further in the following section, with particular reference to its relevance in the context of PE.

Physical education as a core site for corporeal regulation

Drawing upon the work of Foucault (1980), Kirk and Colquhoun (1989) acknowledge "a shift in the locus of social control within capitalist societies from mass, external control of the body to an individual, internal mode of corporeal control" (p. 418). This move towards encouraging individual responsibility, autonomy, self-surveillance and control has also been noted by other theorists (e.g. Evans et al., 2004; Tait, 2000) and has contributed to the development of an established link between the body, physical activity and corporeal power (e.g. Evans, 1986, 1988a,b; Foucault, 1980, 1991; Kirk, 1993, 1998; Azzarito and Solmon, 2006; Hunter, 2005). This association is a significant one when considering learners and popular physical culture, as it facilitates an understanding of how the dominant social and cultural values and ideologies, prevalent within popular culture and embedded in the discourses of PE and health, can be transmitted to and embodied by young people in schools. An increasing recognition of this state of affairs has led theorists within the field of PE to focus their attention on how social and cultural influences are impacting upon young people's embodiment of particular values and ideologies, both broadly through educational discourses and, more specifically, through the PE curriculum. Evans and Davies (2004), for example, draw heavily upon the work of Bernstein (1996, 2001) to argue that body *performance* and *perfection* codes are clearly reflected within pedagogic modalities that dominate curricula within the fields of PE and health. In doing so, they attempt to "explore how the distribution of power and principles of control in society translate into pedagogic codes and pedagogic modalities within schools; and, thereafter, how these codes and their modalities are acquired, shape pedagogic consciousness and … are embodied" (p. 207).

Encouraging young people to embrace these discourses of physicality and healthism has significant implications for their development of habitus (the acquisition of tastes, values and dispositions) and construction of embodied identities. Moreover, as recent studies indicate, there are implications for the reinforcement and reproduction of restrictive, harmful, or inequitable practices through, for example, the promotion of healthy eating discourses, gendered bodily ideals, or leisure and class divisions (Evans et al., 2004; Oliver and Lalik, 2000; Rich et al., 2004). Far from empowering individuals, social practices such as those described above may leave young people feeling powerless, labelled, alienated from their identities (and, perhaps, their bodies), and believing that they have little or, worse still, no control over base essential elements of their lives. Though they are not without power, young people are, of course, less able than adults/teachers to resist or contest the conditions of their school that may be detrimental to their health, or leave them feeling disengaged. As others have pointed out, the contemporary conditions of schooling amplify the distinction between the child and adult as they afford young people little agency (Postman, 1994), being positioned instead as "incompetent social actors" (Wyness, 1999). At worst, this can leave pupils "fixated on" failure and having a "sense of being imprisoned or controlled by schools" (Lynch, 2001).

Young people, physical culture, and physical education: competing influences on the learning experience

Recent research indicates that young people's engagements with the school site can influence their learning and impact upon their construction of embodied identities. However, it should be noted that the field of school does not stand alone within society but is embedded within a larger system of social relations (Wren, 1999; Wyness, 1999). As such, in a society in which schooling can be seen to represent much of young people's social and cultural experiences, it is important not to discount "the complex social, cultural, political and environmental contexts in which schools operate" (Kirk, 1999b, p. 165). A number of authors have also discussed this in relation to the notion of PE, and contend that although this context is as a core site for embodied learning (e.g. Kirk, 1999c; Light, 2001; Oliver and Lalik, 2000) it should not be forgotten that there are also significant overlaps with popular culture and other social contexts. In this respect, the term physical culture is a valuable one to employ here, as it encompasses those practices and discourses associated not only with PE, but also with the broader contexts of physical activity, recreation and leisure.

In addition to a prescriptive curriculum, it is argued that traditional understandings within the discipline of PE have resulted in a somewhat narrow definition of the term itself. However, this does not reflect a recognition of the complex and multidimensional nature of young people's social experiences, in which they both shape and are shaped by their engagement with various social "fields" (Holroyd, 2003). The value of regarding the social world as a multidimensional space, is that it allows for the fact that "young people have many identities and live within a variety of contexts – all of which contribute to their development of self" (Kivel, 1998: 38). Moreover, when it is considered that social fields do not stand independently ring-fenced but can co-exist both temporary and spatially within the wider social environment, it facilitates an understanding of individuals' experiences as intercontextual. A recognition of this within recent studies has led some physical education researchers to look more closely at the links between the body, schooling and culture, and to suggest that it is a mistake to assume that young people are free from socio-cultural values when learning (e.g. Azzarito and Ennis, 2003; Chen, 1999; Kirk, 1993). In other words, it should be recognized that when young people are within the school environment they remain under the influence of the discourses, norms, and regulatory controls of other amorphous fields such as the media, peers, and physical culture. Moreover, when young people enter the school environment, they bring with them the learning that they have acquired and accumulated from these additional social sites. What, then, are some of the implications of this situation for young people's learning in regard to physical culture?

As a field in which the development and display of bodies can be recognized as a fundamental element of practice, physical culture is understandably upheld as a primary site for the construction of embodied identities (Kirk, 1999c; Kirk and Tinning, 1994; Shilling, 1991; Sparkes, 1997). Through their engagement with the discourses of physical culture, individuals' learning is shaped by the implicit assumptions underlying various practices, relating to issues such as gender, class or bodily ideals, which then become embodied as an element of habitus (Theberge, 1991; Vertinsky, 1992). One of the key associations connected with the field of physical culture, for example, is the link between physical activity, health and fitness (Flintoff and Scraton, 2001; Kirk and Colquhoun, 1989; Kirk and Tinning, 1994; Tinning and Fitzclarence, 1992; Vertinsky, 1992), the implications of which are discussed elsewhere in this chapter. It is argued that an acceptance of the discourses of physical culture can help young people acquire physical capital through the construction of socially acceptable bodies (Shilling, 1991). For example, as research has shown, the slender body is often exemplified as the "ideal" within contemporary Western culture, and is associated with various social qualities such as fitness, morality, self-control and self-worth (Featherstone et al., 1991; Kirk, 1993; Oliver and Lalik, 2001). Given these associations, it is perhaps not surprising that young people have been shown to embrace the obligation to take part in self-disciplining physical activities and body maintenance techniques in order to achieve the slender ideal. Although these discourses are transmitted through social sites outside of the school, it has been suggested that PE as a discipline at worst embraces, at best does little to challenge, some of these powerful yet potentially harmful messages.

Another key implication for the multidimensional nature of young people's learning, is that there is potential for conflict and confusion when the nature and structure of the school environment does not match up to students' values or expectations, or if the content of the PE curriculum is deemed by young people to be socially or culturally irrelevant (Conrad and Ennis, 1998; Ennis, 1999; Ennis et al., 1997). Evidence suggests that there is a strong association between young people's engagement with their peers, the media and physical culture (Brettschneider, 1992; Holroyd, 2003; Kirk, 1999c), and that material possessions, clothing in particular, are perceived as important resources both for the "presentation of self" (Goffman, 1990) and for the construction of embodied identities. Not only is appropriate clothing deemed to signify young people's tastes and interests, but it is also a means by which they can gain significant physical capital among their peers. This, in part, helps to provide an understanding of the resistance that some young people show to the compulsory and prescriptive nature of the school uniform. Researchers such as Frost (2001) and Holroyd (2003) argue that this opposition stems from the fact that the image a uniform affords young people is often far from the "ideal" image that counts for physical (and hence social) capital within the peer group.

The issue of clothing is also a significant one in relation to PE. The compulsory nature of prescribed PE uniforms is oft-cited in research, particularly within the UK, as having a major detrimental impact on young women's attitudes to school physical activity; yet the practice remains within many schools and many students still deem their school sports attire to be inappropriate (Flintoff and Scraton, 2001; Frost, 2001; Williams and Bedward, 2001). However, research concerning the complex, interrelated, and multidimensional experiences of young people, such as that outlined above, has highlighted the need to relax the strict regulations on this issue of dress, and to allow for young people to construct identities in line with popular physical culture if this will encourage participation. In addition, studies have shown that giving young people an opportunity to make their own choices regarding the clothing worn for physical activity, albeit within broad guidelines, not only allows them to feel more comfortable but can also reduce the possibility of resistance by recognizing their need to be self-determining (Flintoff and Scraton, 2001).

This issue of being self-determining is a significant one for young people in contemporary society, for research has shown that, thanks to an improved financial position and extended freedom from work responsibilities, young people are now more able than ever to exercise agency in making their own choices. Young people now command considerable weight as consumers, and companies and organizations have responded to this situation by using the media field to brand and target elements of popular culture specifically for and at the youth market. Physical activity and leisure are no exception here, and given that the pervasive and powerful influence of the media field is well-established (Giddens, 1991; Kellner, 1992; Ralph et al., 1999) it is perhaps not surprising that recent research shows young people to be clearly influenced by these discourses of popular physical culture (e.g. Chen, 1999; Flintoff and Scraton, 2001; Miles et al., 1998; Wright and Macdonald, 2005). Researchers agree that youth sport and physical activity is something of a social phenomenon (De Knop and De Martalaer, 2001; Roberts, 1996; Thomson, 2000; Wright et al., 2003), and that sport can now be seen to occupy a primary position among young people's choice of leisure time activities. Moreover, sporting activities, orientations and accessories have become increasingly important elements within the pluralization of youth cultures (Brettschneider, 1992). In relation to this, the promotion of particular activities and associated images through the media have contributed to the growing trend among young people for involvement in more diverse, informal, or individual-type activities such as in-line skating, skateboarding, and mountain biking. However, bearing in mind that the media in consumer culture plays a critical role in young people's subjectivities and sense of themselves (Kirk, 1993) it should be remembered that representations of activities offered by the media do not stand alone but are imbued with meaning and attempt to produce specific identities through association with certain traits and values (Kellner, 1992; Miles and Anderson, 1999). As such, young people's engagements with these activities represent more than a simple leisure choice; they are, in effect, an affiliation to an activity culture that involves a particular image, behaviour, and ideology. There are obvious implications here for their embodied learning, but has this been recognized by the physical education field?

Adopting a broader definition of physical culture

It is recognized, particularly within the UK, that PE has contributed to the growth in recreational lifestyles among young people and families, thanks primarily to the "Sport for All" ideology that led to individuals experiencing a broader range of activities within the curriculum (Roberts, 1996). Nevertheless, it is also accepted that on the whole PE as a discipline has failed to acknowledge or account for the wider dimensions of young people's lives in relation to their current and future patterns of participation in physical activity (for an overview of these issues see Green, 2004). Researchers have argued that a narrow definition of physical education, with its focus on traditional sports and team games, has not allowed for recent trends within young people's engagement with physical culture, nor has it recognized young people's need to generate capital among the peer group and to exercise some degree of agency. Earlier in this chapter it was shown how, in response to a growing recognition of the multidimensional lives of young people and the broad and complex context of young people's leisure and lifestyles, the notion of physical culture has been suggested as a more appropriate means of making sense of young people's engagement with physical activities. The discussion above would appear to endorse this, and point to the significance of adopting the notion within the discipline of PE.

Perhaps the main implication of this for policy and practice is that educational institutions could offer opportunities for young people to bring their learning from wider physical culture settings into the field of PE. As researchers such as Roberts (1996) point out, this may well need to involve the inclusion of more informal or non-traditional activities in the curriculum (see also Brettschneider, 1992; Green, 2004; Thomson, 2000). In relation to this, there is perhaps also a more fundamental need for physical educators and policymakers to readdress their perceptions of physical activity, and to encompass a broader understanding of physical culture that allows for a spectrum of sport, exercise and leisure practices, both formal and informal, to be perceived as overlapping communities of practice (Lave and Wenger, 1991). Evidence suggests that this would allow for a more comprehensive, and perhaps more accurate, picture of young people's leisure activities, and provide opportunities in which they can be encouraged to engage in healthy lifestyles without the restrictive and prescriptive guidelines that, as several studies have shown (e.g. Flintoff and Scraton, 2001; Williams and Bedward, 2001) are perceived to characterize contemporary physical activity programmes. As Roberts (1996) has commented, "sport and leisure policies are always more likely to succeed when they flow with and harness broader tides" (p. 56).

Young people's agency

One of the key issues that has appeared frequently in the above discussions is that of young people's agency. Recent shifts within the social studies of childhood literature have seen a move away from theoretical frameworks that perceive young people as a homogeneous social group, positioned simply as objects of research. Instead, more reflexive approaches have been adopted that recognise young people as competent social agents, capable of generating and articulating their own construction of self and society (Alderson, 1995; Christensen and James, 2000; James and Prout, 1997; James et al., 1998). However, traditional approaches in physical education research, policymaking and practice have generally not acknowledged or allowed for young people's agency, although this oversight is now beginning to be addressed. In addition to generating links between researchers, policymakers and practitioners, recent work within the field of physical education research, such as that conducted by Oliver and Lalik (2000, 2004), is also highlighting the significance of involving students as researchers within the inquiry process. It has been suggested that significant knowledge gains can result when young people's active involvement in research is deliberately solicited, and when their views and perspectives are both acknowledged and accepted (Alderson, 1995; Fontana and Frey, 2000). In this way, increasing the involvement of young people within the research process can also be regarded as both liberating and empowering (Oliver and Lalik, 2000; Punch, 2002). Recent studies have suggested that another practical way of granting young people more agency regarding their learning within PE is through the introduction of critical inquiry into the curriculum and the solicitation of young people's thoughts regarding their own learning. For example, Burrows (2004) suggests that one way of de-privileging the centrality of mainstream competitive sports in schools might be through engaging with students themselves about what they would like to learn in PE. As the next section shows, research on young people's engagement with PE has begun to highlight the potential of these approaches in terms of challenging traditional practices.

Critical inquiry in the curriculum

The above discussion has highlighted the interest in and significance of the implicit discourses that are transmitted through the hidden curriculum of the PE context, and which are perceived to contribute to the reproduction and reinforcement of dominant, and often inequitable, ideologies. Although much research has attempted to challenge this state of affairs through a closer examination of these cultural discourses, there are still calls for more critical inquiry, including critical thinking regarding movement cultures and ideologies, to be employed within PE research (e.g. Gillespie and Culpan, 2000). This reinforces a belief that it is important to challenge the ideologies attained through popular physical culture, if they dissuade young people from participation. In line with a move to involve students within the research process, recent studies have begun to use critical inquiry to facilitate an exploration of the PE curriculum (e.g. Fernández-Balboa, 1997; Gillespie and Culpan, 2000; Oliver and Lalik, 2000, 2001, 2004). The theory behind this move is that including more opportunities for critical inquiry within the PE curriculum will help to expose the discourses of the hidden curriculum, and open up possibilities for students in terms of challenging inequalities or potentially harmful ideologies. Oliver and Lalik (2000), whose work with adolescent girls represents an excellent example of how critical inquiry can be used to examine and challenge inequalities, also suggest that this technique offers a real opportunity for cross-curriculum development.

PE may well have an important role to play in encouraging young people to read, in a critical way, the imagery that is offered to them within popular physical culture. Intervention programmes can encourage young people to challenge the potentially damaging effects of imagery (Chapkis, 1986) and reconceptualize the meanings of received information, in particular how it relates to thinking about male and female roles (Omizo and Omizo, 1992). For example, programmes such as "Body Talk" in the USA are designed to help women develop more positive attitudes towards their physical selves; to become more aware of the way in which culture is defining what it means to be female; to develop healthier eating and exercise habits; to increase ease of expression of feelings towards peers and family; and to develop assertiveness. Of course, such programmes, whilst extremely important and valuable as educational means of contesting media imagery,

may have little impact on young people if such imagery is considered, as it is by some, as a positive resource, a source of confidence and esteem. In relation to physical culture and PE, then, we perhaps need a clearer understanding of how discourses of slenderness, of negative physical culture, are transmitted via the cultures and epistemic communities of schooling, and are interpreted by young people as they co-mingle with other aspects of their lives embedded within popular culture. A growing body of critical pedagogy literature within PE (e.g. Burrows and Wright, 2001; Ennis, 1996; Evans et al., 2004; Fernández-Balboa, 1997; Gard, 2001; Kirk, 1986; Kirk, 1998; McWilliam and Taylor, 1996; Oliver and Lalik, 2000; Thorpe, 2003; Wright, 1996) is evidence in itself of the significance of these issues to theorists. Moreover, texts such as Wright et al. (2004) indicate the wealth of research, past, present, and prospective, that is attempting to assess the role of critical thinking and critical pedagogy within contemporary PE contexts.

Re-evaluation of physical education programmes

The research outlined above would appear to reinforce the need for, and importance of, PE programmes that allow for learning to be situated, relevant and contextual. It is here that research approaches drawing on constructivist and postmodern learning theories are being usefully translated into alternative PE programmes. A number of researchers have argued for a new approach to PE, which takes into account the various learning cultures and life experiences of young people who are growing up in social contexts often very different from those who have the power to "define" and "construct" physical education (Wright et al., 2004). As Kirk (1997) suggests, this is to construct curriculum and learning processes that "both reflect and contribute more directly to popular physical culture" (p. 58).

It is necessary not only to acknowledge and allow for the fact that young people are extending the contexts of their learning (e.g. Macdonald, 2002) but also that both young people's learning and the PE context need to be linked more closely with the socio-cultural dynamics of society (e.g. Azzarito and Ennis, 2003; Chen, 1999; Kirk, 2004). The success of programmes such as Sport Education (Siedentop, 1994), Sport for Peace (Ennis, 1999; Ennis et al., 1997), and the Personal Social Responsibility Model (Hellison, 1995) all highlight the significance of creating PE contexts that are socially and culturally relevant. Similarly, Fernández-Balboa's (1997) call for postmodern and social constructivist pedagogical approaches, encourages students to construct personal meanings by understanding their experiences in PE in relation to their lives, including the wider physical cultures with which they engage. By creating situations in which acceptance, co-operation, and conflict resolution are encouraged, programmes such as these allow for a more constructive and productive learning experience for young people. Moreover, it has been argued that they can also afford young people an opportunity to learn and develop skills that will facilitate their membership in wider communities of practice within physical culture, and hence help to encourage life-long learning. In relation to this, recent research also highlights the need to avoid those practices that can discourage young people from participating, hence limiting their opportunities to become part of these wider practice communities (e.g. Himberg et al., 2003).

Some of these changes are already underway within the field of physical education, but what more can be done? The final section of the chapter now moves on to look at some of the implications of the issues under discussion here for the discipline of PE, and identifies some of the future directions that may help to guide research, policy development and practice in this area.

Future directions for research

Despite moves to address the perceived "crisis" in physical education, and specifically towards identifying, examining, and challenging the implicit discourses transmitted via the PE context that impact on embodied learning, it is clear that there remain many issues in need of subsequent research. Moreover, the dynamic nature of social and cultural life ensures the continuous emergence of additional avenues for inquiry. In this final section, we now move on to identify and discuss some of the issues that represent current or emerging core areas within the broad fields of young people, education, and physical culture.

One of the key issues, highlighted both implicitly and explicitly by a number of researchers, is the need for more relational analyses within research endeavours (e.g. Macdonald, 2002). There is a growing recognition among both educational and physical educational researchers of the complex and multidimensional lives of young people, which has led, perhaps understandably, to calls for more attention to be paid to young people's learning outside of the school environment (e.g. Wright et al., 2005). Moreover, the interrelated nature of social contexts has helped researchers to recognize the possibilities for "joined-up" learning across social sites, and has identified a need to develop more links between schools, homes and communities (e.g. Azzarito and Ennis, 2003; Ennis, 1999; Housner, 1996; Macdonald, 2002). Hurley and Lustbader (1997), for example, have identified the importance of building bridges between families, schools, community

agencies and young people, so that intervention programmes will not have the limitation of being context specific.

As such, developing partnerships between key groups of individuals, namely schools (DCMS, 1999), community agencies (Kraft and Wheeler, 2000), parents (Martinek and Hellison, 1997) and young people themselves (Steer, 2000), not only allows for maximizing the efficiency of resources but can also help to build bridges, break down barriers, and develop more effective communities of practice. The BSkyB 'Living for Sport' project and HSBC Education Trust projects (including the HSBC/Outward Bound Partnership project) represent two current examples from within the UK of this process of "partnership in action". These projects are intervention programmes that, through partnerships between educational and corporate organizations, seek in some way to use physical activities as a means of prompting behavioural improvement among young people within schools (Sandford et al., 2004). Through adopting a multiagency approach in the development of such programmes and initiatives, physical education research can also be seen to answer the call for researchers to pay more attention to, and account for, the social and cultural spaces in which young people spend time (Brettschneider, 1992; Hendry et al., 1998; Macdonald, 2002). In order to discover more about young people's engagement with popular physical culture and their construction of embodied identities, it is also important for PE researchers to develop their own cross-disciplinary partnerships, allowing for the sharing of ideas and information with, for example, researchers from the fields of youth studies, educational studies, or media studies. Such partnerships will facilitate a more holistic approach, and can only contribute to a deeper understanding of young people's social worlds.

Recent research indicates that mentoring is becoming increasingly popular as a learning and support strategy in education (e.g. Colley, 2003; Reid, 2002), with the principal intention being to assist young people's learning through the modelling of positive values, behaviours, and attitudes. The use of adult and peer mentoring has also been suggested as a valuable way in which to develop positive relationships with and among young people in a PE context, particularly for more "challenging" young people, such as those who are disaffected, disadvantaged, or disengaged (e.g. Danish, 2002; Sandford and Armour, 2004; Sandford et al., in press). The notion of addressing the problem of youth disaffection and the need for behavioural improvement through physical activity programmes is currently something of a "hot topic" within the PE literature (see, for example, Bailey, 2005; Cameron and MacDougall, 2000; Coalter, 2002; Gatz et al., 2002;

Hellison, 1995; Merton and Parrott, 1999), and given current public and political concern over the deleterious state of youth within Western society it is likely to remain so. Future research in this area can perhaps benefit from looking more closely at the mechanisms involved in this process of mentoring and role modelling, and the ways in which young people learn to develop appropriate behaviour, values, and aspirations through a process of embodied learning.

In this respect, the notion of "habitus" can perhaps be seen to offer a means of understanding more deeply young people's constructions of embodied identities. As noted, some research has already begun to utilize adaptations of Bourdieu's theory of habitus to facilitate an understanding of how social and cultural influences are written into the body through the learning process. As much of this research has emerged through the medium of doctoral and postdoctoral studies (e.g. Holroyd, 2003; Hunter, 2002; Light, 1999), it would appear that there is evident potential for the further development of this concept in relation to the process of young people's embodied learning within PE. In addition, the related notion of physical capital would also appear to be a valuable theoretical tool, particularly in relation to understanding young people's engagement with popular physical culture and the influence that this has upon their development of tastes, interests and leisure choices (Holroyd, 2003).

In summary, the above discussion points towards the need for greater links between research and practice, in order to develop pedagogies that can relate to, and draw upon, young people's diverse experiences of popular physical culture. There are perhaps implications here for teacher education, which could be considered an apposite context through which to facilitate such change. For example, as Rich (2004) suggests, this might entail encouraging teachers to reflect upon the ways in which physical culture could impact upon their students' engagement with PE. Such a process may help to challenge established assumptions about the relevance of physical activity in young people's lives, and facilitate the development of more culturally relevant forms of PE.

References

Adler, P.A. and Adler, P. (1998). *Peer power: Preadolescent culture and identity*. New Brunswick, NJ: Rutgers University Press.

Alderson, P. (1995). *Listening to children: Children, ethics and social research*. Ilford: Barnados.

Armour, K.M. (1999). The case for a body focus in education and physical education. *Sport, Education and Society, 4(1)*: 5–16.

Armstrong, N. and McManus, A. (1994). Children's fitness and physical activity: a challenge for physical education. *The British Journal of Physical Education, 25*: 20–26.

Azzarito, L. and Ennis, C.D. (2003). A sense of connection: toward social constructivist physical education. *Sport, Education & Society, 8(2)*: 179–198.

Azzarito, L. & Solman, M.A. (2006). A Feminist Poststructuralist View on Student Bodies in Physical Education: Sites of Compliance, Resistance, and Transformation. *Journal of Teaching in Physical Education, 25*, 200–225.

Bailey, R. (2005). Evaluating the relationship between physical education, sport and social inclusion. *Educational Review, 57 (1)*: 71–90.

Bain, L.L. (1975). The hidden curriculum in physical education. *Quest, 24*: 92–101.

Bain, L.L. (1985). The hidden curriculum re-examined. *Quest, 37*: 145–153.

Bain, L.L. (1990). A critical analysis of the hidden curriculum in physical education. In D. Kirk and R. Tinning (Eds), *Physical education, curriculum and culture: critical issues in the contemporary crisis* (pp. 23–42). Lewes: Falmer Press.

Beck, U. (1992). *Risk society: towards a new modernity*. London: Sage.

Bernstein, B. (1996). *Pedagogy, symbolic control and identity: Theory, research and critique*. London: Taylor & Francis.

Bernstein, B. (2001). From pedagogies to knowledges. In A. Morais, I. Neves, B. Davies and H. Daniels (Eds) *Towards a sociology of pedagogy* (pp. 363–368). New York: Peter Lang.

Bordo, S. (1993). *Unbearable weight: feminism, western culture and the body*. London: University of California Press.

Bourdieu, P. (1977). *Outline of a Theory of Practice*. Cambridge: Cambridge University Press.

Bourdieu, P. (1978). Sport and social class. *Social Science Information, 17,(6)*: 819–840.

Bourdieu, P. (1986). The forms of capital. In J. Richardson (Ed.), *Handbook of Theory and Research for the Sociology of Education* (pp. 241–258). New York: Greenwood Press.

Bourdieu, P. (1990). *In other words: Essays towards a reflexive sociology*. Cambridge: Polity Press.

Bourdieu, P. and Wacquant, L.J.D. (2002). *An Invitation to Reflexive Sociology*. Cambridge: Polity Press.

Brettschneider, W-D. (1992). Adolescents, leisure, sport and lifestyle. In T. Williams, L. Almond and A. Sparkes (Ed.), *Sport and physical activity: Moving towards excellence – The proceedings of the AIESEP World Convention* (pp. 536–550). London: Spon.

Brettschneider, W-D. (1994). Youth and sport in Europe: implications for physical education. *British Journal of Physical Education, 25(1)*: 30–34.

Brettschneider, W-D. and Heim, R. (1997). Identity, sport & youth development. In K.R. Fox (Ed.), *The physical self: From motivation to well-being* (pp. 205–227). Champaign, IL: Human Kinetics.

Bromnick, R. D. and Swallow, B. L. (1999). I like being who I am: a study of young people's ideals. *Educational Studies, 25(2)*: 117–128.

Brown, D.H.K. (2001). Living Links and Gender Resources: The social construction of masculinities in teaching Physical Education. Unpublished PhD thesis. Loughborough University.

Brustad, R. (1997). A critical-postmodern perspective on knowledge development on human movement. In J-M Fernández-Balboa, (Ed.), *Critical postmodernism in human movement, physical education, and sport* (pp. 87–98). Albany, NY: State University of New York Press.

Burrows, L. (2004). Understanding and investigating cultural perspectives in physical education. In J. Wright, D. Macdonald and L. Burrows (Eds.), (2004) *Critical inquiry and problem solving in physical education* (pp. 105–119). London: Routledge.

Burrows, L. and Wright, J. (2001). Developing children in New Zealand school physical education. *Sport, Education and Society, 6 (2):* 165–182.

Calhoun, C. (1998). On Pierre Bourdieu, Outline of a theory of practice: Sociology's other poststructuralism. In D. Clawson (Ed.), *Required reading: Sociology's most influential books* (pp. 79–84). Amherst: University of Massachusetts Press.

Cameron, M. and MacDougall, C. (2000). *Crime prevention through sport and physical activity* (trends & issues in crime and criminal justice no. 165). Canberra: Australian Institute of Criminology.

Chapkis, W. (1986). *Beauty secrets.* London: The Women's Press.

Chen, A. (1999). The impact of social change on inner-city high school PE: An analysis of a teacher's experiential account. *Journal of Teaching in Physical Education, 18 (8):* 312–335.

Christensen, P. and James, A. (Eds.). (2000). *Research with Children: Perspectives and Practices.* London: Falmer Press.

Coakley, J.J. (2002). Using sports to control deviance and violence among youths. In M. Gatz, M.A. Messner and S.J. Ball-Rokeach (Eds.), *Paradoxes of youth and sport* (pp. 13–30). Albany, NY: State University of New York Press.

Coalter, F. (2002). *The Social Role of Sport: Opportunities and Challenge.* Center for Leisure Research, University of Edinburgh, John Smith Institute.

Colley, H. (2003). Engagement mentoring for disaffected youth: A new model of mentoring for social inclusion. *British Educational Research Journal, 29(4):* 521–542.

Connell, R.W. (1995). *Masculinities.* London: Polity Press.

Conrad, D.J. and Ennis, C.D. (1998). Curricula of Mutual worth: Comparisons of students and teachers' curricular goals. *Journal of Teaching in Physical Education, 17:* 307–326.

Danish, S.J. (2002). Teaching life skills through sport. In M. Gatz, M.A. Messner and S.J. Ball-Rokeach (Eds.), *Paradoxes of Youth and Sport* (pp. 49–59). Albany, NY: State University of New York Press.

Department for Culture Media and Sport (DCMS) (1999). Policy Action Team 10: Report to the Social Exclusion Unit, Arts and Sport. London: HMSO.

Department of Health (2003). Annual Report of the Chief Medical Officer 2002. London: DoH.

De Knop, P. and De Martelaer, K. (2001). Quantitative and qualitative evaluation of youth sport in Flanders and the Netherlands: A case study. *Sport, Education and Society, 6(1):* 35–51.

Dussel, I. (2004). Fashioning the schooled self through uniforms: A Foucauldian approach to contemporary school policies. In B.M. Baker and K.E. Heyning (Eds) *Dangerous coagulations? The uses of Foucault in the study of education* (pp. 85–116). New York: Peter Lang.

Ennis, C. D. (1999). Creating a culturally relevant curriculum for disengaged girls. *Sport, Education and Society, 4(1):* 31–49.

Ennis, C.D., Cothran, D.J., Davidson, K.S. et al. (1997). Implementing curriculum within a context of fear and disengagement. *Journal of Teaching in Physical Education, 17:* 58–72.

Evans, J. (Ed.) (1986). *Physical education, sport and schooling: Studies in the sociology of physical education.* London: Falmer.

Evans, J. (1988a) Body matters: Towards a socialist physical education. In H. Lauder and P. Brown (Ed.), *Education in search of a future.* London: Falmer.

Evans, J. (Ed.) (1988b). *Teachers, teaching and control in physical education.* London: Falmer.

Evans, J., Davies, B. and Wright, J. (Eds) (2004). *Body knowledge and control: studies in the sociology of physical education and health.* London: Routledge.

Evans, J. and Davies, B. (2004). Endnote: The embodiment of consciousness. In J. Evans, B. Davies and J. Wright (Eds.), *Body knowledge and control: Studies in the sociology of physical education and health* (pp. 207–217). London: Routledge.

Evans, J. and Penney, D. (2002). Introduction. In D. Penney (Ed.), *Gender and physical education: contemporary issues and future directions* (pp. 3–12). London: Routledge.

Featherstone, M. (1982). The body in consumer culture. *Theory, Culture and Society, 1:* 18–33.

Featherstone, M., Hepworth, B. and Turner, B. (Eds.). (1991). *The body: Social process and cultural theory.* London: Sage Publications.

Fernández-Balboa, J-M. (Ed.). (1997). *Critical postmodernism in human movement, physical education, and sport.* Albany, NY: State University of New York Press.

Flintoff, A. and Scraton, S. (2001). Stepping into active leisure? Young women's perceptions of active lifestyles and their experiences of school physical education. *Sport, Education and Society, 6(1):* 5–21.

Fontana, A. and Frey, J.H. (2000). The Interview: From Structured Questions to Negotiated Text. In N.K. Denzin and Y.S. Lincoln (Eds.), *Handbook of Qualitative Research* (pp. 645–672). Sage.

Foucault, M. (1977). *Discipline and Punish: The birth of the prison.* London: Allen Lane.

Foucault, M. (1980). *Power/knowledge: Selected interviews and other writings 1972–1977.* New York: Pantheon.

Foucault, M. (1991). *Discipline and punish: The birth of the prison.* Harmondsworth: Penguin.

Frank, A.W. (1990). Bringing bodies back in: A decade review. *Theory, Culture and Society, 7:* 131–162.

Frost, L. (2001). *Young women and the body: A feminist sociology*. New York: Palgrave Macmillan.

Gard, M. (2001). Dancing around the problem of boys and dance. *Discourse: Studies in the Cultural Politics of Education, 22(2)*: 213–225.

Gard, M. and Wright, J. (2001). Managing uncertainty: Obesity discourses and physical education in a risk society. *Studies in Philosophy and Education, 20*: 535–549.

Gard, M. and Wright, J. (2005). *The Obesity Epidemic: Science, Morality and Ideology*. London: Routledge.

Gatz, M., Messner, M.A. and Ball-Rokeach, S.J. (Eds.). (2002). *Paradoxes of youth and sport*. Albany, NY: State University of New York Press.

Giddens, A. (1991). *Modernity and self-identity*. Cambridge: Polity Press.

Gillespie, L. and Culpan, I. (2000). Critical thinking: Ensuring the "education" aspect is evident in physical education. *Journal of Physical Education New Zealand, 33(3)*: 84–96.

Goffman, E. (1959). *The Presentation of Self in Everyday Life*. New York: Doubleday Anchor.

Green, K. (2004). Physical education, lifelong participation and 'the couch potato society'. *Physical Education and Sport Pedagogy, 9(1)*: 73–86.

Hall, T., Coffey, A. and Williamson, H. (1999). Self, space and place: Youth identities and citizenship. *British Journal of Sociology of Education, 20(4)*: 501–515.

Hellison, D. (1995). *Teaching responsibility through physical activity*. Champaign, IL: Human Kinetics.

Hendry, L.B., Kloep, M. and Olsson, S. (1998). Youth, lifestyles and society: A class issue? *Childhood: A Global Journal of Child Research, 5(2)*: 133–150.

Himberg, C., Hutchinson, G.E. and Roussell, J.M. (2003). *Teaching secondary physical education in the 21st century: Preparing adolescents to be active for life*. Champaign, IL: Human Kinetics.

Hodkinson, P. (2001). *Reworking subculture: Young people and elective affiliations of substance*. Paper presented at a British Sociological Association seminar, January 17, 2001.

Holroyd, R. (2002). 'Body work': Physical capital, habitus and the field of school, *Paper presented at British Educational Research Association Conference*, Exeter, September 2002.

Holroyd, R.A. (2003). *Fields of experience: Young people's constructions of embodied identities*. Unpublished PhD, Loughborough University.

Hopkins, S. (1999). 'Schoolies week': Re-thinking risk. In C. Symes and D. Meadmore (Eds.), *The extra-ordinary school: Parergonality and pedagogy* (pp. 197–209). New York: Peter Lang.

Housner, L.D. (1996). Innovation and change in physical education. In S.J. Silverman and C.D. Ennis (Eds.), *Student learning in physical education* (pp. 367–389). Champaign, IL: Human Kinetics.

Hunter, L.T. (2002). *Young people, physical education, and transition: Understanding practices in the middle years of schooling*. Unpublished PhD, University of Queensland.

Hunter, L. (2004). Bourdieu and the social space of the PE class; reproduction of doxa through practice. *Sport Education and Society, 9(12)*: 175–192.

Hunter, L. (2005). Who gets to play? Kids, bodies and schooled subjectivities. In J.A Vadeboncoeur and L.P. Stevens (Eds.), *Re/Constructing "the adolescent" sign, symbol and body* (pp. 181–210). New York: Peter Lang.

Hurley, L.P. and Lustbader, L.L. (1997). Project support: Engaging children and families in the educational process. *Adolescence, 32(127)*: 523–531.

Jackson, P.W. (1968). *Life in classrooms*. New York: Holt, Rinehart and Winston.

James, A. and Prout, A. (Eds.). (1997). *Constructing and reconstructing childhood*. London: Falmer Press.

James, A., Jenks, C. and Prout, A. (1998). *Theorizing childhood*. Cambridge: Polity Press.

Jarvie, G. and Maguire, J. (1994). *Sport and leisure in social thought*. London: Routledge.

Jenkins, R. (1996). *Social identity*. London: Routledge.

Jowell, T. (2004). Presentation to the Tackling Obesity in Young People Conference, London, 25th February.

Kellner, D. (1992). Popular culture and the construction of postmodern identities. In S. Lash and J. Friedman (Eds.), *Modernity and identity* (pp. 141–177). Oxford: Blackwell.

Kirk, D. (1992). Physical education, discourse, and ideology: Bringing the hidden curriculum into view. *Quest, 44*: 35–56.

Kirk, D. (1993). *The body, schooling and culture*. Geelong: Deakin University Press.

Kirk, D. (1994). Making the Present Strange: Sources of the Current Crisis in Physical Education Discourse. *The Australian Journal of Educational Studies, 15*, 46–63.

Kirk, D. (1998). *Schooling bodies: School practice and public discourse*. London: Leicester University Press.

Kirk, D. (1999a). Embodying the school/schooling bodies: Physical education as disciplinary technology. In C.M. Symes and D. Meadmore (Eds.), *The extra-ordinary school: Parergonality and pedagogy* (pp. 181–196). New York: Peter Lang.

Kirk, D. (1999b). Health, the body and the medicalisation of the school. In C.M. Symes and D. Meadmore (Eds.), *The extra-ordinary school: Parergonality and pedagogy* (pp. 163–180). New York: Peter Lang.

Kirk, D. (1999c). Physical culture, physical education and relational analysis. *Sport, Education and Society, 4(1)*: 63–73.

Kirk, D. (2004). Towards a critical history of the body, identity and health: Corporeal power and school practice. In J. Evans, B. Davies and J. Wright (Eds.), *Body knowledge and control: Studies in the sociology of physical education and health* (pp. 52–67). London: Routledge.

Kirk, D. and Colquhoun, D. (1989). Healthism and physical education. *British Journal of Sociology of Education, 10(4)*: 417–434.

Kirk, D. and Macdonald, D. (1998). Situated learning in physical education. *Journal of Teaching in Physical Education, 17(3)*: 376–387.

Kirk, D. and MacPhail, A. (2002). Teaching games for understanding and situated learning: Re-thinking the Bunker-Thorpe model. *Journal of Teaching in Physical Education, 21(2)*: 177–192.

Kirk, D. and Tinning, R. (Eds.). (1990). Physical education, curriculum and culture: Critical issues in the contemporary crisis (pp. 23–42). Lewes: Falmer.

Kirk, D. and Tinning, R. (1994). Embodied self identity, healthy lifestyles and school physical education. *Sociology of Health & Illness, 16(5)*: 600–625.

Kivel, B.D. (1998). Adolescent identity formation and leisure contexts: A selective review of the literature. *Journal of Physical Education, Recreation and Dance, 69(1)*: 36–38.

Kraft, N.P. and Wheeler, J.W. (2000, 20–27 October). *Service-Learning and resiliance in disaffected youth: A research study.* Paper presented at the 2nd Annual International Service Learning Research Conference, Vanderbilt University, Nashville, TN.

Laberge, S. (1995). Towards an integration of gender into Bourdieu's concept of cultural capital. *Sociology of Sport Journal, 12(2)*: 132–146.

Langley, D.J. (1997). Exploring student skill learning: A case for investigating subjective experiences. *Quest, 49(2)*: 142–160.

Lave, J. and Wenger, E. (1991). *Situated Learning: Legitimate Peripheral Participation.* Cambridge: Cambridge University Press.

Light, R. (1999). *A comparative study of the social dimensions of young men's experiences in and through elite level high school rugby in Japan and Australia.* Unpublished PhD, University of Queensland.

Light, R. (2001). *The body in the social world and the social world in the body: Applying Bourdieu's work to analyses of physical activity in schools.* Paper presented at the Australian Association for Research in Education, Freemantle.

Lynch, K. (2001). *Equality in education – The three R's, (re)distribution, recognition and representation.* Paper presented at the International Sociology of Education Conference: Class, Race, Gender and Disability: Points of commonality and difference, Sheffield.

Macdonald, D. (2002). Extending agendas: Physical culture research for the twenty-first century. In D. Penney (Ed.), *Gender and physical education: Contemporary issues and future directions* (pp. 208–222). London: Routledge.

Marsland, D. (1993). *Understanding youth: Issues and methods in social education.* St. Albans: Claridge Press.

Martinek, T.H. and Hellison, D.R. (1997). Fostering resiliency in underserved youth through physical activity. *Quest, 49(1)*: 34–49.

McRobbie, A. (1994). *Postmodernism and popular culture.* London: Routledge.

Merton, B. and Parrott, A. (1999). *Only Connect: Successful practice in educational work with disaffected young adults.* London: NIACE.

Miles, S. (1998). *Consumerism as a way of life.* London: Sage.

Miles, S. and Anderson, A. (1999). 'Just do it?': young people, the global media and the construction of consumer meanings. In S. Ralph, J. Langham Brown and T. Lees (Eds.), *Youth and the global media: Papers from the 29th University of Manchester Broadcasting Symposium* (pp. 105–113). Luton: University of Luton Press.

Miles, S., Cliff, D. and Burr, V. (1998). 'Sticking out and fitting in': Consumption, consumer meanings and the construction of young people's identities. *Journal of Youth Studies, 1(1)*: 81–96.

Oliver, K.L. and Lalik, R. (2000). *Bodily knowledge: Learning about equity and justice with adolescent girls.* New York: Peter Lang.

Oliver, K.L. and Lalik, R. (2001). The body as curriculum: Learning with adolescent girls. *Journal of Curriculum Studies, 33(3)*: 303–333.

Oliver, K.L. and Lalik, R. (2004). "The beauty walk": Interrogating whiteness as the norm for beauty within one school's hidden curriculum. In J. Evans, B. Davies, and J. Wright (Ed.), *Body knowledge and control: Studies in the sociology of physical education and health* (pp. 115–129). London: Routledge.

Omizo, S.A. and Omizo, M.M. (1992). Eating disorders: The school counselor's role. *The School Counselor, 39*: 217–224.

Penney, D. (Ed.). (2002). *Gender and physical education: Contemporary issues and future directions* (pp. 208–222). London: Routledge.

Penney, D. and Chandler, T. (2000). Physical education: What future(s)? *Sport, Education and Society, 5(2)*: 71–87.

Penney, D. and Evans, J. (1999). *Politics, policy, and practice in physical education.* London: Routledge.

Postman, N. (1994). *The disappearance of childhood.* New York: Vintage Books.

Punch, S. (2002). Research with children: The same or different from research with adults. *Childhood: A Global Journal of Child Research, 9(3)*: 321–341.

Ralph, S., Langham Brown, J. and Lees, T. (Eds.). (1999). *Youth and the global media: Papers from the 29th University of Manchester Broadcasting Symposium.* Luton: University of Luton Press.

Reid, K. (2002) Mentoring with disaffected pupils. *Mentoring and Tutoring, 10(2)*: 153–169.

Rich, E. (2003). 'The problem with girls': liberal feminism, 'equal opportunities' and gender inequality in physical education. *British Journal of Physical Education, 34(1)*: 46–49.

Rich, E. (2004). Exploring teachers' biographies and perceptions of girls' participation in physical education. *European Physical Education Review, 10(2)*: 220–245.

Rich, E., Holroyd, R. and Evans, J. (2004). Hungry to be noticed: Young women, anorexia and schooling. In J. Evans, B. Davies, and J. Wright (Eds.), *Body knowledge and control: Studies in the sociology of physical education and health* (pp. 173–190). London: Routledge.

Roberts, K. (1996). Young people, schools, sport and politics. *Sport, Education and Society, 1(1)*: 47–57.

Rønholt, H. (2002). 'It's only the sissies …': Analysis of teaching and learning processes in physical education:

A contribution to the hidden curriculum. *Sport, Education and Society, 7(1)*: 25–36.

Rovegno, I. and Kirk, D. (1995). Articulations and silences in socially critical work on physical education: Toward a broader agenda. *Quest, 47*: 447–474.

Sandford, R. and Armour, K. (2004). Evaluating the role of adult mentors within a youth physical activity programme. Paper presented at the AIESEP Pre-Olympic Conference, University of Thessaloniki, Greece.

Sandford, R., Armour, K. and Bowyer, S. (2004). *It might be fashionable but does it 'work'?: Physical activity, behaviour management and impact.* Paper presented at the British Educational Research Association Annual Conference, Manchester University, September 2004.

Sanford, R.A., Armour, K.M. and Warmington, P.C. (2006). Re-engaging disaffected youth through physical activity programs. *British Educational Research Journal, 32(2)*: 251–271.

Schwager, S.M. (1997). Critical moral issues in teaching physical education. In J-M. Fernández-Balboa (Ed.), *Critical postmodernism in human movement, physical education, and sport* (pp. 139–156). Albany, NY: State University of New York Press.

Siedentop, D. (Ed.) (1994). *Sport education: Quality PE through positive sport experiences.* Champaign, IL: Human Kinetics.

Shilling, C. (1991). Educating the body: Physical capital and the production of social inequalities. *Sociology, 25(4)*: 653–672.

Shilling, C. (1993). *The body and social theory.* London: Sage Publications.

Smith, A., Green, K. and Roberts, K. (2004). Sports Participation and the 'Obesity/Health Crisis': Reflections on the case of young people in England. *International Review for Sociology of Sport, 39(4)*: 457–464.

Sparkes, A.C. (1997). Reflections On the Socially Constructed Physical Self. In K.R. Fox (Ed.), *The Physical Self: From Motivation To Well Being* (pp. 83–110). Champaign, IL.: Human Kinetics.

Symes, C. and Meadmore, D. (1999). Force of habit: The school uniform as a body of knowledge. In C. Symes, and Meadmore, D. (Eds.), *The extra-ordinary school:*

Parergonality and pedagogy (pp. 171–191). New York: Peter Lang.

Tait, G. (2000). *Youth, sex, and government* (Vol. 3). New York: Peter Lang.

Theberge, N. (1991). Reflections on the body in the sociology of sport. *Quest, 4(3)*: 123–134.

Thomson, R. (2000). Physical activity through sport and leisure: Traditional versus non-competitive activities. *Journal of Physical Education New Zealand, 33(1)*: 34–39.

Thorpe, S. (2000). *The politics of educational crisis.* Unpublished PhD, Deakin University.

Thorpe, S. (2003). Crisis discourse in physical education and the laugh of Michel Foucualt. Sport, *Education and Society, 8(2)*: 131–151.

Tinning, R. (1985). Physical education and the cult of slenderness. *ACHPER National Journal, 107*: 10–13.

Tinning, R., and Fitzclarence, L. (1992). Postmodern youth culture and the crisis in Australian secondary school physical education. *Quest, 44*: 287–303.

Turner, B.S. (1996). *The body and society: Explorations in social theory* (2nd ed.). London: Sage.

Vertinsky, P.A. (1992). Reclaiming space, revisioning the body: The quest for a gender-sensitive physical education. *Quest, 44(3)*: 373–397.

Williams, A. and Bedward (2001). Gender, culture and the generation gap: Student and teacher perceptions of aspects of national curriculum physical education. *Sport, Education and Society, 6(1)*: 53–66.

Wright, J. (1997). The construction of gendered contexts in single sex and coeducational physical education lessons. *Sport, Education and Society, 2(1)*: 55–72.

Wright, J., Macdonald, D. and Groom, L. (2003). Physical activity and young people: Beyond participation. *Sport, Education & Society, 8(1)*: 17–33.

Wright, J., Macdonald, D. and Burrows, L. (2004). *Critical inquiry and problem solving in physical education.* London: Routledge.

Wren, D.J. (1999). School culture: Exploring the hidden curriculum. *Adolescence, 34(135)*: 593–596.

Wyness, M.G. (1999). Childhood, agency and educational reform. *Childhood: A Global Journal of Child Research, 6(3)*: 353–368.

3.7 Development and learning of motor skill competencies

NATALIE WALLIAN AND CHING WEI CHANG

Introduction: "motor learning", an evolving concept

Within a constantly evolving society, an individual's adaptation to the environment is a perennial problematic. While entry to the autonomous adult world is always deferred, the question of educational objectives becomes crucial: one moves from modelling a subject to a defined working task to the development of adaptation competencies. So, the common notions of learning, problem solving and responsible decision-making must be revised. Defined as an active long-term process, learning is a significant-for-the-subject experience where an adaptation problem has to be solved within a particular situation. This complex learning process involves symbolic representations and intentions, and produces motor skill competencies.

Human development is a long-life complex process, which involves at the same time the maturation of the brain structures and the functional achievement of the central nervous system. It depends fully upon genetic and environmental factors. There is the interplay of two determining dynamics as the individual develops: (1) internal factors, linked with the structural and functional characteristics of the person, and (2) external factors, emerging from a dialogue and experience with the environment. So, the processes of growth, maturation and learning interact with an individual's experiences throughout life. An individual's ongoing interaction with the environment helps develop the nervous structuring of the organism, and the functional improvement of these systems. Growth and development of bio-neural systems promotes learning by adapting behaviour within and to environment constraints, and assist individuals to become more competent and efficient in complex situations.

At school, learning has a specific meaning, because it occurs within a normative social context that repr sents for a student many opportunities for growth. A student's social position within the school and access to opportunities to learn will be determined in part by negotiation of the normative social context. So, conceptions of learning determine fundamentally the status of knowledge and the relationship between the teacher and the student. An integrative conception of the student supposes a pluridisciplinary approach of motor learning theories: this suggests the need for a thematic approach instead of an approach based on the exploration of successive and crossed scientific fields.

Motor learning is a particular form of learning directed towards improvement or mastery of new motor behaviours (motor skills, coordination and conditional abilities). Motor learning implicates the mobilization of every social, cognitive, affective and motor dimension of a person, and so contributes to his/her balanced development and to the achievement of physical competencies. One indicator for the quality of motor learning is the respective degree of the achieved body control and the pertinence of strategies involved. In this context, motor skills as modules represent clusters of cue perception capabilities, cognitive strategies and intentions, prior knowledge and representations, and techniques that are activated together in situated learning conditions (Kirk and MacPhail, 2002). Various theories consider the optimal organization of motor learning from the teacher's point of view. They integrate the contributions of different sciences like philosophy of mind, genetic psychology, cognisciences, semiotics, ergonomics and didactics.

We propose in this chapter to analyse the present conceptions of motor learning within an integrative and pluridisciplinary conception of the individual student. We will try to integrate motor development and mental processes involved, by linking action with intention and strategies. The first section of the chapter will provide a historical retrospective of motor learning conceptions within particular theories. Then, these associated concepts will be linked with the problematic of motor learning and pedagogical intervention at school. Finally, we will sketch some scientific and practical issues for the research on physical education and physical education teacher education.

Historical overview of key concepts within motor learning

The evolution of conceptions of learning allows us to understand the shift of pedagogical methods within teaching/learning systems. This evolution must be linked with different scientific paradigms and assumptions inspiring practices, and in returned produced by them. Figure 3.7.1 represents the evolution of conceptions of learning in relation to theories and authors, physical education practices and assumptions. Scientific knowledge production and educational practices are linked all along the chronological frieze with the influence of authors at a precise moment of their main publication. Of course, there is a time delay between concept production and impact on science and practice, but it is interesting to notice the evolution of the educational mind in an evolving scientific and philosophical context.

The Cartesian paradigm, an emerging "knowledge archaeology"

The occidental dualist theory (Descartes, 1667) is grounded on the idea that body is the tool of mind, and that these two elements function separately. In this perspective, body is under the control of thought processes. A second Cartesian assumption is that for studying a phenomenon, one must divide the whole reality in elementary particles, so that reality can be decomposed and described as rationally as possible.

Refuting this dualism after Pascal (1660), Searle (1995) assumes that mental states are caused by cerebral processes and occur within the brain. There is no obstacle for claiming that body and mind are one. Intellectual faculties do not exist independently from the matter on which they operate. Cognitive activities consist of biological and mental processes that involve knowledge of world and of ourselves. The radical materialist theory, promoted by Place, Smart and Feigl, inscribes mind and body within an identity rapport: mind is brain and vice versa. Elsewhere, neurological investigations claim that a mental state (thinking, perceiving, feeling) corresponds to a cerebral state (a physicochemical activity) (Lockman and Thelen, 1993). According to the

neurophysiologist Damasio (1995), there is no unique centre to integrate human mental functions, because there is no specific brain area that processes information simultaneously produced by all sensorial modalities.

This conception of reality has many implications in scientific fields as well as in pedagogical practices. It postulates the pre-existence of an order that depends upon simplification and reduction. In order to organize learning, a teacher is thus required to dissemble elementary movements into their components parts, which are then practiced separately, and then to re-assemble these components back into the whole movement at a final global stage.

Four complementary learning conceptions

We can note a shift in conceptions learning, from an external conception of the factors involved to a more internal implication of the subject structures. This shift means that we give progressively more importance to the personal dynamic of development and learning than before, where the context constraints and particularly the teacher played a determinant rule. But these conceptions are now prevalent in the physical education teacher's practice. Meanwhile, regarding complex learning and decision-making tasks, scientific studies nowadays lean more on student-subject activity, on the prior knowledge and representational system involved, on the cognitive activities of information interpretation, and on the decision making strategies and mental processes. The "constructivist didactic" named by Terhart (2003: 32) is expected to develop comprehensive conceptions of the learning process such as the character of content instructions, instructional situation and interactions, teacher tasks and so on.

Behaviourism and positive reality

Traditional behaviouristic understanding of learning starts with purely external control, and deliberately ignores internal mental processes, because of its allegedly uncontrolled subjective nature. If learning is determined by external factors, the teacher is strongly implicated as organizer and manager of learning tasks. Knowledge, contents, abilities and motor skills are being acquired or "digested" if the presented knowledge is first reduced, simplified and dissembled by the teacher. Therefore, this paradigm focuses research on the manipulability of learning by means of appropriate stimulus constellations, memorization and assessment. In this perspective, the study objects are teacher-centred and deal with task-constraint systems, instructional settings, assessment tools, and feedbacks. Of course, with programmes and content knowledge, the purpose is

Figure 3.7.1 The evolution of conceptions of learning

	SPORT PEDAGOGY RESEARCH	PROCESS-PRODUCT STUDIES	MOTOR LEARNING/MOTOR SKILLS		ECOLOGICAL COMPLEX APPROACH
	Modeling «the» good teacher		Content-knowledge-centered studies	Ecological teacher effectiveness	Managerial/instructional systems
Conceptions of research in PE (Siedentop, 2002)	- Understand teacher effectiveness and classroom life (teaching as work: skills strategies, performances, action planning…) - Identify a repertoire of teaching skills - Applying with appropriate sensitivity to context - Educational research and psychological	- How to observe positively the teacher activity - To understand the broad dimensions of actions - Explaining student achievement: functional value or adaptative significance of behaviours METHODS: Systematic observational grids	- Content-valid outcome measures - Academic learning time - Successful practice in tasks - Authentic assessment of performance during practice	- Routines/disruptions - Ethnographic observational methods - Low-inference observation system - Teacher's knowledge of the taught activities - Student understanding and evaluations - Teacher believes related to the espoused theories of instruction	- Teacher knowledge of content - Task systems/instructional task system - Skill/tactical focus - Enacted theories of instruction - Knowledge-in-action and implicit experienced knowledge - Task negotiation and ambiguity METHODS: Crossed data (videotapes, notes, post units interviews, planned lessons…)
Conceptions of motor learning	"Black" Box"	Learner as an instruction / executer	Information processing / Learner as a dynamic system		Active knowledge co-construction
PARADIGMS	STRUCTURALISM	FUNCTIONALISM	SYSTEMISM (complex thinking)		CONNECTIONNISM
SOCIOLOGY	Ditthey, Malinowski, Machado, Vico, Pascal, Descartes	Merleau-Ponty,	Bourdieu, Bernstein		
Science	Wittgenstein, Popper				
History	1940	1960	1930		2000
PHILOSOPHY of MIND	REALISM / NATURALISM PHENOMENOLOGY	HERMENEUTICS	Morin (75) …… Simon (83)		
LANGUAGE SCIENCES	Information Theory Shannon & Weaver (46) Turning Theory of communication Sperber & Wilson, Chomsky.	Speech act theory Austin (62), Searle (63)	Reception semiotics Quine Iser, Jauss, Eco, Fayol	Conversation pragmatics	
COGNITIVE PSYCHOLOGY	CENTRALISM simon & Newell (56) Bruner, Miller, G. Bruner, Miller, G	CYBERNETICS Macy Conferences (59) Von Neuman, Wiener (58)	PERIPHERISM Bateson (72), Palo-Alto School, Watzlawick SYSTEMICS Dialectic constructivism Newell (76) Rorty (78) Ecologic theory	Dynamic system theory	
Motor development	Behaviourism Hull, 1945 Gestahlt theory	Bounded rationality Von Bertalanffy (68) Simon (69)	Prigogine (83), von Forester (81) Simon (69)	Fodor , Cobb von Foerster (81), von Glasersfeld, Barel	Varela (93), Gibsori, Houdé, Vignaux
GENETIC PSYCHOLOGY	Vygotsky, Bakhtine, Leonbiev Piaget,; Wallon (67),	Genetic epistemology (70)			
PE Theorie Outcomes	Head fitting metaphor deconstruction/reconstruction Inhibition/latence Transfer Repetition effect of exercise Task simplification/curricula programs Assessment/ Feedbacks/Motivation/Goal impact Learning by trials Optimal difficulty Proximal Zone of development Rupture and problem solving Cognitive dissonance Prior knowledge/basic learning Process-oriented approaches Stages of development Biological rythms Construction/	Stereotypes Cognitive/social representations Environment impact Individual profiles Patterns	Awareness Task constraint system Instructional settings Peer tutoring Information processing Language and mind Social negociation used for solving knowledge claim	Debate of ideas settings (DIS) Affordance Problem solving settings Situated learning Distributed cognition Language exchange impact	Phenomenon as experienced by the subject Knowledge-in-action Interpretation strategies Co-construction of knowledge Knowledge as a meaning construction

to create all favourable and "objective" conditions for learning, in order to reduce perturbing external variables and to focus the student attention on good aspects of the task to be fulfilled.

A key purpose of the behaviourist approach is to formulate general learning laws, like repetition, feedback impact, instructional setting variables, and curriculum planning. These preoccupations tend to describe external factors involved within learning in a so-called "positive and objective" way.

Structural/functional theories ("stages"/Gestahlt theory/ Bildung theory)

According to the Adams (1992) closed-up theory, visual perception organizes the specificities of the environment out of informational "forms". Perception of the world is not the sum of separate elements. Our perception is made up of ensembles organized into global forms that give sense to what is perceived. So, perceiving consists in projecting on reality "forms" or already known configurations in order to recognize them. A "form" is a structure equipped with meaning, signification. For any mental act, meaning emerges from the perception of the whole situation, and escapes when we decompose and add each thinner element that is included within a gesture or movement. For instance, perception of a movement is not the successive perception of each gesture that composes it, but the perception of global gestures that constitutes it.

Within Schmidt's (1988) theory, motor skills are determined on one hand by a general programme of movements (based on "recall schema"), and on the other hand by rules that parameterize the specific movement ("recognizing schema"). These schemas represent knowledge systems that are modified and adapted during experiences. In this perspective, the main parameters of motor learning are effective practice quantity and variability of practice. The teacher's task consists of conceiving task arrangement systems where the student has to manage contextual interferences by adapting his or her behaviour. Within this perspective, we can distinguish between "random practice" and "blocked practice".

Structural and functional studies on subjects conceived as producing actions prompted scientists to shift the focus of their analysis on to effective processes developed while interacting with contexts, engaging them with more systemic theories.

Systemic theories

The "cognitive revolution" began with emergence of a constructivist approach. Terhart (2003: 29) assumes that "The theory of autopoïetic self-referential systems uses radical constructivist, neuro-biological, and cybernetic-information-concepts to develop a general system theory". Systemic theories assume that a system obeys laws of equilibrium. The dynamism of a system consists of preserving order by developing adaptation strategies. So, a system shifts successively from one stable stage to another, trying to reduce major perturbations by modifying internal organization.

Information-processing theory is based on a neuronal network metaphor that compares the similarities of neuronal structures to computer programs (Shannon and Weaver, 1949; Sanders, 1990). The postulate is that there is an analogy between human functioning and computers. Two different forms of information processing can be distinguished: (1) situated *bottom–up* process directed by informational environment, and (2) *top–down* process determined by personal concepts and representations Weil-Barais, 1999: 297). Computational theory analyses the logic of the required qualities for a system that is requested to accomplish a given task. It consists of describing different stages of information processing from perception to interpretation (i.e. recognizing an object). The functional architecture of neuronal systems can be linked with different central areas where thought takes place (Kosslyn and Koening, 1992).

This transmission model induces a teaching style based on a "teacher-talk-student-listen" approach. The student is compared with a black box and arrows. These arrows represent relationships between encoded (inputs) and decoded (outputs) messages, and the student's task consists of processing the right information, as much and as quickly as possible (Sanders, 1990; Temprado and Famose, 1993). So, univocal information is considered as objective data that exist independently from subject knowledge (Dretske, 1981, 1988). Efficient action (outputs) results from three stages of information processing based on a logic of "uncertainty reduction": (1) perceptive stage, (2) decision-making stage where the right answer is selected, and (3) effective stage where an answer is planned (recalling a generalized motor program and specification according to environmental conditions).

But this conception of information-processing is refuted by Goldman (1986). For this author, an event carries informational value as a condition of the subject meaning attribution. In this perspective, physiologist Berthoz (1997) assumes that perception is a simulated action, because it can be defined as judgement, decision-making, and anticipating action issues. So, information processing must be linked with the action representational system. A subject must not only recognize pertinent stimuli in a given context, but must also anticipate the significant probable events. Perception is thus linked with intended actions, and information processing consists of searching the expected information that validates intentions of action.

The difficulty of such a theory is that a computer is only able to simulate mental states; simulating does not mean reproducing. It is fundamental, within our conception of reality, to distinguish between things that exist independently from an observer (a force, a weight, etc.), and things that exist only for an observer (language, values and concepts, etc.). When one moves from a conception of learning as information-processing to a conception based on co-construction of knowledge and meaning attribution, the person is no longer compared with an analogical computer connected in series.

Situated learning theories support the assumption that dialogue between learner and context is a determinant for knowledge construction (Lave and Wenger, 1991; Clancey, 1997). The main idea is that, with regards to the uniqueness of context, all learning depends upon the situation in which it takes place; learning takes place in particular sets of circumstances, in time and space. It is not possible to extract general laws from observed facts, and all studies must be case studies, with narrow possibilities of generalization. In return, when an action involves several different effects according to the situation where it takes place, a person must discriminate the characteristics of the situation in order to interpret and to redefine the meaning of an action according to intentions and processes involved.

Thus, each situation being singular and unique, learning is fundamentally situated in a here-and-now. The teacher's task consists of setting up educative environments in which the learning subject produces self-adaptations. While interpreting the context, a learner is therefore allowed to find and to choose his or her own way. Classroom ecological theories can also be included within this grouping of situated learning theories, since among other things they illustrate the importance of dialogue with context (Doyle, 1986).

Complexity theories

Complexity theories assume that simplifying instructional settings and corresponding problems consist of misrepresenting the authentic complexity of total context. For example, Newel's (1991) dynamical systems theory puts the stress on perception/action coupling. Action describes exploring the perceptual-motor space of task constraints. Understanding and problem solving requires taking account of the overall relationship of elements involved (Whitall, 1991). The situatedness of learning, concerned with the natural authentic conditions of life in which learning occurs, stresses the importance of concrete experiences. A difficulty Newell notes with the situated nature of learning is that, with these situations being unique and highly contextualized, there may be limited generalization to learning in other situations.

Ecological theory, first developed by Gibson (1979, 1984, 1988), formulates the concept of "affordance". The concept of affordance refers to the notion that what is perceived of an object depends upon the actions a subject can grasp from it. The concept of affordance accounts for functional relations between actor and environment. Ecological psychology assumes that motor advancement can be observed by the emergence of new motor patterns and that the development of motor skills is determined by dialogue between organism and environment.

Cognition depends upon relationships between the subject's experience and "his/her" world (Yussen, 1985; Suchman, 1987; Flavell, 1987; Cobb, 1994; Fosnot, 1996; Kishner and Whitson, 1997). Constructivism is a general philosophical orientation towards knowledge, derived from phenomenology and hermeneutics. It includes a broad and heterogeneous bundle of concepts and theories, and is not limited to cognitive aspects of learning, but takes the whole individual into account. It casts a subject student as being actively involved in co-constructing his/her own understandings of problem solving. Piaget's theory is grounded on the following assumption: the object is the basic unity of reality construction. So, functional alternation between person and environment serves as a basis for self-socio-construction of the person. From experiences emerge successive representations of world, which serve as a basis for interpreting it. In return, these representations are modified by exploration. Radical epistemic implications assume that there can be no warrant for claiming access to knowledge that either is mediated through personal interpretation of human experience, and deny the existence of any real objective (and objectivable) world. This assumption does not mean that, given the essential incapacity for acceding to another subject world, one must refrain from trying to understand the student's functioning and reasoning while acting. It means that we must be aware of the pathetic position that consists of placing limitations on the attention to very well observed facts and behaviours.

Core concepts and associated theories

In this section, we will define usable concepts associated with motor learning. Indeed, cross-fertilization between different scientific findings helps redefine commonplace terms in new contexts, and clarify their use within current scientific theories. The aim is to extract from philosophy of mind, genetic psychology, cognitive sciences, neurosciences, semiotics, ergonomics and pedagogy, the core concepts useful for understanding motor learning processes.

The postulate of the educability of intelligence

Drawing upon nativist theories, we can consider respectively the subject (1) as determined from birth, and so endowed with competencies (Herrnstein and Murray, 1994), or (2) as potentially competent according to the opportunities of the environment. Herrnstein et al. concluded that minorities are intellectually inferior. This study was deeply questioned by the prestigious National Academy of Sciences of the United States of America (Duyne and Tomkiewicz, 1999) because of its determinist opinion that asserted that social position is determined by intelligence. On the contrary, the nativist theory assumes that the environment is a determinant condition for developing intelligence. But nowadays, it remains difficult to identify the importance of each factor, especially because it is difficult to know exactly what aspects of intelligence tests measure (i.e. the Binet and Simon QI test). So, the fundamental postulate of "educability" must remain the ground of every educational intervention, otherwise education has no meaning and so no proper existence.

The definition of intelligence is the object of numerous theories. Sternberg (1994) sustains the "triarchist theory of intelligence". He distinguishes three kinds of intelligence: (1) analytic intelligence, which is abstract and deductive, (2) creative intelligence (which includes being tolerant of ambiguity, risks and uncertainty), and (3) social and practical intelligence. Problem solving involves all these intelligences. The interest in physical education of this distinction lies in highlighting the two kinds of intelligence that play a major role for decision making in sport practices. Indeed, the tolerance for uncertainty is a mental disposition that favours learning, and practical intelligence is related to knowledge-in-action.

Plasticity represents a system's capacity for modifying its own structure and acquiring new skills in order for it to be more durable. In the face of unusual situations, it is an organism's capability of responding in order to develop new resources which will in turn allow a better adaptation of the subject to the situation. For beginners, adaptation may have led to the installment of many routines that represent their essential resources. A routine is an internal operation used by a player that becomes automatic and is based on principles of economy and speed (Gréhaigne et al., 2002). Such routines have been constructed by impregnation, and without relation to previous experiences.

The developmental dynamic, between rhythms and stages

The performance observed within certain complex motor learning depends on the development of cognitive capabilities, which makes this learning possible for a child. Piaget (1956) proposes an evolutionist conception of intelligence where concepts and categories are constructed all along the child development and the individual maturation life-course. For Piaget, learning is an idiosyncratic process that proceeds according to its own laws and rhythms. He attributes great importance to the sensori-motor stage as a basis for developing intelligence by the means of action: one learns first the gesture necessary to act on an object, and it is during this interaction that the properties of that object are identified. Adaptation is the result of the conjunction of "accommodation", which consists of integrating the constraints of the world, and "assimilation" which consists of transforming and interpreting the real according to mental frames. The sensori-motor stage takes place for one year and a half, then the symbolic stage helps a child represent objects, actions and persons in their absence. During this stage, a child is able to produce language and mental images, to draw and to imagine. The case of the permanence of an object (which characterizes the piagetian stage of a 2-year-old child) is questioned as well (Meltzoff and Moore 1998): knowing that a dissimulated object remains does not indicate how to coordinate the movements for reaching this object. A 7–12-year-old child is then able to reason on concepts at the stage of concrete operations, which is followed by the formal operation stages where abstract deductions are possible. The chronology of the piagetian stages is now questioned, but this framework remains quite solid. Meanwhile, recent knowledge generated by psychological research goes further.

"Learning by doing" is a postulate that is developed by the "nativist" school. This school believes that knowledge is present from birth, and thus independent from any interaction with the world: what is present for a 4-month-old infant cannot be issued from learning. In his paper "How To Build a Baby", Mandler (1988) questions these determinist conceptions of development. The recent psychological investigations on babies (Wynn, 1992), considered as competent and intelligent, renew our knowledge of human development. A dynamic development theory proposes that new learning emerges from the reorganization of previous knowledge (Geert, 1994). When a critical level is reached, the existing patterns become unstable, letting new patterns emerge (Thelen and Smith, 1994).

Recent studies reveal the presence of sophisticated perceptive and functional aptitudes (i.e. olfaction, face recognition, non-verbal exchanges, etc.) from an early age. A baby can be considered as an intelligent subject capable of (1) orienting the attention, (2) perceiving details changing in the environment, and (3) elaborating forms of representations in order to understand laws determining the neighbouring world (i.e. physical properties of objects, regular social laws of interactions, etc.). Baillargeon (2000) formulates the "paradigm of disappointed wait", where 4-month-old babies show a faculty for identifying an event which is structured, new or strange. From these three rules emerges knowledge and the piagetian postulate of prehension–vision coordination as a basis for understanding the world is questioned. What appears in these findings is that babies have the faculty of relationship learning, where young subjects are able to (1) extract invariants, to (2) construct categories, and to (3) distinguish what is appertaining to those categories or not.

To summarize, one admits nowadays that young babies possess certain early forms of representation and abstraction. The frontiers between pre-reflexive and symbolic thinking are not so clearly identified and separate. Thinking is a multiple competency that evolves according to peculiar rhythms. Bruner (1987) distinguishes an "inactive" representational system (linked with action) and an "iconic" system that serves as a basis for the symbolic representational system. Karmiloff-Smith (1992, 2001) distinguishes two processes involved within subject development: (1) a progressive modularization (which consists of specializing the general capacities) and (2) a re-describing process (where implicit information becomes progressively explicit to the cognitive system). Three-year-old children show an implicit knowledge of notions like the gravity centre but cannot explain it. While interacting with the environment, the child explores a "personal action theory" where objects are experienced as balanced on their gravity point. The stages of development which follow let the implicit knowledge be "re-described" and generalized, so that they become conscious and accessible to reasoning according to the situated context. Building on Gesell's theory of "reciprocal interweaving" (1933), Fagard and Pezé (1997) develop studies on the alternating phases of developmental dissociation between action and perception and the growth of interdependence between the activities of the body parts.

Finally, development is conceptualized as a non-linear process of acquisition, made of ruptures, latencies, discontinuities (Roberton and Langendorfer, 1980) and inhibition phenomena. One can formulate the idea that mental operations must be understood and mastered several times during development in order to be acquired in various contexts. All the developmental stages suggest that during the different reorganizations of the structural phases, the child becomes sensible to new environmental changes while he/she explores new modes of perceptive treatment. The brain is continuously in formation, in relation with new perceptions and new perceptivo-motor learning. So, new learning implicates a mutual reorganization of the perceptive, cognitive, affective and sensori-motor systems, which are interdependent.

From these findings emerge several implications for a physical education teacher. First, one must accept the idea that development can no longer be thought of as a continuous and passive process; if growing is not sufficient for being in the mood for learning, then organizing favourable dispositions for learning is no more efficient. The difficulty is to integrate the subject activity into a set of adaptation strategies, where the subject develops motor learning through action. Secondly, it is necessary to build this knowledge on the previous structures at disposal from birth.

Which role does prior knowledge play for expert-novice students? How to reconsider the "error" status?

All learning begins with an already existing knowledge, so called "prior knowledge". So, the postulate of a "newborn" student is disallowed, because one must take into account the prior structures that determine perception and interpretation. Knowledge construction never starts from ground zero; it is structured into networks organized around powerful ideas, personal and cultural experiences (Rovegno, 1999). Prior knowledge influences how students integrate new knowledge, its restructuring and its grounding (Good, 1996). Prior knowledge may facilitate learning, but sometimes also slows it down. In this case, it becomes necessary to first inhibit prior knowledge and to question the previous found solutions in order to find a new reasoning. For problem solving, contextualized skills are not equally intelligent according to the experience one disposes. Being intelligent presumes being able to face a novel situation, and automating the assimilated information both at a certain time. The rule of routines consists of lightening the weight of the mental charge.

Hoc (1987) observes that novice computer programmers have the tendency to imagine particular cases and to treat each case separately. On the contrary, experienced programmers elaborate categories of cases characterized by common properties and by more general problem solving procedures. The difficulty for the physical education teacher is to identify and to recognize the existence and the structure of previous knowledge. In a teacher-centred attitude, the natural posture is to refuse to recognize the existence of that previous knowledge, so that the intervention can be justified. The classical procedure consists of defining the subject motor behaviour by the technical failures and by a negative description of "what is not acquired or realized".

For the constructivist approach, on the other hand, the existence of prior knowledge is linked with the logic of the subject. So, the notion of "error" is non-permissible. Within the self-regulated learning conception, so-called errors have a specific status and play an important role. The idea of "correction" itself is dropped to zero, because each behaviour, each produced movement appears to be significant from the producer/actor point of view. As a consequence, the purpose of assessment is neither to determine what is right or wrong, nor to privilege a suitable solution from an external point of view. Each produced act being considered as meaningful and so valuable, the difficulty lies in interpreting these productions that inform the teacher about the process and the product engaged while learning. It does not mean that self-evaluation is the natural and automatic issue for appreciating the student's learning outcomes; it means that one must consider the produced acts in relation with the singular, the intended actions, and the underlying strategies. Adopting this attitude, the teacher has to interpret not only the behaviour, but to speculate on the relation between aspects of the meaningful action. This speculation consists in formulating a plausible hypothesis of action foundation and variables from a unique student's point of view. These hypotheses are validated or not during the following actions by crossing all indices of learning. In return, the student is not required to anticipate being rewarded for an idea or a motor production, but discovers that there are more or less adapted answers, and that, according to the constraint system, there are different solutions linked with several decisional opportunities. From these mental speculations on action emerges a knowledge-in-action valuable at a certain moment of the subject development. According to these assumptions, one must reconsider the notion of error as a "mistake" indicative of a key stage of learning and neither as a failure to find the right answer nor as a gap from the expected norm.

Perceiving is interpreting a situated action

Perception is the capacity that helps an organism to interpret action. It serves as a basis for recognizing the environment according to information given by the senses (Varela, Thompson and Rosch, 1991). The evolution of perceptual processes is widely determined by the nature of sensorial experiences (Schmuckler, 1993). Information not only needs to be employed automatically for motor control, but also needs to be interpreted in terms of objects and events.

Corbetta and Thelen (1996) formulate the hypothesis that there is a difference between "perceiving for detecting information" and "perceiving information useful for acting". The function of

information determines the way it is interpreted and incorporated within action; perception is fundamentally linked with action projects and intended actions (Turvey and Fitzpatrick, 1993). Every motor act, directed according to an object, needs to be recognized and identified before, during, and after the action progress. Recent contributions of semiotics move the language conceptions from the rapport between words and things (i.e. the question of the reference and of the univocal meaning of a word) to the intersubjective relationship of a subject to a situated action (Gernsbacher, 1994). Arnheim (1966), for instance, asserts "object forms do not exist, they are perceived".

The order principle is a property of the human thought:

> We call order the coincidence, partial or complete, of the perceiving with a model. From this results that an image can be ordered by one onlooker (who disposes of the model) and is not ordered by another one (who does not disposes of this model). It is the reader who constructs the interpretation. (Groupe μ, 1992: 41)

Finally, perceiving is the semiotic act of a "meaning-maker", and the notion of form and of object is not objective: it is at best a compromise of the environmental reading.

Thus, human perception and knowledge are doubly determined by object and interpretation, by the claim of the subject matter and of the perceiver's perspective. Information on object colours, for example, is not contained within their physical description, as complete as it may be, but is reserved for subjects to experience them. This is the case for Daltonian persons who "translate" the visual lack of red and green colours in greys of different degrees of darkness. Without experiencing the colours, they cannot choose their suits according to the same subjective taste as others.

One can distinguish three stages of the perception: (1) coding information at a non-conscious level, (2) bringing together and structuring information, (3) emerging representations from a cognitive process. For example, a subject recognizes more easily his/her own walk represented by moving point joints than someone else's. This means that a subject can transpose motor information onto visual representations, without being able to justify and to explain precisely or consciously the conditions of this process. Conceptions of time or of space, which deeply determine game strategies, for instance, have to be constructed within action. If time or space is a learned experienced construction, the subject constructs these conceptions in relation with associated pragmatic action strategies.

According to Searle (1980), the capability of producing representations exists within human brain.

This author used a brilliant example (called the "Chinese Room") to explain the notion of understanding by means of construction. A subject placed within a closed room is expected to answer questions about a story formulated in Chinese. An experimenter transmits his/her Chinese written questions, knowing that the subject does not know Chinese. But a handbook explaining rules of sentence construction helps associate answering characters with questioning characters. It is probable that the subject will be able to give meaningful answers without ever understanding the Chinese characters, but we cannot consider that he/she understands Chinese! According to that example, we can assume that a subject may be able to answer questions pertinently without being able to understand the discourse.

The same process can be transposed to motor learning. The student involved in an action may produce gestures without being able to attribute a meaning to them. This may happen when a drill to develop motor skills by repetition and error corrections is proposed to a basketball player (i.e. realizing a tactical combination, shooting toward the basket, etc.). In this case, the repeated gesture seems to be acquired, but when required in a more general context (i.e. during a basketball match), it becomes inappropriate. That is the reason why researchers now try to access the subject meaning attribution on the situated context while players make decisions. To explore this topic, cognitive representations have to be extracted and studied.

A representation is an interiorized model of the environment from a subject point of view. The model concerns objects, actions, or concepts and values. These models contain useful information about the world, and serve as a basis for interpreting, planning and regulating behaviour. In this context, the representations can be partially clarified and verbalized. Cadopi et al. (1997) showed for instance the importance of these representations in the gym and the choreographic domains. In such morpho-cinetic practices where mental images have to be linked with the memorization of long-duration sequences (encoded according to different verbal, visuo-spatial, kinesthesic modes), and with internal models of action, the learning of new movements is determined by the working memory (Baddeley, 1996: 343).

There are three modalities of cognitive representations: mental images, concepts and actions. Mental images are linked with visual perception (i.e. forms, colour, height, space orientation of an object). Conceptual representations are linked with language and concern concepts like movement, speed, stress, dynamic forces. These cognitive processes help interpret the world and are specific for the subject who constructs his/her reality. They are produced by dialogue with the environment, and they define conditions for interpreting this world. Representations are organized in a systemic network that evolves along with experience. A learning organism compares the present situation with former situations, and then there emerges a personal representation of environment and of action on it. In this way, he/she assimilates new information and accommodates knowledge. Rivière and Lécuyer (2002) distinguish three levels of representations: (1) "analogical" representation which is a trans-coded copy of the stimulus, (2) "abstract" representation which allows identification of certain object characteristics (i.e. forms, colours, volumes, etc.) and (3) "symbolic" representation which forms a relationship between a represented object and its arbitrary boundary. It is necessary to seek the level of representation of knowledge in order to know at which age it may occur.

Brentano (1966) assumes that mind representations are not always close to the observed world, but may be "false, absent, incomplete, or create obstacles …". For instance, representing a unicorn (the mythological animal) does not mean that it exists in reality, but that one can represent a certain reality from a certain point of view. In physical education, representations are determinant for motor development, because they organize and orient decision-making. If learning consists of "going from one representation to another", being more complex and more appropriate, the difficulty for the teacher is to identify these representations one at a time in order to take them into account, and to make them evolving. For young students, attributing an intention to an object in order to explain a phenomenon is a typical situation. For example, a novice swimmer learning how to equilibrate on deep water may be afraid of the water "which may swallow him/her". After experiencing actively the Archimedian Principle, this representation evolves into a dynamic notion of body equilibrium, where immersion is active and equilibrium is submitted to efficient action rules.

So, competency for learning motor skills presumes preliminarily transforming representational system so that new possibilities of action may rise up. But representational system is also linked with intentions of action.

Which links are there between intentions and metacognition?

"Intensio" is the property of mental processes that consists in figuring external objects, even if they are not present. Consciousness is mental (as a subjective activity) and physical (a brain property). Thinking, desiring, feeling are the subject's own; no external observer can directly have an understanding of these sensations. Making explicit an intended action helps the subject memorize it (Kosslyn et al., 1990; Hall et al., 1997). Yussen (1985) defines metacognition as mental activity where other mental processes become objects of reflection. Metacognition represents cognition on cognition. Flavell (1987) distinguishes four categories of meta-knowledge: (1) representations of persons and of oneself as student or thinking subject, (2) representations of task constraints, (3) knowledge of strategies, and (4) relationships between these three objects. This definition assumes that prior spontaneous intuitions about personal reasoning, problem-solving, knowledge and competences, represent an authentic knowledge, experienced and assessed while learning activities. A subject developing metacognitive competencies must understand and make explicit links between the procedures of problem-solving, the task objectives, and the realized performance (McBride, 1991). This way, a subject re-elaborates the matter of metacognitive experiences at a higher conceptual level.

Making explicit collective action modes helps enrich metacognitive procedures of reasoning. Awareness competencies developed through metacognitive practices facilitate awareness of actions and emancipation from problem setting (Grangeat, 1997). The subject does not stop with describing the area for problem setting, but reformulates it abstractly in order to distance it from experience. So, the student extracts him/herself from immediate emotion and shifts to a more hypothetico-deductive reasoning for decision making.

In this perspective, language helps develop metacognitive competencies, because it has two functions of representation and communication. According to Bruner (1987), language participates in the constitution of mind, social relationships, to the development of consciousness and the acquisition of reflective activity. Thinking presumes playing with a more or less abstract sign, and calls for vocabulary, terminologies and representations. Knowledge is first grounded on these mental operations. All languages are meaningful, and the culture consists of sense construction (Courtès, 2003). So, language facilitates the conduct of some practices on behalf of the subject according to the pertinent-for-him expressed world.

Mental operations Involved within action: imitation/decision making/generalizing/ inhibiting/memorizing

Traditionally, learning by imitating is considered as a simple operation of copying a ready-made solution. The description of processes involved suggests that this operation is based on observation and reproduction of gesture forms. This conception of learning by imitating is quite basic, and considers only its great time cost. The internal processes involved are rarely understood at a deep level, and one considers usually this mode of knowledge transmission as secondary and low level in respect to its cognitive aspects.

But nowadays we cannot underestimate the complexity of this imitation process. This mental operation consists of (1) observing the motor production, (2) extracting useful and meaningful information, (3) constructing a significant representation of this class of problem, (4) reproducing the understood form of production, and (5) comparing the produced form with the original in order to correct oneself. When confronted with a situation similar to the previous one, the subject is able to recognize the structural similarity and to recall in memory the adapted representation. On the contrary, when confronted with a situation presenting a significant difference, this student will have to find new solutions. So, the former notion of "imitation" is renewed according to a more dynamic conception of learning that does not order these ways of learning at the bottom of the hierarchy of mental operations. But yet the problem of learning-by-imitating is not solved. In fact, when for instance a student tries to reproduce the same gesture as an observed one (i.e. the teacher producing a motor demonstration, a peer explaining by doing, a video data of high-level sportsmen, etc.), the mental processes involved are complex as well.

The mental operation of extracting from a global context the pertinent elements necessary to find solutions and make decisions is more complex as it first appears. While confronted with a problem (Richard, 1998), a subject mobilizes several competencies that concern the plan, the anticipation of the action issue, the formulation of inferences which links effects with causes (i.e. deductive/inductive reasoning) and deal with action guidance. For Fayol (1994), a strategy consists of an integrated sequence of procedures selected in order to be mobilized intentionally. According to Richard, a natural tendency is to import within a new situation the same known procedures adapted to an identified analogous situation. In that case, implicit competencies concern the capacity for modifying one's own point of view about the available information, so that other original solutions may emerge. This changing of the representation of a situation prompts an impasse where no action is possible until the subject is unable to change the representational system. In that case, the condition for finding a solution supports the change of the situation interpretation, and mobilizes the "divergent mental operation". This creative process proposes elaborating new links for finding unexpected solutions. Richard assumes that the efficient subjects are the ones able to memorize the impasse situation, to recognize this status, and to memorize the solutions in order to avoid a reappearance of the impasse. So, reasoning efficiently consists of being aware of critical moments where useful and determinant information is available. These moments often arise in the case of discordance between projected events and observed events. But the case of similar situations, where ready-made solutions may be used, must be studied too.

If intellectual skills consist of applying general rules to varied situations, the process is not the same for motor skills. In fact, the movements acquired within a general programme are all specific of a particular context, and relatively few are transferable from one sport to another, from one motor skill to another (i.e. passing a ball in game play situation, match situation, exercise situation, etc.), and from one situation to another one. So, the transfer of learning is considered by psychologists as possible only when there is a certain degree of structural similarity between a new learning situation and the original learning situation (Weil-Barais, 1999; Le Moigne, 1999). Situated learning is always bound to the current, the given situation. The questions of transfer and generalizations remain unsolved and limited because cumulative systematic learning is not stabilized. Every co-ordination appears to be specific to a given motor skill, and so cannot be applied generally to the neighbouring ones. The perceptive effects of practice are less specific and general to similar situations than expected. So, the notion of "generalization" of motor skills helps in understanding how a subject modulates the action according to the pertinent-for-him aspects of the context; this learning expresses a "relative variability" of the activity when the situations are quite similar and interpreted so. The acquisitions must be linked with the context and used according to certain variability instead of being reproduced as ready-made answers. The teacher represents the task to help students identify the similarities and common characteristics of a situation. The difficulty for the teacher is to verify whether they are accessible or not for all of the students. The solution in this context is not teaching movements, but generic knowledge linked with the characteristics of the situation (Newell and Barclay, 1982).

The second main idea is that we can no longer consider learning as the simple progressive acquisition of knowledge (Houdé, 1992; Bjorklund and Harnishfeger, 1995), but instead as mobilizing the capability for inhibiting the processes limiting the expression of an emerging knowledge. These interfering processes can be considered as resistances of the representational system for modifying the present functional process. For example, certain representations prevent the student's capability from producing new adaptations. The difficulty is to deconstruct this reasoning for the emergence of more adapted representations favourable to the motor skill evolution. In swimming for instance, a young student must experience the Archimedian principle for accepting to find and construct a static equilibrium on the water surface; the representation of a "deep water where it is possible to sink, to fall down, or to be eaten" has to be inhibited as a condition for learning new competencies. But if the learning emerges from meaning attribution and decision-making, what role does memory play?

Memory and action

The first studies concerning memory focused on the conditions of optimal memorization, and on the identification of its determinants (i.e. repetition frequency, errors, quantity of remembered information, etc.). In this perspective, motor skill acquisition depends upon both the quality of the movements (i.e. efficiency, coordination, synchronization, etc.) and the repetition of the movements. The target is to automate the movement in order to reduce the attention and the informational costs of the task. This basic assumption grounded in the "practice effect" on learning is nowadays completed by the notion of comprehension. This process consists of comparing the obtained results with the projected results of action, and supposes a variability of the practice by means of increasing the complexity level of the task. Edelman (1992) and Changeux (1983) formulate the theory of "neuronal Darwinism" which considers the brain as an evolving and adaptable system subjected to the classical evolution process: variability, selection and withholding appropriate answers. According to these authors, the first selection occurs during human development, and the second one occurs during individual experiences throughout life. The experiences take place within cerebral maps that correspond to representations; their organization evolves constantly according to the previous configurations and the present context. Therefore, memory is sometimes an imaginative construction and a dynamic reconstruction of the experienced world.

The aim of more recent studies lay in determining the memory impact on (1) perception of the present, (2) anticipation shaping, (3) novelty identification, and (4) situation interpretation. Presently, one considers that there exist several different memories according to their nature and their function and to their abstract properties. Memory is no longer considered as a place where information is stored within the brain, but as a property distributed in a network within the complete system. The former dualist conception of memory gives rise to the theory of "working memory" which links verbal and visuo-spatial memories. Three operations can be identified for permanent memory: (1) an "encoding" phase which transforms and stores the perceptive information into durable traces, (2) an "organization" phase, and (3) a "reactivation" phase where traces are recovered.

Two kinds of memories can be identified (Tulving, 1983). Within long-term memory, there is the "semantic" memory and the "episodic" memory. *Semantic memory* concerns a general knowledge not depending upon the variation of the context. Alternatively, *episodic memory* is strongly linked with a timed and a located context. Present results of research put the stress on memory that appears to be grounded on abstractions generated from concrete lived episodes. For instance, a word like "[to] run" progressively acquires its semantic properties through the multiple contexts encountered. In return, "understanding" its meaning implicates a great diversity of contexts and a repetition of contextual episodes containing in each a part of the whole sense. This distinction has an implication for the distinction between "declarative knowledge" and "procedural knowledge".

If learning outcomes are individually constructed, how is it possible to assess the whole and its parts? On a constructivist basis, there is no unique conceivable reference point and no system of measurement based on objectified comparisons of achievement. This does not mean that assessing learning is impossible. Some authors consider that a solution is peer observation (Gréhaigne and Godbout, 1998). But giving a student the power to appreciate peer's produced behaviour assumes that the student him/herself constructs relevant indicators of progress and of achievement, and is able to interpret the processes involved from his/her point of view. Through comparison, different interpretations (teacher, observer and concerned practitioner points of view) may emerge as "plausibly right" judgement on motor production. The difficulty is not to accede to *the* truth about the observed motor skills, but to compose a plausible interpretation by crossing the observed facts with intentions, cognitive strategies, prior knowledge, representational systems, critical events, emotional and energetic aspect – in a few words – the subject single logic of action. From these complex speculations, the teacher extracts a personal interpretation that will direct decision-making as the teacher devises ways to tap into how a student constructs his/her own learning.

Social interactions, shared meaning and co-construction of knowledge

Vygotsky (2000) gives great importance to sociocultural influences on the learning process. For the early 20th Century Russian School, language is developed first through a social phase where a child learns vocabulary and the grammar structures, and then develops an internalization phase where concepts are constructed. The meaning construction links a dialogue between (1) the intentions and the thinking formation of the message producer, and (2) elaboration by the interpretant, linking prior knowledge, intentions and expectations, felt emotions (Wellman, 1990), the representational system available, and the relationship with the transmitter (Fayol, 1997). Lave and Wenger (1991) introduce the notion of "legitimate peripheral participation in communities of practice". We can assume that meaning is co-constructed because meaning is shared during the interactions with the meaningful social context.

These ideas hold major implications for physical education. The instructional setting is not only the produced teaching act, but is appropriately re-interpreted by the student who, doing this operation, gives the teacher information about its understood meaning. In return, the teacher reformulates, or not, the instructions in order to reduce the ambiguity of the situation. By this reciprocal process a shared system of expectations is developed where students and teacher seek to reduce the ambiguity of the intended learning, and reduce the level of meaning uncertainty.

The hermeneutic paradigm generated by the recent philosophy of mind (Peacocke, 1983) helps understanding how a person constructs meanings in relation with the context. The research domain concerns "mind reading" where mental states are studied, foreseen and inferred for explaining the intentional behaviours. This mind theory designates the subject capability for understanding and generating representations (Flavell, 1988). Every language act must be interpreted, read, decoded, and included with a signification network within a singular context. That is what one calls the "semiotic of reception" (German Constanz School). It is the interpretative activity of the subject that allows him/her to attribute a sense to the perceived forms, according to his/her own framework of references, and to the interpretative competency (Barbier et al., 2000). This assertion postulates the singular character of the reception of any message. Perceiving and interpreting the teaching activity (i.e. gesture, verbal instructions, etc.) depends upon the student reading competencies. These competencies are acquired, elaborated and constructed by learning and are eminently social and cultural (Vallacher and Newak, 1997). They represent a proper knowledge of the "learner job" (Perrenoud, 1995).

In this context, learning can be re-defined as a participative production of construction in relation with the context. The interpretation process leans on the structured/structuring perception that models and orders the meaning within the semantic area at the subject's disposal. This meaning elaboration depends on the construction by the subject of a semic model. The semiotic German School of "Aesthetic of reception", formulates the concept of "*expectation horizon*" (Iser, 1975; Jauss, 2001). This concept is based on the following assumption: every interpretative act consists in anticipating actively the sequences of language production, and in reading the plausible meanings of the communication according to the produced effects. The reception of an object does not first match an organized knowledge, but instead felt impressions and sensations.

In the theory, the student includes the teacher's instructions within an expectation horizon that allows him/her to speculate on an action and on the purchased content knowledge. The interpreting subject attributes a meaning and a particular expectation to the available message within the environment he/she interprets. This way, he/she structures the information according to his/her representations and experiences, his/her knowledge, and finally according to his/her interpretative competences. When confronted with other interpretation systems produced by peers, a student has to re-elaborate the thinking while speaking and expressing oneself, in order to be understood, to exchange reflections, to interact for finding common solutions, to confront action strategies, to argue or to convince and so on. The key to this pedagogical process lies in the sharing of this semantic co-constructed world. It assumes the existence of a common code of communication that is co-elaborated throughout the teaching/learning process (i.e. in swimming, where a teacher has to use non verbal codes of communication for giving feedback to immerged swimmers).

Towards a change of status in PE research on motor learning

In this section, we will discuss possible modifications to physical education research required by the recent shift of the scientific paradigm outlined above.

From an internal to an external validity of research (from experimental psychology to a phenomenological approach)

The *positivist school* attributes to the material environment an existence in itself. The access to the "world out there" is a discovery made possible with experimental appropriated methods; the science purpose is to conduct positively the rational way to give order to this world. Following this approach, human thinking would be content to extract information from supposed reality: science produces knowledge independent from opinions and beliefs. In contrast, the *idealist school* postulates that truth is in principle unattainable and that the world is a subject interpretation and construction. All interpretation is built and produced by thinking; perception is a semiotic process. Since reality in any objective sense is in principle inaccessible to human beings, there can be no absolute truth and no absolute knowledge. This knowledge emerges from the experienced world (the "inner-world"), is highly contextualized, and depends upon the subject's reality construction.

Nowadays, the efficiency of a motor skill is no longer attributed to the gesture itself, but to the precision of the functioning of the different cognitive operations that contribute to their construction. The scientific interests shift from the study of the gesture techniques (i.e. describing elementary movements in terms of segment moving and of motor skills) to the identification of the different processes involved (i.e. the context interpretation, the knowledge-in-action used, the intended strategies, the representational cognitive system, etc.). Although phenomenological epistemology and semiotics can serve as theoretical bases for constructivism, their potential for enriching constructivist theory and research in physical education has only recently begun to be explored. Access to language (verbal as motor productions) is a determinant tool for understanding the functioning learner. If language is not indispensable for thinking, as studies on aphasic persons show, one cannot reach a symbolic level of operations without language. So, language creates neither thought nor abstraction, but it is a formidable tool for exploring the mental universe of the subjects.

The development of discursive pragmatics as a science helps us understand the relationship between signs and interpretations. An interpreter of a language act (like a gesture) determines its meaning within a particular context, but the interpretation attributed by this subject often goes beyond its narrow limits in a linguistic sense. So, the signification of an utterance is the result of a process that consists more of meaning creation than of information selection. Language is a set of strategies used by a subject in order to structure social action, to control and to realize the exploration of the social world by means of communication (Bernicot, 1992; Reboul and Moeschler, 1994; Verschueren, 1995). The communicative intention must be considered according to the Grice "principle of pertinence". This theory assumes that each successful language production (verbal and non-verbal language) corresponds with the speaker's communicative intention; the consequence is that a non-literal communication must be unambiguous and studied according to the produced effects of the indirect language acts (Nachon and Mahut, 2002).

These scientific studies open up the physical education research paradigm to understanding student activity from the student point of view. Indeed, new investigation methodologies for investigation are being elaborated, which link thinking and learning (Vermersch, 1995; Griffey, 1996; Chi, 1997).

Importance of the authentic complex context

The definition of the context widens the simple focus on the teacher's effect as *the* condition for learning. In fact, the teaching/learning system contains the conception of a dynamic where knowledge is co-constructed within the interaction. So, the traditional representation of a teacher providing the "ready-to-learn knowledge" to a passive student is updated. The context represents a resources/constraints system where a student confronted with a task has to elaborate adaptation strategies. The effective-environmental performance is linked to the action strategy (i.e. the rapport of strength emerging from a game play) and is the condition of this success. Alternatively, the isolated-skill performance (like a two-hand overhead pass) is considered as inoperative when extracted from the environmental needs of the play. The context presents different natures of constraints: physical (i.e. normalized space, aquatic element, etc.), emotional (i.e. subjective risks, competitive stress, etc.), social (i.e. interacting with others in order to plan a collective strategy), energetic (i.e. mobilizing energetic resources during a physical effort), and cognitive (i.e. analysing a problem area, speculating on plausible action outcomes, sustaining the awareness). The authentic learning context, organized and shaped by the teacher, is re-interpreted by the student who defines the right-for-him/her strategy.

Application to practice/policy: action theory in physical education – towards a renewal of the teaching/learning system?

The motor learning domain must now transform questions of concepts and processes into those of practice and perspectives. This challenge supports consideration of professional practices in physical education not as the application of the products of scientific research, but in a dialectic relationship between action and theories. One can define the teaching process as the set of decisions, intentionally conceived, planned and regulated by a teacher, oriented to the facilitation of motor learning. In

return, learning builds from a reading process, and consists of interpreting the task system in order to develop a strategic reflection linked with action.

Learning as a new temporal stability/disequilibrium/ reconstruction

The thermodynamic principle of homeostasy assumes that a system spends more energy by maintaining a common functioning than by accepting to change (Atlan, 1979; Geert, 1994, 1998). Considering the student as an "autopoietic system", this economy principle works on the human being; the student often spends more energy by resisting to learning (and accepting a provisory change) than by learning something new. So, in accordance with constructivist theory, one can consider that introducing a problem within informal student activity is a fundamental condition for modifying his/her behaviour. The constructivist authors speak of "rupture, disorder, problem, obstacles, noise …" and defend the assumption of the necessary disequilibrium organized by the teacher so that the student is forced to adapt by reorganizing prior knowledge. The difficulty, however, is to conceive a "problem solving setting" (Chi, 1987; Brousseau, 1998).

A renewal of the status of content knowledge and subject matter

The questions of "what subject matter is pertinent, how to structure it in difficulty levels and learning times, what is the teacher role while giving instructional settings, etc." cannot be a central problem any longer. The purpose is to move off structured programmes and planned content knowledge for the benefits of the processes involved and of the transformation dynamics. The recent outcomes of scientific studies suggest moving our attention from environment characteristics to student activity, the cognitive competencies involved, the intentions orientating actions, the previous knowledge-in-action, the symbolic representations based on language production and the mental strategies in relation to action. This does not mean that one must pick and choose unconnected collections of subjective impressions. The purpose is to incorporate this precious information about the subject activity into a teaching system.

Objects of knowledge/knower of objects

The knowledge construction process never starts at zero, but always has its basis in an already-existing structure. This conception is radically different from an all-ready-made knowledge pre-constructed by the teacher. In fact, postulating the pre-existent prior knowledge presumes that it will serve as a basis for interpreting and constructing former knowledge. The reflexive comprehension of one's own learning process becomes both a dynamic and a structuring element in learning itself. In return, the emerging knowledge becomes the basis for future learning. Thus, according to the radical empiricists, knowledge does not pre-exist to the student activity, but is constructed within action.

The consequence of such a learning conception is that the active participation of the student is required. In these conditions, the contents to be learned are motivating when linked with the inner experiences of the student. The difficulty is to find a significant relationship between previous knowledge and new knowledge. McPherson (1993a,b) and Abernethy et al. (1993) distinguish between (1) *declarative knowledge* ("What to do") and (2) procedural knowledge ("How to do"). *Declarative knowledge* corresponds to facts, theories, events and objects as sports rules, technique vocabulary, gameplay strategies, and history of body techniques. It includes nodes (facts, concepts, or theories) that connect with other nodes relationally and hierarchically in networks. This knowledge can be mobilized out of action context. *Procedural knowledge* concerns the way a task must be realized. It is considered to be production systems arranged as condition–action pairs that operate as if–then conditional propositions. It is analysed in terms of hypothetico-deductive reasoning: "if" I produce this action (conditional rules), "then" the corresponding action effects may be … (consequences). This hypothetico-deductive reasoning being intentional or not, consciously or explicitly, exists independently from the expertise level of practice. But its complexity level is indicative of a certain degree of experience, of maturity and of expertise. So, status of knowledge is different according to the theoretical conception. The consequence is a modification of the status of the student.

From a reproducing student to a "creative" actor

The mental activities involved while elaborating action strategies support several cognitive operations like analogy, hypothetico-deductive formulation, induction/deduction, knowledge generalization, and memorization of situated cases. These operations help determine the action strategies and validate their pertinence in context.

The consequence of such a change is that the student's attitude moves from a reproductive intention to a creative attitude. The mental operation of creation consists of extracting oneself from the pre-established reasoning in order to find original ways of reasoning. The creation of new ways of learning mobilizes the "divergence mental operation" (Richard, 1998) that considers the establishment of new links between prior knowledge and the present situation. So, being creative presumes the existence of methodical habits of reasoning and the production of unusual solutions from which one modifies the net of meaning connections. The dialectic process consists to giving up the former functioning and to produce original links. This reasoning helps to elaborate means–ends issues that are dialectical, privileging the linking of prior experiences with plausible heuristics (Perelman, 1970; Grize, 1983; Peirce, 1984). The argumentation called in order to justify and to ground the decision-making process represents a proper object of study where the theoretical frameworks are extracted from argumentative rhetorics.

From a manager-teacher to a reflective practitioner

As we have argued, the teacher's attitude must be centred on the learning processes and not only on the acquisition of "correct" answers. Organizing the learning process does not consist of preparing a perfect instructional setting by foreseeing the variable mastering and validating the correct answers (which gives the teacher security), but of being aware of the necessity for adapting with student reasoning to promote evolving understanding.

According to this conception of learning, teaching strategies consist in proposing to students (1) the discovery of *the* tactical skill that applies in a specific situation or (2) the suitable personal tactical skills. The first option would be associated with an indirect teaching approach, combining both a centred subject matter and a student-centred perspective. Knowledge is an external reality and exists independently of the student's cognitive activity. In this perspective, the teacher's purpose is to manipulate the variables of the task system (i.e. identifying the nature and the impact of the variable, prioritizing the level of the task constraint, grading the level of the task difficulty, etc.), in order to make the right motor skills appear.

Within the radical constructivist conception, the teaching strategy consists of proposing to students the construction of suitable personal tactical skills that apply in a specific situation (there may be more than one from the student point of view). The knowledge constructed is the result of the interaction between the cognitive activity and environmental interpretation. In this highly situated action, the subject explores different plausible solutions to solve the constraints of a particular task. The consequence is that it is harmful to try to structure the student learning on the basis of a transmission/reception model by means of instructions. Meanwhile, the learning may be facilitated by the opportunity given by the teacher to construct/deconstruct/reconstruct knowledge and meaningful acts.

So, the professional conception of the physical education teacher is radically different. On one side, the practitioner is considered as a class manager and plan elaborator, where uncertainty is reduced at the benefits of the emergence of the desired motor skill. Conversely, the practitioner is a reflective interpreter of the student learning outcomes, where the expertise consists of defining the area of the problem to be solved and of elaborating a hypothetico-deductive reasoning on intended effects and observed facts. Therefore, the teacher's expertise is no more defined as being able to realize the projected pre-established plans, but as co-constructing the knowledge with the student. The implications for physical education teacher training and recruitment are most important.

Major trends and future directions

The effort for integrating the renewed learning theories gave rise to a large number of publications centred on the teaching process. Allison and Barrett (2000) try to help teachers construct a meaningful educational experience with children's physical education. Calling upon the constructivist approach as a theoretical framework, they produce "teacher practice stories" in order to expand their understanding of the pedagogical concepts. But the target remains on the relation between the produced actions and the exercises being planned during the following lessons. Their expanded movement framework (outlined in Figure 3 of Allison and Barrett, 2000, p. 49) consists of describing a movement from an external point of view, according to the four categories expansion (body, space, effort and relationships). Once again, the teacher describes the learning activity.

A renewal of physical education teacher education

Teaching behaviours are traditionally focused on "how" to teach, and these actions are identified and modelled within the physical education teacher's education programme. Several professional competencies can so be described. For instance, "providing appropriate feedbacks to students" belongs to these preoccupations, and focusing on the description of their forms, frequency, ideal moment, and nature.

"Framing the pedagogical content knowledge within a developmental perspective" identifies the pertinent content, prioritizing the emergencies, elaborating a progression from the simple to the complicated, taking into account the child development, and constructing assessment tools. "Managing a class group" takes into account the relationship and the motivations of each student. All these teacher preoccupations are focused from a professional point of view (knowledge, beliefs, values and perceptions), and try to give answers to the encountered problems of the teaching practice. Allison and Barrett (2000: 28) assume that "meaning derived from functional movements is related to its use in achieving its stated purpose". According to these authors, learning is considered as valuable if it corresponds with the teacher's projected actions.

Challenging these authors' interpretations, we might argue instead that a constructivist approach to learning does not consist of answering the following question, "Are the students making personal meaning from the educational experiences that I plan and provide?" The question is, "How does a student construct the pertinent-for-him strategy, and how can we assist him to achieve the efficient-for-him actions?" So, the constructivist approach is based on the analysis of the student activity, from the student's point of view. The basic principle is that the teacher's logic of expectations is divergent from the student's logic of action strategies. The consequence is that if one makes these logics meet, one must relocate the proper reasoning and take the risk of interpreting the situation differently.

The professional activity of a teacher is nowadays considered by ergonomics and working psychology as a workstation where problems extracted from the practice must be solved (Barbier, 1996; Pastré, 2002). The former modelling of this job, based on the student task planning and on a quite rational conception of the professional activity, leads to a more "fuzzy logic" where "knowledge-in-action" is involved. In this perspective, teaching does not consist of reducing the uncertainty of the student behaviour (i.e. correcting the unwanted behaviour), but of interpreting the student activity and of providing improvement situations in relation with the encountered problem. So, understanding of the "problem area" (Schön, 1983, 1987, 1991) is a key determinant for elaborating a solution.

In this perspective, a pedagogical setting can be redefined as (1) a structured *configuration* that is described while the teacher defines the instructional setting, and (2) a *potential* that is the teacher/student disposition of different evolving factors (Jullien, 1996). In this setting, the teacher's expertise consists of identifying the favourable factors present within the evolving setting in order to draw up an action plan. In this paradigm, the "functioning register" (Barbier, 2000) represents the way a practitioner confronted with a task, develops solving strategies according to previous frames of reference, prior knowledge, representational system, former memorized experiences and so on. This competency determines regularities that allow a certain form of foreseeable decisions. In return, this register helps position the practitioner within a field of professional and practical specific preoccupations. One can model different levels and domains of functioning registers according to the category of the problem being solved. In return, it is possible to predict the problem-solving strategy of a practitioner if the problem-solving setting presents similar conditions with the previous experience (Mahut et al., 2000).

Limits of the cognitive approaches: central NS approach/interactive situated learning

Learning that is exclusively oriented to singular useful situations cannot be the purpose of the school, which has to produce "decontextualized" subject matter. The consequence is that students, who do not understand nor accept learning "out-of-context knowledge" at the expense of "ready-made knowledge", may be at odds with that logic, and consequently be labelled as an academic failure.

Conclusion

If physical education is more than the development of physical skills, then cognitive and emotional implications should be of paramount importance considering a holistic view of the subject. A physically educated child develops through his or her life span, the competencies for understanding and decision-making in relation with the evolving environment and the personal resources at a given time; the learning process succeeds when it never ends. The rather heterogeneous background of theories and productions about motor learning provides an agglomeration of interactive – somewhat mutually compatible, sometimes partly contradictory – epistemologies. For instance, there is a full co-operation of the cognitive and the sensori-motor functions, which gives way to the complementarities of the ecologic and the cognitive theories.

The relationship between major findings and practices are complex and dialectic, so that the scientific knowledge produced helps in understanding educational facts in their complexity, and that these influence reciprocally the scientists posture. As Terhart says (2003: 41–42), "there is no new theoretical approach in general didactics … 'new' constructivist didactics in the end is merely an assembly of long-known teaching methods (albeit not practiced!)".

But one can now consider that the needs of praxis may turn into useable concepts of action, and vice versa. The present scientific knowledge as it emerges helps support practices with new justifications and illuminations!

References

Abernethy, B., Thomas, K. and Thomas, J. (1993). Strategies for improving understanding of motor expertise. In J. Strakes and F. Allard (Eds.), *Cognitive issues in motor expertise* (pp. 159–188). Amsterdam: Elsevier Science.

Adams, J.A. (1992). *Revue historique et critique de la recherche sur l'apprentissage, la rétention et le transfert d'habiletés motrices.* Paris: Revue EPS.

Allison, P.C. and Barrett, K.R. (2000). *Constructing childrens physical education experiences.* Needhal Heights MA : Allyn & Bacon.

Allison, S. and Thorpe, R. (1997). A comparison of the effectiveness of two approaches to teaching games within physical education. A skills approach versus a games for understanding approach. *The British Journal of Physical Education,* Autumn, 9–13.

Arnheim, R. (1966). In Groupe μ. (1992). *Traité du signe visuel. Pour une rhétorique de l'image.* Paris: Seuil.

Atlan, H. (1979). *Entre le cristal et la fumée.* Paris: Seuil.

Baddeley, A. (1996). La mémoire de travail. Interface entre mémoire et cognition. In D.L. Schacter and E. Tulving (Eds.), *Systèmes de mémoire chez l'animal et chez l'homme* (pp. 343–357). Marseille: Solal.

Baillargeon, R. (2000). La connaissance du monde physique par le bébé. Héritages piagétiens. In O. Houdé and C. Meljac (Eds.), *L'esprit piagétien* (pp. 55–87). Paris: PUF.

Barbier, J.M. (1996). *Savoirs théoriques et savoirs d'action.* Paris: PUF.

Barbier, J.M., Clot, Y., Dubet, F. et al. (2000). *L'analyse de la singularité de l'action.* Paris: PUF.

Bernicot, J. (1992). *Les actes de langage chez l'enfant.* Paris: PUF.

Berthoz, A. (1997). *Le sens du mouvement.* Paris: Odile Jacob.

Bjorklund, D.F. and Harnishfeger, K.K. (1995). The evolution of inhibition mechanisms and their role in human cognition and behavior. In F.M. Dempseter an C.J. Brainerd (Eds.), *Interference and inhibition in cognition.* San Diego, CA: Academic Press.

Brentano, F. (1930/1966). *The True and the Evident,* transl. by Roderick Chisholm, Ilse Politzer, and Kurt Fischer. London: Routledge.

Brousseau, G. (1998). *Théorie des situations didactiques.* Paris: La pensée sauvage.

Bruner, J. (1987). *Le développement de l'enfant, savoir faire, savoir dire.* Paris: PUF.

Cadopi, M., Jean, J., Ille, A. and Albert, J.C. (1997). Mental practice and improvement of motor skills by young gymnasts working on the uneven bars. *European Yearbook of Sport Psychology,* 1: 200–216.

Changeux, J.P. (1983). *L'homme neuronal*. Paris: Fayard.

Chi, M.T.H. (1987). Representing knowledge and metaknowledge: implications for interpreting metamemory research. In F.E. Weinert and R.H. Kluwe (Eds), *Metacognition, motivation and understanding* (pp. 239–266). Hillsdale, NJ: Lawrence Erlbaum Associates.

Chi, M.T.H. (1997). Quantifying qualitative analyses of verbal data : a practical guide. *The Journal of Learning Sciences, 6*: 271–315.

Chi, M.T.H., Bassrock, M., Lewis, M.W., Reimann, P., and Blaser, R. (1989). Self-explanations: how students study and use examples in learning to solve problems. *Cognitive Science, 13*: 145–182.

Clancey, W.J. (1997). *Situated cognition: on human knowledge and computer representations*. Cambridge: University Press.

Cobb, P. (1994). Constructivism in mathematics and science education. *Educational Researcher, 23*: 4.

Corbetta, D. and Thelen, E. (1996). The developmental origins of bimanual coordination: a dynamic perspective. *Journal of Experimental Psychology: Human Perception and Performance, 22*: 502–522.

Courtès, J. (2003). *La sémiotique du langage*. Paris: Nathan.

Damasio, A. (1995). *L'erreur de Descartes*. Paris: O. Jacob.

Descartes, R. (1667/1979). *Méditations métaphysiques*. Paris: Flammarion.

Dodds, P. (1994). Cognitive and behavioural components of expertise in teaching physical education. *Quest, 46*: 153–163.

Doyle, W. (1986). Classroom organization and management. In M.C. Wittrock (Ed.), *Handbook of Research on Teaching*. New York: Macmillan.

Dretske, F. (1981). *Knowledge and the flow of information*. Cambridge: The MIT Press.

Dretske, F. (1988). *Explaining behavior. Reasons in a world of causes*. Cambridge: The MIT Press.

Duyne, M. and Tomkiewicz, S. (1999). How can we boost IQs of "dull children"?: A late adoption study. *Proceedings of National Academy of Sciences, 96*, 8790–8794.

Eco, U. (1988). *Sémiotique et philosophie du langage*. Paris: PUF.

Edelman, G.M. (1992). *Biologie et conscience*. Paris: O. Jacob.

Ennis, C.D. (1994). Knowledge and beliefs underlying curricular expertise. *Quest, 36*: 164–175.

Ericsson, L. and Simon, H. (1993). *Protocol analysis. Verbal reports as data*. Cambridge (MA): The MIT Press.

Fagard, J. and Pezé, A. (1997). Age changes in interlimb coupling and the development of bimanual coordination. *Journal of Motor Behavior, 29*: 199–208.

Fayol, M. (1994). From declarative and procedural knowledge to the management of declarative and procedural knowledge. *European Journal of Psychology of Education, 9*: 179–190.

Fayol, M. (1997). *Des idées au texte. Psychologie cognitive de la production verbale, orale et écrite*. Paris: PUF.

Flavell, J. (1988). The development of childern's knowledge about mind. From cognitive connections to mental representations. In J. Astington, P. Harris and D. Olson (Eds.), *Developping theories of mind*. New York: Cambridge Press University.

Flavell, J.H. (1987). Speculation about the nature and the development of metacognition. In J. Weinert and R. Kluwe (Eds.), *Metacognition, motivation and understanding*. London: Lea.

Flemming, S. (1994). Understanding "understanding": making sense of the cognitive approach to the teaching of games. *Physical Education Review, 17(2)*: 90–96.

Fosnot, C. (1996). *Constructivism: theory, perspectives, and practice*. New York: Teachers College Press.

Geert, P. van (1994). *Dynamic systems of development: change between complexity and chaos*. New York: Harvester Wheatsheaf.

Geert, P. van (1998). A dynamic system model of basic developmental mechanisms: Piaget, Vygotsky and beyond. *Psychological Review, 105(4)*: 634–677.

Gernsbacher, M.A. (1994). *Handbook of psycholinguistics*. New York: Academic Press.

Gesell, A. (1933). Maturation and the patterning of behavior. In C. Murchison (Ed.), *A handbook of child psychology* (pp. 209–235). Worcester, MA: Clark University Press.

Gibson, E.J. (1979). *An ecological approach to visual perception*. Boston MA: Hougton-Mifflin.

Gibson, E.J. (1984). Perceptual development from the ecological approach. In M. Lamb, A. Brown and B. Rogoff (Eds.), *Advances in developmental psychology III* (pp. 243–286). Hillsdale, NJ: Erlbaum.

Gibson, E.J. (1988). Exploratory behaviour in the development of perceiving, acting and the acquiring knowledge. *Annual Review of Psychology, 39*: 1–41.

Good, T. (1996). Teaching effects and teacher evaluation. In J. Sikula, T.J. Buttery, and E. Guyton (Eds.), *Handbook on research on teacher education* (2nd edition). New York: Simon & Schuster Macmillan.

Goldman, A. (1986). *Epistemology and cognition*. Cambridge: Harvard University Press.

Grangeat, M. (1997). *La métacognition, une aide au travail des élèves*. Paris: ESF.

Gréhaigne, J.-F., and Godbout, P. (1995). Tactical knowledge in team sports from a constructivist and cognitivist perspective. *Quest, 47*: 490–505.

Gréhaigne, J.G. and Godbout, P. (1998). Observation, critical thinking and transformation: three key elements for a constructivist perspective of the learning process in team sport. In R. Feingold, C. Roger Rees, G.T. Barette, L. Fiorentino, S. Virgilio, and E. Kowalski, (Eds.), Education for life. *Proceedings of the AIESEP World Sport Science. Congress* (pp. 109–118). New York: Adelphi University Press.

Gréhaigne, J.F., Richard, J.F., Mahut, N. and Griffin, L. (2002). Reflections on player competencies in team sport. *Journal of Sport Pedagogy, 8(2)*: 22–37.

Griffey, D.C. (1996). The study of teacher cognition in sport pedagogy. In P.G. Schemp (Ed.), *Scientific development of sport pedagogy* (pp. 103–122). Münster/New York: Waxman.

Grize, J.B., Borel, M.J. and Mielville, D. (1983). *Essai de logique naturelle*. Berne: Peter Lang.

Groupe μ. (1992). *Traité du signe visuel. Pour une rhétorique de l'image*. Paris: Seuil.

Hall, C.R., Moore, J., Annett, J. and Rodgers, W. (1997). Recalling demonstrated and guided movements using imaginary and verbal rehearsal strategies. *Research Quaterly for Exercise and Sport, 68(2)*: 136–144.

Herrnstein, R.J. and Murray, C. (1994). *The bell curve: intelligence and class structure in American life*. New York: Free Press.

Hoc, J.M. (1987). *Psychologie cognitive de la planification*. Grenoble: PUG.

Houdé, O. (1992). *Catégorisation et développement cognitif*. Paris: PUF.

Iser, W. (1975). The reading process a phenomenological approach. *In New literary history, 3, 1971-1972. In Warning, R. & co., Munich*: Rezeptionsästetik: Theorie und Praxis.

Jauss, H.R. (2001). *Pour une esthétique de la réception*. Paris: Gallimard.

Jullien, F. (1996). *Traité de l'efficacité*. Paris: Poche.

Kamm, K., Thelen, E. and Jensen, J.L. (1990). A dynamic systems approach to motor development. *Physiology Therapy, 70(12)*: 763–775.

Karmiloff-Smith, A. (1992). *Beyond modularity: a developmental perspective on cognitive science*. Cambridge, MA: MIT Press.

Karmiloff-Smith, A. (2001). *Pathways to language: from foetus to adolescent*. Harvard University Press: Cambridge, MA.

Kant, E. (1965/ 1787). *Critique of pure reason*. New York St Martin's Press.

Kirk, D. and Mc Donald, D. (1998). Situated learning in physical education. *Journal of Teaching in Physical Education, 17*: 376–387.

Kirk, D. and Mc Phail, A. (2002). Teaching games for understanding and situated learning: rethinking the Bunker-Thorpe model. *Journal of Teaching in Physical Education, 21*: 177–192.

Kishner, A.C. and Whitson, D.H. (1997). *Situated cognition. Social, semiotic, and psychological perspectives*. Mahwah, NJ: Lawrence Erlbaum.

Kosslyn, S.M. and Koening, O. (1992). *Wet mind. The new cognitive neuroscience*. New York: Free Press.

Kosslyn, S.M., Margolis, J.A., Barett, A.M., Golknopf, E.J. and Daly, P.F. (1990). Ages differences in imagery abilities. *Child Development, 61*: 995–1010.

Lave, J. and Wenger, E. (1991). *Situated learning: legitimate peripheral participation*. Cambridge: University Press.

Le Moigne, J.L. (1999). *Les épistémologies constructivistes*. Paris: PUF.

Lockman, J.J. and Thelen, E. (1993). Developmental biodynamics: brain, body, behavior connections. *Child Development, 64(4)*: 953–959.

Mahut, N., Outrey, E., Mahut, B. and Gréhaigne, JF. (2000). Professional knowledge and decision making in scholar settings: comparative study on four teacher populations in swimming. *Proceedings of AIESEP* Rockhampton World Conference (AU), 2–6 September.

Magill, R.A. (1994). Introduction. *Quest, 46*: 267–269.

Mandler, J.M. (1988). How to build a baby: on the development of an accessible representational system. *Cognitive development, 3*, 113–136.

McBride, R.E. (1991). Critical thinking- An overview with implications for physical education. *Journal of Teaching in Physical Education, 11*: 112–125.

McBride, R.E. and Cleland, F. (1998). Critical thinking in physical education. *JOPERD, 69(7)*: 42–52.

McPherson, S.L. (1993a). Knowledge representation and decision-making in sport. In J.L. Strakes and F. Allard (Eds.), *Cognitive issues in motor expertise* (pp. 159–188). Amsterdam: North Holland.

McPherson, S.L. (1993b). The influence of player experience on problem solving during batting preparation in baseball. *Journal of Sport and Exercise Psychology, 15*: 304–325.

Meltzoff, A.N. and Moore, M.K. (1998). Object representation, identity, and the paradox of early permanence: steps toward a new framework. *Infant Behaviour and Development, 21(2)*: 201–235

Murray, C. and Herrnstein, R. (1994). *The Bell Curve: intelligence and class structure in American life*. New York: Free Press.

Nachon, M. and Mahut, N. (2002). Lecture et interprétation dans les situations sportives : Approche sémiotique pour la recherche qualitative en sciences du sport. *Recherches Sémiotiques/Semiotic Inquiry, (22)1,2,3*: 71–85.

Newell, K.M. (1991). Motor skill acquisition. *Annual Review of Psychology, 42*: 213–237.

Newell, K.M. and Barclay, C.R. (1982). Developing knowledge about action. In J.A.S. Kelso and J.E. Clark (Eds.), *The development of movement control and coordination* (pp. 175–212). Chichester, UK : John Wiley & Sons.

O'Sullivan, M. and Doutis, P. (1994). Research on expertise: guideposts for expertise and teacher education in physical education. *Quest, 46*: 176–185.

Pascal, B. (1660). *Pensées, oeuvres complètes*. Paris: Seuil.

Pastré, P. (2002). L'analyse du travail en didactique professionnelle. *Revue Française de Pédagogie, 138*: 9–17.

Peacocke, C. (1983). *Sense and content. Experience, thought, and their relations*. Oxford: Clarendon Press.

Perrenoud. P (1995). *Le métier d'élève*. Paris: ESF.

Pillips, D.C. (1995). The good, the bad and the ugly: the many faces of constructivism. *Educational Researcher, 24(7):* 5–12.

Piaget, J. (1956). *La psychologie de l'intelligence*. Paris: Armand Colin.

Piattelli-Palmarini, M. (Ed.) (1980). *Language and learning: the debate between Jean Piaget and Noam Chomsky*. Cambridge, MA: Harvard University Press.

Pierce, C.S. (1984). *Textes anti-cartésiens*. Paris: Aubier.

Perelman, C. and Olbrechts-Tytega, L. (1970). *Traité de l'argumentation: la nouvelle rhétorique*. Paris: Vrin.

Perrenoud, P. (1995). *Le métier d'élève*. Paris: ESF.

Reboul, A. and Moeschler, J. (1994). *Dictionnaire encyclopédique de pragmatique*. Paris: Seuil.

Richard, J.F. (1998). *Les activités mentales*. Paris: Armand Colin. (3rd ed.).

Rivière, J. and Lécuyer, R. (2002). Spatial cognition in young children with spinal muscular atrophy. *Developmental Neuropsychology, 21(3)*: 273–283.

Roberton, M.A. and Langendorfer, S. (1980). Testing the motor development sequences across 9–14 years. In

C.H. Nadeau, R. Halliwell, M. Newell and C. Roberts (Eds.), *Psychology of motor behaviour and sport* (pp. 268–279). Champaign, IL: Human Kinetics.

Rovegno, I. (1999). What is taught and learned in physical activity programs: the role of content. In J.F. Gréhaigne, D. Marchal, and N. Mahut (Eds.), *AIESEP Conference proceedings*, Besançon, France.

Sanders, A.F. (1990). Issues and trends in the debate on discrete/continuous processing of information. *Acta Psychologica, 74*: 123–167.

Schempp, P.G. (1996). Scientific development of sport pedagogy. München/New York: Waxmann.

Schmidt, R.A. (1988). *Motor Control and Learning: A Behavioral Emphasis.* (2nd ed.) (pp. 482–489). Champaign, IL: Human Kinetics.

Schmuckler, M.A. (1993). Perception-action coupling in infancy. In G.J.P. Salvelsbergh (Ed.), *The development of coordination in infancy* (pp. 137–172). Amsterdam: Elsevier Science Publisher BV.

Schön, D.A. (1983). *The reflective practitioner. How professionals think in action.* New York: Basic Books.

Schön, D.A. (1987). *Educating the reflective practitioner.* San Francisco: Jossey-Bass.

Schön, D.A. (1990). *Educating the reflective practitioner: toward a new design for teaching and learning in the professions.* San Francisco, CA : Jossey-Bass.

Schön, D.A. (1991). *The reflective turn: case studies in and educational practice.* New York: Teachers College Press.

Schwager, S. and Labate, C. (1993). Teaching for critical thinking in physical education. *JOPERD,* May-June.

Searle, J.R. (1980). Minds, brain and programs. *Behavioural Brain Science, 3*: 417–457.

Searle, J.R. (1995). *La construction de la réalité sociale.* Paris: Gallimard.

Shannon, C.E. and Weaver, W. (1949). *The mathematical theory of communication.* Urbana, IL: University of Illinois Press.

Sternberg, R.J. (1994) *Encyclopedia of human intelligence.* New York: Macmillan.

Suchman, L. (1987). *Plans and situated actions: the problem of human-machine communication.* Cambridge, UK: University Press.

Terhart, E. (2003). Constructivism and teaching: a new paradigm in general didactics? *Journal of Curriculum Studies, 35(1):* 25–44.

Tête, A. (1994). The mind-body problem. In B. Feltz and D. Lambert (Eds.), *Entre le corps et l'esprit.* Liège: Mardaga.

Thelen, E. (1995). Motor development. A new analysis. *American Psychology, 50(2):* 79–95.

Thelen, E. and Smith, L.B. (1994). *A dynamic systems approach to the development of cognition and action.* Cambridge: The MIT Press.

Temprado, J.J. and Famose, J.P. (1993). Analyse de la difficulté informationnelle et description des tâches

motrices. In J.P. Famose (Ed.), *Cognition et performance.* Paris: INSEP Publication.

Tishman, S. and Perkins, D.N. (1995). Critical thinking and physical education. *JOPERD,* August.

Turner, A.P. and Martinek, T.J. (1992). A comparative analysis of two models for teaching games. *International Journal of Physical Education, 29(4):* 15–31.

Turvey, M.T. and Fitzpatrick, P. (1993). Commentary: development of perception-action system and general principles of pattern formation. *Child Development, 64*: 1175–1190.

Tulving, E. (1983). *Elements of episodic memory.* Oxford: University Press.

Rivière, J. and Lécuyer, R. (2002). Spatial cognition in young children with spinal muscular atrophy. *Developmental Neuropsychology, 21(3).*

Roberton, M.A. and Langendorfer, S. (1980). Testing the motor development sequences across 9–14 years. In: C.H. Nadeau, R. Halliwell, M. Newell and C. Roberts (Eds.), *Psychology of motor behaviour and sport* (pp. 268–279). Champaign, IL: Human Kinetics.

Vallacher, R. and Nowak, A. (1997). The emergence of dynamical social psychology. *Psychological Inquiry, 8(2):* 73–99.

Varela, F., Thompson, E. and Rosch, E. (1991). *The embodied mind: cognitive science and human experience.* Cambridge, MA: MIT Press.

Vermersch, P. (1995). Du faire au dire (l'entretien d'explicitation). *Cahiers Pédagogiques, 336:* 27–32.

Verschueren, J., Östman, J.A. and Blommaert, J. (1995). *Handbook of pragmatics.* Amsterdam: John Benjamins Publishing Company.

Vygotski, L. (2000). *Pensée et langage.* Paris: La Dispute.

Weil-Barais, A. (1993). *L'homme cognitif.* Paris: PUF.

Weil-Barais, A. (1999). *L'homme cognitif.* Paris: PUF.

Wellman, H. (1990). *The child's theory of mind.* Cambridge: The MIT Press.

Werner, P., Thorpe, R. and Bunker, D. (1996). Teaching games for understanding. *JOPERD, 67(1):* 28–33.

Whitall, J. (1991). The developmental effect of concurrent cognitive and locomotor skills: timesharing from a dynamical perspective. *Journal of Experimental Child Psychology, 51:* 245–266.

White, S.R. (2002). Organization model of a constructivist community: a Teilhardian metaphor of educators. *Journal of Educational Tought, 36(2):* 111–128.

Wynn, K. (1992). Addition and subtraction by human infants. *Nature, 358:* 749–750.

Yussen, S.R. (1985). The role of metacognition in contemporary theories of cognitive development. In D.L. Forrest-Presley, G.E. Mackinnon and T.G. Waller (Eds.), *Metacognition, cognition and human performance*, Vol. I (pp. 253–283). Orlando, FL: Academic Press.

3.8 Assessment for learning in physical education

PETER J. HAY

Introduction

Many educationalists, both general (for example, Black and Wiliam, 1998a; Gipps, 1994, 1996; Shepard, 2000) and specific to physical education (for example, Melograno, 1994; Smith, 1997; Veal, 1992a, 1995) acknowledge the significance of assessment in curriculum and pedagogy. Great diversity, however, is evident in the understanding of its definition and purpose in physical education reflecting, to a large extent, the absence of consensus on the constitution and purpose of physical education (Naul, 2003). Irrespective of such divergent perceptions and perspectives, assessment is increasingly becoming an important point of practice, research and philosophical focus within education discussion, the depth and extent of which is not as readily apparent within the physical education academic community. Throughout this chapter a number of key themes are evident which are technically distinct but which must be understood conjointly in order to comprehend the complexities and implications of assessment practice and theory. These themes include perspectives on assessment within contemporary understandings of learning theory, the broad impact of accountability on curriculum and assessment reform and pedagogy, and technical assessment considerations of assessment for learning.

Assessment fundamentally involves the collection of information (Smith, 1997). This information varies in scope and depth, reflecting the process used to collect the information and the purpose for that collection. Veal (1988, 1992a) and Desrosiers et al. (1997) described assessment as the collection of information throughout the teaching and learning process, predicating the interdependence of assessment, curriculum and pedagogy, and learning. Siedentop and Tannehill describe assessment as "a variety of tasks and settings where students are given opportunities to demonstrate their knowledge, skill, understanding and application of content in a

context that allows continued learning and growth" (2000: 179). This is somewhat contrary to the perceptions of some physical education teachers who view assessment as a process for determining grades or levels of achievement through items, tasks or observations at the end of a unit of work (Olrich, 2002; Veal, 1992a).

A distinction needs to be made between assessment, evaluation, and measurement, acknowledging that within practice and within the academic literature semantic contention is evident in the use and understanding of these terms (Black and Wiliam, 1998a,b; Terwilliger, 1998; Wiggins 1998a,b). Tinning et al. (2001) suggest that assessment is a component of the broader concept of evaluation. They define evaluation as the judgement of worth in a broad operational sense including, but not restricted to, programmes, teacher effectiveness and learning quality. Conversely, Veal (1992a) describes a more narrow definition of evaluation, linking it with the collection of summative information, at the completion of a unit work, exemplified by end of unit examinations. Similarly, Melograno (1994) suggests that evaluation refers to the determination of value through the examination and interpretation of information collected via assessment, where assessment is understood as the process of gathering information. Measurement is described by Linn and Gronlund (1995) as the "process of obtaining a numerical description of the degree to which an individual possesses a particular characteristic" (p. 6), often associated with "product" assessment, as opposed to 'process' assessment (Veal, 1995). While acknowledging the necessity for distinction, for the purpose of this chapter, assessment is defined as the collection of information, contextualized by the use of that information.

An uncontested understanding of the purpose of assessment is no less elusive than its definition, the diversity of which reflects the perspectives and interests of a range of educational stakeholders.

Broadfoot and Black (2004) suggest that the purpose of assessment, reflected in policy and practice, is essentially underpinned by context. Decisions concerning who is to be assessed, what is to be assessed, and how the assessment is to occur reflect social, cultural and political contexts and differ according to changes in context. For example, in the classroom assessment provides information for the purpose of giving feedback and enhancing learning. Within the system context assessment provides information on the degree to which students are meeting established standards and as such fulfils the purpose of ensuring teacher accountability for the implementation of the prescribed curriculum. Such differences in purpose may result in different assessment modes being utilized in schools; however, Gipps (1996) suggests that various objectives can be satisfied by the same assessment task.

Two purposes of assessment, broadly and loosely but not necessarily distinctly, within the academic literature are described as assessment for accountability and assessment for learning. Stiggens (2002) suggests that politicians use assessment to increase teacher and student effort. The collection of systemic data holds teachers accountable for their practice and to the dictates of the system authorities. Broadfoot and Black (2004) support this view and suggest that systemic assessment regimes are powerful mechanisms of control. Blackmore (1988) is somewhat stronger in her description of assessment as a political instrument of power. Assessment for accountability is often manifest in large-scale standardized testing (MacNeill and Silcox, 2002; Pearson et al., 2001; Vaughan, 2002). However, recent developments have utilized school-based assessment, founded in contemporary theories of learning, for the purpose of accountability as well as other high-stakes purposes such as certification (Koretz, 1998; Rink and Mitchell, 2002). Assessment for learning was developed as both a reaction to psychometric-based standardized testing (Wiggins, 1998a) and as a result of advances in learning theory in which formative assessment is understood as providing information for feedback, and in which the task itself becomes a learning experience that challenges the students' existing knowledge structures and beliefs, and fosters the active construction of meaning by the students (Shepard, 2000). An assessment for learning paradigm advocates for authentic assessment which refers to contextually relevant and connected tasks that develop and challenge students' higher-order knowledge and skills that can be transferred to contexts beyond the classroom.

Although this chapter is concerned with assessment for learning in physical education, assessment serves purposes beyond assessment for learning that have significant consequences for curriculum, pedagogy and learning in physical education. Besides certification, selection, direction (Natriello, 1987), motivation (Martin et al., 2002), and diagnosis (Carroll, 1994; Mohnsen, 2003), Rink and Mitchell (2002) identify assessment as a powerful influence on curriculum reform, impacting on the definition of the subject area. Similarly, Smith (1997) and Arbogast (2002) identify assessment as a key factor in the definition of physical education. Olrich (2002) supports this understanding of the link between assessment and curriculum definition suggesting that assessment provides information on the degree to which the purposes of physical education have been realized, implying that those purposes are defined by the measures.

A further implication of assessment, implicit to its reformatory role, is the articulation and identification of the valued aspects of the specific and global curriculum. Assessment, particularly in a summative sense and high-stakes context may be viewed as a mechanism through which value is attributed to subjects or aspects of subjects. The connection between the value of a subject and assessment is further substantiated and extended by Hardman and Marshall (2000) who equated the lower status of physical education internationally, with a "lack of official assessment" (p. 15). This point is reiterated by Rink and Mitchell who suggest that "One unintended outcome of the standards, assessment and accountability movement is that any program not included in high stakes state level assessment, for all practical purposes, does not 'count'" (2002: 209). Where this is the case the implications of assessment for learning need to be understood with these broad, potentially competing, implications in mind.

The purpose of this chapter is to review the research and academic theorizing and discussion concerning assessment for learning in physical education. In light of the information presented, suggestions will be made with respect to possible future research directions with a view to better understanding the process and practice of assessment in physical education, enhancing the quality of student learning, and consolidating the place of physical education within schools.

Brief historical perspective

Considering the recognized impact that assessment has on curriculum reform (Hargreaves et al., 2002), the articulation of the valued constructs of a subject (Veal, 1992a), student learning (Shepard, 2000), and future engagement in learning, it is somewhat strange that assessment in physical education has been somewhat neglected by academic researchers. This is further ironic given the substantial interest in assessment in general education research. The following historical perspective on research on assessment in physical education highlights a tendency for research to focus on the practice of assessment as opposed to the impact that assessment has on student learning. Furthermore, researchers have tended to collect data for the investigation of assessment in physical education through surveys, questionnaires and interviews.

Research on assessment in physical education during the 1980s largely focused on the extent to which teachers engaged in assessment practices and the modes of assessment that were being employed by teachers in both the primary and secondary school contexts. For example, Carroll and Macdonald (1981) examined male physical education teachers' perceptions of exams. The research focused on the extent to which examinations were included in male teachers' practice and the perceived value of examinations in physical education. The perceptions of 414 male teachers (predominately from secondary schools) were captured using questionnaires. Assessment was understood as the basis for evaluating the effectiveness of instruction and determining grades. It assumed that learning is dependent upon the curriculum context and content provided by the teacher, ignoring the implications of students' background and prior knowledge as implicating on both learning and the demonstration of the knowledge and skills indicative of learning.

Imwold et al. (1982), in a similar study to Carroll and Macdonald, surveyed 270 physical education teachers, examining the extent to which teachers conducted assessment, the types of assessment employed, and approaches used to determine student grades. This study also found that student grades where largely determined on the basis of observed dispositions. This finding is not dissimilar to those of Hensley et al. (1987) whose research of the assessment practices of 1396 teachers described participation, effort, attitude, sportsmanship and attendance as key factors in the determination of levels of achievement, forming the basis of assessment in physical education. Once again the research methods employed included questionnaires. The research focus on teacher assessment practice, and the constructs used for the determination of grades, was continued by Matanin and Tannehill (1994) who used questionnaires to investigate the perceptions of 11 secondary physical education teachers of the assessment processes and purposes of assessment, the procedures used to assess students, and the consistency between teachers' actions and their beliefs about the assessment process.

Matanin and Tannehill's (1994) interest in the consistency of teachers' practice with their beliefs reflects the research questions of Kneer (1986) and Veal (1988). Kneer, through the use of a series of questionnaires and observations/interviews of 128 teachers, found that the use of formal assessment was lacking in teacher practice. Kneer concluded

that this was due to time constraints, a general disbelief in the necessity of assessment in physical education, and a gap between teachers' knowledge of assessment theory and practice. These findings were substantiated by Veal (1988) who, through observations and formal and informal interviews, also observed a gap between teachers' understanding of assessment theory and practice. Veal (1988), consistent with the findings of Imwold et al. (1982) and Matanin and Tannehill (1994), found that student effort was highly valued by teachers in relation to the determination of student grades.

Research in the 1990s continued to examine teachers' assessment practices, including the extent of assessment practice in physical education classes, the focus of assessment and the modes of assessment utilized, such as research conducted by Kalohn et al. (1992) focusing on the accuracy, validity and reliability of criterion-referenced assessment of tennis skills. Veal (1992b) conducted further research, through two case studies, investigating the congruency of teachers' theories of assessment and their practice. The method involved observations and interviews of two physical education teachers from a middle school in the United States. Also in the USA, Pate et al. (1995) collected data, as part of the "School Health Policies and Programs Study", on school physical education at a state, district, school and classroom level. The majority of states (82.4%) were found to have written curricular and guidelines for physical activity, which were monitored for compliance, to varying degrees. Pate et al. (1995) further report that 72% of the states administered standardized tests, 16.7% of which included physical education topics in the tests.

During the mid 1990s research on assessment in physical education was framed by emerging alternative curriculum approaches such as Sport Education and Teaching Games for Understanding. Greater emphasis on situated learning (Kirk and MacPhail, 2002) and alternative approaches to assessment was also evident. For example, Desrosiers et al. (1997) conducted research specifically on the formative assessment practices of physical education teachers. The focus of their research was on how secondary teachers integrated assessment into the teaching–learning process, the aspects of learning captured by the assessment instruments employed, and the characteristics of the assessment instruments used. However, as exemplified by research conducted by Taggart (1995) on the impact of Sport Education on teacher assessment practices, the focus of the research was largely on the nature or procedure of assessment rather than on the impact of assessment on learning. Taggart et al. (1995) found, through a case study approach, that the Sport Education model provided a framework for one school to develop assessment practices that were more authentic in nature. The other two participating schools were somewhat more resistant to alternative approaches to assessment, regardless of the alternative curriculum approach.

At a similar time, Macdonald and Brooker (1997a) reviewed the impact of a high-stakes curriculum reform based on Arnold's (1985) dimensions of movement on the assessment practices of senior (years 11 and 12) secondary physical education teachers. The principles of authentic assessment were foundational to the assessment structure of the new subject. The research involved in-depth interviews of 27 teachers from 11 schools; interviews of 10–15 students from each pilot school and a document analysis of the pilot Senior Physical Education syllabus. The document analysis focused on, among other significant factors, the breadth, depth and characteristics of the subject matter itself, i.e. the intended learning. While this research focused on teachers' use of authentic assessment, the connection between the assessment used and its impact on the nature and extent of learning in Senior Physical Education was not explored.

Research conducted by Richard et al. (1999) examined teachers' perceptions of the use of a performance peer-assessment procedure for team sports. They found that peer assessment was useful in developing the students' own tactical awareness in game performance and stimulated student interest in learning about their performance. Further contemporary research, such as that conducted by Castelli and Rink (2003) and Rink and Mitchell (2003) has focused on the impact of the introduction of a high-stakes accountability framework for physical education. The data were collected largely through surveys and interviews. Once again the research has been concerned with the pragmatics of teacher practice, including the determination of the factors affecting teacher compliance with the reforms and teachers' ability to utilize the mandated assessment procedures reliably.

Core concepts

Educational accountability is by no means a new concept (Blackmore, 1988; Vaughan, 2002), however its significance has been consolidated within Western society and exemplified in Western education systems to such an extent that Ranson (2003) suggests "accountability is no longer merely an important instrument or component within the system, but constitutes the system itself" (p. 459). Accountability is an operational feature of educational bureaucracies in which those functionaries operating at the lower levels of the education system give account, often through student performance data, to those more powerful within the bureaucracy originally responsible for the operational decisions made (Ranson, 2003). Macdonald and

Brooker (1997b) and Levin (1998) have identified the imperative that Western governments placed, and continue to place, on educational accountability, which reflects a perceived link between fiscal investment in education, the success of their education systems, the skills of the workforce, and future economic stability and growth. The flow of accountability for education in schools is multifarious and may be represented in different degrees of formality and currency (e.g. students to teachers; teachers to students, parents and system; system to government; system and government to community; etc.). As such, the delineation of the lines of answerability (implicit to notions of accountability) is complex (Ranson, 2003). Irrespective of the diversity, complexity and currency of accountability, assessment is an important mechanism for providing information for accountability. In many contexts systemic accountability regimes have been served by large-scale standardized tests, developed by psychometricians. Bates (1984) suggests that these evaluative techniques are meritocratic in nature, legitimated through a purported scientific objectivity (Richardson and Johanningmeier, 1998; Pearson et al., 2001) that assumes scholastic ability. While standardized testing has not had a direct impact on assessment in physical education, its rise has served as a catalyst for alternative perspectives on assessment for learning (Wiggins, 1993).

An assessment for learning paradigm emerged during the late 1970s and early 1980s as educationalists responded to problems and limitations of behaviourist theories of learning, traditional assessment approaches and a growing standardized testing and accountability movement. Traditional methods of educational assessment were criticized as individualistic, based in scientific objectivity and promoting a meritocracy which falsely assumes both the equality of educational opportunity and inherent "ability" (Bates, 1984; Blackmore, 1988). Evidence for learning within this paradigm is collected mainly through written and performance tests. These assessment practices reflect associationist and behaviourist theories of learning in which learning is thought to occur through the sequential accumulation of atomized "bits" of knowledge which are hierarchical in nature (Shepard, 2000). Rink (1999) suggests that "step by step success orientated models of instruction have their roots in behavioural psychology" (p. 152). Within this learning paradigm tests serve the purpose of identifying and ensuring the learner's mastery of objectives, which must be met before the learner can progress. Furthermore, summative testing perpetuates the "mechanistic thinking of Cartesian science, whose proponents believed that the whole could be analysed by studying the parts" (Wideen et al., 1998: 168). Traditional approaches to assessment, particularly those utilized for summative and accountability purposes act to divest the curriculum of its richness and breadth through teachers' preoccupation with defining measurable parameters (Stiggins, 2002), and providing instructional contexts that enhance the opportunities for students to be best represented against the valued constructs of the systemic accountability regimes. As a result of concerns over the educational value and ecological validity of such measures (Kirk and O'Flaherty, 2004), moves towards alternative assessment forms such as portfolios of achievement, more reflective of authentic assessment and congruent with constructivist theories of learning (Shepard, 2000) have emerged.

Assessment for learning is fundamentally grounded in constructivist perspectives on learning (Brooks, 2002; Shepard, 2000). Constructivist and situated perspectives of learning (see Chapters 3.4 and 3.5) recognize that learning occurs as a result of interactions between learners and within contexts, and that students actively appropriate and adapt new knowledge in relation to former understandings and cognitive structures. Learning is not a passive process of knowledge transmission, but rather is a complex process dependent upon previous knowledge, the context, and the task. In contrast to behaviourist approaches to teaching and learning, which advocate for the provision, by the teacher, of small achievable learning steps, constructivist approaches advocate that learning tasks or experiences be broader and demand higher-order thinking (Lambert, 1996). Within this approach learning involves "the use and transfer of problem solving skills in which the pupils are the prime movers in the learning process, and which enable the learner to see the relationships between content and construct 'cognitive maps' for what has been learned" (Mawer, 1999: 91).

"Educative assessment" (Wiggins, 1998b) "formative assessment" (Torrance and Pryor, 1998) "authentic assessment" (Wiggins, 1993), "performance assessment" (Glatthorn, 1999; Oosterhof, 1996) are terms that are associated with assessment that has a learning focus, however these are not discrete categories of assessment or modes of assessment. Neither are they necessarily different from each other. Formative assessment is particularly connected with the notion of assessment for learning. A definition proposed by Black and Wiliam (1998a) describes formative assessment as "encompassing all those activities undertaken by teachers and/or by their students, which provide information to be used as feedback to modify the teaching and learning activities in which they are engaged." (p. 8). Brooks (2002) further suggests that formative assessment involves intervention during the learning process as opposed to information collection at the end. He proposes that unless the information collected is used for feedback and to inform ongoing change to the learning process, then the assessment cannot be regarded as formative. From a constructivist perspective, this feedback is important for students to engage with so that they can monitor and adequately plan for their own learning. Sadler (1998) supported this idea and suggested that feedback was an essential aspect of meaningful and useful formative assessment. However, Sadler warns that feedback only has meaning and use for students if they understand what to do with the information. In order for the feedback to be meaningful to the students Black and Wiliam (1998b) suggest that the desired learning outcomes be explicit, describe where the student is positioned in relation to the desired outcomes, and provide students with strategies to move from their current position to the desired outcome.

The notion of authentic assessment, first described by Archbald and Newmann (1988) (cited in Wiggins, 1998a) was developed to challenge the lack of connectedness and meaning of standardized performance testing for schools, teachers and learners. Archbald and Newmann (1988) discussed an ideal in which assessment in schools required students to demonstrate, and effectively and elaborately communicate, an in-depth understanding of subject matter. The notion of "authentic" assessment refers to connectedness to the world (Shepard, 2000). That is to say, the learning experiences that form the medium for information gathering have application and meaning for students' lives and are not abstract or disassociated. Wiggins (1993, 1998b) suggests that authentic assessment should be realistic, replicating the manner in which the knowledge and processes being assessed are utilized in real-life contexts. He suggests that such practice exemplifies the notion of ecological validity. The tasks should also require students to demonstrate a range of knowledge and skills beyond what is taught. The assessment processes themselves contribute to an improvement in students' learning and teachers' practice. At the heart of authentic assessment is the link between the enacted curriculum and the information gathered about and by the students. From this perspective, the nature of the assessment practice should be reflective of the nature of the subject, in both content and experience. In discussing a constructivist perspective on formative assessment Torrance and Pryor (1998) suggest that the teacher and the student should be jointly part of the assessment process. Drawing on Vygotsky's concept of the zone of proximal development, Tinning et al. (2001) suggest that the interactions between students in the learning process, may be of similar significance to the teacher–pupil interaction.

Numerous academics have advocated for the use of authentic assessment in physical education (Melograno, 1994; Mohnsen, 1997, 2003; Smith, 1997; Smith and Cestaro, 1998) citing an integral link between meaningful assessment and learning.

Whereas authentic assessment was initially described in reaction to standardized testing based on the psychometric principles of intelligence and ability (Wiggins, 1993), authentic assessment in physical education has developed, to some degree, in reaction to the testing and grading of discrete and decontextualized sport-specific skills and fitness components. As such, the notion of authentic assessment has had considerable support from those academics who advocate for contextual and games-based curriculum approaches such as Sport Education (Siedentop and Tannehill, 2000; Taggart et al., 1995). Authentic assessment in any curriculum area is dependent upon the authenticity of the curriculum and pedagogies adopted. Thus authentic assessment in physical education should be based in movement and capture the cognitive and psychomotor processes involved in the competent performance of physical activities. Furthermore, assessment should redress the mind/body dualism propagated by traditional approaches to assessment, curriculum and pedagogies in physical education, through tasks that acknowledge and bring to the fore the interrelatedness of knowledge, process (cognitive and motor), skills and the affective domain.

At the same time, it may be inappropriate to suggest that improvement in teachers' formative assessment knowledge and skills, apart from changes in classroom curriculum and pedagogy, will improve learning. Shepard (2000) suggests that assessment for learning really only has meaning in classroom contexts in which a learning culture has been cultivated.

Major findings

As mentioned previously, research on assessment in physical education has focused largely on teachers' perceptions and practice, rather than the impact of assessment on student learning. Kirk and O'Flaherty (2004) note, in relation to literature on assessment in physical education, the absence of discussion of the nature of learning. Research from more general perspectives has endeavoured to explore the proposed connection between formative assessment and student learning. Crooks (1988) and Black and Wiliam (1998a) in their reviews of research of formative assessment demonstrated that learning gains were achieved where teachers adopted formative assessment within their classrooms. For example, Black and Wiliam (1998a) cite research by Fontanna and Fernandes (1994) who found a marked improvement in students' mathematics achievement as a result of formative self-assessment intervention. They concluded that assessment was vital for informing students of their current knowledge and directing future directions.

Nuthall and Alton-Lee (1995) confirmed this finding and demonstrated that teaching for understanding, incorporating formative assessment practices, results in long-term retention of learning. Wiliam et al. (2004) found that formative assessment conducted throughout a unit resulted in improved student academic achievement.

Desrosiers et al. (1997) conducted research focused on teachers' practice of formative assessment in physical education, the aspects of learning addressed by the assessment instruments and the characteristics of those instruments. They noted that experienced teachers generally used multiple assessment techniques to gather data on student achievement in physical education. Furthermore, they found that almost a quarter of the teachers observed conducted formative assessment at the beginning of the unit, with 62.9% of all assessment items utilized representing formative assessment, at varying points within the unit. Summative assessment was used exclusively at the end of the unit for the purpose of determining a grade. Various techniques were utilized by practitioners such as observation, peer assessment (using prescribed checklists) and written tasks. While not addressed specifically, Desrosiers et al. suggested that "although these data do not make it possible to determine to what extent there was … reflective learning on the part of the students … they do indicate there was authentic assessment" (1997: 224). The learning implications are difficult to determine other than to perpetuate the theory that formative assessment must improve learning in physical education. Other research, such as that conducted by Veal (1988), while not specifically focusing on the impact of assessment on learning, concluded that the purpose and utility of assessment needs to be viewed and understood by teachers and researchers more broadly than as a summative mechanism for the purpose of generating grades to satisfy accountability demands. Assessment should be part of the pedagogical process, occurring throughout the teaching-learning process.

Richard et al. (1999) examined the impact of a formative assessment mode on students' learning. They examined teachers' perceptions of the use of a performance assessment procedure for team sports. The procedure was based on two parameters: (a) how a player gains possession; (b) how a player disposes of the ball. The procedure purportedly captures and quantifies an individual's offensive performance, reflecting both the technical and tactical aspects of the game. Richard and colleagues found that peer assessment enhanced students' tactical awareness in game performance. The effect was larger where students conducted the assessment compared with students who were receiving feedback.

The determination of a level of achievement or "grade" within the authentic assessment for learning/formative assessment paradigm in physical education is something of a contentious issue (Melograno, 1994; Mohnsen, 2003). Where authentic assessment principles have been utilized for the construction of accountability regimes, the pertinence of grades to the learning context has risen as the grades often represent the currency of accountability within these structures. The significance of the factors affecting the determination of grades is augmented where the grades impact upon the educational and vocational futures of the students. Trouilloud et al. (2002) examined the influence of teacher expectations on student achievement in physical education. They found a significant link between teacher expectation and student achievement in which higher teacher expectancy correlated with higher student achievement. Trouiloud et al. (2002) suggest that this is because teacher perception and expectations were found to be mainly accurate, rather than the expectations being self-prophetic. However some results did suggest that teacher expectation had a self-prophetic impact in which teachers' perceptions of students directly influenced student outcomes. This finding is consistent with research by Bibik (1999), who also suggested that teacher expectations influence students' self-perceptions of their abilities.

Applications to practice and policy

A range of assessment techniques are described in the literature, serving the multiple purposes of assessment alluded to earlier. Traditional assessment techniques include fitness test scores and motor-skills tests for accuracy (Mohnsen, 1997; Metzler, 2000), primarily representing product assessments (Veal, 1995) which are often decontextual and thus "inauthentic". In the USA, fundamental motor skills are assessed in elementary school, reflecting the articulation of these valued aspects in the National Association for Sport and Physical Education (NASPE) standards. The rationale for such a focus, Olrich (2002) suggests, rests in the thought that these movements are foundational to proficiency in more complex movements. Other traditional techniques include tests of rules, tactics and history, and psychometric scales and inventories (Metzler, 2000). These traditional approaches to assessment in physical education reflect traditional approaches to curriculum construction and pedagogy. The summative and formal evaluative techniques largely reflect teacher-centred and didactic pedagogies and curricula based on the development of discrete skills, fitness, and health and fitness knowledge.

Alternative assessment for learning approaches, authentic in nature (Wiggins, 1998b) and grounded in constructivist pedagogies (Brooks, 2002), include observations, open-ended questioning, student logs, journals, role-plays and peer assessments (Butler and Hodge, 2001), the evidence of which is often recorded in student portfolios (Mohnsen, 1997). Peer assessment, while questioned by psychometricians in relation to validity and reliability, is firmly underpinned by constructivist notions of learning as such modes promote the active engagement of students with each other through negotiation, reflection and adaptation (Metzler, 2000). Furthermore, alternative assessments allow for a range of responses and interpretations not accommodated for through traditional assessment modes which demand the accuracy and consistency of responses across a cohort of students.

Portfolio assessment involves "the purposeful and systematic collection of student work that shows individual effort, progress, and achievement in one or more areas of learning. Students must be involved in selecting and judging the quality of their own work including self-reflection" (Melograno, 1994: 52). The active appropriation and selection of evidence of learning, by students, reflects the tenets of cognitive and constructivist pedagogies and may promote higher-order thinking such as evaluation and metacognition, although there is little empirical evidence to suggest this is the case (Black and Wiliam, 1998a). Information is systematically collected via multiple methods such as observations, performance samples and specified tasks (Wiggins, 1998b), representing a more informal mode of assessment. Portfolios can be both cumulative or contain representative samples of student work from across units or courses. This approach to assessment implies a change in the teacher's pedagogical approach, requiring a shift from didactic instruction to facilitation, further reflecting constructivist pedagogies in which the teacher offers choice and students take greater responsibility for what is learnt and how it is represented. The shift in responsibility may be achieved through the establishment of a portfolio goal for which students identify samples of their own work that they believe contribute to the realization of the goal (Siedentop and Tannehill, 2000).

Assessment based on observation, particularly in relation to the physical activity context involves the assessment of student work through the use of checklists and rating scales (Metzler, 2000). Observation as an assessment process is a criterion-referenced assessment mode. Given that a judgement, concerning student learning, is made, implies a criterion. This criterion may be explicit and formal or within the mind of the assessor (Veal, 1988). Fundamentally, criterion-referenced assessment involves the description or referencing of an individual's performance in relation to specified criteria, as opposed to reference to the performance of others. Various approaches to criterion-referenced assessment represent this mode, the breadth of which encompasses both the collection of information on student performance and the determination of grades or levels of achievement. Much is written in instructional texts about the establishment of criteria for judging performance in physical education (Siedentop and Tannehill, 2000), however little is discussed about standards and the descriptors that differentiate between different levels. The connection between students' understanding and engagement with criteria and improved academic performance is well established. Torrance and Pryor (1998) discuss the benefits of sharing the criteria with the students, helping the students to unpack the criteria to enhance their understanding of what is required of them. They further suggest that students and teachers should share the process of assessment and that this was one means of achieving a shared understanding and accountability for assessment. One must be careful in equating knowledge of the criteria with learning. The connection between knowledge of criteria and student learning (including intended and unintended learning) is far less substantiated, if reliably established at all.

The accountability movement, and emergent theories of learning, have had an impact on the assessment agenda in physical education (Macdonald and Brooker, 1997a). Wood (1996) suggests that "the very survival of physical education in the public school system will depend, in part, on how well we define the purposes and outcomes of our programs and the methods we use to document the successes of our students and teachers within those programs" (p. 199). Macdonald and Brooker (1997b) suggest that such changes in curriculum content and assessment occurred in response to the perceived diminished status of physical education in schools. The lower status of physical education has been due, largely, to a devaluing of the practical aspect of physical education against traditional "academic subjects" (Kirk and Tinning, 1990), the sentiment of which reflects the notion of a mind/body dualism, and a hierarchy of knowledge (Blackmore, 1988).

The responses of physical education reformers internationally to claims of diminished rigour have resulted in curriculum reform and attention to assessment practices which have had divergent consequences for the representation of curriculum in physical education and the constitution of learning in the subject. Some curriculum reforms in physical education have consolidated the mind/body dualism through assessment practices that examine the "theoretical" aspects of human movement/sports science (Carroll, 1998), devaluing the physical aspects of physical education through the absence of assessment of the quality of movement. Other

systems have sought to validate the place of physical education in the curriculum on the basis of its contribution to individual and community health (Rink and Mitchell, 2002). This approach has significant and potentially problematic accountability consequences for physical education. Macdonald and Brooker (1997b), however, describe a curriculum approach in which the focus is on the integration of movement concepts and movement itself, based on Arnold's (1985) dimensions of movement. The complexity and sophistication of the cognitive processes involved in the competent performance of movement in various contexts, and the principles and processes that underpin, and are implicit to that movement are recognized through this approach. This philosophical position has given rise to a viable secondary school physical education, in Queensland, Australia, that is characterized by school-based, high-stakes alternative assessment. Langendorfer (2001) supports such initiatives and qualifies physical education's inclusion in high-stakes assessment regimes through the development of an academically rigorous curriculum and sound assessment practices.

A brief description of assessment in the Senior Physical Education course is provided to demonstrate an initiative that has attempted to negotiate the potential tension between assessment for accountability and assessment for learning. The Senior Physical Education course for senior (years 11 and 12) secondary-school students in Queensland, Australia represents an example of a sophisticated school-based, high-stakes assessment regime founded upon the principles of authentic assessment (Queensland Studies Authority [QSA], 2004). The regime is loosely based on a portfolio system in which evidence of student learning is collected continuously across the 2 years of the course. This evidence contained in the folios is selectively updated, acknowledging that evidence collected at an earlier date might no longer be representative of student achievement, recognizing the dynamic nature of learning (Rovegno and Kirk, 1995). The syllabus emphasizes the congruence of the learning experiences with the assessment tasks, both of which are to be grounded in "integration" and "personalization". Integration, based upon Arnold's (1985) model of learning in, through and about physical activity, refers to the way in which content focus areas, including "learning physical skills" (the subject matter of which encompasses motor learning, sport and exercise psychology and biomechanics); "process and effects of training" and "sport, physical activity and exercise in the context of Australian society", are engaged with, by students "in", "through" and "about" movement. The notion of integration attempts to counter the mind/body dualism instantiated by a separation of "theory" and "performance" in many physical education contexts. Personalization consolidates the situated, constructivist approach intended in the syllabus, referring to the requirement of teachers to provide students with opportunities to "make meaning of complex understanding by providing connections with their real-life contexts" (QSA, 2004: 2).

A unit (usually about 10 weeks in length) should involve the integration of a focus area (the subject matter of which is determined by the teacher) with a physical activity, the selection of which must be made within the guidelines of the syllabus. Within each unit (four in a school year), teachers are responsible for the design and implementation of assessment tasks that are also integrated and personalized in nature and allow students to demonstrate the criteria, outlined in the syllabus (QSA, 2004), of acquire (involving the "retrieval and comprehension of information and the reproduction of learned physical responses" (p. 5), apply (involving the "application of acquired information and learned physical responses" (p. 5), and evaluate (involving the utilization of information, understandings and skills previously gained in acquiring and applying to make decisions, reach conclusions, solve problems and justify solutions and actions (p. 6), at the standards specified by the statutory authority, in the syllabus. The criteria against which students' work is referenced and grades determined are based on Bloom's (1956) taxonomy of educational objectives. The use of the same criteria for making judgements of student performance in both physical and written tasks highlights the recognition of the cognitive processes involved in "intelligent performance" (Kirk, 1983, 1988). Student's written work (the focus area concepts understood through the physical activity) and their performance in the physical activity is referenced against task-specific criteria and standards, developed by the teachers from the generic set represented in the syllabus. The criteria define the aspects of a subject that are to be measured (for example, "acquire" or "apply" or "evaluate"). Standards represent (symbolically) the distribution of quality along a specified continuum (from highest expected quality to lowest expected quality). The standards descriptors articulate that quality for each criterion that the students' work will be measured or judged against (Sadler, 1987).

The syllabus describes the purpose of assessment in physical education as formative with respect to learning that has occurred and summative in recognition of its contribution to the generation of an exit level of achievement (or grade). Formative assessment is understood in the syllabus as enabling "students and teachers to identify the students' strengths and weaknesses so students may improve their achievement and better manage their own learning" (QSA, 2004: 38). Furthermore the formative techniques should mirror those used for summative assessment to ensure that students are familiar with the techniques as well as the subject matter that constitutes a unit. Teachers are required to utilise a variety of assessment techniques, such as oral assessments, journals, and research assignments that reflect the notions of integration and personalisation and are, by implication, authentic. The assessment involves the engagement of students across the unit and should be supported by, and support, the learning experiences in the unit.

The following examples of learning/assessment experiences, taken directly from the syllabus (QSA, 2004), exemplify the notions of integration and personalisation. These are examples only and teachers are required to develop their own learning/assessment experiences that are of a similar nature.

Through participation in and observation of single- and mixed-gender games in basketball sudents evaluate socio-cultural factors that impact upon participation and performance. From this evaluation they recommend changes that should improve participation and performance of individuals and teams. To complete this task students may:

- identify socio-cultural factors that impact upon participation and performance in basketball
- collect data through observation/development or surveys or checklist of basketball games
- apply knowledge of socio-cultural influences to explain participation outcomes
- recommend and understand changes to improve participation/performance in basketball
- justify from a personal and research base, recommendations made.

(p. 32)

Students:

- participate in a generic training program for their selected track or field event. They will experience training principles and methods and technical and psychological effects associated with the training program
- reflect on each training session in a journal
- evaluate the programs success in terms of improvement (gauged through performance on the event and on specific fitness tests) and propose changes to the program based on their personal reflections and the application of underlying training principles.

(p. 33)

Students design a personal learning plan for their partner based on an analysis of their partner's performance [in Touch Football]. The plan must be justified in terms of the information-processing model of skill learning, factors affecting the rate of skill learning and the stage of skill learning of their partner.

(p. 35)

These examples highlight the sophisticated learning expected of students and the importance of the movement context in students' engagement with the focus area subject matter. Characteristic of each of the examples is the interdependence of the learning experiences and the assessment highlighted by the extended, process-orientated tasks. That is to say, "normal" class experiences are important in providing the information upon which students complete the "assessment task". Students' existing knowledge is challenged by the task itself and the requirement of students to apply and evaluate their knowledge and performance in physical activity.

In relation to the physical performance specifically, the syllabus is quite explicit in requiring that assessment of student performance should be conducted throughout the unit of work providing both formative information for improvement and an indication of the standards achieved in relation to each of the three criteria. Students are required to demonstrate their proficiency of movement and their tactical awareness in both simple and complex performance environments. The complex environment, described as "a new or unrehearsed situation" (QSA, 2004: 28), requires students to apply their knowledge, tactics and strategies in unpredictable circumstances such as a game context. Thus the assessment recognizes the cognitive operations of effective and intelligent performers. Intelligent performance is clearly linked to Arnold's three dimensions of movement. Kirk's (1983, 1988) notion of intelligent performance is particularly descriptive of Arnold's (1985) contextual objective, a subcategory of the "in" dimension of movement which relates to the tactics and strategies involved in meaningful performance in physical activities.

The course described above provides an example of how constructivist and situated assessment practices can be used to collect high-stakes information for purposes such as selection, certification and accountability. The assessment approach is situated within the learning context and allows for a range of responses and interpretations expected of students from, at times, diverse backgrounds and experiences. However, little empirical evidence has been collected on the impact that such assessment practices have had on the transfer of learning to other contexts, or the nature of the learning that has occurred.

Major trends and future directions

While research into the impact of formative or educative assessment has been conducted in other disciplines (for example, Crooks, 1988; Nuthall and Alton-Lee, 1995; Wiliam et al., 2004), such research in physical education has been comparatively limited. Furthermore, much of the research in general education that has been conducted, for example on feedback in the learning process, has largely conformed to behavioural assumptions of learning (Shepard, 2000). Research that has been conducted on formative assessment in physical education has focused on teacher practice rather than the impact of assessment on students' learning. Research within this area may involve exploring how students engage the feedback generated through various formative classroom assessments. Mawer (1999) suggests that learning, from a constructivist perspective, is transferable across contexts. An examination of various modes of formative assessment purported to capture and contribute to learning of this nature would be invaluable in improving teacher practice and enhancing the quality of student learning.

There is little doubt that accountability frameworks will be a significant characteristic of future Western education systems (Vaughan, 2002). This has implications for both the constitution of physical education, the assessment practices of teachers, and the use of the information collected via those practices. While the educative assessment paradigm, within the literature, is largely focused towards learning rather than measuring and accounting for learning, educational bureaucracies are increasingly endeavouring to use the principles of assessment for learning as the structural basis for the development of large scale, high-stakes accountability regimes (QSA, 2004; Castelli and Rink, 2003). Thus an assessment paradigm that was initially positioned as an essential contributor to the learning process becomes the mechanism by which the product of that process is accounted for.

It is a reasonable assumption that the mandated employment of more authentic assessment in physical education is both theoretically and philosophically more beneficial than traditional modes of assessment, however, research needs to be conducted to determine whether the theoretical and philosophical ideals of assessment for learning are realized in a systemic assessment regime designed for such purposes as collection of information for accountability. Implicit in such research would be the investigation of the degree to which eugenic notions of ability and disability continue to pervade thinking in relation to student achievement within these assessment frameworks. The potential danger is that the problems that have been identified with large-scale accountability structures may be concealed by assessment for learning rhetoric, and perpetuated through ignorance. Research may involve critical reflection on the type of evidence that is collected for portfolios, the value ascribed to, and represented by, the evidence, and the means by which the evidence of student learning is generated. A critical perspective in relation to alternative assessment accountability regimes may also involve an examination of the reformatory action of assessment on curriculum scope and depth in physical education.

A further focus may be to examine the "pedagogical work" (Tinning and Glasby, 2002: 117) that assessment performs on students. This would involve examining the impact that an emphasis on assessment (irrespective of the paradigm) on students' understanding of the goals of education and the way the students value learning itself. Whether the goal of physical education is to influence students' dispositions to physical activity and healthy lifestyles, or provide a context in which students' develop "understandings and skills to become critical consumers of physical culture" (Tinning et al., 2001: 149), or both, one must question the impact of an increased salience of assessment in the learning context on the realization of these intentions. The risk is that as teachers focus on the assessment of student performance in their classes, the students begin to engage in learning for the sake of improving their achievement opportunities, rather than the intrinsic value of learning itself. There is also the risk that students may disengage because they don't value educational "success" as described by high achievement on assessment, or the high achievement standards referred to and valued by the teacher seem impossible for them to achieve.

More often than not, discussion in the literature and conclusions from research describe assessment in terms that give the impression that it is unproblematic (Blackmore, 1988). However, little research has challenged practice and the implications of assessment on a range of issues in education. Further research is needed from a critical perspective to inform meaningful practice in schools, and to understand the processes and implications of assessment in student learning and schooling. Carroll (1994) reports that physical education curriculum reformers in the United Kingdom encountered resistance from "influential individuals". Evans (1976), an opponent of examinations, noted that physical education is a process characterized by variability in the development of students' skills and movement patterns. He proposed that establishing standards marginalizes students outside the defined "norms" of individual growth and development. He argued further that the compartmentalization of physical education, which results from the defining of assessment parameters, is not reflective of the essence of physical education. Evans was particularly severe on product assessment and standards suggesting that the validity of standardized measures were undermined by the fact that students develop at different rates, and questioned the purpose of the collection of such data, attacking the postulation that such measures would raise the status of the subject. These still have legitimacy in the absence of empirical evidence to suggest otherwise.

Connected with the notion of the pedagogical work of assessment is the impact that assessment has on the construction of "abilities". Evans' (2004) sociology of ability presents a further conceptual framework for research of assessment in physical education. Evans suggests that ability may be understood as the consistency or comparability of a person's embodied and prevailing dispositions, or habitus (Bourdieu, 1996), with the "values, attitudes and mores prevailing within a discursive field". (p. 100). Assessment may be understood and conceptualized as the means by which those values, etc., are articulated and to some degree imposed upon students. The identification of the means by which assessment acts as a mechanism for the construction of ability presents a potential research direction. Further theorizing, under-girded by the collection of empirical evidence will be valuable in broadening our understanding of assessment and the impact that it has on students' future educational opportunities and engagement in learning. Implicit to such a focus would be an exploration of which abilities are constructed and valued in physical education through the assessment practices used by teachers.

This chapter has focused on assessment for learning in physical education but other salient and contemporary issues concerning assessment have been woven through. Formative and authentic assessment is widely accepted, by those who adhere to cognitive, constructivist and situated perspectives on learning as fundamental to student learning. Grounded in this understanding is the acknowledged interdependence of curriculum, pedagogy and assessment. Teachers, increasingly, have to contend with greater accountability demands that will only increase as physical education stakeholders promote the educational and social significance of physical education in schools. Evidently more research is needed to substantiate assessment for learning theory and to better comprehend the impact of a range of competing assessment demands on teacher practice and student learning.

Acknowledgement

The author wishes to express his gratitude to, and acknowledge the work of David Kirk and Mary O'Flaherty whose conference paper entitled *Learning Theory and Authentic Assessment in Physical Education*, presented at the Annual Conference of BERA, Edinburgh, September 10–13 was invaluable in providing the conceptual and theoretical basis for the content of this chapter.

References

Arbogast, G.A. (2002). Assessment issues and the elementary school-age child, Part 1. *Journal of Physical Education, Recreation and Dance, 73(1)*: 21–25.

Archbald, D.A. and Newmann, F.M. (1988). *Beyond standardised testing: Assessing authentic academic achievement in the secondary school.* Reston: National Association of Secondary School Principals.

Arnold, P. (1985). Movement, physical education and the curriculum. *Bulletin of Physical Education 16(1)*: 5–9.

Bates, R.J. (1984). Educational verses managerial evaluation. In P. Broadfoot (Ed.), *Selection, certification and control. Social issues in educational assessment* (pp. 127–143). London: The Falmer Press.

Bibik, J.M. (1999). Factors influencing college students' self-perceptions of competence in beginning physical education classes. *Journal of Teaching in Physical Education, 18(3)*: 255–276.

Black, P. and Wiliam, D. (1998a). Assessment and classroom learning. *Assessment in Education, 5(1)*: 7–73.

Black, P. and Wiliam, D. (1998b). *Inside the black box: Raising standards through classroom assessment.* London: School of Education, King's College.

Blackmore, J. (1988). *Assessment and accountability.* Geelong: Deakin University Press.

Bloom, B. (1956). *The taxonomy of educational objectives: The classification of educational goals.* New York: David Mckay Company.

Bourdieu, P. (1996). On the family as a realized group. *Theory, Culture and Society, 13(3)*: 19–26.

Broadfoot, P. and Black, P. (2004). Redefining assessment? The first 10 years of assessment in education. *Assessment in Education, 11(1)*: 7–27.

Brooks, V. (2002). *Assessment in secondary schools. The new teacher's guide to monitoring, assessment, recording, reporting and accountability.* Buckingham: Open University Press.

Butler, S.A. and Hodge, S.R. (2001). Enhancing student trust through peer assessment in physical education. *The Physical Educator, 58(1)*: 30–39.

Carroll, R. (1994). *Assessment in physical education, A teachers' guide to the issues.* London: Falmer Press.

Carroll, R. (1998). The emergence and growth of examinations in physical education. In K. Green and K. Hardman (Eds.), *Physical education – A reader* (pp. 335–352). Aachen: Meyer and Meyer.

Caroll, R. and Macdonald, A.I. (1981). Male physical education teachers' opinions about physical education examinations in schools. *Bulletin of Physical Education, 17(1)*: 23–30.

Castelli, D. and Rink, J. (2003). A comparison of high and low performing secondary physical education programs. *Journal of Teaching in Physical Education, 22(5)*: 512–532.

Crooks, T.J. (1988). The impact of classroom evaluation practices on students. *Review of Educational Research, 58(4)*: 438–481.

Desrosiers, P., Genet-Volet, Y. and Godbout, P. (1997). Teachers' assessment practices viewed through the instruments used in physical education classes. *Journal of Teaching in Physical Education, 16(2)*: 211–228.

Evans, J. (1976). An argument against examinations. *British Journal of Physical Education, 7(1)*: 110.

Evans, J. (2004). Making a difference? Education and 'ability' in physical education. *European Physical Education Review, 10(1)*: 95–108.

Fontana, D. and Fernandes, M. (1994). Improvements in mathematics performance as a consequence of self-assessment in Portuguese primary school pupils. *British Journal of Educational Psychology, 64(3)*: 407–417.

Gipps, C. (1994). *Beyond testing: Toward a theory of educational assessment.* London: The Falmer Press.

Gipps, C. (1996). Assessment for learning. In A. Little and A. Wolf (Eds.), *Assessment in transition. learning, monitoring and selection in international perspective* (pp. 251–262). Oxford: Elsevier Science Ltd.

Glatthorn, A.A. (1999). *Performance standards and authentic learning.* New York: Eye on Education.

Hardman, K. and Marshall, J.J. (2000). *World-wide survey of the state and status of school physical education.* Manchester: University of Manchester.

Hargreaves, A., Earl, L. and Schmidt, M. (2002). Perspectives on alternative assessment reform. *American Educational Research Journal, 39(1)*: 69–95.

Hensley, L.D., Lambert, L.T., Baumgartner, T.A. and Stillwell, J.L. (1987). Is evaluation worth the effort?. *Journal of Physical Education, Recreation and Dance, 58(6)*: 59–62.

Imwold, C.H., Rider, R.A. and Johnson, D.J. (1982). The use of evaluation in public school physical education programs. *Journal of Teaching in Physical Education, 2(1)*: 13–18.

Kalohn, J.C., Wagoner, K., Gao, L-G., Safrit, M.J. and Getchell, N. (1992). A comparison of two criterion-referenced standard setting procedures for sport skills testing. *Research Quarterly for Exercise and Sport, 63(1)*: 1–10.

Kirk, D. (1983). A new term for a vacant peg: Conceptualising physical performance in sport. *Bulletin of Physical Education 19(3)*: 38–44.

Kirk, D. (1988). *Physical education and curriculum study: A critical introduction.* New York: Croom Helm.

Kirk, D. and MacPhail, A. (2002). Teaching games for understanding and situated learning: Rethinking the Bunker-Thorpe mode. *Journal of Teaching in Physical Education, 22(2)*: 177–192.

Kirk, D. and O'Flaherty, M. (2004). *Learning theory and authentic assessment in physical education.* Paper presented to the physical and sport education SIG as the Annual Conference of BERA, Edinburgh, September 10–13.

Kirk, D. and Tinning, R. (1990) *Physical education, curriculum and culture: Critical issues in the contemporary crisis.* London: The Falmer Press.

Kneer, M. (1986). A description of physical education instructional theory/practice gap in selected secondary schools. *Journal of Teaching in Physical Education, 5(2)*: 91–106.

Koretz, D. (1998). Large-scale portfolio assessment in the US: Evidence pertaining to the quality of measurement. *Assessment in Education, 5(3)*: 309–334.

Lambert, L. (1996). Goals and outcomes. In S.J. Silverman and C.D. Ennis (Eds.), *Student learning in physical education. Applying research to enhance instruction* (pp. 149–169). Champaign, IL: Human Kinetics.

Langendorfer, S.J. (2001). Should the physical education grade be included in a high school student's GPA?. *Journal of Physical Education, Recreation and Dance, 72(8):* 9.

Levin, H.M. (1998). Educational performance standards and the economy. *Educational Researcher, 27(4):* 4–10.

Linn, R.L. and Gronlund, N.E. (1995). *Measurement and assessment in teaching.* New Jersey: Prentice Hall.

Macdonald, D. and Brooker, R. (1997a). Assessment issues in a performance-based subject: A case study of physical education. *Studies in Educational Evaluation, 23(1):* 83–102.

Macdonald, D. and Brooker, R. (1997b). Moving beyond the crises in secondary physical education: an Australian initiative. *Journal of Teaching in Physical Education, 16(2):* 155–175.

MacNeill, N. and Silcox, S. (2002). Overcoming a perception of failure in public schools. *The Practising Administrator, 24(1):* 30–33.

Martin, J.J., Hodges Kulinna, P. and Cothran, D. (2002). Motivating students through assessment. *Journal of Physical Education, Recreation and Dance, 73(8):* 18–30.

Matanin, M. and Tannehill, D. (1994). Assessment and grading in physical education. *Journal of Teaching in Physical Education, 13(4):* 395–405.

Mawer, M. (1999). Teaching styles and teaching approaches in physical education: Research developments. In C.A. Hardy and M. Mawer (Eds.), *Learning and teaching in physical education* (pp. 83–104). London: Falmer Press.

Melograno, V.J. (1994). Portfolio assessment: documenting authentic student learning. *Journal of Physical Education, Recreation and Dance, 65(8):* 50–61.

Metzler, M.W. (2000). *Instructional models for physical education.* Boston, MA: Allyn and Bacon.

Mohnsen, B. (1997). Authentic assessment in physical education. *Learning and Leading with Technology, 24(7):* 30–33.

Mohnsen, B. (2003). *Teaching middle school physical education: A standards-based approach for grades 5–8.* Champaign, IL: Human Kinetics.

Natriello, G. (1987). The impact of evaluation processes on students. *Educational Psychologist, 22(2):* 155–175.

Naul, R. (2003). Concepts of physical education in Europe. In K. Hardman (Ed.), *Physical education: Deconstruction and reconstruction – issues and directions.* Berlin, Germany: ICSSPE.

Nuthall, G. and Alton-Lee, A. (1995). Assessing classroom learning: how students use their knowledge and experience to answer classroom achievement tests in science and social studies. *American Educational Research Journal, 32(1):* 185–223.

Olrich, T.W. (2002). Assessing fundamental motor skills in the elementary school setting. *Journal of Physical Education, Recreation and Dance, 73(7):* 26–34.

Oosterhof, A. (1996). *Developing and using classroom assessments.* New Jersey: Prentice-Hall.

Pate, R.R., Leavy Small, M., Ross, J.G., Young, J.C., Flint, K.H. and Warren, C.W. (1995). School physical education. *Journal of School Health, 65(8):* 312–318.

Pearson, P.D., Vyas, S., Sensale, L.M. and Kim, Y. (2001). Making our way through the assessment and accountability maze. Where do we go now? *The Clearing House, 74(4):* 175–182.

Queensland Studies Authority (2004). *Senior syllabus in physical education.* Brisbane: Queensland Studies Authority.

Ranson, S. (2003). Public accountability in the age of neo-liberal governance. *Journal of Education Policy, 18(5):* 459–480.

Richard, J-F., Godbout, P., Tousignant, M. and Grehaigne, J-F. (1999). The try-out of a team sport performance assessment procedure in elementary and junior high school physical education classes. *Journal of Teaching in Physical Education, 18(3):* 336–356.

Richardson, T. and Johanningmeier, E.V. (1997). Intelligence testing: the legitimation of a meritocratic educational science. *International Journal of Educational Research, 27(8):* 699–714.

Rink, J. (1999). Instruction from a learning perspective. In C.A. Hardy and M. Mawer (Eds.), *Learning and teaching in physical education.* London: Falmer Press.

Rink, J. and Mitchell, M. (2002). High stakes assessment: a journey into unknown territory. *Quest, 54(3):* 205–223.

Rink, J. and Mitchell, M. (2003). Introduction. State level assessment in physical education: the South Carolina Experience. *Journal of Teaching in Physical Education, 22(5):* 471–472.

Rovengo, I. and Kirk, D. (1995). Articulations and silences in socially critical work on physical education: Toward a broader agenda. Quest, *47(4):* 447–474.

Sadler, R. (1987). Towards a working model for criteria and standards under ROSBA. Discussion paper 13. Board of Secondary School Studies, Brisbane.

Sadler, D.R. (1998). Formative assessment: Revisiting the territory. *Assessment in Education, 5(1):* 77–84.

Shepard, L. (2000). The role of assessment in a learning culture. *Educational Researcher, 29(7):* 4–14.

Siedentop, D. and Tannehill, D. (2000). *Developing teaching skills in physical education.* Mountain View, CA: Mayfield Publishing Company.

Smith, T.K. (1997). Authentic assessment: using a portfolio card in physical education. *Journal of Physical Education, Recreation and Dance, 68(4):* 46–52.

Smith, T.K. and Cestaro, N.G. (1998). *Student-centered physical education: Strategies for developing middle school fitness and skills.* Champaign, IL: Human Kinetics.

Stiggins, R.J. (2002). Assessment crisis: The absence of assessment for learning. *Phi Delta Kappan, 83(10):* 758.

Taggart, A., Browne, T. and Alexander, K. (1995). Three schools' approaches to assessment in sport education. *The ACHPER Healthy Lifestyles Journal, 42(4):* 12–15.

Terwilliger, J.S. (1998). Rejoinder: response to Wiggins and Newmann. *Educational Researcher, 27(6):* 22–23.

Tinning, R. and Glasby, T. (2002). Pedagogical work and the 'cult of the body': Considering the role of HPE in the context of the 'new public health'. *Sport, Education and Society, 7(2):* 109–119.

Tinning, R., Macdonald, D., Wright, J. and Hickey, C. (2001). *Becoming a physical education teacher.* Sydney: Prentice Hall.

Torrance, H. and Pryor, J. (1998). *Investigating formative assessment: Teaching, learning and assessment in the classroom.* Buckingham: Open University Press.

Trouilloud, D.O., Sarrazin, P.G., Martinek, T.J. and Guillet, E. (2002). The influence of teacher expectations on student achievement in physical education classes: Pygmalion revisited. *European Journal of Social Psychology, 32(5):* 591–607.

Vaughan, A.C. (2002). Standards, accountability, and the determination of school success. *The Educational Forum, 66(3):* 206–213.

Veal, M-L. (1988). Pupil assessment practices and perceptions of secondary teachers. *Journal of Teaching in Physical Education, 7(4):* 327–342.

Veal, M-L. (1992a). The role of assessment in secondary physical education – a pedagogical view. *Journal of Physical Education, Recreation and Dance, 63(7):* 88–92.

Veal, M-L. (1992b). School-based theories of pupil assessment: A case study. *Research Quarterly for Exercise and Sport, 63(1):* 48–59.

Veal, M-L. (1995). Assessment as an instructional tool. *Strategies, 8(6):* 10–15.

Wideen, M., Mayer-Smith, J. and Moon, B. (1998). A critical analysis of the research on learning to teach: Making the case for an ecological perspective on inquiry. *Review of Educational Research, 68(2):* 130–178.

Wiggins, G. (1993). Assessment: Authenticity, context, and validity. *Phi Delta Kappan, 75(3):* 200–214.

Wiggins, G. (1998a). An exchange of views on "semantics, psychometrics, and assessment reform: a close look at 'authentic' assessments". *Educational Researcher, 27(6):* 20–21.

Wiggins, G. (1998b). *Educative assessment. Designing assessments to inform and improve student performance.* San Francisco, CA: Jossey-Bass Inc.

Wiliam, D., Lee, C., Harrison, C. and Black, P. (2004). Teachers developing assessment for learning: impact on student achievement. *Assessment in Education, 11(1):* 49–65.

Wood, T.M. (1996). Evaluation and testing: the road less travelled. In S.J. Silverman and C.D. Ennis (Eds.), *Student learning in physical education: Applying research to enhance instruction.* Champaign, IL: Human Kinetics.

3.9 Students' perspectives of physical education

BEN DYSON

Introduction

If aliens from another world landed on planet earth and consulted the professional literature to learn about our education system, it would be quite possible for them to overlook the perspectives of students in the entire process. Ironically, the two groups most intimately involved in the day-to-day function of education, teachers and students, have rarely been asked for their thoughts by researchers (Brooker and Macdonald, 1999; Cohn and Kottkamp, 1993; Corbett and Wilson, 1995, 2002). In handbooks of research on teaching there is little research on students' perspectives in the classroom or in the physical education gymnasium (Graber, 2001; Richardson, 2001; Travers, 1973; Wittrock, 1986). An illustration of the lack of attention paid to this area is the fact that in the most widely used education research handbook, Graber (2001) does not refer to students' perspectives as a line of inquiry but rather places the research on students' perspectives under one of three categories: student characteristics, students' social system, or curricular goals. Cothran and Ennis (1999) argued that the "lack of information about students' perspectives greatly reduces physical educators' ability to design intervention and reform efforts to increase student engagement" (p. 236). This chapter explores the research carried out *with* students in an attempt to access *their voices*.

After a lifetime of research, Siedentop (2002) stated that we only started learning more accurately about what was going on in physical education when we began to systematically observe what students were doing in the gymnasium. Graham (1995) argued that "we just do not know how students feel about physical education programs – what they like, do not like, value, would like to have included or excluded in their programs" (p. 364). Students as early as "five years old, are able to express their feelings, needs, and thoughts about what is taught in physical education"

(p. 481). Perhaps physical educators find themselves caught up in organizing large numbers of students in the large open spaces in the gymnasium and start teaching "numbers" and forget that each student has thoughts and feelings and opinions about what is being taught (Graham, 1995). There were very few research studies based on students' perspectives until Graham's monograph in 1995. Pissanos and Allison (1993) argued that there was a lack of concentrated inquiry on students' perspectives in educational research related to curricular practice. "Insight from continued inquiry into students' construction and reconstruction of meaning will help us be better informed school practitioners and teacher educators" (Pissanos and Allison, p. 434).

Smith (1991) emphasized a "child-orientated" pedagogy for physical education. He questioned our ability to keep "the child in view" in our research endeavors and the extent to which we are committed to improving pedagogical practices that offer children "genuine help" (p. 51). Smith (1991) asked: how can we improve physical education in the 21st century without accessing the students in the physical education classes or physical activity settings? Thirty years ago wise counsel from Locke (1977) suggested that student wants and needs should not dictate what is taught in physical education but students' voice should inform teachers' practice. Pissanos and Allison (1993) recognized that student perspective had largely been ignored in curricular practice. They proposed that more researchers have begun to recognize student input and experience as valuable insights and influential contributions to analyzing the teaching and learning process. They found that students had similar responses related to their physical education program. "The fact that the students all had the same recollection regarding the teacher's program goal" (p. 433) suggested that this is a valuable form of inquiry.

The review of literature in this chapter will focus on research conducted in K-12 schools on students' perspectives, viewpoints, opinions and/or judgments. This is a student-centered approach to research to determine the students' views relative to their experiences of the curriculum. The basic premise of this chapter is that researchers can develop more insightful understandings of the teaching and learning environments that exist in schools by studying the subjective meanings that are constructed by students in their physical education experiences. This chapter explores the research carried out 'with students' rather than research 'on students,' in order to gain a more accurate view of what students value and believe about their physical education experiences and their physical activity. Students' perception research that is grounded in motivation theory and achievement motivation (Duda and Nichols, 1992) is not presented here. Nor does this chapter discuss the broad term of students' attitudes to physical education that have mainly been assessed through psychometric testing. These topics are covered in Chapters 2.4 and 3.3. The studies presented and discussed here are inductive qualitative research compared to other forms of research that tend to be more deductive and quantitative in nature.

By its very nature students' perspectives research is student-centered. The thoughts and opinions of students are the focus of this area of study. All of the researchers cited in this chapter spent extended periods of time with students, ranging from one semester to multiple years. Many of the studies are mini-ethnographies. The research is set in school-based contexts. In addition to research in the naturalistic physical education setting, many researchers have asked students to talk about different instructional models, such as Sport Education, Cooperative Learning, and Adventure Education. In many projects the research on student voices is part of a multiple-method approach to the study of physical education. Therefore, the majority of the work draws on methods such as non-participant observation, interviews, and field notes of students within schools. The purpose of the research is often to determine students' views relative to student engagement, student meaning, student relevance, and the authenticity of student learning. Student cognition, which will not be discussed here, is covered in Chapters 2.4 and 3.3.

This chapter presents a brief historical perspective or background to students' perspectives. This is followed by methodological issues in this research, the theoretical underpinnings of students' perspectives, and then by major findings from the research, which include students' perspectives from innovative curriculum in physical education. The chapter concludes with the application to practice, policy, and implications for future research on students' perspectives, and major trends, future directions and issues for research on teaching in physical education.

Brief historical perspective/ background

In the early 1960s Spindler (1963) was critical of the bulk of educational research carried out at that time. He advocated a redirection towards investigations of what actually occurs in schools and what norms and values are represented by teachers and their students explicitly and implicitly. At the same time in physical education, Bill Anderson recommended school-based research using descriptive-analytic research techniques (observing, interviewing, describing, and analyzing), which at that time were given limited recognition among physical educators as legitimate research tools. Anderson (1971) valued the investigations of this nature as a means of gaining a clearer understanding of what occurred in the "real-world" of student–teacher interactions in the gymnasium. The research focus was now on "what the student was doing" in the gymnasium (Anderson and Barrett, 1978). In the second *Handbook of Research on Teaching*, Nixon and Locke (1973) discussed the emerging field of research on teaching physical education but stated that "descriptive research in physical education is in its infancy" (p. 1226). Later in the 1970s Locke (1977) argued for a systematic and quantitative approach to research on teaching physical education in his *QUEST* article, "Research on teaching Physical Education: New hope for a dismal science".

With the rise of qualitative studies from the early 1980s, more attention was paid to qualitative methodologies and students' perspectives (Evans and Davies, 1986; Hendry, 1996, Kollen, 1981; Pissanos and Allison, 1993; Underwood, 1988; Wang, 1977). Critique of research on physical education stated that knowledge was based on large-scale surveys of participants that were "rather unsophicated and generalized" (Evans and Davies, 1986: 12). The profession had failed to take a reflective attitude towards practices and rationales that establish and maintain physical education. Evans and Davies (1986) argued for cultural sensitivity and recommended qualitative methodology to research the processes that occur in the physical education setting. Hendry (1986) proposed that physical education had educational potential to develop social awareness and interpersonal understanding for students through its potential to change students' attitudes and values. In the mid-1980s Underwood (1988) studied four secondary schools and found that students provided support for the contention that physical education should be enjoyable. The majority of the students interviewed expressed enthusiasm and enjoyment for physical education. Underwood (1988) used member checks to verify that students' comments in the interviews were consistent over time. He found that immediately after lessons students provided similar responses while their experiences were "still fresh in their minds" (p. 212). "All students considered they could cooperate with others, help the less able, and derive pleasure and satisfaction in physical education" (Underwood, 1988: 166).

In 1991 in his review of research on teaching in physical education, Silverman did not place students' perspectives as a research stream or substream. It was not until George Graham's monograph in the *Journal of Teaching in Physical Education* in 1995 that student voices emerged as a legitimate area of inquiry in mainstream physical education research.

The study of students' perspectives is a recent phenomenon in the area of research on teaching in physical education. However, two early dissertations that attempted to represent the student voice were Wang (1977) and Kollen (1981). Wang (1977) used an ethnographic approach to study one physical education class over a 4-month period. She was a participant observer and collected data using field notes and formal and informal interviews with 5th- and 6th-grade students. The categories of importance to students that emerged from the data were: free play, tumbling club, field day, leadership, entry into a game, and gym class in the total curriculum. Wang (1977) concluded through student interview and observation that a student-imposed hidden curriculum appeared through the subtle expression of symbolic rituals. The hidden curriculum instructed students in a code of behavior contradicting the physical education teacher's ideal teaching model described in teacher interviews as motor skill development and cooperative skill development in the gymnasium. The students' curriculum sponsored through implicit actions was described as discrimination, stratification, and segregation of individuals.

In another dissertation, Kollen (1981) studied the experience of movement in physical education classes from a phenomenological approach. She wanted to remedy the lack of concern in the literature for the meaning of physical education experience for students. Kollen (1981) focused on the reports and experiences of students. "Being open to the perspective of our students will help us acknowledge how *all* the actors in the educational process are significant" [emphasis added] (Kollen, 1981: 12). She discovered a paradox as she interviewed K-12 students. The students gave a "fairly positive overall evaluation of their physical education experience despite describing much of it as meaningless, boring, and alienating" (Kollen, 1981: 31).

There is also a paucity of research on students' perspectives in the classroom. Erikson and Shultz (1992) argued that helping students find and use their voice is in conflict with the traditional view of the role of students in schools. "It is a nuisance, a

distraction, to think that different students, together with their teachers and fellow students might be inhibiting and constructing profoundly different subjective worlds as they encounter what school presents as a standardized curriculum" (Erikson and Shultz, 1992; 467). Corbett and Wilson (1995) proposed that little is known about the subjective experiences of students in core content areas in general education and the same is true for physical education (Graham, 1995). However, recently, experts would agree that gaining students' perspectives can provide insights into curriculum reform (Corbett and Wilson, 2002; Fullan, 1991, 1999; Rudduck et al., 1997). Moreover, Corbett and Wilson (1995) suggested that if we want "true reform" in schools it makes good sense to include students' subjective experiences in partnership with other key players in the reform process. Erikson and Shultz (1992) argue that little attention has been paid to students' subjectivities particularly with respect to policy changes in schools:

> In our judgment, student experiences have been treated in partial and incidental ways, as researchers, teacher educators, and policy analysts consider relatively thin slices of classroom life, usually from a single perspectival angle. None of these slices have been multidimensional enough to capture students' subjective worlds as phenomena. (p. 466)

Methodological considerations

Student perspective research is qualitative inquiry grounded in students' subjective realities. This research requires extended periods of time spent with students in their naturalistic environment. The majority of the work draws on methods such as non-participant observation, interviews, field notes, and document analysis.

Erikson and Shultz (1992) explain that the traditional positivist deductive research techniques of direct instruction, limited response questionnaires, and statistical analysis fail to recognize students as the "insiders" regarding their schooling experience and the subjective meanings that those experiences hold. It is only through a multiple-method approach that values and respects student voice that an understanding of the students' "under-life" can be revealed through skilful observations in richly described contexts. "Detailed investigation [interpretive work] is necessary, for without it one cannot develop a coherent theoretical picture of the natures and varieties of student experiences" (Erikson and Shultz, 1992: 479).

Early research in physical education that incorporated student interviews within the data collection process provided the investigator with deeper understanding of the contexts and a richer description of class events (Evans and Davies, 1986; Hendry, 1996;

Kollen, 1981; Wang, 1977). Since those early studies many researchers have suggested that we need to use qualitative analysis such as interviews with children to enable us to clarify children's perspectives and views (Amis, 2005; Brooker and Macdonald, 1999; Chen and Cone, 2003; Graham, 1995; Morey and Goc Karp, 1998). Despite its problem with ambiguity, the interview is one of the most powerful techniques to begin to understand our fellow human beings (Fontana and Frey, 1994). However, making accurate interpretations of students' experiences in physical education requires a labor-intensive process to hear a more authentic voice from students. Researchers need to spend extended periods of time to get connected to a school culture, gain the trust of students, and ask the right questions.

One reason that there is a low prevalence and priority on research involving students is that working with students in schools is "messy, unpredictable, and constrained by bureaucratic and ethic restrictions" (Johnson and Howard, 1997: 1). Group interviewing has been identified as possible methodology to researchers in this labor-intensive process since it is "inexpensive, data rich, flexible, stimulating to respondents, recall aiding, and cumulative elaborative" (Denzin and Lincoln, 1998: 55). Ratliffe et al. (1992) studied *"What kids really think about their physical education classes"* (p. 32). They used three different methods of data collection: drawing and writing exercises, a questionnaire, and interviews with 22 grade 1, 2, 3, and 5 students. Ratliffe et al. (1992) found that "interviewing provided the most interesting and in-depth information" (p. 34). They stated that unfortunately this was the most time-consuming procedure and therefore difficult for teachers to incorporate into their physical education program. They argue, however, that teachers should take the time to listen to their students' views and opinions.

Trust is an essential requirement to attain authentic voice. "Gaining trust is essential to an interviewer's success and even once it is gained trust can be very fragile indeed; any faux pas by the researcher may destroy days, weeks, or months of painstakingly gained trust" (Denzin and Lincoln, 1998: 59–60). In response to the potential controlling role of the interviewer, qualitative interviewing has moved toward increasing attention to the voices and feelings of those being interviewed (Amis, 2005; Carlson, 1995; Dyson, 1995; Hunter, 2002; Nilges, 2004). In order to obtain the "real experiences" and perspectives of young people, a variety of methods can be used. Obtaining authentic voice is the first step towards gaining authentic student representation in the teaching and learning process as opposed to superficial or insincere tribute or respect (Anderson, 1998). In addition, schools often marginalize students' views and diminish their contribution to instruction and curriculum; indeed the culture within schools and among teachers does not lend itself to student input being valued (Brooker and Macdonald, 1999; Corbett and Wilson, 2002; Erikson and Shultz, 1992).

Over twenty years ago Jan Wright (1995) presented a feminist poststructuralist methodology to investigate the production and reproduction of gender in physical education. She suggested textual analysis adopting systematic linguistics as an analytical tool (Halliday, 1985). Wright (1995) commented at that time that this was a shift away from a broad ethnographic approach to focus more on classroom interactions in depth. She suggested taking field notes and interviewing students and teachers to understand the school context and to substantiate interactions. "Transcripts of the audiotapes were analyzed using methods developed from systematic functional linguistics (Halliday, 1985), together with more conventional qualitative coding methods for identifying important themes in textual material" (p. 14). Wright (1995) suggested that "In creating such texts through their use of language, space, gestures, dress, touch, and so on teachers and students reproduce specific discourses, social relations, and practices of culture … that circumscribe what can be done in a 'normal' physical education lesson." (p. 16). Feminist poststructuralist methodology have been used by researcher who work in described later in this chapter (Azzarito and Solmon, 2006; Azzarito, Solmon, and Harrison, in press; Oliver and Lalik, 2004).

In other school based research Nilges (2004) used an alternative subjective epistemology with transcendental phenomenology as the theoretical framework to study 19 5th grade students in a suburban city in the southeastern United States. Data collection included videotaped classes, student homework, researcher journals, field notes, and in-depth multiple interviews. The students participated in a creative dance unit in their physical education class, which focused on effort (force, time, space, flow). Nilges (2004) developed primary and secondary data codes, triangulated the data through crosschecking, source checking, negative case analysis, and analyzing the data using the theoretical framework. She created five dimensions of movement meaning: *Expressive, Sensory, Experiential, Competency,* and *Inter-subjective.* In each dimension themes emerged from the data, such as: "Mixing Perception and Imagination," "Moving and being moved", "Like lint on a sweater," "Being good and being seen being good," and "Meaning through the conscious mind of others." In the sensory dimension, Bethany stated she enjoyed moving fast and free: "it feels like I am on a porch swing. I like to get on my swing and put the pillows down by my arms … It feels like I'm floating fast and sort of free like" (p. 308). Robby found in the *experiential* dimension that he "enjoyed moving with strong force and an indirect space pathway [in hockey]. You also have to use strong force, like if you're trying to get the puck from someone and they are stronger than you" (p. 309). For Valerie, the inter-subjective direction of meaning was more positive. "[I like] strong force better because most of the time strong force is more Tommy Girl like me. I feel comfortable doing it because I am it. I am a Tommy Girl" (p. 311). "The results of this study provide a window into the meanings and associations students have with movement and may assist educators in helping students better recognize the personal meanings they derive from participating in physical activity" (p. 312). Nilges (2004) attempts to show that *Ice Can Look Like Glass* or there are always two sides of meaning to a given movement. Students in this study were challenged to find their own subjective meaning in movements outside of their peers' opinions and influence. She reflected that students perceive certain aspects of physical education as highly individualized. Nilges (2004) used journaling, projection techniques, think-aloud exercises, and probing questions to capture the "subtleties and sophistication of meaning" (p. 312) represented in the findings. She reflected that "students needed guidance, to critically reflect on movement" (p. 313) and strongly recommended creative dance as valuable content area in physical education. Nilges (2004) believed that there "appears to be room for a happy marriage between phenomenology, as a highly individualized way of coming to know, and the more subjective goals of physical education" (p. 313). This is a valuable perspective to approach the study student voice.

In our research efforts it would also be prudent to explore other forms of inquiry like narrative. Connelly and Clandinin (1990) have used narrative inquiry to tell others' stories. Narrative research is a form of writing that has rarely been used to tell the stories of young people, or those in physical education research (Oliver, 1998). Connelly and Clandinin (1990) warned us to be as alert to the stories that are not told as to those that are told and emphasized.

Teachers often feel reluctant to increase student input and responsibility. Since teachers usually believe that they are responsible for guiding students as learners, they often feel that student input is not a priority (Hunter, 2002). However, administrators and teachers who dismiss the appropriateness of the student perspective miss the opportunity to create quality programs with students (Brooker and Macdonald, 1999; Corbett and Wilson, 1995, 2002; Fullan, 1991).

A theoretical framework for students' perspectives

It could be argued that students' perspectives research takes a social constructivist approach. Constructivists believe that students are implicitly engaged in the process of knowledge generation guided by their perspective and action through the use of their energy and mental effort over time (Hendry et al., 1999). Perkins (1999) emphasized three tenets of constructivism: the active learner, the social learner, and the creative learner. As active learners students are not passive recipients of knowledge but are involved in tasks that stimulate decision-making, critical thinking, and problem solving. As social learners, students construct knowledge through social interaction with their peers, facilitated by their teachers. As creative learners, students are guided to discover knowledge themselves and to create their own understanding of the subject matter. Individuals draw on prior knowledge and experiences to construct knowledge. Researchers working within this perspective have attempted to access student voice relative to the student as an active, social, and creative learner. This research is based on a rationale that the study of educational experiences should take a student-centered approach.

Social constructivist theories have been endorsed as providing a potentially useful reconceptualization of existing approaches to teaching and learning in physical education (Azzarito and Ennis, 2003; Chen and Cone, 2003; Chen and Rovegno, 2000; Dodds et al., 2001; Ennis, 2000; Kirk and Macdonald, 1998; Rovegno and Kirk, 1995). Situated learning theory has been represented as one example of a social constructivist approach to learning (Kirk and Macdonald, 1998). Situated learning provides an authentic framework in which to position the study of students' perspectives in physical education. Social and cultural contexts contribute to and influence what is learned and how learning takes place (Lave and Wenger, 1991). Kirk and Macdonald (1998) presented situated learning as a theoretical approach to the study of physical education. Kirk and MacPhail (2002) extended this work to reconceptualize teaching games for understanding in a situated learning framework. Dyson et al. (2004) discussed both Sport Education and Tactical Games and in addition, they argue that Cooperative Learning in physical education is an instructional model that can be studied under the theoretical framework of situated learning. Situated learning theory investigates the relationships among the various physical, social, and cultural dimensions of the context of learning (Lave and Wenger, 1991). Taking time to discover students' perspectives can lead to a better understanding of relations in physical education through a situated learning theoretical framework.

Further detail on these theoretical frameworks can be found elsewhere in Chapters 3.4 and 3.5.

Major findings

In this chapter, studies will be highlighted that present students' perspectives in physical education classes. After a review of the research findings on students' perspectives in physical education, a conscious effort was made to include students' voice by presenting students' quotes. This represents the actual words of the students within their physical education contexts.

Students' view of the physical education curriculum and instruction

Cothran and Ennis (1999) studied students' perspectives on school membership looking specifically at students' meaning of relevance and connection to an urban high school physical education curriculum. They collected field notes and used informal and formal interviews of 16 students during a semester of required physical education. Similar to other research (Tousignant and Siedentop, 1983; Tjeerdsma, 1997), this study found that teachers do not explicitly convey their goals to students and students were left with a vague rationale for the curriculum. These high school students believed the curriculum was not relevant. Justin commented that the fitness course is "just stupid stuff. I don't need no aerobics or anything" (p. 240). In addition, students felt little connection to the curriculum. Stacy stated that her teachers should "tell us real life stuff and not just the book ... They should tell us how to use stuff we learn in school in the future" (p. 238). And negative experiences turned students off from participating in physical education. "I don't play no more. I tried to play once, and they just yelled at me. I was embarrassed. I just quit playing" (Dana, p. 243).

An understandable conclusion from this research is that "when students understand and believe in the subject matter, engagement is more likely" (p. 244). Cothran and Ennis (1999) argue that if we understood more about students' participation and enjoyment we would be more likely to effect change in schools. Cothran and Ennis (1999) revealed that students believed that teachers did not operate in a fair or logical manner and students reported that many of the class rules were not valuable or legitimate.

A study conducted by Gagnon et al. (2000) found numerous injustices with the delivery of physical education curriculum. Students were put in situations where teachers punished or scolded students who had done nothing wrong, students were belittled by their teachers, teachers treated students differently, and teachers' evaluations of students were too harsh or unfair. Boy: "In nearly every class my physical education teacher picks the same person to put away and take out the equipment." Girl: "When he picks someone to show how something is done in a game, I am not picked very often" (p. 59).

Other research has also uncovered many inequities in the gymnasium related to gender and ability in physical education (Azzarito and Solmon, 2006; Carlson, 1995; Hunter, 2002; Kirk, 2002; Portman, 1995). Gagnon et al. (2000) found that more than 60% of 5th- and 6th-grade students believed that at some time they were treated unjustly by their physical education teacher. These students were under the impression that they had no influence on the behavior of their teachers and did not believe that students could get teachers to treat students in what they considered a more appropriate fashion. In a follow up study Martel et al. (2002) concurred that students do not have a voice in physical education classes and they are often placed in situations where they are apprehensive to participate fully in the learning process. "This attitude of resignation and the fear of freely expressing their thoughts to the physical education teacher are clear indications of the impasse in which students find themselves" (p. 56). Martel et al. (2002) argue that physical educators should become acquainted with the main sources of dissatisfaction of their students.

Hunter (2002) studied Australian students' transition to middle school to gain an understanding of their perspective. She "hung-out" at schools for extended periods of time, taking field notes, writing reflections, and interviewing students about their physical education curriculum. Students indicated the important place one's subjectivity had in the transition from primary to secondary school and the learning that took place during this process. Hunter (2002) uncovered that this was in relation to how they were constructed and constituted as students and learners, and their social position within a class group. The students' perspectives were often associated with the material and symbolic body, which included sport, health and fitness, gender and sexuality, and pleasure. Students reported a lack of formal "voice" in curriculum, pedagogical, and governance issues within their schooling, stating that they would not be "heard" unless they paralleled the dominant adult line of thought (Hunter, 2002).

In New Zealand, Burrows et al. (2002) studied children's responses to the National Education Monitoring Project (NEMP). Grade-4 and grade-8 student responses were collected from four tasks: one-on-one interviewing, station work, team and independent work, and open space physical activity assessments. Burrows et al. (2002) cited that students seemed to value exercise and proper nutrition and saw the relationship to their health. However, they proposed that the relationship between eating particular kinds of food and regular exercise to health is problematic. They make the case that this curriculum has developed the construction of a "guilt complex" for students. If students do not conform to the "accepted norms" this creates constant guilt and self-consciousness. Burrows et al. (2002) reported that children rarely mentioned pleasure in their responses. They commented that perhaps we have developed an overly "moralistic position which suggests that someone who cannot demonstrate a slim body shape is in some ways unworthy, undisciplined, lazy, a couch potato … and some of the students' responses are already indicative of this" (Burrows et al., 2002: 46). Educators are aware that boys and girls readily develop a socially constructed view of "the ideal body". Burrows et al. (2002) proposed that physical educators examine the ways in which practices are implicated in reproducing social meanings and experiences for students that contribute to the guilt complex associated with the desire to achieve a socially desirable body shape.

In a critical inquiry of girls' experiences in physical education, Azzarito et al. (2006) present a feminist post-structural perspective on girls in physical education. Interviewing 15 female students in a high school, they found that students enjoyed and valued physical activity. Students chose to participate or resist participation in their physical education classes through their negotiated gender and race relations. Physical education classes were considered "contested terrain" where girls supported the notion of equal opportunity in physical activity but often perceived the limits on their choices compared to their male peers. As Kirk (2002) has suggested, the problem does not necessarily reside with the girls but with the historically constructed and maintained "gender order" that has existed in physical education for the last 100 years.

Oliver and Lalik (2004) provided an example of poststructuralist feminist work in schools with girls' physical education classes.

Oliver and Lalik (2004) utilized alternative methodologies to study grade 7, 8, and 9 girls' physical education classes to examine the development and implementation of an innovative curriculum using the theme of girls' understanding of their bodies. Oliver and Lalik (2004) utilized a number of different methods of data collection: journal entries, collages, photographic essays, and other textual and visual artifacts. In addition, they asked the girls to work in pairs to conduct interviews. Findings suggested that students could produce creative and well-developed artifacts. Grade 9 students produced strong critiques of inappropriate messages about the female body and eagerly contributed to class discussions.

Adding to this work and grounded in a feminist poststructuralist perspective, Azzarito and Solmon (2006) utilized a qualitative ethnographic design to study students' perspectives of their bodies in physical education classes. Twenty-one students (9 girls and 12 boys) were interviewed individually. Two majors themes emerged from the data from physical education classes: Students were either compliant to dominant gendered body discourses, which was represented as the "Comfortable Body" and the "Bad Bodies", or they rejected the dominant gendered body discourses presented as "resistance" or "transformation" to mainstream notions of the body. The body ideal was represented as the feminine slender and the masculine muscular body (Kirk, 2002). To stimulate conversations the researcher showed students a portfolio of body images drawn from sport, fitness, and fashion magazines. Students were asked to look at the images, comment on which images they identified with, explain why, and tell how physical education might help them become like the body image with which they identified. In terms of comfortable bodies only three girls perceived themselves as having comfortable bodies compared to nine boys. Sean stated that physical education could be valuable: "I mean, if you don't do it in physical education or some kind of workout, there is no way you can look like that [photograph number 8]" (p. 210). Six girls and three boys expressed dissatisfaction with their body image. Helen expressed a "bad body image" when she commented: "I'm not skinny enough, you know … I don't consider myself skilled or fit" (p. 212). Vonda lamented: "I think that big people, people probably don't want to be like big people because some people like laugh at you, or talk about you when you're big" (p. 213). In contrast, a boy Trevor wanted to be more muscular: I'm not very strong and stuff, I'm a little weaker than most average people are and skinnier … cause I can't lift a lot of weight or anything like that" (p. 214). Six girls and one boy resisted the dominant gendered body discourses. This was represented as "Sites of Resistance" or "Sites of Transformation". In poststructuralist terms this was described as "borderland bodies". Michael was described as resistant: "… they [the other boys] want to look muscular because of the sports they want to play … and have the muscles and power" (p. 216). Precious viewed physical education as the potential to be transformative for her. Azzarito and Solmon (2006) explained her situation. "Instead of labeling her body as comparatively bad, Precious constructed a body narrative recognizing her physicality as different but valuable, Precious weighed over 200 pounds, and she explained during the interview that obesity runs in her family. Because she 'lives in the middle of nowhere,' as she said, physical education is the only space available to her for exercise" (p. 217).

From another perspective Suomi et al. (2003) studied the factors that have a positive or negative effect on the experiences of students who are "thriving" (doing well), "struggling" (having problems), or "had disabilities" in an integrated kindergarten and 4th-grade class. Six students from kindergarten and six students from 4th grade were categorized by their physical educators to be observed and interviewed. They found that the social experience of students clearly varied depending on their social or cultural grouping, that is, whether they were thriving, struggling, or classified as having a disability. The students' comments demonstrated how the immature social behaviors could have a deleterious effect on relationships in the elementary school curriculum. Two fourth-grade students confided: "Well, basically Gail [student with disability] is kind of a little cuckoo because she always says peekaboo. She doesn't pay attention and goofs around a lot". In addition, Joshua commented that "when we were playing the Prison Ball game, I saw Gail was not getting a ball to throw, others [other students] would jump in front of her to get the ball."

It is interesting to note that the physical education teachers in this study, who were considered "highly skilled and empathetic teachers who used a progressive curriculum" (p. 200), were unaware of the consequences of poorly developed social skills. When the researchers looked more closely at the learning environment there were factors that negatively affected the social experiences of all students, especially the strugglers and those students with disabilities. For example, in tag games the struggling students or students with disabilities were left out, embarrassed, and/or had their feelings hurt. "The manner in which students choose partners and the level of individual social skill development had a negative effect on the social experiences of the struggling students and those with disabilities" (Suomi et al., 2003: 200). They suggested improving students' social skills through peer teaching and cooperative learning or other more student-centered approaches to teaching and learning. These instructional models could enhance the experiences of struggling and disabled students and increase their chances of acceptance.

Cothran, Kulinna, and Garrahy (2003) interviewed 182 students from 14 different high schools (Grade 6–12) schools across the United States to address the lack of information related to students' voice on class management. More specifically, Cothran et al. (2003) were interested in how the students would describe effective and ineffective class managers. The students were interviewed alone and in groups of 2–3 friends. Despite the wide variety of school contexts and student backgrounds, students provided similar explanations of teacher behaviors that improved or impeded effective class management in their gymnasiums. Students reported that teachers need to set their expectations, rules, and regulations early: "this is kind of giving the secret away, but you've gotta lay down rules on the very first day … Don't let us break the rules and then try the rules later 'cause no one will pay attention" (Joelle, p. 437). Students agreed that teachers who were too lenient or too strict were also ineffective class managers. Latoya agreed: "… but you know

there's a time for you to play and a time for you to learn. She is going to take you out of class if you don't" (p. 439). In addition, students reported that the most effective managers also have relationships with their students. "If you have a relationship with your students, they're gonna trust you more and they're gonna respect you more and then they'll be nicer to you" (Sonya, p. 439). Students also felt that teachers who genuinely cared for and respected their students' needs and wishes were the best managers. Cothran et al. (2003) concluded that "These students' experiences and reports act as personal educational theories that support and broaden educators' conceptions of what makes an effective class manager" (p. 440).

Cothran and Kulinna (2006) examined students' perspectives on direct, peer, and inquiry teaching strategies in seven school districts. Seventy middle school students (21 in 6th grade, 25 in 7th grade, and 24 in 8th grade) from one large urban school district and six smaller suburban districts from a large metropolitan area in the United States participated in the study. Prior to the interviews, researchers developed short physical education class scenarios to represent basketball lessons using direct, peer, and inquiry teaching strategies. Students were given the scenarios and illustrations during an interview and were asked what they thought of the teaching strategies. The students were then asked to "rank order the three strategies with regard to the best way to teach physical education and to explain why they ordered the strategies in that manner" (p. 169). No statistical significance was revealed in relation to the teaching strategy ranking. However, the interview responses revealed a variety of perspectives: the affective climate of each strategy, and beliefs about knowledge. Alex believed that preferences for a strategy were primarily based on students' priorities. He explained: "I'd rather learn more than have fun and talk. Most middle school students want to have fun at this age, and maybe learning isn't as important to them. I think learning is more important, but having fun is like a higher priority than learning for most kids" (p. 171).

The social aspect of peer instruction made it "a clear fun favorite for many of the students" (p. 172). Students' views of having to perform a skill in public affected their choice of strategy. For example, in direct instruction students were more likely to have to publicly display a skill. As Julia commented, a low-skilled student would not like the strategy because, "they're getting kind of like they have to do it right in front of the teacher, so they might not like to do it because they might not give a lot of effort" (p. 173). In contrast, some students preferred direct instruction because of the direct exchange of knowledge from the teacher. Melinda commented, "You can get the material done and get it into your brain because you're seeing it and then doing it yourself, and someone is telling you who has the really trained eye" (p. 174). Peer teaching was also seen more positively than inquiry in regards to knowledge, "because many students thought working with others would be fun" (p. 174). Tana did not like the peer teaching strategy because she felt the teacher would not really be teaching, therefore not doing his/her job. Likewise, Jessica did not feel that the teachers using inquiry instruction would be doing their jobs: "I really don't feel the teacher is teaching" (p. 175). Special students and independent learners preferred peer and inquiry strategies to direct instruction because it gave them the opportunity to learn from others. Cothran and Kulinna (2006) reported that students provide both concerns and preferences that can inform the teacher consideration of different instructional models.

Working in the middle schools, Dyson, DiCesare, Coviello, and Stover (in review) carried out 21 separate student interviews with small focus groups (76 students). The purpose of this study was to describe and interpret students' perspectives in four urban middle school physical education programs in the mid-south of the U.S. Additional data collection included frequent class observations using field notes over an 18-week period, and researchers wrote a reflective journal. Inductive analysis and constant comparison methods were used to organize the data throughout the research process. This study attempted to represent "student voices" in their naturalistic physical education setting. Eight themes emerged from the student voice: "I like to eat and watch T.V.," "We want to play," "If our class was a bit smaller," "You get new friends out of it," "The testosterone level gets a little high," "It pumps you up," "PE is not challenging," and "Teachers are uptight." Students appeared to understand the benefits of being physically active. However, findings suggest that overcrowding in the gymnasium, repetitive boring exercises, gender inequity, and the lack of challenging content impeded students' participation in their physical education classes. This study suggests that teachers need to tap into students' interests, provide equitable and inclusive opportunities, and provide choice to increase the likelihood that students will be physically active during and outside physical education classes.

Marginalization in physical education

Siedentop and O'Sullivan (1992) warned the profession that physical education in schools is marginalized and deteriorating. Even more disturbing, Martinek and Griffith (1994) found that in today's schools many students believe that they are not very skilled or cannot learn skills, and hesitate to participate in physical activity. Some even refuse to participate in physical activity because of the negative experiences in physical education (Martinek and Griffith, 1994).

Walling and Martinek (1995), Portman (1995), and Carlson (1995) presented research that portrayed learned helplessness, inequity, and alienation in physical education. Walling and Martinek (1995) described learned helplessness as a phenomenon that has emerged with individuals whose feelings of incapability can become a static condition in which individuals acquire a feeling of helplessness in attempting a number of different tasks. That is, learned-helpless individuals perceive little control over their achievement during physical or academic tasks. Utilizing a case-study methodology Walling and Martinek (1995) provided an in-depth understanding of a middle-school student who was learned-helpless. They analyzed her situation through observation and interview and then proposed an intervention targeting physical education to start to impact her motivational patterns. Their proposal to improve the student's control and confidence involved: stressing effort and improvement over outcome, structuring the learning environment for maximum participation, encouraging the student to engage in physical activity outside the class and school time, and creating leadership and responsibility roles for the student.

Portman (1995) studied the experiences of low-skilled 6th graders (11 girls and 2 boys). This researcher demonstrates the power of non-participant observations and interviewing in school-based research.

Being low skilled was an unhappy experience for all 13 students. They were rarely successful in any unit, experienced little assistance in developing the necessary motor skills, tended to be left alone during skilled practice, received the brunt of critical comments in all competitive situations, and they recognized a 'skill pecking order' in the class, preferring anonymity to being publicity identified as low skilled. (p. 448)

The same students reported that they liked physical education when they were successful. Field notes confirmed that there was a lack of teacher-initiated feedback to low-skilled students. All 13 students felt that they would have been more successful in class if they were not publicly criticized by their peers, especially in competitive situations. Fiona remarked: "Sometimes when you are playing you get nervous and you are afraid that you are going to goof up and that everyone is going to think that you are a jerk or something" (p. 451). The knowledge that they were low skilled when compared to the performances of others, combined with the teacher's low expectations, caused the students to believe that success was unattainable. When they failed they usually attributed their failure to a lack of their own ability and thus perpetuated their perceived status. "Most of the low-skilled students in this study bore this understanding [that they were learned helpless] quietly" (Portman, 1995: 452). Only a few blamed the nature of the class, the content, or the situation in their environment for their lack of success.

Carlson (1995) illuminated a common problem in middle- and high-school physical education: student alienation. She defined alienation as students' persistent negative feelings that may have their origins in one or several of three affective states: meaninglessness, powerlessness, and isolation. The students Carlson (1995) interviewed talked of lack of personal meaning, lack of control, and isolation. They had all developed strategies to avoid aversive experiences in physical education. A student, May, confirmed her negative attitude to physical education: "Sometimes I might change and just mope around and not really do what they want me to do, or I might just sit down and say, 'Don't bug me, I don't want to do this. It's not worth it'" (p. 474). She found 20% of the students did not enjoy physical education. Some of these students, as Portman (1995) and Walling and Martinek (1995) found in their respective studies, felt that they could not succeed in physical education. Carlson (1995) reminded us that alienation in any form exists as a result of a complex equation or set of events that appears more frequently than we would like to admit in physical education. The lack of student voice can lead to student disengagement in classroom activities and program goals. In this chapter student perspective primarily is discussed in terms of research with student, voice contributing to our knowledge base, however, as Carlson (1995) reminds us, student viewpoint can be used by teachers to improve their practice. In her optimistic manner she challenges us to create a positive learning environment with students. "What may be possible is to envision a form of physical education that includes *all* and alienates none" [emphasis added] (Carlson, 1995: 475).

Students' likes and dislikes in physical education

Other studies have examined what aspects of physical education students enjoy or do not enjoy. Sanders and Graham's (1995) study highlighted the fact that students had unfavorable feelings regarding the repetition of tasks, specifically the stretching that occurred at the beginning of every lesson. Tabitha complained that, "We always do the same activities" and Brett stated that it was "silly and boring stuff" (p. 380). However, students would talk at length about what they enjoyed in their physical education experience. For example, in the manipulative activities, Holly exclaimed "We play, play, play, with the balls" (Sanders and Graham, 1995: 380). This was an example of what Sanders and Graham (1995) described as "the relentless persistence for play", which was defined as "a natural characteristic of children to change, alter, or adapt a task that does not meet their current skill or interest level into a task or tasks that better meets their current abilities or interests" (p. 376). After Sanders and Graham's (1995) extended observations of kindergarteners in schools and interviewing students, they believed the term relentless persistence for play aptly depicts kindergarteners in a physical education program.

Hopple and Graham (1995) studied how children think, feel, and what they understand about physical fitness testing. Interviewing 54 students in 4th and 5th grade they discovered that most students did not have a clear understanding of why they take physical fitness tests, particularly the mile-run. Hopple and Graham (1995) found that for many students, the mile-run test was the test to avoid. Students stated overt methods of dodging the mile-run that included faking a variety of illnesses or injuries, being absent on the days the test was being administered, or producing a written note from a doctor or parent. Students commented that, if provided with the opportunity, they would change the mile-run to make it more fun. Physical educators will not be surprised to learn from students that: "the pressure that came from competing against an external standard was not motivating" (Hopple and Graham, 1995: 414). The challenge for the field is to examine issues surrounding these results to determine how curriculum and instruction (fitness testing, content, assessment) can be made more meaningful and relevant for students. If we as educators have the fitness education of our students as a goal, we must access what students "think, value, and feel" in order to present more effective curriculum and instruction. Hopple and Graham (1995) "remind educators that children are not miniature adults" (p. 416) and therefore we need to be cognizant that we cannot simply apply strategies that may work with adults "on" students.

In a dance unit Hastie and Pickwell (1996) stated that students were highly skilled at finding ways to minimize work and have fun, but do enough to pass the course. The high school students did not enjoy the dance experience. The teacher seemed to trade off lower levels of participation in the instructional task system to "gain and maintain the cooperation of the students" (Siedentop et al., 1994). This diminished students' achievement in the instructional system but enhanced the students' social agenda (Hastie and Pickwell, 1996). Students talked about "giving the teacher what she wanted" (Hastie and Pickwell, 1996: 179) and described in detail how they avoided participation in the class.

Tjeerdsma et al. (1996) studied students' perceptions, values, and beliefs prior to, during, and after badminton instruction. Students could identify that this unit was taught differently from their normal physical education classes because it was longer in length (a 6-week unit compared to a 3-week unit) and because the teacher purposefully taught a skill, tactical, and combination approach to instruction, providing feedback and interaction with students throughout the unit. All 44 students said that they liked physical education classes that tried to teach them about skills and tactics in an unfamiliar content badminton. The students participating in this study liked participating in sports and did so on a regular basis. The reasons they gave for participating in sports were: fun, teamwork, social interaction, fitness, health benefits, and challenges.

Morey and Goc Karp (1998) studied why some students who are good at physical education dislike it so much. Interviews were carried out with each student in a 10th-grade intact class. They confirmed that students considered physical education as a break from more important academic subjects. However, students felt dissatisfied with their physical education program and this created a negative perspective toward physical education and physical activities. Frankie: "We don't like to do drills and you know we're not going to be perfect ... we want to play" (p. 94). Penny: "Um I just don't like exercising with other people, it gets kind of embarrassing" (p. 96). Morey and Goc Karp (1998) discovered that teachers knew very little about the home lives of their students and these contextual considerations had an impact on student performance and effort.

Cothran and Ennis (2001) interviewed and observed three teachers and 16 students at a large urban high school to "examine the potential multiple meanings assigned to a curricular change effort in a secondary physical education program" (p. 1). Two themes emerged from the data: the value of physical education and learning in physical education. A majority of students felt that there was no value in physical education and were frustrated that they were required to take the physical education class. Julie stated, "Shouldn't have to take it at all. It takes time away from what you should be studying" (p. 3). Lori agreed with Julie: "Like me, I don't think I need it. I might take PE if I needed to exercise but I don't" (p. 3). In contrast, the students who valued physical education, valued it because "it provided a pleasant break from the routine" (p. 3). The students who agreed with their teachers about the value of physical education were the students in the dance or personal fitness class." The new personal fitness class was met with animosity by the students. Carrie said "it's almost like a real class. It's not right." The students refused to dress out or bring their notebooks and showed significant negative attitudes toward the class and teachers. Some students

somewhat enjoyed the fitness classes and another group really thought it helped them develop physically active lifestyles: "it's about taking care of your body and yourself. You got to know about exercise and things. It's a lot more than regular PE class. You can use this stuff forever." (p. 4).

Students' perspectives of innovative curriculum

Much of the research on student perspectives has been carried out on the growing number of innovative instructional models in physical education. Several research studies have explored students' perspectives of innovative programs in physical education (Carlson and Hastie, 1997; Dyson 1995, 2001, 2002; Hastie, 1996, 1998, 2000; Kinchin and O'Sulivan, 2003; Tjeerdsma et al., 1996). Generally, students report having positive experiences in adventure education settings (Dyson, 1995; Hastie, 1995), in Sport Education units (Carlson and Hastie, 1997; Hastie, 1996, 1998, 2000; Kinchin and O'Sullivan, 2003; McPhail, Kinchin, and Kirk, 2004; Mowling, Brock, and Hastie, 2006) and in cooperative learning (Dyson 2001, 2002; Dyson and Strachan, 2000).

Dyson (1995) studied students' perspectives of Project Adventure in two alternative elementary schools. Students' voices emerged from 106 students in grades 3 and 5. Dyson (1995) found that when the researcher spends extended periods of time in a school setting and then sits down at students' level and talks to them, he or she can begin to explore their realities and reveal their experiences and perceptions of the world. In this adventure education-based curriculum, students spoke with a positive attitude towards physical education. The themes the students mostly talked about were: cooperating with others, challenging, taking risks, having fun, not having fun, trust, problem solving, and communication. Sally explained that in physical education "everyone was screaming and laughing and I just thought that it was really nice that they were having fun, because school-work is sort of fun and sort of boring. Gym is nicer" (p. 399).

In a study of an outdoor adventure camp Hastie (1995) found that the students' experience was "in significant contrast to the school setting" (p. 93). There were high levels of fun and achievement of tasks even though there was no formal accountability. The students were challenged at their level and the students' social agenda drove the social tasks and supported the students participating in the adventure activities. For a comprehensive coverage of the ecology of the gymnasium defining managerial, instructional, and social task system see Chapter 3.2.

Pope and Grant (1996) studied students' perspectives in a 28-lesson sport education touch rugby unit. Themes that emerged were student union, student liberation, and the team as a productive unit. Cooperation was a significant outcome for many students with student voices exclaiming "significant personal progress" (p. 111). The students felt liberated by the structure of Sport Education. Glen stated "you are 90% in control of everything that you do" (p. 112). Students commented that responsibility and effort were as important as winning. Cooperative teams promoted student success and gains in learning. The structure of Sport Education and the cooperative nature of the unit allowed students to become more invested in the learning process. Students were able to help with team planning, work on team skills and tactics, referee the games, and increase knowledge about the sport under study. Pope and Grant (1996) argue that students can become capable of decision making at early ages. They suggest that if we took more notice of student voice then we may be better able to deal with the "dysfunctional" nature of much that occurs in physical education (Kirk, 1996; Locke, 1992; Siedentop et al., 1994).

In a study of students' social system in a Sport Education unit, Carlson and Hastie (1997) found that socialization emerged as an important behavior in physical education classes. Three high-school classes were studied in coeducational netball and touch rugby units. A number of themes emerged relating to the learning environment: team work, cooperation, leadership responsibilities, refereeing responsibilities, changing perceptions of roles, and students' preference for student coaches. John took on a leadership role with his group: "I think it is really great because … if someone is not doing well you can teach them, and then they like it better and better, and you get enjoyment out of that." (p. 187). When talking about refereeing, Nadia stated that: "It was a good feeling, because you could tell them what to do, and you could blow the whistle, and you know you felt free" (p. 185). Students' responses to the situation were generally positive and the students stated that they preferred peers as coaches rather than their physical education teacher. Rita was adamant that students were the best teachers: "I think we learned more because teachers can only teach you so much. They've got to get around big groups and they can't get over to you individually and spend a lesson just showing you where you are going wrong" (p. 187).

Carlson and Hastie (1997) discussed an extension of the word and concept of "fun" that was evident in reports from students in this study. Fun included responsibility for refereeing, organizing schedules, or playing suitable positions. Fun referred to working as a team, cooperating, and learning new skills. Similar results have been found in other research (Dyson 2001, 2002; Grant, 1992; Hastie, 1998; Pope and Grant, 1996). Carlson and Hastie (1997) discovered that students had expanded "the term *fun*

to include teamwork, improving skills, as well as socializing" (p. 193). Hastie (1998) discovered that in a 20-lesson unit on floor hockey, girls commented that they enjoyed playing on mixed-sex teams and taking responsibility for the unit, even though they believed some of the boys sometimes dominated decision making and the major roles of captain and referee. Hastie (1998) examined the involvement and opinions of 6th-grade girls during a season of floor hockey that followed a Sport Education format. Twenty lessons were observed and field notes were taken throughout this unit focusing on whether girls received more practice opportunities in this unit versus a traditional physical education format. It was concluded that girls preferred the Sport Education experience because they were motivated and worked harder. Hastie (1998) found that, consistent with other findings from Sport Education studies, "the girls particularly enjoyed taking roles other than player" (p. 167).

Hastie (2000) studied the ecology of Sport Education. Student interviews revealed that students had fun, learned to "get along", developed teamwork, learned from observing others play, and learned roles in order to self-manage each other in their team. Hastie (2000) found that a student, Marcus, could take on the leader role as a "second teacher". Marcus developed task responsibility for management with his own accountability system that he called "keeping everyone happy". When students talked about Marcus they stated "He didn't fuss at us, but he tried to keep us on task" (student team interview, Hastie, 2000: 14). Mary explained the benefits of being on the same team for 20 lessons: "you got to know people better, and the whole program taught us to come together to win as a team, and lose as a team. That only happened because we were together for the whole season" (Hastie, 2000: 368). Students learned to get along with other students that they would not normally spend time with. "I would not be friends with the people I am friends with if we were not on the same team for a long time. There are people on the team that I would not normally get along with, even talk to" (Hastie, 2000: 368). Students reported that they preferred having students as coaches rather than their regular teacher, which is similar to the findings of other studies (Carlson and Hastie, 1997; Dyson, 2002; Dyson and Strachan, 2000). The data from this study regarding the student social system replicated findings from Carlson and Hastie (1997) where the students' social agendas were consistent with the teacher's goal for the unit. In contrast, research suggests that in traditional physical education classes, the teachers' and students' goals are not always congruent (Hastie and Pickwell, 1996; Tjeerdsma, 1997; Tousignant and Siedentop, 1983; MacPhail, Kinchin, and Kirk, 2004; Mowling, Brock, and Hastie, 2006).

The innovative curriculum "Sport for Peace" was derived from Sport Education and specifically designed for urban schools (Ennis et al., 1999). In studying this curriculum, the researchers utilized field notes and student and teacher interviews for 30 weeks in a high-school program. A physical education program was dramatically changed to increase motivation and engagement of urban students. Students were grouped into teams and were involved in scheduling and formulating practices in sport roles. In Sport for Peace more emphasis was placed on exhibiting peaceful relationships with peers and teammates. This year-long study concluded that students began to develop an affiliation with their team, similar to a family atmosphere. One coach explained, "When they do it wrong, I learned that you can't yell at them. You have to teach them" (p. 282). The analysis of the program through field notes and interviews revealed that these students were more successful and more interested during the Sport for Peace curriculum than during the traditional approach to PE. "Highly skilled students were unable to gain respect through dominant play. Instead, they earned respect through thoughtful decision making, effective teaching, and positive support for every player" (p. 283). As the 9-week unit continued, the teachers were surprised at the level of responsibility and camaraderie developed in the classes. In the Sport for Peace curriculum, it appeared that students developed respect for self and others, and gained trust and a "sense of family" through thoughtful decision-making and a supportive learning environment.

Kinchin and O'Sullivan (2003) studied student support for and resistance to a curricular innovation in high-school physical education. They found that 9th- and 10th-grade students generally responded positively to features of a cultural studies unit that was a modified form of Sport Education. Kinchin and O'Sullivan (2003) had similar findings of other research using Sport Education (Carlson and Hastie, 1997; Ennis et al., 1999; Grant, 1992; Hastie, 1998, 2000). The purpose of the unit was to have students become critical consumers of sport and physical activity and critique issues of social justice. Students appreciated the shift from teacher-centered to student-centered instruction. Students talked about helping other classmates, and spoke positively about decision-making and problem solving during the unit. In addition, students learned roles and took ownership for leading others in instruction and managing and organizing the learning environment. Kinchin and O'Sullivan (2003) reported that marginalized students were motivated to participate through team cohesion, working together, and positive encouragement. Students perceived physical education as having purpose and meaning during a unit where they developed better skills and strategies for volleyball, which was similar to the findings of

Ennis et al. (1999). Life skills of leadership, responsibility, cooperation, communication, and support and encouragement for others appeared to be nurtured. Students reported that the unit was an opportunity to fully participate in physical education in a critical manner. However, Kinchin and O'Sullivan (2003) uncovered strong resistant behaviors from the students: goofing-off, interrupting the teacher, and overt completion of unrelated school-work. These inappropriate behaviors were fueled by the teacher lecturing, having periods of inactivity, expecting homework, and adjusting to the new instructional format of Sport Education. To teach an innovative curriculum the researchers emphasized the need for thorough and meticulous planning of the content and careful selection of teaching methods to deliver effective instruction.

MacPhail, Kirk, and Kinchin (2004) used Sport Education (SE) as the framework, and interviewed students and teams throughout the season to determine if team membership or affiliation affected students' physical education experience. Researchers found in their study of 76 year-five students "that the opportunity to become affiliated with a team was an attractive feature of the pupils' physical education experience" (p. 106). Students at the school saw the benefits of having increased interaction time with the same teammates. "I like being in a team since Christmas because ... you don't have to keep swapping teams so you get to know them and play with them" (p. 114). The students wanted to be a part of their team and felt "you're in a team you feel like the team needs you" (p. 115). MacPhail et al. (2004) observed students investing in their teams and developing a sense of loyalty to their teammates. One team, The Invaders, were specifically impacted by the team affiliation. Initially the team members did not like their team and the students complained about the teammates. By the end of the unit Billy commented: "it was fun and we didn't think we would get to the final. I think we are a pretty good team" (p. 118). Students talked about creation of new friendships and discontinuing negative comments to other students.

Mowling, Brock, and Hastie (2006) asked 4th grade students to draw pictures after participating in a Sport Education soccer unit. Through the student illustrations, they wanted to determine what students believed was most important during their soccer season. The study had two main objectives: to determine whether student representations would follow the components of sport education (e.g. season, team affiliation, formal competition, record keeping, festivity, culminating event); and to determine whether student focus shifted as the sport education season progressed. Mowling et al. (2006) found that students' primary agenda throughout the unit was winning the competitions. Even from the beginning, in drawings, students always drew their team in a scenario where their team held banners, won games, depicted scoreboards, and expressions of winning. Similar to the findings of McPhail et al. (2004) students also showed a strong focus on the affiliation and festivity component which "somewhat minimized the possible negative effects of winning and losing during the competitive phase of the season" (p. 31). For example, the teams who were knocked out of the tournament often expressed enthusiasm for their half time show participation. One student described his picture of their half-time performance: "We are doing the half time show, who rocks the house, the five musketeers rock the house. We are doing it for half-time, because we are not in the playoffs, and because after the final we do the half time show ... We are cheering for our team because we almost won and we did good ..." (p. 19).

In Sport Education Hastie (1998, 2000) and Siedentop (2002) recommend that each student be assigned a specific role and assume that particular role, but in this study, Mowling et al. (2006) found that "only one student showed herself in a nonplaying role, and there was no evidence in any drawings of students in the role of referee" (p. 32). This minimal role representation or responsibility was attributed to very little time being devoted to learning and practicing roles, the developmental level of the students, and the lack of student interest.

Another physical education program that students found relevant and meaningful used the instructional model of cooperative learning. In a study of 8th- and 11th-grade students, Dyson and Strachan (2000) reported that students had positive attitudes towards cooperative learning in two handball units. More specifically, students stated that the program encouraged learning motor skills and strategies, participating actively, communicating, having fun, and working as a team. Students enthusiastically talked about their motor skills and tactics. Sheri, a low-skilled student exclaimed: "I got two goals and two assists today. It seems that every time I play I get better" (p. 26). Brenda talked about how different students have different contributions: "Working together, one person knows one thing, another person knows something else. It's more fun and easier to work together" (p. 33). In addition, Dyson and Strachan (2000) reported that students learned to respect their peers, accept responsibility, and develop close attachments to each other. One student, Tricia stated that "Everyone gets along, everyone communicates", and Donna added, "We have become really close-knit. My best friends come from phys. ed. class" (p. 34). These findings are similar to the findings of the Sport for Peace Curriculum (Ennis et al., 1999) in that students reported physical education as pertinent and having an important effect, which was in contrast to Cothran and Ennis (1999) who uncovered that students in traditional physical education programs were suffering from disillusionment and lack of connectedness to physical education.

In further research on cooperative learning, Dyson (2001) studied fifth- and sixth-grade students during volleyball and basketball cooperative learning units. Students appeared to hold similar beliefs to their teacher and talked about: their motor skills, their social skills, working together as a team, helping each other improve their skills, and taking responsibility for their own learning. Emily stated that her improved skill had led to her increased confidence, enjoyment, and participation in physical education:

> I remember last year I used to not really participate in the games, because I was afraid I'd mess up, but this year I like participating more and I like having the ball and shooting. I was just always afraid I'd mess up, and now I'm not so afraid ... I'm getting better in the games. And also I used to not get passed to, and now I can do everything better than I used to, so now I get passed to. (p. 271)

Dyson (2001) argued that one of the benefits of cooperative learning was that students learned to analyze skill. When students watched others in their group with a task sheet, they commented that it often helped them improve their own skills. James said, "sometimes if someone else on your team also makes a mistake, it shows you 'oh, maybe that's what I was doing and that's why the ball's not going over here'" (p. 271).

In these lessons cooperative learning roles became important. Roles, such as coach and encourager, gave students a purpose in the class and provided a structure for students. Nicholas explained the role of the coach during skill practice in a volleyball lesson: "If a person makes a mistake, the coach corrects the person's mistake." Similar to other research findings (Carlson and Hastie, 1997; Hastie, 1998, 2000) students learned to teach other students and often preferred students as their coaches compared to their regular teachers. Another role, encourager, is often used in cooperative learning. Most educators would agree that students need to learn how to encourage each other. Dyson (2001) found that students learned to be active encouragers in their classes. Greg provided his understanding of the role of encourager: "I was the encourager, so I had to encourage people ... If they do something good, you usually praise them for it ... It's fun to be an encourager" (p. 271).

In research on the implementation of cooperative learning in 3rd and 4th grades, Dyson (2002) found that students had definite opinions about this teaching and learning process. In the first year of the research project, units on striking, educational gymnastics, and throwing and catching were observed and in the second year units on throwing and catching, kicking, and orienteering were observed. Data collection included interviews of a physical education teacher and students, non-participant observation, field notes, a teacher journal, and documents. The students generally had positive responses to the implementation of cooperative learning into their physical education classes but there were a range of comments from the students. Similar to research on Sport Education (Carlson and Hastie, 1997; Hastie, 1998, 2000) students in this study learned the role of the coach (Dyson, 2002). Many students enjoyed the role of coach. Jill recalled, "We just worked together and gave encouraging words when we were coach. [Like] 'bring your arm back' and 'bring the ball into your stomach when you catch the ball' and 'aim for your target' because that is really helpful." In addition, students developed a keen sense of responsibility. After 2 years of cooperative learning Andrea reported that: "When you write it down [sign your name to the task sheet] it means you practiced it and are good enough to do it [perform the skill] in front of the class and then you could sign the paper" (p. 78). At the end of the second year, Audrey demonstrated her understanding of the importance of the task sheets when her partner, Drew, wanted to check her off when she felt she was not ready. She said to him: "Don't check me off because I haven't done it yet" (p. 79). Audrey had learned to hold herself accountable for the activity. Many physical educators believe in the development of student responsibility as an important goal in their programs (Ennis et al., 1999; Cothran and Ennis, 1999; Hellison, 1996). However, their enacted curriculum can fall short of providing a clear and consistent social responsibility message to students (Cothran and Ennis, 1999). This study and others provide support for cooperative learning as a structure for increasing student responsibility (Dyson, 2001; Dyson and Strachan, 2000; Pope and Grant, 1996; Suomi et al., 2003).

The implementation of cooperative learning was not smooth or trouble free. Dyson (2002) discovered that students were quick to explain that communication broke down when group members did not listen or speak clearly to each other. In the second unit of the study, Melanie said that "I was the coach and the group was yelling and talking too loud and people weren't listening to me. I don't know why" (p. 79). These words highlight the importance and difficulty of communication and small-group skills in cooperative learning. The quotes also demonstrate that students were constructing their own meaning about listening and its importance to the success of the task. Although these grade 3 and 4 students were able to articulate a clear understanding of working together, they were not always able to do it. Ronnie was not happy when his group did not listen to him. "When we were drawing the obstacle course they were all

deciding and I barely got to help. I said 'I have an idea' and they said 'what?' and then they just skipped me. I felt left out, mad, and sad" (p. 81). Nonetheless, there were groups that had a strong understanding of what it meant to be cooperative in the gymnasium. During the second year of the study Chelsea commented that "Our group worked well together. We knew what we wanted to get and we all chose our different roles. We all wanted different roles. So we all worked together to make the course" (Dyson, 2002: 82).

Recently, through the use of cooperative learning in physical education Grenier (2004) discovered that persons with severe disabilities could be included in many ways in a "truly" inclusive 3rd-grade physical education program. The students voiced their support for the inclusive cooperative learning environment created by their teacher. "I want to say something about Jack. I think it's really neat how she [the teacher] could think of something neat to do for Jack because you know he's in a wheelchair. And it's kind of clever that he had feet to do, that he got eight or seven [turns]" (Kara). In another example we see the caring nature of the students in the cooperative learning groups: "We read the team contract over before we were even running. It said that we should work together and try to solve our problems on our own and a few other things that we should have done as a group. And so when James told us he had sunburn on his shoulders and neck so Kendra helped him out."

Azzarito and Ennis (2003) studied two effective middle-school physical education teachers who demonstrated a social constructivist pedagogy within their physical education curriculum. Students reported that they had a sense of connection with the physical education program. In a group interview students stated that it "helps us learn to get along with other people" (Azzarito and Ennis, 2003: 194). They commented about the new style of reciprocal teaching: "Yeah, I would say [when you work with your peers] you learn more, because you get to learn how the teacher would have it, and also classmates would explain it" (p. 187). Students took on leadership roles, were responsible for equipment and tasks, and learned to be decision makers in the gymnasium. "Yeah, when we are leader we just can't pick our friends, we can't just leave people out, we have to pick [include peers in the group equally] ... basically what's good for our team and what's good for them" (p. 189). In addition, students made a connection to life outside the gymnasium. "Maybe you'll work for a business when you're older and a business is based mostly on team work" (p. 193). Even though life in the urban school is not easy, students can get enthusiastic and feel connected to the physical education content. "Despite the hardship in both students' and teachers' experiences, social constructivist pedagogy can enhance a sense of connection among students, and students' and teachers' communities" (Azzarito and Ennis, 2003: 195).

Implications of students' perspectives research

Teachers often assume that they know and understand the needs and interests of their students (Graham, 1995). The challenge for everyone involved in education is to deal with the wide range of student differences that face teachers in the 21st century. However, it is disconcerting to learn that in many school gymnasiums "physical education programs, especially at the secondary level, have remained unchanged since World War II" (Graham, 1995: 480). There appears to be a plethora of literature to support the notion that many physical education programs are not effective (Kirk, 1996; Locke, 1992; Tinning and Fitzclarence, 1992; Siedentop et al., 1994). There are indications that a growing number of students find physical education less relevant, boring, and not an enjoyable experience (Carlson, 1995; Cothran and Ennis, 1999; Morey and Goc Karp, 1998; Tinning and Fitzclarence, 1992).

As Graham (1995) discovered, one of the obvious implications from students' perspective research is the need for teachers to understand how all their students (of all abilities, genders, and races) feel about their physical education programs. However, generally interviewing is too labor intensive, time consuming, and difficult to schedule for teachers to be practical (Denzin and Lincoln, 1998; Ratliffe et al., 1992). Researchers need to discover better ways for teachers to access student voice, so this knowledge can better inform their practice. In addition, interviewing could serve as a means to make students in physical education classes more sensitive to the wide range in abilities, opinions, emotions, and interests in a typical class. Interviewing has the potential to reveal more of the complexities of teaching and learning environments.

Erikson and Shultz (1992) argue for student voice in the education process, stating that often students are not seen as part of the reform process. "Student experience and its possible diversity do not appear as a phenomenon of interest in culture debates on education policy and research" (Erikson and Shultz, 1992: 467). Fullan (1991) reminds us that reformers "rarely think of students as participants in a process of change and organizational life" (p. 170). In addition, Corbett and Wilson (1995) suggest that we should "make a difference **with,** not for students", [emphasis added] (p. 12). They provide an alternative view to curriculum reform based on change in schools implemented in partnership with students. We should be working with students as partners in

education not imposing on them what they should "soak up like a sponge" from their teachers.

Corbett and Wilson (2002) included students' voice in education reform efforts being implemented in Philadelphia. They interviewed inner-city middle-school students annually for 3 years while their schools were undergoing a district-wide reform. Corbett and Wilson (2002) reported that students were aware of many of the issues that arise in school-based reform; after all, they are an integral part of the school culture. Their interviews with students in high-poverty schools suggested that these adolescents do care and that students are more perceptive than many adults give them credit for; the students stated that they cared about their education, they cared about the teachers' instruction, they could recognize effective teachers, and they were not satisfied with teachers who were not competent.

Research that includes student voice does take extended periods of time and it is obviously complicated by context factors. Graham (1995) highlighted that one of our major challenges in physical education is to deal with differences. How do students of different races, genders, skill levels, economic levels, interpersonal skills, and/or cognitive ability feel about what happens in physical education? We need to ask different students in varied contexts at different grade levels to begin to better understand students' subjective realities that we know are often different from their parents' and their teachers' perspectives (Hunter, 2002).

Brooker and Macdonald (1999) challenged the profession in their discussion of student voice. Grounded in a post-structuralist and feminist analysis they critiqued how student voice was positioned in a high-school curricular innovation. "While the curriculum supposedly exists to serve the interest of learners, their preferences, if sought at all, are marginalized and their voices are mostly silent in curriculum making" (Brooker and Macdonald, 1999: 84). They presented questions pertinent to any analysis of students' perspectives: "Why must students speak? For whose benefit? What use will be made of the speech after it is heard? Who gives voice to whom? Is it safe for the students to speak?" (Brooker and Macdonald, 1999: 87). They argue that not only should student representatives be added to curriculum-making committees but that students need to feel comfortable enough to express their views, providing them an "active voice" in the gathering and reporting of an authentic student contribution. They suggest techniques that could facilitate this process. Students could conduct peer interviews or provide other responses that are not tied to an interview protocol or data-collection time-frame and students could act as volunteer cases whose experiences of the curriculum could be tracked. As Brooker and Macdonald (1999) suggested, the framing of the questions, the selection of particular "voices" for interview, and the construction of power relationships between the interviewer and the interviewee throughout the interview process are extremely important research considerations. The issue of capturing breadth and depth of representation of students' perspectives remains problematic (Brooker and Macdonald, 1999).

If we are open to listening to the students' voice then the teacher can move from director of instruction to the facilitator of learning activities. However, this will require a conceptual shift for teachers (Dyson et al., 2004; Fullan, 1991, 1999). This would allow for a more holistic education of students in physical education and physical activity settings. Students talk enthusiastically about innovative instructional models such as Sport Education, Adventure Education, and Cooperative Learning, and other innovative curricula. In these programs, research demonstrates that students can learn roles, take responsibility, lead others, self-manage, work together, critique issues of social justice, and get along in a caring manner (Carlson and Hastie, 1997; Dyson, 1995, 2001, 2002; Dyson et al., 2004; Ennis et al., 1999; Hastie, 1995, 1996, 1998, 2000; Kinchin and O'Sullivan, 2003; Oliver and Lalik, 2004; Dyson and Strachan, 2000). Perhaps this positive student voice on innovative instructional models is leading us to a future direction in physical education (Metzler, 2000).

Major trends and future directions and issues of gaps in the research

The majority of research on student voice has been carried out in isolated studies and in a fragmented manner. Many studies focus on a particular instructional model such as Sport Education (Carlson and Hastie, 1997; Ennis et al., 1999; Hastie, 1996, 1998, 2000; Kinchin and O'Sullivan, 2003), Cooperative Learning (Dyson, 2001, 2002), and Adventure Education (Dyson, 1995; Hastie, 1995). There is no clear line of inquiry on students' perspectives in physical education that exists over a period of time. Neither do longitudinal studies exist. It is likely that this trend will continue due to the labor-intensive nature of accessing student experiences of the curriculum and the lack of value placed on students' perspectives by the reform and policy movement (Corbett and Wilson, 1995, 2002; Brooker and Macdonald, 1999; Erikson and Shultz, 1992, Fullan, 1991; Rudduck et al., 1997). Policy research in physical education is non-existent (O'Sullivan et al., 2004). O'Sullivan et al. (2004) proposed a direction for policy research in physical education. I would argue that future policy research in physical education should be informed by classroom research and

should include students' voice in this emerging area of inquiry.

We do have a foundation for research on accessing students' subjective worlds. In Research on Teaching in Physical Education there are a number of studies at the elementary level (Dyson, 1995, 2001, 2002; Graham, 1995; Hopple and Graham, 1995; Portman, 1995; Sanders and Graham, 1995); and a number of studies at the high-school level (Azzarito et al., in press; Carlson, 1995; Carlson and Hastie, 1997; Cothran and Ennis, 1999; Ennis et al., 1999; Kinchin and O'Sulivan, 2003; Morey and Goc Karp, 1998; Oliver and Lalik, 2004). In addition, there are emerging studies at the middle-school level (Azzarito and Ennis, 2003; Hunter, 2002; Walling and Martinek, 1995). Future research should extend the work done at the elementary- and high-school levels and focus on accessing students' perspective at the middle level so as to contribute significantly to curricular reform.

Research in the classroom does not appear to strongly support the value of "student voice" in the classroom-based research literature (Corbett and Wilson, 1995, 2002; Erikson and Shultz, 1992; Fullan, 1991; Rudduck et al., 1997) and therefore perhaps we are well positioned in physical education and physical activity research to lead the way on research in this area of inquiry. Since physical education learning environments lend themselves to more social interaction, physical educators are in a unique position to learn a great deal about their students' perspectives. Since physical education is a content area that can be closely linked to the interests, media, and the culture of students (Tinning and Fitzclarence, 1992), it appears that physical education is "uniquely situated in the school environment to promote student attachment to peers and the school" (Cothran and Ennis, 1999: 245).

In a recent chapter on student learning Solmon (2003) implied that in future research educators could listen to their students more frequently. In addition, listening to student voice was emphasized as an "important aspect in learning how to design and implement quality physical education programs that are meaningful and valuable to all students" (Solmon, 2003: 160). There appear to be many connections to student perception research, particularly in achievement motivation research (Solmon and Lee, 1996; Li and Lee, 2004). Why are students not interested in physical education? What can we do to "spark" students' motivation in physical education and physical activity? Future research agenda could explore the connectivity to the two different research paradigms.

The questions still remain: How do we access more student voice? How do we "truly represent" student voice? What can we learn form student voice? This is a challenging enterprise for future research on student perspectives.

Conclusion

Fullan (1991) poses that question, "What would happen if we treated the student as someone whose opinion mattered?" (p. 70). The challenge for our field is to move beyond superficial understanding within physical education and physical activity settings and for educators to tease out the theoretical constructs, contradictions, and articulations among and between the different contexts to better inform our practice (Rink, 2001). This process has the potential to ultimately provide a more comprehensive understanding of physical education contexts but only if we also more accurately access students' own perspectives.

How have students' perspectives impacted our practice and research in physical education and have we learned from the students' voices? I would argue that we have a limited, but growing, understanding of students' viewpoints, opinions, and/or judgments. Through the process of asking students their perspectives, we might better enhance possible insights into the "really lived worlds" of each student as an individual (Tinning and Fitzclarence, 1992). Since educational environments are multifarious and complex it behooves us to do a better job of accessing the voices of students in physical education and physical activity settings. As educators suggest, policy and reform initiatives need to include student voice to enable schools to be more effective and avoid the epidemic of "innovation without change" that has plagued much school reform to date (Sparkes, 1991). Listening to students can provide valuable perspectives and new insights into the complexities of teaching and learning that can then be applied to improving the quality of physical education in our schools.

References

Amis, J. (2005). The art of interviewing for case study research. In D. Mason, D. Andrews and M. Silk (Eds.) *Qualitative Research Methods for Sports Studies*. Oxford & New York: Berg.

Anderson, G.L. (1998). Towards authentic participation: Deconstructing the discourse of participatory reforms in education. *American Educational Research Journal, 35*: 571–606.

Anderson, W. (1971). Descriptive-analytical research on teaching. *Quest, 15*: 1–8.

Anderson, W.G. and Barrett, G.T. (1978). What's going on in the gym: Descriptive studies of physical education classes. *Motor Skills: Theory into Practice, Monograph 1.*

Azzarito, L. and Ennis, C.D. (2003) A sense of connection: Toward social constructivist physical education. *Sport, Education, and Society, 8*: 179–198.

Azzarito, L. and Solmon, M.A. (2006). A feminist poststructuralist view on student bodies in physical education:

Sites of compliance, resistance, and transformation. *Journal of Teaching in Physical Education, 25*: 200–225.

Azzarito, L., Solmon, M.A. and Harrison, L., Jr. (2006). '… If I had a choice I would…' A feminist post-structural perspective on girls in physical education classes. *Research Quarterly for Exercise and Sport, 77*: 222–239.

Brooker, R. and Macdonald, D. (1999). Did we hear you?: Issues of student voice in curriculum innovation. *Journal of Curriculum Studies, 31*: 83–97.

Burrows, L. Wright, J. and Jungersen-Smith, J. (2002). 'Measure your belly.' New Zealand Children's Constructions of Health and Fitness. *Journal of Teaching in Physical Education, 22*: 39–48.

Carlson, T.B. (1995). We hate gym: Student alienation from physical education. *Journal of Teaching in Physical Education, 14*: 467–477.

Carlson, T. and Hastie, P. (1997). The student social system within sport education. *Journal of Teaching in Physical Education, 16*: 176–195.

Chen, W. and Cone, T. (2003). Links between children's use of critical thinking and an expert teacher's teaching in creative dance. *Journal of Teaching in Physical Education, 22*: 169–185.

Chen, W. and Rovegno, I. (2000). Examination of expert teachers' constructivist-orientated teaching practices using a movement approach to physical education. *Research Quarterly for Exercise and Sport, 71*: 357–372.

Cohn, M.M. and Kottkamp, R.B. (1993). *Teachers: The missing voice in education*. Albany, NY : State University of New York Press.

Connelly, F.M. and Clandinin, D.J. (1990). Stories of experience and narrative inquiry. *Educational Researcher, 19*: 2–14.

Corbett, D. and Wilson, B. (1995). Make a difference with, not for students: A plea to researchers and reformers. *Educational Researcher, 24*: 12–17.

Corbett, D. and Wilson, B. (2002). What urban students say about good teaching students. *Educational Leadership, 60*: 18–22.

Cothran, D.J. and Ennis, C.D. (1999). Alone in a crowd: Meeting students' needs for relevance and connection in urban high school physical education. *Journal of Teaching in Physical Education, 18*: 234–247.

Cothran, D.J. and Ennis, C.D. (2001). "Nobody said nothing about learning stuff": Students, Teachers, and Curricular Change. *Journal of Classroom Instruction, 36*: 1–5

Cothran, D.J. and Kulinna, P.H. (2006). Students' Perspectives on Direct, Peer, and Inquiry Teaching Strategies. *Journal of Teaching in Physical Education, 25*: 166–181.

Cothran, D.J., Kulinna, P.H. and Garrahy, D.A. (2003). *Teaching and Teacher Education, 19*: 434–444.

Denzin, N.K. and Lincoln, Y.S. (Eds.) (1998). *Collecting and interpreting qualitative materials*. Thousand Oaks, CA: Sage.

Dodds, P., Griffin, L.L. and Placek, J.H. (2001). A selected review of the literature on the development of learners' domain-specific knowledge. *Journal of Teaching in Physical Education [Monograph], 20*: 301–313.

Dyson, B.P. (1995). Students' voices in two alternative elementary physical education programs. *Journal of Teaching Physical Education, 14*: 394–407.

Dyson, B. (2001). Cooperative learning in an elementary school physical education program. *Journal of Teaching in Physical Education, 20*: 264–281.

Dyson, B. (2002). The implementation of cooperative learning in an elementary school physical education program. *Journal of Teaching in Physical Education, 22*: 69–85.

Dyson, B., DiCesare, E., Coviello, N., and Stover, B. (in review). Students' perspectives in four urban middle schools. *Physical Education and Sport Pedagogy.*

Dyson, B., Griffin, L. and Hastie, P. (2004). Sport education, tactical games, and cooperative learning: Theoretical and pedagogical considerations. *Quest, 56*: 226–240.

Dyson, B. and Strachan, K. (2000). Cooperative learning in a high school physical education program. *Waikato Journal of Education, 6*: 19–37.

Duda, J.L. and Nichols, J.G. (1992). Dimensions of achievement motivation in schoolwork and sport. *Journal of Educational Psychology, 84*: 290–299.

Ennis, C.D. (2000). Canaries in the coal mine: Responding to disengaged students using theme-based curricula. *Quest, 52*: 119–130.

Ennis, C.D., Solmon, M.A., Satina, B., Loftus, S.J., Mensch, J. and McCauley, M.T. (1999). Creating a sense of family in urban schools using the 'Sport for Peace' curriculum. *Research Quarterly for Exercise and Sport, 70*: 273–285.

Erickson, F. and Shultz, (1992). Students' experience of the curriculum. In P. Jackson (Ed.), *Handbook of research on curriculum* (pp. 465–485). New York: MacMillian.

Evans, J. and Davies, B. (1986). Sociology, schooling and physical education. In J. Evans (Ed.), *Physical education, sport and schooling: Studies in sociology of physical education.* London, England: The Falmer Press.

Fontana, A. and Frey, J. (1994). Interviewing the art of science. In N. Denzin and Y. Lincoln, (Eds.), *Handbook of qualitative research* (pp. 361–376). Thousand Oaks, CA: Sage.

Fullan, M. (1991). *Change Forces.* London: Falmer Press.

Fullan, M. (1999). *Change forces: The sequel.* London: Falmer Press.

Gagnon, J., Martel, D., Dumont, S., Grenier, J. and Pelletier-Murphy, J. (2000). Le pouvoir de l'eleve sur l'agir de l'enseignant ou l'enseignante: un constant d' impuissance. *AVANTE, 6*: 37–50.

Graber, K.C. (2001). Research on teaching in physical education. In V. Richardson (Ed.), *Handbook of research on teaching* (pp. 491–519). Washington, DC: American Educational Research Association.

Graham, G. (1995). Physical education through students' eyes and in students' voices: Introduction. *Journal of Teaching in Physical Education, 14*: 364–371.

Grant, B.C. (1992). Integrating sport into the physical education curriculum in New Zealand secondary schools. *Quest, 44*: 304–316.

Grenier, M. (2004). *Inclusion in physical education for students with severe disabilities.* Unpublished doctoral dissertation, The University of New Hampshire.

Halliday, M. (1985). *An introduction to functional grammer.* London: Edward Arnold.

Hastie, P.A. (1995). An ecology of a secondary school outdoor adventure camp. *Journal of Teaching in Physical Education, 15*: 79–97.

Hastie, P.A. (1996). Student role involvement during a unit of sport education. *Journal of Teaching in Physical Education, 16*: 88–103.

Hastie, P.A. (1998). The participation and perceptions of girls within a unit of sport education. *Journal of Teaching in Physical Education, 17*: 157–171.

Hastie, P.A. (2000). An ecological analysis of Sport Education Season. *Journal of Teaching in Physical Education, 19*: 355–373.

Hastie, P.A. and Pickwell, A. (1996). Take your partners: A description of a student social system in a secondary school dance class. *Journal of Teaching in Physical Education, 15*: 171–187.

Hellison, D. (1996). Teaching personal and social responsibility in physical education. In S. Silverman and C.D. Ennis (Eds.), *Student learning in physical education: Applying research to enhance instruction* (pp. 269–286). Champaign, IL: Human Kinetics.

Hendry, G.D. (1986). Changing schools in a changing society. In J. Evans (Eds.), *Physical education, sport and schooling: Studies in sociology of physical education.* London, England: The Falmer Press.

Hendry, G.D. (1996). Constructivism and educational practice. *Australian Journal of Education, 40*: 9–45.

Hendry, G.D., Frommer, M. and Walker, R.A. (1999). Constructivism and problem based learning. *Journal of Further and Higher Education, 23(3)*: 359–371.

Hopple, C. and Graham, G. (1995). What children think, feel, and know about physical fitness testing. *Journal of Teaching in Physical Education, 14*: 408–417.

Hunter, L. (2002). *Young people, physical education, and transition: Understanding practices in the middle years of schooling* (p. 374). Unpublished doctoral thesis, School of Human Movement Studies. Brisbane, The University of Queensland.

Johnson, B. and Howard, S. (1997). *Researching children: Ethical and practical inhibitors.* Paper presented at the Australian Association for Research in Education Conference, Brisbane, Australia.

Kinchin, G.D. and O'Sullivan, M. (2003). Incidences of student support for and resistance to a curricular innovation in high school physical education. *Journal of Teaching in Physical Education, 22*: 245–260.

Kirk, D. (1996). The crisis in school physical education: An argument against the tide. *The ACHPER Healthy Lifestyles Journal, 43*: 25–27.

Kirk, D. (2002). Physical Education: a gendered history. In D. Penny (Ed.), *Gender and physical education. Contemporary issues and future directions* (pp. 24–37). New York: Routledge.

Kirk, D. and Macdonald, D. (1998). Situated learning in physical education. *Journal of Teaching in Physical Education, 17*: 376–387.

Kirk, D. and MacPhail, A. (2002). Teaching games for understanding and situated learning: Rethinking the Bunker-Thorpe model. *Journal of Teaching in Physical Education, 21*: 117–192.

Kollen, C. (1981). *The experience of movement in physical education: A phenomenology.* Unpublished doctoral dissertation, Anarbor, MI: University of Michigan,

Lave, J. and Wenger, E. (1991). *Situated learning: Legitimate peripheral participation.* New York: Cambridge University Press.

Li, W. and Lee, A.M. (2004). A review conceptions of ability and related motivated constructs in achievement motivation. *Quest, 56*: 441–464.

Locke, L. (1977). Research on teaching in physical education: New hope for a dismal science [Monograph]. *Quest, 28*: 2–16.

Locke, L. (1992). Changing secondary school physical education. *Quest, 44*: 361–372.

MacPhail, A., Kirk, D., and Kinchin, G. (2004). Sport Education: Promoting Team Affiliation Through Physical Education. *Journal of Teaching in Physical Education, 23*: 106–122.

Martinek, T.J. and Griffith, J.B. (1994). Learned helplessness in physical education: A developmental study of causal attributions and task persistence. *Journal of Teaching in Physical Education, 13*: 108–122.

Martel, D., Gagnon, J. and Tousignant, M. (2002). Physical education teachers' and students' views of injustices in the gymnasium. AVANTE, 8: 55–68.

Metzler, M. (2000). *Instructional models for physical education.* Boston, MA : Allyn and Bacon.

Mowling, C.M., Brock, S.J., and Hastie, P.A. (2006). *Journal of Teaching in Physical Education, 25*: 9–35.

Morey, R.S. and Goc-Karp, G. (1998). Why some students who are good at physical education dislike it so much? *The Physical Educator, 55*: 89–100.

Nilges, L.M. (2004). Ice Can Look Like Glass: A Phenomenological Investigation of Movement Meaning in One Fifth-Grade Class during a Creative Dance Unit. *Research Quarterly for Exercise and Sport, 75*: 298–314.

Nixon, J.E., and Locke, L.F. (1973). Research on teaching physical education. In R. Travers (Ed.), *Second handbook of research teaching* (pp. 1210–1242). Chicago, IL : Rand McNally.

Oliver, K.L. (1998). A journey into narrative analysis: A methodology for discovering meaning. *Journal of Teaching in Physical Education, 17*: 244–259.

Oliver, K.L. and Lalik, R. (2004). Critical inquiry on the body in girls' physical education classes: A critical poststructural perspective. *Journal of Teaching in Physical Education, 23*: 162–195.

O'Sullivan, M., Lee, M. and Wallhead, T. (2004). *Opening Pandora's Box of state-wide policies in physical education: Possibilities and unintended consequences.* Paper to be presented at the Special Interest Group: Research on Instruction and Learning in Physical Education at the American Education Research Association, San Diego, CA.

Perkins, D. (1999). The many faces of constructivism. *Educational Researcher, 57*: 6–11.

Pissanos, B.W. and Allison, P.C. (1993). Students' constructs of elementary school physical education. *Research Quarterly for Exercise and Sport, 64*: 425–436.

Pope, C.V. and Grant, B.C. (1996). Student experiences in sport education. *Waikato Journal of Education, 2*: 103–118.

Portman, P.A. (1995). Who is having fun in physical education classes? Experiences of sixth grade students in elementary and middle schools. *Journal of Teaching in Physical Education, 14*: 445–453.

Ratliffe, T., Imwold, C. and Conkell, C. (1992). What do your kids really think about their physical education class?: Procedures teachers can use to find out. *Florida Journal of Health, Physical Education, Recreation, Dance & Driver Education, 30(3)*: 32–35.

Rink, J. (2001). Investigating the assumptions of pedagogy. *Journal of Teaching in Physical Education, 20*: 112–128.

Richardson, V. (Ed.). (2001). *Handbook of Research on Teaching* (4th Ed.). Washington, DC: American Educational Research Association.

Rovegno, I. and Kirk, D. (1995). Articulations and silences in social critical work on physical education: Towards a broader agenda. *Quest, 47*: 447–474.

Rudduck, J., Day, J. and Wallace, G. (1997). Students' perspectives in school reform. In A. Hargreaves (Ed), *Rethinking educational change with heart and mind.* (pp. 73–91). Alexandria, VA: ASCD.

Sanders, S. and Graham, G. (1995). Kindergarten children's initial experiences in physical education: The relentless persistence for play classes with the zone of acceptable responses. *Journal of Teaching in Physical Education, 14*: 365–372.

Siedentop, D. (2002). Sport education: A retrospective. *Journal of Teaching in Physical Education, 22*: 401–48.

Siedentop, D. and O'Sullivan, M. (Eds.). (1992). Secondary school physical education [Special Issue]. *Quest, 44(3)*: 285–288.

Siedentop, D., Doutis, P., Tsangaridou, N., Ward, P. and Rauschenbach, J. (1994). Don't sweat gym. An analysis of curriculum and instruction. *Journal of Teaching in Physical Education, 13*: 375–394.

Smith, S.J. (1991). Where is the child in physical education research? *Quest, 43*: 37–54.

Solmon, M.A. (2003). Student issues in physical education classes: Attitude, cognition, and motivation. In S. Silverman and C. Ennis (Eds.), *Student learning in physical education: Applying research to enhance instruction* (pp. 147–164). Champaign, IL: Human Kinetics.

Solmon, M.A. and Lee, A.M. (1996). Entry characteristics, practice variables, and cognition: Student mediation of instruction. *Journal of Teaching in Physical Education, 15*: 136–150.

Spindler, G.D. (1963). Anthropology and education: an overview. In G. Spindler (Ed.), *Education and culture:*

Anthropological approaches (pp. 53–83). New York: Holt, Rinehat and Winston.

Sparkes, A.C. (1991). The culture of teaching, critical reflection and change: Possibilities and problems. *Educational Management and Administration, 19*: 4–19.

Suomi, J., Collier, D. and Brown, L. (2003). Factors affecting the social experiences of students in elementary physical education classes. *Journal of Teaching in Physical Education, 22*: 186–202.

Travers, R. (Ed.) (1973). *Second Handbook of Research Teaching* (2nd ed.). Chicago, IL: Rand McNally.

Tinning, R. and Fitzclarence, L. (1992). Postmodern youth culture and the crisis in Australian secondary physical education. *Quest, 44*: 287–303.

Tjeerdsma, B. (1997). A comparison of teacher and student perspectives of tasks and feedback. *Journal of Teaching in Physical Education, 16*: 388–400.

Tjeerdsma, B., Rink, J. and Graham, K. (1996). Student perceptions, values, and beliefs prior to, during, and after badminton instruction. *Journal of Teaching in Physical Education, 15*: 464–476.

Tousignant, M. and Siedentop, D. (1983). A qualitative analysis of tasks structures in required secondary physical education classes. *Journal of Teaching in Physical Education, 3*: 47–57.

Underwood, G.L. (1988). *Teaching and learning in physical education: A social psychological perspective.* London, England: The Falmer Press.

Walling, M. and Martinek, T.J. (1995). Learned helplessness: A case study of a middle school student. *Journal of Teaching in Physical Education, 14*: 454–466.

Wang, B.M. (1977). *An ethnography of a physical education class: An experiment in integrated living.* Unpublished doctoral dissertation, Greensboro, North Carolina: University of North Carolina at Greensboro.

Wittrock, M.C. (Ed.) (1986). *Handbook of Research on Teaching* (3rd ed.). New York: Macmillan.

Wright, J. (1995). A feminist poststructuralist methodology for the study of gender construction in physical education: Description of a study. *Journal of Teaching in Physical Education, 15*: 1–24.

3.10   Student learning within the *didactique* tradition

CHANTAL AMADE-ESCOT

Introduction

Student learning in the *didactique* tradition is a subarea of the so-called research which has been developed within the perspective of a better knowledge of the functioning of the "didactic system" which links teacher, content knowledge and students in classroom and gymnasium. In the *didactique* tradition of research the topics include: What is taught and learned? How it is taught and learned? Why it is taught and learned? By whom it is taught and learned? Research on didactics in physical education has focused primarily on teaching and most of the work concerns the analysis of didactic interactions in the aim of enlightening the teacher's role (Amade-Escot, 1999, 2000a). Contrary to didactics of some school disciplines (physics, biology, social studies) the topic of student learning in didactics of physical education has lurked in the shadows of research in teaching, despite (or because of) a widespread interest in other sport sciences such as motor learning, psychology, social psychology (see Vanden-Auweele et al., 1999, textbook endorsed by the European Network of Sport Sciences in Higher Education). In fact, the issue of student learning in physical education has long been an exclusive topic of research in sport psychology notably in France. When researchers in didactics began to investigate student learning from a didactical viewpoint, in the early 1980s, the influence of social psychology was noticeable. A few studies were conducted within the framework of "social representations" of sports and physical activities and their influence on learners' activity. Then despite the presence of considerable literature devoted to students' social representations among physical education teachers and teacher educators (see Clément, 1996) some investigations were conducted to describe students' conceptions (or misconceptions) and their role in the learning process during physical education lessons. For the last decade the interest in student learning within the *didactique* tradition has grown again. Today, this trend in didactic research is invigorating but the need to go deeper into the issue must be underscored.

The scope of the review in this chapter is intended to serve as (1) a summary of the theoretical framework of research within the *didactique* tradition, with special emphasis on studies related to student learning in physical education; and (2) a statement of what is known about learners' difficulties and obstacles in physical education, as well as what the new insight is on their learning processes highlighted by this line of research. The coverage is by no means exhaustive. The emphasis, rather, has been on identifying significant themes and findings in the research to help readers to have a better knowledge of this stream of research. The chapter is divided into four major units. The first section provides a brief historical perspective of the *didactique* tradition. The second section outlines the conceptual and theoretical underpinnings to the topic of student learning in this program of research. The third section gives an overview of the findings. The fourth section concludes with a summary of the major themes emerging from the review and suggests some possible developments for future research.

The *didactique* stream in the French-speaking world of educational research

The *didactique* tradition of educational research in Europe has been developed for 35 years. Beyond its pejorative meaning in the English language the term "didactic" has to be considered from the Greek "Didaktos: 'taught, able to be taught (…) fitted or intended to teach'" (*Webster's Third New International Dictionary*, 1981, p. 628). In German educational language and in most European languages, didactics concerns the practice of teaching and its methods in general and/or related to specific subject matter (for a controversial discussion, Terhart, 2003; Vasquez-Levy, 2002). In the French-speaking world of educational research, the noun "didactics" and the adjective "didactic, didactical" are to be understood in terms of research that studies teaching and learning processes with a special focus on the content knowledge taught. On the contrary to what is usually thought the *didactique* tradition does not promote a subject-matter centered model, but studies the way in which the subtleties of content knowledge are organized and presented to students, how they interpret them, what forms of teacher/students interactions are developed concerning the unit of knowledge at stake, in order to have a better understanding of the teaching/ learning process (Amade-Escot, 1996). The word "*didactique*" was chosen in the early 1970s by Brousseau (a researcher in mathematics education) to label an emergent research area. He borrowed the word from Comenius (1627/2000), the Czech philosopher who defended the idea of an autonomous science to study educational phenomena in schools.

> One of the fundamental hypotheses of Didactics consist of claiming that only the global study of situations presiding over the manifestation of knowledge [for any individual/i.e. in the student's work] allows us to choose and connect knowledge from different origins (…) [and] the derivation or modification of the necessary concepts currently imported from other scientific fields (Brousseau,[1] 1986/1997: 24).
>
> The object of didactics studies [is] the description and explanation of activities connected with the communication of knowledge and the transformations, intentional or not, made by the protagonists in this communication [i.e. the teachers, the students], and the transformations of the knowledge itself (Brousseau, 1986/1997: 34).

In the French-speaking world of educational research the concept of *didactique*, is strongly related to: (1) the study of the content and its function in the teaching/learning process; (2) the way it is embedded in instructional tasks and brought into play during the interactive teaching/learning process. The *didactique* program of research focuses on the features of teaching that are specific to the knowledge to be taught and learned in schools (Amade-Escot, 1996, 2000a). Its purpose is to capture and understand the complexity of teaching and learning, with an assumption that the content knowledge to be learned and thus taught is the

decisive element that lies at the heart of teachers' and students interactions as situated action (Kirk and Macdonald, 1998). For this reason in this paper the French word "*didactique*" will be used to denote the field of research in order to avoid the pejorative English meaning and also to focus on the most contemporary meaning of the concept.

Historical perspective

Research first began in *didactique* in France during the early 1970s in mathematics, experimental sciences education (physics, biology, etc.) followed immediately by other school disciplines like the French language (writing, reading, literature) and other humanities. For the last 10 years there has been a wide expansion of this stream of research inside the community of educational researchers and many international and national congresses and seminars have taken place. At the beginning the didactics of school disciplines evolved independently. Since the mid 1990s researchers from different subject-matter areas or school disciplines have begun to exchange and co-operate with the aim of providing a clearer understanding of the common phenomena they are investigating This was facilitated by a common conceptual framework around a few core concepts which help to unify the field (Raisky and Caillot, 1996). A new orientation named "comparative *didactique*" has recently emerged. Its aims are to provide epistemological reflection and findings on the generic and the specific phenomena of the teaching and learning process in various educational institutions and venues (Mercier et al., 2002; Loquet et al., 2002). This evolution of the field has an influence on the ongoing research in physical education.

In PE the first *didactique* research was launched at the beginning of the 1980s. Its development within the French-speaking world is heterogeneous but is currently growing in countries like Switzerland, Tunisia, Canada (Quebec) and some Spanish-speaking countries. In France the program of research is considered as "an expanding new field" (David et al., 1999). Two English-language literature reviews provide a good insight into the whole field (Amade-Escot, 2000a; David et al., 1999). Recently on the occasion of the 20 years of research on didactics in physical education the state of the art of the field was published (Amade-Escot, 2003a). This chapter will only focus on the findings on student learning as a subarea within this tradition.

---

[1] Brousseau is considered as a pioneer in the field of *didactique*. Most of his theoretical contribution to the field, originated in didactics of mathematics, has been translated into English and published in 1997, as collected papers in a book at Kluwer Academic Publishers. In this text the date of the original French version is specified, followed by the English translation (i.e. Brousseau, 1986/1997); in the reference list only the 1997 book is listed.

Conceptual and theoretical framework of the *didactique* tradition of research

Broadly speaking, the research into didactics refers to studies which investigate the features of teaching and learning as social processes that are specific to an element knowledge to be taught and learnt in context. The topic of *didactique* has thus a relationship with instruction within a constructivist background.

The theoretical object of the research into *didactique*

Research into *didactique* studies the functioning of the "didactic system" which is defined as the irreducible three-way relationship linking teacher, students and a piece of knowledge to be taught and learned (Amade-Escot, 2000a; Brousseau, 1986/1997). Within the didactic program any study of one term of the didactic system (the student, the teacher, the knowledge) cannot have any meaning without taking into account the other two. This seminal assumption has some methodological consequences. It implies that student learning cannot be studied without taking into consideration the knowledge involved in the task, the context (material, social, institutional) in which the learning process is developed, and the teaching strategy that is used by the teacher. Thus the empirical object on which data are collected must have a certain size and cannot be reduced to one pole of the three-way relationship. This makes a difference between the approach of researchers into *didactique* and that of researchers into psychology when studying student learning. This preliminary remark introduces the idea (defended originally by Comenius, 1627, then developed by Brousseau, 1986/1997 in mathematics and further ahead by many researchers into *didactique*) that the understanding of student learning (for instance in PE) cannot be deduced from motor learning research, psychology research, social psychology research even though all these areas of research have a lot of interest for PE teachers. Many scholars in the world of sport pedagogy have already pointed out the issue (Siedentop, 1989/2002, 1998/2002, 1999/2002; Silverman, 1991). But the key point introduced by the *didactique* tradition is to define the level of complexity needed for a didactical approach to student learning phenomena. The kind of reduction done in *didactique* is based on conventional elements and a theoretical framework that consider the didactic system as an irreducible triadic relation. The focus of didactic research is thus to study the dynamics and the evolution of didactical interactions between students and teacher a propos of the content knowledge embedded in the learning environment. Moreover when for research purposes the student learning is studied outside of the classroom, the researcher should consider in absentia what the knowledge intended to be taught and learned was, what the strategy of the teacher was, what the context of the learning was. All these are necessary conditions in which a didactical signification can be given to the data collected.

Methodological consequences

The assumption of an irreducible triadic system has some consequences when studying learners' activity in PE. Within the scope of this chapter only some methodological implications are summarized. Student learning in the *didactique* perspective is studied through questionnaires or interviews, or by observational means. Section 3.9 in this handbook will provide all information regarding the first method. This section will briefly enlighten the second way of investigation (for a development see Amade-Escot, in press). Classroom observation conducted from a quasi-ethnographic viewpoint is at the heart of the methodology. The aim is to understand in depth the construction of meaning that the students and the teacher (partners of the classroom interactions during the teaching–learning process) attribute to their experience, and the complex dynamic of the functioning of the didactic system in which they are immersed. A brief description is provided below. The data collection combines interviews and videotape observations. The basic components of data encompass: (1) pre-lesson interview with the teacher, (2) lesson videotaped with a cordless microphone connected to the camera, (3) students' short interviews audio-taped, (4) post-lesson interview with the teacher, and (5) post-lesson interview with the students (for a development see Amade-Escot, 2005). These qualitative data sources are based on four principles:

- First, didactic observations focus on the content knowledge actually presented to students and its ongoing evolution during academic work through the flow of interactions and implicit negotiations which occur between students and teacher all along their many attempts to achieve the instructional goals of the task through shared practice.
- Second, the investigation concerns the functioning of the didactic system, which implies that data are collected on all three components of the system (students' activity, content knowledge embedded in the process, teacher's activity). Trustworthiness and validity are based on constant triangulation between these three components informed by the data gathered through interviews as well as videotape transcripts.
- Third, the interpretation of the interrelated and ongoing process of teaching and learning a specific content knowledge is based on a

dialectic stance between intrinsic data (the voice of the participants) and extrinsic data (the viewpoint of the researcher).

- Fourth, the data must be interpreted by comparing and contrasting the "a priori analysis" with post-observation. The a priori analysis consists of an analysis of the design of the learning environment with the aim of identifying through teacher interviews and researcher analysis (e.g. including the constant comparison between the intrinsic viewpoint of the teacher and the extrinsic viewpoint of the researcher) what the content embedded in the task is and its relation to the didactic intent of the teacher. This analysis serves to highlight or predict the kind of response or strategy expected from the students and the potential alternative responses that may appear. The term a priori is utilized to emphasize that the analysis is conducted independently of the observation in order to provide a point of reference for subsequent didactic interactions. The a posteriori analysis concerns the events that occur during the observed lesson. Interpretation results from a comparison between the opportunities provided by the learning environment (a priori analysis) and the observed effects of the interaction as achieved by the participants. The result of the interpretation is to highlight the difference between the content to be taught, the content really at stake and the content learned and to provide understanding about how and why these differences occur.

The core concepts in the *didactique* tradition of research

Three majors concepts are at the heart of student learning studies in didactics: "didactic transposition", "didactic contract" and "student's individual relation to knowledge".

Didactic transposition

This concept highlights the fact that the knowledge to be taught and the knowledge actually taught and learned undergo complex transformation processes at various stages of selection and teaching. This issue was discussed in Amade-Escot (2000a). It includes the idea that the content knowledge for physical education (the knowledge, understanding, skill, know-how, and disposition that are to be learned by students) is a shared construction that implies individuals and societal concerns and values. This point was also underlined by Kirk (1993); Kirk and Almond (1999); Kirk and Macdonald (1998); Siedentop (1989/2002) and Tinning (2002). The concept of didactic transposition highlights the inevitable chain of transformation, elaboration and reconstruction of the knowledge, from the social practices taken as a reference, the academic knowledge to the school knowledge taught and, finally, to the knowledge really learned by students. Indeed, with the aim of covering a specified aspect of the curriculum, the presentation of content knowledge always isolates certain elements taking them more or less away from the network of cultural and social activities which provide their meaning, motivation and use. That is why Brousseau (1997) considers that the didactic transposition is inevitable but necessary and thus must be kept under epistemological surveillance. The concept of didactic transposition assists in considering the problems, the roles and the consequences of what Shulman quotes as "pedagogical reasoning and action" (Shulman, 1987: 13). It underscores the fact that reorganization of the subject-matter knowledge into the pedagogical content knowledge may have some undesirable effects. The *didactique* tradition of research has shown that these necessary and inevitable transformations might also have some negative effects on students' achievement. A substantial number of studies on student learning in PE within this tradition have been carried out on the difficulties and the obstacles encountered by students due to this phenomenon. This will be developed in the section related to findings.

Didactic contract

The second major concept in the *didactique* tradition is the "didactic contract". The concept was introduced in didactics of mathematics by Brousseau (1988/1997) who stressed the triadic nature of the teaching relationship (within the didactic system) which is bound by an "implicit contract" that concerns reciprocal and specific expectations with regard to the element of knowledge taught and learned. The concept of "didactic contract" (Brousseau, 1988/ 1997) needs to be clarified. The term is used to identify the set of negotiations, more often than not implicit, between teacher and students about the content taught in a given task. The didactic contract is the result of tacit and implicit negotiations among students, an instructional environment (the "didactic milieu") and a teacher about the content knowledge to be taught and learned. Thus the didactic contract specifically concerns the content taught and cannot be confounded with class management or "treaties" (Hampel, 1993: 36–37) or what has been called the "teaching/learning contract" (Hansen, 1991) which concerns, in the North American literature, the negotiations between students and teachers in order to sustain an environment in which instruction and learning can occur as theorized by Doyle (1986). The author of this chapter has discussed the relationships between the ecological perspective on PE (Hastie and Siedentop, 1999; Siedentop, 1998/2002) and the research into *didactique* (Amade-Escot, 2000b). Undeniably there are connections between the two programs of research, the major one is to consider the dynamics of classroom life through the implicit negotiations being at work during academic work: how students and teacher interact, how they negotiate and navigate the instructional tasks, with what influences on the learning outcomes. Moreover both approaches are based on ethnographic (or quasi-ethnographic) observational methods (Amade-Escot, 2005; Siedentop, 1999/2002). The interest of the concept of the didactic contract is to help in focusing on the part of the negotiations that concerns the knowledge at stake in academic work. In particular, the *didactique* tradition seriously tends to take into consideration what Doyle called the "primary vector of action" and his expectation: "subject matter needs to be included more explicitly in research on classroom management" (1986, p. 406).

Characteristics of the didactic contract

The concept of the didactic contract emerges within a theory of learning which emphasizes that learning is an active process in which the student seeks out information in relation to the task at hand and the environmental conditions (including social relations with peers) and tests out her/his own capabilities within the learning context in which the content is brought into play by the teacher. In this framework the teacher becomes a resource to enhance students' learning. Researchers consider that the didactic contract is the continuation in action of the didactic transposition.

The key to understanding the concept of the didactic contract is to consider that it is not a formal contract but an implicit attempt to find a common meaning on what is at stake in the teaching/learning process. Brousseau (1986/1997) describes it as a relationship between student(s), teacher and the content knowledge which determines – explicitly to some extent, but mainly implicitly – what each partner, the teacher and the student(s), will be mutually responsible for. According to Brousseau (1997) this system of reciprocal obligations resembles a contract, but this contract is specific to the targeted content knowledge. Because these reciprocal obligations are mostly implicit, the didactic contract remains silent. In fact, it appears when it breaks down. Brousseau adds "it is in fact the breaking of the contract that is important" (1997: 32).

> The theoretical concept in didactics is therefore not the contract (the good, the bad, the true, or the false contract) but the hypothetical process of finding a contract. It is this process which represents the observations and must model and explain them. (Brousseau, 1986/1997: 32)

The breaches of the didactic contract

Interpretation in the *didactique* perspective highlights the point that the real content is not the primary content embedded in the learning environment provided to the students, but that which results from the incredible amount of interactions and implicit negotiations during academic work. That is why the functioning and the evolution of the didactic contract in the classroom are ongoing across its successive breaches. What is the force behind these breaches? The theoretical framework posits that the meanings teacher and students attribute to the task from their own background are at the heart of their relationships and, furthermore, underpin the evolution of the didactic contract. This explains why the content taught and learned in PE emerges most often as the result of unpredictable and unstable processes. The notion of a breach acknowledges the fact that content is contingently unfolding as a result of a shared construction of meanings in the situation where the content knowledge or know-how is at stake. The teacher and the students must share, at a minimum, a common background regarding what is expected during the academic work. This concerns mostly the meaning that each of them gives to the knowledge, their "individual relation to knowledge" (see below). But reaching a common meaning is an idealistic viewpoint, classroom interactions still continue in spite of some mismatches, discrepancy of meanings, not to say some misunderstandings or misrepresentations as shown by different studies (Amade-Escot, 1998, 2003b; Amade-Escot and Léziart, 1996; Amade-Escot and Marsenach, 1995; Goirand, 1998; Loquet, 2003; Marsenach, 1995; Roustan, 2003; Thépaut, 2002; Verscheure and Amade-Escot, 2004). The results underpin the subtle negotiations and trade-offs that occur in the instructional system. The consequences of these continuous negotiations result in slight modifications in the content taught. Thus, the teaching/learning process goes on with successive breaches of the didactic contract. Some are necessary and critical (for example, when the teacher introduces a new object of learning), some are problematic (for example, when the breaches have a negative influence on students' achievement). The purpose of didactic studies is to describe these phenomena. Results of this line of research are summarized later.

Epistemological and theoretical tenets

The didactic contract has some epistemological commonalties with the theory of symbolic interactionism which underscores the need for common backgrounds in order to make communication possible between people (Goffman, 1967; Wood, 1983). Interactionists assume that people are constantly in a process of interpretation and definition as they move from one situation to another. The didactic contract is a specification of this phenomenon within the teaching/learning processes. Characterized by an unsteady equilibrium (because of its inevitable breaches) the functioning of the didactic contract is, according to Brousseau (1997), somewhat paradoxical. The purpose of research is to describe the mechanisms through which teacher and students decipher their respective expectations. Defining the interplay of the mutual expectations between teacher and students as a "contract" (even though implicit) is a way of accounting for the social conditions that enable the acquisition of the school knowledge. In the classroom, the meaning that participants attribute to the situation in which they are involved depends on their status and role in the immediate context, as well as in the social and institutional context in which the micro-context takes place (Schubauer-Leoni and Grossen, 1993). This last remark introduces the third major group of concepts in student learning within the *didactique* perspective: student relations to knowledge.

Student relation to knowledge

This subsection is about student characteristics and their influence on the teaching and the learning. Student characteristics play an important role as shown by the mediating paradigm as well as the ecological paradigm in research on teaching (for an overview of research paradigms, see Shulman, 1986; Silverman, 1991) (see also Section 3.2 and 3.3 in this handbook. In recent years there has also been considerable interest, especially among psychologists, to underscore the impact of the student characteristic on teaching. Investigators clearly stated that it is impossible to completely understand student learning without accounting for what students bring to the situation. As indicated earlier in this chapter the first studies regarding student learning in the didactic program were conducted in the framework of social representations, a concept borrowed from social psychology. The research was based on the assumption that the meaning and the understanding of the content by the students might be related to their social representation of the subject matter (David, 1993, 1995; Bouthier et al., 1990). Further discussion and controversies (see Bouthier and Griffet, 1992; Bouthier et al., 1990; Cadopi, and Durand, 1996) highlighted the fact that social backgrounds and social representations of sports play an undeniable role, but operational representations are to be taken into account (Bouthier, 1993). The notion of operational representations was borrowed

from cognitive ergonomics (Leplat, 1985). What comes out of these studies as a whole is that students' representations (social and operational) could be at the origin of difficulties during the teaching/learning process. Moreover the findings highlighted also the need for better attention to be given to students' voice and experience.

These early findings initiated some studies on students' conceptions and misconceptions and the obstacles generated by them within the didactic system. The terms "conceptions" and "misconceptions" were first introduced by researchers in didactics of science (for an overview in *didactique*, see Bednarz and Garnier, 1989). The two notions point out the fact that conceptions and misconceptions are not simply images or mental representations of the world but useful knowledge, know-how, and body language organized to solve a concrete learning problem. In this framework student conceptions become a tool that can be used by the teacher to provide meaningful learning environments. Giordan (1996) has utilized the notion of "allosteric learning" to account for how teachers can organize the learning conditions sometimes in conjunction with students' conceptions, sometimes in opposition to them.

In recent years the next conceptual stage in this line of research has been the notion of "one's individual relation to knowledge". The term appeared at the end of the 1980s in different areas of educational research including didactics (Charlot, 1997; Chevallard, 1989, 1992). It tries to encompass the different aspects of the previous research by integrating different elements like the student's experience, skill level, disposition, knowledge, conception, beliefs and representation which are all involved in the learning process. This broad concept helps to make visible the taken-for-granted inequalities in the access to the content knowledge at the micro level of the teaching and learning situation in the classroom, as well as the fact that any unit of knowledge activates individual and different meanings.

After having portrayed the methodological and conceptual framework of research it could be pointed out that *didactique* tradition is rooted in anthropological studies. The next section provides an overview of their findings.

What we know about student learning through the didactic approach

In this section the major findings are presented according to four areas of investigation on student learning. The first subsection summarizes what is highlighted by the line of research on students' social representations, students' conceptions and misconceptions, and their individual relation to knowledge.

The next stage specifies some teaching strategies that enhance student learning from the didactic viewpoint. The third subsection examines the problem of students' difficulties and learning obstacles from observation in classroom. The issue of progress and heterogeneous outcomes is discussed. The last point gives an overview of students' negotiations within the conceptual framework of the didactic contract. Some recent results on gender in physical education are then discussed. The section concludes with the major findings emerging from the review which establish the enacted characters of content knowledge in physical education as a shared construction process through didactic interactions.

Student relations to knowledge: the learner's perspective in *didactique*

Understanding the local meanings that individuals construct from experience is the central focus in student learning within the *didactique* tradition. As indicated earlier students' social and operational representations, students' conceptions and the student's individual relation to knowledge are the key concepts of this line of research. The data collected during the earliest research were interpreted in terms of "social representations" of physical activities and sports as part of the national curriculum. David (1989) and Bouthier (1989) introduced the theme during a national congress on teaching in physical education. They drew attention to the links between the "initial social representations" of physical activities and motor learning process. Bouthier and David (1989) examined by means of a test of word associations the representations of rugby in a large population of students (middle and high school). Their findings suggested that the initial representations of the game (tactical versus technical; emotional versus social; energetic versus violent) have an impact on students' strategies, actions, and performances during the learning process. In order to help teachers design learning tasks, the authors emphasized the need for collecting the students' initial representations in various physical activities. The first studies clearly demonstrated that students' representations differ from one group of students to another: beginner versus experienced, low skilled versus high skilled (David, 1989, Bouthier and David 1989); boys versus girls (David, 1995).

The idea that the representations of a team sport have an influence on the way students interpret the situation is linked with the notion of "action rules" (Gréhaigne and Godbout, 1995). For these authors "action rules" are related to the tactical knowledge constructed by the students and represent "a punctual truth" which "can become obstacles to progress in other occasions" (p. 496). Investigations were conducted in different sport areas. Implementing a volleyball curriculum, Tanguy (1992) suggested taking into account the different social and operational representations of volleyball among boys and girls in order to design an adaptive learning environment and to facilitate their understanding of the game. Aubert (1997) identified eight components that structure the social representations of gymnastics: esthetic, mastery, obedience, physical factors, risk, show, vertigo and, virtuosity. Her findings suggested that in the context of physical education learning tasks related to a particular gymnastic skill: the upside-down standing posture, each student activates various components in order to achieve the academic work. From classroom observation she described five styles of students' behavior when performing the gymnastic upside-down standing posture: (1) "the refusal", (2) "the bent back", (3) "the block", (4) "the throwing of the legs", and (5) "the dissociate". Each style is associated with a combination of some components of the social representations of gymnastics (Aubert, 2003). The findings indicated clearly the impact of the various tasks on the activation of one or the other components of the social representation of each student and her/his motor behavior. Marsenach and her associates (see Dhellemmes, 1995; Goirand, 1998; Marsenach et al., 1991; Loquet, 1996) asked students to draw themselves performing a learning task in order to grasp their "operational representations" (i.e. how they think they have to behave to succeed). Findings in gymnastics, handball, hurdles, rhythmic gymnastics, swimming and, volleyball indicated that students' operational representations of what they have to perform have a big impact on learning strategies. For example, students (French equivalent of 7th grade) drew themselves tossing the ball in front of their nose when doing a volleyball overhead pass (and not leaning back one's head) (Marsenach, 1995). Loquet (1996) asked students to draw themselves during a throw and catch task during a unit of rhythmic gymnastics. Their sketches represent them pushing the ball (or the hoop) far away in front of them (and not toward the vertical line of their movement). Classroom observations showed that sketches drawn by students were mostly congruent with the motor behavior performed in the learning task (Dhellemmes, 1995; Goirand, 1998; Marsenach, 1995; Loquet, 1996).

Students' conceptions (or misconceptions) of movement concepts would seem to have an important impact on learning strategies and learning outcomes. Some support for this view was found in studies which described the learning obstacles (findings will be presented later) encountered by students due to their own conceptions (Loquet, 1997, 1999, Marsenach, 1995, Refuggi, 1994, 1999, 2003). The data also underlined that the student's individual relation to the knowledge at stake in the didactic situation is continuously enacted through didactical interactions (Amade-Escot, 2000b, Garnier, 2003; Loquet, 2003; Uchan and Amade-Escot, 2002, Verscheure, 2001, 2003).

Some attempts have been made recently to describe student's individual relation to knowledge. In this line of research Sauvegrain and Terrisse (2003) explored student activity during a coed unit of wrestling. The study underscored the complexity of the student's individual relation to knowledge and its consequences on learning achievement. Data were collected through long and deep interviews and classroom observation of three students. Findings pointed out a big gap between the knowledge embedded in the learning tasks during the unit and the knowledge used by students during the fighting games in the application part of content development (Rink, 1993). This case study provides an analysis of different strategies in terms of one's relation to knowledge. Different resources are at the core of students' activity during the unit: technical, strategic, affective and, bio-informational (Sauvegrain and Terrisse, 2003). Depending on their own school biography, their individual relation to physical education as a school discipline, and their gender identity, all three students negotiated individually the way of being a wrestler. Claire complied with the demand of the teacher, Roxane always tried to avoid the core content and used alternative know-how, Florent behaved as he wanted during the whole unit but invented some personal techniques to win all the fights. Taking a slightly different focus, Garnier (2003) examined the interplay between the individual relation to knowledge of a teacher and one of his students. She followed through an ethnographic observation all the interactions between the teacher, the student and each element of knowledge embedded in the different learning stations of a long gymnastic unit (8 weeks) in a French middle school (equivalent of 8th grade). She held deep interviews with both the teacher and the student in conjunction with video recall of each lesson and for all the learning stations. This case study confirmed that the individual relation to knowledge of both teacher and student are continuously interdependent, even discrepant, because of the situated context of shared practice which characterizes classroom interactions. From a phenomenology viewpoint Garnier highlighted the fact that student learning outcomes are the result of social construction of meanings and knowledge through the inevitable breaches of the didactic contract (Brousseau, 1988/1997).

In summary, from broad inquiries exploring the initial representations (social and operational) of students in physical education to more ethnographic approaches of students' conceptions and students' individual relations to knowledge, the past decade has been marked by a growing interest of this topic in *didactique*. The research tries to understand the complexity of individual characteristics that could explain student learning trajectories. The findings established some discrepancy between the knowledge taught and the knowledge really learned by students during the academic work due to their representations, conceptions and meanings. These results are consistent with those provided by studies conducted on students' conceptions as presented in Section 3.9 of this handbook. Finally, one's relation to knowledge (i.e. that special amalgam of one's individual experience, skill level, disposition, representation, conception, beliefs and subjectivity that enables students to bear a relation to the content taught) underlies the functioning of the didactic system (Chevallard, 1989). This underscores the crucial or decisive role played by the knowledge taught and learned. It emphasizes the hidden phenomena of didactic transposition which is partly under the control of the teacher (for a discussion in relation to PCK, see Amade-Escot, 2000a) but continues implicitly when the content knowledge is brought into play in situations and activities in the classroom and puts constraints on the teaching and learning process. The question is what are the implications for practice?

Student learning processes: implementing teaching key strategies

According to the fact that students' perception and meaning given to the content knowledge embedded in the learning contexts have an impact both on teaching and learning some scholars try to foresee the implications for practice. Most of the authors quoted above have noted that research on students' representations, students' conceptions and student's individual relation to knowledge has implications for teaching strategies. In this view, the learner is seen as someone who actively creates her/his own personal construction of what is meaningful (David, 1989; Dhellemmes, 1995; Goirand, 1998; Gréhaigne and Godbout, 1995, 1998; Marsenach et al., 1991). Thus the teaching strategies enhanced by the *didactique* literature are based on constructivist perspectives and curricula which promote essentials rather than basics. Traditional curricula are based on elemental fragments of knowledge while the didactic curriculum approach promotes learning environments conceived as rich, meaningful, whole experiences. The idea is to help students search for meaning as suggested by contemporary curriculum theories (Kirk, 1993). It is argued that when teachers themselves adopt a reflective attitude toward the content they teach, they engage themselves in a process of rendering problematic or questionable those aspects of teaching generally taken for granted: the content knowledge embedded in learning environments.

Thus, in accordance with a constructivist theory of learning (broadly influenced by the Piagetian tradition) researchers in *didactique* advocated teaching through problem-solving tasks and insisted that the content emerge from relevant meaningful contexts. This is related to the idea developed by Kirk (2002) that teaching and learning in physical education are situated in the sense that teachers and learners participate in a "community of practice". The didactic notion of "social practices taken as a reference" (Amade-Escot, 2000a: 87) clearly suggests that the source of the didactic transposition has to be determined among "one or more communities of practice" which provide students with opportunities for making sense of their learning. The "didactic engineering" program of studies performed over 10 years at the Institut National de la Recherche Pédagogique (INRP: French National Institute for Pedagogical Research) experimented and provided concrete tools for designing meaningful environments to teach physical activities and sports most commonly found in middle-school curricula (Dhellemmes, 1995; Goirand, 1998; Loquet, 1996; Marsenach, 1995).

More recent studies implemented a semioconstructivist teaching approach in physical education in order to promote meaningful student learning (Gréhaigne, 2003; Nachon, et al., 2001). These authors were cautious about introducing the "debate of ideas" as a key strategy to develop students' construction of understanding. Some support for this view was found in studies on badminton, table tennis and different team games (Chevalier et al., 2004a,b; Darnis et al., 2004; Deriaz et al., 1998; Gréhaigne and Godbout, 1998; Wallian and Gréhaigne, 2004). The assumption is to consider that language is a mediating object which guides the student learning process through critical thinking. In these studies the conceptual framework combines the situated theory of "speech acts" and a semiotic theory of "expectation horizon" (Wallian and Gréhaigne, 2004: 259–260). From this perspective there is a certain degree of affordance between language, thought, and action. With research evidence (see section above) suggesting that students might perceive meanings that are different from those of teachers the authors argue for asking students as often as possible to verbalize and to comment their action (Wallian and Gréhaigne, 2004). According to Nachon et al. (2001) "the knowledge constructing in action can be defined as a semiotic activity of representation's reworking" (p. 114). In this line of research, the "debate of ideas" is thus a "didactic tool" (Gréhaigne and Godbout, 1998; Gréhaigne, 2003: 86) which helps the teacher to transform the student reading of a play's configuration. As a result of these studies, the authors provide models for verbal reports of player in action at various stages of the teaching and learning

process which differ from advanced beginners and experienced students (Deriaz et al., 1998; Nachon et al., 2001). For a student, to debate an idea with peers regarding her/his action becomes a means to free herself/himself from the emotional and the immediate feeling and thus help in construing through verbalization the efficient "action rules" needed to perform in the didactic situation (Wallian and Gréhaigne, 2004: 265). In this context the role of the teacher is to design a contextualized environment that allows students and teacher to debate. Within the limitation of these studies which were conducted in teaching and learning decision making strategies in team sport (Gréhaigne et al., 2001) this line of research is of particular interest and should be developed in the future for a better understanding of the role of language and verbal interactions as a didactic means in physical education. However it should be noted that classroom observations suggest within a different focus that verbal interactions might play a role in producing some unexpected outcomes. Doyle (1986) already pointed out this issue when speaking about the "whole-class format characterized by question-answer drills over content" (p. 403). The risk of conventional transactions conducted by the teacher and its consequences in terms of problematic breaches of the didactic contract has been already pointed out (Amade-Escot, 2000a).

Learner outcomes: obstacles and progress

As indicated in the first section of this chapter research into *didactique* began in the early 1980s at the INRP. The concerns of the pioneers were to understand the difficulties encountered by teachers in teaching physical education. The first studies focused on teacher activity and her/his role in terms of didactic transposition (for an overview, see Amade-Escot, 2000a, Amade-Escot and Marsenach, 1995). But tracking teacher activity in physical education teaching through the functioning of the didactic system (the irreducible triadic relationship) empowered investigators to analyze students' difficulties and obstacles. As said before students' difficulties were initially interpreted as the effects of students' social and operational representations on learning effectiveness. However, within a different assumption the need for a better knowledge of the relation between didactic transposition and learning obstacles appeared quickly. A national large-scale research project was conducted from 1986 to 1991 at INRP by Marsenach and her colleagues (see Marsenach et al., 1991). The research project was to identify and describe the major obstacles encountered by teachers and students in day-to-day lessons. This study associated 55 physical education teachers and more than 150 units of physical education lessons were analyzed. The conceptual framework about learning obstacles was borrowed from Bednarz and Garnier (1989) with reference to Bachelard (1938/1983) and Brousseau (1989/1997). From a constructivist viewpoint these authors consider that students learn through adaptation: "The student learns by adapting him/herself to a milieu which generates contradictions, difficulties and disequilibria" (Brousseau, 1986/1997: 30). Teaching therefore requires the teacher to provoke the expected students' adaptation by a judicious choice of "problems" embedded in a meaningful learning environment. To highlight this issue Brousseau provided the term of "didactic milieu" (1988/1997: 227–249). But it remains that students' expected adaptation is never gained and some resistance might appear due to "learning obstacles". That is why research into *didactique* tries to identify the major obstacles which might interfere with the teaching/learning process. The concept of obstacle in physical education had to be specified. To do this, Marsenach et al. (1991) analyzed in depth 90 critical didactic incidents (CDI) (for a development on CDI, see Amade-Escot, 2005). The CDIs were collected from direct observation of lessons conducted by 55 teachers. Qualitative data provided a rich, detailed description of the obstacles which limit student learning during physical education lessons with specification among various physical activities (dance, gymnastics, handball, rhythmic gymnastics, swimming, track and field and, volleyball: see Marsenach et al., 1991). Following Brousseau (1989/1997) the investigators identified three types of obstacles that interfere with the whole process of teaching and learning: (1) "ontogenetic obstacles", (2) "epistemological and technical obstacles", and (3) "didactical obstacles" (Amade-Escot and Marsenach, 1995: 60–61).

- Ontogenetic obstacles refer to some limitation in motor learning due to student maturation, for example the coincidence-anticipation deficit in motor ability of young children. The need for more scientific knowledge in sport sciences to inform researchers into *didactique* was pointed out.
- Epistemological and technical obstacles in physical education are related to the notion of epistemological obstacles developed by Bachelard for science education (1938/1983). Obstacles belong to the learning process itself. They cannot be avoided. Learning in physical education implies a restructuring of motor behavior in order to increase adaptation. For instance an epistemological and technical obstacle in learning swimming for a beginner is to accept the restructuring of her/his motor and perceptual locomotion pattern within an emotional water environment, namely to transform her/his habit of a vertical posture (as

when walking) to a horizontal body position to move in the water (Refuggi, 1999). Moreover it must be pointed out that in many physical activities and sports the epistemological and technical obstacles may be found in the historical evolution of the sport techniques. The social and historical construction of efficient skills of sport techniques and the context of their appearance might allow teachers to select or not relevant content knowledge to be taught.
- Didactical obstacles refer to the difficulties that appear during the learning process in relation to the implementation of specific contents. Some learning outcomes can help the student at a certain stage of her/his learning, while this adaptation might be an obstacle for the development of further skills. The existence of didactic obstacles illustrates some of the inevitable effects of the didactic transposition.

There is some evidence (Amade-Escot and Léziart, 1996; Dhellemmes, 1995; Goirand, 1998; Loquet, 1996; Marsenach et al., 1991) that the combination of these three types of obstacles might be at the origin of students' failure or difficulties in physical education. For example the forearm pass is widely taught as a basic skill to play volleyball. Is this skill relevant for students? Following Marsenach's studies (1991, 1995) it appeared that: (1) This manipulative skill might increase students' difficulties because teachers often decontextualize the skill from its initial meaning and context and teach it as a drill rather than as tactical knowledge relevant for the understanding of the game and meaningful for students' experience (for a similar discussion see Rovegno, 1995; McCaughtry and Rovegno, 2001); (2) Its teaching is counterproductive because this "basic" and fragmented sport technique reinforces the epistemological and technical obstacle to be overcome by beginners. Why? Usually individual manipulative patterns are structured for manipulating the various objects in a self-space sector situated just in front of the upper body. Construing the volleyball overhead pass implies that students overcome this obstacle. Teaching the forearm pass is thus contradictory with the construction of the postural pattern needed to achieve an overheard pass; (3) The volleyball forearm pass is an efficient sport technique which appeared in the mid 1950s as an inventive players' adaptation to defend float serves. Indeed this historical recall allows Marsenach to ascertain that teaching the forearm pass is also useless in the context of the type of serve usually performed by beginners in a school context. The development of this long example illustrates how epistemological and technical obstacles combined with ontogenetic obstacles could very well crystallize students' difficulties. Similar findings were analyzed within different forms of practice of school sports (Loquet, 1996, 1997, in rhythmic gymnastics;

Dhellemmes, 1995, in hurdles, javelin and triple jump; Goirand, 1998, in gymnastics).

Observing the recurrent difficulties and obstacles in student learning the issue of progress and heterogeneous outcomes of students in physical education have been raised by many scholars and practitioners. The theme of students as "perpetual beginners" emerged at the end of the 1980s with emphasis growing within the debate around the new national physical education curriculum.[2] What kind of progress and valuable learning outcomes are expected from students? In what kinds of educational experiences? How can we think about content knowledge together with value-laden, educational ends and personal and social development? How can we take into account students' diversity and specific needs and at the same time reach a "common culture in physical activities and sport" (MEN, French national PE curriculum, 1996, 2000)? How does one help students to construct meaningful experiences in physical activities and sport that promote transferability in other contexts and for lifelong physical activity? All these questions are recurrently addressed to the physical education curricula models. Within the *didactique* perspective the question of students' progress through diversity was taken into consideration during the "didactic engineering" program held at INRP. The project was to follow and assess the impact of the experienced teaching sequences on students' achievement. Besides the systematic data collection on students' outcomes, the researchers (e.g. Dhellemmes, 1995; Goirand, 1998; Loquet, 1996; Marsenach, 1995) wrote monographs about a few students observed all along the study. In the research design students were considered as informants as in the ethnographic method. The teacher indicated to the researcher three students: low-skilled, high-skilled and intermediate-skilled. The monographs consisted of day-to-day, lesson-to-lesson written logs on how each student behaved, what she/he felt, her/his appropriate level of engagement in the learning environments, her/his success and failure in the stated tasks, the transformation of her/his motor skill (even very tiny). Qualitative data and accounts were collected through videotape, field notes and short interviews. The observation in depth of the three students nuanced the results by giving an overview of the type of progress that can be encountered among the diversity of students' interest and ability. Loquet (1996) and Marsenach (1995) proposed the notions of "minor progress" versus "major progress" to acknowledge the various students' achievements, which are for low-skilled students often denied by observers. All the authors in the "didactic engineering" project pointed out that the difficulties of some

students, in terms of learning obstacles should be better known. The information given by each student's monograph allowed the researchers to show that low-skilled students accumulate tiny progresses. They control the toss of the ball better in volleyball (Marsenach, 1995). They can co-ordinate the throw and the catch in rhythmic gymnastics on a small space (Loquet, 1996). They are able to perform a gymnastic element in a safe and protected context (Goirand, 1998). But the tiny progressions observed through the monograph do not enable some students to demonstrate "major progress" (i.e. to overcome the learning obstacle). Dhellemmes (1995) used the term of "stage of adaptation" to described students' progressions in track and field activities. These studies drew attention to the fact that learning in physical education implies a restructuring of motor ability which differs among individuals and needs various pace and time. This factor supports a case for a long unit or season as defended in the Sport Education model (Siedentop, 1994). This point was clearly demonstrated in the important program of didactic research conducted by Marsenach and her associates. It suggests that more attention must be given to the diverse learning processes and outcomes (even tiny) constructed by students during physical education lessons in order to create appropriate learning contexts, to design meaningful physical activity experiences even at the micro level of the didactic milieu.

Student negotiations of the didactic contract

Micro-ethnographic studies have underscored the complexity of content knowledge as emergent outcomes jointly constructed by teachers and students in time and space through a process of situated action, negotiation and subjective interpretation. Content knowledge as transaction is at the core of the important line of research presented in the last part of this chapter. The analysis of didactic interactions (i.e. interactions which are specific to the content taught and learned) is an important and increasing sector of research into the *didactique* of physical education. In the previous sections, little attention was given to the process involved when the students and the teacher determine the evolution of the academic work in actual classes. Discussion on the findings of this line of research is now the focus of this review. Based on classroom observation (see the section on Method) an important amount of research focused on how students and teacher co-manage the didactic contract (Amade-Escot, 2000b, 2004; Brousseau, 1988/1997) and thus jointly transform the content knowledge. It has been clearly stated that the dynamics of the

---

[2] It must be pointed out here for international readers that since the early 1980s the national PE curriculum in France has been based on a very similar curriculum framework to the Sport Education model (Siedentop, 1994).

functioning of the didactic system is continuously dependent on the implicit didactic contract that underlies the academic work. As presented in the theoretical section the results of these implicit negotiations only appear when the didactic contract is broken. Thus researchers can only observe the breaches of the didactic contract when the teacher for her/his part and the students for their part modify the content embedded in the didactic milieu. Some of the breaches are necessary, namely when the teacher develops the content (Rink, 1993) or introduces new content in her/his lesson. But many breaches of the didactic contract appear incidentally and have discrepant consequences for student learning (for an example, see Amade-Escot, 2000a: 89, 92–93). The implicit negotiations of the didactic contract emerge in action and continually change the content taught. Most of the time teachers are not aware of these critical moments which consequently are not under their control (Amade-Escot, 1993, 1998, 2000b, 2003b, 2004; Amade-Escot and Léziart, 1996; Costes 2003; Dhellemmes, 1995; Garnier, 2003; Loquet, 1996, 2003; Marsenach, 1995; Roustan, 2003; Thépaut, 2002, Uchan and Amade-Escot, 2002, Verscheure, 2001, 2005; Verscheure and Amade-Escot, 2004, Wallhead, 2004). There is some evidence that physical education is achieved through a rather subtle and tacit process of negotiation.

Student and teacher negotiations within the didactic system

Content knowledge is enacted by teacher and students during a specific segment of academic work through the triadic interaction that occurs within the didactic situation. A didactic situation has two components: (1) a didactic intention borne by the teacher (the content knowledge to be taught and learned) and, (2) a didactic milieu that is a problem space defined by a set of instructions, resources, social and material setting in which some key variables are chosen to maximize students' learning. In the flow of the ongoing lesson researchers have underscored the need for fine-grained observation to sort out what teacher and students shared practices are. Indeed, breaches of the didactic contract are initiated neither by the teacher, nor by students, but instead evolve through joint, tangled co-activities that modify the initial content to be taught and learned. Studies have identified some typical breaches which chart the evolution of the didactic contract as developed below.

Student modifications of the key variables of the didactic milieu

When the teacher implements new content in the ongoing lesson she/he usually fixes the critical elements of the learning environment (the didactic milieu) in order to facilitate the students' construction of knowledge. Among these elements are some key variables which are decisive. Studies have shown that students transform ingeniously the key variables of the didactic milieu (see Amade-Escot, 2000a: 89). These transformations might be very tiny (Amade-Escot, 1993, 1998, 2000b; Garnier, 2003; Thépault, 2002; Marsenach, 1995; Loquet, 2003; Wallhead, 2004). Most of the time the teacher does not pay attention to these small modifications because the students' level of engagement in the academic work is still high. But the consequences of the whole are a change in the content knowledge actually taught and learned that might sometimes lead to the submergence of learning. This factor must not be confused with findings of studies from the ecological perspective (Doyle, 1986; Hastie and Siedentop, 1999, Siedentop, 1998/2002, Section 3.2 in this handbook). The main results in the ecological tradition of research stated that the ecology of physical education focuses on cooperation rather than on academic work. Teachers maintain cooperation by reducing the demands in the instructional system due to disruption in the student social system (for a review, see Hastie and Siedentop, 1999). As far as this is concerned the didactic approach focuses on students who participate consistently in academic work. Its contribution stresses that even in a context of students' strong commitment to the task the issue of the knowledge really taught and learned still remains problematic.

Student interpretation of teacher's expectations

In order to help the students, teachers may select specific content and design a related "learning experience" (Rink, 1993: 64) in which some assignments or instructions are combined to provoke a greater level of students' engagement in the task, or to highlight some particular aspect of the content knowledge at hand. Thus the didactic milieu may have two or more interconnected key variables. For instance in gymnastics (Uchan and Amade-Escot, 2002) a relevant learning environment may include two components: the aesthetic and the acrobatic. Students are asked to fulfill the two (or more) requirements at the same time in order to participate in a rich, meaningful learning process. Studies have revealed that students might interpret the task or the expectation of the teacher in a way very different than the one expected. They might favor one of the components of the assignment, not only because they try to reduce the demand of the task, but because there is a mismatch between what they think they have to do, or what they think the teacher expects them to do. In the previous gymnastics example girls may favor the aesthetic component of the task neglecting the acrobatic one. A discrepancy, not to say a misunderstanding, thus appears as the result of the respective expectations that are never really expressed but underlie many regrettable but tacit breaches of the didactic contract. Studies have described such phenomena in different areas like badminton, basketball, football, gymnastics, volleyball (Amade-Escot, 1998; Amade-Escot and Léziart, 1996; Costes, 2003; Garnier, 2003; Roustan, 2003; Thépault, 2002; Uchan and Amade-Escot, 2002; Verscheure, 2001) and at different school levels (primary school, middle school and high school). The need for and the uncertainty of common backgrounds underpinning didactic interactions were thus established.

Student and teacher verbal interactions

In order to enrich the learning environment and promote cultural understanding, group interaction, and cognitive skills, teachers use verbal phases in their teaching like questioning or using the debate of ideas (see above). These teaching strategies are very pertinent to develop personal and social responsibility as learner outcomes, but, as said before, do not always have positive consequences (see Wright, 1993, 1997 for the implications of the system of meanings expressed through teachers discourses on the construction of gender and other social relations). Analyses of verbal interactions during physical education lessons have underscored some unexpected effects on the evolution of the didactic contract. In questioning phases teachers tend to acknowledge the one part of the answer that they want to hear (Amade-Escot, 2000a). Students are very clever in anticipating their demand and very often give back the verbal cues expected even though they have not experienced them. This type of didactic contract appeared with great regularity. Since the early 1980s this form of classroom management has been described as a "whole-class format characterized by question–answer drills over content" (Doyle, 1986: 403) but the didactic approach stresses a new form of classroom communication which appeared recently when teachers intended to set up constructivist exchanges between students, but unconsciously pilot the communication to the answers expected (Amade-Escot, 2003; Amade-Escot and Léziart, 1996; Loquet, 1996; Roustan, 2003). Classroom studies suggest moreover that the dynamics of these interactions are very different according to each student and her/his status in the classroom (Costes, 2003, Verscheure, 2001, 2005, Verscheure and Amade-Escot, 2004). Recent research that has taken a semiotic approach to student–teacher interactions has drawn attention

to some consequences of language use for the social construction of gender (Wright, 1997).

Gender issues in PE as a result of a differentiated didactic contract

A large amount of research in physical education has established evidence of inequities that are part and parcel of teachers' interactions with girls and boys. A few studies have shown that a gendered curriculum might mitigate these effects (see Section 6.4 in this handbook). In *didactique* little attention was given to the issue of girls' and boys' learning in physical education (excepted David, 1995; Davisse, 1991). The need for a better understanding of the gendered student learning process was at the origin of some recent research on the gender issue from a didactic viewpoint (Amade-Escot et al., 2002). The theme was explored through the notion of the "differentiated didactic contract" defined by Schubauer-Léoni (1996). She considers that the didactic contract is not implicitly negotiated with all the students of the classroom but with some "groups of students which have diverse status in the classroom (…) status which are related to the diverse hierarchy of excellence and are partially tributary of students' social origins" (Schubauer-Léoni, 1996: 160). From this perspective the notion of the differentiated didactic contract contributes to the understanding of the diverse students' achievement. Within this framework a few authors (Amade-Escot et al., 2002; Costes, 2003, Uchan and Amade-Escot, 2002; Verscheure, 2001, Verscheure and Amade-Escot, 2004) have made the assumption that gender learning in physical education might be highlighted through microdidactic observations. To illustrate the differentiated process they established chronicles as narrative records of the didactical interactions. Their exploratory studies confirmed that girls and boys interact differently with the learning environment provided by the teacher due to their specific representations, and gendered identities. To avoid gender bias due to teaching styles the observed teachers were chosen on the basis of the equally gendered physical education curriculum implemented in their class. The findings pointed out the subtle way in which girls' and boys' achievements are enacted through the dynamic of the differentiated didactic contract and gave some insight into the phenomena. Each student (girl or boy) occupies specific niches within the didactic contract. Each of them interprets the task at hand and the teacher assignments depending on her/his individual relation to knowledge. For example girls, but also low-skilled boys in football (Costes, 2003), seem to apply the learning cues asked by the teacher without integrating them into the whole process. The teacher willing to help these students may not require them to overcome the difficulties but reinforces their "minor progress" (see earlier) through differentiated interactions. Nevertheless the studies indicated also that on the continuum of gendered behavior (from a feminine sport stereotype to a masculine sport stereotype) as described by Amade-Escot et al. (2002) girls and boys might occupy different status. Verscheure (2005) introduces the concept of "gender position" to indicate this specific habitus at the heart of dialectical interactions. The results of the studies indicated that subtle differentiation in the learning process appeared between girls and boys (Verscheure, 2005; Uchan and Amade-Escot, 2002) combined sometimes with the skill level of each (Costes, 2003). Studies were conducted in different sports: a feminine one (gymnastics), a more masculine one (football) and, a neutral one (volleyball). Further research is needed for a better knowledge of the co-constructed activities at the basis of gender differences in student learning.

To sum up this topic, the didactic contract is primarily the part of the negotiations, usually implicit, that concerns specifically the content knowledge embedded in a learning environment. The dynamic of the didactic contract and its differential evolution allows the teaching/learning process to go on because activities and content knowledge are jointly constructed (co-constructed in situ) by the students and the teacher. All the studies underscored the importance of the background in the differential dynamics of the didactic interactions. They also gave some support to the theoretical tenet which considers that the didactic contract is a specification of the communication contract as developed in social interactionism (Goffman, 1967). Hastie and Siedentop stated in their review on the ecological perspective that "research on ambiguity, risk, negotiation and trading-off within physical education is scarce" (1999: 19). The research into *didactique* has contributed to bridging some aspect of the gap raised by these authors. In fact there is some evidence nowadays that the content knowledge embedded in a learning environment is slightly modified during academic work while students' involvement in the managerial system or the student social system is congruent with the demands of academic work. According to the ecological paradigm authors, the issues of subject-matter content and management come together in ways that are not easily separated. But evidence can be found that the specific behavior of students depends on the way they understand or are related to knowledge embedded in the didactic milieu. In other words, didactic perspective confirms that "there is accountability intrinsic to the manner in which the activities develop and the goals are to be achieved" (Hastie and Siedentop, 1999: 16). The didactic perspective specifically studies the modification of the "content-embedded accountability" when the managerial and student social systems are not problematic. It assumes that the student's individual relation to knowledge plays a role in the modification

of the task, has an influence on both teacher and student work and consequently on student academic achievement. The didactic contract appeared as one of the key concepts to describe and understand the whole process.

Conclusion and possible future developments for the *didactique* of physical education

The number of studies on student learning in physical education within the *didactique* tradition has grown since the first appearance of this stream of research. From surveys on students' representations to more phenomenological approaches of the co-activities of teacher and students in single learning environment, the characteristics of this research are to provide a deep insight into student learning in physical education from a triadic lens. Using a variety of conceptual and methodological tools investigators have drawn up the complexity of the theme. This body of research supplies a rich knowledge base for a better understanding of physical education practices. "The knowledge, its transposition and the successive didactic contracts governing how it is brought into play, are all co-straints that cannot be avoided since they weave connections at the very foundation of the didactic relation" (Amade-Escot, 2000a: 93). It is because of these constraints that students' learning outcomes undergo subtle processes of transformation and elaboration of knowledge. These processes emerge as a result of shared construction of knowledge through didactic interactions within the situated teaching and learning context. The major findings emerging from the review establish the enacted characters of content knowledge in physical education. This review also tries to indicate some links and commonalty with other traditions of contemporary research in the world of sport pedagogy.

As a new and expanding field of research it is time to conclude by noting some issues and directions for further developments:

- Promising research on students' learning obstacles emerged during the first decade, but this line of work seems silent today. At the same time the quality of physical education should meet the needs of all students – girls and boys, high skilled and low skilled, gifted and less gifted, all social and cultural backgrounds. The need for specific research on the difficulties and obstacles encountered by diverse learners must be pointed out.
- Effort needs to be devoted to the development of semiotic and language models to study verbal interactions and classroom debate in physical education. Specific issues seem to arise from recent research, but future development is

clearly suggested in connection with the didactic contract theme. The research reviewed here indicates also that gestural (body language) and non-verbal aspects of didactic interactions play a role in the semiotic process and thus have to be studied jointly with verbal interactions. Their function on the knowledge taught and learned has also to be deepened.

- In physical education different types of knowledge are interconnected. Beyond the motor aspect of learning outcomes, social, cultural, and value-laden contents are to be studied together to have a better understanding of the contribution of school discipline to student development.
- Student learning in economically and socially deprived contexts has to be known better from a didactic viewpoint in order to examine what kind of specific constraints weigh on the functioning of the didactic system. Learning physical activities within the "community of practice" (Kirk, 2002) has a role to play in these areas and should be studied in depth.
- Sport pedagogy literature encourages some new orientations based on situated theories which advocate their impact on student learning outcomes. Studies should be developed in order to identify what kind of knowledge and values are really taught and learned and what types of new constraints force the didactic system. For example, peer teaching and its effect on student learning is probably the weakest focus of didactic research (except the recent work of Wallhead, 2004). It must seriously be taken into consideration that changes in teaching have always an influence in terms of didactic transposition and thus should be analyzed.
- At least and from a methodological perspective even the need for articulating both qualitative and quantitative studies is suggested, more longitudinal studies with a micro-ethnographic design have to be developed at different stages of the school system, as well as case studies to confirm the recent findings.

In order to progress in our understanding of the dual movement of teaching and learning, we shall conclude here by insisting upon the benefit of working at the heart of the didactic system, towards a clinic of teaching and learning exchanges in order to have a better observation and understanding of the processes of constructing that intersubjectivity which is unique in its own way. It is indeed these processes that ultimately generate a situation in which one student allows him/herself to take a place in the culture while another stays outside the game.

References

Amade-Escot, C. (1993). Procédures de régulation didactique en EPS : étude de quelques modalités de gestion des situations didactiques chez les enseignants novices [Procedure of didactict re-adjustment in PE: study of some forms of management of didactic situations by novice teachers]. In G. Bui-Xuan and J. Gleyse (Eds.), *Enseigner l'éducation physique et sportive* (pp. 61–73). Grenoble, France: AFRAPS.

Amade-Escot, C. (1996, November). *French trends in Pedagogical Content Knowledge Analysis: The didactic paradigm.* Paper presented at the AIESEP International Seminar, Lisbon, Portugal.

Amade-Escot, C. (1998). Apport des recherches en didactique à l'analyse de l'enseignement de l'EPS. Une étude de cas : le contrat didactique [Contribution of didactics research to teaching analysis in PE. A case study: the didactic contract]. In C. Amade-Escot, J.P. Barrué, J.C., Bos, F. Dufor, M. Dugrand and A. Terrisse (Eds.), *Recherches en Education Physique et Sportive: Bilan et perspectives* (pp. 253–266). Paris: Editions de la Revue Education Physique et Sports, Recherche et Formation.

Amade-Escot, C. (1999, April). *Teacher's role in didactic interactions.* Paper presented at AIESEP World Congress, Besançon, France.

Amade-Escot, C. (2000a). The contribution of two research programs on teaching content: PCK and Didactics of physical education. *Journal of Teaching in Physical Education, 20*: 78–101.

Amade-Escot, C. (2000b, April). *How students manage the didactic contract? Contribution of the didactic perspective to research in the physical education classroom.* Paper presented at AERA Congress, New Orleans, LA (ERIC Document Reproduction Service N° ED442786).

Amade-Escot, C. (2003a). *Didactique de l'éducation physique. Etats des recherches [Didactics of Physical education: state of the art].* Paris: Editions de la Revue Education Physique et Sports, Recherche et Formation.

Amade-Escot, C. (2003b). La gestion interactive du contrat didactique en volley-ball : agencement des milieux et régulations du professeur [The management of the didactic contract in volley ball: teacher lay-out of the didactic milieu and regulations]. In C. Amade-Escot (Ed.), *Didactique de l'éducation physique – Etat des recherches,* (pp. 255–278). Paris: Editions de la Revue Education Physique et Sports, Recherche et Formation.

Amade-Escot, C. (2004). Contenus d'enseignement et aléas de la relation didactique en éducation physique et sportive [Teaching content and uncertainty of didactic relationship in PE]. In G. Carlier (Ed.), *Si l'on parlait du plaisir d'enseigner l'éducation physique* (pp. 227–239). Montpellier, France: AFRAPS

Amade-Escot, C. (2005). The critical didactic incidents as a qualitative method of research to analyze the content taught. *Journal of Teaching in Physical Education, 24:* 127–148.

Amade-Escot, C. and Léziart, Y. (1996). *Contribution à l'étude de la diffusion de propositions d'ingénierie didactique auprès de praticiens. Analyse de cas d'enseignants d'éducation physique et sportive* [Contribution to the study of circulation of new content design from didactic research: case study of PE teachers], (Rapport de recherche N°30506). Paris, INRP.

Amade-Escot, C. and Marsenach, J. (1995). *Didactique de l'éducation physique et sportive : questions théoriques et méthodologies* [Didactics in physical education: Theoretical and methodological aspects]. Grenoble, France: La pensée sauvage/INRP.

Amade-Escot, C., Uchan, K. and Verscheure, I. (2002, December). *La question des inégalités de genre en éducation physique et sportive: Intérêt de l'approche didactique* [The issue of gender inequities in PE: interest of the didactic approach]. Paper presented at the Colloque ARIS on "Cultures Sportives et Artistiques. Formalisation des Savoirs Professionnels. Pratiques, Formations, Recherches", Rennes, France.

Aubert, J. (1997). *Représentations sociales et comportements en gymnastique d'élèves de collège* [Social representations and behavior of middle school students in gymnastics]. Unpublished doctoral dissertation, Université Joseph Fourier, Grenoble, France.

Aubert, J. (2003). Représentations et conduites d'élèves de collège en gymnastique scolaire [Representations and students' conduct in school gymnastics]. In C. Amade-Escot (Ed.), *Didactique de l'éducation physique – Etat des recherches* (pp. 309–323). Paris: Editions de la Revue Education Physique et Sports, Recherche et Formation.

Bachelard, G. (1938/1983). *La formation de l'esprit scientifique* [The development of scientific thought] (12nd ed.). Paris: J. Vrin, Librairie philosophique.

Bednarz, N. and Garnier, C. (1989). *Construction des savoirs. Obstacles et conflits* [The construction of knowledge: obstacles and conflicts]. Ottawa: Editions Agence Arc.

Bouthier, D. (1989). Contribution à la transformation des représentations fonctionnelles des élèves en EPS [Contribution to the change of students' operational representations in PE]. In SNEP (Ed.), *L'EPS aujourd'hui ce qui s'enseigne* (pp. 303–308). Paris: SNEP.

Bouthier, D. (1993). *L'approche technologique en STAPS: représentations et actions* [Technological research in STAPS: representations and actions]. Unpublished Note de synthèse pour l'Habilitation à Diriger des Recherches. Université de Paris XI, Paris, France.

Bouthier, D. and David, B. (1989). Représentation et action: De la représentation initiale à la représentation fonctionnelle des APS en EPS [Representation and action: from initial representation to operational representation of exercise and sport in physical education]. In G. Bui-Xuan (Ed.), *Méthodologie et didactique de l'éducation physique et sportive* (pp. 233–249). Clermont-Ferrand: AFRAPS.

Bouthier, D., Davisse, A., Fleurance, P. and Lafont, L. (1990). Controverse: Les représentations en EPS [Representations in physical education: a controversial issue]. *Echanges et controverses, 2*: 103–122.

Bouthier, D. and Grifflet, J. (1992, Eds.) *Representation et action en activites physiques et sportives* [Representations and actions in physical activities and sport]. Paris Universite de Paris XI, France

Brousseau, G. (1997). *Theory of Didactical Situations in Mathematics.* N. Balacheff, M. Cooper, R. Sutherland and V. Warlfield (Eds.), collected papers. Dordrecht: Kluwer.

Clément, J.P. (1996). *Représentations et conceptions en didactique: Regards croisés sur les STAPS* [Representations and conceptions in didactics: cross glances into STAPS (Sciences and Techniques of Activities and Sport)]. Strasbourg: CRDP.

Cadopi, M. and Durand, M. (1996). Représentations et actions dans l'apprentissage et l'enseignement des activités physiques et sportives [Representations and actions in learning and teaching physical activities and sports]. In J.P. Clément (Ed.), *Représentations et conceptions en didactique: Regards croisés sur les STAPS* (pp. 101–107). Strasbourg: CRDP

Charlot, B. (1997). *Du rapport au savoir: Eléments pour une théorie* [From relation to knowledge: Elements for a theory]. Paris: Anthropos.

Chevallard, Y. (1989). *Le concept de rapport au savoir: rapport personnel, rapport institutionnel, rapport officiel* [The concept of relation to knowledge: personal relation, institutional relation, official relation] (Document interne, n°108). Séminaire de didactique des mathématiques et de l'informatique, Université Joseph Fourier, Grenoble, France.

Chevallard, Y. (1992). Fundamental concepts in didactics: perspectives provided by an anthropological approach. In R. Douady and A. Mercier (Eds.), *Research in didactics of mathematics.* Selected papers, (pp. 131–168). Grenoble, France: La pensée sauvage.

Chevalier, G., Gréhaigne, J.F. and Nachon, M. (2004a). *Interaction et construction de connaissances en badminton: analyse et sens de l'action par la verbalisation* [Interaction and knowledge construction in badminton: analysis of action meaning through verbalization]. Paper presented to the international congress on "Faut-il parler pour apprendre?", Arras, France.

Chevalier, G., Gréhaigne, J.F., Nachon, M. and Wallian, N. (2004b). *Interlocutions et apprentissage en sports collectifs à l'école: une logique sémiolinguistique en basket-ball* [Interlocution and learning in games sports: a semioli guistic logic in basket-ball]. Paper presented to the inte national congress on "Faut-il parler pour apprendre?", Arras, France.

Comenius, J. (1627/2000). Didactica magna. Paris: Ed. Klinsieck.

Costes, L. (2003). *Dynamiques différentielles des apprentissages en Football : une étude selon le sexe et le niveau d'habileté en classe de 6eme* [Differential dynamics in learning football in 6th grade. A study on gender and level of skill]. Unpublished master's thesis, Université Toulouse Le Mirail, Toulouse, France.

Darnis, F., Lafont, L. and Menaut, A. (2004, March). *Verbalisation en dyades dans une situation de coopération et d'affrontement en EPS* [Verbalization within dyades in a cooperative and opponent game in PE]. Paper presented to the international congress on "Faut-il parler pour apprendre?", Arras, France.

David, B. (1989). Représentations et actions [Representations and actions]. In SNEP (Ed.), *L'EPS aujourd'hui, ce qui s'enseigne* (pp. 295–298). Paris: SNEP.

David, B. (1993). *Place et rôle des représentations dans la mise en œuvre d'une APS: l'exemple du rugby* [Place and role of the representations in teaching a physical activity: the example of rugby]. Unpublished doctoral dissertation. Université de Paris XI, Paris, France.

David, B. (1995). Rugby mixte en milieu scolaire [Co-education in rugby at school]: in school. *Revue Française de Pédagogie, 110*: 51–61.

David, B., Bouthier, D., Marsenach, J. and Durey, A. (1999). French research into the didactics and technology of physical activities and sports: An expending new field. *Instructional Science, 27*: 147–163.

Davisse, A. (1991). Au temps de l'école: l'éducation physique et sportive des filles [From school time: physical education for girls]. In A. Davisse and C. Louveau (Ed.), *Sport, école et société: la part des femmes* (pp. 174–263). Paris: Editions Actio.

Dhellemmes, R. (1995). *EPS au collège et athlétisme* [PE in middle school and track and field]. Paris: INRP.

Deriaz, D., Poussin, B. and Gréhaigne, J.F. (1998). Le débat d'idées [Debate of ideas]. *Education physique et Sport, 273*: 80–82.

Doyle, W. (1986). Classroom organization and management. In M.C. Wittrock (Ed.), *Handbook of Research on Teaching* (3rd ed.), (pp. 392–431). New-York: Macmillan.

Giordan, A. (1996). Représentations et conceptions [Representations and conceptions]. In J.P. Clément (Ed.), *Représentations et conceptions en didactique: regards croisés sur les STAPS* (pp. 11–32). Strasbourg: CRDP.

Garnier, A. (2003). *Le rapport au savoir du professeur: entre contraintes et autonomie. Une étude de cas lors d'un cycle d'enseignement de la gymnastique au collège* [Teacher's relation to knowledge: between constraints and autonomy. A case study during a gymnastic unit in middle school]. Unpublished doctoral dissertation. Université Paul Sabatier, Toulouse, France.

Goffman, E. (1967). *Interaction ritual.* New York: Doubleday.

Goirand, P. (1998). *EPS au collège et gymnastique* [Physical Education in Middle School and Gymnastics]. Paris: Editions de l'INRP.

Gréhaigne, J.F. (2003). Vers une didactique constructiviste en sport collectif [Toward constructivist didactics in team games]. In C. Amade-Escot (Ed.), *Didactique de l'éducation physique - Etat des recherches,* (pp. 79–102). Paris, Editions de la Revue Education Physique et Sports, Recherche et Formation.

Gréhaigne, J.F. and Godbout, P. (1995). Tactical knowledge in team sports from a constructivist and cognitivist perspective. *Quest, 47*: 490–505.

Gréhaigne, J.F. and Godbout, P. (1998). Observation, critical thinking and transformation: three key elements for a constructivist perspective of the learning process in team sports. In R. Feingold, R. Rees, G. Barrette, L. Fiorentino, S. Virgilio and E. Kowalski (Eds.), *Education for life* (pp. 109–118). New York: Adelphi University.

Gréhaigne, J.F., Godbout, P. and Bouthier, D. (2001). The teaching and learning of decision making in team sports. *Quest, 53*: 59–76.

Hampel, R.L. (1993). Historical perspectives on academic work: the origins of learning. In T.M. Tomlison (Ed.), *Motivating students to learn. Overcoming barriers to high achievement* (pp. 21–39). Berkely, CA: MrCutrhan Publishing Corporation.

Hansen, A.J. (1991). Establishing a teaching/learning contract. In C.R. Christensen, D.A. Garvin and A. Sweet (Eds.), *Education for judgement. The artistry of discussion leadership* (pp. 123–135). Boston, MA: Harvard Business School.

Hastie, P. and Siedentop, D. (1999). An ecological perspective on physical education. *European Physical Education Review, 5*(1): 9–29.

Kirk, D. (1993). Curriculum work in physical education: Beyond the objectives approach? *Journal of Teaching in Physical Education, 12*: 376–387.

Kirk, D. (2002, December). *Physical education as it was, as it is and as it might be: Situated learning as a framework for theoretical synthesis and practice-referenced research.* Paper presented at the Colloque ARIS on "Cultures Sportives et Artistiques. Formalisation des Savoirs Professionnels. Pratiques, Formations, Recherches", Rennes, France.

Kirk, D. and Almond, L. (1999, April). *Sport education as situated learning in physical education: Making links to citizenship, leadership, and critical consumerism.* Paper presented to the AIESEP International Congress, Besançon, France.

Kirk, D. and Macdonald, D. (1998). Situated learning in physical education. *Journal of Teaching in Physical Education, 17*: 244–265.

Leplat, J. (1985). Les representations fonctionnelles dans le travail [Functional representations in work setting]. *Psychologie Française, 30*(3–4): 269–275.

Loquet, M. (1996). *EPS au collège et gymnastique rythmique et sportive* [PE in middle school and rhythmic gymnastics]. Paris: INRP.

Loquet, M. (1997). Conception des contenus d'enseignement en Gymnastique Rythmique et Sportive, apport de l'analyse mécanique: le cas des lancer-rattraper d'engins [Conceptions about teaching content in Rhythmic Gymnastics, contribution of mechanic analysis: the throwing apparatus case study]. *Science et Motricité, 31*: 36–45.

Loquet, M. (1999, April). *Knowledge taught: between school constraints and social meaning of the activity.* Paper presented at the AIESEP World Congress, Besançon, France.

Loquet, M. (2003). Scolariser une pratique sociale. Apports d'une recherche d'ingénierie didactique: le cas de la gymnastique rythmique [How to implement a social practice in the curriculum. Contribution of didactic engineering: the case of Rhythmic Gymnastics]. In C. Amade-Escot (Ed.), *Didactique de l'éducation physique – Etat des recherches,* (pp. 137–168), Paris: Editions de la Revue Education Physique et Sports, Recherche et Formation.

Loquet, M., Garnier, A. and Amade-Escot, C (2002). Transmission des savoirs en activités physiques, sportives et artistiques dans des institutions différentes: enseignement scolaire, entraînement sportif, transmission chorégraphique [Knowledge transmission in physical activities: school teaching, sport coaching, ballet choreographing]. *Revue Française de Pédagogie, 141*: 99–109.

Marsenach, J. (1995). *EPS au collège et volley-ball* [Physical education in middle school and volleyball]. Paris: INRP.

Marsenach, J. (1998). Dix ans de recherches en EPS à l'INRP. Bilan et perspectives [Ten years of research at INRP. Contribution and perspectives]. In C. Amade-Escot, J.P. Barrué, J.C. Bos, F. Dufor, M. Dugrand and A. Terrisse (Eds.), *Recherches en Education Physique et Sportive: Bilan et perspectives* (pp. 57–66). Paris: Editions de la Revue Education Physique et Sports, Recherche et Formation.

Marsenach, J., Dhellemmes, R., Lebas, A. et al. (1991). *EPS: Quel enseignement ?* [PE : what kind of teaching]. Paris: INRP.

McCaughtry, N. and Rovegno, I. (2001). Meaning and movement: exploring the deep connections to education. *Studies in Philosophy and Education, 20*: 489–505.

Mercier, A., Schubauer-Léoni, M.L. and Sensevy, G. (2002). Vers une didactique comparée [Toward comparative didactics]. *Revue Française de Pédagogie,* (special issue), 141.

MEN (1996). *Programme d'EPS de la classe de sixième des collèges* [National PE curriculum for middle-schools] Arrêté du 18-6-1996, BO du MEN, N°29 du 18 juillet 1996.

MEN (2000). *Programmes des enseignements de la classe de seconde et première : Éducation physique et sportive* [National PE curriculum for high-schools] BO Hors série, N° 6 et BO Hors série N° 7 du 31 août 2000.

Merriam-Webster. (1981). *Webster's Third New International Dictionary of the English Language Unabridged.* Springfield, MA: Merriam-Webster.

Nachon, M., Mahut, N., Mahut, B. and Gréhaigne, J.F. (2001). Students' construction of strategies in table tennis: design of the expectation horizon within debate of ideas. In K. Nyit Chin and H. Jwo (Eds.), *AIESEP International Conference Proceedings* (pp. 114–120). Taipei: National Taïwan Normal University.

Raisky, C. and Caillot, M. (1996). *Au-delà des didactiques, le didactique: débats autour de concepts fédérateurs* [Beyond didactics of school disciplines: debate around federative concepts]. Bruxelles: De Boëck, Perspectives en éducation.

Refuggi, R. (1994). Obstacles à l'enseignement par résolution de problèmes en EPS [Obstacles in teaching with problem-solving tasks]. *Impulsions, 1*: 13–31.

Refuggi, R. (1999, April). *Students' conceptions as obstacle to learning crawl swimming.* Paper presented at the AIESEP World Congress, Besançon, France.

Refuggi, R. (2003). Apprendre à transformer sa nage pour mieux la connaître. Rôle des conceptions du monde physique en EPS [Learning how to transform the stroke to improve swimming. Impact of students' conception of the physic world in PE]. In C. Amade-Escot (Ed.), *Didactique de l'éducation physique – Etat des recherches* (pp. 325–338). Paris: Editions de la Revue Education Physique et Sports, Recherche et Formation.

Rink, J.E. (1993). *Teaching physical education for learning.* St Louis. MO: Mosby.

Roustan, C. (2003). *La mise en place d'un milieu pour l'étude d'une activité physique et sportive au CP: le cas du badminton* [The setting of a milieu for studying a physical activity: the badminton case study]. Unpublished doctoral dissertation, Université d'Aix-Marseille I, Aix en Provence, France.

Rovegno, I. (1995). Theoretical perspectives on knowledge and learning and a student teacher's pedagogical content knowledge of dividing and sequencing subject matter. *Journal of Teaching in Physical Education, 14*: 284–304.

Sauvegrain, J.P. and Terrisse, A. (2003). Analyse de la décision d'élèves à l'épreuve du combat: une étude de cas dans un cycle de lutte en EPS [Analysis of students' decisions in a fighting event: a case study during a unit of wrestling in PE]. In C. Amade-Escot (Ed.), *Didactique de l'éducation physique – Etat des recherches* (pp. 339–366). Paris: Editions de la Revue Education Physique et Sports, Recherche et Formation.

Schubauer-Léoni, M.L. (1996). Etude du contrat didactique pour des élèves en difficulté en mathématiques. Problématique didactique et/ou psychosociale [Study of the didactic contract for students in difficulties in mathematics. Didactic or/and social psychology issue]. In C. Raisky, and M. Caillot (Eds.), *Au-delà des didactiques le didactique: débats autour de concepts fédérateurs* (pp. 159–189). Bruxelles: De Boëck, Perspectives en éducation.

Schubauer-Leoni, M.L. and Grossen, M. (1993). Negotiating the meaning of questions in didactic and experimental contracts. *European Journal of Psychology of Education, 4*: 451–471.

Shulman, L.S. (1986). Paradigms and research programs in the study of teaching: a contemporary perspective. In M.C. Wittrock (Ed.), *Handbook of research on teaching,* (pp. 3–36). New York: Macmillan.

Shulman, L.S. (1987). Knowledge and teaching: Foundation of a new reform. *Harvard Review, 57*: 1–22.

Siedentop, D. (1989/2002). Content Knowledge for Physical Education. *Journal of Teaching in Physical Education, 21*: 368–377.

Siedentop, D. (1994). The sport education model. In D. Siedentop (Ed.), *Sport education: quality PE through positive sport experiences* (pp. 3–16). Champaign, IL: Human Kinetics.

Siedentop, D. (1998/2002). Ecological perspectives in teaching research. *Journal of Teaching in Physical Education, 21*: 427–440.

Siedentop, D. (1999/2002). Lessons learned. *Journal of Teaching in Physical Education, 21*: 454–464.

Silverman, S. (1991). Research on teaching in physical education. *Research Quarterly for Exercise and Sport, 62*: 352–364.

Tanguy, G. (1992). Le volley : un exemple de mise en œuvre didactique [Volleyball: a didactic approach]. *Echanges et controverses, 4*: 7–20.

Thépaut, A. (2002). *Echec scolaire et éducation physique et sportive à l'école élémentaire. Etude des interactions maître-élèves dans la construction des savoirs. L'exemple de l'apprentissage de la passe en basket-ball* [Academic failure in PE in primary school: Studies of the teacher and students interactions during the students' learning of the basket ball pass]. Unpublished doctoral dissertation, Université de Rennes II, Rennes, France.

Terhart, E. (2003). Constructivism and teaching: a new paradigm in general didactics. *Journal of Curriculum Studies*, *35*(1): 25–44.

Tinning, R. (2002). Engaging Siedentipian perspectives on content knowledge for physical education. *Journal of Teaching in Physical Education*, *21*: 378–391.

Uchan, K. and Amade-Escot, C. (2002, December). *Les contrats didactiques différentiels filles et garçons au collège: le cas de l'appui tendu renversé* [Differential didactic contracts between girls and boys in middle school: the case of the gymnastic handstand]. Paper presented during the symposium on gender in PE, Colloque ARIS on "Cultures Sportives et Artistiques. Formalisation des Savoirs Professionnels. Pratiques, Formations, Recherches", Rennes, France.

Vanden-Auweele, Y., Bakker, F., Biddle, S., Durand, M. and Seiler R. (1999). *Psychology for physical educators*. Champaign, IL: Human Kinetics.

Vasquez-Levy, D. (2002). Bildung-centered didaktik: a framework for examining the educational potential of subject matter. *Journal of Curriculum Studies*, *34*(1): 117–128.

Verscheure, I. (2001). *Analyse exploratoire des contrats didactiques en relation avec la différence des genres: le cas de l'attaque en volley-ball* [Exploratory analysis of didactic contract in relation to gender: the case study of attack in volleyball]. Unpublished Master's thesis. Université Toulouse Le Mirail, Toulouse, France.

Verscheure, I. (2005). *Dynamique différentielle des interactions didactiques et co-construction de la différence des sexes en Education Physique et Sportive: Le cas de l'attaque en volley-ball en lycées agricole* [Dynamic differentiation of didactical interactions and the social construction of sex differences in physical education: The case of the attack in volley ball in a lycée agricole (High school)]. Unpublished doctoral dissertation, Université Paul Sabatier, Toulouse, France.

Verscheure, I. and Amade-Escot, C. (2004). Dynamiques différentielles des interactions didactiques selon le genre en EPS. Le cas de l'attaque en volley-ball en seconde [Dynamics of differential didactic interactions among gender in PE. The case of the attack in volleyball in a 10th grade classe]. *Revue STAPS*, *66*: 79–97.

Wallian, N. and Gréhaigne, J.F. (2004). Vers une approche semioconstructiviste des apprentissages moteurs [Toward a semio-constructivist approach to motor learning]. In G. Carlier (Ed.), *Si l'on parlait du plaisir d'enseigner l'éducation physique* (pp. 257–268). Montpellier, France: AFRAPS.

Wallhead, T.L. (2004). *A didactic analysis of student content development during the peer-assisted learning tasks of a unit of sport education*. Unpublished doctoral dissertation. The Ohio State University, Columbus.

Wood, P. (1983). *Sociology and the school. An interactionist viewpoint*. London: Routlege, Kegan Paul.

Wright, J. (1993). Regulation and resistance: the physical education lesson as speech genre. *Social Semiotics*, *3*(1): 23–56.

Wright, J. (1997). The construction of gendered contexts in single sex end co-educational. *Physical Education Lessons in Sport. Education and Society*, *2*(1): 55–72.

SECTION IV
Teachers, Teaching and Teacher Education in Physical Education

Teachers and teacher educators internationally have come under enormous scrutiny in recent years. Numerous reports have highlighted the failure of students to thrive and achieve in schools, as measured by a series of standardized achievement tests. These failures, regardless of their veracity, have been attributed in part to poor teaching and teacher education programs that fail to prepare teachers for the realities and challenges of contemporary schools.

In similar fashion, reports documenting physical activity and nutrition levels of children have suggested that poor quality physical education experiences are partly responsible for what some have called a rising tide of overweight and inactive youth around the world. Recent public health documents in several countries report physical education as part of the problem and a potential solution to this "crisis". The accuracy of such claims made about education, teacher education, and public health should be read, understood and contested by students and scholars of physical education. This is part of what this handbook and this section attempt to do.

While priorities of our educational, political, social, economic and democratic systems influence what is taught and learned in schools and on playing fields, there is no denying how individual teachers and coaches can be significant change agents in the lives of young people. The chapters in this section of the handbook focus on research related to physical education teachers, coaches, teacher educators and teacher education and how they impact, directly or indirectly, student learning and achievement.

What teachers/coaches and students/athletes say and do in school classrooms/athletic fields are key factors in how students/athletes choose to be physically active and what they come to know and value about physical activity and its role in their lives and in society more broadly. Physical educators' knowledge, beliefs, and experiences, as well as their professional preparation and continuing professional development interact and impact what and how teachers teach and coach and the goals they have for their interactions with students/athletes.

The first four chapters of the section focus on the research on prospective teachers and their learning to teach. The section begins with a critique by Tinning of the major theoretical perspectives used in physical education teacher education programs and research on aspects of these programs. He calls for greater engagement by scholars with the core ideas that form the central tenets of teacher education studies. He suggests greater engagement with "first order" theorists by PETE scholars will open up new possibilities in the practice of and research on teacher education and be less restrained by current educational discourses. Collier discusses research on models and instructional methods used in physical education teacher education. She calls for a more democratic curricular process in the design and delivery of teacher education that allows for the development of caring teachers who take time to develop the emotional dimensions of their pedagogical approaches and who cultivate equitable practices. Behets and Vergauwen investigated the research on the role of field experiences in the development of prospective physical educators and highlight the paucity of strong theoretical and evidentiary bases of what is done in the name of fieldwork in physical education. Stroot and Ko reviewed the research on a pre-service teacher's transition to teaching noting the need for a more seamless and collaborative (between the school and the teacher education program) model of learning to teach that includes the induction phase.

In his chapter Byra described the diversity of teaching styles used in teaching physical education and reviewed the research on teaching styles. His review can inform our understanding of the alignment (or lack thereof) between programme and lesson objectives and the experiences of students during physical education classes.

The next four chapters focus on research on physical education teachers' narratives, beliefs, knowledge and instructional pedagogies and research on continuing professional preparation of practicing teachers. Armour's chapter focuses on teacher's lives beyond the first years of teaching presenting research methods such as life history, life story, autoethnography, and narrative techniques. She argues such research provides forms of "story" and "storying" that can be used as a dynamic tool to help teachers and ultimately students learn.

Originally the co-editors invited Tsangaridou to write a chapter focusing on the research related to teachers' knowledge and beliefs. The growth of research in recent years forced us to separate the literature into two chapters. We understand a distinction between teacher knowledge and teacher belief is somewhat arbitrary and readers should treat this division of the literature as a solution to chapter length and not some theoretical perspective about knowledge and beliefs. Tsgangaridou highlights the complexities of these constructs and research methodologies that make it difficult to develop a theoretically coherent knowledge base to inform teacher education or continuing professional development initiatives.

The chapter on coaching and coach education by Trudel and Gilbert was placed in this section as many physical education teachers choose to both coach and teach and the issues of professional preparation for such instructional activities are not unconnected. There has been a growing interest in coach education and coach education research is slowly emerging as a substantive field of study. There has been relatively little overlap in the teacher and coach education literature. Placing the chapter is this section was our effort to encourage conversations and cross-disciplinary research across somewhat arbitrary boundaries in sport and physical education research.

The chapter on policy and policy research in teaching and teacher education by Dodds is recognition of the growing significance and intrusion of government on the professional lives and practices of physical educators at both the school and college level. This is an international phenomenon. At the local and national levels, health and education policies increasingly prescribe standards for teacher and coach preparation and certification, content standards for school health and physical education curricula, and performance standards for teacher and coach professional development. Even though the research base is small in this area, the proliferation of policies is not. This chapter should alert students and scholars of research on teaching and teacher education in physical education to the growing policy arena and need for increased research activity.

Reforming teacher education, continuing professional development, or improving the quality of school physical education for all children and youth will not be resolved solely on the basis of the evidence, however valid and valuable it may be. It is important we debate the nature of ideological and political aspects of reform agendas and policies together with the evidence we have about teachers, teaching, learning, and students so we can better understand the complexities of educational reform (Cochran-Smith, 2002; Dunkin, 1987).

There are calls for value-added accountability models for teacher education, the design of evidence based teacher education programs with student learning placed at the centre of this enterprise (Richardson, 2001). The authors describe the challenges of these and other claims for teachers and teacher educators. They describe and question research already conducted, shed light on areas that require more research, and suggest emergent areas or approaches to research on teacher education. It is our collective attempt to contribute substantively to that debate.

References

Cochran-Smith, M. (2002). Teacher education, ideology, and Napoleon. *Journal of Teacher Education. 53*, 3–5.

Dunkin, M. (1987). *The international encyclopedia of teaching and teacher education*. Oxford, Pergamon Press.

Richardson, V. (2001). *Handbook of research on teaching* (4th ed). Washington, DC: American Educational Research Association.

4.1 Theoretical orientations in physical education teacher education

RICHARD TINNING

Introduction

Handbook reviews are supposed to present a "state of the art" review of a selected topic. They conjure up an image of the disinterested scholar searching the databases and distilling the vast literatures into an accessible account that represents the "state of the art". But scholarship is seldom like that. Given the scope of the literature, decisions (read judgements) must be made regarding what to include, what to leave out, what to emphasize, what to background, how to classify different literature, and how to arrange the narrative of the review. Much of this work is subjective and will be influenced by the values and experiences that the author brings to the task. Accordingly this chapter presents an interpretation, one of many possible interpretations, of the topic "theoretical orientations in physical education teacher education (PETE)".

In this chapter I discuss the major theoretical perspectives that have oriented the programmes of PETE and research into PETE. I also discuss the links between the ways in which research has been conceived and the programmes that have been the objects of the research. At root here are the paradigmatic ways of thinking about knowledge that underpin both research and practice within PETE.

Of course when I talk of PETE exactly whose PETE am I referring to? This is an English language handbook and although its major audience will be from English-speaking countries (especially the USA) it is important to note that PETE exists in most developed countries and they may have orientations to their programmes and research that do not mirror those of the USA. However, it is also noted that the volume of English-language literature on PETE from the USA is huge and the available literature from non-English-speaking countries that is written in English is minimal (and for good reason considering the difficulty of writing academic work in a second language).

Moreover, since many teacher educators and researchers from Asian countries such as Korea, Taiwan, Indonesia, the Philippines and Japan have done their doctoral degrees in the USA, the influence of American ways of thinking about PETE and the issues they choose to research in PETE have come to dominate in many Asian countries as well. Accordingly, I will draw attention to literature from beyond the USA where possible.

Orientations

The task of this chapter is to provide an account of the theoretical orientations in PETE. But what exactly is an orientation? Among the different meanings for orientation given by *The Shorter Oxford Dictionary* we find that orientation is a direction or compass bearing to guide progress. Accordingly such questions as: Where is PETE heading? What are the main theories, ideas and concepts that give it direction? Who or what determines its heading? are pertinent questions when considering the theoretical orientations in PETE.

The American B.O. Smith, in his much quoted *Model for a School of Pedagogy*, reveals very clearly what he considered should be the principal orientation of teacher education: "The pre-service student should not be exposed to theories and practices derived from ideologies and philosophies about the way schools should be. The rule should be to teach thoroughly, the knowledge and skills that equip beginning teachers to work successfully in today's classrooms" (1980: 23). However, some 6 years before Smith's statement, Spodek (1974) claimed that "All teacher education is a form of ideology. Each program is related to the educational ideology held by a particular teacher educator or teacher education institution, even though the relationship may not be made explicit. There is no such thing as a value free education for children" (p. 8). Clearly there is a significant difference of opinion between Smith and Spodek and, in some ways their difference of opinion also reflects a real difference of orientation within PETE in regard to the purpose of teacher education.

Trying to find a way to organize this chapter proved to be a difficult task. The handbook editors suggested a chapter structure that included a brief historical perspective, core concepts, major findings, and major trends and future directions. My initial attempt was to write an integrated account of programmes and research. In the process of writing it soon became obvious that although there was overlap between the theoretical orientations for programmes and research, it would be better to deal with each separately. In what follows I have constructed two sections: the first has as its focus the theoretical orientations in PETE programmes themselves; the second has as its focus the theoretical orientations to research into PETE. In discussing programme orientations I will also make reference to the broader contemporary educational context.

Theoretical orientations in PETE programmes

In 1985 Vendien and Nixon's edited collection *Physical Education Teacher Education: Guidelines for Sport Pedagogy* was published. The book is instructive in many ways not the least of which is the insight into the issues topical in PETE two decades ago. In Section 5 of the book is a collection of models of selected undergraduate teacher education programmes in physical education. None of the 11 models presents even the briefest account of the theoretical orientations that might underpin the programme. Representations of the various PETE programmes were all based on details of course offerings, programmes structures and mandatory requirements. This emphasis on description of structural elements with little or no consideration of the theoretical underpinnings was not just a concern related to programme development and implementation. It also related to research.

How can we make sense of the volume of literature on PETE? What organizing themes can frame our analysis? In considering a useful arrangement for this analysis I began by looking at the ways that others in PETE and in teacher education in general classified orientations. Within the teacher education literature there have been the reviews of the field by scholars such as Zeichner (1983), Peck and Tucker (1973), Feiman-Nemser (1990), Doyle (1990), and within the field of PETE by Bain (1990), O'Sullivan (1996), Kang (2003), as well as other useful analyses by Vendian and Nixon (1985), Rink (1993), Fernandez-Balboa (1997), Macdonald (1997) and

others. Since most of the contemporary analyses of PETE (e.g. O'Sullivan, 1996, 2003; Rink, 1993) have used orienting frameworks borrowed from teacher education I consider it worthwhile to give a brief account of these frameworks before considering the specific PETE versions.

Feiman-Nemser (1990), in a chapter on the structural and conceptual alternatives in teacher preparations written for the *Handbook of Research on Teacher Education,* claimed that the dominant conceptual orientations give an insight into the ways of thinking about teacher education that underpin a programme. The conceptual orientations she identifies include: *academic; practical; technological; personal and critical.* O'Sullivan (1996) suggests that this framework is "useful in providing insight into the diversity of what is valued in the preparation of beginning teachers" (p. 318) and she makes use of the Feiman–Nemser model for her thoughtful analysis of PETE.

Rink (1993) also used the Feiman-Nemser framework to analyse PETE and suggested that *an academic orientation* (focus on subject matter of games, sport, dance, fitness, etc.), *a practical orientation* (which places a heavy reliance on field experience and practice), a *technological orientation* (which emphasises research-based teacher effectiveness skills), *a personal orientation* (emphasis placed on personal meaning for personal growth as a teacher), and a *critical/social orientation* (with an emphasis on the moral basis of teaching and on issues of equity and social justice) covered the various possibilities for PETE.

Importantly, the Feiman-Nemser (1991) categories resonate with the categorizations offered by other leading teacher education analysts. Doyle (1990), for example, suggests five themes that orientate programmes in teacher education (TE). Dolye's five themes are:

> *Good employer* (TE should have a "real world" focus, apprenticeship model, technical, experiential, master teacher)
> *Junior professor* (TE should emphasize academic content, content knowledge, high standards, suspicious of pedagogical knowledge)
> *Fully functioning person* (TE should have a personal development emphasis, maximizing self-potential, psychological maturity)
> *The innovator* (TE for school renewal, TE should present the latest research, apprenticeship viewed with suspicion)
> *Reflective practitioner* (TE should foster reflective capacities, research and theory not for rules of practice, emphasis on teaching as a moral craft).

We can also see overlaps here with Zeichner's (1983) earlier categorization of orientations (which he called

Table 4.1.1   Similarities in orientations

Feiman-Nemser (1990)	Doyle (2001)	Zeichner (1983)
Practical	Good employee	Traditional/craft
Academic	Junior professor	–
Personal	Fully functioning person	Personalistic
Technological	–	Behaviouristic
–	Innovator	–
Critical	Reflective practitioner	Critical inquiry

perspectives) in teacher education. According to Zeichner there are four perspectives that seemed to orient teacher education programmes: the *behaviouristic perspective; personalistic perspective; traditional/craft perspective;* and the *critical inquiry perspective.*

Table 4.1.1 shows how each of these three teacher education categorizations interrelate and collectively they provide a useful framework for thinking about orientations in PETE.

For this discussion I will use Zeichner's four orienting perspectives to think about our field of PETE. It needs to be recognized, however, that programmes most likely as not are not "pure" representations of a particular orientation. Notwithstanding the official, explicit curriculum of a programme, individual faculty will bring to their teaching particular commitments and preferences and this will result in variability, and at times confusion (for PETE students).

Rink (1993) makes a similar observation when she explored the potential of integrating the results of earlier research on teaching with recent work stemming from both naturalistic inquiry and theoretical work in cognitive science. She suggests that although different, perhaps even antagonistic, in their underpinning philosophical assumptions, these theoretical orientations can find a place beside each other in an eclectic teacher education programme. Accordingly, in the discussion that follows I am referring to rather idealized orientations knowing that "on the ground" programmes might be rather more eclectic of various orientations.

Traditional/craft orientation

PETE programmes that are based on the modelling of co-operating/supervisory teachers' practice comprise Zeichner's *traditional/craft perspective,* Doyle's *good employee,* and Feiman–Nemser's *practical orientation.* In this orientation students are seen as receivers of knowledge with little input into shaping their own professional development. Interestingly, programmes with this orientation while originally

common place in the 1960s and 1970s are becoming more popular in the contemporary educational context. Mawer's (1996) book *Mentoring in Physical Education* is testimony to the rising interest in partnerships in school-based teacher training within the UK in particular during the late 1990s. A discussion of the contemporary educational context is offered later in this chapter but it is significant to note that as advocates of economic rationalism turned their attention to teacher education, this orientation has become increasingly attractive to bureaucrats.

Behaviouristic orientation

Programmes that have a *behaviouristic* orientation (including Feiman-Nemser's *technological*) privilege the positivistic epistemology of behavioural psychology as exemplified by the Competency Based Teacher Education (CBTE) programmes of the 1970s. Programmes in this orientation focus on developing specific, observable teaching skills that were known (or assumed) to be associated with pupil learning. The criteria for success are "… made explicit and performance at a pre-specified level of mastery is assumed to be the most valid measure of teacher competence" (Zeichner, 1983: 4). Program content is meant to be derived from research into teacher effectiveness. Although Larry Locke (1984) claimed that in the early 1980s "there is little evidence that programs have made use of existing knowledge [of teacher effectiveness]" (p. 5) Anderson's (1980) *Analysis of Teaching Physical Education* and then Siedentop's (1983) *Developing Teaching Skills in Physical Education* became influential texts in the development of PETE programmes that engaged the growing teaching effectiveness literature of the time. Siedentop's own programme at The Ohio State University (OSU) was probably the best exemplar of this behaviouristic orientation, the effectiveness of which was monitored by a sequential programme of PETE research during the 1980s (see Siedentop 1981, 1983, 1991).

In the 20 years since Locke's comments the findings from the research literature on teaching effectiveness have, through the process of recontextualization (Bernstein, 1971), increasingly become part of the instructional discourse (Kirk et al., 1997) within PETE. This is represented in texts like Silverman and Ennis' (1996, 2003) *Student Learning in Physical Education: Applying Research to Enhance Instruction.*

Personalistic orientation

The *personalistic perspective,* synonymous with Feiman–Nemser's *personal* and Doyle's *fully functioning person,* is based on the foundations of phenomenological epistemology and perceptual and developmental psychologies. Programme content is based on such things as students' self-perceived needs in a developmental sequence (e.g. Fuller and Bown, 1975; Iannaccone, 1963); application of cognitive developmental theories, or the application of the ideals of humanistic psychology, which seek development of the self as the key to competent teaching. Although there are key differences between programmes utilizing these theoretical frames, they all seek to develop psychological maturity, and teaching competence is predicated upon such maturity. Interestingly, although there are few representations of this model in the literature (see, for example, Vendien and Nixon, 1985) the focus on student concerns has been the major focus of research into PETE (see the section on research) over the past 20 years.

Critical orientation

Programmes that privilege the *critical inquiry* orientation are based on the belief that all education is ideological (a'la Spodek, 1974). Accordingly teacher education should help prospective teachers to understand the socially constructed nature of schooling and to challenge the taken-for-grantedness of the status quo. Technical teaching skills are not valued (or pursued) as ends in themselves but rather as practices that carry hidden messages related to power and control. The critical inquiry perspective challenges the positivistic underpinnings of behaviouristic programmes, the individualist orientation of the personalistic perspective, and the utilitarian tendencies of the craft/traditional perspective.

There is no doubt that discourse on critical pedagogy (as a particular manifestation of the critical inquiry perspective) has become increasingly popular in PETE over the last 20 years. However, although advocacy for critical pedagogy orientation to PETE is relatively easy to find (see for example, Tinning, 1987; Kirk, 1986; Bain, 1990; Gore, 1990; Dewar, 1990; Fernandez-Balboa, 1995; Macdonald

and Brooker, 1999; Penny and Waring, 2000) many of these same advocates have also written accounts of the limitations and difficulties of critical pedagogy in practice (see in particular Gore, 1990; Devis-Devis and Sparkes, 1999, Tinning, 2002; Muros and Fernandez-Balboa, 2004).

Academic orientation

Programmes with an *academic* focus (Feiman–Nemser) or the *junior professor* orientation (Doyle) were not captured in Zeichner's model but are nonetheless useful to consider in the context of PETE. Up until the 1960s, all higher-education programmes in physical education were PETE programmes. They were developed solely to prepare teachers for work in school settings. At that time the debate was over the type of practical subject matter content that should comprise the programme (e.g. what sports should be featured, how much gymnastics, etc.). This academic orientation is explained by Rink (1993) as the focus on the subject matter of games, sport, dance, fitness, etc. This orientation was behind Locke et al's. (1981) argument for a subject matter centred model of teacher education for physical education.

We are all now familiar with the rise of the sub-disciplines and the broadening of the field to what we currently recognize as kinesiology, human movement studies or sport and exercise science. Accompanying these developments have been many challenges to PETE programmes including considerable debate over the nature and relevance of the subject matter content knowledge (Shulman, 1987) that is now known as discipline studies (see Henry, 1964; Newell, 1990; Kirk, 1990; Kirk, Macdonald and Tinning, 1997; Krahenbuhl, 1998; Kirk and Macdonald, 2001).

Commenting on the challenges to PETE in the early 1980s Locke (1984) was far from sanguine about the rise of a scientific sub-discipline knowledge base for PETE. He claimed that in the 1960s "an academic elite burst upon us waving Research Quarterly ... and proclaiming themselves the prophets of truth about preparing teachers and coaches (which were to become scientific-based professions rather than mere crafts)". Locke went on to say "Today, others are heard speaking the powerful, universalistic tongue of science to legitimise their vision of teacher education" (p. 9). But the science to which Locke is referring is not the science of teaching that became associated with teaching effectiveness research and increasingly powerful in the development of programmes within the behaviouristic orientation. Locke was concerned at the time with the rise of the sub-disciplines as *essential* knowledge for teachers of physical education.

Most contemporary PETE programmes comprise subject matter content knowledge that includes physical activity and also what has been broadly termed the biophysical and sociocultural sub-disciplines of the field of kinesiology (exercise physiology, motor control/learning, biomechanics, history of sport, sociology of sport, etc.). There are however, challenges to the centrality of sub-discipline knowledge of sport and exercise science for the preparation of teachers of physical education. For example, Australia's Edith Cowan University (ECU) offers a programme that has placed knowledge of the "client" (young people, children, adolescents) to be of central importance for PETE students rather than advanced knowledge of the disciplines that typically comprise the field of kinesiology/human movement studies (see details on the website http://www.ecugreatcareers.com/searchFrame.htm).

Reflection: another orientation or a sub-category?

There is no doubt that one of the major trends in teacher education and PETE over the last decade has been the rise of reflection as a dominant concept. There are even PETE programmes that have been explicitly oriented around the concept of developing *reflective* teachers (see, for example, the Bachelor of Physical Education degree at the Auckland College of Education; Ovens, 2003). Feiman-Nemser (1990), however, suggests that "reflective teacher education is not a distinct paradigmatic emphasis but rather a generic professional disposition" (p. 221) that is found in different forms within the different program orientations. Although reflection might not warrant the label of orientation it is nonetheless a major contemporary discourse within PETE that deserves attention in this chapter.

In Table 4.1.1 we saw that Doyle (2001) included the *"reflective practitioner"* as one of his orienting perspectives for teacher education. The way that Doyle describes the reflective practitioner has sympathies with Zeichner's (1987) *critical inquiry* and Feiman-Nemser's (1990) *critical orientations.* However, there are numerous versions of reflection (see Carr and Kemmis, 1986; Tripp, 1987; Grimmett and Ericksen, 1988). Van Manen's (1977) distinctions between *technical, practical* and *critical* forms of reflection underpins most of the versions that find currency in the teacher education and PETE literatures.

There have been many attempts by various authors to clarify the numerous interpretations and uses of reflection and reflective teaching. Significantly there is no consensus over the meaning of the term (Ovens, 2002; Tsangaridou and Siedentop, 1995). As Tsangaridou and Siedentop (1995) suggest, "reflective teaching has different meanings, different approaches towards implementation and little consensus on what ought to be the

object of reflection" (p. 213). Technical versions of reflection can be found in some programmes that privilege a behaviouristic orientation while critical reflection tends to be associated with programs with critical orientations (see Tinning, 1995).

Hellison and Templin (1991) expressed a concern that reflective teaching had become a buzzword in the educational community and Martinez (1990) was concerned that even by the end of the 1980s critical reflection was becoming "the patchwork panacea of teacher educators of all theoretical persuasions" (p. 20). However, notwithstanding the ubiquitous use of the term, the explicit privileging of *critical* reflection finds expression in texts for undergraduate PETE students such as *Improving Teaching in Physical Education* (Tinning, 1987); *A Reflective Approach to Teaching Physical Education* (Hellison and Templin, 1991); *Becoming a Physical Education Teacher: Contemporary and enduring issues* (Tinning et al., 2001). Further, as mentioned above, there are some PETE programmes that are clearly, and explicitly, oriented around critical reflection (Ovens, 2004).

The European PETE context

It is important to understand that the scholars mentioned in the section above were focusing their thoughts and attention on PETE predominantly within the USA. As mentioned in the introduction focusing only on the USA produces a distorted vision of PETE. But so does focusing only on knowledge from the UK or other English-speaking countries. Fortunately, there is now a small number of European scholars who are writing about their PETE research in English language journals and engagement with what they have to say is of considerable benefit to we Anglophones who must spend their entire career within the English speaking world of PETE.

Crum (1996) conducted an interesting study of the nature of PETE programmes in European countries. He surveyed the conceptual orientations in PETE institutions from 13 European countries and reported that there were real differences in programme orientation across countries that resulted from divergent views of the body, and the nature and purposes of physical education. Crum reported his concern that some programmes were oriented by a "physicalist view of human movement and a decontexualized technical view of sport". Many viewed PE as an "education through the physical" and as a "training of the physical". He considered that such an orientation leads to objectives of PE that cannot be sustained under the conditions of contemporary schooling (see Crum, 1993 for a discussion as to why Crum considered this situation problematic). Crum was particularly concerned that few European PETE programmes had a critical-social orientation underpinning their programmes and that "curricular knowledge and pedagogical content knowledge are relatively neglected domains" (p. 19). Although expressing his disappointment, Crum argued that "a recommendation to strive for full convergence and standardization would be out of place." Moreover, " [c]onceptual divergences may result from differences in well-considered normative positions" (p. 20) and that they should be accepted and made explicit.

Hanke (2001), in his review of PETE research published in German in 1999 and 2000, claimed that the contemporary situation is similar to what it was in 1986 when German research into PETE was largely hermeneutic in nature with little empirical base. This was seen to be in contrast to the vast descriptive empirical literature published in the USA in the 1980s, most of which, according to Crum (1989), lacked theoretical reflection.

Currently across Europe it seems that there is increasing international pressure to introduce comparable standards (in terms of programme length and content) in order to increase student mobility across countries and improve employment mobility (Hanke, 2001). This trend to standardization is also occurring in non-European countries as PETE programmes in particular and universities more generally, respond to the contingencies of changing community (stakeholder) expectations. Indeed, teacher education in general, and PETE in particular, are shaped and reshaped by enduring and contemporary educational discourses which are themselves located in a broader economic-social-political context. Accordingly it is instructive to give a brief account of some of these trends and discourses.

The broader educational context

Commenting on the state of play in PETE within the USA in the mid 1980s Daryl Siedentop wrote in the forward to Vendien and Nixon's 1985 text:

anybody who has lived through or been associated with a preservice teacher education program in physical education during the past several decades knows first hand the degree to which programs have responded to issues both within and outside the university that are, at best, only tangentially related to fundamental issues such as improved schooling, better teaching, and an improved physical education experience for students. Although these forces, and new ones that are likely to be just as potent, are still operative, it is clear that teacher education in physical education is finally in a position to stand on its own and to respond to these forces with a collective voice that says "No we will not succumb to these influences to the extent that they require us to divert our attentions from more fundamental issues. (p. vi)

Two decades later however and we cannot be confident about our ability to stand firm in the face of external "influences". Indeed, as we see below in the contemporary context the spaces for innovation in PETE programmes have become fewer rather than more since the 1980s.

More and more, teacher education programmes across many Western countries are governed by policies that are manifestations of neo-liberal ideologies with respect to schooling as a marketable commodity (see Bates, 1994). Luke (2002) is trenchant in his critique of the trend for education becoming increasingly conceptualized and driven by a logic underpinned by "a now internationally rampant vision of schooling, teaching and learning based solely on systemic efficiency at the measurable technical production of human capital" (p. 1). Indeed in many parts of the Western world "... the earlier evolution of liberal-progressive forms of teacher education has been displaced by a new, more prescriptive managerialist and economic rationalist position on teacher education. It is as if a new paradigm for teacher education is emerging." (Knight et al., 1993: 25).

Increasingly, stakeholders beyond the university are having a greater voice in determining the nature of teacher education. The rise of interest in mentoring in the UK (see Mawer, 1996) is a manifestation of this trend. As Furlong (1994) argued, the rise of the mentor in the British initial teacher training context has been an outcome of the new right discourses in education in general and teacher education specifically. According to Furlong (1994) " ... by far the most significant change to initial teacher education in the last ten years [in the UK] has been the growing insistence by the government that schools take on a greater and more consistent involvement in the training process [of student teachers]" (p. 6).

Another trend is the recent move in many countries (following trends in the UK and the USA) to develop a national set of competencies for teacher education (for example, the National Board for Professional Teaching Standards (NBPTS) in the USA). The thrust of the National Board for Professional Teaching Standards (NBPTS) in Physical Education is clearly upon self-assessment and self-renewal positing the responsibility for self-monitoring with the individual teacher while at same time using performative mechanisms of public submissions and appraisal as evidence of reflective practice (Macdonald and Tinning, 2003).

The construction (usually inaccurately called identification) of graduate outcomes, specific skills and competencies, specific criteria for assessment, etc., can be interpreted as attempts to regulate for *certainty* of pedagogical outcomes (Kelly et al., 2000). However, although Giddens (1991) argued that in an increasingly complex and uncertain world the sceptre of certainty is an anachronism, PETE programmes across the world are still having to respond to these pressures. Accordingly, the choice of a theoretical orientation underpinning a PETE programme will be constrained by this broader educational context. It will be a forced choice from limited options.

Key theoretical orientations for research in PETE

It is sometimes difficult to disentangle research on teaching physical education from research on teacher education since they often have overlapping concerns (e.g. the characteristics that "make" a good teacher). Notwithstanding attempts to provide a clear operational definition of what constitutes each, distinctions do overlap as Doyle (1990) clearly reveals in his "Themes in teacher education research" chapter for the *Handbook of Research on Teacher Education*.

Locke and Dodds (1985) claimed that a summary of research on teacher education in physical education (ROTR/PE) at the time was not possible because "we are only at mid stream" (p. 129) but, "with luck and diligence a comprehensive overview … will soon be available". They lamented that, at the time, "ninety-nine percent of all ROT/PE [research on teaching PE] is produced by graduate students as requirements for completion of the Masters or Doctoral degree" (p.119). Significantly they claimed that this was not the case in mainstream (non PE) teacher education research.

PETE research at the time of the 1980s is best characterized by such publications as Anderson's (1980) *Analysis of Teaching Physical Education*; Siedentop's (1983) *Developing Teaching Skills in Physical Education*; Cheffers' (1977) *Observing Teaching Systematically*, and Pease's (1975) *Competency Based Teacher Education*. In their analysis Locke and Dodds (1985) used the variables that were representative of the research on teaching (ROT) literature of the time (you might recognize them from the Dunkin and Biddle model of 1974): presage variables (trainee characteristics); context variables (programme characteristics); content variables (what is learned); process variable (such as student teaching, microteaching); and product variables (programme impact on trainee and teacher behaviours). They also included the two additional categories: research (methods of inquiry and management of the knowledge base); and change (how programmes evolve, adapt and innovate).

Some 5 years later Bain (1990) produced a comprehensive review that was published in the *Handbook of Research on Teacher Education* (Houston et al., 1990). In particular Bain summarized research derived from what she identified as the three orienting perspectives; behaviour analysis; occupational socialisation; and critical theory. Although she included many of the Locke and Dodds (1985) variables in her analysis she did so under somewhat broader and less ROT-inspired language. Bain included: participants in teacher education (including teacher education students and teacher educators); preservice teacher education programmes (including programme content [organized as content knowledge, pedagogical content knowledge, curricular knowledge]; programme design (including hidden curriculum); inservice teacher education (including induction and inservice programmes).

Macdonald (1997) reviewed PETE research (including 15 empirical studies, 29 interpretive studies and eight critical) published in key journals from 1990–97. She concluded that the "predominant, identifiable literature bases and frameworks were those of socialisation, Shulman's knowledge framework and constructivism" (p. 25).

In what follows I present some work that is *indicative* of the four major organizing perspectives represented in Table 4.1.2. However, I have also included a category called *knowledge*, since it is a special focus of PETE research not adequately captured by the other four categories. The logic underpinning my ordering is the connection between knowledge and human interests (see Habermas, 1972; Carr and Kemmis, 1986). It was Habermas (1972) who argued that all human knowledge is connected to human interests in a constitutive sense. This means that human interests make knowledge what it is, and human knowledge is always constitutive of human interests. Table 4.5.2 illustrates the relationship between the various orientations and the knowledge forms and research paradigms that underpin their application to research and programme conceptualization.

In reviewing the literature I trawled databases such as ERIC and SPORT DISCUS. I also reviewed major textbooks and conference contributions. However, in this process it became apparent that not all papers could be conveniently placed into these four categories. In particular some of the influential literature in PETE is actually in the form of commentary on research and/or practice (e.g. O'Sullivan et al., 1992) rather than a report of a particular research project. Some takes the form of advocacy for a particular orientation (e.g. Kirk, 1986; Fernandez- Balboa, 1997). Many of the papers that focus their attention on knowledge (e.g. Rovegno, 1995; Rossi and Cassidy, 1999) do not easily locate themselves within any of the four chosen categories. Papers dealing with student concerns and those

Table 4.1.2   Knowledge, PETE, human interests and research

Orientation	World view	Purpose of teacher education	Human interests	Research paradigm
Behaviouristic	Objective reality Science for a better world	Prepare skilled technicians of teaching	Technical Prediction Control	Empirical-analytical, Natural science
Personalistic	Multiple realities Subjectivity meaning	To develop the individual teacher as a person	Practical Interpretive understanding	Hermeneutic Interpretive Phenomenological
Traditional/ craft	Reality exists in 'the field' not in theory Practice is best	Prepare teachers for the current system	Practical Technical mastery	Simple descriptive modelling
Critical inquiry	Reality is socially constructed Social inequities, power and oppression	Challenge the school system where necessary	Criticism Liberation Emancipation Critical theory	Action research Case study Feminist Poststructuralist

focused on socialization probably fit into both the personalistic and traditional/craft categories.

Behavouristic orientations in PETE research

Certainly Siedentop and his colleagues and graduate students from OSU were the first to clearly pursue behaviouristic orientations for PETE. Their early work (for example, the doctoral dissertations of Rife, 1974; Hutslar, 1977; Darst, 1974;) was characterized by the development of systematic observation instruments, by the identification of discrete teaching skills, and the application of specified interventions within the PETE context. While space prohibits a detailed account of these specific studies (and others like them), they essentially found that, using behaviour modification techniques, the behaviour of student teachers and co-operating (or supervising) teachers could be changed in the desired direction. Underpinning these early studies was the explicit desire to develop a science of teaching that was amenable to human intervention and control.

A review of behaviour analysis research in physical education by Ward and Barrett (2002) provides an excellent discussion of the use of behaviouristic orientation to research in PETE. They reported on four groups of studies using behaviour analysis in physical education: studies focusing on teacher training interventions; studies focusing on class management interventions; studies focusing on instruction; and studies focusing on participants

with disabilities. They reported 18 studies using behaviour analysis into PETE and this represented the largest category in their review.

A recent example of the behaviouristic orientation to research in PETE is Sharpe et al.'s and (2002) study of the "Comparative effects of sequential behaviour feedback and goal-setting across peer-teaching and field-based practice teaching". This study uses applied behaviour analysis research methods (including multiple baseline design). The authors suggested that their results demonstrated substantial improvement in select teacher and student practices in the school-based setting but a limited effect in the peer-based setting. This study endorsed a collaborative field-based approach to teacher education.

Another example of the application of applied behaviour analysis for PETE research is Kahan's (2002) study into "The effects of a bug-in-the-ear device on intra-lesson communication between a student teacher and a cooperating teacher". While this intervention might sound bizarre to some, it is a theme that can be traced back to the early work of van der Mars (1987). This case study of a student teacher and her cooperating teacher used similar applied behaviour analysis research methods to Sharpe et al. (2002) and found that the radio device/intervention did not differentiate communication characteristics from baseline or reversal phases. However, both student teachers and co-operating teachers identified the audio-cue as a discrete and immediate communication tool that promoted student teacher "with-it-ness" and autonomy.

Personalistic orientations to research in PETE

Matanin and Collier (2003) conducted a longitudinal analysis of pre-service teachers' beliefs about teaching physical education. The purpose of the study was to explore and describe the beliefs of three pre-service teachers as they evolved throughout a 4-year teacher preparation programme. Data collection spanned 5 years and included formal interviews, open-ended questionnaires, and document analysis of reflective writings. Matanin and Collier reported that their results indicated that participants assimilated program messages into their beliefs about teaching physical education relative to elementary content, teaching effectiveness, and the importance of planning. The authors claim that the data suggest that participants' K-12 school experiences as well as their lived experiences play a powerful role in the formation of their beliefs about teaching physical education

Banville (2002) provided a review of the literature on the student teaching experience. The review focused on studies into the student teaching experience in the physical education field; more specifically, the supervision processes. The student teaching experience is a very well-researched topic and Banville's conclusion that co-operating teachers need better training so that they can better provide student teachers with specific and relevant feedback is certainly not new.

Hynes-Dusel (1999) is the latest in a long line of teacher educators who have followed Fuller's 1969 framework for investigating student concerns. It is interesting to ponder on why the issue of "student concerns" continues to be such a popular topic. Certainly the contemporary trend of considering education as a commodity and students as clients (as mentioned earlier) has implication for giving attention to "client concerns". It is ironic that the personalistic perspective to teacher education that was grounded in the interpretive hermeneutic tradition with its focus on developing the individual as a person (see Table 4.5.2) is now being co-opted in the cause of a neo-liberal political orientation that is underpinned by a free-market logic and "the production of human capital" (Knight et al., 1994: 1). The reader who is interested in this trend in education might like to enter this literature through the works of authors such as Marginson (1995), Kenway et al. (1993), Kenway and Bullen (2001).

In considering the limitations of the "student concerns" model, Peter Sacks' (1996) *Generation X Goes To College* provides an alternative perspective. Sacks (actually a pseudonym) provides an eye-opening account of college teaching in postmodern America and the particular confrontations he had with Generation X students (born between 1965 and 1980). In his account of teaching journalism students he tells how, following the brutal student evaluations in his first year, he decided to give the students what they wanted … which was minimal academic expectations and maximum grades. Following his "sand pit experiment" as he called it, student evaluations were very positive and his tenure facilitated. For Sacks, the Generation X students he was teaching had a different value system than baby-boomers like himself. They expected to achieve without hard work, and listening to "student concerns" merely pandered to their laziness. Although Sacks' provocative account is about journalism students it is easy to read the resonances with teaching certain PETE students. It is a book worthy of attention even if you might find his analysis overly "forceful".

Traditional/craft orientations to research in PETE

Two areas of focus in PETE research that represent the traditional/craft orientation are student teaching and mentoring. Many of these studies are "slippery" in their category because they sometimes have aspects that connect them to one of the broader four categories. However, for the purposes of this chapter what follows are some examples of each focus area.

As mentioned earlier, mentoring has become particularly popular in the UK where, inspired by neo-liberal sentiments, the government has moved to place initial teacher education back in schools and thus remove the influence of liberal, "left-leaning" university-based teacher educators. Mawer's edited book *Mentoring in Physical Education: Issues and Insights* (1996) provides testimony to the significance of this area of PETE study in the late 1990s. The move to school-based teacher training is also gaining strength in the USA where currently some school districts (e.g. Houston, Texas and a number of other US urban areas), have received state accreditation to run their own professional development programmes for teachers and can now licence teachers without any connections to a university. Perhaps this will provide an interesting research "space" for teacher education researchers over the next decade as the impact of this trend is monitored and assessed.

Hardy's (1999) UK-based study into pre-service teachers' perceptions of learning to teach in a predominantly school-based teacher education program is one empirical study that investigates this area. Sixty-two pre-service teachers completed a questionnaire to examine their perceptions of how the school-based experiences within a predominantly school-based PETE programme, helped them learn to teach. Hardy found that the pre-service teachers placed considerable emphasis on the accumulation of experiences and "coming to terms" with the realities of teaching. He concluded that although some university–school partnerships were helping pre-service teachers to look beyond the immediate context, the quality of the collaborative venture was being affected by the variability in mentoring processes, school contexts, and the personal histories of both mentors and pre-service teachers. Hardy suggested that the continual extension of school-based experiences is not only privileging the practical over theory and emphasizing doing more than thinking, but is replacing complexity with simplicity.

Critical orientations to research in PETE

The works of Bain (1990), Dewar (1990), Wright (1990), Kirk (1986), Hellison (1988), Evans (1993), Gore (1990), Fernández-Balboa (1995), Tinning, 1988), and more recently Macdonald and Brooker (2000), Hickey (2001) and Penny and Waring (2000) are indicative of accounts into critical orientations research within PETE.

Muros and Fernández-Balboa (2004) provide a very recent example of work that is oriented by critical orientations. Their paper, titled "Implicit Theories of PETEs Regarding Their Practice of Critical Pedagogy", was an account of Muro's doctoral research project (Muros, 2004). In Muros' study she interviewed seventeen Spanish physical education teacher educators in 15 separate programmes. Their conclusion was that despite claiming to practice critical pedagogy, 6 of the 17 physical education teacher educators did not have a clear definition of critical pedagogy nor had they thought of its pedagogical principles. They conclude by wondering whether many of these participants (i.e. teacher educators) were actually capable of implementing critical pedagogy.

The most powerful (in terms of influence) of the published critiques of the critical orientation was delivered by O'Sullivan et al. (1992) in their *Quest* article "Towards collegiality: Competing viewpoints among teacher educators". They begin their critique by indicating that their reaction to the "radical" discourse (as they called critical pedagogy) is mixed. "We agree with much of what they aspire to for physical education. However, several of their accusations about work within the dominant discourse and some of the assertions about the new discourse have at times made us frustrated, uncomfortable, and even angry" (p. 268).

O'Sullivan et al. (1992) proceeded to challenge the often "overzealous" (their word) language used by some "radicals" in the prosecution of their critical pedagogy "mission", the perceived high moral ground taken by them, and the lack of evidence to support many of their claims. As suggested elsewhere (see Tinning, 2002) on many counts this critique is valid, however it does fail to consider the

context and motivation for the critical discourse. Of course since the writers' specific context and motivation were not explained in that article, readers would not be expected to understand "where they were coming from". Notwithstanding this significant issue of representation, McKay et al.'s (1990) "Beyond the limits of technocratic physical education", published in *Quest*, provided a good example of the style of discourse that was intended to provoke readers to seriously consider the hegemony of technocratic discourse within physical education. To the extent that their paper provoked strong reactions, their work was partially successful. Their intentions were polemic and not to provide solutions to the perceived problem. A good deal of the literature on critical pedagogy has had similar polemic purpose.

Fernández Balboa's (1997) edited book *Critical Postmodernism in Human Movement, Physical Education & Sport* provided an important voice for the emerging interest in postmodernism within the field of kinesiology/human movement studies. Fernández Balboa's own chapter on "Physical education teacher preparation in the postmodern era: Toward a critical pedagogy" provided an advocacy account for critical pedagogy and joined Kirk (1986) and others who argued for a critical orientation to PETE.

One of the few empirical studies on the implementation of critical pedagogy within PETE available in the literature is that of Hickey (2001). He reported on the introduction of a critical orientation to an undergraduate PETE programme and, using case study methodology, described and analysed two student-teachers' engagement with a range of critical social discourses during a year-long course. Hickey discussed some of the ways these students engaged with the theory and practice of a critical orientation to teaching and learning in physical education. He concluded with tempered optimism about the potential for critical inquiry to guide PETE in practical ways.

Tinning (2002) discussed the difficulties of "doing" critical pedagogy with postmodern students and presented an argument for working toward what he called a "modest pedagogy" that takes seriously the problematization of knowledge and schooling yet avoids some of the pitfalls of Enlightenment thinking and the neglect of student subjectivity.

Knowledge as a focus of research in PETE

As mentioned earlier, there is some literature that is difficult to categorise into any of the four chosen orientations. Studies that focus on the topic of knowledge is a case in point. Although Niki Tsangaridou has a chapter in this Handbook specifically devoted to "Teachers' Knowledge" (Chapter 4.8) consideration of knowledge as an orienting focus for PETE research is warranted in this section. Shulman's seminal work in the 1980s published in 1986, 1987 and 1991 provided the analytic framework eagerly appropriated by PETE scholars including Siedentop (1989), Tinning (1992), Rovegno (1993, 1995) and Jenkins and Veal (2002).

For example, Rovegno's (1995) paper on "Theoretical perspectives on knowledge and learning and a student teacher's pedagogical content knowledge of dividing and sequencing subject matter" describes and interprets a student teacher's decisions about task content and content progression and those aspects of his pedagogical content knowledge that he used to explain and justify his decisions. Taken-for-granted perspectives that knowledge and learning are molecular are questioned, and the potential of more holistic, non-linear perspectives were considered.

Jenkins and Veal (2002) described the kinds of knowledge exhibited by eight student teachers during coaching activities, and how the roles of teacher and coach contributed to knowledge development during an elementary physical education field-based methods course. Data collection included observations, post-lesson conferences, and daily written reports. They revealed that pedagogical content knowledge (PCK) developed differently in the roles of teacher and coach. Growth in the teaching role resulted initially from interaction of two knowledge components (i.e. students and pedagogy), and later from interaction of three or more components (subject matter, environmental context, and general pedagogical knowledge).

Research into knowledge within PETE also includes studies such as Rossi and Hooper's (2001) account of the use of personal construct theory (PCT) and narrative methods to facilitate reflexive constructions of teaching physical education. They reported on two lengthy studies in PETE conducted independently but which are epistemologically and methodologically linked. They described how (PCT) and its associated methods provided a means for PETE students to reflexively construct their ideas about teaching physical education over an extended period. Data are drawn from each study in the form of a story of a single participant to indicate how this came about. The authors suggested that PCT might be both a useful research strategy and an effective approach to facilitate professional development in a teacher education setting.

Another variation on the study of knowledge in PETE is represented by Macdonald et al. (1999) in their investigation into the social construction of the physical activity field at the school/university interface. Using Bernstein's (1986) notions of classification, framing, and regulatory discourse as their analytic frame Macdonald et al. introduced aspects of the production, reproduction, adaptation, and modification of educational discourse as students move from school physical education into university human movement studies. Understanding how knowledge is recontextualized and given pedagogical form within PETE is an important contribution of this line of research.

Fernández-Balboa's (1997) work advocated for a new knowledge base for PETE. He argued that PETE is partly responsible for a contemporary crisis in school physical education because it does not prepare teachers to be transformative agents. He proposed an alternative knowledge base to that articulated for PETE by NASPE (i.e. Beginning Teacher Standards). His alternative is based on considering knowledge to be partisan[1] and dynamic and hence should be conceptualized within a multidimensional sociocultural matrix including ethical and political matters. He also suggested that teachers should become transformative intellectuals (not technicians merely transmitting their subject matter) able to engage in professional reform.

Another variant of knowledge research in PETE is O'Sullivan and Doutis's (1994) overview of research on expertise in which they offered some guideposts for expertise and teacher education in physical education. They critique the concept of expertise and substituted the term virtuoso to describe those who engage expertly with students in the teaching–learning process. Teachers who are virtuosos are described as not only having sophisticated content knowledge and pedagogical content knowledge structures but also demonstrating a commitment to the social, political, and moral agendas of teaching physical education. Implications of this redefinition were presented for what it might mean to teach expertly and to prepare prospective teachers to do so. They offered a critique of the efforts and limitations of current directions, methods, and findings of the expertise literature and also discuss implications for teacher education in terms of research and teaching.

Concluding comments

In reviewing the literature for this chapter I must admit to a certain disappointment with both the nature and focus of much of what I read. I have not included reference to many articles that, though scholarly in their craft (that is they were written in a style and format which clearly conveyed what they researched) lacked a clearly developed theoretical position. I do not mean that all studies must apply a

---

[1] Fernández-Balboa is using this term in the sense of referring to the connection between knowledge and particular political/ideological investments. See Table 4.1.2 for the relationship between knowledge and human interests.

particular theory or use a particular theorist to underpin the work. This is necessary for some work but not for others. In too many studies we rely too heavily (often totally) on the work of "second-order" scholars who have themselves developed or taken ideas from "first-order" theorists. One of the problems with this is that we might be merely compounding limited thinking. Of course the perfunctory reference to some "leading or in vogue" theorists is also to be avoided. What is necessary, however, is an engagement with the theorising *behind the ideas* that form the central tenet of the study.

In 1996, commenting on PETE presentations at an AIESEP conference in Lisbon, Tousignant (2000) claimed that there is "… the absence of a recurring theory" (p. 263) Moreover, she asserted that "Research in PETE appears theoretically disorganized!" (p. 263). My disappointment is less about coherence and organisation (a search for order) than about restricted and underdeveloped thinking. Issues of coherence (of focus or agenda) are a reflection of the politics of problem-setting (see Lawson, 1984 and Tinning, 1991) an accordingly inherently difficult to control, even if that was the intention. Of course that raises issues of who would do the controlling and, as Law (1994) points out, it is a very slippery and dangerous slope into "perfect order" (demonstrated, for example, in Nazi Germany and the McCarthy era in the USA). Personally I am happy with eclecticism of theory in the field of PETE.

An example of my particular concern for the theoretical "health" of PETE scholarship is found in relation to the category of personalistic orientation. I was interested to note that there was so much interest in PETE student opinions and concerns (about their programmes). In the contemporary educational context in which an ideology of user-pay, student-as-client pervades, teacher educators obviously need to be seen to be attending to student concerns. But that does not explain why this topic has been so popular for almost 30 years! The concern I have with many such studies is that most of them lacked any engagement with much of the contemporary literature relating to identity, the self and the post-modern "condition" (e.g. McDonald, 1999). If PETE researchers continue to use the psychologized, developmentalist literature (such as the over-used Fuller 1969 Development Theory of Student Teacher Concerns) to provide the theoretical lens for their work they will continue to miss other generative ways of thinking about these issues. There is important theorising on issues of the self and identity by scholars in such fields as education, cultural studies, youth studies, feminist studies that deserve the attention of PETE scholars who continue to focus on student concerns and opinion (for example, see Butler, 1999; Lupton, 1998; McDonald, 1999; McNay, 2000).

The continued interest in the student teaching practicum is another feature of any review of published articles in PETE. Apart from some of the literature from the UK (e.g., Mawer, 1996) most of this literature involves the search for answers to the question "how can the practicum be improved?" While this is a laudable focus given that we always should be searching for ways to improve the pedagogical experiences of students in our PETE programmes, too often these studies employ a technocist approach in which questions of means overshadow (or worse, preclude) consideration of issues relating to the purposes or ends of the educational experience. Engaging theorising related to the broader education context (e.g. Luke and Carrington, 2001) in which the practicum is located with the micro-level concerns of students and cooperating teachers in schools might be a more illuminating and generative approach.

In far too many cases the literature on PETE is basically a rehash of what has been circulating for many years (the case of student teacher concerns is an example here). One contributing factor to this is that a high proportion of the literature is an account of doctoral dissertations from the USA. The sheer number of PhD graduates in PETE from the USA compared with other countries is part of the issue here. By numbers alone we would expect to read a disproportionately large number of US doctoral studies in the PETE literature. The context is also significant. Although there are many notable exceptions, and recognising the improvements that have been made over the past decade or so, the doctoral model of coursework and dissertation predominant in the USA, tends to produce theses that are often less theoretically grounded than doctorates from, for example, UK, continental Europe, Australia or New Zealand where the degree is awarded solely on the basis of the dissertation. Accordingly, this difference underpins the published version of these studies.

What was also of interest was the variability of the published work relating to PETE. Of course this reinforces what we already know about our field; namely that not all refereed journals are of equal merit. They have different standards with respect to the scholarship they are prepared to publish. This will always be the case and presumably researchers consciously chose their target journals with this knowledge. I do not want to be misunderstood here. I am not suggesting that it is not appropriate to target particular journals because of the audiences they serve. For example, a professionally oriented journal with a readership of predominantly professional practitioners might be the most appropriate target audience for certain research. And perhaps (most probably) such an audience will not be interested in the more sophisticated analyses and or theorising that might be of interest to professional academics. But the fact remains that much of the PETE literature is a recycling (with some new data) of issues well researched in previous years.

Notwithstanding these criticism of some of the research in PETE, I do believe that contemporary PETE scholars, including many PhD students in the area, are better informed regarding educational theorising than was the case a generation ago. Although this is an encouraging trend, I am however increasingly less sanguine regarding the consequences of the context in which PETE must operate – a context that is increasingly shaped by discourses and stakeholders that restrict rather than open what is possible in PETE programmes. In my view program orientations will probably become less eclectic, more conservative and less adventurous. For example, it is hard to imagine a PETE programme in an Australian university that does not foreground the discourses of outcomes-based assessment (including how to do it and how to create school PE programmes that embrace it) since both the various state education systems and, not surprisingly, their respective Teacher Registration Boards privilege this orientation to assessment. Commenting on the USA context, O'Sullivan (2003) remarked that "NCATE's shift to performance-based standards for teacher education programmes will require teacher education programmes to share evidence about the knowledge, skills, and dispositions that teacher candidates have acquired during their teacher preparation" (p. 286). Institutions like Boards of Teacher Registration and NCATE are by nature conservative institutions and they work in and for a context of conservative educational discourse. Although performance-based standards and outcomes-based assessment are not necessarily conservative, the operationalisation of these concepts within teacher education programmes will probably orient towards conservatism. The extent to which that makes for more conservative and less adventurous PETE graduates is something that future PETE researchers might consider a worthwhile focus of their attention.

O'Sullivan (2003) writes that "A widespread view in government circles is that research on teacher preparation has been of low quality and incapable of producing knowledge that improves educational policy and practice" (p. 289). She is absolutely right that many bureaucrats and commentators have a low regard for the impact of educational research. However, while low-quality research is easy to find and hardly defensible, the claim regarding the production of knowledge to influence policy and practice is more problematic. Yes some PETE research should be able to inform policy and, in time that may influence practice. But not all PETE research should be oriented by pragmatics.

Let me finish with reference to two articles from a recent edition of the *Journal of Teaching in Physical Education* (Jan, 2004) that demonstrates this point. McCaughty (2004) researched the emotional dimension of one teacher's pedagogical content knowledge. It is an interesting study. But his findings are unlikely to effect policy or practice (at least not in the foreseeable future). They do, however, stimulate us to think in some new ways about the possible connections that might exist between emotion and pedagogical work. It also offers a fruitful topic for future study. I can imagine such a study might gain research grant support (e.g. from a government funding agency) and probably the grant proposal would outline possible "implications for policy and practice". But beyond those articulated aspirations, the probability of this outcome is slim. However, that does not mean that the study is not worthwhile, nor that it cannot help us to better understand the PETE process.

The other article (Brown and Evans, 2004) describes their study of the ways in which particular embodied gendered dispositions of student teachers are part of an intergenerational "cultural conduit" that acts as a channel for reproducing particular gendered relations within physical education. Using life-history methodology, their research portrays an important phenomenon that could have potential implications for policy regarding the recruitment of prospective physical education teachers. However, since their findings are challenging at some deeply structural levels, Most likely, those invested with making policies regarding recruitment of PE teachers would not register its implications as worthy of policy change.

In some ways it comes back to the claim made earlier regarding knowledge and human interests. Yes, it might be appropriate to orient PETE research and programmes towards particular ends, such as performance-based standards and outcomes-based assessment, but we should always try to understand the broader logic behind such ends. Such logic will always be underpinned by certain human needs (for example, greater prediction or control of educational outcomes). Those of us involved in PETE have an obligation not just to serve the interests of the vocal and powerful stakeholders. While we might have to "play the tune" that those who "pay the piper" expect, we must also be bold enough to follow research leads and program possibilities that are informed by marginalized ideas and discourses if we consider that such leads have the potential to reveal the shortcomings of the limited or restrictive perspectives advocated by certain stakeholders. Brown and Evans' (2004) study is an example of such work. In an educational landscape increasingly dominated by concerns over standards and performance PETE needs studies who "play the tune" and also those that "play to a different tune".

References

Anderson, W. (1980). *Analysis of Teaching Physical Education*. St Louis, C.V. Mosby.

Auckland College of Education at URLhttp://www. ace.ac.nz/progs/teacher/bpe/index.asp (accessed 3rd September, 2004).

Bain, L. (1990). Physical education teacher education. W.R. Houston, M. Haberman and J. Sikula (Eds.), *Handbook of Research on Teacher Education.* (pp. 758–782) New York: Macmillan.

Banville, D. (2002). Re-defining the student teaching experience: a review of the literature. *Avante, 8(3)*: 30–38.

Bates, R. (1994). Teacher education: An international perspective. Paper presented at the New Zealand Council for Teacher Education National Conference, Wellington.

Bernstein, B. (1971). On the classification and framing of educational knowledge. In M.F.D. Young (Ed.), *Knowledge and Control*, London: Collier-MacMillan.

Brooke-Schmitz, N. (2002). Building today for tomorrow: developing effective teachers. *Journal of the International Council for Health, Physical Education-Recreation, Sport & Dance 38(3)*: 15–21.

Brown, D. and J. Evans (2004). Reproducing gender? Intergenerational links and the male PE teacher as a cultural conduit in teaching physical education. *Journal of Teaching in Physical Education, 32(1)*: 48–71.

Butler, J. (1999). *Gender Trouble: Feminism and the subversion of identity.* New York: Routledge.

Carr, W. and Kemmis, S. (1986). *Becoming critical: Education, knowledge and action research.* London: Falmer Press.

Cheffers, J. (1977). Observing teaching systematically. *Quest, 28*: 17–28.

Crum, B. (1989). *The itself reproducing failing of physical education.* Paper presented at the AIESEP 'Movement and sport – a challenge for life-long learning', Jyvaskyla, Finland.

Crum, B. (1993). Conventional thought and practice in physical education: Problems of teaching and implications for change. *Quest 45(3)*: 339–356.

Crum, B. (1996). Conceptual divergences in European PE teacher & sport coach education programmes: A pilot study. Paper presented to the Danish Sport Confederation, Copenhagen.

Curtner-Smith, M. (1999). Influence of biography, teacher education, and entry into the workforce on the perspectives of first-year elementary school physical education teachers. *European Journal of Physical Education, 3(1)*: 75–99.

Darst, P. (1974). *The effects of competency-based intervention on student-teacher and pupil behaviour,* Unpublished PhD thesis, The Ohio State University, Columbus, Ohio.

Devis-Devis, J. and A. Sparkes (1999). 'Burning the book: A biographical study of a pedagogically inspired identity crisis in physical education.' *European Physical Education Review, 5(2)*: 135–152.

Dewar, A. (1987). Knowledge and gender in physical education. J.S. Gaskell and A.T. McLaren. (Eds.), In *Women and education: A Canadian perspective.* (pp. 265–289) Calgary: Detselig Enterprises.

Dewar, A. (1990). Oppression and privilege in physical education: Struggles in the negotiation of gender in a university program. D. Kirk and R. Tinning (Eds.), In *Physical education, curriculum and culture: Critical issues in the contemporary crisis.* (pp. 67–100) Basingstoke: The Falmer Press.

Doyle, W. (1990). Themes in teacher education research. In W.R. Houston (Eds.), In *Handbook of research on Teacher Education.* (pp. 3–24). New York: Macmillan.

Dunkin, M. and B, Biddle (1974). *The Study of Teaching.* New York: Holt, Rinehart and Winston.

Edith Cowan University at URL http://www.ecugreatcareers.com/searchFrame.htm (accessed 30 September, 2004).

Feiman-Nemser, S. (1990). Teacher preparation: Structural and conceptual alternatives. *Handbook of Research on Teacher Education.* W.R. Houston, M. Haberman and J. Sikula. New York: Macmillan, 212–233.

Fernández-Balboa, J.-M. (1995). Reclaiming physical education in higher education through critical pedagogy. *Quest 47*: 91–114.

Fernández-Balboa, J.-M., (Ed.) (1997). *Critical postmodernism in human movement, physical education and sport.* Albany, NY: SUNY.

Fuller, F. (1969). Concerns of teachers: A developmental conceptualization. *American Educational Research Journal, 6*: 207–226.

Furlong, J. (1994). The rise and rise of the mentor in British initial teacher training. In R. Yeomans and J. Sampson (Eds.), *Mentorship: The primary school* (pp. 6–18). London, Falmer Press.

Giddens, A. (1991). *Modernity and self-identity. Self and society in the late modern age.* Cambridge: Polity Press.

Gore, J.M. (1990). Pedagogy as text in physical education teacher education: Beyond the preferred reading. D. Kirk and R. Tinning (Eds.), In *Physical education, curriculum and culture: Critical issues in the contemporary crisis.* (pp. 101–138). Basingstoke: The Falmer Press.

Grimmett, P. and G. Erickson (Eds.) (1988). *Reflection in teacher education.* New York: Teachers College Press.

Habermas, J. (1972). *Knowledge and human interest.* London: Heinemann.

Hanke, U. (2001). Research on physical education teacher and coach education (published in German) 1999–2000. *International Journal of Physical Education – A Review Publication, 38(1)*: 17–24.

Hardy, C. (1999). Preservice teachers' perceptions of learning to teach in a predominantly school-based teacher education program. *Journal of Teaching in Physical Education, 18(2)*: 175–198.

Hellison, D. (1988). Our constructed reality: some contributions of an alternative perspective to physical education pedagogy. *Quest, 40*: 84–90.

Hellison, D. and T. Templin (1991). *A reflective approach to teaching physical education.* Champaign, Illinois, Human Kinetics.

Henry, F. (1964). Physical education – An academic discipline. *Journal of Health, Physical Education and Recreation, 35*: 32–33.

Hickey, C. (2001). I feel enlightened now, but … : the limits to the pedagogic translation of critical social discourses in physical education. *Journal of Teaching in Physical Education, 20(3):* 227–246.

Houston, W., Ed. (1990). *Handbook of Research on Teacher Education.* New York: Macmillan.

Hutslar, S. (1977). *The effects of training cooperating teachers in applied behaviour analysis on student teacher behaviour in physical education.* Unpublished PhD thesis, The Ohio State University, Columbus, Ohio.

Hynes-Dusel, J. (1999). Physical education student teacher concerns. *The Physical Educator, 56(1):* 33–48.

Kahan, D. (2002). TI: The effects of a bug-in-the-ear device on intra-lesson communication between a student teacher and a cooperating teacher. *Journal of Teaching in Physical Education, 22(1):* 86–104.

Kang, S. (2003). *Beyond the challenges of physical education teacher education (PETE): Research and development of PETE.* The New Challenges and Possibilities for Physical Education in the 21st Century, Seoul, Korea, Seoul National University.

Kelly, P., Hickey, C. and Tinning, R (2000). Producing knowledge about physical education pedagogy: Problematising the activities of expertise. *Quest, 52(3):* 284–296.

Kenway, J., Bigum, C., Fitzclarence, L. and Collier, J. (1993). Marketing education in the post-modern age. *Journal of Education Policy, 8(2):* 105–122.

Kenway, J. and Bullen, E. (2001). *Consuming children: Education-entertainment-advertising.* Buckingham: Open University Press.

Kirk, D. (1986). A critical pedagogy for teacher education: Toward an inquiry-oriented approach. *Journal of Teaching in Physical Education, 5(4):* 230–246.

Kirk, D. (1990). Knowledge, Science and the Rise and Rise of Human Movement Studies. *The ACHPER National Journal,* March, 8–18.

Kirk, D. and Macdonald, D. (2001). The social construction of PETE in higher education: Towards a research agenda. *Quest, 53(4):* 440–457.

Kirk, D., Macdonald D. and Tinning, R (1997). The social construction of pedagogic discourse in physical education teacher education. *The Curriculum Journal, 8(2):* 271–298.

Knight, J., Lingard, B and Bartlett, L. (1994). Reforming teacher education policy under Labor Governments in Australia. *British Journal of Sociology of Education, 15(4):* 451–466.

Krahenbuhl, G. (1998). Higher education in the 21st century: The role of kinesiology and physical education. *Quest, 50(2):* 108–116.

Law, J. (1994). *Organizing Modernity.* Oxford, Blackwell.

Locke, L. (1984). Research on teaching teachers: Where are we now? *Journal of Teaching in Physical Education.* Monograph 2, pp. 1–86.

Locke, L. and P. Dodds (1985). Research on pre-service teacher education for physical education. In C. Vendien and J. Nixon (Eds.), *Physical education teacher education: Guidelines for sport pedagogy,* (pp. 113–134). New York: Collier Macmillan.

Locke, L., C. Mand and Siedentop, D. (1981). The preparation of physical education teachers: A subject-matter-centred model. *Progress Through Diversity* (pp. 33–54). Washington, DC: American Alliance for Health, Physical Education, Recreation and Dance.

Luke, A. (2002). Curriculum, ethics, meta-narrative: Teaching and learning beyond the nation. *Curriculum Perspectives, 22(1):* 49–55.

Luke, A. and Carrington, V. (2001). Globalisation, literacy, curriculum practice. In R. Fisher, M. Lewis and G. Brooks (Eds.), *Language and Literacy in Action.* London: Routledge/Falmer.

Lupton, D. (1998). *The emotional self: A sociological exploration.* London: Sage.

Macdonald, D. (1997). Researching PETE: An account of explicit representations and covert knowledges. J. Wright (Ed.), *Researching in physical and health education* (pp. 23–39). Wollongong: Faculty of Education, University of Wollongong.

Macdonald, D. and R. Brooker (1999). Articulating a critical pedagogy in physical education teacher education. *Journal of Sport Pedagogy, 5(1):* 51–63.

Macdonald, D. and R. Tinning (2003). Reflective practice goes public: Reflection, governmentality and postmodernity. *The Future of Physical Education: Building a New Pedagogy.* A. Laker (Ed). London: Routledge, 82–102.

Macdonald, D., Kirk, D. and Braiuka, S. (1999). The social construction of the physical activity field at the school/university interface. *European Physical Education Review, 5(1):* 31–51.

Marginson, S. (1995). *Markets in Education.* Sydney: Allen & Unwin.

Martinez, K. (1990). Critical reflections on critical reflection in teacher education. *The Journal of Teaching Practice 10(2):* 20–28.

Matanin, M. and C. Collier (2003). Longitudinal Analysis of Preservice Teachers' Beliefs about Teaching Physical Education. *Journal of Teaching in Physical Education 22(2):* 153–68.

Mawer, M. (Ed.) (1996). *Mentoring in physical education: Issues and insights.* London: Falmer Press.

McCaughtry, N. (2004). The emotional dimensions of a teacher's pedagogical content knowledge: Influences on content, curriculum and pedagogy. *Journal of Teaching in Physical Education, 23(1):* 30–48.

McDonald, K. (1999). *Struggles for subjectivity: Identity, action and youth experience.* Cambridge: Cambridge University Press.

McKay, J., Gore, J. and Kirk, D. (1990). Beyond the limits of technocratic physical education. *Quest, 42(1):* 52–75.

McNay, L. (2000). *Gender and agency: Reconfiguring the subject in feminist and social theory.* Cambridge: Polity Press.

Muros, B. and Fernández-Balboa, J.-M. (2004). *Implicit theories of PETEs regarding their practice of critical pedagogy.* Paper presented to the PE SIG, American Educational Research Association annual meeting, San Diego,CA.

Muros, B. (2004). Teorías implícitas del profesorado universitario español en Educación Física respecto a su práctica de la pedagogía crítica. Unpublished PhD thesis, Universidad de Granada, Spain.

Newell, K. (1990). Physical education in higher education: Chaos out of order. *Quest, 42*: 227–242.

Nixon, J. and L. Locke (1973). Research on teaching in physical education. R. Travers (Ed.), In *Second Handbook of Research on Teaching.* (pp. 1210–1242). Chicago IL, Rand McNally.

O'Sullivan, M. (1996). What do we know about the professional preparation of teachers? S. Silverman and C. Ennis (Eds.), In *Student learning in physical education: Applying research to enhance instruction* (pp. 315–339). Champaign, IL, Human Kinetics.

O'Sullivan, M. (2003). Learning to teach physical education. S. Silverman and C. Ennis (Eds.), In *Student learning in physical education: Applying research to enhance instruction.* (2nd edition pp. 275–295). Champaign: IL, Human Kinetics.

O'Sullivan, M. and P. Doutis, (1994). Research on expertise: Guideposts for expertise and teacher education in physical education. *Quest, 46(2)*: 176–185.

O'Sullivan, M., Siedentop, D. and Locke, L. (1992). Toward collegiality: competing viewpoints among teacher educators. *Quest, 22*: 266–280.

Ovens, A. (2002). *Discourse communities and the social construction of reflection in teacher education.* Paper presented at the HERDSA Conference, Perth.

Ovens, A. (2004). The (Im)Possibility of Critical Reflection: The Lived Experience of Reflective Practice in Teacher Education. Unpublished PhD thesis, The University of Queensland, Brisbane, Australia.

Pease, D. (1975). Competency based teacher education. *JOHPERD 46*(5): 20-22.

Peck, R. and J. Tucker (1973). Research on teacher education. R. Travers (Eds.), *Second handbook of research on Teaching* (pp. 940–978). Chicago, IL: Rand McNally

Penny, D. and M. Waring (2000). The absent agenda: Pedagogy and physical education. *Journal of Sport Pedagogy, 6*(1): 4–38.

Rife, F. (1974). *Modification of student teacher behaviour and its effect on pupil behaviour.* Unpublished PhD thesis, The Ohio State University, Columbus, Ohio.

Rink, J.E. (1993). Teacher education: A focus on action. *Quest, 45*: 308–320.

Rossi, A. and T. Cassidy (1999). Knowledgeable teachers in physical education: A view of teachers' knowledge. C. Hardy and M. Mawer (Eds.) (pp. 188–202), *Learning and teaching in physical education.* London, Falmer Press.

Rossi, T. and T. Hopper (2001). Using personal construct theory and narrative methods to facilitate reflexive constructions of teaching physical education. *Australian Educational Researcher, 28*(3): 87–116.

Rovegno, I. (1995). Theoretical perspectives on knowledge and learning and a student teacher's pedagogical content knowledge of dividing and sequencing subject matter. *Journal of Teaching in Physical Education, 14*(3): 284–305.

Sacks, P. (1996). *Generation X Goes to College: An eye-opening account of teaching in postmodern America.* Chicago, Open Court.

Sharpe, T., So., H. Marvi, H, and Brown S. (2002). Comparative effects of sequential behavior feedback and goal-setting across peer-teaching and field-based practice teaching. *Journal of Teaching in Physical Education, 21*(3): 337–360.

Shulman, L. S. (1986). Those who understand: Knowledge growth in teaching. *Educational researcher* (February): 4–14.

Shulman, L.S. (1987). Knowledge and teaching: Foundations of the New Reform. *Harvard Educational Review, 57(1)*: 1–21.

Shulman, L.S. (1991). Ways of seeing, ways of knowing: ways of teaching, ways of learning about teaching. *Journal of Curriculum Studies, 23*(5): 393–395.

Siedentop, D. (1981). The Ohio State University supervision research program summary report. *Journal of Teaching in Physical Education* (Introductory Issue): 30–38.

Siedentop, D. (1983). *Developing Teaching Skills in Physical Education.* Mountain View, Mayfield Publishing Co.

Siedentop, D. (1983). *Developing Teaching Skills in Physical Education.* Palo Alto: CA, Mayfield.

Siedentop, D. and D. Tannehill (2000). *Developing teaching skills in physical education.* Pal Alto: CA, Mayfield.

Silverman, D. and C. Ennis (Eds). (1996). *Student learning in physical education: Applying research to enhance instruction.* Champaign, IL: Human Kinetics.

Silverman, D. and C. Ennis (Eds.) (2003). *Student learning in physical education: Applying research to enhance instruction.* 2nd Edition. Champaign, IL: Human Kinetics.

Smith, B. (1983). Teacher education in transition. In D. Smith (Ed.), *Essential knowledge for beginning teachers.* Washington, DC: American Association of Colleges for Teacher Education.

Spodek, B. (1974). Teacher education: Of the teacher, by the teacher, for the child. *Journal of Teacher Education. 34*(3): 3–9.

Tinning, R. (1987). *Improving Teaching in Physical Education.* Geelong, Deakin University.

Tinning, R. (1988). Student teaching and the pedagogy of necessity. *Journal of Teaching in Physical Education 7*(2): 82–89.

Tinning, R. (1991). Teacher education pedagogy: Dominant discourses and the process of problem solving. *Journal of Teaching in Physical Education* 11: 1–20.

Tinning, R. (1995). We have ways of making you think, or do we? Reflections on 'training' in reflective teaching In C. Pare (Ed.) (pp. 21–52), *Training of teachers in reflective practice of physical education.* Trois-Rivieres, Universite du Quebec a Trois-Rivieres.

Tinning, R. (2000). Unsettling matters for physical education in higher education: Taking seriously the possible implications of 'new times. *Quest, 52*(1): 32–49.

Tinning, R. (2002). Towards a 'modest' pedagogy: Reflections on the problematics of critical pedagogy. *Quest 54*(3): 224–241.

Tinning, R., Macdonald, D. Wright, J. and Hickey, C. (2001). *Becoming a physical education teacher: Contemporary and enduring issues.* Sydney: Prentice-Hall.

Tousignant, M. (2000). Synthesis of the section devoted to research on teacher education. *Research on Teaching and*

Research on Teacher Education: Proceedings of the International Seminar, Lisbon, 1996. F. Carreiro da Costa, J.-A. Diniz, L.-M. Carvalho, (Eds.), Faculty of Human Movement Sciences, University of Lisbon, 261–264.

Tsangaridou, N. and D. Siedentop (1995). Reflective teaching: A literature review. *Quest, 47*: 212–237.

Tsangaridou, N. and O'Sullivan M. (1997). The role of reflection in shaping physical education teachers' educational values and practices. *Journal of Teaching in Physical Education, 17*: 2–25.

Tripp, D. (1987). Teachers, journals and collaborative research. J. Smyth (Ed.), In *Educating Teachers: Changing the Nature of Pedagogical Knowledge*. London: The Falmer Press, 179–193.

van der Mars, H. (1987). Effects of audio-cueing on teacher verbal praise of student managerial and transitional task performance. *Journal of Teaching in Physical Education, 6*: 157–165.

Van Manen, M. (1977). Linking ways of knowing with ways of being practical. *Curriculum Inquiry 6*: 205–228.

Vendien, C. and Nixon J. (1985). *Physical education teacher education: Guidelines for sport pedagogy*. New York: John Wiley & Sons.

Ward, P. and Barrett, T. (2002). A review of behaviour analysis research in physical education. *Journal of Teaching in Physical Education, 21*(3): 242–266.

Wright, J.K.R. (1990). "I say what I mean," said Alice: An analysis of gendered discourse in physical education. *Journal of Teaching in Physical Education 10*: 210–225.

Zeichner, K. (1983). Alternative paradigms of teacher education. *Journal of Teacher Education 34*(3): 3–9.

4.2 Models and curricula of physical education teacher education

CONNIE COLLIER

Introduction

The purpose of this chapter is to discuss the research on models and curricula of Physical Education Teacher Education (PETE). The research on models of PETE describes the programmatic nature of helping teachers learn to teach, including information on program structure and curricular content. The section on curricula examines ways teacher educators use pedagogical methods to promote teacher professional development that aim to positively influence student learning. The intent is to represent the current knowledge base on teacher preparation in physical education including relevant core concepts and how the major research findings might guide future policy and practice. PETE research informs the bulk of this chapter however, research on teacher education (TE) assists with framing the issues and challenges common to all teacher preparation programs.

As the author of this chapter, I would like to acknowledge its limitations. This account advantages sources readily available in the most prominent journals as well as papers deemed worthy of recognition by our professional associations. In addition, it is important to recognize the many voices marginalized by the culture of academe, despite the validity of their contribution including but not limited to women, practitioners, and minority populations. I would also like to acknowledge my own bias of writing from a position of being a US citizen, as my experience limits my breadth of knowledge of the international perspective as well as my ability to address relevant research without accessible English translations. My espoused values as a teacher educator include a blend of perspectives that emphasize the preservice teacher's role in becoming a student of teaching, with a focus on the role of inquiry in learning to teach, all of which pose a certain prejudice within my writing.

Impact of history on PETE

It is important to take a brief historical retrospective to gain an understanding of how the most prominent issues of our past may have some bearing on the current state of affairs in PETE and provide possible insights and future directions for research and practice.[1] Considering the range of political and cultural influences transcending our histories, three themes surfaced as significant issues in the life of PETE as a field of inquiry. Themes shaping PETE's current program orientations, structure, curricular content, and pedagogical practices were selected. The representative themes include PETE's promotion of competition and physical prowess, gender politics in PETE, and the struggle for status within academe.

Physical prowess and competition

The purpose or aim of physical education within every culture influences the way in which physical educators are prepared and the content included in the curriculum shapes their professional development. Physical education has consistently taken on a scientific functionalist aim, which promotes physical prowess and competition (Kirk, 1992). While the overarching role of schools and school physical education is to improve society, being overly responsive to whimsical trends of society warrants caution. Kirk and Tinning (1990) warn us as a profession of the dangers associated with the act of social responsiveness without the companion social critique. Political agendas and dominant cultural views historically infuse a strong influence on the social construction of physical education. In turn, those definitions of physical education shape what core content is included in PETE. Kirk and Tinning (1990) maintained that scientific functionalism is the dominant world-view of physical education. They characterized this perspective as an "unquestioning belief in the status of quantitative, objective information focusing on the physical and physiological functioning of the body" (Kirk and Tinning, 1990: 10).

The early influences in the 1800s of the German gymnastic traditions of Jahn and the Swedish gymnastic movement of Ling were evident across much of Europe and the USA (Kirk, 1992). These traditions proposed various strands of curricula emphasizing systems of physical training. David Kirk (1992) provides a detailed account of the gymnastic movement and its evolution in postwar Britain in his text on defining the subject matter of physical education. Some of the earliest documented PETE curricula in the USA demonstrate evidence of the German influence within Brooklyn's Normal School under the direction of Turner in 1886 and the Swedish influence at the Boston Normal School of Gymnastics under the direction of Hemenway and Homans (McCullick and Lomax, 2000).

Embedded within the dominant German gymnastic movement of the late 1800s, was a focus on strength and competitive Olympic gymnastics, while the Swedish system was favored by female teachers and incorporated intricate flexions and extensions (Kirk, 1992). For many countries, this gymnastics and fitness movement was a response to the politics of war, where military training models became a part of physical education, employing pedagogical techniques focused on mass exercise routines (Kirk, 1992; Lumpkin, 2002). This aim of a physically strong society is evident in Hitler's definition of the Aryan body (Naul, 2002) and in America during the push for fitness testing in the 1940's-60's under the direction of Eisenhower and Kennedy (Sage, 2003).

An effort to broaden the aim of physical education to include sport and games is also evident in the history of physical education. The original intent of the sport and games movement was grounded in educational developmentalism and the work of John Dewey (Sage, 2003), yet it failed to capitalize on the moral and social agendas pioneered by Jesse Feiring Williams and Thomas Woods of Teachers' College Columbia University. The spirit of nationalism and competing for world power in the sporting arena refocused physical education on performance initiated by the physical training models. During the early 19th century, sport and games dominated the British private schools and their sport programs became a primary socializing agent (Kirk, 1992; Sage, 2003) for what was labeled "athleticism." Early in PETE's history, the sport curriculum, even though its intent was to broaden physical education's aim to include social responsibility and citizenship, embraced the deeply entrenched values of competition and performance evolving from Olympic and professional sport. Competition and elitism associated with competitive

sport contributed to a discourse of performance (Tinning, 1997) as opposed to a discourse valuing participation and inclusion. This performance based discourse continues to shape the teaching and learning in many PETE programs in the USA and internationally (Laker, 2003; Tinning, 1991, 1997). Throughout the mid and later 1900s, despite frequent attempts to define physical education within a broader framework associated with enjoyment, play, leisure, sport performance, and character building, the sport and performance mantra maintained its functionalist position within most cultures (Kirk and Tinning, 1990).

Changes associated with the global economy, cold war politics, and the concurrent developments of technologies have shifted many societies' foci toward an information economy. Some teacher education programs in Australia, USA, and England have begun to consider a broader socio-cultural knowledge of sport and physical activity that uses a critical perspective to expand scientific functionalism. These perspectives promote the examination and critique of "humans as thinking and feeling entities who must have social and cultural features as part of their existence" (Laker, 2003: 27). While these alternative conceptions of physical education are beginning to receive more attention, progress is slow. The reason for this slow recognition may be that practice based curricular examples that represent what it means to teach school physical education applying a critical lens have only recently become available (Kinchin and O'Sullivan, 2003; Oliver and Lalik, 2004; O'Sullivan and Kinchin, 2005). Reform of physical education policy and syllabi at the national level in Australia have also provided a more holistic perspective on physical education which integrates human development and movement with issues of physical literacy, embodied identity, and critical evaluation of physical culture (Burrows, 2004; Kirk and Macdonald, 1999).

Evidence exists in the early twenty first century suggesting "survival of the fittest" continues to hold an important role for physical education in countries other than the USA and England (McNeill et al., 2003; Sage, 2003). In the year 2004, popular media is satiated with articles on the "battle of the bulge" or the war against obesity whether it be in the USA or Australia (Evans, 2003b). With this increased attention, many physical education professionals have interpreted the role of physical education in line with a health club model, which closely resembles the military model of training and fitness. Classrooms have become places where lines of exercise cycles and step machines replace the squad lines for calisthenics, representing a narrow definition of physical education (Laker, 2003). This trend impacts the curriculum of PETE, as teachers now are being taught how to use heart rate monitors, generate funds for expensive equipment and operate computer applications to compile fitness testing data. This return to an emphasis on physical prowess is another example of physical education's social responsiveness without sufficient examination of the relevance or significance of our mission as educators.

The idea that physical education will successfully address social problems such as obesity and inactivity with a curriculum focused on competitive sport and fitness warrants our attention (Evans et al., 2004; Kirk and Tinning, 1990; Laker, 2003). The widespread marginalization of students who do not fit the mold of the competitive sports person or do not possess the physique of a fit person suggests that a broader interpretation of physical education as a moral and social enterprise is long overdue. PETE programs historically have not given serious consideration to cultural appreciation for or the aesthetics of content such as dance, or taken into consideration the need to understand the highly complex social and psychological perspectives of a healthy body (Evans, 2003b; Kirk and Macdonald, 2001; Laker, 2003). The socially responsive curricula in physical education privileges the performance domain and as an after thought addresses some critical perspectives (Fitzclarence and Tinning, 1990).

Gender politics in PETE

Another theme playing a particularly important role in the history of PETE is the prominence of males in sport and physical education (Bain, 1990). Men dominated the world of work in industrialized societies, translating to more men in positions of power throughout working cultures including universities. Couple the male presence in society overall with the dominance of males in sport and the stage was set for men to hold powerful positions in PETE. This early foothold of male dominance has been long standing and despite attempts at social change, the "cult of masculinity" (Kirk and Tinning, 1990) sustains itself in school physical education as well as in PETE (Bain, 1990). This dominance of the male culture while waning in higher education continues to impact what content is privileged and the nature of pedagogical experiences within PETE. Females often provide field-intensive supervision of student teachers and methods courses (Bain, 1990). Research on gender equity in all areas of academe suggest a greater number of women hold part time positions and issues of bias in tenure decisions and salary disparities tend to favor males despite recent progress (Valian, 2004).

For most of the century, males and females were trained at separate institutions or within separate departments (Bain, 1990). Women were not absent in the early days of PETE, however their contributions were not as visible or well recognized. Women's contributions did not have the luxury of

the intercollegiate sport coaching connection therefore their work was confined to the departments of women's physical education. In the women's department, teaching and the construction of curriculum were emphasized versus administration and coaching (Lumpkin, 2002). McCullick and Lomax (2000) record the women's contribution of the Boston Normal School of Gymnastics (BNSG) as the earliest female PETE program of record, which provided a substantial model for teacher preparation curricula. BSNG's curriculum included theory courses on anatomy, physiology, gymnastics balanced with their "participation in daily drills in pedagogical gymnastics, games, and a class that could be termed as a methods of teaching course" (McCullick and Lomax, 2000; 55). The BNSG program closely resembles many contemporary PETE curricula in the USA and other countries in the early 21st century whereby a mixture of performance courses, foundational content, pedagogy, and internships comprise their curricula.

While the issue of gender receives much attention in primary and tertiary schools (Brown and Evans, 2004), the analysis of gender bias and a culture of masculinity appears to be an area currently receiving only cursory attention in PETE. The gendered nature of school physical education (Griffin, 1985; Laker et al., 2003) suggests that gender politics within university communities are socializing teachers and we must refocus our attention in order to challenge the existing patriarchal system that shapes curricula and workplace practices (Dewar, 1990). The research on the socialization of PETE women (Dodds, 2002) sheds some light on how women's experiences in their doctoral programs and early career choices shaped their professional identities. More attention is needed to fully capture how PETE faculty are recruited, prepared, and socialized (Locke, 2003) if PETE hopes to foster workplace values that challenge the patriarchal discourse emphasizing competition and legitimization of capitalism within academe.

Certainly a history of research that challenges inequitable practices in physical education exists within PETE (Dewar, 1990; Fernández-Balboa, 1995; Tinning, 2002b; Wright, 1997) helping keep the issues of diversity, in particular gender and homophobia (Griffin, 1985), amidst our discourse on the hidden curriculum (Bain, 1990). The impact of inequities related to gender is only one area of diversity deserving the attention of PETE researchers. The promotion and reliance on scientism continues in many PETE programs without an accompanying critical perspective (McKay et al., 1990). Valuing a wide variety of theoretical orientations is important in shaping democratic governance structures and equitable personnel policies. Institutionalized traditions that have helped maintain the status quo of PETE need to be viewed through a critical lens if PETE's future is to promote and implement curricula valuing social justice.

Struggle for legitimacy

PETE's struggle for status in academe is the third historical theme. The kinesiology debate in the USA, initiated with Franklin Henry's publication of "Physical Education as an Academic Discipline" in 1964, marks a turning point in the history of PETE (Bain, 1990). The discourse shifted from physical education as a profession to physical education as a discipline focusing on a multidisciplinary view of human movement. The kinesiology degree offered options, other than teaching, to students interested in the area of sport science and related fields. While the profession and discipline debate continues to receive attention, many in the field of physical education accept that there is more to physical education than teacher education. As a result of this shift towards kinesiology, a preponderance of propositional knowledge in the related sciences such as physiology and biomechanics began to serve as a foundational layer for many PETE programs (Fitzclarence and Tinning, 1990).

Choosing to use the scientific paradigm as a way to legitimize physical education has caused a disconnect in the curricular content of PETE programs and the content of physical education in schools (MacDonald et al., 2002). If physical education is defined according to the scientific biophysical paradigm, the PETE curriculum includes sport psychology, biomechanics, sport physiology, and sport sociology, and school physical education reflects the likes of net games, invasion games, gymnastics, swimming, dance, and track and field. The change in focus from the subject matter of physical education to kinesiology is perceived by some scholars to be based upon faulty logic and promotes the preparation of physical education specialists ill prepared in their specialty content (Griffey, 1987; Huffman, 1988a; Siedentop, 2002). Lack of consensus on purpose and definition of what constitutes physical education parlays into similar trials and tribulations in school physical education. Public and private school physical education has historically been left out of the examinable subjects and professionals in the schools are assigned a much lower status based upon the types of duties assigned, privileges afforded, and resources allocated to their programs (O'Sullivan, 1989; Stroot et al., 1994). The question that continues to confound the alignment of PETE programs and school physical education curriculum is how to define the essential knowledge of physical education and its underlying mission. In addition, how might PETE deliver such knowledge?

Despite progress in promoting the value of physical education, physical education teachers and teacher educators continue to experience marginalization of their subject matter (Johns and Dimmock, 1999; O'Sullivan, 1989). Physical educators at all levels continue to fight for recognition as an academic subject (Fitzclarence and Tinning, 1990). Physical education is not specifically a part of the most recent USA legislation on educational reform, No Child Left Behind Act (NCLB) signed by President Bush in an effort to improve education for all children in the USA (Paige, 2001). Despite the lack of recognition for the centrality of physical education to the education of children in the USA, countries such as Australia, England, and Wales include physical education as an examinable subject and it is a formal part of the national curricula in the United Kingdom.

Questions surrounding the content and purpose of PETE plague our effort for status and continue to be of extreme importance as we articulate for ourselves, our students, and society the nature and scope of physical education's contribution in the lives of future generations. We need to be able to prepare teachers, who possess the knowledge and skills to make a difference in the lives of children and youth. To strengthen and systematically improve teacher education in physical education, it is imperative that we analyze our history, incorporate current research, and anticipate how to be active stakeholders in the process of political reform and policy generation. As Penny and Chandler (2000) recommend, we need to be addressing our visions of and for the future.

Theoretical foundations in PETE programs

Central to understanding the vision of a teacher education program is the examination of its associated theoretical perspectives. Theoretical perspectives are important because they establish the origins and traditions for interpreting the language used to describe methods and curriculum in teacher education. As Cochran-Smith and Lytle (1999) suggest conceptions of teacher learning "lead to very different ideas about how to improve teacher education and professional development, how to bring about school and curricular change, and how to assess and license teachers over the course of their professional life span" (p. 249).

In the PETE literature, Rink (1993) draws on the work of Feiman-Nemser (1990) and suggests four orientations for interpreting PETE programs, including the academic, practical, technological, and critical social perspectives. The academic orientation relates most closely to the view that the production of knowledge is a scientific venture and learning to teach relies on conveying a codified set of principles or truths to novice teachers. Those codified principles stem from the effective teaching literature in physical education (Siedentop and Tannehill, 2000). The academic orientation sets the stage for a program to prepare teachers by first providing them with learning experiences that would enhance their subject matter preparation, eventually allowing them to teach this subject matter to students. The practical orientation represents programs that are field based and rely heavily on the integration of knowledge and practice. A decision in both England and Wales to situate the majority of initial teacher training (ITT) practices within schools perhaps best represents the practical orientation. The technological orientation focuses on the individual and emphasizes the importance of each teacher's own personal and professional development as the key to quality teaching and learning. Lastly, the social or critical orientation rests upon the premise that teaching is an inherently moral practice. Teacher candidates need to examine inequities within school practices so they might help schools serve an emancipatory role within society. Research in PETE which examines the emotional dimension of teaching informs the social critical orientation by helping teacher candidates empathize with students to create more equitable experiences for all (McCaughtry, 2004; McCaughtry and Rovegno, 2003).

O'Sullivan (2003) foregrounds the work of Cochran-Smith and Lytle (1999) as another way to analyze PETE programs. Cochran-Smith and Lytle in the teacher education literature utilize a new epistemology for analyzing teacher development using three perspectives on knowledge. They use this epistemology to expand the notion of learning to teach to include professional development and the assumption that teacher education extends well into the induction years (Cochran-Smith and Lytle, 1999). The first conceptualization is "knowledge for practice" which aligns with Shulman's (1987) taxonomy of knowledge and the approach to teacher development focused on transmission of knowledge from experts to the novice. The second perspective is "knowledge in practice," which places the emphasis on the shared construction (Ball, 2000) of knowledge in the workplace and the localized nature of pedagogy (Laker, 2003). Cochran-Smith and Lytle's third conception is "knowledge of practice," which embraces the transformational ideals proposed within critical pedagogy and is similar to the calls for a postmodern[2] perspective within PETE (Fernández-Balboa, 1995, 1997b; Tinning, 2002b).

Initially examining the orientations as discrete entities appears simple, but the difficulty arises because few programs implement them in mutually exclusive ways. Rink (1993) makes the case for the coexistence of more than one orientation within one teacher education program. She suggests too much energy is spent debating the value of discrete

theoretical perspectives when the essential task of PETE faculty is to examine their own visions and create a program with a coherent and clearly articulated mission.

The intent is to not to debate the merits of any single orientation but to understand the theoretical underpinning of each position. I would like to acknowledge the cautions of other scholars (Ennis, 1997; O'Sullivan et al., 1992) who suggest the value is in understanding the shared meanings versus the dangers of dichotomizing the perspectives. The primary intent of this chapter is to dissect the conceptions so that we may best serve students in PETE and in school physical education. A thorough presentation and critique of theoretical orientations is available in Chapter 4.1. Understanding the conceptions of teacher education helps construct solutions to the fundamental question of how learners best learn or in the case of teachers, what frames the instructional approaches and curricular content that best supports the processes of learning to teach.

PETE's charge has for most of its history been defined as a functionalist role (Kirk, 1992; Tinning, 1991). Learning to teach physical education using the scientific biophysical knowledge base privileges that way of knowing at the expense of the interpretive ways of knowing (Fitzclarence and Tinning, 1990). While a select number of international PETE programs and a few scholars in the USA may espouse the importance of theories of constructivism, humanism, and critical theory, the majority of PETE programs systematically preserve the scientific functionalist aim, a curriculum advantaging the culture of masculinity and a conceptual framework that positions physical education as one of the "ologies" (Fernández-Balboa, 1997b). PETE professionals who identify themselves within departments of Kinesiology or Sport Science instead of Physical Education have played an active role in creating a theoretical identity aligning with scientism and technocratic rationality. While some would argue it is just a name change,[3] others (Tinning 1997; McKay et al., 1990) would suggest language does matter and the discourse surrounding PETE legitimizes the dominant position of scientism therefore marginalizing the voices of social reconstruction (Tinning, 1997) and post-modernity (Fernández-Balboa, 1999). The historical trends outlined at the start of this chapter help explain how scientism has played a central role in PETE and how many of the reform agendas that represent alternative perspectives seldom made a dent in this dominant view. This reliance on one way of knowing and informing our practices has led us to a place of false certainty particularly in the current climate of uncertainty (Tinning, 2000) as described in theories of post modernism (Fernández-Balboa, 1997a; Penney and Chandler, 2000).

The current context for teacher education is situated amidst this changing world of information explosion, issues of global economy, and increased institutional change (Cheng, 2001; Tinning, 2000). In an attempt to be responsive to the changing times, teacher educators have adopted constructivist discourses to make sense of teaching and learning (Chen, 2001). Laker (2003) notes that the trend is "toward a more holistic sense of education," whereby education becomes an interactive process of knowledge construction and occurs within and is influenced by the social world or community (p. 32). While constructivist discourse was originally intended to explain individual learning and not necessarily the bigger picture of schooling or deliberate teaching, the use of the constructivist perspective has dominated teacher education (Davis and Sumara, 2002). While various interpretations of constructivism exist in the literature[4], social constructivism tends to be the perspective most commonly used to frame educational studies (Chen, 2001; Davis and Sumara, 2002). Social constructivism places emphasis on shared meaning and social interactions. Taking into consideration the contextual complexities of each teacher education program, the culture in which it is situated, and their underlying values are keys to shaping quality teacher preparation programs espousing a constructivist discourse.

Attempting to understand the nuances and complexities of individual programs and multiple identities of teacher candidates within those programs causes much uncertainty for those attempting to create a new teacher education. As Tinning (2000) suggests these "new times" and unsettling matters require different ways of theorizing about teacher education. He recommends that we look beyond PETE to better understand PETE and use contemporary literature in the social sciences "relating to self, identity, and the postmodern condition" (Tinning, 2001: 14).

One of the fundamental principles underlying teacher education programs espousing perspectives of constructivism is that knowing your students is essential to good teaching (Feiman-Nemser and Remillard, 1996). One of the common mantras in the constructivist literature of teacher education is that instructors need to build upon learner's prior experiences in order to make learning meaningful. While the language of social constructivism is embedded within many TE and PETE program mission statements, behavior based teacher education continues to gain the most wide spread acceptance (Fitzclarence and Tinning, 1990; Kirk and Tinning, 1990; Tinning, 1997). Will a model of PETE for the "new times" come to fruition? Perhaps so if dissatisfaction with current practice becomes increasingly more unsettling. Scholars in PETE (Fernández-Balboa, 1997b; Lawson, 1990; Tinning, 2000) have warned us about these unsettling matters for years, but uncertainty about the practical

implications of how to build a model of PETE that addresses these complexities and uncertainties continues to plague our progress (Hellison, 1997). Progressive work by Ken Alexander at Edith Cowan University is underway as he leads an effort to create a "Health and Physical Education curriculum with an emphasis on personal development, self-management, and decision-making" within the discourse of sport and physical activity (Tinning, 2004: 231).

Research on models and methods

The word "model" by definition refers to a structural design or framework or an exemplar (Merriam-Webster, 2004). Models within an educational context often allude to teaching models (Joyce and Weil, 1996) or instructional models, which according to Metzler (2000: 14) can be described as "a comprehensive and coherent plan for teaching that includes: a theoretical foundation, statements of intended learning outcomes, teachers' content knowledge and expertise, developmentally appropriate and sequenced learning activities." Cruickshank (1985) defined models by means of structural components of teacher education and describes how those structures prioritize curricular content under the umbrella of teacher education. In *Models for the Preparation of America's Teachers*, Cruickshank (1985) argued that teacher education is best understood as part of the bigger picture of higher education including the general education or liberal arts component as well as the professional education curricula, which encompasses content specific courses, theories on teaching and learning, practica, field experiences, and internships. The localized nature of research on TE challenges researchers attempting to describe best practice or to construct a model to serve as an exemplar (Cochran-Smith, 2001; Wilson et al., 2001).

Some of the best teacher education programs are contextualized by particular theoretical orientations, situated within localized cultures, and serve an audience with specific needs, all of which make the meta-analyses of research on the range of programs very difficult to synthesize (Wilson et al., 2001). Therefore, descriptions of the research findings (Cochran-Smith, 2001; Wilson et al., 2001) tend to revolve around relevant questions followed by a range of possible answers guided by research findings.

Cochran-Smith (2001) categorizes the questions into the broad themes of teacher attributes, effectiveness, knowledge, and learner outcomes. These categories assist in generating questions to frame the next section of the chapter for research on models and methods in PETE and include: What role should

PETE candidates' attributes play in the PETE curriculum? What programmatic structures or curricular frameworks (5-year, 4-year, graduate programs, and alternative programs) offer the most promise for preparing effective teachers? How should we define and deliver subject matter within PETE? What pedagogical strategies within PETE promote effective teaching? What is the relationship between effective PETE and student achievement in physical education? Some of these questions appear to be dated and cynical readers might suggest that there is little use in examining the same old questions. Cochran-Smith (2001) reminds us that the political tapestry has changed and these same "ole" questions deserve new attention.

What role should teacher candidates' attributes play in the PETE curriculum?

What do we know about teacher candidates and why their attributes are important relative to informing best practice in PETE? Teacher quality and the well-documented teacher shortage represent the demographic imperative (Zeichner, 2003) which is the focus of educational reform agendas in many countries (Committee for Teaching and Teacher Education, 2003) and in the USA in particular (Darling-Hammond, 2000). The primary strategies for addressing teacher quality revolve around recruiting and more importantly retaining high quality teacher candidates (Darling-Hammond, 2002; Ingersoll, 2003).

US researchers in TE policy (Darling-Hammond, 2000; Ingersoll, 2003; National Commission on Teaching and America's Future, 2003) highlight the need to recruit and particularly retain a more diverse preservice teacher population. The National Education Association report on teacher demographics (2000–2001) describes the USA teaching force as 90% white, 79% female, average age 46 years old, while more than half hold a master's degree. When the high percentage of white middle class females who wish to return and teach in a school similar to their own is contrasted with the increasing diversity of student populations in urban public schools, the inherent mismatch causes quite a dilemma for TE (Howey and Zimpher, 1989). Similarly demographics of teacher candidates from Hong Kong indicate a significant female to female ratio 6.5:1. A large portion of these teacher candidates come from homes with low family income and insufficient study conditions (Forrester, 2003). To enhance the quality of education for our school children and youth, addressing the issue of whom we recruit for the teaching force and how we might find this information useful in designing TE is of importance.

The research on teacher socialization in PETE addresses the teacher attributes question by recognizing the importance of physical education teacher candidates' subjective warrants (Dewar and Lawson, 1984; Lortie, 1975) and suggests the information we glean about these recruits should help guide the design and sequence of our curricular programs (Lawson, 1983). The coaching orientation (Curtner-Smith, 1998) is one lens PETE research uses to understand recruits and how the dual roles (Bain and Wendt, 1983) of teacher and coach may negatively influence the effectiveness of teachers to carry out both roles.

Hutchinson and Buschner's (1996) research describes the profiles of delayed-entry recruits using qualitative case studies, while O'Bryant et al. (2000) used teacher candidates in a fifth-year program as participants to inform PETE faculty attempting to plan curricula for non-traditional teacher candidates in a graduate level teacher education program. Research on socialization into teacher education provides us with the life experiences recruits bring to our programs (Templin et al., 1982), the reasons for choosing to teach physical education (Belka et al., 1991; Dewar and Lawson, 1984), and people and events influencing those decisions (Lawson, 1983; Placek et al., 1995). Research on PETE and teacher beliefs suggests teacher education programs are not "strong enough interventions" (Graham, 1991) and few if any of recruits' original dispositions are transformed as a result of their education (Matanin and Collier, 2003; Placek et al., 1995). See also the chapter by Tsangaridou on teacher knowledge and values in this handbook.

Many of the socialization studies used limited samples and failed to provide a larger profile of the PETE recruit, making generalizations about who our teacher candidates are and determining what information is helpful in designing and informing PETE programs a difficult task. Placek and her colleagues (1995) were an exception. They examined 476 PETE recruits' beliefs and backgrounds relative to the purpose of physical education (Placek et al., 1995). This study gives us a glimpse of PETE candidates in the USA where 97% of the teacher candidates were Caucasian, 58% were male, and most were first-generation college students. Reinforcing this profile of PETE recruits, Macdonald et al., (1998) findings indicated the majority of their Human Movement Studies students were traditionally aged college students between 17–20 years of age, 97% were Australian, 65% of the teacher education strand were male and chose the major primarily for the opportunity to continue their interest in physical activity.

In 2003, Petersen et al. reported on a PETE program which is the largest major on a Midwestern, American campus with 700–800 students overall and 60–70 student teachers each semester. The purpose of the study was to describe the teacher candidates' knowledge about physical fitness and their respective fitness capacity but the data provides a glimpse of the student population at one of the larger USA PETE programs. Sixty-three student teachers made up the sample, with 53% male and 47% female. Seventy-three percent ($n = 46$) were between the ages of 20–25; 17.5% ($n = 11$) were between 26–30; approximately 10% ($n = 6$) were over 30 years old.

When examining a demographic profile of PETE recruits in the USA, Australia appears to differ from our TE counterparts with respect to gender, as a balance of male, and females exist while physical education candidates are similar relative to the high percentage of Caucasians. Other countries had no published research reporting on the profiles of their PETE recruits, making a broader international profile of PETE impossible to sketch.

Little information is available describing the market demand in the public schools for physical education teachers beyond the broad interpretation that urban schools are more likely for economic reasons to hire beginning teachers with less experience. Perhaps this gap in the PETE literature is due in large part to the fact there does not appear to be a documented shortage of physical education teachers but rather an over abundance of physical educators in some regions of the USA (Randall, 1986) and countries such as Germany (Naul, 2002). If the teacher shortage conundrum does not apply to PETE with regard to recruitment, certainly the issue of retention is valid (Hebert and Worthy, 2001; Macdonald, 1995). We have numerous accounts of the low status given to the work of physical educators (O'Sullivan, 1989) and the lack of relevant professional development opportunities (Armour and Yelling, 2002, 2004) both of which lead to attrition within the first 5–10 years on the job (Macdonald, 1995).

Fundamental to good teaching and good teacher education is the assumption that teachers or teacher educators know their students. Understanding the attributes of PETE recruits is fundamental to constructing meaningful learning experiences at the course level and programmatic features that address the diversity or homogeneity of the student population (Feiman-Nemser and Remillard, 1996). The literature on teacher beliefs in PETE suggests that recruits' beliefs require direct challenge (Matanin and Collier, 2003; Placek et al., 1995). Issues of studentship (Graber, 1995) continue to mask PETE candidates' intentions to improve their own practice (Carlson and Parry, 2003). Understanding how to encourage PETE candidates to question their own deeply entrenched beliefs about teaching and learning in physical education continues to be a dilemma for many teacher educators (Graber, 1996; Matanin and Collier, 2003).

Perhaps recruiting PETE candidates who represent beliefs and philosophical orientations that are similar to program goals might be easier than trying to significantly alter the beliefs of recruits once they enter teacher preparation programs. However this might exacerbate the dilemma of constructing PETE programs that recruit teacher candidates with dispositions already akin to a pedagogy of performance (Tinning, 2002a). Further research on the role of dispositions and beliefs of PETE candidates remains important as we search for ways to influence the socialization process and enhance the quality of physical education for children and youth.

Recognition and awareness of diversity issues by all PETE professionals is critical to better understanding the homogeneity of PETE recruits. More emphasis on research by PETE professionals, needs to be directed at better understanding and altering the lack of diversity associated with our preservice teacher population (Macdonald, 1998). In a profession where the study of marginalization and oppression has a long standing history (Brown and Evans, 2004; Flintoff and Scranton, 2001; Griffin, 1985; Wright, 1997), attention to issues of multicultural education and provisions for diversity in our PETE student population is obviously one of our "black holes" (Locke, 2003). The issue may reside in the institutional racism of the entry requirements and recruitment plans or within the overt or covert bias of teacher educators themselves. Whatever the case, efforts are needed to prepare teachers who are more diverse and/or possess the ability to celebrate and foster the diversity (Burden et al., 2004; O'Bryant, 1996; Stanley, 1997) of current and future generations of school children (Brown and Evans, 2004; Flintoff and Scranton, 2001). While research on anticipating student teacher success (Martens, 1987) produced mixed results, perhaps rethinking what data are most pertinent to this question would be most helpful. Instead of focusing on grade point average and skill and fitness scores, teacher educators could begin to determine which dispositions are most important in the process of recruiting PETE candidates, particularly those dispositions related to moral and ethical practice (Tinning, 1991). The moral (Laker, 2003) and emotional dimensions of teaching (McCaughtry, 2004) while they play a part in PETE program curriculum, tend to play a tertiary role to content knowledge and pedagogical skill (Tsangaridou and O'Sullivan, 1994).

It is important to consider the gaps in our current findings on teacher recruit's dispositions as we continue to ask what we believe to be the role of the PETE student in the process of learning to teach. The research on biography and life history (Sparkes, 1999, 2000) continues to make significant contributions to the PETE literature on socialization. However, studies informing PETE programs about the strengths and weaknesses of the demographic profiles of candidates may help those programs attract a more diverse student population or at the very minimum speak to the ever-widening cultural gap between teacher candidates and students in public schools (Burden et al., 2004). Studies on the ethnicity and culture of PETE candidates are scarce, therefore, more information on the status of PETE's profile and how to infuse our programs with multicultural values and perspectives is an important future direction. Related chapters in this handbook on teacher socialization by Stroot and teachers' biographies by Armour can better inform this area of inquiry.

What structures facilitate the preparation of qualified teachers?

What types of teacher education programs contribute to a more qualified teaching force? Nearly all countries and all subjects are in search of a new kind of teacher education (Cheng, 2001) and PETE is no exception (Laker, 2003). Each decade teacher education programs come under the scrutiny of some type of top down institutional or governmental agendas. In the USA, (Carnegie Commission on the Improvement of Teaching, 1986; Holmes Group, 1986; National Commission on Teaching and America's Future, 1997) and elsewhere (Department of Education and Science, 1988) education reforms regularly call for changes in the ways teachers learn to teach and what they will teach in schools. In 1984, Larry Locke, in his address to PETE researchers, cautioned that "efforts to improve PETE with good data might be guided by good intentions" but the likelihood of change in PETE based upon their research would be marginal. He based this caution on the trend in TE and PETE to be under the influence of social policies guided by political agendas and fluctuating economic times. The policy climate for PETE in the early twenty-first century is proving to be historically consistent with Locke's projection.

Political reforms and subsequent polices have affected nearly every country. There have been a multitude of publications on teacher education in general and some with specific implications for PETE programs. The range of reforms have impacted education in Australia, USA, Singapore (McNeill et al., 2003), Hong Kong (Cheng, 2001), and most of Europe (Naul, 2002). In the USA, the most recent version of political policy addressing the quality of teachers in schools is the No Child Left Behind Act, signed into law by President Bush in 2001. Various other reform agendas in the USA (Holmes Group, 1986) and in England (Department of Education and Science, 1988) have pushed and pulled at teacher education resulting in multiple formats for learning

to teach. For a complete review of policies affecting PETE refer to Chapter 4.10.

In Europe, the once uniform and traditional practices of teacher education possess more diverse systems than at any other time in history (Buchberger, 1994). Despite this diversity, many programs possess some of the following similarities (Buchberger, 1994: 16)

- Education studies/studies in educational sciences
- Academic subject studies
- Studies in subject matter methodologies/subject didactics and
- Teaching practice.

In some countries a blend of theoretical and practical experience is orchestrated by those in charge of university curricula, while countries such as England have moved much of the teacher education processes to field based programs (Capel, 2001; Hardy, 1999). In the US, there are options for earning a bachelors degree or gaining licensure within a graduate program (Darling-Hammond et al., 2002; Yinger, 1999). England, Wales, Scotland, Northern Ireland, and Australia have teacher education options that are primarily a graduate venture and typically couple teaching physical education with a teaching certificate in an academic subject. In the aforementioned countries, there are few options for a bachelor of education. The basic premise for the move to graduate licensure stems from the concern that teachers need to know more about their subject matter. The answer for improved content knowledge expertise is to prolong the length of teacher education in many countries (Darling-Hammond et al., 2002). Reports in the USA on teacher quality (National Commission on Teaching and America's Future, 1997, 2003) state many beginning teachers who are fully prepared in their discipline and in general studies of education are rated using the contested label of "highly qualified." Highly qualified is a distinction primarily determined by passage rates on subject matter licensure exams, however recently this distinction has been relaxed to include a broad range of possibilities many of which lack the same rigor (Barnett et al., 2004).

The disheartening aspect of the reform cycle is that little systematic evidence exists on which teacher education programs prepare teachers who are most likely to improve student achievement. Defenders of rigorous teacher education contend that subject matter knowledge is not enough and suggest "the research literature on teacher quality sends a clear message to policy makers and practitioners that teachers need to know their subject matter and how to teach it" (Barnett et al., 2004: 688). This appears to be due in part, to the range of stakeholders involved in TE and their ability to avoid the accountability issue once the political tides change. With numerous reform programs spanning several countries, accountability for change in teacher education, is seldom cast on the revolving team of policy writers and reform advocates but rather in the laps of teacher educators. Critics have harshly reprimanded teacher educators[5] (Education Commission of the States, 2000; The Abell Foundation, 2001) for their failure to carefully research the effectiveness of teacher education and deliver more highly qualified teachers. Respondents to the critics (Darling-Hammond et al., 2002; Wilson et al., 2001) defend model programs that make an impact on teacher candidates. The challenge of preparing a strong teaching force has in many instances produced mixed results as far as student learning is concerned (Education Commission of the States, 2000; The Abell Foundation, 2001) warranting some criticism.

In PETE, O'Sullivan (2003) cautions professionals to be more introspective about their own programs. She contends the missing link in the PETE literature is a failure to connect the processes of teacher education and the conceptions of student learning (O'Sullivan, 2003) and believes this to be one of the most significant challenges facing PETE professionals. Attempting to understand the issues and problems associated with teacher education requires specific knowledge about policy and educational reform. PETE professionals have begun to engage in the politics of policy debate but a closer examination seems desirable. The most comprehensive review of policy on PETE reform in the UK is available in Penny and Evans (1999).

The competing trend opposing lengthy and rigorous teacher preparation programs is the growing attention for alternative certification (AC) programs as an answer to the teacher shortage (Darling-Hammond et al., 2002). The market for teachers with particular expertise is so great that doors have been opened for those interested in a fast track to teacher certification in math, science, technology, second language education, and special education. The balance of the market driven response to teacher licensure and the demands for higher quality teachers is a fine line to walk and careful scrutiny of AC is necessary. However, these alternative routes do appear to possess relative benefits including fostering a more diverse population of teacher candidates who come into the teaching profession. Shen (1998) reported that more minorities enter through AC programs than traditional ones and AC teachers take teaching positions in urban schools with high percentages of students of color.

Given the multitude of possibilities for teacher preparation, defining the standards for what it means to prepare quality teachers is a reasonable request of the critics (Darling-Hammond et al., 2002). While no model for teacher preparation exists, there are characteristics of model programs available in the research on TE and in PETE (National Commission

on Teaching and America's Future, 1997, 2003). The six dimensions of high quality teacher preparation programs outlined by the NTCAF include:

- Careful recruitment and selection of teacher candidates
- Strong academic preparation
- Strong clinical practice to develop effective teaching skills
- Entry level teaching support in residencies and mentored induction
- Modern learning technologies
- Assessment of teacher preparation.

In PETE, Graham (1991) outlines four dimensions that support the positive influence on preservice teacher candidates' perspective on teaching.

1. A shared vision of teacher preparation by all involved in the process (cooperating teachers, clinical faculty, and university personnel).
2. An inquiry approach to teaching is valued. Student and instructors critically examine the nature of their values and beliefs.
3. The structure and content of the experiences represent the theoretical perspectives under girding the program.
4. A critical approach to curriculum and instruction is promoted so that schools are viewed as places for transforming society's injustices.

According to Wilson et al. (2001), in their review of the current gaps in teacher preparation research, the structure of teacher preparation appears to be of much less importance than the characteristics of teacher preparation that are informed by research. Wilson and colleagues (2001) suggest that future research needs to implement multi-institutional studies with strong research designs, seek to clarify the role of subject matter expertise, define what characterizes quality pedagogical and clinical experiences, and examine how specific parts of teacher preparation affect teaching practice and student achievement. These recommendations for improving research on teacher education are derived from the review of over 300 peer-reviewed research reports, however cautions are offered for these interpretations due to the sponsorship of this research by the Committee on Teacher Education (CTE). The CTE has a vested interest in quantifiable research outcomes that exemplify the role of policy in teacher education (Cochran-Smith, 2004).

Subject matter of PETE programs

Comparing agendas from TE and PETE, the one dimension that receives much attention in the general teacher education literature is the notion of strong academic preparation. Embedded in the notion of strong academic preparation is the issue of subject matter preparation. The subject matter issue is of utmost interest and concern to TE in general (Wilson et al., 2002) and increasingly to PETE professionals (Siedentop, 2002; Tinning, 2002a). Conceptualizing the role of subject matter knowledge in teacher preparation continues to be a dilemma for PETE professionals.

The disciplinary debate initiated by Henry in 1964, continues to perplex PETE curriculum designers as they search for ways to attend to both the biophysical curriculum of kinesiology and the subject matter knowledge most closely connected to school physical education (sport, games, gymnastics, fitness, dance, etc.). Similar to the research findings in the general TE literature, PETE scholars believe that lacking full understanding of subject matter impedes good teaching (Hoffman, 1988a; Siedentop, 2002). Siedentop (2002) goes one step further and suggests that PETE programs will likely prepare pedagogically skillful teachers who are "ignorant" of the content of physical education.

Results from a recent survey of PETE programs implies that there are discrepancies relative to what constitutes movement content and how much emphasis or space is given to the movement based curriculum in the USA (Bahneman and McGrath, 2004). Bahneman and McGrath surveyed one half of the 537 institutions in the USA having physical education programs about their requirements for essential activity courses regarding sport, movement, and fitness. Less than half of the participating institutions required a fitness activity course. This lack of consensus can be found across various countries. Some PETE programs continue to pursue sport, yet in a form that is more equitable and profitable for all students (Griffin et al., 1997; Mitchell, et al., 2003; Siedentop, 1994). Advocates for a PETE curriculum that is more inclusive and sensitive to the needs and interests of all students tend to caution against sporting curriculum as it tends to represent an elitist, competitive male model of physical activity (Fitzclarence and Tinning, 1990; Tinning, 1997, 2002a).

Determining what should represent the essential movement core for PETE programs is a long standing issue. This problem is confounded by our own inability to resolve the content debate and the lack of status and academic prestige afforded movement courses by institutions of higher education. Locke, et al. (1981) offered a subject-matter-centered model for the preparation of teachers that foregrounds the subject matter of school physical education in the PETE program. This model outlines a teacher education program whereby sport, games, dance, exercise, and outdoor activities are the subject matter. The model provides multiple

and sequential opportunities to engage with the subject matter leading to the development of performance skills and knowledge about the subject beyond the introductory level. For example, courses might include introductory, intermediate, and advanced net games. While the subject of physical education is at the center of this model, it also includes essential knowledge about school cultures, teacher socialization, development of pedagogical skills, and on-going support for teacher learning (Locke et al., 1981).

Alternative teacher certification programs attempt to address and simplify the complexity of the subject matter question by suggesting candidates interested in becoming a teacher need only have a degree in the discipline or major in which they will teach. What would be the core content for alternative certification programs in physical education? The likely subject matter degree would be in human movement science or kinesiology with the bulk of the courses vaguely resembling the subject of school physical education. The research on AC programs suggests success in recruiting a more diverse pool of teachers and mixed results for equipping teachers with adequate subject matter (Wilson et al., 2001). The potential for physical education AC ventures will hinge on strict guidelines for admission and careful scrutiny of prior experiences to ensure adequate subject matter preparation.

Efforts of the Holmes Group in the USA attempted to force many institutions into fifth year Master's programs thereby creating 5-year MED programs with the first 4 years focused on subject matter and the fifth year of the PETE curriculum containing a pedagogical sequence and internship. Some relatively strong PETE programs were dismantled as a result of the Holmes Group agenda only to be rebuilt some 5 years later. This represents another clash between educational reform and market trends and higher education institutions' emphasis on an entrepreneurial agenda of increasing enrollment over sustaining best professional practice. Given the lack of a research base on how much what kind of subject matter knowledge and how much is essential to good teaching more research is needed to inform future program curricula (O'Sullivan, 2003).

One of the notable teacher education scholars (Shulman, 1986) advocates the integration of subject matter and pedagogy. Shulman has been credited with the definition of pedagogical content knowledge (PCK) as "ways of representing and formulating the subject that make it comprehensible to others" (Shulman, 1986: 9). Others (Ball, 2000; Feiman-Nemser and Parker, 1990) who have made the subject matter issue the center of their research agendas in TE are quick to articulate the complexities of fostering teacher learning of a subject in ways that impact student achievement. Many believe the idea of preparing teachers to possess strong subject matter expertise goes beyond the addition of courses (Ball, 2000; Wilson et al., 2001) or securing disciplinary degrees but should focus on the implementation of knowledge in practice (Griffin and Dodds, 1996; McCaughtry and Rovegno, 2003; Placek and Griffin, 2001). O'Sullivan (2003) proposed that the content knowledge question can be best understood by drawing on the growing body of literature on practical knowledge (Martinek and Hellison, 1997) in addition to the substantive growing research base on PCK in PETE (McCaughtry and Rovegno, 2003; Rovegno, 1992, 1993). Issues surrounding PCK are perhaps best understood in the knowledge domain and expert novice literature in other chapters of this handbook. See also summaries by Amade-Escot (2000) and emerging research on PCK by Rovegno and McCaughtry and Rovegno (2003). Descriptions of PETE curricula that meld the subject matter and the practical application of the subject in a movement context (Oslin et al., 2001) represent attempts by professionals to situate activity courses within curricular frameworks consistent with how they would be taught in public school physical education. However, determining which methods foster the types of skills and knowledge that are central to creating high quality PETE programs (O'Sullivan, 1990) is an area of the current literature that deserves more attention (O'Sullivan, 2003).

What programmatic features contribute to quality PETE programs?

The majority of PETE research resides within the realm of field experiences, internships or student teaching. All reports on quality teacher preparation programs (Darling-Hammond et al., 2002; Holmes Group, 1986; National Commission on Teaching and America's Future, 1997; The Abell Foundation, 2001) emphasize the importance of clinical experiences that align with the conceptual orientation guiding the program's mission. Many studies in PETE examine the roles and responsibilities of the members of the supervision triad and the experiences and concerns of student teachers (Capel, 2001; Hardy, 1999; Tannehill, 1989; Veal and Rikard, 1998). Comprehensive research reviews on cooperating teachers (Banville, 2002) and early field experiences (You and McCullick, 2001) are readily available that specifically address the research in PETE. See also Chapter 4.3.

Tinning (2001) in a review of research on teacher and coach education conveyed a certain disappointment by saying the field of PETE appears theoretically disorganized. Tinning's most critical reflections on the teacher education literature focus on the role of student teacher concerns (Capel, 1997; Wendt and Bain, 1989). While recognition of student opinions and concerns might serve the client driven climate of entrepreneurial academe, Tinning suggests that after thirty years we might be missing other "generative ways" of looking at these issues (2001: 14). His recommendations entail moving beyond the reproductive nature of studying teacher concerns from the insular perspective of PETE recruits and pursuing the contemporary literature on identity, self and post modernism (Tinning, 2001). Brown and Evans' (2004) research on the intergenerational links of gender reproduction provide a glimpse of how a relational view of learning to teach can inform teacher preparation. Their study identifies "key moments in the process of cultural reproduction" that help make sense of the transmission of gender orientations and practices within physical education. This rich description of how male teachers formulate gendered practices "considers the implicit and embodied construction and reconstruction across generations of physical education teachers and pupils" (p. 50).

Research on different configurations and structures for the student teaching experience has begun to accumulate. Attempts have been made to study a day-long inquiry seminar as a means of fostering group inquiry and reflective practice, in developing a different set of skills and knowledge needed if student teachers are to become change agents in schools (Collier, 2001). Evidence exists showing that some PETE programs value collaboration (Knop et al., 1997) as a means of improving teaching skills and knowledge during student teaching. Some studies offering new perspectives include those using peer coaching (Jenkins and Veal, 2002) or student teaching and learning in a cohort setting (Melnychuk, 2001; Oslin and Collier, 2003). The need to consider the collaborative arrangements for field work come from a practical stand point of sheer work load and the research on professional learning that conveys the need to provide an appropriate balance of support and challenge (Tang, 2003). In Canada, Melnychuk's (2001) research on student teaching cohorts has shown positive results as five physical education teacher candidates were placed in one secondary department which created a supportive learning environment that fostered reflective practice, joint thought, and collaborative action.

For a novice teacher, the role of peer assessor can be a daunting task, however it holds the potential to develop skills and knowledge associated with a culture of collaborative change (Bullough and Gitlin, 2001). The peer assessment model also tends to alleviate the hierarchical power of the traditional triad (Tannehill, 1989; Veal and Rikard, 1998). This idea of peer coaching (Jenkins and Veal, 2002) certainly is not new (Dodds, 1979) but is receiving more support as the ideals associated with communities of practice gains momentum (Lave and Wenger, 1991).

The review of literature on field experiences by Patt Dodds (1984) has been a guiding force for structuring clinical experiences in PETE. She delineated the importance of debunking the myths of field work and in 1989 reported the following recommendations for developing more effective experiences: (a) participants involved in the clinical experience need to share basic principles in order to impact the student's learning; (b) the design of the clinical experiences needs to be sequential, deliberate and aligned with the programmatic philosophy of the PETE program; (c) dialog on issues and impact of sport such as social injustice and equity must be a part of the discussion with PETE candidates; and (d) reflective processes need to play a central role in the programmatic design and implementation of clinical experiences.

You and McCullick (2001) revisited and reexamined the EFE literature and found a lack of longitudinal research, therefore calling for studies that would inform teacher candidates performance in courses following EFE's as well as follow-up studies to measure the impact on career choices in subsequent years of teaching. The research indicated that quality of the experiences and supervisory practices included a wide range of configurations and accountability. To address the accountability issue, they (2001) recommended research on supervisor certification programs and referred to the literature on PETE program assessment (Metzler and Tjeerdsma, 2000) in order to design better assessments capable of supplying programmatic feedback about the effectiveness of EFEs. For an in depth review of research on field experiences in PETE, refer to the chapter in this handbook by Behets and Vergauwen.

What methods within PETE help prepare quality teachers?

The ability to reflect and problem solve is viewed as central to effective teaching (Calderhead, 1989; Schon, 1987). The research on reflective teaching gained support as teacher educators began to shift attention from the behavioral paradigm to cognitive psychology and the study of teacher thinking (Dodds, 1993a). The language of reflective teaching was evident in the early 1960s in Germany stemming from the emphasis on critical theory and the scholarly contributions of Jurgen Habermas, promoting an alternative view to the model of technical rationality so widely accepted in PETE (Crum, 1993; Tinning, 1991).

The premise underlying reflective practice is that schools and classrooms are increasingly uncertain entities, which in turn demand teachers become better problem solvers and in some instances problem setters (Lawson, 1993; Tinning, 1991). The range of literature on teacher reflection is broad (Macdonald and Tinning, 2003) but the conception most frequently used in the PETE literature (O'Sullivan and Tsangaridou, 1997; Tsangaridou and O'Sullivan, 1994) refers to definitions of reflection posed by Schon (1987) and to some extent Van Manen (1977).

In PETE, developing reflective praxis is extremely valuable from the standpoint that physical educators often work in isolation. The physical education specialist must rely on the self reflexive process to respond to the complexities of gymnasium life and to develop their own theories which guide their actions (Tsangaridou and O'Sullivan, 2003). Modest progress has been made promoting reflective practice of PETE candidates (Curtner-Smith and Sofo, 2004; Tsangaridou and O'Sullivan, 1994) to focus beyond the technical aspects of teaching and to address issues of equity in physical education (Burden et al., 2004; Oliver, 2001). However, more work remains before the process can substantively contribute to the wide spread transformation of social injustices referred to by advocates of the critical postmodern perspective (Fernández-Balboa, 1997b; Kirk and Tinning, 1990; Macdonald and Tinning, 2003).

One method possessing promise for advancing reflection and critical thinking in PETE is the case method. The case method has been touted as useful in bridging the gap between theory and practice (Shulman, 1987). Case method also enables the analysis of problems from multiple perspectives (Boyce, 1993; Collier and O'Sullivan, 1997). Scholars in general teacher education maintain that the case method provides opportunities for teacher candidates to develop their own knowledge (Hammerness et al., 2002) by reflecting upon and examining the intricacies of teaching cases (Merseth, 1996; Richert, 1991).

The case method promotes the conception of teacher learning referred to by Lytle and Cochran-Smith (1999) as "knowledge of practice". The case for the case method hinges on the argument that novices need to learn "how to develop conceptual understandings" or the recognition of meaningful patterns of information so they might begin to possess richer more substantive cognitive representations of subject matter, instructional strategies, and students, similar to experts (Dodds, 1994). High-quality case materials have the potential to provide PETE candidates a more in-depth focus that leads to conceptual understanding or conditionalized knowledge (Bransford et al., 1999). Conditionalized knowledge affords the learner understanding of the context in which such knowledge is useful rather than simply memorizing content independent of real world situations (Bransford et al., 1999). The fostering of conditionalized knowledge supports those scholars advocating the value of situated learning theory (Lave and Wenger, 1991) as it holds potential for promoting more meaningful physical education for students in schools (Kirk and Macdonald, 1998; Laker, 2003).

Research on the case method in PETE (Bolt, 1998; Collier and O'Sullivan, 1997) has shown potential for encouraging reflection and cognitive growth of teacher candidates; however further investigation is needed to substantiate claims that cases hold the key to better problem solving and improved theories of action for PETE candidates. The enhanced capacities of information technology and the trend toward multi media cases (Beck et al., 2002) offer promise. Also the shift toward cases constructed by and for teacher candidates as they reflect upon their own work as teachers is a method worth exploring (Hammerness et al., 2002).

Complimenting the research on teacher reflection is the focus on action research (Levin and Rock, 2003; Locke et al., 1999). PETE's historical disconnect of theory from practice has been well defined in our literature (Lawson, 1990; Martinek and Hellison, 1997). Action research expands the notion of transforming practice that is embedded in the reflective teaching literature and provides a framework for a cycle of change (Macdonald and Tinning, 2003; Tinning, 1992). As part of a strategy to promote change, a version of action research that would engage practitioners, scholars, and students of teaching in a collaborative process (Bullough and Gitlin, 2001; Levin and Rock, 2003) could begin to mend the disconnect of theory and practice. Lytle and Cochran-Smith's (1999) "inquiry as stance" perspective suggests that "inquiry communities" are central to school improvement. These communities would help make "consequential changes in the lives of teachers and, as important, in the lives of students and in the social and intellectual climate of schools and schooling" (Cochran-Smith and Lytle, 1999: 295).

Another trend in the broader teacher education literature that promotes the civil and moral dimensions of teacher learning is service learning. Service learning has the capability of solving part of the "disconnect" between the classroom and the "real world" by simultaneously integrating academic study and community service (Parker et al., 2004). Examples of service learning projects (Kahan, 1998; LaMaster, 2001; Parker et al., 2004) within PETE programs are beginning to surface and deserve our attention if the field is serious about the values associated with the emancipatory role of universities in schools and communities (Collier and Lawson, 1997). Service learning or academic community service has the potential to connect the typically dichotomous worlds of research and practice (Martinek and Hellison, 1997) by focusing scholars on the most relevant issues and problems in their surrounding communities. This perspective provides a pivotal avenue to foreground practical applications of the theories of the critical postmodern world by engaging collaborative teams in the messy social world. Designing collaborative solutions will require us to take a multi disciplinary approach versus the insular disciplinary avenues of our past (Collier and Lawson, 1997; Lawson, 1990). Walton and LaVine (2005) propose a multidisciplinary approach to teaching and learning about obesity using a case based approach titled Challenging Obesity: Media Powered Experiences To Engage Students (COMPETES). COMPETES promotes the analysis of obesity from a multidisciplinary perspective using problem-based learning. Digital images and video stimulate competing perspectives on what it means to be healthy, hopefully causing students to question their taken for granted assumptions about health and fitness.

We are entering a time when it would be quite easy to slip into our comfortable historical shoes and embrace scientism as a potential solution to obesity devoid of moral and ethical concerns (Evans et al., 2004). PETE needs caring teachers who take time to develop the emotional dimensions of their pedagogical approaches and who cultivate equitable practices (Dodds, 1993b; McCaughtry, 2004; O'Sullivan, 2003). The discourse on obesity places the bodies of children and youth on center stage, thus creating the pressing need for a cautious and comprehensive approach to understanding the issues. If students are to have access to enjoyable programs of physical activity within schools a critically reflexive approach is needed to examine policies, curricula, and media reports associated with the public health agenda within physical education. We cannot afford to foreground physical education as the panacea for one of society's most complex issues (Evans et al., 2004; Locke 2003). Ethical issues associated with the public health agenda within physical education requires special attention of PETE professionals so that heightened fitness testing and weekly weigh in stations do not become the norm in schools. Competing perspectives on the role of public health exist within the PETE literature (O'Sullivan, 2004). These discussions have important contributions to make for those with a vested interest in PETE curricula. The critical perspectives offered by our colleagues in the social sciences provide a valuable perspective (Evan et al., 2004). The renewed interest in physique and fitness could easily return to the narrow physiologic solutions of our past (Kirk, 1992). As Thomas cautions, physical education teachers are already "finding themselves trying to ride to the rescue while holding on by a thread" (2004: 150) and a teachers must become better informed about their role in the physical inactivity problem.

Future directions

PETE currently maintains a relatively weak position amidst the information economy led by mathematics, science, and technology (Cheng, 2001; Laker, 2003; Tinning, 2004). The NCLB policy in the US which encourages highly qualified teachers for all children excludes physical education. In addition, classroom teachers teach specialized physical education content to elementary children in several countries, including Australia and regions in the US. Some public schools in the US are replacing physical education requirements with experiences in marching band and interscholastic athletics (Lee and O'Sullivan, 2004). It is up to PETE professionals to position physical education within policy-making environments and become more astute in the political agendas influencing teacher preparation (Locke, 2003). For an in-depth analysis of policy in PETE, see Chapter 4.10. One important aspect of promoting physical education's longevity and centrality within the educational and political debate is the preparation and retention of quality teachers who can make a difference in student learning.

To improve PETE curricula and methods the following recommendations are offered for future research and practice: (a) consider student achievement in the assessment and preparation of qualified physical educators; (b) prepare physical educators who possess adequate and meaningful subject matter knowledge; and (c) develop communities of inquiry in PETE that can sustain and inform quality teaching.

To gain momentum in our struggle for legitimacy, the preparation of qualified teachers who are capable of influencing gains in student achievement is essential. If we are to effectively show gains in student achievement we must be clear, about what our program goals are and what assessments we will use to judge their effectiveness. O'Sullivan (2003) contends the missing link in the PETE literature is a failure to connect the processes of teacher education and the conceptions of student learning. She believes this to be one of the most significant challenges facing PETE professionals.

PETE professionals across the world must be clear on what constitutes physical education's subject matter within their local context in order to make meaningful contributions to schools and the lives of children. The relationship of good teaching and student achievement hinges on clear definitions of subject matter and its underlying conceptual orientations. Subject matter debates about whose curriculum counts are counterproductive. PETE needs to engage the voices of students, teachers, and university professionals in a more democratic curricular process. This process needs to emphasize the student learning dimension, while alleviating concerns and biases of individual teachers and pedagogy scholars. The goal of PETE should be to prepare teachers who are capable of developing curricula that stop trying to be all things to all people and better serve local communities, and honors the voices of stakeholders including community members, family members, teachers and especially students. This will take a shift in thinking, particularly in those countries where the national curricula guides much of school physical education.

Shaping the goals and values of school physical education needs to be a collaborative venture of PETE professionals, experienced and novice teachers so that communities of inquiry can begin to produce knowledge that can be immediately applied to the delivery of physical activity for today's children and youth. This scope of physical activity options needs to reflect our students' personal interests, school culture, and community resources (Fitzclarence and Tinning, 1990; Laker, 2003; Tinning, 2002a).

Improving health and increasing physical activity in our respective countries is not as simple as the "move more eat less" mantra resonating in popular media. A multidisciplinary approach is recommended that encompasses several disciplines and engages experts of multidisciplinary teams who can study the human body from a variety of perspectives including medical, pedagogical, and cultural. This multidisciplinary approach can help increase visibility of physical education professionals across campus and within communities. Physical education professionals can engage in research, practice, and service projects with colleagues from the arts and sciences, the humanities, and community agencies. These collaborative ventures set the stage for multisite research programs that have the potential to draw funding that will support much needed longitudinal investigations on learning to teach.

The "inquiry as stance" perspective on teacher learning (Cochran-Smith and Lytle, 1999) views knowledge construction as a highly interactive process where teachers and students learn to collaboratively deconstruct situations, analyze issues, and build uniquely situational knowledge. PETE professionals continue to focus attention on a "new teacher education" as a stronger intervention (Graham, 1991) or course assignments that develop teachers into active problem setters and solvers. Is there a transformational process to be co-constructed within practice and academe that might foster a better understanding among professionals and be representative of an inquiry community for PETE? As our counterparts in TE suggest "teacher learning for the next century needs to be understood not primarily as an individual professional accomplishment but as a long-term collective project with a democratic agenda" (Cochran-Smith and Lytle, 1999, 296).

Larry Locke queried the PETE audience at the 2003 conference in Baton Rouge, by asking how many of us were confident our PETE candidates would be of sufficient quality to teach our own children? There was no applause or confident verbal response from the audience. Perhaps some folks were sitting in quiet optimism, my best guess it that we were more than likely silently contemplating the huge challenge that lies ahead in the name of quality models and methods for PETE.

Notes

1 For a more complete historical rendition of the research in PETE specific to the United States, see Linda Bain's review of teacher education in the W.R. Houston's Handbook of Research on Teacher Education (1990).

2 I would like to acknowledge that post-modernity and critical theories possess differing ideologies. For the sake of this paper, the general intent of these perspectives conveys calling to question the inequities of power in an effort to initiate emancipation and transformation to a more just society.

3 This is not the space or place to engage in the name debate, for further explanation of the consequences of the disciplinary splintering of the title physical education, see "The dispersal of the department at Teachers College: The Diaspora," continues by Shirl Hoffman (1998).

4 See Davis and Sumara (2002) for a thorough critique of constructivist discourses. They analyze constructivist theory, in particular the contemporary theories of situated cognition as well as cultural and critical theories most closely aligned with educational issues. Cautions are provided that suggest constructivist discourse provide insight but are not coterminous with formal education.

5 Both the Educational Commission Education Commission of the States (2000) and the Abell Foundation (2001) reports have been criticized heavily by scholars in TE for basing their claims on faulty research findings, primarily Darling-Hammond (2002).

References

Amade-Escot, C. (2000). The contribution of two research programs on teaching content: "Pedagogical content knowledge" and "Didactics of physical education." *Journal of Teaching in Physical Education, 20*(1): 78–101.

Armour, K. and Yelling, M. (2002). Time for a change: Providing effective continuing professional development for physical education teachers. *PE and Sport Today* (10): 13–15.

Armour, K. and Yelling, M. (2004). Continuing professional development for experienced physical education teachers: Toward effective provision. *Sport, Education, and Society, 9*(1): 95–114.

Bahneman, C. and McGrath, J. (2004). *Analysis of the undergraduate physical education teacher certification activity requirements within the United States.* Paper presented at the American Alliance of Health, Physical Education, Recreation, and Dance, New Orleans, Louisiana.

Bain, L.L. (1990). Physical education teacher education. In W.R. Houston (Ed.), *Handbook of research on teacher education* (pp. 758–781). New York: Macmillan.

Bain, L.L. and Wendt, J.C. (1983). Undergraduate physical education majors' perceptions of the roles of teacher and coach. *Research Quarterly for Exercise and Sport, 54*(2): 112–118.

Ball, D.L. (2000). Bridging practices: Intertwining content and pedagogy in teaching and learning to teach. *Journal of Teacher Education, 51*(3): 241–247.

Banville, D. (2002). Re-defining the student teaching experience: A review of the literature. *AVANTE, 8*(3): 30–38.

Barnett, B., Hoke, M. and Hirsh, E. (2004). The search for highly qualified teachers. *Phi Delta Kappan, 85*(9): 684–670.

Beck, R., King, A. and Marshall, S. (2002). Effects of video-case construction on preservice teachers' observations of teaching. *The Journal of Experimental Education, 70*(4): 345–352.

Belka, D., Lawson, H. and Lipnickey, S. (1991). An exploratory study of undergraduate recruitment into several major programs at one university. *Journal of Teaching in Physical Education, 10*(3): 286–306.

Bolt, B. (1998). Encouraging cognitive growth through case discussions. *Journal of Teaching in Physical Education, 18*(1): 90–102.

Boyce, A. (1993). *Case study approach for pedagogists.* Paper presented at the American Alliance for Health, Physical Education and Dance, Washington, DC.

Bransford, J., Brown, A. and Cocking, R. (1999). *How people learn: Brain, mind, experience, and school.* Washington, DC: National Academy Press.

Brown, D. and Evans, J. (2004). Reproducing gender? Intergenerational links and the male PE teacher as a cultural conduit in teaching physical education. *Journal of Teaching in Physical Education, 23*(1): 48–70.

Buchberger, F. (1994). Teacher education in Europe – diversity versus uniformity. In M.J. Galton and B. Moon (Eds.), *Handbook of teacher training in Europe* (pp. 14–50). London: David Fulton Publishers.

Bullough, R.V. and Gitlin, A. (2001). *Becoming a student of teaching: Linking knowledge production and practice* (2nd ed.). New York: Routledge Falmer.

Burden, J., Hodge, S., O'Bryant, C. and Harrison, L., Jr. (2004). From colorblindness to intercultural sensitivity: Infusing diversity training in PETE programs. *Quest, 56*: 173–189.

Burrows, L. (2004). Understanding and investigating cultural perspective in physical education. In J. Wright, D. Macdonald and L. Burrows (Eds.), *Critical inquiry and problem solving in physical education* (pp. 105–119). London: Routledge.

Calderhead, J. (1989). Reflective teaching and teacher education. *Teaching and Teacher Education*, 5(1): 43–51.

Capel, S. (1997). Changes in students' anxieties and concerns after their first and second teaching practices. *Educational Research*, 39(2): 211–228.

Capel, S. (2001). Secondary students' development as teachers over the course of a PGCE year. *Educational Research*, 43(3): 247–261.

Carlson, T. and Parry, S. (2003). A reflective framework from a preservice teacher's perspective. *Physical Educator*, 60(4): 208–221.

Carnegie Commission on the Improvement of Teaching. (1986). *A nation prepared: Teachers for the twenty-first century.* New York: Carnegie Coporation.

Chen, S.H.L. (2001). Constructing a constructivist teacher education: A Taiwan experience. In Y.C. Cheng, K.W. Chow and K.T. Tsui (Eds.), *New teacher education for the future* (pp. 261-290). Hong Kong: Kluwer Academic Publishers.

Cheng, Y.C. (2001). *New teacher education for the future: International perspectives.* Hong Kong: Kluwer Academic Publishers.

Cochran-Smith, M. (2004). Ask a different question, get a different answer: The research base for teacher education. *Journal of Teacher Education*, 55(2): 111–115.

Cochran-Smith, M. (2001). Constructing outcomes in teacher education: policy, practice, and pitfalls. *Education Policy Analysis Archives*, 9(11): 1–59.

Cochran-Smith, M. and Lytle, S. (1999). Relationships of knowledge and practice: Teacher learning in communities. *Review of Research in Education*, 24: 249–305.

Collier, C.S. (2001). Can less be more? Structural and ideological shift in a student teaching program. *Chronicle of Physical Education in Higher Education*, 12(1): 5, 16–17.

Collier, C.S. and Lawson, H.A. (1997). Toward academically based community scholarship: Ideals, realities, and future needs. *Quest*, 49(4): 380–393.

Collier, C.S. and O'Sullivan, M. (1997). Case method in physical education higher education: pedagogy of change? *Quest*, 49(2): 198–213.

Committee for Teaching and Teacher Education. (2003). *Australia's teachers: Australia's future advancing innovation, science, technology and mathematics.* Canberra: Commonwealth of Australia.

Cruickshank, D. (1985). *Models for the preparation of america's teachers.* Bloomington, Indiana: The Phi Delta Kappa Educational Foundation.

Crum, B. (1993). *The urgent need for reflective teaching in physical education.* Paper presented at the AIESEP, Trois-Rivieres, Quebec, Canada.

Curtner-Smith, M.D. (1998). Influence of biography, teacher education, and organizational socialization on the perspectives of first-year physical education teachers: Case studies of recruits with coaching orientations. *Sport, Education and Society*, 2: 73–94.

Curtner-Smith, M.D. and Sofo, S. (2004). Influence of a critically oriented methods course and early field experience on preservice teachers' conceptions of teaching. *Sport, Education and Society*, 9(1): 115–142.

Darling-Hammond, L. (2000). Teacher quality and student achievement: A review of state policy evidence. *Education Policy Analysis Archives*, 8(1), 1–50.

Darling-Hammond, L. (2002). The challenge of staffing our schools. *Educational Leadership*, 58(8): 12–17.

Darling-Hammond, L., Chung, R. and Frelow, F. (2002). Variation in teacher preparation: How well do different pathways prepare teachers to teach. *Journal of Teacher Education*, 53(4): 286–302.

Davis, B. and Sumara, D. (2002). Constructivist discourses and the field of education: Problems and possibilities. *Educational Theory*, 52(4), 409–428.

Department of Education and Science. (1988). *Education Reform Act: Circular 7/88.* London: DES.

Dewar, A. (1990). Oppression and privilege in physical education: Struggles in the negotiation of gender in a university programme. In D. Kirk and R. Tinning (Eds.), *Physical education, curriculum and culture* (pp. 67–99). London: Falmer Press.

Dewar, A. and Lawson, H. (1984). The subjective warrant and recruitment into physical education. *Quest*, 36(1): 15–25.

Dodds, P. (1979). *A peer assessment model for student teacher supervision.* Paper presented at the Research Quarterly.

Dodds, P. (1984). *Delusions of "worth-it-ness": Field experiences in elementary physical education programs.* Paper presented at the Physical Education Professional Preparation: Insights and Foresights, Orlando, Florida.

Dodds, P. (1993a). *Reflective teacher education (RTE): Paradigm for professional growth or only smoke and mirrors?* Paper presented at the AIESEP, Trois Riveres, Quebec, Canada.

Dodds, P. (1993b). Removing the ugly 'isms' in your gym: Thoughts for teachers on equity. In J. Evans (Ed.), *Equality, education and physical education* (pp. 28–42). London: Falmer Press.

Dodds, P. (1994). Cognitive and behavioral components of expertise in teaching physical education. *Quest*, 46: 153–163.

Dodds, P. (2002). *Third-stage professional socialization into the professoriate: Women sport pedagogy faculty experiences with doctoral programs.* Paper presented at the American Educational Research Association, New Orleans, Louisiana.

Education Commission of the States. (2000). *New imperatives for teacher preparation.* Denver, CO.

Ennis, C.D. (1997). Defining the dreaded curriculum. In J.-M. Fernández-Balboa (Ed.), *Critical postmodernism in human movement, physical education and sport* (pp. 207–220). Albany, NY: State University of New York.

Evans, J. (2003a). Changing lifestyles: A major responsibility for physical education. *Education Links*, 66/67: 50–54.

Evans, J. (2003b). Physical education and health: A polemic or 'let them eat cake!' *European Physical Education Review*, 9(1): 97–101.

Evans, J., Davies, B. and Wright, J. (2004a). *Body knowledge and control: Studies in the sociology of education and physical culture.* London: Routledge.

Evans, J., Rich, E. and Davies, B., (2004b). The emperor's new clothes: Fat, thin, and overweight. The social fabrication of risk and ill health. *Journal of Teaching in Physical Education*, 23: 372–391.

Feiman-Nemser, S. (1990). Teacher preparation: Structural and conceptual alternatives. In R. Houston (Ed.), *Handbook of research on teacher education* (pp. 3–24). New York: MacMillan.

Feiman-Nemser, S. and Parker, M. B. (1990). Making subject matter part of the conversation in learning to teach. *Journal of Teacher Education*, 41: 32–43.

Feiman-Nemser, S. and Remillard, J. (1996). Perspectives on learning to teach. In F.B. Murray (Ed.), *The teacher educator's handbook: Building a knowledge base for the preparation of teachers* (pp. 63–91). San Francisco, CA: Jossey-Bass.

Fernández-Balboa, J.-M. (1995). Reclaiming physical education in higher education through critical pedagogy. *Quest*, 47(1): 91–114.

Fernández-Balboa, J.-M. (1997a). *Critical postmodernism in human movement, physical education, and sport.* Albany, NY: State University of New York.

Fernández-Balboa, J.-M. (1997b). Knowledge base in physical education teacher education: A proposal for a new era. *Quest*, 49(2): 161–181.

Fitzclarence, L. and Tinning, R. (1990). Challenging hegemonic physical education: Contextualizing physical education as an examinable subject. In D. Kirk and R. Tinning (Eds.), *Physical education, curriculum and culture* (pp. 169–191). London: Falmer Press.

Flintoff, A. and Scranton, S. (2001). Stepping into active leisure? Young women's perceptions of active lifestyles and their experiences of school physical education. *Sport, Education and Society*, 6: 5–22.

Forrester, V. (2003). Tertiary learning: The case of student teachers in self-research. In Y.C. Cheng, K.W. Chow and K.T. Tsui (Eds.), *New teacher education for the future: International perspectives.* Hong Kong: Kluwer Academic Publishers.

Graber, K.C. (1995). The influence of teacher education programs on the beliefs of student teachers: General pedagogical knowledge, pedagogical content knowledge, and teacher education course work. *Journal of Teaching in Physical Education*, 14(2): 157–178.

Graber, K.C. (1996). Influencing student beliefs: The design of a "high impact" teacher education program. *Teaching and Teacher Education*, 12(5): 451–466.

Graham, K.C. (1991). The influence of teacher education on preservice development: beyond a custodial orientation. *Quest*, 43: 1–19.

Griffey, D. (1987). Trouble for sure, a crisis perhaps. *Journal of Physical Education, Recreation and Dance*, 39: 174–178.

Griffin, L. and Dodds, P. (1996). Pedagogical content knowledge for teachers. *Journal of Physical Education, Recreation & Dance*, 67(9): 58.

Griffin, L., Mitchell, S. and Oslin, J. (1997). *Teaching sport concepts and skills: A tactical games approach.* Champaign, IL: Human Kinetics.

Griffin, P. (1985). Teachers' perceptions of and responses to sex equity problems in a middle school physical education program. *Research Quarterly for Exercise and Sport*, 56(2): 103–110.

Hammerness, K., Darling-Hammond, L. and Shulman, L. (2002). Towards expert thinking: How case-writing contributes to the development of theory-based professional knowledge in student-teachers. *Teaching Education*, 13(2): 219–243.

Hardy, C.A. (1999). Preservice teachers' perceptions of learning to teach in a predominantly school-based teacher education program. *Journal of Teaching in Physical Education*, 18(2): 175–198.

Hebert, E. and Worthy, T. (2001). Does the first year of teaching have to be a bad one? *Teaching and Teacher Education*, 17: 897–911.

Hellison, D. (1997). A practical inquiry into the critical-postmodernist perspective in physical education. In J.-M. Fernandez-Balboa (Ed.), *Critical postmodernism in human movement, physical education, and sport* (pp. 197–205). Albany, NY: State University of New York Press.

Hoffman, S. (1988a). The Holmes Group and 5th year licensure. In *Big Ten Leadership Conference Report* (pp. 61–71). Champaign, IL: Human Kinetics.

Hoffman, S. (1998b). The dispersal of the department at Teachers College: The Diaspora continues. *Chronicle of Physical Education in Higher Education*, 9(2): 1, 12–13.

Holmes Group. (1986). Tomorrow's teachers: A report of the Holmes Group. East Lansing, MI.

Howey, K. and Zimpher, N. (1989). *Profiles of preservice teacher education: Inquiry into the nature of programs.* Albany, NY: SUNY Press.

Hutchinson, G. and Buschner, C. (1996). Delayed-entry undergraduates in physical education teacher education: Examining life experiences and career choice. *Journal of Teaching in Physical Education*, 15(2): 205–223.

Ingersoll, R. (2003). *Is there really a teacher shortage?* University of Pennsylvania: CTP Research Report.

Jenkins, J.M. and Veal, M.L. (2002). Preservice teachers' PCK development during peer coaching. *Journal of Teaching in Physical Education*, 22(1): 49–68.

Johns, D.P. and Dimmock, C. (1999). The marginalization of physical education: Impoverished curriculum policy and practice in Hong Kong. *Journal of Educational Policy*, 14(4), 363–384.

Joyce, B. and Weil, M. (1996). *Models of teaching* (5th ed.). Englewood Cliffs, NJ: Prentice-Hall.

Kahan, D. (1998). When everyone gets what they want: A description of a physical education-teacher education service-learning project. *Action in Teacher Education*, 19(4): 43–60.

Kinchin, G. and O'Sullivan, M. (2003). Incidences of student support for and resistance to a curricular innovation in high school physical education. *Journal of Teaching in Physical Education*, 22(3): 245–260.

Kirk, D. (1992). *Defining physical education: The social construction of a school subject in Postwar Britain.* London: The Falmer Press.

Kirk, D. and Macdonald, D. (1998). Situated learning in physical education. *Journal of Teaching in Physical Education*, 17(3): 376–387.

Kirk, D. and Macdonald, D. (1999). Imagining beyond the present: Recent developments and future prospects for physical education in Australian primary schools. *Teaching Elementary Physical Education*, 10(6): 25–28.

Kirk, D. and Macdonald, D. (2001). The social construction of PETE in higher education: Toward a research agenda. *Quest*, 53(4): 440–456.

Kirk, D. and Tinning, R. (1990). *Physical education, curriculum, and culture: Critical issues in the contemporary crisis*. London: Falmer Press.

Knop, N., LaMaster, K., Norris, M., Raudensky, J. and Tannehill, D. (1997). What we have learned through collaboration: A summary report from a National Teacher Education, *Physical Educator* (Vol. 54, pp. 170–181).

Laker, A. (2003). *The future of physical education: building a new pedagogy*. London: Routledge.

Laker, A., Laker, J.C. and Lea, S. (2003). School experience and the issue of gender. *Sport, Education and Society*, 8(1): 73–89.

LaMaster, K.J. (2001). Enhancing preservice teachers field experiences through the addition of a service-learning component. *Journal of Experiential Education*, 24(1): 27–33.

Lave, J. and Wenger, E. (1991). *Situated learning: Legitimate peripheral participation*. New York: Cambridge University Press.

Lawson, H. (1983). Toward a model of teacher socialization in physical education: the subjective warrant, recruitment and teacher education. *Journal of Teaching in Physical Education*, 2(3): 3–16.

Lawson, H. (1990). Beyond positivism: Research, practice, and undergraduate professional education. *Quest*, 42(2): 161–183.

Lawson, H. (1993). Dominant discourses, problem-setting, and teacher education pedagogies: A critique. *Journal of Teaching in Physical Education*, 12: 149–160.

Lee, M. and O'Sullivan, M. (2004). Physical educators must collaborate to improve physical education policy in Ohio. *Future Focus*, 25(2): 13–19.

Levin, B. and Rock, T. (2003). The effects of collaborative action research on preservice and experienced teacher partners in professional development schools. *Journal of Teacher Education*, 54(2): 135–149.

Locke, L. (2003). *Preparing teachers to grab the brass ring: Lessons from the carousel at Missoula*. Paper presented at the Physical education teacher education conference, Baton Rouge, Louisiana. Retrieved October 2004 from http://www.unlockresearch.com/content/article/8/0/

Locke, L., Mand, C. and Siedentop, D. (1981). The preparation of physical education teachers: A subject-matter-centered model. In *Progress through diversity* (pp. 33–54). Washington, DC: American Alliance of Health, Physical Education, and Dance.

Locke, R., Minarik, L. and Omata, J. (1999). Gender and the problem of diversity: Action research in physical education. *Quest*, 51: 393–407.

Lortie, D. (1975). *Schoolteacher: A sociological study*. Chicago, IL: University of Chicago Press.

Lumpkin, A. (2002). *Introduction to physical education, exercise science, and sport studies* (5th ed.). New York: McGraw-Hill.

Macdonald, D. (1995). The role of proletarianization in physical education teacher attrition. *Research Quarterly for Exercise and Sport*, 66(2): 129–141.

Macdonald, D. (1998). Who are "you"? Identity and religion in physical education teacher education. *Sociology of sport online*, 1(1).

Macdonald, D., Abernathy, P. and Bramich, K. (1998). A profile of first-year Human Movement Studies Students: A case study in Australia. *Chronicle of Physical Education in Higher Education*, 9(2): 7, 16–19.

MacDonald, D., Hunter, L., Carlson, T. and Penney, D. (2002). Teacher knowledge and the disjunction between school curricula and teacher education, *Asia-Pacific Journal of Teacher Education* (Vol. 30, pp. 259–275).

Macdonald, D. and Tinning, R. (2003). Reflective practice goes public: Reflection, governmentality and postmodernity. In A. Laker (Ed.), *The future of physical education: Building a new pedagogy* (pp. 82–101). London: Routledge.

Martens, F. (1987). Selection of physical education students and success in student teaching. *Journal of Teaching in Physical Education*, 6(4): 411–424.

Martinek, T. and Hellison, D. (1997). Service bonded inquiry: The road less traveled. *Journal of Teaching in Physical Education*, 17(1): 107–121.

Matanin, M. and Collier, C. (2003). Longitudinal analysis of preservice teachers' beliefs about teaching physical education. *Journal of Teaching in Physical Education*, 22(2): 153–168.

McCaughtry, N. (2004). The emotional dimensions of a teacher's pedagogical content knowledge: Influences on content, curriculum, and pedagogy. *Journal of Teaching in Physical Education*, 23: 30–47.

McCaughtry, N. and Rovegno, I. (2003). Development of Pedagogical Content Knowledge: Moving from Blaming Students to Predicting Skillfulness, Recognizing Motor Development, and Understanding Emotion. *Journal of Teaching in Physical Education*, 22: 355–368.

McCullick, B.A. and Lomax, M. (2000). The Boston normal school of gymnastics: An unheralded legacy. *Quest*, 52(1): 49–59.

McKay, J., Gore, J. M. and Kirk, D. (1990). Beyond the limits of technocratic physical education. *Quest*, 42: 52–76.

McKay, J., Gore, J. and Kirk, D. (1990). Beyond the technocratic limits of physical education. *Quest*, 42(1): 52–76.

McNeill, M., Sproule, J. and Horton, P. (2003). The changing face of sport and physical education in post-colonial Singapore. *Sport, Education and Society*, 8(1): 35–56.

Melnychuk, N. (2001). A cohort practicum model: Physical education student teachers' experience. *Alberta Journal of Educational Research*, 47(3): 259–275.

Merriam-Webster, I. (2004). *Merriam-Webster On-line Dictionary*.

Merseth, K. (1996). Cases and case methods in teacher education. In J. Sikula, T. Buttery and E. Guyten (Eds.),

Handbook of research in teacher education (2nd ed., pp. 722–744). New York: Macmillan.

Metzler, M. (2000). *Instructional models for physical education*. Boston: Allyn and Bacon.

Metzler, M. and Tjeerdsma, B. (2000). The physical education teacher education assessment project. *Journal of Teaching in Physical Education, 19*(4): 1–556.

Mitchell, S., Oslin, J. and Griffin, L. (2003). *Sport foundations for elementary physical education: A tactical games approach*. Champaign, IL: Human Kinetics.

National Commission on Teaching and America's Future. (1997). *What matters most: Teaching for America's future*. New York.

National Commission on Teaching and America's Future. (2003). *No dream denied: A pledge to America's children*. Washington, D. C.

National Education Association. (2000–2001). *The status of American public school teacher*. Washington, D. C.

Naul, R. (2002). Physical education teacher training. In R. Naul and K. Hardman (Eds.), *Sport and physical education in Germany* (pp. 99–112). London: Routledge.

O'Bryant, C. (1996). *Choosing physical education as a profession: Stories of three African American women*. Unpublished Dissertation (Ph.D.), Ohio State University, Ohio State University, 1996, Columbus, OH.

O'Bryant, C., O'Sullivan, M. and Raudensky, J. (2000). Socialization of prospective physical education teachers: The story of new blood. *Sport, Education and Society, 5*: 177–193.

Oliver, K.L. (2001). Images of the body from popular culture: Engaging girls in critical inquiry. *Sport, Education and Society, 6*(2): 143–164.

Oliver, K.L., and Lalik, R. (2004). The beauty walk: Interrogating whiteness as the norm for beauty within one school's hidden curriculum. In J. Evans, B. Davies and J. Wright (Eds.), *Body knowledge and control: studies in the sociology of Physical Education and Health* (pp. 115–129). London: Routledge.

Oslin, J. and Collier, C. (2003). *Redefining student teaching*. Paper presented at the Physical Education Teacher Education Conference, Baton Rouge, LA.

Oslin, J., Collier, C. and Mitchell, S. (2001). Living the curriculum. *Journal of Physical Education, Recreation and Dance, 72*(5): 47–51.

O'Sullivan, M. (1989). Failing gym is like failing lunch or recess: Two beginning teachers' struggle for legitimacy. *Journal of Teaching in Physical Education, 8*: 227–242.

O'Sullivan, M. (1990). Physical education teacher education in the United States. *Journal of Physical Education, Recreation and Dance, 61*(2): 41, 43.

O'Sullivan, M. (2003). Learning to teach physical education. In S.J. Silverman and C.D. Ennis (Eds.), *Student learning in physical education: Applying research to enhance instruction*. Champaign, IL: Human Kinetics.

O'Sullivan, M. (2004). Possibilities and pitfalls of a public health agenda for physical education. *Journal of Teaching in Physical Education, 23*: 392–404.

O'Sullivan, M. and Kinchin, G. (2005). Cultural perspectives. In J. Lund and D. Tannehill (Eds.), *Standards-based curriculum development in physical education*. Sudbury, MA: Jones and Bartlett.

O'Sullivan, M., Siedentop, D. and Locke, L. (1992). Toward collegiality: Competing viewpoints among teacher educators. *Quest, 44*(2): 266–280.

O'Sullivan, M. and Tsangaridou, N. (1997). The role of reflection in shaping physical education teachers' educational values and practices. *Journal of Teaching in Physical Education, 17*(1): 2–25.

Paige, R. (2001). *No child left behind: A blueprint for education reform*. Washington, DC: Eric Document Reproduction Service.

Parker, M., Doty, J., Collins, D., Black, J. and Drake, J., Grable, K. (2004). *Service learning, youth sport, and graduate education: A trio for learning*. Paper presented at the American Alliance of Health, Physical Education, Recreation, and Dance, New Orleans, LA.

Penney, D. and Chandler, T. (2000). Physical education: What future(s)? *Sport, Education and Society, 5*(1): 71–87.

Penney, D. and Evans, J. (1999). *Politics, policy, and practice in physical education*. London; New York: E & FN Spon.

Petersen, S., Burne, H. and Cruz, L. (2003). The reality of fitness for pre-service teachers: What physical education majors 'know and can do'. *Physical Educator, 60*(1): 5–14.

Placek, J., Dodds, P., Doolittle, S., Portman, P., Ratliffe, T. and Pinkman, K. (1995). Teaching recruits' physical education backgrounds and beliefs about purposes for their subject matter. *Journal of Teaching in Physical Education, 14*: 246–261.

Placek, J. and Griffin, L. (2001). The understanding and development of learners' domain-specific knowledge: concluding comments. *Journal of Teaching in Physical Education, 20*(4): 401–406.

Randall, L.E. (1986). Employment statistics. A national survey in public school physical education. *Journal of Physical Education, Recreation and Dance, 57*(1): 23–28.

Richert, A. (1991). Case method and teacher education: Using cases to teach teacher reflection. In B. Tabachnick and K. Zeichner (Eds.), *Issues and practices in inquiry-oriented teacher education* (pp. 130–150). London: Falmer Press.

Rink, J.E. (1993). Teacher education: A focus on action. *Quest, 45*: 308–320.

Rovegno, I. (1992). Learning to teach in a field-based methods course: The development of pedagogical content knowledge. *Teaching and Teacher Education, 8*(1): 69–82.

Rovegno, I. (1993). Content knowledge acquisition during undergraduate teacher education: Overcoming cultural templates and learning through practice. *American Educational Research Journal, 30*(3): 611–642.

Sage, G. (2003). Foreword. In A. Laker (Ed.), *The future of physical education: Building a new pedagogy*. London: Routledge.

Schon, D. (1987). *Educating the reflective practitioner*. San Francisco, CA: Jossey-Bass.

Shen, J. (1998). Alternative certification, minority teachers, and urban education. *Education and Urban Society, 31*(1): 30–41.

Shulman, L.S. (1986). Those who understand: knowledge growth in teaching. *Educational Researcher, 15*: 4–14.

Shulman, L.S. (1987). Knowledge and teaching: Foundations of the new reform. *Harvard Educational Review, 57*(1): 1–22.

Siedentop, D. (1994). *Sport education: Quality PE through positive sport experiences.* Champaign, IL: Human Kinetics.

Siedentop, D. (2002). Content knowledge for physical education. *Journal of Teaching in Physical Education, 21*(4): 368–377.

Siedentop, D. and Tannehill, D. (2000). *Developing teaching skills in physical education* (Vol. 4th). Mountainview, CA: Mayfield.

Sparkes, A. (1999). Exploring body narratives. *Sport, Education and Society, 4*(1): 17–30.

Sparkes, A. (2000). Autoethnography and narratives of self: Reflection on criteria in action. *Sociology of Sport Journal, 17*: 21–43.

Stanley, L.S. (1997). Preservice physical educators' attitudes toward cultural Pluralism: A preliminary analysis. *Journal of Teaching in Physical Education, 16*(2): 241.

Stroot, S., Collier, C., O'Sullivan, M. and England, K. (1994). Contextual hoops and hurdles: Workplace conditions in secondary physical education. *Journal of Teaching in Physical Education, 13*: 342–360.

Tang, S. (2003). Challenge and support: the dynamics of student teachers' professional learning. *Teaching and Teacher Education, 19*: 483–498.

Tannehill, D. (1989). Student teaching: A view from the other side. *Journal of Teaching in Physical Education, 8*(3): 243–253.

Templin, T., Woodford, R. and Mulling, C. (1982). On becoming a physical educator: Occupational choice and the anticipatory socialization process. *Quest, 34*: 119–133.

The Abell Foundation. (2001). *Teacher certification reconsidered: Stumbling for quality.* Baltimore, MA: Abell Foundation.

Thomas, K.T. (2004). Riding to the rescue while holding on by a thread: Physical activity in schools. *Quest, 56*: 150–170.

Tinning, R. (1991). Teacher education pedagogy: Dominant discourses and the process of problem setting. *Journal of Teaching in Physical Education, 11*(1): 1–20.

Tinning, R. (1992). Reading action research: Notes on knowledge and human interests. *Quest, 44*(1): 1–14.

Tinning, R. (1997). Performance and participation discourses in human movement: Toward a socially critical physical education. In J.-M. Fernández-Balboa (Ed.), *Critical postmodernism in human movement, physical education, and sport* (pp. 99–119). Albany: NY: State University of New York.

Tinning, R. (2000). Unsettling matters for physical education in higher education: implications of "new times." *Quest, 52*(1): 32–48.

Tinning, R. (2001). A review of research on physical education teacher and coach education (1998–2000). *International Journal of Physical Education*, 3–16.

Tinning, R. (2002a). Engaging Siedentopian perspectives on content knowledge for physical education. *Journal of Teaching in Physical Education, 21*(4): 378–391.

Tinning, R. (2002b). Toward a "modest pedagogy": Reflections on the problematics of critical pedagogy. *Quest, 54*(3): 224–240.

Tinning, R. (2004). Conclusion: Ruminations on body knowledge and control and the spaces for hope and happening. In J. Evans, B. Davies and J. Wright (Eds.), *Body knowledge and control: Studies in the sociology of physical education and health* (pp. 218–238). London: Routledge.

Tsangaridou, N. and O'Sullivan, M. (1994). Using pedagogical reflective strategies to enhance reflection among preservice physical education teachers. *Journal of Teaching in Physical Education, 14*(1): 13–33.

Tsangaridou, N. and O'Sullivan, M. (2003). Physical education teachers' theories of action and theories-in-use. *Journal of Teaching in Physical Education, 22*(2): 132–152.

Van Manen, M. (1977). Linking ways of knowing with ways of being practical. *Curriculum Inquiry, 6*: 205–228.

Valian, V. (2004). Creating equity. *Gender Equity Project.* Retrieved on November 15, 2004 from http://www.hunter.cuny.edu/genderequity/resources.html

Veal, M.L. and Rikard, L. (1998). Cooperating teachers' perspectives on the student teaching triad. *Journal of Teacher Education, 49*(1): 108–119.

Walton, T. and LaVine, M. (2005). *Competes (Challenging obesity: Media powered experiences to engage students).* Presentation at the American Alliance of Health, Physical Education, Recreation, and Dance Annual Conference in Chicago, IL.

Wendt, J.C. and Bain, L.L. (1989). Concerns of preservice and inservice physical educators. *Journal of Teaching in Physical Education, 8*(2): 177–180.

Wilson, S., Floden, R. and Ferrini-Mundy, J. (2001). *Teacher preparation research: Current knowledge, gaps, and recommendations.* Seattle, Washington: Center for the Study of Teaching and Policy in collaboration with Michigan State University.

Wilson, S., Floden, R. and Ferrini-Mundy, J. (2002). Teacher preparation research: An insider's view from the outside. *Journal of Teacher Education, 53*: 190–204.

Wright, J. (1997). The construction of gendered contexts in single-sex and co-educational physical education lessons. *Sport, Education and Society, 2*(1): 55–72.

Yinger, R. (1999). *Models of Teacher Education.* Retrieved January 25, 2004, from http://www3.baylor.edu/SOE/Models/sld015.htm

You, J. and McCullick, B.A. (2001). Rethinking and reconstructing of early field experiences in physical education teacher education. *International Journal of Physical Education, 38*(1): 24–33.

Zeichner, K. (2003). The adequacies and inadequacies of the three current strategies to recruit, prepare, and retain the best teachers for all students. *The Teachers College Record, 105*(3): 490–519.

4.3   Learning to teach in the field

DANIËL BEHETS AND LIEVEN VERGAUWEN

Introduction

Reviews on specific subsets of the literature do not stand alone and can build on existing precursors. For this handbook on physical education and in the section on teacher education, we can rely on handbooks on generic research on teachers and teacher education (Houston, 1990; Richardson, 2001; Sikula et al., 1996) and on specific reviews of the field of physical education (Bain, 1990; Graber, 2001; O'Sullivan, 1996, 2003; Rovegno, 2003; Silverman and Ennis, 1996, 2003). With respect to the generalizability of classroom research, scholars in physical education have built upon this general body of knowledge. We began our review in the 1990s. The main point of this chapter is to investigate the role of field experiences in the development of prospective teachers (PTs). Our analysis of the available literature will reveal the current state of research on field experience and provide suggestions for future research as well as program reform. Within the constraints of this chapter we limit ourselves to field experiences as an integral part of the teacher preparation program.

The finding that a theoretical framework or clear set of goals is missing in teacher education programs as a whole applies also the development and implementation of field experiences (McIntyre et al., 1996). The historical ineffectiveness of teacher education may be due to the disjointedness of program goals and curricula. The setting of national standards for teacher education across the world (National Association for Sport and Physical Education standards in the US: NASPE, 2001; Post Graduate Certificate of Education in the UK: Hardy, 1999) can compel teacher educators to adopt models with purposes, processes, and outcomes of teacher education programs. There appears to be a trend emerging toward programs that develop teachers who are reflective decision makers, not mere technicians, resulting in a movement where the positivist orientation is broadened with a more constructivist approach. Student-teachers within

this framework will learn from relevant problematic situations in which the learner makes decisions. This emergence of constructivist teacher education programs has resulted in a movement toward developing reflective teachers, or reflective practitioners. This new focus will lead to the restructuring of all field experiences. PTs will not only practice reflectivity and perform reflective assignments, but also observe experienced teachers practicing reflectivity. The traditional conflict between theory and practice in teacher education programs is felt most strongly in the area of field experiences. When student teaching is seen as an apprenticeship, student-teachers are expected to copy their mentor teacher. When, on the other hand, student teaching is a laboratory experience, student-teachers try out different ways of teaching, reflect on the outcomes and make modifications accordingly.

Reviewing research in the field of physical education teacher preparation requires knowledge of certain specific historical perspectives. Bain (1990) summarized the following elements influencing PETE research: the marginal status of physical education in schools and universities, the segregation by sex of the physical education programs, and the dominant sport culture shaping the experiences of physical education teachers (coaches) and their students. Although the field is in transition, this picture is still valid and we wonder if PETE is still more traditional than conceptual.

Introducing the context of field experiences

The school – the place to be – constitutes the rich environment where PTs will learn a great deal of their job. Although the placement of PTs in schools is crucial in teacher preparation, too often it is based on convenience rather than on any other consideration of what would provide a quality learning experience (McIntyre et al., 1996). The ecology of the school setting – pupils, physical environment, curriculum, and community – is a major influence on PTs development, and all too frequently this influence is not positive. Revealing several benefits for early field experiences, we also identify several interfering factors. In a physical education setting, teacher educators are aware of potentially more difficult and complex learning environments in schools, such as large classes with heterogeneous groups of students (skill, race, gender, …), poorly equipped gym rooms, no existing curricular planning, inadequate physical education departments, absence of managerial rules and routines. We will discuss the major role of the cooperating teachers in the student teaching context as individual teachers with their own beliefs and conceptions, as members of the school team and the physical education department, and in collaboration with the university teachers and the PTs.

Efforts to transform the student teaching context include the so-called professional development schools, introducing cohort groups of students who proceed through their field experiences together, increasing the number and variety of teaching sites, and the implementation of reflective field experience programs (McIntyre et al., 1996).

Some of the disadvantages of increasing the number and length of field experiences could be socializing novice teachers, adjusting to routines, and encouraging inappropriate behaviors. Hardy (1999) argued that the quality of the field experiences can be affected by the variability of the mentor processes and different school contexts. Increasing the length of school-based experiences is replacing complexity with simplicity. Only part of the job of teaching is learned through field experiences. Despite the overwhelming positive feelings about the efficacy of field experiences, there are insufficient research data to suggest or to give preference to any particular format of school teaching practice. It appears that what occurs during the field experience is more important than the length of that experience (McIntyre et al., 1996). Increased practice alone does not always lead to analysis, reflection, and growth on the part of the novice teacher (Hardy, 1999). Even when teacher educators can modify their traditional formats for teaching practices, research on the effects of the various components is minimal at the present.

Historical perspective

The history of field experiences in student teaching is closely related to the development and evolution of supervisory models. From the beginning systematic supervision has been accepted to be an integral part of the student teaching experience. This is taken as evidence that student teaching is the most important part of teacher preparation, and that changes in teacher behavior are not always in the desirable direction. Several models of supervision have been described (Randall, 1992) and vary

according to the focus or content of supervision together with the style of supervision. This evolution is parallel to the shift in research paradigms in sport pedagogy. Early supervisory models emphasized observable teaching behaviors which were closely related to teacher effectiveness. Supervisors were expected to observe, control, and redirect the teaching behaviors of their student teachers in a directive approach, based on quantitative data (Metzler, 1990). This approach resulted in objective teaching standards and teacher competencies with different models of clinical supervision.

A shift in the research from behavior analysis to studying teacher thoughts and cognitions was accompanied by more individually adapted counseling approaches for the supervisors in the teacher education programs. In this approach teacher competencies are broadened with reflective abilities leading to the production of reflective and critical practitioners. The focus of teacher education is redirected from effective teacher behaviors to the knowledge base of the prospective teacher, including their thought processes and decisions. Pedagogical content knowledge and teachers' practical knowledge are the features under study (Calderhead, 1996; Rovegno, 1993). This eclectic approach is characterized by combining supervision with self-analysis and peer evaluation based on teacher competencies, and modeling the reflective practitioner.

When field experiences are conceptualized as apprenticeship, supervisors assist students in acquiring teaching techniques. The second conception is more akin to a laboratory experience where the student teacher receives supervisory assistance in developing skills for personal inquiry and reflection about actual teaching.

Core concepts

Field experiences for physical education students during teacher preparation are also called prior or early teaching experiences, teaching practice or practicum, and student teaching. Early field experiences typically begin with school visits, structured observations in the gymnasium, discussions with teachers, tutoring of individual students. Eventually they include teaching parts of lessons to small groups of students. Placement in the school is limited, and most usually of short duration. Student teaching involves more extended practice in one setting and a progressive increase to full-scale teaching responsibility for the student-teacher in particular classes. Field experiences vary on the timing within the program where the initial placement occurs, the number and variety of placements, the duration and total number of hours, the frequency of visits by supervisors, and the evaluation procedures.

Student teaching is the critical element in teacher education programs, as it is the place where teacher competencies are developed. This immediately induces the tension between theory and practice, as exemplified by the organization, the content and the persons involved in this learning environment.

The integration of learning experiences for prospective teachers has been influenced by new insights in learning psychology. The organization of the teaching practicum within the framework of the teacher education program involves struggling to keep the balance between theoretical courses and the on-campus and the in-school experiences and with questions about consecutive or concurrent scheduling of lessons about theory and practice. The length of the teaching practicum has long been and continues to be a point of argument. Meanwhile discriminating and differentiating between good and bad teaching remains essential for effective learning. The content of learning experiences is focused on practical teaching skills within the competency based teacher education model. It can be broadened to encompass teachers' cognition and knowledge as characterized by the use of the term "reflective practitioner".

All participants, preservice teachers (PTs) or student-teachers, university teachers (UTs), and mentors or cooperating teachers (CTs) are in full agreement that the teaching practicum is the most important and effective learning experience in a physical education teacher education (PETE) program. It should be noted that this triad itself also creates some tensions. The dominant influence of the CT pushes the student teacher into an apprenticeship model where he is told what to do and how to do it. There the attention is focused on actual teaching problems, leaving little space for experimenting with new ideas and restricting the use of innovative teaching approaches. The need for selection and training of CTs is urgent, as the role of the university supervisor is limited due to the low frequency of visits. Reflective strategies are prefered for the processes of mentoring and supervision which is congruent with the professionalization of teacher education.

Within all these tensions and discussions one convergent idea has the potential to address some of the problems. Collaboration between secondary schools and universities, between CTs and UTs has been concretized in the concept of the "professional development schools" (PDS). The PDS can bridge theory and practice, and can offer student teachers opportunities to experience good theories in practice.

Development of teachers' professional knowledge

Beginning teacher competencies can be conceptualized in the preactive, interactive and postactive teaching tasks (Behets, 2000; Graber, 2001;

Reynolds, 1992). Kagan (1992) defined the professional growth as changes over time in the behavior, knowledge, images, beliefs, or perceptions of PTs. Field experiences are considered an essential part of the teacher preparation program with plenteous positive and negative experiences for the PTs. The recent literature in cognitive psychology and on learning-to-teach research provides a conceptual framework for exploring teacher development in terms of a constructivist approach (Richardson, 1997). This cognitive movement has resulted in a shift of the focus of attention in the research on teaching from teachers' behaviors to the underlying teachers' cognitions. This change was also stimulated by qualitative research methods. The cognitive concepts of teachers' knowledge and beliefs raised questions like: what constitutes teachers' professional knowledge, how it might be represented, how it relates to practice (Calderhead, 1996), as well as what is the nature of teachers' knowledge and how it is constructed (Rovegno, 2003)? In the next section we focus on knowledge development of teachers, especially the kind of knowledge structures which changes during field experiences.

Recent studies on teacher education have labeled teachers' knowledge with different categories. Pedagogical content knowledge has gradually evolved into a generic term for teachers' professional knowledge (Amade-Escot, 2000).

Two major types of teacher knowledge are distinguished. Formal knowledge, primarily produced by the researcher, is described as knowledge for the teacher. Practical knowledge is knowledge of the teachers and is generated by the teachers themselves as a result of their teaching experiences and their reflections. It is an amalgam of all of the teachers' cognitions, such as declarative and procedural knowledge, beliefs, and values, which influences their preactive, interactive and postactive teaching activities (Zanting et al., 2001).

Within the constructivist approach a crucial learning outcome of PTs' field experiences should be the development of practical knowledge. A description of the main features of this type of knowledge illuminates its complex nature (Meijer, 1999; Rovegno, 2003).

- Each teacher's practical knowledge is unique and describes the idiosyncratic nature of what a teacher knows. It reflects an individual teacher's biography, values, knowledge, and experiences in the school context and reflects personal and emotional dimensions.
- Teachers' practical knowledge is based on experience; it develops with experience in school settings. Reflection on experience is an important aspect of the nature of teachers' practical knowledge.
- This kind of practical knowledge is typically implicit or tacit, and teachers may not know they have it or find it difficult to articulate.

- Practical knowledge is a product of the activities and situations in which it is produced. The individual, the activity and the environment are interrelated and will be treated as a unit. Knowledge is always under construction and is acquired in specific situations. It is contextually developed knowledge.
- Practical knowledge guides teachers' actions in their classroom.
- Practical knowledge is content-related; it is connected with the subject that is taught.

Understanding the nature of teachers' practical knowledge, researchers examined how this knowledge is constructed and is developing during field experiences.

A constructivist approach to teacher education

A constructivist approach to teaching and learning in teacher education has been widely accepted by many researchers in the field (Richardson, 1997). Teachers build new knowledge on the basis of their prior knowledge and experiences, they actively construct new meanings. The traditional approach – the transmission model – promotes the passive intake of new information (listening to others or reading a textbook) and doesn't explain the relations between prior and new knowledge, involving an active engagement of the learner. In the framework of the complex nature of constructivist theories we describe the development of teachers' knowledge during field experiences, with respect to the role of prior knowledge, the influence of others in social constructivism, the relevance of formal knowledge, teachers' knowledge of themselves, and of their students.

Preservice teachers' prior knowledge

As constructivist theory describes new knowledge is built on pre-existing knowledge and experiences. PTs already have experiential knowledge and beliefs about teaching and physical education. This prior knowledge is influenced by the long history of the PT as a student. These cognitions, called preconceptions, are often misconceptions and can constrain the development of new knowledge. Teacher educators have to address these "preconceptions" in order to reconstruct the professional knowledge base (Allison et al., 2000; Kagan, 1992; Rovegno, 2003).

Mayer-Smith and Mitchell (1997) found many teacher education programs adopting the constructivist perspective. They emphasized that such an approach involves considerable conceptual change to the training program. The beliefs of PTs were influential in mediating this process. The scholars reported mixed results in promoting changes in PTs' beliefs and practices. Reasons cited included the short duration of course and program interventions, the critical timing of field and university experiences, conflicting pedagogical perspectives at universities and schools, academic backgrounds of the candidates, mismatches in the theories and strategies espoused in teacher education programs, and the powerful socializing influence of the school culture. Winitzky and Kauchak (1997) advocate openly challenging teacher candidates' misconceptions about teaching and learning in discussion seminars. Teacher educators need more knowledge about the prior knowledge of their students. Reviewing the studies on PTs' growth Kagan (1992) documented the stability and inflexibility of preexisting beliefs and images in early teacher education programs. She concluded that prior beliefs must be modified and reconstructed as a prerequisite for professional growth. A more recent review on learning to teach (Wideen et al., 1998) supports the findings that teacher education programs have little effect upon the firmly held beliefs of the beginning teachers; it also provides examples of successful programs. Deep and meaningful cognitive changes in PTs are difficult to realize, and without changes in beliefs changes in performance will be superficial (Richardson and Placier, 2001).

Prior knowledge and experiences in particular subject matters and sport can have equally positive or negative effects on the learner. In summarizing the literature in physical education, Rovegno (2003) stated that prior knowledge and experiences sometimes constrain teachers' knowledge construction and sometimes do not. Within the concept of recognizing and redirecting PTs' prior knowledge and beliefs Allison et al. (2000) argue for the development of epistemological bases that direct goals, curriculum, instructional practices, and evaluation processes and that interact with the views of the PTs. Insisting on the importance of strong PETE programs, they focused on the construct of skillfulness as a main goal of physical education in schools. Rovegno (1993) illustrates the difficulties of PTs when learning a new movement approach, their prior knowledge being a major resource of confusion. The lack of teacher program impact on prospective physical educator recruits' beliefs is illustrated by the fact that PTs filter new experiences through the screen of their earlier belief systems (Graham, 1991; Doolittle et al., 1993; Matanin and Collier, 2003).

The social constructivist context

Where the first issue of prior knowledge was found in the PTs, the second issue of constructivism can be found in the learning context. The process of constructing and reconstructing meaning is either guided by the individual itself or by the interaction of different individuals. The social constructivist approach is suited for the early teaching experiences of PTs. The sociocultural context is formed with the CTs, the UTs and the school context (Richardson, 1997). Rovegno (2003) reviewed the role of the school context in knowledge construction in physical education. The community, peers and administrators, and also the students can have positive or negative effects on teachers' knowledge development. The main theme emerging from the research on the practicum setting is the tension between teacher educators and PTs in their attempts to bridge the cultures of the school and the university (Wideen et al., 1998). The CTs' practical knowledge conflicts with the formal knowledge of the university supervisors. The PTs move somewhere in between, teaching in a curricular zone of safety (Rovegno, 1994). The tension between the demands to experiment with nontraditional teaching strategies and the reality of the conservative school system typically brings the PTs to routine rather than reflective action. Research suggests close collaboration is needed between the participants in student teaching. Good examples of such applications can be found in the professional developmental schools (see Book, 1996), in teams consisting of CTs and PTs (Wideen et al., 1998), and in working groups of PTs (Korthagen, 2001).

Formal knowledge

To what extent PTs do need a base of formal knowledge when they start their teaching practicum? In the constructivist approach some researchers dispute the relevance of abstract knowledge derived from systematic studies to teacher education. When meaning is formed and reformed on the basis of an interaction between prior knowledge and new experiences, an individual's understanding will be more or less idiosyncratic. All practical knowledge is context-related. Knowledge from textbooks will be understood in many different ways (Richardson, 1997). The balance in importance for PTs between theoretical and practical knowledge is not yet clear. Research suggests that understanding of general principles provides the knowledge foundation that transfers to a variety of situations (Winitzky and Kauchak, 1997). Novice teachers should acquire procedural knowledge first, especially managerial routines and not theoretical knowledge (Kagan, 1992). Research findings do not support the implicit theoretical approach or the presentation of propositional knowledge as the basis of teacher education (Wideen et al., 1998).

Teachers' knowledge of themselves and of students

The central role played by a novice's image of himself as a teacher is summarized by Kagan (1992).

Candidates enter the teaching practicum with images of themselves as teachers that have been derived in part from their own experiences as learners. The growing knowledge of pupils and classrooms is used to adapt and reconstruct their images of self as a teacher. Without cognitive dissonance, knowledge acquired during preservice teacher education will be superficial. Only after novices resolve their images of self as teacher can they focus on students. Learning how to teach is a deeply personal activity in which the individuals concerned have to deal with their prior beliefs in the light of the expectations from a university, a school, and a society, and in the context of teaching (Wideen et al., 1996). Well-constructed early field experiences and student teaching can have a significant impact on PTs' perceptions of teaching and of themselves as teachers (O'Sullivan and Tsangaridou, 1992). The construction of knowledge about students during teaching practicum is inherent to a constructivist learning approach to teaching. This knowledge is an integral part of the pedagogical content knowledge and includes PTs' conceptions, beliefs, self-concept, learning styles and experiences (Reynolds, 1992). PTs have difficulty to integrate this knowledge in their preactive, interactive, and postactive teaching as they are primarily concerned with themselves (Behets, 1990). An inquiry-based approach can refocus and refine PTs on students' characteristics (Woods et al., 2000). When novices try to teach with little knowledge about students, the tendency is for them to grow increasingly authoritarian and custodial (Kagan, 1992). McCaughtry and Rovegno (2003) identified three main shifts in preservice physical education teachers' knowledge about students: predicting skill level of their students, recognizing motor development, and understanding student emotions.

Teacher development and field experiences

The essence of constructivism is the learners' knowledge building process. This process of change, growth, development or knowledge construction in individual teachers can be described as voluntary and naturalistic changes within stages of development, and as influenced by formal teacher preparation programs (Richardson and Placier, 2001).

Voluntary changes by teachers occur all the time and may be prompted, promoted, or supported by different kinds or sources of information. For the PTs the information resources are multiple. The personal contacts during the teaching practicum occur with peers, UTs and supervisors, CTs and students. They read books, articles, and other written materials. Their teaching knowledge is constructed with formal and practical knowledge. The direction of change is not always determined. Naturalistic research suggests that biography, experience, personality, and context play a role in the change choices that individuals make. These changes can lead to tacit or practical knowledge and become expressed only through reflection.

Different models of stages of development are described and shift from rigid and deterministic stages to more flexible stage theories. Kagan (1992) integrates Fuller's developmental model of teacher concerns and Berliner's model of teacher development from novice to expert teacher. Professional growth consists of at least five components:

- An increase in metacognition: Novices become aware of what they know about pupils and classrooms and how this knowledge is changing.
- The acquisition of knowledge about pupils: This knowledge is used to reconstruct the novice's image of self as teacher.
- A shift in attention from self to the design of instruction to pupil learning.
- The development of standard procedures and routines.
- Growth in problem solving ability.

Teacher development from preservice to novice and expert teachers can be conceptualized as transformations in teachers' knowledge structures as they gain experience and expertise (Sebren, 1995). Experts' knowledge is more differentiated, more organized, and more connected or integrated. This principle of advanced knowledge acquisition has been confirmed within physical education (Rink et al., 1994; Rovegno, 2003; Sebren, 1995).

McCaughtry and Rovegno (2003) documented shifts in teachers' thinking and identified problematic stages or pitfalls which teachers encounter during their development. The facilitating and inhibiting factors in knowledge development concern personal, cultural and contextual elements. Rikard and Knight (1997) examining PTs' beliefs and perceptions during their internships, formulated constraints and obstacles for teacher development: interns' desire to fit in, get along, and be real teachers.

Kagan (1992) underlies that preservice programs should address the developmental needs of novices. These include more procedural, as opposed to theoretical knowledge, the relevance of self-reflection, extended interaction with pupils, cognitive dissonance confronting one's own beliefs and images with experienced teachers' knowledge, obsession with class control, developmental readiness, and questioning the relevance of theory. Grossman (1992) criticizes the focus on mastery of procedural routines and advocates maintaining a balance between the technical aspects of teaching and its intellectual and moral demands.

Formal teacher education programs, characterized by deliberate processes of preparing teachers for teaching, have shifted from considering behaviors to considering various forms of cognition. The critical question in this line of research is "to what degree do teacher education programs affect deep and meaningful cognitive changes in PTs?" Despite the difficulty of changing beliefs, changes in performance will be superficial without changes in beliefs (Richardson and Placier, 2001).

Quantitative and qualitative research designs have produced large amounts of prescriptive and descriptive data in the field of teacher effectiveness studies and teacher education. The paradigm shift has affected the way we think about teaching and teacher education. The constructivist perspective could raise questions about the context specificity and the authenticity of educational events. Can we provide directions for teaching and for teacher education? Rink (1993) explores the potential of integrating the positivist and the naturalistic inquiry. The teacher is a thoughtful practitioner using declarative and procedural knowledge in a two-way interaction between thought and action. Critical pedagogues propose a knowledge base in physical education for the future, where the teachers and consequently teacher education are seen as agents of change (Fernández-Balboa, 1997; Kirk, 1997). Linking knowledge changes to program experience is critical. Learners construct meaning on their own terms no matter what teachers do. The link between teacher designed learning and student outcomes is not simple. Constructivism is still looking for theories of instruction which propose optimal learning environments. Winitzky and Kauchak (1997) describe two alternate approaches. The first model is a theory of skill learning, explaining how declarative knowledge evolves towards procedural knowledge and into a smoothly coordinated process. Knowledge is acquired through repeated efforts to solve a problem. Implications for teacher education might be extending field experiences in a single setting for PTs with the provision of feedback from different resources, especially from their own students. The second model focuses on declarative knowledge and directly challenges candidates' misconceptions by studying prior knowledge through concept mapping, journaling, and biography. Cochran-Smith and Lytle (1999) linked three prominent conceptions of teacher learning with initiatives in teacher education. The first conception, knowledge-for-practice, produces knowledge base books, emphasizing what teachers and teacher educators need to know. The knowledge-in-practice conception promotes the idea of the teacher as a valid knower of practical knowledge. PTs are placed with experienced CTs, and grounded in socially constructed learning theory. In the same line of thinking are the many initiatives PTs are invited and offered guidance on how to reflect on their teaching experiences. The knowledge-of-practice concept finally is characterized by making teacher learning more critical. This knowledge emanates from teachers' systematic inquiries regarding their own teaching and that of others. Preservice programs use critical reflection, action research, learning communities and professional development schools as teacher learning sites.

The problematic relationship between theory and practice in teacher education is illustrated by three major causes of the transfer problem: first, the role of prior knowledge or preconceptions and their resistance to change; secondly the feed-forward problem, indicating that teachers must have personal concerns or must have encountered concrete problems; and finally the nature of relevant knowledge (Korthagen and Kessels, 1999). The evolution from campus-based to school-based teacher education implies that PTs should gain more concrete experiences first and that teacher educators have new roles to play in coaching reflective experiences. Teacher educators are invited to redirect the focus of preservice teaching practice. Realistic practices from the field should be sheduled early in the program and closely related to theoretical seminars. When moving from practice to theory to create a knowledge base, theory will be more situation specific.

Reflective and inquiry-oriented field experiences

According to the constructivist view PTs develop their professional knowledge in a process of reflection on practical situations. Field experiences offer optimal chances for growth of reflective skills and inquiry-oriented activities (Korthagen, 2001).

Reflection

Advocacy for reflection in teacher education programs is based on the general acceptance of the complexity of teaching, resulting in the image of a teacher as a thoughtful decision maker. Teachers cannot be prepared for every situation they may encounter, so it is preferable to help them become reflective practitioners (Tsangaridou and Siedentop, 1995). The assumption that PTs can learn to be more reflective, and that reflective teachers will be better teachers is critical within this context (Placek and Smyth, 1995).

Reflection is defined by Korthagen (1999) as a mental process of structuring or restructuring an experience, a problem or existing knowledge or insights. Fundamental to his conceptualization of the reflection process is the close relationship between PTs' teaching and their learning from this teaching.

Field experiences hold great potential for providing opportunities for reflective practice. Therefore, PTs must be initiated in the practice of learning to reflect before they begin their student teaching experiences, and they must be guided in structured reflection processes during teaching practicum. Because learning to reflect takes time and a certain measure of peace and quiet, student teaching, characterized by a lot of survival concerns, is not the ideal learning period. Reflection must be learned beforehand in method courses, seminars and early field experiences. Certain teachers have difficulty reflecting or writing in logbooks. Internally oriented PTs want to learn by reflecting on their experiences, while externally oriented PTs want instructions and guidelines from the teacher educator. The latter type needs a careful strategy with a gradual approach, structure and safety. By making the learning orientations explicit, those students can change their orientations in a more learner directed way (Korthagen, 2001).

A variety of specific strategies have been used by teacher educators to enhance the reflective capabilities of PTs during field experiences; writings, curriculum inquiry, supervisory approaches, action research, ethnography, and reflective teaching (Tsangaridou and Siedentop, 1995). The writing of journals, logs, logbooks and portfolios is a common strategy to encourage reflection (Melograno, 1998; Senne and Rikard, 2002, 2004). It should be noted that keeping a logbook is not in itself sufficient. A stepwise approach is recommended when using the teachers' logbook as an instrument in helping them to become self-directed learners (Korthagen, 1999). In the logbook the PTs record their own reflections on a particular lesson or meeting. Starting with concrete events, systematic examination is facilitated by answering specific questions (What did I want? What did I feel? What is the problem?). Individual guidance from the supervisor is indispensable in learning to reflect and also in logbook writing. So the logbook or portions thereof should be made available to the teacher educator. In order to structure and guide the process of reflection, Korthagen (2001) describes a spiral process of five phases called the "ALACT-model". It is represented by a circle starting with the Action, followed by Looking back at the action, Awareness of the essential aspects, Creating alternative methods and finally ending with a new Trial. Within each phase exemplary questions are formulated to help and guide the PTs through a structured and spiral reflection process.

In the supervisory approaches supervisors and CTs help the PTs to reflect about the practice of teaching, stimulating them to analyze and look more critically at their teaching performance (Byra, 1996). Reflection sessions are organized in a safe, supportive, and nonjudgmental environment, in small groups or individually, and participants are provided with sufficient time. PTs can choose their own focus of reflection, mostly determined by their concerns. Reflection sessions are characterized by open-ended questions, encouraging the participants to describe, reconstruct, and consider the many factors and details that influenced their teaching.

Focus of reflection

The critical role of reflection in teacher development is influenced by the orientation towards reflection which is adopted within the teacher education program. This orientation directs what PTs will learn about teaching (Sebren, 1994). Reflection can be focused on students and student learning, on the subject matter, on teaching strategies, or on the social and political aspects of teaching. Studying the content or the product of reflection mirrors the stage of development of the reflective person. Tsangaridou and Siedentop (1995) distinguish four traditions of reflective teaching:

- The academic tradition emphasizes the teacher's role as a specialist on the subject matter, addressing reflection on subject matter and its transformation to students.
- The social efficiency tradition emphasizes that the knowledge base from scientific study and reflection should focus on the intelligent use of generic teaching skills and strategies suggested by this research.
- In the developmentalist tradition the learner's natural development provides the bases for teachers' decisions and as a consequence reflection should focus on students.
- The social reconstructionist tradition interprets teacher education as agencies for the creation of a more humane society.

Tsangaridou and O'Sullivan (1994) proposed a reflective framework for teaching in physical education describing the focus and the level of teachers' reflections. The reflection focus can be technical, situational, or sensitizing.

- Technical reflection is concerned with instructional or managerial aspects of teaching.
- Situational reflection deals with the contextual issues of teaching.
- Sensitizing reflection represents reflection upon social, moral, ethical, or political aspects of teaching.

The level of reflection can be represented by description, justification, or critique.

- Description provides descriptive information of an action about some aspects of teaching.
- Justification provides the rationale or logic of an action related to teaching.
- Critique provides an explanation and evaluation of various teaching actions.

Reflective writings show the dominant messages of the teacher education program. While critical reflections with moral and ethical dimensions must be examined, entirely technical reflections concerning managerial and instructional practices are reported frequently (O'Sullivan and Tsangaridou, 1992; Tsangaridou and O'Sullivan, 1994). The idea

that the supervisory process is critical in promoting PTs' reflective abilities was worked out by Byra (1996). A trained supervisor organized postlesson conferences under either a directive approach (teacher tells–student listens) or a collaborative approach (student tells–teacher listens/questions). The supervisor approach and the students' assignments seemed to influence the focus of the PTs, changing from technical to situational and sensitizing issues of teaching. O'Sullivan and Doutis (1994) warn against developing prescriptions for PETE in the light of teaching expertise. The limited focus of the cognitive processing paradigm on the notion of teaching as an academic enterprise ignores the social, political, and moral dimensions of teaching. Moore (2003) concluded that, despite consistent efforts by university professors, the orientation of PTs' reflection tended to shift to procedural concerns and routine tasks. Korthagen (1992) states that the focus of reflection should be the relationships between concepts, promoting the restructuring of inadequate teacher cognitions. For Kagan (1992) the necessary and proper focus of a novice's attention and reflection may be inward: on the novice's own behaviors, beliefs, and image of self as a teacher.

Action research

The process of systematically reflecting on ones practice in order to improve it leads to action research. Several authors have called for engaging PTs in action research activities based upon the concept of teaching as inquiry. In order to make teacher learning more critical, a number of efforts, initiatives, and strategies at the preservice level are noted; investigating ones biography, critical reflections, ethnographies, teacher research and action research, networks and inquiry communities. The establishment of professional development schools offers enormous potential to stimulate research communities (Cochran-Smith and Lytle, 1999).

Kagan (1992) noted that novices may need structured research experiences resulting in changing their preconceptions about teaching and students. Woods et al. (2000) proposed an inquiry based model in PETE programs as a viable constructivist learning approach for PTs. To improve the efficacy of this learning approach they suggest:

- implementing mini research projects early in the teacher education programs
- focusing on questions about all types of experiences and assignments
- emphasizing the development of time management skills
- cooperation between PTs and CTs who are engaging in teacher research
- confronting formal and practical knowledge of PTs.

The authors believe implementing these suggestions will enhance the PTs' knowledge base and will serve to develop teachers who have the skills to continue to learn and grow throughout their career.

Many PETE programs claim they foster reflective activities (Carlson, 2001; Cutforth and Hellison, 1992; Hellison and Templin, 1991; Paré, 1993). Some professional programs highlight the critical, inquiring teacher (Graham, 1991; Sebren, 1995; Tsangaridou and O'Sullivan, 1994, 1997). Few, however, have empirically evaluated their efforts, especially in the physical education literature. Data indicated that changes in reflective thoughts and teaching were difficult (Placek and Smyth, 1995; Rovegno, 1992), and there was evidence for positive influences (Byra, 1996; Tsangaridou and O'Sullivan, 1994, 2003).

Participants in field experiences

The classic triad in field experiences is composed of the student-teachers or preservice (prospective) teachers (PTs), the cooperating teachers (CTs) and the university teachers (UTs).

PTs bring their own experience as primary and secondary school students to physical education classes and as university students in the PETE program. Teacher education faculty or UTs bring knowledge gained through teaching and research. The CTs bring subject matter and practical knowledge gained from their experience as practitioners and as undergraduates (McCullick, 2001).

The belief that practice teaching is an essential part of teacher training is generally shared by all participants. PTs experience practical training as real teaching and real learning. CTs also stress the value of the teaching practices. UTs will not deny the existence of the learning opportunities, but they are more concerned about the conservative effects of this training (Zanting et al., 1998).

A well documented study by Hardy (1999) on PTs' perceptions of their teaching practicum revealed several important items; questions on extending or limiting school-based and integrated field experiences, the problem of the discrepancy in mentoring quality between CTs and UTs, school context constraints, and PTs' prior beliefs. The research domain on PTs' concerns during teaching practicum has received a lot of attention in physical education (Behets, 1990; Capel, 1998; Meek, 1996). PTs go through different developmental stages, from focusing on themselves, the act of teaching, and the students' learning. It seems that these stages of concern are not as static as proposed in Fullers' model. A dynamic approach involves PTs, CTs, and Uts being aware of those concerns and taking into consideration that they can change in direction and magnitude (Behets and Meek, 1999).

The conflicts reported between PTs, CTs, and UTs refer to the specific culture of schools and university, misunderstandings developed through the socialization process about each other's role, incongruent thoughts about learning to teach, and divergent expectations and decisions (McCullick, 2001). The tensions between the participants will negatively affect learning (Kahan, 1999). Several forms of collaboration have been suggested (Wideen et al., 1998). A shared vision on teacher education and a conceptually coherent program will lead to a delineation of the roles and responsibilities between university and school partners, and will result in clearly written and negotiated competencies required for each member of the triad (Hardy, 1997, 1999; McIntyre et al., 1996; Siedentop and Locke, 1997).

Mentoring and supervision

The concept of mentoring is a topic of current interest but has remained vague. Different roles, models, styles and functions have been ascribed to mentors, and one result is that there is no standard definition of mentoring. Individual teachers interpret their own roles and therefore the nature of mentoring is idiosyncratic (Zanting et al., 1998). Different forms of mentoring emerge in different contexts. Formal expectations, working conditions, selection, and preparation all create a set of constraints and opportunities that shape how mentors define and enact their role (Feiman-Nemser and Parker, 1993). Rikard and Veal (1996) identified three distinct supervisory styles, reflecting the CTs' beliefs about learning to teach, labeled as (a) do it my way and learn from a proven success, (b) do it your way and learn from trial and error, and (c) we'll do it together so we can learn and improve from each other. Direct and indirect styles of supervision refer to prescriptive, interpretive, and supportive approaches (Randall, 1992).

The mentor is an experienced person working with a younger person, with the intention of helping to shape the growth and the development of the protégé (Wright and Smith, 2000). In the domain of teacher education the role of the mentor is implemented by the CT and is often referred to as the mentor-protégé dyad (Hodge, 1997). Mentoring is assisted performance where the mentor in a cooperative activity scaffolds the learning of the PTs by co-planning and co-teaching (Feiman-Nemser and Beasley, 1997). The dual role of assessing and assisting PTs can provoke an area of tension for the mentor (Feiman-Nemser and Parker, 1993). For some teacher educators these functions should be separated. The involvement of the PTs in their own evaluation can maybe help to solve this problem.

In the literature one can distinguish between the traditional and the reflective approach to mentoring. The first emphasizes the teaching performance and the actual teaching practice, and the second focusing on reflection on teaching or thinking about and learning from teaching.

The traditional approach to mentoring in physical education is widely implemented (see Metzler, 1990 and Randall, 1992) and identifies the following supervisory duties (Coleman and Mitchell, 2000). In the preclass briefing, the supervisor or CT can provide effective models, preplan or discuss PTs' planning intentions. During the lesson teacher and pupil behaviors are observed, data are collected, and salient items are noted by the observer. In the post teaching conference the relevant data are analyzed, feedback is provided, modifications for the next lesson are suggested, and the teaching act can be evaluated. The clinical supervision model, close to this behavioral approach, involves collecting objective and reliable data on observable teaching behaviors with some type of systematic observational instrument. Data-based feedback is oriented to increase levels of desirable behaviors (Smith et al., 1993). Alternative supervisory models, self-assessment supervision and collaborative supervision have been investigated by Brawdy and Byra (1995). The provision of feedback to PTs in post-lesson conferences (Coulon and Byra, 1997; Mitchell and Schwager, 1993) is supplemented and supported by the use of computer and communication technology during and after the data collection process (Boyce and Kelly, 1992; Everhart, 1997; Kahan, 2002; Sharpe, 1997; Sharpe et al., 1997; Smith and Steffen, 1994; St Pierre, 1998).

In contrast to the traditional mentoring, a more dynamic approach is based on the developmental processes of the PTs. Furlong and Maynard (1995) describe four phases with specific supervisory functions. In the beginning PTs learn rules, routines and authority, and the CT models these behaviors. Next, attention is focused on competencies, while the mentor, as coach, stimulates the PTs to reflect. In the third phase the PTs are focused on pupil learning and the CT has the role of "critical friend". Finally, the political, social, and moral dimensions are related to teaching. CT and PTs are equal partners and function as "co-enquirers". They expound upon their practical professional knowledge.

Capel (1998) stresses the need for mentors to take account of PTs' stage of development and their needs at different stages. This implies a number of different types of learning experiences. PTs can observe CTs as models, followed by collaborative planning and teaching. PTs being observed by the mentor are encouraged to develop their own teaching style. CTs make their thinking processes explicit. Finally, mentors' feedback changes from a focus on teaching skills to a focus on developing the PTs' reflective skills. PTs are encouraged to think about the needs of the pupils and to reflect on their observations. In this strategy the role of the PTs is systematically and progressively increased, with more responsibility in terms of teaching and organizing activities (Smith, 1998). The mentor-protégé relationship can be poor when CTs and PTs focus on different areas, when their concerns between teaching versus learning diverge, when they have conflicting perceptions on the use of routines, the teaching of lessons, the involvement of the PTs, the CT as a model, and the goals regarding physical education (Askins and Imwold, 1994; Hardy, 1995). Within the reflective approach Zanting et al. (1998) reveal an interesting extension of the mentors' role, explicating their practical knowledge. The mentors' practical knowledge remains hidden from PTs as their conversations too often are focused on teaching behaviors instead of thinking about and analyzing teaching and learning from experiences. The mentors can make explicit their own thinking by discussing PTs' lessons, by reflecting on their own lessons with PTs, and by jointly planning, giving, and analyzing lessons. They stimulate PTs to develop an attitude of inquiry, to question the teacher, and by applying research techniques like interview, concept mapping and stimulated recall interviews (Zanting et al., 2001).

The reflective approach implies a new role for the teacher educator, requiring the following competencies (Korthagen and Kessels, 1999):

- create suitable learning experiences
- promote awareness and reflection on teaching experiences
- offer theoretical notions from empirical research, and
- train PTs to act productively.

The proposed ALACT-model for PTs' reflection (Action, Looking back, Awareness, Creating alternatives, and Trial) is completed and complemented with specific teacher educator competencies; finding useful experiences, creating a safe learning environment by means of acceptance, empathy, and genuineness, stimulate concreteness, help in finding solutions, and finally during the new trial help in continuing the learning process.

Selection and training of cooperating teachers

The critical role played by the CTs should involve a serious selection and training of candidates (Hardy, 1999). They require new skills because their work differs from the normal teaching activities (Feiman-Nemser and Parker, 1993). For teacher training institutes the selection process does not seem a major priority, but instead a rather arbitrary situation. CTs are often selected because there is a lack of placements. Teaching expertise is not always an effective criterion (Tannehill and Goc-Karp, 1992). The willingness to supervise PTs is not primarily the monetary rewards. Relevant incentives are mentioned as a win–win situation for PTs and CTs; the opportunity to learn new ideas, interest in supervising PTs, and a professional attitude of critically thinking about their own teaching. Most CTs have no formal preparation and perceive their role as supervisor primarily from memories of their own student teaching supervision and their experience as teachers (Rikard and Veal, 1996).

The existence of collaborations between teacher education institutions and schools could orient the selection process. The shared vision on teacher education could be strengthened by involving CTs in the teacher education program (Hynes-Dusel, 1999). A screening strategy which analyzes the observation focus and conference targets can identify CTs whose ideas are congruent with teacher education program goals (Coleman and Mitchell, 2000). The need for careful selection of student teaching practice sites is demonstrated as PTs are sensitive to positive feedback from their students and from the CTs in relation to the confirmation of their career choice (Jones, 1992).

Several studies have shown that CTs can be trained to be effective supervisors (see Coleman and Mitchell, 2000). Systematic supervision training is the exception to the rule. The requested competencies of the mentor will mirror the behavioral or reflective concept of the program. The models proposed by Metzler (1990) and by Randall (1992) are well supported by data and observational techniques from research on teacher effectiveness. This behavioral approach involves mentor skills like modeling, observation, data collection, and analysis focused on feedback provision. The training of teacher educators with a reflective approach will focus on supervision and reflective skills built on the needs and concerns of the PTs and their practical experiences (Korthagen, 2001).

Mentoring and learning outcomes

All participants agree that the CTs have the most significant influence on PTs, especially on their attitudes. The teaching behaviors of the PTs even closely reflect the methods used by their CTs rather than the methods from the PETE program (Coleman and Mitchell, 2000).

Studying the learning outcomes of mentoring activities on PTs, the traditional behavioral approach is focused on discrete teaching behaviors, while the more reflective approach assesses the reflective strategies and the development of PTs' pedagogical knowledge.

Several studies investigated the effects of different supervisory models and schedules on specific teaching behaviors of PTs (Brawdy and Byra, 1995; Coulon and Byra, 1997; McCullick and Coulon,

1998; Smith and Steffen, 1994; Smith et al., 1993). The majority of these studies suggested that supervision with feedback which is delivered frequently and consistently, can improve teachers' instructional behaviors.

Few studies are to be found which investigated the effects of supervision on PTs' reflective practices. Byra (1996) experimented with two postlesson conferencing strategies, the directive and the collaborative supervision. Both strategies seemed to facilitate the development of PTs' reflective thoughts on teaching.

The involvement of peers in the mentoring process is characteristic of the reflective approach and is based on social constructivist ideas. In the peer coaching model (Jenkins and Veal, 2002) PTs act alternately as teacher and as coach. In the postlesson conference the role of the observer-coach was to encourage rather than tell the teacher what to do. Both roles of teacher and coach were complementary and helped to develop PTs' pedagogical content knowledge. Peer involvement includes peer teaching support, classroom research, a peer group seminar, developing teaching cases, and qualitative data collection (Korthagen, 2001; Poole, 1994). The idea of creating cases based on PTs' reflective writing from their own student-teaching experiences is intriguing (Wilson and Williams, 2001; for case methods see also Collier and O'Sullivan, 1997). Proactive seminars (Rhea, 1999) help PTs to develop problem solving skills by sharing experiences with peers and provide extra information for the university supervisor about the PTs practical knowledge. The minimal role of the UTs in the supervision process is reflected in the few publications on that topic (see Goc-Karp and Williamson, 1993; Williamson, 1993). McIntyre et al. (1996) summarized a number of studies, concluding that the UTs have little effect on PTs' attitudes or behavior. UTs and CTs do not apply a shared knowledge base during discussions. UTs seem to play a role in organizing PTs progress in their teacher curriculum and in tuning the uncritical relationships between CTs and PTs. Alternative models have been tested like the concept of clustering PTs in schools and setting up teacher supervision groups made up of the CTs, the building principal, and the UTs. The involvement of CTs as faculty members with supervising duties for specific groups of PTs seems a promising avenue to us.

Implications for practice

Based on our synthesis of the key findings from the research base on field experiences and student teacher mentoring, we provide some implications for the format, provision, and supervision of field experiences in PETE programs. There is no debate that for PTs field experiences are the central part of their teacher preparation program. We focus on the following ideas characterizing new trends: a theoretical framework with teacher competencies, in a constructivist learning environment based on reflection.

Teacher education programs are structured within a theoretical framework and a constructivist approach. All participants share the same vision on teaching and communicate this shared understanding in close collaboration. Program goals are well-defined and accepted.

The required teacher competencies are explicitly laid out in (national) teacher standards, shifting from teacher skills to teacher cognitions. Teacher job profiles formulate the required competencies in terms of knowledge, skills and dispositions. The search for complex teaching skills and the respective training techniques, as predicted by Bain's review in 1990 is stagnant. PTs are involved in action research and reflective inquiry in which they attempt to improve educational practice through analysis, dialogue, and strategic action.

The development of teacher thinking skills is embedded in a constructivist environment. The dominant role of PTs' preconceptions and beliefs about physical education, teaching and learning requires more dynamic and flexible models of developmental stages. As the influence of CTs and especially of UTs is still under discussion, contextual changes are focused on the collaboration between the participants in forms such as cohorts of prospective teachers, professional development schools, inquiry and learning communities. Structural changes, and in particular, the timing of field experiences, are suggested in order to integrate formal knowledge and practical knowledge.

The concept of teacher reflection is a key premise within this dynamic process of change. Increased practice without analysis and reflection does not lead to professional growth. The degree of assistance and mentoring which are needed from all participants and from the context are still under study. The use of portfolios, reflective journals and reflective assignments, in which PTs document their own professional development, reveal alternative and more authentic evaluation procedures for PTs' field experiences, replacing the traditional evaluation methods and observational categories.

Conclusions and recommendations

We will not summarize research findings in PETE concerning field experiences with cliché statements. We will not plead for better quality research. Scholars with inferior perceptions of the academic status of our research domain and of our subject physical education itself often follow a pattern of individualistic "research wildcating". They tend to jump on the latest educational fad without adequate attention to either proper conceptualization of the problem or development of reliable tools for data collection (Graber, 2001). For these reasons, we prefer to formulate a limited number of positive research recommendations.

We summarized a selected number of studies in Table 4.8.1. The selection in alphabetical order is limited to empirical studies in field experiences in the PETE research from 1990 in the *Journal of Teaching in Physical Education* and in the journal *Research Quarterly for Exercisce and Sport*. Most participants under study were prospective teachers (PTs). The qualitative nature of data analysis limited the number of PTs. The content analysis of several different written documents and resources is a common and accepted research strategy. This is also apparent in the study focus, where teacher cognition (beliefs, perceptions, concerns, and knowledge) are favorite items. Descriptive studies emphasize the complexity of the teaching-learning experiences, while intervention studies mostly claim positive effects.

Most scholars argue for long term planning of research projects with a well-conceived theoretical base for studying learning effects in field experiences (McIntyre et al., 1996). Fenstermacher (2002) advocates more extended programs of scholarship, but also reports on the tension between large-scale social science research and interpretive and narrative research in the field of teacher education. The application of results from large-scale research is possible only when the lost context, complexity, and intentionality is restored.

Shulman (2002) does not allow us to forget the moral message of the process–product research. Our research field's critique of this paradigm made us shift from behavior to thought, from observable performance to strategy and understanding, and from simple models of stimulus and response to more complex models involving context, content, and cognition. In doing so, as researchers, we also managed to lose sight of the key principle of product-process research: linking teaching to learning, connecting teacher knowledge and student achievement.

We will need to develop instrumentation to monitor teacher growth in ways that can guide teacher educators and teachers themselves. The continuing application of qualitative methods to research and evaluation of field experiences will sustain this ongoing process.

The highlighting of reflection in teacher education, hyped-up as the ultimate mean and goal is a prime example of data-free advocacy (Graber, 2001; Tsangaridou and Siedentop, 1995). In physical education we need long term studies in the area of reflection, focused on teaching and learning, and

Table 4.3.1 Selected studies

Author	Participants/Methodology	Study focus	Results
Allison et al. (2000)	25 PTs Inductive data analysis	epistemology of PETE	epistemologies of skillfulness
Behets (1990)	110 PTs Questionnaire and logbook	teacher concerns	indistinct stages of concerns idealistic and realistic concerns
Byra (1996)	14 PTs Levels of reflection	postlesson strategies reflective practice	reflection on technical and other issues of teaching
Coleman and Mitchell (2000)	18 CTs Video, notes, interview	CTs' observation focus; CTs' conference targets	discriminating instrument for supervisory skills
Doolittle et al. (1993)	3 PTs Questionnaire, interview	PTs' beliefs	persistence of beliefs lack of program impact
Graber (1995)	20 PTs, 7 UTs, 8 CTs Interview	teacher knowledge	incorporation of general pedagogical and less content knowledge
Hardy (1999)	62 PTs Questionnaire	perceptions of learning to teach	complexity of field experiences not only quantity but quality
Jenkins and Veal (2002)	8 PTs Observations, reports	teachers' knowledge peer coaching	roles of coach and teacher were complementary
Kahan (2002)	1 PT and 1 CT Questionnaires and interview	intralesson communication bug-in-the-ear radio device	positive effects
Matanin and Collier (2003)	3 PTs Document analysis	longitudinal teacher beliefs	differentiated assimilation of program messages
McCaughtry and Rovegno (2003)	4 PTs Observation and document analysis	pedagogical content knowledge	three main shifts identified in teacher knowledge
McCullick (2001)	18 PE teachers Inductive analysis of interviews	perspectives on characteristics needed by PTs, UTs and CTs	a shared technical culture in PE
Meek (1996)	77 PTs Questionnaire	teacher concerns instrumentation	need for more sensitive questionnaires
O'Sullivan and Tsangaridou (1992)	39 PTs Critical incidents and questionnaires	PTs' perceptions	emphasis on technical aspects of teaching
Paese and Zinkgraf (1991)	35 PTs Specific questionnaires	teacher efficacy and stress	various changes during student teaching

(Continued)

Table 4.3.1 (Continued)

Author	Participants/Methodology	Study focus	Results
Rikard and Veal (1996) model	23 CTs Inductive analysis of interviews	CTs' preparation, beliefs and practices	need for a supervision and training of CTs
Rikard and Knight (1997)	46 PTs Interviews and questionnaire	beliefs and perceptions professional development	identification of obstacles and concerns
Rovegno (1993)	12 PTs Qualitative document analysis	pedagogical content knowledge	inaccurate development and acquisition of knowledge
Rovegno (1994)	2 PTs Observation and interview	pedagogical content knowledge	teaching within a curricular zone of safety
Rovegno et al. (2003)	4 PE teachers Video, interviews	pedagogical content knowledge teaching dribbling	learning orientation: holistic and cognitive
Sebren (1995)	7 PTs Content analysis of documents	reflections and knowledge	reflection may influence knowledge development
Senne and Rikard (2002)	67 PTs Test and questionnaire	two portfolio models moral judgment	professional growth different reflective practices
Senne and Rikard (2004)	9 PTs Interviews and questionnaires	teaching portfolio moral/ethical judgment	positive developmental intervention
Sharpe et al. (1997)	4 PTs Behavioral observation	sequential behavior feedback	positive changes
Tsangaridou and O'Sullivan (1994)	6 PTs Interviews and documents	pedagogical reflective strategies reflective framework for teaching	positive influence
Tsangaridou and O'Sullivan (2003)	4 PTs Observations and documents	theories of action versus theories-in-action learning about students	theories are strong and consistent
Woods et al. (2000)	26 PTs Inductive analysis of documents	PTs' perceptions	positive effects challenging preconceptions

developing sound assessment instruments. We suggest the following research items:

- Are reflective physical education teachers better teachers?
- What is the relationship between the teaching and learning style of physical education PTs and their reflection skills?
- How can they develop the required reflection skills?
- How can we assess or stimulate this learning process, how can we intervene?
- Which personal and contextual variables influence reflectivity and teaching efficiency?

Given that the beliefs and conceptions from prospective teachers, from cooperating teachers and university teacher educators are resistant to change, physical education teacher education programs will continue to be more traditional than conceptual for the time being. This review, nevertheless, offers some interesting avenues for the future.

References

Allison, P.C., Pissanos, B.W., Turner, A.P. and Law, D.R. (2000). Preservice physical educators' epistemologies of skillfulness. *Journal of Teaching in Physical Education, 19*: 141–161.

Amade-Escot, C. (2000). The contribution of two research programs on teaching content: "Pedagogical content knowledge" and "didactics of physical education." *Journal of Teaching in Physical Education, 20*: 78–101.

Askins, J.C. and Imwold, C.H. (1994). The existence of conflicting perceptions in a secondary physical education student teaching experience. *The Physical Educator, 51*: 35–46.

Bain, L.L. (1990). Physical education teacher education. In W.R. Houston (Ed.), *Handbook of research on teacher education* (pp. 758–781). New York: Macmillan.

Behets, D. (1990). Concerns of preservice physical education teachers. *Journal of Teaching in Physical Education, 10*: 66–75.

Behets, D. (2000). Physical education teachers' tasks and competencies. In F. Carreiro da Costa, J.A. Diniz, L.M. Carvalho and M.S. Onofre (Eds.), *Proceedings of the Lisbon AIESEP international seminar on research on teaching and research on teacher education* (pp. 208–212). Lisbon: University of Lisbon.

Behets, D. and Meek, G. (1999) Physical educators' concerns. In Y. Vanden Auweele, F. Bakker, S. Biddle, M. Durand, and R. Seiler (Eds.), *Psychology for Physical Educators* (pp. 479–499). Champaign, IL: Human Kinetics.

Book, C.L. (1996). Professional development schools. In J. Sikula, T.J. Buttery and E. Guyton (Eds.), *Handbook of research on teacher education: A project of the association of teacher educators* (pp. 194–210). New York: Macmillan.

Boyce, B.A. and Kelly, L. (1992). Developing pedagogical skills of preservice teachers through goal setting and computer generated feedback. *The Physical Educator, 49*: 213–218.

Brawdy, P. and Byra, M. (1995). Supervision of preservice teachers during an early field teaching experience. *The Physical Educator, 52*: 147–159.

Byra, M. (1996). Postlesson conferencing strategies and preservice teachers' reflective practices. *Journal of Teaching in Physical Education, 16*: 48–65.

Calderhead, J. (1996). Teachers: Beliefs and knowledge. In D.C. Berliner and R.C. Calfee (Eds.), *Handbook of educational psychology* (pp. 709–725). New York: Macmillan.

Capel, S. (1998a). Experiences of physical education students in learning to teach. *European Physical Education Review, 4*: 127–144.

Capel, S. (1998b). PE students' stages of development as teachers: Part 2: The mentors' perspective. *British Journal of Physical Education, 29*(4): 10–20.

Capel, S. and Katene, W. (2002). Secondary PGCE students' perceptions of their subject knowledge. *European Physical Education Review, 6*: 46–67.

Carlson, T.B. (2001). Using metaphors to enhance reflectiveness among preservice teachers. *Journal of Physical Education, Recreation and Dance, 72*(1): 49–53.

Carreiro da Costa, F. (1993). Teaching teachers: Aims, methods and contents. In J. Mester (Ed.), *Sport sciences in Europe – Current and future perspectives* (pp. 484–505). Aachen: Meyer und Meyer Verlag.

Cochran-Smith, M. and Lytle, S. (1999). Relationships of knowledge and practice: Teacher learning in communities. *Review of Research in Education, 24*: 249–305.

Coleman, M.M. and Mitchell, M. (2000). Assessing observation focus and conference targets of cooperating teachers. *Journal of Teaching in Physical Education, 20*: 40–54.

Collier, C.S. and O'Sullivan, M. (1997). Case method in physical education higher education: A pedagogy of change? *Quest, 49*: 198–213.

Coulon, S.C. and Byra, M. (1997). Investigating the postlesson dialogue of cooperating and student teachers. *The Physical Educator, 54*: 2–10.

Cutforth, N. and Hellison, D. (1992). Reflections on reflective teaching in a physical education teacher education methods course. *The Physical Educator, 49*: 127–135.

Doolittle, S., Dodds, P. and Placek, J. (1993) Persistence of beliefs about teaching during formal training of preservice teachers. *Journal of Teaching in Physical Education, 12*: 355–365.

Everhart, B. (1997). Using e-mail in student teaching. *Journal of Physical Education, Recreation and Dance, 68*(6): 36–38.

Feiman-Nemser, S. and Beasley, K. (1997). Mentoring as assisted performance: A case of co-planning. In V. Richardson (Ed.), *Constructivist teacher education: Building new understandings* (pp. 108–126). London: Falmer Press.

Feiman-Nemser, S. and Parker, M.B. (1993). Mentoring in context: A comparison of two U.S. programs for beginning teachers. *International Journal of Educational Research, 19*: 699–718.

Fenstermacher, G.D. (2002). A commentary on research that serves teacher education. *Journal of Teacher Education, 53:* 242–247.

Fernandez-Balboa, J.M. (1997). Knowledge base in physical education teacher education: A proposal for a new era. *Quest, 49:* 161–181.

Furlong, J. and Maynard, T. (1995). *Mentoring student teachers: The growth of professional knowledge.* London: Routledge.

Goc Karp, G. and Williamson, K. (1993). PETE faculty at work: The reciprocal nature of organizational structures and identity. *Journal of Teaching in Physical Education, 12:* 413–423.

Graber, K.C. (1993). The emergence of faculty consensus concerning teacher education: The socialization process of creating and sustaining faculty agreement. *Journal of Teaching in Physical Education, 12:* 424–436.

Graber, K.C. (1995). The influence of teacher education programs on the beliefs of student teachers: General pedagogical knowledge, pedagogical content knowledge, and teacher education coursework. *Journal of Teaching in Physical Education, 14:* 157–178.

Graber, K.C. (2001). Research on teaching in physical education. In V. Richardson (Ed.), *Handbook of research on teaching* (pp. 491–519). Washington, DC: American Educational Research Association.

Graham, K.C. (1991). The influence of teacher education on preservice development: Beyond a custodial orientation. *Quest, 43:* 1–19.

Grossman, P.L. (1992). Why models matter: An alternate view on professional growth in teaching. *Review of Educational Research, 62:* 171–179.

Hardy, C. (1995). Problems in the supervision of the practicum. *European Physical Education Review, 1:* 163–172.

Hardy, C. (1997). Perceptions of mentoring in physical education classes: The subject mentors' view. *The British Journal of Physical Education, 28(1):* 12–16.

Hardy, C. (1999). Preservice teachers' perceptions of learning to teach in a predominantly school-based teacher education program. *Journal of Teaching in Physical Education, 18:* 175–198.

Hellison, D. and Templin, T. (1991). *A Reflective approach to Teaching Physical Education.* Champaign, IL: Human Kinetics.

Hodge, S.R. (1997). Mentoring: Perspectives of physical education graduate students from diverse cultural backgrounds. *The Physical Educator, 54:* 181–195.

Houston, W.R. (1990). *Handbook of research on teacher education.* New York: Macmillan.

Hynes-Dusel, J.M. (1999). Cooperating teachers' perceptions about the student teaching experience. *The Physical Educator, 56:* 186–195.

Jenkins, J.M. and Veal, M.L. (2002). Preservice teachers' PCK development during peer coaching. *Journal of Teaching in Physical Education, 22:* 49–68.

Jones, R. (1992) Student teachers: Incidents that lead them to confirm or question their career choice. *Physical Educator, 49:* 205–212.

Kagan, D.M. (1992). Professional growth among preservice and beginning teachers. *Review of Educational Research, 62:* 129–169.

Kahan, D. (1999). Characteristics of and explanations for cooperating teachers' immediate supervisory comments: A pilot study using the thinking-out-loud technique. *The Physical Educator, 56:* 126–137.

Kahan, D. (2002). The effects of a bug-in-the-ear device on intralesson communication between a student teacher and a cooperating teacher. *Journal of Teaching in Physical Education, 22:* 86–104.

Kirk, D. (1997). Thinking beyond the square: The challenge to physical educators in new times. *Quest, 49:* 182–186.

Korthagen, F.A.J. (1992). Techniques for stimulating reflection in teacher education seminars. *Teaching and Teacher Education, 8(3):* 265–274.

Korthagen, F.A.J. (1999). Linking reflection and technical competence: The logbook as an instrument in teacher education. *European Journal of Teacher Education, 22:* 191–207.

Korthagen, F.A.J. (Ed.) (2001). *Linking practice and theory: The pedagogy of realistic teacher education.* Mahwah: Lawrence Erlbaum associates.

Korthagen, F.A.J. and Kessels, J.P.A.M. (1999). Linking theory and practice: Changing the pedagogy of teacher education. *Educational Researcher, 28(4):* 4–17.

Laker, A. (1994). A teachers' guide for supervising student teachers. *The British Journal of Physical Education, 25(4):* 31–33.

Livingston, C. and Borko, H. (1989). Expert-novice: Differences in teaching: A cognitive analysis and implications for teacher education. *Journal of Teacher Education, 40:* 36–42.

Livingston, L. (1996). Re-defining the role of physical activity courses in the preparation of physical education teaching professionals. *Physical Educator, 53:* 114–121.

Matanin, M. and Collier, C. (2003). Longitudinal analysis of preservice teachers' beliefs about teaching physical education. *Journal of Teaching in Physical Education, 22:* 153–168.

Mawer, M. (Ed.) (1996). *Mentoring in physical education: Issues and insights.* London: Falmer Press.

Mayer-Smith, J.A. and Mitchell, I.J. (1997). Teaching about constructivism: Using approaches informed by constructivism. In V. Richardson (Ed.), *Constructivist teacher education: Building new understandings* (pp. 129–139). London: Falmer Press.

McCaughtry, N. and Rovegno, I. (2003). Development of pedagogical content knowledge: Moving from blaming students to predicting skillfulness, recognizing motor development, and understanding emotion. *Journal of Teaching in Physical Education, 22:* 355–368.

McCullick, B.A. (2001). Practitioners' perspectives on values, knowledge, and skills needed by PETE participants. *Journal of Teaching in Physical Education, 21:* 35–56.

McCullick, B.A. and Coulon, S.C. (1998). The effects of varying supervisory conference on pre service teachers' specificity, pedagogical focus and implementation of written behavioral objectives. *The Physical Educator*, 55: 38–49.

McIntyre, D.J., Byrd, D.M. and Foxx, S.M. (1996). Field and laboratory experiences. In J. Sikula, T.J. Buttery and E. Guyton (Eds.), *Handbook of research on teacher education: A project of the association of teacher educators* (pp. 171–193). New York: Macmillan.

Meek, G.A. (1996). The TCQ with preservice physical educators in Great Britain: Being concerned with concerns. *Journal of Teaching in Physical Education*, 16: 20–29.

Meijer, P.C. (1999). *Teachers' practical knowledge: Teaching reading comprehension in secondary education*. Leiden: University Leiden.

Melograno, V.J. (1998). *Professional and student portfolios for physical education*. Champaign, IL: Human Kinetics.

Metzler, M.W. (1990). *Instructional supervision for physical education*. Champaign, IL: Human Kinetics.

Mitchell, M.F. and Schwager, S. (1993). Improving the student teaching experience: Looking to the research for guidance. *The Physical Educator*, 50: 31–38.

Moore, R. (2003). Reexamining the field experience of preservice teachers. *Journal of Teacher Education*, 54: 31–42.

Munby, H., Russell, T. and Martin, A.K. (2001). Teachers' knowledge and how it develops. In V. Richardson (Ed.), *Handbook of research on teaching* (pp. 877–904). Washington, DC: American Educational Research Association.

National Association for Sport and Physical Education. (2001). Standards for initial programs in physical education teacher education. AAHPERD.

Neide, J. (1996). Supervision of student teachers: Objective observation. *Journal of Physical Education, Recreation and Dance*, 67(7): 14–18.

O'Sullivan, M. (1990). Physical education teacher education in the United States. *Journal of Physical Education, Recreation and Dance*, 61(2): 41–45.

O'Sullivan, M. (1996). What do we know about the professional preparation of teachers? In S.J. Silverman and C.D. Ennis (Eds.), *Student learning in physical education: Applying research to enhance instruction* (pp. 315–337). Champaign, IL: Human Kinetics.

O'Sullivan, M. (2003). Learning to teach physical education. In S.J. Silverman and C.D. Ennis (Eds.), *Student learning in physical education: Applying research to enhance instruction, second edition* (pp. 275–294). Champaign, IL: Human Kinetics.

O'Sullivan, M. and Doutis, P. (1994). Research on expertise: Guideposts for expertise and teacher education in physical education. *Quest*, 46: 176–185.

O'Sullivan, M., Siedentop, D. and Locke, L. (1992). Toward collegiality: Competing viewpoints among teacher educators. *Quest*, 44: 266–280.

O'Sullivan, M. and Tsangaridou, N. (1992). What undergraduate physical education majors learn during a field experience. *Research Quarterly for Exercise and Sport*, 63: 381–392.

Paese, P.C. and Zinkgraf, S. (1991). The effect of student teaching on teacher efficacy and teacher stress. *Journal of Teaching in Physical Education*, 10: 307–315.

Paré, C. (Ed.) (1995). Better teaching in physical education. Think about it? *Proceedings of the international seminar on Training of Teachers in Reflective Practice in Physical Education*. Trois-Rivières, Quebec: University du Quebec à Trois-Rivières.

Placek, J.H. and Smyth, D.M. (1995). Teaching preservice physical education teachers to reflect. *The Physical Educator*, 52: 106–112.

Poole, J.R. (1994). Finding more teaching opportunities for physical education teacher education. *The Physical Educator*, 51: 53–56.

Randall, L. (1992). *Systematic supervision for physical education*. Champaign, IL: Human Kinetics.

Reynolds, A. (1992). What is competent beginning teaching? A review of the literature. *Review of Educational Research*, 62: 1–35.

Rhea, D.J. (1999) Proactive seminars for student teachers. *Journal of Physical Education, Recreation and Dance*, 70(8): 46–49.

Richardson, V. (1997). Constructivist teaching and teacher education: Theory and practice. In V. Richardson (Ed.), *Constructivist teacher education: Building new understandings* (pp. 3–14). London: Falmer Press.

Richardson, V. (Ed.) (2001). *Handbook of research on teaching*. Washington, DC: American Educational Research Association.

Richardson, V. and Placier, P. (2001). Teacher change. In V. Richardson (Ed.), *Handbook of research on teaching* (pp. 905–950). Washington, DC: American Educational Research Association.

Rikard, G.L. and Veal, M.L. (1996). Cooperating teachers: Insight into their preparation, beliefs, and practices. *Journal of Teaching in Physical Education*, 15: 279–296.

Rikard, G.L. and Knight, SM. (1997). Obstacles to professional development: Interns' desire to fit in, get along, and be real teachers. *Journal of Teaching in Physical Education*, 16: 440–453.

Rink, J. (1993). Teacher education: A focus on action. *Quest*, 45: 308–320.

Rink, J., French, K., Lee, A.M., Solmon, M.A. and Lynn, S.K. (1994). A comparison of pedagogical knowledge structures of pre-service students and teacher educators in two institutions. *Journal of Teaching in Physical Education*, 13: 140–162.

Rovegno, I. (1992). Learning to reflect on teaching: A case study of one preservice physical education teacher. *Elementary School Journal*, 92: 491–510.

Rovegno, I. (1993). The development of curricular knowledge: A case of problematic pedagogical content knowledge during advanced knowledge acquisition. *Research Quarterly for Exercise and Sport*, 64: 55–68.

Rovegno, I. (1994). Teaching within a curricular zone of safety: School culture and the situated nature of student teachers' pedagogical content knowledge. *Research Quarterly for Exercise and Sport*, 65: 269–279.

Rovegno, I. (2003). Teachers' knowledge construction. In S.J. Silverman and C.D. Ennis (Eds.), *Student learning in physical education: Applying research to enhance instruction, second edition* (pp. 295–310). Champaign, IL: Human Kinetics.

Rovegno, I., Chen, W. and Todorovich, J. (2003). Accomplished teachers' pedagogical content knowledge of teaching dribbling to third grade children. *Journal of Teaching in Physical Education, 22*: 426–449.

Schempp, P.G. and Graber, K.C. (1992). Teacher socialization from a dialectical perspective: Pre-training through induction. *Journal of Teaching in Physical Education, 11*: 329–348.

Sebren, A. (1994) Reflective thinking – Integrating theory and practice in teacher preparation. *Journal of Physical Education, Recreation and Dance, 65*: 23–59.

Sebren, A. (1995). Pre-service teachers' reflection and knowledge development in a field-based elementary physical education methods course. *Journal of Teaching in Physical Education, 14*: 262–283.

Senne, T.A. and Rikard, G.L. (2002). Experiencing the portfolio process during the internship: A comparative analysis of two PETE portfolio models. *Journal of Teaching in Physical Education, 21*: 309–336.

Senne, T.A. and Rikard, G.L. (2004). A developmental intervention via the teaching portfolio: Employing the teaching/learning framework. *Journal of Teaching in Physical Education, 23*: 88–104.

Sharpe, T. (1997). Using technology in preservice teacher supervision. *The Physical Educator, 54*: 11–19.

Sharpe, T., Lounsbery, M. and Bahls, V. (1997). Description and effects of sequential behavior practice in teacher education. *Research Quarterly for Exercise and Sport, 68*: 222–232.

Shulman, L. (2002). Truth *and* consequences? Inquiry and policy research on teacher education. *Journal of Teacher Education, 53*: 248–253.

Siedentop, D. and Locke, L. (1997). Making a difference for physical education: What professors and practitioners must build together. *Journal of Physical Education, Recreation and Dance, 68*(4): 25–33.

Sikula, J., Buttery T.J. and Guyton E. (Eds.) (1996). *Handbook of research on teacher education: A project of the association of teacher educators.* New York: Macmillan.

Silverman, S.J. and Ennis, C.D. (Eds.) (1996). *Student learning in physical education: Applying research to enhance instruction.* Champaign, IL: Human Kinetics.

Silverman, S.J. and Ennis, C.D. (Eds.) (2003). *Student learning in physical education: Applying research to enhance instruction, second edition.* Champaign, IL: Human Kinetics.

Smith, M.D. (1993). An examination of a generic field experience from a physical education perspective. *The Physical Educator, 50*: 151–168.

Smith, M.D., Kerr, I.G. and Meek, G.A. (1993). Physical education teacher behaviour intervention: Increasing levels of performance and motivational feedback through the utilization of clinical supervision techniques. *Physical Education Review, 16*: 162–172.

Smith, M.D. and Steffen, J.P. (1994). The effect of different schedules of feedback on the management time of student teachers. *The Physical Educator, 51*: 81–92.

Smith, T.K. (1998). A mentoring strategy for cooperating teachers. *Journal of Physical Education, Recreation and Dance, 69*(5): 55–58.

Solmon, M.A. and Boone, J. (1993). The impact of student goal orientation in physical education classes. *Research Quarterly for Exercise and Sport, 64*: 418–424.

St. Pierre, P. (1998). Distance learning in physical education teacher education. *Quest, 50*: 344–356.

Strand, B.N. (1992). A descriptive profile of teacher preparation practices in physical education teacher education. *The Physical Educator, 49*: 104–112.

Tannehill, D. and Goc Karp, G.G. (1992). The student teaching practicum: Placement trends and issues. *The Physical Educator, 49*: 39–48.

Tsangaridou, N. and O'Sullivan, M. (1994). Using pedagogical reflective strategies to enhance reflection among preservice physical education teachers. *Journal of Teaching in Physical Education, 14*: 13–33.

Tsangaridou, N. and O'Sullivan, M. (1997). The role of reflection in shaping physical education teachers' educational values and practices. *Journal of Teaching in Physical Education, 17*: 2–25.

Tsangaridou, N. and O'Sullivan, M. (2003). Physical education teachers' theories of action and theories-in-use. *Journal of Teaching in Physical Education, 22*: 132–152.

Tsangaridou, N. and Siedentop, D. (1995). Reflective teaching: A literature review. *Quest, 47*: 212–237.

Wideen, M., Mayer-Smith, J. and Moon, B. (1998). A critical analysis of the research on learning to teach: Making the case for an ecological perspective on inquiry. *Review of Educational Research, 68*: 130–178.

Williamson, K.M. (1993). A qualitative study on the socialization of beginning physical education teacher educators. *Research Quarterly for Exercise and Sport, 64*: 188–201.

Wilson, S. and Williams, J.A. (2001). Student-created case studies for teacher education. *Journal of Physical Education, Recreation and Dance, 72*(2): 49–53.

Winitzky, N. and Kauchak, D. (1997). Constructivism in teacher education: Applying cognitive theory to teacher learning. In V. Richardson (Ed.), *Constructivist teacher education: Building new understandings* (pp. 59–83). London: Falmer Press.

Woods, M., Goc Karp, G. and Escamilla, E. (2000). Preservice teachers learning about students and the teaching-learning process. *Journal of Teaching in Physical Education, 20*: 15–39.

Wright, S.C. and Smith, D.E. (2000). A case for formalized mentoring. *Quest, 52*: 200–213.

Zanting, A., Verloop, N., Vermunt, J.D. and Van Driel, J.H. (1998). Explicating practical knowledge: An extension of mentor teachers' roles. *European Journal of Teacher Education, 21*: 11–28.

Zanting, A., Verloop, N. and Vermunt, J.D. (2001). Student teachers eliciting mentor's practical knowledge and comparing it to their own beliefs. *Teaching and Teacher Education, 17*: 725–740.

4.4 Induction of beginning physical educators into the school setting

SANDRA A. STROOT AND BOMNA KO

Socialization into the teaching profession occurs over the entire scope of a teacher's career. Varying definitions of socialization resulted in differing interpretations of outcomes for teachers. For example, Lortie (1975) defined socialization as, "… a subjective process – it is something that happens to people as they move through a series of structured experiences and internalize the subculture of the group" (p. 61). Lacey (1977) described socialization as "…the process of change by which individuals become members of the teaching profession" (p. 634). Socialization, as described by Van Maanen and Schein, (1979) is a process where an individual is " …taught and learns what behaviors and perspectives are customary and desirable within a professional role" (p. 212). Finally, Macdonald and Kirk (1996) defined socialization as "…a subjective process with the goal being for the teacher to build and maintain a sense of personal identity, self-worth and professional competence within the constraints of occupational standards, ethics and regulations" (p. 60).

Different definitions of socialization may be explained by Zeichner and Gore's (1990) description of three main traditions in teacher socialization research: functionalist, interpretive, and critical. They explained that, "Each [tradition] is characterized by a theoretical orientation which shapes the questions that are asked, the way the research is conducted and the interpretation of the data collected"(p. 1).

The phase of teacher socialization addressed in this chapter is the induction into the school setting, or the transition from teacher preparation to the first few years of teaching. Huling-Austin and colleagues described induction as "…a transitional period in teacher education between teacher preparation and continuing professional development during which assistance may be provided and/or assessment may be applied to beginning teachers" (Huling-Austin et al., 1989: 3). It is during the induction phase of teacher development, that the lessons learned in the preservice programs are tested within the reality of the class settings to which the teachers were assigned. Observation data and information gleaned from specific teachers' stories have helped to bring their realities to the forefront, as researchers all over the world have studied this field of inquiry.

The socialization process for physical educators may not be the same as for classroom teachers, as the status and rewards of physical education teachers are not the same as for teachers of other disciplines (Sarason, 1972; Smyth, 1995; Stroot, 1993; Templin and Schempp, 1989; Williams and Williamson, 1998). Macdonald (1995) reminds us about the complexity of socialization in physical education, as it "…not only reflects the expectations and constraints generated by the society, educational organizations, and bureaucracies but also the pervasive influences of working with and within sport" (p. 129).

History of the study of socialization in physical education

The study of socialization into the field of education was heavily influenced by literature from the medical profession (Becker et al., 1961). Borrowing from medical models, socialization research in general education, and then in physical education became organized around three distinct stages: anticipatory socialization, professional socialization, and entry into the workplace. Several articles targeted teachers' socialization into physical education during the 1970s and early 1980s (e.g. Pooley, 1972, 1975; Templin, 1979; Templin et al., 1982), and spawned interest in studying the process of socialization, particularly the recruitment into teaching and the socialization process of student teachers. In the early 1980s, the two-article series published by Lawson (1983a,b) acted as a renewed catalyst for discussion and additional research in socialization across the continuum of teacher development. In this series, Lawson described how the 'socialization of physical education teachers may be seen as a life-long process' (1983a; 3). Lawson's first article (1983a) highlighted the relationship between the subjective warrant, recruitment, and teacher education. He described three kinds of socialization important for teachers: (a) acculturation, which begins at birth, and helps individuals develop their values and beliefs about their role in life; (b) professional socialization, which is the process for developing the values, beliefs, knowledge and skills for success in the profession; and (c) organizational socialization, which is the process by which teachers "…acquire and maintain a custodial ideology and the knowledge and skills that are valued and rewarded by the organization" (p. 4). Lawson stated that these processes of socialization may occur simultaneously and are often incompatible, making socialization problematic, not automatic. Lawson's second article (1983b), the one most closely related to induction into the workplace, examined the socialization for teachers who have completed their preservice preparation and are moving into the school setting. The article discussed entry into the schools, highlighted various role orientations, and finally prompted examination of how and why teachers were able to remain in teaching over long periods of time. Lawson applied Van Maanen and Schein's (1979) theory of organizational socialization to physical education teachers and their workplace, connecting six tactical dimensions identified by Van Maanen and Schein to socialization outcomes (e.g. custodial and innovative) for physical educators. The authors identified tactics associated with custodial orientations, designed to maintain the status quo; tactics with innovative orientations were more likely to result in change from the status quo in an organizational structure.

Socialization into physical education

The book, *Socialization into Physical Education: Learning to Teach* (Templin and Schempp, 1989), was organized around the three phases of socialization similar to the medical model mentioned previously, recruitment into teaching, professional preparation, and the influence of the school setting and related agencies. The authors presented a shift in thinking from a functionalist to a dialectic perspective, where teachers were viewed as playing an active role in the socialization process. Research syntheses and new perspectives were presented with chapters on apprenticeship of observation (Schempp), recruitment (Dewar), and the effect of workplace conditions on teachers (Lawson; Templin). Additional themes such as gender as a socializing agent (Griffin), classed and gendered career opportunities (Evans and Williams), and teaching culture and ideology (Sparkes) emerged into the mainstream of socialization research in physical education.

In 1993, the *Journal of Teaching in Physical Education* monograph targeted socialization of teachers from preservice education through their career pathways (Stroot, 1993). The research field gained depth but the new teachers' entry into the workplace was still relatively unstudied. A review of the research on induction in physical education (Stroot et al., 1993) uncovered only six articles targeting newly graduated physical educators. In this early research, patterns emerged to describe new teachers' experiences and concerns when transitioning from teacher preparation into the school setting. Since 1993, there have been more studies on the induction process in the US, and a few studies from countries outside of the US. Initial patterns that emerged in early research on socialization in physical education have begun to illustrate how some aspects of induction were similar to those found in the general education literature. Other aspects have been different as physical educators were further marginalized than teachers in other subjects (see O'Sullivan, 1989; Schempp and Graber, 1992; Smyth, 1995).

Overview of theories supporting induction

Various theoretical frameworks have been applied in the study of teacher induction into the workplace. Five models used to study induction into physical education will be described in the next section of this chapter: Occupational Socialization (Van Maanen and Schein, 1979), Developmental Stages of Teachers (Fuller, 1969, Fuller and Bown, 1975); Teacher Career Cycle (Fessler, 1985); Dialectical Approach (Hall, 1993; Hegel, 1910; Zeichner, 1979), Identity Theory (Giddens, 1991), and Situated Learning Theory (Lave and Wenger, 1991).

Organizational socialization

Lawson (1986) described the occupational socialization as "all of the kinds of socialization that initially influence persons to enter the field of physical education and that later are responsible for their perceptions and actions as teacher educators and teachers" (p. 107). Five subcategories of occupational socialization were identified: societal, sport, professional, organizational, and bureaucratic. The subcategory of organizational socialization has often been the theoretical framework chosen to support research on physical education teachers' entry into the workplace.

Van Maanen and Schein (1979) described organizational socialization as "a jejune phrase used by social scientists to refer to the process by which one is taught and learns 'the ropes' of a particular organizational role" (p. 211). More specifically, organizational socialization is when "an individual is taught and learns what behaviors and perspectives are customary and desirable within the work setting as well as what ones are not" (pp. 211–212). The socialization process in the organization is explored through the process of learning the organizational culture, particularly when new members with different backgrounds and beliefs enter the workplace. The most common aspect of organizational socialization utilized in physical education research refers to three responses to the socialization process as described by Van Maanen and Schein (1979): custodianship, content innovation, and role innovation.

Custodianship

The most common response when entering the workplace is to assume a custodial stance by accepting the status quo, and rarely questioning information provided by experienced colleagues who have been successful in the current system. The new teacher accepts and supports the overall mission of the role, therefore learns, accepts, and implements the requirements of the job and the customary strategies associated with the definition of successful performance within the role. As a result, the existing system becomes stronger and the continuation of current knowledge, practices, and outcomes is assured.

Content innovation

Content innovation is a second type of response, which is "marked by the development of substantive improvements or changes in the knowledge base or strategic practices of a particular role" (p. 228). This situation is likely to occur if the new teacher entering the organization is not willing to be limited by the current system, but wants to try new teaching strategies learned in a teacher education program or to improve a set of routines that have become part of the ongoing practices within the new program area. The overall goals and objectives of the workplace are not in question, but the newcomer wishes to change the practices and strategies used to accomplish the existing goals. These modifications could change the current system for the better or could result in negative changes that inhibit progress toward meeting the original goal.

Role innovation

When the newcomer completely rejects the current system, he or she may react by "attacking and attempting to change the mission associated traditionally with that role" (p. 228). Most of the time differences in the fundamental belief system between the newcomer and the philosophies supporting the existing system are the cause of the rejection. When that occurs the new teacher may try to completely redefine the role function, modifying the overarching objectives of the system.

Van Maanen and Schein (1979) labeled teacher responses as custodial or innovative, and presented tactics of organizational socialization leading to custodial or innovative role orientations. Tactics of organizational socialization refer to "the ways in which the experiences of individuals in transition from one role to another are structured for them by others in the organization" (p. 230). Tactical dimensions associated with a custodial role orientation include experiences that are collective, sequential, variable, serial, and involve divestiture. Tactics more conducive to an innovative role orientation include experiences that are individual, informal, random, disjunctive, and involve investiture. For further explanation of these tactics, see Van Maanen and Schein (1979) or Lawson (1983b). For a clear description of the organizational socialization model in physical education, refer to Lawson (1983a,b).

Within the physical education literature, organizational socialization has been the most widely used model to study the socialization of physical educators into the school setting, especially in the US. For example, Curtner-Smith (1997, 1998, 2001) has studied physical educators in their preservice program then in their first year of teaching, couching these studies in the occupational socialization framework. In Macdonald's (1995) earlier work she utilized the occupational socialization model to frame her study of teachers entering the profession in Australia. Using this model, both were able to follow the influence of teacher preparation and school context on the beliefs and practices of beginning teachers.

Stage theory

Developmental stage theories found in the teacher education literature described the process of learning to teach and the changes that teachers experience during these processes. They addressed various interrelated domains, including the cognitive (Piaget and Inhelder, 1969), conceptual (Hunt, 1971), ego (Loevinger, 1976), interpersonal development (Selman, 1980), and values or morals (Kohlberg, 1969).

When concepts from these domains were applied to teachers' career development, developmental stages were characterized as distinct phases that described teachers' experiences and tended to be hierarchical in nature. Two models representing stage theory have been utilized when studying the socialization process of physical educators: Teacher Concerns Model (Fuller 1969; Fuller and Bown, 1975), and Katz's (1972) Developmental Stages of Teachers. When developing their respective models, researchers studied different populations and addressed differing aspects of a teachers' career.

Table 4.4.1 Comparison of stage theories: Fuller and Bown (1975) and Katz, (1972)

Fuller and Bown (1975)	Katz (1972)
Preteaching concerns Teacher's concerns focus on the pupils, not on the role of the teacher.	**Survival** Teacher is overwhelmed with the responsibilities of teaching, and faces feelings of inadequacy
Survival concerns Teacher is concerned about adequacy and survival	**Consolidation** Teacher is beginning to reflect on progress, differentiating tasks and skills to be mastered
Teaching situation concerns Teacher's focus is on teaching context, and teaching performance	**Renewal** Teacher has effective strategies, and is looking for challenges to maintain motivation for teaching
Pupil concerns Teacher is concerned about attending to the needs of the pupils in the classroom	**Maturity** Teacher has developed a professional identity, and begins to explore issues reaching beyond the classroom setting

Fuller and Bown studied preservice teachers and teachers early in their careers. In the Developmental Stages of Teachers model, Katz described the developmental stages for teachers in their first through fifth years of teaching. When discussing teachers' stages within each model, there are quite a few similarities. Due to limited space the Teacher Concerns Model (Fuller, 1969; Fuller and Bown, 1975) model was chosen for further expansion.

Teacher concerns model

One of the earliest models for exploring teacher development and concerns during the preservice and early inservice phases of a teacher's career is the Teacher Concerns Model (Fuller, 1969; Fuller and Bown, 1975). Teachers' concerns were identified through preservice and early inservice experiences and clustered into stages of learning. Fuller and Bown (1975) identified a major weakness at that time, claiming that the stages have been "described mainly in terms of what the teacher is concerned about rather than what she is actually accomplishing" (p. 37). Nevertheless, the Teacher Concerns model has been used to explore teachers' concerns throughout their career.

Dominant concerns of teachers at the various career stages were identified and grouped into clusters that reflected teachers' changes as they gained experience (Fuller and Bown, 1975). The authors began with teachers' concerns before they entered the classroom and continued with concerns that emerged through their preservice preparation and entry into the schools. As teachers gained experience their concerns seemed to change, resulting in four clusters: preteaching: concerns, survival concerns, teaching situation concerns, and pupil concerns.

Preteaching concerns

Teachers in the preteaching stage had not entered the classroom to experience the realities of teaching and were often severe critics of the classroom teacher they were observing. These prospective teachers identified with the pupils in the observed class much more closely than they identified with themselves as a teacher, which may have explained their predominant concerns for the pupils.

Survival concerns

As teachers began to teach they had fewer concerns about pupils and became more concerned about their own survival. Novice teachers experienced conflict between new, innovative strategies taught at the university and the traditional, more familiar practices they observed in the school setting. Teachers found this experience to be very stressful, were often frustration with their limited repertoire of teaching strategies, and wondered if they would ever learn to teach. At this stage, teachers were concerned about class control, whether students liked them, others' opinions of their teaching, and their own adequacy and survival. These types of concerns seemed to be more prevalent for preservice teachers than inservice teachers.

Teaching situation concerns

Teachers began to focus on their individual teaching context and began to recognize the pressures to teach, not just to survive. They explored new teaching methods and struggled to learn the content well enough to teach it to their students. Frustrations were caused by situations within the workplace such as having to work with too many students, having additional extracurricular duties, lack of materials, and lack of time. Concerns about the teaching situation were more prevalent for inservice teachers than preservice teachers.

Pupil concerns

Finally, pupil concerns were those which targeted the needs of pupils in the classroom. Teachers began to discriminate and address individual strengths and limitations of students and their social and emotional needs. Teachers were concerned about tailoring content to promote student success, but limitations of the context minimized their ability to meet students' demands. Teachers in this stage became frustrated with limited curricular material, lack of parental support and uncooperative colleagues, and felt inadequate and discouraged.

The Teacher Concerns model was one of the early theoretical frameworks used to study induction into physical education (Wendt and Bain, 1989, Wendt et al., 1981), and was further explored McBride et al. (1986) to frame their study of the concerns of inservice physical educators. Later, McBride (1993) modified the Teacher Concerns model to target physical educators, creating the teacher concerns questionnaire for the physical education setting – the TQE-PE.

Teacher Career Cycle Model

The Teacher Career Cycle refuted the idea that a teacher's career was one of a static or fixed set of stages, but one of dynamic and flexible stages influenced by environmental conditions. Borrowed from social systems theory (Getzels et al., 1968), and utilized in the study of teachers throughout their professional career, the Teacher Career Cycle Model (Burke et al., 1984; Fessler, 1985) was used to study teacher socialization.

The Teacher Career Cycle consists of three categories. The first is the Career Cycle category, which consists of eight stages of teacher development: Preservice; Induction; Competency Building; Enthusiastic and Growing; Career Frustration; Stable and Stagnant, Career Wind-Down; and Career Exit. The authors argued that the teacher's career cycle is influenced by factors such as personal and organizational environments. The Personal Environment category consists of positive and negative factors such as family, positive critical incidents, crises, or individual dispositions. The Organizational Environment category includes factors such as the teachers' union, management style, societal expectations, or professional organizations (see Figure 4.4.1).

Due to the dynamic, interactive forces of the personal and organizational factors, teacher development does not occur in a linear fashion with teachers moving through the stages in a predictable and sequential fashion. It is possible that only one factor or a combination of factors could positively or negatively influence a teacher's place in the career cycle. An organizational environment that provides an atmosphere of trust and support and opportunities for recognition when work is done well could be a positive context for a teacher to move into the enthusiastic and growing phase of the career cycle, and continue to work in a productive and meaningful manner. However, if a teacher is in the midst of a life crisis, such as the death of a loved one, or a difficult divorce, this environment is likely to have a negative impact, perhaps keeping the teacher in a stable and stagnant period while coping with the stress and frustrations of personal life. Another teacher, who is in the career wind-down phase of the cycle, may be required to use technology in the classroom. When learning technology, the teacher may find new, motivating strategies for instructing students, and return to the enthusiastic and growing cycle of the teacher career. In the examples mentioned previously, the teachers' personal or organizational environment influenced their place within the Teacher Career Cycle. According to the assumptions of the Teacher Career Cycle and the unpredictable nature of the personal and organizational environments, it is likely that teachers move in and out of various stages within the Teacher Career Cycle throughout their years in the classroom.

The Teacher Career Cycle Model has not been widely used in physical education, but examples can be found within a series of articles based on the work of Amy Woods and colleagues. Using this framework, Woods and colleagues conducted a longitudinal study of one physical educator's journey from a research-based preservice program into the first decade of the teacher's career (Lynn et al., 2003; Woods and Earls, 1995; Woods and Lynn, 2001). The authors were able to document how perceptions and practices changed over multiple years of a teachers' career cycle.

Dialectical approach

The word dialectic originated with the Greek expression for art of conversation or dialog (Hall, 1993), which emerges as a negotiation between two potentially opposing viewpoints. Hegel's (1910) dialectical model of history was described as having three components: a thesis, an antithesis which negates the thesis, and a synthesis which considers knowledge gleaned from each of the previous perspectives to form an opinion or change the status quo. Within this model there was an assumption of a power struggle (Hegel, 1910), and resistance was created by the struggle between these two entities.

When Hegel's philosophy was applied to more current contexts, participants were encouraged to examine most commonly held views of their respective contexts (those held by the persons in power), explore opposing viewpoints, then synthesize

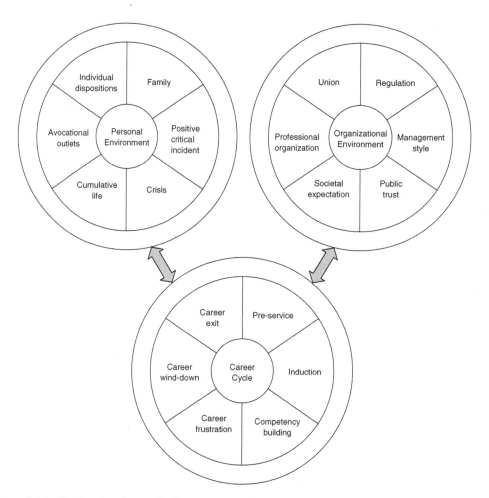

Figure 4.4.1   The Teacher Career Cycle

information to create the observers' own perspectives of the situation (Hall, 1993). A primary concept of dialectical method is the inclusion of contradicting viewpoints to come to consensus on an issue. Falmagne (1995) stated, "Whereas, within the standard view, conceptual unity among objects relies on the commonality of elements, it is the interrelatedness of diverse elements and the integration of opposites that creates unity within dialectics" (p. 207).

When applied to education the dialectical approach was manifest through the dialog that occurred between teachers and social and cultural context in which they worked as a way for educators to negotiate their role or identity within the school context (Zeichner, 1979; Zeichner and Gore, 1990). This dialog provided a means for teachers to gather information to analyze the thesis and antithesis of the status quo, providing a dialectical relationship between the self and the context and an opportunity for teachers to develop their own meaning and identity from this relationship. In this dialectical

relationship the school culture often encouraged reproduction of the dominant society by establishing boundaries to stifle change and continue the status quo (Giroux, 2001). Conflict may have occurred when these boundaries were resisted, the existing culture was questioned, and change was pursued. As change was negotiated, accommodation and resistance in this context occurred as a part of the dynamic dialectical relationship. Giroux (2001) called for a better understanding of this dialectic in the struggle for transformation and change.

The dialectical philosophy was applied in the physical education literature when Schempp and colleagues (Schempp and Graber, 1992; Schempp et al., 1993) studied the political forces imbedded in the induction process of physical educators into their school setting. Schempp and Graber (1992) stated,

When individuals push back against the forces of socialization, covertly or overtly making their own choices based upon the wisdom of their experience, the process may properly be called dialectical – a context of social thesis against individual antithesis. (p. 331)

Using this philosophy, the authors highlighted the potential for how new teachers can resist the status quo, acting as active agents to guide their own destiny in the socialization process (Schempp and Graber, 1992; Schempp et al., 1993).

Identity theory

Similar to the dialectical approach, identity theory is couched in the socialization theories, with the assumption that identity is created through the interrelationship between the context and the self, thereby influencing the personal identity of the individual. Much of this work is guided by Giddens' (1990) concept of high modernity; one aspect of high modernity is the reordering of social relations in light of new knowledge. Giddens (1991) described the changing nature of self-identity, recognizing that self-identity is not a set of traits possessed by an individual but that the individual actively constructs and revises a story of self which provides a basis for self-identity. Identity theory is changed through the concepts of social and personal transformation. Giddens stated "the self is reflexively understood by the person in terms of her or his biography" (p. 53).

Researchers in physical education have criticizes role theory as a framework for studying socialization of teachers because it does not recognize the "dialectical relationship between teachers and the cultural and social context of their work" and tends to "overlook active efforts by teachers as they seek to make sense of their position" (O'Connor and Macdonald, 2002: 41; Schempp and Graber, 1992). Macdonald and colleagues chose identity theory to foreground the importance of this dialectical relationship during the socialization of physical educators in Australia (O'Connor and Macdonald, 2002; Macdonald and Kirk, 1996). Macdonald and Kirk (1996) utilized this theory to explore how the involvement in sport influenced the beginning teachers' identities, and how the notion of surveillance and social regulation were consequential in beginning teachers' negotiation of their identities during socialization into teaching (p. 61).

Situated learning theory

Situated learning theory assumes learning is a function of the instructional activity as well as the context and culture in which the activity is situated (Lave and Wenger, 1991). A key component of situated learning theory is the social aspect of learning

within the relevant instructional context; that knowledge is socially constructed.

Lave and Wenger explained that peripherality "suggests an opening, a way of gaining access to sources for understanding through growing involvement" (p. 37). When applying legitimate periphery of participation to a situation where a beginner attempts to gain entry into an existing community, the beginner enters as a part of the periphery, first observing the learning activities of the community. Through direct involvement in the activities of the community, the knowledge, understanding and skills of the beginner develop and the beginner becomes a full participant within the community as knowledge increases and expertise is developed. Throughout the process of engagement, the situated learning activity that first engaged the beginner in the community has transformed into legitimate peripheral participation and full engagement in the community of practice.

When social learning theory is applied to the socialization of teachers into the teaching profession, the concepts help them to learn about the professional community within their educational context (Wenger, 1998). Teachers begin to understand the practices within the context in which they are applied and the intricacies of that context and culture, which influence teachers' ability to perform the practices in the way they were intended. The experienced teachers act as role models and provide social opportunities to engage in discussion about their teaching practices. Strong, sustained professional relationships develop as novices become a part of the community. As the learners become fully participating members and begin to take on leadership roles, they have greater opportunities to negotiate their role within the group and to influence the culture of the community.

According to Wenger (1998), "…placing the focus on practice has broad implications on what it takes to understand and support learning" (p. 7). Wenger argued that we must rethink learning for individuals, for communities, and for organizations. For *individuals*, it means that learning is an issue of engaging in and contributing to the practices of their communities. For *communities*, it means that learning is an issue of refining their practice and ensuring new generations of members. For *organizations*, it means that learning is an issue of sustaining the interconnected communities of practice through which an organization knows what it knows and thus becomes effective and valuable as an organization (pp. 7–8).

Situated learning theory was included in this review was because of its profound impact in general education, particularly on induction in general education (Feiman-Nemser et al., 1999; Feiman-Nemser, 2001; Moir, 2003), and its potential for use in physical education. Situated learning theory has begun to emerge in the physical education literature (Kirk and Macdonald, 1998; Kirk and MacPhail, 2002). Though no studies on induction of physical educators have used situated learning theory to frame their work, one recent study utilized a "learning community model" which was "informed by an ethic of care" (Nugent and Faucette, 2004: 61) to focus on induction into physical education. The authors recruited four first-year teachers to work as a part of a collaborative learning community by acting as supervisors to two preservice students during a two-day a week internship. Though there were no indications of the effect on practice, teachers valued the collaborative relationship with their colleagues and benefited from the community created to support them in the schools.

Comparison of theoretical frameworks

In their review of the teacher change literature, Richardson and Placier (2001) described two approaches to change, with the first examining "individual or small group cognitive, affective, and behavioral change processes" and the second focusing on "an organizational view of change that links structural, cultural, and political aspects of the school organization to changes in teachers and teaching" (p. 905). The authors explained two disciplinary boundaries informing this literature, with "individual change literature within behavioral, cognitive, and social psychology" and the "organizational literature within sociology, anthropology, political science, and organizational theory" (p. 905). Though there may be linkages between these two bodies of literature, the primary emphasis tends to target either "individual or small group change" or the "functions of the organization and the relationships among aspects of the organization, the context of schools, and teacher change" (p. 907).

With regard to the theoretical frameworks supporting research on induction in physical education, stage theory tends to emphasize individual teacher change; however variation occurs even within different stage theories. Fuller's model focusing on teachers' stages of concern (Fuller, 1969; Fuller and Bown, 1975) and Katz's (1972) model targeting developmental stages of teachers are relatively stable, sequential and hierarchical. Fessler's Teacher Career Cycle (1985), career is more flexible and provides opportunities to acknowledge influences from the organizational and personal environment throughout the teachers' career cycle. When attempting to identify reasons for teachers' change Fessler's model provides a broader context to connect the relationships that may occur between the context in which the teacher works and teacher change. For both the dialectical model (Hegel, 1910; Schempp and Graber, 1992) and identity theory (Giddens, 1991; Macdonald and Kirk, 1996), the focus is on the individual's self-identity, however a clear relationship between the social and cultural context and

the formation of an individual's identity is recognized. A primary difference between the stage theories, the dialectical model and identity theory is that the latter two assume the active role played by the individual in negotiating and defining his or her position in the environment, whereas the stage theories assume a more passive role of the individual in the socialization process.

Both Van Maanen and Schein's (1979) model of organizational socialization and Lave and Wenger's (1991) focus on situated learning within an organizational structure fell within the second approach to change identified by Richardson and Placier (2001). Again, clear differences emerged in the models. In Van Maanen and Schein's model, "new members must be taught to see the organizational world …if the traditions of the organizations are to survive" (p. 211). The intent was to maintain the status quo in the organizational structure. The authors identified the difficulty in changing norms supporting the mission of an organization, stating that an organizationally defined role will only change "when an individual who is innovative in orientation at the outset encounters an essentially benign socialization process which not only does not discourage role innovation, but genuinely encourages it" (p. 254). Lave and Wenger's model provided opportunities for novices, in this case new teachers, to learn about the current context from more experienced colleagues. There were, however, intentional opportunities for new teachers to engage and participate in the learning community, and as they became fully engaged, there were opportunities for leadership to help shape practices within the community. New participants had multiple opportunities to change the community by becoming a part of the process of change.

A major tension between various theoretical models is grounded in the assumptions about the role of the new teacher in the socialization process. The more functionalist approaches, such as stage theories (Fessler, 1985; Fuller and Bown, 1975, Katz, 1972) and Van Maanen and Schein's (1979) organizational socialization, are based on the assumption that the new teacher will be taught cultural norms and expectations in order to be effective within the current organization and to maintain the status quo of that organization. In more constructive approaches such as the dialectical approach (Schempp and Graber, 1992; Schempp et al., 1993), identity theory (Giddens, 1991; Macdonald and Kirk, 1996) and situated learning theory (Lave and Wenger, 1991), it is assumed that the new teacher will be an active agent in constructing his or her place in the organization, and as a result of the new teacher's active involvement in the professional community the current culture and organizational structure could change to accommodate new ideas and beliefs.

Interesting trends have emerged within the induction literature. Though there were some exceptions (Schempp and Graber, 1992; Schempp et al., 1993), most research on induction within the United States utilized a more functionalist approach to study new physical educators as they entered the school setting (e.g. Curtner-Smith, 2001; Lynn et al., 2003). In contrast, research on induction outside of the United States was more likely to be framed within a constructivist approach (e.g. Macdonald and Kirk, 1996). Studies using varying theoretical frameworks have provided important contributions to literature on induction into physical education and have shown how theories guide the type of research and the findings generated from each study. As the induction research base is enhanced and similarities and differences of theoretical models continue to emerge, it is important to be knowledgeable about the frameworks found throughout the relevant literature then make informed choices on theories guiding future research.

Physical education research on induction

Five themes seem to be consistent when studying the socialization of beginning physical education teachers: reality shock, wash out effect, workload, isolation, and marginalization. In addition, classroom concerns focusing on management, individualizing instruction, and assessment continue to be important to new teachers. Though these themes have remained consistent over the last decade, research in multiple contexts has provided greater depth of understanding of each area.

In reviewing research on induction experiences of physical educators, some aspects of the induction process are directly influenced by beginning teachers' experiences in their physical education, teacher education (PETE) programs. In addition, after beginning teachers enter their school setting the impact of the context of the work place has clear implications for their success. Though related, discussion about the induction process for beginning physical educators will be organized in two sections. The first section, exploring the influence of PETE programs, will address some major pedagogical concerns faced by beginning physical educators as well as teachers' ability to overcome reality shock and the wash-out effect. The second section targeting the influence of the school context will discuss workload, isolation, marginalization and the importance of mentoring and support during the first year of teaching.

Influence of PETE programs on beginning teachers' success

Early research identified the concerns of beginning teachers in general education and in physical education, including classroom discipline, student motivation, dealing with student differences and assessment (Stroot et al., 1993; Stroot and Whipple, 2003; Veenman, 1984, Williams and Williamson, 1995). In some instances however, beginning physical educators overcame these struggles in their first year of teaching, especially when they perceived a strong teacher preparation programs. Two beginning teachers, Mike and Kelley, were able to implant a strong management program by successfully infusing rules and routines in their classroom during their first year of teaching (O'Sullivan, 1989). Mary, another new teacher, struggled at the beginning of the year, as her students were misbehaving and she was not able to change the status quo as quickly and easily as she wanted (Solmon et al., 1993). Though she struggled, Mary knew she would be successful. She stated, "I had an excellent supervising teacher [during preservice] and she taught me ways of handling problems that occur" (p. 318). As the year progressed these pedagogical strategies began to take effect. "Mary managed to control her classes", "her students continually became more cooperative", and "almost all the students in her classes demonstrated improved performance on the fitness measures" (p. 319).

Concerns with planning and teaching developmentally appropriate lessons and assessment also emerged for many beginning teachers in physical education (Napper-Owen and Phillips, 1995; O'Sullivan, 1989; Williams and Williamson, 1995). Again, evidence showed that some teacher education programs provided teachers with tools to be successful in these areas. Curtner-Smith (1998) explained that Paul "attempted to teach much as he had been taught during this core PETE programme" (p. 89) and his unit plans were "very detailed and 'just like college'" (p. 90). With the support of the building principal, Paul was also able to change the evaluation procedures for physical education, resulting in different, skill-based, evaluation strategies for the various grade levels, and the inclusion of a PE notebook for note taking (Curtner-Smith, 1998).

Though effective pedagogical strategies were taught in many teacher education programs, not all beginning teachers were able to implement these strategies during their first year of teaching. The shock of the realities faced by these teachers sometimes interfered. Gordon (1990) stated that reality shock is "caused by a combination of realizations by the entry-year teacher of the 'real world' of teaching and of being unprepared for many of the demands and difficulties of that world" (p. 5). Research in physical education seems to indicate that when teachers have had preservice experiences in school settings similar to those found in their school site, they are more likely to be ready for the issues they face during their first year. If teachers do not have similar opportunities, they are likely to experience reality shock.

There is evidence that some physical educators were not ready for the realities of the school sites in which they were hired (Eldar et al., 2003; Smyth, 1995; Solmon et al., 1993; Williams and Williamson, 1995, 1998; Wright, 2001). These teachers were very explicit in the shock and surprise they felt during first year of teaching and the lack of experience and preparation they received during their preservice programs to address issues faced as beginning teachers. There were, however, a few beginning physical educators who found their school experience to be one where they expected the teaching situation to be much as it was, and felt prepared for success. For Mike and Kelly in O'Sullivan's (1989) study, "Little came as a surprise to them during the year, as they felt well prepared for their first year of teaching" (p. 235). Mike stated that, "everything he thought would happen has happened" (p. 240). Kreider (1985) commented, "In all, I felt adequately prepared to deal with my new teaching situation. First-year teaching is a frightening but extremely exhilarating experience. I hope everyone who enters this field for the first time will feel as satisfied with teaching as I do" (p. 265). Ed (Curtner-Smith, 2001) entered his first year "armed with an impressive range of pedagogical skills" (p. 99) and was determined to do well in his school setting. He felt ready for his first year as he "'got the science of teaching down' and gained a 'firm commitment to teaching properly' in the undergraduate program" (p. 95). Ed also stated that the "graduate program was invaluable … It just made me more critical, more reflective as a teacher … I am constantly examining my own thoughts … and I am a stronger teacher because of that" (p. 95). Participants in Macdonald's (1995) study did not experience reality shock as they perceived themselves to be well prepared for teaching and had developed appropriate competencies to meet the challenges faced during their first year. Rather than facing insurmountable challenges in their classroom, these teachers were looking for additional opportunities to eliminate the boredom and routine from their typical teaching day. When describing the paradoxical lives of physical educators Locke (1974) stated, "In the midst of complexity is routine, in the midst of change is repetition, and in the midst of challenge is boredom" (p. 15). Though teachers in Macdonald's study did not experience reality shock and seemed to be well prepared to address immediate classroom needs, they were not challenged by opportunities within their own classroom and looked elsewhere to eliminate boredom.

Teachers' success stories are important to examine, as specific aspects of the PETE program that contributed to the beginning teachers' success can be identified and clarified. Beginning physical educators who were successful in their initial school context seemed to have completed strong, systematic teacher education programs where they learned management and instruction strategies that could be applied in their new setting. Specific PETE programs have been described in the literature. Taggart (1989) described Kelly and Mike's PETE program, and Paul and Ed's teacher education program was detailed by Curtner-Smith (1998), thus giving some insight into the preservice experiences of these successful beginning teachers. In both cases prior to student teaching, methods courses were closely connected to early field experiences, providing multiple opportunities for prospective teachers to practice teaching in different school contexts. Both programs worked collaboratively with highly qualified teachers, resulting in strong, consistent supervision from teachers and university supervisors during field placements. Prospective teachers learned sufficient course content and pedagogical practices to plan and implement their physical education curriculum. In addition, teacher candidates from both programs gathered and analyzed data from their preservice teaching practices, requiring reflection and modification on the effectiveness of their planned lessons, and establishing clear directions for needed improvements in their teaching.

These components of a teacher education program align with those presented by the National Commission for Teaching and Americas Future (NCTAF, 1997). After completing a study of "… seven extraordinary teacher education programs that prepare teachers who are successful at teaching diverse learners effectively" (p. 30), NCTAF shared specific features similar to those mentioned by the successful beginning physical educators:

- A common, clear vision of good teaching that is apparent in all coursework and clinical experiences;
- A curriculum grounded in substantial knowledge of child and adolescent development, learning theory, cognition, motivation, and subject matter pedagogy, taught in the context of practice;
- Extended clinical experiences (at least 30 weeks) which are carefully chosen to support the ideas and practices presented in simultaneous, closely interwoven coursework;
- Well-defined standards of practice and performance that are used to guide and evaluate coursework and clinical work;
- Strong relationships, common knowledge, and shared believes among school- and university-based faculty;
- Extensive use of case study methods, teacher research, performance assessments, and portfolio evaluation to ensure that learning is applied to real problems of practice.

Sometimes, in spite of strong teacher education programs, knowledge learned in a teacher education program does not manifest itself in the beginning teacher's classroom. This phenomenon, the "wash out effect", was described by Zeichner and Tabachnick (1981) as the period of time when the impact of teacher education programs diminish, and by Lawson (1989) as a situation where "School practices progressively erode the effects of teacher education" (p. 148). Research suggested that most physical education teachers understand the components of good curriculum and of good pedagogy learned in their teacher education programs; however, they had varying degrees of success implementing the strategies during their first year of teaching.

Several explanations have been provided in the literature for the wash out effect. Some argued that teacher candidates tend to become more progressive and liberal in their attitudes toward education as they move through their preservice program, and then shift back to more conservative, traditional views of teaching as they move into their first year of teaching (Hoy and Rees, 1977; Templin, 1979). Schempp and Graber (1992) suggested that though it may appear that new teachers' knowledge and insights from the preservice program were washed out, "these teachers probably never appropriated the behaviors and beliefs of the education program" in the first place (p. 337). In other cases, it seemed that the information was not washed out, but the teachers decided to go along with the practices that were currently in place, even though they had learned more effective teaching practices in their teacher preparation programs. In Smyth's (1995) study, participants reported "consciously altering both their teaching behaviors and their teaching objectives so that they would be more congruent with what they perceived to be the norms of their workplace" (p. 210). Smyth explained that most new physical educators graduated from preservice programs where student learning was important, and entered a school environment where student learning in physical education was not a priority for parents, administrators, or even other physical educators. In these situations the new teachers abandoned goals supported in their teacher education program for those more acceptable in the school context. This decision seemed to be an intentional choice for the new teachers who described the adjustment in their teaching, but "indicated a firm belief that if (or when) their situation changed they would (and could) return to their earlier teaching methods" (p. 210). Similar findings emerged in other studies as well (Curtner-Smith, 1997; Williams and Williamson, 1995, 1998). Interestingly, in spite of pressure from colleagues and from students these teachers did not seem to be ready to completely abandon the techniques learned during their teacher education programs. When faced with a context that inhibited their ability to teach in ways they were taught, the teachers intentionally utilized "strategic compliance" (Lacey, 1977), or "strategic adjustment" (Ethridge, 1989) to adjust to their teaching context. They realized they were not utilizing the techniques taught to them but they seemed to believe they

would wait for a more appropriate time to implement their ideas. The question does remain, however, whether an opportune time ever presented itself, or whether the teachers continued the compromise further into their teaching career.

Influence of school context on beginning teachers' success

Though we have some indication a strong teacher education program can make a difference in beginning teachers' readiness for entering a school setting, workplace conditions have a major impact on beginning teachers' ability to make a successful transition into the schools (Feiman-Nemser et al., 1999). Overall, the issues and concerns identified by beginning physical education teachers have changed little in more than a decade. Teacher educators can use these emerging patterns of concern to enhance preparation programs, thus ensuring that prospective teachers leave the university with knowledge and skills necessary for a successful transition into a teaching career. However many issues faced by beginning physical educators emerge within the school context and are difficult to address in teacher preparation.

Similar to the research findings in general education across the United States (NCTAF, 2003), context matters in physical education and contextual factors within the school setting seem to contribute to physical educators' abilities to be successful. Teacher education programs can prepare teachers for their first year in the school setting, but as previously indicated, without ongoing support within the school setting quality practices learned in teacher education programs are difficult to sustain and are "washed out". Four major contextual factors emerged in the physical education literature as having an effect on beginning physical educators' ease of transition into the school setting: teacher workload, marginalization, isolation, and mentoring and support.

Workload

When referring to beginning teachers in the US, Lortie (1975) described the abruptness by which beginning teachers attain full responsibility for their classroom. He explained that the beginning teacher is "fully responsible for the instruction of his students from his first working day" and that he or she "performs the same tasks as the twenty-five-year veteran" with no allowance for the "gradual increase in skill and knowledge", and that the "beginner learns while performing the full complement of teaching duties" (Lortie, 1975: 72).

Smyth (1995) found results supporting Lortie's observations as beginning physical education teachers in her study "were expected to perform the same duties as a 20-year veteran" (p. 207). Not only do many physical educators have the same teaching load as experienced teachers, they often have extracurricular activities, such as coaching or non-teaching duties that further complicate their daily schedules. The two beginning teachers in O'Sullivan's (1989) study had learned strategies for individualizing instruction but were limited in their ability to apply all that they knew as the "class size and lack of allocated time did not allow them to provide quality instruction to individual students" (O'Sullivan, 1989: 239). Bob and Tim, two more beginning physical education teachers described their schedules as "grueling" (Curtner-Smith, 1997: 81) and "murderous" (p. 84). Both started teaching early in the morning, had full teaching schedules throughout the day, and then fulfilled coaching responsibilities in the evening. Teachers in the Schempp et al. (1993) study found the "weight from their responsibilities heavy, and at times crushing" (p. 458). Similarly, Ed felt "confident in his teaching abilities, [but] the additional responsibilities that are part of the job are staggering" (Curtner-Smith, 2001: 91). By the end of the first school year, Ed questioned his ability to maintain the standards learned during his preparation program. He stated, "I am realizing that it is quite difficult to teach the PE side of my classes as I have been prepared to do. There are so many situations that make the teaching of PE a very difficult task. I am thoroughly frustrated" (p. 97).

Outside of the US, workload issues for physical education teachers have varied. In Wright's study (2001), teachers in Singapore had difficult workloads with full teaching schedules and the majority of the participants also held at least two extracurricular activities throughout the year. They reported being "worn out … You totally have no life, no social life. It is like you are married to the school" (p. 220). In contrast, participants from Macdonald's (1995) study in Australia were not overwhelmed with their teaching responsibilities, as they indicated a "readiness and willingness to become involved with more complex demands of teachers' work" (p. 133). By their second year teachers in this study sought strategies to challenge and motivate them. "Teachers' responsibilities frequently associated with sport organization and coaching were a source of challenge and reward" (Macdonald, 1995: 134). In this situation, coaching not teaching seemed to be the reason these teachers stayed in the profession.

Marginalization

Sparkes et al. (1993) stated that "physical educators teach a subject that tends to be defined as peripheral to the central functions of the school; that is, PE is a marginal subject" (p. 387). According to Sparkes et al., this phenomenon is consistent across a multitude of contexts, as "for both male and female PE teachers across generations and working in a variety of schools, their subject is seen as less important than others" (pp. 389–390).

Physical educators continually comment on situations that provide evidence of varying degrees of marginalization of the teacher and of the content. In some cases, physical educators were valued, but not for their ability to enhance student learning. O'Sullivan (1989) found that teachers were recognized for their ability to manage a classroom rather than for their instructional abilities, and Schempp et al. (1993) reported that "Teachers' status was measured in student control and matters removed from classroom instruction" (p. 469). Smyth (1995) commented, "… student learning in physical education is not a primary expectation of the administration, faculty, parents, students, or even physical education teachers themselves" (p. 199). Teachers' stories clearly indicated beginning teachers "were teaching a subject with low status" (p. 209), as physical education was not a valued subject area. Similarly, Ed commented that it is "standard practice for physical education to be assigned secondary status" (Curtner-Smith, 2001: 94). All three beginning physical educators in the Solmon et al. (1993) study shared their struggle for legitimacy. Courtney believed the other teachers in her building perceived her as a supervisor of play. Courtney and Mary believed they were not considered real teachers and struggled to get students to recognize physical education as a legitimate class. Lisa from the Stroot et al. (1993) study felt teachers "value physical education only for the 'prep period' it provided them" (p. 379). Finally, Sue (Smyth, 1995) was explaining the importance of planning to her principal, who stated, "Anyone can teach physical education. Just play games. Basically, she was told 'not to take it so seriously'" (p. 205).

In the studies reviewed from outside the US, physical education and physical educators continued to be marginalized. Wright (2001) claimed that in Singapore physical education was not accepted as a legitimate subject. Participants in this study stated "Most of the schools take PE as just a play session", and teachers commented that, "anyone can teach PE" (p. 220). Even in Australian schools, where physical education carries "full academic (Board) status", derogatory terms, such as "Mickey Mouse subject" were consistently used to describe physical education (Macdonald, 1995: 132). Macdonald (1995) concluded that as long as "physical activity and sport are positioned as manual activity in opposition to mental activity, physical education will continue to be devalued within the schooling agenda, students channeled into the subject will be lower academic achievers, and teachers in the field will continue to be considered as marginal" (p. 139).

Isolation

Early research showed multiple ways teachers were isolated from their colleagues (Lortie, 1975; McPherson, 1972; Sarason, 1982; Silver, 1973; Waller 1932). Beginning teachers often experience physical, social, psychological, and professional isolation (Gordon, 1990; Houston and Felder, 1982; Kurtz, 1983, Macdonald, 1995; Newberry, 1978; Ryan, 1979). Physical isolation for physical educators is often more extreme than for most teachers in the school building. Sometimes, especially at the elementary level, there is only one physical educator in the school building. Mary (Solmon et al., 1993) traveled between schools and as the "only physical educator in either school, she felt isolated without anyone to turn to for support and advice" (p. 318). Jackie was split between a primary and intermediate building, and struggled with her inability to get information about school-based initiatives, as no one communicated with her (Williams and Williamson, 1995). In other cases, the gymnasium was located on the far end of the school, or even in a separate building unattached to the main structure. Natural opportunities for discussions that occurred when colleagues were in close proximity did not happen easily, as physical educators were often physically separated from their colleagues. Secondly, when teachers were in close proximity they were more likely to interact on a social basis. Ed (Curtner-Smith, 2001) was able to form friendships with a group of male classroom teachers, and found them to be a "major source of support" (p. 92). He was able to eat lunch with that group and "discuss issues and exchange ideas" (p. 93). Kelbe (Stroot et al., 1993) was in a very similar situation but felt the lunchtime conversations were primarily negative as teachers complained about their teaching positions and students.

Though many teachers had multiple opportunities for social interaction with their peers before and after school, at lunchtime, and at school meetings, they had little opportunity to pursue professional dialogue. This problem seemed to be exacerbated by the marginalized status of physical education in Smyth's (1995) study. Unlike reading and math teachers, physical educators "did not have to be concerned with covering a specified curriculum or teaching basic concepts and skills to be assessed on standardized tests" (p. 209). Teachers in Smyth's study felt a "growing sense of isolation from the main functions of the school" (p. 209). They commented that school was not a "place where students, faculty, staff, administrators, and community members would interact to form a culture within which they would be a member" (p. 208). Similarly, Batia and Gila (Eldar et al., 2003) struggled for a professional connection to the school staff and Gila "felt alone and isolated" (p. 40).

Limited professional dialog was a major concern for physical educators. Napper-Owen and Phillips (1995) reported that Peter "longed for a peer with whom he could discuss physical education concerns" (p. 325) but did not find teachers with a similar approach to teaching within his district. Tamara also stated, stated, "I learned …what it was like to be alone – to teach and reflect by myself. I learned how to self-assess, but wanted someone to tell me what was good or what I did wrong" (Williams and Williamson, 1995: 34–35). Mike, in O'Sullivan's (1989) study experienced both social and professional isolation. He believed teachers treated him differently than they would a "real teacher", and felt isolated when he entered the teachers' lounge. He was also "very disappointed with the quality and quantity of inservice opportunities at his school district" (p. 233) for physical educators. Mike commented, "It is like intellectual isolation" (p. 234).

Context seemed to contribute to the type of isolation experienced by novice teachers. Australian teachers in a small town found themselves "being watched" in ways that were intrusive (Macdonald, 1995). One teacher stated, "Here, private lives and professional lives are just so intertwined that it becomes really depressing" (p. 136). Another teacher stated, "The worst thing is that you go down to a pub with mates from football and there's students there from school", and "you have to be conscious of what you're eating because students will see the health and phys. ed. teacher eating something they shouldn't" (p. 136). Macdonald and Kirk (1996) also discussed the impact on this type of surveillance on beginning teachers, commenting, "Of central concern to our discussion of the experiences of beginning physical education teachers is the notion of social regulation as a mechanism through which self and social identities are shaped" (p. 64). Macdonald (1995) argued that the "issue of professional scrutiny adds another dimension to the discussion of isolation for physical education teachers. … that they were psychologically isolated" (p. 137).

In some cases, attempts at professional involvement took on a level of hostility, resulting in further isolation when beginning teachers were perceived as a threat and encountered resistance from more experienced colleagues in their setting. Williams and Williamson (1998) stated that the beginning teachers' "…ideas and suggestions were met with suspicion and skepticism by veteran colleagues" (p. 82). Joe, a beginning teacher in the study commented, "I wanted to introduce new ideas, but I didn't know how far I could go without making the other teacher mad" (p. 82). Bob explained how his athletic director made it difficult to focus on quality teaching, as there was "…a problem with trying to do what you were taught to do [i.e. teach] and being loyal to the A.D. [i.e. focus on coaching], especially when the school has hired you to coach" (Curtner-Smith, 1997: 81). Bob as able to "covertly" incorporate "elements of practice he had learned during teacher training when he perceived that doing so would not jeopardize his prospects for being rehired the following year" (p. 82). Schempp et al. (1993) addressed the same issue when discussing the micropolitics of induction. They stated, "Veteran teachers have established traditions and perceptions that the novice must accept, reject, modify, or accommodate. Sometimes the newcomer walked a thin line between alienating these teachers and injecting his or her own brand of pedagogy" (p. 464). Furthermore, the teachers "were afraid to express opinions to peers and administrators that might be considered controversial and thus jeopardize their chances for success and survival in the school" (p. 468). In Wright's (2001) study teachers in Singapore "felt their efforts to teach differently were not appreciated by their colleagues" (p. 224). Vince, a beginning teacher in an urban setting in the US (Williams and Williamson, 1995), stated that his colleague, would say, "'We're going to do this, and this is how we are going to do it'. ... I told her I'll put up the volleyball net and throw the parachute over it to divide the gymnasium so we could do our own thing. She got mad. I guess I insulted her" (pp. 38–39). It seems that experienced colleagues in many of the physical education settings were not interested in supporting the teaching and learning techniques brought to their school by the beginning teachers. Schempp et al. (1993) explained this phenomenon, stating the "current micropolitical climate faced by inductees devalued and discounted the professional preparation received at universities" (p. 469).

Due to the structure of the school setting and professional isolation the majority of teachers' time is spent interacting with children or young adults (Kurtz, 1983; Ryan, 1979). Therefore it is important to recognize the role of students in the beginning teachers' induction process (Zeichner and Gore, 1990). When studying physical educators, Schempp et al. (1993) found that, in "...the isolated confines of a classroom, this feedback [from students] strongly influenced the young teacher's sense of competence and professional value" (p. 466). Bob described how he responded to the students' comments, stating, "the kids complain that they get to play in his [Jeff's] classes, but have to do drills in mine – [Bob] was worn down by the end of the year" (Curtner-Smith, 1997: 83). Smyth (1995) found the "students were barometers by which most of these teachers measured their success" (p. 208). Eldar et al. (2003) provided strong evidence for the importance of pupils in the socialization process when Anna, a successful beginning teacher stated, "... my most important reinforcement came from the pupils. I felt that they loved me. I felt that they loved the subject, and for me, this was very

important" (p. 36). For another participant, "the pupils strengthened the teacher's motivation and imbued her with great confidence in her work, even when support and reinforcement from the principal and colleagues were not forthcoming" (p. 42). For these new teachers, students had a powerful influence on their beliefs and practices.

Mentoring

Several models of mentoring have been used in school settings, representing multiple approaches to the induction of new teachers (Fideler and Haselkorn, 1999; Villani, 2002). The types of programs varied, often depending upon the available funds and primary purpose for induction. Some state mandated programs (e.g. Connecticut's Beginning Educator Support and Training Program) include supervision and support for new teachers with a required assessment component to qualify for licensure (Fideler and Haselkorn, 1999). Similarly, some district Peer Assistance and Review (PAR) programs (e.g. The Columbus Public Schools PAR program in Columbus, OH, and the Toledo Plan in Toledo, OH) incorporate an evaluation component to observe and document teacher performance in the classroom, ultimately determining whether the teacher's contract is renewed for the subsequent year in the district. (Bloom and Goldstein, 2000; Villani, 2002). Anderson and Pellicer (2001) commented, "Although *peer assistance* and *peer review* are two distinct functions, they are most frequently linked in a comprehensive approach to improving teacher quality by providing support and assistance to a broad range of teachers while simultaneously setting and maintaining high standards for teaching performance" (p. 7).

Different induction programs also vary with regard to the time and preparation mentors receive to perform their responsibilities with the new teachers. Some districts provide support to teachers for up to three years (e.g. Glendale Union High School District, Glendale, AZ), whereas most others limit services to one year (Villani, 2002). In addition, some teachers received no release from their teaching duties to perform their mentoring role and others (Villani, 2002) adopt a full-time mentoring role. Though many mentors are offered extensive professional development to prepare them for their role, others receive limited training for their new responsibilities (Feiman-Nemser et al., 1993; Stroot, 2000).

The quality of the induction program may have an important influence on the quality of the support received by the beginning teacher. Moir (2003) has provided a list of core elements of a quality induction program (see Table 4.4.2) that can be used to guide the development and assessment of induction programs in multiple contexts.

She supported the need for high-quality mentors as, "Mentors have an impact on new teachers in

Table 4.4.2 Core elements of a quality induction program (Moir, 2003)

1. Programs should be staffed with innovative, full-time program administrators with the training, time, and resources to establish and run excellent programs
2. Mentoring should take place during the school day, in-class and one-on-one, with sanctioned time for both mentors and beginning teachers
3. Mentors should be selected for their ability to work with adults, their expertise in pedagogy and content areas, their leadership qualities, and their commitment to collaborative work
4. Mentors need ongoing training and support to be the most effective "teacher of teachers"
5. New teachers, with help from their mentors, should systematically identify areas for growth, set personal performance goals, and develop the skills needed to attain these goals
6. New teachers and mentors should be trained to collect classroom data, analyze data, and use the results to guide instruction
7. Site administrators must understand the needs of beginning teachers, provide them with resources, and learn techniques for evaluation that build teacher practice
8. New teacher guidance and self-assessment must take into account the acceptance of state standards for what teachers need to know and be able to do
9. Induction program should be expected to help teachers excel, not just survive
10. Additional support is necessary for areas with minority students and English language learners, since beginning teachers are so often placed in schools serving these students
11. Workshops and training sessions help novices overcome the traditional isolation of teachers
12. Working with teacher unions, policy-makers should ensure that new teachers are not routinely placed with the hardest-to-serve students in high-priority schools

ways that no amount of training can. The real-life classroom presents questions that only real-life experience can answer. Mentors help provide those answers" (p. 3). Research in general education (Bey and Holmes, 1990, 1992; Huling-Austin, 1990; Huling-Austin et al., 1989; Serpell and Bozeman, 1999; Stroot et al., 1999) has shown the positive benefits of a supportive induction program yet very few physical education teachers have a mentor during their first year of teaching (Mawer, 1996; Tannehill and Coffin, 1996). Almost a decade later, there continues to be a limited understanding of the importance of mentoring in physical education.

Both formal and informal mentoring has been described in the physical education literature (Stroot et al., 1993). Lisa was involved in a district-wide formal mentoring program, and was able to find support for her efforts to develop a high-quality physical education program (Stroot et al., 1993). Jesse, another participant benefited from informal induction assistance, as she was able to maintain a mentoring relationship with her former university student teaching supervisor. In both situations, teachers established productive communication with their mentor teacher where they were able to receive emotional support and professional guidance to improve their teaching performance. Andy, a physical educator in Smyth's (1995) study found the support he needed from Jack the head of maintenance at the school site who assisted Andy with entry into the school's social network. In Napper-Owen and Phillip's (1995) study, induction assistance was provided to two beginning physical educators by the primary author who reinforced the teachers' strengths, provided suggestions to assist them in their weak areas and offered emotional

support. Teachers received the message that what they taught and how they taught did matter. The authors stated, "It was important that they understood the knowledge they gained in their undergraduate programs could be applied in their school environment" (p. 324). As a result the teachers were not isolated and were able to improve teaching practices throughout their first year of teaching. Napper-Owen (1996) followed Cathy and Peter into their second year where both teachers reported that induction assistance helped them develop confidence and refined their management, planning and instructional skills, so they became better teachers during their second year. In the Eldar et al. (2003) study, none of the three teachers had a formal mentoring system in place. However, Anna was able to create strong ties with the homeroom teachers in her school. She stated, "I could turn to the homeroom teacher immediately with every problem I had. In most cases, we would sit and together search for the appropriate solution" (p. 37). Katie (Williams and Williamson, 1998) was mentored by one of her physical education colleagues, stating that she "benefited from observing and teaching with him. It was inspirational to work with a person who was innovative and truly cared about outcomes of his efforts" (p. 83). Mentoring programs are as varied as the context in which they are found, with some offering ongoing, systematic support to teachers; some beginning teachers are left with little support and must learn about the complexities of teaching with little support from their colleagues. In spite of the recognized need for mentoring, the majority of the beginning physical educators were not assigned a mentor, nor were they able to find a supportive colleague to help them negotiate the difficulties experienced during their first year. In many cases, if physical educators needed support during their first year, they were left to find their own mentor. Wright and Smith (2000) argued for formalizing the mentoring process. They stated, "Kinesiology and physical education students and beginning professionals have special needs and, therefore, should be provided with mentoring models that cater specifically to them" (p. 211). Hopefully this concept would bring more consistency and rigor to the mentoring process for beginning physical educators.

Application to practice

The need for a collaborative, seamless model for learning to teach

Findings from induction studies indicate that, even in high-quality teacher education programs it is virtually impossible to provide all knowledge and skills necessary for new teachers to be completely successful in their teaching setting. Given the various contexts new teachers experience when they enter the teaching profession, it is hard to completely prepare them within a teacher education program. Feiman-Nemser et al. (1999) stated, "Novices rarely have an extensive, content-specific repertoire of teaching strategies and or local knowledge of students required for such thoughtful and powerful teaching" (p. 8). There is, however, a responsibility to provide a systematic, coherent approach to teacher education, with multiple opportunities for prospective teachers to practice teaching in multiple contexts. Several authors have argued for a seamless continuum stretching from preservice teacher preparation through induction to continued professional development, stating that the induction period has the potential to bring two worlds, the university and schools, together into a true partnership (Feiman-Nemser, 2001; Howey and Zimpher, 1999). If teacher education is viewed as a continuum of teacher development, preservice teacher preparation is only one phase of that process as teachers continue to grow throughout their professional career. Teachers are not "finished products" when they leave the university but still need support during induction and throughout their career. This support results from designing an intentional, systematic strategy to connect teachers' knowledge, skills and philosophies they have when finishing the preservice program, and the type of support they receive when they enter the schools to provide a context for ongoing support and development throughout their career. A continuum of teacher development provides potential for a shared responsibility between the university and schools to support the professional growth of teachers during

their preservice program, as they enter the school site and well into their teaching career, thus creating a seamless transition for beginning teachers.

If there is a shared responsibility for a continuum of teacher education to develop a teaching repertoire expected program outcomes for prospective teachers must bridge the gap between theory and practice. Similarly, if beginning teachers are expected bring new ideas into the schools thereby acting as change agents within their current school setting they must first be provided with the tools to survive within that context. Feiman-Nemser et al. (1999) stated that "we do know that teachers often leave teaching because they feel overwhelmed and unsupported in their early years on the job" (p. 6). Similarly, current induction research on beginning teachers in physical education clearly shows that if teachers cannot apply practical skills to organize and manage their setting and students within that setting, they are frustrated, and achieve limited success in teaching (Stroot and Whipple, 2003; Williams and Williamson, 1995).

It is also important that beginning teachers leave the university with a clear understanding of their core content as identified by their content standards, and learn to organize, present, and assess the content of their lessons in a relevant and appropriate manner. To do these things teacher candidates must have multiple, highly supervised opportunities to practice teaching in schools with diverse, and sometimes difficult contexts. If candidates learned to teach in multiple contexts they would have an easier time transferring these skills into their new setting and could address the specific issues that emerge in their new context. Yet it is difficult to prepare teachers in advance for these issues as they are specific to the particular environmental factors that surround each context. Feiman-Nemser et al. (1999) supported this notion, and suggested we view induction as a process of situated learning. She commented,

> Teachers can acquire knowledge of subject matter, students, learning, curriculum, pedagogy in a variety of settings, including university-based teacher preparation, but using such knowledge in teaching requires information and understandings that cannot be learned in advance or acquired outside of teaching. Teachers teach particular subjects to particular students in particular contexts. Consequently some of the most important knowledge they need is local. (p. 17)

Induction research has shown that some beginning teachers learn effective teaching strategies during their teacher preparation program and want to apply these strategies and act as innovators in their school setting when they feel they are able to do so. Unfortunately, many beginning teachers default to "strategic compliance" in order to survive, as they perceive contextual factors to be limiting their success in their setting. Again, if teacher education is a shared responsibility, teacher educators must work more closely with school-based colleagues to find communities of practice that support high-quality, innovative approaches to teaching physical education. If these communities of practice become a part of the seamless continuum of teacher development the new teacher may begin the legitimate periphery of participation by first observing, then actively participating with, the community of professional physical educators. As stated in the NCTAF report, "Developing good teachers remains essential…. The missing ingredient is finding a way for school systems to organize the work of qualified teachers so they can collaborate with their colleagues in developing strong learning communities that will sustain them as they become more accomplished teachers" (2001: 7). It is through participation in these strong, supportive learning communities that the newcomer can learn and critically analyze current practices, and perhaps ultimately change the practices defining the community of professionals within each respective context. Ironically, though we talk about the benefits of learning to teach as a part of a community the reality seems to be that the teacher is still isolated in the closed-door context of his or her classroom. Perhaps Shulman's (2004) recommendation to open the doors of the classroom and think of teaching as community property should be taken more seriously in the school setting. Rather than isolating new teachers, communities of educators could study the process of teaching, thereby improving the teaching and learning process for all.

Future research on induction for physical educators

Researchers targeting the induction process of physical educators have not addressed several induction themes emerging as national trends in the general field of education. In order to influence and to respond to national trends, it is important that we address these issues in physical education.

It is also important that we understand the unique scenarios that emerge for physical educators, and assist teachers in their efforts to provide valuable education to students in school settings. For that reason, we must continue to study teachers throughout the continuum of teacher development. Though a few physical education studies have shown a clear connection between prospective teachers' experiences in their PETE programs and their success in their first few years of teaching, there is still a need for longitudinal studies to track teachers over time to further understand the relationship between teacher preparation and the transition into teaching, as well as other contextual factors that influence teachers throughout their career (Ward

and O'Sullivan, 1998). Therefore, four themes will be suggested for further study.

Policies targeting induction for physical educators

For over a decade there has been a focus on developing and implementing policies guiding the induction of beginning teachers throughout the world. The need to study the induction period for teachers has taken on a new sense of urgency. In the US, there was a call for accountability in higher education, mandated by the reauthorization of the Higher Education Act (1998), as well as in local school districts, mandated by the No Child Left Behind Act (NCLB) (US Department of Education, 2001). In addition to federal law, agencies focusing on teacher quality have provided empirically based reports and recommendations, which have been widely disseminated and recognized by educators and legislators (NCTAF, 1996, 1997, 2003). In 2003, NCTAF published the document, *No Dream Denied: A Pledge to America's Children*, which acknowledged while teacher preparation programs still need to focus on preparing highly qualified teachers, one of the main contributors to the predicted teacher shortage is the difficulty in retaining teachers once they enter the teaching force. The Commission reported, "teacher shortages will never end and that quality teaching will not be achieved for every child until we change the conditions that are driving teachers out of too many of our schools" (p. 3). Though there were federal and state mandates, programs were locally designed and implemented, therefore the type and quality of programs varied across the country.

In countries other than the US, varying policies have guided the induction process. In England the Teaching and Higher Education Act of 1998 provided a plan for new teachers to transition from teacher training to effective professional practice. Teachers were provided support and assistance by mentors, and induction standards were used to assess Newly Qualified Teachers (NQTs) during their first three terms of teaching (Department for Education and Skills, 2003). During this induction period, NQTs received a minimum of 10% reduction in their teaching schedule in relation to other teachers in their school. Though program was designed to provide individualized support and involved regular reviews of progress toward meeting the criteria defined in the induction standards, not all schools complied with the induction regulations resulting in varying degrees of success (Totterdell et al., 2002). In Japan, the Japanese National Ministry of Education, Science, Sports, and Culture (Monbusho) mandated and financially authorized a new program of teacher induction in 1988 (Nohara, 1997). By 1992, all teachers received 1-year of support during their first year of teaching, which entailed both in-school training (2 days per week – approximately 60 days per school year), as well as training outside of the school setting (1 day per week – approximately 30 days; and an overnight stay of 5 days or longer). Stevenson and Nerison-Low (2002) stated that new teachers in Japan were assigned a master teacher to mentor them during that first year of teaching. The mentor was provided a reduced workload to observe the teacher in the classroom and offer suggestions about the observed practice. In addition, the new teacher had opportunities to utilize a resource center for resource materials and sample lesson plans to assist in lesson development. In New Zealand, all schools were expected to provide local support to beginning teachers by assigning an experienced tutor to mentor each beginning teacher for a 2-year period. Beginning teachers in New Zealand were assigned a lighter teaching load (80% of the time teaching, 20% of the time on induction activities). The induction time provided released opportunities for new teachers to leave the building for inservice or classroom observations (Stephens and Moskowitz, 1997). Contrary to the previous countries, in Germany, there was no formal induction program for beginning teachers. Stevenson and Nerison-Low (2002) reported that the beginning teachers were given full responsibility for their students, and had a high degree of independence during that first year. This arrangement resulted in lack of support for the beginning teacher during their entry into the school setting. Specke (2003) stated "There is no master teacher assigned to assist the beginning teacher during the first roller-coaster year" (p. 312).

In spite of the focus on policies and practices in general education, there has been no research on the impact of these policies on induction for physical educators. Policies advocating reduced workload for new teachers in countries like New Zealand were found (Stephens and Moskowitz, 1997) and England (DfES, 2003), but no research was identified on the impact of policy for physical educators. There has been some recent concern that educational policies in the United States may have a negative impact for physical education (Morse et al., 2004). Given these scenarios, it is important that we study the impact of policies during induction and throughout teachers' professional careers.

In spite of the lack of research from scholars in physical education teacher education (PETE), policies are available to guide the focus of physical education and the impact on children and youth. Policies in the United States (Center for Disease Control and Prevention, 1996) and the Physical Activity and Health (1996) report from the Surgeon General can also inform the physical education profession in the United States. In response to the Surgeon General's call to action to prevent and decrease overweight and obesity (US Department of Education, 2001), Action for Healthy Kids (2002) was formed to create health-promoting schools that support sound nutrition and physical activity as part of a total learning environment. Developed by the Center for Disease Control and Prevention (CDC), The Youth Risk Behavior Surveillance System (YRBSS) was created to determine the prevalence of young people's risk behaviors. These policies, reports and targeted instruments could have an important impact on the quality of physical education in schools, yet to date there have been no data to show the influence of these documents. Potential research questions may include:

- What are the policies guiding teacher induction in your local context?
- What impact do these policies have on teachers' opportunities for professional growth?
- What impact do these policies have on physical education programs where new teachers work?
- What impact do these policies have on teachers' practices?
- What impact do these policies have on students' achievement in physical education?
- Is the impact for physical educators similar or different from the impact for teachers in other content areas?

Teacher retention and support

Ingersoll (2000) reported after 5 years, retention rates are at about 50% for educators across the US, and the turnover rate is almost a third higher in high-poverty schools than for all teachers in all schools. It is also clear that context matters, as a supportive mentoring program can help retain teachers, as "teachers without induction support leave the profession at a rate almost 70% higher than those who receive it" (NCTAF, 2003: 29). Though teacher retention is a major theme in general education research, there is a paucity of research targeting teacher retention of physical educators. The only study found to specifically focus on retention in physical education cited 62% of secondary physical educators in British Columbia leaving the teaching profession (Carre, 1980). NCTAF (2003) referred to teacher attrition as "the leak in the bucket" and that we must "reverse debilitating turnover rates" (p. 10). More specific information must be provided to determine how district-wide mentoring programs support beginning physical educators, and the impact of the support structures on their success in the district. In addition, more research must target the extent to which physical educators are retained, and reasons for retention of physical educators. Suggested research questions may include:

- What is the retention rate for physical educators in your local school context?
- What are the factors that encourage teachers to remain in their current context?

- What are the factors that influence teachers' decision to leave their context?
- Who are the teachers who leave?
- When teachers leave their context, where do they go?

Standards-based instruction

Teacher induction in the US has been greatly influenced by federal legislation and national reports, as they have emphasized the need for funding and documentation supporting initiatives targeting standards-based instruction and guidelines for teacher quality. In spite of this new thrust, the relationship of beginning teachers' knowledge and skills to national standards has been completely absent from the physical education literature. In the US, professional standards guide teacher education programs to ensure prospective P12 teachers are highly qualified and many states are required to identify standards guiding expectations for beginning teacher performance (e.g. Interstate New Teacher Assessment and Support Consortium (INTASC) Standards). In addition, the National Association for Sport and Physical Education (NASPE) has published the second edition of the *National Standards for Beginning Physical Education Teachers* to inform teacher educators and prospective and new teachers about the knowledge, skills and dispositions expected of them as they begin to teach in the schools (NASPE, 2003). Also published by NASPE are content standards for K-12 physical educators to guide content and assessment (NASPE, 1995, 2004), and many teacher education programs are guided by standards developed by the National Council for Accreditation of Teacher Education (NCATE). At this time, no researchers are using a standards-based approach to studying teachers' success during their induction period. Given the standards-based approach to education in the US and other countries, it is crucial that we address this issue within our collective research agenda. Suggested research questions may include:

- To what extent do beginning teachers know and understand national and state standards?
- To what extent are beginning teachers' curricula (i.e. content) aligned with national and state standards?
- To what extent are beginning teachers' practices (i.e. instruction, assessment) aligned with national and state standards?
- To what extent are physical education students achieving the national standards?

Longitudinal studies

When studying beginning teachers, Macdonald's (1995) findings began to show trends indicating that as beginning teachers became more competent in their teaching context they also became bored, and began seeking challenges outside of their classroom setting. What we did not learn from that study, were the specific changes in teachers' competencies and continued challenges relative to teaching and learning in the classroom over the first few years of teaching physical education.

A few longitudinal studies have pursued the successes and challenges of teachers beyond their first year. Curtner-Smith (1997, 1998, 2001) has followed teachers from their preservice teacher education program into their first year of teaching. Ward and O'Sullivan (1998) studied one teacher during his induction year, then 5 years later. Similarly, six teachers participated in study during their induction year (Woods and Earls, 1995), then, the three teachers who were still in teaching, participated in a follow-up study 6 years later (Woods and Lynn, 2001). Though teachers who remained in teaching were able to maintain some quality teaching practices, some struggled with professional isolation, professional boredom, and seemed to accept compromises in their professional goals and teaching practices (Ward and O'Sullivan, 1998). Others needed support through professional development opportunities, a strong relationship with the local college or university and connections to their professional organizations (Woods and Lynn, 2001). Given the limited information to date, it seems that teachers' change over time could lead to a pattern of compromise (Siedentop et al., 1994) resulting in less effective teaching in the classroom and a limited sense of job satisfaction for teachers. In order to fully understand these patterns of change and the factors that contribute to them, we must study teachers over longer period of time. Suggested research questions include:

- How do physical education teachers' perceptions and beliefs about physical education change over time?
- How do physical education teachers' practices change over time?
- Why do these changes occur?
- What types of support do physical education teachers' receive to assist them in their professional growth?

Though we have learned some valuable lessons over the last two decades, greater depth with regard to the number of studies and the level of data collection and analysis is needed to inform our understanding of the induction process for physical educators. Feiman-Nemser et al. (1999) stated that the "…survey and self-report data can document general trends, but more fine-grained analyses are needed to understand where these trends come from, what they mean to those involved, how they unfold" (p. 32). This statement seems to be true for physical educators as well. There is a need for systematic study of teachers as they move from the university into the school setting, and continued study to determine the influence of teacher education and contextual factors on teachers' professional decisions throughout their career. It is expected that the questions guiding future studies on the induction process will range across the "traditions of socialization research" (Zeichner and Gore, 1990), and across various theoretical paradigms supporting these studies. However, the choice of paradigm does not limit the need for a thorough understanding of teacher development over time. Knowledge of the influence of teacher education and contextual factors on teachers' success is necessary to further develop a support system to assist teachers' transition into the school setting. The call for a seamless transition from teacher education into the teaching context is the springboard to a successful, rewarding teaching career. Once in the school setting communities of practice that act as a supportive, professional network for teachers to learn their profession can also act as the mechanism for change, as teachers enhance their knowledge and practices to meet the needs of an ever-changing societal culture.

In addition to a clear focus of teachers' experiences in their classroom setting, findings must also be viewed through the influences of national, state, and local policies guiding teachers' practices. The direct impact of the national legislation has not yet been thoroughly researched, but the potential implications are clear when the policies are examined closely. The No Child Left Behind legislation specifically targets mathematics and literacy as areas needing attention, and holds states and districts accountable for children's performance on high-stakes testing areas (e.g. math, reading, writing, science, social studies). Results are publicly posted on state and district report cards, and decisions are made about the quality of districts, schools, and teachers as a result of these published results. District funding from the federal government is also tied to students' performance on these high-stakes content areas and influences federal dollars coming into each school district. Because, in many cases, physical education is not one of these high-stakes content areas, physical education teachers are not seen as contributors to this mandate. Possible fallout from this mandate could jeopardize the attention and support given to physical education and physical educators.

Finally, some teacher educators have had limited contact with school settings as traditional roles have allowed them to remain in the university and protected them from the daily struggles of teachers. School settings are changing on a daily basis as teachers respond to the policies and contextual factors that must be addressed. New knowledge and practices are necessary to meet these changing needs and higher education has an important role to ensure teachers are prepared for success in their schools. Cross (2004) suggested that teacher education programs in the future will only receive federal funding if their training is aligned with K-12 teaching, curriculum, and testing. If this does occur, the relationship between what happens in schools and what happens in universities will have to be much more closely aligned. There is a shared responsibility to support teachers during their first years in the school setting. NCATE requires teacher education programs to follow their graduates into their school site, and, using external sources such as state licensing exams or evaluations during an induction year, determine the success of the teachers during their first years of practice. Universities and school districts also are encouraged to provide professional support and continued opportunities for teacher development to support and maintain highly qualified teachers. As stated by Feiman-Nemser (2001) "We must recognize that new teachers are still learning to teach, and provide the conditions, support and guidance to help them construct a professional, standards-based practice in the context of their teaching" (p. 2). Collaboration among and between school and university personnel is no longer optional. We must work together to support teachers throughout their career. A thorough understanding of policies, their influence on curriculum, professional support and opportunities for teachers, and the culture of schools where teachers work is necessary to prepare prospective teachers for success. It is only through a collaborative partnership that this can occur.

References

Action for Healthy Kids (2002). *Taking action for healthy kids.* Author. Retrieved November 10, 2004 from http://www.actionforhealthykids.org/about/bkmats.htm

Anderson, L.W. and Pellicer, L.O. (2001). *Teacher peer assistance and review.* Thousand Oaks, CA: Corwin Press, Inc.

Bain, L.L. and Wendt, J.C. (1983). *Transition to teaching: A guide for the beginning teacher.* Reston, VA: The American Alliance for Health, Physical Education, Recreation and Dance.

Becker, H.S., Geer, B. and Hughes, E. (1961). *Boys in white.* Chicago, IL: University of Chicago Press.

Bey, T.M. and Holmes, C.T. (1990). *Mentoring: Developing successful new teachers.* Reston, VA: Association of Teacher Educators.

Bey, T.M. and Holmes, C.T. (1992). *Mentoring: Contemporary principles and issues.* Reston, VA: Association of Teacher Educators.

Bloom, G. and Goldstein, J. (2000). *The peer assistance and review reader.* Santa Cruz, CA: The New Teacher Center.

Burke, P.J., Christensen, J.C. and Fessler, R. (1984). *Teacher career stages: Implications for staff development.* Bloomington, ID: Phi Delta Kappa.

Carre, F.A., (1980). *Summary report of the British Columbia assessment of physical education.* Victoria, BC.: British Columbia Ministry of Education.

Center for Disease Control and Prevention. (1996). *Physical activity and health, A report of the surgeon general.* Author. Atlanta, Georgia.

Cross, C. (2004). Atlanta, Georgia. *Political education: National policy comes of age.* New York: Teachers College Press.

Curtner-Smith, M.D. (1997). The impact of biography, teacher education, and organizational socialization on the perspectives of first-year physical education teachers: Case studies of recruits with coaching orientations. *Sport, Education and Society, 2*: 73–94.

Curtner-Smith, M.D. (1998). Influence of biography, teacher education, and entry into the workforce on the perspectives and practices of first-year elementary school physical education teachers. *European Journal of Physical Education, 3*: 75–98.

Curtner-Smith, M.D. (2001). The occupational socialization of a first-year physical education teacher with a teaching orientation. *Sport Education and Society, 6*(1): 81–105.

Department for Education and Skills. (2003). The induction support programme for newly qualified teachers. Author. Retrieved November 10, 2004 from http://www.teachernet.gov.uk/docbank/index.cfm?id=4866

Dewar, A.M. (1989). Recruitment in physical education teaching: Toward a critical approach. In T. Templin and P. Schempp (Eds.), *Socialization into physical education: Learning to teach* (pp. 39–58). Indianapolis, IN: Benchmark Press.

Dewar, A. and Lawson, H. (1984). The subjective warrant and recruitment into physical education. *Quest, 36*: 15–25.

Eldar, E., Nabel, N., Schechter, C., Talmor, R. and Mazin, K. (2003). Anatomy of success and failure: The story of three novice teachers. *Educational Research, 45*(1): 29–48.

Ethridge, C.P. (1989). Strategic adjustment: How teachers move from university learnings to school-based practices. *Action in Teacher Education, 11*: 31–37.

Falmagne, R.J. (1995). The abstract and concrete. In L.M. W. Martin, K. Nelson and E. Tobach (Eds.), *Sociocultural psychology: Theory and practice of doing and knowing* (pp. 205–228). New York: Cambridge University Press.

Feiman-Nemser, S. (2001). From preparation to practice: Designing a continuum to strengthen and sustain teaching. *Teachers College Record, 103*(6): 1013–1055.

Feiman-Nemser, S., Parker, M.B. and Zeichner, K. (1993). Are mentor teachers teacher educators? In D. McIntyre, H. Hagger and M. Wilkin (Eds.), *Mentoring: Perspectives on school-based teacher education* (pp. 147–165). London: Kogan Page (ERIC Documentation Reproduction Service No. ED 353 251).

Feiman-Nemser, S., Schwille, S., Carver, C. and Yusko, B. (1999). *A conceptual review of literature on new teacher induction.* Washington, DC: National Partnership for Excellence and Accountability in Teaching.

Fernandez-Balboa, J.M. (1990). Helping novice teachers handle discipline problems. *Journal of Physical Education, Recreation & Dance, 66*(7): 50–54.

Fessler, R. (1985). A model for teacher professional growth and development. In P.J. Burke and R.G. Heideman

(Eds.), *Career-long teacher education.* Springfield, IL: Charles C. Thomas.

Fessler, R. (1992). The teacher career cycle. In R. Fessler and J. Christensen (Eds.), *The teacher career cycle: Understanding and guiding the professional development of teachers* (pp. 21–44). Boston, MA: Allyn and Bacon.

Fideler, E. and Haselkorn, D. (1999). *Learning the ropes: Urban teacher induction programs and practices in the United States.* Belmont, MA: Recruiting New Teachers.

Frasz, C. and Kazuo, K. (2003). Teacher preparation and teachers' lives in Japan. In H.W., Stevenson, S-Y. Lee, and R. Nerison-Low, (Eds.). *Contemporary research in the United States, Germany, and Japan on five educational issues: Structure of the education system, standards in education, the role of school in adolescents' lives, individual differences among students, and teachers' lives.* Washington DC: US Department of Education (pp. 315–437). Retrieved November 10, 2004 from http://www.ed.gov/pubs/Research5/index.html

Fuller, F. (1969). Concerns of teachers: A developmental conceptualization. *American Educational Research Journal, 6*: 207–226.

Fuller, F.F. and Bown, O.H. (1975). Becoming a teacher. In K. Ryan (Ed.), *Teacher education 74th yearbook of the National Society for the Study of Education, Part II,* (p. 25–52). Chicago, IL: University of Chicago Press.

Getzels, J.W., Lipham, J.M. and Campbell, R.F. (1968). *Educational administration as a social process: Theory, research and practice. New York:* Harper Row.

Giddens, A. (1990). *The consequences of modernity.* Cambridge, UK: Polity Press.

Giddens, A. (1991). *Modernity and self-identity.* Cambridge, UK: Polity Press.

Giroux, H. (2001). *Theory and resistance in education: Towards a pedagogy for the opposition.* Westport, DT: Bergin and Garvey.

Gordon, S.P. (1990). Assisting the entry-year teacher: A leadership resource. Columbus, OH: Ohio Department of Education.

Hall, R. (1993). Dialectic. In J.O. Urmson and J. Ree (Eds.), *The concise encyclopedia of western philosophy and western philosophers* (pp. 80–81). London: Unwin Hyman.

Hegel, G.W.F. (1910). *Phenomenology of mind* (J.B. Baillie, Trans.). New York: Harper Torchbooks. (Original work published 1807). Retrieved November 10, 2004 from http://www.class.uidaho.edu/mickelsen/ToC/Hegel%20Phen%20ToC.htm

Houston, W.R. and Felder, B.D. (1982). Break horses, not teachers. *Phi Delta Kappan, 63*(7): 457–460.

Howey, K. and Zimpher, N. (1999). Pervasive problems and issues in teacher education. In G. Griffin (Ed.), *The education of teachers, Ninety-eighth yearbook of the National Society for the Study of Education* (pp. 279–305). Chicago, IL: University of Chicago Press.

Hoy, W.K. and Rees, R. (1977). The bureaucratic socialization of student teachers. *Journal of Teacher Education, 28*(1): 23–36.

Huling-Austin, L. (1990). Teacher induction programs and internships. In W.R. Houston (Ed.), *Handbook of research on teacher education,* (pp. 535–548). New York: Macmillan.

Huling-Austin, L., Odell, S.J., Ishler, P., Kay, R.S. and Edelfelt, R.A. (Eds.) (1989). *Assisting the beginning teacher*. Reston, VA: Association of Teacher Educators.

Hunt, D. (1971). *Matching models of education*. Toronto, Ontario: Institute for Studies in Education.

Ingersoll, R. (2000). Teacher turnover and teacher shortages: An organizational analysis. *American Educational Research Journal, 38*: 499–534.

Katz, L.G. (1972). Developmental stages of preschool teachers. *Elementary School Journal, 73* (1): 50–54.

Kirk, D. and Macdonald, D. (1998). Situated learning in physical education. *Journal of Teaching in Physical Education, 17*: 376–387.

Kirk, D. and MacPhail, A. (2002). Teaching games for understanding and situated learning: Rethinking the Bunker-Thorpe Model. *Journal of Teaching in Physical Education, 21*(2): 177–192.

Kohlberg, L. (1969) Stage and sequence: the cognitive-developmental approach to socialization. In D.A. Goslin (Ed.), *Handbook of socialization theory and research*, (pp. 347–480) Chicago, IL: Rand McNally.

Kreider, S. E. (1985). First year teaching: Secondary level. In C.L Vendien and J.E. Nixon (Eds.), *Physical education teacher education: Guidelines for sport pedagogy* (pp. 262–265). Toronto, Canada: John Wiley and Sons, Inc.

Kurtz, W.H. (1983). Identifying their needs: How the principal can help beginning teachers. *NASSP Bulletin, 67*: 42–45.

Lacey, C. (1977). *The socialization of teachers*. London: Methuen.

Lave, J. and Wenger, E. (1991). *Situated learning: Legitimate peripheral participation*. Cambridge University Press.

Lawson, H.A. (1983a). Toward a model of teacher socialization in physical education: The subjective warrant, recruitment, and teacher education. *Journal of Teaching in Physical Education, 2*(3): 3–16.

Lawson, H.A. (1983b). Toward a model of teacher socialization in physical education: Entry into schools, teacher's role orientations, and longevity in teaching. *Journal of Teaching in Physical Education, 3*(1): 3–15.

Lawson, H.A. (1986). Occupational socialization and the design of teacher education programs. *Journal of Teaching in Physical Education, 5*: 107–116.

Lawson, H.A. (1989). From rookie to veteran: Workplace conditions in physical education and induction into the profession. In T. Templin and P. Schempp (Eds.), *Socialization into physical education: Learning to teach* (pp. 145–164). Indianapolis, IN: Benchmark Press.

Lawson, H.A. (1992). Beyond the new conception of teacher induction. *Journal of Teacher Induction, 43*(3): 163–172.

Locke, L.F. (1974). *The ecology of the gymnasium: What the tourists never see*. Proceedings of SAPECW, 38–50, Spring. (ERIC Documentation Reproduction Service No. ED 104–823).

Loevinger, J. (1976). *Ego development*. San Francisco, CA: Jossey-Bass.

Lortie, D.C. (1975). *Schoolteacher: A sociological study*. Chicago, IL: University of Chicago Press.

Lynn, S., Walsdorf, K. and Woods, A. (2003). *Teacher change and stages of development. One teacher's journey from preservice education to mid-career*. Presented at the annual meeting of the American Educational Research Association, April, 2003, Chicago, IL.

Macdonald, D. (1995). The role of proletarianization in physical education teacher attrition. *Research Quarterly for Exercise and Sport, 66*(2): 129–141.

Macdonald, D. and Kirk, D. (1996). Private lives, public lives: Surveillance, identity and self in the work of beginning physical education teachers. *Sport, Education and Society, 1*(1): 59–75.

Mager, G.M. (1992). The place of induction in becoming a teacher. In DeBolt, G.P. (Ed.), *Teacher induction and mentoring: School-based collaborative programs*. (pp. 3–33). Albany, NY: State University of New York Press.

Mawer, M. (1996). *Mentoring in physical education: Issues and insights* (pp. 217–238). London: The Falmer Press.

McBride, R.E. (1993). The TCQ-PE: An adaptation of the teacher concerns questionnaire instrument to a physical education setting. *Journal of Teaching in Physical Education, 12*(2): 188–196.

McBride, R., Boggess, T. and Griffey, D. (1986). Concerns of inservice physical education teachers as compared with Fuller's concern model. *Journal of Teaching in Physical Education, 5*: 149–156.

McPherson, G. (1972). *Small town teacher*. Cambridge, MA: Harvard University Press.

Merton, R.K., Reader, G.G. and Kendal, P.L. (1957) (Eds). *The student physician*. Boston, MA: Harvard University Press.

Moir, E. (2003). Launching the next generation of teachers through quality induction. *National commission on teaching & America's future*. New York (ERIC Documentation Reproduction Service No. ED 479 764)

Morse, L., Wilbur, K. and Ballard, K. (2004). *Unintended consequences: Implications for health and physical education*. Presentation at the No Child Left Behind Forum, February, 20–21, 2004, Reston, VA. Retrieved November 10, 2004 from http://www.aahperd.org/aahperd/nclb/NCLB%20ImplicationsHPE.ppt

Napper-Owen, G.E. and Phillips. A.D. (1995). A qualitative analysis of the impact of induction assistance on first-year physical educators. *Journal of Teaching in Physical Education, 14*(3): 305–327.

National Commission on Teaching and America's Future. (1996). *What matters most: Teaching for America's future*. New York: Teachers College Press.

National Commission on Teaching and America's Future. (1997). *Doing what matters most: Investing in quality teaching*. New York: Teachers College Press.

National Commission on Teaching and America's Future. (2003). *No dream denied: A pledge to America's children*. New York: Teachers College Press.

National Association for Sport and Physical Education. (1995). *Moving into the future. National standards for physical education: A guide to content and assessment*. Reston, VA: Author.

National Association for Sport and Physical Education. (2004). *Moving into the future. National standards for physical education (2nd ed.)*. Reston, VA: Author.

National Association for Sport and Physical Education (2003). *National standards for beginning physical education teachers (2nd ed.)*. Reston, VA: Author.

Newberry, J.M. (1978). The barrier between beginning and experienced teachers. *Journal of Educational Administration, 16*(1): 46–56.

Nohara, D. (1997). The training year: Teacher induction in Japan. In Jay Moskowitz and Maria Stephens (Eds.) *From students of teaching to teachers of students: Teacher induction around the Pacific Rim.* (pp. 95–133) Washington DC: Asia-Pacific Education Forum; U.S. Department of Education. http://www.ed.gov/pubs/APEC/ch4.html.

Nugent, P. and Faucette, N. (2004). Developing beginning teachers through an interactive induction and internship program. *Action in Teacher Education, 26*: 53–63.

O'Connor, A. and Macdonald, D. (2002). Up close and personal on physical education teachers' identity: Is conflict an issue? *Sport, Education and Society, 7*(1): 37–54.

O'Sullivan, M. (1989). Failing gym is like failing lunch or recess: Two beginning teachers' struggle for legitimacy. *Journal of Teaching in Physical Education, 8*(3): 227–242.

O'Sullivan, M. and Tsangaridou, N. (1992). What undergraduate physical education majors learn during a field experience. *Research Quarterly for Exercise and Sport, 63*(4): 381–392.

Piaget, J. and Inhelder, B. (1969). *Psychology of the child.* New York: Basic Books, Inc.

Pooley, J.C. (1972). Professional socialization: A model of the pre-training phase applicable to physical education students. *Quest, 18*: 57–66.

Pooley, J.C. (1975). The professional socialization of physical education students in the United States and England. *International Review of Sport Sociology, Eng3–4*: 97–107.

Richardson, V. and Placier, P. (2001). Teacher change. In V. Richardson (Ed.), *Handbook of research on teaching, (4th ed.)* (pp. 905–950). Washington, DC: American Educational Research Association.

Ryan, K. (1979). Toward understanding the problem: At the threshold of the profession. In K.R. Howey and R.H. Bents (Eds.), *Toward meeting the needs of the beginning teacher* (pp. 35–52). Lansing, MI: Midwest Teacher Corps Network; St. Paul, MN: Minnesota University Press.

Sarason, S.B. (1972). *The culture of the school and the problem of change.* Boston, MA: Allyn and Bacon.

Sarason, S.B. (1982). *The culture of the school and the problem of change (2nd ed.).* Boston, MA: Allyn and Bacon.

Schempp, P.G. (1989). Apprenticeship-of-observation and the development of physical education teachers. In T. Templin and P. Schempp (Eds.), *Socialization into physical education: Learning to teach* (pp. 13–38). Indianapolis, IN: Benchmark Press.

Schempp, P.G. and Graber, K.C. (1992). Teacher socialization from a dialectical perspective: Pretraining through induction. *Journal of Teaching in Physical Education, 11*(4): 329–348.

Schempp, P.G., Sparkes, A.C. and Templin, T.J. (1993). The micropolitics of teacher education. *American Educational Research Journal, 30*(3): 447–472.

Sclan, E. and Darling-Hammond, L. (1992). *Beginning teacher performance evaluations: An overview of state policies.* Washington, D. C.: American Association of Colleges for Teacher Education. (ERIC Document Reproduction Service No. ED 341 689).

Selman, R.L. (1980). *The growth of interpersonal understanding: Developmental and clinical analyses.* Orlando, FL: Academic Press.

Serpell, Z. and Bozeman, L.A. (1999). *Beginning teacher induction: A report on beginning teacher effectiveness and retention.* Washington, DC: National Partnership for Excellence and Accountability in Teaching (NPEAT) (ERIC Documentation Reproduction Service No. ED 448 153).

Shulman, L.S. (2004). *Teaching as community property: Essays on higher education.* San Francisco, CA: Jossey-Bass.

Siedentop, D., Doutis, P., Tsangaridou, N., Ward, P. and Rauschenbach, J. (1994). Don't sweat gym! An analysis of curriculum and instruction. In M. O'Sullivan (Ed.), High school physical education teachers: Their world of work [Monograph]. *Journal of Teaching in Physical Education, 13*(4): 375–395.

Silver, C.B. (1973). *Black teachers in urban schools.* New York: Praeger

Smyth, D. (1995). First-year physical education teachers' perceptions of their workplace. *Journal of Teaching in Physical Education, 14*(2): 198–214.

Solmon, M.A., Worthy, T. and Carter, J.A. (1993). The interaction of school context and role identity of first-year teachers. *Journal of Teaching in Physical Education, 12*(3): 313–328.

Sparkes, A.C., Templin, T.J. and Schempp, P.G. (1993). Exploring dimensions of marginality: Reflecting on the life histories of physical education teachers. In S. Stroot (Ed.), Socialization into physical education [Monograph]. *Journal of Teaching in Physical Education, 12*(4): 386–398.

Specke, U. (2003). Teacher preparation and teachers' lives in Germany. In H.W., Stevenson, S-Y. Lee and R. Nerison-Low, (Eds.). *Contemporary research in the United States, Germany, and Japan on five educational issues: Structure of the education system, standards in education, the role of school in adolescents' lives, individual differences among students, and teachers' lives* (pp. 282–313). Washington DC: US Department of Education Retrieved November 10, 2004 from http://www.ed.gov/pubs/Research5/Germany/teacher_g.html

Stephens, M. and Moskowitz, J. (1997) Teacher induction Policy and Practice Among APEC Members: Results of the Exploratory Survey. In M. Moskowitz and M. Stephens (Eds.), *From students of teaching to teachers of students: Teacher induction around the Pacific Rim.* (pp. 7–45) Washington DC: Asia-Pacific Education Forum.

Stevenson, H.W. and Nerison-Low, R. (2002). *To sum it up: Case studies of education in Germany, Japan, and the United States.* Washington DC: Office of Educational Research and Improvement; U.S. Department of Education. ERIC Documentation Reproduction Service No. (ED 463–240).

Stroot, S.A. (1993). Socialization into physical education [Monograph]. *Journal of Teaching in Physical Education, 12*(4): 337–469.

Stroot. S.A. (2000). PD for PAR: A professional development model. In G. Bloom and J. Goldstein (Eds.), *The peer assistance and review reader* (pp. 99–114). Santa Cruz, CA: The New Teacher Center.

Stroot, S.A., Faucette, N. and Schwager, S. (1993). In the beginning: The induction of physical educators. In S. Stroot (Ed.), Socialization into physical education [Monograph]. *Journal of Teaching in Physical Education, 12*(4): 375–385.

Stroot, S.A. and Whipple, C. (2003). Organizational socialization. In S. Silverman and C.D. Ennis (Eds.), *Student learning in physical education: Applying research to enhance instruction, (2nd ed.)* (pp. 339–365). Champaign-Urbana, IL: Human Kinetics.

Stroot, S. A., Fowlkes, J., Langholz, J. et al. (1999). Impact of a collaborative peer assistance and review model on entry-year teachers in a large, urban school setting. *Journal of Teacher Education, 59*(1): 28–42.

Tabachnick, B.R. (1980). Intern-teacher roles: Illusion, disillusions and reality. *Journal of Education, 15*(1): 122–137.

Taggart, A. (1988). The systematic development of teaching skills: A sequence of planned pedagogical experiences. *Journal of Teaching in Physical Education, 8*(1): 73–86.

Tannehill, D. and Coffin, D.G. (1996). Mentoring within physical education teacher education in the USA: Research trends and developments. In M. Mawer (Ed.), *Mentoring in physical education: Issues and insights* (pp. 217–238). London: The Falmer Press.

Templin, T.J. (1979). Occupational socialization and the physical education student teacher. *Research Quarterly, 50*(3): 482–492.

Templin, T. (1989). Running on ice: A case study of the influence of workplace conditions on a secondary school physical educator. In T. Templin and P. Schempp (Eds.), *Socialization into physical education: Learning to teach* (pp. 165–189). Indianapolis, IN: Benchmark Press.

Templin, T. and P. Schempp (1989). *Socialization into physical education: Learning to teach.* Indianapolis, IN: Benchmark Press.

Templin, T., Woolford, R. and Mulling, C. (1982). On becoming a physical educator: Occupational choice and the anticipatory socialization process. *Quest, 34*(2): 119–133.

Totterdell, M., Heilbronn, R., Bubb, S. and Jones, C. (2002). Evaluation of the effectiveness of the statutory arrangements for the induction of the newly qualified teachers – Final report. London: Institute of Education, University of London. Retrieved November 10, 2004 from http://www.teachernet.gov.uk/docbank/index.cfm?id= 3100

Tsangaridou, N. and O'Sullivan, M. (1994). Using pedagogical reflective strategies to enhance reflection among preservice physical education teachers. *Journal of Teaching in Physical Education, 14*(1): 13–33.

U.S. Department of Education. (2002). *No Child Left Behind Act of 2001.* Washington, DC: Author.

U.S. Department of Health and Human Services. (2001). *The Surgeon General's call to action to prevent and decrease overweight and obesity.* Rockville, MD: U.S. Department of Health and Human Services, Public Health Service, Office of the Surgeon General.

Van Maanen, J. and Schein, E. (1979). Toward a theory of organizational socialization. In B. Staw (Ed.), *Research in organizational behavior* (Vol. 1, pp. 209–261). Greenwich, CT: JAI Press.

Veenman, S. (1984). Perceived problems of beginning teachers. *Review of Educational Research, 54*(2): 143–178.

Villani, S. (2002). *Mentoring programs for new teaches: Models of induction and support.* Thousand Oaks, CA: Corwin Press, Inc.

Waller, W. (1932). *The sociology of teaching.* New York: Russell and Russell.

Ward, P. and O'Sullivan, M. (1998). Similarities and differenced in pedagogy and content: 5 years later. *Journal of Teaching in Physical Education 17*(2): 195–213.

Wendt, J. and Bain, L. (1989). Concerns of preservice and inservice physical educators. *Journal of Teaching in Physical Education, 8*: 177–180.

Wendt, J., Bain, L. and Jackson, A. (1981). Fuller's concerns theory as tested on prospective physical educators. *Journal of Teaching in Physical Education,* Introductory issue: 66–70.

Wenger, E. (1998). *Communities of practice: Learning, meaning, and identity.* Cambridge, UK: University Press.

Williams, J. and Williamson, K.M. (1995). *Beginning to teach physical education: The inside stories.* Dubuque, IA: Kendall/Hunt Publishing Co.

Williams. J.A. and Williamson, K.M. (1998). The socialization strategies of first-year physical education teachers: Conflict and concessions. *Physical Educator, 55*(2): 78–88.

Woods, A.M. and Earls, N.F. (1995). An examination of physical education teachers from a research-based preparation program. *Physical Educator, 52*(2): 78–92.

Woods, A.M. and Lynn, S.K. (2001). Through the years: A longitudinal study of physical education teachers from a research-based preparation program. *Research Quarterly for Exercise and Sport, 72*(3): 219–231.

Wright, S.C. (2001). The socialization of Singaporean physical educators. *Journal of Teaching in Physical Education, 20*: 207–226.

Wright, S.C. and Smith, D.E. (2000). A case for formalized mentoring. *Quest, 52*: 200–213.

Zeichner, K. (1979). Teacher Induction Practices in the United States and Great Britain. 51 pages ED272456.

Zeichner, K. and Gore, J. (1990). Teacher socialization. In R. Houston, (Ed.), *Handbook of research on teacher education* (pp. 329–348). New York: Macmillan.

Zeichner, K.M. and Tabachnick, B.R. (1981). Are the effects of university teacher education 'washed out' by school experience? *Journal of Teacher Education, 32*(3): 7–11.

4.5 Teaching styles and inclusive pedagogies

MARK BYRA

Introduction

Teaching signifies action taken with the purpose of realizing learning in another (Dewey, 1933; Robertson, 1987; Smith, 1987). The aim of teaching is to engage students in meaningful goal-oriented activity with the intent of meeting instructional objectives specific to a given lesson or set of lessons (Mosston and Ashworth, 2002; Rink, 2002). Teaching styles, also referred to as teaching strategies in the literature (Metzler, 2000; Rink, 2002), are planned interactions between teacher and learners that result in the accomplishment of a set of specific outcomes. A given teaching style is distinguishable from another by particular teacher actions and decisions, particular student actions and decisions, and the objectives that the relationship satisfies (Mosston and Ashworth, 2002).

The need for a teacher to use a variety of teaching styles stems from the understanding that (a) student population is diverse, (b) physical education involves objectives from the psychomotor, cognitive, and social learning domains, and (c) subject matter and context at times dictate the employment of a specific approach to instruction (Mosston and Ashworth, 2002; Rink, 2002). Students learn in different ways, come from different cultural backgrounds, and enter physical education with different levels of movement experience. This precipitates different learner needs and aspirations, which in turn precipitates the need for a variety of teaching styles. Objectives from the psychomotor, cognitive, and social learning domains can be achieved in physical education and different teaching styles can help facilitate meeting outcomes across these learning domains. For example, in a peer teaching format students analyze their partner's performance and give feedback based on what they observed. In this teaching style, objectives from the social (peer interaction), cognitive (analysis of movement), and motor (skill performance) domains are met. Finally, subject matter and context at times suggests the employment of a more appropriate teaching style. For example, when teaching a beginning archery unit, a teacher-centered instructional style is likely more effective than a student-centered style of teaching given the safety issues involved with the delivery of such content.

Historical perspective on teaching styles

In the earliest physical education programs in North America teaching styles centered around the teacher (Van Dalen and Bennett, 1971). Teachers were the decision makers in the gymnasium. They demonstrated and selected the exercises and games to be performed. The students followed the lead of the teacher or student leader (who was trained by the teacher) from assigned spots on the floor. The goal for students was to imitate the teacher-demonstrated or student leader-demonstrated activities as precisely and accurately as possible. Terms used to describe this type of teaching include direct, formal, and teacher-centered instruction (Metzler, 2000; Rink, 2002). According to Mosston and Ashworth (2002), this kind of teaching would be comparable to the command or practice styles, two direct teaching styles found within the Spectrum of Teaching Styles as developed originally by Mosston (1966). Given the militaristic nature of the 1880s and early 1900s and the influence of the German gymnastics of Jahn, it is not surprising that the teaching style of this time period emphasized precision and uniformity in learner performance (Van Dalen and Bennett, 1971).

The emphasis of physical education subject matter changed from calisthenics and gymnastics to sports and games during the early and mid 1900s, but changes in teaching styles did not ensue. Teacher-centered instructional approaches that emphasized drill and repetition continued to be the norm up until the 1960s. In the mid 1960s, new teaching styles began to emerge in schools, ones that invited greater student decision making and interactions between teacher and students as well as among students. These included station teaching, peer teaching, small group teaching, and teaching through questions. This change coincided with the demand for university-trained teachers in the field of physical education, the beginnings of research on effective teaching in education which served to generate new ideas about teacher–learner processes, and the general shifts in society that were occurring during this era, specifically the move from a state of conformity in the 1950s to the intense individuality of the younger generation of the 1960s and 1970s (Rice, et al., 1958; Van Dalen and Bennett, 1971).

A further impetus for change in teaching styles specific to physical education transpired with the introduction of Mosston's Spectrum of Teaching Styles. In his book Mosston (1966) introduced a framework of instructional approaches based on teacher and learner decision making. The *Spectrum* was presented as a unifying framework for delineating landmark teaching styles based on the shift of decisions from teacher to learner. According to Mosston's conceptual framework in his original text and in subsequent editions (Mosston, 1966, 1981; Mosston and Ashworth, 1986, 1994, 2002), the *Spectrum of Teaching Styles* proceeds from being highly teacher-centered to highly student-centered. Decision making is dominated by the teacher in the teacher-centered styles. In the student-centered styles, students play a significant role in the decision-making processes. The *Spectrum* is framed by two landmark styles: the command style, where the teacher is the primary decision maker, and the self-teaching style, where the learner is the primary decision maker. Between are nine additional landmark styles (plus alternative approaches that lie between these landmark styles), each defined according to "who makes which decisions about what and when" (Mosston and Ashworth, 2002: 4).

Although teacher-centered instructional styles continue to be the most commonly observed approaches to teaching in physical education classes in the 2000s, other instructional styles are finding a place in the teaching repertoires of physical educators. There are several reasons why this is happening today. In the United States, one relates to the development of national content standards in physical education (National Association for Sport and Exercise (NASPE), 1992, 1995, 2004) and the incorporation of these content standards into a teacher's day-to-day work. Learning outcomes associated with the psychomotor, cognitive, and social learning domains are reflected in the US national content standards in physical education. Physical educators are beginning to recognize that different teaching styles are required to meet the wide array of learning outcomes associated with the national content standards. For example, direct teaching styles (where the teacher models the skill and learners attempt to replicate the modeled skill) can be effective in meeting learning outcomes associated with the psychomotor domain, whereas peer teaching styles (where the student analyzes a partner's performance and provides feedback about the performance) can be effective in meeting learning outcomes associated with the social, cognitive, and motor domains. We are still in the early stages of experiencing national content standards in the US and thus know little about the impact that these standards have on student learning and teachers' practices in physical education.

Teachers are also becoming more cognizant of alternative teaching styles through the research being conducted in physical education teacher education. Variables that have been shown to have a relationship to student learning include amount of time students engage in appropriate content, student motivation, student assessment, informed planning, teacher use of time, teacher management, teacher feedback, and teaching styles. Research findings about appropriate and effective teaching practices are being published in more and more of the journals aimed at practitioners (e.g. *Journal of Physical Education, Recreation, and Dance; Strategies; Teaching Elementary Physical Education*) and in publications (e.g. Assessment Series; Appropriate Practice Documents) produced by US national and state organizations in physical education (e.g. NASPE, AAHPERD, and State AHPERDs). For example, two articles published in the *Journal of Physical Education, Recreation, and Dance* have as a focus evidence-based practical implications specific to the inclusion teaching style (Byra and Jenkins, 2000; Chatoupis and Emmanuel, 2003b). Similarly, in several of the Assessment Series publications, *Authentic Assessment of Physical Activity for High School Students* (Doolittle and Fay, 2002), and *Assessing Motor Skills in Elementary Physical Education* (Holt/Hale, 1999), the authors present evidence-based practical information specific to the implementation of various instructional styles.

Defining teaching styles and inclusive pedagogies

A teaching style in this chapter is defined as a plan that can be used to design and arrange teacher–learner transactions in the physical education class/gymnasium setting. Teaching styles have to do with the "how" and "why" of delivering content, not the "what" (Rink, 2002). Within the instructional setting, students must be provided with developmentally appropriate content, clear instructions for practice, opportunity to practice at an appropriate level of difficulty, opportunity to participate in appropriately designed task progressions, and accurate feedback and assessment about subject matter and role performance (Rink, 2002). Interaction between teacher and learners in a given teaching style results in "a particular teaching behavior, particular learning behavior, and particular sets of objectives ... [being] reached" (Mosston and Ashworth, 2002: 13) during a lesson. The amount of time that the teacher and learners are engaged in a teaching style in a lesson will vary. In some cases the teacher and learners may engage in the same teaching strategy for an entire 30-minute lesson, whereas in other situations the teacher and learners may engage in two or three different teaching styles, one after another, in a 30-minute lesson. The terms "teaching style" and "teaching approaches" will be used interchangeably throughout this chapter.

Inclusive pedagogies are pedagogical practices that "include or tend to include" (*Webster's New World College Dictionary*, 2000) learners in the interactive teaching environment. Inclusive pedagogies facilitate equal opportunities for success for all learners regardless of gender, socioeconomic status, race, ethnic background, or physical and/or cognitive ability. For example, a teacher who employs inclusive pedagogies provides students of lower motor ability the same opportunities to achieve as students of higher motor ability; provides girls with the same opportunities to achieve; and provides students from different ethnic backgrounds with similar opportunities to achieve. Inclusive pedagogies also promote the accomplishment of multiple learning outcomes, concurrently. Physical education is multifaceted. A teaching style that offers students possibilities for achieving multiple goals concurrently reflects the term "inclusion." Inclusive pedagogies promote active learning among learners. Active learners share in the decision making that transpires in the instructional environment. Learners may be invited to make decisions about who they work with, where they work in the gymnasium, level of task difficulty, or the solutions to a problem or question. Inclusive pedagogies promote equal opportunity for success for all students. The ultimate goal of inclusive pedagogies is to ensure continued participation in physical education (Hastie, 2003; Siedentop and Tannehill, 2000).

Teaching styles continuum

When selecting a teaching style or approach, teachers must decide to what degree they want students involved in the decision making that takes place during a lesson. In teacher-centered styles, the teacher controls the decisions about "what the students are learning and how they are learning it" (Rink, 2002). The teacher selects the skill(s) to be presented, demonstrates how the skill is to be performed, structures an appropriate progression of tasks to facilitate the learning of the skill, provides students time to engage in the tasks, gives specific feedback to the learners about their performance, and structures new tasks for future lessons according to what the students have learned (Mosston and Ashworth, 2002; Rink, 2002). Other names used in the literature to describe teacher-centered instructional strategies include direct, formal, interactive, command, and practice teaching. In student-centered teaching structures, decisions about what and how the students are learning is shared between the teacher and learner. Teachers invite the learners to make decisions about use of equipment, space, groupings, level of task difficulty, assessment of performance, and/or the discovery of solutions to movement problems. The degree of sharing in decision making between teacher and learners depends upon the style selected. The decision-making relationship that exists between the teacher and learner within a given teaching style will invariably impact who is at the center of the instructional environment, teacher or learner, and, in turn, impact the potential to reach different learner outcomes.

Major findings from research

Teaching styles range from being highly teacher-centered to highly student-centered. The major findings from the teaching approaches researched in physical education will be organized according to the following titles: (a) direct teaching approaches; (b) peer teaching styles; (c) small-group cooperative learning formats; (d) self-check teaching styles; (e) inclusion teaching style; and (f) discovery teaching styles. In direct teaching styles the teacher is at the center of the instructional setting while in discovery teaching styles the learner is at the center of the instructional setting. In addition to presenting the findings from research, the relationship of these different teaching strategies to inclusive pedagogies will be discussed.

Approximately 50 data-based studies related to teaching styles and conducted in the setting of physical education are reviewed in this chapter. The majority of the articles reviewed are from journals written in English and published in the US (e.g. Human Kinetics, AAHPERD). More than three-quarters were published in *Journal of Teaching in Physical Education* or *Research Quarterly for Exercise and Sport*. Approximately 75% of the studies reviewed were published in the past decade (1993–2003). The other 25% were published between 1982 and 1992. These studies represent quantitative, qualitative, and mixed method research designs (Locke et al., 2004).

Direct teaching approaches

Scenario

After calling the 24 4th graders to their spots, Mr. Johnson instructs them to sit down and observe the demonstration. The new skill of the day is striking with a bat. The critical skill elements for batting a ball are first highlighted by Mr. Johnson and then demonstrated several times from an underhand toss. Following the demonstration, the students are instructed to select a partner, retrieve a bat and a medium-sized foam ball, and to perform the task as demonstrated within their designated area (previously identified). Once the students begin practicing, Mr. Johnson moves from one pair of learners to the next to give positive specific and/or corrective skill-related feedback specific to the critical skill elements presented during the demonstration.

Direct teaching implies a highly structured, teacher-centered and controlled instructional environment. Rink (1996) describes it as follows: "The teacher teaches in small steps; gives explicit directions or instructions on what the student is to do; maintains a task-oriented, teacher-monitored environment with high student engagement with the content; and provides immediate feedback to students" (p. 192).

Research on direct teaching approaches has its roots in classroom-based teaching, specifically in the areas of mathematics and reading (Brophy, 1979; Horwitz, 1979; Rosenshine, 1979; Soar and Soar, 1979). The findings from these many process–product studies in math and reading show that when teachers present the content in a structured, goal-oriented, hierarchical fashion, students learn. Strategies that encompass the described elements of direct teaching approaches have also been shown to facilitate student learning in the subject matter of physical education. When the general elements of direct teaching styles, as described by Rink (1996), are implemented in a movement environment, Harrison et al. (1995) and Gusthart and Sprigings (1989) found that college-aged and elementary-aged students improved their motor skill performance significantly when performing volleyball skills and a fundamental movement skill, respectively. The findings from two more recent studies conducted on college-aged students' volleyball skill performance (Harrison et al., 1999) and elementary-aged learners' fundamental motor skill performance (Sweeting and Rink, 1999) corroborate favorably with the results reported in the previous two process–product studies (Gusthart and Sprigings, 1989; Harrison et al., 1995).

In a study of task presentations and content development of four teachers differing in teaching experience, students taught by an experienced teacher were found to be more effective in performing volleyball skills than those taught by teachers with little experience (Pellett and Blakemore, 1997). The more experienced teacher was able to present the tasks to the students more clearly and meaningfully and able to match the content to the individual needs of the students through the more appropriate use of task progressions than less-experienced teachers.

Results from three additional studies of content development specific to volleyball support the findings from Pellett and Blakemore (1997). Pellett and Harrison (1995) found that students who received refinement tasks during skills progressions were more effective at executing volleyball skills than students who practiced under conditions that included no refinement tasks in skill progressions. Refinement tasks are designed to help students improve quality of skill performance (Rink, 2002). Following is an example of a refining task: "On your next forearm pass, be sure to follow through (shift your weight) to the target." French et al. (1991) and Rink et al. (1992) found 9th graders' motor skill performance specific to the volleyball serve and set to be enhanced when they practiced the skills using task progressions. It was also shown that learning was evident only when the level of difficulty of the task progressions matched the skill level of the student (French et al., 1991).

Two teaching styles specific to Mosston and Ashworth's (2002) *Spectrum* can be categorized as direct teaching approaches. They are the command and practice styles of teaching. In the command style of teaching, students learn to perform a task accurately and quickly when and as described by the teacher (Mosston and Ashworth, 2002). In the practice style of teaching, students learn to perform a task individually, as demonstrated, while receiving individual feedback from the instructor (Mosston and Ashworth, 2002). As is the case in other direct approaches to teaching, the learner is provided a correct model to emulate, adequate time to practice the model, and congruent feedback related to the original model in both the command and practice styles.

The effects of the command and practice styles of teaching on student learning in physical education settings have been examined in a number of research studies. In one of the first *Spectrum* studies, Griffey (1983) found that when practicing the forearm volleyball pass higher-ability students benefited more from the task (practice) style of teaching than the command style of teaching, while lower-ability learners benefited more from the command style of teaching than the task style. All of the high-school students were found to benefit in the same manner when performing the serve during the 2-week unit of instruction. Griffey surmised that time allocated to skill performance was greater in the task style and that higher-ability learners were better equipped (had the knowledge and skill) to engage more productively with assigned tasks.

Goldberger et al. (1982) and Goldberger and Gerney (1986) studied the effects of the practice style of teaching on middle-school children's performance of a hockey accuracy task. The conditions of the practice style of teaching resulted in student skill gains in both studies. The practice style of teaching has also been found to be effective in fostering skill changes in college-aged students as they performed soccer-ball-juggling (Beckett, 1991) and rifle shooting (Boyce, 1992), and in young children as they performed striking with a racquet (Jenkins and Byra, 1996).

Goldberger and Gerney (1990) examined the effect of two different organizational "formats" as presented within the instructional framework of the practice style. Under one format (teacher-rotate) the participants rotated from station to station, in a specific order every few minutes on the command of the teacher. Under the second format (learner-rotate) the fifth graders decided the order of rotation (from station to station), the amount of time to spend at each station, and when to rotate (from station to station). Both formats were found to be effective in fostering student learning. In addition the learner-rotate format was found to be more effective for the low-ability students than the high-ability students. The low-ability learners seemed to benefit from the opportunity to make decisions about amount of time spent practicing at a given station.

Dimensions of direct teaching styles include: goals that direct student learning; teacher decision making; similar activities across all students; use of large group instruction; basic skills; structured practice; and teacher feedback (Mosston and Ashworth, 2002; Rink, 2002; Rosenshine, 1979). Research indicates that students perform well on achievement tests under conditions afforded by direct teaching approaches, particularly when the subject matter is concrete (fixed) and contains mainly facts, rules, and basic skills and knowledge (Peterson, 1979; Rink, 2002). Direct teaching styles are commonly observed in physical education settings because there are benefits to performing motor skills according to precise models. One of the drawbacks of direct teaching styles is that they are unidimensional; that is, a direct teaching style "assumes that the only important educational goal is to increase measurable student achievement [motor skill achievement in physical education] and that all students learn in the same way and thus should be taught in the same way" (Peterson, 1979: 66). Physical education is not unidimensional; rather, it is multidimensional. Meeting the outcomes associated with the psychomotor, cognitive, and affective domains of learning in physical education requires the use of multiple teaching styles. The multidimensionality of physical education necessitates physical educators to employ a variety of different teaching styles in their instructional practices.

Peer teaching approaches

Scenario

"Come on down to your spots," called Mr. Johnson. Once the 8th graders were sitting quietly, Mr. Johnson proceeded with his instructions. "In our second drill today, you will be organized in groups of four. There will be a tosser (places a student on one side of the net), a serve receiver (places another student on the other side of the net), a target (places a student at the net on the same side as the serve receiver), and a *coach* (Mr. Johnson locates himself to the side and in front of the passer). The tosser will toss the ball underhand to the serve receiver and the serve receiver will attempt to forearm pass the ball to the target who will catch the ball and roll it back to the tosser. The *coach* must first analyze the execution of the forearm pass and then give positive and/or correct specific feedback to the passer based on the skill cues we have learned and practiced. Make a record of your partner's task performance on the task sheet. Let's see what it looks like."

After observing Mary's first forearm pass, Mr. Johnson said, "Mary, I like how you kept your elbows locked and shifted your weight to the target – excellent." After the next pass, Mr. Johnson said, "be sure to maintain a wide-base of support."

"Let me remind you that I will only interact with the *coach* as I circulate from group to group. Oh, I almost forgot, rotate from tosser to passer to target to coach to tosser after each five tosses. Do you have any questions about the coach's role or the other roles?"

"Okay, you need to get into your groups. I should see the first toss within 30 seconds."

Peer teaching structures have a rich history in education, particularly in the areas of math and language arts (Delquadri et al., 1986; Fuchs et al. 1994, 1997; Pumfrey, 1986). Within the scheme of peer tutoring, students work in pairs to support each other's learning. This teaching style has been shown to be effective in promoting student cognition and social interaction (Byrd, 1990; Katstra et al., 1987; Olson, 1990). Findings suggest that increases in learner achievement are related to the increase of individualized instruction, opportunity to respond, and provision of specific feedback (Fuchs et al., 1994; Maheady, 1998). Within certain conditions, researchers have found peer tutoring to be more effective in fostering student learning than traditional teaching strategies (Anania, 1983; Russell and Ford, 1983; Sharon, 1980).

In physical education there is a growing body of literature that supports the use of peer teaching structures with normally developing students as well as students with motor and cognitive delays. In adapted physical education, researchers have studied the effects of pairing normally developing students with developmentally disabled students (DePaepe, 1985; Houston-Wilson et al., 1997; Webster, 1987). DePaepe (1985) found that students with moderate developmental disabilities who were paired with 5th-grade peer tutors from the regular student population spent more time in the subject-matter content (ALT-PE) of lessons than similarly disabled students who were practicing in self-contained and mainstreamed environments where instruction was provided by the teacher. The results of this study compare favorably to the work of Webster (1987) who found that peer tutors had a positive influence on the amount of time moderately to severely disabled students engaged in subject-matter content (ALT-PE), regardless of whether the peer tutors were trained or not. Houston-Wilson et al. (1997) support Webster's (1987) contention that trained peer tutors can influence the motor performance of students with developmental disabilities, but not the contention that untrained peer tutors can. This discrepancy may be attributed to the age differences in the developmentally disabled participants and/or the type of educational training provided to the peer tutors. The use of peer tutors in combination with physical education specialists and teacher assistants is endorsed as an educationally appropriate practice in adapted physical education (Block, 1994; Block et al., 1995; Kelly, 1995).

Peer teaching structures have also been studied in regular physical education classes. One group of researchers has systematically examined the number of trials and percentage of correct trials students perform when participating in class-wide peer tutoring. In the first of five studies Ward (1993) compared student opportunity to respond (as reflected in the number of trials performed in a 1-minute time period) in two peer tutoring conditions, dyads partnered to give feedback to each other, and dyads partnered to keep a written record of their partner's performance, to whole-group instruction. In both dyad conditions the students performed more than five times as many skill trials in 1 minute as the students participating in the traditional whole-group instruction setting. Increases in student responses in the dyad conditions were surmised to be the product of the structure of the task and students being placed in pairs. In a follow-up study, Ward and Johnson (1995) examined the percentage of student correct responses throwing a football within a fixed number of trials. The same three study conditions employed in the initial study (Ward, 1993) were used in this study with comparable results. Given that the task was not timed and required students to complete a

fixed number of trials, it is likely that the increases in student responses in the two dyad conditions can be attributed to the students being placed in pairs (Ward and Johnson, 1995).

In the third study, a variation of class-wide peer tutoring was incorporated as a condition (Crouch et al., 1997). This condition, termed peer-mediated accountability (PMA), was based upon the findings from the first two studies (Ward, 1993; Ward and Johnson, 1995) and the research on effective accountability practices (Jones, 1992; Lund, 1992). The elements of PMA include "teacher-established goals, peer recording of performance, public posting of student performance" (Crouch et al., 1997: 29), and the awarding of "fun activities" to represent consequences for improvement. The three conditions were: (a) whole-group instruction, where students moved through the sequence of four stations on their own; (b) peer dyads, where students completed the stations with a partner and the partner's responsibilities included recovering the ball and providing verbal encouragement; and (c) PMA (as previously described). The results revealed that the elementary students performed a greater number of trials (1-minute time period) while in the PMA condition than in the peer-dyads and whole-group instruction conditions. In addition, students generally performed a greater percentage of correct trials in the PMA condition than in the other two conditions. It is unknown whether the results would have been similar if the number of trials were fixed (e.g. ten) rather than those performed in a 1-minute time period.

The next step in this series of studies was to examine the effects of the PMA condition on average-skilled elementary-aged boys and girls and low-skilled girls (Ward et al., 1998). Similar to the previous studies, the PMA condition was found to be effective in promoting student opportunity to respond. In addition, the average-skilled students increased the number of correct trials they performed, but the low-skilled students did not. In a follow-up study of elementary students of differing skill levels, Johnson and Ward (2001) found that the students in the PMA condition performed fewer total trials but a greater percentage of correct trials compared to previous research. In addition, they found that the condition was equally effective for lower- and higher-skilled elementary students. These results do not corroborate with the finding from the previous study (Ward et al., 1998). The differences are likely attributable to one subtle, yet significant, change in the design of the intervention (PMA condition). For the first time, partners were responsible for providing verbal feedback about the correctness of performance. This changed the dynamics of the intervention from simply making a written record of a partner's correct and incorrect skill performance to verbalizing the incorrect performance. Time was now being expended giving the verbal feedback statements and digesting the information provided (before attempting the next skill attempt).

In summary, it is clear that the PMA condition impacts student skill performance in a positive manner, even when giving and receiving specific corrective feedback is not a component of the peer-tutoring teaching strategy. When giving and receiving feedback is incorporated within this peer-tutoring model, it seems to be even more powerful in fostering change in student skill performance.

Other researchers have been studying the impact of a peer teaching style, called the reciprocal style, on student social, cognitive, and motor skill performance (Mosston and Ashworth, 2002). In this style, learners form partners, and, as one learner (doer) performs, the other (observer) gives specific feedback to the doer based on information provided by the teacher (criteria sheet). The extent of peer teaching in the reciprocal style is specifically the provision of feedback from one learner to another. The components of the reciprocal style of teaching are very similar to those espoused in the class-wide peer tutoring model (Delquadri et al., 1986). The only difference is that post-performance awards given for appropriate social and skill behavior are a part of the class-wide peer tutoring model, but not the reciprocal style of teaching.

Skill performance has been shown to improve in different-aged learners across various physical activities when practicing under the conditions of the reciprocal style of teaching (Ernst and Byra, 1998; Goldberger and Gerney, 1986; Goldberger et al., 1982). In addition, interactions between students have been found to be high in number and positive in nature (Byra and Marks, 1993; Ernst and Byra, 1998; Goldberger, 1992). Cox (1986) found that the number of exchanges between pairs in the reciprocal style of teaching is much greater and more positive than the interactions between learners within the command and practice styles of teaching. Byra and Marks (1993) reported that learners gave more specific feedback to partners who were identified as friends, and felt more comfortable receiving feedback from friends than non-acquaintances. These findings support Mosston and Ashworth's (2002) contentions that feedback is provided at a much higher rate when the teaching style requires learners to provide immediate task-related information to a partner, and that learners will interact more when partners are self-selected (i.e. friends). Ernst and Byra (1998) revealed that learners, practicing under the conditions of the reciprocal teaching style, were able to identify a significantly greater number of skill elements in a

given movement than learners practicing under conditions of direct instruction.

In the reciprocal style of teaching students are formally provided opportunity to engage in physical activity in a paired setting, one that promotes social development as elicited by the process of giving and receiving feedback, cognitive development as elicited by the thought processes required to analyze skill performance, and motor skill development as elicited by the "physical performance" and "observation and analysis" of the skill. If the desire is to emphasize the multidimensionality of physical education as reflected by the US national content standards (NASPE, 2004), it is fitting that teachers incorporate peer teaching approaches within their teaching repertoire.

Cooperative learning

Scenario

Ms. MacDonald began class by asking the high-school students to sit within their small, heterogeneous groups. Once settled, she said, "You are going to work on a strategy for defending your goal today. Take a minute to discuss, within your group, what you might do and how you will accomplish it. Be sure that you are working together and each member is contributing. Then practice the strategy selected in preparation for game play today. After incorporating the strategy discussed in today's scheduled game, you will regroup and determine how successful you were in completing the task. I will seek some explanation from your groups about the defensive strategies selected as I circulate during the first part of class. Be sure to remember the social skills needed to successfully participate in your groups. Do you have any questions about what you are required to do?"

Cooperative learning is a teaching structure where small groups of heterogeneous learners work together to complete an assigned task or project. Critical features used to qualify group work as cooperative learning include promotive interaction, positive interdependence, individual and small-group skills, group processing, and individual accountability (Johnson and Johnson, 1991; Kagan, 1990; Slavin, 1990). Leading proponents of cooperative learning indicate that the two most vital conditions needed to qualify group work as cooperative learning are positive interdependence and individual accountability (Johnson and Johnson, 1991; Kagan, 1990; Slavin, 1990). Johnson and Johnson (1991) believe that the three other components, promotive interaction, individual and small-group skills, and group processing, are also important defining criteria for cooperative learning, but not as important as the first two identified.

Cooperative learning structures, commonly observed in teachers' classrooms, are the focus of much research in education (Antil et al., 1998; Johnson and Johnson, 1992; Slavin, 1996). With a history of 30 years, cooperative learning remains one of the most fruitful areas of systematic inquiry in education today (Antil et al., 1998). Literally hundreds of studies have been conducted to examine the effects of cooperative learning structures on student learning in different school settings, with different aged students, and in different content areas (Johnson and Johnson, 1992). These studies indicate that both elementary- and middle-school teachers frequently employ cooperative learning structures in their classroom with positive effects on social and cognitive student learning (Antil et al., 1998; Puma et al., 1993).

There are several reasons why cooperative learning structures have gained such a high level of acceptance among scholars and practitioners alike. First, cooperative learning is designed to accommodate individual differences among students (Johnson and Johnson, 1991). Teachers are searching for teaching styles that will help them manage the challenges of teaching children and youth who enter schools with varied experiences and backgrounds (e.g. different race, ethnicity, cognitive ability, motor ability, social needs, etc.).

Another desirable asset of cooperative learning is its potential to contribute to both cognitive and social learning outcomes. Antil et al. (1998) suggest that with this dual emphasis, cooperative learning "appeals to teachers because it addresses and integrates seemingly diverse goals within a single approach" (p. 420).

Recent applications of constructivist approaches to learning is another reason why researchers and teachers are attracted to cooperative learning formats. Constructivists advocate that learning is "an active process in which the individual seeks out information in relation to the task at hand and the environmental conditions [e.g. social, cultural, grouping contexts] prevailing at any given time, and tests out her or his own capabilities within the context formed by the task and environment" (Kirk and Macdonald, 1998: 376). Teaching styles that foster increased dialogue among learners (i.e. emphasizes the social construction of knowledge), like cooperative learning, have received much attention recently from both researchers and teachers (Antil et al., 1998; Slavin, 1990).

Cooperative learning formats are appealing to physical educators because of their threefold convergence on social, cognitive, and motor outcomes. Although much research has been completed on cooperative learning in different classroom subject areas with different-aged learners, only a few studies have been conducted in physical education. In one of the earlier studies in physical education,

Grineski (1989) observed and systematically recorded kindergarten children's interactive behaviors as they participated in cooperatively and competitively structured group games. He found that the children exhibited a much greater number of prosocial interactions in a cooperatively structured group game setting than in the competitively structured group game setting. Interactions related to sharing, encouraging, protecting, and helping were displayed. Some of the children were interviewed following the games. Their perceptions of the cooperatively structured group games focused on the positive (e.g. help people, fun, play, etc.), whereas their perceptions of the competitively structured group games focused on the negative (e.g. sit down, out, lose, etc.). Other studies support the contention that cooperative learning formats contribute positively to student outcomes associated with the social, cognitive, and motor domains (Barrett, 2000; Johnson et al., 1984; Yoder, 1993).

Dyson, one of the leading researchers of cooperative learning in physical education, is beginning to explore the applicability of cooperative learning structures in different settings, with different participants, and different subject matter. Dyson's efforts represent the beginnings of a program of inquiry on cooperative learning in physical education using qualitative research techniques. Two of the studies were conducted with elementary learners (Dyson, 2001, 2002), while one was conducted with high-school students (Dyson and Strachan, 2000). The elementary teacher reported multiple successes with cooperative learning including achieving social, motor, and cognitive learning outcomes, understanding that working cooperatively in small groups requires much practice time and teacher guidance, and understanding that learning seems to be at its highest when students are actively involved in the process. She also reported her struggles, during this 2 year journey, with implementing a new instructional approach. The students reported that they learned from working together to complete assigned tasks in their small groups. The results from Dyson's (2001) study involving older elementary students reflect the findings associated with the 2002 study. Students perceived success when they "worked together, learned together, and helped each other learn" (Dyson, 2001: 279).

Dyson and Strachan (2000) researched the implementation of cooperative learning strategies in a secondary school physical education setting with 8th- and 11th-grade students. The secondary students and teacher reported that the cooperative learning format promoted the development of both motor (sports skills and strategies) and social skills (cooperation and communication), as was the case with elementary students (Dyson, 2001, 2002).

Dyson and colleagues continue to examine the impact of cooperative learning formats on elementary and secondary-aged learners in physical education. The research indicates that cooperative learning formats facilitate student learning in the social, cognitive, and motor domains. It is critical that physical education teachers explore the use of teaching styles, like cooperative learning, given the development of the US national standards in physical education (NASPE, 1995, 2004) that are based on outcomes associated with the motor, social, and cognitive educational learning domains. Although the implementation of cooperative learning formats is complex and time consuming, the benefits of cooperative learning as reported by students and teachers in physical education are supportive of those described in the general education literature.

Self-check teaching styles

Scenario

Emily, a 3rd grader, is batting a ball from a tee. According to the criteria sheet she is instructed to bat the ball five times while following three skill cues: step, swing the bat in a horizontal plane, and rotate hips, trunk, and shoulders. Mr. Corbett, the teacher, observes three of Emily's trials, each of which results in missing the ball completely. "How are you doing Emily?" Mr. Corbett asks. Emily sadly states that she can't seem to hit the ball and she doesn't know why. Mr. Corbett asks her to read the three critical skill cues from the task sheet. She does. "Do you think you're performing the skill cues as described?" While doing the task again she says, "I'm stepping and rotating my hips, trunk, and shoulders, but, but, my swing isn't level – maybe that's why I'm missing the ball." Mr. Corbett says, "try one more time – think about the horizontal plane." Emily tries again and contacts the ball. "Sure, that must be it, I wasn't swinging level." "Emily, you're beginning to feel your performance and recognize what you are and are not doing. Excellent!" Mr. Corbett moves on to observe Josh.

Self-regulated learners view learning "as something they do for themselves rather than as something that is done to or for them" (Zimmerman, 1998: 1). According to Zimmerman (1998, 2000), self-regulatory learning processes are characterized by the three phases (forethought, performance, and self-reflection) of the academic learning cycle. During the forethought phase, students prepare for performance by using self-regulatory learning processes like goal setting and strategic planning. During the performance phase, students use self-regulatory processes like attention focusing and self-imagery, while during the self-reflection phase of the academic learning cycle students employ processes like self-evaluation/self-checking to prepare for future responses. These processes have been employed by learners to effectively improve academic performance in classroom settings (Newman, 1994; Pintrich and DeGroot, 1990; Zimmerman, 1986). In physical education, strategies like self-talk, imagery, and goal-setting have been used to encourage self-regulated learning (Anderson, 1999). In terms of teaching styles, the self-check strategy is a formal element of Mosston and Ashworth's (2002) self-check and inclusion styles of teaching.

Although little research has been conducted in the area of self-assessment and student learning in physical education, there are two styles within Mosston and Ashworth's (2002) instructional framework that necessitates students to check their own skill performance. The two teaching styles are self-check and inclusion. In both of these teaching styles the learner performs a task and checks his/her work against a criteria sheet. These two teaching styles are exceedingly student-centered in that the learners are given the added responsibility (decision making) of self-checking performance.

To self-check, students must analyze (compare and contrast) their performances against the task criteria (criteria sheet) and draw conclusions concerning what is correct and incorrect. They then apply this information to the execution of subsequent trials which ultimately should lead to improved motor skill performance. The cognitive processes in which students engage when self-checking include understanding, applying, analyzing, and evaluating, within the knowledge dimension of conceptual knowledge (Krathwohl, 2002).

The impact of self-checking has been examined in two studies in physical education (Beckett, 1991; Jenkins and Byra, 1996). Beckett (1991) compared gains in learner knowledge in college-aged students across two of Mosston and Ashworth's (2002) teaching styles, the inclusion style where learners assess their own skill performance, and the practice style where the teacher is responsible for assessing student skill performance and providing specific feedback. Learners who received instruction under the conditions of the inclusion style scored significantly higher on a written knowledge test than students engaged in instruction under the conditions of the practice style. These results are supported by Jenkins and Byra's (1996) findings with elementary-aged students. In their study, student knowledge gains were examined across three of Mosston and Ashworth's (2002) teaching styles, self-check, inclusion, and practice. As per Beckett's (1991) study, the students in the self-check and inclusion teaching styles reported a significantly greater number of critical skill elements during the post–test (knowledge test) than students in the practice style. The findings support Mosston and Ashworth's (2002) contention that learners understand and perform better when taught in a style that requires the learners to assess their own skill performance.

Research supports the contention that self-assessment strategies facilitate cognitive learning (Beckett, 1991; Jenkins and Byra, 1996). This instructional style helps more students become independent learners, which is one of the goals espoused in the US National Standards for Physical Education (NASPE, 1995). However, within this instructional framework the teacher assumes a very different role as does the student. The teacher no longer provides skill-related feedback to the learners, which is a major shift from direct styles of teaching, and the students assume the responsibility of assessing their performance, which also represents a shift away from what they are accustomed to doing.

Inclusion teaching style

Scenario

Ms. Homer's classes in physical education are somewhat different than what is normally observed in a traditional physical education class. While working on the components of physical fitness, her 6th graders do the same exercises, at the same time, however, they choose a level of difficulty for each exercise from pre-set options. For example, her students can complete a set of 9, 12, or 15 push-ups while leaning against the wall (feet out), from a prone position (regular), or from a bench (feet raised on a bench). At another station the students can lift their bodyweight using a traditional chin-up bar (do regular chin-ups or the flexed arm hang) or they can lift their body weight while lying on their back on the floor and pulling-up on a bar located a distance of 2 feet above their shoulders. When it comes to practicing motor skills, the students can also choose a level of difficulty from pre-set options. For example, when practicing the basketball lay-up, the students can do so from two steps, no dribble, from the top of the basketball key (while dribbling), or from the top of the basketball key with an opponent in pursuit. They can work on dribbling while alternating hands and moving in general space, while moving in general space against an opponent who has their hands behind their back, or while moving in general space against an opponent who is guarding "full steam ahead." The students in Ms. Homer's classes make their initial choice of level of difficulty in a task based on their perception of what they can and can not do. When they make subsequent decisions about level of difficulty, choices are based on their initial level of success with the task. While her students are engaged in practice, Ms. Homer monitors their performance and decisions regarding level of difficulty. She also questions them about the critical skill elements to determine whether they are self-checking performance accurately.

The inclusion style of teaching (Mosston and Ashworth, 2002) facilitates the process of individualizing instruction across learners of varying skill ability. Students are provided with legitimate options for practicing a task, options based on factors that make the practice of the given task more or less difficult. As in the self-check teaching style (Mosston and Ashworth, 2002) learners use a teacher-designed criteria sheet to self-assess actual performance. The purpose of this style is to include all learners at their appropriate level of participation and skill. Unlike the direct, peer, cooperative, and self-check teaching structures reviewed in the previous sections, the inclusion style of teaching is specifically designed to accommodate individual learner performance differences. Student decision making is high in the inclusion style of teaching. The inclusion style of teaching is a student-centered instructional approach.

Goldberger et al. (1982) and Goldberger and Gerney (1986) found the inclusion style of teaching effective in producing improvement in learner skill performance, particularly for students of average skill level. These authors found that many of the low- and high-skilled middle-school students chose levels of difficulty in the hockey task that were too challenging or not challenging enough to facilitate learning. This may have been as a result of them being unfamiliar and inexperienced with the inclusion style of teaching or level of task difficulty not falling within the range of student ability.

In a study of college-aged students, Beckett (1991) found the inclusion style to be as effective as the practice style for learner skill improvement, and as suitable for learners of average and exceptional aptitude for learning motor skills. Beckett suggests that differences in students' ages (college students versus 5th-graders), the motor tasks learned (soccer juggling versus floor hockey accuracy task), and the settings in which the research studies were conducted (natural versus laboratory) may help to explain why the findings from his study do not support the findings from Goldberger et al. (1982) and Goldberger and Gerney (1986).

Goudas et al. (1995) examined the motivational effects of the inclusion style on a group of upper elementary-aged learners in track and field. The girls reported a preference for the inclusion style for reasons associated with intrinsic motivation. Specifically, the girls perceived that they had greater control over what they did and the amount of effort they put forth, and less anxiety, as a result of being able to select level of task difficulty. Chatoupis and Emmanuel's (2003a) study of students' perception of athletic competence in the inclusion style of teaching supports the findings of Goudas et al. (1995), particularly those findings specific to females, as self-perception of athletic competence (Harter, 1981) may be influenced by both teaching style and gender.

Byra and Jenkins (1998) examined learner decision making in the inclusion style of teaching with fifth-grade students in a striking (bat) task. They suggest that 5th-graders can select different levels of task difficulty when provided the opportunity, and make task decisions regarding level of difficulty according to their perceptions of success, challenge, and curiosity.

The primary goal of the inclusion style of teaching is to provide students opportunity to engage in activity at an appropriate skill level. Individualizing instruction to permit greater student success is the underlying premise of the inclusion style of teaching (Mosston and Ashworth, 2002). Lee (1997) suggests that an instructional approach like the inclusion style, one that influences learner interest, enjoyment, and personal meaning, likely has a positive impact on learner task engagement that, in turn, mediates achievement. Research on the inclusion style of teaching provides some evidence to support Lee's (1997) instructional approach/model.

Discovery teaching styles

Scenario

After having observed the 6th graders working on the basic skills of basketball in two-on-two games, Mr. Bushner calls them to their spots and says, "I have a problem for you to solve when you go back out in your two-on-two games. Here is the problem: Your partner passes the ball to you. What can you do with it now? Go back to your mini-games and solve this problem – try to find as many solutions to it as possible. I will come around and help you make connections to what you already know about shooting, passing, and dribbling in basketball; this may include me presenting to you a sequence of tasks (scaffolding). Once I observe various solutions to the question, I will call you all in and we will discuss them. Do you have any questions? No, then let's begin."

Akin to discovery teaching styles is the development of critical thinking skills in learners. Beyer (1987) proposes that critical thinking involves evaluation and objective analysis of any "claim, source, or belief to judge its accuracy, validity, or worth" (p. 33). According to Ennis (1987), critical thinking is defined as "reasonable and reflective thinking that is focused on deciding what to believe or do" (p. 10). Lipman (1988) argues that critical thinking involves "skillful, responsible thinking that facilitates good judgment because it (1) relies upon criteria, (2) is self-correcting, and (3) is sensitive to context" (p. 39). All of these definitions propose that to engage in critical thinking, students must be actively involved within the context of a subject area and the teacher must create conditions for participation that allow students to "elaborate, defend, and extend

their positions, opinions, and beliefs" (Garside, 1996: 215). Students must take major responsibility for their own thinking and learning within this student-centered instructional style.

Research indicates that teachers can help facilitate the development of critical thinking skills for students in classroom settings. Hudgins and Edelman (1986) reported that elementary-aged learners were able to offer "supporting evidence"-type statements at a greater frequency after receiving instruction in a teacher-led small-group discussion discovery teaching style. Garside (1996) found small-group discussion better than lecture for facilitating the use of higher-level critical thinking skills, such as analyzing, synthesizing, and evaluating, in college-aged students. Green and Klug (1990) reported that students who worked collaboratively within small groups learned more effectively than students working alone. These students demonstrated thinking aloud, working together to extend their opinions, and defending positions, all of which are elements that characterize critical thinking (Beyer, 1987; Ennis, 1987; Garside, 1996).

The concept of critical thinking was introduced into physical education via the movement education curriculum (Kirchner et al., 1970; Logsdon et al., 1977; Ludwig, 1968) and the *Spectrum of Teaching Styles* (Mosston, 1966). Movement education emphasizes moving, thinking, and feeling through movement exploration and discovery and Buschner (1990) points out that "skillful movement requires skillful thought" (p. 59). The *Spectrum* is a series of teaching options that "foster reproduction of past knowledge" and "invite production of new knowledge" (Mosston and Ashworth, 2002: 10–11). When producing new knowledge, students engage in cognitive operations like applying, analyzing, evaluating, and creating, which leads to the discovery of information new to the learner.

It is only in the past decade that the acquisition of critical thinking skills has become an area of study in physical education. McBride (1988, 1992) presents a theoretical framework for critical thinking while others have described the importance and researched the benefits of critical thinking (Blitzer, 1995; Buschner, 1990; Cleland, 1990; Greenockle and Purvis, 1995; McBride, 1995; Schwagger and Labate, 1993; Tishman and Perkins, 1995; Woods and Book, 1995). McBride (1992) defines critical thinking in physical education as "reflective thinking that is used to make reasonable and defensible decisions about movement tasks or challenges" (p. 115).

Cleland, one of the leading US researchers in this area in physical education, has studied the effects of different discovery teaching styles on the acquisition of critical thinking skills in children in several studies. McBride's (1992) work on critical thinking seems to have been as much of a stimulus for Cleland's research as has Mosston and Ashworth's

(2002) *Spectrum of Teaching Styles*. Cleland and her colleagues have examined the effects of the divergent discovery, convergent discovery, and guided discovery *Spectrum* teaching styles on learners' critical thinking. In her first study Cleland studied the divergent movement patterns of young children to establish baseline information about children's divergent movement patterns, and to examine different factors that might contribute to a child's production of divergent movement (Cleland and Gallahue, 1993). When asked to engage in the discovery process, the youngsters demonstrated that they could modify, adapt, or combine fundamental movement patterns to produce divergent movement. Experience and age were found to be factors that contributed to a child's ability to produce divergent movement patterns.

In a second study of children's divergent movement ability, Cleland (1994) randomly assigned second and third graders to one of three instructional groups (divergent discovery, command/practice, or control, no instruction) to examine the effect of content and specific teaching styles on learner ability to produce divergent movement. The students in the divergent discovery group generated a significantly greater number of divergent movement patterns than those who received treatment under conditions of direct instruction or no instruction.

In a year long study of 5th-grader's critical thinking in physical education, Cleland and Pearse (1995) examined how physical education specialists structured their learning environments to promote critical thinking. Based on systematic analysis of videotapes, the investigators concluded that a student's ability to think critically (to produce divergent movement) "depends on the movement task and the teacher's ability to effectively use indirect [divergent discovery and convergent discovery] teaching styles" (Cleland and Pearse, 1995: 36). According to student interviews, the learners reported that they enjoyed the critical thinking activities employed in the lessons, preferred to engage in tasks that involved small groups, while written movement problems were more difficult to solve. The research of Cleland and her colleagues (Cleland, 1994; Cleland and Gallahue, 1993; Cleland and Pearse, 1995) serves to affirm that critical thinking in children, specifically as it applies to the production of divergent movement, can be fostered through discovery teaching styles (Mosston and Ashworth, 2002).

Discovery styles of teaching reflect a constructivist view of learning. Constructivists postulate that knowledge is actively created in an environment where "learners can experiment, that is, manipulate objects to see what happens, question what is already known, compare findings and assumptions with those of others, and search for their own answers" (Alkove and McCarty, 1992: 21). According to advocates of the constructivist approach, critical thinking skills are best developed in students when they actively participate in the construction of their own knowledge during a lesson, as is the case with discovery teaching styles. Chen (2001) examined how an expert teacher employed a constructivist-oriented teaching approach to promote the learning of critical thinking skills in children during creative dance lessons. Three themes emerged from the video-audio-taped lessons and transcriptions of the teacher and student interviews. Firstly, the inquiry activities employed during constructivist-oriented teaching strategies triggered the children's interest and motivation to create new dance movements. The teacher did this by blending the student's "prior knowledge and experience [using children's literature] with learning the content of creative dance' (Chen, 2001: 373). Secondly, the teacher provided the students with opportunities to actively engage in the processes of discovery and exploration. This was accomplished by "encouraging the students to explore different ways to express ideas through body movement, having them choose their ideas for creating a dance, and encouraging them to create their own dance movement" (p. 374). Thirdly, the students were directed to self-assess and refine their thoughts and actions throughout the process of discovery. Constructivists suggest that the process of discovery fosters a deeper understanding of the content and improves the quality of learning (Prawat, 1992). The results of this study indicate that students do use critical thinking skills to create and discover in a movement setting when the teacher guides them to actively engage in discovery processes (i.e. by sparking their interest in the subject matter, drawing on prior knowledge, integrating new knowledge, and self-assessing performance).

The video-audio-taped lessons and written anecdotal descriptions of the lessons from Chen's study (2001) were re-analyzed to further investigate the teaching strategies used to evoke critical thinking in children during creative dance lessons (Chen and Cone, 2003). Two types of teaching strategies were found to generate divergent and undiscovered movement patterns in the children: teacher scaffolded sequential learning tasks, and teacher presentation of open-ended tasks with questions, demonstrations, and/or verbal cues. Chen (2001) and Chen and Cone's (2003) work confirms that a constructivist-oriented teaching style facilitates the learning of critical thinking skills in children in physical education as reflected by their movement actions and reactions.

Research shows that the strategies associated with discovery teaching styles (Cleland, 1994; Cleland and Gallahue, 1993; Cleland and Pearse, 1995) and constructivist-oriented teaching (Chen, 2001; Chen and Cone, 2003) help to facilitate critical thinking skills in students in physical education as reflected in their movement actions. Within this genre of teaching structures, the teacher's role shifts from one of controlling student decision making to one of inviting students to be problem solvers. Discovery teaching styles are highly student-centered.

Major trends and future directions

The history of research on teaching styles in physical education specific to student learning in the psychomotor domain dates back approximately 20 years. Research specific to student learning in the social and cognitive domains has an even shorter history of approximately 10 years.

It is not surprising that teacher centered teaching structures have the richest and longest research history in physical education. This makes perfect sense given that we in physical education have "followed the lead of educational research" (Rink, 2002: 50), research conducted during the late 1960s and throughout the 1970s and early 1980s that was directed at studying teaching variables related to direct instruction and student learning, and that psychomotor performance is at the core of physical education and is what differentiates it from the other subjects in schools.

Research in physical education indicates that teacher-centered (direct) teaching styles are effective in promoting student motor skill learning. The findings from multiple studies in physical education verify that, when teachers employ the elements of direct instruction in their teaching, significant student achievement gains are made in skill performance. There is a need to conduct research that extends the conditions under which direct teaching styles have been studied. In addition, there is a need to conduct "replication" studies to verify what we already know.

Many physical educators and researchers contend that learning in physical education should not be limited to the psychomotor domain. These individuals believe that cognitive and social learning outcomes contribute as much, if not more, to student learning in physical education as psychomotor outcomes. Teaching approaches that have a dual- or tri-emphasis (e.g. cooperative learning, peer teaching, discovery teaching styles, etc.) are appealing to teachers because they integrate "seemingly diverse goals within a single approach" (Antil et al., 1998; 420). The multidimensionality of physical education necessitates physical educators to employ a variety of student-centered teaching styles in their instructional practices.

In 1995 the National Association for Sport and Physical Education (NASPE) published a document titled Moving into the future: *National standards for physical education.* This has been followed by a second edition (NASPE, 2004). The six US national standards for physical education frame what students should learn from a quality physical education program. This document speaks to the multidimensionality of physical education, and is one of the few, perhaps only, subjects in schools where teachers have the opportunity to enhance student learning in the psychomotor, cognitive, and affective educational domains.

Other nations have committed to multiple goals in physical education as well. For example, in Australia, New Zealand, and the UK, national goals and curricular frameworks reflect the multidimensionality of physical education (Qualifications and Curriculum Authority Physical Education, 1999; Queensland School Curriculum Council, 1999). In an attempt to develop lifelong learners for a changing society, teachers are incorporating sociocultural aspects and cognitive theories of learning into the curriculum aims and goals, and ways of teaching in physical education (Kirk, 2004; Macdonald, 2004; Tinning and Fitzclarence, 1992; Wright, 2004).

If the goal is to teach interaction skills, positive interdependence skills, skills related to giving and receiving feedback or analyzing motor skill performance, and/or inquiry skills while engaged in motor activities, then it behooves physical education teachers to employ student-centered teaching styles. Decision making and critical thinking skills, and the subsequent responsibilities that are coupled with making decisions, are shared between the student and teacher in student-centered teaching styles. Peer teaching, cooperative learning, the self-check and inclusion teaching styles, and discovery teaching styles are student-centered teaching approaches that emphasize social and/or cognitive development within a movement setting. Each of these student-centered teaching styles is dual-or tri-istic in nature; that is, outcomes from two or more of the three learning domains are integrated in one approach. Student-centered teaching styles exemplify the characteristics of inclusive pedagogies.

Research indicates that student learning is not limited to the motor domain in student-centered instructional approaches. Findings from research on peer teaching approaches, cooperative learning formats, self-check and inclusion teaching styles, and discovery teaching styles in the physical education setting are supportive of student social and/or cognitive learning. Researchers, however, have just begun to expose the "tip of the iceberg" on student-centered teaching approaches. Further research is required to explore how these student-centered teaching styles contribute to social and cognitive learning outcomes with different students at different grade levels performing different physical activities. For example, how do changes in task structure or changes in the accountability/incentive systems used in the peer teaching or cooperative learning approaches affect social and cognitive learning in students engaged in physical activity?

In student-centered teaching styles students are afforded the opportunity to learn and practice cognitive and/or social skills while engaged in motor tasks. Given this common characteristic, it seems that researchers of student-centered teaching styles could learn much from one another's investigations. For example, those studying the reciprocal style of teaching (one of several peer teaching instructional approaches) could benefit from reviewing the literature on peer-mediated accountability tutoring schemes (another of several peer teaching instructional approaches). Incorporating the dependent measures used by Ward and colleagues (i.e. number of trials, correct trials, and percent correct trials) when studying the reciprocal teaching style might serve to help us better understand how giving and receiving feedback impacts motor skill performance. Including a dyad intervention that reflects the conditions of the reciprocal style of teaching in a study of the peer-mediated accountability tutoring model might help us better understand feedback within this model. Or, those studying cooperative learning formats might profit from reviewing the research on discovery styles. Both teaching approaches have been found to promote cognitive and social learning in students in physical education settings. Elements of both of these teaching structures lead students to actively participate in the construction of their own learning. It seems that much could be gained from this integration of knowledge across teaching styles research.

Summary

In this chapter research on teaching styles used in physical education has been reviewed. How has this research informed us? Three basic conclusions can be made. Firstly, direct teaching styles remain prominent in the teaching of and research in physical education. Secondly, researchers in physical education are now more interested in studying the effects of inclusive pedagogies (teaching styles in which outcomes from two or three educational learning domains are emphasized). It seems that this change is akin to the US efforts to improve schools (Holmes Group, 1985; National Commission on Teaching and America's Future, 1996; National Education Goals Panel, 1991) and more specifically to the recent development of the US national standards in physical education (NASPE, 1992, 1995, 2004). Finally, this review of research on teaching styles highlights the need for us to broaden our understanding of teaching styles beyond "one". For example, those studying a cooperative learning format can learn from research on discovery teaching styles given the similarities between these two teaching styles. This will help to further develop research methods employed in teaching styles studies.

References

Alkove, L.D. and McCarty, B.J. (1992). Plain talk: Recognizing positivism and constructivism in practice. *Action in Teacher Education, 14(2)*: 16–21.

Anania, J. (1983). The influence of instructional conditions on student learning and achievement. *Review of Educational Research, 46*: 355–385.

Anderson, A. (1999). The case for learning strategies in physical education. *Journal of Physical Education, Recreation, and Dance, 70(1)*: 45–49.

Antil, L.R., Jenkins, J.R., Wayne, S.K. and Vadasy, P.F. (1998). Cooperative learning: Prevalence, conceptualization, and the relation between research and practice. *American Educational Research Journal, 35*: 419–454.

Barrett, T. (2000). *Effects of two cooperative learning strategies on academic learning time, student performance, and social behavior of sixth grade physical education students.* Unpublished doctoral dissertation, University of Nebraska, Lincoln.

Beckett, K. (1991). The effects of two teaching styles on college students' achievement of selected physical education outcomes. *Journal of Teaching in Physical Education, 10*: 153–169.

Beyer, B. (1987). *Practical strategies for the teaching of thinking.* Boston, DC: Allyn and Bacon.

Blitzer, L. (1995). It's a gym class ... What's there to think about? *Journal of Physical Education, Recreation, and Dance, 66(6)*: 44–48.

Block, M.E. (1994). Why all students with disabilities should be included in regular physical education. *Palaestra, 10(3)*: 17–24.

Block, M.E., Oberweiser, B. and Bain, M. (1995). Using classwide peer tutoring to facilitate inclusion of students with disabilities in regular physical education. *The Physical Educator, 52*: 47–56.

Boyce, B.A. (1992). The effects of three styles of teaching on university student's motor performance. *Journal of Teaching in Physical Education, 11*: 389–401.

Brophy, J. (1979). Teacher behavior and student learning. *Educational Leadership, 37(1)*: 33–38.

Buschner, C.A. (1990). Can we help children move and think critically? In W.J. Stinson (Ed.), *Moving and learning for the young child* (pp. 51–66). Reston, VA: AAHPERD.

Byra, M. and Jenkins, J. (1998). The thoughts and behaviors of learners in the inclusion style of teaching. *Journal of Teaching in Physical Education, 18*: 26–42.

Byra, M. and Jenkins, J. (2000). Matching instructional tasks with learner ability: Inclusion style of teaching. *Journal of Physical Education, Recreation, and Dance, 71(3)*: 26–30.

Byra, M. and Marks, M. (1993). The effect of two pairing techniques on specific feedback and comfort levels of learners in the reciprocal style of teaching. *Journal of Teaching in Physical Education, 12*: 286–300.

Byrd, D. (1990). Peer tutoring with the learning disabled: A critical review. *Journal of Educational Research, 84(2)*: 115–118.

Chatoupis, C. and Emmanuel, C. (2003a). The effects of two disparate instructional approaches on student self-perceptions in elementary physical education. *European Journal of Sport Science, 3(1)*: 1–16.

Chatoupis, C. and Emmanuel, C. (2003b). Teaching physical education with the Inclusion style: The case of a Greek elementary school. *Journal of Physical Education, Recreation, and Dance, 74(8)*: 33–38, 53.

Chen, W. (2001). Description of an expert teacher's constructivist-oriented teaching: Engaging students' critical thinking in learning creative dance. *Research Quarterly for Exercise and Sport, 72*: 366–375.

Chen, W. and Cone, T. (2003). Links between children's use of critical thinking and expert teacher's teaching in creative dance. *Journal of Teaching in Physical Education, 22*: 169–185.

Cleland, F. (1990). How many ways can I? Problem solving through movement. In W.J. Stinson (Ed.), *Moving and learning for the young child* (pp. 73–75). Reston, VA: AAHPERD.

Cleland, F.E. (1994). Young children's divergent movement ability: Study II. *Journal of Teaching in Physical Education, 13*: 228–241.

Cleland, F.E. and Gallahue, D.L. (1993). Young children's divergent movement ability. *Perceptual and Motor skills, 77*: 535–544.

Cleland, F. and Pearse, C. (1995). Critical thinking in elementary physical education: Reflections on a yearlong study. *Journal of Physical Education, Recreation, and Dance, 66(6)*: 31–38.

Cox, R.L. (1986). A systematic approach to teaching sport. In M. Pieron and G. Graham (Eds.), *Sport pedagogy* (pp. 109–116). Champaign, IL: Human Kinetics.

Crouch, D.W., Ward, P. and Patrick, C.A. (1997). The effects of peer-mediated accountability on task accomplishment during volleyball drills in elementary physical education. *Journal of Teaching in Physical Education, 17*: 26–39.

Delquadri, J., Greenwood, C., Whorton, D., Carta, J. and Hall, R. (1986). Class-wide peer tutoring. *Exceptional Children, 52*: 535–542.

DePaepe, J.L. (1985). The influence of three least restrictive environments on the content motor-ALT and performance of moderately mentally retarded students. *Journal of Teaching in Physical Education, 5*: 34–41.

Dewey, J. (1933). *How we think: A statement of the relation of reflective thinking to the educative process.* Boston, DC: Health and Company.

Doolittle, S. and Fay, T. (2002). *Authentic assessment of physical activity for high school students.* Reston, VA: NASPE Publications.

Dyson, B. (2001). Cooperative learning in an elementary physical education program. *Journal of Teaching in Physical Education, 20*: 264–281.

Dyson, B. (2002). The implementation of cooperative learning in an elementary physical education program. *Journal of Teaching in Physical Education, 22*: 69–85.

Dyson, B. and Strachan, K. (2000). Cooperative learning in a high school physical education program. *Waikato Journal of Education, 6*: 19–37.

Ennis, R. (1987). A taxonomy of critical thinking dispositions and abilities. In J. Baron and R. Sternberg (Eds.), *Teaching thinking skills: Theory and practice* (pp. 9–26). New York: W.H. Freeman.

Ernst, M. and Byra, M. (1998). What does the reciprocal style of teaching hold for junior high school learners? *The Physical Educator, 55*: 24–37.

French, K.E., Rink, J.E., Rikard, L., Mays, A., Lynn, S. and Werner, P. (1991). The effects of practice progressions on learning two volleyball skills. *Journal of Teaching in Physical Education, 10*: 261–274.

Fuchs, L., Fuchs, D., Bentz, J., Phillips, N. and Hamlett, C. (1994). The nature of student interactions during peer tutoring with and without prior training and experience. *American Educational Research Journal, 31*: 75–103.

Fuchs, D., Fuchs, L.S., Mathes, P.G. and Simmons, D.C. (1997). Peer-assisted learning strategies: Making classrooms more responsive to diversity. *American Educational Research Journal, 34*: 174–206.

Garside, C. (1996). Look who's talking: A comparison of lecture and group discussion teaching strategies in developing critical thinking skills. *Communication Education, 45*: 212–227.

Goldberger, M. (1992). The spectrum of teaching styles: A perspective for research on teaching physical education. *Journal of Physical Education, Recreation, and Dance, 63(1)*: 42–46.

Goldberger, M. and Gerney, P. (1986). The effects of direct teaching styles on motor skill acquisition of fifth grade children. *Research Quarterly for Exercise and Sport, 57*: 215–219.

Goldberger, M. and Gerney, P. (1990). Effects of learner use of practice time on skill acquisition of fifth grade children. *Journal of Teaching in Physical Education, 10*: 84–95.

Goldberger, M., Gerney, P. and Chamberlain, J. (1982). The effects of three styles of teaching on the psychomotor performance of fifth grade children. *Research Quarterly for Exercise and Sport, 53*: 116–124.

Goudas, M., Biddle, S., Fox, K. and Underwood, M. (1995). It ain't what you do, it's the way that you do it! Teaching style affects children's motivation in track and field. *The Sport Psychologist, 9*: 254–264.

Green, C.S. and Klug, H.G. (1990). Teaching critical thinking and writing through debates: An experimental evaluation. *Teaching Sociology, 18*: 462–471.

Greenockle, K.M. and Purvis, G.J. (1995). Redesigning a secondary school wellness unit using the critical thinking model. *Journal of Physical Education, Recreation, and Dance, 66(6)*: 49–52.

Griffey, D.C. (1983). Aptitude X treatment interactions associated with student decision making. *Journal of Teaching in Physical Education, 3:* 15–32.

Grineski, S. (1989). Children, games, and prosocial behavior – insights and connections. *Journal of Physical Education, Recreation, and Dance, 60(3):* 20–25.

Gusthart, J.L. and Sprigings, E.J. (1989). Student learning as a measure of teacher effectiveness in physical education. *Journal of Teaching in Physical Education, 8:* 298–311.

Harrison, J.M., Fellingham, G.W., Buck, M.M. and Pellett, T.L. (1995). Effects of practice and command styles on rate of change in volleyball performance and self-efficacy of high-, medium-, and low-skilled learners. *Journal of Teaching in Physical Education, 14:* 328–339.

Harrison, J.M., Preece, L.A., Blakemore, C.L., Richards, R.P., Wilkinson, C. and Fellingham, G.W. (1999). Effects of two instructional models-skill teaching and mastery learning-on skill development, knowledge, self-efficacy, and game play in volleyball. *Journal of Teaching in Physical Education, 19:* 34–57.

Harter, S. (1981). The development of competence motivation in the mastery of cognitive and physical skills: Is there a place for joy? In G.C. Roberts and D.M. Landers (Eds.), *Psychology of motor behavior and sport-1980* (pp. 3–29). Champaign, IL: Human Kinetics.

Hastie, P. (2003). *Teaching for lifetime physical activity through quality high school physical education.* San Francisco, CA : Benjamin Cummings.

Holmes Group. (1995). *Tomorrow's schools of education.* East Lansing, MI: Author.

Holt/Hale, S.A. (1999). *Assessing motor skills in elementary physical education.* Reston, VA: NASPE Publications.

Horwitz, R.A. (1979). Psychological effects of the open classroom. *Review of Educational Research, 49(1):* 71–85.

Houston-Wilson, C., Dunn, J.M., van der Mars, H. and McCubbin, J. (1997). The effect of peer tutors on motor performance in integrated physical education classes. *Adapted Physical Activity Quarterly, 14:* 298–313.

Hudgins, B.B. and Edelman, S. (1986). Teaching critical thinking skills to fourth and fifth graders through teacher-led small-group discussions. *Journal of Educational Research, 79:* 333–342.

Jenkins, J. and Byra, M. (1996). An exploration of theoretical constructs associated with the Spectrum of Teaching Styles. In F. Carreiro da Costa (Ed.), *Research on teaching and research on teacher education: What do we know about the past and what kind of future do we expect?* (pp. 103–108). Lisbon, Portugal: AIESEP.

Johnson, D.W. and Johnson, R.T. (1991). *Learning together and alone: Cooperative, competitive, and individualistic learning* (3rd ed.). Bostonm, DC: Allyn & Bacon.

Johnson, D.W. and Johnson, R.T. (1992). Positive interdependence: Key to effective cooperation. In R. Hertz-Lazarowitz and N. Miller (Eds.), *Interaction in cooperative groups: The theoretical anatomy of group learning* (pp. 174–199). New York: Cambridge University Press.

Johnson, M. and Ward, P. (2001). Effects of class-wide peer-tutoring on correct performance of striking skills in 3rd grade physical education. *Journal of Teaching in Physical Education, 20:* 247–263.

Johnson, R.T., Bjorkland, R. and Krotee, M. (1984). The effects of cooperative, competitive, and individualistic student interaction patterns on the achievement and attitudes of students learning the golf skill of putting. *Research Quarterly for Exercise and Sport, 55:* 129–134.

Jones, D.L. (1992). Analysis of task structures in elementary physical education classes. *Journal of Teaching in Physical Education, 11:* 411–425.

Kagan, S. (1990). The structural approach to cooperative learning. *Educational Leadership, 47(4):* 12–15.

Katstra, J., Tollefson, N. and Gilbert, E. (1987). The effects of peer evaluation on attitude toward writing and writing fluency of ninth grade students. *Journal of Educational Research, 80(3):* 168–172.

Kelly, L. (1995). *Adapted physical education national standards.* National Consortium for Physical Education and Recreation for Individuals with Disabilities. Champaign, IL: Human Kinetics.

Kirchner, G., Cunningham, J. and Warrell, E. (1970). *Introduction to movement education.* Dubuque, IA: Wm. C. Browne.

Kirk, D. (2004). New practices, new subjects, and critical inquiry: Possibility and progress. In J. Wright, D. Macdonald and L. Burrows (Eds.), *Critical inquiry and problem-solving in physical education* (pp. 199–208). London: Routledge.

Kirk, D. and Macdonald, D. (1998). Situated learning in physical education. *Journal of Teaching in Physical Education, 17:* 376–387.

Krathwohl, D.R. (2002). A revision of Bloom's taxonomy: An overview. *Theory Into Practice, 41:* 212–218.

Lee, A.M. (1997). Contributions of research on student thinking in physical education. *Journal of Teaching in Physical Education, 16:* 262–277.

Lipman, M. (1988). Critical thinking-What can it be? *Educational Leadership, 46(1):* 38–43.

Locke, L.F., Silverman, S.J. and Spirduso, W.W. (2004). *Reading and understanding research* (2nd ed.). Thousand Oaks, CA: Sage.

Logsdon, B., Barrett, K., Broer, M., McKee, R. and Ammons, M. (1977). *Physical education for children: A focus on the teaching process.* Philadelphia, PA: Lea & Febiger.

Ludwig, E.A. (1968). Towards an understanding of basic movement education in the elementary schools. *Journal of Health, Physical Education, and Recreation, 39(3):* 26–28, 77.

Lund, J. (1992). Assessment and accountability in secondary physical education. *Quest, 44:* 352–360.

Macdonald, D. (2004). Understanding learning in physical education. In J. Wright, D. Macdonald and L. Burrows (Eds.), *Critical inquiry and problem-solving in physical education* (pp. 16–29). London: Routledge.

Maheady, L. (1998). Advantages and disadvantages of peer-assisted learning strategies. In K. Topping and S. Ehly (Eds.), *Peer-assisted learning* (pp. 45–65). Mahwah, NJ: Erlbaum.

McBride, R.E. (1988). Teaching critical thinking in the psycho-motor learning environment – A possibility or a passing phase? *The Physical Educator, 46:* 170–173.

McBride, R.E. (1992). Critical thinking – An overview with implications for physical education. *Journal of Teaching in Physical Education, 11:* 112–125.

McBride, R.E. (1995). Critical thinking in physical education … An idea whose time has come. *Journal of Physical Education, Recreation, and Dance, 66 (6):* 21–23.

Metzler, M.W. (2000). *Instructional models for physical education.* Boston, DC : Allyn & Bacon.

Mosston, M. (1966). *Teaching physical education.* Columbus, OH: Merrill.

Mosston, M. (1981). *Teaching physical education* (2nd ed.). Columbus, OH: Merrill.

Mosston, M. and Ashworth, S. (1986). *Teaching physical education* (3rd ed.). Columbus, OH: Merrill.

Mosston, M. and Ashworth, S. (1994). *Teaching physical education* (4th ed.). New York: Macmillan.

Mosston, M. and Ashworth, S. (2002). *Teaching physical education* (5th ed.). San Francisco, CA: Benjamin Cummings.

National Association for Sport and Physical Education. (1992). *Outcomes of quality physical education programs.* Reston, VA: Author.

National Association for Sport and Physical Education. (1995). *Moving into the future: National physical education standards – A guide to content and assessment.* Reston, VA: Author.

National Association for Sport and Physical Education. (2004). *Moving into the future: National standards for physical education* (2nd ed.). Reston, VA: Author.

National Commission on Teaching and America's Future. (1996). *What matters most: Teaching for America's future.* New York: Author.

National Education Goals Panel. (1991). *The national education goals report: Building a nation of learners.* Washington, DC: Author.

Newman, R.S. (1994). Academic help-seeking: A strategy for self-regulated learning. In D.H. Schunk and B.J. Zimmerman (Eds.), *Self-regulation of learning and performance: Issues and educational applications* (pp. 283–301). Hillsdale, NJ: Erlbaum.

Olson, V. (1990). The revising processes of sixth-grade writers with and without peer feedback. *Journal of Educational Research, 84(1):* 22–29.

Pellett, T.L. and Blakemore, C.L. (1997). Comparisons of teaching presentation and development of content: Implications for effective teaching. *Perceptual and Motor Skills, 85:* 963–972.

Pellett, T.L. and Harrison, J.M. (1995). The influence of refinement on female junior high school students' volleyball practice success and achievement. *Journal of Teaching in Physical Education, 15:* 41–52.

Peterson, P.L. (1979). Direct instruction reconsidered. In P.L. Peterson and H.J. Walberg (Eds.), *Research on teaching: Concepts, findings, and implications* (pp. 57–69). Berkeley, CA: McCutchan.

Pintrich, P.R. and DeGroot, E. (1990). Motivational and self-regulated learning components of classroom academic performance. *Journal of Educational Psychology, 82:* 33–40.

Prawat, R.S. (1992). Teacher's beliefs about teaching and learning: A constructivist perspective. *American Journal of Education, 100:* 354–395.

Puma, M.J., Jones, C.C., Rock, D. and Fernandez, R. (1993). *Prospects: The congressionally mandated study of educational growth and opportunity.* Interim Report. Bethesda, MD: Abt Associates.

Pumfrey, P. (1986). Paired reading: Promise and pitfalls. *Educational Research, 28(2):* 89–94.

Qualifications and Curriculum Authority (QCA). (1999). *Physical education: The national curriculum for England.* London: QCA.

Queensland School Curriculum Council. (1999). *Health and physical education: Years 1 to 10 syllabus.* Brisbane: Queensland Publishing Services.

Rice, E.A., Hutchinson, J.L. and Lee, M. (1958). *A brief history of physical education* (4th ed.). New York: The Ronald Press Company.

Rink, J.E. (1996). Effective instruction in physical education. In S.J. Silverman and C.D. Ennis (Eds.), *Student learning in physical education* (pp. 171–198). Champaign, IL: Human Kinetics.

Rink, J.E. (2002). *Teaching physical education for learning* (4th ed.). Boston, DC : McGraw Hill.

Rink, J.E., French, K.E., Werner, P.H., Lynn, S. and Mays, A. (1992). The influence of content development on the effectiveness of instruction. *Journal of Teaching in Physical Education, 11:* 139–149.

Robertson, E. (1987).Teaching and related activities. In M.J. Dunkin (Ed.), *International encyclopedia of teaching and teacher education* (pp. 15–18). Oxford: Pergamon Press.

Rosenshine, B. (1979). Content, time, and direct instruction. In P.L. Peterson and H.J. Walberg (Eds.), *Research on teaching: Concepts, findings, and implications* (pp. 28–56). Berkeley, CA: McCutchan.

Russell, T. and Ford, D. (1983). Effectiveness of peer tutors vs resource teachers. *Psychology in the Schools, 20:* 436–441.

Schwagger, S. and Labate, C. (1993). Teaching for critical thinking in physical education. *Journal of Physical Education, Recreation, and Dance, 64(5):* 24–26.

Sharon, S. (1980). Cooperative learning in small groups: Recent methods and effects on achievement, attitudes, and ethnic relations. *Review of Educational Research, 50:* 241–271.

Siedentop, D. and Tannelhill, D. (2000). *Developing teaching skills in physical education.* Mountain View, CA: Mayfield.

Slavin, R.E. (1990). *Cooperative learning: Theory, research, and practice.* Boston, DC : Allyn & Bacon.

Slavin, R.E. (1996). Research on cooperative learning and achievement: What we know, what we don't know. *Contemporary Educational Psychology, 21:* 43–69.

Smith, B.O. (1987). Definitions of teaching. In M.J. Dunkin (Ed.), *International encyclopedia of teaching and teacher education* (pp. 11–14). Oxford: Pergamon Press.

Soar, R. and Soar, R.M. (1979). Emotional climate and management. In P.L. Peterson and H.J. Walberg (Eds.), *Research on teaching: Concepts, findings, and implications* (pp. 97–119). Berkeley, CA: McCutchan.

Sweeting, T. and Rink, J.E. (1999). Effects of direct instruction and environmentally designed instruction on the process and product characteristics of fundamental skill. *Journal of Teaching in Physical Education, 18:* 216–233.

Tinning, R. and Fitzclarence, L. (1992). Postmodern youth culture and the crisis in Australian high school physical education. *Quest, 44:* 287–303.

Tishman, S. and Perkins, D.N. (1995). Critical thinking and physical education. *Journal of Physical Education, Recreation, and Dance, 66(6):* 24–30.

Van Dalen, D.B. and Bennett, B.L. (1971). *A world history of physical education: Cultural, philosophical, comparative* (2nd ed.). Englewood Cliffs, NJ: Prentice Hall.

Ward, P. (1993). An experimental analysis of skill responding in physical education high school accountability (Doctoral dissertation, Ohio State University, 1993). *Dissertation Abstracts International, 54,* 2950A.

Ward, P. and Johnson, L.A. (1995, July). *Effects of peer-mediated accountability during peer tutoring on skill development in physical education.* Paper presented at the World Congress of the International Council for Health, Physical Education, Recreation, Sport, and Dance, Gainsville, FL.

Ward, P., Smith, S.L., Makasci, K. and Crouch, D.W. (1998). Differential effects of peer-mediated accountability on task accomplishment in elementary physical education. *Journal of Teaching in Physical Education, 17:* 442–452.

Webster, G.E. (1987). Influence of peer tutors upon academic learning time-physical education of mentally retarded students. *Journal of Teaching in Physical Education, 6:* 393–403.

Webster's new world college dictionary (4th ed.). (2000). Foster City, CA: IDG Books Worldwide.

Woods, A.M. and Book, C. (1995). Critical thinking in middle school physical education. *Journal of Physical Education, Recreation, and Dance, 66(6):* 39–43.

Wright, J. (2004). Critical inquiry and problem-solving in physical education. In J. Wright, D. Macdonald and L. Burrows (Eds.), *Critical inquiry and problem-solving in physical education* (pp. 3–15). London: Routledge.

Yoder, L.J. (1993). Cooperative learning and dance education. *Journal of Physical Education, Recreation, and Dance, 64(5):* 47–51, 56.

Zimmerman, B.J. (1986). Development of self-regulated learning: Which are the key sub-processes? *Contemporary Educational Psychology, 11:* 307–313.

Zimmerman, B.J. (1998). Developing self-fulfilling cycles of academic regulation: An analysis of exemplary instructional models. In D.H. Schuck and B.J Zimmerman (Eds.), *Self-regulated learning: From teaching to self-reflective practice* (pp. 1–19). New York: Guilford Press.

Zimmerman, B.J. (2000). Attaining self-regulation: A social cognitive perspective. In M. Boekaerts, P.R. Pintrich and M. Zeidner (Eds.), *Handbook of self-regulation* (pp. 13–39). San Diego, CA: Academic Press.

4.6   The way to a teacher's heart: narrative research in physical education

KATHLEEN M. ARMOUR

When teachers told their stories and responded to others' stories in sustained conversation groups, they came to understand their own practices in new ways. Their participation in these groups led them, many said, to new insights, new restoried knowledge. Many described their experiences in these groups as their most powerful professional development. (Clandinin, 2001, p. viii)

The story begins ...

This chapter is about a range of research methods that use forms of "story" and "storying" to help teachers (and ultimately pupils) to learn. The genre encompasses research approaches such as life history, biography and autoethnography, and employs mainly qualitative methods. However, all the different approaches (and there are many) share a fundamental concern with using narrative techniques to encourage personal analysis, critical understanding and, where warranted, pedagogical change. In this chapter, "narrative research" is used as an umbrella term that can embrace them all. It is also important to recognize that whereas narrative techniques are employed to different extents as part of a range of research approaches, this chapter focuses specifically on research that uses narrative as its primary analytical and reporting medium. Furthermore, underpinning the discussion is a belief that this form of research has an unrivalled capacity to reach teachers – to really engage them – and, as a result, to change them and their practices. In the hands of a skilful researcher, therefore, narrative research has the potential to be a powerful and dynamic research tool. The purpose of this chapter is to demonstrate how and why.

The structure of this chapter is similar to others in this handbook, with sections covering historical background, core concepts and techniques, key findings for physical education, practical application and suggestions about future research directions. However, as Ellis and Bochner (2000: 734) point out, research handbooks can become full of "dry, distant, abstract, propositional essays" and it would certainly be odd if a chapter about the narrative research genre included no stories! So, grounding each section are personal accounts by five practising PE teachers/researchers from four countries, who have used autobiographical techniques to reflect upon and inform their personal pedagogies; thus, narrative research is represented in theory and in action. There is also the question of the position of the chapter author in all this – that's me. Ellis and Bochner (2000) note that even in handbook chapters about autoethnography, authors have struggled with the use of the first person:

> ... the 'I' usually disappeared after the introduction and then reappeared abruptly in the conclusion ... and the authors almost never became characters in the stories they wrote ... Why should we take it for granted that the authors' personal feelings and thoughts should be omitted in a handbook chapter? After all, who is the person collecting the evidence, drawing the inferences, and reaching the conclusions?

It is a good point. The question is: what do you need to know about me in order to make best use of the information I present? I think, perhaps, it is in the context of the teachers' stories that you need to "see" my role most clearly. These aren't just randomly selected teachers. They are eager, hungry learners who have devoured the Master's degree in Physical Education at Loughborough University in England. I teach a core module that uses autoethnography as a form of professional development and these were teachers who were sparked by the genre and who feel that they have learned and changed their pedagogies as a result. They are all continuing with further research on their practice;

indeed, once started, they seem unable to stop the learning process. So, whereas they started out as full-time teachers doing part time research, it might be more accurate now to describe them as full-time teacher/researchers (and I have no idea how they manage it – but the late night emails might provide a clue!). For me, this is what is important. Research in physical education must have a foundational concern with learning: learning about teachers' learning and pupils' learning, and understanding the nature of "better" learning and how to achieve it. Moreover, research must, in some way, engage teachers and schools such that teachers as professional pedagogues can evaluate it and learn from it. Tsangaridou makes a similar point in Chapter 4.8 on developing teacher content knowledge. The alternative position is one where educational research is a sterile, detached activity conducted largely for the benefit of other academic researchers; one of the great strengths of the research approach presented in this chapter is that the detached position simply isn't an option. The teachers whose stories you will read in this chapter agree with me. We learnt together – always me as much as them – and the learning was tangible. It is also important to note, however, that although most teachers on the MSc programme find autoethnography to be valuable and helpful, some do not. This serves as a reminder that no research approach should be viewed as a panacea.

My location in the text, therefore, is as an author who is convinced by the narrative genre, who uses different manifestations of it as a research method and a learning tool with teachers, and who thoroughly admires the PE teachers you will hear from in the sections that follow. On the other hand, I am sensitive to concerns about credible research and continue to struggle with notions of validity, reliability and generalizability in this, as in all forms of social research. Furthermore, a decision has been taken to retain a clear focus on narrative research in the context of teachers' learning, rather than more broadly in social science. It is from that position that I write this chapter and attempt to ensure that it is not an "author evacuated text" (Geertz 1988). The scene is set, therefore, for the story that follows …

Tales from history

So, reader, where do you position yourself as a researcher? If you are a traditional "hard" science type, then you may have moved on to another chapter already, confident that what is presented here is "soft", "unscientific" and unsound; not real research at all. History is littered with such reactions (Denzin and Lincoln, 2000). In order to understand the narrative research genre, however, it is important

to understand what it is (and is not) attempting to achieve. This section traces the history of the genre and, in so doing, exposes some confusion in terminology and, if not confusion, then certainly a very complex range of concepts that appear to mean similar things. So, bear with it, because you will find some clarification of that complexity in the section that follows.

Perhaps the first point to make is that narrative research techniques place a strong emphasis upon the skill of writing. This holds true for the researcher constructing the life story of a teacher and for the teacher writing an autobiography. Richardson (2000) highlights the historical divide between "literary" and "scientific" writing, the former being classified as fiction, thus subjective and "false", while the latter was viewed as objective and "true":

> Thus, by the 19th century, literature and science stood as two separate domains … Given to science was the belief that its words were objective, precise, unambiguous, noncontextual and nonmetaphoric. (p. 925)

The term "social science" was initially linked firmly to science, although during the 20th century, the boundaries between scientific and literary writing were blurred leading some to argue for the term "narrative" to encompass all forms of writing (Richardson, 2000: 926). However, as Richardson also argues, an author makes claims to be writing "fiction" or "science" depending on the audience to be reached. This places narrative research in education in the peculiar position of trying to meet the criteria of social science in the traditional scientific sense, and also literary standards of writing which might include, for example, interest, structure and dramatic intention. It is, thus, an exacting skill and Richardson would argue that few get it right: "Undergraduates, graduates and colleagues alike say they have found much of qualitative writing – yes – boring" (p. 924). It may be the predictability of qualitative writing that has led some to experiment with new forms. In the field of physical education, for example, Sparkes (1996, 2002) has used fictional accounts and poetry (Sparkes et al., 2003) to facilitate data analysis and, importantly, communication. These, and other examples, are considered later.

This leads us to a second key point: narrative research is closely aligned to qualitative, interpretive or ethnographic research traditions. As such, it shares the strengths of that paradigm and is open to similar critiques. While the days of mud-slinging between qualitative and quantitative research traditions are largely over (at least in the educational research literature) there are lingering concerns about warranted conclusions in qualitative research

(Gorard, 2002). As Eisenhart (2001: 19) warns: "the negative perception that ethnography is loosely designed, opportunistically conducted, magically analysed, and notoriously unreliable persists in some quarters". However, Ellis and Bochner (2000) remind us that qualitative research was a much-needed counterpoint to the dominance of scientific knowledge. They point out that writers such as Kuhn (1962), Rorty (1982), Lyotard (1984), Barthes (1977), Derrida (1978) and Foucault (1970) were pre-eminent in questioning traditional scientific forms leaving spaces in social science research for "multiple perspectives, unsettled meanings, plural voices, and local and illegitimate knowledges" (p. 735). Moreover, Becker (1990) simply refuted claims that qualitative research is unscientific by arguing: "we, who are researchers have to deal with that, but we dont have to believe that it poses deep epistemological problems" (p. 235). Yet, further to Eisenhart's earlier point, Ritchie and Spencer (2004: 2) point out that in qualitative research "It was often hard to know how people dealt with the rich, voluminous and often tangled data they had collected". It could be argued, however, that in the case of narrative forms of qualitative research, "stories" of all types are exceptionally well positioned to address this concern. Wolcott (1990) for example, argued that "objectivity is not my criterion as much as what might be termed rigorous subjectivity" (p. 133) and it could certainly be argued that a life history or autoethnographical account has the potential to make transparent links between analysis and the storied life. Sparkes (2000: 23) adds another dimension to this issue by identifying the key problem as one of "how to pass judgement on autoethnography and narratives of self. What differentiates a 'good' one from a 'bad' one?", highlighting again, perhaps, the demands placed on the writing skills of the author/researcher; as Wolcott (1994) puts it, qualitative researchers need to have the skills of a storyteller. The question remains though, is narrative research "real" research? I will return to this question in the final section of this chapter.

Looking more specifically at education research, Carter and Doyle (1996) noted that it was in the 1980s and 1990s that narrative research became prominent. They argued that:

> Overall, work that is grounded in a biographical perspective involves intense and extended conversations with teachers (see Woods, 1985) and is based on the premise that the act of teaching, teachers' experiences and the choices they make, and the process of learning to teach are deeply personal matters inexorably linked to one's identity and, thus, one's life story. (p. 120)

Goodson and Numan (2002) recall that by the 1980s, Goodson was arguing strongly for the use of life history methods of research into teachers' lives and careers, and Atkinson (1990) described life story research as a potent portrayal of individuals. Elbaz (1991) suggested that life story research gives teachers a "voice" enabling the reader to "see connections between the practice of teaching … the institutions of education … and the stories of individual teachers" (p. 3). Two key authors in the field of narrative research, Clandinin and Connelly (e.g. 1990, 1995) pointed to the powerful influence of Schon's (1983, 1987) work on reflective practice, and his arguments against a technical rationalist approach to teacher education. Following Schon, Clandinin and Connelly (1990) set out to:

> rethink curriculum and teaching in terms of a narrative enquiry which draws on classroom observation and participant observation of the practical, along with the bringing forward of personal experience in the form of stories, interviews, rules, principles, images, and metaphors. (p. 245)

However, as Goodson and Numan (2002) point out, this approach to conceptualising teacher learning and knowledge is not widely accepted, and there are examples across the world where standards, testing and accountability approaches to education and teaching leave little space for research that foregrounds teachers in all their active, creative agency. A similar tension can be seen in the professional development literature. Whereas governments tend to view professional development as a functional activity designed to improve teachers' skills, Day (1999) argues that teaching involves "the head and the heart" (p. 47) and so professional development is unlikely to be effective if it is "not based on an understanding of the complexities of teachers' lives and conditions of work, nor upon an understanding of how teachers learn and why they change" (p. 204).

Narrative research in physical education has, to some extent, mirrored its history more broadly in education. Thus, in 1981, Lawn and Barton described teachers as the "great unknowns" (p. 243) of education and it could certainly be argued that physical education teachers were something of a mystery – albeit a stereotyped mystery. Thus, research that could, in Atkinson's (1990) terms, deliver "potent portrayals" of PE teachers was just what was required, and a few of these were beginning to emerge. These included: Sparkes (1987), Sikes (1988), Templin et al. (1988), Templin et al., (1991); Schemmp (1993), Sparkes, (1994, 1996), Dowling Naess (1996) and some of my own work (Armour, 1997). Sparkes has, however, been the most influential writer in narrative research within physical education. His scholarship can be traced from the mid 1980s to today, providing an important link between mainstream education and physical education research. In addition to the studies identified above, in 1992 he authored a research text on alternative visions of research, including chapters on life histories (Sparkes and Templin, 1992) and forms of writing (Sparkes, 1992). In 1995, in response to the publication of a growing number of qualitative research reports in physical education, Sparkes questioned the ways in which the researched were represented and authors/researchers were positioned in the texts. He has continued this work with pioneering writing on poetic representations (Sparkes et al., 2003) and embodied memories (Sparkes, 2002, 2004). Thus, although Sparkes is not the only writer of narrative research in the field of physical education, he is without a doubt the most sustained. The details of his research, and others mentioned above, are discussed in a later section.

So, having ploughed through the history, are you still interested in, or at least curious about narrative forms of research? Rousemaniere (2000) describes an exercise in what she terms "educational autobiography" that she undertakes with teachers, and argues that:

> when teachers reflect on their own schooling experiences through educational autobiography, they can see their own personal and professional development in a new light that can enlighten their current work in the classroom. (p. 87)

Consider, then, this personal account by Ashley Casey, a practising secondary school PE teacher/researcher in England, where he writes about an influential colleague.

Power to the pupils

The first time I heard him speak I thought he was a lost prophet, a zealot preaching a message of 'power to the pupil'. I was a 'Rugby Man', an archetypal product of a middle class school with a highly traditional approach to Physical Education and GAMES – with the emphasis squarely on the games. So what time did I feel like giving to such an idea? Put the pupils in charge and you'll have an unmitigated disaster. Slowly however, as I worked more closely with my prophet I began to comprehend his ideas. Yet it would eventually take more than just ideas to make any sort of change, it would take a re-examination of my life and my teaching – of me – before I could profit from the message.

I had tried things, sure, little ideas that I gleaned from my prophet, but nothing concrete or life changing. Why? Because despite realising that I wanted to change, I didn't fully know what it was that I wanted to change. So I played lip service to these new, to me, concepts and began to realise that my teaching style no longer fitted with my ideals, yet I did nothing of note about it.

By this time – two years down the road – my prophet was a valued friend and mentor who, a year previously, had started a part-time Master's degree. The idea of further study had always appealed but I had never really considered myself to be of 'the right stuff' for postgraduate or higher learning.

Well it turns out that I am. In addition, I also had a story of my own to tell, although I didn't know it when I nervously applied to follow in my friend's footsteps. However, through the use of autoethnography, I was able to undertake the re-examination I needed but just didn't know I needed. It took little steps, tentative peeks into my childhood, my schooling and my pedagogy to find the answers that I had sought for so long and finally to plot the course that had been for so long prophesised.

If, as William Shakespeare wrote, all the world's a stage, and all the men and women merely players, then in my teaching I didn't fully understand when to enter and when to exit or that there were many roles for me to play. I was changing, slowly, but I still wanted the limelight and I was reluctant to become a stagehand, the shadowy figure who didn't hog the centre stage but moved in between scenes to make sure that everything was in place. It was only by examining my journey through my own life that I was able to identify not only the desire to change but also the direction of that change. I was able to decentralise myself and place the pupils at the heart of their own learning. I was no longer the font of all knowledge for my pupils, the expert and the knowledge giver, for I had finally given 'power to the pupils'.

In the case of this teacher, it would appear that Rousemaniere's (2000) point is proven. Engaging in autoethnography has launched Ashley into new pedagogies and purposes. He is endlessly curious in the drive to learn and is restless in his ambition to make PE learning "better" for himself and his pupils. The point he illustrates, quite powerfully, is that there *is* something in all this if, like me, you view educational research as something that must seek to touch teachers and reach pupils. The more contentious claim, perhaps, is that narrative research is more than a personal odyssey, that it has something to offer others – i.e. other than the researcher and researched. As Carlisle Duncan (1998) puts it: "This is the point of storytelling: We express others' voices, yet in so doing we recognize them as our own … This is the truth of the narrative turn" (p. 106–7). It is a claim that is interrogated further as this chapter progresses.

The words we use (core concepts)

As I pointed out earlier, the field of narrative research embraces a bewildering number of different approaches, definitions and concepts. The task here is not to reproduce all that complexity; indeed, I confess that I have found the literature to be somewhat confusing at times and the task of finding a defensible line of understanding through it will help me, the writer, as much as you the reader. Maybe this is a good example of one of Richardson's (2001) "top ten" thoughts about narrative writing: "Writing is a method of discovery" (p. 35). In this section then, we are learning together.

One way to classify the narrative research genre is to specify the research focus. Two broad approaches then become apparent:

- research undertaken by a teacher on him/herself, possibly guided by a researcher (this might include confessional tales written by a researcher on the research process) and
- research undertaken by a researcher on another person (as in life history/biographical approaches).

For the purposes of clarity in this chapter, the former will be located under the heading "autoethnography" and the latter "life story/history", even though it must also be recognized that autoethnographies will include life story/history. Furthermore, Clandinin and Connelly (1996) draw an important distinction between:

- stories of teachers and schools and
- teacher/school stories.

This reminds us that in narrative research, it is not only stories "of" that are important. In the context of schools, stories that are created around schools and teachers are also a key feature of, what Clandinin and Connelly (1995) term "the professional knowledge landscape". Examples of such stories in our own field might include the notion that PE teachers need to be young, fit and active, and the rather confused (but alluring) story about PE and its role in health promotion/illness prevention (Locke, 2003). Finally in this section, I will provide some examples of the specific research methods used to obtain stories, and the different forms of writing (or other forms of representation) that might be used to communicate them.

Autoethnography

Ellis and Bochner (2000) note that terms within the field of autoethnography, like language more broadly, are constantly evolving and so precise definitions are somewhat elusive. They suggest that authoethnography can be regarded as a generic term encompassing methods such as "narratives of the self (Richardson, 1994), self-stories (Denzin, 1989) … personal ethnography (Crawford, 1996) … critical autobiography (Church, 1995), self-ethnography (Van Maanen, 1995)" (p. 739) and a seemingly endless list of variations on the theme. The clear defining point about these terms is that they refer to research on self. In this context, Ellis and Bochner make three important points that are helpful to new narrative researchers:

> Autoethnography is an autobiographical genre of writing and research that displays multiple layers of consciousness, connecting the personal to the cultural … (p. 739)
> Usually written in first-person voice, autoethnographic texts appear in a variety of forms – short stories, poetry, fiction … etc. (p. 739)
> Autoethnographers vary in their emphasis upon the research process (graphy), on culture (ethnos) and on self (auto)'. (p. 740)

Moreover, they give some clues about method:

> I start with my personal life. I pay attention to my physical feelings, thoughts and emotions. I use what I call systematic sociological introspection and emotional recall to try to understand an experience I've lived through. Then I write my experience as a story. (p. 737)

Sparkes (2004) hints at a similar process in his autoethnographic writing about the transition from being an elite sportsperson to an injured one. The important point to be made is that "memories are not the 'truth' of the past. Nor are they the 'facts'. Instead, memory 'refers to the *retelling* of the past from the experience of the present" (p. 158). This, in a nutshell, is what the PE teachers were engaged in as they undertook my MSc module using auto ethnography. In this case the teachers worked within a broad framework, and to a particular focus (professional development). Beyond that, I would accept any style of writing as long as it worked as a piece of academic writing. By this, I meant that while the task of the writers was to tell stories in ways that worked for them, they also had to locate their stories within other stories or writings about the issues they wanted to raise. Not a "pure" form of autoethnography, perhaps (if there is such a thing) but I had in mind a process of "growing" personal stories in such a way that entry into more traditional forms of academic writing would also be eased. Many of these teachers begin their postgraduate studies as tentative, worried learners who need to be convinced, as Ashley described it earlier, that they are "the right stuff" for further study (why, I ask myself?). Once they have the skills and the confidence, however, it is as if a door has been opened. Fiona Chambers, a secondary school PE teacher/researcher in Ireland, describes it like this:

Me, my school and autoethnography

The MSc PE module on autoethnography forced me to reflect on my practice. It made me slow down, from moving through life at one hundred miles per hour, to take time to 'smell the roses', to value my life, my contribution to society and, invariably, to teaching. This reflection through autoethnography has brought me on a journey. I found it all a little uncomfortable at first, talking to my classmates about myself, and sharing my thoughts and ideas with them. I had to undo years of a system where I kept my left arm curled over my work, peeping above as I wrote, to ensure that no one caught a glimpse. Now, autoethnography is part of my practice. I have been keeping a journal of my reflections for the past eighteen months, and have been flabbergasted at the myriad of influences on my teaching, from Vogue magazine articles to 'Red Dog' by Louis de Berniere. I have been reacquainting myself with myself. It has been a very interesting journey so far as it has allowed me the space in my hectic life to look at myself as a 'person-pedagogue' and to understand who exactly is Fiona the teacher? Furthermore it has given me the opportunity to project into the future and to plan my pathway. This reflection may lead me into further research into teacher training in Ireland and, ultimately, I may wish to actively train teachers in this country.

Autoethnography has been infectious in my school too. Many of my colleagues now subscribe to it and it has led to changes in our practice. This change has occurred slowly over the past year. At our subject department meetings, my colleagues and I now trust each other enough to admit when we need guidance and accept the help being offered by colleagues. This has resulted in the pooling of resources and the emergence of team teaching. It has also reduced stress levels and ensured that students receive the best education possible in our classes.

In my experience, autoethnography is a most powerful and accessible form of CPD because it improves teacher learning and ultimately pupil learning through the age-old art of story telling.

As Fiona recalled, in our module we shared teachers' stories as they developed. In a collection of narrative accounts written by teachers in America who had engaged in a shared learning experience, Duckworth (1997) argues that "if one's knowledge is to be useful, one must feel free to examine it, to acknowledge one's confusions" (pp. 2–3). This was something that our MSc PE group did together, becoming powerful supporters and friendly (but exacting) critics of each other's writing. Indeed, the relief was palpable as this group realized that they were all tentative learners with similar concerns. In this instance, narrative research on self was used successfully as a professional development tool. There is more to it though. Duckworth compiled a book of American teachers' learning experiences. The purpose of her programme was to "help the participants to develop their own views of what it means to learn and what it means to know something, and to develop ways of teaching that are consistent with these views" (p. 2). One of the teachers wrote about his struggles to reach a difficult and challenging pupil. He concludes:

This roller coaster ride tires both of us. I'm afraid we'll get to a point where neither of us wants to try anymore. I am left wondering if he will ever experience the joy of learning. It doesn't feel as if the things I did made a difference in his life this year. I wish I knew. (Whitbeck, 1997: 53)

It could be argued that such accounts are more valuable to other teachers than shelves full of "official" behaviour management policies. They support teachers' understandings that teacher knowledge and "effective teaching" are dependent upon so many variables that the qualification "it depends" always seems to apply to questions about what "works" (Clandinin and Connelly, 1996). Perhaps that is why teachers reject so much of what is offered, traditionally, as professional development (Armour and Yelling, 2004a).

Life story/history

In education generally, and in physical education, life story/history research has a stronger tradition than autoethnography and so published examples of the genre are more readily available, especially from the late 1980s onwards. Life story/history research is, essentially, biographical research where a researcher constructs, or co-constructs, a story about a life, or part of a life. The purpose is to better understand that life, to shed light on similar or contrasting lives, and/or to inform an analysis of a particular issue or event. The distinguishing line that has been drawn in this chapter is between autoethnography as research on/by self (possibly with the assistance of another person) and life story/history research as that undertaken by a researcher "on" (or more likely "with") selected individuals. There is also an important distinction to be made between life "story" and life "history" methods. Whereas life stories can be constructed using a range of data about a life, life histories must consciously seek to link such data to historical times, locations and events. Thus, whereas life stories might focus exclusively on teacher agency, life histories are about the interplay of agency and structure as played out in the lives of particular individuals at particular moments in time. Sparkes and Templin (1992) were at pains to take this into account in their work on life histories and PE teachers, noting that they had heeded Goodson's (1988: 80) warning: "The life historian must constantly broaden the concern with personal truth to take account of the wider sociohistorical concerns *even if these are not part of the consciousness of the individual*".

Erben (1998) identifies two purposes to what he terms, "biographical research":

> We may say that biographical research has both *general* and *specific* purposes. The *general* purpose is to provide greater insight than hitherto into the nature and meaning of individual lives or groups of lives. Given that individual lives are part of a cultural network, information gained through biographical research will relate to an understanding of the wider society. The *specific* purpose of the research will be the analysis of a particular life or lives for some designated reason. (p. 4)

Erben also makes four key points about specific methods to be used to gather biographical data:

- 'the variety that is the life of the subject will guide researchers against too rigid a view of methodology' (p. 4)
- a wide variety of documentary evidence may be required
- interviews are likely to be a key research method
- the size of the sample is dependent upon the research purpose. 'The exact size of any sample in qualitative research cannot be ascertained through quantitative methods. It is for this reason that the conspicuously chosen sample must correspond to the overall aims of the study'. (p. 5)

Having collected data for a life story/history, the researcher is left with the task of assembling it into a readable format. One of the most common ways to do this is to segment the data into categories that fit the researcher's purposes. Hence, in some earlier life story research that I undertook on the lives and careers of four PE teachers (Armour, 1997) I reported the research not as four teacher case studies, but under the headings of:

- Family influence
- School experiences
- 'And on to college!'
- Doing the job.

However, in looking back on that writing process, it is possible to criticize the way in which I organized the data to fit the story I wanted to tell. I argued that I had used life stories to generate a better "understanding" of the teachers. Yet, Erben (1998) points out that segmenting lives in this way can also result in a loss of insight; thus, although I had retained a certain chronological understanding (albeit not sufficiently linked into historical events and temporal concerns) I may have lost something important about the holism of those lives. Moreover, in my concern to present an ordered account, I was probably guilty of crafting a traditional story line that could have obscured other important stories. As Usher (1998) puts it, there is a need in all forms of narrative research to "deconstruct the dominant self of the story" (p. 30). Instead, he argues, "Perhaps we just need to get used to living with fragmentation, and rather than endlessly searching for it, accept that the self is in process, continually re-newed and re-invented" (p. 27). If we accept Usher's point then, as Sparkes argues and later demonstrates (1995, 2002, 2004) we need to be more imaginative in the ways in which we write narrative research. This, in turn, might help us to use stories to support teachers' learning in more dynamic ways.

Writing and sharing stories

Usher (1998: 19) comments that in narrative research "The central character of this story is language and more particularly writing and the production of text". Sparkes (1995) made a similar point in the context of physical education research:

> How we as researchers choose to write about others has profound implications, not just for how readable the text is but also for how the people the text portrays are 'read' and 'understood.' (p. 159)

Sparkes (1995) articulates what he terms a "dual crisis of representation and legitimation" in qualitative enquiry. For example, he points out that the "absent author" style of writing used in traditional scientific texts was being reproduced in some qualitative research writing. He also argues that the notion of "giving voice" to research participants through qualitative writing is problematic. Instead, he suggests that qualitative researchers should consider alternative forms of writing that more closely fit the purposes of the research. Hence, he identifies new possibilities such as "confessional tales" (Van Maanen, 1988; Sparkes, 2002) where the researcher retells the experience of doing fieldwork; "impressionist tales" that use literary and metaphorical tools; "narratives of the self" which may include fictional accounts; "poetic representations"; "ethnographic drama"; as a means of communicating emotional and complex stories; and "ethnographic fictions" leading to powerful stories that can offer multiple interpretations. These possibilities lead Sparkes to raise the central issue of legitimation: essentially, how can we convince our audiences that this is "legitimate" research? It is an important question. Yet, I have decided, once again, to postpone further discussion of it until the final section of the chapter. It is an issue best addressed, I feel, once more evidence is in.

Stories and meanings (major findings)

When I began writing this chapter, I thought this would be the easy part; having arrived here, it feels like the most difficult. The brief from the editors was to provide an overview of the major findings from narrative research in PE. However, such a brief appears to rest on the assumption that the findings from different life stories/histories and autoethnographies can be aggregated in some way to produce a specific set of truths that can inform pedagogy and future research. Yet, Carter and Doyle (1996: 139) pose the question: "what is a finding in biographical research?" and I now find myself asking the same thing. Erben (1996) provides a clue. He suggests that narratives allow "the individual life to emerge in the dual nature, first, of its distinctiveness" (person "X" can never be person "Y") and secondly in its connectedness (person "X" can "recognize" person "Y") (cited in Scott, 1998: 35). Terkel (1969) puts it more eloquently:

> Each of the subjects is, I feel, uniquely himself (sic) whether he is an archetypal American figure, reflecting thought and condition over and beyond himself, is for the reader to judge, calling upon his own experience, observations, and an occasional look in the mirror. (Terkel, 1969 cited in Lawn and Barton, 1981: 245)

Judgements about what constitute the major findings from this research genre depend, to some extent then, on the ways in which the findings can reach different readers; in short, how the story told is both unique and shared, or at least connective. The most useful task I can perform, therefore, is to provide an overview of some of the widely read and easily accessible examples of narrative research in the field of physical education. In doing this, I will simply attempt to provide enough detail to tempt you to explore further and read the originals. I acknowledge many limitations. The selection does not include every example of narrative research in PE, nor does it attempt to cover narrative studies in/about sport that might be interesting and relevant to some readers. It could also be argued that the way in which I have grouped the studies is somewhat arbitrary, and that the selection fails to recognize that elements of narrative research can be found in lots of research approaches. A good example is the paper by Benn (1996) on "Muslim women in initial teacher training". However, such papers are too numerous to cover in one short chapter, and so the distinguishing feature of those selected is that they claim to have set out specifically to conduct a form of narrative research and/or writing.

The studies that have been selected can be grouped into three main categories, the first of which is, unsurprisingly perhaps, the largest:

1. Research on physical education teachers' lives and careers.
2. Research on different aspects of gender/sexuality.
3. Research that attempts new forms of analysis, writing and representation.

In each category, I will summarize selected research publications (mainly in date order of publication) pointing to key methodological or "writing" features and identifying some of the narrative threads that link them.

Physical education teachers' lives and careers

Age. It is a theme that flits in and out of the lives and careers research that follows. This may be because, as Sikes (1988) suggests:

> Getting old and, in particular, the physical consequences of aging are perhaps of greater significance to PE teachers than to teachers of other subjects. No matter what individuals may claim for themselves, physical ability declines with age, and teaching physical education tends to be seen to be directly linked with physical ability. (p. 21)

Sikes set out to analyse the ways in which PE teachers view and experience the aging process using "conversation-interviews which took a life history approach" (p. 22). She notes that most studies about PE teachers' careers have been about men, but that her research also focused on women. Sikes presents her data under the headings of initial career thoughts, involvement, promotion prospects and career moves, thus making it difficult to appreciate the lives of the respondents in any holistic sense. She concludes that career development is linked to age and experience, and this presents a problem for PE teachers because at the point at which they could claim to be the most experienced, their age (and attendant physical "decline") tends to lead them out of physical education. In addition, senior positions in PE are dominated by male teachers, leading to a "youthful, male orientation to

PE" (p. 37) that results in a traditional curriculum that is slow to change: "it has changed very little since I, my parents or even my grandparents were at school" (p. 36). Over 25 years later, I could make the same comment.

Age also features in research by Templin et al. (1988). This study focuses on two mid-career PE teachers and attempts a comparison of teachers in two different countries. Templin et al. argue that whereas most studies of teachers' careers are organized around occupational mobility and job commitment, their study views "career" more broadly and is "grounded in a whole life perspective" (p. 58) that recognizes subjectivity and the link between self and context. The data from life history interviews with the two teachers are presented in separate teacher stories, and a summary compares their experiences. The data are rich and the teachers' voices are strongly (albeit selectively) reported. The lead author compares the teachers" profiles and concludes that "Both commonalities and differences appeared to exist as I analyzed their careers" (p. 77). The commonalities included working long hours, seeing PE as a low-status subject in their schools, and valuing education and their role in it. The career differences were about promotion out of PE versus staying in it, i.e. "settling down" to a career with "advancement" or to a career as a PE teacher. In conclusion, the authors claim that their study has "revealed the idiosyncratic biographies of two mid-career female teachers" and they argue that a significant feature of both stories "was the marginality of PE … as a subject and the consequences of this marginality on career direction" (p. 80). They also suggested that further research is needed on PE teachers" careers.

A paper by Templin et al. (1991) begins with the phrase: "All of us age", so the narrative thread continues. It reports a series of life history interviews with one male PE teacher, Danny, to demonstrate how such teachers "negotiate a career" in relation to the aging process. The intention is to "communicate the personal reality of teachers through the description of their stories" (p. 143). Danny has 36 years' experience of PE in a career characterized by "middle class, conservative values, and one centring around personal involvement in sport" (p. 145). However, after an enthusiastic beginning, he became increasingly disenchanted: "Danny's last few years in teaching were characterised by a sense of bitterness that infused his process of disengagement" (p. 154). As the authors comment, this is in stark contrast to Sikes' (1988) notion of "growing old gracefully". Importantly, the authors claim that Danny's story, and the stories of other teachers, "can provide profound insights for many involved in education" (p. 154) and they contend that in this instance they have moved beyond description "to research that is value based as it asks the person

listening or reading the story to assess her or his own values and experience relative to the subject's stories. In this sense, active readership is encouraged and multiple interpretations of the story are invited" (p. 155). Again, they plead for more stories like this to be told.

Following on from the above, is a paper by two of the same authors (Sparkes and Templin, 1992) but a more detailed analysis of life history as method underpins it. The authors suggest that "One very good way to gain a greater understanding of teachers lives is to listen to what Bertaux (1981) has called their life stories" (p. 119) and they suggest that oral accounts are the foundation of this approach. They also point out, echoing the distinction made earlier in this chapter, that if a life *history* is the purpose of the research, then the story must be located broadly "to guard against the production of accounts that focus exclusively upon personal process and experiences at the expense of any consideration of socio-historical structures" (p. 122). In this study, the authors each interviewed teachers at different stages in their careers. They report four aspects of the data. Under the heading "Living with a low status image" they illustrate that "there was an awareness across generations that physical educators had a poor anti-intellectual and non academic image" (p. 125). They then contextualize this issue in an historical context and explore the implications for PE teachers' career opportunities. The main section, however, examines "women physical education teachers and experiences of double marginality", reminding us that teachers are not a homogeneous group. Using lengthy quotes from the teachers they illustrate, vividly, the "strands of oppression" (p. 138) that structured the life of one of the teachers and, they speculate, others like her. They also argue that the approach taken in this research "is able to provide important insights into the nature of teaching, for example, teaching as a gendered profession" (p. 139) although they caution against viewing it as the only valuable method for studying teaching.

In contrast to the last paper, research by Schempp (1993) focused on one high-school teacher, Steve Sommers, using a combination of life history and ethnographic techniques. Schempp notes that "this case study cannot be considered the definitive answer on how teachers construct professional knowledge" but he also suggests that it does "offer a useful glimpse into the knowledge construction of one experienced teacher" (p. 5) and so it may be useful to readers as they make connections between Steve's story and their own. Schempp identifies four main sources of Steve's professional knowledge: the views and expectations of the local community, including parents; the school culture, including students; sources and resources linked to or emanating from the profession, although these were not as influential as might have been expected; and Steve's biography in the form of personal initiative and professional experiences. The study concludes, in a strong echo of the earlier research by Sparkes and Templin (1992) with comments about the low status of physical education as viewed through Steve's story. Although Steve was valued as a sports coach, Schempp argues that "if communities and schools want teachers to teach their children, they must cast teachers in the role of pedagogues first and foremost" (p. 20). Linked to this is a conclusion about professional development. In Steve's case professional development provision was largely unhelpful in informing his professional knowledge and, as Schempp comments "teacher educators, authors, and in-service coordinators may find a larger, more receptive audience of practicing teachers if the knowledge they convey is structured in a format that addresses the needs and conditions teachers face in schools" (p. 21). Interestingly, this point has been strongly reinforced in some of my recent research on PE teachers' professional development needs (Armour and Yelling, 2004b).

Like the previous paper, two papers by Dowling Naess (1996, 2001) are based on the life histories of individual PE teachers. The first paper (1996) is about a male PE teacher, Sven Hoel. Here, the author "problematises the rationality of national curricula as agents of change" (p. 42) and critically appraises the life history approach. The data were collected from regular meetings over a period of 2 years during which time Sven and the author established "a warm and open dialogue" (p. 42). The data are reported in chronological order from childhood and school days through to training, teaching, illness and seeking retirement. Echoing earlier studies, age emerges as an important issue, particularly in the context of illness: "Sven had to face up to the realisation that no employer wants to take on board someone of his age with his case-history" (p. 47). The clear message from the research, however, is that despite the introduction of new curricula and policies throughout his career, Sven remained largely impervious to them and, for most of his career, he retained a sport and physical mastery focus to his pedagogy. Moreover, the author concludes that "Sven had neither the opportunity nor the incentive to develop or share professional knowledge" (p. 49), a point that provides a link to Schempp's (1993) case study reported earlier.

The second paper by this author (Dowling Naess, 2001) focuses on the life history of a 54-year-old female PE teacher, Jorunn Andersen. The author claims that "Jorunn Andersen's career is an interesting case because it reminds us that while teachers may enjoy agency … in their socialization within PE, rarely are the conditions for this agency of the teacher's own choosing" (p. 45). These data are reported differently to the earlier study. Dowling Naess presents Jorunn's life history in three stories;

what Jago (1996) terms a "layered account". Dowling Naess also provides some information about her interest in all this; describing herself (in sharp contrast to Jorunn) as one of the "disillusioned" in PE who left teaching in schools after "countless struggles" borne of "PE's marginal status in society" (p. 46). Thus, her research has centred on understanding better the experiences of other PE teachers "driven by a long-term goal of wanting to enhance the type of physical education experiences we can offer young people in schools" (p. 46). The first story presented is entirely in Jorunn's words, although it has been structured by Dowling Naess. It depicts a happy teacher who has had a wonderful career in PE. Although Jorunn expresses some mild concerns about poor teachers, age and being "over the hill", lack of money, and the sheer number of lessons to teach, she concludes "I love my job and I wouldn't swap it for the world!" (p. 49). In the second story, Dowling Naess provides an analysis of the first, largely in Jorunn's positive terms, describing Jorunn as a vocationally committed teacher. However, in the third story, Dowling Naess provides a much more critical reading of Jorunn's story, focusing on those things which Jorunn "chose to play down and yet which I, positioned as researcher, believe could have been significant factors in her career" (p. 53). Jorunn read this third story and found it 'interesting to be provoked into looking at certain issues in a new light" (p. 53) although she didn't agree with all of it. In essence, Dowling Naess argues that Jorunn may have been a victim of the "double marginality" of being a female teacher in a subject with low status, as was reported in the earlier research by Sparkes and Templin (1992). The author concludes: "Jorunn may well choose to say that subject status and gender issues do not interest her, but she cannot choose to remain unaffected by these structural constraints because she does not live and teach in a vacuum" (p. 56).

The status theme emerges again in a book that originated in my PhD (Armour and Jones, 1998). The book is based upon the life stories of eight physical education teachers, exploring "the complex links between sport, education and physical education" (p. 3). Methodologically, we make the point early on that we do not attempt to generalize from these stories to all physical education teachers. Instead, "Our aim is to ensure that the reader can *understand* these teachers and their philosophies: a task Wolcott (1990, 146) describes as 'a more ambitious activity' than 'merely knowing'" (p. 7). The teachers' stories are presented as individual case studies, written and structured by the authors in largely chronological format and using extensive teacher quotes. The data are analysed in four "themes": the links between physical education and sport, including an analysis of the ways in which language has shaped this issue; low status, focusing on the PE profession's attempts to overcome their marginality and the role of the wider education community in reinforcing it; the notion of 'caring' in physical education and the ways in which this shapes teachers' lives and career opportunities; and career progression, particularly looking at the ways PE teachers "move out" of the profession. A clear link is made, therefore, with the findings of several of the studies presented in this section. Finally, we argued at the time that low status continued to present problems for physical education, but that the profession itself bore some responsibility for this. We concluded: "physical educationists are long on opinion and rather short on substantiated claims about the educational value of their subject" (p. 137). Hence, we argued for "fundamental research" in physical education, described as "painstaking and detailed research" (p. 138) that focuses on teaching and learning and enables physical educators to have more confidence in their knowledge claims. This argument remains relevant almost ten years later.

Gender and sexuality in PE

Two papers in this group focus on the experiences of lesbian physical education teachers. The first by Sparkes (1994) extends his earlier research on teachers' lives and careers, and the concept of marginality, by examining the life history of Jessica, a young, lesbian physical educator. Sparkes argues that little is known about lesbian, gay and bisexual teachers, and even less about these PE teachers. The paper is described as an attempt to "help further interrupt the prevailing 'conspiracy of silence' described by Lenskyj (1991)" (p. 94) and to illustrate "how these ... teachers ... experience 'public' school life in ways that are hard to imagine for those (the majority) who are the beneficiaries of the privileges of heterosexuality" (p. 95). The author positions himself in the research and in relation to Jessica in terms of the social categories to which he belongs (e.g. white, male, heterosexual) and questions his responsibilities as a researcher: "One way that privilege can be used is to provide, for voices that are normally silenced, areas in which they can be heard by a range of audiences that might not otherwise hear them" (p. 96) although the tensions inherent in this aspiration are acknowledged. Jessica's story ranges through experiences of "coming out", reading for a degree, working and travelling, teacher training, and her first teaching post. Reflecting upon her story, Sparkes notes that whereas his earlier research identified the marginality of PE in schools, and the double marginality of female PE teachers, this research points to a "third dimension of marginality" (p. 109) in the lives of lesbian PE teachers. He also points to the public face–private life divide that Jessica feels compelled to maintain. The paper

concludes: "Having recognised the complexities of the dilemmas that Jessica faces, it is important to emphasise that with regard to her own invisibility, silence, and daily denial of self, she feels that in the present cultural climate her situation is likely to get worse rather than better" (p. 114).

The second paper, by Squires and Sparkes (1996) reports life history research undertaken with five lesbian PE teachers at different ages and stages in their careers. The main body of the paper uses extensive quotes from the teachers' stories in order to present authentic (rather than idealistic) stories. Moreover, the authors claim that "The construction of this paper ... needs to be seen as an expression of solidarity with the participants who have shared moments of their lives with Sarah [Squires, who conducted the interviews] in the hope of creating dialogue and facilitating change at both the individual and societal level" (p. 82). The data are reported in two key "themes": relationships with colleagues and relationships with students, and the authors note that daily life in school for these teachers is shaped and "framed by various layers of heterosexism and homophobia" (p. 94). The coping strategies these teachers adopt to hide their sexual identity, and the ways in which they struggle to be themselves are clearly illustrated. The authors argue that evidence such as that presented here suggests that 'taking action against homophobia and heterosexism is the responsibility of *all* teachers regardless of sexual identity' (p. 97).

Some of the issues raised in these papers are discussed further by Clarke (1998) who argues for different forms of sport to ensure justice and equity fors all participants, and Bredemeier et al. (1999) who illustrate ways in which the lesbian PE teachers in their study overcame fear and isolation to gain a sense of community and empowerment. Moreover, Sparkes (1996) notes the lack of empirical data on gay male physical educators, and so points readers to an "ethnographic fiction" that he crafted to represent their dilemmas and struggles (discussed in the third group of papers in this section).

Continuing with the thread of gender identity, a paper by Brown (1999) focuses on gender reproduction through the development and maintenance of masculine identity in teaching physical education. Interviews, using a life history strategy, were conducted with male graduates who were in a teacher-training programme. This paper presents stories about two of these men, illustrating the ways in which they adopt "complicit masculine identities" that reinforce the traditional gender order leading to a dilemma whereby "in spite of a desire to change that order in PE, they are in fact a living part of it" (p. 144). Both main characters, Joe and Derek, are described as "typical" male student PE teachers: "heterosexual, White, mesomorphic, with a history of successful participation in a specific team game"

(p. 149). Their life histories raise issues about school experiences, family, social class and managing their masculine identities in teaching PE. The cycle of gender reproduction is presented as difficult to "interrupt", and the author concludes that initial teacher education programmes need to seek opportunities to offer "alternative practical and physical resources ... so expanding the available range of professional identities in ways that acknowledge and challenge complicity to hegemonic masculinities" (p. 156).

Although not reporting a specific study, the suggestions made in a paper by Hickey and Fitzclarence (1999) are particularly interesting when read in conjunction with empirical evidence from the last by Brown (1999). This paper is built on the premise that males engage in more violence and crime than females, and that physical educators have a role in presenting new forms of masculinity to counter this trend. Hegemonic masculinity is described as being in crisis, and sport is identified as a site where the dominant forms of masculinity are learnt and reproduced. The authors argue, therefore, that "Along the developmental path from boy to man there needs to be some circuit breakers available to those who aspire ... to unsettle the mainstream patterns of enculturation" (p. 54). The narrative method is offered as one possibility that can "provide a means through which individuals and groups can question and remake the dominant story-lines which have framed their understandings" (p. 55). The authors outline the narrative strategies they employ and conclude, from their experiences of research with young males in a range of research projects, that "young males have relatively poor strategies for dealing with conflict and/or rejection" (p. 60) and that the story lines they live leave little space for responses other than violence or aggression. They suggest, therefore, that the narrative method offers "teachers (and teacher educators) and coaches, as cultural workers, a means through which to introduce alternative narratives to challenge the unproblematic production of dominant masculinity" (p. 61). However, if the findings of the previous paper (Brown, 1999) are applicable more widely to male physical education teachers and coaches, this might be quite a challenge.

New forms of analysis, writing and representation

It would be helpful to read the paper by Sparkes (1996), in conjunction with his earlier paper about 'Jessica' (Sparkes, 1994). In the 1996 paper, Sparkes tells elements of Jessica's story, but he also uses ethnographic fiction to create another story about Alexander, a gay, male PE teacher. Both stories are told to "present a view of schooling from a particular standpoint that for the most part has been repressed" (p. 167) and also to illustrate the different experiences of the two teachers. The creation of a fictional character is justified on the grounds that Sparkes "has never met a gay male PE teacher who was explicitly out" (p. 174) and so, if there are concerns about its validity, he suggests readers ask Tierney's (1993) questions of such work, for example: Can you learn from it? Is it plausible? Does it work?

Another example of a fictional account is Tinning's (1997) monograph written specifically to support teachers' learning as they undertook a Master's degree at Deakin University in Australia. He tells the story of a teacher called Pauline and he states: "This monograph has an agenda. It is not intended to be a dispassionate, disinterested account of what stands for research in physical education teaching" (p. 1). Through the monograph, Tinning tells Pauline's story and weaves into it both his own voice as narrator and a wide range of literature as viewed through Pauline's eyes. Similar to the last paper, Tierney's (1993) questions also apply and, as Tinning puts it "you will make, or not make, connections with Pauline's story based on your own history. As a writer, I can't change that reality" (p. 1). Narrative as a method of data analysis is the focus of a paper by Oliver (1998) and in a link to the two accounts above, Oliver uses some illustrative fictional writing techniques. Oliver begins by recounting an opportunity she took to "play around" with some research ideas with teachers and students. It led her to comment: "I was amazed at just how easy it is to forget one of the underlying purposes of educational research, that is, to come to better understand students, teachers, and their complex learning environments in the hope of creating better teacher preparation and physical education programs" (pp. 244–5). Narrative analysis is offered as a way of "accessing and framing" (p. 246) the stories people tell and, centrally, "The lifelikeness, the verisimilitude, of narrative allows for multiple interpretations, and multiple interpretations render multiple educational possibilities" (p. 249). Furthermore, narrative analysis must move beyond telling a story, it must offer insight and explanation using the three key components of setting, character and plot. Oliver concludes that physical education scholarship "needs narratives that touch the hearts and minds of readers" (p. 257). "Hear hear!" is the response from me and the teacher/researchers in this chapter.

There are strong developmental links between the next paper by Nilges (2001) and the previous by Oliver (1998). Here, the author revisits an earlier paper that reported qualitative data to raise questions about the strategies she used for that reporting. The author felt constrained by journal conventions to present her data in an "acceptable" publication format. However, she also wrote an "impressionist tale" (Van Maanen, 1988) where startling images provide the reader with vivid glimpses of the fieldwork (likened to impressionist painting techniques). This writing is presented against a backdrop of a "postmodern era", suggesting that new writing forms can expand our understandings of knowledge and culture in physical education. The write-up of the original study about gender inequalities (Nilges, 1998) is summarized, and then an impressionist tale told. In such tales, although the story is "tightly woven" and has clear structure, the purpose is to locate the author in the telling and invite the reader to engage with the issues and learn reflexively: "A well-written impressionist tale keeps readers close to the tale yet at the same time makes it possible to determine what part of the story is fact and what is fiction" (p. 240). The title of the second telling of the original tale reflects the author's new location within it, suggesting this tale is "participatory" rather than authoritative, and different points of view are presented throughout. There is also an explicit attempt to use "polyphonic voice", "reflecting the postmodern contention that truth is always partial and context dependent" (p. 246). Moreover, the conclusions to each version of the story are different. In the first, more conventional telling, "I clearly establish the final word on how the reader is to interpret that context that was studied" whereas in the second "I rhetorically construct a reflexive conclusion" (p. 252). The author suggests that such new forms of writing offer new understandings within the human movement profession.

Similar to the last paper, Sparkes et al. (2003) question conventional forms of writing in qualitative research. If, as Richardson (2000) argues, writing is a form of enquiry, then the form of that writing bears scrutiny. Focusing specifically on poetic representations, the authors suggest that researchers in sport and physical education should consider "harnessing the power of poetry, using it as a resource for not only understanding their own experiences and the experiences of others but also as a means of communicating to different audiences" (p. 155). Examples of such poetry are included, depicting the authors' experiences as student teachers, surviving oppression, and different elements of teachers' lives and careers. The authors claim that, more than some other forms of writing, poetic representations can engage readers *emotionally*, as they "stimulate and encourage multiple interpretations" (p. 170). It is also acknowledged, however, that researchers in physical education and sport may feel daunted by the prospect of embarking upon poetry, believing that they need to become skilled poets first. Strategies to overcome this are proposed,

including the suggestion that taking lessons in poetry may be necessary.

The final selection is a chapter by Sparkes (2004) from an edited collection of writings about the body (Evans et al., 2004). Sparkes constructs an "autoethnographic tale … to provide a partial, selective, somewhat ragged, and loosely stitched patchwork of memories that relate to my transition from a performing body to an impaired body, and the identity dilemmas this has instigated for me" (p. 158). His intention is to provide a "multi-layered text that draws the reader in" (p. 159) and he invites the reader to address the questions it raises in the contexts of their own lives – or ask new questions. He also poses questions about the learning to be gained from such writings, suggesting one possible answer is "the immense power that 'master' narratives have" (p. 169) – a point that is reinforced in some of the teacher stories about learning that I have used to illustrate this chapter. Sparkes uses hegemonic masculinity as his example, and suggests that the ways in which this, and other narratives, operate within physical education at all levels could be examined further. It is this latter point that I want to take forward into the next section.

Stories and learning (applications)

What can teachers learn from narrative research? Well, answers to that question have been offered by me and by other authors throughout this chapter. So, perhaps it's time to ask another teacher. Kelly Hulme is a primary school teacher in England with a special responsibility for PE throughout the school. She describes her experience of reading narrative research and also doing autoethnography:

Narrative research: my teacher thoughts

Generally we teachers do not view ourselves as researchers. Well, at least I didn't. To me, my job was straightforward! I imparted knowledge, tried to make it interesting and, hopefully, the pupils learnt. I was reflective about my practice in as much as I thought about different ways to present a lesson or organise the children to help them work better. I didn't, however, reflect on my practice as a whole. I didn't question, I didn't have time to question. I didn't really have time to think.

Upon beginning my Masters I did so cautiously, entering the room on that first day, looking around for tweed jackets and highbrow conversation. What I found, however, was very different. We were all quite similar, all of us had different reasons for taking on a Masters, but most of us had the common aim of improving our practice.

Through my studies I have come to understand that research on teaching and learning can be accessible and meaningful. My initial reservations, however, stem from reading research as an undergraduate and not understanding what most of it meant; looking at statistics and thinking, 'how does this have anything to do with teaching?' Once we become teachers, we are even more isolated from academia. Theoretically based literature seems far removed from what we are doing in the classroom, written in some complicated language by some anonymous (or hidden) writer, trying not to bias their work with what they actually think.

'Storying' was, 'a way in' to learning for me. Narrative writing highlighted the human side of research. Furthermore, in reading about autoethnography for a project that I wanted to write in a narrative style, I began to understand the importance of recognising my place in the research process. If the research is about you, then the writing-up process becomes much more than a report of what you have found out, it involves examining yourself, a scary process! Your voice is allowed to be present in the piece because the piece is about you. And you learn from reading the stories of others because you can empathise (and sympathise) with the author or the characters. Their stories provide you with a personal perspective and therefore the research becomes real.

Through all this I have become much more adept at reflecting on my practice. I have begun to understand the important influence that I have on the children's learning. My opinions, my views, my passion, my encouragement, how I see things, all impact on the learning experience. I now have an accessible medium through which I can participate in research giving me a powerful, professional development tool.

Kelly's account resonates strongly with an issue raised by Clandinin and Connelly (1998) about narrative research. They expressed concern that story telling had become something of a "fad" in educational research, and that its potential for learning needed to be restated:

People's lives are composed over time: stories are lived and told, retold and relived ... As we think about our own lives and the lives of teachers and children with whom we engage, we see the possibility for growth and change. (p. 203)

More recently, Keats Whelan et al. (2001) illustrated the ways in which stories are usually used in schools by teachers ("stories to live by" in Connelly and Clandinin's terms, 1999). They argue that certain storylines (difficult pupils, uncooperative parents) are simply *reaffirmed* by professional colleagues in school (in the interests of providing solidarity and support):

What troubles us is that, over the long term, such stories as these can become reified with certain characteristics always storied the same way. (p. 149)

Indeed, I can think of such reified stories in PE: the adolescent girl who loses interest in PE, the disaffected boy who is disruptive in everyone's lessons except ours, the over-ambitious parent who simply can't see that his or her child is not talented, the professional colleagues who don't appreciate PE. Yet, Keats Whelan et al argue that what teachers sometimes need is the opportunity to retell and relive such stories in order to *imagine new storylines*. The teacher in their story had a difficult encounter with a particular parent, and had received moral support from colleagues as a result. However, she also had the opportunity to retell her story in a research group, although even here, the initial response of the group (comprising other teachers) was simply to empathize with her difficulties. Eventually, however, the group responded differently, more reflectively, leading to the possibility for "imaginative retellings" (p. 151). This led to the possibility of learning. As the teacher at the centre of the story commented: "when I'm in school, with the others, telling stories isn't to do with learning, it's to do with diffusing this thing" (p. 153). Keats Whelan et al. conclude that although stories *are* often used in schools as a conservative force, the potential exists for them to be dynamic and revolutionary:

We want, instead, to draw attention to storytelling with diverse responses that leads to restorying with growth and change. In order for this to happen, we realise that teachers and others who live in schools will need to create new places on the professional knowledge landscape of schools. We are arguing for restorying of the landscape, perhaps in ways more like our research community, that is, more like a chosen community. (p. 154)

The PE teachers who feature in this chapter have all had the opportunity to explore their ideas and share their (initially) tentative learning in a professional learning space similar to the research group in Keats Whelan's account. Yet, that space simply doesn't exist in most schools (Newman, 1994; Stokes, 2001). What is interesting, however, are the ways in which teachers can make their own spaces once they are pointed in the right direction, and given the confidence to make a start. Karl Attard is a physical education teacher/ researcher in a secondary school in Malta. He is at an early stage in his career and, as the only physical education teacher teaching a new syllabus in the school, he has often found himself to be professionally isolated. After completing his Master's degree, Karl decided that he wanted to continue to research his own practice. He is now engaged in part-time doctoral studies and he is learning through writing, a tool that he has found invaluable in overcoming his professional isolation. Karl writes continuous reflexive accounts of his personal learning, his professional learning and his pupils' learning. The resulting narratives are detailed, intense and riveting. They chart moment-by-moment teacher learning and they illustrate the web of links that exist between the teacher as person and the teacher as pedagogue (Day, 1999; Armour and Fernandez Balboa, 2001). Karl writes:

Writing to learn

Sometimes I ask myself what have I learned from writing, self-study, and being reflexive. This is a difficult question to answer because learning, in this case, is an ongoing process. To cut a long story short, it is very unlikely (not to say impossible) to see a big difference in your teaching in just a few days; it is more likely that you'll see such changes over the years. However, these are a few things I have learnt.

Teachers are not technicians and like all other professionals, we need to evolve in accordance with our surroundings and our clients. The best way to do this is to learn and understand our clients. I have also learnt to value myself and to understand and listen to my own feelings by examining my emotions. Yet, the most important lesson I have learnt is that I have a lot more to learn. I now realise how important it is for everybody, especially teachers, to learn throughout their lives. The more I learn, the more I realise how much more there is to learn.

My doctoral studies are not helping me to become a better teacher in the sense of acquiring new teaching skills. On the contrary, my present studies are helping me become a better teacher by making me understand that there is no specific point where one can objectively say that one is a 'good' teacher. I'm learning to question everything and this, in turn, has helped me realise that I can always improve. No matter how much I have studied … no matter how much experience I've got … no matter how much I've reflected upon my experience … learning is ongoing and also essential if I am to improve. Thus, I am now realising that my doctoral research will be an unfinished piece of work.

Stories to be told … (future directions)

From my perspective, the list of stories to be told in the future is endless. As the authors in this chapter have argued, crafting stories about self and others can be a powerful learning process for both the teachers and the researchers engaged in it. If that view is accepted, then in physical education I think we need many more stories from which to learn. We also need more and better ways of telling those stories such that teachers can access them. Sparkes (1999) wrote about "body narratives" and identified six areas for future research centred on the premise that "Just as we can think of storied lives, so we can think of storied bodies and storied selves" (p. 26). I, too, have argued for a better understanding of the body in physical education (Armour, 1999) and so, at one level, could support Sparkes' sentiments. I also see interesting new lines of narrative enquiry developing from publications such as that by Macdonald and Kirk (1999) on the body and religious identity in physical education, and Chen (1999) on PE curriculum and pupils' social capital. Yet, perhaps a list of research topics is not the way to end this chapter. Instead, it might be helpful to return to the opening quote:

When teachers told their stories and responded to others' stories in sustained conversation groups, they came to understand their own practices in new ways. Their participation in these groups led them, many said, to new insights, new restoried knowledge. Many described their experiences in these groups as their most powerful professional development. (Clandinin, 2001; p. viii)

Also, earlier I referred to Oliver's (1998) account of how she was reminded of the purpose of physical education research when she spent some time "playing around" with research ideas with teachers and pupils. Maybe it is in these two points that the future lies. Given the opportunity, teacher/researchers and researchers working together can identify the stories that teachers, researchers and pupils need to tell in order to learn. However, it is the *opportunity* that is, too often, the missing link. Finally, I return to the issue I identified, but have dodged, throughout this chapter …

Is it "real" research?

Well, it is to me. And the PE teachers and the researchers you have read about in this chapter are convinced too. Moreover, for the teachers, narrative research is a powerful form of professional development. But some argue that narrative research is more pseudo-therapy than research: more self-indulgence than rigorous science. So, I draw upon two strong (for me) pieces of evidence:

I get impatient with writers who belittle or diminish the therapeutic consequences of stories. They tend to draw a hard and fast distinction between therapy and social research, implying that narratives are only useful insofar as they advance sociological, anthropological or psychological theory. For these critics, narrative threatens the whole project of science ... What they oppose is what they equate with the therapeutic: the sentimental, the mushy, the popular ... Why should we be ashamed if our stories have therapeutic value? Besides, haven't our personal stories always been embedded in our research [*and, I would add, our teaching*]. The question is whether we should express our vulnerability and subjectivity openly in the text or hide behind 'social analysis' ... Why is it so hard to grasp that personal narrative is moral work and ethical practice? (Ellis and Bochner, 2000: 746–7)

The 'fate' of emotions in education has, so far, been largely one of discipline and subjugation. I have hope that this fate is not a determined destiny but a historically specific confluence of social forces which is being altered. But education – specifically relations between educator and student, relationships between peers, and the creative expression within our work – also engenders passion, creativity and joy. (Boler, 1999: xxiv)

What I conclude from all this is that teachers as persons (rather than as robots) are very much present in the teaching process and no amount of pretending that they are not there will make them, or their influence as persons (with emotions and feelings) disappear. As Day (2004) puts it "good teachers invest large amounts of their substantive emotional selves in pursuing their work with students" (p. 12). It seems to me, then, that research that can (a) reach teachers, (b) give them the confidence to learn, (c) help them to change their practices and (d) provide a way in which such learning can be accessed, shared and critically evaluated by other teachers in the context of their own pedagogies is research worth doing. The evidence presented in this chapter suggests that narrative research has that potential. In a nutshell, it is research that begins with "I" but, when made accessible to others, becomes research about "you" and about "we" the profession. I will allow Kyriaki Makopoulou, a PE teacher from Greece, to have the final word:

The more I explore my experiences using stories and relevant literature, the more I see my own pedagogy in a new and, sometimes, negative, light. For writing about my experiences in a creative way turns the familiar into the strange. This situation makes me feel uneasy. I challenge, re-evaluate, and question many aspects of my education, teaching

and learning. At the same time I feel motivated because, for the first time, I can make personal sense of what is happening while teaching, adding depth and meaning to my experiences.

References

Armour, K.M. (1997). Developing a personal philosophy on the nature and purpose of physical education: Life history reflections. *European Physical Education Review*, 3(1): 68–82

Armour, K.M. (1999). The case for a body focus in education and physical education. *Sport, Education and Society*, 4(1): 5–16.

Armour, K.M. and Fernandez-Balboa, J.M. (2001). Connections, pedagogy and professional learning. *Teaching Education*, 12(1): 103–118.

Armour, K.M. and Jones, R.L. (1998). *Physical education teachers' lives and careers: PE, sport & educational status.* London: Falmer Press.

Armour, K.M. and Yelling, M.R. (2004a). Continuing professional development for experienced physical education teachers. *Sport, Education & Society*, 9(1): 95–114.

Armour, K.M. and Yelling, M.R. (2004b). Professional 'development' and professional 'learning': bridging the gap for experienced physical education teachers. *European Physical Education Review*, 10(1): 71–94.

Atkinson, P. (1990). *The Ethnographic Imagination.* London: Routledge.

Barthes, R. (1977). *Image, Music, Text (S. Heath Trans.),* New York: Hill & Wang.

Becker, H.S. (1990). Commentary by H.S. Becker. In E.W. Eisner and A. Peshkin (Eds.), *Qualitative inquiry in education. The continuing debate* (pp. 233–242). New York: Columbia University.

Benn, T. (1996). Muslim women and physical education in initial teacher training. *Sport, Education and Society*, 1(1): 5–22.

Bertaux, D. (Ed). (1981). *Biography and Society.* London: Sage.

Boler, M. (1999). *Feeling power. emotions and education.* London: Routledge.

Bredemeier, B.J.L., Carlton, E.B., Hills, L.A. and Oglesby, C.A. (1999). Changers and the changed: Moral aspects of coming out in physical education. *Quest*, 51(4): 418–431.

Brown, D. (1999). Complicity and reproduction in teaching physical education. *Sport, Education and Society*, 4(2): 143–159.

Carlisle Duncan, M. (1998). Stories we tell about ourselves. *Sociology of Sport Journal*, 15: 95–108.

Carter, K. and Doyle, W. (1996). Personal narrative and life history in learning to teach. In J. Sikula (Ed.), *Handbook of research on teacher education: A project of the association of teacher educators. 2nd Edition,* (pp. 120–142). London: Prentice Hall International.

Chen, A. (1999). The impact of social change on inner-city high school physical education: An analysis of a teacher's experiential account. *Journal of Teaching in Physical Education, 18*(3): 312–335.

Church, K. (1995). *Forbidden narratives: Critical autobiography as social science.* Newark, NJ: Gordon & Breach.

Clandinin, D.J. (2001). Foreword. In C.M. Clark (Ed.), *Talking shop,* (p. viii). New York: Teachers College.

Clandinin, D.J. and Connelly, F.M. (1990). Narrative, experience and the study of curriculum. *Cambridge Journal of Education, 20*(3): 241–253.

Clandinin, D.J. and Connelly, F.M. (1995). *Teachers' professional knowledge landscapes.* New York: Teachers' College Press.

Clandinin, D.J. and Connelly, F.M. (1996). Teachers' professional knowledge landscapes: Teacher stories – stories of teachers – school stories – stories of schools. *Educational Researcher, 25*(3): 24–30.

Clandinin, D.J. and Connelly, F.M. (1998). Asking questions about telling stories. In C. Kridel (Ed.), *Writing educational biography: Explorations in qualitative research.* New York: Garland.

Clarke, G. (1998). Queering the pitch and coming out to play: lesbians in physical education and sport. *Sport, Education and Society, 3*(2): 145–160.

Connelly, F.M. and Clandinin, D.J. (1999). *Shaping a professional identity: Stories of educational practice.* New York: Teachers College Press.

Crawford, L. (1996). Personal ethnography. *Communication Monographs, 63*: 158–170.

Day, C. (1999). *Developing teachers. The challenges of lifelong learning.* London: The Falmer Press.

Day, C. (2004). *A Passion for teaching.* London: Routledge Falmer.

Denzin, N.K. (1989). *Interpretive biography.* Newbury Park, CA: Sage.

Denzin, N.K. and Lincoln, Y. (2000). The discipline and practice of qualitative research. In N.K. Denzin and Y.S. Lincoln (Eds.), *Handbook of qualitative research: 2nd Edition* (pp. 1–29). London: Sage.

Derrida, J. (1978). *writing & difference (A. Bass, Trans).* Chicago, IL: University of Chicago Press.

Dowling Naess, F. (1996). Life events and curriculum change: The life history of a Norwegian physical educator. *European Physical Education Review, 2*(1): 41–53.

Dowling Naess, F. (2001). Sharing stories about the dialectics of self and structure in teacher socialization: Revisiting a Norwegian physical educator's life history. *European Physical Education Review, 7*(1): 44–60.

Duckworth, E [and the experienced teachers group] (1997). *Teacher to teacher. Learning from each other.* New York: Teachers College Press.

Eisenhart, M. (2001). Educational ethnography past, present and future: Ideas to think with. *Educational Researcher, 30*(8): 16–27.

Elbaz, F. (1991). Research on teachers' knowledge: The evolution of a discourse. *Journal of Curriculum Studies, 23*(1): 1–19.

Ellis, C. and Bochner, A.P. (2000). Autoethnography, personal narrative, reflexivity. Researcher as subject. In N.K. Denzin and Y.S. Lincoln (Eds.), *Handbook of qualitative research: 2nd Edition* (pp. 733–768). London: Sage.

Erben, M. (Ed.) (1998). *Biography and education: A reader.* London: Falmer Press.

Evans, J., Davies, B. and Wright, J. (Eds.) (2004). *Body knowledge and control. Studies in the sociology of physical education and health.* London: Routledge.

Foucault, M. (1970). *The order of things: An archaeology of the human sciences.* New York: Random House.

Geertz, C. (1988). *Works and lives: The anthropologist as author.* Cambridge: Polity Press.

Goodson, I. (1988). *The making of curriculum: Collected essays.* Lewes: Falmer Press.

Goodson, I.F. and Numan, U. (2002). Teachers' life worlds, agency and policy contexts. *Teachers and Teaching: Theory and Practice, 8*(3–4): 269–277.

Gorard, S. (2002). Warranted research claims from nonexperimental research evidence. *ESRC TLRP Research Capacity Building Network Occasional Paper 48.* Retrieved March 12th, 2004, from www.cardiff.ac.uk/socsi/capacity at http://www.cardiff.ac.uk/socsi/capacity/Occasional.html

Hickey, C. and Fitzclarence, L. (1999). Educating boys in sport and physical education: Using narrative methods to develop pedagogies of responsibility. *Sport, Education and Society, 4*(1): 51–62.

Jago, B. (1996). Postcards, ghosts and fathers: Revising family stories. *Qualitative Inquiry, 2*(4): 495–516.

Keats Whelan K., Huber, J., Rose, C., Davies, A. and Clandinin, D.J. (2001). Telling and retelling our stories on the professional knowledge landscape. *Teachers and Teaching: Theory & Practice, 7*(2): 143–156.

Kuhn, T. (1962). *The structure of scientific revolutions.* Chicago, IL: University of Chicago Press.

Lawn, M. and Barton, L. (Eds) (1981). *Rethinking curriculum studies.* London: Croon Helm.

Lenskyj, H. (1991). Combating homophobia in sport and physical education. *Sociology of Sport Journal, 8*: 61–69.

Locke, L.F. (2003). Preparing teachers to grab the brass ring: Lessons from the carousel at Missoula. *Summary Address: NASPE PETE Conference,* Baton Rouge, Louisiana, October. Retrieved March 12th, 2004, from http://www.unlockresearch.com/content/article/8/0/

Lyotard, J.F. (1984). *The Postmodern condition: A report on knowledge (G. Bennington and B. Massumi, Trans.).* Minneapolis, MN: University of Minnesota Press.

Macdonald, D. and Kirk, D. (1999). Pedagogy, the body and Christian identity. *Sport, Education and Society, 4*(2): 131–142.

Newmann, F.M. (1994). School-wide professional community. *Issues in restructuring schools. Issue Report 6.* (Spring, pp. 1–2) Center on Organization and Restructuring of

Schools. Wisconsin Center for Education Research. University of Wisconsin-Madison. Retrieved on 12th March, 2004, from http://www.wcer.wisc.edu/archives/completed/cors/Issues_in_Restructuring_Schools/

Nilges, L.M. (1998). I thought only fairy tales had supernatural powers: A radical feminist analysis of Title IX in physical education. *Journal of Teaching in Physical Education, 17*: 172–194.

Nilges, L.M. (2001). The twice told tale of Alice's physical life in wonderland: writing qualitative research in the 21st century. *Quest, 53*: 231–259.

Oliver, K.L. (1998). A journey into narrative analysis: A methodology for discovering meanings. *Journal of Teaching in Physical Education, 17*(2): 244–259.

Richardson, L. (1994). Writing: A method of inquiry. In N.K. Denzin and Y.S. Lincoln (Eds.), *Handbook of Qualitative Research* (pp. 516–529). Thousand Oaks, CA: Sage,

Richardson, L. (2000). Writing. A method of inquiry. In N.K. Denzin and Y.S. Lincoln (Eds.), *Handbook of qualitative research: 2nd Edition* (pp. 923–948). London: Sage.

Richardson, L. (2001). Getting personal: Writing stories. *Qualitative Studies in Education, 14*(1): 33–38.

Ritchie, J. and Spencer, L. (2004). Qualitative data analysis: The call for transparency. *Building research capacity (Issue 7)*. Cardiff: Cardiff University School of Social Sciences.

Rorty, R. (1982). *Consequences of pragmatism (essays 1972–1980)*. Minneapolis, MN: University of Minnesota Press.

Rousemaniere, K. (2000). From memory to curriculum. *Teaching Education, 11*(1): 87–98.

Schempp, P.G. (1993). Constructing professional knowledge: A case study of an experienced high school teacher. *Journal of Teaching in Physical Education, 13*(1): 2–23.

Schon, D.A. (1983). *The reflective practitioner: How professionals think in action*. New York: Basic Books.

Schon, D.A. (1987). Educating the reflective practitioner. London: Jossey-Bass.

Scott, D. (1998). Fragments of a life: Recursive dilemma. In M. Erben (Ed.), *Biography and education: A reader* (pp. 32–45). London: Falmer Press.

Sikes, P.J. (1988). Growing old gracefully? Age, identity and physical education. In J. Evans, (Ed.), *Teachers, teaching & control in physical education* (pp. 21–40). London: The Falmer Press.

Sparkes, A.C. (1987). Strategic rhetoric: A constraint in changing the practice of teachers. *British Journal of Sociology of Education, 8*: 37–54.

Sparkes, A.C. (1992). Writing and textual constructions of realities: Some challenges for alternative paradigms research. In A.C. Sparkes (Ed.), *Research in physical education. Exploring alternative visions* (pp. 271–297). London: The Falmer Press.

Sparkes, A.C. (1994). Self, silence and invisibility: A life history of a lesbian experience. *British Journal of Sociology of Education, 15*(1): 93–119.

Sparkes, A.C. (1995). Writing people: Reflections on the dual crisis of representation and legitimation in qualitative inquiry. *Quest, 47*: 158–195.

Sparkes, A.C. (1996). Physical education teachers and the search for self: Two cases of structured denial. In N. Armstrong (Ed.), *New directions in physical education. Change and innovation* (pp. 157–178). London: Cassell.

Sparkes, A.C. (1999). Exploring body narratives. *Sport, Education and Society, 4*(1): 17–30.

Sparkes, A.C. (2000). Autoethnography and narratives of self: Reflections on criteria in action. *Sociology of Sport Journal, 17*: 21–43.

Sparkes, A.C. (2002). *Telling Tales in Sport and Physical Activity: A Qualitative Journey*. Champaign, IL: Human Kinetics.

Sparkes, A.C. (2004). From performance to impairment: A patchwork of embodied memories. In J. Evans, B. Davies and J. Wright (Eds.), *Body knowledge and control. Studies in the sociology of physical education and health* (pp. 157–172). London: Routledge.

Sparkes, A.C. and Templin, T.J. (1992). Life histories and physical education teachers: Exploring the meanings of marginality. In A.C. Sparkes (Ed.), *Research in physical education. Exploring alternative visions* (pp. 118–145). London: The Falmer Press.

Sparkes, A.C., Nilges, L., Swan, P. and Dowling, F. (2003). Poetic representations in sport and physical education: Insider perspectives. *Sport Education & Society. 8*(2): 153–178.

Squires, S.L. and Sparkes, A.C. (1996). Circles of silence: Sexual identity in physical education and sport. *Sport, Education & Society, 1*(1): 77–102.

Stokes, L. (2001). Lessons from an inquiring school: Forms of inquiry and conditions for teacher learning. In A. Lieberman and L. Miller (Eds.), *Teachers caught in the action. Professional development that matters* (pp. 141–158). New York: Teachers College.

Templin, T.J., Bruce, K. and Hart, L. (1988). Settling down: An examination of two women physical education teachers. In J. Evans, (Ed.), *Teachers, teaching & control in physical education*, (pp. 57–82). London: The Falmer Press.

Templin, T.J., Sparkes, A.C. and Schempp, P.G. (1991). The professional life cycle of a retired physical education teacher: A tale of bitter disengagement. *Physical Education Review, 14*(2): 143–155.

Tierney, W. (1993). The cedar closet. *International Journal of Qualitative Studies in Education, 6*(4): 274–294.

Tinning, R. (1997). *Pedagogies for physical education: Pauline's Story*. Deakin University Press: Geelong, Australia.

Tsangaridou, N. (in press). Teachers' knowledge. In D. Kirk, D. Macdonald, and M. O'Sullivan (Eds), *Handbook of research on physical education*. London: Sage.

Usher, R. (1998). The story of self: Education, experience and autobiography. In M. Erben (Ed.), *Biography and education: A reader* (pp. 18–31). London: Falmer Press.

Van Maanen, J. (1988). *Tales from the field: On writing ethnography*. Chicago, IL: University of Chicago Press.

Van Maanen, J. (1995). An end to innocence: The ethnography of ethnography. In J. Van Maanen (Ed.), *Representation in ethnography* (pp. 1–35). Thousand Oaks, CA: Sage.

Whitbeck, C. (1997). Against all odds: Creating possibilities for children to invent and discover. In E Duckworth [and the experienced teachers group] (Eds.), *Teacher to teacher. learning from each other* (pp. 48–53). New York: Teachers College.

Wolcott, H.F. (1990). On seeing – and rejecting – validity in qualitative research. In E.W. Eisner and A. Peshkin (Eds.), *Qualitative inquiry in education. The continuing debate* (pp. 121–152). New York: Columbia University.

Wolcott, H.F. (1994). *Transforming qualitative data.* London: Sage.

Woods, P. (1985). Conversations with teachers: Some aspects of life-history method. *British Educational Research Journal, 11*(1): 13–26.

4.7 Teachers' beliefs

NIKI TSANGARIDOU

Over the last years, teachers' beliefs has become one of the most important concepts in teaching and teacher education (Calderhead, 1996; Pajares, 1992). In codifying and understanding the complexity of teaching, scholars have suggested that greater attention needs to be paid to the teachers' thoughts and actions and how they affect quality teaching (Borko and Putnam, 1996). A number of scholars have suggested that educational researchers need to shift their research focus from pedagogical strategies and teaching behaviors to the beliefs that prompt teachers to use these strategies and behaviors (Richardson, 1996). As Rovegno (2003) suggested "to understand good teaching, we need to hear teachers' voices and study what good teachers thought, knew, and believed" (p. 295).

Calls for exploring the nature and role of teachers' beliefs in teacher education have proliferated in the literature (O'Sullivan, 1996; 2003; Wilson and Berne, 1999; Zeichner, 1999). O'Sullivan (2003), for example, argued that in quality teacher education programs, teacher educators need to understand the critical role of teachers' beliefs and address them in their programs in order to influence teachers' views of teaching and learning. In contemporary research, teachers' change is assumed to lead to better teaching which implies a better education of students (Richardson and Placier, 2001). Scholars have suggested that the beliefs that teachers hold, serve as filters through which their learning takes place and they are critical targets and major determinants of changes in teaching practice (Borko and Putnam, 1996).

This chapter aims to provide an overview of what do we know about teachers' beliefs in physical education. The content of this chapter is based on a selected number of studies in which teachers' beliefs are explicitly represented. Given the rapid growth of research this chapter is not meant to be exhaustive or even comprehensive. The scope, rather, is to define this body of literature, to represent the basic dimensions and directions of this work, and to make it accessible to the physical education community in general. The chapter is intended to provide an overview of the forms of beliefs teachers hold, how beliefs are developed, and the role of teachers' beliefs on teaching and learning. It is organized around the main area of research on teachers' beliefs and each of its sections examines categories of research conducted on this topic.

More specifically, the first section of the chapter opens with an analysis of the construct of teachers' beliefs and an effort is made to clarify the term. Subsequently, the role of teachers' beliefs in the act of teaching is discussed. Finally, the first section provides a short presentation of the kind of experiences that are influential in the development of teachers' beliefs. In the second section research findings on teachers' beliefs are reviewed and discussed. The third section provides an analysis of major findings and conclusions from this line of research and provides directions for further inquiry and implications for teacher education practices.

Definitions, functions, and origins of beliefs

Defining beliefs

This part of the chapter presents a brief orientation of the meaning of the term teacher beliefs in an attempt to clarify the concept. The construct of teachers' beliefs has been used extensively in the literature and, on many occasions, in quite problematic ways. Distinguishing and defining the concept is a daunting undertaking (Calderhead, 1996; Pajares, 1992). Ennis (1994) observed that beliefs are more difficult to measure directly than is factual knowledge because "an individual's beliefs often must be inferred from statements or actions. They reflect a tacit understanding of personal, social, or professional truths that have been constructed over time through enculturation, education, or schooling" (p. 164).

In his review article, "Teachers' beliefs and educational research: cleaning a messy construct", Pajares (1992) proclaimed that the concept of beliefs is rarely, clearly, defined in educational discourses or used explicitly as a conceptual tool in research studies. Pajares (1992) commenting on the construct of teachers' belief noted:

> Defining beliefs is at best a game of player's choice. They travel in disguise and often under alias – attitudes, values, judgments, axioms, opinions, ideology, perceptions, conceptions, conceptual systems, preconceptions, dispositions, implicit theories, explicit theories, personal theories, internal mental processes, action strategies, rules of practice, practical principles, perspectives repertories of understanding, and social strategy, to name but a few that can be found in the literature. (p. 309)

Nespor (1987) described beliefs as framing or defining tasks, established a view of cognitive processing essential to understand this function, and identified four levels of thought: internal processing, resources, control or metacognitive processes, and belief systems. Nespor (1987) made the argument that in understanding teaching from teachers' perspectives we have to understand the beliefs which define their work. Fang (1996) defined beliefs as the rich store of general knowledge of objects, people, events and the relationships that teachers have that influence their planning decisions as well as their classroom actions. Educational beliefs have been referred to as beliefs about confidence to affect students' performance, about the origin of knowledge, about causes of teachers' or students' performance, about perceptions of personal feelings, about confidence to perform specific tasks, and about specific subject matters or disciplines (Pajares, 1992).

Generally speaking, beliefs has been a global concept with a variety of meanings. Beliefs are rarely clearly defined in studies or used explicitly as a conceptual tool, "but the chosen and perhaps artificial distinction between belief and knowledge is common to most definitions: Belief is based on evaluation and judgment; Knowledge is based on objective fact" (Pajares, 1992: 313). In other words "although beliefs generally refer to suppositions, commitments, and ideologies, knowledge is taken to refer to factual propositions and the understandings that inform skillful action" (Calderhead, 1996: 715).

The functions of beliefs

Most would argue that beliefs are an important concept in understanding teachers' thought processes, classroom practices, change, and learning to teach (Richardson, 1996). Teaching is embedded in explicit and implicit beliefs, mainly because teaching involves evaluation, judgment, and choice. All teachers hold beliefs about their work, their students, and their subject matter which are part of their broader general belief system (Pajares, 1992).

Teachers' beliefs are considered to play an important part in the judgments, understanding, and interpretations they make every day. Nespor (1987) emphasized that teachers' beliefs influence perception, interpretation, and judgment and therefore have important consequences for what teachers do and say. The beliefs teachers hold influence their perceptions and judgments which affect their teaching practices. Teachers' beliefs play a critical role in defining teaching tasks and organizing the knowledge and information relevant to those tasks (Calderhead, 1996).

Teacher's beliefs only recently gained prominent attention in the literature (Richardson, 1996). Understanding the belief structure of teachers is critical to improving the teacher education programs and teaching practices (Calderhead, 1996; Ennis, 1996; Feiman-Nemser and Remillard, 1996; O'Sullivan, in press; Pajares, 1992). According to Richardson (1996) teacher beliefs "are important considerations in understanding classroom practices and conducting teacher education designed to help prospective and in-service teachers develop their thinking and practices" (p. 102). Richardson (1996) continued to suggest that, in such teacher education programs, beliefs of teachers "strongly affect what and how they [prospective and in-service teachers] learn and are also targets for change within the process" (p. 102).

The origin of beliefs

In the literature three major categories of experience are identified as influential in the development of beliefs about teaching. Research studies have shown that teachers' beliefs may have been acquired and formed (a) during their experiences as pupils in schools, (b) from life experiences, and/or (c) by their teacher education professional preparation program (Fang, 1996; O'Sullivan, 2005; Pajares, 1992; Richardson, 1996). As Richardson (1996) pointed out these forms of experience may not be mutually exclusive and at times may be studied together as is the case with several teacher biography and life history studies.

Research findings indicated that different life experiences contribute to the development of strong and enduring beliefs about teaching and learning (Richardson, 1996). It has also been found that teachers hold many untested beliefs that influence how they think about classroom issues and respond to particular teaching and learning situations (Calderhead, 1996). Several scholars have suggested that teacher beliefs must be brought to light, discussed, tested, and reframed during professional preparation programs in order to make significant changes in teaching and schooling (Calderhead, 1996; O'Sullivan, 2005; Pajares, 1992; Richardson, 1996; Schon, 1983, 1987). Readers interested in this issue might examine Chapter 4.3 on field experiences by Behets and Vergauwen.

Research findings

Research studies in physical education indicated that teachers' hold strong beliefs about educational issues. Representative studies of this field of inquiry are reviewed under the following ten major categories: (a) beliefs of recruits and prospective teachers about the purposes of PE, (b) beliefs about learning to teach and teaching experiences, (c) beliefs about effective teaching, (d) classroom teachers' beliefs of teaching PE, (e) beliefs about learners and learning, (f) relationship of beliefs to teaching practices, (g) beliefs about subject matter, (h) beliefs about self and teaching role, (i) beliefs about the nature of their work, and (j) teacher concern based on Fuller's framework.

Beliefs of recruits and prospective teachers about the purposes of PE

In the recent past, Lortie (1975) suggested that prior to entering teacher education programs prospective teachers would have spent over 13 000 hours in observation and apprenticeship in K-12 schools. His influential work has shown that preservice teachers enter professional preparation programs with well-developed beliefs about teaching and most of the time their beliefs are difficult to change. Research in physical education indicated similar findings. Preservice physical education teachers enter teacher preparation programs with a broad spectrum of beliefs about physical education and change little over time (Graber, 2001; O'Sullivan, 2005; Stroot, 1996).

Doolittle et al. (1993) suggested that it is vital to explore and understand recruits' beliefs because "beliefs filter what recruits learn during formal training, most adopting ideas that fit their beliefs and ignoring those that do not. ... Understanding recruits' beliefs is also important for teacher educators to exert maximum impact" (p. 355).

Placek et al. (1995) designed a study that used a large national sample to describe recruits' physical education backgrounds and beliefs about the purposes of physical education. Background findings indicated both a wide range of activities and significant similarities across the total program, with more emphasis on team and competitive sports and fitness. Findings revealed that the most frequent belief about the purposes of physical education was for students to learn motor skills or activities and develop physical fitness. The researchers concluded:

> Clearly, our recruits' beliefs about physical education are shaped through the social institution of the school – teachers, physical education programs, and sport experiences. The messages absorbed through this socialization probably provide even more powerful messages than those of university-based teacher educators. (Placek et al., 1995: 259)

O'Sullivan 2005, summarizing the major results of this line of research, indicated that "the dominant view of new recruits is that they perceive physical education as being primary skill oriented, prefer coaching to teaching, and are more conservative than other teachers" (p. 5).

In the literature there are some studies which described the influence of teacher education programs on the beliefs of preservice teachers. In an initial study, Doolittle et al. (1993) examined three recruits' beliefs about the purposes of physical education and good teaching from entry to exit in one teacher education program. It was found that the participants' beliefs were well established when they entered the professional program, developed during the recruit stage, but did not change markedly during their training program. "Their rejection or adaptation of particular teaching skills offered by this program illustrated how recruits filter new experiences through the screen of their earlier belief systems. They accepted practices that complemented their core beliefs and ignored practices that did not fit" (p. 364). In explaining the lack of program impact on the recruits beliefs system, Doolittle et al. (1993) noted that possibly the program was not as well designed to help preservice teachers deliberately and directly confront their belief systems. The investigators pointed out that:

> Although more teacher educators now recognize the strength of recruits' entering beliefs and the impact these will have on how well recruits absorb program messages, few of us are yet sufficiently skilled in helping recruits articulate, share, discuss, or debate – much less change – their beliefs. (p. 364)

In another study, Graber (1995) explored the beliefs held by student teachers, from two universities, regarding the elements of the teacher education program that most directly guided their practice. Findings suggested that the preservice teachers believed that the practicum experiences were the more valuable aspects of the teacher education program. The participants also believed that professional activity courses (e.g. tennis, basketball) were significant to developing subject matter knowledge. Results also suggested that the prospective teachers had greater difficulties in making a connection between university education courses and the knowledge they believed essential for physical education teachers. Finally, all participants from one university believed one particular teacher educator mainly influenced their beliefs about physical education.

In a longitudinal study, Matanin and Collier (2003) explored three preservice teachers' beliefs as they evolved throughout a 4-year teacher education program. Data collection spanned 5 years and included interviews, open-ended questionnaires, and reflective documents. Findings show that the preservice teachers assimilated only part of the program messages on teaching physical education relative to content, teaching effectiveness, and the role of planning. The participants emphasized students' effort and participation and rejected the program philosophy on assessment of student learning outcomes. Results also indicated that, due to the impact of their biographies, the participants were less likely to assimilate the teacher education program's messages about classroom management and the purposes of physical education. Matanin and Collier (2003) concluded that the preservice teachers' K-12 and personal experiences played a powerful role in the formation of their beliefs about teaching physical education.

The effects of a teacher education program on the beliefs of a beginning teacher were studied by Curtner-Smith (2001). More specifically, he examined the positive influence of one university PETE program on the practices and perspectives of a beginning teacher with a strong teaching orientation. The PETE program's influence was mediated by the teacher's biography and entry into the workforce. Findings indicated that the PETE program and the teachers' biography influenced his pedagogical philosophy and practices to a great extent. Workplace factors (i.e. facilities, classroom teachers, etc.) did not have a negative impact on the teacher. The teacher "was determined to teach as he had been trained even in the face of some serious situational constraints" (Curtner-Smith, 2001: 81).

Beliefs on learning to teach and teaching experiences

Teachers, especially preservice teachers, hold beliefs about professional development and how someone learns to teach (Calderhead, 1996). McIntyre et al. (1996), in a review article, concluded that teaching experiences have been considered by teachers to be the most valuable component of the teacher education programs. The literature suggested that the role of these experiences in the professional development of teachers is not always positive (Bain, 1990; Dodds, 1989; Graber, 2001). Evidence suggested that school experiences stimulate preservice teachers to adopt more rigid attitudes toward teaching and that

preservice teachers become more custodial, authoritarian, and utilitarian (Dodds, 1989; Graber, 2001; O'Sullivan, 2003; Richardson, 1996). Research findings also indicated that prospective teachers' attitudes toward students decreased significantly as they progressed through teaching experiences and aligned with those of the cooperating teachers (McIntyre et al., 1996).

Reviewing findings on the role of teaching experiences, Bain (1990) concluded that "student teachers seem to become more concerned with control and discipline and to feel less responsible for student learning" (p. 768). In addition, findings revealed that prospective teachers are rarely provided with opportunities for analyzing and reflecting on different aspects of teaching and schooling (O'Sullivan, 2003; Tsangaridou and Siedentop, 1995).

Several scholars have pointed out that during the formal teacher education program and teaching experiences, reflective inquiry should be used to help change the custodial ideologies of the preservice teachers. Tinning (1988), for example, indicated that the pedagogy developed by student teachers is a "pedagogy of necessity". He proposed (1988) that teacher educators should employ a critical-inquiry methodology and break the cycle of the pedagogy of necessity, which characterizes student teaching. Similarly, Kirk (1986) emphasized that "teacher education should be concerned with producing teachers who are critically aware of the complexities of the educational process, of their contribution to this process, and of the potential for change" (p. 242). Reflective approaches and strategies that attempt to surface, challenge, and transform teachers' beliefs have been proposed and used by scholars in several teacher education programs (Byra, 1996; Carlson, 2001; Dodds, 1989; Macdonald and Tinning, 2003; McCollum, 2002; McCormack, 2001; Tsangaridou and O'Sullivan, 2003; Tinning, 1988; Tsangaridou and Siedentop, 1995).

Hardy (1999) examined preservice teachers' perceptions of how they felt the school-based experience helped them learn to teach. Findings suggested that the preservice teachers placed a great deal of emphasis on the accumulation of experiences and "coming to terms" with the realities of teaching. Furthermore, the preservice teachers' personal histories, the context of the teaching environment, and the general ecology of the school setting influenced preservice teachers' beliefs and their development as teachers.

Beliefs about effective teaching

Few studies were found on teachers' views and beliefs about effective teaching. Parker (1995) reminds us that much of the research on teacher effectiveness has been process–product studies in which the behavior of the teacher constitutes the process, and student-learning outcome is treated as the product. Based on the fact that studies which describe teachers' voices and personal accounts of effective teaching did not exist, Parker (1995) conducted a study to explore high school physical education teachers' views of effective teaching. Findings suggested that teachers' beliefs of effective teaching reflected a hierarchy of pedagogical practices including organization, management, discipline, and control with student learning being the ultimate goal.

A similar observation was made by McCullick (2001) who pointed out that "in socialization research in PETE, one voice is missing: that of the practitioner" (p. 36). McCullick (2001) explored the perspectives of practicing teachers related to the values, knowledge, and skills required for teaching physical education and training teachers to teach. Results revealed that these practicing teachers believed that future teachers should have a love for physical activity, be physically fit, have a love for children and people, and be flexible. The participants believed that teacher educators' effectiveness in preparing prospective teachers related to being credible, displaying a love for physical activity, and having concern for the growth and development of future teachers.

Classroom teachers beliefs of teaching PE

One aspect that has received little attention is classroom teachers beliefs about teaching physical education. Xiang et al. (2002) designed a study to describe the impact of a field-based elementary physical education methods course on preservice classroom teachers' beliefs. The authors suggested that "the methods course had a positive impact on the preservice teachers' beliefs but no impact on their disposition toward teaching elementary physical education" (p. 145). The preservice classroom teachers shared similar beliefs about the value and purposes of elementary physical education as those held by physical education specialists. More specifically, the participants believed that contributing to the development of the whole child; enhancing students' physical fitness and guiding them to a healthy and active lifestyle; helping students develop personal and social skills, and teaching students motor skills were the four major purposes of elementary physical education. Finally, the authors suggested that the two most important aspects of the course that contributed to the participants' beliefs were teaching physical education in an elementary school setting and observing physical education classes.

In another study, Tsangaridou (2002) described the learning process of an elementary classroom teacher during student teaching. Findings indicated that the preservice teacher designed instructional tasks with an emphasis on students' learning. The teacher also used several student-centered pedagogical strategies during the lessons based on her belief that students' knowledge is more meaningful when it is experiential. The researcher concluded that it is essential and valuable to understand preservice classroom teachers' beliefs and practices of physical education if we are to design teacher education programs which may influence prospective teachers to acquire and refine professional knowledge.

Beliefs about learners and learning

Woods et al. (2000) explored what preservice teachers learned about students in an early field experience that involved them in a structured teacher research project. Results suggested that the research project process helped the preservice teachers to learn more about students' motivation and interests, characteristics, and interactions. The research process forced the preservice teachers to challenge "previous beliefs and assumptions about students, as PTs began making connections between their newfound knowledge of students and its implications for curriculum, instruction, and management decisions" (p. 15).

Allisson et al. (2000) explored the epistemological stances on movement skillfulness of preservice teachers. A constructivist approach, that individuals' meanings are created based on the interaction of their previous knowledge and beliefs with recently experienced phenomena, was used as the framework for inquiry into a teacher education program which put emphasis on the development of skillful movers as the major goal of physical education. The findings revealed that the preservice teachers believed that above average ability, task commitment, and creativity were seen as characteristics of being skillful.

Some studies provide descriptions of experienced teachers' perceptions of how students learn, how instructional practices affect students' learning, and what is important for students to learn in physical education. Veal (1998) investigated secondary teachers' perceptions and practices of pupil assessment in physical education. The findings were categorized into five themes that "represent an umbrella of ideas, beliefs, and concerns about pupil assessment which appear to influence all assessment practices" (p. 332). The themes were named: effort, improvement, individualization, purpose/utility, and efficiency. Veal (1998) reported that teachers' assessment practices were affected by the effort and improvement of their students, and that teachers' individualized assessment strategies. Results of the study also indicated that some teachers use no formal assessment. These teachers believed that "they can see whether a student is learning and that testing was unnecessary. Other themes show that teachers are concerned with efficient use of allocated time and that many of the formal practices are impractical for their situations" (p. 332).

O'Reilly et al. (2001) explored seven female Canadian physical education teachers' perspectives on the experiences they believed important for students to have in their physical education classes. The authors found that "In many cases, 'having fun' became substituted for skill development or even 'challenge' as the most appropriate and the most attainable outcome for their students" (p. 219). The participants believed that the crowded facilities, inadequate equipment, and limited allocated time prevented them from providing constant opportunities for their students to experience profound pleasure in purposeful, focused movement. O'Reilly et al. (2001) pointed out that the conditional restrictions were constant sources of frustration for the participants. They concluded that "despite their desire and efforts to promote lifetime involvement with physical activity, it was most often fun that was highlighted, rather than any attention to skill and challenge" (p. 220).

In another study, Tsangaridou and O'Sullivan (2003) explored experienced teachers' educational theories and found that the teachers held firm and clearly articulated views about student learning and what constitutes a physically educated student. The primary goal of the physical education programs for these teachers was skill development and they believed guided student practice was important for student learning. In addition, the investigators concluded that the teachers' selection and implementation of teaching practices demonstrated their commitments to gender equity and to the needs and abilities of their students.

Relationship of beliefs to teaching practices

Most agree that teachers hold various beliefs about teaching and learning which are part of their broader general belief system. It has been a contestable issue, however, whether or not such beliefs influence their classroom practices (Calderhead, 1996). Researchers of teaching have often overlooked the degree to which beliefs influence the nature of teachers' actions and there is very limited empirical work on the alignment of teacher's beliefs and actions (Fang, 1996; Kulinna et al. 2000; Pajares, 1992; Richardson, 1996; Tinning, 1988; Tsangaridou and O'Sullivan, 2003).

Studies in general education have shown inconsistent results with a few researchers reporting teachers' beliefs related to their practices while other studies have not shown a relationship between teachers' beliefs and teaching (Calderhead, 1996). In physical education results on the alignment of teacher's beliefs and practices are mixed. Some evidence suggests consistent alignment between teachers' beliefs and their practices. Chen and Ennis (1996) investigated the impact of physical education teachers' value systems on their curricula by examining two physical educators' curriculum content and implementation. Results indicated that the two teachers established curriculum goals and addressed aspects of the physical education content that were associated with their individual value orientations. In another study, Tsangaridou and O'Sullivan (2003) described the relationship between teachers' theories of action and theories-in-use and found that the teachers held strong and well-articulated views about teaching and learning, and the teachers' theories-in-use were consistent with their theories of action.

Other research evidence has shown a partial relationship between theories or beliefs and teaching actions. Veal (1992) used a case study design, to examine the practices (enacted theories) and perceptions (espoused theories) of two middle-school teachers who included formal assessment in their teaching. Teachers who held strong beliefs about student assessment were affected by a desire to treat students as individuals. The author also suggested that the teachers' espoused and enacted theories were often congruent, but they were more incongruent in the areas of performance testing and formative record keeping.

Finally, some studies suggest inconsistent results between teachers' theories or beliefs and actions. Using a multiple case study design to examine the teachers' espoused and enacted theories of action, Romar (1995) found that there was a level of discrepancy between teachers' espoused theories and professional practices. Kulinna et al. (2000) investigated the relationship between teachers' belief system toward physical activity and fitness and what was taught in their classes and found that there was no relationship between teachers' belief systems and their teaching behaviors.

Beliefs of subject matter

Some studies have explored physical education teachers' views of their subject matter incorporating a philosophical perspective. Using this orientation, Green (2000) explored the everyday "philosophies" of 35 secondary teachers working in secondary schools in England. He found that the participants' ideologies related to sport, health, academic value, education for leisure, and "sport for all". Enjoyment was a major consideration for the teachers and the emphasis on enjoyment was prominent in all teachers' "philosophies". Green (2000) indicated that the participants seldom had anything that could be called philosophies in the sense of integrated, sound sets of ideas. He indicated:

> Confusion and contradictions were common features of their views. What PE teachers articulated was typically a kind of check-list of aims and practices frequently centering upon words and phrases like 'enjoyment', 'health', 'skills' and 'character'. … Indeed, their 'philosophies' appeared more like justificatory ideologies; that is to say, ideologies that served to vindicate teachers' preferred conceptions of PE. (p. 124)

Green (2000) concluded that the impact of philosophy on teachers' "philosophies" from a figurational perspective was limited. Teachers' "philosophies" according to him are best understood as processes rather than states. He argued that "a figurational sociological approach to making sense of PE teachers' 'philosophies' holds out more promise than a (traditional) philosophical perspective" (p. 126).

In another article Green (2002) analyzed and discussed extensively how the figurational sociological perspective can contribute to our understanding of teachers' physical education "philosophies". He suggested that teachers' "philosophies" need to be viewed in context and "can only be fully understood when teachers are located in the figurations they form with each other – as inescapably interdependent people" (p. 65). Physical education teachers are a group of professionals who "have similar habituses at the personal level and all constrained by similar circumstances at the local and national dimensions of their figurations" (Green, 2002: 79). He concluded,

> The largely normative views of their subject that teachers internalize are, to some extent, transmitted by these teachers to future teachers whilst the later are pupils experiencing school and college PE. Hence, the likelihood that PE teachers' outlook on PE remains to a greater or lesser extent tied to 'yesterday's social reality'. … As such, PE teachers' 'philosophies' tended to be practical 'philosophies'; that is to say 'philosophies' that bore the hallmarks of their prior PE and sporting practice and their contemporaneous practical teaching contexts. (p. 80)

Beliefs about self and teaching role

Biographical research on teachers' lives and socialization research has indicated that preservice teachers come to any learning situation with ideas, knowledge, and beliefs acquired through prior experiences (see Chapter 4.6). These all influence the ways in which preservice teachers think, interpret, and make use of new information (Calderhead, 1996; Stroot, 1996; Stroot and Whipple, 2003; Zeichner and Gore, 1990). Empirical evidence has shown that most of the people who chose physical education as a career, are academically average students who are mostly successful in physical education and sports rather than in academic achievement (Stroot, 1996). They had positive experiences in sports and their physical education teachers and coaches were role models for them. Their experiences in sports during schooling influenced their understanding of what it means to be a physical education teacher (Stroot, 1996).

Research evidence also suggested that the decisions prospective teachers make about their role as teachers are made long before they learn how to teach. Hutchinson (1993), for example, investigated the perspectives on teaching physical education of ten high-school students who had chosen to become physical education teachers. The participants held similar and narrow beliefs about physical education and viewed teaching as a career contingency for coaching. The participants' histories of participating in organized sports or other physical activities prior to teacher education had significantly affected their decisions to choose physical education as their major area of study.

In another study Griffin and Combs (2000) examined physical education interns' perceptions and beliefs about the role of the physical education teacher, their sense of readiness for the student teaching experience, and the consistency of their desire to become physical education teachers during the socialization process. Findings of the study supported the view that individual beliefs are deeply ingrained and neither teacher education programs nor teaching experiences significantly alter them. The researchers stated "it became apparent that the interns either held significant philosophical differences or lacked knowledge about the purpose of teaching physical education" (p. 45).

O'Bryant et al. (2000) investigated what influenced the decision of prospective teachers to become physical education teachers and what were their beliefs about physical education teaching and teachers. The eight participants in the study entered an M.Ed. program in a Holmes institution. They were older than traditional-aged students and several had previous career and educational experiences in areas other than physical education. The participants "were attracted to the field by the love of the content, the dynamics and culture of the work with young people" (p. 191). The prospective teachers believed that their role as a physical education teacher was to be a physically active role model and help students to understand the importance of physical activity, contribute to the development of all students' self-esteem and especially those marginalized in classes, and plan and implement lessons that would reinforce all students to participate in an active way in class. O'Bryant et al. (2000) concluded that:

> This cohort of students was primarily interested in and committed to teaching (as opposed to coaching) and equity in the curriculum and their work with children. These two trends observed in this cohort of students appear to fit core values and shifting paradigms linked to diversity and improved quality of teaching in teacher education programmers. Perhaps faculty in PETE programmes should consider that older, non-traditional students (undergraduate and graduate) bring life experiences (personal and professional) that will enhance their professional socialization. (pp. 191–192)

Teachers' beliefs about the nature of their work

Teacher socialization research described and explored potential factors affecting teachers' work and sought to understand and improve the work of teachers in schools (Stroot and Whipple, 2003; Zeicher and Gore, 1990). In exploring physical education teachers' beliefs about their working lives many investigators have used the occupational socialization framework (Lawson, 1986). Findings from this line of research suggested that the working environment and the nature of physical education teachers' work produced multiple frustrations to physical education teachers. Workplace factors and conditions which affect teachers' work are the low status of physical education teachers and their subject matter, poor communication and interaction with school administration, sexism, work overload, poor facilities, isolation, routinized work, and lack of rewards (Graber, 2001; Macdonald, 1995; Stroot and Whipple, 2003). Readers interested in an extensive review on teacher socialization research might examine Chapter 4.4.

Doune Macdonald and her colleagues used different epistemological traditions (e.g., critical orientation) and different methodological strategies (e.g. life history) to better understand teachers' beliefs. In one study, Macdonald (1995) argued that the professionalization and proletarianization model is another useful framework in understanding teachers' professional work. She pointed out "the tensions between professionalization and proletarianization provide a useful lens through which to understand patterns in beginning teacher attrition" (p. 130). Macdonald (1995) described the frustrations and disappointments for beginning physical education teachers in schools and examined the dissatisfactions that motivated the teachers to leave the profession. She proposed that "rather than being disparate concerns, they can be understood through the dynamic of the proletarianization of teachers' work" (p. 130).

Macdonald (1995) found that some of the situational constraints for physical education teachers, including lack of status, repetitive nature of physical education work and limited decision making was similar to earlier research findings (Graber, 2001; Stroot and Whipple, 2003). Additional concerns included the lack of intellectual stimulation, personal and professional surveillance, and unprofessional staffroom culture. She concluded that the teachers' early phase of socialization reflected the trend of proletarianization, and that the professionalization and proletarianization tension is a useful framework for understanding the perspectives of physical education teachers' attrition. She indicated this perspective can "offer a frame of reference for considering how the nature of teachers' work and their organizational contexts may be changed in order to stem the tide of talented and initially enthusiastic beginning teachers from leaving the profession" (p. 140).

Using the same theoretical lens, Macdonald (1999) examined whether experienced physical education teachers perceived the same frustrations and dissatisfactions as beginning teachers. She found that the participants' work-based frustrations and satisfactions emerged under the general themes of competence, commitment, and authority. Macdonald (1999) found that the participants' working conditions and orientations were more supportive and positive that those reported in other studies by beginning or experienced teachers. The participants' stories differed from other teachers' stories in the following four key ways. "All but one of the experienced teachers: (a) had started their careers in supportive environments; (b) greatly valued their interactions with the students; (c) derived ongoing intellectual challenge from teaching 'Board' physical education; and (d) could influence what they perceived as significant aspects of their work practices and environments" (p. 51). Macdonald (1999) concluded that the professionalization–deprofessionalization tension is a valuable framework at a theoretical and practical level. It allows the exploration of the social regulation and bureaucratic constraints on teachers in different contexts and developmental stages of their careers. Practically, they suggest what work practices should be maintained and "strengthened to support committed, experienced teachers and also what might constitute more satisfying working conditions for beginning teachers" (p. 52).

Macdonald and Kirk (1996), recognizing the role of the dialectical relationship between teachers and cultural context of their work, explored beginning teachers' working dissatisfaction in non-metropolitan school contexts. They found that the participants faced several pressures relating to their isolation, beginning professional status, and personal lifestyle choices. The participants felt that they were under constant and continuous observation in both their public and private lives. Macdonald and Kirk (1996) concluded that teachers' identities as physical educators were shaped by the dual configuration of schooling and sports. They suggested that "the dynamic process of corporeal regulation within the tightly knit communities put pressure on and shaped how the teachers conducted their professional and personal lives, and constructed their identities, which in turn influenced their satisfaction with physical education teachers' working conditions" (p. 65).

In another study, Macdonald and Kirk (1999) explored the students' beliefs and lifestyles, as self-identified Christians, and the tensions they experienced between their beliefs and professional and pedagogical practices. They concluded that the visibility of students' religious beliefs with professional, curricula, and instructional issues is another challenge to current pedagogies. As they pointed out:

> When confronted with contemporary pedagogical principles for health and physical education, the Christian students are faced with dual moral missions; on the one hand, responsibility to their church to proselytize and, on the other hand, responsibility to the socially critical liberal curriculum as defined by the State. For teacher education, this raises questions concerning the breath of beliefs and practices considered appropriate for a graduate moving into contemporary schooling. (p. 140)

The occupational socialization process for physical education teachers has been identified in the literature as complex since "the process not only reflects the expectations and constraints generated by the society, educational organizations, and bureaucracies but also the pervasive influences of working with and within sport" (Macdonald, 1995: 129). O'Connor and Macdonald (2002) used the identity theory to understand how physical education teachers manage their dual teacher/coach roles and the possible tensions that arise through inconsistencies across teaching and coaching responsibilities. They argued that properties of identity theory, such as the dialectical interaction of context and societal influences on personal identities, provide a different way to understand how teachers who work in multiple contexts with multiple responsibilities negotiate their identities in achieving complementarily in their work despite tensions across contexts. O'Connor and Macdonald (2002) studied Australian physical education teacher/coaches' personal philosophies, their dual responsibilities, and the risks and rewards derived from teaching and coaching. Findings suggested that the participants generally enjoyed the dual responsibilities of teaching and coaching. The dynamic tension that existed in

teachers' work was constantly monitored and negotiated by the teachers to reach a level of security. "Teachers constantly negotiated, both self-reflexively and publicly, ways to reduce tensions and maximize complementarily across the responsibilities, and in line with their personal lives" (p. 49). The participants' pedagogical theories and practices involved a commitment across tasks for the benefit of themselves and the students. O'Connor and Macdonald (2002) concluded that the teachers' identities were evolved and established through a reflexive monitoring of action which occurred in light of new information, experience, and knowledge.

Teacher concerns – Fuller's framework

There is much research today documenting how formal or informal social structure of schools affects teachers' perceptions and practices (Stroot and Whipple, 2003; Zeichner and Gore, 1990). Wendt and Bain (1985) suggested that "the informal social structure in certain situations may be more powerful than formal. Success in teaching may depend on accurate perceptions of what is accepted as 'good' and where the power lies" (p. 25).

Over the past several decades, research in physical education has suggested that physical education teachers have a wide range of concerns which affected their teaching practices. Large class sizes, inappropriate facilities, insufficient equipment, increased pupil assessment, external accountability, and new curriculum initiatives are a few of the several variables that influenced their teaching (Meek and Bethets, 1999). Working under such conditions teachers, whether preservice or inservice, undoubtedly have concerns about their teaching and about their capacity to be effective teachers (Meek and Bethets, 1999; Richardson and Placier, 2001).

Teachers' concerns about their teaching as well as their professional progress and development through their careers have attracted the attention of educators for quite some time now (Graber, 2001; Meek and Bethets, 1999; Richardson and Placier, 2001). A number of approaches have been suggested and used to describe teachers' progress and development through their careers. These approaches have been focused on different aspects of the teachers' learning, thinking, and action (Richardson and Placier, 2001). Fuller's model of teacher development and the enormous empirical research upon which it was based underpins concerned-based approaches to research on preservice and inservice teacher education programs. This model is "perhaps the most classic of stage theories in that it was meant to be relatively invariant, sequential and hierarchical" (Richardson and Placier, 2001: 910).

The theoretical foundation of teachers' concerns research focused primarily on the work of Frances Fuller. The primary assumption was that concerns about teaching are an expression of the need to become a more competent teacher (Meek and Bethets, 1999). Fuller's (1969) seminal work of the evolution of teachers' concerns describes the stages that teachers go through as they become teachers. Fuller (1969) defined teachers' concerns as perceived constructive problems, worries, or frustrations when focusing on tasks or challenges. In her model, she suggested three developmental stages of teachers as they gain teaching experience. She indicated that "the evidence seems to support a developmental conceptualization of teacher concerns. We posit three phases of concern: a pre-teaching phase, an early teaching phase and a late teaching phase" (p. 218). Fuller (1969) categorized concerns into three teaching clusters and believed that teachers progress through as they mature in their teaching environment. First, self-concerns are concerns associated with the teachers' ability to teach and dealt with class control and discipline. Second, task-concerns are concerns associated with teaching tasks such as working with big classes, and inadequate instructional materials. Third, impact-concerns focused on the needs of the pupils. Teachers are concerned about themselves as individuals, about the tasks and contents of the teaching process, and about the impact of their teaching on pupil behaviors. Fuller's theory has been used extensively by her associates and other researchers who focused their research effort in the teaching concerns domain. As Meek and Behets (1999) pointed out Fuller's theory "has achieved a status as a developmental paradigm of sorts with concerns frequently being operationalized via George's (1978) Teacher Concerns Questionnaire (TCQ)" (p. 498).

A number a studies explored the nature of physical education teachers' concerns at various career stages using Fullers' framework (Graber, 2001). Studies that adopt a concern-based model include research on both preservice and inservice physical education teachers. Research evidence from these studies on the development of teaching concerns has yielded mixed results. The following are representative of these studies which have used a sample of preservice teachers, a sample of inservice teachers, and a sample of both preservice and inservice teachers.

Preservice teachers

Wendt et al. (1981) attempted to test Fuller's theory of teaching concerns applied to professional preparation of physical educators and found that the theory was not supported by their findings. The cross-sectional results indicated that no change occurred while the longitudinal findings suggested

that self, task, and impact concerns were lowered. They concluded that the Fuller's theory would predict a lowering of self-concerns but heightened task and impact concerns with progression through a teacher education program.

Boggess et al. (1985) examined the level of concern that exists in physical education student teachers with regard to self, task, and impact identified in Fullers' model. In order to detect changes in the participants' concerns patterns the TCQ was administered on three occasions during student teaching: prior to the actual teaching task, at mid-semester, and at the end of the student teaching experience. They concluded that "although the results did indicate a developmental process over the semester, they did not appear to bear out Fuller's theory in the case of preservice teachers" (p. 210).

In exploring the concerns of Belgium physical education student teachers Behets (1990) used two different data collection strategies: (a) a TQ questionnaire and (b) a logbook. Only impact concerns increased significantly and could be documented as a stable variable. The major concerns in the participants' logbooks were concerns about student control and organization. The data from the TCQ and logbooks reflected both idealistic and realistic concerns (Behets, 1990).

Meek (1996) conducted a study to investigate the concerns of British prospective physical education teachers prior to and following teaching experiences. The study had two major purposes (a) to assess the effectiveness of the TCQ with a sample of preservice teachers and (b) to compare the changes in concerns for each preservice cohort as an indicator of developmental shifts in concerns during teaching practice. The author suggested that the TCQ was a poor instrument for the participants. In addition, no significant differences were found on developmental shifts in concerns between cohorts, based on teacher education program and experience.

Capel (1997) described prospective secondary physical education teachers' anxiety and concern after completing two teaching practices. She found that the students experienced moderate levels of anxiety and concern after their first and second teaching practices with no significant differences between the level of anxiety or concern in both teaching practices. She concluded that "the greatest cause of anxiety and concern for these students on both teaching practices was being observed, evaluated and assessed by the teaching practice supervisor" (p. 225).

Another study of testing Fuller's developmental theory of preservice teachers concerns was conducted by Hynes-Dusel (1999). The aims of this study was (a) to describe the concerns of physical education student teachers and (b) to assess the extent to which student teachers expressed concerns that reflect Fuller's theory. Twenty-five physical education students from two different American universities were administered the Teacher Concerns Questionnaire – Physical Education (TCQ-PE) three times during their student teaching experience. Results did not support Fuller's model. At the beginning of the semester the participants were primarily concerned for self, less concerned for impact, and least concerned for task. At the middle of the semester they were concerned for impact, less concerned for self, and least concerned for task. By the end of the semester they were concerned for self, less concerned for impact, and least concerned with task.

Inservice teachers

Research on experience physical education teacher concerns has been limited. McBride et al. (1986) found the participants followed the Fullers' three patterns of development expressing their highest scores on the impact scale, a moderate score on the self scale, and the lowest score on the task scale.

Faucette (1987) used the Concern-Based Adoption Model to describe seven elementary physical education teachers' types and intensities of concerns as they proceeded through an inservice program and to examine their degree of implementation of the proposed changes. The cross case analysis of the data suggested little change and non-use of the innovations. "Individual profile analysis revealed three distinct participation styles among the 7 teachers – resisters, actualizers, and conceptualizers" (Faucette, 1987: 430). Two of the participants, the actualizers, become users of innovations. Three of the participants, named conceptualizers, felt positively disposed to the changes but did not become users during the inservice program. The other two teachers, named the resisters, were negatively disposed to the innovations and failed to implement them.

More than 10 years ago, McBride (1993) observed that concerns research in physical education had used the TCQ instrument extensively in collecting data. He pointed out that "the instrument is based on Fuller's theory and is designed to assess classroom teachers concerns. The instruments therefore may not be as appropriate in the physical education setting" (p. 189). He conducted a three-phase study to identify task items appropriate to a physical education setting for a planned adaptation of the TCQ instrument. Analysis of the data revealed five new task items for use in the Teacher Concerns Questionnaire – Physical Education (TCQ-PE). McBride (1993) concluded that the TCQ-PE instrument was a valuable data collection strategy for physical education teacher concern research.

Preservice and inservice teachers.

A study with both preservice and inservice teachers was conducted by Wendt and Bain (1989). They used cross-sectional data to describe physical education teachers' concerns and found that the experienced teachers had lower self and impact concerns. Longitudinal data revealed only evidence of lower self concerns over time. They concluded that "Fuller's hypothesis has not been fully substantiated. It seems evident that change is occurring over time in concern for self. Both cross-sectional and longitudinal data support this. However, lower concern for impact does not follow. It may be that Fuller's scale is valuable only in predicting self-concerns" (p. 180).

Meek and Behets (1999) conducted a study to examine whether the Teacher Concerns Questionnaire – Physical Education (TCQ-PE) was representative of concerns of a sample of British and Belgian preservice and inservice physical education teachers. Data were analyzed according to nationality and teaching experience. "The results of the confirmatory factor analysis cast doubt on the applicability of the TCQ-PE as a adaptation of the TCQ for physical educators in Belgium and Britain" (p. 503). Meek and Behets (1999) suggested:

> While there is considerable need to develop and validate applications of TCQ-PE within other culturally different and experience-related samples of physical educators, it is predicted here that to determine the processes involved in concern resolution of physical educators it will be necessary to analyze Fuller's concerns conceptualization within developmental and interpretative analysis, not with adaptation of existing questionnaires. (p. 505)

As has been mentioned earlier Frances Fuller's (1969) theory is one of the most classic approaches of teachers' stages of concern and has been accepted by the educational community as a developmental paradigm (Meek and Behets, 1999). Over the past several years we have seen a proliferation of studies using this perspective. More specifically, the vast majority of studies conducted on teachers' work and concerns have used Fuller's framework and the TCQ instrument. Although there is much to be learned from these efforts, findings and conclusions derived from this work need to be interpreted with caution. As Richardson and Placier (2001) indicated, an often unstated assumption of these studies is that the three developmental stages are meant to be generalized to teachers other than those involved in the studies, including teachers in quite different contexts. In addition, these studies seldom address the issue of what causes the change from one stage to another or how a teacher moves along a developmental continuum.

Another concern of these studies relates to the nature of Fuller's conceptual framework as a one-dimensional and linear model (Richardson and Placier, 2001). Few will disagree that nowadays teaching is a complex profession that takes place in complex environments. Based on this assumption, it seems that alternative conceptual and epistemological models that envisage multiple and different paths may be more appropriate at this time for the investigation of teachers' work and concerns. Today, several conceptual, theoretical and epistemological alternatives (e.g. critical theory, conflict theory, symbolic interactionism) as well as multiple research methodologies (e.g. narrative research, life history, biographical research) are available to the research community. Hopefully, a subsequent review in the near future will be able to call upon a sufficient number of studies with a variety of epistemological orientations and research methodologies to not only describe teachers' concerns but also to describe and assess what happens to students learning when their teachers progress through their career and confront specific concerns.

Summary

Although, teachers' beliefs are considered to play a vital role in defining teaching tasks and organizing the knowledge and information relevant to those tasks (Calderhead, 1996) teachers' beliefs have only recently gained prominent attention in the literature (Richardson, 1996). Several scholars suggested that understanding the belief systems of teachers is critical in improving teacher education programs and teaching practices (Calderhead, 1996; O'Sullivan, 2005; Pajares, 1992).

Research studies have shown that teachers' beliefs may have been acquired and formed during their experiences as pupils in schools, from life experiences, or by their teacher education professional preparation program. The physical education literature suggested that preservice physical education teachers enter teacher preparation programs with a broad, yet conservative range of beliefs about physical education. Studies which described the influence of teacher education programs on the beliefs of preservice teachers suggested that preservice teachers' beliefs about teaching may or may not change or become more sophisticated over time.

A number of studies have described the role of teaching experiences and the teachers' beliefs about these experiences. Teaching experiences have been considered by preservice teachers as the most valuable component of the teacher education programs. Research findings have indicated that prospective teachers' attitudes toward students decreased significantly as they progressed through teaching experiences and that their attitudes become more custodial, authoritarian, and utilitarian towards teaching. Little evidence exists currently which describes teachers' voices and personal accounts of effective teaching. Another area which has received little attention in the literature is classroom teachers' beliefs on teaching physical education.

Research evidence has indicated that teachers hold firm beliefs about learners and learning. It has also been demonstrated that inquiry-oriented strategies, reflective strategies, and constructivist approaches can help preservice teachers learn more about students' motivations, needs, interests, and characteristics. Such approaches have been helpful in forcing prospective teachers to alter prior beliefs about students and learning.

Very few studies have investigated the relationship between teachers' beliefs and practices even though it has an important role to play in teaching. Some evidence has suggested a consistent alignment between teachers' beliefs and practices. Other evidence has shown a partial relationship, and some studies have suggested inconsistent results between teachers' beliefs and actions.

Biographical and socialization studies on teachers lives have shown that people who choose to become physical education teachers hold several beliefs in relation to the teaching role. It has also been documented that their prior histories shape the ways in which preservice teachers come to think about teaching physical education.

Many investigators have used the occupational socialization framework (Lawson, 1986) to describe physical education teachers' beliefs about their work while others (Macdonald, 1995) have used other theoretical frameworks (e.g. the professionalization–deprofessionalization tension framework) and approaches (e.g. the identity theory approach). Such newer approaches have highlighted teachers' frustrations and situational constraints included the lack of status, the repetitive nature of physical education work and the limited decision making.

Considerable attention has been given to the study of teachers' concerns about their professional practice for quite sometime now (Fuller, 1969; Graber, 2001; Richardson and Placier, 2001). Research findings indicated that teaching concerns ranged from self-survival issues as teachers face the demands of teaching realities, having an impact on students' needs and progress, and improving the educational system more generally. Today, there are several conceptual alternatives and research methodologies that can be used in describing the concerns that teachers face during their professional lives. Insights gained from this line of research can be helpful in addressing key concerns at appropriate times in teacher education programs.

Conclusions

Thus far, this chapter has discussed the construct of teachers beliefs in relation to its development and its role on teaching. Throughout the chapter, issues of methods, findings, and conclusions of research studies conducted in the area of teachers beliefs were reviewed and discussed. Since this review is based on selective studies, no claim can be make that is inclusive. However, it is neither mutually exclusive although some important work may have been left out. The goal was to portray some of the promising lines of research which have evolved in this area. In this final section, some of the broader issues found in this area of study are addressed.

The recent attention on teachers' beliefs has demonstrated some of the complex dimensions and factors that interrelate in the process of teaching and learning. This chapter begins and ends with the same premise; that is, still there is inadequate research on teachers' beliefs in physical education. Knowledge derived from the teachers' beliefs area of study will have robust impact on teaching practices only when more research findings will reveal the conditions and possibilities of how to change teachers' beliefs. Researchers interested in educational improvement need to further explore how teachers' beliefs are created and under what conditions these beliefs may changed over time.

Several scholars interested in quality education point to changes in teachers' beliefs on the basis of specific non-traditional teacher education programs. For many, the solution to quality education is a move to more globalized teacher education programs that will fully prepare teachers for the extremely complex act of teaching. Of course such efforts will definitely need further exploration.

Implications for teacher education

Research evidence has demonstrated that teachers' beliefs play a critical role in teaching. In addition, it was found that the beliefs teachers hold are difficult to change during professional education programs. More often, teachers' initial beliefs shape the professional knowledge acquired through teacher education programs, instead of initial beliefs being shaped by professional knowledge. Based on these indications, a greater emphasis should be given during teacher education programs to the influential role that beliefs play in educational contexts. As has been suggested by several scholars meaningful change in educational practice may be achieved more easily when teachers' beliefs are brought to the surface and tested through reflection and analytical processes.

Future research directions

Even thought, research on teachers' beliefs has increased during the last ten years it is still in its infancy (Fang, 1996; O'Sullivan, 2005). The first and foremost recommendation, is that more studies in this area of inquiry are definitely needed. Studies, with an emphasis on how teachers' beliefs are manifested in their teaching practices in relation to the complexities and constraints of their context, is a necessary direction of future research.

A second common suggestion is that teachers' beliefs, understanding, judgment, and interpretation should be considered by researchers within the teacher's own context. Therefore, more effort to study and describe the nature of teachers' beliefs need to be placed within the context where such practices occur.

A third recommendation relates to the research methods and designs used to study teacher beliefs. Researchers often describe and record teacher beliefs by detaching them from direct experience or action. Teachers, however, teach within the classroom and school contexts and there is no easy distinction between beliefs and actions. Given the fact that little evidence exists of the relationship between teachers' beliefs and practices there is considerable need to conduct more studies in this area. Investigating the relationship between teacher beliefs and practices empirical knowledge can be generated to inform professional practices. Knowledge deriving from such studies will definitely enhance teacher educators' understanding of the nature, status, and role of teacher beliefs in teaching and learning.

The emerging research work on teachers' beliefs, although valuable, revealed some methodological concerns, which need careful reconsideration in future studies. The difficulties with definitions, inadequate conceptualizations, and different understandings of the manifestation of teachers' beliefs, is an endlessly complex area of inquiry. Some of the existing empirical evidence described the nature of teachers' beliefs but stops short of describing their role and value for the long-term development of teachers. Investigators seem to assume that teachers' beliefs remain the same for a long time. With the exception of a few studies, no rich and longitudinal descriptions exist today, on whether, how, and in what direction teachers' beliefs change over long periods of time. Portraying the essence of beliefs proved to be problematic because they are difficult to articulate, and the subtle, indirect evidence that manifest their existence must be gathered over long periods of time to show stability or evolution (Doolittle, Dodds, and Placek, 1993). Longitudinal studies therefore are needed, to explore teachers' beliefs over their professional development in providing thick descriptions and insights for this area of inquiry. Studying the trajectories of teachers' beliefs, over the years, a knowledge basis can be generated beyond the teachers' self-reported recollections about beliefs. This knowledge can be beneficial to teacher educators in redesigning inservice and preservice education programs.

A final note: No study has yet explored the nature and role of teachers' beliefs as they relate to students' learning outcomes. I strongly agree with Pajares' (1992) proposition that little will have been accomplished if future research into educational beliefs fails to provide insights into the relationships between beliefs, teacher practices and student outcomes.

The review of literature indicated that the study of teacher beliefs is critical to the educational enterprise since beliefs lie at the hard of teaching (Calderhead, 1996; Pajares, 1992). Based on this review it is obvious that methodological and theoretical improvements in educational research during the last decades have helped researchers study teacher beliefs more closely. At the same time this chapter suggests that there is a long way to go in physical education scholarship before we feel confident that we have a clearer picture of the complex construct of teacher beliefs. Future inquiry needs to espouse a diverse range of methodologies (e.g. multivariate designs, narrative research, life history) and theoretical frameworks (teacher identify, sociocultural perspectives) in revealing the complex and unique nature and role of teacher beliefs about the teaching and learning process. Knowledge deriving from these studies should provide insights and help teacher educators contribute to reconstructing teacher education programs. Of course the next decade should speak of our capacity to provide an excellent education to children through excellent teacher education programs.

References

Allison, P., Pissanos, B., Turner, A. and Law, D. (2000). Preservice physical educators' epistemologies of skillfulness. *Journal of Teaching in Physical Education, 19*: 141–161.

Armour, K. (in press). The way to a teacher's heart: Narrative research in physical education. In D. Kirk, D. Macdonald and M. O'Sullivan (Eds), *Handbook of physical education* (pp. 467–486). London: Sage Publications.

Bain, L. (1990). Physical education teacher education. In W. R. Houston, M. Haberman and J. Sikula (Eds.), *Handbook of research on teacher education* (pp. 758–781). New York: Macmillan.

Behets, D. (1990). Concerns of preservice physical education teachers. *Journal of Teaching in Physical Education, 10*: 66–75.

Boggess, T., McBride, R. and Griffey, D. (1985). The concerns of physical education teachers: A developmental view. *Journal of Teaching in Physical Education, 4*: 202–211.

Borko, H. and Putnam, R. (1996). Learning to teach. In D.C. Berliner and R.C. Calfee (Eds.), *Handbook of educational psychology* (pp. 673–708). New York: Macmillan.

Byra, M. (1996). Post lesson conferencing strategies and preservice teachers' reflective practices. *Journal of Teaching in Physical Education, 16*: 48–65.

Calderhead, J. (1996). Teachers: beliefs and knowledge. In D.C. Berliner and R.C. Calfee (Eds.), *Handbook of educational psychology* (pp. 709–725). New York: Macmillan.

Capel, S. (1997). Changes in students' anxieties and concerns after their first and second teaching practices. *Educational Research, 39*(2): 211–228.

Carlson, T. (2001). Using metaphors to enhance reflectiveness among preservice teachers. *Journal of Physical Education Recreation and Dance, 72*(1): 49–53.

Chen, A. and Ennis, C. (1996). Teaching value-laden curricula in physical education. *Journal of Teaching in Physical Education, 15*: 338–354.

Curtner-Smith, M. (2001). The occupational socialization of a first-year physical education teacher with a teaching orientation. *Sport, Education and Society, 6*(1): 81–105.

Dodds, P. (1989). Trainees, field experiences, and socialization into teaching. In T.J. Templin and P.C. Schempp (Eds.), *Socialization into physical education: Learning to teach* (pp. 81–104). Indianapolis, IN: Benchmark Press.

Doolittle, S., Dodds, P., and Placek, J. (1993). Persistence of beliefs about teaching during formal training of preservice teachers. *Journal of Teaching in Physical Education, 12*: 355–365.

Ennis, C. (1994). Knowledge and beliefs underlying curricular expertise. *Quest, 46*(2): 164–175.

Ennis, C. (1996). A model describing the influence of values and context on student learning. In S. Silverman, and C. Ennis, (Eds.), *Student learning in physical education: Applying research to enhance instruction* (pp. 127–147). Champaign, IL: Human Kinetics.

Fang, Z. (1996). A review of research on teacher beliefs and practices. *Educational Research, 38*: 47–65.

Faucette, N. (1987). Teachers' concerns and participation styles during in-service education. *Journal of Teaching in Physical Education, 6*: 425–440.

Feiman-Nemser, S. and Remillard, J. (1996). Perspectives on learning to teach. In F.B. Murray (Ed.), *The teacher educator's handbook: Building a knowledge base for the preparation of teachers* (pp. 63–91). San Francisco, CA: Jossey-Bass.

Fuller, F. (1969). Concerns of teachers: A developmental conceptualization. *American Educational Research Journal, 6*: 207–226.

George, A. A. (1978). Measuring self, task and impact concerns: A manual for use of the teacher concerns questionnaire. The University of Texas, Research and Development Center for Teacher Education, Austin, TX.

Graber, K. (1995). The influence of teacher education programs on the beliefs of student teachers: General pedagogical knowledge, pedagogical content knowledge, and teacher education course work. *Journal of Teaching in Physical Education, 14*: 157–178.

Graber, K. (2001). Research on teaching in physical education. In V. Richardson (Ed.), *Handbook of research in teaching* (4th ed., 491–519). Washington, DC: American Educational Research Association.

Green, K. (2000). Exploring the everyday 'philosophies' of physical education teachers from a sociological perspective. *Sport, Education and Society, 5*(2): 109–129.

Green, K. (2002). Physical education teachers in their figurations: A sociological analysis of everyday 'philosophies'. *Sport, Education and Society, 7(1)*: 65–83.

Griffin, L. and Combs, C. (2000). Student teachers' perceptions of the role of the physical educator. *Journal of Physical Education Recreation and Dance, 71(4)*: 42–45.

Hardy, C. (1999). Preservice teachers perceptions of learning to teach in a predominantly school-based teacher education program. *Journal of Teaching in Physical Education, 18*: 175–198.

Hutchinson, E. (1993). Prospective teachers' perspectives on teaching physical education: An interview study on the recruitment phase of teacher socialization. *Journal of Teaching in Physical Education, 12(4)*: 344–354.

Hynes-Dusel, M. (1999). Physical education student teacher concerns. The *Physical Educator, 56*(1): 33–48.

Kirk, D. (1986). A critical pedagogy for teacher education: Toward an inquiry-oriented approach. *Journal of Teaching in Physical Education, 5*: 230–246.

Kulinna, P., Silverman, S. and Keating, X. (2000). Relationship between teachers' belief systems and actions toward teaching physical activity and fitness. *Journal of Teaching in Physical Education, 19*: 206–221.

Lawson, H. (1986). Occupational socialization and the design of teacher education programs. *Journal of Teaching in Physical Education, 4*: 107–116.

Lortie, D. (1975). *Schoolteacher: A sociological study.* Chicago, IL: University of Chicago Press.

Macdonald, D. (1995). The role of proletarianization in physical education teacher attrition. *Research Quarterly for Exercise and Sport, 66*(2): 129–141.

Macdonald, D. (1999). The 'professional' work of experienced physical education teachers. *Research Quarterly for Exercise and Sport, 70*(1): 41–54.

Macdonald, D. and Kirk, D. (1996). Private lives, public lives: Surveillance, identity and self in the work of beginning physical education teachers. *Sport, Education and Society, 1*(1): 60–75.

Macdonald, D. and Kirk, D. (1999). Pedagogy, the body and Christian identity. *Sport, Education and Society, 4(2)*: 131–142.

Macdonald, D. and Tinning, R. (2003). Reflective practice goes public. In A. Laker (Ed.), *The future of physical education* (pp. 82–101). London: Routledge.

Matanin, M. and Collier, C. (2003). Longitudinal Analysis of preservice teachers' beliefs about teaching physical education. *Journal of Teaching in Physical Education, 22*: 153–168.

McBride, R. (1993). The TCQ-PE: An adaptation of the teacher concerns questionnaire instrument to a physical education setting. *Journal of Teaching in Physical Education, 12*: 188–196.

McBride, R., Boggess, T. and Griffey, D. (1986). Concerns of inservice physical education teachers as compared with Fuller's concern model. *Journal of Teaching in Physical Education, 5*: 149–156.

McCollum, S. (2002). The reflective framework for teaching in physical education: A pedagogical tool. *Journal of Physical Education Recreation and Dance, 73*(6): 39–42.

McCormack, A. (2001). Using reflective practice in teaching dance to preservice physical education teachers. *European Journal of Physical Education, 6(1)*: 5–15.

McCullick, B. (2001). Practitioners' perspectives on values, knowledge, and skills needed by PETE participants. *Journal of Teaching in Physical Education, 21*: 35–56.

McIntyre. D., Byrd, D. and Foxx, S. (1996). Field and laboratory experiences. In J. Sikula, T. Buttery and E. Guyton (Eds.), *Handbook of research on teacher education*, (pp. 171–193). New York: Macmillan.

Meek, G. (1996). The teacher concern questionnaire with preservice physical educators in Great Britain: Being concerned with concerns. *Journal of Teaching in Physical Education, 16*: 20–29.

Meek, G. and Behets, D. (1999). Physical education teachers' concerns towards teaching. *Teaching and Teacher Education, 15*: 497–505.

Nespor, J. (1987). The role of beliefs in the practice of teaching. *Journal of Curriculum Studies, 19(4)*: 317–328.

O'Bryant, C., O'Sullivan, M. and Raudesky, J. (2000). Socialization of prospective physical education teachers: The story of new blood. *Sport, Education and Society, 5*(2): 177–193.

O'Connor, A. and Macdonald, D. (2002). Up close and personal on physical education teachers' identity: Is conflict an issue? *Sport, Education and Society, 7(1)*: 37–54.

O'Reilly, E., Tompkins, J. and Gallant, M. (2001). They ought to enjoy physical activity, you know?: Struggling with fun in physical education. *Sport, Education and Society, 6*(2): 211–221.

O' Sullivan, M. (1996). What do we know about the professional preparation of teachers? In S. Silverman and C. Ennis (Eds.), *Student learning in physical education: Applying research to enhance instruction* (pp. 315–337). Champaign, IL: Human Kinetics.

O' Sullivan, M. (2003). Learning to teach physical education. In S. Silverman and C. Ennis (2nd Ed.), *Student learning in physical education: Applying research to enhance instruction* (pp. 275–294). Champaign, IL: Human Kinetics.

O' Sullivan, M. (2005). Beliefs of teachers and teacher candidates: Implications for teacher education. In F. Carreiro da Costa, M. Cloes and M. Gonzalez (Eds), *The art and science of teaching in physical education and sport*. Lisbon: Universidade De Tecnica.

Pajares, M.F. (1992). Teachers' beliefs and educational research: Cleaning up a messy construct. *Review of Educational Research, 62*(3): 307–332.

Parker, J. (1995). Secondary teachers' views of effective teaching in physical education. *Journal of Teaching in Physical Education, 14*: 127–139.

Placek, J., Dodds, P., Doolittle, S., Portman, P., Ratliffe, T. and Pinkham, K. (1995). Teaching recruits' physical education backgrounds and beliefs about purposes for their subject matter. *Journal of Teaching in Physical Education, 14*: 246–261.

Richardson, V. (1996). The role of attitudes and beliefs in learning to teach. In J. Sikula, T. Buttery and E. Guyton (Ed.), *Handbook of research on teacher education*, (pp. 102–119). New York: Macmillan.

Richardson, V. and Placier, P. (2001). Teacher change. In V. Richardson (Ed.), *Handbook of research in teaching* (pp. 905–947). Washington, DC: American Educational Research Association.

Romar, J.E. (1995). *Case studies of Finnish physical education teachers: Espoused and enacted theories of action.* Abo: Abo Academi University Press.

Rovegno, I. (2003). Teachers' knowledge construction. In S. Silverman and C. Ennis (2nd Ed) *Student learning in physical education: Applying research to enhance instruction* (pp. 295–310). Champaign, IL: Human Kinetics.

Schon, D.A. (1983). *The reflective practitioner.* New York: Basic Books.

Schon, D.A. (1987). *Educating the reflective practitioner.* San Francisco, CA: Jossey-Bass.

Stroot, S. (1996). Organizational socialization: Factors impacting beginning teachers. In S. Silverman and C. Ennis (Eds.), *Student learning in physical education: Applying research to enhance instruction* (pp. 339–365). Champaign, IL: Human Kinetics.

Stroot, S. and Whipple, C. (2003). Organizational socialization: Factors impacting beginning teachers. In S. Silverman and C. Ennis (Eds.), (2nd ed.), *Student learning in physical education: Applying research to enhance instruction* (pp. 311–328). Champaign, IL: Human Kinetics.

Tinning, R. (1988). Student teaching and the pedagogy of necessity. *Journal of Teaching in Physical Education, 7*: 82–89.

Tsangaridou, N. (2002). Enacted pedagogical content knowledge in physical education: A case study of a prospective classroom teacher. *European Physical Education Review, 8(1)*: 2136.

Tsangaridou, N. and O'Sullivan, M. (2003). Physical education teachers' theories of action and theories-in-use. *Journal of Teaching in Physical Education, 22*: 132–152.

Tsangaridou, N. and Siedentop, D. (1995). Reflective teaching: A literature review. *Quest, 47*: 212–237.

Veal, M. (1992). School-based theories of pupil assessment: A case study. *Research Quarterly for Exercise and Sport, 63(1)*: 48–59.

Veal, M. (1998). Pupil assessment perceptions and practices of secondary teachers. *Journal of Teaching in Physical Education, 6*: 327–342.

Wendt, J. and Bain, L. (1985). Surviving the transition: Concerns of the beginning teacher. *Journal of Physical Education Recreation and Dance, 56(2)*: 24–25.

Wendt, J. and Bain, L. (1989). Concerns of preservice and inservice physical educators. *Journal of Teaching in Physical Education, 8*: 177–180.

Wendt, J., Bain, L. and Jackson, A. (1981). Fuller's concerns theory as tested on prospective physical educators. *Journal of Teaching in Physical Education, 1*: 66–70.

Wilson, S. and Berne, J. (1999). Teacher learning and the acquisition of professional knowledge: An examination of research on contemporary professional development. *Review of Research in Education, 24*: 173–209.

Woods, M., Goc Karp, G. and Escamilla, E. (2000). Preservice teachers learning about students and teaching-learning process. *Journal of Teaching in Physical Education, 20*: 15–39.

Xiang, P., Lowy, S. and McBride, R. (2002). The impact of a field-based elementary physical education methods course on preservice classroom teachers' beliefs. *Journal of Teaching in Physical Education, 21*: 145–161.

Zeichner, K. (1999). The new scholarship in teacher Education. *Educational Researcher, 28*: 4–15.

Zeicher, K. and Gore, J. (1990). Teacher socialization. In W. R. Houston, M. Haberman and J. Sikula (Eds.), *Handbook of research on teacher education* (pp. 329–348). New York: Macmillan.

4.8   Teachers' knowledge

NIKI TSANGARIDOU

In the past two decades several reform movements in many countries call for higher standards for teachers and teacher education. The central dilemma facing teacher educators is how to educate teachers who can and will conduct quality programs in schools. Reformers argued that quality education may occur when changes take place in teacher education curricula (Feiman-Nemser and Remillard, 1996; Kirk, 1986; Macdonald et al., 2002a; O'Sullivan, 2003; Richardson and Placier, 2001; Wilson and Berne, 1999; Zeichner, 1999). Concurrent with this call for quality teacher education programs has been a call for more research on teachers' professional knowledge. Until now, what we know about teachers' knowledge is rather mystifying. The question of how teachers and under what conditions they construct their knowledge is clearly a complex enterprise for teacher educators. It is important, however, to give answers to this question since teachers' knowledge affects teaching and learning (Rovegno, 2003). Carter (1990) explained that "for the most part, attention in teacher education has traditionally been focused on what teachers need to know and how they can be trained, rather on what they actually know or how that knowledge is acquired" (p. 291).

Research on teachers' knowledge and how this knowledge is acquired, constitutes a substantial area of inquiry in explorations on the nature of teaching. As Rovegno (2003) suggested teachers are not born with the knowledge to deal with complex work contexts but they construct this knowledge over time and with experience. The nature and development of teachers' knowledge is just beginning to be understood by the present generation of researchers in teaching and teacher education (Calderhead, 1996; Munby, et al., 2001; Richardson, 1996; Rovegno, 2003; Wilson, and Berne, 1999). Scholars emphasize that greater attention needs to be paid to the acquisition of teachers' knowledge and how it affects teaching and learning since the growth of research in this area can open new ways of thinking about teaching and teacher education. As Calderhead (1996) pointed out:

How teachers make sense of their professional world, the knowledge and beliefs they bring with them to the task, and how teachers' understanding of teaching, learning, and children, and the subject matter informs their everyday practice are important questions that necessitate an investigation of the cognitive and affective aspects of teachers' professional lives. (p. 709)

The purpose of this chapter is to present, summarize, and discuss illustrative issues and findings of the research on teachers' knowledge. It is worthwhile to note that since this chapter provides an overview of this line of research, only selected research studies conducted in physical education that are relative to the concepts considered here were reviewed. The chapter is directed to questions about the forms of knowledge teachers have; what teachers know; how this knowledge is acquired; and under what conditions teachers' knowledge is demonstrated.

The chapter is divided into three sections. In the first section the concept of teachers' knowledge is defined and discussed. Then, a presentation of the epistemological traditions and typologies of teachers' knowledge are provided. In the second section, an account of empirical enquiries and findings on teachers' knowledge are presented under the following categories: (a) pedagogical knowledge, (b) content knowledge, (c) pedagogical content knowledge, and (d) expertise and teachers' knowledge. Finally, the third section provides a summary of the main findings, discusses the major conclusions and future directions for research, and points to gaps in research on teachers' knowledge in physical education.

Conceptual and theoretical framework

Defining knowledge

Although widely used in the literature the phrase teachers' knowledge has different meanings for different people. Cognitive psychologists define knowledge as objective, factual information that has been scrutinized and agreed upon within an educational community (Calderhead, 1996). The parameters under investigation are often defined rigidly to delimit and refine the concept for enhanced understanding and parsimony. Knowledge under this tradition of thought can be directly measured (Ennis, 1994).

Alternative definitions of knowledge refer to a more subjective understanding of the knowledge that a person values or believes to be meaningful. These viewpoints and constructs of knowledge consider knowledge as personal constructions based on the relationship of the disciplinary and experiential knowledge (Borko and Putnam, 1996; Ennis, 1994). These alternative constructs of knowledge are attempts to describe teachers' knowledge about teaching and learning in ways that preserve its close and significant connection to the practical nature of teaching from which it arose and in which it is primarily manifested (Calderhead, 1996; Carter, 1990; Cochran-Smith and Lytle, 1999; Rovegno, 2003).

An example of an alternative and more inclusive framework of teachers' knowledge in education is the recent work of Cochran-Smith and Lytle (1999). In an article on teacher learning, they explored the relationships of teachers' knowledge and practice and suggested three interconnected images of knowledge. They proposed a comprehensive framework for theorizing teacher learning based on an alternative construct of teacher knowledge. In their framework they analyzed and documented how these constructs are related to practice and how teachers' knowledge is constructed within communities and other contexts. Inez Rovegno's luminous framework is another alternative representation of teachers' knowledge in the field of physical education. Rovegno (2003) presented four different forms of knowledge which constitute the nature and properties of teachers' knowledge. Her perspective includes a practical, personal, experiential, and situational orientation to teachers' knowledge. In this framework, the construct of teacher knowledge is defined quite differently from traditional cognitive psychologies.

Within the broad field of research on teachers' knowledge, distinct and at times overlapping theoretical approaches exist. As Tom and Valli (1990) indicated "professional knowledge can be generated through more than one epistemological tradition" (p. 374). Distinctions have been made between research that is positivist, interpretive, or critical in orientation, carrying different fundamental assumptions about the nature and priorities of knowledge and the purpose of inquiry (Calderhead, 1996). This chapter begins with a brief account of the historical trends of research on teachers' knowledge and an overview of the epistemological traditions and typologies of knowledge.

Historical perspective

The study of teachers' knowledge has emerged only quite recently in the educational research community (Calderhead, 1996; Carter, 1990; Munby et al., 2001; Rovegno, 2003). The research on teaching in the late 1960s was strongly characterized by a behaviorist view, which described and explored teaching as a sequence of behaviors (Calderhead, 1996). Since the behaviorist tradition dominated the study of teaching and teacher education during that era, knowledge and thinking were considered too mentalistic and abstract for research studies, so the focus was mostly on observable behaviors (Carter, 1990). Over the following two decades, however, researchers paid more attention to how teachers understood their work and the thought processes, judgments, decisions, and interpretations that their work entails (Calderhead, 1996).

The emphasis of systematic research on teachers' knowledge revealed a substantial shift from a preoccupation with behavior and what teachers need to do, to a concern with what teachers know and how that knowledge is acquired and developed through formal education and practical experience (Carter, 1990; Wilson and Berne, 1999). The development of research on teachers' knowledge can be explained by the acceptance of the study of cognition in the social and behavioral sciences and the appearance of qualitative and interpretive studies of teaching phenomena (Calderhead, 1996; Carter, 1990). Teachers' knowledge has received increasing attention in recent years as researchers were motivated to explore the knowledge base of teaching and provide a rich database for teacher education programs and demonstrate the complexity of teaching as a professional activity (Calderhead, 1996; Rovegno, 2003; Tom and Valli, 1990).

Epistemological traditions of knowledge

According to Tom and Valli (1990) what counts as teachers' knowledge, is "vigorously contested" (p. 373) in the education community. Knowledge is a global construct, which creates considerable debate over its nature and properties. What knowledge represents, its purposes and forms, depends to a great extent on underlying epistemological assumptions. In exploring these assumptions, Tom and Valli (1990) provided a theoretical framework of knowledge that has evolved from three epistemological traditions: positivistic, interpretive, and critical.

The *positivistic tradition* focuses attention on the knowledge and skills of teaching derived from the scientific study of teaching practices. Within this tradition:

> Social phenomena are presumed to exist naturally rather than be socially constructed, knowledge of how social variables affect one another is cumulative: thus the concept of a knowledge base (or knowledge bases) fits comfortably in the professional vocabulary of educational positivists. (Tom and Valli, 1990: 375)

Professional knowledge is viewed as a set of law-like generalizations to be explored through classroom research and applied by teachers (Calderhead, 1996). The positivistic orientation is based on the assumption that knowledge can be objective and that this knowledge can adequately explain and predict human behavior. Professional knowledge is as law-like as possible, is cumulative and is different from values. Positivists made a strict distinction between facts and values and purposefully place values outside their systematic line of research (Tom and Valli, 1990).

A central characteristic of *the interpretive tradition* is the use of theory-laden constructs in studying social life. Interpretive researchers reveal the meanings that humans attach to the interpersonal and social aspects of their lives while these meanings and interpretations are viewed as context dependent (Tom and Valli, 1990). Teachers' knowledge is uncovered with the use of case studies and ethnographies and aims to generate ways of viewing situations and solving problems that teachers might encounter within the context of their own classrooms (Calderhead, 1996). Interpretivists try to understand others in their own terms and implicitly accept the values of those being studied. As Tom and Valli, (1990) indicated, "interpretivism melds values and facts together in an attempt to understand the meanings that various actors construct out of educational and other social environments" (p. 376). Although, educational positivism and interprestivism differ significantly in the form and purpose of knowledge both epistemological traditions have trouble approaching the issue of values (Tom and Valli, 1990).

The *critical theory tradition* combines a progressive social vision with a radical critique of teaching and schooling. A central objective of the critical theory orientation "is to bring to consciousness the ability to criticize what is taken for granted about every day life. Class, gender, and race relations become key foci ... A vital concern of those operating within the critical paradigm is social transformation aimed at increasing justice, equality, freedom, and human dignity" (Zeichner and Gore, 1990: 331).

Critical theorists have located values which are at the heart of educational inquiry by exploring the role of knowledge in improving practice. A critical theory perspective aims to understand the relations between values and actions and to change the world for the better (Tom and Valli, 1990). Within this tradition professional knowledge is viewed as problematic because it serves specific interests and reflects particular power relations. A critical theory approach aims "to sensitize teachers to the ways in which knowledge is being used and the values that are implicit within it" (Calderhead, 1996: 715).

Typologies of teachers' knowledge

Over the past several years, it has been suggested that "understanding the organization of teachers' knowledge refines our appreciation of knowledge use by showing how different forms of knowledge permit different kinds of performances" (Feiman-Nemser and Floden, 1986: 513). In the literature several conceptual alternatives, describing a variety of content, forms, and categories teachers' knowledge can take, have evolved in an attempt to delineate the forms of knowledge that teachers possess and how they might be interconnected. Some typologies have also been proposed by scholars to portray ways in which knowledge can be explored as related to practice (Calderhead, 1996; Tom and Valli, 1990). These typologies and categories of knowledge are examined and discussed below.

Craft knowledge

The type of knowledge that teachers acquire during their own classroom practice, the knowledge that informs them to employ the strategies, tactics, and routines that they do, has sometimes been referred to as "craft knowledge" or the "wisdom of practice" (Shulman, 1987; Siedentop, 1991). Calderhead (1996) observed that Schon's work on the reflective practitioner (1983, 1987) was very influential in this line of research. Schon's theory suggests that professionals, through their everyday experiences, have developed a context-specific "craft knowledge" that enables them to face new situations and solve problems. This knowledge is rarely made explicit by teachers and most of the time teachers are not conscious of using it (Calderhead, 1996). According to Siedentop (1991) physical education teachers' craft knowledge, which is based on their personal theories of practice, includes knowledge about teaching, students, parents, and curriculum. These personal theories guide teachers' work and some of them are "good, some fragmented, some no doubt contradictory, and some no doubt sophisticated and elegant" (p. 7). He suggested that the codification of teachers' craft knowledge represented one of the new directions for research on teaching in physical education and a new form of collaboration among researchers and practitioners. In his own words, " I am convinced that systematically investigating craft knowledge will not only enhance the knowledge base for teaching physical education but will also require a new and fruitful form of collaboration" (p. 7).

Practical knowledge

This line of research "deriving from roots in curriculum research and teacher education rather than cognitive psychology, has examined teachers' practical knowledge" (Shulman, 1986; 25) and has developed from a variety of research methodologies including ethnomethodology, phenomenology, and symbolic interactionism. Even though there are often substantial differences among research programs, studies on teachers' practical knowledge and theories have, mostly, consisted of intensive case analysis, and in a few instances self-analyses of classroom episodes (Carter, 1990).

Calderhead (1996) pointed out that the study of teachers' personal knowledge is an approach which has been derived from teachers' "craft knowledge" and focuses on the way teachers' understanding of their world affects the way they structure classroom experience. Studies focused on certain distinctive features of teachers' craft knowledge such as the way teachers understand and approach their work are influenced by the teachers' idiosyncrasies, past experiences, and how they view and interpret teaching.

According to Carter (1990) teachers' practical knowledge "refers broadly to the knowledge teachers have of classroom situations and the practical dilemmas they face in carrying out purposeful action in these settings" (p. 299). Elbaz (1991) emphasized that practical knowledge encompasses knowledge of practice as well as knowledge mediated by practice. She continued to suggest that the defining characteristics of teachers' knowledge should be explored in their work contexts. According to her, the most plausible way of conceptualizing practical knowledge should be via direct examination. A key notion of practical knowledge is that it is experiential, value-laden, purposeful, and oriented to practice. Clandinin (1985) explained that "personal practical knowledge is viewed as tentative, subject to change and transient, rather than something fixed, objective, and unchanging" (p. 364).

In general, the research literature on teachers' practical knowledge "does provide a rich picture of the effects of experience and the conditions under which teachers use their knowledge to make sense of a complex, ill-structured, classroom world of competing goals and actions" (Carter, 1990: 302).

Shulman's content knowledge of teaching

Shulman (1986) suggested that research on teaching overemphasized the organizational and managerial aspects of teaching and underemphasized the role of content knowledge in teaching situations. He suggested that in exploring the complexities of teacher understanding and transmission of content knowledge, research studies should focus on teachers' understanding of their subject matter and the function of this understanding in children's understanding of content.

According to Shulman (1986) teachers' content knowledge consists of three categories: subject-matter knowledge, pedagogical content knowledge (PCK), and curricular knowledge. Subject-matter knowledge refers not only to the valid and acceptable facts or concepts of the discipline but also to how and why these facts or concepts are organized within the discipline in a specific structure. PCK refers to the unique way of representing and formulating the subject matter that make it comprehensible to others. Curricular knowledge refers to the full range of programs and materials designed for particular subject matters and to the most appropriate application of these curricula or instructional alternatives in instructional situations (Shulman, 1986).

Shulman's framework of the knowledge base: emphasis on pedagogical content knowledge

Shulman (1987) extended his theoretical framework of teachers' knowledge base for teaching and teacher education to seven categories: (a) content knowledge, (b) general pedagogical knowledge, (c) curriculum knowledge, (d) PCK, (e) knowledge of learners, (f) knowledge of contexts, and (g) knowledge of educational ends. Although all the above forms of knowledge are necessary for successful teaching, PCK has received the most attention in the educational community. Shulman (1987) argued that "among these categories, pedagogical content knowledge is of special interest because it identifies the distinctive bodies of knowledge for teaching" (p. 8).

PCK has been defined by Shulman (1987) as "that special amalgam of content and pedagogy that is uniquely the province of teachers, their own special form of professional understanding" (p. 8). In this category of teachers' knowledge are included "the most useful forms of representations of those ideas, the most powerful analogies, illustrations, examples, explanations, and demonstrations – in a word, the ways of representing and formulating the subject that makes it comprehensible to others" (Shulman, 1986: 9).

Grossman (1989) combined different forms of knowledge into the term of PCK. An alternative definition of PCK by Grossman (1989):

includes overarching conceptions of what it means to teach a particular subject, knowledge of curricular materials, and curriculum in a particular field, knowledge of students' understanding and potential misunderstanding of a subject area, and knowledge of instructional strategies and representations for teaching a particular topic. (p. 25)

Rovegno's framework of the nature of teacher's knowledge

In a recent review of teachers' knowledge construction, Rovegno (2003) suggested four conceptions of the nature and characteristics of teachers' knowledge. The first conception refers to "teachers' knowledge as practical knowledge". This view of knowledge suggests that practice assists teachers to know what to do, how to do it, and how to face and solve the dilemmas and problems that evolve in specific situations. The second conception refers to "teachers' knowledge of personal knowledge". Viewing knowledge as personal means "it reflects an individual teacher's biography, values, knowledge, and experiences in the school context" (p. 296).

The third conception of teachers' knowledge is "teachers' knowledge as complex". This representation of knowledge indicates that problems in practice are often complex and teachers need to be flexible and reflective in providing solutions to such problems. "Practice is complex, and teachers' knowledge reflects this complexity" (Rovegno, 2003: 296). Situated knowledge is the fourth conception of teacher knowledge. This vision of teachers' knowledge emphasizes that knowledge is situated which means that it operates in practice, develops through practice, is shaped by practice, and shapes practice (Rovegno, 2003).

Research findings

Research on teaching in physical education on teacher knowledge "is still a young field" (Siedentop and Tannehill: 2000; 31). Researchers in physical education have recently recognized the vital role teachers' knowledge has on teaching and learning "because teachers' knowledge plays a critical role in what and how they teach, researchers have begun to study teachers' knowledge and how this knowledge grows out of and reflects practice" (Rovegno, 2003: 295). This section is organized around the major themes and directions of teachers' knowledge researched in physical education. Pedagogical knowledge, content knowledge, PCK, and expertise and teachers' knowledge are the areas.

Pedagogical knowledge

The enormous methodological improvements in educational research over the last decades have helped researchers to study teacher and student behaviors during the interactive phase of instruction (Floden, 2001). A major conclusion is that teachers do make a difference in students' lives (Rink, 2003; Siedentop and Tannehill, 2000). This line of research, which is often called "process–product research" attempts "to explain between-class differences in achievement in terms of differences in teaching processes. The ultimate hope of this kind of analysis is a list of classroom conditions or characteristics known to affect the outcomes of teaching" (Doyle, 1990: 12). A brief review of the most significant findings regarding teacher behavior and student learning, which constitutes the pedagogical knowledge base, are briefly summarized here (for an extensive analysis of the effective teaching literature see Rink, 2003).

Findings from teacher effectiveness research revealed that effective teachers use specific pedagogical behaviors that facilitate student learning. Effective teachers have high-performance expectations and hold their students accountable for learning. They provide appropriate feedback to their students, ask appropriate questions, and give clear instructions, explanations, and demonstrations to them. These teachers establish a set of rules and routines at the beginning of the year, exhibit prevention management techniques, and actively supervise and monitor the class. Contextual variables such as grade level, SES status of learners, and aptitude of learners are always considered by effective teachers during instructional time. Furthermore, effective teachers provide optimum coverage of appropriately sequenced content and maximize academic learning time by actively engaging all students in productive and meaningful work (Rink, 2003, Siedentop and Tannehill, 2000).

Many scholars recognized the significant contribution of research on pedagogical knowledge in helping teachers to be effective though most agree that it alone is not sufficient for excellent teacher education (Floden, 2001; O'Sullivan, 1996).

Content knowledge

Most of the educational research has focused on the pedagogical aspects of teaching and learning. An important omission has been the investigation of teachers' understanding of their subject matter content and characterized by Shulman (1986) as the "missing paradigm". According to Shulman (1987), content knowledge refers to

knowledge, understanding, skills, and disposition that are to be learned by school children. This knowledge rests on two foundations: the accumulated literature and studies in the content areas, and the historical and philosophical scholarship on the nature in those fields of study. (pp. 8–9)

Siedentop (2002) wrote that the subject matter of physical education was ill-defined and invited physical education scholars to reconsider the "physical education missing paradigm". He pointed out that the "content knowledge domain for physical education is not easily identified. In fact, it continues to be a source of serious controversy in our field" (p. 368). In a critique to Siedentop's (2002) article "Content knowledge for physical education", Tinning (2002a) agreed that the knowledge domain for physical education is problematic but he argued that "it is also important to recognize that subject matter content knowledge for physical education includes knowledge that is both practical and theoretical" (p. 379).

Fernandez-Balboa, et al. (1996) also discussed the nature of content knowledge in physical education. They proposed a multiperspective approach to content knowledge of physical education. Teacher education programs, according to them, should expose teachers to a broad array of knowledge and experiences so as to prepare them to make complex decisions about content. They proposed four perspectives on content knowledge in physical education: the programmatic, cognitive, constructivist, and critical perspectives. They concluded that each one of the four perspectives has a place in physical education. In their own words:

> We see them [the four perspectives] as complementary, not as competitive; they all aim at the same target – developing the intellectual and physical acuity of both students in schools and those soon-to-be teachers. Providing students with a sound, multifaceted preparation regarding our content knowledge will most likely ensure their educational success and our future as a profession. (p. 57)

Several physical education scholars have written critiques and analyses on the low academic status of physical education. Kirk and Macdonald (1998), for example, noted:

> Reports of crisis in physical education, students' alienation from the subject, and its continuing marginalization in the curricula of many schools, prompt us to explore new possibilities for theorizing learning. In so doing, we might better understand the nature of the subject matter and what it might contribute to the education of young people who face challenges, risks, and opportunities in the new millennium. (p. 385)

Kirk and Macdonald (1998) proposed that constructivist approaches provide the potential for some sophisticated and powerful thinking about the challenges that physical education was facing.

In a review article Wright (2000) pointed out that the low academic status of physical education relates to the uniqueness of the subject matter and the inability of others to understand its nature and its characteristics. She claimed that "physical education as a practical subject on an educational curriculum is often undervalued because the concept of practical knowledge is not sufficiently understood" (p. 273).

Extensive discussions and debates in the literature expressed intellectual perspectives on the nature and properties of subject matter in physical education. Alternative directions were also offered for the most valuable content in teacher education programs (Bain, 1990; Graber, 2001; O'Sullivan, 2003; Kelly et al., 2000; Kirk, 1986; Macdonald et al., 2002b; Siedentop, 2002; Tinning, 1988, 1991; Wright, 2000). Tinning (2002b) reminded us that a long time ago he advocated a "critical pedagogy" for teacher education curricula that emphasized issues relative to gender equity, equality of opportunity, catering for diversity, and challenging unjust practices. Tinning (2002b) emphasized that putting critical pedagogy into action is not an easy task. He described several difficulties and challenges that he faced as a teacher educator in "doing critical pedagogy with postmodern students" (p. 224).

Macdonald et al. (2002a) also provided a rich analysis of how curriculum initiatives such as those associated with the application of Key Learning Areas (KLA) in Australian schools have portrayed the disjunctions between teacher education programs and contemporary school curricula. The relationship between the content knowledge inherent and dominant in tertiary programs and those that are required are analyzed extensively. In addition, they discussed the ideological and organizational issues and the dynamic relationship of the two dimensions in the creation and reproduction of the "official knowledge". Based on findings from a school-based evaluation of the health and physical education key learning area syllabus, they concluded that modest curriculum initiatives do not address the radical challenges to knowledge structures arising from postmodern trends in globalization and technology. They argued for more attention to postmodern teacher education programs with an emphasis on the social configuration and application of knowledge. The authors provided several examples of how postmodernity can be implemented in teacher education programs. Some of their ideas are highlighted in the following example:

> For example, teacher education programmes need to consider the increasing responsibilities for teachers with respect to broader health and social concerns of young people (such as drug, harmful drinking, child abuse, young suicide) alongside new ways in which knowledge is generated and young people may learn. (p. 272)

Researching different types of pedagogies are imperative in educational communities as they stimulate engagement in new approaches to teacher education. It is also important, however, that such pedagogies be put into action in teacher education programs. Such attempts are still young and the discussions continue to be mostly theoretical with little influence on research and practice (Macdonald et al., 2002b).

Some evidence exists about what physical education teachers know about the subject matter of physical education. Studies by Ohio State doctoral students have explored teachers' content knowledge and its relationship to teachers' PCK, values, and practices. Fortin (1993) described how two nontraditional dance teachers' experiences and knowledge gained throughout their professional career influenced knowledge in action. The two forms of teacher content knowledge, practical (demonstrations) and conceptual (explanations), transformed what the teachers knew into the instructional tasks for dance lessons. The teachers represented their content knowledge purposefully in a sequence of tasks and they were able to describe what content was illustrated in the tasks and why it was essential.

In another study, Romar (1995) found that content knowledge and PCK affected the goals of an instructional unit and the activities designed to achieve these goals. It was also found that teachers used few applying tasks and when these tasks were used they "were not incorporated with work on particular skills, but rather as game play in basketball and final tasks in gymnastics" (p. 211). Romar (1995) suggested that the teachers wanted to teach students to play a game but had little knowledge of the tactics or strategies of the game and instead used isolated tasks in a unit of instruction.

Exploring teachers PCK and theories of content, Doutis (1997) found that teachers' content knowledge was evident in how they chose to progress and sequence lesson tasks. The decisions the teachers made about what and how to teach developed from their content knowledge and PCK. In another study describing teacher knowledge and its relationship to student success in learning gymnastics skills, Kutame (1997) found that content knowledge and PCK influenced teaching practices when teaching introductory motor skills to novice students. Hastie (1996) studied the teaching practices of high school teachers who were categorized as having either high or low subject matter knowledge. Results suggested that the teachers with high subject matter knowledge used more instructional tasks, held students more accountable, and had fewer off task behaviors in their classes than teachers' who had less subject matter knowledge.

Pedagogical content knowledge

Understanding sports and physical activities from a participant's perspective is simply not enough for excellent teaching! Teachers need pedagogical content knowledge (PCK) so that they can "package" everything they understand – about the learners, the activity, the physical education program goals, the instructional strategies, the school the students, and the community – in order to help students learn (Griffin et al., 1996: 58).

During the last decade an extensive body of literature has emerged on teachers' PCK. These studies have tried to describe the nature of teachers' PCK both in general education and physical education. This line of research directly affects the content and structure of teacher education curricula which must meet the profession's requirements and standards (Amade-Escot, 2000; Rovegno, 2003; Shulman, 2002). A series of studies focusing on pedagogical content knowledge explored how physical education teachers acquire, elaborate, and transform their pedagogical content knowledge (Amade-Escot, 2000; Graber, 2001; Rovegno, 2003).

Inez Rovegno was one of the first scholars to explore PCK in physical education and has made a valuable contribution to the field. She has conducted several studies in an effort to delineate the nature and dimensions of preservice physical education teachers' PCK and to describe how PCK emerges and persists in context (Rovegno, 1992, 1993, 1994, 1995). She found that preservice teachers' PCK was inadequate for the realities of schooling (Rovegno, 1992, 1994) and that preservice teachers' PCK of dividing, sequencing, and differentiating subject matter was not always developmentally appropriate for student learning (Rovegno, 1994, 1995).

Graber (1995) designed a study to examine how student teachers believed they incorporated general pedagogical knowledge and PCK into lessons. She found that the degree to which preservice teachers used general pedagogical knowledge in teaching was based on the opportunities that they had to practice teaching prior to the student teaching (early field experiences), the support of the cooperating teacher, the influence of pupils on the student teacher, and the level (elementary or secondary) at which the participants were teaching. Most participants indicated that "they had no specific training for determining what pedagogical strategies were best suited for particular types of physical education subject matter" (p. 169).

In another study Sebren (1995) found a lack of PCK development by preservice teachers during a field-based methods course and concluded that advanced knowledge acquisition in other areas of the knowledge base may need to precede the development of teachers' PCK. Describing and analyzing the nature and development of PCK, Griffin et al. (1996) concluded that developing PCK is an enterprise for highly committed teachers who are willing to address their teaching practice thoughtfully and make substantial changes over time.

Tsangaridou (2002) described the enacted pedagogical content knowledge of an elementary classroom teacher during student teaching and found that during the process of content delivery the student teacher used examples, demonstrations and open-ended questions to develop students' learning and understanding. She concluded that the PCK of the student teacher positively affected her pedagogical actions and practices. Jenkins and Veal (2002) investigated how preservice teachers' PCK evolved during peer coaching experiences and found that PCK developed differently for the teacher and coach roles. In the teaching role, growth resulted, initially, from the interaction of knowledge about students and pedagogy and later from interaction of content, context, and pedagogical knowledge.

McCaughtry and Rovegno (2003) examined how preservice teachers' PCK developed and evolved in response to the realities of the teaching context. There were three significant changes in preservice teachers' knowledge during a 20-lesson unit of instruction. The first shift occurred when they moved from inaccurately blaming students for unsuccessful instruction to realizing the deficiencies in their own knowledge. The second shift happened when the preservice teachers went beyond blaming students and came to a stage of seeing and understanding the complexity of motor development. Finally, the preservice teachers evolved from ignoring students' emotions to understanding and acknowledging the role of emotion in student learning.

The complexity of the development and acquisition of PCK during preservice education has lead researchers to explore the PCK of experienced teachers. The following studies represent some of the research effort during inservice education.

Rovegno et al. (2003) observed that research on PCK has primaryly focused on general elements of PCK with little information about teachers' knowledge of teaching specific content. Thus, they examined experienced teachers' PCK as it was enacted in dribbling lessons to third grade students. They found that accomplished teachers taught dribbling holistically, refined the quality of movement using a limited number of cues, and explicitly taught cognitive processes that were embedded in, and relevant to, dribbling lesson tasks.

McCaughtry (2004) noted that PCK research has mostly focused on an "accurate understanding of students cognition and physical development blends with knowledge of content, curriculum, and pedagogy to facilitate learning" (p. 33). McCaughtry (2004) pointed out that "although enlightening and beneficial, research on pedagogical content knowledge has also been one-sided in not considering teacher knowledge of student emotion as an integral component of their understanding of student learning" (p. 33). Investigating the emotional dimensions of a teacher's PCK and the influences on content, curriculum, and pedagogy McCaughtry (2004) found that understanding student emotion is essential to a teacher's understanding of teaching and to the teacher's PCK. The teacher's understanding and interpretation of student emotion affected the selection, order, and formulation of curriculum units as well as pedagogical approaches and interactions during instruction in order to facilitate students' learning.

Amade-Escot (2000) addressed both PCK and didactics as ways to investigate content issues in the teaching and learning process of physical education. According to her PCK "is situated in the broader area of teachers' thinking" (p. 78). Didactics of physical education emphasizes that "the content taught results from numerous transformation that knowledge undergoes at the various stages of its selection and teaching" (pp. 78–79). She pointed out that although the two lines of research have several similarities "an important difference between the two agendas is the focus of didactics research on the content itself and its major role in the teaching system, whereas PCK research focuses on the teacher cognition variable" (p. 94). A major result of the didactics research is that the content of physical education depends less on experience than on specific competence in terms of didactic knowledge of the physical activity taught (Amade-Escot, 2000). Amade-Escot (2000) concluded that teaching content in physical education is highly specific to physical activities and sports, develops in action, is an important part of professional knowledge and dependent on constraints inherent in the system.

Expertise and teachers' knowledge

The expert novice model appeared in educational research in the mid – eighties and explored the development of teachers' "craft knowledge" or "wisdom of practice" (Berliner, 1986). Berliner (1986) emphasized that an alternative way to enrich the knowledge base of teaching was to compare and contrast expert and novice teachers' knowledge, thinking, and behaviors. In the literature there are a plethora of definitions related to teaching expertise. Dodds (1994) pointed out that "teaching expertise in physical education is a global construct that refers to the ease with which teachers perform their work to maximize student learning". She emphasized that "teaching expertise is not limited to particular teaching perspectives but rather may be grounded in a variety of dispositions, attitudes, beliefs, knowledge, and behaviors that compromise a teacher's world view" (pp. 156–157).

Studies in physical education have investigated the relationship of teaching expertise and teachers' knowledge (Graber, 2001) and the ways that expert and novice teachers respond to teaching situations. Housner and Griffey (1985) investigated the planning process and teaching actions of experienced and inexperienced teachers. They found that inexperienced teachers focused on the interest level of the whole class, while the experienced teachers made more strategic decisions and considered more the individual interests and success of the students. Siedentop and Eldar (1989) described and explored expertise, experience, and effectiveness in physical education. Their study indicated that expertise was highly specific to context, experience was an essential but not sufficient condition for expertise and that high subject matter knowledge and skillfulness were properties of expertise.

Schempp et al. (1998) indicated that "one question that has yet to be addressed pertains to the role subject matter knowledge plays in teachers' expertise" (p. 344). They explored the influence of subject matter expertise on the pedagogical content knowledge of physical education teachers and found that there were significant differences between teachers teaching subjects in which they had expertise and subjects in which they had little or no expertise. Chen and Rovegno (2000) examined the characteristics of expert and novice teachers' constructivist-oriented teaching practices while using a movement approach to elementary physical education. They found that the expert teachers were better able than novice teachers to (a) facilitate students' self responsibility and critical thinking about movement quality, (b) link new learning to students' prior knowledge, and (c) facilitate students' social interaction and cooperation.

Although, the construct of expertise is global, "the teachers' subject matter knowledge, pedagogical content knowledge, and conditional knowledge [includes beliefs and values] constitute much of what is studied under the rubric of teaching expertise" (Dodds, 1994: 159). O'Sullivan and Doutis (1994) suggested that the concept of expertise in teaching needs to go beyond "the academic and developmental agendas to include the social, political, and moral dimensions" (p. 179). Similarly, Dodds (1994) emphasized that researchers of expertise had to pay more attention to the more global dimensions of teaching. As she noted "for instance, part of teaching expertise ought to include creating equity for all students by addressing motor elitism, racism, sexism, homophobia, and other social justice issues in physical education" (p. 163). Based on the review conducted for this chapter, no study was found that has investigated the construct of expertise in its global form that includes sensitive social, political, and moral dimensions of education.

Summary

Inquiry on teachers' knowledge has grown rapidly in recent years in an effort to explore and record the knowledge base of teaching. Several typologies have been proposed by scholars in portraying ways knowledge can be explored as related to practice. Research in physical education on teacher knowledge has focused on pedagogical knowledge, content knowledge, PCK, and expertise and teachers' knowledge.

Pedagogical knowledge has been the focus of several studies in physical education (Rink, 2003). Some evidence exists today of what physical education teachers know about the subject matter of physical education. Results of these studies indicated that teachers' content knowledge is evident in the way teachers select to sequence tasks in lessons and it affects the main goals and activities of instructional units.

Research into teachers' PCK has being going on for at least a decade (Rovegno, 2003). Studies on teachers' PCK in physical education have described how preservice and experienced teachers acquire, elaborate, and transform their PCK. Findings from research studies revealed that prospective teachers had difficulties connecting lesson content to a broader context, were less able to deal simultaneously with different dimensions of teaching, and ignored students' emotions in teaching. In contrast, experienced teachers were found to be able to deal with multiple aspects of content and dimensions of teaching and took into account students' emotions. Results also showed that PCK is embedded in teaching, develops and interconnects to professional competence, and is affected by contextual factors.

The teaching expertise studies in physical education provide insights into the ways expert and novice teachers react to teaching situations. In general terms, results suggest that expert teachers are more able than novice teachers to facilitate students' learning. Expert teachers make more strategic decisions and consider more the individual interests and success of the students. The various studies on expertise have not investigated the construct of expertise in its global form that includes sensitive social, political, and moral issues in education as has been suggested by several scholars (Dodds, 1994; O'Sullivan and Doutis, 1994).

Conclusions

The aim of this chapter was to explore the different perspectives regarding related theory and research on teacher knowledge. An effort was made to define this body of literature and to represent the basic dimensions and directions of this work. Although, not all-encompassing and comprehensive since representative studies were selected here to review, the chapter focused on questions such as what forms of knowledge teachers have about teaching, what teachers know about teaching, and the role of teachers' knowledge in teaching. In this final section, some of the major themes proposed by the review are discussed.

One of the most interesting conclusions of this chapter is that the recent attention to teachers' knowledge has demonstrated some of the complex dimensions and factors that interact in the process of teaching and learning. Research has begun to reveal some of the complex pedagogical processes involved in teaching and the multiple types of knowledge that teachers draw upon in their efforts to help students learn. As the literature review in this chapter suggests, this far the majority of studies have centered on the general properties and characteristics of teachers' knowledge and fewer studies have focused on the acquisition, development, and/or construction of teachers' knowledge. There are also indications in the literature that greater thought need to be given on what actually teachers know, how they come to know, and/or what they think they need to know about teaching and learning. More studies to capture the collective understanding and orientations of the nature and content of teacher knowledge are definitely needed in the near future.

Another concluding message of this review is that teacher knowledge can be conceptualized and investigated in several ways. With the exception of few efforts the majority of studies used traditional theoretical frameworks to investigate teachers' knowledge. There are available to the research community several constructivist and situated approaches (see Chapter 3.4) which seemed to be promising in describing what processes facilitate teachers' construction of knowledge and what factors or conditions facilitate or affect the construction of teachers' knowledge. The emerging empirical work on teacher knowledge can definitely sensitize teacher educators and researchers to both the possibilities and the intricacies involved in the study of teachers' knowledge. Evidence from this literature can significantly add to the knowledge base for teaching and teacher education programs.

Implications for teacher education

Research evidence on teacher knowledge indicates that teacher knowledge is a practical, action-oriented form of knowledge and experience plays a crucial role in knowledge development (Rovegno, 2003). It has been suggested that teacher knowledge is neither highly abstract nor propositional. Nor can this knowledge be formalized into a set of specific skills or predetermined answers to particular problems. Rather teacher knowledge was found to be experiential, procedural, situational, and particularistic. Therefore, it will be necessary for teacher educators and researchers to develop forms of representations that capture these essential features of what teachers know with a high degree of situation and task validity. Frequent progressive, sequential, well-constructed, and well-guided experiences – designed on the basis of analytical and reflective thinking and understanding of teaching events and pedagogical issues – should be used extensively in teacher education programs. Pedagogical approaches which are used to transform professional content for teachers, should aim at revealing educational dilemmas and problems as well as finding ways of thinking and acting about such educational dilemmas and problems. Readers interested in learning more on such pedagogical approaches might examine Chapter 4.2 by Connie Collier where she discusses the rationale for case-based teaching in physical education environments.

Future research directions

Based on the fact that the field of inquiry on teacher knowledge is still young, more research should be conducted to describe and explore teachers' knowledge in physical education settings. Such studies should aim at describing what, how, and under what conditions teachers, with various degrees of experiences working in different settings or in different stages of their teacher education program, know about teaching and learning.

A second suggestion is that contextual factors need to be built in the research designs of studies exploring teachers' knowledge. Recent findings have suggested that contextual factors are promising signs in exploring teacher knowledge. Since, contextual factors seems to shape and define teacher knowledge, it will be advisable that greater emphasis and clarity should be given to these factors.

A third recommendation relates to research methodologies and designs. "Because of the complexity of the area, diverse methodologies are needed, each contributing its own evidence and perspective to an overall understanding of teaching" (Calderhead, 1996: 722). At this point small sample and case studies approaches dominate the research on teachers' knowledge. How one frames the research questions of a study depends to a great extent on how one conceives of what is to be learned and how that learning might take place. It is also acceptable that improvements can take place when more sophisticated and inclusive research approaches are used in educational research. As

Shulman (2002) pointed out we need studies and program of research that combine meaningful, credible, alternative designs and include "good instrumentation, careful measurement, scrupulously faithful ethnographic accounts, and carefully reasoned inferences and arguments" (p. 252). Furthermore, greater thought needs to be given to more sophisticated research questions concerning the improvement of teacher knowledge. An understanding of teacher knowledge might be dramatically enhanced by probing more deeply with questions such as how these forms of knowledges are obtained, under what conditions they are obtained, and how their knowledge changes over time. In a review of literature, on teacher knowledge and learning, Carter (1990) concluded that:

> There is still a tendency in studies of teachers' knowledge to focus on characteristics of what teachers know (e.g. their knowledge is complex, diverse, idiosyncratic, rich, holistic, personal) or on topics about which they think (e.g. they know about routines, students, images, curriculum). Less attention is given to the substance of that knowledge, to what actually teachers know or need to know about classrooms, content, and pedagogy and how that knowledge is organized. The later task is considerably more difficult but is likely to be productive. (p. 307)

Carter's conclusion is as valid today as it was in the 1990s. Based on these methodological problems, it is obvious that more systematic and programmatic research should be conducted on teachers' knowledge. Programmatic and systematic research may help to explore, interpret, and understand teachers' knowledge to a greater extent.

A major gap in research is the lack of empirical evidence on the relationship between teacher knowledge and student learning. At the present time, there are not enough studies that have taken into account the complexities of student learning. In a recent article, Shulman (2002), reflecting on the basic research on teacher knowledge, pointed out that in the 1900s a shift from exploratory, theory driven, research occurred to more product oriented studies. The emphasis of these studies was on the three theoretical constructs – content, cognition, and context. Shulman (2002) suggested that although the shift to the three Cs of content, cognition, and context was a significant improvement, there still a major omission: the fourth C, consequences for students. Shulman (2002) emphasized that a set of well developed and field tested instruments are imperative for documenting and measuring important aspects of teacher learning and development and the opportunities for students to learn.

Campbell et al. (2004) proposed "the differentiated model" to investigate and assess various aspects of teachers' learning and improvement as it might be more valuable than the classic "teacher effectiveness model" (Doyle, 1990) for those searching and assessing valuable and effective educational practices. The researchers emphasized that the constructs of teacher and school effectiveness have developed a "one size fits all" model, based on the assumption that effective teachers and schools are effective with all students in all contexts and in all subject domains. Campbell et al. (2004) suggest that much of the educational research provides a generic profile of teacher behavior and knowledge irrespective of age of student, ability of pupil groups, social and organizational context, or even the subject being taught. Such a conceptualization of effectiveness has led to a simple dichotomy between effective and ineffective teachers and has eschewed the fact that teachers may have strengths and weaknesses in their professional practices. They argued that the field is now ready to examine how far it is possible to build a theory which emphasizes not only teachers' skills and behaviors but also teacher knowledge and student learning.

Although, few studies in mathematics, science, and language have investigated the relationship of teacher knowledge and student achievement (Campbell et al., 2004) there has been no attention to the extent that teacher knowledge affects student learning in physical education settings. Studies which focus on teacher and student improvement across differing school groupings, seem to be a critical area of future inquiry in physical education.

A final recommendation for future research on teacher knowledge is to design studies that incorporate, not only student learning but also students' views of how teachers' knowledge affects them. Such studies might offer important evidence of students' meanings, interpretations, and insights of their experiences during the teaching and learning process. I would like to conclude with an enlightened proposition expressed by Lee (1997) in her review article on research on student thinking. She noted:

> If we view the world through the eyes of our students and hear the messages embedded in their actions, we will learn things we never knew we did not know. There seem to be consistent messages from our students – messages about the content of the curriculum, their value perceptions, and the meaningfulness of their experiences. (p. 274)

References

Amade-Escot, C. (2000). The contribution of two research programs on teaching content: "Pedagogical content knowledge" and "didactics of physical education". *Journal of Teaching in Physical Education, 20*: 78–101.

Bain, L. (1990). Physical education teacher education. In W.R. Houston, M. Haberman and J. Sikula (Eds.), *Handbook of research on teacher education* (pp. 758–781). New York: Macmillan.

Berliner, D. (1986). In pursuit of the expert pedagogue. *Educational Researcher, 15(7)*; 5–13.

Borko, H. and Putnam, R. (1996). Learning to teach. In D.C. Berliner and R.C. Calfee (Eds.), *Handbook of educational psychology* (pp. 673–708). New York: Macmillan.

Calderhead, J. (1996). Teachers: Beliefs and knowledge. In D.C. Berliner and R.C. Calfee (Eds.), Handbook of educational psychology (pp. 709–725). New York: Macmillan.

Campbell, R.J., Kyriakides, L., Muijs, R.D. and Robinson, W. (2004). *Assessing teacher effectiveness: Developing a differentiated model*. London: Routledge Falmer.

Carter, K. (1990). Teachers' knowledge and learning to teach. In W.R. Houston, M. Haberman, and J. Sikula (Eds.), *Handbook of research on teacher education* (pp. 291–310). New York: Macmillan.

Chen, W. and Rovegno, I. (2000). Examination of expert and novice teachers' constructivist-oriented teaching practices using a movement approach to elementary physical education. *Research Quarterly for Exercise and Sport, 71(4)*: 357–372.

Clandinin, J. (1985). *Classroom practice: Teacher images in action*. London: Falmer.

Cochran-Smith, M. and Lytle, S. (1999). Relationships of knowledge and practice: Teacher learning in communities. *Review of Research in education, 24*: 249–305.

Dodds, P. (1994). Cognitive and behavioral components of expertise in teaching physical education. *Quest, 46*: 153–163.

Doutis, P. (1997). Teachers' pedagogical content knowledge and pedagogical theories of content. *Dissertation Abstracts International, 58*(3872). (University Microfilms No. 9813254).

Doyle, W. (1990). Themes in teacher education research. In W.R. Houston, M. Haberman and J. Sikula (Eds.), *Handbook of research on teacher education* (pp. 3–24). New York: Macmillan.

Elbaz, F. (1991). Research on teacher's knowledge: The evolution of a discourse. *Journal of Curriculum Studies, 23*: 1–19.

Ennis, C. (1994). Knowledge and beliefs underlying curricular expertise. *Quest, 46(2)*: 164–175.

Feiman-Nemser, S. and Floden, R.E. (1986). The cultures of teaching. In M.C. Wittrock (Ed.), *Handbook of research on teaching* (pp. 505–525). New York: Macmillan.

Feiman-Nemser, S. and Remillard, J. (1996). Perspectives on learning to teach. In F.B. Murray (Ed.), *The teacher educator's handbook: Building a knowledge base for the preparation of teachers* (pp. 63–91). San Francisco: Jossey-Bass.

Fernandez-Balboa, J.M., Barrett, K., Solomon, M. and Silverman, S. (1996). Perspectives on content knowledge in physical education. *Journal of Physical Education, Recreation, & Dance, 67*(9): 54–57.

Floden, R. (2001). Research on effects of teaching: A continuing model for research on teaching. In V. Richardson

(Ed.), *Handbook of research on teaching* (4th Ed., pp. 3–16). New York: Macmillan.

Fortin, S. (1993). The teaching of modern dance: What two experienced teachers know, value, and do. *Dissertation Abstracts International, 53*(2580). (University Microfilms No. 9238175).

Graber, K. (1995). The influence of teacher education programs on the beliefs of student teachers: general pedagogical knowledge, pedagogical content knowledge, and teacher education course work. *Journal of Teaching in Physical Education, 14*: 157–178.

Graber, K. (2001). Research on teaching in physical education. In V. Richardson (Ed.), *Handbook of research in teaching* (4th ed., 491–519). Washington, DC: American Educational Research Association.

Griffin, L., Dodds, P. and Rovegno, I. (1996). Pedagogical content knowledge for teachers. Integrate everything you know to help students learn. *Journal of Physical Education Recreation & Dance, 67(9)*: 58–61.

Grossman, P.L. (1989). A study in contrast: Sources of pedagogical content knowledge for secondary English. *Journal of Teacher Education, 40*: 24–31.

Hastie, P. (1996). The effect of teacher content knowledge on accountability in instructional tasks. *Research Quarterly for Exercise and Sport, 67*(Suppl.1), A-81.

Housner, L. and Griffey, D. (1985). Teachers cognition: Differences in planning and interactive decision-making between experienced and inexperienced teachers. *Research Quarterly for Exercise and Sport, 56(1)*: 45–53.

Jenkins, J. and Veal, M. (2002). Preservice teachers' PCK development during peer coaching. *Journal of Teaching in Physical Education, 22*: 49–68.

Kelly, P., Hickey, C. and Tinning, R. (2000). Producing knowledge about physical education pedagogy: Problematizing the activities of expertise. *Quest, 52*: 284–296.

Kirk, D. (1986). A critical pedagogy for teacher education: Toward an inquiry-oriented approach. *Journal of Teaching in Physical education, 5*: 230–246.

Kirk, D. and Macdonald, D. (1998). Situated learning in physical education. *Journal of Teaching in Physical Education, 17*: 376–387.

Kutame, M. (1997). Teacher knowledge and its relationship to student success in learning gymnastics skill. *Dissertation Abstracts International, 58*(1637). (University Microfilms No. 9731661).

Lee, A. (1997). Contributions of research on student thinking in physical education. *Journal of Teaching in Physical Education, 16*: 262–277.

Macdonald, D., Hunter, L., Carlson, T. and Penney, D. (2002a). Teacher knowledge and the disjunction between school curricula and teacher education. *Asia-Pacific Journal of Teacher Education, 30(3)*: 259–275.

Macdonald, D., Kirk, D., Metzler, M., Nilges, L., Schempp, P. and Wright, J. (2002b). It's all very well, in theory: Theoretical perspectives and their applications in contemporary pedagogical research. *Quest, 54*: 133–156.

McCaughtry, N. (2004). The emotional dimensions of a teacher's pedagogical content knowledge: Influences on content, curriculum, and pedagogy. *Journal of Teaching in Physical Education*, 23: 30–47.

McCaughtry, N. and Rovegno, I. (2003). Development of pedagogical content knowledge: Moving from blaming students to predicting skillfulness, recognizing motor development, and understanding emotion. *Journal of Teaching in Physical Education*, 22: 355–368.

Munby, H., Rusell, T. and Martin, A. (2001). Teachers' knowledge and how it develops. In V. Richardson (Ed.). *Handbook of research on teaching* (4th Ed., pp. 877–904). New York: Macmillan.

O' Sullivan, M. (1996). What do we know about the professional preparation of teachers? In S. Silverman and C. Ennis (Eds.), *Student learning in physical education: Applying research to enhance instruction* (pp. 315–337). Champaign, IL: Human Kinetics.

O'Sullivan, M. (2003). Learning to teach physical education. In S. Silverman and C. Ennis (2nd ed.), *Student learning in physical education: Applying research to enhance instruction* (pp. 275–294). Champaign, IL: Human Kinetics.

O'Sullivan, M. and Doutis, P. (1994). Research on expertise: Guideposts for expertise and teacher education in physical education. *Quest, 46*: 176–185.

Richardson, V. (1996). The role of attitudes and beliefs in learning to teach. In J. Sikula, T. Buttery and E. Guyton (Eds), *Handbook of research on teacher education*, (pp. 102–119). New York: Macmillan.

Richardson, V. and Placier, P. (2001). Teacher change. In V. Richardson (Ed.), *Handbook of research in teaching* (4th ed., 905–947). Washington, DC: American Educational Research Association.

Rink, J. (2003). Effective instruction in physical education. In S. Silverman and C. Ennis (Eds.) (2nd ed.), *Student learning in physical education: Applying research to enhance instruction* (pp. 165–186). Champaign, IL: Human Kinetics.

Romar, J.E. (1995). *Case studies of Finnish physical education teachers: Espoused and enacted theories of action*. Abo: Abo Academi University Press.

Rovegno, I. (1992). Learning to teach in a field-based methods course: the development of pedagogical content knowledge. *Teaching and Teacher Education, 8*: 69–82.

Rovegno, I. (1993). The development of curricula knowledge: A case of problematic pedagogical content knowledge during advanced knowledge acquisition. *Research Quarterly for Exercise and Sport, 64*: 56–68.

Rovegno, I. (1994). Teaching within a curricular zone of safety: School culture and the situated nature of student teachers' pedagogical content knowledge. *Research Quarterly for Exercise and Sport, 65*: 269–279.

Rovegno, I. (1995). Theoretical perspectives on knowledge and learning and a student teacher's pedagogical content knowledge of dividing and sequencing subject matter. *Journal of Teaching in Physical Education, 14*: 284–304.

Rovegno, I. (2003). Teachers' knowledge construction. In S. Silverman and C. Ennis (Eds.), (2nd ed) *Student*

learning in physical education: Applying research to enhance instruction* (pp. 295–310). Champaign, IL: Human Kinetics.

Rovegno, I. and Dolly, J. (in press). Constructivist perspectives on learning. In D. Kirk, D. Macdonald and M. O'Sullivan (Eds), *Handbook of physical education*, (pp. 242–261). London: Sage Publications.

Rovegno, I., Chen, W. and Todorovich, J. (2003). Accomplished teachers' pedagogical content knowledge of teaching dribbling to third grade children. *Journal of Teaching in Physical Education, 22*: 426–449.

Schon, D.A. (1983). *The reflective practitioner*. New York: Basic Books.

Schon, D.A. (1987). *Educating the reflective practitioner*. San Francisco, CA: Jossey-Bass.

Schempp, P., Manross, D., Tan, S. and Fincher, M. (1998). Subject expertise and teachers' knowledge. *Journal of Teaching in Physical Education, 17*: 342–356.

Sebren, A. (1995). Preservice teachers' reflections and knowledge development in a field-based elementary physical education methods course. *Journal of Teaching in Physical Education, 14*: 262–283.

Shulman, L. (1986). Those who understand: Knowledge growth in teaching. *Educational Researcher, 15*: 4–14.

Shulman, L. (1987). Knowledge and teaching: Foundation of a new reform. *Harvard Review, 57*: 1–22.

Shulman, L. (2002). Truth and consequences? Inquiry and policy in research on teacher education. *Journal of Teacher Education, 53*: 248–253.

Siedentop, D. (1991). The mountain yet to be climbed (pp. 3–9) *Proceedings from the 1991 AIESEP-NAPEHE World Congress*, Atlanta, Georgia.

Siedentop, D. (2002). Content knowledge for physical education. *Journal of Teaching in Physical Education, 21*: 368–377.

Siedentop, D. and Eldar, E. (1989). Expertise, experience, and effectiveness. *Journal of Teaching in Physical Education, 8(3)*: 254–260.

Siedentop, D. and Tannehill, D. (2000). *Developing teaching skills in physical education* (4th ed.). Palo Alto, CA: Mayfield.

Tinning, R. (1988). Student teaching and the pedagogy of necessity. *Journal of Teaching in Physical Education, 7*: 82–89.

Tinning, R. (1991). Teacher education pedagogy: Dominant discourses and the process of problem setting. *Journal of Teaching in Physical Education, 1*: 1–20.

Tinning, R. (2002a). Engaging Siedentopian perspectives on content knowledge for physical education. *Journal of Teaching in Physical Education, 21*: 378–391.

Tinning, R. (2002b). Toward a "modest pedagogy": Reflections on the problematic of critical pedagogy. *Quest, 54*: 224–240.

Tom, A. and Valli, L. (1990). Professional knowledge for teachers. In W.R. Houston, M. Haberman and J. Sikula (Eds.), *Handbook of research on teacher education* (pp. 373–392). New York: Macmillan.

Tsangaridou, N. (2002). Enacted pedagogical content knowledge in physical education: A case study of a prospective classroom teacher. *European Physical Education Review, 8(1)*: 21–36.

Wilson, S. and Berne, J. (1999). Teacher learning and the acquisition of professional knowledge: An examination of research on contemporary professional development. *Review of Research in Education, 24*: 173–209.

Wright, L. (2000). Practical knowledge, performance, and physical education. *Quest, 52*: 273–283.

Zeicher, K. (1999). The new scholarship in teacher Education. *Educational Researcher, 28*: 4–15.

Zeicher, K. and Gore, J. (1990). Teacher socialization. In W. R. Houston, M. Haberman and J. Sikula (Eds.), *Handbook of research on teacher education* (pp. 329–348). New York: Macmillan.

4.9   Coaching and coach education

PIERRE TRUDEL AND WADE GILBERT

Introduction

Presenting an overview of coaching and coach education research as well as suggestions for future study is a tremendous challenge considering the amount of coaching literature. A recent analysis of the scientific articles published between 1970 and 2001 revealed over 600 publications just in English (Gilbert and Trudel, 2004a). To make sense of this amount of information in a limited number of pages we experimented with different ways to classify, regroup, and present the research. Careful attention to the work of key authors helped us to develop a structure that, we hope, will give credit to many of the authors who have contributed to this research field. We have sought to provide a new perspective on that literature that will extend our understanding of coaching both as a science and as an art.

Using Sfard's (1998) metaphors on learning (acquisition and participation) we prepared a visual display (see Figure 4.9.1) showing two ways through which coaches learn how to coach. In the acquisition metaphor, learning means acquisition of concepts to be understood as basic units of knowledge: "The language of knowledge acquisition and concept development makes us think about the human mind as a container to be filled with certain materials and about the learner as becoming an owner of these materials" (p. 5). Once the knowledge has been acquired, the knower can apply, transfer and share with others the "material goods" of the learning process. It has traditionally been the emphasis of large-scale (L-S) programs to deliver these material goods to coaches.

In the participation metaphor, the learner "should be viewed as a person interested in participation in certain kinds of activities rather than in accumulating private possessions" (Sfard, 1998: 6). Thus, learning activities should not be dissociated from the context within which they take place. This is the fundamental tenet of situated learning theories (Brown et al., 1989; Lave and Wenger, 1991) and implies that "learning is social insofar as it may involve interaction between an individual learner

and others" (Kirk and Macdonald, 1998: 380). For Sfard, the differences between the two metaphors involves a shift from the individual mind and what goes "into it" to individuals and their interactions with others. Learning through experience could then be conceived of as a process of becoming a member of a community that "entails, above all, the ability to communicate in the language of this community and act according to its particular norms" (Sfard, 1998: 6).

This chapter is divided in three main sections. The first section deals with the left part of Figure 4.9.1 – how coaches learn to coach through L-S programs. Focusing on L-S programs first provides insight into how the coaching process is understood and viewed around the world. We start this section by providing a brief historical perspective of L-S programs. Based on recent trends in L-S program design, we then suggest a typology of coaching contexts and summarize some of the research on coaches in each context. We conclude the first section of the chapter by discussing the influence of coaching research on L-S program design. In the second section we address the right part of Figure 4.9.1 – how coaches learn to coach through experience. In this section we make the distinction between learning through reflection on experience and learning through participation in social interactions (i.e. the social and cultural process of learning to become a coach). In the third and final section, we conclude by presenting coaching and coach education issues that we believe provide directions for future research.

Learning to coach through large-scale programs (acquisition metaphor)

History of large-scale programs

As thorough accounts of L-S programs around the world are available elsewhere (Campbell, 1993; De

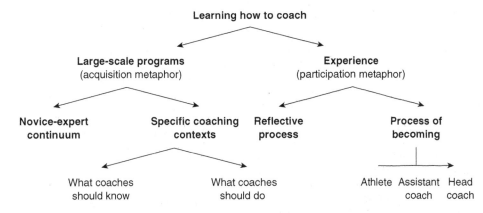

Figure 4.9.1   Learning how to coach

Knop et al., 1996; Dickson, 2001; Lyle, 2002; Mills and Dunlevy, 1997; Sawyer, 1992; Woodman, 1993) only an overview of the common types of L-S programs will be presented. It is difficult to trace the exact origins of L-S programs, although various forms of coach certification have existed in the United States for nearly a century (National Federation of State High School Associations, n.d.). The genesis of L-S programs may be traced to mid-20th century Britain when national sport governing bodies started to develop coaching programs (Campbell and Crisfield, 1994; Douge and Hastie, 1993). In terms of a national coach education program model, most sources cite Canada's National Coaching Certification Program (NCCP) as the first widely adopted model, developed in the mid-1970s. The NCCP has since certified nearly 900,000 coaches in Canada (Coaching Association of Canada, 2005). Canada's NCCP was followed shortly thereafter by the creation of Australia's National Coach Accreditation Scheme (NCAS) in the late 1970s (Dickson, 2001). Although no one national model has been adopted in the US, several L-S programs were created around the same time as the NCAS. For example, the American Coaching Effectiveness Program (ACEP), founded in 1976, delivered courses starting in 1981 (Douge and Hastie, 1993). ACEP has since evolved into the American Sport Education Program (ASEP) and is perhaps the most widely adopted L-S program in America where it is used by nearly 250 organizations from high school to college and national sport governing bodies (Martens, 2004).

The primary impetus for developing L-S programs was to address moral and legal issues (i.e. certification) and to increase coaching competency. Certification to protect against litigation and to protect the safety of the athletes is often cited as a driving force behind the evolution of L-S, particularly in the US (Conn and Razor, 1989; Mills and

Dunlevy, 1997) where there are over 500 000 coaches in the school system alone (Martens et al., 2004). Certification of coaches was considered of such import in the United States that in 1967 a Coaching Certification Task Force was created by the American Alliance for Health, Physical Education, Recreation, and Dance (AAHPERD) (Massengale, 1984). Certification serves as a gatekeeper to coaching, but it has been noted that an emphasis on mandatory certification, particularly at lower levels of athletic participation, may turn some volunteers away from coaching because of the additional cost and time commitment (Conn and Razor, 1989). Although the gatekeeper function of certification is evident, certification's relationship to coaching competence has not been established. This is particularly evident in the United States where, despite numerous L-S programs, coach certification has been described as weak and a failure "because they do not have the force of law" (Massengale, 1984: 7).

Comprehensive L-S programs are now available in many countries around the world (Campbell, 1993; Mills and Dunlevy, 1997; The International Council for Coach Education, n.d.). Coach education has grown to the point where there is now an International Council for Coach Education (ICCE) based at the Wingate Institute for Physical Education and Sport in Israel (www.icce.ws). The mission of the ICCE is to promote coaching around the world as a true profession, and to improve the quality of coaching at all levels of sport. The ICCE aspires to accomplish this mission by creating a global community of coaching practice comprising organizations and individuals responsible for coach education and coaching. In 2003, the ICCE's membership included national organizations providing coach education in 21 countries, and seven international coach conferences were held between 1995 and 2003.

The novice to expert continuum

The first L-S programs were generally designed on the assumption that coaches existed on a continuum from novice (beginner) to expert (master). In other words, there is one body of coaching knowledge and coaches will accumulate the coaching concepts as they progress along the continuum. Thus, knowledge gained from expert coaches and sport scientists is packaged in a curriculum and disseminated to coaches hoping that they will memorize this material and transfer it to their day-to-day coaching activities (Martens, 2004). This view is still pervasive in coach education today where novice coaches are viewed as beginner experts who may someday "progress from a novice to a highly skilled professional, master coach" (National Association for Sport and Physical Education [NASPE], 1995: 6).

Generally most L-S programs include three components: (a) coaching theory, (b) sport-specific techniques and tactics, and (c) coaching practice. Each of these three components is addressed through a multilevel system designed around a novice – expert coaching continuum, usually comprising four or five levels (Campbell, 1993; NASPE, 2001). The first level, designed for volunteer or recreational coaches, generally requires less than 15 hours of coursework focused on creating awareness of basic coaching principles. About the same amount of time is invested in courses on techniques and tactics. The time commitment and specialization increases significantly as one moves higher in coaching education levels. The primary levels of coach education are generally offered through government-based national coaching organizations, although private organizations like ASEP provide most of the coach education in the US. In some countries, coach education is also offered as part of university or college curriculum in sport science. For example, in the United Kingdom 26 colleges offer degrees or diplomas related to sports coaching (Lyle, 2002), and in the United States 163 colleges offer degree programs in athletic coaching education (McMillin and Reffner, 1999).

Although L-S programs have traditionally been classroom based, alternative delivery methods such as videodiscs, Internet, CD-ROM, and distance learning initiatives are increasingly being considered (Campbell and Crisfield, 1994; Coaching Association of Canada, n.d.(a); Human Kinetics, 2004; Seefeldt and Milligan, 1992). This "anywhere, anytime" approach to coach education will rely heavily on Internet delivery (Seefeldt and Milligan, 1992). For example, in the National Federation Interscholastic Coaches Education Program (NFICEP), which is endorsed in over 30 states in the US, coaches have the option of taking courses online or in a traditional class setting (although courses on sport-specific techniques and tactics are only online). Also, in 2003 ASEP started offering online coach education courses in partnership with several sport associations (Human Kinetics, 2004). ASEP plans to release 16 new sport-specific coaching courses between 2005 and 2007, all to be offered exclusively online (Martens, 2004).

On numerous occasions these L-S programs have been criticized for their low ecological validity (Abraham and Collins, 1998; Douge and Hastie, 1993; Gilbert and Trudel, 1999). These critiques have contributed to discussions on program redesign such as taking a specific coaching contexts approach.

Specific coaching contexts

The design of programs for specific coaching contexts takes two forms. In the first form the program is based, like in the novice to expert continuum, on "what coaches should know" but there is a clear recognition of the specificity of the different coaching contexts. For example, in the US, the National Collegiate Athletic Association (NCAA), the National Federation of High Schools (NFHS), the United States Olympic Committee (USOC), and ASEP have joined forces to prepare a blueprint for coach education in America (Martens et al., 2004; National Federation of State High School Associations, n.d.). The proposed National Coaching Credentialing Program is organized into two curriculums – one for volunteer coaches and one for professional (paid) coaches (see Table 4.9.1).

In the second form, the program is based on "what coaches should do" and therefore is often called a competency-based program. A job task analysis is first performed to identify what coaches should be able to do in each coaching context and then the reference material and the delivery system are selected. In Canada, the course-based certification program is in the process of moving to a coaching competency-based program (Coaching Association of Canada, n.d., 2005; Savard, 1997). Eight specific coaching contexts have been identified (see Table 4.9.1). Another example is the National Vocational Qualifications (NVQ)/National Occupational Standards developed for coaches in the United Kingdom (Campbell and Crisfield, 1994; Lyle, 2002) in which five coaching contexts have been identified (see Table 4.9.1). In these two last examples, the programs are structured in such a way that allows sport-specific adaptations.

A problem-based (sometimes called problem-solving) approach has been suggested as an effective instructional method in these new competency-based coach education programs (Savard, 1997). Although this approach is a fairly new idea in coach education, a similar approach referred to as the case method has been used in physical education teacher training for over a decade (Collier and O'Sullivan, 1997). In a problem-based approach, courses start with problems rather than with the presentation of

Table 4.9.1   Sample coaching context typologies

Source	Typology
Coaching Education in America: A White Paper (National Federation of State High School Associations, n.d.)	Professional level – Elite sport – College sport – School-based sport Volunteer level – Community-based youth sport
National Coaching Certification Program – (Coaching Association of Canada, n.d., 2005)	Community sport – Initiation – Ongoing participation Competition – Introduction – Development – High performance Instruction – Beginners – Intermediate performers – Advanced performers
National Vocational Qualifications – (Campbell and Crisfield, 1994)	National level coach (director of coaching) Senior coach (regional coach) Coach (club coach) Assistant coach Precoach (sports leader)
Role of Organized Sport in the Education and Health of American Children and Youth (Ewing et al., 1996)	Agency-sponsored sports Club sports Recreational sports Intramural sports Interscholastic sports
Worldwide Trends in Youth Sport (Wankel and Mummery, 1996)	Community-based youth sport – Representative/travel team – House league School-based sport – Interschool – Intramural – Instructional physical education
Sports Coaching Concepts (Lyle, 2002)	Representative team/group coach Performance coach Participation coach Sport teacher

disciplinary knowledge: "The key to problem-based learning is using material through which students engage with problems in situations as near as possible to 'real life'" (Jarvis et al., 1998: 117). The problem-based approach seems to address many of the critiques of the "traditional" approach to coach preparation and therefore to leave the acquisition metaphor. However, is working with coaches at solving context-specific coaching problems enough to be considered part of the participation metaphor? Due to time constraints, coaches are provided with what is called a "common coaching problem" that they usually have to discuss in sub-groups. They then have to compare what they said they usually do with the "appropriate solution" presented by the course conductor. In the participation metaphor the focus is on the actual practice of coaching in real time. In actual coaching practice: (a) problems are not presented, they have to be recognized and defined (Schön, 1983), (b) problems often have their origin in events that happen weeks, months and even years before (Gilbert and Trudel, 2001), (c) the process of creating a solution includes interactions with other participants in the sport environment (Gilbert and Trudel, 2001), and (d) there is no appointed facilitator to stimulate the reflective process. In brief, in most problem-solving approaches, coaches will only "practice" addressing the kinds of coaching issues they might encounter in the field: "However, the practices that learner engages in are still school tasks abstracted from the community, and this has important implications for the meaning and type of practices being learned, as well as for the individual's relations to those meanings and practices" (Barab and Duffy, 2000: 34).

It is clear that L-S programs now acknowledge that coaches in different coaching contexts need context-specific knowledge and competencies. The number and types of coaching contexts, however, varies widely among programs and scholars (see Table 4.9.1). This discrepancy can be perceived as a way to address the needs of sport systems in different countries or as an indication that a guiding conceptual framework is lacking. The lack of a common typology of coaching contexts hinders the organization of coaching research into a meaningful framework that can be used to inform coach education program design. It would be helpful to have a single typology of coaching contexts to organize the research on the characteristics of coaches in each context because coach characteristics directly influence the coaching process (Côté et al., 1995; Lyle, 2002). Understanding the profile of a typical coach in each type of sport context also provides critical information for making important coach education program delivery decisions. For example, scholars in the United Kingdom have advocated for a flexible program that allows coaches to "pick and mix" from different coaching modules to create a customized program that fits their individual background (Campbell and Crisfield, 1994).

For the purpose of facilitating a review of the coaching research, we are proposing a classification system with three specific coaching contexts. Although based on a review of different typologies

suggested by researchers and the current structure of L-S programs, our classification is most similar to Lyle's (2002) typology of sport leadership roles and organizational contexts. Lyle's typology is the most thoroughly described, is grounded in a comprehensive discussion of the coaching process, and is most consistent with the empirical research on stages of athlete skill development (Bloom, 1985; Côté et al., 2003). The three types of coaching contexts that we will use are (a) recreational sport, (b) developmental sport, and (c) elite sport. Each type of coaching context is defined and research on core coaching concepts in each context is summarized.

The summaries of core concepts for each coaching context are based primarily on a review of over 600 coaching science articles identified by Gilbert and Trudel (2004a). The research on coaches in each context is organized into six core concepts that provide a portrait of the typical coach in each context: (a) coach gender, (b) coach age and coaching experience, (c) athletic experience, (d) reasons for coaching, (e) education, and (f) stress and burnout. The sixth concept, stress and burnout, is excluded from the review of research on recreational sport coaches because there is insufficient research on this concept with this type of coach.

Recreational sport coaching

The recreational sport coaching context includes an emphasis on participation and leisure over competition, basic skill development, low intensity and commitment, formal organization but irregular and local involvement, and athletes are not selected based on skill tryouts (Lyle, 2002; Wankel and Mummery, 1996). If athletes are selected, the purpose is to have balanced teams in the league. For young athletes, this context may be similar to the sampling stage of athlete development (Côté et al., 2003). An example of the recreational sport coaching context is the local youth sport league that is designed for novice athletes, sometimes referred to as the initiation level of sport (Coaching Association of Canada, n.d., 2005). Recreational sport coaches may work with athletes at all ages, from young children to adult (i.e., recreational leagues, adult clubs).

Examples of research that provide data exclusively on the characteristics of coaches in the recreational sport context are extremely rare. Although some published studies do exist (e.g. Silvestri, 1991), almost all of the research considers recreational and development sport coaches together in their analysis, usually under the youth sport coach descriptor (Albinson, 1973; Barber et al., 1996; Gould and Martens, 1979; Gray and Cornish, 1985; Salminen and Liukkonen, 1996; Weiss and Sisley, 1984). Therefore, the following research summary is limited by the lack of a clear distinction between the recreational sport and developmental sport contexts when describing core concepts.

Coach gender

The vast majority of recreational sport coaches are male. The percentage of male coaches usually ranges from 70% (Bratton, 1978) to 100% (Curtis et al., 1979).

Coach age and coaching experience

Most recreational sport coaches are in their mid-30s with an average of 6 years coaching experience (Dwyer and Fischer, 1988a, 1988b; Gould and Martens, 1979; Graham and Carron, 1983; Weiss and Sisley, 1984). As few as 10% of these coaches continue coaching for 10 years or more (Hansen and Gauthier, 1988).

Athletic experience

Almost all recreational sport coaches competed in sport as athletes before they assumed the role of a coach (Barber et al., 1996; Gray and Cornish, 1985; Lee et al., 1989; Ubbes, 1991). Reported percentages always exceed 90% and the majority of the coaches were better than average athletes (Bratton, 1978; Silvestri, 1991). Most of these coaches acquired athletic experience for 5 years or more in the sport they now coach (Bratton, 1978; Dwyer and Fisher, 1988a, 1988b; Silvestri, 1991; Sisley et al., 1990). Even in this introductory context of coaching their athletic playing experience can be quite extensive with one study reporting a mean of 16.4 athletic seasons for novice female coaches (Sisley et al., 1990).

Reasons for coaching

Common reasons cited for coaching include enjoyment and love of the sport, wanting to remain associated with the sport, a desire for helping young people develop skills, and serving as a leader and supervisor for young people (Graham and Carron, 1983; Hansen and Gauthier, 1988; Lee et al., 1989; Sisley et al., 1990). It is very common for these coaches to be parents of athletes on the team they coach (Spallanzani, 1988; Weiss and Sisley, 1984). Generally these coaches have a positive attitude towards coaching and report positive and supportive coaching styles (Curtis et al., 1979; Gould and Martens, 1979; Dwyer and Fischer, 1988a,b; Salminen and Liukkonen, 1996).

Education

On average, 50% or fewer of the coaches in this context have completed any formal coach education coursework (Bratton, 1978; Corso et al., 1988; Weiss and Sisley, 1984) and fewer than 60% have college degrees (Gould and Martens, 1979; Hanson and Gauthier, 1988; Lee et al., 1989; Ubbes, 1991).

Developmental sport coaching

The developmental sport coaching context includes a more formal competitive structure, an increasing commitment from athletes and coaches, a stable relationship between athletes and coaches, and athletes are selected based on skill tryouts (Lyle, 2002; Wankel and Mummery, 1996). Athletes in this context receive specialized sport-specific training, and it is also considered by some the primary context for talent identification to elite levels of sport performance (Côté et al., 2003; Lyle, 2002). This context is similar to Côté et al.'s (2003) specialization stage of athlete development. Examples of the developmental sport coaching context include high school varsity athletics, local or regional sport clubs that restrict participation based on athlete skill level, and adult competitive sport that is neither full-time nor professional. Coaching research provides a fairly detailed portrait of developmental sport coach characteristics. However, much of the research on coaches in this context is limited to high school coaches in the US.

Coach gender

In most cases the majority of developmental sport coaches are male, although the percentage is not as high as found in the recreational sport coaching context and appears to be dependent on the sport and athlete gender. For example, football coaches in the United States (Chng and Field, 1993) and soccer coaches in Greece (Koustelios et al., 1997) are typically 100% male, while males comprise just over 50% of age-group swimming coaches in the United States (Raedeke et al., 2000, 2002). Special population athletics such as Special Olympics report equal or greater percentages of female coaches than male coaches (DePauw and Gavron, 1991; Miller, 1987; Palaestra, 1988). In almost all team sports it is extremely rare for a female to coach a male team (Capel et al., 1987; Cox and Noble, 1989; Sisley et al., 1987; Wilkinson and Schneider, 1991).

Coach age and coaching experience

The mean years of age for coaches in this context is approximately 36 while they typically average just over 9 years of coaching experience. It is not uncommon for coaches in the developmental sport context to coach for several years prior to assuming their current coaching position and they spend approximately four years as assistant coaches (Capel et al., 1987; Dale and Weinberg, 1989; Pastore and Judd, 1993; Penman et al., 1974; Weiss and Stevens, 1993). Although not widely reported, a few studies show that the average age for male coaches is several years older and they have accumulated several more years of coaching experience than female coaches

(Hasbrook et al., 1990; Pastore and Judd, 1993). Regardless of gender, coaches in this context often coach multiple sports (Capel et al., 1987; Cody, 1988; Cox and Noble, 1989; Jacobs and Ballard, 1996; Sisley et al., 1987; Young, 1992).

Athletic experience

Generally over 75% of coaches in the developmental sport context have several years of experience as competitive athletes in the sport they coach (Cody, 1988; DePauw and Gavron, 1991; Dodds et al., 1991; Mistro, 1985; Weiss and Stevens, 1993). There does not appear to be any coach gender trend for athletic experience as some data show female coaches to be more likely to have athletic experience (Eitzen and Pratt, 1989) while other data show just the opposite (Hasbrook et al., 1990). Several studies show that coaches in this context were better than average athletes based on the number of athletic awards received or participation in elite level competition (Dodds et al., 1991; Eitzen and Pratt, 1989b; Hasbrook et al., 1990; Mistro, 1985).

Reasons for coaching

The majority of these coaches report coaching to be fun, and it is one of the primary reasons they coach. The other main reasons cited for coaching are to maintain association with sports, teach sport skills, and provide a service to young people (Dodds et al., 1991; Hastie, 1991; Maurer, 1991; Mistro, 1985; Weiss and Stevens, 1993). Although this is fairly consistent across studies both for male and female coaches, one study did show coach gender differences in reasons for coaching. Maurer (1991) found that after working with young people, the second main reason for coaching among males was to produce a winning team while for females it was to stay involved in sport. Numerous studies provide data on the leadership style of coaches in this context, with most studies showing coaches to be democratic, positive, and offering high levels of praise and social support (Bennett and Maneval, 1998; Brandt and Elam, 1987; Holmes, 1980). This may vary depending upon coaching success, coach gender, athlete gender, and athlete expectancies. There is evidence that more successful coaches – as defined by winning percentage – use a more authoritarian style (Penman et al., 1974). Yet there are other data that show both winning and losing coaches, particularly male coaches, in this context prefer an autocratic style (Chelladurai and Quek, 1995; Pratt and Eitzen's, 1989a,b). At least one study indicates motivational style to vary by athlete gender (Holmes, 1980). Lastly, developmental sport coaches may modify their leadership style based on athlete expectancies. Research shows that coaches provide more praise and instruction to high

expectancy athletes than to low expectancy athletes (Solomon et al., 1998).

Education

Almost all (90%) of developmental sport coaches have college degrees and nearly 35% attained a graduate degree (Capel et al., 1987; Chng and Field, 1993; Dale and Weinberg, 1989; DePauw and Gavron, 1991; Gillentine and Hunt, 2000; Sisley et al., 1987). Although the percentages vary widely from less than 30% (DePauw and Gavron, 1991) to 100% (Hardin, 2000), the most common college field of specialization is physical education (Cox and Noble, 1989; Eitzen and Pratt, 1989; Gaunt and Forbus, 1991; Miller, 1987; Schatzle, 1980). Typically 75% or more of the coaches in this context also complete some formal coach education, either in the form of a clinic, college course, or coaching program (Cody, 1988; DePauw and Gavron, 1991; Klaus, 1986; Miller, 1987; Sisley et al., 1987).

Stress and burnout

Another area that has received considerable research attention for developmental sport coaches is coach stress and burnout. Although at least one study indicates coaches believe coaching in this context to be stressful (Kroll and Gendersheim, 1982), generally developmental sport coaches show a low to moderate level of burnout that places them below population norms (Capel et al., 1987; Chng and Field, 1993; Dale and Weinberg, 1989; Kosa, 1990; Quigley, 1989; Sisley et al., 1987; Young, 1992). However, more research is needed on this topic as at least one study shows coaches to score higher than population burnout norms (Pastore and Judd, 1993) and the influence of coach gender is not clear. Some data reveal male coaches to be more burned-out than female coaches (Dale and Weinberg, 1989), other data show females to score higher than males (Pastore and Judd, 1993), while still other data show no significant gender differences (Young, 1992).

Elite sport coaching

The elite sport coaching context is characterized by the highest levels of athlete and coach commitment, intensive preparation and involvement, public performance objectives, highly structured and formalized competition, coaches who typically work full-time as a coach, and very demanding and restrictive athlete selection criteria (Lyle, 2002). Coaches in this context generally spend most of their time guiding athletes in the investment stage of athlete development (Côté et al., 2003). Examples of the elite sport coaching context include college athletics in many countries, national and Olympic teams, and professional athletics. There is considerable research available on elite sport coaches but again the portrait is highly influenced by research conducted in the US.

Coach gender

Over 60% of the head coaches in the elite sport context are male (Baker-Finch, 1991; Caccese and Mayerberg, 1984; Cunningham and Sagas, 2002; Dunn and Dunn, 1992; Frederick and Morrison, 1999; Hendry, 1974; Kelley, 1994; Kelley et al., 1999; Knoppers et al., 1989; Kuga and Pastore, 1994; Pastore and Judd, 1993; Wang and Ramsey, 1998). However, this is an oversimplification of the coach gender profile in this context as the percentage varies widely and appears to depend upon athlete gender, sport, and level of elite competition. For example, 100% of the professional men's soccer coaches in Kugler et al., (1996) study were males while 36% of the coaches in Stahura and Greenwood's (2000) study of women's college basketball and volleyball coaches were male. Furthermore, Kelley and Gill's (1993) data show 46% of the coaches at the lower competitive divisions of American colleges to be male coaches while data on Australian (Baker-Finch, 1991) and Canadian (Wilson and Bird, 1988) national team coaches show male coaches hold well over 80% of the head coaching positions.

Coach age and coaching experience

The mean age in years for coaches in the elite sport context is 40 (Cheng and Wu, 1987; Cunningham and Sagas, 2002; Frederick and Morrison, 1999; Freischlag and Jacob, 1988; Kelley and Gill, 1993; Kelley et al., 1999; Kuegler et al., 1996; Krueger and Casselman, 1982; Latimer and Mathes, 1985; Pastore, 1991, 1992; Pastore and Judd, 1993). Female head coaches are on average several years younger than their male counterparts (Cunningham and Sagas, 2002; Kelley et al., 1999). It is common for elite development coaches to change coaching positions during their careers as they average nearly 13 years of coaching experience but only 6 years at their current position (Acosta and Carpenter, 1992; Bloom and Salmela, 2000; Cheng and Wu, 1987; Cullen et al., 1990; Frederick and Morrison, 1999; Kelley and Gill, 1993; Kjeldsen, 1981; Krueger and Casselman, 1982; Latimer and Mathes, 1985; Pastore, 1991, 1992; Wilson and Bird, 1988). A few studies show that female coaches generally have fewer years of coaching experience and years at their current coaching position (Pastore and Judd, 1993; Knoppers et al., 1989). Although not widely reported, it appears that most coaches in this context have five or more years of assistant coaching experience before they assume a head coaching position (Braddock, 1981; Cullen et al., 1990; Frederick and Morrison, 1999).

Athletic experience

Typically over 90% of elite sport coaches are former competitive athletes in the sport they coach (Dunn and Dunn, 1992; Knoppers et al., 1989; Krueger and Casselman, 1982; Latimer and Mathes, 1985; Richardson, 1981; Schinke et al., 1995). It appears, however, that female coaches usually are significantly more likely to have played for more years at a higher competitive level and received more athletic awards than their male counterparts (Cunningham and Sagas, 2002; Knoppers et al., 1989; Simpson and Beach, 1986). There does not appear to be any clear relationship between centrality of playing position and elite coaching status. Data are available both to support the importance of playing a central position (Chu and Segrave, 1981; Kjeldsen, 1981; Singell, 1991; Solomon et al., 1996) and the insignificance of playing a central position (Braddock, 1981; Kjeldsen, 1981; Latimer and Mathes, 1985; Simpson and Beach, 1986). Race is a significant factor in at least some sports such as football and basketball where Caucasians are significantly more likely to be selected for elite development coaching positions (Braddock, 1981; Chu and Segrave, 1981; Cullen et al., 1990).

Reasons for coaching

Men appear to have a significantly greater desire to become elite sport head coaches and generally show greater coaching self-efficacy (Cunningham and Sagas, 2002; Cunningham et al., 2003). Reasons for coaching in this context include to stay involved in the sport, to work with elite athletes, and to serve as a role model (Pastore, 1991, 1992). There is no one common leadership or motivational style, yet there seldom are significant differences noted between successful and non-successful coaches (Calloway and Driscoll, 1983; Frederick and Morrison, 1999; Keane and Cheffers, 1978) or between coach genders (Frederick and Morrison, 1999). However, there does appear to be significant leadership style differences at different levels of competition within this context. For example, several studies show that coaches at the highest level of American elite college competition are more autocratic and provide less praise and social support than their counterparts at the lower levels of elite college competition (Chelladurai et al., 1989; Martin, 1985; McGrath and Tipps, 1991). Leadership style may also vary by coaching success as at least one study found that more successful National team coaches were perceived to be significantly higher in democratic behaviors, praise, and social support (Serpa et al., 1991). In addition, a coach's leadership style may be perceived differently by different athletes on the same team. It has been shown that high expectancy athletes usually perceive their coaches to be more positive than do low expectancy athletes (Solomon et al., 1996).

Education

The vast majority of elite sport coaches have at least an undergraduate college degree, although coaches outside of the US consistently show lower percentages of college degrees. Typically 100% of elite development coaches in the United States have a college degree (Cullen et al., 1990; Krueger and Casselman, 1982; Latimer and Mathes, 1985; Pastore, 1991; Pastore and Judd, 1992; Richardson, 1981). Percentages for elite sport coaches in other parts of the world such as Asia, Europe, and South Africa range from 56% to 84% (Cheng and Wu, 1987; Krueger and Casselman, 1982; Singh, 2001). An average of 65% of elite development coaches also attain a graduate degree with an additional 9% completing a doctoral degree (Cullen et al., 1990; Cunningham and Sagas, 2002; Freischlag and Jacob, 1988; Kelley and Gill, 1993; Kelley et al., 1999; Latimer and Mathes, 1985; Pastore, 1991; Pastore and Judd, 1992, 1993; Richardson, 1981). The most common college major is physical education or sport studies (Cullen et al., 1990; Cunningham and Sagas, 2002; Freischlag and Jacob, 1988; Knoppers et al., 1989; Krueger and Casselman, 1982; Pastore, 1991, 1992). A few studies show that nearly all coaches in this context have attended some formal coach education clinics or workshops (Freischlag and Jacob, 1988; Singh, 2001) and these coaches have a very strong desire for continual learning (Bloom and Salmela, 2000). These coaches also appear to highly value personal reflection and experimentation as a method of developing coaching skills (Fleurance and Cotteaux, 1999; Gould et al., 1990; Jones et al., 2004; Krueger and Casselman, 1982; Salmela, 1996).

Stress and burnout

Generally elite sport coaches experience only moderate levels of burnout (Hunt and Miller, 1994; Kelley, 1994; Kelley and Gill, 1993; Pastore and Judd, 1992, 1993). Although burnout levels are moderate and comparable to other professions (Kelley et al., 1999), typically more than 50% of coaches report high levels of stress and anxiety about their job (Singh, 2001; Wilson and Bird, 1988; Yow, 2000). Female coaches, however, commonly report significantly higher levels of emotional exhaustion, lower levels of personal accomplishment and confidence, and a greater intent to leave the coaching profession (Baker-Finch, 1991; Caccese and Mayerberg, 1984; Cunningham and Sagas, 2002; Cunningham et al., 2003; Kelley et al., 1999; Pastore and Judd, 1992). The main reason often cited by females for exiting elite coaching is to spend more time with family (Pastore, 1991, 1992; Theberge, 1992). Regardless of

coach gender, coaching during matches in this context can be very stressful both emotionally and physiologically. Several studies show significant physiological stress during matches, such as increased tension and excitement (Kugler et al., 1996) and elevated heart rate averaging over 200% of resting heart rate (Porter and Allsen, 1978).

Influence of coaching research on large-scale program design

Although there is considerable research on a wide range of coaching concepts it is not evident that this information has been used to inform L-S programs. Several scholars have argued that coaching research in general has had very limited, if any, influence on the way coaches are trained or the content of L-S programs (Abraham and Collins, 1998; Lyle, 2002). One reason perhaps for this research-training gap may be the methods by which coaching research is disseminated. Producers of coaching research typically publish their results in scientific journals written for other scientists, and the application or transfer of the findings to coach training and coaching is seldom described in detail. A second reason suggested for the research-training gap is that coaching scientists may have been asking the wrong types of research questions (Abraham and Collins, 1998; Campbell and Crisfield, 1994). For example, are the research questions driven by basic research agendas, which may or may not have application for coaching (Campbell and Crisfield, 1994), or by practical issues in coach training and coaching? This raises two issues for immediate consideration: what are the main research questions that have been posed in coaching research, and who are the main authors of this research?

Information compiled in Gilbert and Trudel's 2004a comprehensive analysis of coaching research provides insight into these issues. They systematically identified and reviewed all English-language coaching research published in journals from 1970–2001. Analysis of the 610 research articles shows that publication of coaching research has increased substantially across the timeframe in part because of the wide range of journals ($n = 161$) that now consider coaching research for publication. This finding alone may help to explain the possible research-training gap in coaching because it now requires significant research skills and resources simply to identify and retrieve the body of research on a particular coaching concept. Woodman (1993) foresaw this challenge many years ago and hypothesized that coaches and sport clubs would someday require an "information-specialist" to facilitate the assimilation and application of coaching research.

In terms of the types of questions that have been posed by coaching scientists, Gilbert and Trudel

(2004a) organized the coaching research into four research categories (that included 54 unique coaching themes). The four categories were coach behaviors, coach thoughts, coach characteristics, and coach career development. Coaching scientists have historically been most interested in documenting what coaches do (behavior). This is still true in the most recent time period of analysis (1998–2001) in which 55.7% of the coaching research focused on documenting coaching behaviors. Coaching research design clearly has been informed heavily by physical education research design, which has relied extensively on systematic observation methods of data collection (Darst et al., 1989). The most commonly examined themes (i.e. coaching concepts) were general coaching behaviors, coach-athlete relationship, coach effectiveness, leadership style, role of the coach, and coach feedback. Research on coach thoughts has increasingly been the focus of coaching research. Common coaching concepts examined in this category include perceptions, knowledge, attitudes, decision-making, and beliefs. Although they have experienced a decline in numbers of published studies in recent years, research on the other two categories – coach characteristics and career development – was still a research focus of over 350 articles. The most frequently studied coaching concepts in the coach characteristics category were gender, demographics, and qualifications. The most often studied coaching concepts in the career development category were career opportunities, interventions, stress and burnout, and coach education/training.

Other findings from the analysis of coaching research include: (a) an emphasis on quantitative research, (b) reliance on questionnaires as the predominant method of data collection, (c) focus on head coaches with less than 30% of the research including multiple types of sport participants (i.e. coaches and athletes), (d) inclusion of both of male and female coaches, and (e) emphasis on school-based team sport coaching.

Although not published in their review, Gilbert and Trudel (2004a) also analyzed the research database to determine the main contributors to coaching research. Many ($n = 856$) different authors have contributed to the coaching science database from 1970–2001. Six authors have contributed at least ten or more journal publications: D. Pastore ($n = 21$), P. Chelladurai (n=13), J. Salmela ($n = 13$), P. Trudel ($n = 13$), D. Gould ($n = 12$), G. Solomon ($n = 10$). Seventeen authors have all authored or co-authored at least six articles (1% of the database) on coaching science since 1970.[1] Furthermore, many of these 17 scholars are collaborators and frequently co-author papers (e.g. Côté and Salmela; Gilbert and Trudel; Smith and Smoll). However, these 17 authors collectively represent only 2% of the authors who have published articles in the coaching science database. The predominance of

what seems to be a "one-shot" study research enterprise means that few scholars have had a programmatic research line in coaching (Hastie, 1992; Kahan, 1999). This limitation of coaching science was also noted in the early 1990s when Hastie concluded that "research in coaching settings remains in the formative stages" and "most studies start de novo" (p. 27). Unfortunately Gilbert and Trudel's findings indicate that in many cases coaching research still has not progressed beyond the formative stage. As noted elsewhere, this type of trend limits the development and application of a field of research (Dodds and Placeck, 1991).

Thus only a small number of scholars appear to have made a sustained contribution to coaching research. Although few in number, their importance is such that they may be referred to as "elders" (Mitchell, 1992), because this term "describes the individuals who control invisible networks of prestige and who determine what information is accepted for publication in professional journals. These published works stand as the foundation for the knowledge base of a discipline" (p. 426). Another characteristic of this cohort of scholars is they tend to focus on one or two categories of the coaching research database. Thus although scholars from different fields have contributed to coaching research, if there is no effort made to work together and combine the different perspectives we will lose an opportunity to create a holistic understanding of the coaching process, and a better understanding of its complexity (Jones et al., 2002; Potrac et al., 2000).

Summary of section one

In sum, coach education was founded on a technical rationality model focused on the delivery of sport science knowledge out of context and assumed a novice-expert coach continuum. Today, comprehensive L-S programs exist in many countries and there is a trend to separate the content into different coaching levels to address the particular needs of the coaches in specific contexts. Based on a review of the literature we have suggested a general coaching context typology. Our review of coaches' characteristics specific to each of three coaching contexts – recreational sport, developmental sport, and elite sport – highlights some important coach differences that should be considered in L-S program design and delivery. Although there is some debate as to the influence of coaching research on coach education and actual coaching, there is a considerable amount of published coaching research that covers numerous coaching concepts. However, there does not appear to be many significant or sustained lines of coaching research. This surely contributes to the lack of a clear conceptual framework for coaching (Lyle, 2002).

At the same time that program content is now more specific to unique coaching contexts there is also a trend to move from a simple "what a coach should know" to "what a coach should do" approach. Although this change will contribute to make coach training more applied, we are still in the acquisition metaphor in the sense that coaches are expected to apply specific scientific knowledge or skills to solve pre-selected problems common in the particular coaching context. This procedure respects the basis of coaching science: "A branch of study and activity concerned with establishing and systematizing facts, principles and methods in order to create procedures having a factual basis – in this case the coaching process on solid fact, not tradition or opinion" (Percival, 1971: 7). As we have already said, one important limit of the acquisition metaphor approach is that the learning activities are happening outside of the real world. Although coaches have repeatedly said that their day-to-day coaching activities are a major source of knowledge (Fleurance and Cotteaux, 1999; Gilbert and Trudel, 2001; Gould et al., 1990; Salmela, 1996) studies on the "art of coaching" (Cushion et al., 2003) as opposed to the "science of coaching" are in their infancy. Percival (1971) defines the art of coaching as:

> The human ability to make things creative; to take from feeling, knowledge and understanding and create an object, an idea, a concept, a production. The application of a skill to create solutions to problems, to mold ideas and thoughts into forms making or producing a whole from a series of parts, as in creating a play or a symphony. To have empathy toward the created object and the ideal purpose or role of it. To produce through creativity a viable result, in this case an athlete or a team. (p. 7)

Presently we can identify two main avenues to explore the art of coaching or, in other terms, learning to coach through experience. When the term experience refers to specific events researchers are looking at how coaches address problematic situations – how they reflect or think. When the term experience refers to the global participation of an individual, the focus is on the social interactions – the process of becoming a coach.

Learning to coach through experience (participation metaphor)

The reflective coach

To be an effective reflective practitioner one needs to do more than merely experience an activity. The role of reflection has been central in many models of experiential learning (Honey and Mumford, 1992;

Kolb, 1984; Lewin, 1951). Based on Moon (1999), the role of reflection in the professions has been highly inspired by the work of Schön (1983). For Schön, it is inadequate to reduce the task of practitioners to applying scientific theories and techniques to solve problems:

> … with this emphasis on problem solving, we ignore problem setting, the process by which we define the decision to be made, the ends to be achieved, the means which may be chosen. In real-world practice, problems do not present themselves to the practitioner as givens. They must be constructed from the materials of problematic situations which are puzzling, troubling, and uncertain. In order to convert a problematic situation to a problem, a practitioner must do a certain kind of work. (p. 40)

At this point, it is important to indicate the main difference between the problem-solving approach used to prepare teachers/coaches and the reflective practice discussed by Schön. As indicated earlier, when teacher/coach educators use the problem-solving approach, the problem is given to the participants for discussion; they do not have to find it. For Schön, "Such cases may usefully display linkages between features of action, outcome, and context, but they do not reveal the path of inquiry which leads from initial framing of the situation to the eventual outcome" (Schön, 1983: 317). The ability to set a problem is said to be particularly important in professions where problems are ill defined. Coaching is one such profession (Gilbert and Trudel, 2001; Saury and Durand, 1998).

Adopting Schön's (1983; 1987) concepts of reflective practice for understanding how coaches learn to coach is a move from a scientific perspective to an artistic perspective. This means leaving the technical rationality that "holds that practitioners are instrumental problem solvers who select technical means best suited to particular purposes" (Schön, 1987: 3) for an epistemology where coaches are considered artists which "refer to practitioners unusually adept at handling situations of uncertainty, uniqueness, and conflict" (Schön, 1987: 16). This move however does not mean a return to the mystery of coaching or the fatal assumption that successful coaches are born or have some unknown innate ability to coach.

> The dilemma of rigor or relevance may be dissolved if we can develop an epistemology of practice which places technical problem solving within a broader context of reflective inquiry, shows how reflection-in-action may be rigorous in its own right, and links the art of practice in uncertainty and uniqueness to the scientist's art of research. We may thereby increase the legitimacy of reflection-in-action and encourage its broader, deeper, and more rigorous use. (Schön, 1983: 69)

Using Schön's (1983, 1987) theoretical framework and taking into consideration the critiques of Schön's work (Munby and Russell, 1989; Usher et al., 1997) as well as the literature on coaching, Gilbert and Trudel (2001) explored how model youth sport coaches develop knowledge during their day-to-day coaching activities. Coaches used three types of reflection: reflection-in-action (during games or practices), reflection-on-action (after games and practices), and retrospective reflection-on-action (at the end of the season). Because of the research design used, data on reflection-on-action dominated. Results show that coaches will identify a situation as problematic or a coaching issue based on their coaching philosophy, also referred to as their coaching role frame (Gilbert and Trudel, 2001, 2004). When facing a coaching issue, the coach will start a reflective conversation composed of four components: issue setting, strategy generation, experimentation, and evaluation. The selection of options at each stage in a reflective conversation is influenced by access to peers, the coach's stage of learning, the issue characteristics, and the environment (Gilbert and Trudel, 2005). The study clearly shows that model youth sport coaches[2] learn through experience and that reflection on their actions should not be perceived as an isolated activity, but instead as a social activity. The value of head coach consultations with assistant coaches, respected peers and players to check the accuracy of their assumptions has also been found in studies with elite sport coaches (Fleurance and Cotteaux, 1999; Jones et al., 2004; Strean et al., 1997).

The social process of becoming a coach

From a sociocultural perspective interacting with others in context is an important condition for learning. Vygotsky (1978), one of the most influential authors to support the theory that children's cognitive development can not be understood without reference to the social milieu, proposed the concept of "zone of proximal development" in which child development is the result of participation in activities just beyond their competence with the assistance of more skilled others (particularly adults). For Sfard (1998), many studies using sociocultural theories could be categorized as part of an acquisition metaphor: "As long as they investigated learning by focusing on the 'development of concepts' and on 'acquisition of knowledge', however, they implicitly agreed that this process [learning] can be conceptualized in terms of the acquisition metaphor" (p. 6). Among the researchers who extended the work of Vygotsky some focused less on the internally driven maturation and more on the constant inter-action with the world (Stetsenko and

Arievitch, 1997: 160). For example, Rogoff (1995) suggested the concept of "participatory appropriation" in which cognition is not defined: "as a collection of stored possessions (such as thoughts, representations, memories, plans), but rather treats thinking, re-presenting, remembering, and planning as active processes that cannot be reduced to the possession of stored objects" (p. 151).

While studies on child thinking and development were based on a sociocultural approach to cognitive development, studies on the situated nature of learning for adults have been influenced largely by the work of Lave (1982; 1988; Lave and Wenger, 1991) who advocated an anthropological approach to research on learning:

> Although we have a long tradition of importing psychological and linguistic theory into anthropology, it may not be the (only) appropriate course to pursue today. We are in a position to make a useful contribution to the understanding of learning by pursuing an anthropological approach that emphasizes the socially organized nature of learning. (Lave, 1982: 186)

Recently Wenger (1998) extended the work of Lave by explaining in detail the concept of communities of practice defined as "groups of people who share a concern, a set of problems, or a passion about a topic, and who deepen their knowledge and expertise in this area by interacting on an ongoing basis" (Wenger et al., 2002: 4).

In reviewing the literature on the process of becoming a coach, research is available on how coaches learn values and ways to behave (Sage, 1989) and on the development of knowledge related to the coaching process (Bloom et al., 1997). In some studies both types of information are available (Bloom et al., 1998; Jones et al., 2003). It is noteworthy to now find research conducted on the social and cultural nature of the coaching process in many different countries including Australia, United Kingdom, New Zealand (Jones et al., 2003, 2004; Potrac et al., 2002), Canada (Strean, 1995; Trudel and Gilbert, 2004), France (Fleurance and Cotteaux, 1999; Saury and Durand, 1998) and the United States (McCallister et al., 2000).

Perhaps the earliest account of a formal study using a sociocultural perspective in coaching was Sage's (1989) research with developmental sport coaches in the United States. The research was framed specifically in organizational and role theory perspectives that emphasize the function of social interactions and situated learning in the process of acquiring occupational skills, knowledge, and values. Data were collected over a 5-month period observing and interviewing 50 participants. No formally organized experiential learning process, or social interactions among coaches, was evident.

Instead it was found that coaching skills, knowledge, and values were learned through constant observation of and listening to more experienced coaches. This socialization process, which resulted in the development of collective understandings and shared meanings about coaching and its culture, actually began when the participants were athletes many years prior to becoming a coach. Sage referred to this experience as "an informal apprenticeship of prolonged observation" (p. 87).

This informal apprenticeship seems to be typical of most sport coaches (Bloom et al., 1998; Dunn and Dunn, 1992; Knoppers et al., 1989; Krueger and Casselman, 1982; Latimer and Mathes, 1985; Richardson, 1981; Saury and Durand, 1998). Successful developmental sport and elite sport coaches accumulated an average of over 4600 hours as athletes (Gilbert et al., 2006). Furthermore, Gilbert and colleagues found that coaches played an average of four sports per year as athletes, thereby being exposed to many different coaching styles, strategies, and values. It is not known if this pre-coaching experience is correlated with future coaching competency. However, Sage (1989) clearly showed that this apprenticeship of observation (Lortie, 1975) does indeed provides coaches with tacit knowledge about the sport and coaching roles. Coaches draw heavily on their athletic experience while coaching and believe it equips them with the ability to adequately demonstrate techniques which are important in gaining player respect (Hardin, 2000; Potrac et al., 2002).

Coaches, specifically those at the elite sport level, proceed from athletes to assistant coaches, where they may spend five or more years (Braddock, 1981; Capel et al., 1987; Cullen et al., 1990; Dale and Weinberg, 1989; Frederick and Morrison, 1999; Pastore and Judd, 1993; Weiss and Stevens, 1993). This process may be referred to as "legitimate peripheral participation" that is: "a way to speak about the relations between newcomers and old-timers, and about activities, identities, artifacts, and communities of knowledge and practice" (Lave and Wenger, 1991: 29). Based on this definition, the engagement of the assistant coach should not be limited to observing a head coach and waiting for this expert to share parts of their knowledge. Because learning takes place in a participatory framework and not in an individual mind "Teachers, masters, and specific role models can be important, but it is by virtue of their membership in the community as a whole that they can play their roles" (Wenger, 1998: 100). Although most elite sport coaches tend to assume the role of assistant before becoming a head coach, it is not as common at the developmental sport coaching level and it is extremely rare in the recreational sport context where parents are often asked to volunteer because of coaching shortages (McCallister et al., 2000).

When people assume the role of head coach, they will inevitably engage in interactions with "others". At the elite sport level, coaches will exchange ideas on a daily basis with their assistant coaches but they often will also work with sport specialists such as nutritionists, sport psychologists, and athletic trainers (Durand-Bush, 1996; Lyle, 2002). Therefore, it becomes more important to know where and how to find information and guidance than to try to learn everything. Depending of the type of interactions coaches have, these interactions will be referred to as networks of practice, informal knowledge networks or a community of practice. In networks of practice "most members are unknown to one another ... The members hardly meet face-to-face, yet they contribute and help each other out regularly. This type of community readily adapts to the Internet and other communication technologies" (Nichani and Hung, 2002: 50). In the informal knowledge networks, people know one another and exchange information but "they are loose and informal because there is no joint enterprise that holds them together, such as the development of shared tools. They are just a set of relationships" (Allee, 2000: Communities of practice section, para. 8). The existence of an informal knowledge network, and its centrality to learning how to coach, was clearly revealed in Sage's (1989) pioneering study with developmental sport coaches. Members in a community of practice, on the other hand, work together closely and there is a "sense of mission – there is something people want to accomplish or do together that arises from their shared understanding" (Allee, 2000: Communities of practice section, para. 8).

Summary of section two

In sum, an important part of learning how to coach occurs outside L-S programs. This learning through experience – the art of coaching – is more than "doing". Coaches must become competent at setting problems and then developing and evaluating their strategies for solving the problems they have identified. Without this reflective process, coaches might simply accrue experience without becoming more effective coaches (Douge and Hastie, 1993; Gilbert and Trudel, 2001). For many coaches, specifically developmental sport and elite sport coaches, learning how to coach begins many years before becoming a head coach. The progression consists of observing coaches while in the role of athlete and then as an assistant coach. When assuming the role of head coach, coaches will still continue to learn through engagement in social interactions with "others". These interactions will vary in terms of how much these "others" are concerned with the coach's coaching issues, which in turn will influence the form and content of the social interactions.

Conclusion and directions for future research

We have organized this chapter around the two learning metaphors of acquisition and participation. Tension between the two learning metaphors has been present in coaching for many years. For people in the scientific community, the tendency can be to maintain that informal (participation) learning should not be taken seriously because it is less structured and knowledge created through this method is often structured much differently than formal coaching science. Thus, the elaboration of a L-S program that will recognize both the science and the art of coaching is far from obvious. However, for Sfard (1998), the solution could be to recognize both ways of learning how to coach as: "too great a devotion to one particular metaphor can lead to theoretical distortions and to undesirable practices" (p. 4). Considering our analysis of learning to coach through both metaphors "it now seems that we can live neither with nor without either of them" (p. 10).

Determining who should be responsible for coach preparation is a major dilemma in coaching. As presented in the first section of this chapter, in some countries, a national governing body may offer a L-S program and oversee accreditation. But this does not prevent colleges and universities from offering coaching programs that vary from a few college credits to a complete degree. Furthermore, coaches can also now complete L-S programs via the Internet (Human Kinetics, 2004). Is professionalisation of coaching the solution? If being a profession means among other things to have the "capacity to identify a body of knowledge and skills, to educate its initiates, to promote its distinctive values and to defend its boundaries" (Lyle, 2002: xiv), predominance will be given to the science of coaching as opposed to the art of coaching. The same result might occur if higher education institutions assume control of coach education. For example, college physical education departments in many countries (Australia, Canada, United Kingdom, United States) have changed their name (e.g. sport science, exercise science, kinesiology) to appear more scientific. In most cases the name change resulted in curriculum changes "involving pressure to reduce physical activity content to make way for more 'academic' content particularly in the biophysical sciences" (Kirk and Macdonald, 2001, p. 450).

To promote an approach to coach development that recognizes both the science and the art of coaching, researchers must show openness regarding their research paradigms – their ontological, epistemological and methodological perspectives (Culver et al., 2003; Potrac et al., 2000; Sparkes, 1992). The number of research issues in coaching and coach education is in some sense unlimited. We would like, however, to suggest a short list of research issues we believe are important for investigation.

Evaluation of large-scale programs

In a report on the evaluation of the Australian National Coach Accreditation Scheme (Dickson, 2001) it was noted that only one published study was found on evaluating coach education programs (Gilbert and Trudel, 1999). Therefore, there is no evidence to suggest that certification through a coach education program is correlated with coaching competency: "there are governing bodies that certify coaches based on the successful completion of our program, but we don't certify competency of coaches" (Cohen, 1992: 25). Instead, the primary outcomes from coaching certification programs may be coaching confidence and awareness as opposed to coaching competency (Conn and Razor, 1989). It has been consistently shown that coaching efficacy – coaches' belief in their coaching ability – significantly increases immediately after completing a coach education course (Feltz et al., 1999; Malete and Feltz, 2000). Although this is a positive short-term outcome of coach education, there is no evidence that coach efficacy is maintained once coaches enter the field. Furthermore, coaching efficacy is not a measure of coaching competency. Clearly evaluation of coach education effectiveness is a critical need for future research in coaching and coach education. Gilbert and Trudel (1999) discuss the main issues when designing evaluations of coach education programs, and their evaluation framework can be used as a guide for this type of research. A related task that needs to be addressed is to identify and clearly define the dependent variables to use as indicators of effective coaching, specific to each of the three coaching contexts described in the current chapter.

Leaving the novice-expert continuum for a specific coaching context approach

Structuring coach education programs for specific coaching contexts has the advantage of regrouping coaches with similar needs, and therefore it should be easier to develop specific competences. If a problem-solving approach is also used, which favors active participation, then key assumptions about adult learning are respected (Knowles et al., 1998). The recent changes in some L-S programs that include a problem-based approach (i.e. Coaching Association of Canada) are certainly interesting. However, we do not yet have any empirical studies that show if this new approach will be more effective than what we had before. One factor that can limit the potential of the new approach is that program designers often try to condense coach education courses because lack of time is a key concern for coaches in all contexts. Unfortunately, a problem-based approach requires considerable time for participants to define the nature of the problem and how they can deal with it using a variety of resources (Jarvis et al., 1998). If participants are encouraged to work collaboratively in small groups, it is important to give them time to develop trust and rapport. The limited amount of time that beginning coaches have to invest in their preparation has been noted (Abraham and Collins, 1998), and the appropriateness of "weekend education programs" is questionable if we want to facilitate coach development by taking their experience into account (Savard and Brunelle, 1998). Literature in the education field (Barab and Duffy, 2000; Brown et al., 1989; McLellan, 1996), including physical education (Kirk and Macdonald, 1998), on how to design learning contexts in schools that respect the social nature of cognition can provide guidance for research on coach education.

Programs developed on a competency-based model raise another interesting research topic. In the past, coaches were generally assessed mainly through formal exams because the objective was to evaluate "what coaches knew". But now, the evaluation is about "what coaches do" and, to be credible, the evaluation process will have to be done in a real context. Therefore a new group of "experts", the evaluators, will have to be included in the structure. These evaluators will have to be knowledgeable about the specific competences expected of coaches in each coaching context and about how to assess competences. Studies on how to train these evaluators and on how to achieve reliability between evaluators would be very helpful.

The importance of coach refletion on their experiences

If in the field of education (including physical education) there is a general agreement that programs "cannot prepare teachers for every situation they may encounter [and therefore] it is preferable to help them become thoughtful decision makers" (Tsangaridou and Siedentop, 1995: 213) then this measure will be even more important for coaches considering their very limited formal education. However, despite this agreement "reflective teaching has different meanings, different approaches towards implementation, and little consensus on what ought to be the object of reflection" (Tsangaridou and Siedentop, 1995: 213).

The literature on reflective coaching seems almost non-existent. The only study we have

presented (Gilbert and Trudel, 2001) tends to suggest that model youth sport coaches will use a reflective conversation and its quality is influenced by conditions such as access to peers, stage of learning of the coach, the perception of the importance of the issue based on their coaching philosophy and support from the sport organization (Gilbert and Trudel, 2005). Thus, studies on the reflective coaching process of coaches in different coaching contexts are needed.

For those interested in examining the topic of reflection, the work of a few key authors should first be reviewed. Based on Dodds (1995), much of the research conducted by North American scholars has been influenced by Dewey (1938/1963), Schön (1983, 1987), Van Manen (1977), and Kemmis and McTaggart (1988). We would like to also add Zeichner (1981; 1987) to this list. In the field of physical education, Lawson (1980, 1984) and Tinning (1985, 1987) are probably the first to discuss the concept of reflective teaching (Crum, 1995) although "they do not completely agree on the process through which problems are defined" (Rossi and Cassidy, 1999: 190). More recent research on the topic of reflection in physical education has been published by Rovengo (1992), Tsangaridou and O'Sullivan (1994, 1997, 2003), and Tsangaridou and Siedentop (1995).

Limits of the process of becoming a coach

Learning from experience requires the ability to identify and set complex problems and then develop and test a solution. It is also a process of becoming, or learning how to fit within the context by learning the language and cultural norms of coaching. Is that learning always in line with societal expectations? The many scandals evident in sport make us wonder about the value of what coaches learn within the sport context. Each sport has its own sub-culture that is, on certain aspects at least, of questionable value. For example, the sub-culture of violence in youth ice hockey in Canada and the US has been denounced for years by researchers (Smith, 1975; Smith et al., 1997; Vaz, 1979) and medical associations (American Academy of Pediatrics, 2000). Yet those in charge of the game are unable to bring changes and even more tend to resist any suggestions that will change how the game is played (Bernard and Trudel, 2004; Smith et al., 2000). Skepticism regarding the pertinence of modifying conventional sport programs seems to be a common reaction (Green, 1997). Considering the few studies on how coaches learn through interactions with others in their daily activities, more studies are needed to reveal the uniqueness of different coaching contexts, and to identify ways to address the factors that limit learning experiences, specifically for underrepresented groups such as women coaches (Inglis et al., 2000; Landers and Fine, 1996; McCallister et al., 2000; Pastore, 1992; Pastore and Judd, 1992; Sagas et al., 2000) and coaches of color (Anderson, 1993; Knoppers and Anthonissen, 2001; Rosenberg, 1990).

Initiatives to increase knowledge exchanges between coaches have been suggested (e.g. Gilbert and Trudel, 2004b) but studies are needed to assess the effectiveness of the different types of exchange opportunities such as networks of practice, informal knowledge networks, and communities of practice (Culver and Trudel, in press). Some central elements that characterize sport tend to limit the sharing of information and make the development of a coaches' community of practice impossible:

> When winning is what drives coaches, isolationism takes root and coaches see other coaches as enemies not partners. This individualistic approach refrains coaches from engaging with other coaches in their league while searching for solutions to common problems. This context is best described in terms of an individual enterprise instead of a joint enterprise. (Trudel and Gilbert, 2004)

Even in the teaching context where competition is absent, collaboration among teachers in the same department is not guaranteed. Stroot et al., (1994) found that within a physical education department some teachers "taught their own classes in their own teaching stations and had virtually no professional interactions with their co-workers" (p. 358). Can we overcome this problem in coaching?

Combining the two ways of learning how to coach?

As we are describing two ways of learning how to coach, it becomes evident that each has limits. Therefore, should we consider combining them? Just by asking this question, there is a potential debate regarding the logic of even thinking about combining two approaches that differ so much on how learning is defined. But this problem of incompatibility can be reduced if we consider two things. First, as we said before, there is a general agreement that L-S programs, based on a novice-expert continuum and delivered only through lectures, are not very effective. Therefore, as an alternative, new programs for coaches in specific coaching contexts using a problem-based model have been developed. This recent change brings coach education programs closer (but not there yet) to actual practice. Second, learning how to coach that happens through interactions with others (process of becoming) is an inevitable phenomenon. Because we are talking in terms of knowing and not knowledge

(Sfard, 1998), control of the content is impossible. The only thing that can be done is to facilitate the interactions and cultivate a community of practice (Wenger et al., 2002). Therefore, those in charge of coach education programs should recognize and accept that learning will also happen outside of their program (Werthner and Trudel, 2006).

Our problem then is reduced to this question: Is it possible, within a L-S program structured to fulfill the specific needs of coaches, to teach coaches the reflective process that they will use later in their practice and then continue to learn? If coaches' theories of action (what coaches say they do) are similar to their theories-in-use (what coaches do in their professional practice) coach educators could help coaches "bring to light the theories that guide their actions so that these theories and actions can be refined, adjusted, or restructured as appropriate" (Tsangaridou and O'Sullivan, 2003: 148). Unfortunately, studies looking at the adequacy between these two theories for coaches do not reach the same conclusion (e.g. Bernard and Trudel, 2004; Strong, 1992). Reflective pedagogical strategies (journals, portfolios, videos, group discussions, and so on) that have been developed and implemented to teach students how to reflect could be adapted for coaches. However, these strategies require time, commitment and programmatic efforts (Tsangaridou and O'Sullivan, 1994). For Rovengo (1992), "the desire to foster reflection does not carry with it any easy answer" (p. 509). Thus, how much of these strategies can be used with volunteer or part-time coaches taking a coach education program dispensed over one or two weekends? More importantly, under such conditions, will learning how to reflect be used in actual coaching practice once coaches return to the field? For Tsangaridou and Siedentop (1995): "Educators seem to assume that reflective thinking learned via reflective practice would be retained, generalized, and/or transferred in ordinary settings. No evidence exists to support this assumption" (p. 228).

For Schön (1987), the answer to our problem can be found in the reflective practicum defined as "a practicum aimed at helping students acquire the kinds of artistry essential to competence in the indeterminate zones of practice" (p. 18). If this option is to be retained, program designers will have to go back to the drawing table because they will have to "rethink both the epistemology of practice and the pedagogical assumptions on which their curricula are based and must bend their institutions to accommodate the reflective practicum as a key element of professional education" (p. 18). At the center of a reflective practicum there is a dialog of reciprocal reflection-in-action between a student and an instructor (Schön calls him/her a coach). This dialog, which can last over many encounters, has at its starting point a real task performed by the student. Therefore, "a reflective practicum demands intensity and duration far beyond the normal requirements of a course" (Schön, 1987: 311). Thus, one might wonder if the typical youth sport system that relies predominantly on volunteer coaches can afford this type of coach education (Campbell and Crisfield, 1994). As we can see, more research is needed to find out what will be more effective ways to nurture coach development.

Using mentors to foster coach development

We will like to end this short list of future research issues by addressing the role that mentors play (or should play) in coach development. In the last decade, mentoring has often been suggested as a way to improve coach education (Bloom et al., 1998; Campbell and Crisfield, 1994; Cushion et al., 2003; Lyle, 2002; Saury and Durand, 1998). This suggestion finds legitimacy in the results of interviews in which coaches emphasized how much they have learned watching and/or working with a coach they respected and admired. Thus in most cases the mentors were not assigned to coaches, "finding a mentor was often the case of being at the right place at the right time. With a bit of luck and personal persistence, novice coaches were able to find a mentor with whom they shared their passion for their sport and for coaching" (Bloom et al., 1998: 274). Can a formalized and structured mentoring program, where mentors are selected, accredited and to a certain extent imposed on coaches, be effective? More research is needed to better understand the role, the preparation and the impact of mentors considering that mentors can be considered (a) a "research-practice facilitator" (Gilbert and Trudel, 2004b) or an "information-specialist" (Woodman, 1993) who will help coaches retrieve and use the coaching literature, (b) a "supervisor-mentor" who is assigned to a group of coaches to help them master specific competencies and/or reflect on their coaching (Knowles et al., 2001; Krane et al., 1991), (c) a "model-mentor" who as a coach accepts to take a novice coach under his/her wings (Weiss et al., 1991), and (d) a "facilitator-mentor" who will structure and cultivate coaches' communities of practice (Trudel and Gilbert, 2004).

It is our hope that the content of this chapter will contribute to a better understanding of coaching and coach education research. At a time when considerable coaching science is produced (Gilbert and Trudel, 2004a) that can be shared across the world instantly via Internet, learning how to stay current, interpret, and synthesize this body of literature will present new challenges for coaches and coach education designers. Sport coaches, and those who train them, must be "perpetual students" who constantly seek new information, as increased professionalization of coaching will continue to bring closer scrutiny of coaches and L-S programs (Campbell and Crisfield, 1994). Thus there is no shortage of exciting challenges for those conducting research in coaching and coach education.

Notes

1 The following list of authors who have contributed to at least 1% ($n = 6$) of the coaching science database is provided as a guide for conducting literature searches. Many of these authors have also published coaching literature in conference proceedings, books and book chapters: D. Pastore ($n = 21$), P. Chelladurai ($n = 13$), J. Salmela ($n = 13$), P. Trudel ($n = 13$), D. Gould ($n = 12$), G. Solomon ($n = 10$), M. Weiss ($n = 9$), A. Carron ($n = 8$), W. Gilbert ($n = 8$), R. Smith (n=8), F. Smoll (n=8), G. Bloom ($n = 7$), J. Côté ($n = 7$), P. Hastie ($n = 7$), B. Sisley ($n = 7$), R. Weinberg ($n = 7$) and I. Franks ($n = 6$).

2 Model youth sport coaches were defined as coaches who "(a) demonstrated interest in learning about the theory and practice of coaching; (b) respected in the local sporting community for their commitment to youth sport; (c) considered good leaders, teachers and organizers; and (d) kept winning in perspective and encouraged children to respect the rules of the game, their competitors and officials" (Gilbert and Trudel, 2001: 18). Model youth sport coaches were identified through consultation with local sport administrators (i.e. coaching directors).

References

Abraham, A. and Collins, D. (1998). Examining and extending research in coach development. *Quest, 50:* 59–79.

Acosta, R.V. and Carpenter, L.J. (1992). As the years go by – coaching opportunities in the 1990s. *Journal of Physical Education, Recreation and Dance, 63*(3): 36–41.

Albinson, J. (1973). Professionalized attitudes of volunteer coaches toward playing a game. *International Review of Sport Psychology, 8*(2): 77–87.

Allee, V. (2000). Knowledge networks and communities of practice. Journal of the *Organization Development Network, 32*(4). Retrieved July 14, 2004, from http://www.odnetwork.org/odponline/vol32n4/knowledgenets.html

American Academy of Pediatrics. (Committee on Sports Medicine and Fitness). (2000). Safety in youth ice hockey: The effects of body checking. *Pediatrics, 105* (3 Pt 1): 657–658.

Anderson, D. (1993). Cultural diversity on campus: A look at intercollegiate football coaches. *Journal of Sport and Social Issues, 17*(1): 61–66.

Baker-Finch, S. (1991). Women in leadership in Australian sport. *Sports Coach, 14*(4): 13–15.

Barab, S.A. and Duffy, T.M. (2000). From practice fields to communities of practice. In D.H. Jonassen and S.M. Land

(Eds.), *Theoretical foundations of learning environments* (pp. 25–55). Mahweh, NJ: Lawrence Erlbaum Associates.

Barber, H., Sukhi, H. and White, S.A. (1996). The influence of parent-coaches on participant motivation and competitive anxiety in youth sport participants. *Journal of Sport Behavior, 22*: 162–180.

Bennett, G. and Maneval, M. (1998). Leadership styles of elite Dixie youth baseball coaches. *Perceptual and Motor Skills, 87*(3): 754.

Bernard, D. and Trudel, P. (2004). Coaches' and players' values about rule infractions, violence and ethics. In D.J. Pearsall and A.B. Ashare (Eds.), *Safety in ice hockey: Fourth volume, ASTM STP 1446* (pp. 152–166). West Conshohoken, PA: ASTM International.

Bloom, B. (1985). *Developing talent in young people.* New York: Ballantine.

Bloom, G.A., Durand-Bush, N., Schinke, R.J. and Salmela, J.H. (1998). The importance of mentoring in the development of coaches and athletes. *International Journal of Sport Psychology, 29*: 267–281.

Bloom, G.A. and Salmela, J.H. (2000). Personal characteristics of expert team sport coaches. *Journal of Sport Pedagogy, 6*(2): 56–76.

Bloom, G.A., Schinke, R.J. and Salmela, J.H. (1997). The development of communication skills by elite basketball coaches. *Coaching and Sport Science Journal, 2*(3): 3–10.

Braddock, J.H. (1981). Race and leadership in professional sports: A study of institutional discrimination in the National Football League. *Arena Review, 5*(2): 16–25.

Brandt, D. and Elam, R. (1987). A survey of leadership styles of high school head coaches in El Paso County. *Texas Coach, 32*(Sept): 48–50.

Bratton, R. (1978). Why coaches coach. *Canadian Journal of Health Physical Education and Recreation, 45*: 26–29.

Brown, J.S., Collins, A. and Duguid, P. (1989). Situated cognition and the culture of learning. *Educational Researcher, 33*: 32–42.

Caccese, T.M. and Mayerberg, C.K. (1984). Gender differences in perceived burnout of college coaches. *Journal of Sport Psychology, 6*: 279–288.

Calloway, D.J. and Driscoll, M.L. (1983). Leadership style of women basketball coaches. *Women's Varsity Sports, 4*(mar/apr): 7–8.

Campbell, S. (1993). Coaching education around the world. *Sport Science Review, 2*(2): 62–74.

Campbell, S. and Crisfield, P. (1994). Developing and delivering a quality-controlled coach certification programme. In P. Duffy and Dugdale, L. (Eds.) *HPER-Moving toward the 21st century* (pp. 201–211). Champaign, IL: Human Kinetics.

Capel, S.A., Sisley, B.L. and Desertrain, G.S. (1987). The relationship of role conflict and role ambiguity to burnout in high school basketball coaches. *Journal of Sport Psychology, 9*: 106–117.

Chelladurai, P., Haggerty, T.R. and Baxter, P.R. (1989). Decision style choices of university basketball coaches and players. *Journal of Sport and Exercise Psychology, 11*: 201–215.

Chelladurai, P. and Quek, C. B. (1995). Decision style choices of high school basketball coaches: The effects of situational and coach characteristics. *Journal of Sport Behavior, 18*: 91–108.

Cheng, H. and Wu, Y. (1987). Comparison of the personality traits of judo coaches and athletes. *Asian Journal of Physical Education, 9*(4): 23–37.

Chng, C.L. and Field, J.G. (1993). An analysis of perceived burnout among Texas high school football coaches. *Texas Coach, 38*(May): 23–27.

Chu, D. and Segrave, J.O. (1981). Leadership recruitment and ethnic stratification in basketball. *Journal of Sport and Social Issues, 5*(1): 13–22.

Coaching Association of Canada. (2005). *Training and certification.* Retrieved May 16, 2005, from http://www.coach.ca/eng/certification/index.cfm

Cody, C. (1988). The CAHPERD study of Colorado coaches (part 2): Demographic data. *Colorado, 14*(Summer): 7–8.

Cohen, A. (1992, December). Standard time. *Athletic Business,* 23–28.

Collier, C.S. and O'Sullivan, M. (1997). Case method in physical education higher education: A pedagogy of change? *Quest, 49*, 198–213.

Conn, J. and Razor, J. (1989). Certification of coaches – A legal and moral responsibility. *The Physical Educator, 46*: 161–165.

Corso, M., Steffen, J. and Cody, C. (1988). The CAHPERD Study of Colorado Coaches (Part 3): Current preparation to coach and future coaching needs. *Colorado, 14*(Spring), 11.

Côté, J, Baker, J. and Abernethy, B. (2003). From play to practice: A developmental framework for the acquisition of expertise in team sports. In J.L. Starkes and K. Anders Ericsson (Eds.), *Expert performance in sports: Advances in research on sport expertise* (pp. 89–113). Champaign, IL: Human Kinetics.

Côté, J., Salmela, J., Trudel, P., Baria, A. and Russell, S. (1995). The coaching model: A grounded assessment of expert gymnastic coaches' knowledge. *Journal of Sport and Exercise Psychology, 17*(1): 1–17.

Cox, R. and Noble, L. (1989). Preparation and the attitudes of Kansas high school head coaches. *Journal of Teaching in Physical Education, 8*: 329–341.

Crum, B. (1995). Le besoin urgent pour une pratique réflexive [The urgent need for reflective teaching in physical education]. In C. Paré (Ed.), *Mieux enseigner l'éducation physique? Pensez-y!* [*Better Teaching in Physical Education? Think about it!*] (pp. 1–20). Trois-Rivières, Québec: Département des sciences de l'activité physique.

Cullen, F., Latessa, E. and Byrne, J. (1990). Scandal and reform in collegiate athletics: Implications from a national survey of head football coaches. *Journal of Higher Education, 61*(1): 50–64.

Culver, D. and Trudel, P. (in press). Cultivating coaches' communities of practice: Developing the potential for learning through interactions. In R. Jones, *Re-conceptualising the coaching role and how to teach it: New ways of thinking about practice.* London: Routledge.

Culver, D., Gilbert, W. and Trudel, P. (2003). A decade of qualitative research in sport psychology journals: 1990–1999. *The Sport Psychologist, 17*: 1–15.

Cunningham, G.B. and Sagas, M. (2002). The differential effects of human capital for male and female division I basketball coaches. *Research Quarterly for Exercise and Sport, 73*: 489–495.

Cunningham, G.B., Sagas, M. and Ashley, F.B. (2003). Coaching self-efficacy, desire to become a head coach and occupational turnover intent: Gender differences between NCAA assistant coaches of women's teams. *International Journal of Sport Psychology, 34*: 125–137.

Curtis, B., Smith, R.E. and Smoll, F.L. (1979). Scrutinizing the skipper: A study of leadership behaviors in the dugout. *Journal of Applied Behavior Analysis, 64*(4): 391–400.

Cushion, C.J., Armour, K.M. and Jones, R.L. (2003). Coach education and continuing professional development: Experience and learning to coach. *Quest, 55*: 215–230.

Dale, J. and Weinberg, R.S. (1989). The relationship between coaches' leadership style and burnout. *The Sport Psychologist, 3*: 1–13.

Darst, P.W., Zakrajsek, D.B. and Mancini, V.H. (1989). (Eds.). *Analyzing physical education and sport instruction* (2nd ed.). Champaign, IL: Human Kinetics.

De Knop, P., Engström, L-M., Skirstad, B. and Weiss M. (Eds.), (1996). *Worldwide trends in youth sport*. Champaign, IL: Human Kinetics.

DePauw, K. and Gavron, S.J. (1991). Coaches of athletes with disabilities. *The Physical Educator, 48*(1): 33–40.

Dewey, J. (1938/1963). *Experience and education*. NewYork: Collier.

Dickson, S. (2001). *A preliminary investigation into the effectiveness of the national coach accreditation scheme*. Canberra: Australian Sports Commission.

Dodds, P. (1995). La préparation à l'enseignement réflexif: un paradigme pour une croissance professionnelle ou seulement un mirage? [Training for reflexive teaching: A paradigm or a mirage!]. In C. Paré (Ed.), *Mieux enseigner l'éducation physique? Pensez-y!* [*Better Teaching in Physical Education? Think about it!*] (pp. 69–88). Trois-Rivières, Québec : Département des sciences de l'activité physique.

Dodds, P. and Placek, J.H. (1991). Silverman's RT-PE review: Too simple a summary of a complex field. *Research Quarterly for Exercise and Sport, 62*: 365–368.

Dodds, P., Placek, J.H., Doolittle, S., Pinkham, K.M., Ratliffe, T.A. and Portman, P.A. (1991). Teacher/coach recruits: Background profiles, occupational decision factors, and comparisons with recruits into other physical education occupations. *Journal of Teaching in Physical Education, 11*: 161–176.

Douge, B. and Hastie, P. (1993). Coach effectiveness. *Sport Science Review, 2*(2): 14–29.

Dunn, T.P. and Dunn, S.L. (1992). The graduate assistant coach: A preliminary profile of an endangered species. *The Physical Educator, 49*: 189–193.

Durand-Bush, N. (1996). Training: Blood, sweat and tears. In J.H. Salmela (Ed.), *Great job coach: Getting the edge from proven Winners* (pp. 103–139). Ottawa, ON: Potentium.

Dwyer, J.J.M. and Fischer, D.G. (1988a). Leadership styles of wrestling coaches. *Perceptual and Motor Skills, 67*(3): 706.

Dwyer, J.J.M. and Fischer, D.G. (1988b). Psychometric properties of the coach's version of leadership scale for sports. *Perceptual and Motor Skills, 67*(3): 795–798.

Eitzen, D.S. and Pratt, S.R. (1989). Gender differences in coaching philosophy: The case of female basketball teams. *Research Quarterly for Exercise and Sport, 60*: 152–158.

Ewing, M.E., Seefeldt, V.D. and Brown, T.P. (1996). *Role of organized sport in the education and health of American children and youth*. E. Lansing, MI: Institute for the Study of Youth Sports.

Feltz, D.L., Chase, M.A., Moritz, S. and Sullivan, P.A. (1999). A conceptual model of coaching efficacy: Preliminary investigation and instrument development. *Journal of Educational Psychology, 91*: 765–776.

Fleurance, P. and Cotteaux, V. (1999). Construction de l'expertise chez les entraîneurs sportifs d'athlètes de haut-niveau français [Development of expertise in elite athletics coaches in France]. *Avante, 5*(2): 54–68.

Frederick, C. and Morrison, C. (1999). Collegiate coaches: An examination of motivational style and its relationship to decision making and personality. *Journal of Sport Behavior, 22*: 221–233.

Freischlag, J. and Jacob, R. (1988). Developmental factors among college men basketball coaches. *Applied Research in Coaching and Athletics Annual, 3*: 87–93.

Gaunt, S.J. and Forbus, W.R. (1991). Qualifications of high school coaches in Georgia. *Georgia, 25*: 14–16.

Gilbert, W.D., Côté, J. and Mallett, C. (2006). Developmental paths and activities of successful sport coaches. *International Journal of Sports Sciences and Coaching, 1*(1): 69–76.

Gilbert, W. and Trudel, P. (1999). An evaluation strategy for coach education programs. *Journal of Sport Behavior, 22*: 234–250.

Gilbert, W. and Trudel, P. (2001). Learning to coach through experience: Reflection in model youth sport coaches. *Journal of Teaching in Physical Education, 21*(1): 16–34.

Gilbert, W. and Trudel, P. (2004a). Analysis of coaching science published from 1970–2001. *Research Quarterly for Exercise and Sport, 75*: 388–399.

Gilbert, W. and Trudel, P. (2004b). Role of the coach: How model youth team sport coaches frame their roles. *The Sport Psychologist, 18*: 21–43.

Gilbert, W. and Trudel, P. (2005). Learning to coach through experience: Conditions that influence the reflective process. *The Physical Educator, 62*(1): 32–43.

Gillentine, A. and Hunt, B. (2000). Factors affecting the sportsmanship attitudes of interscholastic coaches. *Applied Research in Coaching and Athletics Annual, 15*: 39–54.

Gould, D., Giannini, J., Krane, V. and Hodge, K. (1990). Educational needs of elite U.S. national team, Pan American and Olympic coaches. *Journal of Teaching in Physical Education, 9*: 332–344.

Gould, D. and Martens, R. (1979). Attitudes of volunteer coaches toward significant youth sport issues. *Research Quarterly, 50*: 369–380.

Graham, R.H. and Carron, A.V. (1983). Impact of coaching certification on coaching attitudes. *Canadian Journal of Applied Sport Sciences, 8*(Sept): 180–188.

Gray, G. and Cornish, J. (1985). Values and attitudes of junior sport coaches. *Sports Coach, 9*(2): 39.

Green, C.B. (1997). Action research in youth soccer: Assessing the acceptability of an alternative program. *Journal of Sport Management, 11*: 29–44.

Hansen, H. and Gauthier, R. (1988). Reasons for involvement of Canadian hockey coaches in minor hockey. *The Physical Educator, 45*(3): 147–153.

Hardin, B. (2000). Coaching expertise in high school athletics: Characteristics of expert high school coaches. *Applied Research in Coaching and Athletics Annual, 15*: 24–38.

Hasbrook, C.A., Hart, B.A., Mathes, S. and True, S. (1990). Sex bias and the believed validity of believed differences between male and female interscholastic athletic coaches. *Research Quarterly for Exercise and Sport, 61*: 259–267.

Hastie, P.A. (1991). Evaluation of coaches', players' and parents' attitudes to Aussie footy in Brisbane. *ACHPER, 31*–36.

Hastie, P.A. (1992). Towards a pedagogy of sports coaching: Research directions for the 1990's. *International Journal of Physical Education, 29*(3): 26–29.

Hendry, L. (1974). Coaches and teachers of physical education: A comparison of the personality dimensions underlying their social orientation. *International Journal of Sport Psychology, 5*(1): 40–53.

Holmes, S. (1980). Characteristics of the ideal coach. *New Zealand Journal of Health, Physical Education and Recreation, 13*: 17–26.

Honey, P. and Mumford, A. (1992). *Manual of learning styles* (3rd ed.). Maidenhead: Honey Publications.

Human Kinetics. (2004). *Curriculum overview*. Retrieved July 22, 2004, from http://www.asep.com/courseInfo/curriculum.cfm

Hunt, K.R. and Miller, S.R. (1994). Comparison of levels of perceived stress and burnout among college basketball and tennis coaches. *Applied Research in Coaching and Athletics Annual, 9*: 198–222.

Inglis, S., Danylchuk, K.E. and Pastore, D.L. (2000). Multiple realities of women's work experiences in coaching and athletic management. *Women in Sport and Physical Activity Journal, 9*(2): 1–26.

Jacobs, W. and Ballard, D.J. (1996). A demographic analysis of coaches teaching secondary health education. *Texas Association for Health, Physical Education, Recreation and Dance Journal, 64*: 9–12.

Jarvis, P., Holford, J. and Griffin, C. (1998). *The theory and practice of learning*. London: Kogan Page.

Jones, R.L., Armour, K.M. and Potrac, P. (2002). Understanding the coaching process: A framework for social analysis. *Quest, 54*: 34–48.

Jones, R.L., Armour, K.M. and Potrac, P. (2003). Constructing expert knowledge: A case study of a top-level professional soccer coach. *Sport, Education and Society, 8*(2): 213–229.

Jones, R.L., Armour, K.M. and Potrac, P. (2004). *Sports coaching cultures: From practice to theory*. London: Routledge.

Kahan, D. (1999). Coaching behavior: A review of the systematic observation research literature. *Applied Research in Coaching and Athletics Annual, 14*: 17–58.

Keane, F. and Cheffers, J. (1978). The relationship of sex, leader behavior, leadership style and coach player interaction. *Track and Field Quarterly Review, 78*: 61.

Kelley, B.C. (1994). A model of stress and burnout in collegiate coaches: Effects of gender and time of season. *Research Quarterly for Exercise and Sport, 65*: 48–58.

Kelley, B.C., Eklund, R.C. and Ritter-Taylor, M. (1999). Stress and burnout among collegiate tennis coaches. *Journal of Sport and Exercise Psychology, 21*(2): 113–130.

Kelley, B.C. and Gill, D.L. (1993). An examination of personal/situational variables, stress appraisal and burnout in collegiate teacher-coaches. *Research Quarterly for Exercise and Sport, 64*: 94–102.

Kemmis, S. and McTaggart, R. (1988). (3rd ed.). *The action research planner*. Geelong, Australia: Deakin University Press.

Kirk, D. and Macdonald, D. (1998). Situated learning in physical education. *Journal of Teaching in Physical Education, 17*: 376–387.

Kirk, D. and Macdonald, D. (2001). The social construction of PETE in higher education: Toward a research agenda. *Quest, 53*: 440–456.

Kjeldsen, E.K. (1981). Centrality and leadership recruitment. *Review of Sport and Leisure, 6*(2): 1–20.

Klaus, B. (1986). A status study of the existing educational qualifications of practicing high school coaches in suburban Chicago, Illinois. *Illinois Journal for Health, Physical Education, Recreation and Dance, 22*(Fall): 5–6.

Knoppers, A. and Anthonissen, A. (2001). Meanings given to performance in Dutch sport organizations: Gender and racial/ethnic subtexts. *Sociology of Sport Journal, 18*: 302–316.

Knoppers, A., Myer, B.B., Ewing, M. and Forrest, L. (1989). Gender and the salaries of coaches. *Sociology of Sport Journal, 6*: 348–361.

Knowles, S.M., Holton, E.F. and Swanson, R.A. (1998). *The adult learner*. Woburn, MA: Butterworth-Heineman.

Knowles, Z., Gilbourne, D., Borrie, A. and Nevill, A. (2001). Developing the reflective sports coach: A study exploring the process of reflective practice within a higher education coaching programme. *Reflective Practice, 2*(2): 185–207.

Kolb, D. (1984). *Experiential learning*. Englewood Cliffs, NJ: Prentice Hall.

Koustelios, A.D., Kellis, S. and Bagiatis, K. (1997). The role of family variables on football coaches' burnout. *Coaching and Sport Science Journal, 2*(3): 41–45.

Kosa, B. (1990). Teacher-coach burnout and coping strategies. *The Physical Educator, 47*(3): 153–158.

Krane, V., Eklund, R. and McDermott, M. (1991). Collaborative action research and behavioral coaching intervention: A case study. *Applied Research in Coaching and Athletics Annual, 6*: 119–148.

Kroll, W. and Gendersheim, J. (1982). Stress factors in coaching. *Coaching Science Update*, 23: 47–49.

Krueger, A. and Casselman, J. (1982). A comparative analysis of top level track and field coaches in the U.S.A. and West Germany. *Comparative Physical Education and Sport*, 11(3): 20–29.

Kuga, D.J. and Pastore, D.L. (1994). A status report of women's intercollegiate athletic programs in two year colleges. *JUCO Review*, 46: 18–22.

Kugler, J., Reintjes, F., Tewes, V. and Schedlowski, M. (1996). Competition stress in soccer coaches increases salivary immunoglobulin A and salivary cortisol concentrations. *Journal of Sports Medicine and Physical Fitness*, 36(2): 117–120.

Landers, M.A. and Fine, G.A. (1996). Learning life's lessons in tee ball: The reinforcement of gender and status in kindergarten sport. *Sociology of Sport Journal*, 13: 87–93.

Latimer, S.R. and Mathes, S.A. (1985). Black college football coaches' social, educational, athletic and career pattern characteristics. *Journal of Sport Behavior*, 8: 149–162.

Lave, J. (1982). A comparative approach to educational forms and learning processes. *Anthropology & Education Quarterly*, XII(2): 181–187.

Lave, J. (1988). *Cognition in practice*. Cambridge: Cambridge University Press.

Lave, J. and Wenger, E. (1991). *Situated learning: Legitimate peripheral participation*. Cambridge: Cambridge University Press.

Lawson, H.A. (1980). Beyond teaching and ad Hocracy. *Quest*, 32: 22–30.

Lawson, H.A. (1984). Problem-setting for physical education and sport. *Quest*, 36: 48–60.

Lee, M., Williams, V. and Capel, S.A. (1989). Who are our coaches? *Sport and Leisure*, 29(Jan/Feb): 30–31.

Lewin, K. (1951). *Field theory in the social sciences*. New York: Harper and Row.

Lortie, D. (1975). *Schoolteacher: A sociological study*. Chicago, IL: University of Chicago Press.

Lyle, J. (2002). *Sports coaching concepts: A framework for coaches' behavior*. London: Routledge.

Malete, L. and Feltz, D.L. (2000). The effect of a coaching education program on coaching efficacy. *The Sport Psychologist*, 14: 410–417.

Martin, J. (1985). Leadership behavior and soccer coaches. *Soccer Journal*, 30(May/June): 55–58.

Martens, R. (2004). *Successful coaching* (3rd ed.). Champaign, IL: Human Kinetics.

Martens, R., Flannery, T. and Roetert, P. (2004). *The future of coaching education in America*. Retrieved July 23: 2004: from http://www.nfhs.org/ScriptContent/VA_Custom/va_cm/contentpagedisplay.cfm?Content_ID=265&SearchWord=coach%20education

Massengale, J.D. (1984). The certification of coaches: Considering the lack thereof. *Journal of Teaching in Physical Education*, 3: 6–8.

Maurer, M.R. (1991). A profile of coaches of girls' interscholastic sports. *Tennessee*, 30: 5–6.

McCallister, S.G., Blinde, E.M. and Kolenbrander, B. (2000). Problematic aspects of the role of youth sport coach. *International Sports Journal*, 4(1): 9–26.

McGrath, J.C. and Tipps, C.R. (1991). A comparison of self reported leadership behavior of NCAA Division I, II and III soccer coaches. *Soccer Journal*, 36: 32–34.

McLellan, H. (1996) (Ed.), *Situated learning perspectives*. Englewood Cliffs, NJ: Educational Technology.

McMillin, C.J. and Reffner, C. (Eds.), (1999). *Directory of college and university coaching education programs*. Morgantown, VA: Fitness Information Technology.

Miller, S. (1987). Training personnel and procedures for Special Olympic athletes. *Education and Training in Mental Retardation*, 22(4): 244–249.

Mills, B.D. and Dunlevy, S.M. (1997). Coaching certification: What's out there and what needs to be done? *International Journal of Physical Education: A Review Publication*, 34(1): 17–26.

Mistro, J.S. (1985). Factors influencing female physical educators and coaches in decisions concerning coaching in secondary schools. *Illinois Journal for Health, Physical Education, Recreation and Dance*, 20(Spring): 10–12.

Mitchell, M.F. (1992). A descriptive analysis and academic genealogy of major contributors to JTPE in the 1980s. *Journal of Teaching in Physical Education*, 11: 426–442.

Moon, J.A. (1999). *Reflection in learning & professional development: Theory and practice*. London: Kogan Page.

Munby, H. and Russell, T. (1989). Educating the reflective teacher: An essay review of two books by Donald Schön. *Journal of Curriculum Studies*, 21(1): 71–80.

National Association for Sport and Physical Education. (1995). *National standards for athletic coaches*. Dubuque, IA: Kendall/Hunt.

National Association for Sport and Physical Education. (2001). *Coach education: Designing quality programs*. Dubuque, IA: Kendall/Hunt.

National Federation of State High School Associations. *Coaching education in America: A white paper*. Indianapolis, IN. Author.

Nichani, M. and Hung, D. (July-August, 2002). Can a community of practice exist online? *Educational Technology*, 42: 49–54.

Palaestra. (1988). A survey of ISSOG coaches. *Palaestra*, ISSOG, 58–60.

Pastore, D.L. (1991). Male and female coaches of women's athletic teams: Reasons for entering and leaving the profession. *Journal of Sport Management*, 5(2): 128–143.

Pastore, D.L. (1992). Two-year college coaches of women's teams: Gender differences in coaching career selections. *Journal of Sport Management*, 6(3): 179–190.

Pastore, D.L. and Judd, M.R. (1992). Burnout in coaches of women's team sports. *Journal of Physical Education, Recreation and Dance*, 63(5): 74–79.

Pastore, D.L. and Judd, M.R. (1993). Gender differences in burnout among coaches of women's athletic teams at 2-year colleges. *Sociology of Sport Journal*, 10: 205–212.

Penman, K., Hastad, D. and Cords, W. (1974). Success of the authoritarian coach. *The Journal of Social Psychology*, 92(1): 155–156.

Percival, L. (Ed.). (1971). *Proceedings of the first international symposium on the art and science of coaching.* Willowdale, Ontario: F.I. Productions, Coaching Association of Canada.

Porter, D. and Allsen, P. (1978). Heart rates of basketball coaches. *The Physician and Sportsmedicine, 6*: 85–90.

Potrac, P., Brewer, C., Jones, R.L., Armour, K.M. and Hoff, J. (2000). Toward an holistic understanding of the coaching process. *Quest, 52*: 186–199.

Potrac, P., Jones, R.L. and Armour, K.M. (2002). It's all about getting respect: The coaching behaviors of an expert English soccer coach. *Sport, Education and Society, 7*: 183–202.

Pratt, S.R. and Eitzen, D.S. (1989a). Contrasting leadership styles and organizational effectiveness: The case of athletic teams. *Social Science Quarterly, 70*: 311–322.

Pratt, S.R. and Eitzen, D.S. (1989b). Differences in coaching philosophies between male coaches of male and female basketball teams. *International Review for the Sociology of Sport, 24*(2): 151–161.

Quigley, T. (1989). The levels and possible causes of burnout in secondary school teachers, coaches. *Canadian Journal of Health Physical Education and Recreation, 55*(Jan/Feb): 20–25.

Raedeke, T.D., Granzyk, T.L. and Warren, A. (2000). Why coaches experience burnout: A commitment perspective. *Journal of Sport and Exercise Psychology, 22*(1): 85–105.

Raedeke, T.D., Warren, A.H. and Granzyk, T.L. (2002). Coaching commitment and turnover: A comparison of current and former coaches. *Research Quarterly for Exercise and Sport, 73*: 73–86.

Richardson, H.D. (1981). Academic preparation of athletic coaches in higher educations. *Journal of Physical Education and Recreation, 52*(3): 44–45.

Rogoff, B. (1995). Observing sociocultural activity on three planes: Participatory appropriation, guided participation and apprenticeship. In J.V. Wertsch, P. Del Rio and A. Alvarez (Eds.), *Sociocultural studies of mind* (pp. 139–164). Cambridge: Cambridge University Press.

Rosenberg, E. (1990). Race, position and managerial recruitment in baseball: A methodological critique and reexamination. In V.L. Velden and J.H. Humphrey (Eds.), *Psychology and sociology of sport: Current selected research* (pp. 115–131). NY: AMS Press.

Rossi, T.M and Cassidy, T. (1999). Knowledgeable teachers in physical education: A view of teacher's knowledge. In C.A. Hardy and M. Mawer (Eds.), *Learning and teaching in physical education* (pp. 188–202). London: Falmer Press

Rovengo, I. (1992). Learning to reflect on teaching: A case study of one preservice physical education teacher. *The Elementary School Journal, 92*: 491–510.

Sagas, M., Cunningham, G.B. and Ashley, F.B. (2000). Examining the women's coaching deficit through the perspective of assistant coaches. *International Journal of Sport Management, 1*(4): 267–282.

Sage, G.H. (1989). Becoming a high school coach: From playing sports to coaching. *Research Quarterly for Exercise and Sport, 60*(1): 81–92.

Salmela, J.H. (1996). *Great job coach: Getting the edge from proven winners.* Ottawa, Ontario: Potentium.

Salminen, S. and Liukkonen, J. (1996). Coach-athlete relationship and coaching behavior in training sessions. *International Journal of Sport Psychology, 27*(1): 59–67.

Saury, J. and Durand, M. (1998). Practical coaching knowledge in expert coaches: On-site study of coaching in sailing. *Research Quarterly for Exercise and Sport, 69*: 254–266.

Savard, C. (1997). How coaches acquire competencies. *Coaches Report, 4*(1): 18–21: 26.

Savard, C. and Brunelle, J. (Fall, 1998). Conceptions du savoir et formation en entraînement [Conceptions of knowledge and training of coaches]. *CAHPERD Journal,* 16–20.

Sawyer, T. (1992). Coaching education in North America. *Journal of Physical Education, Recreation and Dance, 63*(7): 33.

Schatzle, W. (1980). A question of professional preparation. *Texas Coach,* Jan, 19.

Schön, D.A. (1983). *The reflective practitioner: How professionals think in action.* New York: Basic Books.

Schön, D.A. (1987). *Educating the reflective practitioner: Toward a new design for teaching and learning in the professions.* San Francisco, CA: Jossey-Bass.

Schinke, R.J., Bloom, G.A. and Salmela, J.H. (1995). The career stages of elite Canadian basketball coaches. *Avante, 1*(1): 48–62.

Serpa, S., Pataco, V. and Santos, F. (1991). Leadership patterns in handball international competition. *International Journal of Sport Psychology, 22*(1): 78–89.

Seefeldt, V.D. and Milligan, M.J. (1992). Program for Athletic Coaches Education (PACE) – Educating America's public and private school coaches. *Journal of Physical Education, Recreation and Dance, 63*(7): 46–49.

Sfard, A. (1998). On two metaphors for learning and the dangers of choosing just one. *Educational Researcher, 27*: 4–13.

Silvestri, L. (1991). Survey of volunteer coaches. *Perceptual and Motor Skills, 72*: 409–410.

Simpson, W. and Beach, C. (1986). Previous playing position, experience and leadership recruitment in women's intercollegiate basketball: A pilot study. *Applied Research in Coaching and Athletics Annual, 1*: 101–108.

Singell, L.V. (1991). Baseball specific human capital: Why good but not great players are more likely to coach in the major leagues. *Southern Economic Journal, 58*(1): 77–86.

Singh, P.C. (2001). The job security of coaches. *S.A. Journal for Research in Sport, Physical Education and Recreation, 23*(1): 65–73.

Sisley, B.L., Capel, S.A. and Desertrain, G.S. (1987). Preventing burnout in teacher/coaches. *Journal of Physical Education, Recreation and Dance, 58*(8): 71–75.

Sisley, B.L., Weiss, M.R., Barber, H. and Ebbeck, V. (1990). Developing competence and confidence in novice women coaches - A study of attitudes, motives and perceptions of ability. *Journal of Physical Education, Recreation and Dance, 61*: 60–64.

Smith, A.M., Stuart, M.J., Wiese-Bjornstal, D.M. and Gunnon, C. (1997). Predictors of injury in ice hockey players: A multivariate, multidisciplinary approach. *The American Journal of Sports Medicine, 25*(4): 500–507.

Smith, A.M., Stuart, M.J., Colbenson, C.M.L. and Kronebusch, S.P. (2000). A psychosocial perspective of aggression in ice hockey. In D.J. Pearsall and A.B. Ashare (Eds.), *Safety in ice hockey: Fourth volume, ASTM STP 1446:* (pp. 199–219) West Conshohocken, PA: ASTM International.

Smith, M.D. (1975). The legitimation of violence: Hockey players' perceptions of their reference groups' sanctions for assault. *Canadian Review of Sociology and Anthropology, 12*: 72–80.

Solomon, G.B., Striegel, D.A., Eliot, J.F., Heon, S.N. and Maas, J.L. (1996). The self-fulfilling prophecy in college basketball: Implications for effective coaching. *Journal of Applied Sport Psychology, 8*: 44–59.

Solomon, G.B., DiMarco, A.M., Ohlson, C.J. and Reece, S.D. (1998). Expectations and coaching experience: Is more better? *Journal of Sport Behavior, 21*: 444–455.

Spallanzani, C. (1988). Profil d'entraîneurs en hockey mineur et motifs de participation et de démission [Profile of participation motives of minor hockey coaches]. *Canadian Journal of Sport Sciences, 13*(2): 157–165.

Sparkes, A.C. (1992). *Research in physical education and sport: Exploring alternative visions.* London: Falmer.

Stahura, K.A. and Greenwood, M. (2000). An empirical examination of coaching representation in women's intercollegiate basketball and volleyball. *Applied Research in Coaching and Athletics Annual, 15*: 55–77.

Stetsenko, A. and Arievitch, I. (1997). Constructing and deconstructing the self: Comparing post-Vygotskian and discourse-based versions of social constructivism. *Mind, Culture and Activity, 4*(3): 159–172.

Strean, W.B. (1995). Youth sport context: Coaches' perceptions and implications for intervention. *Journal of Applied Sport Psychology, 7*: 23–37.

Strean, W.B., Senecal, K.L., Howlett, S.G. and Burgess, J.M. (1997). Xs and Os and what the coach knows: Improving team strategy through critical thinking. *The Sport Psychologist, 11*: 243–256.

Strong, J.M. (1992). A dysfunctional and yet winning youth football team. *Journal of Sport Behavior, 15*: 319–326.

Stroot, S.A., Collier, C., O'Sullivan, M. and England, K. (1994). Contextual hoops and hurdles: Workplace conditions in secondary physical education. *Journal of Teaching in Physical Education, 13*: 342–360.

The International Council for Coach Education. (n.d.). *About the ICCE.* Retrieved July 14, 2004, from http://www.icce.ws/about/index.htm

Theberge, N. (1992). Managing domestic work and careers: The experiences of women in coaching. *Atlantis: A Women's Studies Journal, 17*(2): 11–21.

Tinning, R. (1985: August). *Student teaching and the pedagogy of necessity.* Paper presented at the AIESEP Conference, Adelphi University, NY.

Tinning, R. (1987). Beyond the development of a utilitarian teaching perspective: An Australian case study of action research in teacher preparation. In G. Barrette, R. Feingold, R. Rees and M. Piéron (Eds.), *Myths, models and methods in sport pedagogy* (pp. 113–122). Champaign, IL: Human Kinetics.

Trudel, P. and Gilbert, W. (2004). Communities of practice as an approach to foster ice hockey coach development. In D.J. Pearsall and A.B. Ashare (Eds.), *Safety in ice hockey: Fourth volume ASTM STP 1446* (pp. 167–179). West Conshohoken, PA: ASTM International.

Tsangaridou, N. and O'Sullivan, M. (1994). Using pedagogical reflective strategies to enhance reflection among preservice physical education teachers. *Journal of Teaching in Physical Education, 14*: 13–33.

Tsangaridou, N. and O'Sullivan, M. (1997). The role of reflection in shaping physical education teachers' educational values and practices. *Journal of Teaching in Physical Education, 17*: 2–25.

Tsangaridou, N. and O'Sullivan, M. (2003). Physical education teachers' theories of action and theories-in-use. *Journal of Teaching in Physical Education, 22*: 132–152.

Tsangaridou, N. and Siedentop, D. (1995). Reflective teaching: A literature review. *Quest, 47*: 212–237.

Ubbes, V.A. (1991). Descriptive evaluation of participants who attend coaching certification workshops. *Illinois Journal for Health, Physical Education, Recreation and Dance, 30*: 37–39.

Usher, R., Bryant, I. and Johnston, R. (1997). *Adult and the postmodern challenge: Learning beyond the limits.* London: Routledge.

Van Manen, M. (1977). Linking ways of knowing with ways of being practical. *Curriculum Inquiry, 6*: 205–228.

Vaz, E. (1979). Institutionalized rule violation and control in organized minor league hockey. *Canadian Journal of Applied Sport Science, 4*(1): 83–90.

Vygotsky, L.S. (1978). *Mind in society: the development of higher psychological processes.* Cambridge, MA: Harvard University Press.

Wang, J. and Ramsey, J. (1998). The relationships of school type, coaching experience, gender and age to new coaches' challenges and barriers at the collegiate level. *Applied Research in Coaching and Athletics Annual, 13*: 1–22.

Wankel, L.M. and Mummery, W.K. (1996). Canada. In P. De Knop, L-M. Engström, B. Skirstad and M. Weiss (Eds.), *Worldwide trends in youth sport* (pp. 27–42). Champaign, IL: Human Kinetics.

Weiss, M.R., Barber, H., Sisley, B.L. and Ebbeck, V. (1991). Developing competence and confidence in novice female coaches: II. Perceptions of ability and affective experiences following a season-long coaching internship. *Journal of Sport and Exercise Psychology, 13*: 336–363.

Weiss, M.R. and Sisley, B.L. (1984). Where have all the coaches gone? *Sociology of Sport Journal, 1*: 332–347.

Weiss, M.R. and Stevens, C. (1993). Motivation and attrition of female coaches: An application of social exchange theory. *The Sport Psychologist, 7*(3): 244–261.

Wenger, E. (1998). *Communities of practice: Learning, meaning and identity.* Cambridge: Cambridge University Press.

Wenger, E., McDermott, R. and Snyder, W.M. (2002). *A guide to managing knowledge: Cultivating communities of practice.* Boston, MA: Harvard Business School.

Werthner, P. and Trudel, P. (2006). A new theoretical perspective for understanding how coaches learn to coach. The *Sport Psychologist, 20*: 196–210.

Wilkinson, S. and Schneider, P. (1991). The status of women coaches in the state of Illinois. *Illinois Journal for Health, Physical Education, Recreation and Dance, 29*: 14–15.

Wilson, V.E. and Bird, E.I. (1988). Burnout in coaching – part two: Results from survey of national coaches. *Sports Science Periodical on Research and Technology in Sport, 8*(9): 1–5.

Woodman, L. (1993). Coaching: A science, an art, an emerging profession. *Sport Science Review, 2*(2): 1–13.

Young, D.S. (1992). The status of burnout and Illinois girls' varsity basketball head coaches. *Illinois Journal for Health, Physical Education, Recreation and Dance, 31*: 36–40.

Yow, D.A. (2000). Coaches under stress: Causes, consequences and coping. *Athletic Administration, 35*: 32–35.

Zeichner, K. (1981). Reflective teaching and field- based experience in teacher education. *Interchange, 12*: 1–22.

Zeichner, K. (1987). Preparing reflective teachers: An overview of instructional strategies which have been employed in preservice teacher education: *International Journal of Educational Research, 11*: 565–575.

4.10 Physical education teacher education (PE/TE) policy

PATT DODDS

Introduction

Chapter overview

This chapter is about policy affecting school physical education and teacher education programs, whose unique contribution to human lives is promoting and teaching physical activity (PA). The murky world of policy is complex, convoluted, confusing, and contentious. Here, *policy* will be defined as "...*rules, statements of intent, and specified strategies that are formally adopted by legitimated individuals or agencies to guide collective action.*" (Hawley, 1990: 136). Located at the intersection of several policy fields acting at multiple global to local sites, PE/TE[1] policy embraces policy discourses of education, health, and sport among others. This nexus creates an arena for lively debate, contestation of priorities, and shifting power. This chapter presents sources of influence on PE/TE policy including governmental, non-governmental, professional, advocacy, and philanthropic organizations and individuals. It details education, health, and sport policies influencing PE/TE policies for recruiting, selecting, preparing, licensing, recertifying, supporting, and evaluating PE teachers and teacher educators, and for improving the quality of teaching and TE. Research in traditional and critical perspectives is presented and future research agendas proposed.

Recent international education reform history

Today the policy realm is lively but still relatively unstudied. Since the mid-1980s the global PE/TE policy context has generally lagged behind most educational reforms. A recent international review of teacher education research (West et al., 1996) disappointingly reveals not a single policy analysis among studies considered. Other authors, however, clearly articulate international commonalities, an "education reform triangle", that recently have influenced PE/TE: curriculum standards, student and teacher assessment, and accountability (Rink and Mitchell, 2002, 2003).

Economic and political discourses dominate the language of education reform. A market economy perspective that links higher educational attainment with increased national competitiveness in global markets has led to educational restructuring around the world (Calderhead, 2001; Lee, 2001; Rezai-Rashti, 2003). Calderhead (2001) notes the following policy trends. School *curricular reform* varies from one country to another, with greater centralization (e.g. England and Wales) or lesser centralization (e.g. Spain, Canada) and specific curricular standards. *Increasing internationalization* of education encourages comparisons of student achievement across nations. More "marketization" of schools through *decentralized control* (i.e. site-based management) leads to competition for students (e.g. charter schools in the US, grant-maintained schools in England) and differences in funding levels, in turn resulting in more and less privileged schools. High-stakes testing moves students, schools, and in some places even individual teachers toward greater accountability. Commonly, teachers are informally accountable for more content and higher student attainment as measures of school or teacher effectiveness. *Teacher education reform* pervades the international community, although widespread disagreement exists about how to do it (Calderhead, 2001).

Correlated with raising student achievement though high standards, assessment, and accountability, and integrating P12 and TE reforms, political agendas centralize education with politicians increasingly active in shaping substance and content of education policy. As public attention to education reform grows, education systems are simultaneously blamed for economic and social problems yet paradoxically expected to solve them

(Calderhead, 2001; Lee, 2001; Rink and Mitchell, 2002). Calderhead notes, "…reform efforts themselves have frequently been ill-coordinated and often focus on simple answers to complex problems" (Calderhead, 2001: 778). Because education and teacher education are integrally related enterprises with multiple contexts exerting authority over policies, understanding how policies originate, are modified, and function could be highly productive for researchers, teachers, and teacher educators who wish to influence and fully participate in the governance of their own work.

Two general policy practices appear across the international community: a centralized model of national responsibility (e.g. England and Wales, Scotland, China) or a decentralized model with states/provinces sharing primary policy roles (e.g. Canada, Australia, US) (Calderhead, 2001; Lee, 2001; West et al., 1996). In all countries, PE/TE policies originate in several sectors or communities of practice (cf. Kirk and Macdonald, 2001): national and state/provincial governments specify policy for P12 and TE, higher education institutions initially prepare teachers, school districts and individual schools set regulations, advocacy organizations commission policy studies and special papers, and professional organizations recommend "best practices" in specializations such as PE.

National policies govern PE/TE, by specifying broad conditions and restrictions of funding for P12 and TE for special purposes (special education, curriculum or TE reforms). State/provincial policies specify requirements for initial teacher licensure and recertification and may dictate content requirements within preservice teacher education (PTE)curricula (e.g. diversity/equity, legal issues, clinical teaching practice) and requirements for veteran teachers' continuing professional development (CPD) Universities specify requirements for academic majors. PE time and content requirements are set by states and local school districts. Professional organizations design national standards for PE students (e.g. NASPE, 2004b) and for preparing teachers (e.g. NASPE, 2001).

Major discourses within PE/TE Policy

Policy governs every aspect of PE/TE. Principal discourses that shape PA policies include those within *education, health,* and *sport,* intersecting with *politics* and *global economics.* As Penney notes, "Raising the profile of discourses that have typically remained absent from or marginalized within teaching and learning is an important advancement within arenas of both policy and practice in PE" (Penney, 2003: 304). Increased globalization

supports market economy approaches to education policies (Cochran-Smith, 2001; Penney and Evans, 1999; Rezai-Rashti, 2003) in which higher student achievement on standardized measures means greater international economic capital (education discourses), the health and fitness of national populations are useful to maximize workplace productivity (health discourses) and how athletes perform in international competitions (e.g. the Olympics) shows national superiority (sport discourses).

Education discourses permeate national and state/provincial curriculum documents. Typically, policy language implies equality of learning opportunities for all students, foregrounding democratic values and beliefs that all children deserve the best education possible. Education discourses, through reform documents, detail how schools and teachers must change to meet ever-higher requirements for student achievement. *Health discourses,* rooted in a preventive public health orientation, advocate educating students toward healthy lifestyles and lifelong PA to prevent and combat diseases and chronic health problems, thus saving national budgets from rising health care costs. *Sport discourses* range from foregrounding elitist competitive values such that only the strongest thrive to promoting positive social and individual development through participation. All three realms of discourse influence PE/TE practice: education because the majority of youngsters' time is spent in schools, health because lifetime health habits are formed during childhood, and sport because most PE curricula have significant sport components. Underneath these three discourses that permeate PE/TE policies throughout the world, lie political and economic discourses, both forces that drive all nations toward global superiority and market domination. Understanding these multiple discourses in PE/TE policies positions researchers, teachers, and teacher educators to maximize their stakeholder influences on policy.

Current policy documents, organizations, and influences shaping PE/TE

This section of the chapter briefly describes key policy documents, organizations, and other influences on PE/TE policy. This treatment focuses in some detail on PE/TE policy in the US and more briefly on other countries as well as on important coalition efforts across national boundaries that shape PE/TE policy. The discourses found within education, health, and sport frame this presentation.

Education discourses

United States

US policy currently foregrounds *teachers* as the specific intervention point, building on earlier P12 curriculum, student assessment, and accountability reform policy (Cochran-Smith, 2001; Darling-Hammond, 2001; Darling-Hammond and Sykes, 2003). Internationally, P12/TE policy appears more concerned with P12 *curriculum, assessment, and accountability* with TE reforms associated but backgrounded.

Teacher education policy

The major theme of US efforts seems to be figuring out how to coordinate multiple policy sources to improve the teaching profession, the idea being that better teachers will improve P12 education. Readers are directed to three significant background papers that overview TE policies, detailing historical and contemporary roles and responsibilities of states, the federal government, teacher education programs, P12 school districts, and associated constituents in overall policy processes (Cochran-Smith, 2001; Darling-Hammond, 2001; Darling-Hammond and Sykes, 2003).

TE policies encompass the full range of recruitment, selection, initial preparation, retention, and continued professional development (e.g. Cochran-Smith, 2001; Darling-Hammond, 2001; Darling-Hammond and Sykes, 2003; Holmes Partnership, 1986, 1990, 1995). Darling-Hammond's (2001) metaphoric wobbly three-legged stool of quality assurance for teaching requires compatible policy for accreditation of teacher preparation programs, licensure for individual teachers to practice, and certification recognizing highly competent teachers.

Principal responsibility for US education resides with states, each with its own regulations governing teacher preparation programs, teacher licensure and recertification, and P12 education. Although states' specific policies for high school graduation, teacher preparation, and licensure differ, most now use high stakes testing for P12 students linked with state curriculum frameworks, teacher tests linked with initial licensure, and a periodic recertification system (Education Commission of the States, 2004; state departments of education websites).

National reforms

US education reforms of the mid-1980s resulted from perceived loss of international economic superiority. Among other reports, *A nation at risk* (National Commission on Excellence in Education, 1983) called public attention to poorer student achievement. In response, reports recommending new teacher preparation policies appeared. *A nation prepared: Teachers for the 21st century* (Carnegie Forum on Education and the Economy, 1986) influenced state policies by recommending specific subject matter bachelor's degrees, broad as well as subject-specific knowledge for teaching certification, longer internships and a master's degree prior to initial certification, and a national teacher certification board to certify teaching professionals beyond initial licensure. Both the Education Commission of the States' *New directions for state teacher policies* (1985) and *Tomorrow's teachers* (Holmes Partnership, 1986) recommended similar changes in teacher preparation touted to improve student achievement in the long run.

In the 1990s, *Goals 2000: Educate America Act* (US Congress, 1994) was an early systemic reform policy to improve student opportunities to learn through improved teacher development, increased parental involvement in schools, and better use of technology to enhance learning. Currently, the most prominent national policy is *NLCB* (US Congress, 2001). *NCLB* mandates a highly qualified (fully licensed) teacher in every classroom in core subjects (*not* PE). This law sets parameters for teacher recruitment, selection, and retention, initial and advanced certification; for state accountability (annual state report cards) in tracking these characteristics of the teaching force; and for content mastery and ongoing CPD for experienced teachers.

One strength of *NCLB* is its equity language that calls for state policy to redistribute teachers to advantage poor, high minority districts. If used wisely, this law could help states address teacher recruitment problems, including using high-quality alternative routes to certification (i.e. those not situated in traditional college/university programs). Early reports on the effects of *NCLB* as TE policy are now appearing. *Meeting the highly qualified teachers challenge* indicates that 41 states now have teacher certification and student content standards linked and more than 30 now require teacher testing as part of initial certification (US Dept. of Education, 2003).

The National Commission on Teaching for America's Future

The strongest contemporary influence on US TE policy is now the National Commission on Teaching and America's Future (NCTAF, 2006[2]), primarily through leadership in building coalitions with like-minded organizations. NCTAF's publications, *What matters most* (1996) and *No dream denied* (2003) underscore six key research-based components of teacher preparation: strong content preparation, strong clinical practice and mentoring support during induction, use of current learning technologies, careful recruitment and selection, and assessment of teacher preparation. NCTAF's principal foci are quality assurance for initial teacher licensure, national teacher certification, and accreditation of teacher preparation programs (Darling-Hammond, 2001). NCTAF emphasizes standards for students *and* teachers; schools organized for student *and* teacher success; and equitable distribution of highly qualified teachers to *all* schools (NCTAF, 2003). NCTAF's impact derives from acknowledging that accountability is important at all levels of compliance with educational policy, that local contexts matter in designing state and local policies, and that leadership is essential to rally other organizations to accomplish broad policy goals.

Program accreditation

Two organizations currently set accreditation standards for teacher preparation institutions. The National Council for the Accreditation of Teacher Education (NCATE, 2006) dominates, though the Teacher Education Accreditation Council (TEAC, 2006) is gaining strength. NCATE's performance-based standards for initial teacher licensure require TE programs to demonstrate that teacher candidates meet these standards. Working with 35 specialty professional associations to develop its standards[3], NCATE draws on the expertise of diverse specialists in formulating standards policy and holding responsible parties accountable for implementing TE policy. TEAC's performance-based standards for preservice teachers require individual TE programs to specify particular goals for what teacher candidates should know and be able to do; candidates are then judged on evidence of student learning data (TEAC, 2006).

The American Association of Colleges for Teacher Education (AACTE, 2006) serves institutions with TE programs and carries out important collaborative agendas that influence TE policy, for example by brokering a potential merger of NCATE and TEAC standards (AACTE, 2003). AACTE supports rigorous assessment of preservice teachers' content and pedagogical knowledge, maintains a national data base linking TE impact with P12 student learning, and advocates common assessment and reporting systems. AACTE promotes equity and diversity among teachers and teacher educators, supports accountability to prospective teachers and the public, and advocates using best practice and research to ground teacher preparation.

Licensure of teachers

The Interstate New Teacher Assessment and Support Consortium (INTASC, 2006)[4], overseen by the Council of Chief State School Officers, involves state education agencies and national educational organizations in reforming preparation, licensing, and CPD of teachers. INTASC supports aligning states' education and strong teacher licensure systems to support P-12 standards for students. Teachers, school administrators, state agencies, and teacher educators together develop model policies for states to adapt to particular local contexts. INTASC now has model "core" standards for "… what all beginning teachers should know, be like, and be able to do in order to practice responsibly, regardless of the subject matter or grade level being taught." (Council of Chief State School Officers, 2006). INTASC builds consensus among states while leaving specific policy to them as long as it is within federal guidelines.

The Education Commission of the States (ECS) is a powerful national policy body whose mission is "helping state leaders shape education policy" (Education Commission of the States, 2006). Its website summarizes state actions and policies monthly (ECS, 2002) and it maintains a searchable state policy database for teacher preparation. ECS's *Eight questions on teacher preparation: What does the research say?* (Allen, 2003) exemplifies this organization's commitment to *research-based* TE policy recommendations.

Certification of experienced teachers

While INTASC, NCATE, and TEAC all address initial teacher licensure standards, the National Board for Professional Teaching Standards (NBPTS, 1994) and the American Board for Certification of Teacher Excellence (ABCTE, 2006) provide national certification for outstanding experienced teachers. Now recognized by 49 states, NBPTS has certified more than 24 000 accomplished teachers (Carnegie Foundation, 2003) based on five core propositions with differentiated standards by subject and stages of student development. NBPTS (2006) desires "…to establish high and rigorous standards for what accomplished teachers should know and be able to do." (National Board for Professional Teaching Standards, 2006). Using structured reflection on one's teaching over a 1–3-year timeframe, demonstration of student learning through presentation of a teaching portfolio, and high scores on a teaching examination, NBPTS (2006) certification requires at least three years' experience. NBPTS has commissioned over 150 research studies of its effectiveness (e.g. NBPTS certification's relationships to teacher career pathways, professional development, mentoring, and minority teachers) A recent large-scale study shows increased student achievement in math and reading for North Carolina NBPTS teachers, with particularly strong results for poorer students (Goldhaber and Anthony, 2004).

In contrast, ABCTE is an alternative route to both initial (Passport) and experienced teacher certification, claiming portability state to state of nationally recognized credentials (true also of NBPTS) and cost effectiveness in becoming credentialed (i.e. by avoiding expensive university-based teacher education). ABCTE's foundation in "…subject area mastery and professional teaching knowledge as demonstrated by rigorous testing standards" relies on examination, though its master teacher certification also requires demonstration of student achievement as well as test performance (ABCTE, 2006).

Standards for teacher educators

Predictably lagging somewhat behind student content standards and beginning and experienced teacher performance standards policy, several professional organizations have drafted standards for teacher educators, although little conversation has occurred about formal licensure or certification. The Association of Teacher Educators (ATE) drafted "generic" standards (ATE, 2006) along with indicators, related evidence, and forms of assessment to guide the practice of master teacher educators. Some content-specific organizations also now have teacher educator standards (e.g. reading, math, science, and English), commonly including content and pedagogical knowledge, research, curriculum design, assessment, diversity and equity, and professional development (Placek et al., 2003).

Although many current P12 and TE policy effects are positive, negative impacts also occur. Evidence to date unfortunately indicates that more poor and minority students are taught by teachers who are least experienced, uncertified, or teaching out of field and that the rhetoric of *NCLB* thus far has had little impact on such conditions (Education Commission of the States, 2002; Darling-Hammond, 2001). The very language of *Meeting the highly qualified teachers challenge* clearly reflects conservative political agendas in labeling states' mechanisms for teacher certification "…burdensome and bureaucratic" (US Department of Education, 2003: 7).

PE/TE Policies

The National Association for Sport and Physical Education (NASPE) is the primary professional organization attempting to influence US policy for PE/TE. *Moving into the future: National standards for physical education* (1995) contains content standards for PE student achievement ("what students should know and be able to do", p. vi), distinguishing these from performance standards ("how good is good enough", p. vi). Introduced in marketing (being "internationally competitive", p. vii) and political language (proving PE's "academic standing" in school curriculum),

Moving promotes performance-based, authentic, formative and summative assessments leading to sound data-driven pedagogical practice. The second edition (NASPE, 2004c), contextualized within accountability provisions of *NCLB* (U.S. Congress, 2001), promotes instructional alignment among learning goals, instructional practices, and assessment as the best way to demonstrate program accountability (p. 2).

NASPE (2001d) now has revised standards for initial preparation of teachers in conjunction with NCATE (2001c) and new standards for advanced teacher preparation (2001a), the latter modeled on the NBPTS standards for accomplished physical educators (NBPTS, 1994). The nine initial preparation standards reflect model INTASC standards; the advanced standards reflect the five NBPTS core propositions, including "promoting an active lifestyle".

Without researchers, teachers, and teacher educators deliberately engaging in policy issues, there is little likelihood that PE/TE policy will improve or that the two enterprises will become better aligned in the US Good policy research can underscore the significance of positioning PE/TE in public health policy debates to promote lifetime PA.

International perspectives

England and Wales

At the P12 level, the Education Reform Act (ERA) specified a national curriculum for England and Wales with three core subjects and seven foundation subjects (including PE), each containing programs of study (curriculum frameworks) and attainment targets (student achievement standards) organized in four key stages for students aged 5–7, 7–11, 11–14, and 14–16 years. Implementation occurred for "core subjects" first (not PE). The ERA included adoption of a national curriculum, local school (site-based) management, grant maintained (i.e. formula-funded) schools, and changes in school admission standards. Following the ERA, the National Curriculum in Physical Education (NCPE), now in its third revision since 1992, is overseen by the Office for Standards in Education (OFSTED) (Lacon and Curtner-Smith, 1998). NCPE policies significantly shifted the discourse. While Penney and Evans (1999) argue that this shift refocused from content to be taught (at the local school level) to a technical focus on how to deliver a specified (sport dominated) curriculum in all schools (i.e. instructional strategies), other scholars counter that specific instructional strategies are left to local options (Curtner-Smith and Hasty, 1997; Curtner-Smith and Todorovich, 1998). NCPE policy was developed quickly and largely without teacher input or review, yet demanded more of teachers (Evans et al., 1993). PE teachers could choose different texts based on knowledge of their students and were required to teach six content areas of dance, gymnastics, games, athletics (track and field), outdoor and adventure activities, and swimming. One recent policy development is a pilot Professional Development Board for PE (PDB-PE) intended to improve continuing professional development (CPD) for experienced teachers (Armour and Yelling, 2004).

Scotland

In Scotland, the McCrone Report (2000) sets national priorities through "performance and quality indicators", including for PE. Recommendations have been made that children have at least two hours of quality PE per week and that 80% under age 16 meet minimum PA levels by 2022. A First Stage review of initial teacher preparation describes present programs and structures with respect to key issues (e.g. instructional technology, special needs education, partnership arrangements, recent training of teacher educators). Later stages will include setting priorities for change (Scottish Executive Online, 2006). Equity language is prominent in the values underlying this policy recommendation such as "…equal opportunities and access" for all. Learning and Teaching in Scotland (2004), a government-funded organization providing resources and CPD to support education, also advises the Scottish Executive Education Department and provides web resources for teachers and local education authorities to access national standards, teachers' organizations, education policy and assessment reports, and certification and qualifications authorities.

Ireland

Ireland's National Council for Curriculum and Assessment advises the Minister of Education in matters related to promoting equity, preparing children for the "knowledge society", assuring Irish education maintains its impact on economic development, and creating research informed policy (NCCA, 2006). Like most of the international community, Ireland's key issues for teaching include teacher shortages by subject, underperforming teachers, and high teacher turnover rates in disadvantaged areas (NCCA, 2006).

Australia

The 1999 Adelaide Declaration on National Goals for Schooling in the 21st Century set national education policy directions for Australia (Ministerial Council on Education, Employment, Training and Youth Affairs, 1999). Emphasizing schools as learning communities, partnerships between students/families and wider communities, alignment of curriculum with assessment and with program accreditation and teacher credentialing, the Adelaide Declaration contains strong equity language ("Schooling should develop fully the talents and capacities of all students") and social justice ("students' outcomes from schooling are free from the effects of negative forms of discrimination based on sex, language, culture and ethnicity, religion or disability; and of differences arising from students' socio-economic background or geographic location"). This policy explicitly includes minority groups (e.g. "all students understand and acknowledge the value of Aboriginal and Torres Strait Islander cultures to Australian society"). States/territories devise their own contextually-specific policy statements, based on the Australian national model, a distinct difference from policy functions in the US.

The Australian College of Educators promotes standards for teachers (ACE, 2003). Because Australia's education system is decentralized, ACE provides critical leadership in formulating model (national) teacher standards with states licensing and certifying teachers. For example, New South Wales' teacher professional learning policy includes common elements such as lifelong professional development and school plans for teachers' professional development (NSWDET, 2006), and Queensland's College of Teachers policy contextualizes education in New Times and sets Professional Standards for Graduates which preservice teachers should meet (QCT, 2006).

The curriculum framework for HPE, one of eight Key Learning Areas (KLAs), includes key principles, goals, and values within three strands: (a) Communication, Investigation, and Application (process strand); and (b) Human Functioning and PA and (c) Community Structures and Practices (conceptual strands) (Australian Education Council, 1994a). Accompanying documents specify student learning outcomes (AEC, 1994b) and a work sample approach for assessing student outcomes (AEC, 1997). The national curriculum promotes cross-subject integration, distinguishes between games and sport per se, characterizes HPE as socially constructed with students taking active roles in learning, and provides latitude to challenge traditional conceptualizations of PE (Penney, 1998). Both Queensland (QEA, 2006) and New South Wales (NSWBoS, 2006) state policies illustrate the contested identities of PE (since education, health, and sport discourses are represented in their curriculum frameworks).

New Zealand

Tomorrow's Schools (1989) set the stage for New Zealand's most recent major education reforms by aligning the New Zealand Curriculum (NZMoE,

2006), assessment of learning, and teacher CPD. Seven learning areas designated (all in English and Maori), include Health and Physical Well-being, each with eight levels of learning progressions. Schools also teach core skills (e.g. communication, numeracy, physical, self-management and competitive) and common values (e.g. honesty, tolerance, respect, compassion). Student achievement is a major focus, the Maori culture is recognized and integrated into school curricula, and teacher development is prioritized. Evidence-based practice, improving learning opportunities for diverse students, and foregrounding learning that helps students negotiate the "realities of an interdependent world" are emphasized (Fancy, 2006).

International collaborations

The International Committee of Sport Pedagogy sponsored a World Summit on Physical Education (1999) for 250 participants from 80 countries. Education, sport, and health discourses were linked strongly in the Call for Action's definition of PE: "...a systematic introduction to and progression through the skills and understandings required for life-long involvement in PA and sport and for effective participation in 21st century work, family life, and leisure" (International Committee of Sport Pedagogy, 1999). Calling PE, "... the most effective and inclusive means of providing all children, whatever their ability/ disability, sex, age, cultural, race/ethnicity, religious or social background, with the skills, attitudes, knowledge and understanding for life long participation in PA and sport" (World Summit on Physical Education, 1999), the World Summit generated model PE/TE policy for use by all nations. This policy model emphasizes effective leadership, coordination with parents and organizations, public relations information, and strong connections within schools to other subjects. PE is linked to "sustainable economic development", its status is reinforced as a "human right", and the agenda includes greater cooperation among national, regional, and international entities to promote ethical sport behavior, to assist developing countries with good PE/TE policy, and to preserve cultural heritage physical activities in different nations. Key participants include the United Nations, United Nations Education, Scientific, and Cultural Organization, the World Health Organization, the International Olympic Committee, and nongovernmental organizations. UNESCO's 3rd International Conference of Ministers and Senior Officials Responsible for PE and Sport designed parallel recommendations (ICSSPE, 1999).

International comparisons of education policy should be cautious and respectful of national cultural contexts. For instance, one comparison of school reform initiatives among the US, England, Japan, and Korea concluded that globalization influenced the specific nature of each country's reforms although policies were created to address their unique problems. Cultural differences diverged as US and England's reforms involved increasing academic achievement and raising standards while the Pacific Rim nations' reforms encompassed deregulating schools and promoting whole-person education (Lee, 2001).

Health discourses

Many countries' PE/TE policy contexts rest on a strong health discourse promoting lifetime PA to offset earlier onset of disease, obesity, and diabetes. Alarming statistics about overweight obesity, diabetes, cardiovascular diseases, and other chronic conditions among children, youth, and adults around the world directly correlate to correspondingly high levels of physical inactivity (e.g. Australian Sports Commission, 1996, 2004; Morrow and Gill, 1995; Wanless, 2003, 2004). Some researchers question the accuracy of the obesity and overweight data, seeing these as potentially overestimating the problem, particularly among children (Evans, 2004). Nonetheless, regardless of disagreement over the extent of the problem, these data have sharpened public health policy debates early in the 21st century, prompting numerous policy papers, policies, action strategies, and followup surveillance to judge how effectively these problems are addressed. Since childhood and adult activity patterns are related (Taylor et al., 1999), PE/TE is well-positioned to address these PA initiatives for healthier nations.

United States

In the US, the Center for Disease Control and Prevention's (CDC) weekly *Morbidity and Mortality Weekly Reports* have featured PA for adults and for children 9–13 years (2006a, 2006b), based on responses to the Behavioral Risk Factor Surveillance System (BRFSS) and Youth Media Campaign Longitudinal Survey (YMCLS) data, respectively. The YMCLS report is the first national policy recommendation about kinds and amounts of PA for this "tweener" age group.

Two decades ago, *Healthy People: The Surgeon General's Report on Health Promotion and Disease Prevention* (USDHHS, 1979) first mentioned PA as an integral part of healthy lifestyles, emphasizing increasing exercise, fitness, and sound nutrition. The *Surgeon General's Report* (USDHHS, 1996) urged inclusion of regular moderate PA across the lifespan, summarized research about the role of PA in disease prevention, reported patterns of PA, and proposed multiple policies and interventions for increasing PA. A recent *Journal of Teaching in Physical Education* theme issue analyzes the impact of the 1996 Surgeon General's Report on PE (Blankenship and Solmon [Eds.], 2004).

The *Surgeon General's Call to Action to Prevent and Decrease Overweight and Obesity* (USDHHS, 2001) clarified the need for coordinated actions by families, schools, the health care system, media and communications, and workplaces: "The design of successful interventions and actions for prevention and management of overweight and obesity will require the careful attention of many individuals and organizations *working together through multiple spheres of influence.*" (p. 27, italics mine). Calls to increase PA among youth have snowballed, coming from several policy documents[v]. These policies emphasize carefully coordinated, multifaceted approaches to change among educational, community, and environmental agencies as well as program, family, and individual behavioral changes to increase PA for all. That these strategies are population-based and combine individual, community, and ecological approaches speaks to the growing sophistication of policy making around PA. The prominence of school-based PE as a recommendation challenges the PE/TE community to join this collaborative approach to policy implementation.

Healthy People 2000: National Health Promotion and Disease Prevention Objectives (USDHHS, 1990) established national health objectives in the US to increase healthy lifespans, reduce health disparities among people, and provide greater access to preventive services. Two leading priorities were "physical activity and fitness" and "nutrition". This policy encouraged joint state and community strategies to address priorities, another indication of shifting national policy toward coordinating multiple agencies and strategies to address public policy mandates.

The most recent PA-related US health policy, *Healthy People 2010* (USDHHS, 2000), is based on current research, intended for use by multiple constituents (e.g. individuals, states, professional organizations), and designed to monitor success longitudinally (built-in accountability). Its two primary goals, increasing the quality and years of healthy life and eliminating health disparities, are linked with ten high-priority public health issues, listing "physical activity" and "overweight and obesity" first.

The Centers for Disease Control and Prevention play a huge role in PA-oriented policies and programs, collecting surveillance data, creating health-related programs (many include PA), and preparing sophisticated yet simply worded reports of health trends and program effectiveness for policymakers, educators, health professionals, and the public. CDC's broad goal is to change public health-related behavior on a population-wide scale. CDC is well-connected through coordinated programming and sophisticated websites to other organizations and agencies behind the same public health agendas.

CDC's well-established surveillance data influence policy formulation and can be used to lobby policy makers. Key mechanisms for monitoring information to inform PE/TE policy include the NHIS (CDC, 2006d), the NHANES (CDC, 2006c), the BRFSS (CDC, 2006e), and the YRBS (CDC, 2006f). NHIS, the major database for health issues in the US, now has a Spanish version in response to the changing national demographics. Linked widely with other health-related surveys, NHIS sorts data by socioeconomic and demographic characteristics. NHANES reports on adolescent and adult overweight and obesity. BRFSS, billed as the largest phone survey in the world, has interactive databases including topics like Leisure Time PA, Overweight, and Obesity. YRBS data show, for example, that 30% of high school males and 19% of females are either overweight or at risk of being overweight (CDC, 2006f).

CDC also develops specific programs and public relations campaigns designed to meet current national PA policy objectives. For example, the *VERB: It's What You Do* media campaign is a "national, multicultural, social marketing" directed to tweens aged 9–13, parents, and other "adult influencers" (CDC, 2006g). *VERB* promotes increased, sustained regular PA for early adolescents, particularly targeting racial/ethnic groups through banners, magazines, posters, TV, radio, and the World Wide Web.

Summit meetings often precede large-scale, multi-faceted interventions. Representatives from many public, private, and philanthropic organizations whose interests coincide meet to develop policy recommendations in particular sectors of public life. Action for Healthy Kids (AFHK, 2006), a multi-state, multi-level initiative stemming from the 2002 Healthy Schools Summit (AFHK, 2006), coordinates government agencies (e.g. CDC), state AFHK coalitions, national organizations (e.g. American Diabetes Association, National Coalition for Parent Involvement in Education), and private funding sources (e.g. Robert Woods Johnson Foundation) to improve "… the health and educational performance of children through better nutrition and physical activity in schools" (AFHK, 2006).

PA-related PE/TE policies

NASPE's research-based PA guidelines, (NASPE, 2002a, 2004b), along with its appropriate practice documents for young children (2000b), elementary PE (2000a), middle school PE (2001b), and high school PE (2004a), constitute policy recommendations. They could be linked to PE content standards and beginning/advanced TE program standards to align best instructional practice with PA-related student outcomes.

International comparisons

The World Health Organization's (WHO) *Global Strategy on Diet, PA, and Health* (WHO, 2006) exemplifies international cooperation for health policy, encouraging regular PA in work, transport, domestic tasks, and leisure settings. Calling PA an individual *and* societal problem, WHO's sophist cated analysis "demands a population-based, multisectoral, multidisciplinary, and culturally relevant approach" for each nation with particular emphasis on partnerships among organizations to enhance PA for children at school and in communities.

Many countries' national health policies mirror the intent and provisions of the US's *Healthy People 2010*, including emphases on PA. In Australia this includes *Active Australia* (ASC, 1996) and *A More Active Australia* (ASC, 2004); in England, the Wanless Reports (Wanless, 2003, 2004); Scotland's *Let's Make Scotland More Active* (Scottish Executive Health Department, 2004); Ireland's *New Health Strategy* (DoH&C, 2006), and New Zealand's *Taking the pulse: The 1996/97 New Zealand Health Survey* (Ministry of Health, 2006). All emphasize school and community PA contexts with evidence-based strategies as key elements in addressing obesity, overweight, and early chronic disease onset problems across world populations. The Irish policy echoes the WHO's clear messages of inequities in health care: "Health follows a social gradient: 'poor people get sick more often and die younger'" (DoH&C, 2004); the language of this policy acknowledges the importance of social capital accrued through participation in PA through sports.

National professional organizations promote PA and health discourses in PE. The Australian Council of Health, Physical Education, and Recreation maintains a national database of research on children's fitness and health (ACHPER, 2006). In promoting healthy lifestyles, ACHPER works through both education and commercial programs providing advocacy, professional development, and consulting services to professionals. In New Zealand, SPARC's *Push Play* initiative reports PA data for all age groups (SPARC, 2006a, 2006b). The Canadian Association for Health, Physical Education, Recreation and Dance spells out both Quality Daily PE and Quality School Health curricula with associated school report cards. CAHPER also sponsors a PE Mentors Network for new teachers and supports numerous links to research that supports PE and to websites of like-minded, collaborative organizations promoting PA (CAHPER, 2006). Most industrialized nations have comparable professional teacher organizations that advocate for physical activity (e.g. British Association of Advisors and Lecturers [BAALPE, 2004], Physical Education Association United Kingdom [PEAUK, 2006]).

Sport discourses

International collaboration

The International Olympic Committee's Sport for All Commission sponsors the Sport for All movement, engendering the "Olympic ideal that sport is a human right for all individuals regardless of race, social class, and sex" (IOC, 2006; SportEngland, 2006) and encourages national bodies to provide sports opportunities in their countries for everyone. Biennial theme-based Congresses are held around the world to promote sport internationally (e.g. the 2000 Congress theme was Sport for All and Governmental Policies). The International Youth Sports Congress meets annually as a coalition of youth sports organizations to discuss current global and national issues that influence youth sports (National Alliance for Youth Sport, 2006).

In the US, sport dominates the entire culture. Professional sport leagues for men and more recently for women, college and high school athletics, burgeoning numbers of community and elite traveling youth sport teams, huge numbers of spectators reached live and through media, and infiltration of sport metaphors into American English demonstrate that sport infuses the entire culture. Correspondingly, policies abound for its governance. For example, national legislative policy governs the US Olympic Committee, the National Collegiate Athletic Association (NCAA, 2006) has rules for eligibility of college athletes and for practice hours, and regulations exist for national and local youth sport organizations (e.g. Amateur Softball Association of America, 2006; Little League Baseball, 2006). For P12 education, sports and games dominate the PE curriculum.

Youth sport has become big business in the US Organizations offer coaching courses (Human Kinetics' American Sport Education Program, 2006; Institute for the Study of Youth Sport's (ISYS) Coaches Education, 2004a), promote policy relating to young participants (ISYS, 2006b), and support adults involved with youth sports (North American Youth Sport Institute, 2006; National Alliance for Youth Sports, 2006). NAYS's *National Standards for Youth Sports* (NAYS, 2006), include program standards based on children's well-being; proper sports environments; drug, tobacco, and alcohol-free environments; positive role models; parents' active roles; and providing safe, positive settings for youth sports. NASPE also has formulated *Guidelines for After School PA and Intramural Sport Programs* (2002b) and *Coaches' Code of Conduct* (2001c).

Not to mention Title IX's athletics provisions would be remiss. Among other educational provisions, this

1972 gender equity legislation exerted tremendous pressures on schools and colleges to provide arrangements for girls and women's sports proportionately comparable to those of men (US Government, 2006). Surviving recent attacks (NAGWS, 2006; NOW, 2006), Title IX remains one of the bulwarks responsible for the increased opportunities for females in school sport in the US.

While many positive values can be transmitted through developmentally appropriate sports curricula, unfortunately the most widespread discourses appear to emphasize elitism and competition as underlying values. Regardless of numerous sport policy levels and contexts that impinge on PE/TE, few researchers to date have addressed any US sport policy issues.

International comparisons

Children's sport is increasingly important internationally. In the UK, a key policy paper on revitalizing school sport emphasizes five core (masculine) games (Evans and Penney, 1995). Begun in 1995, the Youth Sport Trust (YST) supports NCPE by promoting opportunities for children (aged 1½–18) "to receive a quality introduction to PE and sport and structured pathways for them to continue participating and progressing" (YST, 1996). Collaborating with other organizations, YST markets materials as a resource for teachers (Penney, 1998). Sport-oriented Specialist Sports Colleges (SSCs), begun in 1994, are secondary schools with sports as the magnet theme, representing a rapidly changing infrastructure for both education and sport (Penney and Houlihan, 2003). *Best Practices in Sports Colleges* (Youth Sport Trust, 2002) lays out expectations that SSCs will collaborate with a variety of other community and education institutions to promote positive youth sport participation. National Junior Sport Programmes target UK teenagers, providing "… opportunities for all young people aged 14 to 18 years to become fully involved in sport and physical recreation …" (English Sports Council, 1997).

Government-sponsored organizations promote youth sport in several countries. SportEngland, the former English Sports Council, implements governmental sports objectives: to get all citizens to start, stay, and succeed in sports (SportEngland, 2006). *A Sporting Future for All: The Government's Plan for Sport* (Department for Culture, Media, and Sport, 2001) promotes sports for youngsters sponsored by national governing bodies, schools, and communities. The Irish Sports Council's "Sport for Life" emphasizes Local Sports Partnerships to increase participation, sport for young people, and positive connections with PE curricula (ISC, 2006). Sport and Recreation New Zealand (SPARC) assists schools, community organizations, sports clubs, and other entities to promote New Zealanders' becoming highly active in sports of their choice. SPARC's campaign, Push Play, encourages children toward higher activity levels through sport (SPARC, 2006a). New Zealand has seen a large growth in sport schools and they vary from support of elite athletes to using sport as an incentive to stay in school (Pope, 2002)

Australian policy makers clearly desired to separate sport from PE: (" … the Aussie Sport program is not a PE program and should not be used by State and Territory education departments to salve their consciences for opting out of their responsibility for the provision of a properly structured PE program" [Senate Standing Committee on Education, Recreation and the Arts, 1992, p. 22]). The policy provides all citizens with access to "… quality participation opportunities to enable them to fulfill their potential and be provided with physical, social, mental, and spiritual benefits regardless of socio-economic status, race, age, or gender, ability, and geographic location" (Australian Sports Commission, 1996: 8). Current sport policy supports special Health Promoting Schools that combat prevalent sport discourses (Penney, 1998).

Potential policy outcomes from competing discourses

The importance of the education, health, and sport discourses to PE/TE policy rests partially on the incompatibility of their respective intended outcomes. To illustrate, health discourses advocate more curriculum time to PE to promote PA so students develop skills to sustain lifetime participation and enjoyment. Sport discourses prioritize games and sports in P12 curricula, arguably excluding some children from lifetime PA commitments because of negative experiences in school PE. Education discourses foreground positive, appropriate, inclusive learning opportunities for all students, a goal that often contradicts some sport discourses' of "winner take all" goals although it seems more compatible with health discourses' goals. Because education reforms mandate good high stakes test scores in "core" subjects, schools naturally devote more curriculum time to those areas, thus disadvantaging marginalized subjects such as PE with less time. The overall result is fewer physically active children with all the attendant short- and long-term aversive outcomes.

Equally important are potential policy clashes within TE. States' program accreditation and teacher licensure stipulations may contradict what is considered best practice for content and instruction by PE/TE professionals and professional organizations, and there is usually insufficient time to include all aspects of preservice preparation desired. PE/TE thus becomes contested terrain where sport, health, and education discourses compete. The 2004 *JTPE* thematic issue (Blankenship and Solmon, 2004) addresses the intersection among these three discourses in the authors' analyses of the 1996 *Surgeon General's Report* (USDHHS, 1996).

Contemporary PE/TE policy research

This section offers exemplar papers presenting primary empirical data, theory, and analysis, not an exhaustive review. PE/TE policy research in the US and most other countries is difficult to find, although policy studies abound in other P12 subjects and teacher education (e.g. *Education Policy Analysis Archives,* 2004). In contrast, PE/TE policy research in the UK offers a rich initial data base on which to build subsequent investigations throughout the international community. Three broad questions could guide future PE/TE policy research; only the first is addressed by current research:

1. How is policy formulated, implemented, revised, coordinated with potentially conflicting policies, and related to practice? How do social, economic, political, historical, and contemporary contexts affect policy?
2. What do PE/TE policies say about school PE, PE teachers, TE, and teacher educators? How do PE/TE policies connect to PE and TE work? What entities influence PE/TE policy
3. What are the best ways to research the design and effects of PE/TE policies? How might teachers and teacher educators best influence policymaking and implementation?

Two policy research perspectives

Traditional policy perspectives

Current policy research appears to be framed in two distinct perspectives (Penney and Evans, 1999). Traditional orientations view policymaking and implementation as separate processes. Policies created at the top of hierarchical bureaucracies by key players (with more power) are transmitted to those lower down to implement (people with less power). Policy makers expect policies to be enacted by practitioners as given so policy practice closely mirrors policy documents. Policy makers, who may be informed by a variety of advocates, periodically review and modify policy. Teachers and teacher educators, those charged with implementation, are rarely consulted in larger nations, although in smaller countries opportunities to influence policy are more common. Professional organizations, advocacy groups, and government commissions frequently produce policy briefs, commissioned papers, or electronic publications intended to influence policy makers. For example, the American Alliance for Health, Physical Education, Recreation and Dance (AAHPERD) generates documents to affect policy making (e.g. NASPE *Concepts and Principles,* 2003; NASPE *Standards,* 2004c) and has increasingly strengthened its national advocacy role (e.g. promoting passage of the Carol M. White (2006) PEP legislation to improve school PE (USD-HHS, 2004) Professional organizations are increasingly savvy about forming coalitions to influence legislation or collectively develop population-based data to influence public policy. AAHPERD, for example, joined other organiztions to support the CDC's VERB Campaign promoting physical activity among adolescents (CDC, 2006g).

Traditional policy perspectives identify major roles and players who influence policy processes and delineate basic policy processes (Rink and Mitchell, 2002). The complexities of overlapping, multiple policy contexts and practitioner agency are sometimes ignored in these analyses. The unidirectionality of traditional perspectives (assumption that policy flows down while implementation flows out to the grassroots level) misses the rich multidimensional, multi-directional influences on policy formulation and practice. In traditional perspectives, government officials dictate structures, processes, and content of PE/TE programs from outside while educators conform to external dictates without substantial authority, control, or ownership of their work. Traditional perspectives on policy imply deskilling of teachers and teacher educators whose roles are confined to receiving and executing policy (Penney and Evans, 1999).

Traditionally oriented policy research

Several researchers are now examining PE/TE policy in the UK and a few in the US. In the UK Curtner-Smith investigated the grass roots effects of National Curriculum Physical Education by mixing quantitative and qualitative approaches. Using systematic observation, he examined both teacher and student behaviors before and during the NCPE. Teachers' value orientations revealed that, while neither gender nor experience accounted for differences, distinct value orientations were associated with activity backgrounds, teachers with traditional backgrounds orienting toward social responsibility and those with nontraditional backgrounds prioritizing learning process. Few teachers' orientations foregrounded disciplinary mastery (most congruent with NCPE). Teachers with self-actualization or social responsibility value orientations may find implementation of NCPE most difficult (Curtner-Smith and Meek, 2000). Teachers' use of teaching styles (Curtner-Smith, and Hasty, 1997; Curtner-Smith et al., 2001a) and rules, routines, and expectations (Curtner-Smith, and Todorovich,

1998; Curtner-Smith, 1999b) were studied before and during NCPE with few differences discovered.

Rural and urban teachers were compared during the first revised NCPE. Most teachers used direct instruction styles and few differences were observed between the teaching contexts (Curtner-Smith et al., 2001). Lacon and Curtner-Smith (1998) reported results from a study comparing urban and rural secondary teachers and replicating the methodologies used in an earlier rural study (Curtner-Smith et al., 1995a). Urban teachers, while differing slightly over most measures of teacher behavior from their rural counterparts, showed similar overall patterns, which Curtner-Smith attributed to the similarity of initial teacher training.

Curtner-Smith's (1999c) qualitative paper, drawing on occupational socialization theory and Sparkes' (1991) technological, ecological, and cultural curriculum change perspectives, found that teachers' different interpretations of NCPE policy depended on gender, participation in sport and PA, experiences in PE and school sport, perceptions of the government's interpretations of the curriculum policy, teacher education, colleagues, and situational constraints of their teaching setting. No real changes were noted in teachers' value and belief orientations nor in their practices following implementation of the NCPE; they merely adapted NCPE policy to be congruent with their current ideologies.

Curtner-Smith and colleagues have explored the effects of the NCPE on teacher behaviors related to students' skill learning (Curtner-Smith et al., 1995b), health-related fitness (Curtner-Smith et al., 1996), and psychosocial development (Curtner-Smith, 1999a; Curtner-Smith et al., 1995a), comparing these with similar studies of teacher behavior effects prior to implementation of NCPE (Curtner-Smith et al., 1995, a,b).

Curtner-Smith's research connecting NCPE policy with classroom-based descriptions of teachers' and students' work in rural and urban settings is important in the progression and complexity it shows. Curtner-Smith's shift toward a more critical policy perspective (2002a,b) raise key questions about policy research in general: Who makes policy and how is it framed? What discourses and whom do official policy texts privilege? If teachers adapt or contest policy, what effects does their work have on students? Extending Curtner-Smith's thinking, additional research should examine the responsibilities of PETE programs to prepare their candidates for policy matters such as advocacy and articulation of model policies that support values around improving PA for all. The special theme issue of *JTPE* (Blankenship and Solmon, 2004) explores such issues.

Armour and Yelling (2004) examined research on continuing professional development for experienced teachers in the UK within a CPD policy context whose "… strong focus on the role of the teacher in improving the standard of pupils' learning" (p. 98) parallels the NCPE's emphasis on development of performance skills for students. Effective CPD is collaborative, aligning with teachers' prior learning, student achievement standards, assessment, and policy. Based on their questionnaire and interview data that describe current CPD models as lacking progression, coherence, and relevance, they propose that CPD radically shift to collaborative inquiry and reflective examination of teachers' own practices, using the constructs of communities of practice and situated learning to address school policy barriers and create new kinds of knowledge in PE. Advocating a pedagogy for learning rather than teaching, Armour and Yelling note increasing presence of online CPD opportunities for PE teachers.

Two traditional examples of policy-oriented research in the US are presented next, one illustrating Berliner's purpose of educational research for "understanding", the other his purpose for "intervention" (Berliner, 1987). It is critical to note that in the US, very little policy research is available in PE, though many studies have policy components or implications.

First, a small-scale survey was designed to examine how time for art, music, and PE was allocated in one state's elementary schools, how these allocations were influenced by high stakes testing policy, and what kinds of relationships existed between time allotments and student test scores (Wilkins et al., 2003). Findings indicated that time allotment and high stakes test scores were not related, that lower special subject time allotments were not related to higher test scores, and that schools did not decrease PE time to provide more time for 'core' subjects appearing on the high stakes tests. These PE data run counter to other research findings that marginal subjects' curriculum time is reduced when high stakes testing policies are in effect. Within this study's limitations, these findings enhance understanding of PE's relationship with generic education reform policy around high stakes testing as a measure of accountability.

In contrast, Rink and colleagues (Rink and Mitchell, 2002, 2003) studied the South Carolina Physical Education Assessment Project, with state-level policy processes at center stage for both initiation and implementation stages (Fullan, 2001). Although the full report centers on various assessment data and the overall model of statewide accountability for secondary PE, the most critical part details efforts of PE/TE constituents to change state policy to include PE on the state report card (Rink and Mitchell, 2003). More detailed analysis of policy strategies is explained in a second paper (Rink and Mitchell, 2002). A third state example, describing political strategies that support PE in Ohio, references the South Carolina project (Lee and O'Sullivan, 2004).

Critical policy perspectives

Critical perspectives on policy research make distinctly different assumptions. Policy is conceptualized as operating at multiple sites without particular hierarchy. Analysis of multi-site policy operations allows discovery of more complex patterns of policy making and implementation. Formulation, adoption, adaptation, modification, and contestation of policy making occur simultaneously at different sites with those in policy roles reciprocally affecting others at different policy sites. Policy is seen as written, spoken, mental, and corporeal texts, the latter particularly relevant to PE/TE since physical capital represents major aspects of our work (Shilling, 1993). Individuals encounter multiple forms of policy texts within their own contexts, adding their own interpretations to policy interactions with others (Penney and Evans, 1999). The flow of policy moves back and forth among people and sites, although policies ultimately are enacted by teachers and students in PE/TE programs:

> The physical texts that pop through the school letterboxes do not arrive out of the blue; they have an interpretational and representational history, and neither do they enter asocial and institutional vacuum. The text and its readers and the context of response all have histories (Ball, 1994 p. 17). In short, schools and teachers are not all equally well positioned or resourced... . (Evans and Penney, 1995: 2)

Critical perspectives use political, ideological, economic, and historical contexts to explain constraints and conditions under which policy is made and changed. Stakeholders holding divergent values and beliefs influence policy. Since stakeholders often invest in differential policy outcomes based on their particular values, policy spaces are always contested. The broader and more comprehensive the realm of potential policy application, the more contested the policy space becomes because more stakeholders are interested in different outcomes.

Critical perspectives (Penney and Evans, 1999) enable researchers to examine particular interests, values, and beliefs using policy texts as evidence. Different discourses at multiple sites are more visible, promoting and privileging particular sets of values, while excluding others; each discourse thus has silences about what is ignored, excluded, subordinated, or marginalized (Penney and Evans, 1999). Since policy texts are never neutral, they should always be examined for implicit values. Policy actors do not have equal policy roles; some are marginalized, others ignored, some have greater power and privilege. Policy content is thus not the sole concern, but who speaks, in which sites, and with what

authorities is also important. Power is thus not a commodity but is "... expressed in the context of social positioning and interaction [among] individuals, groups, and institutions" (Kirk and Macdonald, 2001).

Critical perspectives better account for policy processes and overlapping contexts governing PE/TE, providing richer ways of thinking about interactions among policy stakeholders. A key theme is that "... issues of equity need to be foregrounded in our reflections upon policies and practices, as in privileging particular interests and definitions, developments will inevitably advantage some individuals and disadvantage others." (Penney, 1998: 117). Traditional and critical perspectives can complement each other in PE/TE research designed to discover more powerful ways of examining policy development and implementation.

Research from a critical perspective

Penney, Evans, and their colleagues have examined the NCPE of England and Wales using a critical lens. Early on they argued that ERA and NCPE effectively "marketized" and deregulated education and that the discourse in PE shifted significantly away from equity and equal opportunity issues:

> The emphasis and direction in state public policy...has intentionally changed from issues of employing the local state to overcome social and educational disadvantages, inequity, and difference in material and cultural provision, to that of guaranteeing the individual's choice under the conditions of the 'free market' to secure for herself or himself the services she or he wants and needs. (Evans et al., 1993: 322)

Critical research foregrounds the importance of politics in education. Evans and Penney (1995) critique the ERA as an instrument of the conservative discourse of the New Right (Penney and Evans, 1997). Through surveys and qualitative case studies they examined relationships among state schools, local education authorities (LEAs), and central (national) government. Central government control was greater and LEA functions became merely an "...extension of the state's ideological powers of surveillance and control" (Evans and Penney, 1994: 532) as ERA legislation shifted LEA functions from local advice and assistance to teachers toward record keeping and greater accountability for inspection.

The New Right's influence on NCPE revisions supports "cultural restoration" of sport to dominate the language of NCPE policy, partially influenced by politicians' actions (e.g. posing for photographs with prominent sports figures) who frame the discourse from outside schools (Evans and Penney, 1995). Questioning whether ERA rhetoric about raising standards is found in practice, these authors note that ERA and NCPE "...policies will inevitably be made and remade by teachers within the education system in ways that have intended and unintended negative and positive consequences for both education and its surrounding milieu" (Evans and Penney, 1995: 36) and indicate clear links with teacher preparation policy. Within the broad frame of the worldwide standards—assessment—accountability reforms, it is sad to note the report here of common problems such as the lack of curriculum texts and CPD to help teachers implement assessment for NCPE. Evans and Penney call for ongoing inservice training around implementation of the NCPE if it is to be successful. This paper is unambiguous evidence that "... policy initiatives are rarely unproblematically translated into school practice." (Evans and Penney, 1994: 531)

Penney and Chandler (2000) use the NCPE as an exemplar vehicle to argue for a 21st century "critical pedagogy for social justice" and "....a *thematically oriented, rather than activity-based curriculum*, and a framework that openly privileges what we may term 'themes' or 'strands of learning'" (p. 77, italics original) They propose curricular themes of "movement and physical literacy; PA, health, and fitness; competition and cooperation; challenge" (pp. 79–80) with links among them to challenge all youngsters to be successful, motivated, self-directed, and willing to continue lifelong PA. Proposing a partnership model involving teachers, students, parents, and community agencies as key players, they envision PE as developing "... critically informed citizens who are committed to playing a part in establishing more equitable societies in which all individuals are valued; in which individual, social and cultural differences are celebrated as a richness of society; and in which knowledge is something to be collectively, collaboratively and creatively advanced, rather than pre-defined and 'delivered'" (p. 73).

In a 1998 paper, Penney elegantly presents arguments about education, health, and sport discourses as they appear in NCPE policy statements and implementation. A key point is that while people at all policy sites exert some power, the major surveillance and control work top down from the state (Penney, 1998). In a later paper she argued that the NCPE foregrounds sport discourses of excellence in performance while discourse about educational excellence in PE is weakly developed (Penney, 2000). The strong connections between sport and PE are grounded in the history of the profession, in how curricula are structured, and in the processes through which policy is developed. The NCPE is an example where there was little contribution or review by teachers, on tight timelines, and in a centralized, hierarchical manner. Penney speculates, using a parallel example of music education, about the possibilities of a distinct shift in policy and curricular orientation to one based in educational excellence.

Harris and Penney (2000) examined gender issues around teaching health-related exercise (HRE) within the NCPE. Not surprisingly, their findings confirm differences between men and women department heads in program development at the school level, as well as curricular differences delivered to girls and boys (single-sex classes in Britain). The paper highlights the difficulties of changing policy, curricula, and pedagogical practices, underscoring variability in policy implementation, thus corroborating the active participation of all constituents in policy processes, and reiterating long-term resistance to change in PE practice.

In one of the only papers to link P12 with TE, Penney and Houlihan (2003) consider the growth and positioning of Specialist Sports Colleges (SSCs) with respect to institutions of higher education (IHEs) that have traditionally supplied initial teacher training and continued professional development for veteran teachers. Using a policy frame, they conclude that SSCs are privileged over traditional Institutions of Higher Education (IHEs) and are better positioned to dominate future preparation of PE teachers and coaches in England. Although SSCs could provide opportunities for partnerships with higher education institutions preparing teachers, political constraints and policy shifts toward more centralized governmental control of TE dim these prospects, but may enhance possibilities of SSCs collaborating with other organizations (Penney and Houlihan, 2003).

MacPhail (2004) studied Scottish teachers' social construction of Higher Grade Physical Education (HGPE) in curriculum decision making. HGPE for 16–18-year-olds is parallel to England and Wales' A level examinations and Queensland's Senior Syllabus. MacPhail's questionnaire data indicate that teachers' reasons for making curricular decisions reside more in their school contexts than in their interpretations of HGPE curriculum policy. Drawing on Bernstein's social construction of pedagogic discourse model with primary, recontextualizing, and secondary fields of knowledge production, MacPhail documents the gendered nature of PE (men hold more power and support the sport and biophysical science content of the HGPE than women). She notes that teacher decisions to offer HGPE were based on school context for teaching, teacher expertise and views of HGPE, and how students' needs are addressed. Teachers deciding not to offer HGPE did so because of perceived lack of student interest, preparation, or time.

MacPhail concluded that "…with the advent of certification and examination in PE teachers are no longer able to experience the relative freedom they once commanded over the course design of PE." (p. 70).

At the state level in Australia (Queensland), Macdonald and Brooker (1997) compared a trial secondary PE curriculum with the current curriculum, both enacted, in a direct study of policy implementation. They concluded that the movement-oriented trial curriculum includes key elements of education reform such as clear conceptual frameworks, closely aligned assessments, and a definitive focus on PA as the "authentic medium for becoming physically educated" (Macdonald and Brooker, 1997).

Macdonald et al. (2002) draw attention to the positioning of teacher education practices vis a vis current curriculum policies in Australia, noting their weak connections. Using data from evaluation of the HPE key learning area syllabus, the authors examine how knowledge is organized differently in schools and universities and draws implications about changing practices in teacher preparation and in PE to design and implement the most appropriate PE programs for students. Using Australian examples to show that while P12 and TE policy ought to align, they don't necessarily do so by virtue of different contexts and value systems, Macdonald and colleagues (2002) provide useful questions about policy and argue that 'official knowledge' as represented in P12 and TE curricula may differ because knowledge is organized differently by discipline, department, and subject in the two sites. Since Australian states are now considering teaching standards, Macdonald (2003) presents arguments for and against use of national and state standards. She incorporates comparisons with the NBPTS standards in the US.

Pope's writings on the relationships between education and sport schools in New Zealand take a much more positive perspective. He examines the growth of sports academies (Pope, 2002), reflects on how schools can provide educative experiences in sport (Grant and Pope, 2000; Pope, 2004), argues that good school sport in curricular and co-curricular contexts can help students maintain playfulness characterized in early sport experiences (Pope, 2004), and suggests specific ways to include sport in PE curricula (Pope, 1999).

Policy research themes

Drawing themes from the few studies available would be premature. There is currently more research on P12 than TE topics. Traditional studies examine micro-level effects of policy effects on teachers, while critical studies explore multiple policy sites at once in tracing political and other influences and various discourses in policy actions. Several researchers noted that research confirms old teaching/curricular practices even in light of the NCPE as new policy (Curtner-Smith and colleagues in multiple papers; PIS provide year Evans and Penney, 1994; Penney and Evans, 1999). They acknowledge the international commonality of issues and the slowness of real change as policy is implemented and negotiated at different sites.

Future research agendas

Policy is about competing values, *not* competing data….When social scientists do their work well they can provide policy makers with what might be called "is" data. The policy makers, however, use "ought" data. And you simply cannot go from an "is" to an "ought" … from a statement of fact, to a statement of value. (Berliner, 2004: 7)

Three substantive reasons underscore why good policy – and good policy studies – are critical to the PE/TE community. First, good research from a multiplicity of complementary perspectives illuminates the intricate connections between P12 and TE within PE/TE. Second, understanding policy positions PE/TE professionals to influence agencies and individuals who create policy and to become key policy makers ourselves. PE/TE can support education, public health, and sport initiatives underlying lifelong PA. Though admittedly more difficult as educators and researchers in a "marginal" subject, PE/TEs can learn from general P12 and TE policy, thus becoming experts that other constituents want at the policy making table (Rink and Mitchell, 2002). Finally, PE/TE improvements can result from understanding how different factors shape policy, how policies clash or align, and how policy is proposed, opposed, or adapted to best sustain PA and other elements of PE/TE.

Future research agendas should first be broad and inclusive, encouraging a range from functionally to critically oriented research using sound designs, substantial data sets, and theoretically driven interpretations to enhance the current, rather thin PE/TE policy knowledge base. While individual researchers have contributed considerable bodies of work (e.g. Penney from critical perspectives, Curtner-Smith as a functionalist), more PE/TE researchers could investigate policy issues from other perspectives. For example, interventionist studies could be designed to understand the consequences of deliberate efforts to influence policy formulation. Or case studies could be built to understand policy implementation in local contexts with particular teachers, students, and school sites. Additionally, broad-scale investigations of simultaneous policy making/implementation at multiple sites (i.e. local, state, national, international) could elaborate on the "big picture" of PE/TE policy processes.

One clear theme in the policy world is action through coalition-building. Research agendas should examine how coalitions originate, operate, and are assessed for impact. How do coalitions coordinate multiple organizations to share common goals, collaboratively design initiatives, secure multiple funding sources, collect long-term accountability data, and assess cost effectiveness of delivery vis a vis coalition goals? Understanding such processes better positions PE/TE specialists to participate wisely in policy making (e.g. by knowing that coalition-building is long term and that conceptualizing common agendas across organizations with different goals and values is difficult).

Second, PE/TE policy research agendas should both study and promote advocacy to position PE/TE as more important subject matter in schools, using education, health, and sport discourses, and focusing on how value differences among constituents influence policy formulation and implementation. This should be an internationally collaborative agenda. As Penney and Evans (1999) note, "The issue of who and what are defining PE and controlling the purposes that it serves, and of how particular definitions and elements of 'control' of teaching and learning are being established and reinforced, are matters for those involved in PE world-wide to address." (p. xii)

Third, PE/TE policy research agendas must address equity in policy studies. How does school PE implement policy and what are the consequences in equitable learning opportunities for *all* children? Even unintended consequences of legislation such as *NCLB* in the US or *NCPE* in England and Wales, for example, can disadvantage certain children because of school location or funding. How do gender, race, ethnicity, sexual orientation, social class, and multiple social identities relate to policy implementation in schools where programs significantly differ for children with diverse identities? Distribution of qualified teachers across school districts, systems for assigning teachers to schools, and recruitment and retention schemes for inviting people into teaching careers should be examined for unintended inequities.

Fourth, PE/TE policy research should untangle interconnections among political, education, health, sport, and market discourses as these affect PE/TE policy. The New Right is increasingly powerful in many countries (Evans and Penney, 1995) while liberal influences wane, and education policy (including PE/TE) is more often controlled by politicians than by education professionals. Learning how these constituencies gain and maintain power over policy could offer compelling lessons for PE/TE practitioners in all contexts.

Fifth, PE/TE policy research should include the impact of technology on policy making. The Internet, Worldwide Web, and warp speed of information exchange could provide shortcuts to basic understandings of policy matters for PE/TEs, though the sheer volume and availability of websites, documents, and information can overwhelm neophytes intent on learning about policy. Further, technology provides an effective means of influencing policy makers by exponentially gathering like-minded advocates and communicating messages faster.

In conclusion, the PE/TE policy landscape is a place where constituents, organizations, and functions are never crystal clear, where respective goals often compete, where coalitions are formed and reformed over time, and where power relations constantly shift. If the PE/TE community's goal is creating equitable and fair policy for preparing and supporting skillful teachers who promote life-long healthful PA for all, then NCTAF's *No dream denied* (2003) envisions ideal policies that enhance…

… a chain of shared responsibility for learning that links students, teachers, [parents, communities] administrators, and policymakers….A coordinated system of teacher recruitment, quality teacher preparation, clinical practice, induction, mentorship, and continuing professional development, with accountability built in at each stage, is essential for ensuring high-quality teaching for all students. (p. 143, brackets mine)

Notes

1 PE/TE includes *P12 school physical education* (hereafter PE), *preservice teacher education* (PTE), and *continuing professional development (CPD)* The PE/TE hyphen denotes the strong linkage between PE and PTE/CPD in recent education reforms. P12 denotes P12 education; TE includes PTE and CPD.

2 Websites are cited for current year.

3 NCATE associated organizations: Among these organizations are the American Association of Colleges for Teacher Education (AACTE), the Association of Teacher Educators (ATE), teachers unions such as the American Federation of Teachers (AFT) and the National Education Association (NEA), state and local policy making bodies such as the Council of Chief State School Officers (CCSSO) and the National School Boards Association (NSBA), child-centered organizations (e.g. National Association for the Education of Young Children [NAEYC]), technology organizations (e.g. International Society for Technology in Education

[ISTE]), specialist organizations (e.g. American Educational Research Association [AERA]), administrator organizations (e.g. National Association of Elementary School Principals [NAESP]), teacher certification organizations (e.g. National Board for Professional Teaching Standards [NBPTS]), and subject-specific organizations including the National Association for Sport and Physical Education (NASPE).

4 All URLs were checked multiple times for accuracy on page proofs. Nonetheless, many are subject to rapid change and may not operate at the time this chapter is read.

5 These documents include *Guidelines for School and Community Programs to Promote Lifelong Physical Activity Among Young People* (1997), *Dietary Guidelines for Americans* (2000), *Promoting Better Health for Young People Through Physical Activity and Sports: A Report to the President from the Secretary of Health and Human Services and the Secretary of Education* (2000), and *Guide to Community Preventive Services* (2001).

References

Action for Healthy Kids. (2006). Homepage. Retrieved 06/07/06 from http://www.actionforhealthykids.org.

Allen, M. (2003). *Eight questions on teacher preparation: What does the research say?* Education Commission of the States. Retrieved 06/07/06 from http://www.ecs.org/publications.

Amateur Softball Association of America (2006). Homepage. Retrieved 06/07/06 from http://www.softball.org.

American Alliance for Health, Physical Education, Recreation, and Dance. (n.d.) Home page. Retrieved 06/07/06 from http://www.aahperd.org.

American Association of Colleges for Teacher Education. (2003). *Comparison of NCATE and TEAC processes for accreditation of teacher education.* Washington DC: AACTE.

American Board for Certification of Teacher Excellence. (2004). Home page. Retrieved 06/07/06 from http://www.abcte.org.

Armour, K. and Yelling, M. (2004). Continuing professional development for experienced physical education teachers: Towards effective provision. *Sport, Education and Society, 9(1)*: 95–114.

Association of Teacher Educators. (2006). *Standards for teacher educators.* Retrieved 06/07/06 from http://www.ate1.org.

Australian College of Educators. (2003) *Teacher standards, quality and professionalism project.* Retrieved 06/07/06 from http://www.austcolled.com.au.

Australian Council of Health, Physical Education, and Recreation. (2006) *Active Australia schools network.* Retrieved 06/7/06 from http://www.achper.org.au.

Australian Education Council. (1994a). *A statement on health and physical education for Australian schools: A joint project of the states, Territories and the Commonwealth of Australia.* Carlton, Victoria: Curriculum Corporation.

Australian Education Council. (1994b). *Health and physical education – A curriculum profile for Australian schools.* Carlton, Victoria: Curriculum Corporation.

Australian Education Council. (1997). *Student work samples in health and physical education.* Carlton, Victoria: Curriculum Corporation.

Australian Sports Commission. (1996). *Active Australia: A national participation framework.* Canberra. Retrieved 06/07/06 from http://www.ausport.gov.au.

Australian Sports Commission. (2006). *Backing Australia's sporting ability: A more active Australia.* Retrieved 06/07/06 from http://www.ausport.gov.au/fulltext/2001/feddep/active.ap.

Berliner, D. (2006). Educational psychology as a policy science: Thoughts on the distinction between a discipline and a profession. *Canadian Journal of Educational Administration and Policy,* Issue # 26. RRetrieved 06/07/06 from http://www.umanitoba.ca/publications/cjeap.

Berliner, D. (1987). Knowledge is power: A talk to teachers about a revolution in the teaching profession. In Berliner, D. and Rosenshine, B. (Eds.), *Talks to teachers* (pp. 3–33). New York: Random House.

Blankenship, B. and Solmon, M. (Eds.). (2004). Physical education, physical activity and public health: Learning from the past and building for the future. *Journal of Teaching in Physical Education, 23(4)*: 269–404.

Association for Physical Education (2006). Home page. Retrieved 10/19/04 from http://www.baalpe.org.

Calderhead, J. (2001). International experiences of teaching reform. In V. Richardson (Ed.), *Handbook of research on teaching,* 4th ed. (pp. 777–800). Washington DC: AERA.

Canadian Association for Health, Physical Education, and Recreation. (2004). Home page. Retrieved 06/06/07 from http://www/cahperd.ca.

Carnegie Forum on Education and the Economy. (1986). *A nation prepared: Teachers for the 21st century.* Washington DC: Carnegie Forum on Education and the Economy, Task Force on Teaching as a Profession.

Carol M White. (2006). Retrieved from http://www.ed.gov/programs/whitephysed/index.html.

Centers for Disease Control and Prevention. (1997). Guidelines for school and community programs to promote lifelong physical activity among young people. *Morbidity and Mortality Weekly Report, 46*: 1–36.

Centers for Disease Control and Prevention. (2006a). *Prevalence of overweight among children and adolescents: United States, 1999–2002.* Retrieved 06/06/06 from http://www/cdc.gov/cdc.

Centers for Disease Control and Prevention. (2006b). *Prevalence of overweight and obesity among adults: United States, 1999–2002.* http://www.cdc.gov/cdc.

Centers for Disease Control and Prevention. (2006c). *National health and nutrition examination survey.* Retrieved 06/07/06 from http://www.cdc.gov/cdc.

Centers for Disease Control and Prevention. (2006d). *National health interview survey.* Retrieved 06/07/06 from http://www.cdc.gov/cdc.

Centers for Disease Control and Prevention. (2006e). *Behavioral risk factor surveillance system.* Retrieved 06/07/06 from http://www.cdc.gov/nchs.

Centers for Disease Control and Prevention. (2006f). *Youth risk behavior surveillance system.* Retrieved 06/07/06 from http://www.cdc.gov/nchs.

Centers for Disease Control and Prevention. (2006g). *VERB: It's what you do.* Retrieved 06/07/06 from http://www.cdc.gov/nchs.

Cochran-Smith, M. (2001). Constructing outcomes in teacher education: Policy, practice, and pitfalls. *Education Policy Analysis Archives, 9(11)*: 57. Retrieved 06/07/06 from http://www.epaa.asu.edu/epaa/arch.html.

Council of Chief State School Officers. (2006). Homepage. Retrieved 06/07/06 from http://www.ccsso.org.

Curtner-Smith, M. (1998). Behaviors of inner-city teachers following the introduction of the National Curriculum in Physical Education: A descriptive-analytic study. *The Physical Educator, 55(2)*: 101–111.

Curtner-Smith, M. (1999a). Influence of the National Curriculum for Physical Education on inner-city teachers' behaviors associations with pupils' psychosocial development. *Perceptual and Motor Skills, 89(1)*: 127–136.

Curtner-Smith, M. (1999b). Teachers' rules, routines, and expectations prior to and following the implementation of the National Curriculum for Physical Education. *European Journal of Physical Education, 4(1)*: 17–30.

Curtner-Smith, M. (1999c). The more things change the more they stay the same: Factors influencing teachers' interpretations and delivery of the National Curriculum in Physical Education. *Sport, Education, and Society, 4(1)*: 75–97.

Curtner-Smith, M. (2002a, July). *Research strands and future policy/political work in physical education:* Reflections on UK and USA experiences and issues. Invited paper presented at Loughborough University, Loughborough, UK.

Curtner-Smith, M. (2002b, October). *Policy research in physical education.* Invited paper presented at the 4th Works in Progress Conference, Athens GA.

Curtner-Smith, M. and Hasty, D. (1997). Influence of the National Curriculum in Physical Education on teachers' use of teaching styles. *Research Quarterly for Exercise and Sport 68(1)*: A -75–76 Supplement.

Curtner-Smith, M. and Meek, G. (2000). Teachers' value orientations and their compatibility with the National Curriculum for Physical Education. *European Physical Education Review, 6(1)*: 27–45.

Curtner-Smith, M., and Todorovich, J. (1998). Influence of the National Curriculum in Physical Education on teachers' rules, routines, and expectations. *Research Quarterly for Exercise and Sport 68(1)*: A-88 Supplement.

Curtner-Smith, M., Chen, W. and Kerr, I. (1995). Health-related fitness in secondary school physical education: A descriptive-analytic study. *Educational Studies, 2(1)*: 55–66.

Curtner-Smith, M., Hasty, D. and Kerr, I. (2001). Teachers' use of productive and reproductive teaching styles prior to and following the introduction of the National Curriculum in Physical Education. *Educational Research, 43(3)*: 333–340.

Curtner-Smith, M., Kerr, I. and Clapp, A. (1996). The impact of the National Curriculum in Physical Education on the teaching of health-related fitness: A case study in one English town. *European Journal of Physical Education, 1(1)*: 66–83.

Curtner-Smith, M., Kerr, G. and Hencken, C. (1995a). Influence of the British National Curriculum in Physical Education on teachers' behaviors associated with pupils' psychosocial development: A case study in one English town. *Perceptual and Motor Skills, 81(1?)*: 967–976.

Curtner-Smith, M., Kerr, G. and Hencken, C. (1995b). The impact of the National Curriculum in Physical Education on teachers' behaviors related with pupils' skill learning: A case study in one English town. *British Journal of Physical Education Research Supplement 16*: 20–27.

Curtner-Smith, M., Kerr, I. and Hencken, C. (1995c). Teacher behaviors related with pupil psychosocial development in physical education: A descriptive analytic study. *Educational Research 37(3)*: 267–277.

Curtner-Smith, M., Kerr, I., Kuesel, K. and Curtner-Smith, M.E. (1995). Pupil behaviors in British physical education classes: A descriptive analytic study. *International Journal of Physical Education, 32(1)*: 16–23.

Curtner-Smith, M., Todorovich, J., McCaughtry, N. and Lacon, S. (2001). Urban teachers' use of productive and reproductive teaching styles within the confines of the national Curriculum for Physical Education. *European Physical Education Review, 7(2)*: 177–190.

Darling-Hammond, L. (2001). Standard setting in teaching: Changes in licensing, certification, and assessment. In V. Richardson (Ed.), *Handbook of research on teaching* 4th ed., (pp. 751–776).

Darling-Hammond, L. and Sykes, G. (2003). Wanted: A national teacher supply policy for education: The right way to meet the "highly qualified teacher" challenge. *Education Policy Analysis Archives, 11(33)*: 58 Retrieved 10/19/04 from http://epaa.asu.edu/epaa/v11n33.

Department of Culture, Media and Sport (DCMS). (2006). *A sporting future for all: the government's plan for sport.* London: DCMS. etrieved 06/07/06 from http://www.sportdevelopment.org.uk.

Department of Health and Chidlren (Ireland). (2006). New health strategy. Retrieved 06/07/06 from http://www.doh.ie/hstrat/index.html.

Education Commission of the States. (2006). Homepage. Retrieved 06/07/06 from http://www.ecs.org.

Education Commission of the States. (2006). *No Child Left Behind Policy Briefs: Teaching quality.* Denver: Author (GP-02–04W) Retrieved 06/07/06 from http://www.ecs.org.

Education Policy Analysis Archives. (2006). Homepage. Retrieved 06/07/06 from http://epaa.asu.edu/epaa.

English Sports Council. (1997). *Information sheet 15 – Young people and sport.* London: English Sports Council.

Evans, J. (2004). Making a difference? Education and ability in physical education. *European Physical Education Review, 10(1)*: 95-108.

Evans, J. and Penney, D. (1994). Whatever happened to good advice? Service and inspection after the Education Reform Act. *British Educational Research Journal, 20(5)*: 519–534.

Evans, J. and Penney, D. (1995). Physical education, restoration and the politics of sport. *Curriculum Studies, 3(2)*: 183–196.

Evans, J., Penney, D., Bryant, A. and Hennink, M. (1996). All things bright and beautiful? PE in primary schools post the 1988 Education Reform Act. *Educational Review, 48(1)*: 29–40.

Evans, J., Penney, D. and Bryant, A. (1993). Improving the quality of physical education? The Education Reform Act, 1988 and physical education in England and Wales. *Quest, 45*: 321–338.

Fancy, H. (2006). *Education reform: Reflections on New Zealand experience.* Retrieved 06/07/06 from http://www.minedu.govt.nz/index.cfm?layout=document&documentid=9750&indexid=5451&indexparentid=5437.

Fullan, M. (2001). *The new meaning of educational change (3rd ed.).* New York: Teachers College Press.

Goldhaber, D. and Anthony, E. (2006). Can teacher quality be effectively assessed? Retrieved 06/07/06 from http://www.crpe.org/workingpapers.shtml#quality.

Grant, B. and Pope, C. (2000). Retrospection and ruminations on sport and physical education. *Journal of Physical Education New Zealand, 33(2)*: 64–74.

Harris, J. and Penney, D. (2000). Gender issues in health-related exercise. *European Physical Education* Review. *6(3)*: 249–274.

Hawley, W. (1990). Systematic analysis, public policy making, and teacher education. In W.R. Houston (Ed.), *Handbook of research on teacher education* (pp. 136–156). New York: Macmillan Publishing Co.

Health Education Authority. (1998). *Young and active? Policy framework for young people and health-enhancing physical activity.* London: Health Education Authority. Retrieved 10/19/04 from http://www.nhsinherts.nhs. uk/hp/health_topics/physical_activity/exbooks.asp.

Health Promotions Agency (Northern Ireland). Homepage. Retrieved 06/10/06 from http://www.healthpromotionagency.org.uk.

Holmes Partnership. (2006). *Tomorrow's teachers.* Retrieved 06/07/06 from http://www.holmespartnership.org.

Holmes Partnership. (1990). *Tomorrow's schools.* Retrieved 06/07/06 from http://www.holmespartnership.org.

Holmes Partnership. (2006). *Tomorrow's schools of education.* Retrieved 06/07/06 from http://www.holmespartnership.org.

Human Kinetics. (2006). American Sport Education Program. Retrieved 06/07/06 from http://www.asep.com/

Institute for the Study of Youth Sports. (2004). PACE Coaches Education Program. Retrieved 06/07/06 from http://ed-web3.educ.msu.edu/ysi.

Institute for the Study of Youth Sports. (2004). *Bill of Rights for Young Athletes.* Retrieved 06/07/06 from http://ed-web3.educ.msu.edu/ysi.

International Committee of Sport Pedagogy. (2006). Second World Summit on Physical Education. Retrieved 06/08/06 from hssp://www.icsspe.org.

International Conference (3rd) of Ministers and Senior Officials Responsible for Physical Education and Sport (1999). Retrieved 06/08/06 from http://www.icsspe.org/portal/index.php?seite=project/tx2442.html.

International Olympic Committee. (2006). *Sport for all and governmental policies.* Retrieved 06/08/06 from http://www.olympic.org/uk.

Interstate New Teacher Assessment and Support Consortium. (2006) Retrieved 06/08/06 from http://www.ccsso.org/Projects/Interstate_New_Teacher_Assessment_and_Support_Consortium.

Irish Sports Council. (2006). *Sport for Life.* http://www.irishsportscouncil.ie.

Kirk, D. and Macdonald, D. (2001). The social construction of PETE in higher education: Toward a research agenda. *Quest, 53*, 440–456.

Lacon, S. and Curtner-Smith, M. (1998). Behaviors of inner-city teachers following the introduction of National Curriculum Physical Education: A descriptive-analytic study. *Physical Educator, 55(2)*: 101–112.

Learning and Teaching Scotland. (2006). Retrieved 06/08/06 from http://www.ltscotland.org.uk.

Lee, J. (2001). School reform initiatives as balancing acts: Policy variation and educational convergence among Japan, Korea, England, and the United States. *Educational Policy Analysis Archives, 9(13)*. Retrieved 06/08/06 from http://epaa.asu.edu.

Lee, M. and O'Sullivan, M. (2004). Little League Baseball. *Home page.* Retrieved 10/19/04 from http://www.littleleague.org.

Lowry, R., Brener, N., Lee, S., Epping, J., Fulton, J. and Eaton, D. (2006). Participation in high school physical education: U.S. 1991–2003. *Morbidity* and *Mortality Weekly Reports, 53(36)*: 844–847. Retrieved 06/08/06 from http://www.cdc.gov/mmwr/preview/mmwrhtml/mm5336a5.htm.

Macdonald, D. (2003). Curriculum change and the post-modern world: Is the school curriculum-reform movement an anachronism? *Journal of Curriculum Studies.* Retrieved 06/08/06 from http://faculty.ed.uiuc.edu/westbury/JCS.

Macdonald, D. and Brooker, R. (1997). Moving beyond the crises in secondary physical education: An Australian

Initiative. *Journal of Teaching in Physical Education.* *16(2)*: 155–176.

Macdonald, D., Hunter, L., Carlson, T. and Penney, D. (2002). Teacher knowledge and the disjunction between School curricula and teacher education. *Asia-Pacific Journal of Teacher Education, 30(3)*: 259–276.

MacPhail, A. (2004). The social construction of higher grade physical education: the impact on teacher curriculum decision-making. *Sport, Education and Society, 9(1)*: 53–73.

Massachusetts Department of Education. (2006). Retrieved 06/08/06 from http://www.doe.mass.edu.

McCrone, G. (2000). A Teaching Profession for the 21st Century. Edinburgh, Scotland: Scottish Executive.

Ministerial Council on Education, Employment, Training and Youth Affairs. (1999*). Adelaide Declaration on National Goals for Schooling in the Twenty-First Century.* Retrieved 06/10/06 from http://www.mceetya.edu.au.

Morrow, J. and Gill, D. (Eds.). (1995). The academy papers: The role of physical activity in fitness and health. *Quest, 47(3),* 261–262.

National Alliance for Youth Sports. (2006). *International youth sports congress.* Retrieved 06/10/06 from http://www.nays.org.

National Association for Sport and Physical Education. (1995). Moving into the future: National standards for physical education. Reston, VA: Author.

National Association for Sport and Physical Education. (2000a). *Appropriate practices for elementary school physical education.* Reston VA: Author.

National Association for Sport and Physical Education. (2000b). *Appropriate practice in movement programs for young children.* Reston, VA: Author.

National Association for Sport and Physical Education. (2001a). *Advanced standards in physical education teacher education.* Reston, VA: Author.

National Association for Sport and Physical Education. (2001b). *Appropriate practices for middle school physical education.* Reston, VA: Author.

National Association for Sport and Physical Education. (2001c). *Coaches' code of conduct.* Reston VA: Author.

National Association for Sport and Physical Education. (2001d). *Initial standards in physical education teacher education.* Reston, VA: Author.

National Association for Sport and Physical Education. (2002a). *Active start: A statement of physical activity guidelines for children birth to five years.* Reston, VA: Author.

National Association for Sport and Physical Education. (2002b). *Guidelines for after school PA and intramural Sport programs.* Reston, VA: Author.

National Association for Sport and Physical Education. (2003). *Concepts and principles of physical education: What every student needs to know.* Reston, VA: AAHPERD.

National Association for Sport and Physical Education. (2004a). *Appropriate practices for high school physical education.* Reston, VA: Author.

National Association for Sport and Physical Education. (2004b). *Physical activity for children: A statement of guidelines.* Reston, VA: Author.

National Association for Sport and Physical Education. (2004c). *Moving into the future: National standards* for physical education (2nd ed.). Reston, VA: Author.

National Board for Professional Teaching Standards. (1994). *Standards [including PE specific ones].* Detroit, MI: NBPTS. Retrieved 06/10/06 from http://www.nbpts.org/standards/stds.cfm.

National Collegiate Athletic Association. (2006). Home page. Retrieved 06/10/06 from http://www2.ncaa.org/about_ncaa.

National Commission on Excellence in Education. (1983). *A nation at risk: The imperative for educational reform.* Washington DC: U.S. Government Printing Office.

National Commission on Teaching and America's Future (NCTAF). (1996). *What matters most: Teaching for America's future.* New York: Author, Teachers College, Columbia University. Retrieved 06/10/06 from http://www.nctaf.org.

National Commission on Teaching and America's Future (NCTAF). (2003). *No dream denied: A pledge to America's children.* New York: Author. Retrieved 06/10/06 from http://www. nctaf.org.

National Council for the Accreditation of Teacher Education. (2006). *Standards.* Retrieved 06/10/06 from http://www.ncate.org.

National Council for Curriculum and Assessment (Ireland). (2006). *Publications.* Retrieved 06/10/06 from http://www.ncca.ie.

National Council for Curriculum and Assessment [Ireland]. (2004. *Home page.* Retrieved 06/10/06 from http://www.ncca.ie/j/aims_who.htm.

New South Wales Board of Studies. (2004). *Board of Studies NSW years 7–10 syllabuses and support materials.* Retrieved 10/19/06 from http://www.boardofstudies.nsw.edu.au/syllabus_sc/index.html.

New South Wales Department of Education and Training. (2006). Board of Studies NSW HSC syllabuses. Retrieved 06/10/06 from http://www.boardofstudies.nsw.edu.au.

New South Wales Department of Education and Training. (2006). *Professional support and curriculum.* Retrieved 06/10/06 from http://www.curriculumsupport.nsw.edu.au.

New Zealand Ministry of Education. (1989). *New Zealand curriculum framework.* Retrieved from http://www.tki.org.nz/r/governance/nzcf/index_e.php.

New Zealand Ministry of Health. (2006). *Taking the pulse: The 1996/97 New Zealand Health Survey.* Retrieved 10/14/04 from http://www.moh.govt.nz.

North American Youth Sport Institute. (2006). Home page. Retrieved 06/10/06 from http://www.naysi.com.

National Alliance for Youth Sport. (2004). *National standards for youth sports.* Retrieved 08/16/04 from http://www.naysi.org.

National Association for Girls and Women's Sports. (2004). *Title IX.* Retrieved 06/10/06 from http://www.nagws.org.

National Organization of Women. (2006). *Save Title IX*. Retrieved 06/10/06 from http://www.now.org.

Penney, D. (1998). Positioning and defining physical education, sport, and health in the curriculum. *European Physical Education Review*, 4(2): 117–126.

Penney, D. (2000). Physical education, sporting excellence and educational excellence. *European Physical Education Review*, 6(2): 135–150.

Penney, D. (2003). Sport education and situated learning: Problematizing the potential. *European Physical Education Review*, 9(3): 301–308.

Penney, D. and Chandler, T. (2000). Physical education: What future(s)? *Sport, Education and Society*, 5(1): 71–88.

Penney, D. and Evans, J. (1997). Naming the game: Discourse and domination in physical education and sport in England and Wales. *European Physical Education Review*, 3(1): 21–32.

Penney, D. and Evans, J. (1999). *Politics, policy and practice in PE*. London: E & F Spon (Routledge imprint).

Penney, D. and Houlihan, B. (2003). Higher education institutions and specialist schools: Potential partnerships. *Journal of Education for Teaching*, 29(3): 235–249.

Physical Activity Task Force [Scotland]. (2003). *Let's make Scotland more active: A strategy for physical activity*. Retrieved 06/10/06 from http://www.show.scot.nhs.uk/sehd/PATF/Index.htm.

Physical Education Association of the United Kingdom [PEAAUK]. Home page. Retrieved 10/14/04 from http://www.pea.uk.com/menu.html.

Placek, J., Griffin, L. and Dodds, P. (2003, October). *Store-bought Oreos or Home-made Chocolate Chip Cookies: How to Judge the Goodness of PETE Doctoral Programs*. Paper presented at the NASPE Teacher Education Conference, Baton Rouge, LA.

Pope, C. (1999). A compete students port experience: Getting young people back into sport. *Teaching and Curriculum*, 3: 73–76.

Pope, C. (2002). Plato makes the team: The arrival of secondary school sport academies. *Waikato Journal of Education*, 8: 89–100.

Pope, C. (2004). Realizing the potential of physical activity: Guest Editorial. *Children's Issues*, 8(1): 5–6.

Queensland College of Teachers. (2006). Homepage. Retrieved 06/10/06 from http://www.qct.edu.au.

Queensland Studies Authority (2006) *QSA KLA*, from http://www.qsa.qld.edu.au/yourqsa/newsletters/docs/kla-01.pdf.

Queensland Studies Authority. (2006). *Health & Physical Education [curriculum]*. Retrieved 06/10/06 from http://www.qsa.qld.edu.au.

Rezai-Rashti, G. (2003). Educational policy reform and its impact on equity work in Ontario: Global Challenges and local possibilities. *Education Policy Analysis Archives*, 11(51). Retrieved 06/10/06 from http://epaa.asu.edu/epaa.

Rink, J. and Mitchell, M. (Eds.). (2003). State level assessment in physical education: The South Carolina experience. *Journal of Teaching in PhysicalEducation*, 22(5): 471–608.

Rink, J. and Mitchell, M. (2002). High stakes assessment: A journey into unknown territory. *Journal of Teaching In Physical Education*, 54(3): 205–223.

Scottish Executive Health Department. (2006). *Let's make Scotland more active*. Retrieved 06/10/06 from http://www.show.scot.uk.

Scottish Executive Online. (2006). *Education and training*. Retrieved 06/10/06 from http://www.scotland.gov.uk.

Shilling, C. (1993). The body, class and social inequalities. In J. Evans (Ed.), *Equality, education and physical education* (pp. 55–73). London: Falmer Press.

SPARC [Sport and Recreation New Zealand]. (2006a). *Push play*. Retrieved 06/10/06 from http://www.pushplay.org.nz.

SPARC [Sport and Recreation New Zealand]. (2006b). *SPARC research*. Retrieved 06/10/06 from http://www.sparc.org.nz.

Sparkes, A. (1991). The culture of teaching, critical reflection and change: possibilities and problems. *Educational Management and Administration, 19 (1)*: 4–19.

Sport England. (2006). *About Sport England*. Retrieved 06/10/06 from http://www.sportengland.org.

Taylor, W., Blair, S., Cummings, S., Wsun, C. and Malina, R. (1999). Childhood and adolescent physical activity patterns & adult physical activity. *Medicine and Science in Sports and Exercise*, 31: 118–123.

Teacher Education Accreditation Council. (2006). *About TEAC*. Homepage Retrieved 06/10/06 from http://www.teac.org.

U.S. Congress. (1994). *Goals 2000: Educate America Act*. Retrieved 06/10/06 from http://www.ed.gov/G2K.

U.S. Congress. (2001). *No child left behind*. Retrieved 06/10/06 from http://www.ed.gov/nclb.

U.S. Department of Education. (2003). *Meeting the highly qualified teachers challenge*: The secretary's second annual report on teacher quality. Washington. DC: Author Retrieved 06/10/06 from http://www.title2.org/ADATitleIIReport2002.pdf.

U.S. Department of Education. (2006). Carol M. White Physical Education Program. Retrieved 06/02/06 from http://www.ed.gov/programs/whitephysed/index.html.

U.S. Department of Health and Human Services (USD-HHS). (1979). *Healthy People: The surgeon general's report on health promotion and disease prevention*. Washington DC: U.S. Government Printing Office.

U.S. Department of Health and Human Services (USD-HHS). (1990). *Healthy People 2000*. Washington DC: U.S. Government Printing Office. Retrieved 06/10/06 from http://www.healthypeople.gov.

U.S. Department of Health and Human Services (USD-HHS). (2000). *Healthy people 2010*. Washington DC: U.S. Government Printing Office. Retrieved 06/10/06 from http://web.health.gov/healthypeople.gov.

U.S. Department of Health and Human Services (USD-HHS). (1996). *Physical activity and health: A report of the Surgeon General*. Atlanta: Centers for Disease Control and Prevention, National Center for Chronic Disease Prevention and Health Promotion. Retrieved 06/10/06 from http://www.cdc.gov/nccdphp/sgr/ataglan.htm.

U.S. Department of Health and Human Services (USD-HHS). (2001). *The surgeon general's call to action to* Prevent and decrease overweight and obesity. Retrieved 06/10/06 from http://www.surgeongeneral.gov/topics/obesity.

U.S. Government (ED.gov). (2006). *Title IX: 25 Years of Progress – June 1997*. Retrieved 06/10/06 from http://www.ed.gov/pubs/TitleIX/part2.html.

Wanless, (2002). *Securing our future health: Taking a long-term view*. Retrieved 06/10/06 from http://www.unlock research.com.

Wanless, (2004). *Securing Good Health for the Whole Population*. Retrieved 6/10/06 from http://www.dh.gov./uk/PublicationsAndStatistics.

West, B., Jarchow, E. and Quisenberry, N. (1996). Teacher education research in international settings. In J. Sikula (Ed.), *Handbook of research on teacher education 2nd ed.*, (pp. 1047–1107). New York: Macmillan.

Wilkins, J., Graham, G., Parker, S., Westfall, S., Fraser, R. and Tembo, M. (2003). Time in the arts and physical education and school achievement. *Journal of Curriculum Studies, 35*: 721–734. Retrieved 06/10/06 from http://www.unlockresearch.com.

World Health Organization. (2004). *Global strategy on diet, PA, and health*. Retrieved 06/10/06 from http://www.who.int/hpr/gs.process.document.shtml.

World Summit on Physical Education. (1999). *The Berlin agenda for action for government ministers* Summit Statement. Retrieved 06/10/06 from http://www.the sportjournal.org.

Youth Sport Trust (YST). (2006). TOP prgorammes. Retrieved 06/10/06 from http://www.youthsporttrust. org/

Youth Sport Trust (YST). (2006). *YST and schools*. Retrieved 06/10/06 from http://www.youthsporttrust. org.

SECTION V
Physical Education Curriculum

What gets taught and learned across the curriculum has come under scrutiny as schools are positioned as both the problem and solution in relation to a number of social, health, economic and political issues. More specifically, reports documenting physical activity and nutrition levels of children have suggested that poor quality physical education experiences are partly responsible for what some have called a rising tide of overweight and inactive youth around the world. With this pressure, as one of the three message systems of schooling – curriculum, pedagogy and assessment (Bernstein, 2001) – the curriculum has become a site for increased governmental planning, monitoring, and evaluation. This section of the handbook provides a critical review of what are the curriculum possibilities in physical education and reminds us what may constitute evidence-based physical education.

While definitions of curriculum vary, most share a focus upon the social organization of knowledge for learning (Young, 1998). Thus this section looks at the complex interplay of knowledge (what), context (where) and interaction (how) as dimensions of curriculum study (Kirk, 1988). Following Pinar et al. (1995) in talking about curriculum research, it becomes clear that physical education curriculum study no longer sees the problems of curriculum as "technical" problems or problems of "how to" but rather as "why" problems.

In physical education, the organization of knowledge has traditionally been reported in terms of curriculum models. In 1985 Jewett and Bain outlined that "curriculum models are designed to provide a basis for decisions regarding the selection, structuring, and sequencing of educational experiences" (p. 45). They proceed to discuss seven curriculum models: developmental education; humanistic physical education; fitness; movement education; kinesiological studies; play education; and personal meaning. The following year, Siedentop et al. (1986) wrote about major physical education models as: multiactivity; fitness; sports

education; adventure; social development; concepts; and non-attached time (such as providing intramural and club opportunities).

We too, in Section 5, continue to use physical education curriculum models as an organizing framework around which to review physical education curriculum research. Chapters 5.3 to 5.9 look at research in: sport education; social responsibility; games teaching; health-related fitness; adventure education, youth sport; and dance education. This selection was made on the basis of cohesive and/or sustained lines of research in the field and by no means is intended to be comprehensive. A cursory comparison of models over the past 30 years might suggest that the field has not moved very much. Indeed, some of the chapters in this handbook's Section 6 on Difference and Diversity in Physical Education point to the ways in which the "traditional" curriculum has continued to alienate many students of physical education. That said, the chapters highlight the sophistication of the models and the diversity of practices they bring to physical education.

Before moving into the models, the first two chapters of this section take a broader approach to curriculum issues. The first chapter addresses research in the field of physical education curriculum construction and change. Penney draws on the work of Basil Bernstein to provide a framework around which she addresses power and relationships that shape curriculum inertia and change. This chapter provides a backdrop for the section in that it reminds us that the curriculum is highly contested yet at the same time resistant to change, and that there are many vested interests in the physical education curriculum both within and beyond the field. The second chapter synthesizes research conducted on the elementary or primary school physical education curriculum. This chapter was included for two reasons; as an attempt to highlight some curriculum issues when the subject is not taught by physical education specialists and to give some balance to the subsequent focus on models which, in the majority, draw upon research conducted in middle, secondary or high schools.

The first four models – sport education, personal and social responsibility, games-centred, and youth sport (non-attached time) – have each attracted strong global research interest and focus most explicitly on sport as their curriculum content. In Chapter 5.3 Kinchin reviews sport education, a model introduced to physical educators by Daryl Siedentop in the 1980s. The chapter outlines the core concepts of sport education and demonstrates its application across an increasing range of physical activities, age groups, school subjects, and non-school settings. In the following chapter Hellison and Martinek look at teaching personal and social responsibility as a physical education model that has applications both within and beyond the school contexts. They explain the historical, psychological and social perspectives on the concept of responsibility before looking at the major findings in terms of empirical and philosophical outcomes. Chapter 35 turns to games-centred approaches to physical education that may be familiar to readers as Teaching Games for Understanding, Tactical Games Model, Games Sense, or perhaps Play Practice. As with the preceding two models, games-centred approaches are increasing in the breadth of their applications within and beyond schools. The authors of Chapters 5.3–5.5 argue that while the quality of student outcomes from the models is significant, and the breadth of research applications is welcome, that longitudinal research of the models is needed.

Chapter 5.6 looks at the somewhat "outlying" physical education model which Siedentop et al. (1986) called 'non-attached time' suggesting that physical education should be planned for outside the formal curriculum as extra-curricula physical education or (organized) youth sport. In this chapter Martelaer and Theeboom address issues surrounding youth sport and its relationship to physical education. In doing so, they draw upon on some of the research discussed in the previous three chapters and also the important relationship between physical education, the community, and government policies and services. They consider that this curriculum responsibility raises challenges for physical education teacher education in particular, as educators need the knowledge and skills to work outside the school setting.

The final cluster of three chapters in this section shifts the focus from sport to other forms of physical activity – health-related exercise, dance, and adventure. Ironically, as public discourses call for more effective health-related fitness programs in schools as described by Welk, Eisenmann and Dollman, they are most likely to displace activities such as adventure (Brown) and dance education (Buck). While Welk et al. are concerned with the lack of large-scale longitudinal data on health-related exercise programs in schools, Brown and Buck highlight that there is little research in the adventure and dance curriculum models despite the highly student-centred and diverse applications of the models in schooling.

As with other sections of the handbook, we have tried here to include authors from a range of countries (Australia, Belgium, Britain, New Zealand, and the USA) though we recognize there is a bias towards English-speaking countries. That said, the section reveals aspects of globalization of the physical education curriculum (see Pinar, 2003 for a comprehensive view of school curriculum from a global perspective) whereby research into dominant curriculum models such as fitness, sport education, games sense/teaching and social responsibility is being carried out across continents and cultures.

References

Bernstein, B. (2001). *Pedagogy, symbolic control and identity*. Lanham: Rowman & Littlefield.

Jewett, A. and Bain, L. (1985). *The curriculum process in physical education*. Dubuque: Wm. C. Brown.

Kirk, D. (1988). *Physical education and curriculum study: A critical introduction*. London: Croom Helm.

Pinar, W., Reynolds, W., Slattery, P. and Taubman, P. (1995). *Understanding curriculum*. New York: Peter Lang.

Pinar, W. (2003). *International handbook of curriculum research*. Mahwah: Lawrence Erlbaum.

Siedentop, D., Mand, C. and Taggart, A. (1986). *Physical education teaching and curriculum strategies for grades 5 – 12*. Palo Alto: Mayfield.

Young, M.D. (1998). *The curriculum of the future*. London: Falmer Press.

5.1 Curriculum construction and change

DAWN PENNEY

Introduction

Ward and Doutis (1999) were undoubtedly justified in their observation that:

> Despite significant progress in the field of sport pedagogy, there are few studies that have reported on the implementation and evaluation of curriculum in physical education. Our collective attention in the past three decades has focused more on teacher effects than curriculum effects. (Ward and Doutis, 1999, 393)

Nevertheless, it is fair to say that in recent years there has been considerable research in physical education that has engaged with the processes, politics and implications for teachers and learners of "curriculum construction and change". Curriculum has been a timely focus for researchers in the field, with no shortage of national and local reforms and reviews generating research interest and agendas. The past decade and a half has been a time of unprecedented externally driven curriculum "change" in education and physical education specifically. But as other chapters in this section highlight, it has also been a time of curriculum change instigated by teachers in schools and/or colleagues in tertiary institutions.

Discussion in this chapter reflects the varied scope and nature of curriculum research in physical education, with a number of interests and agendas being pursued by researchers. Some studies have centred on national initiatives. Others have focused on developments at a local government or "system" level, or the curriculum in specific school contexts or tertiary education settings. Some research has been openly *investigative* of construction and change processes, while other projects have been concerned (and frequently, commissioned) to *evaluate* newly constructed and/or changed curricula in relation to the resultant "impact" upon teaching and/or learning in physical education.

It is important to note that the growth in curriculum research has also prompted significant evolution in research design and methodology in physical education, as researchers have endeavoured to engage with the complexities of "curriculum construction and change" that research within and beyond the field has revealed. Many of the studies reported in this chapter have featured the use of multiple methods in several sites involved in curriculum development, and have challenged researchers to maintain parallel lines of inquiry across different sites, while being responsive to evolving situations. Further methodological innovation needs to be encouraged if research is to not only engage with but also *actively inform* future curriculum development in physical education.

The chapter aims to draw particular attention to linkages between research and conceptual considerations relating to curriculum. It also reaffirms that the research act is never a neutral act, but rather, one that will always reflect particular interests in and for the curriculum in physical education (see Griffiths, 1998; Penney, 2003). Selection is inevitable and reoccurring in research and furthermore, in research reviews. Certainly, there is no pretence here to be incorporating each and every line of inquiry in relation to curriculum research in physical education. The review takes a specific conceptual focus that is discussed below. Particularly in addressing government-led curriculum changes, it privileges selected studies conducted in England and Australia that have been directly concerned with advancing conceptualisations of curriculum construction and change. The research discussed tells us much about curriculum construction and change as a political and social process. Doctoral studies also feature prominently in the review, pointing to curriculum as an important emergent line of research development in the field. In many instances, the research cited has focused on secondary or high school curriculum rather than the primary curriculum. The need for this balance to be redressed in future research in the field is acknowledged. Similarly, the curriculum in tertiary based training programmes is identified as in need of further investigation, specifically in relation linkages between training and curriculum construction and change in schools.

Curriculum construction and change: historical perspectives

Beginning with an historical commentary is appropriate. Contemporary curriculum research continues to reveal the significance of history in shaping the future of physical education. Simply stated, research into curriculum construction and change always has to recognise that developments never start from a "blank sheet". Histories – curriculum, institutional and personal – are always destined to be influential, both enabling and constraining change physical education. This section therefore discusses curriculum research that has specifically adopted an historical perspective. Firstly, however, it is important to consider the *history of research* in curriculum construction and change in physical education.

The various studies discussed later in the chapter need to be recognized as an important reference point and foundation for future studies in the same way as they have variously drawn on preceding investigations of curriculum. Key investigations (and thus points of reference for curriculum research) undoubtedly have national specificity. For example, when challenged to identify early milestones in curriculum research, physical educationalists in the UK will typically recall Kane's (1974) report of an enquiry into physical education in secondary schools, together with Underwood's (1983) text focusing on the planning and implementation of the physical education curriculum in secondary schools. Both of these works were large scale studies with a notably technical orientation that generated extensive data about what were, at the time, deemed to be key curriculum issues. In many respects they can be regarded as fact-finding missions, seeking comprehensive details about current curriculum provision and practices in physical education as a basis for future planning. Kane's research was commissioned (by the Schools Council) with the specific task of providing detailed descriptive information that was regarded to be an essential basis for curriculum development. Interest in or demand for curriculum research thus came from an external source and beyond the field of physical education. The remit was to gather information about the following:

(a) The degree of compulsion to take part in some form of physical education at different stages in the secondary school course;

(b) Period [lesson] allocation for physical education in school timetables;

(c) The introduction and range of options [in terms of activity choices];

(d) Out-of-school activities;

(e) Staffing and facilities; and

(f) The criteria by which the physical education curriculum is constructed.

Irrespective of one's familiarity with Kane's study, many of the above points will probably be recognizable as "curriculum issues" that have retained an identity as such both over time and internationally in physical education arenas (see Hardman, 2000, 2001). Within and beyond the profession, a demand for detailed descriptive information about curriculum provision and related resourcing has thus typically accompanied consideration of curriculum change or reform.

Several of the issues pursued in early work such as Kane and Underwood's studies, together with specific comments made in reporting findings can also now be viewed as indicative of the growing dominance of the multi-activity, sport-based conceptualization of curriculum as reported by Kirk (1992, see below). For example, amongst Underwood's (1983) 25 "main findings" were the observations that most teachers assessed the balance of a programme by analysing the time allocation to each (activity-based) aspect of the curriculum, and that nine out of ten teachers were "attempting to integrate within the subject by planning for links between the different activities *that comprise the curriculum*" (p. 132, my emphasis). The research can thus be seen as reaffirming a particular curriculum structure and content, and as concerned with the pragmatics of implementing a physical education curriculum conceived as a collection of activities. Underwood (1983) also identified seven factors influencing planning of the physical education curriculum: school climate; subject procedures; community resources; school resources; societal values; democratic atmosphere; children's abilities and interests. Variously, these will again be recognizable as "curriculum issues" that have been the subject of sustained interest over time. But while many of the contemporary studies discussed later in the chapter have also investigated and/or highlighted these factors, a shift in the orientation of curriculum research is nevertheless discernible in physical education. Alongside the continued concern for comprehensive "facts" of a similar ilk to those demanded and generated by Kane (1974), we have seen the growth of a body of work that has approach curriculum construction and change from interpretive and socio-critical perspectives. It is this more recent history, representative of a period of significant research development in relation to curriculum construction and change in physical education, which is the focus of discussion in the remainder of the chapter.

Before moving on from a historical focus, however, it is important to acknowledge the significance of curriculum research in physical education curriculum that has specifically been undertaken from a historical perspective. This underpins current understandings of the evolution of the subject over time and can also inform our reading of research studies and their findings. Kirk's (1992, 1998, 2003) work, directed towards developments in both the United Kingdom and Australia is notable in this respect. In relation to physical education in the UK, Kirk's (1992) analysis of the historical, social, political, economic and institutional factors variously influential in key changes in the form and content of the physical education curriculum, and related shifts in pedagogical practices throughout the 20th century, has been an unparalleled and is discussed further below.

Core concepts

"Curriculum" is a somewhat problematic term in that it continues to generate a variety of meanings in different educational settings. It thus presents an immediate challenge to researchers; to clarify their conceptualization and thereby establish both a foundation and direction for their work. Indeed, Print (1993) has observed that;

> The search for an appropriate definition of the term 'curriculum'; has become increasingly problematic over time. Rather than achieving consensus and thereby enhancing effective communication the literature reveals continued differentiation and disputation as to an acceptable definition. The result has meant that those writing and teaching about curriculum are well advised to preface their statements about curriculum by *their interpretation of the concept*. (Print, 1993: 7)

In the text *Education, Movement and the Curriculum* Arnold (1988) similarly identified that curriculum "has many connotations of meaning" (p. 117) and went on to clarify his specific use thus:

> In order to be clear I propose to use the term to refer to all those planned activities of a school, whether done formally or informally, and which are encouraged and pursued with the interests of the pupils in mind. It will include education as well as those elements of schooling which are considered both necessary and desirable. This broader approach to the curriculum is defined by Kerr (1969) as "all learning which is planned and guided by the school, whether it is carried out in groups or individually, inside or outside the school" (p. 16). Such a definition provides a more comprehensive basis for curriculum planning and development. (Arnold, 1988, p. 117)

This chapter explores research from the perspective of curriculum conceptualized as *a social, political and relational process*. Curriculum is acknowledged as socially constructed, and the construction is recognised as ongoing. Curriculum is "unfinished", "always in the making"; in the process of (de- and re-) construction and furthermore, contested and contestable throughout what have traditionally been referred to as "stages" of making (or construction) and implementation (or "delivery"). Studies reported here have specifically sought to challenge conceptualizations that reaffirm a distinction between "making" and "implementation". They are representative of a renewed emphasis of "fluidity" and of construction and change as ongoing. In this context the study of curriculum (or curriculum research) has emerged as a study of *texts* and their creation, transformation(s) and transmissions between and within educational settings. "Text" itself is a concept that needs to be problematized. Formal written texts are recognized as only one of the textual forms that curriculum research needs to engage with. Spoken and pedagogical texts equally need to be acknowledged as integral elements of curriculum construction and change, with researchers thus prompted to explore the many and varied forms in which curriculum is expressed in schools and specifically, in the teaching of physical education. The challenge is to provide insights into the factors underpinning the differences that are apparent in curricula experienced by different children in different schools, and to thus advance understandings of curriculum construction and change processes.

Curriculum research can therefore be seen as concerned with "content", "processes" and "contexts" and importantly, the dynamics between these dimensions. Research in physical education has advanced understandings of the ways in which these dynamics are "played out" in curriculum construction and change on national, state, institutional and classroom stages. Increasingly, the concept of *discourse* has been acknowledged as highly effective in shaping explorations of curriculum in ways that will facilitate their engagement with the complexities of "construction and change". Following developments in mainstream educational research, researchers in physical education have employed a conceptualization of discourse that engages with textual content *and* the power-relations that the particular content reflects. In relation to content, it is important to note a concern with what is absent from curriculum as much as what is present. From this poststructuralist perspective, discourse directs our attention to the meanings and values represented and "carried by" language, curricula and pedagogical texts, but also the values and interests that are simultaneously being marginalized and/or denied both by what is "said" (written, enacted, embodied) or not. The concept of discourse enables exploration of the different forms that we see texts taking in the course of curriculum construction but also, the differing degrees to which particular individuals and organizations can influence the form of texts; what say they have in curriculum construction and change. Curriculum construction and change emerges as a politically as well as socially constructed process. It is a process conceptualized in terms of an ongoing and often problematic balance between "opportunities and constraints" in relation to our capacity to produce our own readings, interpretations and adaptations of texts; to actively (re)shape curriculum form and content to suit specific interests, particular school and classroom contexts and individual students' learning needs. Macdonald (2003a) captured this emphasis very effectively in stating that "underpinning curriculum reform is a contest over what is chosen, by what processes, by whom, with what intent, and with what result" (p. 140) and adding that "Struggles over curriculum and its management are, in a sense, struggles over what education is for, and whose knowledge is of most worth – learners', parents', teachers', or curriculum authorities?" (p. 140). Macdonald's comments together with Ball's research in education policy sociology (Ball, 1990, 1993a, b, see below) directs us towards analyses that ultimately render conceptualisations of reform as either "top–down" or "bottom–up" as inherently problematic, and also prompt critical examination of so called "partnership-based" reform.

Meanwhile, talk of "form and content" in relation to curriculum directs us to further conceptual reference points that are pertinent to consider in conjunction with an overview of curriculum research in physical education. While by no means the only work to which curriculum researchers have turned, Basil Bernstein's (1971, 1990, 1996, 2000) writing has provided powerful concepts to utilize in studies seeking to explore curriculum construction and change and understand the dynamics at play in the process. Bernstein's (1990) principles of *classification* and *framing* are key to that process. The two principles relate respectively to the "'what' and 'how' of pedagogic discourse" (Bernstein, 1990: 196); curriculum content and the legitimate means of engagement with it, by teachers and students.

The principle of classification is concerned with "the categories, contents and relationships to be transmitted", while the principle of framing, refers to "the manner of their transmission" (Bernstein, 1990: 196). The principle of classification thus relates to curriculum organization and structural characteristics. Bernstein's emphasis is that it is the boundaries inherent in curricula that provide the structure, but also, far more than that. It is the boundaries that legitimate and reinforce particular curriculum/ knowledge categories and distinguish one category from another. The principle of classification thus generates so-called "recognition rules" for both "transmitters" and "acquirers" in relation to the specialization of their texts. It is at the heart of defining what lies legitimately within, or conversely, outside certain fields and furthermore, what we recognize as content and organizational possibilities when considering curriculum construction and change.

When there is "strong classification" boundaries are firm, emphasising the distinctiveness of each specialism. When boundaries between specialisms become blurred or are crossed, classification is said to be weak.

The parallel principle of framing is concerned with curriculum "transmission". It provides the realization rules for the production of pedagogic texts by defining legitimate and illegitimate modes of communication and relationships between transmitter and acquirer (Bernstein, 1990). As with classification, we can refer to relatively strong or weak framing, with roles, relationships and possible modes of communication either firmly defined or in contrast, more flexible. Other chapters within this section show that there has been no shortage of efforts to instigate "new" or "alternative" approaches to teaching characterised by weaker framing (Bernstein, 1990, 1996). Yet, as discussed below, the multiactivity curriculum model remains firmly in place (entrenched) as *the* dominant model, privileging, legitimating and reproducing the dominance of discourses of performance in sport as core to the curriculum in physical education. Undoubtedly, research in physical education has yet to fully explore the extent to which changes in pedagogical relations provide a means via which to seriously challenge the matters (categories, contents and their relationships) that are defined by the principle of classification.

Research underpinned by a conceptualisation of curriculum inherent in which is acknowledgement of issues of politics and social justice at play, is thus needed. In introducing Goodson's (1997) text *The changing curriculum. Studies in social construction* Kincheloe (1997) highlights Goodson's recognition of power as "a dialectical force that works both on and through people – it empowers and disempowers" (p. xxii). Goodson's (1993, 1995, 1997) work has repeatedly and vividly illustrated the ways in which power operates in and through the dominant categories of curriculum, shaping (limiting) professional thinking, defining professional identities and positioning both knowledge and people in hierarchical relations within schools and wider society. The emphasis Bernstein places upon the principles of classification and framing, and dynamic between them, is thus reflected in Goodson's contention that "educators who are concerned with establishing a socially just curriculum must constantly assert the necessity for an ongoing dialogue around the *reconstruction of knowledge*" (Kincheloe, 1997: p. xxx; my emphasis).

Major findings

In now turning to the findings arising from research in physical education that has focused upon curriculum construction and change, the aim is to illustrate and reaffirm the conceptual points above. In addition, linkages between various studies will be discussed with the key concepts in mind.

Curriculum construction and change as a political imperative

As explained above, in recent years, much of the "drive" for curriculum change in physical education has come from national governments. Particularly in England and Australasia, the development of National Curricula and/or state derivatives of them have been the focus of research projects in physical education that have provided important insights into the processes of curriculum development in government arenas. My work with John Evans addressing the development and subsequent revisions of the National Curriculum in England and Wales, Kay's (1997) work also conducted in England and Glover's (2001) research in Australia have collectively served to highlight key points about the processes within those arenas, and their implications for curriculum developments in physical education. The following summary of research findings endeavours to capture the contribution of a number of projects to conceptual understanding of curriculum construction and change. Progressively, the focus shifts from nationally orientated studies to research that has centred on state and school contexts of curriculum development in physical education.

Competing interests; multiple discourses

The research conducted in national arenas in England and Wales and Australia has demonstrated that physical education (or health and physical education) is a subject (or learning area) that is regarded as potentially contributing to the realisation of multiple political and economic agendas. It has become vividly apparent that discussions about prospective curriculum change or development in national government settings will reflect multiple and diverse interests in and for physical education. Interests in sporting excellence, participation in physically active and/or healthy lifestyles, the development of competitive and cooperative behaviours that are seen to have relevance in many social (and particularly employment) contexts, concerns to dissuade young people from engagement in behaviours that are identified as "antisocial", and crime prevention have all variously been identified as shaping political thinking about contemporary curriculum developments (Evans and Penney, 1995; Kay 1997; Penney and Evans, 1999; Glover, 2001). All have also been shown as remaining as reference points for curriculum construction and change and not only in England and Australian contexts. Referring to developments in New Zealand, Lisette Burrows and Bruce Ross recently reflected that;

It seems that health and physical educators are increasingly being regarded (both by others and themselves) as capable of inoculating young people against an ever-expanding range of risks and problems such as stress, low self-esteem, drugs and alcohol, teenage sex and spiritual decline. (Burrows and Ross, 2003: 15)

Ha et al. (2004) explain that in Hong Kong, the government decision to make physical education a key learning area in both the primary and secondary curriculum reflects the aims "to develop students' knowledge and motor skills through physical activity, to encourage them to have active and healthy lifestyles, and to foster desirable moral behaviour and other generic skills" (p. 422).

Meanwhile, the potential for connections between physical education curriculum development and multiple political agendas has underpinned international research focusing particularly on the time allocated to physical education in schools internationally (Hardman, 2000, 2001). Recently, Richard Bailey and colleagues led an international project (funded by the International Olympic Committee (IOC) and the International Council for Sports Science and Physical Education (ICSSPE)), that specifically sought to generate evidence of physical education programme developments successfully targeted towards one or more of identified "domains" – physical, intellectual, social/moral, organizational/institutional; and sport and lifestyle (see Bailey and Dismore, 2004). The diversity of policy-curriculum connections pursued and revealed by research in physical education is also reflected in the scope of interests pursued in other chapters within this section.

The research conducted by Glover (2001) and Penney and Evans (1999; see also Evans and Penney, 1995; Kay, 1997) has, however, also illustrated that the various interests in and for the subject or learning area do not have an equal bearing upon thinking about curriculum, and nor will they find equal expression in "official texts". The research has revealed that inevitably, but *also quite deliberately*, political attention will be directed towards particular interests in line with current political and economic priorities. Thanks to the range of national and state contexts collectively covered by the research undertaken in physical education, we can also say with confidence that priorities will vary and that we need to be wary of making global (and in a federal state context, also national) generalizations about the dominance of particular discourses in curriculum developments at the government level. For example, while many similarities were evident in the processes tracked respectively by Glover (2001) and Penney (1994), clear differences emerged in the range and relative position of discourses in the national arena in Australia as compared to in England (Penney and Glover, 1998).

Channelling interests; shaping curriculum

National and international commonalities have, however, been very apparent in relation to the *means and mechanisms* via which curriculum "shaping and directing" occurs within and between government arenas (including curriculum "quangos"[1]). The selection of writers, remit given to them, time schedules for writing and consultation, scope and procedures for consultation, have all been shown to be key factors in curriculum construction and change. The research in physical education and health and physical education has provided some vivid illustrations of the ways in which certain curriculum matters (structural characteristics and content) will be effectively non-negotiable in developments. Politicians and/or those instructed to act for them will establish (either overtly or more subtly) specific discursive boundaries in relation to the form that new or modified curricula may legitimately take in a particular national or state, historical and cultural development context. Discursive boundaries have been shown to be fundamental to the privileging of specific discourses in curriculum development in physical education and the marginalization or exclusion of others from curriculum debates (and texts arising). Once again, there is a need to acknowledge that the boundaries will differ across development contexts. What is a legitimate proposal for the physical education curriculum in one context will not be entertained (or be able to be voiced) in another. Comparing, for example, Penney (1994) or Kay's (1997) commentaries with Glover's (2001) findings illustrates national specificity in this regard. The boundaries to legitimate curriculum debate in England have been fundamentally different to those in Australia. These and other studies have highlighted that the same can be said in relation to the dynamics, possibilities and constraints within any particular national or state context. For example, Dinan-Thompson's (2002) and Glasby's (2000) doctoral studies revealed the significance of micropolitics in shaping curriculum development in the state curriculum arena (in Queensland) and in individual schools (see also Macdonald and Glover, 1996, 1997).

Research in the field has thus repeatedly pointed to the critical role of power-relations in curriculum construction and change, and continues to do so. Macdonald's (2003) critical analysis of the implementation of "rich tasks" in the context of what many would view as "radical" curriculum reform in Queensland, is notable in effectively relating the micro-politics and dynamics of curriculum development to macro, historical and global agendas, power and knowledge hierarchies. The paper reports on educational agents in the recontextualizing field (Education Queensland) selecting particular contexts for multidisciplinary tasks that have strong physical fitness components that are not scientifically rigorous (primary field knowledge) but reflect what is perceived as a public response to the "obesity crisis".

Power-relations at play in the construction process

Through the use of archival data originating from government departments, professional associations and institutions, Kirk (1992, 1998, 2003) has vividly illustrated that curriculum construction and change has long been a matter of political interest and intervention and a process in which different interests are accorded different status. His work has demonstrated the way in which practices established in a few elite schools and training institutions were the reference point for curriculum construction nationally, but also internationally. "Transition" points in the dominant form and focus of the physical education curriculum or elements of it (such as gymnastics, see Kirk, 2003) have been shown to be fundamentally linked to shifting interests in "the body" and changing views of the best means to educate/regulate the body (Kirk, 1992, 1998). Furthermore, in spanning decades of curriculum development, Kirk's work has revealed the way in which developments are always and inevitably shaped by past practices. Arguably, the progressive dominance of a "multi-activity", "sport-based" and sport-performance-orientated curriculum during the latter half of the twentieth century and into the twenty-first century has highlighted that the historical influence can be seen as cumulative. Curriculum research has identified that this particular curriculum form has become highly resistant to change (see below). A historical perspective thus remains critical if research is to capture the elements of re-construction and reproduction that feature in and amidst "change".

With a focus on contemporary curriculum change, Glasby's (2000), Glover's (2001), Kay's (1997) and Penney and Evans' (1999) research has collectively demonstrated that the production of curriculum texts in health and physical education (including so-called "official texts" issued by governments or curriculum authorities, but also, texts produced by teachers), is ultimately always a matter of compromise between multiple and competing interests. Producing a compromise involves various discourses being positioned in particular configurations and hierarchical relations. Priorities and hierarchies in relation to discourses in and of physical education thus shape curriculum texts, but the hierarchies are also actively reproduced by the texts. In England and Australia there has been relatively little in the way of research findings to suggest significant challenges or changes to long-established discursive hierarchies, the origins of which have been captured so well by Kirk (1992, 2000, 2003). Power-relations or "relative authority" in the curriculum process have repeatedly been shown to be critical in determining the curriculum proposals and practices (inherent in which will be particular discourses positioned in specific ways) that will be deemed legitimate and desirable in the context of curriculum development; and more specifically, the continued dominance of a multiactivity curriculum form, privileging discourses of sport and performance (see Crum, 1993; Locke, 1992; Penney and Chandler, 2000).

Many of the studies referred to above have highlighted Stephen Ball's (1990: 17) point that "who can speak where, when and with what authority" is fundamental to discourse. Evans and Penney (1999; see also Evans and Penney, 1995), Glasby (2000), Glover (2001) and Kay (1997) have all provided detailed accounts of the processes of curriculum construction in government arenas. In each case the researchers have shown that the competition for position and representation of particular curriculum interests is not a competition among equals, and nor is the curriculum game played on an even playing field. Rather, certain voices, representing particular interests, are accorded a privileged position in developments, while others are excluded or marginalised. The specific representation and positioning of discourses will be context specific. For example, comparative analysis has revealed clear variation in the scope and nature of the interests in "health" that have featured in curriculum developments relating to physical education and the ways in which health interests have been positioned in developments (Penney and Harris, 2003). But the common characteristic across contexts is that all interests do not receive equal consideration in curriculum development and that in important respects "what is thinkable as HPE has already been decided for teachers" (Kirk and Macdonald, 1998, 565) by those influential in government arenas.

Yet in some respects paradoxically, Sparkes' work (1988, 1990, 1991a,b) has led the field in reaffirming that life history studies have an important contribution to make to our understanding of processes of construction, change and resistance in relation to physical education curricula. Sparkes' investigation of the micro-politics and "subjectivities" of curriculum development in schools and an emerging body of research addressing the "lives and careers" of physical education teachers (Armour and Jones, 1998; Brown and Rich, 2002; Sparkes, 1994; Keyworth, 2001) (see below) have served to illustrate that the meanings and realities of curriculum come to fore at the point of interpretation and enactment by individual teachers in specific school settings. This focus in research remains important in countering tendencies to "depersonalize" curriculum and/or underplay the role of teachers and "teacher histories" in curriculum construction in the field.

Cultural specificity and tensions in curriculum construction

Curriculum research in physical education has also highlighted that construction and change needs to be recognised as culturally specific. Researchers have identified ways and instances in which discourses of national and cultural identities have been embedded within specific proposals for the physical education curriculum, with the curriculum openly identified as both a symbolic representation particular national and cultural identities, and a mechanism for the reproduction of those identities. In England and Wales these issues have come to the fore in relation to the "non-negotiable" central position of specific ("traditional") team games in physical education curriculum, and the cultural distinctiveness of Wales actively being pursued in the construction of its curriculum (Davies et al., 1997; Evans and Penney; 1995). Salter's (2000a, b) research in New Zealand has provided an invaluable depth of insight into political and cultural dynamics at play in curriculum construction. Specifically, Salter (1996, 2000a, b) has revealed the contestation and compromises in relation to the ways in which culturally distinct discourses of "health" (Maori and Pakeha) have been represented and combined in the new curriculum framework for Health and Physical Education in New Zealand. His work has further reaffirmed the lack of neutrality of curriculum construction processes as well as texts.

In the arena of curriculum construction in teacher education, Benn's (1998) doctoral research has highlighted the extent of the challenges involved in attempts to directly challenge the marginality of particular cultural and religious interests in developments. Benn's work at the University of Birmingham's Westhill campus to develop a teacher education curriculum that positively embraces discourses of Islam and bring Muslim women into curriculum construction in physical education also raised notable methodological issues. Benn was an "insider" as programme director and lecturer, yet an "outsider" to the key cultural and religious issues that she was focusing upon (Benn, 1998, 2000, 2002).

Curriculum continuity amidst construction and change

The research conducted in England and spanning the initial development and two revisions of the National Curriculum for Physical Education, has shown that discursive boundaries have effectively ensured an ongoing reproduction of the multi-activity model and curriculum structure in physical education. "Official texts" have been identified as reaffirming activity-related specialization and thus a strongly classified curriculum (see above; Bernstein, 1990; Penney, 1994; Penney and Chandler, 2000). In England but also elsewhere, research has revealed the strong degree to which curriculum texts produced by politicians, appointed writers, providers of professional development, teachers and students are informed by established understandings of the form, content and key purposes of the physical education curriculum. Change that extends beyond existing understandings[2] of what physical education (or HPE) should "look like" has been shown to be inherently problematic, because it falls outside of familiar frames of reference. In England this has meant that repeatedly, there have been few opportunities for consideration of alternatives to a strongly classified sport-performance orientated multi-activity curriculum in which "traditional" games are prominent (Evans and Penney, 1995; Kay, 1997; Penney and Evans, 1999).

Research in physical education has also shown that while there is undoubtedly a need to acknowledge the "unfinished" nature of curriculum and "scope for slippage" (Bowe et al., 1992) in and from the "official texts" arising from government arenas, limits are nevertheless effectively "set" for the extent and direction of the slippage that will feature in ongoing and school-based curriculum development. Those limits have been associated with both the government texts and characteristics of the contexts of school-based construction, with curriculum history and teacher life histories coming to the fore as highly influential factors in the maintenance of curriculum status quo (Penney, 1994; Curtner-Smith et al., 1999; Green, 1998, 2002).

At this point it is timely to note a further important and reoccurring feature in Kirk's (1992, 1998, 2003) analyses; namely the inherently gendered nature of the physical education curriculum, tied to historically gendered training institutions and regimes. Others have extended this line of inquiry via historical studies focusing not merely on institutions and their practices, but also individuals within them. Fletcher's (1984) account of the development of the "female tradition" in physical education in England over the course of the century, and subsequent research by Flintoff (1993), has demonstrated a key linkage between institutional and personal histories and important elements of continuity in the physical education curriculum in training institutions.

Yelling's (2002) recent doctoral research has provided further insights into the issues arising when attempts are made to challenge established discourse hierarchies in physical education curricula and specifically, encourage pedagogical developments that weaken classification (Bernstein, 1990; see above). Yelling (2003)'s work captured the dilemmas arising

for both teachers and students attempting to develop learning experiences that focused upon physical activity in games settings. The research revealed clear tensions between physical activity and performance discourses, but at the same time also pointed to important potential for productive compromises to be achieved between "competing" discourses in curriculum and pedagogical development work.

In Australia, quite different tensions and "slippage" has been observed in contexts of (ongoing) curriculum construction. National and state texts that have openly sought to move curriculum thinking and practices beyond the "established and familiar" have been shown to generate repeated problems (for national, state and system-based curriculum authorities, teachers, students and teacher educators) of reconciliation of (radical) new proposals with existing structures and practices. Research in Australia has revealed tensions in national, state and school arenas associated with established school subjects being re-located in curriculum terms, within the new learning area of HPE. Key findings from the HPE National Professional Development Project (NPDP) conducted in Victoria and Queensland, Dinan-Thompson's (2002) research focusing on developments in Queensland, and an evaluation of the HPE 1–10 developments in Queensland (Macdonald et al., 1998) are discussed further below. Before moving on to consider these projects, however, it is important to acknowledge that research has clearly identified "no change" agendas amidst curriculum construction at national, local government and school levels. In relation to the former, Penney (1994) and Glover's (2001) respective doctoral studies drew attention to the ways in which amidst development purportedly directed towards curriculum change, there were clear interests in the maintenance of status quo in curriculum. Political timelines, resource considerations (relating to the provision and training implications of curriculum proposals), but also concerns to minimize anticipated resistance from teachers set to take on the task of implementing new requirements and from politicians and the media, were shown to variously limit the possibilities open to those individuals charged with drafting proposals for the respective national texts. In essence curriculum writers have recounted the pressures and/or imperative for established curriculum content, structures and identities to be clearly visible in new curriculum proposals.

Curriculum construction and change: rushed and little more than rhetoric?

In many respects, the picture emerging from curriculum research in physical education has been one of repeated and unrelenting government-led curriculum change in physical education. The importance of research exploring curriculum from the perspective of teachers and students is captured by Ward and Doutis' comment that:

> ... the study of curriculum in physical education has been largely a theoretical enterprise, focusing on ideology, discourse, and action (Jewett, Bain and Ennis, 1995) ... . our journals are filled with discourse about curricula. If one accepts the enacted curriculum as a "lived" experience for teachers and students, we know very little about what goes on in the name of curriculum in schools ... (Ward and Doutis, 1999: 394)

Research in physical education has, however, highlighted that we should not equate the high volume of new "official texts" with substantial or sustained change in school physical education curricula. A number of studies that have directed their focus to curriculum and pedagogical responses in schools faced with imposed changes to curriculum requirements have been revealing in this respect. For example, the research conducted by Curtner-Smith (1995; Curtner-Smith et al., 1999) in England has captured the ways in which teachers have been able to exploit the inherent conservatism in the official texts and repeatedly accommodate new requirements within essentially unchanging curricula and pedagogical practices. The situation has been read as one of increasing resistance to an ongoing stream of new or revised curriculum requirements, captured by headlines such as "the more things change, the more they stay the same" (Curtner-Smith, 1999). Other researchers have drawn attention to the curriculum experience of physical education in England as still inherently gendered, with the passing of time and introduction of a National Curriculum having seemingly little impact upon historical practices and perceptions in this regard (Cockburn and Clarke, 2002; Williams and Bedward, 1999; 2002). Meanwhile, Harris' (1995, 1997) research focusing specifically on responses to changes in curriculum requirements relating to health-related exercise in physical education has further pointed to a notable "gap" between the rhetoric of new official texts and curriculum practices in secondary schools.

There is, however, a need for some caution in our readings of these reports of apparently very limited change to school physical education curricula and pedagogical practices in physical education. Research to date may well have failed to take due account of the timelag between legislative change and construction and change in school and classroom arenas. Nevertheless, it is notable that Dinan-Thompson's (2002) and others' research in Australia (see for example, Brown, 2005; Fox et al., 1997; Macdonald and Glover, 1997; Macdonald, 2003b) has shown agendas for curriculum re-construction and change inherent in official texts being resisted and re-negotiated as the texts are re-contextualized

in schools and by teachers, with histories, professional identities and interests that have not necessarily matched with those dominant in the official texts. Research in Australia, like that in England, has demonstrated that while we may be correct in viewing the "official" curriculum as structuring teachers' work; "... this is not to suggest a simple, direct and unproblematic connection between the officially sanctioned and defined curriculum, and what teachers do" (Reid, 1999: 188). Garrett and Piltz (1999) provided a particularly strong statement on this matter, contending that their research into teacher's implementation of the national Health and Physical Education texts calls into question the contemporary emphasis on the deskilling of teachers. They stressed the reflexivity inherent in teachers' responses, explaining that;

> ... rather than simply accept or reject HPE and its associated expectations, they use their accumulated wisdom – a theoretical and practical wisdom – to critique imposed curriculum development. They employ this critique to inform ways by which they can shape the curriculum 'product' to overcome its deficiencies, while still meeting some of its non-negotiable requirements. (p. 206)

Garrett and Pilz's claim was that "In this way, teachers are acting (often implicitly) to deconstruct and reconstruct curricula in a manner which is more consistent with the role of curriculum intellectuals than that of curriculum technicians" (p. 206). In a similar vain Cothran and Ennis (1998) identified physical education teachers as being in a position to "select curricular goals that are most congruent with their beliefs about the knowledge of most worth" (p. 309). In many respects the research discussed in other chapters within this section supports the view of teachers as active constructors, not passive implementers of curriculum.

There is considerable evidence to support the view that physical education teachers have been instrumental in constructing their curricula in distinctly new and innovative ways. Yet we can equally reflect that instrumentality has been very evident in teachers actively resisting new directions for curriculum development. Macdonald and Glover (1997), for example, reported the tendencies for curriculum development of the Health and Physical Education Learning Area to be taken forward "within safe subject boundaries" (p. 25) and highlighted that "strong socialisation into a subject can be lived out in a teacher's commitment to retaining their traditional subject matter" (p. 26). In his work with teachers and students undertaking upper secondary school vocational version of physical education, Brown (2005) identified similar tendencies and knowledge hierarchies being played out in curriculum developments in schools. The potential of this version of physical education to provide vocational certification was openly undermined by the low status of the course in the minds of the school, the teachers and students undertaking it.

While studies such as those above reaffirm the active role of teachers in relation to school curriculum, we still can not escape the reality that many of the contexts of government-led contemporary curriculum development have marginalized teachers and seemingly denied them the time and professional resources for creative intellectual engagement with proposals. In both the English and Australian research referred to above, teachers' experiences have frequently been identified as one of frustration and bureaucratic burden, accompanied in some instances, by a perceived threat to established professional identities and long-held curriculum "territory" (see for example, Dinan-Thompson, 2002; Macdonald and Glover, 1996, 1997; NPDP, 1997; Yelling, 2003). Regression to familiar and established patterns of provision has been portrayed more as an essential coping strategy than a proactive response to new requirements. Meanwhile, the physical education curriculum has been identified as inadequately resourced and lacking status on a world-wide scale (Hardman, 2000, 2001). Studies such as that conducted by Johns and Dimmock (1999) in Hong Kong confirm that the scope and tendency for very significant "slippage" between the construction of laudable curriculum aims and/or requirements and the realities of the curriculum that continues to be constructed by teachers in schools is far from unique to Australia and England. Even within what is portrayed as a highly collaborative curriculum development, the *Saber-Tooth Project* (see below), it is acknowledged that "the content of physical education did not change much" (Ward et al., 1999: 457) – although it is emphasized that familiar content is being engaged with very differently (a point also at the core of recent curriculum reform in Queensland, see Macdonald, 2003b, Macdonald et al., 2005).

Curriculum construction and change: collaborative and collegial

Many of the research findings discussed thus far contribute to a view of curriculum construction and change in physical education that is far from a cause for celebration.

Research reported in this part of the chapter extends the range of international contexts considered and provides a welcome counter to that view. Once again it is also important to stress the need to view the research discussed in this chapter in conjunction with the array of studies reported in other chapters within the section. There are numerous examples to be found of research and furthermore, curriculum construction and change characterised by collaboration and collegiality. The extensive number of developments of Sport Education and/or hybrid derivatives of it (See Chapter 5.3) are particularly notable in that regard. Hastie and Buchanen's (2001) development of the model termed *Empowering Sport*, and Ennis' (1999) development of the *Sport for Peace* curriculum both fall into the latter category. They are also significant in openly endeavouring to bring discourses of cooperation, self and social responsibility to the fore in physical education curriculum development.

On a personal note, involvement in the trial phase of the senior physical education syllabus development in Queensland remains an experience that I look back on as a great privilege specifically because of the process that was employed by the Board of Senior Secondary School Studies. Our conclusion as evaluators was that "In the main, the development of a new senior physical education syllabus has been neither imposed, nor rushed and has appeared to recognise that involvement, 'ownership' and time are critical for achieving anything more than 'surface level' or tokenistic change in education" (Penney and Kirk, 1998).

The so-called *Saber-Tooth Project* (Ward, 1999a,b) in the USA was undoubtedly underpinned by a very similar recognition. Given that evaluation studies commissioned to examine the nature of responses to new curriculum frameworks or requirements have stressed the need for curriculum development processes that provide teachers with the quality time and professional support required to respond positively and creatively to developments involving new conceptual challenges (Macdonald et al., 1998; Penney, 1997), it is appropriate to comment further on the *Saber-Tooth Project*. Writing in 1999, Ward described the project as;

> ... an ongoing reform effort involving a university and a district in a collaborative partnership designed to improve physical education for middle school students by improving workplace conditions and engaging teachers in professional development focused on curriculum improvement ... The guiding question of this project is: To what extent and in what ways does this particular partnership enable a school faculty to pursue an agenda of systemic change in their physical education curriculum? (Ward, 1999a: 380)

The project involved three schools and their teachers. Importantly, both teacher and school histories were acknowledged as key to the whole development endeavour.

> The schedule was divided into three phases. For 3 weeks, teacher values and beliefs, student needs, the existing curriculum, and contemporary curriculum issues were examined. For the next 5 weeks, curriculum and instructional models were reviewed, and for the remaining 8 weeks, the group focused on the development of specific curricula for the different grade levels in the school. (Ward, 1999b: 403)

Teacher professional development was thus the mechanism of curriculum reform undertaken within the context of collaboration.

A further encouraging example of the integration of professional development and curriculum development within a context of collaboration arises in Hong Kong (Ha et al., 2004). Ha et al.'s (2004) study was designed to "evaluate the effectiveness of an in-service training program and understand teachers' receptivity to curriculum change in physical education" (p. 421). Faced with a government initiated reform that "is attempting to transform physical education from a skill-oriented discipline that emphasizes the development of motor skills to a more comprehensive health-related curriculum" (p. 422), it is perhaps not surprising that teachers confirmed that "inservice training was needed to equip them to implement a physical education program in line with curriculum reform" (Ha et al., 2004: 421). Encouragingly, the in-service training was a collaborative venture, involving university scholars and teachers in the development of conferences and workshops for local primary school teachers, supported by the Hong Kong Education and Manpower Bureau. In addition to reaffirming the effectiveness of a professional development program involving educators, curriculum planners and peer teachers, the participating teachers identified that to enhance prospects of curricular change, future initiatives should also involve school principals and administrators. They also reflected that apart from the development program, teachers' attitudes and beliefs and school support were "the most important factors for successful curricular change in Hong Kong" (Ha et al., 2004: 430).

The above developments are important illustrations of collaboration between stakeholders in curriculum development. Yet as indicated in the introduction to this chapter, there are dangers that curriculum research overlooks students as key stakeholders and influential figures. As Brooker and Macdonald (1999) pointed out; "Whether students have an opportunity to contribute meaningfully to centrally developed school curricula is a question that deserves close study" (p. 83). Critically reflecting on the positioning and voice of students in the evaluation of the trial Board of Senior Secondary School Studies Physical Education syllabus, Brooker and Macdonald commented that;

> Student data in the formal reports were a distilled version of what the students had said in the course of the evaluation, and individual voices were subsumed into a single reporting 'voice'. There was no alternative for this procedure, because students' views were gathered from group conversations and the identity of individual respondents was not recorded. As a result, student voices were 'homogenized'... (Brooker and Macdonald, 1999: 93–4)

If we regard the curriculum as "co-constructed", with teachers *and* *students* active in shaping its pedagogical form and focus, then we should be as concerned with student histories as teacher histories. It is hard to envisage how we can effectively fulfil stated commitments to develop curricula that are directed towards students' learning needs and interests without establishing a comprehensive understanding of the curriculum that they have experienced to date, within and beyond schools, or acknowledging the values they bring to the curriculum. Cothran and Ennis' (1998) research exploring the nature of teacher and student values, and the dynamic between these, generated important insights into curriculum from the student perspective. In so doing it served to highlight why "educational travel through the curriculum is not always a cooperative, mutually satisfactory process for teachers and students" (p. 307).

Major trends and future directions

The research incorporated in this review presents somewhat mixed and arguably paradoxical messages; of a time of much apparent change and yet seemingly very little *real* change in physical education curriculum. Many may well share the view that perhaps this is because we have yet to devote sufficient research attention to curriculum construction and change that remains ongoing and furthermore, a daily reality, for teachers and their students. Curriculum research from students' perspective and furthermore, that is sustained over time, emerges as in need of development in physical education. Also reaffirmed is the fundamental importance of partnerships if we are seeking innovation in physical education curriculum. From the *Saber-Tooth Project* Ward et al. (1999) observed that "teachers often do not have the knowledge to engage in curriculum planning" (p. 459) – a point echoed more recently by Kirk and Macdonald (2001). Drawing upon the findings of two large-scale curriculum reform projects in Health and Physical Education in Australia, Kirk and Macdonald suggested that;

> The teachers' authoritative voice within these projects was located within the local context of implementation of the reforms and based upon their intimate knowledge of their students, their colleagues, their school structures and the resources available to them. It was from this position that teachers made an invaluable contribution to the curriculum reform process. However, this expertise set limits on the majority of teachers' opportunities to be co-producers of the new versions of HPE at the level of national and state documents. (Kirk and Macdonald, 1998: 552)

Acknowledging this differential, Kirk and Macdonald (1998) are quite clear that "forming partnerships for the duration of curriculum projects is of vital importance" (p. 566). But their comments elude to the fact that it is not merely partnerships that are important here. The collective knowledge and capacity for new curriculum thinking that is inherent in the partnerships is what is important and what we need to nurture in and through more curriculum research. Ennis (2003) has emphasized that physical education "should afford multiple opportunities for students to engage with activities in a positive, stimulating environment" (p. 81). Yet we still lack research that gives a profile to *various ways* in which this may be achieved in curriculum design. Having attempted through this review, to make links between conceptualisations of curriculum and research in curriculum, I contend that the starting point for more and innovative research has to be new conceptualisations of curriculum. Amidst global rhetoric of interest and investment in lifelong learning and learning communities, it is inadequate to view the physical education curriculum as confined to schools, or school years. We urgently need "expanded" conceptualizations of curriculum and research projects that embrace those conceptualizations. Such conceptualisations will rightly refocus attention on students but also prompt more involvement of them in both curriculum development and research in physical education (Macdonald, 2003a). A dual challenge is thus posed from this review; namely to be rethinking curriculum and rethinking research in physical education in response to the changing realities of education and possibilities for education in the 21st century. As Macdonald (2003a) has observed;

> While the literature in the curriculum field recognizes the difficulty in creating meaningful curriculum change within current school structures, the majority of innovations and analyses are blind to the bigger and more significant questions surrounding change: Who are the young people in schools? and What, where and how do they learn? (Macdonald, 2003a, 147)

Notes

1 Quasi non-government organizations.
2 Particularly, but not exclusively, understandings of so-called "key players" in curriculum developments.

References

Armour, K. and Jones, R.L. (1998). *Physical education teachers' lives and careers. PE., sport and educational status.* London : Falmer Press.

Arnold, P.J. (1988). *Education, movement and the curriculum.* London: The Falmer Press.

Bailey, R. and Dismore, H. (2004). Sport in education (SpinEd) Project: Examining the role of Physical Education and sport in education. *British Journal of Teaching Physical Education, 35, 2:* 6–8.

Ball, S.J. (1990). *Politics and policy making in education. Explorations in policy sociology.* London: Routledge

Ball, S.J. (1993a). Education policy, power relations and teachers' work. *British Journal of Educational Studies, Vol. XXXXI, 2,* 106–121.

Ball, S.J. (1993b). What is policy? Texts, trajectories and Toolboxes. *Discourse, 13, 2:* pp. 10–17.

Benn, T. (1998). Exploring experiences of a group of British Muslim women in initial teacher training and their early teaching careers, *Unpublished doctoral thesis,* Loughborough, UK: Loughborough University.

Benn, T. (2000). Towards inclusion in education and physical education. In A.Williams (Ed.), *Primary school physical education* (pp. 118–135). London: Routledge/Falmer Press.

Benn, T. (2002). Muslim women in teacher training: Issues of gender, 'race' and religion. In D. Penney (Ed.), *Gender and Physical education. Contemporary issues and future directions* (pp. 57–79). London: Routledge

Bernstein, B. (1971). On the Classification and Framing of Educational Knowledge. In M.F.D. Young (Ed.), *Knowledge and Control. New Directions for the Sociology of Education.* London: Collier Macmillan.

Bernstein, B. (1990). *The Structuring of Pedagogic Discourse. Volume IV Class,Codes and Control.* London: Routledge.

Bernstein, B. (1996). *Pedagogy, Symbolic Control and Identity. Theory, Research, Critique.* London: Taylor & Francis.

Bernstein, B. (2000). *Pedagogy, Symbolic Control and Identity. Theory, Research, Critique. Revised Edition.* Oxford: Rowman & Littlefield Publishers, Inc.

Bowe, R. Ball, S.J. and Gold, A. (1992). *Reforming education and changing schools. Case studies in policy sociology.* London: Routledge

Brooker, R. and Macdonald, D. (1999). Did we hear you?: issues of student voice in curriculum innovation. *Journal of Curriculum Studies, 31, 1:* 83–97.

Brown, S. (2005). Holding bays or pathways: Vocationalism and physical recreation. Unpublished doctoral dissertation. Brisbane: The University of Queensland.

Brown, D. and Rich, E. (2002). Gender positioning as pedagogic practice in teaching physical education (pp. 80–100). In D. Penney (Ed.), *Gender and Physical Education. Contemporary Issues and Future Directions.* London: Routledge.

Burrows, L. and Ross, B. (2003). Introduction. In B. Ross and L. Burrows (Eds.), *It takes two feet. Teaching physical education and health in Aotearoa, New Zealand.* Palmerston North, New Zealand, Dunmore Press.

Cockburn, C. and Clarke, C. (2002). "Everybody's looking at you!": Girls negotiating the "femininity deficit" they incur in physical education, *Women's Studies International Forum, 25, 6:* 651–665.

Cothran, D. and Ennis, C. (1998). Curricula of mutual worth: comparisons of students' and teachers' curricular goals. *Journal of Teaching in Physical Education, 17*: 307–326.

Crum, B.J. (1993). Conventional Thought and Practice in Physical Education : Problems of Teaching and implications for Change. *QUEST, 45*: 336–356.

Curtner-Smith, M.D. (1999). The more things change the more they stay the same : Factors influencing teachers' interpretations and delivery of national curriculum physical education. *Sport, Education and Society, 4*, 1: 75–97.

Curtner-Smith, M.D., Kerr, I.G. and Hencken, C.L. (1995). The impact of the national curriculum physical education on teachers' behaviours related with pupils' skill learning : A case study in one English town. *British Journal of Physical Education Research Supplement, 16,* Summer: 2–12.

Curtner-Smith, M.D., Todorovich, J.R., Lacon, S.A. and Kerr, I.G. (1999). Teachers' rules, routines and expectations prior to and following the implementation of the National Curriculum for Physical Education. *European Journal of Physical Education, 4*, 1: 17–30.

Davies, B., Evans, J., Penney, D. and Bass, D. (1997). Physical education and nationalism in Wales. *The Curriculum Journal, 8*, 2: 249–270.

Dinan-Thompson, M. (2002). Curriculum construction and implementation: a study of Queensland health and physical education. *Unpublished doctoral thesis*, University of Queensland.

Evans, J. and Penney, D. (1995). Physical education, restoration and the politics of Sport. *Curriculum Studies, 3*, 2: 183–196.

Ennis, C. (1999). Creating a culturally relevant curriculum for disengaged girls. *Sport, Education and Society, 4*, 1: 31–49.

Ennis, C. (2003). What works in physical education: designing and implementing a quality educational program. *Educational Horizons, 81*(2): 77–82.

Fletcher, S. (1984). *Women first: The female tradition in English* physical education, 1880–1980. London: Althone.

Flintoff, A. (1993). Gender, physical education and initial teacher education. In J. Evans (Ed.), *Equality, education and physical education* (pp. 184–204). London: The Falmer Press.

Fox, B., Timmins, R. and Macdonald, D. (1997). Working in the HPE key learning area: Three case studies of curriculum change. *The ACHPER National Journal, 44*, 1: 8–11.

Garrett, R. and Piltz, W. (1999) A Case Study of Curriculum Control: Curriculum Reform in Health and Physical Education (pp. 201–209). In B. Johnson and A. Reid (Eds.), *Contesting the Curriculum*. Australia: Social Sciences Press.

Glasby, P. (2000). Teacher constructions of health: A case study of school Health Education in Queensland. *Unpublished doctoral thesis*, Brisbane: The University of Queensland.

Glover, S. (2001). The social construction of pedagogic discourse in Health and Physical Education: A study of the writing of the National Statement and Profile, 1992–1994. *Unpublished doctoral thesis*, Brisbane: The University of Queensland.

Goodson, I.(1993). *School subjects and curriculum change. Studies in curriculum history.* (3rd Edn.) London: The Falmer Press.

Goodson, I.F. (1995). *The making of curriculum. Collected essays.* (2nd Edn.) London : The Falmer Press.

Goodson, I.F. (1997). *The changing Curriculum. Studies in social construction.* New York : Peter Lang Publishing.

Green, K. (1998). Philosophies, ideologies and the practice of physical education. *Sport, Education and Society, 3*: 125–143.

Green, K. (2002). Physical education teachers in their figurations: A sociological analysis of everyday 'philosophies'. *Sport, Education and Society, 7*, 1: 65–83.

Griffiths, M. (1998). *Educational Research for social justice. Getting off the fence.* Buckingham: Open University Press.

Ha, A., Lee, J., Chan, D. and Sum, R. (2004). Teachers' perceptions of in-service teacher training to support curriculum change in physical education: The Hong Kong experience. *Sport, Education and Society, 9*, 3: 421–438.

Hardman, K. (2000). The world-wide survey of physical education in schools: Findings, issues and strategies for a sustainable future. The Fellows Lecture (part 1). *The British Journal of Teaching Physical Education, 31*, 4: 29–31.

Hardman, K. (2001). The world-wide survey of physical education in schools: Findings, issues and strategies for a sustainable future. The Fellows Lecture (part 2). *The British Journal of Teaching Physical Education, 32*, 1: 29–31.

Harris, J. (1995). Physical education – a picture of health? *The British Journal of Physical Education, 26*, 4: 25–32.

Harris, J. (1997). Physical education: A picture of health? The implementation of health-related exercise in the National Curriculum in secondary schools in England. *Unpublished doctoral thesis*, Loughborough, UK: Loughborough University.

Hastie, P. and Buchanen, A.M. (2000). Teaching Responsibility Through Sport Education: Prospects of a Coalition. *Research Quarterly for Exercise and Sport, 71*, 1: 25–35.

Jewett, A.E. Bain, L.L. and Ennis, C.D. (1995). *The curriculum process in physical education.* Dubuque, IA: Brown and Benchmark.

Johns, D.P. and Dimmock, C. (1999). The marginalization of physical education: Impoverished curriculum policy and practice in Hong Kong. *Journal of Education Policy, 14* (4): 363–384.

Kane, J.E. (1974). *Physical education in secondary schools.* London: Macmillan.

Kay, W. (1997). The New Right and physical education. *Unpublished doctoral thesis*, Loughborough, UK: Loughborough University.

Keyworth, S. (2001). Critical autobiography: 'straightening' out dance education. *Research in Dance Education, 2*, 2: 117–137.

Kincheloe, J. (1997). Introduction. In Goodson, I.F. *The Changing Curriculum. Studies in Social Construction.* New York: Peter Lang Publishing.

Kirk, D. (1992). *Defining physical education: The social construction of a school subject in postwar Britain*. London: Falmer.

Kirk, D. (1998). *Schooling bodies: School practice and public discourse 1880–1950*. London: Leicester University Press.

Kirk, D. (2000). Gender associations: Sport, state schools and Australian Culture, *The International Journal of Sport History, 17* (2/3): 49–64.

Kirk, D. (2003). Towards a critical history of the body, identity and health. Corporeal power and school practice. In J. Evans, B. Davies and J. Wright (Eds.), *Body. Knowledge and control. Studies in the sociology of physical education and health*. London: Routledge.

Kirk, D. and Macdonald, D. (1998) Teacher voice and ownership of curriculum change, *Journal of Curriculum Studies, 33* (5): 551–567.

Kirk, D. and Macdonald, D. (2001). Teacher voice and ownership of curriculum change. *Journal of Curriculum Studies, 33*, 5: 551–567.

Locke, F.L. (1992). Changing Secondary School Physical Education. *QUEST, 44*: 361–372.

Macdonald, D. (2003). A modest attempt at rich task implementation. Modernism meets postmodernism. *Discourse: Studies in the Cultural Politics of Education, 24*(2): 247–262.

Macdonald, D. (2003a). Curriculum change and the postmodern world: Is the school reform project an anachronism? *Journal of Curriculum Studies, 35*, 2: 139–149.

Macdonald, D. (2003b). A modest attempt at rich task implementation. Modernism meets postmodernism. *Discourse: Studies in the Cultural Politics of Education, 24*, 2: 247–262.

Macdonald, D. and Glover, S. (1996). The PE Department Can't Just Take Over!: Physical Education Teachers' Identities in the HPE Area. Paper presented at the *20th Biennial National International ACHPER Conference.*, Melbourne, 14–19 January 1996.

Macdonald, D. and Glover, S. (1997). Subject matter boundaries and curriculum change in the health and physical education key learning area. *Curriculum Perspectives, 17*, 1: 23–28.

Macdonald, D., Penney, D., Hunter, L., Carlson, T. and Gillespie, A. (1998). *Report 3 of the Evaluation of the trial/pilot of the Queensland School Curriculum Council Years 1–10 Health and Physical Syllabus-in-Development*. Department of Human Movement Studies, The University of Queensland.

National Professional Development Program Health And Physical Education Project. (1997). *The Health and Physical Education Project "Reviewing the curriculum in the health and physical education key learning area: A model for professional development using the health and physical education statement and profile for Australian schools. Annual report*. Canberra : DEETYA.

Penney, D. (1994). No Change in a new ERA? The impact of the Education Reform Act (1988) on the provision of PE and sport in state schools. *Unpublished doctoral thesis*, Southampton: University of Southampton.

Penney, D. (1997). *Report of the external evaluation of the health and physical education project "Reviewing curriculum in the health and physical education key learning area: A model for professional development using the health and physical education statement and profile for Australian schools"*. Department of Human Movement Studies, University of Queensland.

Penney, D. (2003). Countering control. Challenging conceptualisations of educational research, *Curriculum Perspectives, 23*, 1: 60–64.

Penney, D. and Chandler, T. (2000). A Curriculum with connections? *British Journal of Teaching Physical Education, 31* (2): 37–40.

Penney, D. and Evans, J. (1999). *Politics, Policy and Practice in Physical Education*. London: FN Spon, an Imprint of Routledge.

Penney, D. and Harris, J. (2003). The Body and Health in Policy: Representations and recontextualisation. In J. Evans, B. Davies and J. Wright (Eds.), *Body, Knowledge and Control* (pp. 96–112). London: Routledge.

Penney, D. and Glover, S. (1998). Contested identities: A comparative analysis of the position and definitions of physical education in national curriculum developments in England and Wales and Australia. *European Journal of Physical Education, 3*, 1: 5–21.

Penney, D. and Kirk, D. (1998). Changing thinking, changing practice in curriculum development. In R. Fisher, C. Laws and J. Moses (Eds.), Active living through quality physical education. Selected Readings from the *eighth European Congress of ICHPER*SD (Europe)*, St.Mary's University College, Strawberry Hill, London, 14–19 July 1998.

Print, M. (1993). *Curriculum development and design*. (2nd edn.) St.Leonards, Australia: Allen and Unwin.

Reid, A. (1999). Controlling the curriculum work of teachers (pp. 186–200). In B. Johnson and A. Reid, (1999) (Eds.), *Contesting the Curriculum*. Australia: Social Science Press

Salter, G. (1996). Curriculum development and reform in New Zealand physical education. Paper presented at the joint *Educational Research Association Singapore and Australian Association for Research in Education Conference*, Singapore, November 1996.

Salter, G. (2000a). Marginalising indigenous knowledge in teaching Physical Education: The sanitising of hauora (well-being) in the new HPE curriculum. *Journal of Physical Education New Zealand, 33*, 1: 6–16.

Salter, G. (2000b). Deciding between cultural identiy or 'success' in physical education: Describing attitudes and values. *Journal of Physical Education New Zealand, 33*, 3: 67–83.

Shaughnessy, J. and Price, L. (1995). Physical education in primary schools. What's been going on since September 1992? *The Bulletin of Physical Education, 31*, 2: 34–42.

Sparkes, A.C. (1988). The micropolitics of innovation in the physical education curriculum. In J. Evans (Ed.), *Teachers, teaching and control in physical education* (pp. 157–173). London: The Falmer Press.

Sparkes, A.C. (1990). Winners, losers and the myth of rational change in physical education: Towards an understanding of interests and power in innovation. In D. Kirk and R. Tinning (Eds.), *Physical education, curriculum and culture: Critical issues in the contemporary crisis* (pp. 193–224). London: Falmer Press.

Sparkes, A.C. (1991a). Curriculum change: On gaining a sense of perspective. In N. Armstrong and A. Sparkes (Eds.), *Issues in physical education* (pp. 1–19). London: Cassell Education Limited.

Sparkes, A.C. (1991b). Exploring the subjective dimension of curriculum change. In N. Armstrong and A. Sparkes (Eds.), *Issues in physical education* (pp. 20–35). London: Cassell Education Limited.

Sparkes, A. (1994). Self, silence and invisibility as a beginning teacher: A life history of lesbian experience. *British Journal of Sociology of Education 15*, 1: pp. 93–118.

Underwood, G. (1983). *The Physical Education curriculum in the secondary school'. Planning and implementation.* London: The Falmer Press.

Ward, P. (1999a). An introduction to the Saber-Tooth Project. *Journal of Teaching Physical Education, 18*:, 379–381.

Ward, P. (1999b). Design of the Saber-Tooth Project. *Journal of Teaching Physical Education, 18*: 403–416.

Ward, P. and Doutis, P. (1999) Toward a consolidation of the knowledge base for reform in physical education. *Journal of Teaching Physical Education, 18*: 382–402.

Ward, P., Doutis, P. and Evans, S. (1999). Lessons, conclusions and implications of the Saber-Tooth Project. *Journal of Teaching Physical Education, 18*: 382–402.

Williams, A. and Bedward, J. (1999). *Games for girls – The impact of recent policy on the provision of physical education and sporting opportunities for female adolescents. Summary report of a study funded by the Nuffield Foundation.* King Alfreds University College, Winchester.

Williams, A. and Bedward, J. (2002). Understanding girls' experience of Physical Education: Relational analysis and situated learning. In D. Penney (Ed.), *Gender and physical education. Contemporary issues and future directions* (pp. 146–160). London: Routledge.

Yelling, M.R. (2002). Physical education, physical activity and the National Curriculum Physical Education: Policy, provision and prospects. *Unpublished doctoral thesis,* Bedford, UK: De Montfort University.

5.2 Research into elementary physical education programs

lisahunter

Introduction

Elementary physical education (EPE) has on the one hand been heralded as important, for benefits such as health, fitness, exercise, social interaction, motor development, skill development and more recently obesity control, yet on the other hand often absent in practice, under-researched, and therefore under-theorised with respect to the rhetoric around claims made to justify its presence within the curriculum. EPE is now commanding the attention of politicians concerned about lifestyle issues (such as lifelong fitness, health, and obesity) as well as a community of academics, professionals, educational policymakers and health and sport advocates who want to justify EPE. This chapter summarizes and critiques the research that focuses on physical education programmes in elementary schools, that is schools that include young people approximating ages four to 11, grades one to six or seven, and sometimes referred to as "primary school". In particular the chapter offers a history of the EPE and its research; the key themes and findings of the research; applications to practice and policy, and; major trends and future directions for research in elementary physical education programs (EPEP).

The EPEP may be understood as being the enacted curriculum, the intended curriculum as defined by a teacher plan, or more generally, all that occurs within the school that is related to physical education. Clearly, if the latter definition were used I would need to incorporate research associated with cross-disciplinary contributions to the curriculum (see Section 2), the learners and learning in physical education (Sections 3 and 6), teachers and teaching (Section 4) assessment (Section 3), and teacher–student relationships. As there is sufficient research relating to these areas in other sections of this handbook, this chapter will focus more specifically on the research associated with the content of the intended curriculum with some reference to who teaches that curriculum, the background of the

teacher often playing a large part in what is or is not included in the programme.

The definition and place of physical education in the elementary programme more broadly will also be discussed, given the increased responsibility being placed upon schools in some countries for the delivery of programmes that create healthy citizens – those who are physically fit and not overweight. This largely reflects the research literature of North American, UK and to some extent Australasian although I have attempted to draw in research from other countries where it has been accessible. Because of the unclear boundaries and definitions of EPE, research that might inform elementary programs might also, but not necessarily, be drawn from overlapping areas of early childhood literature, growth and development, motor learning, health and fitness, school sport, and middle school literature (see, for example, Barney, 2003). Components of these areas of research imply or directly suggest content of EPEP.

A dearth of research reports the conditions and realization of physical education in elementary school programmes (e.g. Hardman and Marshall, 2000; Kirk et al., 1995; Sosnowska and Kostka, 2002), the research being more about justification of physical education through "opportunity", "potential" or "responsibility to create situations" for learning. Reporting of activities that review and evaluate the curriculum (Kirk et al., 1995; Macdonald et al., 2003) exist but have not been prevalent, ongoing or extensive. Programmes and justification for particular forms of EPE seem to be based on assumptions and generalizations made about the transferability of related research to practice with little research examining the difference between the intended and enacted curriculum, the processes, practices and outcomes. As this has become recognized by researchers, and to some extent the broader world of accountability in education, only recently has the huge variety of contexts and complexities of the enacted curriculum been the focus of research.

However, some research related to primary programs continue to also make the weak link between the efficacy of physical education and healthy active lifestyles that go well beyond the physical education classroom (e.g. Gray and Oslin, 2003). Compounding this lack of focused research around elementary programmes is the dominance, instead, of a focus on teachers (Allison and Pissanos, 1994), including teachers' work (Fink and Siedentop, 1989; Graham et al., 1993; van de Mars, 1988), teacher perspectives (Henkel, 1991), and teacher education (Sebren, 1995).

Historical perspective

Research that might be said to be focusing on EPEP has not been substantial, rigorous, prolific and systematic, like, for example, physical education teacher education (PETE), research perspectives or adventure education. This has largely been because of: the relatively minor place that physical education has in the elementary school curriculum; the unclear boundaries, definitions, and nature of EPE; and a lack of clarity over who teaches aspects of what might be included as physical education, including sport, perceptual motor skills pro-grammes, health education, school competitive sport, physical activity fundraisers, play, school camp programmes, and social/local celebratory dance functions. In some research EPE is regarded as, or confused with "play", and "extracurricula sport". Hardman and Marshall (2000) note "In Italian primary schools, 'motor activity' (physical education) is often regarded as free play" (p. 24). As such there is a spread of research *associated* with these different aspects of schooling as well as extensive research on the growth and development of elementary students, not necessarily a part of the EPEP but nevertheless related. Much of the research around fitness, sport and physical activity patterns of engagement by elementary-aged students, motor development, and health focuses more on the students individually, teacher behavior, or one part of a programme rather than the programme as such. Where programmes *have* been the subject of research it has mostly either been toward physical education as a concept generally across schooling and not specific to elementary; as a weakly linked argument for the justification of EPE to be in the school curriculum; or around programmes in senior schooling credited with greater importance for the preparation of school-leavers.

By classifying textbook writers of the twentieth century, Barrett (1988) has noted that historically two views have existed of the subject matter for elementary school physical education – one as human movement that takes into account space and relationships, the other based on sports skills and

games. These reflect the gendered history of physical education (see Chapters 4.7 and 4.8). Traditionally, elementary programmes have tended to be understood or researched through document analysis, adult observations and semi-structured surveys (initially only adults) that indicate shifts, reflecting reforms. For example, the shifts to more western (USA) forms of physical education in Taiwan rather than eastern systems (earlier China), between top-down curriculum and teacher curriculum design and development (see Hardman and Marshall, 2000; Liu, 2003). Others such as Chien-Tai (2003) discuss the influence of Western natural physical education thought on modern Chinese physical education while Kirk (1998) explains the school practices that include those related to EPE in Australia's early development of programmes.

In the 1970s, seminal works such as *Movement activities, motor ability and the education of children* (Cratty, 1970); *Perceptual and motor development in infants and children* (Cratty, 1979) and *Fundamental motor patterns* (Wickstrom, 1970) guided EPE practices and reflected the research focus on perceptual and motor development. By the mid-1980s academic learning time in physical education (ALT-PE) (e.g. Dodds and Rife, 1983; Silverman, 1984) and schema theory motor skills (e.g. Gabbard, 1984) reflected research trends that were said to inform elementary programmes, but not critique or research the programmes themselves. Early sociocultural research using qualitative methods began to emerge in the mid-1970s (Locke, 1975), beginning to question what goes on in the enacted curriculum beyond the positivist and/or quantitative paradigms more commonly used.

However, examples of research tapping into student perceptions of elementary programs and the use of narrative methods in accessing children's experiences (*Journal of Teaching in Physical Education* monograph, 1995; Ratliffe et al., 1994; Solmon and Carter, 1995; Pollard et al., 1997; MacPhail et al., 2003) grew during the 1990s and into this century. An example of recent research that has taken a more coherent and comprehensive approach to an EPE programme is *Physical education grades K-12. Program evaluation 1995–1996. Focus on program evaluation* (Des Moines Public Schools, 1996). It is interesting to note the lack of elementary student representation relative to high and senior students, again perhaps reflecting the relatively minor or limited place of elementary programme implementation and research.

Key themes and major findings

In 1999 quality physical education was noted as "the most effective and inclusive means of providing all children, whatever their ability/disability, sex, age, cultural, race/ethnicity, religious or social background, with the skills, attitudes, knowledge and understanding for life long participation in physical activity and sport" (World Summit on Physical Education, 1999). But as has already been discussed the ambiguity surrounding definition, quality and quantity, also affected by who teaches physical education, makes "quality physical education" difficult to name. As well, others would argue that "lifelong participation in physical activity and sport" is neither a realistic outcome nor reflective of the broader definitions adopted in some schools (for example see Penney, 1998). While much continues to be written about these issues, the key themes reflected in contemporary research associated with EPEP includes the material and symbolic *place of physical education in the school curriculum*, interrelated with the quality and quantity of physical education, the *outcomes of physical education*, the *content* of physical education, the *quality of teaching* and the delivery of what is possible according to who teaches physical education, and the *learning environment* of the physical education class.

These themes represent clusters of research evident in key elementary and physical education research literature found mostly in peer refereed academic journals such as the: *Australian Council for Health, Physical Education and Recreation Healthy Lifestyles Journal*; *British Journal of Physical Education*; *European Physical Education Review*; *Journal of Physical Education, Recreation and Dance*; *Journal of Teaching in Physical Education*; *Teaching Elementary Physical Education*; *Research Quarterly for Exercise and Sport*; *Sport, Education and Society*; and books authored or edited by researchers well recognized in the field. The lists of relevant sources were developed from academic literature database searches using keywords, and combinations of these, including elementary, physical education, primary school, physical activity, sport, elementary curriculum, physical education programs, and health education. Database searches were also cross-referenced with manual searches for relevant research in the above-mentioned journals as these are regarded to be the primary publication sites for research relating to EPEP. I have also attempted to acknowledge some of the research literature relating to EPEP but outside above-mentioned journals, including research conference papers, research from non-English sources but with English interpretations, and from literature such as the *American Journal of Public Health*, *Journal of Classroom Interaction*, and *Pediatric Exercise Science*.

Curriculum place and time allocation

As noted above, what counts as "physical education" and what is an adjunct to physical education is not necessarily clear in elementary schools. As well as a multiactivity programme, focused curriculum formats might include a perceptual motor programme, physical activity, fitness, sport education, adventure education, integrated physical education, developmental physical education, health education, outdoor education, games and sport. These might or might not be named as being physical education. Additionally, Siedentop and Tannehill (2000) suggest recess being structured as an adjunct to physical education classes "so that students have extra time to practice the skills they are learning in physical education classes" (p. 309). Physical education homework, after-school clubs and projects, performance groups, intramural programmes and comprehensive health and physical activity programmes such as the Healthy Lifestyles Elementary School Program, Child and Adolescent Trial for Cardiovascular Health (CATCH) and District Wellness Initiatives, Jump Rope For Heart, all could be included, including or replacing physical education

Currently physical education is considered an integral part of the education system (Hardman and Marshall, 2000; Liu, 2003) for health and wellbeing and socioculturally to produce particular citizens. However, as Hardman and Marshall note:

> only 9 out of 25 countries surveyed offer two hours per week for the age group 6–12 years. A majority of countries reported inadequate training in physical education for primary school teachers, as well an undervaluing of the primary school phase for motor development and motor learning. In essence, in most European countries there is a) insufficient curriculum time for physical education, especially for primary age groups...; and b) the quality of physical education is not, or is insufficiently, controlled. The latter is especially the case in primary schools because of inadequate physical education teacher education. (p. 2)

In Botswana time allocated to EPE was devoted to examination subjects of English and mathematics; up to 85% of primary schools in Western Cape Province (South Africa) having no physical education at all; and in the USA "most States have not adopted the Surgeon General's Report recommendations on daily physical education for all students, K-12 grades" (Hardman and Marshall, 2000: 11). Disparities between state or national requirements and implementation are reflected in many sites such as Ireland, France, Australia and for example, New Brunswick where approximately a third of the national recommendation of 150 minutes and half the provincial guidelines were registered in primary schools (Tremblay et al., 1996). Reduced curriculum time is explained by the lack of teacher expertise, the marginal status of the subject (Johns, 2001) the lack of facilities, and the nature and extent of time allocated for specialists to teach physical education (Graham et al., 2002). "Improved literacy and numeracy are at the forefront of government education policy, an agenda for which included, in 1998, a two-year suspension of physical education from statutory orders for the primary schools' (pupils age 5–11) curriculum in England and Wales" (Hardman and Marshall, 2000: 15).

School reforms in Norway and Netherlands have suggested time allocations be reduced for physical education (Hardman and Marshall, 2000). Paradoxically Sallis et al. (1999) suggest that increased time spent on physical education at the elementary level has no detrimental effect on academic achievement, and may well be positively correlated with improvements in subjects such as mathematics. A significant finding for the justification of physical education time in the curriculum is reflected in Treanor et al.'s work (1997). The study consisted of 76 fourth, fifth and sixth-grade classes with an elementary physical education specialist over eight weeks working on performance and knowledge of three fundamental motor skills of catching, throwing and kicking in a 3-day-a-week or 1-day-a-week physical education class. Gains over the weeks were significant and highest for the girls in the 3-day-a-week classes although boys in this group also had increases in all measures. This very specific research however, does not consider other positive and negative factors that might be operating, and operating differently for the many individuals in the same class. It is in this area of research that little work has progressed within the elementary setting, particularly on a longitudinal and more extensive basis. Notwithstanding the obvious importance of research around quality, quantity and status of EPEP much research reinforces the hegemonic content of what counts as EPE – informed by the "possible" outcomes suggested by research.

Quality physical education experiences for young people in elementary school have been shown to exist although the conditions are not fixed by the content or the type of teacher (generalist/specialist) who works with the students. We know that there are qualities the program should have to ensure maximum benefits to as many students as possible. These include an element of fun (Portman, 1995); distribution of lessons revisiting various topics throughout the year rather than blocking long units (Graham, 1998; Schmidt, 1991); teaching for difference with an awareness by teachers of their stereotypes towards the students, assumptions around gender, sexuality, ethnicity, social class, age, religion, ability, appearance, etc (see related chapters in this handbook). As research located in middle years or secondary schools has shown, the complexity of the context makes it difficult to tease out generalisable influential factors, different students experiencing the same program differently (Barney, 2003; Carlson, 1995). Having said this however, research has pointed to aspects of a program that influence

the quality of experiences of students. For instance, the work of Hastie, Sanders and Rowland (1999) indicated that despite teachers being EPE specialists, due to the large size of classes "while the teachers provided high quality instruction, they were working under considerable hardship and had feelings of marginalization and powerlessness over their students" (p. 277).

Unfortunately, many of these "qualities" are also problematic. For example, the purpose of making EPE "fun" is important although if the sole purpose, its place in a "standards" curriculum becomes questioned and EPE becomes replaced by time for more academically valued subjects such as maths (Hardman and Marshall, 2000). As well, different students' perspectives about the goals of physical education, such as what is fun, differs within a class and is often different to that of the teacher (see Griffin et al., 1993; Portman, 1995; Cothran and Ennis, 1997; Morey and GockKarp, 1998 for more detail about some of these issues). The characteristics of how "quality" might be understood is argued alongside definitions of physical education but has some grounding in the claimed and realized *outcomes* discussed in the research literature.

Outcomes

The purpose or function of EPE is examined and debated in the literature and influences what is researched and researchable. But looking to the research that analyses what *actually happens* in EPE (e.g. Placek, 1982) it is evident there are differences in learning opportunities for different students in EPE. Motor skills, physical fitness and physical activity relevant to the physical domain and the corollary of growth and maturation have been perhaps the most dominant areas of research. However, the diversity of outcomes is reflected in research findings that clusters around four foci:

- Motor skills
- Health and fitness
- Social processes
- Cognitive change.

Each of these will be addressed separately and in more detail, this fragmentation representing research foci, a problem to be discussed further in the final section of the chapter.

Motor skills

Without doubt there is much evidence for the need for organized motor skill programs more generally in primary school programs and for particular populations of children (e.g. disadvantages Hispanic children – Goodway et al., 2003 and rural children–Van Beurden et al., 2002), this evidence used as a justification for particular types of EPE programs (Malina, 1999). However, research by Walkley et al. (1992, as cited in Tinning et al., 1993) indicated that despite comprehensive curriculum programs such as the Daily Physical Education Program, most children's motor skills were *still* poorly developed. Woodard and Surburg (2001) found that elementary children with learning difficulties also had lower levels of locomotor skills, object control skills, and gross motor skills. Although Chase, Ewing, Lirgg and George (1994) focus on a recreational programme there are implications for EPE classes. The correlation between anatomical measures and shooting performance for girls and boys were positive but low most of the variance accounted for by factors other than experience and physical size. Ball size did not affect performance for the task of shooting but authors cautioned transfer of this result to other tasks. Hoop height did affect performance for girls and for some ages and not others.

Hanson (1994), working with 54 fourth grade students participating in a 16 week EPE programme, showed that "instruction focused on the creative movement processes improves general creativity, results in superior performances in motor creativity and motor skills ability". Plenaar (1996) established that in Israeli primary schools motor problems with associated secondary problems exist among children. Through a remedial program there were significant improvements in the students' motor skills, EPE being promoted as the intervention site. Another advocate was Harris and Jones (1982) who, through an extensive study including more than 1000 children, noted "motor performance variables were significantly related to reading and mathematics abilities suggests that motor performance objectives should be included in elementary school physical education curriculum" (p. 21). Likewise Murata (2003) argues the importance of the relationship between children's speech and language development and their motor development, thereby supporting EPE as an:

> ideal setting for the development of language concepts, and provide a number of language augmentation strategies, including: the use of predictable activities; adaptable learning; activity scripting; the use of novel and colourful materials; collaboration; the use of expansion and extension in verbal utterances; task review; and the use of simple language and other forms of communication when necessary. (p. 29)

Health and fitness

The link between movement or motor development and health is taken for granted in much justification for EPE. With the attention given to the social concerns of hypokinetic diseases associated with affluence and lifestyle in the 1970s and the current concerns around inactivity and obesity, the educational purposes of physical education have been subservient to the development of fitness and health with a "new health consciousness" and health-based physical education (HBPE). Programmes such as the Australian Daily Physical Education Program and British Health-Related Fitness (HRF) became commonplace in primary schools. Huang et al. (2003) note that the American Association Schoolsite's Heart Power curriculum demonstrated a:

> significant difference in the level of attraction toward physical activity in liking of exercise, liking of games and sport, perceived health benefits in the post-and follow-up tests ... the Heart Power curriculum is associated with improvements in health-related fitness knowledge and the children's attitude toward physical activity in fourth- and fifth-grade students. (Huang et al., 2003, 46)

Curriculum such as Heart Power may become a default EPE programme or be run separately.

Wong and MacFarlane (1997) found that less than 4% of Hong Kong primary aged children maintained a single 20-minute period of light to moderate physical activity on the day of measurement while Johns (2001) reports "extremely low patterns of passive behaviors in primary school children during discretionary time at home and school recess" (p. 56). In relation to EPE Wong and Macfarlane (1997) indicated that during each of the two compulsory 35-minute EPE classes found in the Hong Kong school curriculum, only 3.4 minutes (10%) of student time is devoted to vigorous activity. This is below recommendations of the "Healthy People 2000" project (USDHHS, 1996) Objective 1.9 that recommends students be active for at least 50% of their physical education class time. Recommendations such as these, set against findings of student inactivity have implications well beyond the EPE programme yet a narrow understanding of EPE and its place within the curriculum nevertheless places the responsibilities around student health at the door of physical education. With Johns (2001) noting that "the patterns of low level habitual physical activity found in the primary student not only remain with the student as he/she enters the secondary school but are now showing signs of decreasing even further" (p. 56) there is clearly a responsibility beyond well beyond EPE.

With the link between EPE and health, several studies investigate the effects of various programs oriented to health outcomes (see, for example, Pieron et al., 1996). The work of Sallis et al. (1997) has often been referred to as they studied the effects of a 2-year physical education programme (SPARK) on physical activity and fitness in elementary-school students. Significant effects were found for girls and according to who taught the programme. Other studies examine the effects of individualized instructional fitness programmes taught in conjunction with the regular physical education curriculum (e.g. Adams, 2003), or as part of EPE with a health focus where the teacher recognized an absence of healthy and active lifestyles amongst students (Gray and Oslin, 2003). In essence, the EPE programme becomes informed or regulated by larger social issues such as health, without extensive research to substantiate some of the positive effects claimed through the inclusion of EPE. Similarly, studies continue to use schools as sites for research into the state of young peoples' health with an aim to promote EPE as an important site for intervention (e.g. Shen, 1997).

Social processes

The *potential* social outcomes of EPE are well documented (for example, see Chapter 3.4 and Section 6) although rarely linked into research attending to ongoing enacted EPEP. Some exceptions include studies that show positive results from a programme focusing on student moral development and fair play behaviour (Gibbons et al., 1995); team building (Gibbons and Black, 1997); modified time-out procedures used to reduce frequency of disruptive behaviours (White and Bailey, 1990); and improved prosocial behaviours (Sharpe, 1996). Importantly, the EPE teacher is the only factor that was found to be a positive influence on the social experiences of all students (Suomi et al., 2003) whereas the social substance of activities, cultures, and the social skills of students differentially affected students' social experiences. Juxtaposed with these positive social outcomes are studies that suggest some of the negative social outcomes of the various forms of EPE programmes found in primary schools where the competitive, elitist model of EPE is enacted "which wasted children's time, was inherently inequitable, and potentially harmed the self-esteem of most of the children" (Thompson, 2003: 42). Despite a number of studies that suggest similar findings and argue for different forms of EPE, there is lack a depth of research that is cohesive, extensive and critiquing of the variety of programs found in primary schools.

Cognitive or psychological change

The cognitive outcomes of EPE programmes have been used to argue for particular forms of physical education, in the elementary to argue for activity based physical education that might enhance cognitive development in academic subjects (Summerford, 2001) and in the secondary to argue for the introduction of theoretical work to the programme or for "thought-based" physical activity such as Teaching Games for Understanding (Kirk, 1989). Other research associated with cognitive development or psychological aspects of learning and participation are not specific to EPEP. For instance,

applicable to physical activity, but not directly related to EPE Martinek (1997: 63) found that "mastery oriented students had significantly higher levels of task persistence than learned helpless students. They were also more task oriented and less ego oriented". Lee et al.'s (1995) research shows that students are more likely to maintain the belief that they have the ability to achieve if they are encouraged to take a mastery view of learning (see also Treasure, 1997). They demonstrate that if teachers adapt learning to the individual students' ability, help students establish realistic goals, and discourage the social comparison process students increase their belief in an ability to achieve, suggesting that "[t]eachers must provide learning environments that allow children to perceive their efforts as being valuable in reaching their goals" (Lee et al., 1995: 392).

The research literature indicates that EPEP predominantly consists of physical activity in the form or games or fitness-based exercise, focusing on competitive sport events including swimming, gymnastics, track and field, basketball, volleyball and soccer. Any scientific planning of the curriculum is heavily based on developmental stages related to motor learning and biophysical measures (Hardman and Marshall, 2000). Despite trends in some countries to take a broader view of physical education, for example in Australia and New Zealand, evidence of transfer to practice and the efficacy of these practices in elementary schools is scant, the world-wide survey's findings still reveal increasing orientations to outside school agencies and competitive sport dominance (Hardman and Marshall, 2000, 57).

Content of programmes

Much argument over what EPE is, what its goals are and what should be included in it has continued throughout the modern era of physical education (see Chapter 2.3). As mentioned above this is played out in the primary school under further complications as to who is responsible for its delivery and to what extent it is justified for time in the curriculum or how its purposes might be captured in alternative time/spaces such as recess and interschool sport. Methodologically the efficacy of any programme cannot necessarily be measured or compared with other programs that may have different or contradictory goals and processes, for example between programmes that emphasize educational goals versus the more dominant programs that emphasise fitness, health or exercise. While there are compelling arguments for a number of contemporary curriculum models such as Teaching Games for Understanding (TgfU), Sport Education (Siedentop, 1994), Sport for Peace (Ennis, 1999), Teaching Personal and Social Responsibility (Hellison, 1995) and Empowering Sport (Hastie and Buchanan, 2000) their application currently is mixed, unsystematic, poorly networked with the research surrounding them in elementary schools not extensive and heavily context-specific in relatively short projects.

However, despite policy and curriculum documents provided at national or more localised levels there is little mandating or accountability in the implementation of physical education in elementary schools and therefore little research on the application or efficacy of such programs. For example in England Benn (1991) stated that:

> The national curriculum working party was recently reminded that physical education includes dance (DES, 1990: 3) and as the programmes of study and attainment targets become a reality [in primary schools] there is a possibility that in the future all children will be entitled to dance in education. (p. 167)

However, the implementation of physical education, let alone the more marginal aspect of EPE such as dance seems to be poorly supported at all levels of education and throughout the world (Hardman and Marshall, 2000). Exacerbating issues of EPE's identity and the constant reworking of curriculum guidelines and frameworks as well as their abstract nature causes difficulties for teachers to interpret and implement translated programmes. In turn, revision and research may reflect more the speed of the change process rather than translation and practice from syllabus documents. This has been illustrated by Shin (2003) with the introduction of the 7th version in Korea. Similar research beyond local levels is sparse but points to poor teacher expertise in the area, poor teacher confidence in implementation, and a lack of structural support and time for teachers to understand and implement the change, particularly in the case of the primary teacher who may be responsible for many curricula areas undergoing reform at the same time. Before discussing the research about programme–teacher relationships however, it is important to locate the research in EPE programmes, as influenced largely by a developmentalist and biophysical paradigm; sport, fitness and health; and the formal curriculum documents that are currently in use to guide programmes.

Major influences on programmes

Traditionally research has been carried out on *students* (their fitness, motor skill development, growth, levels of health, perceptions) in primary school without it necessarily focusing on physical education *programmes* per se. However, findings like "informational feedback is an important factor in facilitating student engagement, fostering positive perceptions of ability, and ultimately improving [motor] performance on a challenging task" (Fredenburg et al., 2001) may *guide* programmes such as physical education. Much of the

research related to elementary school programmes are about physical activity and sport or related to developmentalist paradigms rooted in biology or psychology. One strong area of influence is associated with fundamental motor skills (FMS). In rating the proficiency of primary aged children in FMS Van Beurden et al. (2002) suggests that "The low prevalence of FMS mastery found in this survey suggests that there may be great potential to improve fundamental movement skills of primary aged children" (p. 244) suggesting EPE programmes as one space where this might happen. Likewise, Malina (1999: 65) notes:

> most neural structures are near adult form and most fundamental movement patterns are reasonably well established by 6 to 8 years of age. It might be expected, therefore, that these ages would be ideal for specific instruction and practice in the basic motor skills ... Children refine established motor patterns, and learn new motor skills and sequences of skills as they grow and mature, and with instruction (as in physical education or organized youth sports) and practice.

This implied application to the physical education setting is common in much of the research toted as that attending to elementary school programs, but as Malina also notes:

> Data that deal with physical education as practised in schools are very limited, and outcome variables differ among studies. Studies refer to additional or special physical education, supplementary physical activity, sports classes, added callisthenics, run training or jogging, physical fitness programs, and so on, and rarely to regular physical education programs. (Malina, 1999: 59)

Sport, fitness and health

Historically, strong influences on EPEP include sport and health (see Kirk, 1998; and Chapter 2.3), these dominating and/or competed within the field and at times subsuming physical education. The tensions between the two have been well documented at various organizational levels (for example, Glover and Macdonald, 1997; Kirk and Gray, 1990; Senate Standing Committee on Environment, 1992; Tinning, 1990) generating related research. As an example the Sport Education "movement" (Alexander et al., 1993; Siedentop, 1994) and other sport-based innovations such as *Game Sense* (Brooker et al., 2000; Nakagawa, 1980; Thorpe and West, 1969) and *Teaching Games for Understanding* (TGFU) (McMorris, 1998; Tinning et al., 1993, Turner and Martinek, 1999; Werner, et al., 1996) have triggered research and been promoted by advocates of physical education. In 1995 the Sports Education in Physical Education Program (SEPEP) (Alexander et al., 1995) was launched for Australian schools as a nationally promoted curriculum resource funded by the government's Australian Sports Commission. The government and systemic support for such a program provided avenues for domination by particular forms of EPE at the expense of others. It is for these reasons that some of the tensions within physical education continue (e.g. see Penney et al., 2002) and is played out within programme debates at the elementary level.

The prevalence of documents representing the more narrow, traditional and dominant curriculum, captured for example in the National Association for Sport and Physical Education (NASPE) standards (2004) in the USA and the key stages in the UK (Department of Education and Science, 1991) is challenged by much of the research around EPE. Shifts to broaden and critique traditional curriculum is now on the increase as are discussion around broadening the definition of physical education. Much debate has ensued over the substance and accountability around such national/state curricula, as intended curricula, but relatively little empirical evidence has explored the efficacy of these curricula on classroom practice, or the enacted curriculum, either extensively or in differently nuanced sites. Also, while Brettschneider (1999) cautions the application of findings of research about positive outcomes of physical activity and sport on "development" others are looking to provide evidence on "more-relevant-to-students'-needs" approaches and physical education programs for young people in their elementary schooling. As the conduit for top–down curricula and a major influence on the substance and quality of an EPEP we must also consider the integral influence of the teacher, and the research that informs what is optimal and what is realised.

Quality teaching in physical education

Who teaches EPE influences content and pedagogical possibilities of the programme. Literature associated with who has the responsibility and ability to teach physical education in elementary schools is littered over the last twenty years (e.g. see Buschner, 1984; Lee, 2002). For example the International Council of Sport Sciences and Physical Education (ICSSPE) observed that:

> Too often physical education teachers in primary or elementary schools are untrained for the subject and some conduct physical education lessons as supervised play. Physical education is

> taught by the classroom teacher who usually has had little or no training in physical education. (1999: 119)

Blackburn (2001) concluded that discrepancies in provision and implementation of National Curriculum Physical Education (NCPE) in primary schools in the UK "are dependent upon the type of school, its location and how teachers and other educational policy makers view the subject" (p. 58). However, due to the complexity of understanding what is being learned, what attainment and progress is occurring it is not clear as to the extent to which these discrepancies are significant. Nevertheless Lee (2002) makes the link between teachers and the programme. Through an extensive research program spanning 20 years she concludes that by offering quality instruction in physical education, schools have been identified as a primary institution to promote regular participation in physical activity among young people. In-depth studies using qualitative methods suggest it is critical to recognize teachers as the centerpiece, but not sole factor to change and support efforts to initiate meaningful program reform. Solmon and Carter (1995) and Hunter (2002) showed that a teacher can influence student views and positioning in the class about the value of physical education, teacher practices being linked to students' beliefs about engagement in physical activity. However, with limited evidence to argue for an increase in specialist EPE teachers the assumption that this intervention "would be a significant step forward to achieving effective and successful implementation of the NCPE" (Blackburn, 2001: 61) is weak.

LaMaster et al.'s (2001) results suggest "modifications to physical education frequency, duration, intensity, and content are needed if primary school children taught by classroom teachers are to accrue recommended levels of physical activity for health purposes" (p. 47). Although some countries have specialist EPE teachers it is more usual globally that there is a "generalist" teacher at the elementary level with specialists at the secondary level. In the Philippines and British Columbia, for example, athletes or untrained non-specialist teachers regularly teach physical education, while in Oceania, USA and Canada approximately 20%, 80% and 25% respectively of schools have specialists (Hardman and Marshall, 2000). Hardman and Marshall also note that elementary preservice teachers would have received an average of 26 hours of EPE course work, some with as little as 8 hours. Like in many countries Australian, New Zealand and English schools may leave EPE to the "whim" of the teacher if s/he is not an EPE specialist. Numerous case studies (e.g. Thompson, 2003) illustrate the ambivalent space in which physical education is located, by definition, quality, quantity and status in the elementary curriculum.

Logan et al. (2000) have shown that classes with daily EPE and lower teacher–student ratios score higher on student performance measures, such as locomotor skills, cardiorespiratory efficiency, upper body strength, and abdominal strength and endurance, and on the "best practices observation instrument" than did those with less consistent scheduling and higher teacher–student ratios. Due to the work structure of primary generalist and specialist teachers in many school systems where EPE exists there has been an ongoing discussion as to the efficacy of teacher type and therefore what the EPE programme can be. Research (e.g. Hunter, 2004; Suomi et al., 2003) has established that the teacher is a significant factor in affecting the learning experiences of young people in the EPE program as they make and enact many of the curriculum, pedagogical and assessment decisions. The research is mixed in showing whether an integrated approach with either generalist or specialist, or a focused EPE program delivered by a generalist or a specialist, or combination, is most effective (see for example, Molina, 1994; Behets, 1995; Buchanan et al., 2002). However, there is strong evidence in some of the research that a quality programme can effectively improve children's manipulative skills when delivered by EPE specialists and classroom teachers with substantial training (McKenzie et al., 1998), supporting the employment of specialists and extensive professional development for classroom teachers responsible for physical education (McKenzie et al., 1997). Expertise allows for more flexibility in teaching the subject matter and as noted by Ko et al. (2003), students are provided with developmentally appropriate tasks after verbal explanations, demonstration and then practice situations.

Guidelines may exist to encourage particular values, beliefs and practices by teachers of EPE (for example, see *Australian Council for Health, Physical Education and Recreation, 2001. Professional competencies for beginning teachers of primary physical education – years P-6*) but as Portman (1996) demonstrates, the two largest contributors to elementary preservice teachers' liking or disliking physical education are the curriculum and the teacher. Prior experiences of physical education or physical activity influence the extent and nature of the EPE a teacher will engage with or encourage and therefore the program that is possible. DeVoe (1991) has shown that if a teacher believes that a students' participation is high they received more praise and encouragement "with their ideas accepted by the teacher twice as often as low participators" (p. 9) and that boys receive more attention than girls. Some studies (Hopple and Graham, 1995; Ratliffe et al., 1994; Solmon and Carter, 1995) indicate the large gap between what teachers believe they are teaching and what students demonstrate they learn. Research by Martel et al. (2002: 55) highlights

the need "for teachers to look beyond their pedagogical intentions to see the effects their pedagogical actions have on the well-being and the conduct of the students in their classes". The place of the teacher is clearly very important to the EPE programme (and is dealt with in more detail in Section 4), as are other factors in the learning environment.

Learning environment

Efficacy of a programme cannot just be analysed on its content. It is also important to recognise the influence that other factors such as relationships, class size and EPE frequency has, sometimes referred to as the learning environment. For example, Ratliffe et al. (1994) emphasized the importance of partners, and students choosing their partners with whom they work with in EPE, there being a desire to work with someone they got along with. Ennis (2003) describes the use of humour:

> to emphasize particular content they intended students to remember and apply [students realizing] that humor made the learning environment more relaxing and accessible to both skilled and unskilled students. Humor used within this positive environment appeared to be an effective tool to enhance student learning. (p. 43)

Patrick et al. (1998) describe the successful implementation of a five-part intervention accountability system that imposed consequences for students' social behavior. As part of developing a positive learning environment, van der Mars et al. (1994) found that teachers spend a great deal of time moving and being on the periphery of the class. "This active supervision resulted in student engagement in movement tasks. Students were more inclined to stay on task when teacher feedback was positive" (p. 99). Dyson (2002) advocates for the use of cooperative learning after positive outcomes from its use in an EPE class while White and Bailey (1990) and Locke and Lambdin (2003) show that factors such as prompt sanctioning, clear instructions for action, punishment relating to the inappropriate action, and targeting the responsible student allows for more successful implementation of a programme.

In relation to the learning environment however, Hastie and Saunders (1991) have demonstrated that "changes in class size and the amount of available equipment will affect student lesson involvement" (p. 221). In another study Hastie et al. (1999) note some of the strong impediments to EPE currently, daily EPE implementation being "difficult to achieve with high stakes testing taking priority in curriculum time, a lack of space and equipment for large classes and lack of support for increased specialists to take smaller classes" (p. 277) (see also Graham et al., 2002). They found that despite teachers intentions, space and equipment were insufficient for individualized participation, teachers could not deliver the intended curriculum based on skill themes and movement concepts, and that large classes and minimal time created safety and administration difficulties.

An important shift in research in the area of EPE was in the realization of the importance of understanding students' and parent's perspectives of the programme and learning experiences. Studies such as Coulon and Reif (1994), Folsom-Meek (1992), Gray and Oslin (2003), and Shropshire et al. (1997) give insights into the enacted rather than intended programme. Sulisz (1997) helps us understand that there may be influences outside the programme and school, in the form of the home that needs to be considered when designing a programme. At the same time, building on the strengths, needs and interests of students, once understood, has been pivotal in the findings of research advocating for increased student engagement in schooling more generally (Barratt, 1998) and physical education more specifically (McKenzie, 1994). Nevertheless, the material constraints on teachers and schools to enact "quality" programmes and include EPE in the curriculum, coupled with the lack of systematic, extensive and rigorous research of EPEP across topics, theory and methods when such a curriculum can occur, limits the application of research to practice and policy.

Applications to practice/policy

Depending on which research with which practitioners, teacher educators and policymakers have engaged I could argue that *some* research is being used to inform *some* EPEP. For instance in Australia and New Zealand, research and literature from the social view of health, constructivism, and personal development has informed curriculum and policy documents (for example, see Australian Education Council, 1994) although there is a lack of research evidence of the effect on practice (Macdonald and Hunter, in press). In the USA, epidemiological and motor skill research has heavily influenced the content of standards that inform programmes (see NASPE standards) but again the translation to practice in elementary schools is not evident in the research literature. Little extensive research in any country has focussed largely on EPEPs or their enactment, critique and evaluation. Some related *elements* of programmes, although not necessarily EPEP, have been researched more rigorously, for example, motor skill development (Goodway et al., 2003; Kelly et al., 1989; Treanor et al., 1997;

Woodard and Surburg, 2001). Debate about the efficacy of EPE still seems to fall into permutations of two "old camps" – one based on motor skills, sport and fitness, the other on a more broad definition of health including the importance of the social world, both with selected snippets of research to justify factional content (Barrett, 1988). It would seem however that the research does indicate a need for broader curriculum content and definition if it is to meet the educational needs of the young people participating in EPE.

Research has indicated the marginal position of physical education in elementary schools, the often-neglected teacher education in EPE for generalists, the lack of specialists or their ineffective use, and poor resourcing. These conditions mean that EPEPs may become reactive to contemporary popular knowledge, and be uninformed or misinformed, as in the case of the reaction to childhood inactivity and obesity. This is despite what we currently know about constructing, enacting and evaluating programmes. Practice and policy developed on what research is available, as well as driving more extensive research in EPEP, is clearly necessary.

Other than that research around motor skills in early childhood education much of the programme research focuses on secondary school or physical education more generally, rather than the nuances of elementary programmes. As already mentioned however, particular programmes have been researched, for example, sport education, perceptual motor skill programmes, integrated curriculum, often with many positive outcomes produced, although without these outcomes being produced over time or with a greater number of contexts. It is important to remember however that the possible outcomes of a programme may be multiple and not necessarily observable or measurable, although this should not deter us from seeking informed practice. Although programmes may be under-researched many of the elements of a successful program may be more heavily investigated, such as teacher effectiveness and student perspectives, giving some hints to programming. Sadly, much research has also been ignored such as that surrounding primary to secondary transition, programmes that reflect student interests and needs, contraindications in the use of fitness testing, and the importance of movement in learning more generally.

The research does indicate that the quality of EPEPs can be enhanced by attention to the teachers' ability to develop relationships with the students and enact a reflexive programme that takes into account the needs of the students within a broad conceptualization of what physical education can be. For this to occur however, teachers need to have some expertise in the ways of knowing through, about and of the body and physicality, or access to this expertise. As well, teachers need support to develop programs that integrate various forms of knowledge around movement, both in and outside the classroom context. This implies many permutations of "who" might teach physical education, such as a primary specialist, primary generalist, specialist and generalist working together, generalist and external experts, or generalists with some specialist background.

The research indicates that curriculum control and decision-making that affects the EPEP also requires some depth and breadth of knowledges to make connections between subject knowledges and between the programme and students' lives. Where the expertise is developed in teachers and students and their specific context, they might be guided and informed, rather than constrained by, educational bureaucracies, nevertheless recognizing the important roles of accountability for quality and informed EPEP carried out by these bureaucracies.

Teacher education for preservice generalist teachers would seem to be inadequate in ensuring construction and delivery of a quality EPEP. Teachers require a broader definition of physical education if they are to incorporate much of the "potential" of physical education into the rest of the curriculum but also to value and work towards realising these potentials either individually or in purposeful ways with other specialists. Many of those within the physical education field would argue for the increased numbers of specialists in primary schools as the research has indicated to some extent that this ensures a quality programme. However, this would only be positive if again the programme meets a range of needs of all students, and in many ways also connects with other elements of students' elementary curriculum. Both of these conditions would seem to be unmet when specialists work with very large numbers of students, in narrow forms of physical education, and separately to the generalist teacher.

Major trends and future directions

With the increasing concern around lifestyle-related health and elementary programmes meaning young people are a captive audience we would expect to see an increase in the volume of research around health- and fitness-related EPEP. This may lead to a narrowing of the programme, as seen in the England and Wales curriculum, with functional implementation of more measurable outcomes. This would be juxtaposed against the poor funding for research in elementary physical education programmes although large health and medical research budgets may be tapped into, albeit restraining a focus on the educational outcomes of programmes. This would potentially enhance the research around biophysical measurement as justification for physical education, but with parallel critique of

programmes through sociocultural research that has been increasingly evident, in particular in the UK, New Zealand, and Australia.

Globalization has been effective in the Westernization of some physical education programs, such as in China, Japan and Korea so it will be interesting to monitor the cross-fertilization that may be possible. Although research demonstrates the Westernization of physical education anecdotally, there is also resurgence in interest in how cultural values are played out in non-Western programmes, and indeed how indigenous or traditional activities, philosophies, and strategies may be nurtured. One such example is evident in New Zealand where attempts are being made to value Maori culture. As much EPE research is based on a Western scientific paradigm a large proportion is anglocentric and from economically privileged countries. While EPEP-related research from countries with languages other than English have existed but were less accessible there have been some attempts to present research in a number of languages and to translate and share knowledge. In the future, with technological advances in communication and the increased visitation between those in different cultural practices it would be hoped that a more global interest, such as that fuelled by Hardman and Marshall's (2000) work, would enhance our understanding of possibilities for EPEP as well as how they might be enacted and evaluated in different cultural settings. At the very least this will challenge some of the ideas and values on which dominant forms of physical education are based.

As yet there is not reliable evidence indicating that physical education in the elementary curriculum is a strong predictor for quality of adult life. Long-term follow-up studies only reveal indirect value (Shephard and Trudeau, 2000) and tracking studies indicate persistence of some particular variables with weak to moderate correlation but it is "unclear how far such data can be extrapolated to infer the impact of physical education programs on adult lifestyle" (p. 39).

Another trend in the research has been towards participation in the production, evaluation, and critique of national curriculum that spans across primary and secondary, and even tertiary sectors. As a result there has been a return of attention to transitions between the sectors albeit weighted more heavily towards secondary and tertiary. Nevertheless, as research around middle schooling buffs up against the more functional and rationalist curriculum and questions of educational purpose influences upper primary and lower secondary, or middle schools, I would also expect to see an increase in the research that informs us of the outcomes and experiences of physical education for young people.

The increasing volume of research that refers to student perspectives and perceptions rather than the more historically dominant voices of adults would also support this. Practice-based research will possibly become more prevalent as arguments for taking into account contextual factors of specific physical education class situations and the recognition of the complexity at the site of enactment causes a shift away from single-factor or semi-laboratory analysis. While the methods employed in EPEP research have not been discussed in this chapter they mostly parallel those discussed in secondary programs including a shift in method to qualitative-based work and mixed method to capture the complexity of EPEPs and outcomes. This is not to suggest that quantitative methods have become redundant. Quite the opposite would be expected as a future direction in order to enhance the research pool that monitors overall trends but also explores the nuances, ambiguities, contradictions and complexities of rich methods such as narrative and critical discourse analysis. Given the relatively thin distribution of research in the area of EPEP it would be important to encourage an increase in *all* methods reflective of the questions asked.

With the increased introduction of "outside providers" of physical activity in some countries and the congregation of researchers and funding agents around initiatives such as TGfU and Sport Education we would expect to see an increase in research in these areas, although due to the ad hoc and less stratified system in elementary schools this research might be located more in secondary contexts. We would expect to see an increase in both the justification and critique of these initiatives. Although Brock (2003) only worked with a small population she extends the conversation around programs now more prevalent in physical education programmes. She suggests that "if students only perceive success as winning, then we are simply perpetuating an elite sports model, rather than the intended goals of fair play and equitable participation as set forth for Sport Education" (p 38). While particular curriculum programmes, such as Aussie Sport, TGfU, Games Sense and CATCH can be seen to endorse particular purposes of physical education (arguably directed by political agendas) such as games approaches and health-related fitness, still relatively little is known about how the various approaches and programs are used and why they are used. Areas in an elementary students' life, such as health, human development, play, fitness activity, physical activity, recreation, relationships, and sport are all within but not limited to EPE, and neither might EPE be limited to these areas.

Conclusion

Brettschneider (1999) notes that pphysical activity and sport do not automatically enhance self-esteem, reduce stress, initiate cognitive processes, or create social ties. This is also true of EPEP. "Whether or not positive relationship or even effects evolve depends on the experiences young people have while participating in physical activity and sport. Moreover, the quality of these experiences depends on how physical activity is arranged" (p. 81). Putting aside the fact that this statement reinforces a narrow view (physical activity and sport) of the potential EPE programme it nevertheless emphasizes the warning that has been often ignored in the assumed positive influences of EPE based on inadequate volume and depth of research associated with elementary schools and physical education. As such we would encourage research in general to be increased in this area to explore the importance of, and problems associated with physical education. I conclude with two insightful comments that perhaps sum up this chapter:

> Evidence dealing with the attainment of the "physical objectives" of physical education is suggestive and emphasizes the potential of physical education to favourably influence motor skill, physical fitness, and patterns of physical activity. The key word is potential. The attainment of potential is dependent upon many factors, primary among which are the quality of the physical education program and the teachers involved. (Malina, 1999: 70)

And...

> Many researchers with physical education or sport backgrounds tend to look for the positive associations and are blind to the negative associations. This is inadmissible from the point of view of research ethics, against the background of the need for legitimisation, filtering out the undesirable effects of physical activity is actually counterproductive. It is precisely the ambivalence of some findings regarding the psychological and social outcomes of physical activity and sport that clearly highlights the necessity of educational competence in teaching physical activity, and thus the importance of school physical education. (Brettschneider, 1999: 81–2)

References

Adams, R. (2003). *The effects of an individualized instructional fitness program, taught in conjunction with the established physical education curriculum, upon selected health-related fitness performance scores of fifth grade students.* Oregon, Kinesiology Publications, University of Oregon.

Alexander, K., Taggart, A. and Medland, A. (1993). Sport education in physical education: Try before you buy.

Australian Council for Health, Physical Education and Recreation Journal, (142): 16–23.

Alexander, K., Taggart, A., Medland, A. and Thorpe, S. (1995). *The sport education in physical education program.* Canberra, Australian Sports Commission.

Allison, P. and Pissanos, B. (1994). The teacher as observer. *Action in Teacher Education, 15*(4): 47–54.

Australian Education Council. (1994). *Health and physical education: a curriculum profile for Australian schools.* Carlton, Vic., Curriculum Corporation.

Australian Council For Health Physical Education and Recreation (Victorian Branch). (2001). Professional competencies for beginning teachers of primary physical education ~ years P-6. Melbourne.

Barney, D. (2003). Factors that impact middle school student's attitudes and perceptions in physical education. *Research Quarterly for Exercise and Sport, 74*(1): 36.

Barratt, R. (1998). *Shaping middle schooling in Australia: a report of the National Middle Schooling Project.* Canberra, Australian Curriculum Studies Association.

Barrett, K. (1988). Two views. The subject matter of children's physical education. *Journal of Physical Education, Recreation and Dance, 59*(2): 42–46.

Behets, D. (1995). Specialist and non-specialist teaching behaviour in elementary school physical education. *European Physical Education Review, 1*(2): 148–54.

Benn, T. (1991). A field study investigation into good practice in dance teaching in primary schools. *Physical Education Review, 14*(1): 157–68.

Blackburn, C. (2001). National curriculum physical education implementation in primary schools – A case for specialist teachers. *The Bulletin of Physical Education, 37*(1): 47–62.

Brettschneider, W. (1999). Psychological outcomes and social benefits of sport involvement and physical activity implications for physical education. *World Summit on Physical Activity,* Berlin.

Brock, S. (2003). Students' conceptions of fair play in Sport Education. *Research Quarterly for Exercise and Spor,t 74*(1): 37–38.

Brooker, R., Kirk, D., Braiuka, S. and Bransgrove, A. (2000). Implementing a game sense approach to teaching junior high school basketball in a naturalistic setting. *European Physical Education Review, 6*(1): 7–26.

Buchanan, A., Howard, C., Martin, E. et al. (2002). Integrating elementary physical education and science: A cooperative problem-solving approach. *Journal of Physical Education, Recreation and Dance, 73*(2): 31–36.

Buschner, C. (1984). Teaching elementary physical education: Whose responsibility? *Education,105*(1): 34–39.

Carlson, T. (1995). We hate gym: Student alienation from physical education. *Journal of Teaching in Physical Education, 14*(4): 467–477.

Chase, M., Ewing, M., Lirgg, C. and George, T. (1994). The effects of equipment modification on children's self-efficacy and basketball shooting performance. *Research Quarterly for Exercise and Sport, 65*: 159–168.

Chien-Tai, W. (2003, August). *Influence of western natural physical education thought on modern Chinese physical education.* DAEGU Universiade conference, Yeungnam University, Korea.

Cothran, D. and Ennis, C. (1997). *Curricular accommodation as a consequence of students' and teachers' values.* Annual meeting of the American Educational Research Association, Chicago, IL.

Coulon, S. and Reif, G. (1994). Elementary physical education: A rural school district's perspective. *Rural Educator, 15*(3): 13–17.

Cratty, B. (1970). *Movement activities, motor ability and the education of children.* Springfield, IL: C. C. Thomas.

Cratty, B. (1979). *Perceptual and motor development in infants and children.* Englewood Cliffs, N.J: Prentice-Hall.

Department of Education and Science. (1990) 'John Macgregor announces physical education working group'. Press release, Schools Branch 11.7.1990.

Department of Education and Science. (1991). *Physical education for ages 5–16. Proposals of the secretary of state for education and the secretary of state for Wales.* London, Department of Education and Science.

Des Moines Public Schools. (1996). *Physical education grades K-12. Program evaluation 1995–1996. Focus on program evaluation.* Des Moines Public Schools, IA

DeVoe, D. (1991). Teacher behavior directed toward individual students in elementary physical education. *Journal of Classroom Interaction, 26*(1): 9–14.

Dodds, P. and Rife, F. (1983). *Time to learn in physical education : history, completed research, and potential future for academic learning time in physical education.* Blacksburg, VA: Journal of Teaching in Physical Education.

Dyson, B. (2002). The implementation of cooperative learning in an elementary physical education program. *Journal of Teaching in Physical Education, 22*(1): 69–85.

Ennis, C. (1999). A theoretical framework: The central piece of a research plan. Journal of Teaching in Physical Education, 18, 129-140.

Ennis, C. (2003). Can you hear me now? Expert teachers' use of humor to enhance student learning. *Research Quarterly for Exercise and Sport, 74*(1): 43–44.

Fink, J. and Siedentop, D. (1989). The development of routines, rules, and expectations at the start of the school year. *Journal of Teaching in Physical Education, 8*(3): 198–212.

Folsom-Meek, S. (1992). *A comparison of upper elementary school children's attitudes toward physical activity.* Paper presented at the Annual Meeting of the American Alliance for Health, Physical Education, Recreation and Dance (Indianapolis, IN, April 1992).

Fredenburg, K., Lee, A. and Solmon, M. (2001). The effects of augmented feedback on students' perceptions and performance. *Research Quarterly for Exercise and Sport, 72*(3): 232.

Gabbard, C. (1984). Teaching motor skills to children: Theory into practice. *Physical Educator, 41*(2): 69–71.

Gibbons, S. and Black, K. (1997). Effect of participation in team building activities on the self-concepts of middle school physical education students. *Avante, 3*(1): 46–60.

Gibbons, S., Ebbeck, V. and Weiss, M. (1995). *Fair Play for Kids*: Effects on the moral development of children in physical education. *Research Quarterly for Exercise and Sport*, 66: 247–255.

Glover, S. and Macdonald, D. (1997). Working with the Health and Physical Education statement and profile in Physical Education Teacher Education: Case studies and implications. *The ACHPER Healthy Lifestyles Journal*, 44(3): 21–25.

Goodway, J., Suminiski, R. and Ruiz, A. (2003). The influence of project SKILL on the motor skill development of young disadvantaged Hispanic children. *Research Quarterly for Exercise and Sport*, 74(1): 12–14

Graham, G. (1998). *Children moving: A reflective approach to teaching physical education*. Palo Alto, CA: Mayfield Pub. Co.

Graham, G., Hopple, C., Manross, M. and Sitzman, T. (1993). Novice and expert children's physical education teachers: Insights into their situational decision-making. *Journal of Teaching in Physical Education*, 12: 197–217.

Graham, G., Parker, S., Wilkins, J., Fraser, R., Westfall, S. and Tembo, M. (2002). The effects of high-stakes testing on elementary school art, music, and physical education. *The Journal of Physical Education, Recreation and Dance*, 73(8): 51–54.

Gray, T. and Oslin, J. (2003). Primary school students' choices for a healthy active lifestyle. *The Journal of Physical Education, Recreation and Dance*, 74(6): 52–55.

Griffin, L., Chandler, T. and Sariscany, M. (1993). What does fun mean in physical education? *Journal of Physical Education, Recreation and Dance*, 64(9): 63–66.

Hanson, M. (1994). *Developing the motor creativity of elementary school physical education students*. Eugene, OR: Microform Publications, Int'l Institute for Sport and Human Performance, University of Oregon.

Hardman, K. and Marshall, J. (2000). World-wide survey of the state and status of school physical education: The final report to the International Olympic Committee. Manchester, University of Manchester: 83.

Harris, I. and Jones, M. (1982). Reading, math, and motor performance. *Journal of Physical Education, Recreation and Dance*, 53(9): 21–22.

Hastie, P. and Saunders, J. (1991). How equipment and class size make a difference. *The Journal of Experimental Education*, 59: 212–24.

Hastie, P., Sanders, S. and Rowland, R. (1999). Where good intentions meet harsh realities: Teaching large classes in physical education. *Journal of Teaching in Physical Education* 18(3): 277–289.

Hellison, D. (1995). *Teaching responsibility through physical activity*. Champaign, IL: Human Kinetics.

Henkel, S. (1991). Teachers' conceptualization of pupil control in elementary school physical education. *Research Quarterly for Exercise and Sport*, 62: 52–60.

Hopple, C. and Graham, G. (1995). What children think, feel and know about physical fitness testing. *Journal of Teaching in Physical Education*, 14: 408–417.

Huang, M.-Y., Chou, C.-C. and Ratcliffe, T. (2003). The implementation and effectiveness of the American Heart Association's Schoolsite Heart Power Program with fourth- and fifth-grade students in elementary physical education. *Research Quarterly for Exercise and Sport*, 74(1): 46.

Hunter, L. (2002). Young people, physical education, and transition: understanding practices in the middle years of schooling. Unpublished Doctoral thesis. *School of Human Movement Studies*. Brisbane, The University of Queensland: 374.

Hunter, L. (2004). Bourdieu and the social space of the physical education class: Reproduction of doxa through practice. *Sport, Education and Society*, 9(2): 175–192.

International Council of Sport Sciences and Physical Education. (1999). *Results and recommendations*. *World Summit on Physical Education*. World Summit on Physical Education, Berlin.

Johns, D. (2001). *The determinants of children's physical activity: The case of Hong Kong*. AIESEP International conference, Taiwan.

Kelly, L., Dagger, J. and Walkley, J. (1989). The effects of an assessment-based physical education program on motor skill development in preschool children. *Education and the Treatment of Children*, 12: 152–164.

Kirk, D. (1989). Teaching for understanding: An innovation in the games curriculum. *Australian Council for Health, Physical Education and Recreation* (December): 25–27.

Kirk, D. (1998). *Schooling bodies: School practice and public discourse, 1880–1950*. London, Leicester University Press.

Kirk, D., Emmett, G., Tregenza, K., Juntenen, K. and Coleman, J. (1995). *A map of current primary and secondary school practice in health and physical education against the statement and profile for Australian schools*. Brisbane, Department of Education, Employment and Training.

Kirk, D. and Gray, R. (1990). School health education in Australia. Trends and issues in policy, curriculum and research. *Unicorn*, 16: 68–75.

Ko, M.-S., Sohn, C.-T. and Lee, J.-Y. (2003). *Pedagogical content knowledge of elementary physical education specialists*. DAEGU Universiade conference, Yeungnam University, Korea.

LaMaster, K., McKenzie, T. and Rosengard, P. (2001). Physical activity levels in primary school physical education taught by classroom teachers: Comparisons to National Health Standards. *Research Quarterly for Exercise and Sport*, 72.

Lee, A. (2002). Promoting quality school physical education: Exploring the root of the problem. *Research Quarterly for Exercise and Sport*, 73(2): 118–125.

Lee, A., Carter, J. and Xiang, P. (1995). Children's conceptions of ability in physical education. *Journal of Teaching in Physical Education*, 14(4): 384–393.

Liu, H.-Y. (2003). *Cross-cultural research focused on Taiwanese physical education*. DAEGU Universiade conference, Yeungnam University, Korea.

Locke, L. (1975, Spring). *The ecology of the gymnasium: What the tourist never sees*. Paper presented at the meeting of the Southern Association for Physical Education for College Women, Gatlinburg, TN.

Locke, L. and Lambdin, D. (2003). *Putting research to work in elementary physical education: conversations in the gym*. Champaign, IL: Human Kinetics.

Logan, B., Lambdin, D., Ramirez, T. and Farr, D. (2000). *Documenting and verifying best practice in elementary physical education*. Paper presented at the Annual Meeting of the American Alliance for Health, Physical Education, Recreation, and Dance (March 21–25), Orlando, FL.

Macdonald, D. and Hunter, L. A critical analysis of Rich Tasks in the recontextualization field. Australian Journal of Education.

Macdonald, D., Glasby, P., Hunter, L. and Tinning, R. (2003). Critique of HPE-related rich tasks: Phase 1, Brisbane, School of Human Movement Studies, University of Queensland, St Lucia.

MacPhail, A., Kinchin, G. and Kirk, D. (2003). Students' conceptions of sport and sport education. *European Physical Education Review, 9*(3): 285–299.

Malina, R. (1999). *Physical education and its physical domains*. World Summit on Physical Education, Berlin.

Martel, D., Gagnon, J. and Tousignant, M. (2002). Physical education teachers' and students' views of injustices in the gymnasium. *Avante, 8*(1): 55–68.

Martinek, T. (1997). Goal orientation and task persistence in learned helpless and mastery oriented students in middle school physical education classes. *International Sports Journal*, 1997, (Summer): 63–76.

McKenzie, T. (1994). Assessing children's liking for activity units in an elementary school physical education curriculum. *Journal of Teaching in Physical Education, 13*(3): 206–215.

McKenzie, T., Alcaraz, J. and Sallis, J. (1998). Effects of a physical education program on children's manipulative skills. *Journal of teaching in Physical Education, 17*: 327–341.

McKenzie, T., Sallis, J., Kolody, B. and Faucette, N. (1997). Long-term effects of a physical education curriculum and staff development program: SPARK. *Research Quarterly for Exercise and Sport, 68*(4): 280–291.

McMorris, T. (1998). Teaching games for understanding: its contribution to the knowledge of skill acquisition from a motor learning perspective. *European Journal of Physical Education, 3*(1): 65–74.

Ministry of Education. (1999). *New Zealand Health and Physical Education Statement*. Wellington, Ministry of Education.

Molina, M. (1994). *A comparison of test evaluators and two teaching programs and the development of fitness and skill norms in elementary physical education*. Oregon, Eugene.

Morey, R. and GockKarp, G. (1998). Why do some students who are good at physical education dislike it so much? *The Physical Educator*, Spring: 89–99.

Murata, N. (2003). Language augmentation strategies in physical education. *The Journal of Physical Education, Recreation and Dance, 74*(3): 29–32.

Nakagawa, A. (1980). A test of game sense in rugby football. *Japanese Journal of Physical Education, 25*(1): 21–29.

National Association for Sport and Physical Education (NASPE). (1995). *Moving into the future: National standards for physical education*. St. Louis, MO: Mosby.

Patrick, C.A., Ward, P. and Crouch, D.W. (1998). Effects of holding students accountable for social behaviors during volleyball games in elementary physical education. *Journal of Teaching in Physical Education, 17*: 143–156.

Penney, D. (1998). Positioning and defining physical education, sport and health in the curriculum. *European Physical Education Review, 4*(2): 117–126.

Penney, D., Clarke, G. and Kinchin, G. (2002). Developing physical education as a 'connective specialism' (Young, 1998): Is sport education the answer? *Sport, Education and Society, 7*(1): 55–64.

Physical activity and health: a report of the Surgeon General (Atlanta, GA, U.S. Department of health and Human Services, Centers for Disease Control and Prevention, National Center for Chronic Disease and Prevention and Health Promotion)

Pieron, M., Cloes, M., Delfosse, C. and Ledent, M. (1996). An investigation of the effects of daily physical education in kindergarten and elementary schools. *European Physical Education Review, 2*(2): 166–132.

Placek, J. (1982). Academic Learning Time (ALT_PE) in a traditional elementary physical education setting: A descriptive analysis. *Journal of Classroom Interaction, 17*(2): 41–47.

Plenaar, A. (1996). *The incidence and treatment of motor deficiencies in children six to nine years of age*. Proceedings of the 1995 AIESEP World Congress, Netanya (Israel), The Zinman College, Wingate Institute, Israel.

Pollard, A., Thiessen, D. and Filer, A., (Eds.) (1997). *Children and their curriculum. The perspectives of primary and elementary school children*. London, Falmer Press.

Portman, P. (1995). Who is having fun in physical education classes? Experiences of sixth-grade students in elementary and middle schools. *Journal of Teaching in Physical Education, 14*(4): 445–453.

Portman, P. (1996). Preservice elementary education majors beliefs about their elementary physical education classes. Pt. 1. *Indiana Journal for Health, Physical Education, Recreation and Dance*, Spring: 25–28.

Ratliffe, T., Imwold, C. and Conkell, C. (1994). Third-grade children describe physical education. *The Physical Educator, 51*: 106–111.

Sallis, J., McKenzie, G., Alcaraz, J., Kolody, B., Faucette, N. and Hovell, M. R. (1997). The effects of a 2-year physical education program (SPARK) on physical activity and fitness in elementary school students. *American Journal of Public Health, 87*: 1328–1334.

Sallis, J., McKenzie, T., Kolody, B., Lewis, M., Marshall, S.J. and Rosengard, P. (1999). Effects of health-related physical education on academic achievement: Project SPARK. *Research Quarterly for Exercise and Sport, 70*(2): 127–134.

Schmidt, R. (1991). *Motor learning and performance*. Champaign, IL: Human Kinetics.

Sebren, A. (1995). Preservice teachers' reflections and knowledge development in a field-based elementary physical education methods course. *Journal of Teaching in Physical Education, 14*(3): 262–283.

Senate Standing Committee on Environment, Recreation and The Arts. (1992). *Physical and sport education: A report*. Canberra, The Parliament of the Commonwealth of Australia.

Sharpe, T. (1996). Description and effects of prosocial instruction in an elementary physical education setting. *Education and Treatment of Children, 19*(4): 435–457.

Shen, X. (1997). Analysis on fatty rate of students 7 to 18 years old in Shanghai. *Journal of Shandong Physical Education Institute, 13*(4): 21–25.

Shephard, R. and Trudeau, F. (2000). The legacy of physical education: Influences on adult lifestyle. *Pediatric Exercise Science, 12*: 34–50.

Shin, K.-C. (2003). *Analyzing the elementary physical education curriculum: A critical examination of the curricular document*. DAEGU Universiade conference, Yeungnam University, Korea.

Shropshire, J., Carroll, B. and Yim, S. (1997). Primary school children's attitudes to physical education: Gender differences. *European Journal of Physical Education, 2*(1): 23–38.

Siedentop, D. (1994). *Sport education: Quality physical education through positive sport experiences*. Champaign, IL: Human Kinetics.

Siedentop, D. and Tannehill, D. (2000). *Developing teaching skills in physical education*. Mountain View, CA: Mayfield.

Silverman, S. (1984). Academic Learning Time in elementary school physical education (ALT-PE) for student subgroups and instructional activity units. *Research Quarterly for Exercise and Sport, 55*(4): 365–370.

Solmon, M. and Carter, J. (1995). Kindergarten and first-grade students' perceptions of physical education in one teacher's classes. *The Elementary School Journal, 95*: 355–365.

Sosnowska, S. and Kostka, T. (2002). Realisation of physical education in the youngest children of primary schools at the Wloclawek province. *Medycyna-sportowa-(Warszawa), 18*(2): 69–74.

Sulisz, S. (1997). Physical education in the school as perceived by the parents of children attending the initial classes. *Wychowanie Fizyczne I Sport, 41*(4): 111–117.

Summerford, C. (2001). What is the impact of exercise on brain function for academic learning. *Teaching Elementary Physical Education, 12*(3): 6–8.

Suomi, J., Collier, D. and Brown, L. (2003). Factors affecting the social experiences of students in elementary physical education classes. *Journal of Teaching in Physical Education, 22*(2): 186–202.

Thompson, G. (2003). A parent's case-study of a primary school athletics day. *Journal of Physical Education New Zealand, 36*(1): 42–52.

Thorpe, J. and West, C. (1969). Test of game sense in badminton. *Perceptual Motor Skills, 28*: 159–169.

Tinning, R. (1990). *Ideology and physical education: Opening Pandora's box*. Geelong, Australia: Deakin University.

Tinning, R., Kirk, D. and Evans, J. (1993). *Learning to teach physical education*. New York; Sydney, N.S.W.: Prentice Hall Australia.

Treanor, L., Vanin, S., Nolan, C., Housner, L., Wiegand, R. and Hawkins, A. (1997). The effects of 3-day-a-week and 1-day-a-week physical education on the development of children's motor skills and knowledge in the United States. *Pedagogy in Practice, 3*(2): 3–18.

Treasure, D. (1997). Perceptions of the motivational climate and elementary school children's cognitive and affective response. *Journal of Sport and Exercise Psychology, 19*(3): 278–290.

Turner, A. and Martinek, T. (1999). An investigation into teaching games for understanding: effects on skill, knowledge, and game play. *Research Quarterly for Exercise and Sport, 70*(3): 286–296.

Van Beurden, E., Zask, A., Barnett, L. and Dietrich, U. (2002). Fundamental movement skills – How do primary school children perform? The 'Move it Groove it' program in rural Australia. *Journal of Science and Medicine in Sport, 5*(3): 244–252.

van de Mars, H. (1988). The effects of audio-cueing on selected teaching behaviors of an experienced elementary physical education specialist. *Journal of Teaching in Physical Education, 8*(1): 64–72.

Werner, P., Bunker, D. and Thorpe, R. (1996). Teaching games for understanding: Evolution of a model. *Journal of Physical Education, Recreation and Dance, 67*(1): 28–32.

White, A. and Bailey, J. (1990). Reducing disruptive behaviors of elementary physical education students with sit and watch. *Journal of Applied Behavior Analysis, 23*: 353–359.

Wickstrom, R. (1970). *Fundamental motor patterns*. Philadelphia, PA: Lea and Febiger.

Wong, T. and Macfarlane, D. (1997). Levels of habitual physical activity and exercise intensity during physical education class among 8–13 year old Hong Kong primary school children, cited in Johns (2001). *Research Quarterly for Exercise and Sport, 68*(1).

Woodard, R. and Surburg, P. (2001). The performance of fundamental movement skills by elementary school children with learning disabilities. *Physical Educator, 58*(4): 198–205.

World Summit on Physical Education. (1999). The Berlin agenda for action for government ministers. Berlin.

5.3   Sport education: a view of the research

GARY D. KINCHIN

Introduction

Sport education is a model of curriculum and instruction, which attempts to incorporate many of the features of authentic sport in an effort to offer a culturally relevant and inclusive sport experience for children and youth. The purpose of this chapter is to present a review of empirical research and published professional work concerning the sport education curriculum model. Recent developments are included and suggestions for further research agendas/lines of inquiry are offered.

Brief historical perspective

The model of curriculum and instruction known as "sport education" was conceived by Daryl Siedentop in the United States. As the following will attest Siedentop's conception of sport learning and teaching has extended to many parts of the globe and there is considerable evidence of its impact on students, teachers, and programmes in the United States, Australia, New Zealand and more recently Europe from primary/elementary through to college-level settings.

Siedentop's (2002) detailed retrospective draws attention to the earliest roots of sport education which emerged from his doctoral work in the late 1960s from which sport education would become an evolutionary and progressive step. According to Siedentop and Kinchin (2003) sport education developed in and around Columbus, Ohio with Siedentop working in collaboration with local teachers, many of whom taught at the elementary level. Some of the first units were implemented at 5th and 6th grade in activity areas such as gymnastics. Shortly after a chapter on sport education was included within one middle and secondary methods text (Siedentop et al., 1986) allowing the model both national and international attention. Numerous workshops with teachers, conference papers, and

book chapter contributions followed where the sport education model was further described (e.g. Siedentop, 1987).

Siedentop (2002) cites the 1990 national 10th grade trial established in New Zealand as a major turning point in the model's development with numerous gains and positive outcomes evident (Grant, 1992). Efforts in New Zealand soon prompted sport education to be introduced into western Australia followed by a national trial throughout Australia and several research papers from the Sport and Physical Education Research Centre (Alexander et al., 1993, 1996)

The first edition of the text *Sport Education* was published which included many units developed and tested by teachers in elementary, middle and secondary schools (Siedentop, 1994b). A further series of empirical papers followed detailing how sport education worked in practice and how teachers and their students responded to various aspects of the model (e.g. Hastie, 1996, 1998a, 1998b). Acknowledgement of sport education's evolution would soon be evident in a two-part series in the *Journal of Physical Education Recreation and Dance* (Tannehill, 1998).

Sport education continued its development internationally and by the late 1990s the model captured the attention of physical educators in England and Wales following Almond's (1997) proposal that sport education be given serious consideration in schools. By 1999 some secondary schools commenced pilot work in partnership with Southampton University and Loughborough University and presented their initial outcomes (Kinchin et al., 2001; Youth Sport Trust, 2000).

By the new millennium some 50 articles had been published world-wide (Siedentop, 2002; Siedentop and Kinchin, 2003) and more have appeared in the subsequent years (e.g. Alexander and Luckman, 2001; Clarke and Quill, 2003; Kirk and Kinchin, 2003; MacPhail and Kinchin, 2004; MacPhail et al., 2004; Wallhead and Ntoumanis, 2004; McCaughtry et al., 2004).

Core concepts

Sport education: what is it and why should we consider it?

Many detailed accounts introducing readers to the sport education model and its rationale have been set out in professional journals (Siedentop, 1994b, 1998) and in some textbooks (e.g. Almond, 1997; Laker, 2003; Metzler, 2000; Siedentop, Mand and Taggart, 1986; Siedentop and Tannehill, 2000).

Hastie's (2003b) opening scenario within his recently published text is helpful in conceptualizing sport education in that it clearly illustrates a sharp contrast between recognizable features within a major sporting experience or event and those that are typically present within a physical education sport unit. Such a contrast endorses Siedentop's (1994b) claim that the teaching of sport in physical education has typically been decontextualized and that the experiences students quite often gain in lessons are "incomplete", as the following illustrates:

> Skills are taught in isolation rather than as part of the natural context of executing strategy in game-like situations. The rituals, values and traditions of a sport that give it meaning are seldom mentioned, let alone taught in ways that students can experience them. The affiliation with a team or group that provides the context for personal growth and responsibility in sport is noticeably absent in physical education. The ebb and flow of a sport season is seldom captured in a short-term sport instruction unit. It becomes clear that, too often, physical education teaches only isolated sport skills and less than meaningful games. Students are not educated in sport. (Siedentop, 1994b: 7–8)

Siedentop (1994b) argued that much of the teaching of sport consisted of short units of predominantly isolated skill-based instruction with some form of large-sided team competition appearing at their conclusion. Such learning and teaching in physical education was organised around a multi-activity curriculum model (with units no longer than 4–6 sessions), which some claimed to be the norm in most physical education programmes (Locke, 1992). The extent to which the content could be either acquired and/or applied by students within these organisational arrangements is highly questionable.

A further rationale for sport education was a response to expressed concerns over the teaching of sport in terms of its presentation, potential to be exclusionary, and also questions over its assumed relevance to students. Commentary on who is "served" within and by physical education revealed issues of marginalization and disengagement/ avoidance by some less skilled and less aggressive girls and boys (Ennis, 1999). Worryingly, examples of learners who disliked physical education have also appeared within the literature (e.g. Carlson, 1995a). Further, the presence of student resistance was evident in some lessons due to repetitive and uninteresting work within (Rovegno, 1994) and that much of what was presented and learned was deemed boring and irrelevant to adolescent lives beyond school (Tinning and Fitzclarence, 1992). Some teaching of physical education (particularly that which adopted the multi-activity approach) had made explicit issues of inequity, student segregation and differential playing opportunities and involvement on the basis of gender and skill (Cothran and Ennis, 1999; Ennis, 1996, 1999).

In view of these concerns sport education was designed to offer all pupils a positive, inclusive, engaging, and enjoyable sport experience. Its principle aim is to "… educate students to be players in the fullest sense and to help them develop as competent, literate, and enthusiastic sportspeople" (Siedentop, 1994: 4). In this context a competent sportsperson has developed sufficient skill and strategy to participate within a game, a literate sportsperson understands rules, traditions, and rituals and is able to discern between appropriate and inappropriate sport-like behaviour, and an enthusiastic sportsperson is active in preserving and developing present and new sport cultures (Siedentop, 1994b). The fullest sense would seem to imply the development of educationally worthwhile and relevant "sport-simulated" in-class experiences that more closely relate to the needs and interests of students than might currently be the case.

To contextualize sport in physical education requires identifying, simulating and then maintaining as far as possible the characteristics and features typically found in recreational and competitive/bonafide settings and then facilitating the development of children's knowledge and understanding of those features. To effectively achieve this task requires an awareness of the some of the more troubling elements that one might associate with higher levels of sport and a determination that these neither be characteristics that are supported in class nor reproduced in class *but* are confronted and challenged in class. Siedentop (1994b) acknowledged some of these more unpleasant consequences of sport participation (win-at-all-costs, foul play, arguing with officials, etc.) but saw sport education as an opportunity to reproduce the essential and educationally worthwhile features of the complete sport experience within physical education and thus advance sport education as one "… vehicle through which these abuses can be eliminated as children and youth learn about and experience educationally appropriate competition" (Siedentop, 1994b: 13).

To develop a meaningful and recognizable sport experience, sport education includes six major characteristics/primary features, which are evident and identifiable within authentic sport settings (Siedentop, 1994b):

(a) Activities are arranged in **seasonal formats** with the intent that units of work extend beyond the more traditional blocks of 4–6 lessons to, in some instances, 18–20 sessions.
(b) **Affiliation** is emphasized through establishing and maintaining working groups/teams for the duration of seasons (pupils remain on the same teams). These teams are of a small size to promote maximum participation.
(c) **Formal competition** is enabled using modified arrangements in terms of team size, rules and equipment (e.g. 2 v 2 or 3 v 3) and which is interspersed with student-led and teacher-led practice.
(d) **Records** are kept to form the basis of individual and group attainment. This could include league points for win–losses, fair play, supporting others or for batting averages/shot percentages/shots on goal, match scores, etc.
(e) Seasons conclude with a **culminating event** that might resemble what is typically seen in major sporting events (e.g. World Series, World Cup, Commonwealth Games), from the point of organization, festivity, etc.
(f) **Festivity** is emphasized to mark the occasion of sport, which can be achieved by the use of team names, team uniforms, announcements, spectators, etc.

A unique characteristic not explicit in the previous list is the scope for pupils to adopt roles (with responsibilities) in addition to that of a player – thereby adding to the authenticity within the unit and broadening and extending knowledge and understanding of participation and performance in various sports. While the sustained team enables students to experience the "full season" together (pre-season, practice, no-consequence scrimmages within and against other teams, and formal competition) they also have opportunity to become captains, coaches, equipment managers, timers or umpires, etc. Whilst these roles would normally be evident and visible in an authentic sport experience, their use is necessary in a sport education unit to support a progressive shift in pedagogy from teacher-directed to more pupil-centred instruction across a season, where students are encouraged to work cooperatively as a team in supporting the within-class managerial/organizational and instructional aspects and to:

> … help and learn from each other and carry out their assigned roles to the benefit of their team …become more responsible for contributing to effective classes and for achieving seasonal outcomes. (Siedentop and Kinchin, 2003: 10)

Major findings

Sport education texts

Siedentop (1994b) presented the first text on sport education aimed at getting teachers started. This text provided an introduction to sport education and included several case studies of the model in practice across a range of elementary, middle and high schools. A second edition has recently been published (Siedentop et al., 2004), with an accompanying CD Rom, that is intended to provide a wide range of practical support/planning materials and proformas to help teachers develop sport education across a wide range of physical education programmes.

Penney et al. (2005) will offer the first text, which considers the possibilities for sport education in the context of the national curriculum for physical education in England and Wales. Several chapters present case studies of sport education in action across a broad range of areas of activity (games, gymnastics, track and field, outdoor and adventurous activities, swimming and water-based activities) and all key stages of learning (aged 5–16). Some implications for sport education in terms of assessment, citizenship, and life-long learning are also included.

The availability of practical and support materials

Siedentop (2002) made mention of the greater availability of practical materials for teachers to support their planning and teaching. The professional literature includes several examples of support materials to assist teachers in beginning sport education within their programmes (e.g. Alexander and Taggart, 1995). As mentioned Siedentop et al. (2004) includes a CD ROM resource.

Further support materials comprise outlines of the model and how it works (Siedentop, 1996c, 1998), various chapters in books (e.g. Siedentop, 1996b; Hastie, 2003a,b), examples of 20-day units and shortened schemes of work (Kinchin, 2002; Wardle and Kinchin, 2004; Wardle et al., forthcoming), detailed guidance to assist teachers in designing seasons (Hastie and Kinchin, 2004), how sport education can support the teaching of specific activities, such as dance (Graves and Townsend, 2000), rich descriptions of what sport education lessons might look like (Siedentop and Kinchin, 2003), and other planning and pedagogical support materials (Hastie, 2003b; Mohr et al., 2001b). In England the Youth Sport Trust recently developed a Sport Education Resource Pack, Teacher's Guide, and accompanying videotape aimed at supporting and enhancing the inclusion of sport education within schools (Youth Sport Trust, 2003).

Applications to practice

Impact upon curricular design: breadth and balance

One of the major philosophies of sport education is the greater depth of content coverage. Sport education units are longer than that typically seen in many physical education programmes enabling a strong focus upon tactics and time for students to grow in the various outcomes expected of them (e.g. an ability to support peers and work cooperatively). The extended nature of sport education units clearly asks physical education teachers to think differently about their curricular provision in terms of sequence and balance. Evidence suggests that the adoption of extended units has not greatly disturbed some timetables (Alexander et al., 1996). While sport education units might present logistical problems in terms of curricular design, there is some evidence (while not referring directly to sport education), that extended units do assist in helping children practice more often, improve continuity of their learning, and recall more of what was has been learned (Qualifications and Curriculum Authority, 2002).

As a consequence of perceived curricular restrictions among some teachers in England (wanting to ensure that the physical education provision is recognized by External Inspection from government), shortened sport education units of some 8–9 sessions in length have been recently developed (e.g. Wardle and Kinchin, 2004; Wardle et al., forthcoming) and there are examples of similar unit lengths elsewhere.

Interest at different levels of schooling

The published literature on sport education makes reference to instruction within the elementary/primary range (e.g. Bell, 1998), middle (e.g. Hastie, 1996), and secondary age-range (e.g. Carlson and Hastie, 1997; Jones and Ward, 1998) and it extends to teaching and learning within "at-risk" settings (Hastie and Sharpe, 1999), in college basic instruction programmes (Bennett and Hastie, 1997; Bennett, 2000) and in learning to teach within higher/teacher education (Collier, 1998; McCaughtry et al. 2004).

Issues of activity focus/selection

Siedentop (1994b) advised teachers when considering sport education to introduce sports they knew well to ease their instruction in skill and tactics. Penney et al. (2002) extended the discussion to a range of factors that might influence activity selection as the basis for individual sport education units, which included:

equipment, facilities, timetabling, staff expertise, pupil familiarity with the content, and the ability to address issues of equity and inclusion.

An analysis of the research on sport education highlights a range of activity areas, which have provided the unit focus, but it has not always been clear why such activities were indeed selected. Some have argued that invasion games have tended to dominate activity selection (Penney et al., 2002), however the activity selection of late has become considerably broader: Bicycle safety (Sinelnikov et al., 2005); Ultimate (Hastie, 1998a); netball (Clarke and Quill, 2003); softball (Bennett and Hastie, 1997); dance (Graves and Townsend, 2000); rugby (Kinchin et al., 2004); netball/basketball amalgam (MacPhail et al., 2003); badminton (Brunton, 2003); basketball (Ormond et al., 1995); volleyball (Kinchin, 2001a), swimming/aquatics (Sciverner and Penney, 2005); outdoor and adventurous activities (Penney and Wilkie, 2005).

Differing classroom demographics

The creation of heterogeneous groups is one expectation of the sport education experience. Much of the research on sport education has typically been developed in mixed-sex settings. However, there is less research on sport education in action within single-sex arrangements of students (e.g. Hastie, 1998a). Kinchin et al. (2004) discussed the use of sport education in an all-boys secondary school in England. Three classes ($n = 96$) completed exit questionnaires following a 15-hour unit of either soccer, rugby or basketball. Boys spoke positively of many elements of sport education (being on a team, having a role, having greater ownership of the learning). However, some boys described their feelings of being "left out" and the authors speculated that the all-boys context and choice of activity [male oriented] may have served to make more explicit some issues of exclusion and enabled the dominance of some forms of masculinity over others.

Specific student outcomes from sport education

Much of what has been learned in terms of student outcomes has been as a result of qualitative methods and to a lesser extent anecdotal reporting. A large majority of sport education studies have adopted some form of field note observation of lessons, teacher logs, and interviewing of the participants. Few papers have adopted quantitative techniques (e.g. Hastie, 1998a; Wallhead and Ntoumanis, 2004). A review of student responses to sport education now follows.

It is better than before...

Clearly students have reported that sport education is an attractive model of curriculum and instruction. A preference for sport education when compared to previous time in physical education has regularly been an outcome of the research, with some students expressing a wish that their teachers continue to use sport education in future units/blocks (Alexander et al., 1993; Brunton, 2003; Carlson and Hastie, 1997; Grant, 1992; Hastie, 1998b). General increases in student enthusiasm have been reported across a diversity of settings and a number of boys and girls have indicated that they tend to work harder than they did in their regular physical education lessons (Carlson and Hastie, 1997; Grant, 1992; Hastie, 1998a; Kinchin et al., 2002; Alexander, Taggart and Medland, 1993). Some teachers have reported that the attraction of sport education has made a positive impact upon kit/dressing, attendance, and fewer issues over non-participation (Alexander et al., 1996; Kinchin, 2003). In some extreme cases sport education and specifically their team-mates was the principle reason why one low-skilled adolescent girl came to school rather than played truant/skipped class (Kinchin, 1997).

Being with a team that persists

Sport education's use of persisting teams across an individual unit or series of units has received praise from some students (Hastie, 1998a). The opportunity to become affiliated with team-mates has been a recurring finding across several studies (e.g. Hastie, 1996; MacPhail et al., 2004). Students particularly like being on teams, being with their friends and some have appreciated the opportunity to get to know new class-mates (Kinchin, 2001a). Students have also expressed a sense of loyalty towards their team-mates and did not wish to "let their team down" (Clarke and Quill, 2003). In MacPhail et al. (2004) 9–10-year-old students were interviewed following a 16-week modified basketball and netball unit: they positively discussed the extended time available to get to know team-mates, cultivate friendships, develop loyalty, work through differences and difficulties, and that they came to the realization that working as a team was preferential to maintaining a destabilized position characterized by arguing and unrest.

Learning within extended units

Support has been evident in the use of extended units (Grant et al., 1992). Some students indicated how an extended unit provided more time to play, more time to learn one particular activity in some depth, and more time to socially interact with the same team-mates (Alexander et al., 1996; Brunton, 2003; Carlson and Hastie, 1997; Kinchin and O'Sullivan, 2003; Kinchin et al., 2004).

Notions of peer support, encouragement and social interaction

Some lower skilled students have discussed their appreciation of the encouragement and support they received from high skilled peers on their team (Kinchin, 1997). The social opportunities and social development within sport education teams is commonly cited in a positive manner (Carlson and Hastie, 1997) and this has been most evident from the peer teaching and cooperative learning features of the model. In this respect some students have preferred being taught by their peers rather than the teacher (Hastie, 1996) and in a few instances the social interaction, which was conceived in class has continued beyond class-time (Grant et al., 1992). Sport education certainly enables students to socialize while still taking part in the instructional aspects of the model and that the student social system can be viewed as a prime factor for enabling student work in sport education units.

Being in charge: Having roles ... having responsibility ... having ownership!

The opportunity to take on specific roles as a feature of sport education has been endorsed (Hastie, 1998b). Some studies have identified role preferences (Wilson and Kinchin, 2000). If given the opportunity boys indicated they would prefer to be either the captain or vice-captain (Kinchin et al., 2004). Students have taken the non-playing roles seriously and higher levels of student active engagement and task congruence when fulfilling roles have been observed (Hastie, 1996). Roles have brought a positive sense of "being in charge" (Brunton, 2003).

The student centeredness of sport education has been positively received across a range of settings (Alexander et al., 1996; Kinchin and O'Sullivan, 2003) with endorsements of the opportunities to made decisions about the progression of learning-on a team (Kinchin et al., 2004).

Benefits across the skill/ability range and in the development of competence

Hastie (1998c) commented that small-sided teams, which remain together for the duration of a season of considerable length can support the progress of lower-skilled students. Indeed some students previously considered "lower skilled" have benefited from their experiences in sport education. Some girls have gained in confidence and were more willing to participate (Carlson, 1995b). Others have described more positive dispositions towards physical education, have felt included and valued by their team-mates, were willing to try, were less fearful of others' reactions following unsuccessful attempts (Alexander et al., 1998; Hastie, 1998a,c; Kinchin, 1997) and many were of the view that they had improved in terms of acquiring skill and applying tactics.

There is a paucity of research on the experiences of the higher skilled/gifted and talented pupils. Some anecdotal accounts refer to more able students extending their learning through assisting others and learning about their role (Kinchin et al., 2002). Kinchin (2001a) presented an empirical case study of one high skilled African-American male student during a 20-day volleyball unit. In-class observations and interviews revealed strong initial resistance to the requirements of sport education. As the season progressed the student became more tolerant of his team-mates and less resistant to some of the expectations of the model (working together, helping and encouraging team-mates).

Little research has been undertaken which has specifically looked at the development of competence across a sport education season. Accounts on the development of player competence, while mostly positive, have largely been anecdotal through predominantly teacher and to a lesser extent pupil interviews (Grant, 1992; Carlson and Hastie, 1992; Kinchin, 2003). Hastie (1998a) offers one of the few papers aimed at examining student competence during a sport education Ultimate Frisbee season. Six individuals from across the skill spectrum were tracked. Findings indicated that the two lower-skilled and two higher-skilled students showed significant gains and the lower skilled received significantly more throws during the latter part of the season. These students felt they had improved and that being helped by team-mates was key to developing skill. Ormond et al. (1995) ran parallel basketball units using sport education and non-sport education teaching approaches. At the conclusion of the season culminating games from the respective classes were video-taped and observed by an experienced coach who concluded that games within the sport education class were "better" due to the appropriate use of defence and offence, the ability of the teams to share possession among members, and the opportunities for the lower skilled.

Addressing issues of equity and inclusion

There is inconsistency within the sport education literature on the extent to which the model has addressed issues of equity and inclusion. Some have reported positively upon how boys and girls worked together during practice and competition (Clarke and Quill, 2003) and that the model has the potential to address principles of equity and inclusivity (Alexander et al., 1998). The placement of the student in terms of playing position has been critical to reducing opportunities for some individuals to dominate the game to the detriment of others (Hastie, 1998b). Some girls have expressed a preference for mixed-sex team arrangements (Hastie, 1998a) and others have felt more valued by the boys on their team (O'Donovan, 2003). Some boys have reported feeling "left out" (Kinchin et al., 2004), or have taken on the more "power-oriented roles" such as captain or coach and have ridiculed girls' efforts (Curnow and Macdonald, 1995). There is further evidence that some boys have dominated more (Alexander et al., 1996) and that some isolation and exclusion were more obvious in the competition stages of a unit (Hastie, 1998a). As Kinchin et al. (2001: 43) stated:

> There is need to recognise that there may be dangers of marginalization and exclusion of some pupils in contexts of sport education as there are in more traditionally structured curricula and lessons. Increasing the extent to which children take more ownership for their learning does not always mean these learning experiences will be more equitable.

Sport education with very young learners

Several units have appeared, developed by both specialist elementary physical educators (Bell, 1998; Darnell, 1994) and non-specialists (Strikwerda-Brown and Taggart, 2001). Recent evidence has confirmed that full versions of sport education can be achieved successfully by the equivalent of 5th grade (see McPhail and Kinchin, 2004; McPhail et al., 2003).

Taggart et al. (1995: 16) were of the view that sport education, "… may legitimately claim to be more integral to the central purpose and ethos of primary schooling". Consequently, Kinchin and Kinchin (2005) have encouraged teachers to consider a "foundation" for sport education that would be established in the very early years of primary or elementary education (aged 4–5). Key early year's documentation and statutory guidance within England and Wales states:

> The early years are critical in children's development. Children develop rapidly during this time – physically, intellectually, emotionally and socially. The foundation stage is about developing key learning skills such as listening, speaking, concentration, persistence and learning to work together and cooperate with other children. (DfES/QCA, 2000: 2)

Such a "foundation" could be achieved through the adoption of the following elements: sustained groups and affiliation, developing and using routines, having responsibility – all of which are common features of learning and schooling at this age. There are some isolated trials using adapted/modified versions of sport education with young students. Acknowledgement of some of Metzler's (2000) adaptations led to Lewis (2001) reporting the views of 22 5- and 6-year-olds following an 8-week unit of a modified throwing and catching invasion game. Affiliation, competition, records, and festivity were included within the unit. Roles were assigned on each team including team spokesperson, equipment-person, team uniform-person, and scorer. Team names (e.g. Green Monsters) and coloured uniforms were included. Children talked positively about the roles they performed and were able to distinguish between teams who worked well and those who did not:

Researcher: Did you think your team was the best?
Pupil 1: Yes
Pupil 2: We didn't win all our games.
Pupil 1: I know, but we did pass the ball a lot to each other.
Pupil 3: Yeah and the blue team only passed the ball to the boys, they left the girls out
Pupil 4: And they argued quite a lot, we didn't …
(Lewis, 2001: 52).

Children were able to perform simple duties and their affiliation extended to the cafeteria when they ate, when they lined up, and their play in the playgrounds/recess.

What do teachers say about sport education?

The majority of teachers who have used sport education have come to endorse its pedagogy and in many cases have maintained its visibility within their curriculum (Alexander et al., 1996; Grant, 1992). In arguably the largest study of teachers Alexander and Luckman (2001) reported that of sample of 344 teachers, over 80% believed that sport education produced more student interest within physical education when compared with previous curricular forms.

The release of direct instruction has been difficult in some instances (Kinchin et al., 2001) but in time many teachers have come to appreciate and support their facilitation role (Siedentop, 1995). Teachers

specifically support the freedom from direct instruction, the more opportunities that emerge to support teams, the greater space available to undertake the assessment of pupils, and the chance to reinforce the need for support and sport-like behaviour during team-based practice and competition (see Hastie, 2003a).

Sport education within initial teacher education

There are only a few published examples of how sport education has been used in higher education (Bennett and Hastie, 1997; Bennett, 2000) and there is a paucity of literature concerning the preparation of physical education teachers. Collier (1998) set forth a range of experiences directed at sport education including the use of the model for practical work (see Kinchin, 1999), observation of sport education in schools and teaching sport education under the guidance of a mentor.

Drawing from the suggestions of Collier, Kinchin (2003) employed interviews and written reflections with two pre-service teachers to seek their reactions to the range of sport education input they had received in their 1-year postgraduate program. These student teachers had been exposed to sport education in lectures and university practical work and then completed their student teaching in two different schools (one where they had observed sport education in action and one where they had attempted it for real). Kinchin concluded that the student teachers were initially sceptical of sport education following university-based lectures. Their scepticism was eased when they not only had opportunities to observe teachers using sport education, but then attempted the model "for real" as part of their placement work, with the support of mentors/cooperating teachers. The following quotes illustrate:

Being in a school has helped tremendously. We have seen the benefits of this [sport education] and how they [the department] set this up. I have been exposed to this all the time. (Kinchin, 2003: 41)

The lectures we were given provided a framework for sport education. We then saw this in a practical sense at the school … that has provided us with enough information for us to go away and be able to begin to teach it … (Kinchin, 2003: 41)

Seeing first-hand some of the stated outcomes of sport education as a consequence of their own teaching (while working within a department who had adopted sport education) clearly assisted the bridging of the theory–practice gap.

It is acknowledged sport education is a specific feature in a number of programmes of initial teacher education in physical education. Kinchin et al. (2005) specifically outline the ways in which sport education has been embedded within teacher training at the University of Southampton and Edith Cowan University respectively. Specifically at both institutions initial teacher training has forward as a shared endeavour with continuing professional development opportunities available for school-based mentors. In some instances school-based mentors have joined pre-service teachers for field experience sessions at sites specifically identified for training pre-service teachers in sport education.

Learning to teach sport education

There is a paucity of research, which has focused specifically upon issues of learning to teach sport education, let alone during pre-service training. Pope and O'Sullivan (1998) offered arguably the first paper describing one teacher's efforts to deliver sport education in an urban high school in the United States. These authors concluded that time was crucial for teachers to both learn about and deliver sport education. A determination to succeed is crucial given the pedagogy of sport education is likely to be quite dissimilar to previous ways of teaching sport.

McCaughtry et al. (2004) examined two groups of undergraduate physical education majors during their efforts to learn to teach sport education (one during secondary methods plus field teaching course and the other during an independent teaching placement). The authors foregrounded three major issues of considerable concern:

(a) Delivery of tactical instruction was problematic for the pre-service teachers, choosing instead to retreat to more traditional isolated skill practice and non-instructional games.

(b) Resistance was expressed regarding predictions of future use of sport education and that some of the central features were deemed not worthwhile and would be removed (e.g. use of records and non-playing roles). Student teachers conceptualized their future teaching from the perspective of more traditional curricular forms, deeming sport education to be "too much work" and which reduced student skill acquisition.

(c) Planning mistakenly involved lengthy attention/sessions devoted to skill practice.

The authors concluded that the pre-service teachers lacked tactical knowledge and the ability to teach strategically. They appeared not to value some outcomes possible from some of sport education's inherent features (e.g. festivity). Opportunities to see sport education taught well was recommended as one strategy to assist in their ability to teach the model.

Variations/new derivations of sport education

Siedentop (1994a) pointed to sport education's flexibility to be adapted to meet the needs of individual schools and programmes. This inherent flexibility has also led to the emergence of a small cluster of curriculum models, where sport education has been united with other pedagogical frameworks. Three such examples are now presented.

Empowering sport

Hastie and Buchanan (2000) examined the extent to which the teaching of personal and social responsibility (Hellison, 1995) could form a coalition with sport education. They were particularly interested in the combination of responsible role positions and the development of leadership, fair play and the mutual interest in individuals while they engage themselves and others in physical activity through the inter-relationship of sport, competence in terms of skill and social responsibility. The outcome of a 26-lesson unit in X-ball (an invasion game developed by students in the study modified on Australian Rules Football) was a hybrid of sport education and teaching for personal and social responsibility they termed "Empowering Sport". This hybrid foregrounded specific features of sport education (persisting teams, formal competition) with a united objective being "… personal empowerment through making appropriate personal and social responses" (Hastie and Buchanan, 2000: 34).

Cultural studies

An interest in developing students who are able to question taken-for-granted assumptions about sport and physical education (see Kirk and Tinning, 1990), prompted the development of a cultural studies approach to physical education (Kinchin, 1997; Kinchin and O'Sullivan, 1999; Kinchin and O'Sullivan, 2003; O'Sullivan and Kinchin, 2005; O'Sullivan et al., 1996). This curricular approach consists of an integrated practical and theoretical investigation of a particular sport (e.g. volleyball) adopting sport education in concert with theoretical attention to issues of social justice. Inspired by Siedentop's (1995) call for physical education to develop learners who are critical consumers of sport and physical activity this model enables students to present and defend their ideas on social justice through journals, class discussions, and projects (much of this work is completed in their sport education teams). The cultural studies approach attempts to make a meaningful connection between physical education experiences in school (as a consequence of sport education) and the provisions for sport and physical activity in the school, community and national contexts. Kinchin and O'Sullivan (2003) reported specific features of this approach, which students endorsed [the relevance of discussing gender, sport media and body image issues, team affiliation, student-centred instruction] and aspects of the unit some did not support (some seatwork, some new expectations in class including homework). Given the limited data on this model:

> More research using this approach is needed to better understand the types of learning experiences desired by youth which might reduce and perhaps overcome their resistance while at the same time recapture and sustain their interest in physical education. (Kinchin and O'Sullivan, 2003: 258)

Sport for Peace

Ennis and colleagues (Ennis et al., 1999), following extensive work in some urban locations within the United States, integrated conflict resolution with the essential curricular elements of sport education. Sport education was extended to accommodate concern for and care for others and self and social responsibility. The outcome was a hybrid model aimed at developing an ability in students to negotiate and compromise in response to conflict. The model was termed "Sport for Peace". Initial attention was directed at female disengagement in physical education lessons, however the outcomes of the Sport for Peace approach were positive from the perspective of boys and girls.

Sport education as situated learning

Some writers have explored a theoretical connection between situated learning (Lave and Wenger, 1991) and sport education (Kirk and Almond, 1999; Kirk and Kinchin, 2003; Kirk and Macdonald, 1998). Physical education lessons in particular are seen as locations for the reproduction of various educative aspects of authentic/bona fide sport and so offers the potential for a transfer of learning beyond school. For example, the season format falls more in line with the practice of community-based sport where lessons include training sessions and matches for teams that persist. Sport Education also offers students considerable opportunity to fulfil roles as "legitimate peripheral participants" (Lave and Wenger, 1991) that are not only meaningful to individuals but also to other members of their community, or in this instance the team.

However, some have expressed caution over the potential for transference of learning from within sport education to that within larger community sport cultures, (Penney at al., 2002; Penney, 2003).

There are few published examples, which set out this transfer of sport education to sporting contexts outside of school (e.g. Lister, 2001). This transfer will continue to be limited at best, unless significant efforts are made to affect change in the real world of sport and their attendant situated practices (Oslin, 2002), and that there is also, " ...a shared interest in revisiting the format and nature of experiences provided in community club settings, and, more crucially matters of underpinning rationale" (Penney, 2003: 306).

Some major trends and future directions

Sport education as a catalyst for thinking differently about assessment

Siedentop and Tannehill (2000) and Metzler (2000) outline a range of alternative assessment options available to teachers who might adopt sport education, including checklists, quizzes/tests, journals, portfolios, game performance summaries and statistics and rubrics. An examination of the sport education literature offers a few examples of some of these alternative assessment techniques in practice. Kinchin (2001b) discussed the use of team portfolios and how the role of portfolio manager was quite successfully built into a 15-day volleyball unit with physical education majors. Written journals have also been used to gather the perspectives of pupils on various aspects of sport education, such as being on a team, having a role and so on (e.g. Kinchin, 1997). O'Sullivan and Henninger (2000) described and evaluated the development of a behaviour profile in one urban high school in the United States as one strategy for assessing student teamwork and responsibility.

Expanding research designs and seeking different data collection tools

Recently, the application of different research designs have appeared when investigating aspects of teaching and learning using sport education. Wallhead and Ntoumanis (2004) examined the influence of sport education on students' motivational responses in a high school setting applying arguably the first non-equivalent control group design in the context of sport education research. One class of all-boys received a shortened sport education unit with a parallel class of boys receiving a more traditional format. Significant increases in student enjoyment and perceived effort were observed within the sport education group, however increases in perceived competence were not observed.

MacPhail and Kinchin (2004) offered the first paper using drawings to investigate the perceptions of sport education amongst 46 5th years (9–10-year-olds) in one English primary school. Several major themes emerged via an analysis of the drawings: having fun, teamwork and team allegiance, importance of game play, and the influence of external factors (logos, popular media). The authors concluded that the drawings complemented other data on students' experiences of sport education but provided an additional format for the students to convey their feelings and experiences.

Further progress and development

Siedentop (2002) draws attention to several anecdotal accounts describing how some teachers in New Zealand have attempted to connect the school-based learning from sport education to the sport culture beyond school. Hastie (2003b) makes mention of how sport education is being used to support cross-curricular outcomes in Australia through integration with content areas such as social studies. He also describes one example of the complete United States collegiate football occasion including barbecues, banners, half-time entertainment.

Immersion of sport education principles in non-PE contexts

Kinchin and Hastie (2004) examined the extent to which some of the features of sport education (affiliation, formal competition, records, etc.) support learning and teaching in non-physical education spaces. They describe one head of physical education (with considerable experience using sport education) who has transferred some of the core principles and features of sport education into the teaching of French. Students were placed on table teams, which assembled one lesson per week. Each team had a name (e.g. Team Zidane), with each pupil having a role (in French of course!). Competition was both individual and team-based. A notice board kept records of team-points for completion of homework, being supportive within teams during small group-work, and which publicized the schedule of activities and examples of student work. Survey data pre- and post a 3-month period of instruction was collected. Initial findings were very positive showing a preference for learning French in a "sport education-related" environment amongst one class of boys. The head of physical education spoke of fewer in-class behaviour incidents, more motivated students, and a newfound interest in the teaching of French.

Current work in progress also points to the use of technology to support the development of web-based portfolios with college-aged students (Hastie, personal communication).

Sport education: future research agendas?

Few would dispute the impact sport education has had upon the experiences of children, youth and adult-learners in physical education and a wide examination of the literature indicates that sport education has been introduced successfully into schools in the majority of cases. However, there is much that remains to be learned and perhaps might be developed as new lines of research and inquiry. The following suggestions are by no means complete but offer a little insight into where we might head next.

As evident within this review few papers have documented the impact of sport education upon player competence from a quantitative point of view. In an ever increasing climate of a need to demonstrate the raising of standards in education, such tangible evidence will be necessary to potentially convince more administrators/principals and head of physical education that sport education is indeed worthy of attention. Clearly, instruments such as the Game Performance Assessment Instrument (Oslin et al., 1998) might generate some evidence to support these efforts and answer questions along these lines.

Much of the sport education research has been the outcome of single units. There is a lack of longitudinal work to see if the model's outcomes can be sustained across a series of units in terms of team affiliation, student interest, the development of present roles and the scope to develop new roles and relationships with teachers. Equity and inclusion remain an issue in come contexts, reference to new roles such as "Equity Officer" (Curnow and Macdonald, 1995) would be worth some investigation.

Furthermore, sport education enables students to take more responsibility for the learning within teams, for example when executing their team leadership roles. We need a focus upon how students make use of that independent time, how do they practice, what do they practice, and who decides what is/what is not done or practiced within the team.

If students do claim to work harder in sport education units, then how hard is that? If, as many teachers have indicated, time-on-task/activity appears to increase when sport education is adopted then systematic measurement of time-dependent variables is worth pursuing in concert with levels of physical activity. Making use of computerized observation systems such as BEST (Sharpe and

Koperwas, 1999) will potentially enhance our knowledge and understanding here.

As suggested above, the use of technology is clearly worth pursuing. For example, electronic communication and accessible web-pages might enable team affiliation to be extended across a school or between schools (and perhaps countries) where teachers run parallel sport education units and this technology is used to communicate relevant outcomes from competitions amongst students from a range of schools. This technology could expand the possible roles students might take on and add to the cross-curricular potential some observers have referred to.

How pre-service teachers/those in initial teacher education learn about and then learn to teach sport education certainly needs further investigation. McCaughtry et al.'s (2004) paper has provided a beginning, but has clearly raised substantive issues about trainee knowledge, their apparent misconceptions about sport education, and some disinterest in using the model in future teaching. Concurrent support for pre-service and in-service teachers has revealed some positive findings in terms of the development of sport education within schools.

Research on the extent to which new entrants to physical education teaching can implement and sustain sport education in their first years of teaching warrants some investigation in order to identify the facilitators and potential barriers to this transference and also offer some indication as to what continued professional development these practitioners perceive they might need or what was lacking in their professional preparation. Similarly, an investigation into experienced teachers/sport educators would be helpful in understanding the nature of their curricular and pedagogical knowledge of sport education and how they came to obtain that knowledge – this line of work might also be extended to a systematic examination of physical education teacher educators renowned for their work and expertise within sport education.

This chapter has pointed to current work looking at immersing sport education principles and structures within other classroom subjects (e.g. French), as has been the case within some cross-curricular efforts in some parts of the southern hemisphere. Can the persisting group in sport education be transferred to other subjects for the benefit of student learning and motivation? What potential is there for establishing a foundation to sport education within the early years of schooling and how might this continue through the stages of education?

How can sport education influence and inform the provision of sport and physical activity within the community? There is little progress here, some caution, but also some beginnings. Penney (2003) reports on some examples of sport education going beyond the bell in Australia and Reid (2003) recently identified how the Rugby Football Union in England has taken steps to support a sport education strategy. Reid makes explicit the potential tensions that exist between encouraging and developing the most talented individuals and supporting the educative potential of sport education. These tensions need further re-examination and additional links established if sport education is able to make a contribution to the development of healthy sport cultures.

References

Alexander, K. and Luckman, J. (2001). Australian teachers' perceptions and uses of the sport education curriculum model. *European Physical Education Review*, 7(3): 243–267.

Alexander, K. and Taggart, A. (1995). *Sport education in physical education (SEPEP)*. Belconnen, Australia: Australian Sport Commission.

Alexander, K., Taggart, A. and Medland, A. (1993). Sport education in physical education: Try before you buy. *ACHPER*, 40(4): 16–23.

Alexander, K., Taggart, A. and Luckman, J. (1998). Pilgrims progress: The sport education crusade down under. *Journal of Physical Education, Recreation and Dance*, 69(4): 21–23.

Alexander, K., Taggart, A. and Thorpe, S. (1995). Sport education in Australian physical education. *The ACHPER Lifestyles Journal*, 42(4): 4–5.

Alexander, K., Taggart, A. and Thorpe, S. (1996). A spring in their steps? Possibilities for professional renewal through sport education in Australian schools. *Sport, Education and Society*, 1: 23–46.

Almond, L. (1997). *Physical education in schools*. London: Kogan Page.

Bell, C. (1998). Sport education in the elementary school. *Journal of Physical Education, Recreation and Dance*, 69(5): 36–48.

Bennett, G. (2000). Sport education as an alternative for the basic instruction program. *Chronicle of Physical Education in Higher Education*, 11(3): 3, 9–11.

Bennett, G. and Hastie, P. (1997). A sport education curriculum model for a collegiate physical activity course. *Journal of Physical Education, Recreation and Dance*, 68(1): 39–44.

Brunton, J. (2003). Changing hierarchies of power in physical education using sport education, *European. Physical Education Review*, 9(3): 267–284.

Carlson, T. (1995a). We hate gym: Student alienation from physical education. *Journal of Teaching in Physical Education*, 14: 467–477.

Carlson, T. (1995b). "Now I think I can." The reaction of eight low-skilled students to sport education, *ACHPER Healthy Lifestyles Journal*, 42(4): 6–8.

Carlson, T. and Hastie, P. (1997). The student social system within sport education. *Journal of Teaching in Physical Education*, 16: 176–195.

Clarke, G. and Quill, M. (2003). Researching sport education in action: a case study. *European Physical Education Review*, 9(3): 253–266.

Collier, C. (1998). Sport education and preservice education. *Journal of Physical Education, Recreation and Dance*, 69(5): 44–45.

Cothran, D.J. and Ennis, C.D. (1999). Alone in a crowd: Meeting students' needs for relevance and connection in urban high school physical education. *Journal of Teaching in Physical Education*, 18: 234–247.

Curnow, J. and Macdonald, D. (1995). Can sport education be gender inclusive? A case study in upper primary school. *The ACHPER Healthy Lifestyles Journal*, 42(4): 9–11.

Darnell, J. (1994). Sport education in the elementary curriculum. In D. Siedentop (Ed.), *Sport Education* (pp. 61–71). Champaign, IL: Human Kinetics.

Department for Education and Skills/Qualifications and Curriculum Authority. (2000). *Curriculum Guidance for the Foundation Stage*. London: HMSO.

Ennis, C. (1999). Creating a culturally relevant curriculum for disengaged girls. *Sport, Education and Society*, 4(1): 31–50.

Ennis, C. D. (1996). Students' experiences in sport-based physical education: More than apologies are necessary. *Quest*, 48: 453–456.

Ennis, C.D., Solmon, M., Satina, M., Loftus, S.J., Mensch, J. and McCauley, T. (1999). Creating a sense of community in urban schools using the 'Sport for Peace' curriculum. *Research Quarterly for Exercise and Sport*, 70: 273–285.

Grant, B.C. (1992). Integrating sport into the physical education curriculum in New Zealand secondary schools. *Quest*, 44: 304–316.

Grant, B., Trendinnick, P. and Hodge, K. (1992). Sport education in physical education. *New Zealand Journal of Health, Physical Education and Recreation*, 25(3): 3–6.

Graves, M.A. and Townsend, J.S. (2000). Applying the sport education curriculum model to dance. *Journal of Physical Education, Recreation and Dance*, 71(8): 50–54.

Hastie, P. (1996). Student role involvement during a unit of sport education. *Journal of Teaching in Physical Education*, 16: 88–103.

Hastie, P. (1998a). Skill and tactical development during a sport education season. *Research Quarterly for Exercise and Sport*, 69: 368–379.

Hastie, P. (1998b). The participation and perception of girls within a unit of sport education. *Journal of Teaching in Physical Education*, 17: 157–171.

Hastie, P. (1998c). Applied benefits of the sport education model. *Journal of Physical Education, Recreation and Dance*, 69(4): 24–26.

Hastie, P. (2003a). Teaching sport within physical education. In S.J. Silverman and C.D. Ennis (Eds.), *Student learning in physical education: Applying research to enhance instruction* [2nd ed.], (pp. 227–240). Champaign, IL: Human Kinetics.

Hastie, P. (2003b). Sport education. In A. Laker (Ed.), *The future of physical education* (pp. 121–136). London: Routledge.

Hastie, P. and Buchanan, A.M. (2000). Teaching responsibility through sport education: Prospects for a coalition. *Research Quarterly for Exercise and Sport*, 71: 25–35.

Hastie, P., and Kinchin, G.D. (2004). Design a season of sport education. *British Journal of Teaching Physical Education*, 35(1): 14–18.

Hastie, P. and Sharpe, T. (1999). Effects of a sport education curriculum on the positive social behavior of at-risk rural adolescent boys. *Journal of Education for Students Placed At Risk*, 4(4): 417–430.

Hellison, D. (1995). *Teaching responsibility through physical activity*. Champaign, IL: Human Kinetics.

Jones, D. and Ward, P. (1998). Changing the face of secondary physical education through sport education. *Journal of Physical Education, Recreation and Dance*, 69(5): 40–45.

Kinchin, G.D. (1997). High school students' perceptions of and responses to curriculum change in physical education. Unpublished doctoral dissertation, The Ohio State University, Columbus, OH.

Kinchin, G.D. (1999, October). Implementing seasons of sport education into one PETE institution: What do the participants tell us? Paper presented at the National Association for Sport and Physical Education Conference on Physical Education: Exemplary Practice in Teacher Education, Bloomingdale, IL.

Kinchin, G.D. (2001a). A high skilled pupil's experience with sport education. *The* ACHPER Healthy Lifestyles Journal, 48(3–4): 5–9.

Kinchin, G. D. (2001b). Using team portfolios during a sport education season, *Journal of Physical Education, Recreation and Dance*, 72(2): 41–44.

Kinchin, G.D. (2002). A closer look at sport education. *PE and Sport Today*, 10: 27–30.

Kinchin, G.D. (2003). Sport education at the student teacher. *PE and Sport Today*, 13: 40–42.

Kinchin, G.D. and Hastie, P. (2004, September). Sport education and its perceived impact upon practice: The case of one head of department in and out of the gym! Paper presented at the Annual meeting of the British Educational Research Association conference, Manchester, England.

Kinchin, G.D. and Kinchin, V.K. (2005). Laying the foundation for sport education. In D. Penney, G. Clarke, M. Quill and G.D. Kinchin, (Eds.), *Sport Education in Physical Education: Research-based Practice*. London: Routledge.

Kinchin, G.D. and O'Sullivan, M. (1999). Making high school physical education meaningful for students. *Journal of Physical Education, Recreation and Dance*, 70(5): 40–44, 54.

Kinchin, G.D. and O'Sullivan, M. (2003). Incidences of student support for and resistance to a curricular innovation in high school physical education, *Journal of Teaching in Physical Education*, 22(3): 245–260.

Kinchin, G.D., Penney, D. and Clarke, G. (2001). Teaching national curriculum physical education: Try sport education? *British Journal of Teaching* Physical Education, 32(2): 41–44.

Kinchin, G.D., Penney, D. and Clarke, G. (2002a). Roles and responsibilities in physical education. *British Journal of Teaching Physical Education, 33*(4): 23–26.

Kinchin, G.D., Quill, M. and Clarke, G. (2002b). Sport education in action. *British Journal of Teaching Physical Education, 33*(1): 10–12.

Kinchin, G.D., Wardle, C., Roderick, S. and Sprosen, A. (2004). A survey of year 9 boys' perceptions of sport education in one English secondary school. *Bulletin of Physical Education, 40*(1): 27–40.

Kinchin, G.D., Penneys, D. and Clarke, G. (2005). Sport education in teacher education. In D. Penney, G. Clarke, M. Quill and G.D. Kinchin, (Eds.) *Sport Education in Physical Education: Research-based Practice.* London: Routledge.

Kirk, D. and Almond, L. (1999). Sport education as situated learning in physical education: Making links to citizenship and critical consumerism. Paper presented to the AISEP International Conference, Besancon, France, April 1999.

Kirk, D. and Kinchin, G.D. (2003). Situated learning as a theoretical framework for sport education. *European Physical Education Review, 9*(3): 221–236.

Kirk, D. and Macdonald, D. (1998). Situated learning in physical education. *Journal of Teaching in Physical Education, 17*: 376–387.

Kirk, D. and Tinning, R. (1990). *Physical education, curriculum and culture: critical issues in contemporary crisis.* London: Falmer Press.

Laker, A. (2003). *The future of physical education: Building a new pedagogy.* London: Routledge.

Lave, J. and Wenger, E. (1991). *Situated learning: Legitimate peripheral participation in communities of practice.* New York: Cambridge University Press.

Lewis, J. (2001). Is it possible that Siedentop's sport education model can be used with a key stage 1 physical education class to aid pupil development? Unpublished undergraduate dissertation, De Montford University: Bedford.

Lister, A. (2001). 'SEPEP cricket and school-community links': Taking sport education beyond bell-time. Paper presented at the AARE International Conference, Freemantle.

Locke, L. (1992). Changing secondary physical education, *Quest, 44*: 361–372.

MacPhail, A. and Kinchin, G.D. (2004). The use of drawings as an evaluative tool: students' experiences of sport education. *Physical Education and Sport Pedagogy, 9*(1): 87–108.

MacPhail, A., Kinchin, G.D. and Kirk, D. (2003). Students' conceptions of sport and sport education. *European Physical Education Review, 9*(3): 285–300.

MacPhail, A., Kirk, D. and Kinchin, G.D. (2004). Sport education: Promoting team affiliation through sport education. *Journal of Teaching in Physical Education, 23*: 106–122.

McCaughtry, N., Sofo, S., Rovegno, I. and Curtner-Smith, M. (2004). Learning to teach sport education: misunderstandings, pedagogical difficulties, and resistance, *European Physical Education Review, 10*(2): 135–155.

Metzler, M. (2000). *Instructional models for physical education.* Boston, MA: Allyn & Bacon.

Mohr, D.J., Townsend, J.S. and Bulger, S.M. (2001). A pedagogical approach to sport education season planning. *Journal of Physical Education, Recreation and Dance, 72*(9): 37–46.

Mohr, D.J., Townsend, J.S. and Bulger, S.M. (2001b). Maintaining the PASE: A day in the life of sport education. *Journal of Health, Physical Education, Research and Dance, 73*(1): 36–45.

O'Donovan, T.M. (2003). A changing culture? Interrogating the dynamics of peer affiliations over the course of a season. *European Physical Education Review, 9*(3): 237–252.

Ormond, T.C., DeMarco, G.M., Smith, R.M. and Fischer, K.A. (1995). Comparison of the sport education and traditional approaches to teaching secondary school basketball. Paper presented to the Annual meeting of the American Alliance for Health, Physical Education, Recreation and Dance, Portland, OR.

Oslin, J. (2002). Sport education: Cautions, considerations and celebrations. *Journal of Teaching in Physical Education, 21*: 419–426.

Oslin, J., Mitchell, S.A. and Griffin, L.L. (1998). The Game Performance Assessment Instrument (GPAI): Development and initial validation. *Journal of Teaching in Physical Education, 72*(5): 47–51.

O'Sullivan, M. and Henninger, M. (2000). *Assessing student responsibility and teamwork.* Reston, VA: National Association for Sport and Physical Education.

O'Sullivan, M. and Kinchin, G.D. (2005). Cultural studies curriculum in sport and physical activity. In J., Lund, and D. Tannehill, (Eds.), *Standards-Based Physical Education Curriculum Development.* Sudbury, MA: Jones and Bartlett Publishers.

O'Sullivan, M., Kinchin, G.D., Dunaway, S., Kellum, S. and Dixon, S. (1996). Thinking differently about high school physical education. Paper presented to the Annual meeting of the American Alliance for Health, Physical Education, Recreation and Dance, Atlanta, GA.

Penney, D. (2003). Sport education and situated learning: Problematizing the potential. *European Physical Education Review, 9*(3): 301–308.

Penney, D. and Clarke, G. (2005). New relationships, new futures. In D. Penney, G. Clarke, M. Quill, and G.D. Kinchin, (Eds.) *Sport Education in Physical Education: Research-based Practice.* London: Routledge.

Penney, D., Clarke, G. and Kinchin, G. (2002). Developing physical education as a "connective specialism:" Is sport education the answer? *Sport, Education and Society, 7*: 55–64.

Penney, D., Clarke, G., Quill, M. and Kinchin, G. (2002). Activity selection in sport education. *Journal of Sport Pedagogy, 8*(2): 53–66.

Penney, D. and Wilkie, B. (2005) Sport education and outdoor and adventurous activities. In D. Penney, G. Clarke, M. Quill, and G.D. Kinchin, (Eds.), *Sport Education in Physical Education: Research-based Practice.* London: Routledge.

Pope, C. and O'Sullivan, M. (1998). Culture, pedagogy and teacher change in an urban high school: How would you like your eggs done? *Sport, Education and Society*, 3(2): 201–226.

Qualifications and Curriculum Authority. (2002). PE in schools today. *British Journal of Teaching Physical Education*, 33(4): 6–8.

Reid, P. (2003). More than a game? The role of sports governing bodies in the development of sport education programmes. *European Physical Education Review*, 9(3): 309–318.

Rovegno, I. (1994). Teaching within a curricular zone of safety: School culture and the knowledge of student teachers' pedagogical content knowledge. *Research Quarterly for Exercise and Sport*, 65: 269–279.

Scivener, E. and Penney, D. (2005). Sport education in key stage 4 swimming. In D. Penney, G. Clarke, M. Quill, and G.D. Kinchin, (Eds.), *Sport education in physical education: Research-based practice*. London: Routledge.

Sharpe, T. and Koperwas, J. (1999). *BEST: Behavioral Evaluation Strategy and Taxonomy Software*. Thousand Oaks, CA: Sage Publications.

Siedentop, D. (1987). The theory and practice of sport education. In G. Barrette, R. Feingold, R. Rees and M. Piéron (Eds.), *Myths, models and methods in sport pedagogy* (pp. 79–86). Champaign, IL: Human Kinetics.

Siedentop, D. (1994a). Sport education. Paper presented at the SPARC-ACHPER Conference, Perth: Western Australia.

Siedentop, D. (1994b). *Sport education*. Champaign, IL: Human Kinetics. Siedentop, D. (1995). Improving sport education. *The ACHPER Healthy Lifestyles Journal*, 42(4): 22–23.

Siedentop, D. (1996a). Sport education. *Teaching Secondary Physical Education*, 2(3): 8–9.

Siedentop, D. (1996b). Physical education and education reform: The case of sport education. In S.J. Silverman and C.D Ennis (Eds.), *Student learning in physical education: Applying research to enhance instruction*: Champaign, IL: Human Kinetics.

Siedentop, D. (1998). What is sport education and how does it work? *Journal of Physical Education, Recreation and Dance*, 69(4): 18–20.

Siedentop, D. (2002). Sport education: A retrospective. *Journal of Teaching in Physical Education*, 21: 409–418.

Siedentop, D., Hastie, P A. and van der Mars, H. (2004). *Complete guide to sport education*. Champaign, IL: Human Kinetics.

Siedentop, D. and Kinchin, G.D. (2003). What makes sport education different? *British Journal of Teaching Physical Education*, 34(2): 10–11.

Siedentop, D., Mand, C. and Taggart, A. (1986). *Physical education: Teaching and curriculum strategies for grades 5–12*. Palo Alto, CA: Mayfield Publishing.

Siedentop, D. and Tannehill, D. (2000). *Developing teaching skills in physical education* (3rd ed). Palo Alto, CA: Mayfield Publishing.

Sinelnikov, O.A., Hastie, P.A., Chance, A. and Schneulle, D. (2005). Bicycle safety: Sport education style. *Journal of Physical Education, Recreation and Dance*, 76(2): 24–29.

Strikwerda-Brown, J. and Taggart, A. (2001). No longer voiceless and exhausted: Sport education and the primary generalist teacher. *The ACHPER Healthy Lifestyles Journal,*, 48(3–4): 14–17.

Taggart. A., Browne, T. and Alexander, K. (1995). Three schools' approaches to assessment in sport education. *The ACHPER Healthy Lifestyles Journal*, 42(4): 12–15.

Taggart, A., Medland, C. and Alexander, K. (1995). "Goodbye superteacher!" Teaching sport education in the primary school. *The ACHPER Healthy Lifestyles Journal*, 42(4): 16–18.

Tannehill, D. (1998). Sport education: introduction. *Journal of Health, Physical Education, Recreation and Dance*, 69(4): 16–17.

Tinning, R. and Fitzclarence, L. (1992). Postmodern youth culture and the crisis in Australian secondary school physical education. *Quest*, 44: 287–303.

Wallhead, T. and Ntoumanis, N. (2004). Effects of a sport education intervention on students' motivational responses in physical education. *Journal of Teaching in Physical Education*, 23: 4–18.

Wardle, C., Hastie, P.A. and Kinchin, G.D. (forthcoming) A sport education unit of work: Part 2, *PE and Sport Today*.

Wardle, C. and Kinchin, G.D (2004). Sample sport education units: year 7 tennis. *PE and Sport Today*, 16: 43–46.

Wilson, A. and Kinchin, G.D. (2000). High school students' present and predicted like and dislikes regarding physical education. *Illinois Journal for Health, Physical Education, Recreation and Dance*, [Spring]: 4–8.

Youth Sport Trust. (2000). Towards girl-friendly physical education. The Nike/YST girls in sport partnership project final report. Institute of Youth Sport: Loughborough University UK.

Youth Sport Trust. (2003). '*Step into sport': Sport education resource pack*. Youth Sport Trust: Loughborough University UK.

5.4   Social and individual responsibility programs

DON HELLISON AND TOM MARTINEK

Introduction

This chapter traces our journey through the physical education curriculum research literature related to social and individual responsibility, highlighting conceptual issues, major research findings, applications to policy and practice, and major trends and future directions. This is no easy task, because the core concept, individual and social responsibility, is open to a number of interpretations, blurring the boundaries of our search. Moreover, curriculum research itself has been conceptualized in a number of ways.

To address these issues, we begin with a brief history of the responsibility-related literature in physical education which immediately underscores the importance of defining the core concept. To address this issue head on, this history is followed by a cursory review of the underpinnings and conceptualization of social and individual responsibility in three fields with strong linkages to physical education in order to arrive at supportable definition of individual and social responsibility. We then share our perspective on curriculum research in order to provide a basis for identifying the research questions and methodological approaches that occupy the attention of physical education curriculum scholars interested in social and individual responsibility. thereby providing a framework for describing the physical education responsibility-based curriculum research findings. The chapter concludes with applications to policy and practice and future directions.

History

Although earlier examples of efforts to link physical activity to instrumental goals dot the pages of history – e.g. the Greek "sound mind in sound body", the chivalric ideal of the Middle Ages (Broekhoff, 1968), and "muscular Christianity" in Europe – its most elaborate rationale emerged in England in the mid-1800s. At that time English school sports began to embrace a moral ideology of "athleticism", viewing sports as a vehicle for teaching moral courage, teamwork, "manliness", social control, socialization and, in general "character training." Since private boarding schools were intended to produce future government and society leaders, sports were mostly governed by the students themselves (Sage, 1990).

Although the primary objective of early physical education programs in the United States was physical health, even prior to the twentieth century some American physical educators – for example, Dudley Sargent, some leaders of the German Turners, and the YMCA – envisioned a connection between physical education and social and emotional well-being. For both the Turners and the YMCA, this interest in broadening the focus of physical education was influenced by earlier trends in Europe, for the former the German turnvereine movement and for the latter the European "muscular Christianity" movement. Their ideas, however, were vague, and drew on speculation and personal observations. It was not until after 1900, that "character development" began to vie with physical health for dominance. This new focus received a substantial boost from three forces. First, the American progressive education movement, an extension of "natural" education based on the work of Rousseau and others in Europe, recognized the uniqueness of children and emphasized the whole child. Second, the emergence of sport opened the door to utilizing play, cooperation, and competition for educational purposes. Third, industrialization and urbanization which began to impact society in the nineteenth century, brought urgency to the unique needs of children and youth. By 1930, the slogan "education through the physical," in contrast to education of the physical', become common among physical education leaders such as Thomas Wood, Clark Hetherington, and their students J.B. Nash and Jesse Feiring Williams (and his student Delbert Oberteuffer) and sparked a number of heated debates (Gerber, 1971; Siedentop, 1990).

Although England had promoted self-governed school sport for the upper class, the notion of becoming more socially and individually responsible was infrequently included in the extensive rhetoric of character development and education through the physical in America in the first half of the twentieth century. Miller and Jarman (1988), in their review of this history, cited only two related quotes, both at mid-century: "To give youth some freedom of choice ... so that they may develop the ability to make wise choices by their own judgment" (Cowell and Hazelton, 1955 as cited in Miller and Jarman, 1988: 74). "A well-directed physical education program should [include] ... responsibility for the consequences of [one's] ... behavior" (Manley, 1958 as cited in Miller and Jarman, 1988: 75).

Core concepts

The primary contribution of the early historical record to defining individual and social responsibility in physical education was its focus on physical activity as a medium for social and emotional outcomes. The idea of students being taught to take responsibility for their choices and behavior in physical education appeared here and there but was not central to the themes of the education through the physical movement. It was not until the publication of *Beyond balls and bats* (Hellison, 1978) that a curriculum model for teaching social and personal responsibility (TPSR) was introduced. Hellison was a late entrant to physical education, already having studied history as an undergraduate and sociology as a master's student, worked as a college admissions counselor, and spent a tour of duty in the armed forces before he entered a physical education teacher certificate program. The perspective he brought to the field emerged quickly in the publication of his first book, *Humanistic physical education* (Hellison, 1973). The values explicated in that book were augmented substantially by his regular practice of teaching underserved and so-called at risk youth part-time along with his university duties. These factors and particularly his failure to reach the youth in his charge led to his first version of TPSR. Because he has continued to teach urban youth, TPSR continues to evolve (Hellison, 1985, 1995, 2003; Hellison and Templin, 1991). Hellison's conceptualization of responsibility, derived totally from practice and his own background and values, can be summarized as helping students take responsibility for their own development and well-being and for contributing to the well-being of others. The details of TPSR are described below (see physical education philosophical contributions). (For additional early background, see Hellison et al., 2000; and Hellison, 2003.)

TPSR hovered on the margins of the physical education profession for several years, although a few teachers here and there found in it a kindred spirit. However, as problems with children and youth, whether poor or affluent, escalated, TPSR began to be adopted and adapted in a variety of settings in North America and several other countries. Most of this activity involved altering in-school physical education practices, but extended day programs both in schools and community youth organizations were affected to some extent as well. Occasionally a brave interscholastic youth coach attempted to introduce aspects of TPSR. For many of these pioneers, TPSR was first viewed as a class management approach, but at least some of these teachers found themselves changing their relationships with students and broadening their physical education goals as a result of utilizing TPSR (e.g., Mrugala, 2002). As a result of this activity, TPSR began to be identified as an exemplary curriculum model (Bain, 1988; Kirk, 1992; Steinhardt, 1992) and as an approach relevant for underserved youth (e.g. Siedentop, Mand, and Taggart, 1986).

In 1996, Hellison formed a partnership with five other faculty members who had adapted TPSR to their own work, who taught underserved kids as university professors, and who had developed professional preparation courses and programs focused on serving underserved populations (Hellison and Kallusky, 1999). The partnership promoted TPSR by conducting workshops for teachers and youth workers and publishing a book describing various ways to utilize TPSR in in-school and other settings, and how to use such programs to link universities and communities (Hellison et al., 2000).

The primary contribution of the early historical record to defining individual and social responsibility in physical education is its focus on physical activity as the medium for instrumental social and emotional outcomes. Over the past 30 years, Hellison has built on this legacy by his conceptualization, implementation, and field-testing of personal and social responsibility in physical education. In order to more fully understand the underpinnings and specific components of individual and social responsibility, we turn to a selected review of the literature in three fields closely aligned with physical education: education, psychology, and youth development.

The education literature on social and individual responsibility

We begin by looking at the affective domain. Beane offered an in-depth conceptualization of affect in the curriculum which,

> ... in the broadest sense, is concerned with personal-social development. It includes knowledge, skills, behaviors and attitudes related to personal interests, social relations, and the

integration of the two ... [indicating] that affect is situated in the curriculum in all experiences that involved self-perceptions, values, morals, ethics, beliefs, social predispositions, appreciations, aspirations, and attitudes. (1990: 10)

Beane (1990) also drew upon the work of Wight (1972) to describe an "elaborate set of goals based on self ..., others ..., and the environment ..." (p. 8). His list of goals for the "others" in a person's life included "social responsibility". Although Beane and Wight's ideas are grounded in the broader perspective of personal and social development rather than responsibility, they do lay the affective and social development groundwork for more specific treatments.

Education scholars have specifically cited the need for responsibility in the school curriculum. For example, Sizer (1992: 59) was critical of pedagogical approaches that "thwart opportunities for young people to take responsibility ... [and] develop the habit of delivering on that responsibility". Haberman (2000) agreed, pointing out that urban schools have become preoccupied with control and compliance which are an integral part of the school culture. Bredemeier (1988) found that urban teachers rejected the indoctrination approach, instead favoring student decision-making with attention to consequences, control over their own behavior rather than teacher control, and acceptance of responsibility for their actions. Tappan (1992: 387) also weighed in on the indoctrination issue, pointing out that students need to "discuss, examine, and reflect critically on values and ethical positions within a diverse, complex, and ever-changing society". Jones and Tanner (1981: 497) argued that "training children for freedom requires different kinds of plans and structures than training them for slavery". Kamii et al. (1994) advocated autonomy as the major goal of education, and emphasized self-governing in moral as well as cognitive areas.

Berman's (1997: 12) work is perhaps the most in-depth treatment of social responsibility, which he defined as "a person's relationships with others and with the larger political and social world". He emphasized the development of a social conscience that encompasses concern about social issues, ethical considerations of both justice and caring, and the process of meaning-making and identity formation. Such an agenda cannot be imposed, but since children want to make sense of, and engage in, the world around them, age-appropriate processes need to be utilized to facilitate their engagement. Berman's conceptualization does empower students, but unlike most others who focus on both personal and social responsibility, he restricts his perspective to social responsibility.

An alternative view to responsibility as empowerment was provided in Wentzel's (1991) review of the relationship between social responsibility and academic achievement. The studies reviewed by Wentzel were based on her definition of social responsibility as "adherence to social rules and role expectations" (1991: 2). Using this definition, she concluded that: "social responsibility can facilitate learning and performance outcomes by promoting positive interactions with teachers and peers and, from a motivational perspective, by providing students with additional incentives to achieve" (1991: 1).

The psychology literature on social and individual responsibility

Psychologist deCharms' (1976) developed a theory of motivation closely aligned with children and youth taking personal and social responsibility, which he successfully implemented in a research project with urban elementary school children in the classroom. His theory is based on teaching students to be "origins" rather than pawns in their lives. By that he meant setting internal standards, striving against external forces (even if unsuccessful), and doing as one must rather than as one pleases. The social responsibility of being an origin is to treat others as origins as well, for example by taking responsibility for the consequences of one's actions toward others.

Other psychologists have also advocated responsibility as a core affective and social development concept in schools. Elias and his associates (Elias et al., 1997: 1) argued that everyone wants schools to prepare students "to become knowledgeable, responsible, and caring adults". Their conceptualization of responsibility includes both personal and social dimensions: "For children to become responsible, they must be able to understand risks and opportunities, and be motivated to choose actions and behaviors that serve not only their own interests but those of others" (1997: 1).

The concept of constructivism has recently received attention in both psychology and education. Constructivism often refers to an active learner who constructs knowledge. In teaching, this means "helping learners to engage actively in independent thinking, problem-solving, and discovering ... through an open-ended non-linear process" (Rovegno and Kirk, 1995: 462). Perhaps Ennis best summarized the relation of constructivism to social and individual responsibility:

Curricula structured within a constructivist theory of learning provide students with multiple opportunities to participate, take responsibility for personal and social actions, and facilitate the participation of others. Often this occurs within a personalized environment in which students set goals and monitor their own progress. (1999: 167)

The youth development literature on social and individual responsibility

Youth development scholars have also addressed the importance of responsibility in their work. In Benson's (1997) assets-based approach to today's kids, empowerment, meaning shifting power and decision-making from the teacher or program leader to students, is one of seven types of assets he advocated. One social responsibility benchmark of empowerment is serving in the community regularly. Another Benson (1997: 32) asset type, social competencies, includes "knows how to plan ahead and make choices" and "seeks to resolve conflict nonviolently".

McLaughlin's research on successful community youth organization programs for inner city youth emphasized the importance of trusting and empowering youth (McLaughlin, 2000; McLaughlin et al., 1994), a point reinforced by a review of similar studies of best practices in inner city extended day programs (Hellison and Cutforth, 1997).

The underserved youth resiliency literature (e.g. Wang and Gordon, 1994) focuses on the strength of kids' resistance to environmental forces. That literature, while diverse in its recommendations of positive factors affecting youth, often cites responsibility-related concepts such as empowerment, independent decision-making, and being pro-active.

The critical pedagogy literature on social and individual responsibility

Paulo Freire (e.g. 1970/1993), who spent much of his life fighting oppression and championing liberation, is universally recognized as an early leader in critical pedagogy. He was critical of what he calls the banking concept of education which "erroneously assumes that students are not active agents in the world ... [and] in their own education" (Fowler, 1998: 319). Instead, Freire offered liberation characterized by strategies such as problem-posing, reflection, and dialog. Freire's work can be viewed as a kind of responsibility-based education, although this is true only insofar as the broader educational goals are consistent with Freire's revolutionary objectives (Aronowitz, 1993).

More recently, Rovegno and Kirk (1995) broadened what they call socially critical work beyond rights-based social justice and empowerment to include an ethic of relational caring and responsibility. Although they navigate through a wide range of literature to make their case, their conceptualization of responsibility, unlike caring and social justice, is left vague. However, they do draw on TPSR in the physical education literature (see the history and

philosophical contributions sections) along with other examples to buttress their case. Macdonald and her associates (2002) also refer to TPSR in their discussion of the socially critical perspective's "commitments to social justice, equity, inclusivity, and social change" (p, 140) but argue that, while TPSR and other perspectives "work toward realizing such commitments ... [they do not] frame their research around these assumptions and purposes" (p. 140). Bain (1988) also identified TPSR as a curricular example of critical reflection in physical education

Defining social and individual responsibility

The primary contribution of the early historical record was its focus on physical activity as the medium for instrumental social and emotional outcomes, although Hellison's work over the past thirty years extended beyond this contribution (and is described in detail below). Since social and individual responsibility was not central to early physical educators' conceptualization of social and emotional well-being, we turned to elements of the literature from related fields and found several points of agreement concerning the core concept:

- Personal and social development provides a conceptual foundation for including responsibility in curriculum work.
- Both individual and social responsibility are included in most definitions of responsibility.
- Responsibility entails shifting power to students to help them to make good decisions not only for themselves but in relation to others, to set internal standards, and to plan ahead (to be pro-active).
- Social responsibility requires the development of a social conscience.
- Responsibility also entails being accountable by delivering on one's responsibilities, which often involves striving against external forces.
- Responsibility includes not only behaviors but values, attitudes, and self-perceptions.
- Support for a common conceptualization comes not only from "mainstream" education scholars but those in youth development and psychology as well.

A curriculum research perspective

Having taken a brief excursion into the history and conceptual treatments of our core concept, individual and social responsibility, we now turn to curriculum research that focuses on this topic. However, given the range of, and to some extent controversy surrounding, curriculum research, it is crucial to first share our definition of curriculum research, thereby enabling us to identify the research questions and approaches that occupy the attention of curriculum scholars interested in social and individual responsibility. We agree with curriculum scholar Bill Schubert who stated:

> Curriculum research goes hand in hand with curriculum scholarship … [and] is more broadly conceived [than social and behavioral methodologies] Although it often includes social and behavioral methodologies, curriculum scholarship is more properly denoted by the terms inquiry, studies, theory, and perspectives rather than research. (1982: 420)

Schubert supported this conceptualization by describing in some detail its origins and early research, recent paradigms and categories, and emergent trends. His state-of-the-art curriculum text, *Curriculum: Perspective, Paradigm, and Possibility* (1986), provides further evidence in the form of detailed chapters devoted to philosophy in curriculum, curriculum policy creation, and the paradigms of perennial analytic categories, practical inquiry, and critical praxis. Edmund Short's (1991) book-length treatment of curriculum research, *Forms of Curriculum Inquiry*, includes 17 forms of curriculum inquiry. Among the many methodologies are three forms of philosophical curriculum research including, though data collectors may shudder at the thought, the speculative essay. Among other forms of curriculum inquiry are the scientific, evaluative, ethnographic, phenomenological, theoretic, and aesthetic.

Curriculum research, therefore, can be either philosophical or empirical. Curriculum research is sometimes empirical, because studies are needed to evaluate the fidelity and impact of various curriculum approaches. Curriculum research is sometimes philosophical, because the primary curriculum question is "What kind of knowledge and experience enable a person to lead a good and fulfilling life?" (Schubert, 1986: viii). The branch of philosophy most relevant here is axiology, which "rather than being concerned with what is … focuses on what should be … [I]t looks at specific values … such as the composition of the good life" (Kretchmar, 1994: 16).

Sport philosopher Scott Kretchmar distinguished between empirical and philosophical research by pointing out that philosophers, unlike most of the work in fields such as history, physiology, and sociology "do not take the empirical turn. Rather they look inward to find their data" (1994: 13–14), utilizing reflection, abstraction, judgment. Their tools, then, are reflective in nature rather than empirical.

In our opinion, physical education research has been hampered by two forces: The positivistic experimental paradigm of the flagship subdiscipline exercise physiology, and the subdisciplinary structure itself which encourages replication of the parent discipline's perspectives and methodologies, thereby discouraging innovation and, in Bressan's (1982, 1987) view, true scholarly work. Crum (1986) raised more general questions about the data-based nature of physical education research in the United States, especially in comparison to Europe's more theoretical orientation. We joined in the dissent by developing service-bonded inquiry (1997; Martinek et al., 2004) which builds the development of ideas into the research process, similar to several earlier efforts such as Joseph Schwab's practical inquiry (e.g. 1971) and Kirk's (1991) curriculum as craft. Kirk's argument supports our broad definition of curriculum research in this way:

> If curriculum work is viewed as a precise, technological exercise that involves logical lock-step, sequential reasoning along with rational action and quantitative measurement, then we may be sacrificing quality for mere technical sophistication. It is possible to advocate an altogether different view of design in curriculum work through the view of curriculum as craft, which involves disciplined action, but builds into the exercise the values and beliefs which lead teaching as well as ways of handling uncertainty, spontaneity, creativity, and ambiguity. (1991: 260)

Our view, then, is that curriculum research methods can be broadly classified as either philosophical – which draws primarily on reflection rather than empirical data, or empirical which relies on analyses of quantitative and/or qualitative data.

Major philosophical findings

Based on our interpretation of curriculum research described in the introduction, major findings for physical education curriculum research in personal and social responsibility can be divided into two parts: philosophical and empirical. The research questions and research methodologies differ depending on this classification. Philosophical research inquires into value-based issues such as what is worth while to know and experience and utilizes research methods such as reflection, imagination, conceptual analysis, and theorizing. By classifying curriculum work in this way, innovative reflectively based curricular ideas of physical education teachers such as John Hichwa and Kevin Kaardal (see below), who are not considered nor do they consider themselves curriculum scholars, qualify for inclusion. Our emphasis is on physical education curriculum and instruction contributions but also include sport psychology and adapted physical education.

Physical education curriculum and instruction contributions

Gibbons and Bressan (1991) offered a comprehensive theoretical framework for the affective domain in physical education. Their framework emphasized taking social–moral responsibility which they explained as: "the development of a moral attitude … to be based upon students' acquisition of the ability to balance their decision-making among the competing claims associated with their concept of autonomy, their concept of altruism, and their concept of responsibility" (1991: 87).

The responsibility theme has been continued in more current physical education literature as well. The concept of student empowerment is apparent in Siedentop's Sport Education model (1994), which is the focus of another chapter in this *Handbook*. While the original model (Siedentop,1980) was grounded in play theory and Siedentop's interest in preserving the best of the sport culture, empowerment of students soon became central to its practice and to subsequent descriptions of sport education. Students coach, officiate, keep statistics, and perform other duties related to organized sport while being members of a team for a season (e.g. of soccer, basketball, track and field). Hastie and Buchanan (2000) combined and field-tested a combination of sport education and TPSR (Hellison, 2003). Their "mixed model" placed more emphasis on taking personal and social responsibility in the various sport seasons but did not include transfer outside the sport setting as advocated by TPSR.

Ennis's Sport for Peace model (Ennis et al., 1999) resembles sport education but emphasizes conflict resolution and the role (and plight) of inner city girls in physical education. Students learn to solve conflicts and to include girls, with boys skilled at dominant inner city sports (especially basketball) being given responsibility to help the girls become productive members of their teams. The sport education model facilitates this process by prioritizing the team approach and recording team statistics including wins and losses, thereby pressuring coaches to be effective in their roles. Ennis (1999: 167) also referred to "[taking] responsibility for personal and social actions including goal-setting and monitoring their own progress" as part of her advocacy of a constructivist theory of learning. She also emphasized the need for "trusting and caring teacher–student relationships" (1999: 167) as an important but often ignored factor in curriculum theory, a point also made and elaborated upon by Hellison (2003) in facilitating TPSR.

Noddings (1992) is an unlikely contributor to the physical education literature, yet she directly addressed school physical education, providing a radical departure from traditional practices. She argued for combining several middle and high school departments such as physical education, home economics,

health education, driver training and for eliminating the supervision of sport and exercise, substituting instead learning "to take responsibility for our fitness [by providing] open discussion on issues of fitness" such as the "selfish and unproductive" character of the recent fitness movement and issues of competition and cooperation (1992: 75).

The influence in physical education of Freire's conceptualization of responsibility (as construed above) is apparent in some of the themes that surfaced in Miguel Fernández-Balboa's (1997) edited volume on critical postmodernism in physical education and sport. In that same volume, however, Hellison (1997) raised questions about the transformation of theory into curriculum practice in the critical postmodernist movement. More to the point, Rovegno and Kirk (1995), arguing that the ethic of justice and emancipation is too narrow a theoretical base for socially critical physical education curriculum work, offered a reconceptualization that included an ethic of care and responsibility. Although their argument was presented above in the review of critical pedagogy literature, it needs to be included here as well since they are physical education scholars, and their article appeared in a physical education journal.

Social and individual responsibility also has been extended to include citizenship. Laker (2000) contended that the concept of citizenship consists of three strands: moral responsibility, community engagement, and political literacy. All three strands represent stepping stones for being a desirable citizen in today's society. Laker and others (see Allen, 1997) claimed that many school curricula need to offer a multitude of opportunities for heightening the sense of responsibility and citizenship in youth. Gaining the necessary skills of being a responsible citizen can only occur when the school culture is fashioned in a way that authentically fosters the development of these skills. Schools that are harnessed with test score mandates along with interschool competition for top scores make the foundation for teaching responsibility shaky at best.

Laker (2000) emphasized the importance of physical activity and sport play in cultivating responsibility attitudes and behaviors in children and youth. He reinforced the notion that the interactive nature of sport sets the stage for teaching important life lessons (e.g. fair play, being good losers, including others). He cautioned, however, that like schools, raising the competitive stakes in sport will surely undermine the chances for life skills to be experienced and learned.

Stiehl's (1993) "Becoming Responsible" model conceptualized responsibility as taking care of one's self (for example, making and keeping commitments, setting goals), others (for example, honoring others rights, dignity, and worth; working together on common goals), and the environment (for example, respecting property, recognizing the importance of taking care of the environment). The addition of caring for the environment is not common in the responsibility literature but was a core concept for Wight (1971, 1972 as cited in Beane, 1990). The Becoming Responsible model includes specific steps (or example, learning to use responsibility-based language and behaviors), strategies to become more responsible (for example, changing how the teacher and students talk and act), and an advanced personal responsibility project based on Becoming Responsible principles.

Hellison's (1978, 1985, 1995, 2003) TPSR (teaching personal and social responsibility; also known as the responsibility model) conceptualization of responsibility, augmented by the work of others (e.g. Hellison et al., 2000; Martinek et al., 1999), has made some inroads in the practice of both school-based and agency-based physical education programs for a number of years, as noted in the history section above. In his latest work, Hellison (2003) tried to make clear that this approach is a set of ideas, not a rigid blueprint, which includes these components:

- Physical activity is a potentially powerful vehicle for teaching life skills and values, while at the same time promoting physical activity content learning.
- The overarching purpose is to help students take responsibility for their own well-being and development and for contributing to well-being of others.
- To help students focus on what to take responsibility for, five goals or levels are suggested, along with the caveat to adjust these as necessary: (1) Self-control and respect for others' rights and feelings; (2) participation, effort, self-motivation; (3) self-direction; (4) helping others and leadership; and (5) transfer outside the gym.
- Five themes characterize daily practice: Develop a respectful kids first relationship with students, integrate responsibility with physical activity, gradually empower students, promote group and self-reflection, and teach for transfer outside the gym.
- A daily format is suggested (but not mandated) to facilitate putting the purpose and themes into practice: Relational time, awareness talk, physical activity lesson, group meeting, and reflection time.
- A wide range of specific instructional strategy and assessment ideas are offered as examples of the implementation of personal and social responsibility.

A specific empowerment-oriented conflict resolution strategy compatible with TPSR was developed and field-tested earlier by Horrocks (1978). He called his idea the "Talking Bench". Students who had a conflict went to the talking bench to work out their differences, reporting back to the teacher when the matter has been settled satisfactorily. DeLine's (1991) "no plan no play" strategy, in which students who have difficulty playing with other students are required to submit an improvement plan before reentering the game, is also compatible with TPSR.

Some best practice models of physical education practitioners reflect these teachers' responsibility-based philosophical stance. For example, Hichwa, 1993 National Association of Sport and Physical Education Middle School Teacher of the Year and author of *Right fielders are people too* (1998) emphasized "the 3 Rs in physical education" (p. 35): Respect, responsibility, and resourcefulness. Responsibility is conceptualized as:

- "Condition, quality, fact, or instance of being responsible.
- Obligation, accountability, dependability.
- Responsible … able to distinguish between right and wrong, and to think and act rationally, and hence accountable for one's behavior". (1998: 36)

His definition of respect, "to show consideration for [and] to feel or show honor or esteem for" (1998: 36), could also be considered part of his responsibility conceptualization.

Although he does not use the term responsibility, Kaardal's (2001) "goal-directed physical education" is a best practice approach based on individual responsibility. He defined "success for [the various groups of children in any school] … according to their [chosen] goals and abilities" (2001: 7), rather than specifying those goals for them.

> Physical education needs to provide a range of options, not only of activities, but of the primary motivators of physical activity for different students [such as] … social … competitive, and personal satisfaction … [and] the levels at which they'll participate in those programs (beginning, intermediate, advanced or elite) … Our programs should *empower* students through giving them choice … [our italics]. (2001: 8)

Carefully planned individualized instruction and reflection journals are but two of the many processes Kaardal used to reach his goals.

The Sports Plus model (Beedy, 1997), which is intended as an extended day rather than in-school program, has been adopted by several school districts in collaboration with other agencies (for example, the YMCA, the public library). This model is based on five core values, one of which is responsibility, defined as "being accountable for one's actions to self and others [and] acknowledging duties to self and others" (1997: 20).

Sport psychology contributions

Sport psychologists Shields and Bredemeier (1995) viewed physical education as a "rich environment for dealing with moral issues" (1995: 201), particularly if teachers and coaches share power with students (i.e. empowerment). Their comprehensive review and critique of, as well as their contributions to, moral theory and empirical studies of social–moral development in sport and physical education added significantly to our understanding of social development in physical education. Moreover, some aspects of their work shed light on the moral aspects of responsibility development in physical education as well as youth sport, for example by explicating a process for critically analyzing moral situations, developing moral self-efficacy, and taking moral action.

The Life Development Intervention and Life Skills Orientation is one of two perspectives in a framework designed for prevention and intervention by sport psychologists Hodge and Danish (1999; see also Danish and Nellen, 1997). The purpose of this approach is to develop the "ability to do life planning, be self-reliant, and seek the resources of others" (1999: 64), thereby promoting responsibility. Two of the programs based on this perspective involve sport and physical education, which are used as attractive vehicles for teaching life skills. One program, Going for the Goal (GOAL), uses sport as a metaphor for life skills in ten sessions focused on goal-setting, overcoming obstacles, rebounding from difficulties, and developing a plan to reward themselves. The other program, Sports United to Promote Education and Recreation (SUPER), consists of ten three hour sport clinics designed to teach sport skills, learn life skills that are related to sports such as goal-setting and anger management, and to play the sport.

Adapted physical education contributions

Lavay et al. (1997) offered Becoming Responsible (Stiehl, 1993) and TPSR (Hellison, 2003) (as well as Glasser's reality therapy) as alternatives to behavioral methods of management for adapted physical education students. Adapted physical education textbooks by Sherrill (2004) and Winnick (2000) applied TPSR to adapted physical education.

Summary of the field's philosophical contributions

- Physical education has been envisioned as vehicle for teaching social and individual responsibility by a number of scholars, teachers, and youth program leaders.
- A number of curriculum models focus on, or include, social responsibility and individual goals and strategies, including Sport Education, Sport for Peace, Becoming Responsible, Sports Plus, and TPSR.
- Sport psychology has also contributed responsibility-based approaches to moral development and life skills development.
- Adapted physical education has recently embraced responsibility as an alternative curriculum approach.

Major empirical findings

While philosophical research can answer curriculum questions such as "What kind of knowledge and experience [in physical education] enable a person to lead a good and fulfilling life?" (Schubert, 1986: viii), empirical research is needed to address evaluation questions that require both quantitative and qualitative data collection and analysis, such as whether any of these philosophical approaches work in practice.

Cheffers (1987) was perhaps the first scholar in physical education curriculum and instruction to conduct a systematic program of research on children to take responsibility. Between 1972 to 1982, his research team investigated the efficacy of children's decision-making and found that a structured decision-making approach, with choices and management strategies, fostered shared decision-making better than either a teacher-centered approach or total freedom. They utilized a variety of research methods in this work, including the creation and validation of both psychometric and process–product instruments as well as interviews and field notes.

Three physical education curriculum models described above have received attention from researchers. Siedentop (1994) argued that Sport Education is congruent with authentic assessment, because records kept are authentically connected to the intended outcomes of Sport Education. He gave six specific examples of how such records can be used in the service of assessment. Moreover, empirical studies have supported the model's claims (e.g. Grant, 1992; Hastie and Sharpe, 1999). Recently, Wallhead and Ntoumanis (2004) compared sport education to a traditional physical education class to determine the effect of sport education on motivational responses. Analysis of the data from variety of pre-post psychometric scales and questionnaires indicated that sport education increased perceptions of autonomy and a task-oriented climate in comparison to the control group. (Sport education is the focus of Chapter 5.3) The second curriculum model, Sport for Peace, which can be viewed as a spinoff of Sport Education, also has an empirical base (e.g. Carson, 1992; Ennis et al., 1999) comprised of a variety of qualitative methods. The empirical work of the third model, TPSR, is described in some detail in a separate section below.

Sport psychology research

Sport psychologists Hodge and Danish (1999) addressed the difficulty of evaluating responsibility-based programs:

> Few instruments enable a researcher to measure different outcomes and still have the properties necessary to compare experimental

and control participants, Even fewer consider positive outcomes such as those identified in the Task Force on Education of Young Adolescents (1989) report. Although quantitative measures may permit such analyses, they are labor-intensive, difficult to use, and expensive with large groups. (1999: 70)

For these reasons, Hodge and Danish used Goal Attainment Scaling to measure on a five point scale the level of success that a participant achieves in pursuing a stated goal. They also collected other quantitative and qualitative data for both participants and a control group. Results included participants' achievements in the program such as achieving the goals they set and associated learning as well as improvements outside the program such as better school attendance and fewer health-compromising behaviors compared to controls.

Also in the realm of sport psychology, the structural developmental approach to moral development, while not using the term responsibility, promotes moral decision-making. Romance and his associates (1986) conducted an innovative elementary physical education experiment based on five physical activity-based strategies using the structural developmental approach to moral development. In all of these strategies, children were asked to solve conflicts that derived from implementation of the strategies. During an 8-week program for two fifth grade classes, pre–post interview scores based on Haan's interactional moral development instrument revealed that students in the experimental group improved significantly compared to controls in their ability to reason morally in relation to the conflicts. Other studies (Bredemeier et al., 1986; Gibbons et al., 1995) found similar results.

TPSR model research

A number of studies have been conducted on Hellison's TPSR curriculum model. All of the studies ($n = 26$) that focused on underserved or at-risk children and youth, both published and unpublished and dating from 1978 to 2001, were analyzed and summarized by Hellison and Walsh (2002). All were program evaluations, and 21 of the 26 were case studies based on either qualitative data sources or some combination of qualitative and quantitative data. Four research questions were explored across the 26 studies, three of which involved assessing TPSR outcomes. The other focused on TPSR processes. Findings were grouped into strong and weaker evidence based on the number and quality of the studies and nature of the findings. When the results of these studies across a 23-year time period are compared to the summary of TPSR principles provided above, several conclusions emerge, including:

- Strong support for "Physical activity as a potentially powerful vehicle for teaching life skills and values, while at the same time promoting physical activity content learning."
- Strong support for "The overarching purpose [as helping] students take responsibility for their own well-being and development and for contributing to well-being of others."
- Variable support for program participants improving on the five goals (or levels) that help students focus on what to take responsibility for. Of the 19 studies that investigated this question, 14 studies reported self-control improvement and 12 reported effort improvement, but only eight showed self-direction improvement and only seven supported improvement in helping others. Perhaps surprisingly, of the 11 studies that investigated transfer of these goals outside the program, strong evidence was found for the transfer of several goals. However, the findings were generally stronger in the program, and some evidence showed non-transfer as well. The two studies that investigated the impact of cross-age teaching (older students teaching younger students TPSR in the gym) found strong support for a number of positive outcomes.
- Uneven support regarding the five themes that characterize daily practice and a daily format to facilitate putting the purpose and themes into practice. Exploration of the processes experienced by program participants turned up some evidence for interacting with a caring adult and having fun. However, the design of this review as well as the design of most of the studies were not conducive to answering these process-oriented questions.

A study one one TPSR-based extended day program, published after the above review of research (Hellison and Wright, 2003), was carried out over a nine year period, based on nine years of attendance records and nine years of post-program qualitative student evaluations of the program. Results showed that program retention rates surpassed the average dropout pattern for inner city youth in extended day programs, and in anonymous program evaluations over the nine years consistently showed perceived improvements in personal and social responsibility as consequences of their participation in the program. They also emphasized the importance of having a respectful, caring program leader.

Wright and White (2004) studied the implementation of TPSR with cerebral palsy children, providing empirical evidence concerning its effectiveness and thus testing the philosophical notions of adapted physical education scholars described above. Based on medical records, fieldnotes, and interviews with participants' physicians, therapists, and parents, Wright and White concluded that the intervention increased participants' sense of ability, produced positive feelings about the program and positive social interactions, and had therapeutic relevance.

Recently, Watson and her associates (Watson et al., 2003) developed the Contextual Self-Responsibility Questionnaire based on TPSR and administered the questionnaire to 135 underserved youth who participated in a National Youth Sports Program summer camp. Validity was checked by conducting an exploratory factor analysis, revealing that the participants merged the two advanced TPSR goals, thereby producing "less-than-perfect" alignment between TPSR and the questionnaire items. Regardless, the questionnaire roughly reflected participant perceptions toward TPSR. Since no intervention was involved, the primary contribution of this study was to add a psychometric tool to TPSR methodology. However, descriptive statistics of the results showed that the participants perceived themselves to be taking personal and social responsibility, and the more they perceived TPSR to be emphasized, the more robust the results. In fact, "a significant proportion of affect and attitude were explained by the [questionnaire]" (p. 228). The researchers surmised that the NYSP teaching staff's training in TPSR as part of their university professional preparation program influenced these findings.

Project effort research

Three of the studies reviewed by Hellison and Walsh (2002) were products of a University of North Carolina at Greensboro research and development program based on TPSR called Project Effort, but the responsibility-based research being carried out there is extensive and therefore warrants additional attention. By presenting the methods and findings of specific studies, a more complete understanding of TPSR research can be achieved.

Project Effort is aimed at fostering responsibility values for underserved youth through participation in a values-based sports club guided by TPSR. Empowering students is a centerpiece of the program. Empowerment means giving the club members "choices and voices". This means giving young people meaningful and genuine choices along with opportunity for expression and dialogue. Elementary and middle school students work with the responsibility values and are empowered through a number of learning experiences. These include peer and cross-age teaching opportunities, choices regarding specific activities, and time for personal reflection.

An important extension of the sports club is a mentoring program. University students receive extensive education to enhance their cultural competence and learn strategies for goal setting. The main goal of the mentoring program is to help the students transfer the values learned in the sport club to the school setting. As in the sports club, TPSR serves as a framework to guide the mentor and student in goal setting efforts.

Early evaluation of the mentoring program focused on school performance measures (Hellison et al., 1996; Martinek et al., 1999). Nine-week grades, recorded reprimands, mentor journal entries, and office referrals were obtained from school records. The club members' teachers were also informally asked to comment on how hard they thought they were trying in their daily work. Overall improvement in students' engagement in class work along with increases in grade-point average and with decreases in reprimands and office referrals were reported. Teachers also noted that barriers to preventing positive impact included home (or example, unstable family conditions) and environmental (for example, gang involvement) factors.

In a follow-up study by Martinek et al. (2001), a shift from looking at performance outcomes was made. Instead, the researchers focused on outcomes that more clearly reflected actual transfer of club goals to the classroom. Using a "creative evaluation" strategy (Patton, 1987), teacher and mentor journals, and student exit interviews were analyzed. A "program–goal matrix" was developed to determine the level of performance of each participant. Results indicated that the youngsters were able to apply the goal of "trying hard" in the classroom most of the time. They struggled, however, to transfer some of the other values to the classroom (i.e. self-control and respect for others, self-direction, helping others). One particular problematic area was the club members' inability to set personal goals in the classroom setting. Our own past work (see Martinek and Hellison, 1997, 1998) found that both environmental and personal barriers are main culprits in preventing successful application of responsibility value outside the gym. Similarly, mentors in this study cited the youngsters' personal values as formidable obstacles to goal setting. Devaluing the school experience, possessing combative values, and feeling helpless in meeting teacher expectations were frequently mentioned in the mentor journals.

Another area of evaluation of Project Effort was to find out why young people stay in the program. For years retention has always been an important consideration with program planners. To clear our thinking about why young people "hang in there", Schilling (2001) examined underserved youth perceptions of commitment to Project Effort. Using a case study approach, she described the levels of program commitment of seven veteran club members. She was also interested in identifying the reasons for being committed. The length of involvement in Project Effort among the participants ranged from four to seven years. One-on-one interviews were augmented by focus group interviews which were the primary data sources for her study.

Some of the reasons that kept the participants in the program were the program's activities and organization, relationships with the staff and program leader, and the program's environment (i.e. having fun, being in a positive place, having a snack). They also described the nature of being committed. Things like being "into the program," "always coming to the club", and "having fun" were typically mentioned as indicators. An important aspect underlying these findings was the interconnection between showing responsible behavior and being a good club member.

Barriers to commitment were also highlighted. For a few club members, the type of activities and repetition of things were two inhibitors to program commitment. Schilling's study also reemphasized the importance placed on having program leaders who truly internalize and practice the responsibility values. This seemed to be a primary factor in keeping the kids connected to the program goals of Project Effort. We believe that this is an area that needs considerable attention from program evaluators. Sport Psychologist Scanlon and her colleagues (Scanlon et al., 1993) also underscored the need to look at leader attributes. They claimed that it is probable that certain types of program leaders are particularly successful with values-based models. Knowing what characteristics make leaders effective in values-based sport programs will undoubtedly have important implications in the professional training of future leaders.

We are beginning to see the development of sport programs that encourage adolescent youth to be caring and compassionate leaders – a focus of the more advanced levels of Hellison's model (especially Level Four). Broadening the definition of leadership is fundamental in these programs. Van Linden and Fertman (1998) promoted the notion that leaders need to think for themselves, communicate their thoughts and feelings to others, and help others to act in ethical and socially responsible ways. Such qualities are characterized as those that reflect caring and compassion for others.

Some recent program developers have found that getting young people to acquire these qualities requires early exposure and practice using the responsibility values. Programs like those in Greensboro, Chicago, and Denver have club participants learning a set of skills and attitudes through planned physical activities. Emerging from these programs have been research data describing how adolescent youth respond to the challenges of being responsible for the welfare of others.

For example, Cutforth and Puckett (1999), in a study reviewed by Hellison and Walsh (2002), examined a summer apprentice teacher program at the University of Illinois at Chicago in which a group of urban young people taught basketball to young children attending a summer sports camp. The program captured the interests and talents of the youth who struggled with behavior problems,

truancy, and grades during the school year. Quantitative and qualitative results including interviews and field notes showed that the teachers gained self confidence, concern for others, intrapersonal and interpersonal skills, problem-solving skills, and enthusiasm for learning.

The development of youth leadership ability was also examined in a program called the Youth Leader Corps at the University of North Carolina at Greensboro. Two evaluation studies have emerged from this program. In one study, Schilling and her colleagues (Schilling et al., 2001) examined data from informal observation notes and journal entries. They found that getting adolescent youngsters to be compassionate leaders involved the application of various levels of empowerment. The first level was simply providing an open forum for youngsters to share their ideas. Open dialogue among staff and club participants gave opportunity for expressing perceptions and attitudes. The second level entailed having youth participants make decisions within the program or activity, moving beyond discussion to action. Choices in activity, with whom to work, or even deciding how the program should run were some of the ways in which decision-making was given to the participants. The third level of empowerment was peer teaching. At this level, club members' decisions and actions directly impacted the experiences of their fellow club members. Coaching responsibilities (e.g. running team drills, reinforcing teamwork) were also given to those club members ready to take on more advanced leadership roles. The most advanced level of empowerment occurred at the fourth responsibility level. At this level the club members became involved with cross-age teaching. They took responsibility for teaching younger children in a different environment than the sport club. They planned for and taught in their own sport club, reinforcing the TPSR levels of responsibility.

A fifth level is empowering youth to take control of their own future. It is uncertain as to whether youth leaders ever get to experience this most advance level of empowerment. They will need to be ready to assume the difficult responsibility of making society a better place to live. How this takes place is unclear. Empowerment at this level will be dependent on how well a youngster can successfully manage the responsibilities offered at the previous levels.

In another study on youth leadership, Martinek and Schilling (2003) looked at how youth participants advance in their leadership skills. Similar to earlier investigations, interview, journal entries, and informal observations served as the major data sources. The program attempted to foster the leadership qualities of underserved high school youth, guided by the learned helplessness theory (Martinek and Griffith, 1993) as well as moral development theories (Burns, 1978; Gilligan, 1982; Kohlberg, 1971). The study showed that youth progress in leadership along a continuum of leadership qualities, beginning with personal needs and eventually maturing into a compassionate leader. The stages of development found the leaders either placing emphasis on either: (a) personal needs (stage 1), (b) teaching skills (stage 2), (c) reciprocal learning (stage 3), or (d) compassionate leadership (stage 4). The evaluation also showed that operating at these stages was fluid for the leaders; that is, they fluctuated from level to level depending on their personal struggles outside the program. The developmental framework to ease feelings of uncertainty by giving the staff members a sense of what should come next when setting personal and program goals for the youth leader corps members.

TPSR research in Spain and New Zealand

Escarti and her research team (2005) at the University of Valencia in Spain have been conducting TPSR intervention investigations over the past several years. The first focused on underserved youth in an after-school coaching club (Hellison et al., 2000). The second involved elementary school PE teachers using TPSR. Also in Spain at the University of Madrid, faculty member Pedro Martin (2000) implemented TPSR with low income youth and reported positive changes in their values but frustration with the social and economic barriers they face in improving their lives outside the physical activity setting.

Gordon (2005) conducted a six month implementation of TPSR in a New Zealand secondary school. Two classes were based on TPSR, and two classes acted as controls. All four classes were taught by the same teacher. Both qualitative and quantitative data were collected, including daily notations of student behaviors, number of detentions, goal-setting and self-reflection records kept by the students, interviews with the teacher and selected students from all four classes. Results indicated that behavior, class atmosphere, and relationships with the teacher improved in the TPSR classes but not in the controls. A small number of students in the TPSR classes also transferred what they had learned to other contexts outside the program. Initially the teacher had problems giving up control but eventually stated that TPSR was a success and that she would continue to use it.

Summary of empirical research

The empirical literature on responsibility in physical education and sport programs, while not extensive, does address the concern of scholars who have complained about the absence of data-based research in this area (e.g. Newton et al., 2001; Shields and Bredemeier, 1995). Since Cheffers and his associates' early work (1987), both Hodge and Danish (1999) and Romance and his associates (1986) have produced promising results for their philosophical frameworks, the former for life skills and sport and the latter for applying structural developmental moral reasoning to physical education. Two physical education curriculum models, Sport Education and Sport for Peace, also have an empirical basis, as has the TPSR curriculum model. The most robust and significant line of TPSR research is that of Project Effort. A unique component of Project Effort is the development and utilization of individual mentors for program participants. Empirical studies from Project Effort researchers have for the most part focused on retention in responsibility-based programs, transfer of responsibilities from the gym to the classroom, and the development of youth leadership. In this work, as well as in the other TPSR studies noted above, the results are uneven but promising, especially when taking into consideration the low income minority characteristics of most student participants.

Applications to policy and practice

Practice

Much of the philosophical and empirical research reported above was based on practice and fed back into efforts to improve practice. In fact, rather than theory and research dictating practice, an interplay between the two exists. Some speculative essays cited above, for example, often consisted at least in part of reflections based on experiences in practice. In a similar way, some empirical studies cited above were often conducted by a teacher-as-researcher, thereby linking research and practice in ways that no other approach can match, despite the scoffing of some traditional researchers at such biased and value-oriented inquiry. In fact, almost all TPSR research has used some version of teacher-as-researcher, practical inquiry, or service-bonded inquiry. Fortunately, criticism of this family of research methods is in decline, at least for now.

In addition to Gordon's New Zealand physical education teacher study reported above, Mrugala's (2002) exploratory qualitative internet survey of over fifty school physical educators who claim that they use TPSR shed considerable light on the difficulties of putting such curriculum models into practice. This purposive sample of mostly elementary school teachers heard about TPSR from a number of sources; many never had listened to or read the work of someone whose expertise lies with TPSR. The vast majority adopted this approach to deal with discipline problems and implemented it primarily by posting the "levels" on the gym wall, despite strong cautions about using the model this way (Hellison, 2003). Perhaps the most surprising finding was that some, but certainly not all, of the sample reported improving their relationships with their students and becoming more focused on the whole child, despite their initial motivation to improve discipline and their interpretation of TPSR as posting the levels.

Policy

Kahne's (1996) vision for reframing educational policy provides principled advocacy for more democratic and humanistic policy work and moves the discussion to policies that support responsibility-based curriculum theory and practice. He argued that current policies are based mostly on utilitarian and rights-based theories that prioritize equity, efficiency, and excellence, whether policy makers are aware of these theories or not. Kahne, however, advocated a shift in emphasis toward democratic communitarian and humanistic theories, which offer "powerful critiques of the dominant emphasis on utility and rights" (1996: 3). A shift toward self-actualization and the creation of a democratic community in education policy, while not popular among policy analysts, would in Kahne's view be welcomed by the education community. The upshot would be to promote personal and social development in a systematic way, rather than, as policy makers tend to do, promote a litany of desirable educational ends such as self-esteem, honesty, well-roundedness, critical thinking, even though "there is little evidence that all of these goals can be pursued simultaneously or even on agreement of the meaning of the varied terms" (1996: 5–6).

Specific policy applications of personal and social responsibility can be found in suggested or mandated curriculum documents at both the national and international level, as the following examples show.

One of the seven National Association of Sport and Physical Education's (NASPE) standards (National Association for Sport and Physical Education, 1995) is demonstrating responsible personal and social behavior in physical activity settings. Parker and Hellison (2001), building on TPSR, developed a specific curricular example of this standard. This example described responsibility-based physical education learning outcomes, instructional strategies (including transfer from the physical activity setting to other aspects of students' lives), and assessment ideas. In addressing another of the NASPE standards, "understanding and respect for differences among people in physical activity settings" (p. 28), Doolittle and Demas (2001) offered 23 "positive examples" of this standard in practice. Many of these positive examples of understanding and respect involved students taking social responsibility.

Several Canadian curriculum guides include references to teaching responsibility. For example, Saskatchewan (Nick Forsberg, personal communication, 2003) has embedded TPSR in physical education in all grades except grades nine and ten, which utilize the more holistic wellness subject matter to embed TPSR concepts. Even the terms used in the curriculum documents parallel TPSR language quite closely. The New Foundland– Labrador physical education curriculum framework (Mark Jones, personal communication, 2003) uses responsibility language throughout which is particularly evident in the sections on philosophy, the nature of physical education, essential graduation learnings, and key stage curriculum outcomes. This language is strongest for physical education in the intermediate years.

In New Zealand's curriculum framework (Barrie Gordon, personal communication, 2003), responsibility is included in several of the curriculum's eight groupings of essential skills. Examples include taking responsibility for one's own actions, taking responsibility for one's health and safety, and developing a sense of responsibility for the well-being of others.

England's recent emphasis on social inclusion and disaffected youth has given social responsibility a foothold there as well. Holroyd and Armour (2003) of the Institute of Youth Sport at Loughborough University included responsibility as one of several components comprising a promising physical education curriculum for disaffected youth, citing Sport Education, Sport for Peace, and TPSR as specific examples.

And most recently, several regions of Indonesia are beginning to create community sport programs based on personal-social responsibility ideology (Mutohir, 2003). With economic and human resources hanging in the balance, several local governments are looking at ways to empower its citizens and reconstruct a value system that fosters honesty and sustainable development.

Summary of practice and policy

Much of the responsibility curriculum research is linked directly to practice and reflects an interplay between theory and practice. Mrugala (2002) and Gordon (2004) explored practicing physical education teachers' implementation of responsibility-based curriculum ideas. Responsibility has also appeared, sometimes prominently, in curriculum policy documents in the United States, Canada, New Zealand, and England.

Major trends and future directions

Much remains to be done in physical education responsibility curriculum research. On the other hand, most of the work reviewed here is relatively recent, suggesting an upswing in interest that hopefully will continue. Even more recently, responsibility-based research has begun to be carried out internationally.

Such recency of interest and activity inevitably produces research gaps. Regarding TPSR, Martinek's Project Effort research (e.g. 2001, 2003) is an exemplar in attempting to close some of these gaps by focusing on specific issues such as youth leadership and transfer from the physical education program to the school.

Hodge and Danish's (1999) work on life skills through sport seems to be continuing, thereby building an even stronger data base for their compelling programs. Brenda Bredemeier and David Schields' Mendelson Center for Sports, Character, and Community held two national conferences on the Notre Dame campus, the second one with "sports, character, and responsible citizenship" as the conference theme. Such efforts also promise to yield additional related research.

Hellison and Walsh (2002) concluded their review of a number of TPSR studies with the following (abridged) remarks, perhaps reflecting the current state of the art in all physical education responsibility-based curriculum research:

> The 'is it working' question remains a work in progress due to methodological issues and gaps in the evidence, but these ... studies, however limited, do enhance the theoretical and practical potential of [responsibility-based curriculum models] ... Moreover, future research can focus on the methodological shortcomings and evidence gaps as well as to build on what has already been accomplished. (2002: 304)

References

Allen, G. (1997). *Education at risk*. London: Cassell.

Aronowitz, S. (1993). Paulo Freire's radical democratic humanism. In P. McLaren and P. Leonard (Eds.), *Paulo Freire: A Critical Encounter* (pp. 8–24). London: Routledge.

Bain, L.L. (1988). Curriculum for critical reflection in physical education. In R. S. Brandt (Ed.), *Content of the curriculum: 1988 ASCD yearbook* (pp. 133–147). Washington, DC: Association for Supervision and Curriculum Development..

Bain, L.L. (1992). Sport pedagogy. In J.D. Massengale and R.A. Swanson (Eds.), *The history of exercise and sport science* (pp. 18–37). Champaign, IL: Human Kinetics.

Beane, J.A. (1990). *Affect in the curriculum: Toward democracy, dignity, and diversity*. New York: Teachers College Press.

Beedy, J.P. (1997). *Sports plus: Positive learning using sports*. Hamilton, MA: Project Adventure.

Benson, P.L. (1997). *All kids are our kids: What communities must do to raise caring and responsible children and youth*. San Francisco, CA: Jossey-Bass.

Berman, S. (1997). *The development of social responsibility as a meaning making process: The role of schools*. Albany, NY: State University of New York Press.

Bredemeier, B.J., Weiss, M.R., Shields, D.L. and Cooper, B. (1987). Promoting moral growth in a summer sport camp: The implementation of theoretically grounded instructional strategies. *Journal of Moral Education, 15*: 212–220.

Bredemeier, M.E. (1988). *Urban portraits: Teachers who make a difference*. New York: Lang.

Bressan, E.S. (1982). An academic discipline for physical education: What a fine mess! *NAPHE Proceedings, 7*: 3.

Bressan, E.S. (1987). The future of scholarship in physical education. In J. Massengale (Ed.), *Trends toward the future in physical education* (pp. 25–36). Champaign, IL: Human Kinetics.

Broekhoff, J. (1968). Chivalric education in the Middle Ages. *Quest, 11*: 24–31.

Burns, J.M. (1978). *Leadership*. New York: Harper Collins.

Carson, T.B. (1992). Remembering, forward: Reflections of education for peace. In W. Pinar and W, Reynolds (Eds.), *Understanding curriculum as phenomenological and deconstructed text*. New York: Teachers College Press.

Cheffers, J. (1987). Tuesdays and Thursdays with Boston's inner-city youth. *Quest, 49*: 50–66..

Crum, B. (1986). Concerning the quality of the development of knowledge in sport pedagogy. *Journal of Teaching in Physical Education, 5*: 211–220.

Cutforth, N.J. and Puckett, K.M. (1999). An investigation into the organization, challenges, and impact of an urban apprentice teacher program. The *Urban Review, 31*: 153–172.

Danish, S. and Nellen, V.C. (1997). New roles for sport psychologists: Teaching life skills through sport to at-risk youth. *Quest, 49*: 100–113.

deCharms, R. (1976). *Enhancing motivation: Change in the classroom:* New York: Irvington.

DeLine, J. (1991). Why ... can't they get along? *Journal of Physical Education, Recreation and Dance, 62*: 21–26.

Doolittle, S. and Demas, K. (2001). Fostering respect through physical activity. *Journal of Teaching in Physical Education, 72*: 28–33.

Elias, M.J., Zins, J.E., Weissberg, R.P. et al., (1997). *Promoting Social and Emotional Learning: Guidelines for Educators*. Alexandria, VA: ASCD.

Ennis, C.D. (1999). Communicating the value of active, healthy, lifestyles to urban students. *Quest, 51*: 164–169.

Ennis, C.D., Solmon, M.A., Satina, B., Loftus, S.J., Mensch, J. and McCauley, M.T. (1999). Creating a sense of family in urban schools using the Sport for Peace curriculum. *Research Quarterly for Sport and Exercise, 70*: 273–285.

Escarti, A., Pascual, C., and Gutierrez, Melchor (2005). *Responsibilidad personal y social a traves de la education fisica y el deporte*. Barcelona, Spain: GRAO.

Fernández-Balboa, J.M. (Ed.) (1997). *Critical postmodernism in human movement, physical education and sport*. Albany, NY: State University of New York Press.

Fowler, S.B. (1998). "Under the shade of this mango tree"; Reflections on a pedagogical practice that crosses disciplinary boundaries. *Quest, 50*: 319–322.

Freire, P. (1970/1993). *Pedagogy of the oppressed.* New York: Continuum.

Gerber, E.W. (1971). *Innovators and institutions in physical education.* Philadelphia, PA: Lea and Febiger.

Gibbons, S.L. and Bressan, E.S. (1991). The affective domain in physical education: A conceptual clarification and curricular commitment. *Quest, 43*: 78–97.

Gibbons, S.L., Ebbeck, V. and Weiss, M.R. (1995). Fair play for kids: Effects on the moral development of children in physical education. *Research Quarterly for Sport and Exercise, 66*: 247–255.

Gilligan, C. (1982). *In a different voice.* Cambridge: Harvard University Press.

Glass, R.D. (2001). On Paulo Freire's philosophy of praxis and the foundations of liberation education. *Educational Researcher, 30*: 15–25.

Gordon, B. (2005). *An evaluation of a six month implementation of the responsibility model in a New Zealand secondary school.* Doctoral dissertation, Massey University College of Education, Palmerston North, New Zealand.

Grant, B. (1992). Integrating sport education into the physical education curriculum in New Zealand secondary schools. *Quest, 44*: 304–316.

Haberman, M. (2000). Urban schools: Day camps or custodial centers. *Phi Delta Kappan, 82*: 203–208.

Hastie, P.A. and Buchanan, A.M. (2000). Teaching responsibility through sport education: Prospects for a coalition. *Research Quarterly for Sport and Exercise, 71*: 25–35.

Hastie, P.A. and Sharpe, T. (1999). Effects of a sport education curriculum on the positive social behaviors of at-risk rural adolescent boys. *Journal of Education for Students Placed At Risk, 4*: 417–439.

Hellison, D. (1973). *Humanistic physical education.* Englewood Cliffs, NJ: Prentice-Hall.

Hellison, D. (1978). *Beyond balls and bats: Alienated (and other) youth in the gym.* Washington, DC: AAHPER.

Hellison, D. (1985). *Goals and strategies for physical education.* Champaign, IL: Human Kinetics.

Hellison, D. (1995). *Teaching responsibility through physical activity (1st ed.).* Champaign, IL: Human Kinetics.

Hellison, D. (1997). A practical inquiry into the critical postmodernist perspective in physical education. In J.M. Fernandez-Balboa, (Ed.), *Critical postmodernism in human movement, physical education, and sport* (pp. 197–205). Albany, NY: State University of New York Press.

Hellison, D. (2003). *Teaching responsibility through physical activity* (2nd ed.). Champaign, IL: Human Kinetics.

Hellison, D. and Cutforth, N. (1997). Extended day programs for urban children and youth: From theory to practice. In H. Walberg, O. Reyes and R. Weissberg (Eds.), *Children and youth: Interdisciplinary perspectives* (pp. 223–249). San Francisco, CA: Jossey-Bass.

Hellison, D., Cutforth, N., Kallusky, J., Martinek, T., Parker, M. and Stiehl, J. (2000). *Youth development and physical activity: Linking universities and communities.* Champaign, IL: Human Kinetics.

Hellison, D. and Kallusky, J. (1999). The youth leader project partnership in physical education in higher education. *The Chronicle of Physical Education in Higher Education, 10*: 6, 14.

Hellison, D., Martinek, T. and Cutforth, N. (1996). Beyond violence prevention in inner-city physical activity programs. *Peace and Conflict: Journal of Peace Psychology, 2*: 321–337.

Hellison, D. and Templin, T. (1991). *A reflective approach to teaching physical education.* Champaign, IL: Human Kinetics.

Hellison, D. and Walsh, D. (2002). Responsibility-based youth programs evaluation: Investigating the investigations. *Quest, 54*: 292–307.

Hellison, D. and Wright, P. (2003). Retention in an urban extended day program: A process-based assessment. *Journal of Teaching in Physical Education, 22*: 369–383).

Hichwa, J. (1998). *Right fielders are people too.* Champaign, IL: Human Kinetics.

Hodge, K. and Danish, S. (1999). Promoting life skills for adolescent boys through sport. In A.M. Horne and M.S. Kiselica (Eds.), *Handbook of counseling boys and adolescent males* (pp. 55–71). Thousand Oaks, CA: Sage.

Holroyd, R. and Armour, K. (2003) *Re-engaging disaffected youth through physical activity programs.* Paper presented at the British Educational Research Association Annual Conference, Heriot-Watt University, Edinburgh.

Horrocks, R.N. (1978). Resolving conflict in the gymnasium. *Journal of Physical Education, Recreation and Dance, 49*: 6.

Jones, R.S. and Tanner, L.N. (1981). Classroom discipline: The unclaimed legacy. *Phi Delta Kappan, 63*: 494–497.

Kaardal, K. (2001). *Learning by choice in secondary physical education: Creating a goal-directed program.* Champaign, IL: Human Kinetics.

Kahne, J. (1996). *Reframing educational policy: Democracy, community, and the individual.* New York: Teachers College Press.

Kammi, C., Clark, F.B. and Dominick, A. (1994). Six national goals: A road to disappointment. *Phi Delta Kappan, 75*: 672–677.

Kirk, D. (1991). Curriculum work in physical education: Beyond the objectives approach? *Journal of Teaching in Physical Education, 12*: 244–265.

Kirk, D, (1992). *Articulations and silences in sociallly critical research on physical education: Towards a new agenda.* Paper presented at the AARE Annual Conference, Geelong, Australia.

Kohlberg, L. (1971). Stages of moral development as a basis for moral development. In C.M. Beck, B.S. Crittenden and E.V. Sullivan (Eds.), *Moral education: Interdisciplinary approaches* (pp. 23–92). Toronto, Canada: University of Toronto Press.

Kretchmar, R.S. (1994). *Practical philosophy of sport.* Champaign, IL: Human Kinetics.

Laker, A. (2000). *Beyond the boundaries of physical education.* New York: Rutledge-Falmer.

Lavay, B.W., French, R. and Henderson, H.L. (1997). *Positive behavior management Strategies for physical educators.* Champaign, IL: Human Kinetics.

Martín, P.J.J. (2000). *An intervention model for values education to at risk youth through physical activity and sport.* Doctoral dissertation, Technical University of Madrid, Madrid, Spain.

Macdonald, D., Kirk, D., Metzler, M., Nilges, L.M., Schempp, P. and Wright, J. (2002). It's all very well, in theory: Theoretical perspectives and their applications in contemporary pedagogy. *Quest, 54*: 133–156.

Martin, P.S.S. (2000). *An intervention model for values education to at risk youth through physical activity and sport.* Doctoral dissertation, Technical University of Madrid, Madrid, Spain.

Martinek, T. and Griffith, J.B. (1993). Working with the learned helpless child. *Journal of Physical Education, Recreation and Dance, 64*: 17–20.

Martinek, T. and Hellison, D. (1997). Service-bonded inquiry: The road less traveled. *Journal of Teaching in Physical Education, 17*: 107–121.

Martinek, T. and Hellison, D. (1998) Values and goal setting with underserved youth. *Journal of Physical Education, Recreation, and Dance, 69*: 47–52.

Martinek, T., Hellison, D. and Walsh, D. (2004). Service-bonded inquiry revisited: A research model for the community-engaged professor. *Quest, 56*: 397–412.

Martinek, T., McLaughlin, D. and Schilling, T. (2004). Project effort: Teaching responsibility beyond the gym. *Journal of Physical Education, Recreation, and Dance, 70*: 12–25.

Martinek, T. and Schilling, T. (2003) Developing compassionate leadership in underserved youth. *Journal of Physical Education, Recreation, and Dance, 74*: 33–39.

Martinek, T., Schilling, T. and Johnson, D. (2001). Evaluation of a sport and mentoring program designed to foster personal and social responsibility in underserved youth. *The Urban Review, 33*: 29–45.

McLaughlin, M.W. (2000). *Community counts.* Washington, DC: Public Education Network.

McLaughlin, M.W., Irby, M.A. and Langman, J. (1994). *Urban sanctuaries: neighborhood organizations in the lives and futures of inner-city youth.* San Francisco, CA: Jossey- Bass.

Miller, R.F. and Jarman, B.O. (1988). Moral and ethical character development: Views from past leaders. *Journal of Physical Education, Recreation, and Dance, 59*: 72–78.

Mrugala, J. (2002). *Exploratory study of responsibility model practitioners.* Doctoral dissertation, University of Illinois at Chicago.

Mutohir, A.T. (2003). *Peace, friendship, and sustainable development.* Paper presented at the International Conference on Sport and Sustainable Development, Yogyakarta, West Java, Indonesia.

National Association for Sport and Physical Education. (1995). *Moving into the future: National physical education standards: A guide to content and assessment.* Reston, VA: National Association of Sport and Physical Education.

Newton, M., Sandberg, J. and Watson, D.L. (2001). Utilizing adventure education with the model of moral action. *Quest, 53*: 483–494.

Noddings, N. (1992). *The challenge to care in schools: An alternative approach to education.* New York: Teachers College Press.

Parker, M. and Hellison, D. (2001). Teaching responsibility in physical education: Standards, outcomes, and beyond. *Journal of Physical Education, Recreation, and Dance, 72*: 25–27.

Patton, M. (1987). *Creative evaluation.* Newbury Park, CA: Sage.

Romance, T.J., Weiss, M.R. and Bockoven, J. (1986). A program to promote moral development through elementary school physical education. *Journal of Teaching in Physical Education, 5*: 126–136.

Rovegno, I. and Kirk, D. (1995). Articulations and silences in socially critical work on physical education: Toward a broader agenda. *Quest, 47*: 447–474.

Sage, G.H. (1990). *Power and ideology in American sport: A critical perspective.* Champaign, IL: Human Kinetics.

Scanlon, T.K., Carpenter, P.J., Schmidt, G.W., Simons, J.P. and Keeler, B. (1993). An introduction to the sport commitment model. *Journal of Exercise and Sport Psychology, 15*: 1–15.

Schilling, T. (2001). An investigation of commitment among participants in an extended day physical activity program. *Research Quarterly for Exercise and Sport, 72*: 355–365.

Schilling, T., Martinek, T. and Tan, C. (2001). Fostering youth development through empowerment. In B.J. Lombardo, T.J. Caravella-Nadeau, H.S. Castagno, and V.H. Mancini (Eds.) *Sport in the twenty-first century: Alternatives for the New millennium* (pp. 169–179). Boston, MA: Pearson Custom Publishing.

Schubert, W.H. (1982). Curriculum Research. In H.E. Mitzel (Ed.), *Encyclopedia of Educational Research*, Vol. 1 (5th ed. pp. 420–431). New York: Free Press.

Schubert, W. H. (1986). *Curriculum: perspective, paradigm, and possibility.* New York: Macmillan.

Schwab, J.J. (1971). The practical: Arts of eclectic. *School Review, 79*: 493–542.

Shields, D.L.L. and Bredemeier, B.J.L. (1995). *Character development and physical activity.* Champaign, IL: Human Kinetics.

Sherrill, C. (2004). *Adapted physical activity, recreation, and sport* (6th ed.). Boston, MA: McGraw-Hill.

Short, E.C. (Ed.) (1991). *Forms of curriculum inquiry.* Albany, NY: State University of New York Press.

Siedentop, D. (1980). *Physical education: Introductory analysis* (3rd ed.). Wm. C. Brown.

Siedentop, D. (1990). *Introduction to physical education, fitness, and sport.* Mountain View, CA: Mayfield.

Siedentop, D. (1994). *Sport education: Quality PE through positive sport experiences.* Champaign, IL: Human Kinetics.

Siedentop, D., Mand, C. and Taggart, A. (1986). Physical education: Curriculum and instruction strategies for grades 5–12. Palo Alto, CA: Mayfield.

Steinhardt, M. (1992). Physical education. In P.W. Jackson (Ed.), *Handbook of research on curriculum* (pp. 964–1001). New York: Macmillan.

Sizer, T.R. (1992). *Horace's school: Redesigning the American high school*. Boston MA: Houghton Mifflin.

Stiehl, J. (1993). Becoming responsible: Theoretical and practical considerations. *Journal of Physical Education, Recreation, and Dance, 64*: 38–40, 57–59, 70–71.

Tappan, R.B. (1992). Educating for character: How our schools can teach respect and responsibility. *Journal of Teacher Education, 43*: 386–389.

Van Linden, J.A. and Fertman, C.I. (1998). *Youth leadership: A guide to understanding leadership development in adolescents*. San Francisco, CA: Jossey-Bass.

Wallhead, T.L., and Ntoumanis, N. (2004). Effects of a sport education intervention on students' motivational responses in physical education. *Journal of Teaching in Physical Education, 23*: 4–18.

Wang, M.C. and Gordon, E.W. (Eds.) (1994). *Educational resilience in inner-city America*. Hillsdale, NJ: Lawrence Erlbaum.

Watson, D.L., Newton, M. and Kim, Mi-Sook (2003). Recognition of values-based constructs in a summer physical activity program. *Urban Review, 35*: 221–232.

Wentzel, K.R. (1991). Social competence at school: Relation between social responsibility and academic achievement. *Review of Educational Research, 61*: 1–24.

Wight, A.R. (1972). *Toward a definition of affect*. Salt Lake City, UT: Interstate Educational Resource Center.

Winnick, J. (2000). *Adapted physical education and sport* (3rd ed.). Champaign, IL: Human Kinetics.

Wright, P.M. and White, K. (2004). Exploring the relevance of the personal and social responsibility model in adapted physical activity" A collective case study. *Journal of Teaching Physical Education, 23*: 71–87.

5.5 Game-centered approaches to teaching physical education

JUDY OSLIN AND STEPHEN MITCHELL

Introduction

The purpose of this chapter is to provide a review of research on game-centered teaching (GCA), specifically the literature stemming from the Teaching Games for Understanding model proposed by Bunker and Thorpe (1982). Initially, this chapter's authors were assigned to "review the games teaching and coaching literature," however research on game-centered coaching appears to be in the conceptual stage and contains primarily anecdotal accounts proclaiming the merits of the approach. This is not unlike the GCA literature, thus there is hope that a body of research on games-centered coaching will soon emerge and add to the GCA research base. The chapter begins with an historical perspective of the emergence of GCAs, first as it conceptually evolved and later as it expanded to youth sport initiatives. The next section of the review examines core concepts such as motivation, transfer, decision-making, and theories that have underpinned GCAs, from information processing theory to the integration of situated and constraint theories. This second section also integrates aspects of the motor learning literature particularly as it applies to information processing and decision-making during sport performance. The third section of the review, titled "major findings," begins with a review of GCA studies that focus on comparative analyses of technical and tactical approaches. A review of literature on game performance assessment precedes a review of more recent studies that have investigated the processes involved in GCAs to teaching and learning. Following this portion of the major findings is a segment on responses to GCAs, which includes research on perceptions of preservice teachers, future teacher educators, as well as public school students and their teachers. Finally, this review of GCA literature culminates in a discussion of trends and future directions.

Historical perspectives on GCAs

Growth of competitive sport around the mid 1900s gave impetus to the inclusion of games into the physical education curriculum, particularly at the secondary level. Similar to dance and gymnastics, development of technical proficiency was, and still is, considered to be the primary goal of games education. The technical or skill-based approach, which emphasizes acquisition of skills before the introduction of rules and game play, remains the most commonly used approach by both physical educators and sport coaches.

Bunker, Thorpe, and Almond (1982) posited that technical approaches to games teaching were associated with development of the discipline of physical education in the 1960s. The emphasis of most teacher training programs was, as it is now, on skill acquisition, measurement, and evaluation, which promoted the quantification of isolated techniques. In addition, Bunker and Thorpe suggested that methods courses generally required that lessons be organized so that content could be "easily documented" (e.g. first – an introductory activity; second – skill practice; and last – a culminating activity), which fostered the use of more direct methods of instruction, generally command or task. "Thus the focus of skill acquisition courses and desire for order in methodology may have reinforced an approach which was already well embedded in student teachers who, as skilled performers, had been through highly technique oriented coaching procedures." (p. 27).

The notion that games could be used to help children develop psychomotor skills was first proposed by Maulden and Redfern (1969) in their seminal book *Games Teaching: A New Approach for the Primary School*. Characterizing the rationale for including games in secondary physical education curriculum (e.g. "socializing," "character-building," burn off excess energy, and preparation for lifetime

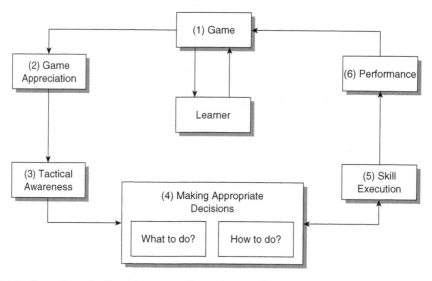

Figure 5.5.1 Procedures for Teaching games for understanding approach (Thorpe et al., 1986)

leisure activities) as "indefensible on educational grounds," Maulden and Redfern (1969) defended inclusion of games in the primary curriculum if, and only if, games could provide educational opportunities for all children.

Based on a developmental perspective and a movement education approach (Laban, 1963), Maulden and Redfern (1969) emphasized teaching the physical aspects of games as well as social, moral, and intellectual components. In addition, Maulden and Redfern proposed: (1) developmental stages in games, leading to the development of skillfulness; (2) use of a problem-solving approach through game-like situations to highlight tactical situations; (3) grouping skills according to generalized constructs (e.g., sending away, gaining possession, and traveling with an object); (4) games categories (net, batting, and running) as a way of addressing similarities and analyzing game play; and (5) games invention, as a means of giving children choice and an appreciation for the value of rules. Maulden and Redfern's (1969/1981) approach to games teaching was directed primarily toward elementary physical education. However, there is no evidence to suggest that these concepts and methods were broadly adopted in secondary physical education.

In 1982, Bunker and Thorpe proposed a game-centered model for secondary physical education called Teaching Games for Understanding (TGfU). This model was reprinted in 1983 and again in 1986. Influenced by the work of Wade (1967) and Maulden's (1981) problem-based approach to teaching gymnastics (Thorpe, 2001), Bunker and Thorpe identified the tendency of games to motivate children and suggested that games could be designed to be developmentally appropriate and

"conditioned" to highlight specific tactical situations. They also proposed that games provided the contextual requirements needed to develop "skillful" performers and therefore games should be the central feature of the lesson. As seen in Figure 5.5.1, Bunker and Thorpe (1982/1983/1986) proposed a framework for "Games Education" that was game-centered and child-centered, with the intent to allow, "… every child to participate in decision-making based upon tactical awareness thereby retaining an interest and involvement in the game" (p. 8). The TGfU framework included: (1) game forms – use of a variety of developmentally appropriate game forms; (2) game appreciation – intentional use of rules to help children understand how rules shape games; (3) tactical awareness – promoting understanding of how tactics should be used in game play; (4) decision-making – helping children understand "what to do" or the ability to recognize cues and predict possible outcomes during a game situation – and "how to do it" or the selection of appropriate responses; (5) skill execution – producing the required movement in the context of the game; and (6) performance – "observed outcome," which should be a "… measure of the appropriateness of the response as well as the efficiency of the technique" (p. 10). As illustrated by this model, Bunker and Thorpe advocated presenting the game (i.e. game appreciation, tactical awareness, and decision-making) before addressing skill execution.

Ellis (1983) and Almond (1986) proposed a thematic approach to games classification, with the intent of categorizing games according to their tactical similarities. Ellis's categories included: territory, field, court, and target games. Similarly,

Almond's (1986) categories included: invasion, net/wall, fielding/run scoring, and target games. Categories in both of these classification systems are essentially the same, yet there are some differences in the subcategories. For example, Ellis breaks down territory games in to goal (e.g. basketball and soccer) and line (e.g. football and rugby) subcategories, where as Almond breaks down invasion games into three sub-categories: handball (e.g. basketball and team handball); football (e.g. soccer and American football); and stick-ball (e.g. hockey and lacrosse). Ellis (1983) suggested that it was important to teach students to understand similarities and differences between games in order to teach students what games were about and to help them understand the benefits of playing games. Furthermore, games categories provided a basis from which to extend the TGfU approach from an alternative lesson format to a means of identifying and sequencing content in the physical education curriculum (Mitchell and Oslin, 2005).

Thorpe et al. (1984) further extended the TGfU model to include: sampling, modification-representation, modification-exaggeration, and tactical complexity. The intent of these principles was to guide teachers in the design of developmentally appropriate games, since many of the teachers lacked understanding and therefore were unable to conceptualize or modify games to highlight important aspects of tactical play. Sampling referred to the selection of games according categories, using games from the same category to demonstrate similarities between games. Through modification-representation, Thorpe, Bunker, and Almond suggested that games should be designed to represent the same tactical structures as the adult game, but with modifications to equipment and reductions in the number of players to accommodate age and developmental abilities of children. Modification-exaggeration is required when primary rules break down or there is a need to emphasize a particular aspect of the game. For example, a long, thin badminton court exaggerates the need to use a clear or drop shot to "create space" on the court and thus score points. For the final principle, tactical complexity, Thorpe, Bunker, and Almond recommended that teachers consider the tactical complexity of games during the process of sampling, noting that children are likely to be introduced to tactically complex games such as soccer prior to less complex games such as badminton.

Influenced by the original TGfU model, the games categories proposed by Almond (1986), and John Kessel's games approach to volleyball, Griffin et al. (1997) developed the tactical games model (TGM). Griffin et al. (1997) discovered that TGfU required considerable knowledge and tactical understanding of games, which prohibited many teachers from using the model, particularly given the extent of games content and constraints of public school physical education (Oslin, 1996). The TGM includes tactical frameworks to help teachers and students identify tactical problems (and solutions) common to games, in and across game categories. In their first text, directed toward secondary level physical education, Griffin et al. (1997) suggested that content selection and instruction ought to be more game specific to allow for greater tactical and skill complexity. The TGM varied from TGfU in that it proposed a progression of games along with tactical- and skill-based practices in a game–practice–game format to accommodate and assist teachers with lesson planning and instruction. Mitchell et al. (2003) extended the TGM to games teaching at the elementary level, by using a thematic approach to emphasize the integration of several games from the same category thus taking advantage of the similarities between games while at the same time accommodating elementary specialists' need for efficiently integrating instructional content.

Play Practice, developed by Launder (2001), is another variation of the GCA. According to Piltz (2003), the evolution of the play practice model occurred "parallel" to the TGfU model and was the result of Launder's "lifetime" of experiences as a teacher, coach, physical educator, and teacher/coach educator. Similar to TGfU, the work of Wade (1967) influenced the play practice approach, thus it has similar elements such as modified and mini games that emphasize development of game sense. According to Piltz, the play practice approach clarifies the specific elements of game play by providing definitions for terms such as technique, skill, and game sense and provides a framework for designing learning experiences. Launder uses principles of shaping play, focusing play, and enhancing play to create play practice progressions.

The appeal of GCA concepts and methods has not been limited to the physical education context, as a number of youth sport initiatives were developed and supported by national initiatives in Britain, Australia, New Zealand, and Canada. For example, Playsport was designed by Thorpe and a research assistant to address the needs of coaches, parents, and teachers who did not know games well enough to implement TGfU. Whereas TGfU proposed that the teacher design games and respond to problems to help students identify and apply solutions, Playsport and "TOP play" do not have these requirements. Instead, a set progression of mini-games is presented, and as children meet the challenges of one game, the coach then presents the next game. The Game Sense approach, recently introduced in Australia and New Zealand, incorporates elements of TGfU and "TOP play." According to Thorpe (2003), the game sense approach promotes questioning and a player-centered approach, which challenges coaches to change their coaching style as well as their approach (Kidman, 2001).

As exemplified in the following sections, current research reflects a growing interest and expanded efforts to explore the potential of GCAs to impact learning and performance in physical education. While GCAs have been applied in youth, adult, and elite sport contexts, results have yet to extend beyond anecdotal accounts.

Core concepts and theoretical underpinnings

All GCAs, TGfU or Game Sense (Bunker and Thorpe, 1982), TGM (Griffin et al., 1997), and Play Practice (Launder, 2001), advocate learners playing the game (modified and/or mini) as the central organizational feature of a lesson. Modified games are designed or conditioned to highlight particular tactics that are found in a variety of games, such as defending a goal or space or advancing the ball toward the goal or target. Game "conditions" relate to rules, methods of scoring, and goal of the game, and serve to give the game structure and purpose. Mini games are defined as smaller versions of full-sided, adult versions of the game (Thorpe, 2001). Proponents of GCAs contend that the game contains a number of essential features that make a tactical model superior to the traditional or technique model, which promotes skill development prior to introducing tactics and strategy: (1) Children are motivated by games, (2) tactical similarities between games increase potential for children to transfer decision-making skills from one game to another games, (3) games promote development of decision-making, and (4) games promote development of decision-makers, which assumes the use of a problem-solving approach.

In the following section, essential features of games will be used to address core concepts and theoretical underpinnings of GCAs. Relative to cognitive development and sport performance, the motor learning literature has advanced considerably in the past twenty years and has underpinned much of the GCA literature in sport pedagogy. The following review will include aspects of the motor learning literature that apply to cognitive development and information-processing – particularly development of expertise in sport performance.

Motivation

Recognizing the potential of games to motivate students, Bunker and Thorpe (1982) proposed that game play as the central feature of a lesson. The potential for games to enhance students' intrinsic desire to play games was also recognized by many teachers with whom Bunker, Thorpe, and Almond worked (Almond and Thorpe, 1988). Thorpe

(1992) noted that while adults who know the game may be motivated to improve their techniques, most children would prefer to play the game using the skills they have. Once in the game, children come to appreciate the purpose and value of good technique and therefore become more motivated to practice (Bunker and Thorpe, 1982). Along with game play, Thorpe (1992) suggested a number of other incentives that could potentially motivate children to play games, such as affiliation, achievement, stress or sensation (factors such as excitement, nervousness, anxiety, etc.), social facilitation, self direction, and perceptual-motor skills (i.e. perception, decision-making, and response).

Transfer

In the original Bunker and Thorpe model (1982), the game was considered necessary to provide a context for presenting a perceptual problem that requires children to seek a solution (decision-making) and then determine a response (Thorpe, 1992). Thus, emphasis was placed on designing and implementing conditioned games that children could play with the skills they possessed, then providing skill instruction when children were ready. For example, if a child cannot perform a forehand drive with a tennis racket, he/she might use an underhand toss to initially solve the problem of keeping the ball in play. It was Bunker and Thorpe's contention that the requirement for skill performance has the potential to keep children from learning the perceptual and decision-making components of game play. However, the recommendation for substituting one skill for another assumes that decision-making features in one game will transfer to another similar game.

Piggott (1982) suggested that performing movement patterns (motor programs) across a variety of contexts was consistent with the underlying premise of schema theory, and thus supported the notion that skills could be transferred (e.g. an overhand throw to overhead racket shots). According to Piggott (1982), schema theory also supported transfer of principles underlying game play. Schemata were seen as being responsible for prescribing details needed for skill execution, whereas decision-making was considered the responsibility of higher centers of the central nervous system. Thus, understanding the higher order rules or tactics in one game had the potential to enhance understanding and application in another game.

Action Systems Theory (Handford et al., 1997; also known as dynamical systems theory) also supports the possibility of transfer, and suggests that the learner's interactions with the environment are dictated by constraints imposed by the environment and the task. Positive transfer can occur even when some of the constraints are modified, if the goal of the game remains the same (Handford et al., 1997).

Research on the effects of blocked and variable practice has also provided support for transfer (Ota and Vickers, 1999; Singer et al., 1989; Wrisberg and Liu, 1991). Based on this body of motor learning literature, Mitchell and Oslin (1999a) investigated transfer of tactical concepts in net games, from badminton to pickleball. High school students demonstrated significant improvement in decision-making from the beginning to the end of the badminton unit. While not significant, the students demonstrated that they were able to maintain and slightly improve their decision-making skills by the end of the pickleball unit (Mitchell and Oslin, 1999a).

In a study of transfer in invasion games (Contreras Jordan et al., 2003), students (10–11-year-olds) demonstrated transfer of dribbling decisions from a generic invasion game to hockey. However, they were unable to transfer passing decisions. Investigators concluded that the length of the hockey sticks may have imposed constraints that were not present in the generic invasion game. Overall, findings from Contreras Jordan et al. and Mitchell and Oslin (1999a) suggest the potential for transfer between games in the same category. This supports the assumptions of Thorpe et al. (1986) regarding the transfer of tactics and suggests that the potential for transfer ought to be a consideration when making curricular decisions about sequencing of games in physical education (Mitchell and Oslin, 1999a).

Decision-making

According to Bunker and Thorpe (1982), to be a proficient games player, the child needs to make decisions regarding "What to do?" and "How to do it?". "What to do?" involves recognizing cues and predicting outcomes. These processes include functions such as, selective attention, perception, and anticipation. "How to do it?" requires the student to choose an appropriate response given the particular environmental constraints. For example, the decision regarding "how to" take a shot on goal is dependent upon how much time is available to shoot, which may (or may not) allow the performer an additional touch to control the ball prior to taking the shot.

As described by Bunker and Thorpe (1982), both "What to do?" and "How to do it?" relate to response selection, which requires procedural knowledge. However, researchers in the sport domain of motor learning have associated "What to do?" with declarative knowledge and "doing it" with procedural knowledge (Magill, 1993). Recognizing the complexity of various types of knowledge used in sports, Abernethy et al. (1993) stated that "how to" could refer to either response selection or response execution, depending upon the tactical complexity of the motor task. During high complex motor tasks both decision-making and skill execution may have procedures, where as with low complexity motor tasks procedural knowledge may relate exclusively to skill execution (Abernethy et al., 1993).

Abernethy et al. (1993), McPherson (1994) and others have suggested that accessibility to procedural knowledge may be more a function of the methods used to examine movement selection processes in contrast to movement execution processes, particularly when investigating decision-making components of high complexity motor tasks. McPherson (1994) proposed a model for conceptualizing and identifying the possible levels of analysis, using the response selection and response execution continuum juxtaposed with the declarative (what to do) and procedural (doing it) continuum (see Figure 5.5.2). This is consistent with Abernethy et al.'s contention that response execution and response selection aspects of decision-making can be both declarative and procedural, depending on the research question and the ways in which that question is addressed. As shown in Figure 5.5.2, components of performance are positioned across the top from left (response selection) to right (response execution). A second continuum is represented vertically, which ranges from declarative knowledge ("What to do") at the top to procedural knowledge ("Doing it") at the bottom. The model uses tennis to illustrate possible levels of analysis, along with potential research questions and the tools for addressing these questions. These continua are positioned within the context of game play, with performers in less game-like situations at the top and more game-like contexts as the continuum extends toward the bottom. According to McPherson, "The points of possibility along each continua are actually representative of a dynamic process in which any change in one level of analysis (e.g. a research question, a tool used to address that question, or experimental context) may produce a change in position along any one continuum" (p. 226). For those interested in examining the cognitive aspects of game performance, this model provides a useful framework for identifying levels of analysis during the conceptual phase of a study as well as a method of analyzing and synthesizing previous research.

The knowledge-based, information-processing perspective has served as the primary theoretical framework from which most of the research on GCAs has been based. Researchers in cognitive psychology originally used an information-processing framework to study differences between expert and novice cognitive knowledge. A summary of these findings, found throughout the motor learning (Chi et al., 1988; Glasser and Chi, 1988; Starkes and Allard, 1993; Thomas et al., 1988) and sport pedagogy literature (Dodds et al., 2001; French

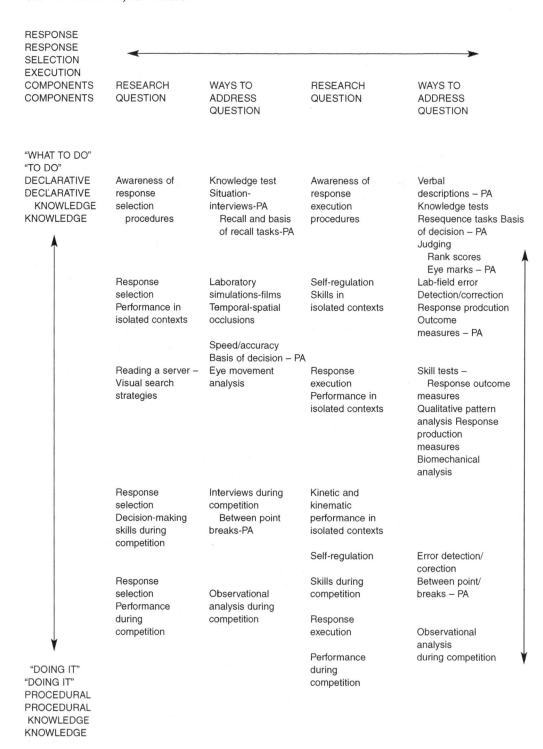

RESPONSE RESPONSE SELECTION EXECUTION COMPONENTS COMPONENTS	RESEARCH QUESTION	WAYS TO ADDRESS QUESTION	RESEARCH QUESTION	WAYS TO ADDRESS QUESTION
"WHAT TO DO" "TO DO" DECLARATIVE DECLARATIVE KNOWLEDGE KNOWLEDGE	Awareness of response selection procedures	Knowledge test Situation-interviews-PA Recall and basis of recall tasks-PA	Awareness of response execution procedures	Verbal descriptions – PA Knowledge tests Resequence tasks Basis of decision – PA Judging Rank scores Eye marks – PA
	Response selection Performance in isolated contexts	Laboratory simulations-films Temporal-spatial occlusions Speed/accuracy Basis of decision – PA	Self-regulation Skills in isolated contexts	Lab-field error Detection/correction Response prodcution Outcome measures – PA
	Reading a server – Visual search strategies	Eye movement analysis	Response execution Performance in isolated contexts	Skill tests – Response outcome measures Qualitative pattern analysis Response production measures Biomechanical analysis
	Response selection Decision-making skills during competition	Interviews during competition Between point breaks-PA	Kinetic and kinematic performance in isolated contexts	
			Self-regulation	Error detection/corection Between point/breaks – PA
	Response selection Performance during competition	Observational analysis during competition	Skills during competition Response execution Performance during competition	Observational analysis during competition
"DOING IT" "DOING IT" PROCEDURAL PROCEDURAL KNOWLEDGE KNOWLEDGE				

Figure 5.5.2 Response selection and response execution continuum (McPherson, 1994)

et al., 1996; Rovegno et al., 2001, Turner and Martinek, 1995), suggest that experts tend to be superior to novices relative to: (a) the organization and structure of declarative and procedural knowledge; (b) decision-making; (c) pattern recognition; (d) anticipation of game events; (e) visual search and selection of cues; (f) retrieval of information from the game environment; (g) retrieval of information from short- and long-term memory, and (h) speed of information processing.

Developing decision-makers

Whereas much of the early GCA research focused on acquisition of cognitive knowledge from an information-processing perspective, the most recent research focused on instructional aspects of the approach, which emphasized the student as an active learner. Compared to the technical approach where the teacher/coach has control over decision-making during game play, GCAs advocate the use of problem-solving to position students in the role of decision-maker. Thus, positioning students as active agents in their own learning has served to align GCAs with constructivist perspectives (Grehaigne and Godbout, 1995; Kirk and Macdonald, 1998; Kirk and MacPhail, 2002; Mahut et al., 2003).

With GCAs, teachers are called upon to construct and implement conditioned games that pose tactical problems for students to interpret and solve, with guidance from the teacher and/or peers. Understanding students' prior knowledge, aids the teacher in constructing meaningful tasks, which require the student to interpret the setting and respond from his/her own point of view (Dodds et al., 2001). Using information processing along with alternative conceptions in science education, Dodds et al. investigated development of domain-specific knowledge in children. Dodds et al. contended that understanding, "…the content of children's prior knowledge and their processes for acquiring new knowledge" [ought to lead to the] "…design of effective instructional practices" that will help learners acquire and incorporate new information with their prior "domain-specific knowledge". (p. 306). Alternative conceptions perspective takes into account the active role of the learner in the learning process, the cumulative effects of learning, the function of prior learning, the hierarchical arrangement of knowledge in memory, as well as the validity of the learning context (see Dodds et al., 2001: 306–307, for an overview of alternative conceptions research in science education. Findings from Dodds et al. are presented in the Major Findings section of this chapter).

Rovegno and her colleagues at the University of Alabama grounded a multidimensional study in situated, constraint, and information-processing theoretical perspectives as a means of understanding the learning and teaching of tactical skills and knowledge. Informed by Clancey (1997) who suggested that multiple perspectives were necessary to account for both action and cognition, Rovegno et al. (2001) contended that use of multiple perspectives provided the study of content, instruction, and learning concurrently in a naturalistic context.

Situated perspective represents a shift from knowledge-based approaches (Clancey, 1997) to the study of knowledge in action (Rovegno et al., 2001). According to Kirk and MacPhail (2002), many of the key assumptions, which underpin information processing theories, particularly assumptions involving interactions between the learner and environment via perception and decision-making, are also common to situated perspective. Rovegno et al. contended that situated perspective includes the individual, activity, and environment as an inseparable unit of analysis. This suggests that, "…a broader view of cognition and context requires that task characteristics and cognitive performance be considered in light of the goal of the activity and its interpersonal and sociocultural context" (Rogoff, 1990: 6).

A second aspect of situated perspective relates to the mutuality of individual and environment, meaning that, "…every human thought and action is adapted to the environment, that is, situated, because what people perceive, how they conceive of their activity, and what they physically do develop together" (Clancey, 1997: 1–2). This notion is consistent with the theory of affordances, as interpreted by Gibson (1986), which suggests that an individual's response is dependent upon their goals and abilities, and thus an individual's perceptions cannot be defined independent of their goals and abilities. An affordance includes the notion of mutuality in that it relates to the relationship between the environment, goals, capabilities, and intended actions of the individual. Therefore, the individual can perceive information directly from the environment rather than processing that information via knowledge-based representations that are stored in memory.

Rovegno et al. (2001) as well as Kirk and Macdonald (1998) pointed out that situated perspective is similar to Newell's (1986) constraint theory. The individual response required to achieve the goal of the task is shaped by the constraining response dynamics imposed by both the constitutive and regulatory rules of the game as well as the implements or equipment used to play the game (e.g., rackets, balls, or bats). While constraint theory (or ecological perspective) does account for the individual, task, and environment together as the unit of analysis, it does not account for "…the roles of individual knowledge and prior experiences or the social and cultural norms and settings" (Rovegno et al., 2001: 349). By integrating multiple perspectives, situated, ecological, and information

Table 5.5.1   Research on game-centered teaching in physical education

Variables of interest Author and date	Theoretical Perspective	Game/ category	Sample	Length of treatment	Variables
Comparative research on game-centered approaches					
Allison and Thorpe (1997)	Information processing	Basketball (Boys) Hockey (Girls)/ invasion Game	40 Year 9 boys and 56 year 8 girls	6/60 min lessons	Skill execution Knowledge Affective domain
French et al. (1996)	Information processing	Badminton/ net Game	48 9th grade	3 weeks 15/25 min lessons	Skill execution Game performance
French et al. (1996)	Information processing	Badminton/ net Game	52 9th grade	6 weeks 30/45 min lessons	Skill execution Knowledge Cognitive representations of knowledge and skill Game performance
Graham et al. (1996)	Information processing	Badminton/ net game	52 9th grade	6 weeks 30/45 min lessons	Skill execution
Gabriele (1995)	Information processing	Squash/ net game	College	6 weeks	Skill execution Decision-making
Griffin et al. (1995)	Information processing	Volleyball/ net game	22 6th grade	9 classes 8/40 min lessons	Skill Tactical knowledge Motivation
Mitchell et al. (1997)	Information processing	Soccer/ invasion game	41 6th grade	9 classes 8/40 min lessons	Cognitive Skill execution – pass/receive and shooting Motivation
Mitchell et al. (1995)	Information processing	Soccer/ invasion game	41 6th grade	9 classes 8/40 min lessons	Support decision-making Skill execution (outcome) Game involvement Game performance

processing, the individual, task, and context become the unit of analysis, and individual actions can be viewed in relation to what the context affords and what the individual perceives to be the relations between the task and context.

An integrated theoretical perspective was also used by Mahut et al. (2003), whereby "situated action" (ecological model) and "reflective attitude" (semioconstructivist model) were used to investigate interpretations of the context from the participant's point of view. The notion of reflective attitude stems from the Parisian Semiotic School, which involves a cycle of reflecting about action (i.e. in a particular game situation) and includes: verbally interpreting the situation, generating an action plan, and then implementing the action plan. Making the learner deconstruct and reconstruct actions results in production of knowledge about action, and allows for examination of the learner's knowledge. According to Mahut et al. (2003), "Reflection about action is a moment where students verbally encode the sense in which they attribute the meaning that they are the only ones able to give to the oppositional relationship. Only the pertinent characteristics of the setting contribute to the knowledge-in-act building" (p. 141).

Table 5.5.1   (Continued)

Variables of interest Author and date	Focus	Game	Sample	Length of treatment	Variables
Development of tactical knowledge					
Griffin et al. (2001)	Information processing Alternative conceptions	Soccer/ invasion game	39 6th grade 18 girls 21 boys	30–40 min interview	Domain-specific declarative procedural knowledge Diff in gender and experience
Nevett et al. (2001)	Multiple perspectives Information processing Situated Ecological	Aerial ball/invasion game	24 4th grade 12 girls and 12 boys	12 lessons	Knowledge of tactics and skills Generation of tactical solutions
Nevett et al. (2001)	Multiple perspectives Information processing Situated Ecological	Aerial ball/invasion game	24 4th grade 12 girls and 12 boys	12 lessons	Game performance Decision-making – passing–cutting Skill execution–sending a catchable pass–catching a pass
Rovegno et al. (2001)	Multiple perspectives Information processing Situated Ecological	Aerial ball/invasion game	24 4th grade 12 girls and 12 boys	12 lessons	Teachers', teacher aids' and researchers' responses to children's learning
Mahut et al. (2003)	Ecological perspective Semiotic perspective	Badminton/ net game	21 boys ages 12–13	8 90-minute lessons	Verbalization of action plans Identifying expectation horizon about opposition relationship Player responses/actions

Major findings

Comparative GCA studies

Much of the early research on GCAs has involved comparative analyses of technical and tactical approaches to games education (see Table 5.5.1). These studies occurred in naturalistic settings and included predominantly middle school students taught by physical education specialists trained to use a TGfU (Allison and Thorpe, 1997; Lawton, 1989; Turner and Martinek, 1992; 1999) or TGM approach (Griffin et al., 1995; Mitchell et al., 1995, 1997). In studies with high school and college age students (French et al., 1996a, 1996b; Gabriele and Maxwell, 1995), one or more of the investigators implemented a TGfU approach (Gabriele and Maxwell, 1995) or a "technique" only, tactic only,

or combination approach (French et al., 1996a, 1996b). In the technique versus tactic approach studies, two of the four games categories (Almond, 1986; Ellis, 1983) were investigated: invasion games – basketball (Allison and Thorpe, 1997), hockey (Allison and Thorpe, 1997; Turner and Martinek, 1992, 1999), and soccer (Mitchell et al., 1995, 1997); and net/wall games – badminton (French et al., 1996a, et al., 1996b; Lawton, 1989), volleyball (Griffin et al., 1995), and squash (Gabriele and Maxwell, 1995). The length of instruction ranged from as few as 8, 40-minute lessons (Mitchell et al., 1995) to 30-45-minute lessons (French 1996). Principal variables included skill execution, tactical knowledge, and game performance. Affective variables such as motivation, pupil enjoyment, effort and involvement, and teacher enjoyment were also included, but to a much lesser extent in the technique

Table 5.5.1 (Continued)

Variables of interest Author and date	Focus	Game	Sample	Length of treatment	Variables
Responses to game-centered approaches					
Allison and Thorpe (1997)	Teachers/ students	Basketball (Boys) Hockey (Girls)/ invasion game	2 physical education teachers – 1 male, 1 female	6/60 min lessons	Perceived pupil effort Perceived pupil involvement in planning and evaluationTeacher enjoyment of the approach Student enjoyment, effort, and planning and evaluation opportunities
Almond (1986)	Teachers	Variety of games taught	Variety of levels	Induction course on TGfU	Teacher response to TGfU as an innovative approach
Brooker et al. (2001)	Teachers	Basketball	1 middle school PE teacher (8th grade)		Teacher response to implementing TGfU in middle school setting
Burrows and Abby (1986)	Teachers students	Badminton	3rd year class	5 lessons	Teacher and student responses to TGfU approach
Butler (1993)	Teachers	Variety of games	Variety of levels	4 weeks of support	Teacher beliefs Teaching methodology Teacher perceptions of student responses
Doolittle (1983)	Teachers	Net and invasion games	Variety of levels	Initial course and follow-up workshop 8 weeks later	Teacher perceptions
Gubacs (2000)	Preservice teachers Future teacher educators	Tennis	13 PTs	8-weeks	Perceptions of PTs of TGM Perceptions of FTEs
Gubacs et al. (1998)	Future teacher educators	Soccer and badminton	3 PETE Doctoral Students	5th and 6th grade	Process used by FTEs to adapt to TGM approach
Howarth and Walkuski (2003)	Pre-service teachers		8 PTs 5 males 3 female		Changes in PT's knowledge of tactical concepts pre and post a tactical concepts class
Light (2003)	Pre-service teachers	Basketball, field hockey, kanga cricket and volleyball	152 respondents 20 randomly selected for interviews	Undergraduate activity course taught via TGfU	Response to TGfU approach

Table 5.5.1   (Continued)

Variables of interest Author and date	Focus	Game	Sample	Length of treatment	Variables
McNeill et al. (2004)	Pre-service teachers	Variety of games	11 PTs	Applied TGM during student teaching experience in 6–8-lesson games unit primary schools	PTs experiences with TGM teaching experience
Mitchell et al. (1997)	Teachers	Soccer	1 teacher 24 students in tactical group 29 students in technical group	6th grade 8 40-minute lessons	Teacher perceptions of TGM Student intrinsic motivation
Sullivan and Swabey (2003)	Pre-service teachers	2 lessons w/each approach	PTs teaching 4/5th	First teaching experience with TGfU approach	Preservice teachers Analyze teaching practices of PTs from 2 diff countries and 2 diff games teaching approaches
Sweeney et al. (2003)	Pre-service Teachers	Invasion games	17 PTs 10 males 7 female in an UG activity-based course	16-week under-graduate activity course taught via TGfU	Attitudes of PTs toward TGfU – Determine how they perceive knowledge and learning
Tjeerdsma et al. (1996)	Students	Badminton	Same sample – extended data set	6 weeks	Student responses
Turner (1996)	Teachers	Field hockey	2 middle school PE teachers		

versus tactic approach studies. Findings from GCA comparative studies will be presented below and will proceed according to the dependent variables examined in this segment of GCA research.

Skill outcomes

All of the studies comparing technical and tactical games approaches included measures of motor skill performance, some outside of game play and in the form of skill tests (Allison and Thorpe, 1997; Lawton, 1989; French et al, 1996a; Gabriele and Maxwell, 1995) and other studies included measures

of skill performance inside game play (Mitchell et al., 1995, 1997; Turner and Martinek, 1992, 1999). With the exception of Turner and Martinek (1999), students receiving technical and tactical games instruction demonstrated significant improvement in motor skills, but no significant differences in motor skill performance were reported between technical and tactical treatment groups. Turner and Martinek (1999) reported that the TGfU group scored significantly higher on control and passing execution during game play than the technical or control groups. The TGfU group also showed a trend toward better dribbling and shooting execution during game play. However, skill test performance measures for skill accuracy showed no significant difference between technical and tactical groups, but the technique group scored significantly higher than the control group on speed. Turner and Martinek (1999) suggested that the technique groups' success was likely the result of similarities between the skill test and the content of the technique group's lessons. While the technique group demonstrated significantly better speed during skill tests, they were unable to control the hockey ball during small-sided game conditions. The TGfU group, however, was able to control and pass the hockey ball more effectively during posttest game play than the technique and control groups. These findings are similar to previous research by French and Thomas (1987), in which skill test scores correlated with success rate in control and motor execution during game play.

Cognitive outcomes

Perhaps the most significant factors differentiating the technique from tactical approaches to games teaching relate to the cognitive components of game play. All of the GCA comparative studies included cognitive measures of tactical understanding, and used paper-pencil tests, or a combination of paper-pencil and a game performance instrument that included a decision-making component (French et al., 1996a, 1996b; Griffin et al., 1995; McPherson and French, 1991; Mitchell et al., 1995; Turner and Martinek, 1992, 1999). Between point interviews were also used to assess decision-making and ongoing changes in the use of cognitive strategies (McPherson and French, 1991).

The technique versus tactical studies that reported paper-pencil protocols, knowledge tests tended to include measures of declarative (i.e. rules, skills, player positions, etc.) and procedural knowledge (i.e. selecting or determining "how to do it" or "doing it" (McPherson, 1994) in a particular game situation). Turner and Martinek (1992) reported no differences over time or between treatment groups on measures of declarative and procedural knowledge. This finding is similar to Lawton's (1989) study of badminton players. The TGfU group scored higher than the control group for declarative and procedural knowledge, with no significant differences found between technique and TGfU groups on procedural knowledge (Turner, 1999). This is similar to findings of French et al. (1996a) who used written tests that included rule, skill technique, and strategy sections and found no significant difference between technique, tactical and combination, but all treatment groups scored significantly higher than the control group. Other comparative studies reported that students instructed through a GCA scored significantly higher on measures of declarative and procedural knowledge than students

receiving technique approaches (Allison and Thorpe, 1997; Gabriele and Maxwell, 1995; Griffin et al., 1995; Mitchell et al., 1997).

Another cognitive measure used in the tactic versus technique studies included decision-making, which was assessed through observing game play (Turner and Martinek; 1992; 1999; Griffin et al., 1995; Mitchell et al., 1995, 1997) or through analysis of between point interviews (French et al., 1996a, 1996b). Findings suggested that tactical games instruction produced significant improvement in decision-making (Allison and Thorpe; Gabriele and Maxwell, 1995; Griffin et al., 1995; Mitchell et al., 1997) as well as response selection and response execution (Turner and Martinek, 1999). Other studies found significant improvement from pre- to post-test, but no differences in cognitive measures between treatment groups (Lawton, 1989; Turner and Martinek, 1992). In studies using a control group, technical and tactical treatment groups demonstrated significant improvement in tactical understanding and scored significantly higher than control groups (Turner and Martinek, 1992).

Game performance

Game performance measures varied from study to study. Turner and Martinek (1992, 1999) adapted an observational tool originally developed by French and Thomas (1987), with control, decision-making, and skill execution components. The decision-making component included measures of response selection (i.e. shoot, dribble, pass, or tackle) as well as response execution (i.e. when to shoot, which direction to dribble, where to pass), control included "successfully and legally stopping the ball," and skill execution required successful execution of open skills (i.e. passing, dribbling, tackling) during game play.

French et al.'s (1996a, 1996b) observation instrument for game play was similarly modified from instruments developed by French and Thomas (i.e. McPherson and French, 1991 (tennis); McPherson and Thomas, 1989 (tennis); French et al., 1995 (baseball); and Turner and Martinek, 1992, 1995), with variations to accommodate specific components of game play in badminton. The badminton game performance instrument included the following components of game play: contact decision, contact execution, shot type, game decisions, and game execution. (See French et al. (1996a) for specific definitions and examples of these components.)

The Game Performance Assessment Instrument (GPAI; Oslin et al., 1998) was used to assess soccer (Mitchell et al., 1995, 1997) and volleyball (Griffin et al., 1995). Game play components included decision-making, skill execution, and support. The Mitchell et al. (1995) study also included measures of game involvement and game performance.

Measures of support play were included to assess quality of off-the-ball movement, such as support movements of offensive players that do not have the ball (i.e. moving to get open to receive a pass). Game involvement combined appropriate and inappropriate skill execution and decision-making, and appropriate support, and game performance scores included the efficiency scores averaged across all three components (see Oslin et al., 1998 for specific definitions, examples, and formula for computing game involvement and game performance scores). The intent of including game involvement is to recognize that low ability students can be involved in a game, regardless of their ability to make good decisions and execute skill efficiently (Mitchell et al., 1995). Game performance measures are arithmetical averages of successful or appropriate skill executions, support movements, and decisions made during game play.

Summary

The degree of variability between content, instructional tasks, instructional methods, instructors, and contexts makes it difficult to determine the superiority of the technical over the tactical methods of teaching games. Results, however do suggest that GCAs tend to result in: improved skill execution within game play (Turner and Martinek, 1999); improved decision-making skills (Allison and Thorpe, 1997; Gabriele and Maxwell, 1995; Griffin et al., 1995; Mitchell et al., 1997) as well as response selection and response execution (Turner and Martinek, 1999) and improved game involvement (Mitchell et al., 1995). As Metzler (2000), Rink (1996), and others have suggested, perhaps the more important issue is to understand the processes that contribute to teaching and learning tactics, rather than determining whether one model is better than another.

Game performance assessment

In addition to the game performance analysis instruments developed by French and Thomas (1987) and Oslin et al. (1998) Grehaigne et al. (1997) developed the Team Sport Performance Assessment Instrument (TSPAI), which combines various measures of game performance such as shooting percentage, number of shots on goal, and relational nature of game play. The intent of the TSPAI is to incorporate measures of game performance and include both the tactical process and technical product. The TSPAI involves observation of a player during game play (soccer) and recording data on an "Observational Grid" – two categories relate to gaining possession of the ball: (1) conquering the ball (CB – steeling the ball from an opponent, or recapturing it after a shot on goal), and (2) receiving the ball (RB – receiving a pass from a partner). Four categories are assigned to disposing

the ball: (1) playing a neutral ball (PB – a pass that does not pose a threat to the opposition); (2) losing the ball (LB); (3) playing an offensive ball (OB – a pass that puts pressure on the opposition and often leads to a shot on goal; and (4) executing a successful shot (SS – a shot scores or is retained by one's team). At the conclusion of the observation, frequencies for each category are summed and combined to produce additional game play scores. (See Grehaigne et al. (1997) for additional information and formula for calculating team and individual performance scores.)

Given the relative infancy of the GCA literature, perhaps it is not surprising that few instruments have been developed to measure game performance. Those presented here appear to be in the initial stages of development, with one developed for a specific game (Grehaigne et al., 1997, soccer) and another in with only preliminary measures of validity and reliability (Oslin et al., 1998). While other highly specialized game performance instruments have been tested (e.g. Grehaigne et al., 1997; Hughes and Jones, 2003; and Suzuki and Nishijima, 2004), these instruments tend to be game specific, complex, and very technical, making them perhaps more appropriate for elite sport coaches and athletes. However, these instruments have potential to provide a greater understanding of the complexity of game performance as well as the variety and combinations of measures that can be used to assess individual and team performance.

Understanding the development of tactical knowledge in students

Some of the more recent studies on GCAs have moved away from comparing teaching methodologies to investigate processes related to teaching and learning tactical knowledge (see Table 5.5.1). A 2001 monograph in the *Journal of Teaching in Physical Education*, co-edited by Griffin and Placek, focused on *The Understanding and Development of Learners' Domain-Specific Knowledge* Grounded in information-processing perspective, the first two studies examined student's prior knowledge of fitness as a low-strategy movement activity (Placek et al., 2001) and prior knowledge of soccer as a high-strategy movement activity (Griffin et al., 2001). Information-processing perspective (along with situated and constraint perspectives) was also used by Nevett et al. (2001) to examine changes in children's tactical understanding and motor skills as a result of a 12–lesson unit of instruction and to examine student knowledge of simple invasion game tactics and skills as well as their ability to generate tactical solutions. In Chapter 2.2 Rovegno, Nevett, Brock, and Babiarz (2001) examined how students learned tactics and how teachers responded to students' learning of tactics. Mahut et al. (2003) used a combination of situated and constraint perspectives (based on constructivist/semi-constructivist theory) to examine how students interpret (i.e. debate) game play and formulate action rules. An overview of the research on development of tactical knowledge in students follows.

Based on learning theory in cognitive psychology, Dodds et al. (Chapter 1.2, JTPE Monograph; 2001) used information-processing theory and alternative conceptions research in science education to investigate children's prior knowledge of specific physical education content (i.e. fitness and soccer). According to the authors, understanding children's prior knowledge informs the process of planning and instruction and thus facilitates learning.

As reported in Chapter 1.4, Griffin et al. (2001) investigated student conceptions of soccer and solutions to tactical problems. Students responded to structured interviews that included open-ended and application questions related to sources of soccer knowledge, personal soccer experiences in and out of school, descriptions of specific aspects of soccer, as well as game play scenarios that required students to solve problems related to offensive and defensive tactics. When provided scenarios, considered "contextualized pieces of the game," students were required to move game pieces and provide a verbal explanation for doing so. According to the authors, the scenarios represented situated, declarative, and procedural knowledge; situated because scenarios reflected isolated situations that occurred within the context of the game and declarative and procedural because students had to move game pieces according to particular offensive or defensive situations and provide verbal explanations for doing so.

Analysis of open-ended interview data revealed four conceptual levels upon which students described the game of soccer: (I) how to play soccer; (II) the purpose of the game; (III) what to do to be a successful player; and (IV) what to do when your team has (or does not have) the ball. From these data, the authors devised a "knowledge taxonomy" to classify levels of thinking about soccer, from level I where students described declarative knowledge such as basic rules, player positions, and skills, to level IV in which students "…described coherent sequences of actions, gave reasons for those actions, and explained tactical options" (p. 326). When confronted with scenarios, level I students were unable to move players into "open space," consider oppositional players, or advance play. Level IV students appeared to have a better understanding of basic offensive tactics than defensive tactics and could arrange more "if-then" statements, inferring the use of production systems associated with procedural knowledge structures. Most of the students clustered around levels II and III, approximately 16% at level I, and approximately 11% at level IV.

Relative to students' soccer backgrounds, the authors reported that students were able to report sources of knowledge (i.e. family, friends, teachers, and media), but were unable to provide specific details regarding where they acquired specific skills or information. Students reported a range of soccer experience, from no soccer experience to several years in formal leagues. Approximately 60% of the students played formally in community programs or physical education classes, 27% reported playing in their neighborhoods with family or friends, and more than 15% reported having no playing experience. The authors concluded that experience was an important factor in the knowledge taxonomy.

Student solutions were categorized as: sound, feasible, and convoluted (Griffin et al., 2001). Students were reported to have provided a wide assortment of solutions to each of the seven tactical problems presented as scenarios. Most of the students scored higher on problems related to attacking the goal, creating space in the attack, and maintaining possession. Students were reported to be less likely to provide sound solutions for defensive problems. Overall, approximately 41% of the solutions were scored as sound, 28% feasible, and 31% convoluted. While experience appeared to be a factor relative to the knowledge taxonomy, experience did not appear to be a factor in the students' ability to solve tactical scenarios. The authors suggested that this difference could be caused by the differences in the types of knowledge being assessed. A significant correlation ($r = 0.47$; $p < 0.01$) was found between the soccer knowledge taxonomy and the solutions to the scenarios.

Similar to the University of Massachusetts studies (Griffin et al., 2001; Placek et al., 2001), the University of Alabama studies focused on students' development of tactical knowledge, but at a fourth- rather than sixth-grade level. Rovegno et al. (2001) designed and implemented a comprehensive study that included multiple measures of student learning and teacher responses to student learning. In Chapter 6 Nevett et al. (2001) reported results of two game performance components, decision-making and skill execution. After a 12-lesson unit of instruction, fourth-graders were reported to have improved their good passing decisions from 52.9 to 66.6% and cutting actions from 45.7 to 64.1%. Most students, even those who did not improve on their overall scores, were able to demonstrate some improvement in passing decisions and cutting actions. The authors reported variability in decision-making and skill execution from one game play situation to another, suggesting the "fragility of newly formed knowledge and tactical skill" (p. 366). This was reported in both low and high-skilled students. The authors' concluded that the students' improvement in decision-making and skill execution indicated development of procedural knowledge.

Students also improved their passing decisions to use a lead pass, from 23.2 to 41.4%, but failed to improve decisions related to the held-ball category (i.e. decision to throw to an open teammate that was close enough to receive a pass). The authors suggested three possible reasons for this failure: (1) they did not see the open player; (2) they did not think they could complete the pass; and (3) they did not want to pass to that player. The latter of these reasons suggests the influence of the student social system, while all three of these possibilities suggest the relational nature of game play.

Relative to cutting, the authors reported that students were more active, particularly the low-skilled students. Low-skilled students also decreased the time spent standing still in space and while slower to perform cuts, they used more V-cuts than high skilled students. The student's ability to send catchable passes also increased after instruction, from 43.5 to 69.5%. Overall, the students catching skills remained unchanged, but only 6–8% of the catches were bobbled or dropped during pre- and post-tests. The authors noted a number of interactions between cutting, passing, and catching. Increases in good passing were associated with good cutting, and increases in good cutting resulted in increases in good catches. The relationship between these three variables suggests the importance of examining these skills within the context of the game, relative to teammates and/or opponents.

Nevett et al. (2001) reported that some of the students demonstrated poor skill execution but were able to make good decisions. Overall, low skilled students demonstrated equal or slightly better passing decisions and slightly lower on cutting-skills, both groups demonstrated improvement from pre- to post-tests. From these findings, the authors were able to conclude that both low and high skilled students were able to learn tactical and decision-making components in an invasion-type game after a 12-lesson instructional unit.

Data related to decision-making (response-selection) components of game performance suggested that fourth-grade students were able to acquire knowledge of simple invasion-game tactics and skills and generate solutions to tactical problems associated with aerial basketball.

A 20-item multiple choice test containing declarative, procedural and simple game tactic questions was given pre- and post-instruction as a measure of student knowledge. In addition, one-on-one knowledge interviews were performed pre and post-instruction and were used to determine student's knowledge of passing and cutting in an invasion game. The authors reported that the fourth-grade students' improved their knowledge of cutting and passing from 44.3 to 53.3% on the knowledge test. Although the students did improve, the authors noted that the overall score was just slightly above 50%.

Based on the results of the interview data, the fourth-grade students were able to access more solutions to tactical problems, but the amount of information and variety of solutions did not change from pre- to post-instructional interviews. Differences in the types of knowledge accessed were reported to have changed, as the students began to use more tactical action concepts following instruction, from 47.3 to 64.2%, and generated a higher percentage overall of tactical action concepts, from 24.7 to 36.2%. After examining some of the individual interview data, the authors reported finding evidence of the "fragility" of newly formed knowledge, which was also supported by performance data related to decision-making during cutting, passing, and catching. The authors stated that the fourth-grade students tended to "piece-meal" solutions together rather than formulate strong action plans or responses to game situations, suggesting that the process of problem-solving is much the same as motor skill learning in that it may take literally hundreds of trials to learn a skill. Although such knowledge development may have appeared fragile, the authors concluded that overall the fourth-graders were able to acquire better knowledge of skills and tactics after the 12-lesson unit of instruction.

Rovegno et al. (2001) reported using a combination of cognitive-processing, situated, and constraint perspectives to describe the teaching and learning of basic invasion-game tactics in fourth-grade students. The "teaching experiment" methodology was used to collect data related to how fourth-grade students learned cutting to receive a pass and sending a pass as well as how the teachers, aides and researchers, all of whom team-taught the unit, responded to student's learning. This methodology put student learning rather than the instructional (games) approach at the center of the investigation and, along with situated and constraint perspectives, researchers were able to focus on the 'mutuality' of the students and their environment.

The teacher, aides, and researchers met at the end of school for all but one lesson. The purpose of the meetings was to "generate descriptive, more comprehensive data" (p. 371) of the student's responses, beyond what could be obtained from pre- and post-test results. Meetings were tape-recorded and served as group interviews, which began with descriptions of students' cognitive, motor, and social interaction responses. At the end of each meeting, the group analyzed the lesson and planned the lesson for the next day.

Data collection also included videotaping students during the 2 days of assessment tasks and 11 of the 12 lessons. Videotapes were viewed and used to confirm descriptions of movement patterns discussed in the after-school meetings. Discussions of the after-school meetings were transcribed using constant comparison methods (Glaser and Strauss, 1967) and resulted in identification of general categories of passing, cutting, offensive/defensive game play, working together in groups, process of designing games, game rules, off-task behavior, class organization, and management.

Rovegno et al. (2001) reported that the "teaching experiment" guided their teaching in a number of ways: (1) it put student learning rather than the instructional approach at the forefront – thus the focus of instruction was on the "mutuality" of the students with their learning environment; (2) constrained by the "economy of teaching" and "in-depth learning," the instructors (i.e. teacher, aides, and researchers) had to determine which aspects of skill learning needed to be implicit and which needed to be explicit; (3) instructors determined that they needed to help students with the social aspects of game play and therefore "explicitly" and "repeatedly" taught various relational aspects of game play, such as the passer's responsibility for sending a catchable pass to a receiver or the receivers responsibility to get "open" to catch a pass; (4) instructors carefully considered constraints of task, learner, and environment to "afford practicing and learning more mature movement patterns" (p. 388); (5) instructors off-loaded cognition and teaching to facilitate "economy of teaching" by imposing environmental constraints that would compel the student to move (or not move) in a specific way – for example, using a hula hoop to keep the student from traveling; (6) instructors "… found that defenders were a task constraint that helped passers and receivers understand the socially structured nature of invasion-game play and provided authenticity to [their] learning cues"; and (7) to create a more inclusive practice space, instructors choose to shift defenders from being competitive to being socially responsible for the learning of others. Overall, the authors reported that situated and constraint perspectives provided insight into teaching and learning of invasion-game tactics that might not have otherwise been provided, and gave them a "profound respect for the complexity of teaching and learning tactics in a school setting" (p. 388).

Similar to Rovegno et al. (2001), Mahut et al. (2003) employed a situated-constraint perspective to examine construction of tactical knowledge in students. The "situated action" or ecological perspective aligns with situated and constraint perspectives in that performance results from an interaction between subject and environment, and therefore ought to be studied in authentic learning contexts. In addition to situated perspective, Mahut et al. combined the "reflective attitude" or semioconstructivist perspective, which suggests that meaning is constructed by interpreting the environment from the student's perspective. This requires the student to generate reflections about strategies, "… making [him/her] deconstruct and reconstruct sense of action and produce knowledge 'in' and 'on' action" (Schon, 1990: 141).

Mahut et al. identified three concepts related to processes used by the learner for interpreting the environment and decision-making: (1) The concept of "expectation horizon" – as the player interprets the environment, he/she actively anticipates the sequence of events and then plans possible responses; (2) the concept of "semic load" – relates to player assignment of "significant weight" to environmental elements and these player-determined significant elements ("semic treats") become the basis upon which he/she interprets the situation and subsequently responds; and (3) the concept of "debate of ideas" – involves the player verbalizing significant elements needed to formulate "action rules" for solving a problem. "This verbalization constitutes a reflective act about action, and allows action determinants to make the subject's point of view explicit" (p. 142). Following the "debate of ideas," the player immediately returns to game play, which provides the player an opportunity to validate his/her interpretations.

The purpose of this study was to examine student interpretations of game play (expectation horizon), specifically the network of elements to which they assign significant weight (semic load), through verbalization of action (debate of ideas). During each of the eight 90-minute lessons students engaged in a 10–minute segment of game play, after which they observed their game play on videotape and "debated about action," and then returned to game play. Videotapes of the debate setting were transcribed by two coders. Investigators designed a "verbal report interpretive map" (Bardin, 1975; Chi, 1997) to aid in the identification of action rules and a "behavior observational motor-skill grid" to analyze game performance before and after the debate of ideas. Initially students used gestures (non-verbal productions), but were able to verbalize more toward the end of the lessons. Eventually students were able to produce more statements that were fluent and used more appropriate terms to describe action. Students' ability to produce and or extract action rules appeared to increase throughout the eight lessons and evolved with the student's expectation horizon. Mahut et al. identified three characteristics of beginners expectation horizon: (1) "Shuttlecock centered" – students focused on the flight of the shuttlecock and various aspects of skill execution; (2) "constraint of court" – focused on the court as well as positioning/repositioning of their opponent (i.e. moving opponent left and right); and (3) "the opponent" – focused on the opponent, however, "… incomplete compared to top players where regulation constraints and adversarial strategies constraints were almost nonexistent" (p. 145). Mahut et al. reported that these characteristics were not the same for all students and tended to emerge at different times. Students were also reported to have had "shifts" in their interpretations of game play as they progressed through the course. These findings are similar to Rovegno et al. (2001) who reported the "fragility" of developing knowledge structures.

In terms of game performance, initially students tended to engage in cooperative exchanges with their opponent, remaining under the shuttlecock with predominantly underhand and overhand hits in the frontal plane. As students' game play evolved, they began to take more cross-court shots, suggesting a more "lateralized view" of their opponents court. This led to more cross-court shots, which were intended to move their opponent left and right. As students progressed, they began to demonstrate a "new rapport of time," which involved varying the speed of the shuttlecock to obtain an advantage over their opponent. At this stage, students began to alternate smash shots deep into their opponent's court and drop shots near the net. Toward the end of the eight-lesson course, students were 'moving and replacing on the court'. This phase was characterized by students' intentional attempts to respond to opponents' actions as well as to re-position after each shot. Mahut et al. (2003) concluded that through verbalization the student was able to identify significant aspects of the setting that allow him/her to understand how events link with tactical solutions. Verbal accounts produced by the students could then be tested when put into action (i.e. when students return to game play), thereby providing an opportunity for the student to validate the action rules that evolved from their "debate of ideas". Once formulated, these action rules can serve as the foundation for interpretation of future actions.

Responses to GCAs

Most studies that have examined responses to GCAs have been quasi-experimental and have used a combination of quantitative and qualitative measures to assess PT's ability to learn tactical concepts (Howarth and Walkuski, 2003), assess changes in physical educator's beliefs about GCAs (Butler, 1993), PTs (Gubacs, 2000; Light, 2003; Sweeney et al., 2003), and future teacher educators (FTEs; Gubacs, 2000; Gubacs et al., 1998), and examine teacher, PT, and FTE, responses to GCAs (see Table 5.5.1). Though early accounts (Almond, 1986; Burrows and Abbey, 1986; and Doolittle, 1983) appear anecdotal, these observations are consistent with recent research related to responses to GCAs by physical educators, PTs, FTEs, and students. Research from 1993 to 2004 utilized a variety of scales, questionnaires, interview techniques, and observation instruments to measure responses to GCAs (see Table 5.5.1).

PT responses to GCA

GCA studies have examined the potential of PTs to learn tactical concepts (Howarth and Walkuski, 2003), shift epistemological beliefs to align with a GCAs (Sweeney et al., 2003), and implement a GCA in a physical education context (Light, 2003; McNeill et al., 2004; Sullivan and Swabey, 2003). PTs reported that they enjoyed being taught via GCAs (Light, 2003) and demonstrated better understanding of tactics by the end of a tactical concepts course (Howarth and Walkuski, 2003). Howarth and Walkuski concluded that while PTs knowledge and application of tactical concepts improved, those who started lower were not able to catch up or close the gap between themselves and participants who were more experienced.

When teaching via a GCA, PTs were initially inconsistent and struggled with transition from technical approaches to GCAs (Gubacs, 1999; Light, 2003; McNeill et al., 2004; Sullivan and Swabey, 2003). Sullivan and Swabey reported that PTs used more questions overall, more probing questions, and the range of cognitive-level questioning was higher than when teaching via a technical approach. In the McNeill et al. study, PTs reported a number of contextual constraints interfered with implementation of a GCA, such as facilities, equipment, and scheduling. Light (2003) also noted that limited support from cooperating teachers interfered with PTs' ability to successfully implement the approach. The PTs who had positive, supportive experiences indicated that their cooperating teachers identified similarities between the GCA and constructivist approaches (Light, 2003).

Responses of PTs to GCAs were quite similar to reactions of FTEs and practicing teachers, in that it took some time for them to adjust from teaching through a traditional approach, develop an understanding of unfamiliar pedagogical content knowledge, and spontaneously pose higher order questions (Brooker et al., 2001; Butler, 1993; Doolittle, 1983; Gubacs, 2000; Gubacs et al., 1998). In an in-depth study of a secondary teacher's initial experience with a GCA, Brooker et al., reported that there were a number of constraints posed by institutionalized physical education and the status of competitive games in the school context (e.g. location and condition of facilities, scheduling, lack of support from colleagues, and misaligned assessment tools).

Teacher and FTE responses to GCAs

Practicing physical educators were initially skeptical of GCAs and challenged by their lack of pedagogical content knowledge, particularly as it related to tactical concepts and the design and implementation of conditioned games. After gaining experience with the GCA, the physical educators' reactions were far more positive (Allison and Thorpe, 1997; Almond, 1986; Brooker et al., 2001; Butler, 1993; Doolittle, 1983). Teachers reported having more time to observe and assess student performance (Allison and Thorpe, 1997) and felt more confident in their ability to plan and implement a GCA (Brooker et al., 2001). Teachers with broader interpretations of games teaching tended to adapt more successfully, as were those who were better able to accurately interpret the game-centered philosophy (Butler, 1993). FTE's were similar to teachers, as their initial period of skepticism was followed by a better understanding of tactical concepts and an appreciation for the student-centered nature of the GCA (Gubacs et al., 1998).

Student responses to GCAs

The only study to directly investigate student responses to a GCA was reported by Tjeerdsma et al. (1996). Students were randomly assigned to instructional groups: skill only, tactics only, combination of skill and tactics, and a control group receiving instruction in softball. Except for the combination group, findings did not suggest superiority of one method of instruction over another. Students in the combination group perceived "slightly greater improvement" than the skill only and tactics only experimental groups.

Most student reactions to GCAs have been reported through teacher perceptions, during or following the teacher's initial experience with a GCA (Allison and Thorpe, 1997; Almond, 1986; Brooker et al., 2001; Burrows and Abbey, 1986; Butler, 1993; Doolittle, 1983; Gubacs, 2000; Mitchell et al., 1997; Turner, 1996). Overall, teachers reported greater student engagement, enthusiasm, and positive attitudes about game play. Students with lower technical ability were reported to have higher levels of enjoyment and effort and were more positive about their ability to play (Allison and Thorpe, 1997; Almond, 1986; Doolittle, 1983). Teachers also perceived that GCAs encouraged students to demonstrate more positive attitudes about physical education in general (Allison and Thorpe, 1997), promoted more engagement in game play activities (Burrows and Abbey, 1986; Butler, 1993, Gubacs, 2000; Mitchell et al., 1997), and appeared to enhance students' ability to think (Gubacs, 2000; Turner, 1996). In contrast to the numerous positive student responses, the teacher in the Brooker et al. (2001) study reported that eighth-grade students were resistant to small-sided games and frequently requested the "real game," which Brooker et al. suggested was influenced students' access to the media and "institutionalized physical education."

Summary

Perhaps more important than the positive responses of teachers and students to GCAs is understanding and appreciation of the change process, and specifically the transformation of teacher knowledge and practice. In what ways does an approach change how and what we teach as well as how and what is learned, and in what context? To have the necessary tools to meet the needs of their students, teachers (as well as PTs and FTEs) need to know a range of instructional approaches, including traditional as well as contemporary approaches to games teaching (Sullivan and Swabey, 2003).

Trends and future directions

In a very short time the literature on GCAs has evolved from comparative analyses of technical and tactical approaches underpinned by knowledge-based theory, to naturalistic inquiries of teaching and learning processes underpinned by multiple, yet overlapping theories of learning. While the more recent literature is broader in perspective, observing both teaching and learning processes (Rovegno et al., 2001), the teacher in context (Brooker et al., 2000), and students' construction of knowledge (Mahut et al., 2003), it is far from the more holistic view prescribed by many who have encouraged rethinking and expanding the original TGfU model (Holt et al., 2002; Kirk and MacPhail, 2002; Light and Fawn, 2002; and others). The integrated theoretical perspectives, research designs and methodologies used in the most recent GCA studies hold promise, as they have potential to allow examination of multiple variables, and thus more holistic interpretations of the child, the game, and the context.

Research designs and methodologies associated with recent research on GCAs provide excellent examples for examining complexities of teaching and processes of learning in physical education. The "debate of ideas" protocol implemented by Mahut et al. (2003), for example, illustrates the use of constructivist pedagogy grounded in both ecological and semiotic perspectives. The protocol involves reflective practice about action, which consists of producing reflections about strategies used to deconstruct and reconstruct action and construct knowledge "in" an "on" action (Schon, 1990 in Mahut et al., 2003). Verbalization throughout the reflective process makes learning processes explicit and therefore makes metacognitive strategies available for analysis and interpretation by the learner, teacher, and researcher. Debate of ideas or similar protocols may also prove useful for investigating the formulation and implementation of teachers' action plans as they respond to students' domain-specific knowledge and/or alternative conceptions contained in student comments as well as interactive processes between the teacher and their students.

The teaching experiment methodology (Cobb et al., 1997; Simon, 1995) implemented by Rovegno et al. (2001) is also underpinned by multiple theoretical perspectives (information processing, ecological perspective, situated learning perspective) and represents yet another framework for investigating the teaching–learning process. The planning– teaching–reflection cycle gives teachers (and researchers) an opportunity to analyze the instructional process and subsequently test assumptions about the learning process, much the same as Mahut et al.'s (2003) debate of ideas protocol. The significance of the teaching experiment is that it provides a means for understanding instruction in terms of the learning theories upon which GCAs are based as well as the student experiences that underlie the learning process. An additional benefit of teaching experiment methodology is that it includes primary stakeholders (e.g. teachers, students, administrators, as well as teacher educators) and allows collaborative efforts that promote physical education as inquiry.

Hopefully, recent studies on GCAs will provide impetus to the inclusion and investigation of additional variables that, as many have suggested (e.g. Holt et al. 2002), contribute to a more holistic perspective of games teaching. For example, Kirk and MacPhail (2002) suggest "rethinking" TGfU from a situated learning perspective, thus emphasizing "...the learners perspective, game concept, thinking strategically, cue recognition, technique selection, and skill development as the clustering of strategies and techniques" (p. 189). Situated perspective also emphasizes the game/learner relationship or what Lave and Wenger (1991) referred to as the "legitimate peripheral participants in a community of practice," thereby acknowledging the impact of cultural interpretations of sport on a student's concept of a particular game and how it ought to be played (Brooker et al., 2001). According to Kirk and MacPhail (2002), "When sport is understood as a complex, multifaceted, and heterogeneous community of practice, it is possible to track players' learning trajectories over time as they begin to understand broader social, cultural, and institutional practices that constitute games." (p. 189). Findings of the Brooker et al. study suggest that institutionalized physical education, environmental conditions, and student interpretations of sport as portrayed in the media can impact the integration of GCAs. Understanding institutional forces that affect innovations is important for games teaching and physical education in general.

Holt et al. (2002) also recommended a more holistic approach to GCAs. They proposed "expanding" the TGfU model to go beyond the cognitive and psychomotor domains to include the affective domain, noting that the affective domain had received little attention in the GCA literature. Holt et al. proposed expanding the TGfU model to fully integrate principles of play (Kirk, 1983; Wade, 1970) and the four pedagogical principles of sampling, modification-representation, modification-exaggeration, and tactical complexity into the original model (Bunker and Thorpe, 1982) This expanded version of TGfU is intended to aid in the design of developmentally appropriate games to enhance affective experiences of learners and increase game appreciation, thus further serving to enhance motivation and continued participation. This is consistent with an extension of the TGfU model posited by Griffin et al. (1997) suggesting that improved game performance leads to more fun and enjoyment as well as increases in students' perceived competence. Findings reported by Daigle (2003, in Lee 2004) indicate a positive direct effect between perceived competence and engagement in physical education as well as greater intent to participate in physical activity outside of class. According to Iso-Ahola (1980), perceived competence, along with positive feedback and self-determination motivates children to continue their involvement in physical activity, whereas perceived incompetence and/or a lack of self-determination may inhibit future involvement. As emphasized by Holt et al., "... the continued participation of learners in games throughout life is of paramount importance," (p. 174) and therefore warrants further investigation into the potential of GCAs to promote fun and enjoyment as well as means of fostering lifelong participation in sport. Recent attempts to provide a more holistic perspective of GCAs have resulted in the integration of TGfU and TGM with other curricula. For example, Dyson et al. (2004) suggest integrating Sport Education, Tactical Games, and Cooperative Learning, as each model endorses a student-centered approach and has the potential to include affective, social, cognitive and psychomotor outcomes. Each of these models recommends use of small groups to establish authentic communities of practice that promote positive social interactions, decision-making, and understanding of games as well as the social-cultural aspects of sport contexts. Integration of sport education and GCAs appears to be an international trend, as many schools, school districts, and countries, such as United Kingdom, Australia, and New Zealand, have adopted sport education and/or GCAs as part of their physical education curriculum. Integration of multiple instructional approaches to games education can result in an expanded curriculum that includes affective and social-cultural aspects associated with game and sport participation. However, it is not clear how GCAs and other approaches can or ought to be linked to address multiple outcomes (Penney and Brooker, 2002). Research will be needed to examine how different instructional approaches are modified and integrated relative to curricular goals.

Expanding the curriculum to include more holistic and authentic sport experiences may indeed provide more meaningful, positive, and inclusive experiences for children "in" physical education, but can and will these experiences be available outside of physical education? (Kirk and Macdonald, 1998;

Penney et al., 2002). A number of youth sport initiatives such as Game Sense in Australia and TOP Sport in Britain and national team coaches, such as Wayne Smith (coach of New Zealand national rugby team in Kidman, 2001), have adopted approaches that have much of the same content and concepts associated with GCAs, suggesting a growing acceptance by the dominant culture. The question is whether these national youth sport initiatives are promoted as a means of gaining a competitive edge in future competitive events (i.e. World Cups), or as a means of providing fun, enjoyable, and equitable experiences that motivate future participation. Can GCAs be used to transform community contexts and the dominant values and practices associated with them? Can we or how can we encourage teachers, students, and significant stakeholders to take "transformative action" or consider such action necessary? The potential to transmit inclusive, fun and enjoyable communities of practice from inside to outside physical education rests upon our willingness and abilities as educators to challenge traditional conventions governing physical education as well as those governing sport. Given the progress of the GCA research methodology, perhaps the time is ripe for extending inquiry into coaching contexts, with the goal of creating positive and inclusive sport experiences "in" and "out" of physical education.

References

Abernethy, B., Thomas, K.T. and Thomas, J.R. (1993). Strategies for improving understanding of motor expertise (or mistakes we have made and things we have learned). In J.L. Starkes and F. Allard (Eds.), *Cognitive issues in motor expertise* (pp. 317–356). Amsterdam: Elsevier.

Alison, S. and Thorpe, R. (1997). A comparison of the effectiveness of two approaches to teaching games within physical education: A skills approach versus a games for understanding approach. *The British Journal of Physical Education, 28*(3): 9–13.

Allison, P. C., Pissanos, P.W., Turner, A.P. and Law, D.R. (2000). Pre-service physical educators' epistemologies of skillfulness. *Journal of Teaching in Physical Education, 19*: 141–161.

Almond, L. (1986). Reflecting on themes: A games classification. In D. Bunker, R. Thorpe and L. Almond (Eds.), *Rethinking games teaching* (pp. 71–72). England: University of Technology, Loughborough, Department of Physical Education and Sports Science.

Almond, L. and Thorpe, R. (1988). Asking teachers to research. *Journal of Teaching in Physical Education, 7*(3): 221–227.

Aspin, D. (1976). Knowing how and knowing that and physical education. *Journal of Philosophy of Sport, 3*: 97–117.

Bardin, L. (1975). L'analyse de contenu [The analysis of content]. Paris: P.U.F.

Barrett, K.R. (1977). Games teaching: Adaptable skills, versatile players. *Journal of Physical Education, Recreation, and Dance, 48*(7): 21–24.

Barrett, K.R. and Turner, A.P. (2000). Sandy's challenge: New game, new paradigm <a correspondence>. *Journal of Teaching in Physical Education, 19*: 162–181.

Bayer, C. (1979). *L'enseignment des jeux sportifs collectives* [The teaching of team sport games']. Paris:Vigot.

Berkowitz, R. (1996). A practitioner's journey: From skill to tactics. *Journal of Physical Education, Recreation, and Dance, 67*(4): 44–45.

Blomqvist, M.T., Luhtanen, P., Laakso, L. and Keskinen, E. (2000). Validation of a video-based game- understanding test procedure in badminton. *Journal of Teaching in Physical Education, 19*: 325–337.

Bouthier, D. (1984). *Sports collectives: contribution a l'analyse de l'activite et elements pour uneformatin tactique essentille. L'exemple du rugby* [Team sports: Contribution to the analysis of the activity and elements of essential tactical learning. The example of rugby]. Paris: INSEP.

Bowring, K. (2003). Developing decision making: Giving the brains back to our players. *British Journal of Phsyical Education, 34*(1): 10–11.

Brooker, R., Kirk, D., Braikua, S. and Bransgrove, A. (2001). Implementing a game sense approach to teaching junior high school basketball in a naturalistic setting. *European Physical Education Review, 6*(1): 7–26.

Brown, A.L. (1992). Design experiments: Theoretical and methodological challenges in creating complex interventions in classroom settings. *The Journal of Learning Sciences, 2*: 141–178.

Bunker, D. and Thorpe, R. (1982). Model for the teaching of games in secondary schools. *Bulletin of Physical Education, 18*(1): 5–8.

Bunkner, D., and Thorpe, R. (1982). Model for the teaching of games in secondary schools. *Bulletin of Physical Education, 19*(1): 5–8.

Bunker, D. and Thorpe, R. (1983). Model for the teaching of games in secondary schools. *Bulletin of Physical Education, 19*(1): 5–8.

Burger, J.M. and Cooper, H.M. (1979). The desirability of control. *Motivation and Emotion, 3*: 381–393.

Burrows, L. and Abbey, W. (1986). A teacher's reactions. In D. Bunker, R. Thorpe and L. Almond (Eds.), *Rethinking games teaching*. England: University of Technology, Loughborough, Department of Physical Education and Sports Science.

Butler, J. (1993). *Teacher change in sport education.* Dissertation Abstracts International, 54(02A).

Butler, J. (1996). Teacher responses to teaching games for understanding. *Journal of Physical Education, Recreation, and Dance, 67*(9): 17–20.

Butler, J. (1997). How would Socrates teach games? A constructivist approach. *Journal of Physical Education, Recreation, and Dance, 68*(9): 42.

Butler, J., Griffin, L., Lombardo, B. and Nastasi, R. (Eds.). (2003). *Teaching games for understanding in physical education and sport.* Oxon Hill, MD: AAHPERD Publications.

Chandler, T. (1996). Teaching games for understanding: Reflections and further questions. *Journal of Physical Education, Recreation, and Dance,* 67(4): 49–51.

Chandler, T. and Mitchell, S. (1990). Reflections on "Models of Games Education". *Journal of Physical Education, Recreation, and Dance,* 61(6): 19–21.

Chang, C.W., Mahut, N., Nachon, M., Hsu, L.H. and Grehaigne, J.F. (2003). *Debate of ideas and action strategies: The case of a 6th grade basketball class.* Paper presented at the 2nd International Conference: Teaching Sport and Physical Education for Understanding, Melbourne, Australia.

Cheffers, J. (1977). Observing teching systematically. *Quest,* 28: 17–28.

Cheffers, J. and Sullivan, E. (2000). *Instruction sheet for the teacher performance criteria questionnaire, TPCQ:* Available through the authors at Boston University.

Chen, W. and Rovegno, I. (2000). Examination of expert and novice teachers' constructivist-oriented teaching practices using a movement approach to elementary physical education. *Research Quarterly for Exercise and Sport,* 71: 357–372.

Chi, M.T.H. (1997). Quantifying qualitative analyses of verbal data: A practical guide. *The Journal of Learning Sciences,* 6: 271–315.

Chi, M.T.H., Glaser, R. and Farr, M.J. (1988). *The nature of expertise.* Hillsdale, NJ: Lawrence Erlbaum.

Clancey, W.J. (1997). *Situated cognition: On human knowledge and computer representations.* Cambridge, UK: Cambridge University Press.

Cobb, P., Gravenmeijer, K., Yackel, E., McClin, K. and Whitenack, J. (1997). Mathematizing and symbolizing: The emergence of chains of signification in one first-grade classroom. In D.Kirshner and J.A. Whitson (Eds.), *Situated cognition: Social, semiotic, and psychological perspectives* (pp. 151–233). Mahwah, NJ: Erlbaum.

Commission, A.S. (1997). *Game sense: Developing thinking players.* Belconnen, Australia: Author.

Contreras Jordan, O.R., Garcia Lopez, L.M and Ruiz Perez, L.M. (2003). *Transfer of procedural knowledge from invasion games to hockey* [Abstract]. Paper presented at the 2nd International Conference: Teaching Sport and Physical Education for Understanding, The University of Melbourne, Australia.

Cooper, J.O., Heron, T.E. and Heward, W.L. (1987). *Applied behavior analysis.* Columbus, OH: Merrill.

Daigle, K. (2003). *Gender differences in participation of physical activities: A comprehensive model approach.* Unpublished doctoral dissertation, Louisiana State University, Baton Rouge.

Dodds, P., Griffin, L.L. and Placek, J.H. (2001). Chapter 2. A selected review of the literature on development of learners' domain-specific knowledge. *Journal of Teaching in Physical Education,* 20(4): 301–313.

Doolittle, S. (1983). Reflecting on an innovation. *Bulletin of Physical Education,* 19(1): 36–38.

Dyson, B., Griffin, L.L. and Hastie, P. (2004). Sport education, tactical games, and cooperative learning: Theoretical and pedagogical considerations. *Quest,* 56: 226–240.

Ellis, M. (1983). *Similarities and differences in games: A system for classification.* Paper presented at the AISEP Conference, Rome, Italy.

French, K.E. and McPherson, S.L. (1999). Adaptations in response selection processes used during sport competition with increasing age and expertise. *International Journal of Sport Psychology,* 30: 173–193.

French, K.E. and Nevett, M.E. (1993). The development of expertise in youth sport. In J.L. Starkes and F. Allard (Eds.), *Cognitive issues in motor expertise* (pp. 255–270). Amsterdam: Elsevier.

French, K.E. and Thomas, J.R. (1987). The relation of knowledge development to children's basketball performance. *Journal of Sport Psychology,* 9: 15–32.

French, K.E., Spurgeon, J.H. and Nevett, M.E. (1995). Expert-novice differences in cognitive and skill execution components of youth baseball performance. *Research Quarterly for Exercise and Sport,* 66: 194–201.

French, K.E., Werner, P.H., Rink, J.E., Taylor, K. and Hussey, K. (1996a). The effects of a 3-week unit of tactical, skill, or combined tactical and skill instruction on badminton performance of ninth-grade students. *Journal of Teaching in Physical Education,* 15(4): 418–438.

French, K.E., Werner, P.H., Taylor, K., Hussey, K. and Jones, J. (1996b). The effects of a 6–week unit of tactical, skill, or combined tactical and skill instruction on badminton performance of ninth-grade students. *Journal of Teaching in Physical Education,* 15(4): 439–463.

Gabriele, T.E. and Maxwell, T. (1995). Direct versus indirect methods of squash instruction. *Research Quarterly for Exercise and Sport,* 66(Suppl.), A–63.

Gibson, J.J. (1986). *The ecological approach to visual perception.* Hillsdale, NJ: Erlbaum. (Original work published 1979).

Glaser, B.G. and Strauss, A.L. (1967). *The discovery of grounded theory: Strategies for qualitative research.* New York: Aldine.

Glasser, R. and Chi, M.T.H. (1988). Overview. In R. Glaser, M.T.H. Chi and M.J. Farr (Eds.), *The nature of expertise* (pp. xv–xxviii). Hillsdale, NJ: Lawrence Erlbaum.

Graca, A. (1994). Os comos e os quandos no ensino do jogo [The hows and the whys in the teaching of games]. In A. Graca and J. Oliveira (Eds.), *O ensino dos jogo desportivos* [The teaching of sport games] (pp. 27–34). Porto, Portugal: CEJD/FCDEF-UP.

Graca, A. and Oliveira A. (1994). *O ensino dos jogos desportivos* [The teaching of sport games]. Porto, Portugal: CEJD/FCDEF-UP.

Graham, G. (1977). Helping students design their own games. *Journal of Physical Education and Recreation,* 48(7): 35.

Graham, K.C., Ellis, S.D., Williams, C.D., Kwak, E.C. and Werner, P.H. (1996). High- and low-skilled target students' academic achievement and instructional performance in a 6-week badminton unit. *Journal of Teaching in Physical Education,* 15(4): 477–489.

Grehaigne, J.F., Bouthier, D. and David, B. (1997). Dynamic-system analysis of opponent relationships in collective actions in soccer. *Journal of Sports Sciences,* 15: 137–149.

Grehaigne, J.F. and Godbout, P. (1995). Tactical knowledge in team sports from a constructivist and cognitivist perspective. *Quest, 47*: 490–505.

Grehaigne, J.F., Godbout, P. and Bouthier, D. (1997). Performance assessment in team sports. *Journal of Teaching in Physical Education, 16*: 500–516.

Grehaigne, J.F., Godbout, P. and Bouthier, D. (2001). The teaching and learning of decision making in team sports. *Quest, 53*: 59–76.

Griffin, L.L., Oslin, J.L. and Mitchell, S.A. (1995). An analysis of two instructional approaches to teaching net games. *Research Quarterly for Exercise and Sport, 66* (Suppl.), A–64

Griffin, L.L., Mitchell, S.M. and Oslin, J.L. (1997). *Teaching sport concepts and skills: A tactical games approach.* Champaign, IL: Human Kinetics.

Griffin, L.L. and Placek, J.H. (2001). Chapter 1. The understanding and development of learner's domain-specific knowledge: Introduction. *Journal of Teaching in Physical Education, 20*(4): 299–300.

Griffin, L.L., Dodds, P., Placek, J.H. and Tremino, F. (2001). Chapter 4. Middle school students' conceptions of soccer: Their solutions to tactical problems. *Journal of Teaching in Physical Education, 20*(4): 324–340.

Gubacs, K., Carney, M.P., Griffin, L.L. and Supapron, S. (1998). "Orderly chaos:" Future teacher educators' learning experiences implementing a tactical approach to games teaching. *Research Quarterly for Exercise and Sport, 69* (Suppl.), A–92.

Gubacs, K. (1999). Action research on a tactical approach to teaching a preservice tennis class. *Research Quarterly for Exercise and Sport, 70*(1), Supplement, 82.

Handford, C., Davids, K., Bennet, S. and Button, C. (1997). Skill acquisition in sport: Some applications of an evolving practice ecology. *Journal of Sports Science, 15*: 621–640.

Hare, M.K. and Graber, K.C. (2000). Student misconceptions during two invasion game units in physical education: A qualitative investigation of student thought processing. *Journal of Teaching in Physical Education, 20*: 55–77.

Holt, N.L., Strean, W.B. and Bengoechea, E.G. (2002). Expanding the teaching games for understanding model: A qualitative investigation of student thought processing. *Journal of Teaching in Physical Education, 21*: 162–176.

Hopper, T. (2003). Four R's for tactical awareness: Applying game performance assessment in net/wall games. *Journal of Teaching Elementary Physical Education, 14*(2): 16–21.

Howarth, K. and Walkuski, J. (2003). Teaching tactical concepts with preservice teachers. In J. Butler, L. Griffin, B. Lombardo and R. Nastasi (Eds.), *Teaching games for understanding* in physical education and sport. Oxon Hill, MD: AAHPERD Publication.

Hughes, M. and Jones, R. (2003). *Patterns of play of successful and unsuccessful teams in men's 7-a-side rugby union.* In Book of abstracts, world congress on science and football 5. (pp. 81–82.). Gymnos: Spain.

Iso-Ahola, S.E. (1980). *The social psychology of leisure and recreation.* Dubuque, IA: Wm.C. Brown.

Jackson, S., Jones, D. and Williamson, T. (1982). It's a different ball game! *Bulletin of Physical Education, 18*(1): 23–31.

Jaegle`, P. and Roubaud, P. (1990). *La notion de re`alite`.* Paris: Messidor, Ed. Sociales.

Kessel, J. (1992). *Volleyball's basic skills.* Pittsburgh, PA: Sports Support Syndicate Inc.

Kidman, L. (2001). *Developing decision makers: An empowerment approach to coaching.* Christchurch, New Zealand: Innovative Pring Communications Ltd.

Kirk, D., Theoretical guidelines for teaching for understanding. *Bulletin of Physical Education, 19*(1), Spring 1983, 41-45.

Kirk, D. and Macdonald, D. (1998). Situated learning in physical education. *Journal of Teaching in Physical Education, 17*: 376–387.

Kirk, D. and MacPhail, A. (2002). Teaching games for understanding and situated learning: Rethinking the Bunker-Thorpe model. *Journal of Teaching in Physical Education, 21*: 177–192.

Laban, R. (1963). *Modern educational dance* (2nd ed.). London: Macdonald and Evans.

Langley, D.J. (1995). Student cognition in the instructional setting. *Journal of Teaching in Physical Education, 15*: 25–40.

Launder, A.G. (2001). *Play practice. The games approach to teaching and coaching sports.* Champaign, IL.: Human Kinetics.

Lave, J. and Wenger, E. (1991). *Situated learning: Legitimate peripheral participation.* New York: Cambridge University Press.

Lawton, J. (1989). Comparison of two teaching methods in games. *Bulletin of Physical Education, 25*(1): 35–38.

Lawton, J. and Werner, P. (1989). A program of badminton/net games which emphasize tactical awareness. *The Physical Educator, 46*: 99–106.

Lee, A. (2004). Promoting lifelong physical activity through quality physical education (Alliance Scholar Lecture). *Journal of Physical Education, Recreation, and Dance, 75*: 21–24, 54–55.

Light, R. (2003). Preser vice teachers' responses to TGfU in an Australian university: "No room for heroes". In J. Butler, L. Griffin, B. Lombardo and R. Nastasi (Eds.), *Teaching games for understanding in physical education and sport: An international perspective.* Oxon Hill, MD: AAHPERD Publications.

Light, R. and Fawns, F. (2003). Knowing the game: Integrating speech and action in games teaching through TGFU. *Quest, 55*: 161–176.

Mahut, N., Chevalier, G., Mahut, B. and Grehaigne, J.F. (2003a). The construction of student tactical knowledge in badminton. In J. Butler, L. Griffin, B. Lombardo and R. Nastasi (Eds.), *Teaching games for understanding in physical education and sport. An international perspective* (pp. 139–154). Oxon Hill, MD: AAHPERD Publications.

Mahut, N., Chang, C.W., Nachon, M., Chevalier, G. and Grehaigne, J.F. (2003). *Student action reading and meaning attribution: Towards a model of interpretation register in game play*. Paper presented at the 2nd International Conference: Teaching Sport and Physical Education for Understanding, Melbourne, Australia.

Malho, F. (1969). *Acte Tactique en jeu* [Tactical action in play]. Paris: Vigot.

Mandigo, J.L. (2003). Using problem based learning to enhance tactical awareness in target games. In J. Butler, L. Griffin, B. Lombardo and R. Nastasi (Eds.), *Teaching games for understanding in physical education and sport: An international perspective* (pp. 15–28). Oxon Hill, MD: AAHPERD Publications.

Mauldon, E. and Redfern, H.B. (1969). *Games teaching: A new approach approach for the Primary School.* London: MacDonald and Evans Ltd.

Mauldon, E. and Redfern, H.B. (1981). *Games teaching: an approach for the Primary School.* London: MacDonald and Evans Ltd.

McMorris, T. (1998). Teaching games for understanding: Its contribution to the knowledge of skill acquisition from a motor learning perspective. *European Journal of Physical Education*, 3: 65–74.

McPherson, S.L. (1991). *Changes in knowledge content and structure in adult beginner tennis: A longitudinal study.* Paper presented at the North American Society for the Psychology of Sport and Physical Activity, Asilomar, CA.

McPherson, S.L. (1992). *Instructional influences on longitudinal development of beginners' knowledge representation between points in tennis.* Paper presented at the North American Society for the Psychology of Sport and Physical Activity, Pittsburgh, PA.

McPherson, S.L. (1993). Instructional influences on player's planning strategies in tennis [Abstract]. *Research Quarterly for Exercise and Sport*, 64(Suppl.), A–78.

McPherson, S.L. (1994). The development of sport expertise: Mapping the tactical domain. *Quest*, 46(2): 223–240.

McPherson, S.L. and French, K.E. (1991). Changes in cognitive state and motor skill in tennis. *Journal of Sport and Exercise Psychology*, 1: 26–41.

McPherson, S.L. and Thomas, J.R. (1989). Relation of knowledge and performance in boys' tennis: Age and expertise. *Journal of Experimental Child Psychology*, 48: 190–211.

Magill, R.A. (1993). *Motor learning: Concepts and applications* (4th ed.). Madison, WI: Brown and Benchmark.

McKinney, D. (1977). But can game skills be taught? *Journal of Physical Education and Recreation*, 48(7): 17–20.

Mesquita, I. (1991). O ensino do voleibol na escola [The teaching of volleyball at school]. *Horizonte*, 43: 31–37.

Mesquita, I. and Graca, A. (2003). Physical education teachers' conceptions about teaching TGfU in Portuguese Schools. In J. Butler, L. Griffin, B. Lombardo and R. Nastasi (Eds.), *Teaching Games for Understanding in Physical Education and Sport: An International Perspective* (pp. 87–98). Oxon, MD: AAHPERD Publications.

Messick, J. (1977). Movement is the medium. *Journal of Physical Education and Recreation*, 48(7): 29–30.

Metzler, M.W. (2000). Instructional models for physical education. Boston: Allyn and Bacon.

Mitchell, S., Griffin, L. and Oslin, J.L. (1994). Tactical awareness as a developmentally appropriate focus for the teaching of games in elementary and secondary physical education. *The Physical Educator*, 51(1): 21–28.

Mitchell, S.A., Griffin, L.L. and Oslin, J.L. (1995). An analysis of two instructional approaches to teaching invasion games. *Research Quarterly for Exercise and Sport*, 66(Suppl.), A–65.

Mitchell, S.A., Griffin, L.L. and Oslin, J.L. (1997). Teaching invasion games: A comparison of two instructional approaches. *Pedagogy in Practice: Teaching and Coaching in Physical Education and Sports*, 3(2): 56–69.

Mitchell, S.A. and Oslin, J.L. (1999a). An investigation of tactical understanding in net games. *European Journal of Physical Education*, 4: 162–172.

Mitchell, S.A. and Oslin, J.L. (1999b). *Assessment in games teaching*. Reston, VA: National Association of Sport and Physical Education.

Mitchell, S., Oslin, J. and Griffin, L. (1995). The effects of two instructional aproaches on game performance. *Pedagogy in Practice: Teaching and Coaching in Physical Education and Sport*, 1: 36–48.

Mitchell, S.A., Oslin, J.L. and Griffin, L.L. (2003). *Sport foundations for elementary physical education: A tactical games approach*. Champaign, IL: Human Kinetics.

Morris, D. (1976). *How to change the games children play*. Minneapolis, MN: Burgess Publishing Co.

Morris, G.S.D. (1977). Let's give the games back to the children. *Journal of Physical Education and Recreation*, 48(7): 26–27.

Morris, G.S.D. and Stiehl, J. (1999). *Changing kids' games* (2nd ed). Champaign, IL: Human Kinetics.

Nachon, M., Mahut, N., Mahut, B. and Grehaigne, J.F. (2001: June). *Student's construction of strategies in table tennis: Design of the expectation horizon within debate of ideas.* Paper presented at the AIESEP Proceedings, Taipei (TW), June.

Nevett, M.E. and French, K.E. (1997). The development of sport-specific planning, rehearsal and updating of plans during defensive youth baseball game performance. *Research Quarterly for Exercise and Sport*, 68: 203–214.

Nevett, M., Rovegno, I. and Babiarz, M. (2001). Chapter 8. Fourth-grade children's knowledge of cutting, passing and tactics in invasion games after a 12-lesson unit of instruction. *Journal of Teaching in Physical Education*, 20(4): 389–401.

Nevett, M., Rovegno, I., Babiarz, M. and McCaughtry, N. (2001). Chapter 6. Changes in basic tactics and motor skills in an invasion-type game after a 12-lesson unit of instruction. *Journal of Teaching in Physical Education*, 20(4): 352–369.

Newell, K.M. (1986). Constraints on the development of coordination. In M.G. Wade and H.T.A. Whiting (Eds.), *Motor development in children: Aspects of coordination and control* (pp. 341–360). Dordrecht, The Netherlands: Marinus Nijhoff.

Oslin, J.L. (1996). Tactical approaches to teaching games. *Journal of Physical Education, Recreation, and Dance, 67*(1): 27.

Oslin, J.L., Mitchell, S.A. and Griffin, L.L. (1998). The game performance assessment instrument (GPAI): Development and preliminary validation. *Journal of Teaching in Physical Education, 17*: 231–243.

Ota, D. and Vickers, J. (1999). The effects of variable practice on the retention and transfer of two volleyball skills in male club-level athletes. *International Journal of Volleyball Research, 1*(1): 18–24.

Penney, D. and Brooker, R. (2002). *Sport education in physical education: An exploration of place, purpose and pedagogy.* Paper presented at the Australian Association for Research in Education Conference, Brisbane. (http://www.aare.edu.au/02pap/pen02258.htm)

Penney, D., Clarke, G. and Kinchin, G. (2002). Developing physical education as a 'connective specialism': Is sport education the answer? *Sport, Education and Society, 7*: 55–64.

Piggott, B. (1982). A psychological basis for new trends in games teaching. *Bulletin of Physical Education, 18*(1): 17–22.

Piltz, W. (2003). Teaching and coaching using a 'Play Practice' approach. In J. Butler, L. Griffin, B. Lombardo and R. Nastasi (Eds.), *Teaching games for understanding in physical education and sport. An international perspective* (pp. 189–200). Oxon Hill, MD: AAHPERD Publications.

Placek, J.H. and Griffin, L.L. (2001). Chapter 9. The understanding and development of learners' domain-specific knowledge: Concluding comments. *Journal of Teaching in Physical Education, 20*(4): 402–406.

Placek, J.P., Griffin, L.L., Dodds, P., Raymond, C. and James, A. (2001). Chapter 3. Middle school students' conceptions of fitness: The long road to a healthy lifestyle. *Journal of Teaching in Physical Education, 20*(4): 314–323.

Richard, J. F., Godbout, P., Tousignant, M. and Gerhaigne, J.F. (1999). The try-out of a team sport performance assessment procedure in elementary and junior high school physical education classes. *Journal of Teaching in Physical Education, 18*: 336–356.

Riley, M. (1977). Teaching original games. *Journal of Physical Education and Recreation, 48*(7): 30–32.

Rink, J. (1996). Tactical and skill approaches to teaching sport and games: Introduction. *Journal of Teaching in Physical Education, 15*(4): 397–398.

Rink, J., French, K.E. and Graham, K. (1996). Implications for practice and research. *Journal of Teaching in Physical Education, 15*(4): 490–502.

Rink, J.E. (2001). Investigating the assumptions of pedagogy. *Journal of Teaching in Physical Education, 20*: 112–128.

Rink, J.E., French, K.E. and Tjeerdsma, B.L. (1996). Foundations for the learning and instruction of sport and games. *Journal of Teaching in Physical Education, 15*(4): 399–417.

Roberton, M.A. (1977). Developmental implications for games teaching. *Journal of Physical Education, Recreation, and Dance, 48*(7): 25.

Rogoff, B. (1990). *Apprenticeship in thinking: Cognitive development in social context.* New York: Oxford University Press.

Rovegno, I. (1995). Theoretical perspectives on knowledge and learning and a student teacher's pedagogical content knowledge of dividing and sequencing subject matter. *Journal of Teaching in Physical Education, 14*: 284–304.

Rovegno, I. (1999). *What is taught and learned in physical activity programs: The role of content.* Paper presented at the Keynote presentation at the AIESEP Conference, Beasancon, France.

Rovegno, I., Nevett, M. and Babiarz, M. (2001). Chapter 5. Learning and teaching invasion-game tactics in 4th grade: Introduction and theoretical perspective. *Journal of Teaching in* Physical Education, 20(4): 341–351.

Rovegno, I., Nevett, M., Brock, S. and Babiarz, M. (2001). Chapter 7. Teaching and learning basic invasion-game tactics in 4th grade: A descriptive study from situated and constraints theoretical perspectives. *Journal of Teaching in Physical Education, 20*(4): 370–388.

Schmidt, R.A. (1975). A schema tgheory of discrete motor skill learning. *Psychological Review, 82*: 225–260.

Schoenfeld, A.L. (1999). Looking toward the 21st century: Challenges of educational theory and practice. *Educational Researcher, 28*: 4–14.

Schon, D.A. (1990). *Educating the reflective practitioner: Toward a new design for teaching and learning in the professions.* San Francisco, CA: Jossey-Bass.

Siedentop, D. (1994). *Sport education: Quality PE through positive sport experiences.* Champaign, IL: Human Kinetics.

Simon, M.A. (1995). Reconstructing mathematics pedagogy from a constructivist perspective. *Journal for Research in Mathematics Education, 26*: 114–145.

Singer, R.N., DeFrancesco, C. and Randall, L.E. (1989). Effectiveness of a global learning strategy practiced in different contexts on primary transfer self-paced motor tasks. *Journal of Applied Sport Psychology, 11*(3): 290–303.

Starkes, J.L. and Allard, F. (Eds.). (1993). *Cognitive issues in motor expertise.* Amsterdam: Elsevier.

Stein, J.F. (1981). *Sports d'opposition, elements d'analyse pour une pedagogie des prises de decisions* [Opposition sports, elements of analysis for a decision making pedagogy]. Paris: INSEP.

Strean, W.B. and Holt, N.L. (2000). Players', coaches', and parents' perceptions of fun in youth sports: Assumptions about learning and implications for practice. *Avante, 6*: 83–98.

Sullivan, E. and Swabey, K. (2001). *Assessment of pre-service teaching practices using a traditional and a teaching games for understanding (TGFU) approach: Pilot date from the United States and Australia.* Paper presented at the Conference Proceedings of the International Congress: Teaching Games for Understanding in Physical Education and Sport, Waterville, NH.

Sullivan, E. and Swabey, K. (2003). Comparing assessment of preservice teaching practices using traditional and TGfU instructional models: Data from Australia and the United States. In J. Butler, L. Griffin, B. Lombardo and R. Nastasi (Eds.), *Teaching games for understanding in physical education and sport: An international perspective* (pp. 99–112). Oxon, MD: AAHPERD Publications.

Suzuki, K. and Nishijima, T. (2004). Validity of a soccer defending skill scale (SDSS) using game performances. *International Journal of Sport and Health Science*, 2: 34–49.

Sweeney, M. and Everitt, A. (2000). *Validation of the learning by connections scale*. Unpublished raw data.

Sweeney, M., Everitt, A. and Carifio, J. (2003). Teaching games for understanding: A paradigm shift for undergraduate students. In J. Butler, L. Griffin, B. Lombardo and R. Nastasi (Eds.), *Teaching games for understanding in physical education and sport: An* international perspective (pp. 113–122). Oxin Hill, MD: AAHPERD Publications.

Tavares, F. (1994). O processamento de informacao nos jogos desportivos colectivos. In A Graca and J. Oliveira (Eds.), *O ensino dos jogos desportivos* [The teaching of sport games] (pp. 35–46). Porto, Portugal: CEJD/FCDEF-UP.

Thomas, J.R., French, K.E. and Humphries, C.A. (1986). Knowledge development and sport skill performance: Directions for motor behavior research. *Journal of Sport Psychology*, 8: 259–272.

Thomas, J.R., French, K.E., Thomas, K.T. and Gallagher, J.D. (1988). Children's knowledge development and sport performance. In R.A. Magill, F.L. Smoll and M.J. Ash (Eds.), *Children in sport* (3rd ed.). Champaign, IL: Human Kinetics.

Thomas, J.R. and Nelso, J.K. (1996). *Research methods in physical activity* (3rd ed.). Champaign, IL: Human Kinetics.

Thomas, K. (1994). The development of sport expertise: From Leeds to MVP legend. *Quest*, 46(2): 199–210.

Thorpe, R., Bunker, D. and Almond, L. (1986). Rethinking games teaching. Loughborough, England: Department of Physical Education and Sports Science University of Technology.

Thorpe, R. (1990). New directions in games teaching. In N. Armstrong (Ed.), *New directions in physical education* (pp. 79–100). London: Human Kinetics.

Thorpe, R. (1992). The psychological factors underpinning the 'teaching for understanding games' movement. In L. Almond T. Williams and A. Sparks (Eds.), *Sport and physical* activity: Moving towards excellence (pp. 209–218). London: E and FN Spon.

Thorpe, R. (2001). Rod Thorpe on teaching games for understanding. In L. Kidman (Ed.), *Developing decision makers: An empowerment approach to coaching* (pp. 22–36). New Zealand: Innovative Print Communication.

Thorpe, R. and Bunker, D. (1986). Is there a need to reflect on our games teaching? In R. Thorpe, Bunker, D. and Almond, L. (Eds.), *Rethinking games teaching.* (pp. 25–34). Loughborough, UK: Department of

Physical Education and Sports Science, University of Technology.

Thorpe, R. and Bunker, D. (1989). A changing focus in games teaching. In L. Almond (Ed.), *The place of physical education in schools.* (pp. 52–80). London, GB: Kogan Page.

Thorpe R., Bunker, D. and Almond, L. (1984a). Four fundamentals for planning a games curriculum. *Bulletin of Physical Education*, 20: 24–28.

Thorpe, R.D., Bunker, D. and Almond, L. (1984b). A change in the focus of teaching games. In In M. Pieron and G. Graham (Eds.), *Sport pedagogy: Olympic scientific congress* proceedings. Champaign, IL: Human Kinetics.

Thorpe, R., Bunker, D. and Almond, L. (Eds.). (1986). *Rethinking Games Teaching.* Loughborough, UK: University of Technology.

Tjeerdsma, B.L., Rink, J.E. and Graham, K.C. (1996). Student perceptions, values, and beliefs prior to, during and after badminton instruction. *Journal of Teaching in Physical* Education, 15(4): 464–476.

Turner, A.P., Allison, P.C. and Pissanos, P.W. (2001). Constructing a concept of skillfulness in invasion games within a games for understanding context. *European Journal of Physical* Education, 6: 38–54.

Turner, A. (1996). Teachers' perceptions of technical and tactical models of instruction. *Research Quarterly for Exercise and Sport*, 67(Suppl.), A–90.

Turner, A.P. and Martinek, T.J. (1992). A comparative analysis of two models for teaching games (technique approach and game centered [tactical focus] approach). *International Journal of Physical Education*, 29(4): 15–31.

Turner, A.P. and Martinek, T.J. (1995). Teaching for understanding: A model for improving decision making during game play. *Quest*, 47: 44–63.

Turner, A.P. and Martinek, T.J. (1999). An investigation into teaching games for understanding: Effects on skill, knowledge and game play. *Research Quarterly for Exercise and Sport*, 70: 286–296.

Wade, A. (1967). *The F.A. Guide to training and coaching.* London: Heinemann.

Walker, J. (2002). *Small-sided developmental games for children under twelve.* Edmonton: Alberta Soccer Association.

Werner, P. (1977). Inexpensive equipment for innovative games. *Journal of Physical Education and Recreation*, 48(7): 28.

Werner, P., Thorpe, R. and Bunker, D. (1996). Teaching games for understanding: Evolution of a model. *Journal of Physical Education, Recreation, and Dance*, 67(1): 28–33.

Wrisberg, C.A. and Liu, Z. (1991). The effect of contextual variety on the practice, retention, and transfer of an applied motor skill. *Research Quarterly for Exercise and Sport*, 62(4): 406–412.

5.6 Physical education and youth sport

KRISTINE DE MARTELAER AND MARK THEEBOOM

Introduction

The aim of this chapter is to describe the relationship between physical education and youth sport. Therefore it is useful to start with a short description of the terminology of physical education (curricular), extracurricular physical education and youth sport as used in this chapter. We approach *physical education* as the compulsory physical activities taught as an integral part of the curriculum for every pupil, described in final attainment levels as qualitative criteria (closed systems) or guidance (open systems) for physical education teachers and schools. Penney and Harris (1997) describe *extracurricular physical education* as "the provision of activities outside of formal physical education curriculum, most often after-school and at lunch-times, but also in some schools, at weekends and/or before school" (p. 42). This extracurricular offering of physical activities in schools or school sport is a collective term for play, sport and movement not compulsory for pupils but offered within the institutional framework of school with or without other sport providers (sports clubs, municipalities, private organisations). In this chapter (*organized*) *youth sport* can be understood as sports for children (under the age of 12) and youth (between 12 and 18 years of age) provided within the framework of a sport club or local municipality. When we want to underline the physical activities or sport participation of youngsters themselves, outside of an organisational context of adults, the term *movement culture* will be used.

The aim in this chapter is to accentuate the link between physical education, extra-curricular physical education and youth sport, which will be done from two approaches:

(a) structural and institutional level
(b) individual and interpersonal level

focusing on the program as well as on the leadership or pedagogy (Figure 5.6.1). The guidance or pedagogy refers, depending on the context, to physical education teachers, youth sport trainers, coaches, supervisors and youth sport coordinators. Figure 5.6.1 summarizes the different aspects to study the link between physical education and youth sport, taking into account the focus on the program and the pedagogy (x-axis), the structural and individual level (y-axis), and the context (z-axis).

Figueroa (1993) underlined that the cultural level provides the "frame of reference" for what follows at structural, institutional, individual and interpersonal levels. We are aware that it is impossible to generalize research findings on physical education and youth sport resulting from national surveys, more in particular predominantly from a European perspective. Nevertheless, examples of good (local) practices together with several international perspectives given in the literature are relevant and will be quoted.

Brief historical perspective of physical education and youth sport

This brief historical perspective gives a short overview of some data on curricular and extracurricular physical education and youth sport, focussing on the evolution of the programme and ways of teaching or guiding children. However, there is a lack of empirical information on extra-curricular physical education. According to Kirk (1998), this is due to the process of "academicization" of the field in higher education institutions as historians and sociologists have abandoned school sport and physical education for the apparently more appealing topics of community-based sport and exercise.

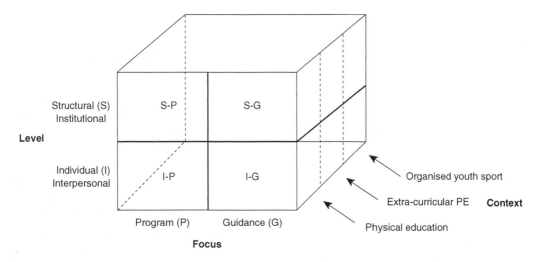

Figure 5.6.1   Overview of the different aspects to study the link between physical education, extra-curricular physical education and organised youth sport

Physical education – program

In history there is an obvious link between the evolution of the approach to sport within and beyond the school. Physical education has always been a reflection of the times (Naul, 1999). After a long period of rigid exercises up until the 1960s, the content of many physical education curricula accentuated a dominant sport curriculum copied from the successful competitive sport programs in some (British) schools, and in leisure time in general. Little by little, the objectives and methods of what was done in sports clubs among adults, such as the growing interest in circuit and power training, was adopted by physical education teachers. This resulted in an image of physical education as a synonym for (competitive) sport (Laporte, 1995). The world-wide survey findings of Hardman and Marshall (2000) reveal increasing orientations to both outside school agencies and competitive sport. As a reaction to this emphasis on performance and rules, a more recreational approach (the New Games Movement) came to influence physical education in the 1970s and 1980s. Forms of activities developed that reflected new and individualized values with action and thrills, but also with risk and fun, such as adventure and aquatic sports. Further, in elementary school programs a movement education framework was used to structure content in games, dance and gymnastics. Here, an understanding of movement concepts through problem solving and discovery was emphasized. According to Naul (1999), in the discussions between traditionalists and reformers, efficiency and performance have been critical points of debate because competition and fun are considered contradictory or incompatible

(see Chapter 2.4 for a more detailed history of physical education).

A third influence came from the perceived need to promote physical well-being, which resulted in an increased attention to fitness in and outside schools. It is no coincidence that physical educators around the world were developing health-based physical education programs at the same time as there was a popular cultural movement towards physical fitness and health (Hardman and Marshall, 2000; Kirk and Tinning, 1990).

The extra-curricular physical education program has traditionally comprised a competition-based sports program for those pupils who are most talented (Penney and Harris, 1997). However, as illustrated in an audit of school sport in Flanders (De Knop et al., 2001), increasingly large-scale recreational activities are also being offered to all pupils.

Physical education – pedagogy

The way experts and teachers believe physical skills are acquired has changed over time. Traditionally, teachers practised a command style method of instruction where learners were thought to be passive recipients of information. Until the middle of the 20th century, militaristic forms of instruction, influenced by the Swedish gymnastics, dominated physical education in Western European schools (Kirk et al., 2002; Stegeman, 2001). When games and sports became popular as content for physical education, the command style remained influential. In the last two decades of the 20th century researchers recognized that developmental and personal differences, as well as cognitive processes, influence how physical skills are learned. From this knowledge, teachers and coaches have begun to adopt a range of teaching styles (see Mosston and Ashworth, 1994). Theories of information-processing and constructivism have positioned the teacher in the role of facilitator (Kirk et al., 2002). Because of the complex cultural positioning of sport as a leisure pursuit, it is also necessary for young people to become critical consumers of youth sport options.

Youth sport – program and pedagogy

During the 20th century a lot of work was done to organise competitive sport on local, national and international levels. Because of the need to harmonize rules, selection criteria and league tables, sports federations have an international foundation. This institutionalization of sport implies that in some countries spontaneous movement activities such as skating or rope skipping have turned into sports as well. Sport has become more specialized and differentiated at the same time as the demands upon performance have increased. Most of the structural and institutional arrangements focus on the competitive orientation to sport. Another trend is the influence of fitness activities and outdoor recreation organized by commercial organizations. They offer possibilities to young people to be physically active in individual and unaffiliated ways, within and beyond the school year (De Knop et al., 1996, 2004a; Freeman, 1997, 1998).

In recent years, more and more initiatives have been taken to stimulate participation for less-talented and underprivileged youth. In the overview of good practices in Europe, Janssens et al. (2004) express their hope that the exchange of experiences and ideas within the scope of the European Year will continue to further the proliferation of good practices in education through sport. However, a lot of initiatives still lack a structural approach, thereby providing limited opportunities for more long-term effects (Janssens et al., 2004). To cite the words of these authors, "Success is by no means a guarantee for continuity" (p. 257). Further, because of the adult domination of youth sport, De Knop et al. (1996, 2004) have indicated it has become more serious and less playful. In many countries there are problems in getting qualified youth sport leaders through challenges in financing, educating and motivating them. The heavy dependency on (untrained) volunteers creates a high turnover and uncertain quality in leadership and coaching (De Knop et al., 1996, 2004).

Core concepts

The conceptual and theoretical underpinnings of school physical education have received substantial attention in the literature, however the same cannot be said for youth sport. Following is an outline of divergent and convergent conceptual thinking in both physical education and youth sport.

Conceptual thinking in physical education

In education, increasing emphasis is placed on the importance of cross-curricular links and holistic education. Arising from this, educational authorities define attainment levels or standards that a majority of pupils should be able to achieve at the end of particular stages during the school career. As well, there are the physical education specific attainment levels consistent with the holistic educational concept. Despite the diversity in the organization of physical education within different countries and national school systems, common objectives specific for physical education can be identified. The recent conceptual thinking in physical education comprises different categories, which include the development of:

- motor competencies;
- safe and healthy lifestyles; and
- positive self-concept and social functioning.

The development of motor competencies is pursued by offering physical activities in different categories such as: gymnastics, games, athletics, dance, outdoor and adventurous activities, swimming and water safety. Nevertheless, other ways of categorisation can be used, based on a common characteristic or aim, for example: "having direct or indirect interceptive contact with others", "individual performance", or "aesthetics". Because of the range existing in each of these categories, most school physical education programmes include only a selection from each category (Kirk et al., 2002).

In the UK the concept of "physical literacy" has been used within the profession for some years now. Whitehead (2001) defined effective "reading" in a physical context as follows: "The physically literate individual, on perceiving the environment, through a range of senses, appreciates, via experience, the relevant components of the display e.g. shape, size, weight, surface, speed, movement of others" (Whitehead, 2001: 8).

The second category in physical education conceptual thinking is the development of a safe and healthy lifestyle. Physical activity, health and fitness centres around the relationship between participation in physical activity and the health and well-being of individuals and societies and the key role that physical education has to play in influencing patterns of activity and health (Penney and Chandler, 2000). Specific material has been developed to inform physical education teachers about measuring physical activity and how to change behaviour (Borms et al., 1999; Pangrazi and Corbin, 2000; QDPE Mentor Program, 2004; Sallis and Owen, 1999). Using individualized programs for (some) pupils is one avenue. According to McKenzie (1999), physical education has the potential to be an optimal vehicle for influencing physical activity habits among youth. While not everyone has accepted health-related goals, Pate and Hohn (1994) indicated that there is a strong movement to adopt health promotion as the primary mission of physical education as seen in Canada, Australia and New Zealand where the learning area is called Health and Physical Education (Stegeman, 2001).

Another objective of physical education is to introduce young people to the world of sport and exercise. In Western sedentary lifestyles, introducing children to movement culture is certainly not something that comes automatically anymore. According to a number of authors, physical education must nurture participation in sensible leisure time activities and pupils must be prepared for active and critical participation in activity and sports culture (Laporte, 1992; McCracken, 2001; Stegeman, 2001). Educating critical sport consumers means: (a) letting them know what kind of activities and organizations are available on the market, (b) teaching them to discover their own capabilities, (c) teaching them to make choices, and (d) learning about values and norms in several sports (events).

The third conceptual category in physical education involves the development of a positive self-concept and social functioning. According to Ommundsen and Bar-Eli (1999), psychological outcomes, such as self-esteem and social behavior, are important in at least two ways. They may result in the pupils having positive experiences of physical education classes that in turn can develop a long-lasting motivation and interest in physical activity. The intervention at individual level is illustrated by means of the "transtheoretical model of behavioural change" (e.g. De Bourdeaudhuij and Rzewnicki, 2001; Sallis and Owen, 1999). Through this model teachers are provided a better insight into the specific stage a pupil is going through with regard to their attitudes towards physical activities.

Competitive sport and development of sport skills have been established as the dominant and defining feature of physical education (Hardman and Marshall, 2000). According to Jones et al. (1999), there is a pressure to compete successfully in inter-school sport, where good results have been associated with the school's general achievements, and that this has an impact upon physical education programs.

Conceptual thinking in youth sport: ethics and quality criteria

In contrast to the conceptual thinking in physical education, less work is done with regard to this area in youth sport. As a result this section will focus more on quality criteria in youth sport, thus desirable approaches in organizing and guiding youth sport will be emphasized. The concern for values and norms in sport in general and in youth sport in particular is growing. There are a few examples of specific publications which dealing with conceptual thinking in youth sport (De Knop et al., 1994; Smoll and Smith, 1996; Steenbergen et al., 2001; Vanden Auweele, 2004).

While the first publications dealing with pedagogical, psychological and/or social aspects of youth sport were published in the 1970s (e.g. Martens, 1978), in the 1990s and in recent years, more frequently and more detailed work has been produced (Brettschneider, 1990; Coakley, 1990; De Martelaer et al., 2001). The discussion about medical and pedagogical aspects of youth sport started several decades ago, while the debate on ethics and rights of children in sport has been more recent (David, 1993, 1999, 2004; De Martelaer, David, De Knop, 2006; Vanden Auweele, 2004). One of the international organizations spreading the sporting rights of the young and a fair play charter is Panathlon International (www.Panathlon.org), member of AGFIS (General Association of International Sports Federations) and of CIPP (International Committee for Fair Play). According to Panathlon International, children and youth have the rights, among others to: practise sports have fun and play like a child, attend training sessions adequate to one's own rhythm, and participate in competitions adequate for one's age.

In September 2004 a satellite conference on ethics in youth sport was organized during the 12th European Congress of Sport Management (EASM). Several experts have focused on children's rights and child abuse in sport. The arguments for reflection and discussion on a European level were:

- in only a few countries appropriate structures and measures exist to prevent or reduce the occurrence of incidents and for dealing with negative consequences,
- a committed sports world should use negative reports to stimulate better documentation on the causes, effects and mechanisms of abuse and question which values are explicitly and implicitly propagated in and by current competitive sport in children and youth,
- a growing awareness that sport does not automatically produce positive or negative effects and that good planning and sustained reflective action is needed to give the positive values of sport a better chance to prevail than the negative ones. (Vanden Auweele, 2004)

Quality criteria for youth sport have to be interpreted taking into account the typical characteristics of sport (Steenbergen and Tamboer, 1998). Steenbergen and Tamboer (1998) emphasized that

Table 5.6.1 Convergent and divergent conceptual thinking in curricular physical education and actual youth sport

Convergent	Curricular physical education	Youth sport
Convergent		
Broad offer	Wide choice in activities is good for child development in general and, more specifically, the physical development of children	Wide choice in activities and organizational context is essential with marketing as a starting point
Interest	Fix on possibilities according to accommodation and resources (in school and neighborhood) and ability of physical education teacher	Fix on local possibilities according to accommodation and resources in municipality and availability of volunteers
Divergent		
Objectives	Course-exceeding standards and/or course-specific final attainment levels in school	Final attainment levels are rare and usually only in case of competition
	'Learning-oriented' → development of: – motor competencies – safe and healthy lifestyle – positive self-concept and social functioning	Continuum between "win-oriented" and "progression-oriented" depending on organization and guidance → development of: – motor competencies
Focus	Stimulate transfer in and between domains of activities	Selecting specific sport activities/training sessions
Age group	Usually children are brought together based on their calendar age and cognitive performances in school	Children are brought together in broader age categories and/or necessary physical performances in the selected sport
Level	Teachers have to adapt the program to the level of the children and provide differentiation	Children are depending on the existence of an appropriate group according to their level of performance

competition, or exceeding the performance of others, is a typical goal for sport. In order to achieve this goal, uniform rules have to be respected together with a system of selection. After all, as indicated elsewhere (De Martelaer et al., 2001), in competitive sport the value of winning is usually one of the most important orientations. In youth sport, and more in particular for young children, a "progression-orientation" should be more important than the "win-orientation" (Buisman et al., 1998). A progression-orientation refers to the importance of improving one's own technical skills, condition, knowledge and insight in the sport characteristics. The question "how could children benefit from sports?" is of value and not "how could sports benefit from children?" (David, 1999).

Table 5.6.1 offers an overview of the most striking convergent and divergent conceptual thinking in curricular physical education and youth sport.

In this overview we did not mention anything about extra-curricular physical education. As defined in the introduction of this chapter, these are the physical activities (play, sport and movement) within the institutional framework of the school whether or not organized together with other sport providers but not compulsory for pupils. Curricular physical education and youth sport seem to have shared conceptual thinking as well as divergent aspects. Because of the status of physical education as a school subject on the one hand and the leisure orientation of youth sport on the other, both do have complementary goals in movement education. Nevertheless, extra-curricular physical education can bridge the gap between physical education and youth sport. In the following section we will not only focus on findings in physical education and youth sport but also on initiatives and data concerning extra-curricular physical education.

Major findings in youth sport

In this section research findings concerning youth sport and extra-curricular physical education will be described. Where possible and meaningful, the focus will be on the program content and pedagogy, although these two items cannot always be separated.

Youth sport

Several authors have described in recent years a number of trends that have occurred with regard to activities in youth sports (De Knop, 1998, 2004a,b; De Knop et al., 1994, 1996; Hartmann-Tews, 1996; Loret, 1995; Renson, 2001; Schwier, 1998; Vanreusel, 1998; Vanreusel and Scheerder, 2000). According to De Knop et al. (1996, 2004a) during recent decades, an increasing number of children have become involved in organized sport all over the world and, as a result, became an important target group. Most of these activities take place in a sport club or in extracurricular training in school. More boys than girls are sports active. This is especially true in traditional and team (competitive) sports. De Knop indicated that soccer is most popular among boys and swimming among girls. Jogging, cycling and walking are the most popular activities outside a sport club. It is interesting to note that there are hardly any sports that are only popular in one particular country. De Knop therefore indicated that the most common sports practiced by youth have become universal. Enjoyment and social reasons appear to be the most important participation motives among youth, while success in competition and better performance is indicated to be less important. Middle class children are over-represented in organized youth sport. Furthermore, sports club membership is related to gender, social class and family situation. That said, girls' organized sport participation has increased, thereby diminishing the difference between girls' and boys' sport participation. This phenomenon is more visible in Nordic countries (i.e. Sweden, Norway, Finland). However, this trend of increased participation in sports clubs among youth appears to have stopped and even diminished in other countries (e.g. Australia, Belgium, Canada, Finland, Germany, New Zealand, Portugal, Spain and Sweden).

According to a number of authors (among others Crum, 1992; Hartmann-Tews, 1996; Renson 2001),

the postmodern movement culture is characterized by a hybridization or internal differentiation of sport. This has been interpreted as a reaction against over-institutionalized and over-competitive sport. It has been indicated that there is a move from regulated sports to non-regulated or differently regulated sports. In other words, style is more important than results. There is flexibility regarding the location, playing rules and equipment; as well as an increased importance of music and clothing. Schildmacher (1998) also reported another trend occurring in the shift from organized sports in clubs and federations to other organizations (e.g. municipal, school sport and private organizations) and an increased freedom and flexibility regarding training times and commitments, and all-round service. The most important change in the movement culture of young people manifests itself in gradual replacement of traditional sports by individual sports and greater freedom of organization as a result of a perceptible process of individualization and differentiation. Commercial training institutes, where people can come and go as they like, have an increased attraction (De Knop et al., 1996). According to Renson (2001), the postmodern "homo ludens" composes his/her private mix of movement activities by zapping from modern sport disciplines to local traditional games, new street games, and movement activities from other cultures.

De Knop (1998) summarized trends in youth sport as follows:

- an increase in possibilities concerning active and passive sport commitment;
- a move from indoor sports to outdoor variants (beach volleyball, street-ball, etc.), frequently coupled to values such as sun, freedom and holidays;
- a move from large teams to smaller teams: volleyball with two players instead of six, basketball with three players instead of five, soccer with five players instead of 11;
- a move from safe sports to activities full of risk for the "kick": adventure sports, extreme skiing and extreme mountain biking, rafting;
- an increasing popularity of so-called "glide sports". Loret (1995) referred in this context to "la génération glisse" ("the gliding generation") in water, air and on snow;
- the youth-friendliness of competitive sport has been threatened because of the hard and sometimes monotonous competitions and training programs starting at early ages.

There is a rapidly growing number of national and world championships for junior athletes. As indicated by Freeman (1998), even within nations the trend is toward year-round, high-performance competition and national/international travel for young teen and pre-teen athletes. To cite in the words of Freeman,

"The child-athlete movie is becoming a Hollywood staple" (p. 55), referring to the child's emulation of a professional athlete's focus and success goals. The problem is that much is made of elite sport and its "showbiz" side, while sport for all is given insufficient consideration within local and national policies (Decker, 2002). Despite this a growing number of governmental/non-governmental organizations are currently increasing their efforts to promote sport participation for all people (Doll-Tepper, 2004) and for youngsters in particular (Flintoff, 2003). For Houlihan (2000) there is a "crowded policy space" in youth sport. Nevertheless keys for future success in implementing the many strategies for being physically active, practising and enjoying sport lie in cooperation amongst the different sectors and disciplines as well as coordinated and comprehensive efforts of all relevant partners, institutions and organizations (Doll-Tepper, 2004).

Western competitive sports have developed a greater degree of seriousness, focusing on results. As indicated by several authors, adult sport has influenced youth sport to a large extent and norms and values of adults are dominating (De Knop et al., 1996; Freeman, 1998). Ethical issues have been raised as psychologists, sociologists and pedagogues are concerned with negative effects such as overuse injuries, stress and burnout, problems related to growth, maturation, and readiness issues (David, 2004; Freeman, 1998; Vanden Auweele, 2005).

De Knop et al. (1996) have stressed the importance of sound youth sport guidance, because of the impact volunteers have in the educational process of children. This can be seen as a strength because of the intrinsic motivation of those adults. However, in many parts of the world there is a lack of qualified youth sport coaches, often as a result of educational and financial problems (De Knop et al., 1996).

All topics mentioned above have to be taken into account when analyzing the challenge or the restrictions in bridging the gap between physical education and youth sport by stressing the importance of decent extra-curricular physical education.

Extra-curricular physical education

In our analysis of the program, the way activities are organized will also be taken into account. Some initiatives to bridge the gap in the triangle between the school, the sports club and the municipality (Figure 5.6.2) are mentioned here, but scientific research in this area is scarce (Janssens et al., 2004).

Eighty percent of the citizens of the European Union agree with the statement that there should be a better co-operation between the educational institutions and sports organizations in their country (European Commission, 2004). Collins and Buller (2000) argued that the post school gap is as much in

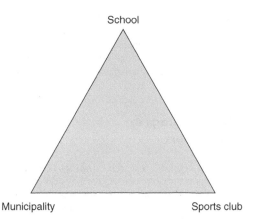

Figure 5.6.2 The local triangle to stimulate sport for children

the system as in participation. "Few children are given consumer skills to find their way through the sport and leisure maze, with its gaps and tenuous links" (Collins and Buller, 2000: 206). According to these authors, the success of agency campaigns "to bridge the gap" between physical education and out-of-/post-school activity has varied greatly. They underlined that the most successful programs have been those in which different agencies have worked in partnership. The problem is there is a lack of research and evaluation of projects (Janssens et al., 2004).

An audit, analyzing the strategic management of the school sport federation in Flanders (the northern Dutch-speaking community of Belgium), revealed that this federation emphasizes their own activities too much (De Knop et al., 2001). On the basis of this action research, recommendations were made in order to stress more local school activities, in co-operation with the municipalities and sports federations. According to their own policy documents, the school sports federation tries to initiate and motivate children in a broad array of sports activities: competitive as well as recreational, traditional as well as new trends (SVS, 2000–2006). Notwithstanding several new recreational initiatives of the federation, there is still a competitive orientation of school sport in Flanders (De Knop et al., 1998a). The researchers stressed that school sport organizers have to take into account that all children, including the less talented, should have the opportunity to try out one or more sports.

A good example of co-operative structural contacts in Flanders is the "Sports Academy", which provides a multi-sport program for local children after school time and without the requirement of membership of a sports club (De Knop et al., 1998b). This is a useful but not yet widespread organizational structure in Flanders. In early 2000 the Flemish government provided an extra budget to finance local youth sport with a distinct co-operation between the municipality, sports clubs and schools on a local level. The aim of the large-scale project, named "Youth Sport Contract", is to stimulate all children, including the non- and less-talented, who are not yet participating to become active in sports. In this project, the municipality is considered as an important link between the given sports actors (sports clubs, schools and municipal sports services) and the participants. The project subsidy stimulates a better use of the available resources such as people, infrastructure, logistics, and budget. In 2001, another initiative was launched by the ministry of sport and education, to try out with 18 physical education teachers a part-time involvement in school physical education combined with a part-time job in the sector of extra-curricular sport (school sport, municipality and/or sports club).

In the UK, a Government's strategy has been launched for "A Sporting Future for All", promising a new deal with governing bodies in sport. The strategy sets out the Government's vision for sport in the 21st century and highlights the importance of coordinating sport between schools and local clubs and organizations. They also plan a radical boost in access to school sport, with a five-point plan to make schools the nurseries of sports stars of the future.

This plan includes:

- a new fund for primary schools to provide 300 new, multi-purpose sports and arts facilities for pupils and the wider community;
- the goal of having 110 specialist sports colleges;
- the establishment of up to 600 school sports coordinators to develop more interschool competitive games;
- developing more after-school sport and physical education;
- encouraging world class performance athletes to volunteer to visit a minimum of schools each year (News and Views, 2000).

With the school sport coordinator program in the UK several of the following outcomes are pursued:

- increased participation amongst school-age children;
- increased participation by girls and young women, black and ethnic minorities, disabled young people and young people in areas of socio-economic disadvantage;
- improved standard of performance by children across a range of sports;
- improved motivation and attitude resulting in an increase in pupils' achievements in all aspects of their school life; and
- increased number of qualified and active coaches, leaders and officials in schools, local primary schools and local sports clubs/facilities (Flintoff, 2003).

The central premise in programs to realize the bridge between youth sport and physical education is the strategic development of networks and partnerships to maximize the quality, quantity and coherence of youth sport and physical education opportunities (Flintoff, 2003).

Because of the link between physical education and youth sport, it is interesting to look at ministries working out the policy of physical education and sport. According to Kirk and Gorely (2000), a large part of the problem at policy level lies in the separate responsibilities of government and their agencies. Sometimes a specialist has the task to link the Ministry of Sport and the Ministry of Education. According to Reeves (2001), building the bridges between the two Ministries is proving to be a mammoth task.

The literature on guidance in extra-curricular physical education and youth sport is also scarce. The personnel involved in a partnership as described for the UK have different roles:

- partnership development manager, is released from teaching timetable for two or three days per week in order to manage the partnership;
- school sport coordinator, is released from teaching timetable for two or three days per week in order to work with an identified primary teacher;
- primary link teacher is released from their teaching timetable for approximately 12 days per year and is responsible for physical education in their school.

Flintoff (2003) explored the perceptions of the teachers involved in the early stages of one School Sport Coordinator partnership about their new role. For the personnel it was of vital importance they could develop the partnerships they felt were important in their local context. According to the interviewees the school sport coordinator program offered opportunities for different kinds of interaction and staff development based on collaboration and cooperation. Part of the challenge of the program was to develop coherent and progressive opportunities for physical education and sport for young people both within and between the primary and secondary phases. The writing of their (three-year) development plan, central to the initial stage of their planning, was experienced as the most challenging and for some, the least interesting (Flintoff, 2003). Observational and interview data suggests that a "sporting" discourse has been dominated in the work so far. To have success in the future the ethos underpinning the coordinated activities has to be first and foremost "educational". According to the author the development of the staff through ongoing training and development will be central to the long-term success of the school sport coordinator program.

Christensen (2003) focused on three professions (physical education teachers, after-school teachers, and coaches), exploring their values and

Table 5.6.2 Major findings in youth sport and extra-curricular physical education

Focus on In the context of	Program	Pedagogy
Youth sport	– a lot of children have become involved in organized sport – broad offerings in leisure and sport activities → more consumer behavior and flexibility – internal differentiation movement culture lost transparency – evolution toward outdoor activities, small teams, extreme and gliding sports – hard competition and training programs starting at early ages	– problems in getting qualified youth sport coaches – heavy dependency on volunteers – ethical questions, too serious and adult-centered
Extra-curricular physical education	– the ethos is often sporting instead of educational – accommodating local needs is necessary for success – making a development plan is a challenge but not an easy job	– working in partnership, between schools (primary and secondary) as well as with outside agencies is central – ongoing training and development is crucial
Physical education	– competitive sport dominance – decontextualized teaching of sport – increasing orientations to outsides school agencies with the danger of non-educational objectives – high-quality PE programs result in psychological outcomes pertaining to enhance self-perceptions – financial restrictions and inadequate facilities, no manageable class sizes influences the quality of PE lessons and lead to reductions in PE programs	– education/training to implement a health-related PE curriculum has effect – PE specialists provide better classes compared to classroom teachers – PETE modules are taught in relative isolation from one another, which interferes with a holistic view on (physical) education – recent evolution in (physical) education prompts the shift from a predominant teacher-led to more pupil-led and from a predominant instructional approach to a management approach

working relationships in sport. The results show that these professions share a relatively common understanding of competencies relevant to their work, while they point to different values in physical education and sport. Moreover, development of partnerships across professions was difficult, mainly because of different cultures of practice and working relationship and different values and concepts in sport.

When physical education teachers are placed in a situation with priorities such as winning sport competitions, their position – being responsible for educational purpose – can be fruitful ground for role conflict (Jones et al., 1999; Jones and Potrac, 1996). Researchers have found more enthusiasm displayed by the practitioners within the coaching environment compared with teaching settings (Chelladurai and Kuga, 1996; Jones et al., 1999; Van

Deest, 2001). Where physical education teachers are co-ordinators in the triangle (school, sports club and municipality), the ethos should be educational and sporting inspired.

Table 5.6.2 summarizes the research findings on youth sport, physical education, and extra curricular physical education.

Applications to practice

Taking into account the challenge to make a well-considered choice keeping the pedagogical vision and practice in balance (Kurz, 1996), we cannot generalize for every country though an effort will be made to generalize some principles and possibilities. As indicated in Figure 5.6.1, focusing on program content and guidance can be done from two main levels: a structural or institutional and an individual and interpersonal one. The potential for change exists in the context of curricular and extra-curricular physical education and youth sport. Some aspects of change require a willingness to challenge thinking and reconsider policy on the part of agencies and ministries. Others change options have to do with the interest and capability of the individual guidance, department, school or local organization. Successively we will give some applications to practice at the:

- individual level of the teacher, the coach or the coordinator;
- local institutional level;
- institutional level of government; and
- institutional level of PETE.

The individual level of the teacher, the coach or the coordinator

Reference can be made to a quote from Christensen (2003) with regard to the school–sports club–municipality triangle.

> In the relation to the development of partnerships across professionals dealing with children's physical activity, different values in sport are both a limitation, because opposite values do not spontaneously inspire engagement in partnerships, and a challenge, because different values cover different needs and interests among the children.(Christensen, 2003: 33)

The main concern of guidance should be young people themselves, their development, their needs and requirement, their attitudes and interests.

It is obvious that due to a broader offering in the movement culture, physical education teachers have to watch over a sound choice. Timmers (2001) described three criteria that can be used to make well-considered choices in the physical education curriculum:

- developmental value: the activity can be gradually built up during different years and developmental phases;
- exemplary value and transfer: typical and similar characteristics for a group of activities regarding intentional, technical, tactical aspects and experiences; what is learned is a stimulus for other activities of the same category;
- experience and sport value: the activities are challenging, interesting and meaningful for the target market in general and young participants in particular.

Because youth sport is typically set up based on isolated and (inter-)nationally accepted sport structures and competitions, the criteria of choice may be restricted to what is offered within the municipality. Extra-curricular physical education frequently reflects the physical education curriculum with the added value of being an interface between the formal curriculum and voluntary youth sport. Depending on the role of the physical education teacher in the extra-curriculum program, they may act to help interface the different sites for young people's engagement.

The local institutional level

School-specific sport curricula provide opportunities for innovation moreso than at state and national levels (Fessler, 2000). Physical educators can focus upon how wider movements in society circumscribe and infuse school-based physical activity (Kirk and Tinning, 1990). Thus schools can become sites for the development of healthy lifestyles across the curriculum such as "moving", "active" or "broad" schools (Fessler, 2000; Janssens et al., 2004; Laeven, 2004). Some campaigns have et al. a broader focus than the encouragement of youngsters to practice more sport or being more physically active. There are some projects set up to stimulate youngsters to become actively involved in the organisation and implementation of sport. A good example is WhoZnext of The Netherlands with the goal to see more youngsters participating in local youth councils and school sport committees (van Groeningen and Meijs, 2004).

The institutional level of government

Nearly one decade ago one of the greatest challenges facing youth sport was to set up a co-operative and coordinated approach by schools, municipalities and clubs (De Knop et al., 1996). A challenge was offering sports in an educational environment for all children, enabling them to develop at their own speed according to their own interests. Recently, in some countries, political stimuli have given concrete form to a structural co-operation between sports organizations. While beyond the scope of this chapter to describe initiatives all over the world, an inventory of good practices would be a useful development. These examples can, once they are evaluated and their effectiveness and efficiency is proven, be implemented on a larger scale.

The institutional level of PETE

In order to bring about changes in policy and practice, PETE and volunteer coaching education have to be considered. Together with the strategic development of networks and partnerships to maximize quality, quantity and coherence of physical education opportunities and youth sport (Flintoff, 2003), those responsible for teacher training have to work out and evaluate an adapted role of physical education teachers. The central problem to "expand or deepen" the sport curriculum exists in the school curriculum as well as in the professional training of physical education teachers (Klinge, 2000). The learning of isolated motor skills should be replaced by a more holistic approach, taking into account the transfer of skills and knowledge across several sport disciplines. Penney and Chandler (2000) suggested establishing programs of study centring upon strands or themes, rather than specific areas or activities. According to these authors, the attention of both teachers and learners would thereby be clearly focused upon the "core learning" or "generic problems" of physical activity thereby facilitating transfer.

It is believed that once both the teaching and coaching settings are more clearly distinguished, teacher/coaching education and preparation programs should include strategies for coping with conflicting demands (Chelladurai and Kuga, 1996). This seems to be necessary taking into account the different values that are perceived depending on the profession and context or subculture in physical education and youth sport.

Pupil-led physical education and the need for a more child-centered approach in youth sport also have implications for physical education teacher education (PETE) programs. PETE programs need to address the changing role of teachers from teacher- to pupil-centered pedagogies (De Martelaer et al., 2004). Increasingly there is also a need to prepare teachers who can function as a member of a team with other physical education teachers, and to communicate, for example, with parents, physicians, and representatives and coaches of sports organisations. The recent initiatives on a structural basis to develop and enhance links between physical education and sporting opportunities in the wider community justify these foci in PETE as an important contributor to the quality of youth sport experiences.

References

Borms, J., Van Assche, E. and Pion, J. (1999). Fysieke activiteit en voeding. Meting en gedragsverandering [Physical activity and food. How to measure and change behaviour] Brussels: BLOSO.

Brettschneider, W-D. (1990). Pedagogical, psychological and social aspects of children's sport. In R. Telama, L. Laakso, and V. Vinko (Eds.), Physical education and life-long physical activity. Reports of physical culture and heath, Jyväskyla, AIESEP World Convention, June 17–22 1989.

Buisman, A., De Knop, P. and Theeboom, M. (1998). Quality of youth sport: towards a pedagogical framework. In P. De Knop. and A. Buisman (Eds.), Kwaliteit van jeugdsport, (pp. 29–61), Brussel: VUB Press.

Chelladurai, P. and Kuga, D.J. (1996). Teaching and coaching: Group and task differences. Quest, 48: 470–485.

Christensen, M.K. (2003). Professions and values in children's sport, International Conference on PE-teaching, learning and research, "What's going on in the gym? (p. 66)". University of Southern Denmark, 20th-22nd Nov. 2003.

Coakley, J.J. (1990). Organized sport programs for children are they worth the effort? In J.J. Coakley, Sport in society. Issues and Controversies. St.-Louis: Mosby College Publishing.

Collins, M.F. and Buller, J.R. (2000). Bridging the post-school institutional gap in sport: evaluating champion coaching in Nottinghamshire. Managing leisure, 5: 200–221.

Crum, B. (1992). Over versporting van de samenleving. Haarlem: De Vrieseborch.

David, P. (1993). Children and sport: accomplishment or exploitation. International Children's Rights MONITOR, 4: 8–12.

David, P. (1999). Les droits de l'enfant dans le sport. Jeunes athlètes en compétition: Exploits et exploitations. In Institut International des droits de l'enfant. Un champion à tout prix? Les droit de l'enfant et le sport (pp. 37–64). Institut International des droits de l'enfant and Institut Universitaire Kurt Bösch.

David, P. (2004). Human rights in youth sport. Oxon: Routledge.

De Bourdeaudhuij, I. and A Rzewnicki, R. (2001). Determinanten van fysieke activiteit [Determinants of physical activity]. In G. Beunen, I. De Bourdeaudhuij, Y. Vanden Auweele, and J. Borms (Ed.), Fysieke activiteit, fitheid and gezondheid (pp. 75–88). Speciale uitgave – Vlaams Tijdschrift voor Sportgeneeskunde en Sportwetenschappen.

De Knop, P. (1998). Jeugdsportbeleid, quo vadis? De noodzaak van kwaliteitszorg [Youth sport policy, quo vadis? The necessity of quality care]. Zeist: Jan Luiting Fonds.

De Knop, P. (2004a). Global trends in youth sport. Paper presented at International Conference on School sport and Physical Activity. Liverpool, UK, 9/12/2004.

De Knop, P. (2004b). Van invaller tot kernspeler. Leuven: Van Halewyck.

De Knop, P., Wylleman, P., Theeboom, M., De Martelaer, K., Van Puymbroek, L. and Wittock, H. (1994). Youth-friendly sport clubs. Developing an effective youth sport policy. Brussel: VUB Press.

De Knop, P., Engström, L.-M., Skirstad, B. and Weiss, M. (Eds.) (1996). Worldwide trends in youth sport. Champaign IL.: Human Kinetics.

De Knop, P., Theeboom, M., Spilthoorn, D., Arnouts, K., Leyers, H. and Leys, E. (1998a). De functie van schoolsport in het secundair onderwijs in Vlaanderen. De visie van leerlingen en leerkrachten. In P. De Knop and A. Buisman (Eds.), Kwaliteit van jeugdsport (pp. 249–263), Brussels: VUB Press.

De Knop, P., Van Der Smissen, M. and Van Look, T. (1998b). De gemeentelijke sportacademie: keuze-mogelijkheden buiten de schoolcontext. In P. De Knop, and A. Buisman, (Eds.), *Kwaliteit van jeudsport* [Quality of youth sport] (pp. 57–67). Belgium, Brussels: VUBPress.

De Knop, P. and Theeboom, M. (1999). Sports stimulation initiatives for underpivileged youth in Flanders (Belgium). *Journal of Education and Training, 20*: 1, 4–48.

De Knop, P., Spilthoorn, D., Theeboom, M., De Martelaer, K., Sannen, R. and Van Den Bergh, K. (2001). *Audit Stichting Vlaamse Schoolsport [Audit of the Flemish School Sport]* Final report. Brussels: Author.

De Martelaer, K., David, P., DeKnop, P. (2006). Rights of children in sport. In Y. Vanden Auweele, C. Malcolm, B. Meulders (Eds.), *Sport and Development*, (pp. 87–94). Lueven, Belgium: Lanoo Campus.

De Martelaer, K., De Decker, S. and Vandaele, B. (2004). Management capacities of the (future) teacher PE. *EASM congress Gent, Book of Abstract*, 181–182.

De Martelaer, K., De Knop, P. and Buisman, A. (2001). Child-oriented sport. In J. Steenbergen, De Knop, P. and A.H.F. Elling (Eds.), *Values and norms in sport. Critical reflections on the position and meanings of sport in society.* (pp. 303–322). Meyer and Meyer Sport.

Decker, R. (2002). Quality physical education and 'open sport', two principles of sport for all. *9th World Sport for All Congress 2002, Book of Abstracts*, 61.

Doll-Tepper, G. (2004). Sport promotion – realities and visions. In *Management capacities of the (future) teacher PE. EASM congress Gent, Book of Abstract*, 22–23.

European Commission. (2004). *The citizens of the European Union and Sport, Special Eurobarometer 213/Wave 62.0 – TNS Opinion & Social.*

Fessler, N. (2000). Curriculum theory in sport (1998–1999) (Publications in German). *International Journal of PE. A review publication, XXXVII*, 3, 94–103.

Figueroa, P. (1993). Equality, multiculturalism, anti-racism and physical education in the National curriculum. In J. Evans (Ed.), *Equality, education and physical education.* London: The Falmer Press.

Flintoff, A. (2003). The school sport co-ordinator programme: Changing the role of the physical education teacher. *Sport, Education and Society, 8*(2): 231–250.

Freeman, W.H. (1997). *Physical education and sport in a changing society* (5th edition). Boston: Allyn and Bacon.

Freeman, W.H. (1998). The trend toward professionalism in youth sport: The implications for educational sport for all. In R. Fisher, C. Laws and J. Moses (Eds.), *Selected readings 8th European Congress ICHPER-SD, "Active living through quality physical education".* (pp. 54–58). UK: St. Mary's University College.

Hardman, K. and Marshall, J. (2000). *World-wide survey of the state and status of school physical education.* Manchester: Campus Print Ltd.

Hartmann-Tews, I. (1996). *Sport für Alle? Strukturwandel europäischer Systeme im Vergleich.* Schorndorf: Hofmann.

Houlihan, B. (2000). Sporting excellence, schools and sports development: the politics of crowded policy spaces. *European Physical Education Review, 6*: 171–193.

Janssens, J., et al. (Eds.) (2004). *Education through sport. An overview of good practice in Europe.* Ministerie van Volksgezonheid, Welzijn en Sport.'s Hertogenbosch. The Netherlands: W.H.J. Mulier Institute.

Jones, R.L. and Potrac, P. (1996). The role of social construction in understanding participant motivation in physical education and inter-school sport. *Bulletin of Physical Education, 32*(1): 28–31.

Jones, R., Potrac, P. and Ramalli, K. (1999). Where sport meets physical education: A systematic observation of role conflict. *International Journal of PE, A Review Publication. 16*(1): 7–14.

Kirk, D. (1998). School sport and physical education in history, international journal of PE. *A review publication, XXXV, 2*: 44–56.

Kirk, D. and Gorely, T. (2000). Challenging thinking about the relationship between school PE and sport performance, *European Physical education Review, 6*(2): 119–134.

Kirk, D., Penney, D., Burgess-Limerick, R., Gorely, T. and Maynard, C. (2002). *A-level physical education. The reflective performer.* Champaign IL.: Human Kinetics.

Kirk, D. and Tinning, R. (1990). Introduction: Physical education, curriculum and culture. In D. Kirk and R. Tinning (Eds.), *Physical education, curriculum and culture: critical issues in the contemporary crisis,* (pp. 1–21). London: The Falmer Press.

Klinge, A. (2000). *Sport Wissenschaft 4*: 443–453.

Kurz, D. (1996). *Bewegungserziehung/Sport in der Lehreraus-und Lehrerfortbildung,* 30–49.

Laporte, W. (1992), Taak van de leraar L.O. in de sportieve opvoeding van de jeugd. *Tijdschrift voor Lichamelijke Opvoeding, 5*: 5–9.

Laporte, W. (1995). De LO in het onderwijs in België van 1842 tot 1990: een vak apart. In D.'hoker, M. and J. Tolleneer (Eds.), *Het vergeten lichaam* (pp. 37–57). Leuven: Garant.

Laporte, W. (1998). Physical education in the European Union in a Harmonisation Process (Part II): The physical education teacher for secondary schools. *ICHPER-SD Journal, 35*(2): 7–9.

Laeven, K. (2004). De sportieve school. *Lichamelijke Opvoeding, 92*(14): 36–39.

Loret, A. (1995). *Génération glisse.* Paris: Éditions Autrement.

Martens, R. (1978). *Joy and sadness in children's sports.* Champaign IL.: Human Kinetics.

McCracken, B. (2001). *It's not just gym anymore.* Champaign IL: Human Kinetics.

McKenzie, T.L. (1999). School health-related physical activity programs: what do the data say? *Journal of Physical Education, Recreation and Dance, 70*(1): 16–19.

Mosston, M. and Ashworth, S. (1994). *Teaching physical education* (4th edition). New York: MacMillan.

Naul, R. (1999). School sport and competition: sports pedagogy, *Perspectives, 1*: 73–83.

News and Views. (2000). A sporting future for all. *The British Journal of Teaching Physical Education, Summer,* 34.

Ommundsen, Y. and Bar-Eli, M. (1999). Psychological outcomes: Theories, research, and recommendations for practise. In Y. Vanden Auweele, F. Bakker, S. Biddle, M. Durand, R. Seiler (Eds.), *Psychology for physical educators,* (pp. 73–113). Champaign IL: Human Kinetics.

Pangrazi, R.P. and Corbin, C.B. (2000). Heath foundations: Towards a focus on physical activity promotion. *International Journal of PE, A review Publication, XXXVII, 2*: 40–49.

Pate, R.R. and Hohn, R.C. (1994). A contemporary mission for physical education. In R.R Pate and R.C. Hohn (Eds.), *Health and fitness through physical education* (pp. 1–8). Champaign, IL: Human Kinetics.

Penney, D. and Chandler, T. (2000). A curriculum with connections? *The British Journal of Teaching Physical Education, Summer,* 37–40.

Penney, D. and Harris, J. (1997). Extra-curricular physical education: more of the same for the more able? *Sport, Education and Society, 2(1)*: 41–54.

QDPE Mentor Program. (2004) www.cahperd.ca/e/qdpe/mentor.html

Reeves, B. (2001). Whither PE? *The British Journal of Teaching Physical Education, Spring,* 48–50.

Renson, R. (2001). Messages from the culture: Significance of sport and exercise in the third millennium, *European Journal of Sport Science,* 1(1): 1–17.

Sallis, J.E. and Owen, N. (1999). *Physical activity and behavioral medicine.* California: Sage Publications.

Schildmacher, A. (1998). Trends and moden im jugendsport. In J. Schwier (Ed.), *Jugend-Sport-Kultur: Zeichen und Codes jugendlicher Sportszenen,* Hamburg: Czwalina Verlag.

Schwier, J. (1998). *Jugend-Sport-Kultur: Zeichen und Codes jugendlicher Sportszenen,* Hamburg: Czwalina Verlag.

Smoll, F.L. and Smith, R.E. (Eds.) (1996). *Children and youth sport. A biopsychosocial perspective,* Madison: Brown and Benchmark.

Steenbergen, J., De Knop, P. and Elling, A. (Eds.) (2001). *Values and norms in sport. Critical reflections on the position and meanings of sport in society.* Oxford: Meyer and Meyer Sport.

Steenbergen, J. and Tamboer, J. (1998). The double character of sport: conceptual dynamics. In J. Steenbergen, A.J. Buisman, P. De Knop and J. Lucassen (Eds.), *Waarden en normen in de sport* (pp. 69–95). Houten/diegem: Bohn Stafleu van Loghum.

Stegeman, H. (2001). *Bewegingsonderwijs: belang en bedoeling.* Zeist: Jan Luiting Fonds.

SVS (2000–2004). Jaarlijks rapport. [*Annual report SVS*]. Brussels: SVS.

Timmers, E. (2001). *Bewegingsdidactiek.* Haarlem: De Vrieseborch.

Van Deest, T. (2001). Schulsport in England. *Sportunterricht, Schorndorf,* 50(7): 201.

Vanreusel, B. (1998). Leerlingen en hun bewegingscultuur. [Pupils and their movement culture] In H. Stegeman and K. Faber, (Eds.). *Onderwijs in bewegen: basisthema's in de lichamelijke opvoeding* (Lichamelijke opvoeding and Sport, theorie en onderzoek), (pp. 115–142). Houten: Bohn, Stfleu and Van Loghum.

Vanreusel, B. and Scheerder, J. (2000). *Sport: cultuur in beweging. Een verkenning van cultuurtrends inde sport,* Samenleving and Sport. Brussel: Koning Boudewijnstichting.

Van Groeningen, H. and Meijs, L. (2004). WhoZnext. In J. Janssens, et al. (Eds.), *Education through sport. An overview of good practices in Europe* (pp. 236–241). 's-Hertogenbosch/Nieuwegein: Mulier Institute/Arko Sports Media.

Vanden Auweele, Y. (2004). *Ethics in youth sport. Analysis and recommendations.* Leuven, Belgium: Lannoo Campus.

Whitehead, M. (2001). The concept of physical literacy. *The British Journal of Teaching Physical Education, Spring 2001:* 6–8.

5.7 Health-related physical activity in children and adolescents: a bio-behavioral perspective

GREGORY J. WELK, JOEY C. EISENMANN
AND JAMES DOLLMAN

Introduction

The health and emotional benefits from regular physical activity have been confirmed in the scientific literature and the majority of the population acknowledges the importance of being physically active. Unfortunately, most people still find it difficult to maintain regular patterns of physical activity. Promoting physical activity in all age groups is a critical public health priority but there has been an increased emphasis placed on understanding and promoting physical activity in youth. Part of the concern stems from the well-documented increase in the prevalence of obesity in youth over the past few decades (Ogden et al., 2002). Patterns are evident in all age groups and in most developed countries including Australia (Booth et al., 2003), Canada (Tremblay and Willms, 2000), China (Chunming, 2000), Spain (Moreno et al., 2000) and the UK (Hughes et al., 1997).

While the clinical manifestations of chronic diseases (e.g. cardiovascular disease, osteoporosis) typically do not occur until mid-adulthood, it is becoming clear that most chronic diseases have their origins in childhood and adolescence. Research also suggests that overweight and obesity may have more immediate health implications for children than previously expected. For example, type II diabetes was commonly characterized as "*adult onset diabetes*" but the emergence of type II diabetes among youth (Kaufman, 2002) has shown this to be a misnomer. The onset of type II diabetes and other metabolic problems in adolescence enhances the severity of problems later in life so it has been suggested that obese children may actually have greater risks in adulthood than individuals who develop obesity as adults (Boreham et al., 2001). This possibility changes the equation considerably and supports the current public health urgency to understand and promote health-related physical activity in youth.

Declines in physical education and/or lack of physical activity in the school day have not been specifically implicated as contributing causes of the increased prevalence of obesity in youth but these school-based programs are clearly viewed as part of the solution (Centers for Disease Control and Prevention, 1997, 2002; The Prevention Institute, 2001; American Academy of Pediatrics, 2003). Schools provide opportunities for children to be active during the day and training on the physical, cognitive and behavioral skills needed to be active later in life. This chapter will review the impact of physical activity on health for youth and document the effectiveness of school-based programming to promote physical activity in youth. The first section titled *Historical Perspective* will provide a brief overview of the chronology of research on health-related physical activity in youth and document the centrality of this research in advancing public health. A section titled *Core Concepts* will describe key issues in understanding health-related physical activity and fitness in youth. The *Major Findings* section will review patterns and trends in physical activity and summarize the effectiveness of school-based programs aimed at promoting physical activity in youth. The section on *Applications to Policy and Practice* will integrate the results from the past sections and highlight promising school-based approaches for youth physical activity promotion. The final section on *Needs for Future Research* will describe priorities for future research that may facilitate the curricular and environmental changes needed to increase participation in physical activity on a population level.

A number of excellent reviews have already been published on physical activity behavior in youth (Kohl and Hobbs, 1998; Sallis et al., 2000; Trost et al., 2002b; Welk, 1999), the relationships between physical activity and health of youth (Boreham et al., 1997; Caspersen et al., 1998; Eisenmann, 2004; Malina, 1995; Twisk, 2001) and on the effectiveness of school-based interventions in youth (Stone et al., 1998). This review adopts a bio-behavioral perspective and highlights the *potential* impact that school-based programs can have on promoting physical activity in youth. We contend that a clearer understanding of the bio-behavioral basis of physical activity is essential for helping physical education reach this potential.

Historical perspectives on health-related physical activity

The study of health-related physical activity in youth has a long history and its progression has been shaped by a variety of forces including political influences, advances in epidemiological research and changes in curricular approaches in physical education. The seminal events or influences that contributed to these shifts are described below.

Political influences

Political pressures during the late 20th century influenced the evolution and growth of the Kinesiology/Exercise Science field and the expansion of school-based physical education programs. In the United States, much of the impetus for studying youth physical activity can be attributed to the Kraus Weber report. This study highlighted the lower levels of motor fitness among American youth compared to European youth. Although the results have been challenged, the report served as a clear "call to action" and contributed to the formation of the President's Council on Physical Fitness and Sports. Similar changes in the evolution and promotion of physical education programs were evident in the UK and Australia following WWII. These political influences contributed to future trends in fitness as well as to a diversification and intensification of research efforts on physical activity and physical fitness.

Scientific influences

The evolution of disciplinary research in kinesiology and exercise science legitimized the study of physical activity as both a behavior and an outcome. While there were many notable findings from the late 1960s and 1970s, one of the more seminal discoveries impacting pediatric research was the discovery of advanced atherosclerotic lesions in the vessels of young soldiers who died in the Korean and Vietnam Wars (Enos et al., 1953; McNamara et al., 1971). The observation that this type of condition could be manifested in young adults brought attention to the need to study lifestyle behaviors and health outcomes in youth. Increased sophistication in research and public health practices led to enhanced surveillance

of health-related outcomes. These surveillance studies provided population-level statistics on important health-related variables and also allowed trends to be examined over time. In the United States, a major study called the National Child and Youth Fitness Survey provided detailed documentation on the status of health related fitness in school aged children (Ross et al., 1985; Pate and Ross, 1987). A similar national survey of Australian youth was conducted at the same time. Measures collected in this survey included a comprehensive array of health-related fitness variables on over 8000 youth aged 9–15 years. Follow-up analyses in this project have revealed substantial increases in body fatness and declines in aerobic fitness among Australian children since the mid-1980s (Booth et al., 2003).

A number of longitudinal studies of growth and physical activity and fitness have also advanced research on pediatric health issues. One such study, the Amsterdam Growth and Health Longitudinal Study, is a unique and rare multi-disciplinary, longitudinal study of the biological and psychosocial determinants of health from adolescence into adulthood that has lasted a quarter of a century (1974 to present). The study was initially planned to study the effectiveness of enhanced physical education on the growth and health of Dutch secondary schoolchildren (13 years of age) in 1974. Since the initial measurements during the teenage years, follow-up measurements have been recorded at ages 21, 27, 29 and 32 years. The ability to follow adolescent subjects into adulthood has allowed this study to analyze changes in health, fitness and lifestyles, determine the relationships between changes in lifestyle and health in a healthy population from age 13 to 36 years of age and examine the stability and predictability of health outcomes. This study and other pioneering studies of growth and fitness, brought attention to the needs to study the development of chronic disease.

In the 1990s, there was a dramatic paradigm shift in physical activity and physical fitness research. The assumption that vigorous intensity physical activity was needed to obtain important health benefits was eroded by epidemiological evidence documenting important health benefits associated with participation in more moderate forms of physical activity. The revised health-related guidelines for physical activity by the Centers for Disease Control and Prevention and the American College of Sports Medicine (Pate et al., 1995a) and the subsequent publication of the Surgeon General's Report on Physical Activity and Health in 1996 (US Department of Health and Human Services, 1996) enhanced the visibility of physical activity research and spurred on changes in research and funding priorities.

Implicit in this new paradigm was the realization that specific efforts were needed to promote physical activity in children. An international consensus conference in 1994 documented the unique needs for physical activity in youth (Sallis and Patrick, 1994). An Expert Consensus Group in the UK (Biddle et al., Cavill, 1998) provided updated documentation on these needs and recommended that youth should accumulate a minimum of 60 minutes per day for optimal health (*'Young and Active'*). Similar recommendations have been developed for Canada and the U.S. (Strong et al., 2005) (www.csep.ca/physical_activity_guide.asp) and new recommendations from Australia are in progress. The consistent message and standards embraced by these documents reveals the strong international consensus that has emerged regarding the importance of health related physical activity for youth. Further review of these documents is recommended for professionals and researchers interested in this topic.

Education/curricular influences

Physical education has an important role in shaping children's overall physical, mental and social well-being. The mission and philosophy of physical education have evolved over time – dictated, in large part, by the political forces and public health influences described above. For example, the increased emphasis on physical activity in the 1990s led to changes in the stated mission of physical education. One frequently cited statement (Pate and Hohn, 1994) described the contemporary mission of physical education as follows: ". . . to promote in youngsters the adoption of a physically active lifestyle that persists throughout adulthood". A similar mission statement is currently used as the basis for the *FIT-NESSGRAM* youth fitness program used throughout the United States (Welk et al., 2002). The definition of a "physically educated person" also emphasizes participation in (and appreciation of) physical activity (National Association for Sport and Physical Education, 2004a).

Curricula in physical education have shifted to focus more directly on the promotion of lifetime physical activity. Contemporary curricula programs now emphasize training on the physical and behavioral skills that children need to be physically active later in life.[1] Improvements in the quality of physical education programming are evident but competing pressures for enhanced academic performance standards in schools have restricted funding and support. These barriers have made it more difficult for physical educators to accomplish their intended objectives.

Summary of historical perspectives

Physical education provides a promising means to impact youth physical activity habits on a large scale. While physical activity is considered to be an important priority among public health researchers it has proven difficult to make systematic changes through school-related programs. An incomplete understanding of associations between physical activity, physical fitness and health in children has likely contributed to the marginalization of physical education in school programming. Many experts have called for the use of evidence-based curricula to increase accountability in school programs. However, challenges in implementing complicated programs and difficulty in documenting programmatic effects with traditional curricula have left holes in the scientific evidence needed to advance the status of physical education. The subsequent section will review key concepts essential to understanding links between physical activity, physical fitness and health in youth and provide the conceptual basis for the remainder of the review.

Core concepts

Relationships between physical activity, fitness and health are inherently complex but the added variability due to growth and maturation during childhood and adolescence further complicates these relationships. The unique social and behavioral characteristics of youth and inherent difficulties associated with measuring physical activity and fitness in youth present additional challenges (Welk et al., 2000). Three models that summarize key concepts in understanding health related physical activity in youth are described below.

Model 1: model of health-related physical fitness

Physical activity and physical fitness are often considered to be synonymous terms but they are fundamentally differences and have unique implications for health. The most fundamental difference is that physical activity is a behavior while health-related fitness (HRF) is a collection of physiological traits. While physical activity contributes to physical fitness the association is not as strong as one would expect – especially in youth (Morrow and Freedson, 1994).

A conceptual model that illustrates some of the possible associations between physical activity, physical fitness and health is provided in Figure 5.7.1. The figure was adapted from the one originally presented as part of the prestigious international consensus conference on physical activity and health (Bouchard and Shepard, 1994). The reciprocal relationships between physical activity and fitness are depicted with bi-directional arrows. The model also suggests that both physical activity and fitness contribute independently to health. For optimal health a person needs to be physically active *and* have reasonable levels of fitness.

It is important to note that physical fitness is not a unitary concept, but rather a multi-factorial

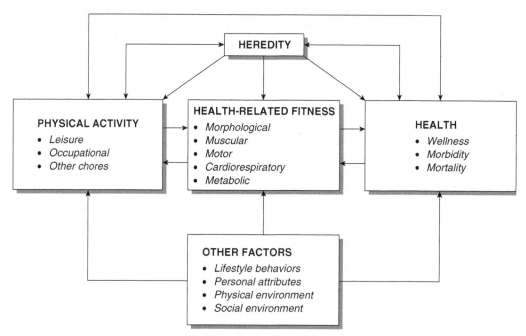

Figure 5.7.1 Multidimensional Model of Physical Fitness (adapted from Bouchard and Shepard, 1984)

representation of components. The five components of HRF in this model include morphological fitness, cardiorespiratory fitness, metabolic fitness, motor fitness and neuromuscular fitness (Bouchard and Shepard, 1994). These five components are categorized as independent factors based on common characteristics. A key principle in this model is that an individual may possess adequate levels of certain components (e.g. cardiorespiratory) but not others (e.g. motor). The multidimensional nature of physical fitness and the challenges involved in assessing physical activity have made it difficult to capture and understand the complex interactions between physical activity, HRF and health. Specific associations between physical activity and the different components of HRF are briefly described below:

Morphological fitness

Morphological fitness includes indicators that represent the structure and composition of the body such as subcutaneous and visceral adipose tissue, body fat distribution and bone mineral density. This component has often been labeled as body composition but the category of morphological fitness provides a more inclusive and broader classification of this component. Body fatness is the most common indicator of morphological fitness and numerous studies have been conducted examining associations between physical activity and body fatness. Results from large scale surveillance studies in the United States (Andersen et al., 1998; Crespo et al., 2001; Eisenmann

et al., 2002; Levin et al., 2003), Australia (Dollman and Martin, 2003; Wake et al., 2003), Canada (Tremblay and Willms, 2003) and Ireland (Boreham et al., 1997) have demonstrated associations between physical inactivity and body fatness or elevated BMI. Two large longitudinal studies in the United States (Berkey et al., 2000; Gordon-Larsen et al., 2002) have recently provided strong evidence that low levels of physical activity and high levels of inactivity are associated with changes in overweight in children, findings that have also been supported in a recent meta-analyses (Rowlands et al., 2000). Bone density is another important indicator of morphological fitness and positive associations have been reported between physical activity and bone mineral density in childhood and adolescence.

Cardiorespiratory fitness

In the composite model of HRF, cardiorespiratory fitness includes the categories of aerobic power, heart functions (blood pressure) as well as lung function. Participation in physical activity that challenges the cardiovascular system (aka aerobic activity) helps to improve cardiorespiratory fitness but the cross sectional associations between habitual physical activity and aerobic fitness are generally low in youth ($r < 0.20$) (Morrow and Freedson, 1994). The data suggest relatively little trainability of maximal aerobic power in children less than 10 years of age (i.e. less than 5% improvements). Among older children and adolescents the responsiveness of aerobic power to training increases considerably, but the absolute magnitude of trainability has been variable among studies (Payne and Morrow, 1993). The relatively limited impact of physical activity on cardiorespiratory fitness indicates that these parameters, while related, should be viewed somewhat independently.

Metabolic fitness

Metabolic fitness includes biochemical indicators of blood lipids and glucose metabolism that are important for cardiovascular disease and type II diabetes. While these indicators are not traditionally viewed as part of "physical fitness" by many professionals they are known to be influenced by physical activity and to relate directly to health. Indicators of metabolic fitness are known to cluster together as part of an overall "metabolic syndrome" that predisposes individuals to cardiovascular disease (Lakka et al., 2002). Recent findings have suggested the emergence of the metabolic syndrome during adolescence (Eisenmann, 2004; Ford et al., 2002). Physical inactivity has been associated with the onset of early cardiovascular disease in children (Boreham et al., 1997; Katzmarzyk et al., 1998, 1999) but it has proven difficult to determine the independent contributions of physical activity/physical inactivity and obesity on metabolic fitness. In adults, physical activity is known to moderate the impact of obesity on health outcomes (Lee et al., 1999; Wei et al., 1999) but this has not been established in youth.

Motor fitness

Motor fitness (also known as skill related fitness) refers to components that can improve the ability to learn and perform complex skills required in some sports and physical activities. The acquisition and improvement of motor skills is often a primary focus of physical education and youth sports but studies have not systematically examined how participation in unstructured physical activity may influence motor fitness development over time. Early exposure to a variety of motor skills is considered essential to facilitate skill learning at older ages.

Muscular fitness

Muscular fitness includes dimensions of power, strength and endurance. While resistance training can improve muscular fitness in adults there has been considerable interest (and debate) regarding the appropriateness of resistance exercise of youngsters. Historically, it was thought that resistance exercise could not improve muscular fitness in youth and could increase the risk of injury and premature closure of the epiphyseal plate. However, professional associations have suggested that pubertal and prepubertal children can gain strength and endurance without injury from a well-designed and supervised resistance training program (National Strength and Conditioning Association, 1996; Stratton et al., 2004). It is important for physical educators and others implementing resistance exercise into a curriculum or sports program to be familiar with youth guidelines regarding resistance training.

Summary of the influence of physical activity on health-related physical fitness

Physical activity has effects on a variety of physiological systems and has been shown to impact each of the different components of HRF. The associations between physical activity and health are quite strong in adults but relationships tend to be weaker in youth. This is largely due to the interacting influences of growth and maturation as well as the increased measurement challenges in this age group. In addition, most youth are relatively healthy so higher levels of physical activity may not impact HRF in the same manner as in adults. While the evidence is still incomplete, public health officials have widely acknowledged the importance of youth physical activity promotion as an important public health goal. This is mainly because of the potential tracking (i.e. the stability of a characteristic over time) of physical activity, physical inactivity and obesity across the lifespan. The next section will summarize research on the tracking of these parameters and how they may influence adult health outcomes.

Model 2: lifespan model of physical activity and health

Because lifestyles exert an influence on health at all ages it is important to adopt a lifespan perspective in studying physical activity, fitness and health. Blair proposed a conceptual model that describes pathways through which physical activity can contribute to health across the lifespan (see Figure 5.7.2). A key aspect of the model is that both physical activity and health-related risk factors have the potential to track into adulthood. Other paths in the model suggest that physical activity during childhood/adolescence may impact adult HRF and that HRF during childhood/adolescence may impact adult physical activity. Finally, the model suggests that childhood physical activity and/or HRF in youth can directly influence adult health outcomes.

Consistent with the previous multidimensional model, the Lifespan Model suggests that the relationships between physical activity and health outcomes are reciprocal (bi-directional arrows). Physical activity is needed for good health, but it is also true that a person must have some amount of health and fitness to be able to participate in physical

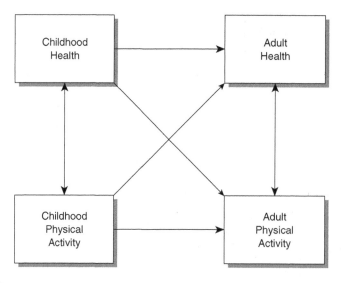

Figure 5.7.2   Lifespan Model of Physical Activity Promotion (adapted from Blair, 1989)

activity. Similarly, physical inactivity is both a cause *and* consequence of overweight and obesity. A key difference in this model is that it implies that good health requires that healthy behaviors be maintained over time. An active child will clearly benefit from physical activity during childhood, but these benefits will not be fully realized unless the child adopts and maintains an active lifestyle throughout adulthood.

Tracking of physical activity and health-related fitness

While it makes conceptual sense that a physically active and fit child will become a physically active and fit adult, longitudinal studies on physical activity have demonstrated only weak to moderate tracking of physical activity across the lifespan (Malina, 2001b). A number of factors, including the age span, age at first observation, significant environmental change and measurement variability all can influence the magnitude of tracking coefficients. Studies over short time frames typically exhibit higher tracking coefficients than studies over longer time frames. Patterns established late in adolescence are also more likely to be maintained so tracking studies beginning in adolescence have also demonstrated tracking effects than studies initiated with young children (Malina, 2001b). Difficulties associated with measuring physical activity may contribute to the weak tracking coefficients.

In contrast to physical activity, biological risk factors such as blood lipids and blood pressure track moderately well, particularly from adolescence to adulthood (Eisenmann, 2004; Guo et al., 1993; Orchard et al., 1983; Webber et al., 1983). It is not clear if the impact of childhood risks on adult health outcomes is mediated directly by biological factors

or due to various lifestyle behaviors that become more entrenched over time.

Effects of motor skills and sports involvement on adult activity patterns

The early to middle childhood years are considered to be particularly important for the development of motor skills and it has been suggested that a foundation of competence in motor skills is a necessary requisite for subsequent enjoyment and involvement in physical activity (Malina, 1995a; 2001a). There is not much empirical evidence linking skill-related fitness to adult physical activity (Beunen et al., 2001; Kemper et al., 2001) but fundamental motor skills have been shown to predict significant amounts of variance in organized physical activity and cardiorespiratory fitness in youth (Okely et al., 2001a,b). Physical education and organized sport provides opportunities for youth to develop motor skills but studies have not been able to document long-term effects from these programs. A report from the Trois-Rivieres Growth and Development Study (Trudeau et al., 2000) revealed no difference in adult levels of aerobic fitness, blood lipids, blood pressure, or body composition between experimental subjects that had daily physical education and control subjects who had less physical education[2].

In general, the complexity of conducting longitudinal studies (and in measuring motor skills and activity patterns over time) has made it difficult to examine these effects. Another consideration is that associations between motor skills and long term physical activity behavior may be mediated by undescribed or unmeasured psychosocial variables. For example, individuals with higher levels of motor

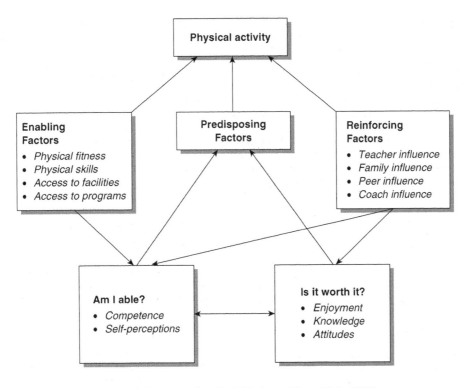

Figure 5.7.3   Youth Physical Activity Promotion Model (adapted from Welk, 1999)

skills and fitness would be expected to have higher perceptions of competence in the physical domain (Eklund et al., 1997; Welk et al., 1998; Welk and Eklund, 2004) and higher perceptions of competence have been associated with physical activity behavior (Crocker et al., 2000). Longitudinal research on possible psychosocial mediators of physical activity is clearly needed.

Summary of tracking studies

Our understanding of the tracking of physical activity and HRF from childhood to adulthood is still incomplete. This is due in part to the inherent challenges associated with measuring these variables over time, but also to the complex interactions that likely exist between physical activity and health. As highlighted in Figure 5.7.2, there are a number of possible pathways through which youth physical activity and health-related physical fitness may influence adult health. Physical activity attitudes and beliefs established early in life may increase the likelihood of subsequent involvement in a physically active lifestyle. Motor skills learned early in life may make it easier to learn and adopt new activities later in life. Body composition and risk factor profiles established early in life may also

carry on into adulthood. While the mechanisms underlying transmission of health benefits across the lifespan cannot be confirmed it is likely that activity patterns during childhood and adolescence have some benefits on adult health. The next section will examine factors that may influence youth activity behavior.

Model 3: The Youth Physical Activity Promotion Model

There are many models and theories used to explain physical activity behavior but few have been developed specifically for youth. The Youth Physical Activity Promotion (YPAP) Model is a social-ecological model that was developed to facilitate the targeting of variables known to influence children's physical activity behavior. The model categorizes factors that influence youth physical activity into three major components – Predisposing Factors, Enabling Factors and Reinforcing Factors (see Figure 5.7.3).

Predisposing factors

Predisposing factors refers to factors that may predispose a child to be physically active. The YPAP model adopts a social cognitive theory (SCT) perspective and reduces physical activity behavior into two fundamental questions: "Is it worth it?" and "Am I able?". The first question ("Is it worth it?") reflects children's attitudes to physical activity and the level of enjoyment they get from movement experiences. Enjoyment, by itself, is not directly captured in any of the mainstream models of physical activity behavior yet it is consistently associated with children's physical activity behavior (Sallis et al., 2000; Welk, 1999). In the YPAP model, children who enjoy physical activity are *predisposed* to be more physically active. The second question ("Am I able?") addresses perceptions of competence toward physical activity. Perceptions of competence have been consistently associated with children's physical activity behavior (Sallis et al., 2000) and recent evidence suggests that the relationship may be causal (Welk and Schaben, 2004). A child can value physical activity but may not want to do it unless s/he feels competent in performing this activity. In the YPAP model, children with good competence are more likely to be *predisposed* to an active lifestyle.

Enabling factors

Enabling factors refers to factors that enable a child to be physically active. These can include environmental variables such as access to facilities, equipment and programs that provide opportunities for physical activity. Access may help to increase the likelihood of activity but it certainly does not ensure participation. Some children may have access but may not choose to participate. However, if children do not have access they may not even have that opportunity. Physical skills and level of physical fitness are also considered enabling factors because these attributes can enable children to perform different sports and activities. These physical attributes may also act to influence activity indirectly by enhancing children's interest and enjoyment in physical activity (through the Predisposing factors). This indirect pathway is supported by a number of studies that have shown that fitness is related to physical self concept (Biddle et al., 1993; Welk et al., 1995) and that low levels of physical self-concept are associated with lower perceptions of competence and lower levels of physical activity (Crocker et al., 2000; Fox, 1997; Welk et al., 1995; Whitehead and Corbin, 1997).

Reinforcing factors

Reinforcing factors refers to support that a child receives from significant others to be physically active. Parents, peers and teachers/coaches can all act to directly influence children's interest and involvement in physical activity by providing opportunities for children to be active through the day. Direct support may reflect the structure that a physical education teacher imparts on a classroom to increase the amount of activity or the way in which a coach organizes a youth sport session. Direct effects from parents include parents being active with their child, parents taking children to parks or playgrounds or parents that enroll their children in programs that provide opportunities to be active during the day. Indirect effects are also emphasized in the YPAP model. The messages that teachers, coaches and parents send to children about physical activity clearly can influence the child's perception of competence and interest in physical activity. There is clear evidence that children's motivation for physical activity is influenced by the nature of interactions with adults (Welk et al., 2003).

Major findings – physical activity in youth

Physical education, as an institution, has been targeted by public health agencies as a promising setting for youth physical activity interventions. The Task Force on Community Preventive Services in the United States reviewed promising intervention approaches for promotion of physical activity in the population. The use of modified curricula and policies to increase physical activity in schools (CDC Task Force on Community Preventive Services, 2001) was "strongly recommended" as a behavioral strategy to promote physical activity in children. Countries have established different standards or goals depending on the position of physical education in their schools but the centrality of physical education in the public health agenda is clear. The Healthy People 2010 goals in the United States have established a goal of children being physically active for at least 50% of class physical education time. A recommendation in Australia has called for at least 100 minutes of total instruction in physical education each week (Brown et al., 1999). The "Young and Active" document from the UK also advocates for increased emphasis on physical education (Biddle et al., 1998).

Surveillance of patterns and behaviors is an important part of the epidemiological framework used in physical activity promotion. This section will first review research findings describing patterns and trends in physical activity and physical fitness. Then, the effectiveness of school based programs aimed at promoting physical activity will be reviewed.

Patterns and trends in physical activity and physical fitness

Levels of physical activity in youth

It is well established that children are the most physically active segment of society (Welk et al., 2000). However, there is considerable public health concern about the progressive decline in physical activity that occurs during late childhood and through adolescence (Welk et al., 2003). This period has been identified as the age range with the largest overall change in physical activity patterns in the lifespan (Sallis et al., 1998; Sallis, 2000). Longitudinal data from the Amsterdam Growth and Health study indicate that activity levels in girls decline by 26% from age 12–13 to age 17–18 (Kemper et al., 1999). Reductions in activity of approximately 20% during the transition from childhood to adolescence were recently confirmed in the NHLBI Growth and Health Study, a longitudinal study of US girls followed from 9–10 years to 18–19 years (Kimm et al., 2000).

Declines in activity patterns with age are expected since this pattern is evident in essentially animal species (Sallis, 2000). As a group, children can only become less active with age since the only direction to go from being the most active is down; however, Rowland (1998) has provided compelling documentation for the biological basis for this decline with age. Young children have an inherent need for regular physical activity for optimal growth, energy homeostasis and development. As children mature, the need for this type of stimulation may decrease and physical activity becomes more of a volitional choice rather than as a result of an internal program. Thus, the decline in physical activity with age may simply be indicative of a reduced physiological or biological need for this type of movement. Explaining the declining patterns of physical activity during adolescence is important but a more fundamental question for public health professionals and researchers is whether children obtain the *recommended amount* of physical activity. The recommendations vary slightly across countries but most have adopted a recommendation that calls for children to accumulate 60 minutes of moderate intensity physical activity every day (Biddle et al., 1998; National Association for Sport and Physical Education, 2004b).

A number of studies have sought to characterize levels of physical activity in youth but it has proven to be difficult to get accurate estimations. The answer to the question of how active children are depends greatly on the way in which physical activity is assessed and expressed (Welk et al., 2000). Studies using self-report instruments have generally concluded that children participate in large amounts of physical activity (Pate et al., 1994). The format of most self-report instruments favors overestimation since they typically ask children to comment on the amount of time spent in different physical activities. Because activity (and play) in youth is sporadic and intermittent, children may spend a lot of time outside or in a game but the intensity of physical activity varies considerably in a game and all of it may not be considered "active".

Capturing the inherently intermittent forms of activity with self-report instruments is quite difficult so research has also been done using other objective methods. Heart rate monitors provide an objective indicator of physical activity and are linearly related to energy expenditure during physical activity but this device is prone to other measurement challenges and artifact. They have been used in many studies (Epstein et al., 2001) but individual variability in the heart rate-energy expenditure relationship and difficulty in controlling for other influences on heart rate (e.g. emotion, temperature) have limited their utility for surveillance purposes.

Accelerometry-based activity monitors are another frequently used device in contemporary surveillance research. A number of studies have obtained data on large samples of youth using accelerometers but variability across studies has made it difficult to draw any definitive conclusions about youth activity patterns. A sample of youth from the Amherst study wore an accelerometer for 7 days and data were processed to determine the number of bouts of moderate and vigorous activity (Trost et al., 2002). Another analyses on the same data reported the percentage of youth achieving public health recommendations for physical activity (Pate et al., 2002). These results suggested that nearly all elementary school children achieved the 60-minute guideline for physical activity and that compliance with this guideline decreased sharply for older youth. Similar results were obtained in a large sample of youth from the European Youth Heart Study (Riddoch et al., 2004). Collectively, these studies demonstrate that youth are more likely to perform bouts of moderate activity that physical activity declines with age and that boys are more physically active than girls. Accurate determinations of the amount of activity that children perform are still not available but the increasing use of accelerometers in these studies suggest that they have promise for surveillance research employing larger, more representative samples of youth. Improvements in the accuracy of calibration equations used to process accelerometer data will enhance the utility of these devices (Welk, 2002).

Pedometers provide a lower cost alternative to accelerometers. This advantage has allowed them to be used in a number of large school based research projects aimed at understanding activity levels in youth. Using descriptive data from a large sample of youth of varying ages, an international team of researchers (Vincent et al., 2003) proposed step count guidelines of 13000 and 11000 steps per day for boys and girls, respectively. These recommendations were revised recently to consider the influence of weight status (normal weight and overweight) on pedometer step counts using a more robust statistical technique and an international sample of nearly 2000 children (Tudor-Locke et al., 2004). The recommended cut-points for activity in this study were 1000 and 12000 steps per day for boys and girls, respectively. There are a number of studies that have reported pedometer step counts but there is not enough data to accurately characterize children's activity patterns in a systematic way. The descriptive data from Vincent et al. (2003) from the three different countries (US, Sweden and Australia) provide the best sample with which to examine youth activity levels using pedometers.

Because there is no established gold-standard measure of physical activity it has proven difficult to reconcile differences between different measures or methods of physical activity. Obtaining more accurate measures of physical activity in children and adolescents is an important research objective to improve our understanding of children's activity patterns. Even without clear evidence, most experts still have concerns about children's activity patterns. These concerns are often based on research that has examined physical *inactivity* as a separate outcome. For example, data from the Youth Risk Behavior Survey in the United States suggest that nearly half of the nation's youth (ages 12–21) are not vigorously active (Kann et al., 2000). Data from the Youth Media Campaign Longitudinal Survey in the United States indicated that 62% of children (ages 9–13) do not participate in any organized physical activity outside of school (Centers for Disease Control and Prevention, 2003). These patterns of inactivity may have independent behavioral correlates and independent effects on health so additional research is needed to understand inactivity.

Secular changes in physical activity and physical fitness

The increasing epidemic of obesity in society has been attributed in large part to declining levels of physical activity among youth. This is a somewhat logical hypothesis but research on secular patterns of physical activity, although limited, have not demonstrated any appreciable changes in recent years (Eisenmann et al., 2004; Pratt et al., 1999). In the United States, data from the Youth Risk Behavior Survey (YRBS) show that there has been no significant change in self-reported vigorous physical activity among adolescents in grades 9–12 between 1993 and 1997 (Pratt et al., 1999). Using data from five Canadian national surveys, it was shown that the mean activity energy expenditure and prevalence of physical activity (i.e., meeting physical activity of 12.6 kJkg^{-1}.day^{-1} or 25.1 kJkg^{-1}.day^{-1}) increased between the 1981 and 1988 surveys and has since remained relatively stable between 1988 and 1998 (Eisenmann et al., 2004). The activity measures from the large population surveys may not have been sensitive enough to detect small changes in levels of physical activity in youth. The results from this study are based on physical activity and it is also possible that levels of physical inactivity may have changed without corresponding changes in the amount of physical activity. While the lack of secular change in physical activity is counter-intuitive to the secular increase in pediatric obesity it is important to remember that obesity is a result of energy imbalance. Additional work is needed to understand secular changes in activity, inactivity and factors that influence these behaviors.

Secular patterns in participation rates of youth sport programs have also been investigated. One study documented declining popularity of sport programs by Australian youth in the past 20 years (Norton et al., 2001). Sport participation declined from a high in the 1980s (82.5% of all children surveyed participated at some level) to approximately 60–64% in the 1990s (Norton et al., 2001). The most dramatic decline was in the percentage of children involved in greater than two sports per year. In 1985, 40% of children played three or more organized sports within the previous 12 months. In 2000, only 11% of children reported playing three or more sports. Sports are clearly a popular activity for youth but changes in the overall participation rates in youth sports may indicate cultural or sociological shifts in the relative importance of sport and physical activity in children's lives.

The difficulties in measuring physical activity may have made it difficult to detect subtle changes in activity patterns over time. However, a recent study has provided compelling evidence documenting international declines in aerobic fitness in recent years (Tomkinson et al., 2003). A meta-analysis was conducted on 55 reports of performance of children and adolescents (aged 6–19 years) in the 20 m shuttle run test between 1981–2000. Rates of change were calculated for 11 countries representing a total of 129882 children and adolescents in 151 age × gender × country slices. Of the 151 performance changes calculated, 106 were negative. The mean change was –0.43% of mean running speed per year. The decline was most marked in the older age groups and declines were similar for boys and girls (Tomkinson et al., 2003). Additional work is needed to better understand secular patterns in physical activity and physical fitness in youth. This type of data will aid in public health surveillance but also is important to understand factors that contribute to children's physical activity patterns.

Health-related physical education programming in schools

Despite the acknowledged importance of physical education, trends from several studies suggest that physical education is in decline (Brown et al., 1999; Pate et al., 1995b; Pratt et al., 1999; Ross, 1994). These trends are troubling considering the potential benefits of enhanced physical education programs for children. The continual challenge is that other competing pressures in schools get more attention and funding. Currently there is a strong argument for more time to be committed to the "core academic" learning areas, such as literacy, numeracy and information technology (Sibley and Etnier, 2003). The lack of documentation of program effectiveness from physical education and the increasing pressures for improved academic performance have made it difficult for decision makers to position physical education strongly enough in the school hierarchy.

Research has consistently shown that additional time spent in physical activity does not detract away from academic performance (Dwyer et al., 1983; Sallis et al., 1999a; Sibley and Etinier, 2003). In fact, some evidence suggests that cognition and attention are actually improved through additional activity time in the day, possibly leading to improved performance. The mechanisms are unclear but may be psychological (e.g. relief from boredom), physiological (e.g. increased cerebral blood flow), or functional (e.g. reduced absenteeism from illness) (Sibley and Etinier, 2003). Whatever the mechanism, it is clear that additional activity can be integrated into the school day while maintaining a strong emphasis on academics. Despite this evidence, major barriers exist in getting schools to add additional physical education into a packed schedule. A variety of innovative programmatic options may provide alternative ways to help students get more physical activity as a part of the school day. Reviews of different physical education interventions and school-based activity programs are described below.

Comprehensive physical education interventions

A number of studies have examined the efficacy of school-based interventions (Sallis and Owen, 1999b; Stone et al., 1998). The highly publicized Child and Adolescent Trial for Cardiovascular Health (CATCH) in the United States evaluated the effectiveness of major curricular and school level changes on children's physical fitness levels in 96 schools across four states. Emphasis was placed on improving the amount of activity provided during physical education but comprehensive curricular changes were also attempted as well as changes in school food service. While the study sought to make a variety of changes, the most noteworthy finding is that intervention schools were able to provide more physical activity during physical education classes than control schools (McKenzie et al., 1996) A number of recent studies have examined the sustainability of versions of CATCH (Hoelscher et al., 2004; Lytle et al., 2003; Kelder et al., 2003), and the results suggest that training and ongoing support for physical education can help maintain the use of evidence-based programs over time.

Broad school-level approaches to physical activity promotion have been tested in some large studies. The Class of 1989 Study involved a peer-led program combined with a 10 lesson health education module among 8th and 10th grade North Americans (Kelder et al., 1993). At 7-year follow-up, intervention girls were more active than girls in the control community, while no differences were observed for boys.

A large South Australian intervention evaluated the effectiveness of comprehensive school programming for populations that may be at greater risk for cardiovascular disease (Gore et al., 1996). The intervention included curriculum components on the benefits of healthy eating and physical activity, and other school-based environmental supports. These involved a shift in food service policies and a lifestyle program for teaching staff. No intervention effects were found in skinfolds, fitness or lipid profiles but the trial did result in lower total cholesterol and triglyceride levels in the treatment schools. There were significant increases in health knowledge in the intervention schools during the first year, but these differences had disappeared after the following year. The authors concluded that previous interventions showing improvements in aerobic fitness and reduced adiposity involved more intensely monitored activity sessions by research teams external to the school. If classroom teachers have responsibility for implementing regular activity for children, it appears that other curriculum demands for classroom time, and perhaps lack of confidence among teachers without PE training, conspire to reduce the health-enhancing quality of the experience (Gore et al., 1996).

While these large-scale studies demonstrated some short-term benefits it has proven difficult to maintain these effects over time. The complexity and structure imposed by these large school-based programs may be too cumbersome for long-term use by teachers barraged with many demands.

Training programs and curricular changes in physical education

Physical education programs can differ in a number of ways but the largest and most critical differences for youth physical activity promotion are arguably in the quality of teaching and the type of curricula that is used. Several studies have shown that the quality of primary school physical education can be enhanced with improved curriculum and specific teacher training and in-servicing (McKenzie et al., 1993, 1997, 2001). Most success has been observed in those programs that emphasize high levels of aerobic activity, are well resourced, and are noncompetitive (Sallis et al., 1999b). Reported enjoyment levels are higher in classes characterized by frequent encouragement and praise, where students do not select teams and where winning is de-emphasized.

Recent North American studies have examined the impact of systematic teacher training on the quality of physical education programs. The Go for Health Study in Texas focused on teacher training and promotion of their own physical activity levels. Active engagement by children in intervention classes represented 40% of lesson time after 2 years of the program, compared with 10% in control schools (Simons-Morton et al., 1991). The SPARK (Sports, Play and Active Recreation for Kids) program in Southern California compared the impact of physical education specialists and trained classroom teachers on active time in class and use of "quality" teaching methods, such as demonstration skills (Sallis et al., 1997). Trained classroom teachers greatly increased their children's active time compared with untrained classroom teacher controls, but the best results were seen in classes conducted by physical education specialists. A 1.5-year follow-up of the SPARK initiative showed that only in those schools where trained classroom teachers received ongoing on-site support were changes in quantity and quality of physical education classes sustained (McKenzie et al., 1997). Similar findings were reported from the dissemination of the CATCH intervention (McKenzie et al., 2003).

Alternative curricular approaches have also been examined as ways to improve physical education outcomes. Concepts-based physical education has also been a growing phenomenon in middle and high school physical education programs. This type of curriculum incorporates classroom lessons and interactive physical activity experiences to teach children the cognitive and behavioral skills needed to be active. A recent study compared the effects of concepts-based physical education and more traditional (activity or game-based) physical education programs (Dale et al., 1998). The results showed that youth in the concepts-based approach were less likely to be sedentary 2 years post intervention than students receiving the traditional curriculum.

Other school level programming efforts to promote activity

There has been increasing attention paid to other creative ways to change activity patterns in school settings. One goal has been to attempt to influence physical activity outside of school. While some studies have shown that classroom curricula can stimulate out of school activity among North American primary schoolers (McKenzie et al., 1996), other studies have shown no effects (Sallis et al., 1997). One recent Australian study (The Switch Off and Play Study) has reported promising links between behavioral modification classes in school and reduction in television viewing in the home (Salmon, 2003). Process evaluation of this ongoing initiative confirms a high level of acceptability among children and parents.

Physical education "homework" has been the focus of some recent interventions – the goal in these programs has been to extend the influence of the school into the home. While some strategies have focused on the cognitive domain, the use of active homework is being increasingly reported in the literature (Smith and Claxton, 2003). Innovative strategies to increase the quantity of active homework (e.g. through calendars with daily "fun" activities) and the quality of movement skill (e.g. through checklists for mastery of specific skills) have been introduced and trialed.

A variety of other programmatic changes have been tried to provide additional opportunities for children to be active during the school day (Jago and Baranowski, 2004). The provision of more structured opportunities during recess breaks has been shown to increase activity levels in elementary school youth (Connolly and McKenzie, 1995; McKenzie et al., 1997a; Scruggs et al., 2003). Providing short physical activity breaks *during* normal class activities has also been shown to increase total amounts of activity (Ernst and Pangrazi, 1999). These strategies may be more successful in promoting physical activity than structured efforts to increase the amount of physical education available to children. If these types of programs were disseminated widely and maintained over time they could make important contributions to children's daily activity levels.

Considerable efforts have also been spent to increase the extent and effectiveness of after school opportunities for youth (Powers et al., 2002). The changing family structures and work rhythms in contemporary society have increased the use of out-of-school hour care during the time between end of school and evening mealtime. Research has shown that this time is a critical predictor of children's overall physical activity behavior (Sallis and Saelens, 2000) but there have been few efforts to enhance the effectiveness of these programs or to integrate it into other school-based programs. An innovative activity promotion program conducted in low SES suburbs of Adelaide, South Australia demonstrated the potential of coordinated after school programming. The program known as GOSH (Get active Out of School Hours) made use of existing school facilities and equipment and involved college students to lead developmentally appropriate games and activities in eight intervention sites, twice a week for eight weeks. Children in the intervention study had free access to all other choices in the center including sedentary activities such as TV and computer games but the availability of these active opportunities reduced the numbers of children inside, and increased the overall amounts of moderate to vigorous activity.

Enhancing the utility of school playgrounds and resources has also shown some promise for increasing physical activity in youth. Several studies have characterized key aspects of the school environment that may be important for future interventions. One study (Sallis et al., 2001) demonstrated that boys and girls tended to be more active in court spaces followed by fields and least active in indoor play areas. Areas with high levels of sports equipment and improvements (basketball hoops, tennis courts, etc.), coupled with high levels of adult supervision, were four to five times more likely to have physically active boys and girls than areas deficient in both (Sallis et al., 2001). In another study (Harten et al., 2002), investigators deliberately manipulated the size of the available play space on different days to examine effects on activity behavior. Activity in boys was found to be negatively impacted by reduced amounts of available space but the effect was not evident in girls. This is consistent with previous reports that boys tend to occupy most space under free play. In high amounts of play space, there was no association of motor skills and physical activity. However, in restricted space, boys with higher levels of motor skills maintained activity levels but youth with lower ability were more easily discouraged. These results indicate that the provision of large and well-organized play spaces is important for enabling children to get the recommended amounts of physical activity.

A final untapped opportunity for activity promotion in schools is active commuting to school (Tudor-Locke et al., 2001). The increased use of automobiles and the increased number of working parents have led to fewer children walking to school and efforts to reverse these trends are promising. Walk to school programs are targeted as one of the most promising approaches. The popularity of these programs has sparked national and international campaigns aimed at promoting walking to school.

Summary of school-based activity programming in youth

Collectively, the general trends in youth physical activity reveal low levels of physical activity, high levels of inactivity and tendencies for the activity profiles to get worse with age. School based programs have shown promise in changing short-term behaviors but it has proven difficult to maintain outcomes over time. While a number of comprehensive physical education interventions have been developed and tested they typically show little or no long term benefits (Estabrooks et al., 2003). This is mainly because teachers find it difficult to maintain the structure imposed by the cumbersome curricula and approaches that are tested in efficacy-based clinical trials. A more promising public health strategy for school-based activity promotion would be to emphasize the use of programs that can be maintained more easily over time. The incorporation of multiple activity breaks during the day and enhanced opportunities for children to be active before and after school are models that may work well with proper site level coordination.

Applications to practice and policy

Humans were clearly meant to move but the sedentary nature of contemporary society makes it difficult for adults and children to obtain sufficient amounts of physical activity. Children are much more active than adults; however, without additional intervention or environmental changes they are likely to grow up to adopt similar values and behavioral patterns as the rest of society. School-based programs provide opportunities for youth to be active and education on the physical and behavioral skills needed to be active later in life. This exposure is critical for optimal physical and social development, but school-based programs can't assume sole responsibility for promoting physical activity and health-related fitness in youth.

To enhance the promotion of physical activity in youth in a more comprehensive way, broader social and environmental changes are needed. In the United States, public health experts have recommended coordinated links between the school, home and community to promote physical activity in youth (Centers for Disease Control and Prevention, 1997). Broader roles for physical education have also been proposed in a number of other public health documents (US Department of Health and Human Services, 2000; Biddle et al., 1998, Bauman et al., 2002). The concept of targeting behavior change efforts at multiple levels of influence is consistent with social–ecological models of health promotion that are currently used to guide many public health initiatives (Booth et al., 2001). Many permutations of these models exist but they share some common characteristics. The models typically incorporate multiple dimensions of influence (individual, interpersonal, organizational, community and policy) and incorporate multiple theoretical perspectives (Sallis and Owen, 1997). Physical education, as an institution, resides at the *organizational* level of the social-ecological framework. Coordinated efforts and policies within a community-based school district dictate the amount of physical education and the type of curriculum that is delivered. Instruction during physical education is considered to be at the *individual* level and interactions between teacher and student can be considered as *interpersonal*. The coordinated delivery and institutionalization of physical education in society is impressive but small funding allocations, overloaded teachers, inconsistent training programs and poor environmental support limit the ability of school based physical education to fully accomplish its mission.

A health promotion setting that parallels the organization and potential impact of school-based programs is worksite health promotion. These programs reach a large percentage of working adults in the same way that school programs reach a large percentage of children. It is well established in worksite health promotion that behavior change programs or awareness campaigns are not likely to be effective without broader administrative and environmental support. In the same way, improvements in physical education curriculum provide only part of the answer to school based health promotion. To advance the promotion of physical activity in schools, physical education programs should be incorporated into more comprehensive school-wide efforts aimed at helping students live healthier and more active lives. Incorporation of more structured recess and activity breaks during the school day, increased access to equipment and resources and more effective after school programming (or intramural programs) are some of the possible ways to create a more active school setting.

Teachers can also extend their influence by encouraging parents to be more involved in promoting activity in their family. As shown in the YPAP model (see Model 3), parents can influence children's activity levels directly by providing access to programs and activity–oriented environments (e.g. parks) or indirectly through encouragement or facilitation of children's activity (Welk et al., 2003). Awareness messages and prompts from teachers would remind parents of the important role that they play in shaping their child's physical development and encourage additional activity. The current generation of parents grew up at a time when children were more likely to play outdoors on their own and when neighborhood games and activities were the rule rather than the exception. Because of the changing nature of society, parents must accept a greater responsibility for providing opportunities for children to be active. Delivering this message through physical education newsletters or reports is one way to get more parents involved. The *FITNESSGRAM* youth fitness program widely used in the United States was established with the inherent goal of enhancing communication and involvement of parents in physical education. Teachers can print individualized reports on children's physical activity and physical fitness levels and send them home to parents with recommendations for how to improve. The delivery of these reports or newsletters is commonplace in many school districts but could be utilized more extensively or more effectively to promote greater parental involvement in physical education.

The next level of outreach from physical education would be to enhance the quality and availability of community recreation and sport programs. These programs are popular among youth but may reach middle or upper socio-economic families. They also may focus too much on performance and competition rather than on building lifelong interest in sport and physical activity. Systematic efforts to redirect the focus of community recreation programs towards maximizing physical activity, competence and enjoyment may promote greater long term adherence than the current skill-based models of instruction. Coordination with school based physical educators trained in effective management skills and instructional techniques would enhance the effectiveness of these programs.

Major trends and future directions

Complex problems clearly require complex solutions – and building physical activity into the fabric of a largely sedentary society is clearly a daunting task. Because of the heavy influence of environmental factors on behavior, it is tempting to want to "wind the clock back" to patterns of living from past generations, but this is clearly not a realistic policy. We cannot return to the environmental conditions of the pre-1970s, when playing and riding bicycles in urban parks and streets were commonplace, and at least one parent was likely to be free during daylight hours to supervise or share free play. Rather, we must think in terms of winding the clock forward. From a societal perspective, the question becomes how can physical activity be maximized in the world in which children currently live, a world in which both parents work, a world of highways and roads not conducive to commuting and a world with engaging multimedia opportunities that compete for our time and interests? From a curricular standpoint, the question becomes how can physical education help children develop positive lifestyles with limited time and resources and in schools that have policies aimed primarily at academic performance? Our primary suggestion is that the role of physical education specialists should be extended beyond the current paradigm of fixed curricular responsibilities, to include physical activity promotion in the broader school context. A broader role for teachers in the school setting would enable the development of a more integrated physical activity program in the school and better outreach into the community. Efforts are also needed to develop systems to facilitate communication between physicians and school health officials so that children (and families) at risk for inactivity or obesity could receive appropriate counseling. These approaches are consistent with social-ecological models of health promotion that have proven effective for other behaviors.

Policies and programs are important but efforts are needed to develop innovative approaches that integrate physical activity promotion into the increasingly complex and integrated society we live in. Companies using well planned marketing strategies to target messages and advertisements at their target audience. The use of more targeted messages and social marketing campaigns aimed at activity promotion may be needed to reach different segments of youth. Preliminary outcome data from the VERB campaign in the United States indicates that these social marketing campaigns can have potent effects. Researchers have recently used clustering techniques to characterize the predominant activity characteristics of different youth social groups (Marshall et al., 2002). Youth categorized as "inactive socializers" may be most effectively targeted with "walk and talk" networks on the school playground that satisfy the need to socialize while increasing energy expenditure from activity. Youth classified as "techno-active" are characterized by dual interests in sports/activity and mediated entertainment and computer games. Interventions aimed at reducing screen time may be most effective with this group since they are already interested in physical activity. Employing these types of social marketing strategies will facilitate the development of programs that fit the unique needs and interests of the target population.

A major gap in the physical education literature is research that can document the overall impact of school environment and policies on levels of physical activity and health related fitness in children and adolescents. Most studies have been done in isolated schools or have experimentally manipulated environments within individual classes or areas at the school to study these effects. To more fully understand the impact of environments and policies it is important to study effects at a macro level. The SHIPPS study in the United States has documented large differences in the way in which P.E. is delivered and promoted; but, studies have not yet linked specific policy variables (amount of physical education or recess) or other school-level variables (programming characteristics or teacher-related behaviors/experience/training) to objective outcomes of physical activity, fitness or fatness. This type of work will enhance our understanding of effective programs and policies for youth and contribute to the use of evidence-based decision making in schools and communities.

Notes

1 Reviews of some PE curricular programs are provided later in the chapter.

2 Some differences were evident in the treatment and control samples at baseline (Trudeau et al., 1998) so design problems may have contributed to these findings.

References

American Academy of Pediatrics. (2003). Prevention of pediatric overweight and obesity. *Pediatrics, 112*: 424–430.

Andersen, R.E., Crespo, C.J., Bartlett, S.J., Cheskin, L.J. and Pratt, M. (1998). Relationship of physical activity and television watching with body weight and level of fatness among children: results from the Third National Health and Nutrition Examination Survey. *Journal of the American Medical Association, 279*: 938–942.

Bauman, A., Bellow, B., Brown, W. and Owen, N. (2002). *Getting Australia active; towards better practice for the promotion of physical activity.* Melbourne, Australia.

Berkey, C.S., Rockett, H.R., Field, A.E. et al. (2000). Activity, dietary intake, and weight changes in a longitudinal study of preadolescent and adolescent boys and girls. *Pediatrics, 105*: E56.

Beunen, G.P., Philippaerts, R.M., Delvaux, K. et al. (2001). Adolescent physical performance and adult physical activity in Flemish males. *American Journal of Human Biology, 13*: 173–179.

Biddle, S., Page, A., Ashford, B., Jennings, D., Brooke, R. and Fox, K. (1993). Assessment of children's physical self-perceptions. *International Journal of Adolescence and Youth, 4*: 93–109.

Biddle, S.J.H., Sallis, J.F. and Cavill, N.A. (1998). *Young and active? Young People and health enhancing physical activity. Evidence and implication.* Health Education Authority: London.

Booth, M., Chey, T., Wake, M. Health Education Authority: et al. (2003). Change in prevalence of overweight and obesity among young Australians. *Journal of Clinical Nutrition, 77*: 29–36.

Booth, S.L., Mayer, J., Sallis, J.F. et al. (2001). Environmental and societal factors affect food choice and physical activity: rationale, influences and leverage points. *Nutrition Reviews, 59*: 21–39.

Boreham, C.A., Twisk, J., Savage M.J., Cran, G.W. and Strain, J.J. (1997). Physical activity, sports participation, and risk factors in adolescents. *Medicine and Science in Sports and Exercise, 29*: 788–793.

Boreham, C., Twisk, J., Murray, L., Savage, M., Strain, J.J. and Cran, G. (2001). Fitness, fatness, and coronary heart disease risk in adolescents: the Northern Ireland Young Hearts Project. *Medicine and Science in Sports and Exercise, 33*: 270–274.

Bouchard, C. and Shepard, R.J. (1994). Physical activity, fitness, and health: the model and key concepts. In C. Bouchard, R.J. Shepard and T. Stephens (Eds.), *Physical activity, fitness, and health: International proceedings and consensus statement* (pp. 77–88). Champaign, IL: Human Kinetics.

Brown, R., Lewis, F., Murtagh, M., Thorpe, S. and Collins, R. (1999). 100 Minutes Project: Researching PE and sport in

DETE schools. Flinders University of South Australia, Adelaide.

Caspersen, C.J., Nixon, P.A. and Durant, R.H. (1998). Physical activity epidemiology applied to children and adolescents. In J.O. Holloszy (Ed.), *Exercise and sport sciences reviews* (pp. 341–403). St. Louis: Williams and Wilkins.

CDC Task Force on Community Preventive Services. (2001). Increasing physical activity: A report on recommendations of the Task Force on Community Preventive Services. *Morbidity and Mortality Weekly Report, 50*: 1–14.

Centers for Disease Control and Prevention. (1997). Guidelines for school and community programs to promote lifelong physical activity among young people. *Morbidity and Mortality Weekly Report, 46*: 1–36.

Centers for Disease Control and Prevention. (2002). *Promoting better health for young people through physical activity and sports.* Atlanta, GA: Centers for Disease Control and Prevention.

Centers for Disease Control and Prevention. (2003). Physical activity levels among children aged 9–13 years—United States, 2002. *Morbidity and Mortality Weekly Report, 52*: 785–788.

Chu, N.-F., Rimm, E.B., Wang, D.-J., Liou, H.-S. and Shieh, S.-M. (1998). Clustering of cardiovascular disease risk factors among obese schoolchildren: the Taipei Children Heart Study. *American Journal of Clinical Nutrition, 67*: 1146.

Chunming, C. (2000). Fat intake and nutritional status of children in China. *American Journal of Clinical Nutrition, 72*: 1368S–1372S.

Connolly, P. and McKenzie, T.L. (1995). Effects of a games intervention on the physial activity levels of children at recess. *Research Quarterly for Exercise and Sport, 66*: A60.

Crespo, C.J., Smit, E., Troiano, R.P., Bartlett, S.J., Macera, C.A. and Andersen, R.E. (2001). Television watching, energy intake and obesity in US children: results from the third National Health and Nutrition Examination Survey, 1988–1994. *Archives of Pediatric and Adolescent Medicine, 155*: 360–365.

Crocker, P.R.E., Eklund, R.C. and Kowalski, K.C. (2000). Children's physical activity and physical self-perceptions. *Journal of Sports Sciences, 18*: 383–394.

Dale, D., Corbin, C.B. and Cuddihy, T.F. (1998). Can conceptual physical education promote physically active lifestyles? *Pediatric Exercise Science, 10*: 97–109.

Dennison, B.A., Strauss, J.H., Mellits, E.D. and Charney, E. (1988). Childhood physical fitness tests: Predictor of adult physical activity levels? *Pediatrics, 82*(3), 324–330.

Dollman, J. and Martin, M. (2003). Physical activity, sedentary behavior and youth adiposity: moderating influence of socioeconomic status. In de Ridder, H. and Olds, T. (Eds.), Kinanthropometry 7. Proceedings of the Seventh Conference of the International Society for the Advancement of Kinanthropometry (pp. 159–174). Potchesfstroom: Potchesfstroom University of CHE.

Dwyer, T., Coonan, W.E., Leitch, D.R., Hetzel, B.S. and Baghurst, P.A. (1983). An investigation of the effects of daily physical activity on the health of primary school students in South Australia. *International Journal of Epidemiology, 12*: 308–313.

Eisenmann, J.C. (2004). Physical activity and cardiovascular disease risk factors in children and adolescents: an overview. *Canadian Journal of Cardiology, 20*: 295–301.

Eisenmann, J.C., Bartee, R.T. and Wang, M.Q. (2002). Physical activity, television viewing and weight status in U.S. adolescents: results from the 1999 YRBS. *Obesity Research, 10*: 379–385.

Eisenmann, J.C., Katzmarzyk, P.T. and Tremblay, M.S. (2004). Leisure-time physical activity levels among Canadian adolescents, 1981–1998. *Journal of Physical Activtiy and Health, 1*: 154–162.

Eklund, R.C., Whitehead, J.R. and Welk, G.J. (1997). Validity of the children and youth physical self-perception profile: A confirmatory factor analysis. *Research Quarterly for Exercise and Sport, 68*: 249–256.

Enos, W.F., Beyer, J.C. and Holmes, R.H. (1953). Pathogenesis of coronary disease in American soldiers killed in Korea. *Journal of the American Medical Association, 152*: 1090–1093.

Epstein, L.H., Paluch, R.A., Kalakanis, L.E., Goldfield, G.S., Cerny, F.J. and Roemmich, J.N. (2001). How much activity do youth get? A quantitative review of heart-rate measured activity. *Pediatrics*, 108, E44.

Ernst, M.P. and Pangrazi, R.P. (1999). Effects of a physical activity program on children's activity levels and attraction to physical activity. *Pediatric Exercise Science, 11*: 393–405.

Estabrooks, P., Dzewaltowski, D.A., Glasgow, R.E. and Klesges, L.M. (2003). Reporting of validity from school health promotion studies published in 12 leading journals, 1996–2000. *Journal of School Health, 73*: 21–28.

Ford, E.S., Giles, W.H. and Dietz, W.H. (2002). Prevalence of the metabolic syndrome among US adults: findings from the Third National Health and Nutrition Examination Survey. *Journal of the American Medical Association, 287*: 356–359.

Fox, K.R. (1997). *The physical self: from motivation to well-being.* Champaign, IL: Human Kinetics.

Gordon-Larsen, P., Adair, L.S. and Popkin, B.M. (2002). Ethnic differences in physical activity and inactivity patterns and overweight status. *Obesity Research, 10*: 141–149.

Gore, C.J., Owen, N., Pederson, D. and Clarke, A. (1996). Educational and environmental interventions for cardiovascular health promotion in socially disadvantaged schools. *Australian and New Zealand Journal of Public Health, 20*(2): 188–194.

Guo, S., Beckett, L.A., Chumlea, W.C., Gardner, J.D. and Siervogel, R.M. (1993). Serial analysis of plasma lipid and lipoproteins from 9 to 21 years. *American Journal of Clinical Nutrition, 58*: 61–67.

Guo, S., Salisbury, S., Roche, A.F., Chumlea, W.C. and Siervogel, R.M. (1994). Cardiovascular disease risk factors and body composition, a review. *Nutrition Review, 14*: 1721–1777.

Harten, N.R., Olds, T.S. and Dollman, J. (2002). The effect of available play space on children's freeplay activity. *Journal of Science and Medicine in Sport, 5*: S112.

Hoelscher, D.M., Feldman, H.A., Johnson, C.C. et al. (2004). School-based health education programs can be maintained over time: results from the CATCH Institutionalization study. *Preventive Medicine, 38*: 594–606.

Hughes, J.M., Li, L., Chinn, S. and Rona, R.J. (1997). Trends in growth in England and Scotland 1972 to 1994. *Archives of Disease in Childhood, 76*: 189.

Jago, R. and Baranowski, T. (2004). Non-curricular approaches for inceasing physical activity in youth: a review. *Preventive Medicine, 39*: 157–163.

Kann, L., Kinchen, S.A., Williams, B.I. et al. (2000). Youth Risk Behavior Surveillance – United States, 1999. *Morbidity and Mortality Weekly Report, 49(SS05)*: 1–96.

Katzmarzyk, P.T., Malina, R.M. and Bouchard, C. (1998). Physical activity and health-related fitness in youth: A multivariate analysis. *Medicine and Science in Sports and Exercise, 30*: 709.

Katzmarzyk, P.T., Malina, R.M. and Bouchard, C. (1999). Physical activity, physical fitness, and coronary heart disease risk factors in youth: The Quebec Family Study. *Preventive Medicine, 29*: 555–562.

Katzmarzyk, P.T., Tremblay, A., Perusse, L., Despres, J.-P. and Bouchard, C. (2003). The utility of the international child and adolescent overweight guidelines for predicting coronary heart disease risk factors. *Journal of Clinical Epidemiology, 56*: 1–7.

Kaufman, F.R. (2002). Type 2 diabetes mellitus in children and youth: a new epidemic. *Journal of Pediatric Endocrinology and Metabolism, 15*: 737–744.

Kelder, S.H., Mitchell, P.D., McKenzie, T.L. et al. (2003). Long-term implementation of the CATCH physical education program. *Health Education and Behavior, 30*: 463–475.

Kelder, S.H., Perry, C.L. and Klepp, K.I. (1993). Community-wide youth exercise promotion: long-term outcomes of the Minnesota Heart Health Program and the Class of 1989 Study. *Journal of School Health, 63*: 218–223.

Kemper, H.C., Post, G.B., Twisk, J.W. and van Mechelen, W. (1999). Lifestyle and obesity in adolescence and young adulthood: results from the Amsterdam Growth And Health Longitudinal Study (AGAHLS). *International Journal of Obesity and Related Metabolic Disorders, 23 Suppl 3*: S34–S40.

Kemper, H.C., de Vente, W., van Mechelen, W. and Twisk, J.W. (2001). Adolescent motor skill and performance: is physical activity in adolescence related to adult physical fitness? *American Journal of Human Biology, 13*: 180–189.

Kimm, S.Y., Glynn, N.W. Kriska, A.M. et al. (2000). Longitudinal changes in physical activity in a biracial cohort during adolescence. *Medicine and Science in Sports and Exercise, 32*: 1445–1454.

Kohl, H.W.I. and Hobbs, K.E. (1998). Development of physical activity behaviors among children and adolescents. *Pediatrics, 101*: 549.

Lakka, H.M., Laaksonen, D.E., and Lakka, T.A. (2002). The metabolic syndrome and total and cardiovascular disease mortality in middle-aged men. *Journal of the American Medical Association, 288*: 2709–2716.

Lee, C.D., Blair, S.N. and Jackson, A.S. (1999). Cardiorespiratory fitness, body composition and all-cause and cardiovascular disease mortality in men. *American Journal of Clinical Nutrition, 69*: 373–380.

Levin, S., Louwry, R., Brown, D.R. and Dietz, W.H. (2003). Physical activity and body mass index among US adolescents. *Archives of Pediatric and Adolescent Medicine, 157*: 816–820.

Lytle, L.A., Ward, J., Nader, P.R., Pedersen, S. and Williston, B.J. (2003). Maintenance of a health promotion program in elementary schools: results from the CATCH-ON study key informant interviews. *Health Education and Behavior, 30*: 503–518.

Malina, R.M. (1995). Physical activity and fitness of children and youth: questions and implications. *Medicine, Exercise, Nutrition and Health, 4*: 123–135.

Malina, R.M. (2001a). Physical activity and fitness: pathways from childhood to adulthood. *American Journal of Human Biology, 13*: 162–172.

Malina, R.M. (2001b). Tracking of physical activity across the lifespan. *President's Council on Physical Fitness and Sports Research Digest, 3*: 1–8.

Marshall, S.J., Sarkin, J.A., Sallis, J.F. and McKenzie, T.L. (1998). Tracking of health-related fitness components in youth ages 9 to 12. *Medicine and Science in Sports and Exercise, 30*: 910–916.

Marshall, S.J., Biddle, S.J.H., Sallis, J.F., McKenzie, T.L. and Conway, T.L. (2002). Clustering of sedentary behaviours and physical activity among youth: A Cross-national study. *Pediatric Exercise Science, 14*: 401–417.

McKenzie T.L., Sallis, J.F., Faucette, N., Kolody, B. and Roby, J. (1993). Effects of a curriculm and inservice program on the quantity and quality of elementary physical education classes. *Research Quarterly for Exercise and Sport, 64*: 178–187.

McKenzie, T.L., Nader, P.R., Strikmiller, P.K. et al. (1996). School physical education: Effect of the child and adolescent trial for cardiovascular health. *Preventive Medicine, 25*: 423–431.

McKenzie T.L., Sallis, J.F., Elder, J.P. et al. (1997a). Physical activity levels and prompts in young children at recess: A two-year study of a bi-ethnic sample. *Research Quarterly for Exercise and Sport, 68*: 195–202.

McKenzie, T.L., Sallis, J.F. and Faucette, F.N. (1997b). Long-term effects of a physical education curriculum and staff development program: SPARK. *Research Quarterly for Exercise and Sport, 68*: 280.

McKenzie, T.L., Sallis, J.F., Kolody, B. and Faucette, N. (1997c). Long term effects of a physical education curriculum and staff development program: SPARK. *Research Quarterly for Exercise and Sport, 68*: 280–291.

McKenzie, T.L., Stone, E.J., Feldman, H.A. et al. (2001). Effects of the CATCH physical education intervention: teacher type and lesson location. *American Journal of Preventive Medicine, 21*: 101–109.

McKenzie, T.L., Li, D., Derby, C.A., Webber, L.S., Luepker, R.V. and Cribb, P. (2003). Maintenance of effects of the CATCH physical education program: results from the CATCH-ON study. *Health Education and Behavior, 30*: 447–462.

McNamara, J.J., Molot, M.A., Stremple, J.F. and Cutting, R.T. (1971). Coronary artery disease in combat casualties in Vietnam. *Journal of the American Medical Association,* 216: 1185–1187.

Moreno, L.A., Sarria, A., Fleta, J., Rodriguez, G. and Bueno, M. (2000). Trends in body mass index and overweight prevalence among children and adolescents in the region of Aragon (Spain) from 1985 to 1995. *International Journal of Obesity,* 24: 925–931.

Morrison, J.A., Barton, B.A., Biro, F.M., Daniels, S.R. and Sprecher, D.L. (1999a). Overweight, fat patterning and cardiovascular disease risk factors in black and white boys. *Journal of Pediatrics,* 135: 451–457.

Morrison, J.A., Sprecher, D.L., Barton, B.A., Waclawiw, M.A. and Daniels, S.R. (1999b). Overweight, fat patterning, and cardiovascular disease risk factors in black and white girls: the National Heart, Lung and Blood Institute Growth and Health Study. *Journal of Pediatrics,* 135: 458–464.

Morrow, J.R. and Freedson, P. (1994). Relationship between habitual physical activity and aerobic fitness in adolescents. *Pediatric Exercise Science,* 6: 315–329.

National Association for Sport and Physical Education. (2004a). *Moving into the future national standards for physical education.* (2nd ed.) Reston, VA: NASPE publications.

National Association for Sport and Physical Education. (2004b). *Physical activity for children: A statement of guidelines for children 5–12.* (2nd ed.) Reston, VA: NASPE Publications.

National Strength and Conditioning Association. (1996). Youth resistance training: postion statement paper and literature review. *Strength and Conditioning,* 18: 62–75.

Norton, K., Dollman, J., Klanarong, S. and Robertson, I. (2001). Kid's sport: who's playing what? *Sport Health,* 19: 12–14.

Ogden, C.L., Flegal, K.M., Carroll, M.D. and Johnson, C.L. (2002). Prevalence and trends in overweight among US children and adolescents 1999–2000. *Journal of the American Medical Association,* 288: 1728–1732.

Okely, A.D., Booth, M.L. and Patterson, J.W. (2001a). Relationship of cardiorespiratory endurance to fundamental movement skill proficiency among adolescents. *Pediatric Exercise Science,* 13: 380–391.

Okely, A.D., Booth, M.L. and Patterson, J.W. (2001b). Relationship of physical activity to fundamental movement skills among adolescents. *Medicine and Science in Sports and Exercise,* 33: 1899–1904.

Orchard, T.J., Donahue, R.P., Kuller, L.H., Hodges, P.N. and Drash, A.L. (1983). Cholesterol screening in childhood: Does it predict adult hypercholesterolaemia? The Beaver County experience. *Journal of Pediatrics,* 103: 687–691.

Paffenbarger, Jr. R.S., Wing, A.L. and Hyde, R.T. (1978). Physical activity as an index of heart attack risk in college alumni. *American Journal of Epidemiology,* 108: 161–175.

Pate, R.R., Freedson, P.S., Sallis, J.F. et al. (2002). Compliance with physical activity guidelines; prevalence in a population of children and youth. *Annals of Epidemiology,* 12: 303–308.

Pate, R.R. and Hohn, R.C. (1994). A contemporary mission for physical education. In R.R. Pate and R.C. Hohn (Eds.), *Health and fitness through physical education* (pp. 1–8). Champaign, IL: Human Kinetics Publishers Inc.

Pate, R.R., Long, B.J. and Heath, G. (1994). Descriptive epidemiology of physical activity in adolescents. *Pediatric Exercise Science,* 6: 447.

Pate, R.R., Pratt, M., Blair, S.N. et al. (1995a). Physical activity and public health: A recommendation from the Centers for Disease Control and Prevention and the American College of Sports Medicine. *Journal of the American Medical Association,* 273: 402–407.

Pate, R.R. and Ross, J.G. (1987). Factors associated with health-related fitness. *Journal of Physical Education, Recreation and Dance,* 58: 93–95.

Pate, R.R., Small, M.L., Ross, J.G., Young, J.C., Flint, K.H. and Warren, C.W. (1995b). School physical education. *Journal of School Health,* 65(8), 312–318.

Payne, W.G. and Morrow, J.R. (1993). Exercise and VO2 max in children: A meta-analysis. *Research Quarterly for Exercise and Sport,* 64: 305–313.

Powers, H.S., Conway, T.L., McKenzie T.L., Sallis, J.F. and Marshall, S.J. (2002). Participation in extracurricular physical activity programs at middle schools. *Research Quarterly for Exercise and Sport,* 73: 187–192.

Pratt, M., Macera, C. and Blanton, C. (1999). Levels of physical activity and inactivity in children and adults in the United States: current evidence and research issues. *Medicine and Science in Sports and Exercise,* 31: S526–S533.

Raitakari, O.T., Porkka, K.V., Taimela, S., Telama, R., Rasanen, L. and Viikari, J.S. (1994). Effects of persistent physical activity and inactivity on coronary risk factors in children and young adults. The Cardiovascular Risk in Young Finns Study. *American Journal of Epidemiology,* 140: 195–205.

Riddoch, C., Andersen, L.B., Wedderkopp, N. et al. (2004). Physical activity levels and patterns of 9 and 15-yr-old European children. *Medicine and Science in Sports and Exercise,* 36: 86–92.

Roche, A.F. (1995). Tracking in body composition and risk factors for cardiovascular disease from childhood to middle age. In K. Froberg, O. Lammert, H. St. Hansen and C.J.R. Blimkie (Eds.), *Children and Exercise XVIII* (pp. 238–255). Odense: Odense University Press.

Ross, J.G. (1994). The status of fitness programming in our nation's schools. In R.P. Pate and R.C. Hohn (Eds.), *Health and fitness through physical education* (pp. 21–30). Champaign, IL: Human Kinetics.

Ross, J.G., Dotson, C.O., Gilbert, G.G. and Katz, S.J. (1985). What are kids doing in school physical education? *Journal of Physical Education, Recreation and Dance,* 73–76.

Rowland, T.W. (1998). The biological basis of physical activity. *Medicine and Science in Sports and Exercise,* 30: 392–399.

Rowlands, A.V., Ingledew, D.K. and Eston, R.G. (2000). The effect of type of physical activity measure on the relationship between body fatness and habitual physical activity in children: a meta-analysis. *Annals of Human Biology, 27*: 479–497.

Sallis, J.F. (2000). Age-related decline in physical activity: a synthesis of human and animal studies. *Medicine and Science in Sports and Exercise, 32*: 1598–1600.

Sallis, J.F., Conway, T.L., Prochaska, J.J., McKenzie, T.L., Marshall, S.J. and Brown, M. (2001). The association of school environments with youth physical activity. *Journal of Science and Medicine in Sport, 91*: 618–620.

Sallis, J.F., McKenzie, T.L., Alcaraz, J.E., Kolody, B., Faucette, N. and Hovell, M.F. (1997). Effects of a 2-year health-related physical education program on physical activity and fitness in elementary school students: SPARK. *American Journal of Public Health, 87*: 1328–1334.

Sallis, J.F., McKenzie T.L., Elder, J.P. et al. (1998). Sex and ethnic differences in children's physical activity: discrepancies between self-report and objective measures. *Pediatric Exercise Science, 10*: 277–284.

Sallis, J. F., McKenzie, B., Kolody, M., Lewis, M., Marshall, S. and Roengard, P. (1999). Effects of health-related physical education on academic achievement:Project SPARK. *Research Quarterly for Exercise and Sport, 70*: 127–134.

Sallis, J.F. and Owen, N. (1997). Ecological models. In K. Glanz, F.M. Lewis and B.K. Rimer (Eds.), *Health behavior and health education* (2 ed., pp. 403–424). San Francisco, CA: Jossey-Bass Publishers.

Sallis, J.F. and Owen, N. (1999). *Physical activity and behavioural medicine.* Thousand Oaks, CA: Sage Publications.

Sallis, J.F. and Patrick, K. (1994). Physical activity guidelines for adolescents: consensus statement. *Pediatric Exercise Science, 6*: 302–314.

Sallis, J.F., Prochaska, J.J. and Taylor, W.C. (2000). A review of correlates of physical activity of children and adolescents. *Medicine and Science in Sports and Exercise, 32*: 963–975.

Sallis, J.F. and Saelens, B.E. (2000). Assessment of physical activity by self-report: status, limitations, and future directions. *Medicine and Science in Sports and Exercise, 71*: S1–S14.

Salmon, J. (2003). *Children's physical activity and obesogenic environments.* The Public Health Association (SA) Forum on Childhood Obesity, Adelaide.

Scruggs, P.W., Beveridge, S.K., Eisenman, P.A., Watson, D.L., Schultz, B.B. and Ransdell, L.B. (2003). Quantifying physical activity via pedometry in elementary physical education. *Medicine and Science in Sports and Exercise, 35*: 1065–1071.

Sibley, B.A. and Etnier, J.L. (2003). The relationship between physical activity and cognition in children: a meta-analysis. *Pediatric Exercise Science, 15*: 243–256.

Simons-Morton, B.G., Parcel, G.C., Baranowski, T., Forthoefer, R. and O'Hara, N.M. (1991). Promoting physical activity and a healthful diet among children: results of a school-based intervention study. *American Journal of Public Health, 81*: 986–991.

Smith, M.A. and Claxton, D.B. (2003). Using active homework in physical education. *Journal of Physical Education Recreation and Dance, 74*: 28–34.

Smoak, C.G., Burke, G.L., Webber, L.S., Harsha, D.W., Srinivasan, S. and Berensen, G.S. (1987). Relation of obesity to clustering of cardiovascular disease risk factors in children and young adults. *American Journal of Epidemiology, 125*: 364–372.

Stone, E.J., McKenzie T.L., Welk, G.J. and Booth, M.L. (1998). Effects of physical activity interventions in youth: Review and synthesis. *American Journal of Preventive Medicine, 15*: 298–315.

Stratton, G., Jones, M., Fox, K.R. et al. (REACH Group) (2004). *Journal of Sports Science, 22*(4): 283–390.

Strong, W.B., Malina, R.M., Blimkie, C.J., Daniels, S.R., Dishman, R.K., Gutin, B., Hergenroeder, A.C., Must, A., Nixon, P.A., Pivarnik, J.M., Rowland, T., Trost, S., Trudeau, F. (2000). Evidence based physical activity for school-age youth. *Journal of Pediatrics, 146*: 732–737.

The Prevention Institute. (2001). *Promoting physical activity among youth.* Columbus OH: The Prevention Institute.

Tremblay, M. and Willms, J. (2003). Is the Canadian childhood obesity epidemic related to physical inactivity? *International Journal of Obesity, 27*: 1100–1105.

Tremblay, M.S. and Willms, J.D. (2000). Secular trends in the body mass index of Canadian children. *Canadian Medical Association Journal, 163*: 1429–1433.

Trost, S.G., Pate, R.R., Sallis, J.F. et al. (2002a). Age and gender differences in objectively measured physical activity in youth. *Medicine and Science in Sports and Exercise, 34*: 350–355.

Trost, S.G., Saunders, R. and Ward, D.S. (2002b). Determinants of physical activity in middle school children. *American Journal of Health Behavior, 26*: 95–102.

Trudeau, F., Laurencelle, L., Tremblay, J., Rajic, M. and Shephard, R.J. (1998). A long-term follow-up of participants in the Trois-Rivieres semi-longitudinal study of growth and development. *Pediatric Exercise Science, 10*: 366–367.

Trudeau, F., Espindola, R., Laurencelle, L., Dulac, F., Rajic, M. and Shepard, R.J. (2000). Follow-up of participants in the Trois-Rivieres Growth and Development Study: examining their health-related fitness and risk factors as adults. *American Journal of Human Biology, 12*: 207–213.

Tudor-Locke, C., Ainsworth, B.E. and Popkin, B.M. (2001). Active commuting to school: an overlooked source of childrens' physical activity? *Sports Medicine, 31*: 309–313.

Tudor-Locke, C., Pangrazi, R.P., Corbin, C.B. et al. (2004). BMI-referenced standards for recommended pedometer-determined steps/day in children. *Preventive Medicine, 38*: 857–864.

Twisk, J. (2001). Physical activity guidelines for children and adolescents: a critical review. *Sports Medicine, 31*: 617–627.

U.S. Department of Health and Human Services. (1996). *Physical activity and health: A report of the Surgeon General.* Atlanta, GA.

U.S. Department of Health and Human Services. (2000). *Promoting better health for young people through physical activity and sports: A report to the president from the Secretary of Health and Human Services and the Secretary of Education.* Washington, D.C..

Vincent, S.D., Pangrazi, R.P., Raustorp, A., Tomson, L.M. and Cuddihy, T.F. (2003). Activity levels and body mass index of children in the United States, Sweden and Australia. *Medicine and Science in Sports and Exercise, 35:* 1367–1373.

Wake, M., Hesketh, K. and Waters, E. (2003). Television, computer use and body mass index in Australian primary school children. *Journal of Pediatric and Child Health, 39:* 130–134.

Webber, L.S., Cresanta, J.L., Voors, A.W. and Berenson, G.S. (1983). Tracking of cardiovascular disease risk factor variables in school-age children. *Journal of Chronic Diseases, 36:* 647–660.

Wei, M., Kampert, J.B., Barlow, C.E. et al. (1999). Relationship between low cardiorespiratory fitness and mortality in normal-weight, overweight, and obese men. *Journal of the American Medical Association, 282:* 1547–1553.

Welk, G.J. (1999). The youth physical activity promotion model: A conceptual bridge between theory and practice. *Quest, 51:* 5–23.

Welk, G.J. (2002). Use of accelerometry-based activity monitors to assess physical activity. In G.J. Welk (Ed.), *Physical activity assessments for health related research* (pp. 125–141). Champaign, IL: Human Kinetics.

Welk, G.J., Babke, M. and Brustad, R.J. (1998). Causal links among determinants of physical activity in children: A structural equation model. *Medicine and Science in Sports and Exercise, 30:* S182.

Welk, G.J., Corbin, C.B. and Dale, D. (2000). Measurement issues for the assessment of physical activity in children. *Research Quarterly for Exercise and Sport, 71:* 59–73.

Welk, G.J., Corbin, C.B. and Lewis, L.A. (1995). Physical self-perceptions of high school athletes. *Pediatric Exercise Science, 7:* 152–161.

Welk, G.J. and Eklund, R.C. (2004). Validation of the children and youth physical self perception profile for young children. *Psychology of Sport and Exercise, 6(1):* 51–65.

Welk, G.J., Morrow, J.R.J., Falls, H.B. and (Eds.) (2002). *Fitnessgram Reference Guide.* Dallas, TX: The Cooper Institute.

Welk, G.J. and Schaben, J.A. (2004). Psychosocial correlates of physical activity in children – a study of relationships when children have similar opportunities to be active. *Measurement in Physical Education and Exercise Science, 16(4):* 310–323.

Welk, G.J. and Wood, K. (2000). Physical activity assessments in physical education: A practical review of instruments and their use in the curriculum. *Journal of Physical Education, Recreation and Dance, 71:* 30–40.

Welk, G.J., Wood, K. and Morss, G. (2003). Parental influences on physical activity in children: an exploration of potential mechanisms. *Pediatric Exercise Science, 15:* 19–33.

Whitehead, J.R. and Corbin, C.B. (1997). Self-esteem in children and youth: The role of sport and physical education. In K.R. Fox (Ed.), *The physical self: From motivation to well-being,* (pp. 175–203). Champaign, IL: Human Kinetics.

Williams, D.P., Going, S.B., Lohman, T.G., Harsha, D.W., Srinivasan, S. and Berensen, G.S. (1992). Body fatness and risk for elevated blood pressure, total cholesterol, and serum lipoproteins ratios in children and adolescents. *Amercan Journal of Public Health, 82:* 358–363.

5.8 Adventure education and physical education

MIKE BROWN

Introduction

The concept of impelling people into adventurous situations to achieve educational goals is not a recent phenomenon. It has been argued that the use of adventurous activities for educational purposes can be traced, in Western culture at least, to the works of Plato (Hunt, 1990). In this century the work of Dewey, Hahn, Lewin, Piaget and others have laid the foundations of the modern adventure education movement. The influence of these theorists and practitioners is well documented (see Kolb, 1984; Miles and Priest, 1990; Warren et al., 1995). Adventure education is based on the experiential learning model which combines direct experience with guided reflection and analysis under the supervision of a group instructor/facilitator/teacher. Adventure education is one branch of an area that is loosely termed outdoor education. As Boyes (2000) points out there is still a lack of agreement about the most appropriate terminology to use in this discipline area; frequently used terms include environmental education, wilderness education, outdoor pursuits, camp and education outside the classroom. As with any socially constructed discipline area the terminology associated with outdoor education has arisen due to different professional conceptualisations and ideologies which practitioners and scholars bring to the field (Martin, 1998). Miles and Priest, two authoritative writers in the field of outdoor and adventure education state that,

> Adventure education involves the purposeful planning and implementation of educational processes that involve risk in some way. ... The defining characteristic of adventure education is that a conscious and overt goal of the adventure is to expand the self, to learn and grow and progress toward the realization of human potential. (1990: 1)

In this chapter the term adventure education is used to describe experiential education programs that are conducted in an outdoor setting and/or involve physical engagement in an activity which provides a sense of challenge to participants. Within adventure education the "action–reflection" cycle is integral to the learning process as it assists the student to focus on the experience and gain valuable insights about one's self and one's relationship to the world (Joplin, 1995; Sugarman et al., 2000). With particular reference to adventure programs conducted within the physical education curriculum, it should be explicitly stated that such programs may be conducted in school gymnasiums or on sports fields – the key point being that the participant is actively engaged in the learning endeavour, preferably in a holistic manner which requires physical, mental and emotional commitment. Whilst it might be argued that adventure education can only be conducted in "natural" or "wilderness settings", in the context of a discussion of adventure and physical education, this restricts adventure education to too narrow a group of programs and too small a potential participant base. The use of adventure education pedagogy (pedagogy employing the experiential approach) in "short" or "lesson-space" periods of time is not without its difficulties if one conceptualizes adventure education as being based on the development of three fundamental relationships: (a) intrapersonal relationships; defined as how an individual relates to themselves (e.g. self-concept, confidence, spirituality), (b) interpersonal relationships (e.g. communication, trust, co-operation), (c) relationship to/with the environment (see Priest and Gass, 1997). It is the third relationship which is potentially the most problematic to convey in school-based programs and the one currently emphasized as adventure/outdoor educators seek to embrace a holistic and ecological approach to the field as the more "traditional" adventurous and personal development outcomes are being increasingly called into question (see Brookes, 2003a, 2003b; Zink, 2003).

Whilst direct experience and reflection are the cornerstones of adventure education, the implementation and practices of educators are not necessarily similar in different localities. The different emphases placed on personal development or team building through "high" adventure activities or the promotion of an increased understanding of the environment and one's place within the ecological sphere reflect different cultural and geographical imperatives. Wattchow (2001) for example expounds the value of a pedagogy of production as a way of embodying knowing through the action of craft in outdoor education. Based on data collected from teachers, Rubens (1999) has provided a conceptualisation of outdoor education which provides a way of demonstrating and classifying the different perceptions of outdoor education. He refers to adventure being broadly classified as "narrowly" or "broadly" conceived. Narrow conceptions are characterised by short duration experiences requiring minimal effort, activities with high "thrill" value and significant levels of anxiety (e.g. abseiling or ziplines/ropes course). In contrast the broad conception involves longer time frames, more effort, varied challenges and the devolution of responsibilities to the students (e.g. a journey or expedition). In this classification 'narrow' adventure education is dedicated to the development of the learner's interpersonal and intrapersonal abilities while the 'broad' notion expands on these elements through its emphasis on the development of a relationship with and for the environment. This "narrow" conception of adventure education is articulated by Priest who states that:

> The process of adventure education involves the use of adventurous activities such as recreational pursuits in the outdoors or the so-called artificial adventure environs (ropes courses and group initiatives). These activities are used to provide a group or an individual with tasks to accomplish. These tasks often involve problem solving and challenge. The problem solving requires decision making, judgement, cooperation, communication, and trust. The challenge may take the form of testing one's competence against mental, social or physical risks. (Priest, 1999: 112)

With the aforementioned comments in mind it may well be more appropriate to call adventure education in the physical education curriculum Adventure Based Learning (ABL), a term which emphasises the potential development of the first two relationships without making potentially spurious and unfounded claims in regard to how we might (or might not be) educating our students about and for the environment. Cosgriff (2000: 90) defines ABL as "the deliberate use of sequenced adventure activities particularly games, trust activities and problem solving initiatives-for the personal and social development of participants".

She highlights the following as key features of ABL programs:

(a) the place of innovative and sequenced physical activity;
(b) the importance of experiential learning;
(c) the interdependence of educational goals and curriculum;
(d) the goal that students become committed and active members of the school and local community.

Bearing in mind the comments made earlier about the difficulty of defining and clearly differentiating adventure education and outdoor education I will refer to both terms (certainly when they are used by others in quotations) interchangeably. However in the context of adventure in physical education I am primarily concerned with the role of adventure activities/programs in achieving educational outcomes relating to intra- and interpersonal domains.

Elements of contemporary adventure education have developed from, and conversely been incorporated into, the broader "camping movement". Recreational camps organised by schools, community and youth groups (e.g. scouts, church congregations) have featured in both educational and recreational endeavours in western societies for well over one hundred years (for a more detailed history of the camping movement see Ewert, 1989; Hammerman, 1980; McRae, 1990). Perhaps the best known international provider of outdoor programs is the Outward Bound movement which was co-founded by German educator Kurt Hahn in Wales during the Second World War.

Outdoor education has not had a prominent position as a key learning area within the formal school curriculum. In Australia, for example, outdoor education is often positioned, if at is mentioned at all, within the physical education curriculum as a series of activities. It is not until the senior years of schooling that it can be chosen as an independent subject in its own right (and then only in one state). As a result outdoor education is often seen as an extracurricular activity in many schools, its continued existence dependent on the enthusiasm and expertise of individual teachers. In contrast to the state education sector there are a large number of independent (private) schools who conduct outdoor education programs which compliment the existing "formal" curriculum. These are often long term (one month to one year) residential programs which integrate "formal" studies with outdoor camping and expeditionary components. These programs are often presented to prospective parents as means to enhance "life skills" or aid in "personal development". As will be discussed in more detail, the measurable outcomes of outdoor education programs are not always easily, defined and recourse to ideas of outdoor education as "building character" (a suitably vague and difficult term to define) are coming under increasing scrutiny.

This chapter will briefly examine the principles of adventure programming prior to discussing the place of adventure education with physical education. This is followed by a review of research con ducted within the broad gambit of adventure/ outdoor education and a summary of the claimed outcomes of adventure programs. In the next section the focus will be on research on adventure education within physical education. Finally, in discussing the major issues, trends and future directions my aim is to draw together some of the key issues faced by both physical education and adventure/outdoor education researchers in an effort to encourage a dialogue that will enhance our understanding of what it is we claim to know and conversely what it is we should be seeking to know to promote adventure education in the physical education curriculum.

Core concepts of adventure programes

Central to adventure education programs is the concept of experiential learning; the belief that learning will occur more effectively if the learner is as involved as possible in the activity. This involvement is maximised if the student is required to commit themselves to the activity mentally, emotionally and physically. Student participation would ideally include involvement in the planning, executing, reflecting and evaluating of the experience. Integral to the experiential process is the provision of direct experience with guided reflection and analysis.

> Broadly defined, experiential education is a philosophical orientation toward teaching and learning that values and encourages linkages between concrete educative activities and abstract lessons to maximize learning. Through these experiences, it is hoped and believed that learners attain a qualitatively superior level of knowing than can be achieved through abstract lessons alone.... (Sakofs, 1995: 149)

However experiential learning is not simply "learning by doing", for as Proudman (1995) points out, repetitively performing a task can become a ritualised and habitual conditioning process rather than an educational undertaking. Experiential education is the intentional planning of learning that requires two components, the provision of an experience for the learner and the facilitation of that experience through reflection. Adventure education programs combine direct experience, through adventurous or challenging activities that are meaningful to the student, with guided reflection

and analysis that offers challenge and calls on them to make decisions and take responsibility (Luckner and Nadler, 1997; Priest and Gass, 1997).

Luckner and Nadler (1997) state that what experiential education does best is to instill a sense of ownership over what is learned, adding interest and engagement for the student and providing the ability to transfer learning to other situations. It is the process that defines a learning experience as experiential rather than the activity that is performed.

> Experiential learning is also based on the belief that change occurs when people are placed outside a position of comfort and into a state of dissonance, or the difference between the current situation and the desired future. In such a state, people are challenged by the adaptations necessary to reach a new state of equilibrium, yet are also supported through such processes by peers and leaders. Reaching these self-directed states produces changes that result in growth and learning. One of the major differences between experiential learning and other formats is that experiential learning is not a product of learning, but a learning process that is implemented under appropriate circumstances. (Priest and Gass, 1997: 136)

A number of educators and researchers (Dewey, 1938; Joplin, 1995; Pfeiffer and Jones, 1980; Priest and Gass, 1997; Walsh and Golins, 1976) have constructed models to explain the essential features of experiential learning, all of which have emphasised the cyclic component of the learning process. Kolb's (1984) four stage model of experiential learning (see Figure 5.8.1) is perhaps the most widely known in adventure education literature.

Luckner and Nadler (1997) point out that although the stages of the experiential learning cycle, are presented in discrete terms, they are interrelated and there is interaction between the various components. The four components of the cycle are: experiencing, reflecting, generalizing and applying.

Once the learning objectives have been identified (for example, team-building, communication) many types of experience(s) can be selected. However, experience alone is not a guarantee that learning will occur. Reflection provides an opportunity to integrate the new experience with past experiences. In the reflection stage the intention is that the student will reflect back on and examine what they felt, observed and thought about during the experience (Luckner and Nadler, 1997). At the third stage the intention is that students share, normally verbally, what they felt, observed and thought during the experience. The intention at this point is to assist students to find out "what happened at a cognitive, affective and behaviour level – before the activity, while the activity was progressing, and after its completion" (Luckner and Nadler, 1992: 2). The

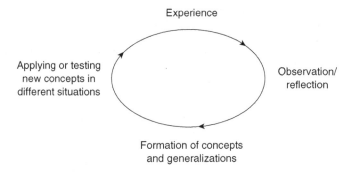

Figure 5.8.1 Adaptation of Kolb's (1984) model of the experiential learning cycle

participant moves from an analysis of what occurred in a specific situation to an understanding of patterns of behaviour across situations. The focus moves from "what happened in this experience" to "what tends to happen when I am placed in situations that mirror this experience". Thus generalizations are made from specific actions or behaviours to ways of acting/behaving. Finally, for experiential learning to be considered effective, participants need to be able to apply what they have learned in one specific situation to other settings. The application of what has been learned feeds back into the next experience, so continuing the cycle.

Priest and Gass (1997) have outlined eight principles of adventure programming that have been developed by the Association of Experiential Education to reflect the ideals of the experiential approach.

(1) Adventure programs should be based on direct and purposeful experiences. Change and growth have experience at their origin and therefore placing the participant close to this experience will enhance learning.

(2) Adventure programs focus on appropriately challenging participants. Adventure education is premised on the belief that change occurs when people are placed in a situation which is challenging and creates a perception of disequilibrium with presently held attitudes or practices. Participants are required to use their abilities and those of their group to regain a state of equilibrium. It is maintained that the quest for equilibrium may require change within the individual resulting in the type of growth clients are attempting to achieve. In order to achieve change, programs are designed to put participants in appropriate environments and situations that encourage a change of attitude.

(3) The activities in the program must have meaningful and natural consequences within an appropriate safety framework. Consequences are a result of

decisions or actions taken by the participants and should be real and immediate.

(4) Consequences that are natural, rather than construed, result in changes that are participant-based rather than leader-determined. This allows participants to determine the level and meaning of their experiences.

(5) Changes that occur within groups or individuals should have relevance not only for the task at hand, but for the future.

(6) Synthesis and reflection are used as elements of the change process. Processing and reflection help to enhance the internalisation of change for the participant. (Carver, 1996; Dewey, 1938; Joplin, 1995; Kolb, 1984; Proudman, 1995)

(7) Participants are called on to be responsible for their involvement – they are impelled rather than compelled. Participants are given power and control over their learning through the "challenge by choice principle". (Rohnke, 1984)

(8) Participants have the opportunity to become actively involved in their learning through adventure activities. They can deal with new situations by applying what they have learned and identified in previous situations.

Adventure education's emphasis on using challenging outdoor/physical activities as a medium in which to learn means that in the process of facilitation, participants need to be able to make connections concerning the applicability of this learning to other non-outdoor/physical settings. For example, learning how to rock climb or canoe is less important than the intra and interpersonal insights gained from these activities; insights that need to be transferable for adventure education to make claims to legitimacy. The important pedagogical features of adventure education include challenge, a sense of uncertainty of outcome and appropriate sequencing of activities which lead to success. Martin and Priest (1986) refer to these features as the "Adventure

Experience Paradigm"; a model which is currently being critiqued and is the subject of further discussion later in the chapter.

The place of adventure education within physical education

In the following section I highlight some of the claims made in regard to the role of adventure/outdoor activities within physical education and discuss how adventure education has been promoted by some physical education specialists as a curriculum innovation model. It is important to stress that many of the assumed benefits or outcomes attributed to an adventure education curriculum are often based on anecdotal evidence rather than empirical research. By way of example, Hammersley states,

> There can be no doubt about the value of adventure education in the mind of anyone who has witnessed the powerful learning experiences of students such as Anne, whose face beamed with accomplishment and a new glimmer of confidence, as she said triumphantly, 'I never thought I could do it'. (1992: 67)

In a similar vein Panicucci (2002: 41) states somewhat evangelically and without an empirical basis, that "The Adventure approach promotes the acquisition and mastery of simple and complex motor skills, allows for real kinesthetic exploration. Adventure can help prepare students for today's world". Rogers (2000) also makes a case for adventure-based learning in the secondary physical education curriculum and states that students who have participated in outdoor adventure activities as part of the school curriculum may continue to participate in such activities throughout life and therefore keep them active. However Rogers does not provide evidence to support this assertion, nor can I find any independent research to back up this claim. Perhaps more debateable is the assertion that as businesses today are demanding more from their employees in the areas of teamwork and group communication skills, "It could be proposed that if high school students had the opportunity to participate in outdoor adventure activities, they would have an advantage in the job market" (Rogers, 2000: 11). A strong correlation has yet to be established which links participation in school based adventure education programs to increased physical fitness, this is despite wishful claims (for example, see Latess, 1986) by some adventure education advocates.

Whilst many of these claims are contestable, adventure education has been promoted within physical education for its student centred pedagogy which is seen as an innovative and holistic approach to movement education and a means of developing

social interaction and personal qualities. In a paper specifically focused on physical education and outdoor education, Bunting (1989) listed social development, improved intrapersonal attitudes, environmental awareness, enhancement of learning, skill development and physical fitness as being objectives common to both OE and physical education. Chen and Ennis (1996) argue that curriculum innovation is an imperative for physical educators and adventure education is seen as a viable alternative model to traditional approaches to physical education. Latess (1986) suggests that it is only a matter of time before we consider adventure activities as an integral component of the 'traditional' physical education curriculum. Panicucci states that:

> Many believe the addition of an Adventure curriculum has kept their PE programs from being eliminated. Whether true or not, all of us who have taught PE using Adventure know that these programs are a contributing factor to many students graduating with a stronger sense of self and a "can-do" attitude that encompasses the physical and transcends it into many other areas of their lives. (2000: 53)

It is issues relating to students' personal, social and physical development that those who have introduced adventure education are hoping to address through the implementation of authentic tasks with real outcomes which involve the students in a holistic manner. Hammersley (1992) cites work by Dunn and Wilson (1991) in which they describe how co-operative learning can result in higher academic performance, greater sense of locus of control, improved social relations and better language skills; all benefits which may result from co-operative learning which is inherent in adventure education. Another integral component of the adventure education approach is the student-centered pedagogy.

> Person-centred learning, in which individuals feel valued and in which trust is communicated between teachers and pupils and between pupils and pupils is in a sense, essential in much of the work in OE. It is essential because of the possibility of physical or psychological harm occurring as a consequence of badly organised and/or poorly taught hazardous activities. ... Consequently, it is not just for ideological but also for pragmatic reasons that OE pedagogy tends to be child-centred. (Humberstone, 1993: 223)

As briefly mentioned earlier, one of the key drivers for the inclusion of ABL into "mainstream" schooling was the advent of Project Adventure (PA). PA was instigated by a Massachusetts High school principal to incorporate the Outward Bound process and philosophy into a public secondary school setting (Hirsch, 1999). PA has been widely promoted as a curricular innovation in physical education classes (Cosgriff, 2000; Cosgriff and Schusser, 1999; Dyson, 1996; Dyson and O'Sullivan, 1998). Initially employing staff with Outward Bound experience and teachers who sought pedagogical innovation, this program introduced a modified curriculum that was focused on physical education with the aim of nurturing "joy in one's physical self and in being with others" (Rohnke, 1984: 9). Additional curricular units were subsequently written for other subject areas. The PA model aims to promote the education of "the total student by developing each child mentally, physically, emotionally, and socially to produce an effective citizen for our society" (Project Adventure, 1991: 6).

The PA approach is characterised by the use of non-wilderness activities including games, initiatives and ropes courses (Hirsch, 1999). For examples of how this approach might be implemented in a class see the following texts (Dyson and Brown, 2005; Schoel et al., 1988). PA has expanded beyond the United States and has become an innovative and influential international adventure training organisation, for example PA concepts such as "full value contract" and "challenge by choice" are widely employed in a variety of non-PA adventure education programs.

While PA has developed a particular "variety" or form of adventure education, students' involvement with the outdoors has also been fostered through school residential camps, summer camping experiences run by charitable or commercial organisations and outdoor pursuit groups run by dedicated and enthusiastic teachers and parents.

Whilst there is considerable rhetoric about the potential value of adventure education programs within physical education, much of which appears to be based on "casual observation" or untested assumptions, it is clear that adventure education is seen as a viable curriculum innovation. Attention will now turn to research findings based within the adventure/outdoor education field followed by a more detailed examination of research of adventure programs in PE.

Major findings in outdoor education research

This section presents a brief overview on how research has been conducted in the wider field of adventure education, highlighting some of the problematic methodological issues, coupled with recent shifts in research approaches as researchers

have attempted to examine not only the outcomes of adventure programs but to also investigate how these outcomes are achieved. This is followed by a discussion of the claimed outcomes of adventure education programs and a section detailing research that has specifically focussed on adventure education within the physical education curriculum.

Approaches to research within adventure education

In this sub-section I will briefly trace the move within the discipline to more "process-oriented" studies that build on earlier researcher's work which had a strong focus on measuring the outcomes of adventure programs. Adventure educators may well, with some understandable reticence, agree with comments by Gass (1993) that the field lacks a strong research base (see Ewert, 1989; Richards, 1997; Warner, 1990). Richards (1997) claims that much of the early research and evaluation in outdoor and adventure education has been of dubious value. Warner (1990) maintains that too much time and effort has been devoted to poorly controlled outcome studies on psychological variables. Early research in the field was limited to and typified by "one-time" outcome studies conducted using pre- and post-treatment questionnaires in order to record changes in designated personality traits and attitudes; traits that are themselves the source of ongoing debate (Bocarro and Richards, 1998). Much of the research in adventure education has tended to concentrate on the dependent variable that could commonly be referred to as "personal development outcomes": self-esteem, self-concept, self-efficacy, self-worth and self-confidence (Ibbott, 1997). Ibbott also notes that not only are these constructs conceptually difficult to define, but the measurement instruments and the effects of adventure programs do not necessarily translate readily into measurable differences. Neill (1997) notes that in this preoccupation with describing positive outcomes individual differences were largely ignored and research tended to gloss over the fact that programs were not always beneficial to all participants.

The rationale behind these outcome-based studies was to determine if outdoor education "worked" (Allison and Pomeroy, 2000; Richards, 1997) and whether the program had an effect on the participants. The two main methodologies in the outcome-based approach were: (a) interviewing the participants at the end of the experience to determine what they thought of the program and had gained from it; and (b) giving participants some form of questionnaire at the start of the program and again at the end (a pre–post test design) and comparing the results (Richards, 1997). This research has received criticism for its "over reliance on self-selected samples and measures using a self-report format" (Ewert, 1989: 17), resulting in claims that such studies are often methodologically flawed (Miles, 1995).

While the outcome-based approach to research may have been of some use in supporting educators' claims about the benefits of adventure education programs and provided external funding agencies with a justification for continuing their support, it has done little to improve practice or the understanding of the experiences of program participants (Allison and Pomeroy, 2000).

The predominance of outcome-based research coupled with the lengthy and protracted debate in adventure education literature concerning appropriate methodological approaches to capturing the "uniqueness" of experiential learning (Ewert, 1987; Kolb, 1991; Richards, 1997; Rowley, 1987), has meant that until relatively recently little research has been conducted on "process", programmatic or instructional issues in adventure education. It is possible that this relative lack of research on "process" reflects the prevailing dominance of researchers and graduate students from psychology departments who bring with them a set of research methods determined by the epistemological perspective in which they operate. This is not to cast doubt on the value of psychological approaches but to indicate that this approach can be complemented by the differing perspectives offered by sociology, linguistics or cultural studies researchers (Brown, 2002b).

Researchers (Allison and Pomeroy, 2000; Richards, 1997) note that while process-oriented studies have not been as prevalent as outcome-based approaches, there is a growing recognition that these studies offer important insights not afforded by outcome-based approaches. There is "the increasing recognition that better outcomes will come from better processes and that therefore understanding processes is the primary route to gaining better outcomes" (Richards, 1997: 245).

The increasing acceptance of process-oriented studies has been the result of a debate within experiential and adventure education circles which centres on the argument that research that is outcome-based and seeks to treat the program or the individual in neatly packaged discrete portions is "philosophically out of tune with experiential theory and practice" (Warner, 1990: 310). In a similar vein Allison and Pomeroy (2000) advocate for a shift in the epistemological basis of existing research and the embracing of a new set of research questions. Like Warner (1990) they argue that an "incongruent epistemology is often employed in research in this field" (Allison and Pomeroy, 2000: 97). They maintain that the experiential approach to learning is based on a constructivist epistemological vision that is not reflected in the outcome-focused objectivist epistemology on which most research in the field is based. Allison and Pomeroy (2000) argue that in the field of experiential and adventure education there is the need to move away from proving that these programs work to develop an understanding of the processes that are involved through the use of ethnography, case studies, phenomenology and biographies. Bocarro and Richards (1998) maintain that there is the continual need to develop new research techniques and measures in order to better understand and deal with the uniqueness of adventure-based experiential learning programs. "This may require a paradigm shift away from what has traditionally been considered the 'correct' way to conduct research" (Bocarro and Richards, 1998: 107). Miles and Priest assert that practitioners

> are only beginning to ask why they do things in a certain way, what the outcomes of their approaches are, what alternatives to their approaches might be. They have little idea which parts of the processes they use result in which effects ... (1990: 2)

In providing this review of approaches to research in adventure education and the various paradigmatic positions adopted I do not want to construct or re-enact the unproductive debate surrounding qualitative verses quantitative research methods. The intention has been to provide a background to the type of research that has been traditionally conducted in adventure education and to foreshadow the changing nature of research in the area and acknowledge that there is a call for, and a valued place, for process-oriented studies in this field.

What has become apparent from the review of literature is that while there are many articles and books on how to organise adventure education programs (and how to conduct "adventurous" activities), and considerable research on outcomes (see Cason and Gillis, 1994; Hattie et al., 1997) there are few studies, with the notable exceptions discussed below, on adventure education within physical education.

Humberstone (1995) claims that researchers and educators in mainstream physical education tend to neglect outdoor education as peripheral to physical education. She claims that when OE does appear on the physical education agenda, in the UK at least, it is usually in relation to its removal from the physical education curriculum.

> The marginalization of outdoor education may partly be a consequence of the paradoxical and perplexing relationship between it and physical education. Both are concerned with physical activities, but their ideological underpinnings are different .... In addition, material issues surround the use of outdoor education. Most other forms of physical activity are more cost effective and offer less exposure to physical risk than do outdoor/adventurous activities. (Humberstone, 1995: 153)

What are the claimed outcomes of adventure programs?

As evidenced in the earlier section, on the place of adventure education within physical education, there is no shortage of literature that makes substantial claims for the educational achievements of outdoor programs in schools. For some people in the field the value of outdoor education programs is self-evident and requires no further justification or proof (Neill, 1997).

> These claims range from the global and comprehensive, for example "that outdoor education is a panacea for ills which pervade our contemporary educational and societal systems" (Gray and Perusco, 1993: 20), to extensive lists of specific physical, social, intellectual, and psychological outcomes. (Neill, 1997: 193)

In an attempt to gain a "big picture" view of the results of outcome-based studies researchers have started using meta-analyses, an analytic method which enables investigators to summarise the results of a large number of independent studies (see Cason and Gillis, 1994; Hattie et al., 1997; Neill and Richards, 1998).

The first published meta-analysis of outdoor education outcomes was conducted by Cason and Gillis (1994). The data analysed was collected from studies of adolescents in outdoor programs (age 11 to freshmen). Forty-three studies were used in the analysis generating 235 effect sizes describing 19 outcome measures. The studies ranged from college courses in outdoor education to three week Outward Bound courses. In their findings they state that adolescents who participated in adventure programs were "better off", that is they exhibited significantly significant differences in seven broad categories of outcome measurements (e.g. self-concept, locus of control, behavioural assessments, attitude surveys, clinical scales, grades and school attendance) than 62% who did not participate. The average of the 147 effect sizes was 0.31, a small to moderate effect size. The authors commented on the limitations of the study including course length, undocumented variables, leadership styles, participants in individual studies, activities undertaken, and the quality of the original measurement instrument.

> The wide variance in findings raises questions about the validity of quantitative research for this field, the reliability of instruments used for assessment of pre- and post program changes, and the host of unknown variables that may be influencing both positive and negative effects of adventure programming. (Cason and Gillis, 1994: 46)

In a later and more comprehensive study Hattie et al. (1997) conducted a meta-analysis which examined the effects of adventure programs on a range of outcomes including self-concept, locus of control and leadership. The study drew 151 samples from 96 studies. They concluded that in general terms the average effects from attending adventure programs was not dissimilar to the effects of innovations in classrooms. "This overall picture appears comforting. The details, however, reveal a different picture. Only some adventure programs are effective, and then on only some outcomes …" (Hattie et al., 1997: 70).

Interestingly the results indicate larger gains for adults than for school-aged students and the outcomes improved as the length of the program increased. Their results also indicate that short or intermediate term gains were followed by additional gains between the end of the program and any follow-up assessment. The researchers claim that adventure programs appear to be most effective at providing participants with a sense of self-regulation. The effects on leadership, personality and adventuresome dimensions were noted but these decrease over time. It should be noted that programs analysed in this study ranged from short, several day experiences to programs of up to 26 days in duration. "Overall, the results suggest that adventure programs can obtain notable outcomes… It is clear, however, that adventure programs are not inherently good. There is a great deal of variability in outcomes between different studies, different programs, and different individuals" (Hattie et al., 1997: 77).

Therefore it is not unreasonable to claim, on the basis of these studies that the overall effects of adventure programs on the outcome measures are at least equivalent to those of typical in-class educational interventions on achievement (Hattie et al., 1997). Neill (1997: 195) argues that outcome studies suggest the "potential of outdoor education to provide effective personal growth experiences for school students. However, the results indicate a low to moderate amount of change is actually achieved, with considerable variability in outcomes between various programs".

Whilst these meta-analyses draw on a large number of studies on the outcomes of adventure programs few empirical studies have examined the processes involved in achieving these outcomes. In a review of the literature on how adventure education program outcomes are achieved McKenzie (2000) identified and examined the following categories as being important to the adventure education process: the physical environment, activities, processing (facilitation), group structure, instructors and the participant. Interestingly she noted that the "current understandings of how adventure education program outcomes are achieved is based largely on theory, rather than empirical research" (McKenzie, 2000: 19). Therefore our practice may well prove to be grounded on assumptions that may or may not be correct. We are in essence working with what Ewert (1983: 27) describes as an "educational black box"; "we know something works but we don't know why or how". McKenzie argues that it is the quality of adventure activities (holistic involvement, challenge which is increased incrementally, mastery, and success/failure) that are responsible for outcomes rather than the specific activities themselves. She suggests that the same outcomes can be achieved using a variety of challenging activities; it is not the activity per se that is important, rather it is the quality or teaching/learning approach employed in adventure activities.

Research in adventure education within physical education

In presenting material relating to research in physical education I have made a somewhat arbitrary distinction between research conducted with participants in school settings or of school age (approximately aged 5–18) and that conducted in university or other tertiary settings. This distinction is done more for reasons of maintaining a semblance of order rather than to suggest that one body of research has primacy over the other.

School level

Whilst this first study (Dyson and O'Sullivan, 1998) primarily sought to describe and interpret the factors that supported and maintained curricular innovation at two elementary schools it is of interest because it featured Project Adventure as the vehicle to facilitate substantive school change. As Dyson and O'Sullivan (1998: 251) note, the reform at these schools,

> was not a subtle transformation of the existing status quo but a radical restructuring of the philosophy, content, and teaching methodology. The teachers and principals ... emphasized a holistic approach to learning by promoting the physical, intellectual, emotional, and social development of their students.

The researchers identified the following factors as supporting school reform: a shared vision, external support for the program, curricula integration, the centrality of physical education, and shared decision making. Dyson and O'Sullivan (1998: 248) reported that interdisciplinary integration was the one of the key elements of the reform.

> [T]his integrated approach allowed the students the opportunity to use their strengths and the environment to improve their limitations. Students may excel at certain physical or academic tasks, or in both; therefore, each discipline interrelates in a way that uniquely supports and develops the Project Adventure concepts.

The research indicated that the use of the Project Adventure approach within the physical education program was an integral component of a substantive curricular reform in these two schools.

Dyson (1995) has also investigated students' perceptions of their physical education classes that were conducted on the PA principles of trust, risk, cooperation, problem solving and challenge. The physical education teachers at the two schools involved in the study sought to build the students' social skills, have them take responsibility, have fun, develop cognitive skills and a healthy attitude toward competition. Dyson (1995) reported that the students claimed to have increased their enjoyment and learning in their modified physical education lessons. Importantly they revealed that they liked to challenge themselves in physical education. In adopting the PA approach students appeared to be less intimidated attempting difficult and risky tasks if trying their best was emphasized by their teachers. "For many students, success was equated with trying hard, instead of being limited to attaining the goal of the activity or having their team win" (Dyson, 1995: 405). Dyson's study is also supported by Rubens (1999) who argues, from motivational research, that reinforcing the importance of student effort is more important to learning than student performance. Students reported positively on the value they placed on being given responsibility and the opportunity to choose their own activities in physical education class. Of particular interest was the alignment between the students' goals and those of their teachers: cooperating, personal challenges, taking risks, having fun and learning new motor skills. Dyson asserts that several lessons can be learned from gaining students' perceptions about their physical education classes. He argues that at these schools, a positive, trusting, and supportive environment allowed students to participate in and enjoy certain activities that they might not otherwise have engaged in (see Dyson and O'Sullivan, 1998).

In a further paper Dyson (1996) examined two physical education teachers' experiences of conducting the Project Adventure approach in physical education. The rationale behind this study was to gain an understanding of the program from the teachers' perspective; to give their experiences "voice". He argues that teachers' personal theories and beliefs impact on classroom practice and curriculum decision making, therefore it is of some importance that we endeavour to understand teachers' underlying beliefs and teaching and learning theories. Data collection and analysis were based on interviews, non-participant observation and document analysis. Data was analysed using constant comparison (Glaser and Strauss, 1967).

Both teachers believed in a holistic approach to education; education for physical, emotional, social and cognitive development. Their common goals were building social skills and self esteem, giving the students the opportunity to take responsibility, creating fun in a learning environment and developing a healthy attitude toward competition. Both teachers believed they employed a student-focused teaching style through the use of co-operative activities and taking a more facilitative than instructional role. To this end the teachers employed extensive use of co-operative activities included peer tutoring and small group initiatives. Dyson contends that even if teachers do not implement a PA program within their school, the innovative strategies used by these teachers may be of benefit in reforming the classroom teaching and learning environment. Dyson states that the goals espoused by the teachers indicate that PA has the potential to be a valuable curriculum approach in elementary physical education programs.

In a research project investigating the construction of gender identities Humberstone (1990) sought to examine whether, in an adventure education context, girls might be more involved in the learning process than is apparent in mixed-sex classrooms. She contends that in mixed-sex classrooms girls are marginalized and their abilities underrated. Using an ethnographic case study (participants aged 13–15) she found that, at least at the residential outdoor education centre where the study was conducted, interaction patterns and forms of communication contradicted those which prevail in mainstream schools. Outdoor education, as practiced in this locality, with its "particular material, social and ideological features … seems to provide a powerful medium through which social change, at least at the level of identity and relations, may be a possibility" (Humberstone, 1990: 200). Humberstone remarked on the importance of positive peer group expectations and the effect which this had upon the girls' involvement and feelings of success. "The particular form of learning made available to girls and boys gave them the opportunity to develop friendships amongst themselves *and* with the other sex. This tended to foster a mutual understanding and trust between the sexes rather than antagonism and contempt" (Humberstone, 1990: 209).

This "particular form of learning" de-emphasized the importance of competition where students who do not "win" feel a sense of inadequacy. Humberstone argues that the creation of "winners" and "losers" may well "engender antagonism between pupils and militate against a context which is conducive to mutual understanding and to co-operation" (1990: 210). In contrast the centre and its staff promoted the positive aspects of competition which are generated from a challenge against perceived difficult circumstances or situations (see comments above concerning effort and performance and Dyson, 1995; Rubens, 1999). Humberstone observed that the teachers exhibited a "child-centred" pedagogy and that they seldom adopted an authoritarian position. "As a consequence of the material conditions, and the imperative for co-operative endeavours, this ideology was more easily realised than in a more restrictive competitive school situation" (Humberstone, 1990: 212). What is of significance from this study is the contrast between "traditional" physical education programs that are mediated through an ideology which supports masculine imagery and superiority (Humberstone, 1990) and that evidenced in the adventure education programs which facilitated behaviours which encouraged collaborative endeavours and non-competitive challenge. She also reported that the girls perceived that the teachers fostered understanding and co-operation between the sexes and that the teachers were concerned to help them overcome their hesitation to participate in unknown endeavours which involved an element of risk. Humberstone suggests that the high teacher–student ratios at the centre gave teachers more freedom to interact individually and with greater equity with the students. The organization of students into co-educational groupings also provided a setting where it was possible for both sexes to challenge gender stereotyping.

In a later paper Humberstone (1995) argued that evidence suggests that by adopting some of outdoor education's features, such as child-centred approaches, smaller class sizes and non-authoritarian pedagogy, physical education may provide a setting that might enhance gender equity. She remarked that the teachers at the outdoor centre at which the study was conducted displayed a pedagogy that was supportive, child-centred, utilizing a non-authoritarian more symmetrical mode of communication.

There is evidence of coeducational groups in outdoor contexts acting as "oppositional educational paradigms" (cf. Humberstone, 1993), in which new skills and knowledge are encountered and through which (a) conventional sex stereotyping is challenged and (b) transformative gender relations (between boys and girls) and power relations (between teachers and pupils) are created. … Yet this evidence is absent from recent feminist discourse on coeducational grouping in physical education (cf. Scraton, 1993) and from physical education discourse more broadly. (Humberstone, 1995: 152)

McCaughtry and Wojewuczki have conducted two recently published studies (2003a,b) which examined the implementation of an adventure education curriculum. The purpose of the first study (McCaughtry and Wojewuczki, 2003a) was to develop and field test an elementary adventure education physical education curriculum as part of a larger project merging the need for "more systematic and field tested adventure education curriculum with recent calls for incorporating social objectives into school physical education" (2003: A-50). The authors developed a 30 lesson unit organized around the social themes deemed to be inherent in education; empathy, co-operation, trust and communication. Data was collected through participant observation, teacher and student interviews and it was analyzed through constant comparison, negative case analysis and member checks. The authors identified three principles related to effective implementation of the curriculum;

(1) The importance of the introduction for setting the stage for social learning. To be effective the lesson should commence with a single well-defined social theme, students' prior knowledge base should be determined and students should be encourage to make connections between this and the upcoming activities.
(2) Need to establish the connections and continuity between the social theme and the upcoming activities. The particular social theme should be embedded within the activity.
(3) Need for thorough debriefings if learning is to be maximised. There is a need for substantive discussion of the social theme and how this theme was experienced in the activity. Linkages should be made to other aspects of students' lives.

McCaughtry and Wojewuczki (2003a) contend that without reference to these principles students had difficulty in identifying instances where these themes emerged during the activities and they were unable to make connections with everyday life.

This study shows the inherent value of adventure content in addressing typically overlooked social objectives, points out valuable mechanisms to facilitate curriculum development, and offers initial, and long overdue, curriculum for school physical education aimed at moving beyond the status quo. (McCaughtry and Wojewuczki, 2003a: A-50)

In the second study (2003b), which was also part of the larger project mentioned above, the researchers used cognitive learning theory as a means to identify the factors that enable or inhibit teachers to learn how to implement an adventure curriculum. Data was collected through field observations and interviews. The authors found that three factors inhibited the teachers' curricular learning and implementation;

(1) Difficulties differentiating between social themes. Teachers tended to use social themes interchangeably and not teach the particular social theme that was the focus of the lesson.
(2) Troubles moving beyond surface level discussions in the debriefing. Depth and detail in discussing social themes was absent. Discussions tended to be vague and superficial and hence opportunities to delve deeper into critical incidents were missed.
(3) Problems becoming familiar and comfortable with the new curriculum. The teaching of social themes initially proved problematic; certain themes caused anxiety and there was fearfulness about where free-flowing discussions might lead and hesitancy about removing competition from the curriculum.

The authors acknowledged that learning a new curriculum model can be problematic, however they assert that this process can be facilitated in a positive manner when troublesome components are identified and specifically addressed to teacher learning and development programs.

Whilst the following two studies (Boyle, 2003; Meyer and Wenger, 1998) were not conducted with students in physical education lessons they have been included as they are examples of how adventure programs have been used in sports teams to assist in the development of teamwork and psychological skills development. Given that physical education professionals are often involved in school sports teams the findings may encourage teachers to advocate for the inclusion of such programs in extra-curricular activities. In one of the few studies of secondary school age athletes (members of a tennis team) in an adventure education program, Meyer and Wenger (1998) sought to determine the effects, both short and long term, that ropes course participation might have on both the individual and the team. Their data indicated that both individual and group benefits were achieved from participation in the ropes course. Reported individual benefits included increases in confidence and concentration, both of which are claimed to be a result of the detailed goal setting and/or contracting stressed by facilitators prior to and during the session. In addition to these individual benefits, the authors reported that group related benefits were achieved as well. The data suggested that involvement in the ropes course allowed the participants an opportunity to get to know and trust one another, thereby increasing their sense of commitment and dedication to the team. Overall, the results of this study were claimed to be consistent with those of other efficacy studies conducted on other populations (Cason and Gillis, 1994) which reported psychosocial benefits from participation in adventure education programs. As one would expect, the authors noted that the ropes course program appeared to have differential impact on the participants and some participants were more effective in their ability to transfer the concepts they had learned.

In another study involving an elite sports team (State netball representatives, age 17–19), Boyle (2003) sought to investigate the major outcomes of participation in an adventure-based program. Using both quantitative and qualitative methods he presented data to support the efficacy of adventure-based training as a valid and viable approach to improve team cohesion and psychological skills development for elite sportspeople. He stated that an unexpected and more significant outcome was the positive impact the adventure experience had on the athletes' performances in competition. Importantly he noted that the "Athlete's accounts of the implementation of skills learnt during the adventure training intervention, gave clear and unequivocal support for the notion of transfer from the adventure setting to netball" (Boyle, 2003: 61). He argued that adventure-based training can make a difference to sporting teams and their performance.

Tertiary level

In a study involving students enrolled in pre-service physical education teacher degree program, Hastie (1994) sought to examine the outcomes of an adventure experience which aimed to increase these students' awareness of the concepts of enjoyment, success, and challenge which he claimed were significant in the planning of physical education activities for school students. Drawing upon the literature Hastie proposed that the "adventure experience has been shown to provide a setting where reflective experiences are promoted", hence his rationale behind using a weekend engaged in a series of outdoor activities was based on their "widespread use as a means to help people reflect upon their personal and professional values" (Hastie, 1994: 29).

At the weekend camp the students were given the opportunity to participate in a high ropes course, climbing wall, group problem solving activities and low ropes elements. The fundamental ethic of the weekend was for the students to "have a go" and they were not formally assessed according to performance criteria. However their reflections were submitted in an assignment which was evaluated. As result of the experience Hastie made the following comments and observations in regard to the students' perceptions of the role of the teacher in the learning process. The pre-service teachers in the study agreed that as teachers they would need to construct learning experiences so that their students have the opportunity to achieve success. They became aware of the need to plan programs that were challenging and enjoyable, whilst developing a positive supportive learning environment in which students would feel comfortable attempting activities they perceived to contain an element of risk. Hastie went on to state that it would appear that the participants in the program were able to identify certain features of physical education teaching they thought were important. "It was evident they had become more thoughtful about what programs in physical education could look like, and they seemed to have a heightened awareness of the need for going "beyond fun" and to provide students with opportunities to experience success" (Hastie, 1994: 32). Of particular significance was the students' recognition that "busy", "happy" and "good" are not a valid measure of teaching. "The students at least recognized that the learner is central in the physical education experience" (1994: 33).

Anderson and Frison (1992) conducted a study with 16 second year university students who were participating in an adventure based program (mixture of academic and practical sessions coupled with an overnight expedition) with the aim of developing students' awareness of how adventure based activities might be incorporated into a physical education or recreation program. The authors sought to identify, through interviews and journals, some of the skills that had developed through these activities and some of the positive effects of participation in such a program. The researchers used participant observation methods and recordings of briefing and de-briefing sessions. Students were also required to write a short reflective summary of their experience. The study indicates that the students:

(1) gained new insights into the role of open communication in proper group functioning;
(2) increased trust in other group members;
(3) felt more comfortable as part of a group;
(4) felt more comfortable voicing concerns and opinions without fear of ridicule, lessening of fear of self-disclosure; and
(5) reported increased self-confidence and a willingness to engage in risk taking behavior.

Carlson and McKenna (2000) expressed concern that pre-service physical education teachers' experiences of physical education in school may serve to construct an understanding of physical education that may not recognize the diverse needs and desires of their future students. This potential lack of congruency between student teachers' perceptions of physical education and the reality for many students presents teacher educators with a considerable challenge; "how to assist student teachers to reconstruct some of their knowledge and beliefs about teaching and learning in physical education to create a supportive environment" (Carlson and McKenna, 2000: 17).

In an effort to raise student teachers' awareness and understanding of the elements that might constitute a supportive physical education environment, Carlson and McKenna conducted an adventure-based experiential learning program. The program was based on the premise that teacher preparation programs should be grounded "in the same practices, principles, and purposes as the education teachers will eventually provide for their students" (2000: 18). The adventure education program involved 40 third-year pre-service teachers who were involved in two sessions at the university, a weekend program at an outdoor centre and an evaluation at the conclusion of the program. The data was collected from student reflective writings and was analysed using constant comparison (Glasser and Strauss, 1967; Lincoln and Guba, 1985 cited in Carlson and McKenna, 2000).

The adventure education program aimed to promote change in student teachers' ideas about the level of support needed for students in the physical education context with the aim of encouraging them to define a supportive environment within this context. To do this the student teachers were placed in an environment where they were required to deconstruct and then reconstruct both the personal and professional paradigms from which they were operating. The activities were chosen to provide students with a powerful "destabilizing" experience with the aim of exposing them to alternative ideas and ways of thinking. It was hoped that this experience would lead to an action–reflection praxis phase.

> In challenging participants, both physically and emotionally, within a carefully maintain supportive environment, they were exposed to the feelings of vulnerable students and the potential impact of certain teachers' behaviours. This exposure served to thaw preconceived notions of teaching and learning. The program offered the participants some strategies to make the "shift" to a new way of approaching certain issues and problems. (Carlson and McKenna, 2000: 24)

A major outcome of the program was the students' exposure to personal feelings of self-doubt. The authors claim that such experiences, accompanied by appropriate facilitation assisted the student teachers to recognize and empathise with feelings of apprehension and unease that their students might experience during physical education classes. Carlson and McKenna claim that "The development of such empathy within future physical educators is paramount to the delivery of effective education" (2000: 24). The authors state that the program had a positive effect on at least some of the participants' learning and therefore offers the potential for the transfer of learning. This research is in general agreement with the work of Hastie (1994) who found that student teachers who participated in an adventure program altered their perceptions about the concepts of enjoyment, success, and challenge.

These studies suggest that the adventure education experience may be a creditable way to assist student physical education teachers to change their perceptions on teaching and learning in physical education.

Issues, major trends and future directions in adventure education

Within adventure/outdoor education literature there is an increasingly critical focus on some of the underlying assumptions that have hitherto been taken for granted in the field. The greater emphasis being placed on the "process" of adventure education pedagogy has resulted in a number of studies which have problematised some of the assumptions upon which adventure education theory has been constructed. One of the main areas that has come under scrutiny is related to the role of the instructor/leader/teacher in assisting the learner in their reflection on an experience (see Bell, 1993; Brown, 2002a, 2003; Hovelynck, 1999). Using transcripts from verbal facilitation sessions, Brown (2002a; 2003) has called attention to how knowledge is articulated and whose knowledge is privileged in these settings, issues which are at the very core of adventure education theory which is premised on the centrality of the learner's experience as the basis for valid knowledge. The challenge that faces us pedagogically is how to provide experiences and reflection on these experiences in ways that allow students to remain the "agents" of their experience and their learning (Hovelynck, 1999). We can no longer simply claim that adventure education permits teachers to "move beyond teacher–student rhetoric to enhance deep learning within students" (Spegel, 1996: 30).

Brookes (2003a,b) has called into question many of the traditional claims relating to adventure education being a site for character-building. Drawing on dispositional social psychology he argues that outdoor adventure programs do not build character, rather they provide situations that elicit certain behaviours. "Character building" he argues, must be seen as a source of bias in the literature rather than a foundation on which we justify our programs (Brookes, 2003b). In a similar vein Leberman and Martin (2003) have questioned the premise on which much adventure education theory is based (see Luckner and Nadler, 1992, 1997; Priest and Gass, 1997); that it is necessary to take people out of their comfort zone to ensure that learning takes place. The findings of their research indicate that the activities in which students felt out of their comfort zones may not necessarily be the activities that are most effective in promoting learning.

Participants in the programs under investigation reported that it was the physical components of the course that pushed them out of their comfort zones yet it was the social, creative and reflective activities that produced the most learning. The authors caution facilitators to recognize that participants' perceptions of risk differ, and with it their zone of comfort, and therefore facilitators should remain responsive to participants needs. Learning may be derived from activities that do not necessarily create the highest perception of risk for participants. As Zink states,

> The ongoing focus on outcomes such as self-esteem and 'character building' that permeate much of outdoor education rhetoric tend to foreground the roles of challenging activities as the means of achieving this.... I suggest there is a need for a great deal more research on students' and teachers' subjective experiences of outdoor education. The current lack of research in this area... limits the ways in which we not only make decisions about what to include in an outdoor education programme, but also makes it difficult to question some of the assumptions that underpin the decisions we do make. (2003: 61)

Whilst one might initially regard such work as "heretical", the basis for these critiques are well researched and indicate an increased level of sophistication and complexity in adventure education research; a sign of a maturation in the field. The increased academic rigour being applied to our discipline area from scholars of diverse backgrounds is a positive step forward for adventure education theory and practice; a process which is well anchored in the reflective practice which we encourage in our learners.

In regard to school-based adventure programs within physical education, Beedie (2000) reports that the educational potential of "internally" lead activities, (facilitated by the students' usual teacher, rather than being contracted out to an external agency or outdoor education center) is likely to be greater due to issues of continuity, the likelihood of transfer to other school-based activities and endeavours and is more empowering for physical education teachers who can build relationships with students in non-traditional teaching and learning situations. Beedie argues that urban outdoor education which is essentially school based, is achievable by any physical education teacher. He argues that a school-based program,

> offers an opportunity for all pupils to have an ou door experiential experience: it becomes a common right and is therefore more egalitarian. ... [A] structured and teacher lead programme can be

> progressive and continuous thereby offering greater potential for learning assessment and evaluation. (2000: 20)

Beedie goes on to state that the economic issues which often hinder students attending residential camps "can be addressed by recognising that programmes can be delivered that require very little technical equipment and do not need wilderness locations to implement" (2000: 20). He argues that instead of "buying in" expertise, schools may be better served by focusing on developing the competencies of their staff so that teachers feel empowered and fulfilled in their relationships with their students. This approach might help to address some of the concerns raised by Burrus-Bammel and Bammel (1990) who reported that teachers indicated that the greatest barriers to OE instruction are lack of instructional resources and misgivings about their level of competence; issues that are surmountable with a move away from "high-adventure" and technical activities which are risk-oriented and expensive to conduct.

Rubens (1999) also provides a caution in regard to adopting too "narrow" an approach to adventure education within existing school structures and timetabling considerations. He argues that teachers need to be aware that the use of "sensational" or performance-based activities requiring skill rather than effort may not cater for all students. Additionally skill-based activities may not allow for the delegation of responsibility to students or incorporate the acquisition of necessary skills and behaviours that such programs ultimately seek to deliver.

Boyes (2000) draws attention to the fact that there is a growing recognition from scholars of outdoor education that our discipline operates within a wider socio-ecological context and the primacy of "adventure" or risk-taking endeavours through the commodification of adventurous activities restricts the possibilities for the field to embrace more balanced sociological and ecological perspectives (see Martin, 1999; Wattchow and O'Connor, 2003). This is a point that Brookes makes when he speaks of his optimism for the future of outdoor education research, especially in areas that look at the "relationships between participants and the experiences they have, that place those experiences thoughtfully in the landscape, and that consider them in the context of the metaphorical landscape of individual lives" (2003a: 23).

The Adventure Experience Paradigm may be useful for explaining and understanding aspects of outdoor education. But as Zink states:

> it also privileges certain ways of thinking about outdoor education. The focus of this model is the experience of the individual student and activities that

are perceived to involve risk and skills based competence, that is, individualised pursuits. This in itself may not be problematic, but when it becomes the dominant way of understanding outdoor education then skills based pursuits are positioned in a privileged position over activities with a different emphasis.... Concepts of outdoor education orientated around this model privileges a focus on the individual student and also outcomes associated with self-esteem and self-confidence related to individual action. (2003: 59)

Conclusion

Whilst ABL might be promoted as an "innovative curricular strategy" (Salter 1999b, cited in Cosgriff, 2000) or an approach that promotes "holistic learning" to assist in the acquisition of life skills (Hodge et al., 1999a cited in Cosgriff, 2000) there is little empirical research *within* physical education literature to support such claims. The empirical evidence from within the adventure and outdoor education discipline area (Cason and Gillis, 1994; Hattie et al., 1997) suggests that adventure programs can have a small to moderate impact on socio-psychological constructs to a similar magnitude as other educational interventions. Of particular note is that there appears to be no evidence that adventure programs increase physical fitness, a claim made repeatedly by many proponents of the inclusion of adventure activities into the physical education curriculum. As Neill notes, "Contrary to common belief, the research evidence does not show that outdoor education is inherently good. Overall, there is evidence for a great deal of variability in outcomes between different studies, different programs, and different individuals" (1997: 198).

What researchers in physical education have accomplished is a sound body of qualitative research based on students' perceptions of participation in adventure programs (Carlson and McKenna, 2000; Dyson, 1995, 1996; Hastie, 1994; Humberstone, 1990, 1993). These attempts to investigate participant "voice" are to be encouraged as they provide insights into programmatic issues that are seldom available in outcome based studies (although programmatic issues were addressed in Hattie et al., 1997).

At present the main research thrust, certainly of a critical nature is coming from those scholars involved in adventure education from the "broader" outdoor education perspective (see Bell, 1993; Brookes, 2003a,b; Brown, 2002a, 2003; Hovelynck, 1999; Humberstone, 1990, 1993; Leberman and Martin, 2003; Martin, 1999). This is not entirely unexpected given outdoor education's long association with "adventure" and the experiential approach

to teaching and learning. The challenge is to forge productive links between these similar, but often disparate discipline areas to create a dialogue which will produce research that will improve our practice and ultimately be of benefit to our students.

The greater emphasis being placed on the "process" of adventure education pedagogy has resulted in a number of studies which have problematised some of the assumptions upon which adventure education theory has been constructed. The increased academic rigour being applied to our discipline area from scholars of diverse backgrounds is a positive step forward for adventure education theory and practice; a process which should be well anchored in the reflective practice which we encourage in our learners. Physical education and outdoor education researchers have a formidable, but not insurmountable challenge ahead of them as they seek to ground "what we know happens" within a strong research base that supports our claims. As Humberstone reports, "[o]utdoor education needs greater recognition both as an area of research and as a valuable part of the physical education program. It is productive to critically compare physical education and outdoor education to provide opportunities for physical and outdoor educators to develop greater understanding of transformative pedagogy" (1995: 154).

If we were to pose the question, "What do adventure education programs achieve in the physical education?", the answer is that we don't yet have the full picture. We can reasonably claim that adventure activities have the potential to affect various socio-psychological constructs in programs ranging from several days to three weeks, but what of "lesson duration" adventure programs conducted in schools as part of the physical education curriculum? We know from the work of Dyson (1995, 1996) that both teachers and students report favorably on their experiences and that inclusion of a PA-based initiative can play a part in school reform (Dyson and O'Sullivan, 1998). It is possible that "student-centred" adventure pedagogy in physical education may enable positive changes in gender relationships (Humberstone, 1990) and, through a focus on effort rather than performance we can help improve students enjoyment of physical education (Dyson, 1995; Rubens, 1999). We also can appreciate the role adventure may play in improving pre-service physical education teachers' understandings of the diversity of students experiences of school-based physical education (Carlson and McKenna, 2000; Hastie, 1994). However unless research and evaluation is included as a fundamental component of adventure education in physical education we will continue to be working on faith rather than evidence in large areas of our practice. It is time to move beyond anecdote and hearsay and seriously consider and empirically examine the effects on physical education students from participating in adventure education programs. It is imperative that practitioners and researchers alike make a concerted effort to document both the outcomes and processes involved in adventure education in physical education to improve the scholarly base of our field and therefore improve the educational experiences of our students.

Acknowledgments

This chapter is dedicated to Teresa Carlson, an enthusiastic teacher and researcher who used adventure in physical education teacher preparation classes. Thanks to Brian Wattchow who read an earlier draft of this chapter.

References

Allison, P. and Pomeroy, E. (2000). How shall we "know?" Epistemological concerns in research in experiential education. *Journal of Experiential Education*, 23(2): 91–98.

Anderson, S. and Frison, D. (1992). The hidden value of adventure based programs: A reflection. *CAHPER Journal*, 58(2): 12–17.

Beedie, P. (2000). Teaching outdoor & adventurous activities: Issues surrounding modes of delivery. *British Journal of Teaching Physical Education*, 31(4): 18–20.

Bell, M. (1993). What constitutes experience? Rethinking theoretical assumptions. *Journal of Experiential Education*, 16(1): 19–24.

Bocarro, J. and Richards, R. (1998). Experiential research at-risk: The challenge of shifting traditional research paradigms. *Journal of Experiential Education*, 21(2): 102–107.

Boyes, M. (2000). The place of outdoor education in the health and physical education curriculum. *Journal of Physical Education New Zealand*, 33(2): 75–88.

Boyle, I. (2003). The impact of adventure-based training on team cohesion and psychological skills development in elite sporting teams. In *13th National Outdoor Education Conference Proceedings* (pp. 42–64). Adelaide, Australia: Outdoor Educators Association of South Australia.

Brookes, A. (2003a). Character building. Why it doesn't happen, why it can't be made to happen, and why the myth of character building is hurting the field of outdoor education. In *13th National Outdoor Education Conference Proceedings* (pp. 19–24). Adelaide, South Australia: Outdoor Educators Association of South Australia.

Brookes, A. (2003b). A critique of Neo-Hahnian outdoor education theory. Part one: Challenges to the concept of "character building". *Journal of Adventure Education and Outdoor Learning*, 3(1): 49–62.

Brown, M. (2002a). The facilitator as gatekeeper: A critical analysis of social order in facilitation sessions. *Journal of Adventure Education and Outdoor Learning*, 2(2): 101–112.

Brown, M. (2002b). *Interaction and social order in adventure education facilitation sessions*. Unpublished doctoral dissertation, University of Queensland, Brisbane.

Brown, M. (2003). Paraphrases and summaries: A means of clarification or a vehicle for articulating a preferred version of student accounts? *Australian Journal of Outdoor Education*, 7(2): 25–35.

Bunting, C. (1989). The compatibility of physical education and outdoor education. *Journal of Physical Education, Recreation and Dance*, 60(2): 35–39.

Burrus-Bammel, L. and Bammel, G. (1990). Outdoor/environmental education- An overview for the wise use of leisure. *Journal of Physical Education, Recreation and Dance*, 61(4): 17–22.

Carlson, T.B. and McKenna, P. (2000). A reflective adventure for student teachers. *Journal of Experiential Education*, 23(1): 17–25.

Carver, R. (1996). Theory for practice: A framework for thinking about experiential education. *Journal of Experiential Education*, 19(1): 8–13.

Cason, D. and Gillis, L. (1994). A meta-analysis of outdoor adventure programming with adolescents. *Journal of Experiential Education*, 17(1): 40–47.

Chen, A. and Ennis, C. (1996). Teaching value-laden curricula in physical education. *Journal of Teaching in Physical Education*, 15: 338–354.

Cosgriff, M. (2000). Walking our talk: Adventure based learning and physical education. *Journal of Physical Education New Zealand*, 33(2): 89–98.

Cosgriff, M. and Schusser, E. (1999). Adventure based learning and the new curriculum. *New Zealand Physical Educator*, 1(1): 14–16.

Dewey, J. (1938). *Experience and education*. New York: Collier.

Dyson, B. (1995). Students' voices in two alternative elementary physical education programs. *Journal of Teaching in Physical Education*, 14(4): 394–407.

Dyson, B. (1996). Two physical education teachers' experience of Project Adventure. *Journal of Experiential Education*, 19(2): 90–97.

Dyson, B. and Brown, M. (2005). Adventure Education in your physical education program. In J. Lund and D. Tannehill (Eds.), Standards based physical education curriculum development (pp. 154–175). Sudbury, MA: Jones and Bartlett.

Dyson, B. and O'Sullivan, M. (1998). Innovation in two alternative elementary school programs: Why it works. *Research Quarterly for Exercise and Sport*, 69(3): 242–253.

Ewert, A.W. (1983). *Outdoor adventure and self-concept: A research analysis*. Eugene, OR: Center of Leisure Studies, University of Oregon.

Ewert, A.W. (1987). Research in experiential education: An overview. *Journal of Experiential Education*, 10(2): 4–7.

Ewert, A.W. (1989). *Outdoor adventure Pursuits: Foundations, models, and theories*. Scottsdale, AZ: Publishing Horizons Inc.

Gass, M.A. (1993). The evaluation and research of adventure therapy programs. In M.A. Gass (Ed.), *Adventure therapy: Therapeutic applications of adventure programming* (pp. 301–310). Dubuque, IA: Kendall/Hunt.

Glaser, B. and Strauss, A. (1967). *The discovery of grounded theory*. Chicago, IL: Aldine.

Hammerman, W.M. (1980). *Fifty years of resident outdoor education (1930–1980): Its impact on American education*. Martinsville, IN: American Camping Association.

Hammersley, C. (1992). If we win, I win. Adventure education in physical education and recreation. *Journal of Physical Education, Recreation and Dance, 63*(9): 63–67.

Hastie, P. (1994). Redefining "enjoyment": Prospective physical education teachers appraisal of "enjoyment" following an outdoor adventure camp. *Journal of Experiential Education, 17*(3): 29–33.

Hattie, J., Marsh, H.W., Neill, J.T. and Richards, G.E. (1997). Adventure education and outward bound: Out-of-class experiences that have a lasting effect. *Review of Educational Research, 67*: 43–87.

Hirsch, J. (1999). Developmental adventure programs. In J.C. Miles and S. Priest (Eds.), *Adventure programming* (pp. 13–27). State College, PA: Venture.

Hovelynck, J. (1999). Facilitating the development of generative metaphors: Re-emphasizing participants' guiding images. *Australian Journal of Outdoor Education, 4*(1): 12–24.

Humberstone, B. (1990). Gender, change and adventure education. *Gender and Education, 2*(2): 199–215.

Humberstone, B. (1993). Equality, physical education and outdoor education ideological struggles and transformative structures. In J. Evans (Ed.), *Equality, education and physical education* (pp. 217–232). London: Falmer Press.

Humberstone, B. (1995). Bringing outdoor education into the physical education agenda: Gender identities and social change. *Quest, 47*: 144–157.

Hunt, J.S., Jr. (1990). *Ethical issues in experiential education*. Boulder, CO: The Association for Experiential Education.

Ibbott, K. (1997). *Adventure/wilderness programs for 'at risk' youth: A school counsellor's perspective*. Unpublished doctoral dissertation, University of New England, Armidale, NSW.

Joplin, L. (1995). On defining experiential education. In K. Warren, M. Sakofs and J. Hunt, Jr. (Eds.), *The theory of experiential education* (3 ed., pp. 15–22). Dubuque, IA: Kendall/Hunt.

Kolb, D.A. (1984). *Experiential learning*. Englewood Cliffs, NJ: Prentice-Hall.

Kolb, D.G. (1991). Meaningful methods: Evaluation without the crunch. *Journal of Experiential Education, 14*(1): 40–44.

Latess, D.R. (1986). Physical education and outdoor adventure: Do they belong together? *Journal of Physical Education, Recreation and Dance, 57*(5): 64–65.

Leberman, S. and Martin, A. (2003). Does pushing comfort zones produce peak learning experiences? *Australian Journal of Outdoor Education, 7*(1): 10–19.

Luckner, J.L. and Nadler, R.S. (1992). *Processing the experience: Strategies to enhance and generalize learning*. Dubuque, IA: Kendall/Hunt.

Luckner, J.L. and Nadler, R.S. (1997). *Processing the experience: Strategies to enhance and generalize learning* (2nd ed.). Dubuque, IA: Kendall Hunt.

Martin, P. (1998). Education ideology and outdoor leadership education: Why ORCA and the AOEC exist. *Australian Journal of Outdoor Education, 3*(1): 1–8.

Martin, P. (1999). Critical outdoor education and nature as a friend. In J.C. Miles and S. Priest (Eds.), *Adventure programming* (pp. 463–471). State College, PA: Venture.

Martin, P. and Priest, S. (1986). Understanding the adventure experience. *Journal of Adventure Education, 3*(1): 18–21.

McCaughtry, N. and Wojewuczki, J. (2003a). Developing and field testing socially critical elementary adventure physical education curriculum. *Research Quarterly for Exercise and Sport, 74*(1 Supplement), A–50.

McCaughtry, N. and Wojewuczki, J. (2003b). Learning to teach socially critical adventure education in elementary physical education. *Research Quarterly for Exercise and Sport, 74*(1 Supplement), A–50.

McKenzie, M. (2000). How are adventure education program outcomes achieved? A review of the literature. *Australian Journal of Outdoor Education, 5*(1): 19–27.

McRae, K. (Ed.). (1990). *Outdoor and environmental education*. Melbourne, Australia: MacMillan.

Meyer, B. and Wenger, M. (1998). Athletes and adventure education: An empirical investigation. *International Journal of Sport Psychology, 29*: 243–266.

Miles, J.C. (1995). Wilderness as healing place. In K. Warren, M. Sakofs and J. Hunt, Jr. (Eds.), *The theory of experiential education* (3rd ed., pp. 45–56). Dubuque, IA: Kendall/Hunt.

Miles, J.C. and Priest, S. (Eds.). (1990). *Adventure education*. State College, PA: Venture Publishing.

Neill, J.T. (1997). Outdoor education in schools: What can it achieve? In T. Gray and B. Hayllar (Eds.), *10th National Outdoor Education Conference Proceedings* (pp. 193–201). Collaroy Beach, Australia: The Australian Outdoor Education Council.

Neill, J.T. and Richards, G.E. (1998). Does outdoor education really work? A summary of a recent meta-analyses. *Australian Journal of Outdoor Education, 3*(1): 2–8.

Panicucci, J. (2000). "This is the first time I ever liked Gym!" A look at PE and adventure. *Zip lines: The voice for adventure education, Summer*, 13–18.

Panicucci, J. (2002). Balancing the project and the adventure: The case for sequenced curriculum in physical education adventure programs. *Zip lines: The voice for adventure education, 44*(Spring): 40–44.

Pfeiffer, J.W. and Jones, J.E. (1980). *The 1980 annual handbook for group facilitators*. San Diego, CA: University Associates.

Priest, S. (1999). The semantics of adventure programming. In J.C. Miles and S. Priest (Eds.), *Adventure Programming* (pp. 111–114). State College, PA: Venture.

Priest, S. and Gass, M.A. (1997). *Effective leadership in adventure programming.* Champaign, IL: Human Kinetics.

Project Adventure. (1991). *Adventure programming workshop manual.* Dubuque, IA: Kendall Hunt.

Proudman, B. (1995). Experiential education as emotionally engaged learning. In K. Warren, M. Sakofs and J.S. Hunt, Jr. (Eds.), *The theory of experiential education* (3 ed., pp. 240–247). Dubuque, IA: Kendall/Hunt.

Richards, G. (1997). Outdoor education: How can we assess its value. In *10th National Outdoor Education Conference Proceedings* (pp. 243–254). Collaroy Beach, Australia: The Australian Outdoor Education Council.

Rogers, K. (2000). Rethinking secondary physical education: Meeting objectives through adventure-based learning. *Kentucky AHPERD, 36*(1): 10–13.

Rohnke, K. (1984). *Silver bullets: A guide to initiative problems, adventure games, stunts and trust activities.* Dubuque, IA: Kendall/Hunt.

Rowley, J. (1987). Adventure education and qualitative research. *Journal of Experiential Education, 10*(2): 8–12.

Rubens, D. (1999). Effort or performance: Keys to motivated learners in the outdoors. *Horizons* (4), 26–28.

Sakofs, M. (1995). Piaget-A psychological rationale for experiential education. In K. Warren, M. Sakofs and J. Hunt, Jr. (Eds.), *The theory of experiential education* (3rd ed., pp. 149–151). Dubuque, IA: Kendall Hunt.

Schoel, J., Prouty, D. and Radcliffe, P. (1988). *Islands of healing: A guide to adventure based counseling.* Hamilton, MA: Project Adventure Inc.

Spegel, N. (1996). Lawyers learning to survive: The application of adventure-based learning to skills development. *Journal of Professional Legal Education, 14*(1): 25–50.

Sugarman, D.A., Doherty, K.L., Garvey, D.E. and Gass, M.A. (2000). *Reflective learning: Theory and practice.* Dubuque, IA: Kendall/Hunt.

Walsh, V. and Golins, G. (1976). *The exploration of the Outward Bound process.* Denver, CO: Colorado Outward Bound School.

Warner, A. (1990). Program evaluation: Past present and future. In J.C. Miles and S. Priest (Eds.), *Adventure education* (pp. 309–320). State College, PA: Venture.

Warren, K., Sakofs, M. and Hunt, J.S. (Eds.). (1995). *The theory of experiential education* (3rd ed.). Dubuque, IA: Kendall/Hunt.

Wattchow, B. (2001). A pedagogy of production: Craft, technology and outdoor education. *Australian Journal of Outdoor Education, 5*(2): 19–27.

Wattchow, B. and O'Connor, J. (2003). *Re(forming) the 'physical' in a curriculum/pedagogy for health: A socio-ecological perspective.* Paper presented at the NZARE/AARE Conference, Auckland, New Zealand. Retrieved June 15, 2004, from http://www.aare.edu.au/03pap/wat 03244.pdf.

Zink, R. (2003). Abseiling at 5, rafting at 10, what do we do with them when they are 15? Why pursuits might seem like an obvious choice for outdoor education. *New Zealand Journal of Outdoor Education, 1*(2): 56–62.

5.9 Teaching dance in the curriculum

RALPH BUCK

Introduction

This chapter looks at how dance has been theorized, and how it has been argued for and conceptualized in curricula, and subsequently the issues that arise when we teach dance in the classroom. Cognisance is taken that dance, though once mostly nurtured by physical education curricula and teachers, is now increasingly found in the arts curricula. This chapter accounts for this trend and its literature. A brief international survey notes the rationale for dance and its placement in various curricula.

The Handbook of Research in Physical Education responds to the fact that physical education curricula and physical education teachers are variously maintaining interest in and advocating for dance in education contexts. This chapter also recognizes the increasing expectation around the world that dance be a formal and mandated part of primary school education. This writer respects school and classroom realities wherein teachers with interests in physical education are often called upon to teach dance. The chapter provides some philosophical insights and rationales as to the current and future directions of dance in schools, and also revisits some of the seemingly traditional barriers for the teaching of dance. The chapter concludes with a review of dance research that reveals curriculum and pedagogical issues, and notes some future needs and opportunities in dance research.

Dance as a way of knowing: assumptions and meanings

Implicit in the inclusion of dance in the curriculum are philosophical, educational and political arguments that dance offers children a way of coming to know, a means for thinking, and a form for expression and understanding of self and others, issues and events (Dewey, 1934; Eisner, 1998; Goodman, 1978).

The ontological stance taken within this chapter is that there is no single way of knowing and, furthermore, that knowledge is always mediated (Eisner, 1993, 1998; Lincoln and Guba, 2000; Schwandt, 2000). Eisner's posits that "the roads to knowing are many" (Eisner, 1985: 24) and like Guba and Lincoln, (1994) reasons, that our understandings of the world are our constructions, apprehended in multiple forms, and socially and experientially based. Such a stance is well supported in the dance research literature (Fraleigh and Hanstein, 1999; Eisner, 1998; Schmidt, 2003; Stinson, 1995). In respect to teaching, teachers may share common experiences about their work, but their "truth" is relative to their perspective of these experiences and, as such, it is their personal construction of their reality that is important to understand (Schwandt, 1994). Implicit in the term "individual" is the created interaction between self and social contexts (Dewey, 1934). The assumption that follows from this position is that meanings of dance in the classrooms are constructed in dialogue with others, events and phenomena (Crotty, 1998; Eisner, 1998; Goodman, 1978; Merleau-Ponty, 1962; Schwandt, 1994).

That meanings of dance are contestable and that curricula, teachers and children play a role in its ongoing definition is well supported in dance education research (Adshead, 1981, Bond and Stinson, 2001; Hanstein, 1999; Shapiro, 1998; Stinson, 1991, 1995; Warburton, 2003). A constructivist orientation towards education, dance and research places emphasis on an active construction of knowledge, meaning that the participants in the process have views, ideas, biases, traditions and bodies that are integral to the dialogue. Such dialogue does not occur in isolation but within social, cultural, historical contexts, where shared understandings, practices, languages and dances provide conceptual frameworks through which the world may be described and interpreted (Eisner, 1998; Schwandt, 2000) Outlining meanings of dance in Western contexts, albeit briefly introduces some of the shared understandings and debates.

What is dance?

Janet Adshead in her influential text *The Study of Dance* (1981) stated, "Since the arguments put forward in this book relate initially to any and all forms of dance no attempt is made to define. It is sufficient to say that whatever is labelled 'dance', and accepted as such by those who do it and watch it, is regarded as 'dance'" (Adshead, 1981: 4). Similarly, the function here is not to define dance, but to give an account of the diversity of thought that shapes the theorising of dance.

Historians, anthropologists, philosophers, dancers, educators, psychologists, and children have asked "what is dance?" and the question remains a source of much writing and debate. Copeland and Cohen acknowledged the key dilemma in defining dance when they asked, "Can we formulate a definition comprehensive enough to cover the wide variety of activities routinely referred to as dance?" (1983: 1). The establishment of "mutual understanding" (Sparshott, 1999: 67) was proposed by way of resolution, where shared, common yet flexible understandings of dance making procedures, customs, histories and institutions might be agreed upon. However, Sparshott was aware of the improbability of establishing a global notion of what constitutes dance. He referred to Wittgenstein's (1953) metaphor of "family resemblance", where there is no one defining resembling feature as a more likely solution.

Dance historian Lincoln Kirstein (1935) wrote of the etymology of dance from Sanskrit (3000 BC) through to current usage, and noted its shifting meaning. Anthropological viewpoints acknowledge "pre-language" dance of aboriginal (world-wide) cultures, where dance is associated with "highly complex social structures, religious practices and art forms" (Kraus et al., 1991: 13; Warburton, 2003). Judith Lynne Hanna, American dance anthropology and education scholar, spoke of the communicative role of dance, and argued that individuals create particular, purposeful and culturally patterned movement that aims to tell and share (Hanna, 1979). Reliance upon "para-language" (Hanna, 1979: 26) symbols of movement requires shared meanings of dance semantics, that is, the use of dance as a signifier relies on another being able to read what it denotes.

Philosophers have debated dance as a language and symbol system (Goodman, 1968; Langer, 1953; Wittgenstein, 1953) and have pointed to the vital criteria of the existence of the establishment of shared meanings in order for a symbol system to operate. Philosophers in aesthetics, and more pertinently aesthetic education, have debated the role of sensuous perception in education (Eisner, 1998a). While aesthetic education is not limited to the arts curriculum and disciplines (Best, 1985; Smith, 1999), giving "form to sensuous and imaginative impressions and feelings – to perceptual experience" (Abbs, 1987: 26) is a unifying process amongst the arts. The arts attend to the histories and qualities of humanity, including qualities of knowing, that can neither be proved nor disproved (Abbs, 1987), but which are nevertheless powerful in evoking response and shared insights.

Concepts of formalism and expressionism (Hirst, 1995) have stirred the aesthetic and artistic debates, inclusive of dance, since the late eighteenth century (Copeland and Cohen, 1983). The expressive nature of dance was the motivating force behind many modern dance artists' work and theories. As Selma Jean Cohen described in relation to Martha Graham, the pioneering American choreographer (1894–1991), "For Graham, dance should be a revelation of experience, regardless of how unpleasant the result may be" (1983: 19). Expressionistic dance recognized the relationship between the dancer's (individual) movement and the dancer's personal experience and whole self. The influential New York critic, John Martin, argued, "it is impossible for everyone to be taught to do the same type of movement. The ideal dance education, therefore, is that which trains the student to find his own type of movement" (1933: 15). Rudolf Laban (1879–1958), perhaps the most influential dance theorist within the dance in education context (Foster, 1977), was also an expressionist. Like Martin, he too valued the individual's dance, and provided an analytical system that outlined the dance's "living architecture" (Laban cited in Foster, 1977: 65). He also took a psychological perspective, recognizing that the whole person danced, not just their body. John Martin emphasized the communicative role of dance, "it [dance] is not interested in spectacle, but in the communication of emotional experiences – intuitive perceptions, elusive truths – which cannot be communicated in reasoned terms or reduced to mere statement of fact" (Martin, 1946: 105).

Aesthetic theorists such as Kant (1966) brought the perspective of the viewer to dance, arguing that what is presented need not have any emotive beginnings and even so, may not communicate them in accordance with the spectator's interpretation (Alter, 1996). The American philosopher Suzanne Langer (1953) distinguished the expressive potential of dance gestures or symbols from what the dancer actually felt. Langer separated the dancing body from the image created by the body and clarified that symbols created the illusion of feeling, not the dancer's actual feeling. According to Langer, the choreographer transforms physical realities into an impression of "interacting forces … [that] move the dance itself" (Langer, 1953). Here "seeing" or "reading" the form as art relies on Kant's theories of aesthetic attitude, wherein the viewer reconstructs the danced symbols as artistic images. It is the viewer or the individual reader that ascribes expressive meaning to the danced symbols. However, it is pertinent to remember Wittgenstein's (1953) reasoning that communication arises from the community's consistent and functional use of symbols that provide for shared meanings. More recently David Best's (1982, 1999) philosophical propositions suggested that the meaning of dance is revealed by the actual action in a particular context, not in some notion of "separate intent". As Best stated, "It is rather that the thinking and rationality are implicit in, inseparable from, and spring from, the activity" (Best, 1999: 116).

Returning the focus of dance theory to the dance form itself, Andre Levinson (1887–1933), the exiled Russian critic turned journalist in Paris, saw the dance for its academic purity (Koegler, 1982), inherent quality – beauty, rather than its representational, intentional or expressive concerns (Carroll and Banes, 1999).

Formalists in dance honour the dance's techniques, structures and patterning that give order and allow for the expression to occur, or as Susanne Langer (1953) argued, the craft of the choreographer is to create illusions of feeling through the structuring of the form. Placing dance's value in its aesthetic, non-utilitarian nature, while appealing at a personal level, does not account for the diversity of dance that has specific ritual and social functions (Adshead, 1981; Hanna, 1999).

Dance exists in a myriad of forms, contexts, cultures and histories. It is undisputed that humans dance and that throughout history peoples all over the world have valued it (Adshead, 1981; Alter, 1996; Brinson, 1991; Copeland and Cohen, 1983; Dewey, 1934; Eisner, 1998; Fraleigh, 1987; Hanna, 1999; Jonas, 1992; Kraus et al., 1991; Williams, 1989). Yet, when we move dance into an education arena characterised by structures such as schools, curriculum and teachers, the question arises, "Is dance a distinct body of knowledge?" (Hanna, 1999: 9). Leaving historical (moral) charges against the propriety of dance to one side (Kraus et al., 1991), can dance claim time and resources comparable to other areas of the curriculum, other areas of knowledge? More importantly, does dance claim uniqueness and value in its contribution to a child's education? Like all domains of knowledge, dance, in claiming membership to the "key learning areas", must articulate its theoretical foundations and also the uniqueness of its offerings. As Williams stated, "Dance in education must be seen as possessing a theoretical basis from which any manifestation of dance could be approached" (1989: 182).

Dance and arts education theories and models

Of particular interest to this chapter is the inclusion of dance within education curricula and the meanings of dance that teachers bring to that context. If one accepts that the curriculum has a degree of influence over what and how dance is taught (Doyle, 1992; Willis and Schubert, 1991), it is useful to review how dance has been theorized as knowledge and argued for in the curriculum. This in turn provides insights and background into issues informing dance education in primary, secondary, and tertiary contexts.

The following section provides a brief account of dominant theories/models that have shaped dance in primary and secondary school classrooms. It then scans dance curricula around the world for an insight into how dance has been argued for and conceptualized on behalf of teachers. Arguably the theories and models that are most influential, as determined by their use, longevity and impact, are Rudolf Laban's Modern Educational Dance model, Janet Adshead's Study of Dance model, Jacqueline Smith Autard's Midway model, Getty Foundation's Discipline Based Arts Education model, Howard Gardner's Theory of Multiple Intelligences, and Somatic Education (Alter, 1996; Brinson, 1991; Hanna, 1999; Haynes, 1987; Kraus et al., 1991; Warburton, 2003; Simon, 2003).

Modern educational dance

Rudolf Laban (1879–1958) is without doubt one of the most influential dance in education theorist (Alter, 1996; Hanstein, 1999; Haynes, 1987). Laban's theories were derived from his direct experience in dancing, teaching dance and observing dance throughout Europe and finally in England where his theories were translated into the educational context and generically referred to as Modern Educational Dance (Laban, 1948). His analysis of movement led to the development of a descriptive vocabulary and a notation system (Laban notation) that allowed for the observation and recording of all dance. Importantly, Laban acknowledged the implicit connections between movement, feeling and thinking, rejecting the ongoing dualistic view of mind/body. This holistic view, that took account of the internal – psychological impulse to move, and the physiological manifestation of movement, informed his categorizing of movement and also laid the foundation for ongoing theoretical development in dance therapy. Laban identified and, more importantly, articulated movement within the components of weight, time, space, and flow, which led to an extensive classification of movement and the development of "effort/shape graphs … [and] sixteen basic movement themes" (Laban, 1948: 25–84) and a comprehensive notation system.

Laban's work influenced the provision of dance within curriculum in England in the 1940s where educationists such as Lisa Ullmann, Valerie Preston-Dunlop, Joan Russell, and Marion North refined Laban's principles and advocated for and implemented dance as a discrete learning area in the curriculum, albeit within the physical education curriculum. Nevertheless, Laban's modern educational dance theory was later criticized for its inability to relate dance to the cognitive and intellectual realms of examinable knowledge when dance became a subject in secondary schools in England in the 1970s, and then within tertiary education (initially within Bachelor of Education) (Haynes, 1987). Laban's work, rooted in practice and experience, did not comply with the emerging conception of knowledge between 1965 and 1980 in England (Adshead, 1981). As Haynes noted, "By the early seventies, a number of influential writers had begun to argue that dance education should shift its attention from the psychological/therapeutic orientation towards the more formal and aesthetic conception as an art form" (1987: 154).

Laban's modern educational dance travelled the world through physical education curricula and teacher training programmes (Brinson, 1991) including New Zealand (Brinson, 1981; Burrows, 1999; Hong, 2001; Smithells, 1974). Both Burrows (1999) and Stothart (1974) described the dominating influences of the English physical education curriculum and teacher training upon New Zealand schools up until the 1950s–60s. In America, Hanna acknowledged Laban as one of the "European thinker-practitioners that had a great influence on the acceptance of dance as education in the United States" (1999: 54). Such influence was similarly noted in England (Brinson, 1991), and Australia (Meiners, 2001). These accounts noted the emergence of Laban's theories that coincided with the progressive philosophies that advocated for shifts away from "drill" to "creativity" in physical education (Haynes, 1987).

The study of dance: choreography, performance and appreciation

Janet Adshead (Lansdale), a teacher and social scientist in England, informed by the work of Laban and his critics, went on to develop a coherent account for the study of dance. In doing so Adshead (1981), provided the theoretical rigour required to sustain dance in educational curriculum at all levels of education. Adshead argued for dance as a discipline (Pring, 1976) comparable to any other within the curriculum, effectively entering dance into the knowledge debate.

Adshead took up Best's (1978) and Reid's (1974) philosophies regarding the correlation and distinction between arts and aesthetic education and strongly advocated that the study of dance concerns dance in ritual, social and artistic functional contexts, all of which have aesthetic concerns. Her arguments also acknowledged the eclectic and diverse nature of dance. In arguing for the value of an aesthetic orientation to the study of dance, Adshead noted that it is within an arts curriculum that dance will be most ably be understood and explored in educational and academic contexts (Haynes, 1987). Adshead's main thesis within the text *The Study of Dance* (1981) is that if dance is to be included in the curriculum then structures and concepts underlying all and any dance must be found and be articulated as appropriate to the study of dance itself.

Adshead developed a conceptual framework around the notions of choreography (making dance), performance (showing dance) and appreciation (reading and analysing dance). These concepts became the centrepiece for her framework that provided the focus for studying all dance within historical, cultural and geographical contexts. In Adshead's (1988) subsequent writings on dance analysis she further articulated choreography, performance and appreciation, drawing attention to the spatial and dynamic qualities (derivatives of Laban's initial analysis). Adshead (1988) developed a model for the analysis of dance that in essence is structured around describing the components of the dance, establishing the form of the dance, interpreting the meaning of the dance, and then evaluating the merit of the dance. This model of analysis is most apparent in secondary school dance syllabus documents such as, New Zealand's National Certificate of Educational Achievement, and each Australian State and Territory's senior syllabus.

The Midway Model

Also in England, Jacqueline Smith (1976) (later known as Smith-Autard) articulated principles and procedures for dance composition based upon the contemporary western theatre dance traditions of the day. Like Adshead, Smith responded to the need for greater academic rigour in the study of dance in educational institutions. Smith also built upon Laban's themes, putting emphasis upon dance as an art form, where students come to know dance as art through actively composing, performing and appreciating dances. Smith's focus upon dance as art drew upon choreographic practices and traditions, pioneered by the likes of Martha Graham, Eric Hawkins, and Merce Cunningham, utilized within the professional dance arena. These practices informing dance in education were derived from a "professional model" (Smith-Autard, 1994: 4) and dominated by an emphasis on developing specific artistic skills and products, reflecting a kickback against the "free, open and child centred approach which has been labelled modern educational dance, creative dance, and the like ... derived from Laban's ideas" (Smith-Autard, 1994: 4). In 1994, Smith-Autard revisited her principles of 1976 and

Table 5.9.1   The Midway Model

Educational	Midway	Professional
Process	Process + Product	Product
Creativity	Creativity Knowledge of	Knowledge of
Imagination	Imagination + public artistic	Theatre dance
Individuality	Individuality conventions	repertoire
Feelings	Feelings + Skill	Skill required
Subjectivity	Subjectivity + Objectivity	Objectivity
Principles	Principles + Techniques	Techniques
Open methods	Open + Closed	Closed Methods
Creating	THREE STRANDS Composition Performance Appreciation OF DANCES leading to ARTISTIC EDUCATION AESTHETIC EDUCATION CULTURAL EDUCATION	Performing

developed the Midway Model that "amalgamates some of the elements of the educational (Modern Educational Dance) and professional models" (Smith-Autard, 1994: 5). The distinguishing feature of Smith-Autard's Midway Model is that it explicitly directed dance in education towards artistic education, aesthetic education and cultural education outcomes. The Midway Model (1994: 26) is outlined in Table 5.9.1.

The model is intended to provide a balanced perspective of what is valued in dance. This model has been cited by Carino (2001) as being helpful in creating a dance curriculum in Singapore that systematically includes cultural dance and creative dance. Similar considerations regarding the inclusion and balance of cultural and "educational" dance in curriculum have been noted in Indonesia (Masunah, 2001) and Korea (Nam, 2001) and Hong Kong (Street, 2001).

Discipline-based arts education (DBAE)

Discipline based arts education (DBAE) is a model sponsored by the Getty Foundation in America and based upon visual arts education practice. DBAE was formed upon and characterized by "four art disciplines – aesthetics, criticism, history and production" (Greer, 1987: 227; Hanna, 1999; Ottey, 1996). Each of these "disciplines" has a recognized body of knowledge

content and mode of inquiry (King and Brownell, 1966) that is interconnected and provides considerable scope for the study of dance.

It is argued that the drive behind the adoption of DBAE is the desire for the arts, including dance, to be seen as having "academic content" (Ottey, 1996: 31) that may be assessed and accounted for in a manner comparable to other disciplines in the curriculum. DBAE successfully and strongly places dance within the academic curriculum and confirms its legitimacy. Yet, I fear DBAE may be a "double-edged sword" that, through its quest to legitimise the arts and dance in academic terms, has unintentionally distanced the teacher from implementing the dance curriculum. There is a gap between the experts' vision, rationale, terminology and standards for dance, and the teachers' practice and experience of dance, a gap that may be quite vast in many teachers' minds and bodies.

Ottey (1996) talks of DBAE shifting the pedagogy of dance towards what Paolo Freire critically described as 'banking' (1972: 46), whereby the teacher provides the knowledge to be learnt or banked by the student. Other concerns relate to DBAE overly formalizing the dance experiences, thereby reducing the liberal nature of the educative experience (Fortin, 1991; Hanna, 1999; Trend, 1992); fragmenting arts practice (Dorn, 1993); undervaluing the relevance of teachers and children's artistic values (Dorn, 1993); losing the holistic experiential qualities that may be accessed through dance; and, valuing achievement outcomes over the child's creativity (Hanna, 1999). Broudy noted the major complaints, yet given the criticisms, he supported DBAE in elementary (primary) school curriculum, because when "classroom teachers are given the opportunity to become familiar with it" (1991: 72) it functions as a useful approach towards overcoming aesthetic illiteracy.

The DBAE model has evolved and been adapted to meet the needs of various curriculum policies in different countries and its influence is evident in the American *National Standards for Arts Education* (Consortium of National Arts Education Associations, 1994), the Australian *Statement on the Arts for Australian Schools* (Curriculum Corporation, 1994), and more recently the New Zealand *The Arts: In the New Zealand Curriculum* (2000). Although these documents have differences, their intent, structure, outcomes and terminology are essentially compatible. Accepting the "curriculum territory" gained by the arguments for dance as advocated for within the DBAE framework, it remains now to "close the gap" between the curriculum intent and the teachers' practice in the classroom.

Theory of multiple intelligences

In 1967 at the Harvard Graduate School of Education, esteemed philosopher Nelson Goodman and colleagues across the behavioural and cognitive sciences, education and the arts, established Project Zero, "a first-of-its-kind think tank on the relationship between the arts, cognitive development, and education" (Warburton, 2003: 9). The core view argued for by the Project Zero team was that artistic practice was cognitive, contesting the predominant view of the time that the arts were primarily emotive, mysterious, and intuitive (Gardner, 1989). In the 1970s this debate set the context for the two research teams at Project Zero: David Perkins directed research by the "cognitive skills" group, and Howard Gardner led the developmental group that focused upon symbol using skills (Gardner, 1989). ARTS PROPEL was the name given to the subsequent phase of research in partnership with the Educational Testing Service and the Pittsburgh Public Schools. The practical implementation of theory in educational settings was studied.

Seeking clarification and understanding of human potential, Gardner questioned popular conceptions of intelligence (Gardner, 1983). In collaboration with anthropologists, geneticists, psychologists, neurobiologists and historians, Gardner synthesized children's symbol-using capacities through his research on the cognitive capacities of individuals with brain damage. In short, the dominant outcome was his theory of multiple intelligences (MI) (Gardner, 1983) that articulated "seven candidate intelligences" (p. xi). These intelligences were named as: Linguistic, Logical –

mathematical, Spatial, Musical, Bodily-Kinesthetic, Interpersonal, and Intra-personal. I have noted Gardner's expression "candidate intelligences" by way of reiterating his view that intelligence is not a thing found or discovered, as he said, 'These intelligences are fictions – at most, useful fictions – for discussing processes and abilities that (like all life) are continuous and with one another" (Gardner, 1983: 70). Since then, Gardner has articulated an eighth intelligence – Naturalist Intelligence (Gardner, 1999). Gardner described these intelligences as "forms of knowing" (Gardner, 1989: 74), and posited that all humans have some capacity in each, and that they may be developed.

Undeniably, as worldwide practice reveals, MI theory has struck a cord of "truth" with teachers (Gardner, 1995, 2000) and dance educators (Green Gilbert, 2003; Sevilla, 2003; Warburton, 2003). The argument that there is no single way to "know" (Gardner, 1983), and that there are multiple entry points into pedagogy (Gardner, 1999) resonates with what many teachers see every day. This is most apparent as teachers re-look at children's intelligences utilized within the realm of artistic and kinaesthetic endeavour.

Somatic education

In the 1990s the movement philosophies grouped under the banner of somatic education increasingly informed tertiary dance programmes and professional dance practice (Fortin, 1998; Kovich, 1996). Somatic practices such as Alexander Technique, Feldenkrais, Ideokinesis, Mind–Body Centring, and Yoga, while not new, have been contemporized by their increasing use in tertiary dance education programmes, within dance company training schedules and in the public arena. Somatics encompasses a holistic perspective of movement that Kleinman referred to as "kinaesthetic phenomenology" (2000: 98). Thomas Hanna described somatics as "the art and science of the inner-relational process between awareness, biological function and environment, all three factors understood as a synergistic whole" (1983: 1).

It can be argued that somatic practice does not yet appear to be directly informing dance curriculum content in schools, however, there is increasing reference to self-awareness and holistic perspectives of the body/mind within curriculum rationale in the arts, and physical education at large (Eisner, 1998; Faire, 2002; Green, 2001; Kleinman, 2000). From an educator's perspective, I suggest, as did Green (2001), that somatic practices reference an ideology similar to the liberal, "progressive", personal, and felt dimensions of dance that were first espoused by Laban. Somatics would support a return to focus upon the child rather than the dance, and if educators have learnt from pedagogical swings of the past, this will include acknowledgement of the relationship between the individual and their contexts, provided by curriculum, teacher and community. As conceptions of knowledge broaden and academia responds to epistemological diversity, disciplines such as dance might then return to championing their inherent practices and rationales.

Somatics may shift dance pedagogy from an "outside-in" phenomenon, where the body has been regarded as a relatively docile site for enculturation (Green, 2001), to an "inside-out" process where the individual may "self fashion ... our dancing body" (Fortin et al., 2002). Within the primary school classroom such a process is desirable if diverse interests and bodies are to be respected and where the emphasis should be upon learning through the dancing body, not training for a dancing body. Somatic practices acknowledge the relationship between the self and their body in the construction of their body and their dance. As noted by Green, somatics is about affirming "what goes on inside the body rather than a sole focus on what the body looks like or how it 'should' behave" (2001: 157).

Review of many current dance curricula in the western world (*Curriculum and Assessment in Scotland National Guidelines: Expressive Arts – Physical Education*, 1992; *The National Curriculum: Physical Education* – England, 1995; *National Standards for Arts Education* – USA, 1994; *A Statement on the Arts for Australian Schools*, 1994; *Physical Education* – Alberta, 2000; *The Arts in the New Zealand Curriculum*, 2000), reveal derivations of these theorists terminologies and concepts, shaped to meet local educational, cultural and political needs. In summary, the above six theories have had a dynamic influence upon dance curriculum and dance pedagogy practice world-wide. It is difficult to account for the influences of these theories upon teachers' practice, and another researcher would most likely give a differing account. Nevertheless, the troika of creating, presenting and appreciating, albeit in differing guises, constantly surface as three core aspects of dance education (Bolwell, 1998). As the above review of literature reveals, this troika is common to several theoretical models, as is Laban's articulation of space, time, weight and flow, and undeniably informs dance curriculum development throughout the Western world. It is timely to look at dance curriculum, and the rationale that various curricula use in support of including dance in children's education.

Dance curricula

Neither dance nor curriculum operate in a vacuum (Willis and Schubert, 1991), but are a product of the socio-cultural-economic community from which they emanate. Curriculum, being "theoretical

models ... and ... idealised structures" (Eisner, 1991: 44), which are informed by research in the academic discipline, teacher research and teacher practice, are subject to debate (Rubin, 1991). Nonetheless, curricula in general share a common role in facilitating learning and aiming to change [educate] the child (Lortie, 1975; Newman, 1990), or as framed by Eisner, "School curriculum is a mind altering device: it is a vehicle designed to change the ways in which the young think" (1991: 42).

The rationale for teaching dance in any curriculum not only has to appease the visionaries, but also appeal to the classroom teacher in such a way as to encourage the implementation of the curriculum. How dance is argued for in the curriculum provides an important link between theory and practice, and also a clear indication of what is valued and meant by including dance in the classroom. Various rationales for dance are reviewed in the following.

As dance moves into the arts globally, its rationale for inclusion in the curriculum is building around common themes. In England, Brinson's arguments for including dance in education included:

- Developing the full variety of human intelligence.
- Developing creativity.
- Education in feeling and sensibility.
- Exploring values.
- Understanding cultural change and differences.
- Developing physical and perceptual skills. (1991: 84)

These qualities seem lost in the *English National Curriculum* (Department For Education) where dance is included in the physical education curriculum which is directed by the following three "requirements" (1995: 2): "To promote physical activity and healthy lifestyles ... To develop positive attitudes ... To ensure safe practice ... " (1995: 2). These requirements provide the rationale for the areas of activity (games, gymnastic activities and dance) in stages 1 and 2 (5–11-year-olds), and in stages 3 and 4 (11–16-year-olds) where dance is more optional and other activities are introduced. This curriculum statement makes for interesting comparison with The Australian document *A Statement on the Arts for Australian Schools*, which advocated for dance along with all of the arts as "symbol systems which communicate in unique and important ways, as part of a broader framework of aesthetic philosophy or understood in terms of recent social and cultural theory" (1994: 3). Dance was cited as contributing to "Aesthetic learning ... Cognitive learning ... Physical learning ... Sensory learning ... [and] Social learning" (1994: 6–7). Before the teacher gets into the classroom or reads anymore of the Australian curriculum content, they are given considerably more scope than their English colleagues.

Encapsulating the "big picture" perspective on the value of the arts, the American document *National Standards for Arts Education* stated:

The arts are one of humanity's deepest rivers of continuity. They connect each new generation to those who have gone before. ... For all these reasons and a thousand more, the arts have been an inseparable part of the human journey; indeed we depend on the arts to carry us toward the fullness of our humanity. We value them for themselves, and because we do, we believe knowing and practicing them is fundamental to the healthy development of our children's minds and spirits. That is why, in any civilisation – ours included – the arts are inseparable from the very meaning of the term 'education'. (1994: 5)

It goes on to say that students studying dance gain knowledge and skills for:

- Understanding past and present human experience.
- Adapting to others and own ways of thinking, working and expressing.
- Learning artistic modes of problem solving and associated analytical tools.
- Understanding the influences of the arts in creating and challenging culture.
- Making decisions in complex, ambiguous, ephemeral and serendipitous situations.
- Analysing non-verbal communication and making informed judgements.
- Communicating thoughts and feelings in a mode that acknowledges the whole self as a medium for expression. (1994: 6–7)

Given this degree of national advocacy, at State level, dance remains predominantly in physical education programmes. Similarly in Australia and Canada each State or Province develops its own curriculum. Dance has a history of being nurtured (and disregarded) in physical education, yet the dominant trend is the location of dance in the arts curricula.

A rationale for the inclusion of dance with in the arts curriculum in Singapore was associated with Singapore's future vision "as a cosmopolis in the next millennium" as referred to in the *Renaissance City Report* (Ministry of Information and The Arts, 2000, cited in Carino, 2001: 87). In brief, this report described Singapore's economic and cultural future as being linked with its creative and artistic activity. Arts education is seen as fundamental to this aspiration. Wong, Senior Minister of State of Education, Singapore, reinforced this view, when she stated, "Arts education ... plays a critical role in securing our future in helping Singapore develop its creative industries" (Wong, cited in Carino, 2001: 95). The ongoing association of "economy", "industry" and "development" is summed up by the "need to nurture creativity and innovativeness in Singapore's education system as a key strategy to release our vision of a developed economy" (Ministry of Information and the Arts, cited in Carino, 2001: 91). Helen Clark, Prime Minister of New Zealand and

Minister for the Arts (1999–), implied the same claim for the arts when she commented, "Welcome to the new New Zealand where culture counts" (Creative New Zealand, 2002: 16). Similarly in Hong Kong and South Korea, dance education leaders are advocating for the development of dance curriculum as part of the arts, distinct from physical education (Nam, 2001; Street, 2001).

England maintains dance as a component of the physical education curriculum. This remains a contentious situation with a good deal of debate revolving around the place of dance in that curriculum (Brinson, 1991; Jobbins, 1998a; Lyons, 1998; Moore, 1997; Paul, 1998). Irrespective of the placement of dance in physical education, it takes on the content and characteristics of an arts orientated curriculum. This is a confusing situation, albeit one where dance is compulsory in key stages 1 and 2 (Lower and upper primary school) which is, one might argue, a very strong position from which dance might grow, or more importantly, a very sure way to ensure that all students gain a certain amount of dance education in their schooling. As several advocates in the UK implied, it does not matter where or how children gain dance experience, just as long as they get it. This is an argument I have also heard in New Zealand.

The Arts in the New Zealand Curriculum (2000) includes dance, drama, music, and visual arts and was mandated for implementation in all New Zealand primary schools from 2003 (Hong, 2001). The key rationale for the arts curriculum at large focuses upon "literacies in the arts" (Ministry of Education, 2000: 10); expression and communication; individual and community awareness; and, awareness of the functions the arts fulfil in societies and histories. Dance is stated as offering "a significant way of knowing, with a distinctive body of knowledge" (Ministry of Education, 2000: 19), and offers "personal" and "social" benefits through the development of confidence in physical expression. Also, "Dance in the NZ curriculum promotes the dance heritages of the diverse cultures within New Zealand" (Ministry of Education, 2000: 19). Further rationales noted that dance is a holistic experience "that links the mind, body and emotions" (Ministry of Education, 2000: 19) and note was taken of the importance of developing critical audiences and fostering students' enthusiasm as viewers or creative participants. In summary, the New Zealand dance curriculum is focused upon developing:

- Students' literacy for engagement with dance practically or theoretically.
- Personal holistic knowledge of self.
- Knowledge of cultural and social diversity in New Zealand.

Dance also remains a component within the current *Health and Physical Education in the New Zealand Curriculum* (Ministry of Education, 1999) the overall focus is upon "personal well-being, the well-being of other people, and that of society as a whole" (Ministry of Education, 1999: 6). Given the variations within the NZ arts and physical education curricula it is safe to say that dance has never been so well supported within NZ schools.

The ongoing call for "creative thinking" and "innovation" is increasingly linked to government policy regarding "knowledge economies", where knowledge is seen as the source of economic productivity (Creativenet, 2001). Commentary on education provision within this "knowledge economy" context calls for change, "Rather than trying to increase skills levels through conventional qualifications, government should take a different approach to educating for creativity" (Creativenet, 2001: 2). Implicit here is a fostering of curricula that purposefully addresses and develops creative thinking and creative application of thinking. All curricula may do this, but the arts explicitly do this (Sylwester, 1998). Debate regarding the rationale of any education in terms of economic need is contentious and ongoing, but it is nonetheless an interesting intersection of minds and needs when educationalists and business leaders both argue a place for arts education and hence dance education, in the curriculum (Barrett, cited in Stiegelbauer, 1999: 394).

Especially in today's outcomes driven education system, parents, teachers, educationalists and politicians want evidence of the benefits to be gained from studying dance. It is fair to say that in the context of education research, dance remains a very under researched discipline (Hanna, 2001). Nonetheless, research that embraces dance in education exists, and reports such as, "Strengthening Communities Through Culture" (Strom, 2001), and "Champions of Change: The Impact of the Arts on Learning" (Fiske, n.d.), noted dance projects and research along with the other arts. These reports have tended to focus upon assessing the value of the arts for their ability to develop cognitive skills and outcomes in other domains of theory and curriculum, especially language literacy and mathematics. They also highlight the contributions the arts make in developing children's essential learning and life skills such as team work, leadership, problem solving, communication and critical thinking. While these values and skills are most publicly argued for in respect to their ability to support other curriculum areas, many arts educators, myself included, believe that the abilities and skills developed are an inherent part of physical and arts education, with stand-alone value.

Implicit within the various dance curricula are differing arts and movement models that reflect different theories, national political agenda's, that skew and shape rationale, content, terminology, objectives, assessment, resources and pedagogy within dance education. Irrespective of the differences, and the place of dance in physical education or arts curriculum, the theoretical place of dance in the school classroom has been well stated (Adshead, 1981; Alter, 1996; Hanna, 1999; Smith-Autard, 1994; Williams, 1989). The above theories, and curriculum rationales articulate dance within schooling contexts, with its own coherent theoretical structures, practices and history that distinguish it as a particular discipline of study. Given the rationales and the rhetoric, Stake et al's comprehensive arts education research in USA revealed that irrespective of curriculum rationales and state policies, the most common perception of arts education practice was "… largely teaching of custom" (1991: 301). That is, ensuring participation, fun and a break from other classroom activity, and sharing and reinforcing cultural customs (often informally known). Stake et al., found minimal evidence of artistic expression (children's as opposed to the teachers), critical engagement, reasoning and problem solving. While dance curriculum are increasingly philosophically clear with arguments for the inclusion of dance well made, in the classroom, dance often remains to be limited to motor skill practice and learning of "product" (Bannon and Sanderson, 2000; Buck, 2003; Hong, 2000).

As a Physical Education teacher myself, and in later years dance curriculum writer and teacher in-service provider, I can attest to the immense support that many PE teachers provide dance in the school context. While national and regional dance curricula emerge world wide, school dance curricula remain to be influenced by the interests and availability of individual teachers who have an interest in dance. This reality was noted in England by Haynes, "… it was ultimately the job of the individual teachers to carve an acceptable place for the subject within their own schools" (1987: 152). As by example, several secondary schools in my home town implement comprehensive dance (arts) programmes with in their schools' physical education programmes. The reality, that dance is supported and administered by secondary school physical education departments and teachers while being structured by arts curricula is a common scenario, and one that presents dance as a potential bridge between arts and sciences. At tertiary level such interdisciplinary connection provides considerable research scope for dance. As dance increasingly becomes accepted as a tertiary entrance subject comparable to any other curriculum area there is increasing demand for dance specialists at the secondary school level. These teachers are trained in the theories and practices of dance that are articulated within specialised dance degrees and dance curricula.

In the primary school context, dance is mostly taught by the generalist teacher. This author's research (Buck, 2003a) of nine primary school teachers meanings of dance in their classroom, found that each teachers' personal experience of learning dance as a child, dancing done and seen, the dance curriculum and their pedagogical habits and style shaped their view of themselves as teachers of dance. It was evident that the teachers dance and physical education histories informed their interpretations of the current dance curriculum.

The theoretical and pragmatic tensions over the place of dance in the curriculum, and who teaches dance, exemplify the fact that curricula change and that education philosophy and attendant pedagogy is in flux. Who should teach dance? In the primary school, every teacher could teach dance. Noting that the focus at primary school is the holistic development of the child and that the classroom teacher is the most qualified to provide the secure "nested" (Gallego et al., 2001) learning context. However, research reveals that several barriers such as, boys, teachers own dance ability, confidence and knowledge base present sufficient barriers to impede the teaching of dance (Buck, 2003a; Moore, 1997; Williams, 1989) At secondary school, it depends on each school's context, teacher's discipline knowledge and pedagogical content knowledge (Fortin, 1993). As stated, many physical education teachers are keen and able to teach dance, however it is accepted that dance specialists are increasingly the norm, and definitely required for children studying at tertiary entrance level.

What the community considers as "dance" and in particular what esteemed arts practitioners create for stage or TV are incredibly influential and part of curriculum and classroom planning. For example, the impact of Isadora Duncan's free-spirited performances in the early 1900s and Michael Jackson's *Thriller* MTV video in the 1980s cannot be underestimated (Hanna, 1999; Jonas, 1992). The interplay between dance in the wider community and dance in the classroom is to be acknowledged. Collaboration between artists, schools, community members provide rich learning experiences, but also challenge and develop meanings of dance in that community (Hong, 2002). In the future, will artists have more informed audiences; will parents see diverse participation and representation of "skill"; and will children see artists challenging social norms, while also appreciating their parents' and grandparents' culture and histories? The community provides a context for each classroom, and of note for teachers, at all levels of education, is to appreciate the community at large and that communities are in flux. Teachers need to keep abreast with educational, aesthetic and social trends, and also learners' interests and concerns, but also know that they are one of the stakeholders that can inform curriculum implementation and change. At the heart of the debate, teachers at all levels need to ask, what do children gain from the inclusion of dance in the curriculum and how can children gain most benefit from its inclusion? Further to the placement of dance in the curriculum, ongoing issues inform its presence in the classroom.

Teaching dance in the classroom

The following literature speaks of teaching dance in the classroom, and where possible focuses upon the primary school classroom by way of advocating for these teachers voices to be heard. This review explores several key issues such as control, content knowledge, relationships between teachers and children and embodied pedagogy.

As stated earlier, curricula do not teach themselves. They are selectively dismantled, interpreted, copied and disregarded by the teacher. Inexperienced or unconfident teachers may closely adhere to the curriculum, while the more confident may glance at it occasionally (Moore, 1997: Buck, 2003a). Of note is that the curriculum is mediated by the teacher and their dance experiences, its delivery is in turn also interpreted by children and their prior dance experiences. Critical and liberatory research in dance, after Stinson (1991, 2001); Shapiro (1998); Marques (1998), affirm the democratic and "humanizing" relationships valued in dance education.

"The model for the traditional dance pedagogue seems to be the authoritarian father" (Stinson, 1998: 27), however, the research literature that focused upon dance pedagogy revealed a growing diversity of practice. Stinson found the theme of control was a common theme in education literature generally, and particularly in the dance literature. "Control is as much an issue in curriculum as it is in dance: we fear that institutions, as well as bodies, will not work without control" (Stinson, 1991: 190). Reflecting upon her own practice and philosophy for teaching dance, Stinson saw the alternative to control as flow and release (Stinson, 1991). She envisaged the relationship between the teacher and the child as being one relying upon teamwork rather than control and power, interaction rather than domination. In seeking a dance metaphor that best described her pedagogical philosophy, Stinson likened her teaching to dance improvisation where one is "creating as one goes along" (Stinson, 1991: 191). Dance improvisation also implies qualities of giving and taking, shared responsibility, risk, respect, acute perception and fun. This metaphor for teaching dance is one I appreciate, as it values the individual qualities that the teacher, the child and the dance bring to the teaching/learning moment, which can be serendipitous, ephemeral and full of meaning.

Cognitive apprenticeship has a considerable history in dance pedagogy. Learning from the "masters" was and remains today a powerful means for what many regard as learning the "best technique" or the "practice of the experts". Cultures and traditions are passed on, both the good and the bad. Fortin (1998) cited dance studies by Clarkson (1988), Gray (1990), and Myers (1989) that all addressed the notion of conformity to traditions in dance pedagogy. Fortin (1993) discussed the common situation within the dance world where a dancer with advanced technical skill – content control, is assumed and expected to be able to teach. This problematic assumption that content knowledge can then be transformed into pedagogical knowledge was noted in her study of dance teachers in the studio setting. Fortin observed the "transformation" of content knowledge into knowledge for teaching as involving much more than a knowledge base of dancing technique and control. My experience is in accord with Fortin's findings and, in the context of the primary school setting I enter contentious ground and suggest that an in-depth knowledge of dance is not prerequisite nor in some cases necessarily advantageous when introducing students to dance education. Nevertheless, I do advocate for secondary school dance specialists with discipline expertise noting that "discipline expertise" does not mean dance technique expertise.

Linda Darling-Hammond's (2000) extensive American study of teacher quality in relation to student achievement noted that the teacher's subject matter knowledge had no consistent relation to student achievement, yet the teacher's knowledge of teaching and learning was shown to have consistent and strong links to student achievement. The view that the teacher's ability to interact and communicate with children is the crucial skill informing dance teacher's effectiveness was supported by Lord (1993). With reference to dance, Zakkai stated, "you do not have to be a skilled mover to be an effective facilitator of movement" (1997: 8). This is not to say that anything goes, in fact my experience tells me it is quite to the contrary and I have said many times in my practice, what is adamantly stated here by Zakkai, "Let's dispel a myth about working with movement and dance. It is not an unstructured experience" (1997: 8). What I do propose is that irrespective of their dance knowledge, primary school teachers must value their generalist pedagogical knowledge and apply it to teaching dance.

It is possible to regard the "teacher as learner" within a paradigm that values the knowledge that they create rather than exclusively relying upon the knowledge transmitted to them by experts (Newman, 1990). It is important to clarify that I am not saying that teachers never need knowledge and experience of dance to be able to teach it. I am however, advocating that a primary school teacher needs to acknowledge their world, their beginning points, their tried and refined pedagogical expertise, and that this is valuable and suitable in commencing a dance programme. Once initiated,

the teacher needs to look to the children and "the dance" to reflect upon and further develop their dance knowledge and the dance programme. Through a reflective process, teachers may ask what works in their teaching, what they value, what do they hope for the children? Stinson spoke from a position of considerable experience when she advocated for teachers to "become wide-awake" (2001: 28) to the choices they make when forming and teaching a dance programme and lesson. With considered and active reflection they will find what they need to know, or as Newman put it "Find our own way" (1990: 1).

It is the personal and conscious enquiry of the teacher that is crucial (Stinson, 2001). Holt stated in regard to children, "knowledge which is not genuinely discovered by children will very likely prove useless and will be soon forgotten" (1964: 125). I believe the same holds true for the teacher. I value the generalist teacher's personal experimentation; trying and re-trying as they establish what they need to know and discover how to find a "personal" way to connect their meaning of dance with the children and the curriculum. I believe conscious enquiry is foundational to the teacher's parallel role of being both "teacher" and "learner", simultaneously developing experience and understanding in both roles (Mayers and Britt, 1995). Holt (1997) suggested that generalist teachers know their children and asserted that it is this knowledge, rather than in-depth subject knowledge, that best enables their teaching of the arts.

Learning is in the experience and doing is at the core of learning (Russell, 1997). Following this logic, teachers learning to teach dance, irrespective of their prior experiences, need to actually do some teaching of dance in order to gain a genuine understanding of what it entails. Researching the impact of somatic practices upon the teaching of modern dance in academic and adult community dance classes, Fortin analysed three dance studio teachers' approaches to their teaching practice. The study found that the teachers' experience with somatics had a great impact upon their teaching. As Fortin stated, the teachers began to, "distance themselves from their 'apprenticeship of observation', develop a personalised dance technique that could be applied to any dance form, and question their own roles as teachers", (1998: 52). Closer reading reveals that the teachers had "critical awareness of their past dance experience as dance students … they integrated their various backgrounds to produce idiosyncratic ways of teaching … they used these [dance steps or somatic exercises] only when needed" (1998: 52). Critical reflection and recognition of personal experience informed these experienced teachers' practice as they broke from dance pedagogy traditions.

Regarding dance in the classroom in a critical and "personalised" way questions traditional dance pedagogy, where the teacher was seen as a "translator" or "funnel" of dance techniques or experiences, which as Stinson (1991) referred to earlier is based upon values of control and tradition. As Shapiro described, "This shift from disembodied knowing to embodied knowing calls into question traditional dance pedagogy" (1998: 15), which in turn impacts upon intent and outcomes of dance programmes, so that "the learning experience moves from one of learning movement vocabulary for the sake of creating a dance to gaining an understanding of the self, others, and the larger world for the possibility of change" (1998: 15). Teachers may find that their own as well as the children's concerns around body (Arkin, 1994; Brown, 1999; Green, 2001), gender (Adair, 1992; Bond, 1994; Brown, 1986; Burt, 1995; Cesan, 2003; Crawford, 1994; Lloyd and West, 1988; MacDonald, 1991; Thomas, 1993), sexuality (Keyworth, 2001; Risner, 2002a) and ability (Cooper Albright, 1997; Hong, 2000), become less of an issue when dance is taught from this pedagogical standpoint.

There is little evidence in the literature of research into how primary school teachers experience the teaching of dance in their classrooms (Hanna, 2001; Moore, 1997). Moore (1997) completed a study in England that explored five primary school teachers' experience of teaching dance as a component of the physical education curriculum. Stake et al., took a broader look at the "reality of arts education in American public schools" (1991: 1). The latter study looked at eight schools and discussed issues surrounding all of the arts, including dance. Both studies described the teachers' experience as they came to grips with teaching dance, and as one would expect, the stories were diverse and unique.

While the teachers' stories in both the American and English studies above were different, they both noted that dance was the least taught of all the arts. There were several reasons cited, including: no music, no time, no training and no expertise. Stake et al., noted, in respect to a Chicago elementary school, "Dance did happen but had a marginal role in the school, not because dance had lower status than the other arts, but because dance education had even fewer qualified to teach" (1991: 115). The teachers' sense of "inability" or lack of confidence to teach dance surfaced in most studies (Hennesy et al., 2001; Jobbins, 1998; MacDonald, 1991; McBride, 1988; Moore, 1997; Paul, 1998). Stake et al., noted that the actual abstract qualities of the form were influential in limiting teachers' access to dance, "as primary materials (space, time, energy) are inherently different from that of common language. Music and dance are accessible to relatively few" (1991: 310). Hence, dance is taught the least and often seen to be a subject taught by specialists. In regard to the dance elements, I believe that once the teacher acquires some familiarity with them, the scope of the discipline becomes apparent and access to participation is maximised for the children. As Stake et al., found, the teachers' perceptions of dance as including unfamiliar and obscure concepts and terminology created barriers to teaching dance.

Hong commented in respect to implementing the dance component of *The Arts in the New Zealand Curriculum,* "The effectiveness of the new curriculum delivery will obviously be very dependent on the ability of teachers in schools to interpret the curriculum from the printed page" (2002: 65).

Teachers have most commonly integrated dance in the curriculum through "activity topics" (Brown, 1986; MacDonald, 1991; Morin, 2001). This has largely been seen as the most time-efficient way of introducing dance experiences and finding a way to draw the students into dance. However, Moore raised the concern "that dance taught in this way is in danger of becoming merely an extension of other work being carried out in the classroom – more of a cross curricular theme – rather than a subject with its own distinctive structure and content" (1997: 161). Several case studies in Stake et al.'s (1991) study referred to the balancing of teacher-led activities and artist-led activities that both linked dance to the other activities and profiled dance as a discipline.

Irrespective of the involvement of artists in the classrooms, Moore (1997) and Stake et al. (1991) concluded, the future of dance in education rests with the teacher. As Charles Leonhard, Director of Research, National Arts Education Research Center, University of Illinois, stated in the foreword of the Stake et al., study, "Among the many lessons to be learned from reading the case studies is that in the final analysis the quality of arts education depends on the sustained efforts of teachers" (1991: 1).

Of note in the latter studies was the reference to the arts, including dance, as being distinct from the "academic subjects". Attention is drawn to the classification of the arts as "non-academic" as it is common (Eisner, 1998a; Kaagan, 1990). Underpinning this perception is the view that the cognitive and the affective states of mind are separate and that the arts are concerned primarily with the affective: emotions, feelings, intuition, perceptions, imagination. Indeed the arts do draw upon the affective state, as do the sciences, social studies, languages and mathematics. The arts are also equally, if not more so, concerned with cognition. As Dewey stated:

> Any idea that ignores the necessary role of intelligence in production of works of art is based on the identification of thinking with use of one special kind of material, verbal signs and words. To think effectively in terms of relations of qualities is as severe a demand upon thought as to think in terms of symbols, verbal or mathematical. Indeed since

words are easily manipulated in mechanical ways, the production of a work of genuine art probably demands more intelligence than does most of the so called thinking that goes on among those who pride themselves on being 'intellectuals'. (1934: 46)

Best (1993, 1996, 1999), Eisner (1991, 1993, 1994, 1998), Goodman (1978), Gardner (1983), Langer (1942, 1982), McKechnie (1998), and Stevens et al., (2001) have well argued the integral role of cognition in the arts, with McKechnie's, Langer's, and Best's work specifically focusing upon cognition in dance.

Dance within the arts curriculum has in theory moved beyond this debate, yet in practice teachers continue to value dance "as a break from academic subjects" or as "fun" (Stake et al., 1991). I don't deny these qualities of dance. The imperative remains, however, that teachers and children see and investigate both the "thinking" and the "fun" of dance (Kahlich, 2001). Fox and Gardiner (1997) researched the impact of the arts on achievement in other curriculum areas, finding that in the early years of primary school, achievement in maths and literacy improved when children were engaged in the arts. Other results revealed that the arts fostered "insight" into problems and fostered solutions, and that the arts were fun, stimulating positive learning, as well as behavioural and attitudinal changes in the classroom. In light of their findings and my belief that a happy classroom is a productive one, I value fun as a rationale for teaching dance.

Notions of fun and fear are wrapped up with participation in dance, tied to exposure of one's body and ideas. Shapiro focused upon the role of the "body" in developing a philosophy for pedagogy in dance education. Drawing upon her personal experience of dance, she initially described the body as "a tool, an instrument objectified for the benefit of the dance" (1998: 9). She then countered this with a critical view of the body as subject "that which holds the memory of one's life, a body that defines one's racial identity, one's gender existence, one's historical and cultural grounding indeed the very materiality of one's existence" (1998: 9). As a result of Shapiro's personal reflection, she began to "own" her body, and see it less as an object to perfect for the aesthetic pleasure of others and her "disembodied self", and more as "a rich source of knowledge" (1998: 9). At the heart of Shapiro's educational philosophy was the focus upon "embodied knowing" rather than "disembodied knowing" (1998: 15). Shapiro described a continuum "moving from a technical language [disembodied knowing] to one concerned with human liberation [embodied knowing]" (1998: 11). Within the classroom context, Shapiro advocated for recognition of the students' diversity and the need to "relate movement vocabulary to the students' experiences whether in pre-school or senior grade levels" (1998: 11).

The importance of establishing an inclusive dance classroom was noted by Musil (1999), especially one that acknowledges different perspectives and involves the student's active creation of meanings around dance. Implicit within such pedagogy is the dialogue between the teacher and the child, where the teacher and the child both draw upon their personal experiences. I believe when teachers teach dance they need to make a connection between their own movement and their life, in the same way that they expect this of the children. In doing this myself 20 years ago and today, I am aware of the personal risk that it requires, and the trust one places in the often unstated vow of classroom respect and privacy. But having made the risk, I have more often found the rewards, as seen in the children's subsequent contributions, equal in all ways to the initial risk.

Ongoing issues and future research

Many issues touched on in this chapter require ongoing research. Several studies (MacDonald, 1991; Stake et al., 1991; Moore, 1997) identified that teacher's lack confidence in interpreting and teaching dance curricula, and yet it remains unclear whether confidence to teach dance would be improved through extended discipline training, or with a focus on pedagogical strategies, or situated experience. Issues surrounding gender loom large in classrooms around the world. Concerns regarding the boys' response to dance, and also maintaining and extending girls' interest are not new, yet remain as some of the dominant barriers for implementing a dance lesson and programme. What dance education and experience would best educate teachers perceptions and assumptions about dance, who dances and why? Do curricula themselves present gendered or cultural barriers? Are teachers preserving stereotypes of how boys participate that are based upon dominant constructs of what masculinity is?

How is a dance programme "grown" within a classroom wherein teachers feel charged to complement curricula directions with children's and their own understandings, critical readings and interests? Do such "home-grown" dance programmes further intimidate teachers or empower them to "give dance a go"?

Research is required if dance education is to grow in a sustainable manner within physical education and other curricula contexts. Initiating dance events, lessons and discrete annual projects are worthy in themselves, but the focus must remain in establishing and improving dance curriculum and the subsequent sustainability of comprehensive dance programmes in our schools.

References

Abbs, P. (1987). *Living powers: The arts in education.* London: Falmer Press.

Adair, C. (1992). *Women in dance: Sylphs and sirens.* London: Macmillan Press Ltd.

Adshead, J. (1981). *The study of dance.* London: Dance Books Ltd.

Adshead, J. (1988). *Dance analysis: Theory and practice.* London: Dance Books.

Alter, J. (1996). *Dance based dance theory.* New York: Peter Lang.

Arkin, L. (1994). Dancing the body: women and dance performance. *Journal of Physical Education Recreation and Dance,* 65(2): 36–38.

Bannon, F. and Sanderson, P. (2000). Experience every moment: Aesthetically significant dance. *Research in Dance Education,* 1(1): 9–26.

Best, D. (1978). *Philosophy and human movement.* London: Lepus.

Best, D. (1982). *Meaning in dance: The objective and the subjective* (pp. 63–71). In M. Howell and P. Barham (Eds.), Proceedings of the VII Commonwealth and International Conference on Sport, Physical Education, Recreation and Dance Brisbane: University of Queensland.

Best, D. (1985). Feeling and reason in the arts. London: Allen and Unwin.

Best, D. (1993). *The rationality of feeling.* London: Falmer Press.

Best, D. (1996). Understanding artistic experience: Some vital pointers for research. *National Association of Drama In Education,* 20(2): 41–52.

Best, D. (1999). Dance before you think. In G. Mcfee (Ed.), *Dance, education and philosophy* (pp. 101–124). Oxford: Meyer and Meyer Sport.

Bolwell, J. (1998). Into the light: An expanding vision of dance education. In S. Shapiro (Ed.), *Dance, power and difference: Critical feminist perspectives on dance education* (pp. 75–96). Champaign, IL: Human Kinetics.

Bond, K. (1994). How 'wild things' tamed gender distinctions. *Journal of Physical Education Recreation and Dance,* 65(2): 28–33.

Bond, K. and Stinson, S. (2000/01). "I Feel Like I'm Going to Take Off!": Young people's experiences of the superordinary in dance. *Dance Research Journal,* 32(2): 52–87.

Brinson, P. (1981). *Dance in New Zealand.* Wellington: Queen Elizabeth II Arts Council of New Zealand.

Brinson, P. (1991). *Dance as education.* London: The Falmer Press.

Broudy, H. (1991). The role of art education in the public school. In G. Willis and W. Schubert (Eds.), *Reflections from the heart of educational inquiry* (pp. 60–73). Albany: State University of New York Press.

Brown, A. (1986). Elementary school dance: Teaching rhythms and educational forms. *Journal of Physical Education Recreation and Dance,* 57(2): 39–45.

Brown, C. (1999). Unpacking the body. *Dance Theatre Journal,* 14(4): 12–16.

Buck, R. (2003). Dance. In J.Whiteoak and A. Scott-Maxwell (Eds.), *Currency companion to music and dance in Australia* (pp. 604–605). Sydney: Currency House.

Buck, R. (2003a). Teachers and dance in the classroom. Unpublished Ph D, University of Otago, Dunedin.

Burrows, L. (1999). *Developmental discourses in school physical education.* Unpublished PhD, University of Wollongong, Wollongong.

Burt, R. (1995). *The male dancer: Bodies, spectacles and sexualities.* London: Routledge.

Carino, C. (2001). Creating a dance elective program: A proposal for Singapore. In S. Burridge (Ed.), *World Dance Alliance 2001 Singapore: Asia Pacific Dance Bridge* (pp. 85–99). Singapore: World Dance Alliance, Singapore.

Carroll, N. and Banes, S. (1999). Dance, imitation and representation. In G. McFee (Ed.), *Dance, education and philosophy* (pp. 13–32). Oxford: Meyer and Meyer Sport (UK).

Cesan, J. (2003). Dancing with the boys. *DANZ,* 16(April), 2–4.

Clarkson, P. (1988). Science in dance. In P. Clarkson and M. Skrinar (Eds.), *Science of dance training* (pp. 17–22). Champaign, IL: Human Kinetics.

Consortium of National Arts Education Associations. (1994). *Dance, music, theatre, visual arts: What every young American should know and be able to do in the arts. National standards for arts education.* Reston: Music Educators National Conference.

Cooper Albright, A. (1997). *Choreographing difference: The body and identity in contemporary dance.* Hanover, Germany: Wesleyan University Press.

Copeland, R. and Cohen, M. (1983). *What is dance?* New York: Oxford University Press.

Crawford, J. (1994). Encouraging male participation in dance. *Journal of Physical Education Recreation and Dance,* 65(2): 40–43.

Creative New Zealand. (2002). Cool culture. *On Arts: nga koreo toi,* 23: 16.

Creativenet. (2001). *Creativenet,* Available: http://www.creativenet.org.uk/ [2001, 10 May].

Crotty, M. (1998). *The foundations of social research: Meaning and perspective in the research process.* London: Sage.

Curriculum Corporation. (1994). *A statement on the arts for Australian schools.* Melbourne, Australia: Curriculum Corporation.

Darling-Hammond, L. (2000). Teacher quality and student achievement: A review of state policy evidence. *Educational Policy Analysis Archives,* 8(1): 1–39.

Department of Education, England. (1995). The national curriculum. London: HMSO.

Dewey, J. (1934). *Art as experience.* Minton: Balch.

Dewey, J. (1938). *Experience and education.* New York: Macmillan Publishing Company.

Dorn, C. (1993). Art as intelligent activity. *Arts Education Policy Review,* 95(2): 2–10.

Doyle, W. (1992). Curriculum and pedagogy. In P. Jackson (Ed.), *Handbook of research on curriculum* (pp. 486–516). New York: MacMillan Publishing Co.

Eisner, E. (1985). Aesthetic modes of knowing. In E. Eisner (Ed.), *Learning and teaching the ways of knowing* (pp. 23–36). Chicago, IL: University of Chicago Press.

Eisner, E. (1991). What the arts taught me about education. In G. Willis and W. Schubert (Eds.), *Reflections from the heart of educational inquiry* (pp. 34–48). Albany, NY: State University of New York Press.

Eisner, E. (1993). Forms of understanding and the future of educational research. *Educational Researcher, 22*(7): 5–11.

Eisner, E. (1994). *Cognition and curriculum reconsidered.* New York: Teachers College Press.

Eisner, E. (1998). *The enlightened eye: Qualitative inquiry and the enhancement of educational practice.* New York: Macmillan.

Eisner, E. (1998a.). *What intelligence looks like in the arts.* Keynote address presented at the New Zealand Association for Research in Education, Dunedin.

Faire, R. (2002). Even smarter bodies? Increasing the somatic literacy of PDHPE teachers. *Healthy Lifestyles Journal, 49*(1):16–20.

Fiske, E. (Ed.), (n.d.). *Champions of change: The impact of the arts on learning.* The Arts Education Partnership (USA) and The President's Committee on the Arts and the Humanities. Available, www.aep-arts.org/Champions. html [2000, 1 July].

Fortin, S. (1991). A retrospective critique of dance education in Quebec, Canada. In S. Stinson (Ed.), *Dance and the child international* (pp. 90–95). Salt Lake City, UT: University of Utah.

Fortin, S. (1993). The knowledge base for competent dance teaching. *Journal of Physical Education Recreation and Dance, 64*(9): 34–38.

Fortin, S. (1998). Somatics: Todays tool for empowering modern dance teachers and transforming dance pedagogy. In S. Shapiro (Ed.), *Dance, power and difference: Critical and feminist perspectives in dance education* (pp. 49–74). Champaign: Human Kinetics.

Fortin, S., Long, W. and Lord, M. (2002). Three voices: Researching how somatic education informs contemporary dance technique classes. *Research in Dance Education, 3*(2): 155–179.

Foster, J. (1977). *The influences of Rudolf Laban.* London: Lepus Books.

Fox, A. and Gardiner, M. (1997). *The arts and raising achievement.* Paper presented at The Arts in The Curriculum, London.

Fraleigh, S. (1987). *Dance and the lived body: A descriptive aesthetics.* Pittsburgh, PA: University of Pittsburgh Press.

Fraleigh, S. (2000). Consciousness matters. *Dance Research Journal, 32*(1): 54–62.

Fraleigh, S and Hanstein, P. (1999). (Eds.), *Researching dance: Evolving modes of inquiry.* London: Dance Books.

Freire, P. (1972). *Pedagogy of the oppressed* (M. B. Ramos, Trans.). Harmondsworth: Penguin Education.

Gallego, M., Hollingsworth, S. and Whitenack, D. (2001). Relational knowing in the reform of educational cultures. *Teachers College Record, 103*(2): 240–266.

Gardner, H. (1983). *Frames of mind.* New York: Basic Books.

Gardner, H. (1989). Zero based arts education: An introduction to ARTS PROPEL. *Studies in Art Education, 30*(2): 71–83.

Gardner, H. (1995). Time to talk turkey. *Educational Quarterly Australia, 3*: 23–25.

Gardner, H. (1999). *Intelligence reframed.* New York: Basic Books.

Gardner, H. (2000). *The disciplined mind: Beyond facts and standardised tests: The K-12 education that every child deserves.* New York: Penguin Books.

Goodman, N. (1968). *Languages of art: An approach to a theory of symbols.* Indianapolis, IN: The Bobbs-Merrill Company Inc.

Goodman, N. (1978). *Ways of worldmaking.* Hassocks: The Harvester Press Limited.

Gray, J. (1990). Dance education in the future: Trends and predictions. *Journal of Physical Education Recreation and Dance, 61*(5): 50–51.

Green Gilbert, A. (2003). Toward best practices in dance education through the theory of multiple intelligences. *Journal of Dance Education, 3*(1): 28–33.

Green, J. (2001). Socially constructed bodies in American dance classrooms. *Research in Dance Education, 2*(2): 153–173.

Greer, W. (1987). A structure of discipline based concepts for DBAE. *Studies in Art Education, 28*(4): 227–233.

Guba, E. and Lincoln, Y. (1994). Competing paradigms in qualitative research. In N. Denzin and Y. Lincoln (Eds.), *Handbook of qualitative research* (pp. 105–117). Thousand Oaks, CA: Sage.

Hanna, J. (1979). *To dance is human: A theory of non-verbal communication.* Austin, Tex: University of Texas.

Hanna, J. (1999). *Partnering dance and education.* Champaign, IL: Human Kinetics.

Hanna, J. (2001). Beyond the soundbite: What the research actually shows about arts education and academic outcomes. *Journal of Dance Education, 1*(2): 81–85.

Hanna, T. (1983). Dictionary definition of the word somatics. *Somatics, 4*(2): 1.

Hanstein, P. (1999). Models and metaphors: Theory making and the creation of new knowledge. In S.H. Fraleigh and P. Hanstein (Eds.), *Researching dance: Evolving modes of inquiry* (pp. 62–88). London: Dance Books.

Haynes, A. (1987). Changing perspectives in dance education. In P. Abbs (Ed.), *Living powers: The arts in education* (pp. 141–162). London: The Falmer Press.

Hennessy, S., Rolfe, L. and Chedzoy, S. (2001). The factors which influence student teachers' confidence to teach the arts in the primary classroom. *Research in Dance Education, 2*(1): 53–71.

Hirst, P. (1995). Education, aesthetic. In D. Cooper (Ed.), *Companion to aesthetics* (pp. 127–130). Cambridge, MA: Blackwell Publishers Ltd.

Holt, D. (1997). Hidden strengths: The case for the generalist teacher of art. In D. Holt (Ed.), *Primary arts education* (pp. 84–95). London: Falmer Press.

Holt, J. (1964). *How children fail.* New York: Dell.

Hong, T. (2000). Developing dance literacy in the postmodern: An approach to curriculum. In J. Crone Willis and J. LaPointe-Crump (Eds.), Proceedings of *Dancing in the Millenium Conference* (pp. 245–251). Washington, DC: Congress on Research in Dance.

Hong, T. (2001). Getting cinders to the ball. *Physical Educator: Te Reo Kori Aotearoa*, 3(1): 4–6.

Hong, T. (2002). Dance artists and the curriculum: an interface. *In Creative New Zealand, Moving to the future Nga Whakanekeneke atu ki te Ao o Apopo* (pp. 64–70). Wellington, N: Creative New Zealand.

Jobbins, V. (1998). Facing the future. *Animated, (Winter)*: 10–11.

Jobbins, V. (1998a). Threats and opportunities: Where is dance? *Dance Matters, 21*(Spring), 1–2.

Jonas, G. (1992). *Dancing*. London: BBC Books.

Kaagan, S. (1990). *Aesthetic persuasion: Pressing the cause of arts in American schools*. Los Angeles, CA: Getty Center.

Kahlich, L. (2001). The challenges in dance education. *Journal of Dance Education*, 1(1): 5–6.

Kant, I. (1966). *Critique of judgement*. (J Bernard, Trans.). New York: Hafner. (Original work published 1790)

Keyworth, S. (2001). Critical autobiography: 'straightening' out dance education. *Research in Dance Education*, 2(2): 117–137.

King, A. and Brownell, J. (1966). *The Curriculum and the disciplines of knowledge*. New York: John Wiley and Sons.

Kirstein, L. (1935). *Dance: A short history of classic theatrical dancing*. New York: G.P. Putnam's Sons.

Kleinman, S. (2000). Summing up: A chronological retrospective or dancing the body electric. *Quest, 52*(1): 89–101.

Koegler, H. (1982). *The concise Oxford dictionary of ballet*. London: Oxford University Press.

Kovich, Z. (1996). *Mind, body, movement and creativity: A somatic epistemology*. Paper presented at the Australian Tertiary Dance Festival. Melbourne: Australian Dance Council.

Kraus, R., Chapman Hilsendager, S. and Dixon, B. (1991). *History of the dance in art and education*. New Jersey: Englewood Cliffs.

Laban, R. (1948). *Modern educational dance*. London: Macdonald and Evans.

Langer, S. (1942). *Philosophy in a new key*. Cambridge: Harvard University Press.

Langer, S. (1953). *Feeling and form*. New York: Scribner's Sons.

Langer, S. (1982). *Mind: An essay on human feeling*. Baltimore, MD: Johns Hopkins University Press.

Lincoln, Y. and Guba, E. (2000). Paradigmatic controversies, contradictions and emerging confluences. In N. Denzin and Y. Lincoln (Eds.), *Handbook of qualitative research* (pp. 163–187). Thousand Oaks, CA: Sage.

Lloyd, M. and West, B. (1988). Where are the boys in dance? *Journal of Physical Education Recreation and Dance, 59*(5): 47–51.

Lord, M. (1993). Reflections on the preparation of effective dance teachers. *The Journal of Physical Education, Recreation and Dance, 64*(9): 39–41.

Lortie, D. (1975). *School teacher: A sociological study*. Chicago, IL: University of Chicago Press.

Lyons, S. (1998). Setting the scene for dance 2. *Dance Matters, 20*(Winter): 6–7.

MacDonald, C. (1991). Elementary school teachers explain why they do not use creative dance in their classrooms. *The Alberta Journal of Educational Research, 37*(2): 157–166.

Martin, J. (1933). *The modern dance*. New York: A.S. Barnes and Co.

Martin, J. (1946). *The dance: The story of the dance told in pictures and text*. New York: Tudor Publishing Company.

Marques, I. (1998). Dance education in/and the postmodern. In S. Shapiro (Ed.), Dance, power and difference: Critical and feminist perspectives on dance education (pp. 171–185). Champaign, IL: Human Kinetics.

Masunah, J. (2001). Traditional dance in formal school education. In S. Burridge (Ed.), *World Dance Alliance 2001 Singapore: Asia Pacific Dance Bridge* (pp. 102–117). Singapore: World Dance Alliance, Singapore.

Mayers, C. and Britt, M. (1995). Constructivism in the mathematics classroom. In J. Neyland (Ed.), *Mathematics education: A handbook for teachers* (pp. 60–69). Wellington, NZ: Wellington College of Education.

McBride, B. (1988). Teaching creative dance as an art form in the primary school. In G. Curl (Ed.), *National Association of Teachers in Further and Higher Education: Collected Conference Papers in Dance* (pp. 71–77). London: National Association of Teachers in Further and Higher Education.

McKechnie, S. (1998). Thinking dancing: matters of art, value, doing and knowing. *Dance forum: Journal of the Australian Dance Council*, 8(3 and 4): 20–22.

Meglin, J. (1994). Gender issues in dance education. *The Journal of Physical Education, Recreation and Dance, 65*(2): 26–27.

Meiners, J. (2001). A dance syllabus writer's perspective: The New South Wales K-6 dance syllabus. *Research in Dance Education*, 2(1): 77–88.

Merleau-Ponty, M. (1962). *Phenomenology of perception* (C. Smith, Trans.). London: Routledge.

Ministry of Education New Zealand. (1999). *Health and physical education in the New Zealand curriculum*. Wellington, NZ: Learning Media.

Ministry of Education New Zealand. (2000). *The arts in the New Zealand curriculum*. Wellington, NZ: Learning Media.

Moore, J. (1997). Dance teaching in the primary school: Voices from the classroom. In D. Holt (Ed.), *Primary arts education* (pp. 142–164). London: Falmer Press.

Morin, F. (2001). Composing dances with children: An instructional model. *Journal of Physical Education Recreation and Dance, 72*(6): 43–60.

Musil, P. (1999). From classroom experience to work of art: Involving dance students in the choreographic process. *Journal of Physical Education, Recreation and Dance, 70*(5): 35–39.

Myers, M. (1989). Dance science and somatic education in dance training. In H. Trotter and J. Dyson (Eds.), *Transitions: Australian Association for Dance Education Biennial Conference* (pp. 13–25). Adelaide: Australian Association for Dance Education.

Nam, J. (2001). Dance education and dance training system in South Korea. In S. Burridge (Ed.), *World Dance Alliance: Asia Pacific Dance Bridge Singapore*

2001 (pp. 118–123). Singapore: World Dance Alliance, Asia Pacific Chapter.

Newman, J. (1990). *Finding Our Own Way: Teachers exploring their assumptions.* Portsmouth, NZ: Heineman.

Ottey, S. (1996). Critical pedagogical theory and the dance educator. *Arts Education Policy Review, 98*(2): 31–39.

Paul, K. (1998). Unleashing the dancer within. *Animated, (Winter),* 28–29.

Pring, R. (1976). *Knowledge and schooling.* London: Open Books.

Reid, L.A. (1974). The arts as a unique form of knowledge. *Cambridge Journal of Education, 4*(3): 153–165.

Risner, D. (2002). Re-educating dance education to its homosexuality: An invitation for critical analysis and professional unification. *Research in Dance Education, 3*(2): 181–187.

Risner, D. (2002a). Sexual orientation and male participation in dance education. *Journal of Dance Education, 2*(3): 84–92.

Rubin, L. (1991). The arts and an artistic curriculum. In G. Willis and W. Schubert (Eds.), *Reflections from the heart of educational inquiry* (pp. 49–59). Albany, NY: State University of New York Press.

Russell, T. (1997). Teaching teachers: How I teach IS the message. In J. Loughran and T. Russell (Eds.), *Teaching about teaching: Purpose, passion and pedagogy in teacher education* (pp. 32–47). London: Falmer Press.

Schmidt, D. (2003). Authentic assessment in the arts: Empowering students and teachers. *Journal of Dance Education, 3*(2): 65–73.

Schwandt, T. (1994). Constructivist, interpretivist approaches to human inquiry. In N. Denzin and Y. Lincoln (Eds.), *Handbook of qualitative research* (pp. 118–137). Thousand Oaks, CA: Sage.

Schwandt, T. (2000). Three epistemological stances for qualitative inquiry. In N. Denzin and Y. Lincoln (Eds.), *Handbook of qualitative research* (pp. 189–214). Thousand Oaks, CA: Sage.

Sevilla, J.M. (2003). One school's application of the theory of multiple intelligences: When one flower blooms. *Journal of Dance Education, 3*(1): 34–44.

Shapiro, S. (1998). Toward transformative teachers: Critical and feminist perspectives in dance education. In S. Shapiro (Ed.), *Dance, power and difference: Critical and feminist perspectives on dance education* (pp. 7–21). Champaign, IL: Human Kinetics.

Simon, D. (2003). *Dance education in New Zealand and Laban's movement theories: Interface and synthesis.* Unpublished Masters Thesis, University of Auckland.

Smith, J. (1976). *Dance composition.* London: A and C Black.

Smith, R. (1999). Justifying aesthetic education: Getting it right. *Journal of Aesthetic Education, 33*(4): 17–23.

Smith-Autard, J. (1994). *The art of dance in education.* London: A and C Black.

Smithells, P. (1974). *Physical education: Principles and philosophies.* Auckland: Heinemann Educational Books.

Sparshott, F. (1999). On what dancing is. In G. McFee (Ed.), *Dance, education and philosophy* (pp. 63–84). Oxford: Meyer and Meyer Sport.

Stake, R., Bresler, L. and Mabry, L. (1991). *Custom and cherishing: The arts in elementary schools.* Urbana – Champaign: Council for Research in Music Education.

Stevens, C., Malloch, S. and McKechnie, S. (2001). Moving mind: The cognitive psychology of contemporary dance. *Brolga: an Australian Journal about Dance, 15*: 55–67.

Stiegelbauer, S. (1999). Without art the world would be a blank piece of nothing. *Curriculum Inquiry, 29*(3): 393–399.

Stinson, S. (1991). Dance as curriculum, curriculum as dance. In G. Willis and W. Schubert (Eds.), *Reflections from the heart of educational inquiry* (pp. 190–196). New York: State University of New York Press.

Stinson, S. (1995). Body of knowledge. *Educational Theory, 45*(1): 43–54.

Stinson, S. (1998). Seeking a feminist pedagogy for children's dance. In S. Shappiro (Ed.), *Dance, power and difference: Critical and feminist perspectives on dance education* (pp. 23–48). Champaign, IL: Human Kinetics.

Stinson, S. (2001). Choreographing a life: Reflections on curriculum design, consciousness and possibility. *Journal of Dance Education, 1*(1): 26–33.

Stothart, R. (1974). *The development of physical education in New Zealand.* Auckland, NZ: Heinemann Educational Books.

Street, S. (2001). New developments in dance education in Hong Kong. In S. Burridge (Ed.), *World Dance Alliance: Asia Pacific Dance Bridge Singapore 2001* (pp. 65–71). Singapore: World Dance Alliance: Asia Pacific Chapter.

Strom, E. (2001). *Strengthening communities through culture.* New Brunswick, NJ: The Centre For Arts and Culture.

Sylwester, R. (1998). Art for the brains sake. *Educational Leadership, November,* 31–35.

The Scottish Office: Education Department. (1992). *Expressive arts 5–14: Curriculum and assessment in Scotland national guidelines.* Edinburgh: The Scottish Office: Education Department.

Thomas, H. (1993). *Dance, gender and culture.* London: The Macmillan Press.

Trend, D. (1992). *Cultural pedagogy.* Westport: Greenwood Publishing Group.

Warburton, E. (2003). Intelligence past, present and possible: The theory of multiple intelligences in dance education. *Journal of Dance Education, 3*(1): 7–15.

Williams, G. (1989). Dance education for young children. A review of principles and practices. *Early Child Development and Care, 47*: 177–203.

Willis, G. and Schubert, W. (1991). *Reflections from the heart of educational inquiry.* New York: State University of New York.

Wittgenstein, L. (1953). *The philosophical investigations.* (G. Anscombe, Trans.). New York: The Macmillan Company.

Zakkai, J. (1997). *Dance as a way of knowing.* Los Angeles: The Galef Institute.

SECTION VI

Difference and Diversity in Physical Education

This final section of the Handbook brings together research that we believe is breaking new ground in physical education. This might seem a rather ironic statement given that some of the topics such as girls and gender, disability, and social class have been around for a long time in the research literature. Our view is, though, that it is in these fields that new theories, methods and forms of representation are occurring. A case in point is research on gender, and on girls in physical education in particular. As Flintoff and Scraton show, researchers working in this field have been among the first to work with new theories such as post-Marxism, poststructuralism, standpoint theory, and so on, as well as new methods such as qualitative and collaborative work.

We have brought together this ground-breaking work under the labels of difference and diversity since it appears to us that it is the effort to think beyond conventions of mainstream research in pedagogy, to include groups who have formerly been excluded, such as young disabled people, lesbian physical educators, or particular ethnic and racial groups, that has prompted new and innovative research. Rather than seeking to normalize and homogenize the diverse populations of young people who engage in varying ways with physical education, this research seeks to recognize and celebrate difference. New conceptual tools, new theories, new frames of mind, and new political agendas are required to undertake these tasks of inclusion and recognizing and celebrating diversity.

Gard compliments Flintoff and Scraton's chapter on girls in physical education by asking some searching questions about the relatively new research focus on boys and the political agendas that underpin an interest in boys in physical education. Harrison and Belcher emphasize the importance of recognizing racial and ethnic difference as legitimate and enriching for physical education, and seek to move our understanding beyond the banalities of multiculturalism that pervade the work of so many physical educators who struggle to serve diverse populations in their schools. On a parallel course, Fitzgerald assists us to understand how particular definitions of disability have pathologized and marginalized young disabled people, and shows how listening closely to the voices of young people with disabilities can illuminate the normalizing tendencies in physical education programmes that seek to legitimate and maintain categories of disability. Meanwhile, Evans and Davies argue that even though social class has been a perennial topic of interest to educational researchers, it remains poorly understood and operationalized in physical education research programs, despite the persistent effects of wealth and poverty on young people's educational opportunities and experiences. Finally, the need for new theories, perspectives and methodologies is clear when we consider the topic of sexuality, which Clarke describes as the last taboo for physical education researchers to confront. Since, as Clarke shows, this is a topic shrouded in silence, myths and misunderstandings, even the task of finding a language that can communicate issues of sexuality in an open and equitable way is a challenge in itself. As Clarke's review shows, however, it is in this area where innovative work is being undertaken as researchers seek to address educational issues in physical education in equitable and inclusive ways.

6.1 Sexuality and physical education

GILL CLARKE

Introduction

The issue of sexuality is perhaps the last taboo as regards open discussion in physical education. Although as I shall argue within this chapter there have been some changes within the pedagogical practices and expectations of physical educators in the two decades since Lenskyj first referred to the "chilly silence" surrounding this issue in the mid 1980s much remains to be done if physical education is to recognize and allow for the sexual diversity of all its participants. Clearly there has been increasing awareness of the importance of addressing issues of sexuality within physical education which has led to a growing corpus of research in this field particularly emanating from North America, Australia and England. Nevertheless, while there may have been a rise in academic study it is questionable what impact this has had on grass roots physical education. Accordingly, there remain considerable gaps in our understanding of what it means to be different within the largely hetero-normative social and cultural context of physical education.

This chapter discusses the practices of physical education in order to demonstrate how these continue to operate around stereotyped notions of what is to be "normal", that is not lesbian, gay, bisexual or transgendered (lgbt) but heterosexual. In doing so this review elucidates the ways in which (hetero)sexual identity is privileged, regulated and controlled. Further, how this intersects with restricted conceptions of gender, (hegemonic) masculinity and (hyper) femininity is revealed. Attention is also directed to considering how heterosexism and homophobia continue to be manifest within physical education. However, it is to "history" and herstory in particular that I turn to to foreground these later discussions.

A brief historical perspective

The term "lesbian" only came in to use when European sexologists in the late nineteenth century began to explore female same sex loving. Faderman (1991: 1) points out that "women's intimate relationships were universally encouraged in centuries outside of our own ... " and "romantic friendships" as they were often called were respected social institutions in America. However, what was once viewed as normal and natural became viewed by the sexologists as a third sex that was abnormal and sick and whose gender was inverted. Further, various religious communities saw such relationships as sinful, and additionally lesbian women were seen as men trapped in women's bodies (Faderman, 1991). Thus, what was in some cases once respected became something not only to be feared but also a condition that required medical treatment. Indeed, it was not until 1967 that male homosexuality was decriminalized in Great Britain and it took a further 7 years before the American Psychiatric Association ruled that homosexuality should be taken off the list of diseases and no longer regarded as a mental disorder (see for instance Smith, 1996; Weeks, 1986).[1]

Much has changed since this pathologising of lesbianism, lesbian women and gay men are now "freer" in certain social and political contexts to both name and define themselves. Yet, this is generally not the case in the context of the conservative world of physical education, for most lesbian teachers go to considerable lengths to conceal their real sexual identities from colleagues, pupils and parents for fear of loss of employment and harassment. Moreover, women who participate in the contexts of physical education and/or sport have traditionally been suspected of being lesbian.

Research by Harris and Griffin (1997: 49) indicated "that most Americans stereotyped women physical educators as masculine, aggressive, athletic, lesbian and unintellectual." From my own now lengthy experiences in physical education and sport I would suggest that similar beliefs would not be uncommon in England and elsewhere. As Sykes (2001: 13) points out "this suspicion has enveloped countless female teachers and coaches in a shroud of oppressive silence – tolerated only as an open secret, an absence presence." Such are the fears and phobias that as will be demonstrated later a further absent presence is gay male physical educators.

In terms of understanding these "teacher absences" in the United Kingdom (UK) it is necessary to reflect on the circumstances leading up to the passing in 1988 of the notorious Section 28 of the Local Government Act and its repealing in 2003 in England and Wales (see Clarke, 1996).[2] Section 28 was passed by the Conservative government during Margaret Thatcher's premiership when the "campaign for family values" was pursued with much vigour, concern was frequently expressed about the well-being of the institution of the family. As Stacey commented:

> An important discourse emerging out of the Thatcher years has been that of sexuality as an increasing threat.... Similarly the ... association of AIDS with so-called sexual perversion and promiscuity has contributed to the notion that sexuality, particularly homosexuality and lesbianism, are threatening to the fabric of British society.[3] (1991: 286)

These threats were to lead, in part, to an increase in state involvement and to greater regulation of sexuality. Homosexuals were depicted as depraved demons whose immoral behaviour and sexual proclivity were regarded variously as perverted, sick, sinful, predatory, and as a threat to children – all attributes directly oppositional to the "naturalness" and moral sanctity of the (heterosexual) family (see Carabine, 1995; Evans, 1993; Smith, 1990). Section 28 stated:

(1) A local authority shall not –

   (a) intentionally promote homosexuality or publish material with the intention of promoting homosexuality;

   (b) promote the teaching in any maintained school of the acceptability of homosexuality as a pretended family relationship.

(2) Nothing in subsection (1) above shall be taken to prohibit the doing of anything for the purpose of treating or preventing the spread of disease. (Smith, 1994: 183)

The passing of Section 28 was an attempt to restore the family to its "rightful" place at the heart of British life, to protect it from attack by lesbians and gay men and to reassert the "moral" high ground in schools. The intention was also to maintain cultural conformity and the omniscience of heterosexual identities, values and institutions whilst at the same time defining, regulating and enforcing sexual boundaries so as to establish what Butler (1990) describes as "gender border control". In order for this to be achieved not only were local authorities targeted as potential purveyors of homosexual propaganda but so too were teachers – both it was argued could use their influence to threaten the authority of the state and the sanctity of the family (see Evans, 1989–90). This legislation exemplified not only legal disapproval of lesbian and gay lifestyles but also illustrated the power of the Conservative moral right to dictate what constituted acceptable/normal sexual identity thereby legitimising dominant discourses of compulsory heterosexuality.

Section 28 undoubtedly had a marked effect on teachers and the teaching of lesbian and gay issues in schools. It is questionable whether its recent repeal will alter this situation. Jenny Broughton (2004 cited in Hastings, 2004: 12), national coordinator for Families and Friends of Lesbians and Gay Men (Fflag) commented "many schools are blithely unaware that anything has changed, or choose to ignore that it has." Globally, the sexual landscape is slowly changing and the right to choose one's sexual identity is now in many countries an issue of civil rights.

In terms of the landscape of research in physical education as I have indicated in the introduction there have been some notable developments since the 1980s which I will draw attention to in a later section on Major findings. However, it is necessary in a section on historical perspectives to summarise the essence of these past studies here. Much of the early research on sexuality was located in North America and was undertaken by two lesbian scholars, Helen Lenskyj (1986) and Pat Griffin (1987). Their pioneering research and that of others (see for instance Hall, 1987) in the early 1980s started to bring the issue of lesbians in physical education and sport out into the open; by and large these researchers examined issues of homophobia and heterosexism with the intention of encouraging open dialogue in education in general and physical education (and sport) in particular. The research was in the main informed by lesbian feminism. Later research analysed in greater depth heterosexuality as a compulsory institution and drew attention to the ways in which it was taken for granted within physical education. Other qualitative research in this domain began to explore through interviews the life histories of lesbian physical education teachers and how they managed their identities within schools (see Griffin, Woods and Sykes in North America and Sparkes, Squires and Sparkes, and Clarke in England). These studies were largely informed by standpoint epistemologies and sought to give voice to silenced and marginal groups, an important feature of this work was the issue of what it means to give voice and what this implies in terms of power and patronage (see also Dewar 1991). In connection with this research it should be noted that Sykes' (2001: 17) work was somewhat different in that she employed a feminist-poststructural approach that incorporated queer theory about identity in order to develop a broader interpretation of sexuality and heteronormativity. This hybrid approach by Sykes has now been extended to include psychoanalytic theorizing (2004).

What continues to be a lacuna in terms of the research undertaken is that regarding gay male physical education teachers, and as will be illustrated Sparkes' fictional ethnography of Alexander remains a notable exception. There has also been a noticeable lack of work that has focused on lesbian physical education students, although Clarke employing a lesbian feminist approach coupled with tenets from postmodernism and poststructuralism did investigate the life stories of lesbian students in three higher education institutions in England in the mid 1990s. This research focused on questions of lesbian identity, life in college and teaching practice experiences including the students' relationships with pupils and teaching colleagues. Flintoff's feminist interpretative research also conducted in the 1990s in England in Initial Teacher Training vividly demonstrated the misogynist and homophobic practices therein. Nixon and Givens (2004) tell "Queer stories from trainee teachers" but their small-scale research in England focused exclusively on Education students although reference is made to Sports Science students, some of whom would likely go on to take a one-year post-graduate teaching certificate in physical education.

Core concepts

At this stage in this review it is perhaps helpful to provide some explanation of the concepts I have referred to previously before expanding upon these in the section that follows. Thus, for the purposes of this discussion I share Robinson and Ferfolja's (2002: 123–4) view of sexuality "as a social relation that is fluid, unstable, complex, contradictory, and culturally and historically constructed. It is considered not to be 'given', but negotiated socially and politically within specific historical contexts (Britzman, 1997)." My concern here is with the contemporary context of physical education, although historically the subject has developed around two distinct and separate male and female sporting cultures both built around particularly narrow ideologies and stereotyped visions of heterosexual masculinity and femininity (see Fletcher, 1984; Scraton, 1992). This gendered legacy of single sex provision for boys and girls remains pervasive insofar as it impacts on restricted expectations of what it is to be a successful boy/girl within the subject. Further, as will be revealed, the spaces to negotiate a sexual identity within schools in general and physical education in particular are constrained by heterosexism and homophobia (see Clarke, 2004).

Heterosexism refers to attitudes and institutional and cultural arrangements predicated on the belief that heterosexuality "is the only normal and acceptable sexual orientation" (Griffin and Harro, 1997: 146). Lenskyj (2003: 4) makes the important point that "Heterosexism remains the dominant perspective of patriarchal culture." The particular cultural and institutional arrangements that are germane here are those that are normalised through the rules, rituals, dress code and expected displays of behaviour within the "gymnasium".[4] Schools are sites of moral and social surveillance wherein young people spend significant time; further they are highly (hetero)sexualized sites with the power to define and regulate what it is to be normal, and to stipulate dominant heterosexual modes of being. Thus largely docile and conforming bodies are produced (Foucault, 1977).

Closely linked to heterosexism is homophobia, indeed, Griffin and Genasci (1990: 213–14) have argued that homophobia is the glue that holds sexism together. Griffin (1998: xv) reminds us that "Fifteen years ago few people outside the lesbian and gay community knew what homophobia was." Homophobia should be viewed as part of a heterosexist system of power and a form of sexual and social control, Sears (1997: 16) defines it as "prejudice, discrimination, harassment, or acts of violence against sexual minorities, including lesbians, gay men, bisexuals, and transgendered persons, evidenced in a deep-seated fear or hatred of those who love or sexually desire those of the same sex." However, Lenskyj (2003: 4) makes the important point that the term homophobia "should not be understood in purely individual or psychological terms" for as will illustrated homophobia is not just about individual acts, rather it is also perpetrated by institutions and institutional practices and operates on a multiplicity of levels.

Any attempt to define terms is inevitably contested, Krane (1996: 238) for instance prefers homonegativism believing it to be a more inclusive term which describes "purposeful, not irrational, negative attitudes and behaviours towards non heterosexuals. Homonegativism incorporates the social context in which negative attitudes towards non-heterosexuals develop and are maintained." Griffin (1998: xv–xvi) explains how she agrees "with the purpose of removing *phobia* from this description", but makes the point that "homophobia is at least recognizable now by many North Americans, and I am reluctant to introduce yet another awkward descriptor to the discussion." I share this sentiment and believe that a similar case would apply in other continents.

Schools have traditionally been entrusted with the education of young and impressionable minds and bodies. As such, the teaching profession has always had a moral responsibility to uphold high standards of conduct in order to fulfil one of its functions that of being a role model for young people. Given the centrality and physicality of the body physical education provides a unique context for the inculcation of particular norms, beliefs and values. These are transmitted both through the formal official and explicit curriculum and the so called hidden curriculum (see Bain, 1990; Fernandez-Balboa, 1993; Kirk, 1992; Laker, 2000; Nutt and Clarke, 2002). However, as Penney has shown in an earlier chapter in this volume the curriculum is socially constructed and always in the making. What appears deeply embedded within the curriculum and counts as valid knowledge is a particular conception of hegemonic masculinity. This conception encompasses sporting prowess, toughness and aggression, and works to marginalize and subordinate other forms of masculinity (and activities) which become constructed as inferior and inadequate, that is those that are not visibly heterosexual. As Fuss (1991: 1) has noted heterosexuality "typically defines itself in critical opposition to that which it is not: homosexuality." As such, homosexuality is defined and constructed as a stigmatised, abnormal and marginal identity that is socially threatening. Thus like other dualisms or binaries these sexual discourses promote (and regulate) a hierarchical order where one of the terms is privileged over the other which is repressed and constrained. In the case of the dialectic of sexuality it is heterosexuality that takes on the privileged, omnipotent position.

For boys successful participation and performance within traditionally male defined activities of the physical education curriculum such as team games provides a form of physical capital that is widely valued, celebrated and reinforced by pupil peer groups. The latter attribute popularity and status to such success and can place "constant pressure on individuals to behave to the expected group norms" (Swain, 2003: 302) factors all contributing to a hierarchy and exalted hegemonic masculinity. Indeed, Renold's (2000, 2002, 2003) ethnographic research with primary aged children (10 and 11 year olds) in England shows that even at a relatively young age unless boys are competent in sport then "their 'heterosexuality' would be called into question and they would often be 'homosexualised' and denigrated as 'gay'" (Renold, 2000: 320); issues I discuss further later in this section.

What I am trying to demonstrate here is how physical education/sport is deemed to make boys into real heterosexual men, and as Pronger (1990: 10) has argued sports (and I would add physical education) provide boys/men with an "apprenticeship in orthodox masculinity". The same can not be said for sporty girls, it is not a rite of passage, sport generally is not deemed to make them into real women, rather the opposite is likely to occur (see Lenskyj, 2003).

That is, if she is a successful sportswoman she can not be a real woman, she has a "femininity deficit" and must be man (see Cockburn and Clarke, 2002). Messner and Sabo (1994: 110) comment "Lesbianism is thus recast by heterosexist culture as an emulation of masculinity. In contrast male homosexuality is considered a negation of masculinity." Clearly socially acceptable and publicly sanctioned forms of masculinity and femininity are intertwined and intimately connected with (hetero)sexuality, but as has been shown masculinity is constructed in sharp contrast to anything deemed to be feminine. Thus if we are to develop a more complete and nuanced understand of the workings out of sexuality and the masculizing processes of physical education it has to be examined in the context and pressures of compulsory heterosexuality (see for instance, Clarke, 1998; Epstein, 1997; Lenskyj, 1986; Renold, 2000; Sykes, 1998).

Discussions about heterosexuality have until recently been largely absent within wider feminist debates. It is somewhat ironic that this task has in the main been undertaken by lesbian theorists such as Butler (1990); Jeffreys (1990); Wilkinson and Kitzinger (1993) and Wilton (1996). These and other theorists have done much to deconstruct and expose the damaging effects of heterosexuality as an institution and practice and also its resultant hegemony over "other" sexualities. It was Rich's (1981: 5) ground-breaking work that drew attention to the need for feminists to critique heterosexuality and to recognize it as a political institution that acted as "a beachhead of male dominance." Hence she argued for the need to view heterosexuality as compulsory for women and to consider the methods by which male power is manifested and maintained. Further, Rich illustrated how women learn to accept compulsory heterosexuality through the idealisation of heterosexual romance and marriage in and through the media, literature, art and so forth.

While it is important to recognize that heterosexuality is experienced differently by different women and men and mediated by a variety of social and cultural factors, just being heterosexual in many countries brings with it certain privileges and legal rights that are denied to lesbian women, gay men or bisexuals, namely: employment and pension rights, marriage, tax allowances and access to other welfare benefits. Thus the state and other institutions such as the church and education reward, subsidise and protect heterosexuality such that it becomes another "regime of truth" (see Foucault, 1977). The resultant dominant discourses by their very exclusions and silences continue to reinforce and legitimize a particular way of being, that is heterosexual. As such heterosexuality is not only legally sanctioned, but also normalised and socially approved. These omissions reinforce commonly held beliefs that homosexuals are not entitled to legal protection and full (sexual) citizenship, and contribute to a situation that Yeatman (1994: 14) has described as "a politics of contested absences". Further, as Connell (1987: 161) notes "Hegemonic heterosexuality … is not a natural fact but a state of play in a field of power and cathexis; at best an ongoing accomplishment." It is therefore essential to recognize how heterosexuality constructs gender and how this impacts on what it is to be a girl/boy; woman/man and how we experience power, subordination and/or oppression within the domain specifically of physical education.

Major research findings

Homophobic and heterosexist oppression

Although my focus is on homophobic and heterosexist oppression it is important to acknowledge the multiplicity and situatedness of oppression and to question the adequacy of oppression as a term. Consequently, I am inclined like Ramazanoglu (1993) to use the term oppression as a relatively loose concept that can be qualified in different situations. Further, I recognize the danger of seeing those who are oppressed as just passive victims (in this case, teachers and pupils) without agency (see Clarke, 2003). Phelan's work is useful in this respect, since she explains that:

Oppression is a word with many contexts and shades … The problems and issues involved in the category of oppression are manifold. When does another impose on me? What sort of power must be involved to make this imposition oppressive? How are we to correct this situation: is it a matter for political action, or a matter for education and social discussion? Are there perhaps many places to deal with aspects of this problem? (1989: 15–16)

This problem manifests itself within the public and highly visible arena of physical education where daily physical performances are open to the scrutiny and judgement of others. Those who fail to perform and/or conform and/or display behavioural characteristics outside of accepted stereotypical heterosexual norms are likely to be ridiculed and subject to homophobic abuse. Boys are judged by their sporting achievements and must prove their heterosexual self – whereas girls are judged less by their physical achievements but rather they are expected to behave in "lady-like" ways and emphasize their femininity (Cockburn and Clarke, 2002). Parker (1996) provides graphic examples of this judgement occurring in boys' physical education, he records that "a practical mistake of any

description … immediately resulted in the children concerned being branded 'fag', 'faggot', or 'queer'". What is increasingly evident is how "The athletic male peer group defines, enforces, and attempts to solidify its boundaries through aggressive misogynist and homophobic talk and actions" (Messner, 2002: 60). Epstein (1997: 113) makes the case convincingly for viewing misogyny and homophobia as inseparable, and as she adroitly says "misogyny is homophobic and homophobia is misogynist". Misogynistic comments are not just made by pupils they may be made by teachers when for example exhorting male pupils to perform better and "not to throw like a girl" or when telling them to stop behaving "like a sissy" or "like a girl".

Another arena where such homophobic and misogynist behaviour can occur is within Initial Teacher Education (ITE). One of the few researchers to draw attention to this was Flintoff (1993, 1998). Her research into secondary initial teacher education in England revealed how male physical education students objectify women, sexualize situations and trivialize other men's performance by suggesting that they "were performing like a 'real nancy' or like a 'girlie'[6] (a derogatory term to describe women PE students)" (p. 81). Further, she revealed how the touching or supporting by men of other men in activities such as dance or gymnastics led not only to questions about their heterosexuality being raised but also homophobic comments being made. Flintoff points out that these comments:

acted to reinforce the display of appropriate "gendered" behaviour by male and female students, but also to make virtually untenable the position of any student (or member of staff) whose sexual orientation is not heterosexual. (1993: 81–2)

Flintoff's research also shows that few male students (the same could be said of boys) actively engaged in dance. This is perhaps unsurprising given that they may be required to display grace and exhibit emotional characteristics in dance all characteristics directly oppositional to those associated with hegemonic masculinity. Yet, as Gard has shown in Chapter 44 although dance continues to be associated by many with femininity and non-heterosexual ways of moving it has the potential to disrupt and contribute to anti-oppressive pedagogies (Gard, 2003a,b). (See also Chapter 39).

My own small-scale qualitative research sought to centre the experiences of nine lesbian physical education students[7] in the 1990s and to make sense of their sexual subjectivities and material realities through life story interviews. Their narratives revealed how they had all been subjected to verbal abuse and harassment by their heterosexual peers (see Clarke, 2000).[8] Comments mostly went unchallenged for fear of making the situation worse, although some of the students at Acresdown stated that they would sit in the front row in lectures in order to avoid comments being made at them and anyone turning round and shouting "lezzie" at them. For these students the verbal abuse they were subjected to often took the form of homo/lesbo phobic jokes as well as comments made about them as "fucking queer" individuals or as the "lezzie group". Adele for example described how the "lads" (their male student peer group) would joke "how can you do without a man?" By and large it was felt that the 'lads' were the main perpetrators of these insults and innuendo. Berni stated that 'the lads in our year can be a bit of a pain …". Eddi also felt that "mostly it is the lads that you get problems off."[9] One of the "problems" Eddi encountered was when one of the lads took her car keys, this followed an incident in the college bar when, as she recalled one of the lads said to Ellie who had been away for a weekend playing hockey in the same team as her said "they are gay, you are, you must be because you hang around there". Although Eddi had seen the lad take her keys she admitted that she "didn't want to make a scene because [I] knew they knew about me and [I] just wanted everything to keep quiet." Keeping quiet meant that she had to walk home as she didn't have her car keys, she later got a call from the college security guard to inform her that her car had been stolen by "the lads" from her year and abandoned outside of Ellie's house. Eddi reasoned that this incident was because she was lesbian and also that Ellie who was heterosexual had "spent a lot of time with the hockey lot and not with him". Berni in trying to explain why the lads behaved as they did remarked "I think they feel really threatened by it and they can't come to terms with it … and it's just like 'oh for god's sake we've been hearing this for four years can you not just give it a rest?' It gets really grating on your nerves."

Although it was the lads who verbally abused these lesbian students Christine pointed out that some of the "girly girls" (that is those who were heterosexual), were on occasions "bitchy" and abusive. She described how the "girly girls have always got boyfriends and their … make up on". The issue at Acresdown was that these "girly girls" were seen as the "worst ones for chatting" about the lesbians. At Longmoor it was the netball team that Helen felt caused "a lot of grief." Helen recalled how in a song the netball club sung to the hockey club finished with "at least we shag the right sex." In reflecting on these comments it is relevant to return to Lees' (1986: 145) early research about sexuality and adolescent girls wherein she found that "many girls expressed marked prejudice against them" [lesbians]. One of her subjects said "Poofs I can tolerate but lesbians I can't. I suppose because it's my own sex" (p. 145).

This is an area that warrants further research insofar us our understanding remains extremely limited about the reasons behind the adopting of such viewpoints.

The students offered some explanations as to why they felt they were seen by their male peers as a real challenge to go out with as opposed to the lesser challenge of going out with a heterosexual student. Dee recalled how the lads had commented to one lesbian student that if she went out with them "it might do you good". Further, Fea outlined how she was approached by one of the lads who said "I can cure you … come with me", she replied that she didn't want to be cured and told him to "sod off". She also described how "some lads in Berni's year … were saying we'd like to go to bed with you, and we'll sort you out." Other students had had similar comments/suggestions made to them. Jay for example remembered how she had been sitting and chatting to one male student on a minibus when some of the lads passed and she:

> … overheard one of them saying … "I don't know why you are bothering to talk to her you know she's not worth the fucking effort."

For some of the students the situation became much worse when they were attacked on their way home from their last disco at college by a male student from the same college. Following the assault and trial the said male student was given a custodial sentence. One[10] of the students wrote to me about the incident reporting how:

> If this was ever to happen it probably happened at the best time. I was about to leave my cosy little nest and I hadn't realised how much college protected me. I had always argued that being honest and open about my sexuality was the correct thing to do but I realise now I had become too blinkered to what really happens. People can justify attacking others because they *think* [sic] you might be gay. At the moment I think I've taken a step back in my self because I always thought if people were educated about homosexuality and we were visible in time they would not just get used to the idea but they'd actually accept it – it wouldn't be a question of hiding everything. However I can no longer believe that …

What is profoundly disturbing about these vivid examples of homophobic violence is that little attempt has been made "to integrate sexual diversity into the teacher education curriculum" (Kissen, 2002: 2). Yet, as Bedford (2002: 134) remarks "teacher education lies at the heart of combating homophobia and heterosexism and faces breaking the culture of silence"[11]. While agreeing with Bedford it also worth noting that some lecturers like many teachers may feel uncomfortable addressing such issues and perhaps more importantly for "queer scholars, [though few would I suspect openly label themselves such in the also conservative world of physical education teacher education] naming one's sexuality may have adverse consequences in relation to tenure, funding, and promotional opportunities" (Epstein et al., 2003: 105). Further, where there have been some attempts by teacher educators to address issues of sexuality and more specifically lesbian and gay issues resistance may occur "due to the controversy and cultural taboos surrounding non-heterosexual or minority sexualities" (Robinson and Ferfolja, 2001: 124). I have also experienced a degree of resistance and of perceived irrelevance when addressing such issues with both undergraduate and postgraduate students. Gard however provides some ground for optimism in terms of the curriculum in Australia:

> Linking physical education with sexuality, gender equity, and social justice has, at least in one respect, become easier ... as most states have moved to integrate physical education with subject material in "health" (usually defined broadly and equated with words such as "well-being") and what is sometimes called "personal development" ... in other countries a growing recognition of the importance of holistic notions of health is reflected in physical education curricula in many parts of the world. In other words, ample scope exists for making a sound and, perhaps more importantly, officially sanctioned case for linking sport, physical activity, and questions of sexism and homophobia. (2002: 53)

This is a case that is long overdue.

Lesbian and gay physical education teachers – an invisible presence?

So far this chapter has focussed on the experiences of pupils and trainee teachers, what is missing are the experiences of lesbian and gay teachers. When I first started to research the experiences of lesbian teachers for my doctorate in the 1990s the limited research that had been published related only to lesbian physical education teachers in North America (Griffin, 1991; Woods, 1992). Further, this research had failed to address directly the impact of compulsory heterosexuality on lesbian teachers' lives (see Rich, 1981).

It is germane to this discussion to note how Griffin in 1991 recorded that fewer than ten studies have focused, at least in part on the experiences of gay and lesbian educators in the United States. Her ground-breaking research (1991, 1992a, 1992b) illustrated how teachers manage their gay or lesbian identities in school, in doing so she outlines four

categories that her research participants described that they employed: passing, covering, being implicitly out and being explicitly out. These were seen as being part of a continuum, from passing being the safest strategy to explicitly out which involved the most risk. Griffin's research was a participatory project insofar as the intention was that her participants would be empowered through collective reflection and action. Woods (1992) (a doctoral student of Griffin) applies a phenomenological approach based on feminist and oppression theory to describe the experiences of lesbian physical educators in the United States. Her work shows how the majority of her participants concealed their sexual orientation. Woods (1992: 92) comments:

> In a society where homosexuals are stereotyped as child molesters who recruit young children to their so-called deviant lifestyles, female physical educators and coaches are prime targets for homophobic suspicions and accusations.

From her data two identity management techniques emerged: strategies to conceal one's lesbian identity and risk-taking behaviours that could disclose one's lesbian identity. She sub-divided the strategies that they used to conceal their lesbian identity into three categories: (i) passing as heterosexual, (ii) personal censoring/self distancing from students, teachers and administrators; and (iii) personal censoring/self distancing from any association with homosexuality. Woods' (1990) intention was that her research should be a catalyst for dialogue and change. There is no doubt that the former has been accomplished, measuring "degrees" of change though is complex given the largely invisible presence of lesbian teachers.

A very small number of English studies were to follow the lead of the aforementioned researchers (Sparkes, 1994, 1995; Squires and Sparkes, 1996; Clarke, 1996). These studies were significant in that they brought issues around lesbian physical education teachers' lives into the public domain. Of the limited published research Sparkes (1994) has written the life history of a lesbian physical education teacher. His research recorded the daily experiences of oppression she faced and highlighted the range of identity management strategies she employed to protect against threats to her substantial sense of self. Sparkes' research while important in its own right and as a valuable stimulus to other research within this domain, only focused on one lesbian life and moreover was written from the privileged (and relatively safe)[12] position of a white heterosexual male. Although Sparkes acknowledges his social positioning and the responsibilities of authorship and his authority to write about an individual who is a member of a group to which he does not belong, I think there is still much to be said for what hooks (1994: 90) calls the "authority of experience" and the "specialness of those ways of knowing rooted in experience". In relation to this notion of the specialness and uniqueness of experience hooks makes reference to black history courses, which to her concern, are taught in some colleges/universities solely by white people. Her concerns are not that they "cannot know these realities but that they know them differently" (p. 90). The same, I would contend, can be said of heterosexual researchers studying lesbian or gay lives.

Returning to research specifically about lesbians in physical education Squires and Sparkes (1996: 79) succeeded in assisting "the process of fracturing the silence that surrounds issues of sexual identity in the world of PE and sport." They focused on the lives of five lesbian physical education teachers and illustrated how this invisibility and silence impacts upon their daily lives in an oppressive manner. They drew attention to the significance of the spatial dimensions of social interaction as well as illuminating how heterosexism and homophobia shape these teachers' lives in school. The notion of space and in particular city versus rural spaces and where teachers locate their lives is an area worthy of further exploration and one that I engage with later in this chapter.

What all these studies share is a desire to bring the debates about sexual identity and in particular lesbianism into the open. Consequently each provide good "thick" descriptions of the lives of lesbian physical education teachers in secondary schools in England while at the same time also offering some analysis of the factors that have contributed to their oppression. Nevertheless, what seemed to be missing from these accounts was a sustained in-depth theoretical discussion and analysis of the notion and politics of difference and a recognition of the usefulness of applying other theoretical paradigms to explain why lesbian teachers are "compelled" to enact most of their lives within the closet of compulsory heterosexuality. Such claims could also be applied to some of the related research that has taken place in the United States. This is not to deny the importance of the work for instance of lesbian researchers Griffin (1991, 1992a,b, 1993, 1998) and Woods (1990, 1992), indeed their work has had considerable impact on researchers in England. A notable exception to these claims about theory is the work of Sykes (1996: 459) in western Canada on the life histories of six lesbian and heterosexual physical education teachers where she has applied (lesbian) feminist and poststructural approaches to researching sexuality as well as calling "for a shift away from individual lesbian identity toward how institutional discourses constrict and construct lesbian identities." Further, Sykes' (1998: 155) recent writing demonstrates that she has now employed queer and

feminist theories to illustrate how these "theories of sexuality can be combined to examine the relations between lesbian sexuality and heterosexualities …". This important work has been developed in a later paper "Understanding and overstanding: feminist-poststructural life histories of physical education teachers' (2001) to incorporate a sophisticated and in places theoretically complex discussion of speech act theory, deconstruction, psychoanalysis and social postmodernism. She explains how she draws on Culler's (1992) "distinction between understanding, which asks questions the text insists upon, and overstanding, which asks questions the text did not pose" (p. 13). For Sykes "speech act theory and social postmodernism led to understanding while deconstruction and psychoanalytic theory contributed to overstanding" (p. 13).

It is notable that the preceding discussion has focused solely on lesbian physical education teachers, it would be pertinent now to devote the same space to discussing research that has focussed on gay male physical education teachers and or students. It is a sad indictment of much of the physical education profession and wider western society that this is impossible. Such is the hyper-masculine, largely homophobic, heterosexist culture of physical education at least in England that discussion is rendered nigh on untenable. We remain indebted to Sparkes (1997, 2002) for constructing an ethnographic fiction of a gay male physical education teacher Alexander. Sparkes (2002: 166) explains "I produced it for pedagogical reasons, and I had critical intentions, in an attempt like that of Duncan (1998), to speak for the absent other – in this case, gay, male physical education teachers." Given this fact I propose to leave this absence albeit paradoxically to speak for itself.[13] Part of the reason for the absence is related to the way in which the spaces we inhabit are neither pure nor innocent, for not only are they gendered, but they are also racialized, sexed and (hetero)sexualized. Space is not neutral, it is as Bell et al. (1994: 32) claim "socially and culturally encoded." For these reasons, it is unsurprising that gay men appear to "choose" not to enter the terrain of physical education departments. Further, while "A whole body of work is emerging in geography that explores the performance of sexual identities and the way that they are inscribed on the body and the landscape" (Bell and Valentine, 1995: 8) with few exceptions (Bensimon, 1992; Clarke, 1998a; Prendergast and Forest, 1997; Shilling, 1991; Thorne, 1993) this analysis has largely escaped the educational context in general and physical education specifically. The ensuing discussion seeks to begin to redress this by revealing the significance that space has for the contestation, construction, and constraining of sexual identities on the educative landscape.

Identity spaces and the heterosexual landscape of physical education

Shilling (1991: 23) in a seminal paper on "Social space, gender inequalities and educational differentiation" made the case that "Space is no longer seen merely as an environment in which interaction takes place, but is itself deeply implicated in the production of individual identities and social inequalities." Hence my interest in how space impacts on sexual identities and how subsequently we come to express ourselves and the places we inhabit. For me, space is not static, rather it is dynamic, fluid and liable to destabilize in the face of queer challenges (see Ingram et al., 1997).[14] So, whilst space may influence and shape who we are, we can act back on space such that the spaces for sexual citizenship can be redrawn and enlarged. Space is more than mere terrain, it is as Blunt and Rose (1994: 5) state "constituted through struggles over power/knowledge." Therefore we need to ask what sort of educative terrain do we have, who controls it and more importantly who has access to it? What does the physical education landscape look like, what could it become? It is clear that the terrain is no smooth landscape; rather it is arguably pitted and hideously scared by a sexual hegemony that puts up borders to maintain the sanctity and normalcy of heterosexuality. These borders necessitate crossing and negotiation, and for some this is a matter of ease, but for those teachers, trainees or pupils on the margins the "right" heterosexual identification papers may be missing, thus the borders that constitute identity may unite or simultaneously divide. In reflecting on the multiple borders that are erected in physical education around ability, performance, appearance, femininity, masculinity and sexual identity we can begin to envisage how those who don't conform to heterosexual hegemonic definitions of what it is to be "normal" feel alienated not only from the subject per se but also potentially from themselves, their bodies and others. The tensions that some must be gripped by as they enter the gymnasium are barely imaginable. It is thus beholden upon us all to make schools, physical education departments and universities safer and more inclusive spaces for all (see Kumashiro, 2002; Remafedi, 1994; Treadway and Yoakam, 1992).

Homophobic bullying and harassment and the power of a name

Rivers' (1995, 2000, 2001) ongoing research demonstrates the widespread extent of bullying in schools of lesbian and gay pupils and those perceived to be

so. Further, the research for the report "*Playing it safe*" (1997) commissioned by the Terence Higgins Trust[15] and Stonewall[16] and undertaken by Douglas et al. (1997) found from a questionnaire survey and telephone interviews with teachers that over eighty per cent were aware of homophobic bullying in their schools. In making sense of their findings Douglas et al. used the following definition of bullying which they rightly acknowledge is fairly narrow, but they wanted to distinguish between other forms of bullying and the type of bullying which their study was concerned with. Thus:

> Homophobic bullying takes place where general bullying behaviours such as verbal and physical abuse and intimidation is accompanied by or consists of the use of the terms such as gay, lesbian, queer or lezzie by perpetrators. (Douglas et al., 1997: 12)

The use of these and other pervasive and derogatory terms warrant closer attention, given as Wallace (2001: 9) notes "The word gay has suddenly become the ultimate putdown in schools – even nursery children are using it to insult each other." Such situations are particularly disturbing as language transmits the moral and heterosexual order and language acts are as Unks (1995: 110) states "acts of power". Thus name calling can be seen as a way of policing the boundaries of heterosexuality.

Physical education is one distinct site where there continue to be rigid ways of being physically and emotionally literate, hence for those who fail or who step out of these boundaries homophobic and heterosexist insults abound, albeit not always well documented (see for example Clarke, 2002; Parker, 1996). Such insults are powerful and effective ways of ensuring that sexual difference remains policed and largely invisible. Rivers' (1995: 37) research reveals that "The school yard was the most likely place for bullying to occur, followed by school corridors … roughly equivalent levels of bullying occurred in … the changing rooms …" (see also Rivers, 2001). Plummer (1999: 242) makes the point that "Change rooms [sic] are also less open to public scrutiny, and the supervision of change rooms can be limited by homophobia – by the risk for teachers of seeming too interested." Yet, verbal abuse remains largely unchecked in schools.[17] As Sykes (2004: 83) contends:

> students' involvement in homophobic name-calling may be more complicated than it first appears. Name-calling can have as much to do with complex, contradictory ways of protecting a vulnerable self as intentionally inflicting harm on others.

Lees' (1987: 177) research revealed that "lezzie" was the worst label that a girl could be called, far worse than a "'slag' (a girl who sleeps around) or a 'drag' (a 'nice' girl who does not …)". Sanders and Burke (1994: 69) also note that "lezzie" is used as an insult and as a means to "pressure the 'other' to conform to stereotypical roles." It is no wonder that given such pressures girls and women frequently disengage from active participation in physical education and sport. Boys are also pressurised into conforming, Lees (1993: 90) claims "that it is far worse for a boy to show feminine qualities than for a girl to show masculine qualities." Masculine identity is constructed in critical opposition to heterosexual femininity and anything deemed to be associated with femininity is subordinated and stigmatised. For a boy to be labelled a "wimp", "sissy", "poofter" and/or "gay"[18] is one of the most virulent forms of insult (Askew and Ross, 1988; Duncan, 1999). A lack of interest in sport can lead to such a label being applied (Thurlow, 2001). Little seems to have changed viz the power of a name, as Paechter argues:

> the abusive form of these terms is of course derived from homophobia; the reason that it can be oppressive to be called 'gay' or 'lesbian', whether you are or not, is that lesbians and gay men are, in fact stigmatised both in and outside school. (1998: 104)

Physical education is unquestionably an arena where homophobic bullying and heterosexist harassment not only of pupils but also of teachers occurs (see Clarke 1996, 1997, 2002). The failure in most cases to respond to this is worrying as schools, that is headteachers and teachers in the UK have a responsibility to prevent any form of bullying (see Renold, 2003).

Although I am unable to describe here the myriad of behaviours that constitute harassment, for the purposes of this research I utilize Halson's (1991: 99) working definition that "Whatever its particular form, the behaviour in question is experienced as humiliating, embarrassing, threatening … It offends, it objectifies, it denies autonomy, it controls." I share Epstein's view (1996: 203) that in order to develop "a fuller understanding of sexist harassment we need to see it within the context of … 'compulsory heterosexuality' …". These points are helpful in that they draw attention to just how powerful the discourses of heterosexuality are and how institutionalised they are within the educative system. Epstein points out how harassment can be understood "as a kind of pedagogy of heterosexuality" (p. 203) "… which schools women and men into normative heterosexuality (but not always successfully)" (p. 207). In other words girls, women, boys and men are schooled within physical education and elsewhere into appropriate ways of behaving sexually, that is heterosexually.

The harassment the lesbian teachers[19] in my research had been subjected to was mainly from pupils, in school this often took the form of name calling, such as "lezzie", "dyke", "homo", and/or "queer" and in some instances graffiti also appeared around the school about a teacher's lesbianism. The women ignored the verbal comments as much as possible for fear of bringing too much attention to themselves. Challenging prejudice for some is not worth the possible risk entailed unlike some of the teachers involved in Sykes' research. Sykes (2004: 75) postulates in a recent and insightful paper about teacher responses to homophobic name calling in physical education that teachers engage in what she calls pedagogies of injury "that is, they recalled their personal experiences of homophobic language to teach students not to use words such as 'fag', 'dyke', and 'queer' … [she] speculates that an unconscious masochistic imperative may also animate this approach to anti-homophobic education".

The performance of sexual identity

Whilst identities are clearly paradoxical I also want to make the case that *all* identities involve acts of performance (see Dhairyam, 1994; Esterberg, 1996; Goffman, 1959) in which we all collude whether willingly or not (Inness, 1997). But at the same time it must be recognized that not all identities are necessarily imbued with the same degree of status or normalcy as heterosexual identities and further these performative acts need to be acknowledged as an inescapable part of lesbian life.[20] Moreover, it is this notion of performance which in the case of sexual minorities might additionally be interpreted as a way of resisting, disrupting and perhaps ultimately contributing to the dismantling of the hegemony of heterosexuality. Such claims provide a means of understanding the ways that some lesbian women and in this particular case lesbian teachers successfully (re)negotiate their sexual identities in the educational context through the performance and enactment of pseudo-heterosexuality. In order to support these contentions I draw selectively on Butler's (1990, 1991, 1993) concept of gender performativity. Although I am unable to analyse the complexities of her work here it does provide a point of departure and a useful metaphor to play with. In connection with this I employ with due caution some of the terms that she uses when she interrogates the process of drag in order to demonstrate that sexual identities can be "appropriated, theatricalized, worn and done" (Butler, 1991: 21). This notion of the theatre is a helpful one as schools and physical education lessons are rather like stages where all sorts of performances are daily engaged in by all the actresses and actors therein.

In considering the metaphor of performance it is also worth paying attention to some of the limitations of such analogies, Jeffreys (1994a) for example raises concerns about the dangers of simply viewing identity as a performance since she believes this could create the situation whereby the oppression of women by men is lost sight of. Additionally, Jeffreys (1994b: 462) sees Butler's notion of performance and drag as being based on largely gay male practices, further she criticises Butler specifically for "… fail(ing) to recognise that lesbians might have different interests, a culture and traditions of their own …". Further, Bell et al. (1994: 33) point out that "Drag may endorse misogyny and reinforce cultural stereotypes, denying that masculinity and femininity are historical not biological facts through virtue of men not being able to dress or 'pass' as well as 'real women.'"

Whilst these are valuable points the concept of performance is still a useful one to employ as it gives us an insight into the lives that many lesbian women are forced to (enact and) live out. Like Connell (1995: 385) I recognize that the emphasis on sexuality as performance does not necessarily involve much more "in the sense of a politics capable of getting rid of the homophobia" that is the ever present reality for many lesbian women. Hence, while it would be a mistake to reduce our understandings of sexual identity to issues solely around the performance of a particular part, the concept of performance must remain as a factor in any analysis of sexual identity and the notion of resistance.

Major trends and future directions … shaping the future

Although the past two decades has witnessed an increasing body of research and writing that has focused on sexuality in physical education this review has demonstrated that the heterosexual status quo remains largely intact. Interrogating the concept of compulsory heterosexuality remains essential if we are to appreciate how sexuality and sexual identities continue to be constructed and constrained within the domain of physical education. Such an understanding serves to demonstrate its pervasive and damaging power to determine the ways in which lives can be lived out in schools. In addition, it has been shown that all identities involve acts of performance and by viewing them as such useful insights can be gained into the ways in which lesbian teachers in particular are "forced" to live out their lives within schools.

The unique context and "space" of physical education with its emphasis on the physical body has also been shown to be a prime site for the manifestation and institutionalization of heterosexism and homophobia in both the teaching and content of physical education. It is imperative to disrupt this

hegemony and recognize the multiplicities of masculinity and femininity if we are to achieve more just, inclusive and anti-oppressive learning environments within physical education. This is not to deny that there has been some progress in the latter particularly in the United States and Australia.

In terms of the direction of future research a number of the issues warrant consideration. Firstly, much of the research cited has focussed on the lives of white able-bodied lesbian women; thus it would be valuable to understand the experiences of lesbian and gay teachers of colour (and those of different social class, age and so forth) within physical education and how this mediates their experiences within schools. However, given the traditions of teacher education and physical education this would be no easy task, further, to locate differently abled lesbian or gay physical education teachers would be almost an impossibility given the able bodied traditions of the subject. Nevertheless, it would be useful to later revisit these same women or men to see whether they are still teaching, and if so, what impact their sexual identity visible or invisible has had on their career pathways. Further, it would be informative to interview "out" heterosexual teachers about their attitudes towards working with lesbian and gay colleagues. What might be most revealing would be to track lesbian and gay physical education students through their training and teaching career. Such research might thereby enable the "testing" of the efficacy of these theoretical frameworks and tools to gain further insights into the lives of lesbian and gay teachers.

Finally, in considering future work in this and related fields of study certain issues are beginning to emerge which are worthy of further in-depth study, these include:

- the impact of space on sexual identities and in particular rural versus city locations;
- the notion of sexual identity as a form of resistance;
- the concept of identity as performance and subversion;
- the power of secrets and silence.

By exploring such issues we may begin to better understand how those on the margins make sense of and live out their lives.

Thus whilst it is evident that sexual boundaries are fluid we need to construct a counter discourse to examine and challenge the privileging of heterosexuality.

Additionally if we value and respect diversity and want to create a climate in physical education where an individual has the right to choose and enact their sexual identity then the goal of social justice together with the pursuit of anti-oppressive pedagogies must be continued if we are to cross boundaries and secure safe spaces for the articulation and celebration of our differences and the destruction of the sexual apartheid which operates within many schools. As Young (1990: 3) suggests "social justice means the elimination of institutionalized domination and oppression." However, this is unlikely to be achieved without cultural transformation (see Irigaray, 1993). In other words until the (heterosexual) values that structure the wider social order and the micro world of physical education are changed many will continue to be denied the right to full sexual citizenship and the spaces within physical education to create a landscape that enables all to define their lives.

Notes

1 Some see homosexuality as a disorder to be treated and cured, see for instance the JIM (Jesus in Me) campaign material, see also note 3 below.

2 This was first repealed in 2003 by the devolved Scottish Parliament.

3 These debates are not dissimilar to those currently being promulgated by some evangelical Christian organizations, see for instance Griffin's (1998) chapter "We prey, they pray? Lesbians and evangelical Christians in sport".

4 I use this term loosely to refer to all locations where physical education is taught.

5 Flintoff (1998: 306–7) explains how this term "was used by male students to describe and control women students in the same kinds of ways that terms like 'slag' are used by boys in school contexts (Halson, 1991; Lees, 1987). The term 'girlie' had two connotations; on the one hand it was used to describe women who were worth 'pursuing' sexually, on the other it was used to describe women's inferior physical abilities. It is significant to note the resilience of such a term within PE ITE: it was in common usage at both institutions, and it is a term which is commonly used amongst students in other ITE institutions, including the one in which I work."

6 This research drew on the life stories of nine white, able-bodied lesbian PE students. The students from Acresdown were aged between 19 and 23 and came from a variety of working and middle class backgrounds. Two were in their second year (Eddi and Fea) and four were in their fourth and final year of study (Adele, Berni, Christine and Dee). These individual interviews all took place in the same student flat over a period of two days. All the participants selected a pseudonym, the only proviso being that they select any name with a specific letter so as to aid me with remembering the sequencing of the interviews. Hence at Acresdown the first interviewee's name began with an "A", the second with a "B" and so forth up to the letter "F". Glenwood Institute of Higher Education was the location for the next interview, this was with a fourth year student Gina who was aged 26. The final two interviews were conducted at Longmoor College of Higher Education, the first took place in a "safe" house, as Helen who was 19 and in her second year of study had not disclosed her sexual identity to all her flatmates. The last interview was with Jay who was 22 and in her fourth year.

The three institutional names are also pseudonyms; the institutions were located in either a city or large town.

7 The evidence of the alarming incidence of campus discrimination, harassment and hate crimes against lesbian and gay students has been well documented by D'Augelli (1989a) and Herek (1989) in the United States and by Trenchard and Warren (1987) and Fahey (1993) in England. See also the more recent work of Rhoads, 1994.

8 D'Augelli (1989b) and Clift (1989) also found in their research that male students had more negative and less tolerant attitudes towards lesbians and gay students than their female counterparts.

9 I have intentionally omitted any name here in order to further protect the identity of the student as her parents were unaware that this assault had occurred.

10 Mathison (1998) provides a useful list of "Actions for Teacher Educators" to enable them to better prepare students to teach gay and lesbian students.

11 It is worth noting that the Tooley (with Darby, 1998) Report on "Educational Research: A critique" (sponsored by OFSTED) critiqued Sparkes' (1994) paper (and others) from the *British Journal of Sociology of Education* and referred to it in some detail in the section "Partisanship in gender and race research" (p. 37). Tooley (1998: 37) states "The paper sets out to show moments of Jessica's life to illustrate the oppression under which she lives. However, if readers had expected many graphic details, they will be disappointed. Hardly anything is related which could possibly qualify as homophobia and oppression." The Tooley Report was widely reported in the press, the *Daily Mail* (23 July 1998: 13) captioned their article "School researchers 'wasting £70m on irrelevant studies'". In this article Halpin reports Tooley's and Darby's findings as well as singling out three studies for "special treatment" namely: "THE LESBIAN", "THE RACIST", "THE EXPERT". The lesbian refers to Sparkes' research.

The research community responded vigorously to this attack, the British Educational Research Association responded via their President Margaret Brown who contributed to the *Independent*'s "Right of reply" column the day after the Tooley Report was published. In a letter to David Blunkett, MP she was also critical of the Tooley Report. Hodkinson (1998: 17) in the British Educational Research Association Newsletter in an article aptly titled "Naivete and Bias in Educational Research: The Tooley Report" wrote "The result, far from an objective, rigorous investigation of research quality is biased, naïve and deeply flawed rhetorical demolition."

I have included comment in some detail here as the Tooley Report and the press reporting of it as it appears in some ways reminiscent of McCarthyism and other "witchhunts"/persecutions of those deemed to be on the margins and/or threatening to the social order. Thus, although I claimed that Sparkes' position was "relatively safe" (since Sparkes' paper was written he has been promoted to a personal chair) undoubtedly this reporting brought attention that he would unlikely have chosen for himself.

12 Sykes (2004) refers to one gay male PE teacher she worked with in North Carolina, albeit we get only a brief view of his life in school.

13 I use the term Queer activists to refer to groups who have begun to fight back through direct (in your face) action and through the formation of such oppositional groups as OutRage in London and Queer Nation in New York. These and other groups have staged various challenges to the assumed heterosexuality of places, spatial pushes in London have included a mass KISS-IN in Piccadilly Circus and a Queer Wedding in Trafalgar Square, both of which were organized by OutRage (see Clarke, 1998a; Bell, 1995). Being queer involves reclaiming an identity and label that was pejorative. It is to be visible, to be playful, to engage in parody and performance; to be queer is to be inclusive, to recognize diversity and to blur the sexual boundaries. It is also the rejection of sexual and gender binaries, labels and "normative" moralities. However, it needs to be asked if queer politics are hostile/oblivious to lesbian feminist politics, and whether the agenda is too narrow and based on a particular "brand of gay male politics?" (Jeffreys, 1994a: 175). For a more detailed discussion see Clarke (1998b).

14 The Terence Higgins Trust is a national HIV and AIDS charity based in London.

15 Stonewall is a national civil rights group working for legal equality and social justice for lesbians, gay men and bisexuals, it too is based in London.

16 Gay, Lesbian, and Straight Education Network (GLSEN) "surveys show that on average, lgbt high school students hear anti-gay epithets twenty-five times a day. A more distressing statistic is that 97 per cent of teachers fail to respond" (Page and Liston, 2002: 72).

17 Duncan (1999: 19) comments "'Gay' seemed to have duality of meaning against boys in much the same way as 'slag', 'cow' or 'dog' were used against girls. The word was recognized as meaning homosexual, but for most purposes it denoted a wider negative male role ... ".

18 The 14 white, able bodied lesbian teachers involved in the research from 1993 to 1995 were from the outset given pseudonyms. They taught in a variety of secondary schools (i.e. mixed comprehensives, girls' schools, church and independent schools) and were aged between 23 and 47, some had just started their teaching careers, whilst others had been teaching for over 25 years. Their schools were located in inner cities, urban and or rural areas. Some were single, some had been married, some were currently in long-standing relationships, and none had children. They came from a variety of working and middle class backgrounds. Making contact and gaining access was difficult due to the prevailing climate of fear of exposure and loss of employment that surrounds lesbian (and gay) teachers and forces many of them to remain an invisible and silent presence within our schools. Contact was therefore initially made through lesbians known to me, who contacted other lesbians, to see if they were willing to talk in confidence about their lives. This created a "snowballing" effect where one woman put me in contact with another and so forth. Contact was also made in this manner because such are the silences and the relative secrecy that it is not always possible to identify through any other method with any degree of certainty those women who are lesbian.

A biographical methodology was utilized as an approach particularly well suited to gaining a closely textured account of lesbian lives within the educational system and for interpreting data generated by the life story interviews. As well as offering a detailed examination of selves in specific settings the research was additionally concerned to make visible the structural and interactional injustices confronting lesbian teachers. For more details about the research process, see Clarke (1997, 1998b,c).

19 I am unable to comment on gay lives.

References

Askew, S. and Ross, C. (1988). *Boys don't cry: Boys and sexism in education*. Milton Keynes, UK: Open University Press.

D'Augelli, A.R. (1989a). Lesbians' and gay men's experiences of discrimination and harassment in a university community *American Journal of Community. Psychology*, 17(3): 317–321.

D'Augelli, A.R. (1989b). Homophobia in a university community: views of prospective research assistants. *Journal of College Student Development, November, 30*: 546–552.

Bain, L.L. (1990). A critical analysis of the hidden curriculum in physical education. In D. Kirk and R. Tinning (Eds.), *Physical education, curriculum and culture: Critical issues in the contemporary crisis* (pp. 23–42). London: Falmer Press.

Bedford, T. (2002). Queer developments in teacher education: addressing sexual diversity, homophobia, and heterosexism. In R.M. Kissen (Ed.), *Getting ready for Benjamin: Preparing teachers for sexual diversity in the classroom* (pp. 133–142). New York: Rowman & Littlefield Publishers.

Bell, D. (1995). Bell, pleasure and danger: the paradoxical spaces of sexual citizenship. *Political Geography, 14*(2): 139–153.

Bell, D., Binnie, J., Cream, J. and Valentine, G. (1994). All hyped up and no place to go. *Gender, Place and Culture, 1*(1): 31–47.

Bell, D. and Valentine, G. Eds. (1995). *Mapping desire: Geographies of sexualities*. London: Routledge.

Bensimon, E. (1992). Lesbian existence and the challenge to normative constructions of the academy. *Journal of Education, 174*(3): 98–113.

Blunt, A. and Rose, G. (Eds). (1994). *Writing women and space: Colonial and postcolonial geographies*. London: Guildford Press.

Butler, J. (1990). *Gender trouble: Feminism and the subversion of identity*. London: Routledge.

Butler, J. (1991). Imitation and gender insubordination. In D. Fuss (Ed.), *Inside/out lesbian theories, gay theories* (pp. 13–31). London: Routledge.

Butler, J. (1993). *Bodies that matter: on the limits of 'sex'*. London: Routledge.

Carabine, J. (1995). Invisible sexualities: sexuality, politics and influencing policy-making. In A.R. Wilson (Ed.),

A simple matter of justice? Theorizing lesbian and gay politics (pp. 91–109). London: Cassell.

Clarke, G. (1996). Conforming and contesting with (a) difference: how lesbian students and teachers manage their identities. *International Studies in Sociology of Education*, 6(2): 191–209.

Clarke, G. (1997). Playing a part: the lives of lesbian physical education teachers. In G. Clarke and B. Humberstone (Eds.), *Researching women and sport* (pp. 36–49). London: Macmillan.

Clarke, G. (1998a). 'Working out: lesbian teachers and the politics of (dis)location. *Journal of Lesbian Studies*, 2(4): 85–99.

Clarke, G. (1998b). *Voices from the margins: lesbian teachers in physical education*. PhD dissertation, Leeds Metropolitan University.

Clarke, G. (1998c). Queering the pitch and coming out to play: lesbians in physical education and sport. *Sport, Education and Society*, 3(2): 145–160.

Clarke, G. (2000) (pp. 75–94). Crossing borders: lesbian physical education students and the struggles for sexual spaces. In S. Scraton and B. Watson (Eds.), *Sport, leisure identities and gendered spaces*. Eastbourne: Leisure Studies Association.

Clarke, G. (2002). Difference matters: sexuality and physical education. In D. Penney (Ed.), *Gender and physical education: Contemporary issues and future directions* (pp. 41–56). London: Routledge.

Clarke, G. (2003). There's nothing queer about difference: challenging heterosexism and homophobia in physical education'. In S. Hayes and G. Stidder (Eds.), *Equity and inclusion in physical education and sport: Contemporary issues for teachers, trainees and practitioners* (pp. 91–104). London: Routledge.

Clarke, G. (2004). Threatening space: (physical) education and homophobic body work. In J. Evans, B. Davies and J. Wright (Ed), *Body knowledge and control. Studies in the sociology of physical education and health* (pp. 191–203). London: Routledge.

Clift, S.M. (1989). Lesbian and gay issues in education: a study of the attitudes of first year students in a college of higher education. *British Educational Research Journal*, 14(1): 31–50.

Cockburn, C. and Clarke, G. (2002). "Everybody's looking at you!": Girls negotiating the 'femininity deficit' they incur in physical education. *Women's Studies International Forum*, 25(6): 651–665.

Connell, R.W. (1987). *Gender and Power: Society, the person and sexual politics*. Cambridge, UK : Polity Press.

Connell, R.W. (1995). Democracies of pleasure: thoughts on the goals of radical sexual politics'. In L. Nicholson and S. Seidman (Eds.), *Social postmodernism: Beyond identity politics* (pp. 384–397). Cambridge, UK: Cambridge University Press.

Dewar, A. (1991). Feminist pedagogy in physical education: promises, possibilities, and pitfalls. *Journal of Physical Education Recreation Dance*, 62(6): 68–71, 75–77.

Dhairyam, S. (1994). Racing the lesbian, dodging white critics. In L. Doan (Ed.), *The lesbian postmodern* (pp. 25–46). New York: Columbia University Press.

Douglas, N., Warwick, I., Kemp, S. and Whitty, G. (1997). *Playing it safe: Responses of secondary school teachers to lesbian, gay and bisexual pupils, bullying, HIV and AIDS education and section 28*. Health and Education Research Unit, Institute of Education: University of London.

Duncan, N. (1999). *Sexual bullying: Gender conflict and pupil culture in secondary schools*. London: Routledge.

Epstein, D. (1996). Keeping them in their place: hetero/sexist harassment, gender and the enforcement of heterosexuality. In J. Holland and L. Adkins (Eds.), *Sex, sensibility and the gendered body* (pp. 202–221). London: Macmillan.

Epstein, D. (1997). 'Boyz' own stories: masculinities and sexualities in schools. *Gender and Education*, 9(1): 105–115.

Epstein, D., O'Flynn, S. and Telford, D. (2003). *Silenced sexualities in schools and universities*. Stoke on Trent, UK: Trentham Books.

Epstein, S. (1993–1994). Gay politics, ethnic identity: the limits of social constructionism. *Socialist Review, May–August*: 9–54.

Esterberg, K.G. (1996). "A certain swagger when I walk": performing lesbian identity. In S. Seidman (Ed.), *Queer theory/sociology* (pp. 259–279). Oxford: Blackwell.

Evans, D.T. (1989–1990). Section 28: law, myth and paradox. *Journal of Critical Social Policy*, 9(3): 73–95.

Evans, D.T. (1993). *Sexual citizenship: the material construction of sexualities*. London: Routledge.

Faderman, L. (1991). *Odd girls and twilight lovers: A history of lesbian life in Twentieth-Century America*. London: Penguin.

Fahey, W.S. (1993). Lesbian and gay men's experiences of peer discrimination and harassment in higher education. Unpublished paper.

Fernandez-Balboa, J-M. (1993). Sociocultural characteristics of the hidden curriculum in Physical Education. *Quest*, 45: 230–254.

Fletcher, S. (1984). *Women first: The female tradition in english physical education 1880–1980*. London: Athlone Press.

Flintoff, A. (1993). One of the boys? Gender identities in physical education initial teacher education. In I. Siraj-Blatchford (Ed.), *'Race', gender and the education of teachers* (pp. 74–93). Milton Keynes, UK: Open University Press.

Flintoff, A. (1998). Sexism and homophobia in physical education: the challenge for teacher educators. In K. Green and K. Harman (Eds.), *Physical education: A reader* (pp. 291–313). Aachen: Meyer and Meyer Publishing.

Foucault, M. (1977). *Discipline and punish: the birth of the prison*. London: Penguin.

Fuss, D. (1991). Inside/out. In D. Fuss (Ed.), *Inside/out lesbian theories, gay theories* (pp. 1–10). London: Routledge.

Gard, M. (2002). What do we do in physical education? In R.M. Kissen (Ed.). *Getting ready for Benjamin: Preparing teachers for sexual diversity in the classroom* (pp. 43–58). New York: Rowman & Littlefield Publishers.

Gard, M. (2003a). Being someone else: using dance in anti-oppressive teaching. *Educational Review*, 55(2): 211–223.

Gard, M. (2003b). Moving and belonging: dance, sport and sexuality. *Sex Education*, 3(2): 105–118.

Goffman, E. (1959). *The presentation of self in everyday life.* New York: Doubleday Anchor Books.

Griffin, P. (1987). *Homophobia, lesbians and women's sports: an exploratory study.* Paper presented at the 95th annual convention of the American Psychological Association, New York.

Griffin, P. (1991). Identity management strategies among lesbian and gay educators. *Qualitative Studies in Education,* 4(3): 189–202.

Griffin, P. (1992a). From hiding out to coming out: empowering lesbian and gay educators. In K.M. Harbeck (Ed.), *Coming out of the classroom closet* (pp. 167–196). New York: Harrington Park Press.

Griffin, P. (1992b). Changing the game: homophobia, sexism, and lesbians in sport. *Quest,* 44(2): 251–265.

Griffin, P. (1993). Homophobia in women's sports the fear that divides us. In G.L. Cohen (Ed.), *Women and sport: Issues and controversies* (pp. 193–203). London: Sage.

Griffin, P. (1998). *Strong women, deep closets: Lesbians and homophobia in sport.* Champaign, IL: Human Kinetics.

Griffin, P. and Genasci, J. (1990). Addressing homophobia in physical education: responsibilities for teachers and researchers. In M.A. Messner and D.F. Sabo (Eds.), *Sport, men and the gender order: Critical feminist perspectives* (pp. 211–221). Champaign, IL: Human Kinetics.

Griffin, P. and Harro, B. (1997). Heterosexism curriculum design. In M. Adams, L.A. Bell and P. Griffin (Eds.), *Teaching for diversity and social justice: A sourcebook* (pp. 141–169). London: Routledge.

Hall, M.A. (Ed.). (1987). The gendering of sport, leisure, and physical education. *Women's Studies International Forum,* 10(4). Special Issue.

Halson, J. (1991). Young women, sexual harassment and heterosexuality: violence, power relations and mixed-sex schooling. In P. Abbott and C. Wallace (Eds.), *Gender, power and sexuality* (pp. 97–113). London: Macmillan.

Harris, M.B. and Griffin, J. (1997). Stereotypes and personal beliefs about women physical education teachers. *Women in Sport and Physical Activity Journal,* 6(1): 49–83.

Hastings, S. (2004). Homophobia. *Times Educational Supplement May 28:* 12–14.

Herek, G.M. (1989). Hate crimes against lesbian and gay men. Issues for research and policy. *American Psychologist,* 44(6): 948–955.

Hodkinson, P. (1998). Naïveté and bias in educational research: the Tooley Report. *British Educational Research Association Newsletter,* 65: 16–17.

Hooks, B. (1994). *Teaching to transgress: Education as the practice of freedom.* London: Routledge.

Ingram, G.B., Bouthillette, A.M. and Retter, Y. (Eds.). (1997). *Queers in space: Communities/public spaces/sites of resistance.* Seattle, DC: Bay Press.

Inness, S.A. (1997). *The lesbian menace: Ideology, identity, and the representation of lesbian life.* Amherst, MA: University of Massachusetts Press.

Irigaray, L. (1993). *Je, Tu, Nous: Toward a culture of difference.* London: Routledge.

Jeffreys, S. (1990). *Anticlimax: A feminist perspective on the sexual revolution.* London: The Women's Press.

Jeffreys, S. (1994a). *The lesbian heresy: A feminist perspective on the lesbian sexual revolution.* London: The Women's Press.

Jeffreys, S. (1994b). The queer disappearance of lesbians: sexuality in the academy. *Women's Studies International Forum,* 17(5): 459–472.

Kirk, D. (1992). Physical education, discourse, and ideology: bringing the hidden curriculum into view. *Quest,* 44: 35–56.

Kissen, R.M. (Ed.) (2002). *Getting ready for Benjamin: Preparing teachers for sexual diversity in the classroom.* New York: Rowman & Littlefield Publishers.

Krane, V. (1996). Lesbians in sport: toward acknowledgement, understanding, and theory. *Journal of Sport and Exercise Psychology,* 18: 237–246.

Kumashiro, K. (2000). Towards a theory of anti-oppressive education. *Review of Educational Research,* 70(1): 25–53.

Laker, A. (2000). *Beyond the boundaries of physical education: Educating young people for citizenship and social responsibility.* London: Routledge Falmer.

Lees, S. (1986). *Losing out: Sexuality and adolescent girls.* London: Hutchinson.

Lees, S. (1987). The structure of sexual relations in school. In M. Arnot and G. Weiner (Eds.), *Gender and the politics of schooling* (pp. 175–186). London: Unwin Hyman.

Lees, S. (1993). *Sugar and spice: Sexuality and adolescent girls.* London: Penguin.

Lenskyj, H. (1986). *Out of bounds: Women, sport and sexuality.* Toronto, Canada: Women's Press.

Lenskyj, H. (2003). *Out on the field: Gender, sport and sexualities.* Toronto, Canada: Women's Press.

Mathison, C. (1998). The invisible minority: preparing teachers to meet the needs of gay and lesbian youth. *Journal of Teacher Education, March-April,* 49(2): 151–155.

Messner, M. (2002). *Taking the field: Women, men and sports.* Minnesota: University of Minnesota Press.

Messner, M. and Sabo, D. (1994). *Sex, violence and power in sports: Rethinking masculinity.* Freedom: The Crossing Press.

Nixon, D. and Givens, N. (2004). "Miss, you're so gay." Queer stories from trainee teachers. *Sex Education,* 4(3): 217–237.

Nutt, G. and Clarke, G. (2002). The hidden curriculum and the changing nature of teachers' work. In A. Laker (Ed.), *The sociology of sport and physical education: An introductory reader* (pp. 148–166). London: Routledge Falmer.

Paechter, C. (1998). *Educating the other: Gender, power and schooling.* London: Falmer Press.

Page, J.A. and Liston, D.D. (2002). Homophobia in the schools: student teachers' perceptions and preparation to respond. In R.M. Kissen (Ed.), *Getting Ready for Benjamin: Preparing teachers for sexual diversity in the classroom* (pp. 71–80). New York: Rowman & Littlefield Publishers.

Parker, A. (1996). The construction of masculinity within boys' physical education. *Gender and Education,* 8(2): 141–157.

Phelan, S. (1989). *Identity politics: Lesbian feminism and the limits of community.* Philadelphia, PA: Temple University Press.

Plummer, D. (1999). *One of the boys. Masculinity, homophobia, and modern manhood.* New York: Harrington Park Press.

Prendergast, S. and Forrest, S. (1997). Hieroglyphs of the heterosexual: learning about gender in school. In L. Segal (Ed.), *New sexual agendas* (pp. 180–195). London: Macmillan.

Pronger, B. (1990). *The arena of masculinity.* New York: St Martins.

Ramazanoglu, C. (1993). *Feminism and the contradictions of oppression.* 2nd. edn. (1st. edn, 1989). London: Routledge.

Renold, E. (2000). "Coming out": gender, (hetero)sexuality and the primary school. *Gender and Education, 12*(3): 309–326.

Renold, E. (2002). Presumed innocence: Heterosexual, heterosexist and homophobic harassment among primary school girls and boys. *Childhood, 9*(4): 415–434.

Renold, E. (2003). "If you don't kiss me, you're dumped": boys, boyfriends and heterosexualised masculinities in the primary school. *Educational Review, 55*(2): 179–194.

Rhoads, R.A. (1994). *Coming out in college: The struggle for a queer identity.* Westport: Bergen and Garvey.

Rich, A. (1981). *Compulsory heterosexuality and lesbian existence.* London: Onlywomen Press.

Rivers, I. (1995). The victimization of gay teenagers in schools: homophobia in teacher education. *Pastoral Care, March*: 35–41.

Rivers, I. (2000). Social exclusion, absenteeism an sexual minority youth. *Support for Learning, 15*(1): 13–18.

Rivers, I. (2001). Playing it safe: addressing the emotional and physical health of lesbian and gay pupils in the U.K. *Journal of Adolescence, 24*: 129–140.

Robinson, K.H. and Ferfolja, T. (2001). "What are we doing this for?" Dealing with lesbian and gay issues in teacher education. *British Journal of the Sociology of Education, 22*(1): 121–133.

Sanders, S.A.L. and Burke, H. (1994). Are you a lesbian Miss? In D. Epstein (Ed.), *Challenging lesbian and gay inequalities in education* (pp. 65–77). Buckingham, UK: Open University Press.

Scraton, S. (1992). *Shaping up to womanhood: Gender and girls' physical education.* Buckingham, UK: Open University Press.

Sears, J.T. (1997). Thinking critically/intervening effectively about heterosexism and homophobia: a twenty-five-year research retrospective. In J.T. Sears and W.L. Williams (Eds), *Overcoming heterosexism and homophobia: Strategies that work* (pp. 14–48). New York: Columbia University Press.

Shilling, C. (1991). Social space, gender inequalities and educational differentiation. *British Journal of Sociology of Education, 12*(1): 23–44.

Smith, A.M. (1990). A symptomology of an authoritarian discourse the parliamentary debates on the promotion of homosexuality. *New formations: A journal of culture/theory/politics, 10*: 41–65.

Smith, A.M. (1994). *New right discourse on race and sexuality: Britain, 1968–1990.* New York: Cambridge University Press.

Sparkes, A. (1994). Self, silence and invisibility as a beginning teacher: a history of lesbian experience. *British Journal of Sociology of Education, 15*(1): 93–118.

Sparkes, A. (1995). Writing people: reflections on the dual crises of representation and legitimation in qualitative inquiry. *Quest, 47*: 158–195.

Sparkes, A. (1997). Ethnographic fiction and representing the absent Other. *Sport, Education and Society, 2*(1): 25–40.

Sparkes, A. (2002). *Telling tales in sport and physical activity: A qualitative journey.* Leeds, UK: Human Kinetics.

Squires, S. and Sparkes, A. (1996). Circles of silence: sexual identity in physical education and sport. *Sport, Education and Society, 1*(1): 77–101.

Stacey, J. (1991). Promoting normality: Section 28 and the regulation of sexuality. In S. Franklin, C. Lacey and J. Stacey (Eds), *Off centre feminism and cultural studies* (pp. 284–304). London: Harper Collins.

Swain, J. (2003). How young schoolboys become somebody: the role of the body in the construction of masculinity. *British Journal of the Sociology of Education, 24*(3): 299–314.

Sykes, H. (1996). Constr(i)(u)cting lesbian identities in physical education: feminist and poststructural approaches to researching sexuality. *Quest, 48*: 459–469.

Sykes, H. (1998). Turning the closets inside/out: towards a queer-feminist theory in women's physical education. *Sociology of Sport Journal, 15*(2): 154–173.

Sykes, H. (2001). Understanding and overstanding: feminist-poststructural life histories of physical education teachers. *Qualitative Studies in Education, 14*(1): 13–31.

Sykes, H. (2004). Pedagogies of censorship, injury, masochism: teacher responses to homophobic speech in physical education. *Journal of Curriculum Studies, 36*(1): 75–99.

Thorne, B. (1993). *Gender play.* Buckingham, UK: Open University Press.

Thurlow, C. (2001). Naming the "outsider within": homophobic pejoratives and the verbal abuse of lesbian, gay and bisexual high-school pupils. *Journal of Adolescence, 24*: 25–38.

Tooley, J. with Darby, D. (1998). *Educational research: A critique. A survey of published educational research.* London: OFSTED.

Treadway, L. and Yoakam, J. (1992). Creating a safer school environment for lesbian and gay students. *Journal of School Health, September, 62*(7): 352–357.

Trenchard, L. and Warren, H. (1987). Talking about school: the experiences of young lesbians and gay men. In G. Weiner and M. Arnot (Eds.), *Gender under scrutiny: New inquiries in education* (pp. 222–230). London: Unwin Hyman.

Unks, G. (Ed.). (1995). *The gay teen: Educational practice and theory for lesbian, gay and bisexual adolescents.* London: Routledge.

Wallace, W. (2001). Is this table gay? Anatomy of a classroom insult. *Times Educational Supplement, 19 January*: 9–10.

War on Want. (1997). *Pride world-wide: Sexuality, development and human rights.* London: War on Want and Unison.

Weeks, J. (1986). *Sexuality*. Chichester and London: Ellis Horwood and Tavistock.

Wilkinson, S. and Kitzinger, C. (Eds.) (1993). *Heterosexuality. A feminism and psychology reader*. London: Sage.

Wilton, T. (1996). Which one's the man? The heterosexualisation of lesbian sex. In D. Richardson (Ed.), *Theorising heterosexuality: Telling it straight* (pp. 125–142). Buckingham, UK: Open University Press.

Woods, S. (1990). *The contextual realities of being a lesbian physical educator: living in two worlds*. EdD dissertation, University of Massachusetts.

Woods, S. (1992). Describing the experiences of lesbian physical educators: a phenomenological study. In A.C. Sparkes (Ed.), *Research in physical education and sport: Exploring alternative visions* (pp. 90–117). London: The Falmer Press.

Yeatman, A. (1994). *Postmodern revisionings of the political*. London: Routledge.

Young, I.M. (1990). *Justice and the politics of difference*. New Jersey: Princeton University Press.

6.2 Race and ethnicity in physical education

LOUIS HARRISON, JR. AND DON BELCHER

Introduction

While discourses of racial and ethnic differences and the unique challenges they bring to teaching and the preparing of future educators is wanting in educational literature (Apple, 1999), it is particularly absent in physical education discussions. Even though it may be politically correct and acceptable to display behaviors and attitudes that embrace racial neutrality, many social scientists and philosophical views indicate that "race matters" (e.g. Coakley, 2004: 283–323; Eitzen and Sage, 2003: 285–306). The role of race, in comparison to gender and class, still remains largely under-theorized (Tate, 2003) and discourse on this topic is long overdue (Carter and Goodwin, 1994). In physical education it is time for frank, constructive, and productive discussion of racial and ethnic issues. Though America prides itself on being a cultural melting pot, noted author and curriculum theorist William Pinar warns:

> We say "we are what we know." But, we are also what we do not know. If what we know about ourselves – our history, our culture – is distorted by delusions and denials, then our identity – as individuals, as Americans – is distorted (Pinar, 1994: 245) All Americans are racialized beings; knowledge of who we have been, who we are, and who we will become is a story or text we construct. (p. 247)

Though it is understandable that researchers may steer clear of controversial topics for fear of uncovering offensive findings, it is the responsibility of the academy to continue in its quest for knowledge. The caution should not focus on what the results may uncover, but on the research perspective, cultural sensitivity of the researcher, and better understanding of the culture of those being studied.

This lack of cross cultural research has created a conspicuous void in the physical education and physical education teacher education (PETE) body of knowledge. The failure to address these issues creates a vacuum that leaves future teachers and students at a major disadvantage in preparing to navigate an ever increasingly diverse world.

Because of the critical mass of research and the authors' expertise, this work is primarily focused on the African-American experience. This in no way is meant to minimize the importance of experiences of other racial/ethnic groups. To the contrary, the intent was to avoid the trivialization and distortion that often occurs when one does not share the perspective of those under study. This is also not to suggest that the research on other people of color in other places does not exist, but the limitations of time, space and expertise serve to limit the scope of this work.

Historical perspective

In most historical accounts of the development of physical education and sport, there is a conspicuous absence of discussions of race and ethnicity. In fact in Van Dalen, Mitchell, and Bennett's book (1953) on the *World History of Physical Education*, the author chronicles the history of the discipline in countries such as India, Italy, Germany, Finland, and others. Other than the mention of Egypt, there is a obvious absence of information regarding countries on the African and Australian continents.

Leonard (1947) in his book *A Guide to the History of Physical Education* alludes to the development of physical education in Negro schools in South Africa but neglects to mention the influence of African-Americans in sport in the US. He points out research on racial differences did not reveal anything of significance. In fact the author states that their research failed to support "superior prowess" (p. 429).

Hackensmith (1966) gives a brief summary of "Negro Institutions" of 1938. Surprisingly the author reports the findings from a Thesis by O.A. Moore in 1938 that found that of the directors of Health and Physical Education in Negro Institutions, 23% were member of AAHPERD (American Alliance for Health Physical Education and Recreation), and 27% had published articles in professional journals (p. 459). Aside from this mention of professional roles the only other minority reference is with regard to the context of slavery.

Dixon et al. (1973) is one of the few authors that addresses the racial factors along with the complexities and opportunities for change that integration brought to sport in the early twentieth century in the US. In the chapter by Munrow (pp. 149–173) the author suggests that racial prejudices were overcome by an emphasis placed on winning in sport. He further stated that interracial understanding was promoted through competitive sport and the value of sport in "breaking down racial barriers" (p. 170). While many would disagree with this conclusion, at least the author attempts to address the issue.

One of the earliest historical accounts fo the African American in sport and physical education was done by E.B. Henderson. Henderson provides a rather detailed chronology of the development of Negro sport leagues as well as the racial integration of African-Americans into American sport. He also discusses the participation of African-Americans in professional writings of Negroes in sport and physical education

Historical and social influences have and continue to encumber people of color's access to education and are interwoven with stereotypical perceptions of their abilities in academic and physical domains. Implied and expressed communications, perceptions, and values reflecting the dominant culture' portrayal of people of color are transmitted through the hidden curriculum in schools (Bain, 1990; Fernández-Balboa, 1993; Kirk, 1992). In the gym the transmission of these ideas have significantly influenced students' and teachers' ways of knowing and practice. Stereotypical messages that are still implicit in physical education curricula, are thought to be constructed to maintain positions of privilege, and enforce discrimination against individuals' participation in specific sports practices or physical activities in physical education classes. Because schools are sites of acculturation, students, teachers and coaches have over the years unconsciously promoted stereotypical views of racialized physical education and sports activities, reinforcing pervasive racial stereotypes regarding physical superiority in particular activities and consequential intellectual inferiority. Because of prevalent stereotypes many students of color may be channeled into participation in a narrow range of physical activities while members of the dominant culture may be steered away from these very activities (Harrison et al., 2004) creating racial physical activity segregation that is often observed in many unstructured gymnasiums and unfortunately, in many unstructured physical education classes.

Historical reviews of research on African Americans indicates that most of the research and on people of African descent revolves around developing explanations for superior performance (Miller, 1998; Wiggins, 1997). Miller contends that this research ignored the long heritage of segregation and racial prejudice that isolated people of color. These isolating arrangements contributed to the development of identifying movement styles and means of expression that distinguished ethnic and racial groups. Most of this research focused on genetic, biological, physiological, or anthropometric variables which in essence disregarded the hard work and discipline as well as creativity involved in sport performance. In their review of racial research in motor development, Barnes et al. (1999) point out a couple of important constructs. The first reminds us that dynamic systems theory diminishes the importance of the race dichotomy in that race is only one of many variables that interact and therefore contribute to one's motor development. These authors also question the initial motivations of previous research on racial differences. If the purpose is to formulate developmental norms by race, given that race is a continuous variable at best and a social variable in the view of many, then for whom are the norms beneficial? This reminds us all to be more aware of the fact that all research has at its root a specific agenda that the conclusions must be re-contextualized within.

Core concepts

Defining race and ethnicity

Defining race as a biological or genetic variable, has a historically ominous and questionable reputation with regard to sport and physical activity (Miller, 1998; Wiggins, 1997). The lines of demarcation between races are at best profoundly blurred and drawn arbitrarily. The investigation of genetic and biological basis for determining racial groups has been deemed futile and consist of "lose and leaky" categories that are inherently inconsistent (Dole, 1995). Even geneticists reiterate the fact that their research does not subscribe to the idea of race as a biological or genetic identity (Census, race and science, 2000). The broad conception of race focuses on one's appearance and common physical characteristics such as skin color, hair texture and facial features.

An ethnic group is a group of individuals organized around a common cultural origin or ancestry. The focus of ethnicity is in the commonality of a groups cultural origin and less on physical characteristics. Ethnicity refers to the cultural heritage of a particular group and is not based on biological or genetic traits but on cultural traditions and background (Coakley, 2004).

The important difference between race and ethnicity is that the perception of race is often based on physical features which in most instances can easily be observed and ascertained. Because these differences are easily observable, people with different physical characteristics are socially identified with belonging to particular races. This, in most cases, makes them easily distinguishable, and susceptible to the social, behavioral, stereotypical, and discriminative social influences that are encountered both consciously and unconsciously. With regard to this chapter, race is considered a social variable that reveals a common socio-political history (LaVeist, 1996). Belonging to a particular racial group has more to do with shared social experiences than shared genetic material. But it is recognized that the physical characteristics lend much to the social consequences of belonging to a particular race.

Works in the realm of race and sport such as Hoberman (1997), and Entine (2000), utilize marginally credulous studies to focus on ostensibly genetic racial factors to reinforce biological determinism and cloud the empirical realities of how racism manipulates and complicates patterns of identity, sport, and social distinction. Few have questioned the way racial categories have been shaped, the agenda of the investigators, nor the social and historical factors that significantly influenced these supposedly value neutral scientific studies (Barnes et al., 1999; Miller, 1998).

Demographic changes

The importance of this topic is amplified when one considers the increasing diversity of the public school population and the corresponding decreasing diversity of the teacher candidates within PETE programs. The most recent census of the United States indicates a decreasing trend in the nations's White population from 75% to 69% and a corresponding increase in minority populations with Latinos representing the fastest growing minority group (Rendon, 2003). The enrollment of minorities in US public schools has risen substantially (National Center for Education Statistics, 1999). Concurrent with student demographic change is the counter trend occurring in teacher preparation programs (Villegas, 1990) where the population of prospective teachers is predominantly White and female.

These opposing trends make evident the necessity to examine PETE programs, practices, and content to answer the call of preparing culturally sensitive teachers (Stanley, 1995) and insuring the creation of positive learning environments for all students. Although the number of students of color are increasing in colleges and universities, there has been no corresponding increase in the number of teachers of color. This increases the probability that many White female novice teachers will be assigned to urban schools where the majority of the students are of a different race, ethnicity or culture (Stroot and Whipple, 2003). Consequently, "Children may perceive that only majority race teachers are qualified and competent to teach and be in instructional and sport leadership positions" (Smith, 1993: 67). Indeed Yeo (1997) thinks that part of the urban education's cycle of failure rests within teacher education programs, which fail to respond to the needs of the schools and may (consciously or unconsciously) encourage negative perceptions of urban teaching. Prospective teachers may become discouraged, uninterested and unprepared to teach in urban schools.

The National Center for Education Statistics (1999) suggests that only 20% of teachers surveyed perceived that they were adequately prepared to work with students from diverse racial, ethnic, or cultural backgrounds. Most beginning teachers are prepared to work effectively mainly with white middle class students. These beginning teachers often think and act in terms of their own schooling experience as white middle class students. This scenario is prevalent in many urban schools and extends a formidable challenge to students and teachers alike (Ennis, 1995). With the small numbers of PETE students of color and current population trends, it appears the racial and cultural divide between teachers and students will continue to grow in the foreseeable future. Physical education's objective of meeting students' movement, fitness, and health needs while preserving relevance and maintaining a sense of identity and connection (Cothran and Ennis, 1999) to the program will be nonexistent if cultural bridges are not built and crossed in preparing future educators.

Major findings

Theoretical and conceptual frameworks

Attempts to explain racial disparity in sport performance and participation patterns in particular sports has been relegated to anthropometric (Meredith and Spurgeon 1980), physiological, biological (Ama et al., 1990), sociological interpretations (Coakley, 2004) and psychosocial explanations (Goldsmith, 2003; Harrison et al., 1999a,b). Anthropometric, biological and physiological theories are thought to be largely unsubstantiated (Hunter, 1998), and few, if any preclude their studies with a clear genetic definition of race or include in their methodology how the race of the participant was determined. Nevertheless, there are still those who hold to the idea of race linked innate physical capabilities. Currently two theoretical bases appear to have the most potential to explain participation patterns; self schemata and racial identity.

Self-schemata

More and more researchers are ascribing to social and pshycosocial rationalizations for the differences in performance and participation patterns in particular sports by race. Sport sociologist Jay Coakley (2004) posits that when there is (1) a history of racial ideology that emphasizes innate, race-based physical abilities; (2) a long history of racial segregation and discrimination that limits opportunities for those who are discriminated against; (3) the existence of many opportunities and encouragement to develop skills in a few sports; then this leads to belief in a biological and cultural destiny to excel in those sports. Furthermore, if this group is motivated to develop the skills needed to fulfill their destiny and are given the necessary motivation and opportunities to develop skill in these limited sports, those with the necessary physical characteristics will be superior athletes in these sports. It is easy to envision the application of this theory to African-Americans in sports such as basketball, football, and track (p. 293).

Some researchers view the disparity in sport participation by race as rooted in the psychological concept of self-schema. Self-schemata are perceptions of one's self stemming from prior experiences. These cognitive structures develop from efforts to explain one's behavior in a particular domain (e.g. sport, physical activity). Self-schemata are derived from repeated evaluations of one's behavior by the self and others and direct the processing of incoming information about the self that in turn summarizes, explains past behavior, and guides future behavior (Markus, 1977). In the domain of sport and physical activity it is easy to see how the influences of one's environment, expectations, stereotypes, and models can act together to develop specific sport or physical activity self-schemata that lead people with similar traits to view themselves participating in particular activities (Harrison, 1995).

Racial identity

Related to the concept of self-schema is emerging research on the influence of racial identity and its relation to sport and physical activity. All people go through a process of delineating themselves in terms of the social significance that accompanies being a part of a particular racial group. The social construction of these groups tend to vary over time, but the experiences of people differ in very important ways depending on the racial category they belong to (Tatum, 1997). Racial identity development is a socialization process shaped and molded by interaction with family, community, school, and social associations. It is formed by undergoing trials,

experiences and tests that serve to make the individual feel centered and stable by making life predictable (Cross, 1995). An individual will likely tolerate or even invite a change in their environment, a change in one's identity will likely be disturbing and unsettling.

Cross (1995) delineates the complex metamorphic process whereby African-Americans "become Black." This process in which American blacks develop a frame of reference for thinking about and evaluating themselves in terms of being "Black" is called Nigrescence (Cross, 1995; Helms, 1985). This process is depicted as a resocializing experience that directs one's pre-existing racial identity from Eurocentric to Afrocentric. Cross's comprehensive model of African-American racial identity development furnishes a reasonable and analytical framework for the understanding of the development of sport and physical activity preferences and participation. This model accomplishes this while supporting the understanding of the relationship of racial identity development and sport and physical activity (Brown et al., 2003; Harrison et al., 2002).

African-American racial identity development

To bring understanding to the actions of students in urban settings, which are largely students of color, it is critical to have an understanding of the students' identity development process. In the case of African-American students, Tatum (1997) suggests that most African-American adolescents have encountered environmental cues that activates an examination of racial issues and activates a quest for racial identity. This sets the stage for entry in what Cross (1995) calls the Immersion-Emersion stage where African-American youth begin to styles of dress and engage in activities that identify their "Blackness." Engaging in physical activities that do not fit into a perceived "black" category may be avoided to avoid "acting white." Also, African-American students at this stage not only tend to display a disengagement from their White peers who "don't get it" and develop closer ties with African-American youth who readily validate and identify with the student's experiences and feelings (Tatum, 1997). This will often be expressed through the desire to engage in physical activities that are perceived as "Black" and a resistance to engage in activities that are labeled as "White" or any activity outside their perception of competence.

European-American racial identity development

European-American youth on the other hand have the opportunity to try on several identities and can still return to the privilege that comes with paler pigmentation (Belcher, 2003b). Similarly Helm (1985) has theorized European American Racial Identity Development into several stages. At "Contact" EA's are unaware of racism and its effects (indeed many may have had little or no actual contact with non-whites) and thus they claim to view people through color-blind lens denying the salience of race. At the next stage "Disintegration" there is an over-reliance on stereotypical rationale for inequality while peers may pressure them to accept myths as facts. But EA's begin to question what they have been socialized to believe about non-whites. Next "Re-integration" calls for the recognition of inequality to lead to blaming the victim for perceived shortcomings with minimal attention to institutional forms of racism. Calls for teaching a "common-culture" and an acceptance of white racial superiority may appear at this juncture. With further critical examination EA's may move to the next stage, "Pseudo-independence" where they acknowledge the political, social, and economic implications of race and can at least intellectualize the negative impact of racism. Further along development calls the stage "Immersion-Emersion" where they explore what it means to be white in a racist society. When EA's can integrate a sense of self as a white person and become proactive in non-racist behavior they have achieved the final stage of Autonomy.

Racial and ethnic preferences for particular sports and physical activities

Available research indicates that racial preferences for particular sports and physical activities exists and are linked to pervasive societal stereotypes (Harrison, 2001). Recent studies on racial influences in sport and physical activity preferences and participation patterns indicates that racial groups display varying proclivities toward and conceptions of appropriateness of particular sports and physical activities (Ainsworth et al., 1992; Bungum and Vincent, 1996; Goldsmith, 2003; Harrison, 1999; Harrison et al., 1999a). In the imagination of many Americans there is no demarcation between what might occur in physical education class and the world of sport. In general, particular sports such as football, basketball and track sprinting are regarded as more appropriate for African-Americans with sports such as golf and hockey deemed more appropriate for European-Americans. The "X-Games" and the "alternative" activities within are quickly becoming an European American venue or refuge. Examples that have been researched are windsurfing and skateboarding (Wheaton and Beal, 2003). Interesting to note that to this point when concerns

about "race and sport" materialize African-Americans have been the focal point of a majority of the research and theoretical reasoning. As Johal (2001) states, "In popular and academic debates focused around sport and race ... the term race is reduced to, or conflated with being black" (p. 155). The focus on African-Americans' sporting ability (Entine, 2000; Hoberman, 1997) has privileged European-Americans' as a norm by which other racial/ethnic categories are to be judged (Carrington and McDonald, 2001). Whiteness has thus escaped sustained examination (Kusz, 2001; Long and Hylton, 2002). Consequently African-American's are hypervisible and European-American's appear to be invisible (Gallagher, 2003). Confounding this "invisibility" are decades of research where participants have been unlabeled in terms of race/ethnicity and many "norms" have been produced with White European-American males as the sample in question yet unquestioned in terms of generalizability to other populations. As Tate (2003) postulates

> The fact that 'whiteness' has gone unexamined for so long is a function of the power of paradigmatic thinking in the social sciences. The predominant viewpoint in the social sciences has been that people of color lack many of the characteristics associated with being white, thus the focus of scholarship has been on documenting these differences or examining interventions designed to remedy these so-called deficiencies. (p. 121)

Even within teacher education this has been problematic. A search of the North American (recognized internationally) *Journal of Teaching in Physical Education* (JTPE) has seldom utilized race as a pertinent reference point for discussion (Belcher, ongoing). Recently, much literature within JTPE has utilized the context of "urban" schools as a means of getting around discussion of race. Unfortunately, this term is utilized not just to mean a densely populated area but may serve as a symbolic code for many detrimental societal effects (low SES, high crime, lack of focus on learning) and a perpetual war zone. Not critically examined is how this urban plight has been created in no small part by White flight.

The concept of racial identity or the application of racial identity theory has not been utilized in physical education research. Interestingly, racial identity theory appears to have potential for explaining the resistance of African-American students in physical classes to engage in activities outside of those stereotyped for African-Americans. Many physical educators express feelings of exasperation when their African-American students, particularly boys, express their desire to engage exclusively in basketball. Obviously a unidimensional curriculum that consists of playing basketball everyday is not in the best interest of students. Unfortunately, many physical educators fail to seek an understanding of this pattern and simply label students as disinterested and uncooperative. Ennis (1996) indicated in her teacher interviews that physical educators that they perceived African-American boys as unskilled in other team and individual sports. These students were easily embarrassed when rendered unsuccessful in public and basketball was a vehicle for displaying athletic talent. For students in this context it would be important to for physical educators to create an environment that is engaging, has meaningful content (Ennis et al., 1997), and develop a curriculum that is culturally responsive to the needs of students (Ladson-Billings, 1995). Ennis (1998) further found that "White teachers often assume that sports typically played by white men are relevant and meaningful for all students. … Students find little meaning in sports not valued within the culture and do not engage in the curriculum" (p. 756).

The issue of competence and racial identity becomes even more complicated when the issue of Black male masculinity is considered. Majors (1998) posits that institutional and other forms of racism have evolved a society where the idea of masculinity has been impressed upon African-American males, but opportunities for legitimate expression are limited. In this frustrating environment African-American males seem to have become obsessed with evidencing their masculinity in the limited venues available. One means of exhibiting masculinity is through creativity in sport. Majors suggests that sport is one of the few places where African Americans perceive equal opportunity. Harrison et al. (2002) proposes that sport is "one of the few places where an African American man can be a man" (p. 131).

Until urban teachers are made aware of these kind of issues, it will be difficult to get beyond the difficulties faced in physical education classes in these settings. Unfortunately, many efforts to provide multicultural education are so watered down and devoid truly useful content. A substantive study of the cultures one will encounter in the physical education class, along with the associated values and beliefs of the students (DeSensi, 1995) are critical to developing a culturally relevant pedagogy and engaging curriculum. Forcing students of color in to a curriculum that consists of activities created by the dominant culture may create an atmosphere of meaninglessness and induce disengagement. When students are simply coerced into activities with no rationale and that are often considered irrelevant, Ennis (1995, 1996) suggest that we may nudge students into a state of noncompliance and even confrontation. At the same time the curriculum should not be allowed to deteriorate to one of "roll out the basketball' mentality. This abdication of responsibility for implementation of a meaningful curriculum

guarantees the participation of an elite group of skilled players, but does nothing to address the needs of lesser skilled students. Moreover, this type of negotiated curriculum fails to meet the true needs of even skilled participants by impeding the acquisition of other skills and knowledge that may better serve them maintaining a healthy lifestyle in their latter years. Without this critical examination of curriculum in-action there is the potential for the perpetuation of myths and stereotypes. The current treatment of multicultural education as "additive" rather than "transformative" within physical education (Chepyator-Thomson and Hsu, 2004) indicates a continued pattern of normalizing a Eurocentric curricular focus (Yeo, 1997).

Major trends and future directions

Sport or physical education: the current dilemma

Several decades ago Lawson (1979) recognized the futility of providing a narrow range of familiar sports as the content and curriculum of a physical education program for African-American (and urban) youth. Even then Lawson recognized that many physical education programs in urban communities consisted of either "play" periods or "pseudo-military training" under the guise of sport (p. 191). These programs serve merely as energy release opportunities for "motor minded" students to experience success (p. 191). While some research, consciously or unconsciously, appears to disparage the urban physical education and sport environment (Pope and O'Sullivan, 2003), few have ventured to understand the context and unique experiences that have led to the development of today's urban "gym scene." The narrow focus of most urban physical education programs may reflect the preferences of students and serve to insure social and skill level segregation. Admittedly, this environment may not be the most conducive for low or unskilled students, but arguable it has produced some of the best athletes in sport. The factors that regulate the urban sport and physical education environment may significantly shape the racial participation levels in some sports (Carlston, 1983).

However, the present focus on lifetime physical activity runs contrary to the typical urban physical education program. This makes a lifestyle of physical activity for these children of color even less likely. School physical education programs can and should provide the foundation for a lifetime of physical activity and improved health status. This is far less likely to occur in the absence of meaningful physical activity instruction and exposure to lifetime physical activities. While mere exposure is inadequate to ensure a lifetime of physical activity, the absence of exposure can significantly decrease the likelihood of students ever engaging in these activities. It is not difficult to realize that one is not likely to continue to play basketball and other vigorous team sports into middle age and older adulthood. When the individual can no longer participate in these activities and there is a perception that no other viable activities exist, the only alternative is a sedentary existence and the health complications that accompany it (Harrison, 1995). Kumanyika and Adams-Campbell (1991) attest that the risk of diabetes, hypertension, and coronary artery disease is markedly elevated in the African-American population. Furthermore, compared to European-Americans, body fat percentages are lower for African-American males up to age 35 when the pattern reverses with African-Americans possessing higher percentages of body fat. It is around this age when participation in vigorous team sports are no longer viable. While the influence of heredity, and diet cannot be ignored, neither can the potential benefits of regular physical activity.

Obesity is more prevalent among minorities, particularly African-Americans, than other ethnic groups. Again, this malady is not confined to adults. African-American children are more likely to be overweight or obese than children in other ethnic groups. The stereotypic conception of African-American youth with regards to physical activity and sports evokes images of physically fit and healthy athletes. The reality, however, is quite different. A recent report from the Surgeon General (1996) and Healthy People 2010 (USDHHS, 2000), indicate that obesity is increasing at a much higher rate among African-American youth than is true of youth in other groups. Contrary to the stereotypical portrayal of the physically fit African-American athlete, these studies report that African-Americans are more sedentary, less fit, experience higher occurrences of hypertension, diabetes, coronary heart disease, and some types of cancer than the majority population. All of these health maladies are closely linked to obesity. Also, it is likely that the stereotypical image of the athletic African-American, despite the contradictory reality, has acted to limit research efforts to address this problem (Harrison, 2001).

Racial issues in physical education teacher education

PETE students

To address demographic changes mentioned earlier and develop culturally sensitive and responsive teachers, PETE programs must make the multicultural facet of the curriculum a priority. Superficial attempts at infusing multiculturalism into PETE programs do little to prepare prospective teachers for the diversity and "reality shock" (Stroot and Whipple, 2003) that beginning teachers experience when employed in urban school districts. DeSensi (1995) stresses the need for the study of cultures, values and beliefs of other cultures, particularly those that prospective teacher will incur, are crucial to the success of the first year teacher. This is particularly important if the teacher has little or no background or exposure to other cultures, races, or ethnic groups. Unfortunately many students in PETE programs have gone through their schooling experience with very little exposure to people of color or people of different socio-economic status. Additionally, many who can claim to have exposure with people of color tend to be in superior status positions. Many students can matriculate through grade school and college having few if any teachers of color. Allport (1954) suggested that to reduce prejudice interactions with individuals of equal status is necessary.

Some report that their teacher education experiences has minimal influence on their racial awareness. While some programs focus on awareness of other cultures, few raise the question of self-racial awareness. When teacher education classes are predominantly White, it is difficult to understand experiences with racism from different perspectives. Further, there is the danger that the discussion will privilege White viewpoints (Johnson, 2002). Limited exposure to other groups will likely lead to development of stereotypical beliefs and inaccurate expectations based on skewed media portrayals and other erroneous sources of information.

This can ultimately to lead to the two extremes of unrealistic optimism or unwarranted pessimism (Proctor et al., 2001). Unrealistic optimism is found in PETE students who display a degree of naivety or patronizing attitude toward children of color that may come from rescue fantasies. These prospective teachers often display a immature racial identity development and insist that they don't notice color. Some scholars suggests that neglecting or refusing to recognize the privilege of being White makes it difficult for teachers to view race as part of the social hierarchy, and thus locate themselves within that hierarchy (Johnson, 2002; Lawrence, 1997). These inexperienced PETE students are prone to early dismay when they don't experience immediate success.

Those that exhibit unwarranted pessimism have embraced the negative stereotypes pervasive in urban settings. They harbor low expectations for student learning and often allow these expectations to illicit self-fulfilling prophecies. Teacher expectations can exert a considerable impact on the students by consciously or unconsciously communicating their views through verbal and nonverbal communication and differential modes of feedback about student performance (Wigfield and Harold, 1992). This is particularly true of young children whose keen observational abilities extract expectations from subtle differences in verbal and nonverbal communication (Babad et al., 1991) while at a stage in which they are especially malleable and will acquiescent to teacher expectations. Culturally inept teachers may harbor low expectations for learning in children of color, but because of pervasive stereotypes, hold high expectations for physical abilities or specific sport performance. Thus perpetuating the racist dialogue that creates and reinforces the binary opposition of intelligence and athletic ability. Either of these may be detrimental to students of color. McMillian (2003) further states that outcome based education proposals such as "No Child Left Behind" may make achievement gaps more pronounced as "achievement is being framed as inferior performance, not inferior treatment" (p. 30) between the interactions of teachers and their racially diverse students.

It would appear that the simple solution to the problem is the development of more teachers of color who can readily address the needs of the growing number of children of color in urban schools. There are some efforts to recruit students of color into teacher education programs, and these efforts do have merit. Diversifying PETE programs can give voice to alternate perspectives and allow White students to experience different world views. Pittman (2003) suggests that most PETE programs include little formal cultural training or informal cultural interaction, thus limiting their ability to produce culturally sensitive teachers. Many universities are also challenged by the accreditation standard IIB of the National Council for Accreditation of Teacher Education (NCATE) that assess the racial composition of teacher candidates (Gallavan et al., 2001). This standard is to insure that the university recruits, admits, and retains a diverse student body. Recent challenges to affirmative action initiatives will likely limit efforts in this realm.

Many researchers are advocating the implementation of diversity training initiatives in PETE program to develop culturally sensitive and responsive teachers (Burden et al., 2004; Johnson, 2002; Proctor et al., 2001). These authors contend that future professionals prepared in ethnocentric programs, that is programs where cultural diversity is either excluded or minimized, have little probability of successful experiences when teaching in urban schools. Potent diversity training that requires PETE students to reflect on the cultural relevancy of their teaching will result in teachers that are better equipped to handle the cultural dissonance White teachers experience when teaching students of color.

Proctor et al. (2001) also recommends the preparation of students for teaching students of color by organizing carefully planned field experiences in culturally diverse school settings. Furthermore, students must also be prepared for these environments to increase opportunities for successful experiences. Students must also have the opportunity to share their experiences so that overly pessimistic or optimistic ideas can be constructively challenged. Students should also be prepared in teaching methodology that fosters coordination and cooperative learning to enhance positive cross-cultural experiences. Cooperative teaching methods such as the "jigsaw classroom" (Aronson and Gonzalez, 1988) can easily be applied to the physical education setting (e.g. Harrison and Worthy, 2001). PETE students should be consistently exposed culturally diverse literature and evaluated on their knowledge of anti-racist teaching techniques and methodology. Articles from practitioner journals (e.g. Harrison and Worthy, 2001; King, 1994; Sparks, 1994) should be used to supplement traditional texts and given as much regard as traditional methods or techniques. If cultural relevant pedagogy is treated as an aside, students will hardly take it seriously.

PETE faculty

One of the difficulties in enhancing the value of diversity in PETE programs is the lack of diversity in PETE faculty. Crase and Walker (1988) labeled African-American physical education faculty an *endangered species*. In a domain where that includes the study of sport and physical abilities coupled with the fascination with racial differences in sport performance and the preoccupation with the Black body (Azzarito and Solmon, 2004; Pinar, 1994), there are conspicuously few African-Americans involved in the research and preparation of physical education teachers.

Diversification of student population is often given high priority in many predominantly White universities while altering the racial and ethnic composition of faculty receives very little attention (Turner, 2002). The reason for this disparity is seldom investigated, but existing evidence suggest that African-American students, once enrolled in PETE graduate programs have more unfavorable experiences and higher attrition rates than their White counterparts (King and Chepyator-Thompson, 1996). Turner et al. (1999) study of faculty of color and Burden et al.'s study of African-American faculty in kinesiology both suggested that faculty of color at predominantly White institutions perceived that they were neglected, not provided with the necessary mentoring, experienced social isolation, disengagement, and were victims of double standards. Frequently, faculty of color find themselves as the *only one* in their departments, perceive their presence as mere tokenism, and are viewed by peers as hired simply to fulfill affirmative action requirements (Hodge et al., 2004). Obviously, experiences and perceptions like these make diversification of PETE faculty extremely difficult. There is little wonder that so many universities find it extremely difficult to satisfy standard III.B of NCATE (Gallavan et al., 2001).

Scott (1993) lists several recruitment strategies with respect to minority faculty that include strategies such as creating a minority visiting scholar programs, postdoctoral fellowships as an enticement to minorities for permanent faculty positions, exchange programs with historically black institutions, hiring minority students from one's own institution, minority vitae banks, and graduate internships. The recent attacks of affirmative action programs may make some of these recommendations difficult, but organizations that place diversity and inclusions as a priority find ways to implement policies and programs to reach those goals.

Recruiting faculty of color is an important but not sufficient endeavor. Once faculty of color are in academic positions they should be given opportunities to be successful. Because faculty of color, like students of color, face more and different barriers to success, efforts should be made to increase their likelihood of success. Scott (1993) also presents several recommendations for retaining faculty of color that include providing a mentors, access to professional networks, support in research and teaching efforts, reduction of teaching and committee loads, and supporting minority-oriented research. Scott also emphasizes the fact that "it is highly unlikely that the recruitment and retention of minority students will improve unless we first succeed in diversifying faculty populations" (p. 80).

Burden, et al. (2004) advocates the inclusion of PETE faculty in diversity training. This will better equip faculty members to instill culturally relevant pedagogy throughout the curriculum. Engaging in diversity training has the potential to equip PETE faculty to integrate ethnorelative pedagogy into their teaching and subsequently impress upon PETE students the value of diversity and culturally relevant pedagogy. A lack of concern for or the undervaluing of diversity will likely be reflected in PETE students. When PETE faculty perceive the inclusion of faculty of color as insignificant or irrelevant to physical education pedagogy, they will likely ignore it in their teaching (Maruyama and Moreno, 2000). Consequently, PETE students will be deprived of the opportunity and understanding of the import of diversity.

Conclusion

Application of research findings across all populations while ignoring the unique differences and problems that people of color denies the importance of these differences. Moreover, it deprives PETE faculty and prospective teachers of the knowledge and competency to provide the best possible physical education for an increasingly diverse student population. Understanding the cultural, ethnic, and racial differences paves the way to development of culturally relevant pedagogy that responds to the unique need of students of color. A culturally relevant pedagogy will foster an improved physical education for students of color and an increased opportunity for successful teaching experiences for PETE prospective teachers.

Often research findings ignore racial, ethnic or cultural differences or fail to include such information and thus denying research consumers valuable information. Since diversity is increasing and most urban schools are comprised of a majority of minority students, and are largely headed by White teachers and administrators, it is imperative that PETE programs respond to the unique needs of a changing school population. There is a heightened need to increase cultural awareness, provide diversity training, and most importantly, increase diversity in PETE students and faculty.

Note

While the authors recognize that scholarship concerning race and ethnicity in physical education is a global phenomena we have limited the discussion to the context in which we can speak more adeptly. Discussion of race and ethnicity makes most sense when it can be taken within a specific context. Readers are encouraged to seek out similar contexts (i.e. post-colonial studies). Although there has been an increase in this area of scholarship it is important to produce even more to create a enlightened dialog.

References

Ainsworth, B.E., Berry, C.B., Schnyder, V.N. and Vickers, S.R. (1992). Leisure-time physical activity and aerobic fitness in African-American young adults. *Journal of Adolescent Health*, 13: 606–611.

Allport, G.W. (1954). The nature of prejudice. Cambridge, MA: Addison-Wesley.

Ama, P.F., Lagasse, P., Bouchard, C. and Simoneau, J.A. (1990). Anaerobic performances in black and white subjects. *Medicine and Science in Sports and Exercise*, 22(4): 508–511.

Apple, M.W. (1999). The absent presence of race in educational reform. *Race, Ethnicity and Education*, 2: 9–16.

Aronson, E. and Gonzalez, A. (1988). Desegregation, jigsaw and the Mexican-American experience. A clear and concise description of the jigsaw classroom technique for reducing overt prejudice and discrimination. In P. Katz and D. Taylor (Eds.), Eliminating racism (pp. 301–304). New York: Plenum.

Azzarito, L. and Solmon, M. (2004). A reconceptualization of physical education: The intersection of race/gender/social class. *Sport, Education and Society*, 10: 25–47.

Babad, E., Bernieri, F. and Rosenthal, R. (1991). Students as judges of teachers' verbal and nonverbal behavior. *American Educational Research Journal*, 28: 211–234.

Bain, L.L. (1990). A critical analysis of the hidden curriculum in physical education. In D. Kirk and R. Tinning (Eds.), *Physical education, curriculum and culture:*

Critical issues in the contempory crisis (pp. 23–42). London: Falmer Press.

Barnes, B.A., Zief, S.G. and Anderson, D.I. (1999). Racial difference and social meanings: Research on "black" and "white" infants' motor development, c. 1931–1992. *Quest, 51*: 328–345.

Belcher, D. (2003a). European Americans and identity development. Presentation at the National AAHPERD Convention, Philadelphia, PA.

Belcher, D. (2003b). White Americans and basketball: Got game? Posing, profiting and policing. Presentation at the Race, Sports and Hip Hop in the New Millennium Symposium, Baton Rouge, LA.

Belcher, D. (Forthcoming). Constructing race within the Journal of Teaching in Physical Education

Brown, T.N., Jackson, J.S., Brown, K.T., Sellers, R.M., Keiper, S. and Manuel, W.J. (2003). "There's no race on the playing field:" Perceptions of racial discrimination among white and black athletes. *Journal of Sport and Social Issues, 27*: 162–183.

Bungum, T.J. and Vincent, M. (1996). Physical activity among adolescent females: Racial differences. *Women in Sport & Physical Activity Journal*, 5: 83–97.

Burden, J.W. Jr., Harrison, L.Jr. and Hodge, S.R. (2003). Perceptions of African American faculty in kinesiology programs at predominantly White American institutions of higher education. Unpublished Manuscript.

Burden, J.W.Jr., Hodge, S.R., O'Bryant, C.P. and Harrison, L. Jr. (2004). From colorblindness to intercultural sensitivity: advocacy for implementing diversity training in PETE programs. *Quest, 56*: 173–189.

Butt, K.L. and Pahnos, M.L. (1995). Why we need a multicultural focus in our schools. *Journal of Physical Education, Recreation & Dance, 66*(1): 48–53.

Carlston, D.E. (1983). An environmental explanation for race differences in basketball performance. *Journal of Sport and Social Issues, 7*: 30–51.

Carter, R.T. and Goodwin, A.L. (1994). Racial identity and education. in: DARLING-HAMMOND, *Review of research in education* (pp. 291–336). Washington DC: American Educational Research Association.

Carrington, B. and McDonald, I. (2001). "Whose game is it anyway?" Racism in local league cricket". In B. Carrington and I. McDonald (Eds.), 'Race', sport and British society (pp. 50–69). New York: Routledge.

Census, race and science (2000). *Nature Genetics, 24*: 97–98.

Chepyator-Thomson, J.R. and Hsu, S.H. (2004). Multiculturalism in secondary school physical education textbooks. Poster presentation at National AAHPERD Convention, New Orleans (April 1).

Coakley, J.J. (2004). *Sport in society: Issues and controversies.* Boston, MA: McGraw-Hill.

Cothran, D.J. and Ennis, C.D. (1999). Alone in a crowd: Meeting students' needs for relevance and connection in urban high school physical education. *Journal of Teaching in Physical Education*, 18: 234–247.

Crase, D. and Walker, H. (1988). The black physical educators: An endangered species. *Journal of Physical Education Recreation, and Dance*, 59: 65–69.

Cross, W.E. (1995). The psychology of Nigrescence: Revising the cross model. In J.G. Ponterotto, J.M. Casas, L.A. Suzuki and C.M. Alexander (Eds.), *Handbook of multicultural counseling* (pp. 93–122). Thousand Oaks; CA: Sage.

DeSensi, J.T. (1995). Understanding multiculturalism and valuing diversity: A theoretical perspective. *Quest, 47*:34–43.

Dixon, J.G., McIntosh, P.C., Munrow, A.D., and Willetts, R.F. (1973). Landmarks in the history of physical education. London: Routledge & Kegan Paul.

Dole, A.A. (1995). Why not drop race as a term? *American Psychologist, 54*: 40.

Eitzen, D.S. (1999). *Fair and foul: Beyond the myths and paradoxes of sport.* New York: Rowman & Littlefield.

Eitzen, D.S. and Sage, G.H. (2003) *Sociology of North American sport.* Boston, MA: McGraw-Hill.

Ennis, C.D. (1995). Teachers' responses to noncompliant students: The realities and consequences of a negotiated curriculum. *Teaching and Teacher Education, 11*: 445–460.

Ennis, C.D. (1996). When avoiding confrontation leads to avoiding content: Disruptive students' impact on curriculum. *Journal of Curriculum and Supervision, 11*: 145–162.

Ennis, C.D. (1998). The context of a culturally unresponsive curriculum constructing ethnicity and gender within a contested terrain. *Teaching and Teacher Education, 14*(7): 749–760.

Ennis, C.D., Cothran, D.J., Davidson, K.S. et al. (1997). Implementing curriculum within a context of fear and disengagement. *Journal of Teaching in Physical Education, 17*: 52–71.

Entine, J. (2000). Taboo: Why Black Athletes Dominate Sports and Why We're Afraid to Talk about It. New York: Perseus Book Group.

Fernandez-balboa, J.M. (1993). Sociocultural characteristics of the hidden curriculum in physical education. *Quest, 45*: 230–254.

Gallavan, N.P., Troutman, P.L.Jr. and Jones, W.P. (2001). Cultural diversity and the NCATE standards: A story in process. *Multicultural Perspectives, 3*: 13–18.

Gallagher, C.A. (2003). Miscounting race: Explaining whites' misperceptions of racial group size. *Sociological Perspectives, 46*(3): 381–396.

Goldsmith, P. A. (2003). Race relations and racial patterns in school sports participation. *Sociology of Sport Journal, 20*: 147–171.

Hackensmith, C.W. (1966). History of physical education. New York: Harper & Row.

Harrison, L. (1995). African americans: Race as a self-schema affecting physical activity choices. *Quest, 47*: 7–18.

Harrison, L., Jr. (2001). Understanding the influence of stereotypes: Implications for the African American in sport and physical activity. *Quest, 53*: pp. 97–114.

Harrison, L. Jr. (1999). Racial attitudes in sport: A survey on race-sport competence beliefs.*Shades of Diversity: Issues and Strategies: A Monograph Series, 2*.

Harrison, L. Jr., Lee, A. and Belcher, D. (1999a). Self – schemata for specific sports and physical activities: The influence of race and gender. *Journal of Sport and Social Issues*, 23: 287–302.

Harrison, L. Jr., Lee, A. and Belcher, D. (1999b). Race and gender differences in the sources of students' self-schemata for sport and physical activities. *Race Ethnicity and Education*, 2: 219–234.

Harrison, L. Jr. and Worthy, T. (2001). Just like all the rest: Developing awareness of stereotypical thinking in physical education. *Journal of Physical Education, Recreation, and Dance*, 72: 20–24.

Harrison, L. Jr., Harrison, C.K. and Moore, L. (2002). African American racial identity and sport. *Sport Education and Society*, 7: 121–133.

Harrison, L. Jr., Azzarito, L. and Burden, J. Jr. (2004). Perceptions of athletic superiority: A view from the other side. *Race, Ethnicity & Education*, 7: 149–166.

Hayes, S. and Sugden, J. (1999). Winning through 'naturally' still? An analysis of the perceptions held by physical education teachers toward the performance of black pupils in school and in the classroom. *Race, Ethnicity and Education*, 21(1): 93–107.

Helms, J.E. (1985). An overview of Black racial identity theory. In J.E. Helms (Ed.), *Black and White racial identity: Theory, research and practice*. New York: Greenwood.

Hoberman, J. (1997). *Darwin's athletes: How sport has damaged black america and preserved the myth of race*. New York: Houghton Mifflin.

Hodge, S.R., Faison-Hodge, J. and Burden, J. Jr. (2004). Politics, pitfalls, and precedents: Going beyond tokenism in diversifying physical education faculty in higher education. *Chronicle of Kinesiology and Physical Education in Higher Education*, 15(2): 6–7, 12–13.

Hunter, D.W. (1998). Race and athletic performance: A physiological review. In G.A. Sailes (Ed.), *African Americans in sport* (pp. 85–101). New Brunswick: Transaction.

Johal, S. (2001). Playing their own game: A south Asian football experience. In B. Carrington and I. McDonald (Eds.), '*Race*', sport and British society (pp. 153–169). New York: Routledge.

Johnson, L. (2002). "My eyes have been opened": White teachers and racial awareness. Journal of Teacher Education, 53: 153–167.

King, S.E. (1994). Winning the race against racism. *Journal of Physical Education, Recreation, and Dance*, 65: 69–74.

King, S.E. and Chepyator-Thompson, J.R. (1996, Early Winter). Factors affecting the enrollment and persistence of African American doctoral students. *Physical Educator*, 53(4): 170–180.

Kirk, D. (1992). Physical education, discourse, and ideology: Bringing the hidden curriculum into view. *Quest*, 44: 35–56.

Kumanyika, S. and Adams-Campbell, L.L. (1991). Obesity, diet and psychosocial factors contributing to cardiovascular disease in blacks. In E. Saunders (Ed.), *Cardiovascular diseases in blacks* (pp. 47–73). Philadelphia, PA: F. A. Davis.

Kusz, K.W. (2001). "I want to be the minority." The politics of youthful white masculinities in sport and popular culture in 1990s America. *Journal of Sport and Social Issues*, 25(4): 390–416.

Ladson-Billings, G. (1995). Toward culturally relevant pedagogy. *American Educational Research Journal*, 32: 465–492.

LaVeist, T.A. (1996). Why we should continue to study race … but do a better job: An essay on race, racism and health. *Ethnicity and disease*, 6: 21–29.

Lawrence, S.M. (1997). Beyond racial awareness: White racial identity and multicultural teaching. *Journal of Teacher Education*, 48: 108–117.

Lawson, H.A. (1979). Physical education and sport in the Black community: The hidden perspective. *The Journal of Negro Education*, 48: 187–195.

Leonard, F.E. (1947). A guide to the history of physical education. Philadelphia: Lea & Febiger.

Long, J. and Hylton, K. (2002). Shades of white: an examination of whiteness in sport. *Leisure Studies*, 21: 87–103.

Majors, R. (1998). Cool pose: Black masculinity and sports. In Sailes (Ed.), African Americans in sport. New Brunswick: Transaction.

Markus, H. (1977). Self-schemata and processing information about the self. *Journal of Personality and Social Psychology*, 35(2): 63–78.

Maruyama, G. and Moreno, J. (2000). University faculty views about the value of diversity on campus and in the classroom. In *Does diversity make a difference: Three research studies on diversity in college classrooms* (pp. 9–35). Washington, DC: American Council on Education and American Association of University Professors.

McMillian, M. (2003). Is no child left behind 'Wise schooling' for African American male students? *High School Journal*, 87(2): 25–33.

Meredith, H.V. and Spurgeon, J.H. (1980). Somatic comparisons at age 9 years for south carolina white girls and girls of other ethnic groups. *Human Biology*, 52(3): 401–411.

Miller, P.B. (1998). The anatomy of scientific racism: Racialist responses to black athletic achievement. *Journal of Sport History*, 25(1): 119–151.

Moody, J. (2001). Race, school integration and friendship segregation in America. *American Journal of Sociology*, 107(3): 679–716.

National Center for Educational Statistics. (1999). *Teacher quality: A report on the preparation and qualifications of public school teachers*. Washington, DC: Author.

Pinar, W.F. (1994). Autobiography, Politics, and Sexuality: Essays in Curriculum Theory 1972–1992. New York: Peter Lang.

Pittman, B. (2003). The Afrocentric paradigm in health related activity. *Journal of Black Studies*, 33(4): 1–14.

Pope, C.C. and O'Sullivan (2003). Darwinism in the gym. *Journal of Teaching in Physical Education*, 22: 311–327.

Proctor, T., Rentz, N., and Jackson, M. (2001). Preparing Teachers for Urban Schools: The Role of Field Experiences. *The Western Journal of Black Studies*, 25 (4): 219–227.

Rendon, L.I. (2003). Foreword. In J. Castellanos and L. Jones (Eds.). *The majority in the minority: Expanding the representation of Latina/o faculty, administrators and students in higher education* (p. ix). Sterling, VA: Stylus.

Scott, M.W. (1993). Faculty diversity–A crucial link to the successful recruitment and retention of minority students. *Journal of Physical Education, Recreation and Dance, 64*(3): 74–76, 80.

Smith, Y.R. (1992). Editorial: Are we preparing health, physical educators and recreators to work effectively with diverse populations? *Journal of Physical Education, Recreation and Dance, 63*(4): 7–8.

Smith, Y.R. (1993). Recruitment and retention of African American and other multicultural physical educators. *Journal of Physical Education, Recreation & Dance, 64*(3): 66–70.

Sparks, W.G. (1994). Culturally responsive pedagogy: A framework for addressing multicultural issues. *Journal of Physical Education, Recreation and Dance, 65*: 33–36, 61.

Stanley, L.S. (1995). Multicultural questions, action research answers. *Quest, 47*: 19–33.

Stroot, S.A. and Whipple, C.E. (2003). Organizational socialization: Factors affecting beginning teachers. In S.J. Silverman and C. D. Ennis (Eds.), *Student learning in physical education: Applying research to enhance instruction* (2nd ed.) (pp. 311–328). Champaign, IL: Human Kinetics.

Tate, W. (2003). The 'race' to theorize education: Who is my neighbor? *Qualitative Studies in Educaiton, 16*(1): 121–126.

Tatum, B. (1997). "Why are all the black kids sitting together in the cafeteria?" And other conversations about race. New York: Basic Books.

Turner, C.S.V., Myers, S., and Creswell, J. (1999). Exploring underrepresentation: The case of faculty in the Midwest. *Journal of Higher Education, 70*: 27–44.

Turner, C.S.V. (2002). Diversifying the faculty: A guidebook for search committees. Washington, DC: Association of American Colleges and Universities.

U.S. Department of Health and Human Services. (1996). *Surgeons General's report: Physical activity and health.* Washington, D.C.: Author.

U.S. Department of Health and Human Services. (2000). *Healthy people 2010: Understand and improving health.* Washington, D.C.: Author.

Van Dalen, D.B., Mitchell, E.D., and Bennett, B.L. (1953). A world history of physical education. New York: Prentice-Hall, Inc.

Villegas, A.M. (1990). *Culturally responsive teaching.* Princeton: Educational Testing Service.

Wheaton, B. and Beal, B. (2003). Keeping it real: Subcultural media and the discourses of authenticity in alternative sport. *International Review for the Sociology of Sport, 38*(2): 155–176.

Wigfield, A. and Harold, R.D. (1992). Teacher beliefs and children's achievement self-perceptions: A developmental perspective. In D.H. Schunk and J.L. Meece (Eds.), *Student perceptions in the classroom* (pp. 95–121). Hillsdale, New Jersey: Lawrence Erlbaum Press.

Wiggins, D.K. (1997). Great speed but little stamina: The historical debate over black athletic superiority. In S.W. Pope (Ed.), *The new American sport history: Recent approaches and perspectives* (pp. 312–338). Urbana, IL: University of Illinois Press.

Yeo, F. (1997). Teacher preparation and inner-city schools: Sustaining educational failure. *The Urban Review, 29*(2): 127–143.

6.3 Disability and physical education

HAYLEY FITZGERALD

Introduction

Unfortunately, society has failed so far to keep in step with the development of sport for the [*sic*] disabled ....Although there has been an awakening of the needs of the [*sic*] disabled in recent years, there is still much to be desired. (Guttmann, 1976: 179)

Sir Ludwig Guttman is considered by many to be the founding father of disability sport through his pioneering work with people with spinal cord injuries. Nearly 30 years ago he claimed that society was failing to adequately address and support sporting opportunities for disabled people. Although he indicated there had been some positive developments these seemed to be incomplete. In the intervening years following Guttmann's observations we have experienced profound social and cultural changes within contemporary society (Wright, 2004). During this time we have also witnessed the vigorous campaigning by disabled activists who have drawn our attention to issues of oppression, civil rights and equal opportunities (Barnes et al., 1999; Campbell, 2002). These activists have sought to challenge professionals and change thinking about the way disabled people are perceived, treated and understood. In part, this lobbying and politicalisation has prompted new legislation and policy developments that continue to impact on many areas of social life (Priestley, 2001). Indeed, within an educational context the proportion of disabled students educated in mainstream[1] settings has increased considerably over the last 10 years. As a consequence of this shift in educational emphasis, and particularly the desire for "inclusion", schools and their inhabitants (governors, teachers, support staff and students) are increasingly exposed to disabled[2] students. It is no longer automatically assumed then that disabled students will be educated in segregated special schools or hidden away in other institutions.

Like all curriculum areas, when considering the inclusion of disabled students, physical education continues to face new kinds of challenges and opportunities. Over 10 years ago Hellison and Templin (1991) posed the following questions to physical education teachers in relation to working with disabled students:

How prepared are you to teach the child with Down syndrome, or the student with muscular dystrophy, or the kid with a congenital heart defect, or the hyperactive student? What are the rights of these students or any other students with disabilities. Do you want to teach these children? Are you legally obligated to teach them? Should they be mainstreamed into your class? (Hellison and Templin, 1991: 33)

In promoting a reflective approach to teaching physical education many of these questions remain equally, or indeed, more relevant to teachers in our schools today. In reviewing research that has been undertaken in relation to physical education and issues of disability this chapter will explore, amongst other things, the extent to which research in this area has helped us to better understand current physical education practice in schools and the ways in which the questions previously posed have been explored and addressed within physical education research.

A brief historical perspective

To a large extent, the historical development of physical education and sport for disabled people was influenced by broader medical understandings of disability and also other developments within physical education that found their roots within the field of medicine (DePauw, 1997, 2000; Sherrill and DePauw, 1997). Indeed, for some time notions of teaching physical education to disabled students were dominated by concerns to address health related problems. In this context, the educational dimension was often lost to that of physiotherapy and other associated medical interventions. In some instances these kinds of therapeutic remedies were seen as the only movement dimension to a school curriculum that disabled students should experience (Halliday, 1993). The marginality of physical education within schools for disabled students was also evident through the training of special school-teachers who frequently did not receive any instruction during their initial teacher education in physical education.

The body of research that developed during this time also focused on medically orientated issues and until the 1980s emphasis was placed on work within the subdisciplines known to us today as exercise physiology, biomechanics, motor learning and motor development (Broadhead and Burton, 1996; Hoover and Wade, 1985; Pyfer, 1986). For example, Pyfer (1986) describes research undertaken between 1930 and 1969 as descriptive in its design and focusing on studies exploring the incidence, evaluation, or correction of postural problems and identifying specific motor problems associated with participation in physical education and sport by young people experiencing particular disabilities. A later review undertaken by Broadhead (1986) confirms the continued interest of researchers to evaluate the "performance" of disabled people. Indeed, a raft of assessment tools have been developed including for example the "Bruininks–Oseretzky Test of Motor Proficiency" (Bruininks, 1974) and the "Test of Gross Motor Development" (Ulrich, 1985) in order to identify the development stages of disabled people. Since the 1950s, in some countries, this kind of research focus continues to be supported by "specialists" within physical education referred to as practitioners of Adapted Physical Activity[3]. Much of this research is positioned within a positivist paradigm and under-pinned by quantitative methods of data collection. From this research perspective disability and "the dis-abled body" has extensively been treated as an object. A number of writers have acknowledged that data generated from this work consequently only provides a partial understanding of the experience of disability and implication for practice (DePauw, 1997, 2000). Indeed, DePauw highlights a key shortcoming by suggesting:

> To most in our field …. The object of our study is the body or specific aspects of the performing body, but traditionally our study has not focused on the body as whole, the body in a social context, or the body in connection with self. (DePauw, 1997: 419)

More recently, the complexion of research relating to physical education and disability has begun to embrace issues relating to participation in a way that understands disability as something more than a biological category. In part, the research agenda has widened as a result of broader changes within society and the need to explore these changes and consider the implications they have for the practice of physical education. In particular, the increasing desire to promote inclusive education has con-tributed to this shift in research emphasis. As we will see later in this chapter research has sought to define and describe inclusive physical education, explore the values and perceptions of teachers and consider the pedagogical implications of inclusive physical education. Although this particular strand of research has inherited some quantitative dimensions from the past it has extended understandings by also adopting a qualitative focus.

Core concepts

In this chapter reference has already been made to the notion of disability and inclusion. As we will see in the following discussion both these concepts have been, and continue to be, understood in different ways.

Understandings of inclusion

Internationally, issues relating to inclusion have become increasingly prominent in government agendas and public policy[4] (Armstrong, 1998). Within Britain the Government's policy commitment to inclusive education was expressed in the Green Paper (DfEE, 1997). Following this the Programme for Action (DfEE, 1998) was established and more recently the strategy document "Removing Barriers to Achievement" (DfES, 2004) was produced. In addition to policy commitments since the 1950s a range of legislative mandates have been put in place to support the rights of disabled people. Some of this legislation specifically addresses issues relating to the education of young disabled people (including in the USA the PL 94-142, the Education for All Handicapped Children Act 1975, PL 105-17 and in the United Kingdom the Education Acts of 1944, 1993 and 1996 and Special Educational Needs and Disability Act 2001). Much of this legislation has promoted a shift from the segregated education of young disabled students to the "inclusion" of young disabled people in mainstream settings. This kind of legislation has also been supported with other inter-national commitments to inclusive education (UNESCO, 1994). More recently, the right of young people, including those with a disability, to experi-ence physical education was unanimously agreed upon during the 1999 "World Summit on Physical Education". The Berlin Agenda for Government Ministers states: "All children have the right to: (1) the highest level of health; (2) free and compulsory primary education for both cognitive and physical development; (3) rest, leisure, play and recreation." (Doll-Tepper and Scoretz, 2001: 115). The Berlin

Agenda was subsequently adopted at the UNESCO World Conference of Ministers and Senior Officials responsible for physical education and sport (MINEPS III).

Within a physical education context the process of inclusion is addressed in a number of ways. At a policy level in England and Wales the National Curriculum (NC) established that all pupils are entitled to a "broad and balanced curriculum" (Department for Education and Employment/ Qualifications and Curriculum Authority, 1999). The NC sets out that teachers must ensure students are enabled to participate and identifies a number of principles that are essential to developing a more inclusive curriculum. These principles include:

1. Setting suitable learning challenges: "Teachers should aim to give every pupil the opportunity to experience success in learning and to achieve as high a standard as is possible."
2. Responding to pupils' diverse learning needs: "When planning teachers should set high expectations and provide opportunities for all pupils to achieve including .... pupils with disabilities."
3. Overcoming barriers to learning and assessment for individuals and groups of pupils: ".... a minority of pupils will have particular learning and assessment requirements which go beyond the provisions described." (DfEE/QCA, 1999: 28–30)

Even before the National Curriculum Physical Education (NCPE) was implemented there was some recognition that this curriculum may not facilitate access for some students to particular physical education activities. Indeed, the NCPE Working Group acknowledged that the delivery of traditional team games was likely to present difficulties to teachers in their effects to include young disabled students in physical education (DES/WO, 1991). Furthermore, following the introduction of the NCPE critics continue to suggest that the discourses of inclusion embedded within this curriculum will remain difficult to achieve as they are set within a context that leaves unchanged other long-established discourses that are unlikely to promote inclusive practice (Penney, 2002).

In recent years, and in part as a result of policy and legislative developments, physical education teachers can now draw on a diverse range of resources to assist them with their practice. For example, national and locally based programmes have been developed, in the United States these include the "I CAN" curriculum (Wessel, 1983), project "ACTIVE" (Vodola, 1978) and "Project UNIQUE" (Winnick and Short, 1985). Similarly, in Australia programmes such as "Willing and Able" (Downs, 1995), project "CONNECT" and Sports Ability[5] have been developed. In the UK "TOP Sportsability" and "Elements" programmes have been implemented in school and community settings. A range of guidelines has also been developed

to support inclusive practice in physical education (Block, 2000; Downs, 1995; Hillary Commission, 1998; NASPE, 1995). This has been coupled with the publication of a number of syllabuses that address, to differing degrees, issues of inclusion (DfEE/QCA, 1999; Ministry of Education, 1999). It is anticipated that all these development will provide positive and inclusive physical education experiences for many young people, including those who happen to be disabled. Indeed, it is claimed inclusive physical education not only contributes to broader benefits (such as those associated with physical, health, cognitive and psychological) but may also offer a number of additional benefits including:

1. Opportunity to develop social skills necessary for interaction with others.
2. Opportunity to develop friendships with peers with and without disabilities.
3. Opportunity to interact with age-appropriate role models among able bodied peers.
4. Decreased isolation.
5. Increased expectations and challenge.
6. Attitude changes among peers and increased acceptance.
7. Increased appreciation of difference.
8. Greater understanding of disability rights and equity. (DePauw, 2000: 363)

Even with extensive programme developments and enhanced understandings, Vickerman (2002) notes there is often confusion about what actually constitutes inclusion or inclusive practices. In part, the confusion arises because of the differing understandings and perspectives regarding the notion of inclusion and other associated concepts such as mainstreaming and integration. According to Farrell (1998) "mainstreaming" is about a disabled student spending part of the school day alongside non- disabled classmates in a mainstream setting. For some, this arrangement may be perceived as inclusive. However, it has been argued by a number of commentators that this kind of arrangement often only promotes the "integration" of disabled pupils. In this respect, the school system remains unchanged and extra provision is made in order the support a disabled student. In contrast, it is suggested that inclusion moves beyond the placement of a disabled student and instead emphasis is placed on inclusion as a process. In this context, inclusion is understood as a means of increasing participation in learning by all students in order that their educational needs can be met (Barton, 1998; Cheminas, 2000; DePauw and Doll-Tepper, 2000; Stainback and Stainback, 1990).

Inclusion is a process. Inclusive education is not merely about providing access into mainstream school for pupils who have previously been excluded. It is not about closing down unacceptable system of segregated provision and dumping those pupils in an unchanged mainstream system. Existing school systems – in terms of physical facilities, curriculum aspects, teaching expectations and styles, leadership roles – will have to change. This is because inclusive education is about the participation of all children and young people and the removal of all forms of exclusionary practice. (Barton, 1998: 85)

According to this account inclusion is a process that is engaged in through changes to various dimensions of a school's structure and practices. The lack of clarity concerning the notion of inclusion is particularly evident when considering disabled students within physical education and school sport. Indeed, what one teacher considers to be good inclusive practice may be interpreted by another teacher very differently. For instance, in a recent study, the following teacher explained how she had promoted inclusion in extra-curricular netball.

Now what we've also done, we've got her [the disabled student] as the mascot for the team. I've explained that she can't take part in the games because the other schools would not take into account her disability …. she knows she's part of the team because she's the team mascot. She's also coming along to the cheer leading as well because again there's no physical contact involved. (Teacher, cited in Institute of Youth Sport, 2003: 32)

There are many questions to ask in relation to this teacher's (inclusive) practice. Is this what inclusive physical education should look like? Why is the teacher so adamant that the student cannot take part in the game? Why does the teacher think the other school would not take account of the student's disability? Why is it that the role of mascot is considered appropriate for the disabled student? Why is it that the student has to accommodate the game rather than the game accommodating the student? As highlighted in the report, it was not evident from the interview if the student had approached the teacher to become the mascot or if the teacher initiated the idea. In either case, perhaps additional consideration should have been given to the consequences of the student adopting this role. For example, the stereotypical image of disability that this may reinforce to other students and members of staff and the kind of impact this role will have on the disabled student's sense of self and identity. It is the notion of disability that this chapter will now turn to by exploring the differing ways in which disability has been conceptualised and understood.

Understandings of disability

Historically and culturally disability has been understood in many different ways. For example, the Masai see the failure to have children as a disabling condition. Ancient Judaism regarded impairments as signs of wrongdoing. In the sixteenth century, the birth of an impaired child implicated the parents as practitioners of witchcraft and other kinds of sinful practices (Barnes et al., 1999; Oliver, 1990). More recently, in the twentieth century the disabled body has been seen as a naturalistic form and defined within medical terms. During this time medical specialists including those focusing on rehabilitation sought to "help" disabled people to cope, or fit in, with "normal" life.

To acquire an impairment is to become the object of professional attention. This "expert" defines an individual's needs and how these should be met. The aim is to overcome, or at least minimize, the negative consequences of the individual's "disability". (Barnes et al., 1999: 21)

As a consequence of the medical profession's concern to diagnose and treat disabled people this view of disability has come to be known as the medical model of disability. The medical influence on disabled people also provided the catalyst for other professionals to make judgements about their lives in relation to education, employment and social welfare. From this perspective, the disabled person is regarded as having limited functioning that deems them to be deficient in some way. Disability then typically becomes a defining feature and this often leads non-disabled people to assume that to be disabled is to be unfortunate, useless, different, oppressed and sick (Hunt, 1966). From this medical model perspective a non-disabled norm prevails (Barnes et al., 1999) and non-conforming disabled bodies are perceived as "spoilt" (Goffman, 1968) and "flawed" (Hevey, 1992).

Internationally, a number of classification schemes of disability have been developed which are underpinned by medical model understandings. The most widely recognised and used scheme has been the International Classification of Impairment, Disability and Handicap (ICIDH) which was devised by the World Health Organization (WHO) in 1980. This system of classification has been used widely within the health care profession, social welfare organizations, education and employers (Pfeiffer, 1998). However, the scheme has not been without its critics and Barnes et al. (1999) and Pfeiffer (1998) highlight in detail significant shortcomings of this classification system. In 2001, and in part as a result of critical dialogue with disabled people this classification scheme was updated and is now known as the International Classification of Functioning and Disability (ICF). It is claimed this new "biopsychosocial" scheme integrates medical model understandings with the kind of social model perspectives of disability that are reviewed later in this chapter.

However, even before this new scheme was adopted there remained some scepticism about the utility of this scheme and more fundamentally the development of any classification system that categorizes and defines disability (Barnes et al., 1999).

In contrast to the medical model of disability an alternative model has emerged that challenges the personal tragedy view of disability. Indeed, the social model has been described by many as the "emancipatory force in the lives of disabled people" (Tregaskis, 2002: 457). It has been argued that this model "'speaks' from the standpoint of disabled people and therefore voices an opinion that has, throughout modernity, been silenced by the paternalism of a non-disabled culture" (Patterson and Hughes, 2000: 35). Central to the social model is the challenge it makes to the naturalistic category of disability. In this context, proponents of the social model believe people with impairments are disabled by a society that is not organized in ways that take account of their needs (Finkelstein, 1980; Oliver, 1990, 1996). From this perspective, physical education and sport are just two of many institutions that are not structured or organised in ways that consider disabled people. Indeed, Barton (1993) argued that the very foundations of sport are based on "ableist" assumptions and little consideration is given to the consequences this may have on those that fail to match up to these ideals.

Recently, a number of commentators have argued that the social model is limited in its ability to articulate disability within society. In particular, it has been suggested that social model accounts of disability ignore the experiences of multiple oppression such as those relating to disability and gender (Lonsdale, 1990; Morris, 1991), ethnicity (Vernon, 1996) and sexuality (Shakespeare et al., 1996). According to these writers the social model fails to sufficiently account for differences between disabled people. Recently, a number of commentators have also argued that by focusing on society as the cause of disability this excludes "the body" from the experiences of impairment (Crow, 1996; Morris, 1991; Pinder, 1995). Indeed, it has been suggested that "within disability studies the term 'body' tends to be used without much sense of bodiliness as if the body were little more than flesh and bones" (Paterson and Hughes, 1999: 600). In this context, Marks (1999: 611) suggests "individual [medical] and social models of disability represent two sides of the same coin". What Marks is suggesting here is that by pathologizing the body (the medical model) and focusing on structural issues (the social model) both models are implicated in failing to consider the individual beyond these restricted understandings. In supporting the need to move beyond the limited understandings that both models articulate, it has been argued that the experiences of disabled people need to be understood from an embodied perspective. Indeed, a small but growing body of literature is now emerging which uses broader social theory relating to embodiment in order to understand experiences of disability (Edwards and Imrie, 2003; Hughes and Paterson, 1997; Hughes, 2000; Hughes et al., 2005; Iwakuma, 2002; Meekosha, 1999; Paterson and Hughes 1999, 2000).

It is clear from this review that understandings of inclusion and disability have changed over time, and indeed, it is likely they will continue to evolve. The next part of this chapter draws on these key concepts and considers the extent and ways in which research within the field of physical education has used these understandings of disability and inclusion.

Research in physical education and disability

Patterns of participation by young disabled people

Over the last twenty years, the number and scale of research projects focusing on patterns of participation by young disabled people has steadily increased (see for example; Borrett et al., 1995; Penney and Evans, 1995; Simeonsson et al., 2001; Sport England, 2001; Stafford, 1989). Prior to this research, medical model understandings of disability dominated and influenced research agendas, and as already indicated, research extensively focused on areas such as exercise physiology, biomechanics, motor learning and motor development (Broadhead and Burton, 1996; Hoover and Wade, 1985; Pyfer, 1986). However, more recently studies have sought to determine patterns of participation and, in doing this, some have also presented comparisons with non-disabled young people. For example, recently a large-scale survey was conducted by Sport England (2001) of 2293 young disabled people in England and Scotland. The data generated by this survey work provides a clear indication that young disabled people fair less favourably in physical education and sport than their non-disabled peers. In particular, this survey found that 53% of primary aged disabled students and 41% of secondary-aged students spend less than one hour in physical education lessons each week. This figure is significantly less than the time spent participating in physical education by non-disabled young people. The survey also found that young disabled people do not have access to as full a range of activities within the NC PE as their non-disabled peers. Echoing previous findings of earlier (Penney and Evans, 1995; Stafford, 1989) and more recent research (Smith, 2004), games activities and athletics were highlighted as activity areas that disabled students were likely to experience to a lesser extent.

The Sport England (2001) survey also revealed that fewer disabled students take part in after-school sporting activities (39% less than non-disabled pupils). According to Smith (2004) this situation is largely a result of broader practices by teachers within school physical education that tend to, more often than not, support after school clubs focusing on games activities that are competitively orientated. This practice within an after school context has led Penney and Harris (1997) to conclude, more generally about after school clubs, that the opportunities offered are "more of the same for the more able" (p. 41).

While acknowledging this recent survey completed by Sport England (2001) is useful, it should also be recognised that this kind of participation data inevitably falls short of providing in-depth understandings of experiences. However, as I have pointed out elsewhere, physical education and sports researchers seem disinterested in exploring insights from the perspectives of young disabled people themselves (Fitzgerald et al., 2003). Indeed, this largely continues to be the case, even though over 10 years ago Barton (1993) signalled that the lack of engagement was perhaps a fundamental weakness in understandings of physical education and sport.

> Merely adopting a curriculum for able-bodied people without some critical dialogue is unacceptable. The voice of disabled people needs to be heard and seriously examined. This is absolutely essential in the teaching of physical education. (Barton, 1993: 52)

Having said this, it should be acknowledged that a small body of research is emerging that engages disabled adults and young disabled people, and contributes to some extent, to our understandings of disabled peoples physical education and sporting experiences.

Disabled adults reflections of sport

Research involving disabled adults has tended to focus on their experiences of sport rather than school physical education. Some of this research highlights the positive qualities associated with participation in sport including enabling "bodies" to be experienced in new and positive ways, improving perceptions of physical characteristics, increasing confidence to participate in new activities and enhancing social integration (Blinde and McClung, 1997; Blinde and Taub, 1999; Martin, 1999). Although this research seems positive it should be remembered that many disabled adults are disadvantaged by what DePauw (1997) describes as the "invisibility of disability in sport". In this context,

participation data (Sport England, 2002) indicates that disabled adults, like disabled young people, are often excluded from participation in sport. Indeed, research has identified a range of issues that may lead to non-participation including inaccessible facilities and programmes, discriminatory attitudes of staff, lack of additional support, negative experiences of physical education and sport, and the treatment of disabled people as a homogeneous group (Disability Rights Commission, 2002; French and Hainsworth, 2001; Health Education Authority, 1999). These kinds of reasons for non-participation illustrate, from a social model perspective, the ways in which society seems to contribute to the lack of participation by developing inaccessible facilities and programmes and holding stereotypical attitudes and prejudices. Importantly, it would seem that previous experiences of physical education can impact negatively on some disabled adults' subsequent decision not to take part in sport later in life.

Research recently undertaken by Brittain (2004a, 2004b) focuses on 12 Great Britain Paralympic track and field athletes' reflective accounts of their physical education experiences. The athletes reveal, amongst other things, that when their physical education teachers exhibited beliefs aligned with the medical model perspective on disability, such as those beliefs reinforcing deficit perceptions, this perspective affected their physical education experiences negatively. The athletes highlighted how this perspective sometimes limited the nature of their experiences in physical education and also, at times, adversely affected their self-confidence to later engage in physical activity and sport. In settings where physical education teachers had positive views of disability it seemed to be the case that physical education experiences would be more positive.

> Interviewer: "How did your PE teachers react to you?"
>
> Athlete: "I think they were pretty good really. I think very much their opinion was that I did everything unless I said otherwise, which was really good really, because I did." (Athlete, cited in Brittain, 2004b: 88)

The importance of teachers' attitudes towards disability has long been known (Lavay, 1987). However, as we will see later in this chapter, many teachers feel unprepared to teach disabled students. The accounts from Brittain's study, along with other autobiographies of disabled athletes (Grey-Thompson, 2001), and research relating to broader life experiences (Disability Rights Commission, 2002; Shelley, 2002; Swain and Cameron, 1999; Viscardi, 2001) provide a range of insights into the way in which physical education and sport can impact on the lives of disabled people. For a long time, this data generated from studies of disabled adults provided the only accounts of disabled people's experiences of physical education and sport. Young disabled people, who currently experience physical education, have seldom participated in research. However, as I highlight in the following section there are a small number of notable studies that are beginning to fill this gap.

Disabled students reflections of physical education and sport

The general failure to engage with young disabled people within the research process is evident in many fields of study. Indeed, it would seem that young disabled people have typically been perceived from a medical model perspective and often considered as lacking the capacity to actively participate within the research process (Priestley, 1999; Shakespeare and Watson, 1998; Ward, 1997). This is not to say of course that young disabled people have not featured in physical education research, but it should be noted that their presence has, in the past, essentially been as "subjects" to be observed and studied rather than engaged with. Within a physical education context it seems somewhat of a missed opportunity that researchers have failed to recognise the value of engaging with young disabled people. Indeed, it seems crucial that future change within physical education must be grounded with insights from the young people this curriculum area is meant to serve.

The research that has generated insights from disabled students provides a real sense of experiences they encounter within physical education. According to Goodwin and Watkinson (2000) disabled students' experiences of physical education can be considered in terms of "bad" and "good" days. A bad day is one in which disabled students are "rejected, neglected, or seen as objects of curiosity by their classmates" (Goodwin and Watkinson, 2000: 151). In contrast, "good" days promote "a feeling of belonging, the chance to share or partake in the benefits of the program, and the opportunity to participate skilfully with classmates" (Goodwin and Watkinson, 2000: 154). During bad days, students often feel a sense of isolation and exclusion from their physical education lesson. This kind of experience is evident in the research undertaken by Borrett et al. (1995) who provided the following commentary for one disabled student's experience of physical education.

> During PE lessons she goes to have special needs tuition on basic literacy skills. She has no PE except for the swimming sessions which, in any case, are not organised by the school. (Borrett et al., 1995: 38)

More recently, other research has also affirmed the exclusion that disabled students experience. It seems physiotherapy continues, for some students, to be a staple substitute for physical education (Fitzgerald and Kay, 2004).

Bad days may also feature episodes of name-calling. Indeed, this was particularly evident in some research I recently completed. Here one student reflects upon his feelings about name-calling.

> Some of them call me. Well I know, it's because of my frame and my walking. They're immature, that's what I think and I'm not bothered, they wouldn't like it, it's not nice and if they call you its not nice. (Student, cited in Fitzgerald, 2005: 52)

Although the student indicated that he was not concerned about this name-calling a later comment was perhaps more telling about the way he felt.

> It doesn't make you feel good about yourself. I get on with things. I ignore them. I sometimes end up shouting and I told Mike his ears stick out [laughs] and they stick out a lot. Let him see what it feels like to be [name] called. (Student, cited in Fitzgerald, 2005: 52)

The name-calling and deliberate exclusion by classmates from physical education activities are experiences that other young people also encounter (Groves and Laws, 2000). However, for many disabled students these kinds of experiences may reinforce dominant discourses of disability, associated with the medical model, that emphasise deficiency, lack and inability (Barnes et al., 1999). On bad days the competence of disabled students may also by questioned. The questioning emerges from many quarters including physical education teachers, non-disabled classmates and the disabled students themselves (Brittain, 2004b; Fitzgerald, 2005; Goodwin and Watkinson, 2000; Taub and Greer, 2000). For example, the comment made by this disabled student indicates a personal sense of inadequacy:

> About everytime I get embarrassed because I can't walk well. I can't run well. I can't do volleyball that well. I can't do any kind of sport well. (Student, cited in Taub and Greer, 2000: 402)

In contrast, good days according to Goodwin and Watkinson (2000) featured characteristics associated with belonging, shared benefits and skillful participation. Belonging seemed to be associated with participation in the physical education class with the physical education teacher and classmates rather than focused work with a support assistant. Indeed, it would seem that students feel particularly isolated from the main physical education class when they are only experiencing physical education with a support assistant (Goodwin and Watkinson, 2000; Fitzgerald and Kay, 2004). According to Goodwin and Watkinson (2000), on good days students are able to articulate the benefits of participation in physical education such as those related to fitness, skill development, knowledge acquisition and other health related benefits. Finally, good days also enabled other classmates to witness the disabled students' skilful participation in an activity. In this respect, students exhibited comparable performances to their non-disabled classmates or made a contribution that was seen as important to the outcome of a game during the physical education lesson.

Much of the research that has engaged with disabled students about their experiences of physical education has drawn on the social model understanding of disability reviewed earlier in this chapter. This work seems to have assumed unproblematically that articulations through this perspective provide the best theoretical grounding for understanding the experiences of disabled students. However, closer scrutiny of the social model reveals its contested and evolving nature. Indeed, as I indicated earlier, the merits of understanding disability from an embodied position have increasingly been supported by a growing number of writers.

In some of my research (Fitzgerald, 2005) I have attempted to move beyond medical and social model understandings by considering the physical education experiences of disabled students from an embodied perspective. In particular, I explored how embodied conceptions of ability are manifest through disabled students experiences of physical education and school sport. The data generated from this study perhaps goes some way to articulating why it may be that disabled students seem to experience "bad" days (Goodwin and Watkinson, 2000) in physical education. My study reveals that a paradigm of normativity prevails in physical education. Indeed, it would seem the physical education habitus[6] serves to affirm this normative presence and is manifest through conceptions of ability that recognise and value certain characteristics and competences more than others. In particular, the disabled students in my study seemed to measure themselves, and perceive others measured them, against a mesomorphic ideal. Normative conceptions of ability were also manifest through articulations of masculinity that value competitive and aggressive forms of activity. For the students in the study, by not participating in activities that overtly promote these mesomorphic characteristics (such as rugby) and by engaging in alterative activities (such as boccia and fitness) they were unable to accumulate physical capital[7]. Finally, the students in this study illustrate how the physical education habitus supports normative conceptions of ability

that are manifest through high levels of motoric competence. For example, one student believed the physical education teacher spent much of his time supporting the "good" footballers, while another student recognized he was not going to be "as good as" many of his peers. It is perhaps not surprising that motoric competences are valued in physical education contexts that are increasingly driven by agendas seeking to identify "performances" rather than retaining a focus on educational aspirations. Interestingly, the skills required to play boccia seemed to be universally rejected as constituting a high degree of motoric competence. In part, though, this rejection may be explained through the absence of any mesomorphic or masculine characteristics associated with boccia. This study found that to deviate from dominant versions of ability was to be seen as different. This expression of difference was essentially seen in negative terms.

Teachers' perspectives and the pedagogy of inclusion

As highlighted earlier in this chapter issues relating to inclusion have become increasingly prominent within physical education discourses. However, as Vickerman (2002) points out, even though there are a myriad of policies and guidance documents in this area, there still remains a lack of clarity regarding what actually constitutes inclusion and inclusive practice.

When considering the experience of teaching David, a disabled student, Bailey offers the following reflective commentary:

> But what about everyday PE lessons? We cannot say it has been easy. There have been times when we have not done what we should. Sometimes the weather, the activity and group do make integration almost impossible. On occasions David himself has chosen what he will do. On occasions he has chosen to participate but perhaps in isolation. He has very rarely opted out. (Bailey, 1997: 18)

Bailey's account provides a sense of the journey a teacher and disabled student embarked on in order to enable physical education to be experienced within a mainstream setting. In this pre-NCPE era it is probably not surprising that Bailey talks of "integration" rather than inclusion. But what are the pedagogic motives driving Bailey's desire to provide physical education for David? Is she concerned to ensure David is integrated into the mainstream (Farrell, 1998), or does she aspire to inclusion (Barton, 1998; Cheminas, 2000; DePauw and Doll-Tepper, 2000; Stainback and Stainback, 1990)? In this instance, we can only speculate about the kinds of outcomes Bailey was seeking to attain and the broader educational philosophy underpinning them.

More recently, Smith (2004) undertook a small scale study of teachers' understandings of inclusion. This research confirms that teachers have differing understandings of what constitutes inclusive physical education. Some teachers conceptualise integration and inclusion as different processes, while other teachers make no distinction between these two notions and articulate them in similar ways. The following comment made by a teacher in Smith's study seems to indicate that disabled students fit more readily into dimensions of the curriculum that include "skills" and "fitness" rather than team games.

> I think the difficult ones to include pupils with disabilities and special needs are team games. It's alright in situations when you are developing skills and fitness but when it comes to the actual game there is not a lot you can actually do. (Teacher, cited in Smith, 2004: 47)

In relation to this point, and other responses from teachers, Smith (2004) concludes that "it would appear that, at present, many pupils with SEN are being required to 'fit' into the curriculum – that is to say, it seems they are being 'integrated' into, rather than 'fully included' in, mainstream PE" (p. 47). As Vickerman (2002) and Smith (2004) note, the difficulty arising from differing understandings of inclusion is the impact this has on the pedagogy that is practiced to include (or integrate) students within physical education.

Although physical education researchers have attempted, to a limited degree, to clarify teachers' understandings of inclusion, more concern seems to have focused on identifying factors contributing to effective inclusive practice. The difficulty in reviewing this research is that much of it fails to adequately define, from the outset, what is considered to be inclusive practice. Much of this research has been driven by a quantitative methodology (see for example, Heikinaro-Johannson and Vogler, 1996; Hodge et al., 2002). For instance, Heikinaro-Johannson and Vogler (1996) found a combination of factors including perceived competence, positive attitudes, specific knowledge and instructional skills each contributed to successful integration[8]. A limited number of other studies (Heikinaro-Johansson et al., 1995; LaMaster et al., 1998; Lienert et al., 2001; Morley et al., 2005; Vogler et al., 2000) have also generated interview data and perhaps shed more light on the factors identified by Heikinaro-Johannson and Vogler (1996) that contribute to effective inclusion in physical education.

LaMaster et al. (1998) considered the experiences of six primary physical education specialists. Through previous research undertaken by the authors each of these specialists had previously been identified as "effective" teachers. The study revealed that the teachers adopted multiple teaching styles when they were attempting to deliver inclusive physical education. For example, some teachers discussed the use of an individualised teaching style and one teacher acknowledged that "The more inclusion you have, the more individualised it would need to be" (LaMaster et al., 1998). Other teaching styles identified included peer teaching, direct teaching and modifications of lesson plans and equipment. In the context of teaching styles adopted it was concluded "It is clear that inclusion has increased the complexity of the teaching environment for these teachers" (LaMaster et al., 1998: 72).

The research conducted by LaMaster et al. (1998) also found that teachers believed the lack of initial teacher training they received in this area adversely affected their ability to deliver inclusive physical education effectively. The issue of insufficient initial teacher training and continued professional development is also evident in other research. Indeed, it has been suggested that even when teachers have received training in this area some still remain concerned about actually teaching disabled students (Lienert et al., 2001; Morley et al., 2005; Vickerman, 2002). A key issue in relation to initial teacher training seems to be related to the balance of practical and theoretical experiences incorporated into courses (Thomas and Green, 1994; Morley et al., 2005). Hodge et al. (2002) conducted a qualitative study of students using self-reflective journaling to explore the meaning of practicum experiences for student-teachers enrolled in a course with an inclusion-based practicum requirement. The authors concluded that student-teachers' attitudes and perceived competency were favourably influenced by what they viewed as challenging, rewarding and meaningful practicum experiences.

A number of research studies have also found that the level of support received during physical education may affect the extent to which effective inclusion is promoted within physical education (Liebert et al., 2001; Morley et al., 2005). Indeed, Morley et al. (2005) recently concluded that support assistants were frequently assigned to other curriculum areas rather than physical education and when assistants support physical education teachers they often lacked training in the area of disability and physical education.

In terms of the breath of activities undertaken by disabled students, research has highlighted that specific activities within physical education are experienced to a lesser extent (Penney and Evans, 1995; Stafford, 1989; Smith, 2004). Echoing these findings, it is evident from the research completed by Liebert et al. (2001) that teachers remain concerned about how they can support inclusive physical education for team based activities. The following comment made by a teacher illustrates this point:

> And they are pretty much able to do the programs that I have for first and second graders, but as they become older and the activities become more complex, like a basketball game, they get lost and start reclusing [sic] themselves. They are not as active because they feel uncomfortable. (Teacher, cited in Liebert et al., 2001)

The issue of activity type has also recently emerged in research undertaken by Morley et al. (2005) who also confirm that activities involving team play provide additional challenges for teachers as they work towards inclusive physical education.

In general, it is claimed that inclusive physical education will contribute to many positive outcomes. Indeed, it has been argued that disabled students and their non-disabled peers may both be the beneficiaries of inclusive practices (DePauw, 2000). However, it has not been until relatively recently that research has begun to explore the nature of these perceived, and often taken for granted, benefits to inclusive physical education. Indeed, Place and Hodge (2001) suggest that the empirical data available in this area still remains somewhat limited. Research underpinned by a quantitative approach, and focusing on the perspectives of non-disabled classmates, indicates that these students perceive inclusion positively (Slininger et al., 2000; Verderber et al., 2003). For example, Verderber et al. (2003) administered a survey underpinned by the theory of reasoned action and found that non-disabled young people had favourable intentions, attitudes, beliefs, and subjective norm influences towards participation in inclusive physical education activities with peers experiencing severe disabilities. In contrast, other studies found that non-disabled classmates perceived inclusive physical education less positively (Ellery et al., 2000). In another study, focusing on teachers' perspectives, it was believed the positive outcomes of inclusion relating to socialization, skill and fitness far outweighed the negative effects (Liebert et al., 2001). Having said this, teachers also indicated that a lack of support during physical education lessons often limited the extent to which these outcomes could be achieved.

Future directions in research

A combination of social, cultural and political changes within contemporary society have heightened the prominence given to issues of inclusion and it is evident that concerns focusing on disability are also firmly embedded within this discourse. As we have seen in this chapter understandings of disability and inclusion change over time, and are likely to continue to evolve. Set within this dynamic

environment it is imperative that researchers continue to centre their concerns on issues around disability within physical education. Although the body of research reviewed in this chapter provides some valuable insights, there remains much that we have yet to learn in order to extend our knowledge and understandings in this area. In concluding this chapter I discuss a number of possible directions future research could take and also highlight other pertinent issues relevant to researchers.

First, it should be acknowledged that often when researchers talk about inclusion within physical education, issues of disability tend to be marginalized in favour of concerns to explore, amongst other things, inclusion in relation to gender, ethnicity and social inequalities. While these dimensions of inclusion are quite clearly important, researchers need to recognise that inclusion also encompasses issues relating to disability. With this in mind, researchers focusing on the multiple dimensions of inclusion need to give due consideration and attention to issues of disability. Indeed, if "difference" is to be considered from an "across the board" perspective (Penney, 2002: 116) it is crucial that issues of disability are incorporated rather than marginalized within research. Of course, researchers who have chosen to focus their concerns on issues of disability and physical education, such as many of those referenced in this chapter, perhaps also need to consider how they can contribute to broader discussions relating to the multiple dimensions of difference and inclusion. By approaching research in this way it would seem the possibilities then open up for the issue of disability to become embedded within wider inclusion research agendas instead of perceived as somewhat separate to the core business of physical education research.

Second, there are some specific aspects of disabled students' physical education experiences that we still know very little about. Either set within a focused study, or broader exploration of inclusion, it would be useful to gain understandings of students' experiences in relation to the following questions:

- what does undertaking physical education and sport mean to young disabled people;
- what value do young disabled people place on physical education and sport;
- what relevance does physical education and sport have to young disabled people within and beyond a school context;
- how do their experiences of physical education and sport inform their sense of self and identity.

Similarly, in the context of teaching and learning, it also seems that we need to build on current insights and gain greater understandings of:

- teachers' perceptions of including disabled students in physical education;
- teachers' practices during physical education.

In the context of students' perspectives and broader understandings of teaching and learning it also seems that there is a need to explore these understandings, for targeted research participants, over a sustained period of time.

Third, given the increasing number of disabled students who are educated in mainstream schools there may be a tendency for researchers to want to locate their work within this context. However, there also continues to be a need to explore the kinds of questions identified above with disabled students and staff from special schools. Indeed, as the support needs required by these students to participate in physical education and sport may be significant this also raises additional questions, such as the extent to which physical education remains a relevant curriculum area for these students, and the nature of the continuity and transition between school and community providers.

Fourth, as I indicated earlier in this chapter, researchers have tended not to engage disabled students within the research process. Indeed, when physical education researchers have done so it has tended to be with physically disabled research participants[9]. I would suggest there is also a real need to consider the views and perspectives of young people experiencing different disabilities, including those experiencing severe learning and multiple disabilities. In order to effectively engage with these young people it may be that as researchers we need to question, or indeed rethink, our approaches to data generation. Interestingly, although some writers have advocated adopting an emancipatory research approach (DePauw, 2000; Oliver, 1997; Stone and Priestley, 1996) these calls seem to have been largely ignored by researchers in physical education. It is particularly ironic that researchers exploring and critiquing issues of inclusion within physical education have yet to consider how their own research practice can become more inclusive.

Although this is my final point, it is perhaps the most important. Aitchison (2003) recently called for researchers to move beyond the discursive boundaries of their field and engage with wider discourses. In preparing this chapter I have attempted to straddle the discursive boundaries of sports pedagogy, sociology, special education, education, disability studies and adapted physical activity. It is a challenge all researchers interested in and committed to issues focusing on disability and physical education must also meet, otherwise any new understandings developed will not be shared or understood between this diverse research community.

Notes

1 Also know as "regular" schools.

2 I acknowledge that the international audience of this text will have different expectations regarding the way in which disability and disabled people are understood. Given that this chapter has been influenced by literature from British Disability Studies I believe it is important that I adopt the understanding of disability found within this field. This includes referring to "disabled people" rather than "people with disabilities". See for example, Barnes et al. (1999) "We will avoid the phrase 'people with disabilities' because it implies that the impairment defines the identity of the individual, blurs the crucial conceptual distinction between impairment and disability and avoids the question of causality." (p. 7). This understanding of disability is also accepted and used by the British Council for Disabled People (BCDP) and the Disabled Peoples' International (DPI).

3 It is not my intention to specifically review the historical development of Adapted Physical Activity research. However, like other related fields to physical education (such as sports pedagogy, sociology, special education, education, disability studies and leisure studies), where relevant, some of the research reviewed in this chapter will be drawn from this broader body of research knowledge.

4 Although inclusion is currently prominent it is worth noting, as Smith (2004) does that the notion of inclusion can be traced back to a longer term social process.

5 See www.ausport.gov.au for more information.

6 "The Habitus is located within the body and affects every aspect of human embodiment" (Shilling, 1996: 129). It is "…. a bridge-building exercise" (Jenkins, 2002: 74) that immerses the relations between structure and agency by incorporating society into the body. According to Crossley (2001), the habitus consists of "dispositions", "schemes", "know-how" and "competency". For Bourdieu social life can only be understood by considering the embodiment of individuals within particular fields, such as physical education, through their habitus. According to Bourdieu an individual will be judged on their ability to deploy the relevant habitus within a particular field. Therefore, if an individual's social action is compatible with the style, manner and customs of the field they are likely to be accepted as a member and support the ongoing reproduction of these conditions.

7 Capital can be "economic", "social" or "cultural". In these forms, capital can be understood as something that is tangible and embodied. This capital can be acquired and converted. In addition to the three forms of capital highlighted above Bourdieu also refers to "physical" capital and suggests this is the embodied state of cultural capital. Physical capital then includes physical attributes and abilities. By focusing on the body in this way Bourdieu is recognizing that the body is "a possessor of power, status and distinctive symbolic forms, which is integral to the accumulation of various resources" (Shilling, 1996: 127).

8 I use the term "integration" here rather than "inclusion" as this is what the authors of this research used in their paper.

9 It should be noted that researchers focusing on motor development often involve people experiencing learning disabilities. However, these participants are not actively involved in the research process i.e. asked for their views.

References

Aitchison, C. (2003). From leisure and disability to disability leisure: developing data, definitions and discourses. *Disability and Society, 18*(7): 955–969.

Armstrong, D. (1998). Changing faces, changes places: policy routes to inclusion. In P. Clough (Ed.), *Managing inclusive education: from policy to experience* (pp. 31–47). London: Paul Chapman.

Bailey, S. (1997). David: a study in integration. *British Journal of Physical Education. Winter*: 17–18.

Barnes, C., Mercer, G. and Shakespeare, T. (1999). *Exploring disability A sociological introduction.* Cambridge: `Polity Press .

Barton, L. (1993). Disability, empowerment and physical education. In J. Evans (Ed.), *Equality, education and physical education* (pp. 43–54). London: Falmer Press.

Barton, L. (1998). *The politics of special educational needs.* Lewes: Falmer Press.

Blinde, E. and Taub, D. (1999). Personal empowerment through physical fitness activity: perspectives from male college students with physical and sensory disabilities. *Journal of Sport Behavior 22*: 181–202.

Blinde, E.M. and McClung, L.R. (1997). Enhancing the physical and social self through recreation activity: accounts from individuals with physical disabilities. *Adapted Physical Activity Quarterly, 14*(4): 327–344.

Block, M.E. (2000). *A teacher's guide to including students with disabilities in regular physical education.* Baltimore, MD: Paul H. Books.

Bourdieu, P. and Wacquant, L.J.D. (2002). *An invitation to reflexive sociology.* Cambridge, UK: Polity.

Borrett, N., Kew, F. and Stockham, K. (1995). *Disability, young people and school sport.* Paper in Community Studies Number 8, Ilkley: Bradford and Ilkley Community College.

Broadhead, G.D. and Burton, A.W. (1996). The legacy of early adapted physical activity research. *Adapted Physical Activity Quarterly, 13*(2): 116–126.

Brittain, I. (2004a). Perceptions of disability and their impact upon involvement in sport for people with disabilities at all levels. *Journal of Sport and Social Issues 28*(4): 429–452.

Brittain, I. (2004b). The role of schools in constructing self-perceptions of sport and ehysical education in relation to people with disabilities',. *Sport, Education and Society, 9*(1): 75–94.

Broadhead, G.D. (1986). Adapted physical education research trends: 1970–1990. *Adapted Physical Activity Quarterly, 3*(4): 104–111.

Broadhead, G.D. (1996). The legacy of early adapted physical activity research. *Adapted Physical Activity Quarterly, 13*(2): 116–126.

Bruininks, R.H. (1974). Physical and motor development of retarded persons. In N.R. Ellis (Ed.), *International review of research in mental retardation.* New York: Academic Press.

Campbell, J. (2002). Valuing diversity: the disability agenda – we've only just begun. *Disability and Society, 17*(4): 471–478.

Cheminas, R. (2000). *Special education needs for newly qualified and student teachers.* London: David Futon Publishers.

Crossley, N. (2001). *The Social Body.* London: Sage.

Crow, L. (1996). Including all of our lives: renewing the social model of disability. In C. Barnes and G. Mercer (Eds.), *Exploring the divide: Illness and disability* (pp. 55–72). Leeds: The Disability Press.

Department for Education and Employment. (1997). *Excellent for all: meeting special educational needs.* London: HMSO.

Department for Education and Employment. (1998). *Meeting special educational needs: a programme for action.* London: DfEE Publications.

Department for Education and Employment/ Qualifications and Curriculum Authority. (1999). *Physical Education: The national curriculum for England.* London: HMSO.

Department for Education and Science. (2004). *Removing barriers to achievement.* London: DfES.

Department of Education and Science/Welsh Office. (1991). *Physical education for ages 5–16. Proposals of the Secretary of State for Education and the Secretary of State for Wales.* London: DES/WO.

DePauw, K. (1997). The InVisibility of DisAbility: Cultural contexts and "Sporting Bodies". *Quest, 49*(4): 416–430.

DePauw, K. (2000). 'Social-cultural context of disability: Implications for scientific inquiry and professional preparation', *Quest, 52*(4): 358–368.

DePauw, K. and Doll-Tepper G. (2000). Toward progressive inclusion and acceptance: Myth or reality? The inclusion debate and bandwagon discourse. *Adapted Physical Activity Quarterly, 17*(2): 135–143.

Disability Rights Commission. (2002). *Survey of young disabled people aged 16–24.* London: Disability Rights Commission Research and Evaluation Unit.

Doll-Tepper, G. and Scoretz, D. (2001). (Eds.), *World Summit on Physical Education – Proceedings.* Schorndorf: Hofmann.

Downs, P. (1995). *An introduction to inclusive practice.* Canberra: Australian Sports Commission.

Edwards, C. and Imrie, R. (2003). Disability and bodies as bearers of value', *Sociology, 37*(2): 239–256.

Ellery, P.J. and Rauschenbach, J. (2000). Impact of disability awareness activities on nondisabled student attitudes towards integrated physical education with students who use wheelchairs. *Research Quarterly for Exercise and Sport, 71 (Suppl. 1)*: A106.

Farrell, M. (1998). *The special education handbook.* London: David Fulton Publishers.

Finkelstien, V. (1980). *Attitudes and disabled people.* New York: World Rehabilitation Fund.

Fitzgerald, H. (2005). Still feeling like a spare piece of luggage? Embodied experiences of (dis)ability in physical education and school sport. *Physical Education and Sport Pedagogy, (10) I*: 41–59.

Fitzgerald, H. and Kay, T. (2004). *Sports Participation by disabled young people in derbyshire. A report for the Derbyshire and peak park sport and recreation forum.* Loughborough, UK: Institute of Youth Sport.

Fitzgerald, H., Jobling, A. and Kirk, D. (2003). Valuing the voices of young disabled people: Exploring experiences of physical education and sport. *European Journal of Physical Education, 8*(2): 175–201.

French, D. and Hainsworth, J. (2001). There aren't any buses and the swimming pool is always cold!: obstacles and opportunities in the provision of sport for disabled people. *Managing Leisure, 6:* 35–49.

Goffman, E. (1968). *Stigma.* Harmondsworth: Pelican.

Goodwin, D.L. (2001). The meaning of help in PE: Perceptions of students with physical disabilities. *Adapted Physical Activity Quarterly, 18*(3): 289–303.

Goodwin, D.L. and Watkinson, E.J. (2000). Inclusive physical education from the perspective of students with physical disabilities. *Adapted Physical Activity Quarterly, 17*(2): 144–160.

Grey-Thompson, T. (2001). *Tannie Grey-Thompson my autobiography – Seize the day.* London: Hodder & Stoughton.

Groves, S. and Laws, C. (2000). Children's experiences of physical education. *European Journal of Physical Education, 5*(1): 19–28.

Guttmann, L. (1976). *Textbook of sport for the disabled.* Aylesbury: HM+M Publishers Ltd.

Halliday, P. (1993). Physical education within special education provision. In J. Evans (Ed.), *Equality, education and physical education.* London: Falmer Press.

Health Education Authority. (1999). *Physical activity 'in our lives': Qualitative research among disabled people.* London: Health Education Authority.

Heikinaro-Johansson, P., French, R., Sherrill, C. and Huuhka, H. (1995). Adapted physical education consultant service model to facilitate integration'. *Adapted Physical Activity Quarterly, 12*(1): 12–33.

Heikinaro-Johansson, P. and Vogler, E.W. (1996) Physical education including individuals with disabilities in school settings. *Sports Science Review, 5*(1): 12–25.

Hellison, D.R. and Templin, T.J. (1991). *A reflective approach to teaching physical education.* Champaign, IL: Human Kinetics.

Hevey, D. (1992). *The creatures that time forgot: Photography and disability imagery.* London: Routledge.

Hillary Commission. (1998). *No exceptions the Hillary Commission's sport strategy for people with a disability.* Wellington: Hillary Commission.

Hodge, S.R., Murata, N.M. and Kozub, F.M. (2002). Physical educators' judgements about inclusion: a new instrument for preservice teachers. *Adapted Physical Activity Quarterly, 19*(4): 435–452.

Hoover, J.H. and Wade, M.G. (1985). Motor learning theory and mentally retarded individuals: A historical review. *Adapted Physical Activity Quarterly, 2*(3): 228–252.

Hughes, B. (2000). Medicine and the aesthetic invalidation of disabled people. *Disability and Society, 15*(4): 555–568.

Hughes, B. and Paterson, K. (1997). The social model of disability and the disappearing body: towards a sociology of impairment. *Disability and Society, 12*(3): 325–340.

Hughes, B., Russell, R. and Paterson, K. (2005). Nothing to be had 'off the peg': consumption, identity and the immobilization of young disabled people. *Disability and Society, 20*(1): 30–17.

Hunt, P. (1966). *Stigma: The experience of disability.* London: Geoffrey Chapman.

Institute of Youth Sport. (2003). *SEN Small Programmes Fund 2002–2003 inclusion training in physical education (PE) and sport for SEN/young disabled people.* Loughborough, UK: Institute of Youth Sport.

Iwakuma, M. (2002). The body as embodiment: An investigation of the body by Merleau-Ponty. In M. Corker and T. Shakespeare (Eds.), *Disability/postmodernity.* London: Continuum.

Jenkins, R. (2002). *Pierre Bourdieu revised edition.* London: Routledge.

Kozub, F.M., Sherblom, P.R. and Perry, T.L. (1999). Inclusion paradigms and perspectives: a stepping stone to accepting learner diversity in physical education. *Quest, 51*(4): 346–354.

LaMaster, K., Gall, K., Kinchin, G. and Siedentop, D. (1998). Inclusion practices of effective elementary specialists. *Adapted Physical Activity Quarterly, 15*(1): 64–81.

Lavay, B. (1987). Is mainstreaming in physical education, recreation and dance working? *Journal of Physical Education, Recreation and Dance, November–December.* 14.

Lienert, C., Sherrill, C. and Myers, B. (2001). Physical Educators concerns about integrating children with disabilities: A cross-cultural comparison. *Adapted Physical Activity Quarterly, 18*(1): 1–17.

Lonsdale, S. (1990). *Women and disability.* London: Macmillan.

Marks, D. (1999). Dimensions of oppression: theorising the embodied subject. *Disability and Society, 14*(5): 611–626.

Martin, J.J. (1999). Predictors of social physique anxiety in adolescent swimmers with physical disabilities. *Adapted Physical Activity Quarterly, 16*(1): 75–85.

Meekosha, H. (1999). Body battles: Bodies, gender and disability. In T. Shakesphere (Ed.), *The Disability Reader* (pp. 163–180). London: Cassell.

Ministry of Education. (1999). *Health and physical education in the New Zealand Curriculum.* Wellington: Learning Media.

Morley, D., Bailey, R., Tan, J. and Cooke, B. (2005). Inclusive physical education: teachers' views of including pupils with special educational needs and/or disabilities in physical Education. *European Physical Education Review, 11*(1): 84–107.

Morris, J. (1991). *Pride against prejudice.* London: Women's Press.

National Association for Sport and Physical Education. (1995). *Moving into the future: National Physical Education Standards. A guide to content and assessment.* Boston, MA: McGraw-Hill Education.

Oliver, M. (1990). *The politics of disablement.* Basingstoke, UK: Macmillan.

Oliver, M. (1996). *Understanding disability: From theory to practice.* London: Macmillan.

Oliver, M. (1997). Emancipatory Research: Realistic goal or impossible dream? In C. Barnes and G. Mercer (Eds.), *Doing disability research* (pp. 15–31). Leeds, UK: Disability Press.

Paterson, K. and Hughes, B. (1999). Disability studies and phenomenology: the carnal politics of everyday life. *Disability and Society 14*(5): 597–610.

Patterson, K. and Hughes, B. (2000). Disabled bodies. In P. Hancock, B. Hughes, E. Jagger et al. (Eds.), *The body, culture and society* (pp. 29–44). Buckingham, UK: Open University Press.

Penney, D. (2002). Equality, equity and inclusion in physical education and school sport. In A. Laker (Ed.), *The sociology of sport and physical education: an introductory reader.* London: Routledge/Falmer.

Penney, D. and Evans, J. (1995). The National Curriculum for physical education: entitlement for all? *British Journal of Physical Education, Winter:* 6–13.

Penney, D. and Harris, J. (1997). Extra-curricular physical education: more of the same for the more able?. *Sport, Education and Society, 2*(1): 41–54.

Pfeiffer, D. (1998). The ICIDH and the need for its revision. *Disability and Society 13*(4): 503–523.

Pinder, R. (1995). Bringing back the body without the blame?: the experience of ill and disabled people at work. *Sociology of Health and Illness, 15*(5): 605–631.

Place, K. and Hodge, S.R. (2001). Social inclusion of students with physical disabilities in general physical education: a behavioural analysis. *Adapted Physical Activity Quarterly, 18*(4): 389–404.

Priestley, M. (1999). Discourse and identity: disabled children in mainstream high schools. In M. Corker and S. French (Eds.), *Disability discourse* (pp. 92–102). Buckingham, UK: Open University Press.

Priestley, M. (2001). Introduction: the global context of disability. In M. Priestley (Ed.), *Disability and the life course global perspectives.* Cambridge: Cambridge University Press.

Pyfer, J. (1986). Early research concerns in adapted physical education, 1930–1969. *Adapted Physical Activity Quarterly, 3*(2): 95–103.

Reid, G. and Prupas, A. (1998). A documentary analysis of research priorities in disability sport. *Adapted Physical Activity Quarterly, 15*(2): 168–178.

Shakespeare, T., Gillespie-Sells, K. and Davies, D. (1996). *The sexual politics of disability.* London: Cassell.

Shakespeare, T. and Watson, N. (1998). Theoretical perspectives on research with disabled children. In C. Robinson and K. Stalker (Eds.), *Growing up with disability.* London: Jessica Kingsley Publishers.

Shilling, C. (1996). *The body and social theory.* London: Sage Publications.

Shelley, P. (2002). *Everybody here? Play and leisure for disabled children and young people.* London: Contact a Family.

Sherrill, C. and DePauw, K. (1997). Adapted physical activity and education. In: J. Massengale and R. Swanson (Eds.), *The history of exercise and sport science.* Champaign, IL: Human Kinetics.

Simeonsson, R.J., Carlson, D., Huntigton, G.S., Sturtz McMillen, J. and Lytle Brent, J. (2001). Students with disabilities: a national survey of participation in school activities. *Disability and Rehabilitation, 3*(2): 49–63.

Slininger, D., Sherrill, C. and Jankowski, C.M. (2000). Children's attitudes towards peers with severe disabilities: revisiting contact theory. *Adapted Physical Activity Quarterly, 17*(2): 176–196.

Smith, A. (2004). The inclusion of pupils with special educational needs in secondary school physical education. *Physical Education and Sport Pedagogy, 9*(1): 37–54.

Sport England (2001). *Disability Survey 2000 young people with a disability and sport, headline findings.* London: Sport England.

Sport England. (2002). *Adults with a Disability and Sport National Survey 2000–2001 Headline Findings.* London: Sport England.

Stafford, I. (1989). Every body active: a sports council national demonstration project in England. *Adapted Physical Activity Quarterly, 6*(1): 100–108.

Stainback, S. and Stainback, W. (1990). Inclusive schooling. In W. Stainback and S. Stainback (Eds.), *Support networks for inclusive schooling.* Baltimore: Paul H. Brookes.

Stone, E. and Priestley, M. (1996). Parasites, pawns and partners: disability research and the role of non-disabled researchers. *British Journal of Sociology, 47*(4): 699–716.

Swain, J. and Cameron, C. (1999). Unless otherwise stated: discourses or labelling and identity in coming out. In M. Corker and S. French (Eds.), *Disability discourse.* Buckingham, UK: Open University Press.

Taub, D.E. and Greer, K.R. (2000). Physical activity as a normalizing experience for school-age children with physical disabilities. *Journal of Sport and Social Issues, 24*(4): 395–414.

Thomas, N. and Green, K. (1994). Physical education teacher education and the "special needs" of youngsters with disabilities-the need to confront PETE's attitude problem. *British Jounral of Physical Education, Winter:* 26–30.

Tregaskis, C. (2002). Social Model Theory: the story so far .... *Disability and Society, 17*(4), 457–470.

Ulrich, D. (1985). *Test of gross motor development.* Austin: Pro-Ed.

United Nations Educational, Scientific and Cultural Organisation. (1994). *Final report: World conference on special needs education: Access and quality.* Paris, France: UNESCO.

Verderber, J.M.S., Rizzo, T.L. and Sherrill, C. (2003). Assessing student intension to participate in inclusive physical education. *Adapted Physical Activity Quarterly, 20*(1): 26–45.

Vernon, A. (1996). A stranger in many camps: the experiences of disabled black and ethnic minority women. In J. Morris (Ed.), *Encounters with strangers.* London: Women's Press.

Vickerman, P. (2002). Perspectives on the training of physical education teachers for the inclusion of children with special educational needs-is there an official line view? *The Bulletin of Physical Education, 38*(2): 79–98.

Viscardi, H. (2001). *Me too! A report by Mencap on play, leisure and childcare for children and young people with a disability in the Metropolitan Borough of Dudley.* Birmingham, UK: Mencap.

Vodola, T. (1978). *ACTIVE research monograph: Competency-based teacher training and individualized-personalized physical activity.* Oakhurst, NJ: Township of Ocean School District.

Vogler, E.W., Koranda, P. and Romance, T. (2000). Including a child with severe cerebral palsy in physical education: a case study. *Adapted Physical Activity Quarterly, 17*(2): 161–175.

Ward, L. (1997). Funding for change: Translating emancipatory disability research from theory to practice. In C. Barnes and G. Mercer (Eds.), *Doing disability research*, Leeds, UK: The Disability Press.

Wessel, J.A. (1983). Quality programming in physical education and recreation for all handicapped persons. In R.L. Eason, T.L. Smith and F. Caron (Eds.), *Adapted physical activity: From theory to application*, Champaign, IL: Human Kinetics.

Winnick, J.P. and Short, F.X. (1985). *Physical fitness testing of the disabled: Project UNIQUE.* Champaign, IL: Human Kinetics.

Wright, J. (2004). Critical inquiry and problem-solving in physical education. In J. Wright, D. Macdonald and L. Burrows (Eds.), *Critical inquiry and problem-solving on physical education.* London: Routledge.

6.4 Girls and physical education

ANNE FLINTOFF AND SHEILA SCRATON

Introduction

In this chapter we provide an overview and synthesis of the current knowledge and developments in understanding girls and physical education (PE). Over the past three decades, there has been a considerable increase in the amount of work focusing on girls' experiences of PE. Over this time, our knowledge and understanding has developed and shifted and become increasingly sophisticated. Theories have developed from viewing girls as a homogeneous group to ones that recognize diversity between girls, and the interconnections of gender, sexuality, race and class.

The chapter begins with a brief historical perspective that explores the changes over time that have occurred with the research on girls and PE. The chapter then outlines the conceptual and theoretical debates relating to girls' PE and how these have underpinned research focusing on the curriculum; teachers and teacher education; teaching styles and approaches, and girls' perceptions and experiences of PE. The final section of the chapter identifies future directions for work in this area.

Brief historical perspective

This section provides a brief historical overview of the major research trends in girls' PE since its early beginnings in the 1970s/1980s. This is followed in the next section by more detailed analysis of how concepts and theories underpinning this research have developed. Early research focused on the historical roots of girls' PE (Fletcher, 1994; Hargreaves, 1979, Vertinsky, 1987) the differential roles of girls and boys in PE, the associated provision of "appropriate" curricula and issues of opportunity and access (Griffin, 1984, Leaman, 1984). Over time the influence of feminist theory shifted the research questions to ones of power relations between the sexes and included research focusing on femininity, sexuality and physicality in school PE (Scraton, 1992), with teachers (Benn, 1996, 2002; Clarke,

1998, 2002) and teacher education (Flintoff, 1993). More recently research, influenced by post structuralist theory, has moved to an exploration of individual girls' experiences of PE and has centralized difference, bodies and subjectivities (Garrett, 2004; Wright, 2004).

The above trends in research in girls' PE reflect more broad theoretical trends in feminist thought. There have clearly been shifts in how gender inequalities have been explained over time yet these different theoretical strands should not be perceived as having clear boundaries and as being totally distinct from each other. As we have discussed elsewhere it may be useful to think of "waves" of theory (Flintoff and Scraton, 2004; and Flintoff, 2002). New theories do not totally replace existing ones but like waves in the sea grow out of and contain aspects of the wave that started further out from the shoreline. Thus liberal feminism developed as a wave of theory reflecting and influencing women's experiences at a certain point in our history in the 1960s and 1970s. Out of this wave developed radical and socialist feminism each of which incorporated some of the arguments from liberal feminism but provided explanations centred on very different understandings and concerns. More recently in the 1990s we have post-structuralist theory once again building from and challenging what has gone before. However, at no point is one theory totally replaced by another. In a similar way although we now have new and exciting research questions, it is important to note that many of the earlier ones are still pertinent to contemporary girls' PE.

Historically research in girls' PE has tended to follow the directions of research on gender and education (Deem, 1980, 1984; Weiner, 1985) and as such could be viewed as "one step behind" the mainstream debates. Because girls' PE has often been seen as marginal to the broader concerns of girls' schooling, it has not always been integrated into research on gender and education. Despite the significant contribution made by research in girls' PE, there remain gaps in our understanding, some of which are highlighted in the final section of this chapter.

Methodologically, since their inception empirical studies on girls' PE have included both quantitative and qualitative approaches. Although there have been no large-scale quantitative surveys specifically on girls and PE, there have been a number of national studies of young people's involvement and participation in sport and physical activity, including school based PE (Australian Bureau of Statistics, 1997; Rowe and Champion, 2000; Sport England, 1995, 2003; United States Department of Health and Human Services (USDHHS), 1996). These studies identify girls' levels of participation as problematic, particularly in relation to health and the need for active lifestyles. The studies that have used qualitative approaches draw on a range of methodologies, including in-depth interviews, observation and ethnography. These studies have focused on a number of schools; a local education authority or higher education institution for data capture (e.g. Benn, 1996, 2002; Scraton, 1992; Wright, 1996, 1997). The use of qualitative and quantitative methodologies are not mutually exclusive, with some of the case study work also incorporating quantitative survey material in order inform more in-depth qualitative analysis (eg. Scraton, 1992; Williams and Bedward, 2001).

In addition, historical studies have used documentary analysis and some life history material. Both Fletcher (1984) and Hargreaves (1979) used extensive archival material and conducted in-depth library research, with Fletcher, also, including some interview data with women in PE.

Unlike the changing foci of research questions there has been no noticeable shift in methodological approach, with many of the recent studies still using the more conventional quantitative and qualitative methods. There is some evidence that some of the newer methodologies such as story telling, narratives, auto-biographies, are beginning to be used in research on girls and PE (Garrett, 2004). However, currently these new methodologies are more evident in the sociology of sport (Markula, 2003; Martin, 2004; Sparkes, 2002).

Concepts and theoretical developments

This section explores the key concepts and shifts in theoretical analyses that have underpinned our understandings of girls and PE. We have identified several key conceptual and theoretical areas: sex/gender distinction; gender power relations; difference and embodiment.

Sex/gender distinction

Work in the 1970s and 1980s began to address the assumptions of biological determination around sex difference, with Ferris (1978) and Dyer (1982) at the forefront of challenging myths around girls' physical inferiorities. This opened up the possibilities for the development of sociological and social psychological understandings of girls' PE. The most significant development was the early distinction between the concepts of sex and gender (Oakley, 1972). This separation of the biological (sex) from the social (gender) opened up possibilities for the critical examination of girls' PE from a social constructionist paradigm. At this time the key conceptual analysis centred on how girls were socialised into specific feminine roles and capabilities. Sex role theory argues that the differences between girls and boys are the result of sex role stereotyping and socialisation practices. Girls and boys learn gender appropriate behaviours, attitudes and roles. PE is seen as one of the most sex-differentiated subjects on the school curriculum that contributes to the social construction of homogeneous gendered categories. Gender is conceptualized as bi-polar opposites of masculinity and femininity. Much of the social psychological research on girls and PE continues to use this conception of gender as its starting point (Lirgg, 1993). Thus most of the work on self-esteem and attitudes towards PE tends to look at girls and boys as separate, oppositional groups (see for example, Chung, 2002; Shropshire, 1997).

Although sex role theory is important for identifying that gender is socially constructed, it has been criticized on a number of points (Hall, 1996). Hall (1996) argues that it is a functionalist conception of gender that focuses attention on individuals and depoliticises questions of power and control. Willis (1974) emphasized the problems associated with a sex difference approach:

> The analytical socio-cultural task is not to measure these differences precisely and explain them physically, but to ask why some differences, and not others, are taken as so important, become so exaggerated, are used to buttress social attitudes or prejudice. (Willis, 1974: 3)

These questions about why some differences are taken as significant and impact on girls' PE provision became the focus of early feminist theoretical analysis. The second wave of feminist thought developed in the 1960s but only began to be applied to education during the 1970s (Weiner, 1994). Central to feminism is the focus on differences as inequality, and how girls and women are oppressed and subordinated in relation to boys and men. A fundamental principle of feminism is the relationship between theory and practice. Feminist praxis seeks to understand inequality and disadvantage and contribute to political and social change (Scraton and Flintoff, 1992).

In PE, Leaman (1984) and the Inner London Education Authority (1984) identified differential opportunities and experiences for girls compared to boys; however the explanations for these began to focus on the social practices of discrimination and stereotyping which create prejudice and ultimately inequality. Drawing on the principles of liberal democracy, the early liberal feminist approach centralised issues of access and equal opportunity. Inequalities were explained as resulting from a lack of access to the same opportunities for girls and boys, rather than a more fundamental approach that questioned the underlying power structures and organisation of PE.

What is missing from a liberal feminist stance is a critical understanding of power relations. Explanations of power have remained central to the different strands of feminist thought that have developed since the 1970s. Theoretical analysis has moved to gender relations rather than sex difference. Increasingly gender relations are defined as relations of power, rather than simply ones of difference as in the earlier feminist accounts.

Gender power relations

Structuralist accounts of power move beyond the level of the individual and see power as both reproduced and resisted through institutions and social practices. Feminism has developed different strands of theoretical analysis centralising structural power relations. These include radical, socialist, and black feminism.

Radical feminism explains inequalities and oppression as the systematic maintenance of male power through patriarchy, whereby men as a group dominate women as a group. Sexuality is explored as a major site of men's domination of women through the social institutionalisation of heterosexuality (Rich, 1980). Radical feminism sees a strong association between gender and sexuality. For Lenskyj (1986, 1994), femininity can be viewed as a code name for heterosexuality, whereby heterosexual attractiveness and availability become central to an acceptable femininity. Radical feminist analyses of PE emphasise the means and processes by which heterosexual femininity is reinforced and reproduced (Clarke, 1998, 2002; Lenskyj, 1997; Scraton, 1992). Girls in PE learn an acceptable femininity that emphasizes appearance, presentation and control, while boys are encouraged to develop a masculinity that is aggressive, dominant and physically strong and assertive. The PE practices that produce and reproduce this acceptable femininity include, for example, the choice of curriculum activities, girls' PE clothing and teacher attitudes and expectations (Cockburn and Clarke, 2002).

Socialist feminism identifies power as located within systems of patriarchy and capitalism. Thus it is the interrelationships between class and gender that are central to understanding women's unequal position. This relationship has been theorized in different ways – as a unified system (capitalist patriarchy (Young, 1981) or as separate systems (Hartmann, 1979). Gendered inequalities are derived from women's class location and the sexual division of labour, as well as male power. Through the sexual division of labour capital benefits from women's unpaid domestic labour, childcare, the day-to-day care of workers, and women's position within the paid work force. The concepts of ideology and hegemony are central to this strand of feminism. Hegemony operates through consent rather than coercion, and is the process by which dominant meanings and interests become accepted as everyday "commonsense" (Hargreaves, 1994). However, hegemony is never total and there is always the possibility of contestation and challenge leading to change. Connell's (1987; 1995) concept of hegemonic masculinity has developed to describe a dominant form of masculinity, constructed, conveyed and internalized through institutions and social practice. Hegemonic masculinity is constructed in relation to subordinated forms of masculinity (for example, gay masculinity) but also in relation to femininity. In Western societies, this dominant form continues to centre on physical strength, dominance, competition and heterosexuality.

A number of authors identify PE as a key site for the maintenance and reproduction of hegemonic masculinity (Bramham, 2003, Fleming, 1991, Light and Kirk, 2000; Parker, 1996). This work shows how hegemonic masculinity operates to reproduce particular kinds of behaviours and attitudes, and how this impacts on both boys and girls in PE. Socialist feminist analysis also highlights the importance of historical analysis in identifying the roots of contemporary teaching. As discussed in the previous section, ideologies of femininity, including those relating to physicality, sexuality and motherhood, underpinned the development of girls' PE. However, the experiences of girls in PE are dependent also on their class location. An example is the material and other kinds of support provided by middle class parents for the provision of transport, team kit and other resources to enhance access and opportunity for their daughters. In contrast, other girls and young women have little access to resources and are constrained by domestic obligations and child care of younger siblings (Flintoff and Scraton, 2001; Scraton, 1992).

Black feminists have identified the ethnocentricity of much feminist work that prioritises the lives and experiences of white women (Brah, 1996; Mirza, 1997). Socialist feminism began to look at the interrelations of gender and class as two axes of power; however, race has been either marginalised or ignored. By focusing only on gendered power relations, white feminist theories have neglected to problematize racial power as central to the production of white feminist knowledge. There is now a wealth of black feminist writing that seeks to centralize black women's experiences and identify racist structures and practices (Hill Collins, 1991; Hooks, 1982, 1984, 1989; Mirza, 1997). In relation to schooling, inequalities tend to be explained through a focus on cultural difference and ethnicity rather than a more critical analysis of race and racism. This mirrors work in relation to gender that focuses on sex difference and sex roles without theorizing structural gender power relations. In PE, this is reflected in a number of studies that have researched the "problems" of religion, culture and ethnicity (e.g. Carrington and Williamson, 1993; Carroll and Hollinshead, 1993). These studies explain the lack of involvement and participation in PE of South Asian pupils, particularly girls, by highlighting the constraints and conflicts perceived to be imposed by religious orthodoxies and family values. There remains some confusion in the use of the terms ethnicity, religion and culture, and studies have tended to universalise categories such as "Asian" or "Muslim". All too often ethnicity and culture are used as static and rigid concepts. We have chosen to discuss black feminism under this section on power relations because most of the work on girls' PE has tended to take an institutional or structural approach. Elsewhere, work on race, gender and ethnicity has not only identified racist structures as important determining features of black women's lives, but they have also highlighted differences between women, black identities and subjectivities (Brah, 1986; Hooks, 1982, 1984, 1989). More recently, Oliver and Lalik (2004a, 2004b) has attempted to engage young women in problematizng discourses of the feminine body as part of a critical curriculum project in PE.

Difference and embodiment

Difference is a central focus of post structuralist analysis. Within this work, the writings of Foucault (1980, 1983) have been particularly influential. Foucault challenges the structuralist definitions of power (top down and repressive) and considers power as plural and productive in a multiplicity of sites such as the body, discourse, knowledge, subjectivity and sexuality. Discourse is a key concept within post structural thought and relates to

> Practices that systematically form the objects of which they speak. Discourses are not about objects; they constitute them and in the practice of doing so conceal their own invention. (Foucault, 1972: 49)

It is through discourse that meanings and people are made and importantly through which power relations are maintained and changed. Poststructural accounts shift the focus from structural constraints to possibilities of empowerment and resistance (Scraton and Flintoff, 2002).

In PE, the use of poststructuralist theory has focused particularly on the production of knowledge/power; language; identities, subjectivities and the body (Evans et al., 2004; Thorpe, 2003; Wright, 1996). The work of Garrett (2004), Paechter (2003) and Wright (2004) demonstrate how post structural analysis can illuminate the ways in which gendered discourses of the body are learnt through PE. Unlike the early structuralist accounts that tended to focus on how PE reproduced a dominant feminine body (e.g. Leaman, 1984; Scraton, 1992) this work emphasises the complexities and diversity of different gendered bodies, identifying different femininities including those that challenge and resist the "norm". Language and verbal interaction between students, and between teachers and students, is seen to be central for our understanding of the construction of male and female bodies and their physical abilities in relation to one another (Wright, 1996, 1997). Thus, post structuralist analyses have made important contributions to theorizing difference and to the deconstruction of binaries such as boy/girl; masculinity/femininity. However, the criticisms of this work are that it underplays the significance of material and structural inequalities and has shifted the debates to a focus on individuals at the expense of social context (Scraton, 1994).

As the above section demonstrates, feminist theories are diverse and focus on different questions of inequality and power. Nevertheless, it is important to recognize that the different feminisms are not totally independent and do have some areas of overlap; all are concerned with understanding and improving girls' experiences of PE. Some theories have been more readily applied in policy and practice than others, but some authors have lamented that fact that there remains too large a distance between theory and practice (Hall, 1996; MacDonald, 2002).

Major findings

This section overviews key research findings on girls and PE. The section is organised around historical research, research on the curriculum, teachers and teacher education, teaching styles and approaches, and girls' perceptions and experiences. Some of the research discussed provides findings that relate to more than one of these sections.

Historical research

A major contribution to our historical understanding of girls' PE is the work of Fletcher (1984). Her research focuses on the beginnings of girls' formal PE, and traces the development of a separate, female tradition in the late 19th century in Britain. Both Fletcher (1984) and Hargreaves (1979) show how the development of girls' PE was underpinned by powerful images and ideas about women, their roles and capabilities. In late Victorian Britain the dominant image of middle class women was as "incapable and ultimately disabled such that she must be protected and prohibited from serious participation in society" (Duffin, 1978: 26). The medical profession helped create and reinforce the dominant view of women as naturally inferior to men and physically weak and helpless. Women needed to be prepared for their "natural" future role as mothers and care had to be taken to protect their reproductive capacities. As a result, they were excluded from most sports and physical activity and spent their time "learning to be ladies". This of course refers to middle class women; working class women were also excluded from formal sport or exercise opportunities although many were involved in strenuous household and servicing work.

Historical research shows how the development of PE for girls took place in the middle class education institutions that were established in the 19th century in England (Hargreaves, 1979; Scraton, 1992). In the 1850s the first 2-day high schools for girls were founded at North London Collegiate (1850) and Cheltenham Ladies College (1853) (Delamont and Duffey, 1978). The beginnings of PE started with callisthenics which was seen as gentle, appropriate exercise for girls with an aim of developing beauty and grace (Fletcher, 1984). The appointment of a gymnastics teacher from Sweden to the London School Board, Concordia Lofving, led to a system of Swedish exercises developed by Per Ling being introduced into the growing numbers of schools for girls. The formal recognition and acceptance of the Ling "scientific" system of gymnastics was the start of organized PE in schooling. Once established in the schools, this led to the opening of training colleges for teachers of PE, beginning with Madame Bergman-Osterberg's establishment of a college at Hampstead in 1885, later to become Dartford College in 1895. Fletcher's research on the history of Bedford College was important for demonstrating how teacher-training colleges both produced and reproduced a "female tradition" in PE (Fletcher, 1984). This "female tradition" incorporated a comprehensive and balanced PE curriculum, with training in gymnastics, some games, swimming and basic anatomy, physiology and hygiene. Gentle exercises, remedial gymnastics and massage were used to address middle class women's "ailments"'s and these became incorporated into the role of the PE teacher (Hargreaves, 1987). In addition, PE students were encouraged to undertake voluntary and local charity work in factory girls' clubs, elementary schools and local orphanages; as such they were part of the social control of the working classes with a concern for moral standards and their health and well being (Hargreaves, 1994). Underpinning the teaching in the teacher training colleges was an educational philosophy that centred on the development of self-control; neatness; service to others; discipline and respect for authority. These became the "standards" of girls' PE, and formed the basis of both medical and educational inspections of the subject (Fletcher, 1984; Hargreaves, 1979, 1994).

The introduction of team games into the school curriculum mainly took place in the developing public high schools for girls, reflecting developments both in the teacher training colleges and the widening of opportunities for women's recreation more generally. These games – netball, tennis, hockey, and lacrosse – remained within the boundaries of "acceptable" femininity, and avoided the stigma of overt masculinity associated with male games (McCrone, 1982; Scraton, 1992). Their introduction was on the premise that girls needed different activities to those of boys or ones that were adapted or foreshortened versions of "male" games. Girls had limited access to team sports that stressed endurance, physical contact or strength. Thus, the pioneers of PE in girls' secondary schools were careful to tread a fine line between gradually increasing physical freedom without challenging the biologically determined assumptions of femininity and women's future roles as mothers.

The establishment of Swedish gymnastics and the adoption of modified team games formed the basis of a PE curriculum specifically for girls, and established the ethos of differential PE. This notion of different but equal PE for girls continued into the twentieth century as girls' schooling expanded for both working and middle class girls (Hargreaves, 1979, 1994). Ideologies of femininity remained significant in educational policies and within the development of PE for girls through to the 1950s and 1960s. Fletcher's work showed that despite Laban's system replacing the early Ling system of teaching gymnastics and dance, a child-centred educational philosophy remained central to the "female tradition" through to the 1970s. Her work was important for showing how this "female tradition" was slowly subsumed by the traditions and philosophies of men's PE with moves towards co-education throughout the 1970s and 1980s. Kirk (1992), in his research into post Second World War PE, also shows how the male view of PE had become the dominant perspective by the mid 1970s. He argues that this male view of PE was informed by a narrow vision of masculinity and this particular definition of PE did not meet the needs of most girls or many boys.

Most of the historical research focuses on the early developments in girls' PE in Victorian Britain and the impact of this on English speaking Commonwealth countries. A further limitation of much of this work is that it focuses on middle and upper class girls and women, and thus we still have only partial accounts of different girls' PE worldwide. Park (1987) and Vertinsky (1987) have explored the impact of the development of girls' PE in Victorian England on developments in the USA. Similarly in Australia, girls' PE was influenced by a combination of Swedish gymnastics and team games imported from England (Crawford, 1987). Lenskyj's (1986) historical analysis of developments in Canada also shows the influence of ideologies of the female body and sexuality in the development of women's sport and PE. Thus, the historical research findings show how the development of girls' PE in the Western world, although radical on the one hand with a strong "female" tradition that opened up positive opportunities for some girls and young women, was also constrained by powerful expectations and ideologies of femininity. Developments since the late 1970s are reflected in the following discussion of the more contemporary research findings.

Curriculum

Given its separate and different historical development from boys, it is not surprising that a large amount of the research on girls and PE has focused on the nature of the curriculum, and on the types of activities offered to girls. In the 1970s and 1980s early debates and research in gender and PE focused on issues of curriculum access and opportunity. A key concern was the differential access to PE activities by boys and girls, particularly at secondary school (Brown, 1985; Griffin, 1984; Leaman, 1984). Leaman's (1984) work was influential because it was one of the first studies in the UK. This formed part of wider project, Reducing Sex Differentiation in the School Curriculum, coordinated by the Schools Council, the main curriculum development body in the UK between 1964 and 1982 (Weiner, 1994). Leaman's research involved observing PE in a large number of schools in different parts of England and Wales, and conducting interviews with both teachers and children. His work was

> an attempt at understanding why PE is not yet a full partner in most schools that have equal opportunities programmes, and at suggesting ways in which PE teachers could use their skills to better effect in fostering equality. (Leaman, 1984: 7)

Leaman (1984) showed how girls were socialized into "female" activities, for example netball and gymnastics, and boys into "male" activities, for example football and cricket, and argued that girls' differential and restricted PE provision both reflected and contributed to the reproduction of an ideology of femininity, and subsequently to women's inferior position in society. Leaman's work was important for beginning to move beyond a liberal approach of equal access and sex differentiation to one that began to problematize gender ideologies and their reproduction through the PE curriculum.

An important part of Leaman's work was to identify the strategies that teachers use to deal with what was perceived to be girls' lack of interest in PE: confrontation; raising aspirations; compromise and mixed PE. This focus on teachers and the structure and organization of girls' PE was developed further in an in-depth study of girls' PE in the late 1980s by Scraton (1992). This study took a more radical theoretical approach, linking girls' PE to gender power relations. It was also important for its recognition of girls' differing experiences of PE, and of the centrality of class, sexuality and ethnicity in the reproduction of gender relations.

Drawing on a questionnaire survey of all head of girls' PE departments in one local education authority and in-depth case studies of four of the schools (interviews with teachers and observation over a year), Scraton showed how the teachers had clear ideas about appropriate activities for girls based on historical and traditional expectations of their capabilities and roles. In her work femininity was explored in more depth, revealing three key ideologies underpinning dominant notions of femininity: physical ability/capacity; sexuality and motherhood/ domesticity. Scraton (1992) showed that although teachers' expectations about girls' physical capabilities had widened from the narrow assumptions of nineteenth century femininity, contemporary expectations remained underpinned by a powerful reaffirmation of femininity which still deemed girls as weaker, less physically powerful, less aggressive than boys, whilst retaining more grace, poise, finesse, flexibility and balance. Teachers' attitudes to girls' physical capabilities reproduced the notion of specific girls' activities which placed limits on the opportunities for girls to move outside the narrow confines of an "acceptable" physicality. Girls' physicality was not theorized as simply a sex difference, but importantly, understood as part of a wider, unequal power relation between men and women. An important aspect of Scraton's work was to show how girls' PE contributed to the physical aspects of male power and domination (Scraton, 1989). In doing so, she identified a politics of sexuality and the role of girls' PE in the social construction of *heterosexual* femininity. Girls' PE does not only reproduce an ideology of physicality that defines girls as physically less able than boys, but also supports the construction of heterosexual femininity as passive, vulnerable and subordinate. In addition, Scraton's (1987) work made an important link between girls' PE and their future work and leisure lives. Although traditional views of women's domestic roles and responsibilities were no longer seen to explicitly underpin the content and teaching of girls' PE, many PE teachers still held very strong views about girls' future roles as wives and mothers. These attitudes still had a powerful impact on teachers' practices and the development of the curriculum. Whilst Scraton showed that PE contributed to the reproduction of gender relations, she also, importantly, recognised that it had the potential to challenge and resist these, and contribute to the physical and political empowerment of girls and young women.

Concerns about the sex-differentiated curriculum have not necessarily gone away with the introduction of a national curriculum in PE (NCPE) in several countries (Flintoff, 1990; Penney, 2002a). In England and Wales, Penney (2002a) notes that although the Interim Report from the NCPE government working party included a strong section on equal opportunities in PE, this was cut significantly in the version that went into schools (DES, 1992). Despite its lack of explicit commitment to gender equity, Penney (2002a) argues that the NCPE in England and Wales remains implicitly gendered. Its flexibility allows space for teachers to continue to offer a different curriculum to boys and girls. For example, whilst all pupils are required to learn about invasion, net and striking/fielding categories of games, many teachers continue to offer specific games for boys (rugby, football and cricket) and others to girls (netball, hockey, rounders) in single sex groupings (Evans et al., 1996). Penney and Evans (1999) argue that the NCPE privileges discourses of sport and performance, and in doing so, reinforces a male definition of PE. Activities that have the potential to challenge gendered stereotypes, such as outdoor education or dance, have either been marginalized or, as in the case of health-related fitness, are themselves delivered in gender specific versions (Harris and Penney, 2002).

Waddington, Malcolm and Cobb's (1998) research shows differences between male and female PE teachers' attitudes to, and involvement in, the six activity areas of the NCPE[1]. Teachers are less involved in the teaching of dance and outdoor education, compared to the other areas of the NCPE, and these activities are most likely to be viewed as gendered. Male teachers are more likely to perceive dance as a "female appropriate" activity, and female teachers more likely to perceive outdoor education as a "male appropriate" activity.

Harris' research (Harris, 1995; Harris and Penney, 2000, 2002) has explored the nature and extent of health-related exercise (HRE) teaching in the implementation of the NCPE in England. Although her research did not set out to investigate gender issues, these emerged as a strong element in the implementation of HRE. The research used a multi-method approach – a questionnaire survey with heads of departments in 1000 secondary schools and interviews, with participant observation and documentary research in three case study schools. This allowed her to assess the provision of HRE in schools and factors affecting this, as well as teachers' attitudes and views on approaches to teaching this aspect of curriculum. Harris' research revealed the existence of distinct "girls" and "boys" versions of HRE resulting from teachers' attitudes about what was considered "appropriate" for boys or girls (Harris and Penney, 2000). She argues that the flexibility

inherent in the NCPE, together with the fact that HRE is not a specified programme of study, allows for the continuation of this gendered practice. Female teachers are more likely to adopt a more holistic approach to HRE, including relaxation and stress management, compared to male teachers who are more likely to include strength work and fitness testing. Significantly, given the current concerns with rising levels of obesity in young people, weight management is rarely addressed within the HRE curriculum for either girls or boys. In addition to the differences in the theoretical work, there are differences in the types of practical activities offered to pupils, with female teachers more likely to use aerobics or skipping, and male teachers more likely to use cross country running, or weight training. Harris' work is important for highlighting the ways in which this aspect of PE contributes to the reproduction of stereotypically gendered conceptions of the body, and its relationships to physical activity and health.

Another important aspect of the contemporary PE curriculum in England is the growth of examinations, and with this, the increasing gendered uptake of these opportunities (Carroll, 1998; Nutt and Clarke, 2002; Penney et al., 2002). Twice as many boys as girls are currently opting to take an examination in PE, and this gap seems to have remained remarkably constant over a number of years. Nutt and Clarke (2002) argue that the growth of examinations in PE is leading to a shift in the nature of teachers' work, and to a narrowing of conceptions of "ability" in PE. In addition, key questions remain in relation to girls and examination PE. Why do fewer girls than boys opt for an examination in PE? What is the significance of this disparity for girls' future careers and opportunities in PE and sport? These are important questions yet to be answered by empirical research (Carroll, 1998).

In the USA, Title IX, a piece of national education legislation, has had dramatic effects on the participation rates of girls in PE and sport. Introduced in 1972, Title IX aims to eliminate discrimination in educational on the basis of sex, and this has resulted in significant rises in the numbers of girls and young women now taking part in sport (O' Sullivan et al., 2002). However, as O'Sullivan et al. (2002) and others (Greendorfer, 1998; Nilges, 1998; Physical Activity Journal, 2003) note, the impact of Title IX has not been straightforwardly positive. One of its biggest impacts was the mandate that PE classes must be taught in mixed sex groups, and whilst this opened up access for girls to participate in more activities, it has not necessarily improved their experiences (Greendorfer, 1998; Griffin, 1984, 1985; Lirgg, 1993). Griffin (1985), for example, has shown how even experienced teachers struggle with gender equitable practices in coeducational sessions. Girls' experiences of mixed sex groups in PE are discussed in the pedagogy section below. In addition,

Vertinskyj (1992) argues that moving to coeducational PE has resulted in a male model of PE becoming dominant, thus influencing the nature of curriculum activities that are offered to girls.

Teachers and teacher education

The research reviewed above shows, amongst other things, the importance of teachers' attitudes and beliefs in shaping and influencing girls' PE curricula. The training of teachers and their initial teacher education (ITE) curriculum has important implications for the school curriculum. In the 1980s and 1990s there were a number of studies that assessed the role of ITE in challenging gender inequalities and improving girls' access and opportunities (e.g. Equal Opportunities Commission, 1989). However, very little of this work has focused on ITE in PE. Dewar's (1987, 1990) work in North America made an important early contribution, identifying the dominance of scientific knowledge in ITE courses in PE at the expense of social sciences. Studies outside of PE have shown the link between scientific knowledge and male power (Harding, 1986, 1991; Spender, 1981) and Dewar (1987) explores this relationship in ITE in PE. Students viewed scientific knowledge rather than social knowledge as the "really useful" knowledge, since it linked with their perceptions of the major aim of PE – to improve pupils' skill levels in physical activities. So whilst students were introduced to gender issues in elements of their course, the dominance of the scientific over social knowledge led Dewar to conclude that "the links between teaching, learning and the oppression of women in sport remain invisible to many students" (Dewar, 1990: 80). Teachers "learn" a gendered knowledge that perpetuates a sex differentiated curriculum built on perceptions of male and female different physical capabilities.

Flintoff's (1993 a,b) ethnographic study was conducted in two case study institutions in England now delivering coeducational teacher education in PE but with different histories. One had been a former women's PE college, the other a former men's institution. As in Dewar's (1987) work, Flintoff showed the marginalization of knowledge addressing equality issues. However, her work also highlighted the ways in which gender power relations were reproduced through the lecturers' expectations, attitudes and their pedagogy. Good practice owed more to the work of a few committed and energetic individuals than to coherent planning or national requirements. In addition, despite moving to coeducation some years ago, this research revealed a sex differentiated curriculum remained in the practical elements of the courses. This further develops Dewar's (1990) analysis of gendered theoretical knowledge underpinning ITE in PE to include students' preparation to teach practical PE activities. Men and women students learnt to teach

traditionally "girls" and "boys" PE, with single sex classes for major games, and with men being allowed to "opt out" of aesthetic activities such as dance. There was also evidence to suggest that curriculum change was instigated in line with men's "needs" over the women's, such as replacing a generic module on striking/fielding games including cricket, rounders and softball to one with a sole focus on cricket. The rationale for these curriculum differences was linked firmly to a conservative view of the role of ITE – to prepare students to teach in schools "as they are", rather than as they might be. Interviews with lecturers revealed deep-seated attitudes and expectations about the physical capabilities of men and women, mirroring the work of Scraton.

Arguably, since Dewar's and Flintoff's research in the early 1990s, there is now even less space in ITE courses for including a consideration of equality issues. In the UK, the 1980s and 1990s have seen huge changes to ITE, with a shift in emphasis towards practical based competences and skills, and away from reflection and theoretical concerns (Mahony and Hexhall, 1997). Tighter teaching standards have been developed, and there is more centralised control over the content of teacher education programmes. There is little evidence in the UK, or elsewhere, to suggest that the now considerable body of knowledge about gender and PE has had anything but a minimal impact on teacher education and consequently on girls' PE in schools (Wright, 2002a,b).

Although knowledge about gender and PE has had little impact on teacher education or girls' PE in schools, gender and sexuality remain significant to girls' experiences of PE because it has been shown to be central to PE teachers' identities and thus is an integral part of their pedagogy (Brown, 1999; Brown and Evans, 2004; Brown and Rich, 2002; Clarke, 1997, 2002; Rich 2001, 2003; Squires and Sparkes, 1996; Sykes, 1998). Brown and Rich's (2002) research used life history analysis of biographical data gathered through semi-structured interviews with male and female student teachers on a Post Graduate Certificate in Education course in an English University. The research found that the pedagogical practice in teacher education is a strongly gendered process. The life history research showed that the student teachers entering the profession already have established gendered identities. As a result, as students develop their pedagogical skills, they draw on these already established gendered roles and practices in their teaching. Drawing on Connell's (1995) work around the gender order, Brown and Rich discuss how this operates in PE to position individual students relationally within a dominant masculine norm. Data gathered from one female student teacher shows how she is presented with a double bind if she attempts to challenge this gender order through more inclusive or radical pedagogy:

If she challenges the gender order operating in this situation, Christie risks being stigmatized and actively subordinated as a non-complicit female and student teacher. But by not offering a challenge to the order, she accepts a complicit role and implicitly reinforces the established order. (Brown and Rich, 2002: 87)

Thus a gendered PE culture tends to be reproduced in teacher education and reinforced when student teachers become the new professionals in schools. This is not a straightforward process as the student teachers in some instances clearly demonstrated an active challenge to the gender order. However these challenges were difficult to make in a climate where gendered practices were perceived and accepted as the norm by other teachers and pupils. Few alternative strategies were made available to them, so on the whole, student teachers became complicit rather than challenging in their teaching. This work extends the earlier work of Leaman, demonstrating the pervasiveness of gendered power relations in and through PE and highlighting the limitations of individual teacher action.

Although not specifically focusing on girls' PE the work of Clarke (1997, 1998, 2002, 2004), Lenskyj (1991, 1992, 1997); Squires and Sparkes (1996) and Sykes (1998) have explored how homophobia and heterosexism impact on teachers' identities and experiences within PE. Clarke's work, for example, shows how lesbian PE teachers adopt coping strategies to negotiate homophobia and often to conceal their lesbian identity. These include strict self-censorship, avoiding personal conversations, distancing themselves from changing rooms and shower facilities, and "playing" the heterosexual. Lenskyj (1991, 1997) highlights the importance of all PE teachers challenging homophobia in their work.

Teaching styles and approaches

Unlike the curriculum, there has been less sustained focus on teachers' styles and approaches in girls' PE (Davis, 2003; Evans et al., 1996). However, throughout the early 1980s, debates about mixed PE teaching were high on the agendas of both professional and academics (British Journal of Physical Education 1987; Dyer, 1986; Evans, 1984; Evans et al., 1985; Leaman, 1984; MacDonald, 1989). Early rationales for mixed PE centred on issues of equal opportunities offering equal access across all areas of the curriculum (Brown et al., 1983; Talbot, 1993). However, there have been no national developments in mixed sex PE teaching in England, and the rationale for its introduction in many schools has often been more to do with resources or timetabling constraints than for good educational reasons (Evans et al., 1985). For example, in the case study schools in Scraton's (1992) research, she found the majority of

mixed groupings occurred in the upper years of secondary schooling when "optional" activities were introduced. Mixed PE was introduced as an organizational convenience in order to be able to offer a range of activities, rather than because of a clearly thought through educational rationale. This study questioned the assumption that mixed PE equates to equal opportunities, showing how boys can control the learning environment and impact negatively on girls' experiences and opportunities in the lessons. Other studies have reported similar findings (Evans, 1989; Evans et al., 1985; Griffin, 1984; Office for Standards in Education, 1995). An early study by Griffin (1984) in the USA, for example, focusing on the participation styles of girls in a coeducational middle school PE unit of work, showed that the majority of girls adopted one of four non assertive behaviour styles in relation to the boys: giving up; giving away; hanging back or acquiescing. Bain's (1990) work, similarly, explores how children learn the "hidden curriculum" of gender relations through interactions between pupils, and between pupils and teachers, in mixed sex PE sessions. Scraton (1993) argues that there needs to be recognition of the centrality of gender and sexuality in understanding girls' experiences in mixed PE classes:

By placing girls in a situation where ideologies of masculinity (especially those concerning physicality and heterosexuality) are reinforced and reproduced, they are in danger of losing out not only in terms of teacher attention, use of space, and inclusion in activities, but also being the focus of sexual abuse and harassment – both verbal and physical. Both girls and boys can learn in this context that the relations between the sexes are power relations with boys taking up the dominant role and girls expected to retain a subordinate position. (Scraton, 1993: 149)

The retention of single sex PE is not necessarily the answer, Scraton (1993) argues, as here too, gender ideologies can be reproduced and reinforced. She concludes that PE teachers need to question how it can best contribute to challenging gender inequalities, and that considerations about groupings need to be made in this light.

A later survey of PE teachers' attitudes towards gender issues in secondary schools across one local education authority by Flintoff (1996) showed that mixed classes were viewed as a key strategy in providing equal opportunities for boys and girls. However, the research also revealed that teachers held considerable reservations about mixed PE as a pedagogical strategy, and there were differences between male and female teachers' views. Male teachers were more likely to be concerned with the girls allegedly "dragging down the standards" of the boys, particularly in traditionally "male" activities, whereas female teachers were more aware of the possibilities of girls losing out in mixed

PE. As a result of such reservations, some schools have reintroduced single sex PE classes with the aim of providing a more supportive environment for girls (Milosevic, 1995). However, as others have noted (e.g. Wright 1999), this tells us little about whether the behaviours that caused the move back to single sex in the first place are simply continued or challenged.

A different approach to exploring teachers' teaching styles is used by Wright (1997) who adopts a poststructuralist theoretical position that centralizes language and discourse. By doing this, she looks at how language constructs relations of power between teachers and pupils. Data was collected from six teachers from three different secondary schools who agreed to use lapel microphones and to have their lessons video recorded. Sixteen lessons (seven single sex, four coeducational) were analysed in detail for patterns of language use. The study shows how girls and boys are differently positioned by teachers' language, and how this occurs in both single sex and coeducational PE contexts. However, not all girls are positioned in the same way; instead there is a multiplicity of positions available for different girls to take up. Nevertheless, compared to boys, interactions between the teachers and girls are more likely to be in an interpersonal rather than instructional mode, underpinned by expectations that girls will be reluctant to engage positively in the physical activity. Girls are marginalized, and marginalize themselves, from the central discourses of PE lessons that centre on knowledge and values more often associated with masculine, traditional team games. Female teachers used language that expressed a sense of solidarity with the girls about their experiences, whereas male teachers were more likely to use language that confirmed their authoritative position as teacher.

Evans et al.'s (1996) research on the NCPE in England and Wales similarly has gone beyond a focus on the curriculum activity, to explore the relationship between what is taught in PE and how it is taught, drawing on Bernstein's theories of pedagogy. They show how girls and boys may experience not just different curriculum activities, but also different pedagogical styles, depending upon whether their teacher is male or female. Women teachers are more likely to use informal (or problem solving) approaches in their teaching than male teachers, particularly in dance and gymnastics, opening up the possibilities for girls to experience their bodies in a range of different ways. Evans et al.'s (1996) research shows that girls experience both a wider range of curriculum activities *and* pedagogical styles in their PE compared to boys (Evans et al., 1996 – see also OFSTED, 1995). Evans et al. (1996) conclude that whilst boys may be *educationally* disadvantaged by the narrow range of activities and pedagogies offered in their PE, in a patriarchal culture they are nevertheless advantaged by the construction of hierarchy, difference and authority that characterises their teachers' pedagogical styles. Both

Wright's (1997) and Evans et al.'s (1996) work is important for highlighting the significance of pedagogical practices, particularly the use and choice of language, in understanding the different social realities and experiences for girls in PE. Research that has focused on girls' experiences of PE from the viewpoint of the girls themselves is reviewed in the next section.

A number of research projects adopting an action research model have involved working closely with teachers in helping them address gender inequalities. The Nike/Youth Sport Trust (1999, 2000) Girls into Sport Partnership Project was an action research project that aimed to develop and disseminate innovative approaches to the delivery of girls' PE. The research was carried out in 26 English specialist sports colleges[2] with each choosing a partner school to work with. Workshops helped teachers devise a series of intervention strategies aimed at increasing girls' participation and enjoyment of PE. These included, for example, the introduction of new activities into the curriculum; changing teaching styles; improving the changing room environment or running a promotional event. Baseline data were collected so that the impact of the interventions on pupils' attitudes towards physical activity could be measured. The research findings show the difficulty of bringing about sustained change and highlight the importance of teachers working together in that process. Schools that were able to show some improvement in girls' attitudes stressed the importance of support and encouragement from colleagues, particularly senior management, and a strong commitment and sustained effort on the part of teachers to change the traditional curriculum and pedagogical practices in PE.

Wright's (1999) review of the Gender Issues in Physical Activity (GIPA) project in New South Wales, Australia – a professional development and evaluation project – reports similar conclusions. This project had formal recognition and financial support from the state, and formed part of a wider gender equity strategy in the education department. A key element of the project was a series of professional development seminars in which PE teachers were helped to understand gender as a socially constructed process, and the implications of this for their practice, and for the experiences of boys as well as girls in PE. Evaluations revealed that the workshops had been useful in helping teachers reflect on their own practice, and in introducing a number of short term changes for girls, but had been less effective in producing changes to every day PE practices, particularly those that involved working with boys.

Girls' perceptions and experiences of PE

More recently research on girls and PE has moved away from a focus on the curriculum and institutional policies and practices, to girls' differing perceptions and experiences of PE, reflecting the broader theoretical shifts and developments overviewed earlier in this chapter.

Williams and colleagues' large-scale study (see Williams et al., 2000; Williams and Woodhouse, 1996; Williams and Bedward, 2001, 2002) used a multi method research design (questionnaires, observation and in-depth interviews) to examine pupils' perceptions and experiences of the NCPE in England. The quantitative findings showed that, on the whole, PE was well liked by both boys and girls, but that there were clear differences between boys' and girls' preferences for different NCPE activities. Winter team games and dance were the two activity areas that showed the most disparity between the boys and girls, with boys being far more positive than girls towards winter games. Dance was the least liked activity on the NCPE, but particularly by boys. In schools where girls' participation rates in curricular and extra curricular PE were high, noncompetitive activities such as dance, keep fit and swimming were on offer, and specifically valued by the girls. Other comments revealed a lack of continuity between the girls' curriculum PE activities and those that are enjoyed out of schools.

Data gathered from the open-ended questions on the survey, and interview data highlighted the significance of the context in which PE took place. Mixed sex PE was a key area for concern. How their efforts were perceived and commented on by the rest of the group; sexist comments from the teachers and dislike of traditionally "male" or "female" activities were all noted by the girls, as well as numerous comments about the traditional PE clothing. Whilst the study highlights the very differentiated perceptions and experiences of girls in PE, it also notes a generational gap between the attitudes of the girls and their teachers. The girls seemed to have a much more sophisticated understanding of issues of gender and culture than their teachers, which leads Williams and Bedward (2001) to conclude that these generational differences might be more important that the differences between the girls themselves.

Flintoff and Scraton's (2001) research explored young women's lived experiences of PE and physical activity, using individual and group interviews. Several group interviews were conducted in four case study schools selected from a previous study as being proactive in gender equity practices (Milosevic, 1995), with follow up individual in-depth interviews with 21 of the young women. This study aimed to explore the link between young women's experiences of PE and wider, out of school physical activity experiences. The findings challenge those of the large scale quantitative surveys mentioned above, that identify young women's participation levels in sport as problematically low. The young women in this study were active, both in and out of schools, but not always in traditional "sporting" activities as "measured" in quantitative surveys, and they chose when, where and if they became involved. The young women's experiences were very varied in both the nature of the activity selected, and the intensity and extent of their involvement. However, decisions to be active were often made within the wider context of economic and gender relations that had to be negotiated and managed, and these varied between different contexts. For most, school PE was too often seen as irrelevant to their academic school careers, or something to be avoided because of their negative experiences, particularly in mixed groups. Building on Williams and Woodhouse's findings, this research provides further support for the significance of the context for young women learning to become physically active, and of ways in which young women actively manage and negotiate the gender relations impacting on their experiences within these.

Cockburn's (2001; Cockburn and Clarke, 2002) study also highlights the compromises many young women have to make in order to take an active part in PE and physical activity. Cockburn argues that young women who are actively involved in physical activity are forced to live a "split life" and have a "double identity" in a society that constructs polarized conceptions of (heterosexual) masculinity and (heterosexual) femininity:

> A girl can identify herself as a masculinized 'doer' of PE (a 'tomboy') or a feminized ('girlie') 'non-doer' of PE. It is highly unlikely that girls can achieve being both physically active and (heterosexually) desirable, so they are often forced to choose *between* these images. The result is a paradox, a double standard to which teenage girls and young women are subjected. (Cockburn and Clarke, 2002: 661)

What each of these studies reveals is, that despite their differences, young women remain constructed as a homogeneous group – as the "other" (and inferior) to a masculine ideal. A negotiation of gender relations remains central to how, or if, they become involved in physical activity, including school PE, and the nature of those experiences. Although these studies have begun to recognize the significance of exploring *different* young women's experiences of PE, there are still large gaps in our understanding about particular young women. We still know very little, for example, about the PE or other physical activity experiences of young women from ethnic minority backgrounds, particularly young black women[3]. Zaman (1997) and Wray (2002) are examples of work that has begun this process, yet as Penney (2002b) notes, too much of the research on equity and PE has tended to be "single issue" research – focusing on either gender, or class, or sexuality and so on, without a recognition of the complexities of pupils' multiple identities.

Increasingly there is recognition too, of the need to go beyond a focus simply on school PE. Young women's PE experiences cannot be understood as separate from the experiences and negotiations they make in the rest of their lives as they move towards adult womanhood (Coakley and White, 1992). As MacDonald (2002) notes, we need not just to move beyond the binaries of male/female, boy/girl, towards an appreciation of young women's and men's different identities, but also beyond the conception of school as *the* site of meaningful learning. Arguing for a move away from a narrow focus on PE towards one of physical culture that incorporates a wider range of discourses and practices about the body, she calls for more research that would help understansd how physical activity is located within the totality of young people's lives. Wright et al.'s (2003) research has begun to do this. Using a longitudinal research design, these authors are beginning to explore the place and meaning of physically activity in the lives of a range of young people across different physical, cultural and geographical locations. What is evident from the initial findings of this much larger study is the importance of geographical location, and the diversity of positions girls take up in relation to physical activity. However, girls' choices of physical activity involvement are constrained by relations with family, community and school.

Future research directions

This chapter has overviewed the wealth of research now available on girls and PE. This final section identifies future directions for research. The shifts and developments in our theoretical understanding have highlighted new areas for research and analysis.

Difference and diversity

As our theoretical understanding has become more sophisticated, there has been recognition of the importance of understanding and exploring difference and diversity. We need research that goes beyond a view of girls as a homogenous group. For example, we know very little about the PE and physical activity experiences of black or South Asian young women, either in or out of school, or how racialised aspects of gender relations may impact on these experiences. We need to develop theoretical frameworks that can adequately account for the complex interrelationships between gender, class and race, but this work needs to be grounded in empirical research that seeks to explore the lived realities of minority ethnic girls and young women. This is a glaring gap in the research that we urgently need to address (Lovell, 1991; Raval, 1989). The major challenge will be to adequately address difference, whilst not losing sight of shared inequalities (Maynard, 1994; Scraton, 2001). As we have asked elsewhere (Scraton and Flintoff, 2002), how significant are *individual* differences or is difference relevant to our understanding of *groups* of girls and women? (for example, minority ethnic groups,

lesbians, working class women). In other words, can there still be a notion of girls and young women continuing to share inequalities in PE?

Praxis

Despite our increasingly sophisticated theoretical understanding of girls and PE, it is not easy to see how and where this has produced positive change for girls in practice (see Penney, 2002c). MacDonald (2002) suggests one of the reasons for this is the gap between theory and practice has widened and argues for a re-engagement with praxis. Praxis – where theory informs practice, and practice informs theory – is, she notes, best exemplified in research projects that involve partnerships that extend across the boundaries of schools, club, universities, pupils, teachers and so on. She argues that PE needs to build alliances with other professionals and look to learn from other contexts about how and where young people are engaged positively in physical activity. As many of the studies reviewed above have shown, for young women in particular, it appears that out of school physical activity contexts are experienced more positively than those within school. MacDonald (2002) suggests we need to learn more about the nature of these engagements and how young women move across different sites of learning and physical activity.

Contemporary youth sport policy in England is changing rapidly, and new programmes and initiatives have been organized around the development of such partnerships, and "joined up thinking" between different contexts for physical activity. The school sport coordinator programme, for example, develops links between school PE and opportunities for physical activity and sport engagement provided in the community and in clubs, and has a clear aim to increase girls' and young women's participation. Although it is very early in its implementation, there is already some evidence to suggest that the programme overall is not being successful in achieving this goal (OFSTED, 2002; Flintoff, 2003). We need ongoing critical evaluation of new policy initiatives such as this programme, specifically in terms of its impact for girls and young women's physical activity experiences.

Bodies, physical activity and health

The current concerns about increasing levels of inactivity and obesity amongst young people raise important questions for PE professionals. There is still plenty of evidence to suggest that young women's participation levels fall below those of young men (e.g. Sport England, 2003). However, we need to go beyond the quantitative picture presented by this kind of research, and provide more qualitative insights into how gender (including questions around expectations of femininity, physicality, identities, bodies) impacts on young women's experiences of PE and sport. The social construction of an idealised feminine body can influence young women's self-perceptions and esteem, and affect how others interact with them. We need more work like Garrett's (2004) and Gorely et al.'s (2003) research that has begun to explore the complexities and interconnectiveness of bodies, gender and physical identity through young women's own "bodily" stories. In addition, as Evans et al. (2004) note, PE teachers' attitudes and values are influential in constructing and reproducing discourses of health, obesity and the body that are also gendered and these require critical analysis and investigation.

This chapter has provided an overview and analysis of research on girls and PE. It has explored the significance of the historical roots of girls' PE for contemporary practice, and traced the shifts and developments in our theoretical understandings. These shifts, together with changing policy contexts, have led to new questions and research issues emerging. Yet this does not necessarily mean that the older questions are no longer significant and have been surpassed by newer, more relevant concerns. For example, issues of access and opportunities are still pertinent, as there are still less opportunities for girls to participate in extra curricular PE than they are for boys (OFSTED, 1995; Penney and Harris, 1997). Nevertheless, there have been other important questions raised about femininities, identities and bodies, and these will need to be addressed if we are to provide PE capable of addressing some of the very real participation, lifestyle and health issues of today's diverse girls and young women.

Notes

1 The NCPE in England includes six activity areas: Games; Athletics; Swimming; Gymnastics; Dance and Outdoor and Adventurous Activities (DfES, 1999).

2 Specialist Sports Colleges are maintained secondary schools in England that receive additional funding from the Department for Education and Skills to raise standards in PE and sport within its own school, in a local family of schools and in the community. To apply, schools are required to raise £50 000 from private sector sponsorship and submit a 4-year development plan.

3 Although see Benn's (1996, 2002) work which has focused on Muslim women in teacher education in PE. See also De Knop et al. (1996) for a review of Islam and its implications for girls' participation in sport.

References

Australian Bureau of Statistics. (1997). *Participation in sport and physical activities*. Canberra: Australian Bureau of Statistics.

Bain, L. (1990). A critical analysis of the hidden curriculum in physical education. In D. Kirk and R. Tinning (Eds.), *Physical education, curriculum and culture: Critical issues in the contemporary crisis*. Basingstoke, UK: Falmer.

Bedward, J. and Williams, A. (2000). Girls' experiences of physical education – voting with their feet? In A. Williams (Ed.), *Primary physical education: Research into practice*. London: Falmer.

Benn, T. (1996). Muslim women and physical education in initial teacher training. *Sport, Education and Society, 1*(1): 5–21.

Benn, T. (2002). Muslim women in teacher training: issues of gender, 'race' and religion. In D. Penney (Ed.), *Gender and physical education: contemporary issues and future directions*. London: Routledge.

Bramham, P. (2003). Boys, masculinity and PE. *Sport, Education and Society, 8*(1): 57–71.

Brah, A. (1996) *Cartographies of diaspora: Contesting identities*. London: Routledge.

British Journal of Physical Education. (1987).

Brown, D. (1999). Complicity and reproduction in teaching physical education. *Sport Education and Society, 4*(2): 143–160.

Brown, D. and Evans, J. (2004). Reproducing gender? Intergenerational links and the male PE teacher as a cultural conduit in teaching. *Journal of Teaching in Physical Education, 23*, 48–70.

Brown, D. and Rich, E. (2002). Gender positioning as pedagogical practice in physical education. In D. Penney (Ed.), *Gender and physical education: contemporary issues and future directions* (pp. 80–100). London: Falmer.

Brown, J. (1985). Equal opportunity in physical education and sport. *Australian Journal for Health, Physical Education and Recreation, 110*: 6–8.

Browne, P., Matzen, L. and Whyld, J. (1983). Physical education. In J. Whyld (Ed.), *Sexism in the secondary curriculum* (pp. 270–284). London: Harper and Row.

Carrington, B., and Williamson, T. (1988). Patriarchy and ethnicity: the link between school and physical education and community leisure activities. In J. Evans (Ed.), *Teachers, Teaching – and Control in – Physical Education* (pp. 83–96). London: Falmer.

Carroll, B. (1998). The emergence and growth of examinations in physical education. In K. Green and K. Hardman (Eds.), *Physical education: A reader*. Aachen: Meyer and Meyer.

Carroll, B. and Hollingshead, G. (1993). Equal opportunities: race and gender in physical education: a case study. In J. Evans (Ed.), *Equality, Education and physical education* (pp. 154–169). London: Falmer.

Chung, M.H. (2002). The relationship between attitude towards physical education and leisure-time exercise in high school students. *Physical Educator, 59*(3): 126–138.

Clarke, G. (1997). Playing a part: the lives of lesbian physical education teachers. In G. Clarke and B. Humberstone (Eds.), *Researching women and sport* (pp. 36–49). London: Macmillan Press.

Clarke, G. (1998). Queering, the pitch and coming out to play: Lesbians in physical education and sport. *Sport Education and Society, 3*(2): 145–160.

Clarke, G. (2002). Difference matters: sexuality and physical education. In D. Penney (Ed.), *Gender and physical education: contemporary issues and future directions* (pp. 41–56). London: Routledge.

Clarke, G. (2004). Threatening space: (physical) education and homophobic body work. In J. Evans, B. Davies and J. Wright (Eds.), *Body knowledge and control: Studies in the sociology of physical education and health* (pp. 191–203). London: Routledge.

Coakley, J. and White, A. (1992). Making decisions: gender and sport participation amongst British adolescents. *Sociology of Sport Journal, 9*: 20–35.

Cockburn, C. (2001). Year 9 girls and physical education: A survey of pupil perception. *The Bulletin of Physical Education, 37*(1): 5–24.

Cockburn, C. and Clarke, G. (2002). Everybody is looking at you! Girls negotiating the 'femininity deficit' they incur in physical education. *Women Studies International Forum, 25*(6): 651–665.

Connell, R.W. (1987). *Gender and power.* Cambridge: Polity Press.

Connell, R.W. (1995). *Masculinities.* London: Polity Press.

Crawford, R. (1987). Moral and manly: Girls and games in early twentieth-century Melbourne. In J.A. Mangan and R.J. Park (Eds.), *From 'fair sex' to feminism: Sport and the socialisation of women in the industrial and post-industrial eras.* London: Frank Cass.

Davis, K. (2003). Teaching for gender equity in physical education: A Review of the literature. *Women in Sport and Physical Activity Journal, 12*(2): 55–81.

Deem, R. (Ed.). (1980). *Schooling for women's work.* London: Routledge and Kegan Paul.

Deem, R. (Ed.). (1984). *Co-education considered.* Milton Keynes, UK: Open University Press.

De Knop, P., Theeboom, M., Wittock, H. and De Martelaer, K. (1996). Implications of Islam on Muslim girls' sports participation in Western Europe. Literature review and policy recommendations for sport promotion. *Sport, Education and Society, 1*(2): 147–164.

Delamont, S. and Duffin, L. (Eds.). (1978). *The nineteenth century woman.* London: Croon Helm.

Department of Education and Science. (1992). *Physical education in the national curriculum.* London: HMSO.

Dewar, A. (1987). The social construction of gender in physical education. *Women studies international journal, 10*(4): 453–465.

Dewar, A. (1990). Oppression and privilege in physical education: struggles in the negotiation of gender in a university programme. In D. Kirk and R. Tinning (Eds.), *Physical education, curriculum and culture: Critical issues in the contemporary crisis* (pp. 67–99). Basingstoke, UK: Falmer.

Duffin, L. (1978). The conspicuous consumptive: woman as an invalid. In S. Delamont and L. Duffin (Eds.), *The nineteenth century woman* (pp. 34–47). London: Croon Helm.

Dyer, K. (1982). *Catching up with the men: Women in sport.* London: Junction Books.

Dyer, K. (1986). *Girls' physical education and self esteem: A review of research, resources and strategies. Report of the commonwealth schools commission.* Fyshwick: Canberra Publishing and Printing Company.

Equal Opportunities Commission. (1989). *Formal investigation report: Initial teacher education in England and Wales.* Manchester, UK: Equal Opportunities Commission.

Evans, J. (1984). Muscle, sweat and showers: girls' conception of physical education and sport: A challenge for research and curriculum reform. *Physical Education Review, 7*(1): 12–18.

Evans, J. (1989). Swinging from the crossbar: equality and opportunity in the physical education curriculum. *British Journal of Physical Education, 20*(2): 84–87.

Evans, J. (1993). *Equality, education, and physical education.* London: Washington, DC.: Falmer Press.

Evans, J. and Davies, B. (2004). Pedagogy, symbolic control, identity and health. In J. Evans, B. Davies and J. Wright (Eds.), *Body knowledge and control: Studies in the sociology of physical education and health* (pp. 3–18). London: Routledge.

Evans, J., Davies, B. and Penney, D. (1996). Teachers, teaching and the social construction of gender relations. *Sport, Education and Society, 1*(2): 165–183.

Evans, J., Davies, B. and Wright, J. (Eds.). (2004). *Body knowledge and control: Studies in the sociology of physical education and health.* London: Routledge.

Evans, J., Lopez, S., Duncan, M. and Evans, M. (1985). Some thoughts on the political and pedagogical implications of mixed sex PE grouping in the PE curriculum. *British Educational Research Journal, 13*(1): 59–71.

Ferris, E. (1978). *The myths surrounding women's participation in sport and exercise.* Paper presented at the Langham Life 1st International Conference on Women and Sport, London.

Fleming, I. (1991). Sport, schooling and Asian male youth culture. In G. Jarvie (Ed.), *Sport, racism and ethnicity.* London: Falmer.

Fletcher, S. (1994). *Women first: The female tradition in English physical education, 1880–1980.* London: Athlone.

Flintoff, A. (1990). PE, equal opportunities and the national curriculum: crisis or challenge? *European Physical Education Review, 13*(2): 85–100.

Flintoff, A. (1993). Gender, PE and initial teacher education. In J. Evans (Ed.), *Equality, education and physical education.* London: Falmer.

Flintoff, A. (1993a). Learning and teaching in PE: A Lesson in gender? In A. Tomlinson (Ed.), *Gender, sport and leisure* (pp. 49–62). Brighton: Leisure Studies Association.

Flintoff, A. (1993b). One of the boys? Gender identities in physical education initial teacher education. In I. Siraj-Blatchford (Ed.), *'Race', gender and the education of teachers* (pp. 74–93). Buckingham, UK: Open University Press.

Flintoff, A. (1996). Anti-sexist practices in secondary PE. *British Journal of Physical Education, 27*(1): 24–31.

Flintoff, A. (2003). The school sport co-ordinator programme: Changing the role of the physical education teacher? *Sport Education and Society, 8*(2): 231–250.

Flintoff, A. and Scraton, S. (2001). Stepping into active leisure? Young women's perceptions of active lifestyles and their experiences of school physical education. *Sport Education and Society, 6*(1): 5–22.

Flintoff, A. and Scraton, S. (2004). Gender and physical education. In K. Hardman and K. Green (Eds.), An essential reader in physical education (pp. 161–179). London: Sage.

Flintoff, A. and Scraton, S. (2005). Gender and PE. In K. Hardman and K. Green (Eds.), *An Essential Reader in Physical Education* (pp. 161–179). London: Routledge.

Foucault, M. (1972). *The Archaeology of Knowledge.* New York: Pantheon.

Foucault, M. (1980). *Power/knowledge.* New York: Patheon.

Foucault, M. (1983). The subject and power. In H. Dreyfus and P. Rabinow (Eds.), *Michel Foucault: Beyond structuralism and hermeneutics* (pp. 36–43). Chicago, IL: Chicago University Press.

Garrett, R. (2004). Gendered bodies and physical identities. In J. Evans, B. Davies and J. Wright (Eds.), *Body knowledge and control: Studies in the sociology of physical education and health.* London: Routledge.

Gorely, T., Holyroyd, R. and Kirk, D. (2003). Muscularlity, the habitus and the social construction of gender: Towards a gender relevant physical education. *British Journal of Sociology of Education,* 24: 4.

Greendorfer, S. (1998). Title IX, gender equity, backlash and ideology. *Journal of Teaching in Physical Education.* 7(1): 69–93.

Griffin, P. (1984). Girls' participation patterns in a middle school team sports unit. *Journal of Teaching in Physical Education, 4*: 30–38.

Griffin, P. (1985). Teachers' perceptions of and responses to sex equity problems in a middle school physical education programme. *Research Quaterley for Sport and Exercise, 56*(2): 103–110.

Hall, M. A. (1996). *Feminism and sporting bodies: Essays on theory and practice.* Leeds, UK: Human Kinetics.

Harding, S. (1986). *The science question in feminism.* Milton Keynes, UK: Open University Press.

Harding, S. (1991). *Whose science? Whose knowledge?* Milton Keynes, UK: Open University Press.

Hargreaves, J. (1979). *Playing like gentlemen whilst behaving like ladies.* Unpublished Masters thesis, University of London.

Hargreaves, J. (1987). Victorian familism and the formative years of female sport. In J.A. Mangan and R. Park (Eds.), *From 'Fair Sex' to feminism: Sport and the socialisation of women in the industrial and post-industrial eras* (pp. 130–145). London: Frank Cass.

Hargreaves, J. (1994). *Sporting females: Critical issues in the history and sociology of women's sports.* London: Routledge.

Harris, J. (1995). Physical education: A picture of health? *British Journal of Physical Education, 26*(4): 25–32.

Harris, J. and Penney, D. (2000). Gender issues in health-related exercise. *European Physical Education Review, 6*(3): 249–273.

Harris, J. and Penney, D. (2002). Gender, health and physical education. In D. Penney (Ed.), *Gender and physical education: Contemporary issues and future directions* (pp. 123–145). London: Routledge.

Hartmann, H. (1979). The unhappy marriage of marxism and feminism. *Capital and Class, 8:* 17–21.

Hill Collins, P. (1991). *Black feminist thought: Knowledge, consciousness and the politics of empowerment.* London: Routledge.

Hooks, B. (1982). *Ain't I A Woman? Black Women and Feminism.* Boston, Massachusetts: South End Press.

Hooks, B. (1984). *Feminist Theory: From Margin to Centre.* Boston, Massachusetts: South End Press.

Hooks, B. (1989). *Talking Back: Thinking Feminist, Thinking Black.* Boston, Massachusetts: South End Press.

Inner London Education Authority. (1984). *Providing equal opportunities for girls and boys in physical education.* London: Inner London Education Authority College of Physical Education.

Kirk, D. (1992). *Defining physical education: The social construction of a subject in postwar Britain.* Basingstoke, UK: Falmer Press.

Kirk, D. (1999). Physical culture, physical education and relational analysis. *Sport Education and Society, 4*(1): 63–74.

Leaman, O. (1984). *Sit on the sidelines and watch the boys play: sex differentiation in physical education.* London: Longman for Schools Council.

Lenskyj, H. (1986). *Out of bounds: Women, sport and sexuality.* Toronto, cannata: Women's Press.

Lenskyj, H. (1991). Combating homophobia in sport and physical education. *Sociology of Sport Journal, 8,* 61–69.

Lenskyj, H. (1992). Unsafe at home base: women's experiences of sexual harrassment in university sport and physical education. *Women in Sport and Physical Activity Journal, 1*(1): 19–34.

Lenskyj, H. (1994). Sexuality and femininity in sport contexts: Issues and alternatives. *Sport and Social Issues, 18*(4): 357–376.

Lenskyj, H. (1997). No fear? Lesbians in sport and physical education. *Women in Sport and Physical Activity Journal, 6*(2): 7–22.

Light, R. and Kirk, D. (2000). High school rugby, the body and the reproduction of hegemonic masculinity. *Sport Education and Society, 5*(2): 163–176.

Lirgg, D. (1993). Effects of same-sex versus coeducational physical education on the self-perceptions of middle and high school students. *Research Quarterly for Exercise and Sport, 64*(3): 324–334.

Lovell, T. (1991). Sport, racism and young women. In G. Jarvie (Ed.), *Sport, racism and ethnicity.* London: Falmer.

Macdonald, D. (1989). Australian policy on mixed sex physical education. *British Journal of Physical Education, Autumn,* 129–131.

MacDonald, D. (2002). Extending agendas: physical culture research for the twenty-first century. In D. Penney (Ed.), *Gender and physical education: Contemporary issues and future directions* (pp. 208–222). London: Routledge.

Mahony, P. and hexhall, I. (1997). Sounds of silence: The social justice agenda of the teacher training agency. *International Studies in Sociology of Education, 7*(2): 137–156.

Markula, P. (2003). Body dialogues; writing the self. In J. Dennison and P. Markula (Eds.) *Moving writing* (pp. 27–50). New York: Peter Lang.

Martin, M.H. (2004). Generating female freedom upon/among women's relationships in rugby union; narratives of sexual difference. PhD thesis, London, Brunel University, UK.

Maynard, M. (1994). 'Race', gender and 'difference' in feminist thought. In M. Maynard and S. Afshar (Eds.), *The dynamics of 'race and gender: Some feminist interventions* (pp. 9–25). London: Taylor and Francis.

McCrone, K. (1982). Victorian women and sport: the game in colleges and public schools. *Canadian Historical Association*, 1–39.

Milosevic, L. (Ed.). (1995). *Fairplay: Gender and physical education*. Leeds, UK: Leeds City Council.

Mirza, H. (Ed.). (1997). *Black British feminism: A reader*. London: Routledge.

Nike/Youth Sport Trust. (1999). *The girls in sport partnership Project: Interim report*. Loughborough, UK: Institute of Youth Sport.

Nike/Youth Sport Trust. (2000). *Girls into sport: Towards girl-friendly physical education*. Loughborough, UK: Institute of Youth Sport.

Nilges, L. (1998). I thought only fairy tales has supernatural power; a radical feminist analysis of Title IX. *Journal of Teaching in Physical Education*, 17(2): 172–194.

Nutt, G. and Clark, G. (2002). The hidden curriculum and the changing nature of teachers' work. In A. Laker (Ed.), *The sociology of sport and physical education: An introductory reader* (pp. 148–166). London: Routledge/Falmer.

O Sullivan, M., Bush, K. and Gehring, M. (2002). Gender equity and physical education: a USA perspective. In D. Penney (Ed.), *Gender and physical education: Contemporary issues and future directions*. London: Routledge.

Oakley, A. (1972). *Sex, gender and society*. London: Temple-Smith.

Office for Standards in Education. (1995). *Physical education and sport in schools: a survey of good practice*. London: HMSO.

Office for Standards in Education. (2002). *The school sport co-ordinator programme: evaluation of phases 1 and 2, 2001–2003*. London: HMSO.

Oliver, K. and Lalik, R. (2004a). The Beauty Walk: Interrogating whiteness as the norm for beauty in one school's hidden curriculum. In J. Evans, B. Davies and J. Wright (Eds), *Body knowledge and control: Studies in the sociology of physical education and health* (pp. 115–129). London: Routledge.

Oliver, K. and Lalik, R. (2004b) Critical enquiry on the body in girls' PE classes: a critical post structuralist perspective. *Journal of Teaching in Physical Education*, 23: 162–195.

O'Sullivan, M., Bush, K. and Gehring, M. (2002). Gender equity and physical education: a USA perspective. In D. Penney (Ed.), *Gender and physical education: Contemporary issues and future directions* (pp. 163–189). London: Routledge.

Paechter, C. (2003). Power, bodies and identity: how different forms of physical education construct varying masculinities and femininities in secondary school. *Sex Education*, 3(1): 47–59.

Park, R. (1987). Sport, gender and society in a translantic Victorian perspective. In J.A. Mangan and R.J. Park (Eds.), *From 'Fair Sex' to feminism: Sport and the socialisation of women in the industrial and post-industrial eras* (pp. 58–93). London: Frank Cass.

Parker, A. (1996). The construction of masculinity in boys' PE. *Gender and Education*, 8(2): 141–157.

Penney, D. (2002a). Gendered policies. In D. Penney (Ed.), *Gender and physical education: Contemporary issues and future directions*. London: Routledge.

Penney, D. (2002b). Equality, equity and inclusion in physical education. In A. Laker (Ed.), *The sociology of Sport and Physical Education* (pp. 110–128). London: Routledge.

Penney, D. (Ed.). (2002c). *Gender and physical education: contemporary issues and future directions*. New York: Routledge.

Penney, D. and Evans, J. (1999). *Politics, policy and practice in physical education*. London: E and F N Spon.

Penney, D. and Harris, J. (1997). Extra-curricular physical education: More of the same for the more able. *Sport Education and Society*, 2(1): 41–54.

Penney, D., Houlihan, B. and Ely, D. (2002). *Specialist sports colleges national monitoring and evaluation research project: First national survey report*. Institute of Youth Sport: Loughborough University,.

Raval, S. (1989). Gender, leisure and sport: a case study of young people of South Asian descent – a response. *Leisure Studies*, 8: 237–240.

Rich, A. (1980). Compulsory heterosexuality and lesbian existence. *Signs*, 5: 631–660.

Rich, E. (2001). Gender positioning in teacher education in England: new rhetoric, old realities'. *International Studies in Sociology of Education*, 11(2): 131– 154.

Rich, E. (2003). The problem with the girls: Liberal feminism, 'equal opportunities' and gender inequality in physical education. *British Journal of Physical Education* (Spring) 46–49.

Rowe, N. and Champion, R. (2000). *Young people and sport: National survey 1999*. London: Sport England.

Scraton, S. (1987). Boys muscle in where angels fear to tread – girls' sub-cultures and physical activities. In J. Horne, D. Jary and A. Tomlinson (Eds.), *Sport, leisure and social relations* (pp. 160–186). London: Routledge and Kegan Paul.

Scraton, S. (1989). Gender and physical education: the politics of the physical and the politics of sexuality. In S. Walker and L. Barton (Eds.), *Changing policies, changing teachers: New directions for schooling?* (pp. 169–189). Milton Keynes, UK: Open University Press.

Scraton, S. (1992). *Shaping up to womanhood: Gender and girls' physical education*. Buckingham, UK: Open University Press.

Scraton, S. (1993). Equality, co-education and physical education in secondary Schooling. In J. Evans (Ed.), *Equality, education and physical education* (pp. 139–153). London: Falmer.

Scraton, S. (1994). The changing world of women and leisure: feminism, 'postfeminism' and leisure. *Leisure Studies*, 13(4): 249–262.

Scraton, S. (2001). Re-conceptualising race, gender and sport: the contribution of black feminism'. In

B. Carrington and I. McDonald (Eds.), *Race, sport and British society* (pp. 170–187). London: Routledge.

Scraton, S. and Flintoff, A. (1992). Feminist research and physical education. In A.C. Sparkes (Ed.), *Research in physical education and Sport* (pp. 167–187). London: Falmer.

Scraton, S. and Flintoff, A. (2002). Sports feminism: The contribution of feminist thought to our understandings of gender and sport. In S. Scraton and A. Flintoff (Eds.), *Gender and sport: A reader* (pp. 30–46). London: Routledge.

Shropshire, J. (1997). Primary school children's attitudes towards physical education: gender differences. *European Journal of Physical Education, 2*(1): 23–38.

Sparkes, A. (2002). *Telling tales in sport and physical activity: A qualitative journey.* Champaign IL: Human Kinetics

Spender, D. (1981). *Men's studies modified: The impact of Feminism on the Academic Disciplines.* Oxford: Pergamon Press.

Sport England. (1995). *Young people and sport survey.* London: Sport England.

Sport England. (2001). *Young people and sport national Survey 1999.* London: Sport England.

Sport England. (2003). *Young people and sport in england: Trends in participation 1994–2002.* London: Sport England.

Squires, S.L. and Sparkes, A. (1996). Circles of silence: Sexual identity in physical education and sport. *Sport, Education and Society, 1*(1): 77–101.

Sykes, H. (1998). Turning the closets inside/out: Towards a queer-Feminist theory in Women's physical education. *Sociology of Sport Journal, 15*: 154–173.

Talbot, M. (1993). A gendered physical education: equality and sexism. In J. Evans (Ed.), *Equality, education and physical education* (pp. 74–89). London: Falmer.

Thorpe, S. (2003). Crisis discourse in physical education and the laugh of Michel Foucault. *Sport, Education and Society, 8*(2): 131–151.

US Department of Health and Human Services. (1996). *Physical activity and health: A report of the Surgeon General.* Atlanta: US Department of Health and Human Services.

Vertinsky, P. (1987). Body shapes: the role of the medical establishment in informing female exercise and physical education in nineteenth century North America. In J.A. Mangan and R.J. Park (Eds.), *From 'Fair Sex' to feminism: Sport and the socialisation of women in the industrial and post-industrial eras* (pp. 256–281). London: Frank Cass.

Vertinsky, P. (1992). Reclaiming space, revisioning the body: the quest for gender-sensitive physical education. *Quest, 44*: 373–396.

Waddington, I., Malcolm, D. and Cobb, J. (1998). Gender stereotyping and physical education. *European Journal of Physical Education, 4*(1): 34–46.

Watson, B. and Scraton, S. (2001). Confronting whiteness? Researching the leisure lives of South Asian mothers. *Journal of Gender Studies, 10*(3): 265–278.]

Weiner, G. (1985). *Just a Bunch of Girls.* Milton Keynes: Open University Press.

Weiner, G. (1994). *Feminisms in education: An introduction.* Buckingham, UK: Open University Press.

Williams, A. and Bedward, J. (2001). Gender culture and the generation gap: Student and teacher perceptions of aspects of National Curriculum Physical Education. *Sport Education and Society, 6*(1): 53–66.

Williams, A. and Bedward, J. (2002). Understanding girls' experience of physical education: relational analysis and situated learning. In D. Penney (Ed.), *Gender and physical education: Contemporary issues and future directions* (pp. 146–159). London: Rouledge.

Williams, A., Bedward, J. and Woodhouse, J. (2000). An inclusive National Curriculum? The experience of adolescent girls. *European Journal of Physical Education, 5*: 4–18.

Williams, A. and Woodhouse, J. (1996). Delivering the discourse: Urban adolescents' perceptions of physical education. *Sport, Education and Society, 1*(2): 210–213.

Willis, P. (1974). Performance and meaning: a sociocultural view of women in sport. Birmingham, UK: Centre for Contemporary Cultural Studies. *Women in Sport and Physical Education Journal* (2004), *12* (2).

Women in Sport and Physical Activity Journal, Vol. 12, No. 2, Fall, 2002, p. 1–54. Special issue on Title IX.

Wray, S. (2002). Connecting ethnicity, gender and physicality: Muslim Pakistani women, physical activity and health. In S. Scraton and A. Flintoff (Eds.), *Gender and sport: A reader* (pp. 127–140). London: Routledge.

Wright, J. (1996). The construction of complementarity in physical education. *Gender and Education, 8*(1): 61–79.

Wright, J. (1997). The construction of gender contexts in single sex and co-educational physical education lessons. *Sport, Education and Society, 2*(1): 55–72.

Wright, J. (1999). Changing gendered practices in physical education. *European Journal of Physical Education, 5*(3): 181–197.

Wright, J. (2002a). Physical education teacher education: sites of progress or resistance. In D. Penney (Ed.), *Gender and physical education: Contemporary issues and future directions* (pp. 190–207). London: Routledge.

Wright, J. (2002b). Changing gendered practices in physical education: working with teachers. *European Physical Education Review, 5*(3): 181–197.

Wright, J. (2004). Post structural methodologies: the body, schooling and health. In J. Evans, B. Davies and J. Wright (Eds.), *Body knowledge and control: Studies in the sociology of physical education and health* (pp. 19–31). London: Routledge.

Wright, J., Macdonald, D., and Groom, L. (2003). Physical Activity and Young People: Beyond Participation. *Sport Education and Society, 8*(1): 17–34.

Wright, J., Macdonald, D., and Groom, L. (2003). Physical Activity and Young People: Beyond Participation. *Sport Education and Society, 8*: 17–34.

Young, I. (1981). Beyond the unhappy marriage: a critique of dual systems theory. In L. Sargent (Ed.), *Women and revolution* (pp. 7–19). Boston, MA: South End Press.

Zaman, H. (1997). Islam, well-being and physical activity: perceptions of Muslim young women. In G. Clarke and B. Humberstone (Eds.), *Researching women and sport* (pp. 50–67). London: Macmillan.

6.5 More art than science? Boys, masculinities and physical education research

MICHAEL GARD

Introduction

Bodies of research literature are not simply (and, sometimes, not even) accounts of the state of knowledge about something. In retrospect, they may be more profitably understood as artefacts of particular historical events, periods or struggles. This is perhaps especially true in educational research although this is not a view which will be welcomed by all readers. Educational practice and research have usually resembled more closely artistic endeavours than scientific ones and have therefore been all the more subject to the winds of fashion. I should stress that this is to say nothing about the worth or significance of any particular line of research. In many respects art and fashion are far more influential and enduring enterprises than science and we should no doubt be grateful that this is so.

We are now in a position at least to begin to ask whether or not increased academic interest in boys, men and masculinities over the last 10–15 years has simply been a matter of intellectual fashion. As well as offering a review of physical education research into boys and masculinities in this chapter, I will also try to contextualise this research within its historical moment and, yes, to begin to evaluate it as a passing intellectual fashion (as all intellectual movements are). But as I have already indicated, this leaves completely open the question of its worth to those who work within physical education. It could be, for example, that brief intellectual fads (which some have claimed masculinities studies to be) sometimes serve as precious blasts of fresh air before we all return indoors to enervating normality. After all, boys and masculinities research in physical education has not simply been the mirror image of research about boys carried out in other educational fields, but has had its own empirical and political agendas and these will also be explored here. In fact, it has produced a number of challenges and possibilities for school and teacher education, as well as suggesting some alternative ways of answering physical education's enduring "why" question.

Sport, masculinity and physical education

Why should boys and masculinity be interesting to researchers? Naively, we might begin by saying that there are two possibilities. First, it could be that boys as a group face particular problems and that we need to know more about the nature of these problems in order to formulate possible remedies. A second possibility is that some or all boys exhibit behaviours that are harmful to other people. In very general terms, physical education research into boys has advanced the second of these two lines of argument. That is, it is not so much that boys as a group are suffering as a result of their experiences in physical education but rather that it is the process of becoming and being a male that presents physical educators with particular problems.

For the moment, I propose to call this "process of becoming and being male" "masculinity". In other words, masculinity is concerned with what would once have been called the "socialisation" of boys, as well as the identities that boys and men form as a result of this process. In a sense, then, masculinity is the umbrella term we might give to the ideas and behaviours which answer the question "what does it mean to be male?", with all the conceptual imprecision a question of this kind unleashes. I will return to a more detailed discussion of the terms "masculinity" and "masculinities" later in this chapter.

With this as a starting point, it is difficult not to turn first to a discussion of the place of sport both within physical education and masculinity. Not all boys and masculinities research in physical education research has been primarily concerned with sport. However, I would argue that the nexus between sport, masculinity and physical education rests at or near the heart of the moral agendas which have driven research in this area. These agendas have been heavily influenced by feminism so that researchers have tended to see the connection between sport and masculinity as an obstacle to much needed change. Thus, physical education has been added to the list of institutions which are thought to favour the interests of boys over girls. And whether it is research into classroom practice, the content of official school curricula or teacher education, sport and its undeniably idiosyncratic moral universe emerge as indispensable ingredients of dominant and (according to many scholars) problematic ways of thinking about physical education.

In this context the history of organised sport in English-speaking Western countries has provided many of the key theoretical resources for contemporary boys and masculinities research. A number of important historical works (e.g. Adair et al., 1998; Chandler, 1996; Crosset, 1990; Kimmel, 1987, 1990, 1996; Mangan, 1981; Phillips, 1984; Putney, 2001) have described the simultaneous and intertwined appearance of modern sports and the development of new, particularly middle class, codes of masculine behaviour during the nineteenth and early twentieth centuries. The exact nature of these codes varied within and between countries, but they shared a general suspicion of aristocratic ostentation and privileged industry over beauty and the athlete over the aesthete. In many ways, they also brought the self-presentation and sexual proclivities of Western men under new and intense forms of scrutiny and laid the foundations for the extreme forms of Western homophobia which flourished throughout the twentieth century. These studies of Victorian masculinity are important for at least three reasons. First, they show that the close association between competitive sports and becoming and being male in English speaking Western cultures is a relatively recent historical phenomenon and followed a period marked by very different ideas about masculinity. For example, the rise of competitive sports during the middle and later Victorian periods tended to displace and undermine earlier, more aristocratic ideals of male bodily deportment based around refinement, restraint and a certain gentility of movement (Burt, 1995). McLaren (1997) argues that the nineteenth century also saw the intermingling of other new and important social forces such as the expansion of middle-class values and economic power, widespread concern about what industrial urbanisation did to the "virility" of professional class men and the social construction of new forms of legal and psychological "deviancy" and "perversion". Kimmel writes:

> Insecure masculinity is not uniquely American, but rather emerges in the nineteenth century as the bourgeoisie ascends to national political dominance. According to the French historian Michel Foucault, it is the bourgeois preoccupation

> with order and control and with an interminable ordering and disciplining of the natural and social environment that defines the era of bourgeois hegemony. (1987: 244)

The newly codified, organised competitive sports can therefore be seen within a kind of "crisis of masculinity", as an antidote to what was seen as the corrosive effects of modern life on boys and men. As Connell writes:

> The exemplary status of sport as a test of masculinity, which we now take for granted, is in no sense natural. It was produced historically, and ... deliberately as a political strategy. (1995: 30)

It is sometimes argued by those who object to sport being subjected to this kind of academic analysis that the new sports were (and are) understood and experienced by people in many other ways which have little to do with the construction of "virile" masculinity. This is undoubtedly true and the danger of any form of analysis is that it reduces social phenomena to their significance within a particular theoretical framework. However, the case for seeing modern sport as, amongst other things, an expression of "insecure masculinity" has not, as yet, been seriously refuted and it remains an important conceptual device for understanding the present via the past.

Second, this historical work shows that the pre-eminent position of sport within these new codes of masculinity was not universally welcomed. The Victorian "cult of athleticism" had many outspoken critics, precisely because it contradicted earlier codes of masculinity (Crotty, 1998). Smith (1974) shows that these critics tended to see undue emphasis on athletics as a violation of man's "true nature" and a general threat to pious and scholarly decorum. What many people today take to be the perfect fit between sport and boys' and men's "nature" actually has its roots in struggles over what this nature actually is.

Third, this period of history also witnessed the spread of competitive sports into the physical activity programs of most ruling and middle-class schools. It is true that sport and physical education in these schools were not (and still today are not) the same thing. However, it was during this period when sport began to establish itself as *the* form of organised physical activity which was widely seen as most compatible with boys' nature and best suited to schools' task of producing the right kind of men.

Importantly, even at this early stage we can see the cracks in this construction of sport as a maker of men. On the one hand sport is held up as being a natural expression of a pre-given and fixed masculinity, while on the other hand it assumes a crucial role in shaping and preserving masculinity against the perceived degenerating potential of modern Western life. In other words, masculinity is seen simultaneously as both eternal and constantly at risk and under siege.

Other scholars have mapped the struggle for classroom ascendancy amongst different movement traditions during the subsequent transition to mass schooling (e.g. Kirk, 1994, 1998; Polidoro, 2000). It would be wrong to characterize these struggles as completely one-sided or finally resolved. However, a good deal of contemporary research suggests that, in the minds of many teachers and students, it was sports participation and the development of sporting skill which increasingly came to be seen as the primary reason for doing physical education throughout the twentieth century. As Kirk (1994: 47) writes in the Australian context: "'Physical education' was, and has continued to be, an invention, which has served mainly to legitimate the practice of competitive sport in schools."

While a historical perspective might help us to understand how we got to where we are now, this does not answer the question of why it should be of interest to people concerned with contemporary physical education practice. For the most part, boys and masculinity researchers have premised their interest in sport's enduring connection with physical education on a feminist politic. This is not to deny that some feminist scholars have viewed boys and masculinities research with suspicion and doubted its relevance to the goals of feminism (Kenway, 1998; Skelton, 1998; Wearing, 1996). For the moment, however, my interest here is in what boys and masculinities researchers say about their research, not whether these claims are justified.

Core concepts, theories and findings

The new "crisis of masculinity"

A reasonable case could be made to the effect that school-based physical education has always had at its core the problematic of the "boy". For example, if we accept that post-Enlightenment formal education has predominantly taken boys rather than girls to be its primary raw material, the production of the "educated" citizen has either explicitly or implicitly centred on making boys into certain kinds of men. This appears to have been as true in education for the mind as for the body.

However, this line of argument is not without its problems. For example, feminine traditions in physical education have been more overlooked than non-existent, a situation which has been partially addressed by feminist scholars (Bouchier, 1998; Lenskyj, 1990; Verbrugge 1997; Welch, 1986).

Nonetheless, as Wright (1996a) has suggested, what counts as legitimate and valuable movement in physical education classrooms has shifted across time and space. Wright argues that the twentieth century saw the eventual marginalization of physical education's feminine traditions in the English-speaking West by masculine traditions, particularly in the form of competitive team sports and athletics. Certainly, it could scarcely be doubted that other movement disciplines such as dance and gymnastics now struggle to receive significant classroom time and that this is partly explained by their association with femininity (Brennan, 1996; Flintoff, 1994; Gard and Meyenn, 2000; Keyworth, 2001; Wright, 1996b). All this is to say that the content of physical education classes and curricula is as inflected by the flows of culture and power, in this case gendered power, as any other area of schooling.

This is an insight which flows directly out of the work of feminist scholars such as Bryson (1987, 1991), Hargreaves (1982), Scraton (1990) and Sherlock (1987) (and a small number of feminist inspired male scholars such as Kidd, 1987; Sabo, 1985; Sabo and Runfola, 1980) who were the first to offer a critique of sport and physical education's gendered knowledge base and practices.

In passing, it is worth keeping in mind that a number of branches of physical education research have at least problematised gender and, as a result, provided insights into boys' experiences and aspirations within physical education. One of these fields is what we might call "gender differences" research, with its primary (although not exclusive) focus on quantitative data concerning boys' and girls' "perceptions", "beliefs", "attitudes" and sources of "motivation" (e.g. Lee et al., 1999; Satina et al. 1998). Research into the merits of same-sex and coeducational physical education classes could also be included here (e.g. Griffin 1983, 1984, 1985; Lirgg, 1994). As useful as this work has been, it is not discussed in this review. In general, gender differences research has taken the categories of "boys" and "girls" as givens and proceeded to argue that teachers need to take account of these differences when planning their teaching. As such, it leaves mostly untouched the categories themselves. By contrast, the remainder of this chapter will deal with research which in different ways problematizes the category "boy".

Weaver-Hightower (2003) has provided a sustained commentary on what he calls the "boy turn" in educational research. He proposes a list of factors which helped to bring boys issues to the attention of educational researchers from the early 1990s onwards. These factors include the rise of explicitly anti-feminist "backlash" politics, upheavals in the world of work including the demise of traditionally male areas of employment and the sheer intellectual novelty value of something new.

However, there is one important factor which Weaver-Hightower includes in his discussion which is not applicable, at least in any straightforward sense, to physical education. In recent years a great deal has been written and said about the performance of boys in the high status academic domains of English and mathematics or, as they are often called, literacy and numeracy. In fact, something approaching a fully blown "moral panic" has emerged, with the media and a series of popular books announcing a "boys crisis". Complex and often acrimonious debates about boys' levels of success in these areas, both in absolute terms and in comparison to girls, have unfolded in the context of a new "crisis of masculinity". As Weaver-Hightower points out, there has been a tendency amongst those within the academic educational research community to see *generalized* concerns about boys' literacy and numeracy performance at schools as misplaced, arguing that it is not at all clear that boys as a group are struggling.

It is worth taking a moment to consider the idea of a "crisis of masculinity". Immediately a number of questions present themselves. Is there *really* a crisis? If there is, for whom are the consequences most acute? Put another way, what is the nature of the crisis? What are its causes and potential sources of amelioration? Some argue that the crisis is real and has been brought about by an increasingly feminized world – in the workplace, in the home, in schools – which has left boys and men out of place and out in the cold. In the student literacy debates, proponents of this line of argument have pointed to a wide range of factors, including the high percentage of female teachers in primary schools and secondary English departments and the emergence of more reflective writing tasks in English assessment. It is important to note that this position rests on a series of generalizations and fixed categories. For example, it asserts that it is in boys' nature to want black and white yes/no answers rather than to reflect and see things (such as the meaning of a novel) from a variety of points of view. It also asserts that it is not in boys' nature to respond to texts in ways which call for emotional engagement with plots and characters.

It could hardly be argued that physical education research about boys was inspired by a general concern about boys' performance in this subject area. First, what counts as "success" in physical education is in some respects an even more conceptually complex and contested notion than it obviously is in subject areas like English and mathematics. For example, there are those who will argue that sheer effort as opposed to, say, physically skilful performance should be the most important marker of student success in physical education. If anything, this situation is probably part cause and part consequence of the traditionally low status of this subject area; if few people really care about what happens in physical education it is unsurprising if no dominant vision of "success", however arrived at, emerges. Second, and probably more important, there exists a long-standing "common sense" assumption that boys enjoy natural advantages over girls, both physical and emotional, which lead to superior performance in physical education. And although both the mass-media and large sections of the academy appear to be convinced that today's young people are a physically inferior crop compared to previous generations (not, it has to be said, a particularly new or empirically defensible proposition), the idea of generalized decline amongst young people does not seem to have cross-fertilized with the idea of a "crisis of masculinity". This does not mean that the idea that sport and physical education play an important part in keeping boys "masculine" is, by any stretch of the imagination, dead. For example, some people clearly do still see sport and physical education as a buffer against the presumably harmful effects of the rest of school life. To this end, some elite school principles have argued that boys are being denied competitive sport in schools and that their natural masculinity is not being acknowledged by a feminised curriculum (Bonnor, 1998).

Gender theory and physical education

During the late 1980s and 1990s masculinities research, led by a small group of mostly (but not only) male theorists (Bordo, 1999; Connell, 1987, 1990, 1995; Kaufman, 1987; Mac an Ghaill, 1996; Morgan, 1992), increasingly attracted academic interest right across the social sciences. Many of these scholars argued that continued progress towards gender equality would require boys and men to take active roles in the change process. While feminism had opened up new vocational and interpersonal trajectories for girls and women, boys and men had clung to older ways of being, mainly because it was (at least in some ways) in their interest to do so.

The work of Connell and others (e.g. Brod, 1987; Brod and Kaufman, 1994; Hearn and Morgan, 1990) also sought to highlight the way both popular and academic discussion about "males" and "masculinity" often assumed an unproblematic unity and coherence about these categories. Connell (1987), in particular, argued that this unitary view owed much to the dominance of sex role theory, dating as far back as the 1930s (also see Carrigan et al., 1987; Edley and Wetherell, 1996; Lehikoinen, 1997 for discussions on the shortcomings of role theory). Despite some concerted efforts to modernise sex role theory (most notably Pleck, 1981), Connell pointed to its methodological flaws (particularly its use of pencil and paper questionnaires and numerical scales of "masculinity" and "femininity"), rigid categories and structuralist tendencies to see gender identity as a pre-existing script to be learnt. In short, it was a theoretical tradition which saw variation in gender identity as fundamentally constrained by existing "scripts" and offered a basically benign account of the politics of gender. That is, people became particular kinds of men and women because these "kinds" were all that were on offer.

Connell and his contemporaries were writing during, and contributing to, the emergence of post-structuralism as the dominant theoretical paradigm within gender theory. Within this new paradigm gender identity was seen as more fluid. In fact, identity itself was seen as a far more problematic idea, such that it became necessary to talk of people moving between various identities across time and space. The idea of a sex role gave way to scepticism about the possibility of ever achieving coherence; being a man or a woman was now something people only ever achieved imperfectly and was always at risk of being exposed as a kind of charade or, in the language of the paradigm, performance.

The question of what motivated people to become particular kinds of males and females also took on a new kind of complexity. Rather than the sheer necessity of social acceptance (as implied by the term "socialization"), post-structuralists tended to argue that pleasure and power were at the centre of things, that different identities promised different sorts of dividends and that resistance to change was not just a matter of blind convention.

In this context theorists proposed that we talk about "masculinities" and "femininities" and that we take account of the politics of identities; that being male and female concealed a complex and active weaving together of different ideas and practices and that the most valued or "dominant" modes of being male and female held the possibility, at least, of certain dividends. It was with a view to describing culturally dominant modes of masculinity, and the dividends that these modes attracted, that the idea of "hegemonic masculinity" became commonplace in gender theory. To take a straightforward example, sporting prowess for boys and men is often seen as a highly valued and prestigious attribute within Western cultures. Amongst its perceived and potential rewards we might include enormous financial reward, the development of a sexually desirable and publicly celebrated body shape and association with commonly "understood" ideas and myths about sport, notably that sport makes one a better person. While some boys may reject or ignore these rewards and fashion non-sporting masculinities, many do so at some social, physical or emotional cost. However, gender theorists have tended to argue that we live in a fundamentally sexist world and that, all other things being equal, being male is invariably

privileged over being female. Whether or not readers concur with this argument, the central point is that, whatever kind of relationships individual boys form with competitive sports, that a relationship should exist seems inescapable. While most boys in the English-speaking West can get through life without having to engage or actively disengage with chess, stamp collecting, ballroom dancing or Russian literature, detached ignorance of sport is virtually impossible (Burstyn, 1999; Plummer, 1999). A number of excellent ethnographic studies have documented the central role sport plays in shaping boys' identities and personal relationships, both inside and outside schools (e.g. Fine, 1987; Foley 1990; Light and Kirk, 2000).

Beginning in the late 1980s and early 1990s with contributions such as George and Kirk (1988) and Skelton (1993), some scholars began to argue that physical education, both in teacher education and school contexts, was increasingly out of step with changes in educational theory, its diverse student base and the changing societies in which it operated. Skelton (1993) claimed that physical education was especially resistant to liberal educational goals which de-emphasized aggressive competition and placed a high value on sensitivity, enjoyment, equal opportunity, co-operation, student autonomy and individually relevant criteria for success. According to this line of argument, physical education's sporting lineage had bequeathed a culture of masculine athleticism, where sporting prowess, aggressive heterosexuality and rampant sexism reigned. Perhaps more significantly, this translated into classroom practices which favoured boys who were more likely to be interested and proficient in competitive sports. A related point which was made less often is that, quite apart from whether or not a sports-dominated curriculum is considered a good or bad thing, physical education classes were (and are) dominated by game playing. After all, there are many ways in which we might teach sporting skills to children and it is not at all inevitable that competitive game playing best suits the goals articulated in curriculum documents.

But here again a historical perspective is useful. Proponents of the Victorian "cult of athleticism" believed passionately that the game itself was the teacher. *Participation* in these newly hyper-rational and rule bound games was seen as sufficient for physical and moral development to occur. As we have seen, this idea that sport is a form of magic, imbued with transformative powers not present in other areas of human endeavour, had originally been formulated with ruling and middle-class boys exclusively in mind. But as Kirk (1998) has argued, twentieth century physical educators tended to see no reason why this magic could not work for all students, a trend which no doubt accelerated as physical education traditions based on dance and gymnastics lost ground (Paechter,

2000; Wright, 1996a). Belief in the magical powers of sport are, if anything, stronger than ever today. In Australia, for example, both state and federal governments have spent significant sums of taxpayers' money on programs which bring elite sportspeople onto school premises in the belief that their mere presence will "inspire" children to lead more physically active and healthy lives.

Following and in conjunction with feminist sport and physical education scholars, the 1990s yielded a number of studies focused exclusively on boys, the construction of different masculinities in physical education and how these shaped what we might call the "movement cultures" of schools. Parker's (1996a) research is a useful case in point. He writes:

> It is accepted that young people enter schools as sexual and gendered objects, having already experienced the formal and informal learning networks of the family environment, peer groups, and the media. But, moreover, I argue that educational environments provide an additional arena within which individuals might contest and negotiate their own sex/gender identity. (1996a: 143)

In particular, Parker suggests that different subject areas make available and provide space for the expression of different kinds of identities and behaviours. For example, "... because of its relatively 'informal' and 'spacious' appeal, physical education appeared to provide more opportunity than other lessons for the enactment of such (violent) behaviours" (Parker, 1996a: 145). This is an important finding because it suggests ways in which physical education classes may privilege and marginalise different masculinities and in different ways to other subject areas. For example, Martino's research shows that success in subject English is seen by some boys as incompatible with being a "cool" or "normal" (read heterosexual) boy (Martino, 1995, 2000). In contrast, Bramham's (2003) study of boys' physical education classes showed that it was *non-conformity* (either through not bringing correct "kit" to school or a lack of skill or interest in the more popular sports) amongst a relatively small number of "resistors" which marked them as less masculine in the eyes of other boys. Parker's study, as with a number of others (Bramham, 2003; Foley, 1990; Gard and Meyenn, 2000; Martino, 1999), shows that, rather than being an expression of some essential, universal masculinity, physical education and sport actually highlight the diversity which exists. For example, both Parker's and Bramham's data, collected in England, show how Western and Asian masculinities diverge to produce different and competing hierarchies around such things as body shape, movement style, physical aggression and the level of importance boys afford to sport and academic school work. It is worth remembering also that diversity within and between ethnic and class-based masculinities had already been amply demonstrated in classic ethnographic studies of school culture such as those conducted by Willis (1977), Walker (1988) and Mac an Ghaill (1994). Mac and Ghaill's study, in particular, showed how ethnicity and class shape boys' and girls' understandings of "appropriate" masculine behaviour. In addition, boys' bodies, including their deployment in school sport and physical education, were important markers for whether they "pass" as "straight" or not.

All of these studies are significant because they confirm the work of other scholars who have argued that physical education is not always a safe place for students or a place where the bodies and movement aspirations of all students are equally valued (Clarke, 1998; Wright, 1996b). As Parker writes:

> Experiences of schooling also tend to show that if children cross over taken for granted "biological sporting boundaries", they may well find themselves the subjects of intense peer group ridicule, particularly in relation to notions of sexuality. (1996b: 127)

In straightforward terms this means that quite apart from the many other obstacles students may face in physical education, "boundaries" around what boys and girls should and should not do with their bodies and the risks associated with "inappropriate" gender performance are all too real, despite the fact that they are social constructions in the purest sense. This can mean that entire fields of physical activity are simply closed for some male and female students (see Chepyator-Thompson and Ennis, 1997 for an example of qualitative research in which boys and girls articulate both conformity and resistance to these boundaries). But as Wright (1996b) argues, in a world which privileges masculinity over femininity, these boundaries are particularly constraining for boys. Wright's study showed that girls were more likely to feel able to "transgress" physical activity boundaries than boys. So just as we have seen in society in general, it has proved much easier to get girls and women interested in sport than boys and men interested in gymnastics and dance, a situation which should not surprise anyone if we accept that gender boundaries do not separate two equally valued halves. For example, the boys in Gard and Meyenn's (2000) study generally saw dance as not only "gay" but also "pointless", an interesting construction which may, in fact, be a kind of code for "not as useful for proving one's masculinity" or "unlikely to secure the same cultural dividends as sports". While a small number of boys found sport "pointless", they were a distinct minority.

What these studies also suggest is how thoroughly constructed the capacities and pleasures of our bodies might be. For example, when some of the boys in Gard and Meyenn's (2000) study say that much of the pleasure of contact sports comes from the rough bodily contact and that they "hate" dance, we need to at least consider these feelings as if they were "true", regardless of whether one is inclined to see these remarks as masculine performance. Why should some people derive pleasure from different forms of physical activity and why should boys experience such discomfort when, say, asked to move in a rhythmical or emotionally expressive way? In my view, the most compelling line of argument here is to discount the idea that any form of physical activity is always experienced in some specific way. Put another way, we might argue that our job as physical educators is not so much to find forms of physical activity to which particular children are inherently "suited", but to find ways of creating contexts in which boundaries might be crossed.

There also exists a small but compelling literature which, like Skelton's (1993) paper, considers the role of teacher education in reproducing physical education's "masculine tradition". Although a detailed discussion of this literature is somewhat outside the scope of this chapter, these researchers argue that the culture of physical education teacher education (PETE) leaves the privileged place of competitive sport effectively unchallenged, while actively undermining alternative visions. Leann Brown (1998) calls PETE "boys' training" while Flintoff (1991, 1994) and Keyworth (2001) have written about the strong resistance amongst male PETE students to dance. Interestingly, the ethnographic work of Skelton (2000) and Renold (1997) suggests that in primary schools at least a kind of "boys' club" can emerge in which male students and teachers collaborate to make traditionally male sports the most valued form of school physical activity and to trivialize and marginalize the interests and talents of female students. Renold shows how this "boys' club" of students and teachers bolsters hegemonic sporting masculinities and feminizes boys who are not high achievers in sport. Drawing on life-history interviews with recent male PETE graduates, Brown (1999) places the male physical education student who grows up to be the male physical education teacher at the centre of "gender order" reproduction in sport and physical education. He claims that:

> ... complicity to a hegemonic norm represents a form of masculine teaching identity that facilitates the reproduction of hegemonic forms of masculinity and patriarchy in PE and school sport. The data illustrate that in managing their masculine teaching identities to accommodate the social expectations placed upon them, the participants draw upon their background experience and in so doing shift their teaching identities towards a complicit masculine teaching identity. Although unintentional this situation represents a dilemma that serves to perpetuate a link between generations of PE discourse and practice helping to reproduce and legitimize hegemonic masculinity and the gender order in physical education. (1999: 143)

It is important to stress here that, although Brown talks about the reproduction of something called "the gender order in physical education", at the heart of this issue is the experience of children in schools. At stake is the question of who's bodies matter in physical education classes and who's do not. While the term "physical education" potentially suggests an opening up of "physical" possibilities, the existence of a gender order may stifle the kinds of experiences that teachers feel prepared to offer and students feel able to try. A gender order may mean that classrooms become, in effect, stages for the enactment of particular identities rather than spaces in which the body's movement potential is cultivated. But more than this, the charge here is that physical education is both victim and engineer of this gender order because it privileges certain kinds of identities over others. While academics may talk about education "in, about and through the physical" and modern syllabus writers recommend new, liberal, student-centred, "culturally relevant" approaches to teaching, physical education has its own history which lives in the present. An important part of this history is a belief in the universal appeal of sport and the transformative power of game playing. What physical education's "boy turn" suggests is that not only is this view limited and likely to favour the tastes and aspirations of male students, but that it is complicit with a long held belief that some recognizable essence called "masculinity" exists somewhere in the mind and/or body of all boys.

Changing masculinities

A small number of scholars have built upon the insights generated by gender research in physical education to propose specific pedagogical interventions. For example, the feminist outdoor educator Barbara Humberstone (1990, 1995) has argued that more egalitarian relationships and less stereotypically masculine identities can be fostered amongst male students by varying the content of physical education. Humberstone articulates very much an experiential approach to physical education; it is not so much that students are made to think explicitly about their identities, but rather that outdoor education can be a qualitatively different experience from competitive sport. For boys, this means engaging in activities in which girls may outperform them and where teachers (or instructors) explicitly discourage "macho" and overtly competitive behaviour. This is a strategy which speaks directly to the work of physical education scholars (discussed above) who implicate (particularly male) teachers in the perpetuation of masculinist physical education. That is, the fact that physical education teachers generally *do* come from competitive sporting backgrounds and tend to see competitive sports as the "natural" domain of physical education *is* significant in shaping the experiences students are offered.

The work of Hickey and Fitzclarence (1999, see also Fitzclarence et al. 1998) takes a different approach. To begin with, they concur with other scholars who have suggested that sports, particularly team sports, have the potential to foster both positive and negative qualities amongst boys. For example, they have highlighted the way male sporting team cultures are sometimes marked by conformity, contempt for weakness, sexist and homophobic attitudes and a kind of masculine group solidarity. They point to similarities and draw connections between the group dynamics of male team sports and the violent, abusive and risk taking behaviour of some other male peer groupings. With specific reference to schools, they also discuss the way sport helps to create divisions amongst boys, so that categories such as "cool" or "nerd", "tough" or "fag", "popular" or "loser" map closely (although never perfectly) onto boys' level of affiliation with sports. These are not trivial matters. In the world of schools where social acceptance is valued almost above all else, Hickey and Fitzclarence argue that students', but particularly boys', relationships, mental health and physical safety are at stake.

Hickey and Fitzclarence have also argued that physical education is an appropriate place to begin to address these issues precisely because of this subject area's obvious and widely understood connection with sport. Sport is, as they say, "where the boys are" so it is in the context of sport where we need to act. In Hickey and Fitzclarence (1999) they suggest that the principles of narrative therapy may be useful in developing "pedagogies of responsibility" for working with boys in physical education. They propose a question driven approach to create spaces for students to tell stories about their life, to distance themselves from particular events or attitudes and, as they put it, to re-narrativise themselves. But rather than this process being one in which boys are expected to confess their sins, these researchers argue that talk and stories in supportive environments can connect actions, behaviours and people. That is, this process asks boys to reflect. Also making use of stories, Pringle (2004) has recorded men's reflections on the way they did or did not willingly engage in rough contact sport as boys and then crafted these reflections into composite or "collective stories"; single stories which weave together elements from multiple stories. An important part of Pringle's motivation here is to listen to males talking about pleasure, pain and, interestingly, fear in the context of sports like rugby. That is, while popular discourse is full of the "natural" masculine desire to throw one's body around a football field and in the path of other (often much larger) bodies, male fear, while no doubt common, is rarely publically celebrated and has the potential to strike an oppositional note. Some of the males in Pringle's research also expressed resentment that they were expected to be footballers at all and described the strategies they developed to appear involved while (at the same time) studiously avoiding physical contact.

Elsewhere, Gard (2001a,b; 2003) takes his lead from Martino's research (discussed above) into masculinities in the English classroom. Both researchers argue that students come to school already well versed in the "rules" of gender. In the case of physical education in Australia, a number of states have introduced syllabus documents which link physical education with health education and conceptualize "wellness" as including physical, mental, social, emotional and spiritual dimensions. Gard's argument is that these syllabuses open up spaces for teachers to use texts, video, artefacts from popular culture and students' existing "common sense" knowledge to problematize the categories of "girl" and "boy". Gard's specific area of interest has been the marginal place of dance within physical education. But as well as suggesting that students might use classroom time to think about and discuss, say, prevailing negative stereotypes about boys who dance (and the never far away homophobic ideas which underpin these stereotypes), he is also concerned with dance as a specific kind of bodily practice. Is it possible, for example, that dance experiences have the potential for boys to use their bodies in ways they would not normally do and, in effect, to enact a new identity? Might it be possible to use dance as a space in which students question (through movement) or even parody the rules of gender as they apply to bodies and movement? In short, Gard asks a question which is simultaneously delicate and imprecise: who are we when we move differently?

It is worth remembering that boys' misgivings about dance have been addressed by a number of other authors (Crawford, 1994; Dymoke, 1998; Lloyd and West, 1988; Pool, 1986) but that these contributions tend to suggest that we avoid using the word "dance" or that we make boys' dance experiences more like sporting experiences. It is precisely this approach Gard questions and which is rendered problematic by research into boys and masculinities. Dance is potentially valuable to us as physical educators *because* it is not sport and because it has the potential to take all of us out of our "comfort zones".

It is not (in most cases) a matter of life and death that students have opportunities to question what it means to be male and what "real" males do with their bodies. But if physical education is simply a place in which the bodily codes and moral imperatives of competitive sport are re-enacted and reinforced, it will have added very little to students' understandings about the world they live in (where images of sport and sporting bodies are already ubiquitous) and a small window into another world of embodied identities will have been closed.

Finally, a word of caution is necessary here. As the tenets of critical pedagogy and post-structuralist theory have infiltrated educational research, it is noticeable that when researchers have turned their hand to suggesting pedagogical responses, they have often fallen back on their theories. For example, while (it is claimed) poststructuralist gender theory has helped us to understand the construction of gender in physical education classes and in educational practice more generally, many writers have argued that students should be taught how to do this deconstructive work for themselves. Here the suggestion seems to be that, if only students could be taught to think like researchers, they too would then see the undesirability of current gender relations. In my view, this is a naïve position and has lead to some unrealistic, mechanical and, frankly, less than stimulating ideas for classroom practice. In effect, researchers (myself included) have been inclined to ask teachers to ask students to problematise their identity, their pleasures and the very things that give their lives meaning, all in the name of "gender reform". This is a point which should be borne in mind no matter how distasteful these identities, pleasures and meanings might appear to some. Not enough work has gone into thinking about how we might more skilfully, playfully, pleasurably and subtly weave critical ideas about gender into our pedagogical responses. Too often the suggestion of researchers has been to turn away from the activity we are supposed to be teaching, so that critical physical education scholars will ask that teachers devote time to discussion, writing and reading tasks in order to address gender. This is in no way to dismiss the potential of these strategies, although, to be fair, their impact is something (as with many important educational initiatives) we are unlikely ever to be able to quantify. However, critical gender work in physical education classes needs to be both bitter and sweet if gender reform in physical education is ever to move substantially beyond rhetoric into practice.

Future developments?

Will physical education scholars be concerned about boys and masculinity in the future? Is research on boys now an established field of enquiry which will develop and "mature"? If it is true that physical education research about boys was merely a reflection or a symptom (depending on one's assessment of its worth) of developments in gender theory and educational research, then we might expect research interest in boys to wane. After all, research agendas in education are rarely, if ever, exhausted on account of all its important questions having been answered. It is not as if questions are answered, ticked off and replaced by new ones in some logical working through of the issues that face us. Instead, different agendas emerge as societies change and different questions simply do not look important any more.

However, the last 20 years or so has witnessed a re-intensification of debate about the role of men in Western societies, the emergence of new scientifically endorsed forms of biological determinism (which purport to show, amongst other things, that males really are all the same) and a general waning in the overtly political influence of feminism. At the same time, the damage that "hegemonic masculinity" can do to girls, boys, women and men has never been so clearly documented, enunciated and, in my view, popularly understood. And despite the recent splash of "new-ladism" in advertising and popular culture, masculinity *is* changing in both trivial and profound ways. Not only do male students douse themselves with sweet perfumes of one kind or another before coming to my classes, many seem genuinely puzzled that anyone would see dancing as incompatible with being male or competitive sport as being incompatible with being female. In fact, it may be that when physical education's gender theorists talk of a "gender order", they are referring to a world which has already disappeared or is at least disappearing. This is not to say that there are no more "gender rules" which need to be challenged, but rather that modern media, consumer and technological cultures have produced new student identities (or as Green and Bigum (1993) put it, "aliens") about which our theories have not very much to say. But what boys research will have helped to reinforce (it certainly could not be suggested that it broke the news) is that the terms "boy" and "masculinity" both signify sites of cultural contestation rather than eternal, stable entities. It almost goes without saying that if masculinity was, in fact, eternal there would be no reason to defend it or worry about its erosion. And in the same way, masculinity will always be in a state of perpetual crisis so long as it is assumed to be stable and eternal and, just as importantly, so long as there are certain forms of cultural power and privilege that flow from it.

References

Adair, D., Nauright, J. and Phillips, M. (1998). Playing fields through to battle fields: the development of

Australian sporting manhood in its imperial context. c. 1850–1918. *Journal of Australian Studies, 56*: 51–67.

Bonnor, C. (1998). Teaching boys how to be real men. *Education Review*, June: 7.

Bordo, S. (1999). *The male body: A new look at men in public and in private.* New York: Farrar, Straus and Giroux.

Bouchier, N.B. (1998). Let us take care of our field: the National Association for physical education of college women and World War II. *Journal of Sport History, 25*(1): 65–86.

Bramham, P. (2003). Boys, masculinities and PE. *Sport, Education and Society, 8*(1): 57–71.

Brennan, D. (1996). Dance in the Northern Ireland physical education curriculum: a farsighted policy or an unrealistic innovation. *Women's Studies International Forum, 19*(5): 493–503.

Brod, H. (Ed.) (1987). *The making of masculinities: The new men's studies.* Boston, MA: Allen & Unwin.

Brod, H. and Kaufman, M. (Eds.) (1994). *Theorizing masculinities.* London: Sage.

Brown, D. (1999). Complicity and reproduction in teaching physical education. *Sport, Education and Society, 4*(2): 143–159.

Brown, L. (1998) '"Boys' training": the inner sanctum. In C. Hickey, L. Fitzclarence and R. Matthews (Eds.), *Where the boys are: Masculinity, sport and education* (pp. 83–96). Geelong, Australia: Deakin Centre for Education and Change.

Bryson, L. (1987). Sport and the maintenance of masculine hegemony. *Women's studies international forum, 10*(4): 349–60.

Bryson, L. (1991). Challenges to male hegemony in sport., In M.A. Messner and D.F. Sabo (Eds.), *Sport, men, and the gender order: Critical feminist perspectives* (pp. 173–184). Champaign, IL.: Human Kinetics.

Burstyn, V. (1999). *The rites of men: Manhood, politics, and the culture of sport.* Toronto, Canada: University of Toronto Press.

Burt, R. (1995). *The male dancer: Bodies, spectacle, sexualities.* London: Routledge.

Carrigan, T., Connell, B. and Lee, J. (1987). Hard and heavy: toward a new sociology of masculinity. In M. Kaufman (Ed.), *Beyond patriarchy: Essays by men on pleasure, power and change* (pp. 139–184). Toronto: Oxford University Press.

Chepyator-Thomson, J.R. and Ennis, C.D. (1997). Reproduction and resistance to the culture of femininity and masculinity in secondary school physical education. *Research Quarterly for Exercise and Sport, 68*(1): 89–99.

Chandler, T.J.L. (1996). 'The structuring of manliness and the development of rugby football at the public schools and Oxbridge, 1830–1880. In T.J.L. Chandler and J. Nauright (Eds.), *Making men: Rugby and masculine identity* (pp. 13–31). London: Frank Cass.

Clarke, G. (1998). Queering the pitch and coming out to play: lesbians in physical education and sport. *Sport, Education and Society, 3*(2): 145–160.

Connell, R.W. (1987). *Gender and power.* Sydney, Australia: Allen and Unwin.

Connell, R.W. (1990). An iron man: the body and some contradictions of hegemonic masculinity. In M.A. Messner and D.F. Sabo (Eds.), *Sport, men, and the gender order: Critical feminist perspectives* (pp. 83–95). Champaign, Il.: Human Kinetics.

Connell, R.W. (1995). *Masculinities.* St. Leonards, NSW: Allen and Unwin.

Crawford, J.R. (1994). Encouraging male participation in dance. *Journal of Physical Education, Recreation and Dance, 65*(2): 40–43.

Crosset, T. (1990). *Masculinity, sexuality, and the development of early modern sport.* In M.A. Messner and D.F. Sabo (Eds.), *Sport, men, and the gender order: critical feminist perspectives.* pp. 45–54. Champaign, IL: Human Kinetics.

Crotty, M. (1998). There's a tumult in the distance, and a war-song in the air: violence and sport in the Australian public school of the late nineteenth and early twentieth century. In D. Hemphill (Ed.), *All part of the game: Violence and Australian sport* (pp. 1–18). Melbourne: Walla Walla Press.

Dymoke, K. (1998). Premier league. *Animated, Spring:* 28–29.

Edley, N. and Wetherell, M. (1996). Masculinity, power and identity. In M. Mac an Ghaill (Ed.), *Understanding masculinities: Social relations and cultural arenas* (pp. 97–113). Buckingham, UK: Open University Press.

Fine, G.A. (1987). *With the boys: Little league baseball and preadolescent culture.* Chicago, IL: University of Chicago Press.

Fitzclarence, L., Hickey, C. and Matthews, R. (1998). Learning to rationalise abusive behaviour through football. In C. Hickey, L. Fitzclarence and R. Matthews (Eds.), *Where the boys are: Masculinity, sport and education* (pp. 67–81). Geelong, Australia: Deakin Centre for Education and Change.

Flintoff, A. (1991). Dance, masculinity and teacher education. *The British Journal of Physical Education, Winter:* 31–35.

Flintoff, A. (1994). Sexism and homophobia in physical education: the challenge for teacher educators. *Physical Education Review, 17*(2): 97–105.

Foley, D.E. (1990). The great American football ritual: reproducing race, class, and gender inequality. *Sociology of Sport Journal, 7*(2): 111–135.

Gard, M. (2001a). Dancing around the 'problem' of boys and dance. *Discourse: Studies in the cultural politics of education, 22*(2): 213–225.

Gard, M. (2001b). I like smashing people, and I like getting smashed myself: addressing issues of masculinity in physical education and sport. In W. Martino and B. Meyenn (Eds.), *What about the boys?: Issues of masculinity in schools* (pp. 222–235). Buckingham, UK: Open University Press.

Gard, M. (2003). Being someone else: using dance in anti-oppressive teaching. *Educational Review, 55*(2): 211–223.

Gard, M. and Meyenn, R. (2000). Boys, bodies, pleasure and pain: interrogating contact sports in schools. *Sport, Education and Society, 5*(1): 19–34.

George, L. and Kirk, D. (1988). The limits of change in physical education: ideologies, teachers and the experience of physical activity. In J. Evans (Ed.), *Teachers, teaching and control in physical education*. London: Falmer Press.

Green, B. and Bigum, C. (1993). Aliens in the classroom. *Australian Journal of Education*, 37(2): 119–141.

Griffin, P.S. (1983). Gymnastics is a girl's thing: student participation and interaction patterns in a middle school gymnastics unit. In T.S. Templin and J. Olson (Eds.), *Teaching physical education* (pp. 71–85). Champaign, IL: Human Kinetics.

Griffin, P.S. (1984). Coed physical education: problems and promise. *Journal of Physical Education, Recreation, and Dance*, 55(6): 36–37.

Griffin, P.S. (1985). Girls' and boys' participation styles in middle school physical education team sport classes: a description of practical applications. *The Physical Educator*, 42: 3–8.

Hargreaves, J. (Ed.) (1982). *Sport, culture, and ideology*. London: Routledge & Kegan Paul.

Hearn, J. and Morgan, D.H.J. (Eds.) (1990). *Men, masculinities and social theory*. London: Unwin Hyman.

Hickey, C. and Fitzclarence, L. (1999). Educating boys in sport and physical education: using narrative methods to develop pedagogies of responsibility. *Sport, Education and Society*, 4(1): 51–62.

Humberstone, B. (1990). Warriors or wimps? Creating alternative forms of physical education. In M.A. Messner and D.F. Sabo (Eds.), *Sport, men, and the gender order: Critical feminist perspectives* (pp. 201–210). Champaign, IL.: Human Kinetics.

Humberstone, B. (1995). Bringing outdoor education into the physical education agenda: gender identities and social change. *Quest*, 47(2): 144–157.

Kaufman, M. (Ed.). (1987). *Beyond patriarchy: Essays by men on pleasure, power and change*. Toronto: Oxford University Press.

Kenway, J. (1998). Masculinity studies, sport and feminism: fair play or foul? In C. Hickey, L. Fitzclarence and R. Matthews (Eds.), *Where the boys are: Masculinity, sport and education* (pp. 155–169). Geelong, Australia: Deakin Centre for Education and Change.

Keyworth, S.A. (2001). Critical autobiography: 'straightening' out dance education. *Research in Dance Education*, 2(2): 117–137.

Kidd, B. (1987). Sports and masculinity. In M. Kaufman (Ed.), *Beyond patriarchy: Essays by men on pleasure, power and change* (pp. 250–265). Toronto: Oxford University Press.

Kimmel, M. (1987). The cult of masculinity: American social character and the legacy of the cowboy. In M. Kaufman (Ed.), *Beyond patriarchy: Essays by men on pleasure, power and change* (pp. 235–249). Toronto: Oxford University Press.

Kimmel, M.S. (1990). Baseball and the reconstitution of American masculinity, 1880–1920. In M.A. Messner and D.F. Sabo (Eds.), *Sport, men, and the gender order: Critical feminist perspectives* (pp. 55–65). Champaign, IL.: Human Kinetics.

Kimmel, M.S. (1996). *Manhood in America: A cultural history*. New York: Free Press.

Kirk, D. (1994). Making the present strange: sources of the current crisis in physical education. *Discourse: Studies in the cultural politics of education*, 15(1): 46–63.

Kirk, D. (1998). *Schooling bodies: School practice and public discourse 1880–1950*. London: Leicester University Press.

Lee, A.M., Fredenburg, K., Belcher, D. and Cleveland, N. (1999). Gender differences in children's conceptions of competence and motivation in physical education. *Sport, Education and Society*, 4(2): 161–174.

Lehikoinen, K. (1997). Fragile masculinities and the sex role theory in dance for boys: a critical discourse. Paper published in *The Call of Forests and Lakes*, proceedings of the 7th International Dance and the Child Conference, Kuopio, Finland. pp. 195–202.

Lenskyj, H. (1990). Training for "true womanhood": physical education for girls in ontario schools, 1890–1920, *Historical Studies in Education*, 2(2): 205–223.

Light, R. and Kirk, D. (2000). High school rugby, the body and the reproduction of hegemonic masculinity. *Sport, Education and Society*, 5(2): 163–176.

Lirgg, C.D. (1994). Environmental perceptions of students in same-sex and coeducational physical education classes. *Journal of Educational Psychology*, 86(2): 183–192.

Lloyd, M.L. and West, B.H. (1988). Where are the boys in dance. *Journal of Physical Education, Recreation and Dance*, 59(5): 47–51.

Mac an Ghaill, M. (1994). *The making of men: Masculinities, sexualities and schooling*. Buckingham, UK: Open University Press.

Mac an Ghaill, M. (Ed.) (1996). *Understanding masculinities: Social relations and cultural arenas*. Buckingham, UK: Open University Press.

Mangan, J.A. (1981). *Athleticism in the Victorian and Edwardian public school: The emergence and consolidation of an educational ideology*. Cambridge: Cambridge University Press.

Martino, W. (1995). Deconstructing masculinity in the English classroom: a site for reconstituting gendered subjectivity. *Gender and Education*, 7(2): 205–220.

Martino, W. (1999). Cool boys, 'Party Animals', 'Squids' and 'Poofters': interrogating the dynamics and politics of adolescent masculinities in school. *British Journal of Sociology of Education*, 20(2): 239–263.

Martino, W. (2000). The boys at the back! Challenging masculinities and homophobia in the English classroom. *English in Australia*, 127–8: 35–50.

McLaren, A. (1997). *The trials of masculinity: Policing sexual boundaries 1870–1930*. Chicago, IL: The University of Chicago Press.

Morgan, D.H.J. (1992). *Discovering men*. London: Routledge.

Paechter, C. (2000). *Changing school subjects: Power, gender and curriculum*. Buckingham, UK: Open University Press.

Parker, A. (1996a). The construction of masculinity within boys' physical education. *Gender and Education*, 8(2): 141–157.

Parker, A. (1996b). Sporting masculinities: gender relations and the body. In M. Mac an Ghaill (Ed.), *Understanding masculinities: Social relations and cultural arenas* (pp. 126–138). Buckingham, UK: Open University Press.

Phillips, J.O.C. (1984). Rugby, war and the mythology of the New Zealand male. *New Zealand Journal of History*, *18*(2): 83–103.

Pleck, J.H. (1981). *The myth of masculinity*. Cambridge, MA.: MIT Press.

Plummer, D. (1999). *One of the boys: Masculinity, homophobia, and modern manhood*. New York: Harrington Park Press.

Polidoro, J.R. (2000). Sport and physical activity in modern America. In J. Polidoro (Ed.), *Sport and physical activity in the modern world* (pp. 54–89). Boston, MA: Allyn and Bacon.

Pool, J.A. (1986). Dance for males in education. paper published in *Dance: The study of dance in society*, proceedings of the VIII Commonwealth and International Conference on Sport, Physical Education, Dance, Recreation and Health, Glasgow: London: E. & F.N. Spon. pp. 174–181.

Pringle, R. (2004). Sporting practices within schools: collective stories, masculinities and transformative possibilities. Paper presented to the *Forum on boys education: The construction of masculinity in practice-oriented subjects*, Sydney University, December 16th.

Putney, C. (2001). *Muscular Christianity: Manhood and sports in protestant America, 1880–1920*. Cambridge, MA: Harvard University Press.

Renold, E. (1997). All they've got in their brains is football. Sport, masculinity and the gendered practices of playground relations. *Sport, Education and Society*, *2*(1): 5–23.

Sabo, D. (1985). Sport, patrirachy and male identity: new questions about men and sport. *Arena Review*, *9*(2): 1–30.

Sabo, D. and Runfola, R. (Eds.). (1980). *Jock: Sports and male identity*. Englewood Cliffs, NJ: Prentice Hall.

Satina, B., Solmon, M.A., Cothran, D.J., Loftus, S.J. and Stockin-Davidson, K. (1998). Patriarchal consciousness: middle school students' and teachers' perspectives of motivational practices. *Sport, Education and Society*, *3*(2): 181–200.

Scraton, S. (1990). *Gender and physical education*. Geelong, Australia.: Deakin University.

Sherlock, J. (1987). Issues of masculinity and femininity in British physical education. *Women's Studies International Forum*, *10*(4): 443–451.

Skelton, A. (1993). On becoming a male physical education teacher: the informal culture of students and the construction of hegemonic masculinity. *Gender and Education*, *5*(3): 289–303.

Skelton, C. (1998). Feminism and research into masculinities and schooling. *Gender and Education*, *10*(2): 217–227.

Skelton, C. (2000). A passion for football: dominant masculinities and primary schooling. *Sport, Education and Society*, *5*(1): 1–18.

Smith, W.D. (1974). *Stretching their bodies: The history of physical education*. Melbourne: Wren Publishing.

Verbrugge, M.H. (1997). 'Recreating the body: women's physical education and the science of sex differences in America, 1900–1940. *Bulletin of the History of Medicine*, *71*(2): 273–304.

Walker, J.C. (1988). Louts and legends: Male youth culture in an inner-city school. Sydney: Allen & Unwin.

Wearing, B. (1996) *Gender: The pain and pleasure of difference*. Melbourne: Longman.

Weaver-Hightower, M. (2003). The "boy turn" in research on gender and education. *Review of Educational Research*, *73*(4): 471–498.

Welch, P. (1986). The relationship of the women's rights movement to women's sport and physical education in the united states 1848–1920. *Proteus*, *3*(1): 34–40.

Willis, P.E. (1977). *Learning to labour: How working class kids get working class jobs*. Farnborough: Saxon House.

Wright, J. (1996a). Mapping the discourses of physical education: articulating a female tradition. *Journal of Curriculum Studies*, *28*(3): 331–351.

Wright, J. (1996b). The construction of complementarity in physical education. *Gender and Education*, *8*(1): 61–79.

6.6   Social class and physical education

JOHN EVANS AND BRIAN DAVIES

Introduction: class matters?

Physical education is a complex social process occurring in a variety of social settings. It refers to the many forms of play, games, sport, gymnastics, leisure and health knowledge(s) that feature formally and informally inside schools and other institutions of organized education. It also refers to those forms of physical activity found in family life, among peers, in clubs and associations and expressed in various media (for example, web sites, newspapers, magazines, radio and TV) that influence people's lives. It is in the relationships within and between these and other sites of social and economic practice and their attendant representations of physical culture that the social class identities that concern us are shaped and formed. Any or all may impact individuals' capacities for intelligent involvement in physical culture, their feelings and ideas about their own and others' corporeality and perceptions as to what "the body" is and ought to be. Physical education inevitably socializes as it skills people, it helps lay down the rules of belonging to a culture and class.

Acknowledging that physical education occurs informally and formally in contexts outside, as well as inside, schools signals that we need to see pedagogic practice as wider than solely classroom relationships between teacher and taught. They include, for example: those between parent/guardian and child; doctor and patient; counsellor and client; coach and player; and individual and TV or PC screen. We look at these contexts relationally, asking, for example, how the media portrays "health" and "fitness", or how parents or guardians invest in physical education both formally and informally out of school hours. Both (parents/guardians and the media) may have a bearing on how children's corporeality is recognized, treated and developed by teachers and others in and out of schools and, in turn, how children interpret and approach physical education in such settings. In them, we may ask how social class acts as a constitutive influence forged by economic forces and

relations constituted, formed and framed by others within, across and between discursive fields. These are fields in which the differences *within* a class, for example, between "new" and "old" middle classes, may be as important as those *between* them in determining individuals' relationships to their own and other's bodies. In Bernstein's terms:

> Educational knowledge is a major regulator of the structure of experience…one can ask, 'How are forms of experience, identity and relation evoked, maintained and changed by the formal transmission of educational knowledge and sensitivities?' (1975: 85)

All forms of physical education inevitably involve a selection from the variety of knowledge forms and physical cultures prevailing locally, nationally and internationally. They are never arbitrary or value free. Selections of which knowledge is worthwhile reflect class and other interests, such as gender and race, mediated by relations of power, authority and control (see Chapter 2.2). According to Bernstein (1975: 85) we can think of processes of selecting worthwhile knowledge in terms of three message systems, which at the level of content or the curriculum, "defines what counts as valid knowledge"; at the level of pedagogy, defines "what counts as valid transmission of knowledge" and; at the level of evaluation, "defines what counts as the valid realisation of this knowledge on the part of the taught". Particular forms of organization, administration and governance shape and define these processes.

In our view, class is a fundamental category of exclusion and identity formation, produced and reproduced in a variety of ways through the content, social context and forms of educational transmission that occur in and outside schools. It is reflected as much in patterns and levels of participation in higher education as it is in behaviours, opportunities and choices in sport, leisure and health. In and through education many working class children persistently learn "to lose" and "how to lose" (Arnot, 2002: 200) even though they may have the "ability" to succeed. In physical education this process of learning to succeed or lose refers not just to "performance" in physical activity and sport but also to the standards of corporeal propriety and "perfection" increasingly required by its subject matter (see Evans and Davies, 2004).

Class, like gender, race and ability relations, constitutes hierarchies in which material and symbolic power is based and differentially distributed. In struggles over knowledge, power, authority and control, these relations are likely to converge (Arnot, 2002, Azzarito, 2005). A focus on social class should not, then, reduce the complexity of identity, opportunity and equity to class issues alone. Indeed, how we articulate these relationships is an important part of class analysis in mainstream sociology and the sociology of education (for examples, see Arnot, 2002; Skeggs, 1997; Walkerdine, 1997) all too rarely reflected in research in physical education(Azzarito and Solomon, 2005). This chapter reflects this lacuna and our endeavour (see also, Green et al., 2005; McDonald, 2003b; O'Flynn, 2004) to reinstate class not only as an important "object" of enquiry in research but as a relevant narrative for policymakers and practitioners in education and PE.

The limited attention given to class matters in the UK and elsewhere, certainly for most of the last 30 years, reflects in part the culture of individualism that has come to pervade Western and Westernized societies. In the UK, this was nurtured and celebrated by successive Conservative governments from the end of the 1970s to 1997 and reconfigured but retained in essence by New Labour. As Kingdom pointed out,

When (Margaret) Thatcher (former British Prime Minister) made her imperious declaration that "there was no such thing as society" she not only captured the essence of a political mission, in a breath she also challenged the very foundations of people having a union or belonging to a 'class'. (1992:1)

Thatcher all but removed "class" from the discursive terrain of politics and education, her sentiments echoing the eccentric nineteenth century genius of Jeremy Bentham for whom society was but a fictitious body, unlike his own, still preserved. These tendencies were reflected in a raft of education policies intended to bring market principles into formal education (Ball, 1990; Penney and Evans, 1999). At their heart lay the assumption that, if parents were given greater "choice" of schools, the "best" schools would thrive and survive as children moved out of the "bad" ones into the "good". This seemed to overlook certain features of a market in compulsory education where "choice" and "mobility" (the capacity of parents to penetrate and manipulate the rules of "choice", including moving

to areas in which "the best" schools are found) are unevenly and differently experienced across social class divides. Although configured rather differently, these tendencies have been reflected in "marketizing" education policies in many societies (Bates, 2003; Luke, 1999). They were also expressed in social theoretical terms by those who eschewed grand narratives, among other things, of class and gender, preferring to see individuals comprised of multiple identities, makers of their own destiny in all aspects of life (Holton and Turner, 1994). Others announced "the death of class" altogether (Pakulski and Waters, 1996) arguing that "new times" and "high modernity" had changed the basis upon which inequality is constituted.

It is not our intention here to document the nuance and detail of these arguments, though they should engage our attention as researchers of class in physical education (see Arnot, 2002; Ball, 2003; MacDonald; 2003; Skeggs, 1997). A retreat from class analysis, whether by policymakers or researchers, is distinctly disturbing and unhelpful if social progress in society, schools and physical education are our chosen goals. As Skeggs pointed out, when a retreat is being mounted we should always ask:

whose experiences are being silenced, whose lives are being ignored, and whose lives are being considered worthy of study?.... to ignore or make class invisible is to abdicate responsibility (through privilege) from the effects it produces. To think that class does not matter is only a prerogative of those unaffected by the deprivations and exclusions it produces. Making class invisible represents a historical stage in which the identity of the middle classes is assumed. (1997: 7)

To make such an assumption is to avoid unpalatable questions relating to the material consequences of capitalism and its attendant inequalities in wealth, including material, symbolic and physical resources and how these are produced, reproduced and reconfigured in society and schools.

Core concepts: but what is class?

The Oxford English Dictionary defines class as "the rank order of society ... the existence of classes as a social factor ... and any set of persons or things differentiated, especially by quality from others" (Allen, 1990: 207). The label social class, then, implies not just a categorization or classification of people with reference to some "quality" (for example, in relationship to the means of economic production, or lifestyle) but an invidious, hierarchical ranking of people which is inherently value laden. Such categories get their meaning comparatively. As Reay (2004: 32) reminded us, "In Bourdieuan terms, the working classes both historically and currently are discursively constituted as an unknowing, tasteless mass from which the middle classes draw their distinction". Apple (2001: 117) too, contended that the very meaning of "working class" is dependent on its relationship to other classes and class fractions. "The same is true of race. Blackness has no meaning unless it is related to the unacknowledged arrogation of the 'white' as the human ordinary" (ibid, 2001: 117). In speaking and writing of class, therefore, we unavoidably invoke or bring into existence its hierarchies and value systems as we speak of "lower", "middle", "upper" (Ball, 2003b). This is not always apparent in "official" classifications of "class" (see below). Silence on these matters, however, does not remove material inequalities and injustices from the fabric of people's lives. At the same time, if the notion of "the working classes" connotes, at bottom, merely a structure of positions in the work place, should it be stretched or reified beyond such meaning, ignoring their fluidity or the nuances of meaning lost in such classifications?

In the UK the practice of officially classifying the population according to occupation has a long history and began in 1851 (Rose, 2003), the idea of including an occupational element being first mooted by the Assistant Registrar General in 1887. He argued that, for mobility analyses, the population ought to be divided into broad groups based on "social standing". The Registrar General's Annual Report of 1911 subsequently included a summary of occupations designed to represent "social grades", later referred to as "social classes" used for the analysis of mortality data and the 1911 Census tables on Fertility and Marriage (Rose, 2003: 2). Following a major revision of the scheme in 1921, a new classification emerged resting on the assumption that society was a graded hierarchy of occupations summarized as:

1. Professional occupations.
2. Managerial and technical occupations.
3. Skilled occupations. (N) non manual, (M) manual.
4. Partly-skilled occupations.
5. Unskilled occupations.
6. Armed forces.

Although many minor changes have been made to this scheme since 1921, its overall shape remained unchanged until 2001. Following a major review of the Registrar General Social Class (RGSC) and with reference to the variety of other classificatory schemes used by governments and academics, particularly the scheme associated with the work of Goldthorpe and Hope (1974), the need for a new social classification "more fitted to the needs of the twenty first century" (Rose, 2003: 10) was recognized.

A new occupational scale, The National Statistics Socio-Economic Classifications (NS-SEC) replaced the Registrar General's Scale. This scheme recognized greater distinctions within previous categories, allowing for differences between employment and self-employment, the scale and degree of supervisory responsibility and the existence of non-work.

The National Statistics Socio-economic Classifications (NS-SEC)

1. Higher managerial and professional occupations.

    1.1 Employers an managers in larger organisations (e.g. company directors, senior company managers, senior civil servants, senior officers in police and armed forces).

    1.2 Higher professionals (e.g. doctors, lawyers, clergy, teachers and social workers).

2. Lower managerial and professional occupations (e.g. nurses and midwives, journalists, actors, musicians, prison officers, lower ranks of police and armed forces).

3. Intermediate occupations (e.g. clerks, secretaries, driving instructors, telephone fitters).

4. Small Employers and own account workers (e.g. publicans, farmers, taxi drivers, window cleaners, painters and decorators).

5. Lower supervisory, craft and related occupations (e.g. printers, plumbers, television engineers, train drivers, butchers).

6. Semi-routine occupations (e.g. shop assistants, hairdressers, bus drivers, cooks).

7. Routine occupations (e.g. couriers, labourers, waiters and refuse collectors).

8. Plus an eighth category to cover those who have never had paid work and the long term unemployed. (Hewett, 2003: 1)

Class, however, is not simply a discursive artefact, a construction of either Governments' or academics' classificatory schemes. It is a visceral reality, a set of social and economic relations that strongly influence, if not determine and dominate, people's lives. And while such classificatory systems "merely" endeavour to register one relatively easily measured aspect of its complexity, inevitably simplifying "class" in the process, class theories and theorists have more complex explanatory goals.

Classical theories of social class are regarded as having their origins in the writings of Karl Marx. A German, writing in 19th century England, Marx saw all history as one of class struggle. He viewed the industrialization unfolding before him as riddled with inevitable conflict between exploited workers (the proletariat) and an upper class (bourgeoisie or "capitalist class") who owned the means of economic production and set the terms of economic and knowledge relations. Others were later to refine this thinking. Max Weber, for example, conceptualised class as not only an *economic* but also a *cultural* relationship in which status and prestige were considered as integral to economic and material relationships which Marx had privileged in defining class. The honour or standing that we are accorded, where and how we live, our manner of speech, our bodily deportment, our consumption and leisure habits, the way we behave and think, together define our life opportunities and whether we perceive ourselves, or are perceived as, having high status or not. Our official "class" categories ought to, indeed, more properly be regarded as expressions of socio-economic status (SES), a mix of "work" (economic) and reputational (cultural) aspects of our position in the social hierarchy.

Although the work of Marx and Weber, along with other 19th and early 20th century social theorists, such as Durkheim, Mead, Mills, Parsons and Elias, has been variously revised, re-worked, rejected and re-discovered by countless social theorists ever since (see Ritzer and Smart, 2001; Shilling, 2003, 2004b), it has rarely made an impact directly on research in physical education. However, when mediated by the work of more contemporary social theorists, particularly the theories of Basil Bernstein, Pierre Bourdieu and Michel Foucault, class has had an important bearing on the research agendas both of sociology of education and physical education (see Evans et al., 2004; Hargreaves, 1986; Kirk, 1993; Shilling, 2003, 2004; O'Flynn, 2004, Green et al., 2005). For example, many of those researchers who have adopted a socially critical or deconstructive approach to the study of physical education (Evans et al., 2004; Fernandez-Balboa 1997; Rovegno and Kirk, 1995) have sought to document and analyse how class interests and prevailing distributions of power, authority and control have influenced our understanding not only of curriculum form and content but processes of socialisation, differentiation and stratification. Some have illustrated how the interests of "capital" are implicated in the production of modern-day "risks", for example, such as those surrounding the "obesity crisis" which, putatively, is facing the Western world (see Gard and Wright, 2001; Pronger, 2002). Others have shown how particular class orientations towards "the body" are reflected in health curricula now featuring in schools, or in processes that may be re-creating "old" hierarchies in new ways around conceptions of the "body", slimness, exercise and food (Evans et al., 2004).

While class theory and recent attempts to incorporate race and gender within such analyses have become important activities within sociology they have yet to be adequately reflected in research in physical education (for overviews, see Hayes and Stidder, 2003; Rovegno and Kirk, 1995; McDonald,

et al., 2003; and Chapters 2.2). This is perhaps unfortunate given that, in the changing contexts of global capitalism, of multinationals and the fragmentation of the work force, it is now more difficult than ever to locate the nature and origins of power and control, as well as to draw social or geographical boundaries around a work force or educational work place.

In this context it is perhaps more important than ever that we identify and know what "class" is, how it is being reconfigured through social and economic practices, reflected in the polices and practices of education, physical education and sport (see McDonald, 2003; Green, Smith and Roberts, 2005) and embodied (see, Shilling, 2004b). Ironically, such social changes have led some observers to suggest that class analysis no longer matters. In the UK, the demise of major, "heavy" industries, like steel and coal, alongside the privatization of most of the remainder of the former "productive" public sector, including transport and utilities in general, has greatly weakened their associated unionised work forces. In the core public sector that remains, such as the National Health Service (NHS), "new managerialism" (Clarke et al., 2000) dominates. In education, the teaching force has been excluded from ordinary industrial relations, let alone policy making. In rapidly declining manufacturing industry and even in many expanding service sectors, multinationals reign. Individualization and globalization have, it is claimed, led to the dissolution of collective identities so that inequalities, like differences, have become personal, "with the result that non-class relations are formed, often briefly, as and when threats appear" (Collins and Kay, 2003 16; see also Beck, 1992; Castells, 1997; Savage, 2000).

While not eschewing class analysis, others have suggested that, as a result of such social changes, increasingly we are all, in certain respects, becoming middle class. Cahill (1994), for example, rightly points to the fluidity in individuals' self-assignations to, and views of, social class. The collective mood, notwithstanding the stubborn existence of the "socially excluded", may have shifted away form "we are all working class now", based in large part on higher and, to some degree, converging consumption patterns, to the view that we are more middle class (for which "class is dead" is often an euphemism). Objectively, more of us in the post-industrial West certainly are. We are also an older, less likely to stay in the same job or family for extended periods, better educated, more gender-equal and a more ethnically diverse population. Higher, converging consumption (alongside its relative lack among our least fortunate 20%) is only part of a hugely complex ensemble of rather poorly mapped social, including class, changes at work.

Among the limited data that we have on such matters, Roberts (1999), for example, has argued that in the UK we now enjoy something of a "leisure democracy" in the sense that members of all strata do similar things in their leisure lives, although he adds "democracy" is not the same thing as equality. The "privileged classes" are distinguished by their ability to do more, which they exercise in virtually all areas of out of home leisure:

> Money is now at the root of the main differences between the uses of leisure in different social strata, and the leisure differences between them are basically and blatantly inequalities rather than alternative ways of life. (Roberts, 1999: 87; in Collins and Kay, 2003: 18)

We are not yet in a position to know whether "democracy" has arrived in physical education in schools, though if participation in the broadening range of activities on offer in schools' sports curricula in the UK is anything to go by, the overview of survey research by Roberts (1996), in the wake of *Sport, Raising the Game* (Department of National Heritage, 1995), suggests that we are less elitist than formerly. Although the National Curriculum in physical education, instituted in 1991, was intended at least to advance the subject in the direction of greater equity, with all schools enjoined to give all pupils aged 5–16 access to "the same" range of curriculum across schools in England and Wales, it did not and could not guarantee the same "quality of provision" across them. National surveys of participation in and facilities for school sport in the mid-90s indicated "schools were extending rather than cutting back on their sports teaching" (Roberts, 1996: 49). Virtually all physical education and headteacher respondents to the surveys regarded physical education as important and were in the process of providing more extra-curricular facilities. Most also anticipated the further expansion of facilities and provision. However, others have pointed out that the effect of cutbacks on school budgets over the last decade or so in the UK, along with the constraints placed on resources available to schools, leading to the sale of school playing fields in some areas, has adversely affected the opportunities available to pupils from working class areas to benefit from the wide ranging National Curriculum physical education (see, McDonald, 2003b: 117). Contrasting images are tempting, of working class boys and girls playing tag rugby on the pock-marked, tar-macadam, chalk-lined, playing surfaces of their inner city schools, unlikely to experience rugby or any other school sport, for that matter, in the same way as their "middle class" counterparts roaming the well-kept acres of grass playing fields in England's top comprehensives, grammar, or fee-paying private schools.

Even if "the same" social and sporting activities are now configured in similar ways across the school system, "the classes" may not derive the same meaning

or significance from them. Shilling (1993) and Horne, and Tomlinson and Whannel (1999) have claimed that different classes derive different kinds of "profit" from sport in terms of health, relaxation, and social relationships, according to the "capital" they already possess. This is not just economic but cultural, symbolic and physical capital, acquired by virtue of primary socialisation within the family and the home. Culturally, while class may seem to matter less in terms of people's leisure choices, individuals may continue to experience "the same" physical activity very differently and enjoy very different opportunities to engage in such practices, given differences in income, mobility and possibility of access to different leisure locations and schools (see Hunter, 2004).

Even, then, if the conceptual quagmires in which class is embedded often means that sometimes "one hardly knows what one is talking about" (Foucault, 1996: 447) and conceptions of class, class analysis and class society are "notoriously vague and stretched because they inevitably contain issues of semantics and substance" (Pakulsky and Waters, 1996: 2), class theorizing and analysis must form an essential element of analysis in research in physical education. Along with Ball we suggest that we

> Use and trouble these concepts at the same time and hold some ambivalence toward their usefulness, set against a very strong sense of the presence of class within the politics and practices of contemporary education. (2003a: 6)

We might productively consider "class" as signalling not only an embodied relationship to the means of economic production (see, Shilling 2004b), a structural position but also a cultural identity and a lifestyle, a set of perspectives on the world and relationships in it.

> Class in this sense is productive and reactive. It is an identity based upon modes of being and becoming, or escape and forms of distinction that are realised and reproduced in specific social locations. Certain locations are sought out, others are avoided. We think and are thought by class, it is about being something and not being something else. It is relational. Class is also a trajectory, a path through space and time, a history of transactions. (Wlatzer, 1984, in Ball, 2003a: 6)

Class is not, then, just an allocated category, or explanatory variable, one amongst many (alongside, "gender" or race), or "simply" a relation. Instead, class is a set of constitutive practices (Ball, 2003a,b; Reay, 2004) that are struggled over in the daily lives of families and individuals. Indeed, if class is considered to no longer matter either as an object of enquiry or as a lived experience, we might reasonably ask, why do the "middle classes" continue to invest so heavily in its reproduction and maintenance in and outside schools? Why are balanced ability entries to schools so difficult to engender, social class compositions of student bodies so resistant to change and both so deeply implicated in school popularity and choice? These matters and their concomitants should rest high on our agendas if class is our concern in research in physical education.

Major themes and findings

Class patterns

The attempt to operationalize systems of class categories to determine "who belongs where", or "who does what" by the way of sport, leisure and physical activity, in and out of schools, in ways that can be used for correlational, comparative, or mobility research has been the best resourced element of our understanding of how class is reflected in society and schools. Stroot (2002: 140) for example, drawing on United States census data, offers information on participation patterns of people representing a range of income levels during the year 1999. Her data reveal that children had different opportunities to participate in physical activity depending on the income level of their parents. Income also affected their ability to become spectators of sport. In the UK, Roberts (1996) has painted a similar, though subtly different, picture with reference to a variety of survey data on participation in physical activity and facility use in and outside schools (see also, Green, 2002; Green et al., 2005). Roberts found that the overall *level* of sports activity, as reported by secondary schools and their students, especially amongst boys, was well above the average for previous decades, such that participation "could not have been the prerogative of any social group", though none of the three surveys upon which his analysis drew either collected or reported social class information (pp. 53–4). He suggested that changes in the structure of education in the UK had led to the majority of children being educated in comprehensive schools, with more young people staying on in full time education beyond 16. Along with increased opportunities to participate in enhanced local authority and voluntary provision, such trends blurred social class boundaries in leisure provision, in and outside schools. Other investigations, however, (Collins, 2003; De Knop and Elling, 2001; Hendry et al., 1993, Kay, 2000, 2003; Nagel and Nagel, 2001; Roberts and Parsell, 1994; Van Der Meulin et al., 2001) suggested that young people's social class backgrounds were still associated with leisure differences in the UK and elsewhere. Roberts, too was clear that "young people of middle class background have higher levels of sports participation

than those in working class locations" and family encouragement and expenditure on the sporting and other activities of their offspring differed from their pre-school years, concluding that:

> the main social class differences are no longer in whether young people play any sport, but how often. It remains the case that sports participation is closely related to age, sex and social class but it is no longer true that nearly all participants are young, male and middle class. (Roberts, 1996: 54)

Other researchers, mainly working within the discipline of psychology, have begun to detail the different physical activity levels of children from different socio-economic groups, reflecting global concerns for children's health (for an overview, see Duncan et al., 2002). In the UK, using "free school meals" as a proxy for economic status (somewhat crudely identifying those families in the UK who receive income support, and therefore, are less "well off" financially), they revealed that children from higher socio-economic groups report greater levels of average daily expenditure of time on "moderate and vigorous activity". Given the long-term benefits of such activity, they suggest that, at least in the UK, children from "lower socio-economic groups may be a cause for concern" (Duncan et al., 2002: 42); although they emphasise the pattern described is not universal but varies across countries and cultures, and that caution is needed when interpreting these data (p. 40). Nevertheless, it may be the case that class differences such as these, established at an early age and, perhaps, consolidated through schooling, are further reflected in the body of evidence built up over a number of years in the UK, Australia, USA and elsewhere. It reveals striking disparities in "health" between groups in the population, where people of low socio-economic status experience worse health than those of higher socio-economic status for almost every major cause of mortality and morbidity (Royal College of Physicians, 2004; Social Health Atlas of Australia, 2003).

Studies such as these have undoubtedly helped illustrate the ways in which "class" and the interests and resources of "the family" and home intersect with those of formal education to either facilitate or prohibit involvement in physical activity and achievement in physical education, potentially with long-term consequences for health. What goes on in families and their ability to invest in education and physical education has a bearing on how children relate to, and what levels of involvement they sustain in, physical activity in and outside schools (Kay, 2003). As Gruneau (1999) pointed out, desire, choice and possibility are likely to be influenced, at least in part, by the differential resource that families can bring to bear on life situations as a result of class position. These resources have their impact upon opportunities to access culturally valued activities, including physical activity and health. The effects of differential resources are to be measured not just in terms of whether or not they permit access to physical culture but "the greater collective power of some agents to 'structure' play, games, and sports in certain ways and to contour the range of meanings and significations associated with them" (Gruneau, 1999: 29). Yet we have little data documenting these processes in physical education.

These few, predominantly quantitative, survey studies that we have map a few of the contours of social class and have made some contribution to debates about class and opportunity, challenging some of the rhetoric that surrounds education, sport and physical education. But they tell us very little of the ways in which patterned class relations and their outcomes in terms of "ability", health and participation are produced, reproduced and reconfigured. These would require analysis of the complex web of meanings, governance, organizational practice, curriculum, teaching, assessment procedures and other social processes that feature in education and physical education. Only this would convey a real sense of the differences that reside within class categories, for example, how the "new" and "old" middle class may differently invest in and interpret the activities of physical education, or how Asian and "white" working class adults and children, males and females, may experience and perceive opportunity and access to physical activity and health rather differently within particular cultures and countries. Some studies employing more qualitative methodologies have begun to throw light on processes such as these.

Class processes and values

Some of the earliest allusions to social class in research in physical education centred, rather crudely it now seems, on the way in which "middle class values" brought to school by virtue of teachers' social backgrounds and training alienated working class pupils (see, Evans, 1986, 1988; Whitehead and Hendry, 1976). Such work raised important questions about schools' pedagogic and organizational practices, for example, as to whether teacher–pupil interactions, or grouping, setting, and streaming policies sieved out children for success and status as much by class and cultural values as by any other more educationally driven definitions of "ability" and "skill". Others, however, prompted a more sophisticated consideration of whether physical education and sport "realigned" and readjusted rather than simply "reproduced" relationships between class fractions through a far more complex set of dynamics between schools and class cultures (see, Corrigan, 1979; Hargreaves, 1986; Willis 1997).

In the UK, Roberts (1996) added to this debate, illustrating empirically how patterns of opportunity and differentiation seem to be changing somewhat in the 1990s, alongside changes in the organisation of schooling.

However, it remains the case that we have all too few studies internationally of how "class values" intersect with other social relations, such as: ethnicity (see Benn, 1996; Zaman, 1997) or gender (see Gilroy, 1997; Hunter, 2004) and are "embodied" and reflected in interactions between pupils, teachers, coaches and other adults involved in the education of children in schools or teacher education; or of how physical education department policies, for example, on "inclusion" (see McDonald, 2003b), grouping and assessment are classed; or of how definitions of "ability", "skill" and "competence" are differently configured and conceptualized around class and other relations at various levels of the education system. We do not know enough of how these processes, especially conceptions and discursive definitions of "the body", vary across contexts or sites of physical culture, and how they are embodied. For example, is the development and embodiment of physical culture within the homes of West Indian, Asian or white, working class children endorsed or "interrupted" but the physical cultures of physical education departments in schools? (see Oliver and Lalik, 2004; Zaman, 1997).

These are not just issues of access, of who gets to experience what forms of physical activity but of process, raising questions as to how "the body", or rather, "different bodies" are classed, valued, recognized and rewarded in physical education processes. In recent years a good many researchers in physical education have begun to throw light on these issues. Fletcher (1984), Hargreaves, (1986), Hargreaves A. (1994), Kirk (1992), Mangan (1981) and Penn (1999), have centred attention on how historically the physical education curriculum and sport have been classed and gendered, and provide some indication as to how "middle class values" have entered the school system to define what is to count as physical education for "different classes" and how such definitions have changed over time. Others have centred on pupil-teacher interaction, revealing differences in the teaching styles of middle class women and men (Wright, 1996; Evans et al., 1996). Yet others have drawn attention to the way in which innovations in health education curricula are encoded with class values (see Evans and Davies, 2004), or how discourses around "risk" (see Wright, 2004; Leahy and Harrison, 2004), "obesity" and corporeality are "classed" (Evans et al., 2005; Rich et al., 2004; Hunter, 2004) and potentially alienate and damage children's well- being and health.

These studies have gone some way towards documenting the social processes by which class is, and has been, enacted and encoded in the message systems of school or Initial Teacher Education PE (ITEPE). However, while these studies allude to "class" as an important element of explanation and analysis, class remains a shadowy presence. It is often no more than an under- or unexplicated caricature of hegemonic (ruling class interests represented as universal interests) authority, power, and control, a backdrop against which the interests of "working class" children are simply and neatly juxta- or counterposed. Even in "socially critical" research (see Evans et al., 2004; Fernandez-Balboa, 1997; MacDonald et al., 2002; Wright et al., 2004), where class hierarchies and interests are often implicitly assumed, there has been little attempt to make explicit, either conceptually or empirically, the complexity of class identity; how "class" and other social relations and hierarchies, for example, gender, "race" and "ability", intersect through educational processes. The current work of Wright (2003), Macdonald (2003a) and their co-workers in Australia is proving some exception to this rule.

Neither this line of qualitative research nor the research centred on patterns of class opportunity alluded to in the section above take us sufficiently close to knowing how, in the fast changing social circumstances of the postmodern world, class interests are being produced, realigned and reconfigured through the message systems of physical education, their systems of organization, governance and administration, and the wider pedagogic contexts in which these are embedded, in and outside schools. Given the attention afforded by researchers in physical education to the expression of middle class interests in the pedagogic discourse and curriculum of school physical education, we cannot claim, as Ball (2003a,b) does of the sociology of education that, in research in physical education, the history of class analysis is a history of the working classes. Yet, in one sense, Ball is correct. Although research has centred on the way in which school physical education has been constructed around the values and interests of "middle class" men and women, it has inadvertently told us more about the nature of working class failure: how children from "other" ethnic backgrounds and classes are less involved in physical activity in and outside schools rather than about the complexity of the identities, factions, relations and strategies of "the middle classes" and how they ensure their continued status and "success" in education and health. Ball has pointed out that only recently in the UK have "the middle classes" entered the sociological fray as worthy of attention because there are now so many of them. The "middle class" now accounts for roughly a third of the population (Roberts, 2001: 121, in Ball 2003a: 5), whose actions either produce or contribute to the perpetuation, inscription and reinvention of social inequalities, both old and new.

How is physical education implicated in processes such as these? What are the processes by which "the middle classes" use physical culture to retain a class advantage, to mark out their distinction and difference from "others"? (see Bourdieu, 1984). How are these processes reflected in consumption choices relating to physical culture, in investments in physical activity in and outside schools and in the meanings attached to different forms of "body work" relating, for example, to diet, exercise and food? Equally we might consider whether, even if middle class interests are expressed in the message systems of education and physical education, they necessarily disbenefit or disadvantage "other" cultures.

None of this emphasis on "the middle classes" should divert attention away from detailing the actions and interests of "other" classes through physical education in families and schools or from documenting how, within a class, different conceptions and processes of embodiment prevail. Viewing the body as a form of "physical capital" (Bourdieu, 1984, 1986; Shilling, 2003, 2004b) has, in recent years, usefully highlighted the ways in which formal education is involved in the production of corporeal inequalities which are both classed and gendered (see Evans, 1988; Gilroy, 1996; Hunter, 2004; Kirk, 1993; Shilling, 1993). We need more research in physical education that focuses upon the achievement or reproduction of class advantage and the different ways of mobilizing power through "the body" for purposes of staking claims to resources, opportunities, status and reward (Parkin, 1979: 5, in Ball, 2003a: 18).

Class and policy

Class does not always enact itself straightforwardly or obviously (see McDonald, 2003a,b) through the message systems of education and physical education and rarely, we suspect, simply by way of a value dissonance between "middle class" teachers and "working class" children (Hargreaves, 1986). If class interests are to endure they must be embedded in policy texts that will shape and define the form, content and purposes of physical education, becoming integral to its instructional and regulative practices, a "taken for granted" presence in a school's or department's discursive terrain. In Lavalette and Mooney's (2000: 9, see Ball, 2003b: 13) terms, "(C)lass provides the context within which policies are developed", acting both *on* policy and reflected *in* policy (both in terms of what *is* and *is not* included in its texts, see McDonald, 2003b), potentially shaping the educational and social experiences of every teacher and child. If past and present policies relating to physical education and health in schools may be read as expressions of struggles over the interests and values of "class", then they have often been "very immediate and down to earth struggles for opportunity, advantage, and closure, over the distribution of scarce resources" (Ball, 2003b: 13) in which all parties are unlikely to enjoy "equal" power, authority, or resource, to influence outcomes (Penney and Evans, 1999). Accepting this, how are we to interpret the emphasis placed on: sport education in the USA; sport in the National Curriculum physical education in England and Wales (see Penney and Evans, 1999); "health" in the physical education curriculum (Penney and Harris, 2004) across Europe (Fisher, 2003) the USA (Pronger, 2002), Australia (Macdonald and Kirk, 2003) and elsewhere (Duncan, 2002); or "social inclusion" through physical education in the UK (McDonald, 2003b)? Whose and what social, political and educational values are reflected in policy initiatives of this kind? What and whose interests do they serve? Furthermore, policy is not simply enacted upon pupils and teachers, it is mediated through different sites of social and educational activity and, in the process, struggled over, made and remade. Researchers have begun to conceptualise this process but not always in ways that speak sufficiently directly of class issues or recognising class interests and struggles (see Kirk, 2003; Penney and Evans, 2004). What are the social class relations of policy production? Who is "able" and "invited" to be involved? How is policy constituted, shaped and formed, struggled over, contested, changed and adapted as it progresses from its point of production, through the processes of recontextualisation that make it fit for reproduction by teachers and with what consequences for the identities and corporeality of teachers and pupils in schools? Do policies build on, accommodate, reflect or reject certain class values and what social movements and changes locally, internationally and globally do they reflect and serve? As Ball (2003a: 30) has pointed out, education reform is now a global movement; we are seeing "new and generic modes of organisation, governance and delivery of state education globally". We are witnessing the globalization of policy and curriculum content reflected, for example, in the attention given to health issues in physical education curricula across the Westernized world. Why is this happening and with what consequences for children and teachers in schools, bearing in mind that these changes are not just about new contents but "new structures, opportunities and incentives, these policy moves bring about new forms of social relationships, cultures and values" (Ball, 2003a). If it is the case that educational polices are primarily aimed at satisfying the interests of the middle classes then we do need to ask, how policy thinking is classed in ways that give them strategic advantage (Ball, 2003a). Are such tendencies evident in the plethora of policy texts that have impacted physical education in very many countries in recent years? Whose interests *are* served in the processes, practices and policies of physical education?

Conclusion: future directions

We should not conclude from this analysis that schools and other institutions of formal education are simply reflective or reproductive of society's hierarchies, class, economic or health relations or that physical education is merely a conduit for the transmission of the meanings, values and competences of the middle or ruling classes. This would be crude and unhelpful analysis suggesting not just that nothing has changed but nothing can change in the processes and outcomes of physical education in schools. There are those (see, for example, the innovative work of Helison, 2003; Lawson, 2005) who see and use physical education and sport explicitly as vehicles for social change. They aim for "inclusion", building individual self-confidence, community renewal, repairing the damage done by impoverishment in all its varied forms. But rarely are such actions sufficiently well articulated in terms of structural and cultural issues relating to "social class". On this score, we would do well to learn from the painstaking work undertaken in other school subject areas, particularly that of Morais, Neves and their associates in devising a "mixed pedagogy" capable of improving the performance of all, including lower working class students, in school science (see Chapter 2.2, note 2.2).

Schools and physical education within them are not simply the sites of reproductive social processes (see Hargreaves, 1986), they are also productive of culture and, potentially at least, have the capacity to act as forces for innovation and change (see Wright et al., 2004). But to understand this potential and its limitations we need to embed our view of physical education in one of broader change and class structures and then relate them to theory of pedagogic discourse that offers "more precise and explicit guides to research" (Bernstein, 1996: 2). This would entail more conceptual and empirical work not just on patterns, processes and polices but, fundamentally, on how class is framed and formed over and within many sites of physical education in the family (see Kay, 2000), home and elsewhere, and embodied. We need "relational studies" of class and physical education (see Chapter 2.2). Many years ago Bernstein emphasized that

> the school's academic curriculum, if it is to be effectively acquired, always required two sites of acquisition, the school and the home. Curricula cannot be acquired wholly by time spent at school. (1990: 77)

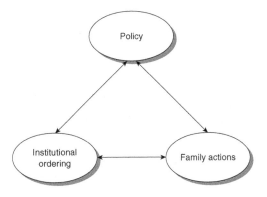

Figure 6.6.1 Interlocking inequalities (from Ball, 2003b: 7)

Given that most of our aims can be summed up in Bernstein's (1990: 75) notion that we seek to produce students who "will eventually have access to the principles of their own discourse", our research needs to take the pedagogic discourse of the family (fundamentally, that relating to embodiment and physical culture) as seriously as that of formal education so as to investigate the ways in which they (children, pupils, students) are "produced" in complex interaction between the cultural, social and material sites of the home, school and restless policy requirements. In this way we may register what Ball (2003b:7) refers to as the "interlocking of inequalities". (see Figure 6.6.1).

Class is not, then, just a category of explanation but a dynamic process that has to be worked on within and across many social sites or fields (Bourdieu, 1986; Hunter, 2004). These are contexts in which orientations to the body are nurtured, expressed, or rejected, others assimilated, affirmed and endorsed. Again, we emphasize we are unlikely to appreciate this complexity unless we adopt a relational perspective. Indeed, it may be more important than ever that we now so do, given that societies are becoming increasingly dependent on their schools as the primary arena of education, even while pedagogical activity occurs across many locations and we are each expected to self regulate, inform our behaviours (for example, on food, diet, exercise) through the family, the media and other "new" technologies that enter our lives, as well as via the message systems of schools. In this "totally pedagogised society" (see Bernstein, 2002 and Tyler, 2004) class reproduction may be becoming even more important. We need, therefore, to consider how these processes are reflected in the policies, practices and processes of physical education at all levels, and how they bear on individual development and embodiment in and out of schools (see, Kirk et al., 1998; Kay, 2003; Burrows and Wright,

2004). Our secondary school curriculum in the UK is moving from "discrete" subjects to curricular "regions" and generic training whose pedagogies represent knowledge as a transferable commodity (see Penney and Chandler, 2000). In Bernstein's (1996) terms, this represents a shift, perceived as meeting political and economic requirements for flexible workers, from knowledge viewed as a specific output, text or product (projected identities) to knowledge as the manifestation of some inner attribute of competence (introjected identities). But as Muller points out, in urging us to analyse what, when and where is pedagogically effective, Bernstein was quite sure that the present, official emphasis on "trainability" presupposes

> a prior regulative and discursive introjection resting on a particular social order … The insidious effect of "trainability" is that it renders invisible (or inaudible) the requirement of prior identity induction into a moral and discursive order that is overwhelmingly still provided in the home and school for the middle class and almost solely at school for the old and new poor. We may say that the perniciousness of 'trainability' lies in its camouflage of the renewed importance of the school for the production of specialized identities and in the false, because unattainable, allure that attaches itself to "trainability" as a consequence. (2004: 5)

This perhaps explains why, ironically, class has gone out of fashion in some quarters, and become less visible in policies bearing on education and physical education (McDonald, 2003b), just as the regulation of the work place, the gap between rich and poor worldwide and the successes of the middle classes in education and health are becoming more visible than they have been for decades. It also shows us why we must move from one-sided, externally determined views of pedagogic process to ones that recognise its own voice in both the production and reproduction of hierarchy, equality and equity.

References

Allen, R.E. (1999). *The Concise Oxford Dictionary*. London: BCA.

Apple, M. (2001). Gender meets new liberalism. *Discourse: studies in the cultural politics of education*, 22(1): 115–119.

Arnot, M. (2002). *Reproducing gender*. London: Routledge.

Azzarito, L. and Solomon, A. (2005). A reconceptualization of physical education. The intersection of gender/race/social class. *Sport, Education and Society*, 10(1): 25–49.

Ball, S.J. (1990). *Politics and policy making in education. Explorations in policy sociology*. London: Routledge.

Ball, S.J. (2003a). *Class strategies and the education market. The middle classes and social advantage.* London: Rouledge/Falmer.

Ball, S.J. (2003b). *The more things change. … educational research, social class and 'interlocking' inequalities'.* London: Institute of Education.

Ball, S. (Ed.). (2004). *The Routledge/Falmer Reader in the sociology of education.* London:Routledge/Falmer.

Bates, R. (2003). *On the governance of education.* Paper presented to the NZARE/AARE Conference, Auckland, New Zealand, November 29 – December, 3.

Beck, U. (1992). *Risk society. Towards a new modernity.* London: Sage.

Benn, T. (1996). Muslim women and physical education. *Sport, Education and Society,* 1(1): 5–23.

Bernstein, B. (1975). *Class, codes and control. Volume 3. Towards a theory of educational transmission.* London: Routledge and Kegan Paul.

Bernstein, B. (1977). *Class, codes and control, Vol 3. Towards a theory of educational transmission.* London: Routledge & Kegan Paul.

Bernstein, B. (1990). *The structuring of pedagogic discourse. Volume IV class, codes and control.* London: Routledge.

Bernstein, B. (1996). *Pedagogy, symbolic control and identity. theory, research, critique.* London: Taylor & Francis.

Bernstein, B. (2001). From pedagogies to knowledge. In A. Morias, I. Neves, B. Davies and H. Daniels (Eds.), *Towards a sociology of pedagogy. The contributions of Basil Bernstein to research.* New York, Peter Lang.

Bourdieu, P. (1984). *Distinction,: A social critique of the judgement of taste.* London: Routledge.

Bourdieu, P. (1986). The forms of capital. In J. Richardson (Ed.), *Handbook of theory and research for the sociology of education.* New York: Greenwood Press.

Burrows, L. and Wright, J. (2004). The Good Life: New Zealand children's perspectives on health and self. *Sport, Education and Society,* 9(2): 193–207.

Cahill, M. (1994). *The new social policy.* Oxford: Blackwell.

Castells, M. (1997). *The power of identity. Volume II the information Age: Economy, society and culture.* Oxford: Blackwell.

Clarke, J. Gerwitz, S. and McLaughlin, E. (2000). *New managerialism, new welfare?* London: Sage Publications.

Collins, M. (2003). Social exclusion from sport and leisure. In B. Houlihan, (Ed.), (2003). *Sport and society. A student handbook.* London.

Collins, M. and Kay, T. (2003). *Sport and social exclusion.* London: Routledge.

Corrigan, P. (1979). *Schooling the smash street kids.* London: MacMillan.

De Knop, P. and Elling, A. (2001). (Eds.). *Values and norms in sport.* Aachen: Meyer and Meyer Sport.

De Knop, P. and Martelaer, K. (2001). Quantitative an qualitative valuation of youth sport in Flanders and the Netherlands: A case study. *Sport, Education and Society,* 6(1): 35–51.

Department of National Heritage (1995). Sport. Raising the Game. London: Department of National Heritage.

Duncan, M., Woodfield, L., Al-Nakeeb, Y. and Nevill, A. (2002). The impact of socio-economic status on the physical activity levels of British secondary school children. *European Journal of physical education,* 7(1): 30–45.

Evans, J. (1986). *Physical education, sport and schooling. Studies in the sociology of physical education.* Lewes: Falmer Press.

Evans, J. (1988). Body matters. Towards a socialist physical education. In H. Lauder and P. Brown (Eds.), *Education in search of a future.* Lewes: Falmer Press.

Evans, J. and Davies, B. (2004). Endnote: the embodiment of consciousness. In J. Evans, B. Davies and J. Wright (Eds.), pp. 207–238.

Evans, J. Davies, B. and Penney, D. (1996). Teachers, teaching and the social construction of gender relations. S*port, Education and Society,* 1(2): 165–185.

Evans, J. Davies, B. and Wright, J. (Eds.). (2004). *Body knowledge and control. Studies in the sociology of physical education and health.* London: Routledge.

Evans, J. Rich, R and Holroyd, R. (2004). What schools do to middle class girls? Education and eating disorders. *British Journal of Sociology of Education,* 25(2): 123–143.

Fernández-Balboa, J.M (1997). *Critical postmodernism in human movement physical education and sport.* Albany: State University of New York Press.

Fisher, R. (2003). Physical education in Europe. Policy into practice. In K. Hardman (Ed.), *Sport science studies, physical education: Deconstruction and reconstruction – issues and directions. 12,* Berlin, ICSSPE.

Fletcher, S. (1984). *Women first: The female tradition in English physical education.* London: Athlone.

Foucault, M. (1996). *Foucault live: Collected Interviews, 1961–1984* (edited by Lotringer, S.). New York: Semiotext.

Gard, M. and Wright, M. (2001). Managing uncertainty. Obesity discourse and physical education in a risk society. *Studies in Philosophy and Education,* 20(6): 535–49.

Gilroy, S. (1996). Working on the body. Relationships between sport and social power. In G. Clarke and B. Humberstone (Eds.), *Researching women and sport.* London: MacMillan Press.

Goldthorpe, J.H. and Hope, K. (1974). *The social grading of occupations: a new approach and scale.* Oxford: Clarendon Press.

Green, K. (2002). Physical education and the Couch potato society. *European Journal of physical education,* 7(2): 95–108.

Green, K., Smith, A. and Roberts, K. (2005). Social class, young people, sport and physical education. In K. Green and K. Hardman. *Physical education. Essential issues.* London: Sage.

Gruneau, R. (1999). *Class, Sports and social development.* Leeds: Human Kinetics.

Hardman, K. (Ed.). (2003). *Sport science studies, physical education: Deconstruction and reconstruction – Issues and Directions, 12,* Berlin, ICSSPE.

Hargreaves, J.E. (1986). *Sport, power and culture – A social and historical analysis of popular sports in Britain.* Cambridge: Polity Press.

Hargreaves. J.A. (1994). *Sporting Females, critical issues in the history and sociology of women's sports.* London: Routledge.

Hayes, S. and Stidder, G. (Eds.). (2003) *Equity and inclusion in physical education and sport.* London: Routledge.

Hellison, D. (2003). *Teaching responsibility through physical activity.* Champaign, IL: Human Kinetics.

Hendry, L.B., Shucksmith, J., Love, J.G. and Glendenning, A. (1993). Young people's leisure and lifestyles. London: Routledge.

Hewett. (Sociology at) (2003). The national statistics socio-economic classification, hhtp://www.hewett. Norfolk.sch.uk/curric/soc/class/NS.htm

Holton, R. and Turner, B. (1994). Debate and pseudo-debate in class analysis, some unpromising aspects of Goldthorpe and Marshall's Defence. *Sociology, 28*(3): 799–804.

Horne, J., Tomlinson, A. and Whannel, G. (1999). *Understanding sport.* London: E&FN Spon.

Hunter, L. (2004). Bourdieu and the social space of the PE class: Reproduction of Doxa through practice, *Sport, Education and Society, 9*(2): 175–192.

Kay, T. (2003). The family factor in sport. A review of family factors affecting sports participation. *Institute of Sport and Leisure Policy,* Loughborough University.

Kay, T.A. (2000). Leisure, gender and the Family. The influence of social policy context. *Leisure Studies, 19*(4): 247–265.

Kingdom, J. (1992). *No such thing as society.* Buckingham: Open University Press.

Kirk, D. (1992). *Defining physical education, the social construction of a school subject in post war Britain.* London: Falmer.

Kirk, D. (1993). *The body, schooling and culture.* Geelong, Australia: Deakin University Press.

Kirk, D. (2003). The social construction of physical education, legitimation crises and strategic intervention in educational reform. In K. Hardman (Ed.), *Sport Science Studies, physical education: Deconstruction and reconstruction – Issues and Directions, 12,* Berlin, ICSSPE.

Kirk, D, Penney, D, Clarkson, T and Braiuka, S. (1998). *Socio-economic determinants of junior sport participation in Queensland.* Department of human movement studies: The University of Queensland.

Lavalette, M and Mooney, G. (Eds.), (2000). *Class struggles and social welfare, Buckingham.* Milton Keynes: Open University Press.

Lawson, H. (2005). Empowering people, facilitating community development, and contributing to sustainable development; The social work of sport, exercise and physical education programs. *Sport, Education and Society, 10*(1): 135–161.

Leahy, D. and Harrison, L. (2004). Health and physical education and the production of the 'at risk self'. In J. Evans, B. Davies and J.Wright (Eds.), *Body knowledge and control. Studies in the sociology of physical education and health* (pp. 130–140). London: Routledge.

Luke, A. (1999). *Education 2010 and new times: Why equity and social justice still matter, but differently.* Prepared for Education Queensland online conference, 20/10/99, Queensland, University of Queensland.

MacDonald, D. (2003a). *Families and physical activity: fortification, facilitation and a 'forbidden thing'.* Paper presented at the NZARE/AARE conference Educational Research Risks and Dilemmas, Auckland, November.

MacDonald, I. (2003b). Class, inequality and the body in physical education. In S. Hayes and G. Stidder (Eds.), *Equity and inclusion in physical education and sport* (pp. 169–185). London: Routledge.

Macdonald, D. and Kirk, D. (2003). Deconstruction, reconstruction and futures for Australian health and physical education teacher education. In K. Hardman (Ed.), *Sport science studies, Physical Education: Deconstruction and Reconstruction – Issues and Directions, 12* (pp. 73–85). Berlin: ICSSPE.

Macdonald, D. Kirk, D, Metzler, M. Nilges, L.M, Schempp, P. and Wright, J. (2002). It's all very well in theory: Theoretical perspectives and their application in contemporary pedagogical research. *Quest, 534*(2): 116–133.

Mangan, J.A. (1981). *Athleticism in the Victorian and Edwardian public school.* Cambridge: Cambridge University Press.

Morais, A., Neves, I. and Pires, D. (2004). The *what and how* of teaching and learning: Going deeper into sociological analysis and intervention. In J. Muller, B. Davies and A. Morais (Eds.), *Reading Bernstein, researching Bernstein* (pp. 75–91). London: Routledge/Falmer.

Muller, J. (2004). Introduction: The possibilities of Basil Bernstein. In J. Muller, B. Davies and A. Morais (Eds.), *Reading Bernstein, researching Bernstein* (pp. 1–15). London: Routledge/Falmer.

Muller, J. Davies, B. and Morais, A. (Eds.). (2004). *Reading Bernstein, researching Bernstein.* London: Routledge/Falmer.

Nagel, M. and Nagel, S. (2001). *Social background and top performance sport.* Paper presented to ECSS congress, July, 24–28, Cologne.

O' Flynn, G.H. (2004). *Young women's meanings of health and physical activity: The body, schooling, and the discursive constitution of gendered and classed subjectivities.* PhD Thesis, Australia, University of Woollongong.

Oliver, K. and Lalik, K. (2004). The beauty walk. Interrogating whiteness as the norm for beauty within one school's hidden curriculum. In J. Evans, B, Davies and J.Wright (Eds.), *Body knowledge and control. Studies in the sociology of physical education and health* (pp. 115–130). London: Routledge.

Pakulski, J. and Waters, M. (1996). *The death of class.* London: Sage.

Parkin, F. (1979). *Marxism and class theory. A bourgeois critique.* London: Tavistock.

Penn, A. (1999). *Targeting schools: Drill, militarism and imperialism.* London: Woburn Press.

Penney, D. and Chandler, T. (2000). Physical education: What future(s)? *Sport, Education and Society, 5*(1): 71–87.

Penney, D. and Evans, J. (1999). *Politics, policy and practice in physical education.* London: E&FN Spon.

Penney, D. and Harris, J. (2004). The body and health in policy: representations and recontextualisations. In J. Evans, B. Davies and J. Wright (Eds.), *Body knowledge and control. Studies in the sociology of physical education and health* (pp. 96–113). London: Routledge.

Pronger, B. (2002). *Body fascism.* London: University of Toronto Press.

Reay, D. (2004). Finding or losing yourself? Working class relationships to education. *Journal of Education Policy, 16*(4): 333–346.

Rich, E., Holroyd, R. and Evans, J. (2004). Hungry to be noticed, young women, anorexia and schooling. In J. Evans, B. Davies and J. Wright (Eds.), *Body knowledge and control. Studies in the sociology of physical education and health* (pp. 173–191). London: Routledge.

Ritzer, G. and Smart, B. (2001). *Handbook of social theory.* London: Sage.

Roberts, K. and Parsell, G. (1994). Youth culture in Britain: The middle class takeover. *Leisure Studies, 13*: 33–48.

Rose, D (2003). *Social research update, Issue Nine,* http://www.soc.surrey.ac.uk/sru/SRU9.html

Rovengo, I. and Kirk, D. (1995). Articulations and silences in socially critical work on physical education: Toward a broader agenda. *Quest, 47*(4): 447– 475.

Royal College of Physicians. (2004). *Storing up problems. The medical case for a slimmer nation.* London: Royal College of Physicians.

Roberts, K. (1996). Young people, schools, sport, and government policy. *Sport, Education and Society, 1*(1): 47–57.

Roberts, K. (1999). *Leisure in contemporary society.* Oxford: CABI Publishing.

Roberts, K. (2001). *Class in modern britain.* Basingstoke: Palgrave.

Savage, M. (2000). *Class analysis and social transformation.* Buckingham: Open University Press.

Shilling, C. (1993). The body, class and social inequalities. In J. Evans (Ed.), *Equality, education and physical education.* Lewes: Falmer Press.

Shilling, C. (2003). *The body and social theory. Second edition.* London: Sage.

Shilling, C. (2004). Educating bodies: schooling and the constitution of society. In J. Evans, B. Davies and J. Wright (Eds.), *Body knowledge and control. Studies in the sociology of physical education and health* (pp. xv–xxiii). London: Routledge.

Shilling, C. (2004b). *The body in culture, technology and society.* London: Sage.

Skeggs, B. (1997). *Formations of class and gender.* London: Sage.

Social Health Atlas of Australia (2003). http://www.publichealth.go.au/atlas.htm

Stroot, S.A. (2002). Socialisation and participation in sport. In A. Laker (Ed.), *The sociology of sport and physical education. An introductory reader.* London: Routledge.

Tyler, W. (2004). Silent, invisible, total: Pedagogic discourse and the age of information. In J. Muller, B. Davies and A. Morais (Eds.), *Reading Bernstein, researching Bernstein* (pp. 15–30). London: Routlege/Falmer.

Van der Meulin, R., Kraylaar, G. and Utlee, W. (2001). *Lifelong on the move. An event analysis of attrition in Non-elite sport.* Paper to ECSS Congress, 24–28, July, Cologne.

Walkerdine, V. (1997). *Daddy's girls: Young girls and popular culture.* London: Macmillan Press.

Whitehead, N. and Hendry, L.B. (1976). *Teaching physical education in England.* London: Lepus Books.

Willis, P.E. (1977). *Learning to labour. How working class kids get working class jobs.* London: Saxon House.

Wlatzer, M. (1984). *Spheres of justice. A defence of pluralism and equality.* Oxford: Martin Robertson.

Wright, J. (1996). The construction of gendered contexts in single sex and co-educational physical education lessons. *Sport, Education and Society, 2*(1): 55–73.

Wright, J. (2003). *Becoming somebody. Changing priorities and physical activity.* Paper presented at the NZARE/AARE conference Educational Research Risks and Dilemmas, Auckland, November, 2003.

Wright, J. (2004). *Poststrucuralist methodologies: the body, schooling and health.* In J. Evans, B. Davies and L.Wright (Eds.), *Body knowledge and control. Studies in the sociology of physical education and health* (pp. 19–33). London: Routledge.

Wright, J., Macdonald, D., and Burrows, L. (Eds.). (2004). *Critical inquiry and problem-solving in physical education.* London: Routledge.

Zaman, H. (1997). Islam, well being and physical activity: Perceptions of Muslim young women. In G. Clarke and B. Humberstone (Eds.), *Researching women and sport* (pp. 50–68). Basingstoke: Macmilllan Press.

Index